CHILDREN'S CATALOG

THIRTEENTH EDITION

1976

STANDARD CATALOG SERIES

ESTELLE A. FIDELL, GENERAL EDITOR

CHILDREN'S CATALOG
FICTION CATALOG
JUNIOR HIGH SCHOOL LIBRARY CATALOG
PUBLIC LIBRARY CATALOG
SENIOR HIGH SCHOOL LIBRARY CATALOG

CHILDREN'S CATALOG

THIRTEENTH EDITION 1976

EDITED BY

BARBARA E. DILL

NEW YORK
THE H. W. WILSON COMPANY
1976

Library of Congress Cataloging in Publication Data

Wilson, H. W., firm, publishers
Children's catalog.

(Standard catalog series)

Includes index.
1. Children's literature—Bibliography—Catalogs. i. Dill,
Barbara E., ed. ii. Title.

Z1037.W7752   1976   [PN1009.A1]   028.52   76-26525

ISBN 0-8242-0601-0

PREFACE

The Tale of Peter Rabbit had been published only seven years when the first edition of Children's Catalog appeared in 1909. A brief note in the Catalog said the story was "very popular" and, as everybody now knows, this inaugural effort of Beatrix Potter has become a classic. After its appearance in the first edition, "Peter Rabbit" has been listed in each successive edition of Children's Catalog, including the present. Few children's books written seventy-five years ago have fared so well. Some have been favored for a generation or two and then, subjected to the whim of popular taste and the demands of the latest educational theory, have disappeared from the Catalog. Others, like "Peter Rabbit," have established themselves firmly in almost every list of favorite children's books. The record of this history, with its admixture of old and new, is once more extended with this edition of Children's Catalog.

In preparing this work, The H. W. Wilson Company has again engaged the services of an advisory committee. The committee reexamined the previous edition of Children's Catalog and its supplements and proposed new titles for the Catalog. The comprehensive voting list that developed from the committee's deliberations was then sent to a group of experienced children's librarians from dispersed geographical areas, who did the actual election of titles. The Catalog covers books for children from preschool through the sixth grade. In addition to the thirteenth edition itself, the service unit includes four annual supplements to be published in 1977, 1978, 1979, and 1980.

Purpose and scope. This edition has been prepared to coordinate with the third edition of Junior High School Library Catalog, published in 1975. Although it can be considered a basic collection, the list may have to be supplemented by those libraries serving large systems, and those that must satisfy the special needs of their users. The thirteenth edition includes 5,415 titles and 13,375 analytical entries. Out-of-print books have not been included, but titles brought back into print later will be considered for inclusion in one of the four supplements.

The Catalog retains the general format of past editions, but some new features have been added and some sections strengthened. Foreign language and bilingual editions are listed when available from the publisher of the English-language version. Paperbound editions are also listed when available from the publisher of the hard-cover edition. Another new feature of the thirteenth edition is the use of uniform titles. All variant forms of individual folk and fairy tales are brought together under one heading. These headings have been established from the second edition of Mary H. Eastman's *Index to Fairy Tales, Myths and Legends* (Faxon, 1926) and its two supplements published in 1937 and 1952, respectively.

There is considerable strengthening of professional books for the librarian. Titles are included to accommodate the revived interest in the history and development of children's literature. As a further aid to the librarian, new materials on book selection and the operation of media centers are provided. Among the expanded listings for periodicals are journals in library science and education, as well as reviewing media, including several from England and one from Canada.

Organization. The Catalog is organized for effective use. It consists of three parts: Classified Catalog—Author, Title, Subject, and Analytical Index—Directory of Publishers and Distributors. To gain the greatest benefit from the Catalog it is advisable to peruse the next section: How To Use Children's Catalog.

Acknowledgments. To those publishers who generously supplied copies of their books and provided information on prices and editions, The H. W. Wilson Company acknowledges its debt. And to the two groups who gave liberally of their time and energy: the advisory committee and the consultants, the publisher is sincerely grateful.

The advisory committee comprised:

James M. Bray, Children's Librarian
    Public Library
    Rochester, Minn.

Patricia Finley, Children's Services
    Consultant
    Onondaga Library System
    Syracuse, N.Y.

Margaret Miller, Supervisor
    Library Services
    City Schools
    Los Angeles, Calif.

Priscilla L. Moulton, Director
    School Library Services
    Public Schools
    Brookline, Mass.

Anne Pellowski, Director-Librarian
    Information Center on Children's
    Cultures
    New York, N.Y.

Henrietta M. Smith, Assistant Professor
    School of Education
    Florida Atlantic University
    Boca Raton, Fla.

Della Thomas, Former Director
    Curriculum Materials Laboratory
    Oklahoma State University
    Stillwater, Okla.

The following consultants participated in the voting:

Annie Jo Carter, Library Supervisor
    Metropolitan Public Schools
    Nashville, Tenn.

Laurie Dudley, Coordinator of Children's
    Services
    Public Library
    Abilene, Tex.

Edith Edmonds, Former Elementary
    School Librarian
    Winnetka Public School Libraries
    Winnetka, Ill.

Beth Greggs, Area Children's Librarian
    King County Library Department
    Seattle, Wash.

Elvajean Hall, Former Supervisor of
    Library Services
    Division of Instruction
    Newton Public Schools
    West Newton, Mass.

Amy Kellman, Graduate School of Library
    and Information Services,
    University of Pittsburgh
    Pittsburgh, Pa.

Kathlyn King Lundgren, Librarian and
    Children's Literature Instructor
    Nebraska Western College
    Scottsbluff, Neb.

Freddy Schader, Elementary School
    Library Consultant
    Arkansas Library Commission
    Little Rock, Ark.

Nancy Schimmel, Children's Librarian
    San Mateo County Library
    Belmont, Calif.

Marian Schroether, Children's Librarian
    Public Library
    Waukegan, Ill.

Helen Tyler, Media Services Specialist
    Eugene School District
    Eugene, Ore.

Caroljean L. Wagner
    Public Library
    Milwaukee, Wis.

Jane B. Wilson, Public Library
    Consultant on Children's Services
    Chapel Hill, N.C.

TABLE OF CONTENTS

HOW TO USE CHILDREN'S CATALOG

CHILDREN'S CATALOG is arranged in three parts: Part 1. Classified Catalog; Part 2. Author, Title, Subject, and Analytical Index; Part 3. Directory of Publishers and Distributors.

USES OF THE CATALOG

CHILDREN'S CATALOG is designed to serve several purposes:

As an aid in purchasing. The CATALOG is designed to assist in the selection and ordering of titles. Annotations are provided for each title and information is given concerning publisher and price as well as varying editions. Since Part 1 is arranged by the Dewey Decimal Classification, the CATALOG may be used as a checklist to determine those parts of the library collection which are weak and require additional material. It is important to mention that many books are susceptible to classification in more than one area. If a particular title is not found where it might be expected in the Classification, the Index in Part 2 should be checked to make certain the title is not classified elsewhere in the schedules.

It is not expected, nor would it be advisable, for a library to depend upon a single aid in book selection. Each library will have to take into account the special character of its own school and community.

As a cataloging aid. For this purpose full bibliographical information is provided in Part 1. This includes recommended subject headings based upon *Sears List of Subject Headings* and a suggested classification based upon the Abridged *Dewey Decimal Classification*.

As a reference aid. Reference work is facilitated both through the annotations in Part 1 and by the subject and analytical approach in Part 2.

As an aid in rebinding, discarding, and replacing. It is possible to see what other titles on a subject are available, a factor which often influences the decision whether to discard, rebind, or replace a book.

As an aid in library schools. The CATALOG is of use in courses which deal with book selection, particularly on the preschool and elementary levels.

Part 1. Classified Catalog

The Classified Catalog is arranged with the non-fiction books first, classified by the Dewey Decimal Classification in numerical order from 000 to 999. Fiction books follow and are designated by the symbol "Fic." These are then followed by the short story collections denoted by the symbol "S C" and finally the easy books which are marked "E."

Each book is listed under its main entry, which will usually be the author. For some books, however, the main entry will be under the editor, and, for others, under title. The following is a typical entry:

> **Hautzig, Esther**
> Let's make more presents; easy and inexpensive gifts for every occasion; illus. by Ray Skibinski. Macmillan Pub. Co. 1973 150p illus $5.95 (4-7)   **745.5**
>
> 1 Handicraft   2 Gifts
>
> Companion volume to the author's: Let's make presents
>
> The author presents 70 easy-to-make gifts which can be constructed from inexpensive, readily available materials. Step-by-step instructions are given for making personal presents; gifts for children, the home, and holidays; and a variety of cookies and candies. There are also special sections on sewing and wrapping
>
> "A bonanza for the crafty kid. . . . Mothers will be pleased to find the book contains safety and sanitation advice. Mr. Skibinski's drawings are as direct and economical as the instructions." Pub W

In this entry the name of the author is given in the form in which it appears on the title page of the book. It is inverted and is printed in dark or bold face type.

The first part of the main body of the entry gives the title of the book *Let's make more presents*.

The information that the book is published by Macmillan Pub. Co. follows (reference to Part 3 will show that this publisher is Macmillan Publishing Company, Inc. located at 866 3d Av, New York, N.Y. 10022). This information, with the price, is useful in ordering books. The date 1973 is the date when this book was published. Further information records that it contains 150 pages and illustrations. It currently sells for $5.95. As the CATALOG grows older, however, prices should be rechecked with the publisher for possible changes. The figures (4-7) indicate that this book is useful for children in the 4th to 7th grades. It is difficult to make generalizations as to the reading ability of children and for this reason the grading given is rather flexible. Most listings are graded, except for Easy books, professional tools for the librarian, and some reference books.

At the end of the last line in the body of the entry is the figure 745.5 in dark type. This is the classification number according to the Abridged *Dewey Decimal Classification*. 745.5 is the classification for Handicrafts.

The line "1 Handicraft 2 Gifts" gives the recommended subject headings for this book. All subject headings are based upon *Sears List of Subject Headings*.

Sometimes the subject or subjects assigned to the entire book will not show that there are portions of the book which deal with more specific subjects. In this case analytics are made. The book listed above contains a section dealing with Sewing. In Part 2 there will be an entry for this portion of the book under the subject heading Sewing.

There are then two notes giving a brief description of the book and its contents. The descriptive note for this example was written by a Wilson staff member and the critical note was taken from Publisher's Weekly. Annotations are useful in evaluating books for book selection. They are also useful in determining which of several books on the same subject are best suited for the individual reader.

Part 2. Author, Title, Subject, and Analytical Index

This is an alphabetical index of all the books entered in the CATALOG. Each book is entered under author, title if distinctive, subject, and under joint author and illustrator if any. Also included are the subject, author and title analytics for the books analyzed. The classification number is the key to the main entry of the book in Part 1. The following are index entries for the book cited above:

Author	**Hautzig, Esther** Let's make more presents (4-7)	**745.5**
Title	**Let's make more presents. Hautzig, E.**	**745.5**
Subject	**Handicraft** Hautzig, E. Let's make more presents (4-7)	**745.5**
Subject Analytic	**Sewing** *See pages in the following book:* Hautzig, E. Let's make more presents p10-19 (4-7)	**745.5**
Illustrator	**Skibinski, Ray** (illus.) Hautzig, E. Let's make more presents	**745.5**

Examples of other types of entries:

Joint Author	**Lembo, Diana** (jt. auth.) Gillespie, J. Introducing books	**028.1**
Author Analytic	**Olcott, Francis Jenkins** The most magnificent cook of all *In* Sechrist, E. H. ed. It's time for story hour p85-90	**372.6**
Title Analytic	**The most magnificent cook of all. Olcott, F. J.** *In* Sechrist, E. H. ed. It's time for story hour p85-90	**372.6**
Uniform Title	**Bremen town musicians** De La Mare, W. The musicians *In* De La Mare, W. Tales told again p25- 32	**398.2**

Grimm, J. The Bremen town musicians

398.2

also in Grimm, J. About wise men and
    simpletons p111-15   **398.2**
also in Haviland, V. comp. The fairy tale
    treasury p110-13   **398.2**
Grimm, J. The four musicians
  In Arbuthnot, M. H. comp. The Arbuth-
    not Anthology of children's literature
    p200-02   **808.8**
Grimm, J. The traveling musicians   **398.2**
McMurray, L. B. The street musicians
  In Association for Childhood Education
    International. Told under the green
    umbrella p67-73   **398.2**
    See also Jack and the robbers

Part 3. Directory of Publishers and Distributors

The name of the publisher or distributor is given in abbreviated form in each entry. This Directory lists the abbreviation and then provides the full name and address of the publisher or distributor.

PART 1

CLASSIFIED CATALOG

OUTLINE OF CLASSIFICATION

The following is the Second Summary of the Dewey Decimal Classification which is reproduced from the tenth abridged edition (1971) of Dewey Decimal Classification and Relative Index, by permission of Forest Press Division, Lake Placid Education Foundation, owner of copyright. The non-fiction titles in Part 1 of this Catalog are arranged according to this outline, which will therefore serve as a table of contents to this portion of the Catalog. Please note, however, that the inclusion of this outline is not to be considered as a substitute for consulting the Dewey Decimal Classification itself.

000	**Generalities**		**500**	**Pure sciences**
010	Bibliographies & catalogs		510	Mathematics
020	Library & information sciences		520	Astronomy & allied sciences
030	General encyclopedic works		530	Physics
040			540	Chemistry & allied sciences
050	General serial publications		550	Sciences of earth & other worlds
060	General organizations & museology		560	Paleontology
070	Journalism, publishing, newspapers		570	Life sciences
080	General collections		580	Botanical sciences
090	Manuscripts & book rarities		590	Zoological sciences

			600	**Technology (Applied sciences)**
100	**Philosophy & related disciplines**		610	Medical sciences
110	Metaphysics		620	Engineering & allied operations
120	Knowledge, cause, purpose, man		630	Agriculture & related technologies
130	Popular & parapsychology, occultism		640	Domestic arts & sciences
140	Specific philosophical viewpoints		650	Managerial services
150	Psychology		660	Chemical & related technologies
160	Logic		670	Manufactures
170	Ethics (Moral philosophy)		680	Miscellaneous manufactures
180	Ancient, medieval, Oriental		690	Buildings
190	Modern Western philosophy		**700**	**The arts**
			710	Civic & landscape art
200	**Religion**		720	Architecture
210	Natural religion		730	Plastic arts Sculpture
220	Bible		740	Drawing, decorative & minor arts
230	Christian doctrinal theology		750	Painting & paintings
240	Christian moral & devotional theology		760	Graphic arts Prints
250	Local church & religious orders		770	Photography & photographs
260	Social & ecclesiastical theology		780	Music
270	History & geography of church		790	Recreational & performing arts
280	Christian denominations & sects		**800**	**Literature (Belles-lettres)**
290	Other religions & comparative		810	American literature in English
			820	English & Anglo-Saxon literatures
300	**The social sciences**		830	Literatures of Germanic languages
310	Statistics		840	Literatures of Romance languages
320	Political science		850	Italian, Romanian, Rhaeto-Romanic
330	Economics		860	Spanish & Portuguese literatures
340	Law		870	Italic languages literatures Latin
350	Public administration		880	Hellenic languages literatures
360	Social pathology & services		890	Literatures of other languages
370	Education		**900**	**General geography & history**
380	Commerce		910	General geography Travel
390	Customs & folklore		920	General biography & genealogy
			930	General history of ancient world
			940	General history of Europe
400	**Language**		950	General history of Asia
410	Linguistics		960	General history of Africa
420	English & Anglo-Saxon languages		970	General history of North America
430	Germanic languages German		980	General history of South America
440	Romance languages French		990	General history of other areas
450	Italian, Romanian, Rhaeto-Romanic		**Fic**	**Fiction**
460	Spanish & Portuguese languages			
470	Italic languages Latin		**S C**	**Story collections**
480	Hellenic Classical Greek			
490	Other languages		**E**	**Easy books**

CHILDREN'S CATALOG

THIRTEENTH EDITION, 1976

CLASSIFIED CATALOG

000 GENERALITIES

001.54 Communication

Amon, Aline
Talking hands; Indian sign language; written and illus. by Aline Amon. Doubleday 1968 80p illus map $4.95, lib. bdg. $5.70 (3-6)   001.54
    1 Indians of North America—Sign language
    ISBN 0-385-08891-4; 0-385-09425-6
"Beginning with the names of the fingers and basic positions of the hands, the author shows how to put words together into sentences, ask questions, tell stories and carry on conversations in sign language. The illustrations throughout are clear and explicit, and the index lists slightly more than 200 words." Sch Library J
"Irresistible as a combination of fun and education, [this book] is a godsend to both harried parents and restless offspring." N Y Times Bk Rev

Hofsinde, Robert
Indian sign language; written and illus. by Robert Hofsinde (Gray-Wolf) Morrow 1956 96p illus lib. bdg. $4.32 (3-6)   001.54
    1 Indians of North America—Sign language
    ISBN 0-688-31610-7
"This book shows how to form the gestures representing about five hundred words [in Indian sign language] ranging from familiar terms, such as 'man,' 'beaver,' and 'rapids,' to modern addictions like 'motion picture' and 'coffee.' The key words are printed in heavy type, and are accompanied by concise directions and explanatory sketches. Words related in meaning are arranged in groups, and there is an alphabetical index." Ontario Library Rev

Lubell, Winifred
Picture signs & symbols, by Winifred & Cecil Lubell. Parents Mag. Press 1972 64p illus maps lib. bdg. $4.59 (2-4)   001.54
    1 Signs and symbols
    ISBN 0-8193-0577-4
"A Stepping-stone book"
The authors "explain the use of pictures as symbols of information and communication. Beginning with a general introduction, the concise and clearly written text progresses to highway signs, Olympic game symbols, Indian signs, etc. Why flags, mascots, animals, and hands are used in symbols is discussed. There are also chapters on holiday and map symbols and a final section of the newly created ecology signs." Library J
"Clear and attractive drawings are carefully integrated with the text in a book that is useful as well as interesting, and that may stimulate readers to a further interest in symbols and communication." Chicago. Children's Bk Center

Neal, Harry Edward
Communication; from stone age to space age; illus. with photographs. [Rev. ed] Messner 1974 192p illus $6.25, lib. bdg. $5.79 (5-7)   001.54
    1 Communication—History
    ISBN 0-671-326511; 0-671-32652-X
    First published 1960
This historical survey of human communications describes the development and functions of languages, alphabets, numbers, writing, printing, newspapers, radio, telegraph, various forms of telecommunication, visual arts, and music
    Bibliography: p183-84. Sources of further information: p185

Rinkoff, Barbara
Red light says stop! Illus. by Judith Hoffman Corwin. Lothrop 1974 unp illus $4.75, lib. bdg. $4.32 (1-3)   001.54
    1 Communication 2 Signs and symbols
    ISBN 0-688-41588-1; 0-688-51588-6
"Bright colors and bold lines make the pictures in this communications primer attractive. And Ms. Rinkoff's text is easy for the beginning reader to handle. Investigated here are ways in which signals are used instead of speech or writing: a shrug of the shoulders means 'I don't know,' a slam of the door means 'I'm angry.' But we find the conclusions arbitrary: Couldn't a shrug mean one doesn't care? . . . The Morse code, the semaphore, Braille, sign language, smoke signals and drumbeats are all discussed, as well as other nonverbal messages." Pub W

001.6 Data processing

Berger, Melvin
Computers; illus. by Arthur Schaffert. Coward, McCann & Geoghegan 1972 43p illus (The Science is what and why bks) lib. bdg. $4.49 (1-3)   001.6
    1 Computers
    ISBN 0-698-30053-X
"Contains the essential facts and provides correct and appropriate illustrations to introduce the grade school child to computer processing. . . . With a minimum of words, the author has shown some of the most important current uses of computers. The space program, data processing, weather predicting, postal sorting, and traffic control are mentioned. Some simple notions of computer operation and programming are given." Sci Bks

Those amazing computers! Uses of modern thinking machines; illus. with photographs. Day 1973 189p illus lib. bdg. $5.95 (5-7)   001.6
    1 Computers
    ISBN 0-381-99637-9
"In an accurate, well-written book with good illustrations, Berger introduces the application of compu-

Berger, Melvin—*Continued*

ters to the younger set. In the first chapter he discusses the basic terminology and principles of computers. Each following chapter illustrates the aid the computer is providing in specific areas. . . . Examples are also given of the computer's ability to play games. Not only are the good points of the computer described, but some problems which have occurred because of computers are explained. A small chapter describes a computer club for young people known as the R.E.S.I.S.T.O.R.S." Sci Bks

Further reading: p183-84

Halacy, D. S.

What makes a computer work? By D. S. Halacy, Jr. Pictures by Nat Goldstein. Little 1973 64p illus lib. bdg. $3.95 (2-4)　　　　　　　001.6

1 Computers

ISBN 0-316-33830-3

"An Atlantic Monthly Press book"

This "survey explains computer functions to beginners. The essential mechanisms of computer operations—arithmetic, memory, input-output, and control—are outlined while short explanations of the binary number system, the programming process, the development of counting machines, and some jobs of modern computers are given. For use in classrooms, particularly as a push-off point for study undertaken at higher age levels. Black-and-white drawings supplement the text; a combination index and glossary is appended." Booklist

Srivastava, Jane Jonas

Computers; illus. by James and Ruth McCrea. Crowell 1972 32p illus (Young math bks) $4.50, lib. bdg. $5.25 (2-4)　　　　　　　001.6

1 Computers

ISBN 0-690-20850-2; 0-690-20851-0

The author "introduces the young reader to the computer, explaining its units, the role of the programmer, the feeding of data and the use of a flowchart. The latter gives instructions for 'counting giraffes met on the way to school,' an example of the light style of writing. The text serves adequately to explain a complicated subject, not going into the subject of the binary system or giving too much detail about computer languages." Chicago. Children's Bk Center

001.9　Controversial and spurious knowledge

Branley, Franklyn M.

A book of flying saucers for you; illus. by Leonard Kessler. Crowell 1973 72p illus $5.95, lib. bdg. $6.70 (2-4)　　　　　　　001.9

1 Flying saucers

ISBN 0-690-15188-8; 0-690-15189-6

The author describes and offers some explanations of unidentified flying objects, and considers the possibility of life on other planets

"Cheerful, appealing wash drawings full of point, looking rather like the paintings on the schoolroom walls, and a clear, brief text to match make up this small book for young grade school readers. There are photographs of flying hats and a Mars crater and useful lists of the dates of bright planet apparitions and meteor showers. The whole vexed topic—hoaxes, the will to believe, Ezekiel, balloons, St. Elmo's fire and all—is spelled out in simple language without either rancor or credulousness. . . . The experienced astronomical author has made a model of honest approach and genuine content." Scientific Am

Liss, Howard

UFOs, unidentified flying objects. Hawthorn Bks. 1968 64p illus $4.95 (4-6)　　　　　　　001.9

1 Flying saucers

ISBN 0-8015-8190-7

Title on spine: Unidentified flying objects

"This brief book recounts many UFO sightings, both those that have been explained and those still under investigation. The author explores the difficulties and improbabilities of interplanetary flight and the possibility of interplanetary communication to let the reader draw his own conclusion. Well organized and interestingly written." Adventuring With Bks. 2d edition

Place, Marian T.

On the track of Bigfoot; illus. with photographs. Dodd 1974 156p illus map $4.25 (5-7)　　　　　001.9

1 Sasquatch

ISBN 0-396-06883-9

This is a "book about 'monsters' of the Pacific Northwest, which have long been the object of much curiosity and search by many people, including some scientists. [The creature is] variously known as Bigfoot, Sasquatch and Oh-Mah. . . . [It] is, reportedly, huge (over 8 ft. tall), human-like, two-legged, covered with hair, a resident of remote forests and very shy of humans." Sci Bks

"By collecting many of the stories people have been telling each other about the bigfoot over the years and retelling them in readable detail, Marian T. Place has produced a fascinating book for young readers. . . . [Her] accounts—without much attempt at scholarly assessment—become redundant; but, for once, that is part of the point: If all of those different people at all those different times were hallucinating, why did they all describe such similar creatures? In fact the book has substance." N Y Times Bk Rev

Bibliography: p151-52

White, Dale

Is something up there? The story of flying saucers. Doubleday 1968 166p illus $4.95, lib. bdg. $5.70 (4-7)　　　　　　　001.9

1 Flying saucers

ISBN 0-385-00787-6; 0-385-02314-6

This "introduction to unidentified flying objects not only examines the history of sightings from 1947 to the recent ones at Exeter but also differentiates between those of known and unknown origin. Included are some famous UFO photographs and some diagrams showing how natural phenomena can be mistaken for UFO's." Library J

"An extensive account of UFO phenomena. The role of the Air Force in investigating reports shows concern for a reasoned approach to studying reported sightings. The style is vivid and very readable, making this a highly interesting and lively book." Adventuring With Bks. 2d edition

Bibliography: p159-60

011　General bibliographies

The Booklist

Reference and subscription books reviews; 1956-1974. A.L.A. 1961-1975 8v　　　　　　　011

1 Reference books—Bibliography 2 Book reviews

Reprinted from issues of The Booklist, listed below

Volumes covering the years 1956-1968 published with title: Subscription Books Bulletin reviews

Volumes 1956-1960, 1960-1962 o.p. 1975; 1962-1964 pa $2 (ISBN 0-8389-0061-5); 1964-1966 pa $2.25 (ISBN 0-8389-0062-3); 1966-1968 pa $2.25 (ISBN 0-8389-0063-1); 1968-1970 pa $3 (ISBN 0-8389-0092-5); 1970-1972 pa $4 (ISBN 0-8389-0143-3); 1972-1974 pa $8.50 (ISBN 0-8389-0194-8)

The Booklist—*Continued*

These reviews prepared by the Reference and Sub-scription Books Review Committee of the A.L.A. describe and evaluate encyclopedias, dictionaries, biographical reference works, atlases and gazetteers, directories, yearbooks and annuals and statistical compendia as well as bibliographical reference sources and periodical indexes

The Booklist. A.L.A. $20 per year   011

1 Books and reading—Best books 2 Book reviews
ISSN 0006-7385

A semi-monthly guide to current books except for August, which has a single issue—the annual index. The Booklist was first published 1905 with title: A.L.A. Booklist. It combined September 1956 with Subscription Books Bulletin. In September 1969 it resumed the title: The Booklist

"Contains brief notes on a wide variety of books and some nonprint materials that are suitable for children, young adults, and adults. About 11,000 books are evaluated each year. No articles are included in the journal. Each issue prints long descriptive and evaluative reviews for one or two reference books. These are cumulated and reprinted as bound volumes every two years [with title: Reference and subscription books reviews, entered above]. The other sections list adult books in classified arrangement, adult fiction, pamphlets and paperbacks, recordings, 16mm films, filmstrips, books for young adults, children's books, and government documents. Each issue selects some 15 adult titles and 10 children's books for the small library. The nonbook columns are printed regularly although some columns are published on an alternating basis. There is an index to authors and titles in each issue. Entries give complete bibliographic and cataloging data, as well as price. Generally regarded as an impeccable source of book reviews, it has been criticized for its conservative policies (see 'Magazines for Libraries', 2d ed., p. 116). Nonetheless, it remains one of the most influential review journals, especially for school and small public libraries." Wynar. Guide to Ref Bks for Sch Media Centers

Books for children, 1960-1965; as selected and reviewed by The Booklist and Subscription Books Bulletin, September 1960 through August 1965. A.L.A. 1966 [c1965] 447p $10   011

1 Catalogs, Classified 2 Children's literature—Bibliography 3 Books and reading—Best books
ISBN 0-8389-0016-X

A compilation of 3,068 titles listed and recommended for purchase in the Children's Books section of: The Booklist and Subscription Books Bulletin. The original "Booklist" information is given for each title

"Arranged by a modified Dewey Decimal classification, with a separate biography section and two sections on fiction, one being on easy and picture books, it provides a useful source of bibliographical information, with annotations of content and a critical and comparative evaluation for each title. Reader interest, grade level, classification number, and subject headings are also supplied. A dictionary index to author, subject, and title is appended." Cur Ref Bks

Kept up to date by annual paperbound compilations published with title: Books for children, preschool through junior high school

The Elementary school library collection; a guide to books and other media, phases 1-2-3. Bro-Dart Foundation $24.95   011

1 Catalogs, Classified 2 Children's literature—Bibliography 3 Audio-visual materials—Catalogs 4 School libraries—Catalogs

Annual. First published 1965

General editor 1st-8th edition: Mary V. Gaver; 9th edition edited by Phyllis Van Orden, assisted by Mary V. Gaver and others

"This bibliography lists 7,635 trade books, 1,743 audio-visual titles, plus periodicals, reference books, and professional tools. Keyed for first, second, and third purchase, it is arranged by Dewey classification. Entries provide bibliographic information, a brief annotation, approximate reading level, and suggested subject headings to be used by the cataloger. Three separate indexes appear in Section II: Author Index, Title Index, and Subject Index." Peterson. Ref Bks for Elem and Jr High Sch Libraries [Review of 1973 edition]

Junior high school library catalog. 3d ed. 1975. Ed. by Ilene R. Schechter and Gary L. Bogart. Wilson, H. W. 1975 991p $42   011

1 Catalogs, Classified 2 School libraries—Catalogs 3 School libraries (High school)—Catalogs
ISBN 0-8242-0553-7

"Standard catalog series"

Kept up to date by annual supplements which are included in the cost of the main catalog

First published 1965

Contents: Part 1. Classified catalog; Part 2. Author, title, subject, and analytical index; Part 3. Directory of publishers and distributors

The third edition catalogs 3,791 books and includes 10,673 subject and author and title analytical entries. The voting list for this edition was compiled by an advisory committee of distinguished librarians and was then submitted to a group of consultants who made the final selection of titles

This catalog "attempts to bridge the gap between elementary and senior high level reading materials. In this volume the analytical entries in the Author, Title, Subject, and Analytical index are valuable for locating specific titles in collected works." Peterson. Ref Bks for Elem and Jr High Sch Libraries [Review of 1970 edition]

Rosenberg, Judith K.

Young people's literature in series: publishers' and non-fiction series; an annotated bibliographical guide [by] Judith K. Rosenberg & Kenyon C. Rosenberg. Libs. Unlimited 1973 280p $10   011

1 Literature—Bibliography
ISBN 0-87287-058-8

Companion volume to the authors': Young people's literature in series: fiction, entered in class 016.8

This evaluative guide for readers in grades 3-12 lists about 6,000 entries. Whenever possible annotations indicate quality of series, reading level, special features and other major characteristics

"Valuable because of the need it answers for descriptions and evaluations, however brief, of the flood of informational books currently put out in series. . . . Unfortunately, age levels are not consistently indicated. Titles in print and published through 1972 are listed in this useful selection tool for school and public librarians. Includes author and title indexes." Booklist

015   Bibliographies and catalogs of works from specific places

Children's books in print. Bowker $20   015

1 Children's literature—Bibliography
ISSN 0069-3480

Children's books in print—*Continued*

Annual. First published 1969, expanded from and replacing: Children's books for schools and libraries

"Three separate alphabets are incorporated in the volume: author index, title index, and illustrator index. The entries in each section are arranged alphabetically by word. Difficulties in the grouping of some authors' names is experienced due to computer limitations. All entries include author, co-author, co-editor, illustrator, translator, title, price, imprint, publisher, year of publication, plus other data where warranted (e.g., order number, ISBN, edition, number of volumes, grade range, type of binding). A key to abbreviations is in the front of the volume, along with an instructive 'How to Use' section. An alphabetical index of publishers is in an unpaged section at the end that provides short form, full name, address, and ISBN prefix." Wynar. Guide to Ref Bks for Sch Media Centers

Subject guide to Children's books in print. Bowker $20   015

1 Children's literature—Bibliography 2 Catalogs, Subject

ISSN 0000-0167

Annual. First published 1970

A subject arranged companion to Children's books in print, entered above. Headings used are derived from the Sears list of subject headings, entered in class 025.3

"The author and title entries provide full bibliographic, price, and binding data—the same as that given in 'Children's Guide to Books in Print.' A key to abbreviations is at the front, and a directory of publishers is located at the back of the volume. The 'Subject Guide' has been criticized for inconsistencies in headings and their assignment and for a dearth of cross references." Wynar. Guide to Ref Bks for Sch Media Centers [Review of third edition]

Vertical file index; a subject and title index to selected pamphlet material. Wilson, H.W. pa $11 a year   015

1 Pamphlets—Bibliography 2 Pamphlets—Indexes

First published 1932 with title: Vertical file service catalog

Issued monthly except August

This index is a subject and title index to selected pamphlets considered to be of interest to general libraries. It is not intended to be a complete list of all pamphlet material, nor does inclusion of a pamphlet constitute recommendation. Each issue contains a list of current, available pamphlets, booklets, leaflets, and mimeographed material arranged alphabetically by subject; each entry includes title, paging, publisher, publication date, descriptive note, and price or condition under which it may be obtained. A title index, giving the subject heading under which each title may be found, follows the subject list. Each issue contains a list of subject headings used, which is cumulated each quarter

Weekly Record. Bowker $10 per year   015

1 American literature—Bibliography—Periodicals

ISSN 0094-257X

Weekly. Formerly issued as part of Publishers Weekly (entered in class 070.505) this periodical was first published as an independent publication in 1974

This magazine provides LC card cataloging information for current American book publications. The arrangement is alphabetical by main entry

016   Subject bibliographies

Peterson, Carolyn Sue

Reference books for elementary and junior high school libraries. 2d ed. Scarecrow 1975 314p $10   016

1 Reference books—Bibliography

ISBN 0-8108-0816-1

First published 1970

"A general guide designed to help librarians and teachers in building a basic reference collection. . . . Entries give information on title, author, publisher, place, date, price, and edition together with descriptive but noncomparative annotations from a few lines to a page in length. Arrangement is by type of reference book: general encyclopedias, English language dictionaries, fact books and yearbooks, indexes, atlases, biographical dictionaries, foreign language dictionaries, hobbies, bibliographies, and reference books in the subject areas of English, geography, history, social science, science and mathematics, and philosophy, music, and art. Subject and author-title indexes." Booklist [Review of 1970 edition]

Wynar, Christine L.

Guide to reference books for school media centers. Libs. Unlimited 1973 473p $17.50   016

1 Reference books—Bibliography 2 School libraries

ISBN 0-87287-069-3

This volume contains 2,575 annotated entries for reference books and selection tools for use in elementary, junior, and senior high schools. The subjects treated are those generally included in school curricula plus extracurricular topics such as pets, hobbies, clubs, etc. Entries are arranged alphabetically by author under 54 main subject headings. Paperback editions and prices are shown. Index includes author, title and subject entries

"The main advantage here will be breadth and up-to-dateness. . . . One could quibble that some titles are too specialized for school libraries or that some very useful titles are omitted. However, this will be a useful list for collection building and for reminding librarians or patrons of sources to use on particular problems." Cur Ref Bks

016.028   Bibliographies of reading and reading aids

Perkins, Flossie L.

Book and non-book media; annotated guide to selection aids for educational materials. Revision of: Book selection media. Natl. Council of Teachers of English 1972 298p pa $4.25   016.028

1 Reference books—Bibliography 2 Bibliography—Bibliography 2 Audio-visual materials—Bibliography

ISBN 0-8141-4808-6

First published 1966 with title: Book selection media, compiled by Ralph Perkins

More than 250 annotated listings of bibliographies and other selection aids for books, films, recordings, pamphlets, photos, toys and games, and other education-related materials, covering elementary school through college and adult interests. Alphabetically arranged by title, the listings also provide author, publisher, publication date and price. Annotations describe the work's purpose, scope, subjects, similar tools, special features and usefulness. There are indexes to those references deemed helpful for

Perkins, Flossie L.—*Continued*
children, teenagers, college students and adults, teachers and parents, and librarians. Includes an author-publisher index, but no subject index

016.03 Bibliographies of encyclopedias

General encyclopedias in print; a comparative analysis. Bowker $12.50   016.03
1 Encyclopedias and dictionaries—Bibliography
ISSN 0072-0739
First published 1963 by Reference Books Research Service. Frequently revised to bring material up to date. Compiler: 1963-   S. Padraig Walsh
"As a practical guide for evaluating enclyclopedias, this small handbook describes in detail the arrangement, age, suitability, history, subject coverage, reviews, etc., of the main general knowledge encyclopedias published. A consensus of opinion chart, by professional librarians and educators, lists those encyclopedias recommended and those not recommended." Ref Bks for Small and Medium Sized Libraries. 2d edition

016.05 Bibliographies of serials

Katz, Bill
(ed.) Magazines for libraries; for the general reader, and school, junior college, college, and public libraries. 2d ed. [Edited by] Bill Katz and Berry Gargal, science editor. Bowker 1972 822p $22   016.05
1 Periodicals—Bibliography
ISBN 0-8352-0554-1
First published 1969
"Some 4,500 titles are annotated in this [volume]. . . . Nearly all subject areas of importance to large school libraries, medium-sized public libraries, junior college libraries, and four-year college libraries are treated. Entries give concise descriptive annotations plus evaluative comments and some highly subjective comments, as well as bibliographic information and prices. There is a title and subject index. It is a very useful reference source on general magazines for school and other small and medium-sized libraries." Wynar. Guide to Ref Bks for Sch Media Centers
   Bibliography: p763-82
   For fuller review see: The Booklist, June 1, 1974

   (ed.) Magazines for libraries; for the general reader, and school, junior college, college, and public libraries. 2d ed. supplement. [Ed. by] Bill Katz and Berry Gargal, science editor. Bowker 1974 328p $16.50   016.05
1 Periodicals—Bibliography
ISBN 0-8352-0761-7
This supplement lists approximately 1,800 periodicals and journals published since the second edition cut-off date in Spring 1972, and journals and magazines published prior to 1972 that for one reason or another were not included in the second edition. Some publications are covered again if there were major changes in ownership, publication schedule, or editorial policy. A combined index to both the supplement and the second edition is included

Periodicals for school libraries; a guide to magazines, newspapers, and periodical indexes. Rev. ed. Comp. and ed. by Marian H. Scott. A.L.A. 1973 xxi, 269p pa $4.95   016.05
1 Periodicals—Bibliography 2 School libraries
ISBN 0-8389-0139-5
First published 1969
"The directory is a buying list of recommended periodicals for all grade levels, K-12. . . . The alphabetically arranged list of periodicals is supplemented by an annotated list of periodical indexes and a subject index. Entries give address, grade level, frequency, price, annotation describing general content, and where abstracted. Highly selective it will be most valuable in small libraries." Wynar. Guide to Ref Bks for Sch Media Centers

016.301 Bibliographies of sociology

Reading ladders for human relations. 5th ed. [by] Virginia M. Reid, editor, and the Committee on Reading Ladders for Human Relations of the National Council of Teachers of English. Am. Council on Educ. 1972 346p $10.50, pa $4.50
          016.301
1 Human relations—Bibliography 2 Intercultural education—Bibliography 3 Children's literature—Bibliography
ISBN 0-8268-1375-5; 0-8268-1373-9
First published 1947. 1st-3d editions edited by Margaret M. Heaton. 4th edition edited by Muriel Crosby
   The books annotated in this work "develop four themes. The themes explore the individual's concept of himself; his relationship to his family, peers, and others, or his alienation from these groups; his appreciation or lack of appreciation of persons from other socioeconomic, cultural or ethnic groups; and his need to cope with change, including all of the traumatic experiences change can produce. . . . Within each theme books are arranged by maturity level and then listed alphabetically by author. The assignment or cross-reference of a given title to a given ladder or a given sequence is only suggestive; any complex work will have more facets than can be reflected here." Design of the Reading Ladders

016.3014 Bibliographies of social groups

The Black experience in children's audiovisual materials. Sponsored by North Manhattan Project, Countee Cullen Regional Branch. . . . N.Y. Pub. Lib. 1973 32p pa $1   016.3014
1 Negroes—Audio-visual aids 2 Audio-visual materials—Bibliography
ISBN 0-87104-610-5
Compiled by Diane DeVeaux, Marilyn Berg Iarusso and Viola Jones Clark
   "Designed as a supplement to 'The Black Experience in Children's Books' [entered below] this bibliography is a well organized list of audiovisual materials depicting Black life. It is divided into the following sections: records and cassettes, films, filmstrips, and multi-media kits. It also contains a directory of sources. Each section lists materials held by the North Manhattan and Countee Cullen branch libraries which have proved popular with children and which

The Black experience in children's audiovisual materials—*Continued*
are still available for purchase." Peterson. Ref Bks for Elem and Jr High Sch Libraries

The Black experience in children's books; selected by Barbara Rollock. N.Y. Pub. Lib. 1974 122p pa $2.50   016.3014
1 Negroes—Bibliography
ISBN 0-87104-614-8
First published 1957 with title: Books about Negro life for children. Previous editions were compiled by Augusta Baker
"This booklist contains selected stories portraying Black life for children from preschool to age twelve. Arranged geographically (United States, South and Central America, the Caribbean, Africa, and England), the list is further subdivided by subjects with titles alphabetically arranged under each heading. Subjects include picture books, readers, stories for younger children, stories for older boys and girls, folklore, poetry and verse, music and art, sports, science, Civil Rights, Frederick Douglass, Dr. Martin Luther King, Jr., biography, history, the way it is, references, and periodicals. Each entry gives the title, author, illustrator, publisher, date, price, and brief annotation." Peterson. Ref Bks for Elem and Jr High Sch Libraries

Child Study Association of America/Wel-Met. Book Review Committee
Family life and child development; a selective annotated bibliography. The Association pa $2.50
                                                016.3014
1 Family—Bibliography 2 Child study—Bibliography
First published 1904. 1969 edition published with title: Recommended reading about children and family life
"An annotated list of 289 books and pamphlets selected to aid parents in their study of marriage and family life, child development, sex education, schools and learning, and social, physical and emotional problems. Titles are grouped by the above topics with subdivisions. There is an author and title index. Revised periodically, it offers a wide range of materials." Wynar. Guide to Ref Bks for Sch Media Centers [Review of 1972 edition]

The Chinese in children's books. N.Y. Pub. Lib. 1973 [c1965] 30p illus pa $2   016.3014
1 China—Bibliography 2 Chinese literature—Bibliography 3 Children's literature—Bibliography
ISBN 0-87104-612-1
Prepared by Angela Au Long and others
A selective list of books on China and the Chinese that includes books in Chinese and books in English with chapters on: Picture books; Stories for younger children; Stories for older children; Folk tales; People and places; Arts and culture; The Chinese in the United States

Enoch Pratt Free Library, Baltimore
Black is . . . The Library 1972 58p illus pa 75¢
                                                016.3014
1 Negroes—Bibliography
"This list includes most of the black-interest books contained in the active collections of children's books in the Enoch Pratt Free Library of Baltimore." Introduction

016.371   Bibliographies of the school

EL-hi textbooks in print. Bowker $22.50   016.371
1 Textbooks—Bibliography
ISSN 0070-9565

Annual. First issued in 1872 as part of Publisher's Weekly. Formerly published with titles: The American educational catalog, and later, Textbooks in print. First published under present title 1970
This volume lists "elementary, junior high, and senior high texts, published by . . . American textbook companies, plus data on programmed learning materials in book form, professional books for teachers and auxiliary AV aids. The subject index lists texts under curriculum headings . . . providing author, title, grade level, publication date, binding, ISBN, price, related teaching material, and publisher. Series are grouped together under the series title. Author, title, and series indexes and a directory of publishers are also provided." Wynar. Guide to Ref Bks for Sch Media Centers

George Peabody College for Teachers, Nashville, Tenn.
Free and inexpensive learning materials. The College pa $3   016.371
1 Teaching—Aids and devices—Bibliography
2 Pamphlets—Bibliography
Biennial. First published 1941
This annotated "well-known guide to inexpensive instructional aids contains some 3,000 items. . . . The contents are arranged alphabetically under curriculum-related categories, from Africa to Weather and Climate. Within each category the names and addresses of organizations, associations, and other sources are given. A list of the items available from each source on the topic follows. Covers pamphlets, offprints, prints, charts, maps, and paperback books." Wynar. Guide to Ref Bks for Sch Media Centers [Review of the 16th edition]

016.3713   Bibliographies of teaching methods

Educational Film Library Association
Film evaluation guide. The Association 016.3713
1 Moving pictures—Catalogs
Volume covering 1946-1964 o.p. 1975 (available in microfilm from University Microfilm Inc.); Supplement covering September 1, 1964-August 31, 1967 and Supplement two covering September 1, 1967-August 31, 1971 each $12
The basic volume is a compilation of 4500 evaluations of 16mm films. Annotations provide "information on subject, running time, price, distributor, age level, possible audience, and rating. Intended for universities, school systems, public libraries, church groups, labor organizations, and youth-serving agencies with film libraries or film programs. . . . Monthly sets of evaluation cards are available to members of the association." Pub W

Educators guide to free films. Educators Progress Service $12.75   016.3713
1 Moving pictures—Catalogs
ISSN 0070-9395
Annual. First published 1941
"This list of sponsored films available to schools free (or for cost of postage) is well annotated. It is indexed by title and by subject." Ref Materials for Sch Libraries

Landers Film Reviews. Landers Associates $35 a year   016.3713
1 Moving pictures—Reviews
ISSN 0023-785X
Published monthly except July and August. First

Landers Film Reviews—*Continued*
published 1956 with title: Bertha Landers Film reviews

Loose-leaf, with binder

"In addition to coverage of instructional films of all types for kindergarten through adult viewing, it includes training films, experimental films, TV documentary and short subject films, and children's fiction films. About 700 to 800 titles from nearly 600 producers (major companies and small independent firms) are reviewed annually. . . . Arrangement of 16mm films is alphabetical by title; other media are arranged by producer. Entries give title, producer /distributor (address is included if the name is not listed in the Source Directory), year of release, running time, sound, color/black and white, price (sale, rental, or free loan), credits, intended audience (e, jh, sh, c, ad), subject area, purpose, and review of about 150 words. Each review provides a synopsis of the film, followed by a short evaluation. Title and subject indexes are included in each issue, and annual cumulative indexes are provided in the last issue of the volume." Wynar. Guide to Ref Bks for Sch Media Centers

McDaniel, Roderick

(ed.) Resources for learning; a core media collection for elementary schools. Bowker 1971 365p $16.50
016.3713

1 Audio-visual materials—Catalogs
ISBN 0-8352-0401-4
"This collection consists of 4,000 titles including 16mm films, 8mm films, filmloops, filmstrips, phonodiscs, study prints, and some slides. The two major sections are: Media Indexed by Subject, with some 1,600 headings, and Media Indexed by Title and Author. At the end is a directory to over 300 producer /distributors and an index of subject headings. The Introduction discusses selection criteria; all entries received recommendation in at least one of the sources listed. A complete entry plus short annotation is provided in the title/author index and a brief entry is used in the subject index. An asterisk indicates that the title was recommended in three sources and is considered an important first purchase. Of the 576 titles in this 'Nucleus Collection,' 123 are 16mm films. The collection is a significant first attempt at a broadly based selection of AV materials for elementary schools." Wynar. Guide to Ref Bks for Sch Media Centers

National Information Center for Educational Media
[NICEM Indexes to nonbook media] The Center
016.3713

1 Audio-visual materials—Catalogs
Contains indexes to: 16mm educational films (3v) $99.50: 35mm filmstrips (2v) $78.50: Educational overhead transparencies (2v) $68.50: Educational audio tapes $42.50: Educational video tapes $26.50: Educational records $42.50; 8mm motion cartridges $42.50; Educational slides $38.50; Producers and distributors $19.50; Psychology—multimedia $26.50; Vocational and technical education—multimedia $26.50; Health and safety education—multimedia $26.50; Black history and studies—multimedia $19.50; Ecology—multimedia $19.50

Also available is an updated subscription service, called Update of nonbook media $388.50 for ten yearly volumes beginning in 1973

New York Library Association. Children's and Young Adult Services Section

Films for children; a selected list. Prepared by New York Library Association, Children's and Young Adult Services Section. Committee: Films for children, Mrs. Madalynne Schoenfeld [and others]. 2d ed. The Association 1969 32p pa $1
016.3713

1 Moving pictures—Catalogs

First published 1966

"Included in this list are about 100 well-chosen 16mm films considered to be of outstanding quality. Alphabetically arranged by title, the entries give the title, producer/distributor, date, running time, color or black and white, sales price, and rather complete annotation. Preceding the main text is an introduction telling how to plan and execute a successful film program. A bibliography, a subject index, and a directory of distributors are also included." Peterson. Ref Bks for Elem and Jr High Sch Libraries

Previews; non-print software & hardware news & reviews. Bowker $5 a year
016.3713

1 Audio-visual materials—Periodicals 2 Audio-visual materials—Reviews
ISSN 0000-0051
Monthly (September through May). First published 1972 with title: LJ/SLJ Previews

"Consists primarily of reviews of various types of audio-visual materials which, before September 1971, appeared in separate columns in 'Library Journal.' Covered in reviews are 16mm films, 8mm silent films, 35mm filmstrips, transparencies, slides, prints, maps, charts, games, and multimedia kits. About 130 titles appear in each issue. The 'Audiovisual Guide: A Multimedia Subject List' announces new titles in advance of their release dates." Peterson. Ref Bks for Elem and Jr High Sch Libraries

Rice, Susan

(ed.) Films kids like; a catalog of short films for children. Comp. and ed. by Susan Rice; assisted by Barbara Ludlum. Published for Center for Understanding Media, Inc. by A.L.A. 1973 150p illus pa $5.50
016.3713

1 Moving pictures—Catalogs
ISBN 0-8389-0152-2
"This collection of 229 short films for children up to age twelve was selected by the staff of the Children's Film Theater in New York. Arranged alphabetically by film title, the list contains rather long annotations often based on the children's reactions. Each entry gives, besides title and annotation, a technical description, distributor, and the country where it originated. Films are not curriculum oriented but most could be used advantageously in the classroom." Peterson. Ref Bks for Elem and Jr High Sch Libraries

Taggart, Dorothy T.

A guide to sources in educational media and technology. Scarecrow 1975 156p $6
016.3713

1 Audio-visual education—Bibliography 2 Teaching—Aids and devices—Bibliography
ISBN 0-8108-0781-5
This bibliography of educational media material contains chapters covering selection of media materials, facility planning, instructional film and television, programed instruction, computer assisted instruction, design and production of instructional materials and media in curriculum design, select bibliography of periodicals on educational media, professional organizations, and indexes

Includes addresses of publishers, as well as indexes of both authors and titles

016.398 Bibliographies of folklore

Folklore of the North American Indians; an annotated bibliography; comp. by Judith C. Ullom, Children's Book Section. Library of Congress [for sale by the Supt. of Docs.] 1969 126p illus map $4.05
016.398

1 Folklore, Indian—Bibliography 2 Indians of North America—Legends—Bibliography

Folklore of the North American Indians—*Continued*

"The Children's Book Section of Library of Congress compiled this selective bibliography for the compiler or reteller of these folktales, for the storyteller or librarian serving children, and for the child's own reading. Stories included were chosen on the basis of the following criteria: (1) a statement of sources and faithfulness to them; (2) a true reflection of Indian cosmology, and (3) a written style that retains the spirit and poetry of the Indian's native manner of telling. Entries are arranged by geographic locale and alphabetically by author in each section. In addition to the rather detailed annotations, each entry lists complete bibliographical data." Peterson. Ref Bks for Elem and Jr High Sch Libraries

016.5   Bibliographies of science

Appraisal. [Published by] The Children's Science Book Review Committee $4 a year   016.5
1 Science—Bibliography—Periodicals 2 Book reviews
ISSN 0003-7052
Triennial. First published 1967
"The unique feature of this journal is its dual reviews. Each of the 50 to 75 titles covered in each issue is reviewed first by a librarian and then by a subject specialist. Each review is 50 to 100 words long accompanied by a grade-level range and a rating code (unsatisfactory to excellent). Includes books on elementary through high school levels. All reviews are signed." Wynar. Guide to Ref Bks for Sch Media Centers

016.505   Bibliographies of science—Periodicals

Science Books & Films. Am. Assn. for the Advancement of Science $16 per year   016.505
1 Science—Bibliography—Periodicals 2 Book reviews 3 Moving pictures—Reviews
ISSN 0036-8253
Quarterly. First published 1965 with title: Science Books: a quarterly review
This periodical reviews trade books, textbooks, reference books and 16mm films in the pure and applied sciences "for all age/grade levels, primary through adult. Arrangement is by Dewey Decimal numbers. Entries provide full bibliographic data, including a grade level code and evaluative annotations aimed at laymen." Wynar. Guide to Ref Bks for Sch Media Centers

016.7899   Bibliographies of recordings

New York Library Association. Children's and Young Adult Services Section
Recordings for children; a selected list of records and cassettes. 3d ed. The Association 1972 40p pa $3   016.7899
1 Phonograph records—Bibliography 2 Magnetic recorders and recording—Bibliography
"Committee: Recordings for Children. Marilyn

Iarusso, co-chairman; Mary Nicholaou, co-chairman; Mary Strang [and] Clara Hulton." Title page
First published 1961
"Approximately 450 highly selective titles are included in this subject arranged bibliography. Both disc recordings and cassettes are chosen for children ranging in age from preschool to age 13. Prepared with emphasis on recordings for home and recreational use, the list covers a wide range of subjects and includes both musical and nonmusical recordings. Entries give album title, composer/author, performing group, narrator, producer/recording company, record number, and a brief annotation." Peterson. Ref Bks for Elem and Jr High Sch Libraries

016.8   Bibliographies of literature

Hotchkiss, Jeanette
European historical fiction and biography for children and young people. 2d ed. Scarecrow 1972 272p $8.50   016.8
1 Europe—History—Fiction—Bibliography 2 Europe—Biography—Bibliography
ISBN 0-8108-0515-4
First published 1967 with title: European historical fiction for children and young people
This bibliography "lists 1,341 books set in the British Isles and continental Europe, including some juvenile history as well as fiction and biography, grouped under geographical regions by historical period. Titles, selected on the basis of historical accuracy, literary merit, readability, and good taste, are briefly annotated, with general age level given. Separate author, title, and biographical indexes are appended." Booklist

Rosenberg, Judith K.
Young people's literature in series: fiction; an annotated bibliographical guide [by] Judith K. Rosenberg & Kenyon C. Rosenberg. Libs. Unlimited 1972 176p $7.50   016.8
1 Fiction—Bibliography
ISBN 0-87287-060-X
Companion volume to the authors': Young people's literature in series: publishers' and non-fiction series, entered in class 011
This bibliography listing 1,400 titles is "a step-saver for every librarian serving fiction to [young readers]. . . . The bibliographers have listed and annotated every fictional juvenile series for grades three through nine published since 1955 and point out that Frank Gardner's 'Sequels' (London, Library Assn.) covers most series published before that date. Older series with new titles published after 1955 are noted and the bottom-of-the-barrel old chestnuts with occasional additions or reprintings (Hardy Boys, Ms. Ames, Ms. Drew, the Bobbseys, the Peppers and Oz) are omitted. There is a series title index and an individual title index, but the main body of the book is the alphabetical author listing with each author's series arranged in chronological order. . . . The annotations are short critical evaluations because the bibliography is intended as a selection aid." Library J

016.807   Bibliographies of literary awards

Children's books: awards and prizes. Children's Bk. Council pa $4.95   016.807
1 Literary prizes—Bibliography 2 Children's literature—Bibliography

Children's books—Continued

Biennial. First published 1969

This is "a handy compilation of 'honors awarded in the children's book field by organization, schools, universities, publishers, and newspapers. Major international and foreign awards of English-speaking countries are included' (Introduction). Awards are listed alphabetically and entries give a short history of the awards, followed by a list of all winners. A table of contents lists the 53 awards; an author/illustrator index and a title index are also provided." Wynar. Guide to Ref Bks for Sch Media Centers [Review of 1971 edition]

016.813 Bibliographies of American fiction

Hotchkiss, Jeanette

American historical fiction and biography for children and young people. Scarecrow 1973 318p $8.50
                                                            016.813

1 U.S.—History—Fiction—Bibliography 2 U.S.—Biography—Bibliography 3 America—History—Fiction—Bibliography

ISBN 0-8108-0650-9

"An annotated bibliography of 1,600 titles, designed to aid teachers, librarians, and students themselves in locating authentic and exciting novels and biographies concerning the history of both Americas. Arranged chronologically in the first section and topically in the second one, the list contains symbols indicating reader ability and interest levels from kindergarten through high school." Peterson. Ref Bks for Elem and Jr High Sch Libraries

016.9 Bibliographies of history

Metzner, Seymour

World history in juvenile books: a geographical and chronological guide. Wilson, H.W. 1973 356p $12
                                                            016.9

1 History—Bibliography 2 Historical fiction—Bibliography 3 Biography—Bibliography

ISBN 0-8242-0441-7

Companion volume to: American history in juvenile books, entered in class 016.973

"This bibliography lists around 2,700 titles for elementary and junior high school age groups relating to political and social aspects of world history. Each of ten chapters covers a large geographical area (e.g., Africa). The last chapter covers subjects of international interest. Books under each country are categorized as fiction, nonfiction and biography. Where there are many books available, chronological subheadings are used. Author, title, publisher, year, grade level and a brief annotation (when needed to disclose the subject) are provided. Selection was made from 'Books in Print', publishers' catalogs, and review journals, and all were available in the spring of 1970." Cur Ref Bks

016.92 Bibliographies of biographies

Kerr, Laura J.

(comp.) Who's where in books; an index to biographical material. Mich. Assn. of School Librarians 1971 313p $6
                                                            016.92

1 Biography—Bibliography 2 Biography—Indexes

"An analytical index to collective biographies for elementary, junior, and senior high school readers, it is produced in loose-leaf format for easy updating to reflect a library's collection. Some 4,000 biographies are referenced. Part one is an alphabetical listing of 551 collective biographies arranged by author or editor. Each entry is assigned a letter-number symbol and each gives the title, publisher, date, and a blank space for a call number. Part two is an index to subjects and to biographees, arranged in alphabetical order (under each letter subjects are listed first, followed by biographees). The symbols shown for each entry refer to books listed in part one; however, no page references are provided." Wynar. Guide to Ref Bks for Sch Media Centers

016.9701 Bibliographies of American Indians

Byler, Mary Gloyne

(comp.) American Indian authors for young readers; a selected bibliography. Comp. and with an introduction by Mary Gloyne Byler. Assn. of Am. Indian Affairs [distributed by Interbk. Inc.] 1973 26p pa $1
                                                            016.9701

1 Indians of North America—Bibliography 2 Indian literature—Bibliography

ISBN 0-913456-59-4

This bibliography has been compiled with the aim of providing alternatives to children's books which stereotype the American Indian. Limited to books written by American Indian authors, this annotated list of approximately two hundred titles is alphabetically arranged by author. Tribal affiliation is noted. A list of publishers' addresses is supplied

Stensland, Anna Lee

Literature by and about the American Indian; an annotated bibliography for junior and senior high school students. Natl. Council of Teachers of English 1973 208p pa $3.95
                                                            016.9701

1 Indians of North America—Bibliography 2 Indian literature—Bibliography

ISBN 0-8141-4203-7

Although designed primarily for junior and senior high school students this bibliography also includes material useful for students in the upper elementary grades

Descriptive and critical annotations of books are arranged into the following sections: myth, legend, oratory, and poetry; fiction; drama; biography and autobiography; history; anthropology and archaeology; modern life and problems; music, arts and crafts; and aids for the teacher. There are also study guides to 8 books, bio-bibliographies of 25 American Indian authors, and a list of basic books for a library collection. Sources of additional materials, a directory of publishers, and author and title indexes are appended

016.973 Bibliographies of American history

Metzner, Seymour

American history in juvenile books; a chronological guide. Wilson, H.W. 1966 329p $10   016.973

1 U.S.—History—Bibliography 2 U.S.—Biography—Bibliography

ISBN 0-8242-0003-9

Metzner, Seymour—*Continued*

Companion volume to: World history in juvenile books, entered in class 016.9

"More than 2,000 trade books, both fiction and non-fiction, relating to American history, are arranged chronologically with topical subheadings. A comprehensive list for elementary and junior high school students, it includes for each entry the full bibliographical information, the suggested grade level span, and a brief annotation if the title does not indicate the book's subject. This guide is invaluable for enriching the social studies program." Peterson. Ref Bks for Elem and Jr High Sch Libraries

016.9733   Bibliographies of the American Revolution

Coughlan, Margaret N.

(ed.) Creating independence, 1763-1789; background reading for young people; a selected annotated bibliography. Lib. of Congress [for sale by the Supt. of Docs.] 1972 62p illus pa 75¢   016.9733

1 U.S.—History—Revolution—Bibliography
ISBN 0-8444-0029-7

Compiled by the Children's Book Section, General Reference and Bibliography Division of the Library of Congress

This "attractively designed publication is an invaluable resource for librarians and teachers. Scholarly, readable annotations indicate the importance of the works selected and testify to meticulous research. The Preface by Virginia Haviland lists the criteria used for selection. The significance of these criteria is further developed in the pithy introduction by Richard B. Morris . . . which sets the American Revolution in historical perspective. Of particular interest to educators are the instructions for ordering photocopies of all illustrations—including reproductions of colonial currency—from the Library's photoduplication department. A unique contribution; a fundamental acquisition." Horn Bk

020.75   Book collecting

Blanck, Jacob

Peter Parley to Penrod; a bibliographical description of the best-loved American juvenile books. Mark Press 1974 [c1938] 153p $15   020.75

1 Book collecting 2 Children's literature—Bibliography

First published 1938 by Bowker

"A selected bibliography of about 115 American children's books, published from 1827 to 1926, that are book collectors' items. General cataloging information, collation, descriptions of format of first editions, and brief notes are included. Literary quality was not a factor in the selection." Booklist

Quayle, Eric

The collector's book of children's books. Photographs by Gabriel Monro. Potter, C.N. 1971 144p illus $8.95   020.75

1 Book collecting 2 Children's literature—History and criticism

The author "has created a unique history of children's literature from the earliest juvenile book (1578) through the beginning of the 20th century. Magnificent illustrations (many in color) reproduced from the author's own extensive collection, vividly portray the

customs and costumes of children from the late 16th century onwards. In addition to recounting the historical development of children's literature, the author describes each individual work including the bibliographical details as well as interesting facts about the author, illustrator, and publisher. Quayle's collection includes not only early printed books, but toy books, periodicals, and 'penny dreadfuls,' each of which is described in text and illustration." Choice

Bibliography: p138

Rosenbach, A. S. W.

Early American children's books; with bibliographical descriptions of the books in his private collection. Foreword by A. Edward Newton illus

020.75

1 Book collecting 2 Children's literature—Bibliography

Some editions are:
Kraus Reprint Co. $14.50 (ISBN 0-527-77002-7)
Smith, P. $7.50 (ISBN 0-8446-0239-6)

First published 1933 by Southworth Press

"The book contains titles, with descriptive and historical notes, for 816 books, with 104 illustrations. Each title is complete with city of publication, publisher and date, size, number of leaves, signature numbers, illustrations, binding and record of mention in Sabin or Evans; there is a fine set of indexes." N Y Her Trib Bks

"Dr. Rosenbach's introduction is amusing and informative, and his notes describe the contents and character of each of the items in his collection, with copious and well-chosen quotations." Times (London) Lit Sup

Targ, William

(ed.) Bibliophile in the nursery; a bookman's treasury of collector's lore on old and rare children's books. Scarecrow [1969 c1957] 503p illus $17

020.75

1 Book collecting 2 Children's literature—History and criticism

ISBN 0-8108-0269-4

Reprint of the title first published 1957 by World

"A miscellany of writings on children's literature, introduced by the editor's enthusiastic essay on collecting rare children's books, both old and modern. Paul Hazard, Marchette Chute, Richard Altick, Iona and Peter Opie, and Ellery Queen are a few of the authors represented, and their topics include education in Chaucer's day, uncovering biographical evidence on Sir Thomas Malory, the story of the Brothers Grimm, side lights on 'Little Women', reading fare offered to Puritan children and to children in the nineteenth century, illustrators, Book Week, and the Newbery and Caldecott medals. A book to delight all those who have a particular interest in children's books; unfortunately its reference use is restricted by the lack of an index." Booklist

021   The library and society

Bomar, Cora Paul

Guide to the development of educational media selection centers [by] Cora Paul Bomar, M. Ann Heidbreder and Carol A. Nemeyer. A.L.A. 1973 102p illus (ALA Studies in librarianship) pa $5   021

1 Instructional materials centers
ISBN 0-8389-0123-9

This "report proceeds on the assumption that all kinds of media are important. . . . An effort is made to avoid duplicating many of the details supporting the significant findings recorded in the Phase I report:

Bomar, Cora Paul—*Continued*
'Educational Media Selection Centers' [entered below under Rowell]. . . . The 'Guide' is not intended as a blueprint for establishing uniform media centers, nor should it be construed as a set of standards. The ideas and data offered here should, however, stimulate creative thinking about ways to improve existing centers and begin new ones." Preface

Rowell, John
Educational media selection centers; identification and analysis of current practices [by] John Rowell and M. Ann Heidbreder. A.L.A. 1971 177p (ALA Studies in librarianship) pa $4.50   021
1 Instructional materials centers
ISBN 0-8389-0088-7
"The object of the study is to identify and record the current practices and attitudes in some 440 leading educational media selection centres throughout the United States and to make recommendations for their more effective operation as a preliminary information gathering process prior to publishing a 'Guide to the development of educational media selection centers' [entered above under Bomar]." Australian Library J
"Though this work obviously will be of only limited value to most educators, it gives an excellent overview of the present state of selection centers and suggestions for future centers for those educators interested or involved in planning them." A.L.A. RQ

025.17   Treatment of special materials

Hicks, Warren
Developing multi-media libraries, by Warren B. Hicks [and] Alma M. Tillin. Bowker 1970 199p illus $12.50   025.17
1 Audio-visual materials
ISBN 0-8352-0265-8
Handling and integrating non-book materials into existing collections by means of book-based library skills is the subject of this guide for librarians

025.3   Cataloging

ALA Rules for filing catalog cards; prepared by the ALA Editorial Committee's Subcommittee on the ALA Rules for filing catalog cards. Pauline A. Seely, chairman and editor. 2d ed. abridged. A.L.A. 1968 94p pa $2.25   025.3
1 Files and filing
ISBN 0-8389-0001-1
First unabridged edition published 1942. This is an abridgement of the 2d edition, also published 1968
"Consists of the same basic rules as the full version, but with most of the specialized and explanatory material omitted. It should be adequate for the needs of most small and medium-sized general libraries, and also be useful as the basic tool for teaching filers in any size library. . . . The basic order recommended in this edition is straight alphabetical, disregarding punctuation, with just a few exceptions." Preface

Akers, Susan Grey
Simple library cataloging. 5th ed. Scarecrow 1969 345p illus $7.50   025.3
1 Cataloging
ISBN 0-8108-0255-4

First published 1927 by American Library Association
This manual of library classification and cataloging has been designed for the inexperienced or untrained librarian working in a small library, although it can also serve as an introduction for library school students. Fundamental classification and cataloging rules are presented with numerous illustrations and an appendix of sample catalog cards. The volume surveys the use of the Dewey Decimal Classification tables, Sears List of Subject Headings, the Anglo-American Cataloging Rules, and the A.L.A. Rules for Filing Catalog Cards. There is also a section dealing with centralized and cooperative cataloging
Bibliography: p332-34

Anglo-American cataloging rules. Prepared by the American Library Association, the Library of Congress, the Library Association, and the Canadian Library Association. North American text with supplement of additions and changes. A.L.A. 1970 xxii, 409p $10, pa $5   025.3
1 Cataloging
ISBN 0-8389-3011-5; 0-8389-3119-7
First published 1967
Supersedes the A.L.A. cataloging rules for author and title entries, and includes a revision of the Rules for descriptive cataloging in the Library of Congress
General editor: C. Sumner Spalding
"Each rule dealing with a specific problem is to be understood in the context of the more general rules. . . . The rules are divided into three main parts, the first two dealing with books and book-like materials. Part I is concerned with entry and heading; Part II with description. The chapters of Part III are devoted to specific types of non-book materials and the rules in each chapter are normally grouped into rules of entry and rules of description. The rules in each group are primarily those that are either additional to or different from those for book-like materials. In no case is a chapter of Part III completely self-contained." Introduction
This is "the definitive codification of cataloging rules for author and title entries. Appendices include a glossary, abbreviations used in headings, rules of style for headings, and transliteration tables." A.L.A.

Piercy, Esther J.
Commonsense cataloging; a manual for the organization of books and other materials in school and small public libraries. 2d ed. Rev. by Marian Sanner. Wilson, H.W. 1974 233p illus $9   025.3
1 Cataloging
ISBN 0-8242-0009-8
First published 1965
Designed as a practical manual for the beginning cataloger, the book proceeds from the general to the specific, from principles to practice. The appendixes include routines, a glossary and a bibliography

Sears List of subject headings. 10th ed. Edited by Barbara M. Westby. Wilson, H.W. 1972 xlvi, 590p illus $12   025.3
1 Subject headings
ISBN 0-8242-0445-X
New edition in preparation
First published 1923 with title: List of subject headings for small libraries, by Minnie Earl Sears
A list of headings "which follows the Library of Congress form of headings, abridged and simplified to meet the needs of smaller libraries." Cheney. Fundamental Ref Sources
Contents: Subject headings: principles and applications of the Sears List; Sample page of checking; Directions for use [summary]; List of subject headings: Appendix: Black subject headings

Sears List of subject headings—*Continued*
This is the list of subject headings used for this catalog

Weihs, Jean Riddle
Nonbook materials; the organization of integrated collections [by] Jean Riddle Weihs, Shirley Lewis [and] Janet Macdonald, in consultation with the CLA/ALA/AECT/EMAC/CAML Advisory Committee on the Cataloguing of Nonbook Materials. Can.Lib. Assn. 1973 107p illus $7   025.3
1 Cataloging—Audio-visual materials
ISBN 0-88802-091-0
Also available from A.L.A. (ISBN 0-8389-3144-8)
This book "has been written for all types of libraries and media centres which wish to have an omnimedia catalogue, i.e., one in which the entries for all materials, both book and nonbook, are interfiled. In order to integrate all entries successfully the same cataloguing principles should apply to all media. . . . Therefore, 'Nonbook Materials' has developed its rules according to the precepts of Parts I and II of the 'Anglo-American Cataloging Rules,' varying these rules only when the nature of the material demands it. It is impossible to predict new media which may be developed in the future. These rules have been written to encompass the cataloguing of new formats of existing media without the confusion and time lapse which attends the adoption of new rules. This book presupposes a knowledge of book cataloguing and basic cataloguing principles. Throughout its text, references are made to the 'Anglo-American Cataloging Rules,' [entered above] which is to be used for the detailed construction of main and added entries, dates, format of notes, etc." Introduction

025.4   Classification

Dewey, Melvil
Abridged Dewey Decimal classification and relative index; devised by Melvil Dewey. Edition 10. Forest Press 1971 529p $12   025.4
1 Classification, Dewey Decimal
ISBN 0-910608-13-X
Also available from The H. W. Wilson Company
First abridged edition published 1894
"Designed primarily for small general libraries, especially elementary and secondary school and small public libraries, in English-speaking countries, libraries with up to 20,000 titles that do not expect to grow much larger. . . . As well as having shorter numbers, the present abridged edition in some places presents different classification policies and slightly different numbers from those in [the unabridged] Edition 18." Publisher's Foreword
This is the classification system used for this catalog, with modifications where necessary to conform to past Wilson Company practice

027.05   Libraries— Periodicals

Wilson Library Bulletin. Wilson, H.W. $11 per year   027.05
1 Libraries—Periodicals 2 Books and reading
ISSN 0043-5651
Monthly except July and August. First published 1914 with title: The Wilson Bulletin
"Along with 'Library Journal,' [this is] the only national library magazine published by an independent publisher. It shows. Under the Eshelman editorship the magazine has grown in its importance to all types of libraries. Each issue is usually given to a single topic from sex education for children to survey articles on the state of the literature in everything from art to zoology. The writing style is professional, lively, informative, and quite often controversial. There are many departments, including excellent reference book reviews and government document surveys. The makeup from the cover to the last page is as imaginative as are the contents." Katz. Magazines for Libraries

027.6   Libraries for special groups

The Right to read and the nation's libraries; ed. by the Right to Read committees of the American Association of School Librarians, Children's Services Division [and the] Public Library Association. A.L.A. 1974 109p illus pa $5.50   027.6
1 Right to Read program
ISBN 0-8389-0193-X
"Published for the American Association of School Librarians and the Public Library Association"
This book opens with excerpts from a speech by the late James E. Allen, former U.S. Commissioner of Education, calling for a national commitment to a "Right to Read" program aimed at the 25% of the U.S. population which is functionally illiterate. An introductory essay, by Grace T. Stevenson, on the library reading program is followed by reports on "Right to Read" programs in school and public libraries and adult education centers
"Information is provided on materials, staff, physical facilities, and cooperation with other community organizations. A number of special projects are described as examples of the involvement of libraries and adult education centers with special emphasis on tailoring the program to fit community needs. The list of sources of materials and a bibliography should prove helpful to anyone planning or wishing to expand a literacy program." Booklist

027.62   Libraries for children

Broderick, Dorothy M.
An introduction to children's work in public libraries. Wilson, H.W. 1965 176p $6   027.62
1 Libraries, Children's 2 Children's literature
ISBN 0-8242-0027-6
Building a proper collection of books for children and insuring maximum use of that collection is the subject of this book, the first half of which treats the philosophy of service to children, problems of book selection, organization and administration of children's rooms, and the relation of the library to the community. The second half deals with the various areas in children's literature, and closes with a chapter on books about children's books, an appendix listing books mentioned in the text, and an index
"Written in the author's usual inimitable style, this book will be useful for library education classes and independent study. State and regional consultants will find it invaluable for in-service training." Library Q
Includes bibliographies

Burke, J. Gordon
(ed.) Children's library service: school or public? Ed. by J. Gordon Burke and Gerald R. Shields. Scarecrow 1974 131p $5   027.62
  1 Libraries, Children's—New York (State) 2 School libraries—New York (State)
  ISBN 0-8108-0688-6
  This book includes four essays in reaction to the 1970 report by the New York State Commissioner of Education's Committee on Library Development which recommended that all library services to children be transferred to school media centers. Appendices include the recommendations of the Regents of the University of the State of New York for library service, and the guidelines for library services to children developed by the Task Force on Library Service to Children
  "The eminence of the contributors and the timeliness of the subject make this invaluable to all who are concerned about 'Where Will All the Children Go?' " Ref Services Rev
  Bibliography on public/school library cooperation: p113-27

Hill, Janet
  Children are people; the librarian in the community. Crowell [1974 c1973] 163p illus $6.95   027.62
  1 Libraries, Children's 2 Libraries and community 3 Children's literature
  ISBN 0-690-00475-3
  First published 1973 in England
  "The author, a London children's librarian, shares her insight on the work of the librarian in the community, with suggestions on storytelling, book selection and concerns of minority groups." Wis Library Bul
  "The book is interesting because the author has done a fine job in her career as a children's librarian in Lambeth, but the problems of British librarians are not the problems of those in the U.S.A. Her philosophy, however, is one that librarians everywhere can adopt, 'taking library services out to those who use them least and possibly need them most.' " Cath Library World

Long, Harriet G.
  Public library service to children: foundation and development. Scarecrow 1969 162p $6   027.62
  1 Libraries, Children's—History 2 Library service 3 Cleveland. Public Library
  ISBN 0-8108-0291-0
  "An overview that puts public library service to children in a historical context, showing how this phase of public library work in the U.S. was shaped by the political, social, and economic environment since the Colonial period. A final chapter is devoted exclusively to work with children in the Cleveland Public Library and other of Cleveland's agencies and institutions during the nineteenth and early twentieth centuries." Booklist
  Selected bibliography: p155-58

027.6205   Children's libraries— Periodicals

Top of the News. A.L.A. $15 per year   027.6205
  1 Libraries, Children's—Periodicals
  ISSN 0040-9286
  Quarterly. First published 1942
  "Journal of the Children's Services Division and the Young Adult Services Division of the American Library Association"

"This and 'School Library Journal' are the best general magazines covering the field of school librarianship from the elementary through high school scene. It has improved with the years, and while the writing is uneven, the overall feeling is of dedication with a dash of realism, and a larger dash of cynicism about instant cures for anything. Most of the authors are practicing librarians who know of what they speak. One of the best features for readers of this compilation is the magazine column which gives succinct, usually critical reviews of newer magazines. On occasion a group effort is launched, e.g., cycle magazines, which evaluates a number of similar titles. The short book reviews are equally good." Katz. Magazines for Libraries

027.8   School libraries

Davies, Ruth Ann
  The school library media program: a force for educational excellence. 2d. ed. Bowker 1973 484p illus $12.50   027.8
  1 School libraries
  ISBN 0-8352-0641-6
  First published 1969 with title: The school library
  "Defining the school librarian as team teacher, media programming engineer, and curriculum energizer, the author suggests requisite approaches and program methods for realizing this composite role and provides basic sample curriculum guides and other aids. Evaluation of library program effectiveness and supervisor's role are also covered. . . . Derived from the author's University of Pittsburgh course for both education and library students." Booklist [Review of first edition]
  "Five curriculum areas are discussed in light of the media center. This is done thoroughly and should be most helpful to educators interested in the total involvement of students, teachers and librarians. The appendixes are also worthwhile, including self-evaluating checklists, book evaluation guidelines, sample policy statements, even a guide for constructing mini-courses." Cath Library World
  Bibliography: p467-76

Gillespie, John T.
  Creating a school media program [by] John T. Gillespie [and] Diana L. Spirt. Bowker 1973 236p $11.50   027.8
  1 School libraries 2 Instructional materials centers
  ISBN 0-8352-0484-7
  This book is intended as a "text on both the principles and practices of creating, organizing, and administering a school media center. . . . The focus of the book is on practical considerations for establishing and operating the media center within a single school. The authors have tried to emphasize the elements that distinguish a media center from the conventional school library and in so doing have attempted to anticipate difficulties that media personnel might encounter in trying to convert from one type of center to another. . . . Only brief mention is made of such technical services techniques as cataloging because the authors believe these routines are best performed through the use of commercial processing sources or district-wide preparation centers. . . . While the authors have discussed the principles and criteria for choosing selection aids, they have omitted a detailed listing of bibliographies and review sources because so many of these lists already exist. There is, however, extensive coverage, particularly in the appendixes, of the characteristics, strengths and weaknesses, and evaluative criteria connected with the selection and use of various educational materials and equipment." Preface
  Selected readings: p223-26

Gillespie, John T.—*Continued*

The young phenomenon: paperbacks in our schools [by] John T. Gillespie [and] Diana L. Spirt. A.L.A. 1972 140p (ALA Studies in librarianship) pa $5

027.8

1 Paperback books 2 School libraries
ISBN 0-8389-0133-6
Companion volume to: Paperback books for young people, entered in class 070.5

"A survey of the use of paperbacks in elementary and secondary schools based on an interpretation and analysis of the computer data from a 1967 school paperback survey conducted by the School Improvement Committee of the American Association of School Librarians, augmented by a 1970 follow-up survey designed by the authors to update the earlier questionnaire. The book highlights effective programs and treats book selection, administration of paperback collections, and the sale of paperbacks in schools. A practical guide to dealing with paperbacks this . . . will be useful . . . for librarians, teachers, and others concerned with paperbacks." Booklist

Selected bibliography: p113-18

Lowrie, Jean Elizabeth

Elementary school libraries. 2d ed. Scarecrow 1970 238p $6

027.8

1 School libraries
ISBN 0-8108-0305-4
First published 1961
Partial contents: Curriculum supportive experiences in the middle grades; Reading guidance in the middle grades library program; "How do I find—"; The teacher and the school library; Role of the school administrator; Community relationships; Children's books mentioned in text; Bibliography

Nickel, Mildred L.

Steps to service; a handbook of procedures for the school library media center. A.L.A. 1975 124p illus pa $4.50

027.8

1 School libraries 2 Instructional materials centers
ISBN 0-8389-0161-1
This manual is "designed as a source of immediate help and guidance to inexperienced and beginning professionals, as well as a review for experienced professionals seeking to reevaluate their programs. . . . [It] treats such basic concerns as budget, evaluation and selection of materials, ordering and receiving, processing, use of materials, mending, rebinding, discarding, inventory, reports, supplies, personal service, instruction in the use of media, staff relationships, and others. The work also discusses recent technological developments as they affect the school library media center." Publisher's note

Includes a directory of publishers, producers and suppliers

Glossary: p109-12

Sullivan, Peggy

Problems in school media management. Bowker 1971 245p (Bowker Ser. in problem-centered approaches to librarianship) $12.95

027.8

1 School libraries 2 Instructional materials centers
ISBN 0-8352-0427-8
The author presents thirty case studies for librarians and library students reviewing current problems involving the administration and organization of school media programs

"Undoubtedly the book will prove invaluable as a supplementary text, as it can provide the basis for discussions, for role playing, and for simulation exercises. It covers a vast range of problems, from those related to teaching library skills to censorship, and covers numerous critical areas. The cases are germane and representative, but are not intended to be comprehensive." Sch Library J

Ward, Pearl L.

(comp.) The school media center; a book of readings; comp. by Pearl L. Ward and Robert Beacon. Scarecrow 1973 299p $8.50

027.8

1 School libraries 2 Instructional materials centers
ISBN 0-8108-0618-5
A collection of readings on the important aspects of media centers. Subjects covered include federal legislation, standards, budgeting, administration and personnel. The newer media such as cassette tapes, film loops and remote access are also discussed

Bibliography: p282-83

027.805   School libraries— Periodicals

SLJ/School Library Journal; for children's, young adult, and school librarians. Bowker $10.80 per year, 2 years $18.35, 3 years $25.90   027.805

1 School libraries—Periodicals 2 Book reviews
ISSN 0000-0035
Monthly September through May. First published 1954 with title: Junior libraries

"The best of the magazines devoted to work with children and teen-agers in libraries. . . . Articles cover all aspects of work with young people, but the magazine has gained a deserved reputation for publishing material (both from librarians and from staffers) which leads, rather than follows, the movements and surges in the library field. There are usually four or five excellent, well-written articles per issue, a number of departments (news, professional reading, recordings, screenings, etc.), and first-rate book reviews. The reviews in themselves make the magazine a must for any library. They are equal to, and often superior to, those found in other sources." Katz. Magazines for Libraries

School Librarian. School Library Assn. $4.50 per year   027.805

1 School libraries—Periodicals 2 Book reviews
ISSN 0036-6595
Quarterly. First published 1937

"Although this publication is the journal of the English School Library Association, between 60 and 70 pages jof each issue are devoted to book reviews. Geared for librarians, the signed reviews are well written, descriptive, evaluative, and often critical. Emphasis is placed on British books for children and young adults, but several books on librarianship and new reference materials are also included. Reviews are grouped by subject and by age level. Bibliographic references—author, title, publisher, price, date, pagination, and special features—are supplied for each review item. An index, arranged alphabetically by author, facilitates the search for a particuar selection." Katz. Magazines for Libraries

School Media Quarterly. A.L.A. $15 per year

027.805

1 School libraries—Periodicals 2 Instructional materials centers—Periodicals
First published 1972. Formerly School libraries

"Journal of the American Association of School Librarians"

"There are four or five articles, usually by practicing librarians, a number of departments, book reviews, and, of course, news of the Association. The articles are deeply involved with change in the elementary and high school library. And they are important. Along with School Library Journal

School Media Quarterly—*Continued*
[entered above] and Top of the news [entered in class 027.6205] this is a must for school libraries." Katz. Magazines for Libraries

028.1 Book reviews

Chicago. University. Graduate Library School
Bulletin of the Center for Children's Books. Univ. of Chicago Press $8 per year   028.1
1 Book reviews 2 Children's literature—Periodicals
ISSN 0008-9036
Monthly except August. First published 1945
"Both recommended and not recommended titles are included in this review periodical. Highly regarded for its critical evaluations of books, this source contains reviews for about 70 books in each issue. Entries contain grade level indications and ratings including the following: recommended, additional book of acceptable quality for collections needing more material in this area, marginal book that is slight in content or weak in style or format, not recommended, subject matter or treatment will tend to limit the book to specialized collections, and a book that will have appeal for the unusual reader only." Peterson. Ref Bks for Elem and Jr High Sch Libraries

Children's Book Review Service. Edited and distributed by Ann L. Kalkhoff, 220 Berkeley Pl, Brooklyn, N.Y. 11217 $25 per year   028.1
1 Book reviews 2 Children's literature—Periodicals
ISSN 0090-7987
Monthly. First published 1972
"Evaluative, short, signed reviews of current titles for children (elementary through junior high school). Nicely augments such standards as 'Center for Children's Books Bulletin' [entered above under Chicago. University. Graduate Library School] and 'School Library Journal' [entered in class 027.805]. . . . The librarian reviewers tend to stress comparison between a new title and an older one. Most of the emphasis is on evaluation, not on giving a full summary of the plot. One novel feature: where there is a difference between the reviewers, several viewpoints are stated. All types of books are considered, and the reviewers are aware of new developments in titles for women, minority groups, etc." Katz. Magazines for Libraries. 2d edition. Supplement

Gillespie, John
Introducing books; a guide for the middle grades, by John Gillespie and Diana Lembo. Bowker 1970 318p $12.50   028.1
1 Book reviews 2 Literature—Stories, plots, etc.
3 Books and reading
ISBN 0-8352-0215-1
Companion volume to Juniorplots, entered below
This book "gives plot analysis, thematic material, book talk material, and additional suggestions for eighty-eight books, all arranged under eleven life-goal themes, such as getting along with the family, making friends, forming a world view, respecting living creatures, and even appreciating books. . . . [Also included are lists] of related books and films, filmstrips and pictures to enliven the book talks. . . . Price and other bibliographic data are supplied for each." Cur Ref Bks
Indexed by authors, titles and subjects

Juniorplots; a book talk manual for teachers and librarians, by John Gillespie and Diana Lembo. Bowker 1967 222p $10.95   028.1
1 Book reviews 2 Literature—Stories, plots, etc.
3 Books and reading
ISBN 0-8352-0063-9
The purpose of this book is to "serve as a guide for those who give book talks to a young adult audience . . . and to aid teachers and librarians in giving reading guidance to children and young people between the ages of nine and 16. Because most book talks are planned around a theme, a thematic approach has been used in this volume. The titles have been arranged by what the authors feel to be the most important goals of adolescent reading. . . . This volume is neither a work of literary criticism, nor a listing of the best books for young adults. It is a representative selection of books that have value in a variety of book talk situations." Preface
Plot analysis, thematic material, book talk material and suggestions of similar titles are given for each of the 80 books covered
Indexed by authors, titles and subjects

The Junior Bookshelf; a review of children's books. Marsh Hall $6 per year   028.1
1 Book reviews 2 Children's literature—Periodicals
ISSN 0022-6505
Six issues per year. First published 1936
"An English magazine which reviews some 125 to 150 children's books (i.e., preschool through about the 8th grade). The reviews are well written, critical, and descriptive. Most, although not all, titles are published in England. There are excellent articles on all aspects of children's reading and books." Katz. Magazines for Libraries

Kirkus Reviews. Kirkus Service apply to publisher for price   028.1
1 Book reviews
Juvenile reviews may be subscribed to separately
Loose-leaf
Semimonthly. First published 1934
"Highly critical reviews of about 70 children's books and 140 adult books are contained in each issue of this book review service. A major advantage of this source is that it reviews titles early, often before publication of the book. Each issue is indexed with indexes cumulating at three and six month intervals." Peterson. Ref Bks for Elem and Jr High Sch Libraries

The New York Times Book Review. N. Y. Times Co. illus $13 per year   028.1
1 Book reviews
Weekly. First published 1896
"'The New York Times Book Review' is a section of the Sunday 'New York Times' and is available separately by subscription. The coverage is broad, aiming at new adult books of literary and cultural interest and books on contemporary political, economic, and social problems. Biography, popular history, and literature are emphasized. A moderate number of children's books are also reviewed. . . . All reviews give author, title, place and publisher, pages, price, and name of the reviewer. The young reader's page reviews from two to six books each week (about 200 or more books per year) plus additional titles contained in two Special Children's Book Issues. Picture books, fiction, and nonfiction are all included. The purpose of these reviews is to inform parents, children's librarians, and bookstore operators of those children's books most likely to be favorites or at least substantial choices for a child's home reading; some books that receive less than favorable evaluation are also reviewed." Wynar. Guide to Ref Bks for Sch Media Centers

Sutherland, Zena
(ed.) The best in children's books; the University of Chicago guide to children's literature, 1966-1972. Univ. of Chicago Press 1973 484p $12.50, pa $6.50   028.1
1 Books and reading—Best books 2 Book reviews
ISBN 0-226-78057-0; 0-226-78058-9

Sutherland, Zena—*Continued*

"A compendium of fourteen hundred reviews . . . arranged alphabetically by author and numbered sequentially for each reference from six indexes. The books are indexed by title, developmental values, curricular use, reading level, subject matter, and type of literature. Publishers, dates, and prices are indicated; and when the information has been available, British publishers and prices have been included." Horn Bk

"The book has not been planned as a balanced list in respect to an individual grade or age, or to subject or genre. The editor's selections have been made primarily on the basis of literary quality, with representation of subjects as a secondary consideration." Introduction

028.5   Reading of children

Andrews, Siri

(ed.) The Hewins lectures, 1947-1962; introduction by Frederic G. Melcher. Horn Bk. 1963 375p $10, pa $5   028.5

1 Children's literature—Addresses and essays 2 American literature—Addresses and essays
ISBN 0-87675-054-4; 0-87675-056-0

Suggested in 1946 by Frederic G. Melcher, this is "a series of lectures on New England books for children, by New England residents. . . . The first fifteen are included in this volume, and invite both a backward and forward look at children's literature. All but one of the Lectures are on some aspect of writing for children; the one exception is that on New England folklore." The author

Arbuthnot, May Hill

Children and books. 4th ed. [By] May Hill Arbuthnot [and] Zena Sutherland. Scott 1972 836p illus $14.95   028.5

1 Children's literature—History and criticism
ISBN 0-673-07609-1

First published 1947

"This edition of the standard textbook on children's books . . . provides discussions of children's needs, types of materials with a heavy emphasis on synopses and some analyses of stories, reproductions of illustrations from books, and lists of books and authors in each category. Part I covers topics relating to children's needs, book selection, and book illustration; Part II covers trends in children's literature and folklore; Part III covers poetry; Part IV, realistic fiction; Part V, biography and informational books; and Part VI, techniques for using books with children. Part VII . . . discusses research, school media centers, and issues concerning minorities, censorship, and TV. Its emphasis is on acquainting teachers with forms of literature and with specific titles, authors and illustrators of books for children from preschool through junior high school. An extensive bibliography section, a pronunciation guide for names, and an author-illustrator title index (no subject index) are at the end." Wynar. Guide to Ref Bks for Sch Media Centers

Bauer, Caroline Feller

Getting it together with books; a teletext. Ore. Educ. & Pub. Broadcasting Serv. 1974 250p illus pa $7   028.5

1 Books and reading 2 Children's literature—Bibliography

This is a viewers guide to a television course on library programs for children. It is designed to help librarians and teachers who are involved with building libraries and reading programs. The book discusses program planning and gives sample programs on various subjects such as holidays, parties, animals and crafts

Bechtel, Louise Seaman

Books in search of children; speeches and essays; selected and with an introduction by Virginia Haviland. Macmillan (N Y) 1969 xx, 268p illus $6.95
                                                                              028.5

1 Children's literature—Addresses and essays 2 Books and reading

"The growth and diversity of publishing for children is reflected in the pieces chosen to celebrate the 50th anniversary of the Children's Book Department of the Macmillan Company which was the pioneering effort of Louise Seaman Bechtel. After a graceful introduction by Virginia Haviland touching on the highlights of Bechtel's career, the selections, from 'Horn Book', 'Library Journal', and other periodicals and from her speeches, cover individual authors and illustrators, the heritage of children's literature, preparation of a publisher's catalog, and books for children under five years. The title essay is a study of the professions that contribute to books for children. Illustrations are taken from early Macmillan catalogs for boys and girls." Booklist

Index of titles, authors and artists: p256-68

Boy Scouts of America

Reading. The Association illus pa 55¢   028.5

1 Books and reading 2 Books and reading—Best books

"Merit badge series"

Intended as a guide for Boy Scouts working toward a merit badge in reading, this pamphlet encourages balance in the book fare of older boys in news, technical fields, travel, fiction, poetry and other areas

Broderick, Dorothy M.

Image of the Black in children's fiction. Bowker 1973 219p illus $13.25   028.5

1 Children's literature—History and criticism 2 Negroes in literature and art
ISBN 0-8352-0550-9

"Over 100 children's books from 1909 to 1968 are analyzed by Dr. Broderick to determine the image of blacks presented in juvenile writings. She concludes that most of them were condescendingly racist and gave a distorted picture of the black heritage. . . . The early books analyzed in the study were listed in Jacob Blanck's popular juvenile bibliography 'Peter Parly to Penrod: A Bibliographic Description of the Best-Loved American Juvenile Books, 1827-1926 (Bowker, 1938) [entered in class 020.75]. Other children's titles are from the 1908 to 1968 editions of the H. W. Wilson Company's 'Children's Catalog.' . . . Notes, a lengthy bibliography, and an index are additional valuable features of this well-researched work." Wynar. Guide to Ref Bks for Sch Media Centers

Cameron, Eleanor

The green and burning tree; on the writing and enjoyment of children's books. Little 1969 377p $6.95, pa $2.95   028.5

1 Children's literature—History and criticism
ISBN 0-316-12524-5; 0-316-12522-9

"An Atlantic Monthly Press book"

"The essays collected here were written out of joy and in appreciation of the distinguished and sometimes extraordinary books discovered throughout a lifetime. My chief reason for putting down these thoughts, aside from satisfying a compulsion, is that I have been preoccupied with the craft of writing since the age of eleven, and since my teens with the question of what makes a book memorable." Foreward

Partial contents: Fantasy; Writing itself; The child and the book; References; Bibliography

Chicago. University. Graduate Library School
A critical approach to children's literature; the thirty-first annual conference of the Graduate Library School, August 1-3, 1966. Ed. by Sara Innis Fenwick. Univ. of Chicago Press 1967 129p (Univ. of Chicago Studies in lib. science) $6.50   028.5
  1 Children's literature—History and criticism
  ISBN 0-226-24161-0
  Analyzed in Essay and general literature index
"Twelve essays ranging from such general topics as poetry for children and a psychologist's view of children's literature to such specialized subjects as children's responses to humor, machine animism in children's literature, and current reviewing of children's books. . . . Originally published as the January 1967 issue of 'Library Quarterly.' " Booklist

Cleary, Florence Damon
Blueprints for better reading; school programs for promoting skill and interest in reading. 2d ed. Wilson, H.W. 1972 312p $14   028.5
  1 Books and reading 2 Reading
  ISBN 0-8242-0406-9
  First published 1957
This book explores ways teachers and librarians can improve their reading programs in areas of selection and evaluation of books and other instructional materials
"Part I identifies the problems involved in improving reading guidance programs, and describes the forces and factors that influence the reader and the understandings required of the person who guides the reading of youth. Part II delineates the kind of organization and schedules essential in promoting effective reading guidance programs in the schools, lists the criteria for the selection and evaluation of learning materials, and explores and describes a variety of directive and nondirective approaches to reading guidance. Part III describes programs, procedures, activities, and devices for teaching young people to read critically, to acquire and use information and knowledge, to build values, appreciations, and the attendant skills that promote lasting habits of reading and reflection." Preface
  Includes bibliographies

Darton, Frederick J. H.
Children's books in England; five centuries of social life. 2d ed. Cambridge 1958 367p $15   028.5
  1 Children's literature—History and criticism
  ISBN 0-521-04774-9
  First published 1932
"A scholarly survey covering the literature from the fables of the Middle Ages to the early 20th century. Devoted to printed works 'produced ostensibly to give children spontaneous pleasure, not primarily to teach them. . . .' Thus schoolbooks are omitted." Winchell. Guide to Ref Bks. 8th edition
  Includes chapter bibliographies

Egoff, Sheila
(ed.) Only connect; readings on children's literature; ed. by Sheila Egoff, G. T. Stubbs, and L. F. Ashley. Oxford 1969 471p illus pa $5.95   028.5
  1 Children's literature—History and criticism
  ISBN 0-19-540161-1
  Analyzed in Essay and general literature index
This is a collection of forty essays, most of which were first published in various periodicals in the 1960s
"Anyone creating, selecting, reviewing, or teaching children's literature [will find] this compilation . . . distinctive, rich, and truly critical. . . . Two sections consider genres of writing for children: fantasy, the realistic animal story (a Canadian specialty), historical fiction . . . teen-age fiction, and science fiction, as perceptively viewed by Sheila Egoff herself.

Two concluding summaries concern the state of children's books today—Townsend's 'The Present State of English Children's Literature' and Miss Egoff's new 'Precepts and Pleasures: Changing Emphasis in the Writing and Criticism of Children's Literature' . . . . A most welcome volume." Horn Bk
  Selected bibliography: p453-57

The republic of childhood; a critical guide to Canadian children's literature in English. 2d ed. Oxford 1975 335p $10.95, pa $6.95   028.5
  1 Children's literature—History and criticism
  2 Children's literature—Bibliography 3 Canadian literature—History and criticism
  ISBN 0-19-540231-6; 0-19-540232-2
  First published 1967
Covering important children's books published to October 1974 this study is divided as follows: Indian and Eskimo legends; Folktales; Fantasy; Historical fiction; The realistic animal story; Realistic fiction; History and biography; Poetry and plays; Illustration and design; Picture-books and picture-storybooks
"Written by a distinguished children's librarian this excellent guide provides lengthy analysis and criticism of children's books by Canadian authors. . . . Both American and English books are drawn into the discussion to emphasize areas of weakness or strength of Canadian works. Annotated lists at the end of each chapter are limited to Canadian titles." Wynar. Guide to Ref Bks for Sch Media Centers [Review of 1967 edition]
  Includes an index of authors, titles and illustrators

Eyre, Frank
British children's books in the twentieth century. [Rev. & enl. ed] Dutton [1973 c1971] 207p illus $7.95   028.5
  1 Children's literature—History and criticism
  2 Books and reading—Best books
  ISBN 0-525-27230-5
  First published 1952 with title: 20th century children's books. This edition first published 1971 in England
"The author has examined main trends in the development of British children's books—including Australian, Canadian, and other Commonwealth productions—during the first seventy years of this century and has called attention to outstanding books. The study is confined to original imaginative works. . . . Chapter I, 'Historical Survey,' scans developments which have advanced the publishing of children's books and fostered the critical acceptance of the 'better book for children.' . . . Successive chapters deal with 'Books with Pictures,' 'The In-Between Books,' and 'Fiction for Children.' " Horn Bk
"Though the field of the 'good' children's book has now been well trodden, Mr Eyre's account of it is quite interesting (though perhaps too abundant in minor names) and his literary assessments shrewd." Times (London) Literary Sup
  Bibliography: p187-95

Halsey, Rosalie V.
Forgotten books of the American nursery: a history of the development of the American story-book. Singing Tree 1969 244p illus $8.50   028.5
  1 Children's literature—History and criticism
  ISBN 0-8103-3483-6
  A reissue of the title first published 1911 by Goodspeed
"A historical survey covering the period of 1647-1840, touching upon many authors and publishers, and replete with interesting and appropriate quotations from U.S. and British critics. A very readable and important landmark in the history of children's literature." Pellowski. The World of Children's Lit

Haviland, Virginia

(ed.) Children and literature; views and reviews.
Lothrop [1974 c1973] 468p illus $7.95   028.5
1 Children's literature—History and criticism
ISBN 0-370-01595-9
First published in paperback in 1973 by Scott,
Foresman
"An excellent background book for students and
teachers of children's literature, the author-compiler
has assembled, in one handy volume, essays, articles,
and excerpts from books on the history, development,
and evaluation of children's literature. . . . Sendak's
'Mother Goose's garnishings,' Walter de la Mare's
essay on Lewis Carroll, and Frances Clarke Sayers'
stinging commentary on Walt Disney are only a few of
the many spirited articles that add sprightliness and
vigor to the book. Perennial controversial topics such
as fantasy vs. realism, literary works vs. pedestrian
writing and comics, and standards for children's reading, are presented. Criticism and reviewing of children's books as well as the awards given writers and
illustrators both here and abroad—are all covered in
detail." Choice
Includes bibliographical references

(ed.) Yankee Doodle's literary sampler of prose,
poetry, & pictures. . . . Selected from the rare book
collections of the Library of Congress and introduced
by Virginia Haviland & Margaret N. Coughlan.
Crowell 1974 466p illus $18.95   028.5
1 Literature—Collections 2 Children's literature—
History and criticism
ISBN 0-690-00269-6
"Being an anthology of diverse works published for
the edification and/or entertainment of young readers
in America before 1900." Title page
"Included are the familiar and the little known in a
chronological assortment of readings expected to be
instructive and entertaining to the young. Initially
influenced by British models, the assertion of indigenous American character and style is shown early.
The collection provides a composite introduction to
the quality and variety available to children prior to
the twentieth century from a growing book industry as
well as in juvenile magazines. Facsimile pages with
original illustrations, some in color, add charm to a
sourcebook that also offers insights into earlier social
and moral values." Booklist
Selected bibliography: p451-58

Hazard, Paul

Books, children & men; tr. by Marguerite Mitchell.
[4th ed] Horn Bk. 1960 xxvi, 176p $6.50, pa $3.50
       028.5
1 Children's literature—History and criticism
2 Books and reading
ISBN 0-87675-050-1; 0-87675-051-X
Translation of a book on children and children's
books which appeared 1932 in France. First American
edition 1944
"Literature for children is given its place among the
literatures of the world in this series of brilliant
essays, by a distinguished French scholar, who discusses, with evident enjoyment, children's books in
terms of the cultures of various peoples." N Y Pub
Library
Bibliography: p173-76

Hoffman, Miriam

(ed.) Authors and illustrators of children's books;
writings on their lives and works [ed. by] Miriam
Hoffman and Eva Samuels. Bowker 1972 471p
$14.95   028.5
1 Children's literature—History and criticism
2 Authors 3 Illustrators
ISBN 0-8352-0523-1

A collection of articles, culled from periodicals and
newspapers, about fifty authors and illustrators of
children's literature
"The title is somewhat misleading, since illustrators
who are not also authors are omitted, as are poets.
Although a number of journals are represented, the
bulk of the articles originally appeared in 'Elementary
English.' The articles are arranged alphabetically by
biographee. Editors' notes following each article offer
some updating, although this is not always consistently handled. Notes also indicate honors and awards
given to the biographees and books published since
the date of the original article. An appendix lists each
author-illustrator's works. In spite of the wide variation in coverage, style, and length of the articles, this
biographical reader is of importance to all children's
literature collections." Wynar. Guide to Ref Bks for
Sch Media Centers

Horn Book Reflections on children's books and reading; selected from eighteen years of The Horn Book
Magazine—1949-1966; ed. by Elinor Whitney
Field. Horn Bk. 1969 367p $6.50, pa $3.50 028.5
1 Children's literature—History and criticism
ISBN 0-87675-032-3; 0-87675-033-1
Companion volume to A Horn Book Sampler on
children's books and reading, entered below
A collection of "articles and essays relating to various aspects of children's reading and literature
includes material by authors, illustrators, parents,
teachers, and librarians. Sections devoted to authors'
own descriptions of writing experiences and to recollections of visits to famous authors are especially
engaging." Booklist

A Horn Book Sampler on children's books and read-
ing; selected from twenty-five years of The Horn
Book Magazine, 1924-1948. Ed. by Norma R.
Fryatt; introduction by Bertha Mahony Miller.
Horn Bk. 1959 261p $6.50, pa $3.50   028.5
1 Children's literature—History and criticism
ISBN 0-87675-030-7; 0-87675-031-5
Companion volume to Horn Book Reflections on
children's books and reading, entered above
Analyzed in Essay and general literature index
"Articles, editorials, book reviews, and a few poems
reprinted from the 'Horn Book' from its founding in
1924 to 1948. The sampler includes essays by authors
on how certain of their stories came to be written,
evaluations of the work of such illustrators as Kate
Greenaway, Arthur Rackham, and Leslie Brooke,
criticisms of single books and of trends in children's
literature, discussions of fairy tales and books for
small children, and a group of papers addressed to
parents. Appended to two of the selections are 1959
commentaries by the original authors. Of particular
interest to children's librarians and connoisseurs of
children's literature." Booklist
"Miss Fryatt has exercised a very nice sense of the
relationship of these papers to each other. . . . Insight is I think, the key word to this sampler." N Y
Times Bk Rev

Huck, Charlotte S.

Children's literature in the elementary school. 2d
ed. [By] Charlotte S. Huck [and] Doris Young Kuhn.
Holt 1968 xxiii, 792p illus $13.50   028.5
1 Children's literature—History and criticism
ISBN 0-03-066330-X
First published 1961
"An excellent guide for teachers and librarians,
covering criteria for selection of books in many fields,
children's characteristics and interests at various ages,
ways of using books with children, and extensive subject bibliographies. Supplementary material includes
children's book awards, children's book clubs, and
other topics related to children's books." Hodges. Bks
for Elem Sch Libraries

Issues in children's book selection; a School Library Journal/Library Journal anthology; with an introduction by Lillian Gerhardt. Bowker 1973 216p $9.95   028.5
1 Book selection 2 Children's literature—History and criticism
ISBN 0-8352-0688-2
"Twenty-nine articles, first printed in 'School Library Journal,' underscore recent issues of children's book selection for librarians: the tension between censorship and selection; bias and prejudice in children's books; genre defenses and criticisms. By juxtaposing articles of different perspectives, the book provides a starting point for discussion and evaluation. . . . As an introduction to the problems of book selection or as an account of the gamut of issues affecting the contemporary children's book world, the compilation only lacks an indication that the quality of the book as a piece of literature might be an issue in children's book selection." Horn Bk

Jacobs, Leland B.
(ed.) Using literature with young children. Teachers College 1965 63p illus pa $1.95   028.5
1 Children's literature
ISBN 0-8077-1557-3
Contents: Enjoying literature with young children, by L. B. Jacobs; Providing good literature for young children, by R. E. Green; Reading aloud to young children, by K. Vandergrift; Telling stories to young children, by L. B. Jacobs; Presenting poetry to children, by L. B. Jacobs; Doing choral speaking, by S. L. Root, Jr; Relating creative experiences to literature, by E. Wenzel; Dramatizing literature with young children, by W. Zinsmaster; Enjoying literature visually, by C. F. Reasoner; Relating literature to other school learnings, by F. Shipley; Making the teacher the model in the literature experience, by J. E. Higgins; Evaluating young children's experiences with literature, by C. C. McCutcheon
Includes bibliographies

Jan, Isabelle
On children's literature; ed. by Catherine Storr; with a preface by Anne Pellowski. Schocken 1974 189p $6   028.5
1 Children's literature—History and criticism
ISBN 0-8052-3564-7
Original French edition published 1969. This translation first published 1973 in England
The author considers the sources and types of children's literature, with particular emphasis on such themes as the hero, animals, adventure, and the family
This book reads "like a series of lectures, each one perceptive and persuasively argued, but lacking a central unity. Professor Jan's strength lies in her range. She cites relevantly and with ease examples from a dozen countries. The depth of her critical penetration varies greatly. . . . As usual with critics in this field, her judgments rest on psychological and sociological principles rather than on stylistic qualities." Times (London) Lit Sup

Jordan, Alice M.
From Rollo to Tom Sawyer, and other papers; decorations by Nora S. Unwin. Horn Bk 1948 160p pa $3.50   028.5
1 Children's literature—History and criticism
ISBN 0-87675-058-7
Analyzed in Essay and general literature index
"Three essays in the book concern children's magazines of the Nineteenth Century, one is a lecture given by Miss Jordan in 1940, and five essays are about important [19th century] authors and editors of children's books." Sch Library J

Karl, Jean
From childhood to childhood; children's books and their creators. Day 1970 175p $6.50   028.5
1 Children's literature—History and criticism
ISBN 0-381-98131-2
The author "describes some of the characteristics of a group of successful children's book writers and how they get their works down on paper, following their work from manuscript to mill, including the functions of literary agents, book designing and some fascinating information about the illustrations and the problems of matching illustrators with authors. She also offers a fine section on the history of children's books, which really began when an 18th century printer-bookseller, John Newbery, issued 'A Pretty Little Pocketbook.' " Pub W
Bibliography: p171-75

Kingman, Lee
(ed.) Newbery and Caldecott Medal books: 1956-1965; with acceptance papers, biographies & related material chiefly from The Horn Book Magazine. Horn Bk. 1965 300p illus $10   028.5
1 Newbery Medal books 2 Caldecott Medal books 3 Children's literature—History and criticism 4 Authors 5 Illustrators
ISBN 0-87675-002-1
"Horn Book Papers"
This compilation continues the coverage begun in: Newbery Medal books, 1922-1955 and Caldecott Medal books, 1938-1957 both entered below under the editorship of Bertha Mahony Miller
"The pattern in the new collection is the same as in the earlier [ones]: a brief description of format, a short book note, the acceptance speech, and a biographical note. . . . An added bonus is the listing of runners-up from the beginning of each medal through 1965. . . . [This book] will be useful to librarians, teachers and other adults interested in children's books. It will also be used by some older boys and girls who are readers of the books, especially those who want to know more about the authors." Top of the News

(ed.) Newbery and Caldecott Medal books: 1966-1975; with acceptance papers, biographies and related material chiefly from The Horn Book Magazine. Horn Bk. 1975 xx, 321p illus $15   028.5
1 Newbery Medal books 2 Caldecott Medal books 3 Children's literature—History and criticism 4 Authors 5 illustrators
ISBN 0-87675-003-X
This volume brings up to date the compilations entered below under Bertha Mahony Miller and the one entered above covering the years 1956-1965. The format of this book is similar to its precedents, but it includes full-color illustrations from the Caldecott Medal books, as well as photographs of all the winning authors and artists. Three evaluative essays are also included

Lanes, Selma G.
Down the rabbit hole; adventures and misadventures in the realm of children's literature. Atheneum Pubs. 1971 239p illus $7.95   028.5
1 Children's literature—History and criticism
ISBN 0-689-10394-8
This "informative collection of essays on picture books and children's stories, is a handsomely illustrated, thoroughly indexed source for parents and teachers who want to know more about the expanding field of children's literature. Much attention is given to illustrators, with separate essays on fairy tales, series books, and books with black themes." Wis Library Bul
Bibliography: p214-31

Larrick, Nancy
A parent's guide to children's reading. 4th ed. With illustrations from fifty favorite children's books. Doubleday 1975 432p illus $8.95   028.5
1 Books and reading 2 Children's literature—History and criticism 3 Children's literature—Bibliography
ISBN 0-385-02564-5
First published 1958
In addition to providing bibliographies the author covers such topics as television and children, oral language in early childhood, developing children's interests, poetry, the audio-visual bridge to reading, how reading is taught, using reference books, buying books and building a home library, the paperback bonanza, magazines, and audio-visual materials

Lepman, Jella
A bridge of children's books; tr. from the German by Edith McCormick, with a foreword by J. E. Morpurgo. A.L.A. 1969 155p $5   028.5
1 Libraries, Children's 2 Libraries—Germany 3 Children's literature—History and criticism
ISBN 0-8389-0070-4
Original German edition, 1964
"In an anecdotal, personal account of her efforts to build international understanding through children's books [the author] reconstructs the events leading to the 1946 Munich International Children's Book Exhibition, the establishment of the International Youth Library in Munich, and the subsequent founding, in 1951 in Switzerland, of the International Board of Books for Young People, which now awards the Hans Christian Andersen prize." Library J
"The campaign for children's books after World War II, which has never before been described, has an important place in the history of children's literature. Since it is interwoven with the unusual experiences of an extraordinary woman and reported with great vitality, the result is an absorbing book." Horn Bk

MacCann, Donnarae
(ed.) The Black American in books for children: readings in racism; ed. and with an introduction by Donnarae MacCann and Gloria Woodard. Scarecrow 1972 223p $7.50   028.5
1 Negroes in literature and art 2 Children's literature—History and criticism
ISBN 0-8108-0526-X
"Intended to make schools and libraries more conscious of their responsibilities in 'alleviating the negative racial attitudes and behavior of white Americans toward black Americans and to nurture the self-esteem and racial pride of black Americans,' these 23 reprints of articles from library and education journals of the late '60's and early '70's include such well-known contributors as Augusta Baker, Binnie Tate, and Nancy Larrick. Minority publishing and the portrayal of the Black in children's literature are the principal themes, treated in both general terms and in the analysis of individual works, such as 'The "Real" Doctor Dolittle.' Indexes to titles and authors of children's books mentioned in the articles are appended." Ref Serv Rev
"Though the articles vary greatly in style, coherence, logic, and polemics, the selection is an important one for anyone who is interested in what is considered racist in children's books." Horn Bk

McGuffey, William H.
Old favorites from the McGuffey readers, 1836-1936. Ed. by Harvey C. Minnich. Associate editors: Henry Ford [and others]. Singing Tree [1969 c1936] 482p $10   028.5
1 Children's literature—Collections 2 Readers
ISBN 0-8103-3854-8

First published 1936 by the American Book Co.
This "is an anthology of selections from the famous Readers which substituted healthy if preachy morality for the gloomy theological selections of the day." Booklist

Meigs, Cornelia
(ed.) A critical history of children's literature. . . . Rev. ed. by Cornelia Meigs [and others]. Decorations by Vera Bock. Macmillan (N Y) 1969 xxviii, 708p $12.95   028.5
1 Children's literature—History and criticism
First published 1953
"A survey of children's books in English, prepared in four parts under the editorship of Cornelia Meigs." Title page
Contents: Part 1 Roots in the past, up to 1840, by C. Meigs; Part 2 Widening horizons, 1840-1890, by A. T. Eaton; Part 3 A rightful heritage, 1890-1920, by Elizabeth Nesbitt; Part 4 Golden years and time of tumult, 1920-1967, by R. H. Viguers
"While it is obviously a valuable reference book for libraries, schools, and teacher-training institutions, it makes fascinating reading not only for those adults who were fortunate enough to have grown up among books, but for those parents who wish to provide such a background for their own children." Cath World
Includes bibliographies

Miller, Bertha Mahony
(ed.) Caldecott Medal books: 1938-1957; with the artist's acceptance papers & related material chiefly from The Horn Book Magazine. Ed. by Bertha Mahony Miller and Elinor Whitney Field. Horn Bk. 1957 329p 20 plates $10   028.5
1 Caldecott Medal books 2 Illustrators 3 Children's literature—History and criticism
ISBN 0-87675-001-3
"Horn Book Papers"
"A companion volume to the editors' 'Newbery Medal books: 1922-1955' [entered below]. A short study of Randolph Caldecott, for whom the award is named, prefaces the chronological listing of the award books. With this listing are given the acceptance speech of each artist and a biographical sketch of each. The illustrations—one from each book—are grouped together in the middle of the volume. In the concluding chapter Esther Averill evaluates the award books as picture books." Booklist
1956-1965 and 1966-1975 compilations, edited by Lee Kingman, entered above

(ed.) Newbery Medal books: 1922-1955; with their authors' acceptance papers & related material chiefly from The Horn Book Magazine. Ed. by Bertha Mahony Miller and Elinor Whitney Field. Horn Bk. 1955 458p illus $10   028.5
1 Newbery Medal books 2 Authors 3 Children's literature—History and criticism
ISBN 0-87675-000-5
"Horn Book Papers"
"The first volume of a series . . . [of] papers originally published in numbers of the 'Horn Book' that are now out of print. This collection constitutes a history of the Newbery Medal awards to date [1955]; the winning books are presented in chronological order, and for each there is a book note [a short excerpt] and an acceptance paper. [There are also brief biographies of the authors.] Introductory essays on Frederic Melcher and John Newbery add to the value of a book that will be prized by librarians and connoisseurs of children's literature." Booklist
1956-1965 and 1966-1975 compilations, edited by Lee Kingman, entered above

Moore, Anne Carroll
My roads to childhood; views and reviews of children's books; introduction by Frances Clarke Sayers. Decorations by Arthur Lougee. Horn Bk. 1961 399p $6.50, pa $3.50 **028.5**

1 Children's literature—History and criticism 2 Children's literature—Bibliography
ISBN 0-87675-055-2; 0-87675-052-8
First published 1939 by Doubleday
Contains the complete texts of: Roads to childhood (1920); New Roads to childhood (1923); and, Crossroads to childhood (1926)
"Here, so happily designed and so well printed that it is a delight to look at and to hold in the hand, is a book of charm and significance. . . . It is [Miss Moore's] faith in human nature, this belief in things of the spirit that makes the reading of 'My Roads to Childhood' an exhilarating experience. It is a book that no one who has anything to do with children and young people can afford to neglect." N Y Times Bk Rev
A representative list of children's books published 1926-1938: p339-66

Sayers, Frances Clarke
Summoned by books; essays and speeches; comp. by Marjeanne Jensen Blinn; foreword by Lawrence Clark Powell. Viking [1968 c1965] 173p pa $1.35 **028.5**

1 Children's literature 2 Books and reading 3 Libraries, Children's
ISBN 0-670-00218-6
Analyzed in Essay and general literature index
First published 1965
This collection includes four speeches on librarianship, two covering the field in general, the others treating work with children. Two portraits of pioneer children's librarians follow. Additional essays discuss the art of story telling, story writing for children, picture books, and children's classics
A "stirring affirmation of faith in fine books for children from a remarkable woman who, like de la Mare, believes that 'only the rarest kind of best of anything can be good enough for the young'—and who stands up to say so." Pub W

Smith, Dora V.
Fifty years of children's books, 1910-1960: trends, backgrounds, influences. Designed by Norma Phillips. Natl. Council of Teachers of English 1963 149p illus $2.95 **028.5**

1 Children's literature—History and criticism
"Beginning with the children's book world of 1910, this author traces literature available to children for the next fifty years. She describes trends, influences upon, and the changes which occurred during the half-century. Lists significant books of 1910-1959, based on author's judgment (date, author, title, publishers, grades). Lists author index and bibliography of other books." Berson. Children's Lit
"Reading this quick but not hasty appraisal is most enjoyable; many old book friends make their appearance. . . . Book lists and indexes invite use for reference purposes, and the choice illustrations from the books discussed invite browsing." Wis Library Bul

Smith, James Steel
A critical approach to children's literature. McGraw 1967 442p $10.50 **028.5**

1 Children's literature—History and criticism
ISBN 0-07-058455-9
Includes "sections on adult literature as a part of children's literature, humor in children's books, and the cultural context of children's reading. The last chapter is devoted to practical suggestions—how to use reviews, book sources, finding and using children's literature outside of books. Index of authors, artists and titles." Berson. Children's Lit
Includes bibliographies

Smith, Lillian H.
The unreluctant years; a critical approach to children's literature. A.L.A. 1953 193p $5 **028.5**

1 Children's literature—History and criticism 2 Book selection
ISBN 0-8389-0065-8
"The aim of this book is to consider children's books as literature and to discover some of the standards by which they can be so judged." Foreword
Contents: The case for children's literature; The lineage of children's literature; An approach to criticism; The art of the fairy tale; Gods and men; Heroes of epic and saga; Poetry; Picture books; Stories; Fantasy; Historical fiction; Books of knowledge; Envoy
Includes bibliographies

Thwaite, Mary F.
From primer to pleasure in reading; an introduction to the history of children's books in England from the invention of printing to 1914 with an outline of some developments in other countries. Horn Bk. 1972 340p illus $12.50 **028.5**

1 Children's literature—History and criticism
ISBN 0-87675-275-X
First published 1963 in England with title: From primer to pleasure
"The main object of this comprehensive work is 'to provide a general introduction to scholarly histories of the subject for the benefit of [people] interested in the link between children's books of today and those of the past.' This it does very well. Chronologically following the developments of children's books and their different genres, the author puts them into proper historical perspective, highlights especially influential works and makes comparative evaluations. The prolific nineteenth century is interestingly analyzed, using a classified arrangement (e.g. fairy lore and fantasy, the tale of adventure, periodicals, etc.). The main body of this work focuses on England, drawing occasional parallels to German and French events. . . . [This] is a thoroughly researched and stimulating reference tool for the student and teacher of children's literature." Top of the News
Bibliography: p283-313

Townsend, John Rowe
A sense of story; essays on contemporary writers for children. Lippincott 1971 215p $6.95 **028.5**

1 Children's literature—History and criticism
ISBN 0-397-31331-4
Analyzed in Essay and general literature index
This introduction to the work of nineteen English-language writers for children consists of essays on L. M. Boston, John Christopher, Eleanor Estes, Leon Garfield, Madeleine L'Engle, and others. It includes brief biographical details of the writers, notes by the authors on themselves and lists of their books
"There is nothing haphazard about this collection of essays, even though Mr. Townsend has chosen—'on a personal basis'—to write about 'authors whose work particularly interests him and about whom he feels he has something to say.' . . . Urbane and pleasurable to read, the essays are expressions of sagacity and common sense." Horn Bk

Written for children; an outline of English-language children's literature. Lippincott [1975 c1974] 368p illus $10.95 **028.5**

1 Children's literature—History and criticism
ISBN 0-397-31528-7

Townsend, John Rowe—*Continued*

First published 1965 in England. First American edition published 1967 by Lothrop. This edition first published 1974 in England

The author "covers fiction from England, the United States, Australia, and a few other parts of the English-speaking world, as well as poetry, picture books, and the art of book illustration. . . . The book ends with notes on the sources of all quotations, an impressive seven-page bibliography of works on children's literature, and an index." Horn Bk

"The writing style is very relaxed and almost chatty with the author providing anecdotes and personal comments and reactions which make the book very alive and entertaining reading. It is for the serious student of children's literature, but one most all of them will enjoy." Children's Bk Rev Serv

028.505   Children's reading— Periodicals

Bookbird. Jugend und Volk Verlagsges $5 per year
028.505

1 Children's literature—Periodicals 2 Books and reading—Best books 3 Book reviews
ISSN 0006-7377

Quarterly. First published 1962

Issued by the International Board on Books for Young People and the International Institute for Children's Literature and Reading Research

This periodical "contains articles of interest to anyone working in the field of children's books. Lists of recommended books for translation . . . appear regularly in almost each issue. There is also a very helpful review of recent publications about children's books and libraries. . . . Awards, congresses, special meetings, exhibits, seminars and many other types of activities throughout the world are reported on in brief news items. Occasional longer articles cover the various aspects of children's books in depth." Pellowski. The World of Children's Lit

Children's Book Review. Five Owls Press $7 per year
028.505

1 Children's literature—Periodicals 2 Book reviews
ISSN 0009-1626

Bimonthly. First published 1971

"Recent issues [of this journal] have offered articles on poetry for children, books for the minority child, fantasy in children's books, and critical essays on specific authors and illustrators. Added features of the journal are a regular classified list of forthcoming books and a detachable section containing annotated subject lists. A wider awareness, through CBR, of British publishing for children and young people may just be the means by which we will have more of the fine books published in Britain brought into this country." Library J

Children's Literature. Temple Univ. Press $15, pa $4.95
028.505

1 Children's literature—History and criticism

Annual. First published 1972 by the English Department of the University of Connecticut

Journal of the Modern Library Association Seminar on Children's Literature and the Children's Literature Association

An annual collection of essays that "covers all aspects of children's literature and interests from pregraders through junior high and high school. ('Children,' as a term, is used freely to include any literature this side of the adult novel.). . . The close to 30 articles in the offset 256 pages are almost all by teachers of English in various American, English and European universities. A few have library back-

grounds, but most do not, and the majority are more involved with the importance of children's literature as literature not as 'kiddy lit'—and this position is well stated in the editor's introductory remarks. What follows completely supports her argument. There are articles on science fiction and the adolescent, a comparison of Heidegger and E. B. White, 'The Wizardness of Oz,' puppet immortals, and bits and pieces on such things as the child in Shakespeare. Add to this: some first rate review articles (the feminist in fairy tales, to a note on contemporary soviet fantasies), shorter book and magazine reviews, tips on teaching of children's literature. Not only is the writing scholarly, but it is lively, usually original, and totally free of the 'kiddy lit' jargon." Katz. Magazines for Libraries. 2d edition sup

Children's Literature Abstracts. Published by the Sub-section on Library Work with Children of the International Federation of Library Associations. [Distributed by C. H. Ray, 45 Stephenson Tower, Station St, Birmingham B5 4DR, Eng] $6.50 per year
028.505

1 Children's literature—Periodicals 2 Children's literature—Indexes

Quarterly. First published 1973

"CLA is attempting to provide a key to writings on 'Children's Literature, reading, authorship, illustration and publishing' on an international scale. . . . Included in the first issue were 52 abstracts from 32 journals (22 of them English language). The coverage was increased to 83 abstracts from 31 journals (22 of them English) in the second issue. Judging from the sample of the first two issues, the emphasis appears to be on literature in journals directed to library service, education, and book trade audiences. The editors are interested in expanding the number of titles, and in this expansion lies the greatest usefulness of this service." Library J

Children's Literature in Education. APS Publications, Inc. $12 per year
028.505

1 Children's literature—Periodicals
ISSN 0045-6713

Quarterly. First published 1970

"Here's one for every children's librarian, and for anyone teaching elementary and junior high students. Although published in England, it is worldwide in scope and interest. . . . Each 60 or so page issue is devoted to a number of articles on the more enduring qualities of children's literature. . . . There are frequent bibliographies . . . opinion pieces, editorials, and generally a high quality of writing rarely found in magazines of this type. As the publisher rightly says: 'The journal provides serious, sustained criticism of writing for children, and is concerned with the interrelationship of literature, imagination and learning.' It is, in short, an effort to elevate 'kiddy lit' to the position it deserves as meaningful, important literature." Katz. Magazines for Libraries. 2d edition. Supplement

Growing Point. Edited and distributed by Margery Fisher, Ashton Manor, Northampton NN7 2JL, Eng. $4 per year
028.505

1 Book reviews 2 Children's literature—Periodicals
ISSN 0046-6506

9 issues per year. First published 1962

This is "Margery Fisher's regular review of books for the growing families of the English reading world, and for parents, teachers, librarians and other guardians"

The Horn Book Magazine. Horn Bk. $7.50 per year
028.505

1 Children's literature—Periodicals 2 Books and reading—Best books 3 Book reviews
ISSN 0018-5078

The Horn Book Magazine—*Continued*
Bimonthly. First published 1924 with title: The Horn Book
"This is one of the most important publications in the field of children's literature. It includes [signed] reviews of current children's books. These are classified by subject and age level. Reproductions of many illustrations from the newest books are incorporated into the text. Articles about authors, illustrators, award books, history of children's literature are frequently featured." Huck. Children's Lit in the Elem Sch

In Review; Canadian books for children. Provincial
Library Service $3 for 3 years 028.505
1 Children's literature—Periodicals 2 Canadian literature—Periodicals 3 Book reviews
ISSN 0019-3259
Quarterly. First published 1967
"Critical, signed reviews of Canadian books, pamphlets, and even documents suitable for children. Also, some short articles on Canadian literature and profiles of authors are included. The 70 to 80 critical appraisals in each issue are by librarians and specialists, are signed, and usually run from 150 to 300 words. The reviewer clearly indicates whether he or she thinks the book should be purchased. The writing is good to excellent, the criticism just that, and the total effect is a profit to just about any librarian, in or out of Canada." Katz. Magazines for Libraries

Interracial Books for Children Bulletin. Council on
Interracial Books for Children $15 per year
028.505
1 Children's literature—Periodicals 2 Minorities—Periodicals 3 Book reviews
ISSN 0020-9708
8 issues per year. First published 1970
"Concerned with children's literature for minority groups, 'Interracial Books for Children' contains articles as well as reviews of books. Reviews are forcefully written and do not reflect the opinions of other review sources (e.g., reviews of 'The Cay' and 'Sounder'). This periodical is valuable for selecting books through junior high school." Peterson. Ref Bks for Elem and Jr High Sch Libraries. 2d edition

Phaedrus: a journal of children's literature research.
Phaedrus, Inc. $9 per year 028.505
1 Children's literature—Periodicals 2 Children's literature—History and criticism
ISSN 0300-3612
Biannual. First published 1973
"Covering studies and research, here is a welcome new addition to the recently growing number of titles given over to children's literature as a serious literary form. Primary emphasis is on research reports 'for those whose professional concerns are directed towards theoretical inquiry into the media environment of the child and adolescent.' . . . Translated into content: a short article on a research society, two pages of annotated notes on children's literature journals, three pages of reports on selected dissertations (1972), a subject listing of articles from recent journals, recent bibliographies and studies, and a concluding page on booksellers. A must for all libraries concerned." Katz. Magazines for Libraries. 2d edition sup

Signal; approaches to children's books. Thimble Press
$5 per year 028.505
1 Children's literature—Periodicals
ISSN 0037-4954
3 issues per year, January, May and September. First published 1970
"The editor states that [this journal] 'is being published to provide a voice for writers whose ideas about, and interests in, children's books cannot be contained in brief reviews and articles, or in periodicals whose purposes are basically pragmatic or educational.' Although the articles are concerned primarily with British poets, authors, and illustrators, there is no indication that this national emphasis will continue as a matter of editorial policy. The informative, scholarly presentations in this unique journal should be of interest to anyone concerned with children's literature, and particularly of value to students and teachers." Katz. Magazines for Libraries

028.52 Reading and reading aids—Bibliographies and catalogs

Africa: an annotated list of printed materials suitable for children; selected and annotated by a Joint Committee of the American Library Association, Children's Services Division, and the African-American Institute. U.S. Com. for UNICEF. Information Center on Children's Cultures 1968 76p pa $1
028.52
1 Africa—Bibliography
A selective guide to over 300 English-language items, published in nine countries. The materials are arranged by general regions of the continent and by country. Each entry gives grade level (pre-school through junior high), price, and quality of the item. Includes a list of publishers and an author, title and subject index
"The annotations in this helpful 76-page bibliography indicate content, scope, and use of each item and point out weaknesses as well as strengths; materials not recommended for use in American public and school libraries for children though junior high school age are so noted." Booklist

American Library Association. Children's Services
Division. Book Evaluation Committee
Notable children's books. A.L.A. pa 10¢ 028.52
1 Books and reading—Best books 2 Children's literature—Bibliography
Reprints of the annual annotated list appearing in American Libraries and its predecessor ALA Bulletin since 1940

American Library Association. Children's Services
Division. Book Reevaluation Committee
Notable children's books, 1940-1959. Prepared by the Book Reevaluation Committee. Children's Services Division. American Library Association. Rosemary E. Livsey, chairman. A.L.A. 1969 39p pa $1.50 028.52
1 Books and reading—Best books 2 Children's literature—Bibliography
ISBN 0-8389-3052-2
"The annual Notable Children's Books lists provide the basis for this selection of nearly 300 children's books. Each of the titles has been re-evaluated after at least a five-year period of use. Those of enduring worth and interest to children are included in this twenty-year reappraisal. Annotations from the original annual list appear for each title. Arranged by author and indexed by title." A.L.A.

American Library Association. Library Service to
The Disadvantaged Child Committee
I read, you read, we read; I see, you see, we see; I hear, you hear, we hear; I learn, you learn, we learn. A.L.A. 1971 104p pa $2 028.52
1 Books and reading 2 Socially handicapped children 3 Audio-visual materials—Bibliography
ISBN 0-8389-3124-3

American Library Association—*Continued*
Title on spine: I read, I see, I hear, I learn
Here are listed "poems, stories, films, and recordings under four broad age-level categories: preschool, ages 5-8, 8-11, and 12-14. The briefly annotated titles, with prices supplied, are followed by useful suggested program aids for adults." Cur Ref Bks

Association for Childhood Education International
Bibliography: books for children. The Association pa $2.75   028.52
1 Books and reading—Best books 2 Children's literature—Bibliography
Biennial. First published 1937. Editors vary
This is a selected list of books, classified and annotated. The books are grouped by subject or form and suggested age levels are given. An index of titles and authors and a directory of publishers are included

Good and inexpensive books for children. The Association illus pa $2   028.52
1 Children's literature—Bibliography 2 Paperback books
Biennial. First published 1947 with title: Children's books for seventy-five cents or less
This bibliography consisting largely of paperback books is arranged in the following categories: Picture books; Fiction, Easy; Fiction, Intermediate; Fiction, Older; Rhymes and verses; Fairy tales and legends; Biography; Social studies; Science; Recreation, Hobbies; Parents and teachers
Includes an author and title index and a list of publishers

Books for mentally retarded children; list developed by Public Library of Cincinnati and Hamilton County. Public Library of Cincinnati and Hamilton County Exceptional Children's Division 1973 34p pa 50¢   028.52
1 Mentally handicapped children, Books for—Bibliography
The books on this list were tried out with one or more classes of retarded children in Cincinnati during a two-year demonstration of Library Services to Exceptional Children

Child Study Association of America/Wel-Met. Children's Book Committee
Children's books of the year. The Association pa $2.50   028.52
1 Children's literature—Bibliography
Annual. First published 1913
"This is a selective list of over 600 children's books, published during the previous year. . . . Titles are arranged under four age-level categories (three to nine years) and then subdivided by subject. Additional categories are special interests, books for parents and children, reprints and new editions, and a list of paperbacks. At the end is a title index. Entries are briefly annotated and give suggested age level." Wynar. Guide to Ref Bks for Sch Media Centers [Review of 1973 edition]

The **Children's** Book Showcase, sponsored by The Children's Book Council. The Council illus $5.95
028.52
1 Books and reading—Best books 2 Illustration of books
Annual. First published 1972
A catalog of the Showcase exhibit of the best designed and illustrated children's books published in the United States during the preceding year

Children's books. Library of Congress [for sale by Supt. of Docs.] pa 40¢   028.52
1 Children's literature—Bibliography 2 Books and reading—Best books
ISSN 0069-3464
Annual. First published 1964
Compiled by Virginia Haviland and Lois B. Watt with the assistance of a small committee
This annotated list of books for preschool through junior high school age children is arranged by categories and reading levels are indicated

Children's books too good to miss [by] May Hill Arbuthnot [and others]. Press of Case Western Reserve Univ. illus $2.95   028.52
1 Books and reading—Best books 2 Children's literature—Bibliography
First published 1948. Periodically revised
"A highly selective list with critical appraisals of 230 books 'of outstanding merit.' Introductory matter discusses the evaluation of children's books. Another section briefly discusses 'the artist and children's books.' Small format. Illustrated with black and white reproductions from children's books." Wynar. Guide to Ref Bks for Sch Media Centers [Review of 1971 edition]

Feminists on Children's Media
Little Miss Muffet fights back; a bibliography of recommended non-sexist books about girls for young readers. Rev. ed. The author [distributed by Feminist Book Mart] 1974 62p illus pa $1   028.52
1 Women in literature and art—Bibliography
First published 1971
"The books recommended in this bibliography were chosen because they show girls and women as vital human beings—active, assertive, clever, adventurous, brave, creative—or because they show some understanding of the social conditions that encourage meaningful choices toward self-fulfillment, or that prevent women from being all they might be. . . . We have sought to present a representative sample of good books about girls and women available; to show the variety of books to read and heroines to read about. No one book on the list can exemplify all the aspects of any girl's life. Our aim has not been to set ourselves up as arbiters of a list of indisputably 'approved' books, but rather to share the knowledge we have gained through reading, reviewing and discussing children's books from a feminist viewpoint." Introduction

Field, Carolyn W.
(ed.) Subject collections in children's literature; consultants: Virginia Haviland [and] Elizabeth Nesbitt, for the National Planning Committee for Special Collections, Children's Services Division, American Library Association. Bowker 1969 142p $8.50
028.52
1 Children's literature—Bibliography
ISBN 0-8352-0230-5
"A guide to 500 special collections in children's literature held by 156 institutions, arranged under 175 subject headings with many cross references. Contains brief descriptive information about the collections, primarily about subject matter and size, whether cataloged, and if available for inter-library loan and photocopying. A directory of collections gives the address, subject under which each collection is entered, and the name of the person in charge of the collection. Institutions and individuals are indexed geographically. Appended is a bibliography of books and articles about special collections." Wynar. Guide to Ref Bks for Sch Media Centers

Fisher, Margery
Matters of fact; aspects of non-fiction for children.
Crowell 1972 488p illus $11.95   028.52
1 Books and reading—Best books 2 Children's
literature—History and criticism
ISBN 0-690-52537-0
"This British publication consists mainly of analyses
of information books and the criteria necessary to
make them works of distinction. Utilizing specific
topics to illustrate general discussions, the author
approaches non-fiction books in the following
categories: Foundations (bread, the postal system,
Holland, honeybees, cowboys, time); The Multiple
Subject (London, atoms); Biography (Johann Sebastian Bach, Helen Keller, Abraham Lincoln); Careers
(nursing, Journalism). Each topic is followed by long
bibliographies of related titles. Writers and parents as
well as teachers and librarians will benefit from studying the criteria listed in this book for outstanding
nonfiction books for children." Peterson. Ref Bks for
Elem and Jr High Sch Libraries

For younger readers: braille and talking books. Pub-
lished for the Library of Congress, Division for the
Blind and Physically Handicapped by the American
Foundation for the Blind. pa gratis   028.52
1 Blind, Books for the—Bibliography 2 Talking
books
First published 1964
This is a periodically published listing of juvenile
braille and talking books available from the Library of
Congress, Division for the Blind and Physically
Handicapped

Greene, Ellin
(ed.) A multimedia approach to children's literature; a selective list of films, filmstrips, and recordings based on children's books; comp. and ed. by Ellin
Greene and Madalynne Schoenfeld. A.L.A. 1972
xxvi, 262p pa $4   028.52
1 Children's literature—Bibliography 2 Audio-
visual materials—Bibliography
ISBN 0-8389-0121-2
"Designed as a buying guide to book-related non-
print materials for use with children from preschool to
grade 8 this lists approximately 425 books, 175 16mm
films, 175 filmstrips (sound and silent), and 300
recordings (33rpm disc and tape cassette) with brief
annotations and buying information. The list is
arranged alphabetically by book title with films, filmstrips, and recordings based on the book following
each; a directory of distributors follows the list. The
guide also suggests related readings, selection and
program aids, and realia for displays and exhibits and
contains six separate indexes for easy access to the
material." Booklist

(comp.) Stories; a list of stories to tell and to read
aloud. [6th ed.] N.Y. Pub. Lib. 1965 78p pa $2
          028.52
1 Children's literature—Bibliography 2 Storytelling—Bibliography
ISBN 0-87104-167-7
First published 1933
The purpose of this annotated list "is to introduce
the beginning storyteller to folk and fairy literature
which children have acclaimed, and to lead him to
source material which will help him develop his art.
. . . Picture books have been included only when the
story can stand without pictures. A main entry has
been listed from an out of print book when it is considered the best version of the story but always a
secondary entry has been listed from a book in print
which includes the same story. . . . The section 'For
the Storyteller' includes recordings." Foreword
Includes subject and name indexes

Griffin, Louise
(comp.) Multi-ethnic books for young children;
annotated bibliography for parents and teachers.
[Natl. Assn. for the Educ. of Young Children 1970]
74p illus pa $2   028.52
1 Children's literature—Bibliography 2 Minorities
—Bibliography
"An ERIC-NAEYC publication in early childhood
education"
This bibliography is arranged in the following
categories: American Indians and Eskimos; Appalachia and the Southern Mountains; Afro-
Americans, Hawaii and the Philippines; Latin-
American derivation; Asian derivation; Jewish derivation; European derivation; and Adult books for
parents and teachers

Haviland, Virginia
(ed.) Children's books of international interest; a
selection from four decades of American publishing.
A.L.A. 1972 69p pa $2.50   028.52
1 Children's literature—Bibliography
ISBN 0-8389-0130-1
This "is a briefly annotated list of over 300 titles
selected by a committee from annual lists entitled
'Books Recommended for Translation,' issued by ALA
since 1955. The books listed have been produced in
the U.S. during the past forty years. Within the
categories of picture books, first reading books, fiction, folklore, biography, history, science, and the
arts, books are arranged alphabetically by author. This
list will be useful for students of children's literature
and for anyone interested in promoting international
understanding through children's books." Cur Ref
Bks

Jordan, Alice M.
Children's classics; with list of recommended editions by Helen Adams Masten. 4th ed. Horn Bk. 1967
15p pa $1   028.52
1 Children's literature—Bibliography 2 Children's
literature—History and criticism
ISBN 0-87675-115-X
"This article first appeared in 'The Horn Book
Magazine,' of February 1947. The booklist of classics
first prepared by Alice M. Jordan was revised by
Helen Adams Masten in 1952, 1960, and 1967." Facing title page
"An aid in selecting editions of the classics to buy
for school or library. The list contains an article by
Miss Jordan, illustrations from some of the books, as
well as a list of recommended editions compiled by
Miss Masten, with publication dates and prices
[given]." Library J

Keating, Charlotte Matthews
Building bridges of understanding between cultures. Palo Verde Pub. Co. 1971 233p $7.95 028.52
1 Children's literature—Bibliography 2 Minorities
—Bibliography
The author examines books "dealing with race relations, with minority groups, with social realities. . . . She has concerned herself with those books
that can give a child or teenager, from ghetto or barrio
or white suburbia, a growing understanding not only
of himself as an individual but of the paradox of a free
society—that valuing the individuality of others
increases the worth of his own, that the more one
respects cultural diversity the more one discovers
how much people have in common." Preface
Partial contents: Black Americans; Indians and
Eskimos; Spanish-speaking Americans; Asian Americans; Nationality groups and religious minorities;
Books for bilingual/bicultural children; African;
Caribbean

Kujoth, Jean Spealman

Best-selling children's books. Scarecrow 1973 305p $8.50 028.52

1 Children's literature—Bibliography 2 Best sellers—Bibliography

ISBN 0-8108-0571-5

This best sellers guide "identifies and describes 958 children's trade books now in print. To qualify, a book must have sold 100,000 copies since its publication. Books are listed by author, title, illustrator, year of publication, number of copies sold, type of book, subject category, and age level. Full information (including a brief synopsis) is provided in the author entry." Wynar. Guide to Ref Bks for Sch Media Centers

Let's read together; books for family enjoyment. 3d ed. Selected and annotated by a Special Committee of the National Congress of Parents and Teachers and the Children's Services Division, American Library Association. A.L.A. 1969 103p pa $2 028.52

1 Books and reading—Best books 2 Children's literature—Bibliography

ISBN 0-8389-3096-4

First published 1960

An annotated bibliography grouped under such categories as: Mother Goose, A B C, and counting books; Picture books; Folk and fairy tales; Tall tales, myths, and legends; Funny books for funny bones; Stories about animals; Other lands and people; Youth in today's world; Special days. Includes title and author index

"Books in this list have been placed in age brackets covering three or four years, sometimes more if the subject is one in which books listed have a wide age appeal. . . . The titles that follow have been chosen to help parents select with greater confidence books for family reading aloud, books for individual reading, and books for a child's own library." Foreword to Parents

National Council of Teachers of English

Adventuring with books; 2,400 titles for pre-K—grade 8. 2d ed. Prepared by Shelton L. Root, Jr., and a committee of the National Council of Teachers of English. Citation Press 1973 395p pa $1.95 028.52

1 Books and reading—Best books 2 Children's literature—Bibliography

ISBN 0-590-09702-4

First published 1950 by the Council

"Contains annotated entries for 2,400 recommended in-print books selected by a committee of the NCTE which '. . . combine the qualities of entertaining reading with literary merit.' (Foreword). Arrangement is by broad categories: picture books (288 titles), fiction (879 titles), biography (171 titles), social studies (190 titles), biological sciences (190 titles), sports and hobbies (33 titles), and others. Entries give bibliographic data, price, suggested grade span. Annotations are usually descriptive, with occasional evaluative comments. Includes a directory of publishers, an author index, and a title index." Wynar. Guide to Ref Bks for Sch Media Centers

National Council of Teachers of English. Picture Book Committee

Picture books for children [by] Patricia Jean Cianciolo, editor, and the Picture Book Committee, National Council of Teachers of English. A.L.A. 1973 159p illus pa $6.50 028.52

1 Picture books for children—Bibliography 2 Books and reading—Best books

ISBN 0-8389-0157-3

"Devised as a book selection tool for teachers, librarians, and those concerned with children's picture books, this graded, annotated bibliography contains more than 375 titles for the pre-schooler through the [young] teenager. The books chosen exemplify story and illustration acting in combination emphasizing aesthetic as well as educational value. Cianciolo has written a 22-page introduction followed by a booklist arranged in broad categories such as 'Me and My Family,' 'Other People,' 'The Imaginative World.' There is an index of authors, illustrators, and titles." Cur Ref Bks

New York. Public Library

Children's books and recordings suggested as holiday gifts. The Library pa 85¢ 028.52

1 Books and reading—Best books 2 Children's literature—Bibliography 3 Children's literature—Discography

Annual. First published 1911 with title: Children's books suggested as holiday gifts

This list of an exhibition held annually in the Central Children's Room of the New York Public library includes not only a selection of new publications, but also a few of the favorites among children's books of former years in new editions. Recordings included comprise a selection of materials recently released

Libros en español; an annotated list of children's books in Spanish, by Mary K. Conwell and Pura Belpré. The Library 1971 52p pa 50¢ 028.52

1 Children's literature—Bibliography 2 Spanish language editions—Bibliography

ISBN 0-87104-601-6

Annotated in both English and Spanish, this bibliography is arranged in the following categories: Picture books; Young readers; Books for the middle age; Books for older boys and girls; Folklore, myths and legends; Songs and games; Bilingual books; Books for learning Spanish; Anthologies

Includes a list of sources and an author title index

Palmer, Julia Reed

Read for your life; two successful efforts to help people read and an annotated list of the books that made them want to. Scarecrow 1974 510p illus $15 028.52

1 Socially handicapped children, Books for—Bibliography 2 Socially handicapped children—Education 3 Books and reading 4 Children's literature—Bibliography

ISBN 0-8108-0654-1

"Part I, 'Real Cool or a bright future?', describes two successful efforts at teaching people to read and write. Following this is a further discussion of library techniques in disadvantaged areas and specific suggestions for helping. Part II consists of an annotated book list. Part III gives author, title, and bibliographic indexes, and indexes to books of interest to blacks, Chicanos, Orientals, American Indians and Puerto Ricans." Ref Serv Rev

Rollins, Charlemae

(ed.) We build together; a reader's guide to Negro life and literature for elementary and high school use. Charlemae Rollins, chairman of the Committee for 1967 revision of We build together. Contributors: Augusta Baker [and others]. Natl. Council of Teachers of English 1967 xxvii, 71p pa $1.65 028.52

1 Negroes in literature and art 2 Negroes—Bibliography 3 Books and reading—Best books 4 Children's literature—Bibliography

First published 1941

"The introduction by the author describes the changing role of blacks in the field of literature and in American society and discusses guidelines for evaluat-

Rollins, Charlemae—*Continued*

ing books. Such topics as illustrations, stereotyping, dialect, and racially potent words are examined. The booklist is selective and contains only 228 titles, omitting adult books for young adult readers and books on African history. Arranged by broad categories (picture books, fiction, biography, and sports), it covers materials for preschool through grade 9. Annotations are lengthy and critical, pointing out weaknesses and suggesting possible uses for the books. Index of biographees, author-title-editor index, and directory of publishers are provided. This guide was published prior to the great publication rush of books by and about blacks, but it stands as an excellent guide to books and evaluation criteria." Wynar. Guide to Ref Bks for Sch Media Centers

Stories to tell to children; a selected list. Published for Carnegie Library of Pittsburgh Children's Services by the Univ. of Pittsburgh Press illus $5.95, pa $3.50   028.52
1 Children's literature—Bibliography 2 Storytelling 3 Holidays—Bibliography
First published 1916. Periodically revised. Editors vary
"An invaluable guide for pre-service and inservice teachers as well as for librarians, the book is logically arranged, beginning with an extensive listing of stories appropriate for three age groups: preschoolers, children from six to ten, and older boys and girls. Stories for Holiday Programs offers an excellent potpourri of tales for all seasons, while a classified list of stories—incorporating such diverse subjects as Afro-Americans, Ecology, Ghosts, Toys—indicates both the range as well as the relevancy of the collection. Also included is a selective list of Aids for the Storyteller—a short guide to articles and books treating various aspects of selection and presentation. Professionally sound, attractive in format and price, the compilation should satisfy many needs." Horn Bk
Includes an alphabetical and a classified list of stories

Welch, D'Alté A.

A bibliography of American children's books printed prior to 1821. Am. Antiquarian Soc. 1972 lxvi, 516p $45   028.52
1 Children's literature—Bibliography 2 Rare books
ISBN 0-8271-7133-1
First published in six parts in the proceedings of the American Antiquarian Society, 1963 through 1967
"Listing some 1,478 titles, in an uncounted number of editions [this volume's] comprehensiveness places it head and shoulders above its forerunners, though even d'Alté had to limit its scope. This, he states was 'primarily . . . narrative books written in English, designed for children under fifteen years of age' that were intended to be read 'at leisure for pleasure.'. . . Describing each work with full title (or, for later editions, as much as is needed to do them justice), detailed collations, notes on sources and typographic peculiarities . . . and bibliographical references (albeit somewhat arbitrarily selected), d'Alté's methods will bring joy to the librarian, collector, and bookseller." New Eng Q

Withrow, Dorothy E.

Gateways to readable books. . . . 5th ed. By Dorothy E. Withrow, Helen B. Carey [and] Bertha M. Hirzel. Wilson, H.W. 1975 299p $12   028.52
1 Reading—Remedial teaching—Bibliography 2 Children's literature—Bibliography
ISBN 0-8242-0566-9
First edition, 1944 by Ruth Strang, Alice Checkovitz, Christine Gilbert and Margaret Scoggin
"An annotated graded list of books in many fields

for adolescents who are reluctant to read or find reading difficult." Subtitle
This bibliography lists over 1,000 titles in broad subject categories, giving full bibliographic information and grade level of difficulty for each book. Indexed by author, title and grade level of reading difficulty

Yonkers, N. Y. Public Library. Children's Services

A guide to subjects & concepts in picture book format. Oceana 1974 166p $7.50   028.52
1 Picture books for children—Bibliography
ISBN 0-379-00131-4
"Intended as a finding tool, not a buying guide for material, this index is limited to titles specifically classified as 'picture books' in the Yonkers (N.Y.) Public Library. Divided into 52 categories and subdivisions, some 2,000 entries cover title, author, publisher, and year of publication. . . . As a supplement to the card catalog for parents, teachers, and library school students, this book is recommended for comprehensive collections." Cur Ref Bks
Bibliography: p165-66

028.7   Use of books and libraries as sources of information

Beck, Margaret V.

Library skills, by Margaret V. Beck, Vera M. Pace [and] Marion L. Welken. Denison 1964-1967 5v illus ea $5.95   028.7
1 Library service 2 Libraries and readers
Accompanied by A guidebook for teaching Library skills and a pupils workbook
Contents: Getting acquainted with the library (ISBN 0-513-00152-2); Book 1: Using the card catalog (ISBN 0-513-00153-0); Book 2: Using the Dewey Decimal System (ISBN 0-513-00155-7); Book 3: Using reference material (ISBN 0-513-00157-3); Book 4: Using the school library (ISBN 0-513-00160-3)

Cleary, Florence Damon

Discovering books and libraries; a handbook for the upper elementary and junior high school grades. Wilson, H.W. 1966 119p illus pa $1.50   028.7
1 Library service 2 Reference books
ISBN 0-8242-0012-8
Designed to build an appreciation of books and study skills through the use of library tools, each of this handbook's eleven chapters comprises a library lesson and is followed by a summary and/or a review section
"The pamphlet should prove a boon to those school librarians who feel that their first responsibility is to work with teachers in developing in each student the spirit and skills of individual inquiry." Cur Ref Bks

Mott, Carolyn

Children's book on how to use books and libraries by Carolyn Mott & Leo B. Baisden. 3d ed. Scribner 1968 illus pa $4   028.7
1 Library service 2 Reference books
ISBN 0-684-51539-3
A workbook is also available pa $1.40 (ISBN 0-684-51539-3)
First published 1937
A text designed to acquaint young people with the more important aspects of books and libraries. Includes classification systems, the parts of a book and their significance, reference sources, the card catalog, maps etc.

Whitney, David C.
The first book of facts and how to find them; illus.
by Edward Mackenzie. Watts, F. 1966 66p illus lib.
bdg. $3.90 (4-6)   028.7
1 Reference books
ISBN 0-531-00527-5
"Small, inexpensive, illustrated in color, 'The First
Book of Facts' is a fine introduction to reference work.
It illustrates various kinds of facts and shows what
kinds of tools will locate them. It explains clearly the
kinds of alphabetical arrangement, the differences in
forms of names, and shows how facts can be used in
critical thinking." Peterson. Ref Bks for Elem and Jr
High Sch Libraries

031   American encyclopedias

Britannica Junior encyclopaedia for boys and girls.
Encyclopaedia Britannica Educ. Corp. 15v illus
maps apply to publisher for price   031
1 Encyclopedias and dictionaries
First published 1934 in 12 volumes
"The set is organized into 15 separately paged
volumes, using the unit letter plan (one or more complete letters per volume). Articles are arranged
alphabetically letter by letter. Volume 1 is the Ready
Reference Index containing, in addition to the 664-
page index, the list of contributing editors and writers
and a nine-page introduction to the index. . . . Annual revisions are made in some articles and the reference index is also revised yearly. Much illustrated
matter is included in the encyclopedia. In fact, few
pages are without some color or black and white
photo, sketch, map, graph, or diagram. Color is also
used to highlight the fact boxes in an attempt to
brighten such usually drab presentations of data.
However, state flowers, symbols, etc., in articles on
the states—usually colorful features in juvenile
encyclopedias—are small and unattractive. Maps are
liberally distributed through the set to show political
/physical features, distribution of people, land use,
and economic factors. Volume 15, in addition to containing letters X, Y, and Z, offers a complete world
atlas section with its own index." Wynar. Guide to Ref
Bks for Sch Media Centers
For a fuller review see: The Booklist, September 1,
1973

Childcraft: The how and why library. Field Enterprises 15v illus maps apply to publisher for price
031
1 Encyclopedias and dictionaries
First published 1934
Each volume in the set can be shelved under the
appropriate classification number
Contents: v 1 Poems and rhymes; v2 Stories and
fables; v3 Children everywhere; v4 World and space;
v5 About animals; v6 The green kingdom; v7 How
things work; v8 How we get things; v9 Holidays and
customs; v10 Places to know; v11 Make and do; v12
Look and learn; v13 Look again; v14 About me; v15
Guide for parents
"Designed for use by and with pre-school and primary level children, its contents are carefully selected
on the basis of young children's interests and
curiosities as indicated by existing research. The
material included substantiates the editor's claim in
this respect, and also reflects the judgments of the
outstanding educational and library consultants who
are associated with the set. . . . Distributed throughout the set are hundreds of illustrations, many in full
color and many being excellent photographs. Generous use of illustrations by outstanding children's
artists, including many Caldecott Medal winners,

enhances the quality of illustrative material. The format of the set has commendable features: sturdy,
rainbow-colored binding; durable, high quality paper;
and clear, legible print. All in all, while 'Childcraft' is
not an encyclopedia, it contains such a wealth of material valuable to teachers and children that it should
definitely be considered as a basic reference source.
Its information and appeal easily justify the expense."
Peterson. Ref Bks for Elem and Jr High Sch Libraries,
2d edition
Supplemented by: Childcraft annual
For fuller review see Booklist, June 15, 1975

Collier's encyclopedia; with bibliography and index.
Macmillan Educ. Corp. 24v illus maps apply to
publisher for price   031
1 Encyclopedias and dictionaries
First published 1949-1951 by Crowell-Collier
Educ. Corp.
The articles in this set "are well developed, well
presented, and well illustrated. Arrangement is
alphabetical, letter by letter. The scholarly, signed
articles vary in length according to importance of
subject treated. The set is especially useful for its
coverage of politics, biography, fine arts, religion,
philosophy, the classics, science, and technology.
Small topical maps and large (many multi-colored)
maps with adjacent gazetteer information accompany
articles on states, provinces, and countries. The list of
contributors appears in Volume 1 and notes the qualifications and writings of each specialist. Volume 24
contains the bibliography; a comprehensive, analytical index; and a study guide designed to aid the reader
seeking to enlarge his knowledge on a particular subject. Bibliographies are listed under broad subject
fields, explicitly sub-divided, with title entries
arranged under broad or narrow subjects according to
the scope of the books listed; generally the books
begin at high school level and progress through college and postcollege levels, with easier or general
works treated first. Continuous revision program,
with several printings a year, assures up-to-dateness."
ALA Ref Bks for Small and Medium-Sized Pub Libraries
"Principally designed to be used by junior and
senior high school, college and university students, it
appeals to and can readily be used by upper elementary grade children. . . . It is probably the easiest
adult set for children to use and therefore provides a
smooth transition from encyclopedias coordinated
with school curricula to those designed for mature
users." Peterson. Ref Bks for Elem and Jr High Sch
Libraries
Supplemented by: Collier's encyclopedia year book
For a fuller review see: The Booklist, June 1, 1973

Compton's Encyclopedia and fact-index. Compton
26v illus maps apply to publisher for price   031
1 Encyclopedias and dictionaries
First published 1922 with title: Compton's Pictured
encyclopedia
"Arrangement of articles is alphabetical, letter by
letter. At the beginning of each volume is a section,
'Here and There in This Volume,' that serves as a
guide to some of the more interesting items and that
provides a stimulus to browse. The remainder of each
volume is divided into text and Fact-Index. The Fact-
Index provides references to the exact location of
related information in all volumes of the set; it is
handy as a ready reference tool because it includes
dictionary-type information on specific topics that do
not merit inclusion as regular articles. . . . In each
article basic information is given first, followed by a
progression toward more complex areas of specializa-
tion. Following many of the main text articles are
reference outlines and bibliographies. There are
study guides and reading guides that lead the reader

Compton's Encyclopedia and fact-index—*Cont.*
to a systematic survey of fields of interest too large or too detailed to have been included in a single article."
Wynar. Guide to Ref Bks for Sch Media Centers
"Extensive use of photographs, drawings, graphs, maps (with liberal use of color) add interest and provide experience in learning from illustrations. As usual, the text is well organized, clear in style, and concise. The books, as always, are packed with excellent learning aids." Sci Teacher
Supplemented by: Compton Yearbook
For a fuller review see: The Booklist, January 15, 1972

Kane, Joseph Nathan
Famous first facts; a record of first happenings, discoveries and inventions in the United States. 3d ed. Wilson, H.W. 1964 1165p $25   031
1 Encyclopedias and dictionaries
ISBN 0-8242-0015-2
First published 1933
This volume "includes 6,652 first happenings, discoveries and inventions in the United States, listed and described under general subject-headings, with appropriate subheads; an index by years, from 1007 to July 10, 1962, the date of the first trans-oceanic television program; an index by days of the month, so useful in planning displays and exhibits; an index to personal names; and a geographical index. . . . Reference librarians may wish that there were more citations to the sources of information, but the compiler's long years of effort, involving, in many cases, unpublished sources, inspire a good deal of confidence in the volume as a source of ready reference." Cur Ref Bks

The Lincoln library of essential information. Frontier Press 2v illus maps apply to publisher for price
                    031
1 Encyclopedias and dictionaries
First published 1924
"Articles are grouped by specific subject fields into 12 divisions. An explanatory note setting forth the scope, importance, and usefulness of a subject precedes each major topic. Within the large divisions material is organized either chronologically, geographically, or topically. Specific points and supplementary information can easily be located through the detailed 'Cross Reference Index.' . . . Information is clearly and concisely presented in the text, with many charts, diagrams, and tables. . . . To supplement each major section there are several thousand review test questions useful for measuring comprehension. Definitions of terms are included with many subjects. . . . The 'Lincoln Library' has particularly strong sections on literature and the fine arts, including a full exposition on music and a valuable major section on education. The biography section discusses over 4,000 of the world's most noted men and women. Also included are valuable charts and lists, such as Nobel Prize winners, tables of literature, and genealogy of royal families. For condensation, and often for side-by-side comparison, a tabular presentation of information is used. The 'Lincoln Library' frequently uses this method not only for statistical data but for other facts that may be grouped to indicate relationships or chronological sequence. All in all, this is an excellent two-volume encyclopedia." Wynar. Guide to Ref Bks for Sch Media Centers
For a fuller review see: The Booklist, June 15, 1972

Merit students encyclopedia. Macmillan Educ. Corp. 20v illus maps apply to publisher for price   031
1 Encyclopedias and dictionaries
First published 1967 by Crowell-Collier Educ. Corp.

This encyclopedia "is created for children from fifth grade through high school and is geared to curriculum materials from all states. Its subject coverage, while outstanding in all areas, is especially strong on states and countries, particularly Canada, science, technology, fine arts, literature, and vocational guidance. The articles are clearly written and are prepared primarily for the grade levels at which the subject is taught. Exceedingly accurate, each article is reviewed or written and signed by one of the many contributing specialists. The encyclopedia is continuously revised and is reprinted at least once each year to include important happenings. . . . Articles, arranged alphabetically letter by letter under specific entry, each begin with a dictionary definition, including pronunciation. Using extensive cross references to link related material, the set includes a 400-page index with 125,000 entries. 'Fact Boxes' and 'Student Guides' further assist in quick location of essential data. Bibliographies of graded titles appear with major articles. The outstanding format features clear printing with bold headings on fine quality paper." Peterson. Ref Bks for Elem and Jr High Sch Libraries
Supplemented by: Merit students year book
For fuller review see: The Booklist, Dec. 15, 1973

The New book of knowledge; the children's encyclopedia. Grolier 20v illus maps apply to publisher for price   031
1 Encyclopedias and dictionaries
Supersedes The Book of knowledge. This title first published 1966
"It is designed primarily for the elementary grades, but it can also be of some assistance to slower developing children in junior high schools. The material is arranged alphabetically, letter by letter, by broad topics. Each volume contains an index that is cross-referenced to the entire content of the set. In addition to the conventional entries, this index also contains many brief notes and informational items, particularly useful for quick reference. The Dale-Chall readability formula is used to test the reading level of every article and, in general, the material is presented in clear and simple style, with helpful pronunciation guides. . . . In terms of revision policy, 'The New Book of Knowledge' follows the policy of continuing revision; the set is printed three or four times a year to incorporate some of the most important information. All in all, this is one of the best encyclopedias for this age group; it is highly recommended by all major reviewing journals." Wynar. Guide to Ref Bks for Sch Media Centers
"This children's encyclopedia is strongly oriented toward the sciences and mathematics throughout and has many suggestions for individual projects and teaching procedures. Although the text is intended primarily for students in Grade 3 and upward, younger children can use the set to advantage." The AAAS Sci Bk List for Children
Supplemented by: The New book of knowledge annual
For fuller review see: The Booklist, April 15, 1973

Soule, Gardner
Surprising facts about our world and beyond. Putnam 1971 158p illus lib. bdg. $4.69 (5-7)   031
1 Curiosities and wonders
ISBN 0-399-60622-X
A collection of surprising but true facts about man's achievements, animals, nature, science, and technology
Partial contents: Medicine chest; Space data; Animal kingdom; The latest on UFO's; Some surprising statistics; Footnotes on history; Faster and farther; First men on the moon; Weather report; Machines and computers; Some unsolved mysteries; Nature wonderland; The future

The World book encyclopedia. Field Enterprises 22v illus maps apply to publisher for price   **031**

1 Encyclopedias and dictionaries

First published 1917-1918

"A good encyclopedia for young people from elementary grades through high school, and popular also as a general adult encyclopedia. Articles are written at the school level for which specific subjects are likely to be studied. Arrangement is alphabetical, word by word. Articles are clear, concise, and factual, the length depending on the importance of the subject treated, and they are signed. The list of contributors in volume 1 gives the title of articles each specialist has contributed to the set. Well-illustrated, multicolored maps have their own index on adjacent pages. While there is no index to the set, there are copious cross references. Major articles contain study aids: lists of related articles, frequently an outline, pertinent questions for understanding comprehension, and separate lists of books for further reading for young readers, and for older readers. Also features different visual aids. Especially useful for scientific subjects, literature, art, and biography. Maintains a continuous revision program." A L A Ref Bks for Small and Medium-Sized Libraries

Supplemented by: The World book year book

For a fuller review see: The Booklist, Dec. 15, 1973

032   English encyclopedias

Guinness Book of world records [ed.] by Norris and Ross McWhirter. Sterling illus $7.95   **032**

1 Encyclopedias and dictionaries 2 Curiosities and wonders

First published 1955 in England with title: The Guinness Book of records; in the United States, 1962. Frequently revised

Lists records of all kinds, including the smallest fish ever caught, the most expensive wine, the greatest weight lifted by a man, the world's longest horse race and the longest river in the world

A "compilation of facts, including both the significant and trivial which young people may find intriguing." Booklist

050   Periodicals

Dobler, Lavinia

(ed.) The Dobler World directory of youth periodicals; comp. and ed. by Lavinia Dobler [and] Muriel Fuller. 3d enl. ed. Citation Press 1970 108p pa $4.25   **050**

1 Periodicals—Directories

ISBN 0-590-08924-2

"The successor to the Dobler International List of Periodicals for boys and girls published in 1960." Foreword

"Nearly 1,000 periodicals are included in . . . [this directory]. The first section of the book, 'Youth Periodicals in the United States,' is arranged by subject and curriculum interest. Entries include title, circulation, advertising, number of issues, number of pages, price, age range, editor, publisher, type material purchased and prices, main emphasis. Part II, 'Periodicals in English Published Outside the United States,' gives essentially the same information. Two other sections are called 'Agents to Foreign Periodical Subscriptions' and 'Periodicals Published in Non-English Languages.' A section in the back lists cessations and title changes. A title index is also present. The list itself is helpful but is too old to be totally accurate as to titles still in publication and their prices." Peterson. Ref Bks for Elem and Jr High Sch Libraries. 2d edition

Sources and references: p12-13

051   American periodicals

Abridged Readers' guide to periodical literature. Wilson, H.W. $17 per year   **051**

1 American periodicals—Indexes

ISSN 0001-334X

First published July 1935. Monthly except June, July, and August (The indexing for these months is included in the September issue) Permanent bound annual cumulations

Indexes 44 periodicals of general interest which have been chosen by the subscribers to the index from the approximately 160 periodicals covered by the unabridged Readers' Guide to Periodical Literature. The form of indexing is the same as that used in the unabridged Readers' Guide, with all the bibliographic information provided that is necessary for locating any article

An index "designed especially for school and small public libraries unable to afford the regular Readers' guide." Winchell. Guide to Ref Bks. 7th edition

How to use the Readers' guide to periodical literature. Wilson, H.W. pa gratis   **051**

1 Readers' guide to periodical literature

First published 1962. Frequently revised

This pamphlet is designed for teaching the use of Readers' guide to elementary and secondary school students. Reasonable quantities for class use are free

Subject index to children's magazines. Edited and distributed by Gladys Cavanagh, 2223 Chamberlain Av, Madison, Wis. 53705 $10.50 per year   **051**

1 American periodicals—Indexes 2 Children's literature—Periodicals—Indexes

ISSN 0039-4351

Monthly August through May. First published 1949

Formerly published by Meribah Hazen, now edited and published by Gladys Cavanagh

"This monthly periodical index is essential for an elementary school library. Using the same form of entry as the 'Readers' Guide,' it indexes the valuable children's publications which contain invaluable information. Its list includes the juvenile weekly newspapers, e.g., 'Newstime' and 'My Weekly Reader;' varied titles, such as 'Boys' Life,' 'Jack and Jill,' 'Cricket,' 'Humpty-Dumpty,' 'Highlights for Children,' 'Arizona Highways,' 'Man and His Music,' 'Ranger Rick's Nature Magazine;' and regional historical magazines, for example, 'Illinois History' and 'Wisconsin Trails.' Indexing stories, poems, and plays as well as factual material, 'Subject Index to Children's Magazines' is an indispensable tool for both children and teachers." Peterson. Ref Bks for Elem and Jr High Sch Libraries. 2d edition

060.4   General rules of order

Powers, David Guy

The first book of how to run a meeting; illus. by Peter P. Plasencia. Watts, F. 1967 62p illus lib. bdg. $3.90, pa $1.25 (5-7)   **060.4**

1 Parliamentary practice 2 Clubs

ISBN 0-531-00553-4; 0-531-02302-8

"A brief but very useful book on the basics of parliamentary procedure. The typical parts of a club meeting are outlined and explained. Types of motions and their presentation are made clear as well as how they may be amended. Committees and their work, elections, voting, and 'rules to live by' (constitutions and by-laws, with samples) are also included. A handy glossary of parliamentary terms is appended as well as

Powers, David Guy—*Continued*
a simplified chart of motions. The humorous, cartoon-type illustrations are aimed at young readers." Sch Library J

Robert, Henry M.
Robert's Rules of order; newly rev. A new and enl. ed. by Sarah Corbin Robert, with the assistance of Henry M. Robert III, James W. Cleary [and] William J. Evans. Scott 1970 xlii, 594p $7.50   060.4

1 Parliamentary practice
ISBN 0-673-05714-3
First published 1876 with title: Pocket manual of rules of order for deliberative assemblies
"This book embodies a codification of the present-day general parliamentary law (omitting provisions having no application outside legislative bodies). The book is also designed as a manual to be adopted by organizations or assemblies as their parliamentary authority." Introduction
"A 48-page section of 'charts, tables, and lists' printed on tinted paper has been inserted in the middle of the volume for easy reference." Winchell. Guide to Ref bks. 8th edition. 3d Supplement

070   Journalism

Goldreich, Gloria
What can she be? A newscaster [by] Gloria and Esther Goldreich; photographs by Robert Ipcar. Lothrop 1973 47p illus $4.50, lib. bdg. $4.14 (3-5)
070

1 Radio broadcasting—Vocational guidance 2 Television broadcasting—Vocational guidance 3 Women as journalists
ISBN 0-688-41540-7; 0-688-51540-1
"One of a series of books that show contemporary women in various careers, this describes the day-by-day activities of Barbara Lamont, newscaster on a New York program, 'Black News.' Combining her career successfully with being a wife and mother, Ms. Lamont leads a busy and constructive life." Chicago. Children's Bk Center
"Realistically, the news events are neither inherently exciting nor action-packed; the interest value lies in photographs on every page and verbal descriptions of the technicalities and functions of the job." Booklist

Henriod, Lorraine
I know a newspaper reporter; illus. by Jane A. Evans. Putnam 1971 48p illus lib. bdg. $3.86 (3-5)
070

1 Journalism 2 Reporters and reporting
ISBN 0-399-60286-0
"A Community helper book"
The young reader is introduced to the newspaper world in this story of how a young girl accompanies her reporter-sister to the newspaper office where she meets the staff and learns the function of each "desk"
Glossary: p47

070.5025   Publishing— Directories

Gillespie, John T.
Paperback books for young people; an annotated guide to publishers and distributors [by] John T. Gillespie [and] Diana L. Spirt. A.L.A. 1972 177p pa $5
070.5025

1 Publishers and publishing—Directories 2 Paperback books
ISBN 0-8389-0131-X

Companion volume to: The young phenomenon: paperbacks in our schools, entered in class 027.8
"The purpose of this book is to give libraries, teachers and others concerned with young people's reading an introduction to important paperback publishers. It lists and describes the leading publishers and their imprints, paperback distribution by state, and in addition to addresses, gives specialty of the publishers, series (if any) for young people, pricing and other information including statements as to whether a publisher's paperbacks can be ordered directly." Wis Library Bul

Literary market place: LMP; with Names & numbers; the directory of American book publishing. Bowker pa $19.95   070.5025

1 Publishers and publishing—Directories
ISSN 0075-9899
A combined edition of the titles first published 1940 and 1952/1953 respectively, and issued annually
"Eighty-two alphabetically arranged sections provide names, addresses, phone numbers and other data on literary agents, associations, book manufacturers, review services, editorial services, exporters, book clubs, typesetters, book wholesalers, and many other specialized production and promotional services of essential interest to the trade. Librarians will be more concerned with the directory information on American and Canadian publishers, lists of awards, associations, and prizes." Wynar. Guide to Ref Bks for Sch Media Centers

070.505   Publishing— Periodicals

Publishers Weekly. Bowker $25 per year   070.505
1 Publishers and publishing—Periodicals 2 Book reviews
ISSN 0000-0019
Weekly. First published 1872 with title: The Publishers' and Stationers' Weekly Trade Circular
This journal provides news of the book industry and trade. Its features cover publishing news throughout the world and its forecasts section contains reviews of forthcoming adult, juvenile and paperback titles

100   PHILOSOPHY

133   Parapsychology and occultism

Cohen, Daniel
In search of ghosts; illus. with photographs and reproductions. Dodd 1972 182p illus $4.95 (6-7) 133
1 Psychical research 2 Ghosts
ISBN 0-396-06485-X
Here is a description of alleged occurrences of ghosts and other supernatural phenomena, and an account of psychical research, including seances, tracking poltergeists, and taking spirit photographs
The author has broadened "the traditional definition of ghosts to include almost any alleged occurrence involving 'spirits'. . . . For anyone seeking an introduction to various views of life 'beyond the grave' there are certainly some intriguing snippets of infor-

Cohen, Daniel—*Continued*
mation (and some well-chosen illustrations) here."
N Y Times Bk Rev
   A selected bibliography: p174-78

133.1   Apparitions. Ghosts

Kettelkamp, Larry
   Haunted houses; written and illus. by Larry Kettelkamp. Morrow 1969 94p illus $4.95, lib. bdg. $4.59
(4-6)   133.1
   1 Ghosts
   ISBN 0-688-21377-4; 0-688-31377-9
   The author "analyzes 10 documented cases of
hauntings and poltergeist activity in England and
America and discusses various scientific theories
which have been suggested as possible explanations
for such phenomena. Illustrated with black-and-white
drawings and three authentic photographs of ghosts."
Booklist
   "As a matter-of-fact look at spectral phenomena,
the book serves its purpose. . . . It's all bound to be
interesting to a young reader on the phantom trail, but
don't look for goose pimples." N Y Times Bk Rev

133.3   Divinatory arts

Aylesworth, Thomas G.
   Astrology and foretelling the future; illus. by J. H.
Breslow. Watts, F. 1973 63p illus lib. bdg. $4.33
(5-7)   133.3
   1 Astrology 2 Fortune telling
   ISBN 0-531-02606-X
   "A Concise guide"
   The author describes the principles of astrology and
the zodiac, explaining how to prepare a simple horoscope. He also provides information about reading
tarot cards and tea leaves, as well as predicting the
future with dominoes. One chapter contains brief
definitions of over twenty-five more obscure kinds of
fortune telling and divination
   "Since a mystic lurks in almost every young person
these days, the book should attract much interest. The
illustrations are marvelous." Pub W

Horwitz, Elinor Lander
   The soothsayer's handbook: a guide to bad signs &
good vibrations. Lippincott 1972 158p illus $5.75, pa
$1.95 (5-7)   133.3
   1 Fortune telling 2 Extrasensory perception
   ISBN 0-397-31538-4; 0-397-31215-6
   A guide to reading character and telling fortunes
using ESP, astrology, palmistry, numerology, playing
cards, tarot, dice, dominoes, tea leaves, and crystal-
gazing

133.4   Magic, witchcraft, demonology

Cohen, Daniel
   Curses, hexes, & spells. Lippincott 1974 125p illus
(The Weird and horrible lib) $5.50, pa $1.95 (5-7)
                                 133.4
   1 Charms 2 Occult sciences
   ISBN 0-397-31493-0; 0-397-31494-9

   The author tells of curses on families, creatures,
places, wanderers and ghosts. He also discusses black
magic, amulets and talismans
   "Most of the author's examples of creepy
phenomena are old hat (the Bermuda Triangle, the
Kennedy tragedies, the Hapsburg curse, etc.).
. . . What is interesting in this book is that Cohen
gives a picture of the society and culture that apparently 'needs' curses and superstitions. His explanations of how the modern fascination with the occult
originated is delivered logically and with no moralizing." Pub W
   Suggestions for further reading: p121-22

Kohn, Bernice
   Out of the cauldron; a short history of witchcraft.
Holt 1972 119p illus $4.95, lib. bdg. $4.59 (5-7)
                                 133.4
   1 Witchcraft
   ISBN 0-03-080229-6; 0-03-080231-8
   "A concise, easy-to-read survey of witchcraft, its
origins in pagan religion, its practices, and the witch
hysteria that swept Western Europe in the fifteenth
and sixteenth centuries and Salem in the seventeenth.
The author describes the lore of the coven and the
sabbat, very briefly profiles some famous witches and
warlocks, and gives a few charms and recipes from
white and black magic concluding with a quick look at
witchcraft today. Appended are several pertinent
documents, a glossary, and a bibliography." Booklist

133.8   Extrasensory perception

Kettelkamp, Larry
   Sixth sense; written and illus. by Larry Kettelkamp.
Morrow 1970 95p illus lib. bdg. $4.59 (5-7)   133.8
   1 Estrasensory perception 2 Clairvoyance
   ISBN 0-688-31463-5
   "The author clearly explains the nature of
telepathy, clairvoyance, and precognition, and also
discusses psychometry, retrocognition, astral projections, mediums, possession, psychokinesis, psychic
photography and healing, and the tricks of phony
mediums and mentalists. . . . [He gives] a generally
accurate and balanced picture of present knowledge
about parapsychology." Sch Library J

150   Psychology

Kohn, Bernice
   A first look at psychology, by Bernice Kohn under
the supervision of G. David Weinick; illus. by Aldren
Watson. Hawthorn Bks. 1969 88p illus $4.95 (4-6)
                                 150
   1 Psychology
   This introduction to the science of psychology
describes how psychologists use experiments, tests
and observations to learn about human behavior and
personality
   "The pencil drawings are excellent. . . . The book
has been prepared in consultation with a number of
psychologists. As an introduction, it establishes basic
ideas at a very elementary level. It supplies a
vocabulary and sketches the field in very broad
strokes." Sci Bks
   Glossary: p77-80. Advanced vocabulary: p81-82

152.1   Sensory perception

Brenner, Barbara
   Faces; photographs by George Ancona. Dutton
1970 unp illus $5.95 (k-2)   152.1
   1 Senses and sensation

Brenner, Barbara—*Continued*
"Big, clear photographs illustrate with joyous vitality the things we see, hear, smell, and taste, and show how each sense operates separately, so that we can shut off perception and use some parts of our faces for different things. More subtly, the book points out the kinship of all peoples. It can be read aloud to very young children and used as a springboard for discussion, but the easy vocabulary, large print, and short sentences make the book an excellent choice for independent readers." Sat Rev

152.4   Emotions and feelings

LeShan, Eda
What makes me feel this way? Growing up with human emotions; illus. by Lisl Weil. Macmillan (N Y) 1972 128p illus $4.95 (3-6)   152.4
1 Emotions
The author uses specific situations involving such emotions as love, hate, fear, anger and jealousy to illustrate the conflicts and confusion every child experiences and to help the child understand and accept his feelings
"This book is an excellent treatment of a rarely taught subject for elementary-age children. It may help some young people who read to understand that certain feelings are shared by others. The illustrations invite the reading of the text." Appraisal

153.7   Perceptual apprehension and understanding

Bendick, Jeanne
Observation; written and illus. by Jeanne Bendick. Watts, F. 1972 71p illus (Science experiences) lib. bdg. $4.90 (2-4)   153.7
1 Perception
ISBN 0-531-01440-1
Using reader-participation pictures and questions, the author discusses how man observes the world around him, examining what senses he uses and what qualities are important in the perception of objects—including shape, color, size, motion, temperature, weight, smell and sound. The concept of change and some techniques of observation and record keeping are also considered
"The reader becomes a detective looking for the answers to posed questions. The illustrations are well drawn and aid the written material. Because it is a question and answer book with no set answers, a child can read it over and over and still find it an enjoyable experience." Appraisal

154.6   Sleep phenomena. Dreams

Kettelkamp, Larry
Dreams; written and illus. by Larry Kettelkamp. Morrow 1968 94p illus $4.95, lib. bdg. $4.59 (5-7)   154.6

1 Dreams
ISBN 0-688-21245-X; 0-688-31245-2
This account "includes a history of attitudes toward dreams, from ancient Egypt to modern psycho-

analysis; a . . . report on contemporary sleep research; a discussion of parapsychology; and some practical suggestions for the interpretation of one's own dreams." Commonweal
"A good first book on the subject. . . . In discussing both the psychological aspects of dreaming and the studies of physiological processes, the author goes into the subjects only enough to make them comprehensible, so that the amount of information given is not too heavy for the understanding of the intended audience." Chicago. Children's Bk Center

Silverstein, Alvin
Sleep and dreams [by] Alvin Silverstein and Virginia B. Silverstein. Lippincott 1974 159p illus map $5.50 (6-7)   154.6
1 Sleep
ISBN 0-397-31325-X
The authors describe research on the slow-wave and rapid eye movements (REM) using electroencephalograms, the sleeping habits of animals and people, sleep deprivation, dreams, insomnia and the use of sleeping pills, and hibernation
"The authors have come up with an informative and well-written summary of . . . new data, which they have presented clearly and non-technically and yet in sufficient detail to answer questions arising in the minds of readers. . . . Photographs and charts are well selected and helpful. This slender volume is excellent as collateral reading and for classroom use as an introduction to the subject." Sci Bks

155.5   Adolescents

LeShan, Eda
You and your feelings. Macmillan Pub. Co. 1975 117p $5.95 (6-7)   155.5
1 Adolescence 2 Emotions
"Some reassuring insights for adolescents who are trying to cope with roller coaster feelings. Family, school, peers, dating, sex, love, drugs, alcohol, and other teen troubles are tackled; responsibility for actions is also stressed on how to develop and cope with adult problems. In a few areas—e.g., sex and drugs—books for further reading are suggested. Other books on teenage feelings are usually more like standard psychology tests: LeShan's use of quotes from young adults gives this a personal tone, a sense of immediacy, and greater validity." Sch Library J

156   Comparative psychology

Freedman, Russell
Animal instincts [by] Russell Freedman and James E. Morriss. Holiday House 1970 159p illus $5.95 (5-7)   156
1 Instinct 2 Animals—Habits and behavior
ISBN 0-8234-0001-8
This book "deals with those functions, actions or activities an animal 'knows how to do' or does instinctively, sometimes even automatically, in response to an appropriate 'signal' or stimulus. The various chapters explore the nature of instinct, offer suggestions for studying instinct, explain migration and suggest how the reader can conduct and participate in migration studies. . . . The last chapter, 'Blueprint for survival,' mentions some of the fundamentals of genetics, natural selection, and behavior. The discussions are documented by citations from the

Freedman, Russell—*Continued*
literature. . . . Perhaps one of the chief merits of this book is that it deals with many familiar animals the young reader recognizes by sight, and offers him explanations of some of their actions and reactions that he may have observed but has not hitherto understood, and points out still other features that may have escaped his attention." Sci Bks
For further reading: p153-55

How animals learn [by] Russell Freedman and James E. Morriss. Holiday House 1969 159p illus $5.95 (5-7)   156
  1 Animal intelligence
  ISBN 0-8234-0050-6
The authors discuss the difference between animal instinct and learning while describing the pioneer work of Skinner, Pavlov and Lorenz
"Fine photographs harmonize well with the text, and a book list and simple experiments to be done with animals are included for especially interested readers. An entertaining exposition, particularly useful in school libraries." Sch Library J

170   Ethics

Black, Algernon D.
The first book of ethics; drawings by Rick Schreiter. Watts, F. 1965 66p illus lib. bdg. $3.90 (5-7)   170
  1 Ethics
  ISBN 0-531-00526-7
An "introduction to the principles and significance of ethics in the conduct of life. . . . The author describes the moral codes and concepts concerning right and wrong action which have evolved through the ages and covers in detail four basic commandments common to the great philosophical and religious teaching of the past and present. He discusses personal and current social ethical issues suggesting ways for making choices in life." Booklist
The text "is not too well organized. . . . Too bad, because the topic is important and interesting, the approach is sensible and sensitive, and the writing style is quite good." Chicago. Children's Bk Center

200   RELIGION

220.3   Bible—Dictionaries

Northcott, Cecil
Bible encyclopedia for children. Designed and illus. by Denis Wrigley. Westminster Press 1964 174p illus $5.95 (5-7)   220.3
  1 Bible—Dictionaries
  ISBN 0-664-20494-5
"A readable book of reference which seems to achieve its purpose of providing basic information about 'the chief people, the main events, and the leading ideas of the Bible.' A wealth of background material is adroitly contained within the concise entries which despite their brevity have clarity and sufficient liveliness to encourage children to read further in the Scriptures. Bible references are chiefly to the Authorized Version. Cross references . . . enhance the book's usefulness." Toronto Boys and Girls House

Young readers dictionary of the Bible; for use with the Revised Standard Version of the Bible. Abingdon 1969 321p illus maps $5.95   220.3
  1 Bible—Dictionaries
  ISBN 0-687-46829-9
This "dictionary contains definitions of names and terms with pronunciations. . . . Illustrations, maps and a chronology of kings of Israel are included." Wynar. Guide to Ref Bks for Sch Media Centers

220.5   Bible. Modern versions

Bible
The Holy Bible; containing the Old and New Testaments; tr. out of the original tongues; and with the former translations diligently compared and rev. by King James's special command, 1611. Oxford prices vary   220.5
The authorized or King James version originally published 1611

The Holy Bible. Revised standard version; containing the Old and New Testaments. . . . Reference ed. with Concise concordance. Nelson 1959 2v in 1 maps prices vary   220.5
"Translated from the original tongues; being the version set forth A.D. 1611, revised A.D. 1881-1885 and A.D. 1901, compared with the most ancient authorities and revised A.D. 1946-1952." Title page
"In this Reference Edition, cross references that refer the student of the Bible to passages having a common motif or theme are placed in the center column of each page. There is also a Concise Concordance divided into references to key words and references to proper names, and there are twelve maps in color. The concordance was compiled with the aid of Univac." Pub W

Bible. Selections
A first Bible; illus. by Helen Sewell [Selected and arranged by Jean West Maury] Walck, H.Z. 1934 109p illus $5 (4-7)   220.5
  ISBN 0-8098-2302-0
First published by Oxford
"Fourteen stories from the Old Testament and almost twice as many from the New, told in the words of the King James Bible." Booklist
"Helen Sewell has provided illustrations which are peculiarly appropriate to the stories. . . . The stories selected are those 'which time has proved to be the most interesting and inspiring to youth of every age.' " Wis Library Bul

Small rain; verses from the Bible; chosen by Jessie Orton Jones; illus. by Elizabeth Orton Jones. Viking 1943 unp illus lib. bdg. $5.95, pa 95¢ (k-3)   220.5
  ISBN 0-670-65265-2; 0-670-05088-1
"The title is from Deuteronomy, the complete verse appearing on the end papers. The selections are from various books of both Old and New Testaments and are those which embody ideas rather than story content. . . . Altogether a book of rare quality, expressing the beauty and wonder which should be part of religious experience." Wis Library Bul
"The compiler could hardly have found a more effective way of introducing children to their cultural heritage: the great poetry of the Bible. . . . In her drawings of children . . . in ginghams and overalls, Elizabeth Jones has brought some of the most beautiful passages of the King James Version into the child's own experience." Sat Rev

Bible. Selections—*Continued*

Wings of the morning; verses from the Bible; selected by Robin Palmer; illus. by Tony Palazzo. Walck, H.Z. 1968 unp illus $3.75 (1-4)   **220.5**

ISBN 0-8098-1150-2

Verses from the Bible are interpreted through illustrations of animals and birds in full-color and brown and white

220.8   Special subjects treated in the Bible

Bible. Selections

Animals of the Bible; a picture book by Dorothy P. Lathrop; with text selected by Helen Dean Fish from the King James Bible. Lippincott 1937 65p illus lib. bdg. $4.50 (1-4)   **220.8**

1 Animals—Stories 2 Bible—Natural history

ISBN 0-397-31536-8

Awarded the Caldecott Medal, 1938

Illustrations of the animals mentioned in the Bible. "The creatures sometimes appear in double-page procession, as when they enter the Ark with a pair of tortoises cheerfully trotting at the head of the line, or as they emerge from the mists of creation; sometimes humans are in the picture, as with Elijah's ravens or the Peaceable Kingdom; sometimes there are angels, as with Balaam and the ass." N Y Her Trib Bks

"Dorothy Lathrop's love and understanding of animals, the sensitiveness and joy with which she draws them, make her the ideal artist for such a volume. It is more than a beautiful picture book, for she has studied the fauna and flora of Bible lands until each animal and bird, each flower and tree, is true to natural history." N Y Times Bk Rev

Farb, Peter

The land, wildlife, and peoples of the Bible; illus. by Harry McNaught. Harper 1967 171p illus maps $4.95, lib. bdg. $5.49 (5-7)   **220.8**

1 Bible—Natural history

ISBN 0-06-021863-0; 0-06-021864-9

This book provides "scientific data on the land, people, plants and animals of the Bible lands. . . . [The] author used the Bible as a guide and constantly related what he observed on his trip to the Holy Land to incidents in the Bible. Useful in geography, history and literature classes." Bruno. Bks for Sch Libraries

The author "knows the land well, and . . . writes about the Holy Land with authority and good sense. He is especially informative when he discusses the animals and birds of the Bible, and in this he is helped by the wonderfully precise drawings." N Y Times Bk Rev

Suggested readings: p160-62. Index of Biblical references: p163-64

220.9   Bible geography, history and stories

Gwynne, J. Harold

The rainbow book of Bible stories; illus. by Steele Savage. World Pub. 1956 319p illus $4.95, lib. bdg. $5.21 (4-7)   **220.9**

1 Bible—Stories

ISBN 0-529-04618-0; 0-529-04672-5

"A collection of many of the best known stories retold from Old and New Testaments of the King James version. . . . Illustrations add greatly to the book; the colored plates are not as well done as the black-and-white drawings, which are unusually attractive." Library J

"Gwynne has done an excellent piece of work, writing simply and with dignity. He writes in the transitions and explanations and quotes the exact words of the Bible whenever possible." N Y Her Trib Bks

Jones, Mary Alice

Bible stories for children; illus. by Manning de V. Lee. Rand McNally 1952 113p illus $4.95 (3-6)   **220.9**

1 Bible—Stories

ISBN 0-528-8215-3

Originally published with title: Bible stories

A collection of stories from the Old and New Testaments, featuring Abraham, Peter, Gideon, Elijah, Jesus, and others. Illustrations are in color and in black and white

Northcott, Cecil

People of the Bible; designed and illus. by Denis Wrigley. Westminster Press 1967 157p illus $4.95 (5-7)   **220.9**

1 Bible—Stories 2 Bible—Biography

ISBN 0-664-20764-2

"A companion to the author's Bible Encyclopedia for Children [entered in class 220.3] this . . . collection of stories is based on the Revised Standard Version and is organized around significant biblical personalities . . . [in] both the Old and New Testaments from Genesis to Revelation. . . . Each story [is] preceded by an appropriate biblical quote." Library J

Peale, Norman Vincent

Bible stories; told by Norman Vincent Peale; with illus. by Grabianski. Watts, F. 1973 247p illus $7.95 (5-7)   **220.9**

1 Bible—Stories

ISBN 0-531-02634-5

"A straightforward retelling of Bible stories from the Creation to the Crucifixion by the well-known pastor. Miracles are neither side-stepped nor explained, and there is no theological bias. Historical allusions are added and contemporary lessons drawn." Sch Library J

"A beautiful book. Grabianski's free and spontaneous water colors truly illustrate the Bible messages." Best Sellers

Turner, Philip

Brian Wildsmith's Illustrated Bible stories; as told by Philip Turner. Watts, F. [1969 c1968] 134p illus lib. bdg. $8.95 (2-6)   **220.9**

1 Bible—Stories

ISBN 0-531-01529-7

First published 1968 in England

The author's "Biblical adaptations, compact and dignified, give the Old and New Testament stories in a sweeping chronological continuum." Sutherland. The Best in Children's Bks

This "is a combination of art work and text which is almost too good to be true. [Wildsmith's] jewel-like illustrations, pen-and-ink drawings, rainbow washes, explosions of brilliant color, are matched by a beautiful text." N Y Times Bk Rev

221.9   Bible. Old Testament

Bolliger, Max

Joseph; illus. by Edith Schindler; tr. by Marion Koenig. Delacorte Press 1969 109p illus $4.95 (4-6)   **221.9**

1 Joseph, the patriarch 2 Bible. Old Testament—Stories

ISBN 0-440-04255-0

"A Seymour Lawrence book"

Original German edition, 1967

Bolliger, Max—_Continued_
An adaptation of the Biblical story about a boy whose older brothers sold him into slavery
"Children who are familiar with the story of Joseph and his brothers will be struck by the effectiveness of the retelling. . . . Special mention must be made of the illustrations: Line drawings, they portray the rugged Canaanites and the highly civilized and sensuous Egyptians, and capture the slight young boy as he becomes a man, and then a prince." Horn Bk

Noah and the rainbow; an ancient story retold by Max Bolliger. Tr. by Clyde Robert Bulla; with pictures by Helga Aichinger. Crowell 1972 unp illus $4.50, lib. bdg. $5.25 (k-3)   221.9
1 Noah's ark 2 Bible. Old Testament—Stories
ISBN 0-690-58448-2; 0-690-58449-0
Original German language edition published in Switzerland
"A beautifully rhythmic text, Biblical in cadence, retells the ancient story of the flood. . . . The Austrian artist's eleven full-page paintings face spaciously set verses. Stylized animals, a cubist Mount Ararat, and a brilliant climactic rainbow emerge with grandeur from sweeping lines and colors, which change from dark tones and deep greens to soft aqua and apricot." Horn Bk

Bulla, Clyde Robert
Jonah and the great fish; illus. by Helga Aichinger. Crowell 1970 unp illus $4.50, lib. bdg. $5.25 (k-3)   221.9
1 Jonah, the prophet 2 Bible. Old Testament—Stories
ISBN 0-690-46430-4; 0-690-46431-2
"A simple, moving retelling of the biblical story of Jonah, presented in picture-book format with striking, atmospheric pictures in bright or somber colors that capture the varying moods of the story." Booklist

Joseph the dreamer; illus. by Gordon Laite. Crowell 1971 unp illus $4.95, lib. bdg. $5.70 (2-4)   221.9
1 Joseph, the patriarch 2 Bible. Old Testament—Stories
ISBN 0-690-46554-8; 0-690-46555-6
"The biblical story of Joseph is retold in an easy-to-read text and illustrated with forceful black-and-white and colored drawings. . . . The book is faithful to the incidents of the Old Testament account, telling of Joseph's being sold into slavery by his jealous brothers, his rise to power in Egypt through his interpretation of the pharaoh's dream, and the confrontation between Joseph and his brothers when they come to Egypt to buy food during the years of famine." Booklist

DeJong, Meindert
The mighty ones (great men and women of early Bible days) Pictures by Harvey Schmidt. Harper 1959 282p illus lib. bdg. $6.89 (6-7)   221.9
1 Bible. Old Testament—Stories
ISBN 0-06-021521-6
Using Hebrews 11 as a focal point—"Now faith is the substance of things hoped for, the evidence of things not seen" the author tells the stories of those men and women for whom these words were true. Here are Noah and his sons, Abraham, Isaac, Sarah, David, Cain, Abel, and many others—living men and women whose faith was the evidence of things not seen

De La Mare, Walter
Stories from the Bible; illus. by Edward Ardizzone. Knopf 1961 420p illus $4.95, lib. bdg. $6.39 (5-7)   221.9
1 Bible. Old Testament—Stories

ISBN 0-394-81676-5; 0-394-91676-X
First published 1929 in England
Here are thirty-four stories retold from the first nine books of the Bible. "New drawings in Ardizzone's typical pen-and-ink style, although not so dramatic as the stories themselves, make an attractive volume. The retellings are outstanding for the beauty of their prose style, rendered with Biblical cadence and dignity fitting the many passages interwoven from the King James Bible. Unsurpassed for stories of the Garden of Eden, Noah's Ark, and such Old Testament heroes as Joseph, Moses, and David." Horn Bk

De Regniers, Beatrice Schenk
David and Goliath; illus. by Richard M. Powers. Viking 1965 unp illus lib. bdg. $4.95 (1-4)   221.9
1 David, King of Israel 2 Bible. Old Testament—Stories
ISBN 0-670-25816-4
"This dramatic Old Testament story, based on the King James version of the 'Bible,' has been carefully retold, and brilliant crayon illustrations add to the strength of the text. David's killing of the bear and the lion to protect his sheep, and his slaying of Goliath are simply and tastefully presented. The illustrations do not show the scenes in which David, using the giant's sword, beheads Goliath and presents the head to King Saul." Sch Library J

Graham, Lorenz
David he no fear; pictures by Ann Grifalconi. Crowell 1971 unp illus $4.50 (1-4)   221.9
1 David, King of Israel 2 Bible. Old Testament—Stories
ISBN 0-690-23264-0
Text first published 1946 as part of the author's: How God fix Jonah
This is the Biblical story of David and Goliath retold in Liberian English dialect
The "bold, imaginative woodcut illustrations add to the spirit and flavor of the African speech and background." Pub W

Singer, Isaac Bashevis
The wicked city; pictures by Leonard Everett Fisher; tr. by the author and Elizabeth Shub. Farrar, Straus 1972 unp illus $4.50 (3-6)   221.9
1 Sodom 2 Lot (Biblical character) 3 Bible. Old Testament—Stories
ISBN 0-374-38426-6
The author retells the Biblical story of the destruction of Sodom and its inhabitants with the exception of Abraham's nephew Lot and his family
"The drama of the story is heightened by the deep-red monotone of the full-page illustrations. With details supplied only by a skillful use of white lines and cross-hatching, the illustrations are particularly effective in character portrayal, and together with the somber story, form a remarkable unified whole." Horn Bk

Tresselt, Alvin
Stories from the Bible; retold by Alvin Tresselt; with lithographs by Lynd Ward. Coward, McCann & Geoghegan 1971 60p illus lib. bdg. $5.39 (3-6)   221.9
1 Bible. Old Testament—Stories
ISBN 0-698-30329-6
The author has retold twelve of the traditional Old Testament stories, including those about Noah; Abraham; David and Goliath; Joseph and his brothers; Shadrach, Meschach, and Abednego; Moses; Esther; and Samson
"There have been many adaptations of Bible stories for children, but few have kept the spirit and the beauty of Biblical language as this does. The prose has been artfully simplified, retaining the sonorous and

Tresselt, Alvin—*Continued*
poetic quality of the Old Testament. The illustrations, reverent and handsome lithographs, are in harmony with the text, and the format does justice to both." Chicago. Children's Bk Center

222 Historical books

Asimov, Isaac
The story of Ruth. Doubleday 1972 102p maps $3.95, lib. bdg. $4.70 (5-7)   222
1 Bible. Old Testament. Ruth
ISBN 0-385-08594-X; 0-385-05208-1
Maps by Rafael Palacios
The "Biblical story of Ruth and her mother-in-law Naomi is the subject of detailed analysis and interpretation in a book which explores both the laws and customs of the times and the historical antecedents of the story." Horn Bk

229 Dead Sea scrolls

Palmer, Geoffrey
Quest for the Dead Sea scrolls; with illus. by Peter Forster. Day [1965 c1964] 88p illus lib. bdg. $3.69 (5-7)   229
1 Dead Sea scrolls
ISBN 0-381-99741-3
First published 1964 in England
"The story of the discovery of the first scrolls by the Arab goatherd in 1947 introduces an account of further discoveries and of the difficulties and misunderstanding before the scrolls were identified and accepted. Varying theories about the age of the scrolls, who wrote them, why they were hidden, why they are important, are discussed as well as the methods used in finding answers to these questions." Toronto
"The content of the most important manuscripts is interestingly discussed. Each page of the well-produced volume is decoratively bordered with sketches." Horn Bk
Bibliography: p[91]

Rappaport, Uriel
The story of the Dead Sea scrolls; illus. by Milka Cizik. Harvey House [1968 c1967] 128p illus maps (A Story of science ser. bk) lib. bdg. $5.49 (5-7)   229
1 Dead Sea scrolls
ISBN 0-8178-3942-9
First published 1967 in Israel
Through maps, drawings, photographs, and text which includes quotations from the Dead Sea scrolls themselves, the author traces the mystery of the discovery of these important archeological finds of the 20th century, the unraveling and deciphering of their contents, and the history of the period in which they were written
"The excellent description of the treatments the scrolls undergo by experts' hands in order to be read and understood contains many precise and well-explained details." Sci Bks
Glossary: p120-23. Bibliography: p124

231 God

Fitch, Florence Mary
A book about God; illus. by Leonard Weisgard. Lothrop 1953 unp illus lib. bdg. $5.49 (k-3)   231
1 God
ISBN 0-688-51253-4

"Beautiful doublespread pictures in color, with brief text, each describing some manifestation of God's love—the sky, the rain, the sun. . . . Both pictures and text give an effect of quiet reverence." Horn Bk
"Written for believers of all faiths, it necessarily shuns specific doctrines, such as the uniqueness of Christ. It provides a foundation on which any parent can help his child build a more definite structure of faith." N Y Times Bk Rev

232.9 Life of Jesus Christ

Aichinger, Helga
The shepard. Crowell [1967 c1966] unp illus $4.95 (k-3)   232.9
1 Jesus Christ—Nativity
ISBN 0-690-73021-7
Original German edition published 1966 in Switzerland
This retelling of the Christmas story "is a simple one. A single shepherd seeks the Christ child, first in a beautiful town, then in a magnificent castle, finally finding him in an old hut. The illustrations [by the author] . . . exude the warmth inherent in the Christmas story." Horn Bk

Bible. New Testament. Selections
The Christ child; as told by Matthew and Luke; made by Maud and Miska Petersham. Doubleday 1931 unp illus $4.49, lib. bdg. $5.70 (k-3)   232.9
1 Jesus Christ—Biography
ISBN 0-385-07260-0; 0-385-07319-4
"The artists, Maud and Miska Petersham, who . . . spent several months in Palestine have interpreted through pictures the spirit of the Holy Land which was the background of the childhood of Jesus. With the exception of the prophecy from the book of Isaiah, the text is from the gospels of Matthew and Luke. A picture book of unusual beauty." Cleveland
The "simplicity [of the Bible text] unspoiled by adaptation. . . . The paper, type, and entire make-up of the book show an almost perfect accord of subject matter and format." Booklist

The Christmas story from the Gospels of Matthew & Luke; ed. by Marguerite Northrup. Metropolitan Mus. distributed by N.Y. Graphic 1966 32p illus $4.95   232.9
1 Jesus Christ—Nativity
ISBN 0-87099-047-0
First published 1950 by Pantheon Books
"A very handsome book indeed, the text comprising selections from the King James Version of the Bible. The layout is spacious and dignified, each page that has print on it being faced by a full-page reproduction in color of a painting appropriate to that part of the Christmas story being told. The page of print has, in addition to the title of the painting, a small reproduction of a woodcut in black and white." Sutherland. The Best in Children's Bks

Branley, Franklyn M.
The Christmas sky; illus. by Blair Lent. Crowell 1966 unp illus $4.50, lib. bdg. $5.25 (3-6)   232.9
1 Star of Bethlehem 2 Jesus Christ—Nativity 3 Magi
ISBN 0-690-19342-4; 0-690-19343-2
"Basing his text on the annual Christmas show at New York's Hayden Planetarium, the author explains in simple language the various theories which

Branley, Franklyn M.—*Continued*
astronomers have advanced to explain the Christmas
star." Hodges. Bks for Elem Sch Libraries
"The tone is reverent; the approach is scientific; the
book is quietly impressive." Sutherland. The Best in
Children's Bks
"Striking illustrations in sandswept hues of gold and
blue hold all the mystery and majesty of the firma-
ment." N Y Times Bk Rev

Brown, Margaret Wise
Christmas in the barn; pictures by Barbara Cooney.
Crowell 1952 unp illus $4.50, lib. bdg. $5.25 (k-2)
232.9
1 Jesus Christ—Nativity 2 Bible. New Testament—
Stories
ISBN 0-690-19271-1; 0-690-19272-X
A retelling of the Nativity story. . . . The text is
in simple rhyme; the pictures are large and detailed
There is "use of modern dress in the pictures
instead of the traditional Biblical costume, but this
does not detract from the spirit of Barbara Cooney's
illustrations. They are lovely." Library J

Graham, Lorenz
Every man heart lay down; pictures by Colleen
Browning. Crowell 1970 unp illus $4.50 (1-4)
232.9
1 Jesus Christ—Nativity 2 Bible. New Testament—
Stories
ISBN 0-690-27134-4
Text first published 1946 as part of the author's:
How God fix Jonah
Retold in Liberian English dialect, this is the story
of the birth of Jesus
"Told with great dignity, vitality, and simplicity.
The African speech patterns and the striking pictures
give a new meaning and beauty to the timeless story."
Commonweal

Hanser, Richard
Jesus: what manner of man is this? Simon & Schuster 1972 191p lib. bdg. $4.95 (5-7)   232.9
1 Jesus Christ—Biography
ISBN 0-671-65200-1
"An effective retelling of the life of Jesus, with
some space devoted to the phenomenon of the modern Jesus movement among the young. Obviously,
the author has done his homework in the Bible and has
based his account on the Gospels which tell us all we
know about Christ. Appended are quotes which show
that Jesus attacked the Establishment of His day and
of ours. There are also parables, prayers and references to the New Testament which reaffirm the
Christmas message of love, brotherhood and peace."
Pub W

Jüchen, Aurel von
The Holy Night; the story of the first Christmas;
illus. by Celestino Piatti; tr. from the German by
Cornelia Schaeffer. Atheneum Pubs. 1968 unp illus
$5.50 (k-3)   232.9
1 Jesus Christ—Nativity 2 Bible. New Testament—
Stories
ISBN 0-689-20338-1
"Stunning illustrations, chiefly in dark-bright
tones, portray the pastoral scenes of the first Christmas; especially lovely are the pictures of Mary and
Joseph riding to Bethlehem through the blue night
shadows. The writing is occasionally stilted, but this is
a quite simple retelling of the story of the journey to
Bethlehem, the birth of the Child, and the appearance to the shepherds of the Heavenly Host. There is
no mention of the Kings." Chicago. Children's Bk
Center

242   Prayers

Farjeon, Eleanor
A prayer for little things; pictures by Elizabeth
Orton Jones. Houghton 1945 unp illus $2.50 (k-3)
242
1 Prayers
ISBN 0-395-06749-8
"A prayer about some of the little things so important in the small child's world—fledglings, seeds,
drops of rain, lambs, foals, and all small creatures.
Each of the five verses is illustrated with appealing
pictures." Booklist
"Little children will understand this little book, and
the grown-up who reads the words as the listener
follows its affectionate pictures will do well to give
himself up, for the moment at least, to their frame of
mind." N Y Her Trib Bks

Field, Rachel
Prayer for a child; pictures by Elizabeth Orton
Jones. Macmillan (N Y) 1944 unp illus $5.95, pa 95¢
(k-3)   242
1 Prayers
Awarded the Caldecott Medal, 1945
One of Rachel Field's "greatest legacies to [chil-
dren] has been this [brief] prayer. It was written for
her own daughter, but now belongs to all boys and
girls everywhere. It is a prayer, beautifully written
and . . . bespeaking the faith, love, hopes, and the
trust of little children." Library J
"The pictures have a freshness and childlikeness
which match the text perfectly." Boston Globe

First prayers; illus. by Tasha Tudor. Walck, H.Z.
1952 48p illus $2.95 (k-3)   242
1 Prayers
ISBN 0-8098-1951-1; 0-8098-1952-X
Companion volume to: First graces, entered in
class 249
First published by Oxford
"Although its small size makes it more suitable for
home purchase, many libraries will want this tiny gem
of a book. There are prayers for morning, evening,
and meals, some less familiar, but all within the
understanding of a child. Delicately and tenderly
illustrated." Booklist
Available in both Catholic and Protestant editions

Vipont, Elfrida
(comp.) Bless this day; a book of prayer for children;
illus. by Harold Jones. Harcourt 1958 95p illus $5.95
(2-5)   242
1 Prayers
ISBN 0-15-208734-6
Divided into four categories of prayers for waking,
for bedtime, of thanksgiving, and of praise
"An unusually varied and rewarding selection of
brief prayers that will have meaning and beauty for
young readers. . . . The selections are profusely and
charmingly illustrated by Harold Jones. Many of the
drawings are in color and all blend gaiety with dignity
and delight in the natural world of people, animals
and landscape with reverence for things spiritual."
N Y Times Bk Rev
Index of first lines: p93-[96]

Yates, Elizabeth
(comp.) Your prayers and mine; decorations by
Nora S. Unwin. Houghton 1954 64p illus $3.95 (5-7)
242
1 Prayers
ISBN 0-395-07212-3
A collection of prayers taken from the Old and New

Yates, Elizabeth—*Continued*
Testaments, from St Augustine and St Francis, from Rabbi Gamaliel, Socrates, and Mohammed, from ancient Gaelic runes, the Navajo Indian, and the Breton fisherman—all of these prayers reflect feelings and needs which people have shared through centuries

246   Christian symbolism

Daves, Michael
Young readers book of Christian symbolism; illus. by Gordon Laite. Abingdon 1967 128p illus lib. bdg. $5.95 (4-6) 246
1 Christian art and symbolism
ISBN 0-687-46824-8
"Beginning with a very clear discussion of symbolism in general, Mr. Daves then traces visual religious symbols following the Old Testament from the Creation through the Apostles. Intended for Protestant children, although the author never states this, the book manages to transcend denominational differences. In general, the writing is simple and appropriate to the subject, while the stylized illustrations in muted shades of red and blue are most attractive and suitable for the text. . . . Well-indexed." Sch Library J

249   Christian worship in family life. Grace

First graces; illus. by Tasha Tudor. Walck, H.Z. 1955 47p illus $2.95 (k-3) 249
1 Prayers
ISBN 0-8098-1953-8
Companion volume to: First prayers, entered in class 242
First published by Oxford
A "diminutive book, delicately and appealingly illustrated, containing 22 graces and prayers of thanksgiving from both old and contemporary sources." Booklist
Available in both Protestant and Catholic editions

289.3   Latter-Day Saints (Mormons)

Elgin, Kathleen
The Mormons; the Church of Jesus Christ of Latter-Day Saints; written and illus. by Kathleen Elgin; with a foreword by Ray Knell. McKay 1969 96p illus maps (The Freedom to worship ser) $4.95, lib. bdg. $4.50 (4-7) 289.3
1 Mormons and Mormonism
ISBN 0-679-20118-1; 0-679-25091-3
The author traces the development of Mormonism in the United States, discusses its status today, describes its organization, and answers questions frequently asked about its beliefs. A long chapter on Charles Coulson Rich, an early Mormon leader, is included
"This is sympathetic, detailed, and extremely useful, especially in religious education collections." Chicago. Children's Bk Center
Bibliography: p94

289.6   Society of Friends (Quakers)

Elgin, Kathleen
The Quakers; the Religious Society of Friends; written and illus. by Kathleen Elgin; with a foreword by Richmond P. Miller. McKay 1968 96p illus map (The Freedom to worship ser) $4.50, lib. bdg. $3.89 (4-7) 289.6
1 Friends, Society of
ISBN 0-679-20156-4; 0-679-25115-4
"After a brief explanation of Quaker beliefs and involvement with social reform movements, a biographical sketch of Levi Coffin is presented, telling of his role in the development of the Underground Railroad. Then a history of the Quaker movement is given. Closing sections explain religious doctrine and the impact the Quaker movement has had on American life." Keating. Building Bridges of Understanding Between Cultures
This is "a useful, handsome, and tastefully designed book, the black and white pictures adding distinction to a clear and informative text." Sutherland. The Best in Children's Bks

289.8   Shakers

Faber, Doris
The perfect life; the Shakers in America. Farrar, Straus 1974 215p illus $6.95 (6-7) 289.8
1 Shakers
ISBN 0-374-35819-2
A history of the Shakers who "came to America to found communities based on religious idealism. And from the time Mother Ann Lee of Manchester sailed from England in 1774, Shaker settlements in New York, New England, and Ohio expanded and developed through the nineteenth century. But by the beginning of the twentieth century, these communities began to dwindle until the women remaining at Canterbury, New Hampshire, decreed—in 1964—an end to all Shaker recruiting. Based on the principles of celibacy, communal living, and obedience to a spiritual leader, reinforced by personal contacts with Deity and by songs and dancing in worship, the Shakers regarded the perfect life as attainable by women as well as by men, by blacks as well as by whites." Horn Bk
"This book is a delight to read. It is interesting [and] informative. . . . The Shaker way of life is sympathetically recreated, and the personalities of Shaker leaders are portrayed with vigor and realism." Children's Bk Rev Serv
Shaker museums and public collections: p201-05. Suggestions for further reading: p207-08

291   Comparative religion and religious mythology

Bulfinch, Thomas
Bulfinch's Mythology: The age of fable; The age of chivalry; Legends of Charlemagne (6-7) 291
1 Mythology 2 Folklore—Europe 3 Charlemagne—Romances 4 Chivalry
Some editions are:
Crowell $6.95 (ISBN 0-690-57260-3)
Modern Lib. (Modern Lib. Giants) $4.95 (ISBN 0-394-60714-7)

Bulfinch, Thomas—*Continued*

This book contains the myths of Greece, Rome, Egypt, and the Far East, as well as German and Norse myths, and the legends of King Arthur, Charlemagne and Mabinogion

Fitch, Florence Mary

Their search for God; ways of worship in the Orient; illus. with photographs selected by Edith Bozyan, Beatrice Creighton and the author. Lothrop 1947 160p illus lib. bdg. $5.81 (4-7)   291

1 Religions 2 Asia—Religion
ISBN 0-688-51599-1

"Beautiful photographs of followers of the Hindu, Confucian, Taoist, Shinto, and Buddhist religions illustrate a straightforward account of their religious practices." Asia. A Guide to Bks for Children

"This excellent book provides the necessary information to begin a study of Oriental religious history, philosophy, and traditions." Keating. Building Bridges of Understanding Between Cultures

Green, Roger Lancelyn

A book of myths; selected and retold by Roger Lancelyn Green; illus. by Joan Kiddell-Monroe. Dutton 1965 184p illus $5.50 (5-7)   291

1 Mythology
ISBN 0-525-26968-1

"Children's illustrated classics"

"Though lacking distinction in literary style this [collection of twenty myths] is a valuable book which will appeal to children who like mythological tales and also serve as a comparative study showing the parallels and variants in myths about the creation of the world, the making of gods and man, and the change of seasons." Booklist

Kettelkamp, Larry

Religions, East and West. Morrow 1972 128p illus $5.50, lib. bdg. $4.81 (5-7)   291

1 Religions
ISBN 0-688-21926-8; 0-688-31926-2

The author surveys the history, beliefs, similarities and differences of Hinduism, Buddhism, Taoism, Confucianism, Zoroastrianism, Judaism, Christianity, and Islam. The religion of ancient Egypt, present-day psychical research, and archeological findings relevant to the study of religions are also described

Price, Christine

One is God; two old counting songs; illus. by Christine Price. Warne 1970 unp illus music lib. bdg. $4.95   291

1 Religions 2 Folk songs
ISBN 0-7232-6075-3

The author has illustrated each verse of the Christian folk song "Green grow the rushes, oh!" and the Jewish folksong "Who knows one?" The symbol each verse represents is clearly explained. The common origin of Judaism and Christianity and the similarities between the songs are discussed. There are notes on each song and musical accompaniment

Seeger, Elizabeth

Eastern religions; illus. with photographs. Crowell 1973 213p illus map $6.95 (6-7)   291

1 Religions 2 Asia—Religion
ISBN 0-690-25342-7

"Giving full due to the mythological concepts native to India, China, and Japan [the author] has traced the rise and development of Far Eastern philosophical or mystical religions as revealed by the lives and teachings of the Buddha, Confucius, or Laotse. Doctrines and principles are quoted as well as exemplified in occasional poems strategically placed;

and stories and anecdotes are chosen to illustrate the tenets of the various Oriental religions and beliefs. Carried on in a vital geographic and historical context, the discussions give an account of the spread of Buddhism in the Far East as well as a sense of the significance of Western influence on Oriental life and thought. Ramakrishna and Gandhi are presented as modern exemplars of Hinduism; and the mythology of Shintoism is related to aspects of life in modern Japan. The book is pervaded by understanding and respect." Horn Bk

Books for further reading: p201-04

Wolcott, Leonard

Religions around the world, by Leonard and Carolyn Wolcott. Abingdon 1967 191p illus lib. bdg. $6.95 (5-7)   291

1 Religions
ISBN 0-687-36026-9

This "study of religious history and belief identifies the founders of religious movements, summarizes the tenets of the major religions, and mentions the customs, practices, and sacred writings of each. A concluding chapter deals with several newer denominations and sects as well as dogmas which are substitutes for religion." Booklist

The World's great religions, by the editorial staff of Life. Special ed. for young readers. Golden Press 1958 192p illus maps $6.95, lib. bdg. $7.50, pa $3.95 (5-7)   291

1 Religions
"A Deluxe Golden book"
First published by Simon & Schuster

"An overview of six great contemporary religions, adapted for young readers from the original edition which was based on the series of articles in 'Life Magazine.' Christianity, Judaism, Hinduism, Buddhism, Islam, and the philosophy of China (a blending of Buddhism, Taoism, and Confucianism) are described. Oversize pages adorned by handsome photographs in color illustrate the religious art, the houses of worship, the festivals, and the solemn rites of each religion. The longest section of the book is devoted to Christianity and to denominations within the Christian religion." Chicago. Children's Bk Center

"Picture selections excellent, text superficial but accurate except for minimizing diversity among faiths." Library J

291.03   Mythology—Encyclopedias

New Larousse Encyclopedia of mythology; introduction by Robert Graves. Putnam [1968 c1959] 500p illus $17.95   291.03

1 Mythology—Encyclopedias
ISBN 0-399-10570-0

First published 1959 by Prometheus Press with title: Larousse Encyclopedia of mythology

"Translated by Richard Aldington and Delano Ames and rev. by a panel of editorial advisers from the Larousse mythologie génerale edited by Felix Guirand." Verso of title page

This compendium includes Egyptian Assyro-Babylonian, Roman, Celtic, Teutonic, Persian, Hindu, Oriental, African and American Indian mythology

"Not an encyclopedia in the usual sense of the term as the material is presented in essay form with no easy approach to specific points. Includes various aspects of folklore, legend, and religious customs." Winchell. Guide to Ref Bks. 8th edition

Further reading list: p486-87

Sedgwick, Paulita
Mythological creatures; a pictorial dictionary. Holt 1974 unp illus $6.95 (5-7)   291.03
 1 Mythology—Dictionaries 2 Animals, Mythical—Dictionaries
 ISBN 0-03-012946-X
"Characters from familiar Greek, Roman, and Norse mythology are joined in this volume by creatures from the folklore of cultures as diverse as Libya, Peru and the Netherlands. The inclusion of animals as commonplace as toads and pelicans which have traditionally been endowed with extra-ordinary connections does indeed give a mythology fan much new territory to explore. . . . This would be a much more valuable tool if the definition included the name of the myth or folklore tradition where the creature is mentioned, or perhaps an index in which the creatures were divided by country of origin." Mass YA Coop Bk Rev Group
"The fanciful pen illustrations, reminiscent of the drawings in medieval bestiaries, add to the book's browsing appeal." Library J
Includes a selected bibliography

292 Classical religion and religious mythology

Asimov, Isaac
Words from the myths; decorations by William Barss. Houghton 1961 225p illus $6.95 (6-7)   292
 1 Mythology, Classical 2 English language—Etymology
 ISBN 0-395-06568-2
The author's "informal retelling and discussion of the myths to point out the scores of words rooted in mythology and to explain their usage in the English language provide a fresh look at the myths and a better understanding of the words and expressions derived from them." Booklist
Mythological index: p222-25

Aulaire, Ingri d'
Ingri and Edgar Parin d'Aulaire's Book of Greek myths. Doubleday 1962 192p illus map $7.95, lib. bdg. $8.70 (3-6)   292
 1 Mythology, Classical
 ISBN 0-385-01583-6; 0-385-07108-6
A "book for first readers in the field of mythology. . . . [The myths] are related as one continuous story, roughly divided into four sections: The Titans, Zeus and his Family, Minor Gods and Goddesses, and Mortal Descendants of Zeus." Best Sellers
"Written in a smooth, uncluttered style, the stories are brief, though not spare, and will probably have more appeal than the more ornate traditional retellings presently available in most libraries. Though the text is well written, this volume is most notable for its illustrations. Some of the lithographs are in soft colors, and a number are full-page. The d'Aulaires' distinctive stylized technique is ideally suited to the subject and captures the strength, grandeur, and heroism of these tales. . . . A distinguished piece of bookmaking." Sch Library J

Benson, Sally
Stories of the gods and heroes; illus. by Steele Savage. Dial Press 1940 256p illus $6.95 (5-7) 292
 1 Mythology, Classical
 ISBN 0-440-8291-8
This is "a fine collection of Greek myths based on Bulfinch's 'Age of Fable', some edited and others entirely rewritten." Adventuring With Bks. 2d edition

Bulfinch, Thomas
A book of myths; selections from Bulfinch's Age of fable; with illus. by Helen Sewell. Macmillan (N Y) 1942 126p illus $5.50 (5-7)   292
 1 Mythology, Classical
"Thirty Greek myths, the text adapted with few changes from Bulfinch's Age of Fable, including such well known myths as 'The golden fleece' and 'Perseus' as well as many less easily available to boys and girls, such as 'Castor and Pollux' and 'Niobe'. . . . A book every library should have." Ontario Library Rev
"Without illustrations, this would be a most usable collection of Greek myths. . . . With the illustrations, this is a truly distinguished book, Helen Sewell's clear-cut, sculptural lines achieve a modern and a classical effect at the same time, in perfect keeping with the text; they, too, are simple, restrained, and dignified." Library J

Colum, Padraic
The Golden Fleece and the heroes who lived before Achilles; illus. by Willy Pogany. Macmillan (N Y) 1962 [c1949] 317p illus $5.50 (5-7)   292
 1 Argonauts 2 Mythology, Classical
A reissue of a book first published 1921; copyright renewed 1949
Contents: The voyage to Colchis; The return of Greece; The heroes of the quest
"With the adventures of Jason, who sought the famous golden fleece, are interwoven other myths and hero stories—of Orpheus the minstrel, who knew the ways and histories of the gods, of Pandora, the Golden Maid, and Atalanta, the huntress of Peleus who won a bride from the sea, and of Theseus who slew the Minotaur." Pittsburgh
"Mr Colum preserves the spirit of the Greek tales and weaves them into a magic whole. In this he is aided by the spirited drawings." Booklist

Farmer, Penelope
Daedalus and Icarus; illus. by Chris Connor. Harcourt 1971 unp illus $4.95 (3-6)   292
 1 Daedalus 2 Icarus
 ISBN 0-15-221212-4
A retelling of the Greek myth "of the inventor Daedalus, who is offered hospitality by King Minos in return for building a labyrinth to house the King's monster son, the Minotaur. When the monster is slain, Daedalus is imprisoned in the labyrinth himself. [He] escapes with his son Icarus, builds wings and learns to fly." N Y Times Bk Rev
"Dynamic recreation of the myth in vigorous, poetic text and stylized, vibrantly colored illustrations." Sch Library J

The story of Persephone; illus. by Graham McCallum. Morrow 1973 unp illus $4.50, lib. bdg. $4.14 (3-5)   292
 1 Demeter 2 Persephone
 ISBN 0-688-20084-2; 0-688-30084-7
"The strong and simple prose in this effective retelling of the ancient [Greek] myth conveys the drama of goddess Demeter's loss of her lovely daughter Persephone. Accompanying illustrations, which alternate between stark black-and-white and brilliant color spreads, evoke the surreal quality of this myth on the changing of the seasons." Library J

Gates, Doris
The golden god: Apollo; illus. by Constantinos CoConis. Viking 1973 110p illus lib. bdg. $5.95 (4-7)   292
 1 Apollo
 ISBN 0-670-34412-5
"Sixteen stories involving Apollo which treat his

Gates, Doris—*Continued*

birth, his victory over the serpent, Python, his fruitless pursuit of Daphne, the loss of his son Phaethon, and his relationship with his twin sister Artemis." Library J

"The illustrations emerge as the most significant accomplishment for they sometimes capture the horror and the strength of the myths, which the text often fails to convey." Horn Bk

Glossary: p109-10

Lord of the sky: Zeus; illus. by Robert Handville. Viking 1972 126p illus lib. bdg. $5.95 (4-7)   292

1 Zeus
ISBN 0-670-44051-6

A retelling of myths in which Zeus plays a part. Included are stories about Io, Deucalion, Baucis and Philemon, Europa, Cadmus, Theseus, Ariadne, Minos, and Dionysus

"Although the myths related to Zeus are many, complicated, and often erotic, Gates has managed to distill readable stories without distorting the spirit of the original too much." Booklist

Glossary: p125-26

Two queens of heaven: Aphrodite [and] Demeter; illus by Trina Schart Hyman. Viking 1974 94p illus lib. bdg. $5.95 (4-7)   292

1 Aphrodite 2 Demeter
ISBN 0-670-73680-5

A retelling of some Greek myths in which the goddesses of love and fertility play a major role. Included are the stories of Adonis, Anchises and Aphrodite, Pygmalion, Atalanta, Cupid and Psyche, Hero and Leander, Pyramus and Thisbe, Demeter and Persephone, and Aphrodite's birth from the sea foam

"Trina Hyman's artistic conception of the deities is classical, and her fine-boned, bared figures, executed in flowing pencil drawings, actively project the emotional pitch of the text." Booklist

Glossary: p93-94

The warrior goddess: Athena; illus. by Don Bolognese. Viking 1972 121p illus lib. bdg. $5.95 (4-7)   292

1 Athena
ISBN 0-670-74996-6

A retelling of the story of Athena's birth along with other myths in which the Greek goddess plays a part. Included are stories about Aglauros, Perseus, Medusa, Andromeda, Bellerophon, Jason, Heracles, Medea, and Arachne

"A simplified, highly readable version of Greek myths. . . . Strong, black-and-white pictures accompany the text." Pub W

Glossary: p119-21

Guerber, H. A.

The myths of Greece & Rome. Rev. by Dorothy Margaret Stuart; with forty-nine reproductions from famous pictures and statues. London House & Maxwell 1963 316p illus maps $8.95   292

1 Mythology, Classical
ISBN 0-8277-0035-0

First published 1907 by Harrap

Contents: The beginning: Zeus; Hera; Athene; Apollo; Artemis; Aphrodite; Hermes; Ares; Hephaestus; Poseidon; Pluto; Bacchus (Dionysus); Demeter and Persephone; Hestia; Ceyx and Halcyone; Aeolus; Herakles; Perseus; Theseus; Jason and the Golden Fleece; The Calydonian Hunt; Oedipus; King of Thebes; Bellerophon; The Trojan War; The Adventures of Odysseus; Agamemnon and his family; Virgil's "Aeneid"; The lesser Gods of the Romans; Interpretation; Glossary and Index; Map of Greece of the myths; Map of Mediterranean countries in mythical times; Genealogical table

Hamilton, Edith

Mythology; illus. by Steele Savage   292

1 Mythology, Classical 2 Mythology, Norse
Some editions are:
Little $7.95 (ISBN 0-316-34114-2)
Watts, F. lib. bdg. $12.50 Large type edition. A Keith Jennison book (ISBN 0-531-00246-2)

First published 1942

Tales from classical and Norse mythology including famous and less well known stories of gods and men. A glossary is included

There is a "sense of the contemporary in the . . . notes and in the retelling of the stories. The section on the writers of mythology is a valuable estimate of the sources." N Y Pub Library

Hawthorne, Nathaniel

A wonder-book, and Tanglewood tales; illus. by Gustaf Tenggren. Houghton 1951 421p illus $4.95 (5-7)   292

1 Mythology, Classical
ISBN 0-395-07079-1
"Riverside bookshelf"
First published 1853

Contents: A wonder book; The Gorgon's head; The Golden Touch; The Paradise of children; The three golden apples; The miraculous pitcher; The Chimaera

Tanglewood tales: The wayside; The Minotaur; The Pygmies; The dragon's teeth; Circe's palace; The pomegranate seeds; The Golden Fleece

Hodges, Margaret

Persephone and the springtime; a Greek myth; retold by Margaret Hodges; illus. by Arvis Stewart. Little 1973 32p illus (Myths of the world) lib. bdg. $5.95 (k-3)   292

1 Persephone
ISBN 0-316-36786-9

This is the retelling of the myth of Persephone, how she was abducted to Hades by Pluto, and how her return to earth for part of the year became our springtime

"Here the focus is not on the anguished goddess Demeter hunting the daughter who has disappeared, taken as a captive bride to Pluto's underworld kingdom, but on Persephone." Chicago. Children's Bk Center

"An excellent retelling, with rich, detailed illustrations." New Bks for Young Readers

Newman, Robert

The twelve labors of Hercules; told by Robert Newman; illus. by Charles Keeping. Crowell 1972 150p illus (Crowell Hero tales) $4.50 (4-6)   292

1 Hercules
ISBN 0-690-83920-0

Included in this retelling of the twelve labors imposed on the Greek god Hercules are his killing and flaying of a lion whose skin is impenetrable; his slaying of the nine-headed Hydra; and his cleaning of the huge Augean stables in a single day

The tale is told "in readable format with dramatic drawings." N Y Pub Library. Children's Bks & Recordings, 1972

Glossary: p146-50. Map on lining-papers

Proddow, Penelope

Demeter and Persephone; Homeric hymn number two; tr. and adapted by Penelope Proddow; illus. by Barbara Cooney. Doubleday 1972 unp illus $5.95, lib. bdg. $6.70 (3-6)   292

1 Persephone 2 Demeter
ISBN 0-385-05966-3; 0-385-06726-7

A "combination of text and illustrations, this book is an adaptation of the classic myth about the kidnapping

Proddow, Penelope—*Continued*
of Persephone by Hades, King of the Dead (sometimes called Pluto). He carries her to her underworld home, leaving her mother, Demeter, to grieve. The distracted goddess sears the earth so that it doesn't yield and it seems that all humans will die of hunger. On the command of Zeus, Hades yields, at last, and allows Persephone to return but for only part of each year." Pub W
"Told in narrative verse, the story is illustrated with color pictures that are classical in style and design. Characters and places are identified in an appended list." Booklist

Dionysos and the pirates; Homeric hymn number seven; tr. [and adapted] by Penelope Proddow; illus. by Barbara Cooney. Doubleday 1970 unp illus lib. bdg. $4.95 (3-6)   292
1 Dionysus
ISBN 0-385-03193-9
This story comes from a collection of hymns known as the Homeric Hymns which Greek minstrels used as introductions to their longer songs. The story tells of the kidnapping by pirates of Dionysos, son of Semele and Zeus, who was the god of grapevines, ivy flowers and some of the forest animals
"The action of the poem is reflected in the dynamic and richly colored pictures that accompany the text." Horn Bk

Serraillier, Ian
A fall from the sky; the story of Daedalus; illus. by William Stobbs. Walck, H.Z. 1966 [c1965] 61p illus $4 (4-6)   292
1 Daedalus 2 Icarus
ISBN 0-8098-2361-6
First published 1965 in England
"A master storyteller has retold the ancient legend of Daedalus, the master craftsman of ancient Athens who was perhaps the forerunner of today's aeronautical engineers and pilots." Cincinnati
"Without doing violence to the basic outlines of various stories related to Daedalus, the author has established a logical sequence and well-developed plot. Literary style, format, and strong, simple illustrations are in keeping with the subject." Sch Library J
Bibliography included in Acknowledgments: p5

The Gorgon's head; the story of Perseus; illus. by William Stobbs. Walck, H.Z. 1962 [c1961] 71p illus $4 (4-6)   292
1 Perseus
ISBN 0-8098-2047-1
First published 1961 in England
"The author returns to the original Greek and Latin sources: Hesiod, Aeschylus, Apollonius of Rhodes, and Ovid, and, in simple, direct prose, he retells the major events in the life of Perseus from the imprisonment of Danae through the slaying of Medusa, the rescue of Andromeda, to the end of Perseus himself. Print, format, and handsome illustrations, which combine classical material with modern dash and vigor, blend to make the mythological marvels and the exciting adventures a joy to read." Sch Library J

Heracles the strong; woodcuts by Rocco Negri. Walck, H.Z. 1970 102p illus $4 (4-6)   292
1 Hercules
ISBN 0-8098-2071-4
This is "the story of heroic Heracles, son of Zeus and Alcmena, Princess of Thebes. Drawn from authentic literary sources and presented in a clear, well-developed narrative, the story describes Heracles' slaying of a serpent as an infant, his tragic fit of madness induced by the jealous Hera, his penitential

12 labors, and other incidental adventures, ending with his death and admittance to the company of Olympian gods. An inviting single volume on Heracles appropriately illustrated with woodcuts." Booklist

The way of danger; the story of Theseus; illus. by William Stobbs. Walck, H.Z. 1963 [c1962] 86p illus $4 (4-6)   292
1 Theseus
ISBN 0-8098-2367-5
First published 1962 in England
"This story of Theseus presents him both as a hero in Greek mythology and in his semihistorical role uniting the tribes of Attica under Athenian rule. The best-known legends involving him—the adventure of the Procrustean bed, the slaying of the Minotaur, the descent into the Underworld—are here, but strung together with more obscure deeds in an uneven biographical narrative. While the journey by land to Athens is recounted too prosaically, the black-sail incident, Aegus' death, and the descent to Hades are dramatically told." Booklist
"The brief chapters with . . . distinctive and handsome black and white pictures make this short book attractive to children who would not willingly attempt an equally excellent account of Theseus' life as part of a long book." N Y Her Trib Bks

Tomaino, Sarah F.
Persephone: bringer of spring; pictures by Ati Forberg. Crowell 1971 unp illus $5.50, lib. bdg. $6.25 (2-5)   292
1 Persephone
ISBN 0-690-61448-9; 0-690-61449-7
"A retelling of the Greek legend in which Persephone, stolen by Hades and taken to his underworld home, is brought back to earth and to her grieving mother, Demeter, for part of each year." Sutherland. The Best in Children's Bks
The "familiar Greek myth is narrated with a graceful simplicity, beautifully complemented by striking illustrations in which color is used with restraint and, on alternate pages, black-and-white pictures have dramatic vigor. . . . Good for reading aloud to younger children and for independent reading." Sat Rev

Turska, Krystyna
Pegasus [retold and illus. by] Krystyna Turska. Watts, F. 1970 unp illus lib. bdg. $4.90 (2-4)   292
1 Pegasus 2 Bellerophon
ISBN 0-531-01857-1
"The Pegasus legend is retold in a dignified style, and more fully developed than in many children's collections of Greek mythology. . . . A good addition to all library collections, this will be especially welcomed by storyteller." Library J
This "is a lavishly coloured version of the story. . . . It is certainly spectacular, with great sugar pink skies and tremendous scenes of battle and shipwreck, and the impressions of Greek light and landscape are very strong. The more sensitive child might find it vulgar, perhaps, but the pictures have great verve and the classical detail is good." Times (London) Literary Sup

White, Anne Terry
The Golden Treasury of myths and legends; adapted from the world's great classics; illus. by Alice and Martin Provensen. Golden Press 1959 164p illus $5.95 (5-7)   292
1 Mythology, Classical 2 Legends
ISBN 0-307-60747-X
Contents: Gods and heroes; Prometheus steals fire

White Anne Terry—*Continued*
from heaven; Miracle on Mount Parnassus; Phaeton
and the horses of the sun; Bride of Pluto; Echo and
Narcissus; Orpheus and Eurydice; Gorgon's head;
Heracles; Golden fleece; Daedalus; Theseus and the
Minotaur; Oedipus; Beowulf; Battle of Roncevaux;
Tristram and Iseult; Rustem and Sohrab; Sigurd of the
Volsungs

292.03   Classical mythology— Dictionaries

Tripp, Edward
Crowell's Handbook of classical mythology.
Crowell 1970 631p maps (A Crowell Reference bk)
$11.95   292.03
  1 Mythology, Classical—Dictionaries
  ISBN 0-690-22608-X
This alphabetical guide to the myths of Greece and
Rome includes characters, events, and the places
mentioned in the myths, the constellations named for
mythological personages, and brief descriptions of the
principal classical works in which the myths are found
  "I can without hesitation recommend this title as a
worthy addition to reference collections dealing with
the imaginative world of the ancient Greek pantheon.
It is thoroughly comprehensive, and, though admittedly aimed at the general reader, it will nonetheless
prove useful to teacher, student, and librarian." Library J
  Pronouncing index: p611-31

293   Germanic religion and mythology

Aulaire, Ingri d'
Norse gods and giants [by] Ingri and Edgar Parin
d'Aulaire. Doubleday 1967 154p illus $7.95, lib. bdg.
$8.70 (4-6)   293
  1 Mythology, Norse
  ISBN 0-385-04908-0; 0-385-07235-X
Illustrated by the authors, this collection of Norse
myths depicts raging giants, horrible monsters, and
all-too-human gods. It includes stories about such
personages as one-eyed Odin, mischievous Loki,
enormous Thor and the beautiful Freya
  The illustrations "reveal the d'Aulaires' intimate
acquaintance with Nordic landscape and folk art and
establish brilliant pictorial atmosphere. . . . All the
creatures in the mythological hierarchy are clearly
established, and their stories are told in a smooth,
colorful prose." Horn Bk
  "It is not usual that a book which is essentially a
good reference volume can be recommended as a
storybook as well. . . . There is a 'Reader's Companion'
that is both glossary and index. . . . The d'Aulaires'
new volume is a big, handsome book and fit companion to their excellent [Book of Greek myths, listed in
class 292]." N Y Times Bk Rev

Colum, Padraic
The children of Odin; the book of Northern myths;
illus. by Willy Pogany. Macmillan (N Y) 1968 [c1920]
271p illus $5.50 (5-7)   293
  1 Mythology, Norse
A reissue in new format of a book first published
1920
  Contents: Dwellers in Asgard; Odin the wanderer:

Witch's heart; Sword of the Volsungs and Twilight of
the gods
  "Padraic Colum has given a free rendering of the
myths of the poetic and the prose Eddas. Mr Colum
tells us that he has done his work directly from the
Eddas and in consultation with Norwegian scholars."
Bookmark
  "The stories of the Norse sagas, from the twilight of
the gods to the destruction of Asgard, are told in a
connected narrative that flows in a simple rhythmic
prose sometimes poetic. Four color plates and several
line drawings." Booklist

Hosford, Dorothy G.
Thunder of the gods; illus. by Claire & George
Louden. Holt 1952 115p illus lib. bdg. $2.92 (5-7)
                                                      293
  1 Mythology, Norse
  ISBN 0-03-036090-0
  "A retelling of the Norse myths . . . which
recreates the spare beauty and simple dignity, the
humor and pathos of these stories as they are told in
the Eddas. In this version, the terse, dramatic form of
the folk tale is used throughout, yet the heightened
langauge in which they are told preserves the remoteness necessary to mythical stories of the gods."
Ontario Library Rev
  Line drawings "catch and emphasize the spirit of
the legends. A book to suggest for home libraries as
well as public and school libraries." Library J
  Includes: Note on the Norse myths [and] Pronunciation of proper names

296.4   Judaism—Public services, rites, traditions

Cone, Molly
The Jewish New Year; illus. by Jerome Snyder.
Crowell 1966 unp illus (A Crowell Holiday bk) $4.95,
lib. bdg. $5.70 (1-3)   296.4
  1 Rosh ha-Shanah 2 Yom Kippur
  ISBN 0-690-46040-6; 0-690-46041-4
  "A simple but dignified telling of why the Jewish
people celebrate the New Year in the autumn, the
customs that are part of the celebration and the meaning of these ancient rites today. Striking illustrations
add to a book that can be read and understood by
children of all faiths and backgrounds." Sch Library J

  The Jewish Sabbath; illus. by Ellen Raskin. Crowell
1966 unp illus (A Crowell Holiday bk) $4.95, lib. bdg.
$5.70 (1-3)   296.4
  1 Sabbath 2 Jews—History
  ISBN 0-690-46111-9; 0-690-46112-7
The author discusses the history of the Sabbath and
of the Jewish people, legends of the Sabbath, and the
customs of traditional celebration
  "The wonderfully special feeling of the Jewish Sabbath is sensitively portrayed. All Sabbath days serve
the same purpose, and this similarity among faiths is
brought out. The stunning woodcuts add to a well-
crafted text." Adventuring with Bks. 2d edition

  Purim; illus. by Helen Borten. Crowell 1967 unp
illus (A Crowell Holiday bk) $4.95, lib. bdg. $5.70
(1-3)   296.4
  1 Purim (Feast of Esther) 2 Esther, Queen of Persia
  ISBN 0-690-65921-0; 0-690-65922-9
  "Through a simple retelling of the story of Esther,
the author explains the origin and significance of
Purim, followed by a description of the special foods
and ceremonies with which the Jewish day of rest is
celebrated." Hodges. Bks for Elem Sch Libraries

Epstein, Morris
All about Jewish holidays and customs; illus. by Arnold Lobel. Rev. ed. Ktav 1970 142p illus $4 (4-6)
296.4
1 Fasts and feasts—Judaism
ISBN 0-87068-500-7
First published 1959
This collection of Jewish holidays reveals the joys and the sorrows, the traditions and the ceremonies of the customs of the Jewish people
Partial contents: The Jewish year; Everything starts with a calendar; The synagogue; Bar Mitzvah; The Jewish home; The world of Jewish books; Bibliography

Morrow, Betty
Jewish holidays, by Betty Morrow and Louis Hartman; illus. by Nathan Goldstein. Garrard 1967 64p illus (A Holiday bk) lib. bdg. $3.69 (2-5)   296.4
1 Fasts and feasts—Judaism
ISBN 0-8116-6560-7
The author presents the history and customs of seven Jewish holidays: the Sabbath; Rosh Hashanah; Yom Kippur; Sukkot; Hanukkah; Purim; and Passover
"A beautifully illustrated book. . . . The spirit of freedom rings throughout paralleling the American wish for freedom. The similarities of religious holidays of the world are also revealed." Bruno. Bks for Sch Libraries, 1968

Purdy, Susan Gold
Jewish holidays; facts, activities, and crafts. Lippincott 1969 94p illus $5.95, lib. bdg. $5.93 (4-7) 296.4
1 Fasts and feasts—Judaism 2 Handicraft
ISBN 0-397-31076-5; 0-397-31077-3
"Each holiday is described, both as to its origins and in the traditional ways in which it is celebrated. Each is followed by directions for some project associated with the holiday: a table decoration, a toy, a recipe, puppets and costumes, greeting cards, etc. The instructions are clear, with a note that adult supervision is needed for handling any sharp tools. The body of the text is preceded by a Jewish calendar and a brief discussion of the Jewish religion. Notes on pronunciation are included; a list of materials and foods used in the projects, and an index are appended. Particularly useful for religious education or for craft groups." Chicago. Children's Bk Center

Simon, Norma
Hanukkah; illus. by Symeon Shimin. Crowell 1966 unp illus (A Crowell Holiday bk) $4.95, lib. bdg. $5.70 (1-4)
296.4
1 Hanukkah (Feast of Lights)
ISBN 0-690-36952-2; 0-690-36953-0
The author has told the story of Hanukkah, the Festival of Lights, which commemorates the battle of the Maccabees for religious freedom—its history, customs, and significance
The information is "presented with dignity in a simple text and pleasing black-and-white and colored drawings." Booklist

Passover; illus. by Symeon Shimin. Crowell 1955 unp illus (A Crowell Holiday bk) $4.95, lib. bdg. $5.70 (1-3)
296.4
1 Passover
ISBN 0-690-61093-9; 0-690-61094-7
"Simply written and attractively illustrated, this is a good addition to the series of books about holidays. The author describes the origin of the Passover celebration, and explains in detail the procedures of the ritual dinner; there is a brief description, also, of observances in Israel and in Jordan today." Chicago. Children's Bk Center

297 Islam

Fitch, Florence Mary
Allah, the God of Islam; Moslem life and worship; illus. with photographs selected by Beatrice Creighton and the author. Lothrop 1950 144p illus lib. bdg. $5.81 (4-6)   297
1 Islam
ISBN 0-688-51257-7
The story of Islam (Mohammedanism) is that of a great historical conquest as well as a religion. Moslems include among their followers small groups in the British Isles, the Soviet Union, and the United States, as well as the masses of people in the true Moslem countries which stretch from Morocco on the African coast through Arabia, Syria, Turkey, and Persia to the north of India
"Readable text and excellent photographs. . . . Useful not only from the religious angle but as an aid to understanding the culture of Moslem people." Chicago. Children's Bk Center

299 Other religions

Brindze, Ruth
The story of the totem pole; illus. by Yeffe Kimball. Vanguard 1951 62p illus $4.95 (4-7)   299
1 Totems and totemism 2 Indians of North America—Northwest, Pacific
ISBN 0-8149-0277-4
Miss Brindze "writes of the origins and uses of the poles, and of the American Indians of the Northwest who carved them. She includes also brief stories about specific poles and even some information on how to read the carvings. The illustrations are striking and in themselves make a valuable addition to books about America." Horn Bk

300 SOCIAL SCIENCES

301.11 Social interaction

Sechrist, Elizabeth Hough
It's time for brotherhood, by Elizabeth Hough Sechrist and Janette Woolsey; illus. by John R. Gibson. [Rev. ed.] Macrae Smith Co. 1973 296p illus lib. bdg. $6.97 (5-7)   301.11
1 Social work 2 Human relations 3 Biography
ISBN 0-8255-8191-5
First published 1962
This book discusses organizations and individuals that have worked to promote the concept of brotherhood, including religious and charitable organizations, civil rights movements, service agencies, foundations, exchange programs, and the United Nations
Bibliography: p271-79

301.16 Mass communication

Adler, Irving
Communication [by] Irving and Ruth Adler. Day 1967 48p illus lib. bdg. $4.47 (4-6)   301.16
1 Communication—History
ISBN 0-381-99973-4

Adler, Irving—*Continued*
"The Reason why books"
"A survey of the development of communication from the first cave pictures of prehistory through the development of writing, the movable type that led to wider use of books, the signaling apparatus for instant messages, the symbols used in special trades or disciplines, and the various contemporary media and devices for stored communication or instantaneous long-distance communication." Chicago. Children's Bk Center
Word list: p47

301.2   Culture and cultural processes. Anthropology

Cooke, David C.
The tribal people of Thailand. Putnam 1972 71p illus lib. bdg. $4.39 (5-7)   301.2
1 Ethnology—Thailand
ISBN 0-399-60740-4
"An account of the ancient tribal people in the remote hills of northern Thailand. [The author] describes the origin of beliefs and nomadic customs and how the principal tribes, Meos and Karens, build houses, smoke pipes and construct crossbars. A chapter is devoted to marriage and the festivities at which young people meet each other." Sch Library J

301.31   Human ecology

Gregor, Arthur S.
Man's mark on the land; the changing environment from the stone age to the age of smog, sewage, and tar on your feet; illus. with photographs, maps, and charts. Scribner 1974 120p illus maps $5.95 (4-7)   301.31
1 Man—Influence on nature 2 Human ecology
ISBN 0-684-13740-2
"Maps, charts, and illustrations by Jean Simpson." Verso of title page
In this historical look at man's interaction with his environment, the author discusses the discovery of farming, the coming of the city, and the rise of civilization. He then describes the effects each had on the environment
"His writing is descriptive, and it is well sprinkled with pictures and illustrations to hold the elementary reader's attention. Gregor briefly covers most major cultures of the world. He has undertaken a written history which just skims a few ideas but is educational and of value to the student." Sci Bks
Dictionary for the environment: p112-15. For further reading: p116-17

Miles, Betty
Save the earth! An ecology handbook for kids; illus. by Claire A. Nivola. Knopf 1974 91p illus lib bdg. $5.57, pa. $2.50 (4-7)   301.31
1 Pollution 2 Conservation of natural resources 3 Ecology
ISBN 0-394-92658-7; 0-394-82658-2
This book contains information and "activities for children on topics of town planning, paper waste, space vs. population, pollution of air and water, noise control, and home conservation practices. Some activities are short ones, such as keeping a log of water use, planning a 'new town,' and identifying noise pollution sources. Others are long-range, such as tak-

ing daily photographs of industrial pollution." Sci and Children
"The book's major strength is in its emphasis on involvement for change. The author encourages students to fight pollution not only as individuals but as citizens working through a variety of channels. Samples of ways to proceed are included. The text is somewhat choppy, but the book contains specific information which is helpful—a chart measuring common sounds in decibels, a list of ecology organizations, and a bibliography which includes newsletters. It is well-organized, and the format is interestingly varied with squiggly line drawings and well-selected black-and-white photographs." Appraisal

301.32   Populations

Asimov, Isaac
Earth: our crowded spaceship. Day 1974 160p illus $6.95 (5-7)   301.32
1 Population 2 Conservation of natural resources
ISBN 0-381-99625-5
"Asimov discusses how Earth became overpopulated and measures for coping with and/or putting a stop to population growth (new forms of energy, major wars, etc.). The psychology of having babies and the need to educate people about the necessity of birth control are explained, however, methods are not. Although written in a casual style, the text is full of carefully indexed facts, statistics (given in metric measures with a conversion table appended), and definitions of terms such as 'standard of living' and 'gross national product.' Although the author's advocacy of birth control may run counter to that of some groups, this timely book is . . . useful." Sch Library J
Bibliography: p155

301.34   The community

Corcos, Lucille
The city book; written and illus. by Lucille Corcos. Golden Press 1972 93p illus map $5.95 (k-2) 301.34
1 Cities and towns
"Panoramic views of New York City accompany an easily read text covering just about all the activity in a huge metropolis. The work of teachers, firemen, the police, postal workers, et al. is discussed, plus ways people get to and from work, where they live, and a host of other facets of life in the big city. The illustrations are interestingly detailed, and there are helpful endpaper map drawings." Pub W

Pitt, Valerie
Let's find out about the community; pictures by June Goldsborough. Watts, F. 1972 48p illus $3.90 (3-5)   301.34
1 Community life
ISBN 0-531-00080-X
The author describes the characteristics, services, and functions of a community and its members

Schwartz, Alvin
Central city/spread city; the metropolitan regions where more and more of us spend our lives. Macmillan Pub. Co. 1973 132p illus maps lib. bdg. $4.95 (5-7)   301.34
1 Metropolitan areas 2 Regional planning
"A depressing, yet true picture of the living and working conditions existing in most central cities and their surrounding suburbs. Although not called by

Schwartz, Alvin—Continued

name, the inner city and suburbs described are in the vast metropolitan area surrounding Philadelphia, where five million people live and work. Dilapidated and inadequate housing, lack of schools, playgrounds, health services and jobs, and the rising crime rate (especially crimes against persons) sum up the sense of futility and frustration of the seven hundred thousand predominantly black people who live in the inner city (Tioga-Nicetown neighborhood). Contrasting with this bleak picture are the conditions, different but also depressing, in the 'typical' new, almost all white suburbs (Upper Merion Township) of split levels and ranch houses, apartments, vast shopping centers, industrial parks, rising crime rates (mostly crimes against property) and boredom for most young people. Some small rays of hope are offered for the future, through the possibilities of good planning. . . . The book is liberally illustrated with photographs, maps and charts; and a supplementary reading list of over one hundred references [both nonfiction and fiction] is appended, including many specifically directed toward teachers." Sci Bks

301.41 The sexes and their relations

Carlson, Dale

Girls are equal too; the women's movement for teenagers; decorations by Carol Nicklaus. Atheneum Pubs. 1973 146p illus $6.95 (6-7)   301.41

1 Woman—Social conditions 2 Woman—Civil rights 3 Women's Liberation Movement
ISBN 0-689-30106-5

This a "discussion of what causes sexist attitudes and how females are discriminated against in their personal, academic, professional, and social roles." Chicago. Children's Bk Center

"The section on the history of the movement is superb and comprehensive with excellent relevant statistics. The last section discusses topical information for the teenage girl (boys, marriage, work, etc.) with exceptional insight. And throughout [the author's message] (that what women are fighting for is the freedom of personal choice) comes through loud and clear." Children's Bk Rev Serv

"Carol Nicklaus' amusing pen-and-ink drawings spark this provocative treatment of the women's movement." Sch Library J
Suggested reading: p144-46

Ingraham, Claire R.

An album of women in American history [by] Claire R. & Leonard W. Ingraham. Watts, F. 1972 88p illus $4.90 (4-7)   301.41

1 Women in the U.S. 2 Woman—Social conditions 3 Woman—Civil rights
ISBN 0-531-01515-7

"This brief survey discusses women in the United States from Indian women at the time of colonization to the current drive for equal rights." Notable Children's Trade Bks (Social Studies)

"Many biographies are noted, but individuals are always viewed as part of women's larger fight for equality. The numerous drawings and photos effectively break up the text and make it a good reference source . . . however the reading list is aimed at older grades." Sch Library J
Suggestions for further reading: p81-82

Levenson, Dorothy

Women of the West. Watts, F. 1973 88p illus lib. bdg. $3.90 (4-7)   301.41

1 Women in the West 2 Frontier and pioneer life— The West 3 The West—History

ISBN 0-531-00793-6
"A First book"
"This covers the role of 19th-Century women—primarily blacks and native American Indians—in the Western U.S. No individual woman is discussed in depth, and only a few receive one or two paragraphs. The lives of these pioneer women are treated realistically, especially the hardships of the prairie, and the U.S. Army's harsh treatment of the Indians is also described. The text is clear and unbiased, and the focus on minority women will be particularly useful." Sch Library J
Bibliography: p86

301.42 Family

Gardner, Richard

The boys and girls book about divorce; with an introduction for parents; foreword by Louise Bates Ames; illus. by Alfred Lowenheim. Aronson, J. 1970 159p illus $7.95 (4-7)   301.42

1 Divorce
ISBN 0-87668-032-5
First published by Science House

"Although marred by excessive repetition, this book is frank and honest in treatment and fills the needs of providing children with valid information and guidance for dealing with divorce situations. . . . Gardner's clear, candid discussion of common childhood fears and worries attendant on divorce is designed to help the child understand his disquieting thoughts and feelings and to face his problems realistically. . . . Illustrated with amusing supplemental drawings." Booklist

Pitt, Valerie

Let's find out about the family; illus. by Gloria Kamen. Watts, F. [1971 c1970] unp illus $3.90 (1-3)   301.42

1 Family
ISBN 0-531-00065-6
The author demons rates the value of the family as a social unit and the importance of family relationships. Different types of contemporary families are used as examples

301.45 Nondominant groups

Clifton, Lucille

The Black B C's; illus. by Don Miller. Dutton 1970 45p illus $4.50 (k-2)   301.45

1 Negroes 2 Alphabet books
ISBN 0-525-26596-1

"Brief verses for each letter of the alphabet, appropriately illustrated, lead into short commentaries about black Americans and their contributions to our national life. Other minorities are included in the text and illustrations, but black personalities and accomplishments are stressed. Excellent for Black Studies at elementary levels." Keating. Building Bridges of Understanding Between Cultures

De Garza, Patricia

Chicanos; the story of Mexican Americans; illus. with photographs. Messner 1973 96p illus lib. bdg. $5.29 (4-6)   301.45

1 Mexicans in the U.S.
ISBN 0-671-32594-9

"A very brief overall view of Mexican Americans which attempts to encompass their 400-year history in addition to the Indian background of most members

De Garza, Patricia—*Continued*

of this group in the United States. Using fictional prototypes, de Garza describes the initial Spanish settlement in the American Southwest, the effects of the Gold Rush, the 'braceros' (farm workers) and 'wetbacks' and modern life in urban 'barrios' and in the migrant stream. The author cites Anglo persecution of Mexicans living in the Southwest in the 1840's and the extreme prejudice against Latins in the gold fields and agricultural areas of California. Unfortunately, she omits or slights a great deal of historical material and occasionally distorts facts. . . . The efforts of Cesar Chávez, 'Corky' Gonzales, and Reies Lopez Tijerina are lauded without pointing out that some Mexican Americans disapprove of their activities. A useful list of prominent Mexican Americans and clear photographs supplement the text." Library J

Dowdell, Dorothy

The Chinese helped build America [by] Dorothy and Joseph Dowdell; illus. with photographs and drawings. Messner 1972 96p illus lib. bdg. $4.79 (4-7)   301.45
   1 Chinese in the U.S.
   ISBN 0-671-32488-8
In their study of Chinese immigration to America, the authors discuss the reasons the Chinese had for coming, the low-paying jobs they were forced to take, the prejudice they encountered, their everyday life, holidays and festivals, their achievements, and their contributions to American society

The Japanese helped build America, by Dorothy and Joseph Dowdell; illus. by Len Ebert and with photographs. Messner 1970 96p illus lib. bdg. $4.79 (4-7)   301.45
   1 Japanese in the U.S.
   ISBN 0-671-32257-5
"The experiences of the Sugimoto family provide an entertaining way to inform children about the movement of Japanese to our country and their contributions to our society. Social-studies teachers will find the book valuable as a supplement to standard texts. It has clearly been written and designed to attract boys and girls. Marriage customs, farming techniques, bicultural social patterns, and festivals are among the subjects discussed. Prejudice and discrimination which led to the establishment of relocation centers during World War II are lucidly explained. Children who enjoy nonfiction will find it appealing for recreational reading." Keating. Building Bridges of Understanding Between Cultures

Gay, Kathlyn

The Germans helped build America; illus. with photographs and old drawings. Messner 1971 96p illus $4.50, lib. bdg. $4.29 (4-7)   301.45
   1 Germans in the U.S.
   ISBN 0-671-32391-1; 0-671-32392-X
The author discusses the reasons for German immigration to the United States from the 17th century to the present, as well as the contributions German-Americans have made toward various aspects of life in this country

Goldhurst, Richard

America is made Jewish. Putnam 1972 127p illus lib. bdg. $4.29 (5-7)   301.45
   1 Jews in the U.S.
   ISBN 0-399-60019-1
The author traces the major waves of Jewish immigration to the United States from colonial times to World War II. He highlights the Jewish contribution to the fields of education, business, journalism, labor, cinema, science, politics, music, and sports

The author "popularizes and interprets the American-Jewish experience with vigor and warmth. His book is full of fascinating historical highlights, details, anecdotes, quotes and colorful editorial comments. . . . The book is especially valuable because it explains areas of misunderstanding to non-Jews; e.g., why Jews become merchants and go into business for themselves." Library J
For further reading: p123

Henderson, Nancy Wallace

The Scots helped build America; illus. by Martin [sic!] Besunder. Messner 1969 96p illus $3.95, lib. bdg. $3.64 (4-7)   301.45
   1 Scotch in the U.S. 2 U.S.—Civilization
   ISBN 0-671-32149-8; 0-671-32150-1
The author discusses the roles the Scotch have played in America from its beginnings to the present. She also describes individuals of Scottish descent—including Alexander Hamilton, John Paul Jones, Andrew Carnegie, Daniel Boone, Alexander Graham Bell and Douglas MacArthur—who have contributed to American politics, science, industry, and the arts

Jackson, Florence

The Black man in America. Watts, F. 1970-1975 6v illus lib. bdg. ea $3.90 (6-7)   301.45
   1 Negroes—History 2 Slavery in the U.S. 3 U.S.—History—Civil War 4 Reconstruction
   Contents: v 1 1619-1790, by Florence and J. B. Jackson (ISBN 0-531-01839-3); v2 1791-1861 (ISBN 0-531-01965-9); v3 1861-1877 (ISBN 0-531-02022-3); v4 1877-1905 (ISBN 0-531-02611-6); v5 1905-1932 (ISBN 0-531-02667-1); v6 1932-1954 (ISBN 0-531-02799-6)
Illustrated with contemporay drawings and photographs, these volumes trace the history and culture of Black Americans from their arrival at Jamestown in 1619 through the Supreme Court decision to desegregate schools in 1954. Slavery, emancipation, civil rights, education, religious life, the Harlem Renaissance, as well as Black businessmen, cowboys, scientists, actors, soldiers and athletes are among the topics considered

Johnston, Johanna

Together in America: the story of two races and one nation; illus. by Morton Kunstler. Dodd 1965 158p illus $3.95, pa 95¢ (5-7)   301.45
   1 Negroes 2 U.S.—Civilization
   ISBN 0-396-05106-5; 0-396-06463-9
This book is "an attempt to show that people of both European and African descent have contributed to America's discovery, growth and strength from the beginning—that the contributions of some who have labored under brutal disadvantages have been remarkable; and that the needs and pressures of the times have played a part in what happened and what was accomplished in every era." Author's note
"Miss Johnston has a style which is fluent and convincing." Best Sellers
Suggested readings: p151-52. Bibliography: p153-54

Jones, Claire

The Chinese in America. Lerner Publications 1972 95p illus (The In America ser) lib. bdg. $4.95 (5-7)   301.45
   1 Chinese in the U.S.
   ISBN 0-8225-0223-2
The author discusses the reasons behind the immigration of the Chinese to the United States, describing also the problems they have met here and the contributions they have made to American life

Jones, Jayne Clark

The Greeks in America. Lerner Publications 1969 78p illus maps (The In America ser) lib. bdg. $4.95 (5-7)   301.45

1 Greeks in the U.S.

ISBN 0-8225-0215-1

This book traces the history of Greek emigration from classical times to the present day, emphasizing the problems of Greek immigrants in the United States and their contributions to America's history and culture

Katz, William Loren

Early America, 1492-1812; illus. with photographs. Watts, F. 1974 88p illus (Minorities in American history, v 1) lib. bdg. $4.33 (5-7)   301.45

1 Minorities 2 U.S.—Race relations

ISBN 0-531-02676-0

This is the first of a six volume series covering the history of minority groups in America from 1492 to the 1970's. It deals with the treatment of the native population by the first explorers and settlers, slavery, religious persecution, attitudes toward immigrants of various ethnic backgrounds, the legal status of Blacks after the American Revolution and the role of Indians and Blacks in the War of 1812

"Reporting incidents from the victim's angle gives a different view of our infamous past. A 'current events' news item is blocked into the text here and there to give a contemporary tone to the series." Best Sellers

Bibliography: p86

From the progressive era to the great depression, 1900-1929; illus. with photographs. Watts, F. 1974 87p illus (Minorities in American history, v4) lib. bdg. $4.33 (5-7)   301.45

1 Minorities 2 U.S.—Race relations

ISBN 0-531-02716-3

The author documents early 20th century discrimination against American racial and ethnic minorities, including European, Indian, and Japanese immigrants, Blacks, Hispanic Americans, and American Indians, as well as natives of new American-occupied territories

"The author incorporates interesting anecdotes and excerpts from writings of minority authors into the narrative which, supported with black-and-white photographs, does provide many refreshingly unfamiliar depictions of immigrant life during the period of progressivism and World War I. Although the culture of ethnic minorities is not discussed at any length, this is still worth reading as a history of the oppression of nonwhites and immigrants." Library J

Bibliography: p84

Modern America, 1957 to the present; illus. with photographs. Watts, F. 1975 64p illus (Minorities in American history, v6) lib. bdg. $4.33 (5-7)   301.45

1 Minorities 2 U.S.—Race relations

ISBN 0-531-02821-6

"In this well-written, carefully researched conclusion to the series, Katz delineates minority groups' struggles for basic rights, equality, economic opportunity, full participation in American society, and identity since 1957. Particular attention is given to César Chávez and Chicano agricultural workers, Black Power and the 'white backlash' of the 1960's, women's liberation, and ghettos—including those of Asian Americans. Also included is a discussion of white ethnic Americans and their present-day search for identity and greater security." Sch Library J

Bibliography: p64

Reconstruction and national growth, 1865-1900; illus. with photographs. Watts, F. 1974 87p illus (Minorities in American history, v3) lib. bdg. $4.33 (5-7)   301.45

1 Minorities 2 U.S.—Race relations

ISBN 0-531-02715-5

This book describes the discriminatory treatment of Blacks, Chinese, Hispanic Americans, European immigrants, and Indians during Reconstruction, westward expansion, and industrial growth in the late 19th century

"The emphasis is on information, not analysis, but the tragic description is validated by quotes from speeches and various private and public documents. A matter-of-fact look at the darker side of American history, a view any balanced history collection needs." Booklist

Bibliography: p84

Slavery to Civil War, 1812-1865; illus. with photographs. Watts, F. 1974 87p illus (Minorities in American history, v2) lib. bdg. $4.33 (5-7)   301.45

1 Minorities 2 U.S.—Race relations

ISBN 0-531-02677-9

Covering the period from the early 19th century to the end of the Civil War, this book surveys the treatment of Blacks under slavery and as free men; European immigration to the United States and the rise of nativism; the Mexican-American War; the treatment of Indian, Mexican, and Chinese minorities; events leading to the Civil War; and the role of minorities in that war

Bibliography: p84

Years of strife, 1929-1956; illus. with photographs. Watts, F. 1975 85p illus (Minorities in American history, v5) lib. bdg. $4.33 (5-7)   301.45

1 Minorities 2 U.S.—Race relations

ISBN 0-531-02785-6

This survey of the history of American minorities from the depression to the Montgomery bus boycott covers "such issues as Japanese internment, segregation in the armed services, and laboring agricultural workers." Booklist

"Mr. Katz presents history in the perfect student's style—concise, readable, interesting, easy to outline, easy for grasping quickly the idea under discussion. And, again, the icing on such a good presentation is the collection of news items, letters, personal comments, advertisements, all from the times under study, giving a sense of being there." Best Sellers

Bibliography: p81

King, Martin Luther

We shall live in peace: the teachings of Martin Luther King, Jr.; ed. and with commentary by Deloris Harrison; illus. by Ernest Crichlow. Hawthorn Bks. 1968 64p illus $4.95 (4-6)   301.45

1 Negroes—Social conditions

ISBN 0-8015-8436-1

"Well chosen excerpts from the speeches of Dr. Martin Luther King, Jr., are arranged here in generally chronological order beginning with the Montgomery bus boycott and extending to Dr. King's assassination. A biographical summary, placed at the front of the book, supplies the readers with the major events of King's life. . . . Juxtaposing King's impassioned language and the editor's objective analysis of each situation results in intensified emotional impact, and what emerges is the image of an inspired leader completely dedicated to the struggle for freedom. Numerous black-and-white pencil drawings appropriately reinforce the effective text." Sch Library J

Kurtis, Arlene Harris

The Jews helped build America; illus. with photographs. [Rev. ed.] Messner 1974 95p illus lib. bdg. $4.64 (4-7)   301.45

1 Jews in the U.S.
ISBN 0-671-32707-0
First published 1970

"An account of the Jewish experience in America from the early days of the German and East European immigration to the present. Includes information about Jewish customs, holidays, and leaders. A helpful reference for both the Jewish and non-Jewish child." Wolfe. About 100 Books

LaGumina, Salvatore J.

An album of the Italian-American; William Loren Katz, consulting editor. Watts, F. 1972 85p illus $4.90 (4-7)   301.45

1 Italians in the U.S.
ISBN 0-531-01514-9

"This informal account illustrated with numerous photographs highlights the experiences and contributions of Italian Americans from the days of the explorers to the present. LaGumina discusses the problems of poverty and prejudices which Italian immigrants had to overcome and their accomplishments in various areas of American life with special reference to outstanding Italian Americans past and present. He also touches on their efforts to combat the Mafia image. An informative and useful addition to books on American ethnic origins." Booklist

McDonnell, Virginia B.

The Irish helped build America; illus. with photographs and drawings. Messner 1969 96p illus $3.95, lib. bdg. $3.64 (4-7)   301.45

1 Irish in the U.S.
ISBN 0-671-32420-9

"The story of one Irish family's migration to America serves to explain the economic and social conditions that caused many to seek haven in this country. Colorful history." Keating. Building Bridges of Understanding Between Cultures

The book includes information on the contributions of famous as well as lesser-known Irish-Americans

Meltzer, Milton

(ed.) In their own words; a history of the American Negro. Crowell 1964-1967 3v illus ea $5.95 (6-7)   301.45

1 Negroes—History
Contents: v 1 1619-1865 (ISBN 0-690-44691-8); v2 1865-1916 (ISBN 0-690-44692-6); v3 1916-1966 (ISBN 0-690-44693-4)

A "history of the American Negro from 1619 to [1966] is told in his own words through selections from letters, diaries, journals, speeches, and other documents. Helpful background information and commentary introduce each of the pieces, some of which have been edited for easier reading, and the source is given at the end of each document. A calendar of Negro history . . . and an annotated reading list are appended [in each of the three volumes]." Booklist

"The collection is occasionally distinguished by a simple eloquence and despite the underlying sadness, is notably lacking in bitterness. . . . [Many will find] inspiration to work for solutions to current problems." Horn Bk

Murphy, Eugene

An album of the Irish Americans [by] Eugene Murphy and Timothy Driscoll; William Loren Katz, consulting editor. Watts, F. 1974 87p illus lib. bdg. $4.33 (5-7)   301.45

1 Irish in the U.S.
ISBN 0-531-01519-X

"This notes Irish contributions to the U.S. while explaining the mix of circumstance and national character that shaped the Irish experience in America: the strong Catholicism and democratic leanings that led to eras of Irish domination in church, labor, and political activities; the subsequent rising incomes that enabled the brawling drunk or overworked scrubwoman stereotypes to be left behind; and today, the almost complete Irish-American assimilation, somewhat bemoaned by the authors." Booklist
Bibliography: p84

Reit, Seymour

Rice cakes and paper dragons; photographs by Paul Conklin. Dodd 1973 79p illus lib. bdg. $3.95 (3-5)   301.45

1 Chinese in New York (City)
ISBN 0-396-06735-2

This is the story of Marie Chan, a Chinese-American girl who lives in New York City's Chinatown, and of the activities leading up to the Chinese New Year's celebration

Sung, Betty Lee

The Chinese in America. Macmillan (N Y) 1972 120p illus map $4.95 (5-7)   301.45

1 Chinese in the U.S.

"An informative account enlivened by anecdotes of the Chinese in America from the earliest days of immigration during the Gold Rush to the present. She describes the contributions made by the Chinese in settling the West, their persecution by whites, and the inequitable immigration laws; and delineates the customs, foods, festivals, and life-styles of the Chinese in the U.S. concluding with a hopeful look at their role in American society today and brief profiles of several successful Chinese-Americans. A short list of books for further reading is appended." Booklist

Swift, Hildegarde Hoyt

North star shining; a pictorial history of the American Negro; illus. by Lynd Ward. Morrow 1947 44p illus $6.50 (5-7)   301.45

1 Negroes—History
ISBN 0-688-21904-7

Brief pictorial history of the Negro in the United States from early slave days to the 1940's, written in free verse, and picking out a succession of great moments to carry the theme. The illustrations are lithographs

"The many characters make this useful for verse choir, individual dramatic readers, or assembly programs." We Build Together

Young, Margaret B.

The first book of American Negroes; illus. with photographs. Watts, F. 1966 86p illus $3.90, pa $1.25 (4-7)   301.45

1 Negroes
ISBN 0-531-02306-0

This book "discusses the history of the American Negro with candor, not rancor, stressing that black Americans 'are' Americans, closely tied to our total social structure. Population distribution, the reasons for the development of urban ghettos, differences in educational facilities leading to the need for legal action to desegregate schools, and problems in employment are covered. Contributions of Negroes in science, industry, education, government, art, music, sports, and the theater are stated. Chapter six traces the civil-rights movement from 1791 to the [mid-1960's]." Keating. Building Bridges of Understanding Between Cultures

317.3   General statistics of the U.S.

Information please almanac; atlas and yearbook. Planned and supervised by Dan Golenpaul Associates. Simon & Schuster pa $5.95   317.3
1 U.S.—Statistics   2   Statistics—Yearbooks
3 Almanacs
ISBN 0-671-21878-6
Annual. First published 1947 by Doubleday
Editor: 1947-1953 John Kieran. 1954-   D. Golenpaul
"There are special timely articles in each volume; reviews of the year in Washington, sports, theater, fiction, screen, music, etc., written by specialists; statistical and historical descriptions of the various countries of the world; sports records; and many kinds of general information. Sources for many of the tables and special articles are noted." Winchell. Guide to Ref Bks. 8th edition
"Another useful annual compilation of facts which supplements the 'World Almanac,' [entered below] each including information not in the other. More legible than the latter, and therefore easier to consult." Enoch Pratt Free Library. Ref Bks, 1970

The Official Associated Press Almanac. Almanac Pub. Co. [distributed by Quadrangle Bks] $5.95, pa $2.75   317.3
1 U.S.—Statistics   2   Statistics—Yearbooks
3 Almanacs
"Successor to The New York Times Encyclopedic Almanac [first published 1969 by The New York Times]." Title page
Annual. First edition 1973, published 1972
Editorial coordinator 1973- Dan Perkes; editor-in-chief 1973- Laurance Urdang
Partial contents: People/places/issues, Finance/industry/labor, U.S. crime summary, Civil rights/race, Stars/planets/space, Communications/language, History: ancient/modern, Arts: popular/classical, Prizes /awards, Disasters/catastrophes, Sports: facts/figures, Obituaries

The World almanac and book of facts. Newspaper Enterprise Assn. [distributed by Doubleday] $5.95   317.3
1 U.S.—Statistics   2   Statistics—Yearbooks
3 Almanacs
ISBN 0-385-07724-6
Annual. First issued 1868
"The most comprehensive and most frequently useful of the American almanacs of miscellaneous information. Contains statistics on social, industrial, political, financial, religious, educational, and other subjects; political organizations; societies; historical lists of famous events, etc. Well up to date and, in general, reliable; sources for many of the statistics are given. A useful handbook. . . . Alphabetical index at the front of each volume." Winchell. Guide to Ref Bks. 8th edition

323.4   Civil rights

Kohn, Bernice
The spirit and the letter; the struggle for rights in America. Viking 1974 175p illus $6.95 (5-7)   323.4
1 Civil rights 2 U.S. Constitution—Amendments
ISBN 0-670-66301-8
This discussion of civil rights as guaranteed by the

Constitution and its Amendments examines individual issues of freedom of worship, speech, privacy, and assembly, as well as the problem of segregation and rights of Blacks
"The inherent flexibility of the Constitution and the changing nature of public and judicial opinion are emphasized throughout. Also, such . . . matters as the Watergate wire-taps, the Pentagon Papers, and the proposed Equal Rights Amendment are filtered through the author's philosophy, consistent with that of the Warren court. With the Declaration of Independence and the Constitution appended, this volume can serve as valuable discussion material for school projects." Booklist
Bibliography: p167-68

Wise, William
American freedom and the Bill of Rights; illus. by Roland Rodegast. Parents Mag. Press 1975 64p illus lib. bdg. $4.59 (2-4)   323.4
1 U.S. Constitution—Amendments 2 Civil rights
ISBN 0-8193-0747-5
"Finding-out books"
"The background and chronological development of the twenty-five amendments to the Constitution, and the Equal Rights Amendment as a possibility, are described in a lively, readable style. Although some concepts may be difficult for this age group to grasp, realistic examples and colorful, eye-catching illustrations should help spark interest." Babbling Bookworm

323.44   Freedom of action

American Library Association. Office for Intellectual Freedom
Intellectual freedom manual; comp. by the Office for Intellectual Freedom of the American Library Association. A.L.A. 1974 xxx, various pagings $12.75, pa $5   323.44
1 Intellectual freedom 2 Libraries—Censorship
ISBN 0-8389-3151-0; 0-8389-3181-2
Looseleaf binding
"This manual is designed to answer the many practical questions that confront librarians in applying the principles of intellecual freedom to library service. It is our hope that every librarian will keep this volume on his desk as a convenient reference work." Preface
Contents: Library Bill of Rights; Freedom to read; Intellectual freedom; Intellectual freedom and the law; Assistance from ALA
Includes bibliography

Newsletter on Intellectual Freedom. A.L.A. $6 per year   323.44
1 Intellectual freedom—Periodicals 2 Censorship —Periodicals
Bimonthly. First published 1952
"A 20-page newsletter which attempts to give objective current information on censorship. There are usually one or two introductory articles, and then 'Censorship Dateline' which traces activities in various regions and states. 'From the Bench' gives current legal opinions, followed by 'Is it Legal?' and 'Success Stories.' There is a minimum of ALA business. Unfortunately, this does not enjoy a wide circulation. It should be brought to the attention of nonlibrarians, and certainly is a required item in any library, regardless of size, type, or location." Katz. Magazines for Libraries

324.73   Electoral processes— U.S.

Lindop, Edmund

The first book of elections. Rev. ed. Illus. by Gustave E. Nebel. Watts, F. 1972 84p illus lib. bdg. $3.90 (4-7)   324.73

1 Elections—U.S.

ISBN 0-531-00521-6

First published 1968

This book "analyzes the American election process, explaining who has the right to vote; what an election is; what is involved in local, state, and national elections; and why the Australian ballot was adopted for use in the United States. The author discusses why some people fail to vote or lose their right to vote when they move; however, no mention is made of criminals losing their right to vote." Library J

"Cartoon-style drawings add little that is informative, but gives some glimpses of familiar scenes that enliven the . . . approach of this timely book." Sat Rev

Stevenson, Janet

Women's rights; illus. with prints & photographs. Watts, F. 1972 90p illus lib. bdg. $3.90 (5-7) 324.73

1 Woman—Civil rights 2 Woman—Suffrage 3 Women in the U.S.

ISBN 0-531-00763-4

"A First book"

Including brief biographies of famous suffragists, the author follows the struggle for women's rights in America, beginning with Lucretia Mott and the forming of the Declaration of Women's Rights, and continuing through 1920 with the ratification of the Nineteenth Amendment

"The photographs are interesting, the writing measured, objective, and clear, and the text particularly valuable for its discussion of the nature of the forces marshalled against suffrage." Chicago. Children's Bk Center

Bibliography: p85

326   Slavery and emancipation

Buckmaster, Henrietta

Flight to freedom; the story of the underground railroad. Crowell 1958 217p $6.95 (5-7)   326

1 Slavery in the U.S. 2 Underground railroad

ISBN 0-690-30846-9

"An historical survey of the formation and operation of the Underground Railroad that is made more vivid by fictionalized examples of escape episodes. . . . The status of slavery and growth of the abolition movement . . . the leadership of men and women of both races, and the role of the Negro after the Civil War are described." Chicago. Children's Bk Center

"Equally interesting are the stories of the great figures . . . Garrison, Douglass, Lovejoy, Wendell Phillips, etc.—and of the many less familiar men and women who played dramatic and heroic roles in the long struggle." Horn Bk

Bibliography: p209-11

Commager, Henry Steele

The great Proclamation; a book for young Americans. Bobbs 1960 112p illus $4.50 (6-7)   326

1 Emancipation Proclamation 2 Slavery in the U.S. 3 Lincoln, Abraham, President U.S.

ISBN 0-672-50304-2

This book covers "the background of Abraham Lincoln's writing of the Emancipation Proclamation; his boyhood feelings about slavery, the Lincoln-Douglas debates, and the great dilemmas facing the President in the midst of Civil War. Told partly in Lincoln's own words or in the words of contemporary documents." Pub W

"This book, fair and just in its appraisal of slavery, and containing many fine reproductions of paintings and photographs, is a valuable aid to understanding the man and the issues." N Y Times Bk Rev

Ingraham, Leonard W.

Slavery in the United States; illus. with photographs and drawings. Watts, F. 1968 89p illus lib. bdg. $3.90, pa $1.25 (5-7)   326

1 Slavery in the U.S.

ISBN 0-531-00630-1

"A concise history of slavery in the U.S. from 1619 to 1865 designed to fill the need for objective, accurate information. The straightforward serviceable account covers the slave trade, the life of both slave and free Negroes, slave rebellions, the Abolitionist Movement, and the role of slavery in the Civil War." Booklist

"The book is enhanced by capsule sketches of distinguished black men and women, by numerous well-correlated photographs, drawings and diagrams, and by quotations from original sources." Library J

Suggestions for further reading: p85-86

Latham, Frank B.

The Dred Scott decision, March 6, 1857; slavery and the Supreme Court's "self-inflicted wound"; illus. with contemporary prints. Watts, F. 1968 54p illus lib. bdg. $3.90, pa $1.25 (6-7)   326

1 Slavery in the U.S. 2 Scott, Dred

ISBN 0-531-01000-7; 0-531-02329-X

"A Focus book"

"A concise, detailed history of the Dred Scott case discusses the issues involved in relation to various aspects of the impassioned controversy over slavery and shows the effects of the Supreme Court's decision on the existent tensions between the North and South. Mainly of value as a supplementary reference for history students." Booklist

Bibliography: p52

Lester, Julius

To be a slave; illus. by Tom Feelings. Dial Press 1968 160p illus $5.95 (6-7)   326

1 Slavery in the U.S.

ISBN 0-8037-8955-6

"Through the words of the slave, interwoven with strongly sympathetic commentary, the reader learns what it is to be another man's property; how the slave feels about himself; and how he feels about others. Every aspect of slavery, regardless of how grim, has been painfully and unrelentingly described." Rdng Ladders

"Striking black-and-white drawings add to the mood and effectiveness of the presentation." Booklist

Bibliography: p159-60

327.73   U.S. foreign policy

Vaughan, Harold Cecil

The Monroe Doctrine, 1823; a landmark in American foreign policy. Watts, F. 1973 65p illus maps lib. bdg. $3.90 (6-7)   327.73

1 Monroe Doctrine 2 U.S.—Foreign relations

ISBN 0-531-02461-X

"A Focus book"

This is a "review of conditions which led to the

Vaughan, Harold Cecil—*Continued*

stand taken by the U.S. in the Monroe Doctrine. . . . Vaughan examines simply and clearly the revolts against Spain in her Latin American colonies, U.S. relations with Spain in regard to the boundaries of the Louisiana territory and Florida, Russia's claim on the Pacific coast from Alaska to northern California, and Britain's claim to Oregon. He stresses the important role John Quincy Adams played as Secretary of State under President Monroe and quotes from the letters of Jefferson and Madison who wrote to Monroe when he asked for their opinions about the presence of European nations in the Americas." Booklist

Bibliography: p62

328 Legislation

Weiss, Ann E.

Save the mustangs! How a federal law is passed; illus. with photographs. Messner 1974 96p illus lib. bdg. $6.29 (3-5)   328

1 Horses—Laws and regulations 2 Legislation
ISBN 0-671-32648-1

A class of fourth graders wages a "pencil war" by writing to their Congressman to introduce a strong save-the-mustangs bill. The author of this book takes readers behind the scenes of this project "as she documents the bill's journey through congressional houses and committees until its signing into law by President Nixon. The plight of the mustangs—sent by 'mustangers' to pet food factories at the going rate of six cents a pound—will serve well in holding the interest of those trying to absorb their lessons in the mechanics of federal government legislation." Booklist

"The author has done a lucid job of explaining the federal lawmaking process, while dealing with an issue which has meaning to young readers. Numerous photographs of the horses and people who supported the bill add to the book's readability." Babbling Bookworm

Glossary: p91-93

328.73 Legislative branch of U.S. government

Coy, Harold

The first book of Congress; pictures by Helen Borten. Rev. ed. Watts, F. 1965 59p illus lib. bdg. $3.90, pa $1.25 (6-7)   328.73

1 U.S. Congress
ISBN 0-531-00509-7; 0-531-02309-5

First published 1956

"A handy guide to Congress with clear concise information on how its members are elected and what their work is. One section is called 'The Story of a Bill' and gives the history of the bill from its introduction to its passing or its defeat. The work of committees is discussed, and a glossary is included." Horn Bk

Stevens, Leonard A.

How a law is made; the story of a bill against air pollution; illus. by Robert Galster. Crowell 1970 109p illus $4.50 (5-7)   328.73

1 Legislation 2 Air—Pollution
ISBN 0-690-40609-6

In this account of a state law against air pollution, the process of law-making takes nearly two years of work by a citizens' committee and legislators. There are times when party politics, public apathy, and pressure from industrial interests threaten to undermine the bill. Compromise is necessary. Step by step, the author shows how citizens can change the law and thereby improve the environment in which they live

"This is an intelligent book for youngsters seeking an understanding of the political process on the state level." Library J

329 Practical politics. Political parties

Cook, Fred J.

The rise of American political parties. Watts, F. 1971 90p illus lib. bdg. $3.90 (5-7)   329

1 Political parties 2 U.S.—Politics and government
ISBN 0-531-00741-3

"A First book"

This book examines the American political system as it evolved from the views of Jefferson and Hamilton in the early days of the republic to the current basic two-party structure. Political parties of historical note, including the Federalists, Whigs, Populists, Know-Nothings and today's Democrats and Republicans, are discussed

"Reproductions of many contemporary drawings and photographs add interest." Booklist

Gray, Lee Learner

How we choose a President: the election year. 2d rev. ed. Illus. by Stanley Stamaty. St Martins 1972 175p illus $5.50 (5-7)   329

1 Presidents—U.S.—Election

First published 1964

The author describes and explains the activities of the Presidential election year including the search for candidates, the nomination of candidates, the campaign, and election day. He also presents an historical background of the laws which affect the election process

This book "provides an unbiased, concise account of what happens during presidential election years. . . . Short, simple chapters, previews and reviews, and full-page cartoons get the information across clearly." Library J

Glossary: p141-47

Markun, Patricia Maloney

Politics; illus. by Ted Schroeder. Watts, F. 1970 62p illus lib. bdg. $3.90 (4-6)   329

1 Politics, Practical 2 U.S.—Politics and government
ISBN 0-531-00692-1

"A First book"

"An introduction to politics as 'the practical exercise of self-government' reveals some of the ways people with opposing interests work to get what they want through political action. Avoiding theoretical description of the U.S. system of government, the author concentrates on the role of citizens and power groups in influencing political decisions and on campaigning practices and voting patterns. Many examples are drawn from typical . . . situations. A competent discussion, illustrated with cartoon-like drawings." Booklist

331.5 Migrant workers

Weiner, Sandra

Small hands, big hands; seven profiles of Chicano migrant workers and their families. Pantheon Bks. 1970 55p illus $4.50, lib. bdg. $5.69 (4-7)   331.5

1 Migrant labor 2 Mexicans in the U.S.
ISBN 0-394-80442-2; 0-394-90442-7

Weiner, Sandra—*Continued*

The seven profiles in this book are based on taped interviews with Mexican-American migrant workers ranging in age from eleven to sixty-seven. Through photographs and first-person accounts, the life of a farm laborer in this country is portrayed

"In some cases, the photographs reveal more than the text does. This kind of first-hand, primary source information is valuable to have: children are enabled to see the facts and draw their own conclusions. The text is within the grasp of third-grade readers, but the book will probably be much more useful for slightly older children with incipient social consciences." Library J

331.7   Labor by industry and occupation

Colby, C. B.

Night people; workers from dusk to dawn. A new and rev. ed. Coward, McCann & Geoghegan 1971 48p illus lib. bdg. $4.29 (3-5)   331.7

1 Occupations 2 Work

ISBN 0-698-30257-5

First published 1961

Described are some of the many jobs that must be performed each night. Black and white photographs present policemen, firemen, taxi drivers, bakers, computer programmers and dock workers, among others

Schwartz, Alvin

The night workers; photographs by Ulli Steltzer. Dutton 1966 64p illus $4.95 (2-5)   331.7

1 Occupations 2 Work

ISBN 0-525-35899-4

An explanation "of the various occupations of people who work at night. By means of numerous photographs and brief, concise text, the 12-hour period between six o'clock in the evening and six o'clock in the morning is covered to show the activities of the policeman on night duty, the nurse, waiter, tugboat captain, baker, printer and many others." Sch Library J

"An appropriate purchase for units of study on community helpers, with the reluctant reader particularly in mind." Minnesota

332.1   Banks and banking

Paradis, Adrian A.

How money works; the Federal Reserve system. Hawthorn Bks. 1972 90p $4.95 (5-7)   332.1

1 Federal Reserve banks

ISBN 0-8015-3678-2

"A simple, lucid explanation of U.S. money and the banking system. The author sketches very briefly a history of money, banks, and checks and tells how the Federal Reserve System came into being. Using appropriate examples he considers the work of the Federal Reserve Bank, its board of governors, the Inter-district Settlement Fund, and the Federal Open Market Committee and suggests a solution to the problem posed by the rapidly growing volume of checks which he states even electronic machines will soon not be able to handle." Booklist

Glossary: p77-85

332.6   Investment finance

Axon, Gordon V.

Let's go to a stock exchange; illus. by Frank Aloise. Putnam 1973 41p illus lib. bdg. $3.86 (5-7)   332.6

1 Stock exchange 2 Securities

ISBN 0-399-60813-3

When they visit a stockbroker's office, two children learn the basic principles behind the sale of stocks and bonds, the functions of a stockbroker, and the operation of the stock exchange

Glossary: p[46]. Other books about the stock exchange p[47]

333.7   Land utilization

Colby, C. B.

Park ranger; equipment, training and work of the National Park rangers. New and rev. Coward, McCann & Geoghegan 1971 48p illus lib. bdg. $4.29 (3-6)   333.7

1 U.S. National Park Service 2 National parks and reserves—U.S.

ISBN 0-698-30278-8

First published 1955

This book describes the training, equipment, and actual duties of the rangers, who are responsible for guarding federally owned parks, seashores, monuments, and other historic sites

Duffey, Eric

Conservation of nature. McGraw [1971 c1970] 128p illus lib. bdg. $4.72 (6-7)   333.7

1 Conservation of natural resources

ISBN 0-07-018016-4

"International library"

The author begins his account by telling how man began to change his natural environment. He then discusses the problems, specific areas of concern and what, if any, attempts at conservation are being made. Included are chapters on forestry and farming on land; water and life; wildlife conservation and management; and pollution of the environment

"The book's interest and attractiveness is enhanced . . . by many excellent photographs from international sources, that serve to indicate vividly the global aspects of the concern for the preservation of our natural resources." Sci Bks

Further reading: p126

Shuttlesworth, Dorothy E.

Disappearing energy; can we end the crisis? By Dorothy E. Shuttlesworth with Lee Ann Williams. Doubleday 1974 95p illus $5.95, lib. bdg. $5.70 (5-7)   333.7

1 Power resources 2 Force and energy

ISBN 0-385-04862-9; 0-385-04863-7

"This is a good resource book presenting factual data on the use and misuse of energy. Interesting descriptions of how coal, oil, and other fuels are searched for and found are included. The reader is left with an idea of not only the need for but also the 'how' of exploring for energy-producing fields. The authors spend significant time on the topic of conservation and energy misuse, although the development of this subject is more a review of what has been done rather than an inquiry into what could be done in the future to solve the problem. The photographs are dated and do not add much to the book." Sci and Children

Smith, Frances C.
The first book of conservation. Rev. ed. Illus. by Mary DeBall Kwitz. Watts, F. 1972 85p illus lib. bdg. $3.90 (4-7)   333.7
1 Conservation of natural resources 2 Ecology 3 Nature conservation
ISBN 0-531-00510-0
First published 1954
This book "explains the interrelationships in nature and what happens when these relationships are upset, points out the results of man's past carelessness and exploitation of our country's natural resources, outlines the work of conservationists today, and tells what the individual can do to help." Booklist
"A well-organized, easy-to-read, informative introduction to conservation and ecology which fosters readers' understanding and concern for the environment. . . . The simple illustrations adequately convey environmental interrelationships." Library J
Conservation terms: p77-78. Other books to read: p79

333.9   Utilization of other natural resources

Brindze, Ruth
The sea; the story of the rich underwater world; illus. with photographs. Harcourt 1971 96p illus maps $5.95 (5-7)   333.9
1 Marine resources 2 Oceanography—Research
ISBN 0-15-271041-8
"The author presents the technological advances made in the use of oceans for man's future support, with photographs to identify the various projects. The idea of a possible future life in the ocean with hotels, homes, gardens, hospitals, and electric plants is discussed. The book cites the U.S. Navy's attempts to live on the sea bottom and describes new rescue craft which can be used to save lives in submarine disasters. Other important projects discussed are the mining of the sea for gold, oil, salt, sulphur and magnesium, and the work of increasing the fish crop and the F.P.C. (fish protein concentrate) to fight protein malnutrition in the world. Chapters also include information on how to desalt water and how the world can share the sea's wealth. This book will alert readers to a timely subject in an entertaining and informative manner. There is a bibliography and an index." Appraisal
"The author has done a workmanlike job of assembling a miscellaneous lot of material into an acceptable volume. Errors are few and unimportant, and the book will probably be a useful addition to school libraries." Sci Bks

Fenten, D. X.
Harvesting the sea. Lippincott 1970 63p illus $3.95 (4-6)   333.9
1 Marine resources
ISBN 0-397-31119-2
"The natural resources found in the sea, present methods of harvesting them, and prospects for the utilization of the sea in the future are described in a brief but adequate account. The author includes information on various methods used to catch fish, to produce fresh water from salty seawater, and to collect minerals and oil. Numerous photographs and drawings illustrate the short, simple sentences of the text. Useful for easy-to-read basic information on the subject." Booklist

338.1   Agriculture. Food supply

Raskin, Edith
World food. McGraw 1971 160p illus lib. bdg. $4.72 (5-7)   338.1
1 Food supply 2 Agriculture
ISBN 0-07-051203-5
"A good beginning book for children who need an introduction to man's responsibility to improve and increase the world supply of food from available resources to fight world hunger. The need to understand individual differences in food habits, religions, and customs to different peoples is introduced as well as the need to encourage developments in domesticating wild animals, using weeds as food, and the helpful role of technocracy on solving this problem for the third world." Appraisal

Tannenbaum, Beulah
Feeding the city, by Beulah Tannenbaum and Myra Stillman; illus. by Marta Cone. McGraw 1971 63p illus maps (Science in the city) lib. bdg. $4.72 (2-4)   338.1
1 Food supply
ISBN 0-07-062888-2
"This presents basic information about how food is transported from rural areas to the city and how it is then prepared for market. Several simple experiments . . . are included; answers to the questions incorporated in the text and a list of the equipment needed for experiments are provided in the back of the book. The material is well organized and the black-and-white line drawings and photographs add to the value of the text." Library J

340.23   Law as a profession

Goldreich, Gloria
What can she be? A lawyer [by] Gloria and Esther Goldreich; photographs by Robert Ipcar. Lothrop 1973 39p illus $4.75, lib. bdg. $4.32 (1-3)   340.23
1 Women as lawyers 2 Law as a profession
ISBN 0-688-41521-0; 0-688-51521-5
This book "describes the types of cases that are handled by Ellen Green, a lawyer who has a young son and works at home. There is a brief mention of the facts that some lawyers specialize and that they must go to law school and pass an examination, but the focus is on Ellen Green: calls on clients, reference work at libraries, court appearances, work at home, discussions with professional friends, and consultations with other lawyers." Chicago. Children's Bk Center
"The informative text is simple enough for young readers to understand, though some may not be able to read it themselves. Photographs of the cases Ellen Green encounters clarify her work without glamourizing it." Library J

341.23   United Nations

Epstein, Edna
The United Nations. Watts, F. illus maps lib. bdg. $3.90 (4-7)   341.23
1 United Nations
ISBN 0-531-00657-3

Epstein, Edna—*Continued*

First published 1959 with title: The first book of the United Nations. Periodically revised to keep information up to date

This book explains what the UN is by discussing its charter, organs, the political groups within it, its enforcement action, and its role in specific world crises

It "is all a 'first book' on this important subject should be, brief, informative, fair and yet not dry." N Y Her Trib Bks

Includes a glossary

Larsen, Peter

The United Nations at work throughout the world; devised and photographed by Peter Larsen; ed. by Egon Larsen; illus. with 130 photographs. Lothrop 1971 127p illus $5.50, lib. bdg. $4.81 (4-6)　341.23

1 United Nations

ISBN 0-688-41239-4; 0-688-51239-0

First published 1970 in England

"Through a concise text and many photographs, Larsen shows how the various sections and agencies of the United Nations are working to improve the living conditions of people throughout the world. First describing the formation and the structure of the U.N., he tells of some of the specific projects and the general goals of the Food and Agricultural Organization, World Health Organization, United Nations Children's Fund, and other similar organizations." Booklist

Sasek, M.

This is the United Nations; published with the co-operation of the United Nations. Macmillan (N Y) 1968 60p illus $5.95 (3-6)　341.23

1 United Nations

"An entertaining guide to the United Nations, the organization of which is briefly explained. The various rooms, art objects, and items of interest—like gifts from member countries—are pictured, and stories told about them. A chart shows the flags of the 122 nations that make up the United Nations [1968]; and the specialized agencies—UNESCO, UNICEF, WHO, and the rest—are listed and identified." Horn Bk

"As always, M. Sasek is smoothly passing along the odd bits and pieces of data children seem to enjoy. . . . But there is plenty of basic historical information in the slim volume. The style is whimsical but not so whimsical that the read-aloud experience is a bore. Inevitably U.N. fans will grumble that there is . . . not enough about the unique status of the U.N.'s staff as international civil servants, or the U.N.'s Peace Force accomplishments in the Middle East and Cyprus and the Congo. But this is such an attractive introduction to the U.N. it seems a pity to carp. It's gay. It's informative. A book to be read once and again, handed down in the family, borrowed— and returned." N Y Times Bk Rev

Savage, Katharine

The story of the United Nations. Rev. and enl. ed. Maps by Richard Natkiel. Walck, H.Z. 1970 272p illus maps $6.50 (6-7)　341.23

1 United Nations

ISBN 0-8098-3094-9

First published 1962

The author relates the history of the United Nations from its earliest wartime meetings to its present-day problems. The construction of the United Nations, how it functions and its employees all over the globe are described. The major crises facing the United Nations today are linked to their historical backgrounds

Bibliography: p263-64

342.2　U.S. Constitution

Commager, Henry Steele

The great Constitution; a book for young Americans. Bobbs 1961 128p illus $4.50 (6-7)　342.2

1 U.S.—Constitutional history

ISBN 0-672-50299-2

This description of the Constitution tells of the work and ideals of George Washington, James Madison, Alexander Hamilton, and the others who were a part of its creation. It describes the many difficulties of preparing a document that would provide a better government than the Articles of Confederation had, and indicates the attitudes of the states to the new Constitution

The "style is informal, as the author tries to make the members of the Constitutional Convention real individuals, and the issues as exciting and the discussions as lively to young Americans as they ought to be. . . . [There are] many direct quotations from source materials, and the book is amply illustrated-in black and white. . . . The text of the Constitution itself is not included in the book." Sch Library J

"A unique and valuable approach to the study of our history." N Y Her Trib Bks

Katz, William Loren

The constitutional amendments, by William Loren Katz and Bernard Gaughran; illus. with contemporary prints and photographs. Watts, F. 1974 87p illus lib. bdg. $3.90, pa $1.25 (4-7)　342.2

"A First book"

This book describes each of the twenty-six amendments to the Constitution. The historical background and the rights and privileges guaranteed by each amendment are discussed as well as the process of amending the Constitution

Bibliography: p84

Morris, Richard B.

The first book of the Constitution; pictures by Leonard Everett Fisher. Watts, F. 1958 68p illus map lib. bdg. $3.90, pa $1.25 (5-7)　342.2

1 U.S.—Constitutional history 2 U.S. Constitution

ISBN 0-531-00511-9; 0-531-02310-9

"Succinct and colorful discussion of how the American Constitution evolved: its background in the weaknesses of the Articles of Confederation; the arguments, fights, and compromises of the able men at the Philadelphia Convention; and the problems of ratification. Strong scratchboard drawings have the effect of wood-cut portraits as they illustrate men in action." Horn Bk

"An excellent presentation for children. . . . Index and simplified outline of the Constitution add usefulness to a book that is a 'must' for every library." Library J

Peterson, Helen Stone

The making of the United States Constitution. Garrard 1974 96p illus (American Democracy ser) lib. bdg. $3.28 (4-6)　342.2

1 U.S.—Constitutional history

ISBN 0-8116-6509-7

"A satisfactory recounting of the Constitutional Convention of 1787 in which 55 delegates conceived, debated, drafted, and finally adopted the Constitution. Black-and-white reproductions of people, places, and documents coupled with an index add to the usefulness of this book." Sch Library J

345.7 Criminal trials

Aymar, Brandt
Laws and trials that created history, by Brandt Aymar and Edward Sagarin. Crown 1974 214p illus $6.95 (6-7) 345.7
1 Trials—History
ISBN 0-517-50535-5
Partial contents: Joan of Arc; Galileo Galilei; The impeachment trial of Andrew Johnson; Captain Alfred Dreyfus; Nicola Sacco and Bartolomeo Vanzetti; The Nuremberg Trials; Jomo Kenyatta; Adolf Eichmann; Philip Berrigan and the Harrisburg Seven
"An excellent, picture-book size, non-fiction account of 22 trials, arranged chronologically from Socrates in 399 B.C. to Angela Davis in 1972. Well-researched, well-written, notably unbiased, and reasonably priced. . . . Although there is an excellent bibliography for each individual or group being tried, the book lacks an index." Children's Bk Rev Serv

347 Civil procedure

Carroll, Sidney B.
You be the judge; illus. by John Richmond. Lothrop 1971 48p illus lib. bdg. $4.81 (4-7) 347
1 Law—U.S.
ISBN 0-688-51508-8
"Pointing out in the introduction that the judges' decisions in legal cases must reflect the feelings of the majority of the people about right and wrong if the laws are to be respected and obeyed, Carroll presents short summaries of 11 civil suits and two criminal cases and asks the reader to make a judgment in each case. The actual decision reached by the court and the reasons for it are printed upside down after each case." Booklist
"Notable for its novel approach, its lively, cartoon-style pen-and-ink drawings, and its selection of precedent-setting cases which should serve as the basis of exciting classroom discussions of the law." Sch Library J

353.007 Specific federal government administrative activities

Neal, Harry Edward
The story of the Secret Service. Grosset 1971 123p illus $4.95 (5-7) 353.007
1 U.S. Secret Service
ISBN 0-448-02655-4
"A former assistant chief in the U.S. Secret Service discusses the history, responsibilities, and organization of the Secret Service since its beginning in 1865 in an account enlivened with many reports of actual cases and investigations involving the Secret Service. Hints on how to recognize counterfeit money, career information, and brief biographies of all of the chiefs of the U.S. Secret Service are also included." Booklist

353.9 State governments

Hoopes, Roy
What a state governor does. Day 1973 94p illus lib. bdg. $7.95 (4-7) 353.9
1 Governors
ISBN 0-381-99788-X

"To show you what it is like to be the Governor of one of our states, we will focus on four Governors. One is from an eastern state, one from a southern border state, one from a mid-western state, and one from the far west. Two are Republicans; two are Democrats. All are in their fifties. Two are lawyers; one a professor of literature; one an architect and businessman. They all have the reputation of being capable administrators presiding over good state governments . . . [The men are] Governor Francis Sargent of Massachusetts; Governor John Gilligan of Ohio; Governor Marvin Mandel of Maryland; Governor John Love of Colorado." The author: p7

355.09 Military art and science— History

Wakin, Edward
Black fighting men in U.S. history; illus with photographs. Lothrop 1971 192p illus lib. bdg. $5.11 (5-7) 355.09
1 Negro soldiers 2 U.S.—History, Military
ISBN 0-688-51264-X
In this assessment of the Black man's role in American wars, the author shows that while Blacks have taken part in every major war, battle and campaign, their rights were abused even while they fought—and died. And when the battle was done, the Black man was forgotten, his contribution to the country overlooked
"Suggestions for further reading, including two bibliographies on the Negro, are appended. Will be useful in U.S. history classes and for leisure reading." Booklist

355.8 Military equipment and supplies

Colby, C. B.
Fighting gear of World War II; equipment and weapons of the American G.I. Coward-McCann 1961 48p illus lib. bdg. $3.99 (4-7) 355.8
1 U.S. Army—Ordnance and ordnance stores 2 World War, 1939-1945—U.S.
ISBN 0-698-30078-5
"On the following pages [of this photographic essay] you will find displayed and described some of the vast inventory of fighting gear of our GIs who slogged into combat afoot or clanked into battle inside metal monsters, or toiled behind the lines." p3

359.3 Organization of naval forces

Van Orden, M. D.
The book of United States Navy ships; illus. with photographs. 2d ed. fully rev. Dodd 1973 96p illus lib. bdg. $4.95 (5-7) 359.3
1 U.S. Navy 2 Ships 3 Warships
ISBN 0-396-06850-2
First published 1969
The most representative types and classes of U.S. Navy ships—carriers, battleships, cruisers, frigates, destroyers, submarines, mine sweepers, amphibious

Van Orden, M. D.—*Continued*
warfare ships—are discussed and illustrated. Included also is Navy terminology, the rules and requirements for naming ships and specifications of individual ships arranged by type

"Succinct and easy-to-use, this will be popular with military ship enthusiasts." Sch Library J

361.7   Private welfare work. Red Cross

Rothkopf, Carol Z.
The Red Cross; illus. with photographs. Watts, F. 1971 65p illus lib. bdg. $3.90 (4-6)   361.7
1 Red Cross
ISBN 0-531-00736-7
"A First book"
"A discussion of the formation, ideals, organization, and activities of the International Red Cross is followed by a history of the American National Red Cross, a review of its services during time of war and peace, and an account of the programs of the Junior Red Cross and Red Cross Youth. Illustrated with a number of well-chosen photographs." Booklist
"This clear, accurate overview . . . will be a useful addition to career-motivation collections, especially for slow readers." Library J

362.1   Physical illness. Hospitals

Kay, Eleanor
The clinic; illus. with photographs. Watts, F. 1971 54p illus lib. bdg. $3.90 (4-7)   362.1
1 Medical centers
ISBN 0-531-00721-9
"A First book"
"The text discusses the ways in which a clinic prepares for its patients, explains how a clinic differs from a hospital or a private physician's office, and describes some of the specialized and institutional clinics, including those of the World Health Organization and of the Armed Forces. The book concludes with a description of a child's first general examination in a clinic. Not comprehensive, but accurate and informative, with clear photographs, most of which are useful. An index is appended, its entries not always using the terminology of the text." Chicago. Children's Bk Center

The emergency room; illus. with photographs. Watts, F. 1970 65p illus lib. bdg. $3.90 (4-7) 362.1
1 Hospitals 2 First aid
ISBN 0-531-00712-X
"A First book"
"Crisp, informative, and direct, this companion volume to The Operating Room [entered in class 617] is well-organized and is illustrated with clear photographs. The text describes some typical emergency room patients and the care they receive, discusses the staff and equipment of emergency services, and reports on the handling of a community disaster and on a volunteer rescue squad, specially trained, in an area that has no hospital nearby. The book closes with some advice to those who may be unacquainted with emergency room care, a list of some of the terms and titles that may be encountered in an emergency room, and an index." Chicago. Children's Bk Center

Let's find out about the hospital; illus. by William Brooks. Watts, F. 1971 48p illus lib. bdg. $3.90 (k-2)   362.1
1 Hospitals
ISBN 0-531-00072-9
The author "explains hospital facilities, personnel

and terminology that the young patient will observe and be involved with during a stay in the hospital. The explanations are clear, and the illustrations on alternate pages facing the text are quite good. The book will be helpful if read to preschool children by parents or others, and a second-grader can probably read it himself with a little help." Sci Bks

Weber, Alfons
Elizabeth gets well; pictures by Jacqueline Blass. Crowell 1970 28p illus $5.95, lib. bdg. $6.70 (k-3)
362.1
1 Hospitals
ISBN 0-690-25838-0; 0-690-25839-9
Originally published 1969 in Switzerland
Elizabeth must go to the hospital to have her appendix out. Since she has never been in the hospital before, she is a bit frightened. This book, written to allay the child's fear of hospitals, describes Elizabeth's experiences before her operation and during her recovery

"An interesting account that can be read to small children or which others can read. The text is on the left-hand pages and on the right-hand pages are reproduced watercolors which let the reader see what is happening at each stage of the story. Each step is explained: the process of admission, examination, going to the operating room, awakening after it is all over, intravenous feeding, recovery, a precautionary chest x-ray, the meeting of new friends, and the joyous return home." Sci Bks

362.4   Physical handicaps and disablements

Wolf, Bernard
Don't feel sorry for Paul; written and photographed by Bernard Wolf. Lippincott 1974 94p illus $6.95 (3-6)   362.4
1 Physically handicapped children
ISBN 0-397-31588-0
Written in the form of a documentary, [this book] presents the highlights of several weeks in the life of Paul Jockimo, a child born without a right hand and foot, and with a deformed left hand and left foot. In stark pictures, with accompanying text, we see Paul's deformities and watch as he puts on the three prosthetic devices. We follow him bicycling, playing, going to school, celebrating his seventh birthday, and, finally, winning second prize in a horse show. We also follow him through a session at the Institute for Rehabilitative Medicine after he has broken two of his prostheses, and we learn how artificial devices that substitute for feet are made." N Y Times Bk Rev
"Photographs of superb quality illustrate a text written with candor and dignity. . . . No mincing of words, no sentimentality, no appeal for sympathy in this text. It's a fine way to acquaint readers with the problems of the handicapped; even more, it is a beautifully conceived book." Chicago. Children's Bk Center

363.3   Maintenance of public safety

Beame, Rona
Ladder Company 108; written and photographed by Rona Beame. Messner 1973 62p illus lib. bdg. $5.29 (3-5)   363.3
1 Fire departments 2 New York (City)—Fires and fire prevention
ISBN 0-671-32642-2

Beame, Rona—*Continued*
"This details the activities of Ladder Company 108 in New York City over a three-day period. The dangers and discomforts involved in fire fighting are brought out and on-the-scene black-and-white photographs are provided." Sch Library J
"The straightforward and informal text and clear, unposed photographs describe the division of labor within the unit, the way the men spend their time in the firehouse, the company's response to different kinds of alarms, from time-consuming false alarms to refuse fires and big fires that necessitate life-saving and calling in other units." Chicago. Children's Bk Center

364.12 Criminal investigation (Detection)

Millimaki, Robert H.
Fingerprint detective. Lippincott 1973 96p illus lib. bdg. $4.95 (5-7)   364.12
1 Fingerprints
ISBN 0-397-31484-1
After giving a brief history of fingerprinting, the author shows how to make a set of prints and classify them. He also discusses the importance of fingerprints in criminal investigations and describes how to locate, develop, lift, classify and analyze prints
"The subject will no doubt appeal to young sleuths inundated with TV detective work, but just how far they'll get will depend on their perseverance. . . . Classifying the prints is intimidating, and only dedicated would-be technicians will master the numerical system; this is not to fault the presentation but merely to indicate that readers can do as much or as little as they wish and still have learned about the subject." Booklist

367 General clubs

Bailard, Virginia
So you were elected! 3d ed. Prepared in consultation with Ruth Strang, by Virginia Bailard and Harry C. McKown. McGraw 1966 264p illus lib. bdg. $4.72 (6-7)   367
1 Clubs
ISBN 0-07-00362-6
First published 1946
This book explains the function of many club activities—from publicity campaigns to planning parties and utilizing parliamentary procedure. The authors detail the duties of club officers, but active participation of each member of the organization is stressed. Includes suggestions for implementing many group activities
"Has ideas not only for school programs but gives a summary of parliamentary law which is easier to understand than the adult titles that are in most young people's collections." Library J
Books you'll like: p259-60

369.43 Boy Scouts

Blassingame, Wyatt
Story of the Boy Scouts; illus. by David Hodges. Garrard 1968 96p illus lib. bdg. $3.58 (4-7) 369.43
1 Boy Scouts—History 2 Boys Scouts of America
ISBN 0-8116-6753-7

"Here is a book which should interest most young boys and certainly their scoutmasters. Mr. Blassingame successfully traces the beginnings of scouting in several nations, showing how various similar groups were eventually merged into the present-day Boy Scout organization. Several true stories of rescues, hiking, and even an Antarctic exploration are included, while helping others, attending jamborees, and working on conservation projects are portrayed as those activities of scouting which lead to international understanding and friendship. The lack of an index dampens neither the appeal of nor the need for this book, as the subjects until now [have] been covered solely in official Scout handbooks." Sch Library J

Boy Scouts of America
Bear Cub Scout book. The author illus pa $1 (3-4)
369.43
1 Boy Scouts—Handbooks, manuals, etc.
Copyright 1967. Frequently reprinted with minor revisions
This is a Cub book for the 9 year old Scout containing Cub literature and including a parents' supplement

Fieldbook; for Boy Scouts, explorers, scouters, educators and outdoorsmen. [2d ed] The author 1967 565p illus maps pa $2.50   369.43
1 Outdoor life
ISBN 0-8395-3201-6
Also available from McGraw for $4.95 (ISBN 0-07-006968-9) lib. bdg. $4.72 (ISBN 0-07-006969-7)
First edition 1944 by James E. West and William Hillcourt published with title: Scout field book. Subtitle varies with reprintings
"This excellent guide covers hiking, camping, swimming, safety, and first aid, survival, nature, conservation, astronomy, weather, and many other topics. Illustrated with outstanding photographs on nearly every page, this book is not limited to use by Boy Scouts, but is universal in content and appeal. Following the explicit instructions, even an amateur could perform well. Well organized and easy to use, it contains an extensive bibliography and a detailed index." Peterson. Ref Bks for Elem and Jr High Sch Libraries

Scout handbook. The author illus pa $2 (5-7)
369.43
1 Boy Scouts—Handbooks, manuals, etc.
First published 1910 with title: Official handbook for boys. Frequently revised with varying titles
A standard handbook which defines Boy Scout requirements and ideals, with instructions on how to progress from a Tenderfoot to an Eagle Scout. Woodcraft, health, camping, handicraft, first aid, facts about the United States, a bibliography and games are included

Webelos Scout book. The author illus pa $1 (4-5)
369.43
1 Boy Scouts—Handbooks, manuals, etc.
Copyright 1967. Frequently reprinted with minor revisions
This handbook is designed for the 10 year old boy who is between Cub Scouting and Scouting and includes all the literature on the program

Wolf Cub Scout book. The author illus pa $1 (2-3)
369.43
1 Boy Scouts—Handbooks, manuals, etc.
Copyright 1967. Frequently reprinted with minor revisions
This handbook of Cub Scout information for the 8 year old includes a parents' supplement

369.463 Girl Scouts

De Leeuw, Adèle
The Girl Scout story; illus. by Robert Doremus. Garrard 1965 95p illus lib. bdg. $3.58 (2-5) 369.463
1 Girl Scouts—History 2 Girl Scouts of the United States of America
ISBN 0-8116-6750-2
"A simply written history of the Girl Scout movement, stressing its importance in promoting international good will." Hodges. Bks for Elem Sch Libraries

Girl Scouts of the United States of America
Brownie Girl Scout handbook. The author 1963 224p illus pa $1.50 (1-3) 369.463
1 Girl Scouts—Handbooks, manuals, etc.
ISBN 0-88441-300-4
Also available in a Spanish language edition for $1 (ISBN 0-88441-305-5)
This handbook contains all the information a 6-8 year old girl needs to be a Brownie Girl Scout

Junior Girl Scout handbook. The author 1963 371p illus pa $1.50 (4-7) 369.463
1 Girl Scouts—Handbooks, manuals, etc.
ISBN 0-88441-301-2
This handbook is designed to help 9-11 year old girls master Junior scouting skills. It outlines ideas and activities for choosing and earning Junior badges

World Association of Girl Guides and Girl Scouts
Trefoil round the world; girl guiding and girl scouting in many lands. The author [distributed by the Girl Scouts of the United States of America] illus pa $2.50 369.463
1 Girl Scouts
First published 1958. Periodically revised
This history of girl scouting tells how the World Association of Girl Guides and Girl Scouts began, and includes words of promise and law, mottos, and programs of the 90 member countries

369.47 Camp Fire Girls

Camp Fire Girls, Inc.
Adventure. The author 1973 181p illus music pa $1.25 (4-6) 369.47
1 Camp Fire Girls—Handbooks, manuals, etc.
"Written by Laurie James. . . . Illustrated by Beth Charney." Verso of title page
This book outlines the Camp Fire Adventure program, its aims and activities, designed for girls in the 4th, 5th or 6th grades

The Blue Bird wish. The author 1970 64p illus music pa $1.25 (1-3) 369.47
1 Camp Fire Girls—Handbooks, manuals, etc.
"Written by Laurie James, illustrated by Margaret A. Hartelius." Verso of title page
This book is designed for six, seven or eight year old girls who want to be Blue Birds. It outlines the history of the organization and describes meetings and activities

The Camp Fire Blue Bird Series; written by Lila Phillips Walz; illus. by Margaret A. Hartelius. The author 1973 3v illus pa $1 ea (1-3) 369.47
1 Camp Fire Girls—Handbooks manuals, etc.
Contents: bk.1 It's all about me; bk.2 Here I am; bk.3 I can do lots of things!
These three books include activities and projects designed for girls aged six, seven and eight

Discovery, written by Laurie James. The author 1971 95p illus music pa $1.35 (6-7) 369.47
1 Camp Fire Girls—Handbooks, manuals, etc.
This book is designed for 7th and 8th grade girls who are members of the Discovery Club. It outlines the club's activities and aims as well as those of the national organization of Camp Fire Girls of which it is part

370.5 Education—Periodicals

Childhood Education: a journal for teachers, administrators, church-school workers, librarians, pediatricians. Assn. for Childhood Educ. $12 per year 370.5
1 Education—Periodicals 2 Kindergarten—Periodicals
ISSN 0009-4056
Monthly September through May. First published 1924
"This journal, while covering many aspects of childhood education in scholarly articles, contains sections of book reviews. The rather long reviews are arranged by broad subjects in the curriculum." Peterson. Ref Bks for Elem and Jr High Sch Libraries

Instructor. Instructor Publications $10 per year 370.5
1 Education—Periodicals 2 Teaching—Periodicals
ISSN 0020-4285
Nine times yearly with May/June and August/September issues. First published 1891
"Directed primarily to the elementary school teacher, principal, and special staff. The large, colorful format is familiar to almost any librarian or teacher. Each issue includes articles 'dealing with trends in educational theory and practice, and sections on arts and crafts and teaching suggestions for all subjects.' Each area is supplemented with diagrams, illustrations, and photographs." Katz. Magazines for Libraries

Learning; magazine for creative teaching. Education Today Co., Inc. $10 per year 370.5
1 Education—Periodicals 2 Teaching—Periodicals
ISSN 0090-3167
Nine issues a year. First published 1972
This periodical is designed for "elementary and junior high school teachers looking for new ideas on how to teach. . . . Articles, usually by teachers, tell of successful curriculum planning, 'how-to-do-it' ideas, and methods of dealing with typical problems. A good feature: profiles and interviews with the world's leaders in education. Also, a concerted effort is made through the writings of well-known authorities to consider basic questions of education and society, e.g., there have been articles on drugs in the school, sexism, and a theory of values. In addition to book reviews, there are notes on new equipment and teaching materials. The magazine is lively, [and] well illustrated." Katz. Magazines for Libraries

Teacher. Macmillan Professional Magazines, Inc. $10 per year 370.5
1 Education—Periodicals 2 Teaching—Periodicals
ISSN 0017-2782
Monthly except July and August (May-June combined issue). First published 1883. Publisher varies.
Former title: Grade teacher
"Includes articles on all subject fields in elementary and junior high schools." Camp. Guide to Periodicals in Educ

371.1 Teaching and teaching personnel

Fisher, Leonard Everett
The schoolmasters; written & illus. by Leonard Everett Fisher. Watts, F. 1967 47p illus (Colonial Americans) lib. bdg. $3.90 (4-7) 371.1
1 Teachers 2 Education—U.S.—History
ISBN 0-531-01034-1
"A brief history of education in Colonial America, describing the dame schools, itinerant schoolmasters, private tutors, and neighborhood schools. Illustrations show a horn book, the New England primer, typical schoolroom scenes, and the schoolmasters and mistresses themselves, some with a comic touch." Hodges. Bks for Elem Sch Libraries
This book "gives ample background for discussing the role of the colonial schoolmaster, since it describes the change of attitude about education and the changes in society's attitudes toward learning and the common man. . . . The illustrations are starkly handsome, the writing style straightforward." Chicago. Children's Bk Center

371.33 Audio and visual materials for teaching

Audio visual market place; a multimedia guide. Bowker pa $21.50 371.33
1 Audio-visual education—Directories 2 Teaching—Aids and devices
ISBN 0-8352-0683-1
Annual. First published 1969
Editor: 1969- Olga S. Weber
Designed primarily for educators, this directory of the audio visual industry "brings together information on the U.S. companies, associations, and services dealing with films and other nonprint materials . . . . Listings cover professional and commercial associations, [producers and distributors], educational radio and television, film libraries, 'hardware' manufacturers, pertinent books and other reference sources, review services, and miscellaneous services. Listings in some sections are also classified by type of media." Booklist

Media programs: district and school. Prepared by the American Association of School Librarians, ALA and Association for Educational Communications and Technology. A.L.A./Association for Educational Communications and Technology 1975 128p pa $2.95 371.33
1 Audio-visual education 2 Audio-visual materials 3 Instructional materials centers
ISBN 0-8389-3159-6
Replaces: Standards for school media programs
"In addition to describing the services such media programs should provide, the standards give the requirements for personnel, resources facilities, and expenditures. These are presented both for a unified media program on the district level and for separate libraries and AV centers on the building level. Focusing sharply on the vital liaison between quality education and a school library media program, these new qualitative and quantitative standards are an essential guide for judging a school's present program and planning for the future. Though particularly germane to school librarians, administrators, and teachers, they are no less important to everyone concerned with better schools." A.L.A.
Terminology: p109-13

371.3305 Audio and visual materials for teaching— Periodicals

Audio Visual Instruction. Assn. for Educational Communications and Technology $18 per year 371.3305
1 Audio-visual education—Periodicals
ISSN 0004-7635
Monthly September through May with combined June-July issue. First published 1956
"Includes articles, reports, and other information intended to help improve instruction through more effective use of audio-visual materials and technology. Each issue contains articles devoted to a single theme. . . . Ten to fifteen major articles are published per issue. Book and film reviews are included." Camp. Guide to Periodicals in Educ

Media & Methods; exploration in education. North American Pub. Co. $9 per year 371.3305
1 Audio-visual education—Periodicals 2 Teaching—Periodicals
ISSN 0025-6897
9 issues a year September through May. First published 1965
This "is a first choice for any library, and while of primary interest to the schools, should be considered by public libraries too. Teachers are primary contributors, tend to write articles which shakeup the established view of education. There is a great emphasis on new approaches to learning. And while a good deal of the material covers films, video, television, etc., there are usually one or two articles on the book. In fact, the book is never forgotten, and what makes this magazine fascinating is that it can stress audiovisual without resorting to dumping everything for the machine. Nor is it all pie in the sky. The articles tend to be practical, give down to earth hints on materials, methods and practices. There are regular departments which review both feature and educational films, television programs, recordings, tapes, books, etc." Katz. Magazines for Libraries. 2d edition

372.1 The elementary school. Methods of instruction

Mulac, Margaret E.
Educational games for fun. Harper 1971 180p $6.95 372.1
1 Games
ISBN 0-06-013099-7
"A collection of individual and team games primarily for children of elementary school age, including exercises in math, spelling, history, geography, nature, and science, and a variety of word games. Each game is graded and the suggested variations range from simple to more difficult forms. While intended for use by both teachers and recreational leaders, the material is largely didactic in substance and will be more useful for classroom diversion than as party fun." Booklist

372.21 Preschool education

Hurd, Edith Thacher
Come with me to nursery school. Photographs by
Edward Bigelow. Coward-McCann 1970 71p illus lib.
bdg. $4.68   372.21
  1 Nursery schools
  ISBN 0-698-30050-5
The author introduces the pre-school child as well
as his parents to the activities of a nursery school class.
Photographs depicting children from a wide range of
economic and ethnic backgrounds were taken at the
Child Study Center at the University of California
during a summer pre-school action program

I saw a purple cow, and 100 other recipes for learning,
  by Ann Cole [and others]. Illus. by True Kelley.
  Little 1972 96p illus $6.95, pa $2.95   372.21
  1 Nursery schools
  ISBN 0-316-15174-2; 0-316-15175-0
This book "is geared to the important first six years
of children's lives and attempts to help the untrained
mother during this period. The table of contents is
keyed to indicate which activities are appropriate for
such special situations as 'Sick in bed,' 'Traveling or
waiting,' 'Math readiness,' and 'Reading readiness.'
Especially needed is the section entitled 'The Basics'
which gives recipes for paste, finger paint, fun dough,
and cornstarch clay. The authors show how such simple ideas as a stroll around the block or a visit to the
supermarket can be good learning-by-observing
experiences. The helpful section on music and
rhythm includes dramatic games and simple instructions for more advanced projects. Ideas for party
decorations, food, and games that young children can
help prepare are included. The illustrations are busy
but add to the text." Sch Library J

372.405 Reading—Periodicals

The Reading Teacher. Int. Reading Assn. $15 per
  year   372.405
  1 Reading—Periodicals
  ISSN 0034-0561
  8 issues a year October through May. First published 1947
"Deals with all aspects of the teaching of elementary and secondary reading, but concentrates on the
elementary level. Each issue carries signed articles
which range from scholarly studies of reading habits
to semi-popular contributions on the woes and joys of
teaching the subject. Regular departments include
notes on current research, magazine articles and
books worth examining, a list of materials particularly
suited for children, 'Crossfire,' 'Interchange,' 'Critically Speaking,' 'ERIC/CRIER' and 'The Membership Card.' Particularly useful for the teacher who is
searching for new methods of improving reading."
Katz. Magazines for Libraries

372.6 Language arts (Communication skills) Storytelling

Carlson, Bernice Wells
Listen! And help tell the story; illus. by Burmah
Burris. Abingdon 1965 176p illus $6.50   372.6
  1 Storytelling—Collections
  ISBN 0-687-22096-3

"Pre-schoolers learn first to listen and then to participate in these finger-plays, action verses and poems
with sound effects and choruses which may be used
with either a single child or any sized group." Ontario
"Though Miss Carlson states that the book is for the
child's own use, its basic value will be to teachers and
parents. . . . The art work is uneven in quality but
has the merit of showing racial integration." Library J

Colwell, Eileen
(ed.) A second storyteller's choice; a selection of
stories, with notes on how to tell them, by Eileen
Colwell; with drawings by Prudence Seward. Walck,
H.Z. 1965 160p illus $5.50   372.6
  1 Storytelling—Collections
  ISBN 0-8098-2378-0
  Companion volume to: A storyteller's choice
In this "book the English librarian-storyteller has
selected stories which are relatively easy to tell, and
appeal to a younger age group than those in the first
collection. Although made up mainly of traditional
tales, the collection has great variety. As in the earlier
book, an afterword includes wise and practical suggestions for the storyteller; and notes for each story give
telling time, age of the audience, helpful points on
preparing and telling the story and background material that will add significance to the story and pleasure
to the telling." Horn Bk

(ed.) A storyteller's choice; a selection of stories
with notes on how to tell them; with drawings by Carol
Barker. Walck, H.Z. 1964 [c1963] 223p illus $5.50
                                372.6
  1 Storytelling—Collections
  ISBN 0-8098-2369-1
  First published 1963 in England
The editor "offers a selection of 18 stories and two
poems which she has told to children. . . . In an
appendix she gives advice on storytelling in general
and helpful guidance on each of the stories in this
book. Of first importance to storytellers, the discriminating collection will also be enjoyed by the
individual reader." Booklist
"One criticism of the collection as a whole might be
that for children today there is very little that links this
world of the storyteller to their own time." Times
(London) Literary Sup

Davis, Mary Gould
(ed.) A baker's dozen; thirteen stories to tell and to
read aloud; decorated by Emma Brock. Harcourt 1930
207p illus $5.95   372.6
  1 Storytelling—Collections
  ISBN 0-15-205691-2
Each story in this collection "has stood the test of
the children's interest and approval. They have all
been told again and again to the boys and girls who
come to the public libraries of New York for the Story
Hour." Foreword
The book "might easily lead to a further reading of
the authors included." Booklist

Dobbs, Rose
(ed.) Once upon a time; twenty cheerful tales to
read and tell; selected, ed. and sometimes retold by
Rose Dobbs; illus. by Flavia Gág. Random House
1950 117p illus $2.95, lib. bdg. $4.99   372.6
  1 Storytelling—Collections
  ISBN 0-394-81462-2; 0-394-91462-7
"The whole contents include some stories from
folklore sources, such as a Grimm tale as Wanda Gág
told it, others as modern as a Rootabaga story. Well
printed and quaintly illustrated, these cheerful tales
are sure to give entertainment to little children in the
home as well as in the story hour." Horn Bk

Hardendorff, Jeanne B.

(ed.) Just one more; selected and retold by Jeanne B. Hardendorff; illus. by Don Bolognese. Lippincott 1969 169p illus $4.50, lib. bdg. $4.39 (3-6) 372.6

1 Storytelling—Collections 2 Folklore
ISBN 0-397-31078-1; 0-397-31079-X

This collection of stories, intended to provide material for storytelling, consists largely of fables, fairy tales and folk tales from around the world, including American Indian and Eskimo tales, as well as tales from Russia, Poland, India and Tibet

"This is a widely varied collection, good for independent reading or reading aloud as well as for telling; an appendage gives the source for each tale, the audience level, and the time each takes in the telling—half of the forty taking three minutes or less." Sutherland. The Best in Children's Bks

Moore, Vardine

Pre-school story hour. 2d ed. Scarecrow 1972 174p illus $6 372.6

1 Storytelling
ISBN 0-8108-0474-3
First published 1966

This book discusses "some of the essentials required to relate a story and conduct a program; story hour location; some recommended physical arrangements; practical measures to deal with the perennial problem of what to do with parents; specific techniques and examples of program planning and extended activities; what makes a story good to tell, in terms of subject and interest areas, type of material, format, and design of the books; and an extensive bibliography of recommended stories and 'related activities.' In the last, the author details a short but effective collection of finger plays, action stories and games with an appended list of recommended books and recordings." Sch Library J

"Even experienced storytellers can benefit from the inspiration and practical advice covering all aspects of this recognized important type of programming." ALA. CSD. Mother Hubbard's cupboard [Review of 1966 edition]

Ross, Eulalie Steinmetz

(ed.) The lost half-hour; a collection of stories; illus. by Enrico Arno. Harcourt 1963 191p illus $5.95 372.6

1 Storytelling—Collections
ISBN 0-15-249360-3

The editor "has told all seventeen of these stories again and again to children. . . . They are not difficult for the beginning storyteller to prepare, and their success with children has been proved. . . . Concluding the book is a valuable and practical essay on storytelling." Horn Bk

Sawyer, Ruth

The way of the storyteller. Viking 1962 360p $4.50, pa $2.95 372.6

1 Storytelling 2 Storytelling—Collections
ISBN 0-670-75244-4; 0-670-00176-7
First published 1942

"This is not primarily a book on how to tell stories; it is rather the whole philosophy of story telling as a creative art. From her own rich experience the author writes inspiringly of the background, experience, creative imagination, technique and selection essential to this art." Booklist

"This book is the expression of a generous spirit. . . . The book will appeal to the creative artist in any field. The storyteller will welcome the group of [eleven] selected stories for telling, and the reading lists which reflect the range and variety of the author's interests." N Y Pub Library

Sechrist, Elizabeth Hough

(ed.) It's time for story hour; comp. by Elizabeth Hough Sechrist and Janette Woolsey; illus. by Elsie Jane McCorkell. Macrae Smith Co. 1964 258p illus lib. bdg. $5.97 372.6

1 Storytelling—Collections
ISBN 0-8255-8211-3

"A fine anthology of 40 stories—some humorous, some romantic, and others about strange happenings —which the [editors] . . . have found from their own experience as storytellers to be favorites with children. Enjoyable for individual reading and particularly suitable for library storytelling and for reading aloud. Illustrated with attractive line drawings." Booklist

Shedlock, Marie L.

The art of the story-teller; foreword by Anne Carroll Moore. 3d ed. rev. with a new bibliography by Eulalie Steinmetz. Dover 1952 [c1951] xxi, 290p front pa $2.50 372.6

1 Storytelling 2 Storytelling—Collections
ISBN 0-486-20635-1
First published 1915

"Suggestions for selecting and for telling stories are included as well as eighteen of Miss Shedlock's own favorites." Horn Bk

With much advice "illustrated by the author's own experiences and by many quotations from literature." Wis Library Bul

Siks, Geraldine Brain

Creative dramatics; an art for children. Harper 1958 472p illus $11.95 372.6

1 Drama in education
ISBN 0-06-046160-8

A guide for those working with varied groups of children. The author sets forth the philosophy, methodology and techniques of working with differing age levels in creative dramatics programs

Bibliography: p405-12. Material for creative dramatics: p413-61

Tashjian, Virginia A.

(ed.) Juba this and Juba that; story hour stretches for large or small groups; with illus. by Victoria de Larrea. Little 1969 116p illus $5.95 372.6

1 Storytelling—Collections
ISBN 0-316-83230-8

"A useful source of chants, poetry and rhyme, stories, finger plays, riddles, songs, tongue twisters, and jokes. The selections accompanied by lively orange and black illustrations, are all suitably silly. They require and inspire audience participation." Sch Library J

"The short, funny tales and games are guaranteed to dispel restlessness, relax listeners, and add variety to any story hour. The illustrations are as full of fun and nonsense as the book." Horn Bk

(ed.) With a deep sea smile; story hour stretches for large or small groups; illus. by Rosemary Wells. Little 1974 132p illus music $5.95 372.6

1 Storytelling—Collections
ISBN 0-316-83216-2

This is a collection of chants, poetry, rhymes, stories, finger plays, riddles, songs, tongue twisters and jokes planned for use as story hour activities. They are taken from a wide variety of sources

"Hints are offered on using the material. Prefacing each selection, and of even greater value, are specific suggestions for stimulating participation. Lively illustrations capture the fun of the contents, making the book attractive to children as well as to adults." Horn Bk

Includes an index of titles

Ward, Winifred

(ed.) Stories to dramatize; selected and ed. by Winifred Ward. The Children's Theatre Press 1952 389p $6   372.6

1 Drama in education 2 Literature—Collections

"This excellent collection of stories, chosen from classic and modern literature, is arranged by age levels from kindergarten through junior high school. There are suggestions for evaluating stories for dramatization and pointers on dramatizing them. Useful to camp counselors and recreation leaders as well as teachers of creative dramatics." Booklist

Bibliography: p381-83. Some good books for integrated projects: p384-86

372.9 Elementary education— History

Sloane, Eric

The little red schoolhouse. Doubleday [1973 c1972] unp illus $4.95, lib. bdg. $5.70 (4-7)   372.9

1 Education, Elementary—History 2 School buildings

ISBN 0-385-07689-4; 0-385-04297-3

First published 1972

The author describes the American "one-room school of the 1700s and 1800s covering such topics as architecture, furnishings, heating and wood supply, discipline, and punishment. He comments on the three R's which he asserts were reading, 'riting, and religion and stresses the importance of morality and penmanship in early education. Sloane discusses the status of the teacher in the community, his low pay, and his need to moonlight and suggests that the effects of present-day progress in education may well be pondered. Generously illustrated with pencil sketches." Booklist

380 Transportation

Hofsinde, Robert

Indians on the move; written and illus. by Robert Hofsinde (Gray-Wolf) Morrow 1970 95p illus lib. bdg. $4.32 (4-6)   380

1 Indians of North America—Social life and customs 2 Transportation

ISBN 0-688-31615-8

"A concise, readable introduction to Indian modes of travel presented in clear, simple text, drawings, and diagrams. . . . [The author] discusses the daily, seasonal, and migratory movement of various tribes, the design and construction of equipment used to transport people and goods, and the tribal customs and environmental circumstances that influenced type and method of transportation. He concludes with a chapter on Indian travel today." Booklist

380.5 Transportation services

Hellman, Hal

Transportation in the world of the future. New, rev. ed. Evans, M.&Co. 1974 187p $6.95 (5-7)
                                                              380.5

1 Transportation

ISBN 0-87131-155-0

First published 1968

This discussion of the function and operation of a variety of vehicles that may be in use in the future includes chapters on rail rapid transit, high speed ground transportation, tunnels and tubes, the electric car and aircraft

Bibliography: p177-80

McLeod, Sterling

How will we move all the people? Transportation for tomorrow's world, by Sterling McLeod and the editors of Science Book Associates; with photographs. Messner 1971 176p illus (Tomorrow's world ser) lib. bdg. $4.29 (6-7)   380.5

1 Transportation

ISBN 0-671-32380-6

"Pointing out that quiet, clean, uncrowded, dependable, and fast methods of transportation are desperately needed to solve the problems of moving millions of people from place to place, the author discusses new experimental forms—fast trains on rails, air cushion vehicles for land and water, Gravity Vacuum Transit underground, and safe, emission-free automobiles. He also describes future automated highways and more convenient airports, gives arguments for and against the SST, and considers spacecraft and space stations. A short bibliography is appended. Many clear photographs and drawings add to the book's usefulness." Booklist

Swallow, Su

Cars, trucks and trains; illus. by Michael and Ann Ricketts. Grosset 1974 c1973 27p illus $2.95 (1-3)
                                                              380.5

1 Transportation

ISBN 0-488-11766-5

"Beginner's world"

First published 1973 in England with title: Cars, lorries and trains

"A mini-encyclopedia covering transportation-related topics—e.g., 'In the street,' 'Roads,' 'Making cars,' 'Motor racing,' etc. Most double-page spreads feature a large picture with simple text surrounded by several smaller pictures with slightly more advanced texts. . . . Some of the Anglicisms here have not been altered for an American audience (e.g., car park, omnibus)." Sch Library J

380.503 Transportation— Encyclopedias

Zehavi, A. M.

(ed.) The complete junior encyclopedia of transportation. Watts, F. 1973 [c1972] 280p illus maps lib. bdg. $8.87 (5-7)   380.503

1 Transportation—Encyclopedias

ISBN 0-531-02596-9

"A compendium of signed articles covering numerous modes of transportation, e.g., automobiles, airplanes, bicycles, and hydrofoil boats, as well as the related areas of maps and globes, passports and visas, driver's education, etc. . . . The designation 'junior' in the title is misleading since much of this information is more technical than that found in standard encyclopedias. However, material on overland trails, the Erie Canal and Pan American Highway, and latitude and longitude supplement social studies curriculums." Library J

380.5074 Transportation— Museums

Jackson, Robert B.

Waves, wheels and wings; museums of transportation; illus. with photographs. Walck, H.Z. 1974 62p illus $4.95 (4-6)   380.5074

1 Transportation—History 2 Museums

ISBN 0-8098-2098-6

Jackson, Robert B.—*Continued*

The author describes the exhibits at four United States transportation museums: Mystic Seaport in Connecticut, Strasburg Railroad in Pennsylvania, Harrah's Automobile Collection in Nevada, and Old Rhinebeck Aerodrome in New York

"This is not an essential purchase but does provide a tangible focus for a brief sketch of transportation history. Black-and-white photos illustrate the text, and travel directions, hours, and prices are included at the end of each chapter." Booklist

383 Postal communication

Adams, Samuel Hopkins

The pony express; illus. by Lee J. Ames. Random House 1950 185p illus $2.95, lib. bdg. $4.39 (5-7)
383

1 Pony express 2 The West—History
ISBN 0-394-80307-8; 0-394-90307-2
"Landmark books"
"All the excitement of Indian attacks, holdups by outlaws, and buffeting by storms is caught in this story of the riders who carried the mail from Missouri to California." Hodges. Bks for Elem Sch Libraries

The history of the Pony Express "is brought out vividly and with careful attention to the meager facts known." N Y Times Bk Rev

Map on lining-papers

Moody, Ralph

Riders of the pony express; illus. by Robert Riger; maps by Leonard Derwinski. Houghton 1958 183p illus maps $2.95 (5-7)
383

1 Pony express 2 The West—History
ISBN 0-395-07246-8
"North Star books"
This is a "mile-by-mile account of the first run of the Pony Express, with emphasis on courage and fortitude of the riders. Concluding chapters on outstanding riders and the historic ride to bring the news of Lincoln's election to California. Distinctive drawings and maps. . . . Worthwhile addition to collections needing more history of the West." Library J

Pinkerton, Robert

The first overland mail; illus. by Paul Lantz. Random House 1953 185p illus $2.95, lib. bdg. $4.27 (5-7)
383

1 Postal service—U.S. 2 Butterfield, John
ISBN 0-394-80340-X; 0-394-90340-4
"Landmark books"
"A narrative history of the first overland delivery of mail by stagecoach from Missouri to California, and of John Butterfield—the man who undertook the impossible—to cover the 2,800 mile route in 25 days—and succeeded." Booklist

384 Other systems of communication

Coggins, Jack

Flashes and flags; the story of signaling; written and illus. by Jack Coggins. Dodd 1963 88p illus lib. bdg. $4.50 (5-7)
384

1 Signals and signaling
ISBN 0-396-06555-4
An "account of the signals which were used for sending prearranged messages in the days before advanced methods of communication and of those in use today. Hand signals, flag systems, the many uses of the Morse code, semaphore flags, semaphore arms, traffic signals used on sea, land, and in the air and the signals used in sports are described and clearly pictured. Illustrated in color with many diagrams and drawings." Booklist

"Much reference information is included but the organization of the book does not make it easy to use as a reference tool." Library J

384.55 Television broadcasting

Shay, Arthur

What happens at a television station. Reilly & Lee 1969 unp illus $5.95 (2-4)
384.55

1 Television broadcasting 2 Television stations
ISBN 0-8092-8604-1
"The author takes readers behind the scenes in TV studios to give them some understanding of TV workers, their jobs and equipment; a number of the pictures depict employees at the Bozo's Circus studio. Briefly mentioned are the sound man, director, assistant director, producer, prop men, cameramen, stagehand electricians, carpenters, painters, writers, artists, reporters and cast members, along with the equipment they use. Also described simply are the TV camera's 'image orthicon' (a light-sensitive tube), the process of sending programs, the master control room, and the news department. The many photographs are generally clear, and the text (printed in large, glaring type) is quite informative." Sch Library J

385 Railroad transportation

Behrens, June

Train cargo; photographs collected by Lou Jacobs, Jr. Childrens Press 1974 64p illus (Transportation and trade ser) lib. bdg. $4.39 (3-5)
385

1 Railroads 2 Freight and freightage
ISBN 0-516-07522-5
"An Elk Grove book"
"With numerous black-and-white photographs and a clearly written text Behrens explains the role of railroads as cargo carriers. She describes kinds of cargo and introduces types of rail cars and their functions. Also covered is the rail terminal process of sorting loaded cars and making up trains, as well as a brief identification of key train jobs such as switchman, brakeman, fireman, etc. For those who need useful material for transportation units or want an up-to-date look at freight trains." Booklist

385.09 Railroad transportation—History

Elting, Mary

All aboard! The railroad trains that built America. [Rev. ed.] Four Winds [1971 c1969] 127p illus maps lib. bdg. $5.72, pa $1.25 (4-7)
385.09

1 Railroads—History
ISBN 0-590-07178-5; 0-590-08709-6
First published 1951 by Garden City Books with title: The real book of trains, under the pseudonym

Elting, Mary—*Continued*

Davis Cole. The 1971 edition was first published 1969 in paperback by Scholastic.

In this history of America's trains "there's a lot of different information . . . such as why tracks are laid on crossties and crushed rock, what torpedoes are, why Casey Jones's locomotive was known as a model 4-6-0, how the first tunnels were dug, when and why Standard Time was adopted. There's a Ralph Nader in the story too. His was Lorenzo Coffin, and he was most active in the 1870's trying to force the railroads to use safer equipment: George Westinghouse's automatic air brake was one example. All these elements make Miss Elting's account exceptionally interesting, and not just for young people." N Y Times Bk Rev

"Illustrated with many excellent photographs and engravings this is an inviting book which conveys the adventure and excitement as well as the importance to the country's development of railroads and railroading." Booklist

Holbrook, Stewart H.

The golden age of railroads; illus. by Ernest Richardson. Random House 1960 182p illus maps $2.95, lib. bdg. $4.39 (5-7)   385.09

1 Railroads—History
ISBN 0-394-80393-0; 0-394-90393-5
"Landmark books"

A "review of the growth of American railroads and their effect on the development of the country in the years between the first trip of the first American-built locomotive in 1830 and the advent of the internal combustion engine in the 1920's. . . . The author describes the building of the major railroads, the pioneers who built them, the invention of safety measures, holdups and robberies, disasters, and the adoption of standard time." Booklist

"With some good maps showing the length of completed railroads at successive periods, and some rather routine pictures in gray and bright yellow. This book has zest, and reads as if the author were filled with enthusiasm for the subject." N Y Her Trib Bks

Bibliography: p178

Latham, Frank B.

The transcontinental railroad, 1862-69; a great engineering feat links America coast to coast. Watts, F. 1973 90p illus map $3.45 (5-7)   385.09

1 Union Pacific Railroad 2 Central Pacific Railroad
ISBN 0-531-01025-2
"A Focus book"

This book describes the building of the first transcontinental railroad and its subsequent effects on American society

This study is "excellent for individualized consideration of [an] historical incident usually glossed over in General History books with one or two paragraphs. The political and financial machinations that primed the pump for transcontinental transportation by rail are as contemporary as any government-industrial conflicts today. Colorful trivia . . . spice the telling." Best Sellers

Bibliography: p88

386   Inland water transportation. Canals

Boardman, Fon W.

Canals. Walck, H.Z. 1959 139p illus maps $5 (5-7)   386

1 Canals—History
ISBN 0-8098-3025-6
"An informative survey of canals in which the

author . . . describes inland waterways of the world, both ancient and modern, giving some technical details [and information about the men involved] and noting use and importance. The Erie, Suez, and Panama Canals are discussed in individual chapters. Of special interest are the many photographs, reproductions of old drawings, maps, and diagrams, valuable for reference use." Booklist

Franchere, Ruth

Westward by canal. Macmillan (N Y) 1972 149p illus map $4.95 (5-7)   386

1 Canals—History 2 U.S.—History—1783-1865
"Map by Rafael Palacios." Verso of title page

"In a lively and informative account of the beginning of the canal era, the author describes the construction of the canals, the people who initiated the plans and those who took part in the digging, and the life on and around the waterways. The canal era, a brief but important period in this country's history, is treated as an influential factor in the westward migration from the crowded eastern seaboard and in the mass emigration from other countries to this land." Top of the News

For further reading: p145-46

387.2   Ships

Colby, C. B.

Sailing ships; great ships before the age of steam. Coward-McCann 1970 48p illus lib. bdg. $3.99 (3-6)   387.2

1 Ships—History
ISBN 0-698-30301-6

A pictorial history of sailing ships of all types, from all ages. The illustrations range from ship models at the Smithsonian to restored ships at Mystic, Connecticut, to contemporary crafts. Information about rigging, masts, and sails is included

Knight, Frank

Ships. Crowell-Collier Press [1971 c1969] 63p illus $4.95 (5-7)   387.2

1 Ships—History
ISBN 0-02-75089

First published 1969 in England

"Brisk text copiously illustrated with black-and-white and colored photographs traces the evolution of water transport in reverse chronological order beginning with nuclear submarines and specialized cargo carriers of today and going back through the eras of steam and sail to the galleys of ancient Rome and the dugout canoes and basket boats of primitive man. Although broad rather than thorough in coverage, the book contains many enlightening historical facts which highlight some of the social, economic, and practical considerations as well as technological advances that affected the development and use of ships." Booklist

"Though the photographs and reproductions are small, they are excellent and numerous, many in full color, with explanatory notes. In fact, the illustrations are worth the price of the book because there are few volumes with such visual appeal for this age level." Sch Library J

Ward, Ralph T.

Ships through history; illus. by Samuel F. Manning. Bobbs 1973 143p illus maps $7.95 (6-7) 387.2

1 Ships—History 2 Naval history
ISBN 0-672-51663-2

Emphasizing their influence on commercial and territorial development, the author traces the de-

Ward, Ralph T.—*Continued*
velopment of ships from those without keels used by the Pharaohs to the American clippers
"This scholarly but always readable narrative combines history, navigation and shipbuilding effectively. . . . [There are] excellent drawings. . . . An extensive glossary and a bibliography are included." Pub W

Zim, Herbert S.
Cargo ships [by] Herbert S. Zim [and] James R. Skelly; illus. by Richard Cuffari. Morrow 1970 62p illus lib. bdg. $4.32 (3-6)   387.2
1 Ships 2 Merchant marine
ISBN 0-688-31143-1
The authors describe "the construction and equipment of cargo ships and the ways in which they may be powered, the function and operation of the three basic cargo ships in use today—freighter, tanker, and bulk carrier—and the duties of the crew and career possibilities on cargo ships. The writing style is clear and simplified, the information specific, the print large; the precise line drawings on almost every page are an essential feature of the book." Booklist

387.7 Air transportation

Olney, Ross R.
Air traffic control. Nelson 1972 124p illus $5.25 (6-7)   387.7
1 Navigation (Aeronautics) 2 Aeronautics—Safety measures
ISBN 0-8407-61546
The author describes the equipment, techniques, duties and training of an air traffic controller as well as the inner workings of the various services that direct today's air traffic, including radio and radar

388.4 Urban transportation

Tannenbaum, Beulah
City traffic, by Beulah Tannenbaum and Myra Stillman; illus. by Marta Cone. McGraw 1972 64p illus (Science in the city) lib. bdg. $4.72 (3-5)   388.4
1 City traffic
ISBN 0-07-062890-4
The authors explain the attempts already activated to solve city traffic problems and describe proposals for future solutions
Partial contents: Traffic lights; Expressways; Signs and lanes; Emergency streets; Parking; Pollution; Traffic is people
"An experiment on pollution and instructions for making a traffic light are included, and the imaginative black-and-white illustrations add a humorous touch." Sch Library J

389 Metrology and standardization

Bendick, Jeanne
Measuring; written and illus. by Jeanne Bendick. Watts, F. 1971 71p illus (Science experiences) lib. bdg. $4.90 (3-5)   389
1 Mensuration
ISBN 0-531-01435-5
This book "introduces the reader to what measure-

ment is, how measurements are made, and how measurements can be used. An initial presentation on the history of measuring clearly demonstrates the need for standard units of measure. Inches, feet, and yards are introduced as standards, and these are compared with standard units in the metric system. The functional process approach involves the reader in using measuring techniques. Carefully designed experiences cause the student to interchange feet and inches, inches and centimeters, feet and miles, etc." Appraisal
"By using many open-ended questions and by clever two-color illustrations that she makes as she writes the text, Mrs. Bendick leads the readers through the various exercises in a manner that is exciting and engenders a sense of accomplishment. Especially appropriate is the treatment of the metric system and its advantages." Sci Bks

Branley, Franklyn M.
Measure with metric, illus. by Loretta Lustig. Crowell 1975 33p illus $4.50, lib. bdg. $5.25 (2-4)   389
1 Metric system
ISBN 0-690-00576-8; 0-690-00577-6
"A direct approach to the challenge of familiarizing students with metric measurement. Readers can, in minutes, make a cardboard meter stick, a simple balance with homemade gram weights, and a plastic bag-lined liter box for liquid measurement. After measuring familiar household items with the help of this book, children will have some functional understanding of metrics. Illustrated with cheerful black-and-white and color pictures." Booklist

Think metric! Illus. by Graham Booth. Crowell [1973 c1972] 53p illus maps $4.95, lib. bdg. $5.25 (3-6)   389
1 Metric system
ISBN 0-690-81861-0; 0-690-81862-9
The author explains how the metric system works and "describes its advantages over our present system of measurement both in terms of efficiency and of translation. The text begins with historical background, goes on to the establishment of the metric system, and presents translation problems that can familiarize the reader with the metric system." Chicago. Children's Bk Center
"Problem solving and examples are well integrated into the text, and English-metric equivalents are listed at the end. The clarity of the writing and of the often amusing illustrations make this a good introduction." Booklist

Fey, James T.
Long, short, high, low, thin, wide; illus. by Janie Russell. Crowell 1971 32p illus (Young math bks) $4.50, lib. bdg. $5.25 (1-3)   389
1 Mensuration
ISBN 0-690-50549-3; 0-690-50550-7
"This is a clear and simple introduction to measurement, the illustrations matching the text nicely. By showing the reader the problem in measuring if there is no established unit or standard, the author makes clear the necessity for having such units. The text explains the ways in which early units of measurement were established, and describes both the metric system and our own units of inch, foot, yard, and mile." Chicago. Children's Bk Center

Gallant, Roy A.
Man the measurer; our units of measure and how they grew. Doubleday 1972 111p illus $4.95, lib. bdg. $5.70 (4-7)   389
1 Mensuration
ISBN 0-385-05676-1; 0-385-09115-X
Measurement as a scientific tool is explored as the

Gallant, Roy A.—*Continued*

author describes its history and gives examples of the many forms of measurement used by scientists today

"The contents fit neatly into three parts: a selective history of measurement units, measuring, and the metric system. Each section includes several experiments that students can carry out. Mr. Gallant obviously has a command of his subject and can make his ideas clear to his readers. Although he steers clear of some of the subtle problems associated with measurement, the book has value for teachers too. . . . Of particular interest is the binary nature of the ancient Egyptian system in which liquid measurement units double in size." Sci Bks

Hahn, James

The metric system, by James and Lynn Hahn. Watts, F. 1975 63p illus lib. bdg. $3.90 (5-7)   389
1 The metric system
ISBN 0-531-00834-7

"A First book"

This book contains an "account of the history of metrics accompanied by some practical, use-oriented material. The authors wisely warn against relying on cumbersome conversion methods while learning the system, although they supply conversion tables for those who wish to use them. A brief survey of current use of metrics puts the other information into perspective. Suggested readings, plus organizations and agencies to write to for information, are listed. Illustrated with black-and-white photographs." Booklist

Hirsch, S. Carl

Meter means measure; the story of the metric system. Viking 1973 126p lib. bdg. $5.95 (5-7)   389
1 Metric system
ISBN 0-670-47365-0

In this book "the controversies and efforts that have occurred in initiating the use of the metric system as a universal measuring standard are described. . . . The influence of persons like Thomas Jefferson, John Quincy Adams, Alexander Graham Bell, Albert Michelson and others is shown in historical perspective as America moves toward the utilization of the metric system of measure." Top of the News

"Well-researched and readable, this also explains the pressures and counter-pressures involved in the reluctance of the United States to adopt the metric system—a dimension which is not covered by other books on the subject." Library J

Suggestions for further reading: p121

Moore, William

Metric is here! Putnam 1974 94p illus $5.95 (6-7)
  389

1 Metric system
ISBN 0-399-20407-5

"Like the other books on the metric system . . . this gives an explanation of the system, discusses the problems of conversion, and gives many examples of areas of our lives that will be affected. Although there are some minor weaknesses in the material (. . . a caption that is confusingly like the text because of the type-size and placement, a table not adequately labelled) the text has good organization, clear explanations, and competent writing style. This gives less historical background about measurement systems than do most of the other books, but it has many tables of equivalents and many opportunities for the reader to practice using metric measurements." Chicago. Children's Bk Center

Pine, Tillie S.

Measurements and how we use them, by Tillie S. Pine and Joseph Levine; pictures by Harriet Sherman. McGraw 1974 48p illus lib. bdg. $4.33 (2-4)
  389

1 Mensuration 2 Measuring instruments
ISBN 0-07-050084-3

"This delightful book attracts the reader's attention with its bright colors and imaginative layout. The book begins with examples of measurement problems encountered in everyday life. . . . The authors deal with spatial measurements time, weight and temperature. In each case, the reader is told exactly how to use the measuring device to determine the quantity of units desired. The authors also describe how each measuring device is constructed. In addition, they cite several experiments that can be performed when primary measuring tools are not available. . . . Many examples are cited showing the importance of measurement in a variety of jobs." Sci Bks

"Sherman's cartoon-like pen-and-ink illustrations complement and enliven the text. . . . This [book] will fill the need for concept and skill development material in an easy-to-read format." Library J

Srivastava, Jane Jonas

Weighing & balancing; illus. by Aliki. Crowell 1970 32p illus (Young math bks) $4.50, lib. bdg. $5.25, pa $1.25 (1-3)   389
1 Weights and measures
ISBN 0-690-87114-7; 0-690-87115-5; 0-690-87120-1

"A brief, uncomplicated text and attractive, often humourous drawings ably explain the difficult concepts of weight, balance, and density to young children. Directions are given for making a simple balance, and the reader is encouraged to experiment with it using marbles, pennies, pencils, and objects of known weight to discover which object is heavier. An easy-to-do experiment using the balance, a stick, a stone, and a glass of water to demonstrate density is also included." Booklist

Zim, Herbert S.

Metric measure [by] Herbert S. Zim [and] James R. Skelly; illus. by Timothy Evans. Morrow 1974 63p illus maps $4.50, lib. bdg. $4.14 (3-6)   389
1 Metric stytem
ISBN 0-688-20118-0; 0-688-30118-5

The authors discuss the history and applications of the metric system of measurement and give examples of its use in common situations. They explain how scientific standards of measurement have been developed for determining length, weight, time and temperature and tell briefly about other units of measurement

391   Costume

Baylor, Byrd

They put on masks; illus. by Jerry Ingram. Scribner 1974 46p illus $5.95 (1-4)   391
1 Masks (for the face) 2 Indians of North America
ISBN 0-684-13767-4

The "text describes the masks used by some Indian tribes, chiefly those of the Southwest, in their ceremonial rites and dances, giving details about the way the masks are made as well as about how they are used. . . . The text incorporates some of the beautiful song poetry that is used by the masked dancers, but it does more than that; it explains how the masks evoke the spirits of those they portray, how wearing a mask invests the person with the powers of the god or the creature he has become." Chicago Children's Bk Center

"This truly outstanding book is beautifully illustrated by Jerry Ingram with dozens of Indian figures and actual masks in brilliant colors and of authentic design. The intangible spirit of beauty and love of the soil which motivate the Indian people are remarkably captured in this book. Children of all ages, and adults

Baylor, Byrd—*Continued*

as well, will learn of a variety of Indian customs from many tribes and with masks as the theme, as well as actual chants which accompany the rituals in which the masks appear. After seeing the many types of masks, the child will be able to copy the ones illustrated, recreate Indian lore for himself, and finally design a personal mask with individual meaning." Reading Teacher

Cummings, Richard

101 costumes; for all ages, all occasions; illus. by Opal Jackson. McKay 1970 194p illus $4.95 (5-7)

391

1 Costume

ISBN 0-679-20135-X

Here are garment patterns, and instructions on the selection, cutting and sewing of materials, and the making of costume accessories, from jewelry to papier-mâché armor. Two complete plays and outlines for several costume pageants and tableaux are included

"While the directions, which are in the nature of suggestions rather than the explicit, step-by-step type, require ingenuity and experience in application, the book is valuable for its wealth of ideas, made easily accessible through several costume indexes." Booklist

Bibliography: p188

Fox, Lilla M.

Costumes and customs of the British Isles; illus. by the author. Plays, Inc. 1974 64p illus map $3.95 (4-7)

391

1 Costume 2 Great Britain—Social life and customs

ISBN 0-8238-0154-3

"A short specialized title covering occupational and festival costumes of England, Scotland, Wales, and Ireland from medieval times to the present. There are brief descriptions of customs, dances, and costumes —many illustrated with small but clearly detailed ink drawings. No other juvenile books are available on this subject." Sch Library J

Gilbreath, Alice

Making costumes for parties, plays, and holidays; pictures by Timothy Evans. Morrow 1974 93p illus $5.50, lib. bdg. $4.81 (4-6)

391

1 Costume

ISBN 0-688-20103-2; 0-688-30103-7

This book contains step-by-step instructions for constructing twenty-one costumes from readily available materials. Presented in their order of difficulty, there are directions for making ghost, scarecrow, octopus, robot, gingerbread boy, valentine, firecracker, and poodle costumes

"Clear directions, accompanied by black-and-white drawings and diagrams, provide all necessary information." Booklist

Hofsinde, Robert

Indian costumes; written and illus. by Robert Hofsinde (Gray-Wolf) Morrow 1968 94p illus lib. bdg. $4.32 (3-6)

391

1 Indians of North America—Costume and adornment

ISBN 0-688-31614-X

"The distinctive costumes of ten different North American Indian tribal groups are here illustrated, showing their ceremonial, warring or everyday apparel. Black and white drawings help in explaining how they were made." Bruno. Bks for Sch Libraries, 1968

The tribes represented are the Apache, Blackfoot, Crow, Iroquois, Navaho, Northwest Coast Indians, Ojibwa, Pueblo, Seminole and Sioux Indians

"The decorations extend to tribal paints on the face and body as well as clothes and Indian ponies." Christian Sci Monitor

Hunt, Kari

Masks and mask makers [by] Kari Hunt and Bernice Wells Carlson. Abingdon 1961 67p illus $4.50 (5-7)

391

1 Masks (for the face)

ISBN 0-687-23705-X

"An interesting survey of different types of masks worn by man since primitive times. The authors tell what peoples have used the various masks, and what social and symbolic functions masks have served. Legends and ceremonies associated with their use are described, and instructions are given for homemade masks." The AAAS Sci Bk List for Children

"Could be much used by teachers . . . and by the boys and girls themselves in accelerated lower grades for special reports. Whether interested in theatre, art, or ethnology, there is something here for older readers, too." Library J

Includes bibliography

Leeming, Joseph

The costume book; drawings by Hilda Richman. Lippincott 1938 123p illus lib. bdg. $5.75   391

1 Costume

ISBN 0-397-30052-2

Title on cover: The costume book for parties and plays

Descriptions and illustrations are given for folk costumes of twenty-seven nations, for fanciful and fairy tales costumes, and for historic costumes of Ancient Egypt, Palestine, Greece and Rome, Medieval Europe, Sixteenth century Europe and Elizabethan England, Seventeenth century Europe and America, Eighteenth century Europe and American colonial, Early nineteenth century or empire period, Mid-Victorian England, and American Civil War period

"There are practical directions for making costumes, on how to cut and use a pattern, and hints on inexpensive material that will give the desired effect. . . . Black-and-white drawings illustrate the costumes." Booklist

Parish, Peggy

Costumes to make; illus. by Lynn Sweat. Macmillan (N Y) 1970 111p illus $3.95 (4-6)   391

1 Costume 2 Sewing

A "book that gives instructions for making very simple costumes, many of them using in part a basic commerical pattern and describing only the frills or accessories. For a toy soldier, for example, the costume is based on a pajama pattern, with instructions given for trim and for making a hat. While the step-by-step directions are clear, and the costumes uncomplicated, the user would need to be familiar with patterns and sewing." Chicago. Children's Bk Center

"The directions are neither so brief that important information is left out or assumed to be known, nor so complex that heads spin and arms flail in exasperation. The 50 costumes are childlike—Indian boys and girls, cowboys, angels and a long list of storybook characters starting with Mother Goose and ending with animals of different kinds. The drawings are appealing to the browser and illuminating to the seamstress." Sch Library J

Purdy, Susan

Costumes for you to make. Lippincott 1971 121p illus $7.95 (4-7)

391

1 Costume

ISBN 0-397-31317-9

There are "directions for each costume part, including collars, cuffs, wings, hats, capes, tunics, medals,

Purdy, Susan—_Continued_

and even wolf muzzles and dog snouts. Every item is accompanied by detailed drawings, directions for measuring and for reducing patterns in some cases." Library J

"Presenting suggestions for all types of costumes, the book contains brief sections on theatrical make-up and costume material. . . . Excellent ideas and simple instructions for theatrical productions or for parties." Horn Bk

391.09   Costume—History

Cunnington, Phillis

Costumes of the seventeenth and eighteenth century. Plays, Inc. [1970 c1968] 120p illus $4.95
391.09

1 Costume—History
ISBN 0-8238-0086-5
Copyrighted 1968 by the author. The English edition has title: Your book of seventeenth and eighteenth century costume

The author describes the style and design of the basic garments worn by English men, women and children of varied social classes in the seventeenth and eighteenth centuries. Accessories such as hats, shoes and trimmings are also featured. The text is accompanied by quotations from the writings of that period about the fashion trends of the day

Medieval and Tudor costume. Plays, Inc. 1968 77p illus $4.95   391.09

1 Costume—History
ISBN 0-8238-0137-3
English edition has title: Your book of mediaeval and Tudor costume

This survey of the clothes worn by English men, women and children is arranged chronologically by chapters, covering the period from the Norman Conquest to 1603. The author discusses fashion trends during the years and relates them to the historical and economic transitions of the times. Pictures are copies of contemporary illustrations

Fox, Lilla M.

Folk costume of Southern Europe; illus. by the author. Plays, Inc. [1973 c1972] 64p illus maps $4.95
(4-7)   391.09

1 Costume—History
ISBN 0-8238-0088-1
First published 1972 in England
The author "describes in detail the costumes of Italy, Switzerland, Spain, and the Mediterranean Islands." Library J
The author's "illustrations are excellent and very detailed, and her text is simple and clear. She provides an index and a map of the region and one of the Swiss Cantons." Jr Bookshelf

Folk costume of Western Europe; illus. by the author. Plays, Inc. [1971 c1969] 64p illus map $4.95
(4-7)   391.09

1 Costume—History
ISBN 0-8238-0087-3
First published 1969 in England
"Presenting a wide range of the traditional folk dress of Western Europe, this book is particularly useful as a guide for the costuming of folk dances and plays. Fox describes how climate, geography and historical events influenced styles of national expression and points up the diversity of costumes within the same country. . . . Great Britain, France, Belgium, the Netherlands, Western Germany, Denmark, Sweden, Norway, Finland, and Lapland are each treated in a separate chapter; however, . . . Fox concentrates on regional rather than national dress. Though the author's line drawings, done in black and white with touches of red and yellow, sometimes fail to capture the distinctiveness of the costumes, a helpful map of Western Europe with the relevant regions indicated is a redeeming accompaniment to the brief, authoritative text." Sch Library J

Lubell, Cecil

Clothes tell a story; from skin to space suits, by Cecil and Winifred Lubell. Parents Mag. Press 1971 64p illus lib. bdg. $4.59 (2-4)   391.09

1 Costume—History
ISBN 0-8193-0452-2
"A Stepping-stone book"
"An introductory chapter comparing what a child of the 1850's had to wear with what a child of today puts on [is] followed by sections on the animal-skin clothes of cave dwellers; clothing made out of wool, flax, cotton and silk; the specific attire—past and present—of different peoples around the world. . . . The authors present the importance of dress generally in understandable, if simplified terms, and with illustrations that are clear and pleasing." Library J

392   Customs of life cycle and domestic life

Price, Christine

Happy days; a UNICEF book of birthdays, name days and growing days; written and illus. by Christine Price. Dutton [1970 c1969] 128p illus $4.50 (4-6)   392

1 Birthdays 2 Rites and ceremonies
ISBN 0-525-31453-9
"By organizing the material by type of event rather than by country or location Price gives a cultural perspective on observances and rituals that differ widely but share common themes—celebration of a child's birth, various significant states in his development, or his initiation into adulthood. The text is enriched by effective illustrations in color and black and white and by poetry and chants connected with some of the celebrations. An appendix includes the music for several birthday songs, a section on children's names around the world, and suggestions for further reading." Booklist

393   Death customs. Mummies

McHargue, Georgess

Mummies. Lippincott 1972 160p illus map (The Weird and horrible lib) lib. bdg. $4.95, pa $1.95 (5-7)   393

1 Mummies
ISBN 0-397-31516-3; 0-397-31417-5
A discussion of natural and embalmed mummies from the frozen mastodons of Siberia to the mummies of ancient Egypt, Polynesia, South America and Europe. The author describes why mummies were made, how they have been preserved and found, and attitudes and superstitions about them

"The many photographs, some rather gruesome, complement a concise overview which concludes with a look at a few present-day mummies and cryonic sleep." Booklist

Suggestions for further reading: p155

Pace, Mildred Mastin

Wrapped for eternity; the story of the Egyptian mummy; Egyptologist and content consultant: Kenneth Jay Linsner; line drawings by Tom Huffman. McGraw 1974 192p illus map $6.95 (5-7)   393

1 Mummies 2 Egypt—Antiquities
ISBN 0-07-048053-2

In this study of mummification, the author "describes the highly advanced embalming techniques used by the Egyptians, the religious significance of the burial ceremony, and the historical and medical facts that have been discovered with the unearthing and unwrapping of these ancient remains." Babbling Bookworm

"The writing style is crisp and informal, the organization of material into and within chapters is logical, and the easily-incorporated research is evident in the extensive bibliography." Chicago. Children's Bk Center

Zim, Herbert S.

Life and death [by] Herbert S. Zim [and] Sonia Bleeker; illus. by René Martin. Morrow 1970 63p illus lib. bdg. $4.32 (4-7)   393

1 Death
ISBN 0-688-31553-4

The text is "invested with the attitude that the cessation of life is a part of life itself. The authors consider man's life span in relation to other living things, having discussed the nature of the latter; they describe the processes of aging and dying, the technicalities of burial and cremation, and some of the funeral practices of other times and other lands. The one significant piece of information that is not included is the fact that the services of a funeral director and the choice between cremation and earth burial are not absolute, but that it is possible to bequeath a body to an institution for medical research. An index is appended." Sutherland. The Best in Children's Bks

"Psychologists, psychiatrists, educators, members of the medical professions, social workers, and parents were among those consulted by the authors. This worthwhile book has been needed for a long time." Sci Bks

394.2 Special occasions. Holidays

Barksdale, Lena

The first Thanksgiving; illus. by Lois Lenski. Knopf 1942 57p illus $2.50, lib. bdg. $4.99 (3-5)   394.2

1 Thanksgiving Day
ISBN 0-394-81156-9; 0-394-91156-3

"Hannah, who lives with her parents and older brothers in Maine, comes down to Massachusetts to make the acquaintance of her cousins and to eat Thanksgiving dinner with Grandma and Grandpa. After the dinner is over she hears Grandma tell the story of that first Thanksgiving in which she and Grandpa had taken part, all of forty years ago, in Plymouth." Wis Library Bul

"The book is warmly human and the pictures by Lois Lenski are full of the atmosphere of New England." Bookmark

Barth, Edna

Hearts, cupids, and red roses; the story of the Valentine symbols; illus. by Ursula Arndt. Seabury 1974 64p illus $5.50 (3-6)   394.2

1 Valentine's Day 2 Signs and symbols
ISBN 0-8164-3111-6

"Beginning with the origins of St. Valentine's Day, Barth traces the celebration of the holiday from the Roman 'Lupercalia' (a pagan festival) to present-day practices. Included are descriptions of the many different types of valentines and the meanings of the colors red, white, and pink as well as such symbols as flowers, doves, hearts, and cupids." Sch Library J

"Interesting, concise text and lists of stories, poems and sources about St. Valentine's Day make this [book] superior." Minnesota

Holly, reindeer, and colored lights; the story of the Christmas symbols; illus. by Ursula Arndt. Seabury 1971 96p illus $5.50 (3-6)   394.2

1 Christmas 2 Signs and symbols
ISBN 0-8164-3023-3

"A collection of Christmas customs from around the world. . . . The book considers each of the symbols, traces its historical roots—whether pagan, Christian, or mythological—and tells of the part it plays in present-day Christmas celebrations. The customs associated with plants, flowers, foods, and lights are just a few of the traditions explained. The book also contains many Christmas legends." Horn Bk

"The well-written text is concise and interesting and the two-colored marginal drawings are festive. A selected list of books containing Christmas stories and poems is appended." Booklist

Lilies, rabbits, and painted eggs; the story of the Easter symbols; illus. by Ursula Arndt. Seabury 1970 63p illus $4.95 (3-6)   394.2

1 Easter 2 Signs and symbols
ISBN 0-8164-3036-5

"By revealing the ancient—often pagan—roots of Easter traditions, the book [indicates] how similar man's desires have always been, especially in the celebration of the miracle of new life in artistic and religious ways. [It] also explains Easter games, chants, and rituals as performed all over the world. . . . Some of the stories are funny, some dramatic; all will add to the appreciation of the season. The small pen drawings which illustrate the symbols and the celebrations will please the children, and an index and a bibliography of other Easter books will please the librarian." Horn Bk

Witches, pumpkins, and grinning ghosts; the story of the Halloween symbols; illus. by Ursula Arndt. Seabury 1972 95p illus $5.50 (3-6)   394.2

1 Halloween 2 Signs and symbols
ISBN 0-8164-3087-X

"This discusses the origins of Halloween and the way it is celebrated today in different countries. Witches (male and female), bats, toads, ghosts, traditional foods, and other customs and symbols related to All Saints's Day are covered. Barth also touches on the incorporation of pagan beliefs into Christianity." Sch Library J

"A diverting as well as useful account appropriately illustrated with drawings in black and orange." Booklist

Stories for Halloween: p95

Bartlett, Robert Merrill

Thanksgiving Day; illus. by W. T. Mars. Crowell 1965 unp illus (A Crowell Holiday bk) $4.95, lib. bdg. $5.70 (1-3)   394.2

1 Thanksgiving Day 2 Pilgrim Fathers
ISBN 0-690-81044-X; 0-690-81045-8

Here is "a simple, brief history of the custom of giving thanks at harvest time from the days of ancient Greece to the present with emphasis on the Pilgrims, and their thanksgiving celebrations of 1621 and 1623." Booklist

A "book to use as an introduction to further study and discussion of the early settlers in our country." Wis Library Bul

Belting, Natalia

Christmas folk; illus. by Barbara Cooney. Holt 1969 unp illus $4.95, lib. bdg. $4.59 (2-5)   394.2

1 Christmas—Great Britain 2 Christmas poetry
ISBN 0-03-072375-2; 0-03-072380-9

In poetic, partly rhymed lines, this book describes the traditions and folklore of Christmas as it was celebrated in Elizabethan times. From November 30 (St Andrew's Day) to January 5 (Twelfth Night), the author portrays such daily holiday activities as mumming and carol singing

"The artist, with her devotion to historical accuracy and meticulous detail, has brought the text wonderfully to life with full-color illustrations; the indoor scenes are marked by an overflowing warmth and vitality; the outdoor views by a remarkable sense of space." Horn Bk

Borten, Helen

Halloween; written and illus. by Helen Borten. Crowell 1965 unp illus (A Crowell Holiday bk) $4.95, lib. bdg. $5.70 (1-3)   394.2

1 Halloween
ISBN 0-690-36313-3; 0-690-36314-1

"The magic and fun of Halloween is found in this attractively illustrated book which covers the early customs and superstitions and our own modern celebrations." Chicago

Bulla, Clyde Robert

St Valentine's Day; illus. by Valenti Angelo. Crowell 1965 unp illus (A Crowell Holiday bk) $4.95, lib. bdg. $5.70 (1-3)   394.2

1 Valentine's Day
ISBN 0-690-71743-1; 0-690-71744-X

"A brief and simple text about the origins of the legends and celebration of St. Valentine's Day and about the way the holiday is observed today." Chicago. Children's Bk Center

Burnett, Bernice

The first book of holidays. Rev. ed. Watts, F. 1974 87p illus $3.90 (4-7)   394.2

1 Holidays
ISBN 0-531-00548-8
First published 1955

This book "not only covers standard American holidays but also celebrations of ethnic minorities in the U.S. and holidays in foreign nations—e.g., Mexico, Canada, France, Japan. In describing the origins of these traditions, Burnett shows how vestiges of the past have been incorporated into present-day celebrations, and excellent black-and-white illustrations and photos add authenticity. A list of holidays around the world, a bibliography, and a thorough index complete the coverage." Sch Library J

Cantwell, Mary

St Patrick's Day; illus. by Ursula Arndt. Crowell 1967 unp illus (A Crowell Holiday bk) $4.50, lib. bdg. $5.25 (1-3)   394.2

1 St Patrick's Day 2 Patrick, Saint
ISBN 0-690-71672-9; 0-690-71673-7

"The author tells the origin of St. Patrick's Day, how he became a much-loved saint and how his day has been celebrated by different countries. The illustrator brightens his story with pleasant sketches." Pub W

Cavanah, Frances

(ed.) Holiday roundup; selected by Frances Cavanah and Lucile Pannell; illus. by Elsie McCorkell. Rev. ed. Macrae Smith Co. 1968 335p illus lib. bdg. $5.97 (4-6)   394.2

1 Holidays—Stories
ISBN 0-8255-7041-7
First published 1950 with editors' names in reverse order

"An anthology of stories for all holidays, birthdays, and the Sabbath. For children of all denominations." Adventuring With Bks

Cooney, Barbara

Christmas; written and illus. by Barbara Cooney. Crowell 1967 unp illus (A Crowell Holiday bk) $4.95, lib. bdg. $5.70 (2-4)   394.2

1 Christmas
ISBN 0-690-19201-0

A "lovely and thoughtful book, which begins with the traditional preparations for the holiday; tells very simply of the birth of Christ, pursues the story into its Jewish background, and ties in some of our customs to the Roman Saturnalia. At the end the book returns to modern holiday customs in various lands, including our own." Bruno. Bks for Sch Libraries. 1968

Cooper, Paulette

Let's find out about Halloween; illus. by Errol Le Cain. Watts, F. 1972 unp illus lib. bdg. $3.90 (k-2)   394.2

1 Halloween
ISBN 0-531-00075-3

"In brief, simple sentences, this . . . book presents an almost complete overview of all aspects of Halloween, from the ancient Druids to today's trick-or-treat antics. The humorous illustrations in the usual colors of Halloween, black and orange, along with some spreads in dark blue and white will find much favor with children." Sch Library J

Dalgliesh, Alice

(comp.) Christmas; a book of stories old and new. Illus. by Hildegard Woodward. [Rev. ed] Scribner 1950 244p illus $5.95 (4-7)   394.2

1 Christmas stories
ISBN 0-684-12667-2
First published 1934

"The stories and poems which are included in this Christmas anthology are those which have been enjoyed by children. The Christmas legend has given way to realistic or slightly fanciful tales. The four divisions of the material is into the headings: Christmas stories and wonder tales, The first Christmas, Christmas in old time America, Christmas in other lands." Wis Library Bul

An "excellent collection. . . . The illustrations are particularly childlike, appropriate and charming." N Y Times Bk Rev

The Thanksgiving story; with illus. by Helen Sewell. Scribner 1954 unp illus map $5.95 (k-2)   394.2

1 Thanksgiving Day 2 Pilgrim Fathers
ISBN 0-684-12330-4

A "picture book that tells the story of Thanksgiving through the experiences of one family on the Mayflower, the hardships of their first winter, the birth of the new baby, spring, planting, harvest, and the giving of thanks." Wis Library Bul

"It is told briefly and directly in the words that will be easy for the youngest readers to enjoy for themselves and in pictures which are in the character of American primitives and at the same time have strength and drama. From the somber tones of the earlier heart of the story the pictures work up to a climax of glowing autumn colors in the illustration for the Thanksgiving feast." Sat Rev

Dobler, Lavinia

National holidays around the world; illus. & designed by Vivian Browne. Fleet Press 1968 234p illus $6.50 (5-7)   394.2

1 Holidays
ISBN 0-8303-0044-9

"Arranged by day under each month, national holi-

Dobler, Lavinia—*Continued*

days of 137 countries are described in this . . . very useful reference tool. Miss Dobler includes a brief history of each land and how its independence was gained, including important dates, how it is governed today, how the holiday is celebrated, the appearance of its flag and emblem or seal, and the title of its national anthem." Sch Library J

Bibliography: p231

Eaton, Anne Thaxter

(comp.) The animals' Christmas; poems, carols, and stories; decorated by Valenti Angelo. Viking 1944 124p illus $4.95 (4-7)   394.2

1 Christmas stories 2 Christmas poetry 3 Animals—Stories 4 Animals—Poetry

ISBN 0-670-12800-7

An anthology of Christmas poems and stories, in each of which animals have an important role

The compiler "has brought together here a collection of such legends, in both prose and verse, making a distinguished addition to the shelf of Christmas material. . . . The decorative illustrations in green and white . . . have a pleasing simplicity." Wis Library Bul

Bibliographical references included in Acknowledgments

Epstein, Sam

European folk festivals, by Sam and Beryl Epstein; illus. by Joseph A. Smith. Garrard 1968 64p illus (A Holiday bk) lib. bdg. $3.69 (2-4)   394.2

1 Festivals—Europe

ISBN 0-8116-6561-5

"This is an attractive and useful presentation of information on customs related to the traditional celebrations of May Day . . . Whitsuntide, Midsummer, harvest festivals, and some miscellaneous colorful sports events. The material is not easily available in other books for this age group and is sufficiently detailed here to satisfy the audience to which it is directed. While some illustrations are only decorative, others enrich the explanations of the text." Sch Library J

Fisher, Aileen

Arbor Day; illus. by Nonny Hogrogian. Crowell 1965 unp illus (A Crowell Holiday bk) $4.95, lib. bdg. $5.70 (1-3)   394.2

1 Arbor Day

ISBN 0-690-09615-1; 0-690-09616-X

"In simple poetic prose the author shows the reason [Arbor Day] was established and how it is observed." Chicago

Easter; illus. by Ati Forberg. Crowell 1968 unp illus (A Crowell Holiday bk) $4.95, lib. bdg. $5.70 (1-3)   394.2

1 Easter 2 Jesus Christ

ISBN 0-690-25235-8; 0-690-25236-6

An "account of the events of Holy Week and of the ways in which they are observed is preceded by a more general discussion of Easter customs in the Christian faith. Some of these, seeming secular, have religious origins; some have been incorporated from pre-Christian celebrations of the springtime." Chicago. Children's Bk Center

"Large, clear print on yellow and white pages and many bright, stylized drawings make it an attractive book which conveys the optimism and happiness of the season." Bruno. Bks for Sch Libraries, 1968

Human Rights Day, by Aileen Fisher and Olive Rabe; illus. by Lisl Weil. Crowell. 1966 unp illus (A Crowell Holiday bk) $4.95, lib. bdg. $5.70 (1-3)   394.2

1 Civil rights 2 United Nations

ISBN 0-690-42348-9; 0-690-42349-7

The authors explain the significance of this holiday. They describe the various steps in the battle for equal rights—the Magna Carta, the American and French Revolutions, the freeing of the slaves—steps leading up to the United Nations' Declaration of Human Rights in 1948

Foley, Daniel J.

Christmas the world over. . . . Line drawings by Charlotte Edmands Bowden. Chilton Co. 1963 128p illus $7.95, pa $4.95   394.2

1 Christmas

ISBN 0-8019-1277-6; 0-8019-6363-X

"How the season of joy and good will is observed and enjoyed by peoples here and everywhere." Title page

Includes celebrations and customs from the United States, Australia, and many countries of Europe, Latin America, and Asia

"A useful addition to holiday collections because of its unusually broad coverage." Booklist

Guilfoile, Elizabeth

Valentine's Day; illus. by Gordon Laite. Garrard 1965 62p illus (A Holiday bk) lib. bdg. $3.69 (3-4)   394.2

1 Valentine's Day

ISBN 0-8116-6556-9

This book provides "information on the origin and celebration of Valentine's Day, attractively illustrated and easy to read." Hodges. Bks for Elem Sch Libraries

Harper, Wilhelmina

(com.) Easter chimes; stories for Easter and the spring season; illus. by Hoot von Zitzewitz. New, rev. ed. Dutton 1965 253p illus $5.95   394.2

1 Easter—Stories

ISBN 0-525-29037-0

First published 1942

"A collection of stories [legends] and a few poems for Easter, with emphasis on seasonal rather than religious stories. . . . The book will undoubtedly fill a need in libraries for holiday material." Booklist

(comp.) Ghosts and goblins; stories for Halloween; illus. by William Wiesner. New, rev. ed. Dutton 1965 250p illus $5.95   394.2

1 Halloween—Stories 2 Ghost stories

ISBN 0-525-30516-5

First published 1936

"A welcome collection of [twenty-six] tales [and some poems] with a shiver in them, drawn from the folklore of several different countries. Many of them are for young children." Horn Bk

"Its use will doubtless not be restricted to this season alone. . . . There is no element of terror in these stories to leave its mark of fear and nightmare on sensitive minds, but each has its share of magic and mystery to stir the imagination." N Y Times Bk Rev

(comp.) The harvest feast; stories of Thanksgiving, yesterday and today; illus. by W. T. Mars. New, rev. ed. Dutton 1965 256p illus $4.95   394.2

1 Thanksgiving Day—Stories

ISBN 0-525-31510-1

First published 1938

This anthology includes "poems and stories by many well known authors on the theme of Thanksgiving. The first part contains stories of long-ago Thanksgivings; the second part is made up of Thanksgiving stories of today. The collection is suitable for reading aloud or for story telling." Wis Library Bul

Harper, Wilhelmina—*Continued*

(comp.) Merry Christmas to you; stories for Christmas; illus. by Fermin Rocker. New, rev. ed. Dutton 1965 254p illus $5.95   394.2

1 Christmas stories
ISBN 0-525-34852-2
First published 1935

An anthology "of Christmas stories and poems, many old favorites, for telling and reading aloud. The wide variety includes miracle, fairy, and modern tales written by many distinguished authors." Adventuring with Bks. 2d edition

It is noted when a story is suitable "for younger readers or listeners. Contains a two-page list of Christmas books for boys and girls." Wis Library Bul

Ickis, Marguerite

The book of festivals and holidays the world over; with drawings by Richard E. Howard. Dodd 1970 164p illus $5   394.2

1 Holidays 2 Fasts and feasts 3 Festivals
ISBN 0-396-06250-4

"Includes only 'holidays and festivals that are current and give promise of continuing indefinitely.' . . . Its 12 chapters, covering New Year's, Epiphany, winter festivals, Lent, Holy Week, Easter, early and late spring, summer, and fall festivals, Advent and Christmas briefly describe the customs in various parts of the world, indexed under country, [and] name of festival. . . . Its international scope and clear, though brief, descriptions make it a good addition to a collection on holidays." Cur Ref Bks

Johnson, Lois S.

(ed.) Christmas stories round the world; ed. and with introductions by Lois S. Johnson; illus. by D. K. Stone. Rand McNally 1970 103p illus $4.95 (3-5)   394.2

1 Christmas stories
ISBN 0-528-82175-X
First published 1960

Each of these twelve stories is prefaced with a few paragraphs about the observance of Christmas in the country of the story following

Illustrated "with 12 large, full-color pictures and a number of small, black-and-white spot drawings." Sch Library J

Lenski, Lois

Lois Lenski's Christmas stories; written and illus. by Lois Lenski. Lippincott 1968 152p illus $6.95 (3-6)   394.2

1 Christmas stories
ISBN 0-397-31031-5

"A collection of Christmas stories, most of which have been excerpted from the author's books, with some poems and a play not previously published. . . . The separation of tale and commentary gives the book a utilitarian air, but the variety (in time, locale, and ethnic or economic focus) of backgrounds makes the book indeed useful and interesting." Sutherland. The Best in Children's Bks

Les Tina, Dorothy

Flag Day; illus. by Ed Emberley. Crowell 1965 unp illus (A Crowell Holiday bk) $4.95, lib. bdg. $5.70 (1-3)   394.2

1 Flag Day 2 Flags
ISBN 0-690-30420-X; 0-690-30421-8

This book "gives the history of the United States flag, the origin of Flag Day, and rules for handling and displaying the flag." Hodges. Bks for Elem Sch Libraries

"The Pledge of Allegiance is included. The text is continuous; material is neatly organized; the style is quite straightforward (with the Betsy Ross story given as a possible event rather than as a fact) although the appropriate note of patriotism is just a bit heavily laid on in a place or two." Chicago. Children's Bk Center

May Day; illus. by Hope Meryman. Crowell 1967 unp illus (A Crowell Holiday bk) $4.95, lib. bdg. $5.70 (1-3)   394.2

1 May Day
ISBN 0-690-52644-X; 0-690-52645-8

"An interesting résumé of the ways in which May Day has been celebrated through the centuries, with special emphasis on the Roman rites and the traditional customs of rural England. There is also a brief mention of the fact that the first of May is celebrated in some places today by worker's marches, and several pages are devoted to May Day customs in countries around the world. The illustrations, attractive woodcuts, are sedate in color but full of movement." Chicago. Children's Bk Center

Luckhardt, Mildred Corell

(ed.) Christmas comes once more; stories and poems for the holiday season; illus. by Grisha Dotzenko. Abingdon 1962 176p illus $4.95 (3-6)   394.2

1 Christmas stories 2 Christmas poetry
ISBN 0-687-07804-0

Contains 43 stories, poems, excerpts from books, and carols from all over the world as well as directions for making an Advent wreath. Among the authors represented are Anne Carroll Moore, Hans Christian Andersen, Elsie Binns, Christina Rossetti, Rachel Field, Phillips Brooks, Jesse Stuart, Amy Steedman, and Eleanor Farjeon

"Most of the stories and poems in this collection have not appeared in previous anthologies. . . . The soft gray tones of the illustrations are in keeping with the mood." Sch Library J

(comp.) Thanksgiving; feast and festival; illus. by Ralph McDonald. Abingdon 1966 352p illus $7.95 (4-7)   394.2

1 Thanksgiving Day
ISBN 0-687-41404-0

"An anthology of prose and poetry about the Thanksgiving holiday in the United States and about other observances of giving thanks or of harvest time. The first section of the book is entitled 'The Pilgrims and Thanksgiving'; the second, and longer, section is called 'Thanksgiving and Harvest Time, Near and Far.' Some of the excerpts from books have been abridged or adapted; there are some pages of background information about holiday customs by the editor. Most of the selections are good, and the book should be useful as an additional source of material; it is weakened somewhat by the pedestrian illustrations. A bibliography and an author-title index are appended." Chicago. Children's Bk Center

McGovern, Ann

Squeals & squiggles & ghostly giggles; illus. by Jeffrey Higginbottom. Four Winds 1973 unp illus $4.75, lib. bdg. $4.88 (2-5)   394.2

1 Halloween 2 Magic 3 Ghost stories

"A Halloween book, with spooky games, poems, scarey ghost stories, clever tricks and fortunes to tell, 'limer-eeks,' and even a skit with ghouls and demons." New Bks for Young Readers

"The four short stories are appropriately spooky and well suited to retelling. Diagrams for tricks are clear, and the black-and-white illustrations depict large-faced, floppy-haired children engaged in amusing antics. While there is no general discussion of Halloween, this collection offers good fun for that holiday and all year round." Sch Library J

Manning-Sanders, Ruth

(ed.) Festivals; comp. by Ruth Manning-Sanders; illus. by Raymond Briggs. Dutton [1973 c1972] 188p illus $5.95 (3-6)   394.2

1 Festivals 2 Holidays

ISBN 0-525-29675-1

First published 1972 in England

"This anthology is a month-by-month journey through major celebrations throughout the world. The young reader learns about Christmas in India, Guy Fawkes Day in England, Easter in Athens and so on. The book includes poetry and prose by Tennyson, Dylan Thomas, Robert Herrick, Jan and Rumer Godden, P. L. Travers, Laura Ingalls Wilder and the anthologist." Pub W

This book "is a delicious dip even for some of the more reluctant readers. . . . It can hardly fail to please many children, and would be a marvellous ideas book for an enterprising but hard-pressed primary school teacher. Brigg's pictures are aptly cheerful and festive in feel." Times (London) Literary Sup

Marcus, Rebecca B.

Fiesta time in Mexico, by Rebecca B. Marcus and Judith Marcus; illus. by Bert Dodson. Garrard 1974 95p illus (An Around the world holiday bk) lib. bdg. $3.58 (4-6)   394.2

1 Festivals—Mexico 2 Mexico—Social life and customs

ISBN 0-8116-4953-9

"A description of Mexican holidays, national and religious, begins with the celebration of the Day of the Dead in November and goes through the year's festive days. The facts about each holiday include explanations of the ways in which it is celebrated and the occasion that is commemorated." Chicago. Children's Bk Center

"Color illustrations, a pronunciation guide, and an index are included, and though the regional customs of the Aztec and Mayan Indians are not covered fully enough, this successfully portrays life style and holiday attitudes of most Mexicans." Sch Library J

Marnell, James

Labor Day; illus. by Clare Romano and John Ross. Crowell 1966 unp illus (A Crowell Holiday bk) $4.95, lib. bdg. $5.70 (1-3)   394.2

1 Labor Day

ISBN 0-690-48099-7; 0-690-48100-4

"The story of Labor Day begins with a few facts about Peter McGuire who conceived the idea for the holiday and arranged the first parade in New York in 1882. There are colorful descriptions of the part others played on behalf of the rights of workers, the rise of labor unions, child labor laws, and other laws to protect workers." Sch Library J

Meyer, Robert

Festivals U.S.A. & Canada [by] Robert Meyer, Jr. Rev. ed. Washburn 1970 280p $5.95   394.2

1 Festivals—U.S. 2 Festivals—Canada

ISBN 0-679-24020-9

A revised and expanded edition of: Festivals U.S.A. published 1950

This guide to annual festivals and events celebrated in various states and in Canada is arranged by categories or type of festival, such as agricultural festivals, community festivals, drama festivals. There is also a listing of festivals by state and province

Nickerson, Betty

Celebrate the sun; a heritage of festivals interpreted through the art of children from many lands. Lippincott 1969 128p illus $6.95 (5-7)   394.2

1 Festivals 2 Holidays

ISBN 0-397-31059-5

In this book "two introductory chapters discuss the psychology and universality of children's art, giving a rationale for its use here, and the relationship of festivals to the fears, myths and religions of man. The body of the book is divided into four seasonal sections, each introduced with an overview of the origin and evolution of that season's characteristic celebrations. Within each section, a page discussing one aspect of the season faces a related child's painting." Library J

"A fascinating book for browsing and a stimulating supplement for art classes and for social studies units on foreign countries and international understanding." Booklist

Bibliography: p124-25

Parents' Magazine's Christmas holiday book. . . . [By] Yorke Henderson [and others]; illus. by Oscar Liebman. Parents Mag. Press 1972 xxi, 320p illus $6.95   394.2

1 Christmas

ISBN 0-8193-0558-8

"The story of Christmas with a treasury of favorite reading, music, cookery, and holiday activities." Subtitle

Colored illustrations throughout include pictures of religious paintings, period prints, and early Christmas cards

Patterson, Lillie

Christmas feasts and festivals; illus. by Cliff Schule. Garrard 1968 64p illus (A Holiday bk) lib. bdg. $3.69 (3-4)   394.2

1 Christmas

ISBN 0-8116-6562-3

"A simple account of some of the customs and folklore that have grown up around the world in celebration of the birth of Christ. Included are traditions from pagan holidays that have contributed almost as much as Christian innovations to the season's observance. Especially useful for elementary school assignments." Booklist

Halloween; illus. by Gil Miret. Garrard 1963 63p illus (A Holiday bk) lib. bdg. $3.69 (3-4)   394.2

1 Halloween

ISBN 0-8116-6552-6

The origins of many facets of Halloween are related, supplemented by old tales, chants and verses

Partial contents: How it all began; Ghosts, ghosts, ghosts; Witches and black cats; Wee folk; Halloween customs from many lands; Halloween comes to America

"An easy-to-read account of Halloween customs from the ancient Celts and Romans to the present day." Hodges. Bks for Elem Sch Libraries

Phelan, Mary Kay

Election Day; illus. by Robert Quackenbush. Crowell 1967 unp illus (A Crowell Holiday bk) $4.95, lib. bdg. $5.70 (1-3)   394.2

1 Election Day 2 Suffrage

ISBN 0-690-25661-2; 0-690-35662-0

"Written in a straightforward manner, this book includes information about how the American system of voting on election day has developed, the importance of this day, and its ancient precedents. Unfortunately missing is the present role of the mass media." Adventuring With Bks

The Fourth of July; illus. by Symeon Shimin. Crowell 1966 unp illus (A Crowell Holiday bk) $4.95, lib. bdg. $5.70 (1-3)   394.2

1 Fourth of July

ISBN 0-690-31414-0; 0-690-31415-9

"This account begins with a brief history of the

Phelan, Mary Kay—*Continued*

events leading up to the Declaration of Independence and mention of some of the key leaders in the Continental Congress. How news of the Declaration was spread throughout the colonies and celebrations by the people are described. There is also mention of many events that have taken place on the anniversary of Independence Day." Sch Library J

"Symeon Shimin's light wash illustrations are soberly, historically patriotic." N Y Times Bk Rev

Purdy, Susan

Festivals for you to celebrate. Lippincott 1969 192p illus $5.95, lib. bdg. $5.82 (4-7)   394.2

1 Festivals 2 Handicraft
ISBN 0-397-31071-4; 0-397-31072-2

"An attractive and useful round-up of craft projects associated with the holidays; those included are holidays most widely observed in the United States (with the exclusion of patriotic holidays), according to the preface, many of them of foreign origin. The material is grouped by seasons, with suggestions for group activities preceding the body of the text. Written with crisp clarity, the directions for craft projects are easy to follow; the information about each holiday is succinct, usually giving both the origins of the holiday and a description of the way or ways in which it is celebrated. A list of mteraisl is included; a bibliography, activities subject index, and an index are appended." Sutherland. The Best in Children's Bks

Reeves, James

(comp.) The Christmas book; illus. by Raymond Briggs. [2d ed] Dutton 1970 189p illus $7.50 (4-6)   394.2

1 Christmas stories 2 Christmas poetry 3 Christmas
ISBN 0-525-27821-4
First published 1968

"A welcome Christmas anthology of prose and poetry, varied in every way: genre, style, form, mood, and period. The black and white illustrations are very effective, the selections well chosen for the level of the reader, although much of the book is suitable for reading aloud to younger children. A good source for holiday storytelling, the book offers a range of authors from Ransome and Dickens to Dylan Thomas and Michael Bond." Sutherland. The Best in Children's Bks

Rollins, Charlemae

(comp.) Christmas gif'. . . . Line drawings by Tom O'Sullivan; book design by Stan Williamson. Follet 1963 119p illus $7.95 (4-7)   394.2

1 Christmas 2 Negro literature 3 Negroes in literature and art
ISBN 0-695-81190-8

"An anthology of Christmas poems, songs, and stories, written by and about Negroes." Title page

This book "gets its title from a joyful Christmas Day custom widespread among the plantation slaves. Included are . . . some special recipes, many of . . . [which] come from the [compiler's] grandmother who was born a slave. A lovely collection of the new and the old enhanced by spirited line drawings." Pub W

Includes author and title indexes

Sawyer, Ruth

Joy to the world; Christmas legends; illus. by Trina Schart Hyman. Little 1966 102p illus $5.95 (3-6)   394.2

1 Christmas stories 2 Legends 3 Carols
ISBN 0-316-77177-5

Ancient Arabia, Serbia, Ireland and Spain are the sources for these six Christmas stories, each accompanied by a carol

These are "unusual and varied Christmas legends. . . . Narrations convey the cultural tone of each country; some of the shorter selections will make good holiday dramatizations." Wis Library Bul

"The illustrations in black and white and tones of golden tan make a book that matches in appearance the glowing spirit of the tales. A beautiful book for family sharing." Horn Bk

Sechrist, Elizabeth Hough

(ed.) Christmas everywhere; a book of Christmas customs of many lands; written and comp. by Elizabeth Hough Sechrist; illus. by Elsie Jane McCorkell. New rev. and enl. ed. Macrae Smith Co. 1962 186p illus $6.50, lib. bdg. $5.97   394.2

1 Christmas
ISBN 0-8255-8130-3; 0-8255-8131-1
First published 1931

Stories of Christmas customs and celebrations in Palestine, Mexico, Servia, Holland, France, England, Spain, Germany, Sweden, Norway, Belgium, Switzerland, Roumania, Italy, India, Philippines, Japan, China, Singapore, Ceylon, Syria, Bagdad, Persia, Turkey, Abyssinia, Australia, Peru, Chile, Brazil, Argentina, United States. The South, New England, New Mexico, among the Shakers, among the Pennsylvania Germans, Puerto Rico, among the Moravians

"Activities, food, and beliefs of the people make this a good resource book." Adventuring with Bks

(ed.) It's time for Christmas; written and comp. by Elizabeth Hough Sechrist and Janette Woolsey. Decorations by Reisie Lonette. Macrae Smith Co. 1959 256p illus $6.50, lib. bdg. $5.97 (4-7)   394.2

1 Christmas
ISBN 0-8255-8222-9; 0-8255-8223-7

"In trying to 'present Christmas as Christ's birthday rather than from the Santa Claus point of view', the authors start off with the story of the Nativity according to St. Luke and continue with a history of Christmas, legends and traditional stories about St. Francis, La Befana, St. Nicholas, and others. . . . [Includes a] section on Christmas customs [and symbols] the words of 10 favorite carols and how they came to be written and finally [a] . . . collection of poems and stories." Chicago Sunday Tribune

"This collection is a welcome addition in planning the true celebration of Christmas in the home, classroom, or club. Indexed." Lutheran Educ

(ed.) It's time for Easter; written and comp. by Elizabeth Hough Sechrist and Janette Woolsey; illus. by Elsie Jane McCorkell. Macrae Smith Co. 1961 255p illus $6.50 (4-7)   394.2

1 Easter
ISBN 0-8255-8198-2

"Beginning with a shortened version of Biblical Easter story as told in the Gospels an excellent and welcome anthology gives a brief history of Easter, explains the origin and meanings of Easter symbols, describes Lenten and Easter customs around the world, and includes Easter legends, music, poems, and stories. Illustrated with attractive line drawings, some in color." Booklist

Most of the material "should be very useful to teachers and group leaders. So may the section composers of Easter music and authors of famous hymns, although it is not very inspiringly presented. The section of fiction is for a rather younger audience than is the first part of the anthology but good stories of Easter are hard to find and this includes some charming ones." N Y Times Bk Rev

(ed.) It's time for Thanksgiving; written and comp. by Elizabeth Hough Sechrist and Janette Woolsey. Decorations by Guy Fry. Macrae Smith Co. 1957 251 illus lib. bdg. $5.97 (4-7)   394.2

1 Thanksgiving Day
ISBN 0-8255-8215-6

Sechrist, Elizabeth Hough—*Continued*

"Pleasant stories, producible plays, traditional and modern poems, recipes, and games for Thanksgiving are brought together here in a useful . . . volume. The [editors] have frequently turned author to give us some always needed, fresh holiday material." Library J

Red letter days; a book of holiday customs; illus. by Elsie Jane McCorkell. Rev. ed. Macrae Smith Co. 1965 253p illus $6.50, lib. bdg. $5.97   394.2

1 Holidays

ISBN 0-8255-8162-1; 0-8255-8163-X

Beginning "with a chapter on the story of the calendar, there follow interesting accounts of the holidays, their historical significance, and some explanation of the methods of celebration in different parts of the world. The days [are arranged] in chronological order. . . . A bibliography and index add to the usefulness [of the book]." Wis Library Bul

Showers, Paul

Indian festivals; illus. by Lorence Bjorklund. Crowell 1969 unp illus (A Crowell Holiday bk) $4.95, lib. bdg. $5.70 (2-4)   394.2

1 Indians of North America—Social life and customs 2 Rites and ceremonies 3 Holidays

ISBN 0-690-43697-1; 0-690-43698-X

The author describes the festivals and holidays of American Indian tribes such as the Seminoles, Zuñis, Sioux and Cheyennes, and the religious beliefs which they reflect

"Transitions are occasionally abrupt, but the text is clear and non-fictionalized. Soft flesh-colored and black crayon drawings adequately depict customs, costumes and individual faces." Sch Library J

Spicer, Dorothy Gladys

46 days of Christmas; a cycle of Old World songs, legends and customs; illus. by Anne Marie Jauss. Coward-McCann 1960 96p illus lib. bdg. $4.99 (4-7)   394.2

1 Christmas

ISBN 0-698-30091-2

Some of this material has been adapted from the author's Festivals of Western Europe, published 1958

Christmas "celebrations in 18 European and Asiatic countries. Arranged in chronological order from Saint Barbara's Day in Syria on December 4th, to the old Twelfth Night, January 18, in England. A . . . carol, prayer, or hymn precedes each chapter." Library J

Indexed by countries, song titles, and special days

Tudor, Tasha

(ed.) Take joy! The Tasha Tudor Christmas book; selected, ed. and illus. by Tasha Tudor. Collins 1966 157p illus music $7.95, lib. bdg. $7.71   394.2

1 Christmas

ISBN 0-529-04961-9; 0-529-00208-6

"A collection of Christmas stories, poems, customs, and carols and their music, celebrating both the religious and the secular aspects of the holiday. Included are the particular traditions and recipes of the Tudor family." Adventuring with Bks. 2d edition

Generously illustrated with tenderness and reverence in full-color and black-and-white pictures. . . . Of special interest to children who enjoy homely, old-fashioned pleasures, parents and grandparents wanting to preserve family Christmas traditions, and to Tasha Tudor fans of all ages." Booklist

395 Etiquette

Bendick, Jeanne

What to do; everyday guides for everyone, by Jeanne Bendick and Marian Warren; illus. by Jeanne Bendick. McGraw 1967 160p illus lib. bdg. $4.72 (5-7)   395

1 Etiquette

ISBN 0-07-004468-6

This "book is a sensible guide to basic etiquette and personal management. It contains suggestions for the whole family regarding the wise handling of money and living within the community and lists community services such as health care available in most localities. Its greatest value will be to young people needing simply stated guidelines to acceptable, rather than highly refined, behavior." Booklist

Hoke, Helen

Etiquette; your ticket to good times; pictures by Carol Wilde. Watts, F. 1970 66p illus lib. bdg. $3.90 (3-5)   395

1 Etiquette

ISBN 0-531-00686-7

"A First book"

"Briefly, in an easy, encouraging manner, the author explains to young children the rules of etiquette for making introductions, dining out, being a house guest, giving and attending parties, writing letters, and speaking on the telephone, and points out some manners that apply only to boys or only to girls. Quizzes are given at the end of each chapter so the reader may test himself. The format of the book is open and inviting and the black-and-white drawings most attractive." Booklist

Joslin, Sesyle

What do you do, dear? Pictures by Maurice Sendak. Young Scott Bks. 1961 unp illus lib. bdg. $3.50 (k-3)   395

1 Etiquette

ISBN 0-201-09387-1

Companion volume to the author's: What do you say, dear?

A "handbook of etiquette for young ladies and gentlemen to be used as a guide for everyday social behavior." The author

"The propriety of what the well-mannered child will do is related to extraordinary situations, as for example: The Sheriff of Nottingham interrupts you while you are reading, to take you to jail; you will, naturally, 'Find a bookmark to save your place.' Sendak's pictures account for a great share of the fun." Horn Bk

A "wonderful spoof on manners in a hilarious picture-book made for laughing aloud." Child Study Assn of Am

What do you say, dear? Pictures by Maurice Sendak. Addison-Wesley 1958 unp illus lib. bdg. $3.50 (k-3)   395

1 Etiquette

ISBN 0-201-09391-X

"Young Scott Books"

"A handbook of etiquette for young ladies and gentlemen to be used as a guide for everyday social behavior." Preceding title page

"A rollicking introduction to manners for the very young. A series of delightfully absurd situations—being introduced to a baby elephant, bumping into a crocodile, being rescued from a dragon—are posed and appropriately answered. The illustrations are among Sendak's best—and funniest." Chicago. Children's Bk Center

Joslin, Sesyle—*Continued*

This "funny and imaginative picture book . . . may stimulate children to invent situations of their own." Booklist

Pitt, Valerie

Let's find out about manners; pictures by Olivia H. H. Cole. Watts, F. 1972 30p illus $3.90 (2-4)   395

1 Etiquette

ISBN 0-531-00082-6

The author demonstrates the importance of manners in daily life by describing situations where their lack makes it difficult for people to live together. Following is a discussion of good manners in our own culture as well as others

Post, Elizabeth L.

The Emily Post Book of etiquette for young people. Funk 1967 238p illus $6.95 (5-7)   395

1 Etiquette

ISBN 0-308-50002-4

"Broad guidelines to behavior and personal development, reflecting the changing concepts about what is correct. Commonsense advice on everyday manners, grooming, correspondence, dating, travel, and entertaining." Hodges. Bks for Elem Sch Libraries

398   Folklore

Emrich, Duncan

398.1

(comp.) The hodgepodge book; an almanac of American folklore. . . . Illus. by Ib Ohlsson. Four Winds 1972 367p illus lib. bdg. $7.95   398

1 Folklore—U.S.

ISBN 0-590-07250-1

"Containing all manner of curious, interesting, and out-of-the-way information drawn from American folklore, and not to be found anywhere else in the world; as well as jokes, conundrums, riddles, puzzles, and other matter designed to amuse and entertain; all of it most instructive and delightful." Title page

"Children, who love the absurd, will be pleased by the size of the volume and its twenty-one alluring topical areas such as Cumulative Stories ('The Little Old Lady Who Swallowed a Fly'), Love and Kisses ('I Love You Better Than a Pig Loves Slop'), and Mind Your Manners! ('Temper, Temper!'). Following the folklorist's notes for the various sections, an impressive fifty-two-page bibliography of sources is appended for scholars. References are keyed to a list of folklore journals. The scribbly pen-and-ink sketches are pert and suitably appropriate to the text." Horn Bk

793.7

(ed.) The nonsense book of riddles, rhymes, tongue twisters, puzzles and jokes from American folklore; illus. by Ib Ohlsson. Four Winds 1970 266p illus $6.95, lib. bdg. $6.34 (3-7)   398

1 Folklore—U.S.

An "extensive collection of traditional American nonsense, funsense, and sentiment. Whatever the occasion or mood, there is a verse or a chant to fit it—from the tongue-tingling tangler 'This is a zither' to the unabashed sentimentality of 'When in my lonely grave I sleep/And bending willows o'er me weep,'/'Tis then, dear friend, and not before,/I think of thee no more, no more.' The compiler . . . has enhanced the value of the collection with a succinct, incisive summary of the history of nonsense together with an extensive bibliography of studies relating to its various forms. But, as the introduction points out,

the compilation is first of all 'a reminder of the wonderful world of play and rhyme and beautiful nonsense.' The skillfully executed line drawings add to the fun." Horn Bk

Helfman, Elizabeth S.

Maypoles and wood demons; the meaning of trees; drawings by Richard Cuffari. Seabury 1972 128p illus lib. bdg. $6.95 (3-6)   398

1 Plant lore 2 Trees

ISBN 0-8164-3085-3

The author explores the folklore of trees, and relates tree legends and ceremonies from different parts of the world, from ancient to modern times

"This is an educational and absorbing book, with lively pictures." Pub W

Books for further reading: p123-24

Signs & symbols of the sun. Seabury 1974 192p illus $8.95 (5-7)   398

1 Sun 2 Folklore

ISBN 0-8164-3122-1

"A Clarion book"

The author describes the symbolic representation of the sun in mythology, science, religion and art. Examples of sun lore extend from earliest times to present, and issue from such diverse cultures as ancient Egypt, the Orient, and the Mayas

Books for further reading: p189

Hofsinde, Robert

The Indian medicine man; written and illus. by Robert Hofsinde (Gray-Wolf) Morrow 1966 94p illus lib. bdg. $4.32 (4-7)   398

1 Indians of North America 2 Medicine man

ISBN 0-688-31618-2

Discussed are "the importance and training of the Indian medicine man; the specific curative practices of the Sioux, Iroquois, Apache, Navaho, Ojibwa, and Northwest Indian tribes; and the status of the medicine man today." Booklist

A "concise and interesting book. . . . The black and white drawings are excellent in giving details of costumes, buildings, and artifacts but are awkward in depicting people." Chicago. Children's Bk Center

McHargue, Georgess

The beasts of never; a history natural & unnatural of monsters mythical & magical; illus. by Frank Bozzo. Bobbs 1968 112p illus $4.95 (5-7)   398

1 Animals, Mythical

ISBN 0-672-50217-8

"This is a book about legendary animals, especially those whose history is connected with western Europe and the country near the Mediterranean Sea. The various species of the beasts and their evolution are explored; their myths are explained in terms of the people by whom they were invented. A thoroughly fascinating account of almost-true magical beasts including unicorns, dragons, phoenix, basilisks, winged and sea monsters and the Loch Ness monster." Wis Library Bul

"An oversize book (8 5/8'' x 11 3/8'') with full page illustration for each chapter and numerous smaller drawings within the text." Library J

Bibliography: p108-09

The impossible people; a history natural and unnatural of beings terrible and wonderful; illus. by Frank Bozzo. Holt 1972 169p illus lib. bdg. $5.95 (5-7)   398

1 Folklore

ISBN 0-03-012541-3

"Useful as a reference source to librarians and fascinating reading for folklore enthusiasts, this is a sol-

McHargue, Georgess—*Continued*

idly conceived and well-researched study of giants, pixies, elves, demons, werewolves, mermaids, and other mythological people. Drawing primarily from American and European folklore, but also including examples from Asian and African mythology, McHargue discusses the appearance, behavior, and distinguishing characteristics of the imaginary beings and recounts various theories based on medicine, anthropology, archaeology, and zoology of their possible origins. Supplements the author's 'The beasts of never; a history natural & un-natural of monsters mythical & magical' [entered above]." Booklist

Bibliography: p159-62

Opie, Iona

The lore and language of schoolchildren, by Iona and Peter Opie. Oxford [1960 c1959] 417p illus map $12.50, pa $5   398

1 Folklore—Great Britain
ISBN 0-19-827206-5; 0-19-881121-7

"Rhymes, riddles, incantations, jeers, torments, parodies, nicknames, holiday customs, and other types of lore that is current among school children today and is transmitted orally, some of it over a period of hundreds of years. The basic study was made in Great Britain and detailed analysis of geographic usage is made for Great Britain but some usage in other countries is also noted. Chiefly of interest to folklorists, teachers, librarians, and others who work with children but some nostalgic appeal for the general reader." Booklist

Includes index to first lines, and geographical index

Schwartz, Alvin

(comp.) Cross your fingers, spit in your hat; superstitions and other beliefs; collected by Alvin Schwartz; illus. by Glen Rounds. Lippincott 1974 161p illus $4.95, pa $2.25 (4-7)   398

1 Superstition
ISBN 0-397-31530-9; 0-397-31531-7

This is a compilation of superstitions about such subjects as love and marriage, food and drink, witches, travel, the human body, ailments and curses, plants and animals, and death

"This delightful book reveals the sometimes humorous but always interesting ideas people have about what's happening. There's even an explanation of the 12 signs of the zodiac plus a brief description of their particular characteristics for budding astrologists. Comically illustrated by Glen Rounds, this book will give hours of fun and fascinating information about people and their beliefs." Children's Bk Rev Serv

Bibliography: p154-60

Withers, Carl

(comp.) A rocket in my pocket; the rhymes and chants of young Americans; illus. by Susanne Suba. Holt 1948 214p illus $4.50 lib. bdg. $3.97 (3-6) 398

1 Folklore—U.S. 2 Nonsense verses 3 American literature—Collections
ISBN 0-03-032765-2; 0-03-036105-2

" 'Over four hundred of the rhymes, chants, game songs, tongue-twisters and ear-teasers current in our time among youngsters living in many different regions of the United States.' A well-designed and illustrated book." N Y Pub Library

"More comprehensive than most books on the subject; some of the material is printed here for the first time. Includes a brief essay on this kind of folklore and an index of first lines. Will be of more interest probably, to folklorists and to adults concerned with the social growth and development of children than to children themselves." Booklist

"Suba's line drawings catch the deadpan eagerness

with which children join games, the animation of dogs, cows, horses, and cats. Here's fun for the young." Chicago Sun

398.2 Folk literature

Sagas, romances, legends, ballads, and fables in prose form and fairy tales, folk tales, and tall tales are included here, instead of with the literature of the country of origin, to keep the traditional material together and to make it more readily accessible. Modern fairy tales are classified with Fiction or Story collections (S C)

Aardema, Verna

Behind the back of the mountain; Black folktales from southern Africa; retold by Verna Aardema; pictures by Leo and Diane Dillon. Dial Press 1973 85p illus $4.95, lib. bdg. $4.58 (4-6)   398.2

1 Folklore—Africa, Southern
ISBN 0-8037-0613-8; 0-8037-0617-0

A collection of "folk legends from half a dozen language groups of South Africa; trickster tales, witches outwitted, talking animals and magical skymaidens, stories of love and charity and hunger that reflect the concerns of people who live close to the land and are governed by the mores of their cultures." Chicago. Children's Bk Center

The stories "may have a touch of violence—about on a par with Hansel and Gretel—but they open up exotic vistas. . . . Here, too, are frameable illustrations—gray, black and white in primitive-style patterns on patterns." Christian Sci Monitor

Glossary: p81-82

Tales from the story hat; illus. by Elton Fax; introduction by Augusta Baker. Coward-McCann 1960 72p illus lib. bdg. $4.89 (3-6)   398.2

1 Folklore—Africa 2 Animals—Stories
ISBN 0-698-30348-2

"Nine African tales of clever animals who outwit their adversaries are retold with zest and illustrated with humor. Helpful notes for the storyteller, a glossary, and a bibliography are included." Hodges. Bks for Elem Sch Libraries

Alegría, Ricardo E.

The three wishes; a collection of Puerto Rican folktales; selected and adapted by Ricardo E. Alegría; tr. by Elizabeth Culbert; illus. by Lorenzo Homar. Harcourt 1969 128p illus $5.50 (4-6)   398.2

1 Folklore—Puerto Rico
ISBN 0-15-286871-2

A collection of 23 tales which reflect the blend of Taino Indian, African, and Spanish influences in Puerto Rican culture. "Included are animal stories, stories of witchcraft, accounts of princesses and peasant boys, and several tales which feature the popular humorous hero, Juan Bobo, or Simple John. Versions of four of the stories have appeared previously in Pura Belpre's 'Perez y Martina' and 'The Tiger and the Rabbit and Other Tales' [both entered below]; most will be unfamiliar to readers." Sch Library J

"In making the stories available to English-speaking children and storytellers, the translator, herself an experienced storyteller, has lost none of the rhythm or humor of the originals." Horn Bk

Aliki

The eggs; a Greek folk tale, retold and illus. by Aliki. Pantheon Bks. 1969 unp illus $3.95 (k-3)

                                                        398.2

1 Folklore—Greece, Modern
ISBN 0-394-81091-0

Aliki—*Continued*

"A tale about a rascally innkeeper who overreaches himself. When an honest sea captain returns to pay for a meal of four fried eggs that he had been forced by a storm to rush away from six years ago, the innkeeper attempts to collect 500 gold pieces for the chicken farm he might have had. His faulty logic, however, is cleverly refuted by another trickster, a lawyer, and the sea captain is free to sail on his way." Sch Library J

"The style of the retelling is excellent, with no distractions in the way of excess verbiage, direct in approach and natural in dialogue. The illustrations have vigor and humor." Chicago. Children's Bk Center

Three gold pieces; a Greek folk tale retold and illus. by Aliki. Pantheon Bks. 1967 unp illus lib. bdg. $5.19 (k-2)   398.2

1 Folklore—Greece, Modern
ISBN 0-394-91737-5

"A Greek folktale concerning a peasant who, after working for 10 years far from home, exchanges his total earnings of three gold pieces for three pieces of advice. So well does he heed the good advice that he avoids death twice and returns home with pockets and bundle filled with gold." Booklist

"Colorful and bright, [the illustrations] give one the feeling of Greece and its people." Pub W

Ambrus, Victor G.
The three poor tailors. Harcourt 1966 c1965 unp illus $5.95 (k-2)   398.2

1 Folklore—Hungary 2 Tailors—Fiction
ISBN 0-15-286847-X

First published 1965 in England

"A picture book version of a folk tale from the author-illustrator's native Hungary. Retold in a simple, flat style is the story of the three tailors who rode to town on a goat, ran into debt, and had to stay in prison until they had mended the clothes of all the townspeople. The illustrations are quite delightful, painted in brilliant colors and having a great deal of vitality and humor." Chicago. Children's Bk Center

"Awarded the Kate Greenaway medal (in the United Kingdom) for the most distinguished illustration in its year." Children's Bks 1966

Anderson, Jean
The haunting of America; ghost stories from our past; illus. by Eric von Schmidt. Houghton 1973 171p illus $4.95 (6-7)   398.2

1 Ghosts 2 Legends—U.S.
ISBN 0-395-17518-6

The author presents accounts of ghosts, poltergeists and supernatural beings who have become part of American folklore. Among those included are Ocean-Born Mary, the Golden Girl of Appledore Island, the Lady in Black of Boston Harbor, the ghost of Abraham Lincoln, the Galloping Ghost of Laramie, Bigfoot, and Marie Laveau, Queen of the Voodoos

"The ghosts collected here hail from a variety of times and places, and all should intrigue fanciers of the supernatural. . . . Anderson makes no claims to authenticity but only tantalizingly relates what 'old-timers' recall and what scientific investigations have been unable to explain." Booklist

Appiah, Peggy
Ananse the spider; tales from an Ashanti village; pictures by Peggy Wilson. Pantheon Bks. 1966 152p illus $3.75, lib. bdg. $4.99 (4-7)   398.2

1 Folklore, Ashanti 2 Folklore—Ghana 3 Spiders—Stories
ISBN 0-394-81143-7; 0-394-91143-1

Thirteen tales of Kwaku Ananse, the rascal spider whose exploits are celebrated in legends and folk tales

of the Ashanti tribe of Africa's Gold Coast. These stories also appear in the folk literature of Negroes living in the West Indies

"For introducing the Ananse stories through oral telling, the Arkhurst and Courlander collections are to be recommended. This collection might be useful to older children for folklore content or for purposes of comparison. The illustrations are excellent, based on traditional motifs." Africa

Arbuthnot, May Hill
(comp.) Time for old magic; comp. by May Hill Arbuthnot and Mark Taylor; illus. by John Averill [and others]. . . . Scott 1970 389p illus $9.95 398.2

1 Folklore 2 Storytelling—Collections
ISBN 0-673-05844-1

An expansion of the section: Old magic, in Arbuthnot's: Time for fairy tales, old and new, first published 1952

"A representative collection of folk tales, fables, myths, and epics to be used in the classroom, home, or camp; especially planned for college classes in children's literature; with section introductions, headnotes for the individual stories, and a special section titled 'Old Magic and Children.' " Title page

Bibliography: p366-83. Glossary and pronunciation guide: p384-86

Arkhurst, Joyce Cooper
The adventures of Spider; West African folk tales; retold by Joyce Cooper Arkhurst; illus. by Jerry Pinkney. Little 1964 58p illus lib. bdg. $5.50 (2-5) 398.2

1 Folklore—Africa, West 2 Spiders—Stories
ISBN 0-316-05016-3

"Spider (usually called Anansi), popular and cunning trickster of West African folk tales, is the hero of six humorous how-and-why stories. . . . Modern illustrations, many in bold color, amplify Spider's amusing character and the West African background." Horn Bk

These Anansi tales "are slightly simpler than the retellings by . . . Courlander. . . . The less difficult text, open format, and attractive illustrations will encourage some children to read them who would not be attracted to other editions. Quite suitable for storytelling, although Courlander's are still the preferred versions." Sch Library J

Arnott, Kathleen
African myths and legends; retold by Kathleen Arnott; illus. by Joan Kiddell-Monroe. Walck, H.Z. 1963 [c1962] 211p illus (Oxford Myths and legends) $6 (4-7)   398.2

1 Folklore—Africa 2 Legends—Africa
ISBN 0-8098-2362-4

First published 1962 in England

Here are thirty-four "well-retold tales, characteristic of [nineteen countries and] a number of different tribes south of the Sahara. Some are animal stories, some are stories of wise and wicked humans, and several are 'why' stories. . . . Distinguished in illustration and format." Horn Bk

Bibliography: p[212]

Animal folk tales around the world; retold by Kathleen Arnott; illus. by Bernadette Watts. Walck, H.Z. [1971 c1970] 252p illus map $7.50 (4-6)   398.2

1 Folklore 2 Animals—Stories
ISBN 0-8098-2415-9

First published 1970 in England

"Hyenas, hippos, butterflies, foxes, pelicans—all kinds of animals, birds, insects, and serpents romp through this medley of [39] folk tales, meticulously gathered from the far reaches of the world . . . South Africa to the Solomon Islands, Palestine to Persia,

Arnott, Kathleen—*Continued*
more than 30 countries are represented. Thurber-like pen-and-ink drawings appear on nearly every page, enhancing the simplicity and essential humor of the tales." Sch Library J
Includes bibliography

Artzybasheff, Boris
Seven Simeons; a Russian tale; retold and illus. by Boris Artzybasheff. Viking [1961 c1937] unp illus $3.95 (3-6)   398.2
1 Folklore—Russia
ISBN 0-670-63574-X
A reissue of a book first published 1937
This is an old Russian folk tale about great King Douda and seven brothers with remarkable abilities. The King commissioned six of the brothers to find him a princess, but the seventh he locked up. However, without the seventh Simeon the brothers would never have been able to give the King beautiful Princess Helena
"The airy delicacy of the drawings in three colors, the beauty of paper and print, all complement the romantic, gay and ironic tale." Sch Library J

Aruego, Jose
A crocodile's tale; a Philippine folk story, by Jose & Ariane Aruego. Scribner 1972 unp illus lib. bdg. $4.95 (k-3)   398.2
1 Folklore—Philippine Islands 2 Crocodiles—Stories
ISBN 0-684-12806-3
Illustrated by the authors
A crocodile decides to eat Juan, the boy who has just saved his life. Juan's appeals to a worn-out basket and a hat which float by are received without sympathy, because both have suffered from man's ingratitude. Saved at last by a clever monkey, Juan shows that he has learned the importance of being grateful
"An amusing Philippine folktale written in clear colloquial langauge. . . . Warm browns, greens and oranges predominate in the cartoon-like illustrations of the jungle and the village." Wis Library Bul

Asbjörnsen, Peter Christen
East of the sun and west of the moon, and other tales; collected by P. C. Asbjörnsen and Jörgen E. Moe; illus. by Tom Vroman. Afterword by Clifton Fadiman. Macmillan (N Y) 1963 136p illus lib. bdg. $3.95 (5-7)   398.2
1 Folklore—Norway 2 Fairy tales
"The Macmillan classics"
"Twelve of the best-loved folk and fairy tales of the Scandinavian countries retold by two folklorists and illustrated in color." Hodges. Bks for Elem Sch Libraries

Norwegian folk tales; from the collection of Peter Christen Asbjornsen [and] Jorgen Moe; illus. by Erik Werenskiold [and] Theodor Kittelsen; tr. by Pat Shaw Iversen [and] Carl Norman. Viking 1960 188p illus $5 (4-7)   398.2
1 Folklore—Norway 2 Fairy tales
ISBN 0-670-51609-0
"This new translation of thirty-[five] of the old tales collected by Asbjornsen and Moe seems to have all the flavor of the classic translation by George Dasent and is even smoother reading for the present day. An excellent introduction gives background for the tales. . . . A good collection of the Norwegian tales has always been indispensable for the story teller or for anyone who would appreciate the cultural inheritance of Norway. This edition, with pictures—as vigorous and earthy as the stories—on almost every page, will be invaluable in the browsing collections of those libraries fortunate enough to have them, as well as on their circulating shelves." Horn Bk

The squire's bride; a Norwegian folk tale; originally collected and told by P. C. Asbjornsen; illus. by Marcia Sewall. Atheneum Pubs. 1975 unp illus lib. bdg. $5.95 (1-4)   398.2
1 Folklore—Norway
ISBN 0-689-30463-3
This "version of a Norwegian folktale is based on the H. L. Broekstad translation and is illustrated with pencil drawings that have warmth, vitality, and a great sense of the comic. The pictures suit the tale admirably, since the story of an obdurate peasant girl who outwits an equally determined elderly suitor ends on a note of comedy. The story, which is as good for storytelling as it is for reading aloud or alone, gives the reader that special pleasure of being in on the joke, since only the squire assumes that the bride who is being forcibly summoned and dressed for the wedding is the girl; everyone else knows it's a horse." Chicago. Children's Bk Center

The three Billy Goats Gruff [by] P.C. Asbjornsen and J. E. Moe; pictures by Marcia Brown. Harcourt 1957 unp illus $6.95, pa $1.65 (k-3)   398.2
1 Folklore—Norway 2 Goats—Stories
ISBN 0-15-286399-0; 0-15-690150-1
For other versions of this story see entries under Three billy goats gruff, in Part 2
Taken from the translation of G. W. Dasent
Another version of the familiar tale of the troll who attempts to devour each of three goats but who meets his match in Big Billy Gruff
The tale is presented in picture book form. With the originality and imagination which she brings to all her work the artist has interpreted the story in striking pictures which admirably reflect the strength, simplicity, and excitement of the tale." Booklist

Association for Childhood Education International
Told under the green umbrella; favorite folk tales, fairy tales, and legends; selected by the Literature Committe of the Association for Childhood Education International [formerly the International Kindergarten Union] Macmillan Pub. Co. 1930 188p illus $6.95 (1-4)   398.2
1 Folklore 2 Fairy tales
"The Umbrella books"
"This collection includes twenty-six familiar stories which range in length and difficulty from 'The pancake' to 'The princess on the glass hill.' Acceptable versions have been used throughout. . . . Good format and many illustrations." Booklist

Aulaire, Ingri d'
D'Aulaires' Trolls [by Ingri and Edgar Parin d'Aulaire]. Doubleday 1972 62p illus $5.95, lib. bdg. $6.70 (3-6)   398.2
1 Folklore—Norway
ISBN 0-385-08255-X; 0-385-01275-6
Illustrated by the authors
The d'Aulaires "present a kind of dissertation on trolls, and children will revel in the glorious array: forest trolls and water and sea trolls, along with their troll-hag wives and their troll-brat offspring; little, mischievous gnome-trolls; and the biggest, most nightmarish of all—the mountain trolls, often twelve-headed, which had magical powers and the strength of fifty men. . . . The commodious pages—black-and-white stone lithographs alternating with full-color illustrations prepared on acetate overlays—are alive with vigor and imagination and a full measure of grotesque detail." Horn Bk

East of the sun and west of the moon; twenty-one Norwegian folk tales; ed. and illus. by Ingri and Edgar Parin d'Aulaire. Viking 1969 224p illus $6.95 (3-6)   398.2
1 Folklore—Norway 2 Fairy tales
ISBN 0-670-28748-2

Aulaire, Ingri d'—*Continued*

First published 1938. The 1969 edition is a reissue with revised text

"These tales have been adapted from the Dasent translation of the collection of Asbjörnsen and Moe." Verso title page

This collection of Norwegian folk tales tells of trolls, water sprites, giant horses, talking cats and mountains made of glass

Aulnoy, Comtesse d'

The White Cat, and other old French fairy tales; arranged by Rachel Field and drawn by E. MacKinstry. Macmillan (N Y) [1967 c1928] 150p illus $4.95 (3-6)   398.2

1 Folklore—France 2 Fairy tales

A reprint of the title first published 1928

"More romantic and less elemental than the classic retellings of French folktales by Perrault are the original tales told by Madame D'Aulnoy, first recorded in the late 1600's." Bruno. Bks for Sch Libraries, 1968

"Charming book. . . . [The] full-page illustrations have the romantic, rather bloodless grace that is in the tradition of seventeenth century France. The [five] tales themselves are old favorites." N Y Evening Post

Babbitt, Ellen C.

Jataka tales; animal stories re-told by Ellen C. Babbitt; with illus. by Ellsworth Young. Prentice-Hall 1940 92p illus $4.25 (1-3)   398.2

1 Folklore—India 2 Fables

ISBN 0-13-509729-0

First published 1912 by Century with title: Jataka tales retold

The Jatakas are fables about Buddha in his various incarnations, mostly in animal form. Many of them are humorous and all teach a lesson. Eighteen of these fables are retold here

"They are simply and acceptably told for children and illustrated with delightful silhouettes." Booklist

Baker, Augusta

(comp.) The golden lynx, and other tales; illus. by Johannes Troyer. Lippincott 1960 160p illus lib. bdg. $3.93 (3-6)   398.2

1 Folklore 2 Fairy tales

ISBN 0-397-30495-1

"Tales of spells and enchantment, of the tasks to be done, of the cunning outwitting the strong, all in true folklore tradition, have been selected from many out-of-print collections by a well-known storyteller. An attractive edition with sixteen stories representing seven different nationalities." Ontario Library Rev

(comp.) The talking tree; fairy tales from 15 lands; illus. by Johannes Troyer. Lippincott 1955 255p illus lib. bdg. $3.39 (3-6)   398.2

1 Fairy tales 2 Folklore

ISBN 0-397-30316-5

"A selection of twenty-eight stories gathered from out-of-print collections. . . . There are old favorites such as 'Tom Tit Tot' and 'Cinderella' that are easily obtainable, and there are others that are to be found in the out-of-print volumes only. The stories are grouped by country or culture; twelve countries are represented by two stories each; two countries have one story each, and there are two Jewish stories. The stories represent varying degrees of appeal and usefulness, but on the whole this is a very good collection and an outstanding contribution to the shelf of story-telling literature." Chicago. Children's Bk Center

"The strong folk quality of the pictures makes them exactly right for the book." Horn Bk

Baker, Betty

At the center of the world; based on Papago and Pima myths; illus. by Murray Tinkelman. Macmillan Pub Co. 1973 53p illus lib. bdg. $4.95 (4-6)   398.2

1 Papago Indians—Legends 2 Pima Indians—Legends 3 Creation

"A stately narrative of six myths woven together by the author from records made by early anthropologists. These include Southern Arizona Indians' stories about how the world was created by Earth Magician, how Coyote caused a great flood, how Eetoi, son of Earth and Sky, saved men from an evil pot and a monster eagle, how he was later judged and killed for his misdeeds, and finally how he returned from the Underworld to win the first war. The illustrations have a dark, epic quality, and the text is smoothly-paced for reading in Indian and comparative mythology studies." Booklist

Baldwin, James

The story of Roland; illus. by Peter Hurd. Scribner 1930 347p illus $10 (6-7)   398.2

1 Roland (Legendary hero) 2 Legends—France 3 Charlemagne

ISBN 0-684-20731-1

"The Scribner Illustrated classics"

"Roland, the nephew of the Charlemagne of romance, and his companion in all great enterprises, is unknown to history. Yet he is the typical knight, the greatest hero of the middle ages. His story, as I shall tell it to you, is not a mere transcript of the old romances. The main incidents have been derived from a great variety of sources, while the arrangement and the connecting parts are of my own invention." Foreword

The story Z "is told in a stirring narrative and illustrated with richly colored paintings." Hodges. Bks for Elem Sch Libraries

The story of Siegfried; with pictures by Peter Hurd. Scribner 1931 279p illus $10 (6-7)   398.2

1 Siegfried 2 Legends, Germanic

ISBN 0-684-20732-X

"The Scribner Illustrated classics"

First published 1882

Here is the story of the adventures of Siegfried, or Sigurd, the Germanic hero whose exploits are described in the sagas of many Northern lands. Apprenticed to a master smith as a young prince, Siegfried forges the sword Balmung and goes forth to fight evil and defend the weak. He slays the dragon Fafnir, gains a gold hoard, wins a beautiful princess, and is treacherously slain

"In spite of the fact that Baldwin used many versions to bring together the complete story, the writing has unity. The language is not that of the saga but it does reflect its spirit." Ontario Library Rev

Barth, Edna

Jack-o'-lantern; pictures by Paul Galdone. Seabury 1974 unp illus $5.95 (2-4)   398.2

1 Folklore 2 Halloween—Stories

ISBN 0-8164-3120-5

"A Clarion book"

The author "retells an old European tale brought to the United States by some of our first settlers. Jack, a stubborn blacksmith, is kind one day to an old man, who is St. Peter in disguise. Given three wishes, Jack desires not the good of his soul but the ability to trick his fellows. He uses his new power to best the Devil's children and finally the Devil himself. After Jack is dead, he tries to sneak into heaven, but St. Peter rejects him. Jack makes his way to Hell, but the Devil locks the gate against him, relenting only enough to give him a few coals to light his path. Jack wanders the world forever, his glowing embers encased in a pumpkin. Although this is presented in a picture book for-

Barth, Edna—*Continued*

mat, the tale is enjoyed by children of all ages and by adults and is an excellent choice for storytelling. Paul Galdone's pictures in orange and brown add humor and atmosphere to this Halloween-oriented version." Reading Teacher

Baumann, Hans

The stolen fire; legends of heroes and rebels from around the world; tr. by Stella Humphries; illus. by Herbert Holzing. Pantheon Bks. 1974 150p illus $4.95, lib. bdg. $5.49 (4-6)   398.2

1 Folklore
ISBN 0-394-82675-2; 0-394-92675-7
First published 1972 in Germany

These twenty-seven "legends are about heroes who fight dragons, resist the oppressor and conquer fear—adventures where everyone must prove himself in his own way. . . . They come from Africa and India, China and Australia, North America and Mexico, Russia and Polynesia. They tell of Sumerian, Indian, Kara-Kirghiz, Tibetan, Ainu and Pygmy heroes, not forgetting the heroines of the various continents. Just as Siegfried and Theseus kill terrifying monsters, so do Mbega and Onkoito, Kara Khan's daughter and Nana Miriam." Introduction

"The stories are brief and fast-paced, retaining their ethnic flavor without additional literary flourishes from the author. Some of the unfamiliar selections are symbol-laden myths, while a few are didactic fables; others, particularly the Slavic and Asian stories, are more suitable to general storytelling sessions." Booklist

Belpré, Pura

Dance of the animals; a Puerto Rican folk tale. Paul Galdone drew the pictures. Warne 1972 30p illus lib. bdg. $4.50 (k-3)   398.2

1 Folklore—Puerto Rico 2 Animals—Stories
ISBN 0-7232-6039-7
Text first published 1946 in Pura Belpré's: The Tiger and the Rabbit, and other tales, entered below

"A lion and his lioness are desperately hungry for meat; their favorite prey, goats, have been too wily for them. But Senor and Senora Lioness have a plan: they invite all the forest animals to a dance and fill a pit with a roaring fire into which they hope to maneuver the goats." Pub W

The illustrator "elaborates Belpré's pithy animal satire with black-and-white and color sketches. He employs sly humor in the animals' posture and facial characteristics (e.g., the smirk on the triumphant dog's face, the grace of the dancing donkeys) but he doesn't anthropomorphize them. In all, an enjoyable addition to Caribbean folklore collections." Sch Library J

Once in Puerto Rico; illus. by Christine Price. Warne 1973 96p illus map $4.95 (3-6)   398.2

1 Folklore—Puerto Rico
ISBN 0-7232-6101-6

These 17 tales "are a mixture of historical and magical incidents. The stories of heroes and the supernatural . . . will have appeal for story hours or for individual reading. Other tales about specific places—Ponce, San Juan, and certain small villages—and about the historical conflicts of Indians and Spaniards will hold particular interest for young Puerto Ricans. In the storyteller's informative opening chapter, she sketches the background of these legends which are a mixture of Indian, Spanish, and Negro lore." Horn Bk

Oté; a Puerto Rican folk tale; retold by Pura Belpré. Paul Galdone drew the pictures. Pantheon Bks. 1969 unp illus $3.95, lib. bdg. $5.19 (1-4)   398.2

1 Folklore—Puerto Rico
ISBN 0-394-80809-6; 0-394-90809-0

Also available in a Spanish language edition, lib. bdg. $5.19 (ISBN 0-394-90454-0)

A "folk tale about a devil, a wise old woman, and a poor peasant who is something of a loser. When Oté, the peasant, encounters the nearsighted devil in the forest and tries to beat him at his own game, he loses and must take the devil home for dinner—and breakfast—and lunch—. Before the family can rid themselves of their obnoxious guest, their tiniest son must take matters into his own hands. The pen-and-ink drawings in bright splashes of color poke fun at hapless Oté and portray with relish a perfectly nasty devil." Horn Bk

Perez and Martina; a Portorican folk tale; illus. by Carlos Sanchez. M. [New ed] Warne [1961 c1960] unp illus $4.95 (1-4)   398.2

1 Folklore—Puerto Rico 2 Mice—Stories 3 Cockroaches—Stories
ISBN 0-7232-6017-6
Also available in a Spanish language edition for $4.95 (ISBN 0-7232-6018-4)
First published 1932

This Puerto Rican folk tale describes the adventures of the sprightly Senorita Martina, a Spanish cockroach of high degree, and her many suitors. After turning away the suitors she did not like, Senorita Martina married Perez the gallant mouse and they were very happy until Perez came to grief

"Here is a picture book with an authentic background, for this droll nonsense tale has long been beloved of Spanish-speaking children. . . . The pictures are full colored and decorative while keeping the realistic quality to which young children always respond." N Y Her Trib Bks

The tiger and the rabbit, and other tales; illus. by Tomie de Paola. Lippincott 1965 127p illus $4.95 (4-6)   398.2

1 Folklore—Puerto Rico
ISBN 0-397-31591-0
First published 1946 by Houghton with illustrations by Kay Peterson Parker

"As in all folklore, the customs of the people, the climate, the food, the ways of living, the measure of wit, the very philosophy of life are all a fascinating part of the stories. Some of the [18 Puerto Rican] stories, such as the one which gives the book its title, share a common heritage with Uncle Remus, with Grimm, and other familiar sources. . . . The stories come easily to the tongue for telling, and have the feeling of having been written down as they were heard." N Y Her Trib Bks

Belting, Natalia

Calendar moon; illus. by Bernarda Bryson. Holt 1964 unp illus lib. bdg. $4.37 (4-7)   398.2

1 Legends 2 Months 3 Quotations
ISBN 0-03-046690-3

Miss Belting "has gathered twenty-six folk beliefs related to the months of the year. From all parts of the world they derive, each explaining a name given to a month or moon: legends of the friendly-moon of the Japanese, the Maoris' grumbling-moon . . . and others. Again, this is poetry, with mood in the words as well as in the lucent illustrations. A silvery blue with the grays of soft pencil describe moonlight on cold snow peaks, strange natural formations, trees, and other ghostly figures." Horn Bk

"A lovely book to hold and look at, to read aloud or hear." Sch Library J

The stars are silver reindeer; illus. by Esta Nesbitt. Holt 1966 unp illus lib. bdg. $3.27 (4-7)   398.2

1 Legends 2 Stars 3 Quotations
ISBN 0-03-055655-4

Belting, Natalia—*Continued*

This book is comprised of "simple, poetic interpretations of some primitive myths relating to the constellations." Best Bks for Children, 1967

"The selections are imaginative, varied, and poetic; some are from lore as old as Babylonian, others from more modern, albeit often, primitive, sources." Chicago. Children's Bk Center

The sun is a golden earring; illus. by Bernarda Bryson. Holt 1962 unp illus lib. bdg. $3.27 (4-7)
398.2

1 Legends 2 Universe 3 Quotations
ISBN 0-03-035505-2

A "collection of folk sayings [and legends] of the world—mythological metaphors about the sun and other celestial phenomena that come from the North American Indians, India, Malaya, Siberia, and many other places." Wis Library Bul

"Exquisite drawings on yellow, blue, gray, or white pages are combined here with the poetically conceived folk sayings. . . . An unusual, lovely, and perfectly integrated picture book." Horn Bk

Whirlwind is a ghost dancing; illus. by Leo and Diane Dillon. Dutton 1974 unp illus maps $7.50 (3-6)
398.2

1 Indians of North America—Legends 2 Indian poetry
ISBN 0-525-42625-6

Poetic versions of American Indian lore from tribes including the Iroquois, Shoshoni, Dakota and Micmac

"Since each brief piece is identified by nation and general location, the influence of environmental conditions is readily apparent. . . . Each of these vivid images is matched by handsome, stylized illustrations developed from authentic Indian motifs; the colors are rich and deep, suggesting the natural dyes available to the Indians." Horn Bk

Berger, Terry

Black fairy tales; drawings by David Omar White. Atheneum Pubs. 1969 137p illus lib. bdg. $5.50, pa $1.25 (4-7)
398.2

1 Folklore—Africa, Southern 2 Fairy tales
ISBN 0-689-20622-4; 0-689-70402-X

Adapted from "Fairy tales from South Africa" by E. J. Bourhill, published 1908 in England

These ten folk and fairy tales from the Swazi, Shangani, Msuto and other Black peoples of South Africa "are filled with ogres, enchanted beasts, and giants. A glossary explains unfamiliar words. These stories would be of particular interest to those preparing Black Heritage curricula." Keating. Building Bridges of Understanding Between Cultures

"The stories, some of them familiar, tell of the customs and of the daily life of South African people, while the superb black-and-white illustrations add their own distinct touch." Pub W

Berson, Harold

How the Devil gets his due; adapted and illus. by Harold Berson. Crown 1972 unp illus lib. bdg. $4.95 (1-3)
398.2

1 Folklore—France 2 Devil—Fiction
ISBN 0-517-50551-7

An "adaptation of a French folk tale. Alone in his brokendown castle, the devil finds himself overworked; he strikes a bargain with a gullible peasant boy: whichever of them complains gets beaten. The boy becomes exhausted by the tasks the devil sets; fearing punishment, he is silent. When the boy's clever brother takes his place, the devil is outfoxed and driven off." Sat Rev

"This is a version that is appropriate for storytelling and reading aloud as well as for individual reading.

. . . The story has action and humor that are echoed in the pictures, frolicsome and lively." Chicago. Children's Bk Center

Bertol, Roland

Sundiata; the epic of the Lion King; retold by Roland Bertol; illus. by Gregorio Prestopino. Crowell 1970 81p illus $3.95 (4-7)
398.2

1 Legends—Africa
ISBN 0-690-79340-5

"A retelling of the 13th-Century African legend concerning a speechless crippled dwarf/prince who rose to become a glorious King, free his people from evil powers, and build the mighty empire of Mali." Library J

"This dramatic version of the ancient legend, written in a superb literary style, includes Arab tales, Islamic philosophy, chilling descriptions of witchcraft and mystic touches which will tempt youngsters. A 'must' for Black Studies programs." Keating. Building Bridges of Understanding Between Cultures

Black, Algernon D.

The woman of the wood; a tale from old Russia; told by Algernon D. Black; illus. by Evaline Ness. Holt 1973 unp illus lib. bdg. $5.95 (k-3)
398.2

1 Folklore—Russia 2 Fairy tales
ISBN 0-03-007436-3

An adaptation of a Russian folktale is handsomely illustrated with pictures that are simply composed, intricate in detail, and subtle in their soft, strong colors. Although the end of the story has a twist of magic that is somehow anticlimactic the tale is nicely told, and the harmony between text and pictures is outstanding. A woodcarver, a tailor, and a teacher share in the creation of a beautiful woman. Each falls in love with her and claims her, the carver because he made her, the tailor because he dressed her beautifully, the teacher because he taught her to speak and think. An elderly sage to whom they have brought their problem decrees that the woman belongs to none of them, since nobody can ever really own anybody else. The woman then chooses the sage; when she touches him his wrinkles disappear and he becomes young and handsome." Chicago. Children's Bk Center

Bloch, Marie Halun

Ivanko and the dragon; an old Ukrainian folk tale; from the original collection of Ivan Rudchenko; tr. [and retold] by Marie Halun Bloch; illus. by Yaroslava. Atheneum Pubs. 1969 unp illus lib. bdg. $5.95 (k-3)
398.2

1 Folklore—Ukraine 2 Dragons—Stories
ISBN 0-689-20581-3

"A childless old couple place a stick of wood in a cradle and rock it and sing to it and love it so much that it turns into a little boy. When Ivanko is grown, he goes fishing to help his parents and is carried off by a she-dragon. Of course, his merry wits keep him out of the roasting pan and return him safe home, but there is sufficient suspense to make storyhour listeners hold their breath." Horn Bk

"From the Poltava region of the Ukraine, [here is] a patterned example of the genre, a bit stilted (whether in the original or because of the translation) and illustrated with pictures that have a poster-like simplicity of design, lovely costume details, and clear, bold colors." Chicago. Children's Bk Center

(ed.) Ukrainian folk tales; ed. and tr. by Marie Halun Bloch, from the original collections of Ivan Rudchenko and Maia Lukiyanenko; illus. by J. Hnizdovsky. Coward-McCann 1964 76p illus lib. bdg. $3.86 (4-6)
398.2

1 Folklore—Ukraine 2 Animals—Stories
ISBN 0-698-30383-0

Bloch, Marie Halun—*Continued*

Eleven stories illustrated with "forcefully drawn figures. . . . Brief animal tales rich in direct, childlike, peasant humor." Bk Week

"Although the stories contain many familiar elements and motifs of European folklore, they have [a] distinct national individuality." Horn Bk

Boggs, Ralph Steele

398.

Three golden oranges, and other Spanish folk tales; by Ralph Steele Boggs and Mary Gould Davis; pictures by Emma Brock. McKay 1936 137p illus $4.50 (5-7)   398.2

1 Folklore—Spain 2 Fairy tales
ISBN 0-679-20210-2
First published by Longmans

Ten Spanish folk tales retold for young readers. The stories were collected and rewritten in Spain and were drawn in the main from Andalusia

"Delightful variants of familiar stories. . . . These versions preserve the full flavor of authentic folklore and reflect the atmosphere of place. . . . For the story-teller and a wide range of readers from ten years on." Booklist

"Emma Brock's drawings, made in Spain, have captured not only its general atmosphere but something of that gusty humor in the sly wink of a peasant." N Y Times Bk Rev

Borski, Lucia Merecka

398.21

The jolly tailor, and other fairy tales; tr. from the Polish, by Lucia Merecka Borski and Kate B. Miller; illus. by Kazimir Klepacki. McKay 1957 [c1928] 158p illus $3.50 (4-6)   398.2

1 Folklore—Poland 2 Fairy tales
ISBN 0-679-20086-X

A reissue of a book first published 1928 by Longmans

"Wit and humor, fun and laughter characterize these [ten Polish folk] tales." N Y Her Trib Bks

One tale: Story of Princess Marysia, the black swan, and an iceberg, might be considered racially offensive to some readers

Glossary: p157-58

Bowman, James Cloyd

398.

Tales from a Finnish tupa; by James Cloyd Bowman and Margery Bianco; from a translation by Aili Kolehmainen; pictured by Laura Bannon. Whitman, A. 1936 273p illus $4.50 (5-7)   398.2

1 Folklore—Finland 2 Fairy tales
ISBN 0-8075-7756-1

Forty-three "folk tales and legends translated from authentic Finnish sources, arranged under the headings: Tales of magic, Droll stories, Fables. Some are easily traced variants of well-known tales from other countries, others are fresh and unusual in plot and characterization. The unfamiliar proper names may offer some hindrance to children's own reading, which will not exist if the stories are read or told to them. Attractive, highly imaginative illustrations." Booklist

Brenner, Anita

398.

The boy who could do anything, & other Mexican folk tales; retold by Anita Brenner; illus. by Jean Charlot. Young Scott Bks. 1942 134p illus lib. bdg. $4.95 (4-6)   398.2

1 Folklore—Mexico
ISBN 0-201-09133-X

"A book of [twenty-five] folk tales, both legendary and contemporary, distinguished for authentic idiom, and the evocation of Mexico and the Mexican people. The illustrations . . . intensify the spirit of the text." N Y Pub Library

Brown, Marcia

Backbone of the king; the story of Paka'a and his son Ku. Scribner 1966 180p illus map $5.95 (5-7) 398.2

1 Legends—Hawaii
ISBN 0-684-20747-8

"Based on The Hawaiian story of Pakaa and Kuapakaa, the personal attendants of Keawenuiaumi . . . collected, assembled, selected, and edited by Moses K. Nakuina, Honolulu, n. d. Translation from the Hawaiian by Dorothy M. Kahanaui." Verso of title page

"This story of a courageous Hawaiian boy who helped to restore his father to his rightful place in the King's court is told in distinguished style and illustrated with stunning linoleum prints by the author. Suggested for reading aloud at story time, or as background reading in the study of the fiftieth state." Hodges. Bks for Elem Sch Libraries

Glossary: p165-80

398

The bun; a tale from Russia. Harcourt 1972 unp illus $6.50 (k-2)   398.2

1 Folklore—Russia
ISBN 0-15-213450-6

"The author-illustrator retells a long-time favorite folktale and captures the essence of its Russian background in her hearty bright drawings. A rollicking read-aloud tale of the runaway bun, a counterpart of the Gingerbread Man and Johnny Cake." Wis Library Bul

"The amount of text and illustration varies on each page. Brown, gold, and turquoise drawings, some with bright scarlet added for accent, give a superb sense of movement and spirit." Horn Bk

398.

Dick Whittington and his cat; told and cut in linoleum by Marcia Brown. Scribner 1950 unp illus lib. bdg. $5.95 (k-3)   398.2

1 Legends—Great Britain 2 Whittington, Richard
ISBN 0-684-13210-9

For other versions of this story see entries under Dick Whittington and his cat, in Part 2

This retelling of the English legend about the merchant Dick Whittington who became Lord Mayor of London tells how young Dick achieved fame and fortune by selling his cat to a king who was plagued by rats

"The print, black and clear, balances the bold lines of the linoleum blocks; the pictures combine strength of line, and a sense of design with vigorous action. The version is complete in the thread of the story but simpler and less wordy in places than in some of those given in the fairy tale collections." Ontario Library Rev

The author "writes a simple, flavorsome prose, sparked with plenty of conversation [and an illustration for each paragraph of text] to give young children a feeling of reality of actually knowing the people." N Y Times Bk R

398

The flying carpet. Scribner 1956 unp illus lib. bdg. $5.95 (2-5)   398.2

1 Folklore—Arabia 2 Fairy tales

The "Arabian Nights" magic carpet story "in a handsome picture-story format ablaze with oriental-rug colors and Eastern motifs. Based on Richard Burton's translation of the much longer story, 'Prince Ahmed and Fairy Paribanou,' this presents the Sultan, his three sons and niece, the flying carpet and the archery contest that determined which prince should marry the princess. . . . The story-telling is rich in words to create images in the listener's mind. . . . A distinguished achievement [by this adapter-illustrator]." Horn Bk

Brown, Marcia—*Continued*
The neighbors; told and pictured by Marcia Brown. Scribner 1967 unp illus $5.95 (k-2)   398.2
1 Folklore—Russia 2 Animals—Stories
ISBN 0-684-20744-3
This adaptation of a Russian tale by Afanas'ev "has the vivacious illustrations children love. Rabbit shares his house with fox, but fox takes over and will not even let rabbit come in. Foxy is finally ousted by the brave rooster. The simple story line has just enough excitement." Bruno. Bks for Sch Libraries, 1968
"The large size of the illustrations make the book especially suitable for the picture-book hour." Booklist

Once a mouse; a fable cut in wood. Scribner 1961 unp illus lib. bdg. $5.95 (k-3)   398.2
1 Folklore—India 2 Fables
ISBN 0-684-12662-1
Awarded the Caldecott Medal, 1962
At head of title: From ancient India
A "fable from the Indian 'Hitopadesa.' There is lively action in spreads showing how a hermit 'thinking about big and little' suddenly saves a mouse from a crow and then from larger enemies by turning the little creature into the forms of bigger and bigger animals—until as a royal tiger it has to be humbled." Horn Bk
"The illustrations are remarkably beautiful. The emotional elements of the story . . . are conveyed with just as much intensity as the purely visual ones." New Yorker
"For children the pleasure is in the transformations; older children will understand the meaning of the fable. For adults, some of the interesting features of this book are its color, its pictorial economy, and the method of reproduction." Sat Rev

Stone soup; an old tale; told and pictured by Marcia Brown. Scribner 1947 unp illus lib. bdg. $5.95, pa 95¢ (k-3)   398.2
1 Folklore—France
ISBN 0-684-92296-7; 0-684-12631-1
"When the people in a French village heard that three soldiers were coming, they hid all their food for they knew what soldiers are. However, when the soldiers began to make soup with water and stones the pot gradually filled with all the vegetables which had been hidden away. The simple langauge and quiet humour of this old folk tale are amplified and enriched by gay and witty drawings of clever lighthearted soldiers, and the gullible 'lightwitted' peasants." Ontario Library Rev

Brown, Margaret Wise
Brer Rabbit; stories from Uncle Remus, by Joel Chandler Harris, adapted by Margaret Wise Brown, with the A. B. Frost pictures redrawn for reproduction by Victor Dowling. Harper 1941 132p illus lib. bdg. $4.79 (3-5)   398.2
1 Folklore, Negro 2 Animals—Stories 3 Rabbits—Stories
ISBN 0-06-020876-7
"We have isolated [twenty-four of] those stories about Brer Rabbit from 'Nights with Uncle Remus' and 'Uncle Remus, his songs and his sayings' that seem most suitable for young children, and have left the stories to stand alone as they did in the beginning." Foreword
"The spirit and language of the stories are retained but the more difficult dialect has been simplified for easier reading and telling." Children's Booklist for Small Pub Libraries

Bryson, Bernarda
Gilgamesh; man's first story; written and illus. by Bernarda Bryson. Holt [1967] 112p illus $4.95, lib. bdg. $4.27 (5-7)   398.2
1 Gilgamesh
ISBN 0-03-055610-4; 0-03-055615-5
This book relates the ancient story of the Sumerian king, Gilgamesh, "and his friendship with Enkidu, the half-beast half-man originally created by the gods to destroy him. . . . Included are the adventures of Enkidu and Gilgamesh in slaying the evil giant Humbaba and the Bull of Heaven, their insulting of the goddess Ishtar, and Gilgamesh's arduous journey to his immortal ancestor Utnapishtim, the Babylonian Noah, who recounts the story of the flood but refuses to help Gilgamesh bring the dead Enkidu back from the underworld. The story ends with Gilgamesh willing himself to die so that he may join his friend." Sch Library J
"A powerful rendering of the legend, done with beauty and style. . . . Magnificent water color and pastel illustrations." N Y Times Bk Rev

Campbell, Camilla
Star Mountain, and other legends of Mexico. 2d ed. Illus. by Frederic Marvin. McGraw 1968 92p illus lib. bdg. $4.72 (4-7)   398.2
1 Legends—Mexico 2 Indians of Mexico—Legends
ISBN 0-07-009681-3
First published 1946
"Twenty tales, tersely told, aptly illustrate the mingling of Indian and Spanish cultures that is modern Mexico. . . . This far-ranging collection includes mythological tales from the Aztecs, the Toltecs, the Mixtecs, and the Mayas; legends of the Conquest based on historical accounts; romantic and religious stories from the long colonial period; and a folktale or two. Their brevity and simplicity make them more useful as supplements to intermediate grade social studies than as storytelling material. New for this edition are drawings . . . in blue and black that, while striking in themselves, owe very little to pre-Columbian art or to the peerless Mexican art of the 20th Century." Sch Library J

Carpenter, Frances
African wonder tales; illus. by Joseph Escourido. Doubleday 1963 215p illus $4.50 (3-6)   398.2
1 Folklore—Africa
ISBN 0-385-02258-1
Twenty-four folk tales of animal and human adventures from West Africa. Egypt, Central Africa, Nigeria, Liberia, the Sudan, the Kafir Country, Madagascar, Basuto Land, Algeria, the Gold Coast, Senegal, South Africa and Morocco
"Drawing upon secondary sources, [Carpenter] tells her folk tales warmly in an uncluttered style that retains their flavor. . . . An overuse of anticipatory phrases and rather quickly resolved problems are occasional weaknesses." Sch Library J
"These stories should tell easily, especially to the younger children who are sometimes at a loss to understand the more cryptic wit of Courlander's African stories." Horn Bk
Some African names of people, places, and things and how to pronounce them: p214-15

People from the sky; Ainu tales from Northern Japan; told by Frances Carpenter; illus. by Betty Fraser. Doubleday 1972 107p illus $4.95, lib. bdg. $5.70 (4-6)   398.2
1 Folklore—Japan 2 Ainu
ISBN 0-385-08186-3; 0-385-00397-8
The seventeen "tales are framed by conversational interludes and interrupted by young Toki and

Carpenter, Frances—*Continued*

Haruko, by their tattooed grandmother, and by the storytelling grandfather Ekashi, who is 'chief of the model village of Hokkaido' (or Ainu Land, the original home of the aborigines of Japan). Ekashi comments on the history and culture of his people as he relates the old tales of the Kamui gods who lived in the sky country; of their creation of man and animals; of warriors, little people, and powerful demons. . . . Although attached to a framework, the stories are independent and distinct enough for good storytelling." Horn Bk

"Contrasts are made frequently between the present way of life on the island and the way in which the Ainu lived in the past. The scarcity of material for children on the Ainu makes this book a valuable addition to folklore collections and useful supplementary reading material for units on Japan." Booklist

Tales of a Chinese grandmother; illus. by Malthé Hasselriis. Tuttle 1973 261p illus pa $2.95 (5-7)
398.2

1 Folklore—China 2 Fairy tales
ISBN 0-8048-1042-7
"Tut books"
A paperback reprint of the title first published 1937 in hardcover by Doubleday
"Thirty Chinese folk stories and legends from various sources are retold with the full flavor of the Orient. . . . They are told to a boy and girl by their grandmother on occasions in their daily life which suggest a story. Useful for storytelling." Booklist
"Phrased with grace and charm, the stories are revelatory of Chinese beliefs in years past, and of customs and home life. Drawings in color and black and white." N Y Libraries

Carter, Dorothy Sharp

(ed.) Greedy Mariani, and other folktales of the Antilles; selected and adapted by Dorothy Sharp Carter; illus. by Trina Schart Hyman. Atheneum Pubs. 1974 131p illus $5.50 (3-7)   398.2

1 Folklore—West Indies
ISBN 0-689-30425-0
"A Margaret K. McElderry book"
"Here are twenty folktales from the group of islands which include Jamaica, Haiti, Cuba, Puerto Rico, and the Dominican Republic. One finds among these stories a few familiar faces and variants of timeless themes—a wily Jamaican Annancy, a Montserrat Brer Rabbit, a classic fool named Juan Bobo, and the doctor who made a deal with Death." Booklist
"One of the most delightful collections of folktales to appear in a long, long time, these stories from the West Indies are illustrated with black and white drawings that are handsome and dramatic. The stories are entertaining in themselves, but they are made delectable by the adapter's style, which captures to perfection the conversational tone of the oral tradition, extracts every ounce of humor from the stories, and handles deftly the use of other languages in dialogue." Chicago. Children's Bk Center

Chafetz, Henry

Thunderbird, and other stories; illus. by Ronni Solbert. Pantheon Bks. 1964 41p illus lib. bdg. $4.99 (4-6)   398.2

1 Indians of North America—Legends
ISBN 0-394-91747-2
"Three Indian myths explaining lightning and thunder, the entry of malice into the world and the Great Spirit's gift of the peace pipe are retold in this collection of stories." Cooperative Children's Bk Center. Materials on Indians of North Am
"Designs in the style of Navajo sand paintings, done in burnt orange, black and white on tan pages, are the dramatic illustrations. . . . If there is a flaw in the book it is the absence of a note for the Indian-wise children and storytellers as to the origins of the stories." Pub W

Chase, Richard

(ed.) Grandfather tales; American-English folk tales; selected and ed. by Richard Chase; illus. by Berkeley Williams, Jr. Houghton 1948 239p illus $5.95 (4-7)   398.2

1 Folklore—Southern States
ISBN 0-395-06692-1
Folklore gathered in Alabama, "North Carolina, Virginia and Kentucky. Written down only after many tellings, these [twenty-four] humorous tales are told in the vernacular of the region with added touches of local color provided by the storytellers as they meet together to keep Old-Christmas Eve. . . . Of special interest to storytellers." Booklist
"Here is a real contribution to American folklore, one of the many made by Mr. Chase, who has gathered old songs and tunes, rhymes and stories from the mountain people. There is an interesting appendix which gives the source for each story as well as some parallels, types and suggestions for the telling of the tales." N Y Her Trib Bks

Jack and the three sillies; pictures by Joshua Tolford. Houghton 1950 39p illus lib. bdg. $5.95 (k-3)
398.2

1 Folklore—U.S.
ISBN 0-395-06693-X
This American folk tale tells about foolish Jack who started out to sell a cow and swapped with everyone he met until he arrived home with only a stone. Then Jack's wife went out to find three people sillier than Jack, found them, and got their money back. The story combines elements of the German tales Hans in luck and the English tale The three sillies
"It would be hard to find a story that would create more merriment among boys and girls, or among grown-ups for that matter, than this one. Tell it or read it aloud in the swinging, rhythmic phrases that Richard Chase gives it and then let them have Joshua Tolford's drawings, in color and in black and white." Sat Rev

(ed.) The Jack tales. . . . Set down from these sources and ed. by Richard Chase; with an appendix comp. by Herbert Halpert; and illus. by Berkeley Williams, Jr. Houghton 1971 201p illus lib. bdg. $5.95 (4-6)   398.2

1 Folklore—Southern States
ISBN 0-395-06694-8
First published 1943. Copyright renewed 1971
"Told by R. M. Ward and his kindred in the Beech Mountain section of Western North Carolina and by other descendants of Council Harmon (1803-1896) elsewhere in The Southern Mountains; with three tales from Wise County, Virginia." Title page
"Humor, freshness, colorful American background, and the use of one character as a central figure in the cycle mark these 18 folk tales, told here in the dialect of the mountain country of North Carolina. A scholarly appendix by Herbert Halpert, giving sources and parallels, increases the book's value as a contribution to American folklore. Black-and-white illustrations in the spirit of the text." Booklist
These stories "show how European tales took on coloration of their new background." Library J
Glossary: p201-[02]

Child Study Association of America

Castles and dragons; read-to-myself fairy tales for boys and girls; illus. by William Pène du Bois. Crowell 1958 299p illus $5.95 (3-6)   398.2

1 Fairy tales
ISBN 0-690-18135-3

Child Study Association of America—*Continued*

A "volume containing 18 fairy tales. Some of them are very familiar, others are less well known but no less entertaining. An excellent book for beginning readers since the story form is familiar while much of the material is fresh and unhackneyed." Pub W

"Particularly attractive is the format with the print and the lucid charming pictures . . . beautifully harmonized." N Y Her Trib Bks

Colum, Padraic

The girl who sat by the ashes; illus. by Imero Gobbato. Macmillan (N Y) 1968 117p illus $3.95 (4-6)
398.2

1 Fairy tales

A reissue in a new format of a title first published 1919

The author presents his own version of the Cinderella story with a Celtic flavor. Girl-go-with-the-goats becomes the Matchless Maiden and wins the heart and hand of the prince. In this version the traditional fairy godmother appears as an ancient dame dressed in a cloak of crow feathers. Irish turns of speech are employed, and some new details are added, but the main features of the old story are preserved

"Beautiful literary style and imaginative story telling have created a marvelous version of the Cinderella story. The illustrations in this new edition . . . are placed perfectly within the story to enhance a truly charming telling." Bruno. Bks for Sch Libraries, 1968

The King of Ireland's Son; illus. by Willy Pogany. Macmillan (N Y) 1962 [c1944] 275p illus lib. bdg. $4.95 (5-7)
398.2

1 Folklore—Ireland 2 Fairy tales

A reissue in new format of a book first published 1916

Includes seven romantic adventure tales about the dashing son of the King of Ireland, who encounters enchanters and ogres as he tries to win his true love

"A book of uncommon beauty in form and content . . . [exhibiting Colum's] genuine simplicity." Bookman's Manual

The Stone of Victory, and other tales of Padraic Colum; foreword by Virginia Haviland; illus. by Judith Gwyn Brown. McGraw 1966 119p illus $3.95, lib. bdg. $4.72 (3-5)
398.2

1 Folklore—Ireland 2 Fairy tales

ISBN 0-07-012100-1; 0-07-012101-X

This is a "collection of 13 delightful stories newly chosen by the author from seven of his books, six of which are out of print. Some of the tales are traditional, others original. Appropriately illustrated in black-and-white drawings." Booklist

Colwell, Eileen

Round about and long ago; tales from the English counties; retold by Eileen Colwell; illus. with linocuts by Anthony Colbert. Houghton 1974 [c1972] 124p illus $4.95 (3-6)
398.2

1 Folklore—Great Britain

ISBN 0-395-18515-7

First published 1972 in England

"Almost all the stories in this book have been retold from collections of folklore made in the period between 1840 and 1900 from oral tradition. I have tried to retain the directions and flavour of the original while at the same time telling the stories in a more modern idiom so that present-day children may enjoy them as did their ancestors so long ago." Author's note

"There is a most appealing distinctive bluntness, an earthiness, a doggedness about these stories along with the usual dose of humour and tenderness; difficult to pin down, but it's there all right. Anthony Colbert's fine strong lino-cuts of boggarts and giants and green children define this mood too. All in all, this is a well-written, well-illustrated and well-produced book." New Statesman

Cooney, Barbara

The little juggler; adapted from an old French legend and illus. by Barbara Cooney. Hastings House 1961 46p illus $4.95 (3-6)
398.2

1 Legends—France 2 Christmas stories

ISBN 0-8038-4239-2

This is the story of the little orphaned juggler of Notre Dame who, having no other gift to bring to Mary and the Child, entertained them with his juggling

"The story is told in simple, dignified, faintly archaic English and is well illustrated with the delicate, formalized precision of a medieval missal. It would be hard to find a story in subject and spirit more appropriate to Christmas." Times (London) Literary Sup

Courlander, Harold

The cow-tail switch, and other West African stories, by Harold Courlander and George Herzog; drawings by Madye Lee Chastain. Holt 1947 143p illus lib. bdg. $3.27 (4-6)
398.2

1 Folklore—Africa, West 2 Folklore, Ashanti

ISBN 0-03-035745-4

"The seventeen stories, mostly gathered in the Ashanti country, are fresh to collections and are told with humor and originality. Their themes, chosen with discrimination, are frequently primitive explanations of the origin of folk sayings and customs, or show examples of animal trickery and ingenuity." Horn Bk

Includes notes and glossary

The fire on the mountain, and other Ethiopian stories, by Harold Courlander and Wolf Leslau; illus. by Robert W. Kane. Holt 1950 141p illus lib. bdg. $3.27 (4-6)
398.2

1 Folklore—Ethiopia

ISBN 0-03-035250-9

"A fine collection of [twenty-four] Ethiopian folk tales retold from stories which the authors heard in Ethiopia. Some have variants in the folklore of other countries; others, they say, 'bear the mark of local invention, and virtually all of them have been so colored by the life and customs of the Ethiopian people that they have a unique flavor.' Entertaining reading and excellent material for the storyteller. Appropriate and pleasing format." Booklist

"The introductory chapter is valuable and the notes at the conclusion of the tales seem to be a built-in teaching device both for a teacher and for the individual reader. A glossary and pronunciation guide are included." Africa

The hat-shaking dance, and other tales from the Gold Coast, by Harold Courlander with Albert Kofi Prempeh; illus. by Enrico Arno. Harcourt 1957 115p illus. $5.50 (3-6)
398.2

1 Folklore—Ghana 2 Folklore, Ashanti 3 Spiders—Stories

ISBN 0-15-233615-X

Here are twenty-one tales from the Ashanti people of the Gold Coast (now Ghana) about the "wiley spider, Anansi. Storytellers and students of folklore will appreciate this additional highly tellable material and be glad for the section of notes concerning origins and variants of the tales. Each [story] . . . portrays the amoral character of Anansi, his perennial gluttony and ruthless guile, in 'how' stories, 'tall tales,' and riddle stories, with fable-like lessons or reasons why today certain animals or things are as they are. . . . Clever and decorative sketches." Horn Bk

Courlander, Harold—*Continued*

The king's drum, and other African stories; illus. by Enrico Arno. Harcourt 1962 125p illus $5.95, pa 75¢ (4-7)   398.2

    1 Folklore—Africa

    ISBN 0-15-242925-5; 0-15-647190-6

"A good collection of [twenty-nine] African folk tales, each very short, told in a style that has restraint and simplicity. Some of the tales are quietly humorous: some are realistic, some are fables; many are perceptive commentaries on the foibles of the human race. Good for reading aloud, and a good source for storytelling. The tales come from many parts of the continent; an appendage gives excellent notes on each story; sources, adaptations, and background information." Chicago. Children's Bk Center

Olode, the hunter, and other tales from Nigeria, by Harold Courlander with Ezekiel A. Eshugbayi; illus. by Enrico Arno. Harcourt 1968 153p illus $4.50 (4-6)   398.2

    1 Folklore—Nigeria 2 Folklore, Yoruba

    ISBN 0-15-257826-9

"These tales are mostly from the Yoruba people with a few from the Ibos and Hausas. There are stories of Ijapa the tortoise, who in Nigeria plays the role given to Anansi the spider in other African cultures. Many of the tales illustrate proverbs, others are how and why stories. All are beautifully retold with the simplicity of true folk tales which brings out the universality of the themes." Sch Library J

"There is a concluding section of notes on the stories, in some cases, comparing them with similar ones in other cultures. Glossary and pronunciation guide. The pictures strongly convey the spirit of the stories." Pub W

People of the short blue corn; tales and legends of the Hopi Indians; illus. by Enrico Arno. Harcourt 1970 189p illus $6.95 (5-7)   398.2

    1 Hopi Indians—Legends

    ISBN 0-15-26025-8

"These 17 tales and legends of the Hopi Indians reflect the many ways these ancient people met the hardships of desert life. They tell of the creation of the world, of magic and sorcery, of courage and folly." Pub W

"In the general Notes on Hopi Oral Literature, the compiler indicates the background of the Hopi people and their myths, legends, and history. He speaks of certain elements and motifs which recur frequently; foot racing, gambling, sorcery, and Spider Grandmother. . . . Njotes on the Stories accounts for the contents of each individual tale and its relationship to other stories." Horn Bk

    Pronunciation guide and glossary: p185-89

The piece of fire, and other Haitian tales; illus. by Beth and Joe Krush. Harcourt 1964 128p illus $4.95 (4-6)   398.2

    1 Folklore—Haiti

    ISBN 0-15-261610-1

A collection of twenty-six Haitian folk tales, among them "are animal fables; tales of trickery, wisdom, and foolishness; and wildly exaggerated tall tales. An abundance of peasant humor, as well as excellent notes from the author's scholarly research, makes the collection equally valuable for the young reader, the storyteller, and the folklorist." Horn Bk

(ed.) Ride with the sun; an anthology of folk tales and stories from the United Nations; ed. by Harold Courlander for the United Nations Women's Guild; illus. by Roger Duvoisin. McGraw 1955 296p illus $4.95 (4-7)   398.2

    1 Folklore 2 Legends 3 Fairy tales

    ISBN 0-07-065930-3

"A Whittlesey House publication"

"Each of these [60] representative, well-loved tales has been approved by the U.N. delegation of the country it represents. A varied and enjoyable collection." Booklist

Terrapin's pot of sense; illus. by Elton Fax. Holt 1957 125p illus lib. bdg. $3.27 (4-6)   398.2

    1 Folklore, Negro 2 Animals—Stories

    ISBN 0-03-049710-8

"A collection of American Negro folk tales, gathered first hand from the rural areas of Alabama, New Jersey, and Michigan. They include plantation tales and animal and tall tales, and vary in type from moralistic to simple humorous. The dialect has been modified, but speech rhythms and patterns have been preserved. The notes on the stories at the end of the book give origins and sources of different versions of each story and will be of interest to the folklorist and storyteller." Top of the News

The tiger's whisker, and other tales and legends from Asia and the Pacific; illus. by Enrico Arno. Harcourt 1959 152p illus $5.25 (4-6)   398.2

    1 Folklore—Asia 2 Folklore—East (Far East)

    ISBN 0-15-287652-9

Included here are thirty-one tales collected from Korea, Burma, China, India, Kashmir, Japan, Arabia, Persia, Laos, Indonesia, Malaya, Polynesia, and Yap, followed by notes on the stories

The "stories, short, humorous or subtle with meaning, reflect the culture of regions from which it is so often difficult to find storytelling material. Notably lacking in sorcery, supernatural creatures, and magic which are common in European folklore, the tales present human and animal characters as heroes, tricksters, fools or villains. Good for telling and most welcome in library folklore collections. Able line drawings by Enrico Arno add luster to the stories." Library J

Credle, Ellis

Tall tales from the high hills, and other stories; illus. by Richard Bennett. Nelson 1957 156p illus $3.95, lib. bdg. $3.80 (4-7)   398.2

    1 Folklore—U.S.

    ISBN 0-8407-6088-4; 0-8407-6089-2

"Twenty tales gathered from the folk of the Blue Ridge Mountains and handed down from one generation to another. Two of them, about pioneer days, have been written by Miss Credle, but the rest are [retellings]." Ontario Library Rev

"Chiefly they tell of poor farmers and their wives and children in hilarious domestic comedies dealing with animals and agricultural problems. . . . With color in the rich vernacular as well as in the subjects themselves, these tales are superb for telling and reading aloud to groups combining younger and older listeners." Horn Bk

Curry, Jane Louise

Down from the lonely mountain; California Indian tales; retold by Jane Louise Curry; illus. by Enrico Arno. Harcourt 1964 128p illus $5.95 (3-5)   398.2

    1 Indians of North America—Legends 2 Animals—Stories

    ISBN 0-15-224142-6

"A dozen tales, told of the world when it was new and of animals that helped to shape it, present American Indian legends with unusual charm and liveliness. . . . Filled with humor and drama, told with economy, color, and an easy flow, all the stories will serve the storyteller well and will be enjoyed for reading aloud." Horn Bk

Davis, Robert

Padre Porko, the gentlemanly pig; illus. by Fritz Eichenberg. Holiday House 1948 197p illus $3.95 (4-6)   398.2

1 Folklore—Spain 2 Pigs—Stories 3 Animals—Stories

ISBN 0-8234-0085-9

First published 1939

These eleven tales from Spanish folklore tell about the chivalrous pig who uses his wisdom to aid both animals and humans in distress

"Davis has kept the fluency of the voices which told him these stories. He has kept the humor, the emotion of despair, the elation of those who work together, the spiritual and earthy qualities of everyday life. Each of the Padre's rescues is so quietly thrilling that you long for a Spanish grandmother who knows more and more of his tales." Chicago Sun

"An excellent reading aloud book." Wis Library Bul

Davis, Russell

The lion's whiskers; tales of high Africa, by Russell Davis and Brent Ashabranner; with illus. by James G. Teason. Little 1959 191p illus map $4.95 (5-7) 398.2

1 Folklore—Ethiopia

ISBN 0-316-17655-9

"Thirty-one stories from the highlands of East Africa which the authors heard from old village storytellers or school children while in Ethiopia. . . . Interspersed with the tales which are representative of nine major tribes are incidents from the author's personal experiences and observations on the country, its people, their way of life, and their folklore. While the storytelling may not be the most expert the tales are fresh and entertaining and the added information of value." Booklist

Dayrell, Elphinstone

Why the sun and the moon live in the sky; an African folktale; illus. by Blair Lent. Houghton 1968 26p illus $3.75, lib. bdg. $3.40 (k-2)   398.2

1 Folklore—Nigeria 2 Sun—Fiction 3 Moon—Fiction

ISBN 0-395-06741-3; 0-395-06742-1

First told by the author in his book: Folk stories from Southern Nigeria, West Africa, published 1910 in England

"When the Sun and the Moon extended an invitation to Water and his people to visit their earthly home, they underestimated the number of Water's followers and thus were forced to seek a habitation in the sky." Sch Library J

"It was an inspiration to bring [this tale] back with Blair Lent's illustrations, for its fanciful, childlike quality offers marvelous scope for his creative talents. Here are the superb sense of design and color, originality and humor that distinguished his earlier books. . . . Pictures in mustard yellow and brown, blue and green, reflect the whole range of African art but are uniquely the artist's own: they tell the story as though it were acted out by African tribesmen dressed to represent the sun and the moon, the water and its creatures." Book World

De La Iglesia, Maria Elena

The cat and the mouse, and other Spanish tales; with pictures by Joseph Low. Pantheon Bks. 1966 unp illus $3.50, lib. bdg. $4.99 (2-4)   398.2

1 Folklore—Spain 2 Fables

ISBN 0-394-81145-3; 0-394-91145-8

"Short fables and amplifications of proverbs are illustrated with amusing line drawings, some of them washed with color. The stories are typical of the humor and wise sayings of Spain, and the retelling is delightfully direct and unadorned and does not con-

form to vocabulary limits. The youngest readers, attracted by the brevity and intrigued by the pointedness of the stories, are more likely to be delighted than discouraged by occasional unfamiliar but appropriate words." Horn Bk

De La Mare, Walter

(ed.) Animal stories; chosen, arranged, and in some part rewritten by Walter De La Mare. Scribner 1940 lvi, 420p illus $5.95   398.2

1 Folklore 2 Animals—Stories 3 Fairy tales

ISBN 0-684-20797-4

"De La Mare has selected and arranged some forty animal folk tales and as many appropriate rhymes taken from many sources. The stories are for the most part familiar. . . . Taken from Perrault and Grimm and Jacobs and changed very slightly. But a few modern imaginative tales have been included. Illustrations are decorative, three-hundred-year-old woodcuts of animals. The long introduction tracing the history and describing the characteristics of folk literature is of particular interest to teachers and students of children's books." Library J

Tales told again; illus. by Alan Howard. Knopf 1959 [c1927] 207p illus $3, lib. bdg. $5.39 (4-7)   398.2

1 Fairy tales 2 Folklore

ISBN 0-394-81728-1; 0-394-91728-6

First published 1927 with title: Told again. The 1959 edition is a reissue with new illustrations

"It is a practically perfect collection of fairy tales containing 19 beautifully-written modern versions of the world's best known, most popular stories. It is a good-looking book." Pub W

De Regniers, Beatrice Schenk

(ed.) The giant book; drawings by William Lahey Cummings. Atheneum Pubs. 1966 188p illus $4.75, lib. bdg. $4.37 (4-6)   398.2

1 Folklore 2 Giants—Fiction

ISBN 0-689-20077-3; 0-689-20078-1

Stories from the Bible, legends, and fairy tales are included in this collection of tales about giants

"Flavorful retellings [of] . . . tales interspersed with a few less well known and odd bits of giant lore. Black-and-white drawings, while rather static, emphasize the great size of giants." Booklist

Red Riding Hood; retold in verse for boys and girls to read themselves; drawings by Edward Gorey. Atheneum Pubs. 1972 42p illus $5.95 (1-3)   398.2

1 Folklore 2 Wolves—Stories 3 Stories in rhyme

ISBN 0-689-30036-0

For other versions of this story see entries under Little Red Riding Hood, in part 2

Retold in verse, this "is stronger fare than the standard version told to nursery age children. Here, Red Riding Hood suffers the same fate as Grandmother, but is saved by the hunter. . . . The wolf gets his comeuppance and the story ends matter-of-factly without a moral. Fittingly accompanied by Edward Gorey's illustrations (pen-and-ink sketches in gray with red accents) of the wonderfully sly, wicked wolf and the plain little girl, this brisk retelling in simple words will brighten the 'easy reading' shelves." Sch Library J

DeRoin, Nancy

(ed.) Jataka tales; with original drawings by Ellen Lanyon. Houghton 1975 82p illus $5.95 (3-5) 398.2

1 Fables 2 Animals—Stories

ISBN 0-395-20281-7

The author has selected thirty of the Jataka tales, "animal fables attributed to the Buddha. Their morals speak of vices and foibles with varying effectiveness to

DeRoin, Nancy—*Continued*

a reader more used to Aesop's directness. There is sharp irony in the story of a drunken dung beetle who challenges an elephant to a battle and is quickly squelched not by an elephant foot, but a giant dropping. Other stories are more subtly indicative of their Eastern origins. . . . But such differences in flavor shouldn't deter librarians from purchasing this introductory group of tales largely unfamiliar to U.S. audiences . . . Illustrated with brown-and-white drawings which have some awkward angles of perspective but project a feel of age and echo the stories' Indian setting." Booklist

Dobbs, Rose

No room; an old story retold by Rose Dobbs; illus. by Fritz Eichenberg. McKay [1966 c1944] unp illus $3.25, lib. bdg. $3.11 (2-4)   398.2

1 Folklore

ISBN 0-679-20129-7; 0-679-25099-9

A reissue of the title first published 1944 by Coward-McCann

A retelling of the story of the selfish peasant who did not want to share his little house with his daughter and her family, and what happened when he consulted the wise man

"Such a tale is only as old as its latest version and this one is droll enough to please any one—and to inspire some of the most vivacious drawings of that inspired humorist, Fritz Eichenberg." N Y Her Trib Bks

Domanska, Janina

Look, there is a turtle flying; story and pictures by Janina Domanska. Macmillan (N Y) 1968 unp illus $4.95 (k-2)   398.2

1 Fables 2 Turtles—Stories

King Powoj of Poland "is accused of talking too much by his century-old pet turtle, Solon. But it is Solon, in his ambition to fly, who demonstrates that he is the one who talks too much and is made wiser by the discovery." Bk World

"Many countries have variants of this folktale, and here, in one of the most sprightly versions yet, the blithe humor of the text is echoed in the gay and graceful illustrations." Sat Rev

The turnip; story and pictures by Janina Domanska. Macmillan (N Y) 1969 unp illus $5.95, pa $1.25 (k-2)   398.2

1 Folklore—Russia 2 Turnips—Stories

For other versions of this story see entries under Turnip, in Part 2

A retelling of "the familiar Slavic [Russian] folk tale about the monstrously overgrown turnip, which by harvest time requires the tug-of-war line-up of Grandfather, Grandmother, little boy, and all the farm animals to unearth it. Folk-style illustrations, with embroidery motifs in the background, bring color, drama, and humor to the simple, cumulative story." Horn Bk

Du Bois, William Pène

The hare and the tortoise & The tortoise and the hare [by] William Pène du Bois and Lee Po; illus. by William Pène du Bois. Doubleday 1972 48p illus $4.95, lib. bdg. $5.70 (1-4)   398.2

1 Fables 2 Rabbits—Stories 3 Turtles—Stories 4 Bilingual books—Spanish-English

ISBN 0-385-02350-2; 0-385-06778-X

A bilingual picture book in which "alternate pages, divided to accomodate English and Spanish versions

of two stories, are accompanied by full-page illustrations. The first story is based on the familiar [Aesop] fable of how the tortoise beat the hare in a race. . . . The second story, based on oriental folklore, is the story of a hare who outwitted a tortoise when the hare was enticed under sea [in an attempt to obtain his liver for use in curing a wound incurred by the Queen of all Fish]." Horn Bk

"Pène du Bois's lively, good-natured narrative pits a traditionally cocksure hare against an unexpectedly adventurous tortoise. . . . Lee Po reverses the characterizations—the tortoise is sly, the hare guileless. . . . Both stories also appear in good idiomatic Spanish, but with a few regrettable errors that could confuse a reader not thoroughly fluent." N Y Times Bk Rev

Duvoisin, Roger

The three sneezes, and other Swiss tales, written and illus. by Roger Duvoisin. Knopf 1941 244p illus lib. bdg. $5.99 (4-6)   398.2

1 Folklore—Switzerland

ISBN 0-394-91746-4

Thirty-seven tales "made up partly of variants of familiar stories and partly of those that are purely local. Many of the latter are short legends explaining the origin of an unusual mountain, lake, or stream." Library J

"The stories are divided into 'Swiss French Tales' and 'Tales from German Switzerland' [and] all have a hearty peasant flavor. Simple, dramatic and full of humor, they will be welcomed by children and by the story teller. Mr. Duvoisin, who was brought up in Switzerland and heard these tales as a child, has caught their lively humor in his drawings." N Y Times Bk Rev

Map on lining-papers

Elkin, Benjamin

Six foolish fishermen; based on a folktale in Ashton's Chap-books of the eighteenth century, 1882; illus. by Katherine Evans. Childrens Press 1957 unp illus lib. bdg. $3.95 (1-3)   398.2

1 Folklore

ISBN 0-516-03601-7

"In simple fashion for beginning readers . . . [this book] describes how a small boy relieves the bewilderment of six fishing brothers who fear one of their number is lost because each, counting in turn, overlooks himself. Folk-style drawings in full color considerably enhance the humor of the tale and the attractiveness of the book." Horn Bk

Such is the way of the world; illus. by Yoko Mitsuhashi. Parents Mag. Press 1968 unp illus lib. bdg. $4.59 (k-3)   398.2

1 Folklore—Ethiopia

ISBN 0-8193-0348-5

"A retelling of an Ethiopian folktale . . . . Desta, a small boy who is proudly guarding his father's cattle, loses his pet monkey when a dog suddenly barks; the dog's owner gives Desta a game board. The boy trips over a saddle and the board falls into a fire; the owner of the saddle gives Desta a pot. 'Such is the way of the world,' each man says, as the series of gifts and mishaps comes full circle and Desta retrieves his pet at last." Chicago. Children's Bk Center

"The story follows a universally popular pattern, but is enlivened by the exotic appeal of African characters and objects. The colorful, attractively stylized illustrations successfully employ many Ethiopian design motifs." Sch Library J

Elkin, Benjamin—*Continued*

The wisest man in the world; a legend of ancient Israel; retold by Benjamin Elkin; pictures by Anita Lobel. Parents Mag. Press 1968 unp illus $4.95, lib. bdg. $4.59 (1-4) 398.2

1 Legends—Israel 2 Solomon, King of Israel 3 Sheba, Queen of

ISBN 0-8193-0353-4; 0-8193-0354-2

"A folktale of Israel, based on a story about King Solomon and the Queen of Sheba, is amplified and brought to life through picturesque language and colorful full-page pictures. When the Queen comes to test King Solomon's wisdom, he easily answers all her questions but almost fails the last test until he is helped by a bee, whose life he had previously spared." Sch Library J

"Anita Lobel's drawings capture the whimsical character of the riddle-filled legend: nothing gloomy here!" Christian Century

Evans, C. S.

Cinderella; retold by C. S. Evans and illus. by Arthur Rackham. Viking 1972 110p illus $5.95 (3-5) 398.2

1 Fairy tales

ISBN 0-670-22255-0

"A Studio book"

A reissue of the title first published 1919 in England

Here is the fairy tale about the poor, beautiful, but mistreated kitchen maid who wins the heart of the prince with the aid of her fairy godmother. A briefer version of the tale is entered below under Charles Perrault

"C. S. Evans elaborated the old folktale of Cinderella into a miniature novel for older children. . . . The original Rackham silhouette illustrations . . . are still fresh and appealing." Booklist

The sleeping beauty; told by C. S. Evans and illus. by Arthur Rackham. Viking 1972 110p illus $5.95 (3-5) 398.2

1 Fairy tales

ISBN 0-670-65096-X

"A Studio book"

A reissue of the title first published 1920 in England

This is an expanded, novel-length version of the popular fairy tale about the beautiful princess who is put into an enchanted sleep for one hundred years, until the kiss of a prince awakens her. Earlier, briefer versions of the story appear in the collected tales of Charles Perrault and the Brothers Grimm

This edition contains "the black-and-white (mostly) illustrations which Rackham prepared in silhouette fashion for the edition he originally illustrated. It . . . is charming." Best Sellers

Evans, Katherine

The boy who cried wolf; retold by Katherine Evans; illus. by the author. Whitman, A. 1960 unp illus lib. bdg. $3.95 (k-2) 398.2

1 Fables

ISBN 0-8075-0863-2

"A spirited retelling of Aesop's story of the shepherd whom nobody helped when a wolf appeared because he had called 'Wolf! Wolf!' too often in jest. The wisdom of the adage 'A liar will not be believed even when he tells the truth,' comes through beautifully." Bks for Deaf Children

Fairy tales from many lands; illus. by Arthur Rackham. Viking 1974 121p illus. $6.95 (4-6) 398.2

1 Fairy tales 2 Folklore

ISBN 0-670-30562-6

"A Studio book"

A reissue of a book first published 1916 by Lippincott with title: The Allies' fairy book

"Thirteen folk tales told in a traditional way. . . . The florid, formal style of such classics as Joseph Jacobs' 'Jack the Giant-Killer' and Perrault's 'Sleeping Beauty' stand colorfully beside a robust Russian 'Frost,' three spare Japanese tales, and the complexly ethical, haunting Belgian story of 'The Last Adventure of Thyl Ulenspiegel.' These are all complemented in Rackham's masterful, unique manner with numerous black-and-white line drawings and 12 full-color plates." Booklist

"It should be noted . . . that these are original versions of the traditional tales, and contain some gory sequences." Pub W

Feagles, Anita

Autun and the bear; an old Icelandic legend; retold by Anita Feagles; with illus. by Gertrude Barrer-Russell. Young Scott Bks. 1967 unp illus lib. bdg. $4.95 (2-4) 398.2

1 Sagas 2 Northmen

ISBN 0-201-09109-3

"Long before the medieval Icelandic sagas were recorded, they had been handed down by oral tradition. From such an ancient source, the story is told of Autun, a humble farm hand, who crossed the seas to Denmark and Norway and whose forthright honesty earned him the affection of two powerful warring kings. The style of the retelling, like that of the [original] sagas, is bald, simple, and factual; the effect is wonderfully enhanced by the striking three-color illustrations that combine impressionistic beauty with medieval detail." Horn Bk

Felton, Harold W.

Bowleg Bill, seagoing cowpuncher; illus. by William Moyers. Prentice-Hall 1957 174p illus lib. bdg. $4.75 (5-7) 398.2

1 Legends—U.S. 2 Bowleg Bill 3 Sea stories 4 Cowboys—Fiction

ISBN 0-13-080424-X

The author "has, with permission, used ideas and some of the language of Jeremiah Digges' 'Bowleg Bill, the Sea-Going Cowboy' (Viking, 1938). Children . . . will make a place for Bowleg between Pecos Bill and Stormalong. For Bowleg Bill is an eight-foot-tall cowboy from Wyoming who, in logically wacky fashion, finds himself on a succession of deep sea voyages. His adventures grow from ignorance of his new environment and attempts to cope with his surroundings by cowboy methods. And he never fails! But the book's humor lies as much in the telling as in the plots; the phonetic spelling and jargon may make the story hard for children below sixth grade to read themselves, but even young children will enjoy hearing it." Horn Bk

John Henry and his hammer; illus. by Aldren A. Watson. Knopf 1950 82p illus lib bdg. $4.99 (5-7) 398.2

1 Legends—U.S. 2 John Henry 3 Railroads—Fiction

ISBN 0-394-91291-8

"The vigorous tale of the American folk hero, whose magnificent strength and skill with the hammer helped build the country's railroads, is matched by dramatic drawings in black, gray, and white. . . . The book ends with the completion of the Big Bend Tunnel and John Henry's death after his contest with the steam drill." Booklist

"The swing of John Henry's hammer echoes in this rhythmic telling of his mighty deeds. The illustrations and the format add to the book's distinction. This

Felton, Harold W.—*Continued*
version lends itself to the storyteller's art." N Y Pub
Library
"A John Henry ballad": p[83-85]

Mike Fink, best of the keelboatmen. . . . Tastefully
amplified and illus. by Aldren A. Watson. Dodd 1960
159p illus $4.50 (5-7)   398.2
  1 Legends—U.S. 2 Fink, Mike
  ISBN 0-396-04344-5
"Being a revealing and trustworthy account of
events in the life of the renowned riverman, Indian
scout, and relentless enemy of divers and sundry
outlaws. Containing facts, anecdotes, history, legend,
and folk-lore of the unique and justly famed hero;
including his experiences in his inimitable craft, the
Lightfoot. Taken from ancient, original sources by
Harold W. Felton." Title page
"This smooth combination of biography and tall
tales presents the ring-tailed roarer of the Ohio and
Mississippi in his more genial moods—no eye-
gouging, just clean shootings and pranks." N Y Times
Bk Rev
"Told in dialect and illustrated with humorously
exaggerated pictures." Hodges. Bks for Elem Sch
Libraries

New tall tales of Pecos Bill; illus. by William
Moyers. Prentice-Hall 1958 164p illus lib. bdg. $4.95
(5-7)   398.2
  1 Legends—U.S. 2 Pecos Bill 3 Cowboys—
  Fiction
  ISBN 0-13-615849-8
"Admirers of Pecos Bill [the fabulous Texas cow-
puncher] will applaud his daring and skill in these
stories. . . . Such stories as Bill's struggle with the sea
monster Sochdolager, a fight to the finish in which the
State of California was pulled out of shape, or his
leaping the Grand Canyon, demonstrate [his]
astounding courage and vigour. The author tells the
stories with the same nonchalance that typifies his
hero." Ontario Library Rev
"Especially good storytelling material." Horn Bk

Pecos Bill and the mustang; pictures by Leonard
Shortall. Prentice-Hall 1965 unp illus $4.95, pa 95¢
(k-3)   398.2
  1 Legends—U.S. 2 Pecos Bill 3 Cowboys—
  Fiction
  ISBN 0-13-655589-6; 0-13-655597-7
"In short, declarative sentences, Mr. Felton retells
the story of Pecos Bill, how he was lost, his upbringing
by the coyotes, his becoming the first cowboy, and his
taming of the Famous Pacing Mustang of the
Prairies." Sch Library J

Pecos Bill, Texas cowpuncher; illus. by Aldren Auld
Watson. Knopf 1949 177p illus. lib. bdg. $4.99
(5-7)   398.2
  1 Legends—U.S. 2 Pecos Bill 3 Cowboys—
  Fiction
  ISBN 0-394-91487-2
"Using existing material as source material and
adding heretofore unknown facts, the author tells in
an appropriately offhand manner, the life story of the
great legendary cow-puncher. . . . The robust illustrations have a decided western flavor. Contains a comprehensive bibliography of books, articles, poetry,
drama, music, and art in which Pecos Bill is featured."
Booklist

Fenner, Phyllis R.
  (comp.) Giants & witches and a dragon or two; with
illus. by Henry C. Pitz. Knopf 1943 208p illus $3, lib.
bdg. $5.69 (4-6)   398.2

  1 Folklore 2 Fairy tales
  ISBN 0-394-81183-6; 0-394-91183-0
A collection of seventeen stories from various countries involving magical creatures such as the Russian
Baba Yaga, Scandinavian trolls and Welsh giants. "All
in excellent versions, from such sources as Pyle, Mac-
Manus, Lang, and Jacobs. Attractive in title, make-up
and selection." Ontario Library Rev
"Good story-telling material, especially for occasions like Hallowe'en. . . . Some are the familiar tales
you would expect; others are new." Wis Library Bul
"This is one of the best. . . . All made pleasantly
scary with marvelous drawings." Bk Week

  (comp.) Princesses & peasant boys; tales of
enchantment; illus. by Henry C. Pitz. Knopf 1944
188p illus $3, lib. bdg. $4.99 (3-6)   398.2
  1 Folklore 2 Fairy tales
  ISBN 0-394-81521-1; 0-394-91521-6
"Eighteen folk and fairy tales drawn from such
sources as Andersen, Grimm, Andrew Lang, Howard
Pyle, and Seumas MacManus, all variations on the
romantic theme of the poor boy who wins the princess." Wis Library Bul
"A well-selected group of favorite tales." Booklist

Field, Edward
  (ed.) Eskimo songs and stories; collected by Knud
Rasmussen on the Fifth Thule Expedition; selected
and tr. by Edward Field; with illus. by Kiakshuk and
Pudlo. Delacorte Press 1973 102p illus $6.95 (3-7)
                                                         398.2
  1 Folklore, Eskimo 2 Eskimo poetry—collections
  ISBN 0-440-02336-X
"A Merloyd Lawrence book"
"This collection contains 34 brief free-verse translations taken from the Eskimo oral tradition as recorded
in the annals of a historic Arctic expedition during the
1920s." Booklist
"By excellently arranging the poems, the author
moves from stories of creation to tales of sickness, of
death, and of afterlife. Even though constructed on
such universal themes, many of the items may seem
oblique to readers unfamiliar with the customs and
lore of the Eskimo, and the book probably will have to
be introduced and read aloud to children. The bold
stonecuts by two Eskimo artists intensify the legends,
adding a stark beauty to the book." Horn Bk
  Suggested reading: p101-02

Fillmore, Parker
  The laughing prince; a book of Jugoslav fairy tales
and folk tales; with illus. and decorations by Jay Van
Everen. Harcourt 1921 286p illus $3.95 (4-6) 398.2
  1 Folklore—Yugoslavia 2 Fairy tales
  ISBN 0-15-243639-1
"A collection of fourteen stories drawn from Slavic
sources full of imagination, humor and extravagant
adventure, suitable for story-telling and the children's
own reading." Booklist

Finger, Charles
  Tales from silver lands; woodcuts by Paul Honoré.
Doubleday 1924 225p illus $4.95, lib. bdg. $5.70, pa
95¢ (5-7)   398.2
  1 Folklore—South America 2 Indians of South
  America—Legends
  ISBN 0-385-07513-8; 0-385-04815-7; 0-385-
  07929-X
  Awarded the Newbery Medal, 1925
The author "has here transcribed legendary stories
out of South America, based upon tales that he took
down at first hand from the Indians he met in his
wanderings. . . . There are nineteen tales in this book
and all reflect the flavor of the lands of their origin.

Finger, Charles—*Continued*

Mr. Finger's service in gathering them is a valuable one, and in the telling he remains a self-effacing troubadour, never diverting the interest of the reader from his story to himself." N Y Her Trib Bks

"The wood cuts by Paul Honoré are exceedingly fine, and carry an atmosphere of the country." Bookman

Fischer, Hans

Puss in Boots; a fairy tale as told by Hans Fischer; adapted from Charles Perrault, and provided with the appropriate explanations and pictures. Harcourt 1959 unp illus $6.50 (k-2)   398.2

   1 Folklore—France 2 Fairy tales
   ISBN 0-15-264224-2

An adaptation of the French fairy tale about the clever cat who by his wit and daring obtains for his poor master a castle to live in and a princess to marry

"Contrary to fairy-tale tradition by which all things are possible, the author shows, in humorous asides, 'what the story does not tell,' such as how Puss had to learn to wear boots and walk on two legs. However, the freshness and merry tone of the translation and the free, enchanting drawings will attract many readers." Booklist

"Storytellers will want this delightful book for small children on their shelves." Sat Rev

Fisher, Anne B.

Stories California Indians told; illus. by Ruth Robbins. Parnassus Press 1957 109p illus map $4.95, lib. bdg. $4.77 (3-5)   398.2

   1 Indians of North America—Legends
   ISBN 0-87466-026-2; 0-87466-067-X

Twelve "stories telling how the Great Spirit created California; how light, fire and the mountains were made; and how the god Coyote helped the people overcome the hardship of their lives." Hodges. Bks for Elem Sch Libraries

They are "retold with animation and presented in a well-designed, effectively illustrated book." Booklist

Fournier, Catharine

The coconut thieves; adapted by Catharine Fournier, illus. by Janina Domanska. Scribner 1964 unp illus lib. bdg. $5.95 (k-3)   398.2

   1 Folklore—Africa 2 Animals—Stories
   ISBN 0-684-13454-3

This story "tells how Dog and Turtle outwit Leopard, who selfishly thinks he can claim all the coconuts from a coconut grove that does not belong to him anyway." Sat Rev

"Janina Domanska has made very precise pen and ink sketches of the animals against a white background on which fairly small areas of tan or dull green suggest distant scenery. Their faces are fashioned like primitive masks and their coats are stiffly patterned or splashed with tan and green. We have rarely seen illustrations that conveyed better both the fabulous and the human characteristics of animal folk-heroes. A fine book." Bk Week

Gaer, Joseph

The fables of India; illus. by Randy Monk. Little 1955 176p illus $4.95 (5-7)   398.2

   1 Folklore—India 2 Fables
   ISBN 0-316-30153-1

The fables of India which are retold in this book have been selected from three great collections: The Panchatantra, or The book of five headings; The Hitopadesa, or The book of good counsel; The Jatakas, or The book of Buddha's birth stories

"Originally told orally to instruct the young, they are rich in source material for the story-teller in search of animal folklore. They make a fine supplement to the Greek fables of Aesop, the French fables of La Fontaine, and the Indian fairy tales collected by Joseph Jacobs." Sat Rev

   Books to read: p173-76

Gág, Wanda

Gone is gone; or, The story of a man who wanted to do housework; retold and illus. by Wanda Gág. Coward-McCann 1935 unp illus lib. bdg. $3.99 (k-3)   398.2

   1 Folklore—Bohemia
   ISBN 0-698-30179-X

The author retells a humorous folk tale which she heard as a child in Bohemia. "Told in informal conversational style, it follows one catastrophe after another as they happen in the brief space of a morning when a peasant farmer takes over what he calls the 'puttering and pottering' of housework in order that his wife might toil in the fields and learn how hard 'his' work is. The full flavor of the tale is conveyed in the numerous small drawings by the author. Excellent version for use in story-telling." N Y Libraries

Galdone, Paul

Androcles and the lion; adapted and illus. by Paul Galdone. McGraw 1970 unp illus lib. bdg. $4.72 (k-3)   398.2

   1 Fables
   ISBN 0-07-022699-7

In this adaptation of the fable, Androcles, a slave, is rescued from a cruel fate by the very lion to whom he had shown a kindness

"A pagan version [of the legend, which] . . . has a light touch. If there's nothing especially memorable about the writing or the pictures, neither is there anything objectionable, and some would say that a story of simple virtue rewarded still has a place in the world." N Y Times Bk Rev

The gingerbread boy. Seabury 1975 unp illus lib. bdg. $6.95 (k-2)   398.2

   1 Folklore 2 Fairy tales
   ISBN 0-8164-3132-9

   "A Clarion book"

"A lively version of the tale of the gingerbread boy who sprang into action as soon as he was baked and gleefully eluded all would-be captors until he was finally outwitted by a fox. The artist's gingerbread boy is a strong-legged, cocky individual, who sets out on a merry race through the countryside. The action of the tale is well-paced; large, humorous illustrations with stone fences, a covered bridge, and hearty rural folk suggest a New England background, while the triumphant fox is the epitome of all slyness." Horn Bk

Henny Penny; retold and illus. by Paul Galdone. Seabury 1968 unp illus $5.95 (k-2)   398.2

   1 Folklore 2 Chickens—Stories 3 Animals—Stories
   ISBN 0-8164-3022-5

This retelling of the story also known as Chicken Little follows "the animals who set out to take the message of the falling sky to the king. Henny Penny, Cocky Locky, Ducky Lucky, Goosey Loosey and Turkey Lurkey are clearly and individually portrayed with characteristic details and expressive facial features." Sch Library J

"The text differs from the original Jacobs and also from the Flora Annie Steel version, substituting pleasanter names." Horn Bk

Little Red Riding Hood; adapted from the retelling by the Brothers Grimm [by] Paul Galdone. McGraw 1974 unp illus $5.95, lib. bdg. $5.72 (k-2)   398.2

   1 Folklore—Germany 2 Wolves—Stories
   ISBN 0-07-022731-4; 0-07-022732-2

Galdone, Paul—*Continued*

Illustrated by the adapter, this is a retelling of the German folk tale about a little girl and her unfortunate meeting with a wolf as she goes through the woods to visit her sick grandmother

"The telling is dramatic, and the lively illustrations star the wolf with his many expressions and poses. While there are almost as many versions of this tale as there are story tellers, Paul Galdone has given us another needed book suitable for pre-school story hours." Children's Bk Rev Serv

The monkey and the crocodile; a Jataka tale from India. Seabury 1969 unp illus $6.95 (k-2) 398.2

1 Folklore—India 2 Fables 3 Monkeys—Stories 4 Crocodiles—Stories

ISBN 0-8164-3044-6

"A Clarion book"

Illustrated by Galdone, this is a retelling of one of the Jataka fables about Buddha in his animal incarnations. "The crocodile wants a meal of monkey, but the intended prey is far wilier than his antagonist. When the monkey eludes the crocodile one more time, by telling him to open his mouth (which means that he must close his eyes), the monkey leaps on to his head, and from there to the river bank, his tree, and safety." Sch Library J

The story "has the humor, plot, and movement to make it a good book for any young child, even one unused to stories; the brilliant colors, clear pictures, and brief text should make it very successful for sharing with groups of children." Horn Bk

Three Aesop fox fables. Seabury 1971 unp illus $6.95 (k-3) 398.2

1 Fables 2 Foxes—Stories

ISBN 0-8164-3070-5

In two of the three fables retold and illustrated by Galdone: The fox and the grapes and The fox and stork, the fox is outsmarted. In The fox and the crow, however the fox's cunning triumphs

"Paul Galdone's bright-eyed fox is the quintessence of merry cunning. . . . The pictures, full of movement and humor, are especially good for showing to a group because of the large animal figures and simple composition." Sat Rev

The three Billy Goats Gruff. Seabury 1973 unp illus $6.95 (k-1) 398.2

1 Folklore—Norway 2 Goats—Stories

ISBN 0-8164-3080-2

In this retelling of the old Norwegian folk tale, "the goats flummox the wicked troll and send him over the rickety bridge to a watery grave." Pub W

"Galdone's illustrations are in his usual bold, clear style. The three Billy Goats Gruff are expressively drawn, and the troll looks appropriately ferocious and ugly. The large, lively, double-page spreads are sure to win a responsive audience at story hour; however, storytellers may prefer the version illustrated by Marcia Brown [entered above under Asbjornsen] as the text is written in more colorful language." Sch Library J

The three little pigs. Seabury 1970 unp illus $5.95 (k-2) 398.2

1 Folklore—Great Britain 2 Pigs—Stories 3 Wolves—Stories

ISBN 0-8164-3071-3

A retelling of the classic English folktale about two little pigs whose poorly built houses are inadequate to protect them from a hungry wolf and their brother whose sturdily constructed brick house enables him to survive and triumph over the wolf

"The illustrator has adapted Joseph Jacobs' well-loved version of the tale and brought it to life in vibrant line-and-watercolor drawings. . . . Small touches—the framed illustrations of each pig building his house, the portraits of Mama and his two brothers on the third little pig's wall, and the four-leaf clovers hidden on the dust jacket and in the end papers—help make for a balanced, sunnily attractive picture book." Horn Bk

The town mouse and the country mouse. McGraw [1971] unp illus $5.95, lib. bdg. $5.72 (k-2) 398.2

1 Fables 2 Mice—Stories

ISBN 0-07-022694-6; 0-07-022695-4

This version, adapted and illustrated by Paul Galdone, is based on the one found in Select fables of Esop and other fabulists published 1764 in England.

On a visit to the city mouse, the country mouse learns that luxury and abundant food cannot compensate for the unfamiliar dangers he finds in the city. He returns, once again content, to his plain but cozy cottage

"Through his superb full-color paintings, Galdone portrays the contrast between quiet country life and gay but precarious city life. Double-spreads of the green-eyed cat with fangs exposed, the yapping, snapping dog, and the appealing characterizations of the mice will delight young readers and listeners." Sch Library J

Garner, Alan

(ed.) A cavalcade of goblins; illus. by Krystyna Turska. Walck, H.Z. 1969 227p illus $8.50 (4-7) 398.2

1 Folklore 2 Fairies

ISBN 0-8098-2407-8

Published in England with title: The Hamish Hamilton Book of goblins

A "selection of traditional tales about goblins and other awesome creatures together with some eerie poems, old and new, and historic anecdotes recording personal encounters with the supernatural. Drawn from the folklore of the North American Indians and from that of the British Isles, Japan, Norway, India, and other parts of the world." Booklist

"Some stories appear in their original form while others have been freely adapted; all move very quickly and sustain the mood. . . . Skillful black line drawings intensify the drama." Sch Library J

Notes and sources: p222-26

Gerson, Mary-Joan

Why the sky is far away; a folktale from Nigeria; retold by Mary-Joan Gerson; illus. by Hope Meryman. Harcourt 1974 unp illus $4.95 (1-3) 398.2

1 Folklore—Nigeria

ISBN 0-15-296310-3

"Vigorous woodcuts in black and bright blue, accented by white, add excitement to a compelling fantasy. African legend has it that the sky, long ago, was close to the earth and that it provided all the food humans needed. One had only to reach up and break off a piece of blue that tasted sometimes like stew or corn, sometimes like delectable pineapple. But the sky grew angry when people began wasting his bounty, taking more than they needed and creating garbage. Thus it was that the sky moved far out of reach and man was forced to plant and reap, to work for his daily bread." Pub W

Gillham, Charles E.

Beyond the Clapping Mountains; Eskimo stories from Alaska; illus. by Chanimun. Macmillan (N Y) 1943 134p illus $4.95 (3-6) 398.2

1 Folklore, Eskimo 2 Animals—Stories

This volume includes thirteen "animal folk tales, illustrated by an Eskimo girl and written by a United

Gillham, Charles E.—*Continued*
States government biologist who heard the stories
from the Eskimos of Alaska. These Eskimos, it seems,
used to believe that the wild creatures were people
who like to dress up to look like animals or birds. The
tales of Miss Mink (a dainty lady wearing a mink
parka), of Mr. Crow, Miss Emperor Goose, and the
others, are therefore very human; they are also funny
with a humor which might be called a cross between
that of the 'Just So Stories' and of Thurber's animal
fables." New Yorker

Ginsburg, Mirra
How the sun was brought back to the sky; adapted
from a Slovenian folk tale; pictures by Jose Aruego
and Ariane Dewey. Macmillan Pub. Co. 1975 unp
illus $6.95 (k-2)   398.2
    1 Folklore, Slovenian 2 Sun—Fiction
    ISBN 0-02-735750-3
"Several chicks and friends (a snail, a duck, a rabbit
and other animals) ascend to the heavens to learn why
the sun has disappeared. They find the sun ashamed
to be seen, for clouds have dirtied its countenance and
made the great star irritable. So the little band of
helpers sets to work to take away all the smudges and
coax the sun to shine again." Pub W
"Brilliant, full-color pictures outlined in pen and
ink and executed in the artists' characteristically lux-
uriant color, are the compelling feature of a slight but
appealing cumulative picture-story. The simple saga
. . . is more universal than Slovenian." Horn Bk

(ed.) The Kaha bird; tales from the steppes of Cent-
ral Asia; tr. and ed. by Mirra Ginsburg; drawings by
Richard Cuffari. Crown 1971 159p illus $4.95 (4-6)
    398.2
    1 Folklore—Asia, Central 2 Folklore—Siberia
    ISBN 0-517-50264-X
"These nineteen stories come from twelve separate
tribes or cultures of southern Siberia and Central
Asia—lands of khans, beys, and yurt-dwellers." Horn
Bk
"Some of the tales are heroic, some earthy, some
explanatory . . . and many have a robust, sly peasant
humor. The style of the retelling is smooth and flavorful, so that the book is as useful and enjoyable for
reading aloud as it is for storytelling." Chicago. Children's Bk Center
    Map on lining-papers

(ed.) The lazies; tales of the peoples of Russia; tr.
and ed. by Mirra Ginsburg; illus. by Marian Parry.
Macmillan Pub. Co. 1973 70p illus $4.95 (3-5) 398.2
    1 Folklore—Russia
"Fifteen variations on the theme of laziness have
been culled from the folklore of the U.S.S.R. . . . That
indolence is not limited to the rich, to the poor, or to
human beings is revealed in the selections, which
include talking-beast tales, drolls, and fables as well as
stories of princesses and peasants." Horn Bk
"The retellings are brisk, sprightly and complemented by amusing black-and-white line drawings." Sch Library J

(comp.) One trick too many; fox stories from Russia;
tr. by Mirra Ginsburg; pictures by Helen Siegl. Dial
Press 1973 39p illus $5.95, lib. bdg. $5.47 (1-3)
    398.2
    1 Folklore—Russia 2 Foxes—Stories
    ISBN 0-8037-6670-X; 0-8037-6671-8
This collection includes nine Russian fox stories
"derived from both European and Asiatic sources.
The style is bright and succinct, and the cunning of
the fox is evident in all of the tales as he succeeds in
outwitting the peasants and the other animals.

Although sometimes, as in the stories of 'The Red Fox
and the Walking Stick' and 'The Fox and the Quail,' he
attempts one trick too many and loses out altogether.
Full-page woodcuts in handsome shades—
predominately red and yellow—give lively expression
to each tale." Horn Bk

The proud maiden, Tungak, and the Sun; a Russian
Eskimo tale; retold by Mirra Ginsburg; illus. by Igor
Galanin. Macmillan Pub. Co. 1974 31p illus lib. bdg.
$4.95 (1-3)   398.2
    1 Folklore—Russia 2 Folklore, Eskimo
    ISBN 0-02-736260-4
A retelling of A Russian Eskimo folk tale which
illustrates the cycle of arctic days and nights. Tungak,
the evil spirit, is destroyed and the proud maiden
finds happiness in her marriage to the Sun
"A sense of remoteness is vividly conveyed in full-
page and doublespread illustrations, whose blues and
whites suggest the arctic chill. Although a slightly
stylized treatment is given to all the figures, only
Tungak has a frightening mask for a face." Horn Bk

Godden, Rumer
The old woman who lived in a vinegar bottle; illus.
by Mairi Hedderwick. Viking 1972 unp illus lib. bdg.
$4.95, pa $1.50 (k-3)   398.2
    1 Folklore—Great Britain
    ISBN 0-670-52318-6; 0-670-05087-3
    Text copyright 1970
A retelling of an English "folk tale about a woman
who saves the life of a magic fish. The fish promises to
grant the old woman whatever she wants, but she
becomes so greedy and ungrateful that she eventually
loses everything. Longer and more fully developed
than the similar 'The fisherman and his wife' by the
Brothers Grimm." Booklist
"Illustrated with soft, fresh pictures that have a
sprightly combination of sophisticated detail and
bucolic charm. The tale is told with grace in a fluid
prose that is a pleasure to read aloud." Sat R

Graham, Gail B.
The beggar in the blanket, & other Vietnamese
tales; retold by Gail B. Graham; illus. by Brigitte
Bryan. Dial Press 1970 95p illus $4.95, lib. bdg. $4.58
(2-5)   398.2
    1 Folklore—Vietnam 2 Fairy tales
    ISBN 0-8037-0663-4; 0-8037-0664-2
"Though drawn from a common folk literature, this
book and the one by VoDinh, [entered below] differ
in style and flavor. The present collection contains
eight romantic fairy tales of love and devotion
selected from French sources in Vietnam, gracefully
retold and harmoniously illustrated with lovely black-
and-white drawings. . . . [Most of] the stories extol
patience and resignation in the face of adversity and
are imbued with a pensive, melancholy air. Four of
the stories relate the sufferings of husbands and wives
separated by war or some other catastrophe and one is
a Vietnamese Cinderella story." Booklist

Green, Kathleen
Leprechaun tales; illus. by Victoria de Larrea. Lippincott 1968 127p illus $4.50, lib. bdg. $3.39 (3-5)
    398.2
    1 Folklore—Ireland 2 Fairy tales
    ISBN 0-397-31025-0; 0-397-31026-9
"These flawless tales have been created by a
storyteller blessed with a gift for rich, fresh invention
and a style to match it in flavor and humor. Cut to the
patterns of ancient lore, these purely Irish creations
introduce the cobbler-leprechauns, banshees,
pookas, and human beings whose foolish ambitions

Green, Kathleen—*Continued*

and searches for cures are answered by magic spells and counter spells." Horn Bk

Greene, Ellin

(comp.) Clever cooks; a concoction of stories, charms, recipes and riddles; illus. by Trina Schart Hyman. Lothrop 1973 154p illus $5.95, lib. bdg. $5.11 (3-6) 398.2

1 Folklore 2 Cookery

ISBN 0-688-41519-9; 0-688-51519-3

This collection of folk and fairy tales involving clever cooks and food is interspersed with charms, riddles and recipes for items such as butter cookies, cherry dumplings, marzipan, roast chicken, pancakes, pumpkin pie and hearty soup

"The pen-and-ink illustrations are crisp and lively, and the collection—the only one with this theme—makes a good addition to the folk lore shelf." Sch Library J

Grimm, Jacob

About wise men and simpletons; twelve tales from Grimm; tr. by Elizabeth Shub; etchings by Nonny Hogrogian. Macmillan (N Y) 1971 118p illus $5.95 (3-6) 398.2

1 Folklore—Germany 2 Fairy tales

"Newly translated from the first edition [with one exception] of the Grimms' stories, this collection includes such favorites as 'Hansel and Gretel,' 'The Bremen Town Musicians,' and 'Rumpelstiltskin.' The versions are brief, less ornamented than they are in familiar versions, and chosen because, Elizabeth Shub says in her preface, 'here, even more than in later editions, the storyteller's voice is omnipresent.'" Sutherland. The Best in Children's Bks

"The translator has presented three short narratives under the heading of 'About Elves' and four more under the heading of 'About Simpletons,' so that she has really translated [seventeen stories]." Horn Bk

"Nonny Hogrogian's etchings, spare and deft, are beautifully appropriate for the ingenuous simplicity of the writing." Sat Rev

The Bremen town musicians; from the collection of the Brothers Grimm; Paul Galdone drew the pictures. McGraw 1968 32p illus lib. bdg. $4.72 (k-3) 398.2

1 Folklore—Germany 2 Animals—Stories

ISBN 0-07-022705-5

For other versions of this story see entries under Bremen town musicians, in Part 2

"With new warm rhythmic illustrations Paul Galdone revives Grimm's tale of the four lonely old animals, about to be done away with, who, for a place to live, rout some robbers from their den. The illustrations of the ass, dog, cat, and cock have form, body and substance as they plod on their way or relax near a tree. The eyes of the robbers and the animals are unusually expressive. Excellent for story telling." Bruno. Bks for Sch Libraries, 1968

The complete Grimm's Fairy tales; introduction by Padraic Colum; folkloristic commentary by Joseph Campbell; 212 illustrations by Josef Scharl. Pantheon Bks. [1974 c1972] 863p illus $12.95 (4-7) 398.2

1 Folklore—Germany 2 Fairy tales

ISBN 0-394-49415-6

A reissue of the edition first published 1944 with title: Grimm's Fairy tales. Copyright renewed 1972

"The text of this edition is based on the translation of Margaret Hunt. It has been thoroughly revised, corrected and completed by James Stern." Verso of Title Page.

"A standard edition of the collected household tales. A discussion of folk literature, with examples from the Grimm's stories, adds to the value of the book." Chicago. Children's Bk Center

This "complete, and lovely Grimm should be in every school, that the teacher may learn anew the magic art of story-telling." Cath World

One tale in this collection: The Jew among thorns, might be considered anti-Semitic in tone

The four clever brothers; a story by the Brothers Grimm; with pictures by Felix Hoffmann. Harcourt 1967 unp illus $6.95 (k-3) 398.2

1 Folklore—Germany 2 Fairy tales

ISBN 0-15-229100-8

German language edition of this version originally published 1966 in Switzerland

"Four brothers, sent into the world by a poor father, learn four separate trades to rescue the King's daughter, they pool their skills (stargazer, thief, hunter, and tailor) and outwit the dragon. Unable to agree on the traditional award, the hand of the princess, the four brothers gallantly agree to accept a fourth of the kingdom each." Sutherland. The Best in Children's Bks

"It's a wise and humorous tale and Hoffmann's portrayal of the brothers is wonderfully sly and full of wit. His colors are magnificent and beautifully reproduced—rich blue of sky, changing greens of grass, tree, sea and fearful dragon, with accents of gold and red." Bk World

The goose girl; a new translation illus. by Marguerite de Angeli. Doubleday 1964 31p illus lib. bdg. $4.95 (2-4) 398.2

1 Folklore—Germany 2 Fairy tales

ISBN 0-385-05148-4

This is "the Grimms' tale about the princess who tended the geese while the serving maid who betrayed her married the prince." Booklist

"Lovely picture book with many full-color illustrations and a few pencil sketches done in the typical manner of the artist. The translation [by De Angeli] adheres to the usually accepted ones of this popular fairy tale. This will be useful in introducing younger children to the world of Grimm." Sch Library J

Grimms' Fairy tales, by the Brothers Grimm; tr. by Mrs. E. V. Lucas, Lucy Crane and Marian Edwardes; illus. by Fritz Kredel. Grosset 1945 373p illus $3.95 (4-6) 398.2

1 Folklore—Germany 2 Fairy tales

ISBN 0-448-05809-X

"Illustrated junior library"

The volume contains fifty-five of the well loved tales illustrated in color and black and white

Grimm's Fairy tales; twenty stories; illus. by Arthur Rackham. Viking 1973 127p illus $6.95 (3-6) 398.2

1 Folklore—Germany 2 Fairy tales

ISBN 0-670-35532-1

"A Studio book"

A collection of "20 familiar stories illustrated by Rackham from the out-of-print 1909 Constable edition of Grimm's fairy tales. The selections keep their original form, and the sometimes harsh opposition of good and evil is faithfully left unsoftened." Booklist

"The illustrations include some full-color plates, some black and white drawings, some silhouettes. More romantic and conventional than Sendak's interpretation [in The juniper tree, and other tales from Grimm, entered below], Rackham's pictures have a beauty and—in some pictures—a vigor that are perennially delectable." Chicago. Children's Bk Center

Grimm, Jacob—*Continued*

Hansel and Gretel; story by the Brothers Grimm; illus by Arnold Lobel. Delacorte Press 1971 37p illus $5.95, lib. bdg. $5.47 (1-3)   398.2

1 Folklore—Germany 2 Fairy tales
ISBN 0-440-03465-5; 0-440-03466-3

First published 1970 in England. Text copyright by Kathleen Lines

This is a retelling of the traditional German tale about two children who are captured by a wicked witch when they become lost in the forest

"In moss green or ocher washed drawings, the illustrator . . . captures the element of intuitive mystery in the story without over-emphasizing the possible element of horror: The pictures of the children listening in the loft to their stepmother's plan to get rid of them, of the finding of the witch's little house in the deep forest, of the fattening of the children for the witch's feast, and of the final destruction of the witch herself are skillfully controlled and successfully lead to the protection and warmth of the reunion scene between father and children. A quiet, completely effective interpretation." Horn Bk

The house in the wood, and other fairy stories; with drawings by L. Leslie Brooke. Warne 1944 141p illus $3.50 (3-5)   398.2

1 Folklore—Germany 2 Fairy tales
ISBN 0-72232-0559-0

This collection of ten fairy tales was first published 1909

"Many cheerful illustrations and clear type make this an attractive book for young children's own reading." Four to Fourteen

Household stories; from the collection of the Bros. Grimm. Tr. from the German by Lucy Crane, and done into pictures by Walter Crane. illus (4-6)   398.2

1 Folklore—Germany 2 Fairy tales
Some editions are:
Dover pa $2.50 (ISBN 0-486-21080-4)
Smith, P. $4.75 (ISBN 0-8446-2167-6)

This collection of over fifty fairy tales "is an unabridged republication of the work first published by Macmillan and Company in 1886." Verso of title page

It "preserves the flavor of the original and is illustrated by a famous nineteenth-century artist." Hodges. Bks for Elem Sch Libraries

The juniper tree, and other tales from Grimm; selected by Lore Segal and Maurice Sendak. Tr. by Lore Segal; with four tales tr. by Randall Jarrell; pictures by Maurice Sendak. Farrar, Straus 1973 2v (332p) boxed set $15 (4-7)   398.2

1 Folklore—Germany 2 Fairy tales
ISBN 0-374-18057-1

"Through 27 selections, Segal and Sendak brilliantly expose the underside of Grimms' fairy tale world. The happily-ever-after tinkering re-tellers will gasp at some of the grizzly goings-on—a stepmother slices and stews her son for dinner in the title story. . . . However, the collection, which contains many unfamiliar tales, is not monotonously morbid. Peasants still marry princes; simpletons find success and fame; and devils get their due. . . . The translations, smooth and chatty, echo the tales' oral origins, but it is the artwork which is unforgettable. The superbly detailed pen-and-ink drawings are reminiscent of German woodcuts. . . . Sendak pictures his people in provocative poses—viewers eavesdrop on a startled and semi-nude couple; the devil's grandmother cradles sleeping Satan in a mock Pietà. . . . Although not for the timid, this is a truly towering achievement in good book-making for children." Sch Library J

King Thrushbeard; a story by the Brothers Grimm; with pictures by Felix Hoffmann. Harcourt 1970 unp illus $5.95 (1-3)   398.2

1 Folklore—Germany 2 Fairy tales
ISBN 0-15-242940-9

German language edition of this version originally published 1969 in Switzerland

"A beautiful and haughty princess mocks the suitors presented to her, so her father forces her to marry the first vagabond who comes to the palace door. Once she has been systematically humbled by being made to live as a peasant wife and kitchen servant, her husband reveals himself as King Thrushbeard, one of the noble suitors she formerly disdained." N Y Times Bk Rev

"The elegance of the storytelling is matched by the handsome illustrations with their subtle color, strong perpendicular lines, and emphasis on pattern and design." Horn Bk

Little Red Riding Hood; a story by the Brothers Grimm; with pictures by Harriet Pincus. Harcourt 1968 unp illus $5.95 (k-3)   398.2

1 Folklore—Germany 2 Fairy tales
ISBN 0-15-247132-4

"A humorously stocky, pudding-faced Little Red Riding Hood comes to her encounter with the wolf via the usual forest route carrying her basket of cakes and honey. At Grandmother's house she is eaten in one gulp, the text reports, by the wolf who has just dispatched her grandmother in the same way. In the end, a passing huntsman slits open the wolf to release the still-spry prisoners and kills the beast. . . . The retelling is longer and more robust than that of 'The Renowned history of Little Red Riding-Hood' [entered below under title]." Booklist

"The captivating illustrations for this old tale are filled with droll humor. . . . The delicate blending of soft color gives the effect of textural variety." Sch Library J

More Tales from Grimm; freely tr. and illus. by Wanda Gág. Coward-McCann & Geoghegan 1947 257p illus $6.95 (4-6)   398.2

1 Folklore—Germany 2 Fairy tales
ISBN 0-698-20093-4

A collection of 32 tales from Grimm including many lesser-known tales "presented with this author's fresh and zestful interpretation, freely translated yet retaining the essence of the original tales. This is the book which Wanda Gág was working on at the time of her death. Although the translation of the text was ready for the press, the drawings were in varying stages of completeness. . . . Many of the drawings which existed only in their preliminary stages have been included without any retouching or correction." Booklist

The pictures are "drawn with humor and charm. Finely made, the book is a pleasure to hold in the hand and a joy to read." Horn Bk

Rapunzel; a story by the Brothers Grimm; with pictures by Felix Hoffmann. Harcourt 1961 [c1960] unp illus $5.50 (1-4)   398.2

1 Folklore—Germany 2 Fairy tales
ISBN 0-15-265656-1

German language edition of this version originally published 1949 in Switzerland. This translation first published 1960 in England

The classic folk tale of a beautiful girl named Rapunzel, held prisoner at the top of a high tower by a witch, and how by means of her long golden hair, a prince was able to rescue her

The artist's lithographs "are often beautiful; they combine clarity of line and colouring with a romantic strangeness, a sense of distance and time. . . . But Mr.

Grimm, Jacob—*Continued*
Hoffmann also responds to what is harsh and cruel."
Times (London) Literary Sup

Rumpelstiltskin, by the Brothers Grimm; pictures
by Jacqueline Ayer. Harcourt 1967 unp illus $5.95
(k-3)   398.2
1 Folklore—Germany 2 Fairy tales
ISBN 0-15-269525-7
A story "about the miller's daughter whom the king
ordered to spin gold out of straw. The girl never could
have managed without help from a little man to whom
she promised to relinquish her first child after she
became queen unless she could guess his name." Bk
World
The tale "is freshly conceived in a 15th-century
castle setting. . . . The text follows closely Lucy
Crane's 1886 translation from the German, recast at
times in more simple and direct language. Imaginative use of color, striking costume designs, and a
smooth prose style make this an appealing edition."
Library J

Rumpelstiltskin; a story from the Brothers Grimm;
illus. by William Stobbs. Walck, H.Z. [1971 c1970]
30p illus $4.95 (k-3)   398.2
1 Folklore—Germany 2 Fairy tales
ISBN 0-8098-1181-2
Another version of the title entered above

The seven ravens; a story by the Brothers Grimm;
with pictures by Felix Hoffman. Harcourt 1963 unp
illus $6.95 (k-3)   398.2
1 Folklore—Germany 2 Fairy tales
ISBN 0-15-272920-8
German language edition of this version first published 1962 in Switzerland
"The tale of a man whose impatient curse changed
his seven boys into ravens. Their little sister, who had
been the unwitting cause of their misfortune, traveled
a weary way to break the spell." America
"A delightfully illustrated version of an old favorite;
the pictures are invariably lovely, but have variety in
their mood and execution, some of the illustrations of
the ravens being strong and bold while those of the ice
palace and the walk to the end of the world have a
charming fragility." Chicago. Children's Bk Center

The shoemaker and the elves, by the Brothers
Grimm; illus by Adrienne Adams. Scribner 1960 unp
illus. lib. bdg. $5.95, pa 95¢ (k-3)   398.2
1 Folklore—Germany 2 Fairy tales
ISBN 0-684-12982-5; 0-684-12634-6
"The tale of the kind shoemaker and the elves who
helped him is presented in a smooth translation."
Hodges. Bks for Elem Sch Libraries
"The pastel drawings, set in Tudor times, capture
exactly the spirit of the story, and add detail and
depth." Christian Sci Monitor

Snow White and Rose Red [by] the Brothers
Grimm; illus. by Adrienne Adams. Scribner 1964 unp
illus lib. bdg. $5.95 (1-3)   398.2
1 Folklore—Germany 2 Fairy tales
ISBN 0-684-20717-6
Here is the "tale of the two sisters, the kind brown
bear who is a prince under a wicked enchantment, and
the ungrateful dwarf, illustrated in delicate colors
with charm and significant detail." Children's Bks,
1964

Snow White and the seven dwarfs; freely tr. and
illus. by Wanda Gág. Coward-McCann 1938 43p illus
lib. bdg. $3.99 (1-4)   398.2
1 Folklore—Germany 2 Fairy tales
ISBN 0-698-30320-2
The beloved story of the little princess who wandered into the home of the seven dwarfs and of how

she eluded the schemes of her wicked step-mother,
bent on destroying her
Miss Gág "has gone to the German for her text and
with her own inimitable drawings, and a translation
faithful to the original, has kept the spirit and the
beauty of the tale." Wis Library Bul

Snow-White and the seven dwarfs; a tale from the
Brothers Grimm; tr. by Randall Jarrell; pictures by
Nancy Ekholm Burkert. Farrar, Straus 1972 unp illus
$5.95 (k-3)   398.2
1 Folklore—Germany 2 Fairy tales
ISBN 0-374-37099-0
"In a large picture book of beauty and distinction,
the traditional fairy tale is given a setting of noteworthy stature. All but one of the illustrations—
medieval in tone, mood, and detail—cover two-page
spreads. . . . Richly detailed medieval motifs are used
to decorate the end papers and the illustrations, and
the colors used throughout have both clarity and
depth. The text is true to its Germanic sources; and
the end is not softened." Horn Bk

Tales from Grimm; freely tr. and illus. by Wanda
Gág. Coward-McCann 1936 237p illus $6.95 (4-6)
                                                                  398.2
1 Folklore—Germany 2 Fairy tales
ISBN 0-698-20139-6
"Sixteen of the Grimm fairy and household tales
ranging from the familiar Cinderella, Rapunzel, and
The fisherman and his wife, to the less known Six
servants . . . and Lean Liesl and Lanky Lenz." N Y
Libraries
"Miss Gág has made a thoroughly satisfying book,
and one that children will at once feel belongs to
them. In her translations and in her drawings Miss
Gág has caught the essence of the folktale, its drama,
its wonder, its humor, its joy, and with a fine freshness and zest she is bringing these qualities to boys
and girls." N Y Times Bk Rev
Includes glossary

Three gay tales from Grimm; freely tr. and illus. by
Wanda Gág. Coward-McCann 1943 63p illus lib. bdg.
$3.49 (2-5)   398.2
1 Folklore—Germany 2 Fairy tales
ISBN 0-698-30366-0
"For this entertaining little book, Wanda Gág has
selected three lesser known tales and with her lively
translation has made them far more readable than
most tales from the Brothers Grimm seem to us
today." Bk Week
The "black and white drawings, scattered through
the pages of this square book, match the gay absurdity
of the text." Bookmark

Tom Thumb; the story by the Brothers Grimm;
with pictures by Felix Hoffmann. Atheneum Pubs.
1973 unp illus $7.95 (k-3)   398.2
1 Folklore—Germany 2 Fairy tales
ISBN 0-689-30318-1
"A Margaret K. McElderry book"
German language edition of this version first published 1972 in Switzerland
"Tom, the wish-fulfillment child of poor farmers, is
tiny in size but large in cunning. He persuades his
parents to sell him to two sharpies who plan to feature
him in a sideshow. He has his own plans for outwitting
his owners and they are successful, as are his other
schemes for getting the best of other adversaries and
incidentally getting rich." Pub W
"The illustrator's animals are sturdily lifelike, his
rustic characters full of spirit, his panoramas and
treatment of changing light masterful. Children will
be captivated by the invention of window-like views
of Tom inside his captors." Horn Bk

Grimm, Jacob—*Continued*
The traveling musicians; a story by the Brothers
Grimm; with drawings by Hans Fischer. Harcourt
1955 unp illus $6.50 (k-3)   398.2
1 Folklore—Germany 2 Animals—Stories
ISBN 0-15-232183-7
German language edition of this version first published 1944 in Switzerland
For other versions of this story see entries under
Bremen town musicians, in Part 2
This is the folk tale of four clever beasts, a donkey, a
hound, a cat, and a rooster who took to the road to seek
their fortunes as musicians until an encounter with
robbers changed their plans
"Hans Fischer here gives us a book lively in form
and color, witty, free and jolly—altogether a work of
art." N Y Times Bk Rev

The wolf and the seven little kids; a story by the
Brothers Grimm; with pictures by Felix Hoffmann.
Harcourt 1959 unp illus $6.95 (k-3)   398.2
1 Folklore—Germany 2 Goats—Stories 3 Wolves—
Stories
ISBN 0-15-299108-5
This translation first published 1958 in England
The tale of a clever mother goat who, assisted by the
youngest of her seven little kids, recovers the other six
from the wolf
"A distinguished picture book by a noted Swiss
artist. Interpreting the beloved folk tale with just the
right blend of fantasy and realism, the beautiful
lithographs are strong and simple in line and
restrained in color. A pure delight for young children." Booklist

Gunterman, Bertha L.
(ed.) Castles in Spain, and other enchantments;
Spanish legends and romances. Comp. and ed. by
Bertha L. Gunterman; illus. by Mahlon Blaine.
McKay [1968 c1956] 261p illus $4.95 (4-6)   398.2
1 Folklore—Spain 2 Legends—Spain
ISBN 0-679-20035-5
A reissue of a book first published 1928 by Long-
mans. Copyright renewed 1956
"Here are collected a group of [sixteen] interesting
legends. The material is original and striking, and the
Spanish atmosphere and feeling most successfully
maintained throughout the book without any undue
straining toward ultra-exotic language." Nation [1928]

Haley, Gail E.
A story, a story; an African tale retold and illus. by
Gail E. Haley. Atheneum Pubs. 1970 unp illus $5.95,
lib. bdg. $7.29 (k-3)   398.2
1 Folklore—Africa 2 Spiders—Stories
ISBN 0-689-20510-4; 0-689-20511-2
Awarded the Caldecott Medal, 1970
"The story explains the origin of that favorite African folk material, the spider tale. Here Ananse, the
old spider man, wanting to buy the Sky God's stories,
completes by his cleverness three seemingly impossible tasks set as the price for the golden box of stories
which he takes back to earth." Sutherland. The Best in
Children's Bks
"The magnificent, big woodcut illustrations in rich,
bold colors and the poetic text . . . combine to make a
truly distinguished version of an ancient African tale."
Commonweal

Hardendorff, Jeanne B.
The little cock; story and illus. by Joseph Domjan;
retold by Jeanne B. Hardendorff. Lippincott 1969
unp illus $4.95 (1-4)   398.2
1 Folklore—Hungary 2 Roosters—Stories

ISBN 0-397-31084-6
In this Hungarian folktale a little cock finds a
diamond half penny which is taken from him by a
selfish Turkish Emperor. The cock wants the diamond
piece for his mistress—a poor Hungarian peasant—so
following the Emperor to court he employs all his
wiles toward its retrieval
"Mr. Domjan's illustrations . . . are so rich and
dazzling, they threaten to overpower the simple folk
tale." Pub W

The Hare and the tortoise; pictures by Paul Galdone.
McGraw 1962 unp illus lib. bdg. $4.72 (k-3)
                                              398.2
1 Fables 2 Turtles—Stories 3 Rabbits—Stories
ISBN 0-07-022713-6
"Whittlesey House publications"
A fable about the boastful, swift hare who, because
he is overconfident and stops to take a nap, loses a race
to the slow but steady tortoise
"An ingratiating picture-book treatment of Aesop's
fable. The drawings mingle lively forest animals with
flowers and grasses done in green, brown, and yellow.
Although a little undisciplined in composition, the
double-page spreads provide plenty of visual entertainment. Text, in large print, is from Joseph Jacobs."
Sch Library J

Harper, Wilhelmina
The Gunniwolf; retold by Wilhelmina Harper;
illus. by William Wiesner. Dutton 1967 unp illus
$6.95 (k-1)   398.2
1 Folklore
ISBN 0-525-31139-4
A retelling of the folktale about Little Girl who
ignores her mother's warnings, wanders into the
jungle searching for pretty flowers, and encounters
the fierce Gunniwolf
"Pictures are green and orange with numerous
black lines." Bruno. Bks for Sch Libraries, 1968

Harris, Christie
Once more upon a totem; illus. by Douglas Tait.
Atheneum Pubs. 1973 195p illus $5.95 (4-7) 398.2
1 Indians of North America—Legends
ISBN 0-689-30088-3
The following three legends of the Indians of the
Pacific Northwest are prefaced by brief introductions
with background information on culture and tradi-
tions: The prince who was taken away by the salmon;
Raven traveling; Ghost story
"Striking illustrations accompany the stories, which
reveal the Indians' humor, strong family ties, exem-
plary noblesse oblige, profound veneration of all life
(including their prey and the spirit world), ecologically perceptive religion, and acceptance of death."
Sch Library J

Hatch, Mary C.
More Danish tales, retold by Mary C. Hatch; illus.
by Edgun. Harcourt 1949 237p illus $3.75 (3-5)
                                              398.2
1 Folklore—Denmark 2 Fairy tales
ISBN 0-15-255453-X
"Retold from an English translation of Svend
Grundtvig's Folkeaeventyr made by the illustrator."
Verso of title page
These fifteen "gay and humorous tales abound with
princesses and trolls, the magic of fairyland and the
wit of farm boys and country bumpkins. Edgun's
amusing drawings have the right Scandinavian touch
and the print and bookmaking are excellent. Storytellers and lovers of fairy tales will be glad to have this
fresh collection." Horn Bk

Hatch, Mary C.—*Continued*

13 Danish tales, retold by Mary C. Hatch; illus. by Edgun. Harcourt 1947 169p illus $4.50 (3-5)   398.2

1 Folklore—Denmark 2 Fairy tales
ISBN 0-15-285683-8

A collection of thirteen tales based on J. C. Bay's Danish fairy & folk tales, published in 1899

The stories "deal largely with everyday objects touched with magic-talking pots, enchanted cats and knapsacks that are never empty." Christian Sci Monitor

"Engaging and humorous. . . . They are the real 'peasant' tales—homely, funny, sometimes a bit sly and cryptic. It is a gay-looking book with apt illustrations." Sat Rev

Haviland, Virginia

(comp.) The fairy tale treasury; [illus. by] Raymond Briggs; selected by Virginia Haviland. Coward, McCann & Geoghegan 1972 192p illus lib. bdg. $7.99 (k-3)   398.2

1 Fairy tales
ISBN 0-698-30438-1

Companion volume to: The Mother Goose treasury entered in class 398.8 under Mother Goose

"Thirty-two fairy tales chosen from many sources, but chiefly from Perrault, Jacobs, Grimm, and Andersen. In addition to many well-known tales ('The Story of the Three Little Pigs,' 'The History of Tom Thumb,' 'Puss in Boots,' and 'The Ugly Duckling'—to name only a few), there are two African stories and the by-now-familiar Japanese 'One-Inch Fellow.' . . . Pictures on practically every page—either filling the wide margins, or appearing in doublespread or full-page drawings—alternate color with black and white; and much caricaturing of character and activity is used to embellish the narratives with humor." Horn Bk

Favorite fairy tales told in Czechoslovakia; retold by Virginia Haviland; illus. by Trina Schart Hyman. Little 1966 90p illus $4.95, lib. bdg. $5.55 (3-5)   398.2

1 Folklore—Czechoslovak Republic 2 Fairy tales
ISBN 0-316-35083-4; 0-316-35066-4

"The illustrations—some in black and white, others in tomato red, olive green, and black—combine finely detailed drawing with strong, vigorous characterizations which heighten the forthright drama and the humor of the stories; the use of Slavic patterns and designs adds a sense of rightness and authenticity. Three of the tales are familiar favorites: 'Kuratko the Terrible' (magnificently pictured as a great strutting tyrant), 'The Shepherd's Nosegay,' and 'The Twelve Months'; the other two, 'The Wood Fairy' and 'The Three Golden Hairs of Grandfather Know All,' contain many traditional folklore motifs." Horn Bk

Favorite fairy tales told in Denmark; retold by Virginia Haviland; illus. by Margot Zemach. Little 1971 90p illus $4.95, lib. bdg. $5.55 (3-5)   398.2

1 Folklore—Denmark 2 Fairy tales
ISBN 0-316-35057-5; 0-316-35058-3

These "six Danish stories depict greed, craftiness, and common sense." Christian Sci Monitor

"A certain generosity of spirit and good humor pervade the collection, along with a very definite sense of justice. . . . The pencil-sketched line drawings with their plum and mustard washes perfectly reflect the good-natured mood of the stories." Horn Bk

Favorite fairy tales told in France; retold from Charles Perrault and other French storytellers, by Virginia Haviland; illus. by Roger Duvoisin. Little 1959 91p illus lib. bdg. $5.95 (2-5)   398.2

1 Folklore—France 2 Fairy tales
ISBN 0-316-35054-0

"Five French fairy tales translated from original sources and retold by the author with style and grace. . . . Beautiful illustrations . . . are in perfect complement with the text." Library J

Favorite fairy tales told in Germany; retold from the Brothers Grimm, by Virginia Haviland; illus. by Susanne Suba. Little 1959 83p illus lib. bdg. $5.50 (2-5)   398.2

1 Folklore—Germany 2 Fairy tales
ISBN 0-316-35075-3

"Virginia Haviland has shortened and simplified the text considerably, using slightly flatter but more easily understood modern words and turns of phrase than the older adapters and translators." N Y Her Trib Bks

"Printed in clear, beautiful type with Suba's expressive line drawings, the [seven] old stories offer new satisfactions to 7-11 year olds who want to read to themselves." Chicago Sunday Trib

Favorite fairy tales told in Greece; retold by Virginia Haviland; illus. by Nonny Hogrogian. Little 1970 90p illus $4.95, lib. bdg. $5.55 (2-5)   398.2

1 Folklore—Greece, Modern 2 Fairy tales
ISBN 0-316-35059-1; 0-316-35060-5

"Among the eight representative Greek tales in this collection are a version of the story about the king's daughter who 'loved her father like salt,' a variant of 'The three sillies,' and several stories in which the exquisite Greek fairies either gain control over a mortal by magic or lose their magic powers to a mortal who acquires possessions of one of their personal belongings. This welcome addition to Haviland's popular series of traditional tales for younger readers is illustrated with piquant line drawings some of which are accented with color." Booklist

Favorite fairy tales told in India; retold by Virginia Haviland; illus. by Blair Lent. Little 1973 95p illus lib. bdg. $5.95 (2-5)   398.2

1 Folklore—India 2 Fairy tales
ISBN 0-316-35055-9

These eight tales tell of clever jackals who outwit lions, tigers, and alligators; a cat who discovers the danger of eating everything you see; a pot-maker who accidentally becomes the saviour of his kingdom; a magical little man who helps a soldier's son win a princess; a blind man and a deaf man who overcome demons and accidentally cure each other

The selections have been "chosen from late-nineteenth and early-twentieth century versions of Hindu folk tales and fables. . . . The stories are marked by the humorous situations and the ingenious solutions of universal folklore. The handsome illustrations by the winner of the 1972 Caldecott Award range from the meticulous to the bold. Black-and-white line drawings alternate with three-color illustrations in cream, green, and mauve. Foliage, architecture, and decorative motifs suggest the exuberance of Hindu art." Horn Bk

Favorite fairy tales told in Ireland; retold from Irish storytellers by Virginia Haviland; illus. by Arthur Marokvia. Little 1961 91p illus lib. bdg. $5.95 (2-5)   398.2

1 Folklore—Ireland 2 Fairy tales
ISBN 0-316-35051-6

A collection of 5 tales involving humans, animals and a leprechaun. The stories can be read independently by the children in the age range to which they appeal, and they serve as an incentive to explore further as reading ability improves." Library J

Haviland, Virginia—*Continued*

The illustrations "are exuberant and colorful." Horn Bk

Favorite fairy tales told in Italy; retold by Virginia Haviland; illus. by Evaline Ness. Little 1965 90p illus lib. bdg. $4.95 (2-5)   398.2

1 Folklore—Italy 2 Fairy tales
ISBN 0-316-35076-1

This retelling of six stories selected from older sources which are out of print has "attractive illustrations and format that entice the young reader. In this volume, three stories follow particularly familiar story patterns: 'Cenerentola,' a Cinderella story; 'The Three Goslings,' reminiscent of the three pigs; and 'Bastianelo,' about three sillies." Horn Bk

Favorite fairy tales told in Japan; retold by Virginia Haviland; illus. by George Suyeoka. Little 1967 89p illus $4.95, lib. bdg. $5.55 (2-5)   398.2

1 Folklore—Japan 2 Fairy tales
ISBN 0-316-35091-5; 0-316-35074-5

"A fine literary and visual experience for younger readers. The retellings . . . have retained their oriental aspects, and the full-page illustrations in orange, green, black, and white are up to the standard expected for this series." Sch Library J

Favorite fairy tales told in Norway; retold from Norse folklore by Virginia Haviland; illus. by Leonard Weisgard. Little 1961 88p illus $5.50 (2-5)   398.2

1 Folklore—Norway 2 Fairy tales
ISBN 0-316-35053-2

These seven "stories have been adapted from the 1859 translation by Sir George Webb Dasent of Norwegian folk tales gathered by Peter Christian Asbjornsen and Jorgen E. Moe." Verso of title page

Compared with several other of Miss Haviland's collections, "the Norwegian volume is, perhaps, the prettiest with its neat precise pictures some of which recall designs in Scandinavian folk art." Pub W

Favorite fairy tales told in Poland; retold by Virginia Haviland; illus. by Felix Hoffmann. Little 1963 90p illus $5.50 (2-5)   398.2

1 Folklore—Poland 2 Fairy tales
ISBN 0-316-35048-6

These six Polish tales "are versions of traditional ones of many types. Some are familiar; others deserve to be better known. Many preserve the characteristics of oral literature and would be well suited for reading aloud." Chicago Sch J

Favorite fairy tales told in Russia; retold from Russian storytellers by Virginia Haviland; illus. by Herbert Danska. Little 1961 86p illus $5.50 (2-5) 398.2

1 Folklore—Russia 2 Fairy tales
ISBN 0-316-35049-4

"Five old tales, retold skillfully so that the vigor and wiliness so characteristic of Russian folklore are retained. The bold illustrations in red, violet, and black, by Herbert Danska, provide a proper setting." Horn Bk

Favorite fairy tales told in Scotland; retold by Virginia Haviland; illus. by Adrienne Adams. Little 1963 92p illus lib. bdg. $4.95 (2-5)   398.2

1 Folklore—Scotland 2 Fairy tales
ISBN 0-316-35061-3

"Six lively tales of peasants and pages, serpents and fairies in this useful series of stories." Ontario Library Rev

"The retelling is direct and simple, the print is large and clear, the illustrations are attractive. Sources for the tales are cited, and the book should be as useful for storytelling as it is for the individual reader." Chicago. Children's Bk Center

Favorite fairy tales told in Spain; retold by Virginia Haviland; illus. by Barbara Cooney. Little 1963 87p illus $5.50 (2-5)   398.2

1 Folklore—Spain 2 Fairy tales
ISBN 0-316-35047-8

These six tales concern such characters as an enchanted mule, four wise and foolish brothers, a flea, and a half-chick

"As in other volumes in the series, this collection of retellings is handsomely illustrated and is printed in large, clear type. The stories are told with a true feeling for the genre and a true feeling of the country of origin; the style is direct and vivacious. A good book for storytelling, for reading aloud, or for independent reading." Chicago Children's Bk Center

Favorite fairy tales told in Sweden; retold by Virginia Haviland; illus. by Ronni Solbert. Little 1966 92p illus $5.50 (2-5)   398.2

1 Folklore—Sweden 2 Fairy tales
ISBN 0-316-35052-4

"Plain, plucky heroes—peasant or prince—gain good fortune with good sense in six tales told with simplicity and humor. The Swedish stories are less well-known than some, but their themes will be familiar. Vigorous, sweeping lines intensified with vibrant yellow and orange suggest the rustic strength and blazing brilliance of a land of the midnight sun." Horn Bk

"Excellent for storytelling." Sch Library J

Hawkins, Quail

Androcles and the lion; retold from Apion; illus. by Rocco Negri. Coward-McCann 1970 unp illus $4.95, lib. bdg. $4.69 (1-3)   398.2

1 Fables
ISBN 0-698-20005-5; 0-698-30012-2

A story from ancient Rome about the slave Androcles and how his friendship with a lion eventually saves his life

"The storytelling, avoiding fussy overstatement and unnecessary embroidery, is smooth, straightforward, and dignified; and the handsome doublespread woodcuts in red, black, and golden yellow show Androcles' miserable plight, the poignancy of friendship between man and beast, and the pomp and splendor of imperial Rome. For the fun of literary parallels and contrasts, the book would make an interesting story-hour combination with Daugherty's Andy and the Lion [entered in class E]" Horn Bk

Hazeltine, Alice I.

(ed.) Hero tales from many lands; illus. by Gordon Laite. Abingdon 1961 475p illus $9.95 (5-7)   398.2

1 Folklore 2 Legends
ISBN 0-687-16943-7

"An excellent collection of thirty tales chosen from classic retellings for young people of the world's heroic literature. Selected with discrimination, the tales may well lead the reader to interest in the original volumes; this collection makes available much material that is no longer in print. The illustrations (some in color, some in black and white) are good; a list of suggestions for further reading is appended; the index and glossary—both of which give pronunciation—are extensive." Chicago. Children's Bk Center

Heady, Eleanor B.

When the stones were soft; East African fireside tales; illus. by Tom Feelings. Funk 1968 94p illus $4.95 (4-6)   398.2

Heady, Eleanor B.—_Continued_

1 Folklore—Africa, East
ISBN 0-308-80225-X

This collection of sixteen folk tales from East Africa tells "about how animals got their tails, why people are different colors, stories of enchantment and of the little people, etc. The frequent inclusion of simple Swahili words enhances the idiomatic presentation." Sch Library J
"The volume has distinctive full-page line-and-wash paintings in soft grays, by a young Negro artist who has worked in Ghana. One for each tale, plus a frontispiece—they not only project an atmosphere greatly enhancing the stories but also show specific elements of African culture and wildlife." Horn Bk

Hieatt, Constance

The Joy of the Court; retold by Constance Hieatt; illus. by Pauline Baynes. Crowell 1971 71p illus $3.95, lib. bdg. $4.70 (4-7)   398.2

1 Arthur, King
ISBN 0-390-46572-6; 0-390-46573-4

"A retelling of a portion of the Arthurian cycle. . . . While hunting a white stag, the young knight Erec rides off to avenge the cruel treatment of a court maiden and returns with the beautiful Enid, who had been a captive of the same Yder who had mistreated the queen's attendant. Erec, who refused to leave his bride to join the knights in a quest, was dubbed a coward; in his wrath he then sought adventure and in a series of dangerous encounters, proved his courage." Chicago. Children's Bk Center
"While some details differ from those in the 'Arthurian Romances' of Chrétien de Troyes as translated by Comfort, the retelling is a concise version of the prodigious tale and is true to the spirit of the original. . . . Attractive black-and-white illustrations by a Kate Greenaway medal winner add another facet to a distinguished piece of storytelling." Horn Bk

The knight of the cart; retold by Constance Hieatt; illus. by John Gretzer. Crowell 1969 85p illus $3.95, lib. bdg. $4.70 (4-7)   398.2

1 Lancelot 2 Arthur, King
ISBN 0-690-47531-4; 0-690-47532-2

The author "confesses to adding her own interpretations to the versions of Chrétien de Troyes and Malory, thus giving a fresh and vivid cast to the familiar Arthurian legends. The king, already troubled by the disappearance of many good men of Camelot, is struck with dismay when a messenger comes to report that the queen and her ladies have been taken captive by the evil Sir Malagant and transported to the Land of Gorre. Sir Lancelot, hot in pursuit, submits to the indignity of riding in a cart (a disgrace usually meted out to criminals) to save his queen, an episode that is only the first of his adventures. The writing style is wonderfully fluent and appropriately romantic." Sutherland. The Best in Children's Bks
"The lively and effective black, white, and gray illustrations seem to be somewhat indebted in style to Evelyn Ness." Horn Bk

Sir Gawain and the Green Knight; retold by Constance Hieatt; illus. by Walter Lorraine. Crowell 1967 unp illus $3.95, lib. bdg. $4.70 (4-6)   398.2

1 Arthur, King
ISBN 0-690-74086-7; 0-690-74087-5

"The story of King Arthur's noble knight Gawain has been turned into splendid prose. . . . The old sorceress Morgan le Fay created the magic of this quest, which sent Arthur's nephew, the 'least' of his brave followers, to meet the gigantic Green Knight, testing both Gawain's courage and his honesty. Without superfluous words or archaic expressions, this brief retelling upholds the atmosphere of wonder surrounding the quest." Horn Bk

"Much of the introductory and descriptive material of the original 14th-century poem is omitted here and emphasis is placed on Sir Gawain's actions. The story moves rapidly and should hold a young reader's interest. Appropriate illustrations in tones of green." Sch Library J

Hirsh, Marilyn

Could anything be worse? A Yiddish tale retold and illus. by Marilyn Hirsh. Holiday House 1974 unp illus lib. bdg. $4.95 (k-3)   398.2

1 Folklore, Jewish
ISBN 0-8234-0239-8

"A tale found in many cultures, here adapted from the Yiddish version, is nicely told and illustrated. Dissatisfied with the way his family behaves, a man takes the advice of a friend and goes to the Rabbi for counsel. The Rabbi will answer no questions, but tells the man to bring chickens into the house, then a cow, then some relatives. The small house is noisy and crowded. Again the man goes to the Rabbi; the relatives are sent off, then the cow, then the chickens. The family throws open the windows and cleans and polishes, and settles down in peace. . . . One of the most durable of the count-your-blessings tales, gently humorous, is pleasant to read alone or aloud, although the format indicates wider read-aloud use." Chicago. Children's Bk Center

Hodges, Elizabeth Jamison

Serendipity tales; drawings by June Atkin Corwin. Atheneum Pubs. 1966 179p illus $3.95, lib. bdg. $3.81 (4-7)   398.2

1 Folklore—Asia 2 Fairy tales
ISBN 0-689-20164-8; 0-689-20165-6

"When the princes of 'The Three Princes of Serendip' [entered below] reached Persia, the Emperor Vahram was gravely ill. They recommended that 'the greatest storyteller in each of the seven largest cities of the land' visit the emperor so that the telling of stories might 'help to drive away the unhappiness' which had made him ill. The stories are mentioned but are not told in the earlier book. Instead they are gathered here as told by the young men after return to the palace of their father in Serendip (Ceylon). . . . They derive from many sources and from the imagination of an author well steeped in the geography, history, and folklore of Ceylon, India, and the Middle East. As in the first book, an original pantoum follows each chapter. Ornate in plot, smoothly written, and rich in the atmosphere of eastern tales, the stories read aloud well and will be excellent for library storytelling." Horn Bk
"Atkin Corwin's tapestry-like drawings help to set the scene." Christian Sci Monitor
Sources: p177-78

The three princes of Serendip; drawings by Joan Berg. Atheneum Pubs. 1964 158p illus $3.95, lib. bdg. $3.81 (4-7)   398.2

1 Folklore—Asia 2 Fairy tales
ISBN 0-689-20166-4; 0-689-20167-2

"Retold 'from an 18th-century English version of an old Persian story set in the days of the Sassanid Emperors, this fairy tale is the odyssey of three princes of Ceylon (called Serendip then). Their quest, spurred by their father, King Jaiya of Serendip, was to find a scroll with the magic formula for a potion called 'Death to Dragons.' . . . Many were their adventures in Persia and India, where their cleverness, kindness and understanding brought unexpected and unsought reward (hence our word serendipity)." Bk Week
"The graceful fantasy, smoothly told and Oriental in feeling, should have a great deal of appeal to the older fairy-tale audience. Each chapter ends with a charming original pantoum—a poetic form unfamiliar

Hodges, Elizabeth Jamison—_Continued_
to many—adding pleasure for the more creative readers. The drawings are decorative, but lack the authenticity of the text." Horn Bk
Bibliography included in Notes: p155-56

Hodges, Margaret
The Fire Bringer; a Paiute Indian legend; retold by Margaret Hodges; illus. by Peter Parnall. Little 1972 31p illus $5.95 (2-5)   398.2
1 Paiute Indians—Legends 2 Fire—Fiction
3 Coyotes—Stories
ISBN 0-316-36783-4
Adapted from the version by Mary Austin in: The basket woman, published 1904
"The coyote is the true hero of the tale, as he helps the Paiute boy who is his friend alleviate the winter suffering of his tribe. Choosing the hundred best runners, who are stationed at intervals along the trail to the mountain of the Fire Spirits, Coyote steals a burning brand, runs to the first station, and passes the fire on; the runners speed along in relay fashion, the Fire Spirits chase to no avail." Chicago. Children's Bk Center
"The Promethean myth is frequently found in American Indian folklore. However, unlike other tellings in which animals form the relay team and humorous elements are stressed, this version emphasizes the nobility of the deed. Peter Parnall's handsome pen-and-ink drawings washed with flat spreads of muted color contrast the stark coldness of the world to the power and beauty of the stolen fire." Sch Library J

The wave; adapted from Lafcadio Hearn's Gleanings in Buddha-fields; illus. by Blair Lent. Houghton 1964 45p illus $3.50, lib. bdg. $3.23 (3-5)   398.2
1 Folklore—Japan
ISBN 0-395-06817-7; 0-395-06818-5
This "Japanese folktale was designed for reading aloud. It tells of an old man who set fire to his own rice fields to warn a village of an approaching tidal wave." Wis Library Bul
"Strong, dramatic illustrations in muted colors have the feeling and flow of Japanese art and turn the story into a handsome picture book." Horn Bk

Hogrogian, Nonny
One fine day. Macmillan (N Y) 1971 unp illus $5.95, pa $1.25   398.2
1 Folklore—Armenia 2 Foxes—Stories
Awarded the Caldecott Medal, 1971
"A picture story book based on an Armenian folk tale is illustrated [by the author] with bold, simple compositions in soft colors, the pictures echoing the humor of the story. Nicely told, the tale uses a familiar cumulative pattern: when a fox drinks all the milk from an old woman's pail, she cuts off his tail; he begs her to sew it on so that his friends won't laugh at him. She agrees—if he will return her milk. So the fox goes from one creature to another, each asking for a reciprocal favor, until a kind man takes pity, and gives him grain to take to the hen to get the egg to pay the peddler, etc. A charming picture book that is just right for reading aloud to small children, the scale of the pictures also appropriate for group use." Sutherland. The Best in Children's Bks

Rooster Brother. Macmillan Pub. Co. 1974 unp illus lib. bdg. $5.95 (k-2)   398.2
1 Folklore—Armenia
ISBN 0-02-743990-9
In this retelling of an Armenian folk tale, illustrated by the author, "a small but clever boy vows he will make three robbers who steal his cooked rooster pay for their misdeed. This he does by outwitting them at their own game and leaving cryptic notes to the effect

that 'Rooster Brother' had been there." Children's Bk Rev Serv
"The brightly colored, engaging caricatures are familiar looking and capture the whimsy of tricksters being tricked. The open, attractive format and simple folk feeling of the story make this a pleasant choice for telling or independent reading." Sch Library J

Hoke, Helen
(comp.) Dragons, dragons, dragons; pictures by Carol Barker. Watts, F. 1972 240p illus lib. bdg. $5.88 (4-7)   398.2
1 Dragons—Stories
ISBN 0-531-02036-3
Here are twenty-five stories and two poems about dragons ranging from the one slain by St. George and the ill-tempered Chinese one, Chi'ien T'ang, to dragons from Greece, Spain and Denmark, including some fairly pleasant dragons. Some authors included are Andrew Lang, Lewis Carroll, E. Nesbit, the Grimms, and Jorge Luis Borges
This collection "celebrates the lore and legend of dragons—the good as well as the most fearful and bloodthirsty. . . . The many handsome black-and-white illustrations are wonderfully appropriate to the mood of the selections." Booklist

Holladay, Virginia
Bantu tales; ed. by Louise Crane; woodcuts by Rocco Negri. Viking 1970 95p illus lib. bdg. $4.95 (4-6)   398.2
1 Folklore, Bantu 2 Folklore—Zaïre
ISBN 0-670-14798-2
"Nineteen folk stories from the Bantu tribes of the Kasai district of the Congo, originally collected in 1930 by an American teacher of a school for missionary children in Lubondai and edited by a former pupil of the school. While reflecting the wisdom and ways of life which the Baluba and Lulua tribes considered important to teach the young, the short tales deal with universal values that transcend their local setting. The antics of men, animals, and mythical beings portray sharply and sometimes poignantly the strengths and weaknesses of human character and the joys and hardships of life. A pronunciation guide is appended and the book is handsomely illustrated with woodcuts." Booklist

Hooke, Hilda Mary
Thunder in the mountains; legends of Canada; illus. by Clare Bice. Oxford 1947 223p illus $7.50 (5-7)   398.2
1 Indians of North America—Legends 2 Legends—Canada
ISBN 0-19-54003-7
A collection of seventeen Canadian folk tales gathered from existing source material. The book is arranged in three sections. In the first: The garden of Gitche Manitou, the author retells the Indian legends of the early inhabitants of the garden created by Gitche Manitou, the Great Spirit. The second section has three tales of the coming of the white men to Canada; and the third section deals with the white men's stories of magic, witches, pixies, saints and the legend which explains why Montreal is such a windy city.
"The book fills a gap in our national folklore collections." Library J

Hosford, Dorothy
By his own might; the battles of Beowulf; drawings by Laszlo Matulay. Holt 1947 69p illus lib. bdg. $3.27 (5-7)   398.2
1 Beowulf
ISBN 0-03-035610-5
A "retelling of this oldest of English epics, in which

Hosford, Dorothy—*Continued*

Beowulf slays the monster Grendel and his wicked mother, becomes king of the Danes, and finally meets his death in combat with a dragon." Hodges. Bks for Elem Sch Libraries

"Because of its comparatively simple plot and motivation 'Beowulf' makes a good introduction to hero stories for younger boys and girls, but this version carries so much of the conviction and force of the original that it could be given with confidence to any one." Horn Bk

Source material: p66

Houston, James

Tikta'liktak; an Eskimo legend, written and illus. by James Houston. Harcourt 1965 63p illus $6.25 (4-6)
398.2

1 Legends, Eskimo
ISBN 0-15-287745-2

The author retells a "legend that celebrates man's will to survive. Tikta'liktak, a young hunter, is trapped on an ice floe and marooned on a barren island. Feeling certain that the island is to be his grave, he prepares a stony coffin. A dream foretells the lucky appearance of an unlucky seal, restoring the hunter's strength and desire to live. . . . [He] survives freezing weather, an attack by a polar bear and the long journey that brings him safely home." N Y Times Bk Rev

"A book that has all the appeal of the Crusoe situation plus the embellishment of the exotic setting. The illustrations, strong and stark in black and white, enhance the mood of solitude and isolation." Sutherland. The Best in Children's Bks

Hume, Lotta Carswell

Favorite children's stories from China and Tibet; illus. by Lo Koon-chiu. Tuttle 1962 119p illus $5.95 (3-6)
398.2

1 Folklore—China 2 Folklore—Tibet
ISBN 0-8048-0179-7

"Nineteen traditional stories from various sections of China and from Tibet, heard and retold by an American woman who lived for 22 years in central China. Most of these enjoyable tales, filled with humor and wisdom are about animals, and many have counterparts in other countries. Illustrated with many attractive black-and-white drawings and full-color pictures done in the Chinese brush style. Suitable for storytelling." Booklist

Hürlimann, Bettina

William Tell and his son; illus. by Paul Nussbaumer. Harcourt [1967 c1965] unp illus $6.50 (2-5)
398.2

1 Legends—Switzerland 2 Tell, William
ISBN 0-15-297340-0

Originally published 1965 in Switzerland. This edition is translated and adapted from the German by Elizabeth D. Crawford

The story of the legendary 13th century Swiss patriot who with the aid of his brave son opposed the tyranny of a governor sent by the Austrian Emperor. The events are presented from the viewpoint of the nine-year-old boy

"Mr. Nussbaumer's illustrations, most of them full page and in full color, leave lasting impressions. Jagged gray mountains reach for a clouded sky; dark, dense forests lie below; and in the closely clustered village, the citizens radiate a ruggedness that scorns submission. Splendidly moving and unmistakably Swiss." Horn Bk

Hürlimann, Ruth

The cat and mouse who shared a house; retold with pictures by Ruth Hürlimann; tr. from the German by Anthea Bell. Walck, H.Z. [1974] c1973 unp illus $6.95 (k-3)
398.2

1 Folklore—Germany 2 Cats—Stories 3 Mice—Stories
ISBN 0-8098-1214-2

Original German language edition first published 1973 in Switzerland. This translation first published 1973 in England

A retelling of the story by the Brothers Grimm, in which a greedy cat devours the winter provisions set aside for herself and the mouse with whom she lives

"The pictures are bold, colorful, and humorous, good for using with a group as well as with individual children." Chicago. Children's Bk Center

Hutchinson, Veronica S.

(ed.) Candle-light stories; selected and ed. by Veronica S. Hutchinson; with drawings by Lois Lenski. Putnam 1928 146p illus lib. bdg. $6.86 (2-4)
398.2

1 Folklore 2 Fairy tales
ISBN 0-399-60081-7

These seventeen "tales are lively, humorous folk and fairy tales drawn from standard sources, and in most cases slightly and wisely adapted by the editor. Big print adds more than most editors think to the pleasure of small readers and this alone would make the book a welcome one." Sat Rev

(ed.) Chimney corner fairy tales; collected and retold by Veronica S. Hutchinson; with drawings by Lois Lenski. Putnam 1926 183p illus lib. bdg. $6.86 (3-5)
398.2

1 Folklore 2 Fairy tales
ISBN 0-399-60090-6

"A selection of thirteen fairy tales selected from the best folk sources. These stories have been slightly adapted and are illustrated with . . . line drawings and several colored plates. A companion book to 'Chimney corner stories' [entered below] but suitable for slightly older children." Booklist

(ed.) Chimney corner stories; tales for little children; collected and retold by Veronica S. Hutchinson; illus. by Lois Lenski. Putnam 1925 149p illus lib. bdg. $6.86 (2-4)
398.2

1 Folklore 2 Fairy tales
ISBN 0-399-60091-4

Companion volume to the author's: Chimney corner fairy tales, entered above

A collection of sixteen easy-to-read folk tales

(ed.) Fireside stories; selected and ed. by Veronica S. Hutchinson; with drawings by Lois Lenski. Putnam 1927 150p illus lib. bdg. $6.86 (2-4)
398.2

1 Folklore 2 Fairy tales
ISBN 0-399-60171-6

"Jolly and intriguing animals scattered all over jacket, cover, title page and end-papers, this book for youngest readers brings together tales from many and varied sources—Mother Goose, English fairy tales, nursery stories from Russia, Denmark and other lands —which Miss Hutchinson has slightly adapted to fit them more exactly to this purpose. Lois Lenski is responsible for the jolly animals, for more than a hundred illustrations in black and white and for six in color, all of them of charming quality and a delicate, roguish sense of humor." N Y Times Bk Rev

Index to fairy tales, myths and legends [comp] by Mary Huse Eastman. 2d ed. rev. and enl. Faxon 1926 610p (Useful reference ser) $11
398.2

1 Folklore—Indexes 2 Fairy tales—Indexes 3 Legends—Indexes 4 Mythology—Indexes
ISBN 0-87305-028-2

First published 1915 by the Boston Book Company

Index to fairy tales, myths and legends—*Continued*

This reference work indexes about 700 collections of "fairy tales and fables, the stories from Greek and Norse mythology which seemed most likely to be called for, also hero stories and some [popular] modern stories like the 'Leak in the dyke.' . . . A special effort has been made to include folk stories of as many nationalities as possible. . . . Since inquiries for stories are mainly by title this is first of all a title index. When the same story appears under various titles, it is indexed under the best known or under the one that seemed most descriptive of the story, and references are made from all the other titles. . . . [There are also selected] cross references from subjects—holidays, stars, flowers, etc." Preface

There are also a list of books analyzed, a geographical and racial index to collections analyzed, and a bibliography

Index to fairy tales, myths and legends; supplement [comp] by Mary Huse Eastman. Faxon 1937 566p (Useful reference ser) $11   398.2
1 Folklore—Indexes 2 Fairy tales—Indexes 3 Legends—Indexes 4 Mythology—Indexes
ISBN 0-87305-061-4
This volume indexes 500 volumes published from 1926 to 1937, as well as some older books omitted from the second edition. New features include catch word title cross references and a title list of books indexed. Subject indexing has been expanded. The subjects now appear in a separate Subject List, with the exception of a few, like holidays, which still appear in the main body of the index

Index to fairy tales, myths and legends; second supplement [comp] by Mary Huse Eastman. Faxon 1952 370p (Useful reference ser) $11   398.2
1 Folklore—Indexes 2 Fairy tales—Indexes 3 Legends—Indexes 4 Mythology—Indexes
ISBN 0-87305-082-7
Indexes 270 volumes published since the first supplementary volume
"The lists of stories for holidays and other days have been moved from the Title Index to the Subject List. However titles beginning with the subject 'catch word' . . . have been omitted." Preface

Index to fairy tales, 1949-1972; including folklore, legends, & myths, in collections [comp] by Norma Olin Ireland. Faxon 1973 xxxviii, 741p (Useful reference ser) $18   398.2
1 Folklore—Indexes 2 Fairy tales—Indexes 3 Legends—Indexes 4 Mythology—Indexes
ISBN 0-87305-101-7
Compiled as a continuation of Eastman's Index to fairy tales, and the first and second supplements
"406 books have been indexed, under title and subject, with authors included only when specifically mentioned in the collection. Stories in collections 'only' are included, not individual-story books. We have included a few older titles which have come out in new [editions] or were not included in the earlier indexes. . . . Variant titles are cross-referenced only if mentioned in the books indexed; Eastman has a very complete list of variants and should be referred to, if needed. Our first innovation is the comprehensive subject indexing of stories. . . . All entries are combined into a single alphabet, unlike the Eastman books, as we feel that such an arrangement is easier to use. . . . We have tried to analyze stories according to the 'importance' of subjects (not always every subject) and towards that purpose we have personally read most every one of these stories." Foreword

Ish-Kishor, Sulamith
The carpet of Solomon; a Hebrew legend; pictures by Uri Shulevitz. Pantheon Bks. 1966 57p illus lib. bdg. $4.99 (4-6)   398.2
1 Solomon, King of Israel 2 Legends, Jewish
ISBN 0-394-91131-8
"Discarding a diabolical gift which gave him a false sense of omnipotence, King Solomon learns the value of humility in a symbolic series of mystical adventures. Rare sensitivity in visual and textual imagery." Top of the News

Jacobs, Joseph
(ed.) English folk and fairy tales; folk and fairy tales from many lands; illus. by John D. Batten. 3d ed. rev. Putnam [n.d.] 277p illus $5 (4-6)   398.2
1 Folklore—Great Britain 2 Fairy tales
ISBN 0-399-20045-2
First published 1890 in England. First U.S. edition published 1891 with title: English fairy tales
"As outstanding as the best collections of fairy tales of any country, are those of the folk-lore of the British Isles made by Joseph Jacobs. In his re-writing of the [forty-one] stories, he has preserved their humour and dramatic power, and while simplifying dialect, has retained its full flavor. He intends his stories to be read aloud, and while children enjoy them for their own reading, this makes them invaluable for the story-teller who appreciates a colloquial, conversational style." Toronto
Includes notes and references

The fables of Aesop; selected, told anew, and their history traced by Joseph Jacobs; illus. by David Levine; afterword by Clifton Fadiman. Macmillan (N Y) 1964 115p illus $3.95 (4-7)   398.2
1 Fables
"The Macmillan classics"
A collection of over 80 fables "in an attractively illustrated edition." Hodges. Bks for Elem Sch Libraries

Hereafterthis; adapted from a folktale by Joseph Jacobs; Paul Galdone drew the pictures. McGraw [1973] unp illus $4.95 lib. bdg. $4.72 (k-3)   398.2
1 Folklore—Great Britain
ISBN 0-07-022690-3; 0-07-022691-1
"Jan the farmer takes a wife, only to have her precipitate one domestic disaster after another. The final blow comes when Jan tells his wife that a bag of coins is for 'Hereafterthis.' The next day, a robber introduces himself as 'Hereafterthis' and makes off with the money. The couple's successful efforts to retrieve their fortune with the aid of their last remaining possession, the front door, make for hilarious reading. Paul Galdone injects rollicking fun into this traditional English folk tale with his slyly humorous pen-and-ink and watercolor illustrations. The double-page spreads are filled with action. . . . This is sure to delight children at story hour." Sch Library J

Hudden and Dudden and Donald O'Neary; adapted by Joseph Jacobs; illus. by Doris Burn. Coward-McCann 1968 unp illus lib. bdg. $4.99 (k-4)   398.2
1 Folklore, Celtic
ISBN 0-698-30195-1
Penniless Donald O'Neary lived on a barren strip of land. Unfortunately his rich neighbors, Hudden and Dudden, wanted to be richer and schemed night and day to steal away Donald's cow and land. How Donald outwitted his greedy neighbors is told in this story
"The robust Irish humor of this old favorite is echoed in the bold black-and-white drawings, as handsome as they are dramatic." Sat Rev

Jacobs, Joseph—*Continued*
(ed.) Indian fairy tales; selected and ed. by Joseph Jacobs; illus. by John D. Batten. (4-6) 398.2
1 Folklore—India 2 Fairy tales
Some editions are:
Dover pa $2 (ISBN 0-486-21828-7)
Smith, P. $4.50 (ISBN 0-8446-0723-1)
A reprint of the title first published 1892 in England. A Putnam edition, o.p. 1975, had title: Indian folk and fairy tales
"From all these sources—from the Jatakas, from the Bidpai, and from the more recent [19th century] collections—I have selected those [twenty-nine] stories which throw most light on the origin of Fable and Folk-tales, and at the same time are most likely to attract English children. . . . The stories existing in Pali and Sanskrit I have taken from translations." Preface
Includes notes and references

Jack the Giant-Killer; illus. by Fritz Wegner. Walck, H.Z. [1971 c1970] 45p illus $4.95 (k-3) 398.2
1 Folklore—Great Britain 2 Fairy tales
ISBN 0-8098-1185-5
First published 1970 in England
Clever and daring Jack, a farmer's son from Cornwall, slays one giant after another. His adventures eventually take him to Wales where he meets King Arthur's son and helps him exorcise and woo a beautiful lady possessed by evil spirits. King Arthur makes him a Knight of the Round Table and presents him with a castle and a duke's daughter in marriage
"Jacobs' successful retelling of this English folk tale, originally issued in the 18th Century in chapbook form, is here combined with Fritz Wegner's very well done black and white and color drawings. . . . The violence potential in giant killing, Griffin conquering, etc. is balanced by the fantasy which is inherent in the tale itself and brought out in Joseph Jacobs' retelling. . . . [The author uses] Old and Middle English words and phrases which could precipitate an early interest in language for children so inclined." Library J

Johnny-cake; illus. by Emma L. Brock. Putnam [1967 c1933] unp illus lib. bdg. $3.97 (k-3) 398.2
1 Folklore—Great Britain
ISBN 0-399-60324-7
A reissue of a book first published 1933
A "lively cumulative nursery tale of the johnny-cake that leaps out of the oven to outrun the farmer, his wife, his little boy, and a succession of other human and animal characters until he meets the fox—and disaster. Emma Brock's black-and-white drawings express the homely quality of the English folk tale. A basic book for storytelling with younger children." Sch Library J
The American counterpart of this story is generally known as The gingerbread boy

(ed.) More English folk and fairy tales; collected and ed. by Joseph Jacobs; illus. by John D. Batten. Putnam [n.d.] 268p illus $5 (4-6) 398.2
1 Folklore—Great Britain 2 Fairy tales
ISBN 0-399-20172-6
First published 1894 with title: More English fairy tales
"A perfect treasure-trove of [forty] fairy tales that has done for the British Isles a service similar to that of the brothers Grimm for Germany. Mr J. D. Batten's illustrations are nearly as delightful as the stories themselves." Pittsburgh
Includes notes and references

Munachar & Manachar; an Irish story as told by Joseph Jacobs; with pictures by Anne Rockwell. Crowell 1970 unp illus $4.50, lib. bdg. $5.25 (k-3) 398.2
1 Folklore—Ireland
ISBN 0-690-56584-4; 0-690-56585-2
"Munachar and Manachar go out to pick raspberries, but as many as Munachar picks, Manachar eats, so Munachar goes off to find a rod to make a gad (rope) to hang Manachar. Before he can have the rod he must get an ax to cut the rod, a flag to edge the ax and so on, which he does only to discover, that, in the meantime, Manachar has burst." Booklist
"Rescuing an amusing story from comparative oblivion, [the artist] has made rollicking, gaily colored pictures that greatly emphasize the inherent humor and nonsense; her two protagonists look as delightfully mindless as Tweedledee and Tweedledum." Horn Bk

Jagendorf, M. A.
Folk stories of the South; illus. by Michael Parks. Vanguard [1973 c1972] xx, 355p illus $6.95 (4-7) 398.2
1 Folklore—Southern States 2 Legends—Southern States
ISBN 0-8149-0000-3
"The noted folklore anthologist has selected 95 items from the 11 states of the old Confederacy. . . . [Included are] a potpourri of pirate tales, Indian legends, ghost stories, Civil and Revolutionary War stories, and local anecdotes. Some tales, like 'The Arkansas Traveler' and that of 'Kate, the Bell Witch' are well known; others are recognizable variants or widely told; but most here have not appeared before at this level. Many would enliven a story hour. . . . Arrangement is alphabetical by state; format is attractive; and Jagendorf's notes are helpful and suggest further sources." Sch Library J

The gypsies' fiddle, and other gypsy tales, by M. A. Jagendorf and C. H. Tillhagen; illus. by Hans Helweg. Vanguard 1956 186p illus $5.95 (5-7) 398.2
1 Folklore, Gypsy
ISBN 0-8149-0339-8
"Some of the nineteen fairy tales and legends have no parallel elsewhere, but a few are variants of the widespread 'noodle stories' about foolish peasants. They . . . reveal many gypsy characteristics." Horn Bk
Includes sources

New England bean-pot; American folk stories to read and to tell; illus. by Donald McKay; introduction by B. A. Botkin. Vanguard 1948 272p illus $5.95 (5-7) 398.2
1 Folklore—New England 2 Legends—New England
ISBN 0-8149-0336-3
"A collection of New England folklore which will be of special interest to storytellers and folklorists. . . . Short retellings; dry humor." Booklist
These "are legends, tales, yarns, jokes, incidents arranged as [46] 'Folk Stories' to read and tell. For that reason they are salted with folksayings and larded with sidelights of the localities from where they come. I have added proverbs, customs, and weather lore, and sometimes even local happenings." Foreword
"There are merry stories of the devil confounded, discomfited witch-hunters, sailors and pirates which have not hitherto appeared in juvenile collections and for which we are the richer. Donald McKay has illustrated them with imagination and skill." N Y Times Bk Rev

Jagendorf, M. A.—*Continued*

Noodlehead stories from around the world; with illus. by Shane Miller. Vanguard 1957 302p illus $5.95 (4-6)
398.2

1 Folklore 2 Wit and humor
ISBN 0-8149-0329-0

This collection contains 64 humorous stories selected from the folk tales of 36 lands and peoples. These stories, all meant for laughter, are about the fools who are sometimes wise, and the wise who are sometimes foolish

Tyll Ulenspiegel's merry pranks; illus. by Fritz Eichenberg. Vanguard 1938 188p illus $5.95 (4-6)
398.2

1 Eulenspiegel 2 Legends—Germany 3 Legends— Flanders
ISBN 0-8149-0337-1

Tyll Ulenspiegel is "a legendary figure of Germany and Flanders. . . . There are thirty-seven stories or episodes, in all of which Tyll plays his jokes and discomforts his enemies, but is always kind and helpful to the poor and the good people with whom he comes in contact." Library J

"The eight full-page illustrations and smaller decorative drawings by Fritz Eichenberg have caught exactly the jovial humor of the tales and add a fine flavor of the period." N Y Times Bk Rev

Jameson, Cynthia

The clay pot boy; adapted from a Russian tale; pictures by Arnold Lobel. Coward, McCann & Geoghegan 1973 unp illus lib. bdg. $4.69 (k-2)
398.2

1 Folklore—Russia
ISBN 0-698-30479-9

This is a retelling of a Russian folktale about "a childless couple who create a son out of clay. The clay pot boy comes alive and greedily swallows everything and everyone in sight. However, he gets his comeuppance when a billy goat smashes him to bits and frees all that he has gobbled. The boy's cumulative boasting makes the story easy to master; however, this same repetition factor limits the development of the theme." Sch Library J

"A favorite tale for storytellers is nicely adapted here and given added dimensions by the illustrations. Lobel's clay pot boy looks like a piece of pottery, and he grows larger and larger as he goes on his voracious path." Chicago. Children's Bk Center

Jones, Hettie

Coyote tales; adapted by Hettie Jones; illus. by Louis Mofsie. Holt 1974 49p illus lib. bdg. $4.95 (3-5)
398.2

1 Indians of North America—Legends
2 Coyotes—Stories
ISBN 0-03-088346-6

The stories "are adapted from Assiniboine, Dakota, and Skidi Pawnee tales (no reference is made as to which story comes from which tribe); as Jones informs us they are similar to those told by other tribes. . . . The tales have vitality and are presented in a pleasing format; the pictographic black-and-white illustrations are uneven in quality—at their best in portrayal of animals but awkward in representing people. A worthwhile addition to folklore and storytelling collections." Booklist

"Four North American Indian tales about Coyote. In 'Coyote Steals the Summer,' Coyote gains his ability to fool people by getting rid of year-round winter. He uses this trickster ability to help others in 'Coyote Rescues the Ring-Girl' (after he is at fault for her disappearance) and 'Coyote Conquers the Iya'; but, because of his selfishness, he is the one to be fooled in 'Coyote Loses His Dinner.' " Sch Library J

Longhouse winter; Iroquois transformation tales; adapted by Hettie Jones; illus. by Nicholas Gaetano. Holt 1972 unp illus $5.95, lib. bdg. $5.59 (4-6)
398.2

1 Iroquois Indians—Legends
ISBN 0-03-086745-2; 0-03-086746-0

Adapted from stories in: Myths and legends of the New York State Iroquois, by Harriet Maxwell Converse, published 1908

"The first story is about a young brave who becomes a robin and the harbinger of spring, the second about a beautiful girl who loves a fish-prince and joins him in his watery home; the third is an explanation of how some murdering Indians became snakes, the fourth about the young man who was so kind to the fauna of the woods that they brought him back to life when he had been scalped and killed." Chicago. Children's Bk Center

"In a brief Foreword, the scene is set for storytelling as it was practiced among the Iroquois, who told the tales of their people during the winter months only 'around the longhouse fire.' The elements of magic and poetry are strong in these four transformation tales. . . . The book is elaborately illustrated in watercolor; every beautiful page has a border of geometric designs (many of them based on Indian motifs); and full-page stylized illustrations accompany the stories." Horn Bk

Keats, Ezra Jack

John Henry; an American legend; story and pictures by Ezra Jack Keats. Pantheon Bks. 1965 unp illus $3.95, lib. bdg. $5.19 (k-3)
398.2

1 Legends, Negro 2 John Henry
ISBN 0-394-81302-2; 0-394-91302-7

"John Henry lived and died with a hammer in his hand. Mr. Keats has adapted legends into a picture-book introduction to the famous Negro folk hero and his high-spirited adventures. The dynamic power with which he wields his hammer is matched by the strong illustrations: brilliant oranges and reds contrast with grays and blacks that are often silhouettes; unusual backgrounds produce startling effects. A good picture-story to show to a group." Horn Bk

Kelsey, Alice Geer

Once the Hodja; illus. by Frank Dobias. McKay 1943 170p illus lib. bdg. $3.59 (4-6)
398.2

1 Nasr al-Din, khwajah 2 Legends—Turkey
ISBN 0-679-25101-4

First published by Longmans

"A delightful collection of humorous folk tales from Turkey. The central character is one Nasr-ed-Din Hodja, a simple, kindly fellow who, because he is both wise and foolish, gets into and out of trouble with equal ease. This is real Turkish folklore, spontaneous and funny." Booklist

"The tales blend history and legend and reflect the customs and folkways of the people. Amusing animated black and white drawings." Bookmark

Kijima, Hajime

Little white hen; a folk tale adapted by Hajime Kijima; illus. by Setsuko Hane. Harcourt 1969 unp illus $5.95 (k-2)
398.2

1 Folklore—Japan 2 Chickens—Stories
ISBN 0-15-247902-3

Original Japanese edition published 1967 with title: Lovely wise hen

"The little white hen of this delightful old folk tale . . . is a close relative of the familiar red hen, for she too saves herself from becoming a hungry fox's dinner by using her ever-handy scissors, needle, and thread. Strong full-color pictures dramatize the con-

Kijima, Hajime—*Continued*
flict and the ultimate victory of the little white hen."
Booklist

Kim, So-un
The story bag; a collection of Korean folk tales; tr.
by Setsu Higashi; illus. by Kim Eui-hwan. Tuttle 1955
229p illus pa $2.50 (4-7)   398.2
1 Folklore—Korea
ISBN 0-8048-0548-2
Original Japanese edition, 1953
This collection contains retellings of thirty Korean
folk tales including ones about animals which repay
human kindness, the origins of earthquakes and
eclipses, a conspiracy by stories to destroy the man
who has kept them confined in a bag, insects who get
drunk at a feast, a warrior who rescues three princesses from an ogre, a little mouse whose care for its
blind mother leads to a spoiled girl's reformation, and
others

Kirkup, James
The magic drum; told by James Kirkup; illus. by
Võ-Dinh. Knopf 1973 58p illus $4.50, lib. bdg. $5.49
(3-5)   398.2
1 Folklore—East (Far East)
ISBN 0-394-82672-8; 0-394-92672-2
A tale set in ancient China, adapted from the traditional Japanese Noh play: Tenko. The son of a peasant
couple, whose birth was miraculously foretold in a
dream involving a magic drum, finds his destiny
linked to the drum both in life and after death
"A number of strong, impressionistic wash drawings by a Vietnamese-born artist add to the beauty of
the book. The perfect telling makes this a unique story
to share with children on a special occasion. Its
strangeness and its poetry will linger." Horn Bk

Lang, Andrew
(ed.) Arabian nights; collected and ed. by Andrew
Lang; illus. by Vera Bock; with a foreword by Mary
Gould Davis. Large type ed. complete and unabridged. Watts, F. [1967 c1946] 303p illus lib. bdg.
$7.95 (5-7)   398.2
1 Folklore—Arabia 2 Fairy tales
ISBN 0-531-00308-6
"A Keith Jennison book"
First published 1898 by Longmans with the title:
The Arabian nights entertainments. This is a large
type reprint of the 1946 Longmans edition which
omitted a few of the less popular stories from the
original Lang collection and added two stories from
his Blue fairy book, as well as new illustrations
In these stories Shahrazad (or Scheherazade)
relates the fables and romances of Arabia and the East
"Vera Bock is a perfect choice as illustrator and her
black and white drawings and decorations give the
book that beauty of design which 'Arabian Nights'
surely deserves." Bk Week

(ed.) The blue fairy book; with numerous illus. by
H. J. Ford and G. P. Jacomb Hood. Dover 1965 390p
illus pa $2.75 (4-6)   398.2
1 Folklore 2 Fairy tales
ISBN 0-486-21437-0
A reprint of the title first published 1889 by
Longmans
A collection of thirty-seven fairy tales from various
countries, consisting largely of old favorites from such
sources as Perrault, the Brothers Grimm, Madame
D'Aulnoy, Asbjornsen and Möe, the Arabian Nights,
and Swift's Gulliver's travels

(ed.) The green fairy book; with numerous illus. by
H. J. Ford. Dover 1965 366p illus pa $2.50 (4-6)
                                                    398.2
1 Folklore 2 Fairy tales
ISBN 0-486-21439-7
A reprint of the title first published 1892 by
Longmans
This collection of forty-two fairy tales from various
countries includes many from the Brothers Grimm
and several by the Comte de Caylus. Other sources
include Madame D'Aulnoy, Paul Sebillot, Charles
Deulin, Fénelon, and traditional tales from Spain and
China

(ed.) The red fairy book; with numerous illus. by H.
J. Ford and Lancelot Speed (4-7)   398.2
1 Folklore 2 Fairy tales
Some editions are:
Dover pa $2.50 (ISBN 0-486-21673-X)
Smith, P. $3.50 (ISBN 0-8446-0756-8)
A reprint of the title first published 1890 by
Longmans
"This book includes a wide assortment of fairy tales
from French, Scandinavian, German, and Rumanian
folklore sources, including tales of the Brothers
Grimm and Madame d'Aulnoy. Accompanying the 37
stories are 100 line drawings." Adventuring With Bks.
2d edition

(ed.) The yellow fairy book; with numerous illus. by
H. J. Ford (4-7)   398.2
1 Folklore 2 Fairy tales
Some editions are:
Dover pa $2.50 (ISBN 0-486-21674-8)
Smith, P. $3.50 (ISBN 0-8446-0758-4)
A reprint of the title first published 1894 by
Longmans
A collection of 48 tales from Eastern Europe, Rus-
sia, Germany, France, Iceland, and the Indians of
North America

Leach, Maria
How the people sang the mountains up; how and
why stories; illus. by Glen Rounds. Viking 1967 159p
illus lib. bdg. $5.95 (3-6)   398.2
1 Folklore 2 Legends 3 Animals—Stories
ISBN 0-670-38264-7
"A collection of myths and legends about the origins
of natural phenomena, primarily of distinctive patterns of behavior or appearance in flora and fauna.
The tales are grouped (plants, constellations, animals,
et cetera) and a bibliography and list of notes on
sources are appended. The selections come from
around the world; many are of American Indian origin, very few are European. The style of the retelling
is crisp, humorous, and usually brief: good storytelling material." Chicago. Children's Bk Center
These stories "develop in the child an awareness of
and appreciation for the various interpretations different cultures have given of the same phenomenon.
. . . Small black-and-white sketches decorate the
pages of this handsomely designed book." Horn Bk

Whistle in the graveyard; folktales to chill your
bones; illus. by Ken Rinciari. Viking 1974 128p illus
$5.95 (4-6)   398.2
1 Folklore 2 Ghost stories
ISBN 0-670-76245-8
These "stories, drawn from many cultures and far-
distant lands, deal with bogeys and bugaboos, ghosts,
witch lore, supernatural manifestations, and haunted
places from the White House to the Tower of London.
Directions for playing 'a scary game' in the dark of a
Halloween night appear at the end of the book. Of
interest to adults are the bibliography and the ample
notes." Horn Bk

Leach, Maria—*Continued*

The author "has authenticated each tale, and Rinciari's pen-and-ink sketches add a spine-tingling touch." Sch Library J

Lent, Blair

John Tabor's ride; story and pictures by Blair Lent. Little 1966 48p illus map $3.75 (k-3)   398.2

1 Legends—New England 2 Sea stories 3 Whales—Stories

ISBN 0-316-52086-1

"An Atlantic Monthly Press book"

"A tall tale based on a New England legend about a shipwrecked sailor from Nantucket. Picked up by a strange old man, John Tabor was taken on a long, wild ride on the back of a whale. . . . John played cribbage with King Neptune and came to a lighthouse manned by a walrus and an albatross. Eventually he was delivered by the whale to the very heart of town; grateful, John Tabor had his whale towed back to the sea and freedom." Sutherland. The Best in Children's Bks

"The pictures are as full of fun and movement as the story and catch both the sea in action and the look of Nantucket." Sch Library J

Lester, Julius

The knee-high man, and other tales; pictures by Ralph Pinto. Dial Press 1972 28p illus $5.95, lib. bdg. $5.47 (k-3)   398.2

1 Folklore, Negro 2 Animals—Stories

ISBN 0-8037-4593-1; 0-8037-4607-5

"Rural scenes in quiet colors are a background for nicely-detailed creatures in an appealing collection of six animal stories from black folklore. The clever Mr. Rabbit outwits Mr. Bear and a farmer in two of the tales; two are 'Why' stories, another proves that you should never trust a snake, and the sixth is on the familiar theme of the person (sometimes it's an animal) who is dissatisfied with himself, tries to change, and gratefully accepts what he can't do anything about—in this case, the knee-high man resigns himself after consultation with a wise owl." Chicago. Children's Bk Center

"These are excellent for story telling and should be so presented for the greatest impact. . . . Handling the book is pleasurable as the pictures, rich in warmth and color, compliment the text and trigger an emotional empathy with the stories." N Y Times Bk Rev

Lexau, Joan M.

Crocodile and Hen; retold by Joan M. Lexau; pictures by Joan Sandin. Harper 1969 unp illus $4.95, lib. bdg. $5.49 (k-1)   398.2

1 Folklore—Congo (Brazzaville) 2 Fables

ISBN 0-06-023866-6; 0-06-023867-1

"An adaptation of the tale entitled 'Why the crocodile does not eat the hen.' " Verso of title page

Based on a folktale from Africa, in which the hen deters the crocodile from eating her by always calling him brother. The crocodile puzzles over their brotherhood until a lizard explains it to him

"Both text and pictures are simple in presentation but rich in suggestion." Sch Library J

The Little red hen [illus. by] Paul Galdone. Seabury 1973 unp illus $5.95 (k-1)   398.2

1 Folklore 2 Chickens—Stories

ISBN 0-8164-3099-3

"In a light-hearted interpretation of the old tale, a domesticated little hen, complete with mobcap and apron, busies herself in a picturesquely shabby cottage while her three house mates—a cat, a dog, and a mouse—doze blissfully. The industry of the little hen produces a cake; and only when 'a delicious smell

filled the cozy little house,' do her lazy companions come to life." Horn Bk

"The large, clear, colorful pictures perfectly suit the book for pre-school story hours; the simple text, with one or two lines per page, will make it a success with beginning readers." Sch Library J

Little red hen; pictures by Janina Domanska. Macmillan Pub. Co. 1973 unp illus $4.95 (k-1)   398.2

1 Folklore 2 Chickens—Stories

"To illustrate a terse and compact telling of the old nursery tale, the artist has made some of her most animated pictures. The enterprising hen busies herself with planting the wheat; cutting, threshing, and carrying it to the mill; and finally baking the flour into bread; while the uncooperative cat, goose, and rat stage a side show of high jinks and capers. Still characteristically stylized, with bold geometric patterns against brilliant reds, yellows, and greens, the illustrations clearly display a welcome vitality and humor not often found in the artist's beautifully designed pages." Horn Bk

Maas, Selve

The moon painters, and other Estonian folk tales; retold by Selve Maas; illus. by Laszlo Gal. Viking 1971 143p illus $4.95 (4-6)   398.2

1 Folklore—Estonia

ISBN 0-670-48832-1

These folk tales and legends, "so plainly indigenous to a northern forested land with long, cold Baltic winters, exhibit aspects of magic related to Finnish and several neighboring folklores. Among others, they tell of such characters as Illmarine, the master smith, and Ahti, 'ruler of the waters in Finnish mythology.' Vanapagan, the devil, the monster Northern Frog, and wolves introduce darker elements into the stories; and gentler forms of the supernatural—a magic mirror or a magic ring—govern the fortunes of maidens, princes, peasants, and kings." Horn Bk

"The clear, readable style is eminently suitable for storytelling, and the tales are attractively illustrated with many full-page charcoal drawings." Sch Library J

McCormick, Dell J.

Paul Bunyan swings his axe. Caxton Ptrs. 1936 111p illus $3.50 (4-6)   398.2

1 Legends—United States 2 Bunyan, Paul 3 Lumber and lumbering—Fiction

ISBN 0-87004-093-6

Tales about the legendary exploits of the giant logger and his blue ox, Babe

"Paul's pranks blithely play havoc with the natural laws. . . . Science teachers may not approve, but these stories, retold with gusto and embellished with drolly imaginative drawings, are a tremendous lot of fun." N Y Times Bk Rev

McDermott, Gerald

Anansi the spider; a tale from the Ashanti; adapted and illus. by Gerald McDermott. Holt 1972 unp illus $5.95, lib. bdg. $5.27 (k-3)   398.2

1 Folklore—Ghana 2 Folklore, Ashanti 3 Spiders—Stories

ISBN 0-03-080234-2; 0-03-080236-9

The adaptation of this traditional tale of Ghana is based on an animated film by McDermott. It tells of Anansi, a spider, who is saved from terrible fates by his six sons and is unable to decide which of them to reward. The solution to his predicament is also an explanation for how the moon was put into the sky

"This folk tale is illustrated with strikingly stylized, boldly colored designs based on the traditional geometric forms of Ashanti art." Sat Rev

"The simplicity of the writing style makes this a

McDermott, Gerald—_Continued_
good adaptation for reading aloud to young children or
as a source for storytelling." Chicago. Children's Bk
Center

Arrow to the sun; a Pueblo Indian tale adapted and
illus. by Gerald McDermott. Viking 1974 unp illus
$6.95 (1-3)   398.2
    1 Pueblo Indians—Legends
    ISBN 0-670-13369-8
    Awarded the Caldecott Medal, 1974
    This myth tells how Boy searches for his immortal
father, the Lord of the Sun, in order to substantiate
his paternal heritage. Shot as an arrow to the sun, Boy
passes through the four chambers of ceremony to
prove himself. Accepted by his father, he returns to
earth to bring the Lord of the Sun's spirit to the world
of men
    "The simple, brief text—which suggests similar
stories in religion and folklore—is amply illustrated in
full-page and doublespread pictures. . . . The strong
colors and the bold angular forms powerfully accompany the text; and even on those pages where there is
no text, both colors and form are visually eloquent."
Horn Bk

The magic tree; a tale from the Congo; adapted and
illus. by Gerald McDermott. Holt 1973 unp illus
$5.95, lib. bdg. $5.59 (k-3)   398.2
    1 Folklore—Zaïre
    ISBN 0-03-086716-9; 0-03-086717-7
    "The brilliant colors, the stunning designs based on
African motifs, and the dignity of the stylized figures
combine to illustrate effectively a Congolese tale that
has many elements traditional in the folk genre.
Rejected, a young man whose twin brother has been
loved and favored leaves home. He releases an
enchanted people from the magic tree in which each
had been a leaf, and he weds the princess and lives in
wealth, having promised never to reveal this. Visiting
his family, Mavungu tells of his experiences: suddenly
he remembers that he has sworn secrecy and he
rushes back to his wife and the beautiful village she
magically created. But there is nothing left—only a
grove of silent trees. The adaptation is terse and simple, the ending abrupt but with great visual impact."
Chicago. Children's Bk Center

The stonecutter; a Japanese folk tale; adapted and
illus. by Gerald McDermott. Viking 1975 unp illus
lib. bdg. $5.95 (k-3)   398.2
    1 Folklore—Japan
    ISBN 0-670-67074-X
    "Tasaku is a poor stonecutter. One day, he sees a
prince and his rich retinue ride by, and makes the
wish that he might equal the noble youth in wealth
and power. The spirit of the mountain where Tasaku is
working grants the stonecutter's wish. But . . . Tasaku
is unsatisfied. He wants more power—to be the sun,
then the cloud which can obscure the sun and, at last,
the mountain. . . . At last, the once lowly stonecutter
feels that, as the mountain, he will stand forever,
strong and immutable. Then he feels a stonecutter
chipping away at his base. . . ." Pub W
    "A restrained text, suggesting the subtle brevity of
haiku, is combined with brilliant, four-color illustrations. Utilizing the motifs of traditional Japanese
prints, the artist has produced a dazzling picture-
story, reminiscent of its folklore origin yet contemporary in feeling and original in execution. Designed
initially as an animated film, the tale—for which no
source is given—adapts easily from one visual
medium to another." Horn Bk

McDowell, Robert E.
    (ed.) Third World voices for children; ed. by Robert
E. McDowell and Edward Lavitt; illus. by Barbara
Kohn Isaac. The Third Press [distributed by Viking]
1971 146p illus $5.95 (4-7)   398.2
    1 Folklore 2 Negro literature
    ISBN 0-89388-020-5
    "Odakai books"
    This is a "collection of short stories, folk tales,
poems, and songs from the Third World, including
Africa, New Guinea, the West Indies, Puerto Rico,
and Black America. Selections are grouped geographically; each section is preceded by an introduction which provides background information." Sch
Library J
    "The selections vary greatly in the quality of the
writing—some are excellent, some inept; and the
volume seems more of a pastiche than a unified collection with any traceable theme. Yet, the total collection
serves as an interesting introduction to the motifs of
third-world writing. . . . The strength of the volume is
in its total composition, the combination of all the
stories and drawings." Horn Bk

McGovern, Ann
    Too much noise; illus. by Simms Taback. Houghton
1967 44p illus lib. bdg. $5.95 (k-3)   398.2
    1 Folklore 2 Noise—Fiction 3 Animals—Stories
    ISBN 0-395-1810-0
    "The too crowded house of a familiar old tale
becomes a too noisy house in this entertaining picture-book story. Bothered by the noises in his house,
an old man follows the advice of the village wise man
by first acquiring and then getting rid of a cow, donkey, sheep, hen, dog, and cat. Only then can he
appreciate how quiet his house is. The simplicity and
straightforwardness of the folktale are evident in both
the telling of the cumulative story and in the amusing
colored illustrations." Booklist

MacLeod, Mary
    The book of King Arthur and his noble knights
(5-7)   398.2
    1 Arthur, King
    Some editions are:
    Lippincott (Lippincott classics) $5.95 Introduction by
        Angelo Petri; illustrations by Henry C. Pitz (ISBN
        0-397-30145-6)
    Macmillan (N Y) (The Macmillan classics) $4.95 Illus-
        trated by Herschel Levit; afterword by Clifton
        Fadiman. Has title: King Arthur
        First published 1900 in England
    Stories from Sir Thomas Malory's Morte d'Arthur
retold in modern English

MacManus, Seumas
    The bold heroes of Hungry Hill, and other Irish folk
tales; retold by Seumas MacManus; illus. by Jay Chollick. Farrar, Straus 1951 207p illus $3.25 (5-7) 398.2
    1 Folklore—Ireland 2 Fairy tales
    ISBN 0-374-30858-6
    "Twelve Irish folk tales, told with humor, charm
and delightful Irish flavor. . . . These stories will be
useful for story telling, for reading aloud, and for boys
and girls to read. Many of the stories are parallels. The
format is attractive." Pittsburgh

Hibernian nights; introduced by Padraic Colum;
illus. by Paul Kennedy. Macmillan (N Y) 1963 263p
illus lib. bdg. $5.95 (4-7)   398.2
    1 Folklore—Ireland 2 Fairy tales
    "The 22 Irish folk and fairy tales in this superior
collection were chosen by a master storyteller as the
cream of his story lore. . . . Told with a strong and
charming Irish flavor and handsomely printed and

MacManus, Seumas —*Continued*
illustrated, these stories of the little people, kings and
queens, cruel stepmothers, and youngest sons will be
a delight to read, to read aloud, or to tell." Booklist

Malcolmson, Anne
(ed.) Song of Robin Hood; selected & ed. by Anne
Malcolmson; music arranged by Grace Castagnetta;
designed & illus. by Virginia Lee Burton. Houghton
1947 123p illus music $12.50 (5-7)　　　　398.2
1 Robin Hood 2 Ballads, English 3 Legends—Great
Britain
ISBN 0-395-06895-9
"Eighteen ballads from the Robin Hood cycle are
given here chosen with regard for the sources and
accompanied by traditional tunes." N Y Pub Library
A "harmonious piece of bookmaking, this version of
Robin Hood will probably be of chief interest where
there is a special folklore collection or a strong interest
in art. These are the original ballads presented with
judicious modernizing, cutting, and omission. Each of
the 500 or more verses is illustrated, with the action
carried along in stylized marginal decoration executed
with painstaking detail." Booklist

Yankee Doodle's cousins; illus. by Robert McClos-
key. Houghton 1969 267p illus $4.95 (4-7)　　　398.2
1 Legends—U.S.
ISBN 0-395-06896-7
First published 1941. Copyright renewed 1969
These are retellings of stories about some of the real
and legendary characters who have become part of
American folklore. Among the twenty-eight stories
are tales of Captain Kidd, Ichabod Paddock, Johnny
Appleseed, Mike Fink, Daniel Boone, Pirate Jean
Laffite, Brer Rabbit, Pecos Bill and Paul Bunyan. The
tales are arranged by region: the East, the South, the
Mississippi Valley, and the West
The tales "are part of the legendary lore of every
young America. Their robust humor, absurdities, and
exaggerations are a never-failing delight, and Robert
McCloskey's drawings reflect these qualities to per-
fection." Children's Bks Too Good To Miss
Glossary: p261-[68]

Manning-Sanders, Ruth
A book of charms and changelings; illus. by Robin
Jacques. Dutton [1972 c1971] 124p illus $5.50 (3-6)
　　　　398.2
1 Folklore 2 Fairy tales
ISBN 0-525-26775-1
First published 1971 in England
A "collection of worldwide fairy stories dealing with
the dual themes of charms and changelings. . . .
Although many familiar symbols and motifs are called
up, these particular stories are not commonly available. In [some stories] . . . charms—a piece of
amber, a handmill, the bones of an ox, and an amulet
respectively—work for their owners' good. In other
stories, the spells are of evil intent." Sch Library J
These fifteen tales are illustrated with "deft and
distinctive black and white drawings. . . . Like other
compilations by Manning-Sanders, this is a joy to read
aloud; the magical fairy changelings and human pawns
are described in a light, flavorful style that has a sense
of humor even when the tales are not humorous.
Good for storytelling, too." Chicago. Children's Bk
Center

A book of devils and demons; illus. by Robin Jacques. Dutton 1970 124p illus $5.50 (3-6)　　　398.2
1 Folklore
ISBN 0-525-26795-6
"Drawn from the folklore of nine countries, an
entertaining collection of 12 stories, skillfully told and
appropriately illustrated. Although the devils and

demons in a few of the tales are helpful to humans,
most are full of trickery and guile. The origin of each
story and an explanation of the difference between
devils and demons are included in the foreword."
Booklist
"Monster lovers especially will like the stories, and
storytellers will find them zestful additions for story
hour." Sch Library J

A book of dragons; drawings by Robin Jacques.
Dutton [1965 c1964] 128p illus $5.50 (3-6)　　398.2
1 Folklore 2 Fairy tales 3 Dragons—Stories
ISBN 0-525-26824-3
First published 1964 in England
This volume "contains fourteen fairy tales—many
of them unfamiliar—gathered from Greece, China,
Japan, Macedonia, Rumania, Ireland, Germany and
Slovakia. No sources are listed but all are good tales,
interesting and unusual in their use of incident. . . .
Some of the stories are concerned with kindly dragons
while others are about dragons bad and savage, to be
either killed or outwitted." Toronto
"Smooth storytelling versions attractively illus-
trated." Children's Bks, 1965

A book of ghosts & goblins; illus. by Robin Jacques.
Dutton [1969 c1968] 126p illus $5.95, pa $1.25
(3-6)　　　　398.2
1 Folklore 2 Ghost stories
ISBN 0-525-26883-9; 0-525-45014-9
First published 1968 in England
A collection of twenty-one stories, funny or
frightening, about all kinds of ghosts and goblins
"Lively content, smooth storytelling, and inviting
format will make the collection of twenty-one stories,
gathered from many different nations, highly popular. The foreword lists the origin of all the stories by
country—from Africa to Siberia, from Spain to Ireland. . . . The humor, eeriness, and suspense of the
book create a superior collection for sharing aloud or
for a child's own reading. Two thirds of the selections
are about ghosts—restlessly seeking to right a wrong,
to regain something missing, or merely wandering.
The goblin tales, including three amusing ones from
Estonia, are particularly entertaining. The illustrator's skillful line drawings give apt individuality to
the characters, and supply humorous detail." Horn Bk

(ed.) A book of magical beasts; illus. by Raymond
Briggs. Nelson 1970 244p illus $4.95 (3-6)　　398.2
1 Folklore 2 Fairy tales 3 Animals—Stories
ISBN 0-8407-6008-6
First published 1965 in England with title: The
Hamish Hamilton Book of magical beasts
An "anthology of 24 tales and 13 poems from around
the world in which magical beasts appear. Introductory paragraphs to each selection give information on
author or collector and on source or variant." Booklist
"Although some old favorites ('The Tinder Box,'
'Jabberwocky') are included, this is a far from humdrum anthology. The sources are wide, the choices
discriminating, the prefatory notes enjoyable. In
addition, the black-and-white drawings are delightful
and the print large and readable." Sat Rev

A book of mermaids; illus. by Robin Jacques. Dutton [1968 c1967] 127p illus $5.50 (3-6)　　　398.2
1 Folklore 2 Fairy tales
ISBN 0-525-26941-X
First published 1967 in England
"Sixteen tales of mermaids and mermen are retold
here in sprightly style; they are varied and eminently
suitable for reading aloud or storytelling as well as for
independent reading; they are from a dozen countries, and they are illustrated with effective black and
white pictures. Many are tales of mortals who loved or

Manning-Sanders, Ruth—_Continued_
were loved by the merpeople; one very amusing story
is about a young mermaid who fell in love with a whale
who was exceedingly irritated by her unwelcome
attentions; another is on the familiar theme of the
beautiful girl mistreated by her stepmother." Sutherland. The Best in Children's Bks

A book of ogres and trolls; illus. by Robin Jacques.
Dutton [1973 c1972] 127p illus $5.95 (3-6)   398.2
1 Folklore 2 Fairy tales
ISBN 0-525-26998-3
First published 1972 in England
These 13 "folk tales from Russia, Iceland, Sicily and
other European countries prove that agreeable ogres
are a rarity, while trolls, though mischievous, often
help humans out of trouble and even into wealth."
Pub W
"Excellent stories. . . . All are retold in the selec-
tor's characteristically rhythmic and folksy style.
Teamed with Robin Jacques' comic pen-and-ink drawings, this is a book to be shared." Sch Library J

A book of princes and princesses; illus. by Robin
Jacques. Dutton [1970 c1969] 127p illus $5.50 (3-6)
                                                398.2
1 Folklore 2 Fairy tales
ISBN 0-525-27024-8
First published 1969 in England
A "collection of 13 traditional stories about princes
and princesses from Italy, Sicily, the Ukraine,
Archangel (in Russia), etc. The stories—dealing with
royal protagonists in love, in danger, in interactions
with ogres, dragons, etc.—are for the most part
unfamiliar." Sch Library J
The narrative is "expert and lively, the illustrations
old-fashioned (that is, credible), spirited, and of such
dedicated care as to repay study with a magnifying
glass. Every story has a happy ending, every silvery
picture a moving dramatic message of its own. First
class." Christian Sci Monitor

A book of sorcerers and spells; illus. by Robin Jacques. Dutton [1974 c1973] 125p illus $5.95 (3-6)
                                                398.2
1 Folklore 2 Fairy tales
ISBN 0-525-27040-X
First published 1973 in England
"Loosely grouped by the omnipresent folktale
themes of spells and sorcery, these 12 stories are held
together by the distinct vitality with which they have
been recounted. One finds an Irish version of 'Beauty
and the beast' in 'The great bear of Orange' as well as
several other tales of people transformed into animals
or fantastic beings. Evil and good sorcerers are pitted
against each other in the Sudanese 'Foni and Fotia,'
while a North African Anansi story, 'The mossy rock,'
finds the well-known trickster under the spell of a
magicked stone. Throughout, the writing is clever and
quick, and many characters are individualized."
Booklist

A book of witches; drawings by Robin Jacques.
Dutton [1966 c1965] 126p illus $5.95 (3-6)   398.2
1 Folklore 2 Fairy tales 3 Witches—Fiction
ISBN 0-525-27054-X
First published 1965 in England
"The bad witches in this collection of twelve stories
are the kind children expect to encounter on Halloween. Some—the witches in 'Rapunzel' and 'Hansel
and Gretel'—are already known, while others are not
as familiar but just as scary. . . . The tales come from
several European countries." Horn Bk
"A nicely illustrated compilation. . . . The writing
style is smooth and colloquial, with just enough of that
turn of phrase appropriate to the genre to give the

stories color without burdening them with either
quaintness or floridity. Useful for reading aloud or for
storytelling." Sutherland. The Best in Children's Bks

A book of wizards; drawings by Robin Jacques.
Dutton [1967 c1966] 126p illus $4.50 (3-6)   398.2
1 Folklore 2 Fairy tales
ISBN 0-525-27082-5
First published 1966 in England
"The wizards who figure in this collection of folk
tales [from various countries] vary in personality, and
the artist has caught their individual characters in
situations that bring out their humor and beneficence
as well as their fearfulness and evil. . . . The eleven
stories are told freely in a direct and lively manner.
The national background of each tale is stated in the
preface, but written sources are not specified." Horn
Bk
"Some of these stories can be found in other collections, but not all, and, for the storyteller, it is especially nice to have so many wizard stories in one
volume." Sch Library J

A choice of magic; illus. by Robin Jacques. Dutton
1971 318p illus $7.50 (3-6)   398.2
1 Folklore 2 Fairy tales
ISBN 0-525-27810-9
"Delicate illustrations mirror the romantic mood of
an anthology in which four new stories have been
added to tales chosen by Ruth Manning-Sanders from
her earlier collections. The tales are from various
parts of the world, primarily European, and they
constitute as discriminating, flavorful, and varied a
collection of folk and fairy tales as the most devoted
reader of the genre could wish." Sat Rev

Gianni and the ogre; illus. by William Stobbs. Dutton [1971 c1970] 191p illus $4.95 (4-6)   398.2
1 Folklore—Mediterranean region 2 Fairy tales
ISBN 0-525-30540-8
First published 1970 in England
"Eighteen tales from Mediterranean sources are
included in . . . [this anthology which] is illustrated
with vigorous, dramatic pictures in black and white.
Many of the story patterns are familiar: the spurned
ragamuffin who returns a wealthy suitor and wins the
sultan's daughter; an ogre outwitted by the lad he
sought to trap; the stepmother who sends her own
daughter off to gain the same wealth that her step-
daughter brought home. The style of the retelling is
delightful, the conversational tone livened by dry wit
and felicitous phrasing. A good book to read alone or
aloud, and a fine source for story-telling." Chicago.
Children's Bk Center

Marriott, Alice
American Indian mythology [by] Alice Marriott and
Carol K. Rachlin. Crowell 1968 211p illus $10.95
                                                398.2
1 Indians of North America—Legends 2 Folklore,
Indian
ISBN 0-690-07201-5
"A fascinating collection of myths, legends and contemporary folklore which the authors have obtained
in most cases directly from Indians. . . . With each tale
there is a brief introduction to the tribe. Subjects
include myths of creation; the world and the hereaf-
ter; 'how-and-why' stories told to children; historic
legends and witchcraft. Among the tribes represented
are Cheyenne, Modoc, Ponca, Hopi, Kiowa, Co-
manche and Zuñi." Pub W
The authors "seek to present the best of two worlds,
accurate background on the main Indian groups in
America, and a sort of literary telling of their myths
and legends. The viewpoint is that of the anthropologist rather than of the folklorist. The stories do not

Marriott, Alice—*Continued*

have an Indian flavor but this makes for somewhat smoother reading." Library J

Bibliography: p207-11

(comp.) Winter-telling stories; illus. by Richard Cuffari. Crowell [1969 c1947] 82p illus $4.50, lib. bdg. $5.25 (3-6)   398.2

1 Kiowa Indians—Legends

ISBN 0-690-89635-2; 0-690-89636-0

First published 1947 by William Sloane Associates, illustrated by Roland Whitehorse

"Based on the Kiowa Indian stories about Saynday, the man who made the world the way it is, this is a delightful collection of brief stories of the good and sometimes bad things Saynday brought to the Indians." Pub W

Pleasing format with many attractive black-and-white drawings. The writing style is informal and full of colloquial dialogue, which, along with the appealing subject and humor, make this useful for junior high remedial reading as well as good entertainment for older elementary school children. The quality of the stories varies throughout, but always remains in the average to superior range." Sch Library J

Matsutani, Miyoko

The crane maiden; illus. by Chihiro Iwasaki; English version by Alvin Tresselt. . . . Parents Mag. Press 1968 unp illus $4.95, lib. bdg. $4.59 (k-3)   398.2

1 Legends—Japan 2 Cranes (Birds)—Stories

ISBN 0-8193-0207-4; 0-8193-0208-2

"This book translated from 'Tsuru No Ongaeshi' originally published by Kasei Sha, Tokyo, Japan." Title Page

An old Japanese tale about a crane who takes a human female form when freed from a trap by a poor woodcutter. She repays the kindness of the woodcutter and his wife, and fills their home with joy and laughter. But in the end, because of a promise broken, she must become a crane once more

"This is a distinguished picture book for storytelling and surely a beautiful legend to read and reread. Glowing and luminous watercolors in lavenders and pink." Wis Library Bul

Mayne, William

(ed.) William Mayne's Book of giants; stories ed. by William Mayne; illus. by Raymond Briggs. Dutton [1969 c1968] 215p illus $4.95 (4-6)   398.2

1 Giants—Fiction

ISBN 0-525-42810-0

First published 1968 in England with title: The Hamish Hamilton Book of giants

This collection of stories by such authors as Eleanor Farjeon, Nathaniel Hawthorne, Jonathan Swift, and Oscar Wilde tells about well-meaning giants as well as evil-minded ones

"A delightful collection, with a light-hearted preface by the compiler, notes on author and story preceding each selection, handsome illustrations, and big, clear print. For reading aloud, for storytelling, or for independent reading." Chicago. Children's Bk Center

Mehdevi, Anne Sinclair

Persian folk and fairy tales; retold by Anne Sinclair Mehdevi; illus. by Paul E. Kennedy. Knopf 1965 117p illus lib. bdg. $5.99 (4-6)   398.2

1 Folklore—Persia 2 Fairy tales

ISBN 0-394-91496-1

"This is a fine collection of [eleven] stories straight out of the oral tradition, retold with grace and authority. . . . Storytellers will recognize variants of Euro-

pean and English stories in ['The pumpkin child' ('Cinderella')] 'Mistress Cockroach' ('Perez and Martina') and 'Simpletons' ('The Three Sillies'). Some stories have an 'Arabian Nights' flavor, some [are] beast tales." Sch Library J

"Unusually compatible illustrations lend cultural as well as artistic distinction. Patterned after old Persian paintings, they have flowing lines and intricate designs." Horn Bk

Melzack, Ronald

The day Tuk became a hunter & other Eskimo stories; retold by Ronald Melzack; illus. by Carol Jones. Dodd [1968 c1967] 92p illus $3.95 (3-6)   398.2

1 Folklore, Eskimo 2 Legends, Eskimo

ISBN 0-396-05656-3

Ten "unusual Eskimo tales, simply retold, are enhanced by beautiful illustrations and attractive book design. Varied and representative stories describe daily life, origin of birds, animals, the sun and stars, animal tales of trickery and wisdom and tall tales that capture the unique spirit of Eskimo culture." Bruno. Bks for Sch Libraries, 1968

Merrill, Jean

High, Wide and Handsome and their three tall tales, by Jean Merrill & Ronni Solbert. Young Scott Bks. 1964 unp illus lib. bdg. $4.50 (1-4)   398.2

1 Folklore—Burma 2 Animals—Stories

ISBN 0-201-09225-5

This is a "Burmese version of an old folk tale about the city slicker who matches his wits with three country rascals who are plotting to steal the clothes off his back. The country rascals (a monkey, a pig, and a fox) challenge a hound to a storytelling contest, the winner to get the loser's clothes." Asia: A Guide to Bks for Children

"The tall tales are amusing and the outcome of the contest only partially predictable. Ronni Solbert's pictures are peculiarly delightful, the pages have luminous backgrounds of transparent watercolor washes of subtle pink, with warm light brown and orange for the pen and ink and color drawings. The scenes and animal figures are highly humorous, especially the hotrod dog, Rolling Stone, in his sports car." Bk Week

Shan's lucky knife; a Burmese folk tale retold by Jean Merrill; illus. in color by Ronni Solbert. Scott, W.R. 1960 unp illus lib. bdg. $4.95 (3-5)   398.2

1 Folklore—Burma

ISBN 0-201-09341-3

A colorful picture-story book, combining "a folktale plot with pictures arranged in flowing doublespreads. . . . Shan, the story's hero, a country boy from the hills of Burma, makes his chance to row down the Irrawaddy to the Rangoon bazaar on a trading boat and manages by a clever trick to outwit the wily boatmaster who would cheat him of his just pay. Captures the flavor of Burmese river life and city trading." Horn Bk

Mosel, Arlene

The funny little woman; retold by Arlene Mosel; pictures by Blair Lent. Dutton 1972 unp illus $5.95 (k-2)   398.2

1 Folklore—Japan

ISBN 0-525-30265-4

Awarded the Caldecott Medal, 1972

Based on Lafcadio Hearn's The old woman and the dumpling

"A Japanese folk tale about a funny little woman who laughs 'Tee-he-he-he' all the time and makes rice dumplings. One of her dumplings rolls away and she chases it into the domain of the fearful 'oni,' a mon-

Mosel, Arlene—*Continued*

ster. The 'oni' sets the giggling woman to work, cooking for him and his friends, until the day she escapes
with their magic paddle that lets her create a potful of
rice with only one grain." Pub W

"The tale unfolds in a simple tellable style. . . .
Using elements of traditional Japanese art, the illustrator has made marvelously imaginative pictures. . . .
All the inherent drama and humor of the story are
manifest in the illustrations: the toothy, fearsome
'oni'; their weird, watery-green subterranean house
contrasting with tiny drawings of the deserted little
house above-ground; the swirling [underground]
river . . . and the ever merry, dauntless figure of the
little woman in her gay orange kimono." Horn Bk

Tikki Tikki Tembo; retold by Arlene Mosel; illus. by
Blair Lent. Holt 1968 unp illus $4.95, lib. bdg. $4.59
(k-2)   398.2
  1 Folklore—China 2 Names, Personal—Fiction
  ISBN 0-03-067935-4; 0-03-067940-0
A "Chinese folk tale about a first son with a very
long name. When Tikki Tikki Tembo-No Sa Rembo-
Chari Bari Ruchi-Pip Peri Pembo fell into the well, it
took his little brother so long to say his name and get
help that Tikki almost drowned." Hodges. Best Bks
for Elem Sch Libraries

"In this polished version of a story hour favorite,
beautifully stylized wash drawings of serene Oriental
landscapes are in comic contrast to amusingly
visualized folk and the active disasters accruing to the
possessor of a 21-syllable, irresistibly chantable
name." Best Bks of the Year, 1968

Ness, Evaline

Long, Broad & Quickeye; adapted and illus. by
Evaline Ness. Scribner 1969 unp illus $5.95 (1-4)
                                                              398.2
  1 Folklore—Bohemia 2 Fairy tales
  ISBN 0-684-20897-0
"The artist has adapted the story skillfully, keeping
the flavor of the Andrew Lang version of a Bohemian
fairy tale. . . . [It tells] the story of the prince who
found the girl he wanted for his wife and broke her
enchantment with the help of his extraordinary companions. . . . The strong, handsome illustrations are in
attractive, muted tones of green, tan, and orange. The
book will be a delight to read aloud to one or two
children looking at the pictures as the story is read."
Horn Bk

Nic Leodhas, Sorche

By loch and by lin; tales from Scottish ballads; illus.
by Vera Bock. Holt 1969 130p illus $4.95, lib. bdg.
$4.59 (4-7)   398.2
  1 Folklore—Scotland 2 Ballads, Scottish
  ISBN 0-03-076450-5; 0-03-076455-6
"Well-told prose versions of two ancient Scottish
lays and eight 'twopenny ballads' dating from the
seventeenth and eighteenth centuries, preceded by
an introduction that explains the origin and characteristics of these old poems. Reflecting the grandiose
spirit and romantic flavor of the originals, the stories
recount the adventures of heroes, noblemen, and
common folk in which grace and courage are
rewarded and the wise triumph over the foolishly
cocksure." Booklist

"Vera Bock's handsome, witty drawings, some of
them symbolic rather than representational, enrich
the book in crystal grays." Christian Sci Monitor

Gaelic ghosts; illus. by Nonny Hogrogian. Holt
[1964 c1963] 110p illus lib. bdg. $3.27 (4-7)   398.2
  1 Folklore—Scotland 2 Ghost stories
  ISBN 0-03-035910-4
"A delightful collection of Scottish tales about

ghosts, friendly ghosts for the most part, both human
and dogs. . . . Humorous rather than hair-raising. . . .
Striking jacket and woodcuts complete a handsome
book." Pub W

"Would be wonderful for informal fireside storytelling as well as for library story hours." Horn Bk

Heather and broom; tales of the Scottish Highlands; illus. by Consuelo Joerns. Holt 1960 128p illus
lib. bdg. $3.07 (4-7)   398.2
  1 Folklore—Scotland 2 Fairy tales
  ISBN 0-03-035280-0
These eight stories "are peopled with such engaging humans as kind lairds and brave lassies, princesses
and farmers and clever women; and such supernatural
beings as fairies, brownies, goblins, witches, bogles,
and the wonderful seal people from the Kingdom of
Ron." Horn Bk

"In a long preface, sources for the retelling are cited
and an interesting explanation is given of the distinguishing qualities of the Highland folk tale. The style
has a combination of forthright dialogue, Scottish
terms, and robust humor that is most attractive. A
good book for reading aloud, also, to younger children." Chicago. Children's Bk Center

Thistle and thyme; tales and legends from Scotland;
illus. by Evaline Ness. Holt 1962 143p illus lib. bdg.
$3.27 (4-7)   398.2
  1 Folklore—Scotland 2 Fairy tales
  ISBN 0-03-035210-X
Companion volume to: Heather and broom,
entered above

Among the ten "stories are six 'sgeulachdan' tales
composed and told by accomplished storytellers as
part of the entertainment at a wedding, wake, christening, or the like. Filled with romance, magic, and
humor and superbly told with a rich Gaelic flavor,
these tales and legends will delight readers and
storytellers alike. Illustrated with striking woodcuts
eminently suited to the text." Booklist

"Children who have wide vocabularies and are
interested in words will love this book, which will
introduce them to a great many picturesque Scottish
words and names." Pub W

Twelve great black cats, and other eerie Scottish
tales; illus. by Vera Bock. Dutton 1971 173p illus
$5.95 (4-7)   398.2
  1 Folklore—Scotland 2 Ghost stories
  ISBN 0-525-41575-0
This collection of ten Scottish tales includes stories
of ghosts, hauntings and odd happenings. Eight of the
stories were written by the author before her death;
the last two were written by the author's niece Jenifer
Jill Digby from notes the author had left

The tales "are told with a fine feeling for the dramatic as well as for the eerie, and with a rhythm and
swing that makes them excellent for storytelling."
Horn Bk

"Vera Bock's black-and-white wash drawings
accented in charcoal and pencil perfectly set the mood
for each story." Sch Library J

Glossary: p163-64

O'Faolain, Eileen

Irish sagas and folk-tales; retold by Eileen O'Faolain; illus. by Joan Kiddell-Monroe. Walck, H. Z.
1954 245p illus (Oxford Myths and legends) lib. bdg.
$6 (5-7)   398.2
  1 Folklore—Ireland 2 Folklore, Gaelic 3 Fairy tales
  ISBN 0-8098-2317-9
  First published by Oxford
The collection begins with such heroic sagas as: The
children of Lir, Cattle-raid of Cooley; The death of
Cuchullin, etc. Then come the tales of Finn and

O'Faolain, Eileen—*Continued*
Fianna, and finally there are the Chimney-corner
tales of the little people
"In her English version, Eileen O'Faolain preserves the authentic rhythm of the Gaelic in which the
tales were told. And even in the section of more
modern stories she has the good sense to allow country story-tellers to use their own idioms." N Y Times
Bk Rev
Glossary: p244-45

The Old woman and her pig; pictures by Paul Galdone. McGraw 1960 32p illus lib. bdg. $4.72
(k-2)   398.2
1 Folklore
ISBN 0-07-022721-7
"Whittlesey House publications"
"A retelling of the old [cumulative] tale about the
woman who had difficulty getting her pig home from
market and had to enlist the aid of a cat, a rat, a rope, a
butcher, an ox, water, fire, a stick, and a dog." Pub W
"Paul Galdone has done an outstanding piece of
work in providing the delightful illustrations and artistic book design for this dearly loved folk tale. The
whole is dramatic in appearance, appropriately
quaint, and full of warm-hearted humor. Young children will enjoy it and many will memorize the text.
Highly recommended." Library J

Olenius, Elsa
(comp.) Great Swedish fairy tales; illus. by John
Bauer; tr. by Holger Lundbergh. Delacorte Press
1973 238p illus $10 (4-7)   398.2
1 Folklore—Sweden 2 Fairy tales
ISBN 0-440-03043-9
"A Merloyd Lawrence book"
Original Swedish edition published 1966
"A double delight for American readers—21 Swedish fairy tales virtually unknown in this country with
artwork by a major Swedish illustrator. Of the nine
authors whose tales reflect 19th-Century morality,
Elsa Beskow is best known. . . . The illustrations
which are reminiscent of Bauer's contemporary,
Arthur Rackham, have a wonderful clarity of detail
even though most depict dark scenes of night, caves,
and deep forests. Like the tales, the pictures swarm
with princes and princesses, harmless tomte; and
vicious, wild trolls. The only complaint is that a few
tales for which illustrations appear . . . are not
included in the present collection." Sch Library J

Opie, Iona
(ed.) The classic fairy tales [ed. by] Iona and Peter
Opie. Oxford 1974 255p illus $13.95   398.2
1 Fairy tales
ISBN 0-19-211559-6
This "surely must be the definitive scholarly edition
of the classic fairy tales, those 24 tales that are the
most familiar. For the first time in one volume, the
reader is able to find the earliest known printed versions of these tales as well as brief but packed analyses
of the origins and histories of the stories. Not necessarily for today's children (several of these are taken
from somewhat bawdy 18th-century chapbooks), this
book will delight every adult who cares about authentic folk material and recognizes its impact on Western
thinking. In addition to the faultless text, the reproductions (woodcuts, wood engravings, oils, etc.) of
some of the greatest illustrators of these tales (Evans,
Doré, Cruikshank, Dulac, Crane, and others) make
this book one that must be owned by every library.
Helpful indexing, bibliography, list of sources of
illustrations." Choice

Otsuka, Yuzo
Suho and the white horse; a legend of Mongolia;
illus. by Suekichi Akaba; tr. by Yasuko Hirawa. Bobbs
1969 unp illus $5 (1-4)   398.2
1 ¡legends—Mongolia
ISBN 0-672-50519-3
Original Japanese edition, 1967
"The story of the origin of the horse-head fiddle is
the tale of Suho the shepherd boy and the white horse
that he raises, only to lose through a cruel betrayal."
Horn Bk
"Beautifully illustrated with dramatic, yet sensitive
full-color paintings that sweep across the oversize
pages." Booklist

Palmer, Robin
Dragons, unicorns, and other magical beasts. . . .
Illus. by Don Bolognese. Walck, H.Z. 1966 95p illus
$5.95 (4-6)   398.2
1 Folklore 2 Animals, Mythical
ISBN 0-8098-2389-6
"A dictionary of fabulous creatures with old tales
and verses about them." Title page
"More than sixty-five mythical beasts from the folklore of Europe, Africa, Asia and America—from playful creatures like the Irish pooka or the Japanese
tanuki to the noble phoenix and the fearsome
werewolf—are identified, described, and pictured.
Eight folk tales from around the world and four
delightful poems (by Elinor Wylie, Vachel Lindsay,
William Rose Benét, and John Greenleaf Whittier)
further place a dozen of these strange beasts against a
legendary or literary background." Horn Bk

Pearce, Philippa
Beauty and the beast; retold by Philippa Pearce;
illus. by Alan Barrett. Crowell 1972 unp illus $4.50,
lib. bdg. $5.25 (3-5)   398.2
1 Folklore—France 2 Fairy tales
ISBN 0-690-12561-5; 0-690-12562-3
A retelling of "the story of the beautiful young girl
who is prepared to sacrifice her happiness to save her
father's life, and whose compassionate kiss breaks the
spell that binds the prince who has been her captor in
the guise of an ugly, beastlike creature. The author's
explanation of the sources of the tale and of the revision she has made is appended." Chicago. Children's
Bk Center
"All the enchantment of this fairy tale with its
theme of love and compassion appears in a truly lovely
picture book. Abridgements in the retelling tighten
the essential story, and added inventions are in perfect harmony. Several distinctive colors are used as
backgrounds for each page, and the illustrations—
some full-page, some doublespread—have a quality
of mystery that enhances the magic." Horn Bk

Perrault, Charles
Cinderella; or, The little glass slipper. A free translation from the French of Charles Perrault; with pictures by Marcia Brown. Scribner 1954 unp illus lib.
bdg. $5.95, pa 95¢ (k-3)   398.2
1 Fairy tales
ISBN 0-684-12676-1; 0-684-12788-1
Awarded the Caldecott Medal, 1955
This is the classic story of the poor, good-natured
girl who works for her selfish step-sisters until a fairy
godmother transforms her into a beautiful "princess"
for just one night
"A distinguished picture book. . . . The story can be
used for telling, but it is perfect for the picture-book
hour. With soft, delicate colors and lines that subtly
suggest, Miss Brown creates a thoroughly fairyland
atmosphere, at the same time recreating the sophistication of the French Court with its golden coach,

Perrault, Charles—*Continued*
canopied bed, dazzling chandeliers, liveried footmen, curled and pompadoured ladies, and peruked [bewigged] courtiers." Library J

Famous fairy tales; pictures by Charles Mozley; tr. by Sarah Chokla Gross. Large type ed. complete and unabridged. Watts, F. [1967 c1959] 160p illus lib. bdg. $7.95 (4-6)   398.2
  1 Folklore—France 2 Fairy tales
  ISBN 0-531-00185-7
"A Keith Jennison book"
A large type edition of the collection first published 1959 with title: Famous French fairy tales
Contains nine of the French writer's stories: The sleeping beauty; Puss-in-Boots: Blue Beard; Hop o'my Thumb; Ricky with a tuft; Little Red Riding Hood; Diamonds and toads; The three wasted wishes; Cinderella

The little Red Riding Hood; illus. by William Stobbs. Walck, H.Z. [1973 c1972] 25p illus $4.95 (k-3)   398.2
  1 Folklore—France 2 Wolves—Stories
  ISBN 0-8098-1202-9
"Some minor modifications have been made in this retelling of Perrault's tale based on Stambler's translation, but the original ending in which both the grandmother and Red Riding Hood are eaten by the wolf is retained. Stobbs' illustrations in black and white and in color aptly portray an innocent, trusting little girl led astray by a cunning, savage wolf." Booklist
"Kathleen Lines explains in an afterword that Perrault's tales were intended to instruct as well as to entertain, and a happy ending would weaken the moral." Sch Library J

Perrault's Complete fairy tales; tr. from the French by A. E. Johnson and others; with illus. by W. Heath Robinson. Dodd 1961 183p illus $4.50 (4-6)   398.2
  1 Folklore—France 2 Fairy tales
  ISBN 0-396-04493-X
"Of the fourteen tales which comprise the present volume, the first eleven are from the master-hand of Charles Perrault. . . . Three of the tales, 'The Ridiculous Wishes,' 'Donkey Skin' and 'Patient Griselda' . . . are reproduced here by paraphrase rather than literal translation [of their original verse form]. . . . To the eleven tales of Perrault, three others have been added here: 'Beauty and the Beast,' by Mme. Leprince de Beaumont (1711-1781) . . . [and] 'Princess Rosette' and 'The Friendly Frog' . . . from the prolific pen of Mme. d'Aulnoy (1650-1705)." Prefatory note
"This is an excellent group to have in one well-printed volume, especially as the 'moralities' of Perrault have not been omitted, and as the fine old illustrations of W. Heath Robinson are used." N Y Her Trib Bks

Puss in Boots; a free translation from the French; with pictures by Marcia Brown. Scribner 1952 unp illus lib. bdg. $6.95 (k-3)   398.2
  1 Folklore—France 2 Fairy tales
  ISBN 0-684-12988-4
This is the story of the poor miller's son, whose fortune was made by the cleverness of his loyal cat
"A beautiful, gay, very French picture book. Miss Brown has made her own free translation, which is humorous and spirited. She has created such a Master Sly-boots as never before has helped to turn a youngest son into a marquis." N Y Her Trib Bks
"The colors, chiefly coral pink, yellow and gray, are brilliantly handled, lush without being in the least vulgar. This effect is one of gaiety and wit." N Y Times Bk Rev

Picard, Barbara Leonie
Stories of King Arthur and his knights; retold by Barbara Leonie Picard; with wood engravings by Roy Morgan. Walck, H.Z. [1966] 291p illus $5.50 (5-7)
398.2
  1 Arthur, King
  ISBN 0-8098-3008-6
  First published 1955 by Oxford
"Miss Picard consulted many sources for this retelling of the Arthurian legends, and, without using archaic words, has turned phrases to recall the grace and vigor of an earlier idiom. Since Arthur's reign is her primary concern, only a few chapters are devoted to his birth and rise to the throne. . . . But to include too many stories would be to crowd out the detail which makes the adventures real, and the best-known stories of the knights are all here. This will make an excellent introduction to Camelot for children who find the language of Lanier's Malory and of Howard Pyle still too difficult. . . . The wood engravings, gray-green on black and white, are fittingly strong and medieval." Horn Bk

Price, Christine
The valiant chattee-maker; a folktale of India; retold by Christine Price. Warne 1965 unp illus $3.50 (k-3)   398.2
  1 Folklore—India
  ISBN 0-7232-0348-2
"Through a series of accidents the [village potter] . . . earns a reputation for bravery and is mistakenly considered a hero." Chicago
"Handsome, lively illustrations that include a magnificent golden tiger complement the story." Horn Bk

Pyle, Howard
King Stork; illus. by Trina Schart Hyman. Little 1973 48p illus $5.95 (k-3)   398.2
  1 Fairy tales
  ISBN 0-316-72440-8
Text first published 1888 in the author's collection: The wonder clock, entered below
Pyle's story of a poor drummer youth who wins a beautiful but wicked princess "with the help of King Stork's magic and 'tames' her with a beating is fluidly illustrated with medieval scenes. . . . [It is] a story in the devious-female, dominating-male tradition." Booklist
"The illustrations fit the various moods of the story. . . . The princess is scantily-clad yet certainly beautiful. Children will enjoy the detailed illustrations and the simplicity and magical qualities of the story." Sch Library J

The merry adventures of Robin Hood of great renown in Nottinghamshire, as written and illus. by Howard Pyle. Scribner 1946 250p illus $7.50 (5-7)
398.2
  1 Robin Hood 2 Legends—Great Britain
  ISBN 0-684-20915-2
  First published 1883. Contains the original drawings of Pyle without the decorative borders
Twenty-two stories of Robin Hood and his adventures with the king's foresters in Sherwood Forest. This band of outlaws made a practice of robbing the rich to help the poor. Set during the reign of Henry II of England
"Of all the books of Robin Hood this is best for literary style, adherence to the spirit and events of the old ballads and wealth of historical background." Toronto
"The author illustrates [this adventure] in a most appropriately picturesque style for young people." Baker's Best

Pyle, Howard—*Continued*
Pepper & salt; or, Seasoning for young folk; prepared by Howard Pyle. Harper 1913 109p illus lib. bdg. $4.79 (4-6)　　　　398.2
1 Folklore 2 Fairy tales
ISBN 0-06-024811-4
A companion volume to: The wonder clock, entered below
First published 1885
This book, with its eight modern retellings of old fairy tales, interspersed with ballads and rhymes and its drawings by the author, has long been a favorite with children and with storytellers

Some merry adventures of Robin Hood of great renown in Nottinghamshire; written and illus. by Howard Pyle (5-7)　　　　398.2
1 Robin Hood 2 Legends—Great Britain
Some editions are:
Scribner lib. bdg. $4.95, pa $2.45 (ISBN 0-684-13066-1; 0-384-71873-1)
Watts, F. $7.95 Large type edition. A Keith Jennison book (ISBN 0-581-00283-7)
First published 1954 by Scribner
Adapted by Pyle from his longer work: The merry adventures of Robin Hood, entered above. This contains 12 stories while the other has 22. Although some of the remaining stories are shortened or condensed, the style and spirit remain the same and the changes make this edition easier reading than the original version

The wonder clock; or, Four & twenty marvelous tales, being one for each hour of the day; written & illus. by Howard Pyle. Embellished with verses by Katharine Pyle. Harper 1915 318p illus lib. bdg. $4.79 (4-6)　　　　398.2
1 Folklore 2 Fairy tales
ISBN 0-06-024821-1
First published 1887
"Tales told by the puppet figures of an old clock found in Time's garret." Hodges. Bks for Elem Sch Libraries
"Pyle adapted tales from Grimm and other legends in his own lively and humorous way." Adventuring With Bks. 2d edition

Quigley, Lillian
The blind men and the elephant; an old tale from the land of India, re-told by Lillian Quigley; illus. by Janice Holland. Scribner 1959 unp illus lib. bdg. $5.95, pa 95¢ (k-3)　　　　398.2
1 Folklore—India 2 Fables
ISBN 0-684-13276-1; 0-684-12782-2
"Retelling of the Indian fable of six blind men who cannot agree on a single description of an elephant, which underlines the sage moral that to get a true picture of the whole one must include all its parts." N Y Times Bk Rev
"The tale takes on new humor and charm. The journey of the six men to the palace of an Indian Rajah is delightfully comic, yet the world which frames the journey is filled with exquisite colors and the ornate designs of Indian architecture and fabrics." Chicago Sunday Trib

Rackham, Arthur
(comp.) Arthur Rackham Fairy book; a book of old favourites with new illustrations. Lippincott 1950 286p illus $7.50 (3-6)　　　　398.2
1 Folklore 2 Fairy tales
ISBN 0-397-30218-5
First published 1933
Twenty-three "old favorites gathered from Grimm, Andersen, Arabian nights, Perrault, Washington

Irving and other sources. Exquisite new Rackham illustrations, eight in color, 53 in black and white, interpret the spirit and action of the tales." N Y Libraries

Ransome, Arthur
The Fool of the World and the flying ship; a Russian tale retold by Arthur Ransome; pictures by Uri Shulevitz. Farrar, Straus 1968 unp illus $4.95 (k-3)　　　　398.2
1 Folklore—Russia
ISBN 0-374-32442-5
"An Ariel book"
Awarded the Caldecott Medal, 1969
Text first published 1916 in Ransome's Old Peter's Russian tales, entered below
The Fool of the World, was the third and youngest son whose parents thought little of him. When the Czar announced that his daughter would marry the hero who could bring him a flying ship, Fool of the World went looking and found one. Aided in surprising ways by eight peasants with magical powers, he then had to outwit the treacherous Czar
This "is a fascinating tale, told with humor and grace and brought vividly to life by Uri Shulevitz's illustrations. Using a palette of rainbow colors, [he] has set the Fool and his ship against a large airy format—helping create a book that will impress grownups and delight the young." N Y Times Bk Rev

Old Peter's Russian tales; with illus. by Dmitri Mitrokhin. (3-6)　　　　398.2
1 Folklore—Russia 2 Fairy tales
Some editions are:
Dover pa $2 (ISBN 0-486-22406-6)
Smith, P. $4.75 (ISBN 0-8446-0867-X)
First published 1916 by Stokes
"The twenty-one stories in the book are such as Russian peasants tell their children and each other. . . . The author says that the stories selected for this volume are 'not for the learned nor indeed for grown-up people at all. No people who really like fairy stories ever grow up altogether. Their reading will convey some idea of the mental processes of the race inhabiting the broad plains and distant forests of half-mysterious Russia, and throw light on the Russian peasant's interpretation of natural phenomena and the abode of his mythology.'" Springf'd Republican

Reeves, James
English fables and fairy stories; retold by James Reeves; illus. by Joan Kiddell-Monroe. Walck, H.Z. 1954 234p illus (Oxford Myths and legends) $6 (4-7)　　　　398.2
1 Folklore—Great Britain 2 Fairy tales
ISBN 0-8098-2318-7
First published by Oxford
A "collection of nineteen English tales, told in language beautiful for either reading or telling. Several familiar tales are included with old favorites such as 'Molly Whipple,' 'Dick Whittington,' and 'Jack and the Beanstalk.'" Secondary Educ Board
These stories "do not make use of the vernacular found in Jacobs' [English folk and fairy tales, entered above] a factor which sometimes puzzles young readers. Style is more polished, similar to that of Perrault." Library J

The Renowned history of Little Red Riding-Hood; illus. by Nonny Hogrogian. Crowell 1967 unp illus $2.95, lib. bdg. $3.70 (k-3)　　　　398.2
1 Folklore
ISBN 0-690-49946-9; 0-690-49947-7
"An old rhymed version of the familiar tale is newly illustrated with delicate watercolors showing a homely but winsome Little Red Riding-Hood. . . . A moral, also in verse, ends the story by warning the

The Renowned history of Little Red Riding-Hood
—*Continued*
reader against confiding in a stranger who may be a
'knave in artful disguise.' The book's small format
complements the dainty illustrations." Booklist

Reyher, Becky
My mother is the most beautiful woman in the
world; a Russian folktale retold by Becky Reyher;
pictures by Ruth Gannett. Lothrop 1945 39p illus lib.
bdg. $4.81 (1-4)   398.2
1 Folklore—Russia
ISBN 0-688-51251-8
A Russian folktale about a little peasant girl, lost in
the wheat fields, who tried to describe her mother as
the "most beautiful woman in the world." When an
exceptionally ugly woman claimed the little girl, they
remembered the proverb: "We do not love people
because they are beautiful, but they seem beautiful to
us because we love them"
"Though its people are Russian peasants a long time
ago, and though Ruth Gannett has brought them to us
in brilliant, convincing pictures, there is not a little
listening child to whom it is read that will not claim it
for his own. These are just the right pictures for a story
told in just the right way." N Y Her Trib Bks

Robbins, Ruth
Baboushka and the three kings; illus. by Nicolas
Sidjakov; adapted from a Russian folk tale. Parnassus
Press 1960 unp illus music $3.95, lib. bdg. $3.96
(1-4)   398.2
1 Legends—Russia 2 Christmas stories
ISBN 0-87466-038-6; 0-87466-006-8
Awarded the Caldecott Medal, 1961
"A retelling of the Christmas legend about the old
woman who declined to accompany the three kings on
their search for the Christ Child and has ever since
then searched for the Child on her own. Each year as
she renews her search she leaves gifts at the homes
she visits, acting, in this respect, as a Russian equivalent to Santa Claus
"Mystery and dignity are in the retelling. . . . At the
end of the book is the story in verse set to original
music. Extraordinary modern drawings, some in rich
colors, and a handsome type face . . . combine to
make a beautiful picture book." Horn Bk

Taliesin and King Arthur; written and illus. by Ruth
Robbins. Parnassus Press 1970 unp illus $4.25; lib.
bdg. $4.11 (3-5)   398.2
1 Legends—Wales 2 Taliesin 3 Arthur, King
ISBN 0-87466-055-6; 0-87466-027-0
"Ornately detailed and deftly composed illustrations show the small figures of a feudal court, stylized
and romantic. The young poet Taliesen has come
[from northern Wales] to Arthur's court at Caerlon,
delighting the king and his retinue with strange tales
and with his rare wisdom. At the Grand Contest of
Poets on Christmas Eve, Taliesin tells the dramatic
and magical story of his birth, King Arthur proclaims
him the greatest bard of all, and the audience rejoices.
The story mingles fact and legend, the style is poetic,
and the tale within a tale should please readers
addicted to folklore and legend." Chicago. Children's
Bk Center

Robertson, Dorothy Lewis
Fairy tales from Viet Nam; retold by Dorothy Lewis
Robertson; illus. by W. T. Mars. Dodd 1968 93p illus
$3.50, lib. bdg. $4.50 (4-6)   398.2

1 Folklore—Vietnam 2 Fairy tales
ISBN 0-396-05681-4; 0-396-05682-2
This collection of tales based on "versions, written
in schoolboy English, supplied by [Mrs Robertson's]
Vietnamese foster son, [includes] legends, talking
animal stories, nature myths, Confucian-influenced
tales of human relationships, and romantic tales of
magic." Library J
The book "will please the young Occidental reader
fully as much as they delight the young Vietnamese."
N Y Times Bk Rev
"While painstaking scholarly research is hardly
required for a children's book, still it is disconcerting
that the sketches show Cambodian rather than Vietnamese temples and generalized Oriental rather than
a distinctly Vietnamese dress." Christian Sci Monitor

Robinson, Adjai
Singing tales of Africa; retold by Adjai Robinson;
illus. by Christine Price. Scribner 1974 80p illus
music $5.95 (3-5)   398.2
1 Folklore—Africa 2 Songs, African
ISBN 0-684-13683-X
"Each of the seven tales, evidently from the
author's Nigeria homeland, has a folklore setting and a
moral ending resembling Aesop's fables. The stories
are prefaced with or include songs that have a catchy
lilt, and some are in the African language." Reading
Teacher
"Humor and wisdom are the keynotes of each selection. Complemented by handsome woodcuts." Children's Bk Rev Serv

Rockwell, Anne
Befana; a Christmas story. Atheneum Pubs. 1974
unp illus lib. bdg. $4.95 (1-3)   398.2
1 Folklore—Italy 2 Befana 3 Christmas stories
ISBN 0-689-30417-X
"A moving retelling of the [Italian] legend of
Befana, the lonely old woman who travels through the
Christmas night, seeking the newborn King in Bethlehem. Because she does not know the way, she stops
in every town and leaves a gift from her basket for
each sleeping child; then she carefully tidies up with
her broom before rushing on. The small volume has
alternate pages of text and illustration, each black-
and-white drawing imaginatively framed with a varied
red-and-white border. Spare in style, the tale lends
itself to reading aloud; and the understated pictures
convey the emotion of the story." Horn Bk

When the drum sang; an African folktale; written
and illus. by Anne Rockwell. Parents Mag. Press 1970
unp illus lib. bdg. $4.59 (k-3)   398.2
1 Folklore—Africa
ISBN 0-8193-0425-5
"In a note at the end of the book, we are told that
tales about the 'zimwis,' greedy ogres with enormous
appetites, are popular, entertaining stories with no
religious or instructive purposes behind them. In this
version, the zimwi assumes the shape of a man and
steals Tselane, a small child, from the riverbank
where she is singing as she fills her calabash with
water. Holding her captive in a huge drum, the ogre
forces Tselane to sing as though she were the voice of
the drum. The child's songs are so plaintively lovely
that the zimwi is gladly fed in each village at which he
plays. . . . In the end, Tselane is rescued by her
parents and the ogre is punished; but the charm of the
book is not so much in the plot as in the sun-filled
watercolors that illustrate it. The intimately
developed mood portrayals are the core of this successful picture-book rendition of folk material." Horn
Bk

Rounds, Glen

Ol' Paul, the mighty logger. . . . [Rev] Holiday House 1976 93p illus $4.95 (3-6)   398.2

1 Legends—U.S. 2 Bunyan, Paul 3 Lumber and lumbering—Fiction

ISBN 0-8234-0082-4

First published 1936

"Being a true account of the seemingly incredible exploits and inventions of the great Paul Bunyan, profusely illustrated by drawings made at the scene by the author, Glen Rounds, and now republished in this special fortieth anniversary edition." Subtitle

Notable for "its tone of mock authenticity and the liveliness of its style and appearance." Bks for Boys and Girls. 3d edition

Roy, Cal

The serpent and the sun; myths of the Mexican world; retold, and with decorations, by Cal Roy. Farrar, Straus 1972 119p illus $5.95 (4-7)   398.2

1 Indians of Mexico—Legends

ISBN 0-374-36742-6

These Mexican myths—eight of Aztec origin, two Mayan and two from present day Indian tribes—illustrate the struggle between opposing forces associated with the god of rain and learning and the god of the sun and war. They tell of the world's creation, the rain dwarfs, monkey musicians and wicked ants, and Hummingbird, god of the warriors

"Roy's excellent, black-and-white illustrations recreate the symbols of the ancient civilizations. . . . Young readers who enjoy the mythology of Greece, Rome, and Asia will want to explore the heritage of Mexico and will find much ground for comparison. The quick pace of these simple stories along with the easy-to-read style should make this book a favorite with reluctant readers." Sch Library J

Sakade, Florence

(ed.) Japanese children's favorite stories; illus. by Yoshisuke Kurosaki. [2d ed. rev] Tuttle 1958 120p illus $6.25 (2-4)   398.2

1 Folklore—Japan 2 Fairy tales

ISBN 0-8084-0284-X

First published 1953

A collection of twenty folk tales "traditionally told to Japanese children. The gay illustrations will appeal to younger children." Asia: A Guide to Bks for Children

Sawyer, Ruth

Journey cake, ho! Illus. by Robert McCloskey. Viking 1953 45p illus lib. bdg. $5.95 (k-2)   398.2

1 Folklore

ISBN 0-670-40943-X

In this new version of the old folk tale about Johnny-cake, Johnny has to leave his mountain home because his foster parents are too poor to keep him. But his parting present, a journey cake, leads the boy into adventures and brings him back home along with a flock of pursuing animals. The cake is then renamed Johnny-cake

Johnny is "drawn with that rollicking bold humor that has made Mr. McCloskey popular. The story is rather odd, but probably good fun for small children who will laugh at a cake that rolls and sings a repeated verse." N Y Her Trib Bks

Say, Allen

Once under the cherry blossom tree; an old Japanese tale; retold and illus. by Allen Say. Harper 1974 31p illus $4.50, lib. bdg. $4.11 (1-3)   398.2

1 Folklore—Japan

ISBN 0-06-025216-2; 0-06-025217-0

"A miserly old landlord sat grumbling on a fine spring day, watching the villagers dance and sing; he swallowed a cherry pit, and a tree grew out of his head. In desperation he pulled it out, leaving a cavity where fish soon appeared. Angry at some boys who were fishing in his head, the old man jumped up, tripped on a rock, and tumbled. His feet went into his head, and soon nothing was left of him but a pond, a lovely pond near which the villagers danced and sang." Chicago. Children's Bk Center

"The intricately textured pen drawings are finely done with the same odd humor that makes this tale unique." N Y Times Bk Rev

Schiller, Barbara

The Vinlanders' saga; illus. by William Bock. Holt 1966 71p illus map lib. bdg. $3.59 (4-6)   398.2

1 Northmen 2 Sagas 3 America—Discovery and exploration

ISBN 0-03-059915-6

"Written by unknown authors in the 13th century about their ancestors of about 930-1030, these sagas extoll the exploits of Eric the Red and his sons, Leif the Lucky, Thorwald, and Thorsten. Around these men is woven a rich fabric of background involving their families, friends, and enemies. A veil of mysticism rests upon the realistic adventures and the excellent pen-and-ink drawings have caught the mystical spirit, giving the book distinction." Sch Library J

The white rat's tale; illus. by Adrienne Adams. Holt 1967 unp illus $3.50, pa $1.45 (k-3)   398.2

1 Folklore—France 2 Fairy tales

ISBN 0-03-065655-9

"A pet white rat is changed via fairy magic into a Royal Princess. Then follows a search for the proper suitor for her marriage. This graceful retelling of a French folktale, with its droll humor and beautiful illustrations, will be fun to share with children in the story hour." Top of the News

"The uncluttered illustrations . . . are among Miss Adams' best, with the luminous coloring and delicately detailed, impossible flora and fauna which are her specialties and are so well suited to a fairy tale." Sch Library J

Schwartz, Alvin

Whoppers; tall tales and other lies; collected from American folklore by Alvin Schwartz; illus. by Glen Rounds. Lippincott 1975 127p illus $5.95, pa $2.95 (4-7)   398.2

1 Folklore—U.S.

ISBN 0-397-31575-9; 0-397-31612-7

Excerpted and adapted from a variety of sources, this is an "assemblage of tall tales and whoppers from American folklore. They range from brief one-liners, some of which are strung into tall stories, to rambling discourses on preposterous turns of events. The humor is marked with both sly subtlety and broad slapstick. . . . Curious readers will find the appended notes and sources thoughtfully informative, and storytellers who aren't intimidated by the various dialects will find good raw material for telling." Booklist

The tales are "divided by topics such as people, animals, weather, and Rounds' scribbly sketches add a quiet folksy humor of their own." Sch Library J

Bibliography: p119-25

Sechrist, Elizabeth Hough

Once in the first times; folk tales from the Philippines, retold by Elizabeth Hough Sechrist; illus. by John Sheppard. Macrae Smith Co. 1969 213p illus map $6.50, lib. bdg. $5.97 (4-6)   398.2

1 Folklore—Philippine Islands

ISBN 0-8255-8140-0; 0-8255-8141-9

First published 1949

Sechrist, Elizabeth Hough—*Continued*

These fifty-one "tales range from the simple why and how myths . . . to the more sophisticated stories including variants of some familiar western tales. The book is accordingly divided into two sections: the first and most lengthy deals with the stories of the early peoples of the islands from the Negritos to the Malayan and Chinese settlers; the second reflects Spanish and American influences. . . . Sources (Igorot, Tagalong, Visayan, etc.) are given for almost every tale. Pen and ink sketches enhance the attractive format, making this good folktale fare for libraries not possessing the now out of print 1949 edition" [from which one story has been deleted]. Sch Library J

Serraillier, Ian

Beowulf the warrior; illus. by Severin. Walck, H.Z. 1961 47p illus $5 (6-7)   398.2

1 Beowulf 2 Legends—Great Britain

ISBN 0-8098-3039-6

First published 1954 in England

A retelling of the Old English verse epic about the Scandinavian warrior who in his youth delivers Hrothgar the Dane and his people from the menace of the monster Grendel, and in his old age fights a victorious but fatal battle against a terrible dragon to save his own people, the Geats

Illustrated with "strong and appropriate black and white illustrations. The author has simplified the language yet maintained . . . [the] heroic mood." Chicago. Children's Bk Center

The seven voyages of Sindbad the sailor; illus. by Philip Reed. Atheneum Pubs. 1962 57p illus lib. bdg. $3.81 (4-6)   398.2

1 Folklore—Arabia

ISBN 0-689-20363-2

Tales from the Arabian nights about the merchant/sailor who is frequently shipwrecked and cast ashore to face incredible dangers but returns from each voyage wealthier than before

"There is a charming and appropriately old-fashioned look to this small volume which contains all of the Sindbad adventures, with tidy multicolor wood engravings suggestive of earlier bookmaking. The text (no editor or translator is named) also has an archaic flavor, with frequently elaborate and colorful sentences in keeping with the source." Horn Bk

Shapiro, Irwin

Heroes in American folklore; illus. by James Daugherty and Donald McKay. Messner 1962 256p illus lib. bdg. $6.29 (4-7)   398.2

1 Legends—U.S.

ISBN 0-671-32054-8

This book contains five tales about legendary American heroes originally published as separate volumes: Casey Jones and Locomotive No. 638; How old Storm-along captured Mocha Dick; John Henry and the double-jointed steam drill; Steamboat Bill and the captain's top hat; Joe Magarac and his U.S.A. citizen papers. Includes the original illustrations

The author writes "in a vigorous style well suited to heroic deeds. . . . James Daughterty and Donald McKay must have grown up with these heroes, judging from their free swinging rollicking, whoopin' and hollerin' illustrations." Chicago Sunday Trib

Shephard, Esther

Paul Bunyan; illus. by Rockwell Kent. Harcourt 1941 233p illus $6.50 (5-7)   398.2

1 Legends—U.S. 2 Bunyan, Paul 3 Lumber and lumbering—Fiction

ISBN 0-15-259749-2

First published 1924

"Tall tales of the mighty exploits of the legendary hero of American lumberjacks; of Teeny, his daughter; Babe, his great blue ox; and other woodsmen who range the forests from Maine to the Northwest. The robust vigor of the tales is graphically reproduced in the illustrations by Rockwell Kent. Another edition for the younger reader is "Ol' Paul, the Mighty Logger" by Glen Rounds [entered above]." Children's Bks Too Good To Miss

Sherlock, Sir Philip

Anansi, the spider man; Jamaican folk tales; told by Philip M. Sherlock; illus. by Marcia Brown. Crowell 1954 112p illus $5.50 (4-6)   398.2

1 Folklore—Jamaica

ISBN 0-690-42987-8

Fifteen West Indian stories about the Caribbean folk hero Anansi "who was a man when things went well, but who became a spider when he was in great danger. They are of West African origin, and the animal characters include Tiger, 'the strongest of all,' Snake, Kisander the cat, Old Owl, Rat and Turtle. The author tells the stories simply and directly, with respect for their 'folk' quality. Line illustrations by Marcia Brown are excellent, and have caught the gaiety of the tales." Ontario Library Rev

This collection has been "retold in a form that will be useful for the storyteller and fun for independent reading." Chicago. Children's Bk Center

The iguana's tail; crick crack stories from the Caribbean; illus. By Gioia Fiammenghi. Crowell 1969 97p illus $3.95 (3-5)   398.2

1 Folklore—West Indies 2 Fables

ISBN 0-690-42987-8

"The author recalls childhood stories he heard while growing up in the West Indies as the basis of this collection. All are animal ["how" and "why"] stories, told on successive nights by various jungle animals as they travel to more fertile land." Pub W

"A simplicity in writing and fluid literary style make the tales highly entertaining, but not necessarily desirable for reading aloud. . . . The flavor of the West Indian idiom is less apparent than in earlier Sherlock collections. [The] illustrations add dimensions of humor and vitality." N Y Times Bk Rev

West Indian folk-tales; retold by Philip Sherlock; illus. by Joan Kiddell-Monroe. Walck, H.Z. 1966 151p illus (Myths and legends ser) $6 (4-6)   398.2

1 Folklore—West Indies

ISBN 0-8098-2392-6

"Twenty-one tales of the ancient peoples, the Caribs and the Arawaks, are intertwined here with the folklore of the African slaves. Simply structured and ably retold, the collection includes the familiar 'pourquoi' (why) stories, several tales of Anansi, the spiderman, and other legends that recount the trials and successes of the West Indian birds and animals." Sch Library J

Shulevitz, Uri

The magician; an adaptation from the Yiddish of I. L. Peretz. Macmillan (N Y) 1973 32p illus $3.95 (k-2)   398.2

1 Elijah, the prophet 2 Legends, Jewish 3 Passover—Fiction

In this story based on a Yiddish folk legend about the prophet Elijah, "a ragged magician appears in a village on the eve of Passover and astounds a pious, needy couple by giving them all they need for the feast." Chicago Pub Library. What's New In Bks

Shulevitz's drawings "are snapshot-sized meticulously executed in black and white [and] . . . occasionally spotlighted by patches of untouched white paper. . . . [They] provide archetypal vignettes of a now-

Shulevitz, Uri—*Continued*
extinct Jewish community life. At once both somber
and gay . . . bleak yet exuding an ethnic warmth, the
illustrations have a dreamlike, mythic quality." N Y
Times Bk Rev
"Nicely retold . . . a story to read alone, read
aloud, and tell." Chicago. Children's Bk Center

Singer, Isaac Bashevis
Mazel and Shlimazel; or, The milk of a lioness;
pictures by Margot Zemach; tr. from the Yiddish by
the author and Elizabeth Shub. Farrar, Straus 1967
42p illus $6.95 (2-5)   398.2
1 Folklore, Jewish
ISBN 0-374-34884-7
"An Ariel book"
The happiness of Tam, a poor peasant lad, and
lovely Crown Princess Nesika depends upon the outcome of a battle of wits between Mazel, the spirit of
good luck, and Shlimazel, the spirit of bad luck
This story "is based on a Jewish folk tale. . . . The
way Shlimazel contrives to win the wager is a witty
surprise, and how, moreover, the storyteller arranges
to have the story end happily after all is also ingenious
and satisfying. The colored illustrations . . . have the
flavor of folk art but, like the text, are anything but
artless." New Yorker

When Shlemiel went to Warsaw & other stories;
pictures by Margot Zemach; tr. by the author and
Elizabeth Shub. Farrar, Straus 1968 115p illus $5.95
(4-7)   398.2
1 Folklore, Jewish
ISBN 0-374-38316-2
"An Ariel book"
"A fine collection of five retold traditional Yiddish
folk tales and three original stories. The foolish people
of Chelm, that indomitable Eastern European town
known for its inverted wisdom, are so lovingly presented that readers will laugh with and not at them:
Utzel, whose daughter Poverty's feet grow larger in
proportion to the time wasted by his lazy refusals to
work; Lyzer the Miser, who learns that if a silver
tablespoon can give birth to a teaspoon, silver candle-
sticks can die; and, of course, Shlemiel himself, whose
attempted trip to Warsaw has incredible repercus-
sions. The original stories—'Tsirtsur and Peziza'
'Rabbi Leib and the Witch Cunegunde,' and
'Menaseh's Dream'—blend well with the reworked
tales, and Margot Zemach's delightful black-and-
white illustrations fittingly capture moods and protagonists." Sch Library J
"The writing has a cadence that is especially evident
when the tales are read aloud; the length, the style,
and the humor make them a happy source for storytelling." Chicago. Children's Bk Center

Zlateh the goat, and other stories; pictures by
Maurice Sendak; tr. from the Yiddish by the author
and Elizabeth Shub. Harper 1966 90p illus $6.95, lib.
bdg. $6.43 (4-7)   398.2
1 Folklore, Jewish
ISBN 0-06-025698-2; 0-06-025699-0
These seven tales which draw upon the Jewish folklore of Poland "will have wide appeal for the excellence of their interpretation: they have the poetic
power of folk tales—a quality of timelessness in the
wisdom imparted and a feeling for the essense of
human nature. Devils and everyday people, adults
and children inhabit stories about the first shlemiel;
the village of Chelm, 'a village of fools'; the devil who
made a mistake on Hanukkah; the lovely goat that
survived a snowstorm on her way to the butcher."
Horn Bk
"Their humor, mysticism, and a quiet acceptance of

fate are perfectly interpreted in Sendak's fine-line
sketches." Children's Bks 1966

Sleator, William
The angry moon; retold by William Sleator, with
pictures by Blair Lent. Little 1970 45p illus $6.95, lib.
bdg. $7.55 (k-3)   398.2
1 Tlingit Indians—Legends
ISBN 0-316-79735-9; 0-316-79736-7
"An Atlantic Monthly Press book"
"The original legend . . . was first recorded by Dr.
John R. Swanton in Bulletin 39 of the Bureau of
American Ethnology, Tlingit myths and text"
"An adaptation of a legend of the Tlingit Indians of
Alaska, the writing simple and staccato; the illustrations combine colorful, sometimes misty backgrounds
and details of costumes or totems that are based on
Tlingit designs. When Lapowinsa laughs at the moon,
she disappears, leaving her friend Lupan desolate. He
shoots arrows at the stars . . . and they form a ladder
up which Lupan climbs. With the help of the
grandmother of a tiny sky boy, he rescues Lapowinsa,
using the four magic objects the grandmother had
given him to foil the angry moon in pursuit of his
escaped prisoner. An attractive book and an interesting legend useful for storytelling, but rather stilted
when read aloud." Sutherland. The Best in Children's
Bks

Small, Ernest
Baba Yaga; illus. by Blair Lent. Houghton 1966 48p
illus lib. bdg. $6.95 (k-3)   398.2
1 Folklore—Russia
ISBN 0-395-16975-5
"Little Marusia searching for turnips in the forest
comes on the house of a wicked witch. . . . Baba Yaga
takes little Marusia captive, but Marusia shows herself more than a match for the witch's evil . . . ways.
The story is a composite of many of the Baba Yaga
stories told to Russian children." Christian Sci
Monitor
"While rather cursory this tale is redeemed by
illustrations that sweep, tumble and soar through the
environs of Baba Yaga's haunted forest." N Y Times
Bk Rev

Soldier and Tsar in the forest; a Russian tale tr. by
Richard Lourie; pictures by Uri Shulevitz. Farrar,
Straus 1972 unp illus $5.95 (k-3)   398.2
1 Folklore—Russia
ISBN 0-374-37126-1
A translation of a story from Aleksandr Afanas'ev's
Russian folktales
This tale concerns "a Russian peasant soldier who
runs away from the army because of unjust punish-
ment and who, while hiding out in the forest, unwit-
tingly saves the life of the Tsar by decapitating the
robbers who attack him." Booklist
"Under willing enchantment, one surrenders to old
Mother Russia in this expansively illustrated [tale].
. . . [There is] an authentic feel not just for woodland
wilds and peasant rusticity, but for dazzling onion-
domed citadels as well. Richard Lourie has provided a
pleasingly colloquial translation . . . but to Uri
Shulevitz must go the major credit for drawing young
listeners into a magical yet real world." Bk World

Spicer, Dorothy Gladys
The owl's nest; folktales from Friesland; illus. by
Alice Wadowski-Bak. Coward-McCann 1968 124p
illus lib. bdg. $4.99 (4-6)   398.2
1 Folklore, Friesian
ISBN 0-698-30277-X
"Seven folktales from the northernmost province of
the Netherlands, told in a direct and rather contemporary style, simply structured and with a mature—

Spicer, Dorothy Gladys—*Continued*
but not demanding—vocabulary. The writing has
vitality and typical folktale humor; most of the stories
have a robust cheeriness and many of them have
familiar themes. Pleasant to read alone or aloud, and
useful as a source for storytelling." Chicago. Children's Bk Center
"The attractive black-and-white illustrations enliven the texts." Sch Library J

Stalder, Valerie
Even the devil is afraid of a shrew; a folktale of
Lapland; retold by Valerie Stalder; adapted by Ray
Broekel; illus. by Richard Brown. Addison-Wesley
[1972] unp illus $5.95 (k-3)   398.2
1 Folklore—Lapland 2 Devil—Fiction
ISBN 0-201-07188-6
"An Addisonian Press book"
"Pava Jalvi is a peaceful man whose life is made
miserable by the bad temper and nagging of his
shrewish wife. One day he takes the opportunity of
pushing her down a deep hole. Peace! But he is conscience-stricken. He ties some strong plants together
to make a rope. . . . Up comes the devil, delighted to
get away from the shrew, but the devil's subsequent
mischief leads Pava Jalvi to try a trick: he pretends his
wife has gotten free and frightens the devil back
below ground." Chicago. Children's Bk Center

Stephens, James
Irish fairy tales; illus. by Arthur Rackham. Macmillan (N Y) [1968 c1948] 318p illus lib. bdg. $6.95, pa
$1.95 (6-7)   398.2
1 Folklore—Ireland 2 Fairy tales
First published 1920; copyright renewed 1948
The collection includes ten hero tales and legends
from Ireland. Among them are tales of Fionn and
Fianna, the Carl of the Drab Coat, and Becuma

Stoutenburg, Adrien
American tall-tale animals; illus. by Glen Rounds.
Viking 1968 128p illus $3.95 (4-6)   398.2
1 Folklore—U.S. 2 Animals—stories
ISBN 0-670-12066-9
"Whiffle-poofles, gillygaloos, bears of incredible
size and wit, talented rattlesnakes, fur-bearing trout,
water-toting, humped-backed desert fish, and spirited hoss-mackerel are among the curious creatures
that appear in Miss Stoutenburg's collection of fantastic American fauna. Drawn from old newspapers,
periodicals, out-of-print books and authentic regional
sources, these entertaining descriptive accounts of
rare animal life and unique hunting tactics add a new
dimension to American folklore." Booklist
"Many of these stories can be found scattered
throughout B. A. Botkin's 'A Treasury of American
Folklore,' but . . . [Stoutenburg's] carefully
organized, entertainingly folksy retellings and Glen
Rounds' amusing, backwoodsy sketches add greatly to
their appeal for children." Sch Library J

Sturton, Hugh
Zomo, the Rabbit; drawings by Peter Warner.
Atheneum Pubs. 1967 [c1966] 128p illus $3.95, lib.
bdg. $3.81 (4-6)   398.2
1 Folklore—Nigeria 2 Folklore, Hausa 3 Rabbits—
Stories 4 Animals—Stories
ISBN 0-689-20429-9; 0-689-20430-2
These are adaptations of eleven "stories that were
told for many years in Hausaland (now Northern
Nigeria). When the Hausa people came to America as
slaves, they brought their stories with them . . . and
brought Zomo, a rascal of a rabbit—really a hare—to
father our Br'er Rabbit." Pub W
"In the bush country of Northern Nigeria, Zaki the

Lion rules over an animal kingdom in which assorted
talking beasts caricature our human frailties. . . .
Although closely related to Br'er Rabbit's and Anansi's, Zomo's pranks may seem funnier and more plausible to children than those of his crafty cousins. . . .
While imparting a sense of African spirit and vernacular, the telling, nevertheless, is robust and modern,
filled with subtle surprises and punctuated with colorful name-calling. The eleven tales read or tell superbly and are enhanced by amusing illustrations highly
suggestive of Zomo's elusive cunning or the personalities of his antagonists." Horn Bk

Sutcliff, Rosemary
Tristan and Iseult. Dutton 1971 150p $5.95 (5-7)
          398.2
1 Tristan 2 Legends, Celtic
ISBN 0-525-41565-3
Based on Celtic legend, this story tells how Tristan
wins the Irish princess, Iseult, for his uncle, King
Marc of Cornwall, and discovers too late that he and
Iseult have fallen in love with each other, with tragic
results
"To one of the great love stories of all time Rosemary Sutcliff brings the felicity of historical detail and
the lyric, flowing style of a master storyteller. Her
version of the tale omits the love potion, ascribing the
sudden admission of their passion to the fact that
Tristan and Iseult touch for the first time when he
carries her ashore while seeking harbor during the
voyage to Cornwall." Chicago. Children's Bk Center
"The presentation is deceptively childlike, but
evokes much more mature emotions." Best Sellers

The **Tall** book of nursery tales; pictures by Feodor
Rojankovsky. Artists and Writers Guild, Inc. [distributed by] Harper 1944 120p illus $2.95, lib. bdg.
$4.43 (k-2)   398.2
1 Folklore 2 Fairy tales
ISBN 0-06-025065-8; 0-06-025066-6
"Twenty-four well told traditional tales. The illustrations, with the 'tall' pages used to the best advantage, are . . . fresh and delightful. . . . The table of
contents with vignettes for each title is as much fun as
the rest of the book. Perfect table book if shelving is a
problem." Booklist

Tashjian, Virginia A.
Once there was and was not; Armenian tales retold
by Virginia A. Tashjian. Based on stories by H.
Toumanian; illus. by Nonny Hogrogian. Little 1966
83p illus $4.95, lib. bdg. $5.55 (3-6)   398.2
1 Folklore—Armenia
ISBN 0-316-83244-3; 0-316-83225-1
"There are familiar elements in many of the [seven]
stories—the animal who puts up a façade of wealth for
his master, the poor man who is saved by the animal
he had befriended, the noodlehead who is easily
hoaxed, the coward who is precipitated into the role of
a hero. . . . The book is a pleasure to read aloud and a
good source for storytelling." Sutherland. The Best In
Children's Bks
The stories "flow naturally and simply and should
be easy for the beginning storyteller to prepare and
tell. The humor and special flavor of the tales is
accented in the striking illustrations—line drawings
washed with jewel-like colors. A very beautiful book."
Horn Bk

Three apples fell from heaven; Armenian tales
retold by Virginia A. Tashjian; illus. by Nonny Hogrogian. Little 1971 76p illus $4.95 (3-6)   398.2
1 Folklore—Armenia
ISBN 0-316-83231-6
Companion volume to the author's: Once there was
and was not, entered above

Tashjian, Virginia A.—*Continued*

These "tales poke fun at the weaknesses of simple folk—laziness, envy, foolishness, and greed—and rejoice in occasional triumphs through cleverness and trickery. . . . Many of the stories follow familiar patterns and are obvious variants of tales found all over the world." Horn Bk

"Nonny Hogrogian's amusing, graceful, drawings, some in pleasing watercolors, complement the stories most attractively. In short, both storytellers and children will be delighted by this [book]." Sch Library J

Thompson, Vivian L.

Hawaiian myths of earth, sea, and sky; illus. by Leonard Weisgard. Holiday House 1966 83p illus lib. bdg. $5.95 (3-6)   398.2

1 Folklore—Hawaii
ISBN 0-8234-0042-5

The twelve "tales are concerned with the gods Hina, Maui, Pele, Kane, God of creation, and others; old beliefs of the creation, the sun, moon, and stars, the volcanoes, the winds and other natural phenomena are related. An interesting group of stories tells how tapa cloth was first made." Library J

This "is a useful supplementary book for school units on Hawaii. The Weisgard illustrations in orange, green, and black are a nice complement to the book." Wis Library Bul

Includes glossary and bibliography

Hawaiian tales of heroes and champions; illus. by Herbert Kawainui Kane. Holiday House 1971 128p illus lib. bdg. $5.95 (4-6)   398.2

1 Folklore—Hawaii
ISBN 0-8234-0192-8

Included among these twelve tall tales of Old Hawaii are stories of shape-shifters who could change their form from one object to another; the supernatural kupua who roamed the islands, challenging kings and chiefs, tricking men, women and boys; and men with rare and special weapons

"The feats of chiefs and gods are recounted in a straightforward, dignified manner and illustrated in dark sepia wash drawings with strong line and Polynesian detail by an artist who once lived in Hawaii." Horn Bk

Glossary: p122-26. Bibliography: p127-28

The Three bears [illus. by] Paul Galdone. Seabury 1972 unp illus lib. bdg. $6.95 (k-1)   398.2

1 Folklore 2 Bears—Stories
ISBN 0-8164-3072-1

This is a retelling of the familiar nursery tale of Goldilocks (pictured here missing a front tooth) and the three bears

"Big clear drawings that can be seen easily from a distance make it a good choice for groups as well as for lap-sitters. The use of print size that is correlated with wee, middle-sized, and great big voices will help incipient readers learn to identify words." Sat Rev

The Three little pigs; in verse; author unknown; illus. by William Pène du Bois. Viking 1962 32p illus lib. bdg. $4.95, pa 85¢ (k-1)   398.2

1 Folklore—Great Britain 2 Pigs—Stories 3 Wolves—Stories 4 Stories in rhyme
ISBN 0-670-70812-7; 0-670-05042-3

This rhymed version of the English folktale is one remembered from childhood by a Viking Press editor

"The very attractive little book is well designed and looks like an old-fashioned small-sized picture book. Full-color illustrations are also done in an old-fashioned manner" Sch Library J

The Three wishes; pictures by Paul Galdone. McGraw 1961 32p illus lib. bdg. $4.72 (k-2) 398.2

1 Folklore 2 Fairy tales
ISBN 0-07-022714-4

"A Whittlesey House publication"

"The Three Wishes dates all the way back to Greek mythology. . . . This telling is from 'More English Fairy Tales,' edited by Joseph Jacobs." Verso of title page

"The old folk-tale about a woodman receiving three wishes for sparing an oak tree is illustrated with drawings that echo the simplicity and humour of the story to perfection." Ontario Library Rev

Titus, Eve

The two stonecutters; freely adapted from the Japanese by Eve Titus; illus. by Yoko Mitsuhashi. Doubleday 1967 unp illus lib. bdg. $4.50 (k-3)
                                                398.2

1 Folklore—Japan
ISBN 0-385-07744-0

"When the Forest Goddess granted seven wishes to the stonecutters the selfish elder brother took six and having finally wished to be a stone was saved by the unselfish brother's only wish." Ontario Library Rev

The author is a "master storyteller whose words burst with fresh metaphors. . . . Yoko Mitsuhashi has created perfect pictures that are at once boldly stylized and free." N Y Times Bk Rev

Tolstoy, Alexei

The great big enormous turnip; pictures by Helen Oxenbury. Watts, F. [1969 c1968] unp illus lib. bdg. $3.90 (k-2)   398.2

1 Folklore—Russia 2 Turnips—Stories
ISBN 0-531-01684-6

A newly illustrated edition of the Soviet writer's version of the old folk "tale about the man who grew a turnip so huge he had to get wife, granddaughter, dog, cat and mouse to help him pull it up." Times (London) Literary Sup

This book "owes its success to its marvelous, brightly-colored illustrations. . . . [They] show highly individualized, distinctive turnip-pullers of extraordinary character in various positions and from numerous perspectives." Sch Library J

Tom Tit Tot; an English folk tale illus. by Evaline Ness. Scribner 1965 unp illus lib. bdg. $5.95 (k-3)   398.2

1 Folklore—Great Britain 2 Fairy tales
ISBN 0-525-43470-4

"The English version of Rumpelstiltskin is boisterously interpreted with woodcuts giving unrestrained expression to the tale's brash humor. Goaded by false pride, a bawling country woman weds her dull and awkward daughter to a greedy, gullible king. . . . When it comes time to earn her exalted station in life, the lazy girl accepts the costly magic of a black imp, a bulbous, nondescript 'thing' with a twirling tail. . . . To children, characters may sometimes seem obscured by strong design in costume and background; but the illustrations make the dialect and folksy expressions of Jacobs' telling more comprehensible and bring the story within the grasp of a younger audience than might otherwise be the case." Horn Bk

Toye, William

How summer came to Canada; retold by William Toye; pictures by Elizabeth Cleaver. Walck, H.Z. 1969 32p illus $4.50 (k-3)   398.2

1 Micmac Indians—Legends 2 Folklore—Canada 3 Seasons—Fiction
ISBN 0-8098-1153-7

"A legend of the Micmac Indians of eastern Canada is retold in simple rhythmic prose. The people of a once fertile land held in the grip of Giant Winter are

Toye, William—*Continued*
saved by their lord Glooskap who goes in search of Summer, the Queen of 'where it is always warm.' Double page illustrations are alive with rich, glowing colors." Cane. Selected Media about the Am Indian for Young Children

Traven, B.
The creation of the sun and the moon; illus. by Alberto Beltrán. Hill & Wang 1968 65p illus $3.95 (5-7)   398.2
    1 Indians of Mexico—Legends 2 Sun—Fiction 3 Moon—Fiction
    ISBN 0-8090-3700-9
The first part of this retelling of a Mexican Indian legend "recounts the adventures of Chicovaneg who, aided by the Quetzal bird and the Feathered Serpent, borrows light from the stars to rekindle the sun destroyed by evil spirits; the second part tells how his son Hauchinog-va-neg, with the help of the rabbit Tul, creates a moon to bring light and comfort to mankind at night." Booklist
"Traven's sonorous prose, the spirited illustrations in black and terracotta by the Mexican artist Alberto Beltrán, and the attractive format make this an outstanding book that belongs in all folklore collections." Library J

Tresselt, Alvin
The legend of the willow plate, by Alvin Tresselt and Nancy Cleaver; with pictures by Joseph Low. Parents Mag. Press 1968 unp illus lib. bdg. $4.59 (1-4)   398.2
    1 Legends—China
    ISBN 0-8193-0222-8
A "picture-book version of a popular legend of unknown origin which interprets the dramatic Chinese scene depicted on the famous blue-and-white willow pattern dinnerware first manufactured in England around 1780." Booklist
"A commoner runs away with the betrothed daughter of a nobleman. Instead of living happily ever after, they are hunted by the disappointed suitor; the husband is killed and the wife immolates herself. A goddess intervenes and turns husband and wife into doves." Adventuring With Bks. 2d edition
"Joseph Low successfully suggests the familiar figures without literally reproducing them. Double-page spreads at front and back of the book show the design in blue, but the rest of the pages are enlivened with touches of green, yellow, and red." Sch Library J

The mitten; an old Ukrainian folktale, retold by Alvin Tresselt; illus. by Yaroslava. Adapted from the version by E. Rachev. Lothrop 1964 unp illus $5.50 (k-2)   398.2
    1 Folklore—Ukraine 2 Animals—Stories
    ISBN 0-688-41053-7
"On the coldest day of the year a little Ukrainian boy loses his fur-lined mitten, which becomes so overcrowded with animals seeking a snug shelter that it finally bursts. Brightly colored pictures show the animals dressed in typical Ukrainian costumes." Hodges. Bks for Elem Sch Libraries

Turska, Krystyna
The woodcutter's duck. Macmillan (N Y) [1973] c1972 unp illus $5.95 (k-3)   398.2
    1 Folklore—Poland
    First published 1972 in England
This retelling of a Polish folktale shows how "Bartek, a poor woodcutter, prevents his pet duck from becoming a meal for an army's commander by using the wonderful magic given him by the King of the Frogs." Horn Bk
"The author's illustrations are a delight, making

imaginative use of the style of the early woodcut to produce stunning decorative and humorous effects." Times (London) Literary Sup

The Twelve dancing princesses; illus. by Adrienne Adams. Holt 1966 unp illus lib. bdg. $3.59, pa $1.65 (k-3)   398.2
    1 Folklore—France 2 Fairy tales
    ISBN 0-03-059880-X; 0-03-088502-7
In this retelling of a fairy tale based on the French version included in Andrew Lang's Red fairy book, entered above, a young cowherd uses a cloak of invisibility to free twelve princesses from a mysterious enchantment.
This is "longer and more romantic [than the Grimm version]. . . . The illustrations, in colors that are rich and warm, are as romantic as the story." Horn Bk

Uchida, Yoshiko
The dancing kettle, and other Japanese folk tales; retold by Yoshiko Uchida; illus. by Richard C. Jones. Harcourt 1949 174p illus $5.50 (3-5)   398.2
    1 Folklore—Japan 2 Fairy tales
    ISBN 0-15-221622-7
"In retelling the 14 tales, told to her in her own childhood, the author has not translated literally from the Japanese versions but has 'taken the liberty of adapting them so they would be more meaningful to the children of America.'" Preface
"The stories possess dramatic quality, humor and a gently insinuated doctrine of human kindness and generosity. They are told with directness and economy in good storytelling style." N Y Times Bk Rev
The pictures are "very fine; keeping to a Japanese style, using fascinating detail. Mr. Jones also has re-created action and characters that will amuse younger children." N Y Her Trib Bks
Includes a glossary and a guide to pronunciation

The magic listening cap; more folk tales from Japan; retold and illus. by Yoshiko Uchida. Harcourt 1955 146p illus $6.75, pa $1.25 (3-5)   398.2
    1 Folklore—Japan 2 Fairy tales
    ISBN 0-15-250978-X; 0-15-655119-5
These fourteen Japanese folk tales are retold "with charm and humor and display those universal elements of folk lore that will give them wide appeal. Several of the stories have counterparts in other folk lore. The stories are suitable for reading aloud, or for telling, and will also be of interest to students of comparative folk lore." Chicago. Children's Bk Center
Includes a glossary

Undset, Sigrid
(ed.) True and untrue, and other Norse tales; illus. by Frederick T. Chapman. Knopf 1945 253p illus lib. bdg. $5.69 (4-7)   398.2
    1 Folklore—Norway 2 Fairy tales
    ISBN 0-394-91778-2
"These tales are based on the original stories collected by Moe and Asbjornsen"
"Twenty-seven representative Norwegian folk tales, vivid, simple and straightforward in style and concerned with giants and trolls, with younger sons who go off into the world to try their luck and with wonderful feats of magic in which evil is vanquished and good, brave, generous deeds are rewarded." Bookmark
"It is a good-looking book with a particularly clear, readable type and strong, humorous drawings. . . . Its foreword should make it a 'must' book in any courses that are given on folklore or the literature of story telling." Sat Rev

Vasilisa the beautiful; tr. from the Russian by Thomas
P. Whitney; illus. by Nonny Hogrogian. Macmillan
(N Y) 1970 unp illus $4.95 (k-3)   398.2
  1 Folklore—Russia
"In this Russian equivalent of Cinderella, Vasilisa
has a doll, the gift of her dying mother, instead of a
godmother to advise and help her and the plot is more
inclusive than that of the fairy tale as it is known to
Western readers. By prevailing over the witch Baba
Yaga, to whom she has been sent to fetch a light,
Vasilisa triumphs over her evil stepmother and jealous
stepsisters—and marries the king." Booklist
"From the Afanasiev collection of traditional tales
. . . translated in good style to read smoothly for reading aloud or independently. The illustrations are
handsome: soft colors, comic details, effective composition." Chicago. Children's Bk Center

Vo-Dinh

The toad is the Emperor's uncle; animal folktales
from Viet-Nam; told and illus. by Vo-Dinh. Doubleday 1970 141p illus $3.50, lib. bdg. $4.25 (4-6)
                                               398.2
  1 Folklore—Vietnam 2 Animals—Stories
  ISBN 0-385-08490-0; 0-385-00838-4
"Customs and beliefs of Vietnam are reflected in
these 18 brief traditional tales, many of which tell
humorously of trickery and justice in the animal
world." Children's Bks 1970
These tales "are sharper and livelier than the stories
in Graham, above, and likely to be more popular with
children. . . . [They] combine explanations of animal
traits and natural phenomena with witty precepts on
human behavior. Information on the background and
significance of the stories appears in the Author's
Note at the beginning and along with different stories
throughout the book." Booklist

Walker, Barbara K.

The dancing palm tree, and other Nigerian folktales; woodcuts by Helen Siegl. Parents Mag. Press
1968 112p illus lib. bdg. $4.59 (4-6)   398.2
  1 Folklore—Nigeria
  ISBN 0-8193-0330-5
The folktales in this "collection were told to the
author by a Nigerian student in an American college
whose homeland is Western Nigeria, populated
largely by the Yorubas. Among the 11 tales of kings
and princesses, common people, and animals are several 'why' stories, a trickster tale, and one of magic. All
have morals since storytelling in Nigeria has always
been to instruct as well as to entertain. Appended
notes in the form of a glossary furnish considerable
information on the ways and beliefs of the Yorubas."
Booklist
"Adroit, distinctive writing combined with striking
woodcuts." Keating. Building Bridges of Understanding Between Cultures

Wiesner, William

Turnabout; a Norwegian tale retold and illus. by
William Wiesner. Seabury 1972 unp illus $5.95 (k-
3)   398.2
  1 Folklore—Norway
  ISBN 0-8164-3083-7
"This text has been adapted from the version of
Edouard Laboulaye." Verso of title page
"The artist has drawn many doublespreads which
depict—on the left-hand page—the wife calmly raking row after row in the field, while the husband
smashes eggs, fails to put the stopper in the cider
barrel, and gets stuck in the chimney—a victim of his
own ineptitude. The line drawings—washed in tones
of red, green, blue, yellow, gray, and brown—are
direct, fresh, and sprightly." Horn Bk

Wiggin, Kate Douglas

(ed.) The Arabian nights; their best-known tales;
ed. by Kate Douglas Wiggin and Nora A. Smith; illus
by Maxfield Parrish. Scribner [1974 c1909] 340p illus
pa $3.95 (5-7)   398.2
  1 Folklore—Arabia 2 Fairy tales
  ISBN 0-684-13809-3
"The Scribner Illustrated classics"
A paperback reissue of the title first published in
1909
A collection of ten tales, from the Arabian nights, of
talking birds, genies, Sinbad, Ali Baba, and Aladdin
"Twelve full-page plates, individual, highly
imaginative, and unsurpassed in richness of color."
Pittsburgh

Wildsmith, Brian

The hare and the tortoise; based on the fable by La
Fontaine; pictures by Brian Wildsmith. Watts, F.
[1967 c1966] unp illus lib. bdg. $4.95 (k-2)   398.2
  1 Fables 2 Turtles—Stories 3 Rabbits—Stories
  ISBN 0-531-01533-5
First published 1966 in England
A retelling of the fable about the slow but steady
tortoise who beats the swift but overconfident hare in
a race through the forest
"A simplified version of the original fable, this is
one of Wildsmith's most successful picture books. The
animals have character and personality, and his brilliant colours are very effective in the forest scenes."
Ontario Lib Rev

The lion and the rat; a fable, by La Fontaine; illus.
by Brian Wildsmith. Watts, F. 1963 unp illus lib. bdg.
$5.95 (k-2)   398.2
  1 Fables 2 Lions—Stories 3 Rats—Stories
  ISBN 0-531-01534-3
A retelling of the French fable about the rat who
repaid the lion's kindness by rescuing him from a trap
"A simplified version that is adequate. The illustrations are a joy. They glow with vivid color and movement; both color and design are used with imagination. . . . A book well worth having for the beauty of
the drawings." Chicago. Children's Bk Center

The miller, the boy and the donkey. Watts, F. 1969
unp illus lib. bdg. $4.95 (k-2)   398.2
  1 Fables
  ISBN 0-531-01542-4
"Based on a fable by La Fontaine." Half-title page
Adapted and illustrated by Brian Wildsmith
The miller and his son take their donkey to market
to sell him. To keep him clean they decide to carry
him, but a passing farmer laughs at them and they ride
the donkey instead. Thus begins a series of suggestions from other people they meet as to who should
ride the donkey. The poor miller is utterly confused
trying to please everyone and in the end decides that
next time he will only please himself
"A spirited and attractive picture book." Children's
Bks 1970

The North Wind and the Sun; a fable by La Fontaine; illus. by Brian Wildsmith. Watts, F. 1964 unp
illus lib. bdg. $5.95 (k-3)   398.2
  1 Fables 2 Winds—Fiction 3 Sun—Fiction
  ISBN 0-531-01536-X
A retelling of the fable in which the North Wind
and the Sun had a wager on which of them could
persuade the horseman to remove his fine new cloak.
Its moral concerns the value of gentleness
"Wildsmith integrates oil, watercolours and
crayon. . . . Every illustration is a striking poster and
yet there is just the proper attention to detail to make
the pictures speak. This bold design and striking jux-

Wildsmith, Brian—*Continued*
taposition of strong and contrasting colours are always pleasing to the eye and make this a truly memorable book." Toronto

The rich man and the shoe-maker; a fable by La Fontaine; illus. by Brian Wildsmith. Watts, F. 1965 unp illus lib. bdg. $4.95 (k-2)   398.2
1 Fables
ISBN 0-531-01538-6
This "fable—the tale of the poor but carefree shoemaker to whom sudden wealth brought only anxiety and distress—has been freely adapted into simple prose. Amplifying the story with an imaginative life of their own, the pictures are full of shapes, angles, and rhythmic patterns, while the sheer glory of dynamic color carries its own emotional impact." Horn Bk

Williams, Jay
The horn of Roland; illus. by Sean Morrison. Crowell 1968 157p illus (Crowell Hero tales) $3.95 (4-6)   398.2
1 Roland (Legendary hero) 2 Legends—France
ISBN 0-690-40218-X
Drawing upon such sources as medieval chanson de geste, ballads, and prose chronicles, this retelling of the adventures of the legendary French hero who was Charlemagne's bravest knight is "a chronological account at Roncesvalles. . . . The long descriptive passages and romantic embellishments characteristic of James Baldwin's 'The Story of Roland' [entered above] are sacrificed to a fast-paced adventure, which may attract more readers." Horn Bk
This "may be especially useful with older but slower readers, since it is clearly written and uses a simple vocabulary. Teachers could easily use these stories in the study of the Middle Ages." Sch Library J
Includes a brief bibliography

Williams-Ellis, Amabel
Fairy tales from the British Isles; retold by Amabel Williams-Ellis; illus. by Pauline Diana Baynes. Warne [1964 c1960] 344p illus $4.95 (5-7)   398.2
1 Folklore—Great Britain 2 Fairy tales
ISBN 0-7232-6026-5
First published 1960 in England
These 48 stories prove "the author's ability to gather, select, and retell folk tales that make a real contribution to our collections for children. Many of the stories are widely known through Jacobs' collections; others ('Fifty Red Night-Caps,' 'The Bear in the Coach') retold from childhood memory are less familiar. The majority of stories are English, but a few good selections from Wales ('The Lake Lady'), Scotland ('The Wee Wee Manie') and Ireland ('Clever Oonagh') round out a pleasing collection. . . . Fifteen pages of notes will be of interest to the storyteller, and good illustrations complement the text." Sch Library J

Withers, Carl
(ed.) I saw a rocket walk a mile. . . . illus. by John E. Johnson. Holt 1965 160p illus lib. bdg. $3.59 (3-6)   398.2
1 Folklore 2 Nonsense verses 3 Literature—Collections
ISBN 0-03-051005-8
"Nonsense tales, chants, and songs from many lands." Title page
"For the esoteric interests of folklorists, the author's generous notes will be illuminating; but for . . . children and storytellers, the stories will be sufficient." Horn Bk
Notes and comments: p153-59

A world of nonsense; strange and humorous tales from many lands; illus. by John E. Johnson. Holt 1968 118p illus lib. bdg. $4.59 (4-7)   398.2
1 Folklore
ISBN 0-03-067990-7
"Nonsensical, tall tale or noodlehead—whatever you wish to call them—these are humorous short-shorts gathered from 'reading several thousand folk-tales from many lands.' Notes, comments and sources are at the back of the book. A treasure house for the story teller who is looking for 'just one more story.' Children will read just for the sheer nonsense." Bruno. Bks for Sch Libraries, 1968
Selections range from boast-topping two-liners and riddles to a few longer tales

Wyndham, Robert
Tales the people tell in China; illus. by Jay Yang; consulting editor: Doris K. Coburn. Messner 1971 92p illus lib. bdg. $5.64 (3-6)   398.2
1 Folklore—China
ISBN 0-671-32428-4
A "collection of 15 simply told Chinese legends, stories, and anecdotes including a traditional tale that, according to Wyndham, has been rewritten for propaganda purposes by the government of the People's Republic of China. In addition, there are stories of scholars, ghosts, generals, peasants, Confucius, and the emperor, and a selection of short sayings. Sources and notes are appended." Booklist
"Gracefully illustrated in the classical Chinese style, the ancient stories offer considerable insight to Chinese culture and customs." Pub W

Yamaguchi, Tohr
The golden crane; a Japanese folktale; illus. by Marianne Yamaguchi. Holt 1963 unp illus $3 (3-5)   398.2
1 Folklore—Japan 2 Cranes (Birds)—Stories
ISBN 0-03-035480-3
"A Wise owl book"
"Toshi, a deaf and dumb child, and his stepfather find a wounded golden crane and nurse it to health. The crane attracts much attention; even the emperor wishes to have it. In order to prevent this happening, several cranes appear and carry Toshi and his stepfather over the ocean horizon." Adventuring with Bks. 2d edition
"A mystical Japanese folk tale . . . sensitively illustrated in black and white." Booklist

Yolen, Jane
The emperor and the kite; pictures by Ed Young. Collins 1967 unp illus $4.95 (k-3)   398.2
1 Folklore—China
ISBN 0-529-00253-1
A retelling of an old Chinese tale. "Princess Djeow Seow, the smallest one, largely ignored by her father the Emperor and her brothers, took solace from her kite. When the Emperor was imprisoned in a tower by wicked men, the tiny girl devised his escape by braiding a rope, attaching it to the kite, and flying it up to her father." Bruno. Bks for Sch Libraries, 1968
This book "is especially distinguished by its Chinese artist's modern use of the Old Oriental paper-cut style. Vividly colored, choreographic figures move across open white pages and grace the equally distinctive poetic rhythm and balance of the text. Small children will be captivated by the emperor's youngest daughter." Bk World

Young, Ella

The wonder smith and his son; a tale from the golden childhood of the world; illus. by Boris Artzybasheff. McKay 1957 [c1927] 190p illus $3.75 (5-7)   398.2

1 Folklore—Ireland 2 Folklore, Gaelic 3 Gobborn Seer

ISBN 0-679-20256-0

First published 1927 by Longmans

Fourteen "glorious adventures of Gubbaun Saor, the master-builder famed in old Irish folk-lore." Chicago

"Tales that have grown out of the folk life of the ancient Gaelic-speaking people of Ireland. They are rich in humor, fresh and uncluttered. Some, Miss Young says, are told almost as recounted to her; others are pieced from gathered fragments; but all are told with absolute respect for the integrity of the folk-tale. The illustrations and decorations reflect the rich symbolism of the tales." Booklist

Zemach, Harve

Duffy and the devil; a Cornish tale retold by Harve Zemach; with pictures by Margot Zemach. Farrar, Straus 1973 unp illus $5.95 (k-3)   398.2

1 Folklore—Great Britain

ISBN 0-374-31887-5

Awarded the Caldecott Medal, 1974

"In this Cornish variation on Rumpelstiltskin Squire Lovel brings the maid Duffy home to help his housekeeper Old Jone, who can no longer do the work that needs 'sharp eyes and quick fingers.' But in truth Duffy can neither spin, knit, nor weave until the devil comes to her aid. They strike a bargain whereby Duffy must discover the devil's name at the end of three years—which she does through the help of Old Jone." Booklist

"The artist employs her typical pastel coloring, but the use of shading and perspective to create entire scenes is highly unusual for her, and the illustrations far surpass anything she has done to date. The author embues the story with wry humor, invented words, and slightly edgy statements, which are perfectly exploited in the illustrations: Duffy sitting 'herself ladylike' on the horse, and the witches taking a swig of beer. The legend of Rumpelstiltskin has probably never seemed as funny as in this version by the author-artist team." Horn Bk

A penny a look; an old story retold by Harve Zemach; pictures by Margot Zemach. Farrar, Straus 1971 unp illus $4.95 (k-3)   398.2

ISBN 0-374-35793-5

"An insensitive and aggressive man has heard about the land of one-eyed people, and he persuades his do-nothing but merciful brother to come along on a trek to get there. Object: to capture one man, bring him back, exhibit him, and get rich. The gentler brother will be allowed to collect penny fees. But the tables are turned: surrounded by one-eyed men, the malfeasant is captured and exhibited, since he is a rarity, a man with two eyes. The brother (even one-eyed men could see he'd never amount to much) is no threat, so he is permitted to collect fees." Sutherland. The Best in Children's Bks

"Zemach's style is low-key and pseudo-serious, his dialogue droll. But it's really his wife Margot who never misses a chance to make you laugh. She has drawn a series of slapstick scenes, like a silent-movie pantomime, that follow the brothers on their Phineas Foggish trek. . . . With a gesture here, a posture there, she draws with a master humorist's touch. . . . Behind the laugh is a lesson: cruelty and avarice don't pay." N Y Times Bk Rev

Too much nose; an Italian tale; adapted by Harve Zemach; illus. by Margot Zemach. Holt 1967 unp illus $3.95, pa $1.65 (k-3)   398.2

1 Folklore—Italy 2 Fairy tales

ISBN 0-03-061525-9; 0-03-086629-4

"Gullibility and cleverness are the secret ingredients of this humorous adaptation of an Italian fairy tale. Three sons are tricked by a clever queen out of their father's inheritance which was able to make each of them invisible, rich, or all-powerful in turn. Magical fruits which can do strange things to noses make for a surprise ending that is hilariously happy. Good for story hours." Wis Library Bul

"Margot Zemach never misses a chance to make us laugh. . . . Harve Zemach's deadpan, pseudo-serious story is an ideal vehicle for [her] talents." Bk Week

Zemach, Margot

The three sillies; a folk tale; illus. by Margot Zemach. Holt 1963 unp illus lib. bdg. $3.07, pa $1.25 (k-3)   398.2

1 Folklore

ISBN 0-03-036135-4; 0-03-091955-X

This is "the ridiculous story of the stupid fellow who would not marry his sweetheart until he found three people sillier than the girl and her parents." Hodges. Bks for Elem Sch Libraries

"The action of this familiar folk tale has been visualized . . . in a comical never-never land where very low-browed peasants in decorative pink and tan costumes show their foolishness and their feelings with gestures of extravagant abandon. We think this is the wittiest, homeliest and prettiest interpretation of this nonsense story we have seen—a modern rendering that reinterprets the ancient comedy without losing the traditional wisdom." Bk Week

398.6   Riddles

Hubp, Loretta Burke

(ed.) Qué será? What can it be? Traditional Spanish riddles collected and arranged, with English translations. Illus. by Mircea Vasiliu. Day 1970 63p illus lib. bdg. $3.48 (3-6)   398.6

1 Riddles 2 Bilingual books—Spanish-English

ISBN 0-381-99779-0

These traditional Spanish riddles are grouped by such topics as nature, animals, music, and food. Literal English translations of riddles and answers are provided with explanations where necessary

Leach, Maria

Noodles, nitwits, and numskulls; drawings by Kurt Werth. Collins 1961 96p illus lib. bdg. $5.71 (4-7)   398.6

1 Wit and humor 2 Riddles 3 Folklore

ISBN 0-529-03662-2

A "collection of time-honored jokes, riddles and funny stories that go way back into the folklore of various countries. There are . . . notes about the origins of these [at the end of the book]." Pub W

"The illustrations have a light humor, and the book is made attractive by good type size and plenty of space on the pages. Not the sort of book for continuous reading, but very useful as a source of material in this genre." Chicago. Children's Bk Center

Bibliography: p96

Riddle me, riddle me, ree; illus. by William Wiesner. Viking 1970 142p illus $4.95 (3-6)   398.6

1 Riddles 2 Folklore

ISBN 0-670-05065-2

Leach, Maria—*Continued*

"A more scholarly collection than most, this is devoted entirely to riddles from around the world. . . . [The more than 200 riddles included] are divided into sections by subject, and the country of origin is given for each one. In addition, each riddle is fully annotated in the 'Notes and Bibliography' section at the back of the book. Told from the viewpoint of the folklorist, some of the riddles will be in a form unfamiliar to American children . . . but the U.S. entries include elephant jokes and state name riddles." Sch Library J

Morrison, Lillian

(comp.) Black within and red without; a book of riddles; illus. by Jo Spier. Crowell 1953 120p illus $3.95 (5-7)   398.6

1 Riddles
ISBN 0-690-14656-6

"This is a collection of almost 200 traditional riddles, most of them in rhyme. . . . There are some 'pun riddles' but the most common are those in which the answers are hidden in metaphors, some strongly imaginative or strangely evocative, others making up in sound or vitality what they lack in sense. . . . The sources of the riddles in this book are shown in the bibliography at the end." Preface

"There is fun and poetry and echoes of the past in these gay riddles, which will keep a child happy puzzling friends and relatives for the answers." Chicago Sunday Trib

Rees, Ennis

Riddles, riddles everywhere; illus. by Quentin Blake. Abelard-Schuman 1964 125p illus lib. bdg. $4.95 (3-6)   398.6

1 Riddles 2 Folklore
ISBN 0-200-71915-7

The author states that "most of the verse riddles included in this book, I have made from prose originals that have for generations been part of American and British folklore." In recreating riddles in rhyme Dr. Rees has tried to capture and further the fun children have experienced when reading and riddling prose riddles. . . . Attractive in format with modern but childishly humorous ink drawings, some with green or orange added, this new collection should prove to be popular. . . . The riddles aren't arranged in any set order, and there is no index." Sch Library J

Schwartz, Alvin

(ed.) Tomfoolery; trickery and foolery with words; collected from American folklore by Alvin Schwartz; illus. by Glen Rounds. Lippincott 1973 127p illus $5.50, pa $1.95 (3-6)   398.6

1 American wit and humor 2 Riddles
ISBN 0-397-31466-3; 0-397-31467-1

"This is a sampling of verbal trickery garnered not only from folklore archives, publications, and folklorists but also from Schwartz's childhood, his children, and other children. Rounds' amusing line drawings add visual interest to the collection which includes wisecracks, riddles, practical jokes, double talk, endless tales, and anecdotes with trick endings. Appended are notes, sources, and a bibliography." Booklist

(ed.) Witcracks; jokes and jests from American folklore; illus. by Glen Rounds. Lippincott 1973 128p illus $4.95, pa $2.50 (4-7)   398.6

1 American wit and humor
ISBN 0-397-31475-2; 0-397-31476-0

A collection of American humor including "riddles, shaggy dog stories, Tom Swifties, hate jokes, noodle-head humor, ethnic humor, and knock-knock jokes." Chicago. Children's Bk Center

"Short explanations about when and why such jokes are told precede each section; copious notes give the origins of jokes and stories; and black-and-white line drawings add to the humor. It is unfortunate, however, that hate or ethnic jokes as well as sick jokes popular in the '50's have been included." Sch Library J

Bibliography: p121-25

Still, James

Way down yonder on Troublesome Creek; Appalachian riddles & rusties; pictures by Janet McCaffery. Putnam 1974 unp illus lib. bdg. $3.96 (3-6)   398.6

1 American wit and humor 2 Riddles
ISBN 0-399-60850-8

"This joke collection presents a fine assortment of riddles and rusties (wise cracks or pranks) that are [in most cases] unavailable elsewhere. Mountain colloquialisms abound giving the spirit of Appalachia. . . . Most unfamiliar terms are defined on the page where they appear, but many riddles are understood easily without any explanation. . . . Janet McCaffery's strong woodcuts illustrate the collection with imagination and humor." Sch Library J

Withers, Carl

(comp.) The American riddle book, by Carl Withers and Sula Benet; illus. by Marc Simont. Abelard-Schuman 1954 157p illus $5.25 (5-7)   398.6

1 Riddles
ISBN 0-200-71842-8

"A collection of over a thousand riddles, conundrums, and other riddling nonsense, old and new, compiled by two anthropologists. . . . Includes numerous special categories such as arithmetic riddles, kinship riddles, Bible riddles, word charades, and Little Moron riddles, and a separate section of representative riddles from other nations, regions, and tribal groups. Amusing illustrations. Of interest to sociologists as well as to children." Booklist

"The title refers to the audience rather than the sources." N Y Times Bk Rev

"The authors have classified the entries for ready reference, but readers may begin on any page for a chuckle." Wis Library Bul

(comp.) Riddles of many lands, by Carl Withers and Sula Benet; illus. by Lili Cassel. Abelard-Schuman 1956 160p illus $4.95 (5-7)   398.6

1 Riddles
ISBN 0-200-00099-3

"Contains eight hundred riddles from over ninety countries, regions and tribal or ethnic groups." The author

This volume is divided into seven major divisions: North America, South America, the British Isles, Europe, Africa, Asia and Oceania. Includes sources

"Children love riddles, and they will love this compiler team for expanding their favorite horizons. Folklorists and teachers of social studies will also welcome such a collection. Lili Cassel's illustrations are gay and pertinent." Library J

Map on lining-papers

398.8 Nursery rhymes

And so my garden grows; illus. by Peter Spier. Doubleday 1969 unp illus (The Mother Goose lib.) $4.95, lib. bdg. $5.70 (k-3)   398.8

1 Nursery rhymes
ISBN 0-385-08757-8; 0-385-05156-5

Pictures from Italian cities, parks, vineyards,

And so my garden grows—*Continued*

monasteries, farms and great estates provide the background to such nursery rhymes as "Mistress Mary, quite contrary," "This is the key to the kingdom," "Rosemary green, and lavender blue," and "Mother, may I go and bathe?"

"As children pore over the extraordinary depth of these pictures, as they surely will, they may even feel that they already have half a foot in this magical land, so brilliantly has it been brought to life in these pages." Times (London) Literary Sup

Blegvad, Lenore

(comp.) Mittens for kittens, and other rhymes about cats; illus. by Erik Blegvad. Atheneum Pubs. 1974 unp illus $5.95 (k-1)   398.8

1 Nursery rhymes 2 Cats—Poetry

ISBN 0-689-50003-3

"A Margaret K. McElderry book"

A selection of 25 brief English rhymes about cats and kittens

The illustrator "has created pages full of his uniquely appealing pictures (some in color, others in black and white) to accompany the verses selected by his wife. . . . The poems are many and various, ranging from the well-known 'Ding, Dong, Bell' and 'I Love Little Pussy' to others which will be new to young readers." Pub W

Bodecker, N. M.

It's raining said John Twaining; Danish nursery rhymes; tr. and illus. by N. M. Bodecker. Atheneum Pubs. 1973 unp illus $4.95 (k-2)   398.8

1 Nursery rhymes

ISBN 0-689-30316-5

"A Margaret K. McElderry book"

These "nursery rhymes are quite different from what we are used to, but they read easily and well. Almost immediately they begin to seem familiar to us in their warmth and simplicity. . . . [The] full-color pictures set different moods to evoke the particular feelings of a rhyme, and which are always rather unexpected. . . . Here are tender, simple, silly nursery rhymes that Danish men and women have grown up with, each specially interpreted for us in an enormously varied and well-constructed picture book. They give us another slant and great pleasure." N Y Times Bk Rev

Briggs, Raymond

Fee fi fo fum; a picture book of nursery rhymes. With a grateful acknowledgement to Iona and Peter Opie. Coward-McCann 1964 unp illus $5.95 lib. bdg. $4.97 (k-1)   398.8

1 Nursery rhymes

ISBN 0-698-20042-X; 0-698-30074-2

"There is a very British air about these [20] humorous nursery rhymes, some well-known, but most of them less familiar. Vigorous, bright paintings and black-and-white line drawings [by Briggs]." Children's Bks, 1964

Cassedy, Sylvia

(comp.) Moon-uncle, moon-uncle; rhymes from India; selected and tr. by Sylvia Cassedy and Parvathi Thampi; illus. by Susanne Suba. Doubleday 1973 32p illus $4.95 lib. bdg. $5.70 (k-3)   398.8

1 Nursery rhymes

ISBN 0-385-07761-0; 0-385-02963-2

A child's view of family, fantasy and nature is reflected in this collection of forty-three Indic nursery rhymes

DeForest, Charlotte B.

The prancing pony; nursery rhymes from Japan; adapted into English verse for children by Charlotte B. DeForest; with "kusa-e" illus. by Keiko Hida. Walker & Co. [1968 c1967] 63p illus lib. bdg. $3.87 (k-3)   398.8

1 Nursery rhymes 2 Japanese poetry

ISBN 0-8348-2000-5

"A Weathermark edition"

First published 1967 in Japan

These fifty-three nursery songs deal primarily with the world of nature

"Working in complete harmony with the poems, Keiko Hida is the perfect illustrator. She works in a new art form she calls 'Kusa-e,' a collage technique using handmade Japanese paper and natural plant dyes that produce subtle shades of red, yellow, purple, indigo, brown and black. Her work, both sophisticated and simple, creates its own poetry of form and line and color." Bk World

Emberley, Barbara

Drummer Hoff; adapted by Barbara Emberley; illus. by Ed Emberley. Prentice-Hall 1967 unp illus $5.95, pa 95¢ (k-3)   398.8

1 Nursery rhymes

ISBN 0-13-220822-9; 0-13-220855-5

Awarded the Caldecott Medal, 1968

In this version of "a rhyming folk verse a cannon is assembled by a team of soldiers, while poker-faced Drummer Hoff stands at the ready [to fire it off] and the ornate headgear of the militia protrudes like ramrods from a trench below. . . . The firing is shown in a double-page spread . . . and the last picture displays a . . . scene in which time has erased all scars and the cannon is covered with flowers and spiderwebs." Sat Rev

"Stylized woodcuts in brilliant hues develop this martial folk rhyme into a sprightly book which the young child will enjoy again and again. The pictures are to be re-examined for their entertaining details (birds, ladybugs, and flowers appear and reappear), and the lines of the brief text are to be chanted for their alliterative nonsense." Horn Bk

Fish, Helen Dean

(comp.) Four & twenty blackbirds; nursery rhymes of yesterday recalled for children of today; illus. by Robert Lawson. Lippincott 1937 104p illus $5.70 (k-3)   398.8

1 Nursery rhymes

ISBN 0-397-31546-5

"A collection of nursery jingles and ballads of yesterday which it is a pleasure to have readily available, especially for reading aloud. . . . For thirteen of the twenty-four, simple airs are included. The source of the jingle and of the version used is given in the table of contents." Booklist

"Robert Lawson's spirited full-page drawings make this a delightful picture book, as well as a source book of nursery songs which are uncommonly hard to find." Atlantic Bookshelf

Heilbroner, Joan

This is the house where Jack lives; illus. by Aliki. Harper 1962 62p illus lib. bdg. $3.79 (k-2)   398.8

1 Nursery rhymes

ISBN 0-06-022286-7

"An I can read book"

"A city apartment building is the setting for this modern version of the old cumulative nonsense rhyme about Jack and his house." Cincinnati

"The illustrations are gay and humorous, echoing in the drawings the cumulative parts of the rhyme." Chicago. Children's Bk Center

The House that Jack built; la maison que Jacques a bâtie. A picture book in two languages [by] Antonio Frasconi. Harcourt 1958 unp illus $6.50 (1-4)
398.8

1 Nursery rhymes 2 Bilingual books—French-English
ISBN 0-15-236300-9
"On each page the lines cumulate separately in French and in English until the end of the tale is reached; then the story is reiterated, with French and English in coupled lines. A third section asks a question in English and answers in French." Chicago. Children's Bk Center
"A refreshing way to learn vocabulary in a second language. . . . Mr. Frasconi's modern woodcuts deserve a review all their own, alive as they are with imaginative action, variety of expression and texture, and expert use of three colors plus black." Horn Bk

I saw a ship a-sailing; pictures by Janina Domanska. Macmillan (N Y) 1972 unp illus $4.95 (k-1) 398.8

1 Nursery rhymes
An illustrated presentation of the traditional Mother Goose rhyme about a magical ship with its delectable cargo, an irrepressible crew of four-and-twenty white mice, and the stalwart captain duck
The book "is illustrated by pictures that are composed with a high sense of design and a deft use of color. The patterns are often geometric, the details intricate, and the bold colors of the ship, her crew, and the cargo effectively set off by the cool pastel shades of water or a patterned background. The illustrations are not primarily humorous, but there are amusing conceits like the clouds that emanate from a giant pipe smoked by the man in the moon." Sutherland. The Best in Children's Bks

If all the seas were one sea; etchings by Janina Domanska. Macmillan (N Y) 1971 unp illus $5.95 (k-2)
398.8

1 Nursery rhymes
The artist has used boldly designed etchings in four colors to illustrate this traditional nursery rhyme
It "is pictured with an airy lightness and a sense of movement. . . . With great distinction, little is made into much." Horn Bk

Ivimey, John W.
Complete version of Ye three blind mice; illus. by Walter Corbould. Warne 1909 31p illus $2.95 (k-2)
398.8

1 Nursery rhymes 2 Mice—Poetry
ISBN 0-7232-0428-4
"The previous history of the famous three (before they encountered the farmer's wife) and their subsequent recovery, told in the same metre with appropriate illustrations." Four to Fourteen

Jeffers, Susan
Three jovial huntsmen; adapted and illus. by Susan Jeffers. Bradbury 1973 unp illus $6.95 (k-2) 398.8

1 Nursery rhymes
ISBN 0-87888-023-2
Title on cover: Mother Goose—Three jovial huntsmen
"The story involves three dimwits who hunt through a forest full of game without ever seeing any. However, viewers will have the pleasure of spotting all the nearly hidden animals the huntsmen either fail to see or mistake for something else." Sch Library J
"It's main attraction lies in the book's physical beauty: The subdued tones of the illustrations—created by yellow, red, blue, and black overlays on pen-and-ink drawings—have been masterfully blended and differentiated. In some of the night

scenes, the twisted branches and muted blues are reminiscent of Arthur Rackham's work." Horn Bk
"A sloppy binding occasionally interrupts beautiful visual effects of the double-page spreads." Booklist

The Life of Jack Sprat, his wife & his cat; Paul Galdone drew them. McGraw [1969] unp illus lib. bdg. $4.72 (k-2)
398.8
1 Nursery rhymes
ISBN 0-07-022703-9
Based on the text of an 1820 chapbook, this Mother Goose nursery rhyme tells about Jack Sprat and his wife Joan and how they lived, from the days of their courtship through the many years of their marriage

Lines, Kathleen
(comp.) Lavender's blue; a book of nursery rhymes; pictured by Harold Jones. Watts, F. 1954 180p illus $7.95 (k-2)
398.8
1 Nursery rhymes
ISBN 0-531-01707-9
Arranged in nine sections under the following headings: Rock-a-bye, baby; Girls and boys come out to play; Old Mother Goose; Lion and the Unicorn; A Apple pie; One, two, buckle my shoe; Here we go round the mulberry bush; House that Jack built; If ifs and ands
"This is a collection of nursery rhymes with a special character all its own. Printed in England, although published here, it is beautifully made. The unusual Harold Jones illustrations, some in warm, subtle colors, some in black and white, all have a charming, haunting quality." Library J
Index of first lines: p175-80

Mother Goose
Brian Wildsmith's Mother Goose; a collection of nursery rhymes. Watts, F. [1965 c1964] 80p illus $5.95 (k-2)
398.8
1 Nursery rhymes
ISBN 0-531-01536-X
First published 1964 in England
These eighty-six verses "are well selected and include many quaint and lesser-known verses." Bk Week
"The artist's wholly original, sophisticated yet childlike interpretation of long-familiar material is revealed in his clever composition, unconventional humor, and characteristic watercolor technique with its use of geometric patterns and brilliant chromatic modulations." Horn Bk
Index of first lines: p80

Hey riddle diddle! A book of traditional riddles [illus] by Rodney Peppé. Holt 1971 unp illus $4.95 (k-3)
398.8
1 Nursery rhymes 2 Riddles
ISBN 0-03-086233-7
Peppé has "illustrated in gaily colored collage 45 favorite traditional riddles [from Mother Goose] such as 'Four stiff-standers, four dilly-danders, two lookers, two crookers, and a wig-wag.' Answers to the riddles are given at the end." Booklist

The large type Mother Goose; pictures by Arthur Rackham. Watts, F. [1970] 164p illus $8.95 (k-2)
398.8

1 Nursery rhymes
ISBN 0-531-00309-4
"A Keith Jennison book"
A large-type edition of Mother Goose nursery rhymes, illustrated by Arthur Rackham (published 1969, o.p. 1975). This version contains the approxi-

Mother Goose—*Continued*

mately 165 rhymes of the original and the black-and-white drawings, but omits the colorplates

Includes an index of first lines

Marguerite de Angeli's Book of nursery and Mother Goose rhymes. Doubleday 1954 192p illus $6.95, lib. bdg. $7.70 (k-2)   398.8

1 Nursery rhymes

ISBN 0-385-07232-5; 0-385-06246-X

Marguerite de Angeli "has compiled and illustrated a beautiful edition that offers nearly 400 rhymes, all the old favorites and the less familiar, and over 250 lovely, imaginative pictures, both in full color and in black and white." Wis Library Bul

Mother Goose and nursery rhymes; wood engravings by Philip Reed. Atheneum Pubs. 1963 57p illus lib. bdg. $6.95 (k-2)   398.8

1 Nursery rhymes

ISBN 0-689-20624-0

A collection of almost 70 "long rhymes, short ones, some most familiar, others less so. . . . The characters are 18th century in costume." Pub W

The selection is "highly individual [and] fresh. . . . The artist-designer has provided beautifully printed wood engravings in six clear colors. With superb execution, quaintness, and humor, they make a volume for the lover of fine books; for the nursery age, [there are] the details and amusing traits of personality." Horn Bk

Index of first lines: p55-56

Mother Goose; or, The old nursery rhymes; illus. in colour by Kate Greenaway. Warne [n.d.] 48p illus $2.95 (k-2)   398.8

1 Nursery rhymes

ISBN 0-7232-0591-4

"This tiny little book contains but a limited number of rhymes but its charming illustrations have delighted many children. The artist, Kate Greenaway, has kept to her usual type of English children rather than adapting herself to the accepted Mother Goose style." Right Bk for the Right Child

Mother Goose; seventy-seven verses with pictures by Tasha Tudor. Walck, H.Z. 1944 87p illus $4.50 (k-2)   398.8

1 Nursery rhymes

ISBN 0-8098-1901-5

First published by Oxford

A lovely "Mother Goose, fresh in its interpretation both as to selection and illustration. . . . The book is smaller than usual for Mother Goose; the pictures in soft colors and in black and white are quaint and charming." Booklist

"Perfect in flavor and spirit for the young child and delightful from the adult standpoint." Library J

The Mother Goose treasury; [illus. by] Raymond Briggs. Coward-McCann 1966 217p illus $8.87 (k-2)   398.8

1 Nursery rhymes

ISBN 0-698-30243-5

The versions of these 408 verses were done by Iona and Peter Opie. They include "from four-liners to 12, 13 and 14-stanza rhymes, such as 'The House that Jack Built' or 'The Old Woman and her Pig' and 'The Twelve Days of Christmas.' Here you will find the complete text of 'The Bells of London,' 'The Death and Burial of Cock Robin,' 'The Love-sick Frog,' 'Little Bo-Peep' to say nothing at all of the many other familiar and not-at-all familiar shorter rhymes. What is special about this edition is that it has been illustrated by Raymond Briggs, who made some 890 draw-

ings and paintings that are a delight, especially in color." Best Sellers

Index to first lines and titles: p[218-20]

One I love, two I love, and other loving Mother Goose rhymes; illus. by Nonny Hogrogian. Dutton 1972 unp illus $4.95 (k-2)   398.8

1 Nursery rhymes

ISBN 0-525-36420-X

Seventeen Mother Goose rhymes chosen for their theme of love. Among those included are: Peter pumpkin eater, Georgie Porgie, and Willy, Willy Wilkin

"Some of the choices ('Daffy-down dilly' for example) seen only remotely related to the scope indicated by the subtitle, but the attractive drawings add appeal to the durable verses, so there seems little for complaint." Chicago. Children's Bk Center

The real Mother Goose; illus. by Blanche Fisher Wright. Rand McNally [1965] 128p illus lib. bdg. $3.39 (k-2)   398.8

1 Nursery rhymes

ISBN 0-8382-0691-3

"Special anniversary edition, with introduction by May Hill Arbuthnot"

First published 1916

This large volume of over 300 Mother Goose verses "is one of the most popular. It has colorful pictures on every page—pictures so clear and simple that they appeal to the young child." Larrick. A Parent's Guide to Children's Reading

Includes a list of titles and an alphabetical list of first lines

Rimes de la Mère Oie. Mother Goose rhymes rendered into French by Ormonde De Kay, Jr. Designed and illus. by Seymour Chwast, Milton Glasser [and] Barry Zaid, of Push Pin Studios. Little 1971 89p illus $8.95 (3-5)   398.8

1 Nursery rhymes 2 Bilingual Books—French-English

ISBN 0-316-17980-9

"In translating into French these 60 Mother Goose rhymes, most of which were taken from the Opies' 'Oxford nursery rhyme book,' [entered below under title] De Kay has succeeded admirably in the difficult task of preserving the meter, rhyme schemes, and the sense of the originals. The rhymes are handsomely presented in a tall volume with elegant page borders, with tiny silhouettes, and with 18 sophisticated but eye-catching colored illustrations by three artists of the Push Pin Studios. The English versions of the rhymes with notes by the translator are appended. Though too special for some children's collections, the book will be enjoyed by children with a knowledge of French and could be extremely useful in the teaching of French." Booklist

The tall book of Mother Goose; pictured by Feodor Rojankovsky. Harper 1942 120p illus $2.95, lib. bdg. $4.43 (k-2)   398.8

1 Nursery rhymes

ISBN 0-06-025055-0; 0-06-025056-9

This tall, narrow book of about 100 of the familiar rhymes is illustrated with over 150 illustrations, more than 50 of them in color

The book's size "makes it easy to hold and look at; its colored pictures are gay, humorous [and] interesting." New Yorker

To market! To market! Illus. by Peter Spier. Doubleday 1967 unp illus (The Mother Goose lib) $4.95, lib. bdg. $5.70, pa $1.25 (k-2)   398.8

Mother Goose—*Continued*

1 Nursery rhymes
ISBN 0-385-08755-1; 0-385-09081-1; 0-385-05352-5

"Nineteen traditional rhymes and proverbs have been woven into a charming tapestry of 19th century American rural life. Countless small details engage the imagination in pictures of water wheels, town squares, smithies, and barnyards, with historical and geographical background provided in a closing section. Most of the rhymes date back to English sources, but they seem quite at home in the New England setting." Sch Library J

Nic Leodhas, Sorche

All in the morning early; illus. by Evaline Ness. Holt 1963 unp illus $3.50, lib. bdg. $3.27, pa $1.65 (k-3)   398.8

1 Nursery rhymes 2 Folklore—Scotland
ISBN 0-03-036080-3; 0-03-036185-0; 0-03-080112-5

"A picture book version of an old Scottish tale; the retelling, in authentic simple folk-style, is in alternate prose and rhyme. Sandy, taking a sack of corn to the miller, meets in turn a huntsman, two ewes, three gypsies . . . and so on. The encounter is described in a few lines of prose; the procession is cataloged in a cumulation that is capped by a rhymed refrain. The author has changed, she explains, some of the Scottish words so that the story will be comprehensible, but some of the vocabulary and all of the flavor of Scottish is retained." Chicago. Children's Bk Center

"This is an outstanding picture book which will be a delight to own and share with the very young. Its format, from the heathery pattern of the end papers to the blue cloth back strip (alas, it is not bound in full cloth), is designed with the care that distinguished . . . Miss Leodhas' other collections of Scottish folk tales." Bk Week

Old Mother Hubbard and her dog; illus. by Evaline Ness. Holt 1972 unp illus $4.95, lib. bdg. $4.59, pa $1.45 (k-2)   398.8

1 Nursery rhymes
ISBN 0-03-091359-4; 0-03-091360-8; 0-03-005721-3

"Using a baker's dozen of verses found in the Opies' 'The Oxford Nursery Rhyme Book' (Oxford) [entered below under title] the artist has produced the most splendid of all picture-book conceptions of the adventures of the incongruous pair. A huge, shaggy white sheepdog dominates the brilliant full-color pictures; and while his gaunt, dead-pan mistress runs about the town buying him all sorts of delicacies, he romps about the house, smoking a pipe, playing the flute, dancing a jig, and standing on his head." Horn Bk

Old Mother Hubbard and her dog; pictures by Paul Galdone. McGraw 1960 32p illus lib. bdg. $4.72 (k-2)   398.8

1 Nursery rhymes
ISBN 0-22723-3

"Whittlesey House publications"

"The entire rhymed tale of Mother Hubbard is illustrated by Paul Galdone in lively, humorous black-and-white pictures with touches of red. Spirited addition to Mother Goose and picture book collections and attractive for reading aloud." Library J

Opie, Iona

(comp.) A family book of nursery rhymes; gathered by Iona and Peter Opie; with illus. by Pauline Baynes. Oxford 1964 [c1963] 220p illus $5.75   398.8

1 Nursery rhymes
ISBN 0-19-500405-1

First published 1963 in England with title: The

Puffin book of nursery rhymes

"This collection of [over] two hundred verses is intended as a companion volume to 'The Oxford Nursery Rhyme Book' [entered below]. The book contains an excellent section of notes on some of the rhymes; within the body of the text there are some instances of comparative versions—seven versions of Humpty Dumpty, for example. The small black-and-white illustrations are appropriate and attractive. A fine and useful book, not divided into sections, but with the selections so arranged that there are affinitive relationships. An index of first lines and an index of principal subjects are appended." Chicago. Children's Bk Center

The **Oxford** Dictionary of nursery rhymes; ed. by Iona and Peter Opie. Oxford 1951 xxvii, 467p illus $12   398.8

1 Nursery rhymes—Dictionaries
ISBN 0-19-869111-4

"A collection of 550 rhymes, songs and riddles which through the years, have come to be associated with childhood. While some are printed here with variations, notes on all of them list approximate age, first appearance in print, literary and historical associations, and parallels in other languages. . . . Arrangement is alphabetical according to the most important word. Nearly 100 reproductions scattered through the text show the changes in illustration of nursery literature during the past two centuries. An index of notable figures and an index of first lines make for easy reference. A comprehensive and authoritative study of the subject, this is an essential tool for all who are engaged in the study or teaching of children's literature." Cur Ref Bks

Bibliography: p xxv-xxvii

The **Oxford** Nursery rhyme book; assembled by Iona and Peter Opie; with additional illus. by Joan Hassall. Oxford 1955 223p illus $10   398.8

1 Nursery rhymes
ISBN 0-19-869112-2

"Gathered here are 800 rhymes and ditties. They are the infant jingles, riddles, catches, tongue-trippers, baby games, toe names, maxims, alphabets, counting rhymes, prayers, and lullabies, with which generation after generation of mothers and nurses have attempted to please the youngest." Preface

"Freely illustrated with reproductions and specially designed wood engravings in the traditional style. Unlike the scholarly 'The Oxford Dictionary of nursery rhymes' [entered above] this is intended mainly for reading to children; it will, however, probably be of more value as a source book." Booklist

Includes: Sources of the illustrations; Index of first lines, refrains, and familiar titles

Petersham, Maud

(comp.) The rooster crows; a book of American rhymes and jingles [by] Maud and Miska Petersham. Macmillan (N Y) 1945 unp illus $4.95 (k-2)   398.8

1 Nursery rhymes 2 Folklore—U.S.
Awarded the Caldecott Medal, 1946

A "collection of the familiar rhymes and jingles known to succeeding generations of children and chanted in their play, such as game rhymes, counting-out rhymes, rope-skipping rhymes." Wis Library Bul

"The Petershams have made delightful pictures in soft harmonious colors, with plenty of humor for these . . . rhymes that American children chant freely. They have made a beautiful book and the publishers have given it clear large type for young readers." Horn Bk

Potter, Beatrix

Cecily Parsley's nursery rhymes. Warne [n.d.] 34p illus $2.50 (k-3) 398.8

1 Nursery rhymes

ISBN 0-7232-0614-7

Illustrated by the author, this book consists of rhymes about Cecily Parsley, a rabbit who "brewed good ale for gentlemen" until she ran away; Goosey, goosey, gander; A little pig who couldn't find his way home; Mistress Pussy; Three blind mice; Little Tom Tinker's dog, etc.

Sendak, Maurice

Hector Protector, and As I went over the water; two nursery rhymes with pictures. Harper 1965 unp illus $4.95, lib. bdg. $5.49 (k-1) 398.8

1 Nursery rhymes

ISBN 0-06-025485-8; 0-06-025486-6

"Sendak has chosen two of the briefest Mother Goose rhymes to expand with drawings, adding 'surprising dimensions.' . . . The little boy Hector Protector works out his hatred of wearing a green suit and being made to visit the queen by acquiring as companions a huge but benign lion and a great snake. In victorious spirit, all present themselves to the queen and the king. The creature conquered in the second rhyme is a boat-swallowing dragon." Horn Bk

He "again proves that the grotesque can be combined with the humorous and appealing in the same creatures." Minnesota

The Snow and the sun; la nieve y el sol; woodcuts by Antonio Frasconi. Harcourt 1961 unp illus $5.95 (1-4) 398.8

1 Nursery rhymes 2 Folklore—Latin America 3 Bilingual books—Spanish-English

ISBN 0-15-276565-4

At head of title: A South American folk rhyme in two languages

"The rhyme is in Spanish and in English (translated by Mr. Frasconi) and is one of the many resembling 'The House that Jack Built,' both in its accumulation and in its series of relationships. But in mood it is very different; 'Cloud that covers the sun,/Sun that melts the snow,/Snow that hurts my feet,/why are you bad?/I am not bad;/the Wind is bad/ that blows me away.' As in his 'The House that Jack Built' [entered above under title] Mr. Frasconi proves again that the repetition of the accumulative folk tales makes them ideal for helping young children to a very natural enjoyment of a second language." Horn Bk

"The book can be used for independent reading, but it may also be used for reading aloud to both English-speaking and Spanish-speaking children." Chicago. Children's Bk Center

"Mr. Frasconi's woodcuts are so evocative that they cause the verse to seem more poetic than it really is." N Y Times Bk Rev

Tom, Tom, the piper's son; pictures by Paul Galdone. McGraw 1964 32p illus lib. bdg. $4.72 (k-2) 398.8

1 Nursery rhymes

ISBN 0-07-022711-X

"Whittlesey House publications"

The version used in this book was published 1850 in London in: A Treasury of pleasure books for young children

This is the old nursery rhyme about Tom the piper's son, who made all creatures dance against their will

"End papers give the words of the more familiar rhyme, and each pair of pages adds a pictured quatrain about Tom's piping bewitchment of animals and humans. Whether black-and-white or three-color the drawings are absorbing with their jolly details and continuity of action." Horn Bk

Wyndham, Robert

(ed.) Chinese Mother Goose rhymes; selected and ed. by Robert Wyndham; pictures by Ed Young. Collins 1968 unp illus lib. bdg. $5.71 (k-1) 398.8

1 Nursery rhymes 2 Chinese poetry

ISBN 0-529-00446-1

"Poetry and nursery rhymes are found in most countries and are surprisingly universal. According to the author there seems to be a common thread of themes: counting toes and fingers, animals, flowers, good and bad children, and many others. The verses in this collection include both new and old translations from China and from this country." Reading Ladders. 5th edition

"A most intriguing collection, the rhymes having both the universal attributes that appeal because of familiarity and the special charm of an unfamiliar variant in the genre. Some of the poems, riddles, and games have been translated for the book. . . . The pages read vertically and are handsomely bordered with columns of Chinese letters; the illustrations are outstanding in the use of color and in design, beautifully adapting modern technique to traditional style." Chicago. Children's Bk Center

Includes a list of first lines

Zemach, Harve

The speckled hen; a Russian nursery rhyme; adapted by Harve Zemach; illus by Margot Zemach. Holt 1966 unp illus $3.50, lib. bdg. $3.27, pa $1.45 (k-2) 398.8

1 Nursery rhymes

ISBN 0-03-055640-6; 0-03-055645-7; 0-03-088512-4

This cumulative nursery rhyme begins when "a speckled egg jumps on the floor and sets off a train of events which ends with grandfather standing on his head in a haystack." Ontario Library Rev

"Little substance, no message, just fun. The illustrations are lively, scratchy, full of vigor and humor." Chicago. Children's Bk Center

400 LANGUAGE

401 Language—Philosophy and theory

Adler, Irving

Language and man [by] Irving and Joyce Adler; illus. by Laurie Jo Lambie. Day 1970 48p illus lib. bdg. $4.47 (3-5) 401

1 Language and languages

ISBN 0-381-99978-5

"The Reason why series"

"A discussion of the importance of speech and of the transmission and diffusion of culture across barriers of time and space, emphasizing the fact that all men are capable of acquiring any language and that infants everywhere make the same sounds, refining their speech to meet approval of the adults with whom they first communicate. There is a competent introduction to the facts that some words resemble each other in many languages and that English has been influenced both by proximity and importation of words from other languages. The writing is clear but staid, the book distracting on a few pages because of the difficulty of reading print against a background of pattern in color." Chicago. Children's Bk Center

Word list: p47

Ludovici, L. J.
Origins of language; illus. by Raymonde Ludovici. Putnam 1965 169p illus map (A Science Survey Bk) lib. bdg. $4.89 (6-7)   401
1 Language and languages
ISBN 0-399-60500-2
"The book presents theories and facts concerning the origin, evolution, and nature of language. It emphasizes the major European languages and English showing the various factors which influenced their development and their similarities and differences. It also explains the physical and mental processes involved in using and understanding speech and explains the attempts to create a universal language. A glossary and list of adult books for further reading are included. A lucid scientific treatment." Booklist

410   Linguistics. Multilingual books

Frasconi, Antonio
See and say; guada e parla, mira y habla, regarde et parle; a picture book in four languages; woodcuts by Antonio Frasconi. Harcourt 1955 unp illus $6.95 (3-7)   410
1 Language and languages 2 Multilingual books
ISBN 0-15-772454-0
"Striking three- and four-color woodcuts in modern design accompany words in English (always printed in black), Italian (blue), French (red) and Spanish (green). The words selected are important to children and their pronunciations are given. The last page, also illustrated, has four parallel columns of everyday expressions. For the very youngest this will succeed as a bright picture book, but it is the next older, more interested today in foreign words, who will find it of special interest, though it is not a book for teaching language." Horn Bk

Hautzig, Esther
At home; a visit in four languages; illus. by Aliki. Macmillan (N Y) 1968 unp illus $4.95 (k-3)   410
1 Language and languages 2 Multilingual books 3 Home
Vocabularies in English, French, Spanish and Russian are presented in this book depicting home scenes "in Chicago, Marseilles, Barcelona, and Leningrad in which families are enjoying each other and the relatives and friends who come to visit. . . . Some additional words and the Russian alphabet are appended and phonetic equivalents are given for all foreign words in the book." Booklist

In school; learning in four languages; pictures by Nonny Hogrogian. Macmillan (N Y) 1969 unp illus $4.95 (k-3)   410
1 Language and languages 2 Multilingual books 3 Schools
The author "introduces children to the Spanish, French, and Russian equivalents of some three dozen words used in the classroom. Hautzig's brief text and Hogrogian's sprightly colored illustrations make it clear that children, whether in San Francisco, San Sebastian, Cherbourg, or Odessa, go to school to study and learn and to have fun, too. Some additional words and the Russian alphabet are appended and a few given names are identified on the endpapers. Phonetic pronunciation is given for all non-English words in the book." Booklist
"The text is stilted and dull; but the pictures are bright and lively, full of humor and mischief, and have universal appeal." Horn Bk

In the park; an excursion in four languages; pictures by Ezra Jack Keats. Macmillan (N Y) 1968 unp illus $4.95 (k-3)   410
1 Language and languages 2 Multilingual books 3 Parks
"A sunny day in the park in New York, Paris, Moscow or Madrid and what to do, see and eat in English, French, Russian and Spanish. The introductory and closing statements are in English and the objects found in the park are presented in all four languages with pronunciation." Library J
"Very simple, very functional, very attractive. . . . The pictures are gay, the word-comparison can be fun, and the universality of children's interests is an implicit additional message. . . . A list of additional words and a pronunciation guide to the Russian alphabet are appended." Chicago. Children's Bk Center

411   Notations. Alphabets

Cahn, William
The story of writing; from cave art to computer, by William and Rhoda Cahn; illus. by Anne Lewis. Reviewed for scientific accuracy by Rhys Carpenter. Harvey House 1963 128p illus maps (A Story of Science Ser Bk) lib. bdg. $5.49 (6-7)   411
1 Writing—History 2 Communication
ISBN 0-8178-3262-9
In text and pictures this book gives "facts not only about the development of [writing and] various alphabets and number systems but also the history of such mechanical aids as the pencil, typewriter and . . . the printing press." Pub W
"A book that covers the subject adequately and is accurate in the facts given, but is weak in writing style. . . . A good bibliography, a brief glossary, and an extensive index are appended, the latter in very small print." Chicago. Children's Bk Center

Dugan, William
How our alphabet grew; the history of the alphabet; written and illus. by William Dugan. Golden Press 1972 69p illus lib. bdg. $5.95 (4-6)   411
1 Alphabet—History
ISBN 0-3076-5771-X
The author traces the development of the 26 letter Roman alphabet in use today. He also shows various changes made when it reached northern Europe during the Middle Ages and discusses improvements brought about by the development of paper and the printing process
Some more books to read: p69

Hofsinde, Robert
Indian picture writing; written and illus. by Robert Hofsinde (Gray-Wolf) Morrow 1959 96p illus lib. bdg. $4.32 (4-7)   411
1 Indians of North America 2 Picture writing
ISBN 0-688-31609-3
"Following a brief history of Indian picture writing, [the author] pictures 248 symbols; some are adapted for modern use. Also included are index to symbols, five sample letters which readers may translate, and the Cree alphabet." Library J
"Fun for children to use for secret message writing and useful in connection with the study of Indians and the history of writing." Booklist

Scott, Joseph

Hieroglyphs for fun; your own secret code language, by Joseph and Lenore Scott. Van Nostrand-Reinhold 1974 79p illus map $6.95 (4-7) 411

1 Hieroglyphics 2 Egyptian language
ISBN 0-442-27523-4

"Clear explanation of the development of ancient Egyptian pictorial language are complemented with examples of common hieroglyphs. After introductory chapters covering picture words, the picture alphabet, and how to draw hieroglyphs, the authors present an adaptation of an Egyptian tale written in hieroglyphs. Students will also enjoy learning how to write secret code messages and how to play an ancient Egyptian game similar to checkers. In all, an excellent supplement for a unit on ancient Egyptian life." Sch Library J

Taylor, Margaret C.

Wht's yr nm? Written and illus. by Margaret C. Taylor. Harcourt 1970 61p illus $5.95 (3-6) 411

1 Writing—History
ISBN 0-15-295529-1

This book "explains the origin and development of written language in lucid, understandable terms. Using the name of Richard as an example, the author traces the possible evolution of the name and describes how it could be interpreted in picture writing, idea writing, sound or rebus writing, and Egyptian hieroglyphics and how it could be written in the Phoenician, Greek, or Roman alphabet. She also encourages the reader to experiment, using his own or other names." Booklist

"Certain theoretical aspects of the book are naive; remarks about the origin of speech are always a problem because they have no basis in historical evidence, and Miss Taylor is too glib about this. However, the information about development of written forms of language is widely accepted. . . . Also, showing children how to write their names in various ancient forms should have particular appeal. A valuable book, especially in school libraries." Sch Library J

419 Verbal language other than spoken or written. Manual alphabet language

Charlip, Remy

Handtalk; an ABC of finger spelling & sign language [by] Remy Charlip, Mary Beth [and] George Ancona. Parents Mag. Press 1974 unp illus lib. bdg. $4.89 419

1 Deaf—Means of communication 2 Alphabet books
ISBN 0-8193-0706-8

"The photographs on every page are so clear that young children (especially third graders who show the most enthusiasm for secret codes and languages) as well as older readers can easily use and learn from it. The first double-page spread [i.e. front end papers] shows the alphabet in finger signs. Each succeeding color photographic spread shows a letter of the alphabet, the finger sign in a corner of the page, some words beginning with the letter spelled out in sign across the bottom of the spread. The exaggerated expressions and mime employed by the finger-spelling deaf are marvelously conveyed by the models for the photographs—hands, faces, and bodies are captured in the effort to communicate. This is a 'breakthrough' book to help serve the often unnoticed, unserved deaf." Sch Library J

420.5 English language— Periodicals

Elementary English. Natl. Council of Teachers of English $15 per year 420.5

1 English language—Periodicals 2 English language—Study and Teaching—Periodicals
ISSN 0013-5968

8 issues a year. First published 1924 with title: Elementary English review

Reading, composition, speaking, and listening skills are emphasized in this journal. Effective teaching is encouraged by coverage of such areas as ethnic studies, humanistic education, language development, and creativity. Among the topics featured regularly are children's literature, educational research, teaching strategies, instructional materials and strategies, plus a children's page

422 English language— Etymology

Adelson, Leone

Dandelions don't bite; illus. by Lou Myers. Pantheon Bks. 1972 58p illus lib. bdg. $5.99 (3-5) 422

1 English language—Etymology
ISBN 0-394-92370-7

"An appealing etymology book for young readers which provides a general overview with interesting specific word histories. Nine chapters discuss the probable beginnings of speech, onomatopoeia, words from other languages, related words with different meanings, new and coined words, words from mythology, new meanings of old words, and how 'The Language Beanstalk' grows and changes. Funny ink cartoons decorate the sprightly text." Sch Library J

Epstein, Sam

The first book of words; their family histories, by Sam and Beryl Epstein; pictures by László Roth. Watts, F. 1954 62p illus maps lib. bdg. $3.90 (5-7) 422

1 English language—Etymology 2 Language and languages
ISBN 0-531-00673-5

The story of English words—how they came to be, how we use them, how in time they change in meaning to suit our needs

"In organization, examples, and pictorial illustration this is an imaginative presentation of the history of language. Adults will find many ways to use it with children and, most important, children will themselves have fun with its ideas and suggestions. Stimulating as an introduction to the study of language, English or foreign. . . . Sketches, in red and black, have humor. A concluding chart shows the development of the alphabet through Phoenician, Greek, and Roman forms." Horn Bk

Kohn, Bernice

What a funny thing to say! Pictures by R. O. Blechman. Dial Press 1974 87p illus $4.95, lib. bdg. $4.58 (5-7) 422

1 English language—Etymology
ISBN 0-8037-9048-1; 0-8037-9079-1

"After a brief but informative survey of the English language's development from its ancient beginnings, the author reveals curiosities of modern usage. She shows how we update by adding foreign words and fabricating others, and deftly explains the differences

Kohn, Bernice—*Continued*
between colloquialisms, slang, and jargon. The 'hippie subculture' may differ with some of Kohn's interpretations of its 1960s' vocabulary, while the ironic comments on Pidgin English may be lost on young readers; however, these discussions and others on cockney rhyming slang, cliches, and pig latin word games provide an informal digression from heavier language study material. A partial table of language families is appended." Booklist
Bibliography: p84

423 English language— Dictionaries

The American Heritage School dictionary. Am. Heritage [distributed by Houghton and McGraw] 1972 xxxii, 992p illus (3-7)   423
1 English language—Dictionaries
Houghton $8.95 (ISBN 0-395-13850-7); McGraw $7.95 (ISBN 0-07-001493-0)
"Intended for use by students in grades 3 to 9, this dictionary lists 35,000 main entries and 50,000 variant forms of words. Clear definitions, simple pronunciation, and sample sentences make this dictionary easy to understand. Entries include pronunciation, part of speech, numbered definitions, illustrative phrases and sentences, and other forms of the word. Using three columns per page, the book's bold yellow center column contains illustrations, word histories, grammar and usage notes, and anecdotal matter to promote understanding and enjoyment of language. The introductory sections, 'The Making of This Dictionary' and 'How to Use Your Dictionary,' provide interesting information for the reader. Extremely attractive, this dictionary will appeal to the intended age group of users." Peterson. Ref Bks for Elem and Jr High Sch Libraries. 2d edition

The Cat in the hat Beginner book dictionary, by the Cat himself and P. D. Eastman. Beginner Bks. 1964 133p illus $4.95, lib. bdg. $5.99 (k-3)   423
1 English language—Dictionaries
ISBN 0-394-81009-0; 0-394-91009-5
Also available in a French language edition (ISBN 0-394-81063-5) and a Spanish language edition (ISBN 0-394-81542-4) for $5.95 each
"A Beginner book"
"A dictionary written only as the Cat Himself can, it is an illustrated explanation of the meanings of words. Simple sentences and pictures explain word meanings. Interest level is not restricted to the primary grade readers." Wynar. Guide to Ref Bks for Sch Media Centers

The Courtis-Watters Illustrated Golden dictionary for young readers. Rev. and expanded by Stuart A. Courtis and Garnette Watters. Allen Walker Read, consultant on pronunciation. Golden Press 1965 666p illus maps $5.95, lib. bdg. $5.95 (2-4)   423
1 English language—Dictionaries
ISBN 0-307-15544-7; 0-307-66544-5
First published 1951 by Simon & Schuster
This "book contains simple, clear definitions for over 10,000 basic words. Usage of the words is indicated by over 20,000 illustrative sentences. No synonyms, antonyms, or derivations are given. Pronunciation symbols are so simple that reference to a key is usually not necessary, but pronunciation keys are given in the front and back of the book. The work is extremely well illustrated with over 3,000 clear black-and-white drawings and a center section of colored illustrations, e.g. flags, birds, animals, etc. Reference to these color illustrations are given throughout the text. There are a few entries for encyclopedic material, e.g., each of the 50 states is given an entry. There are no entries for persons, abbreviations, slang, or foreign words and phrases. An appendix contains some abbreviations, geographical tables plus information on weights and measures and Presidents of the U.S." Sch Library J

Greet, W. Cabell
In other words; a beginning thesaurus [by] W. Cabell Greet, William A. Jenkins [and] Andrew Schiller. Lothrop 1969 [c1968] 240p illus $5.50, lib. bdg. $4.81 (3-6)   423
1 English language—Synonyms and antonyms
ISBN 0-688-41604-7; 0-688-51604-1
"An explanation of the meaning and use of synonyms and antonyms is followed by more than a thousand alphabetically arranged entries based on the 100 words commonly used by elementary school children. Each entry gives a simple definition and illustrative sentences for the main word and several of its synonyms, and lists two or three antonyms. Cross-references are used liberally, and a concluding section on sets presents in pictorial form some of the specialized words for boats, land and water areas, and groups of things, people, and animals. Though the format and the amusing colored pictures indicate a young audience, this is a serviceable thesaurus for use by slow learners in junior high as well as children in grades 3 to 6." Booklist
"An impressive book. . . . [Although the typography] seems overcomplicated, the profuse illustrations in color—some are drawings, others are photographs—make the presentation just about irresistible for junior. The impresario of the book's art work is, alas, anonymous." N Y Times Bk Rev

Junior thesaurus; In other words II [by] W. Cabell Greet, William A. Jenkins [and] Andrew Schiller. Lothrop [1970 c1969] 448p illus lib. bdg. $5.49 (5-7)   423
1 English language—Synonyms and antonyms
ISBN 0-688-51243-7
Companion volume to the authors': In other words, entered above
This book offers over 2000 synonyms and antonyms for 300 words commonly used by upper elementary and junior high school students. The introduction explains how to use the thesaurus. Words can be located either in the main body, arranged alphabetically, or in the Index, where entry words, synonyms and antonyms are listed

My first picture dictionary [by] W. Cabell Greet, William A. Jenkins [and] Andrew Schiller. Lothrop 1970 192p illus lib. bdg. $4.81 (1-3)   423
1 English language—Dictionaries
ISBN 0-688-51385-9
Companion volume to My pictionary, by M. Monroe, and My second picture dictionary, by W. A. Jenkins
"Color-coded, words are arranged in subject areas: people, animals, storybook characters, what we do, things, and places; they are alphabetized within each group, and each word is followed by its plural form and a simple sentence or two, and is illustrated. Cross-references are included. . . . A final section is headed 'Words That Help' and includes words that help tell when, how, how much, where, which one, what kind, what color, etc. An index is appended. The arrangement is logical, the format and print size clear, the pictures usually helpful." Sutherland. The Best in Children's Bks

The Harcourt Brace School dictionary. Harcourt 1972
864p illus $5.70 (4-7)   423
  1 English language—Dictionaries
ISBN 0-15-321148-2
First published 1968
This dictionary "contains 46,000 entries correlated
with modern textbooks. Entries, arranged in a single
alphabet, contain easy to understand definitions and
illustrative sentences. A second color is used to desig-
nate cross references, synonym notes, usage notes,
etymologies, and specific areas of maps and diagrams.
Guide words also appear in color. Preceding the main
text are sections entitled 'How to Use Your Dictionary' (text material for grades four and five) and 'How
to Get the Most from Your Dictionary' (text work for
grades six through eight)." Peterson. Ref Bks for
Elem and Jr High Sch Libraries [review of 1968
edition]

Jenkins, William A.
My second picture dictionary [by] William A. Jen-
kins [and] Andrew Schiller. Lothrop 1975 384p illus
maps lib. bdg. $6.54 (2-4)   423
  1 English language—Dictionaries
ISBN 0-688-51774-9
Companion volume to My pictionary, by M. Monroe, and My first picture dictionary, by W. C. Greet
  First published 1971 under the authorship of W.
Cabell Greet, William A. Jenkins and Andrew
Schiller
This dictionary "is alphabetically arranged and contains material adapted from the 1968 'Thorndike-
Barnhart Beginning Dictionary.' Each entry is in bold
face type, then is divided by syllables. Each contains a
definition, and some have llustrative sentences
which appear in italics. In addition to the Lexicon, this
dictionary contains a gazetteer consisting of the states
of the United States arranged alphabetically, and giving the flag, flower, a map with the capitol, tree, bird,
and fish for each." Peterson. Ref Bks for Elem and
Junior High Sch Libraries. 2d edition

Monroe, Marion
My pictionary [by] Marion Monroe [and] Andrew
Schiller. Lothrop 1975 95p illus lib. bdg. $4.59
(k-1)   423
  1 English language—Dictionaries
ISBN 0-688-51773-0
Companion volume to My first picture dictionary,
by W. C. Greet, and My second picture dictionary, by
W. A. Jenkins
Also available in a bilingual edition, Spanish-
English, entered in class 463 under Mi diccionario
illustrado
  First published 1970 under the authorship of W.
Cabell Greet, Marion Monroe and Andrew Schiller
"A compilation of labeled actions or objects in broad
categories: people, animals, storybook characters,
what we do, things, places, colors, numbers, and
'words that help' (prepositions). Although the pages
are crowded and objects are not always in scale, the
clear pictures and the categorization provide good
orientation for reading readiness. In some cases, both
the singular and plural are given ('goose' and 'geese')
or the names for both young and adult animals ('cat'
and 'kitten'). In 'Things' there is clear grouping: food,
play equipment, household paraphernalia, etc."
Sutherland. The Best in Children's Bks

The Random House Dictionary of the English language. School ed. Stuart Berg Flexner, editor in
chief. Eugene F. Shewmaker, managing editor.
Random House illus maps $7.64 (4-7)   423
  1 English language—Dictionaries
First published 1970. Frequently reprinted with
minor corrections
"Based on the unabridged and college editions of

the 'Random House Dictionary of the English Language,' the School Edition also uses word frequency
lists to determine its entries. It contains a single
alphabetical sequence of more than 47,500 entries,
including biographical and geographical entries,
abbreviations, and contractions. Entries include the
pronunciation, part of speech, definitions, and
examples used in sentences and phrases. Meanings of
words appear in order of frequency with the most
common meaning first. A lengthy section called the
'Student's Guide to the Dictionary' and the 'Explanatory Notes for a Specimen Page' will be beneficial to
the user. The 15 pages of maps by Rand McNally and
the tables of weights and measures further extend the
usefulness of this dictionary. Designed for fourth to
eighth grade students, it should definitely have a
space on the school reference shelf." Peterson. Ref
Bks for Elem and Jr High Sch Libraries [review of
1973 edition]

Schulz, Charles M.
The Charlie Brown dictionary; based on The rain-
bow dictionary by Wendell W. Wright assisted by
Helene Laird. World Pub. [distributed by Random
House] 1973 399p illus $7.95, lib. bdg. $8.99 (k-3)
     423
  1 English language—Dictionaries
ISBN 0-394-83041-5; 0-394-93041-X
"Illustrated with cartoons of Charlie Brown,
Snoopy, Lucy, et al., this picture dictionary will be
chosen by primary students for the popular drawings
alone. They will, however, be getting a bargain for
this dictionary is a new one based on the 'Rainbow
Dictionary' [entered below under Wendell Wright].
Both the illustrations and definitions are new, but in
general the vocabulary is that of the earlier book.
Additions and deletions were made to reflect changes
in the language that children speak, read, and hear,
especially on television. Altogether, this book contains 2,400 entries, consisting of both main entries
and related forms, and has over 580 pictures in full
color." Peterson. Ref Bks for Elem and Jr High Sch
Libraries. 2d edition

Thorndike—Barnhart Advanced junior dictionary, by
E. L. Thorndike [and] Clarence L. Barnhart.
Doubleday illus thumb indexed $8.95 (6-7)   423
  1 English language—Dictionaries
First published 1957. Frequently revised
Designed especially for upper elementary and
junior high school students, this dictionary contains
more than 65,000 entries including biographical, historical and geographical terms, in one alphabet. The
introductory section includes material on how to use
this dictionary and a complete pronunciation key

Thorndike—Barnhart Beginning dictionary, by E. L.
Thorndike [and] Clarence L. Barnhart. Doubleday
illus $6.95 (3-5)   423
  1 English language—Dictionaries
A revision of the Thorndike Century Beginning
dictionary. Frequently revised
This dictionary "contains 20,500 entries and 33,500
meanings. Most of the vocabulary was selected from
words used in text and trade books for grades three
and four. Definitions, which list the most common
meaning first, are illustrated liberally with sentences
and phrases. People and places are included in the
main alphabet. Foreign words and phrases and slang
expressions are omitted. An outstanding section entitled 'How to Use This Dictionary' consists of 58 lessons on locating words, finding meanings, using pronunciations, and using the dictionary for spelling and
writing. The illustrations, large clear print, good
paper, and sturdy binding make this an attractive

Thorndike—Barnhart Beginning dictionary—*Continued*
book." Peterson. Ref Bks for Elem and Jr High Sch Libraries [review of 1972 edition]

Thorndike—Barnhart Junior dictionary, by E. L. Thorndike [and] Clarence L. Barnhart. Doubleday illus maps $6.50, thumb-indexed $7.50 (4-7) 423
1 English language—Dictionaries
A revision of the Thorndike Century Junior dictionary. Frequently revised
"Its more than 43,000 entries contain clear, simple definitions, with the most common meaning first, and with illustrative sentences and phrases. People, places, abbreviations, and slang expressions are incorporated in the main alphabet. It is easy to use and has large clear type; it is heavily illustrated." Peterson. Ref Bks for Elem and Jr High Sch Libraries

Webster's Intermediate dictionary; a new school dictionary. Merriam 1972 50, 910p illus $6.50 (5-7) 423
1 English language—Dictionaries
ISBN 0-87779-179-1
"A Merriam Webster"
This dictionary "is aimed at the young teenager. It has some 57,000 entries. . . . In pronunciation, syllabication, and format this dictionary has the excellence associated with the Merriam-Webster name. An excellent 'Using your Dictionary' section is included. Checking reveals some very current words from various fields of interest to young people. . . . Some definitions seem quite technical, containing words that would have to be looked up themselves." Cur Ref Bks
Includes "supplementary material on presidents, states, nations, and signs and symbols." Wynar. Guide to Ref Bks for Sch Media Centers

Webster's New Elementary dictionary. Merriam 1975 16a, 612p illus $4.95 (4-7) 423
1 English language—Dictionaries
ISBN 0-87779-275-5
A successor to Webster's Elementary dictionary which was first published in 1956
This volume contains over 32,000 entries, directions for using the dictionary, and tables of special information

Webster's New Students dictionary. Merriam illus $6.95 (6-7) 423
1 English language—Dictionaries
"A Merriam-Webster"
First published 1964 with title: Webster's Students dictionary
"Based on 'Webster's Third New International Dictionary' [entered below] and 'Webster's Seventh Collegiate Dictionary.' . . . [It contains] entries selected and defined to meet the needs of junior and senior high school readers. Supplementary material is included. This is the third dictionary in the Merriam-Webster series: it is preceded by the elementary and the intermediate dictionaries [both entered above]." Wynar. Guide to Ref Bks for Sch Media Centers [review of the 1969 edition]

Webster's New World dictionary for young readers. New ed. of the elementary ed. David B. Guralnik, editor-in-chief. Collins 1971 808p illus $7.50 (4-7) 423
1 English language—Dictionaries
ISBN 0-529-04509-5
First published 1961 under title: Webster's New World dictionary; elementary edition
For this dictionary of more than 44,000 terms and

over 1,700 pictures, "the editors studied lists showing the words that students are most likely to see or hear. . . . [There is a] simplified pronunciation key. . . . Of particular interest are the drawings for words like 'scowl, incongruous, cringe,' and 'askew.' " Foreword to 1961 edition
Includes "common idioms such as 'to go Dutch' and to be 'in Dutch' with clear statements that they are a slang phrase." Pub W

Webster's Third new international dictionary of the English language; unabridged. Merriam illus 423
1 English language—Dictionaries
"A Merriam-Webster"
Prices vary according to binding
First published 1828 by S. Converse as: An American dictionary of the English language, by Noah Webster. Also appeared with titles: Webster's Unabridged dictionary, Webster's International dictionary of the English language, and Webster's New International dictionary of the English language. This edition first published 1961. Frequently reprinted with additions and changes to keep it up to date
Editor in chief: 1961, Philip Babcock Gove and the Merriam Webster editorial staff
This work "is evidently intended as a dictionary for our times, for its more than 450,000 entries include 100,000 newly added terms and exclude words obsolete before 1755. Its more than 200,000 quotations illustrate contemporary usage, drawing on many modern writers. Instead of encyclopedic treatment at one place of a group of related terms, each term is defined at its own place in the alphabet with an analytical one-phrase definition. . . . Gone are the biographical and geographical sections, the key to pronunciation at the bottom of each page, while only 3,000 new illustrations replace the 12,000 found in the earlier edition. . . . Thus the dictionary must stand on its true dictionary features—as a source of etymology, pronunciation, syllabication and definition." Cur Ref Bks
"Much is included, often without qualification, which may be regarded by many as colloquial, vulgar, or incorrect. . . . Regardless of varying opinions of editorial judgment, this edition will be wanted in most American libraries, though the 2d edition will be wisely retained as well." Winchell. Guide to Ref Bks. 8th edition
For a fuller review see: The Booklist and Subscription Books Bulletin, July 1, 1963

The World book dictionary; Clarence L. Barnhart, editor in chief. Prepared in cooperation with Field Enterprises Educational Corp. Field Enterprises 2v illus apply to publisher for price 423
1 English language—Dictionaries
"A Thorndike-Barnhart dictionary"
First published 1963 with title: The World book encyclopedia dictionary. Revised annually
"This dictionary was prepared for use with 'The World Book Encyclopedia' [entered in class 031] and for this reason biographical and geographical entries are omitted. In place of such encyclopedic material, the dictionary concentrates on providing word meanings, usage notes, and word history. Supplementary sections cover vocabulary development and use, language rules and references, and a guide to use of the dictionary. . . . The 200,000 entries include idioms, new words and foreign words in general use. Each entry in bold face is followed by the pronunciation (an adaptation of the International Phonetic Alphabet); parts of speech with separate definitions; definitions of various meanings, arranged by frequency; homographs; restrictive labels (e.g., obsolete); inflections; variant spellings; usage notes; illustrative sentences; word origins; synonyms and antonyms. About 2,000 small black and white illustrations placed within the text area are clear. . . . The entries are well prepared, concise, and easy to locate and read. . . . [The supplementary sections contain over 100 pages and] are

The World book dictionary—*Continued*
more simply written than similar ones in other general
dictionaries." Wynar. Guide to Ref Bks for Sch Media
Centers [Review of the 1973 edition]
For a fuller review see: The Booklist and Subscription Books Bulletin Reviews, September 1, 1963

Wright, Wendell W.
The rainbow dictionary, by Wendell W. Wright;
assisted by Helene Laird; illus. by Joseph Low. World
Pub. 1959 433p illus $4.95 (1-4)   423
    1 English language—Dictionaries
    ISBN 0-529-04620-2
    First published 1947
A dictionary in picture book format which "contains
2300 entries consisting of 2000 main entries and
related forms, which children use in speaking and
recognize when reading. The words chosen are those
that occur most frequently in a consolidation of eight
word lists for [young] children." An explanation
"The big pages are not overcrowded, the type is
large and well spaced, and best of all, each page has a
number of small pictures in color to give force to the
definitions." Horn Bk

438   Standard German usage

Cooper, Lee
Fun with German; illus. by Elizabeth M. Githens.
Little 1965 119p illus lib. bdg. $5.95 (4-7)   438
    1 German language
    ISBN 0-316-15588-8
"Using a circus motif [the author] begins with [German] phrases and sentence sequences to introduce
vowel and consonant sounds and a few essentials of
grammar, and then presents stories, games, songs,
and ideas and activities for a German club. Includes a
guide to pronunciation symbols and a German-
English vocabulary." Booklist
An "introduction to the German language. . . . The
phonetic symbols are excellent, especially for those
sounds which do not have exact English equivalents."
Sch Library J

443   French language—
Dictionaries

Fonteneau, M.
Mon premier Larousse en couleurs [par] M. Fonteneau et S. Theureau. Larousse illus $7.50   443
    1 French language—Dictionaries
    First published 1953. Frequently revised
"Nearly 4,000 words are defined in this French
dictionary. Pictures and words are effectively used to
aid the student in understanding meanings. This dictionary is not bilingual but is written entirely in
French with no English equivalents. Designed for
children aged 5 to 8, it includes conjugations of verbs,
and sentences for definitions and plurals." Peterson.
Ref Bks for Elem and Jr High Sch Libraries. 2d
edition

For another French language dictionary see the
note under The Cat in the hat Beginner book dictionary, class 423

448   Standard French usage

Brunhoff, Laurent de
Babar's French lessons; les lecons de Français de
Babar. Random House 1963 14 [i.e. 28]p illus $3.95
(1-3)   448
    1 Bilingual books—French-English
    ISBN 0-394-80587-9
"This is not a new adventure of Babar but a word
and phrase book in French and English in which
Babar teaches fourteen French lessons to the reader.
It is conversational French about such subjects as a
birthday party, fun at the seaside, a morning shower
bath. Probably a very useful and acceptable addition
to the French collection, but must be confined to that.
It would be a disappointment to the child if mistaken
for a new Babar." Toronto

Colyer, Penrose
(comp.) I can read French; my first English-French
word book; illus. by Colin Mier and Wendy Lewis.
Watts, F. 1974 116p illus lib. bdg. $6.90 (2-4)   448
    1 Bilingual books—French-English
    ISBN 0-531-02654-X
    First published 1972 in England
"An unusual, informal approach to conversational
French. Short sentences, largely in present tense,
and individual words from an extensive vocabulary
are printed in English and French beside comical
color representations; these are grouped on a page by
a theme or incident such as 'Mrs. Lejeune chooses a
hat,' 'On vacation,' or 'If I were a millionaire.' The
mood is light and most often humorous; this presentation should encourage a natural, phrase-by-phrase
recognition and use of the language. . . . Some instructional comments and a vocabulary section with numbers, seasons, countries, etc. are included." Booklist

Cooper, Lee
Fun with French, by Lee Cooper and Clifton
McIntosh; illus. by Ann Atene. Little 1963 120p illus
$5.95 (4-7)   448
    1 French language
    ISBN 0-316-15607-8
An elementary text which makes use of pictures,
stories, songs, and phrases to introduce French words
"Humorous drawings on almost every page. Pronunciation key provides excellent approximations of
French sounds." Library J
Le dictionnaire: p100-20

Joslin, Sesyle
There is a dragon in my bed; il y a un dragon dans
mon lit; and other useful phrases in French and
English for young ladies and gentlemen going abroad
or staying at home; illus. by Irene Haas. Harcourt
1961 unp illus $4.95 (3-6)   448
    1 Bilingual books—French-English
    ISBN 0-15-285146-1
"Contains simple English phrases, and their
French equivalents, with a line giving the phonetic
pronunciation and each keyed to a picture, taking
children on an imaginary trip from America to
France." Springf'd Republican
"The book is delightfully humorous: adults will
enjoy reading it aloud and small children will enjoy
having it read aloud. The humor is in the choice of
situation and phrase and in the zany illustrations of
nonsensical situations." Chicago, Children's Bk
Center

458   Standard Italian usage

Cooper, Lee
  Fun with Italian, by Lee Cooper, Marion Greene
[and] Lia Beretta; illus. by Ann Atene. Little 1964
120p illus map lib. bdg. $4.95 (4-7)   458
  1 Italian language
  ISBN 0-316-15617-5
  An elementary book which makes use of pictures,
games, songs, and phrases to introduce Italian words
  "Useful as a supplement to formal instruction and
helpful for the individual learning alone." Booklist
  Vocabolario: p99-120

Joslin, Sesyle
  Spaghetti for breakfast; spaghetti per prima col-
azione, and other useful phrases in Italian and English
for young ladies and gentlemen going abroad or staying at home; illus. by Katharina Barry. Harcourt 1965
unp illus $4.95 (3-6)   458
  1 Bilingual books—Italian-English
  ISBN 0-15-277360-6
  "In the manner of 'There is a dragon in my bed'
[entered in class 448] the Italian phrase, its pronunciation, and English equivalent appear together with a
delightful line drawing showing the occasion for the
phrase." Booklist

463   Spanish language—
Dictionaries

Fonteneau, M.
  Mi primer Larousse en colores [por] M. Fonteneau
y S. Theureau. Traducido y adaptado por Elena
Urquijo y Maria Lucia Cumora. Larousse illus
$6.95   463
  1 Spanish language—Dictionaries
  First published 1958
  Translated and adapted from the French version
entered in class 443, this dictionary lists some 4,000
words. "All entries are defined in one or more illustrative sentences, and many have a color picture. Verb
conjugations are given when appropriate. A single
language dictionary, this one contains no translations
into English." Peterson. Ref Bks for Elem and Jr High
Sch Libraries. 2d edition

  Mi diccionario ilustrado; edición bilingüe. My pictionary; bilingual edition [by] Federico Aquino-
Bermudez [and others]. Lothrop 1972 c1971 96p
illus lib. bdg. $4.59, pa $2.50   463
  1 Spanish language—Dictionaries
  2 Bilingual books—Spanish-English
  ISBN 0-688-50994-0; 0-688-45007-5
  "Following the same format as 'My Pictionary'
[entered in class 423 under Monroe] 'Mi Diccionario
Illustrado' classifies words by subjects. Each Spanish
word is followed by the English word in parentheses.
Variations of Spanish used by Spanish speaking children in America are given. Both Spanish and English
language indexes are included." Peterson. Ref Bks for
Elem and Jr High Sch Libraries. 2d edition

  For another Spanish language dictionary see the
note under The Cat in the hat Beginner book dictionary, class 423

468   Standard Spanish usage

Brunhoff, Laurent de
  Babar's Spanish lessons; las lecciones españoles de
Babar; Spanish words by Robert Eyzaguirre. Random
House 1965 unp illus $3.95 (1-3)   468
  1 Bilingual books—Spanish-English
  ISBN 0-394-80589-5
  This is not another Babar story, but an introduction
to conversational Spanish with Babar conducting the
lessons

Cooper, Lee
  Fun with Spanish; illus. by Ann Atene. Little 1960
118p illus lib. bdg. $5.95 (4-7)   468
  1 Spanish language
  ISBN 0-316-15589-6
  Pronunciation is Mexican rather than Castilian in
this elementary text which makes use of pictures,
stories, games and phrases to introduce over 500
Spanish words
  "Any child who can read English can gallop through
it and at the end find himself reading and speaking
simple Spanish with comparative ease." Horn Bk

  More Fun with Spanish; illus. by Ann Atene. Little
1967 120p illus lib. bdg. $5.95 (4-7)   468
  1 Spanish language
  ISBN 0-316-15616-7
  A second volume to supplement the author's Fun
with Spanish, listed above. This one "is only slightly
more difficult than the first. It contains 11 entertaining stories each of which introduces a new point of
grammar, but without the reader's awareness until
the end of the story when the grammar point is summarized for emphasis. The text is entirely in Spanish,
the only English appearing in the pronunciation guide
and 24-page vocabulary. Copiously illustrated with
lively two-color drawings." Booklist
  El diccionario: p99-117

Joslin, Sesyle
  There is a bull on my balcony; hay un toro en mi
balcón; and other useful phrases in Spanish and
English for young ladies and gentlemen going abroad
or staying at home. Illus. by Katharina Barry. Harcourt 1966 unp illus $4.95 (2-5)   468
  1 Bilingual books—Spanish-English
  ISBN 0-15-285057-0
  "In a series of zany episodes, two boy-travelers in
Mexico introduce Spanish phrases and their English
counterparts." Minnesota
  "Hilarious illustrations . . . make this Spanish
phrase book fun for all ages." Ontario Library Rev

495.1   Chinese language

Wiese, Kurt
  You can write Chinese. Viking 1945 unp illus lib.
bdg. $4.95, pa 95¢   495.1
  1 Chinese language
  ISBN 0-670-25099-6; 0-670-05077-6
  "A picture book—not for little children but for
older ones—to show how some characters of the
national Chinese language are written, and to
demonstrate, in the author-illustrator's clever drawings, the origins of the characters. Boys and girls will
be interested in learning to write even so little Chinese, and their elders will find the book amusing and
entertaining, too." Ontario Library Rev
  "The characters are simple, large, and clear. . . .

Wiese, Kurt—*Continued*
[The Book] should be useful to teachers who teach a unit on China." Library J

500   PURE SCIENCES

500.5   Space sciences

Simon, Seymour
Science at work: projects in space science; illus. by Lynn Sweat. Watts, F. 1971 87p illus lib. bdg. $4.90 (4-7)   500.5
1 Space sciences—Experiments
ISBN 0-531-01997-7
This book contains thirty projects which demonstrate facts and principles related to the science of space travel. Included are sections on: Stabilizing a spacecraft; Experimenting with g-forces; A closed life-support system; Making artificial gravity; Psychological aspects of space travel, and Devising a space language
The book "is written in a non-technical style that encourages the reader to think and to perform the experiments. . . . [It] provides a good source of leisure activities and classroom experiments. There is a fine reading list and a very good list of supply sources at the back of the book. The author also does an excellent job of stressing safety in each experiment." Appraisal

500.9   Natural history

Adventures in the wilderness, by the editors of American Heritage, The Magazine of History. Author: Rutherford Platt; consultant: Horace M. Albright. Am. Heritage 1963 153p illus maps $5.95 (6-7)   500.9
1 Natural history—North America 2 Natural resources—North America 3 America—Discovery and exploration
ISBN 0-06-024760-6
"American Heritage Junior library"
"Illustrated with paintings, prints, drawings, and maps, many of the period." p9
An account of the natural resources, plants, and animals confronting the early explorers and settlers of North America
"A fascinating look. . . . The book describes the geological origins and the natural history of coastal, forest, prairie, mountain, and desert regions. . . . It not only shows how the conquering of the wilderness too frequently resulted in an imbalance of nature and the extent to which conservationists have been successful in saving the wilderness but also makes an implicit plea for the preservation of what remains." Booklist
For further reading: p149

Borten, Helen
The jungle. Harcourt 1968 unp illus $5.75 (3-5)   500.9
1 Nature study 2 Tropics
ISBN 0-15-241355-3
This book describes a day in a hot land near the equator—the jungle plants and animals, sights, sounds, and odors
"Vacillating between poetic description and nature information, this picture book generally combines the two successfully. . . . The finely textured illustrations [by the author] are attractive and express the jungle's mystery in full-page spreads of muted tans, browns, and greens. . . . Impressionistic rather than for instruction." Sch Library J

Busch, Phyllis S.
Exploring as you walk in the city; photographed by Mary M. Thacher. Lippincott 1972 40p illus $4.50 (1-4)   500.9
1 Nature study 2 Cities and towns
ISBN 0-397-31223-7
This book guides the young reader in the exploration of the natural world—animal, vegetable and mineral—surrounding him in the city

Exploring as you walk in the meadow; photographs by Mary M. Thacher. Lippincott 1972 40p illus $3.95 (1-4)   500.9
1 Nature study
ISBN 0-397-31222-9
"Closeup and magnified photographs show the flora and fauna that can be seen on a meadow walk, most of the pictures informative as well as attractive. The author suggests some modest experiments, with such instruments as a thermometer or a compass required. The continuous text moves from topic to topic, sometimes abruptly, closing with a brief description of the plant-animal life cycle." Chicago. Children's Bk Center

A walk in the snow; photographs by Mary M. Thacher. Lippincott 1971 40p illus $4.50 (1-4) 500.9
1 Snow 2 Nature study
ISBN 0-397-31233-4
"Photographs are used both to show the beauty of winter and the ways in which an observant child can find clues to wind directions, read animal tracks, make a plastic copy of a snowflake, test the effect of color on temperature (a piece of dark cloth and a piece of white sink to different depths), or see the evidence of repeated snowfalls in the layers of a snowbank." Sat Rev
"The photographs make this book. It is unfortunate that the text is rather ordinary. Activities are those traditionally used in most elementary schools. Certainly, however, the book does encourage exploration and observation, particularly that of the sounds of different snows. Thus it will be a useful experience." Appraisal

Clark, Ann Nolan
Along sandy trails; photographs by Alfred A. Cohn. Viking 1969 31p illus lib. bdg. $5.95 (2-5)   500.9
1 Natural history—Arizona 2 Deserts 3 Papago Indians
ISBN 0-670-11485-5
"Excellent color photographs combined with poetic text describe the wild plant and animal life observed by a small Papago Indian girl and her grandmother while on a walk in the Arizona desert. Written in the first person, the text expresses the little girl's delight in what she sees and in what her wise grandmother tells her about desert wild life. Identification of the plants included is given at the back of the book." Booklist

Clement, Roland C.
Hammond Nature atlas of America. . . . Hammond 1973 255p illus maps $24.95   500.9
1 Natural history—U.S.
ISBN 0-8437-3511-2
"A Ridge Press book"
This title supersedes: Hammond's Nature atlas of America, by E. L. Jordan
"Reptiles & amphibians, insects, birds, wildflow-

Clement, Roland C.—_Continued_

ers, trees, rocks & minerals, fishes, mammals." Title page

"This book is essentially a color photo sampler covering geologic, botanical, and zoological features of America; clearly written descriptions (about 150 words each) accompany each pictured example. The claim to the title 'atlas' lies in the range maps, which show regional distributions for a sampling of animals, plants, minerals, weather conditions, and physiographic features." Library J

"The illustrations are colorful, accurate, and graphic. Particularly noteworthy are the special maps. . . . Written in clear, succinct language readily understood by the student or layman [this work] is an excellent introduction to the ecology of the United States." Booklist

Glossary: p249. Suggested reading: p251

For a fuller review see: Reference and Subscription Books Reviews, February 1, 1974

Cooper, Elizabeth K.

Science in your own back yard; with illus. by the author. Harcourt 1970 192p illus $5.50 (5-7) 500.9

1 Nature study

ISBN 0-15-270664-X

A reissue of the title first published 1958

A "stimulating out-of-doors book opening up all sorts of nature activities, practicable even on a 50-foot lot. Beginning with soil and rock, it continues with chapters on grass, water, flowers, plant forms, earthworms and insects, birds, clouds, weather, stars, and outer space. Pen-and-ink sketches by the author [with an index included.]" Library J

Day, Beth

Life on a lost continent; a natural history of New Zealand. Doubleday 1971 128p illus $4.95, lib. bdg. $5.70 (5-7) 500.9

1 Natural history—New Zealand

ISBN 0-385-05648-6; 0-385-02466-5

This book deals primarily with the exotic animals which abound on New Zealand's islands, including the only flightless birds extant (i.e. the Kiwi), a three-eyed lizard-like reptile called the tuatara which was a contemporary of the dinosaur, wild pigs, penguins, wallabies, etc. Plant life is touched on briefly and the interaction between New Zealand's settlers, Maori and European, and its wildlife is discussed

Written in a "chatty informal style. Some of the animal life is familiar: rabbits, possums, and sheep; most are exotic. A fascinating book, particularly for animal lovers." Chicago. Children's Bk Center

Maps on lining-papers

The Doubleday Nature encyclopedia [ed. by] Angela Sheehan. Doubleday [1974 c1973] 173p illus $6.95, lib. bdg. $7.70 (3-6) 500.9

1 Natural history

ISBN 0-385-07031-4; 0-385-07045-4

First published 1972 in England with title: Parnell's Discovering nature

Contents: Discovering nature; Prehistoric life; The world of animals; Where animals live; How animals live; The world of plants; Man and nature

"This is a well-designed, single-volume encyclopedia for the young reader. The coverage is comprehensive, though general because of space limitations, including descriptions of the major classifications of plants and animals, adaptations to various habitats from polar regions to the tropics, life functions, and man's influence on the natural world. . . . The illustrations are numerous, informative and attractive." Appraisal

Earle, Olive L.

State birds and flowers. Morrow 1961 64p illus maps lib. bdg. $4.32 500.9

1 State birds 2 State flowers

ISBN 0-688-31536-4

A revised reprint of the title first published 1951

This small book is arranged alphabetically by state. Included for each state are a sketch of the state, indicating capital, and black and white illustrations of the indigenous bird or flower. Information is also included about the appearance, growth, and reproduction of the flowers. For birds a description, the activities, and the off-spring of each are given

"Excellent introduction to the geography of the states as well as a book for nature lovers of all ages." Library J

Farb, Peter

Face of North America; the natural history of a continent. Introduction by Stewart L. Udall; illus. by Bob Hines and Jerome Connolly; with 36 photographs. Young readers' edition. Harper 1964 254p illus maps $10, pa $2.95 (6-7) 500.9

1 Natural history—North America 2 Physical geography—North America 3 U.S.—Description and travel

ISBN 0-06-070746-1; 0-06-090128-4

An adaptation of the longer, 1963 edition

"An absorbing account of the physical features of North America and the plant and animal life of the continent, profusely illustrated with maps, diagrams, drawings, and photographs. Includes a list of outstanding natural areas and suggestions for further reading." Hodges. Bks for Elem Sch Libraries

Howell, Ruth Rea

A crack in the pavement; photographs by Arline Strong. Atheneum Pubs. 1970 unp illus lib. bdg. $4.75 (2-4) 500.9

1 Nature study 2 Cities and towns—U.S.

ISBN 0-689-20668-2

"Even in large cities wherever there is a patch of soil such as in a crack in the pavement one is apt to see a growing dandelion, a weed, or a tuft of grass. Some people have window boxes in which they grow flowers and other plants. Similarly the reader is introduced to other plants and animals he might find—trees, birds, insects, mushrooms, earthworms. . . . Even learning to recognize animal tracks in the snow can be an interesting diversion." Sci Bks

"The photographs are clear and nicely placed; the text moves easily from one subject to another. . . . While there is never a minatory tone, the author makes frequent suggestions for safety (don't eat mushrooms, don't touch wild creatures) and both text and illustrations show children observing and learning with absorption and care." Chicago. Children's Bk Center

Kane, Henry B.

Four seasons in the woods; written and illus. by Henry B. Kane. Knopf 1968 59p illus $3.50, lib. bdg. $5.39 (3-5) 500.9

1 Natural history 2 Seasons

ISBN 0-394-81139-9; 0-394-91139-3

"Small, precise drawings and sharp black and white photographs show the flora and fauna of the woods in an attractive book that should appeal especially to the nature lover. The author does not attempt to be comprehensive, but to give a picture of the appearance of the woods in each season and to describe the sorts of activities that take place in the animal world and the sorts of changes that occur in the plant world. The writing is simple and direct, the organization of material random, and the information interesting if not

Kane, Henry B.—*Continued*

unusual. A good general book for nature study, and one that can be used by adults for discussions with younger children." Chicago. Children's Bk Center

The tale of a meadow; written and illus. by Henry B. Kane. Knopf 1959 108p illus (Borzoi Nature study bks) lib. bdg. $5.39 (4-6)　　　　500.9

1 Natural history
ISBN 0-394-91718-9

"In the introductory chapters the author shows the various stages the meadow underwent from the ice age period until it gained its present proportions and its numerous wild life inhabitants. Bird, mammal, insect, reptile and plant life are seen through the eyes of a boy who delights in the surprises and wonders offered by nature. . . . The information is straightforward, accurate and readable. . . . Illustrated with splendid photographs and small sketches. Well indexed." Ontario Library Rev

The tale of a wood; written and illus. by Henry B. Kane. Knopf 1962 112p illus (Borzoi Nature study bks) $3.50, lib. bdg. $5.39 (4-6)　　　　500.9

1 Natural history
ISBN 0-394-81721-4; 0-394-91721-9

"The natural history of a temperate forest is unveiled through the eyes of a curious and imaginative boy. Plants receive equal treatment with animals, both being explored in an interesting, instructive way." The AAAS Sci Bk List for Children

"The book is worth owning for its exceptional photography alone. . . . Fine drawings, with many caption details, supplement the camera work in adding information to chatty text." Horn Bk

Kirk, Ruth

Desert life; with photographs by Ruth and Louis Kirk. Natural Hist. Press 1970 unp illus $4.95 (k-3)
　　　　500.9

1 Desert animals 2 Desert plants 3 Deserts
ISBN 0-385-02446-0

"Published for the American Museum of Natural History"

This book is an "introduction to the plants and animals of the southwestern United States and northern Mexico. . . . [Included is] information about pack rats, peccaries, ringtail cats, Joshua trees, saguaro cactus, kangaroo rats and kitfoxes." N Y Times Bk Rev

"Of special interest are the close-up and brief description of the kangaroo rat because of the animal's similarity to a popular new rodent pet, the gerbil. Text is minimal, printed in large type and fairly easy to read; it emphasizes the adaptation of plants and animals to a climate of little rainfall." Sch Library J

Parker, Bertha Morris

The new Golden Treasury of natural history. Golden Press 1968 384 illus $6.95, lib. bdg. $7.95 (5-7)
　　　　500.9

1 Natural history
ISBN 0-307-17853-6; 0-307-67853-9

First published 1952 by Simon & Schuster with title: The Golden Treasury of natural history

"Concise, authoritative information on the prehistoric period on the earth through the beginning of life. The last half of the book is devoted to plant life, and at the end are . . . charts of the various orders of animal, insect, and plant life. Well indexed. Illustrations in full color. Really remarkable book but, like most of its kind, not too inclusive." Library J

Perry, Roger

The Galápagos Islands; illus. with photographs and a map. Dodd 1972 92p illus map $4 (5-7)　　　500.9

1 Galápagos Islands 2 Natural history—Galápagos Islands
ISBN 0-396-06576-7

The author "traces the volcanic formation and history of the islands, treats their flora and fauna paying particular attention to the tortoises, and describes the current status of the islands. Perry's appreciation of the islands and their native creatures is apparent as is his dismay at the animals' decimation and, in some cases, extinction through human exploitation. Enhanced by many clear photographs . . . this is a crisp informal introductory account." Booklist

Simon, Seymour

Science in a vacant lot; illus. by Kiyo Komoda. Viking 1970 64p illus lib. bdg. $4.95 (2-5)　　　500.9

1 Nature study
ISBN 0-670-62163-3

Given here are "many ideas for natural science projects in urban vacant lots. Several of the ideas could be adapted to the suburban backyard also. Subjects explored are rocks and soil, insects, plants, birds, and other animals, and the questions raised are open ended. That observations can be made at a site being bulldozed is one interesting suggestion for a science study. The reproductions of pencil sketches that illustrate the book are pleasant and helpful. Some children will be stimulated to begin scientific observation by this book, most will use it best if there is teacher or parental encouragement. It should be useful for class projects in the middle grades." Sci Bks

Books for reading and research: p61-62

Sterling, Dorothy

Fall is here! Illus. by Winifred Lubell. Natural Hist. Press 1966 96p illus $4.95 (4-6)　　　500.9

1 Autumn 2 Natural history
ISBN 0-385-05856-X

"Published for the American Museum of Natural History." Title page

"Accurate scientific information is given simply and interestingly on what happens to sunshine, trees, leaves, seeds, birds, and animals in the fall and why." Adventuring With Bks. 2d edition

"The plant illustrations are generally better than those of animals. . . . A good feature is the section, 'Things to do in the fall.'" Sci Bks

501　Science—Philosophy and theory

Moorman, Thomas

How to make your science project scientific. Atheneum Pubs. 1974 94p illus $3.50 (5-7)　　　501

1 Science—Methodology
ISBN 0-689-30436-6

This book describes the scientific method of experimentation, including its use in simple experiments, controlled experiments, case study, blind and double-blind experiments, naturalistic observation and survey methods. There is a discussion of statistics, record keeping and reporting to others

"This is an easily read book that treats a topic about which there is much talk but not much real effort on the part of many students. . . . There are line drawings and charts which illustrate the examples developed in the text." Sci Teacher

Glossary: p80-88. Bibliography: p91-92

503   Science—Encyclopedias and dictionaries

Asimov, Isaac
More Words of science; decorations by William Barss. Houghton 1972 267p $6.95   503
1 Science—Terminology 2 English language—Etymology
ISBN 0-395-13722-5
Companion volume to the author's: Words of science, and the history behind them, entered below
"This work contributes page-long explanations of 250 words that go beyond . . . [the first volume] in three ways: 1) they were omitted from the earlier work; 2) they are old words with new meanings (e.g., pollution, ecology); or 3) they were only invented in the last decade or so (e.g., laser, pulsar)." Cur Ref Bks
"Asimov's clear and lively prose is informative and enjoyable even when the terms are known to the reader." Chicago. Children's Bk Center

Words of science, and the history behind them; illus. by William Barss. Houghton 1959 266p illus $6.95   503
1 Science—Terminology 2 English language—Etymology
ISBN 0-395-06571-2
A book "both for the reader interested in science and the reader interested in language and words. Two hundred and fifty words [arranged alphabetically] are given one-page explanations, but each word is used as a starting point for giving the histories and derivations of other words related by concept or etymology. The choice of words is, of necessity, rather arbitrary, but the selection is well-balanced and comprehensive; the author has defined his field broadly. . . . Format is attractive, and [there is an] excellent index." Chicago. Children's Bk Center

The Book of popular science. Grolier 10v illus maps apply to publisher for price   503
1 Science—Encyclopedias 2 Natural history—Encyclopedias 3 Technology—Encyclopedias
First published 1924. Revised annually
The information in this set is classified under such broad categories as: the universe, the earth, plant life, animal life, man, health, mathematics, matter and energy, transportation, communications, science through the ages, life, and projects and experiments
"This outstanding set for general background reading in all phases of science and technology undergoes substantial annual revisions. . . . Volume 10 contains various useful appendices, a detailed reading list, and a comprehensive index." Sci Bks

505   Science—Serial publications

Science year; the World book science annual. A review of science and technology during the [preceding] school year. Field Enterprises illus apply to publisher price   505
1 Science—Yearbooks 2 Technology—Yearbooks
Annual. First published 1965
The first section of this volume contains over a dozen signed "special reports" about recent scientific and technological developments. The second section, Science file, presents over 40 signed, briefer articles in alphabetical order which survey fields from agriculture and anthropology to transportation and zoolo-

gy. An annotated bibliography is included. The section entitled Men and women of science offers descriptions of the work of two scientists, lists and descriptions of major science awards, and a necrology. There is also a 3 year cumulative index
For a fuller review see: The Booklist and Subscription books bulletin, April 1, 1966

507.05   Science—Study and teaching—Periodicals

The Science Teacher. Natl. Science Teacher's Assn. $25 per year   507.05
1 Science—Study and teaching—Periodicals
ISSN 0036-8555
Monthly September through May. First published 1934
"Includes articles which relate to the teaching of science, administration and supervision of science programs, and science teacher education." Camp. Guide to Periodicals in Educ

507.2   Science—Experiments

Cobb, Vicki
Science experiments you can eat; illus. by Peter Lippman. Lippincott 1972 127p illus $5.95, pa $2.50 (5-7)   507.2
1 Science—Experiments 2 Cookery 3 Food
ISBN 0-397-31487-6; 0-397-31179-6
"Few cooks think of themselves as chemists, but Vicki Cobb is one who did. The result is an excellent 'lab manual' of experiments utilizing readily available materials and frequently seen processes. Ms. Cobb demonstrates physical states such as solution, suspension and emulsion by giving recipes for popsicles, borscht and strawberry bombe, while discussing the Tyndall effect and suppression of freezing point by solute. She also presents chemistry experiments (in recipe form) to demonstrate such processes as protein denaturation (sour milk biscuits) and coagulation (custard), and the sol-gel transformation (jello). There's also a section on biology, using such experiments as striped celery (by osmotic pressure), color changes in spinach chlorophyll (use of buffered boiling solutions), and measuring moisture content of seeds (diameter of popped corn). And best of all, when the experiments are finished, the young scientist can eat them! (There are a few exceptions, but Ms. Cobb is careful to use clear warnings of safety.) All in all, the book is a delightful combination of learning by doing, and of relating common activities to basic scientific principles." Sci Bks

Gardner, Martin
Science puzzlers; illus. by Anthony Ravielli. Viking 1960 127p illus lib. bdg. $5.95 (6-7)   507.2
1 Science—Experiments 2 Scientific recreations
ISBN 0-670-62113-7
In this book "the author was guided by two principles: 'First, avoid experiments requiring special equipment that cannot be found in the average home. Second, concentrate on experiments that, in addition to being amusing, astonishing or entertaining, also teach something of importance about science.' Ravielli's drawings wonderfully illustrate and ornament the text." The AAAS Sci Bk List for Children
Subjects treated are physiology, psychology,

Gardner, Martin—*Continued*
mechanics, hydraulics, geometry, atmosphere and light
Selected references on recreational science: p[128]

Milgrom, Harry
Adventures with a cardboard tube; illus. by Tom Funk. Dutton 1972 31p illus (First science experiments) $4.95 (k-2) 507.2
1 Science—Experiments
ISBN 0-525-25150-2
This book "spells out simple activities designed to reveal the properties and possibilities of a cardboard tube. Besides being a cylinder, it rolls in a straight line, acts like a spring, bounces, and can act as a weight-mover, light-blocker, sound-collector, and sound-maker." Appraisal
The author's "technique of asking and answering questions would be particularly effective if the book were used with supervision; the child could attempt to answer the questions himself before seeing Milgrom's answers. The most elaborate activity described is the construction of a balance scale which is ingenious and leads to other scientific activity. A summary at the end of the book lists the surprisingly numerous ideas presented." Sci Bks

Adventures with a paper cup; illus. by Leonard Kessler. Dutton 1968 32p illus (First science experiments) $4.95 (k-2) 507.2
1 Science—Experiments
ISBN 0-525-25113-8
This book contains "an assortment of simple experiments devised to awaken an interest in scientific exploration and discovery in young children. . . . A cone-shaped paper cup is used to demonstrate movements of the earth around the sun, air resistance, friction, and sound amplification and to make a hot-air engine, a top, a pinhole camera, and a water clock. Entertaining and stimulating activities for use with kindergarten and primary-age children." Booklist

Adventures with a straw; illus. by Leonard Kessler. Dutton 1967 32p illus (First science experiments) $4.95 (k-2) 507.2
1 Science—Experiments
ISBN 0-525-25229-0
"This is a greatly needed participation book which leads a child to observe, reason, and discover. A straw is used to show simple science concepts. Such as that light travels in a straight line, that air takes up space, that a vibrating column of air can produce a sound, and that air has pressure. The clear text is expanded in clever, informative illustrations, and there is a concluding summary in words and pictures of the concepts offered." Library J

Rosenfeld, Sam
Science experiments with air; illus. by James E. Barry. Harvey House 1969 191p illus lib. bdg. $6.27 (5-7) 507.2
1 Science—Experiments 2 Air
ISBN 0-8178-4402-3
"The text first presents a three-page background, 'A word about air,' followed by twelve questions. . . . The general purpose of . . . [each] experiment is described, there is a list of materials needed, then a description of the 'method,' and finally open-ended questions to find out what has been learned from the experiment, or series of experiments. At the end of the chapter is a 'self-test' with answers in the back of the book. Working through the book, the young experimenter will learn solidly the composition of air, the relation of temperature to volume and pressure, the law of the conservation of matter, principles of oxydation and reduction, buoyancy, the principles of aerodynamics, etc. He will also learn to construct simple instruments which are useful in conducting the experiments." Sci Bks
Glossary: p181-85. Bibliography: p186-87

Schwartz, Julius
It's fun to know why; experiments with things around us. 2d ed. Illus. by Edwin Herron and Anne Marie Jauss. McGraw 1973 159p illus lib. bdg. $4.72 (4-7) 507.2
1 Science—Experiments
ISBN 0-07-055733-0
First published 1952
"Coal, paper, salt, soap, and plastic are some of the resources and commodities Schwartz focuses on in an interesting look at various natural resources and their commonplace value. He describes the source of each product, then proceeds to structure several well-illustrated and delineated experiments to give the concrete basis needed to understand each product's component structure along with the particular process used in developing it to its present-day level of sophistication. These projects, which can all be performed with easily-accessible household equipment prove good vehicles for gaining direct knowledge of how the materials are made and used." Booklist

Simon, Seymour
Science at work: easy models you can make; illus. by Valli Van de Bovenkamp. Watts, F. 1971 65p illus lib. bdg. $4.90 (4-6) 507.2
1 Science—Experiments 2 Scientific apparatus and instruments
ISBN 0-531-01972-1
"Among the 20 models described in this book for young artisans and experimenters are a telescope, a 'Cartesian diver,' a homemade battery, a scintilloscope which measures radioactivity, a Foucault pendulum to illustrate the rotation of the earth, an altimeter, and an earth-moon rotation model. All of the models are teaching devices, for the student learns scientific principles by making them and from the experiments in which he uses them. Directions are minimum yet sufficiently explicit. Open-ended questions abound to stimulate thinking and experimentation. Wherever necessary, the author has inserted warnings so that the student will not injure himself by thoughtless acts. The materials that are needed for making the models will be available in the average household or can be secured easily." Sci Bks
For further reading: p62

Webster, David
How to do a science project; illus. with photographs and drawings. Watts, F. 1974 61p illus lib. bdg. $3.45 (4-7) 507.2
1 Science—Experiments
ISBN 0-531-00817-7
"A First book"
The author "outlines the three major types of projects that could be selected—reports, demonstrations and research, gives suggestions for each category and then proceeds to carefully and sequentially outline how to go about carrying out the project. The print of the book is especially clear and uncrowded. Each chapter heading is prominent and the subheadings in these chapters are also obvious. The illustrations are excellent and varied, ranging from photographs, to cartoons, to graphs and charts. All give the child help in planning, doing and presenting his own project. There is a large bibliography at the end which would be of great help when a particular project has been chosen." Sci Bks

White, Laurence B.
Investigating science with coins, by Laurence B. White, Jr. Addison-Wesley 1969 95p illus $4.50 (4-7) 507.2

1 Science—Experiments
ISBN 0-201-08654-9
"An Addisonian Press book"
"A considerable number of investigations are described which produce interesting phenomena using coins and a few common household items. The effects are directly related to such ideas as surface tension, sensory perception, chemical reactions of metals, energy, momentum, friction, refraction, and several mathematical concepts. The explanations are generally adequate (some of the chemistry is questionable), but are sometimes too quickly offered and too final. Some good-natured chicanery adds to the fun without detracting from the science. Illustrations are effective." Sci Bks

Investigating science with nails, by Laurence B. White, Jr. Addison-Wesley 1970 108p illus lib. bdg. $4.50 (4-7) 507.2

1 Science—Experiments 2 Nails and spikes
ISBN 0-201-08651-4
"In this book young scientists are using nails in a number of experiments ranging from heat transfer to magnetism to magic. The text is clearly written with great pedagogical insight, and the illustrations cannot be misunderstood." The AAAS Sci Bk List for Children

Investigating science with paper, by Laurence B. White, Jr. Addison-Wesley 1970 123p illus $4.50 (4-7) 507.2

1 Science—Experiments 2 Paper
ISBN 0-201-08658-1
"Activities through which children can learn about paper and explore important ideas of science and engineering using paper and a few other common household items are described. Experiments in papermaking, absorption, chromatography, filtration, invisible ink, and topology are included." Sci Bks
The author "also includes mathematical puzzles, fingerprinting and the construction of a Moebius strip. Illustrated with line drawings, the book, which encourages independent scientific investigation, will be useful for science classes and for leisure-time activities." Booklist

Investigating science with rubber bands, by Laurence B. White, Jr. Addison-Wesley 1969 95p illus $4.50 (4-7) 507.2

1 Science—Experiments
ISBN 0-201-08656-5
"In a clear, unpretentious style, simple experiences are set up to illustrate surface tension, chemical bonds, Hooke's Law, sound, molecular models, physiology and the production of 'rubber' from milkweed or dandelions. The experiences 'invite themselves' to be performed, and the simple diagrams illustrate the materials needed and what is to be done." Sci Bks

Wyler, Rose
The first book of science experiments; rev. and rewritten by Rose Wyler; illus. by Sanford Kleiman. Watts, F. 1971 72p illus lib. bdg. $3.90 (4-6) 507.2

1 Science—Experiments
ISBN 0-531-00623-9
First published 1952
Here are directions for simple experiments with air, water, plants, weather, electricity and magnetism, chemistry and light—all done with equipment easily available in the home or at the neighborhood drug store

"The experiments are good, instructional and interesting. Many of them are safe, but some should be performed in front of children by responsible adults only." Appraisal

Prove it! By Rose Wyler and Gerald Ames; pictures by Talivaldis Stubis. Harper 1963 64p illus (A Science I can read bk) $2.95, lib. bdg. $3.79 (1-3) 507.2
1 Science—Experiments
ISBN 0-06-020050-2; 0-06-020051-0
Simple experiments performed with ordinary objects
"Beginners will have no difficulty in reading and following the instructions—and certainly they will be pleased with the illustrations, which are not only clear but original in concept and in use of color." Horn Bk

What happens if . . . ? Science experiments you can do by yourself; pictures by Daniel Nevins. Walker & Co. 1974 48p illus $4.95, lib. bdg. $4.87 (2-4) 507.2

1 Science—Experiments
ISBN 0-8027-6167-4; 0-8027-6168-2
The author "has compiled some home demonstrations that really are easy, safe, and clearly explained. The text is divided into five areas: experiments with balloons, mixtures, flashlights, shadow pictures, and ice. Materials are simple: a balloon, an empty milk carton, a bulb, a battery, aluminum foil, etc. The instructions are clear; the cartoon-style illustrations, reminiscent of Jeanne Bendick's, lively and informative." Chicago. Children's Bk Center

509 Science—History

The Universe of Galileo and Newton, by the editors of Horizon Magazine. Author: William Bixby. Consultant: Giorgio de Santillana. Illus. with paintings, drawings, and documents, many of the period. Am. Heritage [distributed by Harper] 1964 153p illus lib. bdg. $6.89 (6-7) 509
1 Science—History 2 Galilei, Galileo 3 Newton, Sir Isaac
ISBN 0-06-020521-0
"A Horizon Caravel book"
This is a science history which provides an account of Galileo's discoveries in physics and astronomy and Newton's formulation of mathematical principles which altered man's concept of the solar system
It "presents an absorbing account of the discoveries of these two pioneers. Mr. Bixby provides a sober report on their simple reach toward truth in widely different 17th-century environments. The ecclesiastical difficulties of Galileo and the intrigues of the British scientific society in which Newton lived are carefully handled . . . excellent paintings and drawings." Bk Week
Further reference: p151

510 Mathematics

Asimov, Isaac
How did we find out about numbers? Illus. by Daniel Nevins. Walker & Co. 1973 63p illus $4.95, lib. bdg. $4.85 (4-6) 510
1 Numerals
ISBN 0-8027-6135-6; 0-8027-6136-4
The author "allows the reader to go back in time and examine the interesting history of numbers, then proceed to the point when our now familiar Arabic numerals became the accepted symbols throughout the

Asimov, Isaac—*Continued*

world. He tells how primitive man employed fingers, sticks, etc., using a one-to-one correspondence. Since this was a rather clumsy way to keep track of things, man had to work out a marking system of sorts, which he did almost 5000 years ago. The Sumerians, Egyptians, and Chinese first made use of writing symbols to stand for various numbers. These sumbols, called numerals, changed over the thousands of years. Asimov explores the history of Roman numerals and, finally, the Hindu-Arabic numerals, especially important for the concept of zero. . . .The author's accuracy and gift for writing make this a book about numbers not to be missed!" Appraisal

510.3   Mathematics— Encyclopedias and dictionaries

Bendick, Jeanne

Mathematics illustrated dictionary; facts, figures and people including the new math, by Jeanne Bendick and Marcia Levin. In consultation with Leonard Simon; illus. by Jeanne Bendick. McGraw 1965 223p illus $5.95, lib. bdg. $4.72 (4-7)   510.3

1 Mathematics—Encyclopedias

ISBN 0-07-004460-0; 0-07-004461-9

"Some 2,000 mathematical terms with definitions, explanations, and examples as well as thumb-nail sketches of ancient and contemporary mathematicians are listed alphabetically with many cross-references in a handy tool for the student. Tables of mathematical symbols, formulas, weights and measures, the metric system, square roots, and logarithms are appended." Booklist

511   Generalities

Bendick, Jeanne

Names, sets and numbers; written and illus. by Jeanne Bendick. Watts F. 1971 65p illus (Science experiences) lib. bdg. $4.90, pa $1.25 (2-5)   511

1 Set theory 2 Mathematics

ISBN 0-531-01463-3; 0-531-02321-4

"In an informal, simply written explanation, Bendick explores the importance of names and numbers and then introduces some basic concepts of set theory, including empty sets and subsets. Exercises which utilize the concepts presented or stimulate further thinking are interspersed throughout the text; answers are given in the back of the book. Illustrated with lively, occasionally humorous drawings." Booklist

Lowenstein, Dyno

Graphs; written and illus. by Dyno Lowenstein. Watts, F. 1969 63p illus lib. bdg. $3.90 (5-7)   511

1 Graphic methods 2 Statistics—Graphic methods

ISBN 0-531-00679-4

"A First book"

"The book begins by illustrating how the world population explosion can be dramatically and accurately represented through line graphs and pictographs. In similar ways, bar graphs including composite and sliding types, and pie graphs are discussed utilizing interesting statistical data on such events as rainfall in Chicago, Babe Ruth's home run records, heights of boys and girls, weekly earnings, and similar type data. The book is filled with many illustrative

graphs which are both mathematically accurate and attractive in appearance." Sci Bks

513   Arithmetic

Adler, Irving

Integers: positive and negative; illus. by Laurie Jo Lambie. Day 1972 47p illus lib. bdg. $4.47 (4-7)   513

1 Number theory 2 Arithmetic

ISBN 0-381-99988-2

"The Reason why books"

This book explains the meaning and uses of integers, describing how numbers may be positive or negative by comparing them with rewards and penalties. It shows how to add and subtract integers using checkers, arrows, and a number line. Directions for making a slide rule and a simple adding machine are also given

"The author must be complimented for his skillful treatment of this basic topic, and the publishers for producing a sturdy and attractive little book." Sci Bks

Numerals; new dresses for old numbers [by] Irving and Ruth Adler. Day 1964 48p illus lib. bdg. $4.47 (4-6)   513

1 Arithmetic 2 Number theory

ISBN 0-381-99960-2

"The Reason why books"

This is a "guide to counting in groups other than 10. The processes of translating a number from a base 10 numeral system to systems with other bases, adding and multiplying the new numbers, and translating them back to base 10 numerals are thoroughly and understandably explained in simple text and many tables and charts. Problems for the reader to work are supplied for each operation." Booklist

A "rapid overview . . . [which] fills a void in materials for children about this topic. . . .However, reading it requires a background in certain aspects of mathematics such as the use of exponents." Sch Library J

Sets and numbers for the very young [by] Irving and Ruth Adler; illus. by Peggy Adler. Day 1969 47p illus lib. bdg. $4.47 (k-2)   513

1 Arithmetic

ISBN 0-381-99956-4

"Big but crowded pages are filled with very simple, multiple examples—in words and drawings—to make clear to the very young child the cardinal and ordinal numbers [1 to 10] and the concept of sets, with counting introduced late in the text." Chicago. Children's Bk Center

Bendick, Jeanne

Take a number; new ideas + imagination = more fun [by] Jeanne Bendick [and] Marcia Levin; pictures by Jeanne Bendick. McGraw 1961 63p illus map lib. bdg. $3.83 (4-6)   513

1 Arithmetic 2 Number theory

ISBN 0-07-004485-6

"Whittlesey House publications"

Contents: What is a number; The first numeration system; What the Hindu-Arabic system gave us; Rules about numbers; Bases for the numerals we use; The binary system and computers; How many numbers are there; Special numbers; Fun with numbers; Who needs numbers

"The explanations are clear although the text has occasional jocose digressions that are irrelevant, but the attitude of the authors is happily communicated—numbers are exciting. The amount of material

Bendick, Jeanne—*Continued*

covered and the magnitude of some of the concepts indicates that the book's best audience is the reader with a special interest . . . or the teacher who can use some of the topics to stimulate and channel discussion." Chicago. Children's Bk Center

Charosh, Mannis

Number ideas through pictures; illus. by Giulio Maestro. Crowell 1974 33p illus (Young math bks) $3.95, lib. bdg. $4.70 (2-4)   513

1 Number theory

ISBN 0-690-00155-X; 0-690-00156-8

Using pictures of familiar things, this book presents information on several number concepts. "Even-odd number states are defined and explored briefly; square numbers are constructed, based on consecutive adding of odd numbers; and triangular numbers are made by the consecutive addition of even and odd numbers. Various relationships of arithmetic squares and triangles are discussed and diagrammed." Booklist

"This book is a lovely introduction at an elementary level to some important concepts in number theory. . . . The text reads nicely and is handsomely complemented by good illustrations. All in all, a very nice job and a fine addition to the elementary school literature in good mathematics." Sci Bks

Dennis, J. Richard

Fractions are parts of things; illus. by Donald Crews. Crowell 1971 33p illus (Young math bks) $4.50, lib. bdg. $5.25, pa $1.25 (2-4)   513

1 Arithmetic

ISBN 0-690-31520-1; 0-690-31521-X; 0-690-31522-8

The author "makes clear by the clever use of colored mathematical shapes the relationships that are one-half, one-third, two-thirds, one-fourth, and three-fourths. The text contains questions, suggests activities, and invites discussion and group learning." Sci Bks

Froman, Robert

Bigger and smaller; illus. by Gioia Fiammenghi. Crowell 1971 33p illus (Young math bks) $4.50, lib. bdg. $5.25, pa $1.25 (1-3)   513

1 Size and shape 2 Mensuration

ISBN 0-690-14195-5; 0-690-14196-3; 0-690-14197-1

"One can tell whether an object is big or small by comparing it with another object. So begins the general theme of this . . . book, which asks young readers to make their own decisions. They also learn that it is possible for the same object to be big in relation to a second object and small in relation to a third (an elephant is big compared to a man but small compared to a dinosaur). The child will be stimulated to undertake endless comparisons, as to size, of the objects around him, and of the unfamiliar in the illustrations." Sci Bks

"The concept of relative size is presented here with a good deal of imagination and liveliness. . . . Throughout this stimulating introduction the reader is asked to make decisions and at the end is encouraged to explore the concept further. Humorous colored or black-and-white drawings on every page." Booklist

Linn, Charles F.

Estimation; illus. by Don Madden. Crowell 1970 34p illus (Young math bks) $4.50, lib. bdg. $5.25, pa $1.25 (2-4)   513

1 Arithmetic

ISBN 0-690-27027-5; 0-690-27028-3; 0-690-27033-X

"By a series of open-ended experiments the young reader is taught to check his estimates of dimensions, quantity, distance and number. Questions are asked that emphasize importance and practical uses of estimates in human activity. Some of the questions may require help from the teacher or parent in analyzing them." The AAAS Sci Bk List for Children

O'Brien, Thomas C.

Odds and evens; illus. by Allan Eitzen. Crowell 1971 33p illus (Young math bks) $4.50, lib. bdg. $5.25, pa $1.25 (2-4)   513

1 Arithmetic 2 Number theory

ISBN 0-690-59069-5; 0-690-59070-9; 0-690-00207-6

"Instead of defining odd and even numbers and discussing their properties, [the author] encourages the reader to discover for himself the differences between the two types of numbers and some of their characteristics through the examples, questions, and experiments that are presented in the book." Booklist

"The book will perhaps be more fun if an older person shares it with a child, or a group of children. The reading is a little difficult for nursery school and kindergarten youngsters yet they can comprehend the illustrations and participate in the exercises." Sci Bks

Whitney, David C.

Let's find out about addition; pictures by Harriet Sherman. Watts, F. 1966 unp illus lib. bdg. $3.90 (1-3)   513

1 Arithmetic

ISBN 0-531-00073-1

"Let's find out series"

"Introduces numbers, the number line, and sets with clear explanations and attractive illustrations intended to clarify the young child's understanding of beginning arithmetic." Hodges. Bks for Elem Sch Libraries

513.028   Arithmetic—Apparatus and equipment

Dilson, Jesse

The abacus: a pocket computer; drawings by Angela Pozzi. St. Martins 1968 143p illus $6.95, pa $2.95 (5-7)   **513.028**

1 Abacus

"A practical introduction to the use of the abacus, along with an anecdotal history of the device is provided in this entertaining book. There are ample clear diagrams, including a chapter showing the young reader how to build his own abacus with beads, wire, and a cigar box. One of the more interesting sections explains how one can do binary calculations on an abacus using the same number systems employed in modern computers. There is a good amount of simple mathematics in this little book." Sci Bks

514   Topology

Froman, Robert

Rubber bands, baseballs and doughnuts; a book about topology; illus. by Harvey Weiss. Crowell 1972 33p illus (Young math bks) $4.50, lib. bdg. $5.25 (2-4)   514

1 Topology

ISBN 0-690-71353-3; 0-690-71354-1

"A clear introduction to topology for primary school

Froman, Robert—*Continued*

children. Simple experiments reveal the concepts of distortion and invariance, and the genus concept. . . . Although the topic of topology is peripheral to most elementary curriculums, this would provide enjoyable recreational reading for young math buffs." Sch Library J

This book "reaps all the advantages that come from being the first to explain an extremely complex subject to a layman. In some cases—and this is one—no amount of erudite exposition can beat a little playing around with rubber bands, balloons, and a teacup or two. . . . Froman manages to convey with intelligence some basic principles of topology." Bk World

516 Geometry

Bendick, Jeanne

Shapes; written and illus. by Jeanne Bendick. Watts, F. 1968 70p illus (Science experiences) lib. bdg. $4.90, pa $1.25 (2-4)   516

1 Size and shape 2 Geometry
ISBN 0-531-01433-9; 0-531-02322-2

"This informal introduction to geometry leads the elementary-grade child from the basic concepts of line, point, and plane to three-dimensional figures and an explanation of symmetry. Frequent examples are given. Questions are asked of readers and are followed by discussion which will help children link the geometrical concepts to objects in everyday life. In most instances the material is clearly stated and the plain illustrations provide good support for the textual explanation of shapes." Sch Library J

Charosh, Mannis

The ellipse; illus. by Leonard Kessler. Crowell 1971 33p illus (Young math bks) $4.50, lib. bdg. $5.25 (2-4)   516

1 Geometry
ISBN 0-690-25856-9; 0-690-25857-7

The author describes the ellipse and, through a series of experiments to be performed by the young reader, explains its relationship to straight lines and to other curves—hyperbolas, parabolas, and circles

The book "is delightful. The illustrations are amusing; the faces within the curves, the animals formed only by the use of the ellipse, and the diagrams all deserve special commendation." Sci Bks

Straight lines, parallel lines, perpendicular lines; illus. by Enrico Arno. Crowell 1970 33p illus (Young math bks) $4.50, lib. bdg. $5.25, pa $1.25 (2-4) 516

1 Geometry
ISBN 0-690-7792-5; 0-690-77993-3; 0-690-77994-1

"Using string, a checker set and board, pencil, and paper, the reader can follow suggestions for investigating straight, parallel, and perpendicular lines. The text, brisk and straight-forward, also points out some of the familiar objects that illustrate these phenomena: the edge of the table, the corner of a rug, the opposite sides of a blackboard. The illustrations, like the print, are large and clear, with good correlation between pictures and text." Chicago. Children's Bk Center

Diggins, Julia E.

String, straightedge, and shadow; the story of geometry; illus. by Corydon Bell. Viking 1965 160p illus maps $5.95 (6-7)   516

1 Geometry—History
ISBN 0-670-67858-9

The author "relates how early scientists used only three simple tools—the string, the straightedge, and the shadow—to discover the basic principles of geometry, and tells how these discoveries affected the civilizations of ancient Egypt, Greece, and Mesopotamia." Hodges. Bks for Elem Sch Libraries

"Some of the illustrations are informative, some merely decorative. The geometric principles and problems are presented as though their discoverers were explaining them." Chicago. Children's Bk Center

Suggestions for further reading: p156

Freeman, Mae

Finding out about shapes; illus. by Bill Morrison. McGraw 1969 47p illus $3.95, lib. bdg. $4.72 (k-3)   516

1 Size and shape
ISBN 0-07-021958-3; 0-07-021959-1

"Colorful pictures and a text impart the knowledge that most objects have a special shape which is appropriate to their intended use, and that such shapes have their own names. Various activities and exercises are suggested which will teach the various terms, concepts, and characteristics of all of the many shapes that may be observed in familiar and unfamiliar objects. This is not a textbook, but it is good material for supplemental use in the classroom for teaching reading and basics of science and mathematics. It is similar to but somewhat easier for young children than Jeanne Bendick's 'Shapes' [entered above]." Sci Bks

Russell, Solveig Paulson

Lines and shapes; a first look at geometry; illus. by Arnold Spilka. Walck, H.Z. 1965 31p illus $4.95 (2-4)   516

1 Geometry 2 Size and shape
ISBN 0-8098-1112-X

"The author introduces the young reader to geometry by guiding him to examine his environment for lines and shapes. Simple, clear statements, such as 'When a line or a number of lines enclose space, a shape is made' lead the reader from one idea to related ideas in logical sequence. Some of the related concepts introduced . . . are: perpendicular, horizontal, vertical, parallel; right, acute and obtuse angles; triangle, rectangle, square, and other polygons; circle, oval, crescent, arc, semi-circle, sphere, cone, pyramid, and cube." Sch Library J

"Certainly this initial glimpse should prove useful —not to say exciting—to children . . . for they are shown how to observe line and shape in every area of the world around them. Arnold Spilka's line drawings are lively and helpful." America

Sitomer, Mindel

Circles, by Mindel and Harry Sitomer; illus. by George Giusti. Crowell 1971 33p illus (Young math bks) $4.50, lib. bdg. $5.25, pa $1.25 (2-4)   516

1 Size and shape
ISBN 0-690-19430-7; 0-690-19431-5; 0-690-00206-8

"Basic mathematical principles of circles are explored. . . . [The book] explains, by examples, the meaning of the terms circle, radius, diameter, and semicircle, gives a number of experiments to do and designs to make using a compass and ruler, and shows how squares, right angles, regular hexagons, and triangles can be formed from circles." Booklist

"Attractive drawings, simple and large-scale, illustrate clearly the ideas presented in a good introduction to the manipulative charms of the 'perfect' figure. . . . The text is straightforward and lucid, an admirable example of science writing." Chicago. Children's Bk Center

Sitomer, Mindel—*Continued*

What is symmetry? By Mindel and Harry Sitomer; illus. by Ed Emberley. Crowell 1970 33p illus (Young math bks) $4.50, lib. bdg. $5.25, pa $1.25 (1-3) 516

1 Symmetry

ISBN 0-690-87612-2; 0-690-87613-0; 0-690-87618-1

"The authors present for young children an understandable explanation of the nature and occurrence of line, point, and plane symmetry. The explicit, well-developed text is complemented by apt pictorial examples and enlivened with drawings of playful alligators demonstrating some important points. The book will be most effective when used with adult help." Booklist

Srivastava, Jane Jonas

Area; illus. by Shelley Freshman. Crowell 1974 33p illus (Young math bks) $3.95, lib. bdg. $4.70 (2-3) 516

1 Mensuration

ISBN 0-690-00404-4; 0-690-00405-2

The author "touches upon such diverse topics as units of measurement (both British and metric) and the measurement of surface areas, both planar and spherical. The book consists largely of brief statements followed by unanswered questions. . . . The author's use of the term 'standard unit of measurement,' while technically correct, is at variance with the conventional one with which the student may already be familiar. As enrichment material, especially in the classroom, the book does suggest some useful activities." Sci Bks

The "illustrations visualize the concepts explained in the text and are especially helpful in showing readers how to construct and use graph paper." Sch Library J

519.2   Probabilities

Linn, Charles F.

Probability; illus. by Wendy Watson. Crowell 1972 33p illus (Young math bks) $4.50, lib. bdg. $5.25 (2-4) 519.2

1 Probabilities

ISBN 0-690-65601-7; 0-690-65602-5

"An elementary introduction to the probability theory including several experiments for the reader to try." Minnesota

"A light, informal style and lucid explanations are used in conjunction with humorous pictures in cartoon-strip style. . . . The materials are simple, the instructions for doing the experiments, keeping records, and drawing inferences are clear, and the text covers enough material to enable young readers to grasp basic principles but not so much that they may feel overwhelmed." Chicago. Children's Bk Center

519.5   Statistical mathematics

Srivastava, Jane Jonas

Statistics; illus. by John J. Reiss, Crowell 1973 31p illus (Young math bks) $4.50, lib. bdg. $5.25 (2-4) 519.5

1 Statistics

ISBN 0-690-77299-8; 0-690-77300-5

The author introduces the mathematical concepts of statistics and tells "how to assemble numerical facts, classify them into significant information, display findings, and interpret results in addition to drawing up and using various types of graphs." Booklist

"The uses as well as the dangers of statistics . . . are explained in the clear and simple text which is accompanied by John Reiss' amusing, colorful pen-and-ink drawings." Sch Library J

523   Descriptive astronomy

Gallant, Roy A.

Exploring the universe. Rev. ed. Illus. by Lowell Hess. Doubleday 1968 64p illus $4.95 (5-7) 523

1 Astronomy

ISBN 0-385-0110-5

First published 1956 by Garden City Books

"The beliefs of ancient civilizations, theories and discoveries of early astronomers, present day concepts and facts about the universe, and research methods are discussed in clear, interesting text and striking colored illustrations in an oversized book." Booklist

"Gallant's style is entertaining and informal. Lowell Hess's illustrations are, as per usual, superb." Library J

Includes a one-page index

Zim, Herbert S.

Stars; a guide to the constellations, sun, moon, planets, and other features of the heavens, by Herbert S. Zim and Robert H. Baker. Illus. by James Gordon Irving. 150 paintings in color. [Rev. ed.] Golden Press 1956 160p illus maps (A Golden Nature guide) lib. bdg. $4.95, pa $1.50 (5-7) 523

1 Astronomy 2 Stars—Atlases

ISBN 0-307-24493-8

First published 1951 by Simon & Schuster

"A gem of a field guide for the novice, this little book tells how to scan the heavens, where to look and when. Authoritative, carefully organized, here is a wealth of data for quick reference. Divided into three sections: stars, constellations, and solar system. Every page is beautifully illustrated. . . . Binding good for the size." Library J

Includes a bibliography

523.1   Universe

Branley, Franklyn M.

A book of outer space for you; illus. by Leonard Kessler. Crowell 1970 56p illus $5.95, lib. bdg. $6.70 (3-5) 523.1

1 Outer space

ISBN 0-690-15474-9; 0-690-15474-7

The author "tells of the enormity of the solar system, of the vast distances that separate its members, of the composition of the atmosphere of the earth up to 20 miles, and of the rarified atmosphere of outer space. He explains why airplanes cannot be used to navigate in outerspace, to which man can travel only by rockets." Sci Bks

"The format (continuous text, very large print) seems a bit juvenile for the vocabulary and the difficulty of some of the concepts." Chicago. Children's Bk Center

Zim, Herbert S.

The universe. Newly rev. ed. Illus. with drawings by Gustav Schrotter and René Martin and photographs. Morrow 1973 63p illus maps lib. bdg. $4.32, pa $1.25 (4-6)　　　　523.1

1 Universe 2 Astronomy

ISBN 0-688-30096-0; 0-688-25096-3

"Zim surveys man's conception of the nature and size of the universe from ancient times to the present. He clearly and accurately discusses such topics as galaxies, clusters, variable stars, and how vast distances are measured. . . . [Includes] material on radio telescopes . . . moon landings and interplanetary probes." Sch Library J

523.2　Solar system

Branley, Franklyn M.

Comets, meteoroids, and asteroids; mavericks of the solar system; illus. by Helmut K. Wimmer. Crowell 1974 115p illus (Exploring our universe) $5.50 (6-7)　　　　523.2

1 Solar system

ISBN 0-690-20176-1

A "book about the many other smaller bodies that move among our nine planets and their thirty-two satellites. This is the book for one who is looking for concise, accurate descriptions of meteorites, asteroids, tektites, comets, the zodiacal light, the solar wind, and cosmic rays." Best Sellers

"The author introduces these relatively well-known phenomena, surveys myths, theories, and studies, and offers knowledgeable arguments on some scientific issues. Excellent black-and-white drawings and photographs, useful charts, and careful instructions for observing and recording the presence of meteors complete this resource, which will supplement astronomy studies. Suggestions for further reading are appended." Booklist

Gardner, Martin

Space puzzles: curious questions and answers about the solar system; illus. with diagrams and photographs; drawings by Ted Schroeder. Simon & Schuster 1971 95p illus $4.95, lib. bdg. $4.73 (6-7) 523.2

1 Solar system

ISBN 0-671-65182-X; 0-671-65183-8

Each chapter of this book deals with a separate aspect such as: the earth, the moon, space flight, and comets. Following the short introductions containing basic information on each topic there are several questions and puzzles which the reader can use to test his knowledge

"Many conflicting theories are presented as alternative explanations for astronomical phenomena, thus giving the reader a feeling for the never settled state of astronomical knowledge and theory. An interesting aspect is the frequent discussion of theories and titles from science fiction, considering both their valid points and their flaws." Wis Library Bul

523.3　Moon

Branley, Franklyn M.

The moon; earth's natural statellite. Rev. ed. Illus. by Helmut K. Wimmer. Crowell 1972 117p illus (Exploring our universe) $4.50, lib. bdg. $5.25 (6-7)　　　　523.3

1 Moon

ISBN 0-690-55415-X; 0-690-55416-8

First published 1960

The text includes information on moon rocks, radioactivity, and gases. Lunar motion, orbit, atmosphere, temperature, mass and density are explained. The book is illustrated with recent photographs of the earth side, far side and two polar regions of the moon

"Technical terminology is balanced with concise, readable writing. Illustrations include a variety of charts, diagrams, and photographs. [There are] contemporary and historical accounts of moon study, myths, and superstitions traditionally associated with the moon." Adventuring With Bks. 2d edition

Further readings: p112

Shapp, Martha

Let's find out about the moon, by Martha and Charles Shapp; pictures by Brigitte Hartmann. Rev. full-color ed. Watts, F. 1975 43p illus lib. bdg. $4.90 (1-3)　　　　523.3

1 Moon 2 Space flight to the moon 3 Apollo project

ISBN 0-531-00101-6

First published 1965

Here is an easy-to-read description of the surface features and environment of the moon and its relationship to the earth and sun. The story of the Apollo 11 mission is the vehicle for presenting these facts

523.4　Planets

Asimov, Isaac

Jupiter; the largest planet; illus. with photographs. Rev. ed. Lothrop 1976 224p illus $6.95, lib. bdg. $5.81 (6-7)　　　　523.4

1 Jupiter (Planet)

ISBN 0-688-40044-2; 0-688-51728-5

"Asimov delves into every aspect of what is known about Jupiter, theories of the past, present knowledge, and conjectures about future probes and findings. The text is firmly organized and is written with a lucid informality. . . . Jupiter is compared to other planets in reference to whiteness, oblateness, speed of rotation, axial tilt, mass, density, orbital speed, etc. The same close scrutiny is applied to the planet's satellites, and all of the information is summarized in tables, fifty-four of them. There are discussions of the problems yet to be explored, descriptions of what is visible from Jupiter's surface and from its satellites, and theories of Jupiter's formation. A thorough treatment, a good introduction for the layman, and a demonstration of how exciting scientific inquiry can be." Chicago. Children's Bk Center

Glossary: p214-19

Branley, Franklyn M.

The nine planets. Rev. ed. Illus. by Helmut K. Wimmer. Crowell 1971 86p illus (Exploring our universe) $5.50 (6-7)　　　　523.4

1 Planets

ISBN 0-690-58397-4

First published 1958

"This is a very basic description of the major planets in our solar system, one of a competent series from the Hayden Planetarium. Its strong advantages are its easy readability, coherent story design, and relative absence of ambiguity or equivocation." Sci Bks

"Charts are frequent and adequately placed for easy reference. The charts of sizes and distances of planets are supplemented in the text with examples of analogous sizes of everyday objects and commonly used distances. . . . Although most scientific concepts, such as density and mass, are clearly and simply

Branley, Franklyn M.—*Continued*
explained, a certain vocabulary (e.g., molecules) is assumed. No glossary is offered. There is a fairly good bibliography, and the index is quite comprehensive. The illustrations, without being too elaborate, add greatly to the book's appeal. Scientific data are supplemented with interesting historical and mythological facts, which keep the text from becoming dry." Appraisal

Knight, David C.
The first book of Mars; an introduction to the Red Planet. Rev. ed. Watts, F. 1973 82p illus lib. bdg. $3.90 (6-7)   523.4
1 Mars (Planet) 2 Mariner project
ISBN 0-531-00797-9
"A First book"
First published 1966
This book "covers the treatment of Mars in folklore and fiction, the findings of earthbound astronomers, and the results of the recent Mariner spacecraft flights. Since 1966, when only one space craft (Mariner 4) had made it to Mars, three other craft which carried much better instrumentation (Mariners 6, 7, and 9) have also collected and sent back to earth data about Mars. The inclusion of these newer findings makes this a useful . . . book." Sch Library J

The tiny planets; asteroids of our solar system; with 21 photographs and diagrams. Morrow 1973 95p illus $4.75, lib. bdg. $4.32 (4-7)   523.4
1 Planets, Minor
ISBN 0-688-20072-9; 0-688-30072-3
"The author defines asteroids and then launches into a history of their discovery and naming, noting that after the excitement attending the first flurry of their discovery between 1890 and 1940, their novelty waned. The specifics of their physical nature and theories of origin are outlined, and a final chapter describes their usefulness to contemporary astronomical investigations." Booklist
"The subject is introduced in a stimulating manner and developed logically. Mr. Knight adheres totally to facts and is painstakingly careful to explain new terms or concepts. His information is scientifically accurate. He has produced a work which will inform some members of his intended audience. Others it will surely stimulate to further study and will linger as a reference." Appraisal
Glossary: p88-91

Nourse, Alan E.
The asteroids. Watts, F. 1975 59p illus lib. bdg. $3.90 (5-7)   523.4
1 Planets, Minor
ISBN 0-531-00822-3
"A First book"
Nourse "describes how asteroids were discovered, what is known about them, current theories of their origin, and the hope that asteroids will yield evidence about the origin of the solar system. . . . This is an accurate and readable introductory book on astronomy." Sch Library J
Additional reading: p55

The giant planets. Watts, F. 1974 62p illus lib. bdg. $3.95 (5-7)   523.4
1 Planets
ISBN 0-531-00816-9
"A First book"
"An imaginary space voyage to the giant planets is described in this book which introduces one to the vocabulary, such as planet, orbit and ellipse, by citing examples of origin or explaining the terms. In the descriptions of the various planets, it is of particular interest that their atmospheres, surface temperatures

and cloud covers are compared with the more familiar domain of Earth. In presenting various facts about the closer planets to the Earth, time and speed comparisons are presented to illustrate possibilities of space travel. In addition to the telescope, other means of gathering information regarding the planets, such as the radio-radar telescope and rockets, are explained." Sci Bks
"This is a highly readable, five-chapter book for the young astronomer. . . . Black and white photographs enhance the text material." Sci Teacher

523.7   Sun

Asimov, Isaac
What makes the sun shine? Illus. by Marc Brown. Little 1971 57p illus lib. bdg. $4.95 (4-6)   523.7
1 Sun
ISBN 0-316-05462-3
"An Atlantic Monthly Press book"
"Simple experiments throughout the text on the formation of the solar system complement the step-by-step explanation of what the sun's energy consists of, how it works, and what it does. The glossary/index and the illustrations offer further clarification." Appraisal
"The questions that this excellent book will raise in the minds of young readers will tax even our better teachers. The book puts the elementary student on the brink of inquiry into cosmology, quantum theory, and chemistry." Sci Bks
Index and glossary: p55-57

Branley, Franklyn M.
Eclipse; darkness in daytime; illus. by Donald Crews. Crowell 1973 33p illus (Let's-read-and-find-out science bks) $4.50, lib. bdg. $5.25 (2-4)   523.7
1 Eclipses, Solar
ISBN 0-690-25413-X; 0-690-25414-8
The author "explains the phenomenon of the total solar eclipse, defining terminology and explaining why it is possible for the moon to obscure the larger sun. There's some discussion of the effect of the eclipse on animals and on the people of ancient times, and a home demonstration project that will enable the reader to see the image of the eclipse in safety. Succinct, lucid, and authoritative, the text is attractively illustrated." Chicago. Children's Bk Center

Shapp, Martha
Let's find out about the sun, by Martha and Charles Shapp; pictures by Stephanie Later. Rev. full color ed. Watts, F. 1975 39p illus lib. bdg. $4.90 (1-3)
523.7
1 Sun
ISBN 0-531-00047-8
First published 1965
This book tells of the dependence of all living things on the sun for light and warmth. The earth's rotation on its axis about the sun and the changing seasons are also explained through text and pictures

523.8   Stars

Branley, Franklyn M.
The Big Dipper; illus. by Ed Emberley. Crowell 1962 unp illus (Let's-read-and-find out science bks) $4.50, lib. bdg. $5.25 (k-2)   523.8
1 Stars
ISBN 0-690-14088-6; 0-690-14089-4
"This book for the youngest skywatchers gives

Branley, Franklyn M.—*Continued*
directions for locating the Big Dipper and the Little
Dipper, explains how they show direction, and relates
facts and legends concerning the two constellations."
Hodges. Bks for Elem Sch Libraries
"While the scope of subjects exceeds that indicated
by the title, it is not too complicated for the age of the
reader. The text is, however, not always clarified by
the illustrations." Chicago. Children's Bk Center

A book of stars for you; illus. by Leonard Kessler.
Crowell 1967 unp illus $5.95, lib. bdg. $6.70 (2-4)
523.8
1 Stars
ISBN 0-690-15721-5; 0-690-15722-3
The author "explains the place and importance of
the solar system in the galaxy; the numbers, distances,
motions, and properties of stars; and even describes
something of the way stars are formed and evolve.
. . . Some younger children may require explanation
of some of the technical terms." Sci Bks
"Overwhelming as any consideration of astronomy
may seem, when introduced in a concise picture-book
style the subject has a fascinating appeal for a child
just beginning to understand something of the vastness of our universe." Cincinnati

Rey, H. A.
The stars; a new way to see them. Enl. world-wide
ed. Houghton 1967 160p illus maps $7.95 (5-7)
523.8
1 Stars
ISBN 0-395-08121-1
First published 1952
In addition to charts and line drawings that suggest
to the reader the mythological figures for which the
constellations were named, this book "contains 40
charts showing the sky throughout the year as far
north as Alaska and as far south as Australia and New
Zealand." Pub W

523.9 Satellites of planets

Knight, David C.
Thirty-two moons; the natural satellites of our solar
system; illus. with photographs, drawings by Pamela
Carroll, and diagrams by Ellen Cullen. Morrow 1974
95p illus $3.95, lib. bdg. $3.78 (5-7)   523.9
1 Solar system
ISBN 0-688-20110-5; 0-688-30110-X
"This survey of our solar system's moons describes
historical and contemporary research findings on both
the satellites and their primaries, or planets around
which they revolve. The well-designed volume provides clearly labeled diagrams along with descriptive
material on each moon's discovery, physical nature,
and spatial relationships to neighboring satellites. In
addition, many controversial theories on the origin,
composition, and interaction of certain bodies in our
solar system are explored in context. This should be
considered a companion work to less specialized
volumes, particularly since it assumes a degree of
familiarity with some basic concepts on the part of the
reader." Booklist
Glossary: p90-92

525   Earth (Astronomical geography)

Branley, Franklyn M.
The end of the world; illus. by David Palladini.
Crowell 1974 39p illus $5.50, lib. bdg. $6.25 (5-7)
525
1 End of the world 2 Earth
ISBN 0-690-26607-3; 0-690-26608-1
The author describes the inevitable natural
destruction of our planet by means of energy flashes
from other stars, aging from the sun's rays, or changes
in the earth's relationship to the moon. He believes
that by the time this happens man will have found
another life-supporting planet
"Informative, depressing, authoritative, and fascinating, the book is illustrated with imaginative and
dramatic pictures." Chicago. Children's Bk Center

Sunshine makes the seasons; illus. by Shelley
Freshman. Crowell 1974 33p illus maps (Let's-read-
and-find-out science bks) $3.95, lib. bdg. $4.70
(2-4)   525
1 Seasons
ISBN 0-690-00437-0; 0-690-00438-9
"This picture book for younger readers explains the
cycle of seasons as an effect of the earth-sun relationship. . . . The text is generally clear in describing the
progress of the tilted earth and the changes in
amounts of daylight and dark or heat and cold as we
revolve around the sun. Large black-and-white and
three-color illustrations and diagrams help make the
abstract concepts accessible." Booklist

Cartwright, Sally
The tide; illus. by Marilyn Miller. Coward-McCann
1971 46p illus (The Science is what and why bks) lib.
bdg. $4.49 (1-3)   525
1 Tides
ISBN 0-698-30367-9
"The difficult concept of tidal movement is presented here simply and understandably. In some 15
illustrated pages with minimal text on each, the
author discusses phenomena a child can observe for
himself at the ocean side (high tide, low tide, etc.).
From this logical beginning she leads readers farther
away to the moon's changing influence. Now the text
becomes longer, scientifically correct but still uncomplicated and never taking up more than half a page."
Sch Library J
"Delightful, almost poetic prose has been successfully combined with appealing illustrations." Sci Bks

Polgreen, John
Sunlight and shadows [by] John and Cathleen Polgreen. Doubleday 1967 57p illus $4.50 (1-3)   525
1 Shades and shadows 2 Solar radiation 3 Seasons
ISBN 0-385-05222-7
"The Polgreens have written a straightforward, no-
nonsense presentation of the subject. Changing
shadows are explained in terms of the changing location of the sun, and the changing locations are related
to rotation and revolution of the earth. The authors
suggest things to do: to chart the shadows, and to
observe the sun safely with a viewing box." The AAAS
Sci Bk List for Children
"Realistic illustrations in color and black-and-white
provide excellent clarification of the text in this concept book. . . . This is an attractive picture book for use
in the primary grades." Library J

Ravielli, Anthony

The world is round; written and illus. by Anthony Ravielli. Viking 1963 45p illus $5.95 (2-5)   525

1 Earth

ISBN 0-670-78533-4

"After defining a circle and a sphere, the author explains why the world seems flat to man and shows how learned men discovered that it is round. He then explains for the beginner how the Space Age is at last permitting us actually to see the curvature of the earth." The AAAS Sci Bk List for Children

"The history of the changing concepts of the earth's shape is briefly sketched in clear text and beautiful pictures in color. A handsome science picture book for the early elementary school ages." Horn Bk

Tresselt, Alvin

It's time now! Illus. by Roger Duvoisin. Lothrop 1969 unp illus $5.50, lib. bdg. $4.81 (k-2)   525

1 Seasons 2 Cities and towns

ISBN 0-688-41619-5; 0-688-51619-X

The author portrays the sights, sounds, and smells of the changing seasons in the city

"The illustrations, bright with color and movement, show city streets and parks; the text has a light and easy tone as it describes seasonal activities: the games, the holidays, the family outings, and the changing weather and foliage." Chicago. Children's Bk Center

526   Mathematical geography. Cartography

Brown, Lloyd A.

Map making; the art that became a science. Little 1960 217p illus maps $6.95 (5-7)   526

1 Map drawing 2 Maps

ISBN 0-316-11115-5

"An outstanding survey of the development of cartography from earliest times to the beginning of the twentieth century. The discussion takes into account discovery and geography, measuring instruments, compasses, clocks, navigation by the stars and related topics. Authenticated with reproductions of old prints." Sci Bks

McFall, Christie

Maps mean adventure. Rev. and enl. ed. Dodd [1973 c1972] 160p illus maps $5.95 (5-7)   526

1 Maps 2 Map drawing

ISBN 0-396-00614-3

First published 1961

In this survey of the history and uses of maps and the techniques of map making, different kinds of projections, scales, mapping agencies and projects are described. Many kinds of maps are considered, including topographic, geodetic, celestial, nautical, geologic, economic, treasure, census, and transportation

"Clear illustrations and examples of different maps and map-making techniques, and a list of addresses for obtaining maps round out the excellent coverage." Sch Library J

Oliver, John E.

What we find when we look at maps; illus. by Robert Galster. McGraw 1970 39p illus maps lib. bdg. $4.72 (3-5)   526

1 Maps 2 Map drawing

ISBN 0-07-047677-2

"A good book for encouraging spatial awareness and careful observation as well as for introducing the basic concepts used in map-making. The idea of a map is very deftly presented by the first few photographs, which show a close-up of a baseball diamond, then a view from high in the stands, then a view from a helicopter and last, the final view translated into a map. This comparison of photographs and diagrams proves useful several times during the book, as the author explains the use of symbols, scale drawing, grids and labels, and the various things that maps show, such as location, dimension, direction, etc." Chicago. Children's Bk Center

529   Time

Adler, Irving

The calendar [by] Irving and Ruth Adler. Day 1967 48p illus lib. bdg. $4.47 (3-5)   529

1 Calendars

ISBN 0-381-99975-0

"The Reason why books"

This "introduction to the calendar explains solar and lunar cycles and relates mathematical attempts to make days, weeks, months, and years coincide with these cycles. Directions for making a 50-year calendar and many diagrams and sketches are included. Slightly more matter-of-fact than is Brindze's 'The story of our calendar' [entered below] but otherwise similar in scope and coverage." Booklist

Time in your life; illus. by Ruth Adler. [Rev. ed] Day 1969 130p illus lib. bdg. $3.69 (5-7)   529

1 Time 2 Rhythm

ISBN 0-381-99982-3

First published 1955

"A comprehensive account of natural and man-made clocks and the relevance of time for man. Deals with many aspects of the subject, including the rhythms of nature, the history of the modern calendar, time zones, the use of clocks to estimate the age of the earth, and time in music and dancing." The AAAS Sci Bk List for Children

Bendick, Jeanne

The first book of time. Watts, F. 1963 70p illus maps lib. bdg. $3.90 (4-6)   529

1 Time

ISBN 0-531-00653-0

Illustrated by the author

Beginning with the idea that time, like space, is a dimension in which things can be measured, this book explains the complex concept of time. The history of measuring time is described as are various time-keeping devices. The book also deals briefly with Einstein's theory of relativity and geologic time

The book "written as a continuous narrative and exposition for pleasure reading as well as study, is guaranteed to clarify many aspects of the subject for any one and organize their thinking on time and space." N Y Her Trib Bks

Bradley, Duane

Time for you; illus. by Anne Marie Jauss. Lippincott 1960 110p illus lib. bdg. $3.39 (4-6)   529

1 Time 2 Clocks and watches

ISBN 0-397-30526-5

A "book about the devices that man has invented for the measurement of time. In historical arrangement, Mr. Bradley describes the systems evolved by ancient cultures, and he traces the development of modern devices to the day of mass production, with brief mention at the close of the book of the atomic clock. Unindexed." Chicago. Children's Bk Center

"Written in clear simple language with many illus-

Bradley, Duane—*Continued*
trations and diagrams." The AAAS Sci Bk List for
Children

Brindze, Ruth
The story of our calendar; illus. by Helen Carter.
Vanguard 1949 63p illus maps $4.95 (4-7)   529
   1 Calendars
   ISBN 0-8149-0278-2
"An expedition back into time to explore the real
story behind the neat little calendar we use today.
There are some nice bits of information about the
early races who were concerned with the calendar—
the Babylonians, the Egyptians and the Romans. The
illustrations in blue with touches of yellow carry out
the calendar's link with the heavens." Ontario Library
Rev
"Useful in reference work, this book is also a pleasure to handle." Horn Bk

Zarchy, Harry
Wheel of time; illus. by René Martin. Crowell 1957
133p illus $4.50 (6-7)   529
   1 Time 2 Calendars
   ISBN 0-690-88002-2
"The development of the concept of time and the
instruments invented to discover it is the theme of
this clearly written text. . . . Explanation is made of
the evolution of the calendar from the earliest to the
present plan for a World Calendar. There are chapters
on early types of timekeepers, the invention and
growth of mechanical clocks, and watches. Emphasis
is on time and its relation to science and on modern
achievements in timekeeping." Top of the News

530   Physics

Wilson, Mitchell
Seesaws to cosmic rays; a first view of physics; illus.
by Eva Cellini. Lothrop 1967 96p illus $5.95 (5-7)
                                          530
   1 Physics
   ISBN 0-688-41124-X
"An introduction to the basic ideas and fields of
physics, written by a research physicist and illustrated
with some ornamental pictures and a greater number
of useful diagrams. The chapters are on such subjects
as heat, light, the quantum theory, color, electronics,
et cetera; background information about theories and
scientists is given throughout the book." Chicago.
Children's Bk Center
Suggestions for additional reading: p89-91

530.1   Physics—Theories

Bendick, Jeanne
Space and time; written and illus. by Jeanne Bendick. Watts, F. 1968 66p illus (Science experiences)
lib. bdg. $4.90, pa $1.25 (2-4)   530.1
   1 Relativity (Physics)
   ISBN 0-531-01434-7; 0-531-02323-0
The author-illustrator delves into different notions
of space, emphasizing its close bond with time. In this
book space is considered in the sense of location or
position rather than astronomically.
The experiments are very simple, sometimes
requiring no equipment at all, and consist largely of
questions which develop concepts in logical order.
Spaced for easy reading, the cartoon-style illustra-

tions, clear text, and accents of bright blue contribute
to functional format." Library J

530.4   Physics—States of matter

Simon, Seymour
Wet & dry; illus. by Angie Culfogienis. McGraw
1969 39p illus (Let's try it out) $4.50, lib. bdg. $4.72
(1-3)   530.4
   1 Water 2 Matter
   ISBN 0-07-057425-1; 0-07-057426-X
"Children enjoy playing in water and with water.
Mr. Simon's book with its clever illustrations will help
them discover the properties of water, why things get
wet, how and why wet things dry, all about absorption
and evaporation, and other interesting facts. Open-
ended questions stimulate the experimental and
learning process." Sci Bks

530.72   Physics—Experiments

Mark, Steven J.
A physics lab of your own; illus. by Charles Wilton.
Houghton 1964 185p illus $3.95 (5-7)   530.72
   1 Physics—Experiments
   ISBN 0-395-06897-5
Included in this book are "seventy relatively simple
experiments in the various areas of physics which can
be performed in a home laboratory with easily procured material. For each experiment the author . . .
lists the equipment needed, describes the procedure
step by step, and explains, satisfactorily in most cases,
the results observed and the laws of physics demonstrated. Illustrated with numerous line drawings.
Some sources for the purchase of science supplies are
noted in the introductory chapter." Booklist

Stone, A. Harris
Take a balloon, by A. Harris Stone and Bertram M.
Siegel; illus. by Peter P. Plasencia. Prentice-Hall
1967 62p illus lib. bdg. $4.75 (3-6)   530.72
   1 Physics—Experiments 2 Balloons
   ISBN 0-13-882555-6
"The reader takes a balloon and by following the
instructions does any number of tricks or stunts from
electrostatics, propulsion (a balloon in space), sound
and pitch (a balloon inflated and deflated several
times), elasticity and thrust." Appraisal
"The authors endeavor to demonstrate basic scientific phenomena and the scientific method. Many of
the activities are significant and well within the ability
of most children. . . . The explanation and diagrams
seem inadequate in the experiment on 'the Bernoulli
Effect' and in the one on thrust. However, these
slight deficiencies do not seriously detract from the
overall usefulness of the book." Sch Library J

531   Mechanics

Adler, Irving
Energy; illus. by Ellen Viereck. Day 1970 48p illus
lib. bdg. $4.47 (3-5)   531
   1 Force and energy
   ISBN 0-381-99992-0
"The Reason why books"

Adler, Irving—Continued
"Covered are energy's many different forms: inertia, force, friction, heat, electrical, chemical, and nuclear—all adding up to the energy of work. Illustrations are simple and helpful. There is also a word list, as well as a very useful, specific table of contents—really needed since the book is so crammed full of information." Sch Library J

Bendick, Jeanne
Motion and gravity; written and illus. by Jeanne Bendick. Watts, F. 1972 70p illus (Science experiences) lib. bdg. $4.90 (3-5)   531
1 Motion 2 Gravitation
ISBN 0-531-01434-7
Using questions and simple examples, the author discusses such aspects of motion and gravity as: What makes things move? What effect does friction have on motion? Why do things slow down and stop moving? How can motion be measured?
"Those who know this author's previous simple outlines of natural phenomena . . . will welcome this addition with its humorous illustrations which are calculated to take the sting out of learning. Her books are good because they ask questions without giving all the answers, thus forcing the eight-year-old to think for himself, perhaps doing simple experiments in order to reason out the solution." Jr Bookshelf

Why things work; a book about energy; pictures by Jeanne Bendick with Karen Bendick. Parents Mag. Press 1972 64p illus lib. bdg. $4.59 (2-4)   531
1 Force and energy
ISBN 0-8193-0575-8
"A Stepping-stone book"
"All types of energy and their sources are presented in a simple, well-rounded text highlighting the cycles of the earth and sun, and showing how machines use and change energy." Chicago

Branley, Franklin M.
Gravity is a mystery; illus. by Don Madden. Crowell 1970 33p illus (Let's-read-and-find-out science bks) $4.50, lib. bdg. $5.25 (1-3)   531
1 Gravitation
ISBN 0-690-35071-6; 0-690-35072-4
"The force of gravity is explained with the aid of amusing color illustrations. The differences in gravitational forces on the sun, on the earth, and on other planets are carefully explained." The AAAS Sci Bk List for Children
"Mainly of value as a supplemental science book which primary-grade children can read for themselves, the account describes basic concepts." Booklist

Weight and weightlessness; illus. by Graham Booth. Crowell [1972 c1971] 33p illus (Let's-read-and-find-out science bks) $4.50, lib. bdg. $5.25 (1-3)   531
1 Gravitation 2 Weightlessness
ISBN 0-690-87329-8
The author provides a simple explanation of the subjects of gravity and weightlessness, drawing examples from both everyday life and the world of space. The principles behind how a spaceship is sent into orbit are also discussed
"There are few science books for children which can effectively simplify a difficult concept with a creative approach to the topic. This is one of the few. . . . [It combines] succinct text and appealing and clear pictures. . . . There is no comparable book on the subject for this grade level and few science books with such universal appeal." Sch Library J

Hellman, Hal
The lever and the pulley; illus. by Lynn Sweat. Evans, M.&Co. distributed in association with Lippincott 1971 45p illus $3.95 (3-5)   531
1 Machinery 2 Mechanics
ISBN 0-87131-072-4
"The text leads easily from the basic principles of the lever into its use in the seesaw and into other applications in scissors, pliers, pumps, beam balances, wheelbarrows, bottle openers, nutcrackers, the human arm, and various toys like bats and golf clubs. The reader is helped to see the lever in a ship's or car's wheel, a faucet handle, a screwdriver, and a door knob. . . .The concept of the pulley is next introduced and its advantages in flexibility of applications to moving loads is illustrated with experiments to be carried out with a single fixed pulley, a movable pulley, and with other more complicated arrangements." Sci Bks
"Clear diagrams, well-placed in relation to textual references to the principles they illustrate, add to the usefulness of a text that is simple and clear." Chicago. Children's Bk Center

Kaufmann, John
Streamlined; written and illus. by John Kaufmann. Crowell 1974 33p illus (Let's-read-and-find-out science bks) $3.95, lib. bdg. $4.70 (2-4)   531
1 Aerodynamics 2 Hydrodynamics
ISBN 0-690-00273-4; 0-690-00565-2
The author explains the nature of streamlining as it occurs in nature and as man has applied it to vehicles. Experiments are given to show how shape affects motion through air and water
"A well-focused, self-contained presentation that explains a fundamental physical concept. . . .The text offers simple explanations and is coordinated with uncomplicated drawings." Booklist

532 Mechanics of fluids

Branley, Franklin M.
Floating and sinking; illus. by Robert Galster. Crowell 1967 unp illus (Let's-read-and-find-out science bks) $4.50, lib. bdg. $5.25 (1-3)   532
1 Hydrodynamics
ISBN 0-690-30917-1; 0-690-30918-X
The author "invites the young reader to experiment and so to discover why things float and sink. Information for this age group is simplified in the text and attractively and effectively presented in illustrations." Adventuring With Bks. 2d edition

Corbett, Scott
What makes a boat float? Pictures by Victor Mays. Little 1970 43p illus lib. bdg. $4.95 (3-5)   532
1 Hydrodynamics 2 Boats and boating 3 Marine engineering
ISBN 0-316-15713-9
"An Atlantic Monthly Press book"
"The physical properties of water, gravity, density and the principles of buoyancy are explained as the fundamentals of naval engineering, and in particular for designing hulls for various types of surface and subsurface vessels. Good drawings clarify a well-written text. Good collateral reading for elementary science students." Sci Bks
Index and glossary: p39-42

534　Sound and related vibrations

Branley, Franklyn M.

High sounds, low sounds; illus. by Paul Galdone. Crowell 1967 unp illus (Let's-read-and-find-out science bks) $4.50, lib. bdg. $5.25, pa $1.25 (1-3)　534

1 Sound

ISBN 0-690-38017-8; 0-690-38018-6; 0-690-00638-1

"This book describing sounds and how they are made also contains several experiments that illustrate the basic concepts of physics involved." Chicago

"Humorous illustrations reinforce the ideas expressed in a very simple text."Booklist

535　Visible light (Optics)

Adler, Irving

Shadows, by Irving and Ruth Adler. [Rev. ed] Day 1968 48p illus lib. bdg. $4.47 (3-5)　535

1 Shades and shadows

ISBN 0-381-99955-6

"The Reason why books"

First published 1961

This book "maintains interest by progressing logically from the simple and familiar (one's own shadow) to the more complex (eclipses, cameras). Explains how to measure heights, tell time and judge texture and shape with the use of shadows, and encourages the reader to experiment." The AAAS Sci Bk List for Children

Word list: p48

Freeman, Ira M.

Light and radiation; illus. by George T. Resch. Random House 1968 125p illus (Random House Science lib) $3.50, lib. bdg. $4.99, pa $1.50 (5-7)　535

1 Light 2 Radiation

ISBN 0-394-80938-6; 0-394-90938-0; 0-394-81885-7

First published 1965 with title: All about light and radiation

"The way light travels, how we use it, invisible light and rays, and new developments such as masers and lasers are covered in this . . . survey." Children's Bks, 1965

"A clear, concise introduction . . . [in which] numerous photographs and diagrams pertinently illustrate textual concepts." Booklist

Healey, Frederick

Light and color; illus. by Patricia Hamilton. Day 1962 48p illus (Finding out about science) lib. bdg. $3.96 (3-5)　535

1 Light 2 Color

ISBN 0-381-99800-2

"The basic physical properties of light are revealed in this discussion of visible light. Helpful experiments and instructive illustrations give insights into reflection, refraction, color blending, and other light phenomena. A greater appreciation of the sun as man's ultimate source of energy is gained." The AAAS Sci Bk List for Children

Includes a glossary

Kettelkamp, Larry

Shadows; written and illus. by Larry Kettelkamp. Morrow 1957 63p illus lib. bdg. $4.59 (3-6)　535

1 Shades and shadows　　2 Shadow pantomimes and plays

ISBN 0-688-30122-3

This book "deals with shadows from the viewpoints of both amusement and usefulness. Suggestions are given for shadow animals made with the hands, cardboard figures for Chinese shadow plays, a shadow stage, and human shadow plays. The second half of the book discusses, and illustrates with experiments, their uses to science, such as in measuring time, in astronomy, X ray, and aerial photography. Clear, instructive illustrations; large print." Booklist

Tricks of eye and mind; the story of optical illusion; with illus. by the author. Morrow 1974 127p illus $4.75, lib. bdg. $4.32 (4-6)　535

1 Optical illusions

ISBN 0-688-21829-6; 0-688-31829-0

"By explaining the physiological processes that result in optical illusions, the author provides valuable information on perception in general. This book is not merely an enjoyable collection of visual tricks; it describes the parts of the eye, tells of well-known experiments in perception, then gives examples of various types of illusions and ways in which they are achieved. A final section mentions some of the practical uses of illusion, from animal camouflage to slide projection and graphic arts." Booklist

"There are a lot of ideas here for individual or class projects, experiments, and library research; a balanced blend of science, art, and entertainment. The illustrations are black and white." Sci and Children

Simon, Seymour

Light & dark; illus. by Angeline Culfogienis. McGraw 1970 47p illus lib. bdg. $4.72 (1-3)　535

1 Light 2 Shades and shadows

ISBN 0-07-057428-6

"Let's-try-it-out"

"First concepts of shadows and reflections are dramatized in a picture-book of simple experiments. . . . The book presents everyday observations, each made meaningful by a series of questions." Sch Library J

Ubell, Earl

The world of candle and color; photographs by Arline Strong. Atheneum Pubs. 1969 49p illus $4.75, lib. bdg. $4.87 (4-6)　535

1 Light

ISBN 0-689-20446-9; 0-689-20447-7

In this book the author describes "the properties of light. Brief sections introduce readers to sources of light, shadows, colors, mirror images, lenses, the speed of light, and the effect of light on life." Sch Library J

This is "an informative text for young readers and will create a desire for additional information. There is no list of books given for further reading, however." Sci Bks

535.072　Visible light (Optics)—Experiments

Beeler, Nelson F.

Experiments in optical illusion [by] Nelson F. Beeler and Franklyn M. Branley; illus. by Fred H. Lyon. Crowell 1951 114p illus $4.50 (5-7)　535.072

1 Optics—Experiments 2 Optical illusions

ISBN 0-690-27507-2

"A fascinating book, both instructive and entertaining. Following a description of the mechanism of the eye are pages of experiments and diagrams presenting

Beeler, Nelson F.—*Continued*
and explaining optical illusions which are a part of everyday seeing." Booklist

Freeman, Mae
Fun and experiments with light, by Mae and Ira Freeman. Random House 1963 58p illus $3.95, lib. bdg. $3.99 (5-7)   535.072
1 Light
ISBN 0-394-80285-3; 0-394-90285-8
"Thirty-two entertaining experiments with light, described in clear text and photographs. Most of the materials needed can be found around the house." Booklist

Schneider, Herman
Science fun with a flashlight, by Herman and Nina Schneider; pictures by Harriet Sherman. McGraw 1975 unp illus lib. bdg. $5.72 (1-4)   535.072
1 Science—Experiments 2 Shades and shadows 3 Light
ISBN 0-07-055455-2
By using a flashlight and the simplest equipment, readers can experiment to learn about light, shadows, colors, filters and the sources of light in outer space

535.6   Color

Adler, Irving
Color in your life; illus. by Ruth Adler. Day 1962 127p illus lib. bdg. $4.29 (5-7)   535.6
1 Color
ISBN 0-381-99995-5
The author explains "the basic structure and characteristics (e.g.: reflection and diffraction) of light, and the more complex phenomena (polarization, the Doppler effect, etc.). [He] discusses sources of color in nature and the role of color in printing, television, and photography. Scientific explanations are given for phenomena such as the coloring of soap bubbles, [and] the sunset." The AAAS Sci Bk List for Children
Another of the author's "accurate, clear, and entertaining books based on recent scientific knowledge and theory. . . . [He] touches on aspects of organic chemistry and quantum theory without overwhelming or talking down. He gives abundant examples and a few experiments. Good, clear drawings." Library J
"Unlike most science books, it should appeal strongly to young people who have an artistic bent." Pub W

Emberley, Ed
Green says go. Little 1968 32p illus lib. bdg. $4.95 (k-3)   535.6
1 Color
ISBN 0-316-23599-7
The author "first shows primary, secondary and complementary colors and then demonstrates how the addition of black or white can darken or lighten colors. The second part of the book plays with some of the color-associated terms in common use . . . and points out various ways in which color is used for communication." Sat Rev

536   Heat

Adler, Irving
Heat and its uses [by] Irving and Ruth Adler. Rev. ed. of "Heat." Day 1973 48p illus lib. bdg. $4.47 (4-6)   536
1 Heat
ISBN 0-381-99638-7

"The Reason why books"
First published 1964 with title: Heat
The authors discuss the conduction, measurement, molecular movement, and uses of heat

Hot and cold; illus. by Peggy Adler. Rev. ed. Day 1975 128p illus lib. bdg. $5.95 (4-6)   536
1 Heat 2 Cold 3 Temperature
ISBN 0-381-99990-4
First published 1959
The author "explains the nature of heat and cold, examines theories of heat and its behavior, discusses methods of producing and practical uses of very high and very low temperatures, and describes devices used in measuring temperature. A methodical and understandable treatment of the subject." Booklist [review of the 1959 edition]

Balestrino, Philip
Hot as an ice cube; illus. by Tomie de Paola. Crowell 1971 33p illus (Let's-read-and-find-out science bks) $4.50, lib. bdg. $5.25 (k-3)   536
1 Heat
ISBN 0-690-40414-X; 0-690-40415-8
"Basic information about heat and cold is clearly and simply presented in attractive picture-book format. Balestrino explains that there is heat in everything, even icebergs, discusses the relationship between heat and molecular motion, and gives several easy experiments. He also tells why some objects expand when heated and mentions that heat flows from a hot object to a cooler one." Booklist

537.072   Electricity—Experiments

Feravolo, Rocco V.
Junior science book of electricity; illus. by Evelyn Urbanowich. Garrard 1960 61p illus (Junior science bks) lib. bdg. $3.12 (3-5)   537.072
1 Electricity
ISBN 0-8116-6151-2
"A basic treatment of static and current electricity. Characteristics of electricity are investigated through simple experiments with circuits. Some of the topics covered are fuses, dry cells, short circuits and electromagnets." The AAAS Sci Bk List for Children
"Easy directions and informative illustrations clarify the basics of a complex subject for young children." Hodges. Bks for Elem Sch Libraries

Stone, A. Harris
Turned on: a look at electricity, by A. Harris Stone and Bertram M. Siegel; illus. by Peter P. Plasencia. Prentice-Hall 1970 64p illus $4.75 (4-7)   537.072
1 Electricity 2 Magnetism 3 Scientists
ISBN 0-13-933093-3
"This book presents, through a combination of brief, factual information, provocative questions, and instructive drawings, open-end experiments which demonstrate scientific principles or laws discovered by William Gilbert, Van Guericke, Volta, Faraday, Einstein, and others. The suggested experiments are designed to stimulate individual thought and research on magnetic and electrical phenomena and use materials and equipment which are comparatively easy to obtain or construct but require care in handling; 6 of the 13 experiments contain cautionary warnings or suggest adult help." Booklist
Glossary: p59-64

538　Magnetism

Adler, Irving

Magnets [by] Irving and Ruth Adler. Day 1966 48p illus $4.47 (3-5)　　　　538

1 Magnetism 2 Magnets

ISBN 0-381-99962-9

"The Reason why books"

The authors present a "clear picture of all the different types of magnets by which we are surrounded. These include our earth, the sun, and the stars, as well as the more familiar bar magnets, horseshoe magnets, and electromagnets. As we delve into the atoms and molecules which make up these materials, it becomes very clear why a magnet acts as it does. An excellent primer [which] . . . should excite the imagination." The AAAS Sci Bk List for Children

"The Adlers never skimp anything important even in simplifying." Horn Bk

Branley, Franklin M.

North, south, east, and west; illus. by Robert Galster. Crowell 1966 unp illus map (Let's-read-and-find-out science bks) $4.50, lib. bdg. $5.25 (1-3)　　　538

1 Compass

ISBN 0-690-58608-6; 0-690-58609-4

In this book "the young reader learns that left is left and right is right no matter what direction he is facing, up is away from earth and down is toward the earth no matter whether he stands on his feet or on his head, and down continues to the center of the earth. Then directions are taught by the position of the rising and setting sun. Observation of shadows and their changing direction during the day is the 'do-it-yourself activity' that reinforces learning. Finally the reader is introduced to the magnetic compass and the compass 'rose' on maps that indicates North." Sci Bks

The book consists of "simple text and cheery, strong drawings." Scientific Am

Feravolo, Rocco V.

Junior science book of magnets; illus. by Evelyn Urbanowich. Garrard 1960 64p illus map (Junior science bks) lib. bdg. $3.12 (3-5)　　　538

1 Magnets 2 Electromagnets

ISBN 0-8116-6155-5

"The properties and uses of magnets and electromagnets are described clearly and accurately, with the aid of easy experiments." The AAAS Sci Bk List for Children

"Large, black type, wide margins, attractive informative black-and-yellow illustration." Library J

539.7　Atomic and nuclear physics

Gallant, Roy A.

Explorers of the atom. Doubleday 1974 79p illus $4.95, lib. bdg. $5.70 (6-7)　　　539.7

1 Atomic energy

ISBN 0-385-03583-7; 0-385-06459-4

This book includes an "introduction to what the atom really is, the development of the atomic theory from Democritus to Heisenberg, and a particularly engrossing account of the uses and misuses of atomic energy today. Succinct, clear, full of well-placed explanatory diagrams, this book provides a valuable introduction to the knowledge about atoms. Detailed index." Appraisal

Hyde, Margaret O.

Atoms today & tomorrow. 4th ed. by Margaret O. Hyde and Bruce G. Hyde; illus. by Ed Malsberg. McGraw 1970 141p illus lib. bdg. $4.72 (6-7)　539.7

1 Atomic energy

ISBN 0-07-031570-1

First published 1955

Explains in simple terms how atomic energy is produced and discusses its present and future peacetime uses in medicine, agriculture, space and industry

"This is an interesting, accurate, and readable account of the atomic age and its future. . . . The author makes no attempt to be quantitative. . . . The book concludes with advice for the reader on how he may be part of the atomic age either as a participant or part of an informed public." Sch Library J

Glossary of atomic language: p129-36. Sources of additional information: p137-38

540　Chemistry

Freeman, Ira M.

The science of chemistry, by Ira M. Freeman and A. Rae Patton; illus. by Zenowij Onyshkewych. Random House 1968 131p illus (Random House Science lib) lib. bdg. $4.99, pa $1.50 (5-7)　　　540

1 Chemistry

ISBN 0-394-90994-1; 0-394-81084-8

"A good general view is provided of the many different facets of the science of chemistry at the advanced elementary level, and this book is designed to whet the appetite of those young readers who might eventually find careers in this field. . . . The printing is excellent and format and illustrations are good. Photographs are clear and well chosen. Where formulas are introduced, they are simply explained in proper context with presentation of relevant theory. The book starts with the story of the beginnings of chemistry, followed by a discussion on atoms, molecules and compounds. This leads to a look at oil; then steel; then the chemistry of living matter and the development of chemotherapy; and the use of chemical methods in the development of fibers, plastics, and rubber. It ends with a look at the future. Some of the factual material has been simplified to make it more appealing to young readers, and the parts on biological chemistry lose some accuracy because of this." Sci Bks

540.1　Chemistry—Philosophy and theory

Aylesworth, Thomas G.

The alchemists: magic into science. Addison-Wesley 1973 128p illus $4.75 (6-7)　　　540.1

1 Alchemy

ISBN 0-201-00143-8

"An Addisonian Press book"

"This is a well-written account of the rogues, rascals, magicians and scientists who from ancient Egypt to contemporary times have been smitten (for a number of reasons) with the desire to change metals into precious gold. The author presents brief biographies of notorious alchemists and describes interesting situations involving them and their discoveries, including chemicals used in dyes, medicine, glass, waterproofing, sleeping potions and a pain-killing drug. The author points out that the age-old attempt to develop a little man grown in a bottle, the feverish search for the philosopher's stone and the hope of

Aylesworth, Thomas G.—*Continued*

discovering an elixir of life are not such crazy ideas in the light of what modern science is accomplishing today." Sci Bks

"It's an engrossing book, written with verve and wit; the period illustrations are arresting." Pub W

Bibliographic references included in Acknowledgements: p123-24

540.72 Chemistry— Experiments

Shalit, Nathan

Cup and saucer chemistry; illus. by Charles Waterhouse. Grosset [1972] 93p illus $3.95, pa $2.95 (4-6)   **540.72**

1 Chemistry—Experiments

ISBN 0-488-02818-2; 0-448-11690-1

The author provides "an opportunity to explore and investigate chemical elements and compounds in common foods and cleansing agents. Precise directions, which call for ingredients found in storage cupboards and in the refrigerator, are given for some exciting chemical determination for reactants, acids, bases, salts, precipitates, crystalizations, formation of gases and some fun things such as mystery writing." Sci Bks

Here are "chemical experiments intended for young scientists at the kitchen sink, but also suitable for the classroom. . . . The experiments are clearly illustrated, explained, and simple, but most still require supervision and not all are guaranteed successes." Sch Library J

541 Physical and theoretical chemistry

Bronowski, J.

Biography of an atom, by J. Bronowski and Millicent E. Selsam; illus. with pictures by Weimer Pursell and with photographs. Harper 1965 43p illus lib. bdg. $4.79 (4-7)   **541**

1 Atoms 2 Carbon

ISBN 0-06-020641-1

"This is the biography of a single atom—what it is like, where it came from, and its place in the world. There are about one hundred different kinds of atoms, but this story will be about an atom of carbon because carbon is found in every living cell, and its atoms therefore enter into your life and mine." p6

"The very best kind of science writing: simple, lucid, dignified, well-organized and stripped of non-essentials. The diagrams are placed and labelled carefully and there is, out of this matter-of-fact and scientific approach, an honest feeling of wonder communicated: a sense of the marvel of design and continuity in the world about us." Chicago. Children's Bk Center

548 Crystallography

David, Eugene

Crystal magic; pictures by Abner Graboff. Prentice-Hall 1965 unp illus $5.95, pa 95¢ (k-2)   **548**

1 Crystallography

ISBN 0-13-194977-2; 0-13-194969-1

"This book develops the concept of what a crystal is with very simple examples. Clear directions are given for making a salt crystal garden and rock candy. Most of the illustrations are clear and childlike. . . . The vocabulary is well chosen for listening in the pre-school or for the second-grade reader." Sch Library J

Gans, Roma

Millions and millions of crystals; illus. by Giulio Maestro. Crowell 1973 33p illus (Let's-read-and-find-out science bks) $3.95, lib. bdg. $4.70 (2-4)   **548**

1 Crystallography

ISBN 0-690-54029-9; 0-690-54030-2

An introduction to the characteristics, formation, and uses of crystals. Examples include sugar, salt, snowflakes, sand, jewels, and rock crystals which are found in caves in the form of stalagmites and stalactites

"The black-and-white line drawings are a perfect complement to and extension of the text. Simple activities are described, such as pulling off layers of mica with a pin and examining sugar and salt crystals on dark paper in the sunlight or through a magnifying glass. This is a fine book, highly recommended as a supplementary classroom book and for pleasure reading." Sci Bks

Sander, Lenore

The curious world of crystals; illus. by John Kaufmann. Prentice-Hall 1964 64p illus $4.95 (4-7)   **548**

1 Crystallography

ISBN 0-13-195586-1

"Junior research books"

An "introduction to crystallography, giving adequate background material about the forms of matter and giving clear explanations of the qualities that distinguish crystalline structure. The text describes the way in which crystals grow and gives instructions for simple home demonstrations in which crystals can be grown. The author does not go into too much detail about molecular structure: she refers briefly to some of the identification techniques and to some of the uses of crystalline substances. The illustrations vary in usefulness." Chicago. Children's Bk Center

549 Mineralogy

Fenton, Carroll Lane

Rocks and their stories; by Carroll Lane Fenton and Mildred Adams Fenton. Doubleday 1951 112p illus $5.95, lib. bdg. $6.70 (4-6)   **549**

1 Mineralogy 2 Rocks 3 Petrology

ISBN 0-385-07470-0; 0-385-07113-2

"An introduction to petrology, distinguishing rocks, stones, and minerals; explaining methods of identification; and discussing 40 basic minerals." Hodges. Bks for Elem Sch libraries

"Its brief 112 pages contain fine information under alluring titles and the many photographic illustrations are superbly chosen and reproduced." N Y Her Trib Bks

Loomis, Frederic Brewster

Field book of common rocks and minerals. . . . [Rev] with 47 colored specimens and over 100 other illus. from photographs by W. E. Corbin and drawings by the author. Putnam 1948 352p illus (Putnam's Nature field bks) $5.95 (5-7)   **549**

1 Mineralogy 2 Rocks

ISBN 0-399-10286-8

First published 1923

"For identifying the rocks and minerals of the

Loomis, Frederic Brewster—*Continued*
United States and interpreting their origins and
meanings." Subtitle
"A useful guide to observation, collection, and
study which requires little background or equipment.
The minerals are grouped according to their chemical
composition, appearance, specific gravity, and many
other distinguishing characteristics. Uses, natural
combinations and important national deposits are discussed. The rocks are then taken up and grouped by
origin, giving their composition, visible features, and
natural occurrence." The AAAS Sci Bk List for Young
Adults
   Bibliography: p270-71

Pough, Frederick H.
   A field guide to rocks and minerals. 3d ed. Houghton 1960 349p illus maps (The Peterson Field guide
ser) $8.95   549
   1 Mineralogy 2 Rocks
   ISBN 0-395-08106-8
   First published 1953
"A complete explanation of collecting and testing
methods, physical and chemical properties, and types
and geographic distribution of rocks. A well-
organized and detailed description of many common
minerals follows, in which are given the environment,
physical properties, composition, tests, interesting
facts about, and occurrence of each. Slightly more
advanced than Loomis's 'Field Book,' [entered above]
and with more emphasis on minerals." The AAAS Sci
Bk List for Children
   Glossary: p333-38. Bibliography: p339-40

Shuttlesworth, Dorothy
   The story of rocks; illus. by Su Zan N. Swain. Rev.
ed. Doubleday 1966 57p illus (Nature bks. for young
people) $4.95, lib. bdg. $5.70 (5-7)   549
   1 Rocks 2 Mineralogy
   ISBN 0-385-06928-6; 0-385-06929-4
   First published 1956
This book for the rock collector not only tells how
rocks are formed and gives various tests for their
identification, but also discusses beautiful and practical minerals, metals with strange properties, and rock
oddities
   "A well written, beautifully illustrated and practical
book, packed with information." Chicago Sunday Trib
   Books to take on collecting trips for good reading:
p55. Likely hunting grounds: p56

Simon, Seymour
   The rock-hound's book; illus. by Tony Chen. Viking
1973 80p illus lib. bdg. $5.95 (4-6)   549
   1 Mineralogy 2 Rocks—Collection and preservation
   ISBN 0-670-60240-X
The text "deals with some of the elementary facts
and concepts about rocks, minerals and ores. Definitions of 'mineral,' 'rock' and 'ore' and explanations of
the formation of igneous, sedimentary and metamorphic rocks are given. The author describes searching
for novel rocks, using tools to take rock samples,
avoiding fracturing rocks unnecessarily and making
rock collections. There are also discussions of clues for
identifying rocks and minerals and use of Mohr's scale
for detecting hardness. The book ends with a 'mineral
check list' for identification." Sci Bks
   "Safety precautions are given, and information is
reinforced by occasional repetition. Also included are:
an index, reading list, and a section on where to buy
materials. The book is well designed with wide margins, ample spacing between lines, and handsome
titles. The minerals and rocks are shown in full color,
while other illustrations of . . . children are in black,
gray, and white." Sch Library J

Zim, Herbert S.
   Rocks and minerals; a guide to familiar minerals,
gems, ores and rocks, by Herbert S. Zim and Paul R.
Shaffer; illus. by Raymond Perlman. Golden Press
1957 160p illus maps (A Golden Nature guide) lib.
bdg. $4.95, pa $1.50 (4-7)   549
   1 Mineralogy 2 Rocks
   ISBN 0-307-63502-3; 0-307-24499-7
   First published by Simon & Schuster
A pocket "handbook that is educational for
amateurs and useful for quick reference for professionals. Introductory material on the earth and its
rocks gives basic geological information and activities
for amateurs are suggested in identifying, collecting
and studying rocks and minerals. Colored diagrams
and pictures of specimens aid in identification.
Description [of over 400 specimens] include information on formation, structure, use and importance."
Chicago. Children's Bk Center
   More information: p156. Museums and exhibits:
p157

551   Physical and dynamic geology

Ames, Gerald
   The earth's story, by Gerald Ames & Rose Wyler.
Creative Educ. Soc. in cooperation with the Am.
Mus. of Natural Hist. 1967 224p illus map (Creative
science ser) lib. bdg. $6.95 (4-7)   551
   1 Geology
   ISBN 0-87191-012-8
   First published 1957
The contents of this volume include: The ever
changing land; Building and rebuilding; The parade of
life; Treasures of our planet; Guides to discovery
   Glossary: p221

Bendick, Jeanne
   The shape of the earth; written and illus. by Jeanne
Bendick. Rand McNally 1965 72p illus maps $3.95
(4-6)   551
   1 Earth
   ISBN 0-528-80065-5
An "introduction to the earth giving basic facts
about its origin, shape, and composition. [It] explains
the influence of the earth's shape on seasons and
weather and describes how the surface of the earth is
changed by internal shifts in its structure and surface
erosion. There are also two brief chapters on early
exploration and map making." Booklist
   "The author's own illustrations are closely integrated with the text to facilitate comprehension. This
book will not fail to whet the scientific interest and
aptitude of young readers." The AAAS Sci Bk List for
Children
   Definitions of some of the words in this book: p4-7

Branley, Franklyn M.
   The beginning of the earth; illus. by Giulio Maestro. Crowell 1972 33p illus (Let's-read-and-find-out
science bks) $4.50, lib. bdg. $5.25 (1-3)   551
   1 Earth 2 Geology
   ISBN 0-690-12987-4; 0-690-12988-2
The author "presents theories of the earth's formation from clouds of dust and gasses billions of years
ago at about the time other planets and the sun were
forming. He conveys a sense of immense time by his
slowly built descriptions of the earth's materials packing together, cooling under constant rains, and hard-
ening into solid rock on the surface. . . . The illustra-

Branley, Franklyn M.—*Continued*
tions in purple, blue, and black show amorphous masses changing into more identifiable shapes." Booklist

"While there is no extraneous material in this description of the evolution of the earth through the long millennia of whirling dust, heat and rain, the text has an almost lyric cadence and is imbued with an appreciation of the slow, slow passage of time during which the earth formed." Chicago. Children's Bk Center

Lauber, Patricia
This restless earth; illus. by John Polgreen. Random House 1970 129p illus maps (Random House Science lib) $3.50, lib. bdg. $4.99, pa $1.50 (5-7)
551

1 Geology
ISBN 0-394-80802-9; 0-394-90802-3; 0-394-80803-7
Replaces the author's: All about the planet earth, published 1962
This account of the sources that shape and change the earth discusses volcanoes, earthquakes, continents, folded mountains, ridges and rifts. It also describes the birth of the island of Surtsey off the coast of Iceland
"Lacking in this otherwise good book is a list of references of selected readings." Sci Bks

Matthews, William H.
The earth's crust, by William H. Matthews III; illus. with photographs. Watts, F. 1971 92p illus maps lib. bdg. $3.90 (5-7)
551

1 Geology
ISBN 0-531-00724-3
"A First book"
This book describes "the nature of the earth's crust including data from space, probes of what lies below, deformation by earthquakes and volcanoes, the history of the earth as gathered from clues, and the resources found in it." Appraisal
"The information on each subject is brief, but the presentation is clear and the numerous diagrams, maps, and photographs are helpful." Booklist
Glossary: p84-87

The story of the earth, by William H. Matthew III; illus. by John E. Alexander. Harvey House 1968 124p illus (A Story of science ser. bk) lib. bdg. $5.49 (5-7)
551

1 Geology
ISBN 0-8178-3932-1
"A concise and accurate introductory geology book. Covered are minerals, rocks, volcanoes, earthquakes, mountains, erosion, and the geologic calendar. The illustrations are helpful drawings and photographs, some of the latter in color. The material is presented simply, the volume is easy to handle, and the entire package makes a satisfactory addition to the growing collection of books in this field for young readers." Library J
Some books to read: p113-14. Glossary: p115-20

Ruchlis, Hy
Your changing earth; illus. by Janet and Alex D'Amato. Harvey House 1963 40p illus (A Science parade bk) lib. bdg. $4.29 (2-4)
551

1 Earth
ISBN 0-8178-3462-1
"Beginning with the origin of the earth and solar system, the author tells how the land, sea, and air developed, how mountains formed and changed, and how landscapes are transformed as a result of natural forces." The AAAS Sci Bk List for Children
"With pictures on almost every page . . . and over-

simplified text, this will be useful as a first book on the subject for primary grades." Sch Library J

551.2 Earthquakes. Volcanoes

Brown, Billye Walker
Historical catastrophes: earthquakes, by Billye Walker Brown and Walter R. Brown. Addison-Wesley 1974 191p illus $4.95 (5-7)
551.2

1 Earthquakes
ISBN 0-201-00546-8
"An Addisonian Press book"
This is a "chronological account of earthquakes from the Lisbon quake of 1755 to the Alaskan disaster of 1964. In addition to discussion of ancient beliefs and theories of tremors and quakes, scientific explanations of the causes of earthquakes are also provided. The black-and-white photographs are interesting." Sch Library J

Lauber, Patricia
Earthquakes; new scientific ideas about how and why the earth shakes; illus. with maps and diagrams by Cal Sacks and with photographs. Random House 1972 81p illus maps $3.95, lib. bdg. $5.39 (4-6)
551.2

1 Earthquakes
ISBN 0-394-82373-7; 0-394-92373-1
"Covered are the origins of earthquakes, tsunami, Pangaea, and the history of earthquakes in Alaska, California and Japan. Definitions of terms are provided in the text." Sch Library J
The book "provides remarkably current coverage of recent developments in one of the fastest moving fields of the earth sciences. Errors are few and insignificant; the arrangement and balance of the presentation is commendable. . . . [Readers] who want to know what new earth science terms like 'continental drift' and 'plate tectonics' are all about, will come away from this well illustrated and easily read volume with a much improved appreciation of this ever-changing planet and an understanding of why these earthquake-caused changes will always be with us." Sci Bks

Marcus, Rebecca B.
The first book of volcanoes & earthquakes. Rev. ed. Watts, F. 1972 86p illus maps lib. bdg. $3.90 (5-7)
551.2

1 Volcanoes 2 Earthquakes
ISBN 0-531-00799-5
"A First book"
First published 1963
The author discusses the reasons for volcanoes and earthquakes, their effects on the earth and its inhabitants, and the methods used by man for studying them. The text is supplemented with black-and-white photographs, diagrams, and maps. The appendix lists some of the great volcanic eruptions and destructive earthquakes." Appraisal
Glossary: p78-82

Matthews, William H.
The story of volcanoes and earthquakes, by William H. Matthews III. Harvey House 1969 126p illus maps lib. bdg. $5.49 (4-6)
551.2

1 Volcanoes 2 Earthquakes
ISBN 0-8178-4522-4
This book answers such questions as "What causes earthquakes? Why do we have volcanoes? Are volcanoes and earthquakes capable only of destruction—or is there some useful aspect to these great natural forces?" Preface

Matthews, William H.—*Continued*

"Most of the information presented here has appeared in similar books for young people. . . . However, since the pictures and text are of superior quality, libraries in which there is much interest in earth science would want to add the Matthews title to their collections." Sch Library J

Some books to read: p116-17; Glossary: p118-22

551.3   Glaciers. Icebergs

Gans, Roma

Icebergs; illus. by Bobri. Crowell 1964 unp illus (Let's-read-and find-out science bks) $4.50, lib. bdg. $5.25 (1-3)   551.3

1 Icebergs

ISBN 0-690-42774-3; 0-690-42775-1

The text explains "for the young child what icebergs are, where they come from, and the dangers they present to ships." Hodges. Bks for Elem Sch Libraries

Young children "will welcome a book they can read themselves. . . . Bold illustrations augment the text nicely." Library J

Lockard, Roget

Glaciers, illus. by Stefan Martin. Coward-McCann 1970 45p illus (The Science is what and why bks) lib. bdg. $4.49 (1-3)   551.3

1 Glaciers

ISBN 0-698-30176-5

There are places on earth where no plants grow and the sun never warms the land because thick sheets of ice called glaciers cover the earth. This book tells where glaciers come from, how long they have been on earth, how they form, and what effect they have had on the earth

Matthews, William H.

The story of glaciers and the ice age, by William H. Matthews III. Harvey House 1974 142p illus maps lib. bdg. $5.79 (5-7)   551.3

1 Glaciers

ISBN 0-8178-5142-9

The author "examines the theories of formation and movement of glaciers together with the influence of glaciers on the topography and fauna. . . . The sections on the formation and movement of glaciers include many theories of these processes, with excellent explanations of each of the theories and a discussion of the validity of each. The treatment of the fauna of the pre-glacial and glacial periods should be of special interest." Sci Bks

"The book has a colorful and attractive cover and is generously illustrated with photos, maps, and diagrams. It has a glossary of over 100 terms, is well indexed, and includes a relatively complete list of other books on the topic. It will best serve as a reference source in the earth sciences; however, a student will pick up the book as an assignment and find himself reading for pleasure." Sci and Children

551.4   Geomorphology

Atwood, Ann

The wild young desert; text and photographs by Ann Atwood. Scribner 1970 unp illus lib. bdg. $5.95 (4-6)   551.4

1 Deserts

ISBN 0-684-12625-7

The author depicts the desert's slow cycle of geologic change, the effects of wind and water, and the plants and animals which have adapted to the desert environment

"The text is sensitively, even poetically, written and will stir the imagination of some children; others may find it too generalized and unspecific and wish for more factual detail. There won't be any disagreement over Miss Atwood's dramatically juxtaposed color photographs, majestic long views alternating with close-ups of dazzling flowers, formations of agate and quartz, animals resting in shadows out of the sun. They are superbly beautiful and excellently reproduced." N Y Times Bk Rev

Berger, Melvin

The new water book; illus. by Leonard Kessler. Crowell 1973 111p illus $5.50 (4-6)   551.4

1 Water 2 Water—Pollution

ISBN 0-690-58146-7

"A treatment of the subject that is comprehensive in scope, simple in style, lucid in explanation, and given added interest by the inclusion throughout the text of home demonstrations, helpfully illustrated and clearly outlined. The text discusses the composition of water, its three states (liquid, solid, and gas), and some of the unusual properties of water; it describes the need for water in plants, human beings, and other animal life; it surveys water in agriculture and industry, describes the water cycle, and discusses the water supply and water pollution." Chicago. Children's Bk Center

"A list of more advanced books for further reading is appended." Booklist

Oceanography lab. Day 1973 126p illus maps (Scientists at work) lib. bdg. $5.95 (4-6)   551.4

1 Oceanography—Research 2 Oceanography as a profession 3 Woods Hole, Mass. Oceanographic Institute

ISBN 0-381-99940-8

"Woods Hole Oceanographic Institution on Cape Cod is the setting for the story of what an oceanographer does. . . . The early chapters discuss the reasons for establishing research bases, how research projects are initiated, how developed and how financed. The succeeding chapters each discuss the work of one type of scientist: the geologist, the bacteriologist, the chemist, the biologist, etc. There is a chapter on a ten-day expedition aboard the research vessel 'Knorr'; another on the work of the submarine 'Alvin'." Appraisal

"Excellent photographs of the Institute and its research activities on Cape Cod and at sea add to the effectiveness of this generally well-conceived and well-executed presentation." Library J

Further reading: p123-24

Branley, Franklyn M.

Shakes, quakes, and shifts: earth tectonics; illus. by Daniel Maffia. Crowell 1974 33p illus $5.50, lib. bdg. $6.25 (5-7)   551.4

1 Continental drift

ISBN 0-690-00422-2; 0-690-00423-0

"Mr. Branley explains how our planet is still shifting and changing as it has been doing for millions of years due to atmospheric gases and the inner core of the earth itself. He devotes much of the text to a discussion of geologists' ideas of how the land was once one mass, Pangaea, how it split off into separate continents, and how it is still moving at the rate of about one inch a year. . . . It is a very short book and as such only whets the appetite for more." Appraisal

Bibliography: p29

Brindze, Ruth

The rise and fall of the seas; the story of the tides; illus. with photographs and with diagrams by Felix Cooper. Harcourt 1964 96p illus maps $5.95 (4-7)

     551.4

1 Tides

ISBN 0-15-267380-6

An "explanation of tides, and the effect of the moon's and sun's gravity on air, water, and the land masses of earth. Methods for predicting tides, the hazards of tides, and their potential value to man are presented." Children's Bks, 1964

"In this brief book, beautifully illustrated, the author [writes] in a clear and interesting manner. . . . Young readers will find how the effects of the tide can be easily observed at the seashore. . . . It is a well written, instructive book." Best Sellers

Carson, Rachel L.

The sea around us. A special edition for young readers; adapted by Anne Terry White. Golden Press 1958 165p illus maps $6.95 (6-7)

     551.4

1 Ocean

ISBN 0-307-16745-3

Original edition published 1951 by Oxford. This edition first published by Simon and Schuster

"An excellent adaptation. . . . Oversize pages display to advantage an impressive collection of drawings, photographs, maps and charts; most of these are in color. Many young readers who might not otherwise read this fine book will be attracted by the format. . . . Some of the topics explored are the formation of oceans, the tides and currents, marine flora and fauna, the ocean floor and volcanic activity, products obtained from the sea, and many others." Chicago. Children's Bk Center

Clemons, Elizabeth

Waves, tides, and currents; illus. with maps, diagrams & photographs. Knopf 1967 112p illus maps $3.75, lib. bdg. $4.99 (4-6)

     551.4

1 Tides 2 Ocean waves 2 Ocean currents

ISBN 0-394-81824-5; 0-394-91824-X

"A general definition of the tide is followed by a discussion of the force of gravity that leads into an explanation of the causes of the tides, their ranges and differences. Wave action, ground swells, tsunamis, and currents are explained." The AAAS Sci Bk List for Children

"This beginners' book on oceanography delights the eye with its unity of text, illustration and design." N Y Times Bk Rev

Glossary: p105-06. Bibliography: p107-08

Gans, Roma

Water for dinosaurs and you; illus. by Richard Cuffari. Crowell 1972 33p illus (Let's-read-and-find-out science bks) $4.50, lib. bdg. $5.25, pa $1.25 (1-3)

     551.4

1 Water 2 Water supply

ISBN 0-690-87026-4; 0-690-87027-2; 0-690-00202-5

"Stressing the use and reuse of water over millions of years, this is . . . [an] account of the water cycle. The sources of water—oceans, lakes, rivers, underground water, rain—are simply described. Pollution is also briefly covered." Appraisal

"The pictures are generally accurate; and the text descriptions are excellent in spite of the necessarily limited vocabulary." Sci Bks

Goetz, Delia

Deserts; illus. by Louis Darling. Morrow 1956 64p illus maps lib. bdg. $4.32 (3-6)

     551.4

1 Deserts 2 Natural history

ISBN 0-688-31232-2

Also available in a Spanish language edition (ISBN 0-688-31794-4) for $4.32

"A simple introduction to the desert lands of the world, describing their formation, the weather conditions, and ways in which nomadic tribes, and desert animals and plants adapt themselves to their rigorous environment. Sepia drawings by Louis Darling complement the text." Ontario Library Rev

It is "informally descriptive, substantial enough though brief in text. . . . Younger children will find the large type easy to read." Horn Bk

Grasslands; illus. by Louis Darling. Morrow 1959 62p illus maps lib. bdg. $4.32 (3-6)

     551.4

1 Prairies 2 Pastures 3 Natural history

ISBN 0-688-31356-6

The author "tells about the plants and animals of the prairies, steppes, and savannas, and of the changes in these grasslands that man has brought about." Pub W

"Young readers will want to go on from this beginning to learn more about the places and eras that the author glances at briefly." Sat Rev

"Format excellent." Library J

Lakes; illus. by Lydia Rosier. Morrow 1973 64p illus $4.50, lib. bdg. $4.14 (3-5)

     551.4

1 Lakes 2 Natural history

ISBN 0-688-20058-3; 0-688-30058-8

The author discusses the various ways lakes are formed and how they age, the plant and animal life in and around them, and the efforts being made to control their pollution

Mountains; illus. by Louis Darling. Morrow 1962 64p illus lib. bdg. $4.32 (3-6)

     551.4

1 Mountains

ISBN 0-688-31478-3

The author "gives the location and formation of the world's important mountains and explains briefly how they have affected man's religion, freedom of movement, mineral needs, and recreation." The AAAS Sci Bk List for Children

"The vivid writing, coupled with the abundant illustrations, makes this an enjoyable and informative book." Chicago Sch J

Rivers; illus. by John Kaufmann. Morrow 1969 63p illus $4.75, lib. bdg. $4.32 (3-6)

     551.4

1 Rivers 2 Natural history

ISBN 0-688-21180-0; 0-688-31480-5

The author "describes the formation and characteristics of rivers and river wildlife . . . and touches on ancient beliefs about rivers, some important rivers of the world, and man's use and abuse of natural inland waterways." Booklist

"A straightforward, knowledgeable exposition, in primary-level vocabulary, of basic facts about rivers. The material on life and ecology along the riverbank, and on the development and effects of pollution, is particularly timely and useful. The Potomac, not often depicted for children, is used as an example for many of the facts presented; helpful, clarifying, and attractive illustrations appear on nearly every page." Library J

Swamps; illus. by Louis Darling. Morrow 1961 63p illus lib. bdg. $4.32 (3-6)

     551.4

1 Marshes 2 Natural history

ISBN 0-688-31484-8

The author "describes the ways in which swamps form and change, the differences between kinds of swamps and their flora and fauna, and some of the ways in which men have adapted to swamps." Chicago. Children's Bk Center

"Although emphasis is on the Everglades, swamps in other lands are also described. Clearly drawn illus-

Goetz, Delia—_Continued_

trations, on almost every page enhance the simple, informative account." Booklist

May, Julian

The land beneath the sea; illus. by Leonard Everett Fisher. Holiday House 1971 unp illus maps lib. bdg. $4.50 (3-5)   551.4

1 Oceanography

ISBN 0-8234-0183-9

The author describes the contours of the earth and "the early explorations of the ocean depths. Other profiles portrayed and explained show the relationships of the continent to continental shelf, to continental slope, to deep-sea floor or abyss. . . . 'See-through' profiles show the effects of continental drift, volcanic action, and earthquakes." The AAAS Sci Bk List for Children

"The book is descriptive in presentation, relating facts without giving any detailed explanation of how they were deduced. There are, of course, general references to trawls, echo sounders, and deep-sea exploring craft; but the author very sensibly avoids discussing abstract physics. The book should remain useful in any primary-school library without becoming dated for a good many years." Horn Bk

Pringle, Laurence

This is a river; exploring an ecosystem. Macmillan (N Y) 1972 55p illus $4.95 (4-6)   551.4

1 Rivers 2 Ecology 3 Water—Pollution

"A useful introduction. As its subtitle suggests, the author sketches the interdependencies of the creatures in and around rivers—including man—and shows rivers to be not mere bodies of water connecting points on a map, but total life systems embracing fish, fowl, animals, vegetables, minerals, and human beings far beyond their banks." Book World

"Straightforward writing style, well-organized material, and authoritative information simply presented make 'This is a river' an excellent introduction to the subject." Chicago. Children's Bk Center

Glossary: p50-52. Further reading: p53

Selsam, Millicent E.

Birth of an island; illus. by Winifred Lubell. Harper 1959 42p illus $3.95, lib. bdg. $4.79 (3-5)   551.4

1 Islands

ISBN 0-06-025285-5; 0-06-025286-3

The author has told "the story of how a bare mass of rock resulting from an undersea volcano became a green and pleasant island. Particularly interesting is the description of the animal life that gradually made its home there, and the explanation of why there can develop unusual kinds of birds, reptiles, insects and plants which are peculiar to one island and are not to be found anywhere else." Horn Bk

"Described in text that, despite its simplicity, communicates a sense of excitement at the wonder of natural processes. . . . Illustrations are striking, using one or two vibrant colors with bold black and white." Chicago. Children's Bk Center

Simon, Seymour

Science at work: projects in oceanography; illus. by Lynn Sweat. Watts, F. 1972 87p illus lib. bdg. $4.90 (5-7)   551.4

1 Oceanography—Experiments

ISBN 0-531-02580-2

"This series of simple experiments is designed to help the young scientist understand the chemical and physical properties of the ocean, the life sustained by the sea, and man's utilization of the earth's waters." Appraisal

"Several laboratory manuals are available for the high school student, but this is one of the first pre-

pared specifically for use in the elementary school classroom. The projects selected for inclusion have been wisely chosen; when taken collectively they effectively represent a notable cross-section of oceanic phenomena and characteristics. Mr. Simon avoids the use of 'laboratory-type' scientific equipment for experiments; rather he has chosen to utilize everyday 'household' items which are familiar to the elementary school student. . . . Every elementary school attempting to include environmental science as a classroom topic should insure that this book is available in their library." Sci Bks

Wiesenthal, Eleanor

Let's find out about rivers, by Eleanor and Ted Wiesenthal; pictures by Gerry Contreras. Watts, F. 1971 45p illus lib. bdg. $3.90 (k-2)   551.4

1 Rivers

ISBN 0-531-00074-5

This elementary introduction to rivers "has excellent illustrations that vividly depict the meaning of the written word and in fact add a great deal of information. The book begins on a curious note, 'Have you ever wondered how a river begins?' As the story unfolds from brooks and creeks to large streams and rivers that eventually empty into the sea, there is a basic concern for man's use of the rivers." Science Bks

Williams, Jerome

Oceanography. Watts, F. 1972 79p illus maps lib. bdg. $4.33 (5-7)   551.4

1 Oceanography

ISBN 0-531-00775-8

"A First book"

"This account treats the topography of the ocean floor, currents, waves and tides, marine agriculture, water pollution and environmental studies, the question of sea monsters, etc. The brief sections under bold subject headings (none of which are longer than two pages) make for easier introductory reading. . . . Therefore, this book will be helpful in elementary school libraries where children often want just a few facts about some ocean-related phenomena." Sch Library J

Glossary: p69-72

Yolen, Jane

The wizard islands; illus. by Robert Quackenbush; includes photographs, old documents, and maps. Crowell 1973 115p illus maps $4.95 (5-7)   551.4

1 Islands

ISBN 0-690-89671-9

"Some fact and some fiction are included in eleven stories about islands, ranging from a completely factual description of Surtsey to discussions of islands whose existence has been claimed but is doubtful, from the mystifying art of Easter Island to stories of island-based events that have had ghostly legends added to fact." Chicago. Children's Bk Center

The book "is informative . . . generally thought provoking. The colorful jacket and black and white book illustrations are excellent and very appropriate to the storytelling mood that the author establishes." Reading Teacher

For further reading: p110-11

Zim, Herbert S.

Waves; illus. by René Martin. Morrow 1967 62p illus maps $4.75, lib. bdg. $4.32 (3-5)   551.4

1 Ocean waves

ISBN 0-688-21479-7; 0-688-31479-1

"A very simple account of ocean waves, describing their origin, physical characteristics, and the natural forces that modify them. . . . The author discusses techniques that scientists use to measure waves and programs they have developed to handle the vast

Zim, Herbert S.—*Continued*
amounts of sand that are continually being shifted along the shore. One section is devoted to a description of the tsunami or tidal wave resulting from a seismic disturbance." Sch Library J

551.5 Meteorology

Adler, Irving
Air [by] Irving and Ruth Adler. [Rev. ed] Day 1972 48p illus $4.47 (3-5) 551.5
1 Atmosphere 2 Air
ISBN 0-381-99997-1
"The Reason why books"
First published 1962
This book describes "the composition, origin, functions and uses, phenomena, and pollution of the atmosphere. [It] explains combustion, the nitrogen cycle, weather, the upper atmosphere, smog and other aspects of the air. [Also included are] safe, simple projects and experiments." The AAAS Sci Bk List for Children
Word list: p48

Bell, Thelma Harrington
Snow; with drawings by Corydon Bell. Viking 1954 55p illus $5.95 (3-6) 551.5
1 Snow
ISBN 0-670-65366-7
This book describes how snowflakes are formed, the types and sizes of the flakes, how snow is helpful and dangerous to man. There is also an account of such related phenomena as frost, rime, glaze, sleet, and hail. The book ends with the history of a typical snowflake from its birth to the time it falls to earth
"The Bells' book is beautifully printed in dramatic tones of dark blue and bright blue, against which shines the white of snow scenes or the exquisite designs of snowflakes." N Y Her Trib Bks

Bendick, Jeanne
How to make a cloud. Parents Mag. Press 1971 64p illus lib. bdg. $4.59 (1-3) 551.5
1 Clouds 2 Meteorology
ISBN 0-8193-0441-7
"A Stepping-stone book"
In order to explain "how to make a cloud," the author-illustrator presents a brief discussion on the composition of air as well as the phenomenon of hot air rising and cold air sinking. Included also are sections devoted to simple experiments, the identification of major types of clouds, and directions for "making" rain, smog, sleet and snow
"What may seem an oversimplified explanation of clouds, their formation, appearance and effects on the weather is adequate for the age intended and can be read independently. . . . Black, white and blue cartoon-like drawings support the text. An index makes this a possible reference tool for the very young scientist." Appraisal

Branley, Franklin M.
Flash, crash, rumble, and roll; illus. by Ed Emberley. Crowell 1964 unp illus (Let's-read-and-find-out science bks) $4.50, lib. bdg. $5.25 (k-3) 551.5
1 Thunderstorms 2 Lightning 3 Rain and rainfall
ISBN 0-690-30562-1; 0-690-30563-X
"This reassuring book makes thunderstorms interesting instead of frightening by explaining their causes, nature, and effects. Includes safety rules and directions for telling how far away a storm is." Hodges. Bks for Elem Sch Libraries

Rain and hail; illus. by Helen Borten. Crowell 1963 unp illus (Let's-read-and-find-out science bks) $4.50, lib. bdg. $5.25 (k-3) 551.5
1 Rain and rainfall 2 Hail
ISBN 0-690-66844-9; 0-690-66845-7
An elementary explanation of what causes rain and how hail forms. Pictures and text tell of the part played by clouds, droplets and water vapor, in these processes

Snow is falling; illus. by Helen Stone. Crowell 1963 unp illus (Let's-read-and-find-out science bks) $4.50, lib. bdg. $5.25 (k-3) 551.5
1 Snow
ISBN 0-690-74299-1; 0-690-74300-9
An explanation of what makes snow, the shape of snowflakes, the appearance and uses of snow, and how it affects plants and animals
"Attractively illustrated, a good science book for beginning independent readers. . . . [An] introduction to the topics of weather or seasons." Chicago. Children's Bk Center

Brindze, Ruth
Hurricanes; monster storms from the sea; illus. with photographs. Atheneum Pubs. 1973 106p illus maps lib. bdg. $4.50 (5-7) 551.5
1 Hurricanes
ISBN 0-689-30422-6
"A Margaret K. McElderry book"
Contents: When Great Hurricane Camille hit the Gulf Coast; What we know about hurricanes; Columbus discovered hurricanes; Some hurricanes that shaped American history; A tour of the National Hurricane Center; Flights into hurricanes; Can earth's greatest storms be tamed; Anyone can track the course of a hurricane; Official safety rules; Terms to know; Lists of names used for hurricanes
The book's "chapters are well done and might serve to entice a student into some further inquiry into the historical events mentioned. The book reinforces the notion that science and technology stem from social needs and interactions with the natural world. . . . Hurricanes, like volcanoes and other major natural occurrences, are intrinsically interesting to children, and this book should lead them to a better understanding of such events." Sci Bks

Brown, Billye Walker
Historical catastrophes: hurricanes & tornadoes, by Billye Walker Brown and Walter R. Brown. Addison-Wesley [1972] 223p illus lib. bdg. $5.50 (5-7) 551.5
1 Hurricanes 2 Tornadoes
ISBN 0-201-00777-0
"An Addisonian Press book"
"Beginning with the destruction of Galveston in 1900 by a hurricane the authors . . . show how over the years the development of a tracking and warning system has saved many lives when hurricanes and tornadoes have struck, and graphically describe the major storms from 1935 to 1970. They discuss the work of the Hurricane Hunters and scientific experiments with seeding a hurricane to decrease its violence and explain how hurricanes and tornadoes probably develop." Booklist
"Interesting stories about the effects of storms on people make this a good bet for older reluctant readers." Sch Library J

Buehr, Walter
Storm warning; the story of hurricanes and tornadoes; written and illus. by Walter Buehr. Morrow 1972 62p illus $4.75, lib. bdg. $4.32 (3-6) 551.5
1 Hurricanes 2 Tornadoes 3 Storms
ISBN 0-688-21921-7; 0-688-31921-1

Buehr, Walter—_Continued_

The author describes hurricanes he has encountered, explains the conditions that can spawn a tropical storm, and discusses the techniques that have been developed to establish effective storm forecasting

"Not a comprehensive treatment, but a good introduction to the topic, written in an informal but dignified style." Chicago. Children's Bk Center

Jennings, Gary

The killer storms; hurricanes, typhoons, and tornadoes. Lippincott 1970 207p illus maps $6.95 (5-7)
551.5

1 Hurricanes 2 Typhoons 3 Tornadoes
ISBN 0-397-31128-1

The author "describes briefly the creation of these storms and then details interesting phenomena associated with them. . . . The description of the physics of storm formation is brief and quite clear. Concludes with a description of forecasting tracking facilities of the Environmental Science Services Administration and the U. S. Air Force and a few things you may do to survive a killer storm." The AAAS Sci Bk List for Children

"Excellent photographs and drawings elucidate the text." Library J

Weiss, Malcolm E.

Storms—from the inside out; illus. by Lloyd Birmingham, and with photographs. Messner 1973 96p illus maps lib. bdg. $5.79 (4-6)
551.5

1 Storms
ISBN 0-671-32612-0

This is an "introduction to cloud-storm relationships, causes and effects of lightning, tornado and hurricane formation, and cold/warm front interaction." Sch Library J

"This reviewer wishes there had been more material on formation processes and global weather patterns. . . . The illustrations and photographs are well conceived and executed, and the word descriptions of the formation of the weather processes tie in well with the pictures." Sci Bks

Glossary: p89-90

551.6 Climatology and weather

Berger, Melvin

The National Weather Service. Day 1971 124p illus maps (Scientists at work) lib. bdg. $5.95 (4-7) 551.6

1 National Weather Service 2 Weather forecasting
ISBN 0-381-99943-2

"In providing an interesting, informative, and up-to-date account of the weather service's activities, the author explains the work of technicians and forecasters, and describes instruments and equipment used —weather balloons, radar, teletype, facsimile machines, and computers. The work of tornado, flood, and (the newest) air pollution forecasters, climatologists, hurricane hunters, and spaceflight meteorologists are covered. Research into weather control (cloud seeding) is touched upon. The many varied black-and-white photographs add interest to the straightforward text." Sci Bks

Further reading: p121-22

Bova, Ben

The weather changes man. Addison-Wesley 1974 139p illus lib. bdg. $5.50 (5-7)
551.6

1 Climate 2 Man—Influence of environment
ISBN 0-201-00555-7

"An Addisonian Press book"

The author "explores the effect of weather on man: the original formation of a liveable environment on earth, the weather's role in agriculture, the physiological effects of climate, and some recent discoveries about weather's influence on modern living." Booklist

May, Julian

Weather; illus. by Jack White; cover illus. by Alex Ebel. Follett [1967 c1966] 29p illus (Follett Beginning science bks) $2.50, lib. bdg. $2.97 (2-4)
551.6

1 Weather
ISBN 0-695-89210-X; 0-695-49210-1

In this introduction to the scientific study of weather, the author discusses such subjects as cold and warm air masses, tornadoes, the three forms of water, humidity, weather instruments, clouds, precipitation, and weather forecasting

"Although written in a simple style for elementary students, this book uses many technical words that will be new to almost all such readers. The vocabulary listed at the end is included to facilitate comprehension, but the vocabulary must be learned first. This suggests the need for a teacher. For that reason and because of 'things to do' at the end, the book would be very useful as a challenging and interesting classroom project, but would probably discourage the young reader trying to acquire some knowledge of weather on his own. A remarkable quantity of technical material is presented, and is essentially correct." Sci Bks

Milgrom, Harry

Understanding weather. Rev. ed. Illus. by Lloyd Birmingham. Crowell-Collier Press 1970 84p illus map $4.95 (5-7)
551.6

1 Weather 2 Weather forecasting
First published 1959 by Capitol Pub. with title: The adventure book of weather

This book "is informative, inspirational and experimental, providing good background in the how and why of the weather, the water cycle, the classification of clouds and a cloud chart, explanations of the principles of meteorological instruments, and a description of the organization and work of meteorological services. . . . Information on the use of weather satellites and . . . suggestions to anyone interested in exploring meteorology as a career [are also included]. . . . The black-and-white illustrations are well labeled and are keyed to the text." Sci Bks

For further reading: p79-80

551.7 Historical geology

May, Julian

They lived in the ice age; illus. by Jean Zallinger. Holiday House 1967 unp illus lib. bdg. $4.95 (1-3)
551.7

1 Glacial epoch
ISBN 0-8234-0117-0

"A good introduction to the story of the Ice Age for the quite young reader. . . . The author describes the glacial coverage of the four Ice Ages, discusses the movements of men and animals across the land bridge that then existed and explains some of the traces of glacial action and of life in the Ice Ages that can still be seen today." Chicago. Children's Bk Center

"Softly drawn, precise illustrations add to the attractiveness and the utility of this excellent introduction to a fascinating period in prehistory." Sat Rev

552 Rocks (Petrology)

Branley, Franklyn M.

Pieces of another world; the story of moon rocks; illus. by Herbert Danska. Crowell 1972 58p illus $5.50, lib. bdg. $6.25 (5-7)   552

  1 Lunar petrology

  ISBN 0-690-62565-0; 0-690-62566-9

"The title of this attractively produced book refers to the material brought back by Apollo 11, 12 and 14, and Luna 16. The astronauts' tools and collection methods and the quarantine and analysis procedures employed at the Lunar Receiving Laboratory are described. Current theories about the origin of the samples and of the moon itself are discussed. The illustrations are well chosen and executed; the exposition is clear and well organized." Sch Library J

"Jules Verne himself would revel in this fascinating account of the moon rocks. There is a sense of real discovery on every page. An absolute must for the young geologist, astronomer or space scientist, the book gives insight into the interplay of the most precise scientific work and the theories this work promotes." Appraisal

  For further reading: p55

Gallob, Edward

City rocks, city blocks, and the moon; photographs by the author. Scribner 1973 48p illus lib. bdg. $6.95 (3-5)   552

  1 Rocks 2 Lunar petrology

  ISBN 0-684-13542-6

This photoessay brings "elementary geology to the city dweller's doorstep by leading readers to the streets to search out such items as granite curbstones, marble steps, or sandy brownstones. These and other commonly encountered stone surfaces serve as easily accessible illustrations of igneous, sedimentary, and metamorphic rocks—the three broad rock groupings Gallob describes. Within each group the author explains the ongoing formative processes and illustrates various specific rock types, including man-made and moon rocks. Not an in-depth book, but an attractive starting point for budding rock hounds confined to an urban setting." Booklist

McFall, Christie

Wonders of stones. Dodd 1970 64p illus maps $4.50 (5-7)   552

  1 Stone 2 Rocks

  ISBN 0-396-06795-6

  "Dodd, Mead Wonders books"

The author "presents a survey account of how rocks are formed, and describes the distinguishing characteristics of gravel, crushed rock, and building stone. Then he tells us how building stones—limestone, marble, granite, and others—are quarried, and how stones are dressed and carved. . . . The discussion deals also with the effects on stones of bacteria, lichens, mosses, weather, and contaminants in the air. Many of the illustrations are the author's own drawings, which key in expertly with the text; some are photographs from various sources." Sci Bks

Ruchlis, Hy

How a rock came to be in a fence on a road near a town; illus. by Mamoru Funai. Walker & Co. [1974] c1973 unp illus $4.50, lib. bdg. $4.41 (2-4)   552

  1 Rocks

  ISBN 0-8027-6161-5; 0-8027-6162-3

"The story traces the development of sedimentary rocks from their origin to the kinds of rocks in the fence. It begins with the layers of shells at the bottom of the sea and continues with the elevation of the bottom of the sea, the weathering of exposed rock,

and the movement of pieces of rock by glaciers. The collection of rocks is then arranged in a fence row by a farmer and his sons who farm the land and need to clear it of the rocks." Sci and Children

"Written with simplicity and grace, nicely illustrated. . . . The text is accurate but does not digress to discuss such subjects as the different kinds of rocks or the cause of the land rising from the ocean floor, although the illustration shows volcanic action. Deftly compartmentalized in treatment, the book gives a good picture of the slow, inexorable changes in nature." Chicago. Children's Bk Center

Shuttlesworth, Dorothy

The Doubleday First guide to rocks; illus. by James Caraway. Doubleday 1963 30p illus $1.95, lib. bdg. $2.70 (2-3)   552

  1 Rocks

  ISBN 0-385-01796-0; 0-385-03386-9

"An excellent introduction to geology which will teach the child how to identify common rocks such as granite and mica. Attractively illustrated; includes a pronunciation guide." Jr Booklist

553 Economic geology

Adler, Irving

Coal [by] Irving and Ruth Adler. Rev. ed. Day 1974 47p illus lib. bdg. $4.47 (3-6)   553

  1 Coal

  ISBN 0-381-99974-2

  "The 'Reason why' books"

  First published 1965

A "highly informative account of coal mining processes and history. . . . [A] chapter—on safety in the mines—reflects today's concern in this area." Sch Library J

Chaffin, Lillie D.

Coal: energy and crisis; illus. by Ray Abel. Harvey House 1974 47p illus map $3.99 (3-5)   553

  1 Coal 2 Coal mines and mining

  ISBN 0-8178-5202-6

"This brief but informative survey of coal covers the formation, types, locations, and uses of this valuable energy source as well as the lives of miners and their families, dangers of strip mining and pollution. Black-and-white line drawings clearly illustrate the text, but unfortunately, the small type may put off some young readers. Still this is a succinct, thoughtful introduction to the subject which is especially valuable because it updates standard titles." Sch Library J

Chase, Sara Hannum

Diamonds; illus. with photographs. Watts, F. 1971 90p illus lib. bdg. $4.33 (4-7)   553

  1 Diamonds

  ISBN 0-531-00722-7

  "A First book"

"The text includes sections of historical information about diamonds in general and specifically the Koh-i-noor, the Orloff, and the Regent diamonds. Diamond mining in Africa and South America is described and there is an interesting treatment of diamond cutting. Industrial uses of diamond are described as well as the synthesis of diamond in the laboratory." Sci Bks

  Glossary of important diamond terms: p80-85

Freeman, Mae Blacker

Do you know about water? Illus. by Ernest Kurt Barth. Random House 1970 24p illus (A Very first science bk) $2.95, lib. bdg. $3.99 (1-3)   553

  1 Water

  ISBN 0-394-80619-0; 0-394-90619-5

Freeman, Mae Blacker—*Continued*

"Through the use of common experience this book gives the elementary school child in the lower grades a good introduction to the three states of water and a water cycle. It can whet the appetite of an inquisitive child since it leaves room for self investigation. The line drawings are well done and pertinent to the text. The only disturbing thing about this book is the simplistic way it introduces the idea of a molecule." Sci Bks

Goldin, Augusta

Salt; illus. by Robert Galster. Crowell [1966 c1965] unp illus (Let's-read-and-find-out science bks) $4.50, lib. bdg. $5.25 (1-3)   553

1 Salt

ISBN 0-690-71814-4; 0-690-71815-2

"Starting with a simple experiment to demonstrate how salt crystals can be grown, this book proceeds to explain the importance of salt, where it is found, how it is mined and its uses. An attractively illustrated [book]." Ontario Library Rev

Heaps, Willard A.

Birthstones. Hawthorn Bks. 1969 138p $5.95 (5-7)   553

1 Gems 2 Precious stones

ISBN 0-8015-0666-2

"Each of the 12 gems is treated from many angles; ancient lore and legends, superstitions, history, chemical properties, rarity, and value are among the aspects the author explains. Stories are included of some of the world's most famous gems, and an index, historic table, and references add to the usefulness of this unusual, well-organized book. Illustrations are unfortunately lacking, but the fascinating information offered will appeal to a wide range of readers." Sch Library J

References: p126-27

560 Paleontology. Paleozoology

Aliki

Fossils tell of long ago. Crowell 1972 33p illus (Let's-read-and-find-out science bks) $4.50, lib. bdg. $5.25 (1-3)   560

1 Fossils

ISBN 0-690-31378-0; 0-690-31379-9

"Emphasizing what fossils are, how they were formed, and what they reveal about past life, the author . . . describes various ways in which fossils can be formed, tells where to look for them, and suggests making an instant fossil—a handprint in clay." Booklist

"Lively and amusing drawings [by the author] add to the informational value of a good introduction to the subject of fossils, the writing and the scope of the book making it simple enough to read to preschool children although it is intended for the independent reader." Chicago. Children's Bk Center

Colbert, Edwin Harris

Millions of years ago; prehistoric life in North America; illus. by Margaret M. Colbert. Crowell 1958 153p illus $4.50 (5-7)   560

1 Fossils

ISBN 0-690-54064-7

Colbert tells "how fossils are recovered and identified, and describes the fishes and animals which have inhabited our continent from Devonian times to the coming of man, 10,000 years ago. . . . Cautious in

his statements, the author does not attempt to trace the development of any form of life, man included, from earlier forms, though he occasionally points out relationships. Nor does he assign specific reasons for the disappearance of various forms." Best Sellers

"The lucid scientific survey is enlivened by the author's graphic reconstruction of prehistoric life. Handsome drawings complement the text." Booklist

Fenton, Carroll Lane

In prehistoric seas [by] Carroll Lane Fenton and Mildred Adams Fenton. Doubleday 1962 127p illus lib. bdg. $3.50 (4-7)   560

1 Fossils 2 Marine animals

ISBN 0-385-09070-6

"For the serious young paleontologist and collector, the Fentons show the relationship between the shells to be found on any modern seashore and the wide range of fossils which can readily be identified in inland rocks, once the beds of ancient seas. Names of fossils and the geologic age of their species accompany the excellent photographs and wonderfully meticulous drawings; for further clarity and interest there is a summary of nine major groups of the animal kingdom and a calendar of the ancient ages in which they lived." Horn Bk

Holden, Raymond

Famous fossil finds; great discoveries in paleontology; illus. by John Martinez. Dodd 1966 100p illus maps lib. bdg. $4.50 (5-7)   560

1 Fossils

ISBN 0-396-06590-2

"In the explanation of what are considered fossils, and their importance in helping solve the knowledge gap of a billion years' span of development, the author presents several great discoveries in palaeontology. Amazing fossil finds include the mammoth, dinosaur eggs, first true bird, Peking Man and the giant sloth." Bruno. Bks for School Libraries, 1968

"The book's greatest strength may lie in its appeal to browsers who may become interested enough to go on to more advanced books on the subject." Sch Library J

A selected bibliography: p95-96

Hussey, Lois J.

Collecting small fossils, by Lois J. Hussey and Catherine Pessino; illus. by Anne Marie Jauss. Crowell [1971 c1970] 57p illus $4.50, lib. bdg. $5.25 (3-6)   560

1 Fossils—Collectors and collecting

ISBN 0-690-19733-0; 0-690-19734-9

"Simply written and well organized, this short how-to-do-it manual describes the formation of fossils, their likely locations, necessary equipment and procedures for collecting them. The general instructions are practical. . . . Drawings are accurate, there is a good annotated bibliography, and addresses for obtaining topographic and geologic maps are included." Sch Library J

Rhodes, Frank H. T.

Fossils; a guide to prehistoric life, by Frank H. T. Rhodes, Herbert S. Zim and Paul R. Shaffer; illus. by Raymond Perlman. Golden Press 1962 160p illus (A Golden Nature guide) lib. bdg. $4.95, pa $1.50 (6-7)   560

1 Fossils

ISBN 0-307-63515-6; 0-307-24411-3

At head of title: 480 illustrations in color

"Introductory material on fossil hunting is followed by a survey of life of the past; then invertebrate and vertebrate animal fossils are described and a brief account of fossil plants is given." The AAAS Sci Bk List for Children

Rhodes, Frank H. T.—*Continued*

"The last section, a rather condensed treatment of fossil plants, could easily have been enlarged. However, this book is crammed full of information for the fossil collector and is recommended for any school or public library as an inexpensive, colorful guidebook." Library J

561   Paleobotany

Cosgrove, Margaret

Plants in time; their history and mystery; written and illus. by Margaret Cosgrove. Dodd 1967 63p illus $3.95, lib. bdg. $4.50 (4-6)   561

1 Plants, Fossil

ISBN 0-396-05477-3; 0-396-07157-0

"The author presents the story of the evolution of plants beginning with the primordial cell and progressing through the development of the first true stems, first roots, first leaves, Gymnosperms, and finally the Angiosperms which branch into the dicotyledons and monocotyledons. . . . A final chapter explains the process of fossilization and as an activity, tells how to make clay models and plastic casts to simulate fossils." Sci Bks

"Much is speculation based on fossil evidence, but all of it, including the many drawings, presents an intriguing record of the development of our earth." Christian Sci Monitor

568   Fossil reptiles

Aliki

My visit to the dinosaurs. Crowell 1969 33p illus (Let's-read-and-find-out science bks) $4.50, lib. bdg. $5.25, pa $1.25 (k-3)   568

1 Dinosaurs

ISBN 0-690-57401-0; 0-690-57402-9; 0-690-57403-7

Illustrated by the author, this "first-person account of a little boy's visit to a museum, presented in clear pictures and easy-reading text, gives simple facts about the work of paleontologists and the skeletal structure, appearance, and eating habits of such dinosaurs as the brontosaurus, allosaurus, stegosaurus, and triceratops. Limited in scope but contains useful introductory information." Booklist

Cole, Joanna

Dinosaur story; illus. by Mort Künstler. Morrow 1974 unp illus $3.95, lib. bdg. $3.78 (k-3)   568

1 Dinosaurs

ISBN 0-688-21826-1; 0-688-31826-6

"Beginning with scientists' work on bones, the author gives facts about 10 different dinosaurs, relating them to each other in terms of food cycle and time period. Each prehistoric animal is pictured in accurate, black-and-white drawings projecting a sense of action." Booklist

"This will be helpful to fill requests of the very young who never have enough dinosaur books. Style and clarity will interest adults reading aloud to preschoolers and older children able to read on their own." Children's Bk Rev Serv

Darling, Lois

Before and after dinosaurs; written and illus. by Lois and Louis Darling. Morrow 1959 95p illus map lib. bdg. $4.59 (5-7)   568

1 Reptiles, Fossil

ISBN 0-688-31077-X

"The evolution of vertebrate animals is traced for hundreds of millions of years, emphasis is on Class Reptilia and its five subclasses: turtles, mammal-like reptiles, icthyosaurs, sauroteryglans, and the ruling reptiles which included the dinosaurs." The AAAS Sci Bk List for Children

Includes pronunciation list. "Good pictures, charts, and readable text. . . . This is a good addition to a collection." Library J

Ipcar, Dahlov

The wonderful egg. Doubleday 1958 unp illus $4.95, lib. bdg. $5.70 (k-2)   568

1 Dinosaurs

ISBN 0-385-07764-5; 0-385-07780-7

"This picture storybook uses the thread of what kind of an animal laid the wonderful egg that lay in the big green jungles of long ago to introduce 14 prehistoric animals." Wis Library Bul

"For the most part the pictures are reasonably accurate although the colors that have been used for some of the animals make this a book for fun rather than an informational book on dinosaurs." Chicago. Children's Bk Center

"Not the most scientific presentation available on the subject, but an imaginative and exciting introduction to dinosaurs. A picture-table showing comparative sizes and a guide to pronunciation are appended." Booklist

Ipsen, D. C.

The riddle of the stegosaurus. Addison-Wesley 1969 95p illus $4.95 (5-7)   568

1 Stegosaurus

ISBN 0-201-03160-4

"An Addisonian Press book"

"An account of the identification and reconstruction of the stegosaurus from fossilized bones found in the western U.S. in the latter part of the nineteenth century. In tracing the pioneer investigations of Leidy, Cope, and Marsh and the subsequent activities of other scientists involved in the study of the stegosaurus, Ipsen touches on the personalities of the men as well as their working methods and throws light on the problems and techniques of the science of paleontology. Of more interest to neophyte scientists than to dinosaur enthusiasts, the book is illustrated with photographs and sketches and includes a list of museums having stegosaurus exhibits." Booklist

Ibsen emerges "as one of the most readable writers of science books for the young. . . . He tells us more about . . . Stegosaurus than most of us care to know. But in his hands, we do care. . . . [He] makes paleontology, which can be dry as bones, read like fiction." Christian Sci Monitor

Jackson, Kathryn

Dinosaurs; paintings by Jay H. Matternes. Natl. Geographic Soc. 1972 31p illus (k-3)   568

1 Dinosaurs

ISBN 0-87044-123-X

Obtainable only as part of a set for $6.95 with: Dogs working for people, by Joanna Foster, class 636.7; Lion cubs, by the National Geographic Society, class 599; and Treasures in the sea, by Robert M. McClung, class 910.4

"Books for young explorers"

Prepared by the Special Publications Division of the National Geographic Society

Title on spine: Days of the dinosaurs

This book describes the various types of dinosaurs which evolved in the distant past and what scientists learn about them by studying fossils

McGowen, Tom
Album of dinosaurs; illus. by Rod Ruth. Rand
McNally 1972 60p illus $4.95, lib. bdg. $4.79 (3-5)
568
1 Dinosaurs
ISBN 0-528-82024-9; 0-528-82025-7
"Following an introductory sketch of the history
and general characteristics of dinosaurs, each of
twelve succeeding chapters focuses upon a particular
genus—its peculiarities, presumed habits, and relationships to contemporary life." Sci Bks
"The mention of differing scientific opinions
regarding the habits and behavior of dinosaurs as well
as tales of some noteworthy fossil finds heighten the
educational value of this book. . . . The colorful,
full-page illustrations and smaller, black-and-white
drawings accurately portray prehistoric creatures."
Sch Library J

Parish, Peggy
Dinosaur time; pictures by Arnold Lobel. Harper
1974 30p illus $2.50, lib. bdg. $2.92 (k-2)   568
1 Dinosaurs
ISBN 0-06-024653-7; 0-06-024654-5
"An Early I can read book"
"Excellent illustrations, big print and not too much
of it, good page layout, and a simple, accurate presentation make a fine first book on the subject. There's a
bit of background information, and then specific
material on eleven dinosaurs, each topic beginning
with the pronunciation ('BRACHIOSAURUS. This is
how to say it—brack-ee-oh-SAW-russ.') and describing each kind of dinosaur." Chicago. Children's Bk
Center

Pringle, Laurence
Dinosaurs and their world; illus. with photographs
and drawings. Harcourt 1968 63p illus lib. bdg. $4.50
(3-5)   568
1 Dinosaurs 2 Fossils
ISBN 0-15-223520-5
"A well-researched and carefully written narrative
illustrated with photographs of paintings, restorations, fossils, field sites, and museum preparations.
There are explanatory drawings of anatomical features
and a geological timetable. It is easy to read and the
lucid descriptions should hold the interest of any
young reader. The text describes evolutionary history, morphology, representative specimens field
work, and museum study methods: The final chapter
lists museums of North America that have dinosaur
exhibits." Sci Bks
"Of particular interest is the description of how
fossil clues are used by paleontologists to reconstruct
the appearance and trace the life cycles of dinosaurs."
Library J

Shuttlesworth, Dorothy E.
Dodos and dinosaurs. Hastings House 1968 64p
illus map lib. bdg. $3.99 (4-6)   568
1 Dinosaurs 2 Fossils
ISBN 0-8038-1532-8
"Famous museums"
"By narrating the history of some unusual exhibits
in the American Museum of Natural History, Mrs.
Shuttlesworth relates clearly and concisely the story
of the now extinct dodos and auks. She also tells of the
famed early 20th-Century dinosaur hunts headed by
Dr. Barnum Brown and Dr. Roy Chapman Andrews,
searches which resulted in the uncovering of dinosaur
skeletons, Protoceratops eggs, and a mummified
Trachodont, all of which are now in the museum.
Well-chosen, carefully placed photographs enhance
the text . . . and hint at the formidable obstacles
encountered by the dinosaur hunters. The accounts of
the expeditions are dramatic, and the author's accurate, unemotional description of the extinction of auks
and dodos is effective." Sch Library J

To find a dinosaur. Doubleday 1973 113p illus
$4.95, lib. bdg. $5.70 (5-7)   568
1 Dinosaurs 2 Fossils
ISBN 0-385-02233-6; 0-385-08890-6
Illustrated with drawings and photographs
"Beginning with an account of recent fossil foot-
print discoveries in New Jersey and Connecticut, the
book goes on to review the history of 'dinosaur hunting' from earliest discoveries in England to the results
of landmark expeditions in North America and Asia,
with a brief and general account of the procedures
involved in transforming dinosaur fossils into finished
museum exhibits." Appraisal
"The author, who has long worked in the field of
natural history, writes with easy competence and
communicates her sense of excitement about the
satisfactions of fossil-collecting. A relative index is
appended." Chicago. Children's Bk Center

Zim, Herbert S.
Dinosaurs; illus. by James Gordon Irving. Morrow
1954 64p illus map lib. bdg. $4.32 (4-6)   568
1 Dinosaurs 2 Fossils
ISBN 0-688-31239-X
"Explains how the story of dinosaurs has been
pieced together by scientists, describes the different
kinds of dinosaurs and how they lived, shows how
they changed throughout the Age of Reptiles, and
advances theories on why dinosaurs became extinct."
Booklist
"The writing is simple, vivid, and direct. James
Gordon Irving's excellent drawings parallel the text
on every page. Very attractive format . . . with large,
clear type, good paper and binding." Library J

569   Fossil mammals

McGowen, Tom
Album of prehistoric animals; illus. by Rod Ruth.
Rand McNally 1974 60p illus $4.95, lib. bdg. $4.79
(4-7)   569
1 Mammals, Fossil
ISBN 0-528-82032-X; 0-528-82033-8
"McGowen has collected brief, realistic and very
interesting narratives about the giraffe-camel, giant
sloth, mammoth, great cave bear and the tiny eohippus, as well as other less well-known archaic mammals. The effect is excellent. Each of the stories
vividly displays the daily life of these creatures as they
tried to survive in a world completely different from
our own. Young readers should find the stories entertaining, informative and even fascinating. McGowen
wisely has chosen to call the animals by their scientific
names (megatherium, glyptodon, alticamelus, etc.)
and has provided a pronunciation guide at the book's
conclusion. . . . Each of these animals, and many
others besides, are illustrated in pastel and charcoal
drawings by Rod Ruth. They are uniformly excellent
and most ably coordinated with the narrative of the
text. The book is well worth adding to any elementary
school collection." Sci Bks

572   Human races

Cohen, Robert
The color of man; with an afterword by Juan Comas;
illus. by Ken Heyman. Random House 1968 109p illus
$3.95, lib. bdg. $5.99, pa $1.95 (5-7)   572

Cohen, Robert—*Continued*

1 Race 2 Color of man

ISBN 0-394-81039-2; 0-394-91039-7; 0-394-82306-0

This "volume provides a sound, objective introduction to the physical and social significance of skin color. Cohen dispels the myths of color prejudice with facts which explain the biological basis of skin color, the evolution of color variations throughout the world, and the historical background of many false concepts about race. A brief afterword by a noted Mexican anthropologist stresses the need for racial understanding." Booklist

"A lucid book, the writing straightforward and the material rather loosely organized. The photographs are truly impressive, pictures of people from many parts of the world, pictures that amplify the text's message of brotherhood." Sutherland. The Best in Children's Bks

McKern, Sharon S.

The many faces of man; illus. with photographs. Lothrop 1972 192p illus $6.50, lib. bdg. $5.49 (5-7)
572

1 Race 2 Anthropology

ISBN 0-688-40062-0; 0-688-50062-5

The author "explains the techniques utilized by physical and cultural anthropologists and discusses the facts and theories concerning racial differences and similarities revealed by their findings. McKern cites some of the factors which influence physical and cultural differences and stresses the fallacy of looking upon these differences as an indication of either superiority or inferiority. The account is lucidly presented, contains numerous interesting facts about different behavior patterns, and is well illustrated with photographs." Booklist

Further reading: p187-88

May, Julian

Why people are different colors; illus. by Symeon Shimin. Holiday House 1971 unp illus lib. bdg. $5.95 (2-4)
572

1 Race

ISBN 0-8234-0108-4

"This book examines the major races [mongoloid, negroid, caucasoid, capoid, and australoid] and their variations, suggests possible adaptive values of distinctive body features, and discusses the migrations of human populations known to have taken place in prehistoric and historic times." Appraisal

"Softly-drawn portraits and facial details illustrate a book on racial differences that is written with succinct simplicity. Despite the narrow implications of the title, the text covers a much wider area than color differences; in fact, the substances that cause this are not mentioned, although the relationship between exposure to the sun and skin color is discussed. The book describes many kinds of differentiation; noses, eyes, lips, hair, and size of heads and bodies. The text does not stress the point obtrusively, but makes it clear that all of these adaptations are only superficial distinctions." Chicago. Children's Bk Center

573.2 Organic evolution and genetics of man

Goode, Ruth

People of the Ice Age; illus. by David Palladini. Crowell-Collier Press 1973 151p illus map $6.95 (5-7)
573.2

1 Man—Origin and antiquity 2 Man, Prehistoric

ISBN 0-02-736420-8

"Seven gifts set man apart: upright posture, a long-striding walk, free-moving arms, five-fingered hands, eyes that look forward, a reasoning brain, and the power of speech. The evolution of these attributes and the advances man has made with them are the foundation on which Goode bases this fascinating account of the human species from the first man-ape to the beginnings of prehistoric agrarian society." Booklist

This book is "sure to stimulate a young reader's interest in anthropology. The author's examination of cultural factors is particularly effective. . . . [She presents a] refreshingly clear explanation of the role of mutation and natural selection in the evolutionary process." Sci Bks

May, Julian

The first men; illus. by Lorence F. Bjorklund. Holiday House 1968 unp illus lib. bdg. $4.95 (2-4) 573.2

1 Man—Origin and antiquity 2 Man, Prehistoric

ISBN 0-8234-0035-2

"The brief, simple text and numerous fine drawings explain how scientists analyzed the bone structure and brain size of skeletal remains and the remains of tools to reconstruct the probable appearance and capabilities of five different types of early man." Booklist

574 Biology

Bendick, Jeanne

Living things; written and illus. by Jeanne Bendick. Watts, F. 1969 71p illus (Science experiences) lib. bdg. $4.90, pa $1.25 (3-5)
574

1 Biology 2 Nature study

ISBN 0-531-01432-0; 0-531-02324-9

The characteristics which differentiate living things (human, animal and plant) from each other and nonliving things are introduced in this book. Basic scientific concepts, vocabulary and suggestions for further exploration of the subject are included for each organism discussed

This book "is written in crisp straightforward style and illustrated with lively drawings that are moderately useful. Although the text covers so much ground that it only skims the subject, it gives a good overview." Sat Rev

Carrick, Carol

Swamp spring [by] Carol and Donald Carrick. Macmillan (N Y) 1969 unp illus $4.95 (k-3)
574

1 Nature study 2 Marshes 3 Spring

ISBN 0-02-71732

"Sixteen paintings reproduced in four-color process unfold spring's entry into a marsh. The text is so brief that it is little more than captions, but carries the theme well." Appraisal

Musselman, Virginia W.

Learning about nature through crafts. Stackpole Bks. 1969 128p illus $4.95 (5-7)
574

1 Nature study 2 Handicraft

ISBN 0-8117-0938-8

A "guide to recognizing the different types of trees, flowers, vegetables and shells." Pub W

"The author's aim is to give her readers an awareness of ecology and of the importance of the conservation of our resources. . . . She has accomplished her purpose via crafts. . . . The information in the book is easy to locate as there is a detailed table of contents and two indices. The selection of crafts is excellent, and the instructions are clear and precise. The illustrations are helpful." Sci Bks

Resources: p128

Peattie, Donald Culross

The rainbow book of nature; illus. by Rudolf
Freund. World Pub. 1957 319p illus $4.95, lib. bdg.
$5.21 (5-7)   574

1 Natural history 2 Biology
ISBN 0-529-04615-6; 0-529-04673-3

A guide to life in the forest, desert, sky, and ocean,
and the plants and animals that live in those elements

"If only for its ideas and its writing, this would be a
distinguished, necessary book. But, vitally important,
too, are the more than 250 remarkably fine illustrations in color and black and white, and an appendix
with a long, classified list of reading suggestions,
nature films, and recordings." Chicago Sunday Trib

Books for further reading: p300-17. Films about
nature: p317-19. Recordings from nature: p319

Pringle, Laurence P.

(ed.) Discovering the outdoors; a nature and science guide to investigating life in fields, forests, and
ponds. Natural Hist. Press 1969 128p illus $4.95
(4-7)   574

1 Nature study
ISBN 0-385-05836-5

"Published for the American Museum of Natural
History"

"This book is an introduction to the plant and
animal life . . . [to be found] in nearby fields, forests,
and ponds. It can be used to investigate nature almost
anywhere outdoors—from a city park or weedy lot to a
small suburban swamp or a great forest." p6

"The collection of articles by fourteen writers
which were previously published in 'Nature and Science' magazine were written especially for young
people. Each section clearly and simply describes
how to set about an elementary ecological study of a
particular outdoor area. There are excellent black and
white photographs of plants and animals in the field
and also of young people actually working on nature
projects." Sci Bks

Exploring in books: p120-22

Selsam, Millicent E.

Is this a baby dinosaur? And other science picture-
puzzles; illus. with photographs. Harper [1972 c1971]
32p illus $3.95, lib. bdg. $3.79 (k-3)   574

1 Nature study 2 Biology
ISBN 0-06-025302-9; 0-06-025303-7

First published 1971 by Scholastic in a paper-bound
edition

"In this science book for small children, a photograph of an unidentified object or a portion of one is
followed by a photograph showing the object in context. The photos are accompanied by questions and
answers: e.g., 'Is this an old broken tire? No. It is the
horn of the desert bighorn sheep.' . . . This title
provides an interesting way for young readers to learn
specific facts." Sch Library J

Ubell, Earl

The world of the living; photographs by Arline
Strong. Atheneum Pubs. 1965 40p illus $3.25, lib.
bdg. $3.07 (3-5)   574

1 Life (Biology) 2 Natural history
ISBN 0-689-20448-5; 0-689-20449-3

This "brief discussion is enlivened with excellent
photographs of life forms and of children observing
nature. As a stimulating introductory essay on the
miracle of growth and the diversity of species, it covers with scientific details nature's balance and the
battle for survival, the evolution of useful differences,
and the extinction of species that could not adapt. A
helpful book to be shared when children begin to be
aware of such mysteries in nature." Horn Bk

574.1   Physiology

Asimov, Isaac

How did we find out about vitamins? Illus. by
David Wool. Walker & Co. 1974 64p illus $4.95, lib.
bdg. $4.85 (4-7)   574.1

1 Vitamins
ISBN 0-8027-6183-6; 0-8027-6184-4

"A very readable account of vitamins. Asimov explains the discovery and functions of vitamins, deficiency diseases and their cures, and ongoing research to unravel complex vitamin structures." Sch
Library J

Berger, Melvin

Enzymes in action. Crowell 1971 151p illus $4.50
(6-7)   574.1

1 Enzymes
ISBN 0-690-26735-5

"Following a description of the methods used by
scientists to study enzymes and a summary of what has
been learned about the nature and functions of the
compounds, Berger tells how enzymes are produced
for commercial uses and examines the diverse roles of
enzymes in the human body and other organisms and
in manufacturing processes, laundry products, food
production, and medicine." Booklist

"Lively, informal, and informative, this is not only
good science for the layman, but also a good picture of
scientific method." Chicago. Children's Bk Center

Bibliography: p143-45

Branley, Franklyn M.

Oxygen keeps you alive; illus. by Don Madden.
Crowell 1971 33p illus (Let's-read-and-find-out science bks) $4.50, lib. bdg. $5.25 (1-3)   574.1

1 Respiration 2 Oxygen
ISBN 0-690-60702-4; 0-690-60703-2

"The importance of oxygen to man, animals, and
plants is emphasized in an easy-to-read account which
gives brief, elementary descriptions of human respiration and of photosynthesis in plants, an explanation
of how fish breathe, and a simple experiment to show
the presence of dissolved oxygen in water. The picture book is enhanced by cheerful drawings in color
and in black and white." Booklist

Meeks, Esther K.

How new life begins [by] Esther K. Meeks and
Elizabeth Bagwell. Follett 1969 46p illus (Follett
Family life education program) lib. bdg. $3.48 (k-3)
    574.1

1 Reproduction 2 Growth
ISBN 0-695-43855-7

Illustrated with color photographs, this book "reveals the variety and uniqueness of living things and
the continuous renewal of life through the production
of young. Simple facts about animal reproduction are
given." Booklist

Silverstein, Alvin

The excretory system; how living creatures get rid
of wastes [by] Alvin Silverstein and Virginia B. Silverstein; illus. by Lee J. Ames. Prentice-Hall 1972
74p illus $4.95 (4-6)   574.1

1 Excretion 2 Physiology
ISBN 0-13-293654-2

The authors describe and compare the roles of the
skin, the lungs, the urinary system and the digestive
system in the disposal of waste in man and animals

"Especially useful for reference work on the human
body, this also covers excretion in animals and plants
and relates these waste removal systems to pollution
problems." Booklist

Silverstein, Alvin—*Continued*

The muscular system; how living creatures move [by] Alvin Silverstein and Virginia B. Silverstein; illus. by Lee J. Ames. Prentice-Hall 1972 76p illus $4.95 (4-6)   574.1

1 Animal locomotion 2 Physiology, Comparative 3 Muscles

ISBN 0-13-606947-9

An "examination of the human muscular system and how it works. The Silversteins also discuss locomotion in other animals and in the plant world, making frequent comparisons between the human muscular system and that of lower animals." Booklist

"Although somewhat misleading in title, since movement of plants, ciliated protozoa and various hydraulic structures are included, this is an interesting, quite well-illustrated and very readable account of movement in various species. . . . A very good feature is the large number of simple experiments, using the reader's own body or readily available materials, interspersed through the text." Sci Bks

The respiratory system; how living creatures breathe, by Alvin Silverstein and Virginia B. Silverstein; illus. by George Bakacs. Prentice-Hall 1969 60p illus $4.95 (3-6)   574.1

1 Respiration

ISBN 0-13-774547-8

"A concise, accurate treatment of the respiratory system of man and other life forms. . . . The authors discuss, in logical progression: the purpose of such structures as the nose, epiglottis, bronchi, lungs, and diaphragm; the composition of air; the nature of fish, insect, and plant breathing; gas cycles; etc. Technical terms used are immediately followed by pronunciation aids, and the accompanying illustrations (in black, white and turquoise) are generally well captioned." Sch Library J

The skin; coverings and linings of living things [by] Alvin Silverstein and Virginia B. Silverstein; illus. by Lee J. Ames. Prentice-Hall 1972 90p illus $4.95 (4-6)   574.1

1 Skin 2 Physiology

ISBN 0-13-812776-X

An "introductory explanation of the structure and function of human skin and the outer coverings and inner linings of blood vessels, nerves, and organs of the human body. [The authors] also discuss, in brief, the protective coverings of protozoa, insects, birds, mammals, and plants and touch on current research in human skin grafting and treatment of burns. The account includes the pronunciation of technical terms and is ably complemented by numerous cross-section drawings and diagrams." Booklist

"Well-organized, clearly written, and illustrated with drawings that are carefully captioned and placed." Chicago. Children's Bk Center

574.3 Development and maturation

Cosgrove, Margaret

Eggs—and what happens inside them; illus. by the author. Dodd 1966 63p illus lib. bdg. $4.50 (3-6)   574.3

1 Embryology 2 Eggs

ISBN 0-396-06507-4

"Clear, scientific text and well-labeled drawings explain the life-producing process of eggs and describe the way in which an embryo develops. The book traces the development of different types of eggs from the simple jelly-encased eggs of birds and reptiles to the eggs of mammals. There is a detailed account of the growth of a frog and chicken embryo. The development of insect larva is not given but insect eggs are described. Kinds of eggs which may be studied at home or in school and the methods of embryologists are briefly mentioned. Pronunciation and definition of scientific terms are given in the text and explanations are simple enough to be used with primary children." Booklist

Flanagan, Geraldine Lux

Window into an egg; seeing life begin; with photographs. Young Scott Bks. 1969 71p illus lib. bdg. $5.95 (4-6)   574.3

1 Embryology 2 Eggs

ISBN 0-201-09405-3

Through text and step-by-step photographs, this book describes the development of a chick embryo, from fertilization to hatching

"Many authors have attempted to explain the embryology of the chick for young readers, but none have been so meticulously accurate and successful as Mrs. Flanagan who has used remarkably good photographs from many sources. . . . This book is needed in all school and public libraries—multiple copies, please—and in children's book collections at home." Sci Bks

Selsam, Millicent E.

Egg to chick; pictures by Barbara Wolff. [Rev. ed] Harper 1970 63p illus (A Science I can read bk) $2.95, lib. bdg. $3.79 (k-3)   574.3

1 Embryology 2 Eggs

ISBN 0-06-025289-8; 0-06-025290-1

First published 1946

The author "factually and clearly presents the development of the chicken until its hatching. The narrative is conversational in tone, allowing the author to suggest in a natural sort of way that the fertilization process is universal in the animal kingdom. Simple line drawings of the ubiquitous egg are supplemented by a ten-page photographic section showing a chick actually pecking its way out of the egg, emerging as a wobbly, wet baby bird, and finally standing dry and fluffy beside the broken shell. The author wisely explains why 'you cannot hatch a chick from your breakfast egg' in the early pages of this informative little book." Horn Bk

574.5 Ecology

Atwood, Ann

The kingdom of the forest; text and photographs by Ann Atwood. Scribner 1972 unp illus lib. bdg. $5.95 (4-6)   574.5

1 Ecology 2 Forests and forestry

ISBN 0-684-12914-0

This is a "beautiful photographic essay on the ecology of the forest. The smoothly-written, poetic text relates the plant and animal life that comprise the life cycle of many kinds of forests, including the Olympic rain forest. Exquisite color photographs are definitely the book's major drawing card—the beauty they convey can be enjoyed and appreciated by beginners as well as advanced students." Sch Library J

Batten, Mary

The tropical forest; ants, ants, animals & plants; illus. by Betty Fraser. Crowell 1973 130p illus maps $7.95 (5-7)   574.5

Batten, Mary—*Continued*

1 Tropics 2 Ecology

ISBN 0-690-00138-X

The author "starts by noting what a tropical forest is not—in terms of our commonly-heard clichés—then goes on to enlarge upon the characteristics of tropical forests. Ecology is the connecting thread in the book's discussion of plant relationships, layers of life, techniques for survival, ants, reptiles and amphibians, birds, bats, monkeys, and science and tropical forests. Contrasts are drawn between New World tropics (which have more arboreal animals) and Old World tropics (where there are larger and more terrestrial animals). Throughout the book, black-and-white drawings are both textually enlightening and aesthetically satisfying. One of the most pleasing aspects of the book is the author's ability to develop an idea and then to draw comparisons from it to apply to other situations. . . . The book is very well written; the information presented doesn't get in the way of the flow and readability of the book. It is more than a compendium of well-known facts about the tropics." Sci Bks

For further reading: p125-26

Bendick, Jeanne

Adaptation; written and illus. by Jeanne Bendick. Watts, F. 1971 68p illus (Science experiences) lib. bdg. $4.90 (2-4)   574.5

1 Adaptation (Biology)

ISBN 0-531-01437-1

Through questions and answers, the author discusses how plants, animals and people adapt to where and how they live

"Lively drawings, well integrated with the text, add to the informative value of a book that uses the process approach to stimulate a reader's thinking about the purposes and the effectiveness of adaptations in the plant and animal worlds. . . . This is valuable for its fresh approach and its scientific accuracy. An index is appended." Chicago. Children's Bk Center

Billington, Elizabeth T.

Understanding ecology; illus. by Robert Galster. Warne 1971 88p illus lib. bdg. $4.50 (5-7)   574.5

1 Ecology

ISBN 0-7232-6022-2

First published 1968

Among the topics considered are environment, ecosystems, biomes of the world, habitat, niches, food chains and chemical cycles

"This introduction to ecology will introduce the young biologist to a new approach to the out-of-doors, focusing not on isolated species but on the entire skein of nature. The young reader's horizons will be broadened by this clear approach to a most fascinating field. Not to be overlooked are the numerous practical projects suggested by which the reader may practice developing his or her observational skill and sensitivity to nature's relationships." Appraisal [Review of the 1968 edition]

Bronin, Andrew

The cave: what lives there; illus. by Ben F. Stahl. Coward, McCann & Geoghegan 1972 unp illus lib. bdg. $4.99 (1-3)   574.5

1 Caves 2 Ecology

ISBN 0-698-30437-3

This book describes "the nature of caves and how they are formed, as well as what inhabits their various zones." Booklist

"A good introduction to the ecosystem of the cave handsomely illustrated with pictures in black and white and in cool, dim colors. . . . Simply written in a direct and unpretentious style." Chicago. Children's Bk Center

Cohen, Daniel

How did life get there? Illus. with photographs; drawings by Paul Frame. Messner 1973 96p illus map lib. bdg. $5.29 (3-5)   574.5

1 Geographical distribution of animals and plants 2 Ecology 3 Islands

ISBN 0-671-32574-4

The author investigates the "dispersal of plants and animals . . . on the isolated volcanic islands of Krakatoa, Surtsey, and the Galapagos, and on the island continent of Australia." Outstanding Sci Trade Bks for Children, 1973

Goldstein, Philip

Animals and plants that trap; illus. by Matthew Kalmenoff. Holiday House 1974 118p illus $4.95 (4-7)   574.5

1 Animals—Habits and behavior 2 Plants

ISBN 0-8234-0241-X

An "introduction to numerous trapping mechanisms, this covers the wake-robin, ant lion, Venus flytrap, caddis worm, spider, butterwort, sundew, hydra, bladderwort, anglerfish, pitcher plant, and fungi. . . . Black-and-white drawings and photographs round out the coverage." Sch Library J

This "is an informative and engaging book for intermediate and upper-grade children. Much younger students might find the experiments equally interesting to do, given some help with reading the directions. The narrative style is charming. The science content is accurate, well balanced, and covers the field indicated by the title. . . . The bibliography is well put together and is useful to students doing the experiments described." Sci Bks

Hungerford, Harold R.

Ecology; the circle of life. Childrens Press 1971 92p illus lib. bdg. $6.60 (5-7)   574.5

1 Ecology

ISBN 0-516-00510-3

Illustrated by Tom Dunnington

The author describes some of the important interrelationships which are found in nature and what happens when they are weakened or broken

This book "fills a large gap between natural history books and academic ecology texts. It is essentially a primer. . . . The author illustrates each point with fine black-and-white photographs and line drawings. There is a glossary of terms and an index. The final chapter deals with man's role in nature and the author challenges the reader to develop an ecological ethic." Sci Bks

Lauber, Patricia

Everglades country; a question of life or death; photographs by Patricia Caulfield. Viking 1973 125p illus maps lib. bdg. $6.50 (6-7)   574.5

1 Natural history—Everglades, Fla.   2 Everglades National Park 3 Ecology

ISBN 0-670-30022-5

"Chapter by chapter the author considers various aspects of the flora and fauna of the Everglades, clearly indicating the specific dependence of the organisms on the unusual environment of the area. Man's disruptions of the natural cycles and the potential for complete disaster are well described and documented." Appraisal

"A carefully researched, well organized readable account. . . . The interdependence of life in this area is clearly drawn and will be understood by most young students of ecology. There is an especially informative chapter about man's manipulation of the water supply to the Everglades National Park. Good black-and-white photographs, maps, a selected bibliography,

Lauber, Patricia—*Continued*
and an index augment this up-to-date presentation."
Library J

McClung, Robert M.
Mice, moose, and men; how their populations rise and fall; written and illus. by Robert M. McClung. Morrow 1973 64p illus $4.95, lib. bdg. $4.59 (4-7)
574.5

1 Animal populations 2 Population
ISBN 0-688-20087-7; 0-688-30087-1
This "survey of animal population patterns cites the conditions—good and bad, natural and artificial—that affect nature's cyclic balancing mechanisms. To elucidate the notions of balance and change, [the author] defines the determining factors surrounding fertility rates, life span of species, animal explosions, and invasions into new territories, with specific animal, insect, and bird examples for each concept or fact introduced." Booklist
The book "imparts information through supportive anecdotes of the believe-it-or-not sort that attract middle graders. . . . Clearly illustrated in line drawings." Sch Library J
Suggestions for further reading: p60-62

Pringle, Laurence
Ecology: science of survival. Macmillan (N Y) 1971 152p illus lib. bdg. $4.95 (5-7)
574.5

1 Ecology
"Fundamental principles of ecology such as interaction of organisms and abiotic environment, energy flow, biogeochemical cycles, succession, and population changes are topics for discussion in this book. . . . To illustrate concepts, the author relies heavily on classic examples (e.g., the Kaibab deer herd) mentioned in practically all ecology texts, but also includes results of recent studies and discusses contemporary environmental problems such as eutrophication and DDT poisoning. He convincingly points out the importance of ecological studies in solving these problems and gives the reader a good idea of what ecologists do. The book is amply illustrated and a list of 40 books (each designated simple or advanced) is given for further reading." Sci Bks
Glossary: p140-45

Into the woods; exploring the forest ecosystem. Macmillan Pub Co. 1973 54p illus lib. bdg. $4.95 (5-7)
574.5

1 Ecology 2 Forests and forestry
ISBN 0-02-775320-4
The author "presents an elementary explanation of forest ecosystems. The interrelationships between forest zones and the life they support are described, as well as the process of plant succession and the effects—not always bad—of forest fires. A few words on the national forests and an admonition to care for them and all woodlands round out the smooth presentation, abundantly illustrated with clear, black-and-white photographs." Booklist
"A few concepts are overly sophisticated for young readers, and even some of the simpler ones might be difficult for children more familiar with concrete than with humus." Sch Library J
Glossary: p49-50. Further reading: p51

Shuttlesworth, Dorothy
Natural partnerships; the story of symbiosis; illus. by Su Zan Noguchi Swain. Doubleday 1969 62p illus (Nature bks. for young people) $4.95, lib. bdg. $5.70 (5-7)
574.5

1 Ecology
ISBN 0-385-07671-1; 0-385-09422-1
"Symbiosis in general is explained followed by a

discussion of its various forms, mutualism, parasitism, and commensalism, each illustrated with examples from the plant and animal kingdom. In a final chapter symbiosis is related to the whole of ecology, the interdependence and interaction of plants and animals and their physical environment. The examples are varied, some familiar and others not well known." Sci Bks
"Small diagrams show enlarged specimens (the number of times of magnification carefully stated), while some of the bigger color paintings show action. A strong expression of the importance of ecology for the preservation of wildlife." Horn Bk

574.8   Cells

Silverstein, Alvin
Cells: building blocks of life, by Alvin Silverstein and Virginia B. Silverstein; illus. by George Bakacs. Prentice-Hall 1969 60p illus $4.95 (4-7)   574.8
1 Cells
ISBN 0-13-121715-1
"This comprehensive discussion of cells—both plant and animal—gives young readers an elementary understanding of cells, how they work and grow, and a description of instruments and techniques used to study them." The AAAS Sci Bk List for Children
"Pronunciation and definition of biological terms are incorporated in the lucid text which is complemented by labelled drawings." Booklist

Zappler, Georg
From one cell to many cells; illus. by Elise Piquet; science consultant: Stanley R. Wachs. Messner 1970 54p illus lib. bdg. $4.79 (2-4)   574.8
1 Cells
ISBN 0-671-32251-6
"A Center for Media Development, Inc. book"
"Many, many things happen from the time one cell begins to divide to the time a completely developed living thing is formed. Scientists have studied cells, growth, and development in great detail. This story is about some of the things they have learned." p11

574.92   Marine and fresh-water biology

Buck, Margaret Waring
Along the seashore; written and illus. by Margaret Waring Buck. Abingdon 1964 72p illus map $3.95, pa $1.95 (3-6)   574.92
1 Marine biology 2 Seashore
ISBN 0-687-01114-0; 0-687-01115-9
"This book is for beginning naturalists to help in their understanding of marine life. It describes many of the plants and animals to be found along the Atlantic, Pacific, and Gulf coasts of the United States. . . . The life history of each kind of animal is given and a description of some of the commoner species." p4
"Careful black-and-white drawings. . . . [A] useful book to have at hand when the family is trying to identify a plant or shell found near the summer cottage." Pub W
"Has an excellent index including classification. An extra copy would be useful on the reference shelf." Sch Library J
More to read: p72

Burgess, Robert F.

Exploring a coral reef; illus. by Ronald Himler. Science consultant: Harry Milgrom; experiments and investigations by Leon Dorfman. Macmillan (N Y) 1972 56p illus $4.95 (4-6)   574.92

1 Coral reefs and islands   2 Marine ecology

Contents: Let's look at a reef; Building blocks of the reef; Where does coral grow; The most important plants; Is it a plant or an animal; Creeping, swimming, clinging creatures; Little fish, big fish; The reef at night; Some interesting alliances; The food chain; Experiments and investigations; Glossary

"A descriptive study of the organisms and ecology of a coral reef. . . . The excellent glossary includes pronunciation aids. However, although the black-and-white illustrations and diagrams complement the text, the use of color would have been more effective." Sch Library J

Carrick, Carol

The brook, by Carol and Donald Carrick. Macmillan (NY) 1967 unp illus $4.95 (k-2)   574.92

1 Fresh-water biology

This story "in words, in pictures, [is] the biography of a brook from its beginnings in a rainfall to its meeting with the sea." Pub W

"Although the text is very slight, it expresses the bubbling quality of a spring brook." Bruno. Bks for Sch Libraries, 1968

"Imagistic words . . . and poetic, impressionistic paintings [by Donald Carrick] extend and complement each other." Horn Bk

The pond [by Carol and Donald Carrick. Macmillan (N Y) 1970 unp illus $4.95 (k-2)   574.92

1 Fresh-water biology 2 Nature study

Illustrations by Donald Carrick

The "poetic text and lovely watercolor illustrations effectively depict the atmosphere of a pond and the activities of pond wildlife from sunrise to sunset." Booklist

Clemons, Elizabeth

Tide pools & beaches; illus. by Joe Gault. Knopf 1964 78p illus $2.95, lib. bdg. $4.99 (3-5)   574.92

1 Marine biology

ISBN 0-394-81753-2; 0-394-91753-7

This is "a simply written book explaining how to identify, collect, and preserve the commonest sea animals and plants found along the seashore. Warns about dangerous preservatives and shows specimens in clear drawings." Hodges. Bks for Elem Sch Libraries

Cooper, Elizabeth K.

Science on the shores and banks; with illus. by the author. Harcourt 1960 187p illus $4.95, pa 60¢ (5-7)   574.92

1 Marine biology

ISBN 0-15-270843-X; 0-15-679609-0

A "provocative science hobby book, in which [the author] invites the young reader to do some scientific exploring, observing, and collecting of many forms of small [insect and animal] creatures and plants that live at the water's edge, on bank or shore, and in tide pools. He is encouraged to experiment, following scientific method in handling his problem and also later in setting up displays. Clearly illustrated with line sketches and diagrams; indexed." Horn Bk

"It will be an ideal book for children who spend their summer vacations at the beach, even those whose reading is generally confined to less factual material." Pub W

Goldin, Augusta

The sunlit sea; illus. by Paul Galdone. Crowell 1968 33p illus (Let's-read-and-find-out science bks) $4.50, lib. bdg. $5.25, pa $1.25 (1-3)   574.92

1 Marine animals 2 Marine plants 3 Ocean

ISBN 0-690-79411-8; 0-690-79412-6; 0-690-79413-4

This book "describes the plant and animal life that inhabits the sunlit area of the sea which extends downward from the surface to approximately 200 feet in depth. The simple text and appealing, accurate illustrations depict different types of marine life and indicate the role of each in nature's food chain." Booklist

Kane, Henry B.

The tale of a a pond; written and illus. by Henry B. Kane. Knopf 1960 110p illus (Borzoi Nature study bks) $3.50, lib. bdg. $5.39 (4-7)   574.92

1 Fresh-water biology

ISBN 0-394-81720-6; 0-394-91720-0

"A boy watches the strange and interesting inhabitants of a pond through the four seasons. In words, photographs, and expressive drawings of Mr. Kane, we see the teeming, changing life of fish, frogs, turtles, birds, small animals, insects, and plants and learn how to care for many of these creatures in home terrariums and aquariums." Library J

Milne, Lorus

When the tide goes far out [by] Lorus & Margery Milne; illus. by Kenneth Gosner. Atheneum Pubs. 1970 88p illus lib. bdg. $4.25 (4-7)   574.92

1 Marine biology

ISBN 0-689-20606-2

After explaining what tides are, the authors describe the small plants and animals living on beaches which are alternately being covered and uncovered by the sea

"The best part is the pictures. Here's a drawing of a hermit crab that will haunt your nightmares! And it makes beach fleas look cute. A very informative book. I like it. But it is only a book to start you off. There is a lot it doesn't tell you." Christian Sci Monitor

Bibliography: p83

Pringle, Laurence

Estuaries; where rivers meet the sea. Macmillan (N Y) 1973 55p illus map lib. bdg. $4.95 (4-6)   574.92

1 Estuaries 2 Ecology

Through text and photographs, the book describes the ecosystem of estuarine bays and salt marshes, and the many varieties of plant and animal life found in it—including grasses, snails, oysters, fish and birds

"The text is neatly organized, simply written, lucid, and informative; the quality of the photographs is excellent. A glossary and an index are appended." Chicago. Children's Bk Center

Reid, George K.

Pond life; a guide to common plants and animals of North American ponds and lakes, by George K. Reid, under the editorship of Herbert S. Zim and George S. Fichter; illus. by Sally D. Kaicher and Tom Dolan. Golden Press 1967 160p illus (A Golden Nature guide) lib. bdg. $4.95, pa $1.50 (6-7)   574.92

1 Fresh-water animals   2 Fresh-water plants

ISBN 0-307-63535-X; 0-307-24017-7

This guide "explains the dynamics of a pond or lake, shows some of the plants, animals, insects, and fishes likely to be found in or near it, and tells how to collect specimens." Pub W

For more information: p155

Selsam, Millicent E.

See along the shore; pictures by Leonard Weisgard. Harper 1961 unp illus $3.95, lib. bdg. $4.79 (3-5)

574.92

1 Marine biology 2 Seashore
ISBN 0-06-025335-5; 0-06-025336-3
The author "answers questions that arise when a child goes to the seashore, and suggests some things he can do while there. Queries such as why driftwood burns different colors, why the tides come and go, and why waves glow at night are pursued and some plants and animals of the shore are pictured." The AAAS Sci Bk List for Children
"Illustrated with attractive drawings in color or in black and white on every page the book should encourage firsthand exploration and further reading on the subject." Booklist

Tresselt, Alvin

The beaver pond; illus. by Roger Duvoisin. Lothrop 1970 unp illus $5.50, lib. bdg. $4.81 (k-3)

574.92

1 Fresh-water biology 2 Beavers
ISBN 0-688-41123-1; 0-688-51123-6
"Beautiful pictures in full color, bright and delicate, show the abundance of wildlife in the pond from the first invasion of the industrious beavers who have dammed a small stream, through the changing colors of the season, to the abandonment of the dam years later. The colony grows and prospers, the beavers raise their families and fight enemies, and the friendly animals flourish in a balanced ecology. Written with quiet dignity, this is unobtrusively informative and lovely to look at." Sat Rev

Zim, Herbert S.

Seashores; a guide to animals and plants along the beaches, by Herbert S. Zim and Lester Ingle; illus. by Dorothea and Sy Barlowe. Sponsored by the Wildlife Management Institute. Golden Press 1955 160p illus (A Golden Nature guide) lib. bdg. $4.95, pa $1.50 (5-7)

574.92

1 Marine biology 2 Seashore
ISBN 0-307-63512-0; 0-307-24496-2
At head of title: 458 species in full color
First published by Simon & Schuster
"A comprehensive pocket guide for identifying 'plant and animal life found in North American tidal waters.' Algae, sponges, corals, shellfish, birds, flowering plants, etc. are included with brief descriptive text and illustrations in full color. Index." Horn Bk

575.1 Genetics

Pomerantz, Charlotte

Why you look like you, whereas I tend to look like me; pictures by Rosemary Wells and Susan Jeffers. Young Scott Bks. 1969 64p illus lib. bdg. $4.50 (4-6)

575.1

1 Mendel's law 2 Heredity
ISBN 0-201-09409-6
"Zany poetry and cartoons explain how Mendel's experiments with garden peas led to the modern theory of heredity. Dry discoveries are made interesting and understandable. A description with supporting diagrams of Mendel's cross pollination process and a short biography of his life supplement the verse." Adventuring With Bks. 2d edition

Silverstein, Alvin

The code of life [by] Alvin and Virginia Silverstein; illus. by Kenneth Gosner. Atheneum Pubs. 1972 89p illus $4.50 (6-7)

575.1

1 Genetics 2 DNA
ISBN 0-689-30038-7
The authors investigate the genetic code—in the chromosomes, the genes, the DNA bases—detailing how they, along with RNA, "work together to direct the activities of living cells. They describe the inheritance or mutation of traits from generation to generation and discuss genetic research from the study of fruit flies and work done with clones of bacteria to the isolation of a single gene and the synthesis of genes, concluding with a look at progress and prospects in the growing new science of genetic engineering. Many captioned scientific drawings and diagrams complement the text." Booklist

576 Microbes

Lewis, Lucia Z.

The first book of microbes. Rev. ed. Illus. by Howard Berelson. Watts, F. 1972 83p illus lib. bdg. $3.90 (4-7)

576

1 Microorganisms
ISBN 0-531-00798-7
First published 1955
The author describes the discovery, life cycles, and importance of harmful and beneficial plant and animal microbes, including bacteria, protozoa, fungi, yeasts, molds and viruses. Instructions for six experiments are included
"The experiments are noteworthy because they depend on the growing of microorganisms, rather than on their microscopic study. . . . The many illustrations are used like the illustrations of a story and are not referred to specifically in the text as are figures in a textbook. The pictures are well done." Sci Bks
Glossary: p73-76

Silverstein, Alvin

Germfree life; a new field in biological research [by] Alvin and Virginia Silverstein; illus. with photographs. Lothrop 1970 96p illus lib. bdg. $4.81 (5-7)

576

1 Microorganisms 2 Microbiology—Research
ISBN 0-688-51119-8
"A good survey of the science of gnotobiology—the study of certain microorganisms on life forms that live in a sterile condition, germfree—written in a direct style, serious but not formal. The photographs are clear and informative, the material well organized. The authors discuss the early experiments that sprang from the conflicting theories of Pasteur and Nencki, give adequate background information on bacteria, and go on to discuss some of the experiments that are, through gnotobiology, making available new knowledge, pathological and surgical." Sutherland. The Best in Children's Bks

A world in a drop of water [by] Alvin and Virginia Silverstein. Atheneum Pubs. 1969 58p illus $4.95 (3-5)

576

1 Microbiology
ISBN 0-689-20632-1
An introduction to microbiology which describes the life processes of the amoeba, the paramecium, the hydra, the flatworm and other organisms which live in a drop of pond water
"The superbly detailed photographs of tiny plants

Lewis, Lucia Z.—*Continued*
and animals are worth the purchase price of this
book." Sch Library J

576.072   Microbes—
Experiments

Stone, A. Harris
Microbes are something else, by A. Harris Stone
and Irving Leskowitz; illus. by Peter P. Plasencia.
Prentice-Hall 1969 64p illus $4.95 (4-7)   576.072
1 Microbiology—Experiments 2 Microorganisms
ISBN 0-13-580951-7
"The authors offer instructions for the preparation
of nutrient media, the inoculation and incubation of
cultures, and preparing and staining slides for microscopic study. Activities include examination of organisms from the soil and from natural waters, experiments with germicides, the effect of light, pasteuriza-
tion, fermentation, growth of penicillin, and effects of
decomposition." Sci Bks
The book cannot "be used without a microscope.
. . . Also, as the book warns, an adult must supervise
some of the experiments." Sch Library J
Bibliography included in Sources of materials: p60-
61. Glossary: p62-64

578   Microscopy in biology

Selsam, Millicent E.
Greg's microscope; pictures by Arnold Lobel.
Harper 1963 64p illus (A Science I can read bk) $2.95,
lib. bdg. $3.79 (1-3)   578
1 Microscope and microscopy
ISBN 0-06-025295-2; 0-06-025296-0
"The acquisition of a microscope entices Greg into
looking at anything tiny, so he prepares his own slides
of salt and sugar, water and flour, and bits of many
other household things. Eventually he isolates some
amoebae from his fish tank, but finds himself third in
the microscope line—Mother and Dad are in front."
N Y Times Bk Rev
"There is a lively, here-and-now quality to [the]
conversations and to the drawings." Horn Bk

Simon, Seymour
Exploring with a microscope; illus. with photographs and diagrams. Random House 1969 82p illus
$2.95, lib. bdg. $3.99 (4-7)   578
1 Microscope and microscopy
ISBN 0-394-80157-1; 0-394-90157-6
"This simple introduction to the microscope makes
it easy to explore the world of the very small. Seymour
Simon tells step-by-step how to use a microscope. He
describes many fascinating things to look at and tells
where to find them. He suggests some simple experiments. Many . . . photographs show exactly what to
look for under the lens." Introduction
"The students who have shared this book have been
most enthusiastic in reviewing it. A student does not
have to use a microscope to enjoy the book; although,
if he does possess a microscope there are adequate
instructions on its use and for the preparation of cultures and slides. Full page photos of typical microorganisms, inorganic materials, and even parts of insects
are included as is an explanation of scales and magnification." Sci Bks
Books for reading and research: p80

579   Collection and preservation
of biological specimens

Brown, Vinson
How to make a home nature museum; illus. by Don
Greame Kelley. Little 1954 214p illus $4.95, lib. bdg.
$5.55 (5-7)   579
1 Nature study
"An excellent handbook for the amateur collector
on how to display and give meaning to a nature collection. The author . . . discusses space for and arrangement of the collection, collecting, classifying, mounting, and labelling specimens [such as shells, leaves,
stones, birds' nests, and snake skins], collecting pictures and photographs, and making molds and models, drawings, charts, diagrams, and paintings. The
book also offers suggestions for trading museum
mounts and specimens, sources for supplies, and
ideas for exhibits and improvements, and includes a
substantial bibliography of books on natural history."
Booklist
"Illustrations will suggest patterns the reader may
not think of. Young people will be interested in this
book, as well as adults." Wis Library Bul

How to make a miniature zoo. Rev. ed. Illus. by
Don Greame Kelley. Little 1957 212p illus $4.95, lib.
bdg. $5.55 (5-7)   579
1 Zoological specimens—Collection and Preservation
First published 1956
Much "fascinating information comes packed into
this not very big volume. Its guidance is for anyone—
young naturalist, parent, teacher, club or camp
leader—who wishes to set up an indoor or outdoor
miniature zoo. It will serve also as helpful reference
material on the care of individual species as pets:
insects, rodents, fish, reptiles, amphibians, small
mammals, and birds. How to collect them makes particularly adventurous reading. The sketches of zoo
layouts, traps, aquariums, aviaries and cages, as well
as of the creatures themselves, are helpful." Horn Bk

581   Botany

Baker, Jeffrey J. W.
The vital process: photosynthesis; illus. by Patricia
Collins. Doubleday 1969 63p illus (Living things of
the world) $5.95, lib. bdg. $6.70 (4-7)   581
1 Photosynthesis
ISBN 0-385-02818-0; 0-385-03164-5
Drawing from the three sciences of biology,
chemistry and physics, the authors record "the slow
accumulation of knowledge about the process of
photosynthesis from 1600 to the present. Comments
on the need for continuing research in the face of the
population problem [are included]." Minnesota
"I had assumed that [this book] would be devoted to
explaining in detail a highly complex chemical process; it turned out to be aimed at children whom I
would have thought too young for such a rigorous
concept. . . . [The pictures] were at first concrete
things. . . . But then Mr. Baker really waded in, and
the ideas of radiation quanta and excited electrons
suddenly seemed perfectly clear—and Miss Collins
followed right along. . . . Full marks to this team."
Horn Bk

Bentley, Linna

Plants that eat animals; illus. by Colin Threadgall. McGraw [1968 c1967] 31p illus (A McGraw-Hill Natural science picture bk) lib. bdg. $4.72 (3-6) 581

1 Plants

ISBN 0-07-004817-7

First published 1967 in England

"Following a brief introduction of the various methods utilized by carnivorous plants in capturing their prey, vivid detailed descriptions of each group are presented with imagination and accuracy. The excellent sketches magnifying the particular adaptations of each group are a fine supplement to the text, as are the color illustrations. A good introduction to these plants which augment their mineral supplies from captured animal tissue is given. Coverage is world wide and the listing of botanical gardens where collections of these plants are to be found is a welcome addition." Appraisal

Budlong, Ware T.

Performing plants; illus. by Grambs Miller. Simon & Schuster 1969 96p illus $3.95, lib. bdg. $3.79 (5-7) 581

1 Plants

ISBN 0-671-65042-4; 0-671-65043-2

This "introductory account describes plants that move, grow, or respond to such stimuli as touch, gravity, sound, electricity, cold, and atomic radiation in unusual or little-known ways. The book incorporates reports on . . . scientific experimentation and a few experiments for the reader, and notes areas of possible future research." Booklist

"An excellent bibliography and index are provided. Fine line drawings . . . attractively illustrate the book." Best Sellers

Cole, Joanna

Plants in winter; illus. by Kazue Mizumura. Crowell 1973 33p illus (Let's-read-and-find-out science bks) $4.50, lib. bdg. $5.25 (1-3) 581

1 Trees 2 Plants

ISBN 0-690-62885-4; 0-690-62886-2

"The author describes clearly and simply the different ways that plants have adapted for survival during the adverse conditions of winter. The text explains the function of tree leaves and movement of plant materials and water within the plant. Also discussed are the winter dormancy period, leaf fall which protects the deciduous trees, and the leaf structure and thick, tough coats which protect evergreen plants. Underground roots and stems—bulbs, rhizomes and runners—as well as seeds, which can tolerate cold temperatures, are discussed as adaptations which help plants survive." Sci Bks

"The text is clear and simple and is accompanied by wash drawings. Considering how slight a volume this is, it covers a wide range of plants. . . . This is an attractive and informative introduction to plant life." Appraisal

Davis, Burke

Biography of a leaf; illus. by Jean Zallinger. Putnam 1972 46p illus lib. bdg. $4.49 (3-5) 581

1 Leaves

ISBN 0-399-60746-3

The author "covers the life cycle of trees with an emphasis on leaf formation, how leaves live, and the reason for their autumn abscission. He also explains the effects animals have on leaves and how leaves bolster animal survival. Beginning naturalists can gain from the clear, simple text and the accurate diagrams which show the parts of a leaf and the different stages of development." Sch Library J

Earle, Olive L.

Pond and marsh plants; written and illus. by Olive L. Earle. Morrow 1972 64p illus lib. bdg. $4.32 (3-6) 581

1 Fresh-water plants

ISBN 0-688-31779-0

"An easy-to-read reference on wild water plants. Explicit information and accurate black-and-white drawings help young readers understand these plants and identify which ones have edible parts. Examples are culled from a wide range of pond and marsh plants, including those that grow in, near, on and under water. Unfortunately, Earle does not indicate where plants are commonly found. The 45 plants included are indexed by common name; scientific names are not used." Sch Library J

Hutchins, Ross E.

Strange plants and their ways; with 60 photographs by the author. Rand McNally 1958 96p illus $3.95 (6-7) 581

1 Plants

ISBN 0-528-80375-1

"After first explaining how ordinary plants live, grow, and reproduce [the author] describes in animated text and excellent photographs the strange habits of such plants as the yucca tree, Venus flytrap, pitcher plant, mistletoe, lichen, mangrove tree, slime mold, and jumping bean, and offers some helpful suggestions for making a hobby of plant study." Booklist

Lubell, Winifred

Green is for growing, by Winifred and Cecil Lubell. Rand McNally 1964 64p illus $2.95 (3-5) 581

1 Growth (Plants)

ISBN 0-528-8021-8

This "nature picture book written in rhythmic prose, tells in simple language the facts about many growing plants, starting with algae. It goes on to fungi, lichen, moss, ferns and flowering plants, explaining the difference between plants which are reproduced by seed and those that grow from spores." Sch Library J

"Without so stating formally, the text makes evident the profligate variety of the plant world and the innumerable ways, direct and indirect, in which plants are necessary to mankind: both text and illustrations give indications of ecological importance." Chicago. Children's Bk Center

Poole, Lynn

Insect-eating plants, by Lynn and Gray Poole; illus. by Christine Sapieha. Crowell 1963 87p illus $4.50 (3-6) 581

1 Plants

ISBN 0-690-44052-9

"Written from personal research and experience this is a clear, fascinating description of a number of insectivorous plants—their appearance, growth habits, and methods of attracting, trapping, and digesting their insect prey. The book also gives instructions on how to set up a terrarium, how to raise and observe insect-eating plants, and how to keep a record of their growth and eating habits. A list of commercial suppliers is appended." Booklist

"The clear black-and-white line drawings complement the text." Instructor

Zim, Herbert S.

What's inside of plants? Illus. by Herschel Wartik. Morrow 1953 32p illus lib. bdg. $4.32 (2-4) 581

1 Botany

ISBN 0-688-31490-2

"A general discussion of plants and their roots,

Zim, Herbert S.—*Continued*

stems, leaves, flowers and fruits. The pages are alternately in large and small type, the former intended for beginners and the latter offering slightly more advanced information." The AAAS Sci Bk List for Children

"The material is expertly geared to children's interest in these subjects and presented in concise text and in excellent illustrations." Booklist

581.072   Botany—Experiments

Rahn, Joan Elma

Seeing what plants do; illus. by Ginny Linville Winter. Atheneum Pubs. 1972 58p illus $4.95 (3-5)
581.072

1 Plants 2 Botany—Experiments
ISBN 0-689-30034-4

The author offers "twenty-one basic experiments which will provide information about the functioning parts of plants. The experiments are graded from simple to complex. All are easy to perform and require little specialized equipment. Through the directions for setting up the experiments the child is also introduced to the correct botanical names for the parts of plants. The approach is not didactic; instead, Ms. Rahn's well-placed questions encourage the young experimenter to develop a discovery method approach to botanical studies. The answer section which follows the last experiment enables the child to check his or her own responses. The concluding statement encourages the readers to experiment further in the area of botany." Sci Bks

Selsam, Millicent E.

Play with plants; pictures by James MacDonald. Morrow 1949 62p illus lib. bdg. $4.81 (3-6) 581.072

1 Plants 2 Botany—Experiments
ISBN 0-688-31488-0

"This book of plant experiments, presented in simple, detailed explanations . . . has both informational and entertainment value. There are experiments with plants which grow from roots, stems, leaves, and seeds, and others showing how seeds grow, how plants use water and respond to light. There is also a brief chapter on conducting experiments. Materials needed are readily available in the home and all experiments can be performed without an outdoor garden." Booklist

"The directions are clear and the diagrams are an important aid in directing the young botanist." Ontario Library Rev

581.5   Botany—Ecology

Selsam, Millicent E.

Birth of a forest; illus. with pictures by Barbara Wolff and with photographs. Harper 1964 unp illus lib. bdg. $4.43 (4-6)   581.5

1 Botany—Ecology 2 Forests and forestry
ISBN 0-06-025276-6

"The fact that 'the world of nature is always changing' is demonstrated through the story of the progression of plant life in a meadow pond. Beginning with the minute plants floating in the waters of the pond, the author traces the slow changes through which the pond gradually fills with plants, becomes a swamp which is able to support a swamp forest, until, in the course of time these trees are superceded by the 'beech-maple forest,' which is the 'climax community'

of the area. Photographs and delicate pen-and-ink-drawings complement the text which is clear and straightforward." Toronto

Wright, Robert H.

What good is a weed? Ecology in action. Lothrop 1972 128p illus lib. bdg. $5.11 (4-6)   581.5

1 Weeds 2 Botany—Ecology
ISBN 0-688-51467-7

"Brief chapters about 15 types of weeds are introduced by a description of their use in the total life cycle." Minnesota

"Photographs, many showing microscopic detail, add greatly to the text. This is clever, factual writing which will put weeds into a new perspective for most readers. . . . Technical language is not a hindrance to readers. A listing of scientific terminology and page references is given at the end of the book. Teachers will find this a valuable and unique resource for planning outdoor lessons in plant ecology, soil erosion, and conservation." Appraisal

581.6   Economic botany

Beck, Barbara L.

Vegetables; illus by Page Cary. Watts, F. 1970 63p illus lib. bdg. $3.90 (4-6)   581.6

1 Vegetables
ISBN 0-531-00717-0

"A First book"

This book "traces the historical development of common vegetables and brings in some interesting folklore to their use as food by man. The vegetables are grouped according to their botanical classification. . . . The book has no photos, but contains excellent drawings of all the vegetables mentioned." Sci Bks

Fenton, Carroll Lane

Plants we live on; the story of grains and vegetables [by] Carroll Lane Fenton [and] Herminie B. Kitchen; illus. by Carroll Lane Fenton. [Rev. and enl. ed] Day 1971 128p illus map lib. bdg. $4.29 (4-6)   581.6

1 Plants, Edible 2 Grain 3 Vegetables
ISBN 0-381-99819-3

First published 1956 with title: Plants that feed us

This book tells the story of grains and vegetables, of the people who grew them in ancient times and of the influence of these food plants on the progress of mankind

"The material is treated in a nontechnical manner yet it provides the essential facts for developing the curiosity of the young." Sci Bks

Books, articles, and illustrations: p124-25

Limburg, Peter R.

Watch out, it's poison ivy! Photographs by the author; drawings by Haris Petie. Messner 1973 96p illus lib. bdg. $5.29 (3-6)   581.6

1 Poison ivy
ISBN 0-671-32564-7

This book "serves both as an identification source and as a compilation of information about recognizing symptoms and treating poison ivy. The text stresses safety measures in both treatment of poisoning and in eradicating the plant, and warns repeatedly of the necessity of getting professional attention if the case is severe or the poison is near a victim's eyes. There is also discussion of other plants that are harmless but resemble poison ivy and of poison oak and poison sumac, with both text and pictures giving details that enable the reader to recognize each plant." Chicago. Children's Bk Center

"Clearly written and profusely illustrated

Limburg, Peter R.—*Continued*

with . . . drawings, and photographs, this account offers broader coverage of the subject than is found in scout, camping, and first aid handbooks or in more general treatments of plant life." Sch Library J
Glossary: p91-92

Rahn, Joan Elma

Grocery store botany; illus. by Ginny Linville Winter. Atheneum Pubs. 1974 54p illus $4.95 (3-5)
581.6

1 Plants, Edible 2 Botany—Experiments
ISBN 0-689-30414-5

"Basic plant anatomy is explained by investigating plants generally found around the kitchen. Each anatomical part of plants is illustrated with some common examples (roots—carrots, beets; stems—broccoli, asparagus) and some not-so-well-known examples (roots—ginger, licorice; stems—kohlrabi, white potato). Each chapter has several 'Something to Do' sections which include mostly cutting, looking and, occasionally, growing. The book tackles a very difficult subject in trying to explain flowers, fruits and seeds. (Why is an apple really a stem and not a fruit? Why is a kernel of corn a fruit and not a seed? And so on.) Some children may be confused and might be less discouraged if the author had pointed out that sometimes even botanists don't agree on what is the fruit and what is the seed. The illustrations are clear, simple line drawings with all essential details. The text and illustrations form a tight unit." Sci Bks

Schaeffer, Elizabeth

Dandelion, pokeweed, and goosefoot; how the early settlers used plants for food, medicine, and in the home; with illus. by Grambs Miller. Young Scott Bks. 1972 94p illus $4.50 (4-7)
581.6

1 Botany, Economic 2 Botany, Medical 3 Plants, Edible
ISBN 0-201-09304-9

"Not all the wild plants known and used by early settlers in North America were native; some had been deliberately imported while others had made the journey to the New World as hitchhikers. In this book, the plants are first divided by habitat into three groups: woodland, pastureland, and swampland. In each section the plants are further grouped according to the purpose for which they were gathered: medicine, food, or household use. Historical allusions and nature lore are included in the general descriptions and in the explanations of Latin and common names. . . . A Bibliography and an Index are to be found in the well-researched, carefully prepared, and accurately illustrated book." Horn Bk

Selsam, Millicent E.

Plants that heal; illus. by Kathleen Elgin. Morrow 1959 96p illus $4.81 (4-6)
581.6

1 Botany, Medical
ISBN 0-688-31486-4

" 'The plant kingdom was man's only drugstore for countless centuries.' Thus opens a brief and fascinating history of man's use of roots, stems, leaves, and seeds of plants to heal (and some to poison, too). A résumé of superstitions and magic, prescriptions in medieval herbals and Indian folk medicine (now being studied anew) precedes description of recent discoveries of antibiotics and vitamins. Clear botanical sketches, a list of common and scientific plant names, and an index." Horn Bk

582   Seed-bearing plants

Allen, Gertrude E.

Everyday trees. Houghton 1968 47p illus $3.50 (2-4)
582

1 Trees
ISBN 0-395-06549-6

"To acquaint children with a few of the most common trees of the U.S., the author . . . devotes several pages of pictures and text to each of seven varieties: apple, maple, willow, birch, oak, pine, and fir. She describes the bark, flowers, leaves, and seeds of the trees and their seasonal changes. The drawings have a soft, slightly misty quality which adds appeal without obscuring their identifying features." Booklist

Buff, Mary

Big tree, by Mary & Conrad Buff. Viking 1946 79p illus $3.50 (5-7)
582

1 Sequoia
ISBN 0-670-16425-9

"In the forest of giant redwoods in California, one stands biggest and oldest of all. This tree has been chosen by Mary and Conrad Buff as the subject of a moving and dramatic interpretation of five thousand years of earth history. From its marks and scars they picture the effect of the great natural forces; they imagine its start far back when the pyramids were building in Egypt; they tell of the many tenants, friendly and unfriendly, who have found shelter within its branches, the animals that have crouched near by. . . . Most impressive are the beautiful illustrations, bringing out in the pattern of the forest the semblance of a mighty cathedral." Horn Bk

Bulla, Clyde Robert

A tree is a plant; illus. by Lois Lignell. Crowell 1960 unp illus (Let's-read-and-find-out science bks) $4.50, lib. bdg. $5.25, pa $1.25 (k-2)
582

1 Trees
ISBN 0-690-83529-9; 0-690-83530-2; 0-690-00201-7

"The text presents very simply the fact that there are many kinds of trees, that they reproduce by seeding and that an apple tree will be chosen as an example of a tree. The cycle of growth and the seasonal changes, the structure and the functioning of the parts are then described in terms of the apple tree. . . . The greatest asset of the book is in the limitation of information: there is no extraneous information or terminology that might confuse the reader." Chicago. Children's Bk Center

"Lois Lignell's illustrations, each stretching across two pages, are informative as well as beautiful in color and design." Horn Bk

Carle, Eric

The tiny seed. Crowell 1970 unp illus $4.95, lib. bdg. $5.70 (k-3)
582

1 Seeds
ISBN 0-690-84642-7; 0-690-82643-5

"Beautiful collage paintings [by the author] and simple poetic text effectively tell a story that artistically dramatizes the beauty of the changing seasons and the life cycle of a flowering plant." Adventuring With Bks. 2d edition

Collingwood, G. H.

Knowing your trees, by G. H. Collingwood and Warren D. Brush. Am Forestry Assn. illus maps $7.90
582

1 Trees—U.S.

First published 1937. Revised with each printing

"The appearance of the tree is described, its economic importance is indicated, and its range is shown on a small map of the United States. Good

Collingwood, G. H.—*Continued*
photographs show a mature tree and the leaf and bark. Deciduous broadleafed trees are pictured in summer and winter. Index of scientific and common names." Am Forests

Cooper, Elizabeth K.
A tree is something wonderful, by Elizabeth K. Cooper and Padraic Cooper; photographs by Padraic Cooper. Golden Gate 1972 unp illus lib. bdg. $4.95 (2-4)   582
1 Trees
ISBN 0-516-08702-9
"The book contains vivid descriptions, accompanied by excellent photographs, of a wide variety of trees and their habitats. The reader is shown trees growing in desert soil, on cliff edges; city trees in 'cages' on downtown sidewalks; trees, the largest and oldest in nature, protected in our western national parks; trees to climb and swing from and to lounge under shaded from the noonday heat; trees that shelter the nests of birds; and trees that young students can grow from seeds in glass jars." Sci Bks

Dowden, Anne Ophelia T.
Look at a flower; illus. by the author. Crowell 1963 120p illus $6.95 (6-7)   582
1 Flowers 2 Botany
ISBN 0-690-50656-2
This book presents "the evolution, structure and reproduction of common North American plants and flowers, grouped into ten families." Toronto
"Exquisitely detailed botanical drawings will lead the holder of this book first to read the pictures and thus to find introduction to a highly scientific and readable text. It is an excellent treatment of basic botany . . . in a handsomely produced volume, complete with general index and an index of plants referred to in illustration and text." Horn Bk

Wild green things in the city; a book of weeds; illus. by the author. Crowell 1972 56p illus $5.95 (4-7)
                                                                                582
1 Wild flowers 2 Weeds
ISBN 0-690-89067-2
The author describes "city weeds and their development—roots in April, leaves in May, flowers in June, composites and grasses in summer, and seeds in autumn. She discusses plant survival in a manmade environment and man's dependence on oxygen-manufacturing plant life." Booklist
"Beautifully illustrated with meticulously realistic drawings of plants and plant parts, this is not only an excellent book for identification and appreciation of weeds, but gives a great deal of information about botanical structure, photosynthesis, and propagation. The plants described are those found in three urban areas: Manhattan, Denver, and Los Angeles. Lucidly written, the text is followed by lists of plants for each of the three areas, each list divided into rare, common, and very common weeds. An index is appended." Chicago. Children's Bk Center

Earle, Olive L.
Nuts, by Olive L. Earle with Michael Kantor; illus. by Olive L. Earle. Morrow 1975 63p illus. $4.75, lib. bdg. $4.32 (3-6)   582
1 Nuts
ISBN 0-688-22025-8; 0-688-32025-2
"The authors list 34 of the more familiar nut species, telling where they are found, how they grow, and what they are used for. A beginning chapter explains the botanical terminology that appears throughout and clarifies the scientific definition of the term 'nut.' Illustrated with Earle's pencil sketches

showing the leaves, flowers, and nuts of each plant." Booklist
"This will be of interest considering the upsurge in natural foods and forest foraging." Sch Library J

State trees. Newly rev. ed. Written and illus. by Olive L. Earle. Morrow 1973 unp illus lib. bdg. $4.32 (4-7)   582
1 State trees
ISBN 0-688-31956-4
First published 1960
"Describes in brief text the appearance, growth, [legends about] and use of the [39] trees chosen as state trees and shows in detailed drawings the seed, flower, leaf, bark, and shape of the tree. While the same information can be found in encyclopedias many libraries will find it convenient to have the material in a single volume. Arranged alphabetically by tree with an index by state." Booklist [Review of 1960 edition]
"A good book for the young naturalist who has tramped beyond the novice field. . . . Lucid text and dignified drawings." N Y Times Bk Rev [Review of 1960 edition]

Fenton, Carroll Lane
Trees and their world, by Carroll Lane Fenton and Dorothy Constance Pallas; illus. by Carroll Lane Fenton. Day 1957 96p illus lib. bdg. $3.69 (4-7)   582
1 Trees
ISBN 0-381-99815-0
"An introduction to the study of trees 'the largest plants in the world and the most familiar.' Tree families, how trees grow, their fruit, propagation, uses and other questions on tree life are answered in a scientific yet informal manner. Well supplemented with line sketches." Ontario Library Rev

Gallob, Edward
City leaves, city trees; photographs and photograms by the author. Scribner 1972 64p illus lib. bdg. $6.95 (3-6)   582
1 Trees—U.S. 2 Leaves
ISBN 0-684-12808-X
"The trees in this book are to be found in the New England, Middle Atlantic, and North Central states." Facing title page
"A guide to tree identification in the city which includes brief descriptive passages accompanied by photographs of various trees and, on facing pages, photographs of their leaves, flowers, winter buds, fruit, seeds, etc." Sch Library J
"The artistic photograms and photographs are esthetically appealing in design and texture as well as clear in their presentation of information; they will induce children to recognize and to collect leaves, and to make leaf photograms." Top of the News

Guilcher, J. M.
A fruit is born, by J. M. Guilcher and R. H. Noailles. Sterling 1960 111p illus (Sterling Nature ser) $4.50 (4-7)   582
1 Fruit 2 Seeds
ISBN 0-8069-3508-1
Original French edition, 1951
"Unusually fine, enlarged photographs show the life cycle of fruit. The brief text explains and shows in diagrams the structure of a pistil, follows the development of the fruit from flower to seed, and explains seed dispersal." Hodges. Bks for Elem Sch Libraries

A tree is born, by J. M. Guilcher and R. H. Noailles. Sterling 1960 100p illus (Sterling Nature ser) $4.50 (4-7)   582
1 Trees
ISBN 0-8069-3510-3

Guilcher, J. M.—*Continued*

This book "takes up the life cycle of four trees; horse chestnut, oak, walnut, and pine. Well illustrated with 127 photographs which are exceptionally well reproduced. Printed in France, it makes a welcome addition to information already available on the subject." Library J

"The close-up photographs of tree structures are excellent and greatly assist in an understanding of the text. Title is inappropriate." The AAAS Sci Bk List for Children

Hammond, Winifred G.

The riddle of seeds. Coward-McCann [1966 c1965] 63p illus lib. bdg. $4.69 (3-5)   582

1 Seeds

ISBN 0-689-30293-1

"A significant primary science book on seeds and their importance to man of particular use in school libraries. The simple explicit directions for several projects and experiments not only show the shape, size, growth, travel, and food value of seeds but also introduce the young child to various ways of scientifically testing and recording information. The text includes pronunciation of scientific terms and is copiously illustrated with excellent photographs and diagrams." Booklist

Hutchins, Ross E.

The amazing seeds; photographs by the author. Dodd 1965 159p illus lib. bdg. $4.50 (5-7)   582

1 Seeds

ISBN 0-396-06478-7

Starting with an initial chapter on seedless plants, the book then "describes pollination, seed production, germination, plant growth, dispersal of seeds, and other botanical processes. Many forms of common and uncommon seeds are described and illustrated, and the book closes with a brief instruction of collecting wild flower seeds." Sci Bks

Jordan, Helene J.

How a seed grows; illus. by Joseph Low. Crowell 1960 unp illus (Let's-read-and-find-out science bks) $4.50, lib. bdg. $4.25, pa $1.25 (k-2)   582

1 Seeds

ISBN 0-690-40644-4; 0-690-40645-2; 0-690-40646-0

"Begins by explaining that the seeds of different plants are different and grow differently. Then suggests that the student plant and care for some bean seeds in order to observe how they develop; thus it effectively teaches the beginner how a seed grows into a plant." The AAAS Sci Bk List for Children

"For beginning independent readers. Large print, plenty of white space, and information given with simplicity implement the appropriate level of sentence length and vocabulary difficulty." Chicago. Children's Bk Center

Seeds by wind and water; illus. by Nils Hogner. Crowell 1962 unp illus (Let's-read-and-find-out science bks) $4.50, lib. bdg. $5.25 (k-2)   582

1 Seeds

ISBN 0-690-72452-7; 0-690-72453-5

This is "an elementary explanation of the variety of ways in which seeds are distributed. [It] shows how wind, animals, water and even airplanes carry seeds from place to place. Color and black-and-white drawings of each seed and plant help in identifying the plants discussed." The AAAS Sci Bk List for Children

"A very brief account . . . useful for elementary science projects." N Y Times Bk Rev

Kieran, John

An introduction to trees; illus. by Michael H. Bevans. [New ed] Doubleday 1966 77p illus $5.95 (5-7)   582

1 Trees—North America

ISBN 0-385-06035-1

First published 1954 by Hanover House

This book for beginners "is offered as a help in learning to recognize and name the more common trees of our city streets, suburban lawns, country lanes, valley farms, and the great forests of North America." Foreword

"Gives identifying facts and shows tree, leaves, and seeds in color paintings." Hodges. Bks for Elem Sch Libraries

Milne, Lorus J.

Because of a tree [by] Lorus J. Milne & Margery Milne; drawings by Kenneth Gosner. Atheneum Pubs. 1963 152p illus $3.95, lib. bdg. $4.08 (4-6)   582

1 Trees 2 Ecology

ISBN 0-689-20280-6; 0-689-20281-4

An ecological study, "emphasizing the interdependence among trees and various insects, plants, and animals. Various chapters consider the apple, sugar maple, fir and spruce, palm, bald cypress, redwood, aspen, and saguaro [cactus] trees." Sch Library J

Nature facts "organized for upper elementary-school children. . . . Inviting format." Horn Bk

Books for additional reading and reference: p151-52

Petrides, George A.

A field guide to trees and shrubs. . . . Illus. by George A. Petrides [and] Roger Tory Peterson. 2d ed. Houghton 1972 xxxii, 423p illus $6.95, pa $4.95 582

1 Trees—North America 2 Shrubs 3 Climbing plants

ISBN 0-395-13651-2; 0-395-17579-8

."The Peterson Field guide series"

First published 1958

"Field marks of all trees, shrubs, and woody vines that grow wild in the northeastern and north-central United States and in southeastern and south-central Canada." Title page

"Written primarily for the amateur naturalist who wants a quick method of identifying woody plants based on easily observed characteristics. . . . The extensive coverage of shrubs and woody vines adds greatly to the value of this guide. . . . There are silhouettes of tree shapes for many common trees, a key to the hickories, and keys for winter identification. Important information on wildlife values, and uses for furniture, dyes, and emergency food add to the readability of the volume." Choice

Podendorf, Illa

The true book of weeds and wild flowers; pictures by Mary Gehr. Childrens Press 1955 47p illus lib. bdg. $3.95 (1-3)   582

1 Weeds 2 Wild flowers

ISBN 0-516-01261-4

The author identifies the weeds of the dooryard, the roadside, the garden, the fields and the woods and tells why weeds are harmful. She also shows the beauty of the wild flowers of early spring, of fall, of winter

"Beginning readers will like the simple format and colorful illustrations of this introduction to botany." Library J

Rahn, Joan Elma

How plants travel; illus. by Ginny Linville Winter. Atheneum Pubs. 1973 58p illus $4.95 (4-6)   582

1 Seeds

ISBN 0-689-30118-9

"A conversational approach makes this book about plant dissemination inviting and readable. Skillful questions followed by discussion well within the interest and experience of young children identify many kinds of disseminules produced by plants, and describe the great variety of ways in which they are distributed. Anecdotes enliven the exposition, and a wealth of clear line-drawings add information and interest. Disseminules that travel in the wind, by water, and with the help of animals and human beings are described. Recommended for accuracy, clarity, and liveliness." Horn Bk

Riedman, Sarah R.

Trees alive; illus. by Giulio Maestro. Lothrop 1974 128p illus $5.50, lib. bdg. $4.81 (5-7)   582

1 Trees

ISBN 0-688-41574-1; 0-688-51574-6

The author "presents fascinating information about one of our greatest resources. The history of the use of trees is examined, as well as latest scientific findings. Chapters explore such topics as: structure and function of tree parts; how trees breathe, grow, reproduce, age, and die; how they convert solar energy to chemical energy; and the process by which trees purify and renew our air. The concluding chapter poses a sober question for us all: Will trees forever remain a renewable resource if continued cutting depletes our forests?" Sci Teacher

Suggestions for further reading: p125

Selsam, Millicent E.

The apple and other fruits; photographs by Jerome Wexler. Morrow 1973 48p illus $5.50, lib. bdg. $4.81 (3-5)   582

1 Fruit 2 Trees

ISBN 0-688-20089-3; 0-688-30089-8

The book combines photographs "with clear, uncompromising explanations of the apple blossoms' pollination, the fruit's growth from a flower's ovary, grafting and budding, and the comparable development of pears, peaches, plums, cherries, and oranges." Booklist

This is "a model of botanical instruction. . . . There is no extraneous text, and the magnified photographs are handsome, clear, and nicely placed." Chicago. Children's Bk Center

Maple tree; photographs by Jerome Wexler. Morrow 1968 46p illus lib. bdg. $4.81 (2-4)   582

1 Maple

ISBN 0-688-31496-1

"Using the Norway maple to demonstrate the principles of growth, the author and photographer describe the step-by-step development of a seed into a tree from the winged fruit which puts roots into the ground, produces buds, leaves and stems to the trunk and branches." Pub W

"Clear photographs, many enlarged close-ups in black and white and some in color (and beautiful), add to the appeal of a lucid and informative botany book for the primary grades reader." Chicago. Children's Bk Center

"In describing the life cycle of the maple, the author is not rhapsodic about the beauty of the flower or the wonder of reproduction, but lets the reader see for himself the perennial miracle of seed and bud." Sat Rev

Stupka, Arthur

Wildflowers in color, by Arthur Stupka with the assistance of Donald H. Robinson. Harper 1965 144p illus $8.95   582

1 Wild flowers

ISBN 0-06-071860-9

This is "a combination field guide to identification and full-color picture book portraying 250 species common in the eastern United States, with full botanical information and an excellent color photograph of each." Hodges. Bks for Elem Sch Libraries

"True, the wildflowers listed and notes here are found mostly in the Southern Appalachian Mountains, (in the Shenandoah, Blue Ridge, and Great Smokey National Parks); but they occur frequently enough in a large number of instances further north into New York State and Massachusetts for this to be a helpful guide. The pictures with their accompanying notes, are presented in rather haphazard order, it would seem, but can be located by the Index." Best Sellers

Suggested readings: p135-36

Zim, Herbert S.

Flowers; a guide to familiar American wildflowers, by Herbert S. Zim and Alexander C. Martin; illus. by Rudolf Freund. 134 paintings in full color. Sponsored by the Wildlife Management Institute. Golden Press 1950 157p illus maps (A Golden Nature guide) lib. bdg. $4.95, pa $1.50   582

1 Wild flowers

ISBN 0-307-63511-2; 0-307-24491-1

First published by Simon & Schuster

"This is an extremely practical beginner's guide. . . . To facilitate identification the flowers are arranged in four groups according to color. Each flower is pictured in color with a range map. . . . Brief descriptive text gives characteristics, habitat, growing season and family." Booklist

"It is not only a very informing book. It is attractive and easy to carry in a coat pocket." Sat Rev

Trees; a guide to familiar American trees, by Herbert S. Zim and Alexander C. Martin; illus. by Dorothea and Sy Barlowe. 143 species in color. Sponsored by the Wildlife Management Institute. [Rev. ed] Golden Press 1956 160p illus maps (A Golden Nature Guide) lib. bdg. $4.95, pa $1.50   582

1 Trees

ISBN 0-307-24494-6; 0-307-63509-0

First published 1952 by Simon & Schuster

"A beginner's pocket-size guidebook, uniform with . . . other titles in the Golden Nature series; illustrates in color and describes . . . American trees, pointing up the features important in identification—form and height of tree, leaves, bark, fruit, flowers, buds—and including, in most cases, a range map." Booklist

"The authors' aim is to make tree study easy. . . . The nature fan has to read only about 100 words to get complete information about a tree he's trying to identify." Chicago Sunday Trib

582.072 Seed-bearing plants— Experiments

Selsam, Millicent E.

Play with seeds; illus. by Helen Ludwig. Morrrow 1957 93p illus lib. bdg. $4.81 (3-6)   582.072

1 Seeds

ISBN 0-688-31489-9

Selsam, Millicent E.—*Continued*
"Excellent informative introduction to the study of plants and seeds. . . . Traces their evolution on earth from their beginnings 100 million years ago. Clear explanations, accompanied by detailed black-and-white drawings show the development of the seed in a wide variety of plants. The travel of seeds, both useful and harmful, aided by birds, wind, and man, is described with interesting details. Numerous simple but enlightening experiments are suggested. Index adds to the usefulness." Library J

Play with trees; pictures by Fred F. Scherer. Morrow 1950 64p illus lib. bdg. $4.81 (3-5)   582.072
1 Trees
ISBN 0-688-31495-3
"A good introduction to the study of trees [and how they grow] showing how they can be distinguished by their shapes, bark, buds and leaves. It gives the methods for collecting and preserving leaves and twigs, and it is illustrated by numerous black and white drawings." Ontario Library Rev
"Growing a miniature forest in a windowsill-size aquarium glass is one of the most fascinating experiments included in this book. . . . There are many other experiments too and much information for the gradeschool science classes either in city or country schools." Horn Bk

583   Dicotyledons

Earle, Olive L.
Peas, beans, and licorice; written and illus. by Olive L. Earle. Morrow 1971 63p illus $4.75, lib. bdg. $4.32 (4-6)   583
1 Legumes
ISBN 0-688-21570-X; 0-688-31570-4
This "introduction to the small plants and the trees of the legume family . . . describes the distinguishing characteristics of legumes and the appearance and practical and ornamental uses of different species. In addition to the three species mentioned in the title, the book covers alfalfa, loco weed, wisteria, peanuts, Scotch broom, the laburnum tree, and many other legumes. A service supplement to plant studies and, with the author's clear, accurate drawings, a helpful guide to identification." Booklist

The rose family; written and illus. by Olive L. Earle. Morrow 1970 63p illus $4.75, lib. bdg. $4.32 (4-6)   583
1 Roses
ISBN 0-688-21491-6; 0-688-31491-0
"Clearly written survey of the wide variety of members of the rose family. . . . The text points out the similarities and differences among the 20,000 species, illustrating these with exotic as well as familiar flowers, bushes, and trees." Sat Rev
"Each page of the book includes an illustration appropriate for the text on that page. The drawings, by the author, are accurate, labeled, and offer added interest to the text. A discussion on the economic uses of the members of the rose family helps children realize that although many rose family plants are usually appreciated solely for aesthetic beauty, they also may have practical uses as wood products and food sources. For example, a consideration is provided of rose family fruits that belong to the botanical groupings known as drupes, true berries, and pomes. [The author] indicated many botanical terms and their origins that are of concern when offering a scientific account of the rose family." Sci Bks

Selsam, Millicent E.
Milkweed; photographs by Jerome Wexler. Morrow 1967 48p illus lib. bdg. $5.11 (2-4)   583
1 Milkweed
ISBN 0-688-31888-6
"Text and pictures follow the growth of the milkweed plant, the process of cross-pollination, the maturing of the seed pods, and the dissemination of the seeds." Horn Bk
Details of plant anatomy are "shown by appropriate labeling of illustrations. This is . . . [a] model of an interesting, factual, and appropriate science book for small children." Sci Bks

Peanut; photographs by Jerome Wexler. Morrow 1969 46p illus lib. bdg. $5.11 (2-4)   583
1 Peanuts
ISBN 0-688-31803-7
"A clear, accurate text and outstanding close-up photographs, seven in color, describe the development of the self-pollinating peanut plant from seed to maturity. This excellent science book . . . also notes the peanut's value as food, some of its other uses, and the harvesting of peanuts." Booklist

584   Monocotyledons

Selsam, Millicent E.
Bulbs, corms, and such; photographs by Jerome Wexler. Morrow 1974 48p illus $4.95, lib. bdg. $4.59 (2-5)   584
1 Bulbs 2 Botany
ISBN 0-688-21822-9; 0-688-31822-3
This book explains "the reproductive, life-sustaining function of the fleshy, underground parts of non-seedbearing plants. Spring flowers like daffodils and hyacinths serve to illustrate bulbs; gladiolas, begonias, canna plants, sweet potatoes, and dahlias are examples of corms, tubers, rhizomes, and tuberous roots. Directions for growing each flower are appended." Booklist
The book is illustrated with "full-color pictures of plants in bloom contrasting dramatically with black and white pictures—often with plant parts cut away—of stages in the growth of bulbs, corms, tubers, tuberous roots, and rhizomes. . . . This is an example of the best kind of science writing: clear and informative, with the text and illustrations nicely integrated." Chicago. Children's Bk Center

586   Seedless plants

Hutchins, Ross E.
Plants without leaves; lichens, fungi, mosses, liverworts, slime-molds, algae, horsetails; photographs by the author. Dodd 1966 152p illus lib. bdg. $4.50 (5-7)   586
1 Plants
ISBN 0-396-06653-4
"Algae, fungi, slime-molds, lichens, liverworts, mosses, and horse-tails can be quite exciting when examined by a 10-power hand lens, preferably in the woods during the rainy season. Mr Hutchins explains their growth habits, uses to man, and manner of survival. His excellent macrophotographs add depth to the lively text." Sch Library J
Lists of manuals for further study of leafless plants: p145-47

587 Ferns

Guilcher, J. M.

A fern is born, by J. M. Guilcher & R. H. Noailles. Sterling 1971 96p illus (Sterling Nature ser) $4.50 (5-7)   587

1 Ferns

ISBN 0-8069-3512-X

Translated from the original 1957 French edition by Rhea Rollin and adapted by E. W. Egan

The close-up photographs in this book reveal the process by which ferns reproduce themselves—one generation sexually and the succeeding one asexually, over and over again. Each familiar fern plant is the offspring of a totally dissimilar and inconspicuous parent—the prothallium, which in turn grew from a tiny spore borne on the underside of a fern leaf. The authors explain how to grow prothallia from spores and ferns from prothallia and how to watch first hand the life of these fascinating plants

589 Thallophyta

Froman, Robert

Mushrooms and molds; illus. by Grambs Miller. Crowell 1972 33p illus (Let's-read-and-find-out science bks) $4.50, lib. bdg. $5.25 (1-3)   589

1 Mushrooms 2 Molds (Botany)

ISBN 0-690-56602-6; 0-690-56603-4

The book gives "information on fungi covering their growth from mycelium, their manufacture of soil for green plants, and their reproduction by spores. Suggestions for growing bread molds and making mushroom spore patterns are intriguing and practical for small children." Booklist

"The definitions included within the text are scientifically accurate, yet very simple. The drawings on each page clearly show what the author is explaining. Because there is little available on the subject, this will provide good supplementary material for elementary science collections." Sch Library J

Kavaler, Lucy

The wonders of algae; illus. with photographs and with drawings by Barbara Amlick and Richard Ott. Day 1961 96p illus lib. bdg. $4.50 (5-7)   589

1 Algae

ISBN 0-381-99771-5

The tiny organisms called algae are the most primitive form of life on earth, yet they are uniquely suited to the space age. This book tells of their many uses, all over the world, today and in the future, as a source of oxygen, food, and medicine, as an industrial raw material, and in other areas. The uses of plankton are also discussed

"A good example of the stimulating science book, this one is so filled with exciting ideas that it must surely impel the reader to rush out to communicate his enthusiasm of discovery." Horn Bk

The wonders of fungi; illus. with photographs and with drawings by Richard Ott. Day 1964 128p illus lib. bdg. $4.50 (5-7)   589

1 Fungi

ISBN 0-381-99770-7

An introduction to "the study of molds, mushrooms, yeasts, and other kinds of fungi, explaining their useful and harmful effects in food and medicine." Hodges. Bks for Elem Sch Libraries

"A final chapter conjectures about the fungi that may be found in space." Chicago. Children's Bk Center

"The informative scientific account is enlivened by a smooth, informal writing style and the author's apparent enthusiasm for her subject." Booklist

Kohn, Bernice

Our tiny servants; molds and yeasts; illus. by John Kaufmann. Prentice-Hall 1962 62p illus $4.95 (3-6)   589

1 Molds (Botany) 2 Yeast

ISBN 0-13-644427-X

"Lively, interesting text explains the many uses and characteristics of molds and yeasts. Miracle molds, enemy molds, and food of the future will be understandable to young readers. A few experiments include growing penicillin and baking a loaf of bread." Sch Library J

590.74 Zoological gardens

Bridges, William

Zoo careers. Morrow 1971 157p illus $5.50, lib. bdg. $4.81 (6-7)   590.74

1 New York (City) Zoological Park 2 Zoology as a profession

ISBN 0-688-21811-3; 0-688-31811-8

"Following a description of the organization of a typical zoo staff and general advice to zoo job aspirants on preparation, background reading, and setting up a basic personal library, [the author] relates his first-hand observations of the activities of various workers at the Bronx Zoo, including curators, veterinarians, and keepers, and those involved with exhibitions and graphics, publications, publicity, photography, and education. Illustrated with numerous well-chosen photographs." Booklist

Fisher, James

Zoos of the world; the story of animals in captivity. Natural Hist. Press 1967 253p illus maps (Nature and science lib) $6.95, lib. bdg. $7.70 (5-7)   590.74

1 Zoological gardens

ISBN 0-385-08351-3; 0-385-08723-3

"Published for the American Museum of Natural History"

The author discusses the history of zoos from the very earliest times; considers future prospects with respect to research and development; and describes present-day zoos with their problems of obtaining, transporting, feeding, and housing large numbers of animals

"Excellent detail. The author tries to prove that 'zoos are a part of man's deepset strivings to understand the world around him.' " Bruno. Bks for Sch Libraries, 1968

List of zoos and aquariums: p236-45

Perry, John

Zoos; illus. with photographs. Watts, F. 1971 86p illus lib. bdg. $3.90 (4-6)   590.74

1 Zoological gardens

ISBN 0-531-00754-5

"A First book"

In this book "a logical sequence is presented from the arrival of a new animal to its exhibition through behind-the-scenes activities of a zoo and its personnel. The reader is taken on an imaginary trip around the zoo to visit the animals as well as to learn about the people who care for them and do other related jobs. Throughout the book, explanation of activities, operations, and animals is simplified but enough basic scientific information is given to make the book worthwhile. . . . [The author] presents new ideas and developments in zoo management and maintenance.

Perry, John—*Continued*

He explains the trend toward open zoos and toward providing the animal with facsimiles of the natural habitats. . . . [He also] stresses the importance of ecology, behavior, and survival." Sci Bks

Other books to read: p82

Shannon, Terry

New at the zoo; animal offspring from aardvark to zebra, by Terry Shannon and Charles Payzant; illus. with photographs. Golden Gate 1972 79p illus lib. bdg. $4.95 (5-7)   590.74

1 Animals—Infancy 2 Zoological gardens

ISBN 0-516-08836-X

In this description of the care and rearing of zoo-born baby animals, the authors show one aspect of modern zoos and animal parks. Most of the 57 featured animals are mammals. Feeding, some habits, special breeding projects for rare and endangered species, and educational services to the public are considered

"Excellent photographs, informative text and collaboration with some of America's finest zoos and zoo people make this an outstanding little book. The design, role and activities of a modern zoo are nicely emphasized." Appraisal

591 Zoology

Caras, Roger

The bizarre animals; foreword by Roger Tory Peterson. Barre/Webster Bks. distributed by Crown 1974 64p illus $3.95   591

1 Zoology

ISBN 0-517-517884

"Sixty-odd photographs of animals have been coupled with a paragraph or two of description for each. The animals—crab, sea fan, platypus, pelican, chameleon, etc.—were chosen because to our human eyes they seem extraordinary in shape and color. The accompanying paragraphs are moderately informative, are often amusing and are more commentary than exposition." AAAS Sci Bks & Films

Pringle, Laurence

(ed.) Discovering nature indoors; a nature and science guide to investigations with small animals. Natural Hist. Press 1970 128p illus $4.95, lib. bdg. $5.70 (5-7)   591

1 Zoology 2 Nature study

ISBN 0-385-05126-3; 0-385-01000-1

"Like the compiler's 'Discovering the outdoors' [entered in class 574] this book is comprised of articles from 'Nature, and Science' magazine. Dealing with snails, turtles, guppies, mealworms, cockroaches, houseflies, ants, shrimp, gerbils, mice, and other small animals it offers information on how to keep them successfully and suggests projects and investigations for studying them. It also includes instructions on how to make and use a microscope. With many clear photographs and diagrams, a helpful and stimulating book. A list of books for further reading and the names and addresses of supply houses are appended." Booklist

Schwartz, Elizabeth

When animals are babies, by Elizabeth and Charles Schwartz; illus. by Charles Schwartz. Holiday House 1964 unp illus lib. bdg. $4.95 (k-3)   591

1 Animals—Infancy

ISBN 0-8234-0132-4

Differences between families and species are con-trasted for 28 young animals. Also detailed are their relative size, growth patterns, feeding habits and need for protection

"The illustrations are in soft tones of green, brown, and black. At the back of the book are two lists, one giving the common names of the adult animals, the other, the names used for the baby animals." Sch Library J

Selsam, Millicent E.

All kinds of babies; pictures by Symeon Shimin. Four Winds [1969 c1967] unp illus $3.95, lib. bdg. $3.89 (k-3)   591

1 Animals—Infancy

ISBN 0-590-17156-9; 0-590-07156-4

First published 1953 by Scott with title: All kinds of babies and how they grow. Helen Ludwig was the illustrator

"An attractive picture book for the very young explains and shows, by means of attractive illustrations, that the young of many species closely resemble their parents (particularly most mammals), but the young of other species do not resemble their parents at all (butterflies, frogs, eels). However, no matter what the young look like, 'Every kind of living thing in the world makes more of its own kind. This is true of fish, insects, birds, and every kind of animal.' Fundamental biological facts are acquired pleasantly by the child." Sci Bks

Benny's animals, and how he put them in order; pictures by Arnold Lobel. Harper 1966 60p illus (A Science I can read bk) $2.95, lib. bdg. $3.79 (1-3)   591

1 Zoology—Terminology 2 Animals

ISBN 0-06-025272-3; 0-06-025273-1

"Benny, whose passion for tidiness rather worried his mother, became curious about animals after bringing some specimens home from the beach. With some guidance from a museum zoologist, Benny and his friend learned something about the major divisions in zoological classification." Chicago. Children's Bk Center

"This is a readable book, basically accurate and informative. . . . It teaches fundamental processes of observation, comparison, classification, and reasoning." Sci Bks

When an animal grows; pictures by John Kaufmann. Harper 1966 64p illus (A Science I can read bk) $2.95, lib. bdg. $3.79 (k-3)   591

1 Growth 2 Animals—Infancy

ISBN 0-06-025460-2; 0-06-025461-0

"In concurrent narratives which compare the babyhood and maturation first of a gorilla and a lamb, and then of a sparrow and a mallard duck, the author describes some basic factors common to all growing animals as well as variations in rate of growth and time of dependency on parental care in different species. The attractive, realistic illustrations [in black and white] supplement the text and add to the book's appeal." Booklist

Ylla

Animal babies. Story by Arthur Gregor; designed by Luc Bouchage. Harper 1959 unp illus $4.95, lib. bdg. $4.79 (k-3)   591

1 Animals—Pictorial works 2 Animals—Infancy

ISBN 0-06-026740-2; 0-06-026741-0

"These artistically sympathetic, uncluttered photographs of animal babies with their mothers will be studied with wonder and enjoyment by kindergarten and primary age children, who find the reality of uncolored photographs absorbing in a way that the younger picture-book ages do not. And the older child's greater familiarity with the animals of farm and

Ylla—*Continued*

zoo will give him an interest with which to approach this beautiful book." Horn Bk

"Accompanying each photograph are a few lines of text which do little more than identify the animals." Booklist

Whose eye am I? Story by Crosby Bonsall, planned by Charles Rado, designed by Luc Bouchage. Harper 1968 unp illus $4.95, lib. bdg. $4.79 (k-3)   591

1 Animals—Pictorial works 2 Eye
ISBN 0-06-020563-6; 0-06-020564-4

"A small boy sees the eye of an animal 'in a hole in a fence on a farm.' He goes around the farm seeking the owner of the eye and having conversations with the animals he encounters. . . . Black-and-white pictures, from full-page to very small, are stunning—superbly contrasted, cleverly angled, and marvelously successful in evoking the different animal personalities. . . . A fine read-aloud for preschoolers, this will appeal to independent readers in the second and third grades too." Sch Library J

591.03   Zoology—Encyclopedias and dictionaries

Davis, Joseph A.

Five hundred animals from A to Z; [illus] by Tibor Gergely with text by Joseph A. Davis. Am. Heritage 1970 93p illus $4.95 (3-7)   591.03

1 Animals—Encyclopedias
ISBN 0-07-023153-3

A guide to animals, arranged alphabetically from aardvark to zorille, that have been selected from the million or so animals alive in the world today because they are among the most interesting or beautiful or, typical. The drawings are accompanied by brief facts about each animal

591.1   Animal physiology

May, Julian

Living things and their young. Follett 1969 48p illus (Follett Family life education program) lib. bdg. $3.48 (4-6)   591.1

1 Reproduction
ISBN 0-695-45294-0

This book details "the process of reproduction in a variety of animals, from those with one cell to complex mammals." Princeton Pub. Library. Hello, Baby

The author "stresses the importance of the family in the care and protection of the young. Illustrated with photographs and schematic drawings; a glossary is appended." Booklist

591.3   Animal development and maturation

Silverstein, Alvin

Metamorphosis: the magic change [by] Alvin and Virginia Silverstein. Atheneum Pubs. 1971 74p illus $6.25 (4-6)   591.3

1 Animals—Habits and behavior 2 Growth
ISBN 0-689-20645-3

This is an account of the "kind of growth process

which has enabled seven varied species to survive—butterflies, bees, dragonflies, frogs, salamanders, starfish and eels." N Y Times Bk Rev

"Clear photographs add to the usefulness of a book that is written informally and crisply, is well organized, and emphasizes the process of metamorphosis as a change that gives young animal forms an advantage in the struggle for survival." Chicago. Children's Bk Center

Glossary: p73-74

591.4   Animal anatomy and morphology

Mason, George F.

Animal clothing. Morrow 1955 94p illus lib. bdg. $4.32 (4-7)   591.4

1 Anatomy, Comparative 2 Animals
ISBN 0-688-31032-X

The author "discusses the kinds of protective covering among animals—hair, feathers, skin, scales, shells, and external skeletons. The reader learns how feathers help birds fly and keep warm, how some animals change color, how insects, birds, and reptiles molt, and other facts about 'animal clothing.'" The AAAS Sci Bk List for Children

"Almost as valuable as the text are the [author's] line drawings which range from a comparison of a chrysalis with an Egyptian mummy to the reason why a frog's color turns from green to yellow. One-fourth of this slim volume is devoted to illustrations." Sat Rev

Animal feet; written and illus. by George F. Mason. Morrow 1970 95p illus lib. bdg. $4.32 (4-7)   591.4

1 Foot 2 Animal locomotion 3 Anatomy, Comparative
ISBN 0-688-31033-8

"This is an inclusive survey touching on evolution, the ways in which an animal's feet are adapted to its environment, descriptive anatomy, the uses of animal feet, and, briefly, some information on human feet. The writing is explicit, and the illustrations elucidate the interesting facts, both common and unusual." Sch Library J

Animal tails; written and illus. by George F. Mason. Morrow 1958 95p illus lib. bdg. $4.32 (4-7)   591.4

1 Tail 2 Anatomy, Comparative 3 Animals
ISBN 0-688-31037-0

This is an "account of the many different roles that the tails of animals play in their lives. The author describes the use of tails for balance, protection, food storage, decoration, and numerous other functions. Many drawings." Library J

"A clear-cut presentation. . . . Small line drawings by the author give the book a pleasantly old fashioned look." Chicago Sunday Trib

Animal teeth; written and illus. by George F. Mason. Morrow 1965 96p illus lib. bdg. $4.75 (4-7)   591.4

1 Teeth 2 Anatomy, Comparative 3 Animals
ISBN 0-688-21038-4

This "informative introduction to the dentition of fishes, reptiles and mammals is prepared in an elementary and yet scientific manner. The correlation is made between the kinds and shapes of teeth in relation to feeding habits." The AAAS Sci Bk List for Children

Vocabulary: p89-90. Dentition of mammals: p91-93

Mason, George F.—Continued

Animal tools. Morrow 1951 94p illus lib. bdg. $4.32
(4-7)   591.4

1 Anatomy, Comparative 2 Animals
ISBN 0-688-31039-7

"From the mosquito's delicate surgery equipment
to the beaver's tail, the animal world is full of ingenious 'tools' which enable their possessors to perform
the specialized and often highly complicated acts
which are vital to their existence. Mason shows how
teeth, claws, mouth and tail parts, and other appendages and organs are put to work, with his usual clear,
authoritative style and excellent illustrations." The
AAAS Sci Bk List for Children

Animal vision; written and illus. by George F.
Mason. Morrow 1968 94p illus $4.75, lib. bdg. $4.32
(4-7)   591.4

1 Vision 2 Animals 3 Anatomy, Comparative
ISBN 0-688-21042-2; 0-688-31042-7

The author "has examined the gross eye structure of
many different animal species, showing how each has
adapted its vision to its environment and needs. The
book shows how the overall behavior of the animal is
related to the position of the eye, the type of pupil,
the relative number of rods and cones, and the ability
to see at low levels of illumination. Some folklore is
mingled with scientific fact, but is kept distinct
enough to avoid confusion: the young reader's interest
is thus enhanced, as it is also by the many excellent
illustrations of unusual animals." Sci Bks

Animal weapons. Morrow 1949 94p illus lib. bdg.
$4.32 (4-7)   591.4

1 Anatomy, Comparative 2 Animals—Habits and
behavior
ISBN 0-688-31043-5

"Accurate drawings and clear text explain how animals' defensive mechanisms develop and how they
are used." Hodges. Bks for Elem Sch Libraries

The author discusses "weapons that aid in animal
survival—horns, hoofs, claws, teeth, poison, odor,
stings, quills." Kansas Sch Naturalist

A "little volume for the nature-lover's bookshelf. . . . The youngest will have no difficulty with
this author's clear terse prose and practical line drawings, while the mature reader will be humbled to
realize how little he has understood the mechanism of
animal weapons." N Y Times Bk Rev

Zim, Herbert S.

What's inside of animals? Illus. by Herschel Wartik. Morrow 1953 32p illus $4.95 (2-5)   591.4

1 Anatomy, Comparative
ISBN 0-688-21518-1

"The comparative anatomy of representatives of
various animal phyla, with simplified internal and
external views. Contains information about each animal's structure, habitat, and life cycle. Colorful,
attractive format helps the child understand how life
developed, and man's place in the animal kingdom."
The AAAS Sci Bk List for Children

591.5 Animal ecology

Aruego, Jose

Symbiosis; a book of unusual friendships. Scribner
1970 unp illus $3.95 (1-3)   591.5

1 Animals—Habits and behavior
ISBN 0-684-20727-3

"Bold, humorous, three-color drawings and brief
text depict the mutually beneficial relationship that
exists between nine pairs of dissimilar creatures such

as the blue butterfly and ants, the crocodile and the
plover, goatfish and wrasse, and the sooty shearwater
and the tuatara. An engaging and informative nature
picture book." Booklist

Bendick, Jeanne

Why can't I? Written and illus. by Jeanne Bendick.
McGraw 1969 48p illus $4.95, lib. bdg. $4.72 (1-4)
                                               591.5

1 Animals—Habits and behavior
ISBN 0-07-004490-2; 0-07-004491-0

"In conversational style, such phenomena are considered as: birds fly, fish live underwater, flies can
walk on ceilings, some animals sleep all winter, cats
can see in the dark, caterpillars change their shape,
turtles carry their houses, fireflies light up. The scientific principles for each are explained (and readers
comforted with the advantages of being the way they
are) in a very brief, simple text enlivened by the
humorous, cartoon-like drawings in black, yellow and
blue. The information is sufficient to satisfy young
readers to whom these ideas are new; reluctant readers will appreciate the amount of information given by
such a sparse text." Sch Library J

Berrill, Jacquelyn

Wonders of animal migration; illus. by the author.
Dodd 1964 96p illus maps lib. bdg. $4.50 (5-7)
                                               591.5

1 Animals—Migration
ISBN 0-396-06585-6

"Dodd, Mead Wonders books"

"A study of the homing instincts of animals and
birds and the mysterious sense by which birds, fish,
and other animals navigate." Hodges. Bks for Elem
Sch Libraries

"Meticulous drawings add greatly to the value of
the book." Horn Bk

Wonders of the woods and desert at night; illus. by
the author. Dodd 1963 78p illus lib. bdg. $4.50
(4-6)   591.5

1 Animals—Habits and behavior
ISBN 0-396-06395-0

The author "describes and illustrates animals who
sleep by day and forage for food by night. . . . There
are owls . . . skunks, mice, wood and pack rats,
coyotes, cougars, opossums and bobcats. But there
are also animals, birds, and insects one sees by day as
well, such as frogs, foxes, ground squirrels, moose,
bears and deer." Christian Sci Monitor

The illustrations "are bold, strong, attractively
designed portraits of a great variety of animals, every
hair or feather in place. Those done on black in white
line are especially effective." N Y Her Trib Bks

Branley, Franklyn M.

Big tracks, little tracks; illus. by Leonard Kessler.
Crowell 1960 unp illus (Let's-read-and-find-out science bks) $4.50, lib. bdg. $5.25 (k-2)   591.5

1 Tracking and trailing 2 Animals—Habits and
behavior
ISBN 0-690-14372-9; 0-690-14371-0

"A first exercise in nature detection. Author and
illustrator make [a] game of watching for and identifying animal tracks and those of humans too." N Y Times
Bk Rev

"This volume is clearly written, attractively illustrated, and full of the excitement of first explorations
in science." Sat Rev

Brown, Vinson
How to understand animal talk; with illus. by William D. Berry. Little 1958 205p illus $4.95 (5-7)
591.5
1 Animal communication
ISBN 0-316-11191-0
Described are "the characteristic sounds, signs, and movements which convey a wide variety of feelings, emotions, and messages of many domestic and wild animals." The AAAS Sci Bk List for Children
Bibliography: p197-99

Buck, Margaret Waring
Where they go in winter; written and illus. by Margaret Waring Buck. Abingdon 1968 72p illus maps $4.95, pa $1.95 (3-6) 591.5
1 Animals—Habits and behavior
ISBN 0-687-45176-0; 0-687-45177-9
The "author-illustrator, tells how various creatures survive the winter months. The six sections—insects and spiders, fishes, amphibians, reptiles, birds and mammals—describe the winter habits of various species with drawings that border the pages depicting them as they are usually seen and as they look during the winter." Pub W
"The illustrations are detailed enough to be used as identification guides, and maps indicate usual habitat." Adventuring with Bks. 2d edition
More to read: p72

Buff, Mary
Elf owl, by Mary & Conrad Buff. Viking 1958 72p illus lib. bdg. $4.95 (1-4) 591.5
1 Desert animals 2 Owls
ISBN 0-670-29178-1
"A water hole at the foot of a giant cactus, or saguaro in which an elf owl and its mate have their nest and raise their young, is the focal point of this descriptive narrative about a wildlife community of an American desert. The comings and goings of the animals around the water hole are recounted in sensitive verselike prose and handsome sepia drawings which harmoniously reflect the beauty and moods of the desert and convey the drama of the seasons as they affect the lives of the desert inhabitants and surroundings." Booklist
"Both text and illustrations make excitingly real the harshness and the beauty of the desert scene." Chicago. Children's Bk Center

Carthy, John
Animal camouflage; illus. by Colin Threadgall. McGraw [1974 c1972] 32p illus (A McGraw-Hill Natural science picture bk) $4.72 (3-5) 591.5
1 Camouflage (Biology)
ISBN 0-07-010180-9
First published 1972 in England
"The disguises animals have to make themselves appear less visible or more threatening to their enemies are presented in this book, with the help of attractive color and black and white illustrations. As children turn the pages they may have to look twice to see a flatfish against its mottled background of pebbles and soil, or a walking stick insect on a twig. . . . Included in the animal disguises are the use of false eyes (which apparently scare away birds) by some caterpillars and butterflies; the relatively quick change of color of flounders, frogs, and chameleons to match their backgrounds and the slower change from brown to white of the Arctic fox with the change of season [and] the mimicry by 'tasty' insects to make them resemble unpalatable ones. . . . Younger children, with the help of an adult, will enjoy puzzling over the illustrations; older children will be engaged by the text as well." Sci and Children

Cartwright, Sally
Animal homes; illus. by Ben F. Stahl. Coward, McCann & Geoghegan 1973 46p illus (The Science is what and why bks) lib. bdg. $4.49 (1-3) 591.5
1 Animals—Habitations
ISBN 0-698-30492-6
Selecting the habitations of the squirrel, porcupine, woodchuck and beaver as representative of various homes in the forest, the author describes both the materials used to build the homes and the lives of the creatures which inhabit them
"This is a good introduction which emphasizes that each animal home suits the animal who uses it. The warm and earthy illustrations will help young children visualize the interiors of the animal homes, and there is an excellent chart on the dwelling habits of other small forest creatures." Sch Library J

Cloudsley-Thompson, J. L.
Animals of the desert; illus. by Colin Threadgall. McGraw [1971 c1969] 32p illus map (A McGraw-Hill Natural science picture bk) lib. bdg. $4.72 (3-5)
591.5
1 Desert animals 2 Deserts
ISBN 0-07-011387-4
Title on spine: The desert
First published 1969 in England
The author describes a variety of desert animals and how they are able to survive the desert's intense heat during the day, cold nights, and constant scarcity of water
"With an interesting terse style, the author introduces cultural facts, such as the nature of the biblical 'manna,' amid a great amount of vivid scientific information. . . . The excellent text is enhanced by superb black-and-white and color renditions of the animals." Sci Bks

Cohen, Daniel
Night animals; illus. by Haris Petie. Messner 1970 95p illus lib. bdg. $4.79 (4-6) 591.5
1 Animals—Habits and behavior
ISBN 0-671-32259-1
The author introduces his book with a description of two unusual displays at the Bronx Zoo in New York which use special lighting to give visitors the opportunity of observing, during daylight hours, the active night-time period of nocturnal animals. He then discusses these "animals, and their activities, the diurnal rhythms of life, biological 'alarm clocks,' the adaptation of eyes to vision at night, hearing as a substitute for vision in some animals, kinesthetic senses, echo location, bioluminescence, and other topics. Experimental evidence is offered in support of some discussions. The survey is very rapid, yet will certainly interest the reader who is aided in understanding the technical terms by reference to the glossary. Since many young readers will desire to read more information, there should be a list of references, but there is not. The book is indexed. The illustrations are good." Sci Bks

Watchers in the wild; the new science of ethology; illus. by John Hamberger. Little 1971 178p illus $5.95 (6-7) 591.5
1 Animals—Habits and behavior
ISBN 0-316-15006-1
The author defines ethology as the study of how animals behave under natural conditions, and in the seven following chapters describes the behavior of the stickleback, the herring gull, the jackdaw, the greylag goose, the baboon, the gorilla and the chimpanzee. The last chapter concerns man and aggression
"The subject is interesting, the writing only moderately so, but the author does maintain a balanced view and is careful to distinguish among information,

Cohen, Daniel—*Continued*

myth, and conjecture. . . . Since there's little else available on the topic for young people, this would be a good addition to larger collections." Library J

Selected bibliography: p169-71

Earle, Olive L.

Scavengers; written and illus. by Olive L. Earle. Morrow 1973 62p illus $4.75, lib. bdg. $4.32 (3-5) 591.5

1 Animals—Habits and behavior

ISBN 0-688-21933-0; 0-688-31933-5

This book "describes the appearance and behavior of insects, mammals, and birds that perform a valuable function in nature." Sci and Children

The "book is dramatically illustrated with black-and-white pictures of various creatures. Some are easily recognized like the jackal and the hyena of Africa and Asia. . . . Others are less well known." Pub W

Feldman, Anne

The inflated dormouse; and other ways of life in the animal world; photo research by Anne Feldman; text by Jean Ely. Natural Hist. Press 1970 112p illus $4.50, lib. bdg. $5.25 (6-7) 591.5

1 Animals—Habits and behavior

ISBN 0-385-00903-8; 0-385-05186-7

"An informal, fascinating look at a few of the million or more kinds of animals that share this planet. Photographs identify the animals and a brief accompanying text describes such aspects of their lives as feeding habits, reproduction, care of young, or methods of defense. The photographs are excellent and the text, though often condescending, is animated and humorous. While it contains a 13-page table giving information on size, habitat, food, and how to find the animals, the book is more suitable for browsing than for study." Booklist

Freschet, Berniece

Year on Muskrat Marsh; illus. by Peter Parnall. Scribner 1974 unp illus $5.95 (3-5) 591.5

1 Animals—Habits and behavior 2 Marshes 3 Ecology

ISBN 0-684-13748-8

"This book traces the annual life cycle of some of the principal animal species of a Northern marshland. These creatures are portrayed as wild things and, for the most part, are free of the burden of anthropomorphic personalities. Death and consumption of creatures by co-inhabitants of the marsh are dealt with matter-of-factly. A bullfrog, a watersnake and muskrats provide the main elements of continuity." Sci Bks

"The author suggests the endless drama and beauty inherent in nature—a theme extended and enriched by the elegant, meticulous pen-and-ink drawings. An aesthetic presentation for elementary-school nature enthusiasts." Horn Bk

Frisch, Otto von

Animal migration. McGraw 1969 125p illus maps lib. bdg. $4.72 (6-7) 591.5

1 Animals—Migration

ISBN 0-07-067604-6

"International library"

The author "discusses the migration of animals, birds, fish, insects, and reptiles. He explains methods of tracing animal movement, describes experiments testing sense of direction and timing, and points out gaps in the current knowledge of animal travels. Occasional digressions weaken the organization of the text, but the information presented there and in the many color and black-and-white photographs and colored maps is useful, particularly for a comparative look at different species." Booklist

Further reading: p124

Gross, Ruth Belov

What is that alligator saying? A beginning book on animal communication; pictures by John Hawkinson. Hastings House 1972 48p illus lib. bdg. $4.95 (2-4) 591.5

1 Animal communication

ISBN 0-8038-8055-3

"Illustrated by beautifully detailed watercolor pictures, this is an excellent introduction to the subject of animal communication. It is simple, succinct, well-organized and informative, describing the ways in which animals call for help or warn of danger, give signals for mating or for warning others away from an established territory, or lay a trail to a source of food. A few experiments are described, such as the one that determined that it is the sound of a chick's peeping rather than the sight of the chick that brings a response from the mother hen." Chicago. Children's Bk Center

Hess, Lilo

Animals that hide, imitate and bluff; story and photographs by Lilo Hess. Scribner 1970 64p illus lib. bdg. $5.95 (3-5) 591.5

1 Camouflage (Biology)

ISBN 0-684-12525-0

The author "explores woods, fields and jungles to discover animals, insects, reptiles and birds that use camouflage as protection against predators." Pub W

"The author's own excellent photographs illustrate her book that describes animal camouflage. Such forms of camouflage as protective coloration, mimicry, feigning death, seasonal changes in coloration, etc. are carefully explained with examples drawn from various representatives of the animal kingdom. The photographs can be used to teach biological principles to small children and also to sharpen their own observations of life out of doors." Sci Bks

Hopf, Alice L.

Misunderstood animals. McGraw 1973 128p illus lib. bdg. $4.72 (4-7) 591.5

1 Animals—Habits and behavior

ISBN 0-07-030312-6

"Filled with interesting anecdotes, this well-researched book discusses animals often disliked by man—the octopus, wolverine, red bat, killer whale, spotted hyena, Indian dhole, and others. Hopf shows clearly the roles they play in our ecology, and how they are not as fearsome or awful as they appear. Although she occasionally strays from the point . . . in general, her writing is well paced and informative; included is an excellent bibliography." Sch Library J

Hutchins, Ross E.

How animals survive; photographs by the author. Parents Mag. Press 1974 64p illus lib. bdg. $4.59 (3-6) 591.5

1 Animals—Habits and behavior

ISBN 0-8193-0754-8

"Finding-out books"

"The ways in which animals defend themselves and their environment are clearly and simply explained. Defenses such as body armour, stings, poisons, claws, horns, speed, shelters, vision, and camouflage are amply illustrated in clear black-and-white photographs." Sch Library J

"Some subjects, like camouflage, have been examined at greater length in other titles, but their succinct consideration here allows a functional over-

Hutchins, Ross E.—*Continued*
view that will find good use on elementary science shelves." Booklist

Hyde, Margaret O.
Animal clocks and compasses; from animal migration to space travel; illus. by P. A. Hutchison. McGraw 1960 157p illus maps lib. bdg. $4.72 (5-7)
591.5

1 Animals—Habits and behavior 2 Animals—Migration
ISBN 0-07-031593-0
"Whittlesey House publications"
"The uncanny sense of time and direction observed in animals and to a slighter degree in humans is reviewed, as illustrated in certain birds, fish, insects and mammals. These, the author tells us, affect migration, hibernation, honeybee swarming and dancing, bat-flight and the springbuck-lemming mass suicide. Some of the theories advanced to account for these conditions are briefly indicated. And the possibilities which hibernation holds for space travel are examined. The final chapter suggests a few easy science projects along this line which the interested reader may engage in at home. Whether he does or not, he will find useful material for his general science class and interesting information about natural phenomena." Best Sellers
Bibliography: p153

Kirn, Ann
Let's look at more tracks; written and illus. by Ann Kirn. Putnam 1970 46p illus lib. bdg. $3.97 (k-3)
591.5

1 Tracking and trailing 2 Animals—Habits and behavior
ISBN 0-399-60380-8
Companion volume to: Let's look at tracks, entered below
This book "presents the tracks of 10 more common wild animals of North America, [rabbit, skunk, deer, beaver, opossum, bear, otter, porcupine, raccoon, and fox] arranged in . . . alternate spreads: the first shows the tracks and gives several hints to help identify their maker; the next pictures the animal and includes additional information about him." Library J

Let's look at tracks; written and illus. by Ann Kirn. Putnam 1969 48p illus $3.97 (k-3)   591.5

1 Tracking and trailing 2 Animals—Habits and behavior
ISBN 0-399-60381-6
"A slight, bright, attractive nature book invites small children to look at animal tracks, observe their patterns, guess who made them, and learn a little about each animal. Since the track-makers included here are such everyday creatures as a cat, dog, mouse, squirrel, sparrow, turtle, and a human, the material is applicable to a city situation as few nature study books are." Moorachian. What is a City?
"The drawings are uncomplicated and pleasantly colored. They alternate from the left to the right sides of the pages so that children on either side of the reader get their turn on the picture side." Sci Bks

Laycock, George
Wild travelers; the story of animal migration. Four Winds 1974 110p illus maps lib. bdg. $5.95 (5-7)
591.5

1 Animals—Migration 2 Birds—Migration
ISBN 0-590-07312-5
The author "shows the diversity of wildlife migratory patterns by examining various animal groups and their instinct-charted journeys through air, land, or water. Besides noting the often observed migrations of bird species, he calls attention to the seasonal

movements of elk, caribou, bats, seals, whales, fish, and various insects. Dangers that can plague these animals heighten amazement at their sometimes incredible feats of endurance and instinctual compassing. A chapter on the methodology used to document travel patterns rounds out the informative survey, illustrated with black-and-white photos picturing migratory species." Booklist

McClung, Robert M.
How animals hide. Natl. Geographic Soc. 1973 40p illus (k-3)   591.5

1 Camouflage (Biology)
ISBN 0-87044-144-2
Obtainable only as part of a set for $6.95 with: Honeybees, by Jane Lecht, class 595.7; Namu, by Ronald M. Fisher, class 599; and Pandas, by Donna K. Grosvenor, class 599
"Books for young explorers"
Prepared by the Special Publications Division of the National Geographic Society
In color photographs and text, this book shows how animals can hide to avoid their enemies or to trap their prey by using their color and shape to blend in with their environment or by using other types of disguise and protection
"It takes photographers as skilled and well-directed as the contributors to this book to reveal the beauty and mastery of nature's works of camouflage. In stunning color, the pictures offer a broad but graspable scope of biological wonders, from the varying hare to the crab spider and from the peacock flounder to the magnificent pink and white flower mantid. . . . The text is simple, straightforward, and uncompromising in informational value and support of the illustrative matter. An elegant book, its visual impact is unfortunately marred by a binding that resists page-flattening." Booklist

Mason, George F.
Animal baggage; written and illus. by George F. Mason. Morrow 1961 94p illus $4.75, lib. bdg. $4.32 (4-7)   591.5

1 Animals—Habits and behavior
ISBN 0-688-21031-7; 0-688-31031-1
This book "collects a variety of animals and insects, from all parts of the world, that carry things—food, objects, and their own young. . . . Kangaroos, opossums, honeybees, ants, earthworms, koala bears, and swans are a few of the creatures whose ways are pictured and described." Christian Sci Monitor
"This well-written and enlightening addition to the Mason 'Animal' series divides their various kinds of 'baggage' into three sections: materials, such as their shells or houses; food; and their young." The AAAS Sci Bk List for Children

Animal habits; written and illus. by George F. Mason. Morrow 1959 93p illus lib. bdg. $4.32 (4-7)
591.5

1 Animals—Habits and behavior 2 Animal intelligence
ISBN 0-688-31034-6
"Various aspects of animal behavior—instinct, intelligence, communication, neatness and cleanliness, affection and grief, nest building, and survival—are informally and briefly examined in short chapters filled with enjoyable anecdotes; the interpretations of animal behavior presented here are admittedly the author's own." Booklist
"Full-page drawings highlight many of the interesting and amusing incidents this author has observed firsthand." Library J

Mason, George F.—*Continued*

Animal homes. Morrow 1947 96p illus lib. bdg. $4.32 (4-7)　　591.5

1 Animals—Habitations

ISBN 0-688-31035-4

"Describes and shows in the author's full-page, detailed drawings the almost endless variety of shelters constructed by animals: nests, lodges, burrows, dens, etc." Hodges. Bks for Elem Sch Libraries

"A handy guide for locating and studying wildlife in the field, as well as interesting and factual reading for the armchair naturalist." The AAAS Sci Bk List for Children

Animal sounds. Morrow 1948 96p illus lib. bdg. $4.32 (4-7)　　591.5

1 Animal communication

ISBN 0-688-31036-2

"Bird songs, the roars of lions, the sounds made by singing mice, insect music—the author describes these and other animal sounds and discusses how and why they are made. Illustrations by the author show some of the mechanisms which produces the sounds." Hodges. Bks for Elem Sch Libraries

Animal tracks. Morrow 1943 95p illus lib. bdg. $4.32 (4-7)　　591.5

1 Tracking and trailing 2 Animals—Habits and behavior

ISBN 0-688-31041-9

"A guidebook designed to aid in the identification of the tracks of more than 40 common North American animals. There is a full-page drawing [by the author] of each animal, with descriptive text on its tracks, habits, and range. Tracks are pictured in marginal drawings, giving dimensions and showing both the perfect footprints and those of the animal in motion." Booklist

May, Julian

How the animals came to North America; illus. by Lorence F. Bjorklund. Holiday House 1974 37p illus maps lib. bdg. $4.50 (2-4)　　591.5

1 Animals—North America 2 Animals—Migration 3 Evolution

ISBN 0-8234-0234-7

"The content is interwoven around the precise and accurate illustrations of various animals presented throughout this book in one continuous story. The author has recorded in an entertaining and informative way how the Earth gradually separated into several continents and how various animals spread from one land mass to another, thus inhabiting the land in North America. The theory of continental drift is used to explain why some wild animals had to swim or fly from continent to continent. The book also provides an explanation of how the Ice Ages contributed to the dissemination of species on the North American continent. The reader is introduced to the idea that many tame animals were brought to North America by the first settlers from Europe." Sci Teacher

Murie, Olaus J.

A field guide to animal tracks. Text and illus. by Olaus J. Murie. 2d ed. Houghton 1975 [c1974] xxi, 375p illus $6.95, pa $4.95　　591.5

1 Tracking and trailing 2 Animals—Habits and behavior

ISBN 0-395-08037-1; 0-395-18323-5

First published 1954

"The Peterson Field guide series"

This is a "handbook of the tracks, droppings, trails, and nests of many common mammals, birds, insects, reptiles, and amphibians of the Western Hemisphere. Each animal is fully described and illustrated, showing how to identify tell-tale evidence of its

presence." The AAAS Sci Bk List for Children [Review of the first edition]

"A comprehensive volume which serves as both an identification handbook and a manual of ecology." Booklist [Review of the first edition]

Bibliography: p359-67

Rounds, Glen

Wildlife at your doorstep; text and drawings by Glen Rounds. . . . Holiday House 1974 [c1958] 96p illus $4.95 (4-7)　　591.5

1 Animals—Habits and behavior 2 Nature study

ISBN 0-8234-0238-X

"An illustrated almanac of curious doings . . . dealing with wasps . . . spiders . . . snakes . . . toads . . . birds . . . ants . . . squirrels and other kinds of small wildlife that can be found working at complicated trades within sight of my doorstep." Title page

A reissue of a title first published 1958. "The full-page pen-and-ink drawings which appeared in the 1958 edition have been reduced here to spot size and delicately complement these observant sketches of animal life." Sch Library J

Sarasy, Phyllis

Winter-sleepers; illus. by Edna Miller. Prentice-Hall 1962 64p illus $4.95 (3-5)　　591.5

1 Animals—Hibernation

ISBN 0-13-961490-7

This book "tells where snakes and groundhogs, turtles and carp go in winter, how bats and humming-birds conserve fuel by lowering their own body temperatures while asleep, and introduces the use of cold sleep for people undergoing surgery without anesthetics." N Y Times Bk Rev

"With abundant and attractive sketches of wildlife, this little book for younger readers is straight information on hibernation. . . . The tale is direct and conversational, with a good sense of adventure and suspense." Christian Sci Monitor

Selsam, Millicent E.

Animals as parents; illus. by John Kaufmann. Morrow 1965 96p illus $4.95 (5-7)　　591.5

1 Animals—Habits and behavior

ISBN 0-688-21044-9

"There are as many different ways of caring for the young as there are different animals. Chapter one will give a glimpse of the overall pattern of parental behavior among animals. The rest of the book is devoted to parental care among birds and mammals." Introduction

"Mrs Selsam writes in a straightforward style, moving easily from one topic to the next; the material is well-organized and nicely illustrated; most important, there are repeated references to scientific principles." Chicago. Children's Bk Center

Suggestions for further reading: p93-94

Hidden animals; illus. with photographs. [Rev. ed] Harper 1969 63p illus (A Science I can read bk) $2.95, lib. bdg. $3.79 (k-3)　　591.5

1 Camouflage (Biology)

ISBN 0-06-025281-2; 0-06-025282-0

First published 1947

By searching for the stonefish hidden in the coral, or the snowshoe rabbit in his winter habitat, young readers learn the concepts of protective coloration and natural selection as they apply to these and many other animals

"The photographs are effective in encouraging readers to discover insects and animals in their surroundings." Pub W

Selsam, Millicent E.—*Continued*
How animals live together; illus. by Kathleen
Elgin. Morrow 1963 95p illus lib. bdg. $4.81 (5-7)
591.5
1 Animals—Habits and behavior
ISBN 0-688-31408-2
This book "discusses some of the many kinds of
animal relationships: grouping together for warmth
and protection, classes and 'pecking orders,' the
organization of herds and other mammal groups,
insect societies, and association between species
(symbiotic and parasitic)." The AAAS Sci Bk List for
Children
"Mrs. Selsam is consistently outstanding for honesty, clarity, interest, and respect for the integrity and
capacity of her audience. . . . Illustrations are attractive and informative, type and design excellent."
Horn Bk
Bibliography: p91-92

How animals tell time; illus. by John Kaufmann.
Morrow 1967 94p illus $5.50, lib. bdg. $4.81 (4-7)
591.5
1 Animals—Habits and behavior 2 Time
ISBN 0-688-21407-X; 0-688-31407-4
"In a fascinating study of biological clocks, Mrs.
Selsam discusses the relationship between the earth's
daily, seasonal, and tidal rhythms and animal breeding, hibernation, migration, and other behavior. Her
simple, lucid analyses of numerous scientific experiments explains current theories about time-related
behavior and describes research being done on the
unsolved problem of the internal location of biological
clocks. Contains clear, accurate drawings and diagrams and a short list of books for further reading."
Booklist

The language of animals; illus. by Kathleen Elgin.
Morrow 1962 96p illus lib. bdg. $4.81 (5-7)   591.5
1 Animal communication
ISBN 0-688-31515-1
In this study the "author examines the means by
which animals communicate emotion and information, stressing the fallacy of thinking that animals
communicate in the same manner and for the same
purposes as human beings." Hodges. Bks for Elem
Sch Libraries
"Good scientific writing: objective, simple, dignified, but never dry. Mrs. Selsam gives to the
reader, in addition to the information in the text, a
consistency of scientific attitude that is most
valuable. . . . A bibliography is appended; the index
is starred to indicate location of illustrations."
Chicago. Children's Bk Center

Shuttlesworth, Dorothy
Animal camouflage; illus. by Matthew Kalmenoff.
Natural Hist. Press 1966 63p illus $3.95, lib. bdg.
$4.70 (4-7)   591.5
1 Camouflage (Biology)
ISBN 0-385-03950-6; 0-385-06061-0
"Published for the American Museum of Natural
History"
"One must have sharp eyes to see many of the fish,
insects, birds, and mammals that are protected by
nature's coloration and countershading; other animals
hide by changing color, by mimicry, or by masking
techniques. Mrs. Shuttlesworth's interesting text is
enhanced by numerous life-like illustrations and full-
page spreads." Sch Library J

Animals that frighten people; fact versus myth;
illus. with photographs. Dutton 1973 122p illus $4.95
(5-7)   591.5

1 Animals—Habits and behavior
ISBN 0-525-25745-4
"Some members of the animal world have long
lived with reputations for being dangerous and
frightening. In these ten chapters the author presents
the basis for these myths and the facts as we know
them today. Some of the dreaded creatures included
are the tarantula, scorpion, wolf, octopus, and bat.
The accounts make good reading and the black-and-
white photographs add to the book's appeal. This is a
good browsing item. An index makes it useful as a
source of specific information." Appraisal

Silverstein, Alvin
Animal invaders; the story of imported wildlife [by]
Alvin and Virginia Silverstein. Atheneum Pubs. 1974
124p illus $5.95 (4-7)   591.5
1 Geographical distribution of animals and plants
2 Ecology
ISBN 0-689-30146-4
This book describes animals which man has
introduced into new environments, accidentally or
deliberately, as pets, or as predators to control existing problems. Because these animals lack natural
enemies in their new environments, they eventually
cause damage to the ecosystem. The authors cite cases
involving birds, mammals, fish, insects and snails
"This is a provocative and informative introduction
to an overlooked aspect of ecology." Sch Library J

Webster, David
Track watching; illus. with photographs and drawings. Watts, F. 1972 89p illus lib. bdg. $5.88 (4-7)
591.5
1 Tracking and trailing 2 Animals—Habits and
behavior
ISBN 0-531-02030-4
"Suggesting that many interesting stories are
revealed when one learns to interpret tracks of animals, persons, or vehicles . . . [the author] challenges
readers by asking questions about photographs of
tracks. Although answers to many questions are
appended, helps to solutions are also found in the text
as Webster explains how various animals make tracks,
how vehicle wheels behave, and how to interpret
human tracks. He suggests that the reader make a
collection of tracks by using ink, plaster, wax, or a
camera." Booklist
"The format provides immediate reinforcement to
learning: photographs showing tracks that may be
found on beaches, in backyards, and on snow-covered
meadows are accompanied by logical explanations or
are offered as mystery tracks with answers in the back
pages. . . . [This book is] an exciting source of pleasure since it will give new meaning to camping and
excursions at the beach or in the snow." Sci Bks

Zim, Herbert S.
Armored animals; illus. by René Martin. Morrow
1971 64p illus lib. bdg. $4.32 (3-5)   591.5
1 Animals—Habits and behavior
ISBN 0-688-31051-6
"A Rogewinn book"
This "is a survey of the Animal Kingdom with
emphasis on protection by means of some form of
armor covering the animal. The varied ways in which
both vertebrates and invertebrates cope with the dangers of their environment through the use of external
protective coverings are interestingly described. The
profuse black and white illustrations contribute to the
story. Fossils, as well as living forms, are included."
Appraisal

591.9 Zoology—Geographical treatment

Arundel, Jocelyn
The wildlife of Africa; illus. by Wesley Dennis. Hastings House 1965 120p illus map (The Hastings House World wildlife conservation ser) lib. bdg. $4.17 (5-7)   591.9
1 Zoology—Africa 2 Wildlife—Conservation
ISBN 0-8038-8022-7
The author traces "the evolution of wildlife in Africa, and rather dramatically gives highlights of the wanton exploitation and destruction of those important resources. She surveys the efforts at conservation and the programs that have been developed and are currently in progress. It is an exciting narrative for the novice reader." Sci Bks
Glossary: p110-12. Bibliography: p113-16

Dorian, Edith
Animals that made U.S. history [by] Edith Dorian and W. N. Wilson. McGraw 1964 112p illus lib. bdg. $4.72 (5-7)   591.9
1 Animals—U.S. 2 Zoology, Economic 3 U.S.—History
ISBN 0-07-017636-1
"The stories of the eleven animals that dominate these chapters, a few of them domestic, most of them wild . . . [present] a pageant of American history: the adventurous peopling of a vast wilderness and the forging of a mighty nation." p11
"How beavers created fertile meadows for future pioneers and the role of codfishermen in the winning of the Civil War are examples of the many fascinating and useful bits of information in this book." N Y Times Bk Rev
Other books to read: p108

Dugdale, Vera
Album of North American animals; illus. by Clark Bronson. Rand McNally 1966 112p illus $4.95, lib. bdg. $4.79 (4-7)   591.9
1 Animals—North America 2 Mammals
ISBN 0-528-82059-1; 0-528-82061-3
Companion volume to: Album of North American birds, class 598.2
This oversize book describes and pictures twenty-six North American mammals. "Information on life history, behavior, geographic distribution, and past and present abundance of these mammals is woven into . . . natural episodes relating each animal to its unique environment." Foreword
"The life-like drawings [create] . . . a lively setting for Miss Dugdale's sympathetic and readable text. . . . A good beginning reference book." Christian Sci Monitor

Nayman, Jacqueline
Atlas of wildlife; illus. by Adrian Williams & David Nockels; maps by Geographical Projects, London. Consultant: Maurice Burton. Day 1972 124p illus maps $10 (5-7)   591.9
1 Geographical distribution of animals and plants
ISBN 0-381-98162-2
This work deals mostly with mammals but also includes a few birds, reptiles, amphibians and lungfishes. The opening chapter is a "discussion of the origin of the continents and thus of the six major regions. Each region receives a chapter with up to three double-page maps . . . [showing] the distribution of the most characteristic animals, many of which have been illustrated in colour in the text; for each region there is also a chart indicating the occurence of the animals in other regions. Two final chapters deal with Antarctica and with certain islands or island groups, followed by a map of the 200 major wildlife parks in the world." Times (London) Literary Sup

The Rand McNally Atlas of world wildlife; with a foreword by Sir Julian Huxley. Rand McNally 1973 208p illus maps $25   591.9
1 Geographical distribution of animals and plants 2 Ecology
ISBN 0-528-83014-7
"Produced in consultation with the Zoological Society of London and with contributions from leading zoologists throughout the world." Verso of title page
This book "presents tremendous amounts of material on the eight zoogeographical regions of the earth. Fourteen pages are devoted to species inhabiting reefs and islands of the oceans; one section analyzes the effects of man's activities on wildlife. Special features include panoramas of some key species in each region treated, endangered species, and maps showing major parks and reserves. The quality of reproductions, paintings, graphs, charts and photographs of animals and plant associates are outstanding. The only difficulty that some people may experience is correlating colors and keys with maps and graphs. In some cases, the colors are too much alike in tone for easy differentiation. No similar publication is as extensive as this one as far as subject matter is concerned. This atlas should be made available to students in grade schools. . . . It will be of great value to anyone interested in geography, oceanography, or ecology, as well as any phase of wildlife resources." Choice
Glossary: p205. Sources of reference: p207-08

Shuttlesworth, Dorothy E.
The wildlife of South America; illus. by George Frederick Mason; foreword by Philip K. Crowe. Hastings House 1974 120p illus maps (The Hastings House World wildlife conservation ser) lib. bdg. $6.95 (5-7)   591.9
1 Animals—South America 2 Wildlife—Conservation
ISBN 0-8038-8069-3
First published 1966
An "overall picture of South American fauna is communicated verbally, and the author weaves in timely information and commentary on wildlife destruction and conservation. A list of rare and endangered species and a map indicating national parks of South America are included." Booklist
Bibliography: p116-17

Wellman, Alice
Africa's animals; creatures of a struggling land. Putnam 1974 191p illus map lib. bdg. $4.97 (6-7) 591.9
1 Animals—Africa
ISBN 0-399-60838-9
The author "traces the fate of the animals from the first non-African notice of them by Greeks and Romans, through their near-extermination by white hunters, to their partial recovery in wildlife parks and preserves. The book is based on six African ecosystems: thornbush, rain forest, grassed plains, swamps and bodies of water, highlands, and open bush and woodlands. For each system she describes the location and topography, the weather and seasonal changes and the typical vegetation. The material on the animals follows and is enlivened by some discussion of their behavior. For each system, one or two species are described in some depth and the choices are good. The book is enriched by the unusual effective animal photographs." Sci Bks

591.92   Marine zoology

Jacobs, Lou

Wonders of an oceanarium; the story of marine life in captivity [by] Lou Jacobs, Jr. Illus. with photographs; foreword by David H. Brown. Golden Gate 1965 78p illus lib. bdg. $4.95 (3-7)   591.92

1 Marine animals 2 Marineland of the Pacific, Palos Verdes Estates, Calif.
ISBN 0-516-08870-X

"A brief text and more than 75 outstanding photographs give an inside view of an oceanarium—its function and personnel and the capture, care, training, and exhibition of its inhabitants. The oceanarium described is Marineland of the Pacific in California." Booklist

List, Ilka Katherine

Questions and answers about seashore life; woodcuts by the author; line drawings by Arabelle Wheatley. Four Winds [1971 c1970] 123p illus $6.95, lib. bdg. $5.62 (4-6)   591.92

1 Marine animals 2 Marine plants
ISBN 0-590-17182-8; 0-590-07182-3

"Marine plants and invertebrates from the northeastern coast of the United States are used as subjects to skillfully introduce young persons to the ways and habits of seashore life. With a question-answer format, the author anticipates the questions a reader might ask and answers them in an articulate and scientifically correct manner. The relations of the organisms to one another and to their physical environment are cited as well as other biological principles (e.g. evolution, adaptation, reproduction)." Sci Bks

"The text is expanded by helpful, precisely drawn and labeled line illustrations and by the author's decorative woodcuts—which are, however, drawn on a different scale. Neither text nor illustrations indicate the size of the seashore animals." Library J

Selsam, Millicent

See through the sea, by Millicent Selsam and Betty Morrow; pictures by Winifred Lubell. Harper 1955 unp illus lib. bdg. $4.79 (2-4)   591.92

1 Marine animals 2 Ocean
ISBN 0-06-025456-4

" 'In each part of the sea, the plants and animals are different. Turn the pages of this book, and you will see through the sea where it is shallow, deeper and deepest.' A description of the teeming life [mainly animals and fish] of the sea, from the sea-shore, down through the various levels of the ocean, to its depths. It is amplified by arresting pictures and diagrams in predominating tones of green, yellow and black." Ontario Library Rev

"The artist's contrasts between surface light and dark depths create atmospheres of beauty and wonder and suggest the excitement of diving with goggles, helmet, or bathysphere." Horn Bk

592 Invertebrates

Rhine, Richard

Life in a bucket of soil; illus. by Elsie Wrigley. Lothrop 1972 96p illus $4.95, lib. bdg. $4.59 (5-7)   592

1 Invertebrates
ISBN 0-688-41514-8; 0-688-51514-2

The author describes soil inhabitants which can be found in the average backyard, such as beetles, worms, snails, spiders, and centipedes. He tells how they live and interreact, how they affect the soil, and how they can be collected and studied

"Ms. Wrigley has drawn excellent reproductions of the animals discussed as well as labelled their various parts. This fits in wonderfully with Mr. Rhine's scientific discussion of each animal. . . . The young reader will find in this book information and activities to bring him to a greater understanding of the relationship between the soil and its inhabitants." Appraisal

Further reading: p94

593   Amoebas, corals, starfishes

Hurd, Edith Thacher

Starfish; illus. by Lucienne Bloch. Crowell 1962 unp illus (Let's-read-and-find-out science bks) $4.50, lib. bdg. $5.25 (k-3)   593

1 Starfishes
ISBN 0-690-71885-3; 0-690-71886-1

"An easy introduction to the world of starfish. Touches on the feeding habits, life cycle, structure and power of regeneration of these interesting creatures." The AAAS Sci Bk List for Children

"The full-page illustrations are like sections of a decorative mural in greens, grays, and mauve. The information is concise, interesting, and authentic, with the emphasis on personal discovery. The whole has a poetic feeling associated with beachcombing and the sea." Christian Sci Monitor

Morrison, Sean

The amoeba; photomicrographs by Nina Stromgren Allen; consultant: Robert D. Allen. Coward, McCann & Geoghegan 1971 46p illus (Science is what and why) lib. bdg. $4.69 (3-6)   593

1 Amoeba
ISBN 0-688-30010-6

"The life history, morphology, physiology, and ecology of 'Amoeba proteus' are explained by the use of good photographs and photomicrographs with appropriate legends, and labeling of anatomical detail where necessary. Because the amoeba is such a primordial animal, the explanation of its biological makeup and its feeding and reproductive processes have provided the author with an opportunity to give a brief introduction to microscopy and to explain some of the basic elements of cytology. Scientific terms are used where needed throughout the book and are defined in a glossary. The book is carefully indexed. Its excellence is proof that accurate scientific writing can interest children. This is an essential book for children's libraries and will be very useful in elementary science classrooms for collateral study and reference." Sci Bks

Zim, Herbert S.

Corals; illus. by René Martin. Morrow 1966 63p illus maps lib. bdg. $4.59 (3-5)   593

1 Corals
ISBN 0-688-31186-5

The author "describes these interesting animals, their habitat, representative living and fossil specimens, the location of major coral islands and reefs, and some of the other invertebrates and fishes that live in association with the corals, and the formation of coral reefs and atolls." Sci Bks

"Coral animals that look like flowering plants are depicted in drawings of photographic clarity and supplemented by readable text." Sch Library J

594　Mollusks and shells

Abbott, R. Tucker

Sea shells of the world; a guide to the better-known species; under the editorship of Herbert S. Zim; illus. by George and Marita Sandström. Golden Press 1962 160p illus maps (A Golden Nature guide) lib. bdg. $4.95, pa $1.50　　　594

1 Shells 2 Shells—Collection and preservation
ISBN 0-307-63514-7; 0-307-24410-5

At head of title: 790 illustrations in color of 562 species

This book offers information about collecting and preserving shells and outlines the geographical areas of shell distribution. It then describes various species of marine shells, including mollusks, limpets, top shells, cowries, conches, whelks, oysters, clams, and volutes

"This guide is necessarily a brief sampling of the many thousands of marine shells. Because it is a guide for collecting we have emphasized attractive and better-known species." Foreword

Includes bibliographies

Clemons, Elizabeth

Shells are where you find them; illus. by Joe Gault. Knopf 1960 86p illus (Nature study bks) $2.75, lib. bdg. $4.99 (2-4)　　　594

1 Shells 2 Shells—Collection and preservation
ISBN 0-394-81609-9; 0-394-91609-3

"Many suggestions about shell collecting are given for the novice. Includes items such as where to find shells, how to carry them, how to prepare them, and how to classify them. The second portion contains pictures of, and information about some specific shells." The AAAS Sci Bk List for Children

"The brief text and excellent black and white pictures make possible positive identification of many shells found on the beaches of the North American continent." Chicago

Goudey, Alice E.

Houses from the sea; illus. by Adrienne Adams. Scribner 1959 unp illus lib. bdg. $5.95, pa 95¢ (k-3)　　　594

1 Shells
ISBN 0-684-12458-0; 0-684-12783-0

"A scientifically accurate introduction to shells . . . which is at the same time an idyllic tale of two children filling their pails with these treasures while playing at the beach. The short lines of rhythmic prose describe a great variety of shells; their names, how they look, and how they serve as houses for animals of the sea. . . . Even without pictures the text would give clear impressions; but the handsome, detailed color drawings of seashore life and activity turn it into a valuable and distinctive science picture book for kindergarten and beginning readers. Teachers have shown special interest in it." Horn Bk

There is "a quality of delicacy in both writing and the pastel shades of sky, sea and shells. All the shells collected by the children are pictured and labeled at the end of the book." Bookmark

Hess, Lilo

A snail's pace. Scribner 1974 48p illus lib. bdg. $4.95 (3-5)　　　594

1 Snails
ISBN 0-684-13568-9

Beginning with the land snail, this survey of snails covers "the variations of the species, its anatomy, diet and mating habits." Pub W

The author's "beautifully detailed black-and-white photographs are the highlights of this combination pet-keeper's and nature student's source book on snails. The text is clear and thoughtfully selective . . . but it is frequently not well-coordinated with the illustrations and digresses to extended discussions on the relatives of snails and on sea shell collecting. Despite its loose organization, however, the book will be valuable for juvenile naturalists." Booklist

Hogner, Dorothy Childs

Snails; illus. by Nils Hogner. Crowell 1958 81p illus $4.50, lib. bdg. $5.25 (3-5)　　　594

1 Snails
ISBN 0-690-74228-2; 0-690-74229-0

"The text not only describes many species of snails and their habitats and explains their life cycle, but also suggests how to have fun keeping land snails in a 'snailery' and water snails in an aquarium. Many soft-pencil drawings, lovely in effect but detailed, too, with diagrammatic anatomical sketches, add value to the book." Horn Bk

Shaw, Evelyn

Octopus; pictures by Ralph Carpentier. Harper 1971 61p illus (A Science I can read bk) $2.95, lib. bdg. $3.79 (1-2)　　　594

1 Octopus
ISBN 0-06-025558-7; 0-06-025559-5

"The habits and behavior and the life cycle of the octopus are accurately described . . . in an easy-to-read narrative about one individual octopus." Booklist

"A good first science book. Although the behavior of an octopus is described in sequence . . . this is not fictionalized. The writing is direct and simple, the information interesting, the illustrations attractive but not always clear in detail." Chicago. Children's Bk Center

Zim, Herbert S.

Snails [by] Herbert S. Zim [and] Lucretia Krantz; illus. by René Martin. Morrow 1975 64p illus $4.95, lib. bdg. $4.59 (4-7)　　　594

1 Snails
ISBN 0-688-22012-6; 0-688-32012-0

"Physical characteristics of snails, including the interesting process of shell formation, are clearly described with scientific terms well defined. There are many detailed diagrams, and the line drawings depicting distinctive shapes of land and ocean species will be useful to shell collectors. Utilitarian in appearance (there are no color photographs though the beautiful hues of the shells are frequently mentioned) this is otherwise quite thorough and informative." Sch Library J

595　Other invertebrates

Bason, Lillian

Spiders. Natl. Geographic Soc. 1974 32p illus (k-3)　　　595

1 Spiders
ISBN 0-87044-156-6

Obtainable only as part of a set for $6.95 with: Cats: little tigers in the house, by Linda McCarter Bridge, class 636.8; Creepy crawly things, by the National Geographic Society, class 598.1, and Three little Indians, by Gene S. Stuart, class 970.1

"Books for young explorers"

Prepared by the Special Publications Division of the National Geographic Society

This book illustrates the physical appearance, habitats, behavior and natural enemies of spiders. Construction of webs and trapdoors as means of catching food are also described

This book "offers remarkable color photographs, a

Bason, Lillian—*Continued*
brief, general text of considerable value, and a minimum of gimmickry." Booklist

Chenery, Janet
Wolfie; pictures by Marc Simont. Harper 1969 63p illus (A Science I can read bk) $2.95, lib. bdg. $3.79 (k-3) 595
1 Spiders
ISBN 0-06-021261-6; 0-06-021264-0
"Engagingly illustrated, a good first science book in which the story and the information about spiders are smoothly integrated. . . . Harry and George zealously guard their pet from the interfering advances of a little sister; Harry tells Polly that she can see Wolfie (a wolf spider) if she brings him a hundred flies. The boys learn about spiders and about how to take care of Wolfie from a worker at the Nature Center; going out one dark night to give Wolfie some water, Harry finds Polly, also visiting Wolfie, a consolation. Next morning Polly is thrilled by permission, at last, to feed Wolfie." Sutherland. The Best in Children's Bks

Conklin, Gladys
Tarantula; the giant spider; illus. by Glen Rounds. Holiday House 1972 unp illus $4.50 (1-3) 595
1 Tarantulas
ISBN 0-8234-0208-8
The author describes the life cycle of the male and female California tarantula. Not poisonous to man, this spider is portrayed as a gentle, useful member of the natural world
"The text is simple, understandable and convincing. . . . [The] illustrations, in black-and-white, add immensely to the appeal of the story." Pub W
Bibliography included in Author's note

Cook, Joseph J.
The nocturnal world of the lobster; illus. with diagrams and drawings by Jan Cook and with photographs. Dodd 1972 80p illus lib. bdg. $4.50 (4-6) 595
1 Lobsters 2 Crayfish
ISBN 0-396-06420-5
"In a straightforward, rather stolid style that is occasionally lightened by informality, Cook describes the structure of the lobster, its life cycle, the ways in which different species live, and the ways in which the crustaceans are trapped and—since the lobster supply is shrinking—the ways in which they are now being selectively bred and tagged. One catch-all chapter describes 'The Lobster and Crayfish in Fact and Fiction,' with many small and not always relevant bits of information, but there is some truly fascinating material scattered throughout the book." Chicago. Children's Bk Center
"For those who have never tasted lobster as a delicious delicacy, reading about it vicariously is the next best thing. Riding the lobster boats, pulling up the traps and marketing lobsters is an extremely fascinating occupation for students to read about." Sci Bks
Selected bibliography: p78

Darling, Lois
Worms [by] Lois and Louis Darling. Morrow 1972 64p illus $4.59 (1-3) 595
1 Earthworms
ISBN 0-688-31773-1
Illustrated by the authors, this book explains the structure of the earthworm, describes its behavior and provides instructions on how to keep earthworms alive in a container
"The drawings are both imaginative and informative, and beautifully integrated with the clear, simple text." Horn Bk

Goldin, Augusta
Spider silk; illus. by Joseph Low. Crowell 1964 unp illus (Let's-read-and-find-out science bks) $4.50, lib. bdg. $5.25 (1-3) 595
1 Spiders
ISBN 0-690-76074-4; 0-690-76075-2
"The story of how a spider spins his web and uses it to trap insects and cradle its eggs makes fascinating reading." Chicago. Children's Bk Center
"This tells the whole story very well. The pen-and-ink sketches with color wash are most effective." Sch Library J

Hawes, Judy
My daddy longlegs; illus. by Walter Lorraine. Crowell 1972 31p illus (Let's-read-and-find-out science bks) $4.50, lib. bdg. $5.25 (1-3) 595
1 Daddy longlegs
ISBN 0-690-56655-7; 0-690-56656-5
"Big print, engaging style, lively illustrations and fascinating information combine to make this an altogether charming book. The reader is urged to catch a few Daddy Longlegs and is told how, when, and where to do this, how to observe them, what to look for and how to build a home for them while the study is in progress. Youngsters may well find this an embarkation point for an enthusiastic study of nature." Appraisal

Shrimps; illus. by Joseph Low. Crowell [1967 c1966] unp illus (Let's-read-and-find-out science bks) $4.50, lib. bdg. $5.25 (1-3) 595
1 Shrimps
ISBN 0-690-73589-8; 0-690-73590-1
"The remarkable life cycle of shrimp, their habits and growth, clearly written for the young readers." Chicago
"A small subject receives a thorough, colorful treatment." Horn Bk

Hogner, Dorothy Childs
Earthworms; illus. by Nils Hogner. Crowell 1953 51p illus $4.50, lib. bdg. $5.25 (1-4) 595
1 Earthworms
ISBN 0-690-25164-5; 0-690-25165-3
This book "explains how earthworms eat, see, and hear and discusses their importance to agriculture. Includes instructions for setting up an earthworm farm." Hodges. Bks for Elem Sch Libraries
"This easily-read study of the common earthworm leaves the reader in no doubt about the importance of its service as 'nature's plow' and as a source of fertilizer. . . . Black-and-white sketches are clear." Horn Bk

Holling, Holling Clancy
Pagoo; illus. by the author and Lucille Webster Holling. Houghton 1957 86p illus $4.23 (4-7) 595
1 Crabs 2 Marine animals
ISBN 0-395-06827-4
"The life cycle of the hermit crab and a close-up of the teeming life of the tide pool are presented, as in the author's earlier books, in an animated narrative, scientifically detailed marginal drawings, and handsome full-page colored pictures. Although adults are likely to feel that the crab is too humanized and to be irritated by the facetious, overly colorful writing, children will find the story of Pagoo both exciting and informative." Booklist

Nespojohn, Katherine V.
Worms; illus. by Haris Petie. Watts, F. 1972 84p illus $3.90 (4-6) 595
1 Worms
ISBN 0-531-00766-9

Nespojohn, Katherine V.—*Continued*
"A First book"
This "is a book of unquestionable merit, designed for young readers. [The author] encourages her readers to study the worm world by experiment and observation, and shows how to draw up simple charts to record these results. The descriptive text is interspersed with questions and the reader is directed to the answers by way of experiment, observation and logic. The first three chapters attempt to answer the question: what is a worm. . . . Succeeding chapters discuss specific kinds of worms: planaria, flukes and tapeworms, roundworms, earthworms, and other annelids. . . . The final chapter deals with worms and man in relation to each other, their environment and the balance of nature. This book is written in a manner which arouses the young reader's interest, and it succeeds in being informative at the same time." Sci Bks

Pringle, Laurence
Twist, wiggle, and squirm; a book about earthworms; illus. by Peter Parnall. Crowell 1973 33p illus (Let's-read-and-find-out science bks) $4.50, lib. bdg. $5.25 (1-3)   595
1 Earthworms
ISBN 0-690-84154-X; 0-690-84155-8
"A well-designed, uncluttered book that relates the facts about earthworms—their movements, regenerative powers, skin breathing apparatus, mating habits, enemies, and value to plants and soil." Booklist
"Artist Peter Parnall's view of life in the underground is enormously appealing. His sinewy earthworms dig long tunnels through the soil, curl up sleepily in their burrows at wintertime, wiggle to the surface of the earth [and] tie themselves in knots." Christian Sci Monitor

Shuttlesworth, Dorothy E.
The story of spiders; illus. by Su Zan N. Swain. Doubleday 1959 55p illus $5.95, lib. bdg. $6.70 (4-6)   595
1 Spiders
ISBN 0-385-02284-0; 0-385-02286-7
"Garden City books"
This "well written book should do much toward clearing up misconceptions about spiders and interesting young naturalists in studying them. The varieties, physical characteristics, habits, habitats, and spinning ability of spiders and their value or harmfulness to mankind are examined. . . . Of special interest are the descriptions of kinds of webs and their uses and the many excellent colored drawings." Booklist
Books for further reading about spiders: p[57]

Simon, Seymour
Discovering what earthworms do; illus. by Jean Zallinger. McGraw 1969 47p illus lib. bdg. $4.72 (3-5)   595
1 Earthworms
ISBN 0-07-057404-9
"The earthworm is an interesting creature to young children and this book will answer many of their questions and stimulate them to find answers to other questions through a number of simple observations and experiments. Simon describes his subject in adequate detail for his young reader and tells them how to keep earthworms, study their food habits, their regeneration ability, and their reaction to different environments and learning situations. The simple style of the text and the good illustrations will sustain the reader's interest." Sci Bks

Zim, Herbert S.
Crabs, by Herbert S. Zim and Lucretia Krantz; illus. by René Martin. Morrow 1974 63p illus $3.95, lib. bdg. $3.78 (3-5)   595
1 Crabs
ISBN 0-688-20114-8; 0-688-30114-2
"The authors introduce young readers to the many crab families and tell how the different species live. In non-technical language, they describe the general physical structure of crabs and some of the basic facts about their behavior. The authors explain how crabs court and mate, raise their young, feed, secure oxygen, and protect themselves. The molting process is described in interesting detail as in the crab's regeneration of a lost appendage. The authors conclude with a brief discussion of the industry which harvests and markets edible crabs commercially. Realistic pen and ink drawings contribute much to the informational value of the text." Science and Children

595.7   Insects

Anderson, Margaret J.
Exploring the insect world. McGraw 1974 160p illus lib. bdg. $4.72 (5-7)   595.7
1 Insects
ISBN 0-07-001625-9
"Several of the 15 chapters focus on environmental settings (e.g., 'Insects on the Night Shift,' 'Exploring a Pond'), others on a few species of particular interest (e.g., bees and wasps, ants, dragonflies, caddisflies), and still others are used to round out the picture (e.g., general anatomical features, friends, enemies). But the real value of the book is not merely in its content (fine as it is) but in the way the material is presented. Ms. Anderson is an engaging writer and particularly adept at leading the reader to significant questions that are answerable by diligent observation or simple experimentation. The tools and equipment needed for the suggested experiments are readily available, for the most part, in any kitchen or garage. . . . The illustrations are straightforward and useful, the bibliography is simple and the index extensive enough to be useful." Sci Bks

Ault, Phil
Wonders of the mosquito world; illus. with photographs and charts. Dodd 1970 64p illus lib. bdg. $4.50 (5-7)   595.7
1 Mosquitoes
ISBN 0-396-07154-6
"Dodd, Mead Wonders books"
This is the story of one of nature's villains and of man's fight to conquer it. The author delves into the history of the mosquito, which goes back millions of years, and examines the insect's body structure, as well as its role as a carrier of yellow fever, malaria, and other diseases
"The life cycle of mosquitoes is explained, including the sex differences. Three principal species are differentiated: the yellow-fever mosquito, the malaria mosquito; and the ordinary nuisance house mosquito of temperate zones. There is a historical summary of control programs, but the most interesting part is a description of experimental work at Notre Dame." The AAAS Sci Bk List for Children

Brenner, Barbara
If you were an ant. . . . Pictures by Fred Brenner. Harper 1973 unp illus lib. bdg. $4.43 (k-2)   595.7
1 Ants
ISBN 0-06-020619-5
This book "provides an excellent opportunity for

Brenner, Barbara—*Continued*
fantasy based on accurately and concisely presented facts. Size, color, shape, diet, activities, habitat and social life of an ant are shown in bold green, blue and brown illustrations. This is an interesting book for the young beginning reader, and an alert teacher or parent could use it as the beginning of a more detailed study." Sci Bks

Bronson, Wilfrid S.
Beetles; written and illus. by Wilfrid S. Bronson. Harcourt 1963 160p illus $5.50 (4-7)   595.7
  1 Beetles 2 Beetles—Collection and preservation
  ISBN 0-15-206260-2
This study of beetles introduces the reader to the different varieties, including the Scarab, the death-watch beetle, the firefly and glowworm, the water-beetle, and the locust. The author also gives information on collecting, preserving and showing specimens
  The author is "humorous, and chatty in telling of his 'bugs' and has a gift for passing along serious scientific information in an almost casual way, full of anecdotes and informal experiments." Christian Sci Monitor
  Includes bibliography

Cole, Joanna
Cockroaches; illus. by Jean Zallinger. Morrow 1971 62p illus lib. bdg. $4.14 (3-6)   595.7
  1 Cockroaches
  ISBN 0-688-31177-6
Although the cockroach is an unloved insect, the author contends that its reputation may be worse than it deserves. She describes the origins of the cockroach, its various species, and its life cycle. She also explains why it is the ideal creature for scientific research and briefly summarizes the experiments in which it has proved useful
  "Clearly written and copiously illustrated with accurate drawings on almost every page, the brief study is absorbing despite its unpopular subject." Booklist

Fleas; illus. by Elsie Wrigley. Morrow 1973 62p illus lib. bdg. $4.14 (3-6)   595.7
  1 Fleas
  ISBN 0-688-31844-4
The author "discusses the evolution of fleas, the varieties (separate kinds for cats, dogs, man, etc.), the pestilence caused by fleas, and flea circuses (which are horrible). Marvelous and frequent illustrations accompany the text. When drawings are enlarged, actual size is so noted." Appraisal

Conklin, Gladys
The bug club book; a handbook for young bug collectors; illus. by Girard Goodenow. Holiday House 1966 96p illus $4.50 (3-6)   595.7
  1 Insects
  ISBN 0-8234-0017-4
"The author's easy-to-follow directions for collecting, raising, preserving, mounting, studying, and displaying insects will be useful to many young amateurs. The organization of clubs to study insects, suggestions for involvement of parents, and the preparation of exhibits for public display are useful." Sci Bks
  More books to read: p93

I like butterflies; pictures by Barbara Latham. Holiday House 1960 24p illus lib. bdg. $5.95 (k-3) 595.7
  1 Butterflies 2 Moths
  ISBN 0-8234-0055-7
"The running text could be a child's voice describing his experiences as he finds one exquisite butterfly after another, each one (twenty-six in all) pictured against a natural background in full color. The common names of butterflies and moths are included in the back of the book so that each can be identified by the child old enough to be interested." Horn Bk

I like caterpillars; pictures by Barbara Latham. Holiday House 1958 unp illus lib. bdg. $5.95 (k-3)
     595.7
  1 Caterpillars
  ISBN 0-8234-0056-5
"A most arresting book. . . . The wealth of bright green leaves, pink and yellow flowers and caterpillars carefully shown in their own exotic colors are decorative in a lush and tangled fashion. Fun, information and interest for the youngest. We predict visits to the home and primary classrooms of many a Wooly Bear, Horned Devil and Arctid with white bristles standing out all around its tail and head, for the young do like caterpillars." N Y Her Trib Bks

Insects build their homes; illus. by Jean Zallinger. Holiday House 1972 unp illus lib. bdg. $5.95 (1-4)
     595.7
  1 Insects
  ISBN 0-8234-0207-X
"In a readable and interesting text, the author introduces the young naturalist to the habits of a variety of insects. Some live on land and some in water; they are bees, ants, dragonflies, diving beetles, wasps and spittlebugs, among many others. The pictures are authentic and, combined with the text, offer suggestions of what to look for on a walk in the country, at the edge of a pond, and in trees." Pub W

When insects are babies, pictures by Artur Marokvia. Holiday House 1969 unp illus lib. bdg. $4.95 (k-3)   595.7
  1 Insects
  ISBN 0-8234-0134-0
"The praying mantis, spittle bug, pine sawyer beetle, green tiger beetle, cicada, hornet, black wasp, bumblebee, caddis fly, bagworm, earwig, grasshopper, lacewing, dragonfly, firefly, and furry moth are very briefly introduced. The text is dominated by lovely accurate pastel colored illustrations of each of the insects in various developmental stages from egg to adult. The pictures cover two thirds of each of the two pages devoted to each insect. In a familiar style the author mentions habitat, diet, growth pattern and appearance." Sci Bks

Doering, Harald
An ant is born; by Harald Doering (photographer) and Jo Mary McCormick (writer) Sterling 1964 96p illus (Sterling Nature ser) $4.50, lib. bdg. $4.59 (4-7)   595.7
  1 Ants
  ISBN 0-8069-3500-6; 0-8069-3501-4
In this book "the photographs, many times enlarged are equal in importance to the text. The 'story' includes the birth of an ant, its daily life, food, nest, varieties of ants and their function in the community. The photographs are outstanding, showing the structure of the ants' bodies, and their activities both with friends and enemies. . . . The text is sufficiently detailed to be suitable for older readers, yet simple and lucid [for the younger ones]." Toronto

A bee is born; tr. and adapted by Dale S. Cunningham. Sterling 1962 96p illus (Sterling Nature ser) $4.50, lib. bdg. $4.59 (4-7)   595.7
  1 Bees
  ISBN 0-8069-3502-2; 0-8069-3503-0
"Excellent magnified and close-up photographs augment this life history of bees: hatching of eggs,

Doering, Harald—*Continued*
development of the several classes of bees, social
structure of the bee community, and activities in the
hive." Hodges. Bks for Elem Sch Libraries

Earle, Olive L.
Praying mantis. Morrow 1969 48p illus lib. bdg.
$4.32 (2-4)   595.7
1 Praying mantis
ISBN 0-688-31528-3
Illustrated by the author
This book manages "to pack in a remarkable
number of facts: why the mantis is classed as an insect,
its unusually flexible head, its peculiar swaying
motion, changing eye color, territorial range, non-
vegetarian diet and cannibalistic penchant. In the
final section, the author offers suggestions for close-
up study by telling how she kept one of these insects
as a pet, feeding it on raw hamburger and water." N Y
Times Bk Rev
"Softly drawn pictures, scrupulously detailed, add
to both the attractiveness and the informational value
of a book that is simply written, accurate, and interesting. The clean pages and large print are assets."
Chicago. Children's Bk Center

Ewbank, Constance
Insect zoo; how to collect and care for insects; illus.
by Barbara Wolff. Walker & Co. 1973 96p illus $4.50,
lib. bdg. $4.41 (4-7)   595.7
1 Insects
ISBN 0-8027-6145-3; 0-8027-6146-1
The author describes the characterstics of various
types of insects and offers instructions for the collection, care, and study of living and dead specimens.
True bugs, beetles, water insects, noisy insects, butterflies and moths are among the insects considered
Illustrated with "clear black-and-white drawings.
. . . There is just enough interesting information
given about the insects to inspire one to want to begin
'insect watching.' This book would be helpful for a
budding entomologist, an individual child, a class of
youngsters, or an interested adult." Appraisal
Bibliography: p91

George, Jean Craighead
All upon a sidewalk; illus. by Don Bolognese. Dutton 1974 unp illus $6.95 (2-4)   595.7
1 Ants
ISBN 0-525-25462-5
The author describes a day in the life of a common
yellow ant, " 'Lasius Flavus', who searches the city
streets for a treat to bring home to her queen. Climbing out of a crack, over a huge bottle cap, 'Lasius' lays
down a chemical scent which she counts on to guide
her home. But what perils are in her path as she tracks
down the treasure! She's trapped in a soda straw,
attacked by a bee and by a sparrow, involved in a fight
with ants of another species." Pub W
"This ant's eye view of a city sidewalk presents
ecology to children in a palatable fashion. The author,
Jean George, has a way with words. . . . Good readers will find this factual yet creative account absorbing
and challenging. Less able readers will surely find
pleasure in the superb illustrations." Reading Teacher

All upon a stone; illus. by Don Bolognese. Crowell
1971 unp illus $3.95, lib. bdg. $4.70 (1-3)   595.7
1 Crickets
ISBN 0-690-05532-3; 0-690-05533-1
This is "the story of a mole cricket who crawls from
the earth deep under the stone, spends a summer day
exploring, and after a brief, festive encounter with a
host of other mole crickets, returns." Horn Bk
This book "reveals unsuspected color and life in a
seemingly barren rock. . . . [The] illustrations make

an uninterrupted block print of fabric, weaving the
pages into a background for the mole cricket's
universe." Christian Sci Monitor

The moon of the monarch butterflies; illus. by Murray Tinkelman. Crowell 1968 40p illus $3.95, lib. bdg.
$4.70 (3-5)   595.7
1 Butterflies
ISBN 0-690-55555-5; 0-690-55556-3
"The Thirteen moons"
The author describes a "female monarch's journey
up the Mississippi Valley from Arkansas to Michigan.
The changing ecological world around her is sensitively and minutely described. Murray Tinkelman's
black and white drawings are in complete harmony
with the mood of the text." Appraisal
"This book is adequately and accurately descriptive
of the monarch butterfly. However, it does lack the
more detailed substance as well as the activity and
research suggestions for children in other books on
this insect." Sci Bks

Goudey, Alice E.
Butterfly time; illus by Adrienne Adams. Scribner
1964 unp illus $5.95 (1-3)   595.7
1 Butterflies
ISBN 0-684-20833-4
A book that is "as lovely . . . [as it is] accurately
detailed. . . . Author and artist reproduce the world
of 'winged beauty' in all its exquisite variety of color
and pattern. The poetic, imagistic text and naturalistic
four-color illustrations describe twelve butterflies
commonly seen through the summer and into the fall.
Included are a note on the life cycle of butterflies and
a summary of their identification." Horn Bk
"A handsome book, useful for first units in nature
study and perfect for home collections." Chicago.
Children's Bk Center

Harris, Louise Dyer
Flash; the life story of a firefly, by Louise Dyer
Harris and Norman Dyer Harris; illus. by Henry B.
Kane. Little 1966 57p illus lib. bdg. $3.95 (1-3)
                                               595.7
1 Fireflies 2 Bioluminescence
ISBN 0-316-34810-4
The author "traces the life of the firefly through the
states of egg, glowworm, pupa, and beetle." Hodges.
Bks for Elem Sch Libraries
The "details of an easy text and the delights of
beautiful illustrations colored in yellow and green . . .
will heighten wonder and understanding." Horn Bk

Hawes, Judy
Bees and beelines; illus. by Aliki. Crowell 1964 unp
illus (Let's-read-and-find-out science bks) $4.50, lib.
bdg. $5.25, pa $1.25 (k-2)   595.7
1 Bees
ISBN 0-690-12739-1; 0-690-12740-5; 0-690-12745-6
"Young children are told how bees can go great
distances, find their way home, and then dance a
message about where the nectar is to be found."
Pub W
"An amazing little book in that it gives so much
information about a very specific subject in simple
language. . . . The line drawings of bees are both
attractive and scientifically correct." Sch Library J

Fireflies in the night; illus. by Kazue Mizumura.
Crowell 1963 unp illus (Let's-read-and-find-out science bks) $4.50, lib. bdg. $5.25 (k-3)   595.7
1 Fireflies
ISBN 0-690-30065-4; 0-690-30066-2
The author "fills this sprightly little volume [on
fireflies] with information about their history, their

Hawes, Judy—*Continued*

biological functions and even directions on how to make a firefly lantern." N Y Times Bk Rev

"A most satisfying presentation of a subject unfamiliar to most very young children. . . . The pictures are lovely." Bk Week

Ladybug, ladybug, fly away home; illus. by Ed Emberley. Crowell 1967 unp illus (Let's-read-and-find-out science bks) $4.50, lib. bdg. $5.25, pa $1.25 (k-3)   595.7

1 Ladybugs

ISBN 0-690-48383-X; 0-690-48384-8; 0-690-00200-9

The author "tells of the importation of ladybugs from Australia, where they had been found to be instrumental in controlling the pest that was damaging orange trees; and briefly describes their morphology and habits." Sat Rev

"A good first book about the small beetle familiar to most children; the text is written in a crisp, informal style with an occasional note of pleasantry. The illustrations are quite effective: large, clear diagrams or attractive embellishments that make good use of black, white, red, and green." Chicago. Children's Bk Center

Hess, Lilo

The praying mantis, insect cannibal; story and photographs by Lilo Hess. Scribner 1971 47p illus lib. bdg. $5.95 (3-6)   595.7

1 Praying mantis

ISBN 0-684-12317-7

"The excellent photographs are enough to justify acquisition of this book; although black and white, they clearly and interestingly illustrate the different characteristics of the praying mantis. The text is at times cumbersome but, nevertheless, informative, as it covers appearance, habitat, diet, superstitions about the mantis, the mantis as a pet, etc. Children of intermediate age will enjoy the book for pleasure reading and will certainly find it useful when studying insects." Library J

Hogner, Dorothy Childs

Grasshoppers and crickets; illus. by Nils Hogner. Crowell 1960 61p illus $4.50, lib. bdg. $5.25 (2-5)   595.7

1 Locusts 2 Crickets

ISBN 0-690-35035-X; 0-690-35036-8

"Differentiates between grasshoppers, locusts and crickets with the aid of labelled diagrams showing the principal anatomical features, and relates important details of their natural history." The AAAS Sci Bk List for Children

"Good science writing: simple, succinct, and accurate; illustrations are clearly detailed. . . . Large print." Chicago. Children's Bk Center

Water beetles; illus. by Nils Hogner. Crowell 1963 57p illus $4.50, lib. bdg. $5.25 (2-5)   595.7

1 Water-beetles

ISBN 0-690-87008-6; 0-690-87009-4

"The author describes the anatomy, physiology, and life cycle of water beetles in general and the identifying characteristics and habits of 10 different beetle families. She also offers suggestions for setting up and caring for an aquarium and collecting specimens for observation." Booklist

"This is good science writing; simple and to the point with clearly detailed illustrations; the large print and organization into brief sections on limited topics make this book well suited for youngsters." Sch Library J

Huntington, Harriet E.

Let's look at insects; written and illus. with photographs by Harriet E. Huntington; drawings by J. Noel. Doubleday 1969 60p illus $4.95, lib. bdg. $5.70 (1-4)   595.7

1 Insects

ISBN 0-385-02248-4; 0-385-08145-6

The author "describes the distinguishing characteristics of insects, insect development from egg to adulthood, and the function of insect legs, feet, eyes, antennae, and other body parts." Booklist

"The excellent, close-up photographs picture insects so enlarged that such tiny anatomical details as eyes, antennae, mouth parts, etc. are plainly seen. Occasional line drawings in the margins further elucidate the text. While anatomy receives the main emphasis, much information about the development and habits of insects is also given. The photos here are superior to those in most children's books." Sch Library J

Hussey, Lois J.

Collecting cocoons [by] Lois J. Hussey and Catherine Pessino; illus. by Isabel Sherwin Harris. Crowell 1953 73p illus $4.50, lib. bdg. $5.25 (4-6)   595.7

1 Moths—Collection and preservation

ISBN 0-690-19697-0; 0-690-19698-9

This book "describes the four stages in the development of the moth, how cocoons are made, where and when to look for cocoons, how to collect and care for them, how to breed moths, and how to keep a collection of cocoons. The last half of the book consists of identification data on 19 moths. . . . A good basic book for beginners." Booklist

Where to go for other information: p70

Hutchins, Ross E.

The bug clan; illus. with photographs by the author. Dodd 1973 127p illus lib. bdg. $5.50 (5-7)   595.7

1 Insects

ISBN 0-396-06771-9

"This comprehensive and well-organized survey of the insect orders Hemiptera and Homoptera provides a ready reference guide and superb magnified photographs that can be used for identification. The author, after making distinctions between the true bug and other orders of insects, methodically describes the families of the two orders of bugs, giving facts about the life cycle, habitat, habits, and the usefulness (or harmfulness) to people or plants. Succinct and lucid, the text is a model of its kind: a classification outline, a bibliography, and an index are appended." Chicago. Children's Bk Center

Caddis insects; nature's carpenters and stonemasons; illus. with photographs by the author. Dodd 1966 80p illus lib. bdg. $4.50 (5-7)   595.7

1 Caddis-flies

ISBN 0-396-05267-3

The author "describes the life cycle and habits of the unique caddis insects—builders of protective cases of twigs and pebbles—and tells where to obtain caddis flies for aquariums." Hodges. Bks for Elem Sch Libraries

"For closeup photography, entomologist Ross E. Hutchins has few peers." Christian Sci Monitor

The carpenter bee; illus. by Richard Cuffari. Addison-Wesley 1972 48p illus $5.50 (2-5)   595.7

1 Bees 2 Wasps

ISBN 0-201-03098-5

"An Addisonian Press book"

"Despite the title, this treats the Monobia wasp as well as the carpenter bee. Information about the life

Hutchins, Ross E.—*Continued*
cycles of these insects is related in a fictional
framework through Ephraim, a boy who is growing up
in the Smoky Mountains. . . . Along with Eph, readers observe the life cycle of the carpenter bee. Later,
'house-renter' wasps, the Monobia, take over the
abandoned tunnels of the carpenter bees, demonstrating how this insect is dependent upon the other."
Sch Library J
   "The attractive illustrations amplify the text; a page
of 'scientific notes on carpenter bees' and an index are
appended." Chicago. Children's Bk Center

   Insects in armor; a beetle book; illus. with photographs by the author. Parents Mag. Press 1972 64p
illus lib. bdg. $4.59 (3-6)   595.7
   1 Beetles
   ISBN 0-8193-0487-5
   "A Stepping-stone book"
This is an "elementary introduction to the beetle
with scientific terms explained within the text. After
tracing the beetle's life cycle Hutchins describes 30
types of useful, harmful, and unusual beetles and
their habits and habitats, concluding with experiments showing the beetle's muscular strength."
Booklist

   The mayfly; illus. by Jean Day Zallinger. Addison-
Wesley 1970 48p illus $5.50 (3-5)   595.7
   1 May-flies
   ISBN 0-201-3100-0
   "An Addison Press book"
"Centering his life history of the mayfly on genus
Ephemerella that lives in streams in the Great Smoky
Mountains, entomologist Hutchins describes, in narrative style, the habitat, appearance, enemies, habits,
and growth of this moth-like insect from egg to fully
developed adult. Scientific notes on mayflies are
appended. Pencil drawings, some of which are in
color, depict the mayfly in its natural habitat with
charm and accuracy." Booklist

   Paper hornets; illus. by Peter Zallinger. Addison-
Wesley 1973 44p illus $4.75 (3-5)   595.7
   1 Wasps
   ISBN 0-201-02986-3
   "An Addisonian Press book"
"This book depicts the life cycle of a paper hornet as
a story, following the hornet's growth and development through the four seasons of the year. The text is
interesting, and the author uses a vocabulary the
young reader can grasp. The bald-faced hornet of this
story is found in the Great Smoky Mountains of Tennessee where the author has often observed them at
work. His description of the relationship of hornets to
the environment and to other organisims in the environment is ecologically sound and instructive. There
is a section at the end of the text entitled 'Scientific
Notes' which is quite interesting and is primarily
meant for older readers." Sci Bks

   Scaly wings; a book about moths and their caterpillars. Parents Mag. Press 1971 64p illus $4.95, lib. bdg.
$4.59 (2-4)   595.7
   1 Moths 2 Caterpillars
   ISBN 0-8193-0440-9
   "A Stepping-stone book"
"Following an explanation of the differences between moths and butterflies and a discussion of the
life cycle of moths [the author] describes 37 different
types of moths and their caterpillars, including four
types each of millers, tiger moths, and giant silkworm
moths; three varieties that are helpful to plants and
five that are considered pests; and several moths
whose caterpillars are poisonous and dangerous to
handle." Booklist

"Excellent close-up photographs aid in the identification of the lepidoptera, meaning scaled winged.
. . . This book is an excellent introduction the subject
and a good reference source for its intended readers."
Appraisal

   The world of dragonflies and damselflies; illus. with
photographs by the author. Dodd 1969 127p illus
$4.50, lib. bdg. $4.50 (5-7)   595.7
   1 Dragonflies 2 Damsel flies
   ISBN 0-396-07163-5; 0-396-05912-0
This introduction to the life cycles of the dragonfly
and damselfly describes their coloration and distribution and the giant dragonflies of the past. It also
includes instructions on collecting and identifying
these insects as a hobby
"This life history and ecological study of dragonflies
and damselflies is typical since the subject is sufficiently limited in scope to facilitate handling in adequate depth. It contains directions for those who wish
to collect and mount these insects for study; keys and
identification of families, and references for more
detailed study. Libraries who are building good
natural history collections for young people should
purchase it." Sci Bks

Ipsen, D. C.
   What does a bee see? Addison-Wesley 1971 89p
illus $5.50 (5-7)   595.7
   1 Vision 2 Bees 3 Color sense
   ISBN 0-201-03165-5
   "An Addisonian Press book"
This account of honey bee vision and perception of
color "guides young people . . . through the experiments of scientists who contributed most of our
knowledge of what a bee sees. Readers learn about the
use of colored papers by the earlier scientists [and] a
more recent instrument which sends forth an electric
signal to measure how an animal's eye reacts to light,
etc. Emphasis is placed on how scientists test theories
by experiment and how each adds to a growing field of
knowledge." Library J
This work "is so specialized it would be easy to
dismiss it altogether. Don't. It is well researched,
documented and presented—a good example for pre-
and early teens of what can be done when one is
sincerely interested in a topic. It is an excellent book."
Christian Sci Monitor

Kaufmann, John
   Insect travelers. Morrow 1972 126p illus maps
$5.95, lib. bdg. $5.11 (6-7)   595.7
   1 Insects—Migration
   ISBN 0-688-20036-2; 0-688-30036-7
"This covers how and why insects travel, distances
they attempt, their power of flight, and how they find
their way. . . . The account is well written and
absorbing on the whole and will be useful for libraries
trying to build a large, diversified collection of insect
lore." Sch Library J
   Bibliography: p119-21

Klots, Alexander B.
   A field guide to the butterflies of North America,
east of the Great Plains; illus. with color paintings of
247 species by Marjorie Statham and 232 photographs
by Florence Longworth. Houghton 1951 349p illus
$5.95   595.7
   1 Butterflies
   ISBN 0-395-07865-2
   "The Peterson Field guide series"
The author describes and tells the reader how to
identify butterflies found east of the Great Plains
from Greenland to Mexico. He tells about the habits,
the range, the food plant of the caterpillar and the

Klots, Alexander B.—*Continued*

type of country in which the butterfly is likely to be found

"It is scientific without being pedantic." N Y Times Bk Rev

Bibliography: p301-08. Checklist of butterflies: p308-28

Lecht, Jane

Honeybees. Natl. Geographic Soc. 1973 31p illus (k-3)   595.7

1 Bees

ISBN 0-87044-141-8

Obtainable only as part of a set for $6.95 with: How animals hide, by Robert M. McClung, class 591.5; Namu, by Ronald M. Fisher, class 599; and Pandas, by Donna K. Grosvenor, class 599

"Books for young explorers"

Prepared by the Special Publications Division of the National Geographic Society

In color photographs and text, this book describes the life of a honeybee hive, noting the differences between the queen bee, the drone and the worker. It tells how bees gather nectar to make honey and pollinate flowers, and deals briefly with man's treatment of bees

"The superb, color macrophotographs, clear, large print and explanatory illustrations are boldly arranged in poster-style format. Each page reaches out to the reader in a way similar to but even more aggressive than some of the best of television for children. This book represents an exciting approach to science for the younger set and demonstrates the information resource capacity of the picturebook medium." Booklist

Lutz, Frank E.

Field book of insects of the United States and Canada, aiming to answer common questions. 3d ed. rewritten to include much additional material; with about 800 illus. many in color. Putnam 1935 510p illus (Putnam's Nature field bks) $5.95   595.7

1 Insects

ISBN 0-399-10289-2

First published 1918

This "is intended to be an introduction to commonly observed species and to the larger groups (genera and particularly families) of insects. Although the species mentioned are, for the most part, inhabitants of northeastern United States, many of them have a wide distribution in this country and some of them in other continents. . . . I have made an effort in this book to record the real names correctly and have given the nicknames when I knew them." Introduction

"Though not intended for children this is a most valuable handbook for younger as well as older amateur entomologists." Toronto

McClung, Robert M.

Bees, wasps, and hornets and how they live; written and illus. by Robert M. McClung. Morrow 1971 64p illus $4.95, lib. bdg. $4.59 (3-6)   595.7

1 Bees 2 Wasps 3 Hornets

ISBN 0-688-21075-9; 0-688-31075-3

The author explores the differences and similarities of the membrane winged insects, dividing them into four groups: parasitic wasps; solitary hunting wasps; social wasps; and, bees. He concludes with a chapter on the ecological value of bees and wasps

"Packed with relevant information, easy to read, it has the plus of a pleasing format and well-captioned, detailed illustrations." Sch Library J

Caterpillars and how they live; written and illus. by Robert M. McClung. Morrow 1965 63p illus $4.59 (2-4)   595.7

1 Caterpillars

ISBN 0-688-31152-0

"The anatomy and life of the caterpillar, the many different kinds of caterpillars, methods of controlling the harmful varieties, and how to raise caterpillars—all aspects are covered." Horn Bk

"The information on shelter, protection and camouflage is good, as is the brief mention of useful and harmful caterpillars. The final chapter on raising caterpillars is commendable." Sci Bks

"Clear, soft-pencil drawings of caterpillars, in all stages of the life cycle, enhance the [book's] scientific value." Children's Bks 1965

Luna; the story of a moth; written and illus. by Robert M. McClung. Morrow 1957 unp illus $4.59 (2-4)   595.7

1 Moths

ISBN 0-688-31523-2

This is a life cycle story of the Luna moth as it evolves from its cocoon, lays hundreds of eggs, and lives just a few days. Because of the constant danger from other insects and small animals, only one of the six eggs laid on the walnut tree survives to become a caterpillar and pupa

"A beautiful and poetic treatment. . . . Each page or double page is effectively designed with type and decoration as a unit, and the information, told simply enough for younger children, is authentic enough for any age." Christian Sci Monitor

Mendoza, George

The digger wasp; pictures by Jean Zallinger. Dial Press 1969 48p illus $4.95, lib. bdg. $4.58 (2-5)   595.7

1 Wasps

ISBN 0-440-1936-1; 0-440-1959-0

"The life cycle of the solitary digger wasp, who searches the dunes until she finds just the correct spot on which to dig the incredible tunnel that will house her eggs. Mendoza tells how the eggs, as larvae, feed on grasshoppers poisoned and paralyzed for them by their mother; how, after 10 full months, they become the offspring that the mother wasp never lives to see. In turn, the young females will experience their 'mysterious urge to search, to dig, to hunt, and kill among the leaves,' while the males will frolic away their short life span. The black-and-white illustrations and diagrams detail anatomy precisely, and are clear complements to the informative, compellingly narrated, factual material." Sch Library J

Glossary: p47-48

Mitchell, Robert T.

Butterflies and moths; a guide to the more common American species, by Robert T. Mitchell and Herbert S. Zim; illus. by Andre Durenceau. 423 illus. in full color. Golden Press 1964 illus (A Golden Nature guide) lib. bdg. $4.95, pa $1.95 (4-7)   595.7

1 Butterflies 2 Moths

ISBN 0-307-63524-4; 0-307-24413-X

"So numerous are North American species that only about three per cent have been included, but these were selected to include the most common, widespread, important, or unusual kinds. . . . [Includes] range maps which show distribution." Foreword

"No other book shows so many butterflies and moths with their caterpillars, chrysalises, and cocoons. The oft neglected states west of the Rockies appear to be fully covered." Sch Library J

Books: p18

Pringle, Laurence

Cockroaches: here, there, and everywhere; illus. by James and Ruth McCrea. Crowell 1971 32p illus (Let's-read-and-find-out science bks) $4.50, lib. bdg. $5.25 (k-3) 595.7

1 Cockroaches

ISBN 0-690-19679-2; 0-690-19680-6

"The presentation given the roach is simple and straightforward. It starts with history and proceeds through the ecological place of the roach to the inevitable conclusion that the roach will be living with mankind for the future. Both good and bad points in the life of the roach are given. Precautions are given in relation to food spoilage. The book is well-illustrated." Sci Bks

Ripper, Charles L.

Mosquitoes; written and illus. by Charles L. Ripper. Morrow 1969 63p illus lib. bdg. $4.59 (3-5) 595.7

1 Mosquitoes

ISBN 0-688-31801-0

This book describes the research work and control methods used on mosquitoes and gives a "detailed description of anatomy, appearance and life cycle of 3 genera. Excellent illustrations." Minnesota

Roberts, Hortense Roberta

You can make an insect zoo; photographs and cages by Francis Munger. Childrens Press 1974 64p illus lib. bdg. $5.85 (3-5) 595.7

1 Insects

ISBN 0-516-07628-0

"An Elk Grove book"

The author "explains how to build cages for butterflies, moths, crickets, ladybugs, aphids and ants. She provides excellent photographs of both the insects and the completed projects." Sci Bks

"This is an outstanding book from several points of view. It gives clear, distinct directions for keeping and observing insects, as well as suggesting more complex tasks that could be carried out by kids who want to do more than observe growth and development. The illustrations and the figures showing cage designs are all useful as well as part of a thoughtful and attractive design. It will be most useful in elementary and middle school science rooms." Sci and Children

Selsam, Millicent E.

Questions and answers about ants; pictures by Arabelle Wheatley. Four Winds 1967 75p illus lib. bdg. $4.46 (2-5) 595.7

1 Ants

ISBN 0-590-07054-1

This book answers such questions as: How do you watch ants? What do ants eat? How does the ant lay a trail? Do the ants take care of the eggs and young because they "love" them? Which ants do what? What is mating time? How do ants sleep? Can ants learn?

"The text is concise and is enlivened by occasional references to the author's own experiences, and the illustrations on almost every page are clearly drawn. At the end of the inviting book Selsam gives suggestions on how to keep ants for observation at home." Booklist

Terry and the caterpillars; pictures by Arnold Lobel. Harper 1962 64p illus (A Science I can read bk) $2.95, lib. bdg. $3.79 (k-2) 595.7

1 Caterpillars

ISBN 0-06-025405-X; 0-06-025406-8

Also available in a Spanish language edition (ISBN 0-06-025409-2), lib. bdg. $3.79

"A little girl finds three caterpillars, puts them into a jar, and watches all the stages of their life: caterpillar to cocoon to moth to egg and back to caterpillar again." Hodges. Bks for Elem Sch Libraries

"The child gets a good idea of the continuity of reproduction . . . and the attractive presentation may persuade him to do some collecting himself." Library J

"A good sensible easy science book with lively pictures." N Y Her Trib Bks

Shuttlesworth, Dorothy E.

All kinds of bees; illus. by Su Zan Noguchi Swain. Random House 1967 62p illus $2.95; lib. bdg. $4.99 (4-6) 595.7

1 Bees

ISBN 0-394-80143-1; 0-394-90143-6

"Gateway books"

"An overall summary of the families of bees; their anatomy, ways, dances, and relationship to plants and animals. The book has just enough of the facts yet makes interesting reading. The drawings even though black and white, are excellent." Appraisal

"An appendix on classification gives scientific names for all of the families and some of the species of bees." Booklist

This "is a good systematic reference book for young readers." N Y Times Bk Rev

The story of ants; illus. by Su Zan N. Swain. Doubleday 1964 60p illus $4.95, lib. bdg. $5.70 (4-7) 595.7

1 Ants

ISBN 0-385-06676-7; 0-385-05370-3

The author "describes the organization of an ant colony and the characteristics and behavior of its inhabitants, including such fascinating aspects as slavery among ants and ant armies." Hodges. Bks for Elem Sch Libraries

"The artists' method of drawing the insects larger than life size to show detail and putting beside each a small drawing to show actual life size is most effective. Scientifically accurate, this book seems to have more detail about more species than other books on ants, and the handsome format is quite striking." Library J

Simon, Hilda

Dragonflies; illus. by the author. Viking 1972 95p illus lib. bdg. $4.95 (5-7) 595.7

1 Dragonflies 2 Damsel flies

ISBN 0-670-28147-6

The author explores every aspect of the life of a dragonfly and includes an identification guide to North American dragonflies

"Seventy realistic and colorful drawings perfectly complement the text. Although this is a rather technical subject and the writer has aimed at young readers, there is no trace of condescension. The facts are stated simply, accurately, and adequately." Sci Bks

Sterling, Dorothy

Caterpillars; illus. by Winifred Lubell. Doubleday 1961 64p illus lib. bdg. $3.50 (3-6) 595.7

1 Caterpillars

ISBN 0-385-07910-9

This "introduction to caterpillars describes informally the life cycle of a butterfly or moth, the anatomical structure of a caterpillar, its eating habits, silk spinning, enemies, and means of survival. The book also tells how to catch, observe, and raise caterpillars." Booklist

"Truly excellent nature writing: crisp, enthusiastic, accurate, and comprehensive. Even some touches of humor in the side headings. The illustrations are precise and informative, and they are lovely." Chicago. Children's Bk Center

Books about caterpillars: p62

Sterling, Dorothy—*Continued*

Insects and the homes they build; with photographs by Myron Ehrenberg. Doubleday 1954 125p illus lib. bdg. $4.95 (5-7)   595.7

1 Insects

ISBN 0-385-03608-6

In this book "chief attention is paid to [insects'] ingenious methods of building homes. Grouped according to the materials they use—silk, bubbles, mud, paper, wax, wood and plants—there are wasps, spiders, the froghopper and praying mantis, ants and bees. The story of their life cycle and domesticity, and particularly of their individual styles of carpentry and masonry, makes a book of ageless interest. The photographs, with interior scenes and cross-sections of homes, add greatly to the book's scientific value." Horn Bk

Stevens, Carla

Catch a cricket; about the capture and care of crickets, grasshoppers, fireflies and other companionable creatures; photos by Martin Iger. Young Scott Bks. 1961 95p illus lib. bdg. $3.95 (k-2)   595.7

1 Insects

ISBN 0-201-09151-8

A "book which instructs young children in the care and feeding of crickets, grasshoppers, caterpillars, worms, fireflies and other tiny creatures that can be temporarily housed in glass jars, while their habits are studied by the very youngest naturalists." Pub W

"Each page of the text faces a full page photograph showing a boy hunting for, catching, caring for, and releasing a worm, a firefly, a cricket, a grasshopper, and a caterpillar. Each small creature is strikingly introduced by a bright red hand and arm stretching across two white pages." Library J

Teale, Edwin Way

The junior book of insects; illus. with photographs and drawings by the author. 2d rev. ed. Dutton 1972 266p illus $6.95 (6-7)   595.7

1 Insects

ISBN 0-525-32925-0

First published 1939 with title: The boy's book of insects

"The habits of such insect families as the ants, butterflies, moths, wasps, and beetles are discussed, as are methods of studying insects in nature or in captivity. Though the author unfortunately directs his comments to boys . . . both sexes will be engrossed by the anecdotes and little-known details of insect life and by the interesting and practical suggestions for observing and collecting. This will be a useful addition to basic collections on entomology." Sch Library J

Bibliography: p251-59

Villiard, Paul

Insects as pets; with photographs by the author. Doubleday 1973 143p illus $4.95, lib. bdg. $5.70 (5-7)   595.7

1 Insects 2 Pets

ISBN 0-385-07700-9; 0-385-06423-3

The author gives "reasons for keeping insects and the information needed for their care. Beginning with honey bees and ants he explains the makeup of their societies and describes the construction of observation cages, food, and desirable temperature and humidity for them and for ant lions, mantis, mealworms, crickets and six other varieties of insects. He also tells how or where these can be obtained and includes detailed instructions for mounting butterflies and moths, only mentioning, however, the mounting of other insects. Well illustrated with photographs." Booklist

Wong, Herbert H.

My ladybug, by Herbert H. Wong and Matthew F. Vessel; illus. by Marie Nonnast Bohlen. Addison-Wesley 1969 30p illus (Science ser. for the young) $4.95 (k-3)   595.7

1 Ladybugs

ISBN 0-201-08721-9

"An Addisonian Press book"

"The author presents information on the ladybug, its eating habits, its life cycle, its economic value, and different types of ladybugs." Sci Bks

The book has "delightful color illustrations taking up most of each page. [The text is] very short and simple." Christian Sci Monitor

Zim, Herbert S.

Insects; a guide to familiar American insects, by Herbert S. Zim and Clarence Cottam; illus. by James Gordon Irving. Sponsored by The Wildlife Management Institute. 224 species in full color. [Rev. ed] Golden Press [1961 c1956] 160p illus maps (A Golden Nature guide) lib. bdg. $4.95, pa $1.95 (4-7)   595.7

1 Insects

ISBN 0-307-63504-X; 0-307-24492-X

First published 1951 by Simon & Schuster

"Two hundred and twenty-five species of common, important and showy insects are described here with brief texts and colored illustrations for the novice insect collector." N Y Pub Library

"An excellent handbook for the young naturalist. A Key to Insect Groups is included to help in identification and there are colored pictures on every page. Many authorities in the field have been consulted to assure the accuracy of the book." Horn Bk

596   Vertebrates

Cosgrove, Margaret

Bone for bone; written and illus. by Margaret Cosgrove. Dodd 1968 128p illus $3.95, lib. bdg. $4.50 (5-7)   596

1 Vertebrates 2 Anatomy, Comparative 3 Evolution

ISBN 0-396-05706-3; 0-396-06724-7

The author "examines the relationship between major classes of vertebrates as revealed through a study of living animal forms, fossils, and embryological development. The informative, discursive text describing skeletal structure, muscles, and internal body systems is supplemented with numerous two-color drawings and diagrams." Booklist

"A clear account. . . . Students of the biological sciences will find this volume to be an excellent introduction to comparative anatomy and the simplicity of approach will enable the student to handle more difficult materials." Best Sellers

Glossary: p123

Livaudais, Madeleine

The skeleton book; an inside look at animals, by Madeleine Livaudais and Robert Dunne. Walker & Co. [1973 c1972] 31p illus $4.95, lib. bdg. $4.85 (3-6)   596

1 Vertebrates 2 Anatomy, Comparative

ISBN 0-8027-6125-9; 0-8027-6126-7

"The authors present stark photographs—white bones against a black background—of the skeletons of a snake, fish, whale, turtle, frog, bird, penguin, bat, giraffe, horse, elephant, cat, gorilla, and human. Distinguishing features of each are singled out, and readers are encouraged to make their own comparisons between related skeletal types." Booklist

597 Fishes. Amphibians

Aliki

The long lost coelacanth: and other living fossils; written and illus. by Aliki. Crowell 1973 31p illus (Let's-read-and-find-out science bks) $3.95, lib. bdg. $4.70 (1-3)   597

1 Coelacanth
ISBN 0-690-50478-0; 0-690-50479-9
The author describes the coelacanth, a fish thought to have been extinct for 70 million years until one was discovered in 1938, and other "living fossils" such as the horseshoe crab and the Galápagos tortoise

"The simple text gives a clear explanation of how fossil finds enable naturalists to recognize living fossils, and mentions some of the familiar creatures that—although they may have changed in size—are essentially the same as their ancestors of millions of years ago." Chicago. Children's Bk Center

Cook, Joseph J.

The nightmare world of the shark, by Joseph J. Cook and William L. Wisner; illus. with photographs and diagrams. Dodd 1968 96p illus lib. bdg. $4.50 (4-7)   597

1 Sharks
ISBN 0-396-06354-3
Both a "factual and fanciful history of sharks is presented. . . . Several species are identified and the characteristics of sharks as dangerous predators to seamen and swimmers, challenging prey for sportsmen, and a source of many products useful to man are discussed by the authors." Booklist

"Many excellent photographs and several simple line drawings complement the text as does the index. The book will interest both serious and casual readers, as well as swimmers who have the normal amount of healthy fear, but it does not include a bibliography or references to enable further study." Sch Library J

Fletcher, Alan Mark

Fishes dangerous to man; illus. by Jane Teiko Oka and Willi Baum. Addison-Wesley 1969 47p illus $4.95 (4-6)   597

1 Fishes
ISBN 0-201-02056-4
"An Addisonian Press book"
"The electric eel, great white shark, piranha, stingray, lionfish, and puffer are among the 'shockers,' 'biters,' 'stingers,' and poisonous-to-eat fishes assembled here. The short . . . account identifies approximately 25 fishes and describes the ways in which they are dangerous to man." Booklist

The illustrations "are realistic and appropriately labeled." The AAAS Sci Bk List for Children

Unusual aquarium fishes. Lippincott 1968 143p illus $5.50 (5-7)   597

1 Fishes
ISBN 0-397-31049-8
"Scientifically accurate but delightfully interesting information about 30 fishes, each of which has some unique trait such as kissing, shooting down insects with streams of water, or producing an electric charge. Many photographs actually show the strange creatures performing their distinct acts." Bruno. Bks for Sch Libraries, 1968

Some helpful books and magazines for people interested in fishes: p135. Definitions of some words used in this book: p137-39

George, Jean Craighead

The moon of the salamanders; illus. by John Kaufmann. Crowell 1967 39p illus $3.95, lib. bdg. $4.70 (3-5)   597

1 Salamanders
ISBN 0-690-55564-4; 0-690-55565-2
"The Thirteen moons"
The author describes "a blue-spotted salamander on his annual nuptial journey back to a pond in early springtime. The scene is well staged: a rainy night. The cast of characters is well chosen: from snails to fairy shrimp, screech owls to downy woodpeckers, peepers to beetles to spring flowers. The story is rich in relationships between animals and their environment." Appraisal

"The author's keen observations of nature and her gifts for telling a moving story are greatly in evidence here, and the illustrations are equally as lively." Sci Bks

Hawes, Judy

What I like about toads; illus. by James and Ruth McCrea. Crowell 1969 33p illus (Let's-read-and-find-out science bks) $4.50, lib. bdg. $5.25, pa $1.25 (k-3)   597

1 Frogs
ISBN 0-690-87576-2; 0-690-87577-0; 0-690-87582-7
In easy text the author "describes the appearance, habits, and life cycle of toads, dispels the false notion that toads cause warts, and points out the valuable service which these insect-eating amphibians perform for farmers. The appearance and characteristic behavior of a toad are cleverly depicted in the black-and-white and three-color illustrations." Booklist

"Easy enough for very young or reluctant readers, informative and entertaining for all. . . . Pen-and-ink drawings by James and Ruth McCrea complement the text very well, capturing the seemingly smug, introspective look of toads." Sch Library J

Why frogs are wet; illus. by Don Madden. Crowell 1968 35p illus $4.50, lib. bdg. $5.25, pa $1.25 (k-3)   597

1 Frogs
ISBN 0-690-88925-9; 0-690-88926-7; 0-690-00640-3
A "scientific introduction to the life of frogs, their adaptation since prehistoric times, physiology, growth cycle and feeding." Sch Library J

"An easy-to-read, straightforward text with the marvelously humorous drawings of Don Madden. The result is irresistible—even to the most hesitant young reader." Bk World

Hess, Lilo

Sea horses; story and photographs by Lilo Hess. Scribner 1966 46p illus lib. bdg. $5.95 (1-3)   597

1 Sea horse
ISBN 0-684-12446-7
"A captivating book because of the many photographs of the small, engaging sea horse, a fish that has an external skeleton, a prehensile tail, and eyes that move independently. The author describes the habits and the reproductive process of the sea horse, the latter unusual because the eggs of the female are deposited in the male's pouch for gestation. The book closes with instructions for raising sea horses in a home aquarium. The photographs are intriguing, the text straightforward and crisp, the print large and clear." Sutherland. The Best in Children's Bks

Morris, Robert A.

Seahorse; pictures by Arnold Lobel. Harper 1972 60p illus (A Science I can read bk) $2.95, lib. bdg. $3.79 (k-2)   597

1 Sea horse
ISBN 0-06-024338-4; 0-06-024339-2
The text provides "information about the strange seahorse which makes its home in the deepest waters where the sea is calmer. During storms and to hide from bigger fish, the seahorse clings to seaweed which

Morris, Robert A.—*Continued*

provides good camouflage. . . . The author discusses the curious mating and breeding habits of the sea-horse." Pub W

"The soft pastel illustrations of seahorses and oceanscapes, the book's outstanding feature, provide yet another example of the illustrator's sensitivity to design and diversity of style." Horn Bk

National Geographic Society

Wondrous world of fishes. New enl. ed. The Society 1969 373p illus (Natural science lib) $4.95 (5-7)
597

1 Fishes 2 Fishing
First published 1965
Editor and art director: Leonard J. Grant
"Colorfully illustrated articles on underwater exploration in and around North America from New-foundland to Hawaii." Ref Materials for Sch Libraries

Partial contents: Fishes and how they live, by L. P. Schultz; Angling in the United States, by L. Marden; Ice fishing's frigid charms, by T. J. Abercrombie; America's first park in the sea, by C. M. Brookfield; Florida meets a walking catfish, by C. P. Idyll; Aquarium fishes: enchanting entertainers, by T. Y. Canby; Gallery of sharks and Hawaiian fishes; Guide to fish cookery, by J. A. Beard

Ommanney, F. D.

Frogs, toads & newts; illus. by Deborah Fulford. McGraw [1975 c1973] 48p illus (A McGraw-Hill New biology) lib. bdg. $5.33 (4-6)
597
1 Frogs 2 Salamanders
ISBN 0-07-047705-1
First published 1973 in England
This book briefly discusses the evolution and characteristics of amphibians and then describes the habitats, physical characteristics, mating, reproduction and life cycles of frogs and toads, and of newts and other types of salamanders

"An especially interesting and attractively designed survey. . . . Besides general characteristics of the phylum and its larger subgroups, unusual aspects of common British and U.S. species and examples of lesser-known animals in other countries are called to the reader's attention through clear textual descriptions and exact, full-color illustrations. Captions give generic and scientific names and frequently indicate the animal's actual size in relation to the picture. Wide margins and large type will be helpful to beginning readers." Booklist

Simon, Seymour

Discovering what frogs do; illus. by Jean Zallinger. McGraw 1969 47p illus lib. bdg. $4.72 (2-4)　597
1 Frogs
ISBN 0-07-057422-7
The book contains information on how to go frog hunting, how to capture frogs and bring them home without hurting them, and how to keep them well-fed and happy in a home-made aquarium. It also describes the development of the frog and offers instructions for unharmful experiments

"A good introduction to the topic. . . . The information given is useful, the illustrations adequate; the writing is marred by an occasional excursion into exclamation points and by some patronizing questions. . . . A final page, headed 'A Note on the Names of Frogs' gives the common and scientific names for the leopard frog described in the text, and for three others." Chicago. Children's Bk Center

Waters, John F.

Hungry sharks; illus. by Ann Dalton. Crowell 1973 33p illus (Let's-read-and-find-out science bks) $4.50, lib. bdg. $5.25 (1-3)
597

1 Sharks
ISBN 0-690-00127-4; 0-690-00144-4
"A brief examination of the various senses a shark uses to locate food. The shark's sense of smell as a principle means is accompanied by a short profile of the anatomy of a shark's nose. The shark's ability to feel the water movements created by live food is explained via its lateral line system. Likewise, a shark's capacity to hear the vibrations of the water movements and how it sees the food are added to the presentation. . . . As brief as the book is, it definitely conveys the importance of scientific observation and experimentation in a low-keyed way. The authenticity is effectively augmented by a graphic style which is free flowing and communicative." Sci Teacher

Wong, Herbert H.

My goldfish, by Herbert H. Wong and Matthew F. Vessel; illus. by Arvis L. Stewart. Addison-Wesley 1969 30p illus (Science ser. for the young) lib. bdg. $4.95 (k-2)
597
1 Goldfish
ISBN 0-2010-8720-0
"An Addisonian Press Bk"
"A book that describes within a fictional framework how a goldfish breathes, sleeps, and eats. A few other facts are given, and the boy, who has won his fish at a school fair, decides that he would rather have his own pretty goldfish than his uncle's impressive collection of fish. The illustrations are very attractive, the text useful both as a beginning science book and as an example of caring for pets. . . . But the text is stiff and not pleasing when read aloud." Chicago. Children's Bk Center

Zim, Herbert S.

Fishes; a guide to fresh- and salt-water species, by Herbert S. Zim and Hurst H. Shoemaker; illus. by James Gordon Irving. 278 fishes in full color. Golden Press 1957 160p illus (A Golden Nature guide) lib. bdg. $4.95, pa $1.50
597
1 Fishes
ISBN 0-307-63508-2; 0-307-24499-7
First published 1956 by Simon & Schuster
"A pocket identification guide with suggestions for collecting, classifying, and photographing fishes." Hodges. Bks for Elem Sch Libraries

The book contains "a glossary of scientific names and a list of public aquaria. The descriptions include interesting and helpful natural history notes." The AAAS Sci Bk List for Children

Books to read: p153-54

Frogs and toads; illus. by Joy Buba. Morrow 1950 unp illus map lib. bdg. $4.32 (2-5)
597
1 Frogs
ISBN 0-688-31316-7
"The many fascinating aspects of frog and toad life are presented in a lively, informative manner. Discusses their methods of defense and camouflage and their unique food-getting apparatus. The section on amphibian reproduction is thorough and well written. Common misconceptions about frogs and toads are dispelled." The AAAS Sci Bk List for Children

The "illustrations, beautifully executed, are a very helpful addition to the interesting text." N Y Times Bk Rev

Sharks; illus. by Stephen Howe. Morrow 1966 63p illus $4.75 (2-5)
597
1 Sharks
ISBN 0-688-21810-5
"A descriptive account of the evolution of sharks is followed by mention of their chief anatomical features compared with those of bony fishes. A condensed sketch of their activities and feeding habits, individual

Zim, Herbert S.—*Continued*
illustrations and descriptive notes on some of the principal species of sharks, an account of the menace of some species to human life, and other interesting information are included." Sci Bks

"The accuracy of the author's opening statement that 'Sharks are the largest . . . creatures in the sea,' can be questioned; this distinction seems to belong to whales. Nevertheless, this is an interesting, informative, well-illustrated account." Sch Library J

598.1 Reptiles

Brenner, Barbara
A snake-lover's diary; illus. with photographs. Young Scott Bks. 1970 90p illus lib. bdg. $5.50 (4-7) 598.1
1 Snakes
ISBN 0-201-09349-9

"The author, the mother of a young herpetologist, records her son's experiences as if he had described them in a journal. Mark began by discovering a garter snake one April day and decided then and there to 'start a scientific study of snakes, and keep a diary of [his] findings.' Having won over his mother, been abetted by his father, and accompanied and advised by a college-age companion in some of his collecting excursions, Mark enjoyed a spring and summer that netted a number of species. The scientific names, differences, and eating habits of snakes are carefully recorded in a text that contains a mine of fascinating facts relayed informally and with humor. . . . Excellent photographs of collecting scenes and species enliven the book. A glossary, a bibliography, and a list of herpetological organizations are appended." Horn Bk

Conant, Roger
A field guide to reptiles and amphibians of Eastern and Central North America; illus. by Isabelle Hunt Conant. 2d ed. Houghton 1975 429p illus maps (The Peterson Field guide ser) $10, pa $6.95 598.1
1 Reptiles 2 Amphibians
ISBN 0-395-19979-4; 0-395-19977-8

"Sponsored by the National Audubon Society and National Wildlife Federation." Title page

First published 1958 with title: A field guide to reptiles and amphibians of the United States and Canada east of the 100th meridian

This book begins with chapters on catching and caring for specimens and the problem of snakebite. It then describes the physical appearance, habitats, range, subspecies and other characteristics of amphibians and reptiles in North America as far west as Texas and the Dakotas in the United States and Manitoba and Keewatin in Canada. "When all species 'and' subspecies are counted, 574 different kinds of reptiles and amphibians are included, and the vast majority of these are illustrated. There are 472 reproductions of photographs in full color and 174 in black and white on 48 plates grouped at the center of the book. In addition, to show features that are useful in the identification of various species and subspecies, there are 353 line drawings, which appear on the endpapers or are scattered through the text and legend pages. There are also 311 distribution maps arranged near the back of the book." Introduction

Glossary: p351-53. References: p354-61

Darling, Lois
Turtles, by Lois and Louis Darling. Morrow 1962 64p illus lib. bdg. $4.59 (3-5) 598.1
1 Turtles
ISBN 0-688-31547-X

"Every teacher who has had a turtle in the classroom will find this the perfect answer to all those questions children ask, for it covers the history and structure of turtles, the life cycle, and the problems of their survival, and ends with an indispensable chapter on turtle keeping with complete and specific instructions which tell why turtles need to be cared for in certain ways." Chicago Sch J

The book is "compact, and lively. . . . [It] is beautiful to look at because of the variety and excellence of the illustrations. The anatomical drawings are particularly useful and interesting." Horn Bk

Fenton, Carroll Lane
Reptiles and their world, by Carroll Lane Fenton and Dorothy Constance Pallas; illus. by Carroll Lane Fenton. Day 1961 126p illus lib. bdg. $3.96 (4-7)
598.1
1 Reptiles 2 Snakes
ISBN 0-381-99816-9

This book "describes the physical characteristics, habits, behavior, habitats, range, and usefulness of reptiles—turtles and tortoises, lizards, snakes, and crocodilians." Booklist

"Good black and white illustrations and an informal style. Pronunciation of new words given." Ontario Library Rev

Freschet, Berniece
Turtle pond; illus. by Donald Carrick. Scribner 1971 unp illus lib. bdg. $6.95 (k-3) 598.1
1 Turtles
ISBN 0-684-12326-6

After two months in a dry, sandy hole near the pond, eleven turtle eggs hatch. The author tells of the dangers the eleven little turtles encounter on their short trip to the water

"A lovely picture book about pond life. . . . In an easy, natural way, the author helps readers understand the many facets of life in one small habitat, including the fact that some animals fall prey to others. . . . The realistic illustrations are beautiful in soft colors, with marvelous natural detail." Sch Library J

George, Jean Craighead
The moon of the alligators; illus. by Adrina Zanazanian. Crowell 1969 40p illus $3.95, lib. bdg. $4.70 (3-5) 598.1
1 Alligators 2 Everglades, Fla.
ISBN 0-690-55534-2; 0-690-55535-0

"The Thirteen moons"

"October is chosen as the month for a vignette of the alligators of the Florida Everglades. The general style and format is similar to others in the series—dynamic little ecological studies sufficiently narrow in scope to permit depth in detail." Sci Bks

Goode, John
Turtles, tortoises, and terrapins; illus. by Alec Bailey. Scribner [1974 c1971] 63p illus $5.95 (4-6)
598.1
1 Turtles
ISBN 0-684-13760-7

First published 1971 in Australia with title: Tortoises, terrapins and turtles

"Dealing with many species from around the world, this covers the turtle's bony structure, evolutionary history, adaptations, and reproduction. A final chapter on turtles as pets stresses large outdoor enclosures and ponds rather than small terrarium-aquarium habitats. The text is lucid and filled with interest-catching detail; pen-and-ink drawings are clear and accurate. . . . Darling's 'Turtles' [entered above] is

Goode, John—*Continued*
similar in reading level but emphasizes North American species." Sch Library J
Glossary: p59-61

Hess, Lilo
The remarkable chameleon; story and photographs by Lilo Hess. Scribner 1968 45p illus lib. bdg. $5.95 (3-5)   598.1
1 Chameleons
ISBN 0-684-12677-X
Through photographs and text the author clarifies common misconceptions about this variety of lizard and gives scientific background and instructions for those who would like to raise their own chameleons
"Expert black-and-white photography is the striking aspect of this clear study of the chameleon." Wis Library Bul

Huntington, Harriet E.
Let's look at reptiles; written and illus. with photographs by Harriet E. Huntington; drawings by J. Noël. Doubleday 1973 106p illus $5.95, lib. bdg. $6.70 (4-6)   598.1
1 Reptiles
ISBN 0-385-08273-8; 0-385-04853-X
"The author explains the reproductive cycles peculiar to lizards, crocodiles, alligators, turtles, and snakes. Descriptions of characteristics are combined with a discussion of eating, sleeping, self-preservation, and growth patterns for each reptile." Booklist
"Plentifully illustrated with marvelous photos, this is a model of clarity and organization. Even without an index, it should prove useful for elementary school reference." Sci and Children

Johnson, Fred
Turtles and tortoises. Natl. Wildlife Federation [1974] c1973 29p illus (Ranger Rick's best friends) $2.50 (1-3)   598.1
1 Turtles
ISBN 0-912186-10-0
This book contains two stories in which Ranger Rick makes a plea for wildlife conservation in addition to descriptions of different kinds of turtles and tortoises

National Geographic Society
Creepy crawly things; reptiles and amphibians. The Society 1974 32p illus (k-3)   598.1
1 Reptiles 2 Amphibians
ISBN 0-87044-157-4
Obtainable only as part of a set for $6.95 with: Cats: little tigers in your house, by Linda McCarter Bridge, class 636.8; Spiders, by Lillian Bason, class 595; and Three Little Indians, by Gene S. Stuart, class 970.1
"Books for young explorers"
Prepared by the Special Publications Division of the National Geographic Society
In text and color photographs, this book describes some aspects of anatomy, behavior, habitats and reproduction of salamanders, frogs, toads, alligators turtles, lizards and snakes
This book "speaks directly to an eager readership in giving generally superb photographic representations of a variety of reptiles and amphibians. The dramatic format, occasionally overdone with slightly askew print or photos, is clean and shows up the animal examples well. . . . A brief text contains factual items of interest." Booklist

Ricciuti, Edward R.
The American alligator; its life in the wild; illus. with photographs. Harper 1972 70p illus map $5.95, lib. bdg. $5.79 (5-7)   598.1

1 Alligators
ISBN 0-06-024995-1; 0-06-024996-X
The author "discusses the evolution of the crocodilian order, traces the effect of civilization on the alligator, and gives a vivid description of the sights and sounds of the diverse areas of the Southeast wetlands that make up the animal's range. Noting that much is unclear about the alligator's life cycle he records what is known about breeding, nesting, and feeding habits and stresses the importance of the alligator's ecological role." Booklist
"Good [black and white] photographs of alligators and swampland add to the value of an informative survey. . . . The material is well organized, the writing measured and direct. A list of books suggested for further reading and an index are appended." Chicago. Children's Bk Center

Scott, Jack Denton
Loggerhead turtle; survivor from the sea. Photographs by Ozzie Sweet. Putnam 1974 unp illus $6.95 (4-6)   598.1
1 Turtles
ISBN 0-399-20379-6
"The account focuses on the mating and egg-laying of the female [loggerhead turtle] and then shifts to describe the overwhelming dangers from predators, including man, that conservation groups such as Florida's 'Turtle Boys' are trying to offset. Stunning black-and-white photographs document each of the activities encompassed in the text, and the end result is a stately tribute to the loggerhead's 'miracle of survival.'" Booklist

Shapp, Martha
Let's find out about snakes, by Martha and Charles Shapp; pictures by René Martin. Watts, F. 1968 54p illus lib. bdg. $3.90 (1-3)   598.1
1 Snakes
ISBN 0-531-00043-5
"This title, with its simple text and informative illustrations, will be a good addition to elementary school libraries. First mentioning some general biological features of snakes: they are cold-blooded, change their skin, are covered with scales, smell with their tongues, etc., the authors go on to discuss specific snakes, both poisonous and non-poisonous. Each one, with its particular skin pattern, is depicted by the illustrator." Sch Library J

Shaw, Evelyn
Alligator; pictures by Frances Zweifel. Harper 1972 60p illus (A Science I can read bk) $2.95, lib. bdg. $3.79 (1-2)   598.1
1 Alligators
ISBN 0-06-025556-0; 0-06-025557-9
A description of "an alligator's life cycle in narrative form. The female prepares a nest, lays her eggs and covers them with mud and plants; two months later the baby alligators hatch, but—a natural and convincing moment of suspense—the mother is at that moment in hiding from hunters and cannot get back to the nest to uncover the babies. A larger alligator frightens the hunters away, and the mother is able to get back to the nest and rescue the forty babies. The book ends with the young alligators old enough to go off on their own." Chicago. Children's Bk Center
"The drawings and pictures illustrate the environment in which the alligator lives and include both predators and prey. The primary student will find this an interesting reference book on alligators as well as an exciting adventure story." Sci Bks

Simon, Hilda

Snakes; the facts and the folklore; illus. by the author. Viking 1973 128p illus lib. bdg. $6.95 (5-7)
598.1

1 Snakes
ISBN 0-670-65315-2
The author "discusses the role of snakes in Bible stories and in mythology, their evolution from lizards and the behavior patterns of a great variety of snakes. She does much to dispel the universal loathing these creatures inspire but also warns against the deadly nature of some species. A guide to the care of snakes as pets closes the book." Pub W

"Nearly 80 detailed illustrations, most in color, are an excellent addition to the interesting text." Sch Library J

Waters, John F.

Green turtle mysteries; illus. by Mamoru Funai. Crowell 1972 33p illus (Let's-read-and-find-out science bks) $4.50, lib. bdg. $5.25 (1-3)
598.1

1 Turtles
ISBN 0-690-35994-2; 0-690-35995-0
"The author of this book explains what green turtles are, where they live and mate and lay their eggs. He points out the unsolved mysteries surrounding the turtle's habits . . . and questions: How do baby turtles always find their way to the ocean on hatching even though they cannot see it? Where do they go once they reach the sea? How do they find the beach of their birth as adult females ready in their turn to lay eggs? Like many other children's books, this one ends with a strong plea for preserving this turtle which is perhaps on its way to extinction." Appraisal

"It is good to see a book which makes a point of presenting questions about nature to which scientists have not yet found solutions. . . . 'Green Turtle Mysteries' is short . . . well-illustrated, and has a brief text in large type." Sci Bks

Zim, Herbert S.

Alligators and crocodiles; illus. by James Gordon Irving. Morrow 1952 62p illus lib. bdg. $4.32 (4-6)
598.1

1 Alligators 2 Crocodiles
ISBN 0-688-31012-5
"Distinguishes alligators from crocodiles, tells where both species are found, and describes their habits and peculiarities. Illustrations add interest and information." Hodges. Bks for Elem Sch Libraries

The "author manages a surprising coverage of his subject by introducing the reader to the Central and South American caiman and the Asian gavials as well as the Floridian variety." Library J

598.2 Birds

Anderson, John M.

The changing world of birds; illus. with photographs. Holt 1973 122p illus $5.95, lib. bdg. $5.59 (6-7)
598.2

1 Birds
ISBN 0-03-011191-1; 0-03-091302-2
"A changing world book"
The author "considers bird habitats, life cycles, behavior, special adaptations, and mortality stressing throughout the disastrous effects of man-made environmental changes, pesticides, oil spills, and wholesale slaughter. In an afterword he gives tips on bird watching. . . . The book also contains a glossary, a list of books for further reading, and a bibliography." Booklist

"The author's literate style, sense of the dramatic, and obvious wide familiarity with his subject combine to make this a most suitable text or reference for sixth to tenth grade classes, or school activity groups; and all but the advanced amateur ornithologist will find here much new information and research findings. The abundant and uniformly excellent [black and white] photographs are mildly supportive of the text and, in themselves, will add greatly to the appeal of the book." Sci Bks

Audubon, John James

The birds of America; with a foreword and descriptive captions by William Vogt. Macmillan (NY) 1937 XXVI p, 435 plates $15
598.2

1 Birds—North America 2 Birds—Pictorial works
The 435 plates in this volume were originally published by Audubon, in London, during the years 1827-1838

"William Vogt has written an excellent introduction and a brief descriptive note for each plate. The names, both common and scientific, accompanying each plate, are those found in the 'Check-List' of the American ornithologists' union. Index is to common names only. Fine format." Booklist

Blough, Glenn O.

Bird watchers and bird feeders; pictures by Jeanne Bendick. McGraw 1963 48p illus lib. bdg. $4.72 (1-3)
598.2

1 Birds
ISBN 0-07-006127-0
"Lively text and colorful drawings introduce bird observation and study to young readers. Covers types of feeders, food, banding, migration, and state birds." Hodges. Bks for Elem Sch Libraries

Brady, Irene

Owlet, the great horned owl; written and illus. by Irene Brady. Houghton 1974 40p illus lib. bdg. $4.95 (2-4)
598.2

1 Owls
ISBN 0-395-18519-X
This book chronicles the life cycle of a great horned owl, from the time he is hatched until he mates and begins his own family

Brenner, Barbara

Baltimore orioles; pictures by J. Winslow Higginbottom. Harper 1974 62p illus (A Science I can read bk) $2.95, lib. bdg. $3.43 (k-2)
598.2

1 Orioles
ISBN 0-06-020664-0; 0-06-020665-9
"Describing one oriole family during the cycle of a year, the text covers courtship, mating, nest-building, hatching, the care and feeding of baby birds, and predators. The print is large, the prose rather more choppy than in many books in this series . . . but the facts are accurate and the book useful both for the information it gives and as an encouraging reading experience." Chicago. Children's Bk Center

"An attractively illustrated account . . . which should appeal to the young reader and may well stimulate more careful observation of bird behavior in general." Appraisal

Cook, Joseph J.

Wonders of the pelican world [by] Joseph J. Cook and Ralph W. Schreiber; illus. with photographs by Ralph W. Schreiber. Dodd 1974 64p illus lib. bdg. $4.50 (4-7)
598.2

1 Pelicans
ISBN 0-396-06935-5
"Dodd, Mead Wonders books"
"The authors present an excellent and concise life story primarily of the brown pelican. The book begins

Cook, Joseph J.—*Continued*

with a description of the habitat, physical characteristics, courtship behavior, breeding, nest-building, and hatching and care of the chicks. Beautiful black and white photographs show different patterns of behavior of this majestic bird. Information is presented which relates the pelican to its role in religion, myths, and legends through time. A detailed process of banding the birds for scientific study by scientists is presented. The book concludes with a note of warning for posterity. It suggests the pelicans are destined for extinction because the fish they eat are polluted with increasing concentrations of DDT." Sci Teacher

Darling, Louis

The gull's way; photographs and illus. by the author. Morrow 1965 96p illus maps $9.50, lib. bdg. $8.72 (5-7)   598.2

1 Gulls

ISBN 0-688-21366-9; 0-688-31366-3

"From his own observation of a pair of herring gulls on an island off the coast of Maine, the author describes and illustrates the life cycle and habits of the species. Superior nature writing and illustrating. Includes a reading list." Hodges. Bks for Elem Sch Libraries

"Useful for recreational as well as assigned collateral reading." Sci Bks

Dugdale, Vera

Album of North American birds; illus. by Clark Bronson. Rand McNally 1967 112p illus $4.95, lib. bdg. $4.79 (4-6)   598.2

1 Birds— North America

ISBN 0-528-82102-4; 0-528-82103-2

Companion volume to: Album of North American animals, class 591.9

"A lively, non-technical text gives the essential information about the appearance, life and habits of fifty-two well-known birds. Twenty-six of these are shown full page and full color. A wide variety of species is represented, some unusual ones such as the wild turkey and rare whistling swan, as well as more common ones. Has an excellent index for easy reference." Bruno. Bks for Sch Libraries, 1968

"There are smaller drawings in black and white, precise and delicate, of all the birds. . . . The scientific name for each bird is given." Sutherland. The Best in Children's Bks

Earle, Olive L.

Birds and their beaks; written and illus. by Olive L. Earle. Morrow 1965 64p illus $4.75 (3-6)   598.2

1 Birds

ISBN 0-688-21099-6

In this book the author "discusses forty-six birds and shows how each beak or bill is suited to the particular bird's way of life. The illustrations contribute much to the book's beauty and usefulness." Adventuring With Bks

Birds and their nests. Morrow 1952 60p illus lib. bdg. $4.32 (3-6)   598.2

1 Birds 2 Birds—Eggs and nests

ISBN 0-688-31098-2

Forty-two species of birds and the type of nests they build are presented; for each species, the author describes the nest, where it is built, the eggs, their color and size, song, and habits of the bird." Kansas Sch Naturalist

"Olive L. Earle has made ready reference easy with the index, but the pictures and presentation of the material tempt one to read the whole of this short book." Library J

Eberle, Irmengarde

Penguins live here. Doubleday 1975 36p illus $4.95, lib. bdg. $5.70 (3-5)   598.2

1 Penguins

ISBN 0-385-05437-8; 0-385-05715-6

This "description of the migration, mating, and nesting patterns of the Adelie penguin . . . includes background material about the penguin's adjustment to its environment and about man's discovery of the penguin during exploration of the antarctic continent. The continuous text focuses on the behavior of a single pair of birds." Chicago. Children's Bk Center

"Descriptions of nest building, incubation, natural enemies, and caring for the young are quietly informative; black-and-white photographs face each page of text, and the omission of an index is compensated for by the book's brevity and narrow focus." Booklist

Robins on the window sill; photographs by Myron E. Scott. Crowell 1958 42p illus $3.95 (k-2)   598.2

1 Robins

ISBN 0-690-70678-2

Unusual book showing the hatching and developing of young birds in the nest, made possible when a pair of robins decided on a photographer's window sill as a homesite." Bks for Deaf Children

"A delightful and graphic story. Large print and over thirty large photographs make a good first book on birds for reading aloud and classroom use." Chicago. Children's Bk Center

Eimerl, Sarel

Gulls. Simon & Schuster 1969 64p illus lib. bdg. $3.79 (3-5)   598.2

1 Gulls

ISBN 0-671-65079-3

The author describes the various members of the gull family, their ranges, feeding and hunting habits, migrations, breeding grounds and courtship rites. He also discusses the role instinct plays in the gull's ability to survive

"Graceful design complements the excellent photographs of lovely gulls. Text and photos are well coordinated." Sci Bks

Fisher, Harvey I.

Wonders of the world of the albatross [by] Harvey I. Fisher and Mildred L. Fisher; illus. with photographs by Harvey I. Fisher. Dodd 1974 80p illus lib. bdg. $4.50 (4-7)   598.2

1 Albatrosses

ISBN 0-396-06880-4

"Dodd, Mead Wonders books"

"This book describes the life of the Laysan Albatross, the 'gooney bird' of Midway Island in the Pacific. With black and white photographs and text appropriate for the upper elementary bird enthusiast, the authors introduce the physical characteristics of these largest of sea birds. Topographical, meteorological and other features of the islands inhabited by the albatross are discussed. An interesting part of the book deals with the bird-man encounters on these islands. The life cycle of the albatross is treated in detail. Separate chapters describe nesting, the young chicks, maturation of the fledglings, their departure for the sea, flying skills, securing nesting territory, winning a mate, and the first nesting of the young adults." Sci and Children

"The most delightful aspect of the book, making a pleasure of even the briefest perusal, is the abundant selection of black-and-white photographs. Their clarity, beauty, and even humor more than make up for their lack of color." Appraisal

Freschet, Berniece

The owl and the prairie dog; pictures by Gilbert Riswold. Scribner 1969 unp illus $3.95 (k-4)   598.2

1 Owls 2 Prairie dogs
ISBN 0-684-20828-8

The author "weaves information about the habits of two wild creatures who live in symbiotic harmony into an appealing picturebook nature story about a burrowing owl that builds her nest in an abondoned hole in a prairie-dog town. Illustrations in muted earth shades dramatize the actions of natural friends and enemies in a book suitable for reading aloud and for use in primary grade nature study." Booklist

Gans, Roma

Bird talk; illus. by Jo Polseno. Crowell 1971 33p illus (Let's-read-and-find-out science bks) $4.50, lib. bdg. $5.25 (k-3)   598.2

1 Bird song
ISBN 0-690-14592-6; 0-690-14593-4

"Simply written and attractively illustrated, this gives a young reader the fact that birds make different sounds for different purposes, and it explains what some of those purposes are: mating calls, warning sounds, declarations of territorial rights [and] reactions to a specific predator, et cetera." Chicago. Children's Bk Center

Birds at night; illus. by Aliki. Crowell 1968 33p illus (Let's-read-and-find-out science bks) $4.50, lib. bdg. $5.25 (k-2)   598.2

1 Birds
ISBN 0-690-14443-1; 0-690-14444-X

"This is successful treatment for young listeners and readers of a fascinating subject: how nature has provided for a bird's health and protection. The muted wash illustrations are beautifully matched with large clear type. The interesting text explains and illustrates with simple tables and labelled diagrams such things as why a bird has three eyelids, how a feather is constructed, and the comparative body temperatures of birds and humans." Library J

Birds eat and eat and eat; illus. by Ed Emberley. Crowell 1963 unp illus (Let's-read-and-find-out science bks) $4.50, lib. bdg. $5.25, pa $1.25 (k-2)   598.2

1 Birds
ISBN 0-690-14514-4; 0-690-14515-2; 0-690-00633-0

"With a small amount of easy-to-read text set into full-page decorative sketches, some of the pages in green and blue, a great deal of basic information about birds is given—what they eat and how they eat. The young reader is encouraged to make simple home feeders, too, and to observe for himself." Christian Sci Monitor

Hummingbirds in the garden; illus. by Grambs Miller. Crowell 1969 33p illus maps (Let's-read-and-find-out science bks) $4.50, lib. bdg. $5.25 (1-3)   598.2

1 Hummingbirds
ISBN 0-690-42561-9; 0-690-42562-7

"The ruby-throated hummingbird is the species described in this book, which differentiates between the plumage of males and females, and reviews briefly their morphology, natural history, and flight mechanics. Suggestions are offered as to how hummingbirds may be attracted to a garden and taught to feed on artificial nectar. Their seasonal migration is described." Sci Bks

It's nesting time; illus. by Kazue Mizumura. Crowell 1964 unp illus (Let's-read-and-find-out science bks) $4.50, lib. bdg. $5.25, pa $1.25 (k-2)   598.2

1 Birds—Eggs and nests
ISBN 0-690-45543-7; 0-690-45549-6; 0-690-45544-5

"A lot about nests. . . . The author writes mainly of the materials various birds use in their nests and says very little about egglaying and care of the young." N Y Times Bk Rev

"A very simply written introduction. . . . Some of the illustrations are in black and white, but many are in color and can be used as a help in identification. The book should be an incitement to bird-watching, and it should be useful in a curricular unit on nature study." Chicago. Children's Bk Center

George, Jean Craighead

The moon of the owls; illus. by Jean Zallinger. Crowell 1967 40p illus $3.95, lib. bdg. $4.70 (3-5)   598.2

1 Owls
ISBN 0-690-55561-X; 0-690-55562-8

"The Thirteen moons"

"During the bright January moonlight, the owl awakens and seeks first for food and then for his mate. What he sees and hears is described." Appraisal

Young readers will "get a sense of the beauty of a January night in the mountains, and the illustrations . . . beautifully complement the text." Bk World

The moon of the winter bird; illus. by Kazue Mizumura. Crowell [1970 c1969] 38p illus $3.95, lib. bdg. $4.70 (3-5)   598.2

1 Birds
ISBN 0-690-55570-9; 0-690-55571-7

"The Thirteen moons"

"The twelfth moon is December and the 'winter bird' is a song sparrow that did not leave his summer breeding grounds in Ohio. His 'inner signal' did not function. The sparrow must endure hardships of a season from which he is normally absent. Problems of food and shelter are not as severe as one might believe. There is an abundance of weed seeds and the bird's feathers are insulation against the cold. Encounters include birds such as the junco and woodpecker, and mammals such as the rabbit, squirrel, and a threatening cat. There is no anthropomorphism here. The lyric text weaves a delightful and accurate account of a bird that did not go south." Sci Bks

George, John L.

Bubo, the great horned owl, by John L. George and Jean George; illus. by Jean George. Dutton 1954 184p illus (American woodland tales) $4.95 (4-6)   598.2

1 Owls
ISBN 0-525-27308-5

"Through the exciting narrative account of the bird community in which Bubo and his mate lived, hunted, and struggled to reproduce their kind, the reader gains a knowledge and appreciation of common American birds and other small forest creatures." Booklist

"The Georges have a great talent for writing authentically of animals and birds, without humanizing them, but in such fascinating detail that each character is an individual, and the plot as dramatic as any adventure story's." Horn Bk

"The nature background is well done and the pictures strikingly beautiful." N Y Her Trib Bks

Hogner, Dorothy Childs

Birds of prey; illus. by Nils Hogner. Crowell 1969 132p illus $4.50 (4-6)   598.2

1 Birds of prey
ISBN 0-690-14585-3

The author describes nearly fifty birds of prey, telling where they live and nest, what they eat, how they may be identified, and in what parts of the United States they are found. She also discusses the

Hogner, Dorothy Childs—*Continued*
conservation methods being used to save some of them from complete extinction
"Easily read text, carefully drawn, accurate illustrations, and an open-looking format." Booklist

Hudson, Robert G.
Nature's nursery: baby birds. Day 1971 158p illus lib. bdg. $4.47 (4-7)   598.2
1 Birds
ISBN 0-381-99778-2
The author "explains bird characteristics, groups, and names, gives specific details about the young of 14 different species, and describes types of bird nests, eggs, and such facets of growth as imprinting and feeding. A glossary and reading list are appended and the book is illustrated with numerous excellent photographs. Primary-grade teachers will find this a useful source of information on animal family life and protective care." Booklist

Hurd, Edith Thacher
The mother owl; illus. by Clement Hurd. Little 1974 32p illus lib. bdg. $4.95 (k-3)   598.2
1 Owls
ISBN 0-316-38325-2
This nature book presents the yearly cycle of some screech owls from the birth and care of the four young ones, their break with the family to find new nesting grounds, and the mating once again of the parents. The hunt for food and continual watching for natural predators are also described
"Accompanied by blue-and-brown block prints that capture the quiet mood of the nighttime life of these creatures. The book . . . offers substantial yet not overwhelming information." Sch Library J

Sandpipers; illus. by Lucienne Bloch. Crowell 1961 unp illus (Let's-read-and-find-out science bks) $4.50, lib. bdg. $5.25 (k-2)   598.2
1 Sandpipers
ISBN 0-690-71885-3; 0-690-71886-1
This book describes the sandpipers as they spend the summer on a northern beach and then fly south for the winter. It also tells how when they return to the north a pair of sandpipers build a nest, how their babies are hatched from the mothers's eggs and how they grow during their first summer
"Of particular note are the illustrations, some of the freshest and loveliest of the year, which not only are accurate but also convey a sense of the wonder of nature and the beauty of sea and shore." Booklist

Kaufmann, John
Birds in flight; written and illus. by John Kaufmann. Morrow 1970 96p illus $4.75, lib. bdg. $4.32 (5-7)   598.2
1 Birds 2 Flight
ISBN 0-688-21100-3; 0-688-31100-8
"Text, drawings, and diagrams comprise a fascinating as well as thorough study of bird flight. Kaufmann describes in detail the anatomy of birds and the structure and function of bird wings and feathers. He then discusses them in relation to the principles of aerodynamics, the four major methods of bird flight—gliding, soaring, flapping, and hovering—and basic bird flight maneuvers." Booklist
"This book is good fare for all birdwatchers. . . . It offers some aid in identifying birds in flight." Sci Bks
Bibliography: p92-93

Chimney swift; written and illus. by John Kaufmann. Morrow 1971 63p illus maps $4.75, lib. bdg. $4.32 (3-5)   598.2
1 Chimney swifts
ISBN 0-688-21165-8; 0-688-31165-2

The author "first explains the anatomical features that make the chimney swift, along with the hummingbird, unique and then discusses the flight, mating, nesting, feeding, roosting, and migrational habits of the chimney swift, reporting specifically on scientific studies and knowledge gained by banding the birds. Illustrated with maps, diagrams, and excellent drawings on almost every page." Booklist
"For so small a book there is a great deal of useful and up-to-date information on chimney swifts with occasional allusions to other species. Although quite elementary it is even intelligible to advanced grade school children, and adults could profit from reading it, because there are so many interesting and sometimes not widely known facts about these fascinating birds." Sci Bks

Robins fly north, robins fly south; written and illus. by John Kaufmann. Crowell 1970 unp illus map $3.75 (3-5)   598.2
1 Robins 2 Birds—Migration
ISBN 0-690-70642-1
"Sharp, clear, delicately detailed pictures of robins fill these pages with movement. The text focuses on the thesis that the movements of robins are guided by the sun's position at different times of the day. Migration, while discussed in detail, is treated as part of the robin's life-cycle and its relationship to the environment, all in the simplest of terms and straightforward style." Sat Rev

Kieran, John
An introduction to birds; illus. by Don Eckelberry. Doubleday 1965 77p illus $5.95   598.2
1 Birds—North America
ISBN 0-385-03667-1
First published 1950
A guide "in learning to know the more common birds of our lawns, our fields, our woods, our waterways and our ocean shores." Introduction
Each article gives characteristics and habits of the bird, when and where it is most likely to be seen, and size
"An informal guide to the more common birds, filled with entertaining anecdotes and illustrated with more than 100 full-color pictures." Hodges. Bks for Elem Sch Libraries

Lavine, Sigmund A.
Wonders of the eagle world; illus. with photographs. Dodd 1974 64p illus lib. bdg. $4.50 (4-7)   598.2
1 Eagles
ISBN 0-396-06911-8
"Dodd, Mead Wonders books"
This book relates myths concerning eagles and man's relationship to the birds. It also describes physical characteristics and habits, including hunting methods, migration, courtship, and the raising of young

Wonders of the hawk world; illus. with photographs and diagrams. Dodd 1972 64p illus lib. bdg. $4.50 (4-7)   598.2
1 Hawks
ISBN 0-396-06509-0
"Dodd, Mead Wonders books"
This is an "interesting overview of the lore and legend of the hawk throughout history and description of the bird's physical appearance and behavior patterns with emphasis on those species known to ornithologists as accipiters, buteos, and falcons. A few drawings and many clear photographs, a number of them striking close-ups, enhance the text." Booklist

Lavine, Sigmund A.—*Continued*
Wonders of the owl world; illus. with photographs. Dodd 1971 64p illus lib. bdg. $4.50 (4-7)   598.2

1 Owls
ISBN 0-396-06321-7
"Dodd, Mead Wonders books"
"Many photographs and drawings enhance the interest of a book which rounds up fascinating bits of information on beliefs and superstitions about the owl through the ages, discusses the owl in literature and art, and describes its physical characteristics and habits. The account . . . singles out several species— the snowy, burrowing, barn, and great horned owl— for special mention and touches on the owl's chances for survival." Booklist

Laycock, George
The pelicans. Natural Hist. Press 1970 58p illus $3.95, lib. bdg. $4.70 (3-6)   598.2

1 Pelicans
ISBN 0-385-07954-0; 0-385-02442-8
"Published for the American Museum of Natural History"
The author "covers the pelican's appearance, nests, diet, etc.; discusses attempts to study the bird; and relates anecdotes about people's experiences with particular pelicans. More than 20 full-page, black- and-white photographs are used to stimulate reader interest and understanding." Sch Library J
"The action photographs which the author has col- lected are some of the most remarkable ones that have ever been published." Sci Bks

McClung, Robert M.
Redbird; the story of a cardinal; written and illus. by Robert M. McClung. Morrow 1968 47p illus lib. bdg. $4.59 (2-4)   598.2

1 Cardinals (Birds)
ISBN 0-688-31545-3
"The story of this cardinal follows him from his solitary spring visits to the bird feeder, through court- ship, nest building, egg laying, hatching, teaching the nestlings to fly, their first moult, the first snow, and back to the feeder where the male redbird is once again eating alone." The AAAS Sci Bk List for Children

McCoy, J. J.
House sparrows; ragamuffins of the city; drawings by Jean Zallinger. Seabury 1968 126p illus $5.95 (3-6)   598.2

1 Sparrows
ISBN 0-8164-3025-X
"Bird study may seem a limited activity for city children, but this useful, well-illustrated book shows how even the familiar, aggressive little sparrow can prove a rewarding subject. Besides information on the sparrow's life cycle, the author records his appearance in song and story from the Bible to the present. Of special value is a section on sparrow-inspired projects including photography, sketching, and recording bird calls." Moorachian. What is a City?
Suggested reading: p119. Glossary: p121-23

May, Julian
Wild turkeys; pictures by John Hamberger. Holi- day House 1973 unp illus map lib. bdg. $4.95 (1-4)   598.2

1 Turkeys
ISBN 0-8234-0217-7
This is a survey of the wild turkey's habits, behavior, and survival against weather, disease, and predators. Domestic turkeys are briefly described also

Mizumura, Kazue
The emperor penguins. Crowell 1969 35p illus (Let's-read-and-find-out science bks) $4.50, lib. bdg. $5.25 (k-3)   598.2

1 Penguins
ISBN 0-690-26087-3; 0-690-26088-1
This book "describes the habits and habitat of the Emperor Penguins, with particular attention to their unusual methods of feeding and caring for their young." Chicago. Children's Bk Center
"Pre-school children and beginning readers will especially enjoy this book. After finishing the text, the reader, be he adult or child, will know about as much of the life cycle and ecology of the Emperor Penguin as a regular reader of 'Scientific American.'" Appraisal

National Geographic Society
Song and garden birds of North America, by Al- exander Wetmore and other eminent ornithologists; foreword by Melville Bell Grosvenor. 327 species portrayed in color and fully described. The Society 1964 400p illus (Natural science lib) $11.95   598.2

1 Birds—North America 2 Birds—Pictorial works
The major portion of the book consists of sections on the different "species—nearly all that breed north of Mexico. . . . [There are] 555 illustrations that show each bird to best advantage for identification. Where the female's plumage differs significantly from the male's both sexes are portrayed." Preface
"There are also some general articles on families, and on subjects such as 'Courtship and Nesting Behavior.' A pocket inside the back cover contains a small album of 6 vinyl records presenting songs for 70 species." Library J
Map on lining-paper

Peterson, Roger Tory
A field guide to the birds; giving field marks of all species found east of the Rockies; text and illus. by Roger Tory Peterson. 2d rev. and enl. ed. Sponsored by National Audubon Society. Houghton 1947 xxiv, 290p illus map $6.95, pa $4.95   598.2

1 Birds—North America
ISBN 0-395-08082-7; 0-395-08083-5
"The Peterson field guide series"
First published 1934
"An original, authoritative and useful guide . . . designed to help in identifying live birds at a distance. . . . The text gives field marks, such as range, habits, manner of flight, etc., that can not be pictured. In addition it mentions birds that might in any instance be confused with a given species." N Y Libraries
There are 60 plates in color and black and white and many line drawings. Includes a bibliography

A field guide to Western birds; field marks of all species found in North America west of the 100th meridian, with a section on the birds of the Hawaiian Islands. Text and illus. by Roger Tory Peterson. 2d ed. rev. and enl. Sponsored by the National Audubon Society and National Wildlife Federation. Houghton 1961 xxvi, 366p illus map $6.95, pa $4.95   598.2

1 Birds—The West
ISBN 0-395-08085-1; 0-395-13692-X
"The Peterson Field guide series"
Companion volume to: A field guide to the birds
First published 1941
"This compact, but complete little work employs . . . [a] system of field identification based upon the characteristic features of the birds and facilitating quick recognition at a distance." Springf'd Republican

Peterson, Roger Tory—*Continued*

How to know the birds; an introduction to bird recognition. 2d ed. newly enl. and with 72 new full-color illus. by the author and more than 400 line drawings. Endorsed by the National Audubon Society. Houghton 1962 [c1957] 168p illus $5.95   598.2

1 Birds

ISBN 0-395-08090-8

First published 1949

"A useful handbook on bird identification by silhouette without the use of field glasses, divided into five sections: general characteristics and terminology; drawings by family; habitats; silhouettes of common species; and index." Hodges. Bks for Elem Sch Libraries

Rau, Margaret

The penguin book; illus. by John Hamberger. Hawthorn Bks. 1968 79p illus $3.95 (4-6)   598.2

1 Penguins

ISBN 0-8015-5820-4

"Illustrated with realistic black-and-white drawings and well indexed, this serviceable factual account describes the appearance and habits of about a dozen different species of penguins. . . . An introductory chapter sketches the history of penguins and an epilog mentions past expeditions to obtain specimens and studies currently [1968] being conducted." Booklist

Ripper, Charles L.

Diving birds; written and illus. by Charles L. Ripper. Morrow 1967 63p illus $4.95, lib. bdg. $4.59 (3-6)   598.2

1 Water birds

ISBN 0-688-21241-7; 0-688-31241-1

The author deals here with "four genera of diving birds: the loons, grebes, cormorants, and anhingas. Clearly written and well-organized, the book discusses some general characteristics, then describes in detail several species of each group which make their home in the northern hemisphere." Sch Library J

"Young birdwatchers . . . should find [this] an appealing and informative book. . . . Each page bears one of the author's excellent drawings showing a bird in typical pose." Christian Sci Monitor

Selsam, Millicent E.

A first look at birds, by Millicent E. Selsam and Joyce Hunt; illus. by Harriett Springer. Walker & Co. [1974 c1973] 35p illus $4.95, lib. bdg. $4.85 (1-3)   598.2

1 Birds

ISBN 0-8027-6163-1; 0-8027-6164-X

This book "invites the young child to use his powers of observation and learn to identify birds. Simple questions and matching games encourage the child to notice color, size, shape, feet, and feathers—important factors in bird identification. The illustrations are large, clear and well-labeled. Red and blue are used in the section on colors, but all other illustrations are black and white." Appraisal

"The value of the book lies in its single, uncomplicated purpose and in the simplicity of its approach to the study of birds. A good companion to more colorful, encyclopedic volumes." Booklist

Tony's birds; illus. by Kurt Werth. Harper 1961 64p illus (A Science I can read bk) lib. bdg. $3.79 (k-2)   598.2

1 Birds

ISBN 0-06-025421-1

"Birdwatching is the subject. With the help of his father, Tony learns to use binoculars and a bird guidebook to find and identify birds. Two- and three-color pictures and clear print make an attractive easy-to-read book which makes bird-watching an interesting activity." Horn Bk

Stoutenburg, Adrien

A vanishing thunder; extinct and threatened American birds; illus. by John Schoenherr. Natural Hist. Press 1967 124p illus $3.95, lib. bdg. $4.70 (5-7)   598.2

1 Rare birds 2 Birds, Extinct 3 Birds—Protection

ISBN 0-385-06187-0; 0-385-06953-7

"Published for The American Museum of Natural History"

This "account deals only with extinct and threatened birds native to North America. Based on records and eyewitness reports of explorers and naturalists the book describes the habits of the extinct passenger pigeon, ivorybilled woodpecker, and great auk and the nearly extinct California condor, American egret, and whooping crane and dramatically recounts the story of their extermination or struggle for survival." Booklist

"The book, beautifully written and highly readable, is truly a poetic inscription on the gravestones of a number of bird species. A sense of tragedy permeates the pages as the birds' lives are recounted; their habits, migrations, and interactions with, and destruction by, man, the predator." Natur Hist

Includes bibliography

Thompson, David H.

The penguin: its life cycle. Sterling 1974 64p illus (Colorful nature ser) $5.95, lib. bdg. $5.69 (4-7)   598.2

1 Penguins

ISBN 0-8069-3474-3; 0-8069-3475-1

This book about the Adélie penguin describes its "habitat, breeding habits, courting ritual, plumage, adaption to life in water and on land. The author conducted several experiments to discover how parents and chicks recognized one another after long periods of separation while the parent was at sea. These are detailed for the reader." Sci Bks

The book "is appealing on two levels. First, for young people who might have trouble with the somewhat imposing conceptual and verbal levels of presentation, there is a clear color photograph of some aspect of penguin life on almost every page. Second, for those really interested in penguins, the text presents a generally clear, brief, and obviously knowledgeable description of the yearly cycle of the Adelie penguin." Sci and Children

Turner, Ann Warren

Vultures; illus. by Marian Gray Warren. McKay 1973 96p illus $7.95 (5-7)   598.2

1 Vultures

ISBN 0-679-20231-5

An "informative and fascinating survey of the huge and hideous tribe of feathered scavengers which includes condors and the European griffon as well as vultures. Six American and 12 European vulture variations are differentiated and two or three big, powerful drawings accompany each section of text, to give a wonderful feeling of ponderous flight." Pub W

For further reading: p43

Turner, John F.

The magnificent bald eagle; America's national bird; photographs by the author. Random House 1971 81p illus $3.50, lib. bdg. $4.39 (4-6)   598.2

1 Bald eagle

ISBN 0-394-82061-4; 0-394-92061-9

"This life cycle account of a bald eagle, Tally, covers conservation, the historical role of the American eagle, the mating of the parent eagles, the brooding

Turner, John F.—*Continued*
and hatching of the egg, and the growth and development of the young bird." Sch Library J
"The book is accurate yet simple; language is straightforward and the numerous wildlife photos (by the author) are a most significant feature and asset. . . . The only debit of consequence to this reviewer arises from the publisher's choice of layout. The text is arranged in a continuous flow of short paragraphs appearing much as verses of a narrative poem. The irony is that the book in many ways is a narrative poem, but the textual layout is . . . distracting." Sci Bks

Vevers, Gwynne
Birds and their nests; illus. by Colin Threadgall. McGraw [1973 c1971] 32p illus (A McGraw-Hill Natural science picture bk) $4.72 (1-4)   598.2
1 Birds—Eggs and nests
ISBN 0-07-067414-0
First published 1971 in England
"Here are descriptions and illustrations of a variety of nests: open, stick, weaver-bird, hang-nests, nests of mud and saliva, nests on and in the ground, on water, in tree trunks, in other birds nests, in bowers, in mounds and even penguins' portable ones. One or two examples of birds or families of birds which construct nests of each type are given along with a bit of natural history and geography. On the last page the author discusses conservation. She suggests that one observe and possibly photograph nests but warns against disturbing the nest or the young. The illustrations, colored and black-and-white, all are attractive and realistic." Sci Bks

Voight, Virginia Frances
Brave little hummingbird; illus. by Lydia Rosier. Putnam 1971 63p illus lib. bdg. $3.49 (2-4)   598.2
1 Hummingbirds
ISBN 0-399-60074-4
This "is essentially the flight saga of the rubythroat hummingbird from its home in the Central American jungle to New England. During this spring journey the life cycle of the female is described simply and accurately with all of the awe and excitement of an adventure tale. . . . The book concludes with the flight of the birds' offspring. It provides a story of high interest in the general field of nature appreciation." Sci Bks

Zim, Herbert S.
Birds; a guide to the most familiar American birds, by Herbert S. Zim and Ira N. Gabrielson; illus. by James Gordon Irving. 125 birds in full color. Sponsored by The Wildlife Management Institute. [Rev. ed] Golden Press 1956 60p illus maps (A Golden Nature guide) lib. bdg. $4.95, pa $1.50   598.2
1 Birds
ISBN 0-307-63505-8; 0-307-24490-3
First published 1949 by Simon & Schuster
This book "pictures 129 well-known American birds in full color, with descriptions in the text of additional species, enabling the reader to identify 250 birds. Includes a table of data on migration, eggs, kinds and locations of nests, and natural food for each illustrated bird." The AAAS Sci Bk List for Children

599 Mammals

Adamson, Joy
Elsa. . . . Pantheon Bks. 1961 unp illus $3.50, lib. bdg. $4.99 (2-5)   599
1 Lions
ISBN 0-394-81117-8; 0-391-91117-2
"The true story of a lioness who was brought up from cubhood by Joy Adamson and her husband, a senior game warden; they taught her to stalk and kill for herself so that she could be set free into the African jungle." Title page
"The same story as 'Born Free', simplified for young readers. Illustrated with full-page photographs." The AAAS Sci Bk List for Children

Pippa; the cheetah and her cubs. Harcourt 1970 unp illus $6.95 (1-4)   599
1 Cheetahs
ISBN 0-15-262125-3
"The author adopts a young Cheetah and soon allows it to roam freely between her home and a wild game reserve in East Africa. By the end of the story, the beautiful cat has matured, has mated somewhere in the wild, has given birth in the bush to three litters, and has allowed the author to visit the birth-lairs. The story is told by 65 photos (2 in color) and a brief text. . . . The central message is good: that sensitive humans can occasionally peer into the strange world of nonhuman animals. In the classroom, the book could support discussions of Africa, conservation, hazards of adopting orphan animals, humaneness, mammalian reproduction, and the realities of injury and death." Sci Bks

Alston, Eugenia
Growing up chimpanzee; illus. by Haru Wells. Crowell 1975 unp illus $5.50, lib. bdg. $6.25 (2-4)   599
1 Chimpanzees
ISBN 0-690-00015-4; 0-690-00564-4
"The startlingly human-like primates are presented sympathetically in this book. The black-and-white pictures by Haru Wells add zest to Ms. Alston's easily mastered and engrossing text. . . . The structure of the [chimpanzee] family and its place in society are explored. We learn how the mother cares for her young, how status is achieved in the community and other fascinating facts." Pub W

Annixter, Jane
Sea otter [by] Jane and Paul Annixter; illus. by John Hamberger. Holiday House 1972 63p illus lib. bdg. $4.50 (5-7)   599
1 Sea otters
ISBN 0-8234-0211-8
"A slightly romanticized account of the life cycle of the sea otter. . . . The southern coast of Alaska is the setting, and there is a large amount of factual information presented in an accurate and engaging manner. The authors have either visited the habitat of the sea otter or conferred with someone who has, since the description of feeding, mating, frolicking and social behavior bespeak first-hand observations. As seems to be mandatory in books of this genre, several episodes of contact with human hunters occur. These are the only sections of the book where sentimentality overcomes scientific accuracy." Sci Bks

Arundel, Jocelyn
Little Stripe; an African zebra; illus. by John Kaufmann. Hastings House 1967 58p illus (Preserve our wildlife ser) lib. bdg. $3.95 (2-4)   599
1 Zebras 2 Serengeti Plains
ISBN 0-8038-4245-7
This book is intended "to tell and illustrate the life of a zebra and the dangers he faces from the modern world as well as from his natural enemies in Africa." Pub W
A "beautifully written story. . . . A strong plea for wildlife conservation, the book ends with Little

Arundel, Jocelyn—*Continued*

Stripe, the herd leader, heading for a wildlife preserve. Dramatic black and white drawings catch the essence of Little Stripe's life. Very good format and appropriate print size." Bruno. Bks for Sch Libraries, 1968

Some of the animals, plants and places mentioned in the book: p57-58

Bergman Sucksdorff, Astrid

The roe deer; written and illus. by Astrid Bergman Sucksdorff. Harcourt [1969 c1967] unp illus $5.95 (3-6)   599

1 Deer

ISBN 0-15-268365-8

Originally published 1967 in Sweden

The author "sensitively records, in photographs and accompanying text, the life cycle of the roe deer that inhabit the woodlands of her native Sweden and other parts of Europe. The accurate, informative portrayal was achieved by tracking and observing the deer in all seasons over a period of years. Even without wished-for-color the photographs are beautiful and effective." Booklist

Buff, Mary

Dash & Dart, by Mary & Conrad Buff. Viking 1942 73p illus lib. bdg. $4.95 (k-3)   599

1 Deer

ISBN 0-670-25729-X

"The cycle of a year in the life of twin fawns is told in rhythmic prose." N Y Pub Library

"As a picture book this is very beautiful. Soft brown pictures of deer throughout the book and four double spreads in color, showing the four seasons, would in themselves make the book one to be remembered. . . . Adapted for reading aloud, perhaps at bedtime, two little twin deer are followed from their birth in the spring to their first snowstorm. The print, too, is clear and beautiful, making this an especially lovely book." Bookmark

Burkett, Molly

The year of the badger; illus. by Pamela Johnson. Lippincott 1974 128p illus $4.95 (4-6)   599

1 Badgers

ISBN 0-397-31489-2

This book "is about a British family that runs an animal rehabilitation center. Caring for sick and injured animals began as the family's hobby, but it soon grew into a full-time occupation. The main character is Nikki, a badger, who is nursed back to health, generally has the run of the house, and eventually returns to the wild." Sci and Children

Ms. Johnson's "black-and-white illustrations do better by Nikki and the other animals than with the human beings. She captures Nikki's charm and mischievousness equally well. . . . This gentle story is a plea for care of all animals and fits well with the current emphasis on ecology." Babbling Bookworm

Burt, William Henry

A field guide to the mammals; field marks of all species found north of the Mexican boundary. Text and maps by William Henry Burt. Illus. by Richard Philip Grossenheider. 2d ed. rev. and enl. Sponsored by the National Audubon Society and National Wildlife Federation. Houghton 1964 xxiii, 284p illus $7.95   599

1 Mammals

ISBN 0-395-07471-1

"The Peterson Field guide series"

First published 1952

This "handbook provides information on 378 species to be found in North America and surrounding

waters. Contains up-to-date maps showing present distribution, beautiful and detailed color plates of each animal, and many other aids to quick and accurate identification through tracks, skulls, teeth, nests, and distinguishing physical characteristics. Each description also gives the animals' habits, habitat, economic importance and similar easily-confused species." The AAAS Sci Bk List for Young Adults

"The information has been compiled with skill, care and authority; the drawings, some in black and white, many in full color . . . have the life and vitality that is inherent in the natural world." Christian Sci Monitor

References: p267-72

Conklin, Gladys

Elephants of Africa; illus. by Joseph Cellini. Holiday House 1972 unp illus lib. bdg. $5.95 (2-4)   599

1 Elephants

ISBN 0-8234-0201-0

"This book is an account of the African elephants and begins with an 'author's note' that describes in general the salient facts of the natural history and distribution of elephants and includes a plea for their conservation. The story itself concerns a herd of elephants on migration in Africa, and the main character, a new calf, is called 'Little Elephant.' The story continues as he grows into an independent young bull. This book, like others by the same author, presents life histories of single groups or species of animals in a straightforward, factual manner." Sci Bks

"The illustrations by Joseph Cellini are worth the price of the book. They are more beautiful than color photographs and portray the animals in accurate, lifelike situations." Appraisal

Little apes; illus. by Joseph Cellini. Holiday House 1970 unp illus lib. bdg. $5.95 (k-3)   599

1 Apes 2 Monkeys

ISBN 0-8234-0070-0

"Written very simply, a description of a day in the lives of a baby gorilla, chimpanzee, gibbon, and orangutan provides children with an excellent first book on apes, and one that may make it easier for them to distinguish between apes and monkeys. The four diurnal patterns are quite similar, but the illustrations give the book variety: precisely drawn and uncluttered, they have a humorous fidelity and charm." Sat Rev

Cook, Joseph J.

Blue whale; vanishing leviathan, by Joseph J. Cook and William L. Wisner; illus. with drawings by Jan Cook, photographs, and old prints. Dodd 1973 80p illus lib. bdg. $4.95 (4-7)   599

1 Whales 2 Rare animals

ISBN 0-396-06739-5

"This is an interesting account of the blue whale. Discussed are the evolution, food, anatomy, behavior, and conservation of the earth's largest mammal. The selection of photographs is excellent. . . . This is a timely consideration of a species threatened with extinction." Sch Library J

Cooke, Ann

Giraffes at home; illus. by Robert Quackenbush. Crowell 1972 31p illus (Let's-read-and-find-out science bks) $4.50, lib. bdg. $5.25 (1-3)   599

1 Giraffes

ISBN 0-690-33082-0; 0-690-33083-9

The author deals "with the appearance, behavior, and habitat of giraffes in an easy-to-read account illustrated with black-and-white or colored drawings on every page. Included are simple diagrams of the bone structure of a giraffe's neck and of the position of an unborn giraffe within the mother." Booklist

The book is "appropriate for reading aloud and is

Cooke, Ann—*Continued*

sufficiently interesting and attractive to hold the younger child's attention." Sci Bks

Darling, Louis

Kangaroos and other animals with pockets; written and illus. by Louis Darling. Morrow 1958 64p illus maps lib. bdg. $4.59 (4-6)   599

1 Kangaroos 2 Marsupials

ISBN 0-688-31501-1

"A compact and informative book about marsupial mammals of the world; their evolution from a common ancestor and their isolation on the Australian continent is explained. An unusual feature in this book is the use of paired drawings of marsupial animals and their comparable forms among the pouchless mammals. The distinguishing features and habits of the red kangaroo are described in detail as an example of the marsupial's life." Chicago. Children's Bk Center

"Although easy enough for the beginning reader, it should have appeal for any child interested in these fascinating animals." Library J

Dixon, Paige

Silver Wolf; illus. by Ann Brewster. Atheneum Pubs. 1973 108p illus $4.50 (4-7)   599

1 Wolves

ISBN 0-689-30083-2

"The author gives a most vivid picture of the life of a wolf and his pack. He follows this young wolf through the seasons of one year in the wilderness. Silver Wolf is very young when the book opens and the winter is almost over. The social structure of the pack, the hierarchy, the organization for survival, all are vividly described, as are the search for food, the meeting with enemies, such as man the trapper, man the observer, man the conservator and man the game hunter. . . . There are those who will decide that such a book belongs with fiction and others who feel that such detailed observation and knowledge of wolves warrants placing this tale among books of nature nonfiction. In any case, it is exciting reading." Appraisal

Suggestions for further reading: p107-08

The young grizzly; illus. by Grambs Miller. Atheneum Pubs. 1974 106p illus lib. bdg. $5.50 (4-7)   599

1 Bears

ISBN 0-689-30137-5

This story of two grizzly bear cubs and their mother "is a factual account, beginning before the birth of the cubs, following them both for a while, and then the young male to early adulthood. Data are recorded concerning daily happenings: food, wanderings, quarrels, play, how the mother trains and disciplines her young, and the occasional encounters with their only enemy, man. Actually, the bears are described more realistically than the bear-hating hunter and his nature-loving son; they seem somewhat contrived. There are delightful descriptions of the young cubs playing with their mother and with each other. . . . The dozen or so black-and-white sketches by Grambs Miller add to the interest of the book." Sci Bks

Bibliography: p105-06

Earle, Olive L.

Paws, hoofs, and flippers; illus. by the author. Morrow 1954 192p illus lib. bdg. $4.81 (5-7)   599

1 Mammals 2 Animals—Habits and behavior

ISBN 0-688-31503-8

The book describes the habits, characteristics, and habitats of several different orders of mammals, grouped according to types of feet: claws, hoofs, hoofs and claws, flippers, and nails

"An easily read, informative book . . . illustrated

with many drawings, most of which are excellent." Booklist

Eberle, Irmengarde

Bears live here. Doubleday 1966 61p illus lib. bdg. $4.95 (k-3)   599

1 Bears

ISBN 0-385-06116-1

The author "describes one year in the life of a black bear family in readable text and shows their activities in full-page color photographs. Useful as a read-aloud story or for animal study in primary grades." Hodges. Bks for Elem Sch Libraries

Beavers live here. Doubleday 1972 58p illus $4.50, lib. bdg. $5.25 (1-3)   599

1 Beavers

ISBN 0-385-03945-X; 0-385-05931-0

Here "is an excellent factual account of the life of the beaver; it begins with a young pair setting out to build their first home and dam in a new area and follows through the succeeding generations of young. It is a warm, accurate natural history book for children. The dangers that beavers encounter from other animals, man and the elements are dealt with factually. The illustrations, which have been collected from wildlife photographers, are delightful and are well-chosen to follow the text. These are interspersed liberally to hold the interest of the younger child." Sci Bks

A chipmunk lives here; with drawings by Matthew Kalmenoff. Doubleday 1966 60p illus lib. bdg. $4.95 (k-3)   599

1 Chipmunks

ISBN 0-385-05685-0

"The author tells the dramatic story of a chipmunk's life. In addition to excellent color photographs, there are cutaway drawings showing the chipmunk's burrow." Hodges. Bks for Elem Sch Libraries

"This excellent account of the life cycle of the chipmunk is biologically accurate. It can be read to small children and will serve as solid reading material for older ones." Sci Bks

Elephants live here. Doubleday 1970 59p illus $4.50, lib. bdg. $5.25 (1-3)   599

1 Elephants

ISBN 0-385-02536-X; 0-385-04068-7

"So vivid and revealing is the narrative that the reader has a sense of actually seeing for himself the African elephant who drew apart from the traveling and feeding herd to give birth to her first calf, and how it grew and developed over a period of years until it became an adult. The story describes the migration of elephants to find grazing and water as the seasons change, their resting by day and travel and feeding by night, and encounters with their enemies—including man with his guns and traps. Full page action photographs of elephants, and of other mammals enhance the story. Although the level is for students in the middle grades, the narrative will interest younger children who view and discuss the photographs with the reader." Sci Bks

Fawn in the woods; photographs by Lilo Hess. Crowell 1962 42p illus $3.95, lib. bdg. $4.70 (k-3)   599

1 Deer

ISBN 0-690-29284-8; 0-690-29285-6

"Charming photographs show a fawn from birth through her first year; most of the text describes the ways in which the mother doe teaches and protects the fawn. The text is written in a simple and straightforward style; print is large, photographs clear." Chicago. Children's Bk Center

Eberle, Irmengarde—*Continued*

Koalas live here. Doubleday 1967 59p illus lib. bdg. $4.50, pa 95¢ (1-3)   599

1 Koalas

ISBN 0-385-08719-5; 0-385-06963-4

"Appealing full-page photographs and succinct text describe the characteristics and natural life of the koala and the ways in which man contributes to the protection and survival of these Australian animals in their native habitat." Booklist

Moose live here. Doubleday 1971 59p illus $4.95, lib. bdg. $5.70 (1-3)   599

1 Moose

ISBN 0-385-01293-4; 0-385-05665-6

This book about a year in the life of a bull moose and her calf "pictures the birth of a calf on an island and his early training to feed and avoid dangerous enemies by his mother. The illustrations are excellent and will appeal to any nature lover. They are unusual and depict different animals in poses that illustrate behavior at particular and important moments in their life; such as listening for danger, feeding, etc. The text is an excellent story of the growth of a young calf toward independence. It is a book that will appeal to young and old naturalists." Appraisal

Prairie dogs in prairie dog town; illus. by John Hamberger. Crowell 1974 53p illus $4.50, lib. bdg. $5.25 (3-5)   599

1 Prairie dogs

ISBN 0-690-00534-2; 0-690-00069-3

"Set in one of the nation's state parks, this satisfactory nature study examines the life of a family of prairie dogs: how they communicate through barks and chatterings, their response to such intruders as owls and snakes, and their cooperative relationships." Sch Library J

"This easily readable book has lavish illustrations on nearly every page which will help to hold the interest of young readers or even younger listeners. The book is informative, interesting and recommended." Sci Bks

Eimerl, Sarel

Baboons; illus. with photographs. Simon & Schuster 1968 64p illus $3.95 (3-5)   599

1 Baboons

ISBN 0-671-65030-0

The author "presents some interesting life history and ecological facts concerning baboons, accompanied by remarkable photographic black-and-white illustrations. Although factually accurate the style is . . . tedious, [and] choppy." Sci Bks

Fenner, Carol

Gorilla gorilla; illus. by Symeon Shimin. Random House 1973 unp illus $4.95, lib. bdg. $5.99 (1-4)   599

1 Gorillas

ISBN 0-394-82069-X; 0-394-92069-4

"This book describes the birth and early training of a young male gorilla in the eastern Congo until the hunters trap him and ship him to a large zoo. The adjustment to cage-life at the zoo completes this scientifically accurate portrayal of one gorilla's life experience." Top of the News

"The author's free-form poetic style is very effective and makes it easy to empathize with the gorilla as he struggles to adjust to his imprisonment. The sensitive illustrations by a talented artist help create this excellent book." Sci Bks

Fichter, George S.

Cats; illus. by Arthur B. Singer. Golden Press 1973 160p illus (Golden Nature guides) $1.95 (5-7)   599

1 Cats

ISBN 0-307-24356-7

The author "introduces the varied members of the cat family. There are capsule descriptions of the different breeds of cats, both wild and domestic; physiology, personality, and care of cats; and brief looks at the cat in history, literature, art and legend. The color illustrations are attractive and largely accurate. The work is well organized and indexed with a bibliography for further reading." Appraisal

Fisher, Aileen

Valley of the smallest; the life story of a shrew; illus. by Jean Zallinger. Crowell 1966 161p illus $3.95 (4-7)   599

1 Shrews

ISBN 0-690-85801-9

A "description of a tiny creature weighing no more than a penny and of the animals who live near her in the Rocky Mountains." Children's Bks, 1966

"Written in a smooth narrative style, yet never popularized or sentimental. The tiny shrew is an animal, not a winning personality; in describing her life, fraught with danger, the author gives a fine picture of the whole ecology. The illustrations, handsome and realistic in black and white, have both softness and strength. A list of suggested readings and an index are appended." Sutherland. The Best in Children's Bks

Fisher, Ronald M.

Namu; making friends with a killer whale. Natl. Geographic Soc. 1973 30p illus (k-3)   599

1 Whales

ISBN 0-87044-142-6

Obtainable only as part of a set for $6.95 with: Honeybees, by Jane Lecht, class 595.7; How animals hide, by Robert M. McClung, class 591.5; and Pandas, by Donna K. Grosvenor, class 599

"Books for young explorers"

Prepared by the Special Publications Division of the National Geographic Society

In text and color photographs, this book describes how Namu, a killer whale caught by salmon fishermen in the Pacific Ocean, was brought to the aquarium in Seattle, Washington where his new owner, Ted Griffin, made friends with him and scientists studied him to learn more about whale behavior

Fox, Michael

Sundance coyote. Illus. by Dee Gaets. Coward, McCann & Geoghegan 1974 93p illus $4.95 (5-7)   599

1 Coyotes

ISBN 0-698-20284-8

"While revealing much in general of prairie ecology and man's upsetting of the important balances of nature, [the author] dispels the notion that the coyote is an indiscriminate killer and interprets its remarkable manner of communication. Richly evoking the sounds, colors, and smells of the semi-desert land where the Indian was once master, his story highlights the fight for survival of young Sundance, strongest in a litter of five pups, during his first year. . . . Carefully detailed and sometimes lit with humor are the depictions of Sundance's encounters with wild enemies and also with a protective Indian lad who gradually makes a pet of him. At this point, the account becomes pure fiction. Numerous ink-line drawings attractively complement the text, revealing coyotes as appealing, playful animals." Horn Bk

Fox, Michael—*Continued*
The wolf; illus. by Charles Fracé. Coward, McCann & Geoghegan 1973 95p illus $5.95 (3-6)   599
1 Wolves
ISBN 0-698-20200-7
The author traces the stories of five wolves of Alaska "from the birth of a litter through the first year of their cubs' lives, giving a sequential picture of the care and training of the cubs, the ways in which the young learn to avoid danger, hunt, and acquire the approved patterns of behavior." Chicago. Children's Bk Center
"Fox emphasizes the intelligence of the animals, their affection and respect for one another, the part wolves play in the balance of nature, and the fact that men have hunted wolves from planes just for the pleasure of killing them. In a note at the end he speaks briefly on the need for protecting wolves and the deep satisfaction which people can feel when they hear or see a free wolf." Booklist

Freschet, Berniece
Bear mouse; illus. by Donald Carrick. Scribner 1973 unp illus $5.95 (2-4)   599
1 Mice
ISBN 0-684-13320-2
This is the "story of a meadow mouse that ventures forth in the winter snow to feed herself and thus sustain her nursing brood. She narrowly escapes an owl and a bobcat, and in her frantic effort to hide discovers a lifesaving cache of food." Booklist
"The story of her day with its many small crises, frustrations, and fears makes a moving narrative, vivid because of the precise details of surroundings and actions, and enriched by language both realistic and poetic. Handsome watercolors illustrate the two worlds of the mouse; the hidden world safe beneath the snow; and the cold upper world where fox, owl, hawk, and bobcat are dramatically pictured as threats to her existence." Horn Bk
"This is a quiet book, with neither plot nor anthropomorphization, but it is accurate in the information it gives about the mouse and the food-chain of which she is a part, and it also communicates a sense of affection for wild life and natural beauty." Chicago. Children's Bk Center

Skunk baby; illus. by Kazue Mizumura. Crowell 1973 41p illus $3.95, lib. bdg. $4.70 (2-4)   599
1 Skunks
ISBN 0-690-74194-4; 0-690-74193-6
"Attractively illustrated and simply written, the description of the first experiences of a baby skunk are given just enough of a narrative framework to lend impetus to the book. Smallest of his litter, Skunk Baby investigates his small world with adventurous impunity; he knows no fear but obeys the danger signals his mother gives. Skunk Baby learns what fear is when he first encounters a predatory fox. The fox is young also, and he learns from the confrontation what a powerful weapon skunks have. The text and the illustrations have a quiet fidelity to nature." Chicago. Children's Bk Center

Gardner, Richard
The baboon. Macmillan (N Y) 1972 151p illus map $5.95 (5-7)   599
1 Baboons
The author surveys the history of the baboon and "discusses the physical characteristics of various species, their habitats, social behavior, & relationship to man." Pub W
"The information is well-presented, up-to-date and reasonably complete. The appendix on baboon communication is an interesting and useful addition." Sci Bks
Bibliography: p147-48

George, Jean Craighead
The moon of the bears; illus. by Mac Shepard. Crowell 1967 38p illus $3.95, lib. bdg. $4.70 (3-5)   599
1 Bears
ISBN 0-690-55538-5; 0-690-55537-7
"The Thirteen moons"
Set in the Smoky Mountains of Tennessee, this story tells "how the female bear digs her den, awaits her cubs, and then begins another summer." Christian Sci Monitor
"The setting is graphically described in minute detail, right down to the last bluebottle fly. The birth of the two bear cubs is a skillful piece of narration. The illustrations are most appealing." Appraisal

The moon of the chickarees; illus. by John Schoenherr. Crowell 1968 40p illus $3.95, lib. bdg. $4.70 (3-5)   599
1 Squirrels
ISBN 0-690-55541-5; 0-690-55540-7
"The Thirteen moons"
The author "discusses the activities of the chickaree or red squirrel during the spring when a mother rouses her offspring to full activity." The AAAS Sci Bk List for Children
"The many animals and plants indigenous to the surroundings described [along The Bitterroot River in Montana] are brought into [the story]. . . . The black-and-white illustrations complement the text beautifully and, sometimes, dramatically." Library J

The moon of the fox pups; illus. by Kiyoaki Komoda. Crowell 1968 39p illus $3.95, lib. bdg. $4.70 (3-5)   599
1 Foxes
ISBN 0-690-55547-4; 0-690-55546-6
"The Thirteen moons"
Five fox puppies who live in the Cumberland Valley of Pennsylvania learn from their parents the lessons of survival in the wilderness
"Mrs. George writes of the animal world with knowledge and enthusiasm, her descriptions of wild life untainted by melodrama or anthropomorphism. . . . Slow-paced, and the combination of diffused writing and the lack of index or table of contents means that this book, like others in the series, has browsing interest chiefly for the nature lover." Chicago. Children's Bk Center

The moon of the mountain lions; illus. by Winifred Lubell. Crowell 1968 39p illus $3.95, lib. bdg. $4.70 (3-5)   599
1 Pumas
ISBN 0-690-55559-8; 0-690-55558-X
"The Thirteen moons"
On the slopes of Mount Olympus in Washington a young mountain lion, dependent on the herds of deer and elk for his food supply, prepares to follow them to their winter homes. Along the way, he chooses a mate
His life "is sketched with a fast-moving narrative and good line drawings. Other mountain creatures are afforded tiny vignettes in the story." Sci Bks

The moon of the wild pigs; illus. by Peter Parnall. Crowell 1968 39p illus $3.95, lib. bdg. $4.70 (3-5)   599
1 Peccaries 2 Desert animals 3 Desert plants
ISBN 0-690-55568-7; 0-690-55567-9
"The Thirteen moons"
"Life on the great Sonora Desert of Arizona. . . . Through the eyes of a peccary piglet, the young reader is shown vignettes from the lives of many desert plants and animals. The young peccary becomes separated from its clan and tries to find it

Gardner, Richard—*Continued*

again before it succumbs to the heat of a July day. In the process, it comes across a rattlesnake, a road-runner, an elf owl, and many other creatures indigenous to the desert. There is no anthropomorphism here; the book is as realistic as it is interesting. Peter Parnall's illustrations are excellent." Sci Bks

George, John L.

Masked prowler: the story of a raccoon, by John L. and Jean George; illus. by Jean George. Dutton 1950 183p illus $5.95 (4-6)   599

1 Raccoons
ISBN 0-525-34767-4

"This story of Procyon, a raccoon born in the Michigan forest, follows him through his days of training in gathering food and protecting himself to the adult adventures which make him a legend in his community. Good writing, a sound knowledge of the subject, and excellent illustrations." Hodges. Bks for Elem Sch Libraries

Grosvenor, Donna K.

Pandas; with photographs by the author; paintings by George Founds. Natl. Geographic Soc. 1973 30p illus (k-3)   599

1 Giant pandas
ISBN 0-87044-143-4

Obtainable only as part of a set for $6.95 with: Honeybees, by Jane Lecht, class 595.7; How animals hide, by Robert M. McClung, class 591.5; and Namu, by Ronald M. Fisher, class 599

"Books for young explorers"

Prepared by the Special Publications Division of the National Geographic Society

In color pictures and text, this book describes the habitats and behavior of the giant panda. Included are descriptions of Ling-Ling and Hsing-Hsing, the two young pandas sent as a gift from the people of China to the National Zoo in Washington, D.C.

Hancock, Sibyl

The grizzly bear; illus. by Nancy McGowan. Steck-Vaughn 1974 30p illus map (Endangered animals) lib. bdg. $4.25 (2-5)   599

1 Grizzly bear
ISBN 0-8114-7762-2

The author "has written an excellent children's book about the grizzly bear, its ancestors, relatives, range and senses, intelligence and family life. The illustrations by Nancy McGowan are excellent. The book emphasizes that the grizzly is a wild animal and should be respected. . . . The author mentions that the grizzly bear is an endangered species, but had this fact been emphasized more it would have helped the reader understand the meaning of an 'endangered' animal. The writing style is excellent for children, and the book is interesting as well as informative." Sci Bks

Hess, Lilo

The curious raccoons; story and photographs by Lilo Hess. Scribner 1968 46p illus lib. bdg. $5.95 (3-5)   599

1 Raccoons
ISBN 0-684-12459-9

"When a female raccoon is transported by animal-welfare authorities from the suburbs to the countryside, she makes a new home, mates, and raises a family of three kits. This straight-forward account of one particular raccoon acquaints the reader with the habits and characteristics of the species." Booklist

"Lilo Hess has snapped some truly expressive photographs of a raccoon family (a mother and three kits) as the bandit-masked, ringtailed creatures poke their noses into garbage cans, corn cribs, running brooks and wasps' nests. There's much nature lore

unobtrusively slipped into a sympathetic narrative." N Y Times Bk Rev

Foxes in the woodshed; story and photographs by Lilo Hess. Scribner 1966 illus lib. bdg. $5.95 (2-4)   599

1 Foxes
ISBN 0-684-14328-3

"A family of red foxes whose home is a deserted woodshed is the subject of this simply written but informative book. The author describes in words and photographs the habits and activities of the young foxes from the day they are born until they mate. . . . The format is pleasing and the pictures tell the story with such clarity and continuity that even a very young child could 'read' the pictures." Sch Library J

The misunderstood skunk; story and photographs by Lilo Hess. Scribner 1969 45p illus lib. bdg. $5.95 (3-5)   599

1 Skunks
ISBN 0-684-12360-6

"Miss Hess tells the story, from birth through the first year of life, of a family of skunks who made their home on her farm. She describes their appearance, musk-releasing defense mechanism, maturation process, feeding habits, qualities as pets, etc. Children will especially delight in the many black-and-white photographs, which depict the beautiful, inquisitive little animals both outdoors and in, sleeping, eating, exploring, and playing." Sch Library J

"Even grown-ups can learn much from this informative and well-told little book." Christian Sci Monitor

Mouse and company; story and photographs by Lilo Hess. Scribner 1972 46p illus lib. bdg. $5.95 (3-5)   599

1 Mice
ISBN 0-684-12810-1

This book "is crammed with useful and interesting information, without seeming stuffed. It begins by giving a brief natural history of a female deer mouse, introducing the concept of territory, giving the gestation period and something of the classification; all as a natural part of the story. Other common rodents, especially mice—wild and domestic, and including rats, gerbils and hamsters, are discussed in the balance of the book. The essentials of rodent raising and maze-building are also covered. Mrs. Hess has written a book that doesn't talk down to intelligent young people and includes pictures that will appeal to all." Sci Bks

Hiser, Iona Seibert

The bighorn sheep; illus. by Nancy McGowan. Steck-Vaughn 1973 30p illus maps (Endangered animals) $4.25 (3-5)   599

1 Sheep
ISBN 0-8114-7756-8

A "brief, profusely illustrated title . . . about endangered animals of the Southwest, this covers the physical characteristics of bighorn sheep and their way of life. While the format—large print and short chapters—seems aimed at middle graders, some of the detailed information about branches of the bighorn sheep family is beyond the grasp of this age group. However, since there is a lack of elementary material about the species, this should be a useful addition to conservation collections." Sch Library J

Hiss, Anthony

The giant panda book; pictures by Greg and Tim Hildebrandt. Golden Press 1973 45p illus maps $2.95, lib. bdg. $4.95 (3-5)   599

Hiss, Anthony—*Continued*
1 Giant pandas
ISBN 0-307-13753-8
"A most interesting and attractive children's book on the popular giant panda. The color illustrations by Greg and Tim Hildebrandt are excellent and appropriately illustrate the story in the text. The three parts of the book are: 'The Wild Giant Pandas of Szechwan,' 'The Story of Chi-Chi,' and 'The Story of Ling-Ling and Hsing-Hsing.' In the first part, the author concentrates on the native habitat of the giant pandas and on their zoological relationships; the second part concerns the female panda at the London Zoo; the third part tells the story of the two pandas who now live at the National Zoo in Washington, D.C. An altogether fine book to be read by or to young children." Sci Bks

Hoke, Helen
Whales, by Helen Hoke and Valerie Pitt; drawings by Thomas R. Funderburk. Watts, F. 1973 90p illus lib. bdg. $3.90 (4-7)   599
1 Whales
ISBN 0-531-00779-0
"A First book"
The authors describe the characteristics and habits which all whales share, and the distinctive features of some different kinds of whales, including porpoises and dolphins. There are also chapters on whale hunting and conservation
Written "in a crisp, sensible manner. A glossary, bibliography, index, and section on 'where to see cetaceans and whaling exhibits' add to the text. The type style and 32 pages of drawings and photographs are well designed. The few errors are carry-overs from whale literature. (For example, the gray whale quite certainly does not stand on its tail to shake the food into its stomach!) Since whales are modern symbols of wildness in nature, the book will sharpen the interest of the students wishing to know something about wildlife." Sci Bks

Hopf, Alice L.
Biography of a rhino; illus. by Kiyo Komoda. Putnam 1972 63p illus lib. bdg. $4.49 (2-4)   599
1 Rhinoceros
ISBN 0-399-60745-5
A life cycle story of Fari, a white rhino in a Uganda national park. It tells of her capture by the rangers, her life in the park, her eventual return to the wilderness for mating and motherhood, and her tragic death
"Fari is killed by poachers, an event that gives the author an opportunity to deplore the extermination of threatened species. The narrative framework is handled with skill, with facts about feeding, mating, symbiotic relationships, and other information about the rhinoceros smoothly incorporated." Chicago. Children's Bk Center

Hurd, Edith Thacher
The mother beaver; illus. by Clement Hurd. Little 1971 32p illus lib. bdg. $4.95 (k-2)   599
1 Beavers
ISBN 0-316-38317-1
"A year in the life of a female beaver is depicted in a simple narrative account illustrated with colored linoleum block prints on every page. It describes the birth of a litter in the spring, the activities of the beavers throughout the summer, their preparations for the winter, and the mating of the male and female beavers in the early spring to begin the cycle anew." Booklist

The mother deer; illus. by Clement Hurd. Little 1972 32p illus lib. bdg. $4.95 (k-2)   599
1 Deer
ISBN 0-316-38322-8

"One year in the life of a mother deer: her fawns are born; she feeds and protects them until they are old enough to live on their own. The book also depicts the effects of the changing seasons on the life of the deer. The publishers describe the blockprint illustrations as 'magnificent'—and they are, or as near as makes no difference." Pub W

The mother whale; illus. by Clement Hurd. Little 1973 32p illus lib. bdg. $4.95 (k-3)   599
1 Whales
ISBN 0-316-38324-4
"A description of the life cycle of the sperm whale begins with the birth of a calf, describes the mother's care and the baby calf's growth to independence, the challenge of an old bull by a young male, and the courting and mating of the whale mother that brings, months later, the birth of another baby whale." Chicago. Children's Bk Center
"Although the text is minimal, four to six lines on each of the 32 pages, a great deal of information is given so that the child to whom this is read or who reads it himself will understand how and where the great whales live, who are their enemies and who are their companions, and get a feeling from the prose of the vastness of the oceans and a satisfying amount of information on the sperm whale. The beautiful block prints in blues and greens and black cover every page and add to the atmosphere, although they are more likely to be appreciated by the adult introducing the book." Appraisal

Johnson, William Weber
The story of sea otters; illus. with photographs, prints, and map. Random House 1973 89p illus $4.50, lib. bdg. $5.69 (4-7)   599
1 Sea otters
ISBN 0-394-82403-2; 0-394-92403-7
The book gives "a clear portrayal of the habits of sea otters. The author describes their maternal devotion, their ability to use rocks as tools to pry food loose, their communities in offshore kelp beds, their eating habits, and their relation to river otters and other land mammals. Weber also shows how fur trading along the Pacific Coast in the 18th and 19th Centuries nearly brought about their extinction. . . . Vivid black-and-white photographs of the playful otters and their pups add browsing appeal to the informative text." Sch Library J
"The words are simple enough for a good ten-year-old reader, and the writing—direct, warm, and unaffected—will interest children and adults alike." Christian Sci Monitor
Map on lining-papers

Jordan, E. L.
Animal atlas of the world. Hammond 1969 224p illus maps $16.95   599
1 Mammals 2 Geographical distribution of animals and plants
ISBN 0-8437-1600-2
This book describes the habits and behavior of mammals in the mountains and tundras, deserts and oceans, rain forests and ice caps of the world. It also includes distribution maps, showing the range of the species; a geologic time chart of all orders; an article by the author on the world's major wildlife areas; and a zoological breakdown of the orders of mammals
"The atlas, with an Introduction about the efforts made around the globe to preserve some of the threatened species of wild life . . . is a superb piece of book making. . . . The short account of each of the 182 different species [included] is succinct and greatly informative." Best Sellers

Kaufmann, John

Bats in the dark; illus. by the author. Crowell 1972 33p illus (Let's-read-and-find-out science bks) $4.50, lib. bdg. $5.25 (1-3)   599

1 Bats

ISBN 0-690-11780-9; 0-690-11781-7

"Information is presented about how [little brown] bats secure their food, give birth and raise their young. A longer section tells how bats use ultrasonic sounds to find food and to avoid objects while in flight. There is some information about the diet of other bats that feed upon fish, fruit and nectar." Sci Bks

"The attractive format in which black-and-white representational studies are alternated with more impressionistic, mixed-media illustrations is at once explicit and exciting." Horn Bk

Kohn, Bernice

Raccoons; pictures by John Hamberger. Prentice-Hall 1968 unp illus $4.95, pa 95¢ (1-3)   599

1 Raccoons

ISBN 0-13-749978-7; 0-13-749903-5

The author provides "descriptions of the raccoon's appearance, relationships with other mammals, habits and life history." Sci Bks

"A competent text enhanced by attractive illustrations reproduced in warm colors. The book should prove useful for nature study or for recreational reading." Library J

Lauber, Patricia

Bats; wings in the night; illus. with photographs. Random House 1968 77p illus $2.95, lib. bdg. $4.39 (4-7)   599

1 Bats

ISBN 0-394-80147-4; 0-394-90147-9

"Gateway books"

"The author discusses the classification of bats, and those habits or abilities that distinguish them from other mammals or, within the order of Chiroptera, from each other." Sutherland. The Best in Children's Bks

"There is also a discussion of a few of the scientists who have worked with bats and how these men experimented with the animals. Some of the animals' remaining mysteries are mentioned to arouse the young reader's curiosity. Although the text treats of bats in general (there are 800-900 species), a chapter is devoted to each of the five more unusual ones—the Flying Foxes, Vampire Bats, Cannibal Bats, Flower Bats, and the Fisherman Bats. Excellent black-and-white photographs and an index add to the value as a science book." Sci Bks

Lavine, Sigmund A.

Wonders of the bat world; illus. with photographs. Dodd 1969 64p illus lib. bdg. $4.50 (4-7)   599

1 Bats

ISBN 0-396-06532-5

"Dodd, Mead Wonders books"

This book "introduces the various kinds of bats and describes their distribution and morphology. [The author] describes lucidly their extraordinary senses, particularly their hearing and echo-location, smell, and place memory and, where appropriate, mentions research findings that have provided the foundation for our knowledge. Peculiarities of bat behavior, particularly their hibernation, migration, and feeding habits are discussed. . . . A concluding chapter offers suggestions on observing bats." Sci Bks

MacClintock, Dorcas

A natural history of giraffes; pictures by Ugo Mochi; text by Dorcas MacClintock. Scribner 1973 134p illus lib. bdg. $5.95 (6-7)   599

1 Giraffes

ISBN 0-684-13239-7

"A detailed account that begins with taxonomy and evolutionary history and goes on to cover the physical and behavioral aspects of the giraffe. . . . Glossary and suggestions for further reading appended." Booklist

"This book is distinguished by [Ugo Mochi's] work in the form of 'graphic sculpture': cutouts from single sheets of heavy black paper, somehow suggesting motion and depth in a quite remarkable way. The text is brief; rich and clear, the work of a mammalogist who can write and who has seen giraffes in the savanna." Scientific Am

McClung, Robert M.

Blaze; the story of a striped skunk; written and illus. by Robert M. McClung. Morrow 1969 48p illus $4.95, lib. bdg. $4.59 (1-3)   599

1 Skunks

ISBN 0-688-21107-0; 0-688-31107-5

"Beginning readers can follow the striped skunk, Blaze, through one year of her life. She bears her young, teaches them to hunt, and meets some natural enemies during the course of the story. The child will learn about a skunk's living and eating habits, and how the mother cares for the young." Sci Bks

"Although Robert McClung fails to relate all the common facts known about skunks, the large-print text . . . can be read by young children for its story content." Pub W

Possum; written and illus. by Robert M. McClung. Morrow 1963 47p illus lib. bdg. $4.59 (2-4)   599

1 Opossums

ISBN 0-688-31508-9

"Set in extra-large type, this also has attractive illustration, combining pencil stroke with wash. Green and brown are added to half of the pictures. The story is about Possum, one of nine marsupial babies, and also introduces other animals with pouches and some enemy animals who diminish this opossum family from nine to four children. The most fascinating portion of the life-cycle account has to do with the birth of Possum's babies, their growth in the pouch, and final emergence to ride on Possum's back." Horn Bk

Whitefoot; the story of a wood mouse; written and illus. by Robert M. McClung. Morrow 1961 48p illus lib. bdg. $4.59 (1-4)   599

1 Mice

ISBN 0-688-31512-7

This is the story of a year in the life of Whitefoot, a wood mouse, as she raises her family, helps them to find food, teaches them to know which animals are their friends and which their enemies, and out-smarts a shrew

"Information about nesting habits, food, and habitat are woven smoothly into the writing, with no sentimentality and no personalizing." Chicago. Children's Bk Center

"A simple, direct narrative and attractive drawings, some in color. . . . Large print." Booklist

McDearmon, Kay

A day in the life of a sea otter; illus. with photographs. Dodd 1973 44p illus lib. bdg. $3.50 (k-3)   599

1 Sea otters

ISBN 0-396-06743-3

"An informative account in story form which treats the daily routine of a female sea otter. Topics include care of young, grooming, feeding, and defense against enemies. The black-and-white photographs are adequate but in some instances lack clarity. The success

McDearmon, Kay—Continued

of conservation efforts involving this animal makes the book of special interest to school libraries." Sch Library J

McNulty, Faith

Woodchuck; pictures by Joan Sandin. Harper 1974 64p illus (A Science I can read bk) $2.95, lib. bdg. $3.43 (1-3)   599

1 Woodchucks

ISBN 0-06-024166-7; 0-06-024167-5

"A year in the life of a small creature of fields and meadows is presented with clarity, simplicity, and effectiveness. . . . Accompanied by realistic illustrations containing just enough detail to supplement the text, the activities of a female woodchuck are followed from the end of one hibernation period to the beginning of the next. No hint of anthropomorphism or sentimentality mars the objectivity of the story, as the animal responds to the first stirrings of spring, leaves the security of her underground home to find food, evades enemies, mates, raises a family, and finally, in late autumn, returns once again to another deep, safe sleep." Horn Bk

Martin, Lynne

The giant panda. Young Scott Bks. 1972 69p illus map $4.95 (3-6)   599

1 Giant pandas

ISBN 0-201-09226-3

"The author presents a brief history of pandas as well as information about the complex feeding, care, and mating problems of pandas as they are cared for in Western zoos." Notable Children's Trade Bks in the Field of Social Studies

"Appealing photographs, accurate drawings, and a well-written text about an interesting animal." Minnesota

Bibliography: p[72]

Mason, George F.

The bear family; written and illus. by George F. Mason. Morrow 1960 illus maps lib. bdg. $4.32 (4-7)   599

1 Bears

ISBN 0-688-31072-9

The author features, in turn, the American black bear, the O Kasis brown bear, the grizzly bear and the polar bear. For each, he gives the animal's appearance, habits, and habitat. Also included is a section on the origin of the bear family and a brief description of species in other lands

"The author's many personal experiences and anecdotes make the clear and uncluttered text interesting and entertaining." The AAAS Sci Bk List for Children

Milotte, Alfred

The story of an Alaskan grizzly bear, by Alfred and Elma Milotte; illus. by Helen Damrosch Tee-Van. Knopf 1969 149p illus $3.95, lib. bdg. $5.19 (4-7)   599

1 Bears

ISBN 0-394-81574-2; 0-394-91574-7

"This portrait of a year in the life of . . . [a female] Alaskan grizzly shows how ecological balance is maintained." Children's Bks, 1970

"Beginning when her three cubs were born during late winter hibernation, the story continues through the spring, summer and fall seasons, finally ending when the mother and the two surviving cubs have again bedded down for the winter. The story is well written not only because of the writers' literary competence, but also because they know intimately and have covered thoroughly . . . the locale of the story along the foothill of Mount McKinley and the tundra of the Toklat River Valley." Sci Bks

Mizumura, Kazue

The blue whale. Crowell 1971 32p illus (Let's-read-and-find-out science bks) $4.50, lib. bdg. $5.25 (k-2)   599

1 Whales

ISBN 0-690-14993-X; 0-690-14994-8

The author provides information "about whales in general and about the blue whale in particular which is the largest of all. All of the essentials of the life history of a blue whale are here. . . . [A] two-page spread illustrates how whales swim and how a typical bony fish swims. The birth of a blue whale is illustrated and described, and particularly interesting is the description of a whale nursing—the mother squirts milk into him. . . . There are incidental references to the whaling industry, to the products formerly made of whales (now mostly made of plastics), and to the depletion of the whale resources due to over-exploitation." Sci Bks

"Nicely illustrated and very simply written. . . . There is a rather forced fictional framework (a fishing boat captain tells 'many things about whales') but it detracts little from the book." Chicago. Children's Bk Center

Opossum. Crowell 1974 33p illus (Let's-read-and-find-out science bks) $3.95, lib. bdg. $4.70 (k-2)599

1 Opossums

ISBN 0-690-00396-X; 0-690-00397-8

"A description of the opossum, how and why opossums play dead, where and how they live, and the food they eat. The reader learns about the growth and development of the opossum from birth to the time the young leave the mother. The term marsupial is used and defined. The vocabulary is reasonable for a beginning reader; the illustrations go well with the content. The series of pictures showing the growth and development of young opossums and those showing the feet and tracks are particularly well done." Sci Teacher

Moffett, Martha

Dolphins, by Martha and Robert Moffett; illus. with photographs. Watts, F. 1971 85p illus lib. bdg. $3.90 (4-6)   599

1 Dolphins

ISBN 0-531-00723-5

"A First book"

A straightforward, factual account describes the better known members of the dolphin family, the physical structure, senses, langauge, and social organization of dolphins, and current scientific research on the marine mammals. The authors [also] discuss dolphin intelligence." Booklist

"A ratio of approximately three pages of photographs for each five pages of text help to maintain interest and encourage the reader to pursue the information presented in the text." Sci Bks

Morris, Desmond

The big cats; illus. by Barry Driscoll. McGraw 1965 32p illus (A McGraw-Hill Natural science picture bk) lib. bdg. $4.72 (3-5)   599

ISBN 0-07-043171-X

"Full-page descriptions of the big cats—lion, tiger, leopard, jaguar, and snow leopard—and briefer mention of the small cats—puma, lynx, ocelot, and cheetah—answer such questions as: How do big cats differ from small cats? Where do the big cats live? What do they eat? How are they alike and how do they differ? How can one tell when they are angry? Are the big cats really vicious, savage beasts? How big are the big cats? Well written and well-illustrated. . . . Morris places less emphasis on anatomy and more on habitat." Sch Library J

Weights and measures of the big cats: p32

National Geographic Society

Lion cubs; growing up in the wild. The Society 1972
31p illus (k-3)   599
1 Lions
ISBN 0-87044-121-3
Obtainable only as part of a set for $6.95 with:
Dinosaurs, by Kathryn Jackson, class 568; Dogs working for people, by Joanna Foster, class 636.7; and
Treasures in the sea, by Robert M. McClung, class
910.4
"Books for young explorers"
Prepared by the Special Publications Division of
the National Geographic Society
"Super photographs. Illustrated is a brief story of
lion cubs, their home, dependency on the pride for
two years, and their relationship with other animals.
Included is a two-page spread showing other members of the cat family. This book is beautiful to see
with no depth of information." Appraisal

Wild animals of North America. The Society 1960
400p illus (Natural science lib) $7.75   599
1 Mammals
ISBN 0-87044-020-9
"Edited and prepared by the National Geographic
Book Service . . . 409 illustrations. 258 in full color,
by Walter A. Weber, Louis Agassiz Fuertes, and
other artists and photographers." Verso of title page
Chapters by various writers grouped under the following headings: Animals in fur; The hoofed mammals; The meat eaters; Gnawing mammals; Survivors
of ancient orders; Ocean dwellers
"This is an attractive, informative compilation for
readers of all ages and is especially good for browsing." Booklist
Map on lining-papers

North, Sterling

Little Rascal; illus. by Carl Burger. Dutton 1965
78p illus $5.50 (3-5)   599
1 Raccoons 2 Country life—Wisconsin
ISBN 0-525-33854-3
The original book, Rascal, entered below, has been
specially illustrated and abridged for young readers
The book "describes a year in the life of a boy in
Wisconsin fifty years ago. Rascal is his pet raccoon,
and his exploits are comic and sometimes touching,
and described without sentimentality." Times (London) Literary Sup

Rascal; a memoir of a better era; illus. by John
Schoenherr. Dutton 1963 189p illus $5.95 (5-7) 599
1 Raccoons 2 Country life—Wisconsin
ISBN 0-525-18839-8
A book about Rascal "a young raccoon, Sterling
North's pet the year he was eleven, in rural Wisconsin. . . . The book calls up a series of marvelous pictures; boy fishing in peaceful company of raccoon, boy
riding on bike with raccoon (a demon for speed) standing up in bike basket, raccoon with friend, a prize
trotting horse, raccoon helping boy to win a pie-eating
contest. A central episode is about an idyllic camping
trip." Pub W
"Beyond being a charming true animal story, it is
also an account of life in a Wisconsin village in
1918. . . . Young readers will cherish it." N Y Times
Bk Rev

Patent, Dorothy Hinshaw

Weasels, otters, skunks, and their family; illus. by
Matthew Kalmenoff. Holiday House 1973 95p illus
$4.95 (3-6)   599
1 Mammals
ISBN 0-8234-0228-2
The book describes mammals of the Mustelid fam-
ily: "Carnivorous weasels, ferrets, minks, and mar-

tens; omnivorous skunks, badgers, and wolverines;
and the playful and aquatic sea and river otters. [The
author] discusses their physical characteristics, eating
habits, and reproductive processes, and where necessary, dispels damaging myths about them. She follows
these animals through their daily lives showing how
they seek out other animals, protect themselves, survive in different environments, cooperate with other
animals, and are captured by their predators."
Booklist
"Written with grace and precision. . . . Matthew
Kalmenoff's pictures (starting with the loving otter
mother and baby on the cover) are realistic and reas-
suringly un-Disneylike." Pub W
Suggested reading: p91

Pringle, Laurence

Follow a fisher; illus. by Tony Chen. Crowell 1973
38p illus $3.95, lib. bdg. $4.70 (3-5)   599
1 Weasels
ISBN 0-690-31236-9; 0-690-31237-7
"An introduction to the fisher, a little-known
member of the weasel family. In the form of a simu-
lated journey through the forest to track these elusive
animals, the author covers basic facts about their feeding, mating, and care of the young. Described in
detail are successful projects to return fishers to areas
from which they were driven by man in order to help
bring under control the destructive porcupine population." Library J
"The story's ecological point of view is extremely
pertinent today. The drawings are excellent and
appropriately placed, and both text and illustrations
will hold the enthusiastic attention of children." Sci
Bks

Ripper, Charles L.

Foxes and wolves; written and illus. by Charles L.
Ripper. Morrow 1961 64p illus maps lib. bdg. $4.59
(3-5)   599
1 Foxes 2 Wolves
ISBN 0-688-31310-8
"The wild dogs of North America—foxes, coyotes,
and wolves—are described and contrasted with each
other and with domestic dogs. What they eat and their
place in the balance of nature is investigated and it is
shown how they find or make shelter and rear their
young. Included are maps of their range, diagrams of
tracks and prints, and many accurate sketches." The
AAAS Sci Bk List for Children
"Mr Ripper writes for young readers, but he never
humanizes the subjects of his studies of animals and
birds. . . . The illustrations, pencil drawings on
every page, are very attractive." Horn Bk

Roever, J. M.

The black-footed ferret; written and illus. by J. M.
Roever. Steck-Vaughn 1972 30p illus (Endangered
animals) $3.50 (3-5)   599
1 Black-footed ferret 2 Rare animals
ISBN 0-8114-7749-5
This brief "book is packed with information about
this rare animal, including a map of his territory, uses
of the word 'ferret,' physical characteristics, enemies
and family life. The ecological relationship between
the prairie dog and the ferret is explored, and there is
an excellent illustration of the prairie food chain." Sch
Library J
"From the moment the book is opened it is evident
that this is an extraordinarily well-conceived work; the
illustrations are much more than decorative—they
illustrate the points made on each page. . . . Finally,
the author voices her fears about the possible results
of the predator control measures taken by the U. S.
Government in conjunction with the cattle farmers.
These measures have taken their toll of the lowly

Roever, J. M.—*Continued*
prairie dogs and thus have also harmed the black-footed ferret. After arousing our concern, the author offers two pages of drawings of other endangered American species and suggestions for the ecologically minded." Sci Bks

Ryden, Hope
The wild colt; the life of a young mustang; written and photographed by Hope Ryden. Coward, McCann & Geoghegan 1972 unp illus $6.95 (2-4)   599
   1 Mustangs 2 Horses
   ISBN 0-698-20178-7
"This is the story, told in pictures with extensive captions, of a band of wild horses in Wyoming. The horses live on the Cayuse Ranch True Blood Reserve along with other wild horses which are pure descendants of the Spanish Barb horses brought over and lost by the conquistadors in the sixteenth century. The pictures tell the story of a mustang colt and his life in his father's harem from birth through the first summer of his life. Some of the dangers encountered by the colt are shown, and the reader is given a chance to see a band of wild horses in the place where they actually live." Sci Bks

Schaller, George B.
The tiger; its life in the wild, by George B. Schaller and Millicent E. Selsam; illus. with photographs, drawings and maps. Harper 1969 71p illus maps lib. bdg. $4.79 (4-7)   599
   1 Tigers
   ISBN 0-06-025280-4
"The gist of man's knowledge about tigers is contained in this delightful book. It is accurate and tells how an ecologist goes about studying animals in their natural habitat. The book covers life history, behavior, superstitions and the present distribution and abundance of tigers. The chapters on man-eaters and social life are intriguing, and the entire book reflects the excitement of the author's firsthand experiences." Sci Bks
"The book is handsomely illustrated with black-and-white prints of tigers at the beginning of each chapter, clear photographs, and useful maps." Sch Library J
For further reading: p69

Scheffer, Victor B.
Little Calf; adapted from The year of the whale; decorations by Leonard Everett Fisher. Scribner 1970 140p illus $5.95 (5-7)   599
   1 Whales
   ISBN 0-684-20939-X
The author "tells the story of a year in the life of a sperm whale calf—from its birth in equatorial waters through the first months of its suckling life, its growth, its awareness of the whale herd swimming through thousands of miles of seas (tropical and arctic) and its first recognition of that mysterious creature, man, who comes in ships." Pub W

Schlein, Miriam
What's wrong with being a skunk? Illus. by Ray Cruz. Four Winds 1974 unp illus $3.95 (k-3)   599
   1 Skunks
"From this book the young reader learns that skunks are really good-natured animals and they only use their special protective weapon of odor when they are in a real crisis. Their eating habits, sleeping habits, and how they spend the winter are described as well as growing to adulthood, and their natural enemies." Sci Teacher
"The provocative title introduces youngsters to the skunks—striped, spotted, hooded, hognosed or pygmy. Black-and-white sketches highlight the text.

. . . The informal story format carries the student along, providing interest and motivation through pictures and a readable text. Vocabulary is appropriate and the sentence length varied. The popularity of the animal is mentioned—also its unpopularity—allowing the reader to make his own choice." Sci Bks

Shuttlesworth, Dorothy E.
The story of monkeys, great apes, and small apes. Doubleday 1972 111p illus $4.95, lib. bdg. $5.70 (5-7)   599
   1 Monkeys 2 Apes
   ISBN 0-385-06055-6; 0-385-04724-X
Illustrated with photographs, this book examines many of the members of the ape (chimpanzee, gorilla, orangutan) and monkey (baboon, marmoset, rhesus) world. It discusses their distinguished physical characteristics, their environment and way of life, their proper care and feeding, as well as their role in mythology and folklore
"The book has easy-to-read language and print, is well illustrated with many photographs, and has an index. The book conveys a feeling of concern for the well-being of the apes, in their natural habitat or in zoos." Appraisal

The story of rodents; illus. by Lydia Rosier. Doubleday 1971 95p illus $4.95, lib. bdg. $5.70 (4-6)   599
   1 Rodents
   ISBN 0-385-01323-X; 0-385-04689-8
The book "discusses briefly the physical appearance, behavior, diet, and relationship with man of various species of mice, rats, squirrels, lemmings, beaver, porcupines, and other rodents, and describes the origins of such rodent pets as gerbils, hamsters, and guinea pigs. Black-and-white and colored drawings, more decorative than informative, illustrate the clear, readable text." Booklist

Silverstein, Alvin
Rabbits; all about them [by] Alvin and Virginia Silverstein; with photographs by Roger Kerkham. Lothrop 1973 160p illus $5.95, lib. bdg. $5.11 (4-7)   599
   1 Rabbits
   ISBN 0-688-41564-4; 0-688-51564-9
"This well-organized compendium of rabbit fact and fancy gives the reader far more than other standard works on the subject. After an admirable section on care and feeding of rabbits as pets, the remaining chapters examine both the hare and rabbit as laboratory research subjects, then describe their zoological, behavioral, and ecological characteristics, and end with a tasteful survey of rabbit legend and lore. There is a bountiful assortment of instructive and endearing photographs throughout. The authors are moderately anecdotal without cheapening their straightforward writing style, which is devoid of condescension toward the young audience. Suggestions for further reading are appended." Booklist

Rats and mice, friends and foes of man [by] Alvin and Virginia B. Silverstein. Illus. by Joseph Cellini. Lothrop 1968 96p illus $5.50 (3-5)   599
   1 Rats 2 Mice
   ISBN 0-688-41617-9
Besides providing a blueprint for the care and breeding of mice and rats as pets, this book discusses their role in preserving the balance of nature, their life, methods of migration since ancient times, and their use in laboratory experiments, as well as the harm they do
"While the drawings have more dramatic effect

Silverstein, Alvin—Continued
than scientific value, the text achieves a nice balance between a general and a technical tone." Booklist
Suggestions for further reading: p94

Tee-Van, Helen Damrosch
Small mammals are where you find them. Knopf 1966 148p illus $3.50, lib. bdg. $5.39 (3-6)   599
1 Mammals
ISBN 0-394-81643-9; 0-394-91643-3
"A well-organized, informative and graphically illustrated classification of mammals from the tiniest shrew to the beaver. Each page is headed by a habitat map showing where the animal is found in the United States and often foot-marks or tracks are also shown." Bruno. Bks for Sch Libraries, 1968
"Educationally speaking, this book would be a great asset to any science teacher and an excellent reference book for the pupil. . . . Not only does it educate and entertain, but makes children sensitively aware of the world around them." Best Sellers

Tunis, Edwin
Chipmunks on the doorstep; written and illus. by Edwin Tunis. Crowell 1971 69p illus $4.95, lib. bdg. $5.70 (5-7)   599
1 Chipmunks
ISBN 0-690-19044-1; 0-690-19045-X
"The author as artist has caught his subject pictorially on location in the mountain country of Maryland where Chippy and his many mates are at home on the terrace of a human family. The profusion of small full-color drawings, supporting the author's statement that it is the chipmunk's personality that recommends him, provide clear biological information about Chippy's gaits, tracks, cheek pouches, and eating, drinking, and mating habits." Horn Bk
"Because he is writing informally and affectionately about creatures he loves, the author adds to acuity of observation and meticulous detail in illustration a humor that enlivens the informative text." Sat Rev

Waters, John F.
Camels: ships of the desert; illus. by Reynold Ruffins. Crowell 1974 33p illus (Let's-read-and-find-out science bks) $3.95, lib. bdg. $4.70 (1-3)   599
1 Camels
ISBN 0-690-00394-3; 0-690-00395-1
Comparing the camel's physical characteristics to man's, this book explains how camels withstand the desert sand, heat, and lack of water and food
This "is an excellent addition to the elementary science library. Appropriately illustrated in 'water and sand' colors, the book presents a graphic portrait of the 'ship of the desert.' But it does more; it gives a scientific explanation for and refutes theory and superstition about the camel's storage of water. At the same time the basic science principles pertaining to heat and cold, perspiration, the skin and its function and the processes of elimination are all neatly fitted in. Vocabulary is appropriate; and text and pictures have a wonderful invitational quality, asking questions then answering, but carrying the reader along logically and allowing him to make the discovery rather than telling him in so many trite phrases." Sci Bks

Wildsmith, Brian
Squirrels. Watts, F. 1975 c1974 unp illus lib. bdg. $5.95 (k-2)   599
1 Squirrels
ISBN 0-531-02754-6
"Arresting close-ups of furry orange squirrels are the forte of Wildsmith's latest graphic display. . . . While the minimal text is secondary to the color spreads, it imparts enough factual material to consti-

tute a suitable introduction for young listeners." Booklist

Wise, William
The amazing animals of North America; illus. by Joseph Sibal. Putnam 1971 63p illus lib. bdg. $3.96 (1-3)   599
1 Animals—North America 2 Mammals
ISBN 0-399-60015-9
"A See and read Beginning to read book"
The author describes such North American wild animals as the pronghorn antelope, the mountain goat, the grizzly bear, the wolverine, the lynx, the elk and the bison
"In tune with recent interest in ecology, man is presented as the instrument of change and destroyer of animal life. . . . The realities of man-animal and animal-animal relationships give this book an integrity rarely found in children's books. Excellent informative drawings accompany the text. A key word and animal list provides the proper ending for this beautiful text." Sci Bks

Zim, Herbert S.
Mammals; a guide to familiar American species, by Herbert S. Zim and Donald F. Hoffmeister; illus. by James Gordon Irving. 218 animals in full color. Sponsored by The Wildlife Management Institute. Golden Press 1955 160p illus maps (A Golden Nature guide) lib. bdg. $4.95, pa $1.50   599
1 Mammals
ISBN 0-307-63510-4; 0-307-24497-0
First published by Simon & Schuster
This guide to North American mammals presents the habits and characteristics of bears, badgers, rabbits, deer, seals, whales, mice, wolves, etc. with range maps and family trees. It includes lists of books for further study, zoos and museums to visit, and a list of scientific names, as well as an index
This also describes a few extinct mammals "and ways of preserving specimens and tracks. The small size makes it ideal for taking on field trips." Library J

Monkeys; illus. by Gardell D. Christensen. Morrow 1955 unp illus map lib. bdg. $4.32 (3-6)   599
1 Monkeys
ISBN 0-688-31517-8
"An interestingly written introduction to monkeys. Beginning with a description of the entire group of primates and showing structural similarities and differences, the author then discusses the various types of monkeys and how they resemble, or differ from, each other. The detailed drawings add interest and information to the book. There is helpful material on choosing and caring for a monkey as a pet. A useful book for nature study or hobby groups, as well as for general reading." Chicago. Children's Bk Center

600 TECHNOLOGY (APPLIED SCIENCES)

Keen, Martin L.
How it works; illus. by Lloyd P. Birmingham. Grosset 1972 147p illus $4.95 (5-7)   600
1 Technology 2 Machinery
ISBN 0-448-11611-1
A "concise explanation of the workings of a variety of machines and devices, most in common everyday usage, including telephones, cells and batteries, electric lights, small appliances, radio, television, engines, refrigerators, air conditioners, heaters, ball

Keen, Martin L.—*Continued*

point pens, locks, toilets, and elevators. Careful description of the principles of electricity and magnetism begin the text which is aided throughout by the many clear diagrammatic drawings." Booklist

"Both adult and child will find answers to their questions. . . . And though it's not a repair manual, often an understanding of 'how it works' leads to the solution to 'why it doesn't work.' A glossary of technical terms is included." Library J

The Way things work; an illustrated encyclopedia of technology; special ed. for young people, by T. Lodewijk and others. Simon & Schuster 1973 288p illus $10.95 (6-7)   600

1 Technology
ISBN 0-671-65212-5

An adaptation of the two-volume work with same title published 1967-1971, which was originally published 1963 in Germany

"Teachers constantly seek ways to show the scientific principles underlying everyday things, or, conversely, to show practical applications of science. This volume is one convenient answer to the search for relevant materials. . . . There are 91 short descriptions of physical principles or applications. Each has one or more drawings. The nine major headings range from flying, engines, communications, photography, and television to message handling, objects around the house, and materials like plastics, glass, and wood. . . . This book can well be used as an interest primer and supplement." Sci Teacher

An index is included

602   Technology—Miscellany

Weiss, Harvey

The gadget book. Crowell 1971 60p illus $4.50 (4-7)   602

ISBN 0-690-32124-4

Illustrated with diagrams by the author, this book tells how to make both useful and useless gadgets with instructions which allow the reader to add the finishing touches. Some of the projects include: a sunbeam alarm clock, wind chimes, a simple flashlight, a burglar alarm, weather vanes, a monorail system, and lighthouses

"The directions and diagrams are purposefully general, explaining the basic principles and clarifying difficult parts but leaving many of the details to the reader's creativity and imagination. Mechanically inclined children should have many hours of fun with this stimulating book." Booklist

604.6   Waste technology

Pringle, Laurence

Recycling resources. Macmillan Pub. Co. 1974 119p illus $5.95 (6-7)   604.6

1 Salvage (Waste, etc.)
ISBN 0-02-775310-7

The author considers the problems of refuse disposal and the consequences of squandering mineral and other useful resources. The often conflicting interests and attitudes of the packaging industry, the government, and the consumer are taken into account

Bibliography: p113-14

Shanks, Ann Zane

About garbage and stuff; with photographs by the author. Viking 1973 unp illus lib. bdg. $5.95 (k-3)
                                                             604.6

1 Refuse and refuse disposal 2 Salvage (Waste, etc.)
ISBN 0-670-10050-1

In this book "a discussion of recycling is cleverly approached from the child's viewpoint; it begins with a family shopping for groceries, describes the amount of garbage it throws away each day, and the problem of garbage disposal: what happens when there is too much to use for landfill? The family then separates its glass, metal, etc. and the text describes recycling plants; it concludes by coming back to the two children of the family. What can they do? Use both sides of the paper when drawing . . . use disposable paper instead of plastic, put things in one big bag instead of many small ones, and so on. The pictures are large scale, the text is clear and not too heavy, and tone is brisk and matter-of-fact; we have a problem, here's what we can do. No dire threats, no coaxing." Chicago. Children's Bk Center

609   Technology—History

Cooke, David C.

Inventions that made history. Putnam 1968 70p illus (These made history) lib. bdg. $3.86 (5-7)   609

1 Inventions—History 2 Technology—History
ISBN 0-399-60302-6

Here are thirty-two inventions from printing to the laser which have revolutionized the course of human life. They are placed in historical perspective, and the long years of labor, the frequent failures and the breakthroughs are described

Jupo, Frank

The story of things. Prentice-Hall 1972 64p illus $4.75 (3-5)   609

1 Technology—History 2 Inventions—History
ISBN 0-13-850347-8

This is the story of the development of everyday conveniences (brooms, clocks, forks, hammers, and the like) all of which underwent a lengthy evolution

Reading list: p64

Men of science and invention, by the editors of American Heritage, The Magazine of History; narrative by Michael Blow, in consultation with Robert P. Multhauf. Am. Heritage [distributed by Harper] 1960 153p illus map $5.95, lib. bdg. $6.89 (5-7)
                                                             609

1 Inventions—History 2 Inventors 3 Scientists
ISBN 0-06-020540-7; 0-06-020541-5

"American Heritage Junior library"

"A survey of the scientific and technological advances made in America from Colonial times to the present, centered around the work of pioneering scientists and profusely illustrated with old prints and photographs." Hodges. Bks for Elem Sch Libraries

"Scientific information from leading institutions all over the country is welded neatly together making a fine entertaining account." San Francisco Chronicle

610   Medical sciences

Fisher, Leonard Everett

The doctors; written & .llus. by Leonard Everett Fisher. Watts, F. 1968 47p illus lib. bdg. $3.90 (4-7)   610

Fisher, Leonard Everett—*Continued*
1 Medicine 2 Physicians 3 U.S.—History—Colonial period
ISBN 0-531-01027-9
"Colonial Americans"
The author presents a "factual account of medical practice in Colonial America, largely hit-or-miss quackery and superstition by poorly trained amateurs. . . . The colonial period closed with the appointment of Dr. Benjamin Rush as surgeon general of the continental army, who 'Although he still believed in most of the old methods, he kept an open mind about new medical and scientific events.' He was America's first great medical teacher over a period of 40 years. The book closes with a list of some physicians and surgeons of Colonial America, and an index." Sci Bks
"This book can be read for pleasure as well as information and, of course, will supplement the history curriculum well. The black-and-white scratchboard illustrations are, as usual, excellent." Sch Library J

610.28 Medical sciences— Equipment

Marks, Geoffrey
The amazing stethoscope; illus. by Polly Bolian. Messner 1971 80p illus $4.50, lib. bdg. $4.29 (4-6)
610.28
1 Stethoscope 2 Sound
ISBN 0-671-32451-9; 0-671-32452-7
"A good introductory account of the history, development, and diverse uses of the stethoscope. Aside from medical applications, Marks covers many other uses of the instrument: e.g., monitoring valves of water pipes, listening to electrical transformers, checking automobile engines, etc. Also included is a brief discussion of the nature and conduction of sound. Although there is some talking down . . . the book overall is written in a clear, easy-to-read style and its exclusive focus on the evolution of the stethoscope is not found in any other book for the age group." Sch Library J

610.69 Medical personnel

Rockwell, Harlow
My doctor. Macmillan Pub. Co. 1973 unp illus lib. bdg. $4.95 (k-1)
610.69
1 Medicine 2 Physicians
ISBN 0-02-777480-5
This book is intended to "familiarize children with equipment in a modern doctor's office. Depicted are such items as jars of bandages, a sphygmomanometer and an otoscope, an eye chart, a hypodermic syringe and needle, an opened refrigerator with jars of medicines, wooden sticks for tongue depression, and a stethoscope." Sch Library J
"An uncluttered format, poster-like water-color illustrations, and an economical text are combined in an uncondescending picture-information book for the young child anticipating a routine checkup at the doctor's office. Satisfying and reassuring in its explicit, calm presentation of standard medical office equipment, the book is also noteworthy for avoiding stereotyped roles without blatantly advertising the fact. 'My doctor' is depicted as a woman." Horn Bk

611 Human anatomy

Balestrino, Philip
The skeleton inside you; illus. by Don Bolognese. Crowell 1971 32p illus (Let's-read-and-find-out science bks) $4.50, lib. bdg. $5.25 (1-3)
611
1 Bones
ISBN 0-690-74122-7; 0-690-74123-5
"A very simplified text on skeletal structure this does not describe all the bones in the human body, but discusses the different shapes of bones, something of their structure and their function, cartilage, joints, and ligaments. The text also mentions the foods that are high in calcium, necessary for strong bones, and the fact that bones grow and mend. The writing is matter-of-fact and informal, the amount of coverage right for the primary grades audience. The illustrations are lively and often illuminating." Chicago. Children's Bk Center

Elgin, Kathleen
The human body: the skeleton; written and illus. by Kathleen Elgin. Watts, F. 1971 66p illus lib. bdg. $3.90 (3-6)
611
1 Bones
ISBN 0-531-01180-1
This is a lucid straightforward "explanation of the structure and function of the skeleton. It describes the composition and growth of bones, tells how they move, and names and discusses in a few sentences each of the major bones of the body." Booklist
"Liberal paragraphing, careful placement of the large illustrations, a pronunciation guide following each term as it appears, and a complete index make this book extremely useful as an introduction to the skeleton." Sch Library J

Gallant, Roy A.
Me and my bones. Doubleday 1971 45p illus $4.95, lib. bdg. $5.70 (3-5)
611
1 Bones 2 Anatomy, Comparative
ISBN 0-385-01889-4; 0-385-01898-3
The book discusses "two major subjects: the structure and function of bones and the theory of evolution. . . . Using photographs of human and animal skeletons Gallant points out structural similarities." Sch Library J
"This delightful little book presents some really amazing photographs and . . . a tremendous amount of information delivered in a pleasant, interesting, even cheerful manner. The use of highly personalized pictures to demonstrate the living body and skeleton is most attractive. This will be extremely worthwhile collateral reading for a course in biology or health. The terminology is sufficiently simple to be appreciated by elementary school children whether intermediate or advanced." Sci Bks

Ravielli, Anthony
Wonders of the human body; written and illus. by Anthony Ravielli. Viking 1954 125p illus lib. bdg. $4.95 (4-7)
611
1 Anatomy 2 Physiology
ISBN 0-670-78033-2
"This generously illustrated introduction to anatomy—bones, muscles, nerves, digestive and circulatory systems—will serve better than most existing material to explain many of the miracles of the human body to young people with a scientific interest in physiology. Its text is ample enough and clear, technical in its use of scientific terms, and imaginative in its analogies to machines and familiar objects. Its drawings and diagrams, with montage technique—pictures of whole child, body parts and machines superimposed one upon another—and with catchy

Ravielli, Anthony—*Continued*
labels, are also imaginative and effective. Distinguished in format." Horn Bk
"An excellent book for health and hygiene classes." Chicago. Children's Bk Center

Zim, Herbert S.
Bones; illus. by René Martin. Morrow 1969 63p illus lib. bdg. $4.32 (3-5)   611
1 Bones
ISBN 0-688-31115-6
"A sound, basic explanation of the composition and formation of bones and the parts and function of the human skeleton together with brief comments on the uses of bones, presented in Zim's usual simple lucid style." Booklist
The book "uses René Martin's drawings as pictures —that is, as tools for description—and uses them in striking style. You will never see anyone walking around with his skeleton visible in detail, but after reading this book you should have a pretty good idea of what a person's framework would look like if this were possible." Horn Bk

612   Human physiology

Adler, Irving
Taste, touch and smell [by] Irving and Ruth Adler. Day 1966 48p illus lib. bdg. $4.47 (3-5)   612
1 Senses and sensation
ISBN 0-381-99953-X
"The Reason why books"
The author describes how the senses of touch, smell and taste work through the nervous sytem. He also discusses the purpose served by each of these senses
"The vocabulary is sophisticated, precise, and will expand the language facility of the reader." Sch Library J
Word list: p47

Your ears [by] Irving and Ruth Adler; illus. by Peggy Adler Walsh. Day 1963 48p illus lib. bdg. $4.47 (3-5)   612
1 Ear 2 Hearing
ISBN 0-381-99948-3
"The Reason why books"
"The structure and physiology of the ear, the nature of sound, and the types of deafness are explored in this simple, concise account." Booklist
The authors discuss "deafness and some famous deaf people who have overcome the handicap. Readable text and clear illustrations." Hodges. Bks for Elem Sch Libraries

Your eyes [by] Irving and Ruth Adler. Day 1962 48p illus lib. bdg. $4.47 (3-5)   612
1 Eye 2 Vision
ISBN 0-381-99947-5
"The Reason why books"
"A text that comprises discussions of several aspects of sight: normal and abnormal eyesight, color blindness, education for the blind and the partially-sighted, optical illusions, and the structure and function of the human eye." Chicago. Children's Bk Center
"Illustrated with many diagrams and a few drawings and photographs. A glossary is appended." Booklist

Aliki
My five senses. Crowell 1962 unp illus (Let's-read-and-find-out science bks) $4.50, lib. bdg. $5.25, pa $1.25 (k-2)   612
1 Senses and sensation
ISBN 0-690-56762-6; 0-690-56763-4; 0-690-56768-5

"For beginning independent readers, a simply written book about the senses. The [author's] illustrations are lovely, and with light humor they capture a child's delight as he sniffs a flower and his bliss as, with eyes closed, he licks an ice cream cone. While readers will be already familiar with some of the facts established by the text, they will probably become more conscious of the fact that different senses combine in varied ways dependent on the activity at hand." Chicago. Children's Bk Center

Bendick, Jeanne
The human senses; written and illus. by Jeanne Bendick. Watts, F. 1968 70p illus (Science experiences) lib. bdg. $4.90 (3-5)   612
1 Senses and sensation
ISBN 0-531-01431-2
This book "acquaints the young reader with his five senses and how they work. The method is to ask exploratory questions and then lead the child to discover important facts about his world by using his senses and interpreting what they tell him. Basics of the physiology of vision, hearing, smell, touch, and taste are explained with appropriate imaginative diagrams and pictures." Sci Bks

Berry, James R.
Why you feel hot, why you feel cold; your body's temperature; illus. by William Ogden. Little 1973 48p illus lib. bdg. $4.95 (2-4)   612
1 Temperature 2 Fever
ISBN 0-316-09211-8
This book "explains why you feel hot and cold and why you may have a fever and chills, along with experiments that help explain the ideas. Large type. Helpful illustrations." Sci and Children

Brenner, Barbara
Bodies; with photographs and design by George Ancona. Dutton 1973 unp illus $5.95 (k-2)   612
1 Physiology
ISBN 0-525-26770-0
This book "points out the qualities that make the animal world different from plants or inanimate objects, briefly discusses the components of the human body (blood, flesh, skin, bones—all made of cells) and describes all the things people can do (run, jump, sleep, eliminate, eat, etc.)." Chicago. Children's Bk Center
"Brenner makes clear that though human skin and blood cells are similar, everyone does things in his own way. The crisp, skillfully assembled photographs (including two of undressed children and one of a child sitting on a toilet) are matched by the text which is mature in tone and presents factual material without condescension." Library J

Elgin, Kathleen
The human body: the brain; written and illus. by Kathleen Elgin. Watts, F. 1967 51p illus lib. bdg. $3.90 (3-5)   612
1 Brain 2 Nervous system
ISBN 0-531-01170-4
"This is a very simple introduction to the human brain. It is mainly a vocabulary identification of parts of the brain and how it controls the body functions. Due to oversimplification there is not an adequate explanation of current information on how the different parts of the brain operate. The superior capacity of the human brain over those of animals is pointed out. Illustrations are clear." Sch Library J

The human body: the digestive system; written and illus. by Kathleen Elgin. Watts, F. 1973 72p illus lib. bdg. $3.95 (4-6)   612

Elgin, Kathleen—*Continued*

1 Digestion
ISBN 0-531-01183-6
The digestive process is described from the time food enters the mouth to the excretion of waste materials. Medical terms for the parts of the digestive system are included in the text with pronunciations and definitions

The human body: the heart; written and illus. by Kathleen Elgin. Watts, F. 1968 50p illus lib. bdg. $3.90 (3-5) 612

1 Heart
ISBN 0-531-01174-7
The heart is the powerful pump that sends the blood stream on its way. This is an explanation of how that most critical muscle works to help move the nutrients and oxygen throughout the circulatory system
"An introduction to the topic that is limited in usefulness by some weaknesses of the illustrations, which are very handsome in design, but susceptible to confusion in the way color is used. . . . The text is clear; it is focused on a description of heart action rather than a complete description of the circulatory system." Chicago. Children's Bk Center

The human body: the muscles; written and illus. by Kathleen Elgin. Watts, F. 1973 71p illus lib. bdg. $3.90 (3-6) 612

1 Muscles
ISBN 0-531-01181-0
"The need for muscles in the human body, the types of muscles—smooth, cardiac, and skeletal— with which people are endowed, and a general description of how these work are covered in clear, concise language in the first third of the book. New terms are defined as they are introduced, and the name and pronunciation are given for each skeletal muscle described. A rather small number of pages of text and illustration . . . deal specifically with cardiac and smooth muscles. The remainder of the book is devoted to selected skeletal muscles. Location of the muscle in the body is illustrated, and function is explained. The author shows how people are able to smile, eat, swallow, move eyes, lift arms, use legs, breathe and perform numerous other physical activities by using muscles. Illustrations are simple uncomplicated line drawings, and these are used profusely. Children at intermediate and advanced elementary levels with a curiosity about human muscular activity should find this a helpful reference." Sci Bks

Goldin, Augusta

Straight hair, curly hair; illus. by Ed Emberley. Crowell 1966 unp illus (Let's-read-and-find-out Science bks) $4.50, lib. bdg. $5.25, pa $1.25 (k-2) 612

1 Hair
ISBN 0-690-77920-8; 0-690-77921-6; 0-690-77928-3
Also available in a Spanish language edition for $3.95 (ISBN 0-690-77922-4), lib. bdg $4.70 (ISBN 0-690-77923-2)
To explain why hair can be straight or curly, this "book tells about the cross-sectional shape of hair and about its follicles. It presents genuine experiments . . . [using] hair, Scotch tape, keys and some curiosity." Scientific Am
"An easy-to-read scientific explanation. . . . The humorous drawings add interest to a subject about which most children are curious." We Build Together

Heintze, Carl

The priceless pump: the human heart. Nelson 1972 128p illus $5.50 (6-7) 612

1 Heart 2 Blood—Circulation 3 Heart—Diseases

ISBN 0-8407-6150-3
"This is an excellent source of clear, concise information on all aspects of heart function and the interrelationships of the heart, lungs and circulatory system. Heintze also includes a brief history of man's knowledge of the heart anatomy, a survey of diseases of the heart and their causes, and up-to-date information on treatment of heart malfunctions. All medical and scientific terms are explicitly defined in the text." Sch Library J

Kalina, Sigmund

Your nerves and their messages; illus. by Arabellé Wheatley. Lothrop 1973 48p illus lib. bdg. $4.32 (3-5) 612

1 Nervous system
ISBN 0-688-50045-5
"Less inclusive and less difficult than the Silverstein's' 'The Nervous System: the Inner Networks' [entered below] this covers . . . brain structure, simple reflex acts, the nerve network, and the spinal cord." Sch Library J
"The illustrations, always appealing, are of two sorts: simple scenes in the daily life of children pointing to the function of the nervous system and technical illustrations of nerve cells, nerve pathways and portions of the nervous system. The well-written and accurate text stresses the basic functional unit of the nervous system, the reflex arc." Sci Bks

Riedman, Sarah R.

Hormones: how they work. Rev. ed. of Our hormones and how they work. Illus. by Norman Gorbaty. Abelard-Schuman 1973 222p illus $6.95 (6-7) 612

1 Hormones
ISBN 0-200-00005-5
First published 1956
"Explaining complex interconnections between systems of cells and tissues, organs, and organisms requires great patience, a gift for words, and an understanding of what a reader does or does not know. Dr. Riedman has done a creditable job. . . . She writes without the mawkishness characteristic of many books for young people. Beginning with the rather complex discovery of insulin and continuing through cyclic AMP and the prostaglandins, the author describes the discovery of hormones and their discoveries. . . . The technical aspects of the book, the line drawings in a diagrammatic style, the binding, and type style are good; a useful index is appended." Sci Bks

Schuman, Benjamin N.

The human eye; drawings by Michael K. Meyers. Atheneum Pubs. 1968 78p illus lib. bdg. $5.95 (4-6) 612

1 Eye 2 Vision
ISBN 0-689-20672-6
The author "explains the physiological development of the eye and interprets the phenomenon of sight in terms of the physical action of light. Excellent drawings are invaluable in the step-by-step explanations." Adventuring With Bks. 2d edition

Showers, Paul

A drop of blood; illus. by Don Madden. Crowell 1967 unp illus (Let's-read-and-find-out science bks) $4.50, lib. bdg. $5.25, pa $1.25 (1-3) 612

1 Blood
ISBN 0-690-24525-4; 0-690-24526-2; 0-690-24531-9
"Crisp, straightforward writing and gay, cartoon-like illustrations combine to make this introduction to the topic of human blood clear, simple, and accurate. The author describes circulation and the protective powers of the blood, the types of cells of which blood

Showers, Paul—*Continued*

is composed, and the reassuring fact that there is constant replenishment of the blood supply—although the details of this process are not given." Sutherland. The Best In Children's Bks

Hear your heart; illus. by Joseph Low. Crowell 1968 35p illus (Let's-read-and-find-out science bks) $4.50, lib. bdg. $5.25, pa $1.25 (k-3)   612
  1 Heart 2 Blood—Circulation
  ISBN 0-690-37378-3; 0-690-37379-1; 0-690-00636-5
"Simple, graphic sketches with text illustrate the mechanism of the heart, beating day and night, varying its pace with age and pumping blood out of the arteries into the veins. Included are experiments on hearing the heart beat thru a tube and on counting the pulse at given places." Bruno. Bks for Sch Libraries, 1968

How you talk; illus. by Robert Galster. Crowell [1967 c1966] unp illus (Let's-read-and-find-out science bks) $4.50, lib. bdg. $5.25, pa $1.25 (k-3) 612
  1 Speech 2 Sounds
  ISBN 0-690-42135-4; 0-690-42136-2; 0-690-00637-3
Simple experiments demonstrate "how humans use the lungs, larynx, mouth, tongue, lips, teeth, and nose to produce speech." Minnesota
"The text is simple, the animated drawings are uncomplicated, and the experiments included are both helpful and fun. Parents as well as teachers will find this useful." Booklist

Look at your eyes; illus. by Paul Galdone. Crowell 1962 unp illus (Let's-read-and-find-out science bks) $4.50, lib. bdg. $5.25 (k-2)   612
  1 Eye
  ISBN 0-690-50727-5; 0-690-50728-3
Also available in a Spanish language edition for $4.50 (ISBN 0-690-50729-1), lib. bdg. $5.25 (ISBN 0-690-50730-5)
"The young reader is asked to observe his eyes in a mirror as he reads about the human eyes and the specifics of eyecolor; the function of eyelids, eyebrows, and eyelashes; of tears; and the reason for the changes in size of the pupil." The AAAS Sci Bk List For Children
The book "is lucid in explaining basic facts . . . and the writing is not any more stilted than a book for beginning independent readers must be. It is unusual, also, in the simplicity with which the text and the illustrations show the speaker to be a Negro child; he is quite matter-of-fact about brown eyes, quite matter-of-fact about his friends, whose eyes may be blue or brown. And in the last illustrations, waiting in utter boredom for his mother to get back to the car from her shopping and then seeing his mother's smiling eyes between bundles, he is every child." Chicago. Children's Bk Center

Use your brain; illus. by Rosalind Fry. Crowell 1971 33p illus (Let's-read-and-find-out science bks) $4.50, lib. bdg. $5.25, pa $1.25 (1-3)   612
  1 Brain 2 Nervous system
  ISBN 0-690-85410-2; 0-690-85411-0; 0-690-00204-1
"A good introduction for the young reader, not going into too much detail but giving facts about the structure and function of the brain and some information about the rest of the nervous system. The text explains very simply the response to stimuli and the role of nerves; the illustrations are lively but less informative than the few diagrams. . . . Several pages are devoted to the effect of drugs on the efficiency of the nervous system." Chicago. Children's Bk Center

What happens to a hamburger; illus. by Anne Rockwell. Crowell 1970 33p illus (Let's-read-and-find-out science bks) $4.50, lib. bdg. $5.25 (1-3)   612
  1 Digestion
  ISBN 0-690-87540-1; 0-690-87541-X
This book explains how not only hamburgers but all things we eat are turned into bones and muscles and energy. Simple experiments are included
"A simple but quite adequate explanation of the digestive process, with attractive illustrations that only occasionally veer from the factual—such as a conventional heart-shaped symbol in a diagram of the circulatory system. The text does not give all the facts or terms (there is no mention of enzymes) and it does, in some instances, move into peripheral areas, but on the whole it is a competent, simplified treatment of a phenomenon about which most children are curious." Chicago. Children's Bk Center

Your skin and mine; illus. by Paul Galdone. Crowell 1965 unp illus (Let's-read-and-find-out science bks) $4.50, lib. bdg. $5.25, pa $1.25 (1-3)   612
  1 Skin
  ISBN   0-690-91126-2;   0-690-91127-0;   0-690-00205-X
Also available in a Spanish language edition for $4.50 (ISBN 0-690-91128-9), lib. bdg. $5.25 (ISBN 0-690-91129-7)
"The simple, brief text and attractive illustrations present the basic facts about skin and its functions, including color differences, the dermis and epidermis, hair follicles, pores, sensation and temperature adjustments, etc. The discussion of color differences and the use of boys of different color are natural parts of the text and illustrations. Large print and attractive format." We Build Together
"The information on skin color could be used to develop concepts in the area of racial understanding." Minnesota

Silverstein, Alvin

The digestive system; how living creatures use food, by Alvin Silverstein and Virginia B. Silverstein; illus. by Mel Erikson. Prentice-Hall 1970 74p illus $4.95 (4-7)   612
  1 Digestion
  ISBN 0-13-277152-7
"The book explains why digestion is necessary to all living organisms, describes the complex physical and chemical processes involved in human digestion, and compares human digestion with that of lower animals and plants. Difficult words are defined in the text with the pronunciation given the first time the word is used." Booklist
"Readers will need some acquaintance with chemistry and biology; diagrams are clearly drawn but not explicitly explained, nor is the scale indicated. One chapter discusses a balanced diet and the body's need for minerals and vitamins. The final one deals briefly with hunger in the world, the importance of protein in an infant's diet, and the search for new sources of food—but these vital issues call for greater emphasis. . . . This title will be useful since the subject is not treated this extensively elsewhere." Library J

The endocrine system; hormones in the living world [by] Alvin Silverstein and Virginia B. Silverstein; illus. by Mel Erikson. Prentice-Hall 1971 68p illus $4.95 (4-7)   612
  1 Glands, Ductless 2 Hormones
  ISBN 0-13-277152-7
This is an "account of the endocrine system and the effects of various hormones on the body. Covered are animal hormones, plant hormones, pheromones (hor-

Silverstein, Alvin—*Continued*

mones for communication), and hormone research."
Sch Library J

"This book is a concise and informative overview of endocrinal systems in living organisms. It should be most useful as a source for reports or for those students in search of material supplemental to classroom presentation. The format and print are excellent and highly readable. A table of contents and index are included. Scientific terminology is given phonetic pronunciation within the context when the term appears for the first time. The illustrations by Mel Erikson are adequate but not inspiring, mostly because of the publisher's decision to run them in black and white with one color." Appraisal

The nervous system; the inner networks [by] Alvin Silverstein and Virginia B. Silverstein; illus. by Mel Erikson. Prentice-Hall 1971 64p illus $4.95 (4-7)
612

1 Nervous system
ISBN 0-13-610964-0

"In addition to giving information on the structure and function of the brain, spinal cord, and neurons, the Silversteins compare the human nervous system with that of lower animals and touch on the problem of mental illness." Booklist

The authors "have skillfully employed the analogies of facets of telecommunications systems to assist in explaining the organization and functioning of the human central, peripheral, and autonomic nervous systems. The illustrations are closely integrated with the text and are well-labeled. Neurological terms are printed in italics and pronunciation is indicated immediately following the first use of a term in the book. . . . Throughout the book, insofar as the rather difficult material permits, the young reader is involved by asking him to perform certain exercises, and this device will maintain his interest." Sci Bks

The sense organs; our link with the world [by] Alvin Silverstein and Virginia B. Silverstein; illus. by Mel Erikson. Prentice-Hall 1971 73p illus $4.95 (4-7)
612

1 Senses and sensation
ISBN 0-13-806687-6

This book focuses "on the sense organs, describing the structure and function of human eyes, ears, nose, mouth, and skin receptors and comparing them briefly with those of other animals. The Silversteins also discuss the body's inner senses such as those that help maintain balance, perceive thirst and hunger; and give a number of simple experiments for the reader to perform." Booklist

"For the most part, information is adequate for the very young, but in some instances it is scanty, especially about the middle ear and the elimination of blind spots in our vision. Short chapters are arranged logically. Durable binding, attractive black-and-green illustrations, and large, readable type make for ideal format. The style is interesting and clear, and the book has a very good index." Appraisal

The skeletal system; frameworks for life [by] Alvin Silverstein and Virginia B. Silverstein; illus. by Lee J. Ames. Prentice-Hall 1972 74p illus $4.95 (4-7) 612

1 Bones
ISBN 0-13-812701-8

"The authors discuss the structure and function of the human skeleton, the growth and changes in the bone structure from birth to adulthood, the internal and external skeletons of other animals and insects, and the importance of fossilized bones in revealing information about past life on earth." Booklist

"An excellent introduction to basic anatomy. . . . The inclusion of standard terminology with good definitions as part of the text provides a stepping stone to more detailed works and introduces advanced concepts without 'talking down' to students. This reviewer highly recommends it as an addition to the general science resources shelf." Sci Bks

Simon, Seymour

About your heart; illus. by Angeline Culfogienis. McGraw [1975 c1974] 38p illus lib. bdg. $4.95 (2-4)
612

1 Heart 2 Blood—Circulation
ISBN 07-057440-5

"Let's-try-it-out"

This book describes the human heart and how it functions. Using simple projects, the reader learns about blood circulation and pulse rates, and how age and emotional stress effect them

"The illustrations are colorful, attractive, and explicate the text—with one exception, a diagram illustrating blood flow implies that all arteries are on one side of the body and veins on the other. Scientific labels are, however, kept to an encouraging minimum, making this a fine choice for younger students." Sch Library J

Zim, Herbert S.

Blood; illus. by René Martin. Morrow 1968 63p illus lib. bdg. $4.32 (4-6)
612

1 Blood
ISBN 0-688-31109-1

This study of blood describes its composition and the processes by which the body makes use of it. Other topics included are the uses of vaccines and antitoxins, beliefs and customs concerning blood, and an explanation of blood groups and the Rh factor

"This book is a clearly superior explanation of blood, its components and functions. . . . With few exceptions, the book is quite readable and comprehensible and the illustrations are generally useful in expanding the contents of the text." Appraisal

Our senses and how they work; illus. by Herschel Wartik. Morrow 1956 64p illus $4.75, lib. bdg. $4.32 (4-6)
612

1 Senses and sensation
ISBN 0-688-21550-5; 0-688-31550-X

"An introduction to the senses, what they are, details of the working of the five major senses, and the nervous system in general." Chicago. Children's Bk Center

"Interesting, and concise text with clear drawings. . . . Experiments are suggested." Library J

Your brain and how it works; illus. by René Martin. Morrow 1972 63p illus $4.75 (4-6)
612

1 Brain 2 Nervous system
ISBN 0-688-21922-5

"The author discusses the growth of the nervous system, its microscopic and macroscopic structure, the functions of its parts, and especially emphasizes interrelationships and interdependencies. He illustrates these with common experiences from daily life, thereby helping to develop a concept of mind. He offers a few standard exercises by which the reader can test his perception and finishes with a little wholesome advice which the development of his text has given him every right to offer. Illustrations, both diagrams and pictures, are helpful." Appraisal

Your stomach and digestive tract; illus. by René Martin. Morrow 1973 63p illus $4.75, lib. bdg. $4.32 (3-6)
612

1 Stomach 2 Digestion
ISBN 0-688-21838-5; 0-688-31838-X

"This step-by-step digestive tract tour assumes no prior knowledge of the area; Zim locates and describes

Zim, Herbert S.—*Continued*
the stomach and then backtracks to the mouth where the process begins. From there he traces the path of food from start to finish describes chemical actions along the way, and explains the hows and whys of two of the most common stomach disorders, vomiting and ulcers." Booklist
"Each step of the process is described clearly. . . . This explanation of man's alimentary canal, accompanied by black-and-white drawings, will complement the information found in the Silversteins' 'The Digestive System: How Living Creatures Use Food.' [entered above]. " Sch Library J

612.6 Reproduction, development, maturation

Andry, Andrew C.
How babies are made by Andrew C. Andry and Steven Schepp; illus. by Blake Hampton. Time-Life Bks. [distributed by Little] 1968 unp illus $5.95 (k-3)   612.6
1 Reproduction 2 Sex instruction
"The illustrations give clear physiological information about intercourse, pregnancy and birth, and the text moves from flowers to animals to humans in a brief commentary on each illustration." The AAAS Sci Bk List for Children
"Colorful paper cut-outs illustrate this introduction to reproduction." Princeton Pub Library. Hello, baby

Cole, Joanna
Twins; the story of multiple births, by Joanna Cole & Madeleine Edmondson; with drawings by Salvatore Raciti & photographs. Morrow 1972 64p illus lib. bdg. $4.14 (3-6)   612.6
1 Twins
ISBN 0-688-31981-5
"Beginning with an explanation of the difference between fraternal and identical twins, the authors examine the biological development of twins, Siamese twins and supertwins, discuss the relationship between twins as they grow up, and tell of the importance of twins to scientists studying the effects of heredity and environment on human development. The informative wide-ranging account is enlivened by anecdotes and illustrated with numerous photographs and drawings." Booklist

Day, Beth
The secret world of the baby, by Beth Day and Margaret Liley; illus. with photographs by Lennart Nilsson, Susanne Szasz, and others. Random House 1968 113p illus $3.95, lib. bdg. $5.69   612.6
1 Embryology 2 Infants 3 Sex instruction
ISBN 0-394-81555-6; 0-394-91555-0
"From conception through the first few months after birth the baby's physical development and his changing responses are explored." Princeton Pub Library. Hello, baby
"In this successful collaboration by a pediatrician and a layman, a simply written, authoritative text is given added usefulness by photographs of the infant in utero and added charm by photographs of a newborn and very young babies. . . . The final chapters —on the infant's ways of communicating and on the evidences of mental and physical growth—are particularly interesting." Sutherland. The Best in Children's Bks

De Schweinitz, Karl
Growing up; how we become alive, are born, and grow. 4th ed. Macmillan (N Y) 1965 54p illus $4.50, pa 95¢ (2-5)   612.6
1 Reproduction 2 Sex instruction
First published 1928
An account of the processes of procreation, birth, and early growth. "Well written and thoroughly treated, this book explores the birth process in animals before introducing life and its beginning in humans. Information is treated honestly, simply, and without awkwardness. The photographs accompanying the text have been carefully selected and are in good taste." Adventuring With Bks. 2d edition

Elgin, Kathleen
Twenty-eight days [by] Kathleen Elgin [and] John F. Osterritter; illus. by Kathleen Elgin. McKay 1973 56p illus $4.50 (5-7)   612.6
1 Menstruation
The authors recount the cultural and religious myths and taboos surrounding the menstrual cycle. "Anatomical diagrams and explanations of the reproductive organs are offered, as are discussions of such topics as the menstrual cycle from start to finish, cramps and their alleviation, hormonal changes, and emotional stress." Booklist
Glossary: p53-54

Gordon, Sol
Facts about sex for today's youth. Rev. ed. Illus. by Vivien Cohen. Day 1973 48p illus $4.50, pa $1.90 (6-7)   612.6
1 Sex instruction
ISBN 0-381-99647-6
First published 1969 by the Printing House of Charles Brown with title: Facts about sex for exceptional youth. The 1970 edition by Day had title: Facts about sex; a basic guide
"Brief, straightforward, realistic, and with no moralizing, this . . . [book] covers anatomy, human sexual needs and fulfillment, deviation and sex problems, as well as answers to ten questions frequently asked. . . . Topics often not touched by other books on sex—slang terms, methods of contraception, and explanations of articles used during menstruation— are included. While he does not advocate premarital sex, Gordon recognizes its existence and that knowledge about it is a necessary protection." Sch Library J
"The bibliography is very good, and the book is excellent in every way—brief and to the point." Appraisal

Gruenberg, Sidonie Matsner
The wonderful story of how you were born; with illus. by Symeon Shimin. [Rev. ed] Doubleday 1970 unp illus $4.50, lib. bdg. $5.25 (k-5)   612.6
1 Reproduction 2 Sex instruction
ISBN 0-385-03674-4; 0-385-03680-9
First published 1952 by Hanover House, with illustrations by Hildegard Woodward
The author explains the facts of conception, birth and sexual development of the human being
"Suitable [for] reading to the child from 4 to 7 years of age and for the child to read by himself at least to age 10. The terminology is simple and accurate. The illustrations are excellent and add considerably to the general tone of the presentation. There is an extra bonus in the form of a 'Guide to parents.' The author also provides a listing of other books and information sources." The AAAS Sci Bk List for Children

May, Julian

How we are born. Follett 1969 48p illus (Follett Family life education program) lib. bdg. $3.42 (4-6)
612.6

1 Reproduction 2 Embryology 3 Sex instruction
ISBN 0-695-43955-3

Illustrations by Michael Hampshire

"The lucid text and colorful photographs and drawings in this book . . . provide comprehensive, factual information on reproduction and sex for children. . . . The present book traces the human reproductive process from fertilization of the ovum to birth. A glossary is appended." Booklist

Man and woman. Follett 1969 46p illus (Follett Family life education program) lib. bdg. $3.48 (4-6)
612.6

1 Sex instruction
ISBN 0-695-45517-6

Illustrations by Tak Murakami

"Distinctive differences between the sexes and the physical and social aspects of being male or female are explained. The importance of love and concern in both physical relationships and in family life is also stressed." Booklist

Glossary: p46

A new baby comes; illus. by Brendan Lynch. Creative Educ. Soc. 1970 unp illus lib. bdg. $4.95 (1-4)
612.6

1 Reproduction 2 Embryology 3 Sex instruction
ISBN 0-87191-033-0

An account of the prenatal development of a baby from ovum to birth in simple text and illustrations

"Worthwhile are actual-size sketches of the embryo through the first five months. Emphasized are the family's preparations for the coming of the baby and, finally, pictures of the baby's growth stages to womanhood with a baby of her own." Appraisal

Portal, Colette

The beauty of birth; adapted from the French by Guy Daniels. Knopf 1971 26p illus $3.95, lib. bdg. $4.99 (3-6)
612.6

1 Reproduction 2 Embryology 3 Sex instruction
ISBN 0-394-82287-0; 0-394-92287-5

"Delicate and precise watercolor illustrations show the development of a baby in utero, from ovulation and conception through the embryonic and fetal stages to parturition. Especially interesting are the pages on which the author-artist shows the growth of individual anatomical features such as the hand, changing from a knobbly bud to the articulated perfection of an infant's hand. The text is accurate, straightforward, and lucid." Sutherland. The Best in Children's Bks

Sheffield, Margaret

Where do babies come from? Illus. by Sheila Bewley. Knopf 1973 [c1972] 33p illus $4.95 (k-3) 612.6

1 Reproduction 2 Sex instruction
ISBN 0-394-48482-7

First published 1972 in England

Based on a BBC program used throughout the British primary school system, this book is designed to answer the "questions young children pose about how the sperm fertilizes the egg, how it gets into the mother's body, and how the baby gets out. Nearly all the paintings show nude people—infants, a prepubescent boy and girl, grown lovers, a pregnant mother, a baby growing inside the woman's body, a newborn having the cord cut, and finally, a clothed young couple with their new infant." Sch Library J

"The information is given in serious, forthright style, with all the facts included and with the use of correct terminology. What makes this book different from (and, for the most part, better than) other such books is the tone; without a specific reference to the beauty and intricacy of birth, the mood of reverence for life is created in a harmonious complementing of text and illustration." Chicago. Children's Bk Center

Showers, Paul

A baby starts to grow; illus. by Rosalind Fry. Crowell 1969 33p illus (Let's-read-and-find-out science bks) $4.50, lib. bdg. $5.25, pa $1.25 (k-2)
612.6

1 Embryology
ISBN 0-690-11319-6; 0-690-11320-X; 0-690-11325-0

Unlike Showers' other book: Before you were a baby, entered below, this book does not begin with a description of the sexual act leading to conception. It does, however, "go into greater detail on embryonic growth, in a simple, clear, accurate text accompanied by lively illustrations. The material is very basic and much simplified, the format definitely juvenile, making this unsuitable for use beyond the second grade." Sch Library J

Before you were a baby, by Paul Showers and Kay Sperry Showers; illus. by Ingrid Fetz. Crowell 1968 33p illus (Let's-read-and-find-out-science bks) $4.50, lib. bdg. $5.25 (1-3)
612.6

1 Reproduction 2 Embryology 3 Sex instruction
ISBN 0-690-12881-9; 0-690-12882-7

"Here is a well-illustrated book of human reproduction that begins with a description of the sex organs and the process of fertilization. Then it describes the initial stages of cell division, implantation, gastrulations, and weekly stages in development until about 10 weeks when the foetus is fully formed. There is an excellent colored illustration of each stage; also of the four, six, and eight month old foetus, and finally the birth occurs." Sci Bks

"Without fanfare, mystery, coyness, or superfluous information, this gives the facts . . . in a format that is attractive and in language that is clear and simple. The illustrations of children are beguiling, the diagrams helpful, and the print large; the writing is lucid and matter-of-fact." Sat Rev

Strain, Frances Bruce

Being born; completely new and rev. Hawthorn Bks. 1970 134p illus $4.95 (4-7)
612.6

1 Reproduction 2 Sex instruction
ISBN 0-8015-0588-7

First published 1936 by Appleton

This handbook of sex instruction, illustrated with numerous photographs and diagrams, discusses reproduction and birth, including heredity and prenatal development

Partial contents: Where the egg is made; Where the sperm is made; The baby workshop; From embryo to baby; Coming into the world; The milk supply; Mating and marrying

A list of words and their meanings: p127-34

613.7   Physical fitness

Antonacci, Robert J.

Physical fitness for young champions [by] Robert J. Antonacci and Jene Barr; illus. by Frank Mullins. 2d ed. McGraw 1975 144p illus lib. bdg. $6.84 (5-7)
613.7

1 Physical fitness 2 Exercise
ISBN 0-07-002142-2

Antonacci, Robert J.—*Continued*

First published 1962

After describing ways of testing physical fitness using the Kraus-Weber Test and the President's Youth Physical Fitness Test, the author describes exercises to develop muscle strength, coordination, and speed and suggests activities for keeping fit. Exercise advice for the physically and mentally handicapped is included

Carr, Rachel

Be a frog, a bird, or a tree; Rachel Carr's creative yoga exercises for children; photographs by Edward Kimball, Jr. Illus. by Don Hedin. Doubleday 1973 95p illus $5.95, lib. bdg. $6.70 (1-4)   613.7

1 Yoga 2 Exercise

ISBN 0-385-003390-0; 0-385-02358-8

"An excellent introduction to yoga for children begins with a brief explanation and suggestions for starting exercises, proceeding with a two-page spread for each of 30 poses: the first page has inspiring photographs of children taking the position, and the opposite page has a drawing of the animal or object for which the position is named, such as the cat or hare, and underneath it a simple first-person description of the movements and feelings involved." Booklist

"An appended section of notes for parents and teachers describes working with children, gives instructions for using the book, and—a useful addition—explains what each exercise accomplishes." Chicago. Children's Bk Center

Cheki Haney, Erene

Yoga for children, by Erene Cheki Haney and Ruth Richards; illus. by Betty Schilling. Bobbs 1973 unp illus $5.95 (2-5)   613.7

1 Yoga 2 Exercise

ISBN 0-672-51801-5

A "beginner's handbook [which] teaches 16 poses for an overall body stretch, emphasizing in the introduction the importance of never competing or straining and always relaxing after each exercise. . . . Most of the poses have a double-page spread, the first with a drawing demonstrating similarities between the animal and the yoga position and the other with instructions and illustrative drawings of how to do the exercise." Booklist

"A clearly written yoga manual which is unfortunately marred by an unappealing format. The detailed, step-by-step instructions given for each pose are simple enough for children to follow without adult assistance. However, the orange-and-black drawings portray bug-eyed children with splayed hands and crooked legs joined by stock animals who are supposedly doing the same exercises." Sch Library J

Showers, Paul

Sleep is for everyone; illus. by Wendy Watson. Crowell 1974 33p illus (Let's-read-and-find-out science bks) $3.95 (k-2)   613.7

1 Sleep

ISBN 0-690-00424-9

The author "writes with simplicity and smoothness about an intricate subject. His text discusses the ways in which different forms of living things sleep, the fact that people need sleep and that their behavior becomes aberrant when they feel that need strongly, and that the amount of sleep needed varies among individuals. The illustrations are attractive, adding humor especially to a description of an experiment in which four scientists stayed awake as long as they could. Nicely done." Chicago. Children's Bk Center

Turner, Alice K.

Yoga for beginners; photographs by Meryl Joseph. Watts, F. 1973 64p illus lib. bdg. $3.45 (6-7) 613.7

1 Yoga 2 Exercise

ISBN 0-531-02643-4

"A Concise guide"

"In a book that can be used at home or in conjunction with classes, the author writes enthusiastically and clearly about the disciplines and rewards of 'hatha-yoga'. The reader learns about the history of yogic 'asanas' (positions), exercises that were developed and practiced in India over a thousand years ago. Photographs accompany a text which tells precisely how to perform all the exercises in a beginner's course. A final chapter gives suggestions for further study." Pub W

613.8 Addictions and health

Gorodetzky, Charles W.

What you should know about drugs [by] Charles W. Gorodetzky and Samuel T. Christian. Harcourt 1970 121p illus $5.95 (5-7)   613.8

1 Drugs 2 Narcotic habit

ISBN 0-15-295510-0

"Curriculum-related books"

"Although this gives enough coverage to be useful to adults it is so simply written that it serves as an excellent source of information for the young reader. Separate chapters describe the origins, effects, uses, and abuses of narcotics, marijuana, hallucinogens, sedatives, stimulants, alcohol, and organic solvents such as those found in glue. The tone is dispassionate, the style straightforward. Tables give the generic, trade, and slang names for stimulants and sedatives; a glossary of terms and a relative index are appended." Chicago. Children's Bk Center

"The book refrains from moralizing. . . . The most refreshing aspect of the volume is that it has no axe to grind—its purpose is merely to inform." N Y Times Bk Rev

Hyde, Margaret O.

(ed.) Mind drugs. 3d ed. McGraw 1974 190p $4.95, lib. bdg. $4.72 (5-7)   613.8

1 Drug abuse 2 Drugs

ISBN 0-07-031633-3; 0-07-031634-1

First published 1968

Chapters by the editor and by other contributors describe the social, psychological, and physical effects of marihuana, alcohol, LSD, heroin, and barbiturates. Alternatives to drug abuse are discussed

Suggestions for further reading: p147-49. "Drug"-related terms: p151-59

614.7 Environmental sanitation and comfort. Pollution control

Elliott, Sarah M.

Our dirty air; illus. with photographs. Messner 1971 64p illus lib. bdg. $4.29 (3-5)   614.7

1 Air—Pollution

ISBN 0-671-32468-3

"Car exhaust fumes and factories pollute the air, endangering lives and speeding deterioration of property, while chemical sprays kill or injure animals and plants. The text explains some of the measures that can be taken to alleviate the situation, and suggests ways in which young children can help. Succinct and business-like, this is one of the best of several books on the subject for younger readers." Sat Rev

Elliott, Sarah M.—*Continued*

Our dirty water; illus. with photographs; maps and drawings by the author. Messner 1973 64p illus maps lib. bdg. $4.79 (4-6)   614.7

1 Water—Pollution
ISBN 0-671-32576-0

"The causes of water pollution, the dangers of using dirty water, and the actions being taken to rectify the situation are clearly presented in this well-organized treatment accompanied by black-and-white photographs. Weak, laxly enforced anti-pollution laws on the national and local level, industrial lobbying against such laws, and campaign money given to politicians by big business are mentioned. However, while some industries are identified as major polluters, specific companies are not named. A final chapter includes questions about community treatment plants, an experiment for testing fresh water sources, and other suggestions. Unfortunately, the biological process involved in pollution is scarcely mentioned." Sch Library J

Hyde, Margaret O.

For pollution fighters only; illus. by Don Lynch. McGraw 1971 157p illus $4.95, lib. bdg. $4.72 (5-7)   614.7

1 Pollution 2 Conservation of natural resources
ISBN 0-07-031628-7; 0-07-031629-5

The author "points out the effect of pollution on various ecological systems, discusses the problems of controlling pollution, gives examples of action which has been taken, and suggests positive ways in which the reader can help either as an individual or as part of a group. The loosely organized but persuasive person-to-person account includes suggestions on how to organize a community awareness action program, names and addresses of organizations concerned with conservation and ecology and of state pollution agencies." Booklist

Leaf, Munro

Who cares? I do; written and illus. by Munro Leaf. Lippincott 1971 unp illus lib. bdg. $3.95, pa $2.25 (k-2)   614.7

1 Refuse and refuse disposal 2 Pollution
ISBN 0-397-31521-X; 0-397-31276-8

"As the reader proceeds through this book, he is presented with full-page photographs of horrendous acts of vandalism or littering. On the page facing this environmental obscenity are a few lines of text and a simple sketch of two bewildered observers." Appraisal

"The text is very easy to read and understand, and the illustrations aid in making each point. The photographs are striking, and, in Leaf's usual style, many of the line drawings are clever. The ideas and suggestions are simple enough for young children to follow. While the format of the book isn't very inspiring, it does make its point." Sch Library J

Marshall, James, 1933-

Going to waste; where will all the garbage go? Consultant: Glenn Paulson. Coward, McCann & Geoghegan 1972 92p illus (The New conservation) lib. bdg. $4.99 (5-7)   614.7

1 Refuse and refuse disposal
ISBN 0-698-30427-6

The author "discusses knowledgeably and with supporting statistics the problems caused by the accumulation of solid waste in America. Concentrating on municipal rather than industrial waste he explains current methods which are both costly and inadequate, of collection and disposal, describes such alternatives as composting and recycling, and tells what individuals can do to help combat the problem. In conclusion he asserts that not only should old laws be revised and new ones passed but that the federal government should devote more attention and money to solving the problems of waste accumulation and disposal." Booklist

Milgrom, Harry

ABC of ecology; photographs and design by Donald Crews. Macmillan (N Y) 1972 unp illus $4.95 (k-2)   614.7

1 Pollution 2 Alphabet books

" 'ABC of Ecology' is a somewhat deceptive title; the book deals specifically with urban pollution, not ecology. It runs through the alphabet (A atmosphere, B bottle, etc.) making a brief statement about each example and asking a question or suggesting an activity for the reader. The author has relied heavily on visual impact, using strong black and white pictures and occasionally two colors in the layout. In the back is a section for parents and teachers describing the conditions to be stressed with the child reader. This allows even the most uninformed adult to deal effectively with the subject." Sci Bks

Showers, Paul

Where does the garbage go? Illus. by Loretta Lustig. Crowell 1974 33p illus (Let's-read-and-find-out science bks) $3.95, lib. bdg. $4.70 (1-3)   614.7

1 Refuse and refuse disposal
ISBN 0-690-00392-7; 0-690-00402-8

"Problems of sanitation, conservation, and recycling are seen from the child's viewpoint. . . . The child points out that it's different in the country: garbage goes to the pigs and trash is buried. After discussing the problems of the mess and the vermin of city dumps, the pollution of water from garbage, and the possibilities of separating garbage components for recycling, the text comes back to the child's viewpoint. One can help by making less trash and one can mend old toys." Chicago. Children's Bk Center

"The illustrations are an excellent addition to a good book on the important role that garbage plays in the life cycle of the community." Sci Teacher

Shuttlesworth, Dorothy E.

Clean air—sparkling water; the fight against pollution. Doubleday 1968 95p illus $4.95, lib. bdg. $5.70, pa 95¢ (3-6)   614.7

1 Air—Pollution 2 Water
ISBN 0-385-00979-8; 0-385-03052-5; 0-385-05362-2

The author explains the causes and dangers of air and water pollution in parallel accounts which describe the experiences of a hypothetical city and town situated on opposite sides of a river. She points out the worldwide scope of the problem and discusses current and possible future methods of combating pollution." Booklist

A good treatment "that will be used for units on conservation. . . . The black-and-white photographs are fine complements to the clear text." Sch Library J

Litter—the ugly enemy; an ecology story, by Dorothy E. Shuttlesworth with Thomas Cervasio. Doubleday 1973 61p illus $5.95, lib. bdg. $6.70 (3-5)   614.7

1 Refuse and refuse disposal
ISBN 0-385-01698-0; 0-385-06364-4

The author "describes the progress of Ralph and Rita as they and their classmates embark on a campaign to make their city more beautiful. This takes them through many facets of the garbage problem— its causes, methods of removal, citizen's options for action, community organizing, preventative measures and recycling." Appraisal

"As an introduction to the problem for middle grad-

Shuttlesworth, Dorothy E.—*Continued*
ers, this succeeds in providing practical suggestions
for action, though, unfortunately, the photographs do
little to enlarge the text." Sch Library J

Sootin, Harry
Easy experiments with water pollution; drawings
by Lucy Bitzer. Four Winds 1974 109p illus $5.50, lib.
bdg. $5.12 (5-7)   614.7
1 Water—Pollution 2 Water—Purification 3 Science—Experiments
"The text follows water treatment from the removal
of solids through chlorination and water softening to
aeration. Biodegradability is discussed, as are toxic
metals. Septic tanks are the subject of the final
chapter." Sci Teacher
"In this well-illustrated, well-written guide . . .
Harry Sootin has developed some clever ideas for
science experiments. The teacher can perform them
as classroom demonstrations, or the individual student can perform the described tasks himself. Using a cookbook approach, the author directs the students step-
by-step through a proper and safe way of illustrating
water pollution. Many thought-provoking questions
are asked. The eight basic experiments are lavishly
illustrated in easy to see and understand sketches."
Sci Bks
Glossary: p100-02. Further reading: p103-04

Tannenbaum, Beulah
Clean air, by Beulah Tannenbaum and Myra Stillman; illus. by Marta Cone. McGraw [1974 c1973] 64p
illus maps (Science in the city) lib. bdg. $4.72 (3-5)
                                                614.7
1 Air—Pollution
ISBN 0-07-062892-0
"A clearly written text with a positive approach to
understanding air pollution and its prevention. The
worst pollutants of our air—smoke, soot, sulphur
dioxide, and hydrocarbons—are discussed in separate
sections showing each one's chemical and biological
effect and describing preventive and curative measures in which industry, government, and individuals
should engage. Easy experiments to do in the home or
classroom help to demonstrate some important chemical reactions; a short list of needed equipment and
answers to questions raised during the experiments
are appended. Illustrated with helpful black-and-
white drawings." Booklist

614.8   Safety (Accidents and their prevention)

Gore, Harriet Margolis
What to do when there's no one but you; illus. by
David Lindroth. Prentice-Hall 1974 48p illus $4.95
(2-5)   614.8
1 First aid
ISBN 0-13-955070-4
Through a series of fictional episodes "first aid
treatments for 26 common household accidents are
explained sensibly and easily. The brief text and cartoon drawings treat knife cuts, nose bleeds, burns,
scrapes, eye injuries, etc. The book concludes with an
excellent explanation of artificial resuscitation by the
nose and mouth methods and an index lists all of the
injuries alphabetically." Sch Library J
"The recommended treatment is good medical
practice. The physician will especially appreciate the

frequently repeated advice that in some situations
medical consultation is absolutely necessary. . . . The
language is simple and often spiced with prankish
remarks. There is no lecturing or preaching, yet children will understand that many accidents are their
own fault. The imaginative illustrations intensify the
usefulness of the text." Sci Bks

Shapp, Martha
Let's find out about safety, by Martha and Charles
Shapp; pictures by Carolyn Bentley. Rev. full color
ed. Watts, F. 1975 40p illus lib. bdg. $4.90 (k-2)
                                                614.8
1 Accidents—Prevention
ISBN 0-531-00102-4
First published 1964
"An easy-to-read story about safety at home, at
school, and on the streets." Hodges. Bks for Elem Sch
Libraries
"Carolyn Bentley's bright pastel drawings spark up
this [book]." Sch Library J
Vocabulary list: p40

615   Pharmacology and therapeutics

Zim, Herbert S.
Medicine; illus. by Judith Hoffman Corwin.
Morrow 1974 62p illus $4.50, lib. bdg. $4.14 (4-6)
                                                615
1 Drugs
ISBN 0-688-21786-9; 0-688-31786-3
"Not a survey of the field of medicine but of medicinal products, this discusses the various ways in which
medicines are used (taken by mouth, injected by a
hypodermic syringe, etc.) and the care with which
dosage is decided. Zim describes the dangers of careless use of over-the-counter drugs, while recognizing
the usefulness of these for the treatment and relief of
symptoms and minor illnesses; he discusses such
groups of drugs as antibiotics, tranquilizers, anesthetics, analgesics, etc., in relation to the illnesses for
which they are prescribed. The book contains much
sensible advice, and the material is authoritative and
well organized; the writing style is not difficult to read
because of complexity, but it is sedate and the pages
quite solid with close although large print. A single-
page index is appended." Chicago. Children's Bk
Center

616   Diseases

Cobb, Vicki
How the doctor knows you're fine; illus. by
Anthony Ravielli. Lippincott 1973 48p illus lib. bdg.
$4.95 (2-4)   616
1 Medicine
ISBN 0-397-31240-7
The author "explains the procedure of and reasons
for each portion of a medical examination from the
'outside'—posture, height, skin condition, and geni-
tals—to the 'inside'—eyes, ears, nose, heart and
lungs. Diagrams are drawn and labelled to give a
general understanding of human anatomy." Booklist
"The illustrations are clear, informative and greatly
extend the text." Sch Library J

616.01   Medical microbiology

Asimov, Isaac
How did we find out about germs? Illus. by David Wool. Walker & Co. 1974 64p illus $4.95, lib. bdg. $4.85 (5-7)   616.01
1 Bacteriology—History 2 Microbiology—History
ISBN 0-8027-6165-8; 0-8027-6166-6
This "survey of man's expanding knowledge of germs touches on such highlights as the first microscope, the discovery of bacteria, the theory of spontaneous generation and the experiments by Spallanzani and Pasteur that disproved it. The text also discusses antisepsis and disease, vaccination, and viruses." Chicago. Children's Bk Center
The author "presents the usually dull secondary school biology background material in a readable and fascinating style. The book is simply written yet to the point scientifically. It avoids extraneous terminology and provides information about the origin of the basic terms which are included. Further, longer words are pronounced in a simplified fashion, a boon to the reader encountering them for the first time. A number of halftone illustrations complement the text." Sci and Children

616.9   Other diseases

Hyde, Margaret
VD: the silent epidemic. McGraw 1973 63p illus $4.95, lib. bdg. $4.72 (5-7)   616.9
1 Venereal diseases
ISBN 0-07-031637-6; 0-07-031638-4
"The text describes the major kinds of venereal diseases, their symptoms, their treatment, and the manner in which they are transmitted, and discusses some of the campaigns of help and information that have been mounted by official agencies and volunteers." Chicago. Children's Bk Center
"Hyde's factual approach to venereal disease avoids scare tactics and preaching and provides a very readable account. . . . Intelligent parents should encourage their children to become familiar with the information in this book, and it is a good supplementary source for physical education and hygiene courses." Sci Bks

617   Surgery and related topics

Kay, Eleanor
The operating room; illus. with photographs. Watts, F. 1970 62p illus. lib. bdg. $3.90 (4-7)   617
1 Surgery 2 Hospitals
ISBN 0-531-00690-5
"A First book"
Companion volume to: The emergency room, entered in class 362.1
"Well-organized and written in a concise and competent style, a book that describes the techniques, the tools, the procedures and the purposes of the operative sequence: preparation, the operation itself, and post-operative care. The author also describes the purposes of laboratory tests, hygienic precautions, etc. and introduces the hospital staff members the patient will meet. A useful and informative book; a list of some terms used in the operating room and an index are appended." Chicago. Children's Bk Center

617.6   Dentistry

Barr, George
Young scientist and the dentist; illus. by Mildred Waltrip. McGraw 1970 160p illus lib. bdg. $4.72 (5-7)   617.6
1 Dentistry
ISBN 0-07-003830-9
"In a clear, nontechnical text supplemented by many labeled diagrams, the author . . . describes the structure and function of teeth and explains the techniques and devices utilized by dentists in the preservation and restoration of teeth. Barr covers important advances in the history of dentistry as well as current methods of treatment and guidelines for personal tooth care and touches on dentistry as a profession." Booklist

617.8   Otology and audiology

Levine, Edna S.
Lisa and her soundless world; illus. by Gloria Kamen. Human Sciences Press 1974 unp illus $4.95 (1-3)   617.8
1 Deafness 2 Deaf
ISBN 0-87705-104-6
"Intended to help children understand deafness, this focuses on eight-year-old Lisa whose disability is undetected until a doctor diagnoses it. Levine presents useful facts about how the deaf learn to speak and hear in special schools (through hearing aids, lip reading, feeling vibrations in the throat, sign language) and encourages readers to perform simple exercises that promote awareness of what a deaf person experiences." Sch Library J
"The book accomplishes several things: it makes the deaf child's plight explicit, it makes clear the difficulty a deaf child has in learning to speak, it explains why a child so handicapped may feel angry and unloved, and it stresses the fact that the halting speech of the deaf may be governed by physical limitations, that it is not due to a lack of intelligence." Chicago. Children's Bk Center

621.32   Illumination and lighting

Corbett, Scott
What makes a light go on? Pictures by Len Darwin. Little 1966 56p illus lib. bdg. $4.95 (3-5)   621.32
1 Electric lighting 2 Electricity
ISBN 0-316-15703-1
"An Atlantic Monthly Press book"
"Beginning with electric charges of atomic particles, the text develops a clear understanding of the flow of electrons within wires, flashlights, light bulbs, and even generators. Includes . . . explanations of volts, watts, and other measures of current flow. The emphasis is on understanding of electricity as a form of energy rather than on its application, for example, the role of switches and insulation in controlling the flow of electrons." Sch Library J
"The illustrations are very clear, well placed, and adequately captioned. Mr. Corbett uses lucid analogies and familiar phenomena. . . . The terminology is accurate but is never more complex than is necessary; the text includes a discussion of the

Corbett, Scott—*Continued*

necessity for caution and precaution. A combined index and glossary is appended." Sutherland. The Best in Children's Bks

621.381   Electronic engineering

Bendick, Jeanne

Electronics for young people; including automation, computers, communications, microcircuits, lasers, and more. New 5th ed. by Jeanne Bendick and R. J. Lefkowitz; illus. by Jeanne Bendick. McGraw 1973 206p illus lib. bdg. $4.72 (5-7)   621.381
    1 Electronics
    ISBN 0-07-004495-3
First published 1944 with title: Electronics for boys and girls
This book traces the development of electronics from experiments conducted 2600 years ago to modern technological advances. It describes concepts and operations of electrons, electron tubes, different kinds of waves, transistors, microelectronic circuits, lasers, computers, phototubes, phototransistors, radio and television. It also discusses applications in the health, science and telecommunication fields
    Electronic terms: p187-99

612.382   Wire telegraphy

Nathan, Adele Gutman

The first transatlantic cable; illus. by Denver Gillen. Random House 1959 180p illus maps lib. bdg. $4.27 (5-7)   621.382
    1 Cables, Submarine 2 Field, Cyrus West
    ISBN 0-394-90388-9
    "Landmark books"
"Communication across the Atlantic Ocean becomes reality in this story of the men who through belief and perseverance made ocean cables possible." Adventuring with Bks. 2d edition

621.385   Wire telephony

Darwin, Len

What makes a telephone work? Written and illus. by Len Darwin. Little 1970 58p illus lib. bdg. $4.50 (3-6)   621.385
    1 Telephone
    ISBN 0-316-17352-5
    "An Atlantic Monthly Press book"
A basic experiment using a homemade tin can and string telephone demonstrates the principles of the transmission and reception of sound. The author then moves on to the more complex equipment, detailing those instruments involved in dialing and handling calls. The emphasis is on achieving an understanding of the basic principles of sound and an appreciation of the delicate and complex human ear
    "The vocabulary is intended for a fourth grade level, but the illustrations appear more appropriate for a sixth or seventh grader. While this is something of a disadvantage for the younger reader, it does improve its interest to the more advanced student. In almost every instance, however, the written descriptions are accurate and very well done." Sci Bks
    Glossary: p55-58

O'Connor, Jerome J.

The telephone: how it works. Putnam 1971 94p illus (How it works) lib. bdg. $4.29 (5-7)   621.385
    1 Telephone
    ISBN 0-399-60624-6
The author "describes the operation and function of each part of the telephone, discusses manual and automatic central offices, and concludes with a look at modern methods of voice transmission. Illustrated with photographs, drawings, and diagrams." Booklist
    Glossary: p87-91

621.4   Heat engineering and prime movers

Limburg, Peter R.

Engines. Watts, F. [1970 c1969] 86p illus lib. bdg. $3.90 (5-7)   621.4
    1 Engines 2 Power (Mechanics)
    ISBN 0-531-00705-7
    "A First book"
"This book provides chapters devoted to internal combustion engines, diesel, steam, turbine, and jet engines, and to the problem of classification of engines and some speculation on engines of the future." The AAAS Science Bk List for Children
    Bibliography: p81

Weiss, Harvey

Motors and engines and how they work. Crowell 1969 62p illus $5.50 (5-7)   621.4
    1 Power (Mechanics) 2 Engines
    ISBN 0-690-56478-3
The author discusses the different kinds of motors and engines in today's world. He combines text, photographs, and drawings to illustrate the complexities of the principles and operation of: water engines; wind engines; gravity engines; spring engines; steam engines; electric motors; gasoline engines; jet and rocket engines
    "The clear accurate text is illustrated with diagrams and photographs. Of practical value to the mechanically minded and useful for science projects." Booklist

621.43   Internal-combustion engines

Corbett, Scott

What about the Wankel engine? Illus. by Jerome Kühl. Four Winds 1974 72p illus $6.50 (4-7) 621.43
    1 Wankel engine 2 Gas and oil engines
    ISBN 0-590-07369-9
"Corbett covers the development, advantages, and future use of the Wankel rotary engine. . . . [An] explanation of the mechanics of the Wankel engine is also given with a comparison to the piston engine." Sch Library J
    "Clarifying diagrams are well-drawn, labeled, and usually on corresponding pages of descriptive text. The advantages and disadvantages of both engines are reviewed briefly, as well as the past and potential development of other types. Glossary appended." Booklist

Edmonds, I. G.

Jet and rocket engines: how they work. Putnam 1973 96p illus (How it works) lib. bdg. $4.29 (5-7)
          621.43

Edmonds, I. G.—*Continued*

1 Jet propulsion 2 Rockets (Aeronautics)
ISBN 0-399-60816-8

"This excellent introduction to rockets and jets explains the principles and forms of rocket propulsion. Described are the development of rockets—liquid, solid, and nuclear—their advantages and disadvantages, and current research. Accompanied by profuse drawings, diagrams, and photographs, the text discusses in considerable detail the operational theory of rocket construction, the variations that have been worked out, and such future applications as the now-abandoned 'Grand Tour' project using the NERVA nuclear rocket." Sch Library J

Glossary: p92-94

621.46　Electric propulsion technology

Renner, Al G.

How to make and use electric motors. Putnam 1974 127p illus lib. bdg. $4.97 (5-7)　　621.46

1 Electric motors
ISBN 0-399-60858-3

"Detailed instructions and clear diagrams direct the construction of three types of battery-powered, electromagnetic motors. A special feature is suggestions for varying the materials and design of separate parts after each basic model is put together. The usefulness of this book as a guide in experimentation depends on the availability of supplies—which should not be a great problem—and the reader's curiosity and manual skill. One drawback to the author's teaching method is that he relies almost totally on readers gaining knowledge from making the projects; explanations and definitions of terms are minimal. Some ideas for putting the motors to work are included. Useful for hobbies and school projects." Booklist

621.5　Low-temperature technology

Urquhart, David Inglis

The refrigerator and how it works; illus. by Allan Eitzen. Walck, H.Z. 1972 43p illus $4.95 (3-5)　　621.5

1 Refrigeration and refrigerating machinery
ISBN 0-8098-2081-1

The author traces the development of the refrigerator and explains the scientific principles of its operation

621.8　Machine engineering

Adler, Irving

Machines [by] Irving and Ruth Adler. Day 1964 47p illus lib. bdg. $4.47 (3-5)　　621.8

1 Machinery 2 Mechanics
ISBN 0-381-99963-7

"The Reason why books"

This book "explains wheels, pulleys, levers, and other simple devices and shows how they are used in more complex machinery." Hodges. Bks for Elem Sch Libraries

Ancona, George

Monsters on wheels; written and photographed by George Ancona. Dutton 1974 41p illus $5.95 (3-6)
　　621.8

1 Machinery
ISBN 0-525-35155-8

"Huge-wheeled movers and shakers have been captured for the edification and delight of children . . . interested in the uses and performances of various vehicles. Ancona's black-and-white pictures show the monsters in action; his text is a lucid explanation of their functions. We must add that we have seldom seen a book so handsomely designed. Separate chapters are devoted to the scraper, piggy packer, windrower, tractor, crane, bulldozer, paver, straddle carrier and others, fetching up with a discussion of the lunar rover." Pub W

Pine, Tillie S.

Simple machines and how we use them [by] Tillie S. Pine [and] Joseph Levine; illus. by Bernice Myers. McGraw 1965 48p illus $4.72 (2-4)　　621.8

1 Machinery
ISBN 0-07-050067-3

"Whittlesey House publications"

The book "describes simple machines, such as the wheel and axle, lever, pulley, wedge, and screw, and discusses their application in doing the world's work. Basic information presented in simple text and many pictures." Hodges. Bks for Elem Sch Libraries

Rockwell, Anne

Machines, by Anne & Harlow Rockwell. Macmillan (NY) 1972 unp illus $4.95 (k-1)　　621.8

1 Machinery

Illustrated by the authors, this book describes machines and machine parts: pulley, block and tackle, gear, jackscrew, sprocket

"One of the highlights of the book is the use of full-color watercolor paintings as illustrations of the types of machines. Large primary print is used in describing the simple machines such as the wheel or gears. The sentences are structured for primary usage by introducing the terms such as lever or pulley and not using additional new terminology. A brief explanation of the factors which make machines work is presented. This book would be useful as a source of supplementary information in a unit on simple machines since the reading and comprehension level is well within the average primary child's abilities." Sci Bks

Zim, Herbert S.

Hoists, cranes, and derricks [by] Herbert S. Zim [and] James R. Skelly; illus. by Gary Ruse. Morrow 1969 59p illus lib. bdg. $4.32, pa $1.25 (3-6)　621.8

1 Cranes, derricks, etc. 2 Hoisting machinery
ISBN 0-688-31395-7; 0-688-26395-X

The text "explains in very simple terms the three basic types of lifting machines—hoists, cranes and derricks—the kinds of jobs for which they are normally used and some of the things an operator must do to control them. A fascinating feature is the explanation of hand signals used to instruct the operator. At least one illustration of the subject matter is found on each page of the book, as well as some very simple quizzes about the mechanics of pulleys. There is a table showing capacities of typical cranes and derricks. A brief sketch of the first practical lifting machine built by the Romans about 1500 years ago is also included. The book is indexed and ought to make interesting reading." Sci Bks

621.9   Tools

Adkins, Jan

Toolchest; written, designed, and illus. by Jan Adkins; carpenter in residence, Joseph Karson. Walker & Co. 1973 48p illus $5.95, lib. bdg. $5.83 (5-7)   621.9

1 Carpentry—Tools 2 Woodwork

ISBN 0-8027-6153-4; 0-8027-6154-2

"Meticulously illustrated with drawings that show exact details of tools, hardware, wood grains, and techniques, this is a superb first book for the amateur carpenter. Adkins explains the uses of each tool, the ways in which each variety of saw or chisel is fitted for a particular task, such procedures as dowelling, gluing, or cutting a tenon and mortise, and he describes the uses for each kind of nail and screw. This most useful book concludes with advice on the care of tools. A fine piece of craftsmanship, both in example and in execution." Chicago. Children's Bk Center

Adler, Irving

Tools in your life; illus. by Ruth Adler. Day 1956 128p illus lib. bdg. $3.69 (5-7)   621.9

1 Tools—History 2 Inventions—History

ISBN 0-381-99981-5

"A history of tools, showing how the development of tools has paralleled the advance of civilization and has enabled man to conquer his environment." Hodges. Bks for Elem Sch Libraries

Has "a nontechnical vocabulary, an abundance of clear-cut illustrations, and an invaluable index." Library J

Rockwell, Anne

The toolbox, by Anne & Harlow Rockwell. Macmillan (N Y) 1971 unp illus lib. bdg. $4.95, pa $1.25 (k-1)   621.9

1 Tools

Illustrated by Harlow Rockwell, this book describes the contents of a toolbox and explains the uses of each tool

"A picture book celebrates with unadorned economy of words and illustrations the simple beauty of useful tools. The brief text is printed in clear, handsome type; very little boys—and undoubtedly some girls too—will pore over the appreciative portraits of common implements, which make ingenious use of watercolor to show textures and surfaces of wood and metal." Horn Bk

Zim, Herbert S.

Machine tools [by] Herbert S. Zim [and] James R. Skelly; illus. by Gary Ruse. Morrow 1969 63p illus lib. bdg. $4.32, pa $1.25 (3-6)   621.9

1 Machine tools

ISBN 0-688-31555-0; 0-688-26555-3

This book "shows the development of modern hand tools which evolved from Stone Age tools. Then draft animals, water power, steam, gasoline engines and electricity replaced human power with the resultant capability of performing larger tasks. The machinist and the machine tools with which he works are introduced: the lathe, the giant power press, the twist drill and drill press, shaper, milling machine, planer, multiple or gang drilling machine, boring mill, broaching machine, surface grinders, drop forge, and punch press. There is an illustrated glossary explaining and illustrating the principal mechanical parts of machine tools." Sci Bks

623   Military engineering. Forts

Colby, C. B.

Historic American forts; from frontier stockade to coastal fortress. Coward-McCann 1963 47p illus maps lib. bdg. $3.99 (4-7)   623

1 Fortification

ISBN 0-698-30189-7

An account of the fifteen famous early fortifications of various types illustrated with photographs. Included are: Castillo de San Marcos; Fort Clatsop; Castle Clinton; Fort Frederica; Fort Jefferson; Fort Laramie; Fort Matanzas, Fort McHenry; Fort Necessity; Fort Pulaski; Fort Raleigh; Fort Sumter; Fort Union; Fort Vancouver; Fort Washington

Each description includes a "statement concerning the fort's present physical condition. Although some fine examples of early forts are not included (e.g. Mackinac and Ticonderoga), this is a very good survey." Library J

Peterson, Harold L.

Forts in America; illus. by Daniel D. Feaser. Scribner 1964 61p illus map lib. bdg. $5.95 (4-7)
623

1 Fortification

ISBN 0-684-12890-X

The author "recounts in an interesting and clear manner the role and development of forts built by French, Spanish, English and, later, Americans on what is now U.S. soil. He carefully points out differences between forts in coastal-areas and those in frontier country and includes relevant historical incidents such as the writing of our national anthem. Forts which can be visited are so noted. Terms are carefully explained in the text. Skillfully executed diagrams and drawings. Well indexed. . . . [Readers] who enjoy military and historical books, or those who like to create their own models will like this; useful also in American history." Sch Library J

623.4   Ordnance

Colby, C. B.

Arms of our fighting men; personal weapons, bazookas, big guns. New and rev. ed. Coward, McCann & Geoghegan 1972 48p illus lib. bdg. $3.99 (4-7)   623.4

1 Firearms 2 U.S. Army—Ordnance and ordnance stores 3 Tanks (Military science)

ISBN 0-698-30432-2

First published 1952

This book describes the weapons used by our soldiers: hand guns, shoulder arms, recoilless rifles, grenades, mobile artillery, missiles, and anti-aircraft weapons

Countdown; rockets and missiles for national defense. [New and rev. ed] Coward-McCann 1970 48p illus lib. bdg. $3.99 (4-7)   623.4

1 Rockets (Aeronautics) 2 Guided missiles

ISBN 0-698-30056-4

First published 1960

"The missiles described vary from the small shoulder-fired type of rocket such as the Dragon to the big ICBM; the rockets associated with antiballistic missile systems are also described. The purpose of each missile, its type of launcher, guidance system, etc. are given. The text is brief, but adequately written. The pictures (which constitute three-fourths of the book)

Colby, C. B.—*Continued*
include many rockets in flight. No subject background is required of readers." Sch Library J

Revolutionary War weapons; pole arms, hand guns, shoulder arms and artillery. Coward-McCann 1963 48p illus lib. bdg. $3.99 (4-7)   623.4
1 Firearms 2 U.S. Army—Ordnance and ordnance stores 3 U.S.—History—Revolution
ISBN 0-698-30290-7
Here are photographs and descriptions of weapons used in the Revolutionary War by both sides of the contest as well as by the Indians. Included are spears, lances, halberts, flintlock muskets, pistols, knives, pikes and tomahawks
"It is fortunate that some examples of weapons are still preserved in museums and private collections so that they can be photographed and looked at so many years later. . . . After reading this book, you will have a far better understanding of what the soldier of the Revolution had to be like." p3

Glubok, Shirley
Knights in armor; designed by Gerard Nook. Harper 1969 48p illus lib. bdg. $5.89 (4-7)   623.4
1 Arms and armor—History 2 Knights and knighthood
ISBN 0-06-022038-4
"This tastefully conceived study reveals both the craftsmanship involved in the creation of armor and the customs associated with the wearing of the garb." Wis Library Bul
"The discussion of knighthood and the craftsmanship of medieval armorers has the directness and clarity of expression and the meaningful selection of content of one who knows children well. Equally as impressive as the selection for text is the choice of illustrations. . . . Illuminated manuscripts, paintings, and museum pieces of armor make graphic in book form the training and ideals of knights, details of armor construction, chivalric exploits, and the period pageantry." Horn Bk

Nickel, Helmut
Arms and armor in Africa. Atheneum Pubs. 1971 57p illus map lib. bdg. $5.25 (5-7)   623.4
1 Arms and armor 2 Africa—Civilization
ISBN 0-698-20644-5
The author describes "both contemporary and ancient weapons and armor. The information in the text is related to facts about the cultures of the peoples discussed and the material is divided by region: West Africa, the Sudan, the Congo, East Africa, North Africa, and South Africa." Chicago. Children's Bk Center
"An intriguing compilation of facts about weapons, meticulously illustrated. . . . The writing is straightforward and informal." Sat Rev

Peterson, Harold L.
A history of body armor; illus. by Daniel D. Feaser. Scribner 1968 64p illus $5.95 (4-7)   623.4
1 Arms and armor—History
ISBN 0-684-12361-4
"The thick furs and heavy leather garments of ancient man have given way to the steel helmet and nylon body armor of the present day soldier. The centuries between the appearance of these two extremes have witnessed wonderful achievements in design and craftsmanship as skilled workmen in many countries sought to provide this light, flexible protection. The story of some of their significant creations is the subject of this book." Introduction
"Information is brief and general, making the book of more value for recreational reading than for reference." Booklist

623.74   Vehicles

Cooke, David C.
Famous U.S. Air Force bombers. Dodd 1973 62p illus lib. bdg. $4.50 (5-7)   623.74
1 Bombers 2 U.S. Air Force
ISBN 0-396-06695-X
"Two pages of text and pictures are devoted to each of approximately 30 aircraft, from the MB-1 of 1918 to the B-66 of 1956. The descriptions generally include a brief history of the origin and employment of the craft, production and performance data." Sch Library J

Famous U.S. Navy fighter planes. Dodd 1972 63p illus lib. bdg. $4.95 (5-7)   623.74
1 Fighter planes 2 U.S. Navy
ISBN 0-396-06484-1
"This book is a progressive history of fighter aircraft in the U.S. Navy following World War I. Every plane described and pictured was designed in this country, and every one—including the failures—was a milestone of progress in man's conquest of the air." Foreword
"Despite its narrow scope and lack of an index, the book is clear and up-to-date and will be popular with children interested in planes." Sch Library J

623.82   Nautical craft

Fisher, Leonard Everett
The shipbuilders; written and illus. by Leonard Everett Fisher. Watts, F. 1971 48p illus (Colonial Americans) lib. bdg. $3.90 (4-7)   623.82
1 Shipbuilding—History
ISBN 0-531-01043-0
This account traces the history of shipbuilding in Colonial America and describes with clarity the methods used to construct a wooden sailing ship." Booklist
"Tools are described; technical terms defined; and the many clear illustrations and diagrams graphically detail every aspect of ship construction." Sch Library J

Gilmore, H. H.
Model boats for beginners; pictures and diagrams by the author. Harper 1959 97p illus lib. bdg. $4.43 (5-7)   623.82
1 Ships—Models
ISBN 0-06-021981-5
"Easy-to-follow instructions, illustrated with clear diagrams, for making simplified floating models of 10 boats and ships; included are a motorboat, cruiser, tugboat and barge, ferryboat, ocean liner, sloop, schooner, aircraft carrier, atomic submarine, and Coast Guard cutter. The book also explains how a boat floats and is propelled, shows how to identify boats and the parts of boats, outlines the history of the development of boats, and gives information on navigation aids and a chronological list of a few famous sea adventures." Booklist

Model submarines for beginners; 87 pictures and diagrams by the author. Harper 1962 122p illus lib. bdg. $4.43 (5-7)   623.82
1 Submarines—Models
ISBN 0-06-022011-2
"After presenting briefly the history of the submarine, explaining how a submarine works, and showing how to identify submarines, the author . . . gives easy-to-follow instructions and adequate diagrams for

Gilmore, H. H.—*Continued*
building simplified scale models of 14 submarines from the 'Turtle' of the Revolutionary War period to the nuclear-powered ships of the present." Booklist

Hoyt, Edwin P.
From the Turtle to the Nautilus; the story of submarines; illus. by Charles Geer. Little 1963 134p illus $4.95 (6-7)   623.82
  1 Submarines 2 Submarine warfare
  ISBN 0-316-37667-1
"An Atlantic Monthly Press book"
A history of submarines from the first American submarine, the Turtle, used during the Revolutionary War to the atomic powered Nautilus. The book tells about the men who made and manned the submarines, their important wartime role and undersea rescues
"The illustrations are dramatic. Apart from readers especially interested in the subject, this book will satisfy those who are interested in war stories." Pub W

Icenhower, Joseph B.
Submarines. [Rev. ed.] Watts, F. 1970 72p illus lib. bdg. $3.90 (5-7)   623.82
  1 Submarines
  ISBN 0-531-00645-X
"A First book"
First published 1957 with title: The first book of submarines
The author "describes concisely and compactly the equipment, operation, history, and development of the submarine and the qualifications, training, and life of the submarine sailor. Illustrated with eye-catching two-color pictures and diagrams on almost every page." Booklist

Weiss, Harvey
Ship models and how to build them. Crowell 1973 66p illus $4.50 (4-7)   623.82
  1 Ships—Models
  ISBN 0-690-73270-8
This book contains directions for constructing tugboat, sailboat, riverboat, submarine, hollow hull and powerboat models
The author's "text, clear and matter-of-fact, gives background information first: tools, materials, using and adapting scale drawings, general tips. Each project begins with a list of materials and overall suggestions, then proceeds with a step-by-step explanation; the projects are of increasing difficulty; the diagrams are labelled, explicit, and well-placed. Throughout the book Weiss stresses safety and careful work but no need for perfection, and he encourages the reader who wants to adapt or vary the designs to suit himself." Chicago. Children's Bk Center

623.88 Seamanship

Adkins, Jan
The craft of sail; written, designed and illus. by Jan Adkins. Walker & Co. 1973 64p illus $5.95 (5-7)   623.88
  1 Sailing
  ISBN 0-8027-0401-8
"With pen, ink and wash pictures and accompanying text, [the author] has produced a handsome small primer on sailing that is also a model of brevity, clarity and simplicity. Starting with the Bernoulli effect (which explains how sailboats move to windward), the book ends with anchoring, having passed through everything from knots to points of sail, from rigging to

docking, from man-overboard drills to the rough-weather practice of heaving to. On small craftsmanship and sheer draftsmanship Adkins is hard to beat." Time

623.89 Navigation

Hirsch, S. Carl
On course! Navigating in sea, air, and space; illus. by William Steinel. Viking 1967 156p illus maps lib. bdg. $4.95 (5-7)   623.89
  1 Navigation—History 2 Navigation (Astronautics)
  3 Navigation (Aeronautics)
  ISBN 0-670-52441-7
In this book, "a history of marine navigation, highlighted by accounts of scientists and inventors who contributed improvements to charting and sailing on course, is followed by explanations of air and space navigation which are shown as developments based on skills learned in navigating the seas." Booklist
"Most attractive in format and illustrations, this is a highly readable treatment which can arouse an interest in the subject." Sch Library J
Suggestions for further reading: p151-52

Smith, Arthur
Lighthouses; written and illus. by Arthur Smith. Houghton 1971 146p illus $4.95 (5-7)   623.89
  1 Lighthouses
  ISBN 0-395-12371-2
"From the ancient beacons guiding ships in the Mediterranean Sea, this delightful book proceeds to describe in words and pictures the individual United States lighthouses from Maine to Florida on the Atlantic Coast, from California to Alaska on the Pacific Coast, in the Hawaiian Islands, and on to Midway and Guam before coming back to the lighthouses on those fresh water giants—the Great Lakes. The writing style combines history, technology, geography, sea lore, and anecdotes to hold the reader's interest and attention. . . . The book is certainly useful for collateral reading in seafaring history, construction methodology, and United States geography." Sci Bks

624 Civil engineering

Boardman, Fon W.
Tunnels by Fon W. Boardman, Jr. Walck, H. Z. 1960 144p illus $5 (5-7)   624
  1 Tunnels
  ISBN 0-8098-3030-2
"First there is a discussion of caves and the history of tunnels followed by material on canal, railroad [subway] and automobile tunnels. Concludes with examples of tunnels designed for special purposes such as water supply and defense." The AAAS Sci Bk List for Young Adults
Illustrated with photographs

Doherty, C. H.
Tunnels; illus. by Michael Baker. Meredith [1968 c1967] 115p illus maps $3.95 (6-7)   624
  1 Tunnels
  ISBN 0-8015-7992-9
First published 1967 in England with title: Science and the tunneller
The author "discusses tunnel engineering problems from ancient times to the present with major emphasis on tunnel construction in England, Europe, and America since the eighteenth century. . . . In-

Doherty, C. H.—*Continued*
formative diagrams and photographs are well correlated with the text." Booklist

624.2   Bridges

Peet, Creighton
The first book of bridges. Rev. ed. Watts, F. 1966
66p illus lib. bdg. $3.90 (4-7)   624.2
  1 Bridges
  ISBN 0-531-00489-9
  First published 1953
The text "covers the history of bridges since prehistoric times, the engineering problems of bridge building, types of bridges, and brief sketches of some famous bridges. Illustrated with photographs." Hodges. Bks for Elem Sch Libraries
  Special bridge terms: p61-62. Notable bridges: p63-64

625.7   Roads

Oppenheim, Joanne
Have you seen roads? Young Scott Bks. 1969 unp
illus lib. bdg. $4.95 (k-2)   625.7
  1 Roads 2 Transportation
  ISBN 0-201-09211-5
  Design and picture selection by Gerard Nook
From country roads and city streets to super highways and underwater tunnels, from shipping channels to pathways to the stars, the author describes, in photos and verse, the pathways of the 20th century
  "The writing is poetic and evocative, the photographs carefully selected. The book is handsome to look at, a pleasure to read aloud (save for the reiteration of the title question), and a good launching pad for a discussion of various means of transportation." Sat Rev

Paradis, Adrian A.
From trails to superhighways; the story of America's roads; illus. by Russell Hoover. Messner 1971 96p illus map $4.50, lib. bdg. $4.29 (3-6)   625.7
  1 Roads
  ISBN 0-671-32471-3; 0-671-32472-1
  "Paradis traces the development of roads in the U.S. from the Indian and animal trails used by the first settlers to the superhighways of today. He also explains how corduroy, macadam, asphalt, and other types of roads are built and discusses both the advantages of the construction of more superhighways and the increasing opposition from conservationists and others to them. . . . The book is well organized, simply written, and informative. A glossary is appended." Booklist

627   Hydraulic engineering

Farb, Peter
The story of dams; an introduction to hydrology; foreword by E. C. Itschner; illus. by George Kanelous. Reviewed for scientific accuracy by the U.S. Army Corps of Engineers. Harvey House 1961 127p illus maps (A Story of science ser. bk. for young people) lib. bdg. $5.49 (5-7)   627

  1 Dams
  ISBN 0-8178-3252-1
  "This informal presentation explains the importance, principal types, purpose, construction, and operation of dams, describes some famous American dams, and offers a number of experiments with water and dams, and includes a guide to the location of approximately 200 of the largest dams in the U.S. Many photographs, diagrams, and a few color plates add considerably to the usefulness of the book. Suggestions for further reading are appended." Booklist
  "A chapter at the end of the book suggests some assorted home demonstrations: generating electricity, checking stream sediment, mapping a creek basin." Chicago. Children's Bk Center

627.7   Underwater operations

Shannon, Terry
Windows in the sea; new vehicles that scan the ocean depths, by Terry Shannon and Charles Payzant; illus. with photographs and drawings. Childrens Press 1973 78p illus lib. bdg. $4.95 (5-7)   627.7
  1 Underwater exploration 2 Submarine boats
  ISBN 0-516-08876-9
  "A Golden Gate Junior book"
This book "describes with many photographs and drawings new vehicles used by marine scientists to scan the ocean depths and explore ocean resources." Sci and Children

628.7   Fire-fighting

Colby, C. B.
Space age fire fighters; new weapons in the fireman's arsenal. Coward, McCann & Geoghegan [1974 c1973] 48p illus lib. bdg. $4.29 (3-6)   628.9
  1 Fire departments—Equipment and supplies
  2 Fire extinction
  ISBN 0-698-30531-0
The author discusses new techniques in fighting fires on land, air and sea. He also describes innovative developments in clothing and equipment which resulted from the space program, such as astronaut's suits, rocket torches and jet-axes
  "Numerous black-and-white photoclips . . . [are included in this] up-to-date, adulatory look at a subject with perennial appeal." Booklist

629.13   Aeronautics

Dalgliesh, Alice
Ride on the wind, told by Alice Dalgliesh from "The Spirit of St Louis" by Charles A. Lindbergh; pictures by Georges Schreiber. Scribner 1956 unp illus lib. bdg. $5.95 (2-5)   629.13
  1 Lindbergh, Charles Augustus, 1902-1974
  2 Spirit of St Louis (Airplane) 3 Aeronautics—Flights
  ISBN 0-684-12979-5
  "This is more an interpretation of the longer book than a re-writing for younger readers. Briefly and simply, but quite effectively, the story is told of Lindbergh's childhood dreams of flying and of how those dreams matured into the actual experience of the first nonstop solo flight across the Atlantic. The illustrations are a perfect complement to the text, making

Dalgliesh, Alice—*Continued*
this a distinguished book both in writing and illustration." Chicago. Children's Bk Center
"The subject, the direct narrative style, and the harmonious, distinctive illustrations will also attract older slow and reluctant readers." Booklist

Foster, John T.
The flight of the Lone Eagle; Charles Lindbergh flies nonstop from New York to Paris. Watts, F. 1974 61p illus lib. bdg. $3.45 (5-7)   629.13
1 Lindbergh, Charles Augustus, 1902-1974 2 Spirit of St Louis (Airplane) 3 Aeronautics—Flights
ISBN 0-531-02723-6
"A Focus book"
"A readable account of Lindbergh's historic solo flight from its inception in the young aviator's mind to its completion. The emphasis is on the flight itself and Lindbergh's ups and downs as he recalls them; period setting, biographical material, and details of the airplane's construction are also present in small doses. The author steers away from sensationalism, offering instead fast-paced, dramatic narrative. Black-and-white photographs add immediacy to a text that should painlessly inform as it entertains." Booklist

629.132   Principles of aerial flight

Corbett, Scott
What makes a plane fly? Pictures by Len Darwin. Little 1967 58p illus lib. bdg. $4.95 (3-6)   629.132
1 Aerodynamics 2 Flight
ISBN 0-316-15705-8
"An Atlantic Monthly Press book"
"The author discusses the shape of an airplane and of its wings as they add to—or diminish—drag, lift, and speed, and the functioning of air pressure in relation to wing shape. He describes the various methods used to obtain thrust, the aberrations of flight . . . and the balancing forces of lift, thrust, weight, and drag." Sutherland. The Best in Children's Bks
"Labeled diagrams and drawings further clarify every page of text. Combined index and glossary." Booklist

629.133   Aircraft

Barnaby, Ralph S.
How to make & fly paper airplanes; illus. by the author. Four Winds 1968 70p illus lib. bdg. $4.95 (5-7)   629.133
1 Airplanes—Models 2 Aerodynamics 2 Paper craft
ISBN 0-590-07102-5
"A clearly illustrated, easily understood guide to making and flying paper airplanes. . . . [The author] not only provides explicit directions for making several different models of paper airplanes but also explains the basic principles of flight and flight control, tells how to analyze and correct flying defects of the models, and gives instructions for aerial maneuvers and tips on holding competitions and airshows." Booklist
Glossary: p65-70

Burchard, Peter
Balloons; from paper bags to skyhooks; designed and illus. by the author. With photographs. Macmillan (N Y) 1960 48p illus $4.95 (3-6)   629.133
1 Balloons
ISBN 0-02-71560
This "book presents high lights in the history of ballooning from the eighteenth-century experiments of the Montgolfier brothers to the space balloons of today. With many captioned drawings and photographs to supplement the sketchy text, the book will serve as an interesting introduction to ballooning." Booklist

Elting, Mary
Helicopters at work, by Mary Elting and Judith Steigler; illus. by Ursula Koering. Harvey House 1972 95p illus $5.35 (3-6)   629.133
1 Helicopters
ISBN 0-8178-492-1
"The authors show how helicopters are used in all phases of civilian life—rescue work, fire fighting, pest control, ranching, industrial construction, pipelining and drilling, surveillance, film making and sightseeing—but fail to mention military applications. The flying ability and further training pilots need is mentioned, and readers are encouraged to think about future uses for this versatile machine. A good index provides easy access to details, and the abundant black-and-white illustrations add to reader understanding." Sch Library J

Jacobs, Lou
Jumbo jets, by Lou Jacobs, Jr. Illus. with photographs. Bobbs 1969 64p illus $5.95 (5-7)   629.133
1 Jet planes
ISBN 0-672-50344-1
A "book about the newest in jet aircraft. The first chapter compares the newest aircraft with the first jets. The second chapter describes the building of a jet aircraft with photographs showing various stages in design, construction and testing. Following, individual chapters are devoted to the Boeing 747, the Lockheed 1-1011, the Douglass DC-10, the fabrication of jumbo jet engines, and modifications of airport facilities to accommodate the larger airplanes." Sci Bks
"Competent coverage of a topic of great current interest is made more useful by photographs, drawings, and charts—particularly the charts that compare various types of jumbo jets that are on the drawing boards or in the air." Chicago. Children's Bk Center
Glossary: p[67]

Kettelkamp, Larry
Gliders; written and illus. by Larry Kettelkamp. Morrow 1961 46p illus boards $4.81 (3-6)   629.133
1 Gliders (Aeronautics) 2 Gliders (Aeronautics)—Models
ISBN 0-688-31348-5
"Useful guide that explains to future glider pilots how to build and fly model gliders. Also, describes briefly the history of powerless flight from early experiments in the 1880's to the present. Diagrams and other illustrations in two colors are clear and well done. Excellent format and binding." Sch Library J

Lopshire, Robert
A beginner's guide to building and flying model airplanes. Harper 1967 128p illus $5.95, lib. bdg. $5.49 (5-7)   629.133
1 Airplanes—Models
ISBN 0-06-023998-0; 0-06-023999-9
Illustrated by the author
Partial contents: Four kinds of models; What are

Lopshire, Robert—Continued
the parts called; Why does it fly; Tools; Where shall I
work; How to use your new tools; Make it smooth;
Timber; Ways with wire; Nuts and bolts; How to
solder metals; Power; Let's fly it

"Complete, detailed instructions are given for
building planes from the simple glider to the racer.
Instructions are clear, well-illustrated and simple
enough for the beginner. The book is liberally sprinkled with precautions about the use of special materials such as razor blades, glue and plastic." Bruno.
Bks for School Libraries, 1968

Ross, Frank
Flying paper airplane models [by] Frank Ross, Jr.
Illus. with photographs and drawings. Lothrop 1975
128p illus $5.95, lib. bdg. $5.11 (5-7)   629.133
1 Airplanes—Models 2 Paper crafts
ISBN 0-688-41683-3; 0-688-51683-1

"Helping to fill the ever-present demand for paper
airplane books, Ross has put together a precise, careful instruction guide containing patterns for eight jet
and propeller planes in use today and four flyers of the
future: three hypersonic planes and a space shuttle.
Aids to building the flyable models include clear patterns (not on the same scale), simple slot-and-glue
assembly instructions, and black-and-white photographs of both plane and completed model. Many
readers will be interested in Ross' descriptions of the
actual vehicles and the lists of their physical characteristics." Booklist
Glossary: p121-24. Books for further reading: p125

Historic plane models; their stories and how to
make them [by] Frank Ross, Jr. Illus. with photographs, maps, and drawings. Lothrop 1973 188p illus
maps lib. bdg. $5.11, pa $2.45 (5-7)   629.133
1 Airplanes—Models
ISBN 0-688-50046-3; 0-688-45046-6

The author "tells of some memorable flights and
pilots—Lindbergh, Blériot, Commander Byrd and
Amelia Earhart, among others. Then he provides patterns and directions for creating copies of the planes
discussed. In each case, a photo of the model is
shown, as well as one of the original plane." Pub W

"Ross suggests the use of household materials or
easily and inexpensively purchased supplies and
offers tips on coping with difficult procedures and
making more realistic recreations. . . . The clarity of
instructions on the whole and the capsule flight histories will be useful for model enthusiasts who are
interested in early planes." Sch Library J
Further reading: p183

Simon, Seymour
The paper airplane book; illus. by Byron Barton.
Viking 1971 48p illus lib. bdg. $4.95, pa 75¢ (3-5)
629.133
1 Airplanes—Models 2 Aerodynamics 3 Paper
crafts
ISBN 0-670-53797-7; 0-670-05078-4

"Simple sketches illustrate how to fold a sheet of
paper into a fair representation of an airplane. Several
variations are illustrated and the reader can choose
between an airplane designed for aerobatic maneuvers or one which is a beautiful long-distance glider.
The reader is shown how to make rudders, elevators,
and flaps with simple cuts in the paper and is encouraged to investigate their effects on the model's flight
characteristics." Sci Bks

The directions "are easy to follow, the question and
try-it-and see approach to the experiments is provocative, and the diagrams and drawings showing each
step in the construction of the planes and illustrating
the experiments are unusually clear." Booklist

Slade, Richard
Paper airplanes; how to make airplane models from
paper. St Martins [1971 c1970] 94p illus $4.95 (5-7)
629.133
1 Airplanes—Models 2 Papercrafts
First published 1970 in England with title: Paper
aeroplanes

This book contains "easy-to-follow plans for making
darts and cartridge fuselage models of the Mes-
serschmidt 109, Sopworth Camel, Mikoyan Midget,
and others." Chicago

Urquhart, David Inglis
The airplane and how it works; illus. by Enrico
Arno. Walck, H.Z. 1973 46p illus lib. bdg. $4.95
(3-5)   629.133
1 Airplanes 2 Aerodynamics
ISBN 0-8098-2091-9

The author describes "how the airplane works as he
explains the forces of lift, gravity, thrust, and drag,
and the engines, rudders, flaps, and ailerons that
guide these forces. A brief historical glance at flight is
included, and the airplane is distinguished from other
airborne vehicles such as balloons, kites, rockets,
dirigibles and blimps. In spite of the drab illustrations, this stands as a lucid, comprehensible introduction that will satisfy elementary curiosity." Booklist

When zeppelins flew; in pictures by Ken Dallison.
Editor and designer: Charles Mikolaycak; assistant:
Carole Kismaric; writers: Peter Wood and Edmund
White. Time-Life Bks. [distributed by Little] 1969
51p illus (Spotlight on history) $3.95 (4-6) 629.133
1 Airships

Focusing mainly on the 1930's, the golden age of
the zeppelin, text and illustrations depict the history
and construction of these airships and tell of the
adventures of their commanders

Yolen, Jane
World on a string; the story of kites. Collins [1969
c1968] 143p illus $5.95, lib. bdg. $5.71 (5-7)
629.133
1 Kites
ISBN 0-529-00392-9; 0-529-00394-5

"The history of kites, which began at least 2,000
years ago in China, is given in vivid detail. . . . How
kites have contributed to weather watching, electricity, bridge building, the airplane, aerial photography,
military operations, even rescues; how they have
served as religious symbols, art objects, toys, and for
sporting use is told with style, enthusiasm and authority." Bk World

"Illustrated with photographs. A volume of fascinating content, produced with distinction. . . . The
pages carry a profusion of well-printed reproductions
representing the two-thousand year history of kites.
As if pulled by a kite string, the title words and the
chapter headings are interestingly slanted. The latter
have trailing, string-like initial letters as decorative
devices below the words." Horn Bk
Books for further reading: p137-38

629.136   Airports

Richards, Norman
Jetport. Doubleday 1973 96p illus $4.95, lib. bdg.
$5.70 (4-7)   629.136
1 Aeronautics, Commercial 2 Airports
ISBN 0-385-02749-4; 0-385-02347-2

The author describes the modern airport and its

Richards, Norman—*Continued*
operations; the jobs of the flight and ground crews; and the problems of air traffic control
"The readable text thoroughly covers airport activities and should acquaint readers with the scope of airport/airlines work as well as providing a helpful introduction to the vocation." Sch Library J

629.22 Types of vehicles

Barris, George
Famous custom & show cars [by] George Barris and Jack Scagnetti. Dutton 1973 136p illus $6.95 (6-7)
629.22
1 Automobiles 2 Sports cars
ISBN 0-525-29610-7
"The author, himself a noted customizer, has compiled an entertaining album of famous novelty automobiles. The Voxmobile, Brink's Express, Zingers, and the Phone Booth car are among the 80-odd photos of restyled autos, each accompanied by a descriptive commentary on the car. A section on Detroit show cars, custom Corvettes, custom street automobiles, and luxury cars rounds out the coverage." Booklist

Bendick, Jeanne
The first book of automobiles. 2d rev. ed. Written and illus. by Jeanne Bendick. Watts, F. 1971 72p illus lib. bdg. $3.90 (3-5)
629.22
1 Automobiles
ISBN 0-531-00475-9
First published 1955
This book provides factual material on cars and trucks, their safe operation and the problems of pollution and traffic congestion that they generate
Partial contents: Foreign cars; Sports cars; Racing cars and races; How automobiles work; The first automobiles; Cars have changed America; Trucks are automobiles; How a diesel engine works; Designing new cars; Roads and traffic; The car factory; Car games; When you drive; Build your own

Bergere, Thea
Automobiles of yesteryear; a pictorial record of motor cars that made history—pioneer, antique, classic, and sports models; illus. by Richard Bergere. Dodd 1962 160p illus $4.50 (4-7)
629.22
1 Automobiles—History 2 Automobiles—Pictorial works
ISBN 0-396-04627-4
A survey of the changing design of the automobile from the earliest horseless carriages in 1893 to the super-charged racing models of today. Stanley Steamers, Pierce-Arrows, Stutz Bearcats and Duesenbergs are among those described
"Distinguished pictures, so much more interesting and illuminating than photographs." Horn Bk

Corbett, Scott
What makes a car go? Pictures by Len Darwin. Little 1963 43p illus lib. bdg. $4.95 (3-6)
629.22
1 Automobiles
ISBN 0-316-15695-7
"An Atlantic Monthly Press book"
This book "explains the parts of the car's mechanism and how they work to make the engine run and the wheels move." Horn Bk
Text "and clear diagrams and drawings are combined to give a complete and readily understood explanation. . . . Easy enough for the interested third grader to read independently and helpful for the older reader, adult included, who requires a simplified explanation." Booklist

Edmonds, I. G.
Minibikes and minicycles for beginners. Macrae Smith Co. 1973 153p illus $5.95, lib. bdg. $5.79 (5-7)
629.22
1 Motorcycles
ISBN 0-8255-3002-4; 0-8255-3003-2
This introduction to minibikes and the related minicycles describes riding techniques, safety precautions, two-cycle and four-stroker engines, maintenance and repair work. Tips for prospective buyers are also included
"Safety is Edmonds' overriding emphasis. . . . [This presentation] should be welcome in view of the sports' mushrooming popularity." Booklist
Glossary: p143-45

Gladstone, Gary
Dune buggies; written and photographed by Gary Gladstone. Lippincott 1972 unp illus $3.95 (4-7)
629.22
1 Dune buggies
ISBN 0-397-31292-X
The text and photographs show the development of the dune buggy with special attention to the features of the buggy usually driven on the street

Harris, Leon
Behind the scenes in a car factory; with photographs by the author. Lippincott 1972 unp illus $4.50 (4-6)
629.22
1 Automobile industry and trade 2 Automobiles—Design and construction
ISBN 0-397-31219-9
The author presents, in text and photographs, the many phases involved in manufacturing an automobile, from the initial sketches to the car's arrival in a dealer's showroom. The variety of jobs and the people who perform them are included in the discussion

Henkel, Stephen C.
Bikes; a how-to-do-it guide to selection, care, repair, maintenance, decoration, safety, and fun on your bicycle; illus. by the author. Chatham, distributed by Viking 1972 96p illus lib. bdg. $4.95 (5-7)
629.22
1 Bicycles and bicycling
ISBN 0-85699-033-7
This guide covers such varied aspects of cycling as what size bike to buy, learning to ride it, and the tools and techniques needed for repair operations. Safety on the road is emphasized
"A comprehensive treatment of bikes and bicycling containing clear, concise, accurate information. . . . Although the price information will become dated, this does not detract from the book's overall value. The illustrations are labeled and easy to follow." Library J
Bibliography: p89

Jackson, Robert B.
Classic cars; illus. with photographs. Walck, H.Z. [1974 c1973] 63p illus $4.95 (5-7)
629.22
1 Automobiles—History
ISBN 0-8098-2094-3
"Jackson's latest trip into nostalgia includes photographs of the beautiful automobiles that were so much a part of a glamorous scene in the 1930s. . . . The American Duesenberg, the stately British Bentley, the French Hispano-Suiza and the Italian Isotta-Fraschini are all pictured and discussed among many others, in a text and pictures which illustrate details of their construction and intriguing anecdotes about their inventors." Pub W
The author "pays tribute to the men whose craft-

Jackson Robert B.—*Continued*
manship and creativity produced them. Car buffs will
especially appreciate the chart of mechnical specifications and information on classic car museums and
model kits." Sch Library J

Janeway, Elizabeth
The early days of automobiles; illus. by Hertha
Depper. Random House 1956 192p illus lib. bdg.
$4.39 (4-6)   629.22
  1 Automobiles—History
  ISBN 0-394-90368-4
"Landmark books"
A "history of the automobile: its invention, testing,
difficulties encountered, the performance of the early
automobiles, the beginning of the industry, mass production, the influence of the automobile in the changing American way of life—and the dreamers, tinker-
ers, drivers, and skilled engineers who have had a part
in developing and perfecting the automobile. Car-
minded . . . [readers] will enjoy the mechanical
details and the on-the-road action." Booklist

Lent, Henry B.
Car of the year, 1895-1970; a 75-year parade of
American automobiles that made news. Dutton 1970
158p illus $6.75 (5-7)   629.22
  1 Automobiles—History
  ISBN 0-525-27451-0
"From the more than 1,600 different makes of U.S.
automobiles of the past 75 years the author has
selected a single car for each year as his personal
choice of 'car of the year.' Each car . . . [has a]
description dealing with the manufacturer, the
development, the degree of public acceptance, and
the production years of each model. Horsepower, top
speed, and price are usually indicated along with
some other figures but the specifications are subordi-
nated to the discussion of each car's history." Booklist
"Dragsters, racers and 'funny' cars are not included, which may lose a few potential readers; but
most car buffs and especially antique car buffs will
enjoy it. . . . The writing is clear and concise, with
adequate technical data to stimulate further investigation. The format is good—a spread for each year and
car: the left-hand page has a full-page photograph; the
facing page contains the information. This is more
than just a picture book for idle browsing." Sch Library J

The X Cars; Detroit's one-of-a-kind autos. Putnam
1971 127p illus lib. bdg. $4.97 (5-7)   629.22
  1 Automobiles—Design and construction
  ISBN 0-399-60690-4
X cars are the "handcrafted, usually one-of-a-kind
experimental cars created by automotive engineers
and designers to test new designs and mechanical
features. The author briefly describes 81 of these
ideal or dream cars from the Duryea brothers' history-
making pioneer gas buggy to cars of the future in
which the focus will be on the power plant to find a
way to eliminate air pollution caused by today's
gasoline-burning automobiles. Each car is shown in a
clear photograph." Booklist

Sarnoff, Jane
A great bicycle book, by Jane Sarnoff and Reynold
Ruffins. Rudy "The bicycle man" Veselsky, technical
consultant. Scribner 1973 31p illus lib. bdg. $5.95
(4-7)   629.22
  1 Bicycles and bicycling
  ISBN 0-684-13252-4
This book presents information about bicycle selection, repair, and maintenance as well as rules for
riding, racing and safety
"At last, an off-beat, do-it-yourself guide for bicycle

owners, which conveys useful information with imagination, verve, and humor. In fact, you don't have to
own a bicycle to enjoy it. . . . The book is designed
for the future bike owner anticipating his first two-
wheeler as well as for the more experienced rider.
Clear and precise suggestions . . . are punctuated
with serious and comic bicycle facts and statistics. The
text is complemented with vibrant illustrations in a
kaleidoscope page format." Horn Bk
Other books to read about bicycles: p31

Stambler, Irwin
Unusual automobiles of today and tomorrow. Putnam 1972 95p illus lib. bdg. $4.49 (6-7)   629.22
  1 Automobiles—Design and construction
  ISBN 0-399-60719-6
The author discusses many of today's unusual and
experimental automobiles and the engines that power
them. Included are Granatelli's Lotus STP, Breed-
love's Spirit of America, the VW dune buggies and
cars with various electric and battery-powered
systems
"Photographs and labeled drawings show the
finished models and how they work. For knowledgeable automobile enthusiasts." Booklist

Weiss, Harvey
Model cars and trucks and how to build them; illus.
with photographs, plans, and drawings. Crowell 1974
74p illus $5.50 (4-7)   629.22
  1 Automobiles—Models 2 Trucks—Models
  ISBN 0-690-00414-1
Included here are instructions for making seven
basic wooden model cars and trucks, with ideas for
modifications and improvisations to create such other
vehicles as racing cars, fire trucks, derricks, tractors,
and bulldozers
"The clear text is full of practical suggestions and
reminders and is reinforced by the simple plans and
drawings. The format of the book is comfortable and
convenient, and the photographs of the finished models are a pleasure to behold." Horn Bk

Zim, Herbert S.
Tractors [by] Herbert S. Zim [and] James R. Skelly;
illus. with drawings by Lee J. Ames and photographs.
Morrow 1972 63p illus $4.75, lib. bdg. $4.32, pa $1.25
(3-6)   629.22
  1 Tractors
  ISBN 0-688-21782-6; 0-688-31782-0; 0-688-26782-3
Here is a description of the basic kinds of tractors—
crawlers and wheeled tractors. The authors explain
how they work and survey their agricultural and
industrial uses
"Thorough, up-to-date coverage of tractors and
related heavy equipment. While the print is large, the
text is rather technical on subjects like principles of
traction and hydraulic power. Carefully labelled diagrams of engine and body parts will attract mechanically minded readers." Booklist

Trucks [by] Herbert S. Zim & James R. Skelly;
illus. by Stan Biernacki. Morrow 1970 64p illus lib.
bdg. $4.32, pa $1.25 (4-6)   629.22
  1 Trucks
  ISBN 0-688-31565-8; 0-688-26565-0
"Complete illustrated descriptions are provided of
trucks of all kinds, the adaptation of the truck body
and chassis to the intended cargo is well described. A
section on truck engines differentiates among, and
explains the principles of, the three types—gasoline,
diesel, and gas turbine. An explanation of various
transmission and braking systems follows. There is a
detailed account of the duties and qualifications of the
driver of a big truck, and some of the facilities and

Zim, Herbert S.—*Continued*

requirements of a smoothly operating trucking industry. For a young person who may be interested in learning about trucking as a career, this is a readable eye-opener." Sci Bks

629.28 Operation and repair of vehicles

Kleeberg, Irene Cumming

Bicycle repair; photographs by Meryl Joseph. Watts, F. 1973 60p illus lib. bdg. $4.33, pa $1.25 (5-7)   629.28

1 Bicycles and bicycling—Repairing
ISBN 0-513-02636-1; 0-531-02408-3
"A Concise guide"

This book "will enable bike owners interested in making general repairs and conducting maintenance to do precisely that without wasted effort, aggravation, or unnecessary expense. Information on fixing flats, aligning wheels, gear changing, and many other aspects of repair and maintenance is supported by sufficient illustrations and diagrams. While not the most exhaustive title on the subject, this is an easy-to-use reference for cyclists." Sch Library J
Glossary: p53-54. Further reading: p55

Lawrie, Robin

Under the hood; how cars work and how to keep them working; written and illus. by Robin Lawrie. Pantheon Bks. [1973 c1970] 32p illus $2.50, lib. bdg. $4.39 (4-6)   629.28

1 Automobiles 2 Automobiles—Repairing
ISBN 0-394-82603-5; 0-394-92603-X
First published 1970 in England with title: Under the bonnet

The book explains how the engine, cooling system, transmission and other parts of a car work and describes several malfunctions which can be prevented. It ends with a story about Mr Smith who takes good care of his car, and Mr Brown who neglects to have his car serviced

629.4 Astronautics

Americans in space, by the editors of American Heritage, The Magazine of History. Author: John Dille; consultant: Philip S. Hopkins. Am. Heritage [distributed by Harper] 1965 153p illus maps $5.95 (5-7)   629.4

1 Astronautics 2 Rocketry 3 Mercury project
ISBN 0-06-021680-8
"American Heritage Junior library"

"This book tells the story of the first major step taken by Americans into space, a period of our history that lasted roughly from 1914 to 1963. It was a period of experimentation, frustration, and ultimate triumph. It was opened by [Robert Goddard] a secretive physics professor in Worcester, Massachusetts, whose rockets were regarded in some quarters as little more than public menaces. It was given impetus by the technology of World War II; and it was concluded by the sensational feats of Project Mercury." Foreword

"Through old maps and new photographs, old concepts of the shape of the universe, new use of new materials, the awesome story of space is told." Pub W

Branley, Franklyn M.

A book of moon rockets for you; illus. by Leonard Kessler. Rev. ed. Crowell 1970 165p illus $5.95, lib. bdg. $6.70 (1-3)   629.4

1 Rockets (Aeronautics) 2 Lunar probes 3 Space flight to the moon
ISBN 0-690-15437-2; 0-690-15438-0
First published 1959

This book "furnishes information on what moon rockets are, how they were used to determine the possibilities for man's survival on the moon and what lunar probes were used to gather the information. . . . At the back of the book there is a list of the lunar probes that were successfully launched and what they accomplished." Appraisal

"Remarkable chiefly for its many careful illustrations which explain, with unusual clarity, certain matters which are often difficult to get across." Horn Bk

Experiments in the principles of space travel; illus. by Jeanyee Wong. Rev. ed. Crowell 1973 113p illus $4.50 (5-7)   629.4

1 Space flight 2 Physics—Experiments
ISBN 0-690-27792-X
First published 1955

"Scientists' understanding and proper application of basic principles of science can, according to Branley, determine the success or failure of space exploration. The author's succinct presentation of some of these principles is given in tandem with a highly technical yet comprehensible series of experiments. The experiments discuss the principles behind space measurements, rocket design and streamlining, rocket engines, power and pressure in space, temperature control in space, and gravitational force. Clear explanations, illustrations, and charts expose the reader to the scientific tools and framework needed to develop problem-solving abilities while orienting the reader toward research as well." Booklist

Rockets and satellites; illus. by Al Nagy. Rev. ed. Crowell 1970 33p illus (Let's-read-and-find-out science bks) $4.50, lib. bdg. $5.25 (1-3)   629.4

1 Rockets (Aeronautics) 2 Artificial satellites
ISBN 0-690-70820-3; 0-690-70821-1
First published 1961

This book describes "how rockets and satellites work and how they differ." Hodges. Bks for Elem Sch Libraries

"The illustrations are excellent and go a long way towards explaining the concepts. For example, although it is not stated that the rocket contains the fuel which propels it, the illustrations show the flames emanating from the rocket. . . . The book is quite short and easy for the youngster to follow." Sci Bks

Clarke, Arthur C.

Into space; a young person's guide to space, by Arthur C. Clarke and Robert Silverberg. Rev. ed. Harper 1971 129p illus $3.95, lib. bdg. $4.79 (5-7)   629.4

1 Space flight 2 Outer space
ISBN 0-06-021270-5; 0-06-021271-3
First published 1954 with title: Going into space

The "reader will find a brief sketch of rocket development, an explanation of how rockets work, a step-by-step account of manned space flight, and, finally, the details of the marvelous achievement of man's landing on the moon. The authors conclude by informing us of what we might expect from future space exploration." Best Sellers

Ross, Frank

Model satellites and spacecraft; their stories and how to make them, by Frank Ross, Jr. Illus. with photographs and diagrams. Lothrop 1969 159p illus lib. bdg. $4.81, pa $2.45 (5-7)   629.4

1 Artificial satellites—Models 2 Space vehicles—Models
ISBN 0-688-51193-7; 0-688-45017-2

Ross, Frank—*Continued*

The book provides "clear, easy-to-follow directions for model building. Patterns for the various parts of the crafts are included, all required materials are readily available. The book also includes a brief discussion of the crafts' missions, other simple technical data, sketches, and photographs of completed models." Sch Library J

Books for further reading: p155

629.403   Astronautics—Encyclopedias and dictionaries

Asimov, Isaac

ABC's of space. Walker & Co. 1969 47p illus $4.95, lib. bdg. $4.85 (2-5)   629.403

1 Astronautics—Dictionaries 2 Alphabet books
ISBN 0-8027-6001-5; 0-8027-6002-3

"A space age alphabet book, with words for both upper and lower case letters given: e.g., 'A is for Apollo . . . a is for astronaut,' and brief discussions of the terms included. The words are primarily from technological, rather than theoretical, space science, but the definitions are not oversimplified. . . . There is also an area provided on each page where children can add their own space terms." Sch Library J

"Big, clear photographs and diagrams in a stunning red, white and black layout of background and print make this space primer as goodlooking as it is informative. The writing is direct and the print large. . . . Younger children can enjoy the pictures even if they can't understand every word." Sat Rev

629.43   Unmanned flight

Branley, Franklyn M.

A book of satellites for you. Rev. ed. Illus. by Leonard Kessler. Crowell 1971 unp illus $5.95, lib. bdg. $6.70 (1-3)   629.43

1 Artificial satellites
ISBN 0-690-15581-6; 0-690-15582-4
First published 1958

An explanation of man-made satellites; those that have been launched and those that will be sent into space in the years to come. Such questions as why we send up satellites and what we hope to learn from the messages they send back are answered in terms of the young reader's experience

"While not an easy book for young children to manage independently, the attractive illustrations highlighted in red and blue will hold the interest of first and second graders as it is read to them." Sch Library J

Coombs, Charles

Spacetrack; watchdog of the skies; illus. with 50 photographs and diagrams. Morrow 1969 128p illus maps lib. bdg. $4.59 (5-7)   629.43

1 Radar defense networks 2 Artificial satellites
ISBN 0-688-31561-5

The author reports on the work of Spacetrack, the U.S. Air Force organization which keeps track of the many objects launched into space since the beginning of the space age. The book describes the physical layout in which Spacetrack operates and discusses the radar system that it uses to obtain its data

"In a compact presentation, illustrated by good photographs and explanatory drawings, Coombs has

presented the first composite account for students and nonspecialists of the space tracking and defense warning systems in North Amerca. . . . A map explains the linking of NORAD with various types of radar installations and operations circling the North American Continent. This should be a very popular book among young people." Sci Bks

629.44   Auxiliary spacecraft

Freeman, Mae

Space base; illus. by Raul Mina Mora. Watts, F. 1972 63p illus lib. bdg. $4.95 (3-5)   629.44

1 Space stations
ISBN 0-531-02029-0

A trip to a space base of the future is described: what it looks like, how it remains in space, how travelers reach it, how it is structured so that humans can stay alive on it, and the activities that go on there to keep the base in operation

The illustrations "provide only a general pictorial background. The predictions of future space activities are as well based in fact as the current [1972] state of knowledge permits." Sci Bks

Jacobs, Lou

Space station '80 [by] Lou Jacobs, Jr. Hawthorn Bks. 1973 111p illus $5.95 (5-7)   629.44

1 Space stations
ISBN 0-8015-6984-2

"With the launching of Skylab in 1973 the U.S. space program took a giant step toward achieving its next major goal—putting a space station in orbit by the early 1980s. Here Lou Jacobs has given a concise, illustrated account of the latest developments in space exploration including details of the work done following the Skylab launch when the billion-dollar project was seriously threatened. Some space shuttle systems are described, a picture is painted of what life will be like aboard a space station, and a glimpse is offered of what tomorrow's space exploration will bring to mankind. There are numerous full page photographs and drawings." Best Sellers

Suggested reading: p107-08

629.45   Manned flight

Bergaust, Erik

The next 50 years on the moon. Putnam 1974 94p illus lib. bdg. $4.29 (5-7)   629.45

1 Lunar bases
ISBN 0-399-60851-6

The author projects the use of the moon as a base for further space exploration, and as a colony which will probably be as large as an Earth ctiy—all within a timetable of 50 years

"The book is thoroughly scientific in the sense that it shows how prediction based on knowledge, touched with logically controlled imagination, can help set and lead to the accomplishment of future-oriented goals. . . . Numerous illustrations are imaginative and informative." Sci Teacher

Glossary of lunar terms: p85-93

Branley, Franklyn M.

Man in space to the moon; illus. by Louis S. Glanzman. Crowell 1970 38p illus $3.95, lib. bdg. $4.70 (4-6)   629.45

1 Apollo project 2 Space flight to the moon
ISBN 0-690-51685-1; 0-690-51686-X

The author "gives a detailed and accurate report of

Branley, Franklyn M.—*Continued*
the Apollo 11 mission. There is some discussion of the importance of the data gathered, but the book is primarily devoted to what happened: the stages of flight and the manipulation of modules; how the three astronauts ate, slept, disposed of human waste; the mechanics of landing and communication with Mission Control; investigation on the moon, and the details of the return flight, re-entry, and recovery. One of the best books on the subject, it is dignified enough for slow older readers." Sat Rev
Manned space flights: Vostok 1 to Apollo 11: p33-35

Hill, Robert W.
What the moon astronauts do. Rev. ed. of "What the moon astronauts will do all day." Day 1971 64p illus lib. bdg. $3.96 (6-7)   629.45
1 Apollo project 2 Space flight to the moon
ISBN 0-381-99795-2
First published 1963
The author shows how NASA planned and advanced America's man-on-the-moon mission by describing the preparation, technical principles, astronauts' gear and flights of Project Mercury, Project Gemini and Project Apollo
"The many illustrations . . . are well selected and clearly reproduced. . . . [This book] should prove useful where there is a need for simple background material presented in a fairly attractive format." Library J

631   General agricultural techniques, apparatus, equipment, materials

Buehr, Walter
Food from farm to home; written and illus. by Walter Buehr. Morrow 1970 94p illus lib. bdg. $4.59 (4-6)   631
1 Agriculture 2 Farms
ISBN 0-688-31306-X
"An illuminating introduction to modern food production begins with frontier farming, traces the advancements in transportation and communication that revolutionized American farming in the late nineteenth and early twentieth centuries, and briefly describes present-day methods of producing major farm products, noting the role of scientific research in overcoming problems and improving farming techniques. Buehr concludes his account with a forecast of twenty-first-century farming. Well illustrated with clear drawings." Booklist

Floethe, Louise Lee
Farming around the world; illus. by Richard Floethe. Scribner 1970 unp illus lib. bdg. $5.95 (2-4)   631
1 Agriculture 2 Farms
ISBN 0-684-13948-0
"A brief but informative travel guide to the world of farming, accompanied by bright, interesting pictures. Not all countries are described, but the diversification of farming around the world is here: a small rice paddy is contrasted with a huge pineapple plantation; big Australian grazing stations and the Argentina pampas with small, individual Greek and French farms; plus the communal villages of China, the collective farms of Russia and the kibbutzim in Israel. It is shown that the produce grown on the farms is just as varied—milk in America, coffee in Brazil, tea in Ceylon, and barley in Ethiopia. The concise summary of why all farms do

not produce the same amount of food is especially clear and to the point." Sch Library J
"The information may be a bit too extensive for the younger reader, but the carefully detailed illustrations will hold his attention." Adventuring With Bks. 2d edition

631.4   Soil and soil conservation

Goldin, Augusta
Where does your garden grow? Illus. by Helen Borten. Crowell 1967 unp illus (Let's-read-and-find-out science bks) $4.50, lib. bdg. $5.25 (1-3)   631.4
1 Soils
ISBN 0-690-88357-9; 0-690-88358-7
"A beginning book in natural science, illustrated with pictures in varied techniques and of variable usefulness. The text describes, quite simply and with some repetition, the facts that decaying matter forms humus, that humus added to soil makes the rich topsoil in which plants grow best, that the amount of topsoil varies in different places, and that topsoil is liable to be dissipated by the vicissitudes of harsh weather." Chicago. Children's Bk Center
"The basic information concerning horticulture imparted for beginning readers is good and clearly stated. The illustrations are unrealistic, 'arty' embellishments for the most part." Sci Bks

Keen, Martin L.
The world beneath our feet; the story of soil; illus. by Haris Petie and with photographs. Messner 1974 96p illus $6.25, lib. bdg. $5.79 (4-6)   631.4
1 Soils 2 Soil conservation
ISBN 0-671-32673-2; 0-671-32674-0
"This well-organized volume does a conscientious job of explaining the origins and makeup of soil and the ways in which man and nature can both destroy and protect it. A description of soil formation is followed by chapters which analyze plant and animal content in the earth and show the decay and growth cycles that take place. [Included also are] sections on the farming and grazing practices that lead to soil infertility, the effects of wind and rain on unprotected land, and modern efforts to reclaim and preserve the earth's usefulness." Pub W
"The photographs and diagrams clarify difficult concepts and, overall, this offers an interesting and informative look at the subject." Sch Library J
Glossary: p90-93

The Story of soil, by the editors of Country Beautiful and Dorothy Holmes Allen; illus. by James Milton Smith. Putnam in association with Country Beautiful Corp. 1971 63p illus (The World is nature) lib. bdg. $5.49 (4-6)   631.4
1 Soils 2 Erosion
ISBN 0-399-60612-2
"An attractive-to-look-at book discussing the different kinds of soil, how soil is formed, conservation practices and erosion problems. . . . The illustrations are essentially decorative but they do clarify and extend the text, which is unusually clear and well organized." Sch Library J
Glossary: p58-60. Bibliography: p61

631.5   Cultivation and harvesting

Kohn, Bernice
The organic living book; drawings by Betty Fraser. Viking 1972 91p illus lib. bdg. $5.95, pa $1.25 (4-7)   631.5

Kohn, Bernice—*Continued*

1 Organiculture
ISBN 0-670-52833-1; 0-670-05079-2

Contains "ideas for living in harmony with nature while conserving our natural resources and improving our lot as consumers. In the clear, concise text, the young reader is instructed in the arts of label reading, organic gardening, and cooking with natural foods. Recipes for yogurt, bread, and a few gourmet foods are included. There is a chapter devoted to container gardening for city dwellers and another to the problem of pest control. The final chapter deals with ecology and lists some concrete suggestions for fighting pollution and conserving our natural resources. Directions for activities that promote better living organically are very understandable. Delicate black-and-white line drawings support the text and enhance the book's appearance. A good index and bibliography add to the usefulness of this very attractive presentation of a timely topic." Appraisal

Sullivan, George

How do they grow it? Westminster Press 1968 151p illus map $5.50 (5-7)   631.5

1 Farm produce
ISBN 0-664-32428-2

The author describes the production, packaging, and agricultural methods used in the growing of chocolate, bananas, olives, pepper, rubber, tobacco, cotton, tea, mushrooms, rice, grapefruit, pineapple, cork, peanuts, cloves, tomatoes, grapes, potatoes, sugar, and coffee

"Mr. Sullivan's text will be useful in social studies and science units as well as interesting reading for agricultural-minded students and the just plain curious." Sch Library J
Bibliography: p143-46

631.8   Fertilizers and soil conditioners

Rockwell, Harlow

The compost heap. Doubleday 1974 24p illus $4.95, lib. bdg. $5.70 (k-1)   631.8

1 Fertilizers and manures
ISBN 0-385-06822-0; 0-385-08989-9

"Not a lesson in organic gardening, but a description of the changes in a compost heap comprising leaves, grass, and vegetable garbage. The story is told, very simply, by a small boy who watches the compost change to earth, steaming and sprouting and filled with worms. Then he and his father spread it on their garden." Chicago. Children's Bk Center

The text is "complemented and extended through explicit, poster-like illustrations in soft pastels. An appealing story, which effectively and accurately introduces to preschoolers the wonders of natural phenomena." Horn Bk

632   Plant injuries, diseases, pests

Hogner, Dorothy Childs

Good bugs and bad bugs in your garden; back-yard ecology; illus. by Grambs Miller. Crowell 1974 86p illus $5.50, lib. bdg. $6.25 (5-7)   632

1 Insects, Injurious and beneficial
ISBN 0-690-00119-3; 0-690-00120-7

This introduction to biological control of insect pests in the home garden discusses the use of natural enemies, companion planting, immune strains of plants, and botanical insecticides as alternatives to harmful pesticides

"Amply illustrated, an informative and simply written text is divided by topic rather than chapter, the brief topics listed in the table of contents and grouped so that all of the facts about harmful bugs, about beneficial ones, and about methods of pest control are in sequence." Chicago. Children's Bk Center
Bibliography: p81-82

Weeds; illus. by Nils Hogner. Crowell 1968 117p illus $4.50, lib. bdg. $5.25 (3-6)   632

1 Weeds
ISBN 0-690-87292-5; 0-690-87293-3

"After defining a weed and stating where and how it grows, Mrs. Hogner describes over 40 land and water weeds, their habits, origins and relatives, in a clear and interesting manner. She shows just why these plants are pests and how they can be controlled. . . . The format is attractive and the black-and-white drawings are accurate." Sch Library J

McClung, Robert M.

Gypsy moth; its history in America; written and illus. by Robert M. McClung. Morrow 1974 96p illus $4.75, lib. bdg. $4.32 (4-7)   632

1 Moths
ISBN 0-688-20124-5; 0-688-30124-X

"The history of the gypsy moth in America provides exemplary material for a documentation of animal population control. Since being brought to Massachusetts in the 1860s, the moth has expanded its territory over the New England states, despite a variety of human efforts to exterminate the insect. McClung is careful not to depict the gypsy moth as an 'evil' enemy while he reveals at length research and action programs directed against this vegetation-eater." Booklist

"The problems of maintaining ecological balance are well integrated into the smoothly written text. Well-placed pen-and-wash drawings enhance the pleasant format." Sch Library J
Further reading: p90-92

Pringle, Laurence

Pests and people; the search for sensible pest control. Macmillan (N Y) 1972 118p illus $5.95 (5-7) 632

1 Pest control—Biological control 2 Pesticides and the environment

"In a readable text with many photographs and drawings the author . . . discusses insects as the most abundant of all animal pests and ways to control them. He reports on DDT, the immunity insects build to it, its effect on other life forms, and the substitution of stronger biocides when DDT proves ineffective. He considers such biological controls as predators, parasites, and pathogens and cites numerous successful experiments with them. Pringle states that growers want quick, easy, cheap solutions for pest problems and that to date they seek advice from biocide salesmen. He suggests how the social, economic, and political factors that prevent greater use of biological controls can be eliminated." Booklist
Glossary: p108-11. Further reading p112-14

633   Field crops

Boesch, Mark J.

The world of rice; illus. by William Steinel. Dutton 1967 160p illus maps $4.95 (5-7)   633

Boesch, Mark J.—*Continued*

1 Rice

ISBN 0-525-43377-5

The author "relates the historical development and present status of rice production and use in a most interesting and instructive manner. The early beginnings and spread of rice culture, the important developments in improved crop production and utilization are dramatically portrayed against a background of geography, economics and political science. Illustrations are copious. The first discovery of nutritional deficiency and the methods used to overcome the loss of vitamin B in rice milling are dramatically recounted." Sci Bks

"Containing information relevant to the study of food, farming, nutrition, and health, the book is a useful reference source." Booklist

Brooks, Anita

The picture book of grains. Day 1962 96p illus map lib. bdg. $4.68 (4-6) 633

1 Grain

ISBN 0-381-99934-3

The author states three purposes in writing this book: "The photographs and text are meant, primarily, to be informative. They tell what the various grains are and where they grow. . . . The second purpose is an attempt to show the world at work: a related . . . world of fields and farms, wharves and warehouses, research and experiment, and of the people who raise, process, and ship man's most important food. The third purpose is to illustrate . . . that 'the only self-sufficient unit is the world itself,' and to suggest that within this unit, the interdependency of people and their relation one to another are more important than national distinctions." Preface

"This sort of book could help give reality to those deadly dull 'products' discussions in geographies." N Y Her Trib Bks

Limburg, Peter R.

The story of corn; illus. by Paul Frame and with photographs. Messner 1971 96p illus $4.50, lib. bdg. $4.29 (3-5) 633

1 Corn

ISBN 0-671-32469-1; 0-671-32470-5

The author traces the history of corn from its first cultivation by the American Indians to its present-day growth on huge farms with modern machinery. He points out corn's essential use as livestock feed for the meat industry and the processing of specially-grown varieties into such products as flour, cereals, starch, soap, drugs, adhesives, plastics and oils

"The treatment is done in such a way that the story can be extended to other plants without difficulty. And too, the book nicely introduces the reader to genetics, cytology, physiology, and plant morphology. This little book would be a very useful addition to a science class; the teacher could easily extend the ideas portrayed in the book to more general concepts." Sci Bks

Rinkoff, Barbara

Guess what grasses do; illus. by Beatrice Darwin. Lothrop [1972 c1971] unp illus $4.95, lib. bdg. $4.59 (k-3) 633

1 Grasses

ISBN 0-02-41592-X; 0-02-51592-4

"Emphasizing the importance of grasses to all people, Rinkoff recounts in poetic prose many different ways that grasses have been used around the world. She tells of Apache wikiups made of layers of dried grass, corn husk dolls, Hawaiian ti-leaf slides, and other unusual uses as well as noting the value of grasses as food for animals and humans." Booklist

"A simple, brief text, which is set like short lines of poetry and illustrated on every page by silk-screen prints in one, two, or three colors. Text and illustrations give this informational volume the appearance of an attractive picture book for the youngest." Horn Bk

634 Fruits

Beck, Barbara L.

The first book of fruits; pictures by Page Cary. Watts, F. 1967 64p illus lib. bdg. $3.90 (4-6) 634

1 Fruit

ISBN 0-531-00538-0

"After brief consideration of the formation of seeds, the growing of plants by other methods than seeding, and plant improvement a helpful and inviting book gives, by group or family, botanical and historical facts about the different kinds of edible fruits. In most cases the principal states growing a particular fruit are noted and in a final section fruits popular in other parts of the world are described." Booklist

"Fascinating botanical and historical facts about exotic fruits such as the drupe, the muskmelon and casaba and about all the common ones used today are well documented and amply illustrated with drawings in shades of purple." Bruno. Bks for Sch Libraries, 1968

Fenton, Carroll Lane

Fruits we eat, by Carroll Lane Fenton and Herminie B. Kitchen; illus. by Carroll Lane Fenton. Day 1961 128p illus lib. bdg. $4.68 (4-7) 634

1 Fruit

ISBN 0-381-99820-7

"Contents are divided into various types of fruits, such as 'Fruits with Cores,' 'Composite Fruits,' 'Citrus Fruits,' 'Olives and Palms,' 'Melons,' etc. Tells about where these fruits originated and of their introduction to other regions, the various uses of some fruits, and how taste and texture of some have changed with many years of cultivation." Library J

"The writing style is good, illustrations are profuse and beautifully drawn, and an index is appended." Chicago. Children's Bk Center

634.9 Forestry

Budbill, David

Christmas tree farm; illus. by Donald Carrick. Macmillan Pub. Co. 1974 unp illus lib. bdg. $5.95 (k-2) 634.9

1 Trees

ISBN 0-02-715330-4

The author follows the growth of a Christmas tree, from the spring planting of the seedling, transplanting and pruning, to the fall harvest

"Children whose only acquaintance with the trees is seeing them on open lots in the city will learn that they are produced on farms and are the result of planning and care. Budbill's quiet, matter-of-fact text narrates the process, pictured in Carrick's panoramic, serene watercolor illustrations of one Vermont tree farm." Booklist

Kurelek, William

Lumberjack; paintings and story by William Kurelek. Houghton 1974 unp illus $6.95 (3-5) 634.9

1 Lumber and lumbering

ISBN 0-395-19922-0

"This is an inspired carte-de-visite to the post-War

Kurelek, William—*Continued*
logging camps of Canada's vast wilderness. In a wry
and candid introduction, the Canadian artist explains
his motivation for working in 'the bush' of Quebec and
Ontario, and his text continues in this vein with concise explanations of the rudiments of lumbercamp
life. But it is Kurelek's full-color, full-page illustrations which make this book a masterpiece. Full of
humour and affectionate detail, the primitivist paintings splendidly evoke the atmosphere of the pre-
mechanized lumbercamp." Children's Bk Rev Serv

Rich, Louise Dickinson
The first book of lumbering; illus. by Victor Mays.
Watts, F. 1967 66p illus lib. bdg. $3.90 (4-6)   634.9
1 Lumber and lumbering
ISBN 0-531-00573-9
"Lumbering from colonial times to the present
[1967], from Maine to the West Coast, the changes in
tools and methods and the men who employ them are
concisely described and effectively related to forest
conservation, the subject of the last chapter. Appropriate green and white illustrations." Bruno. Bks for
School Libraries, 1968
"Excellent supplementary book for the social
studies program as well as science." Adventuring
With Bks. 2d edition

635   Garden crops
(Horticulture)

Baker, Samm Sinclair
The indoor and outdoor grow-it book illus. by Eric
Carle. Random House 1966 65p illus $2.95, lib. bdg.
$4.99 (1-6)   635
1 Gardening 2 House plants
ISBN 0-394-81325-1; 0-394-91325-6
"Simple, easy-to-follow instructions in text and pictures for growing plants indoors and outdoors for
pleasure, gifts, food, decoration, and science projects. The book tells how to grow such things as a
pineapple plant, an African violet 'child', herbs, cactus, and insect-eating plants; it gives directions for
such activities as growing a garden in a glass bowl or a
bottle cap, making an indoor greenhouse, and arranging, pressing, or drying flowers; and, finally, it
includes general indoor and outdoor 'grow-it' tips.
The two-color illustrations are clearly drawn and
attractive. Enticing, workable suggestions for both
individual and group projects." Booklist

Cutler, Katherine N.
Growing a garden, indoors or out; illus. by Jacqueline Adato. Lothrop 1973 96p illus $4.95, lib. bdg.
$4.59 (4-7)   635
1 Gardening 2 House plants
ISBN 0-688-21365-0; 0-688-31365-5
"Emphasizing that gardening can be fun and is
accessible to everyone, this is a clear introduction to
indoor and out-door planting. In a straightforward
manner, Cutler explains how plants grow and what
they need to thrive, e.g., she gives the different light
requirements needed for a variety of plants. Both
sections of the book—indoor and outdoor gardening
—contain detailed information that will be helpful to
beginning gardeners. . . . There is also a good glossary, a list of plant and seed catalogs, and a well-
selected bibliography." Sch Library J

Fenten, D. X.
Gardening . . . naturally; line drawings by
Howard Berelson. Watts, F. 1973 87p illus lib. bdg.
$5.88, pa $2.95 (4-7)   635

1 Organiculture
ISBN 0-531-02625-6; 0-531-02338-9
This introduction to organic gardening "includes
advice on composting, mulching, dealing with plant
pests, and soil improvement; it discusses annuals,
perennials, bulbs and tubers, et cetera, and it gives a
calendar as a guide to planned gardening." Chicago.
Children's Bk Center
"Organic gardening enthusiasts should love the
book which offers intelligent advice on caring for
house plants as well as outdoor vegetable and flower
plots. If he makes the fight against insects and diseases sound all too easy, [the author] still makes the
reader feel it's much better to aim a jet of cold water at
a crawling intruder rather than a can of insecticide.
And Berelson's lush illustrations provide all the other
inducements necessary to use one's thumb of
whatever color in gardening organically." Pub W
Glossary of gardening terms: p82-83. Other books
to read: p84

Hudlow, Jean
Eric plants a garden; story and photographs by Jean
Hudlow. Whitman, A. 1971 unp illus lib. bdg. $4.25
(2-4)   635
1 Vegetable gardening
ISBN 0-8075-2136-1
"Clear photographs show, more convincingly than
could any description, the pride and delight of a
young gardener harvesting his [vegetable] crop, and
the satisfaction of accomplishment as he enjoys fresh-
ly-picked salad ingredients. The presentation of the
gardener's ritual—planning, measuring, preparing
the soil, planting, weeding, watering, and hovering
about to watch progress—helps to make this informative, unpretentious photodocumentary a success." Sat
Rev

Johnson, Hannah Lyons
From seed to jack-o'-lantern; photographs by
Daniel Dorn. Lothrop 1974 unp illus $4.75, lib. bdg.
$4.32 (1-3)   635
1 Pumpkin
ISBN 0-688-41644-6; 0-688-51644-0
"The simple text and black-and-white photographs
show ground preparation, planting, and growth stages
of the pumpkin plants, and the author explains the
necessity for weeding and ensuring cross-pollination
so that the plants can produce mature fruits.
. . . Johnson brings the fruit indoors to show how to
carve it and roast its seeds. Those with an inclination
for indoor gardening can send for bush pumpkin
plants that can be grown in a pot." Booklist
The "text is uncluttered and easy to follow, and
we'd like to add that grown-ups can learn from and
enjoy this book as well as children." Pub W

Selsam, Millicent E.
The carrot and other root vegetables; photographs
by Jerome Wexler. Morrow 1971 48p illus lib. bdg.
$4.81 (2-4)   635
1 Root crops
ISBN 0-688-31145-8
The author describes "the growth, development,
and reproduction of representative root vegetables.
The carrot is emphasized but the sweet potato, beet,
turnip, and radish are also presented." Sci Bks
"Millicent Selsam's science writing is exemplary;
clear, authoritative and well-organized, the writing
style simple and direct without being choppy. The
description of the life cycle of biennial root vegetables
is made even more lucid by the sharp, enlarged photographs, and the book made more readable as well as
attractive by the spacious page layout and the large
print." Sutherland. The Best in Children's Bks

258

Selsam, Millicent E.—*Continued*

More potatoes! Pictures by Ben Shecter. Harper 1972 62p illus (A Science I can read bk) $2.95, lib. bdg. $3.79 (1-3) 635

1 Potatoes
ISBN 0-06-025323-1; 0-06-025324-X
Because of a young girl's curiosity, her teacher arranges for the class to visit a warehouse and a farm in order to learn how potatoes are grown, harvested, and distributed
"Illustrations with a pleasantly casual air follow the investigation of Sue and her classmates as they learn all about potatoes. . . . The fictional framework is nicely balanced by the information in an adroitly written book for beginning readers." Chicago. Children's Bk Center

The tomato and other fruit vegetables; photographs by Jerome Wexler. Morrow 1970 47p illus lib. bdg. $4.81 (2-4) 635

1 Vegetables
ISBN 0-688-31493-7
"Various stages of the life cycles of the tomato, snap bean, cucumber and eggplant are described: color and close-up photographs reveal very clearly the developmental stages of floral structure and seedlings and will be useful to more advanced readers." Sch Library J
"The photographs are superb and they help tell an interesting story about plants." Sci Bks

Vegetables from stems and leaves; photographs by Jerome Wexler. Morrow 1972 47p illus $5.50, lib. bdg. $4.81 (2-4) 635

1 Vegetables
ISBN 0-688-20177-2; 0-688-30177-7
The author describes the cultivation and growth of twelve common vegetables belonging to the stem group (asparagus and potatoes) and the leaf group (onions, cabbage, celery, chives, dill, kale and collards, lettuce, mustard, parsley and spinach)
"The clear, sharp photographs illustrate the words. . . . Although most of the photographs are in black and white, some are in color. Included in the text is how the plant reproduces, thus showing the life cycle. An excellent book." Appraisal

635.9 Flowers and ornamental plants (Floriculture)

Abell, Elizabeth
Flower gardening; illus. with photographs and drawings by A. D. Cushman. Watts, F. 1969 84p illus lib. bdg. $3.90 (5-7) 635.9

1 Flower gardening
ISBN 0-531-00533-X
"A good book for the beginner, giving advice on soils, watering and fertilizers, and on the planning and preparation of a garden bed. The text describes bulbs, corms, tubers, and roses in some detail, other flowers are included in general lists such as 'easily-grown perennials' or 'flowers for sunny windows.' There is some discussion of pest control, of starting seedlings, potting, et cetera but none of these is covered in great detail. The emphasis is on plants that are easy to grow." Chicago. Children's Bk Center

Bulla, Clyde Robert
Flowerpot gardens; pictures by Henry Evans. Crowell 1967 48p illus $4.50, lib. bdg. $5.25 (3-5) 635.9

1 House plants
ISBN 0-690-31059-5; 0-690-31060-9

"After a brief chapter of general instructions, the prospective gardener is offered 20 plants that can be cultivated indoors without too much effort, including herbs, and foliage and flowering plants. Instructions are given for raising plants from seeds, bulbs, and cuttings, and each plant is illustrated with an exceptionally attractive full-page drawing. The instructions are simple and precise, for the most part, and only occasionally mention materials that a child would be likely not to have." Sch Library J

Fenten, D. X.
Indoor gardening; illus. by Howard Berelson. Watts, F. 1974 61p illus lib. bdg. $3.90 (4-7) 635.9

1 House plants
ISBN 0-531-02731-7
"A First book"
"The opening chapter lists the basic needs of indoor plants: water, humidity, ventilation, temperature, soil, fertilizer, and containers, and gives advice on how best to provide these. Most of the book is alphabetical listings by Latin name (with the popular name in brackets after it) of recommended flowering or foliage plants. There is a chapter on fruits and vegetables, one on dwarf terrarium plants, another on bulbs, and yet another on cacti and succulents. With each plant listed is an accompanying guide on how to care for it. How to deal with the inevitable plant pest is given in a page and a half at the end of the book." Appraisal
"Full color illustrations would have enhanced the book. The black and white drawings by Howard Berelson, however, are clear. Teachers and young readers who are interested in growing plants in the schoolroom or at home will find the book helpful. There is also included a list of 'Other Books to Read' and an adequate index." Sci and Children

Plants for pots; projects for indoor gardeners. Illus. by Penelope Naylor. Lippincott 1969 128p illus $5.95 (4-7) 635.9

1 House plants
ISBN 0-397-31605-4
The author gives "instructions on how to grow plants from discarded vegetable parts, from cuttings to make gift plants, and from seed and bulbs; how to grow unusual plants and edible fruits and vegetables; and how to grow plants in a terrarium. He also describes gardening projects for each month of the year including hydroponically grown strawberries in August and a living Christmas tree in December. A glossary and a pronunciation guide are appended." Booklist
"Explicit instructions for easy projects and precise, attractive illustrations make this a good book for the beginning gardener, young or not so young." Sat Rev

Hoke, John
Terrariums; illus. with photographs. Watts, F. 1972 90p illus lib. bdg. $3.90, pa $1.25 (4-7) 635.9

1 Terrariums
ISBN 0-531-00777-4; 0-531-02405-9
"A First book"
"An introduction to terrariums which discusses the different types, tell what plants to use, surveys soil selection, describes the kinds of containers which are appropriate, and, most importantly, shows how to care for the completed terrarium. The coverage is thorough and accurate, and the text is clear. The different types of plants are accurately drawn in black and white, and numerous photographs, along with captions giving step-by-step instructions, clearly demonstrate the processes. In addition, Hoke includes a list of suppliers where the materials mentioned in the text may be purchased." Sch Library J
Bibliography: p79

Paul, Aileen

Kids gardening; a first indoor gardening book for children; illus. by Arthur Hawkins. Doubleday 1972 96p illus $4.95, lib. bdg. $5.70 (4-7)   635.9

1 House plants

ISBN 0-385-02492-4; -0-385-02494-0

"A book that gives good coverage, sensible advice, and an encouraging word to the beginning gardener. The directions are clear, although (as in the section on propagation) instructions are not always comprehensive. The author first gives general instructions on preparing potting soils, planting, watering, et cetera, then discusses house plants by type: plants that flower from bulbs, plants with attractive foliage, cacti, waterplants, and so on. . . . Appended are a list of sources for further information, a brief glossary, and a relative index." Chicago. Children's Bk Center

Selsam, Millicent E.

How to grow house plants; illus. by Kathleen Elgin. Morrow 1960 96p illus lib. bdg. $4.81 (4-7)   635.9

1 House plants

ISBN 0-688-31410-4

"Begins with an explanation of the structure of a plant and the function of its parts, then describes a number of house plants especially suitable for the beginner, and gives practical advice on water, light, temperature, soil, and fertilizer; also discusses plant housekeeping, raising plants from cuttings, seeds, and bulbs and suggests ideas for miniature gardens. Illustrated with many clear drawings. Helpful for plant growers at home or at school." Booklist

"It should tempt more experimenting and bring increased results while stimulating a hobby." Horn Bk

Guide to the culture of some common house plants: p91-96. Includes technical names

636   Animal husbandry

Fenton, Carroll Lane

Animals that help us; the story of domestic animals, by Carroll Lane Fenton and Herminie B. Kitchen; illus. by Carroll Lane Fenton. Rev. ed. Day 1973 128p illus lib. bdg. $5.95 (4-6)   636

1 Domestic animals

ISBN 0-381-99822-3

First published 1959

"Introductory remarks give a clear and basic review of the history of domestic animals. Subsequent chapters present additional information on how, when and where specific groups of animals became domesticated, as well as thorough and accurate scientific data regarding individual species. The book is rather remarkable in presenting considerable historical, geological, geographical and biological data in a format that is attractive to the young reader. Dogs are introduced through Pepper, a Border Collie; horses through Runner and his brother during the Stone Age in France; cattle through Apis, a sacred temple bull in Egypt; and guinea pigs as pets of an Indian family in the Andes Mountains of Peru. There are fifty-five illustrations; all are outstanding line drawings. The index is accurate and lists all illustrations." Sci Bks

636.08   Production, mainten-
ance, training of
animals. Pets

Caras, Roger

A zoo in your room; illus. by Pamela Johnson. Harcourt 1975 96p illus $5.95 (4-7)   636.08

1 Pets

ISBN 0-15-299968-X

The author "tells how to keep a comprehensive variety of pet store animals, from fish to mammals, and also smaller animals from the wild—reptiles, amphibians, and insects. . . . He emphasizes what children need to be told incessantly: the maintenance work in keeping pets both alive and 'well'. His advice is thoughtful and candid. . . . The three excellent chapters on habitat terrariums—marsh, desert, and woodland—along with the advice on appropriate food make the book useful for reference." Horn Bk

Bibliography: p91-92

Chrystie, Frances N.

Pets; a complete handbook on the care, understanding, and appreciation of all kinds of animal pets. 3d rev. ed. With illus. by Gillett Good Griffin. Little 1974 xxi, 269p illus $6.95 (4-7)   636.08

1 Pets

ISBN 0-316-14051-1

First published 1953

Contents: Dogs; Cats; Small caged animals; Caged birds; Aquarium and vivarium pets; Wild animals and birds; Farm animals; Ponies and saddle horses; First aid and common diseases

"The author stresses the dependency of pets on their owners and the importance of careful attention to animals' needs. The text is illustrated only with miniscule pen-and-ink drawings, but it provides much useful information on a host of pets from beef steers to woodchucks." Sch Library J

Cooper, Kay

All about rabbits as pets; photographs by Alvin E. Staffan. Messner 1974 64p illus $5.95, lib. bdg. $5.29 (3-6)   636.08

1 Rabbits

ISBN 0-671-32693-7; 0-671-32674-0

"Brief sections are included on physical characteristics, on species of wild rabbits and breeds of domestic ones, and on rabbits in research; these supplement the longer, practical chapters which contain advice on choosing, housing, feeding, and breeding domestic rabbits. Of special value are careful descriptions of mating, pregnancy, and birth as well as directions for sexing rabbits. Explicit black-and-white photographs and a table of information on breeds are included." Booklist

Dobrin, Arnold

Gerbils; written and illus. by Arnold Dobrin. Lothrop 1970 63p illus map lib. bdg. $4.14 (3-6)   636.08

1 Gerbils

ISBN 0-688-51636-X

"Gerbils, first brought into the United States for experimental purposes less than twenty years ago, have rapidly become one of the most popular of small pets. . . . This first book for young people should prove of great interest. The illustrations are precise, and the text gives information on the gerbil's habits in its natural environment, as well as complete information about feeding and caring for the animal in captivity. Included are advice on breeding, recording experiments, and arranging for the gerbil's comfort when the owner is away." Sat Rev

Shuttlesworth, Dorothy E.

Gerbils, and other small pets; illus. with photographs. Dutton 1970 130p illus $4.95 (3-6)   636.08

1 Rodents 2 Pets

ISBN 0-525-30459-2

"Helpful advice on how to keep gerbils, hamsters, squirrels, mice, rats, guinea pigs, and rabbits as pets

Shuttlesworth, Dorothy E.—*Continued*
and how to care for and enjoy them. The author points
out the importance of understanding the nature and
needs of these small rodents in order to keep them
healthy and contented and the opportunity such pets
offer for learning about animal behavior. The easily
read text is enlivened by photographs and a frequent
mention of personal experiences with rodent pets. A
list of books for further reading is appended." Booklist
The author "is careful to say which animals enjoy
being handled and which do not, and which should be
left outdoors." N Y Times Bk Rev

Silverstein, Alvin
Guinea pigs; all about them [by] Alvin & Virginia
Silverstein; with photographs by Roger Kerkham.
Lothrop 1972 96p illus $5.50, lib. bdg. $4.81 (3-6)
636.08

1 Guinea pigs
ISBN 0-688-41664-0; 0-688-51664-5
"This simple book has three sections: 1) a general
orientation about guinea pigs, their origin, morphology, varieties and natural history, including a 'rodent
family tree' showing their relatives; 2) 'Guinea pigs as
pets,' telling how to select, house and care for them
and how to breed them and raise the progeny; and 3)
'Guinea pigs in the laboratory,' describing their use in
testing new drugs and investigating the causes of disease and as experimental animals for germ-free
research in studies of nutrition, intelligence and
heredity." Sci Bks
"Here is an excellent reference book for boys and
girls interested in learning more about guinea pigs
and how to care for them. The photographs are most
appealing. Descriptions of the many uses of guinea
pigs in medical research and genetics add depth to the
contents of this volume." Appraisal

Hamsters; all about them [by] Alvin & Virginia
Silverstein; with photographs by Frederick Breda.
Lothrop 1974 126p illus $5.50, lib. bdg. $4.81
(4-7) 636.08

1 Hamsters
ISBN 0-688-40056-6; 0-688-50056-0
This book is a manual for the hamster owner, with
information on the care, feeding, housing, and breeding of these pets. Types of hamsters and their use in
laboratory research is also discussed
"It's a good, fat volume chock full of excellent
photographs . . . [and] should prove to be as popular
as hamsters themselves." Pub W

Simon, Seymour
Discovering what gerbils do; illus. by Jean Zallinger. McGraw 1971 47p illus lib. bdg. $4.72 (2-5)
636.08

1 Gerbils
ISBN 0-07-057434-0
"This is an excellent book for a boy or girl . . . who
has or is thinking about getting a gerbil as a pet. The
book not only tells the child how to care for the gerbil,
but through open-ended questions allows the child to
discover facts about the gerbil's behavior and living
patterns. The illustrations are excellent. The presentation is well-organized and the type is large and easy
to read." Sci Bks

Stevens, Carla
Your first pet; and how to take care of it; illus. and
based on an idea by Lisl Weil. Macmillan Pub. Co.
1974 122p illus. lib. bdg. $4.95 (2-4) 636.08

1 Pets
ISBN 0-02-788200-4
"Ready-to-read handbook"
In this handbook of house-pet care, the author gives
instructions on the feeding, housing and care of gerbils, guinea pigs, mice, hamsters, goldfish, parakeets,
cats, and small dogs
"The print is large, and the vocabulary is generally
accessible to independent readers, but Stevens
doesn't talk down by oversimplifying terms like
'veterinarian,' 'incisors,' and 'siphon.' Lisl Weil's
drawings, appealing in their cartoon-like simplicity,
illustrate techniques and equipment with which readers may not be familiar." Sch Library J

636.089 Veterinary sciences

Berger, Melvin
Animal hospital. Day 1973 126p illus (Scientists at
work) lib. bdg. $5.95 (4-7) 636.089

1 Veterinary medicine 2 Veterinarians
ISBN 0-381-99941-6
The author "discusses the activities of veterinarians
with emphasis on small animal practice and of
researches in animal medicine. He describes what
goes on in the examination, treatment, laboratory,
X-ray, and operating rooms and the work done by the
veterinarian's assistants." Booklist
"Sixty black-and-white photographs accompany
Mr. Berger's highly informative text. . . . The writing
style is simple and the subject matter is clearly presented. . . . The list of suggested readings is well chosen." Appraisal

636.1 Horses

Anderson, C. W.
C. W. Anderson's Complete book of horses and
horsemanship; with over fifty drawings by the author.
Macmillan (N Y) 1963 182p illus $6.95, pa 95¢ (5-7)
636.1

1 Horses
"Beginning with the history and development of
the horse, the author discusses breeds of horses,
selection, care and training, and techniques of riding.
Anatomically correct drawings." Hodges. Bks for
Elem Sch Libraries
"A fat book of facts and features on the . . . horse,
written with clarity, detail, and the appreciation of the
equine always exhibited in any Anderson volume.
Although much of the basic information is duplicated
in various source books, few write about horses with
Anderson's feeling and flair." Sch Library J
Horsemen's talk: p175-79

Balch, Glenn
The book of horses; cover photo: Zimbel-
Monkmeyer. Four Winds 1967 96p illus $5.95, lib.
bdg. $5.62 (4-7) 636.1

1 Horses 2 Horsemanship
ISBN 0-590-17048-1; 0-590-07048-7
First copyrighted 1958
"The author presents the history, breeds, care and
riding of horses and points out effectively the differ-
ence between English and western styles of riding."
Bruno. Bks for Sch Libraries, 1968
"The photographs are many, varied, and excellent.
The author emphasizes the need for instruction and
experience in handling one's own horse, an important
point, especially for children." Sch Library J

Brady, Irene
America's horses and ponies; written and illus. by
Irene Brady. Houghton 1969 202p illus lib. bdg. $9.95
(5-7) 636.1

1 Horses 2 Ponies

Brady, Irene—*Continued*

ISBN 0-395-06659-X

"This is not a pretentious book and is one that will be frequently consulted in homes and libraries. Adults will enjoy it, young children will be fascinated by the drawings, and young horse lovers will look, read, and dream. The author covers each breed with a pencil drawing (to scale), a table of outstanding conformations, and a short commentary on the breed's 'character' and 'flavor' as well as its history. The commentaries are generally informative, but not heavy reading. The author has a nice easy style. The drawings are excellent, and the 'poses' are fairly constant, so that one might compare the various horses, ponies, etc. There is a short section on the evolution of the horse, a diagram of the parts of the horse, and a table describing points of conformation to be used in a comparative judging." Sci Bks

Bibliography: p202

Henry, Marguerite

Album of horses; illus. by Wesley Dennis. Rand McNally 1951 112p illus $4.95, lib. bdg. $4.97 (4-7)
636.1

1 Horses

ISBN 0-528-82050-8; 0-528-82051-6

"The names of this author and artist and the word 'horse' on the cover are enough to recommend a book to hundreds of Henry-Dennis fans throughout the country. They will not be disappointed in these beautifully illustrated chapters on horses of many kinds, from Thoroughbred racers to Shetland ponies. And mules and burros have their chapters too. Description, history and interesting anecdotes are included. Twenty-six full-page colored illustrations and many marginal drawings in black and white." Horn Bk

Hess, Lilo

Shetland ponies; story and photographs by Lilo Hess. Crowell 1964 57p illus $4.50, lib. bdg. $5.25 (k-3)
636.1

1 Ponies

ISBN 0-690-73234-1; 0-690-73235-X

"The growth and development of two Shetland ponies from their birth in the spring to their first winter, affectionately described in . . . photographs and accompanying brief, narrative text." Booklist

The book contains "some gay, frisking photographs. There is little story line but a fair amount of information about this subject matter, which ranks high in appeal for almost every child." Pub W

Hogner, Dorothy Childs

The horse family; pictures by Nils Hogner. Walck, H.Z. 1953 70p illus $4 (3-6)
636.1

1 Horses

ISBN 0-8098-2316-0

First published by Oxford

"How the horse has developed through breeding and training from prehistoric times to the present. Also includes the horse in mythology and art, [man's use of the horse] and something about the horse's cousins, the tapir and the rhinoceros." Minnesota

"Children interested in horses will find this an easy-to-read and broad study of the horse. . . . Written with authority and illustrated with careful diagrams and drawings." Horn Bk

Ipcar, Dahlov

World full of horses. Doubleday 1955 unp illus $4.95, lib. bdg. $5.70 (k-2)
636.1

1 Horses

ISBN 0-385-07571-5; 0-385-07870-6

"This picture book shows a great variety of horses, those of grandfather's day that drew streetcars, and buses, fine carriages and farm wagons, fire apparatus and cannons. Now, after the advent of automobiles there are still horses—riding, policemen's horses, and circus horses

"It is a brief bit of simplified social history for younger children, with large-type, simple sentences for text, given distinction by its fine design and lovely use of interesting colors, well printed. . . . [The author's] pictures are full of action and detail that will interest younger children, introduce them to phases of our past and make them think about horses today in a new way." N Y Her Trib Bks

Rounds, Glen

Wild horses of the Red Desert; written and illus. by Glen Rounds. Holiday House 1969 unp illus lib. bdg. $5.95 (2-4)
636.1

1 Horses 2 The West

ISBN 0-8234-0146-4

"Against a background of the 'barren land of high rocky ridges and dusty sagebrush flats' . . . [the author] shows and tells the life of the wild horses who make this place their home through the seasons that bring hot winds in summer, deep snows in the winter, a home that is filled with dangers for them, any season, from other animals and from men." Pub W

"Well-illustrated account of how the wild horses live throughout the year in the Badlands of South Dakota. The reader is filled with feelings of adventure and can sense the wilderness atmosphere." Adventuring with Bks. 2d edition

Selsam, Millicent E.

Questions and answers about horses; pictures by Robert J. Lee. Four Winds 1973 62p illus $4.95, lib. bdg. $4.46 (2-4)
636.1

1 Horses

In a question-and-answer format, the author presents an "introduction to how horses evolved, how they live, and how man has made use of them. She also describes the various breeds of horses and how they may be distinguished." Babbling Bookworm

The book "is greatly enchanced and enlarged by brown-and-green water-color paintings and has the text printed in these same colors. Providing browsing material and fodder for simple school reports, this title will also stimulate the interest of older reluctant readers." Sch Library J

Slaughter, Jean

Pony care; photographs by Hugh Rogers. Knopf 1961 115p illus $4.50, lib. bdg. $5.69 (5-7)
636.1

1 Ponies

ISBN 0-394-81515-7; 0-394-91515-1

"The author begins by describing the types of ponies and the purchase of a pony by the young enthusiast. From this point the book is very detailed in the various ways of handling and caring for the pony, treating in separate chapters the elements of feeding and grooming, care during different seasons of the year and the fundamentals of first aid and the signs of illness. The book is intended in the first place for young owners, but it will be enjoyed by young horse lovers if for nothing else than vicarious experience and a better understanding of ponies." Best Sellers

Glossary: p109-10

Wright, Dare

Look at a colt. Random House 1969 unp illus $3.95, lib. bdg. $4.69 (k-2)
636.1

1 Horses

ISBN 0-394-80746-4; 0-394-90746-9

"The life of a young colt is vividly presented in very good photographs. The brief text, usually just a sentence or two on each page is superimposed on the photographs." Sci Bks

Wright, Dare—_Continued_
"Children will not find strange the literary device
that has the colt telling (interestingly) of his birth, his
dependence on his mother, his probable future, the
work of a quarter horse, etc." Library J

636.109   Horses—History

Burt, Olive W.
The horse in America; illus. with photographs. Day
1975 192p illus map $6.95 (5-7)   636.109
1 Horses—History 2 U.S.—History
ISBN 0-381-99630-1
This book deals with the history of the horse in
America and the horse's influence on American history. The author discusses prehistoric fossils, the role
of the horse in America's exploration and settlement,
its influence on the Indians and importance in frontier
life, its relationship to the cowboy, its use in warfare,
its role in transportation, communication and industry, and its place in present-day America
Bibliography: p181-83

Darling, Lois
Sixty million years of horses, by Lois and Louis
Darling. Morrow 1960 64p illus lib. bdg. $4.59
(4-7)   636.109
1 Horses—History
ISBN 0-688-31000-1
This book "tells of the wild ass, the zebra, and the
different breeds of modern horses, the uses of horses
through the years; and then goes back to the little
fossil eohippus and traces the evolution of horses to
modern times." Christian Sci Monitor
"For young readers, the history of the horse provides an easy introduction to the complexities of
evolution. . . . The handsome drawings reflect the
authors point that man always has loved horses and
will continue to, even tho most of our horse power
now comes from machines." Chicago Sunday Trib

636.5   Poultry

Milgrom, Harry
Egg-ventures; first science experiments; illus. by
Giulio Maestro. Dutton 1974 31p illus lib. bdg. $4.95
(1-3)   636.5
1 Eggs 2 Science—Experiments
ISBN 0-525-29160-1
"Using simple kitchen utensils, young readers are
shown how to conduct simple scientific experiments
with eggs. Differences in size, color, weight, and
content are discussed as well as the different parts of
eggs and how chicks hatch. Milgrom also explains how
to tell rotten eggs from fresh ones; how eggs are
graded; and how to decorate shells. Maestro's friendly
tiger family who demonstrate the projects add humor
to this lively presentation which concludes with an
excellent summary of the material." Sch Library J

Zim, Herbert S.
Homing pigeons; illus. by James Gordon Irving.
Morrow 1949 62p illus map lib. bdg. $4.59 (5-7)
                                                636.5
1 Pigeons
ISBN 0-688-31398-1
"A guide book to the raising, flying and racing of
homing pigeons, with plans for building simple lofts
and pens. Further instructions for developing the
hobby will be helpful to individuals or leaders, planning pigeon clubs." Wis Library Bul

636.6   Birds other than poultry

Mowat, Farley
Owls in the family; illus. by Robert Frankenberg.
Little 1961 103p illus $5.95 (4-7)   636.6
1 Owls 2 Saskatchewan
ISBN 0-316-58641-2
"An Atlantic Monthly Press book"
This is the story of "Wol and Weeps, a pair of owls,
who take over a family and a neighborhood and turn
them upside down." Growing Up With Bks
"The setting is Saskatoon, Saskatchewan. It is a
book that will appeal very strongly to children who
really love animals and birds. . . . Though it is written in the first person by the boy hero, it has an adult
air about it." Pub W
Mowat's "story is rich with unobtrusive natural history, and he achieves a rare combination of simplicity,
grace and distinction in the writing. Robert Frankenberg's witty illustrations completely capture the spirit
of the book." N Y Times Bk Rev

Villiard, Paul
Birds as pets; with 75 photographs by the author.
Doubleday 1974 177p illus $5.95, lib. bdg. $6.50
(5-7)   636.6
1 Cage birds 2 Pets
ISBN 0-385-03226-9; 0-385-04337-6
"Helpful information on the care, feeding, housing, breeding, and training of about 40 bird species
which thrive' in captivity (e.g., finches, canaries,
Budgerigars, parrots, love birds). Similar in format to
other pet selection guides by the author . . . the text
is generously illustrated with captioned black-and-
white photographs." Sch Library J

Zim, Herbert S.
Parrakeets; illus. by Larry Kettelkamp. Morrow
1953 59p illus lib. bdg. $4.59 (4-7)   636.6
1 Budgerigars
ISBN 0-688-31544-5
This book contains "everything the young person
needs to know about breeding, raising, and training
parrakeets, including how to teach them to talk and
how to build the right kind of cage for them." Hodges.
Bks for Elem Sch Libraries
This "simply presented information . . . will be
useful to those who already have these amusing pets
and may well encourage others to become owners.
Dr. Zim's explanation of color mutations according to
the rules of genetics will interest serious young scientists. Plainly labeled drawings." Horn Bk

636.7   Dogs

Bethell, Jean
How to care for your dog; illus. by Norman Bridwell. Four Winds [1967 c1964] 64p illus $3.95, lib.
bdg. $3.95 (2-4)   636.7
1 Dogs
ISBN 0-590-17076-7; 0-590-07076-2
Originally published 1964 in paperback by
Scholastic
"Instructions center on the comfort and well-being
of the dog from the first day and night with the new
owner. The author explains as simply as possible
proper methods of feeding, housebreaking, and
grooming, discusses illnesses that require a veterinarian's attention, and gives basic directions for training
a dog to obey and to perform easy tricks." Booklist

Bethell, Jean—*Continued*
This "text looks something like second-grade primers used to, but it makes sense from start to finish. Even the puppy pictures of various breeds are well chosen and captioned." N Y Times Bk Rev

Broderick, Dorothy M.
Training a companion dog; illus. by Haris Petie. Prentice-Hall 1965 72p illus lib. bdg. $4.95, pa $1.25 (4-7)   636.7
1 Dogs—Training
ISBN 0-13-926634-8; 0-13-926626-7
"P-H Junior research books"
"An excellent book on training—explicit, detailed, and sensible. The illustrations are helpful; the text is well-organized and is clear enough to need that help only slightly. The author discusses the need for training a dog, the way a dog learns, and the equipment needed and how to use it correctly. The succeeding chapters then describe, step by step, each procedure in the training program—including what not to do and what to do if the dog does not respond. The last chapter discusses Obedience Trials; an index is appended." Chicago. Children's Bk Center

Bronson, Wilfrid S.
Dogs; best breeds for young people; written and illus. by Wilfrid S. Bronson. Harcourt 1969 96p illus $5.95 (3-7)   636.7
1 Dogs
ISBN 0-15-22335-9
"There are many good books on choosing and training a dog, but this has additional appeal because of the humorous style, the forthright discussion of minor problems of dogs and owners, and the sensible discussion of safety measures, courtesy, preparation for ownership, and responsibilities as well as the major problems of selection and care. Actually, there is little on the topic of best breeds; there are several picture-charts (small, medium, big, and giant dogs) of 'Congenial K-9's for Young Folks.' The illustrations are crude but lively in comic valentine style, and a divided bibliography is appended." Chicago. Children's Bk Center

Cole, Joanna
My puppy is born; with photographs by Jerome Wexler. Morrow 1973 unp illus $4.95, lib. bdg. $4.59 (k-3)   636.7
1 Dogs
ISBN 0-688-20078-8; 0-688-30078-2
"Graphic photos show details of the birth of several [dachshund] puppies and the early days in their lives. The . . . [young girl narrating the story] chooses one she names Sausage and the book ends happily with him growing slowly, eating on his own, ready to leave his mother at eight weeks, and adjusting to a leash." Pub W
"This is a wonderful opportunity for the child who has never seen the miracle of birth: to see the sac emerging, the mother biting the cord and licking the newborn pup, and the helplessness of infant life. It's also a lesson in being gentle with animal babies, and it's charming in portrayal of the beguiling puppies." Chicago. Children's Bk Center

Foster, Joanna
Dogs working for people; photographs by James L. Stanfield. Natl. Geographic Soc. 1972 40p illus (k-3)   636.7
1 Dogs
Obtainable only as part of a set for $6.95 with: Dinosaurs, by Kathryn Jackson, class 568; Lion cubs, by the National Geographic Society, class 599; and Treasures in the sea, by Robert M. McClung, class 910.4

"Books for young explorers"
Prepared by the Special Publications Division of the National Geographic Society
This book describes retrievers, trackers and hunting dogs, cow and sheep-herding dogs, seeing-eye dogs, racing greyhounds, police and guard dogs, circus dogs, and Lassie, the television star

Henry, Marguerite
Album of dogs; illus. by Wesley Dennis. [New rev. ed] Rand McNally 1970 64p illus $4.95, lib. bdg. $4.97 (3-6)   636.7
1 Dogs
ISBN 0-528-82016-8; 0-528-82017-6
First published 1955 with title: Wagging tails
"The Pekingese, poodle, boxer, and Saint Bernard are among the 25 popular breeds, plus the mongrel, that are described in this book. In her typically simple, warm, sympathetic style, the author describes these varied breeds in terms of their appearance and history and relates anecdotes that reveal the general personality traits of each. Properly called an album, this book is by no means an encyclopedia of dogs. Nor is it a manual for dog training and care. It is a very personal weaving of words and pictures, making obvious the author's and illustrator's affection and admiration for man's four-legged friends." Sch Library J

Hürlimann, Bettina
Barry; the story of a brave St Bernard; illus. by Paul Nussbaumer. Harcourt [1968 c1967] unp illus $5.75 (k-3)   636.7
1 St Bernard dogs 2 Alps
ISBN 0-15-205710-2
First published 1967 in Switzerland. Translated from the German by Elizabeth D. Crawford
"This is the true story of Barry, a dog born at the Great St. Bernard hospice in the Swiss Alps during the Napoleonic Wars. . . . Following the tradition for these strong, intelligent animals, this famous St. Bernard was trained by the monks to rescue stranded travelers. Going out in blizzards to lead lost strangers to the hospice, finding men buried by avalanches, Barry became a classic example of the breed—and, in his years of service, saved the lives of 40 people." N Y Times Bk Rev
"The illustrations on the oversize pages are in black and white and in color; the latter are stunning paintings of mountain scenes in icy blues and lowering grays, snow-flecked. Only the dogs or the clothing of the muffled travelers are touched with bright color." Sat Rev

Lauber, Patricia
The story of dogs; foreword by Konrad Lorenz; illus. with map and photographs. Random House 1966 64p illus map $2.95, lib. bdg. $4.39 (3-5)   636.7
1 Dogs
ISBN 0-394-80140-7; 0-394-90140-1
"Gateway books"
A "history of dogs, telling how they may have been domesticated and how different breeds have developed." Hodges. Bks for Elem Sch Libraries
"Written in simple language interspersed with many appealing photographs of different breeds of dogs. [The author] gives information about the dog family, rather than identifying features of different breeds. Large print and wide margins will attract young dog-lovers." Sch Library J

Levin, Jane Whitbread
Bringing up puppies; a child's book of dog breeding and care; photographs by Mary Morris Steiner. Harcourt 1958 62p illus $5.95 (3-6)   636.7
1 Dogs
ISBN 0-15-212493-4

Levin, Jane Whitbread—*Continued*

"This book is intended for all boys and girls and parents who want to breed a dog and raise puppies. . . . It is based on the experience of four children who bred their black cocker, Chip, and watched her whelp four black puppies nine weeks later. It is a true story." Introduction

"The information is well selected and interestingly presented . . . . Photographs by Mary Morris Steiner are excellent. A useful book." Library J

Putnam, Peter

The triumph of the Seeing Eye; ed. by Walter Lord; illus. with 30 photographs, courtesy of the Seeing Eye. Harper 1963 178p illus lib. bdg. $4.79 (5-7)   636.7

1 Guide dogs 2 Blind 3 Seeing Eye, Incorporated, Morristown, N.J.

ISBN 0-06-024776-2

"A Breakthrough book"

The story of Morris Frank, pioneer in the use of guide dogs for the blind, and "of the Seeing Eye organization which includes a description of the education of the dogs before they meet their new masters, and the training of dog and man together." Wis Library Bul

"Young readers will find here an informative tale that will inspire them, as well [as] give insight into the problem of the blind." Best Sellers

Bibliography: p171-73

Rappaport, Eva

"Banner, forward!" The pictorial biography of a guide dog; photographs by the author. Dutton 1969 127p illus $7.95 (5-7)   636.7

1 Guide dogs

ISBN 0-525-26169-9

"The story of a golden retriever and her training as a seeing-eye dog at Guide Dogs for the Blind in San Rafael, California. Banner's education is three-fold: at the age of three months she is sent to a foster home where her training in a family atmosphere begins. Later she returns to the school for intensive training by a qualified instructor. The final month of training involves work with her future mistress. The photographs speak for themselves; the text is not loaded with sentimentality, but in a sensitive way tells a factual and fascinating story." Pub W

Sabin, Francene

Dogs of America, by Francene and Louis Sabin; photographs by William P. Gilbert. Putnam 1967 127p illus lib. bdg. $5.69 (5-7)   636.7

1 Dogs

ISBN 0-399-60131-7

While this book recounts the "story of the evolution and origin of the domesticated dog, its main thesis is a description of the various breeds of domesticated dogs—for various tasks and personal tastes—that have been developed over a very long time from the ancestral tamed wolves. The 115 kinds of purebred dogs recognized by the American Kennel Club are discussed and there are suggestions on the care, feeding and training of dogs." Sci Bks

"Although the writing is in places too colloquial and consciously clever, the admiration the authors show for the dogs should lead the reader to an appreciation of many breeds. Clear photographs of show dogs identify almost every breed included." Booklist

Selsam, Millicent E.

How puppies grow; photographs by Esther Bubley. Four Winds [1972 c1971] unp illus $4.95, lib. bdg. $4.95 (k-3)   636.7

1 Dogs

ISBN 0-590-17190-9; 0-590-07190-4

Originally published 1971 in paperback by Scholastic

"This book traces the growth of a litter of six puppies from when they are one day old until they become self-sufficient at the age of about six weeks. . . . Browsers will find photographs of the puppies nursing and at play endearing." Sch Library J

Written with the author's "usual gift for very simple prose that avoids being stilted; easy enough for beginning independent readers, the text is smooth enough to read aloud well, and can be used with preschool children." Chicago. Children's Bk Center

Unkelbach, Kurt

Both ends of the leash; selecting and training your dog; illus. by Haris Petie. Prentice-Hall 1968 72p illus $4.95, pa 95¢ (3-6)   636.7

1 Dogs 2 Dogs—Training

ISBN 0-13-080275-1; 0-13-080903-9

"A short, concise and useful book. The author presents his personal choice of 10 best breeds for children's pets, explaining why he didn't choose seven other popular breeds. He then deals with the teaching of six basic obedience commands, offers a good chapter on dog shows, and discusses such chestnuts as 'you can't teach an old dog new tricks.'" Sch Library J

Glossary: p65-67

How to bring up your pet dog; choosing, understanding, training, protecting, enjoying; illus. by Sam Savitt. Dodd 1972 119p illus $4.50 (4-7)   636.7

1 Dogs

ISBN 0-396-06488-4

"Drawing on his experiences as a breeder, trainer, and exhibitor of Labrador Retrievers the author gives sensible advice on selecting a healthy pup, caring for and training it, taking basic health and safety precautions, and dealing with common ailments. He includes numerous personal anecdotes and answers many representative questions from prospective or actual dog owners. He also provides detailed instructions for building an outdoor run, simple bench for indoor sleeping quarters, puppy playpen, and doghouse and lists of organizations and journals concerned with dogs. Attractive, accurate, and often amusing black-and-white drawings complement the text." Booklist

636.8 Cats

Besser, Marianne

The cat book; illus. by Shannon Stirnweis. Holiday House 1967 91p illus lib. bdg. $5.50 (4-6)   636.8

1 Cats

ISBN 0-8234-0024-7

"This is a book to introduce a younger audience to the evolution, physiology and types of domestic cats. It is not a how-to-train, feed-and-care-for manual but an appreciation of their qualities and liaison with man. Expressive black and white sketches evoke the personality and individuality of cats." Bruno. Bks for Sch Libraries, 1968

Bridge, Linda McCarter

Cats: little tigers in your house; photographs by Donna K. Grosvenor. Natl. Geographic Soc. 1974 30p illus (k-3)   636.8

1 Cats

ISBN 0-87044-159-0

Obtainable only as part of a set for $6.95 with: Creepy crawly things, by the National Geographic Society, class 598.1; Spiders, by Lillian Bason, class

Bridge, Linda McCarter—*Continued*

595; and Three little Indians, by Gene S. Stuart, class 970.1

"Books for young explorers"

Prepared by the Special Publications Division of the National Geographic Society

This book follows the activities of two kittens from the time they are born until they are two months old and are given to their new owners. It describes how their mother cares for them, their play, their eating and sleeping behavior, and their reactions to other animals

"The main appeal of Bridge's book on cats is its excellent photographic documentation. . . . The text here is moderately factual and liberally laced with conversational narrative." Booklist

Burger, Carl

All about cats; illus. with photographs; with a foreword by William Bridges. Random House 1966 143p illus $2.95, lib. bdg. $4.39 (5-7)　　636.8

1 Cats

ISBN 0-394-80258-6; 0-394-90258-0

"All about books"

"The evolution of the cat, his role in history and folklore, and his characteristics and personality are discussed in an entertaining and informative book. Includes a classification table, a chart of the cat's family tree, and a bibliography." Hodges. Bks for Elem Sch Libraries

Daly, Kathleen N.

The cat book; illus. by Gig Goodenow. Golden Press 1964 unp illus $5.27 (k-2)　　636.8

1 Cats

ISBN 0-307-60837-9

This book contains "enormous, captivating color paintings of cats of all kinds, accompanied by charming text." Bks On Exhibit

Rockwell, Jane

Cats and kittens; illus. with photographs. Watts, F. 1974 76p illus lib. bdg. $3.95 (4-7)　　636.8

1 Cats

ISBN 0-531-00812-6

"A First book"

"More instructive than the average pet care book for the middle grades, this volume offers important items of practical concern and curiosity for cat fanciers. Besides chapters on the history of the species and on general care and feeding, there are sections on anatomy and physiology, social and sexual behavior, choosing and training a kitten, and breeds of cats. Black-and-white photographs and drawings with interesting captions supplement the text, and lists of U.S. cat organizations and cat publications are appended." Booklist

Selsam, Millicent E.

How kittens grow; photographs by Esther Bubley. Four Winds [1975 c1973] unp illus $4.95 (k-2) 636.8

1 Cats

ISBN 0-590-07409-1

First published 1973 in paperback by Scholastic

In text and photographs this book describes the first eight weeks in the lives of four kittens. It tells how their mother nurses them, how they learn to walk and to eat solid food, and how they begin to play with each other and with objects around them

"This is an attractive and informative book which will appeal to young primary graders as well as older reluctant readers." Sch Library J

Stevens, Carla

The birth of Sunset's kittens; photographs by Leonard Stevens. Young Scott Bks. 1969 unp illus $4.95 (k-4)　　636.8

1 Reproduction 2 Cats

ISBN 0-201-09119-3

"A series of photographs show every detail of the always-wonderful sight of tiny, blind-eyed kittens being born. The text explains what is happening with matter-of-fact clarity: the muscles of the cat's uterus are contracting, moving the kitten along the birth canal; the kitten emerges, and the clinging amnion is eaten by the cat. The mother cat gently licks and grooms her new family; the kittens nurse. No cute posed pictures, no saccharine comment, just the miraculous facts." Sutherland. The Best in Children's Bks

"The photographs of Sunset and her litter are more than instructive: they arouse affection for the mother and convey her pleasure in the birth of her kittens." N Y Times Bk Rev

Unkelbach, Kurt

Tiger up a tree; knowing and training your kitten; illus. by Paul Frame. Prentice-Hall 1973 unp illus $4.95 (1-4)　　636.8

1 Cats

ISBN 0-13-921601-4

In story form, the author gives a general presentation of how to keep a kitten clean and healthy, and details what and when to feed it, when it is wise to housebreak a kitten, and simple commands the pet can learn

"Thoughtful instructions on raising a kitten for every young owner who wants a good pet and friend." Children's Bks of the Year, 1973

637　Dairy and related technologies

Aliki

Green grass and white milk; written and illus. by Aliki. Crowell 1974 33p illus (Let's-read-and-find-out science bks) $3.95, lib. bdg. $4.70 (2-4)　　637

1 Dairying 2 Milk 3 Cows

ISBN 0-690-00198-3; 0-690-00199-1

The author "tells the story of milk from the green grass of the pasture to the pasturization process in the dairy. The life of the cow is described with emphasis on the food she eats and how the milk is obtained. The process of handling the milk from the cow to the finished product is described." Sci Teacher

"Attractive illustrations and informative diagrams accompany a simply written text that is informal in style and accurate in content." Chicago. Children's Bk Center

639　Nondomesticated animals

Axelrod, Herbert R.

Tropical fish as a hobby; a guide to selection, care and breeding. Rev. ed. McGraw 1969 300p illus $8.95 (5-7)　　639

1 Tropical fish 2 Aquariums

ISBN 0-07-002606-8

First published 1952

With chapters on How fish get their names, and Aquarium genetics, by Myron Gordon, and a chapter on The balanced aquarium myth, by James W. Atz

"Besides rules for the care, feeding, and breeding of fish, and maintaining a healthy home aquarium,

Axelrod, Herbert R.—*Continued*

there are chapters on fish nomenclature and aquarium genetics. A tabular chart gives popular and scientific name, source, reproduction of type, aquarium temperature, disposition, facts on breeding for more than 100 fish for ready reference. Information for both beginners and more advanced tropical-fish hobbyists." Booklist

Bibliography: p285-86

Tropical fish in your home, by Herbert R. Axelrod and William Vorderwinkler. G. J. M. Timmerman, photographer. [Rev. ed.] Sterling 1960 144p illus $4.95, lib. bdg. $4.89 (5-7) 639

1 Tropical fish 2 Aquariums
ISBN 0-8069-3710-6; 0-8069-3711-4
First published 1956

The authors describe how the beginning aquarist can create a tiny underwater world. They offer information on many varieties of fish from which to choose, citing methods of caring for each. The author's objective is to provide answers for the questions raised by young collectors

Buck, Margaret Waring

Pets from the pond; written and illus. by Margaret Waring Buck. Abingdon 1958 72p illus $3.95 (4-7) 639

1 Aquariums 2 Fresh-water biology
3 Amphibians
ISBN 0-687-30865-8

Covers "the kind of information children require for setting up a home aquarium. Miss Buck suggests ways and means of finding these small aquarium creatures and simple methods for providing natural homes and food for them. Brief life histories of fish, frogs, salamanders, turtles, crayfish and water insects are included, with line drawings showing the various stages of development." Ontario Library Rev

A "complete and minutely detailed book, . . . [It is] an exciting book for youngsters interested in nature. Excellent bibliography of books, bulletins, and magazines, and a good index." Library J

Small pets from woods and fields; written and illus. by Margaret Waring Buck. Abingdon 1960 72p illus $5.50, pa $1.75 (4-7) 639

1 Nature study 2 Animals—Habits and behavior
ISBN 0-687-38653-5; 0-687-38678-0

Divided into three parts: Plants, amphibians, and reptiles; Insects and spiders; and, Small mammals and birds, this book gives details of the appearance, habits, development, and care, of easily obtained small pets, such as frogs, salamanders, snakes, squirrels, birds, etc. Includes information on proper foods, and on the construction and care of terrariums, cages, vivariums, and birdhouses

"A wealth of suggestions for children's nature projects is provided here in the attractive format of the author's earlier books, including the parallel 'Pets from the Pond' [listed above]. . . . Many species are identified, each meticulously sketched in clear ink line. Excellent nature bibliography and an index." Horn Bk

Conklin, Gladys

I caught a lizard; words by Gladys Conklin; pictures by Artur Marokvia. Holiday House 1967 unp illus lib. bdg. $5.95 (k-3) 639

1 Animals—Habits and behavior
ISBN 0-8234-0054-9

"Sixteen common small creatures—lizard, salamander, baby bird, snake, praying mantis, among them—are found or bought, one after the other, by a small boy or girl. Some of the creatures are observed in their own habitat; others are brought home, caged, and fed, but most of these are set free again after a

short period. The easy-to-read conversational text is full of information, and the food requirements of the small pets are recapitulated in a concluding chart." Horn Bk

Hoke, John

Aquariums. Watts, F. 1975 71p illus lib. bdg. $3.90 (4-7) 639

1 Aquariums
ISBN 0-531-02772-4
"A First book"

"Viewing aquariums as artificial ecosystems, Hoke emphasizes the tank set-up—light, air, temperature, etc. Aquarium maintenance is covered in detail, but there is only minimal discussion of the fish themselves." Sch Library J

"A useful if undecorated manual for serious beginning fish hobbyists." Booklist

Turtles and their care; illus. with photographs; drawings by Barbara Wolff. Watts, F. 1970 89p illus lib. bdg. $4.33, pa $1.25 (5-7) 639

1 Turtles
ISBN 0-531-00696-4; 0-531-02406-7
"A First book"

"A general discussion of the morphology and natural history of turtles, both land and aquatic, with descriptions of principal species illustrated by photographs and drawings. The major task is a thorough description of how to keep turtles in a balanced environment outdoors and indoors." The AAAS Sci Bk List for Children

Bibliography: p86

Laycock, George

Wild animals, safe places. Four Winds 1973 178p illus $6.95 (5-7) 639

1 National parks and reserves—U.S. 2 Animals—U.S.
ISBN 0-590-17276-4

The author "tells some of his experiences in Yellowstone, Mount McKinley, and Everglades National Parks and on several of the islands of the Hawaiian Islands National Wildlife Refuge. Besides giving some of the history of the four areas he describes the life, food, habitat, and young of their animals, amphibians, and birds." Booklist

"Embellished with black-and-white photographs by the author and containing an index, this title is recommended as an additional purchase." Appraisal

McCoy, J. J.

Nature sleuths; protectors of our wildlife; illus. with photographs. Lothrop 1969 160p illus lib. bdg. $5.49 (5-7) 639

1 Wildlife—Conservation 2 Game protection
ISBN 0-688-51609-2

"This book tells both of the individuals who killed off completely certain species of animals until federal and state conservation officials tracked them down, and of the people engaged in protecting wildlife through conservation laws and agencies." Sci Bks

Glossary: p154-55. Suggested reading: p156

Mason, George Frederick

The wildlife of North America; illus. by the author. Hastings House 1966 87p illus maps (Hastings House World wildlife conservations ser) lib. bdg. $4.17 (5-7) 639

1 Wildlife—Conservation 2 Animals—North America
ISBN 0-8038-8027-8

"This book gives a brief description of the origin, history and destiny of certain North American wildlife. By revealing some of the situations that caused

Mason, George Frederick—*Continued*

animals to become extinct, the author hopes to give young readers a better understanding of the importance of preserving wildlife now endangered by our spreading civilization." Author's note

"Well-organized, objective account. . . . Includes a chart of geological eras, maps of the U.S. wildlife refuge system and Canadian national parks, as well as numerous attractive, accurate drawings." Booklist

Bibliography: p81-82

Pels, Gertrude

The care of water pets; illus. by Ava Morgan. Crowell 1955 119p illus $4.50, lib. bdg. $5.25 (4-6)
639

1 Aquariums 2 Amphibians
ISBN 0-690-17070-X; 0-690-17071-8

An "informative introduction to the care of water pets of various kinds: fish, both tropical and native; frogs; turtles; snails; and salamanders and newts. Directions for setting up an aquarium, for choosing fish, for caring for the aquarium, for feeding and caring for the plants and animals, for breeding fish, and for building an outdoor pond are all discussed in clear detail. The book will make an attractive, useful addition to nature study collections." Chicago. Children's Bk Center

Ricciuti, Edward R.

Shelf pets; how to take care of small wild animals; photographs by Arline Strong. Harper 1971 132p illus $4.50, lib. bdg. $4.79 (5-7)
639

1 Animals—Habits and behavior
ISBN 0-06-024993-5; 0-06-024994-3

"A how-to book for city and country children. Frogs, salamanders, snakes, turtles, spiders, crickets, guppies, snails, hamsters and guinea pigs are some of the animals described here." Pub W

"This is a useful guide for the young naturalist who wishes to study nature at close range. . . . For each pet the author suggests ways of procuring the animal, methods of providing appropriate housing and kinds of food required. In some cases a brief history of the animal is included. The reader is encouraged to simulate the natural environment as much as possible and is provided with many hints for achieving this end with maximum ease." Appraisal

Recommended books: p127-28

Selsam, Millicent

Let's get turtles; drawings by Arnold Lobel. Harper 1965 62p illus (A Science I can read bk) $2.95, lib. bdg. $3.79 (1-3)
639

1 Turtles
ISBN 0-06-025310-X; 0-06-025311-8

"Billy and Jerry buy turtles for pets and, with some advice from Billy's father but mostly by experimentation, learn how to feed and care for them properly. A pleasant story for beginning readers with helpful information for beginning turtle owners." Booklist

"The boys' childlike conversations make their experiences seem real." Horn Bk

Plenty of fish; illus. by Erik Blegvad. Harper 1960 61p illus (A Science I can read bk) $2.95, lib. bdg. $3.79 (k-3)
639

1 Goldfish
ISBN 0-06-025320-7; 0-06-025321-5

"By observing his own two goldfish brought home from the five-and-ten in plastic bags and by experimenting—with a little help from his father—a small boy learns how fish eat and breathe and how to house and care for them." Booklist

"Outstanding because of the beauty of its format, the excellence of its illustrations by Erik Blegvad, the humor and lack of condescension in its text." Horn Bk

Underwater zoos; illus. by Kathleen Elgin. Morrow 1961 96p illus lib. bdg. $4.81 (4-6)
639

1 Aquariums 2 Marine aquariums 3 Marine animals
ISBN 0-688-31531-3

"Valuable to the youngster who wants to keep an aquarium. The first three chapters tell how to collect salt water specimens, give interesting facts about salt water life and tell how to set up and maintain a salt water aquarium. The last three chapters are a counterpart dealing with fresh water life." The AAAS Sci Bk List for Children

"A most useful book, with clear instructions and helpful suggestions, and with many interesting observations made by the author based on her own experience in collecting and caring for the animals in her own aquarium. Mrs. Selsam has a direct and lucid approach that combines with an enthusiasm about the subject to incite equal enthusiasm on the part of the reader." Chicago. Children's Bk Center

Van Dersal, William R.

Wildlife for America; the story of wildlife conservation. Rev. and enl. ed. Walck, H.Z. 1970 160p illus $6.50 (5-7)
639

1 Wildlife—Conservation
ISBN 0-8098-3090-6
First published 1949

"An excellent presentation of the history and concepts of wildlife conservation and management in the United States. Each verso page deals with one concept; each recto page bears one or two good black and white photographs illustrating the facing concept. Valuable for use in social studies, science and English. Sections on preservation and management of wildlife habitat deal primarily with farmlands. A page each is devoted to the dangers of pesticides and pollution." The AAAS Sci Bk List for Children

Further reading: p150

Villiard, Paul

Exotic fish as pets; with fifty-four photographs by the author. Doubleday 1971 187p illus $4.95, lib. bdg. $5.70 (5-7)
639

1 Aquariums 2 Tropical fish
ISBN 0-385-05043-7; 0-385-07387-9

"The first half of this practical guide is concerned with the setting up and proper maintenance of an aquarium, giving information on the water, plants, foods, snails, breeding, and diseases; the latter half is devoted to fish species suggested for beginning aquarists, describing characteristics and needed care. An appendix discusses some tested and recommended commercial products." Booklist

Reptiles as pets; with photographs by the author. Doubleday 1969 188p illus $4.95, lib. bdg. $5.70 (5-7)
639

1 Reptiles
ISBN 0-385-00297-2; 0-385-06773-9

"The author provides an elementary introduction to herpetology, and then tells where and how to collect and care for [reptiles] as pets, where to buy them, what kind of cage and habitat they need, how to keep them healthy, how to breed them, and how to grow their food." The AAAS Sci Bk List for Children

Wild mammals as pets; with photographs by the author. Doubleday 1972 159p illus $4.95, lib. bdg. $5.70 (5-7)
639

1 Mammals
ISBN 0-385-05042-9; 0-385-02495-9

"Despite the title, this is a handbook that is based primarily on the idea that wild mammals should not become pets; it does, however, give advice on the care, housing, and feeding of such wild creatures as

Villiard, Paul—Continued
may have been found injured or abandoned while too young to care for themselves. The book is permeated by a concern for the animals and the text is specific about avoiding those kindnesses that may make it more difficult for the creature returned to the wild. The suggestions for care are authoritative and detailed; a final chapter gives in a listing by states, the addresses of conservation agencies and, in another list, the animals that are protected or for which a permit is needed." Chicago. Children's Bk Center

Waters, Barbara
Salt-water aquariums [by] Barbara and John Waters; illus. by Robert Candy. Holiday House 1967 161p illus $4.95 (5-7)   639
1 Marine aquariums 2 Marine animals
ISBN 0-8234-0099-9
This is "a readable, detailed, and well-organized guide to setting up a marine aquarium either at home or at school. A profusion of excellent illustrations complements the text. The first chapters explain the whys and wherefores, the needs and musts, for keeping the plants and animals alive. General directions are given, followed by step-by-step instructions. There are suggested experiments with a listing of necessary equipment. Finally, there is a large section devoted to marine animals." Appraisal
Suggested reading: p154-56

Wong, Herbert H.
Our terrariums, by Herbert H. Wong and Matthew F. Vessel; illus. by Aldren A. Watson. Addison-Wesley 1969 31p illus (Science ser. for the young) lib. bdg. $4.95 (k-3)   639
1 Terrariums
ISBN 0-201-08722-7
"An Addisonian Press book"
This book "shows young children how to make an observation habitat for a toad and a lizard." Christian Sci Monitor
"Good elementary science reading." Sci Bks

Zappler, Georg
Amphibians as pets [by] Georg and Lisbeth Zappler; with photographs and drawings by Richard Marshall. Doubleday 1973 159p illus $5.95, lib. bdg. $6.70 (5-7)   639
1 Amphibians
ISBN 0-385-04821-1; 0-385-08581-8
"A thorough introduction to the world of amphibians with clear and detailed description of the characteristics of each kind found throughout the world, and illustrated with precise diagrams. All aspects are covered: range, description, digestive tract, hearing, sight, courtship, reproduction, development, etc. . . . A most useful guide, it gives information on over 40 different ones. The last third of the book is the section devoted to finding your own pet: suggested field trips with notetaking; how to catch tadpoles, prepare tanks, aquariums, and terrariums. There are detailed instructions on the care of the amphibians, on treating a sick pet, on rearing your own flies and other insects for food; and much more. The book closes with one-paragraph descriptions of some exotic foreign species available at pet stores." Appraisal

Zim, Herbert S.
Commercial fishing [by] Herbert S. Zim [and] Lucretia Krantz; illus. by Lee J. Ames. Morrow 1973 64p illus map $4.75, lib. bdg. $4.32, pa $1.25 (3-6) 639
1 Fisheries
ISBN   0-688-20091-5;   0-688-30091-X;   0-688-05267-3

"A skillfully organized explanation of commercial fishing which calls attention to the expanding use of seafood in combating food shortages. Descriptions of the types of boats employed are followed by identification and uses of fish. There is also a section on shellfish. New techniques for locating fish (radio, echo sounders, hydrophones) are discussed along with the familiar hook and line which still works best for catching fish. The text is clear and interesting, and the black-and-white drawings extend the information." Sch Library J

Goldfish; pictures by Joy Buba. Morrow 1947 unp illus $4.75, lib. bdg. $4.32 (2-5)   639
1 Goldfish 2 Aquariums
ISBN 0-688-21340-5; 0-688-31340-X
"Not children alone but older persons who keep goldfish as pets may find a great deal of help and information in this factual and authentic book. The type is large, the text clear and simple, the illustrations accurate and amusing. . . . Dr. Zim writes interestingly about the different kinds of fish, their habits and their requirements, and why they have reached their great popularity." Horn Bk
"Simply written but sound scientifically." Los Angeles Sch Libraries

640.73   Consumer education

Gay, Kathlyn
Be a smart shopper; photographs by David C. Sassman. Messner 1974 64p illus $5.95, lib. bdg. $5.29 (4-6)   640.73
1 Consumer education
ISBN 0-671-32695-3; 0-671-32696-1
"A short, elementary consumer's lesson that emphasizes the importance of careful consideration and selection in the purchase of goods and services. Gay discusses consumer motivations and how they are influenced by advertising, packaging, and display; she also clues young shoppers in on some common pitfalls and warns them to familiarize themselves with merchandise so they can distinguish between real and false bargains. . . . Welcome advice for the legions of young buyers who are often the special targets of manufacturers." Booklist

641.3   Food and foodstuffs

Berry, Erick
Eating and cooking around the world; fingers before forks. Day 1963 96p illus maps $5.95 (5-7)
                     641.3
1 Food 2 Manners and customs
ISBN 0-381-99939-4
"Not a recipe book, but a description of the foods and the cooking, serving, and eating customs of peoples of a dozen countries or regions. The text does not cover all older civilizations, but discusses some which have kept primitive customs or are subject to limitations imposed by climatic or agricultural conditions." Chicago. Children's Bk Center
"The book will make a good introduction to the world of anthropology and add dimensions to social studies. Illustrated with clear, well-selected photographs." Sch Library J

Cooper, Elizabeth K.
And everything nice; the story of sugar, spice, and flavoring; illus. by Julie Maas. Harcourt 1966 80p illus map $5.50 (3-5)   641.3

Cooper, Elizabeth K.—*Continued*
1 Spices 2 Sugar 3 Flavoring essences
ISBN 0-15-203498-6
The growth, harvesting, preparation and "history of spices, sweets, and seasonings down through the years to the present is as fascinating as it is fragrant. . . . For added zest, there are directions for making pomander balls; easy-to-make recipes for mustard, eggnog with nutmeg, cinnamon toast; and, best of all, a wholly new appreciation and understanding of how spices enhance flavor and food." Horn Bk

Fenten, Barbara
Natural foods, by Barbara and D. X. Fenten; illus. by Howard Berelson. Watts, F. 1974 66p illus lib. bdg. $4.33, pa $1.25 (5-7)　　　641.3
1 Food
ISBN 0-531-02675-2; 0-531-02409-2
"A Concise guide"
This book gives guidelines on the selection of natural foods, vitamins, and supplements. The authors tell how to grow and prepare various natural foods and suggest what the inclusion of those foods in the diet can and cannot do for the individual
"A balanced, straight-to-the-point presentation that distinguishes between organic, health, and natural foods and discusses the latter in light of the current concern about overprocessing and chemical additives. . . . No scare tactics here, but a low-keyed reminder that much food bought by Americans is worthless if not harmful and that there is a different way to eat. A few places to buy natural foods are suggested, along with some adult books to read." Booklist

Hays, Wilma P.
Foods the Indians gave us, by Wilma P. Hays and R. Vernon Hays; illus. by Tom O'Sullivan. Washburn 1973 113p illus $4.95 (5-7)　　　641.3
1 Food 2 Indians 3 Agriculture
ISBN 0-679-24025-X
"The authors have prepared an informative and interesting book concerning foods which originated as wild plants, were cultivated by the Indians of North and South America, and were eventually introduced to and enjoyed by many other nations. There are discussions of the probable origins of potatoes (white and sweet), peanuts, beans, tomatoes, pineapple, chocolate and cocoa, seafoods, maize or corn and a variety of other foods. . . . The text stresses the importance of a stable food supply in building a civilization, the genius of the Indian farmers in cultivating wild plants for food and what modern man has done to improve these foods. The last chapter contains 25 simple recipes adapted from the Indian ways of cooking." Sci Bks

Lavine, Sigmund A.
Indian corn and other gifts; illus. with photographs, drawings, and old prints. Dodd 1974 80p illus $3.95 (4-7)　　　641.3
1 Food 2 Indians 3 Agriculture
ISBN 0-396-06777-8
"Dealing with the contributions of American Indians to the Western world's diet, Lavine concentrates on five important natural products: potatoes, corn, maple syrup, and varieties of beans and squash. Besides learning of the Indians' cultivation, gathering, and preparation of these and other edibles, one reads about the plants' appearance in legend, ritual, and artifact and also discovers the nature of the white man's first encounter with the vegetation as food. . . . An annotated list of original territories of tribes mentioned in the test and a bibliography are appended." Booklist
"Illustrated with photos and old prints, Lavine's

book . . . is not only informative but entertaining. . . . Recommended for students and others who wish to learn more about their country and the Indians." Pub W

Meyer, Carolyn
Milk, butter, and cheese; the story of dairy products; illus. by Giulio Maestro. Morrow 1974 96p illus $4.95, lib. bdg. $4.59 (5-7)　　　641.3
1 Dairy products 2 Dairying 3 Cookery
ISBN 0-688-20100-8; 0-688-30100-2
This book discusses the dairy industry and its products. Part one surveys milk production, processing, and nutritional value. Part two tells of specific dairy products including butter, cheese, and ice cream. Recipes are included at the end of each chapter
"This look at dairy products covers ground not likely to be familiar to many young readers. . . . A surprise to some will be the recently discovered fact that certain peoples—especially Africans, Southeast Asians, and Indians of North and South America—after childhood lose the ability to digest milk and so can be made ill by it. Historical facts and a sprinkling of legend also add life to the section on cheesemaking, which describes varying processes." Booklist

Smaridge, Norah
The world of chocolate; illus. by Don Lambo. Messner 1969 92p illus map $3.95 (4-6)　　　641.3
1 Chocolate
ISBN 0-671-32091-2
The story of chocolate and the chocolate industry is traced from the Aztec Indians who introduced it to Hernando Cortez in 1519 to the present
"With diagrams, a map, informative drawings, and an index, this history . . . will fill a need in general collections and may inspire further study of manufacturing and dietetics. Further, the text and illustrations are printed in warm brown ink: a complement for the delicious subject." Sch Library J
Kinds of chocolate and cocoa: p85-87

641.5　Cookery

Better Homes and Gardens Junior cook book; for beginning cooks of all ages. [3d ed. Meredith 1972] 80p illus $2.95 (4-7)　　　641.5
1 Cookery
ISBN 0-696-00070-9
First published 1955
"That cooking can be fun is emphasized in this book edited for the beginner. . . . Bright colored pictures of completed dishes, clear diagrams and directions, simple recipes, guidance on table settings, a glossary of cooking terms . . . and a table of weights and measures (and of the sizes of cans) make this easy to use." Sat Rev

Borghese, Anita
The down to earth cookbook; illus. by Ray Cruz. Scribner 1973 128p illus lib. bdg. $5.95 (4-6)　641.5
1 Cookery
ISBN 0-684-13249-4
"A natural foods cookbook for middle graders. Cooking terms, utensils, and ingredients are explained, and the recipe directions are clear. The tone is realistic and comforting. . . . There is a good index, the line drawings of boys and girls cooking are pleasant, and the book on the whole stresses that cooking is a creative, enjoyable activity." Sch Library J

Camp Fire Girls Mother daughter cookbook, by Jody Cameron; illus. by Phoebe Gaughan. Berkley Pub. Corp. 1974 193p illus pa $1.25 (4-7)   641.5
1 Cookery
ISBN 0-425-02467-9
"A Berkley Medallion book"
This cookbook contains approximately 150 simple recipes with utensils, ingredients, methods of cooking and exact steps listed in each. Also includes information on kitchen safety, measuring, shopping, party and menu planning, as well as table setting
Cooking and baking terms: p183-86

Cavin, Ruth
1 pinch of sunshine, 1/2 cup of rain; natural food recipes for young people; illus. by Frances Gruse Scott. Atheneum Pubs 1973 95p illus $5.95 (4-6)
          641.5
1 Cookery
ISBN 0-689-30099-9
"A variety of easy recipes using whole grains, unrefined sweeteners, wheat germ, and unprocessed meats and vegetables. Also has tips for preparing foods for best nutritional value." Chicago
"This natural foods cook book gives some variations on familiar recipes plus a few unusual ones. . . . The directions are simple to follow and enlivened with humorous illustrations." Library J

Cooper, Terry Touff
Many hands cooking; an international cookbook for girls and boys, cooked and written by Terry Touff Cooper and Marilyn Ratner; illus. by Tony Chen. Crowell in cooperation with the U.S. Committee for UNICEF 1974 50p illus $4.95 (4-7)   641.5
1 Cookery
ISBN 0-690-00536-9
Spiral binding
"An intriguing collection of recipes from all over the world ranging from cocoa and maple snow to Guacamole and African stew. Even the simplest fare has new twists such as adding vanilla to cocoa or making herb butter for sweet corn. Directions are clear; the recipes are graded according to difficulty; and the ingredients are easily available. A grade-A cookbook for young gourmets." Sch Library J
Kitchen terms to know: p xi-xiii

Crocker, Betty
Betty Crocker's Cookbook for boys & girls. Golden Press 1975 160p illus $3.95 (3-7)   641.5
1 Cookery
ISBN 0-307-09617-3
Spiral binding
First published 1957 by Simon & Schuster. Golden Press edition published in 1965 had title: Betty Crocker's New boys and girls cook book
A picture cookbook with step-by-step recipes for breads, main dishes, vegetables, party treats, and snacks

Ellison, Virginia H.
The Pooh cook book. . . . Illus. by Ernest H. Shepard. Dutton 1969 120p illus $5.50 (4-7) 641.5
1 Cookery 2 Cookery—Honey
ISBN 0-525-37404-3
"Inspired by Winnie-the-Pooh and The house at Pooh Corner, by A. A. Milne." Title page
"A rather special book and not essential but one which lovers of Pooh will find both pleasurable and practical. Recipes for some distinctly Pooh dishes such as marmalade on a honeycomb, colored honey, Cottleston pie and Cucumber or Mastershalum leaf sandwiches are interspersed between recipes for scrambled eggs, honey buns, hot potato salad with

tuna fish, blueberry pie, and Christmas nut cookies. Directions are explicit and easy to follow and the book is enhanced w th numerous quotations from 'Winnie the Pooh' and 'The House at Pooh Corner.' " Booklist

Girl Scouts of the United States of America
Cooking out-of-doors. The author 1960 216p illus pa $3.25 (4-7)   641.5
1 Outdoor cookery
ISBN 0-88441-128-1
Spiral binding
First published 1946, this is a revision of Woodland cookery
Compiled by Alice Sanderson Rivoire
Designed for both the novice and the procamper this book of outdoor cookery contains about 250 recipes index-keyed to ingredients, and skill levels

Girl Scout cookbook. Regnery 1971 160p illus $6.95 (4-7)   641.5
1 Cookery
ISBN 0-8092-9144-4
"Edited by Ely List." Verso of title page
"Beginning with recipes for snacks and beverages, this book provides advice on meal planning with information on party and outdoor cooking, including recipes for main dishes, soups, and salads
"A very good book for the cook of intermediate status. . . . [The recipes] are interspersed with general comments and bits of ancillary advice. A brief bibliography precedes the relative index." Chicago. Children's Bk Center

MacGregor, Carol
The storybook cookbook; illus. by Ray Cruz. Doubleday 1967 96p illus $4.95, lib. bdg. $5.70 (3-6)   641.5
1 Cookery
ISBN 0-385-05802-0; 0-385-06329-9
The twenty-two "recipes in this cookbook are for foods that favorite storybook characters have eaten—Heidi's Toasted Cheese Sandwiches, Captain Hook's Poison Cake, Hans Brinker's Waffles, Pinocchio's Poached Eggs, and many more. There are brief descriptions of all the stories, quotes from the books about the foods, and then recipes to follow—for cakes, pies, pretzels, fried chicken, and pot pie." N Y Times Bk Rev
Glossary: p93-95

Moore, Eva
The Seabury Cook Book for boys and girls; easy to read, easy to cook. Pictures by Talivaldis Stubis. Seabury [1971 c1969] 48p illus $4.95 (1-3)   641.5
1 Cookery
ISBN 0-8164-3059-4
First published 1969 in paperback by Scholastic with title: The lucky cook book for boys and girls
"A very good first cook book. It contains nine easy recipes: on one page it lists the ingredients and equipment needed, on the other are listed numbered steps in procedure. The illustrations are big and clear, and safety warnings are given repeatedly. Lists of terms and of tools, also illustrated, are included, and instructions for preparing a dinner and a party (using the recipes in the book) are given." Chicago. Children's Bk Center

Parents' Nursery School
Kids are natural cooks; child-tested recipes for home and school using natural foods; text by Roz Ault; based on the ideas of Liz Uraneck; illus. by Lady McCrady. Houghton 1974 129p illus $5.95, pa $3.95 (3-6)   641.5
1 Cookery

Parents' Nursery School—*Continued*
ISBN 0-395-18508-4; 0-395-18521-1
"This is a cookbook that can be used by independent readers or can be used by adults working with young children. The recipes are sensibly grouped by seasons, using ingredients when they are plentiful and suiting the cooking to the weather—especially useful if the book is used for group projects. The instructions are firm but informal, and the recipes use natural foods; cooks are encouraged to be creative. A set of 'Guidelines for Teachers and Parents' gives suggestions for making cooking enjoyable and informative, for equipment and safety measures, and for substituting ingredients." Chicago. Children's Bk Center

Paul, Aileen
Kids cooking; the Aileen Paul Cooking School Cookbook, by Aileen Paul and Arthur Hawkins. Doubleday 1970 128p illus $4.95, lib. bdg. $5.70 (3-6)   641.5
1 Cookery
ISBN 0-385-06874-3; 0-385-02219-0
"This basic cookbook giving recipes for breakfast, lunch, dinner, dessert and party foods, places importance on the pleasure of cooking by suggesting foods that are established favorites with children. The authors have presented their material in an easily understood format with the ingredients on one page and step-by-step directions opposite." Pub W
"Grouping is by meals or type (dinner or lunch, party or snack dishes), and there are separate prefaces addressed to the adult and the child." Sat Rev

Perkins, Wilma Lord
The Fannie Farmer Junior cook book. New and rev. ed. With illus. by Martha Powell Setchell. Little 1957 179p illus $5.95 (5-7)   641.5
1 Cookery
ISBN 0-316-69932-2
First published 1942
A cook book for young people based on the "Boston Cooking School Cook book" by Fannie Farmer. It includes easy to follow recipes plus helpful hints on mixing, using the stove and descriptions of various kinds of pans and other tools

Rombauer, Irma S.
A cookbook for girls and boys; chapter headings by Marion Rombauer Becker. [Rev. ed] Bobbs 1952 243p illus $4.50 (4-7)   641.5
1 Cookery
ISBN 0-672-50258-5
This book "defines cooking terms and processes, teaches correct methods of measuring and mixing, and gives hundreds of recipes for the new and the experienced cook." Hodges. Bks for Elem Sch Libraries

Shapiro, Rebecca
A whole world of cooking; illus. by the author. Little 1972 70p illus $5.95 (5-7)   641.5
1 Cookery
ISBN 0-316-78286-6
"More for the young amateur than for the beginner, these recipes call for uncomplicated cooking procedures and, despite the international flavor, only standard ingredients. Breezy writing introduces each dish, but the instructions that follow are clear and businesslike. The table of contents is arranged by country, the index by type of dish." Sat Rev

Wide world cookbook; illus. by the author. Little 1962 58p illus $5.95 (5-7)   641.5
1 Cookery
ISBN 0-316-78283-1
"A collection of recipes listed alphabetically by country of origin in the table of contents, and indexed by type of food. There is one recipe from each country (except for the United States). . . . Some of the recipes are quite simple, some a bit more complicated; the directions given for the latter are adequate for a reader with cooking experience, but not always adequate for the beginner. Each recipe is preceded by a few lines about the country or the dish." Chicago. Children's Bk Center

Van der Linde, Polly
Around the world in 80 dishes, by Polly and Tasha van der Linde; pictures by Horst Lemke. Scroll Press 1971 85p illus $5.25 (3-6)   641.5
1 Cookery
ISBN 0-87592-007-1
"Easy-to-follow recipes for 53 dishes from many different countries, which utilize common or readily obtainable ingredients, are presented in a cookbook written by two sisters, ages ten and eight. The cheerfully illustrated book is divided into sections of side dishes, soups, eggs, fish, meats, vegetables and salad, sauces and dressings, desserts, and drinks. There are no indications of the number of servings that each recipe will make, an unfortunate omission for beginning cooks, but the book does include a glossary of cooking terms, notes to parents, general rules, tips for setting the table, an illustrated list of cooking utensils, and the authors' subjective evaluation of the difficulty of each recipe." Booklist

641.6   Cookery of and with specific materials

Perl, Lila
The hamburger book; all about hamburgers and hamburger cookery; illus. by Ragna Tischler Goddard. Seabury 1974 128p illus $5.95 (5-7)   641.6
1 Cookery—Meat
ISBN 0-8164-3106-X
The author traces the history of man's use of ground meat from thirteenth century Russia through our modern hamburger chains. Also included are twenty-two international recipes which use ground meat
"The recipes are varied, and the step-by-step instructions are given clearly. A considerable portion of the text in each section gives background information of moderate interest, usually including some facts about national eating habits or other national dishes." Chicago. Children's Bk Center

641.7   Specific cookery processes and techniques

Hautzig, Esther
Cool cooking; 16 recipes without a stove; pictures by Jan Pyk. Lothrop 1973 unp illus $4.95, lib. bdg. $4.59 (2-5)   641.7
1 Cookery
ISBN 0-688-41532-6; 0-688-51532-0
"Simple kitchen tools (no stove is required) and easily available ingredients will produce no-fail, fun-to-make dishes for budding gourmets in the elemen-

Hautzig, Esther—*Continued*
tary grades. Instructions for the 16 recipes—ranging from 'Grapefruit Cups' to 'Strawberry Mint Julep'—are simple to follow, and even second graders can prepare anything from an appetizer to a dessert.... It is a good additional cooking book with a different viewpoint, perky illustrations, and a lively format." Sch Library J

641.8 Composite dishes

Johnson, Hannah Lyons
Let's bake bread; photographs by Daniel Dorn. Lothrop 1973 unp illus $5.50, lib. bdg. $4.81 (2-5)
641.8

1 Bread
ISBN 0-688-41297-1; 0-688-51297-6
"What could be better than a cookbook that tells the most inexperienced reader exactly what he needs to know, and nothing that he doesn't? Here, with photographs that add to its usefulness, is a text that does just that: takes a neophyte step by step through the several procedures of breadbaking, beginning with utensils and ingredients. The photographs show three children mixing, measuring, kneading, and so on; while the pictures and the simple, clear directions make this a book that young cooks can use alone, the text has no note of coyness, so that older readers may feel encouraged to try their hands as well." Chicago. Children's Bk Center

McDonald, Barbara Guthrie
Casserole cooking fun; illus. by Vee Guthrie. Walck, H.Z. 1967 72p illus $5.95, pa $1.50 (4-6)
641.8

1 Cookery
ISBN 0-8098-2398-5; 0-8098-2915-0
"Practical tips on efficient and safe cooking habits and measuring and a glossary of cooking procedures together with 24 step-by-step recipes for a variety of vegetable, meat, and dessert casseroles make this a notable addition to cookbooks for children. Illustrated with appealing, informative sketches." Booklist
It "has just two dozen recipes, but they are for real foods, and [the author] is unusually clear about procedures, tin sizes, etc." N Y Times Bk Rev

Meyer, Carolyn
The bread book; all about bread and how to make it; illus. by Trina Schart Hyman. Harcourt 1971 96p illus $5.95 (3-6)
641.8

1 Bread
ISBN 0-15-212040-8
"The author describes the importance of bread in early times after giving a conjectural explanation of the discovery of baked grain, discusses its place in religious ceremonies and the many special forms in which it appears, gives some facts about large baking plants and small neighborhood bakeries. And, of course, gives recipes for several kinds of home-baked bread. An index is appended." Chicago. Children's Bk Center
The recipes "are aimed at beginners, but there is no writing down and no fictionalizing. Useful for foods units, holidays and customs units, social studies, and for generally inquisitive readers who like a fast-moving, fact-filled book." Sch Library J
"Throughout the tale of the loaf, the illustrator's humorous pen-and-ink drawings delightfully highlight the universality of man's need for this staple no matter what shape, type, or texture it—or he—comes in. An unusual and eminently satisfying presentation." Horn Bk

Moore, Eva
The cookie book; illus. by Talivaldis Stubis. Seabury 1973 64p illus $4.95 (3-5)
641.8

1 Cookies
ISBN 0-8164-3081-0
The author provides beginning bakers with twelve recipes for such favorites as snicker doodles; animal-shaped butter cookies; Christmas ornament cookies; molasses, peanut butter, and oatmeal cookies; and coconut drops, each suggested for a particular month of the year
"The batches are small and manageable—not over two dozen each—and all of the recipes are basic. Important tips, an illustrated cooking dictionary, and an easy conversational style make this collection of recipes as practical as it is readable." Horn Bk

Paul, Aileen
Candies, cookies, cakes [by] Aileen Paul and Arthur Hawkins. Doubleday 1974 144p illus $4.95, lib. bdg. $5.70 (4-6)
641.8

1 Cookies 2 Confectionary 3 Cake
ISBN 0-385-03019-3; 0-385-03066-5
"This simply written cookbook offers an appealing range of recipes from old standards to easy but unusual treats. A variety of no-cook candies heads the list of manageable projects, while for the adventurous, there is chocolate carrot cake and apricot peanut butter drop cookies. Although a few more drawings depicting methods and finished products would have been helpful, expect this book to absorb its share of edible spills. Includes kitchen rules, and information on basic techniques, equipment, and ingredients. Intended to be used with minimal adult safety supervision." Booklist

646.2 Sewing

Corrigan, Barbara
I love to sew. Doubleday 1974 139p illus $4.95, lib. bdg. $5.70 (4-6)
646.2

1 Sewing
ISBN 0-385-03089-4; 0-385-03163-7
Illustrated by the author
"Attractive, functional items result from these instructive projects that teach sewing basics and require a minimum of stitching expertise. The simplest placemats call for fringing raw edges and perhaps ironing on an applique. Tote bags, purses, belts, and triangle scarves require only straight seams; more impressive looking but just as simple are a set of curtains and a bedspread. Later examples escalate slightly in difficulty by introducing curved seams or simple facings. Commercial patterns are relegated to older sewers, though instructions for using a basic pants pattern are included. A clear, effective guide to first experiences with a needle and thread." Booklist

646.4 Clothing construction

Corrigan, Barbara
Of course you can sew! Basics of sewing for the young beginner; written and illus. by Barbara Corrigan. Doubleday 1971 127p illus $4.95, lib. bdg. $5.70 (5-7)
646.4

1 Sewing 2 Dressmaking
ISBN 0-385-07697-5; 0-385-03241-2
"A sound and practical guide to fundamental sewing techniques presented in explicit text and clear

Corrigan, Barbara—*Continued*
diagrams and drawings. Information about equipment, fabrics, basic hand stitches, and the operation of a sewing machine is followed by instructions for making accessories from straight pieces of material; ponchos or capes based on simple geometric shapes; shifts or robes from Turkish towels; curtains, gowns, or robes from colorful sheets; and gathered skirts; and for using commercial patterns to make simple, sleeveless dresses and blouses." Booklist

649   Child rearing

Samson, Joan
Watching the new baby; photographs by Gary Gladstone. Atheneum Pubs. 1974 65p illus $5.95 (3-5)   649
   1 Infants
   ISBN 0-689-30119-7
"This excellent book on infant development provides the late primary and intermediate child with simple tools for observing the behavior of a new-born baby in his home and understanding the different types of motor and sensory developments occurring in the baby's first 18-24 months of life. Early chapters are devoted to prenatal development, birth, appearance. Subsequent chapters explain developments in touch, movement, sight, and hearing as well as the importance of eating, sleeping, and crying. The book not only informs, but suggests ways in which the reader may actively participate in this growth process. Fine black-and-white photography depicts all family members participating in the infant care process. A chart at the back suggests when a baby may be expected to accomplish various motor/sensory tasks." Appraisal
   Glossary: p62-64. Sources: p65

Saunders, Rubie
The Franklin Watts Concise guide to babysitting; illus. by Tomie de Paola. Watts, F. 1972 63p illus lib. bdg. $4.33 (5-7)   649
   1 Babysitters 2 Children—Care and hygiene
   ISBN 0-531-02563-2
Title on spine: The concise guide to babysitting
"A concise, useful guide to baby-sitting intended for the novice. It treats baby-sitting in a professional manner and deals briefly with each step taken in preparation for the first job. Covered are how to find a job, how much to charge, the sitter's responsibilities, safety precautions to remember, and, of course, the care and feeding of the child. . . . The drawings which accompany the text are amusing." Sch Library J

652.8   Cryptography

Gardner, Martin
Codes, ciphers and secret writing. Simon & Schuster. 1972 96p illus $5.95 (5-7)   652.8
   1 Cryptography 2 Ciphers
   ISBN 0-671-65201-X
"A book that should delight the puzzle fan, this explains how to code and decode messages, moving from fairly simple transposition and substitution ciphers to increasingly intricate examples using symbols and numbers as well as alphabets. One chapter describes code machines such as telephone dials, wheels, and grilles; another is devoted to invisible writing. Many examples of classic codes and messages are included; answers to practice codes and riddles are

not. A divided bibliography is appended." Chicago. Children's Bk. Center

Kohn, Bernice
Secret codes and ciphers; illus. by Frank Aloise. Prentice-Hall 1968 63p illus lib. bdg. $4.95, pa. 95¢ (4-7)   652.8
   1 Cryptography 2 Ciphers
   ISBN 0-13-797399-3; 0-13-797738-7
"After explaining the basic differences between codes and ciphers, the author describes various simple and complex types of both including dictionary and machine codes and concealment, transposition, and substitution ciphers. She documents her account with several historic examples and with the work of famous cryptographers and cryptanalysts. Tables showing English letter and word frequencies are appended and the book is illustrated with amusing black-and-white drawings." Booklist

Peterson, John
How to write codes and send secret messages. Illus. by Bernice Myers. Four Winds 1970 64p illus lib. bdg. $4.95, pa 75¢ (2-4)   652.8
   1 Ciphers
   ISBN 0-590-07056-8; 0-590-02606-2
"A practical little book on encoding and decoding secret messages, specifically geared to the interests of young children. The clear easy text, illustrated with two-color diagrams and drawings, gives directions for writing messages in space, hidden word, Greek, and alphabet codes and in invisible ink made of lemon juice or washing soda. The concluding chapter suggests ways of delivering the secret messages." Booklist

Rothman, Joel
Secrets with ciphers and codes, by Joel Rothman and Ruthven Tremain. Macmillan (N Y) 1969 32p illus lib. bdg. $4.95 (3-7)   652.8
   1 Cryptography 2 Ciphers
   Illustrated by Ruthven Tremain
"Ten different codes are given, from easy to hard, with exercises in encoding and deciphering secret messages. Answers included." Hardgrove. Mathematics Library—Elem and Jr High Sch
"For sheer, basic child appeal, [this book] will probably steal everybody's blood and thunder. . . . [The authors] have devised a charming little how-to-baffle-adults book." N Y Times Bk Rev

658   General management

Amazing Life Games Company
Good cents; every kid's guide to making money, by members of The Amazing Life Games Company (and friends); illus. by Martha Hairston and James Robertson. Houghton 1974 128p illus $6.95, pa $3.95 (4-7)   658
   1 Business 2 Finance, Personal
   ISBN 0-395-19500-4; 0-395-19501-2
"Suggestions here are attractively presented with humorous cartoon-type illustrations that make the projects . . . look like lots of fun. Realistic as to the capabilities of middle graders as well as the marketability of the goods or services suggested, 'Good Cents' really is a sensible manual that should provide incentive for youngsters trying to earn cash." Sch Library J

658.85   Personal selling (Salesmanship)

Fisher, Leonard Everett

The peddlers; written & illus. by Leonard Everett Fisher. Watts, F. 1968 45p illus maps (Colonial Americans) lib. bdg. $3.90 (4-7)   658.85

1 Peddlers and peddling 2 U.S.—Social life and customs—Colonial period

ISBN 0-531-01031-7

The author describes Colonial peddlers, "the wares they carried, the routes they followed, the hazards they encountered, and their importance to the settlers." Booklist

"Even more than the text, the strong scratchboard illustrations convey the struggles and strivings of colonial America and the importance of trade to a frontier society." Sch Library J

664   Food technology

Buehr, Walter

Salt, sugar, and spice. Morrow 1969 78p illus map lib. bdg. $4.81 (3-6)   664

1 Salt 2 Sugar 3 Spices

ISBN 0-688-31569-0

"The first two sections give a brief history of salt and sugar respectively, along with a description of the methods used to obtain and process each. The final section explains the importance of the early spice trade and gives the characteristics and uses of 33 major spices." Booklist

"There is a two-page map showing the Portuguese and Dutch spice routes, the Arab caravan and ship routes, and Columbus' route to the West Indies. The various countries and the spices they supply are also indicated on the map. The attractive book concludes with a descriptive list of spices found in most kitchens. There is an index. This book will be a very useful addition to any collection of children's books." Sci Bks

A spice list: p53-[79]

Hammond, Winifred G.

Sugar from farm to market. Coward-McCann 1967 95p illus maps lib. bdg. $4.59 (4-6)   664

1 Sugar

ISBN 0-698-30344-X

"An overview of the sugar industry is presented with actual photographs and other illustrations that give highlights of the history, growing, processing, and distribution of sugar and sugar products, considering both the beet and cane industries. Each chapter concludes with a project or activity." Sci Bks

Silverstein, Alvin

The chemicals we eat and drink [by] Alvin Silverstein [and] Virginia Silverstein. Follett 1973 112p illus $5.95, lib. bdg. $5.97 (4-7)   664

1 Food additives 2 Food contamination

ISBN 0-695-40372-7; 0-695-40372-9

A "discussion of the natural and artificial poisons that are in the foods we consume is documented by reports of research studies by scientists in or out of governmental agencies and by results of the food-testing programs of manufacturers of foods and drugs. The authors also describe the beneficial effects of some chemical elements, and conclude with chapters on foods of the future and on some of the ways in which individual citizens can improve the situation by changing their own diets and supporting supervisory

legislation and pollution control." Chicago. Children's Bk Center

"Well organized and indexed. . . . Pertinent information, previously available only in periodicals, is made easy to understand in this simplified but scientifically accurate report." Sch Library J

666   Ceramic and allied technologies

Buehr, Walter

The marvel of glass; written and illus. by Walter Buehr. Morrow 1963 95p illus lib. bdg. $4.81 (5-7)   666

1 Glass manufacture 2 Glass

ISBN 0-688-31573-9

This is the story of glass, its history and uses. The author describes glass of ancient times, the different methods of making glass by hand, machine processes of glass making, and modern glass products

"Interesting discussion of uses from insulation to waterproofing and air circulating casts, but most astonishing are the predictions for the future uses of glass. The technological development from hand blown glass goblets to a forty thousand pound mirror is interestingly described." Chicago Sch J

Fisher, Leonard Everett

The glassmakers; written and illus. by Leonard Everett Fisher. Watts, F. 1964 43p illus (Colonial Americans) lib. bdg. $3.90 (4-7)   666

1 Glass manufacture 2 Glass 3 U.S.—Social life and customs—Colonial period

ISBN 0-531-01028-7

The author presents the history of glass, the techniques in making it, and the way colonial glassmakers worked

"Well-written text and strong, vibrant illustrations." Sch Library J

Glassmaking terms: p40-41

The potters; written & illus. by Leonard Everett Fisher. Watts, F. 1969 47p illus map (Colonial Americans) lib. bdg. $3.90 (4-7)   666

1 Pottery, American 2 Potters 3 U.S.—Social life and customs—Colonial period

ISBN 0-531-01032-5

This "book discusses the basic ingredients necessary for, and processes involved in, making pottery. The coarse utensils the American potters wrought lacked the beauty of china or porcelain pieces but served very well the needs of the early colonists. Mr. Fisher utilizes a historical approach to detail early pottery operations and the contributions of . . . men instrumental in maintaining this colonial craft. The author's precise, substantial black-and-white illustrations are an integral part of the book, graphically showing equipment, processes, and techniques." Sch Library J

668.4   Plastics

Hahn, James

Plastics, by James and Lynn Hahn. Watts, F. 1974 65p illus lib. bdg. $3.45 (5-7)   668.4

1 Plastics

ISBN 0-531-02702-3

"A First book"

"The authors skillfully cover the history, chemistry

Hahn, James—*Continued*

and uses of plastics and provide some basic knowledge of the plastics that are being used in ever more unexpected places." Sci Bks

"The text is clear, organized, and illustrated with black-and-white photographs. A glossary and list of suggested readings are appended." Booklist

669   Metallurgy

Burt, Olive W.

The first book of copper; illus. with photographs. Watts, F. 1968 86p illus lib. bdg. $3.90 (4-7)   669

1 Copper
ISBN 0-531-00512-7

"Everything about copper is found here: folklore, history of its discovery, mining, smelting, refining and the uses of copper today." Ontario Library Rev

"Sharp, clear black and white photos extend the comprehensive, businesslike text." Bruno. Bks for Sch Libraries, 1968

675   Leather and fur technologies

Fisher, Leonard Everett

The tanners; written & illus. by Leonard Everett Fisher. Watts, F. 1966 43p illus (Colonial Americans) lib. bdg. $3.90 (4-7)   675

1 Tanning 2 U.S.—Social life and customs—Colonial period
ISBN 0-531-01038-4

"This history and description of the preparation and tanning of hides to manufacture leather and parchment . . . provides young readers with accurate and interesting insights into the development of American crafts and industries. The woodcuts are in the spirit of the work and assist in explaining the text." Sci Bks

Tanners' terms: p40-41

676   Pulp and paper technology

Buehr, Walter

The magic of paper; written and illus. by Walter Buehr. Morrow 1966 95p illus lib. bdg. $4.81 (4-7)   676

1 Paper making and trade 2 Paper
ISBN 0-688-31789-8

"Beginning with the chapter on the need for paper throughout the world, the book continues with chapters about the history of papermaking from the earliest times, a discussion of papermaking today, kinds of papers in use today, and concludes with a chapter on paper in the future." Sch Library J

"The drawings add to explanations of technical processes and enliven the book. Names and dates pinpoint world-wide achievements." Horn Bk

Eberle, Irmengarde

The new world of paper; illus. with photographs. Dodd 1969 79p illus lib. bdg. $4.50 (4-7)   676

1 Paper 2 Paper making and trade
ISBN 0-396-05898-1

"A very clear and well written discussion of paper

and the paper industry. The author begins by describing the many uses of paper today, including the less familiar ones. . . . There are chapters on the history of paper, from its invention in ancient China down to the great modern papermaking machines. The author explores the sources of modern paper in the giant forests of the northwest and Canada. The operations of paper mills are clearly explained, and readers are shown every type of paper, corrugated carton, bag, and waxed container being manufactured at them. Accompanying the concise, accurate text are a variety of good black-and-white photographs." Sch Library J

Fisher, Leonard Everett

The papermakers; written & illus. by Leonard Everett Fisher. Watts, F. 1965 46p illus (Colonial Americans) lib. bdg. $3.90 (4-7)   676

1 Paper making and trade 2 U.S.—Social life and customs—Colonial period
ISBN 0-531-01030-9

The author "explains the techniques of the papermaker and gives a brief glimpse into the historical background, the need for paper in the American colonies and the techniques used by these skilled artisans and patriots." Sch Library J

The book "includes a glossary of terms and identifies a number of paper watermarks. Strong black-and-white illustrations on every other page. Special but attractive." Booklist

677   Textiles

Adler, Irving

Fibers [by] Irving and Ruth Adler. Day [1972 c1964] 47p illus map lib. bdg. $4.47 (3-6)   677

1 Fibers
ISBN 0-381-99969-6

"The Reason why books"

Copyright 1964; brought up to date 1972

This book discusses fibers, natural and manmade, including "flax, cotton, wool, rubber, silk, fiberglass, nylon, rayon, and numerous other less common ones. Traces history of the development, preparation, and uses of the material, and the role each plays in the world market today." Sch Library J

"A useful book, succinct and fact-packed, with illustrations of variable quality." Chicago. Children's Bk Center

Fiber index: p47

Buehr, Walter

Cloth from fiber to fabric; written and illus. by Walter Buehr. Morrow 1965 96p illus lib. bdg. $4.81 (5-7)   677

1 Textile industry and fabrics
ISBN 0-688-31176-8

"The various processes of clothmaking—spinning, weaving, knitting, bleaching, and dyeing—are described by Buehr in this brief historical survey. Different fibers such as wool, linen and cotton, require different methods of preparation. An account of these methods, as well as a description of a modern mill, are included. The text moves rapidly and the information is accurate." Sci Bks

"Clear illustrations and diagrams." Horn Bk

Cavanna, Betty

The first book of wool [by] Betty Cavanna & George Russell Harrison; illus. with photographs. Watts, F. 1966 60p illus lib. bdg. $3.90 (4-6)   677

1 Wool 2 Sheep
ISBN 0-531-00672-7

This "treatment of the subject includes information

Cavanna, Betty—*Continued*
about different animals in various parts of the world that produce fleece; the ways of spinning from ancient times to the present; the shearing, processing and weaving; the special attributes of wool." Sch Library J
"An informative book for children in the middle grades. . . . Excellent photographs." Ontario Lib Rev
Includes a glossary

679 Other products of specific materials

Fisher, Leonard Everett
The wigmakers; written and illus. by Leonard Everett Fisher. Watts, F. 1965 45p illus (Colonial Americans) lib. bdg. $3.90 (4-7)   679
1 Wigs 2 U.S.—Social life and customs—Colonial period
ISBN 0-531-01039-2
"The text is divided into a section on the historical background for the industry and one on the techniques of manufacture. The illustrations are nicely detailed and quite informative. . . . A glossary of terms and an index are appended." Chicago. Children's Bk Center

680 Miscellaneous manufactures

Colby, C. B.
Early American crafts; tools, shops and products. Coward-McCann 1967 48p illus lib. bdg. $3.99 (4-7)   680
1 Art industries and trade—U.S.
ISBN 0-698-30066-1
Photographs "taken at the Colonial Williamsburg, Old Sturbridge Village and Mystic Seaport restorations, add another dimension to [this] study of colonial life. Cabinetmakers, silversmiths, blacksmiths, printers, and others are shown at work as are home craftsmen doing spinning, weaving, and candle-making. Suitable as a survey or a browsing book." Library J

Fisher, Leonard Everett
The homemakers; written & illus. by Leonard Everett Fisher. Watts, F. 1973 48p illus (Colonial Americans) lib. bdg. $3.90 (4-7)   680
1 Art industries and trade—U.S. 2 U.S.—Social life and customs—Colonial period
ISBN 0-531-01047-3
The author explains how in colonial times, "four household items—candles, soap, brooms, and cider— were made by families for their own needs. [He] describes techniques and skills involved in these homemaking chores. [The book has] black-and-white illustrations and diagrams and simple text." Sch Library J

Tunis, Edwin
Colonial craftsmen and the beginnings of American industry; written and illus. by Edwin Tunis. World Pub. 1965 159p illus $3.95, lib. bdg. $4.41 (5-7) 680
1 Art industries and trade—U.S. 2 U.S.—Social life and customs—Colonial period 3 U.S.—Industries
ISBN 0-529-04978-3; 0-529-04979-1
The author describes the working methods and products, houses and shops, town and country trades,

individual and group enterprises by which the early Americans forged the economy of the New World. He discusses such trades as papermaking, glassmaking, shipbuilding, printing, and metalworking, and describes some of the objects that are now heirlooms —silverware of Paul Revere, Queensware pottery, etc.
"An oversize book that is impressively handsome and that should be tremendously useful; well-organized and superbly illustrated, the text is comprehensive, lucid, and detailed. . . . An extensive index is appended." Chicago. Children's Bk Center

681 Precision instruments and other devices

Johnson, Chester
What makes a clock tick? Pictures by Nathan Goldstein. Little 1969 73p illus lib. bdg. $4.50 (4-7) 681
1 Clocks and watches
ISBN 0-316-46738-3
"An Atlantic Monthly Press book"
The author describes how clocks work by examining the function of each piece and the regulation necessary for achieving the precise time. Readers are encouraged to try and rebuild a clock
"The mechanical details of spring-wound clocks and watches, and of weight-and-pendulum movement clocks are written very lucidly in a step-by-step sequence. The drawings that accompany the descriptive text are clear. . . . In the final part of the book there are brief descriptions of electrically-driven clocks and watches, including the timekeeper of ultimate precision, the cesium atomic clock. . . . The book should have excellent reception in all schools and particularly vocational schools." Sci Bks
Index and glossary: p67-73

Reck, Alma Kehoe
Clocks tell the time; illus. by Janina Domanska. Scribner 1960 48p illus map lib. bdg. $5.95 (3-5)   681
1 Clocks and watches
ISBN 0-684-13477-2
This book "shows the development of time-keeping methods and devices from the 'shadow clock' of prehistoric man to the complicated Atomichron which will lose only one second in 3,000 years. . . . A map showing time zones in the U.S. is included." Booklist
"Mrs. Reck's [book] is so attractive looking that it will be a pleasure to add to our shelves. . . . Each brief account has boldly printed headings and delightful drawings by Janina Domanska, suggestive of wood block illustrations in early books, and made decorative not only by their design but by scarlet touches and captions." N Y Her Trib Bks

683 Hardware

Kraske, Robert
Silent sentinels; the story of locks, vaults, and burglar alarms. Doubleday 1969 127p illus lib. bdg. $4.50 (5-7)   683
1 Locks and keys 2 Vaults (Strong rooms)
ISBN 0-385-05485-8
"A history of the devices used to safeguard property against theft traces the development of these safety measures from the Great Pyramid of Cheops to the modern bank vault, from simple key lock to time lock,

Kraske, Robert—*Continued*
from ancient curse to electronic burglar alarm. Written in anecdotal style the account is engrossing as well as instructive, having the appeal of a book on crime detection. Illustrated with photographs." Booklist

Peterson, Harold L.
A history of knives; illus. by Daniel D. Feaser. Scribner 1966 64p illus lib. bdg. $5.95 (4-7)   683
1 Knives
ISBN 0-684-13186-2
"Beginning with knives of primitive men—stone, ivory, horn, and so forth—the account then proceeds to describe the development and types of metal knives: daggers, scramasaxes, bowies (including the recently designed Astro knife), fighting knives, hunting knives, table knives, and pocketknives. A section on care and handling makes a suitable conclusion." Horn Bk
The text is "readable and the illustrations are clear. Recommended for large collections because other material on this subject is scattered, treated either as weapons only . . . or divided in encyclopedias among articles on cutlery, stone weapons, etc." Sch Library J

684   Woodworking

Lasson, Robert
If I had a hammer; woodworking with seven basic tools. Photographs by Jeff Murphy. Dutton 1974 76p illus lib. bdg. $5.95 (4-7)   684
1 Woodwork 2 Tools
ISBN 0-525-32532-8
"The book is divided into two parts. The first is concerned with tools and techniques. Seven tools are described—hammer, try square, saw, C-clamp, tape measure, drill and Surform plane. . . . The second part of the book describes six projects using the tools. They range from a potholder hanger (a short plank of wood with a few screws in it) up to a hanging planter, a carrying box, a pet bed. These are the simplest constructions, basically variations of box forms." N Y Times Bk Rev
"An easy introduction to carpentry that could substitute, if necessary, for what a child should have shown to him by an older person working alongside. Large black-and-white photographs clarify each stage of instruction . . . which are sound and simple enough for independent completion by a child capable of reading the text. General tips on handling tools and wood emphasize careful, clean workmanship." Booklist

684.1   Furniture

Fisher, Leonard Everett
The cabinetmakers; written & illus. by Leonard Everett Fisher. Watts, F. 1966 47p illus (Colonial Americans) lib. bdg. $3.90 (4-7)   684.1
1 Cabinet work 2 Furniture, American 3 U.S.—Social life and customs—Colonial period
ISBN 0-531-01026-0
The author explains that colonial American furniture is a reflection of the social life of the times and of the history of the craftsmen who designed it. He also discusses how cabinetmakers worked, what tools they used, and what skills were employed to bring about the final product
"Partly because Mr. Fisher's distinctive illustrative style lends itself well to the graining of wood, the pictures seem unusually handsome. [Includes] two pages of photographs of colonial furniture." Chicago. Children's Bk Center

685   Leather and fur goods, and related manufactures

Fisher, Leonard Everett
The hatters; written & illus. by Leonard Everett Fisher. Watts, F. 1965 48p illus (Colonial Americans) lib. bdg. $3.90 (4-7)   685
1 Hats 2 Fur 3 U.S.—Social life and customs—Colonial period
ISBN 0-531-01029-5
This book contains an "extensive historical section . . . due to the importance of the beaver pelts in colonial economy and to the legislative restrictions imposed by England. The section on the [hatmaking] industry itself is detailed and interesting, although there are some instances of writing (or captioning of the handsome illustrations) that seem not quite clear." Chicago. Children's Bk Center
Hatters' terms: p46-47

The shoemakers; written & illus. by Leonard Everett Fisher. Watts, F. 1967 44p illus (Colonial Americans) lib. bdg. $3.90 (4-7)   685
1 Shoes and shoe industry 2 U.S.—Social life and customs—Colonial period
ISBN 0-531-01035-X
In the New World, the demand for footwear was immense, and shoemaking early became a flourishing business. Here, the author tells the history of the American shoemakers and gives an account of how they went about their work
Written in a "lucid, graphic manner. . . . A glossary of terms is included and the book is illustrated with carefully drawn, detailed pictures on every other page." Booklist

Hirsch, S. Carl
Stilts; illus. by Betty Fraser. Viking 1972 41p illus lib. bdg. $4.75 (4-7)   685
1 Stilts
ISBN 0-670-67053-7
"With a very interesting approach, this book treats a specific topic—stilts—from historical, utilitarian, literary, and other points of view. The author avoids a pedantic structure and sequence, dealing with the various facets in a refreshing but sometimes confusing eclectic way. The book is well-written, engagingly illustrated, and contains good suggestions for activities." Appraisal

686   Book arts

Bartlett, Susan
Books; a book to begin on; illus. by Ellen Raskin. Holt 1968 unp illus lib. bdg. $3.27 (3-5)   686
1 Books—History
ISBN 0-03-059800-1
The process of bookmaking "is traced from clay tablets and papyrus rolls to modern printing presses." Adventuring With Bks. 2d edition
The coverage is "not comprehensive, but it touches on all important points in the evolution of the book." Sat Rev

Weiss, Harvey

How to make your own books; illus. with photographs and drawings. Crowell 1974 71p illus $5.50 (4-7)   686

1 Books

ISBN 0-690-00400-1

The author "deals first with practical matters: choosing papers, cutting, folding, binding techniques (sewing, stapling, or glueing), and attaching covers. Creating marbleized paper is one of the fascinating how-to's described and made to seem achievable by the amateur. Suggestions of kinds of books to make fill the second half of the volume, ranging from travel journals, albums, and scrapbooks to experimental books, and books of sketches, prints, or rubbings (the last not only from stone or metal but from frozen fish, tree bark, or driftwood)." Horn Bk

"In a clear, conversational style, Harvey Weiss shares his love of all kinds of personal books and his extensive knowledge of how to create them. . . . Photographs of books Mr. Weiss has done for his own pleasure abound along with designing hints, and his step-by-step drawings and instructions are perfect." Children's Bk Rev Serv

686.2   Printing

Barker, Albert

Black on white and read all over; the story of printing; illus. by Anthony D'Adamo and with photographs. Messner 1971 96p illus lib. bdg. $4.29 (4-6)   686.2

1 Printing—History

ISBN 0-671-32394-6

"The text traces the history and development of papermaking from its beginnings in China and then carries along with the history of printing up to modern times, with some speculation on the future of printing. The final chapter outlines the various steps in the writing and publishing of a typical book. The various forms of printing—woodblock, letterpress, lithography, photo-offset, and photogravure—are explained. . . . In general the book is readable and has good continuity. The illustrations are good and add to the enjoyment of the reader. The glossary and index are good and add to the value of the book for collateral reading and reference." Sci Bks

Dean, Elizabeth

Printing: tool of freedom; illus. by Erwin Schachner. Prentice-Hall 1964 64p illus lib. bdg. $4.95 (4-6)   686.2

1 Printing—History

ISBN 0-13-711002-2

"P-H Junior research books"

"The author traces the course of printing over the past 500 years, its methods, value, importance, and achievements. Fine coverage of Gutenberg. Considerable emphasis on the effect of printing on world history. Text and glossary alike offer some well-researched definitions of printing terms. Good looking and informative illustrations in browns and black." Sch Library J

Fisher, Leonard Everett

The printers; written & illus. by Leonard Everett Fisher. Watts, F. 1965 46p illus (Colonial Americans) lib. bdg. $3.90 (4-7)   686.2

1 Printing—History 2 Printers 3 U.S.—Social life and customs—Colonial period

ISBN 0-531-01033-3

"The first part of the text describes the role of the printer-publishers; the second part describes the presses that they used, the making of type-characters, and the procedures of the printing process." Chicago. Children's Bk Center

"Full-page (some double-page) illustrations show accurately and clearly the main details of the equipment and how the printers used it. Pages of early colonial newsletters and books are legibly reproduced." Sch Library J

Printers' terms: p42-43. Some Colonial American printers: p45

686.3   Bookbinding

Purdy, Susan

Books for you to make; written and illus. by Susan Purdy. Lippincott 1973 96p illus lib. bdg. $5.95 (4-7)   686.3

1 Bookbinding 2 Books

ISBN 0-397-31318-7

"While directing readers through the construction of their own books, Purdy introduces bookbinding vocabulary and, briefly, concepts of book design, layout, and illustration. A lengthy section on preparing bindings includes instructions for a multi-signature, full-bound book as well as examples of various simpler approaches to binding. The shift in final chapters to exploring professionally printed books becomes an easy step for readers who have busily put together their homemade versions; here the author's illustrated explanations of letter-press versus offset printing, camera and color separation, and the assemblage of printed pages allows readers a functional glimpse behind the scenes of book-making." Booklist

688   Other final products

Maginley, C. J.

Historic models of early America, and how to make them; illus. with numerous diagrams, by James MacDonald. Harcourt 1947 xx, 156p illus $5.95, pa 60¢ (6-7)   688

1 Models and model making 2 Machinery—Models

ISBN 0-15-234689-9; 0-15-640371-4

This book includes "exact specifications, working diagrams, and clear instructions for making Early American models grouped in four categories: transportation, farms, homes, and villages. Especially useful for history projects." Hodges. Bks for Elem Sch Libraries

An historical sketch proceeds each of the models which range in difficulty from a log canoe to the first Ford

"A really challenging book for a young carpenter. Inexpensive tools and materials are easily obtained." Pub W

Models of America's past, and how to make them; illus. by Elizabeth D. McKee. Harcourt 1969 144p illus $6.25 (6-7)   688

1 Models and model making

ISBN 0-15-255051-8

"This book contains precise directions for building simple wooden models of household furniture, school and meetinghouse buildings and equipment, barns, bridges, wagons, and other objects in common use during the seventeenth, eighteenth, and nineteenth centuries. Advice on specific details of modelmaking and lists of the necessary tools and supplies are given in the introduction, and the step-by-step instructions

Maginley, C. J.—*Continued*
for making each model are supplemented by explanatory diagrams and drawings and preceded by a thumbnail historical sketch of each object. An excellent and practical craft book for home or school use." Booklist

688.6   Nonmotor land vehicles

Stevenson, Peter
The Buffy-Porson; a car you can build and drive, by Peter and Mike Stevenson. Scribner 1973 63p illus $5.95 (4-6)   688.6
1 Automobiles—Design and construction
ISBN 0-684-13436-5
"Clear, sensible directions and a straightforward, informal style characterize an inviting do-it-yourself book produced by a father-and-young son partnership. The Buffy-Porson, 'a small racer of great spirit,' can be constructed with ordinary household tools; but, the young enthusiast is told, 'One building aid that you "will" need once in a while is an Older Person to lend a hand.' Attractive photographs and businesslike diagrams illustrate the proceedings from the very beginning to the point where 'the car stops being a project and starts being a sporting proposition.' Some good lumber and hardware are essential to build a sturdy car and to finish it off with a few stylish accessories; the appendix lists the precise sizes and quantities of the necessary materials." Horn Bk

688.7   Recreational equipment

Glubok, Shirley
Dolls, dolls, dolls; special photography by Alfred Tamarin; designed by Gerard Nook. Follett 1975 64p illus $5.95, lib. bdg. $5.97 (3-6)   688.7
1 Dolls
ISBN 0-695-80483-9; 0-695-40483-0
"Black-and-white photographs and clear, concise text trace the history of dolls from ancient Greece to modern times. This is their story and includes early carved wooden dolls, stylish fashion dolls, clever mechanical dolls, and celebrity dolls such as Shirley Temple and Mickey Mouse. A special section includes dollhouses and some distinctive Oriental, American Indian, and African samples. Anyone who has ever loved a doll will love this book!" Babbling Bookworm

Maginley, C. J.
Make it and ride it; diagrams by Elisabeth D. McKee. Harcourt 1949 120p illus $5.50 (4-7)   688.7
1 Toys 2 Woodwork
ISBN 0-15-251336-1
"Careful directions and clear diagrams for making an intriguing collection of toys to ride will insure this book a hearty welcome. . . . There are 18 projects of varying difficulty, including models of racers for the famous Soap Box Derby. Most of the projects, however, are not the simplest and would require some experience." Library J
Some of the projects included are: wagons, bike trailers, scooters, jeeps, toys for younger children. Hand tools and scrap materials can be used for most of the projects

690   Buildings

Colby, Jean Poindexter
Building wrecking; the how and why of a vital industry; photographs by Corinthia Morss, the author, and others. Hastings House 1972 96p illus lib. bdg. $5.95 (4-7)   690
1 Wrecking
ISBN 0-8038-0717-1
"The comprehensive coverage of demolition includes methods, equipment, types of workers, their duties, slum clearance, preservation of historic buildings, etc. The only book for children on the subject, this is an excellent supplement to social studies curriculums." Sch Library J
Bibliography: p91

Harman, Carter
A skyscraper goes up; illus. with photographs. Random House 1973 137p illus $4.95, lib. bdg. $5.49 (5-7)   690
1 Skyscrapers 2 Building
ISBN 0-394-82147-5; 0-394-92147-X
The author follows the whole process of planning and building one skyscraper—the Exxon Building in New York City. He covers such topics as: selecting a site, architectural planning, building a steel superstructure, and operating the finished building
"The text does not go much beyond the single tower, its parking and supplies, but within those limits it is a most readable and informative narrative. Costs are treated sketchily. . . . Floor plans, block maps, sections, elevator schemes and a good set of photographs made over a period of time add to the verisimilitude of this witness's account." Scientific Am

Tannenbaum, Beulah
High rises, by Beulah Tannenbaum and Myra Stillman; illus. by Marta Cone. McGraw 1974 64p illus (Science in the city) lib. bdg. $4.72 (3-6)   690
1 Apartment houses 2 Building
ISBN 0-07-062886-6
"This book concentrates on the planning and construction of alternative compacted human dwellings via vertical space in order to compensate for the pressing need for land to live on. . . . There are excellent expositions on the respective roles of the large team of specialists who contribute to the final construction and surroundings of high rise buildings with shopping centers and other needed community services. A couple of simple investigations for the young reader to try are woven into the text—effects of earthquakes on buildings built over a fault and the making of concrete. This is a rich resource book for population studies, multiple land use, and the urban man-built environment." Sci and Children
"The steps in the construction of high-rise buildings are explained in a simple text accompanied by clear black-and-white drawings that help visualize the process." Sch Library J

696   Utilities

Zim, Herbert S.
Pipes and plumbing systems, by Herbert S. Zim and James R. Skelly; illus. with drawings by Lee J. Ames and Mel Erikson. Morrow 1974 63p illus $4.25, lib. bdg. $3.94, pa $1.25 (3-6)   696
1 Plumbing
ISBN 0-688-20101-6; 0-688-30101-0; 0-688-25101-3
This overview "covers water, sewer, and gas pipes

Zim, Herbert S.—*Continued*
and home heating systems. The authors then describe plumbing uses in industry; the history of plumbing; the manufacture and use of various valves, pipes, and pumps; the training procedure for plumbers and pipe fitters; and the jobs of inspectors, engineers, apprentices, journeymen, and master plumbers. The line illustrations of pipes, fittings, systems, and pumps are meticulously accurate." Sch Library J

697 Heating

Urquhart, David Inglis
Central heating and how it works; illus. by Patricia Frank Korbet. Walck, H.Z. 1972 42p illus $4.95 (3-6)   697
1 Heating
ISBN 0-8098-2083-3
"The story of heating—how we heat our houses and how (presumably) man first discovered the usefulness of fire—is discussed in this very concise and informative little book. . . . Pollution problems from fossil fuels are noted; but, in the reviewer's opinion, insufficient emphasis is placed on the severe disposal problems of atomic wastes caused by their intense radioactivity and the extremely long half-lives of many fission products. One small error was noted—sulfur was described as having an unpleasant odor when in fact it has no odor at all. (It is the combustion product which is unpleasant.) The book is otherwise quite accurate." Sci Bks

700 THE ARTS

701 Art—Philosophy and theory

Chase, Alice Elizabeth
Looking at art. Crowell 1966 119p illus $6.95 (6-7)   701
1 Art 2 Painting
ISBN 0-690-50869-7
"Profusely illustrated with reproductions of works of art and with illuminating diagrams, this is a fine introduction to artistic interpretation. . . . Miss Chase, who is authoritative, sensible, and lucid, draws upon a wide range of sources and periods." Sat Rev
The author "describes the ways in which artists have seen and interpreted such broad areas of their work as people and space, the human figure, or landscape. Perhaps the most valuable aspect of the book is the discussion, in the first chapter, of what art is." Sutherland. The Best in Children's Bks

Grigson, Geoffrey
Shapes and stories; a book about pictures, by Geoffrey and Jane Grigson. Vanguard [1965 c1964] 65p illus $6.95 (5-7)   701
1 Art
ISBN 0-8149-0311-8
First published 1964 in England
This book "deals with the content of a selected group of pictures, rather than being a history of art or giving biographical information about the artists. The collection of art (largely European) begins with 'Adam naming the beasts' by William Blake, proceeds to individual animals, real or imaginary, then to land-

scapes and architectural subjects. . . . The authors' comments about the pictures and about the artists' intent and craft are well chosen and exciting. . . . Pen, pencil drawings, oils, woodcuts, tapestries, watercolours are represented. . . . The outsize format permits the illustrations (both black and white and in colour) to be large." Toronto

Hughes, Langston
The first book of rhythms; pictures by Robin King. Watts, F. 1954 63p illus lib. bdg. $3.90 (4-7)   701
1 Rhythm
ISBN 0-531-00618-2
"An unusual book, beautifully written, to introduce to children the rhythms that are around them, showing how rhythms are to be found in every aspect of life, in all movement, in sounds, and even in the feel and smell of things. The way in which all things are tied to all other things through rhythms is simply but clearly expressed. . . . Teachers at the elementary level will find the book helpful for their own use to give them ideas of ways in which the idea of rhythms can be presented to young children. Readers at the upper elementary and junior high school level will be able to use the book by themselves." Chicago. Children's Bk Center

702.8 Art—Techniques

Marks, Mickey Klar
Op-tricks; creating kinetic art; kinetics by Edith Alberts; photographed by David Rosenfeld. Lippincott 1972 unp illus lib. bdg. $4.95 (5-7)   702.8
1 Kinetic art 2 Art—Technique
ISBN 0-397-31539-2
"An introduction to kinetic (Op) art for children. After a brief explanation of kinetic art, basic directions for nine techniques are clearly outlined. These are intended for use by youngsters as a basis for creating their own designs." Sch Library J
"Most of the projects require only materials that are easily available, but a few may necessitate purchase of supplies of plexiglass, fishing line, compass, etc. The explanations are clear, the projects not too complicated, the results—as shown in photographs—intriguing." Chicago. Children's Bk Center

704.94 Iconography

Downer, Marion
Children in the world's art. Lothrop 1970 144p illus maps lib. bdg. $5.81 (4-7)   704.94
1 Children in literature and art 2 Art—History
ISBN 0-688-51153-8
Arranged chronologically, this "selection of 79 black-and-white reproductions of paintings, sculpture, drawings, tapestries, and prints in which children appear comprises an inviting introduction to art from the ancient Egyptians to the twentieth-century. A few works from the Orient and North America are included, but the major emphasis is on the periods and styles of European art. The interpretive text comments briefly on the subjects, the artists, and the techniques." Booklist
The author's "writing is clear and interesting, and the book's emphasis should appeal to children. It's profusely illustrated, but the art . . . is not well reproduced." Sch Library J

707   Art—Study and teaching

Borten, Helen

Do you see what I see? Written and illus. by Helen Borten. Abelard-Schuman 1959 unp illus $4.95, lib. bdg. $4.89 (k-2)   707

1 Art—Study and teaching

ISBN 0-200-71301-9; 0-200-71845-2

"The author introduces line, shape, and color in terms a young child can understand and extends her text with multicolor woodcuts." Hodges. Bks for Elem Sch Libraries

"The illustrations are rhythmical and lovely." Adventuring With Bks. 2d edition

708   Galleries and museums

Spaeth, Eloise

American art museums; an introduction to looking. 3d ed. expanded. Harper 1975 xxiii, 483p illus $15   708

1 U.S.—Galleries and museums—Directories

ISBN 0-06-013978-1

First published 1960 with title: American art museums and galleries

"A state-by-state directory of fine arts museums in the U.S. For the confirmed museum goer, Spaeth's guide acts as an inventory to special collections; the newcomer can become familiar with special features, programs, [visiting hours] and [restaurant and] class-room facilities offered." Booklist

"This book is not meant to be a definitive guide, but rather an introduction to looking. Although the space is limited I have tried to cover all the major museums and as many as possible minor-major art museums. . . . The emphasis, but for a few exceptions, is on the 'general' art museum. . . . In choosing university and college museums, I have given preference to those which have their own museum buildings and which act as community museums as well. . . . In a few lines, I have tried to capture the quality, character and mood of the museums listed. Each has its own. In some I have singled out specific works of art; sometimes the works chosen are the museum showpieces, sometimes the choice has been my own. The works discussed belong to the permanent collections. . . . Museum libraries are listed, but frequently they are open to the qualified scholar only—or are reference libraries." Foreword

Weisgard, Leonard

Treasures to see; a museum picture-book. Harcourt 1956 unp illus $6.95 (1-4)   708

1 Art—Galleries and museums

ISBN 0-15-290337-2

"The author explains the purpose of an art museum, its main divisions, and the type of things each contains." Sch Arts

"Excellent drawings. . . . The illustrations are representations of the kinds of things to be found in a museum rather than actual reproductions of works of art. The book should serve a useful purpose in cities where children have access to a museum." Chicago. Children's Bk Center

709   Art—History

Batterberry, Ariane Ruskin

The Pantheon Story of art for young people. A rev. up-to-date ed. Pantheon Bks. 1975 157p illus $12.95 (5-7)   709

1 Art—History

ISBN 0-394-83107-1

First published 1964. Author's name appeared as Ariane Ruskin

A history of art from cave painting to Pop Art, illustrated with reproductions in color and black-and-white. The final chapter briefly discusses non-Western art

"Bountifully illustrated with superb reproductions in color and black and white. Essentially chronological in approach, and incidentally working in a surprising amount of world history. . . . The lack of both an index and a list of artists and illustrations is particularly unfortunate." Horn Bk [Review of first edition]

Craven, Thomas

The rainbow book of art. World Pub. 1956 256p illus $4.95, lib. bdg. $5.21 (5-7)   709

1 Art—History

ISBN 0-529-04614-4; 0-529-04671-7

Covering painting, sculpture and architecture, this "survey—from cave paintings to skyscrapers—provides young people with a stimulating introduction to art, especially to the lives of the Masters and the art capitals of their times." New Yorker

The "anecdotal, untechnical and uncondescending text, by the well-known critic-author, is rich in illuminating examples and analogies to make more understandable and significant achievements in art." Horn Bk

709.01   Art of primitive peoples and ancient times

Baylor, Byrd

Before you came this way; illus. by Tom Bahti. Dutton 1969 unp illus $4.75 (1-4)   709.01

1 Indians of North America—Art 2 Cave drawings

ISBN 0-525-26312-8

"A handsome book, thought-provoking and written with lyric simplicity; the illustrations, on handmade bark paper, are in the style of the prehistoric rock pictures on which the book is based. Walking in the quiet of a canyon in the Southwest, you wonder if you are the first to pass this way . . . then you see that some brother, long-dead, has made a record of his people and their lives: the animals they hunted, the battles and the feasts, the masks of the dancers. The writing style is sensitively attuned to the dignity and mystery of the subject." Sutherland. The Best in Children's Bks

Glubok, Shirley

The art of ancient Mexico; designed by Gerard Nook; special photography by Alfred H. Tamarin. Harper 1968 41p illus $4.50, lib. bdg. $5.89 (4-6)   709.01

1 Indians of Mexico—Art 2 Mexico—Antiquities

ISBN 0-06-022033-3; 0-06-022034-1

This book covers the Indian cultures—such as Aztec, Mixtec, Toltec, Olmec, Zapotec—that flourished in Mexico before the Spanish conquest. The author examines these peoples through their art and introduces the reader to Mexico's past. Temples, religious objects, jewelry, weapons and painted books are shown

"Religious and secular art in stone, clay, and metal introduce the Aztec and pre-Aztec world. Fierce gods and warriors abound in photos surging with the spirit of a bellicose and bloodthirsty people; a lighter touch prevails in artifacts depicting the common man at

Glubok, Shirley—*Continued*
work or play. Heroic and mythical creatures adorn the few examples of architecture." Library J
"The objects are either curious or beautiful enough to provide a varied and interesting picture of the intricacy and craftsmanship of several cultures, although the text is rather choppy." Sat Rev

The art of lands in the Bible; designed by Gerard Nook. Atheneum Pubs. 1963 48p illus $3.95, lib. bdg. $3.79 (4-7)   709.01
    1 Art, Ancient 2 Civilization, Ancient 3 Art—Near East
    ISBN 0-689-20110-9; 0-689-20111-7
    "An introduction to the sculptures, great and small of the ancient Near and Middle East, chiefly of Assyria, Babylonia and Persia." N Y Times Bk Rev
    "Those who are bewildered by too much glory collected together in one museum will rejoice in the carefully chosen, cunningly displayed objects in this book. . . . Friezes and sculpture, vases and pottery are displayed on backgrounds of soft color so skillfully that the hand can imagine the feeling of smooth contours and satisfying balance." Christian Sci Monitor

The art of the North American Indian; designed by Oscar Krauss. Harper 1964 unp illus lib. bdg. $5.89 (3-6)   709.01
    1 Indians of North America—Art 2 Indians of North America—Social life and customs
    ISBN 0-06-022066-X
    An "introduction to North American Indian art. . . . Carved masks, baskets, totem poles, wampum, Kachina dolls, pottery, and sand painting are among the examples of Indian art shown in photographs and briefly described as to material, design, and use." Booklist
    "A most handsome book, with photographs of varied and beautiful objects in a format of dignified simplicity. The text is clear and direct." Chicago. Children's Bk Center

The art of the Northwest coast Indians; designed by Gerard Nook. Macmillan Pub. Co. 1975 48p illus lib. bdg. $7.95 (4-7)   709.01
    1 Indians of North America—Art 2 Indians of North America—Northwest, Pacific
    ISBN 0-02-736150-0
    This book concentrates on the crafts of the Indian groups that live along the Pacific coast of the United States and Canada: the Kwakiutl, Tlingit, Nootka, Haida, Tsimshian, Bella Coola, and Coast Salish. Featured are the decorated totems and house fronts, long canoes, ceremonial masks, feast dishes, baskets, and woven fabrics representative of the artistic heritage of these peoples. Black and white photographs accompany the text

The art of the Southwest Indians; photographs by Alfred Tamarin; designed by Gerard Nook. Macmillan (N Y) 1971 48p illus lib. bdg. $5.95 (4-7) 709.01
    1 Indians of North America—Art 2 Indians of North America—Southwest, New
    "Information about some aspects of tribal cultures is woven into discussions of the works of art of the Apache, Navajo, and Pueblo peoples. The photographs of rock carvings and paintings, pottery and basketwork, weaving, carving, jewelry, sand paintings, ceremonial robes and masks, and kachina dolls are accompanied by an informative . . . text. The large print and dignified design of the pages add to the attractiveness of a useful book." Chicago. Children's Bk Center

Hofsinde, Robert
    Indian arts; written and illus. by Robert Hofsinde (Gray-Wolf). Morrow 1971 95p illus lib. bdg. $4.59 (4-6)   709.01
    1 Indians of North America—Art
    ISBN 0-688-31617-4
    "This account explains the materials and techniques used by different American Indian tribes in the creation of artistic works for decorative, religious, and practical purposes. A final chapter discusses current interest in Indian arts and the types of artwork being produced today. Well illustrated with many black-and-white drawings." Booklist

Samachson, Dorothy
    The first artists, by Dorothy and Joseph Samachson. Doubleday 1970 147p illus $4.95, lib. bdg. $5.70 (5-7)   709.01
    1 Art, Primitive 2 Cave drawings
    ISBN 0-385-04062-8; 0-385-08144-8
    A "survey of cave paintings and engravings, more extensive than the usual treatment of the subject. In addition to descriptions of such famous finds as Altamira and Lascaux, the authors discuss minor examples and they examine the work of cave artists of Australia, Africa and America as well as the more familiar European paintings, including styles, techniques, theories about significance, ethnographic parallels, and abstract or symbolic work. The photographs are good; a glossary and an index are appended." Chicago. Children's Bk Center

709.04   Art—History, Modern period, 1500-

MacAgy, Douglas
    Going for a walk with a line; a step into the world of modern art, by Douglas and Elizabeth MacAgy. Doubleday 1959 unp illus $4.95, lib. bdg. $5.70, pa $1.25 (3-7)   709.04
    1 Art, Modern—20th century
    ISBN 0-385-07804-8; 0-385-07832-3; 0-385-05246-4
    In this art book for young moderns the authors "take the child on a guided tour of pictures done by artists with a fresh viewpoint, the infinite variety of the line pointing the way for aesthetic experience ranging from Henri Rousseau on the first page to Paul Klee on the last." Library J

709.32   History of ancient Egyptian art

Glubok, Shirley
    The art of ancient Egypt; designed by Gerard Nook. Atheneum Pubs. 1962 48p illus $4.95, lib. bdg. $5.57 (4-7)   709.32
    1 Art, Egyptian 2 Egypt—Civilization
    ISBN 0-689-20112-5; 0-689-20113-3
    "Not only is this interesting and beautifully designed book a child's guide to Egyptian art, it is also a pictorial history of the early Egyptian civilization. . . . Objects of sculpture, painting, and pottery from the world's great museums, including the Metropolitan Museum of New York, the British Museum, and the Cairo Museum are pictured and described." Chicago Sch J
    "The rules of Egyptian art are simply yet effectively

Glubok, Shirley—*Continued*
expounded in the coordination between text and illustrations. Excellent format. An outstanding book." Sch Library J

709.37   History of Etruscan art

Glubok, Shirley
The art of ancient Rome; designed by Oscar Krauss. Harper 1965 40p illus lib. bdg. $5.89 (4-7)   709.37
1 Art, Roman 2 Rome—Civilization
ISBN 0-06-022046-5
"Young readers are introduced to the classic art of ancient Rome through a clear description of Roman mosaics and murals, portraits and statuary, monuments and buildings. Heroes, games, warfare, school and family life, and worship are represented." Wis Library Bul
"Illustrated with photographs. Those familiar with the author's preceding studies . . . can visualize the makeup of this companion with its superb reproductions of art." Horn Bk

The art of the Etruscans; designed by Gerard Nook; special photography by Alfred H. Tamarin. Harper 1967 40p illus lib. bdg. $5.89 (4-7)   709.37
1 Art, Etruscan
ISBN 0-06-022058-9
The author "covers the known aspects of the Etruscans and their art; speculation as to their origins, connections with Greece, tomb wall-paintings, urns—works in terra-cotta, bronze, and gold granulation." Christian Sci Monitor
"The creativity and culture of an ancient civilization is reflected in this handsome and well-designed book." Children's Bks. 1967

709.38   History of ancient Greek art

Glubok, Shirley
The art of ancient Greece; designed by Oscar Krauss. Atheneum Pubs. 1963 48p illus $3.95, lib. bdg. $4.57 (4-7)   709.38
1 Art, Greek 2 Civilization, Greek
ISBN 0-689-20114-1; 0-689-20116-8
"This handsomely designed and illustrated book introduces younger children to a carefully selected group of the most beautiful treasures of Greek art. Superior photographs of pottery and sculpture, artfully arranged on the pages with skillful use of color for background, are related to Greek life and thought through the brief but significant test." Horn Bk

709.51   History of Chinese art

Glubok, Shirley
The art of China; designed by Gerard Nook. Macmillan (N Y) 1973 48p illus lib. bdg. $6.95 (4-7)
   709.51
1 Art, Chinese—History
"The text—by meandering in and out of Chinese history, customs, culture, and religion—helps the reader develop an awareness of the variety and excellence of Chinese art. Touching briefly on the various forms of art—bronze ceremonial vessels, pottery, scroll paintings, calligraphy, religious statues, and temples—the book also explains some of the ancient Chinese inventions—porcelain, silk, and lacquer—which made various new art forms possible." Horn Bk
"Designed with discrimination, the book is . . . both handsome and informative, and it should lead readers to further examination of Chinese art." Chicago. Children's Bk Center

709.52   History of Japanese art

Glubok, Shirley
The art of Japan; designed by Gerard Nook; special photography by Alfred Tamarin. Macmillan (N Y) 1970 48p illus lib. bdg. $5.95 (4-7)   709.52
1 Art, Japanese
The author shows how the artistic heritage reflects the history and culture of a country in this "survey of Japanese art from simple teapots to paintings, temples, and gardens." Children's Bks. 1970
This book "panoramically sets forth . . . highlights of Japan's multitudinous, classical art forms. . . . Glubok's text, light as a calligrapher's brush stroke, is economically explicit and designer Gerald Nook ravishes the eye in his clearcut unfussy presentation. The selection of masterpieces cannot be faulted." N Y Times Bk Rev

709.54   History of Indic art

Glubok, Shirley
The art of India; designed by Gerard Nook; special photography by Alfred H. Tamarin and Carol Guyer. Macmillan (N Y) 1969 48p illus lib. bdg. $5.95 (4-7)
   709.54
1 Art, Indic—History
This book "presents a brief introduction to ancient and traditional sculpture and painting, focusing on art objects which represent the three great religions of India. The reader [also] receives . . . a glimpse of the civilization that produced these extraordinary works." Top of the News
"Since almost all Indian art is religious art, most of the text here is either descriptive of the object or structure shown in a photograph or it is an explanation of the religious background. . . . [The book] is handsome in design, clearly written, and extremely useful, since there is comparatively little material available on Indian art for the elementary level. The illustrations are preponderantly sculpture and the lack of color is no limitation, but the miniatures lose effectiveness in black and white." Sutherland. The Best in Children's Bks

709.56   History of Islamic art

Price, Christine
The story of Moslem art; illus. with photographs and with drawings by the author. Dutton 1964 160p illus maps lib. bdg. $4.89 (6-7)   709.56
1 Art, Islamic 2 Civilization, Arab
ISBN 0-525-40291-8
"How the Muslim conquerors employed the craftsmen and artists of their empire is the subject of this attractive book which tells of the spread of Islamic art and the forces that shaped it in the past thirteen centuries." Asia: A Guide to Bks for Children

Price, Christine—*Continued*

"A lucid account . . . [The author] precisely describes the architecture, painting, and crafts of the Moslem-occupied territories . . . and reveals what each has contributed to Moslem art. It is unfortunate that the many effectively arranged photographs and sketches are in black and white only and that many are too small to show the intricate details of the design." Booklist

709.6   History of African art

Glubok, Shirley

The art of Africa; designed by Gerard Nook; special photography by Alfred H. Tamarin. Harper 1965 48p illus $5.95, lib. bdg. $5.89 (4-7)   709.6

1 Art, African 2 Art, Primitive
ISBN 0-06-022035-X; 0-06-022036-8

"A fine presentation of representative examples of art and artifacts of various tribes throughout Africa which is interesting, informative and written at a level which is comprehensible for children. The photographs and format are excellent." Africa

"The art is varied and unusual, often strange to American eyes. Shirley Glubok has chosen [wooden] masks, [bronze and brass] figures, rock paintings, gold weights, carved stools, combs, musical instruments, and other objects to illustrate her book." Pub W

Price, Christine

Made in West Africa; illus. with photographs and drawings. Dutton 1975 150p illus map $6.95 (5-7)
709.6

1 Art, African
ISBN 0-525-34400-4

"A book that introduces West African art has been copiously illustrated with photographs of all kinds of aesthetic forms—sculpture, textiles, pottery, carvings, metalwork. The photographs show examples of present-day craftsmanship as well as of ancient artifacts, and the text discusses the techniques and traditions behind the items. Concluding with a chapter, 'Artists of the New Age,' the book gives a feeling for the overall range of West African art and its metamorphosis through history." Horn Bk

Books for further reading: p147

709.73   History of art in the U.S.

Coen, Rena Neumann

American history in art; designed by Wendell Carroll. Lerner Publications 1966 71p illus (Fine art bks for young people) lib. bdg. $4.95 (5-7)   709.73

1 Art, American 2 U.S.—History—Pictorial works
ISBN 0-8225-0157-0

With photographic illustrations, this book gives a panorama of American history through art

Glubok, Shirley

The art of America from Jackson to Lincoln; designed by Gerard Nook. Macmillan Pub. Co. 1973 48p illus lib. bdg. $6.95 (4-7)   709.73

1 Art, American—History

The author "imparts much information about American artists at work up to the time of the Civil War. The illustrations—in black and white with some

brown tints—include landscapes, rural and urban scenes, individual and family portraits, and photographs showing architectural styles and interior designs and furnishings. Covering only the period from 1820-1860, this concise history provides interesting supplementary material." Sch Library J

The art of America in the early twentieth century; designed by Gerard Nook. Macmillan Pub. Co. 1974 48p illus lib. bdg. $6.95 (4-7)   709.73

1 Art, American—History 2 Art, Modern—20th century
ISBN 0-02-736180-2

The author surveys American art during the first four decades of the twentieth century. Painting is emphasized, but sculpture, architecture and photography are also considered

"The simple text points out various trends and provides an informative commentary on the artists and their work. . . . The reproductions, none in their original color, are sometimes indistinct, but the presentation still works well as basic introductory material." Booklist

The art of America in the gilded age; designed by Gerard Nook. Macmillan Pub. Co. 1974 48p illus $6.95 (4-7)   709.73

1 Art, American—History
ISBN 0-02-736100-4

"Continuing the author's series of books on American art, this volume reflects the growing wealth and diversity of life in the years between the Civil War and the twentieth century. In addition to the work of the masters who studied abroad, there are genre paintings, examples of the new medium of photography, Sullivan's auditorium and the lavish homes of financial barons, Tiffany glass, and other media that were examples of art nouveau. The text describes the objects pictured and relates them to the life of the 'Gilded Age.'" Chicago. Children's Bk Center

"The author's well-chosen illustrations are bound to appeal to youngsters: family scenes, children at play, sports events. Reproductions are in black and white, but occasional splashes of color brighten the pages." Christian Sci Monitor

The art of colonial America; designed by Gerard Nook. Macmillan (N Y) 1970 48p illus lib. bdg. $5.95 (4-7)   709.73

1 Art, American—History

The author presents the artistic heritage of the United States which has its roots in England, Holland, Germany and France. The book is full of representative reproductions of paintings, buildings, furniture and individual objects in pottery, glass, pewter and silver

"Of primary interest for the historical tidbits scattered throughout the book and for the picture they give of life in colonial America." Horn Bk

The art of the new American nation; designed by Gerard Nook. Macmillan (N Y) 1972 48p illus lib. bdg. $6.95 (4-7)   709.73

1 Art, American—History

A presentation of American art from 1776 to 1826. Among the forms highlighted are portraits of America's heroes by Gilbert Stuart and Mather Brown; canvases of Revolutionary battles by John Trumbull; and paintings by Samuel F. B. Morse and Robert Fulton—artists as well as inventors. Included also are public and private buildings, furniture, and silver

"Illustrated with photographs and reproductions. . . . The photographs are excellent, although a few color plates might have added a new dimension; the brief text is competent if unexciting, perhaps because

Glubok, Shirley—*Continued*
so slim a volume can only suggest rather than explore so large a topic. A functional compilation." Horn Bk

The art of the Old West; designed by Gerard Nook. Macmillan (N Y) 1971 48p illus lib. bdg. $5.95 (4-7)
709.73

1 Art, American—History 2 The West
The author has brought together paintings, sculpture and photographs, along with her commentary, that recreate the settling of the West. Some representative artists presented are: George Catlin, Karl Bodmer, Charles "Kid" Russell, and Frederic Remington
Glubok "has assembled a most attractive book. As well designed pictorially as it is intelligent textually, it presents enough but not too much technical, biographic, historic and conceptual detail for the reader to see what is before him." N Y Times Bk Rev

The art of the Spanish in the United States and Puerto Rico; designed by Gerard Nook; photographs by Alfred Tamarin. Macmillan (N Y) 1972 48p illus lib. bdg. $7.95 (4-7)
709.73

1 Art, Latin American
An examination of the Spanish contribution to art and architecture in Florida, Texas, New Mexico, Colorado, Arizona, California and Puerto Rico, including homes, churches, forts, furniture, tinware, weaving and embroidery
"In the readable style and attractive format of Glubok's other titles, this provides an overview of the rich Spanish influence on art and architecture. . . . Of particular interest are the 'santos,' small carved and painted statues representing characters from legends and Bible stories. Brief summaries of these stories add interest to the book which will increase reader understanding and awareness of Spanish art heritage." Sch Library J

709.98   The art of the Eskimo

Glubok, Shirley
The art of the Eskimo; designed by Oscar Krauss; special photography by Alfred H. Tamarin. Harper 1964 48p illus lib. bdg. $5.89 (4-7)   709.98
1 Eskimos—Art 2 Eskimos—Social life and customs
ISBN 0-06-022056-2
This introduction to Eskimo art shows masks, ivory carving, soapstone carving, dolls, decorative pipes, recent graphic arts, and other arts and crafts, covering a span of more than a thousand years
"Once again an excellent selection of museum pieces is displayed in handsome photographs—many set on colored pages—to awaken interest in another culture. . . . Partly because so many Eskimo groups are represented, the text suffers from oversimplification and lack of unity." Horn Bk

711   Area planning

Macaulay, David
City; a story of Roman planning and construction. Houghton 1974 112p illus $7.95 (4-7)   711
1 City planning—Rome 2 Civil engineering 3 Architecture, Roman
ISBN 0-395-19492-X
"By following the inception, construction, and development of an imaginary Roman city, the account traces the evolution of Verbonia from the selection of its site under religious auspices in 26 B.C. to its completion in 100 A.D. A military camp set up by soldiers and slaves becomes the basis for an expanding community, which—in the course of its growth—builds roads, a bridge, walls, water and sewage systems, a marketplace, and a religious and civic center, as well as areas for relaxation and entertainment." Horn Bk
"Like his impressive 'Cathedral,' a Caldecott Honor Book of 1973, [entered in class 726] Macaulay's 'City' is large in concept as well as size, profusely illustrated with fascinatingly detailed drawings, and written with clarity and authority. . . . Younger children . . . may not understand every detail but can browse through the text and pore over the pictures." Chicago. Children's Bk Center
Glossary: p112

720   Architecture

Moore, Lamont
The first book of architecture. Watts, F. 1961 82p illus lib. bdg. $3.90 (5-7)   720
1 Architecture
ISBN 0-531-00471-6
"An interesting and valuable brief introduction to the subject of architecture. Discussing, first, two aspects of the architect's scientific knowledge and aesthetic principles—[the author] then presents series of examples of architecture: for worship, living, earning, governing, and pleasure and learning. These, with well-reproduced photographs and a few diagrams, range all over the world and from Stonehenge to the Guggenheim Museum. Time chart of historical periods and glossary of architectural terms." Horn Bk

720.23   Architecture as a profession

Goldreich, Gloria
What can she be? An architect [by] Gloria and Esther Goldreich; photographs by Robert Ipcar. Lothrop 1974 48p illus $4.50, lib. bdg. $5.10 (2-4)
720.23

1 Women as architects 2 Architecture as a profession
ISBN 0-688-41579-2; 0-688-51579-7
"This is one of a series of books that introduces children to the many careers a woman can pursue. The text and photos of this book focus on one woman as she works as an architect consulting with clients, conferring in her office and visiting building sites—and as she lives with her family. Although most of the book is devoted to her work with two families (building and remodeling their homes), other phases of an architect's work are also explored: apartment projects; consultations with other architects, builders, engineers; preservation work. There is an introduction to the training an architect must have before she can practice. The black-and-white photographs (at least one to a page) are large, clear and useful. The short simple sentences suggest a very young audience, but some words and concepts used (e.g., design, apprentice, Soho district) will be difficult for the youngest age group." Sci Bks

720.9 Architecture—History

Paine, Roberta M.
Looking at architecture. Lothrop 1974 127p illus map $6.95, lib. bdg. $5.81 (4-7) 720.9
1 Architecture—History
ISBN 0-688-41553-9; 0-688-51553-3
This book considers "varied aspects of architecture as exemplified by specific structures: the Parthenon, the Pantheon, the pyramids and temples of Mexico, the Taj Mahal, Gothic churches, and skyscrapers—to mention only a few. . . . The architectural milieus include Africa and Asia as well as Europe and America; and structures of the modern world are discussed as well as those of antiquity, the middle ages, and the Renaissance." Horn Bk
"Profuse black-and-white photographs and reproductions illustrate the text." Booklist
Glossary of building materials: p115-19. Notes on the architects: p120-24. For further reading: p125

721 Architectural construction

Downer, Marion
Roofs over America. Lothrop 1967 75p illus lib. bdg. $4.81 (5-7) 721
1 Roofs 2 Architecture, American
ISBN 0-688-51225-9
This book, introducing the architecture of roofs, is divided into four parts: America's first roofs: seventeenth century; Roofs with a touch of elegance: eighteenth century; City roofs; Modern country roofs
"A handsome book with full-page photographs faced by a spacious page with a few paragraphs of comment or explanation." Sutherland. The Best in Children's Bks
Books recommended for further reading: p75

722 Ancient architecture

Leacroft, Helen
The buildings of ancient Egypt [by] Helen and Richard Leacroft. Young Scott Bks. 1963 39p illus map lib. bdg. $5.50 (5-7) 722
1 Architecture, Egyptian 2 Egypt—Civilization
ISBN 0-201-09141-8
This book describes "architectural details, processes of building, and the furnishing of three different styles of pyramid-tombs and other temples . . . also houses, from reed and mud-daubed huts to the mud-brick house and estate of nobleman and royalty. Particulars of social structure give insight into the way the Egyptians lived." Horn Bk
"Useful as a supplement to study of architecture through the ages." Wis Library Bul

The buildings of ancient Greece [by] Helen and Richard Leacroft. Scott, W.R. 1966 40p illus maps lib. bdg. $5.50 (5-7) 722
1 Architecture, Greek 2 Civilization, Greek
ISBN 0-201-09143-7
The book tells of "the domestic and public architecture of Greece, from prehistoric times to 300 B.C., against a background of early Greek life." Hodges. Bks for Elem Sch Libraries
This work "is more technical than the jacket would suggest. It is about 50 per cent illustration, the text is clear and concise and many of the diagrams are highly detailed. Excellent for budding architects as well as historians." Times (London) Literary Sup

The buildings of ancient man [by] Helen and Richard Leacroft. Young Scott Bks. 1973 39p illus lib. bdg. $5.50 (5-7) 722
1 Architecture, Ancient 2 Architecture, Domestic 3 Civilization, Ancient
ISBN 0-201-09150-X
"How ancient man developed architecture to build homes, fortifications, settlements, as well as religious monuments is described in this concise and readable account. Architectural styles are explained as the history of housing is traced from simple lean-tos to more complex structures with many rooms. The text is well-written, although advanced, and the informative illustrations, many of which are in full color, feature nude or partially-clad figures." Sch Library J

The buildings of ancient Rome [by] Helen and Richard Leacroft. Scott, W.R. 1969 40p illus lib. bdg. $5.50 (5-7) 722
1 Architecture, Roman 2 Rome—Civilization
ISBN 0-201-09145-3
"In concise, graphic text well correlated with many detailed full-color and line drawings, the authors . . . describe the materials, designs, and construction of Roman temples, public buildings, towns, aqueducts, theaters, and private housing. . . . Information is based on the excavations and reports of archeologists and provides sidelights on the life style and attitudes of the Romans as well as explaining their architectural skill." Booklist

726 Buildings for religious purposes

Grant, Neil
Cathedrals; illus. with photographs. Watts, F. 1972 90p illus lib. bdg. $3.90 (4-6) 726
1 Cathedrals 2 Architecture, Gothic 3 Architecture, Romanesque
ISBN 0-531-00755-3
"After defining the word 'cathedral' the author discusses briefly the great medieval period of cathedral building and illustrates the two types of architecture used, Romanesque and Gothic. He notes the secular use of cathedrals during the Middle Ages and explains the meaning behind different, sometimes grotesque types of church decoration. Grant describes in a few words the best-known cathedrals of France, England, Germany, Spain, Russia, and the U.S. plus one in Africa and indicates how architects of modern cathedrals have departed from the Gothic style and are using original designs. Copiously illustrated with photographs." Booklist

Macaulay, David
Cathedral: the story of its construction. Houghton 1973 77p illus $7.95 (4-7) 726
1 Cathedrals 2 Architecture, Gothic
ISBN 0-395-17513-5
This is a description, illustrated with black-and-white line drawings, of the construction of a Gothic cathedral "in southern France from its conception in 1252 to its completion in 1338. The spirit that motivated the people, the tools and materials they used, the steps and methods of constructions, all receive measured factual attention." Booklist
The "drawings, some from ground level, some from high in the building itself, reveal the ongoing stages of

Macaulay, David—*Continued*
construction, the interrelation of the parts and the ingenuity and skill of medieval craftsmanship. . . . The fictional Cathedral of Chutreaux—as those real cathedrals of Chartres, Canterbury, Vienna, Ulm, Paris, York, and all the others—achieved that essential blend of beauty and utility that marks all truly functional architecture of the highest order. It is the great virtue of . . . Macaulay's book to reveal this in a pleasing and convincing way." N Y Times Bk Rev
Glossary: p[80]

Rockwell, Anne
Glass, stones & crown; the Abbé Suger and the building of St Denis. Atheneum Pubs. 1968 80p illus $3.75, lib. bdg. $3.59 (4-7)   726
1 Saint-Denis, France 2 Suger, Abbot of Saint-Denis 3 Church architecture
ISBN 0-689-20375-6; 0-689-20376-4
The author-illustrator tells the story of the "abbot of the monastery of St. Denis near Paris . . . [who] was able to realize the building of [the first great Gothic Cathedral of France]. . . . Against the historical background of 12th Century France, the author introduces some of the rich symbolism of the period, and explains, with diagrams, such characteristics of the Gothic style as stained-glass windows, the pointed arch and rib vaulting." Sch Library J
"Especially fine are the detailed descriptions of the complex symbolism of the twelfth century and of the 'wonderful and mysterious' process of making stained glass." Horn Bk

728   Residential buildings

Hoag, Edwin
American houses: colonial, classic, and contemporary. Lippincott 1964 160p illus $7.50 (6-7)   728
1 Architecture, Domestic 2 Architecture, American
ISBN 0-397-30721-7
"This is a handsome book, handsomely illustrated, comprehensive and competent; it is written in a straightforward style that is informal without being either jocose or patronizing. The author relates developments always to influences of heritage, of materials and climate, of function, or of period-fashion. The text provides a considerable amount of historic background to the story of houses in America; the book should be of some use to younger readers as a limited reference source, particularly for the illustrations." Chicago. Children's Bk Center
Bibliography: p155-56

Hofsinde, Robert
Indians at home; written and illus. by Robert Hofsinde (Gray-Wolf) Morrow 1964 96p illus lib. bdg. $4.32 (4-7)   728
1 Indians of North America—Social life and customs 2 Houses
ISBN 0-688-31611-5
This "book describes how Indian homes were built, from the open chikees of the Seminole in the Everglades to the cozy earth lodges of the Mandan. In addition the reader is allowed to investigate the life and customs that went with each home, and the changes that modern times have made in them." Chicago Sch J
"Neatly organized, straightforward in style, and well-illustrated. . . . A map of linguistic-group distribution precedes the text, and a list of tribes within linguistic groups follows it; an index is appended." Chicago. Children's Bk Center

Myller, Rolf
From idea into house; house designed by Myller & Szwarce; drawings for this book prepared by Henry K. Szwarce. Atheneum Pubs. 1974 64p illus $6.95 (5-7)   728
1 Architecture, Domestic—Designs 2 Houses
ISBN 0-689-30144-8
This book "describes the building process—buying land, drawing up plans, and constructing the house. The author follows one family's efforts from the idea stage through contact with the realtor, architect, contractor, mortgagor, etc. Detailed floor plans and diagrams used by electricians, plumbers, and other subcontractors are included." Sch Library J
"Readers may not understand all the minutiae of the drawings, but they will certainly have a thorough introduction to architectural specifications and the order in which a house is constructed." Chicago. Children's Bk Center
Glossary: p60-64

728.8   Castles

Adkins, Jan
The art and industry of sandcastles; being: an illustrated guide to basic constructions along with divers information devised by one Jan Adkins, a wily fellow. Walker & Co. 1971 xxix p illus map $5.95 (4-7)   728.8
1 Castles
ISBN 0-8027-0336-4
"Designed with an unobtrusive mastery of form and line the text and illustrations together serve both as a sophisticated guide to making sandcastles and as a record of the evolution of castle building in Europe. The explanation of various processes used to make sand structures and to build various kinds of actual castles is given in a pleasing, skillfully presented book for all ages, with information included on the duties of major personnel in the traditional castle." Booklist
"Castles conjure up dreams that are deftly captured on sand-colored paper, with hand-lettered text and ink wash drawings." Brooklyn. Art Bks for Children

Duggan, Alfred
The castle book; illus. by Raymond Briggs. Pantheon Bks. 1961 95p illus $2.50 (4-7)   728.8
1 Castles
ISBN 0-394-81001-5
First published 1960 in England with title: Look at castles
"A castle is a building that tries to do two things at once: to shelter a great man and his family in some comfort—and to keep out his enemies." Thus begins this account of how castles were built and used from Norman times until their decline six centuries later
"An entertaining and informative book . . . written with humor and an occasional jarring flippancy or a reference that may be confusing to the young reader [and] . . . especially useful because it gives the reasons, in describing architectural details, for their existence." Chicago. Children's Bk Center

Unstead, R. J.
British castles. Crowell 1970 92p illus maps $3.50 (5-7)   728.8
1 Castles
ISBN 0-690-16029-1
Originally published in England with title: Castles
This is a "well-illustrated survey of high points in the development of the British castle, its 'slighting'

Unstead, R. J.—*Continued*

under Cromwell, and subsequent demise. . . . Discussed in brief are construction, design, castle life, keeps, attack, defence, and 'Z-plan' castles. The book concludes with suggestions for visiting castles." Sch Library J

Glossary: p91

730 Sculpture

Paine, Roberta, M.

Looking at sculpture. Lothrop 1968 128p illus map $5.95, lib. bdg. $5.11 (4-7)   730

1 Sculpture

ISBN 0-688-41223-8; 0-688-51223-2

The author has selected works ranging from ancient Egyptian and Greek sculpture to the metal constructions of today to give a sense of the variety of forms in sculpture, indicate some of its themes, and show the relation of the design of a work to the materials used

"The superb black and white photographs, ranging through the whole history of sculpture in stone, wood, bronze, clay (and more recent modern materials), are a subtle blend of world masterpieces and intriguing, lesser known works. . . . The text is simple and declarative. . . . It is most valuable for its insights into technique and method. Occasionally problems of aesthetic definition are open to quarrel. But all observations are sound and form an eminently solid base on which a child can begin a relationship with works of art." N Y Times Bk Rev

Glossary: p111-22. Books for further reading: p125

731 Processes and representations of sculpture

Rieger, Shay

Animals in clay. Scribner 1971 unp illus lib. bdg. $5.95 (3-6)   731

1 Modeling 2 Animals in art

ISBN 0-684-12322-3

"Photographs taken in [the author's] studio trace the modeling of one particular sculpture, a lion, from the preparation of the clay to the firing of the sculpture in a kiln. A number of other sculptures are pictured in completed form, along with sketches and photographs of the animals." Booklist

"The text is extremely simple, but the finished terra cotta sculpture, often accompanied by photographs of the model, have a charm all their own and could well inspire young artists." Horn Bk

Gargoyles, monsters and other beasts. Lothrop 1972 62p illus lib. bdg. $5.11 (1-5)   731

1 Sculpture 2 Monsters

ISBN 0-688-50063-3

"This is more inspirational than how-to-do-it. Using photographs of gargoyles, dragons, sphinxes, and other grotesque or mythical creatures and photographs of make-believe beasts and monsters created by herself or by children [the author] encourages creativity in the budding artist." Booklist

731.4 Sculpture—Techniques

Chernoff, Goldie Taub

Clay-dough play-dough; clay-dough creations and drawings by Margaret A. Hartelius. Walker & Co. 1974 unp illus $3.50 (1-4)   731.4

1 Modeling 2 Handicraft

ISBN 0-8027-6178-X

A "book of projects made with clay-dough (uncooked flour, salt, and water). Large color photographs of easy-to-make bracelets, animals, baskets, tiles, toys, and decorations accompany the step-by-step directions. Many of the projects are geared for youngest sculptors." Sch Library J

"The instructions are clear, the projects uncomplicated, the illustrations adequate. The text points out that oven-drying should be done only under adult supervision." Chicago. Children's Bk Center

Leyh, Elizabeth

Children make sculpture. Van Nostrand-Reinhold [1972] 96p illus $5.95 (3-5)   731.4

1 Sculpture—Technique

ISBN 0-442-04771-1

Photographs by Alexandra Blanshard, Stuart Barton, and Hendryk Szterbin

"The book, which consists primarily of photographs and has little text beyond the descriptive captions, shows carving, junk construction, paper sculpture, objects made with clay, plaster, styrofoam, cardboard, pebbles, et cetera. While it may give children—or adults who work with children—some ideas for media, it gives little help with techniques, although some construction is explained." Chicago. Children's Bk Center

Seidelman, James

Creating with clay, by James Seidelman and Grace Mintonye; illus. by Robert William Hinds. Crowell-Collier Press 1967 56p illus $4.95 (4-7)   731.4

1 Clay 2 Modeling

"A guide to clay modeling covering tools, materials, basic instructions, a glossary of claying terms, and a special section on firing, glazing, and painting the finished product. Illustrated with photographs, diagrams, and colored line drawings." Hodges. Bks for Elem Sch Libraries

Creating with papier-mache [by] James E. Seidelman and Grace Mintonye; illus. by Christine Randall. Crowell-Collier Press 1971 56p illus $4.95 (4-6)   731.4

1 Paper crafts

"The instructions are clear and complete. The text discusses types of paper, wet and dry methods, things that can be used for armature or for decoration, making molds and working with pulp, and making masks, animal figures, dolls, etc." Chicago. Children's Bk Center

"The book offers enough ideas, encouragement, and practical help for individual and group projects to make it satisfactory as an introduction to the craft." Booklist

Slade, Richard

Modeling in clay, plaster and papier-mâché; illus. with photographs. Lothrop [1968 c1967] 64p illus $4.95, lib. bdg. $4.59, pa $2.50 (3-7)   731.4

1 Modeling 2 Paper crafts

ISBN 0-688-41376-5; 0-688-51376-1; 0-688-45009-1

First published 1967 in England with title: Your book of modeling

"A no-nonsense, practical guide to modeling with three types of material—clay, plaster, and papier-mâché—with many excellent photographs that help to

Slade, Richard—*Continued*
explain the procedures. Extra housekeeping hints
(such as not pouring waste plaster water down the
drain) are a good addition to this easy, concise, and
clear introduction." Sch Library J
    Books for further reading: p60

Weiss, Harvey
    Clay, wood and wire; a how-to-do-it book of sculp-
ture. Young Scott bks. 1956 48p illus lib. bdg. $4.95
(4-7)   731.4
    1 Sculpture—Technique 2 Modeling
    ISBN 0-201-09159-3
    A how-to-do-it "book of sculpture, progressing
from the simple figure made of pipe cleaners to heads,
figures, masks, mobiles, and constructions made from
clay, plasticene, wire, wood, papier-mache, and plaster. Simple line drawings illustrate step-by-step
directions." Library J
    "An excellent introduction to sculpture for young
artists. . . . [The author] constantly urges the
reader . . . to use his own imagination and to try
other forms in addition to the one suggested here. The
illustrations are examples from the works of sculptors
of all periods, nationalities and schools of art, and add
greatly to the appeal and value of the book." Chicago.
Children's Bk Center
    Other books on sculpture: p47

732   Primitive sculpture

Naylor, Penelope
    Black images; the art of West Africa; with photo-
graphs by Lisa Little. Doubleday 1973 95p illus map
$6.95, lib. bdg. $7.70 (6-7)   732
    1 Sculpture, African
    ISBN 0-385-06025-4; 0-385-07462-X
    This book begins with a short introduction about
the role of sculpture in African life. The bulk of the
text describes West African sculpture, including
masks. The objects are thematically arranged in six
categories: mothers and children, fertility, initiation,
royalty, war, and death
    "The book is graphically stunning; on spacious page
layouts, the pictures are matched with explanatory
and descriptive text and often with poetry." Chicago.
Children's Bk Center
    Bibliography: p[96]

736   Carving and carvings.
Paper cutting and folding

Araki, Chiyo
    Origami in the classroom. Tuttle [1965-1968] 2v
illus ea $4.75 (4-7)   736
    1 Origami 2 Paper crafts
    ISBN Bk I 0-8048-0452-1; Bk II 0-8048-0453-2
    Book I has title: Activities for autumn through
Christmas. Book II has title: Activities for winter
through summer
    Original patterns of graduated difficulty are pre-
sented for various holidays, events, seasons, etc.
Measurements, length of time, and materials necessary are given for most projects

Lewis, Shari
    Folding paper masks [by] Shari Lewis and Lillian
Oppenheimer. Original masks created by Giuseppe
Baggi. Dutton 1965 93p illus $5.50 (3-5)   736

    1 Paper crafts 2 Masks (for the face)
    ISBN 0-525-29999-8
    "A. J. P. Tarcher, Inc. book"
    "Step-by-step instructions are presented with easy-
to-follow illustrations for the construction of 21
masks. Most of these projects require little more than
a piece of paper." Adventuring With Bks. 2d edition
    Included are clown, tiger, rabbit, witch, devil,
hobo and other masks. The authors include advice on
how to use the masks and suggest ways to decorate
them
    Bibliography: p92-93

Sarasas, Claude
    The ABC's of origami; paper folding for children;
illus. by the author. Tuttle 1964 55p illus $4.50
(4-6)   736
    1 Origami 2 Alphabet books 3 Multilingual books
    ISBN 0-8048-0000-6
    First published 1951 in Japan
    Here are "diagramed directions for folding 26
objects from Albatross to Zebra with each heading
[first in English and then] translated into French and
transliterated Japanese. Color illustrations show
finished object against an oriental background." Sch
Library J

Temko, Florence
    Paper cutting; illus. by Steve Madison. Doubleday
1973 64p illus $4.95, lib. bdg. $5.70 (3-6)   736
    1 Paper crafts
    ISBN 0-385-09432-9; 0-385-09444-2
    This "introduction to the art of paper cutting pro-
vides advice on general procedures followed by
explicit, well-illustrated directions for making dancing dolls, trucks, lanterns, animals, decorations, toys,
puzzles, star designs, a monster, masks, and simple
spy disguises. Suggestions on how to use the completed paper objects accompany each project and an
'idea index' is included." Booklist
    "Patterns and diagrams done in ink on pastel col-
ored pages accent the simple, concise directions for
each craft." Sch Library J

    Paper folding to begin with, by Florence Temko
and Elaine Simon; pictures by Joan Stoliar. Bobbs
1968 31p illus $3.50 (1-4)   736
    1 Paper crafts
    ISBN 0-672-50419-7
    "The fan, the paper airplane, the newspaper hat—
these are some of the simple constructions included in
this most basic introduction to the art of paperfold-
ing." Horn Bk
    "Also included are a brief history of paper-folding
and suggested uses for the folded paper toys. This will
be a welcome idea book for adults working with
groups of young children as well as a good book for
children to use on their own." Sch Library J

737.4   Coins

Andrews, Charles J.
    Fell's United States coin book. Fell illus $4.95
                                           737.4
    1 Coins
    First edition published 1949 edited by Jacques Del
Monte. Periodically revised to bring material up to
date
    "Information about coins: collecting, selling and
evaluating them. The coins are United States mint
only, and data is given showing the contemporary
value of every United States coin ever minted." Wis
Library Bul

Browin, Frances Williams
Coins have tales to tell; the story of American coins.
Lippincott 1966 152p illus $7.50 (5-7)   737.4
1 Coins
ISBN 0-397-30861-2
"Here is fine coverage of American coins and American history, with descriptions of rare mintings, barter, foreign coins used in this country before our own were made, and the value of old coins today. The text is crisp and graphic, and brings alive the periods of history discussed." Sch Library J
"Contained in the appendix are a list of U.S. commemorative coins, abbreviations used in numismatics, a list of mint marks, a glossary, and a list of coin displays. Illustrated with photographs, most of them of coins." Booklist

Campbell, Elizabeth
Nails to nickels; the story of American coins old and new; illus. by Leonard Weisgard. Little 1960 58p illus lib. bdg. $4.95 (3-5)   737.4
1 Coins 2 Money
ISBN 0-316-12598-9
In this book for young collectors, the first section, Money of long ago, tells how wampum, tobacco, nails, and tea were used as currency by the Indians and colonists. Then, coins of yesterday are described—foreign coins, tree coins, cents and half cents, Indian head cents, silver dollars, gold coins, and others. The Lincoln penny, Jefferson nickel, and Roosevelt dime are among the present-day coins discussed

Hobson, Burton
Coins you can collect. New and rev. ed. Illus. with photographs. Hawthorn Bks. 1970 128p illus $4.95 (4-7)   737.4
1 Coins
ISBN 0-8015-1374-X
First published 1967
"The purpose of this book is to tell you about and show you the coins you 'can' collect, easily and inexpensively. These are coins that are now in circulation in many different nations and colonies of the world. . . . This book [also] shows you the 'kind' of information you can discover from coins and about coins." Introduction
Coin publications: p19. Glossary: p122-24

Reinfeld, Fred
Coin collectors' handbook. Doubleday illus $4.95   737.4
1 Coins
First published 1954 by Sterling. Frequently revised to bring the material on prices and issues up to date
This book tells how to acquire coins for fun and investment, how to store collections, preserve rarities, and sell coins profitably. In the catalog section of the book are up-to-date values for every condition of every United States and Canadian coin, along with the quantities issued
Includes glossary

How to build a coin collection. Rev. by Burton Hobson. Sterling illus $4.95   737.4
1 Coins
First published 1958. Periodically revised to keep material up to date
Contains information necessary to start, build, and maintain a good coin collection. With a sample collection, the author shows how to select coins, and how to build through careful investment and by replacement with coins in superior condition. How to recognize and identify mint marks; how to grade, classify, and determine the condition of coins; and how to care for and store a coin collection are covered
Foreign coins, price lists and glossary are included

Rosenfeld, Sam
The story of coins; illus. by James E. Barry. . . . Harvey House 1968 126p illus (A Story of science series bk) lib. bdg. $5.49 (5-7)   737.4
1 Coins
ISBN 0-8178-3922-4
"Checked for accuracy by Henry Grunthal, curator of European and modern coins, The American Numismatic Society." Title page
This introduction to the hobby of coin collecting tells the story of coinage, from the beginnings of barter through the development of ancient Greek and Roman civilizations. Included are sections devoted to the techniques of coin collecting and to United States coins
Coin glossary: p116-18. Books about coins: p119-20

738.1   Ceramic arts— Techniques, apparatus, equipment, materials

Elbert, Virginie Fowler
Potterymaking; text and photography by Virginie Fowler Elbert. Doubleday 1974 64p illus (Crafts for children) $5.95, lib. bdg. $6.70 (4-6)   738.1
1 Pottery
ISBN 0-385-08342-4; 0-385-03697-3
"A practical and inviting book on working with clay. Explicit directions and equally clear photographs show how to employ tools found in the home as well as a kitchen oven to fire clay. The potter's wheel is only briefly introduced. The author describes the coil method (building with ropes of clay), the slab method (with a rolling pin), and the use of the hands to model pots, bowls, tiles, pendants, boxes and figures. Glazes are explained for the older craftsman or the adult working with children." Horn Bk

Weiss, Harvey
Ceramics; from clay to kiln. Young Scott Bks. 1964 63p illus (Beginning artist's lib) lib. bdg. $4.95 (5-7)   738.1
1 Pottery
ISBN 0-201-09153-4
"A very good book for the beginner. The explanations and the illustrations are clear, the progression of difficulty well-paced. Mr. Weiss strikes a nice balance between detailed, step-by-step instruction and an encouragement of experimentation and creativity. He suggests simple equipment and modest designs, but suggests to the reader that the more complicated procedures should be understood; the reader is referred, for example, to textbooks on glazing, although the method for adding a simple glaze is given." Chicago. Children's Bk Center
Explanation of terms: p[64]

739   Art metalwork

Miller, Natalie
The story of the Statue of Liberty; illus. by Lucy and John Hawkinson. Childrens Press 1965 30p illus lib. bdg. $4.25 (2-4)   739

Miller, Natalie—*Continued*
1 Statue of Liberty, New York
ISBN 0-516-04637-3
"Cornerstones of freedom"
The story of how the nation's symbol of freedom came to be

739.2   Work in precious metals

Fisher, Leonard Everett
The silversmiths; written & illus. by Leonard Everett Fisher. Watts, F. 1964 46p illus (Colonial Americans) lib. bdg. $3.90 (4-7)   739.2
1 Silversmithing 2 U.S.—Social life and customs—Colonial period
ISBN 0-531-01036-8
In this discussion of the history and techniques of colonial silversmiths "respect for . . . achievement is reflected in striking full-page scratchboard illustrations and in concise, informative text." Horn Bk
Silversmiths' terms: p40-41. Some Colonial American silversmiths and their marks: p42-44

739.7   Arms and armor

Hofsinde, Robert
Indian warriors and their weapons; written and illus. by Robert Hofsinde (Gray-Wolf) Morrow 1965 96p illus lib. bdg. $4.32 (3-6)   739.7
1 Indians of North America 2 Arms and armor
ISBN 0-688-31613-1
"A brief account of the weapons and war tactics of seven famous American Indian tribes." Horn Bk
"Hofsinde's discussion is both authoritative and sympathetic. . . . Good illustrations." Sci Bks

741   Drawing and drawings

Campbell, Ann
Start to draw; written and drawn by Ann Campbell. Watts, F. 1968 48p illus lib. bdg. $4.90 (k-3)   741
1 Drawing
ISBN 0-531-01799-0
"Drawing for young children is treated as an imaginative game in this book about a lively boy who draws himself a world." N Y Pub Library. The Black Experience in Children's Bks
He learns to draw the basic geometric shapes—square, cube, circle, sphere triangle, pyramid, and cone—by drawing familiar objects in his surroundings

741.2   Drawing—Techniques

Borten, Helen
A picture has a special look. Abelard-Schuman 1961 unp illus lib. bdg. $5.95 (k-3)   741.2
1 Art—Technique 2 Drawing
ISBN 0-200-7197-9
"The various media (pencil, crayon, watercolor, collage, etc.) which can be used to create a picture are discussed in simple text and illustrated with the author's effective pictures. Useful to show young children the possibilities in different materials and to encourage art appreciation and diversification in art work." Hodges. Bks for Elem Sch Libraries

Hawkinson, John
Pastels are great! Whitman, A. 1968 48p illus lib. bdg. $4.50 (3-6)   741.2
1 Pastel drawing
ISBN 0-8075-6362-5
"An easy and clear introduction for the young child to the use of pastels as an art media. Eight pastel strokes are explained, with suggestions for use." Wis Library Bul
"A child will benefit most if an adult shares this book on the techniques of using pastel chalks. The various types of strokes are well demonstrated and the blending of colors illustrated." Bruno. Bks for Sch Libraries, 1968

Munari, Bruno
From afar it is an island. [Translated and adapted by Pierrette Fleutiaux] World Pub. [1972 c1971] [38]p illus $3.95, lib. bdg. $4.21 (k-3)   741.2
1 Rocks
ISBN 0-529-01284-7; 0-529-01285-5
First published in Italy 1971
The author explores the aesthetics of stones through photographs and suggests pictures to paint on them

Seidelman, James E.
The rub book, by James E. Seidelman and Grace Mintonye; drawings by Lynn Sweat. Crowell-Collier Press 1968 unp illus lib. bdg. $3.50 (1-3)   741.2
1 Drawing
"An art activity story in which Jeff discovers the fun of making rubbings of familiar objects. . . . Clear directions and simple illustrations may inspire elementary age children to experiment with this art medium." Library J

Slobodkin, Louis
The first book of drawing. Watts, F. 1958 68p illus lib. bdg. $3.90 (5-7)   741.2
1 Drawing 2 Anatomy, Artistic
ISBN 0-531-00516-X
"Many a child will welcome this book. Brief as it is, there is helpful information about basic techniques and materials for using pencil, pen and ink, charcoal, Conte crayon, or brush. Illustrations, which fill a major part of the book, follow the text closely. They demonstrate what may be accomplished by shading, or 'modeling,' to give third dimension, movement, and tone. Perspective, 'a complicated science,' is limited to two pages. Mr. Slobodkin's own style of book illustration with pen and ink, water-color pencil, and wet brush will be recognized and appreciated as an apparently simple, effective technique." Horn Bk
"This should prove to be an encouraging book for the young artist. It gives a positive approach to art either as a pleasant pastime or in the serious business of becoming an artist." Ontario Library Rev

Weiss, Harvey
Pencil, pen and brush; drawings for beginners. Young Scott Bks. 1961 63p illus lib. bdg. $4.50 (5-7)   741.2
1 Drawing
ISBN 0-201-09311-1
The author provides "guidance in basic techniques and media and specific step-by-step directions for first efforts to draw from photographs as models. Different methods for capturing the special quality of a subject are illustrated in the work of several artists shown together. Interspersed are examples of ways to suggest textures and tones. . . . actions, and space. . . . Although the coverage is broad and sketchy, it is recommended for stimulus to creative expression and

Weiss, Harvey—*Continued*
for enjoyment of the illustrations used, from
Leonardo to the moderns." Horn Bk
Other books about drawing: p63

Zaidenberg, Arthur
How to draw with pen & brush; a book for beginners. Vanguard 1965 61p illus $4.95 (3-7)   741.2
1 Pen drawing 2 Drawing
ISBN 0-8149-0441-6
The author demonstrates different effects achieved
with a pen or brush and ink. Scratchboard drawing,
pen sketches, dry brush and stick painting are among
the varieties discussed

741.5 Cartoons, caricatures, comics

Schulz, Charles M.
The Snoopy festival; with an introduction by Charlie Brown. Holt 1974 unp illus $9.95 (4-7)   741.5
1 Comic books, strips, etc.
ISBN 0-03-013161-8
"Snoopy and company meander through the pages
(some full color, the rest black and white) of another
large-format comic strip collection, adding to the
stock of Peanuts books for insatiable fans. Strips presented here are in hard cover for the first time."
Booklist

741.64 Illustration of books and book jackets

Illustrators of children's books: 1744-1945; comp. by
Bertha E. Mahony, Louise Payson Latimer [and]
Beulah Folmsbee. Horn Bk. [1961 c1947] 527p illus
$20   741.64
1 Illustration of books 2 Illustrators 3 Children's
literature—History and criticism
ISBN 0-87675-015-3
"An unabridged republication, without change in
format, of a book first released in 1947." Booklist
Part one consists of 10 chapters by leading
authorities on children's literature, which deal with
the history and development of children's book illustration. Part two contains brief biographies of almost
400 illustrators. Part three includes extensive bibliographies

Illustrators of children's books: 1946-1956; comp. by
Ruth Hill Viguers, Marcia Dalphin [and] Bertha
Mahony Miller. A supplement to Illustrators of chil-
dren's books: 1744-1945. Horn Bk. 1958 299p illus
$20   741.64
1 Illustration of books 2 Illustrators 3 Children's
literature—History and criticism
ISBN 0-87675-016-1
A first supplement to the title entered above
It brings forward through December 1956 the biog-
raphies and bibliographies of the outstanding illus-
trators of children's books. Also included are three
articles: Distinction in picture books, by M. Brown;
The book artist: ideas and techniques, by L. Ward;
The European picture book, by F. Eichenberg

Illustrators of children's books: 1957-1966; comp. by
Lee Kingman, Joanna Foster and Ruth Giles Lon-
toft. Horn Bk. 1968 295p illus $20   741.64

1 Illustration of books 2 Illustrators 3 Children's
literature—History and criticism
ISBN 0-87675-017-X
The second supplement to: Illustrators of children's
books, 1744-1945 and Illustrators of children's books:
1946-1956, both entered above
This volume brings forward through 1966 the biographies and bibliographies of the leading illustrators
in the field of children's books. It includes four articles: One wonders, by Marcia Brown; Color separation, by Adrienne Adams; The artist and his editor, by
Grace Allen Hogarth; and Beatrix Potter: centenary of
an artist-writer, by Rumer Godden

Lawson, Robert
Robert Lawson, illustrator; a selection of his characteristic illustrations; with introduction and comment
by Helen L. Jones. Little 1972 121p illus $7.95
(5-7)   741.64
1 Illustrators
ISBN 0-316-47281-6
"A book that should intrigue Robert Lawson's
young readers and be useful to adults working in the
field of children's literature. Helen Jones was one of
the author-illustrator's editors, and she prefaces each
section of his pictures—which form the major part of
the book—with a discussion of his work in that area. A
final section gives a brief biographical sketch and
discusses his work, including a long description by
Lawson of his technique and approach to illustration."
Chicago. Children's Bk Center
Books illustrated by Robert Lawson: p119-20

MacCann, Donnarae
The child's first books; a critical study of pictures
and texts, by Donnarae MacCann and Olga Richard.
Wilson, H.W. 1973 135p illus $12   741.64
1 Picture books for children 2 Children's
literature—History and criticism
ISBN 0-8242-0501-4
"A carefully written analysis of picture books,
designed for critics and book selectors, emphasizing
the study of both literary and graphic aspects. Beginning with the proposition that during a child's first
eight years no 'cultural or intellectual deprivation
must occur . . . if the child is to reach his full potential in later years,' the authors go on to relate illustration to the graphic arts, and to consider texts and
graphics separately. They provide provocative discussions in chapters entitled: Stereotypes in Illustration;
Graphic Elements; Outstanding Contemporary Illustrators; Book Design; Literary Elements; Outstanding Narrative Writers; Specialized Texts (e.g. alphabet and counting books, concept and nature
books); The Caldecott Award; and The Child, the
Librarian, and the Critic. Backed by a liberal number
of philosophical quotations about art and writing, and
with a bibliography of books recommended in the
study, the work will serve admirably as background
reading for students. The beautifully designed
volume with forty illustrations, seven in full color,
includes two large foldouts." Horn Bk

741.9 Collections of drawings

Holme, Bryan
Drawings to live with. Viking 1966 155p illus
$4.50   741.9
1 Drawings 2 Art appreciation
ISBN 0-670-28413-0
In brief text and captions the author "discusses

Holme, Bryan—*Continued*

drawing, print-making, book illustration, and cartoons with an illuminating selection of pictures reproduced in black and white to reveal different ways of treating the same subject." LC. Children's Bks. 1966

"One wishes that more of the precision so evident in the excellent and unusual array of masterpieces were reflected in the text and that the drawings discussed in terms of color had been reproduced in other than black and white. But the young reader who has been roused by the attractive format and informality will surely return for longer looks. An appealing presentation." Horn Bk

I never saw another butterfly; childrens [sic] drawings and poems from Theresienstadt Concentration Camp, 1942-1944. McGraw [1964] 80p illus $6.95
741.9

1 Children as artists 2 Children as authors 3 Terezín (Concentration camp)
ISBN 0-07-067570-8
First published 1959 in Czechoslovakia
Edited by Hana Volavková
Title on spine: Children's drawings and poems—Terezín, 1942-44

"A collection of eloquent, touching poems and drawings created by Jewish children marked for death who passed through Theresienstadt Concentration Camp during World War II. A gift to the children of the world. . . . Epilogue by Jiri Weil." Keating. Building Bridges of Understanding Between Cultures

743   Drawing and drawings by subject

Emberley, Ed

Ed Emberley's Drawing book: make a world. Little 1972 unp illus lib. bdg. $3.95 (2-6)   743
1 Drawing
ISBN 0-316-23598-9

"Emberley gives directions for drawing, among a myriad of other things, 10 different kinds of cars, 16 varieties of trucks, and animals of all species including anteaters and dinosaurs." Bk World

"The final three pages, which supply suggestions for making comic strips, posters, mobiles and games, help make the volume particularly appealing. For all developing artists and even for plain scribblers." Horn Bk

Ed Emberley's Drawing book of animals. Little 1970 unp illus lib. bdg. $3.95 (2-6)   743
1 Animal painting and illustration 2 Drawing
ISBN 0-316-23597-0

"If children can draw a triangle, a circle and a rectangle, and a few 'Things' such as the 'scratchy scribble' and the 'curly scribble,' and if they can write numbers and letters, then they can, by putting them all together in the book's carefully designated manner, draw any of Ed Emberley's charming animals." Sch Library J

The book "has no literary pretensions at all and may well offend the free-drawing advocates, but it makes an encouraging book for those, adults included, who imagine they can't draw for toffee." Christian Sci Monitor

Ed Emberley's Drawing book of faces. Little 1975 32p illus lib. bdg. $4.95 (3-6)   743
1 Drawing 2 Face 3 Cartoons and caricatures
ISBN 0-316-23609-8

Using a "step-by-step illustrative format . . . Em-

berley shows how to embellish a simple shape so that it becomes an amusing character. . . . One row of instruction shows what to draw and one row shows where to put it. Most people and animal faces are accomplished in six to eight steps and the author maintains that if children can 'draw 7 things, they can draw all kinds of faces.' " Sch Library J

"Also included are sections showing how to put action into full figures and suggestions on how to make cards, posters, masks, puppets and other 'good stuff' from the faces." Pub W

Zaidenberg, Arthur

How to draw the wild West. Abelard-Schuman [1973 c1972] 64p illus lib. bdg. $5.95 (4-7)   743
1 Drawing 2 The West
ISBN 0-200-71847-9

The author gives step-by-step instructions for drawing such things as cowboys, stage coaches, covered wagons, settlers, and various scenes of the Wild West

745   Decorative and minor arts

Gladstone, M. J.

A carrot for a nose; the form of folk sculpture on America's city streets and country roads. Scribner 1974 70p illus $9.95 (4-7)   745
1 Folk art, American
ISBN 0-684-13663-5

The author describes the origins and variety of eight kinds of American folk art: weathervanes, whirligigs, pavement lids, trade signs, gravestones, decoys, carousel figures, and snowmen and scarecrows

"The text is written in a casual, conversational style and is both entertaining and informative; the book is intriguing in itself but also useful for those interested in American history, in art, or in the relationship between creative expression and the culture and/or period from which it emanates." Chicago. Children's Bk Center

745.4   Pure and applied design and decoration

Downer, Marion

Discovering design; illus. with photographs and drawings. Lothrop 1947 104p illus $5.50 (5-7) 745.4
1 Design 2 Design, Decorative
ISBN 0-688-41266-1

"Nine branches of design are discussed, showing how patterns in nature have inspired designs in textiles, furniture, ceramics, and other arts and crafts. Principles of design are stressed and illustrated in color, encouraging observation and the development of critical judgment." Hodges. Bks for Elem Sch Libraries

The story of design. Lothrop 1963 216p illus lib. bdg. $6.54 (6-7)   745.4
1 Design 2 Design, Decorative
ISBN 0-688-51451-0

"Illustrated with museum photographs. . . . Prehistoric, ancient Egyptian and Greek, Oriental, Western, early American, and contemporary design—all are interpreted in terms of influences and individual developments. Brief text, facing or surrounding each of the beautiful examples shown,

Downer, Marion—*Continued*

illumines each of the special qualities: economy, relaxation, motion, mathematical rightness, spontaneity, imagination or mystery." Horn Bk

"The text is not intended, clearly, to be comprehensive; it merely suggests some aspects of—for example—Oriental use of design. The photographs are of excellent quality (all black and white) and fascinating variety." Chicago. Children's Bk Center

Selected bibliography: p216

Ellison, Elsie C.

Fun with lines and curves; with illus. adapted from the author's drawings by Susan Stan. Lothrop 1972 95p illus lib. bdg. $4.81, pa $2.95 (4-7)   745.4

1 Geometrical drawing 2 Design, Decorative

ISBN 0-688-51527-4; 0-688-45527-1

After "explaining the use of ruler, compass, and protractor Ellison gives step-by-step instructions augmented by exemplary drawings for making simple polygons and stars, using only straight lines to produce a curved line working with squares, angles, and circles, and combining techniques to achieve three-dimensional effects." Booklist

"The explanations are expressed in exactly the right terms; clear and accurate statements lead the reader along so cleverly that it is difficult to resist rummaging for the tools to start the designs. . . . With many illustrations and the clear directions children (and teachers) should have no difficulty constructing the designs." Sci Bks

745.5   Handicrafts

Cobb, Vicki

Arts and crafts you can eat; illus. by Peter Lippman. Lippincott 1974 127p illus $4.95, pa $1.95 (4-7)
    745.5

1 Handicraft 2 Cookery

ISBN 0-397-31491-4; 0-397-31492-2

Instructions are included for such creations as chocolate marshmallow scratchboard, inlaid pancakes, stained glass cookies, pulled taffy flowers, a pasta mobile, orange peel pomander, and an edible necklace

"The clear and precise directions make failures unlikely; but if they occur, the author consoles the readers by reminding them that they can always eat their mistakes." Horn Bk

Comins, Jeremy

Art from found objects. Lothrop 1974 illus $5.50, lib. bdg. $4.81 (5-7)   745.5

1 Handicraft

ISBN 0-688-41646-2; 0-688-51646-7

"A wide variety of techniques for creating sculpture and other art from found objects is explained in this unusual book. The author is careful to leave the aesthetic decisions up to the reader while he lists basic materials and gives instructions for assemblage. The many black-and-white photographs of mobiles, collages, pendants, and standing or framed constructions show Comins' very able students' work as well as some adult art. A chapter on vacuum forming may present technical difficulties for younger readers but is not out of range for others. A glossary is appended." Booklist

Latin American crafts, and their cultural backgrounds. Lothrop 1974 128p illus $5.50, lib. bdg. $4.81 (4-7)   745.5

1 Handicraft

ISBN 0-688-41582-2; 0-688-51582-7

"This stresses both an appreciation of native crafts

and ways to make items in both the ancient and modern styles. The history of Latin American art forms and a description of how each was originally done precede instructions on how to reproduce them using common materials such as metal, wood, wax, wool, papier-maché and cloth. Especially attractive are the masks, carvings, appliqué work, needlepoint, embroidery, and string designs. Photographs of the original works and student copies are included along with clear line illustrations and simple, step-by-step directions in this especially useful heritage/how-to book." Sch Library J

Glossary: p121-23. Suggested reading: p124

Cross, Linda

Kitchen crafts, by Linda and John Cross; illus. by Burt Blum; photographs by John Retallack. Macmillan Pub. Co. 1974 120p illus $8.95, pa $3.95 (3-7)
    745.5

1 Handicraft

ISBN 0-02-528940-3; 0-02-009430-2

This book demonstrates a variety of crafts using kitchen ingredients such as flour, pasta, nuts, beans, seeds, fruits, and vegetables. Among the skills taught are macramé, tie-dyeing, batik, candlemaking, soap carving, dyeing with plants, and papier-maché

D'Amato, Janet

African crafts for you to make, by Janet and Alex D'Amato. Messner 1969 65p illus lib. bdg. $4.79 (4-7)   745.5

1 Arts and crafts 2 Folk art, African

ISBN 0-671-32130-7

"Projects giving complete details regarding patterns, construction, and materials are described for items such as musical instruments, miniature houses, dolls, costumes, games, and ceremonial masks." Keating. Building Bridges of Understanding Between Cultures

"Far more than just a collection of diagrams and instructions, this meaty, yet slim volume includes much information on tribal backgrounds and living conditions. While describing the item to be made, the book delves into the significance of the ceremonies and rituals in which the art object is used. Maps of tribal areas add geography to the history, culture, and art which are welded into a compact and intriguing study of a long overlooked area of ancient art forms." Christian Sci Monitor

Suggested further reading: p65. Maps on liningpapers

American Indian craft inspirations, by Janet and Alex D'Amato; illus. by Janet D'Amato; designed by Alex D'Amato. Evans, M.&Co. distributed in association with Lippincott 1972 224p illus $7.95 (5-7)
    745.5

1 Indians of North America—Costume and adornment 2 Handicraft

ISBN 0-87131-031-7

The authors examine the materials and techniques used by the Indians in their crafts, and then outline adaptations for both beginner and expert craftsmen. With emphasis on costume, instructions are included for work with such materials as beads, shells, metals, and bone

"Interesting, well-presented ideas with clear illustrations and instructions. . . . Though authentic, the designs are adapted to easily acquirable materials." Sch Library J

Colonial crafts for you to make, by Janet and Alex D'Amato. Messner 1975 64p illus $6.95, lib. bdg. $6.95 (4-7)   745.5

D'Amato, Janet—*Continued*

1 Handicraft 2 U.S.—Social life and customs—
Colonial period
ISBN 0-671-32705-4; 0-671-32706-2

"This is a book that will appeal strongly to children
who like to make things. Following diagrams, patterns
and instructions presented here, youngsters can
create authentic houses complete with fireplaces,
dolls and their colonial costumes, warming pans,
patchwork furnishings, candle holders and even
period toys. Some help may be needed from adults
who will probably be eager to get in on the projects."
Pub W

Indian crafts [by] Janet and Alex D'Amato.
Foreword by Morton Thompson. Lion 1968 65p illus
$5.95, lib. bdg. $5.49 (4-7)   745.5

1 Indians of North America 2 Handicraft
ISBN 0-87460-004-9; 0-87460-088-X

"Clear, detailed instructions are given for construction of six models of various tribal dwellings, two
canoes and a travois. Directions for clothing, household items, weapons, and objects for ceremony and
ritual include some miniature and some full scale
projects. Tribes from all parts of the United States are
represented. The diagrams and drawings are excellent; the bibliography is short but good and includes
mostly adult titles. Background bits of information
enrich the text and enlarge the scope of the book's
usefulness." Sch Library J

Donna, Natalie

Peanut craft, written and illus. by Natalie Donna.
Lothrop 1974 128p illus $6.50, lib. bdg. $5.49 (4-7)
       745.5

1 Handicraft 2 Peanuts
ISBN 0-688-41567-9; 0-688-51567-3

The author presents "craft ideas using peanuts.
With a few inexpensive supplies, peanuts can be
transformed into animals, dolls, puppets, and flowers. The clear instructions are accompanied by
numerous black-and-white photographs and line
drawings. Also included is an interesting discussion of
the characteristics and multiple uses of the peanut
plant." Sch Library J

"For inveterate crafters as well as for the ecology-
conscious interested in recycling materials. . . . The
projects, many of which are readily adaptable for use
with young children, suggest imaginative possibilities. A useful, well-indexed guide for upper
elementary and older students, teachers, scout leaders, and parents. A comprehensive list of necessary
materials (other than peanuts) and tools is included."
Horn Bk

Facklam, Margery

Corn-husk crafts, by Margery Facklam & Patricia
Phibbs. Sterling 1973 48p illus (Little craft bk. ser)
$3.50, lib. bdg. $3.69   745.5

1 Handicraft
ISBN 0-8069-5274-1; 0-8069-5275-X

Instructions are given for dyeing, softening and
preserving corn husks, and for various craft items
made from the preserved corn husks

Hautzig, Esther

Let's make more presents; easy and inexpensive
gifts for every occasion; illus. by Ray Skibinski. Macmillan Pub. Co. 1973 150p illus $5.95 (4-7)   745.5

1 Handicraft 2 Gifts
Companion volume to the author's: Let's make
presents

The author presents 70 easy-to-make gifts which
can be constructed from inexpensive, readily available materials. Step-by-step instructions are given for
making personal presents; gifts for children, the

home, and holidays; and a variety of cookies and candies. There are also special sections on sewing and
wrapping

"A bonanza for the crafty kid. . . . Mothers will be
pleased to find the book contains safety and sanitation
advice. Mr. Skibinski's drawings are as direct and
economical as the instructions." Pub W

Helfman, Harry

Fun with your fingers; working with sticks, paper,
and string; illus. by Robert Bartram. Morrow 1968
47p illus lib. bdg. $4.59 (3-5)   745.5

1 Handicraft
ISBN 0-688-31320-5

"Eleven projects using paper, sticks and string—
and of course some young fingers—are . . . explained
and illustrated. . . . Among them are weaving on a
cardboard loom, printing with an ink pad and a string-
wrapped block of wood, constructing a string design
by wrapping string around random nails in a board,
and making a paper mobile." Bk World

"The author presents clear instructions for simple
crafts, with illustrations to reinforce each explanation.
. . . All can be found in other craft books but not always
in a format so attractive and understandable to this age
group." Library J

Hunt, W. Ben

The complete book of Indian crafts and lore. Golden Press 1976 104p illus map lib. bdg. $9.15, pa
$2.95 (4-7)   745.5

1 Indians of North America—Costume and adornment 2 Handicraft
First published 1954 by Simon & Schuster with
title: The Golden Book of Indian crafts and lore

"It begins with a short piece on where Indians came
from, how to say their names and goes on to describe
in great detail, both with pictures and text, their
clothes, homes, totem poles, dances, utensils and
designs, together with directions and patterns for
making them." N Y Times Bk Rev

"Includes a table of pronounciation and [a map]
showing distribution of the tribes. Excellent for
Scouts and campers." Hodges. Bks for Elem Sch Libraries

Kerina, Jane

African crafts; illus. by Tom Feelings, with diagrams by Marylyn Katzman. Lion 1970 64p illus $3.95,
lib. bdg. $3.69 (4-7)   745.5

1 Handicraft
ISBN 0-87460-064-2; 0-87460-084-7

This book includes "directions for making a variety
of useful and decorative objects in the tradition of
African craftsmen, including pottery, jewelry, wood
carvings, calabash kitchen-ware, Akuaba dolls, tie-
dyed cloth, a musical instrument, and a simple dan-
shiki and other articles of clothing. The objects, which
utilize easily obtainable materials, are identified as to
their use, history, and region of origin. Clear drawings show the finished objects and some of the steps in
their creation. Since the directions are frequently
sketchy, children may require adult help in making
many of the projects." Bks for Children, 1970-1971

Kinney, Jean

21 kinds of American folk art and how to make each
one [by] Jean and Cle Kinney. Atheneum Pubs. 1972
121p illus $6.95 (5-7)   745.5

1 Folk art, American 2 Handicraft
ISBN 0-689-30030-1

"An inviting introduction to a variety of folk arts for
the art student; the younger craftsmen will need additional help. Among the types of art described are
Eskimo carving, handmade pottery, basketry, dolls,

Kinney, Jean—*Continued*

scrimshaw, tap dancing, comic strips, and mobiles. For each the authors provide brief historical information, photographs of representative examples, and suggestions for creating similar, usually simpler objects." Booklist

Kohn, Bernice

The beachcomber's book; illus. by Arabelle Wheatley. Viking 1970 96p illus lib. bdg. $4.95, pa $1.25 (3-7) 745.5

1 Handicraft 2 Seashore 3 Marine biology

ISBN 0-670-15039-8; 0-670-05052-0

"The book includes advice on shell collecting, a home aquarium, collecting and cooking food, drying flowers, and making objects out of sand, driftwood, pebbles, shells, animal skeletons, et cetera. There are several projects for which adult assistance is suggested, but most of them are fairly simple; some supplies are needed, but these tend to be easily obtainable and not expensive." Sutherland. The Best in Children's Bks

"It is never laboriously instructive, and the wide range of suggestions encourages interests of various kinds. . . . The delicate black-and-white drawings, useful for identification or amplification, are quite charming in themselves." Sat Rev

Some common shells and seaweeds: p86-93. Bibliography: p94

Lee, Tina

Things to do; pictures by Manning Lee. Doubleday 1965 64p illus $3.50, lib. bdg. $4.25 (3-6) 745.5

1 Handicraft

ISBN 0-385-03180-7; 0-385-03683-3

"Directions for making a variety of toys, gifts, party favors, and other attractive articles out of such ordinary, easily obtainable materials as cereal boxes, stiff gauze from foot plasters, freezer plates, tin cans, plastic detergent bottles, stamps, paper, corks, and window envelopes. The instructions are, for the most part, easy to follow and each project is clearly illustrated with one or more line drawings. Good ideas for individual creative play and for group projects." Booklist

Lopshire, Robert

How to make flibbers, etc. A book of things to make and do. Beginner Bks. 1964 61p illus $2.50, lib. bdg. $3.07 (k-3) 745.5

1 Handicraft

ISBN 0-394-80037-0; 0-394-90037-5

This is "a book that first-and second-graders can read and follow directions to successfully make the things suggested. The projects range from paper chains and lanterns to bird feeders made out of milk cartons. Directions are simple, pictures are clear, and junior won't be frustrated." Sch Library J

Mason, Bernard S.

The book of Indian-crafts and costumes; drawings by Frederic H. Kock. Ronald 1946 118p illus $7.95 (5-7) 745.5

1 Indians of North America—Costume and adornment 2 Handicraft

ISBN 0-8260-5720-9

First published by A. S. Barnes

Explicit directions for making various items of Indian costumes: war-bonnets, feather crests, beaded headbands, and many other Indian articles. Drawings illustrate the steps in construction, and photographs of finished products are given

"Excellent for Scouts and campers." Hodges. Bks for Elem Sch Libraries

Nagle, Avery

Fun with naturecraft, by Avery Nagle and Joseph Leeming; illus. by Jessie Robinson. Lippincott 1964 80p illus $4.75 (3-6) 745.5

1 Handicraft

ISBN 0-397-30776-4

This book gives directions for making pictures, place mats, dolls, jewelry, Christmas decorations and other objects from nuts, feathers, plants and seeds, leaves, pine needles, pine cones, flowers, trees and twigs

"Although the instructions, for the most part contained in a single paragraph, are not always explicit enough or sufficiently well illustrated, the book offers many good ideas for entertaining projects of varying degrees of difficulty." Booklist

Newsome, Arden J.

Make it with felt; an art and craft book; written and illus. by Arden J. Newsome. Lothrop 1972 96p illus lib. bdg. $4.97, pa $2.95 (4-7) 745.5

1 Handicraft

ISBN 0-688-45984-6; 0-688-50984-3

The author gives instructions on how to get the best results when working with felt and then follows up with step-by-step directions that steer the reader from raw materials to finished articles. Included are patterns for making games, toys, household articles, gifts, holiday and party items, and accessories for school

"Instructions are easy to follow, the patterns and illustrations are clear, and most of the materials are readily available at home or from one of the sources of supplies listed in the appendix." Booklist

Spoolcraft; illus. by Kathleen McGee and Arden J. Newsome. Lothrop 1970 158p illus $5.49, pa $2.95 (4-6) 745.5

1 Handicraft

ISBN 0-688-51439-1; 0-688-45019-9

Using spools as a basis, this book includes directions for making figures, dolls and doll furniture, toys, knitting and printing projects, games, Indian novelties, gifts, gadgets and decorations

"While most of the materials and tools needed are readily available around the house or in nearby craft shops a list of mail order craft suppliers is appended. The textual directions are easy to follow and the illustrations clearly drawn and helpful." Booklist

Papier mâché, dyeing & leatherwork. Watts, F. 1973 175p illus (Color crafts) $5.95 (3-7) 745.5

1 Leather work 2 Paper crafts 3 Handicraft

ISBN 0-531-02632-9

Original Spanish edition, 1972. Translated by Nicholas Fry

"Beautifully colored how-to illustrations and photographs on each page invite readers to try projects that range from simple papier mâché napkin rings to more complicated leather moccasins. Seventy-six craft ideas are presented, each graded for difficulty by a color symbol. . . . The material on dyeing is especially useful since there is little available on this craft. Despite minor flaws (the so-called index is really only a table of contents; and PVA glue, suggested for practically every project, may be difficult to obtain though there are effective substitutes), this is an explicit, well-organized, and attractive manual that will enhance craft collections." Sch Library J

Parish, Peggy

Let's be early settlers with Daniel Boone; drawings by Arnold Lobel. Harper 1967 96p illus lib. bdg. $4.43 (2-5) 745.5

Parish, Peggy—*Continued*

1 Handicraft 2 Frontier and pioneer life 3 Costume
ISBN 0-06-024648-0

"A brief preface to this how-to-make-it book describes the role of early settlers like Boone, explaining that the projects described are for fun and games but will give the reader an idea of some of the things that the early settlers used. Some of the objects or processes: making dyes, building model flatboats or covered wagons, making items of dress, making a hornbook or a diorama of a log cabin. Although the writing seems over-simplified for the audience, the book has value because the materials suggested are easily obtainable (scissors, paste, pipe cleaners, newspaper, straws, salt, clay, et cetera) and the directions clear; the illustrations are sometimes helpful, sometimes decorative, and always amusing." Chicago. Children's Bk Center

Let's be Indians; drawings by Arnold Lobel. Harper 1962 96p illus lib. bdg. $4.43 (2-5)   745.5

1 Indians of North America—Costume and adornment 2 Handicraft
ISBN 0-06-024651-0

Instructions "on how to make Indian costumes, build model Indian villages, play Indian games, etc. The materials recommended are easily available and inexpensive. Profuse attractive black-and-white drawings." Sch Library J

"The book will appeal to many because it is a stimulus for creativity, and it will certainly be suitable for adult use in guiding younger children." Chicago. Children's Bk Center

Pettit, Florence H.

How to make whirligigs and whimmy diddles, and other American folkcraft objects; illus. by Laura Louise Foster. Crowell 1972 349p illus $6.95 (5-7)
          745.5

1 Folk art, American 2 Handicraft
ISBN 0-690-41389-0

This book contains "instructions for making 17 different types of folkcraft. The author introduces many of the crafts with a short discussion of their history. . . . The projects include two toys, woodcarvings, quilts, candles, cornhusk dolls, decorations composed of seeds, cones, and pods, kachina dolls, and theorem paintings. Pettit also includes suggestions for finding designs and directions for enlarging or reducing designs or changing proportions, and appends a glossary of tools and materials, lists of supply houses [and] museums featuring folk arts." Booklist

"Descriptions for making the objects provide explicit directions accompanied by numerous, attractive, and instructive illustrations." Top of the News

Books you will enjoy: p334-35

Pflug, Betsy

Egg-speriment; easy crafts with eggs and egg cartons. Lippincott 1973 39p illus $4.95 (1-3)   745.5

1 Eggshell craft 2 Handicraft
ISBN 0-397-31460-4

Illustrated by the author

"A collection of art projects which can be done with eggs [mainly blown eggshells] and egg cartons. Using such household supplies as pins, scissors, paper, yarn, and scraps, the author clearly and simply describes how to make items like puppets, dolls, masks, bird feeders, animals, flowers, and party favors. Christmas and Hanukkah decorations are included as well as games constructed from cartons. Colorful line drawings show how the finished product will look." Sch Library J

Razzi, James

Bag of tricks! Fun things to make and do with the groceries; ed. by Thomas S. Roberts. Parents Mag. Press 1971 61p illus lib. bdg. $4.59 (k-3)   745.5

1 Handicraft
ISBN 0-8193-0450-6

The author has put together a collection of simple constructions, toys, magic tricks, optical puzzles and games. The necessary materials are found in a grocery bag and are usually thrown away—egg cartons, milk containers, paper bags

"Useful for confined non-reading youngsters as well as for beginning readers. Both projects and text match the dexterity of this age group. The instructions are very clear for the easy action games, tricks, and objects to be constructed like jewelry, floating ducks, beanbags, etc." Library J

Easy does it! Things to make and do; ed. by Anne Walentas. Parents Mag. Press 1969 61p illus lib. bdg. $4.59 (k-3)   745.5

1 Handicraft 2 Games
ISBN 0-8193-0286-4

A "collection of entertaining constructions, games, magic tricks, and optical puzzles. . . . The 40 simple projects and activities, which utilize such readily available materials as paper, cardboard containers, crayons, soda-pop cans, and bottle caps, are described in easy-to-follow text and drawings." Booklist

Simply fun! Things to make and do; ed. by Patricia Kienzle. Parents Mag. Press 1968 61p illus lib. bdg. $4.59 (k-3)   745.5

1 Handicraft 2 Amusements
ISBN 0-8193-0228-7

"Simple amusements which children can make for themselves are illustrated in orange and blue colors with sometimes amusing, sometimes zany results. Simple castle construction, a comic strip show and a pussy cat mask are some of the hardest projects." Bruno. Bks for Sch Libraries, 1968

"Along with having a good time with these craft projects, children can learn about color, shape, size, texture and simple mechanics." ALA. CSD. Mother Hubbard's Cupboard

Rockwell, Harlow

I did it. Macmillan Pub. Co. 1974 56p illus lib. bdg. $4.95 (1-3)   745.5

1 Handicraft
ISBN 0-02-777550-X

"Ready-to-read"

"A how-to book for the beginning reader has big print, plenty of restful blank space and clean-lined drawings in shades of brown and green. Best of all, it has projects that are truly simple, save for the last, breadmaking, and even that is broken down into easy-to-follow instructions. The projects are varied: making a paper airplane, writing a message in invisible ink, making a picture out of dried foods, making a papier mâché fish, making a paper bag mask, and baking bread. Good format, clear instructions, and a variety of things to do." Chicago. Children's Bk Center

Sattler, Helen Roney

Recipes for art and craft materials; written and illus. by Helen Roney Sattler. Lothrop 1973 128p illus $5.50, lib. bdg. $4.81 (4-7)   745.5

1 Handicraft—Equipment and supplies 2 Artists materials
ISBN 0-688-41557-1; 0-688-51557-6

"A particularly useful sourcebook for all who work

Sattler, Helen Roney—*Continued*

with crafts, whether as hobbyists or as teachers. It contains directions for making a great variety of pastes, modeling and casting compounds, paints and paint mediums, inks, and flower preservatives. Materials needed are inexpensive and easily procured. Directions are succinct, clear, and illustrated with simple, explanatory line drawings." Horn Bk

Sommer, Elyse

The bread dough craft book; illus. by Giulio Maestro. Lothrop 1972 128p illus lib. bdg. $4.81, pa $2.50 (3-6)　　　　745.5

1 Handicraft 2 Modeling

ISBN 0-688-51275-5; 0-688-46275-8

Here is a how-to book describing the old folk craft which uses a white bread and glue mixture as a sculpture medium. The author provides a recipe for making the dough and explains how to preserve, color, shape, dry and varnish it, and offers suggestions for several projects from toys and gadgets to jewelry and holiday decorations

"Imagination does not play a large part in either the writing or the projects chosen for inclusion; however, the book will most certainly be a godsend for harried mothers on rainy days and for desperate Girl Scout and Brownie leaders in need of ideas for inexpensive amusements and gifts. A list of Sources of Supplies is given at the end." Horn Bk

Wirtenberg, Patricia Z.

All-around-the-house art and craft book; photographs by Patricia Z. Wirtenberg. Houghton 1968 103p illus $6.95, pa $3.95 (4-7)　　　745.5

1 Handicraft

ISBN 0-395-07209-3; 0-395-19974-3

"An unusual 'make-it' book that rates special notice because its products are designed to be not merely gifts nor gadgets but bona fide works of art. . . . Text and numerous black-and-white photographs describe fifty imaginative projects that use materials from kitchen, laundry, attic, garage, and yard to create paintings, collages, mosaics, prints, and sculpture. . . . Directions for the projects are specific but 'not' so specific that they preclude creative variations. The aim—and the success—of the presentation is to induce the reader to look at old objects in new ways. The book will provide hours of exciting activity to stimulate the reader-doer's imagination and enhance his appreciation of art." Horn Bk

Wiseman, Ann

Making things; the hand book of creative discovery. Little 1973 159p illus $6.95, pa $3.95 (5-7)　　745.5

1 Handicraft

ISBN 0-316-94847-0; 0-316-94849-7

"The majority of the ingenious projects here are not found in other craft books. Topics covered include paper cutting and construction, printing, painting, rubbing, simple wooden toys, nature study, weaving, easy-to-sew clothing, batik and tie-dye, costumes, puppets, masks, homemade musical instruments, and the like. None of the projects are excessively difficult, and though adult supervision is expected, 10-year-olds could comprehend many of the suggestions. The hand-printed text is attractive to look at, and the excellent lists of craft titles and 'Books on Ways of Learning' constitute valuable reference tools." Sch Library J

745.51　　Wood handicrafts

Seidelman, James E.

Creating with wood [by] James E. Seidelman and Grace Mintonye; illus. by Lynn Sweat. Crowell-Collier Press 1969 56p illus $4.95 (4-7)　　745.51

1 Woodwork 2 Handicraft

"Describes simple wood projects for beginners using toothpicks, woodscraps, reed, balsa, bark, and driftwood. Includes a section on basic tools and a workshop." Pub W

"Clear, entertaining, logically organized, this stresses the versatility, sturdiness, low costs involved in working with wood, and demonstrates how it may be used in sculpture, mobiles, printing blocks (no utilitarian projects here). The illustrations are generally helpful, though the items shown lack labels; there is no glossary. . . . Limited in scope, this title will be most useful in large collections of craft books." Sch Library J

Weiss, Peter

Balsa wood craft; written and illus. by Peter Weiss. Lothrop 1972 96p illus lib. bdg. $4.59, pa $2.50 (3-7)　　745.51

1 Woodwork 2 Handicraft

ISBN 0-688-51526-6; 0-688-45526-3

"After describing the tools and readily available supplies needed and giving general instructions for working with balsa wood, the author presents patterns and simple, clear directions for constructing toys, games, doll furniture, gifts, models, and school projects and tells how to do balsa wood printing and make art novelties and decorations for holidays and parties." Booklist

"A very good book indeed for the neophyte hobbyist, with information about what to use and where to buy it, basic techniques, and safety precautions preceding the major part of the text, which gives instructions for a large range of projects. Instructions are clear, each project including a list of materials needed. An index is appended." Chicago. Children's Bk Center

Wright, Lois A.

Weathered wood craft; illus. with photographs. Lothrop 1973 159p illus $5.50, lib. bdg. $4.81 (4-7)　　745.51

1 Woodwork 2 Handicraft

ISBN 0-688-41562-8; 0-688-51562-2

The author presents suggestions for using weathered wood to create such items as wall plaques and planters, bird feeders, candle holders, wood sculptures, and puzzles. Hints are also given for collecting, cleaning, and treating wood

"A list of materials needed, plus at least one photograph, is given for each project. Several of the items don't seem worth the bother—for example, a potholder rack or toothbrush holder; however, most are very attractive and imaginative. Fairly general directions allow for individual creativity and for differences in shapes and textures of various woods." Sch Library J

745.54　　Paper handicrafts

Alkema, Chester Jay

Creative paper crafts in color. Sterling 1967 179p illus (Sterling Craft bks) $12.95 (3-7)　　745.54

1 Paper crafts

ISBN 0-8069-5086-2

The author explores creative uses of paper in two-

Alkema, Chester Jay—Continued
and three-dimensional forms. Origami, collage, weaving, cutting, pasting and assemblages of all kinds are included, as well as instructions for designing practical and decorative objects from many different types of paper. Illustrated with photographs in color and black and white

Bank-Jensen, Thea
Play with paper. Macmillan (N Y) 1962 48p illus $4.95 (2-6)   745.54
    1 Paper crafts
Translated from the Danish by Virginia Allen Jensen
"To encourage and demonstrate the use of paper for creative play, [the author] presents easy-to-follow instructions for making a variety of objects by folding, cutting, tearing, or sculpturing paper. Among the projects included are a paper city, circus, wedding party, jungle scene, doll house furniture, and mobiles." Booklist
The projects "range from simple cut-outs to rather complicated designs requiring sharp scissors and considerable skill. There are black-and-white photographs and diagrams that are wonderfully clear and precise." Pub W

Chernoff, Goldie Taub
Just a box? Pictures by Margaret Hartelius. Walker & Co. 1973 unp illus $2.95 (k-3)   745.54
    1 Paper crafts
    ISBN 0-8027-6138-0
This "is a workable idea book for stay-at-home days. Using household boxes as the base on which to build, the pictures show how to construct a variety of items such as animals, puppets, villages, boats, planes, and trains." Babbling Bookworm
"The directions are simple enough for pre-schoolers to follow by themselves, and only easy-to-find materials—cardboard, construction paper, as well as a good supply of boxes—are needed. With clear illustrations that show each step and the finished product, this will provide hours of inexpensive fun." Sch Library J

Granit, Inga
Cardboard crafting; how to make things out of cardboard. Sterling [1965 c1964] 96p illus $5.95 (5-7)   745.54
    1 Paper crafts
    ISBN 0-8069-5054-4
Translated by Elsa Bley; adapted by Robert F. Scott
Here are instructions, with diagrams and photographs, for making objects out of shirt cardboard, old gift wrappings, and corrugated paper. Some of the projects included are: tool and jewel boxes, notebooks, portfolios, autograph albums, wastepaper baskets, and road map cases
"The directions, patterns, and photographs are excellent, and the end products have a neat professional look. The format of the book suggests use with children, but the text would be better with young adults, or grown-ups who can wield a sharp knife and work with heavy board." Library J

Lidstone, John
Building with cardboard; photography by Roger Kerkham. Van Nostrand 1968 95p illus $6.95 (4-7)   745.54
    1 Paper crafts
    ISBN 0-442-04791-6
"Sculpture, airplanes, miniature stages, masks and posters are some of the projects invented by children that are included in this arts and craft book." Pub W
"A particularly attractive and explicit how-to-make-it book, with lucid instructions and good, sharp photo-

graphs that illustrate some of the many things that can be made of an inexpensive material. All of the pictures show objects made by children, or in the making. The techniques of working in the medium are clearly explained, and the reader is encouraged to experiment." Sutherland. The Best in Children's Bks

Payne, G. C.
Adventures in paper modelling; with 24 photographs and 103 drawings. Warne 1966 64p illus $4.50 (5-7)   745.54
    1 Paper crafts 2 Models and model making
    ISBN 0-7232-6031-1
"Step-by-step directions for making masks, puppet heads, and a variety of other models such as birds and boats using newspaper, clay, cardboard, wire, balloons, and other inexpensive, easily obtainable materials. The textual instructions are clear and fairly easy to follow and each stage of the construction is well illustrated with drawings or photographs. Particularly useful for schools and clubs." Booklist

Pflug, Betsy
Funny bags. Van Nostrand 1968 40p illus $4.95 (k-3)   745.54
    1 Paper crafts 2 Paper bags
    ISBN 0-397-31549-X
"A colorful, easy-to-use book containing a variety of creative projects that can be made with paper bags, readily obtained or inexpensive decorative materials, and imagination. Masks, puppets, party favors, gift wrap, and games are among the projects presented. Adequate directions are given in a minimum of text and an abundance of helpful drawings [by the author]." Booklist

Sattler, Helen Roney
Kitchen carton crafts; with diagrams by the author. Lothrop 1970 94p illus $5.50, lib. bdg. $4.81, pa $2.95 (3-5)   745.54
    1 Paper crafts
    ISBN 0-688-41133-9; 0-688-51133-3; 0-688-45005-9
This "craft book, aimed at primary or intermediate children, or adults working with them, employs easily available materials—milk cartons, salt boxes, egg cartons, etc. It contains concise directions with excellent diagrams for 45 games, toys, and projects, including many holiday ideas. . . . A welcome compilation, the book features such ideas as recipe racks, bottle cap toss, and bird feeders that suggest workable, well thought out projects; many are adaptable for other projects also." Sch Library J

745.55   Shell handicrafts

Cutler, Katherine N.
Creative shellcraft; illus. by Giulio Maestro. Lothrop 1971 96p illus $5.95, lib. bdg. $5.11, pa $2.95 (4-6)   745.55
    1 Shells 2 Handicraft
    ISBN 0-688-40988-1; 0-688-50988-6; 0-688-45011-3
"A handy book for young craftsmen living in coastal areas or inlanders with a seashell collection from last summer's vacation. The book includes some simple scientific information on shells and hints on collecting, as well as instructions for making shell jewelry, matchbox covers, Christmas tree ornaments and other decorations." Pub W
The author writes "clearly and with enthusiasm in a person-to-person style. . . . [He] distinguishes between collecting for specimens and collecting for shellcraft, urges against taking live shells, and encourages the use of imagination in creating things from

Cutler, Katherine N.—*Continued*
shells. A list of books for further reading and a list of shell suppliers are appended." Booklist

745.56 Metal handicrafts

Lidstone, John
Building with wire; photographs by Roger Kerkham. Van Nostrand 1972 95p illus $6.95 (5-7)
                                                             745.56
1 Handicraft 2 Wire
ISBN 0-442-24793-1
"An experienced art teacher, explains in a conversational style how to find wire and other simple supplies needed, how to work with them, and how to produce bracelets, mobiles, screens, pendants, and abstract sculptural constructs. [The] photos of children in the process of making sculptures equal the text in lucidity. Lack of an index or glossary is not a detriment." Library J

745.59 Making specific objects

Alkema, Chester Jay
Greeting cards you can make; photographs by the author. Sterling 1973 48p illus (Little craft bk. ser) $3.75 (4-7)   745.59
1 Greeting cards 2 Handicraft
ISBN 0-8069-5248-2
This book provides instructions for making greeting cards using a variety of techniques. Glue relief prints, collages, folds, pop ups, montages, vegetable prints and crayon etchings are featured

Monster masks; photographs by the author. Sterling 1973 48p illus (Little craft bk. ser) $3.50, lib. bdg. $3.69   745.59
1 Masks (Sculpture) 2 Handicraft
ISBN 0-8069-5256-3; 0-8069-5257-1
This book offers instructions for making a variety of masks for wearing and for decoration. Among the materials suggested are: crayons, paint, drinking straws, yarn, pipe cleaners, seeds, gravel, egg cartons, fiberboard, plastic foam, tinfoil, aluminum, tooled copper, clay, and cast sand

Puppet-making. Sterling 1971 48p illus (Little craft bk. ser) $3.75 (5-7)   745.59
1 Puppet making
ISBN 0-8069-5174-5
The author demonstrates how to make puppets using paper bags, construction paper, papier-mâché, socks, ice cream sticks, paper cups, toothpicks, foil, yarn, and other common materials

Better Homes and Gardens Holiday decorations you can make. [Meredith Corp. 1974] 208p illus $7.95   745.59
1 Christmas decorations 2 Handicraft
ISBN 0-696-00710-X
"The wealth of Christmas ideas contained in this book runs the gamut from trees, ornaments, stockings, and candlemaking to displays and trimmings for mantels, walls, windows, and outdoors. One chapter is for children between six and 12; a final chapter treats other holidays, including Jewish celebrations. Adequate instructions are given for more than 300 projects (traditional and contemporary) of varying

complexity and that require a wide variety of materials. Lavishly illustrated with eye-catching color photos . . . a useful, worthwhile book." Library J

Brock, Virginia
Piñatas; illus. by Anne Marie Jauss. Abingdon 1966 112p illus $3.75 (4-7)   745.59
1 Paper crafts 2 Christmas stories
ISBN 0-687-31436-4
This "welcome and serviceable addition to holiday and handicraft books gives a brief history of 'piñatas,' suggestions on when and how to use them, explicit instructions supplemented by diagrams for making 11 different 'piñatas' and three stories in which 'piñatas' play an important part. A glossary and pronunciation guide is appended." Booklist

Carroll, David
Make your own chess set. Prentice-Hall 1974 151p illus lib. bdg. $7.95 (5-7)   745.59
1 Chess 2 Handicraft
ISBN 0-13-547802-2
"Carroll gives a brief history of chess, the pieces, and how their size or shape relates to their power. The bulk of the book, however, is devoted to the construction of chess sets made from practically every conceivable material. . . . All the materials are cheap; no soldering is required; and the only special tool needed is a saw for cutting the bases of some sets." Sch Library J
"A perfect complement to game-instruction volumes, this is illustrated with clear black-and-white photographs and includes . . . directions for making a board." Booklist

Coskey, Evelyn
Easter eggs for everyone; drawings by Giorgetta Bell; photographs unless otherwise indicated are by Sid Dorris. Abingdon 1973 191p illus $7.95 (5-7)
                                                             745.59
1 Egg decoration
ISBN 0-687-11492-6
This "compendium of information about Easter eggs begins with customs and legends dating from antiquity and continues with explicit directions for decorating eggs in a great variety of ways. Lists of materials and equipment needed for the simplest to the most elaborate Easter eggs are accompanied by instructions for blowing eggs, dyeing with different materials, scratch carving, and batik processing, and for making the beautiful and difficult pysanky, the traditional Ukrainian Easter egg. Cutout, jeweled, peephole, and collage eggs of various kinds are described, as well as such novelties as candles, mobiles, vases, egg animals, and egg trees." Horn Bk
"Simply and lucidly written, helpfully illustrated by diagrams and adorned by photographs of beautifully decorated eggs, this is a book to be enjoyed in home libraries as well as in school and library collections. A bibliography and index are appended." Chicago. Children's Bk Center

Cutler, Katherine N.
Crafts for Christmas, by Katherine N. Cutler and Kate Cutler Bogle; illus. by Jacqueline Adato. Lothrop 1974 95p illus lib. bdg. $5.49, pa $1.95 (3-7)
                                                             745.59
1 Christmas decorations 2 Handicraft 3 Gifts
ISBN 0-688-51663-7; 0-688-46663-X
The authors have provided an "assortment of holiday craft projects: gifts, functional or ornamental decorations, and recipes. . . . [The directions make] use of 'found' objects such as shells and pine cones; in general the projects are simple. There is enough diversity . . . to give the hobbyist a choice of tech-

Cutler, Katherine N.—*Continued*
niques and materials, and the instructions are clear. The pages are clean and spacious, the illustrations adequate; an index is appended." Chicago. Children's Bk Center

Heady, Eleanor B.
Make your own dolls; illus. by Harold F. Heady. Lothrop 1974 94p illus $4.75, lib. bdg. $4.32 (3-5)

745.59

1 Dollmaking
ISBN 0-688-41570-9; 0-688-51570-3
This book contains "ideas for spool figures; sock dolls and carved soap dolls; as well as dolls made of natural materials such as flowers, grass, and cornhusks." Sch Library J
"Making the 17 kinds of male and female dolls from scratch with the help of this book will provide ungimmicky, creative entertainment. . . . Most of the dolls have costumes which are sewn from patterns included in the instructions. A number of the dolls are complex to make but worthwhile; the author assumes little or no sewing or craft knowledge on the reader's part and adequate diagrams and drawings are included." Booklist

Joseph, Joan
Folk toys around the world and how to make them; illus. by Mel Furukawa; working drawings and instructions by Glen Wagner. Parents Mag. Press 1972 96p illus lib. bdg. $4.59 (5-7)

745.59

1 Toys 2 Folk art 3 Handicraft
ISBN 0-8193-0599-5
"In cooperation with the U.S. Committee for UNICEF"
The author describes a variety of toys from 19 countries, discussing their history and giving directions for constructing them
"A better-than-most book for the craftsman, requiring simple materials but needing a considerable variety of tools. . . . The directions are detailed and clear, with diagrams printed on yellow pages, and the step-by-step sets of instructions concluding in most cases (some do not require it) with a direction for using the toy. A list of sources for material is appended, not addresses but the kinds of stores to which one should go." Chicago. Children's Bk Center

Meyer, Carolyn
Christmas crafts; things to make the 24 days before Christmas; pictures by Anita Lobel. Harper 1974 136p illus $4.95, lib. bdg. $4.79 (5-7)

745.59

1 Christmas decorations 2 Handicraft 3 Cookery
ISBN 0-06-024197-7; 0-06-024198-5
Here are instructions for making two dozen crafted objects appropriate to the Christmas season, including egg ornaments, gingerbread sculptures, St. Lucia buns, piñatas, and pomander balls
"The author has actually collected Advent and Christmas traditions from many cultures; and she describes the religious symbolism, the historical significance, and the folklore associated with each project. Materials used are inexpensive and accessible; instructions are simple and sensible. An abundance of pen-and-ink drawings clarifies the sequence of every procedure and adds beauty to an unusual book for the whole family." Horn Bk

Newsome, Arden J.
Egg craft; written and illus. by Arden J. Newsome. Lothrop 1973 128p illus $5.75, lib. bdg. $4.97, pa $2.95 (4-7)

745.59

1 Egg decoration
ISBN 0-688-41512-1; 0-688-51512-6; 0-688-45112-3
This book "provides easy-to-do projects as well as a meaningful history of the art of egg decoration. The step-by-step instructions are accompanied by clear illustrations, and materials needed for each project are listed at the beginning in recipe form. An index, list of suppliers, and suggested readings round out this interesting and useful craft book, which will be especially appreciated by hobbyists." Sch Library J

Pettit, Ted S.
Bird feeders and shelters you can make. Putnam 1970 80p illus $5.95 (3-6)

745.59

1 Bird houses
ISBN 0-399-20018-5
"A Cub Scout project book"
Illustrated with line drawings by Leon A. Hausman
"A very thorough, clear book of instructions for building many types of bird houses. The author gives the exact dimensions of the required house styles for specific breeds. Instructions for building several kinds of bird feeders are also presented, along with suggestions for appropriate foods and ways of enticing wild birds to eat out of the hand. A chapter on backyard sanctuaries even gives directions for a winter birdbath! A good table of contents and an index make the book easy to use; the black-and-white drawings definitely expand the text." Sch Library J

Purdy, Susan
Holiday cards for you to make. Lippincott 1967 64p illus lib. bdg. $5.95 (5-7)

745.59

1 Greeting cards 2 Handicraft
ISBN 0-397-31574-0
"This colorful book contains instructions for silk screen, stencil, linoleum block, potato, eraser, hand, and string prints, as well as directions on collage, marbleizing, and pressed-flower techniques. Information for cut-out and movable cards is also included. . . . There is a special list of materials needed and a short paragraph on postal mailing regulations. Clear directions and good illustrations make this book a pleasure to use." Sch Library J

Villiard, Paul
Jewelrymaking; with 100 photographs. Doubleday 1973 96p illus $4.95, lib. bdg. $5.70 (4-7) 745.59

1 Jewelry 2 Handicraft
ISBN 0-385-05287-1; 0-385-06138-2
"For inexperienced jewelrymakers, this is a valuable step-by-step guide to creating in leather, enamel, and cast plastic, as well as using sewing notions and macaroni. Sections on handmade necklaces, pins, and earrings are presented along with kit jewelry. Stress is placed upon basic tools and equipment, and the Easy-to-follow directions allow imaginative crafters to express their creativity. Many clear, large photographs elucidate the instructions and add to the appeal of the book." Sch Library J

Weiss, Harvey
Collage and construction. Young Scott Bks. 1970 62p illus (Beginning artist's lib) lib. bdg. $4.95 (4-7)

745.59

1 Collage 2 Sculpture—Technique
ISBN 0-201-09163-1
"Sensible advice on materials and techniques, firm adherence to esthetic precepts, and a broad spectrum of media make this a better-than-most book on art experience. While some of the suggestions are quite concrete, most advance ideas about concentrating on realism, or abstract form, or a theme, or simply on contrast of texture of shape. The writing is informal, serious, and encouraging, and the media discussed include box pictures, paper collage, wire sculpture, and string pictures." Sat Rev

Young, Helen

Here is your hobby: doll collecting. Putnam 1964 128p illus (Here is your hobby ser) lib. bdg. $4.69 (5-7)   745.59

1 Dolls
ISBN 0-399-60246-1

"A welcome book on doll collecting although it devotes more attention to the history of dolls and the techniques of dollmaking than to collecting dolls and organizing and displaying the collection. It gives clear instructions on how to make dolls out of rags, paper, wood, and wax and heads out of papier-mâché, how to dress and repair dolls, and how to make a dollhouse and a paper-doll theater. Illustrated with patterns, diagrams, and photographs." Booklist

Bibliography: p126

745.6 Lettering

Hart, Tony

The young letterer; a how-it-is done book of lettering. Warne [1966 c1965] 63p illus $4.50 (6-7) 745.6

1 Lettering
ISBN 0-7232-6005-2

First published 1965 in England

Hart "presents the materials and basic techniques for lettering with pen and brush, describes ancient and modern styles of letters including type faces, and gives advice on the design and use of hand lettering. Directions for brush-drawn letters are based on the Trajan Roman style alphabet and its variations." Booklist

"The author obviously has a deep feeling for this craft and presents the material in an interesting, informative, and attractive way. . . . Step-by-step drawings and photographs make this easy to understand and a practical handbook for students." Sch Library J

Other books on lettering: p[64]

745.92 Floral arts

Cutler, Katherine N.

From petals to pinecones; a nature art and craft book; illus. by Giulio Maestro. Lothrop 1969 128p illus lib. bdg. $5.49, pa $2.95 (4-7)   745.92

1 Handicraft
ISBN 0-688-51594-0; 0-688-45003-2

"A good, solid, attractively illustrated collection of nature-craft ideas. Emphasizing the use of the natural materials found in each area of the United States, and with an eye on conservation rules, this provides ideas for gift, holiday, and school projects. An excellent list of basic tools, clear instructions for pressing and drying the plant materials used in many of the projects, plus imaginative use of materials make this a useful fund of projects, for city as well as suburban rural children." Sch Library J

Books for further reading: p124

Munari, Bruno

A flower with love; tr. by Patricia Tracy Lowe. Crowell 1974 unp illus $4.95, lib. bdg. $5.70 (4-7)   745.92

1 Flower arrangement
ISBN 0-690-00570-9; 0-690-00571-7

First published 1973 in Italy

"In a book for beginners, the Japanese art of floral arrangements, 'ikebana', is defined as 'both an art and a philosophy. . . . a way of creating beauty out of ordinary things.' Emphasis is placed on looking at natural objects reflectively in order to discover nature's hidden messages and then creating original messages with 'care and love.' Twelve such arrangements have been created by the author and photographed in superb color. The page preceding each photograph usually consists of a descriptive text and line drawings of the materials used. . . . Although 'ikebana' is an art with definite rules, there are no rules for the novice who is introduced to the subject through this book. The whole approach is one of freedom, and arrangements are offered only as ideas, not to be rigidly copied." Horn Bk

746.1 Spinning and weaving

Fisher, Leonard Everett

The weavers; written and illus. by Leonard Everett Fisher. Watts, F. 1966 45p illus (Colonial Americans) lib. bdg. $3.90 (4-7)   746.1

1 Weaving 2 U.S.—Social life and customs— Colonial period
ISBN 0-531-01039-2

"The text gives a brief history of the craft in this country; the second, and major part of the book is devoted to a description of weaving itself: the simplest tools and machines first, then such improvements as the foot-power loom and the flying shuttle. The descriptions of patterns also moves from the simplest plain weave to more complicated patterns, showing the positioning of threads in the loom and giving some samples of pattern drafts." Chicago. Children's Bk Center

"The artist's sharp, familiar style of scratchboard drawing is well suited to show clearly the looms and spinning wheel and the tools for carding, spinning, and weaving." Horn Bk

Weavers' terms: p42-43

746.3 Tapestries

Denny, Norman

The Bayeux tapestry; the story of the Norman conquest: 1066 [by] Norman Denny & Josephine Filmer-Sankey. Atheneum Pubs. 1966 unp illus $7.95 (5-7)   746.3

1 Bayeux tapestry 2 Hastings, Battle of, 1066
ISBN 0-689-20076-5

The 230 foot Bayeux tapestry portrays the conflict between Harold of England and William of Normandy in the Battle of Hastings. The entire tapestry is here reproduced with an accompanying text

"The text uses two kinds of type; one paragraph in large type describes the scene of the panel strip; a second, and longer section in small type gives more details and some background information." Chicago. Children's Bk Center

"Thanks to the excellent quality of the photographs, the color and vigor of the tapestry figures are startling. Written knowledgeably and with zest." Sat Rev

Bibliography contained in Acknowledgements. Map on lining-papers

746.4   Needle- and handwork

Enthoven, Jacqueline

Stitchery for children; a manual for teachers, parents, and children. Reinhold 1968 172p illus $7.95   746.4

1 Needlework

ISBN 0-442-11255-6

Here is stitchery for the pre-schooler to the high school student arranged by age and school grade. There are over 200 diagrams and photographs featuring children's stitcheries, 24 in color. New and easier ways of doing traditional stitches, transferring designs, and threading needles are presented

Hanley, Hope

Fun with needlepoint; photographs by Bob Burchette; drawings by Evelyn Baird. Scribner 1972 95p illus lib. bdg. $5.95 (5-7)   746.4

1 Canvas embroidery

ISBN 0-684-12913-2

The author describes the types of canvas and wool used in needlepoint, how to estimate wool usage, how to apply patterns and choose colors, blocking and basic stitches. She presents 15 projects including pillow covers, a pincushion, a belt, a comb case and a tote bag

"The novice may need assistance in reading directions but the drawings by Evelyn Baird do help in this regard. For beginners of all ages." Best Sellers

Holz, Loretta

Teach yourself stitchery; illus. with photographs and drawings by the author. Lothrop 1974 160p illus $5.50, lib. bdg. $4.81 (4-6)   746.4

1 Embroidery

ISBN 0-688-41571-1; 0-688-51571-1

"A history of embroidery is followed by a discussion of equipment and techniques. Stitches are presented in order of difficulty and both text and illustrations are easy to follow. However, most projects (e.g., scarf, apron, tote bag) require some hand or machine sewing ability." Sch Library J

"Clear diagrams of stitches and designs are as helpful as the text. . . . A section on designing projects plus a list of U.S. supply sources, suggestions for further reading, and the address of a club are appended." Booklist

Lightbody, Donna M.

Introducing needlepoint; illus. with photographs and charts. Lothrop 1973 157p illus $5.95, lib. bdg. $5.11 (5-7)   746.4

1 Canvas embroidery

ISBN 0-688-41550-4; 0-688-51550-9

"The author gives a brief history of needlepoint and different patterns (including the adaptation of American Indian designs) as well as information on materials, equipment, and basic stitches. Twenty-one projects, each short enough to satisfy beginners, are followed in easy, step-by-step instructions accompanied by photographs and diagrams." Sch Library J

Glossary: p145-46. Further reading: p152

Meyer, Carolyn

Yarn—the things it makes and how to make them; illus. by Jennifer Perrott. Harcourt 1972 128p illus lib. bdg. $5.95 (4-7)   746.4

1 Handicraft

ISBN 0-15-299713-X

The author "tells a bit about the history of crocheting, knitting, weaving, and macrame, lists the equipment needed, and gives very clear instructions for the beginning steps in each craft. She suggests simple

items which can be made when the basic skill is mastered and repeats the first directions before adding other steps. The accompanying drawings and diagrams are also clear." Booklist

Miller, Irene Preston

The stitchery book; embroidery for beginners, by Irene Preston Miller and Winifred Lubell; drawings by Winifred Lubell. Doubleday 1965 96p illus $4.95, lib. bdg. $5.70 (5-7)   746.4

1 Embroidery

ISBN 0-385-00759-0; 0-385-05550-1

"Embroidery, from the Bayeux Tapestry to the present day, is the subject of a book including both history and explicit directions for basic stitches. Clear illustrations and suggestions for creative projects." Hodges. Bks for Elem Sch Libraries

Parker, Xenia Ley

A beginner's book of knitting and crocheting; illus. with diagrams and photographs. Dodd 1974 154p illus $4.95 (5-7)   746.4

1 Knitting 2 Crocheting

ISBN 0-396-06862-6

"A compendium of basic information, the text is liberally supplemented with illustrative material and offers encouragement as well as practical advice to neophyte knitters and crocheters. The beginning chapters in each category focus on materials, equipment, and accessories. Detailed directions for the various processes involved include a comprehensive listing of the abbreviations for stitches used in patterns and conclude with the main feature—several easy-to-make, yet currently fashionable, projects: a scarf, a granny square pillow, knitted caps, and a fringed poncho. Explicit and clear, conversational and uncondescending." Horn Bk

Rubenstone, Jessie

Crochet for beginners. Photographs by Edward Stevenson. Lippincott 1974 64p illus $5.95, pa $2.25 (3-5)   746.4

1 Crocheting

ISBN 0-397-31547-3; 0-397-31548-1

The author describes the materials and basic stitches used in crocheting and gives directions for making several articles, including scarves, belts, and pot holders. She also explains how to block, wash, and care for finished items

"A good basic book for beginning crocheters. High contrast black and white photographs are clear." Children's Bk Rev Serv

Knitting for beginners; photographs by Edward Stevenson. Lippincott 1973 64p illus $4.95, pa $2.95 (4-7)   746.4

1 Knitting

ISBN 0-397-31473-6; 0-397-31474-4

"Clear photographs are well placed in relation to the text to show, step by step, how to knit a very simple sample square: casting on, knitting, casting off. The author discusses left-handed knitting, recycling old wool, how to make one's own knitting needles, and how to shop for yarn. The instructions that follow are for objects of increasing complexity, but none is very difficult; instructions for purling, ribbing, and making button loops are included. The book concludes with suggestions for caring for knitted articles and some helpful hints. While it may help to have an experienced knitter guide the beginner, this is as clear a book as such guides can be and really can be used for learning alone." Chicago. Children's Bk Center

Glossary: p64

Wartburg, Ursula von
The workshop book of knitting. Atheneum Pubs. 1973 148p illus $8.95 (4-7)   746.4
1 Knitting
ISBN 0-689-20696-8
The author "begins with basic facts about casting on, row knitting, making a slip knot, et cetera; she also gives information about the different kinds of yarn and needles, and about rectifying errors. The major part of the book is devoted to specific knitting projects, beginning with a bookmark and increasing in complexity." Chicago. Children's Bk Center
"Recommended for intermediate knitters, but helpful to all, the book has a host of features not usually included in works of use to children. . . . On all fundamentals of the craft, the book provides concise information, extended by rarely found tips, amplified with dozens of precise black-and-white photographs and diagrams, and brightened with delightful drawings by both male and female workshop participants. A real treat and a lasting addition to any needlecraft collection." Booklist

Wilson, Erica
Fun with crewel embroidery; illus. with photographs and drawings. Scribner 1965 41p illus lib. bdg. $5.95 (3-7)   746.4
1 Crewelwork
ISBN 0-684-12894-2
Through text and illustrations, the author explains how to make a number of articles by stitching designs on fabric with wool. She demonstrates the types of stitches, progresses from simple to more difficult projects, and gives instructions for sewing various motifs such as mushrooms, trees, rabbits, and birds. Directions are also furnished for enlarging a design
"Attractive illustrations and simple but useful projects should encourage the young to discover the fun in crewel work." Wis Library Bul
Alphabet of stitches: p41-[48]

746.5   Beadwork

Donna, Natalie
Bead craft; written and illus. by Natalie Donna. Lothrop 1972 128p illus $5.95, lib. bdg. $5.11, pa $2.50 (5-7)   746.5
1 Beadwork
ISBN 0-688-41525-3; 0-688-51525-8; 0-688-45525-5
The author lists sources of supplies as well as giving instructions for making such items as doll's clothes, jewelry, desk accessories, belts, and flowers from commercial beads or beads made from straws, spools, flip-top cans, and other easily obtained materials

Hofsinde, Robert
Indian beadwork; written and illus. by Robert Hofsinde (Gray-Wolf). Morrow 1958 122p illus lib. bdg. $4.59 (5-7)   746.5
1 Beadwork 2 Indians of North America—Costume and adornment
ISBN 0-688-31575-5
A "handbook on the various types of beading methods and the articles which can be made using beadwork as decoration—belts, jewelry, purses, knife sheaths, book covers, and moccasins. In each case the author recommends ready made articles to be decorated or tells how to make them. . . . Since the work is fairly intricate, and in some cases requires a special frame or leather, most children would probably need some assistance in getting started. However, the

instructions and diagrams are, for the most part, clear and detailed." Chicago. Children's Bk Center

746.6   Textile printing, painting, dyeing

Deyrup, Astrith
Tie dyeing and batik; illus. by Nancy Lou Gahan. Doubleday 1974 63p illus $4.95, lib. bdg. $5.70 (4-6)   746.6
1 Batik 2 Dyes and dyeing
ISBN 0-385-08483-8; 0-385-03626-4
"Some basic tying patterns are shown to yield circles, stripes, and free designs on muslin pieces, which are then utilized as book covers, hand puppets, mobiles, doll clothing, and other miscellaneous items. Batik techniques include spattering, brush-work, and crackling, as well as printing and working with a tjanting. . . . A concluding chapter encourages experimentation by combining techniques and using different fabrics and dyes; a list of suppliers and dye companies is appended." Booklist
"An attractive introduction to two hobbies for middle grade children (although many primary youngsters could carry out the projects with guidance). . . . Instructions in a step-by-step numbered format are complemented with clear line drawings and photos." Library J
Bibliography: p60

746.7   Hooked rugs

Wiseman, Ann
Rags, rugs and wool pictures; a first book of rug hooking. Scribner 1968 32p illus lib. bdg. $5.95 (5-7)   746.7
1 Rugs, Hooked
ISBN 0-684-13490-X
"Ann Wiseman's approach to the subject of rug hooking is simplified with step-by-step directions and diagrams designed for the younger reader to make rugs, samplers and wool pictures." Pub W
"The author stresses the simplicity and originality in children's art and shows how such drawings can be transformed into pleasing rug patterns. The instructions are clear, but most children will need adult help in finding some of the materials." Library J
Glossary: p32

751   Painting processes and forms

Spilka, Arnold
Paint all kinds of pictures. Walck, H.Z. 1963 unp illus $5.25 (k-3)   751
1 Painting 2 Art appreciation
ISBN 0-8098-1091-3
The author "who is firm believer in the theory that art should be self-expression appeals directly to the picture book age to paint freely from their own impressions and feelings. Illustrations are done in chalk or water color (some in black-and-white) and are labeled funny, scary, pretty, loud, quiet, or lonely and combine to make a fascinating picture book, as well as inspiration for creativity." Wis Library Bul

Spilka, Arnold—*Continued*

"Arnold Spilka is obviously full of purposes—purposes that he admirably fulfills, for here is loveliness, instruction, and some humor as well." Christian Sci Monitor

Weiss, Harvey

Paint, brush and palette. Young Scott Bks. 1966 64p illus (The Beginning artist's lib) lib. bdg. $4.95 (5-7)   751

1 Painting 2 Painting—Technique
ISBN 0-201-09303-0

"An excellent book for the beginner, profusely illustrated with diagrams, charts, sketches and reproductions of works of art. The first half of the book is devoted to color: primary, complementary, and contrasting colors; explanations of values and intensity, of warmth and coolness, and of contrast. The author discusses forms, textures, and shadows. The second half of the book describes media and technique—including a brief explanation of perspective—and gives instructions for making an easel. Not comprehensive, but lucidly written and always encouraging the reader to experiment." Chicago. Children's Bk Center

751.4 Painting—Techniques

Hawkinson, John

Collect, print and paint from nature. Whitman, A. 1963 38p illus $4.25 (3-6)   751.4

1 Water color painting—Technique 2 Nature study
ISBN 0-8075-1272-9

An instruction book "on the use of watercolor in painting flora and fauna, with a few techniques for making prints with media other than the brush. The author does not claim to be teaching everything about painting, but limits himself to instructions on using one medium for one field of subjects. The instructions are very lucid and simple, the illustrations very neatly integrated with the text. The colors are wonderfully clear, a very important asset in a book in which brush strokes and paint saturation are discussed. Particularly useful are the illustrations that show the reader examples of correct and of incorrect brush strokes." Chicago. Children's Bk Center

Seidelman, James E.

Creating with paint [by] James E. Seidelman and Grace Mintonye; illus. by Peter Landa. Crowell-Collier Press 1967 58p illus lib. bdg. $4.95 (4-7)   751.4

1 Painting—Technique

"This creative approach to painting starts with basic information on materials but offers many ideas to get the young artist started. Paper, textures, brushes, and paints are discussed, followed by suggested projects and techniques. It is well-expressed and well-illustrated." Bruno. Bks for Sch Libraries, 1968

Zaidenberg, A.

How to paint with water colors; a book for beginners. Vanguard 1968 60p illus $4.95 (4-7)   751.4

1 Water color painting—Technique
ISBN 0-8149-0440-8

"An ideal book for children who are interested in painting and who have graduated from the crayon stage. . . . [The author] describes techniques and materials in water colors." Pub W

"The written descriptions and instructions are concise and informative. Comparison of these reproductions with color prints of the same pictures will be an interesting and most helpful exercise for students of the art." Sch Library J

759.5 Italian painting

Jacobs, David

Master painters of the Renaissance. Viking 1968 143p illus lib. bdg. $7.95 (6-7)   759.5

1 Painters, Italian 2 Painting, Italian 3 Art, Renaissance
ISBN 0-670-46144-X

This "is an introduction to the art of the Renaissance, presented through the biographies of ten of the artists who were the giants of that era and through reproductions of their best-known works." Pub W

"Fortified by 32 pages of illustrations in excellent color, this introduction to the Renaissance painters of Italy is highly recommended. . . . The text is admirably informative without being didactic, is simple without being silly. . . . A selected bibliography completes this estimable book intended for young readers." Best Sellers

760 Graphic arts. Print making and prints

Rockwell, Harlow

Printmaking. Doubleday [1974 c1973] 60p illus (Crafts for children) $4.95, lib. bdg. $5.70 (4-6) 760

1 Graphic arts
ISBN 0-385-01813-4; 0-385-01816-9

This book gives "step-by-step directions for making twelve different kinds of prints, ranging from the simple hand print to the more exacting two-color woodcut and two-color linoleum print." Horn Bk

"The beginning projects are simple enough for children to do alone; however, later techniques, which involve use of knives and gouges or hot objects, will require adult guidance. The introduction lists where to find supplies and the reproductions of children's own handiwork will add incentive for beginning printmakers." Sch Library J

763 Lithographic processes

Hirsch, S. Carl

Printing from a stone; the story of lithography. Viking 1967 111p illus lib. bdg. $4.95 (6-7)   763

1 Lithography—History
ISBN 0-670-57739-1

"Printing by lithography is traced from its invention by Aloys Senefelder in 1798 until modern times. Illustrations show its use by H. Daumier, Currier and Ives, Picasso and others. Diagrams tell how the process makes beautiful books a reality." Bruno. Bks for Sch Libraries, 1968

Suggestions for further reading: p107-08

769 Prints. Postage stamps

Cabeen, Richard McP.

Standard handbook of stamp collecting. Rev. Crowell 1965 628p illus $14.95   769

1 Postage stamps—Collectors and collecting
ISBN 0-690-76997-0

Cabeen, Richard McP.—*Continued*

First published 1957

"Dividing his material into five sections—Introduction to stamp collecting, Postal history and cover collecting, Miscellaneous subjects, Technical matters, and Classification and identification—the . . . [author] offers a practical, comprehensive handbook to the novice and veteran philatelist. The book contains few illustrations but includes a list of monetary units, a complete table of the world's stamps, data on inscriptions, markings, and symbols, and a glossary of special terms." Booklist

DePree, Mildred

A child's world of stamps; stories, poems, fun and facts from many lands. Parents Mag. Press 1973 126p illus $4.95, lib. bdg. $4.58 (3-5)   769

1 Postage stamps

ISBN 0-8193-0661-4; 0-8193-0662-2

"In cooperation with the U.S. Committee for UNICEF"

"Large, colorful reproductions of postage stamps from all over the world are combined with poetry, stories, recipes, and bits of history in this informal approach to philately." Cleveland Pub Library. Children's Bks for Holiday Giving and Year 'Round Reading

United States Postal Service

Postage stamps of United States. U.S. Govt. Ptg. Off. illus pa $2   769

1 Postage stamps

Cover title: United States postage stamps

Annual since 1970. Supersedes the publication with the same title first issued 1927 by the United States Post Office Department

"This is a comprehensive catalog of all adhesive stamp series issued since the first in 1847, including commemorative stamps and plates. Lists all designers and engravers with their stamps, date of issue and the number in the first issue. Stamp series are arranged chronologically by denomination with information on subject, colors and dates. Indexed by subjects depicted on stamps." Wynkoop. Subject Guide to Government Ref Bks

Villiard, Paul

Collecting stamps; with 77 photographs by the author. Doubleday 1974 191p illus $5.95, lib. bdg. $6.70 (5-7)   769

1 Postage stamps—Collectors and collecting

ISBN 0-385-01774-X; 0-385-08677-6

The author "tells readers first how to care for their stamps—since even the slightest damage almost always results in a lower appraisal value—and then goes on to describe the immense variety of collectible items, including types of plate blocks, revenue stamps, first day covers, and numerous other philatelic items. Integrated throughout are explanations of how and why certain stamps rise in value and suggestions on what to watch for when buying. Names and addresses of services and periodicals of help and interest are sprinkled throughout, and an extensive glossary and index provide easy access to specific points of information." Booklist

Zarchy, Harry

Stamp collector's guide; written and illus. by Harry Zarchy. Knopf 1956 178p illus $3.50, lib. bdg. $5.69   769

1 Postage stamps—Collectors and collecting

ISBN 0-394-81672-2; 0-394-91672-7

"A clear, concise guide to stamp collecting for the beginner. The author begins with a brief history of postal systems, and then discusses kinds of stamps, how to start a collection, preparing stamps for the album, stamp albums (including how to make one), use of a stamp catalog, and types of collections. The final section contains a dictionary of philatelic names and overprints, a stamp identification table, and a glossary. Illustrated with numerous pictures of actual stamps and drawings to supplement the text." Chicago. Children's Bk Center

770   Photography and photographs

Holland, Viki

How to photograph your world; photographs by the author. Scribner 1974 63p illus $5.95 (3-5)   770

1 Photography

ISBN 0-684-13709-7

"Some thoughts on organization and creative approach rather than instructions on how to work a camera. Holland suggests using a simple camera . . . and then discusses such things as composition, props, and planning, as well as making a photograph into a personal statement or record of a special event. An appealing format fortifies the occasionally choppy text, illustrated with numerous helpful black-and-white photos from the author's own collection. A reasonable prep book for beginners." Booklist

770.28   Photography— Techniques

Noren, Catherine

Photography: how to improve your technique. Watts, F. 1973 63p illus lib. bdg. $4.33, pa $1.25 (5-7)   770.28

1 Photography

ISBN 0-531-02640-X; 0-531-02410-5

"A Concise guide"

"In addition to advice on improving photographic technique (focusing, composition, correct exposure, films), Noren provides background information on cameras and lenses; a beginning course in darkroom technique; and suggestions for photographic subjects. The text is clearly written and effectively illustrated with photographs [by the author]. A glossary, index, and sensible suggestions for further reading add to the value of this basic treatment." Sch Library J

Weiss, Harvey

Lens and shutter; an introduction to photography. Young Scott Bks. 1971 120p illus (The Beginning artist's lib) $5.95 (5-7)   770.28

1 Photography

ISBN 0-201-09240-9

"Young photographers can learn much about good photography from a careful study of the many well-chosen photographs by such persons as Ansel Adams, Dorothea Lange, and Edward Weston which illustrate this book as well as from the author's lucid, stimulating text. Following a discussion of equipment and basic techniques [the author] deals with various types of photography, including action shots, portraits and close-ups. He concludes with a section on darkroom work." Booklist

778.5   Motion pictures and television photography

Andersen, Yvonne

Make your own animated movies; Yellow Ball Workshop film techniques. Little 1970 101p illus $6.95 (5-7)   778.5

1 Moving picture cartoons 2 Moving picture photography

ISBN 0-316-03940-3

A "survey of both the preparation techniques in making animated film, and the intricacies of filming itself. Such media as clay figures, cutouts, drawing (directly on the film), pixillation (incorporating live actors), and tearouts are discussed, and the processes of positioning, filming, simulating motion, synchronizing sound and motion, splicing film et cetera are described." Sutherland. The Best in Children's Bks

"All of the techniques are clearly illustrated with black-and-white photos and drawings. The book concludes with lists of film equipment and art supplies plus a filmography. Not for rank amateurs, this is a practical and attractive addition to the hobby shelf, where it will be popular with readers having the requisite interest, time and money." Sch Library J

Horvath, Joan

Filmmaking for beginners. Nelson 1974 162p illus $5.95 (6-7)   778.5

1 Moving picture photography

ISBN 0-8407-6375-1

This book includes "information for ambitious beginners regarding the making of Super 8 and 8mm films. Subjects covered include film gauges, films available for varying shooting conditions, the parts of a camera, speed of filming and projecting, camera brands and capabilities, approaches to writing scripts, kinds of shots, camera angles, camera movements, lighting effects, maintaining proper screen direction, hints on directing the actors, special effects which can be created with the camera and with simple homemade devices, editing, sound, and a chapter on animation techniques." Top of the News

Larson, Rodger

Young filmmakers, by Rodger Larson with Ellen Meade; original photographs by Marcelo Montealegre. Dutton 1969 190p illus $7.95 (6-7)   778.5

1 Moving pictures 2 Moving picture photography

ISBN 0-525-43549-2

This book begins with "descriptions of some of the films that teen-agers are making today and goes on to discuss various techniques, the nature of visual language, types and selection of equipment, the sequence of steps involved in shooting a film, problems of casting and directing, the responsibilities of director and cameraman, editing the film, and ways of creating a sound track." Horn Bk

This "is a 'how-to-do-it' book that points to success in guiding the interested student to take up filmmaking at an early age." Best Sellers

Glossary: p174-83

Weiss, Harvey

How to make your own movies; an introduction to filmmaking. Young Scott Bks. 1973 96p illus (The Beginning artist's lib) lib. bdg. $5.50 (5-7)   778.5

1 Moving picture photography

ISBN 0-201-09310-3

"An introduction to the craft of moviemaking that is comprehensive enough to give a novice an understanding of the ways and means of making a film. Written simply and clearly by an author who has a

string of craft books to his credit, the book could easily be used by grade-school children." Horn Bk

780   Music

Norman, Gertrude

The first book of music; pictures by Richard Gackenbach. Watts, F. 1954 67p illus music lib. bdg. $3.90 (4-7)   780

1 Music

ISBN 0-531-00678-6

This book tells the story of music from its prehistoric beginnings to the present day of symphony orchestras and phonograph records. It contains explanations of how music is conceived and written, of theory, harmony and rhythms, notation and interpretation. The book also includes a few easy pieces to pick out on the piano, as well as brief biographies of some of the composers of today and yesterday. All the instruments of a modern orchestra are described, together with their history and their placement in the orchestra

"For any who cannot read music readily and are unfamiliar with the orchestra, this is a clear introduction." Horn Bk

780.1   Music—Philosophy and esthetics

Siegmeister, Elie

Invitation to music; preface by Virgil Thomson; illus. by Beatrice Schwartz. Harvey House 1961 193p illus music $7.75, lib. bdg. $6.27 (6-7)   780.1

1 Music—Analysis, appreciation 2 Music

ISBN 0-8178-3181-9; 0-8178-3182-7

The author "explains the basic elements of musical structure, form and style, points out the similarities and differences between folk and composed music and gives examples of all manner of compositions. . . . There are a chapter on orchestral instruments, suggestions for building a record library and a bibliography for further reading." N Y Times Bk Rev

"Simple vocabulary, appealing format, sketches of composers, listening tests . . . add to this book's usefulness. Excellent supplementary text for music appreciation courses." Library J

780.3   Music—Encyclopedias and dictionaries

Davis, Marilyn Kornreich

Music dictionary, by Marilyn Kornreich Davis in collaboration with Arnold Broido; illus. by Winifred Greene. Doubleday 1956 63p illus music (6-7) 780.3

1 Music—Dictionaries

ISBN 0-385-07594-4

"There are over 800 concise definitions of musical words, foreign terms, and instruments of common and uncommon use, with many illustrations." Christian Sci Monitor

"The pages are large and easily readable off the music rack. Witty black and white sketches are by Winifred Greene. Despite their good cheer, there never is any doubt that a bassoon is a bassoon or that you can work a kettledrum with a pedal to change its

Davis, Marilyn Kornreich—_Continued_
tuning. The information is serious." Chicago Sunday Trib

Scholes, Percy A.
The Oxford Junior companion to music. Oxford 1954 xxiii, 435p illus music $12.95 (3-7)   780.3
1 Music—Encyclopedias
ISBN 0-19-314301-1
"Written by a distinguished authority, this reference book consists of brief articles on composers, instruments, musical terms and expressions, and church music. Although it leans heavily towards British topics, it is a valuable source book for children from 8 to 16 years old. . . . It has a lengthy pronouncing glossary." Peterson. Ref Bks for Elem and Jr High Sch Libraries

780.96   Music of Africa

Warren, Fred
The music of Africa; an introduction, by Fred Warren with Lee Warren; illus. with photos and line drawings by Penelope Naylor. Prentice-Hall 1970 87p illus music lib. bdg. $4.95 (6-7)   780.96
1 Music, African—History and criticism
ISBN 0-13-608224-6
"In a lucid analysis of the distinctive qualities and characteristics of African music . . . [the author] explains the place of music in traditional African life and the function of melody, rhythm, and form in African music. The Warrens illuminate their account with relevant comparisons to familiar musical patterns and with musical excerpts demonstrating African rhythmic structure. They also describe native instruments and conclude with a discussion of modern African music that evolved through a blending of traditional African forms and western music. The book includes a discography as well as a bibliography and an appendix giving information about some of the musical instruments shown in the illustrations." Booklist

781   Music—General principles and considerations

Hawkinson, John
Music and instruments for children to make, by John Hawkinson and Martha Faulhaber; illus. by John Hawkinson. Whitman, A. [1969] 47p illus (Music involvement ser) $4.50 (k-3)   781
1 Music—Theory 2 Musical instruments 3 Rhythm
ISBN 0-8075-5351-4
The authors show children "how to experiment with sounds and rhythms; how to clap, walk, skip, and run to songs, poems, and nursery rhymes; how to make and play a box harp, pan pipes, drum, and other rhythm instruments; and how to organize a band and create their own music and rhythms. The text is wonderfully lucid; the small drawings of children absorbed in musical fun are appealing. Both children and adults who work with children will find this an exciting 'experimental introduction to music.'" Horn Bk

Rhythms, music and instruments to make [by] John Hawkinson and Martha Faulhaber; illus. by John Hawkinson. Whitman, A. 1970 95p illus (Music involvement ser) $4.95 (3-6)   781

1 Music—Theory 2 Musical instruments 3 Rhythm
ISBN 0-8075-6958-5
"Similar in approach to the authors' 'Music and instruments for children to make' [entered above] but designed for slightly older children, the book combines text, drawings, and charts to give explicit instructions for making and playing a variety of simple percussion, wind, and string instruments including drums, panpipes, box harps, a metallophone, xylophone, and a wooden guitar. Together with examples of music for both single and combinations of instruments, the authors explain pitch, major and minor scales, and musical notation and offer suggestions for inventing original melodies and rhythms. A stimulating presentation for interested individuals or for group and classroom use." Booklist

781.5   Musical forms

Hughes, Langston
The first book of jazz; pictures by Cliff Roberts; music selected by David Martin. Watts, F. 1955 65p illus music lib. bdg. $3.90 (4-7)   781.5
1 Jazz music
ISBN 0-531-00565-8
"An absorbing history of jazz beginning with some of the early music that later contributed to jazz, such as African drums, work songs, jubilees, the blues, etc., and coming up to modern swing and bebop. Much of the story is told through the life of Louis Armstrong, since his life is in itself a kind of history of jazz. . . . The book contains an excellent record listing at the end that will be useful for building library or home collections." Chicago. Children's Bk Center

781.7   Music of ethnic and national orientation

Bierhorst, John
(comp.) Songs of the Chippewa; adapted from the collections of Frances Densmore and Henry Rowe Schoolcraft, and arranged for piano and guitar; pictures by Joe Servello. Farrar, Straus 1974 47p illus music $5.95 (3-6)   781.7
1 Chippewa Indians—Music
ISBN 0-374-37145-8
"The pioneer American ethnographer Schoolcraft collected Indian material in the nineteenth century; less well-known is the ethnomusicologist, Frances Densmore, who worked more than fifty years later. The seventeen songs, originally found near the western shores of the Great Lakes, include lullabies, sacred songs, chants, and love songs; and like most Indian songs, they are brief and precise, encompassing a single idea, emotion, or experience. . . . In a few cases, the original Chippewa words have been retained, but English equivalents are indicated. Schoolcraft recorded words but not music; and the editor has replaced the unknown melodies with tunes carefully selected from Densmore." Horn Bk
"A very valuable and handsomely produced book. . . . Authoritatively edited with a section of valuable notes to explain the various songs, this book can be used in many ways with children and adults who are interested in authentic American music. For each of the 17 songs, the artist has captured the mood in effective pictures that complement the lyrics. A book that will do much to better our understanding of the Indian life style and culture." Children's Bk Rev Serv
Bibliography included in notes: p45-47

Hofsinde, Robert

Indian music makers; written and illus. by Robert Hofsinde (Gray-Wolf) Morrow 1967 94p illus music $4.75 (3-7)　　　781.7

1 Indians of North America—Music 2 Musical instruments

ISBN 0-688-21616-1

An introductory chapter discusses "the wide variety and great importance of music in the life of the American Indian. Explicit details are given on various tribes' methods of making and using tom-toms, drums, rattles, and courting flutes. Using Chippewa tribal life as an example, Mr. Hofsinde includes nine simple musical scores with his discussion of typical songs, their origins, and the occasions for their use. The differences between Indian songs and the white man's songs are explained briefly as well as the modern changes in traditional Indian songs." Sch Library J

"A short and readable book. . . . His information is made more accessible by an index to instrument types, and by bold but practical drawings in ink." Christian Sci Monitor

781.9　Musical instruments

Dietz, Betty Warner

Musical instruments of Africa; their nature, use, and place in the life of a deeply musical people [by] Betty Warner Dietz and Michael Babatunde Olatunji; illus. by Richard M. Powers. Day 1965 115p illus map music $9.95 (6-7)　　　781.9

1 Musical instruments 2 Music, African

ISBN 0-381-97013-2

"For young people interested in making their own music—and even their own instruments—this fully illustrated study shows how native African instruments are made and used. Includes two songs with words and melody and a long-playing record of African music recorded in Africa by Colin M. Turnbull." Children's Bks. 1965

Books for further reading: p111-12. Additional books for adults: p113-14

Kupferberg, Herbert

A rainbow of sound; the instruments of the orchestra and their music; illus. by Morris Warman. Scribner 1973 64p illus lib. bdg. $5.95 (4-7)　781.9

1 Musical instruments 2 Orchestra

ISBN 0-684-13389-X

"An enthusiastic book that attempts to explain the functioning of the orchestra as the sum of its parts, to encourage an awareness of orchestration, and to introduce young people to the peculiar individuality and potentiality of each instrument. Between a general section on the orchestra and a final note on the conductor, the instruments are considered within four major groups: strings, woodwinds, brass, and percussion. A note on recordings and a list of recommended examples concludes the book, which is illustrated with photographs of the various instruments played by young students." Horn Bk

Levine, Jack

Understanding musical instruments; how to select your instrument [by] Jack Levine and Takeru Iijima. [Rev. ed] Warne 1971 124p illus $4.95 (4-7)　781.9

1 Musical instruments

ISBN 0-7232-6024-9

First published 1959 by Sterling with title: What musical instrument for me?

This book describes the characteristics of various musical instruments and suggests recordings featuring each instrument to help young people decide which instrument suits them best

Mandell, Muriel

Make your own musical instruments, by Muriel Mandell and Robert E. Wood; illus. by Margaret Krivak. Sterling 1957 126p illus $4.95, lib. bdg. $4.89 (3-7)　　　781.9

1 Musical instruments 2 Handicraft

ISBN 0-8069-5022-6; 0-8069-5023-4

The author provides "directions and illustrations for making a variety of musical instruments from things around the house and suggestions for forming a rhythm and a calypso band." Hodges. Bks for Elem Sch Libraries

There are "more than 100 ingenious instruments described. . . . The text is concise, the pictures clear, and both are easily understood." Booklist

Posell, Elsa Z.

This is an orchestra. Rev. ed. illus. with photographs. Houghton 1973 90p illus music $5.95 (5-7)　　　781.9

1 Musical instruments 2 Orchestra

ISBN 0-395-17712-X

First published 1950

"An excellent basic title to buy because of the wealth of information on orchestral instruments [by families] plus pointers on how to choose an instrument . . . how to buy an instrument, find a teacher and form successful practice habits. There is a chapter on famous makers of stringed instruments and one on building a home record library. . . . [Includes] a seating chart of the orchestra." Wis Library Bul [Review of 1950 edition]

"Distinguished for its excellent photographs of instruments [and] its clearly written text in large print." Cur Ref Bks [Review of 1950 edition]

Rhodes, C. O.

Let's look at musical instruments and the orchestra; foreword by Sir Malcolm Sargent; illus. by Norma Ost. Whitman, A. [1969 c1968] 64p illus $3.75 (4-6)　　　781.9

1 Musical instruments 2 Orchestra

ISBN 0-8075-4483-3

"A competent, though necessarily limited, survey of the history of music and musical instruments. Numerous sketches illustrate the instruments as they are described in the text. The one-page index consists mainly of names of instruments, composers and conductors." Sch Library J

782.1　Opera

Bulla, Clyde Robert

More Stories of favorite operas; illus. by Joseph Low. Crowell 1965 309p illus $5.50 (5-7)　782.1

1 Operas—Stories, plots, etc.

ISBN 0-690-55910-0

Companion volume to the author's: Stories of favorite operas, entered below

The 22 "condensations here are in past tense, simply written, and certainly useful. Each story is preceded by a paragraph of background; the book closes with cast lists for the operas and with an index." Chicago. Children's Bk Center

Stories of favorite operas; illus. by Robert Galster. Crowell 1964 277p illus $4.95 (5-7)　782.1

1 Operas—Stories, plots, etc.

ISBN 0-690-7765-2

"An attractively illustrated book presents the

Bulla, Clyde Robert—*Continued*

stories of 23 of the best-known and most popular operas; clearly written in present tense in a direct, simplified manner which makes it easy to follow even the most complicated plot. A brief introduction to each gives information about the opera's origin and first performance; the cast of characters for each opera and biographical notes on the composers are appended. A valuable reference book for libraries regardless of size." Booklist

Grimm, William

Hansel and Gretel; a story of the forest by William & Jacob Grimm; music by Engelbert Humperdinck and illus. by Warren Chappell. Knopf 1944 unp illus music $3.25, lib. bdg. $5.69 (3-5)   782.1

1 Operas—Stories, plots, etc.

ISBN 0-394-81221-2; 0-394-91221-7

This libretto follows the familiar tale of the children of a poor wood-cutter lost in the forest and of their encounter with the witch who lived there

"A child's book of the opera, four of whose most melodious airs are reduced to easy playing and put each on a page in a simple piano arrangement." N Y Her Trib Bks

"The pictures in color by Warren Chappell have a heavy, peasant-like quality, the dark shades in which they are reproduced contributing to the dread impression of the forest setting." Wis Library Bul

Montresor, Beni

Cinderella; from the opera by Gioacchino Rossini in a version written and illus. by Beni Montresor. Knopf 1965 unp illus $3.75, lib. bdg. $5.39, pa 95¢ (2-4)   782.1

1 Operas—Stories, plots, etc

ISBN 0-394-81055-4; 0-394-91055-9; 0-394-82619-1

Based on Rossini's opera, Cenerentola, which opened in 1817, this version has the young Cinderella transformed into a lovely bride by the Prince's major domo

The pictures "glow as if the costumes and scenery were in a golden setting, grandiose and artificial but romantic. . . . The tone of the story is more sophisticated than the usual version for the youngest children." Bk Week

Streatfeild, Noel

The first book of the opera; illus. by Hilary Abrahams. Watts, F. 1966 62p illus lib. bdg. $3.90 (4-7)   782.1

1 Opera

ISBN 0-531-00602-6

Published in England with title: Enjoying opera

The author "explains the difference between opera, light opera, operettas, and musical plays, outlines the history of opera, tells how operas are composed and produced, gives notes on well-known operas, composers, and performers, and includes a discography. Because of its brevity and enthusiastic tone this compressed account should serve as a useful introduction to opera. The numerous illustrations are colorful though not outstanding." Booklist

Updike, John

The Ring. Music by Richard Wagner; adapted and illus. by John Updike and Warren Chappell. Knopf 1964 unp illus music $3.50, lib. bdg. $5.39 (4-7)   782.1

1 Opera—Stories, plots, etc.

ISBN 0-394-81544-0; 0-394-91544-5

"This retelling of 'Siegfried,' the third of the four operas in Wagner's Ring cycle, is accompanied by musical themes and appropriate illustrations. An aid in understanding the music and arousing interest in reading the Siegfried legend." Hodges. Bks for Elem Sch Libraries

783.6   Sacred songs. Carols

Ehret, Walter

The international book of Christmas carols; musical arrangements by Walter Ehret. Translations and notes by George K. Evans; illus. by Don Martinetti; foreword by Norman Luboff. Prentice-Hall 1963 338p illus music $15.95   783.6

1 Carols

ISBN 0-013-471607-8

"Arranged by nationality this excellent collection gives the words and music of a generous number of carols from England, the U.S., France, Germany, Scandinavia, the Slavic countries, Italy, and Spain. Five Latin carols are included. Lyrics of foreign-language songs are accompanied by English translations. Other features: a prefatory essay on Christmas and its songs, appended notes, a chart of guitar chords, and a title and a first-line index." Booklist

The friendly beasts (Carol)

The friendly beasts [by] Laura Nelson Baker; illus. by Nicolas Sidjakov; adapted from an old English Christmas carol of the same title. Parnassus Press 1957 unp illus music $2.95, lib. bdg. $3.18 (k-3)   783.6

1 Carols

ISBN 0-87466-045-9; 0-87466-014-9

An adaptation of the 14th century English Christmas carol which tells "the story of the animals that waited in wonder in the stable in Bethlehem and told of the gifts each would give to the Christ child who was to be born that night in the manger. . . . The words and music of the carol appear at the end of the book." Booklist

"Nicolas Sidjakov's illustrations, rich in color and exciting in design, have a stained glass quality and help make the book a small gem for family and connoisseur." Chicago Sunday Trib

Horder, Mervyn

On Christmas day; first carols to play and sing; arranged by Mervyn Horder; illus. by Margaret Gordon. Macmillan (N Y) 1969 unp illus music $5.95 (3-7)   783.6

1 Carols

Here are "thirteen carols with simple piano arrangements . . . presented for unison singing by young children. The well-known American carols 'Away in a manger' and 'We three Kings of Orient are' and the English carols 'The first nowell' and 'I saw three ships' are included but the others are English and French carols less familiar to American children." Booklist

"The half-page and full-page illustrations in their glowing greeting-card colors and stylized but lively designs richly set the stage." Horn Bk

Langstaff, John

(comp.) On Christmas day in the morning! Carols gathered by John Langstaff; illus. by Antony Groves-Raines; piano settings by Marshall Woodbridge. Harcourt 1959 unp illus music $5.95   783.6

1 Carols

ISBN 0-15-257959-1

A "Christmas book for all ages. The compiler has chosen four well-known traditional Christmas carols and set them to familiar music, arranged by Marshall

Langstaff, John—*Continued*

Woodbridge. The many detailed illustrations in soft glowing colors [and medieval style] . . . are lovely and interpret the carols. A brief introduction tells of the folk qualities of Christmas carols which can be acted out as well as sung." Library J

Contents: On Christmas day in the morning; Dame, get up and bake your pies; I saw three ships: The friendly beasts

(comp.) The season for singing; American Christmas songs and carols; with music harmonized and arranged by Seymour Barab for piano or guitar accompaniment. Doubleday 1974 124p illus music $5.95, lib. bdg. $6.70 (3-7)   783.6

1 Carols

ISBN 0-385-06564-7; 0-385-06566-3

This book contains American Christmas carols which reflect the cultural diversity of the nation. Included are folk carols; Shaker, Moravian, Indian, Puerto Rican, and Afro-American carols; shape-note hymns; composed songs; and part songs; all with piano and guitar accompaniments. An index of first lines is appended

"The book will supplement collections exclusively devoted to all-time favorites, providing entertainment and a few diminished lessons in our diverse cultural heritage." Booklist

The Little Drummer Boy (Carol)

The Little Drummer Boy; [illus. by] Ezra Jack Keats; words and music by Katherine Davis, Henry Onorati and Harry Simeone. Macmillan (N Y) 1968 unp illus music $4.50, pa $1.25 (k-2)   783.6

1 Carols

"Katherine Davis' Christmas song, originally called 'The Carol of the Drum,' has become a well-loved favorite with young and old. Now the tender verses, which follow a pattern familiar in Nativity stories and legends, provide the text for a handsome picture book. . . . The drummer's boyish earnestness is beautifully characterized in the pictures; occasional touches of collage add variety and texture to the rich color of the painting. Music and words are printed together at the end of the book." Horn Bk

Includes unaccompanied melody

Pauli, Hertha

Silent night; the story of a song; illus. by Fritz Kredel. Knopf 1943 81p illus music $2.75, lib. bdg. $5.69 (4-7)   783.6

1 Silent night (Carol) 2 Gruber, Franz Xaver 3 Christmas stories

ISBN 0-394-81621-8; 0-394-91621-2

"The story of one of the best loved Christmas carols—how it came to be written on Christmas eve 1818 in an Austrian village, the mystery which surrounded its authorship for so long, and its spread throughout the world." Booklist

Simon, Henry W.

(ed.) A treasury of Christmas songs and carols; ed. and annotated by Henry W. Simon. 2d ed. with guitar chords. Illus. by Rafaello Busoni. Piano arrangements by the editor and Rudolph Fellner. Houghton 1973 243p illus music $8.95, pa $5.95   783.6

1 Carols 2 Songs

ISBN 0-395-17786-3; 0-395-17785-5

First published 1955

This collection contains over one hundred songs and carols, with arrangements for both piano and guitar. Designed for use by small informal groups who will find many of the familiar carols but also a sampling of foreign traditional airs

Divided into these six parts: British and American

carols; Carols from foreign parts; Christmas hymns and chorales; Especially for children; Christmas solo songs; Christmas rounds and canons; Index of titles and first lines; Index of musical and literary sources

"The piano arrangements, except for a few solo songs from the great masters, contain the melody and are both well filled out and easily played. Pleasing illustrations have varied two-color arrangements." Horn Bk [Review of 1955 edition]

Slaughter, Jean

(comp.) And it came to pass; Bible verses and carols; illus. by Leonard Weisgard. Macmillan (N Y) 1971 unp illus music $4.95, pa 95¢ (k-4)   783.6

1 Carols 2 Jesus Christ—Nativity

"Alternating selections from the Gospel of St. Luke and Christmas carols are arranged chronologically to tell the Nativity story. The illustrations, some in pen and ink and some in full-color tempera, are a reverent and graceful extension of the text. Guitar and piano arrangements accompany the carols." Pub W

The **Thirteen** days of Yule; introduction by Anthony Murray; pictures by Nonny Hogrogian. Crowell [1968] unp illus $4.95, lib. bdg. $5.70 (k-2)   783.6

1 Carols

ISBN 0-690-81825-4; 0-690-81826-2

"This is a Scottish version of the carol, 'The Twelve Days of Christmas' that was a dance rather than a carol: the dancers circled a chosen king, as he described the gifts for his lady." Pub W

"Illustrations in fine line and rich colors picture the elegant and strange creatures that the king sent to his lady: partriks, a papingo, plovers, starlings, goldspinks, an Arabian baboon. The text in calligraphy is clear; and though children prefer type, the words would, in any case, have to be read or sung to young children, who will take special delight in poring over the beautiful pictures." Horn Bk

The **Twelve** days of Christmas; in pictures by Ilonka Karasz. Harper 1949 unp illus music $5.95, lib. bdg. $5.79 (1-5)   783.6

1 Carols

ISBN 0-06-023090-8; 0-06-023091-6

"Ilonka Karasz has set the verses of [this] lovely old carol against twelve pictures which combine modern technique with the exuberance of the medieval tradition. The first picture is of one partridge in a pear tree, then to the succeeding pictures is added, in order, each of those gifts which 'my true love sent to me,' until we see in grand finale the twelve drummers drumming, the lords a-leaping, the maids a-milking and all the other thoughtful presents." N Y Times Bk Rev

Presented as "a thing of beauty and a joy forever. . . . The color is soft and rich, and on the last two pages is the music for the song. Here are art and music and an old tradition for young and old, all between the covers of one book." Sat Rev

784 Vocal music

Garson, Eugenia

(ed.) The Laura Ingalls Wilder songbook; favorite songs from the "Little house" books compiled and ed. by Eugenia Garson; arranged for piano and guitar by Herbert Haufrecht; illus. by Garth Williams. Harper 1968 160p illus music $6.95, lib. bdg. $6.49 (3-7)   784

1 Songs, American

ISBN 0-06-021933-5; 0-06-021934-3

Garson, Eugenia—*Continued*

"A former children's librarian has researched, compiled, and annotated 62 of the songs that appear in Wilder's 'Little house' books. The collection, valuable as representative of a period as well as interesting in connection with the series, contains dancing or singing game tunes, patriotic songs, ballads, minstrel-show and music-hall melodies, hymns, and gospel songs. Brief notes with the music indicate the page of the story on which each song appears and gives, when available, information about the song, composer, or lyricist." Booklist

"Garth Williams' charming illustrations, done originally for the 1953 uniform edition of the Wilder books add to the appeal of a volume that will be a welcome addition to any children's collection that includes the 'Little House' books." Sch Library J

784.4 Folk songs

A-hunting we will go (Folk song)

Catch a little fox; variations on a folk rhyme, by Beatrice Schenk De Regniers; pictures by Brinton Turkle. Seabury 1970 c1968 unp illus music $4.50 (k-2)   784.4

1 Folk songs
ISBN 0-8164-3011-X

Accompanied by the traditional melody of "A-hunting we will go," the children capture in turn, a fox, frog, cat, mouse, and smoke-breathing dragon. But the hunters are out-smarted by their prey in a turnabout ending

This book "is a charmer. The words are the old nursery rhyme with a comical, gentle new twist. . . . [The] pastel drawings of animals and dressed-up children are bursting with serious and enjoyable life. It is all quite delightful. It is also cute, but not too cute. These are real people. And besides, humor saves them." Christian Sci Monitor

Oh, a-hunting we will go [by] John Langstaff; pictures by Nancy Winslow Parker. Atheneum Pubs. 1974 unp illus music $6.50 (k-2)   784.4

1 Folk songs
ISBN 0-689-50007-6

"A Margaret K. McElderry book"

The nonsense verses of this folk song trace the hunt for such animals as an armadillo, a fox, and a snake, and describe the imagined treatment of each animal once it is caught

"The 12 stanzas are complemented by Parker's droll crayon illustrations (the fox caught in the box is watching TV), and a score for guitar and piano is appended. An amusing addition to 'song' picture books." Sch Library J

Billy Boy (Folk song)

Billy Boy; verses selected by Richard Chase; drawings by Glen Rounds. Golden Gate 1966 unp illus music $4.95 (k-3)   784.4

1 Folk songs—U.S.
ISBN 0-516-08803-3

The wooing of Miss Mary Jane by the mountain lad, Billy Boy, is told in seventeen verses, accompanied by a piano arrangement

"Children will probably not be familiar with the tragic ballad of Lord Randall that Mr. Chase mentions in his preface . . . but they will follow Billy Boy's courting with enthusiasm and curiosity, even adding a few verses of their own." Horn Bk

"The humor and folk quality of the old song are mirrored in the drawings." Notable Children's Bks. 1966

Boni, Margaret Bradford

(ed.) Fireside book of folk songs; selected and ed. by Margaret Bradford Boni; arranged for the piano by Norman Lloyd; illus. by Alice and Martin Provensen. Simon & Schuster 1947 323p illus music $14.95
784.4

1 Folk songs 2 Songs
ISBN 0-671-25836-2

Companion volume to: The fireside book of favorite American songs, entered in class 784

"One of the most colorful and charming collections for people who like to sing for the fun of it. . . . Outstanding for the selection exercised in compiling this volume of 147 old favorites, sea chanteys, cowboy songs and hymns, railroad songs, spirituals and Christmas carols. Arrangements for the piano by Norman Lloyd are excellent for their simplicity. Each song is prefaced by a brief introduction and these plus brief statements at the beginning of each category, constitute all the commentary. It is meant for a songbook and used as such it will be most successful. The colored illustrations, 500 of them, are very gay." Cur Ref Bks

Includes notation for guitar accompaniment

Carmer, Carl

(comp.) America sings; stories and songs of our country's growing; collected and told by Carl Carmer. Arrangements by Edwin John Stringham. Illus. by Elizabeth Black Carmer. Knopf 1942 243p illus music $5.75, lib. bdg. $8.99 (5-7)   784.4

1 Folk song—U.S. 2 Legends—U.S.
ISBN 0-394-80902-5; 0-394-90902-X

"A notable anthology of folk songs and folk tales reflecting America's work and growing. Here, in stories, songs, and appropriate pictures, are 29 American work-heroes from east, west, north, and south—lumberjacks, cotton pickers, miners, fishermen, cowboys, raftsmen, and the rest." Booklist

"Telling is vivid and direct. . . . Large type and a lovely cover. . . . Gay two-page spreads for each story in suitably garish colors." Library J

Casey Jones (Folk song)

Casey Jones; the story of a brave engineer; verses selected and illus. by Glen Rounds. Golden Gate 1968 unp illus music $4.95 (2-4)   784.4

1 Folk songs—U.S.
ISBN 0-516-08806-8

"Some simple music accompanies the verses that tell the epic story of Casey's last run on the railroad. Rounds' sympathetic pictures enhance the tale." Adventuring With Bks. 2d edition

The Erie Canal (Folk song)

The Erie Canal; illus. by Peter Spier. Doubleday 1970 unp illus map music $4.50, lib. bdg. $5.25, pa $1.25 (k-4)   784.4

1 Folk songs—U.S.
ISBN 0-385-06777-1; 0-385-05452-1; 0-385-05234-0

An American folk song is recreated in full-color scenes. Historical notes, a map of the canal which served as a busy trade route, and the musical arrangement for the song is included

The illustrator "records detail with the meticulous accuracy of the historian and the appreciative eye of the artist. His characteristic full-color pictures—many of them double-spreads—are full of boats, buildings, animals, and people, all involved in the bustling activity on and along the banks of the canal." Horn Bk

Felton, Harold W.

(ed.) Cowboy jamboree: western songs & lore, collected and told by Harold W. Felton; musical arrangements by Edward S. Breck; illus. by Aldren A. Watson; foreword by Carl Carmer. Knopf 1951 107p illus music $3, lib. bdg. $5.99   784.4

1 Cowboys—Songs and music 2 Folk songs—U.S.
ISBN 0-394-81056-2; 0-394-91056-7

Here are the words and music of 20 songs the cowboys sing, together with the legend and lore that enliven the history of the West

"Piano fingering is indicated as well as accompaniments for any instrument on which simple chords can be played, such as the guitar, ukulele and accordion." Wis Library Bul

The Fox (Folk song)

The fox went out on a chilly night; an old song illus. by Peter Spier. Doubleday 1961 unp illus music $4.95, lib. bdg. $5.70, pa 95¢ (k-3)   784.4

1 Folk songs—U.S.
ISBN 0-385-07990-7; 0-385-00231-9; 0-385-01065-6

Set in New England, this old folk song tells about the trip the fox father made to town to get some of the farmer's plump geese for his family's dinner, and how he manages to evade the farmer who tries to shoot him

"A true picture book in the Caldecott-Brooke tradition. Fine drawings, lovely colors, and pictures so full of amusing details that young viewers will make fresh discoveries every time they scrutinize (as they surely will) these beautiful, action-filled pages." Horn Bk

Includes music

Go tell Aunt Rhody (Folk song)

Go tell Aunt Rhody; illus. by Aliki. Macmillan Pub. Co. 1974 32p illus music lib. bdg. $5.95 (k-3) 784.4

1 Folk songs—U.S.
ISBN 0-02-711920-3

"A piano arrangement and lyrics are included in this version of the American folk song about the old gray goose." Reading Teacher

"Rich tasty colors and vivid expressions . . . are found in the illustrations. . . . Capturing unabashedly the rural pleasures of the American past, Aliki has dipped into 18th-century landscapes for just the right settings. The children's faces tell us how it feels to live on a farm, to have an Aunt Rhody and to be excited and a little frightened by the death of a goose." N Y Times Bk Rev

Ipcar, Dahlov

The cat came back; adapted and illus. by Dahlov Ipcar. Knopf 1971 unp illus music lib. bdg. $5.49 (k-3)   784.4

1 Folk songs
ISBN 0-394-92291-3

This is a modernized adaptation of an old folksong about an indestructible cat who underwent every conceivable peril and survived

"A simple arrangement of . . . [the] folksong precedes the rollicking text, which almost sings itself when read aloud. The illustrations have vitality and humor." Sutherland. The Best in Children's Bks

Landeck, Beatrice

(comp.) Songs to grow on; a collection of American folk songs for children. . . . Marks, E. B. [distributed by Morrow] 1950 125p illus music $8.95   784.4

1 Folk songs—U.S.
ISBN 0-688-02505-6

"Assembled with explanatory text and rhythm band arrangements by Beatrice Landeck; piano settings by Florence White; designed and illustrated by David Stone Martin." Title page

This book of 60 American folk songs for children is

planned for use in schools or at home. The material is graded in each song group, suggestions are added after each song for an activity to go with the song, and the musical arrangements are simple

Langstaff, John

Frog went a-courtin'; retold by John Langstaff; with pictures by Feodor Rojankovsky. Harcourt 1955 unp illus music $6.25, pa $1.35 (k-3)   784.4

1 Ballads, Scottish
ISBN 0-15-230214-X; 0-15-633900-5

Awarded the Caldecott Medal, 1956

"Picture book version of the old Scottish ballad [also known as: A frog he would a-wooing go]. . . . Each page has a colorful and humorously detailed picture, usually with two lines of the ballad below. The words given here are a composite of several versions. The ending turns out happily when frog and mouse, safely wed despite the old tom cat's interruption at the wedding party, sail for France. The format makes an attractive picture book and good story telling (or singing) material." Chicago. Children's Bk Center

Illustrated in "vivid colours. . . . The accompanying tune is the one sung in the southern Appalachian mountains." Ontario Library Rev

(ed.) Hi! Ho! The rattlin' bog, and other folk songs for group singing; with piano settings by John Edmunds [and others]; with guitar chords suggested by Happy Traum; illus. by Robin Jacques. Harcourt 1969 112p illus music $5.50 (4-7)   784.4

1 Folk songs
ISBN 0-15-234400-4

"An ample and satisfying collection of fifty-three genuine folk songs for group singing at home, school, or camp: work songs, jig tunes, narrative ballads, counting and riddle songs, lullabies, calypsos, and historical songs—a great range, with further variety provided in their settings by four different composers. . . . The title song is not to be found in any other collection, and some of the other selections will seem new to many. The simple accompaniments will tempt young pianists." Horn Bk

"Brief notes explore [the] origin and meanings [of these songs], arrangements are fresh and original and easy to play. . . . Black and white drawings by Robin Jacques are reminiscent of old-fashioned steel engravings and give added appeal to a very rich collection." N Y Times Bk Rev

Ol' Dan Tucker; retold by John Langstaff; with pictures by Joe Krush. Harcourt 1963 unp illus music $5.95, lib. bdg. $5.95 (1-4)   784.4

1 Folk songs—U.S.
ISBN 0-15-257760-2; 0-15-257762-9

A picture book whose text is the author's version of an old banjo dance tune written by minstrel showman Dan Emmett

"The rustic detail and gusto of the drawings emphasize the folk quality. . . . A gay bit of Americana, said to be Lincoln's favorite song, the book offers . . . the fun of tall-tale nonsense rhymes. Piano music and guitar chord fingerings are included." Horn Bk

Over in the meadow; with pictures by Feodor Rojankovsky. Harcourt 1957 unp illus music $5.95, pa $1.25 (k-2)   784.4

1 Songs 2 Counting books
ISBN 0-15-258854-X; 0-15-670500-1

"This old counting rhyme [based on a folk song] tells of ten meadow families whose mothers advise them to dig, run, sing, play, hum, build, swim, wink, spin and hop. The illustrations, half in full color, show the combination of realism and imagination which little children like best. The tune, arranged simply, is

Langstaff, John—*Continued*
on the last page, and children will have fun acting the whole thing out." Horn Bk

"Mr. Rojankovsky's soft-colored close-ups of the flora and fauna of the meadow seem, somehow, a little static in comparison to his usual robustious pictures. They are, however, very decorative, and they make it easy to count the foxes two, the seven polliwogs and even the spiders nine." N Y Times Bk Rev

The swapping boy; with pictures by Beth and Joe Krush. Harcourt 1960 unp illus music $5.95 (1-4)
784.4

1 Folk songs—Appalachian Mountains
ISBN 0-15-283358-7
"Again, John Langstaff has made available to us an old folk song, based on a universal theme. The words to this wonderful, rollicking swapping song about a foolish boy and his 'swappings' were chosen from various versions. The tune was discovered in the southern Appalachian Mountains by Cecil Sharp, collector of folk music in that section. Colorful, lively illustrations . . . are in perfect accord with the broad humor of the text." Library J

London Bridge is falling down! Illus. by Peter Spier. Doubleday 1967 unp illus music $4.95, lib. bdg. $5.70, pa $1.25 (k-2)
784.4

1 Songs, English
ISBN 0-385-08717-9; 0-385-08718-7; 0-385-08025-5
This picture book illustrated with scenes of eighteenth-century London presents the traditional verses of the Mother Goose nursery rhyme. The musical score is included, as well as a three-page historical sketch of London Bridge through the centuries
"For the child who enjoys big pictures filled with small details, this version of the familiar verses should be a small treasure. Each illustration is a double-page spread teeming with action. The colors are subdued save for a bright red-orange, and the pages are crowded with scenes containing authentic details (in costume, architecture, signs, etc.) as well as amusing caricatures." Sat Rev

Nic Leodhas, Sorche
Always room for one more; illus. by Nonny Hogrogian. Holt 1965 unp illus music $5.95, lib. bdg. $2.96 (k-3)
784.4

1 Folk songs, Scottish 2 Folklore—Scotland
ISBN 0-03-053465-8; 0-03-053470-4
Awarded the Caldecott Medal, 1966
"A picture book based on an old Scottish folk song about hospitable Lachie MacLachlan, who invited in so many guests that his little house finally burst. Rhymed text . . . a glossary of Scottish words, and music for the tune are combined into an effective whole." Hodges. Bks for Elem Sch Libraries
"Pen and ink drawings with chalk and color wash add dimension and humor to the lilting text. An enchanting picture book." Wis Library Bul

Old MacDonald had a farm [illus. by] Robert Quackenbush. Lippincott 1972 unp illus music $4.95 (k-2)
784.4

1 Folk songs—U.S.
ISBN 0-397-31262-8
A "picture-book version of the familiar folk song about 'Old MacDonald and the noisy animals on his farm. As each new animal is mentioned in the lyrics printed on the righthand page, that animal is added to brightly colored pictures of the farm on the lefthand page." Booklist
"A joyful treat . . . complete with music and background notes on the origin of the song." Pub W

One wide river to cross (Folk song)
One wide river to cross; adapted by Barbara Emberley; illus. by Ed Emberley. Prentice-Hall 1966 unp illus music $5.95 (k-3)
784.4

1 Noah's Ark 2 Folk songs—U.S.
ISBN 0-13-636167-6
The illustrator depicts "the animals as they file into the ark—snakes on roller skates, elephants doing tricks, and so on, one by one up to ten by ten. The music for this old folk song is included." Children's Bks, 1966
"Processional black woodcut images on solid, bright-colored paper create an exciting, cumulative design of animals. . . . The character of illustrations is striking, and evokes thoughts of Egyptian hieroglyphics or spiritual Negro art." Wis Library Bul

Ritchie, Jean
(comp.) From fair to fair: folk songs of the British Isles; photographs by George Pickow; piano arrangements by Edward Tripp. Walck, H.Z. 1966 illus music $5.95 (4-7)
784.4

1 Folk songs, English
ISBN 0-8098-2391-8
"Sixteen folk songs of Ireland, Scotland, and England, given an imaginary setting as a minstrel wanders from fair to fair. Words, music, and guitar notations are given for each; photographs show appropriate scenes and activities." Hodges. Bks for Elem Sch Libraries

Jean Ritchie's Swapping song book; photographs by George Pickow; piano arrangements by A. K. Fossner and Edward Tripp. Walck, H.Z. 1964 [c1952] 93p illus music $5 (4-6)
784.4

1 Folk songs—Kentucky
ISBN 0-8098-2374-8
A reissue of the 1952 edition published by Oxford
"Photographs and brief text describing life in the mountains set the scenes for 21 folk songs from Kentucky's Cumberland Mountains. Guitar chords are included with the simple piano arrangements. . . . For school, home, and community singing." Booklist

Rockwell, Anne
(ed.) El toro pinto, and other songs in Spanish; selected and illus. by Anne Rockwell. Macmillan (N Y) 1971 52p illus music $7.95 (1-6)
784.4

1 Folk songs, Spanish
"Brightly colored illustrations give this diversified collection of 30 songs in Spanish from Latin America, Spain and the Southwestern U.S. a cheerful, attractive appearance. Melody, guitar chords, and Spanish words are given for each of the lullabies, carols, and other songs; English translations, not intended for singing, are appended; and the country of origin of each song is indicated in the table of contents. Brief introductory notes and suggestions for using the songs precede the selections." Booklist

(ed.) Savez-vous planter les choux? and other French songs; selected and illus. by Anne Rockwell. World Pub. [distributed by Macmillan Pub. Co] 1969 64p illus music $5.95 (3-6)
784.4

1 Folk songs, French 2 Bilingual books—French-English
A "collection of French songs dating mostly from the eighteenth and nineteenth centuries. . . . The musical settings are within a comfortable singing range and chord symbols are supplied for guitar or possibly piano accompaniment. A note on the selection of the materials, an English translation of each number and appropriate illustrations make this especially suitable for the child learning French." Wis Library Bul

Rockwell, Anne—*Continued*

"Stylized, flat pictures in clear, poster-like colors are full of jaunty figures that look like painted toys or gaily dressed characters in a pantomime. The artist has done careful research: French costumes and architecture appear throughout, and 'wherever possible, these represent the styles of the exact time or place of the particular song's origin.'" Horn Bk

Seeger, Pete

The foolish frog [by] Pete Seeger and Charles Seeger; illus. by Miloslav Jagr; music adapted from an old song; book adapted and designed from Firebird Film by Gene Deitch. Macmillan Pub. Co. 1973 unp illus music $4.95   784.4

1 Folk songs—U.S.

ISBN 0-02-781480-7

A farmer makes up a song about a frog and sings it to the storekeeper of the general store. The latter becomes exuberant, treats the customers to pop and soda crackers, and sets up a chain reaction of revelry

The text "is enlivened by splashy, colorful cartoon drawings. The book's usefulness is enhanced by the catchy lyrics and tune included at the end of the book. Where material on folk songs is desired, this would be an adequate addition." Sch Library J

Seeger, Ruth Crawford

American folk songs for children in home, school and nursery school; a book for children, parents and teachers; illus. by Barbara Cooney. Doubleday 1948 190p illus music $6.95, lib. bdg. $7.70   784.4

1 Folk songs—U.S. 2 Singing games

ISBN 0-385-07210-4; 0-385-07316-X

A big book of 90 folk songs from all parts of the country that may be sung and acted out with many variations. The tunes and piano accompaniments are simple enough for most adults to play. It is a source book for family fun

"Several introductory chapters discussing the value of folk music for children and how to use folk songs with children at home and at school give the book added meaning for parents, teachers, and play-group leaders. Excellent classified indexes and index of titles and first lines." Booklist

(comp.) American folk songs for Christmas; illus. by Barbara Cooney. Doubleday 1953 80p illus music lib. bdg. $4.95   784.4

1 Folk songs—U.S. 2 Carols

ISBN 0-385-08299-1

Contains more than fifty American folk songs based on Christmas themes. Divided into these categories: Stars and shepherds; Mary and the Baby; Praise and festivity

"In the introduction [the compiler] tells about the sources of the songs and the holy-day and holiday celebrations at which they used to be sung. . . . The songs vary in difficulty and children will, of course, need an adult to use the book with them. It offers great possibilities for interesting Christmas programs." Horn Bk

(comp.) Animal folk songs for children; traditional American songs; illus. by Barbara Cooney. Doubleday 1950 80p illus music $6.95, lib. bdg. $7.70   784.4

1 Folk songs—U.S.

ISBN 0-385-07210-4; 0-385-07316-X

Companion volume to: American folk songs for children in home, school and nursery school, entered above

These songs about animals of forest, field, farm and ranch "tell a story as they are sung thus often providing opportunity for dramatization, clapping and dancing." ALA. CSD. Mother Hubbard's Cupboard

Includes simple musical accompaniments

Serwadda, W. Moses

Songs and stories from Uganda; transcribed and ed. by Hewitt Pantaleoni; illus. by Leo and Diane Dillon. Crowell 1974 80p illus music $6.50, lib. bdg. $7.25   784.4

1 Folk songs, Ugandan 2 Folklore—Uganda

ISBN 0-690-75240-7; 0-690-75241-5

This is a collection of storytelling songs from the Luganda, an East African language. "The music is transcribed in Western style; and words are supplied in both English and Luganda, with careful instructions for the pronunciation of Luganda words. To go along with the music, explanations or instructions are included for game songs or for dances. The dynamic two-color woodcuts add strongly to the African flavor of the book." Horn Bk

She'll be comin' round the mountain (Folk song)

She'll be comin' round the mountain; [illus. by] Robert Quackenbush. Lippincott 1973 unp illus music $4.95 (k-3)   784.4

1 Folk songs—U.S.

ISBN 0-397-31480-9

"A picture book in play form, this old railroad song is presented in bold purples and blues, golds and oranges. The animated full-page pictures freely interpret the song: a Wild West show, traveling by train, is coming into Pughtown for a one-night stand. Before the train arrives, Sneaky Pete, Rattlesnake Hank and Crumby Joe attempt to rob it. But, the show's star, Little Annie, snares the robbers with her lasso . . . and the show can go on." Babbling Bookworm

"Quackenbush has amiably included a piano accompaniment and a suitably silly number game to decide Annie's future." Booklist

Sweet Betsy from Pike (Folk song)

Sweet Betsy from Pike; verses selected and illus. by Glen Rounds. Childrens Press 1973 unp illus music lib. bdg. $5.06 (1-3)   784.4

1 Folk songs—U.S.

ISBN 0-516-08855-6

"A Golden Gate Junior book"

Including guitar chords and a simple piano arrangement, this is an illustrated version of the American folk song which "relates the hopes and fears of a young couple who travel to California during the Gold Rush. The 17 verses tell of Betsy and Ike's trek westward and their return to Pike County after panning for gold." Library J

This "is pure Roundsville and, I'd say, the definitive work on Betsy, Ike, the two yoke of cattle, yellow dog, Shanghai rooster and spotted hog. If you think you have had it with this bunch, Rounds will make you see you have never been there at all. With his crazy, quirky eye and line (embodying, of all things, the nagging eccentricity of The New Yorker's George Price and the coziness of a Garth Williams), Rounds 'tells it like it was' (it was hard, rough, exciting, dreary, and above all—hilarious) on that westward trek." N Y Times Bk Rev

Yolen, Jane

(ed.) The fireside song book of birds and beasts; arranged by Barbara Green; illus. by Peter Parnall. Simon & Schuster 1972 223p illus music $9.95   784.4

1 Folk songs 2 Animals—Songs and music

ISBN 0-671-66540-5

For each of the nearly one hundred songs assembled here there is a brief introduction, a musical

Yolen, Jane—*Continued*
arrangement for piano, and guitar chords. The book is
divided into five sections: Farmyard and house, Field
and forest, In the air, In the sea, and Other
phenomena
"A delightful collection, with many old favorites, is
delectably illustrated by the clean-lined drawings of
Peter Parnall. They are just right for the animal songs
to be used by or with children, and the piano accompaniments are not intricate. . . . An index of titles is
appended." Chicago. Children's Bk Center

784.6   Songs for specific groups and on specific subjects

Child, Lydia Maria
Over the river and through the wood; pictures by
Brinton Turkle. Coward, McCann & Geoghegan 1974
unp illus music $5.95 (1-3)   784.6
1 Thanksgiving Day—Songs and music
ISBN 0-698-20301-1
This version of the poem about a family's visit to
their grandparents for Thanksgiving, which first
appeared in 1844 as "The Boy's Thanksgiving Day,"
includes usually omitted verses, as well as a musical
arrangement for piano and guitar
"The pictures, realistic in period detail, are evocative and are framed so that each looks as though it
were in an album. Pictures of the visiting family are in
color and alternate with quiet black and white pictures
of the grandparental preparations (bringing in logs,
rolling the piecrust, setting the long table) and then
the whole family is together." Chicago. Children's Bk
Center

Engvick, William
(ed.) Lullabies and night songs; music by Alec
Wilder; pictures by Maurice Sendak. Harper 1965
77p illus music $10 (k-3)   784.6
1 Lullabies 2 Songs
ISBN 0-06-021820-7
"The editor has selected verses, in addition to some
of his own, from poets as notable and varied as
Eleanor Farjeon, Tennyson, Thurber, Stevenson,
Kipling, Walter de la Mare, and William Blake, as
well as many anonymous, traditional poems like
'Sleep, Baby, Sleep,' 'Wee Willie Winkie,' and 'Now
the Day is Over.'" Horn Bk
"Wilder's contemporary and original music and
simple arrangements are suitable. Sendak's gay
muted color illustrations capture every mood perfectly." Wis Library Bul

Fraser-Simson, H.
The Pooh song book. . . . Words by A. A. Milne;
music by H. Fraser-Simson; decorations by E. H.
Shepard. Dutton 1961 148p illus music $6.95 (1-3)
784.6
1 Songs
ISBN 0-525-37489-2
"Containing: The hums of Pooh [1930] The King's
breakfast [1924] Fourteen songs from When we were
very young [1925]." Title page
This compilation brings together the songs from the
Winnie-the-Pooh stories
Piano-vocal score

Girl Scouts of the United States of America
Sing together; a Girl Scout songbook. 3d ed. The
author 1973 182p illus pa $2.50 (4-7)   784.6
1 Songs 2 Folk songs
ISBN 0-88441-309-8

First published 1949
A collection of over 140 songs, including blues,
jazz, contemporary, folk, popular songs, and songs
from other lands, as well as scouting favorites. Guitar
chords and a glossary of terms and instruments add to
the illustrated text. Designed to provide material for
ceremonial meetings or smaller group gatherings

Kapp, Paul
Cock-a-doodle-doo! Cock-a-doodle-dandy! A new
songbook for the newest singers; pictures by Anita
Lobel. Harper 1966 70p illus music $3.95, lib. bdg.
$5.89 (k-2)   784.6
1 Songs
ISBN 0-06-022386-3; 0-06-022388-X
This "collection includes, in addition to traditional
rhymes, verses by Carroll, Lear, John Bunyan, Blake,
Eugene Field, Keats, Herrick, and Christina
Rosetti." Horn Bk
"The music is contemporary in feeling, easy to play,
and in most cases, easy to sing. For parent or teacher,
this is a delightful addition to a song library." N Y
Times Bk Rev

Langstaff, Nancy
(comp.) Jim along, Josie; a collection of folk songs
and singing games for young children; comp. by
Nancy and John Langstaff; piano arrangements by
Seymour Barab; guitar chords by Happy Traum;
optional percussion accompaniments for children.
Illus. by Jan Pienkowski. Harcourt 1970 127p illus
music $5.95 (k-4)   784.6
1 Folk songs 2 Singing games
ISBN 0-15-240250-0
Here are "eighty-one songs chosen for their freshness and adaptability, with simple piano arrangements, guitar chords, and directions or suggestions
for use. Decorated with lively silhouettes." Top of the
News

Larrick, Nancy
(comp.) The wheels of the bus go round and round;
school bus songs and chants; illus. by Gene Holtan;
music arranged by Patty Zeitlin. Golden Gate 1972
46p illus music $4.95 (1-4)   784.6
1 Songs
ISBN 0-516-08871-8
Here are 32 "old and new ditties to while away the
monotony of bus rides to and from school. As the
author mentions, children have handed these chants
on to each other and most have never been written
down before." Pub W
"The exuberant illustrations in color, while somewhat grotesque, will appeal to children and the book
provides a welcome source of hard-to-find material
for storytellers, scout and recreation leaders, and
field-trip chaperones. A simple piano arrangement is
given for each song." Booklist
Index of first lines: p[48]

Mitchell, Donald
(ed.) Every child's book of nursery songs; arranged
by Carey Blyton; illus. by Alan Howard. Crown [1969
c1968] 175p illus music $3.95 (k-3)   784.6
1 Songs 2 Nursery rhymes
"Young books from Crown"
First published 1968 in England with title: The
Faber book of nursery songs
"A musical anthology of over eighty nursery rhymes
and songs including most of the well-known classics,
but also some . . . unfamiliar songs; an effort has been
made to retain the original form of the verses, printed
here in full text. The musical arrangements give the
simple melodies plus suggestions for group participation that may be coordinated with unpitched percus-

Mitchell, Donald—*Continued*

sion instruments, real or contrived; individual and choral spoken parts are included for optional use." Sch Library J

"Attractively illustrated in black and white and in color, the book is appealing to the eye, and can be easily used by teachers, parents, and others whose piano technique is limited." Booklist

Rounds, Glen

The Strawberry Roan; verses selected and illus. by Glen Rounds. Golden Gate 1970 unp illus music $4.95 (k-4)   784.6

1 Cowboys—Songs and music
ISBN 0-516-08850-5

A picture book version of the ballad of the bow-legged, big-mouthed bronc buster who was defeated by a hard-bitten outlaw horse

"The music with guitar chords and the 21 verses are included at the end. Rounds' deft line and sophisticated caricatures will appeal to cowboy connoisseurs beyond the picture book age." Sch Library J

Sackett, S. J.

(comp.) Cowboys & songs they sang; settings by Lionel Nowak; designed by Walter Einsel. Scott, W.R. 1967 72p illus map music lib. bdg. $5.95 (4-7)   784.6

1 Cowboys—Songs and music 2 Cowboys
ISBN 0-201-09165-8

"More than a book of cowboy music, this collection of a dozen-plus songs (written in the simplest notation) gives a great deal of information about the cowboy and his way of life. Each selection is preceded by some background information and an old photograph or two, some of them fuzzy but all of them flavorful. The writing is simple, infrequently humorous, and pleasantly loquacious. A one-page bibliography and discography are appended." Sutherland. The Best in Children's Bks

Winn, Marie

(ed.) The fireside book of children's songs; collected & ed. by Marie Winn; musical arrangements by Allan Miller; illus. by John Alcorn. Simon & Schuster 1966 192p illus music $9.95 (k-6)   784.6

1 Songs 2 Folk songs
ISBN 0-671-25820-6

The book is divided into five parts: Good morning and good night, Birds and beasts, Nursery songs, Silly songs, and Singing games and rounds

"Over 100 songs for preschool and elementary age children are contained in this most attractive volume. . . . The accompaniments are simple, and guitar chords are provided. . . . Stylized decorations in mustard, rust, and shocking pink add to the overall appeal of the volume. Highly recommended for homes, schools, and public libraries." Sch Library J

Index of song titles and first lines: p191

(ed.) The fireside book of fun and game songs; collected and ed. by Marie Winn; musical arrangements by Allan Miller; illus. by Whitney Darrow, Jr. Simon & Schuster 1974 222p illus music $12.50   784.6

1 Songs
ISBN 0-671-65213-3

The songs are divided into ten catagories which include cumulative and diminishing songs, echo songs, motion and wordplay songs, question and answer songs, and rounds

"Although many of the individual items could be found in other books, some would be almost impossible to locate elsewhere. Musical arrangements and accompaniments are simple, and spirited drawings add to the innocent merriment." Horn Bk

Title and first line index: p[223-24]

Yulya

Bears are sleeping; words and music by Yulya; pictures by Nonny Hogrogian. Scribner 1967 unp illus music lib. bdg. $4.95 (k-1)   784.6

1 Lullabies
ISBN 0-684-13619-8

"This lullaby with words and music by the author is based on an old Russian melody. The illustrations in soft water-colours of blue, brown and white evoke a beautiful wintry feeling." Ontario Library Rev

784.7   National airs, songs, hymns

Boni, Margaret Bradford

(ed.) The fireside book of favorite American songs; selected and ed. by Margaret Bradford Boni; arranged for the piano by Norman Lloyd; illus. by Aurelius Battaglia, introductions by Anne Brooks; with a foreword by the late Carl Van Doren. Simon & Schuster 1952 359p illus music $14.95   784.7

1 Songs, American 2 Folk songs—U.S.
ISBN 0-671-24771-9

Companion volume to: Fireside book of folk songs, entered in class 784.4

This book "includes a wide range of ballads, sentimental songs, gospel hymns, and ragtime songs." Hodges. Bks for Elem Sch Libraries

Browne, C. A.

The story of our national ballads; rev. by Willard A. Heaps. Crowell 1960 314p $5 (5-7)   784.7

1 National songs, American
ISBN 0-690-77707-8

First published 1919

This volume contains stories of patriotic songs and war ballads from Yankee Doodle to songs of World War II with biographies of many of their authors including Francis Scott Key, Julia Ward Howe, Daniel Decatur Emmett, Samuel F. Smith, Stephen Foster, Katharine Lee Bates, and Irving Berlin

Reading list: p287-96

Bryan, Ashley

Walk together children; Black American spirituals; selected and illus. by Ashley Bryan. Atheneum Pubs. 1974 53p illus music $6.95   784.7

1 Negro spirituals
ISBN 0-689-30131-6

"The selector prefaces two dozen spirituals—slave songs and 'sorrow songs'—with a commentary that explains the fusion of African musical culture with free melodic ideas to make 'America's most distinctive contribution to world music.' . . . Melody lines and one or more verses are provided for each selection; and stark, heavy woodcuts illustrate most of the songs." Horn Bk

Hofmann, Charles

American Indians sing; drawings by Nicholas Amorosi. Day 1967 96p illus music lib. bdg. $6.27 (5-7)   784.7

1 Indians of North America—Music 2 Indians of North America—Dances
ISBN 0-381-99792-8

"An extensive study of why and how the Indians made music and how these songs and ceremonies

Hofmann, Charles—_Continued_
were a part of their lives. The reader is introduced to
the instruments used and also to the dances of the
major tribes. Profuse illustrations, photographs, musical scores and an accompanying recording help make
this book even more interesting." Bruno. Bks for Sch
Libraries, 1968
Reading list for students: p92. Reading list for
teachers and parents: p92

Key, Francis Scott
The Star-Spangled Banner; illus. by Paul Galdone.
Crowell 1966 unp illus $4.50, lib. bdg. $5.25 (1-4)
784.7
ISBN 0-690-77281-5; 0-690-77282-3
All stanzas of the national anthem are included
"There is a short historical introduction, but no
music in the book. Two reproductions are included: a
facsimile of Key's handwritten version of the poem
and the earliest known photograph of the original
flag." Sch Library J

The Star-Spangled Banner; illus. by Peter Spier.
Doubleday 1973 unp illus map music $5.95, lib. bdg.
$6.70 (1-4)
784.7
ISBN 0-385-09458-2; 0-385-07746-7
"All of the verses of the national anthem are illustrated. . . . Most of the pictures show the battle scenes
that inspired Francis Scott Key to write the words of
'The Star-Spangled Banner' in 1814, but others reflect
aspects of life in the United States today. Following
the illustrated lyrics are a photograph of the manuscript, a discussion of the War of 1812, the music for
the anthem, and a double-page spread that shows
official flags for government agencies and officers."
Chicago. Children's Bk Center
"At the beginning of the book, the mood is set by
the detailed line drawings of sailing vessels and by the
panoramic doublespreads vigorous with the flight of
rockets. The pastel watercolor tones are never
mawkish or sentimental but convey the dramatic feeling for space made possible by the sizable dimensions
of the book." Horn Bk

Lyons, John Henry
Stories of our American patriotic songs; illus. by
Jacob Landau. Vanguard [1958 c1942] 72p illus music
$5.95 (4-7)
784.7
1 National songs, American
ISBN 0-8149-0354-1
Reissue of a 1942 title in larger format
"The stories behind 10 of America's most popular
patriotic songs—when, why, and by whom they were
written. . . . Words and music are given for each. A
large, flat book, well-illustrated." Booklist
Contents: Star-Spangled Banner; Yankee Doodle;
Hail, Columbia; America; Columbia, the gem of the
ocean; Dixie; Maryland, my Maryland; Battle cry of
Freedom; Battle hymn of the Republic; America, the
beautiful

Sandburg, Carl
(ed.) The American songbag. Harcourt 1927 xxiii,
495p illus music $9.95, pa $4.95
784.7
1 Songs, American 2 Folk songs—U.S. 3 Ballads,
American
ISBN 0-15-106287-0; 0-15-605650-X
"The music includes not merely airs and melodies,
but complete harmonizations or piano accompaniments." Introduction
This is a collection of 280 songs and ballads from
every section of the country which reflect the spirit of
the time and place as well as the mood of the singer—
songs of the Negro, the pioneer, the Irish immigrant,
the southern mountaineer, the Great Lakes barge-
man, the hobo, the section hand, the lumberjack, the

soldier, the college student. The collection is a commentary on American life with sidelights on American
history
"Each song is introduced by Mr. Sandburg who in a
few words gives the story of his discovery or of its
origin. Those notes make fascinating reading, and
they can be enjoyed by those who cannot read notes or
who belong to the minority that does not like to sing—
or hear singing." Springf'd Republican

Schackburg, Richard
Yankee Doodle; woodcuts by Ed Emberley; notes
by Barbara Emberley. Prentice-Hall 1965 unp illus
music lib. bdg. $4.50, pa 95¢ (k-3)
784.7
1 National songs, American
ISBN 0-13-971853-2; 0-13-971879-6
"Using only the primary colors with black and
white, the artist has made illustrations that are vivid,
amusing, and very attractive. The text consists of the
verses of the song, printed in a running line at the foot
of each page; notes on the origin of the lyrics, and of
some of the words used, preface the text; the music is
appended." Chicago. Children's Bk Center

Shaw, Martin
(ed.) National anthems of the world; ed. by Martin
Shaw, Henry Coleman and T. M. Cartledge. [4th ed.
enlarged and rev] Arco 1976 c1975 477p music $20
784.7
1 National songs
ISBN 0-668-03849-7
First published 1943 in England with title: National
anthems of the United Nations and France. This edition first published 1975 in England
This volume contains national anthems of some 165
nations, including melody and accompaniment.
Words are presented in the native language with
transliteration provided where necessary. English
translations are also provided. Brief historical notes
on the adoption of each anthem are included and the
book concludes with a list of national days

Yurchenco, Henrietta
(ed.) A fiesta of folk songs from Spain and Latin
America; illus. by Jules Maidoff. Putnam 1967 88p
illus music lib. bdg. $5.97 (2-6)
784.7
1 Songs 2 Folk songs, Spanish 3 Folk songs, Mexican 4 Singing games 5 Bilingual books—Spanish-
English
ISBN 0-399-60165-1
From Mexico and Spain, "here are 34 folk songs—
singing games and dances, songs for Christmas, and
songs about people, animals and nature." Booklist
"In an attempt to familiarize children with the
Spanish language, the texts are presented with
English translations and with phonetic spellings based
upon Latin American pronunciations. The musical
notation is large and clear; guitar chords are indicated.
. . . Lively descriptive annotations and drawings
accompany each of the songs." Horn Bk

785 Instrumental ensembles and their music

Greene, Carla
Let's learn about the orchestra; illus. by Anne
Lewis. Harvey House 1967 44p illus $5.35, lib. bdg.
$4.29 (1-3)
785
1 Orchestra 2 Musical instruments
ISBN 0-8178-3891-0; 0-8178-3892-9
This is "an informative and inspiring book about the
modern orchestra, containing the history and de-

Greene, Carla—*Continued*
velopment of each group of instruments. [It] concludes with a tribute to the conductor. Illustrations add much to the high quality of this fine introduction to instruments." Adventuring With Bks. 2d edition

787 String instruments and their music

Kettelkamp, Larry
Singing strings; written and illus. by Larry Kettelkamp. Morrow 1958 48p illus music lib. bdg. $5.11 (4-7) 787
1 Stringed instruments
ISBN 0-688-31578-X
This is "an unusual book about the development of stringed instruments and differences between four main groups. The author traces the history of the harps, the piano family, the guitar family, and the violin family; he shows how, from the simpler forms, the instruments used today have evolved. Illustrations are clear, and instructions are given to the reader for making a simple version of each type of instrument from materials that may be found in the home." Chicago. Children's Bk Center
Musical terms: p48

788 Wind instruments and their music

Kettelkamp, Larry
Flutes, whistles and reeds; written and illus. by Larry Kettelkamp. Morrow 1962 illus lib. bdg. $4.81 (4-7) 788
1 Wind instruments
ISBN 0-688-31304-3
The author "discusses the instruments of the flute and reed families and the pipe organ. Briefly but clearly he explains how their sounds are produced, touches on the history of the instruments, and gives directions for making an elderberry whistle, a shepherd's pipe, a simplified version of a reed mouthpiece, and a soda-straw oboe. The simple text is illustrated with many drawings and photographs." Booklist

789 Percussion instruments

Kettelkamp, Larry
Drums, rattles, and bells; written and illus. by Larry Kettelkamp. Morrow 1960 47p illus lib. bdg. $5.11 (4-7) 789
1 Percussion instruments
ISBN 0-688-31247-0
The author "describes the four basic groups of percussion instruments: drums, rattles, bells, and keyboard. For each group of instruments there is a brief description of the earlier forms, an explanation of the way in which this type of percussion instrument is made, and some description of the various types used today. The instructions for making instruments at home require materials that are inexpensive or free, and ones easy to procure; directions for assembling the instrument are clear." Chicago. Children's Bk Center

"For music appreciation, or hobby and craft fun, this is an attractive and useful brief book. . . . Children should readily be intrigued." Horn Bk
Musical terms: p[48]

Price, Christine
Talking drums of Africa. Scribner 1973 unp illus map $5.95 (2-5) 789
1 Drum 2 Yorubas 3 Ashantis
ISBN 0-684-13492-6
This book tells "how various kinds of drums are made and played in a number of countries of western Africa. . . . Poems of the Yoruba people of Nigeria and the Ashanti people of Ghana are interpolated to illustrate uses of the drum for festivals and dances, as well as for messages and summonings." Horn Bk
"Price's rhythmic, repetitive, and mesmerizing prose evokes the sound of drums. The black-and-white prints with bright blue and gold overlays are powerful . . . the interesting format and style make this an attractive addition to African culture collections." Sch Library J

Yolen, Jane
Ring out! A book of bells; drawings by Richard Cuffari. Seabury 1974 128p illus $6.95 (5-7) 789
1 Bells
ISBN 0-8164-3127-2
"A Clarion book"
Legends and stories help document this historical description of using bells for religious, curative, political, communicative, musical, and other purposes. Bellringing and bellmaking are also considered. The final chapter contains poems and songs about bells
"A nicely illustrated book. . . . The text is adequately organized and is printed in one broad column, with italicized notes in the broad margin." Chicago. Children's Bk Center
Bibliography: p123-24

790 Recreational arts

Bancroft, Jessie Hubbell
Games. Rev. and enl. ed. of Games for the playground, home, school and gymnasium. Macmillan (N Y) 1937 685p illus music $9 790
1 Games
First published 1909
A "comprehensive guide to play-activities, games, and sports of all kinds, which has been a standard reference work. . . . [In the index] the games are carefully divided into classifications for age groups and school groups, from the primary groups, to colleges." Boston Transcript
Partial contents: Miscellaneous active games; Social and quiet games; Stunts and contests; Feats and forfeits; Singing games; Games for one or two; Beanbag games; Ball games; Track and field events
Includes "games of all countries, with music, diagrams and pictures where necessary. Though primarily for the teacher, this will be a treasury of entertainment for the children." N Y State Lib

Boston. Children's Hospital Medical Center
What to do when "there's nothing to do"; 601 tested play ideas for young children, by members of the staff of the Boston Children's Medical Center and Elizabeth M. Gregg. Illus. by Marc Simont. Delacorte Press 1968 158p illus (Publications for parents) $4.95 790
1 Play 2 Amusements
ISBN 0-8037-09466-6

Boston. Children's Hospital Medical Center—
Continued
"A Seymour Lawrence book"
The authors demonstrate how mothers can use
easy-to-find household items such as milk cartons,
spools, pipe cleaners, and macaroni to create inexpensive toys for the preschool child, age one month to six
years old
Includes sections on books and records for children
and a bibliography for parents

Hofsinde, Robert
Indian games and crafts; written and illus. by
Robert Hofsinde (Gray-Wolf) Morrow 1957 126p illus
$4.75 (4-7)
790
1 Indians of North America—Games
ISBN 0-688-21607-2
"These detailed instructions for making and playing
12 North American Indian games are clear, the diagrams and illustrations have exact measurements and
the materials to be used are easily obtained."
Bookmark
"The book will thus be useful both for the recreation hour and the craft period in summer camps,
schools and scout groups." Horn Bk

Hunt, Sarah Ethridge
Games and sports the world around; illus. by Max
Heldman. 3d ed. Ronald 1964 271p illus $6.95 790
1 Games 2 Sports
ISBN 0-8260-4565-0
First published 1941 by A. S. Barnes with title:
Games the world around
The author presents "games, sports, and play for
developing an understanding of human relationships.
Each activity is prefaced with headings indicating age
level, number of players, playing area, necessary
equipment, type, and intellectual appeal. Addressed
to teachers and recreation leaders, but useful also to
pupils." Hodges. Bks for Elem Sch Libraries
Definition of terms: p237. Books of games and
sports played in the United States: p242

Lavine, Sigmund A.
The games the Indians played; illus. with photographs and old prints. Dodd 1974 93p illus lib. bdg.
$4.95 (5-7)
790
1 Indians—Games
ISBN 0-396-06846-4
The author describes the games of chance and of
dexterity invented and played by Indians of the
Americas, including dice games, lacrosse, football,
archery, and cat's-cradle
"Many games of chance and skill are described
here, not with a 'how-to' approach but through the
eyes of an informed commentator on Indian ceremony and lore. This is a detailed survey, amplified
with black-and-white photographs and reproductions
of artwork. . . . It will be useful for collections of
Indian studies materials." Booklist

Mulac, Margaret E.
Games and stunts for schools, camps, and playgrounds; illus. by Julianne. Harper 1964 362p illus
music $8.95
790
1 Games
ISBN 0-06-004500-0
This book provides a selection of various types of
games: classroom games and activities; hide and seek;
circle and line games; picnic games and contests; tag
and chase games; dance mixers; group stunts;
sidewalk games; word and spelling games. A piano
score is included for many games
"The book will prove invaluable to parents,
teachers, counselors and recreation workers." Bks of
the Year, 1965

790.19 Activities for specific classes of people

Ellison, Virginia H.
The Pooh get-well book; recipes and activities to
help you recover from wheezles and sneezles;
inspired by the four Pooh books by A. A. Milne; illus.
by Ernest H. Shepard. Dutton 1973 81p illus $5.95
(2-5)
790.19
1 Amusements 2 Sick
ISBN 0-525-37440-X
This "activity book inspired by the Pooh books
includes puzzles, quiet games, and simple crafts
designed to engage the attention of the convalescent
child. Each activity is accompanied by a related quotation from a Milne book and by a familiar illustration.
. . . The section entitled 'Strengthening Things To
Drink and Eat,' . . . [contains recipes for such] foods
as Honey and Lemon Juice for a Squeaky Voice, Hot
Clove Oranges, Crustimoney Proseedcake, and
Bananas With Thistles in Honey and Cream." Horn
Bk
"A subdued and sophisticated format, original
Ernest Shepard line drawings, and numerous refer-
ences to and quotes from Milne's works approximate
the tone evoked in the originals." Booklist

791.3 Circuses

De Regniers, Beatrice Schenk
Circus; photographs by Al Giese. Viking 1966 unp
illus lib. bdg. $5.95 (k-3)
791.3
1 Circus
ISBN 0-670-22272-0
"Color photographs of performing lions, elephants,
clowns, acrobats, and other circus artists together
with a minimum of rhythmic text capture remarkably
well the glitter, the breathless excitement, and enchantment of the circus." Booklist

Great days of the circus, by the editors of American
Heritage, The Magazine of History; narrative by
Freeman Hubbard, in consultation with Leonard V.
Farley. Am. Heritage 1962 153p illus $5.95, lib.
bdg. $6.89 (5-7)
791.3
1 Circus
ISBN 0-06-022630-7; 0-06-022631-5
"American Heritage Junior library"
A book that is "comprehensive, attractive, and nostalgic. . . . [It is] gay and colorful from blue bareback
rider and yellow acrobats on the cover to the old print
of an action-filled circus ring which forms the end
paper. Particularly valuable to have in one book are
the many examples of brilliant circus posters which at
one time dotted our national landscape. The first
chapter describes in detail a typical day when the
circus came to town. Others tell of famous performers
[clowns, trapeze artists] and animal acts, of Barnum,
of the problems involved in moving a circus from
place to place, and much else, all of it fascinating."
Horn Bk
For further reading: p149

Hornby, John
Clowns through the ages; illus. by Siriol Clarry.
Walck, H.Z. [1965 c1962] 60p illus $4 (3-5) 791.3
1 Clowns
ISBN 0-8098-2035-8

Hornby, John—*Continued*
"The Byways library"
First published 1962 in England
"With odd, miscellaneous, and some interesting bits of information, the clown's lineage is traced through the ages from the 'danga' of Pharaoh's court, the 'cicirrus' and 'stupidus' in Rome, the court jesters in medieval Europe to the modern circus clown. Lively cartoons illustrate the text." Sch Library J

791.43   Motion pictures

Edelson, Edward
Great monsters of the movies. Doubleday 1973 101p illus $4.95, lib. bdg. $5.70 (4-6)   791.43
1 Monsters 2 Moving pictures—History
ISBN 0-385-00668-3; 0-385-00857-0
Here is a collection of movie monsters from the dinosaurs of silent film to the teen-age vampires of more recent films, with an historical narration of horror stories and legends. It is also an account of the actors who played famous monster roles
"The extensive use of film stills—including a shot of Lon Chaney as the Phantom, and King Kong perched atop his favorite building—should please all of those who love a monster." Horn Bk

791.45   Television

Harris, Leon
Behind the scenes of television programs; with photographs by the author. Lippincott 1972 48p illus $3.50 (4-6)   791.45
1 Television broadcasting
ISBN 0-397-31220-2
In text and photographs, the author describes the various steps followed to produce a television program, and introduces the reader to the people involved, from the producer to the creators of special effects

791.5   Puppetry. Shadow theaters

Adair, Margaret Weeks
Do-it-in-a-day puppets for beginners; how to make your puppets, create your script, and perform—all in one day. Day 1964 89p illus $5.95 (2-5)   791.5
1 Puppets and puppet plays
ISBN 0-381-97098-1
This book contains everything "necessary for instant production of three puppet plays: scripts, directions for making easy puppets and constructing a stage, and production notes. The plays are: 'Three Billy Goats Gruff,' 'King Midas and the Golden Touch,' and 'The Three Little Pigs.' " Hodges. Bks for Elem Sch Libraries

Folk puppet plays for the social studies [by] Margaret Weeks Adair and Elizabeth Patapoff. Day 1972 120p illus music $6.95 (2-5)   791.5
1 Puppets and puppet plays 2 Folklore
ISBN 0-381-97001-9
This "book contains texts of 16 short plays and shows ways to use puppetry as an explanation of societal origins of peoples of the U.S., Europe, Africa,

and Japan. The introduction describes basic techniques of puppetry as an adjunct to classroom theater, and the concluding chapters give ways to successfully dramatize folk stories, and tell how to use puppets in shadow plays, mock television shows, and in pantomime. Additional information is provided on acting and production tricks as well as on creation of the puppets and related effects. . . . A brief list of readings is appended." Booklist
"An excellent reference book for a classroom where children are responsible for the production of their own plays." Notable Children's Trade Bks (Social Studies)
Includes a bibliography

Andersen, Benny E.
Let's start a puppet theatre. Van Nostrand-Reinhold 1973 91p illus $4.95 (4-7)   791.5
1 Puppets and puppet plays
ISBN 0-442-29986-9
Original Danish edition, 1971
A "charming instruction manual on all sorts of simple puppets, puppet theatres, costumes, materials and where to get them, and everything else you need to know to keep puppetry fun and simple. The illustrations are profuse and pertinent, mostly of children doing things." Ref Serv Rev

Cochrane, Louise
Shadow puppets in color; illus. by Kate Simunek. Plays, Inc. 1972 48p illus (The Puppet lib) $4.95 (2-5)   791.5
1 Shadow pantomimes and plays
ISBN 0-8238-0139-X
Published in England with title: Shadows in colour
"Providing an introduction to shadow puppetry, this book fills a gap for primary-school children. Three main styles—Chinese, Greek, and Javanese—are presented along with very short adaptations of traditional plays. The book contains detailed instructions with patterns to trace, an easy-to-follow guide to making shadow theaters, and suggested production techniques. Cochrane's clear text supported by Simunek's illustrations will be useful in school libraries." Sch Library J

Tabletop theatres; illus. by Kate Simunek. Plays, Inc. [1974 c1973] 48p illus (The Puppet lib) $4.95 (4-6)   791.5
1 Puppets and puppet plays 2 Theaters—Models
ISBN 0-8238-0155-1
First published 1973 in England
This book "gives directions for making four kinds of stages, puppets, and costumes, and includes scripts for plays. . . . The instructions are clear and most of the materials inexpensive and easily obtained; characters include both hand-puppets and marionettes." Chicago. Children's Bk Center
"One of those books useful to libraries and schools, which treats a marginal subject on which little material exists." Times (London) Literary Sup

Engler, Larry
Making puppets come alive; a method of learning and teaching hand puppetry [by] Larry Engler and Carol Fijan; photography by David Attie; demonstration puppets designed by Paul Vincent Davis. Taplinger [1974 c1973] 192p illus $9.95   791.5
1 Puppets and puppet plays
ISBN 0-8008-5074-2
The book "opens with a brief description of puppetry as a performing art, an explanation of what a puppet is and how to make one. Since the text is for beginners, most of the puppets discussed and pictured are those activated by hand, not with rods and

Engler, Larry—*Continued*
strings. Instructions on how to manipulate and control the little fantasy figures are also included." Pub W
Bibliography of recommended books: p190-91

Jagendorf, Moritz
Penny puppets, penny theatre, and penny plays; illus. by Fletcher Clark. Plays, Inc. [1966 c1941] 190p illus $6.95 (4-7)   791.5
1 Puppets and puppet plays
ISBN 0-8238-0071-7
Reissue of a book first published 1941 by Bobbs Merrill
"Besides instructions on how to make and manipulate different kinds of puppets—push, rod, hand, and the five- and seven-string marionette—there are suggestions for the help needed in more difficult procedures. Acting, staging, design, and lighting are dealt with in some detail. The book also includes a selection of nine easy-to-produce plays with helpful production notes for the young puppeteer." Sch Library J

Lewis, Shari
Making easy puppets; illus. by Larry Lurin. Dutton 1967 86p illus $6.95 (3-6)   791.5
1 Puppets and puppet plays
ISBN 0-525-34484-5
"Many different materials, such as apples, squash and paper plates are used in the construction of the puppets; but there are also instructions for paper bag and stick puppets. . . . Directions also for making stages and easily draped bodies. Included is a brief history of puppetry." Bruno. Bks for Sch Libraries
"Careful, informal instructions add to the fun-time atmosphere. . . . The book will be more useful as craft than as puppetry." Sch Library J
Includes bibliography

Mahlmann, Lewis
Puppet plays for young players; 12 royalty-free plays for hand puppets, rod puppets or marionettes, by Lewis Mahlmann and David Cadwalader Jones. Plays, Inc. 1974 194p illus $7.95 (4-7)   791.5
1 Puppets and puppet plays
ISBN 0-8238-0152-7
"Plays written for children are frequently cutesy or with no emotion stronger than boo-hoo. Happily, most of the 12 puppet plays in this collection (most adapted from fairy tales and favorite children's stories) offer humor or fast paced action and, in the Queen in 'Snow White,' a flash of genuine hatred. Production notes for each play and a section on producing a puppet play will be very useful. The plays range from 3-17 puppets (hand, rod, or marionettes) and from simple to quite difficult. Should be great fun." Children's Bk Rev Serv

Mendoza, George
Shadowplay [by] George Mendoza with Prasanna Rao; photographs by Marc Mainguy. Holt 1974 unp illus lib. bdg. $5.95 (3-6)   791.5
1 Shadow pantomimes and plays
ISBN 0-03-007881-4
"Even though readers are encouraged to practice forming these intricate and often stunning shadows with their own hands, this collection of silhouette images functions not as a how-to book but primarily as a record of a fascinating art form. Twenty-six animals, objects, and scenes are created by master artist Prasanna Rao; the silhouette is shown on the right page of the spread, a black-and-white photograph of the hand configuration on the left. A few hand exercises are demonstrated at the end, but even these require more dexterity than most children or adults can boast. The shadows themselves are nearly all too

difficult for a beginner to make successfully; still, this is a rare visual treat." Booklist

Pels, Gertrude
Easy puppets; making and using hand puppets; illus. by Albert Pels. Crowell 1951 104p illus $4.50, lib. bdg. $5.25 (3-6)   791.5
1 Puppets and puppet plays
ISBN 0-690-25377-X; 0-690-25378-8
"The step-by-step processes of making simple puppets and giving puppet plays are clearly explained and illustrated in this practical book. . . . By following the book's diagrams and instructions, children can construct and operate puppets made from such materials as apples, bottle-caps, clothespins, and buttons. Directions for making papier-mâché heads and improvised stages are also included." Library J
"Over-all, this how-to book has a wide appeal and will start many a child off on a creative experience." N Y Times Bk Rev

Punch & Judy; a play for puppets; illus. by Ed Emberley. Little 1965 27p illus $3.95 (1-5)   791.5
1 Puppets and puppet plays
ISBN 0-316-23584-9
"An excellent version of the age old 'Punch and Judy' ready for presentation by young performers. The puppet-play is introduced by a brief history of Punch and an illustrated list of characters." Wis Library Bul
"Breezily drawn figures, crosshatched with jarring colors, go whacking and smacking their way through a performance crowded with fast-swinging comedy." Horn Bk

Ross, Laura
Finger puppets; easy to make, fun to use; illus. by Laura and Frank Ross, Jr. Lothrop 1971 64p illus lib. bdg. $4.81, pa $2.50 (k-3)   791.5
1 Puppets and puppet plays
ISBN 0-688-35014-3; 0-688-45013-X
This book "gives clear step-by-step directions for making nine different types of simple finger puppets. Some of the puppets require only bare hands and paint while others are made from scraps of cloth, cardboard, or other readily obtainable materials. [The author] also includes several folktales and poems and tells how to dramatize them using the finger puppets; a list of books of rhymes, songs, and stories is appended." Booklist

Hand puppets; how to make and use them; written and illus. by Laura Ross. Lothrop 1969 192p illus lib. bdg. $5.81, pa $2.95 (k-2)   791.5
1 Puppets and puppet plays
ISBN 0-688-51615-7; 0-688-45015-6
For beginners as well as those with some experience, this book provides step-by-step directions and diagrams for making simple paper-bag, rod, and papier-mâché puppets. The book also contains instructions for dressing and handling puppets, setting up a stage, and writing and producing one's own puppet show. It also includes three puppet plays: Rumpelstiltskin, Punch and Judy, and A visit from outer space
"This is one of the clearest, most thorough, and easiest-to-follow presentations on the subject for children. While her instructions are explicit the author encourages the reader to modify and improvise." Booklist
List of terms: p14. Some other useful books: p189

Holiday puppets; drawings and diagrams by Frank and Laura Ross. Lothrop 1974 223p illus $6.95, lib. bdg. $5.81 (4-6)   791.5

Ross, Laura—*Continued*
1 Puppets and puppet plays
ISBN 0-688-41556-3; 0-688-51556-8
Using holiday themes, this book features instructions for making several types of puppets and stage properties, as well as appropriate plays and stories. The selected holidays are: Lincoln's and Washington's birthdays, St. Valentine's, St. Patrick's and Columbus Days, Purim, Easter, Halloween, Thanksgiving, and Christmas

"Patterns and photographs clarify the detailed written instructions for puppet-making. Although the plays are far from great drama, they are pleasant and lend themselves to easy productions using a wide variety of appealing puppets and special effects." Sch Library J

Puppet shows using poems and stories; drawings by Frank Ross, Jr. Lothrop 1970 192p illus lib. bdg. $5.81 (3-6)   791.5
1 Puppets and puppet plays
ISBN 0-688-51639-4
"A collection of poems and stories suitable for dramatization using hand puppets, shadow puppets, and pantomime, with production notes for each selection covering technique, cast, setting, and action. Contains nursery rhymes, narrative poems, ballads, fables, folk tales, modern stories and Bible stories. . . . A useful book for both adults working with groups of children and for individual puppeteers." Booklist

The author has selected these materials "with imagination and skill. . . . Her introductory articles concerning the origins and background of puppetry are of particular value." America
Further reading: p191. Index of titles: p192

Tichenor, Tom
Tom Tichenor's puppets. Text, drawings and photographs by Tom Tichenor. Abingdon 1971 224p illus $6.95 (5-7)   791.5
1 Puppets and puppet plays
ISBN 0-687-42363-5
"A practical guide to puppetry includes chapters on hand puppets, and on marionettes, with several plays included for each kind. The photographs are useful, particularly in showing details of costume or of the manipulation of the puppets, and the book includes instructions on making puppets, costumes, and stages, and on mounting the plays. One chapter is devoted to using puppets in the story hour, another to use in the classroom, in movies, and in plays with people. The writing style is informal, with . . . casual and useful bits of advice, drawn from [the author's] experience, on drawing faces, choosing materials, sewing, etc. A bibliography and an index are appended." Sutherland. The Best in Children's Bks

Wiesner, William
Hansel and Gretel: a shadow puppet picture book; adapted from the versions of Ludwig Bechstein and the Brothers Grimm. Seabury 1971 40p illus $6.50 (1-4)   791.5
1 Shadow pantomimes and plays 2 Fairy tales
ISBN 0-8164-3020-9
Presented in the form of a shadow play, this is the tale of the brave children, the gingerbread house, and the wicked witch, with illustrations by the author. Instructions for creating a theatre and puppets and for mounting a production are included along with a list of books about shadows and shadow plays

"A good deal of manual dexterity would seem to be required, which might prove frustrating to many children in the publisher's stipulated age group. This sort of book should inspire children (and teachers) to go on to writing their own scripts and designing their own sets." Pub W

792   Theater (Stage presentations)

Carlson, Bernice Wells
Act it out; illus. by Laszlo Matulay. Abingdon 1956 160p illus $3.50, pa $1.95 (3-7)   792
1 Acting 2 Amateur theatricals 3 Puppets and puppet plays
ISBN 0-687-00713-5; 0-687-00714-3
This book on simple dramatics for children is divided into two parts, the first devoted to acting, the second to puppet performances. Included are examples of acting games, pantomime games and plays, dramatic stunts, tableaux, plays, pageants, and puppet plays with directions for making and using several kinds of puppets

"Brief bibliographies at the back list other, more detailed, books on various aspects of acting and puppetry. A useful book for club and hobby groups." Chicago. Children's Bk Center

Let's pretend it happened to you; a real-people and storybook-people approach to creative dramatics; illus. by Ralph J. McDonald. Abingdon 1973 110p illus $5.95 (k-3)   792
1 Acting 2 Folklore
ISBN 0-687-21503-X
"Intended as a beginning guide in creative dramatics, this also 'encourages the understanding of other people' through acting and attempts to teach self-discipline. Eleven well-chosen tales from around the world can be acted out easily and provide a moral, too. Entertaining, often comical, two-tone drawings accompany each story, which is preceded by an introductory activity that prepares children for the ensuing minidrama. An introduction for teachers explains the [book's] approach and also gives tips on dramatic exercises for young children." Sch Library J
More books to read: p107

Play a part; drawings by Catherine H. Scholz. Abingdon 1970 240p illus $5.95 (3-6)   792
1 Acting 2 Amateur theatricals 3 Drama—Collections
ISBN 0-687-31637-5
Included in this guide for the young actor are instructions on acting and over thirty original puppet plays, playlets, dramatic scenes, skits, real-life dramas and plays. A description of the scene, characters and props precedes each

"Children are told in easy-to-understand language how to understand the play, how to breathe, learn the lines, feel the part and then play it. The importance of research and teamwork is emphasized." Sch Library J
Glossary of a few stage terms: p233-34. Other books to help you: p235-36

The right play for you; illus. by Georgette Boris. Abingdon 1960 160p illus $3.75, pa $2.75 (4-7) 792
1 Amateur theatricals 2 Drama—Collections
ISBN 0-687-36376-4; 0-687-36401-9
"Original and very useful book. Practical, clear suggestions for producing plays [including casting and staging] for adapting them for particular groups, for writing plays from stories, fables, legends, or true events, and for dramatizing jokes or holiday themes. Twenty original plays are given as examples and, except for an occasional slang expression, are well written. Illustrations in black and white by Georgette Boris are suitable." Library J
A few stage terms: p160

Smith, Moyne Rice

Plays &—how to put them on; illus. by Don Bolognese. Walck, H.Z. 1961 169p illus lib. bdg. $5.75 (4-7)   792

1 Amateur theatricals 2 Drama—Collections
ISBN 0-8098-2352-7

"Beginning with an explanation of stage terms, this helpful book offers advice on choosing, planning, organizing, and rehearsing a play and on basic theater equipment. It also suggests stories suitable for dramatization, lists a number of good ready-made plays, and includes the scripts for seven plays, complete with production notes." Booklist

Some helpful books: p169

(ed.) 7 plays & how to produce them; illus. by Don Bolognese. Walck, H.Z. 1968 148p illus lib. bdg. $5.75 (4-7)   792

1 Amateur theatricals 2 Drama—Collections
ISBN 0-8098-2404-3

A selection of "short plays that have been . . . adapted by children from fairy tales and stories including Andersen's 'The swineherd,' Grimm's 'The elves and the shoemaker,' and an episode from Hale's 'The Peterkin papers.' Each play is accompanied by production notes and sketches of stage settings and props." Booklist

"The adaptations are fresh, imaginative, and humorous; the production notes give some clues as to mood and tempo as well as to technicalities; moreover, the plays can be further adapted for larger or smaller casts." Sat Rev

Some helpful books: p148

792.3   Pantomime

Howard, Vernon

Pantomimes, charades & skits; with drawings by Shizu. [Rev. ed] Sterling 1974 128p illus $3.95, lib. bdg. $3.99 (4-6)   792.3

1 Charades 2 Pantomimes
ISBN 0-8069-7004-9; 0-8069-7005-7
First published 1959

The author describes the techniques involved in the silent portrayal of dramatic situations using body language, dramatic gesture, and facial expressions

"Included are over 100 games, most with 10 to 20 or more suggestions for play. Howard is thorough on the subject of mime games (not traditional white-face mime) and provides an imaginative collection of popular stunts and games designed for parties, workshops, and classrooms." Sch Library J

792.8   Ballet

Chappell, Warren

The Nutcracker; adapted and illus. by Warren Chappell. Knopf 1958 unp illus $2.95 (2-5)   792.8

1 Ballets—Stories, plots, etc. 2 Christmas stories
ISBN 0-394-80742-1

"Based on the [Alexandre] Dumas version of E. T. A. Hoffmann's story is the fantasy of the Nutcracker who fights the Mouse King; of the bewitched Princess Pirlipate and her handsome rescuer. All these—and more—adventures are the dreams of Marie, the little girl who received a toy nutcracker for Christmas, and who grew up to wed a handsome young man exactly like the imagined suitor of the Princess." Chicago. Children's Bk Center

"The struggle between the gallant little nutcracker and the wicked seven-headed mouse king is brought to life vividly in this picture book fantasy. . . . The full-page coloured illustrations and black and white border decorations are reminiscent of nineteenth century German woodcuts." Ontario Library Rev

The Sleeping Beauty; adapted and illus. by Warren Chappell; from the tales of Charles Perrault; music by Peter Ilyich Tschaikovsky. Knopf 1961 unp illus lib. bdg. $5.39 (1-4)   792.8

1 Ballets—Stories, plots, etc.
ISBN 0-394-90762-0

A retelling of the fairy tale ballet of the beautiful Princess who is put to sleep for one hundred years until a Prince awakens her

"A companion piece to 'The Nutcracker,' [entered above]. Again we have the story in its simplest form so that it can be read to five-year-olds, and again for each step in the tale a musical phrase is given." N Y Her Trib Bks

"The illustrations, done in deep rich colors, are very handsome, but perhaps somewhat too solid and heavy to convey fairy tales or ballets." Pub W

Draper, Nancy

Ballet for beginners, by Nancy Draper and Margaret F. Atkinson. Knopf 1951 115p illus music $4.95, lib. bdg. $6.99 (5-7)   792.8

1 Ballet
ISBN 0-394-80929-7; 0-394-90929-1

Children's ballet class photographs by Fred Lyon; drawings by Margaret F. Atkinson; music adapted and arranged by Beatrix B. Woolard

"Photographs and charts along with the clearly written text show the basic ballet positions and tell children how to practise. Included also are several pages with music . . . photographs and brief biographical sketches of a few famous ballerinas; a history of the ballet; synopses of some of the ballets especially appealing to young people; and a dictionary of ballet terms." Horn Bk

Bibliography: p113-15

Freeman, Mae

Fun with ballet. Random House 1952 60p illus $2.95, lib. bdg. $3.79 (4-7)   792.8

1 Ballet
ISBN 0-394-80276-4; 0-394-90276-9

"Photographs and clear instructive text demonstrate the five positions and the movements and exercises in ballet dancing. Methods most generally used in the training of beginners are shown; how, why, and where to practice and the object of certain routines are explained, and beginners are warned against attempting toe-dancing before consulting an experienced teacher. Ballet terms with pronunciation are given." Booklist

"Inexpensive and extremely accurate, this is a ballet book for every library where there is interest in the art." Library J

Mara, Thalia

First steps in ballet; basic barre exercises for home practice, by Thalia Mara with Lee Wyndham; illus. by George Bobrizky. Doubleday 1955 64p illus $4.95 (4-7)   792.8

1 Ballet
ISBN 0-385-02432-0
First published by Garden City Bks.

With numerous illustrations, this book explains twelve elementary ballet barre exercises for the beginning student. The correct balletic terms are given in French, with the phonetic pronunciation of each, as well as their meanings; and the purpose and function of each exercise

Streatfeild, Noel

A young person's guide to ballet; drawings by Georgette Bordier. Warne 1975 120p illus $7.95 (6-7) 792.8

1 Ballet
ISBN 0-7232-1814-5

Focusing on two children, Anna and Peter, the author shows how they learn the basic steps of ballet, the book also provides a brief history of ballet, and describes some ballet stories and film ballets, leading dancers, and other forms of dancing

"The author is an expert on her subject. Through her simple, precise text, we learn how much discipline and sweat is required to create the illusion that ballet movements are as easy and natural as breathing. . . . Skillful sketches and photos, along with period illustrations, add to the value of an outstanding contender for shelf space." Pub W

Untermeyer, Louis

Tales from the ballet; adapted by Louis Untermeyer; illus. by A. and M. Provensen. Golden Press 1968 91p illus $7.93 (4-6) 792.8

1 Ballets—Stories, plots, etc.
ISBN 0-307-67852-0

The author "abstracts the plots of 20 well-known ballets, including 'Swan Lake,' 'Billy the Kid,' 'Children's games,' 'Coppelia,' 'Rodeo,' 'The rite of spring,' and 'Fancy free.' . . . A brief introduction sketches the history of ballet, and production notes at the end of the book mention story sources, choreographers, and composers." Booklist

"A big beautiful book. . . . Untermeyer lends a light, warm touch to his recital of the plots . . . putting words into the mouths of his characters that 'suggest what they would say if they could speak.' . . . But it is the Provensens' magnificent illustrations, their finest to date, that evoke the enchantment, poetry, color, humor and drama of ballet and give the book its distinction." Bk World

793 Indoor games and amusements

Carlson, Bernice Wells

Do it yourself! Tricks, stunts, and skits; illus. by Laszlo Matulay. Abingdon 1952 159p illus $3.50, pa $2.25 (4-7) 793

1 Amusements 2 Tricks 3 Skits
ISBN 0-687-11007-6; 0-687-11008-4

A volume for young readers showing how to do a variety of tricks, ranging from the very simple to the more complicated; some stunts, both physical and mental; and some brief dramatizations

"For the planned or impromptu party this collection of tricks, stunts and skits offers fun for both performers and audience." N Y Times Bk Rev

Cassell, Sylvia

Indoor games and activities; with 55 drawings by Sylvia S. Cassell. Harper 1960 115p illus $4.95 (3-7) 793

1 Amusements 2 Games
ISBN 0-06-021150-4

"A variety of indoor projects and amusements that children can enjoy alone or in groups are included in this practical guide. Suggestions for arts and crafts, puzzles, recipes, games, science experiments, and special parties are described in simply written text." Chicago

Harbin, E. O.

Games of many nations. Abingdon 1954 160p illus $3.95 793

1 Games
ISBN 0-687-13990-2

A "collection of about 150 games from nearly 30 nations. Full, clear instructions for playing each game are given and similarities to games of different countries are indicated. Includes a chapter on forfeits, listing 58 forfeit stunts. . . . The U.S. is represented by games of the American Indian." Booklist

"The games vary in difficulty, with diagrams supplied when necessary, and directions for making whatever equipment may be needed for playing. . . . Though the directions are easy enough for the middle age child to read and follow, the book will probably be most useful to leaders of child groups. Two indices, one alphabetical, the other classified by type of game." Horn Bk

Helfman, Harry

Strings on your fingers; how to make string figures [by] Harry and Elizabeth Helfman; illus. by William Meyerriecks. Morrow 1965 47p illus lib. bdg. $4.59 (3-6) 793

1 Games
ISBN 0-688-31582-8

"When you make a 'cat's cradle' on your fingers you are indulging in one of the oldest forms of amusement—this and other intriguing facts about string are accompanied by instructions for constructing string figures." Cincinnati

Bibliography: p[48]

793.2 Parties and entertainments

Ellison, Virginia H.

The Pooh Party book; inspired by Winnie-the-Pooh and The house at Pooh Corner by A. A. Milne; illus. by Ernest H. Shepard. Dutton 1971 145p illus $5.50 (1-5) 793.2

1 Parties 2 Cookery 3 Games
ISBN 0-525-37480-9

Explanatory drawings by Grambs Miller

Here are "ideas for invitations, decorations, favors, games, and food for five Pooh-inspired parties, including an Eeyore birthday party, a spring party, a picnic and expotition party, a honey-tasting party, and a woozle-wizzle snow party (Christmas). Although the directions and supplementary drawings are generally clear, some of the projects and recipes will require adult assistance or supervision. Quotations and illustrations from the Pooh books are interspersed throughout, and large drawings of Pooh and his friends, suitable for tracing, are appended." Booklist

Frame, Jean

How to give a party, by Jean and Paul Frame; illus. by Paul Frame. Watts, F. 1972 90p illus lib. bdg. $3.90, pa $1.25 (4-6) 793.2

1 Parties
ISBN 0-531-00759-6; 0-531-02401-6

"A First book"

"In a helpful guide to party giving from planning to entertaining the guests the authors consider nine themes—among them balloon, circus, monster, and winter parties. For each they provide a list of supplies, practical decorating ideas with specific instructions for carrying them out, and somewhat unimaginative menus complete with simple recipes. They also

Frame, Jean—*Continued*
describe a variety of familiar but fun games, some active, others quiet, and a number for beginning or ending a party. The many clear sketches augment the directions." Booklist

Freeman, Lois M.
Betty Crocker's Parties for children, by Lois M. Freeman; illus. by Judy and Barry Martin. Golden Press 1964 166p illus $6 (1-5)   793.2
1 Parties 2 Games
ISBN 0-307-69603-0
First published 1964
The book includes invitations, refreshments, decorations, party favors, and suggestions for party themes, as well as instructions for over 150 games and other activities
"Colorfully and aptly illustrated. . . . The first 35 pages, on planning and organizing parties, will be a great help to adults who, after all, do throw the parties. Age levels and number of players are designated for the games explained on pages 36-141. Two pages of ideas for parties for handicapped children are of special note." Sch Library J

793.3   Dancing

Baylor, Byrd
Sometimes I dance mountains; photographs by Bill Sears; drawings by Ken Longtemps. Scribner 1973 unp illus lib. bdg. $5.95 (k-3)   793.3
1 Modern dance
ISBN 0-684-13440-3
In this introduction to modern dance, the author puts into words the feelings shown by a young girl in her dancing
"The illustrations are innovative in combining photography and sweeping design." Pub W

Powers, William K.
Here is your hobby: Indian dancing and costumes. Putnam 1966 125p illus (Here is your hobby ser) lib. bdg. $4.69 (5-7)   793.3
1 Indians of North America—Dances 2 Indians of North America—Social life and customs
ISBN 0-399-60249-6
"The 22 chapters include 10 complete dances, basic steps, correct body movements, singing and drumming, appropriate costumes, how to build a dance area and run a pow-wow. There is a complete index, and the classified list of sources includes Indian record companies, various suppliers and museums, along with appropriate books." Sch Library J
"Of interest to the individual hobbyist who wants to participate in Indian celebrations and to school, club, or camp groups." Booklist

793.7   Games not characterized by action. Riddles

Adler, Irving
Magic house of numbers; illus. by Ruth Adler and Peggy Adler. Rev. ed. Day 1974 143p illus lib. bdg. $4.68 (6-7)   793.7
1 Mathematical recreations
ISBN 0-381-99986-6
First published 1957
This book presents mathematical puzzles, riddles, tricks, Fibonacci and Lucas numbers, and number oddities which introduce the basis of our number system. It also shows different methods of counting

Barr, George
Entertaining with number tricks; illus. by Mildred Waltrip. McGraw 1971 143p illus lib. bdg. $4.77 (5-7)   793.7
1 Mathematical recreations
ISBN 0-07-003842-2
Contents: Showmanship—parading your genius; What is your favorite number; Guessing Aunt Tillie's age; Please take a number; The magic of 1089; Sum addition stunts; Fun with cards, tickets, and tags; Those fascinating magic squares; Crazy arithmetic; More baffling tricks; Puzzles, riddles, and nonsense; Let's talk algebra
The author "describes each trick clearly, step by step, explaining the mathematical principle involved and suggesting patter to divert the audience. . . . Line drawings supplement the text." Booklist

Cerf, Bennett
Bennett Cerf's Book of animal riddles; illus. by Roy McKie. Beginner Bks. 1964 62p illus $2.95, lib. bdg. $3.69 (k-3)   793.7
1 Riddles
ISBN 0-394-80034-6; 0-394-90034-0
Title on spine: Animal riddles
A book of easy-reading riddles about animals such as "Why are fish so smart? They always go around in schools"
"The kind of humor that adults find obvious and absurd but most children think hilarious. . . . Roy McKie's boldly madcap illustrations have the same tongue-in-cheek spirit." N Y Times Bk Rev

Bennett Cerf's Book of riddles; illus. by Roy McKie. Beginner Bks. 1960 62p illus $2.95, lib. bdg. $3.69 (k-2)   793.7
1 Riddles
ISBN 0-394-80015-X; 0-394-90015-4
These thirty-one riddles are arranged with the riddles being asked on one page and answered on the next, to keep the element of surprise
"Mr. Cerf has collected riddles which are very funny to a child and pleasantly nostalgic to an adult. He has also avoided using the old crutches, giving new twists to many of the riddles." N Y Times Bk Rev
"Simple cartoonlike drawings use strong colour for their effect." Ontario Library Rev

Charosh, Mannis
Mathematical games for one or two; illus. by Lois Ehlert. Crowell 1972 33p illus (Young math bks) $4.50, lib. bdg. $5.25 (1-4)   793.7
1 Mathematical recreations
ISBN 0-690-52324-6; 0-690-52325-4
Each of these six groups of games—pyramid games, shifting games, checker games, take-away games, nim games, and magic tricks—begins with an elementary version and continues with more complex versions in a way that illustrates the basic logical or mathematical principle so that the reader may develop the game still further
"Lois Ehlert's colorful, lively illustrations add humor and her diagrams help to clarify the text. An enjoyable book which will aid in sharpening perception of pattern and sequence." Sch Library J

Chrystie, Frances N.
The first book of jokes and funny things; pictures—Ida Scheib. Watts, F. 1951 unp illus $3.90 (3-6)   793.7
1 Amusements 2 Wit and humor
ISBN 0-531-00566-6

Chrystie, Frances N.—*Continued*

"Jokes, riddles, games, tongue twisters, and funny things to make and do, with illustrations as laughable as the contents." Hodges. Bks for Elem Sch Libraries

"Many children are going to have a lot of fun with this book. It has just the right sort of nonsense that boys and girls . . . enjoy. The little games and amusing tricks would be helpful when children are recuperating from illness." Library J

Riddle me this; pictures by Elizabeth B. Ripley. Walck, H.Z. 1940 unp illus $3.25, pa $1.35 (2-5)
                  793.7

1 Riddles
ISBN 0-8098-1005-0
First published by Oxford

Many boys and girls have contributed to this collection of riddles for young readers. The questions are in black, the answers in red, and the illustrations are humorous line drawings

De Regniers, Beatrice Schenk

It does not say meow, and other animal riddle rhymes; pictures by Paul Galdone. Seabury 1972 unp illus $5.95 (k-1)   793.7

1 Riddles 2 Animals—Poetry
ISBN 0-8164-3086-1

A "riddle book for the very young in which clues to the identity of each of nine different animals including a cat, elephant, ant, dog, frog, and mice are given in a short rhyming verse and full-page illustration. The correct answer appears in a captioned double-spread picture on the following pages." Booklist

"Young readers will relate to the children in the book who are pictured visiting the zoo, watching birds, playing Indians, etc. The colorful illustrations are appealing." Sch Library J

Doty, Roy

Puns, gags, quips and riddles; a collection of dreadful jokes. Doubleday 1974 unp illus $4.95, lib. bdg. $5.70 (4-6)   793.7

1 Wit and humor 2 Riddles
ISBN 0-385-06051-3; 0-385-06057-2

The author's "irreverent brand of humor will appeal to inveterate joke collectors. The generous selection is spaced two to a page and each gag is surrounded by an apropos cartoon. Most follow a simple question-answer form and are drawn, as the title implies, from a mixed bag of puns and riddles. A good choice for replenishing the well-used joke book shelf." Booklist

Gardner, Martin

Perplexing puzzles and tantalizing teasers; illus. by Laszlo Kubinyi. Simon & Schuster 1969 95p illus $5.95, lib. bdg. $4.79 (4-7)   793.7

1 Puzzles 2 Riddles
ISBN 0-671-65057-2; 0-671-65058-0

"Among the puzzles included are tricky questions, teasers, droodles, handies, palindromes, mazes, typitoons, and illusions." Booklist

"The problems are simple but few have too-obvious answers; there are enough sticklers to tempt the quick child but not so many as to discourage the slow thinker. Illustrations are clear, and answers are given at the back of the book. There are a few answers for which no logical clues have been given, but very few." Chicago. Children's Bk Center

Gilbreath, Alice Thompson

Beginning-to-read riddles and jokes; illus. by Susan Perl. Follett 1967 30p illus lib. bdg. $2.75, pa $1.50 (1-3)   793.7

1 Riddles 2 Wit and humor
ISBN 0-695-37740-X; 0-695-47740-4

"A certain success with beginning readers, this will help fill the never-ending request for joke and riddle books. Susan Perl's unusual and clever illustrations are just right for jokes and riddles." Bruno. Bks for Sch Libraries, 1968

Harshaw, Ruth

In what book? By Ruth Harshaw and Hope Harshaw Evans; foreword by Mildred L. Batchelder. Macmillan (N Y) 1970 130p $4.50   793.7

1 Children's literature—Examinations, questions, etc.

"Here is a handy book of intriguing questions, with answers, about more than 400 well-chosen children's books. The questions, designed to stimulate interest in books and to introduce children to good books, are organized with some deliberate overlapping into four general age groups from children of three to six to children age 12 and up." Booklist

Hoke, Helen

Hoke's Jokes, cartoons & funny things; pictures by Eric Hill. Watts, F. 1975 [c1973] unp illus lib. bdg. $4.90 (1-4)   793.7

1 Wit and humor
ISBN 0-531-02682-5
First published 1973 in England

"An assortment of jokes and nonsense accompanied by colorful, funny illustrations. 'Mock Meanings' is the cleverest section (e.g., 'Pasteurize: Up to your forehead.', 'Intense: Where Boy Scouts sleep.') The 11 tongue-twisters are fresh, but the few traditional selections like Lewis Carroll's 'Tweedle-Dum and Tweedle-Dee' seem out of place. . . . Still, the inviting format and contemporary approach is 'with it' enough for joke fans." Sch Library J

Jokes and fun; pictures by Tony Parkhouse. Watts, F. 1973 47p illus lib. bdg. $3.90 (3-5)   793.7

1 Wit and humor 2 Riddles
ISBN 0-531-02616-7

"A collection of jokes, riddles, tongue twisters, rhymes, limericks, and odds and ends that manages to take off in spite of its cornball tendencies. Aiding the effort are Parkhouse's garishly ludicrous but somehow hilariously appropriate caricatures that are a cross between pop and cartoon art. Such oldies as stepping into rain poodles . . . are blended with one liners like 'Have you lived here all your life? Not yet.' Overall, a good choice to help fill young readers' demand for humor." Booklist

Keller, Charles

The star spangled banana, and other revolutionary riddles; comp. by Charles Keller and Richard Baker; illus. by Tomie de Paola. Prentice-Hall 1974 unp illus lib. bdg. $3.95 (3-5)   793.7

1 Riddles 2 U.S.—History—Revolution
ISBN 0-13-842971-5

"Children's love for outrageously bad puns, riddles, and jokes must, at least, date back to the American Revolution; so it is only fitting that such a group of jokes be collected to commemorate the Spirit of '76. Certainly, the puns and jokes in this selection should cause groans and laughter about everything from the signing of the Declaration of Independence to Paul Revere's ride. . . . [The riddles] do for the Revolution what Art Buchwald does for contemporary American politics." Horn Bk

"De Paola's pencil drawings of the 61 riddles are always a pleasure. His good-natured cartoons take clever pokes at history. . . . Children in their first encounter with American history will relish this slightly irreverent portrayal." Sch Library J

Leeming, Joseph
Fun with pencil and paper; games, stunts, puzzles; pictures by Jessie Robinson. Lippincott 1955 91p illus $6.50 (4-7) 793.7
1 Games 2 Puzzles
ISBN 0-397-30300-9
The author has gathered "pencil-and-paper games —word, drawing, number, and spelling games, stunts, and puzzles. In each case the number of players is indicated, the verbal and pictorial explanations are clear, and answers and solutions are given on the same page with the quizzes and puzzles. The material included varies greatly in degree of difficulty." Booklist

Fun with puzzles. . . . Drawings by Jessie Robinson. Lippincott 1946 128p illus $6.50 (4-7) 793.7
1 Puzzles
ISBN 0-397-30114-6
"A Stokes book"
"Puzzles of every kind for everybody, for fun and mental gymnastics; problems with coins, counters and matches, brain twisters, mathematical and number puzzles, pencil and paper problems, cut-out and put-together puzzles, anagrams and word puzzles." Title page

Riddles, riddles, riddles; enigmas, anagrams, puns, puzzles, quizzes, conundrums; illus. by Shane Miller. Watts, F. 1953 244p illus lib. bdg. $5.88 (4-7) 793.7
1 Riddles
ISBN 0-531-01777-X
"Terrific triple title series"
"There are a few classic examples . . . but for the most part Mr. Leeming has concentrated on the riddle or the conundrum with the quick, short answer— the kind that makes you wonder how you could have missed it. The general merriment is heightened by . . . [the] decorations." N Y Times Bk Rev
"A good addition to the collection for parties or any moment of fun." Library J

Sarnoff, Jane
What? A riddle book, by Jane Sarnoff and Reynold Ruffins; technical consultant: Simms Taback. Scribner 1974 62p illus $5.95 (3-5) 793.7
1 Riddles
ISBN 0-684-13911-1
Illustrated by Reynold Ruffins, this is a collection of over five hundred one-line riddles on a variety of subjects. The last chapter includes a series of riddles in code with instructions for deciphering them
"The clever word play in this collection adds up to unusual juvenile humor in which a distinction has been made between silly and stupid. Although some of the answers may cause groans, and others, perplexity, most are just plain funny. . . . Visual charm adds a big bonus to the text. While browsers may dip in and out of the pages of straight black-and-brown print, they will pore over the color spreads with riddles angled into comic illustrations." Booklist

Walls, Fred
Puzzles and brain twisters. Watts, F. 1970 66p illus lib. bdg. $3.90, pa $1.25 (4-6) 793.7
1 Puzzles
ISBN 0-531-00693-X; 0-531-02403-2
"A First book"
Includes "puzzles with coins, numbers, matches, words; brain twisters and optical illusions. . . . Solutions to the puzzles are given in the back of the book." Sch Library J
"What makes this book both useful and enjoyable is its concern with mathematical problems and its sug-

gestion that many of the puzzles can be solved with friends or used as party games." N Y Times Bk Rev

Wiesner, William
A pocketful of riddles; collected and illus. by William Wiesner. Dutton 1966 119p illus lib. bdg. $5.50 (2-4) 793.7
1 Riddles
ISBN 0-525-37206-7
The author "has made up this collection of over 200 riddles, conundrums, and rebuses by culling old riddle books back as far as the nineteenth century and adding a few riddles of his own. This is a small sized picture book with from one to three riddles with illustrated answers on each page or double spread. For lovers of tiny books and for lovers of riddles." Sch Library J
"Since the answers appear in illustrated columns facing the questions the reader needs a young companion for maximum fun or a group to make it possible to turn the whole business into a game. . . . Bright little drawings." Horn Bk

The riddle pot; collected and illus. by William Wiesner. Dutton 1973 120p illus $4.95 (1-3) 793.7
1 Riddles 2 Wit and humor
ISBN 0-525-38285-2
A "plump little volume containing a generous gathering of riddles, teasers, and a few puzzles, illustrated with cheerful, breezy drawings." Horn Bk

793.8 Magic

Barr, George
Show time for young scientists; entertaining with science; illus. by Mildred Waltrip. McGraw 1965 158p illus $4.95 (5-7) 793.8
1 Scientific recreations 2 Science—Experiments
ISBN 0-07-003788-4
"This is an interesting, well-written text on showmanship in the presentation of stunts and demonstrations based on scientific principles. Included are pointers on stage lighting, the rewards of practice, pacing and timing the program, patter, audience participation, gimmicks, use of microphone and tape recorder. Detailed instructions tell how to construct apparatus for scientific tricks which depend upon simple applications of electromagnetism, the open and closed circuit, air pressure, motion, balance, optical illusions, sound vibration, gravity, etc." Sch Library J
"Since the objective is not education, there are no explanations or discussions of scientific principles." Sci Bks

Helfman, Harry
Tricks with your fingers; illus. by Robert Bartram. Morrow 1967 46p illus $4.95, lib. bdg. $4.59 (3-6) 793.8
1 Magic 2 Tricks
ISBN 0-688-21583-1; 0-688-31583-6
"All one needs is fingers, string, coins, hankies, and marbles to do these ten sleight-of-hand tricks which can be performed almost anywhere. Carefully explained and illustrated, they are easy to do." Wis Library Bul

Kettelkamp, Larry
Magic made easy; written and illus. by Larry Kettelkamp. Morrow 1954 illus lib. bdg. $4.59 (4-7) 793.8
1 Magic
ISBN 0-688-31579-8

Kettelkamp, Larry—*Continued*

"An introduction to magic tricks for young readers. The first tricks are simple ones that can be done with practice and very little equipment. Toward the end of the book some more elaborate tricks are described and some suggestions for patter are given." Chicago. Children's Bk Center

"Although not quite so easy as the title and format would indicate, the tricks in this little book are clearly explained both in text and pictures. . . . Sets down also a few basic rules for all magicians." Booklist

Spooky magic; written and illus. by Larry Kettelkamp. Morrow 1955 64p illus lib. bdg. $4.59 (3-7)
793.8

1 Magic 2 Tricks
ISBN 0-688-31581-X

The author tells "how to perform some spooky tricks, such as raising a human body a few feet in the air, making the table move, finding a ghostly spirit in a catchup bottle. Some of the tricks are very simple, some will need patience." Library J

"Mr. Kettelkamp understands his magic and knows how to explain it to youngsters so that they can follow his instructions, and no expensive or hard-to-obtain props are needed to handle these tricks." Sat Rev

Lamb, Geoffrey

Mental magic tricks. Nelson 1973 89p illus $5.95 (5-7)
793.8

1 Magic 2 Tricks
ISBN 0-8407-6332-8

First published 1972 in England with title: Your book of mental magic

These tricks deal "with illusions which seem to be based on telepathy and clairvoyance. Although a certain amount of memory work is required as well as some facility with number manipulation, most of the tricks are easily performed and only a few require an accomplice. The directions and illustrations are clear; however, readers must follow instructions exactly or risk exposure of the trick's method." Sch Library J

Leeming, Joseph

Fun with magic. . . . Drawings by Jessie Robinson. Lippincott 1943 86p illus $7.95 (4-7)
793.8

1 Magic 2 Tricks
ISBN 0-397-30087-5

First published by Stokes

"How to make magic equipment; how to perform many tricks, including some of the best tricks of professional magicians and how to give successful magic shows." Title page

Diagrams and instructions for mind reading and tricks using handkerchiefs, coins, cards, string, rings, and similar easily obtainable properties. Simple directions for presenting shows are also given. A list of dealers in magicians' supplies is included

More Fun with magic; a book of magic tricks for everyone; drawings by Jessie Robinson. Lippincott 1948 89p illus $4.95 (4-7)
793.8

1 Magic 2 Tricks
ISBN 0-397-31440-X

A "fascinating collection of card, coin and mind-reading tricks for the aspiring young Houdini. Explanations are short, clear and minutely illustrated. In addition there are helpful hints on technique and finesse in showmanship and carefully outlined programs for magic shows." Library J

Lopshire, Robert

It's magic? Macmillan (N Y) 1969 unp illus lib. bdg. $4.50, pa $1.50 (k-2)
793.8

1 Magic 2 Tricks

"In a first-reading-book of the most entertaining variety, Boris, a huge bear, visits a Big Magic Show to witness fourteen easy tricks performed with simple materials by Tad, a great magician-dog. Tad even invites him to be the audience participator. Some of the magic lies in jokes. The results of most are obvious and achieved as illustrated; a few must be tried to satisfy the reader. Children will be entranced into copying the performance for anyone whose attention they can command. The reading alone has entertainment value, for Boris is a naive childlike spectator, repeatedly fooled, and capable of saying. 'I knew it all the time.' " Horn Bk

Mulholland, John

Magic of the world; illus. by Al Hormel. Scribner 1965 190p illus $5.95 (5-7)
793.8

1 Magic 2 Tricks
ISBN 0-684-13649-X

"Beginning with a historical survey of the art of magic, this well-written, well-produced book takes the reader on a magician's journey around the world. Each chapter describes in detail either a traditional trick associated with a particular culture or country, or one developed by a famous prestidigitator of the region. Directions for duplicating the magic, accompanied by explicit drawings, are clear and logical; materials required are simple and readily available." Horn Bk

Severn, Bill

Bill Severn's Big book of magic; illus. by Katharine Wood. McKay 1973 238p illus $6.95 (6-7)
793.8

1 Magic 2 Tricks
ISBN 0-679-20022-3

The author includes card, rope, money and handkerchief tricks as well as close-up and stage magic. He explains the secret, necessary materials, preparation and performance of each trick

"The tricks are as clearly explained as they can be without a live demonstration." Chicago. Children's Bk Center

Magic across the table; illus. by Katharine Wood. McKay 1972 112p illus $4.50 (5-7)
793.8

1 Magic 2 Tricks
ISBN 0-679-20102-5

The author provides step-by-step instructions for performing easy magic tricks using such props as pad and pencil, bottle caps, chewing gum, and various other easily obtained household items

"Unlike many other books on performing magic tricks, Severn's title is not directed toward producing a magic show. The tricks can be performed with minimal preparation and little practice. Most of them are based on substitutions, but these simple feats may lead readers to the more demanding illusions." Sch Library J

Magic in your pockets; illus. by Katharine Wood. McKay 1964 147p illus lib. bdg. $4.50 (5-7) 793.8

1 Magic 2 Tricks
ISBN 0-679-25084-8

"Magic tricks which can be performed anywhere without the benefit of special props." Bks on Exhibit

"Directions are concise and clear, and for each trick they plainly state how it looks, what to say, what you need, how you fix it, what to do. Card tricks are not included nor many of the more common party stunts and puzzles readily found in other books. Much of the magic offered here has a tempting freshness: simple enough to learn quickly and perform smoothly, mystifying enough to captivate any audience." Library J

Van Rensselaer, Alexander
Fun with magic; illus. by John N. Barron. Doubleday 1957 55p illus $4.95 (4-7)   793.8
1 Magic 2 Tricks
ISBN 0-385-02428-2
"After offering some tips on basic techniques and equipment the author . . . gives clear instructions for performing 25 tricks with coins, handkerchiefs, cards, string, and numbers, most of them simple enough for beginners." Booklist
"Each trick has helpful step-by-step illustrations, most colorful and attractive in black, white, and red." Library J

White, Laurence B.
So you want to be a magician? Illus. by Bill Morrison. Addison-Wesley 1972 224p illus lib. bdg. $5.95 (5-7)   ·793.8
1 Magic 2 Tricks
ISBN 0-201-08627-1
"An Addisonian Press book"
"Asserting that a magician's purpose is to entertain and that he does so by being a good actor with well-prepared patter and well-practiced tricks the author tells how to become a successful amateur magician. Describing over 50 tricks, all of which require only common household items and the use of such basic techniques as misdirection and substitution he gives lucid directions, illustrated with clear drawings, for performing each. White also indicates how to appeal to different age groups, encourages the young magician to try original ideas, and includes practical suggestions on planning a magic show." Booklist

Wyler, Rose
Funny magic; easy tricks for young magicians, by Rose Wyler & Gerald Ames; pictures by Talivaldis Stubis. Parents Mag. Press 1972 52p illus $4.95, lib. bdg. $4.59 (1-3)   793.8
1 Magic 2 Tricks
ISBN 0-8193-0584-7; 0-8193-0585-5
"A collection of simple sleight-of-hand and fun tricks for the youngest of magicians. Some of the tricks use a puppet prop made from a handkerchief with a paper face taped on it and some require the assistance of a friend. All are easy to perform and require only easily obtainable materials. Gay, colorful pictures help to clarify the written instructions which include suggestions for putting on a show. Useful ideas for parents and primary-grade teachers as well as young magicians." Booklist

Magic secrets, by Rose Wyler and Gerald Ames; pictures by Talivaldis Stubis. Harper 1967 63p illus $2.95, lib. bdg. $3.79 (1-3)   793.8
1 Magic 2 Tricks
ISBN 0-06-020068-5; 0-06-020069-3
"An I can read book"
"A first book about tricks that can be done by an amateur. . . . The text suggests that an audience sees that to which its attention is directed, and shows the small diversionary tactics that add to illusion." Chicago. Children's Bk Center

Spooky tricks, by Rose Wyler and Gerald Ames; pictures by Talivaldis Stubis. Harper 1968 64p illus $2.95, lib. bdg. $3.79 (1-3)   793.8
1 Magic 2 Tricks
ISBN 0-06-026633-3; 0-06-02634-1
"An I can read book"
Readers can learn such tricks as making ghosts appear, cats sparkle in the dark, girls disappear, and boys float on air
The book has "easy-to-understand instructions. The lively tone of the simple text, the imaginative yet clear, illustrative drawings, and the grouping of the 24 tricks under the headings How to be a spook, Willie the ghost, and Haunted house enhance the enjoyment of the book." Booklist

794.1 Chess

Kane, George Francis
Chess and children. Scribner 1974 165p illus (A U.S. Chess Masters bk) $7.95   794.1
1 Chess
ISBN 0-684-13890-5
This book is intended as a guide for adults who wish to teach chess to children, and assumes little or no prior knowledge of the game on the part of the reader. Teaching methods and relevant illustrative problem-solving tasks are described, using diagrams to show various tactics of the game

Kidder, Harvey
Illustrated chess for children. Doubleday 1970 127p illus $4.95, lib. bdg. $5.70 (4-6)   794.1
1 Chess
ISBN 0-385-057664-4; 0-385-05429-7
"A really fine book for the beginning chess player; although there seems an undue stress on the relationship of each piece to its real-life equivalent (the pawns were pikemen who fought side by side, the knight's move can be remembered as the charge of a leaping horse, etc.) the concept gives the book an added dimension. Each piece and its moves are explained separately, and a blitzkrieg game is illustrated. There are illustrations of games-in-process, with questions and answers about possible moves and why some are preferred. The clear diagrams are very helpful, as is the proceeding from basic moves to more and more complicated problems." Chicago. Children's Bk Center

Leeming, Joseph
The first book of chess; pictures by Doris Stolberg. Watts, F. 1953 92p illus lib. bdg. $3.90 (5-7) 794.1
1 Chess
ISBN 0-531-00498-8
The book "familiarizes the beginner with the chessmen and their moves, explains the most important basic principles, rules, and strategy and includes several practice games." Booklist
The book "although terms are defined when first used within the text, a list of chess terms is conveniently located at the end of the book. The easy-to-follow instructions and clear diagrams will attract would-be chess players of almost any age." Booklist
"The clear explanations and diagrams used to instruct beginners in the fascinating but tricky game of chess begin logically with the setting up of the board and the use of the different chess pieces. Notation and special chess terms, 'combinations,' standard openings, and practice games are carefully outlined." Horn Bk

Reinfeld, Fred
Chess for children; with moves and positions pictured in photo and diagram. Sterling 1958 61p illus $3.95, lib. bdg. $3.99 (5-7)   794.1
1 Chess
ISBN 0-8069-4904-X; 0-8069-4905-8
An "introductory book on chess that can be used alone and will be especially helpful to study as a supplement to personal instruction. The pieces used in the game, the ways in which each piece moves and captures and the conventions of illustration (of the

Reinfeld, Fred—*Continued*
board of moves in diagram) are explained." Chicago.
Children's Bk Center
"Clear explanation with many photographs and
illustrations mark this thoughtfully prepared volume.
The step-by-step presentation is easy to understand
and inclusive enough to satisfy the bright beginner."
Library J

Sarnoff, Jane
The chess book, by Jane Sarnoff and Reynold Ruffins. Consultant: Bruce Pandolfini. Scribner 1973 39p
illus $6.95 (4-6)   794.1
    1 Chess
    ISBN 0-684-13494-2
"Clearly laying out the basic rules of chess, the
setup of the board, the movements of pieces, a sample
game (Scholar's Mate), some simple strategy, and a
few chess problems, the book also captures in its
format and tone the fun and enjoyment found in the
game." Horn Bk
The authors "do a grand job enticing new players
into its spell. The thoughtful designs, precise diagrams and witty illustrations make their book an irresistible invitation to play chess." N Y Times Bk Rev

Weart, Edith L.
The royal game; chess for young people; illus. by B.
Brussel-Smith. Vanguard 1948 64p illus $4.95 (5-7)
                                                       794.1
    1 Chess
    ISBN 0-8149-0436-X
How to play chess set forth partly in story form,
with amusing illustrations but conventional diagrams.
After explaining the moves of the various pieces and
the rules of the game, the author gives a number of
sample games and problems
"The chess figures are personalized making the
chess board a real battlefield. The instructions are
clear and the various plays are well illustrated."
Ontario Library Rev

794.6   Bowling

Dolan, Edward F.
The complete beginner's guide to bowling [by]
Edward F. Dolan, Jr. Doubleday 1974 127p illus
$5.95, lib. bdg. $6.70 (5-7)   794.6
    1 Bowling
    ISBN 0-385-01667-0; 0-385-08156-1
"For novices and intermediate bowlers wishing to
rid themselves of bad habits, this well-written book
may be the next best thing to private lessons. Using
helpful black-and-white photographs to illustrate his
points, the author details proven techniques of stance
and approach, release, and follow-through. Later, he
describes variants of ball delivery and aiming,
demonstrates and corrects common mistakes, and
shows ways to tackle various pin arrangements on the
second roll. Rules of the game and common bowling
terms are among the other matters taken up." Booklist

Liss, Howard
Bowling talk for beginners; illus. by Frank Robbins.
Messner 1973 80p illus lib. bdg. $4.79 (4-7) 794.6
    1 Bowling—Dictionaries
    ISBN 0-671-32568-X
"The jargon used by bowlers is alphabetically
arranged, explained, and often illustrated by clear
drawings. An unusually lucid explanation of how to
keep score is included." Booklist

795   Games of chance

Kettelkamp, Larry
Spinning tops. Morrow 1966 63p illus lib. bdg.
$4.59 (3-6)   795
    1 Top
    ISBN 0-688-31585-2
    Illustrated by the author
A "fresh activity book is this fully illustrated guide
to the making and use of tops. The text introduces
international backgrounds for a variety of tops, some
of which, like the popular yo-yo, have served practical
purposes as well as entertained children. Games and
stunts using hand-spun and string-wound types are
clearly diagramed, and action drawings suggest their
fun. Other pictures show how acorns, gourds, Tinker-
toys, or spools can readily be converted into tops."
Horn Bk

796   Sports

Barr, George
Young scientist and sports; featuring baseball, football, and basketball; illus. by Mildred Waltrip.
McGraw 1962 159p illus lib. bdg. $4.72 (4-7)   796
    1 Sports 2 Physics
    ISBN 0-07-003806-6
    "Whittlesey House publications"
The author "applies such scientific principles as
action and reaction, gravity, and inertia to sports in
general and the three major sports in particular. Useful in science classes as well as in sports." Hodges. Bks
for Elem Sch Libraries

Keith, Harold
Sports and games. 5th ed. rev. Crowell 1969 411p
illus $6.95 (5-7)   796
    1 Athletics 2 Sports
    ISBN 0-690-76216-X
    First published 1941
This introduction to seventeen best-known and
most popular sports sets forth the rules and analyzes
great athletic achievements

Morton, Miriam
The making of champions; Soviet sports for children and teenagers. Atheneum Pubs. 1974 136p illus
$6.25 (5-7)   796
    1 Sports 2 Children in Russia
    ISBN 0-689-30142-1
This book discusses the training programs, schools,
clubs, and circles in the Pioneer program, where
Soviet children and teenagers undergo intensive
structural training in the sport of their choice
"The Soviet children's deep respect for and love of
sports, their determination, and their self-discipline,
all mirrored in numerous black-and-white photographs, can inspire and intrigue readers looking for a
new angle on social studies or physical education."
Booklist

796.03   Sports—Encyclopedias and dictionaries

The Concise encyclopedia of sports; ed. by Keith W.
Jennison; illus. with photographs and drawings.
Watts, F. [1974 c1970] 165p illus lib. bdg. $8.95
(5-7)   796.03
    1 Sports—Encyclopedias
    ISBN 0-531-01961-6

The Concise encyclopedia of sports—*Continued*
First published 1970
Alphabetically arranged, this book describes fifty individual sports. Each entry contains a history of the sport with its rules and regulations, the exact dimensions of the playing area, the official scoring and, in many cases, lessons in playing the sport, and material on sports immortals

The Junior illustrated encyclopedia of sports. [Rev. and enlarged ed]. Willard Mullin, illustrator. Herbert Kamm, ed. Bobbs 1975 681p illus $8.95 (5-7)   796.03
1 Sports—Encyclopedias
ISBN 0-672-52094-4
Cover title: The New Junior illustrated encyclopedia of sports
First published 1960, edited by Willard Mullin
For thirteen major sports, this book provides histories, biographical sketches of outstanding participants, records and statistics, and many photographs and drawings

Menke, Frank G.
The encyclopedia of sports. Barnes, A.S. illus $25   796.03
1 Sports—Encyclopedias
ISBN 0-498-01440-1
First published 1939. Periodically revised to bring material up to date
This is a "standard work. . . . It covers a wide variety of sports, e.g. baseball, boxing, football, basketball, hockey and soccer providing brief history, description, basic rules, names and records of champions. . . . [There is also] a tabulation of all current records and statistics." Am Ref Bks Annual, 1970 [Review of the 1969 edition]

796.1   Miscellaneous games

Bley, Edgar S.
The best singing games for children of all ages; drawings by Patt Willen, piano arrangements by Margaret Chase. Sterling 1957 96p illus music $5.95, lib. bdg. $5.69   796.1
1 Singing games 2 Folk songs
ISBN 0-8069-4450-1; 0-8069-4451-X
"More than 50 musical games, jump-rope jingles, and play party games, with words, musical scores, and directions for action. Arranged by age levels and illustrated with helpful drawings." Hodges. Bks for Elem Sch Libraries

Downer, Marion
Kites; how to make and fly them. Lothrop 1959 64p illus lib. bdg. $4.81 (4-7)   796.1
1 Kites
ISBN 0-688-51227-5
"Illustrated with clear diagrams and interesting photographs, this excellent introduction to kite making gives general information on needed tools and materials and detailed directions for making 11 varieties of flat, bow, and box kites. It also treats color and decoration of kites, how to launch and fly them, safety rules, and kite-flying contests." Wis Library Bul

Fowke, Edith
(comp.) Sally go round the sun; three hundred children's songs, rhymes and games. Doubleday [1970 c1969] 160p illus music $6.95, lib. bdg. $7.70 796.1
1 Singing games

ISBN 0-385-02513-0; 0-385-02956-X
First copyrighted 1969 in Canada
This selection of children's lore includes "singing games, rhymes used for rope skipping, ball bouncing, and clapping, foot and finger plays, taunts and teases, and silly songs. Directions for the games and the foot and finger plays are given in an appended section of notes along with sources and comparative references; piano and guitar accompaniments are provided for some of the songs." Booklist
"Younger children, too, will appreciate the material in this collection, since the book is ideally suited for adult use with small children in groups. The musical arrangements are simple." Sutherland. The Best in Children's Bks

Fowler, H. Waller
Kites; a practical guide to kite making and flying; illus. by Francis A. Williams. Ronald 1953 95p illus (The Ronald Sports lib) $5.95 (4-7)   796.1
1 Kites
First published by A. S. Barnes
The author describes the various types of kites, tells the good and bad points of each type, and explains how the reader can make and fly his own
"This book can contribute to the development of measurement, comparison, and geometric ideas." Hardgrove. Math Library—Elem and Jr High Sch
Additional sources: p92

Glazer, Tom
Eye winker, Tom Tinker, Chin chopper; fifty musical fingerplays; illus. by Ron Himler. Doubleday 1973 91p illus music $5.95, lib. bdg. $6.70 (k-3)   796.1
1 Singing games 2 Finger plays
ISBN 0-385-08200-2; 0-385-09453-1
This collection of 50 songs, with piano arrangements, guitar chords and instructions for finger and body movements, "represent three distinct groups: fingerplay songs, such as 'Eentsy, Weentsy Spider'; familiar action rhymes 'newly set to music,' like 'Here Is the Church' and 'Pat-A-Cake'; and many songs—both new and traditional—set down with totally new fingerplays." Horn Bk
"The illustrations are frolicsome [and] always attractive. . . . Even without the fingerplay, this is a compilation of songs that anyone working with young children, particularly in groups, should find useful, and older children who can play piano or guitar can use the book for the music alone." Chicago. Children's Bk Center

Grayson, Marion
Let's do fingerplays; illus. by Nancy Weyl. Luce, R.B. 1962 109p illus $6.95 (k-2)   796.1
1 Finger plays
ISBN 0-88331-003-1
"Approximately 200 rhymes and songs, with directions for accompanying finger plays, are organized under such headings as Animal Antics, Counting and Counting Out, and Holidays and Special Occasions." Hodges. Bks for Elem Sch Libraries
"Sources are listed, and there is a first-line as well as title index. Format is generous, with the pages well designed and illustrated. Very useful book." Sch Library J

Jacobs, Frances E.
Finger plays and action rhymes; photographs by Lura and Courtney Owen. Lothrop 1941 53p illus music $5.50 (k-2)   796.1
1 Finger plays
ISBN 0-688-41312-9
Using subjects from the child's own range of experiences, the author presents a photograph and rhyme

Jacobs, Frances E.—*Continued*
before showing another picture of the corresponding
finger play actually being performed by a child
For instance "a little boy is shown feeding a rabbit,
then the hand making a rabbit as one does in a shadowplay, then two hands making a rabbit eating a carrot.
. . . Each play has a rhyme and for some of these
[there] is music." N Y Her Trib Bks

Kettelkamp, Larry
    Kites; written and illus. by Larry Kettelkamp. Mor-
row 1959 48p illus lib. bdg. $4.81 (3-6)   796.1
    1 Kites
    ISBN 0-688-31584-4
"Included in this book are directions for building
various kinds of kites as well as pertinent information
on the scientific aspects of kite-flying. The places of
kites in the development of aviation and in the gathering of weather data is also discussed briefly." Adventuring With Bks. 2d edition
"Extra ideas, such as adding attachments to the kite
line or glitter to the kite, spark up the book, as do
accounts of the Japanese kite fighting contests and the
launching of Chinese dragon kites." Chicago Sunday
Trib

Langstaff, John
    Shimmy shimmy coke-ca-pop! A collection of city
children's street games and rhymes, by John Langstaff and Carol Langstaff; photographs by Don Mac-
Sorley. Doubleday 1973 95p illus music $4.95, lib.
bdg. $5.70 (2-5)   796.1
    1 Singing games 2 Games
    ISBN 0-385-05769-5; 0-385-05771-7
This collection of urban children's chants, some
accompanied by music, is divided into 11 sections:
name calling, ball bouncing, sidewalk drawing games,
circle games, who's it, tag games, jump rope rhymes,
action games, follow the leader, hand clapping, and
dramatic play
"Photographs on almost every page capture the
same energetic action and constant motion generated
through the rhymes. For an adult the book will provide interesting insight into contemporary children's
blend of traditional and current lore, while young
readers can see their own games in print and maybe
even learn a few new ones." Booklist

Matterson, Elizabeth
    (comp.) Games for the very young; finger plays and
nursery games. Am. Heritage Press [1971 c1969] 206p
illus music $4.95, lib. bdg. $4.72 (k-1)   796.1
    1 Singing games 2 Finger plays 3 Nursery rhymes
    ISBN 0-07-040941-2; 0-07-040942-0
First published 1969 in England with title: This
little puffin . . .
"Tried and tested finger plays, action games and
nursery songs all bound together to give a choice of
some two hundred activities for individual children or
groups." ALA. CSD. Mother Hubbard's Cupboard
"An excellent selection of rhymes, with diagrams
for the finger plays. The material is divided into
categories that are related to the interests and
activities of very young children. . . . Directions for
playing games are given in italics, and the musical
notation gives the melodic line for songs." Sutherland. The Best in Children's Bks
    Index of first lines: p201-06

Millen, Nina
    (comp.) Children's games from many lands. New
and rev. ed. illus. by Allan Eitzen. Friendship Press
1965 192p illus music pa $3.50   796.1
    1 Games
    ISBN 0-377-45011-1

First published 1943
"This anthology is a survey of two hundred fifty-
eight children's games from sixty-four countries.
Readers will find games reflecting the music and language of people, the way people earn a living, daily
customs and common foods from various countries.
They may also discover the universality of games and
game patterns. Each geographical section of the book
is introduced with comments noting the main characteristics of games of this area." Reading Ladders. 5th
edition

Opie, Iona
    Children's games in street and playground . . . by
Iona and Peter Opie. Oxford 1969 xxvi, 371p illus
maps $10   796.1
    1 Games 2 Folklore
    ISBN 0-19-827210-3
"Chasing; catching; seeking; hunting; racing; duel-
ling; exerting; daring; guessing; acting; pretending."
Title page
"Illustrated with game diagrams and photographs.
. . . This volume concerns the 'games that children,
aged about 6-12, play of their own accord when out of
doors, and usually out of sight.' Compared and
documented both geographically and in relation to
earlier lore are hundreds of examples of starting-out
or counting-out rhymes, ritualistic folk dialogues,
chants of chasing and catching games, and the many
other categories named in the subtitle. These are
helpfully indexed to make the book a useful reference
work as well as fascinating reading." Horn Bk

Rockwell, Anne
    Games (and how to play them). [Text and] pictures
by Anne Rockwell. Crowell 1973 43p illus $6.95, lib.
bdg. $7.70 (k-4)   796.1
    1 Games
    ISBN 0-690-32159-7; 0-690-32160-0
"A compendium of 43 noisy, quiet, indoor, outdoor
activities." N Y Times Bk Rev
"A book that can be used with younger children as
well as by independent readers. The explanations are
brief but clear; the pictures are often informative and
always attractive with animals as characters and with
intriguing details. A small bonus: the humor of
interpretation, such as the kilted rabbit for hopscotch,
or the octopus-sailors having a knot contest." Chicago.
Children's Bk Center

Winn, Marie
    (ed.) What shall we do and Allee galloo! Play songs
and singing games for young children. Collected &
ed. by Marie Winn; musical arrangements by Allan
Miller; pictures by Karla Kuskin. Harper 1970 87p
illus music $5.95, lib. bdg. $5.79 (k-2)   796.1
    1 Singing games 2 Songs
    ISBN 0-06-026538-8; 0-06-026537-X
These "forty-seven play games and songs, both
familiar and less known, have large-print music and
lyrics (piano and guitar accompaniment) and instructions for group participation." Children's Bks. 1970
"A title and first-line index is included, and cheerful, decorative illustrations appear on every page."
Booklist

Worstell, Emma Vietor
    (comp.) Jump the rope jingles; illus. by Sheila
Greenwald. Macmillan (N Y) 1961 55p illus $4.95 pa
95¢ (k-4)   796.1
    1 Singing games
"Amusingly illustrated, a compilation of calls and
jingles used in jumping rope. Several pages of instructions for jump-rope games are appended, as is an
index of first lines. A useful book, and one that can be

Worstell, Emma Vietor—*Continued*
used by an adult with children too young to read the text independently." Chicago. Children's Bk Center

796.32   Basketball

Kaplan, Arthur
Basketball: how to improve your technique; photographs by Meryl Joseph. Watts, F. 1974 61p illus lib. bdg. $3.95 (5-7)   796.32
1 Basketball
ISBN 0-531-02674-4
"A Concise guide"
The author discusses specific ways in which a player can perfect his passing, dribbling, shooting, general defensive and offensive play and overall court strategy
Bibliography: p55-57

Knosher, Harley
Basic basketball strategy; foreword by Rick Barry; illus. with diagrams by Leonard Kessler. Doubleday 1972 102p illus $4.95, lib. bdg. $5.70 (4-7)   796.32
1 Basketball
ISBN 0-385-05804-7; 0-385-00008-1
The author "covers every aspect of basketball strategy that concerns a young player, from basics to advanced techniques, from shooting and dribbling to setting a fast break, switching and gambling on defense." Foreword
"Drawings and diagrams illustrate the right and wrong way to perform various skills. Knosher also discusses the value of conditioning, practice, and drills, shows clearly the various ways in which fouls are committed, and stresses the importance of knowing the rules." Booklist

Liss, Howard
Basketball talk for beginners; illus. by Frank Robbins. Messner 1970 95p illus lib. bdg. $5.29, pa 75¢ (4-7)   796.32
1 Basketball
ISBN 0-671-32299-0; 0-671-29579-9
Accompanied by diagrams and drawings of the action on the court, this book provides explanations both of the rules of basketball and slang expressions used by the players

Monroe, Earl
The basketball skill book [by] Earl Monroe & Wes Unseld; ed. by Ray Siegener. Atheneum Pubs. 1973 114p illus $5.95 (4-7)   796.32
1 Basketball
ISBN 0-689-10528-2
Basic basketball fundamentals such as ball handling, dribbling, shooting, passing, and individual and team offensive and defensive play are introduced through text and numerous photographs

796.33   Football. Soccer

Anderson, Dick
Defensive football [by] Dick Anderson and Nick Buoniconti; ed. by Bill Bondurant. Atheneum Pubs. 1973 146p illus $5.95 (3-6)   796.33
1 Football
ISBN 0-689-10573-8
"Written by two members of the Miami Dolphins, this is intended to give aspiring players tips on defen-sive play. Nick Buoniconti, middle linebacker, handles the defensive line positions; Dick Anderson, safety, describes the defensive back's duties. There are also chapters dealing with tackling, pass coverage, reading keys, meeting runs, interceptions, agility drills, fumbles, and punt returns. Numerous demonstration photographs of Anderson and Buoniconti are included (though some are too small), and there is the usual message about dedication, discipline, etc. Easy to read with many anecdotes and summaries of main points at the end of each chapter." Sch Library J

Coombs, Charles
Be a winner in football. Morrow 1974 127p illus $4.75, lib. bdg. $4.32 (5-7)   796.33
1 Football
ISBN 0-688-20119-9; 0-688-30119-3
"A useful guide to football basics. Coombs puts the reader in a team member's shoes and talks him through various plays, giving rules and pointers on the game. Chapters about getting into shape, playing the various positions, passing, and kicking are included. Beginners and more experienced youngsters will be attracted by the generous print size, good black-and-white photographs of pros in action, and down-to-earth, ungimmicky approach. A glossary is appended." Booklist

Jackson, C. Paul
How to play better football; illus. by Leonard Kessler. Crowell 1972 233p illus $4.50 (4-7)   796.33
1 Football
ISBN 0-690-41567-2
"Covered are the history of the game, basic rules, explanations of offensive and defensive team play, the importance of teamwork, and the skills necessary to execute good play. Descriptions of physical conditioning and proper equipment, a glossary of football terms, and illustrated officials' signals round out the coverage. The large print format, with many diagrams and illustrations, enhances the clearly-written text." Sch Library J

Liss, Howard
Football talk for beginners; illus. by Frank Robbins. Messner 1970 94p illus lib. bdg. $4.79 (4-7)
                                                796.33
1 Football—Dictionaries
ISBN 0-671-32241-9
Numerous diagrams illustrate this dictionary of technical terms and phrases used in football
This book, "virtually a cross-referenced dictionary of football talk, should aid youngsters—and many oldsters, too—in better understanding the game's complexities." Sch Library J

Toye, Clive
Soccer; pictures by Paul Frame. Watts, F. 1968 54p illus lib. bdg. $3.90 (4-7)   796.33
1 Soccer
ISBN 0-531-00633-6
In this book "which covers many aspects of the game [of soccer] both the fan and the player will find explanations (and diagrams) of tactics, techniques, and rules and regulations. There are also a list of great soccer names, a glossary of terms, and an index." Horn Bk

Young, A. S.
Black champions of the gridiron: O. J. Simpson and Leroy Keyes; by A. S. "Doc" Young. Harcourt 1969 120p illus $5.50 (5-7)   796.33
1 Football
ISBN 0-15-208399-5
"Curriculum-related books"

Young, A. S.—*Continued*

The author "recapitulates the careers of O. J. Simpson and Leroy Keyes . . . and gives a game-by-game account of their 1968 season, along with several appendixes." Library J

796.34 Tennis

Coombs, Charles

Be a winner in tennis; illus. with photographs. Morrow 1975 128p illus $5.50, lib. bdg. $4.81 (4-6)
796.34

1 Tennis
ISBN 0-688-32020-7; 0-688-32020-1

The book "starts out with a history of tennis and proceeds to the basics of the game. The explanations are clear; there is a most worthwhile chapter on tennis equipment (ball, shoes, etc.); and many black-and-white photos demonstrate positions and techniques." Sch Library J

Glossary: p124-26

Hopman, Harry

Better tennis for boys and girls. Dodd 1972 95p illus lib. bdg. $4.50 (5-7)
796.34

1 Tennis
ISBN 0-396-06365-9

"A practical guide for the serious beginning player stressing the qualities necessary for success—concentration, discipline, and determination—and sportsmanship. [The author] discusses various grips, strokes, and service; points out the importance of thinking and tactics; and gives suggestions about practice, physical fitness, preparation for a match, and equipment. The photographs and drawings are helpful." Booklist

Tennis terms: p93-95

McCormick, Bill

Tennis. Watts, F. 1973 66p illus lib. bdg. $3.90 (5-7)
796.34

1 Tennis
ISBN 0-531-00803-7

"A First book"

"A diversified look at tennis from various strokes and tactics to a list of past and present greats. . . . Basic playing and scoring information are discussed in simple terms dealing with such items as court dimensions; forehand, backhand, and volley strokes; and tennis etiquette and conditioning. Minor factual errors, such as Chris Evert's incorrect home state, do not detract from the overall appeal of this introductory work." Booklist

Glossary: p62-64

Sullivan, George

Better table tennis for boys and girls. Dodd 1972 64p illus lib. bdg. $4.95 (5-7)
796.34

1 Ping-pong
ISBN 0-396-06643-7

"This gives complete, detailed and, for the most part, clear explanations of equipment, techniques, strategies, and rules of table tennis. Numerous excellent photographs and carefully placed diagrams aid understanding of the often technical text. Photos and discussions of major players of the sport are an effective addition, as is the inclusion of a brief, even-handed treatment of Ping-Pong diplomacy with China in the introduction. Well written with no condescension." Sch Library J

796.352 Golf

Smith, Parker

Golf techniques: how to improve your game; photographs by Meryl Joseph; illus. by Dom Lupo. Watts, F. 1973 63p illus $3.95 (5-7)
796.352

1 Golf
ISBN 0-531-02627-2

"A Concise guide"

This book contains "elementary lessons on basics such as grip, stance, and swing and tips on common trouble shots and putting. . . . The photographs and diagrams are generally well correlated with the text." Sch Library J

Glossary: p56-58. Bibliography: p59

796.357 Baseball

Archibald, Joe

Baseball talk for beginners; written and illus. by Joe Archibald. Messner 1969 90p illus lib. bdg. $4.64 (4-7)
796.357

1 Baseball—Dictionaries
ISBN 0-671-32066-1

In this dictionary, the author explains the game of baseball through the use of definitions, tips on how to play, and baseball history and facts

"Some of the words are obvious—but a number have surprise meanings. The book is a good reference source." Christian Sci Monitor

Illustrated with cartoons by the author

Brewster, Benjamin

Baseball; 4th rev. ed. Pictures by Jeanne Bendick. Watts, F. 1970 59p illus lib. bdg. $3.90 (3-5)
796.357

1 Baseball
ISBN 0-531-00479-1

"A First book"

First published 1950 with title: The first book of baseball

The author presents descriptions of rules, players, equipment, and the major and minor leagues. The jargon of baseball is explained in both the text and a glossary. Diagrams help to explain the duties of the various positions as well as clear up different kinds of plays

Kalb, Jonah

How to play baseball better than you did last season; illus. by Kevin Callahan. Macmillan Pub. Co. 1974 148p illus lib. bdg. $5.95 (4-6)
796.357

1 Baseball
ISBN 0-02-749330-X

The author "discusses each playing position separately, giving tips on how to deal with game situations and how to practice between games. Skills and know-how involved in hitting and base running are also detailed with a commonsense approach based on the author's apparent experience. The black-and-white cartoon-style drawings add less to the book's informational value than the several small diagrams included. A well-organized text and long table of contents somewhat make up for the lack of index." Booklist

Robinson, Jackie

Jackie Robinson's Little league baseball book. Prentice-Hall 1972 135p illus $5.95 (4-7)
796.357

1 Little league baseball
ISBN 0-13-509232-9

"Using a conversational approach and including

Robinson, Jackie—*Continued*

many anecdotal reminiscences . . . [the author] emphasizes the importance of personal attitude, teamwork, and sportsmanship and gives solid advice on improving baseball skills, covering hitting and base running as well as each of the positions in the infield and outfield, pitching, and catching. He also has an admonishing word on the role of the adult, parent and coach, in the functioning of the Little League." Booklist

Rosenburg, John M.

The story of baseball; illus. with photographs. Random House 1972 191p illus $4.95, lib. bdg. $5.99 (6-7) 796.357

1 Baseball—History

ISBN 0-394-81677-3; 0-394-91677-8

"Landmark giant"

First published 1962

A history of major league baseball in the United States which "describes the development of the game, the rise of professional baseball clubs, and a number of pennant races and World Series. It also introduces many baseball personalities of the past and present, making clear their contributions to the world of baseball." Booklist [Review of 1962 edition]

Sports Illustrated Baseball, by the editors of Sports Illustrated; illus. by Ed Vebell. [Rev. ed] Lippincott 1972 93p illus $4.95, pa $1.95 (5-7) 796.357

1 Baseball

ISBN 0-397-00857-0; 0-397-00831-7

"The Sports Illustrated library"

First published 1960 with title: Sports Illustrated Book of baseball. Text revisions by Roy Blount

Contents: Harmon Killebrew on hitting; Dave McNally on pitching; Brooks Robinson on infielding; Tim McCarver on catching; Tommie Agee on outfielding and base-running

The "remarkable drawings showing technique of major league stars accompany tips from the players themselves." Bks for Deaf Children

Sullivan, George

Baseball's art of hitting; illus. with photographs and diagrams. Dodd 1974 128p illus lib. bdg. $4.50 (5-7) 796.357

1 Baseball

ISBN 0-396-06913-4

Companion volume to: Pitchers and pitching, entered below

The author describes grip, stance, and swing techniques of hitting a baseball, the relationship between hitter and pitcher, bats, and the importance of pinch-hitters. He also profiles several notable hitters

"This will be useful for students of the game." Sch Library J

Better softball for boys and girls. Dodd 1975 64p illus lib. bdg. $4.50 (4-7) 796.357

1 Softball

ISBN 0-396-07063-9

Basic techniques of softball are described in this book. Included are advice and diagrams on how to hit, field, pitch, bunt, and run bases, as well as information on equipment and the rules of the game

The author delivers "a straightforward text well illustrated with black-and-white photographs and diagrams." Booklist

Glossary: p64

Pitchers and pitching; illus. with photographs and diagrams. Dodd 1972 123p illus lib. bdg. $4.50 (5-7) 796.357

1 Baseball

ISBN 0-396-06473-6

This book explains and analyzes the art and craft of pitching, describing different types of pitches, grips and deliveries, pitching strategy, control, and how the ball curves. It reveals how pitchers train and keep in condition. Also included are all-time pitching records and brief profiles of baseball's greatest pitchers

Turkin, Hy

The official encyclopedia of baseball, by Hy Turkin and S. C. Thompson. Barnes, A. S. illus $13.95 796.357

1 Baseball—Encyclopedias

ISBN 0-498-01436-3

First edition, called "Jubilee edition," published 1951. Each subsequent volume brings information about players, records and teams up to date

The volume includes historical information on the evolution of baseball; data on players, umpires, managers, major leagues, world series games, and records; playing hints and official playing rules; baseball ballads; and a glossary of slang terms

796.4 Athletic exercises and gymnastics. Olympic games

Antonacci, Robert J.

Track and field for young champions, by Robert J Antonacci and Gene Schoor; illus. by Frank Mullins. McGraw 1974 185p illus $5.95, lib. bdg. $5.72 (4-7) 796.4

1 Track athletics

ISBN 0-07-002135-X; 0-07-002136-8

The authors discuss the history and rules of various track events. They provide tips, drills, and exercises for participation in distance running, relays, hurdles, jumps and vaults, throwing events, and jogging and hiking

This "is designed for reluctant readers who are beginners at this sport, but . . . [the authors] skillfully keep both interest and instructional levels on a high plane. . . . There are handy charts showing youngsters how to compare their efforts in events with norms for particular age levels." Sch Library J

Glossary: p177-81

Walsh, John

The first book of the Olympic games; rev. by Frank Litsky; illus. with photographs. [2d rev. ed] Watts, F. 1971 55p illus lib. bdg. $3.90 (4-7) 796.4

1 Olympic games

ISBN 0-531-00601-8

First published 1963

Here is "the story of the Olympic games from their beginning to the present, and information about some of the great competitors and their records." Hodges. Bks for Elem Sch Libraries

Other books on the Olympics: p52-53

796.54 Camping

Paul, Aileen

Kids camping; illus. by John Delulio. Doubleday 1973 128p illus $4.95, lib. bdg. $5.70 (4-6) 796.54

1 Camping

ISBN 0-385-02937-3; 0-385-02939-X

The author "advises children who have never been camping about the selection of a tent, sleeping bags, and camp equipment. She offers instructions for erecting a tent, laying out the camp site, building a

Paul, Aileen—*Continued*

camp fire, and camp cooking and gives menus for seven days plus a grocery shopping list. The food can be prepared with little effort and several simple recipes have been included. The author mentions special things to consider when camping at the seashore, in Canada, and in Mexico and briefly covers safety precautions in camping. Lists of sources for additional information and a checklist of things needed on a camping trip appended." Booklist

796.6   Cycling

Coombs, Charles
Bicycling; illus. with 59 photographs and diagrams. Morrow 1972 127p illus $4.95, lib. bdg. $4.59 (4-7)
796.6
1 Bicycles and bicycling
ISBN 0-688-30032-4; 0-688-20032-X
This survey begins with a brief history of the two wheeler and goes on to describe how to select, use, and take care of bicycles. Other chapters discuss the use of the bicycle in commerce and industry, and in group and club activities
Glossary: p123-24

Frankel, Lillian
Bike-ways (101 things to do with a bike) by Lillian and Godfrey Frankel. New rev. ed. Sterling 1972 128p illus $4.95, lib. bdg. $4.89 (4-6)   796.6
1 Bicycles and bicycling
ISBN 0-8069-4004-2; 0-8069-4005-0
First published 1961 with title: 101 things to do with a bike
Bike clubs, trips and tours, camping, selecting a bike, accessories, and safety are some of the aspects of bicycles and bicycling covered in this book

Radlauer, Edward
Soap box racing. Childrens Press 1973 32p illus lib. bdg. $5.25 (1-4)   796.6
1 Soap box derbies
ISBN 0-516-07423-7
"Ready, get set, go books." "An Elk Grove book"
Here are directions for building a soap box racer and entering a derby
The "book has prominent black type, a simple text, and lush color photographs facing or accompanying each page of text. . . . [It is] an interest-grabbing reading ladder for beginning or poor readers." Booklist

Sullivan, George
Better bicycling for boys and girls. Dodd 1974 64p illus map lib. bdg. $4.50 (4-7)   796.6
1 Bicycles and bicycling
ISBN 0-396-06845-6
Aspects covered include maintenance and repair, rules of the road and safety, equipment and tips for touring
"There are numerous black-and-white photographs and references to helpful information sources throughout; a list of mainly U.S. cycling organizations is appended. The lack of index is partially compensated for by well-marked sections and subsections." Booklist

796.7   Driving motor vehicles

Cooke, David C.
Racing cars that made history. Putnam 1960 70p illus lib. bdg. $3.86 (5-7)   796.7

1 Automobile racing 2 Automobiles
ISBN 0-399-60529-0
"Full-page photographs, with descriptive text, of thirty-seven famous racing cars dating from 1903 to 1959." Horn Bk

Jackson, Robert B.
Road race round the world; New York to Paris, 1908. Walck, H.Z. 1965 58p illus map $4.95, pa $1.50 (4-7)   796.7
1 New York to Paris Race, 1908
ISBN 0-8098-2038-2; 0-8098-2901-0
This is a "chronicle of the 1908 road race across 1300 miles of the U.S., Asia, and Europe that was staged to demonstrate the dependability of cars." Minnesota
"The many surprisingly clear photographs will further attract the most reluctant reader." Sch Library J

Road racing, U.S.A. Rev. ed. Illus. with photographs. Walck, H.Z. 1972 53p illus $4.95 (4-7)
796.7
1 Automobile racing
ISBN 0-8098-2029-3
First published 1964
Written in a lively style, the text offers the historical background of road racing, compares it with drag and track racing, and conveys vividly the color and excitement of the events. Photographs are clear and integrated smartly with the text." Sch Library J [Review of 1964 edition]

Navarra, John Gabriel
Wheels for kids; photographs by Celeste Navarra. Doubleday 1973 63p illus $4.95, lib. bdg. $4.95 (3-6)   796.7
1 Motorcycles
ISBN 0-385-02693-5; 0-385-04630-8
Photographs and text cover techniques of riding motor bikes, parts, maintenance, safety rules, and races
"Strictly for novices in the use of motorbikes, this touches only lightly on instructions for driving. . . . There are many large, clear photos, but the text is disorganized and safety is preached on almost every page." Sch Library J

Stevenson, Peter
The greatest days of racing; with an introduction by Phil Hill; illus. with photographs. Scribner 1972 189p illus lib. bdg. $6.95 (5-7)   796.7
1 Automobile racing—History
ISBN 0-684-12987-6
"A lively enthusiastic account of the high points in auto racing history which begins with the Gordon Bennett race from Paris to Vienna in 1903. Stevenson concentrates on the engineers whose revolutionary ideas produced the little Peugeot, Bentley, and Porsche as well as on such sensational drivers as Boillot, Nuvolari, Hawthorn, Hill, and McQueen." Booklist

796.8   Karate

Kozuki, Russell
Junior karate; photographs by the author. Sterling 1971 128p illus $4.95, lib. bdg. $4.89 (5-7)   796.8
1 Karate
ISBN 0-8069-4446-3; 0-8069-4447-1
Illustrating with pen and camera, the author "renders karate exercises, stances, blocking techniques, strikes, kicks, contests, and Katas vividly—

Kozuki, Russell—*Continued*
certainly graspable—for young readers." Sch Library J

Karate for young people. Sterling 1974 128p illus $4.95, lib. bdg. $4.89 (5-7) 796.8
1 Karate
ISBN 0-8069-4074-3; 0-8069-4075-1
"Concise instructions and clear photographs of male and female teenage karatekas (practitioners of karate) in action in a basic step-by-step introduction to sport karate in which all blows and kicks are stopped just short of actual contact. Stressing body balance the guide demonstrates the different stances; punching, striking, blocking and kicking techniques; and the three types of sparring: formal basic, semifree, and freestyle. Scoring is touched on briefly in conclusion." Booklist

796.9 Ice and snow sports

Coombs, Charles
Be a winner in ice hockey. Morrow 1974 128p illus $4.75, lib. bdg. $4.32 (5-7) 796.9
1 Hockey
ISBN 0-688-20099-0; 0-688-30099-5
The author covers the fundamentals of ice hockey including techniques for "skating, stick handling and passing and discusses tactics to employ on offense and defense. Black and white photographs are interspersed throughout the text to illustrate certain ice hockey actions. Italics are used to emphasize important information and a glossary is included for some of the sport's terminology." Cath Library World
"While no book can substitute for coached practice, this is an excellent example of a how-to-do-it sports book: logically sequential, practical, clear, and comprehensive. . . . The writing style is lively and informal." Chicago. Children's Bk Center

Gavett, Bruce
Skiing for beginners, by Bruce Gavett and Conrad Brown; skiers: Peter Mumford and Cindy Gavett; photographed by Kim Massie. Scribner 1971 57p illus lib. bdg. $5.95 (4-7) 796.9
1 Skis and skiing
ISBN 0-684-12510-2
The book offers "step-by-step instructions in the American Ski Technique which is the method taught in most ski schools in the U.S. today. The book contains . . . photographs and includes . . . a number of transitional exercises to facilitate the passage from one basic maneuver to the next." Booklist

Liss, Howard
Hockey talk for beginners; illus. by Frank Robbins. Messner 1973 94p illus lib. bdg. $5.29 (4-7) 796.9
1 Hockey—Terminology
ISBN 0-671-32644-9
"A series of definitions and explanations, alphabetically arranged and with cross-references, is useful as a handbook for new hockey fans or players, but it doesn't function well as an introduction to the game because the reader with no background must collate scattered facts while reading. . . . As a companion to a book that explains the game, however, this is very handy." Chicago. Children's Bk Center

Scott, Barbara Ann
Skating for beginners, by Barbara Ann Scott and Michael Kirby. Knopf 1953 106p illus lib. bdg. $5.99 (5-7) 796.9
1 Skating
ISBN 0-394-91632-8
"This combination of explanatory text, photographs and diagrams demonstrates positions and techniques for the attainment of skill and grace. The photographs—of learners of many ages and of the authors themselves, both champions—are particularly helpful when revealing weaknesses in form. It is unfortunate for real beginners who need diagrams that these appear only in later chapters." Horn Bk
Some terms used: p93-95

797 Aquatic and air sports

Radlauer, E.
Racing on the wind, by E. and R. S. Radlauer; illus. with photographs by the authors. Watts, F. 1974 47p illus (Sports action bks) lib. bdg. $4.95 (3-6) 797
1 Aeronautical sports 2 Sailing
ISBN 0-531-02681-7
This book introduces various wind sports: self-soaring, sailplane gliding, ballooning, land sailing, ice boat sailing, and windsurfing
The authors "pair clear color photographs with an informative, conversational text geared to the high interest, low effort reading market. . . . While a combination glossary-index explains key words that have appeared earlier in bold type, the whole manages to avoid sounding like a reading lesson." Booklist

797.1 Boating

Gibbs, Tony
Sailing. Watts, F. 1974 90p illus map lib. bdg. $3.95 (5-7) 797.1
1 Sailing
ISBN 0-531-00820-7
"A First book"
This introduction to sailing in a daysailing sloop describes the boat and its parts; rigging and checking equipment; how to sail; how to care for the boat; and seamanship, safety on the water, and emergencies
"A very comprehensive book with black and white photographs by Gary L. Falkenstern to recommend to an aspiring sailing enthusiast." Cath Library World
Other books to read: p76. Glossary of sailing terms: p77-87

Navarra, John Gabriel
Safe motorboating for kids; photographs by Celeste Scala Navarra. Doubleday 1974 64p illus map $4.95, lib. bdg. $5.70 (4-7) 797.1
1 Motorboats 2 Boats and boating
ISBN 0-385-06512-4; 0-385-07949-4
This book "describes all the steps necessary for an enjoyable water ride, with the emphasis always on safety. How to make ready, get the engine started, avoid collisions and take care of the craft are all covered, along with information on marine engines and other parts of the boat. A nautical dictionary is appended." Pub W
"Easy-to-read supplementary material. . . . Illustrated with up-to-date black-and-white photographs." Sch Library J

797.2   Swimming and diving

Sullivan, George

Better swimming and diving for boys and girls. Dodd 1967 64p illus lib. bdg. $4.50 (5-7)   797.2

1 Swimming 2 Diving

ISBN 0-396-06574-0

"This guide to swimming strokes and springboard dives is designed for the young person who wishes to train for competition. The concise text explains precisely how to perform each style of swimming and diving, while clear sequences of photographs illustrate ideal form." Booklist

Glossary: p64

797.5   Air sports

Halacy, Dan

Soaring; photographed by James Tallon. Lippincott 1972 unp illus $3.95, lib. bdg. $3.79 (3-6)   797.5

1 Gliding and soaring 2 Gliders (Aeronautics)

ISBN 0-397-31248-2; 0-397-31322-5

This book describes the technique of soaring—powerless airflight in crafts known as gliders or sailplanes

798   Equestrian sports

Anderson, C. W.

Twenty gallant horses. Macmillan (N Y) 1965 87p illus $4.95 (5-7)   798

1 Horses 2 Horse racing

Some of these brief horse stories were published 1939, in different versions, in the author's: Black, bay and chestnut

"In handsome full-page lithographs and brief text [the author, who is also the illustrator] portrays a score of the greatest racing and jumping champions of all time, describing the qualities of breeding, courage, and intelligence that accounted for their amazing performances." Booklist

Slaughter, Jean

Horsemanship for beginners: riding, jumping, and schooling; photographs by Michael J. Phillips. Knopf 1952 118p illus $4.50, lib. bdg. $5.69 (5-7)   798

1 Horsemanship

ISBN 0-394-81256-5; 0-394-91256-X

The reader is shown the first steps in the English and eastern school of riding and horsemanship. The horse, equipment, kindness and discipline, mounting, gaits, jumping, clothes, and show riding are discussed

Glossary: p116-18

Sports Illustrated Horseback riding; by the editors of Sports Illustrated. [Rev. ed] Lippincott 1971 [c1960] 94p illus $4.95, pa $1.95 (6-7)   798

1 Horsemanship

ISBN 0-397-00736-1; 0-397-00735-3

"The Sports Illustrated library"

First published 1960 with title: Sports Illustrated Book of horseback riding

Text by Gordon Wright with Alice Higgins. Illustrated by Sam Savitt

This book, designed for the beginning rider, includes instructions on the handling of horses, equipment, and the care and feeding of horses

Sullivan, George

Better horseback riding for boys and girls. Dodd 1969 64p illus lib. bdg. $4.50 (5-7)   798

1 Horsemanship

ISBN 0-396-06404-3

"Many carefully sequenced photographs accompany a clear, informative text. . . . [The book] covers the basics of safe and correct horseback riding for beginners of any age. Each step is clearly developed, including choosing the correct tack and clothing; handling the horse by leading, mounting and riding through the basic gaits; jumping and trail riding; and the personal care of one's own horse." Sch Library J

Glossary: p64

799   Fishing, hunting, shooting

Hofsinde, Robert

Indian hunting; written and illus. by Robert Hofsinde (Gray-Wolf) Morrow 1962 96p illus lib. bdg. $4.32 (3-6)   799

1 Indians of North America 2 Hunting

ISBN 0-688-31608-5

"The division of the text is on the basis of the game being hunted: large game, small game, whales and seals; two sections discuss hunting from canoes and preparing for the hunt. In each section, there are descriptions of the differences in tribal techniques, of traps and weapons, and of the special procedures used with individual animals." Chicago. Children's Bk Center

"An anthropological approach to the hunting and fishing lore of early man. Fine sketches of traps and weapons." Chicago Sch J

799.1   Fishing

Hofsinde, Robert

Indian fishing and camping; written and illus. by Robert Hofsinde (Gray-Wolf) Morrow 1963 92p illus map lib. bdg. $4.32 (3-6)   799.1

1 Indians of North America 2 Fishing

ISBN 0-688-31797-9

"Factual descriptions of Indian and Eskimo camping and fishing are accompanied by detailed accounts of how to make many different items of Indian fishing equipment, of what bait to use, and of how to cook one's catch. Exact, informative illustrations further instruct the reader in these activities." Wis Library Bul

799.3   Archery

Sullivan, George

Better archery for boys and girls. Dodd 1970 64p illus $3.50, lib. bdg. $4.50 (5-7)   799.3

1 Archery

ISBN 0-396-06055-2; 0-396-06056-0

Basic information for the beginning archer is given—how to choose the proper bow and arrow, how to brace a bow, nock, draw, hold, air, release and follow through. Tips are also given on correcting faults, caring for equipment, and safety measures

"One interesting section is devoted to self-correction where several examples of faults are

Sullivan, George—*Continued*
pointed out with simple techniques for eradication of the errors. The principle negative-adaptation in motor learning is well exemplified in this valuable part." Choice

Glossary: p64

800 LITERATURE

803 Literature—Encyclopedias and dictionaries

Brewer's Dictionary of phrase and fable. Centenary ed. Rev. by Ivor H. Evans. Harper [1971 c1970] 1175p front $15 **803**
1 Literature—Encyclopedias 2 Allusions
ISBN 0-06-010466-X
First published 1870, edited by Ebenezer Cobham Brewer
This book "encompasses real, fictitious, and mythical names from history, romance, the arts, science, and fable, and phrases, superstitions, and customs ancient and contemporary. The 20,000 entries include phrases grouped under key words, [i.e.] names of saints, giants. Quotations provide source, etymology, and pronunciation." Wynar. Guide to Ref Bks for Sch Media Centers
"Long on trivia. Grand for browsing. Useful for reference." Choice

The Reader's encyclopedia. 2d ed. Crowell 1965 1118p illus $12.50, thumb indexed $15 **803**
1 Literature—Encyclopedias 2 Art—Encyclopedias 3 Music—Encyclopedias
ISBN 0-690-67128-8; 0-690-67129-6
First published 1948, edited by William Rose Benét
Replaces: Crowell's Handbook for readers and writers, edited by Henrietta Gerwig
"A one-volume literary handbook, it aims to cover the entire field of world literature and arts. It contains articles, arranged alphabetically, on authors, titles, and characters of literary works; literary movements, terms and allusions; people, terms and movements associated with the arts, philosophy, science, religion, and mythology." Wynar. Guide to Ref Bks for Sch Media Centers
It "will serve as a well organized supplementary memory and an explanation of many literary allusions." Cleveland
For a more complete review see: The Booklist and Subscription Books Bulletin, April 15, 1965

808 Rhetoric

Brandt, Sue R.
How to improve your written English; illus. by Carolyn Bentley. Watts, F. 1972 87p illus lib. bdg. $3.90 (4-6) **808**
1 English language—Composition and exercises 2 English language—Grammar
ISBN 0-531-00772-3
"A First book"
This book discusses the differences between spoken and written English and between formal and everyday speech. Aimed at middle-school age children, it has sections on vocabulary building, use of verbs and pronouns, sentence structure, spelling, handwriting, capitalization and punctuation

808.5 Rhetoric of speech

Kettelkamp, Larry
Song, speech, and ventriloquism; written and illus. by Larry Kettelkamp. Morrow 1967 96p illus $4.95, lib. bdg. $4.59 (5-7) **808.5**
1 Voice 2 Speech 3 Singing 4 Ventriloquism
ISBN 0-688-21799-0; 0-688-31799-5
"The mechanism of speech is discussed with explanation of the muscles and actions involved in breathing, vibration of the larynx, and articulation. There is a chapter on singing and one on ventriloquism." The AAAS Sci Bk List for Children
"In this combination of scientific text and how-to-do-it manual, the interrelationships between the two parts are not always made clear. However, the book would be very useful to those interested in the subject and the illustrations and charts admirably support the text." Library J
Glossary of terms: p91-93

808.6 Rhetoric of letters

Joslin, Sesyle
Dear dragon . . . and other useful letter forms for young ladies and gentlemen engaged in everyday correspondence; illus. by Irene Haas. Harcourt 1962 unp illus $4.50 (1-4) **808.6**
1 Letter writing
ISBN 0-15-223052-1
This "volume of instruction in correct social behavior illustrates hilarious situations with completely proper answers in startling contrast. Notes for business, congratulations, thank-you, regret, apology, and acceptance, a bread-and-butter letter, and a get-well note are associated with such activities as holiday traveling on ostrich-back, ordering crocodile shoes, attending a masked ball, and being dropped on a desert island." Horn Bk
"The situations will need some mind-stretching on the part of younger children, but they may think up letters even funnier than these. Irene Haas's pictures are . . . both entertaining and decorative." Sat Rev

808.8 Literature—Collections

Anderson, C. W.
(ed.) C. W. Anderson's Favorite horse stories; collected and illus. by C. W. Anderson. Dutton 1967 192p illus $6.95 (5-7) **808.8**
1 Horses 2 Literature—Collections
ISBN 0-525-25626-1
This collection includes essays and poems as well as stories about horses. Some authors represented are John Masefield, Will James, C. W. Anderson, Enid Bagnold and Eddie Arcaro
"A brief introduction by Mr. Anderson precedes each selection and he has done all but two of the illustrations. Though it's not an outstanding anthology, Anderson's many devotees form an assured audience." Sch Library J

Association for Childhood Education International

Told under the Christmas tree; stories and poems from around the world; selected by the Literature Committee of the Association for Childhood Education International; illus by Maud and Miska Petersham. Macmillan Pub. Co. 1948 304p illus $6.95 (3-6)   808.8

1 Literature—Collections 2 Christmas stories 3 Christmas poetry

"The Umbrella books"

"A fine collection of Christmas stories and verse which includes . . . a group of stories and poems related to Hanukkah, the Jewish Festival of Lights, which falls near the Christmas season. Many of the stories are excerpts from longer ones and describe the customs and traditions of the Christmas celebration in many lands. Listed at the end are the titles, with sources, of Christmas stories which have been published in preceding Umbrella books but which are not included here." Booklist

"The book can be enjoyed by Christian and Jew alike, and perhaps draw the two more closely together through an understanding of each other's beliefs." N Y Times Bk Rev

Arbuthnot, May Hill

(comp.) The Arbuthnot Anthology of children's literature; [comp. by] May Hill Arbuthnot and [others]; 4th ed. rev. by Zena Sutherland; illustrators: Rainey Bennett [and others]. Lothrop 1976 xxii, 1088p illus $22.50   808.8

1 Literature—Collections

ISBN 0-688-41725-6

First published 1953 by Scott

An anthology of selections and excerpts from a wide range of literature for children of all ages, this book was originally intended as a source book for classes in children's literature as well as a collection of materials to be used with children in groups or individually. Part one includes over 500 poems. Part two is a collection of folk tales, fables, myths, epics, hero tales and modern fantasy. Part three consists of selections from realistic stories, historical fiction, biographies, and informational books. Part four contains the following: a chronology of important events in the history of children's literature; "Illustrations in children's books," by Donnarae MacCann and Olga Richard—an historical and critical account accompanied by illustrations, a glossary and a bibliography; "Guiding literary experience," by Sam Sebesta and Dianne Monson—a guide to the selection and use of literature with children, including suggestions for reading aloud, storytelling, dramatization and discussion groups, with subsection bibliographies; a listing of children's book award winners; an annotated bibliography including background and reference sources for adults, sources of audiovisual materials, and lists of books for children corresponding to the organization of Parts I to III. The book contains a glossary, a subject index, and an index of authors, illustrators and titles

Brown, Michael

(ed.) A cavalcade of sea legends; illus. by Krystyna Turska. Walck, H.Z. [1972 c1971] 274p illus $8.50 (5-7)   808.8

1 Sea stories 2 Legends

ISBN 0-8098-2419-1

First published 1971 in England with title: The Hamish Hamilton Book of sea legends

This is a collection of 37 stories and poems dealing with various aspects of the sea, grouped under the headings: Mermaids and monsters; Superstitions and legends; Voyages and adventures

The "Orient, Middle East, and Ancient Greece are represented while most of the selections originate in Northern Europe. Styles of writing vary, many having an old-fashioned flavor of dialect or archaic usage, but all add up to an excellent collection." Library J

Notes on sources: p272-74

Darrell, Margery

(ed.) Once upon a time; the fairy tale world of Arthur Rackham. Viking 1972 296p illus $14.95   808.8

1 Literature—Collections

ISBN 0-670-52574-X

"A Studio book"

This is "a compilation of the full texts of seven works illustrated by Rackham: 'Alice's Adventures in Wonderland,' 'A Christmas Carol,' 'Fables' by 'Aesop,' 'Peter Pan in Kensington Gardens,' 'Rip Van Winkle,' 'Seven Fairy Tales' of the Grimm Brothers and 'Three Tales from Shakespeare,' by the Lambs. The illustrations, in black and white and in color, are valuable both in themselves and for historical reasons, and the editor's preface discusses both Rackham's work and his philosophy of illustration for children." Chicago. Children's Bk Center

Farjeon, Eleanor

(ed.) A cavalcade of kings; collected and ed. jointly by Eleanor Farjeon and William Mayne; illus. by Victor Ambrus. Walck, H.Z. 1965 [c1964] 237p illus $7.50 (5-7)   808.8

1 Kings and rulers 2 Literature—Collections

ISBN 0-8098-2380-2

First published 1964 in England with title: The Hamish Hamilton Book of kings

"A collection of a variety of writings about kings, real and imaginary, including some poems, fairy tales, nursery rhymes, a psalm, and a selection from T. H. White's 'Sword in the Stone.' Sources are primarily English, and many of the authors are familiar: E. Nesbit, G. K. Chesterton, de la Mare, Tennyson. Text is divided into sections called 'Imaginary Stories about Imaginary Kings,' 'Imaginary Stories about Real Kings,' 'Better Not to Be a King' (including two poems and an essay), and 'Some Real Kings.'" Sch Library J

"The reader who expects to find here a systematic anthology of stories about kings will be disappointed. . . . It is instead a wholly creative work." Horn Bk

(ed.) A cavalcade of queens; collected and ed. jointly by Eleanor Farjeon and William Mayne; illus. by Victor Ambrus. Walck, H.Z. 1965 243p illus $7.50 (4-7)   808.8

1 Queens 2 Literature—Collections

ISBN 0-8098-2381-0

Published in England with title: The Hamish Hamilton Book of queens

A companion volume to: A cavalcade of kings, entered above

"There is great variety including nonsense rhymes, fairy tales, bits of history, Fanny Burney's letter to a friend telling her how to behave at court, Kipling's 'Gloriana,' the passage about the Queen of Sheba from the first Book of Kings, and a story by each editor. The introduction and the lively notes about the authors of the [14] pieces reflect the pleasure the collaborators must have had in compiling the collection. Large type and attractive drawings." Horn Bk

Green, Roger Lancelyn

(ed.) A cavalcade of dragons; illus. by Krystyna Turska. Walck, H.Z. [1971 c1970] 256p illus $8.50 (4-7)   808.8

1 Dragons—Stories 2 Literature—Collections

ISBN 0-8098-2413-2

Green, Roger Lancelyn—*Continued*
First published 1970 in England with title: The Hamish Hamilton Book of dragons
In this collection "three divisions—Dragons of Ancient Days, Dragons of the Dark Ages, and Dragons of Folklore—contain traditional material taken from the Greek and Roman myths, the Scandinavian sagas, medieval romances, and the folk and fairy tales of different countries. The fourth division—Dragons of Later Days—presents a more modern view of the 'terrible Worm' in material by writers such as J. R. R. Tolkien, E. Nesbit, C. S. Lewis, G. K. Chesterton, and Andrew Lang." Horn Bk

(ed.) A cavalcade of magicians; illus. by Victor Ambrus. Walck, H.Z. 1973 274p illus $8.50 (4-7)
808.8
1 Literature—Collections 2 Fairy tales
ISBN 0-8098-2422-1
Published in England with title: The Hamish Hamilton Book of magicians
Twenty-one tales and stories and four poems about "good and bad magicians down through the ages are paraded in the author's latest cavalcade. Some, like the Sorcerer's Apprentice, Aladdin, and, of course, Merlin, are familiar, but a good number of the remainder offer fair reading on not so common ground. Green deftly handles most of the retelling [himself], except for those tales involving magicians of more recent vintage, as in E. Nesbit's 'The princess and the cat' or Milne's 'Prince Rabbit.' All told, the whole of these parts offers pleasing possibilities for fanciers of necromancy." Booklist
Notes on sources: p271-73

Gruenberg, Sidonie Matsner
(ed.) Favorite stories old and new. Rev. and enl. ed. Illus. by Kurt Wiese. Doubleday 1955 512p illus $6.95
808.8
1 Literature—Collections 2 Storytelling—Collections
ISBN 0-385-07293-7
First published 1942
This volume contains "many excellent stories and poems, chosen for appeal to children of all ages, useful for storytelling and reading aloud." Hodges. Bks for Elem Sch Libraries

(comp.) Let's hear a story; 30 stories and poems for today's boys and girls; illus. by Dagmar Wilson. Doubleday 1961 160p illus $5.95
808.8
1 Literature—Collections
ISBN 0-385-03316-8
Stories and poems by such authors as: Hardie Gramatky, Miriam Schlein, Eleanor Farjeon, Virginia Lee Burton, Alvin Tresselt, Phyllis McGinley and Marjorie Flack. Some of the subjects are "lively boys and girls, birthday parties, kittens, puppies, kangaroos, horses and elephants, trains, tugboats and grandpas." Introduction
"A read-aloud anthology. . . . Some [inclusions] are appropriate for independent reading by second-grade children. The selection is judicious and the book is useful, although the material is available elsewhere." Chicago. Children's Bk Center

Hoke, Helen
(ed.) Witches, witches, witches; pictures by W. R. Lohse. Watts, F. 1958 230p illus lib. bdg. $5.88 (5-7)
808.8
1 Witches 2 Literature—Collections
ISBN 0-531-01823-7
"Short stories, fairy tales, poetry, and excerpts from books are included in this collection of material about witches. Some of the authors and editors represented are Oliver Wendell Holmes, Sigrid Undset,

the brothers Grimm, Oscar Wilde, Rachel Field, and Eleanor Farjeon. Selection has been made with discrimination." Chicago. Children's Bk Center
"A bonanza for storytellers and Halloween requests. Wonderfully spooky illustrations by W. R. Lohse. Print is clear and well spaced, so 5th-graders on up can read it. All the stories are already in libraries though some in books now out of print, but this is good for those that can afford the luxury of having their witches all together in one brew." Library J

Hope-Simpson, Jacynth
(ed.) A cavalcade of witches; illus. by Krystyna Turska. Walck, H.Z. 1967 [c1966] 225p illus $8.50 (4-7)
808.8
1 Witches 2 Literature—Collections
ISBN 0-8098-2396-9
First published 1966 in England with title: The Hamish Hamilton Book of witches
A collection of poems, stories, excerpts from novels, folklore, and miscellaneous pieces about both ancient and modern witches. Included are accounts of witch-hunts and "confessions" by supposed witches
"An introduction briefly reviews the role of witches in history and literature and numerous notes throughout the book explain the source and significance of the selections. Illustrated with atmospheric drawings in black and white." Booklist

Johnson, Edna
(ed.) Anthology of children's literature; 4th rev. ed. [Edited by] Edna Johnson, Evelyn R. Sickels [and] Frances Clarke Sayers; with black and white illus. by Fritz Eichenberg and full color paintings by N. C. Wyeth. Houghton 1970 xxxviii, 1289p illus $24.95
808.8
1 Literature—Collections 2 Children's literature—Bibliography
ISBN 0-395-10914-0
First published 1935
Partial contents: Around the world in nursery rhymes; Folk tales; Myths and legends; Sacred writings and legends of the saints; Fiction; Poetry; Biography; Travel and history
"Indispensable for anyone who wishes to survey the general field of children's books, who is not looking for a substitute for the books themselves but for a guide that is both practical and inspiring." Horn Bk
Includes appendices on storytelling, the history of children's literature, illustrators of children's books, and children's book awards, as well as graded reading lists, biographical sketches of authors, and bibliographies. There is a pronouncing glossary and, in addition to an author/title index, a listing of contents by ages and grades

Martignoni, Margaret E.
(ed.) The illustrated treasury of children's literature; ed. and with an introduction by Margaret E. Martignoni; comp. with the original illus. under the direction of P. Edward Ernest. Staff editors: Doris Duenewald, Evelyn Andres [and] Alice Thorne. Grosset 1955 512p illus $7.95
808.8
1 Literature—Collections
ISBN 0-448-04101-4
Contained in this anthology "are Mother Goose rhymes, a picture alphabet, and poems, fairy tales, fables, and legends taken from recognized sources, and well-known stories, some complete in themselves and others carefully chosen excerpts. What makes the anthology unique are the hundreds of illustrations, chosen from distinctive editions and reproduced from the original illustrations. Designed primarily for fam-

Martignoni, Margaret E.—*Continued*
ily use and for reading aloud, the book should be tremendously popular in the parents collection." Booklist

Untermeyer, Bryna
(ed.) The Golden Treasury of children's literature; ed. and selected by Bryna and Louis Untermeyer. Golden Press 1966 544p illus $7.95, lib. bdg. $6.95
                                                    808.8

1 Literature—Collections
ISBN 0-307-16522-1; 0-307-66522-4
Selections from the ten previously published volumes comprising: The Golden Treasury of children's literature
Featured here are modern stories, as well as the classics, ancient myths, folk tales and legends

808.81 Poetry—Collections

Adams, Adrienne
(comp.) Poetry of earth; selected and illus. by Adrienne Adams. Scribner 1972 48p illus lib. bdg. $5.95 (3-6)   808.81

1 Nature in poetry 2 Poetry—Collections
ISBN 0-684-13012-2
In this collection of thirty-three poems, such poets as Robert Frost, David McCord, Edna St Vincent Millay, and James Stephens write about the earth and its many creatures
"Handsomely designed and beautifully illustrated with pictures in soft colors, with some of the pages in quiet tones of earth and rock colors, this a compilation of poems that celebrate the beauty of flora and fauna, of the stars and the sea and the snow. The poetry has been chosen with high selectivity. . . . A good choice for reading to younger children as well as for independent readers." Chicago. Children's Bk Center

Brewton, John E.
(comp.) Index to children's poetry. . . . Comp. by John E. and Sara W. Brewton. Wilson, H.W. 1942 xxxii, 965p $20   808.81

1 Poetry—Indexes
ISBN 0-8242-0023-3
"A title, subject, author, and first line index to poetry in collections for children and youth." Title page
An index, in one alphabet, to more than 15,000 poems by approximately 2,500 different authors. The poems, from 130 collections of poems for children and young people, are classified under more than 1,800 subjects. An analysis of the books indexed, noting grade levels of interest, and a directory of publishers are included

(comp.) Index to children's poetry; first supplement. . . . Comp. by John E. and Sara W. Brewton. Wilson, H.W. 1954 xxii, 405p $12   808.81

1 Poetry—Indexes
ISBN 0-8242-0022-5
"A title, subject, author, and first line index to poetry in collections for children and youth." Title page
Following the form of the main volume, entered above, this volume indexes 66 collections, published between 1938 and 1951, of more than 7,000 poems by about 1,300 different authors. Classified under 1,250 subjects. Each collection is analyzed and graded

(comp.) Index to children's poetry; second supplement. . . . Comp. by John E. and Sara W. Brewton. Wilson, H.W. 1965 xxiv, 453p $12   808.81

1 Poetry—Indexes
ISBN 0-8242-0021-7
"A title, subject, author, and first line index to poetry in collections for children and youth." Title page
An extension of the basic volume and of the first supplement, published in 1942 and 1954, respectively, and entered above. This volume indexes 85 collections, published between 1949 and 1963, of more than 8,000 poems by approximately 1,400 authors, classified under more than 1,500 subjects

(comp.) Index to poetry for children and young people, 1964-1969. . . . Comp. by John E. and Sara W. Brewton and G. Meredith Blackburn III. Wilson, H.W. 1972 xxx, 575p $20   808.81

1 Poetry—Indexes
ISBN 0-8242-0435-2
"A title, subject, author, and first line index to poetry in collections for children and young people." Title page
An extension of the basic volume published 1942 with title: Index to children's poetry, and the first and second supplements published 1954 and 1965 respectively, all entered above. This volume indexes 117 collections of more than 11,000 poems by approximately 2,000 authors

(comp.) Under the tent of the sky; a collection of poems about animals large and small; with drawings by Robert Lawson. Macmillan (N Y) 1937 205p illus $5.95 (3-7)   808.81

1 Animals—Poetry 2 Poetry—Collections
A collection of poems grouped under twenty headings such as: Circus cavalcade; I went down to the zoo; Animals never seen in circus or zoo; Let's pretend; In fairy-land; Beneath man's wings; Little folks in the grass; Hurt no living thing
"A charming collection. . . . Children will find much to delight and entertain them. . . . Decorated end pages and pen and ink sketches by Robert Lawson. Indexes of authors, titles and first lines." N Y Libraries

Brewton, Sara
(comp.) Bridled with rainbows; poems about many things of earth and sky; selected by Sara and John E. Brewton; decorations by Vera Bock. Macmillan (N Y) 1949 191p illus lib. bdg. $4.95 (3-7)   808.81

1 Poetry—Collections
Nearly 200 poems, arranged according to subject with author, title, and first line indexes
"The anthology includes verses by modern poets as well as the old favorites that tell of the joys of childhood, the earth and sky, the seasons and school, the sea and ships, the day and night." Wis Library Bul
"This anthology will be a pleasant addition to poetry collections in children's rooms. The compilers have favored the imaginative poems over the humorous or down-to-earth and Vera Bock's excellent black-and-white decorations are very appropriate. Many of the selections are good for reading aloud. Library J

(comp.) Christmas bells are ringing; a treasury of Christmas poetry, selected by Sara and John E. Brewton; illus. by Decie Merwin. Macmillan (N Y) 1951 114p illus $4.95 (4-7)   808.81

1 Christmas poetry
"About 100 poems are included in this inviting and varied anthology of Christmas poetry. Under such headings as In the week when Christmas comes and Who will kneel them gently down, there are selec-

Brewton, Sara—*Continued*
tions for all ages, gay verses as well as reverent poems.
Author, title, and firstline indexes." Booklist
"Good for personal ownership and a valuable addition to school and public libraries." Horn Bk

Cole, William
(comp.) Beastly boys and ghastly girls; poems.
Drawings by Tomi Ungerer. Collins 1964 124p illus
lib. bdg. $4.91 (5-7)   808.81
1 Poetry—Collections
ISBN 0-529-03903-6
Here is "a collection of fiendish rhymes by such
humorists as Gelett Burgess, Hilaire Belloc, Shelly
Silverstein, A. A. Milne, and Lewis Carroll." Children's Bks. 1964
"In these poems is the naughtiest crew of pre-adults
ever assembled. In words and marvelous line drawings they stand ready to gladden the hearts of children." Pub W
Author and title indexes

(ed.) I went to the animal fair; a book of animal
poems; illus. by Colette Rosselli. Collins 1958 45p
illus $4.91 (k-3)   808.81
1 Animals—Poetry 2 Poetry—Collections
ISBN 0-529-03530-8
"Thirty-five poems about animals—from frogs and
grasshoppers to bears and whales—entrancingly illustrated and presented in picture-book format. Humor
and catchy rhythms predominate in the pleasing collection which includes old favorites and many less
familiar verses. Among the poets represented are
Milne, De la Mare, Coatsworth, Lindsay, Aldis,
Laura E. Richards, and William Jay Smith." Booklist
"William Cole, an experienced anthologist, has
chosen well. Like the poems, Colette Rosselli's drawings are simple, humorous and direct." N Y Times Bk
Rev
Title index: p[46]. Author index: p[47]

(ed.) Pick me up; a book of short short poems.
Macmillan (N Y) 1972 183p $4.95 (4-7)   808.81
1 Poetry—Collections
An anthology of over 200 poems, "divided into
seven parts—'Beginnings,' 'The Wit of Poets,' 'The
Poetry of Wit,' 'The Things of Nature,' 'Portraits,'
'Pictures,' and 'Ends.'" Library J
"An excellent book for browsing, for introducing
poetry to those who are not already poetry lovers, and
for classroom use when time is short or when children
might be dismayed by longer poems to read or
memorize." Chicago. Children's Bk Center.
Includes indexes of authors, titles and first lines

Ferris, Helen
(ed.) Favorite poems, old and new; selected for
boys and girls; illus. by Leonard Weisgard. Doubleday 1957 598p illus $6.95 (4-6)   808.81
1 Poetry—Collections
ISBN 0-385-07696-7
An anthology of more than seven hundred poems
divided into eighteen sections related to children's
interests that enable the reader either to browse or to
find a special poem for a special occasion
"This collection with its Leonard Weisgard illustrations is a treasure for the children's library shelves and
for the family to own." Wis Library Bul
Includes indexes of authors, titles and first lines
For a fuller review see: The Booklist and Subscription Books Bulletin, April 1, 1974

Granger's Index to poetry. 6th ed. completely rev.
and enl. indexing anthologies published through
December 31, 1970; ed. by William James Smith.
Columbia Univ. Press 1973 xxxvii, 2223p $80
                                                   808.81
1 Poetry—Indexes
ISBN 0-231-03641-8
First published 1904 by McClurg with title: Index
to poetry and recitations
This "is the best known of poetry indexes. The sixth
edition indexes 514 volumes of poetry anthologies
containing the works of some 12,000 poets and translators. There is a subject index that lists poems under
5,000 headings, an author index, and a combined
first-line and title index." Wynar. Guide to Ref Bks
for Sch Media Centers

Hazeltine, Alice I.
(comp.) The year around; poems for children;
selected by Alice I. Hazeltine & Elva S. Smith; decorations by Paula Hutchison. Abingdon 1956 192p illus
$3.95 (4-7)   808.81
1 Seasons—Poetry 2 Holidays—Poetry 3 Poetry—
Collections
ISBN 0-687-46624-5
A "volume of poems about the seasons, special days
and nature. Divisions are by the four seasons, and
then by the individual months within each season."
Chicago. Children's Bk Center
"The selections are from familiar authors, modern
favorites, and some less-familiar poets, but all with
appeal to children." Sat Rev
"Nicely illustrated with spot drawings. Author and
title index." Booklist

Koch, Kenneth
(comp.) Rose, where did you get that red? Teaching
great poetry to children. Random House 1973 360p
$7.95, pa $2.45   808.81
1 Poetry—Collections 2 Poetry—Study and teaching 3 Children as authors
ISBN 0-394-48320-0; 0-394-71885-1
Following an introductory essay describing Koch's
teaching method, each of the chapters is devoted to
explaining how he taught a particular poem, and gives
examples of poems the children wrote as part of the
lesson. Poets covered include Blake, Donne, Whitman, and Shakespeare among others. An anthology of
more poems to teach and suggestions for teaching
them is also included
"A handbook, anthology, and instructor's guide
combined, Koch's work will instantly endear itself to
writers and to teachers of every age and competence."
Library J

Larrick, Nancy
(ed.) Piping down the valleys wild; poetry for the
young of all ages; ed. with an introduction by Nancy
Larrick; illus. by Ellen Raskin. Delacorte Press 1968
xxiii, 247p illus $4.95, lib. bdg. $4.58   808.81
1 Poetry—Collections
ISBN 0-440-06923-8; 0-440-06953-X
A collection of poems, from all over the world,
arranged in sixteen sections, each one containing
poems dealing with a particular subject or experience
common to young people. Some of the poets included
are: Dylan Thomas, Emily Dickinson, Langston
Hughes, John Updike, and William Shakespeare
"A pleasant, quite comprehensive collection that
includes little unfamiliar material; the selections
range widely in source, somewhat less widely in
mood. . . . An index of first lines and an author-title
index [are] appended. The compiler's introduction is
addressed to adults and discusses reading aloud to the
young; this plus the fact that so much of the poetry is

Larrick, Nancy—*Continued*

for quite young children suggests that the book may be best suited to a home collection, although it should be useful in any collection of books for children." Sutherland. The Best in Children's Bks

(ed.) Room for me and a mountain lion; poetry of open space; illus. with photographs. Evans, M.&Co. 1974 191p illus $5.95 (5-7)   **808.81**
1 Nature in poetry 2 Poetry—Collections
ISBN 0-87131-124-0
This anthology "doesn't merely illustrate a theme, but conveys a feeling of connectedness, of interaction between our inner and outer worlds. The poets represented are mostly contemporary, ranging from Frost and D.H. Lawrence through Roethke and Jarrell to Stafford, Levertov, Kinnell, Swenson (and some lesser names); there are also short selections from Whitman, some Eskimo and Indian songs, [and] an 18th-Century Chinese poem." Library J
It "includes the work of children's poets as well as adult, and although it is perhaps too heavily weighted with William Stafford and, to a lesser degree, Galway Kinnell and Walt Whitman, it is certainly . . . appealing . . . for younger children." N Y Times Bk Rev
Indexes of poems and poets and of first lines are included

Lewis, Richard

(comp.) Miracles; poems by children of the English-speaking world. Simon & Schuster 1966 215p illus $6.95, lib. bdg. $5.70   **808.81**
1 Poetry—Collections 2 Children as authors
ISBN 0-671-47540-1; 0-671-65049-1
Poems on a variety of subjects by children between the ages of 4 and 13. The authors come from such varied backgrounds as the United States, England, Ireland, New Zealand, Kenya, Uganda, and Australia
"Poems chosen with a keen appreciation of the spontaneity of children's creative expression." Childrens Bks 1966

(ed.) Out of the earth I sing; poetry and songs of primitive peoples of the world. Norton 1968 xxi, 144p illus lib. bdg. $4.58 (4-6)   **808.81**
1 Poetry—Collections
ISBN 0-8037-6553-3; 0-8037-6551-7
This volume "brings together the poetry and the art of primitive peoples in a highly creative interpretation of fundamental human concerns and emotions. It draws examples from North American and South American Indian, African, Asian, Pacific, and arctic cultures, expressing man's reactions to earth, sky, and the elements and to living creatures, children, love, and death." Booklist
"A delightful anthology, the dignified layout of pages and the handsome photographs adding to its value; the latter are identified at the close of the book; the songs and poetry are identified on the pages on which they appear. The illustrations are not matched by source but by mood or subject; the poems and songs are simple and moving." Sutherland. The Best in Children's Bks

(comp.) The wind and the rain; children's poems. Photographs by Helen Buttfield. Simon & Schuster 1968 44p illus lib. bdg. $3.79 (3-6)   **808.81**
1 Nature in poetry 2 Poetry—Collections 3 Children as authors
ISBN 0-671-65003-3
"These writings by children explore the moods, sensations and ideas experienced in man's relationship with some aspects of the natural world." Sat Rev
This "is a handsome assemblage, perhaps a little overproduced, as if 10-year-old child prodigies were competing for the Emily Dickinson award. Still, if not

taken in concentrate, the effects can be most pleasant." Christian Sci Monitor
"The poems are accompanied by some spectacular black-and-white photographs." N Y Times Bk Rev

Livingston, Myra Cohn

(ed.) What a wonderful bird the frog are; an assortment of humorous poetry and verse. Harcourt 1973 192p $5.25 (5-7)   **808.81**
1 Humorous poetry 2 Poetry—Collections
ISBN 0-15-295400-7
"A cheerful anthology comprises poems and jingles chosen from authors who range from the fifth century A.D. to contemporary, and from sources other than the English language. Just as varied are the subjects and styles, from haiku and couplets to extracts from plays and mock-serious odes. There's a title index, an author index that includes birth dates, an index of first lines, and—small but significant—an index of translators." Chicago. Children's Bk Center
This book "presents interesting material not found in similar collections for young people. . . . [It] will afford children many hours of pleasurable reading, either independently or in groups." Sch Library J

McEwen, Catherine Schaefer

(comp.) Away we go! 100 poems for the very young; illus. by Barbara Cooney. Crowell 1956 111p illus $3.95 (k-3)   **808.81**
1 Poetry—Collections
ISBN 0-690-11177-0
A collection of poems about learning, noticing, doing; poems about nature and the times of the year; about pets; and about holidays and special days
"It is a very attractively designed and illustrated book." Pub W
Includes a bibliography and indexes of authors, titles, and first lines

Morrison, Lillian

(comp.) Sprints and distances; sports in poetry and the poetry in sport; illus. by Clare and John Ross. Crowell 1965 211p illus $5.95 (5-7)   **808.81**
1 Sports—Poetry 2 Poetry—Collections
ISBN 0-690-76571-1
"The poems included here range from memorable newspaper verse to pieces by Pindar, Virgil, Wordsworth, and Yeats. They vary in form from simple quatrains to intricate modern verse. No attempt was made to include every sport though many are represented, from baseball to falconry." Prefatory note
"A very good poetry anthology; discriminating selection, good format, and—considering the limitations of the subtitle—a surprising range of moods and sources. . . . Sources are cited; appended are indexes by author, by first line, by title, and by sport." Chicago. Children's Bk Center

Parker, Elinor

(comp.) The singing and the gold; poems tr. from world literature; wood engravings by Clare Leighton. Crowell 1962 230p illus $5.95 (6-7)   **808.81**
1 Poetry—Collections
ISBN 0-690-73802-1
"Divided into sections on war and death, friendship, love, seasons and nature, solitude, worship and praise, this collection brings together major and minor poets many hard to find in anthologies. American Indian, African, Russian poets are represented among a world-wide range taken from many sources. Text is enhanced by lovely wood engravings." Sch Library J
"The selections illustrate the universality of human thoughts and emotions." Booklist

Parker, Elinor—*Continued*

Includes indexes of authors and sources, titles, first lines, translators, languages

Plotz, Helen

(comp.) The earth is the Lord's; poems of the spirit; illus. with wood engravings by Clare Leighton. Crowell 1965 223p illus $5 (6-7)   **808.81**

1 Religious poetry

ISBN 0-690-25093-2

"Man's relationship to God and God's to man are celebrated in this sensitive collection of poems from the literature of many people and ages." Booklist

Indexes of authors, titles, first lines

Subject index to poetry for children and young people. Comp. by Violet Sell [and others]. A.L.A. 1957 582p $9   **808.81**

1 Poetry—Indexes

ISBN 0-8389-0059-3

An index to 157 poetry collections "selected with the assistance of children's, young people's, and school librarians. . . . [Subject headings] were derived largely from a study of those in Rue's 'Subject Index to Books for Intermediate Grades.' " Preface

An index to both anthologies and works of individual poets, graded from kindergarten to grade twelve. Each reference gives the poem's title and author, and the page number of each book in which it appears

808.82   Drama—Collections

Burack, A. S.

(ed.) One hundred plays for children; an anthology of non-royalty one-act plays. Plays, Inc. 1970 886p $8.95   **808.82**

1 One-act plays

ISBN 0-8238-0002-4

First published 1949

These plays "appeared originally in 'Plays,' the drama magazine for young people. Providing a varied collection for both classroom and special assembly programs, the four sections cover holidays, legends, historical plays, and a general group of about thirty. A valuable feature is the appended instruction for production with playing time, costumes, properties, and setting given." Cur Ref Bks

(ed.) Popular plays for classroom reading; ed. by A. S. Burack and B. Alice Crossley. Plays, Inc. 1974 xx, 353p $7.95 (4-6)   **808.82**

1 One-act plays

ISBN 0-8238-0151-9

Among the twenty-four one-act plays in this collection are comedies, mysteries, adventure plays, and dramatizations of classic stories and novels

Chicorel Theater index to plays for young people in periodicals, anthologies, and collections; ed. by Marietta Chicorel. Chicorel Lib. Pub. Corp. 1974 489p $49.50   **808.82**

1 Drama—Indexes

ISBN 0-87729-237-8

"Chicorel Index series"

This index "includes many aids to the teacher, the director, and the librarian in listing plays from periodicals and books, for ages from 5 to 16, from the turn of the century to the most recently published plays by contemporary playwrights. Some 15,000 entries are given in a single alphabetical arrangement. The entries are in six forms: the title of the play, the name of the author, periodical title or title of the anthology, translator, adaptor, and editor. The plays have been indexed by subject and identified with appropriate grade level. A few plays available on the recorded media are included. Periodicals are listed with the contents of each. . . . For this alone, the index is already invaluable. It would have been even more admirable if the author had included more contemporary material." Choice

Kreider, Barbara

(comp.) Index to children's plays in collections. Scarecrow 1972 138p $6   **808.82**

1 One-act plays—Indexes

This volume "indexes by author, title, and subject more than 500 one-act plays and skits published in twenty-five collections in the United States from 1965 through 1969. The introduction states that 'no effort was made to select plays on merit.' The author . . . has included a cast analysis, with plays arranged by number of characters, and a directory of publishers indexed in the book." Cur Ref Bks

Bibliography: p135-38

Play index, 1949-1952; an index to 2616 plays in 1138 volumes; comp. by Dorothy Herbert West [and] Dorothy Margaret Peake. Wilson, H.W. 1953 239p $10   **808.82**

1 Drama—Indexes

ISBN 0-8242-0381-X

This volume "includes plays for both children and adults, plays in collections and single plays, one-act plays and full-length plays, radio plays and those written for television, trade editions of Broadway plays and paperbound plays for amateur production." Preface

Part I, arranged in one alphabet, has author, title and subject entries for all plays indexed; Part II lists the collections; Part III is the cast analysis; Part IV, Directory of publishers

"All types of plays are indexed, including translations into English. The dictionary catalog arrangement and the large amount of subject indexing are particularly helpful." Winchell. Guide to Ref Bks. 8th edition

Play index, 1953-1960; an index to 4592 plays in 1735 volumes; ed. by Estelle A. Fidell [and] Dorothy Margaret Peake. Wilson, H.W. 1963 404p $14   **808.82**

1 Drama—Indexes

ISBN 0-8242-0382-8

A supplement to the basic volume, 1949-1952

Play index, 1961-1967; an index to 4,793 plays, ed. by Estelle A. Fidell. Wilson, H.W. 1968 464p $16   **808.82**

1 Drama—Indexes

ISBN 0-8242-0383-6

This volume supplements the previous volumes with a slight change in arrangement

Contents: Part I: Author, title, and subject index; Part II: Cast analysis; Part III: List of collections indexed; Part IV: Directory of publishers and distributors

Play index, 1968-1972; an index to 3848 plays, ed. by Estelle A. Fidell. Wilson, H.W. 1973 403p $20   **808.82**

1 Drama—Indexes

ISBN 0-8242-0496-4

This volume supplements the previous volumes

Plays, the Drama Magazine for Young People. Plays, Inc. $9 per year, 2 years $17   **808.82**

Plays, the Drama Magazine for Young People
—*Continued*

1 Drama—Collections—Periodicals 2 College and school drama—Collections—Periodicals
ISSN 0032-1540

Monthly October through May. First published 1941

"Features eight to ten plays per issue designated for lower, middle grades, junior, and senior high. Most are original, unimaginative one act plays which may be performed in less than an hour. A few plays represent adaptations of better known classics. There are often skit or puppet programs. For each play production notes are included (number and sex of characters, costumes, time, and properties)." Katz. Magazines for Libraries. 2d edition

808.87   Collections of humor

Cole, William
(comp.) The book of giggles; with pictures by Tomi Ungerer. [Collins 1970] unp illus $4.95, lib. bdg. $4.91 (1-4)   808.87

1 Limericks 2 Riddles 3 Humorous poetry
ISBN 0-529-02641-4; 0-529-02642-2

A collection of "giggle" material which includes limericks, jokes, rhymes, nonsense verses and riddles contributed by such people as Shel Silverstein, Jack Prelutsky and Ian Serraillier

"The comical pen-and-ink and brown wash drawings suit the humorous mood and are a delight in themselves. Newly independent readers can handle this with little aid, and it should help fill the need for easy-to-read poetry, as well as for the always in demand riddle books." Sch Library J

Hoke, Helen
(ed.) The big book of jokes; selected and told by Helen Hoke; pictures by Richard Erdoes. Watts, F. 1971 200p illus lib. bdg. $5.88 (4-7)   808.87

1 Wit and humor 2 Riddles
ISBN 0-531-01990-X

A collection of jokes and anecdotes, quips, and scatty stories listed under such categories as: Animal antics; Goofy girls; Kute kids; Legal laughs; Medical madness; Neurotic nonsense; Vacation vagaries; Youthful yarns; Zestful zoology

Kohl, Marguerite
Jokes for children, by Marguerite Kohl [and] Frederica Young; illus. by Bob Patterson. Hill & Wang 1963 116p illus $3.95 (3-5)   808.87

1 Wit and humor
ISBN 0-8090-6181-3

"A collection of more than 650 jokes including jokes told by children as well as jokes selected by them for their school publications and theatrical productions. The book is divided into the following categories: Teachers and pupils, Melissa, Rhymes, Gruesomes, Riddles, The little moron, Whoppers and insults, Puns, Alfie and Archie, Family style, Wildlife, Sign language, and Mishmash. Will fill a need for books of humor." Booklist

808.88   Collections of miscellaneous writings

Bartlett, John
(comp.) Familiar quotations. Little $15   808.88

1 Quotations

First published 1855. Periodically revised and brought up to date. Editors vary

"A collection of passages, phrases and proverbs traced to their sources in ancient and modern literature." Subtitle [of 14th edition]

Authors are arranged in chronological order from ancient times to the present so that the quotations may be considered in the context of the author's work and period. Includes author and key word indexes

"A standard collection, comprehensive and well selected. . . . One of the best books of quotations with a long history." Winchell. Guide to Ref Bks. 8th edition [Review of the 13th edition]

Lewis, Richard
(ed.) Journeys; prose by children of the English-speaking world. Simon & Schuster 1969 215p illus lib. bdg. $4.73 (2-6)   808.88

1 Children as authors 2 Literature—Collections
ISBN 0-671-65088-2

"To show the entire scope of children's capacity to create literature Lewis has compiled a delightful collection of prose. . . . The more than 150 short pieces —descriptions, essays, stories, fantasies—written by children from age four to fourteen from nine English-speaking countries reveal the perceptiveness and candor of children and demonstrate the ability of children to express their thoughts and feelings freely and with imagination." Booklist

"The best use of the collection will probably be to inspire adults to encourage and allow children to express themselves as freely and as fully in prose as in poetry." Horn Bk

Morrison, Lillian
(comp.) Best wishes, amen; a new collection of autograph verses; illus. by Loretta Lustig. Crowell 1974 195p illus $4.95 (5-7)   808.88

1 Epigrams
ISBN 0-690-00579-2

A companion volume to Morrison's earlier collections of autographs, "this comprises over three hundred new bon mots, jibes [and] complimentary verses. . . . There are many that demonstrate the self-conscious humor of young autographers who felt comfortable only when taking a dig at a friend's expense, some impersonal quips, a few that reflect the changing times, and a modest number that admit to affection: in fact, exactly what one finds in children's autograph books." Chicago. Children's Bk Center

"A final section contains Spanish autograph rhymes, plus translations, again gathered from actual albums of Spanish-speaking children in New York City. A guaranteed hit with elementary graders, this won't gather any dust on the shelves—especially at promotion/graduation time." Sch Library J

(comp.) A diller, a dollar; rhymes and sayings for the ten o'clock scholar; illus. by Marj Bauernschmidt. Crowell 1955 150p illus $4.50 (5-7)   808.88

1 Epigrams
ISBN 0-690-23957-2

"A collection of schoolroom plaints and schoolyard taunts, mnemonics, proverbs and parodies, jokes and jingles, admonitions, game rhymes, and chants. Garnered from old-time primers, chapbooks, nursery rhymes, and folk journals, from adults' remembrances of rhymes known in childhood, and from children and teenagers themselves, the rhymes included here were selected on the basis of inventiveness, sound, fun, and freshness today. Arranged under subject categories and decorated with amusing illustrations. Sources given." Booklist

Bibliography: p149-50

Morrison, Lillian—*Continued*
(comp.) Remember me when this you see; a new collection of autograph verses; illus. by Marjorie Bauernschmidt. Crowell 1961 182p illus $5.50 (5-7)
808.88

1 Epigrams
ISBN 0-690-69613-2
This book includes poems about love, friendship, sincerity, and success, as well as nonsense poems. All are suitable for autograph albums
"A new bonanza of the tender sentiments, the jokes, and puns . . . the friendly insults and good advice that our grandfathers and grandmothers may well have written in their albums." N Y Times Bk Rev

Pellowski, Anne
(ed.) Have you seen a comet? Children's art and writing from around the world [ed. by] Anne Pellowski, Helen R. Sattley [and] Joyce C. Arkhurst. Day 1971 120p illus $7.50
808.88
1 Children as authors 2 Children as artists 3 Literature—Collections
ISBN 0-381-99739-1
"In cooperation with the U.S. Committee for UNICEF"
Children of varying ages from many countries, are contributors to this anthology of prose, poetry, and art
"By careful editing and compilation, the editors have successfully interwoven the beautiful artwork and sensitive writings in this remarkable volume. Some of the work is highly subtle, some less adept, but all of it reflects the intelligence and emotional intensity of the creative children." Horn Bk

Schwartz, Alvin
(comp.) A twister of twists, a tangler of tongues; tongue twisters; illus. by Glen Rounds. Lippincott 1972 125p illus $4.95, pa $1.95 (4-7)
808.88
1 Tongue twisters
ISBN 0-397-31387-X; 0-397-31412-X
This is a collection of tongue twisters in both prose and verse, including several in other languages
"A grand gathering guaranteed to gag a gaggle of garrulous gossips, the selection of well-known and not-so-well-known tongue twisters should provide endless hours of elocutionary diversion for young and old alike. . . . A helpful series of notes, sources, and bibliographic references give added dimension to a light-hearted, yet incisive, compilation, highlighted by the jovial line drawings." Horn Bk

Stevenson, Burton
(ed.) The home book of quotations; classical and modern. Dodd $40
808.88
1 Quotations
First published 1934 and periodically revised
"A comprehensive and well-chosen collection of more than 50,000 quotations arranged alphabetically by subject with subarrangement by smaller topics. Usually gives exact citation. Includes an index of authors—giving full name, identifying phrase, and dates of birth and death, with reference to all quotations cited—and a word index, which indexes the quotation by leading words, usually nouns, though in some case verbs and adjectives are also used. Boldface entries are given for some of the smaller subjects. The quotations under these are not indexed separately, and one must, therefore, turn to the subject and run through the entries. This practice must be remembered when using this index." Winchell. Guide to Ref Bks [Review of the 1964 edition]

810.8 American literature— Collections

Free to be . . . you and me; conceived by Marlo Thomas; developed and ed. by Carole Hart [and others]. Editor: Francine Klagsbrun; art director: Samuel N. Antupit. McGraw 1974 143p illus music $7.95, pa $4.95
810.8
1 American literature—Collections
ISBN 0-07-064223-0; 0-07-064224-9
"A project of the Ms. Foundation, Inc." Title page
The theme of this collection of twenty-five songs, stories, poems and a dialogue is that children should develop as individuals and be independent of obsolete sexual and racial role myths. Fifteen of the selections originally were recorded on a 1973 album of the same title
This collection "is a significant step toward filling the need for nonsexist material for children. . . . The total adds up to a qualitatively uneven but still useful endeavor at encouraging children to be themselves." Booklist

Henry, Ralph
(comp.) My American heritage. . . . Collected by Ralph Henry and Lucile Pannell; illus. by John Dukes McKee. Rand McNally 1949 318p illus pa $1.50 (4-7)
810.8
1 American literature—Collections 2 American poetry—Collections
ISBN 0-528-87735-6
"A collection of songs, poems, speeches, sayings and other writings dear to our hearts." Subtitle
"A visit from St Nicholas," "Casey at the bat," "Little Orphan Annie," and "The village blacksmith" are among the 250 pieces included
Includes an Index of authors, titles and first lines

Jordan, June
(comp.) The voice of the children; collected by June Jordan and Terri Bush. Holt 1970 101p illus lib. bdg. $3.59, pa $1.95 (4-7)
810.8
1 American literature—Collections 2 Children as authors
ISBN 0-03-085113-0; 0-03-085174-2
"Growing out of a Saturday morning creative writing workshop in Brooklyn this is a collection of poetry and bits of prose by 25 black and Puerto Rican young people ranging in age from nine to seventeen, but most of them thirteen or fourteen. . . . The selections speak out on subjects meaningful to the young writers: hope for the future, ghetto life, racism, riots, peace, school, blackness, love, nature, and self-identity. . . . Jordan's afterword describes the workshop; photographs of all the contributors are provided." Booklist
"The pride, sadness, bitterness and hope expressed in these writings are eloquent testimony to the courage and talent of these children." Wolfe. About 100 Bks

A St Nicholas anthology; the early years; selected and ed. by Burton C. Frye; foreword by Richard L. Darling. Meredith 1969 439p illus $9.95
810.8
1 American literature—Collections
ISBN 0-696-77906-4
A "selection of stories, poems, articles, and letters from the best-known children's magazine ever published, the material grouped by seasons and the authors including some of the most famous writers for children: Alcott, Kipling, Pyle, Wiggin, and the editor of the magazine, Mary Mapes Dodge. There is also a selection of the work of child contributors in the

A St Nicholas anthology—*Continued*
St. Nicholas League, including such Honor Members as Bennett Cerf, Rachel Field, and Edna St. Vincent Millay. . . . Appended are author and artist, title and artwork, and subject indexes." Sutherland. The Best in Children's Bks

"One is not sure whether this should be directed to the Young People of today or the Oldsters of Yesterday. . . . This was a magazine for Young People that did not patronize them or stoop to them or consider them as second-class citizens. The most modern advancements of the time were subjects of the articles, the best writers were courted for stories and essays and poems. Even some songs were included from time to time with music for those who were learning to play piano. This is a fine anthology." Best Sellers

811 American poetry

Aiken, Conrad
Cats and bats and things with wings; poems. Drawings by Milton Glaser. Atheneum Pubs. 1965 unp illus $6.95 (k-4)   811
1 Animals—Poetry
ISBN 0-689-30017-4
These "poems about sixteen different members of the animal kingdom are all but overshadowed by sixteen astonishingly imaginative drawings. . . . Poem and picture have each a page to themselves; each poem also makes a picture in its typographical arrangement. Conrad Aiken clearly enjoyed writing the verses. [However] here and there the poems peter out at the end." Horn Bk

Aldis, Dorothy
All together; a child's treasury of verse. . . . Illus. by Helen D. Jameson, Marjorie Flack, and Margaret Freeman. Putnam 1952 192p illus $6.45 (k-3)   811
ISBN 0-399-20006-1
"Including selections from Everything and anything; Here, there and everywhere; Hop, skip and jump; Before things happen; with poems previously unpublished in book form." Title page
"These are poems that the author herself has chosen from her store and they are the ones that have been most loved through the years. The joy of childhood lies within these pages, and the pathos; the magic and the energy." Christian Sci Monitor
"Many of the familiar illustrations have been printed in color, adding to the appeal of the book." Library J

Atwood, Ann
Haiku: the mood of earth. Scribner 1971 unp illus lib. bdg. $5.95 (5-7)   811
1 Haiku 2 Nature in poetry 3 Nature photographs
ISBN 0-684-12494-7
"Stating in her brief introductory analysis of Haiku that the oriental verse form is primarily a visual experience which achieves direct contact with nature through the use of specific techniques, the author suggests that the same principles can be applied in art or photography to capture a timeless moment of wonder. She then presents 25 such moments, drawn from the moods of earth and the cycles of the seasons, each consisting of two color photographs, one frequently a closeup or magnification of detail in the other, accompanied by a single unifying Haiku. A striking volume for any young reader inclined toward poetry, photography, or nature." Booklist

My own rhythm; an approach to haiku. Scribner 1973 unp illus $5.95 (5-7)   811

1 Haiku 2 Nature in poetry 3 Nature photography
ISBN 0-684-13248-6
"Introducing this lovely book, Ann Atwood offers a brief history of haiku and points out the differences among the three Japanese masters of the form: Buson, Issa and Bashô. The rest of the book consists of her own haiku, each one her reaction to splendors in nature which she has photographed in full color. This is a volume to treasure." Pub W

Behn, Harry
The golden hive; poems and pictures by Harry Behn. Harcourt 1966 61p illus $4.50 (4-6)   811
1 Nature in poetry
ISBN 0-15-231200-5
These forty-two poems "reflect the poet's joy in the natural world—the wildness of a storm, the charm and humor of small animals, the beauty of growing plants." Cincinnati
"A very pleasant book of poems, many of them on familiar topics. . . . There are, however, many fresh and imaginative poems. Not all of the selections are outstanding, but none (familiar topic or less-familiar) is meretricious. . . . The format has a quiet dignity." Chicago. Children's Bk Center

The little hill; poems & pictures by Harry Behn. Harcourt 1949 58p illus $4.50 (1-4)   811
ISBN 0-15-245966-9
"This small book of poems about nature and familiar things to childhood is unusual both as to the different and unexpected rhythms and the decorative and imaginative drawings." Booklist
"Gardens, raindrops, the merry-go-on, the caterpillar, Undine's garden and Hallowe'en are among the varied subjects included." Horn Bk

The wizard in the well; poems and pictures by Harry Behn. Harcourt 1956 62p illus $4.95 (1-4)   811
ISBN 0-15-298929-3
"A collection of poems for children, most of them dealing with nature or with toys and games that capture the childish imagination. They are all clear. . . . A longer story-poem, 'The Wizard in the Well,' is a little less successful." Pub W

Benét, Rosemary
A book of Americans, by Rosemary and Stephen Vincent Benét; illus. by Charles Child. Holt 1933 114p illus lib. bdg. $4.95 (5-7)   811
1 U.S.—History—Poetry 2 U.S.—Biography—Poetry
ISBN 0-03-015041-8
"Fifty-six poems of varied moods and meters describe cleverly and often with gusto the life and character of famous men and women from Columbus to Woodrow Wilson. Humorously illustrated . . . in red, white and blue, and black and white." N Y Libraries
"The verse bids fair to give fresh life to boys and girls who have been starving for living words of American history. It is a book of fine ideas and true associations, as well as one of amusing characterization of American idiosyncrasies." Atlantic Bookshelf

Bodecker, N. M.
Let's marry said the cherry, and other nonsense poems; written and illus. by N. M. Bodecker. Atheneum Pubs. 1974 79p illus $4.95 (2-5)   811
1 Nonsense verses
ISBN 0-689-50004-1
"A Margaret K. McElderry book"
Here are thirty-two short nonsense poems, ranging from "The Porcupine," about a girl who pats a por-

Bodecker, N. M.—*Continued*

cupine, to "Mr. Beecher," a poem describing an off-beat Spanish teacher

The verses "are immediately inviting for their combination of syllabic nonsense and topsy-turvy logic . . . . Secondly, they are always full of rhyme if not of reason, and their rhythm echoes familiar cadences. The poems are profusely illustrated with line drawings elegantly and humorously expressive, and delicately ornamented with patterns and hatchings. When read aloud, they must be said trippingly on the tongue, lest they trip up the unwary reader." Horn Bk

Brooks, Gwendolyn

Bronzeville boys and girls; pictures by Ronni Solbert. Harper 1956 40p illus $3.95, lib. bdg. $3.79 (2-5)   811

1 Negroes—Poetry
ISBN 0-06-020650-0; 0-06-020651-9

A collection of thirty-six poems about everyday experiences of children. "While the children are black and the place is Chicago, the place might be anywhere and the children, any children." Adventuring with Bks. 2d edition

"The poems are gay, carefree, and serious—but none is sad. . . . Ronni Solbert's sensitive and expressive drawings reflect and extend the mood and beauty of the poetry." Chicago Sunday Trib

Brown, Margaret Wise

Nibble, nibble; poems for children; illus. by Leonard Weisgard. Young Scott Bks. 1959 unp illus lib. bdg. $5.50 (k-3)   811

1 Nature in poetry
ISBN 0-201-09291-3

"A posthumous collection of [25] nature poems, 14 of which are published here for the first time. The pleasingly cadenced verses are fresh and childlike, and the illustrations in black, white, and cool green are lovely; together they make a harmonious, evocative whole which young children will enjoy." Booklist

Carmer, Carl

The boy drummer of Vincennes; illus. by Seymour Fleishman. Harvey House 1972 unp illus map lib. bdg. $4.79 (2-4)   811

1 U.S.—History—Revolution—Poetry
ISBN 0-8178-4932-7

"A narrative poem in first person celebrates a facet of the American Revolution. Based on a true incident, the story is told by a drummer boy on the Western frontier; in 1779, a band of patriotic volunteers led by George Rogers Clarke marched across the soggy lands of Illinois to take from the British a small French outpost they had won—Vincennes. The poem has a swinging rhythm that fits the jaunty mood of the lad who defiantly thumps his drum and it is faithful in its language to the speech of the period. Nice to read aloud, useful for its historical as well as its poetic appeal, the poem incorporates some of the folklore and the contemporary lyrics of the time." Chicago. Children's Bk Center

Caudill, Rebecca

Come along! Illus. by Ellen Raskin. Holt 1969 30p illus $3.95, lib. bdg. $3.59, pa $1.65 (1-4)   811

1 Nature in poetry 2 Haiku
ISBN 0-03-075420-8; 0-03-075425-9; 0-03-088504-3

"Haiku through the year: direct and simple, the poems capture the brief and compact moments of delight in the natural beauty of the seasons, of flora and fauna, and the moods of weather. The illustrations, strong but never harsh, show a small girl and a still smaller boy gazing at golden forsythia, a leaping gleam of scarlet fish, the pristine iciness of winter boughs. Although there are some words and concepts

that impose a challenge, most of the poems can be read to children even younger than the independent reader." Chicago. Children's Bk Center

"Matching the fleeting moods and metaphoric images are splendidly brilliant pictures, each painted on rice paper of a different color; the turning pages reflect the changing seasons with ever-shifting patterns and tonal modulations." Horn Bk

Ciardi, John

I met a man; illus. by Robert Osborn. Houghton 1961 74p illus lib. bdg. $4.95 (1-3)   811

1 Nonsense verses
ISBN 0-395-18018-X

"These poems were written for a special pleasure: I wanted to write the first book my daughter read herself. To bring them within her first-grade range, I based them on the two most elementary word lists in general use. . . . The basic devices of these poems for leading the child to new words are rhyme, riddles, context, and word games." Author's note

Ciardi's "imagination, fluency in rhyme, and delight in plays on words lift the results of his intention above the limitation of the first-grade word lists. . . . The cartoonish drawings admirably suit the moods of his fantastic sequences. . . . An honest and original attempt to make both poetry and learning fun." Horn Bk

The man who sang the sillies; drawings by Edward Gorey. Lippincott 1961 63p illus $4.95, lib. bdg. $4.39 (2-5)   811

1 Nonsense verses
ISBN 0-397-30568-0; 0-397-30569-9

"Twenty-four nonsense poems, appropriately illustrated by exaggeratedly zany line drawings. Some of the selections are flagrant and elaborate playing with words and sounds, others are narrative-nonsense verse in the vein of Lewis Carroll. . . . Variable in quality; none of the verse is mediocre but a good deal of it seems to strain for humorous effect." Chicago. Children's Bk Center

The reason for the pelican; illus. by Madeleine Gekiere. Lippincott 1959 63p illus $4.95, lib. bdg. $3.39 (1-4)   811

1 Nonsense verses
ISBN 0-397-30472-2; 0-397-30473-0

Twenty-three poems "for young readers in delightful nonsense vein. Ranging in subject matter from birds to children, pinwheels to lightning bugs, the poems have fun and laughter as well as wisdom, word play, fine rhythm, and varied rhyme." Library J

"The drawings in ink line are sophisticated abstractions; some with an eccentric grotesqueness suggesting Lear are as right for this new fun as are Lear's for his nonsense, to which some of this is akin." Horn Bk

Someone could win a polar bear; drawings by Edward Gorey. Lippincott 1970 62p illus $3.95, lib. bdg. $3.79 (2-5)   811

1 Humorous poetry
ISBN 0-397-31159-1; 0-397-31160-5

"Though the poems tend to stretch the imagination to the point of incredulity, there is a fine sense of nonsense which holds the book together. . . . Several [poems] need to be read and reread, mulled over and chewed upon. But that, after all, is one of the joys of poetry." Library J

Ciardi's "imagination is . . . wide-ranging. . . . At least two of the poems, 'The Hearsay' and 'The Answer,' have a genuinely classical finish." N Y Times Bk Rev

Ciardi, John—*Continued*

You read to me, I'll read to you; drawings by Edward Gorey. Lippincott 1962 64p illus $5.50, lib. bdg. $3.93 (1-4)   811

1 Humorous poetry

ISBN 0-397-30645-8; 0-397-30646-6

Thirty-five "imaginative and humorous poems for an adult and a child to read aloud together. Written in a basic first-grade vocabulary, the poems to be read by the child alternate with poems to be read by the adult." Booklist

"With few exceptions, the poems are humorous: some in a nonsense vein, some tongue-in-cheek about parents or children, some playing imaginatively with words or ideas. Here and there the poetry seems to strain for effect, but for the most part it is gay and imaginative. The selections are good for reading aloud." Chicago. Children's Bk Center

Clifton, Lucille

Everett Anderson's Christmas coming; illus. by Evaline Ness. Holt 1971 unp illus lib. bdg. $3.95, pa $1.25 (k-3)   811

1 Christmas poetry

ISBN 0-03-089507-3; 0-03-09146-0

The young Black boy "of 'Some of the Days of Everett Anderson' [entered below] gives readers his thoughts and feelings about the Christmas season in nine brief poems. And Evaline Ness has again created the illustrations (three color line-and-wash drawings), that reflect the quiet spirit of Christmas. From his city apartment world, Everett spreads warm wishes and cheer to young readers everywhere." Pub W

Everett Anderson's year; illus. by Ann Grifalconi. Holt 1974 unp illus $4.95 (k-3)   811

1 Months—Poetry

ISBN 0-03-012736-X

In these unrhymed poems, "the reader is guided through a poetic view of Everett's own distinctive outlook on a year in his life. Everett, a seven year old, lives alone with his working mother in apartment 14A. Each month offers him a different kind of excitement, experience, reminiscence, or apprehension. Despite the activity of the moment, one theme persists—love—that's what it's all about." Reading Teacher

"The best of these verses will cause smiles of understanding and feelings of camaraderie with the small black boy. Large woodcuts in black and white with alternating orange and light blue accents and backgrounds are traditional and pleasing to the eye." Booklist

Some of the days of Everett Anderson; illus. by Evaline Ness. Holt 1970 unp illus $3.95, lib. bdg. $3.59, pa $1.25 (k-3)   811

ISBN 0-03-084404-5; 0-03-084405-3; 0-03-086621-9

"A week of days, a poem for each day, and a charming picture of a six-year-old black child whose fears and pleasures have a universal quality." Chicago. Children's Bk Center

"The line, brush, and print techniques of the expertly composed illustrations—brown, gray, and yellow on a cream ground—capture the boy's vibrant week. Excellent for reading aloud as well as for viewing." Horn Bk

De Regniers, Beatrice Schenk

Something special; drawings by Irene Haas. Harcourt 1958 unp illus $5.50 (k-2)   811

ISBN 0-15-277101-8

"A collection of [nine] poems in varied styles. Some are rollicking entertainment, such as the cumulative chanting game, 'What Did You Put In Your Pocket?' with the humor of incongruity; others are gently evocative ('If You Find a Little Feather'); and 'If I

Were Teeny Tiny' is pure fantasy." Chicago. Children's Bk Center

"This is a delightful book of poems that has caught the spirit of a child's world with humor, sounds, smell, and color. The fine drawings complement the text." Atlantic

Dickinson, Emily

Poems for youth; ed. by Alfred Leete Hampson; foreword by May Lamberton Becker; illus. by George and Doris Hauman. Little 1934 unp illus $5.95 (5-7)   811

ISBN 0-316-18418-7

"Poems written by Emily Dickinson for her young niece and nephews serve as an excellent introduction to the poet. Indexed by first lines." Hodges. Bks for Elem Sch Libraries

"The fact that of the seventy-eight poems in this group many were written for special children does not narrow their appeal. On the contrary, it seems to widen it." Boston Transcript

"The illustrations have a grace and delicacy that is most appropriate." N Y Times Bk Rev

Field, Eugene

Poems of childhood; with illus. by Maxfield Parrish. Scribner 1904 199p illus $10, pa $3.95 (3-5)   811

ISBN 0-684-20803-3

"Scribner Illustrated classics"

First published 1896

This is a collection of poems both grave and gay, from "Love-songs of childhood" and "With trumpet and drum." There are eight pictures in color

Field, Rachel

Poems; decorations by the author. Macmillan (N Y) 1957 118p illus $3.95 (2-5)   811

A collection of poems, most of them taken from the author's books, several of which are out of print. A few are reprinted from magazines, and six of the poems are here printed for the first time

"Most of Rachel Field's lilting 'poems' are tiny, about tiny things. . . . Their delicacy is admirably expressed in the agile, silhouetted figures that illustrate them." Christian Sci Monitor

Includes an Index of first lines

Taxis and toadstools; verses and decorations by Rachel Field. Doubleday 1926 129p illus $1.69, lib. bdg. $2.44 (2-5)   811

ISBN 0-385-07520-0; 0-385-07115-9

Poems arranged under the following headings: People, Taxis and thoroughfares, Stores and storekeepers, Salty days, Especially islands, Birds and beasts, Berries and branches, Fringes of fairyland, Reminiscences, A number of things

This is "a gay, alluring little book of poems for children on all sorts of subjects. . . . [It] should prove a happy experience for any boy or girl." Open Shelf

Fisher, Aileen

Cricket in a thicket; illus. by Feodor Rojankovsky. Scribner 1963 63p illus $4.95, pa 95¢ (k-3)   811

1 Nature in poetry

ISBN 0-684-13456-X; 0-684-12784-9

"Poems about grasshoppers, and ladybugs, and ducklings, and turtledoves, and other outdoor things that delight the eye of children." Pub W

Short "poems fitted into capricious categories such as six legs and eight, four legs and two, and warm days and cold, make wonderful read-aloud material. Soft charcoal drawings and easy vocabulary. Variations of

Fisher, Aileen—*Continued*

rhythms and themes stimulate the urge to read the complete volume, and brevity assures it." Chicago Sch J

Includes an index of titles

Do bears have mothers, too? [Illus. by] Eric Carle. Crowell 1973 unp illus $4.95, lib. bdg. $5.70 (k-2)
811

1 Animals—Poetry
ISBN 0-690-00166-5; 0-690-00167-3
This collection of short poems describes "mother-and-child life among the animals. Features are a white swan and her cygnets, a bear and cubs, a deer and her fawn, alligator mom and [babies] along with several others." Pub W

"Eric Carle's distinctive and ebullient collages dominate this poetry book about 12 animal mothers and their young. . . . Although the verses are competent, they are not as spontaneous as many of Fisher's other poems. Used as a lap book, however, this would be good for sharing with a small group of children." Sch Library J

Feathered ones and furry; illus. by Eric Carle. Crowell 1971 37p illus $4.50, lib. bdg. $5.25 (k-3)
811

1 Animals—Poetry 2 Birds—Poetry
ISBN 0-690-29451-4; 0-690-29452-2
"A collection of poems about the animal world in all seasons; cats and kittens, dogs and puppies, ponies, chipmunks, weasels, squirrels, and mice, as well as many kinds of birds from sandpipers to pelicans. Some of the verses are new; some are reprinted from periodicals and from the author's early books. The author sees nature not in its fury and violence but in its gentleness and benign relationship to man. . . . One cannot say that this is great poetry, but in idea and expression, the verses are childlike and appreciative. Seldom is a book of poems so handsomely designed, so beautifully illustrated." Horn Bk

In one door and out the other; a book of poems; illus. by Lillian Hoban. Crowell 1969 65p illus $3.95, lib. bdg. $4.70 (1-3)
811

1 Children in poetry
ISBN 0-690-43555-4; 0-690-43556-8
A selection of poetry which embraces the adventures, joys and frustrations of childhood as it touches upon such subjects as father, mother, playmates, pets, and the wonders of nature

"The poems are aptly illustrated with a profusion of small black-and-white drawings, which young readers will identify with and delight in." Sch Library J

In the woods, in the meadow, in the sky; illus. by Margot Tomes. Scribner 1965 64p illus $4.95 (k-3)
811

1 Nature in poetry
ISBN 0-684-12652-4
A volume of "nature poetry expressing childlike feelings about the charm of trees, wild creatures, the sky, and stars." Children's Bks, 1965

"There is gaiety and a gentle humor in these poems of the outdoors. . . . The drawings are a perfect complement to the verses." Commonweal

My cat has eyes of sapphire blue; pictures by Marie Angel. Crowell 1973 24p illus $4.50, lib. bdg. $5.25 (2-4)
811

1 Cats—Poetry
ISBN 0-690-56637-9; 0-690-56638-7
Twenty-four short poems describe "the multifaceted nature of cats and their activities." Booklist

"A pair of cat-lovers—a poet-naturalist and a nature painter—have combined their talents to create a tour de force that cannot fail to surprise and delight other feline fanciers. . . . The exquisitely meticulous cat portraits—which so easily could have strayed into sentimentality—are totally representational, yet strikingly expressive." Horn Bk

Skip around the year; illus. by Gioia Fiammenghi. Crowell 1967 unp illus $4.95, lib. bdg. $5.70 (1-3)
811

1 Holidays—Poetry
ISBN 0-690-74157-X; 0-690-74158-8
"A Crowell Holiday bk"
"Thoughtful poems appropriate for Jewish, Christian and national holidays are arranged chronologically from New Year's Eve to Hanukkah and Christmas. Different from many holiday books, this emphasizes giving such as spreading seeds for birds on Valentine's Day and leaving May baskets." Bruno. Bks for Sch Libraries, 1968

"The spirited illustrations help the verses to dance across the pages." Adventuring with Bks. 2d edition

Frost, Robert

You come too; favorite poems for young readers; with wood engravings by Thomas W. Nason. Holt 1959 94p illus lib. bdg. $4.50 (5-7)
811

ISBN 0-03-089530-8
This volume features "Frost's own selection of his poems to be read to and by young people." Hodges. Bks for Elem Sch Libraries

Frost's "simplicity, wisdom, and humanity, as well as his craftsmanship, come clear in some half-hundred poems, among them 'Mending Wall,' 'The Death of the Hired Man,' and 'Tree at My Window.' The foreword by Hyde Cox, one of Frost's younger friends, introduces the ageless poet and his poetry with sensitive skill. Format is distinctive, and Thomas W. Nason's wood engravings will surely sharpen reader's pleasure and perception." Library J

Index to titles: p93-94

Garelick, May

Look at the moon; with illus. by Leonard Weisgard. Young Scott Bks. 1969 unp illus lib. bdg. $4.95 (k-3)
811

1 Moon—Poetry
ISBN 0-201-09269-7
"Does everyone see the moon I see, the very same moon that shines on me?" The illustrations, describing different parts of the world in moonlight, and the verse story combine to answer this question

"The dark illustrations, in midnight blue and black with touches of green, show a big full moon shining on a boy, his cat, the forest full of animals, the city, the sea and on other lands, creating a continuity of mood that conveys the general idea perfectly." Sch Library J

Giovanni, Nikki

Spin a soft Black song; poems for children; illus. by Charles Bible. Hill & Wang 1971 unp illus $6.95 (k-3)
811

1 Negroes—Poetry
ISBN 0-8090-8795-2
"A beautifully illustrated book of poems about black children for children of all ages. . . . Simple in theme but a very moving collection nonetheless." Reading Ladders. 5th edition

Hoban, Russell

Egg thoughts, and other Frances songs; pictures by Lillian Hoban. Harper 1972 31p illus $3.95, lib. bdg. $3.79 (k-2)
811

ISBN 0-06-022331-6; 0-06-022332-4
In this collection of poems, Frances the badger focuses "on eggs cooked in various ways, a well-worn

Hoban, Russell—*Continued*

favorite doll, string, homework, little sister Gloria, and other joys and tribulations of childhood. All of the verses are new except for 'Soft boiled' which is taken from 'Bread and jam for Frances' [entered in class E]." Booklist

"Frances' thoughts and observations though not always fluidly expressed, are childlike and unselfconsciously amusing, and the verse is complemented by illustrations that are equally down-to-earth and appealing." Sch Library J

Hoberman, Mary Ann

A little book of little beasts; pictures by Peter Parnall. Simon & Schuster 1973 48p illus $4.50 (k-3)
811
1 Animals—Poetry
ISBN 0-671-65203-6

"Poems about such creatures as ants, snakes, raccoons, moles, mice, worms, rabbits, and turtles are illustrated with clean, fine-line drawings that are accurate and attractive. Some of the poems have humor, some are descriptive, a few are sharply evocative; there are few outstanding selections, but there are none that fall flatly on the ear." Chicago. Children's Bk Center

Nuts to you & nuts to me; an alphabet of poems; illus. by Ronni Solbert. Knopf 1974 unp illus lib. bdg. $5.99 (k-2)
811
1 Alphabet books
ISBN 0-394-92742-7

This book contains a brief rhyme for each letter of the alphabet about such things as ants, balloons, cookies, and ducks

"A blend of lilting rhythms, unforced rhymes, and freshly conceived, child-like imagery cast in a variety of poetic forms. Some of the poems are tongue twisters . . . others are just plain nonsense . . . while still others offer an unexpected yet wondrously logical twist. . . . [The book is] ingenious, unpretentious, and appealing." Horn Bk

Hughes, Langston

Don't you turn back; poems. Selected by Lee Bennett Hopkins; woodcuts by Ann Grifalconi. Knopf [1970 c1969] 78p illus $4.50, lib. bdg. $5.19 (5-7)
811
1 Negroes—Poetry
ISBN 0-394-80846-0; 0-394-90846-5

This selection of Langston Hughes' poetry is divided into four parts: My people, Prayers and dreams, Out to sea, and I am a Negro. The 45 poems "celebrate the dreams and sorrows, the joys and aspirations of his people, prideful of being Black." Best Sellers

"Dramatic woodcuts and dignified format help make this a tribute to a fine poet." Sat Rev

Includes an index of titles and an Index of first lines

The dream keeper, and other poems; with illus. by Helen Sewell. Knopf 1932 77p illus lib. bdg. $5.69 (5-7)
811
1 Negroes—Poetry
ISBN 0-394-91096-6

This volumes contains "the author's own selection of his poems, including lyrics, songs, and several typical Negro blues." Hodges. Bks for Elem Sch Libraries

Jordan, June

Who look at me; illus. with twenty-seven paintings. Crowell 1969 97p illus $8.50 (6-7)
811
1 Negroes—Poetry 2 Negroes in literature and art
3 Paintings, American
ISBN 0-690-88854-6

"Twenty seven paintings of black people are accompanied by poems . . . that speak, on the whole, with piercing clarity of the pathos, beauty, pride, and anger in Negro lives. The format is dignified, and notes on the artists (some of whose work is reproduced in full color) are appended. The author, young and black, has interpreted some of the paintings rather narrowly so that the poems cannot quite stand alone, but these are in the minority." Chicago. Children's Bk Center

Among the prominent American artists, both Black and white, whose paintings are represented are: Charles Alston, Thomas Eakins, Romare Bearden, John Wilson, Ben Shahn, and Andrew Wyeth

Kuskin, Karla

Any me I want to be; poems. Harper 1972 unp illus $4.95, lib. bdg. $4.79 (1-4)
811
ISBN 0-06-023615-9; 0-06-023616-7
Illustrated by the author

These thirty poems "do not describe: instead, the poet has tried—and, with refreshing, edged but gentle humor and not an ounce of condescension, succeeded—'to get inside each subject and briefly be it.' . . . The subjects—and moods and pacing, too—range from a mirror to the moon. . . . There is more than a touch of A. A. Milne here, and a bit of Edward Lear, and a bit of Ogden Nash. But mostly it is Karla Kuskin, who, as any you might like to be, is fun, funny, and therefore wise." Sat Rev

Lawrence, Jacob

Harriet and the promised land. Windmill/Simon & Schuster 1968 unp illus lib. bdg. $6.75 (2-5)
811
1 Tubman, Harriet (Ross)—Poetry
ISBN 0-671-65027-0
Illustrated by the author

"Simple rhymes tell the story of Harriet Tubman, the slave who led many of her people North to freedom." Adventuring With Bks. 2d edition

"The strength of this volume is in the forceful, stylized paintings by the famous black artist, which capture the degradation of slavery." Brooklyn Art Bks for Children

Lenski, Lois

City poems. Walck, H.Z. 1971 118p illus $6.95 (k-3)
811
1 Cities and towns—Poetry
ISBN 0-8098-2414-0

Over 110 poems, with illustrations by the author, capture the noise, rhythm and turmoil of city life

"The poems are short, one or two to a page and their chief attraction is, for the urban child, the familiarity of the sights and activities they describe. . . . The inclusion of such subjects as the local bully, buying things on credit, gangs, and riots reflects the way it is for many children, and the book has a balance of advantages and disadvantages in urban living." Chicago. Children's Bk Center

Includes indexes of titles and first lines

Lindsay, Vachel

Johnny Appleseed, and other poems; illus. by George Richards. Macmillan (N Y) 1928 144p illus $4.50 (4-7)
811
"Macmillan Children's classics"

"Nonsense rhymes and songs . . . historical poems, and selections from The Congo and The Chinese nightingale are included in this selection." Wis Library Bul

This "book is for all boys and girls who love poetry already. They will find all their Lindsay favorites here in a convenient size to carry about and learn by heart. It is also, especially, for those many unfortunate youngsters who think they don't like poetry.

Lindsay, Vachel—*Continued*

. . . [Richards' pictures] are perfect, though the author himself is the only person hitherto, to illustrate his poems." Preface

Livingston, Myra Cohn

The Malibu and other poems; illus. by James J. Spanfeller. Atheneum Pubs. 1972 44p illus $4.25 (4-7)   811

ISBN 0-689-30308-4

"A Margaret K. McElderry book"

"Most of the [40] poems are observations on every-day life, nature, pollution, peace, people, animals, books. The young person's viewpoint is well maintained throughout." Sch Library J

The author "writes with a free-flowing rhythm and an effect of spontaneity. Themes and mood vary, some of the selections light and humorous, others thoughtful. . . . Many of the poems reflect the child's view of self. Although this book is recommended for a particular reading-level span, there are no boundaries for good poetry—adults may enjoy this, and it can be read aloud to younger children." Chicago. Children's Bk Center

Longfellow, Henry Wadsworth

The children's own Longfellow. Houghton 1920 103p illus $4.95 (5-7)   811

ISBN 0-395-06889-4

First published 1908

Includes 8 colored illustrations by various artists

Contents: The wreck of the Hesperus; The village blacksmith; Evangeline [selection]; The song of Hiawatha [selection]; The building of the ship; The castle-builder; Paul Revere's ride; The building of the Long Serpent

Paul Revere's ride; illus. by Joseph Low. Windmill Bks. 1973 unp illus $5.95 (3-6)   811

1 Revere, Paul—Poetry 2 U.S.—History—Revolution—Poetry

ISBN 0-87807-050-8

"Longfellow's familiar poem is set in picture-book form and backed with misty, earthy-hued landscapes peopled by sketchy, cartoonish colonists. The open, lightly washed scenes are in keeping with the poem, but Low's people, especially Paul Revere, are possessed of a comic note somehow incongruous with both the quiet backgrounds and Longfellow's poem. Nevertheless, the book is attractive and may be of special use in elementary collections for its narrative poetic value." Booklist

Paul Revere's ride; illus. by Paul Galdone. Crowell 1963 unp illus $4.95, lib. bdg. $5.70 (3-6)   811

1 Revere, Paul—Poetry 2 U.S.—History—Revolution—Poetry

ISBN 0-690-61235-4; 0-690-61236-2

An illustrated edition of the famous poem about Paul Revere's ride at the start of the American Revolution

"The dashing verses, printed in strong, clear type, have the right complement in the robust figures and moonlit scenes—in black with blue and brick red—of Boston Harbor and colonial streets and countryside. Authentic in detail, as well as interpretative in spirit, the pictures considerably enhance the meaning of the verses." Horn Bk

The song of Hiawatha; with a colored frontispiece and line drawings in the text by [Joan] Kiddell-Monroe. Dutton 1960 214p illus $4.50 (5-7)   811

1 Indians of North America—Poetry

ISBN 0-525-39669-1

"Children's illustrated classics"

First published 1855 by Ticknor and Fields

Founded on a tradition among North American Indians about a person of miraculous powers sent to teach them the arts of peace, this is a narrative poem about an Ojibway Indian who is reared by his grandmother, Nokomis, daughter of the Moon. The poem describes the deeds of the hero in revenging his mother, Wenonah, against his father, the West Wind

McCord, David

All day long; fifty rhymes of the never was and always is. Drawings by Henry B. Kane. Little 1966 104p illus $4.95 (4-6)   811

ISBN 0-316-55508-8

Poems about the haunting delights, surprises and wit of childhood

"The topics are simple but intriguing, the writing has rhythm, humor, and imaginative zest; the black and white illustrations are attractive, many of them also humorous." Chicago. Children's Bk Center

Every time I climb a tree; illus. by Marc Simont. Little 1967 unp illus lib. bdg. $5.95 (1-3)   811

ISBN 0-316-55495-2

Twenty-five of the youngest verse selected from the author's collections: Far and few, Take sky and All day long, all entered separately

"All the Simont drawings coincide happily with the McCord mentality: sassy, inventive, fresh." Bk World

Far and few; rhymes of the never was and always is; drawings by Henry B. Kane. Little 1952 99p illus $4.95 (4-6)   811

ISBN 0-316-55502-9

This book of verse for children takes its title from: The jumblies, by Edward Lear. It contains sixty poems with a great variety of rhythm and ideas, of humor, imagination, and a tinge of sadness in occasional lines

"In the author's words, this book reflects 'a child's self-reliance, his instinctive interest in nature.'" Bks for Deaf Children

For me to say; rhymes of the never was and always is. Drawings by Henry B. Kane. Little 1970 100p illus $4.95 (4-6)   811

ISBN 0-316-55511-8

A "collection that is with few exceptions, light in topic and tone, with breezy humor and relish of word play, and with small, neat illustrations that often implement the poems. Some of the selections are, indeed, word games as well as poetry. . . . The author shows, in a final section . . . [how to write] verse forms. Included here are the ballade, the tercet, the villanelle, the clerihew, the cinquain, and haiku." Sutherland. The Best In Children's Bks

Take sky; more rhymes of the never was and always is; drawings by Henry B. Kane. Little 1962 107p illus $4.95 (4-6)   811

ISBN 0-316-55509-6

A collection of forty-eight humorous poems on various subjects ranging in form from short verses to longer narrative poetry

"Adult help may be needed for understanding the verse-lessons part 'by Professor Swigley Brown' about couplet, triolet, quatrain, and limerick." Sch Library J

"Diversity of imagination and humor makes a volume that bears dipping into again and again for quiet enjoyment and for reading aloud. Henry Kane's pencil drawings make beautiful pages, with great variety in layout." Horn Bk

McGinley, Phyllis

Mince pie and mistletoe; pictures by Harold Berson. Lippincott 1961 unp illus $3.50 (4-7)   811

McGinley, Phyllis—*Continued*
1 Christmas poetry
ISBN 0-397-30573-7
"The book is divided into states or regions of the United States, giving in verse form the Christmas customs of the region, some dependent on circumstance (the limitations imposed by frontier life) and some on the origin of the resident group (the Dutch heritage of New Amsterdam settlers)." Chicago. Children Bk Center
A book of "swinging rhymes. . . . The illustrations are most attractive, filled with action and dozens of objects for young readers to pore over." Pub W

A wreath of Christmas legends; illus. by Leonard Weisgard. Macmillan (N Y) 1967 62p illus $5.95 (5-7)   811
1 Christmas poetry 2 Jesus Christ—Nativity—Poetry
A collection of 15 poems based on medieval legends of the first Christmas
"The black and white illustrations of birds and beasts have a precise grace, and the page layout is dignified. The poems have the felicitous phrasing, the polished simplicity, and the quick shafts of humor that distinguish Miss McGinley's work." Chicago. Children's Bk Center

The year without a Santa Claus; pictures by Kurt Werth. Lippincott 1947 unp illus $5.95 (k-3)   811
1 Christmas poetry
ISBN 0-397-30399-8
The author's verse and "the illustrator's agreeable pictures give new life to an old theme. When Santa Claus announces that he is much too tired for Christmas capers and is going to take his first vacation, the weeping children of the world . . . decide to give Santa a Merry Christmas. What happens when Santa receives his gifts climaxes a story-poem which will be enjoyed by the whole family." Booklist

McGovern, Ann
Black is beautiful; with photographs by Hope Wurmfeld. Four Winds 1969 unp illus $4.95, lib. bdg. $4.88   811
1 Black—Poetry
ISBN 0-590-17155-0; 0-590-07155-6
"A series of photographs (some competent compositions, some hazy shots of children) accompanies a text in which a few poetic lines on eage page reiterate the message of the title. 'Zig-zag of lightning. Thunder crack; Stormy sky; the clouds turn back. Black is beautiful.' " Chicago. Children's Bk Center
"For a book to have as its title such an emotionally loaded slogan is sufficient to make some adults feel apprehensive . . . [but this] picture-book should assuage the fears of even the most timid." Sch Library J
"A child can now see that there are many beautiful things that are black—including people. This book is appropriate for the primary grades because pictures tell the story. There is not an overemphasis on race, but rather a presentation of many beautiful things that are black." Reading Ladders for Human Relations. 5th edition

Mendoza, George
And I must hurry for the sea is coming in. . . . Photographs by DeWayne Dalrymple; design by Herb Lubalin. Prentice-Hall 1969 unp illus lib. bdg. $3.95 (3-6)   811
ISBN 0-13-036517-3
The "verse text describes a black boy's imaginative voyage across a threatening sea. 'It will not break me,' he resolves as he embarks. . . . When the trip ends . . . the book has made a . . . statement about cour-

age in adversity and the transforming power of the imagination." N Y Times Bk Rev
"Full-color photographs show the sweet and serious face of a Negro boy, a boat sailing on a silver-sparkling sea, spray flashing. . . . Evocative but static, the book may be limited in its appeal to the more sophisticated reader or the child who particularly enjoys poetry." Chicago. Children's Bk Center

Merriam, Eve
Finding a poem; illus. by Seymour Chwast. Atheneum Pubs. 1970 68p illus lib. bdg. $5.95 (6-7)   811
ISBN 0-689-20607-0
"There are poems of despair, cries of a poet, 'in a plastic age of time for everything and time for nothing, of masses of people and lonely individuals, of new discovery and numbing sameness.' There are poems as bright as quicksilver that in a few words reveal a mood of awe, of surprise, of wonder. And there is a record, noted down step by step, word by word, of how she created a poem." Pub W
"Uneven in quality and depth of thought but for the most part imaginative, amusing, or thought-provoking." Booklist

Independent voices; drawings by Arvis Stewart. Atheneum Pubs. 1968 79p illus $4.25, lib. bdg. $4.08 (5-7)   811
1 U.S.—Biography—Poetry
ISBN 0-689-20269-5; 0-689-20270-9
These seven "verse biographies of individualistic Americans . . . include Benjamin Franklin, Elizabeth Blackwell, Frederick Douglass, Thoreau, Lucretia Mott, Ida B. Wells, and Fiorella La Guardia." Bk World
"The author says [these poems] 'are intended primarily to be read aloud.' The poems vary greatly in ease of execution and in treatment of the heroes." Sch Library J

It doesn't always have to rhyme; drawings by Malcolm Spooner. Athenuem Pubs. 1964 83p illus lib. bdg. $4.25 (4-7)   811
ISBN 0-689-20671-2
Here is a collection of over 50 humorous poems on a variety of subjects including vocabulary and "the very fun of poetry and its infinite possibilities." Horn Bk

There is no rhyme for silver; drawings by Joseph Schindelman. Atheneum Pubs. 1962 70p illus $3.25, lib. bdg. $3.07 (2-5)   811
ISBN 0-689-20271-7; 0-689-20272-5
A pleasant, mostly humorous, collection of poems for children dealing with such things as kittens, space, flying, asking questions, wishing, summer rain, the Optileast and the Pessimost (imaginary beasts), and exploring
"Joseph Schindelman's drawings are good complements to the poetry." Bookmark

Miles, Miska
Apricot ABC; illus. by Peter Parnall. Little 1969 unp illus $4.95 (k-3)   811
1 Alphabet books 2 Stories in rhyme
ISBN 0-316-57030-3
"An Atlantic Monthly Press book"
"The artist's clean, sharply detailed drawings for a fauna-and-flora ABC give lively action as well as identifiable form to a sequence of natural subjects—from 'A' for 'An apricot tree grew knobby and tall' to 'Yellow sun shines' and 'Rains zig and zag.' Locating the large capital letters could be made a kind of game, for these are interwoven into green, leafy sketches. The even rhyming lines tell of the insects and plants among which an apricot falls, and of a hen with feathers

Miles, Miska—_Continued_

fluffed—a monster to the frightened frog—that finds the fruit a 'magnificent meal' and leaves only a seed. . . . Artistically the author-artist collaboration is successful; the combination of life-cycle and ecological concepts with ABC rhymes raises the level of interest above the usual ABC audience." Horn Bk

Mizumura, Kazue

I see the winds. Crowell 1966 unp illus $4.50, lib. bdg. $5.25 (k-3)   811

   1 Winds—Poetry

   ISBN 0-690-43342-5; 0-690-43433-3

"In haiku-like verse the author-artist has portrayed the many forms of the wind through the seasons of the year." Chicago

"The skillful water colors say as much economically as do the poems. This should be a valuable book to stimulate creative work with children." Sat Rev

If I were a cricket. . . . Crowell 1973 unp illus $4.50, lib. bdg. $5.25 (k-2)   811

   1 Love poetry 2 Animals—Poetry

   ISBN 0-690-00076-6; 0-690-00075-8

"Small creatures such as a spider, firefly, snail, etc. are used to pronounce tender messages of love. . . . The appealing word images and mosaic-like drawings—pastels alternating with spreads done in black, white, and grey—will provide many opportunities for sharing warm feelings with very young children." Sch Library J

Moore, Clement C.

The night before Christmas (k-3)   811

   1 Christmas poetry

   Some editions are:

Grosset $2.95 Illustrated by Leonard Weisgard (ISBN 0-448-02935-9)

Houghton $3.25 With pictures by Jessie Wilcox Smith. Has title: 'Twas the night before Christmas (ISBN 0-395-06952-1)

Lippincott $4.50 Illustrated by Arthur Rackham (ISBN 0-397-30276-2)

McGraw $4.95 Paul Galdone drew the pictures. Has title: A visit from St Nicholas (ISBN 0-07-042900-6)

Rand McNally $4.95, lib. bdg. $4.97 Illustrated by Tasha Tudor (ISBN 0-528-82181-4; 0-528-80144-9)

First published 1823

This popular Christmas poem has been a favorite with American children ever since this professor of Oriental and Greek literature wrote it for his children in 1822. It is from this poem that we get the names for the Christmas reindeer

Moore, Lilian

I thought I heard the city; collage by Mary Jane Dunton. Atheneum Pubs. 1969 unp illus lib. bdg. $4.95 (3-6)   811

   1 Cities and towns—Poetry

   ISBN 0-689-20623-2

A collection of seventeen poems "about trees and birds, rain and snow, the beauty of a bridge at night, a construction project." Sat Rev

This "is poetry that encourages the listener to consider familiar objects with fresh attention. The illustrations match the mood of the poems and help to make a very attractive small volume." Horn Bk

Nash, Ogden

The cruise of the Aardvark; pictures by Wendy Watson. Evans, M.&Co. 1967 unp illus $3.95 (3-5)   811

   1 Aardvark—Poetry 2 Animals—Poetry 3 Noah's Ark—Poetry

   ISBN 0-87131-019-8

Aardvark, thoroughly disgruntled when the weather turned rainy, decided to go on a cruise. His fellow passengers were travelling two by two, and Noah was the captain of the ship. This story in verse recounts the events of this remarkable voyage

O'Neill, Mary

Hailstones and halibut bones; adventures in color; illus. by Leonard Weisgard. Doubleday 1961 59p illus $4.50, lib. bdg. $5.25, pa $1.50 (k-4)   811

   1 Color—Poetry

   ISBN 0-385-07911-7; 0-385-07912-5; 0-385-05314-6

"Stimulating to the imagination and pleasing to the eye is this unusual introduction to color. Twelve simple poems relate thoughts, moods, and images to the colors of the spectrum." Chicago

"What it amounts to, really, is a list of familiar objects that children can identify with colors. These things are very well chosen, however, and the book will be useful to those teaching little children to identify colors." Pub W

Prelutsky, Jack

Circus; pictures by Arnold Lobel. Macmillan Pub. Co. 1974 unp illus $5.95 (k-3)   811

   1 Circus—Poetry

   ISBN 0-02-775060-4

Prelutsky "presents the attractions of the big top in verses and they are made visible in Lobel's witty color pictures. . . . For children who haven't experienced the thrills of the greatest show on earth, this book tells about the performing seals, the acrobats, sword-swallowers, fire eaters, human cannonballs and more." Pub W

"Best for reading aloud, the alliterative poems which move in a fast, bouncing rhythm require a nimble-tongued storyteller. Although the book may be overly long to hold the attention of youngest listeners, Lobel's detailed, full-color drawings add humor and interest to this ode to the big top." Sch Library J

A gopher in the garden, and other animal poems; pictures by Robert Leydenfrost. Macmillan (N Y) 1967 unp illus $3.95 (2-5)   811

   1 Animals—Poetry

Among the animals represented in this collection of verses are a crafty crocodile, a gopher in a garden, a caterpillar, a brindled gnu, a giggling gaggling gaggle of geese, a multilingual mynah bird, a weasel, a giraffe and a pygmy shrew

The author "sustains the fun without a letdown in easy delightful rhymes and rhythms, and with words that call for reading aloud. . . . Broken-line drawings in blue, yellow, green, and black echo the lively spirit of the rhymes." Horn Bk

Richards, Laura E.

Tirra lirra; rhymes old and new; foreword by May Hill Arbuthnot; with illus. by Marguerite Davis. Little 1955 194p illus $5.95 (3-5)   811

   1 Nonsense verses

   ISBN 0-316-74415-8

First published 1932

"These nonsense verses have been selected from the author's early books and from pages of 'St. Nicholas.' " Booklist

This "is still in demand in children's libraries, and treasured in homes. . . . For no one who has ever known the frog who 'lived in a bog, on the banks of Lake Okeefinokee'; the 'elephant who tried to use the telephant'; the owl, the eel and the warming pan who 'went to call on the soap-fat man'; and the other members of the gay Tirra Lirra company is ever likely to forget them." Horn Bk

Riley, James Whitcomb

The gobble-uns'll git you ef you don't watch out! James Whitcomb Riley's "Little Orphant Annie;" illus. by Joel Schick. Lippincott 1975 unp illus $4.95 (1-4)   811

1 Monsters—Poetry
ISBN 0-397-31621-6

This is the classic story poem of ill-mannered children spirited away by the ferocious Gobble-uns, as told by Little Orphant Annie.

"This 1885 poem in Midwest dialect has always given a few chills to those with vivid imaginations. Now the 'Gobble-uns' have been sketched in all their sinister glory—and they look a lot like your average, mean-eyed, snaggle-toothed heavy. Gruesome enough for those who like that sort of thing, but don't offer this book to the timid. The black and white drawings of rotund Annie and the characters in her stories help clarify obscurities in the verse for youngsters." Children's Bk Rev Serv

Sandburg, Carl

Wind song; illus. by William A. Smith. Harcourt 1960 127p illus $4.95, pa $1.25 (4-7)   811

ISBN 0-15-297497-0; 0-15-697096-1

A collection of poems for children and young people chosen from the poet's published works plus sixteen new poems. The poems are grouped under the following headings: New poems; Little people; Little album; Corn belt; Night; Blossom themes; Wind, sea, and sky

"Selected by Carl Sandburg himself for 'young folks.' Well-printed and designed with a black and white drawing for each one of the seven groupings. An original and distinctive book of poems that will be enjoyed by all ages." Ontario Library Rev

Silverstein, Shel

Where the sidewalk ends; the poems & drawings of Shel Silverstein. Harper 1974 166p illus $7.95, lib. bdg. $6.11 (3-6)   811

1 Humorous poetry 2 Nonsense verses
ISBN 0-06-025667-2; 0-06-025668-0

"There are skillful, sometimes grotesque line drawings with each of the 127 poems, which run in length from a few lines to a couple of pages. The poems are tender, funny, sentimental, philosophical, and ridiculous in turn, and they're for all ages . . . [Subjects include] an anti-nose-picking poem and one about belching—but that's life." Sat Rev

"This collection of rather unusual poems will convince the poetry scorners that a poem does not have to be all flowers and fairies. Many of these first appeared as song lyrics or in William Cole's anthologies of poetry for children." Children's Bk Rev Serv

Smith, William Jay

Laughing time; illus. by Juliet Kepes. Little 1955 54p illus $4.50 (k-2)   811

1 Nonsense verses
ISBN 0-316-80134-8

"An Atlantic Monthly Press book"

A book of nonsense verse for the very young

This "is indeed a funny book, one to share with that age when a child's own imaginings are bursting with new ideas about himself, about all sorts of sensual experiences, about strange animals far away." N Y Her Trib Bks

Teasdale, Sara

Stars to-night; verses new and old for boys and girls; illus. by Dorothy P. Lathrop. Macmillan (N Y) 1930 49p illus $3.95 (5-7)   811

1 Nature in poetry

"Great care and thought have gone into this collec-

tion. . . . As the title suggests, many of the poems are about stars, but there are many others in Miss Teasdale's best strain about flowers, birds and the poet's emotional response to nature. Dorothy P. Lathrop has enhanced the verse with her special gift of rare and imaginative decoration." N Y Evening Post

Thayer, Ernest Lawrence

Casey at the bat; illus. by Paul Frame. Prentice-Hall 1964 unp illus lib. bdg. $4.95, pa 95¢ (4-7) 811

1 Baseball—Poetry
ISBN 0-13-120410-6; 0-13-120402-5

"The classic poem that relates how the fate of the Mudville nine came to rest on that paragon hitter, Casey, and then to the disbelief of all that 'mighty Casey' had struck out is here presented in picture book form." Pub W

Tippett, James S.

Crickety Cricket! The best-loved poems of James S. Tippett. Pictures by Mary Chalmers. Introduction by Donald J. Bissett. Harper 1973 83p illus $3.95, lib. bdg. $3.79 (k-2)   811

ISBN 0-06-029118-8; 0-06-026119-6

"Uniformly light and cheerful, the 52 poems here cover a variety of subjects from building with blocks and watching trucks go by to making tracks in the snow. The rhymes are pedestrian and sing-song at times ('The store around the corner/Has groceries to sell./ I go there with my mother;/ I like that very well.' . . . These pleasant selections are easy to comprehend and are adequately complemented by cozy pencil drawings." Sch Library J

Updike, John

A child's calendar; illus. by Nancy Ekholm Burkert. Knopf 1965 unp illus lib. bdg. $4.99 (k-3)   811

1 Months—Poetry
ISBN 0-394-91059-1

"A poem for each month, a picture for each poem; the poetry has simplicity of style and familiarity of subject that are appealing, and has, here and there, a freshly imaginative image. The illustrations are delicate and precise in detail." Chicago. Children's Bk Center

Watson, Clyde

Father Fox's pennyrhymes; illus. by Wendy Watson. Crowell 1971 56p illus $4.95, lib. bdg. $5.70 (k-3)   811

1 Nonsense verses
ISBN 0-690-29213-9; 0-690-29214-7

"A collection of short, original nonsense rhymes, illustrated with a bounty of high-spirited pictures. Some of the verses are impish or boisterous or just plain silly; some are similar to counting-out rhymes and jump-rope jingles; a few are as gentle as lullabies. All are highly rhythmic and reminiscent of the traditional rhymes of folklore. The watercolor-and-ink illustrations are somewhat whimsical in their busyness; tiny pictures printed in sequence—like comic strips—as well as single, full-page pictures are brimming with minute detail and activity." Horn Bk

Whitman, Walt

Overhead the sun; lines from Walt Whitman; woodcuts by Antonio Frasconi. Farrar, Straus 1969 unp illus $4.95 (6-7)   811

ISBN 0-374-35676-9

"A strikingly beautiful book with full-page, multicolored sensitive woodcuts by Antonio Frasconi accompanying 16 of his selections from 'Leaves of Grass.' This brilliant artist captures the mood and dignity of the text and gives an imposing interpretation to it." Top of the News

Worth, Valerie
Small poems; pictures by Natalie Babbitt. Farrar, Straus 1972 41p illus $4.50 (3-6) **811**
ISBN 0-374-37072-9
"In twenty-four poems about such topics as raw carrots, cows, jewels, grasses, and crickets, the author gives added dimensions to the object by a suggestive turn of phrase or an unusual perspective. . . . The illustrations, in perfect harmony with the poems, suggest the possibilities of the items but are never so precise as to limit their potential scope. Both text and illustrations have been housed in a book in which the texture of the pages, the typography, the layout, and even the color of the binding are as understated, but as beautiful, as the text and illustrations." Horn Bk

811.08 American poetry— Collections

Adoff, Arnold
(ed.) I am the darker brother; an anthology of modern poems by Negro Americans; drawings by Benny Andrews; foreword by Charlemae Rollins. Macmillan (N Y) 1968 128p illus lib. bdg. $4.95, pa $1.25 (5-7) **811.08**
1 Negro poetry—Collections 2 American poetry—Collections
"Selections by 28 American Negro poets who reflect on the past, the current social scene, and the hope for the future. . . . In a brief foreword, Charlemae Rollins discusses creativity, poetry, and the Negro." Sch Library J
"A most interesting anthology, with many contributions from such well-known poets as Brooks, Dunbar, Hayden, Hughes, and McKay, and a broad representation of selections from the work of some two dozen other modern authors. The format is dignified and spacious." Chicago. Children's Bk Center
Includes notes, biographies, and indexes to authors and first lines

(comp.) My Black me; a beginning book of Black poetry. Dutton 1974 83p $5.50 (4-7) **811.08**
1 Negro poetry—Collections
ISBN 0-525-35460-3
A collection of fifty poems by Black poets who convey the Black experience and the hope for a better, prouder quality of life. Included are works by Langston Hughes, Don L. Lee, Nikki Giovanni, and Sam Cornish
"There are poems that speak in protest, but as a collection the poems are a positive affirmation of blackness, and they have been wisely chosen for younger readers. Notes on the poets and an index [to first lines] are appended." Chicago. Children's Bk Center

Allen, Terry
(ed.) The whispering wind; poetry by young American Indians; with an introduction by Mae J. Durham. Doubleday 1972 128p lib. bdg. $4.95, pa $1.95 (6-7) **811.08**
1 Indian poetry—Collections 2 American poetry—Collections
ISBN 0-385-07405-0; 0-385-01032-X
This "is a sampling of the work of students at the Institute of American Indian Arts in Santa Fe. All poems are of high quality, the techniques ranging from lyrical metaphors of nature to intricate abstractions, from primitive drumbeat rhythms to the idiom of today's urban youth." N Y Times Bk Rev

Baron, Virginia Olsen
(ed.) Here I am! An anthology of poems written by young people in some of America's minority groups; illus. by Emily Arnold McCully. Dutton 1969 159p illus lib. bdg. $5.95 **811.08**
1 American poetry—Collections 2 Minorities—Poetry 3 Children as authors
ISBN 0-525-31708-2
"The topics include nature, family, dreams, problems, places, situations, and special people. The contributions have come from Alaska, Utah, California, New Mexico, New York and other areas of the United States where economic and racial problems are numerous. The reader will be aware of Black, Puerto Rican, Eskimo, Aleut, Navajo—and the range of moods is extensive." Best Sellers
"From schools all over the United States, the author solicited children's poems and chose approximately one hundred twenty for inclusion in a volume that has some moments of lightness but chiefly comprises candid observations on awareness, isolation, prejudice, and justice—or, more often, injustice. . . . Most of the selections are intensely personal and infinitely moving." Chicago. Children's Bk Center
Includes Index of poets and Index of first lines

Benét, William Rose
(comp.) Poems for youth; an American anthology. Dutton 1925 xxxiv, 512p $6.95 (6-7) **811.08**
1 American poetry—Collections
ISBN 0-525-37234-2
"A generous selection of the most striking poems of American poets old and new, compiled especially for young Americans." Literary Rev
The poets are arranged chronologically from Fitz-Greene Halleck to Hilda Conkling. Notes give bibliographical and critical facts. Includes author and title index

Bontemps, Arna
(comp.) Golden slippers; an anthology of Negro poetry for young readers; with drawings by Henrietta Bruce Sharon. Harper 1941 220p illus $7.95, lib. bdg. $6.27 (5-7) **811.08**
1 Negro poetry—Collections 2 American poetry—Collections
ISBN 0-06-010395-7; 0-06-010404-X
"Containing a representative collection of Negro verse, by such poets as Langston Hughes, Claude McKay, Countee Cullen, Paul Laurence Dunbar, and James Weldon Johnson [this] is not limited in appeal to the young people for whom it was compiled." Wis Library Bul
"Mr. Bontemps' preference for the short lyric with a strong rhythmic pattern makes this anthology a selection young people should enjoy." L.C. Children & Poetry

Downie, Mary Alice
(comp.) The wind has wings; poems from Canada; comp. by Mary Alice Downie & Barbara Robertson; illus. by Elizabeth Cleaver. Walck, H.Z. 1968 95p illus lib. bdg. $6.75 (5-7) **811.08**
1 Canadian poetry—Collections
ISBN 0-8098-2401-9
"An absolutely delightful anthology, some of the selections about things peculiarly Canadian, some on topics of a serious nature, and some of deft absurdity. There are folk-like poems translated from the French, some particularly nice animal poems, and some very conventional selections. The illustrations have a great deal of vitality and are as varied as is the poetry." Chicago. Children's Bk Center

Dunning, Stephen

(comp.) Reflections on a gift of watermelon pickle . . . and other modern verse [comp. by] Stephen Dunning, Edward Lueders [and] Hugh Smith. Lothrop 1967 [c1966] 139p illus $5.95, lib. bdg. $5.11 (6-7)   811.08

1 American poetry—Collections

ISBN 0-688-41231-9; 0-688-51231-3

Text edition of this title first published 1966 by Scott

"From a group of twelve hundred modern poems, three teachers of English have selected one hundred fourteen, many of them by unknown poets, but scattered single ones by such writers as Ezra Pound, Walter de la Mare, and Robert Frost. The subjects range from the wonder of beasts and birds to the equally astonishing phenomena of fireworks, steam shovel, sonic boom, and the multifarious activities of child and man. The language is contemporary and conversational, and the versification generally free. The uniqueness of the collection, however, consists in the pairing—on imaginatively designed pages—of significant, sharp, and beautifully composed photographs with many of the poems." Horn Bk

Includes an author and title index

Emrich, Duncan

(comp.) American folk poetry; an anthology. Little 1974 xxxi, 831p illus $22.50   811.08

1 Ballads, American 2 Folk songs—U.S.

ISBN 0-316-23722-1

This volume includes "songs, poems, and ballads arranged under the broad headings: children's ballads; hymns, religious pieces, and carols; wars and other disasters; songs of occupations and sea, forest, mines; songs of cowboys, Mormons, outlaws." Library J

"The annotated selections, often familiar but sometimes exceedingly quaint . . . show a distinct English, Irish, and Scotch heritage modified by American taste. Texts are given without music but Library of Congress archive numbers are noted for items recorded in its folklore series. Extensive bibliography and indexes by title and first line." Booklist

Hine, Al

(ed.) This land is mine; an anthology of American verse; illus. by Leonard Vosburgh. Lippincott 1965 244p illus $4.95 (6-7)   811.08

1 American poetry—Collections 2 U.S.—History—Poetry

ISBN 0-397-30840-X

"A collection of over 100 poems, with comments by the compiler tracing the history of the United States from Indian days to the present." Adventuring With Bks. 2d edition

"The selections are varied in quality and in kind. . . . An index of first lines and an author index are appended; there is no alphabetical listing of titles." Chicago. Children's Bk Center

Hopkins, Lee Bennett

(comp.) Girls can too! A book of poems; illus. by Emily McCully. Watts, F. 1972 45p illus lib. bdg. $4.90 (k-3)   811.08

1 Girls—Poetry

ISBN 0-531-02587-X

The compiler has selected 19 poems by such poets as Dorothy Aldis, Myra Cohn Livingston, David McCord and Aileen Fisher illustrating various activities typical in a young girl's life

"Delightful collection of poems depicting many of the activities and feelings of children with emphasis on what little girls can experience. The pen and ink illustrations are perfectly charming." Notable Children's Trade Bks (Social Studies)

(comp.) Hey-how for Halloween! Poems selected by Lee Bennett Hopkins; illus. by Janet McCaffery. Harcourt 1974 31p illus $4.75 (2-4)   811.08

1 Halloween—Poetry

ISBN 0-15-233900-0

"This short anthology features 22 poems about ghosts, haunted houses, witches, goblins, etc. by E. E. Cummings, Carl Sandburg, John Ciardi, Carson McCullers, and Maurice Sendak among others." Sch Library J

"The compiler is careful to avoid cuteness and condescension while recognizing the pleasures of creepy imagery and spooky sonorities. All selections are suitable for story hour activities and individual reading, making the volume more valuable than its slim dimensions might indicate. Scratchy, spattery black-and-white illustrations lend atmosphere." Booklist

(comp.) Me! A book of poems; illus. by Talivaldis Stubis. Seabury 1970 30p illus $5.95 (k-2)   811.08

1 American poetry—Collections

ISBN 0-8164-3042-X

This collection contains poems by such contemporary authors as Gwendolyn Brooks, Dorothy Aldis, Aileen Fisher, Charlotte Zolotow, Carson McCullers and others whose subjects are familiar to children

These poems "have been selected with respect for craftsmanship and the pleasure of young listeners or readers. . . . The book is well-designed textually and complemented by charming light sepia washes with a nice quality that bridges reality and fantasy." Library J

Larrick, Nancy

(comp.) Green is like a meadow of grass; an anthology of children's pleasure in poetry; drawings by Kelly Oechsli. Garrard 1968 64p illus lib. bdg. $3.40 (k-4)   811.08

1 American poetry—Collections 2 Children as authors

ISBN 0-8116-4103-1

"The 74 poems contained in this small anthology were written by the six- to 13-year-old pupils of 22 teachers participating in a workshop on poetry for children at Lehigh University. The brief, unrhymed selections too obviously seemed to have been the result of assigned topics; many of them are simple similes conventional in tone. . . . Nevertheless, the book's slim, oblong shape and its low-keyed black line drawings can be used to encourage youthful browsing and emulation." Sch Library J

(comp.) I heard a scream in the street; poems by young people in the city; illus. with photographs by students. Published by Evans, M.&Co. and distributed in association with Lippincott 1970 141p illus $5.95 (5-7)   811.08

1 American poetry—Collections 2 Cities and towns—Poetry 3 Children as authors

ISBN 0-87131-064-3

"From class magazines, workshops and community centers, student newspapers and college poetry projects, from young people in twenty-three cities, Nancy Larrick has chosen almost eighty poems that testify to the perception, vision, and candor of the young." Chicago. Children's Bk Center

"Some readers may blanche at the frankness of the language, the loose attention to meter and rhythm. But many will hear these honest voices with their economy of expression, passion and explicitness, the absence of illusion and the presence of disillusion. . . . Limited to city poetry by the young and largely unknown, with prize-winning photographs by other talented youngsters, it is the natural companion to Miss Larrick's 'On City Streets' [entered below] a

Larrick, Nancy—*Continued*

compilation of city poetry by the famous, illustrated with professional photographs." Sch Library J

Includes an Index of poets and titles and an Index of first lines

(ed.) On city streets; an anthology of poetry; illus. with photographs by David Sagarin. Evans, M.&Co. 1968 158p illus $5.95 (5-7)   811.08

1 American poetry—Collections 2 Cities and towns—Poetry

ISBN 0-87131-080-5

"This anthology of poems compiled by Nancy Larrick, with the help of more than 100 city children, has the perfect, the perfectly exact title. Country and suburban children who read the poems (and look at the photographs) will know what life is like on city streets; children who live on city streets will feel the elation of recognition." Pub W

"Sharp, immediate, full of evocative music . . . the book has poems whose sequences arrive thrilling and smiting at one's life. . . . The short ones, the loving ones, the mysterious ones, the shouting ones, the ones with animals, the ones from other cultures, the ones perhaps most like children—very frail and very strong, like bubbles. . . . [This book] opens up a great landscape of poems that children want." N Y Times Bk Rev

Includes an Index of poets and titles and an Index of first lines

(comp.) Poetry for holidays; drawings by Kelly Oechsli. Garrard 1966 64p illus lib. bdg. $3.40 (1-4)   811.08

1 Holidays—Poetry

ISBN 0-8116-4100-7

Poems for Halloween, Christmas, Saint Valentine's Day, Easter, and other holidays, by such authors as Harry Behn, Marchette Chute, Aileen Fisher, Langston Hughes, Henry Wadsworth Longfellow, and Ruth Sawyer

Includes an index of authors

Weiss, Renée Karol

(comp.) A paper zoo; a collection of animal poems by modern American poets; pictures by Ellen Raskin. Macmillan (N Y) 1968 38p illus lib. bdg. $4.95 (1-4)   811.08

1 Animals—Poetry 2 American poetry—Collections

"Presented in a picture book given an almost psychedelic look by Ellen Raskin's brilliant designs of paper-cut creatures, this small collection invites an audience of very young listeners, to whom its poems about animals will certainly appeal, while at the same time its selections from writing by the first rank of modern American poets is for any age." L.C. Children & Poetry

812   American drama

Behrens, June

Feast of Thanksgiving; the first American holiday; a play. Pictures by Anne Siberell. Childrens Press 1974 31p illus lib. bdg. $5.25 (1-3)   812

1 Thanksgiving Day—Drama

ISBN 0-516-08725-8

"A Golden Gate Junior book"

"The story of the first Thanksgiving is once again told, this time for young children and in play form. . . . Act One concerns a typical Pilgrim family preparing for the great feast. Act Two depicts the happy feast itself. A light plot in which the Pilgrim children

realize that Red Feather, the Indian boy they have feared and distrusted, is really just like them adds a new touch to the familiar story." Reading Teacher

"Teachers charged with putting on a Thanksgiving play in the primary grades will be happy about this title. The dialogue is couched in language primary children will understand. The illustrations are childlike color collages. . . . Elementary librarians will find this traditional story of Thanksgiving useful." Children's Bk Rev Serv

Bennett, Rowena

Creative plays and programs for holidays. . . . Plays, Inc. 1966 448p $8.95 (3-6)   812

1 Holidays—Drama 2 Seasons—Drama 3 Holidays —Poetry 4 Seasons—Poetry

ISBN 0-8238-0005-9

"Royalty-free plays, playlets, group readings, and poems for holiday and seasonal programs for boys and girls." Subtitle

"The short plays composed of simple sentences lend themselves to easy memorization by lower and middle grades. There is a great deal of variety in the subject matter as well as the genre." Sch Library J

Production notes: p439-48

Boiko, Claire

Children's plays for creative actors; a collection of royalty-free plays for boys and girls. Plays, Inc. 1967 368p $8.95 (3-7)   812

1 One-act plays

ISBN 0-8238-0006-7

Here are thirty-five one-act plays, playlets, comedies, fantasies, holiday plays, and fairy tales. Some of the plays feature choral speaking. Included are plays for Christmas, New Years, Washington's and Lincoln's birthdays, Thanksgiving, Halloween, Book Week, Arbor Day, and other special occasions

Carlson, Bernice Wells

Funny-bone dramatics; illus. by Charles Cox. Abingdon 1974 96p illus lib. bdg. $4.95 (k-3)   812

ISBN 0-687-13867-1

"The selection of speak-up riddles, jokes for enactment with puppets, skits and plays (many based on the familiar droll or simpleton motifs of folk tradition) will be a convenient resource for creative dramatics programs. The book progresses from short riddles to multicharacter plays, and the tone is predominantly slapstick." Horn Bk

This book is "designed to polish clarity, timing, acting, and reaction, and other comic acting techniques. . . . With a glossary of acting terms and a short reading list, this . . . will provide good routines for young entertainers." Sch Library J

Fisher, Aileen

Holiday programs for boys and girls. Plays, Inc. 1970 374p $7.95 (4-7)   812

1 Holidays—Drama 2 One-act plays

ISBN 0-8238-0018-0

First published 1953

"A collection of easily produced, nonroyalty plays—some of them in verse—poems, group readings, and recitations for holidays and special occasions observed in schools. . . . [It] will probably be helpful for teachers planning classroom or assembly programs. Production notes are given." Booklist

United Nations plays and programs, by Aileen Fisher and Olive Rabe. Plays, Inc. 1965 285p $6.95   812

1 United Nations—Drama 2 One-act plays

ISBN 0-8238-0021-0

First published 1954

Fisher, Aileen—*Continued*

The aims, purposes, and accomplishments of the United Nations are dramatized in this collection of original program material for young people. This book contains a choice of royalty, free, one-act plays, play-lets, group readings, peoms, songs, recitations, prayers and toasts, with production notes. A wide variety of classroom or assembly programs may be arranged in combinations suitable for various grade levels

Howard, Vernon

The complete book of children's theater; illus. by Doug Anderson and others. Doubleday 1969 544p illus $9.95 (4-7)   812

ISBN 0-385-03682-5

This book includes over 350 non-royalty plays, skits and monologues which can be performed at home or in the classroom. It is also an introduction to theater technique and discusses how non-royalty productions can be adapted to amateur staging

Preston, Carol

A trilogy of Christmas plays for children; music selected by John Langstaff; illus. with music, photo-graphs, and diagrams. Harcourt 1967 135p illus music $5.95 (5-7)   812

1 Christmas plays

ISBN 0-15-290450-6

The three plays "are variations on the Nativity theme. One is contemporary (with Nativity scenes in a play-within-the-play) and one adapted from Medieval folk and miracle plays; the third is based on English miracle plays and old carols. The dialogue is flavored with appropriate idiom and vocabulary without being too quaint; indeed, the plays are in the best of taste. Sources are discussed and quite complete instructions given for staging, lighting, simple choreography, et cetera. An appendix gives information about sources for obtaining appropriate music." Sutherland. The Best in Children's Bks

Thane, Adele

Plays from famous stories and fairy tales; royalty-free dramatizations of favorite children's stories. Plays, inc. 1967 463p $8.95 (4-6)   812

1 One-act plays

ISBN 0-8238-0060-1

"Twenty-eight royalty-free, one act plays are included in this collection of adaptations from well-known folktales, fairy tales, children's classics and old favorites. The dramatizations are simple, often com-pressing into a scene or two several incidents from a book; they are adequately written and some are mod-erately funny. Because of the appeal of the sources, a useful collection. Brief notes on costumes, props, lights, setting, et cetera, are appended." Chicago. Children's Bk Center

812.08   American drama—
Collections

Burack, A. S.

(ed.) Christmas plays for young actors; a collection of royalty-free stage and radio plays. Plays, Inc. 1969 308p $7.95 (3-7)   812.08

1 Christmas plays 2 One-act plays

ISBN 0-8238-0008-3

First published 1950

Twenty-six Christmas plays selected from: Plays, the Drama Magazine for Young People

The collection "has considerable range in point of view, age level, size of cast, length of playing time, etc., and includes production notes to help in stag-ing." Library J

Kamerman, Sylvia E.

(ed.) Dramatized folk tales of the world; a collection of 50 one-act plays—royalty-free adaptations of stories from many lands. Plays, Inc. 1971 575p $8.95 (5-7)   812.08

1 Drama—Collections 2 One-act plays

ISBN 0-8238-0004-0

These "one-act plays, royalty free, include some about folk heroes, some that are based on books . . . and such old favorites as 'Stone soup.' The sources are not given, but the plays are based on tales from twenty-six countries, some being prefaced by an author's note. The dramatization is of variable quality, but the book is useful both as a source for short plays and as a compilation with an international and literary flavor. Production notes are provided." Chicago. Children's Bk Center

"This book is a must, especially for school li-braries." Library J

(ed.) Fifty plays for junior actors; a collection of royalty-free, one-act plays for young people. Plays, Inc. 1966 676p $8.95 (4-7)   812.08

1 American drama—Collections 2 One-act plays

ISBN 0-8238-0034-2

Here are "plays for children in the middle and upper grades which can be performed with simple settings and properties and can be adapted for large or small casts. Comedies, fairy tales, mysteries, science fiction, and dramatizations for special occasions and on various subjects are contained in the serviceable collection of entertaining plays. Helpful production notes are provided at the end of the book." Booklist

(ed.) Little plays for little players; fifty non-royalty plays for children. Plays, Inc. 1969 335p $7.95 (1-6)   812.08

1 American drama—Collections 2 One-act plays

ISBN 0-8238-0035-0

First published 1952. Originally published in Plays, the Drama Magazine for Young People

Here are simple-to-produce plays for the primary grades. "To meet the demands for plays the year round, there is a wide variety of material covering all the important holidays, as well as dramatizations of legends and fantasies which young children love. Often, intangible ideas such as the importance of good health, safety, voting, etc., can be effectively taught through dramatic means, and this book therefore con-tains plays on these subjects." Preface

(ed.) A treasury of Christmas plays; one-act, royal-ty-free plays for stage or microphone performance and round-the-table reading. Plays, Inc. 1975 509p $8.95   812.08

1 Christmas plays 2 One-act plays

ISBN 0-8238-0203-5

First published 1958

"Included in this volume are [forty] traditional and modern one-act plays for young people— contemporary comedies, dramatizations of the Christmas Story, plays with flexible casts, musical backgrounds—all revealing the true spirit of Christ-mas." Preface

817.08 American satire and humor—Collections

Clark, David Allen
(ed.) Jokes, puns, and riddles; illus. by Lionel Kalish. Doubleday 1968 288p illus $4.95, lib. bdg. $5.70 (4-6) 817.08
1 American wit and humor 2 Riddles
ISBN 0-385-09018-8; 0-385-09019-6
Partial contents: Brain teasers; Daffinitions; Insults and wisecracks; Hippies, hairdos, and hermits; Done with a pun; World-wide whimsey; Silly dillies; Historical howlers; Elephants, elephants, elephants
"The happy feature of [this collection] is not only that it's a good reference book but that it's inoffensive in content. A nice, innocous, funny slice of comedy, for any youngster." N Y Times Bk Rev

De Regniers, Beatrice Schenk
(comp.) The Abraham Lincoln joke book; illus. by William Lahey Cummings. Random House 1965 92p illus lib. bdg. $4.59 (4-6) 817.08
1 Lincoln, Abraham, President U.S. 2 American wit and humor
ISBN 0-394-91079-6
"Here are the wit and wisdom of a great American—more than sixty jokes and humorous stories told by and about Abraham Lincoln. He used humor to prove a point, to help answer questions, or to cheer up people around him." p 1

818 American miscellany

Rockwell, Thomas
The portmanteau book; illus. by Gail Rockwell. Little 1974 141p illus $6.95, pa $3.95 (5-7) 818
1 Wit and humor 2 Amusements
ISBN 0-316-75341-6; 0-316-75342-4
This is a collection of humorous stories, poems, and miscellaneous games and amusements including a comic strip, a maze, puzzles, and recipes for such delicacies as entomological soup, liver punishment, and infested spinach
"Designed for sampling rather than continuous reading. . . . Rockwell has put together a treasury that has flair and built-in audience appeal." Sch Library J

Sandburg, Carl
The Sandburg treasury; prose and poetry for young people. . . . Introduction by Paula Sandburg; illus. by Paul Bacon. Harcourt 1970 480p illus $8.95 (5-7) 818

ISBN 0-15-270180-X
"Including 'Rootabaga stories,' 'Early moon,' 'Wind song,' 'Abe Lincoln grows up,' 'Prairietown boy.'" Title page
This volume brings together all of Sandburg's books for young people: his whimsical stories, two books of poetry, a version of his biography of Abraham Lincoln, and portions of his autobiography specially edited for children
Index of titles for stories and poems: p478-80

820.8 English literature—Collections

Mayne, William
(ed.) Ghosts; an anthology. Nelson 1971 187p $6.50 (6-7) 820.8
1 Ghost stories 2 English literature—Collections
ISBN 0-8407-6112-0
The editor has compiled an "anthology of stories, poems and factual accounts of ghosts, goblins, trolls, [and] 'poltergeists.'" Pub W
Although the selections "may be read satisfactorily in any order, it is worth noting the excellent organization of the material. In a brief preface, the editor discusses the arrangement, indicating the stories that are pure fiction, those that are based on legend, and those that are true accounts. Each story is also prefaced by an imaginative paragraph that sets the tone for . . . the selections [which] have a wide range of settings—from England and Scotland, Norway and Sweden, India and China—indicating that ghosts and the belief in them are respecters of no time or place. A substantial, imaginative, and suitably shivery anthology." Horn Bk

821 English poetry

Belloc, Hilaire
The bad child's book of beasts; pictures by B. T. B. Knopf 1965 46p illus lib. bdg. $4.69 (1-4) 821
1 Animals—Poetry 2 Nonsense verses
ISBN 0-394-90958-5
First published 1896 in England; 1923 in the United States. Illustrated by Basil T. Blackwood
This precursor of Ogden Nash wrote "absurd verses . . . presenting the idiosyncracies of such beasts as the Yak, the Dodo and the Cameleopard." Bks for Boys and Girls
"Belloc's nonsense is as funny as ever and a brief and succinct preface by Frances Clarke Sayers makes this reissue an especially welcome volume for libraries." Sch Library J

More beasts for worse children; pictures by B. T. B. Knopf 1966 46p illus lib. bdg. $4.69 (1-4) 821
1 Animals—Poetry 2 Nonsense verses
ISBN 0-394-91415-5
Sequel to: The bad child's book of beasts, entered above
First published 1897 in England, 1923 in the United States
"Antic creatures . . . described in delightfully terse, nonsensical verses. Happily, the illustrations are the original ones." N Y Times Bk Rev

Browning, Robert
The Pied Piper of Hamelin; illus. by C. Walter Hodges. Coward, McCann & Geoghegan 1971 unp illus lib. bdg. $5.29 (3-7) 821
ISBN 0-698-30280-X
"The story of the piper whose revenge for a broken promise resulted in the disappearance of the children of Hamelin is delightfully illustrated by Walter Hodges. His full-color pictures are rich and authentic in detail, the faces varied and the composition dramatic: many of the illustrations bubble with humor and most of them are scenes of action." Sutherland. The Best in Children's Bks

Browning, Robert—*Continued*

The Pied Piper of Hamelin; illus. by Kate Greenaway. Warne 1899 48p illus $5.95 (3-7)   821

ISBN 0-7232-0586-8

This long nineteenth century poem tells of the piper who, employed to rid the town of rats, also pipes the children of the town into the mountain

"With Kate Greenaway's inimitable illustrations, it is a 'must have' for every library. . . . It deserves a place in every children's room, so that the illustrations as well as the poem may become a part of each child's heritage." Library J

Burns, Robert

Hand in hand we'll go; ten poems by Robert Burns; illus. by Nonny Hogrogian. Crowell 1965 28p illus $3.75, lib. bdg. $4.50 (6-7)   821

ISBN 0-690-36668-X; 0-690-36669-8

"Some of the most familiar and also the best loved of Burn's poems are included and a variety of moods is represented. The combination of strength and subtlety, of humor and gentleness in the handsome woodcuts makes the selection a choice introduction to the poet and a beautiful book for all ages." Horn Bk

"For the reader not deterred by the dialect this is an unusually satisfying sampling." Booklist

Glossary p[30-31]

Carroll, Lewis

The hunting of the snark; pictures by Helen Oxenbury. Watts, F. 1970 48p illus lib. bdg. $4.90 (3-6)   821

1 Nonsense verses
ISBN 0-531-01964-0

This nonsense poem recounts the adventures of "the Bellman and his crew who hunt for the Snark." Booklist

"An oversize book affords Helen Oxenbury the opportunity to make big pictures, composed with boldness and imaginativeness, that echo both the nonsensical and the satirical elements in Carroll's rollicking poem." Chicago. Children's Bk Center

The walrus and the carpenter, and other poems; pictures by Gerald Rose. Dutton 1969 c1968 unp illus $2.95 (3-6)   821

1 Nonsense verses
ISBN 0-7232-1813-7

First published 1968 in England with title: Jabberwocky, and other poems

Eleven of Lewis Carroll's "nonsense poems are presented here in picture-book format. . . . In addition to 'You are old, Father William,' 'The Lobster Quadrille,' and other favorites from the Alice books, the collection includes two poems from the lesser-known Sylvie and Bruno stories." Sch Library J

Rose "uses sharp, bright colours that somehow give the impression of immense joie de vivre—a good balance to the occasional slight melancholy in the verse. The only danger, as with so much of Lewis Carroll, is that too many parents will be seduced into buying the poems for children who are still far too young for them." Times (London) Literary Sup

Coleridge, Samuel Taylor

The rime of the ancient mariner (6-7)   821

Some editions are:

Coward McCann$5.95, lib. bdg. $4.97 Illustrated by C. Walter Hodges (ISBN 0-698-20118-3; 0-698-30295-8)

Hawthorn Bks. $3.95 Edited by Mina Lewiton. Illustrated by Howard Simon (ISBN 0-696-77224-8) Written in 1798

This poem "deals with the supernatural punishment and penance of a seaman who heartlessly shot an albatross, a bird of good omen, in the Antarctic regions. The story is told by the Mariner himself—part of his penance is its periodic repetition—to the reluctant, fascinated listener, a man who was on his way to a wedding." Benét. The Reader's Encyclopedia

De La Mare, Walter

Bells and grass; illus. by Dorothy P. Lathrop. Viking 1963 [c1942] 144p illus $4 (3-7)   821

ISBN 0-670-15625-6

A reissue of a book first published 1942

A collection of the author's favorite poems he wrote for children. "Some of them tell of actual and personal memories. Most of them, whether fanciful or not, are concerned with the imagined and the imaginary." Introduction

This "is a book for all ages. Here . . . we find music and humor and a winning absurdity. . . [The]pictures have the moonlit quality of the poems." N Y Times Bk Rev

Index of first lines and titles: p137-44

Peacock Pie; illus. by Barbara Cooney. Knopf 1961 117p illus lib. bdg. $4.99 (4-7)   821

ISBN 0-394-91486-4

First published 1916 in England

This collection of 82 poems leads the reader "to venture into the realms of Earth and Air, Witches and Fairies, Places and People, Boys and Girls, and Beasts of all descriptions." Ontario Library Rev

"This is unquestionably a beautiful edition of a favorite collection. The decorations and the full-page soft drawings have humor, mystery, and feeling; and, while they are in harmony with the poetry, they can be enjoyed as much for themselves as they can for their interpretations of the poems. Walter de la Mare's poetry calls up such vivid images in many reader's minds that for them pictures are not needed. However, it would be a pity to miss these drawings, with or without the poetry." Horn Bk

Rhymes and verses; collected poems for children; with drawings by Elinore Blaisdell. Holt 1947 344p illus $6.95 (4-7)   821

ISBN 0-03-031710-X

This volume contains selections from the published works of this English poet. The poems are arranged under such headings as: Green grow the rashes, O; All round about the town; All creatures great and small; Fairies—witches—phantoms; etc. Indexed by title and first line

Farjeon, Eleanor

The children's bells; a selection of poems; illus. by Peggy Fortnum. Walck, H.Z. 1960 212p illus $7.50 (3-6)   821

ISBN 0-8098-2342-X

First published 1957 in England

"This collection of poems, now brought together for the first time, has been made by Eleanor Farjeon from many of her previous books of prose and verse for children." Half-title page

"With verses about people, places, saints, kings and queens, magic, and the seasons, the collection is rich in imagination, humor, and beauty and makes a delightful companion piece to the author's 'The little bookroom' [entered in class S C]. Illustrated with decorative line drawings on every page." Booklist

Eleanor Farjeon's Poems for children. Lippincott 1951 236p $4.95 (3-5)   821

ISBN 0-397-30193-6

This book contains the complete text of four volumes of verse by Eleanor Farjeon: Sing for your supper (1938); Over the garden wall (1933); Joan's door (1926); and Come Christmas (1927). In addition there are twenty poems from her: Collected poems, which heretofore has been published only in England

Farjeon, Eleanor—*Continued*
"It is a happy choice for the individual child or for a school or public library. Put it on the shelf and do not doubt that the children will find it. It is illustrated with graceful line drawings from the earlier volumes." Sat Rev
Index: p233-36
Then there were three; being Cherrystones, The mulberry bush, The starry floor; verses. Drawings by Isobel & John Morton-Sale. Lippincott [1965] 174p illus $4.95 (4-7) $21
ISBN 0-397-30839-6
This poetry anthology contains The mulberry bush, and two previously published collections: Cherrystones, 1942, and The starry floor, 1949
The poet writes of the assorted fancies, hopes, and amusements of children
"At her best. [Mrs Farjeon's] versification is firm and without slackness or affectation. She has a strong lyric sense, and a certain airy gaiety which has captivated many readers. Her best work is securely based in the English folk tradition, from which she rarely strays far." Times (London) Literary Sup

Greenaway, Kate
Marigold garden; pictures and rhymes by Kate Greenaway. Warne [1910] 56p illus $4.95 (k-2) $21
1 Flowers— Poetry
ISBN 0-7232-0588-4
First published 1885 by Routledge and Sons
"Flower verses written in simple rhyme for very young children. The floral theme is well developed in the design, colour, and arrangement of the pictures." Toronto

Under the window; pictures & rhymes; engraved & printed by Edmund Evans. Warne [n.d.]56p illus $4.95 (k-2) $21
ISBN 0-7232-0587-6
First published 1878 by Routledge and Sons
Similar to: Marigold garden, entered above, in its charming pictures and verses
This is "a collection of simple rhymes on subjects of childhood. The block prints illustrating the verses have gaily solemn figures dressed in large bonnets, slim gowns and smocks, pictured with a delicacy of colour which makes this book precious among picture books." Toronto

Lear, Edward
The complete nonsense book. . . . Ed. by Lady Strachey; introduction by the Earl of Cromer. Dodd 1948 430p illus $5.95 $21
1 Nonsense verses
ISBN 0-396-00886-0
First published 1912
"Containing all the original pictures and verses, together with new material." Subtitle
"This is a choice contribution to the literature of laughter. Limericks, verses of all kinds, alphabets and botanics are as daft and amusing as the pictures." Adventuring With Bks

The dong with a luminous nose. Drawings by Edward Gorey. Young Scott Bks. 1969 unp illus lib. bdg. $4.50 (k-3) $21
1 Nonsense verses
ISBN 0-201-09173-9
This is an illustrated version of the nineteenth century nonsense poem about "the Dong who falls in love with a Jumbly girl 'With her sky-blue hands and her seagreen hair.' . . . The Jumblies sail away from the Chankly Bore in a sieve and the Dong is left searching desperately for his love." Library J
"Lear's lonely Dong . . . is newly captured in

evocative drawings by Edward Gorey—though Lear's own drawings cannot be improved on. But Mr. Gorey is clearly the only modern illustrator to do justice to the Victorian master." Bk World

Edward Lear's The Scroobious Pip; completed by Ogden Nash; illus. by Nancy Ekholm Burkert. Harper 1968 unp illus $4.95, lib. bdg. $5.79 (2-6) $21
1 Animals—Poetry 2 Nonsense verses
ISBN 0-06-023764-3; 0-06-023765-1
The original unfinished text was first published 1953 in the U.S. by the Harvard University Press in the author's: Teapots and quails
"A beautiful book, its large pages filled with pictures of birds, beasts, fish, and insects; handsome in format and design, the book is distinguished by the delicate charm of the illustrations. The Lear verses, left incomplete at his death, have been filled in by Nash; his additions are in brackets. The nonsense poetry bears a subtle message of acceptance, as all the creatures challenge the Pip (a bit of every species, class, genus etc. in one appealing package) to explain what he is; his firm and only response is that he is himself, the Scroobious Pip." Chicago. Children's Bk Center

The Jumblies; drawings by Edward Gorey. Young Scott Bks. 1968 unp illus lib. bdg. $4.50 (k-3) $21
1 Nonsense verses
ISBN 0-201-09249-2
This is a picture book version of one of Lear's favorite nonsense poems immortalizing a motley crew who go out to sea in a sieve, illustrated with 19th Century style cross-hatched line drawings of all their unlikely doings

The Jumblies, and other nonsense verses; with drawings by L. Leslie Brooke. Warne [1954] unp illus $2.95 (2-6) $21
1 Nonsense verses
ISBN 0-7232-0583-3
Here is a selection of nonsense rhymes, including The Owl and the Pussy Cat, taken from: Nonsense songs, entered below
"Superbly funny pictures, some in colour." Four to Fourteen

Nonsense songs; with drawings by L. Leslie Brooke. Warne 1954 unp illus $4.95 (2-6) $21
1 Nonsense verses
ISBN 0-7232-0582-5
This volume includes nineteen of the author's nonsense verses taken from: The Jumblies, and other nonsense verses, entered above, and The pelican chorus & other nonsense verses, entered below
"Ageless and amusing as ever, with perfect illustrations. . . . This excellent reprint will be welcomed by young and old." Secondary Educ Board

The owl and the pussy-cat (k-3) $21
1 Nonsense verses
Some editions are:
Doubleday $2.95 Illustrated by William Réne Du Bois (ISBN 0-385-00077-4)
Little $3.95, lib. bdg. $4.55 Illustrated by Barbara Cooney (ISBN 0-316-51840-9; 0-316-51841-7)
Warne (Stuff & Nonsense Books) $2.95 (ISBN 0-7232-1810-2)
Here is the classic children's nonsense poem about the owl and the cat who went to sea in a peagreen boat

The pelican chorus; pictures by Harold Berson. Parents Mag. Press 1967 unp illus music $4.95 (k-3) $21

Lear, Edward—*Continued*

1 Nonsense verses 2 Birds—Poetry
ISBN 0-8193-0179-5
"Gay and colorful illustrations cleverly interpret the humor and background of Lear's poem about the grand King and Queen of the Pelicans who happily dwell on the banks of the Nile. The inviting book includes a musical score." Booklist

The pelican chorus & other nonsense verses; with drawings by L. Leslie Brooke. Warne [1954] unp illus $2.95 (2-6)   821
1 Nonsense verses
ISBN 0-7232-0584-1
First published 1910?
This is a selection of nonsense rhymes from the larger volume: Nonsense songs, entered above

Milne, A. A.

The Christopher Robin book of verse; with decorations and illus. in full color by E. H. Shepard. Dutton 1967 62p illus $4.50 (k-3)   821
ISBN 0-525-27904-0
"Numerous full color illustrations and some small black and white drawings add charm to these twenty-four poems selected from 'When we were very young' and 'Now we are six' [both entered below]. Small quarto size and big type make the book easier to handle and easier to read than the original." Bruno. Bks for Sch Libraries

Now we are six; with decorations by Ernest H. Shepard. Dutton [1961 c1927] 104p illus $3.95, lib. bdg. $3.91 (k-3)   821
ISBN 0-525-36126-X; 0-525-36127-8
First published 1927. "Reprinted September 1961 in this completely new format designed by Warren Chappell." Verso of title page
Companion volume to: When we were very young, listed below
"The boy or girl who has liked 'When we were very young' and 'Winnie-the-Pooh' will enjoy reading about Alexander Beetle who was mistaken for a match, the knight whose armor didn't squeak, and the old sailor who had so many things which he wanted to do. There are other entertaining poems, also, and many pictures as delightful as the verses." Pittsburgh

When we were very young; with decorations by Ernest H. Shepard. Dutton [1961 c1924] 102p illus $3.95, lib. bdg. $3.91 (k-3)   821
ISBN 0-525-42580-2; 0-525-42581-0
First published 1924. "Reprinted September 1961 in this completely new format designed by Warren Chappell." Verso of title page
Verse "written for Milne's small son, Christopher Robin, which for its bubbling nonsense, its whimsy, and the unexpected surprises of its rhymes and rhythms, furnishes immeasurable joy to children." Right Bk for the Right Child
It is for "very small children (and for their elders who get a surreptitious joy from what is meant for their little ones). . . . Mr. Milne's gay jingles have found a worthy accompaniment in the charming illustrations of Mr. Shepard." Sat Rev

The world of Christopher Robin; the complete When we were very young and Now we are six; with decorations and new illus. in full color, by E. H. Shepard. Dutton 1958 234p illus $7.50 (k-3)   821
ISBN 0-525-43292-2
This "companion volume to: 'The world of Pooh' [entered in Fiction class] contains Milne's two collections of verses. . . . [An] appealing combination volume." Booklist

"These verses are so right that they strike the child who hasn't read them before as both fresh and familiar. Again E. H. Shepard has added some colored drawings but nothing takes the place of the generous quota of [the original] black-and-whites scattered through the pages." N Y Times Bk Rev

Rossetti, Christina G.

Sing-song; a nursery rhyme book for children; illus. by Marguerite Davis. Macmillan (N Y) illus $3.50 (k-2)   821
First published 1872. This is a shortened reissue of the 1924 edition
Contents: In the country; At home; Just for fun; Lesson time; Lullaby, baby; Christmas carols; To Lalla; List of first lines
"Unsurpassed in lyric quality and childlike spontaneity, these verses . . . are excellent to use following Mother Goose." Children's Bks Too Good to Miss

Stevenson, Robert Louis

A child's garden of verses (k-4)   821
Some editions are:
Collins (Rainbow classics) $4.95 Illustrated by Alexander Dobkin (ISBN 0-00-120307-X)
Dutton (The Children's illustrated classics) $3.95 With drawings in colour by Mary Shillabeer and wood engravings by the author (ISBN 0-525-27762-5)
Golden Press $3.95, lib. bdg. $3.95, pa $1.25 Illustrated by Alice and Martin Provensen (ISBN 0-307-13583-7; 0-307-65557-1; 0-307-10873-2)
Grosset $4.95 Illustrated by Gyo Fujikawa (ISBN 0-448-02878-6)
Platt $3.50 (ISBN 0-8228-2009-9)
Scribner (Scribner Illustrated classics) $10 Illustrated by Jessie Wilcox Smith (ISBN 0-684-20949-7)
Walck, H.Z. $7.95 With pictures by Tasha Tudor (ISBN 0-8098-1902-3)
Watts, F. lib. bdg. $6.95 Illustrated by Brian Wildsmith (ISBN 0-531-01531-9)
First published 1885 in England with title: Penny whistles
"Verses known and loved by one generation after another. Among the simpler ones for pre-school children are: Rain; At the Seaside; and Singing." Right Bk for the Right Child
"Poems full of music and rhythm, by a poet who always kept his ability to live in a child's world." A. T. Eaton's Treasure for the Taking

Tagore

Moon, for what do you wait? Poems by Tagore; ed. by Richard Lewis; illus. by Ashley Bryan. Atheneum Pubs. 1967 unp illus lib. bdg. $3.41 (k-4)   821
1 Nature in poetry
ISBN 0-689-20228-8
"The poems which constitute the text of this book are reprinted from 'Stray Birds' by Rabindranath Tagore." Verso of title page
"Distinctive designs in sharp, bright colors interpret seventeen two-line nature poems." Notable Children's Bks, 1967
"Lewis has chosen from Tagore's most compact verse. It is made of flashes that can reach the youngest reader, before he can read." N Y Times Bk Rev

Tolkien, J. R. R.

The adventures of Tom Bombadil, and other verses from The Red Book; with illus. by Pauline Baynes. Houghton 1963 [c1962] 63p illus $4.95 (6-7)   821
ISBN 0-395-08251-X
Spine title: Tom Bombadil
First published 1962 in England
"Verses about trolls, elves, the sea, knights, strange beasts and birds, and a spirited fellow named Tom Bombadil, who weds a river-nymph." Pub W

821.08 English poetry— Collections

Adshead, Gladys L.
(comp.) An inheritance of poetry; collected and arranged by Gladys L. Adshead and Annis Duff; with decorations by Nora S. Unwin. Houghton 1948 415p illus $7.95 (5-7)   821.08
1 English poetry—Collections 2 American poetry—Collections
ISBN 0-395-06537-2
A collection of poetry, mainly English and American, by poets famous and little known, gathered from a great variety of sources. Sonnets, ballads, and hero poems, gay rhymes, songs, and deeply spiritual verses are here
The "selection is fresh but includes both the expected and the unexpected. Divisions are indicated only by a full-page drawing at the beginning of each one, and by the poems in the division. Nora Unwin's illustrations are in the exact mood of the poems. An admirable book—one that will certainly instill in a child a love of poetry. For all ages, from earliest childhood through the teens and beyond." Library J
"It is a fat, sturdy book, pleasing in appearance with large print and the authors have been inspired to compile not only the usual author, title and first line indices but also a source index and an index of musical settings." Ontario Library Rev

Agree, Rose H.
(ed.) How to eat a poem & other morsels; food poems for children; illus. by Peggy Wilson. Pantheon Bks. 1967 87p illus lib. bdg. $4.99 (3-5)   821.08
1 Food—Poetry 2 English poetry—Collections 3 American poetry—Collections
ISBN 0-394-91622-0
"A collection of poems about food, employing delightful uses of rhymes, rhythms, words and ideas. Sources range from fragments of prose works or longer poems, to nonsense verses of writers now out of print." Bruno. Bks for Sch Libraries, 1968
"Some of the contributors are Ciardi, Merriam, McGinley, McCord, Sendak, Farjeon, and Coatsworth; a few short rhymes from Mother Goose are tucked in here and there." Chicago. Children's Bk Center
"Sprightly drawings accentuated with pink and yellow add to the jovial atmosphere. Delicious fare for browsing and to enliven curriculum units on food and health." Booklist
Includes indexes of authors and first lines

Arbuthnot, May Hill
(comp.) Time for poetry . . . comp. by May Hill Arbuthnot and Shelton L. Root, Jr. Illus. by Arthur Paul. 3d general ed. Scott [distributed by Lothrop 1967 c1968] 277p illus $9.95   821.08
1 English poetry—Collections 2 American poetry—Collections
ISBN 0-673-05549-3
First published 1952
"A representative collection of poetry for children, to be used in the classroom, home, or camp; especially planned for college classes in children's literature; with a special section entitled 'Keeping poetry and children together.'" Title page
In addition to articles about poetry and poems about animals, people, plays, seasons, and magic, this includes the full versions of: The Pied Piper of Hamelin, by R. Browning; The A B C Bunny, by W. Gág; A visit from St Nicholas, by C. C. Moore; Paul Revere's ride, by H. W. Longfellow

Association for Childhood Education International
Sung under the silver umbrella; poems for young children; selected by the Literature Committee of the Association for Childhood Education; illus. by Dorothy Lathrop. Macmillan (N Y) 1935 xxiii, 211p illus $4.95 (k-2)   821.08
1 English poetry—Collections 2 American poetry—Collections
A collection of about 200 poems by Christina Rossetti, Laura Richards, Lear, De La Mare, Stephens, Lindsay, many others of like calibre, and many who are contemporary. An excellent introduction about poetry by Padraic Colum
All the poems have been tried out with children. The grouping is by subject: poems about animals, children, out-of-doors, day and night, weather and seasons, fairies, trains and ships, Christmas, etc.
"I hope even those who have a favorite collection of this kind will get this book too. I have spent charmed moments over its quiet uncrowded pages." N Y Her Trib Bks
Includes indexes of authors and first lines

Blishen, Edward
(comp.) Oxford Book of poetry for children; with illus. by Brian Wildsmith. Watts, F. [1964 c1963] 167p illus lib. bdg. $7.95 (4-7)   821.08
1 English poetry—Collections
ISBN 0-531-01537-8
First published 1963 in England
An anthology of English poetry intended to introduce children beyond the nursery rhyme level to "serious" verse
"Childhood's imaginary creatures ride, reel, swim, and swoop right out of the poems to romp through the pages. Included in the jolly host are such characters and creatures as Sir Eglamour's dragon. 'The Forsaken Merman.' the 'Three Knights from Spain.' 'Meg Merrilees,' and Casey Jones with his eight-wheeler. Familiar and less familiar poems by English poets rollick in spirited merriment among the many by 'Anon.' The collection seems to defy organization, but the compiler exercises delightful control with such enigmatic groupings as 'The Moon's in a Fit' and 'O'er Ditches and Mires.' The whole 'enjoyable gathering' is as enticing as a circus where the audience can enter the rings." Horn Bk
Index of authors: p163. Index of first lines: p164

Bogan, Louise
(comp.) The golden journey; poems for young people; comp. by Louise Bogan and William Jay Smith; woodcuts by Fritz Kredel. Reilly & Lee 1965 272p illus $5.95 (4-7)   821.08
1 English poetry—Collections 2 American poetry—Collections
ISBN 0-8092-8689-0
The poems are "grouped in sections by subject: love poems, animal poems, country poems, etc. . . . The illustrations preceding each section are attractive woodcuts in a dark green. The selections are varied, the poems ranging from amusing jingles to classics, and the poets ranging from Skelton and Herrick (clearly a favorite of the compilers) to Walt Kelly. . . . The anthology is nicely balanced in every sense; sources are cited; author and title indexes are appended." Chicago. Children's Bk Center

Brewton, John E.
(comp.) Gaily we parade; a collection of poems about people, here, there & everywhere; illus. by Robert Lawson. Macmillan (N Y) 1940 218p illus $4.95 (3-6)   821.08
1 English poetry—Collections 2 American poetry—Collections

Brewton, John E.—*Continued*

The collection is divided into groups as follows: Come buy; To the shops we go; These make a town; Relatives all; At our house; Neighbors of ours; Willingly to school; Sing ho! Ye sailormen; Beyond far blue hills; Out in the country; We are the music makers; Ring-a-ring o'fairies; Some see this and some see that; At the royal court; Ring around the world; Bells for Christmas ring; Funny folk; Dustman comes; Vespers

"Mr. Brewton has specialized in poems about people. The title is well chosen, for a livelier, more spirited collection could scarcely have been assembled. . . . The authors range from Blake and Keats to Rachel Field and Elizabeth Madox Roberts." Library J

Brewton, Sara

(comp.) Birthday candles burning bright; a treasury of birthday poetry; selected by Sara and John E. Brewton; decorations by Vera Bock. Macmillan (N Y) 1960 199p illus $4.95 (4-7)   821.08

1 Birthdays—Poetry 2 English poetry—Collections 3 American poetry—Collections

An anthology of poems about birthdays—birthdays at different ages, gifts, parties, christenings. There are also poems about twins, youth, growing up, and the birthday of Jesus. Some of the poets are: Walter de la Mare, Phyllis McGinley, Ivy O. Eastwick, A. A. Milne, Mary Mapes Dodge, Walt Whitman, and Aileen Fisher

"Some of the material is very light, most of it is very pleasant . . . with quite a bit of brief and simple poetry that can be used for reading aloud to younger children." Chicago. Children's Bk Center

Indexes of authors, first lines, and titles

(comp.) Laughable limericks; comp. by Sara and John E. Brewton; illus. by Ingrid Fetz. Crowell 1965 147p illus music $3.95, lib. bdg. $4.70 (4-7)   821.08

1 Limericks 2 English poetry—Collections 3 American poetry—Collections

ISBN 0-690-48667-7; 0-690-48668-5

A collection of limericks old and new by such poets as Gelett Burgess, John Ciardi, Lewis Carroll, Robert Louis Stevenson, Ogden Nash, and Edward Lear

The verses are "arranged in groups under such headings as 'Bugs, Bees, and Birds,' 'Crawlers, Croakers, and Creepers,' 'Behavior—Scroobious and Strange,' 'Laughs Anatomical,' and 'School and College.' . . . David McCord concludes the fun with some limericks which give advice on how to write more limericks." Horn Bk

"Black and white line drawings match the fun in this delightful collection of nonsense verses on a multitude of subjects which children of all ages will enjoy." Ontario Library Rev

Index of authors: p140-41. Index of first lines p142-47

(comp.) My tang's tungled and other ridiculous situations; humorous poems collected by Sara and John E. Brewton and G. Meredith Blackburn III; illus. by Graham Booth. Crowell 1973 111p illus $5.50 (3-6)   821.08

1 Humorous poetry 2 Limericks 3 English poetry— Collections 4 American poetry—Collections

ISBN 0-690-57223-9

This collection "includes tongue tanglers, topsy-turvies, poems about the vexations of family life, the peculiarities of animal life, and the contradictions of school life—as well as a liberal sprinkling of just plain nonsense." Horn Bk

"The assortment of authors is impressive: T. S. Eliot, Elizabeth Coatsworth, Theodore Roethke, Hilaire Belloc, Shel Silverstein and John Ciardi are a

few. . . . Small chuckles and big laughs abound here. The illustrations are ridiculously funny." Pub W

Includes title, author and first line indexes

(comp.) Shrieks at midnight; macabre poems, eerie and humorous; selected by Sara and John E. Brewton; drawings by Ellen Raskin. Crowell 1969 177p illus $4.50 (4-7)   821.08

1 English poetry—Collections 2 American poetry—Collections

ISBN 0-690-73518-9

A "collection of spooky, weird, extremely humorous poems, including funny bits of terror by such poets as Lewis Carroll, Ogden Nash, Hilaire Belloc, Langston Hughes, Dorothy Parker, James Reeves, and a few good old 'Author Unknowns.' Puns, epitaphs, and old ballads are represented." Sch Library J

The illustrations "are full of verve and splendid visual puns. . . . Miss Raskin is inventive, amusing, happily horrifying." N Y Times Bk Rev

Index of authors: p167-68. Index of titles: p169-72. Index of first lines: p173-77

(comp.) Sing a song of seasons; poems about holidays, vacation days, and days to go to school; selected by Sara and John E. Brewton; decorations by Vera Bock. Macmillan (N Y) 1955 200p illus $5.95 (3-7)   821.08

1 Seasons—Poetry 2 Holidays—Poetry 3 English poetry—Collections 4 American poetry—Collections

"Dividing the book into eight sections, the Brewtons include one for each season of the year, with nature poems as well as those for the holidays of the season. The other four sections are about morning, evening, birthdays and time itself." Horn Bk

A "welcome collection . . . well arranged and attractively printed; the only illustrations are pleasing decorations preceding each subject division. Indexed by author, title, and first line." Booklist

Cole, William

(comp.) The birds and the beasts were there; animal poems. Woodcuts by Helen Siegel. World Pub. 1963 320p illus lib. bdg. $6.21 (5-7)   821.08

1 Animals—Poetry 2 English poetry—Collections 3 American poetry—Collections

ISBN 0-529-03742-4

These are poems about small animals of the woods and fields, dogs, cats, horses, donkeys, big beasts, wild beasts, leapers and flyers and impossible animals. Some of the poets included are Peggy Bennett, William Blake, Elizabeth Coatsworth, Rachel Field, Arthur Guiterman, Don Marquis, Ogden Nash, James Reeves and Shakespeare

"Funny poems, sad poems, exhilarating flag-waving kinds of poems, all of them about animals, should make poetry-lovers out of animal-lovers. And poetry-lovers, admiring animals as they do already, will find unending delight in this splendid, solid volume with its attractive woodcut illustrations." Christian Sci Monitor

Indexed by author and title

(comp.) A book of animal poems; illus. by Robert Andrew Parker. Viking 1973 288p illus $8.95 (5-7)   821.08

1 Animals—Poetry 2 English poetry—Collections 3 American poetry—Collections

ISBN 0-670-17907-8

This "substantial collection of approximately two hundred fifty poems has been limited to titles not found in other animal anthologies and represents a great variety of subjects. . . . Numerous poems about birds, horses, cats, and dogs are found in indi-

Cole, William—*Continued*

vidual sections. The rest of the poems come under the following headings: The Wild Ones, The Farmyard, Hunters and Other Horrors, Cold-Bloods, Insects . . . and Bat, Animals Together. Verse forms are as varied as the contents are extensive and range from the succinct brevity of haiku . . . to lengthy narrative. The poets included span centuries. Shakespeare is represented by a vivid poem about a horse; the eighteenth and nineteenth centuries are well-represented by John Clare, Thomas Hardy, and Rudyard Kipling; the large number of poems by contemporary writers gives the book the impact of freshness. Distinctive black-and-white line drawings interpret the dominant characteristics of the animals pictured. A splendid volume that should bring joy to animal and poetry lovers alike." Horn Bk

Includes an Index of titles and an Index of authors

(ed.) A book of nature poems; illus. by Robert Andrew Parker. Viking 1969 256p illus lib. bdg. $7.95 (5-7) 821.08

1 Nature in poetry 2 English poetry—Collections
3 American poetry—Collections
ISBN 0-670-18006-8

This anthology, mainly by American and British authors, contains poems, old and new, on the seasons, flowers and trees, lakes and the sea, night and stars, rain and wind. Authors include S. T. Coleridge, Padraic Colum, Ralph Waldo Emerson, Robert Frost, Charles Dickens, Alfred Tennyson, John Updike and others

"The anthology will be of use to teachers and to anyone who has need of a compendium of good nature poetry. The book is well produced and remarkably well indexed [by separate author and title sections]." Horn Bk

(comp.) Humorous poetry for children; illus. by Ervine Metzl. Collins 1955 124p illus lib. bdg. $5.91 (5-7) 821.08

1 Nonsense verses 2 English poetry—Collections
3 American poetry—Collections
ISBN 0-529-03480-8

Here is "a collection of humorous poems, some by well-known and others by obscure poets. Some of the well-known poets have a reputation for light verse; others are better known for their serious verse. The quality varies from slightly better than doggerel to quite good poetry, and there is something here for every taste in humor from the most obvious to quite subtle." Chicago. Children's Bk Center

"Well arranged and indexed." N Y Pub Library

(ed.) Oh, how silly! Poems selected by William Cole; drawings by Tomi Ungerer. Viking 1970 94p illus lib. bdg. $3.95 (3-6) 821.08

1 Nonsense verses 2 English poetry—Collections
3 American poetry—Collections
ISBN 0-670-52095-0

A collection of humorous verse by both English and American poets, past and present. Along with the familiar names of Ogden Nash and Hilaire Belloc, the editor has included such poets as Shel Silverstein, Jack Prelutsky and Alexander Resnikoff

It "is sure to be popular with readers who enjoy the absurd." Booklist

Author index: p91-92. Title index: p93-94

(comp.) Oh, that's ridiculous! Poems selected by William Cole; drawings by Tomi Ungerer. Viking 1972 80p illus lib. bdg. $5.95 (3-6) 821.08

1 Nonsense verses 2 English poetry—Collections
3 American poetry—Collections
ISBN 0-670-52107-8

Here are limericks and nonsense rhymes by various authors, including Gelett Burgess, Ogden Nash, Theodore Roethke, A. E. Housman, and others

"There are a few rhymes that have the tinge of children's doggerel, but most of them are delightfully silly. . . . The illustrations are divinely, fittingly mad." Chicago. Children's Bk Center

Author index: p78. Title index: p79-80

(comp.) Oh, what nonsense! Poems selected by William Cole; drawings by Tomi Ungerer. Viking 1966 80p illus $2.95 (3-6) 821.08

1 Nonsense verses 2 English poetry—Collections
3 American poetry—Collections
ISBN 0-670-52117-5

"Nonsense verses, both naughty and nice, cavort across the pages in company with comical poker-faced characters. Because many of the verses are those of modern poets (Mr. Lear and Mr. Carroll are conspicuous in their absence), the anthology is as fresh as it is gleeful. Also included among the fifty selections are anonymous pieces—words to songs, counting rhymes, jump-rope rhymes. The illustrations are peculiarly amusing, a few of them positively unnerving." Horn Bk

Author index: p77-78. Title index: p79-80

(comp.) Poems for seasons and celebrations; illus. by Johannes Troyer. Collins 1961 191p illus lib. bdg. $5.71 (5-7) 821.08

1 Holidays—Poetry 2 Seasons—Poetry 3 English poetry—Collections 4 American poetry—Collections
ISBN 0-529-03660-6

Arranged chronologically beginning with the New Year, this is a collection of over 140 poems, traditional and modern, English and American, celebrating various holidays and the four seasons. Both an author and title index are included

"Poetry for special occasions is always in demand, but the variety of both mood and form in the poems of this book will make it a delight for any time of the year, in homes as well as libraries. Ranging from the Bible, Shakespeare, and Robert Herrick down to the present, with several poems by two new poets written especially for this book, the collection is fresh and unhackneyed, excellent for reading aloud, and wholly inviting. Charming line drawings." Horn Bk

(comp.) Poems of magic and spells; illus. by Peggy Bacon. World Pub. 1960 224p illus lib. bdg. $5.91 (4-7) 821.08

1 Fairies—Poetry 2 English poetry—Collections
ISBN 0-529-03587-1

"In handsome format, a fine collection of ninety poems, about strange people and magical events. From Jonson and Shakespeare, Blake and Coleridge, to contemporary authors, there is a good range of . . . poets. Of the sixty poets whose work is included, most are represented by one selection; eight anonymous poems are included. . . . The illustrations are perfectly suited to the theme of the book. Separate title and first line indexes are appended . . . . Suitable for reading aloud." Chicago. Children's Bk Center

(comp.) The poet's tales; a new book of story poems; illus. by Charles Keeping. World Pub. 1971 320p illus $6.95, lib. bdg. $6.87 (6-7) 821.08

1 English poetry—Collections 2 American poetry—Collections
ISBN 0-529-00458-5; 0-529-00459-3

First published 1957 with title: Story poems, new and old

The selections in this volume are "grouped into eight categories: 'Strange and Mysterious,' 'Characters and Individualists,' 'Birds, Beasts, and Bugs,'

Cole, William—*Continued*

'Adventures and disasters,' 'Love Stories,' 'Fighting Men,' 'At Sea,' and 'Odd and Funny.' " Library J

"While the anthology has many old favorites and folk ballads, it also includes some new narrative poems. . . . The selection is discriminating, the lively preface is actually addressed to young readers rather than to adults, and the illustrations are striking." Sat Rev

Includes indexes of authors, titles, and first lines

(ed.) Rough men, tough men; poems of action and adventure; illus. by Enrico Arno. Viking 1969 225p illus $5.95 (5-7)   821.08

1 Adventure and adventurers—Poetry 2 English poetry—Collections 3 American poetry—Collections

ISBN 0-670-60863-7

"Represented are 72 different authors, not including the prolific 'Anonymous' author of 32 items. The rough and tough men are cowboys and prospectors, pirates and outlaws, soldiers and sailors, knights of old, railroaders and robbers. It is a treasury that . . . [demonstrates] that poetry is not all soft sighs and swoonings." Best Sellers

Includes indexes of authors and titles

Colum, Padraic

(ed.) Roofs of gold; poems to read aloud; ed. and with an introduction by Padraic Colum. Macmillan (N Y) 1964 179p illus $5.95 (6-7)   821.08

1 English poetry—Collections 2 American poetry—Collections

"For this anthology of poems intended for reading aloud a noted Irish storyteller and poet has selected more than 80 poems outstanding for their visualness, striking imagery, picturesqueness, action and humor, and lack of subjectiveness. . . . Supplemented with notes illuminating the historical background of 14 of the poems and illustrated with a few decorative wood engravings." Booklist

"An anthology that contains very few unusual selections; the poems are chiefly . . . old favorites. . . . A few newer poets are represented—including Mr. Colum. Arrangement is fairly random." Chicago. Children's Bk Center

De La Mare, Walter

(ed.) Come hither; a collection of rhymes & poems for the young of all ages; decorations by Warren Chappell. Knopf 1957 xxxi, 777p illus $10   821.08

1 English poetry—Collections 2 American poetry—Collections

ISBN 0-394-40336-3

First published 1923

"Nearly five hundred selections representing a poet's choice, and including a number from modern writers. There is an introduction, in the form of a story, which shows the development of Mr. De La Mare's own love of poetry from the days of his early boyhood. The many notes 'written about and roundabout the poems' are also of unusual interest." Pittsburgh

It serves as an "outstanding anthology of English poetry." Ontario Library Rev

Author index, title and first line index, and an index of notes

(ed.) Tom Tiddler's ground; a book of poetry for children, chosen and annotated by Walter De La Mare; with a foreword by Leonard Clark and drawings by Margery Gill. Knopf [1962 c1961] 253p illus lib. bdg. $5.39   821.08

1 English poetry—Collections

ISBN 0-394-91757-X

First published 1931 in England. This 1962 American edition was copyrighted 1961 in England

More than 225 "game rhymes and nursery rhymes, lyrics, storytelling poems—poems of all kinds by many different poets are included here. Only a few are so-called poems for children, but the selection was made with children in mind. There are no specific divisions; but often one poem suggests another, and they read pleasantly in sequence. Most of the longer poems have been placed toward the end of the book." Horn Bk

"It is a handsome book, a delight to handle. . . . There are many comments by Mr. de la Mare at the end of the book, quiet seemingly casual remarks as if he were talking to each individual reader trying to show him how added understanding brings increased delight." N Y Her Trib Bks

Includes indexes of authors and first lines

Eaton, Anne Thaxter

(comp.) Welcome Christmas! A garland of poems; decorated by Valenti Angelo. Viking 1955 128p illus lib. bdg. $3.95 (4-7)   821.08

1 Christmas poetry

ISBN 0-670-75708-X

"This useful anthology of [about fifty] Christmas poems and carols includes selections from ancient broadsides and from less familiar verses such as those of William Morris. Modern poets whose verse expresses 'the inner meaning of Christmas' are represented by Walter de la Mare, Katharine Tynan, Dorothy Sayers and others." Bks for Boys and Girls, Supplement to 3d edition

Contains Index of titles and first lines and Alphabetical list of authors

Geismer, Barbara Peck

(Comp.) Very young verses; comp. by Barbara Peck Geismer and Antoinette B. Suter; illus. by Mildred Bronson. Houghton 1945 210p illus $4.50 (k-1)
    821.08

1 English poetry—Collections 2 American poetry—Collections

ISBN 0-395-06779-0

The poems are arranged under subjects: Birds, beasts, and bugs; About me; About other people and things; About going places; About the seasons; About the weather; Just pretend; Just for fun; Prayers. No index

"An anthology of poems chosen for their appeal to children, 'either for their content, rhythm, words, sound or humor.' Intended for children under six; a good selection for reading aloud. Should become a permanent feature in every poetry collection." Wis Library Bul

Grahame, Kenneth

(comp.) The Cambridge Book of poetry for children. New ed. with an unpublished poem by the editor and illus. by Gwen Raverat. Putnam 1933 238p illus $6   821.08

1 English poetry—Collections 2 American poetry—Collections

ISBN 0-399-20027-4

First published 1916

Rhymes and jingles for little children are followed by poems about the seasons and the weather, animals, fairies, and Christmas poems and lullabies for those a little older. Part 2 consists of poems interesting to the junior high school age. Author and first line indexes

An anthology of "lyric poems . . . attractively illustrated with small cuts." N Y Libraries

Hannum, Sara

(comp.) Lean out of the window; an anthology of modern poetry; comp. by Sara Hannum & Gwendolyn E. Reed; introduction by Siddie Joe Johnson. Decorations by Ragna Tischler. Atheneum Pubs. 1965 112p illus lib. bdg. $3.81 (4-7) 821.08

1 English poetry—Collections 2 American poetry—Collections

ISBN 0-689-20359-4

Includes poems by James Joyce, Robert Frost, Elinor Wylie, William Carlos Williams, Robert Graves, and Gwendolyn Brooks, as well as many other modern poets

"In this anthology of modern poetry there is variety, depth, beauty, and wonder, which offers every reader at least one place for stopping, considering, and returning again." Adventuring With Bks. 2d edition

Author-title index: p107-12

Huffard, Grace Thompson

(comp.) My poetry book; an anthology of modern verse for boys and girls. Rev. ed. Selected and arranged by Grace Thompson Huffard and Laura Mae Carlisle in collaboration with Helen Ferris; introduction by Marguerite de Angeli; illus. by Willy Pogány. Holt 1956 504p illus $4.50 (5-7) 821.08

1 English poetry—Collections 2 American poetry—Collections

ISBN 0-03-033630-9

First published 1934

Over "five hundred poems are included in this interesting anthology. . . . They are arranged under broad subject headings indicative of children's interest. . . . Author, title, and first-line indexes, and a glossary of unusual and difficult words." Booklist

The reader "will notice two salient features. The first is the open-mindedness with which its choice of poems has been made; the second is the way in which they all fit somehow into the active or contemplative life of children." N Y Her Trib Bks

Larrick, Nancy

(ed.) Piper, pipe that song again! Poems for boys and girls; illus. by Kelly Oechsli. Random House 1965 85p illus lib. bdg. $4.59 (2-5) 821.08

1 English poetry—Collections 2 American poetry—Collections

ISBN 0-394-91508-9

A poetry collection "appropriate for reading aloud to younger children. Most of the selections are the work of contemporary writers; much of the material is humorous, many of the poems are about nature or about animals. The black and white illustrations are attractive; there is no table of contents; separate author and title indexes are appended." Chicago. Children's Bk Center

Livingston, Myra Cohn

(ed.) Listen, children, listen; an anthology of poems for the very young; illus. by Trina Schart Hyman. Harcourt 1972 96p illus $5.50 (k-4) 821.08

1 English poetry—Collections 2 American poetry—Collections

ISBN 0-15-245570-1

"Sophisticated verses as well as simple ones (but not less effective) are well represented. The poems range from the nonsense of Belloc and Lear to the sensitivity of Emily Dickinson, T. S. Eliot, e.e. cummings, William Butler Yeats and other poets, old and new." Pub W

"The black-and-white drawings on almost every page are remarkably fine visual extensions of the imagery of the poems. And the pictures of the children, the animals and the birds, and the delightfully hairy uglies should invite repeated viewings as the poems should invite repeated readings." Horn Bk

Love, Katherine

(comp.) A little laughter; illus. by Walter H. Lorraine. Crowell 1957 114p illus $4.50 (3-6) 821.08

1 Limericks 2 Nonsense verses

ISBN 0-690-49804-7

"An anthology of light-hearted poetry that one would be glad to have at hand for many an occasion. . . . The selections happily include favorites from Lear, Richards, Belloc, and Eliot, Kenneth Grahame and Walter de la Mare, interspersed with just as happy but less easily found choices from such modern poets as Harry Behn, Palmer Brown, and J. R. R. Tolkien. The pen-and-ink sketches introduce a giddiness of their own, occasionally suggesting Lear's graphic humor." Horn Bk

Indexes of authors, titles and first lines: p109-14

McFarland, Wilma

(ed.) For a child; great poems old and new; illus. by Ninon. Westminster Press 1947 96p illus $4.50 (k-3) 821.08

1 English poetry—Collections 2 American poetry—Collections

ISBN 0-664-32001-5

Here are poems of nature and the seasons, songs of home, family, and childhood pets, verses reflecting the everyday life of a child. Represented are R. L. Stevenson, Lois Lenski, Eleanor Farjeon, Robert Browning, Christopher Morley, Swinburne and many others

"Format and gay, colored illustrations give it the appearance of a picture book." Booklist

Nash, Ogden

(ed.) The moon is shining bright as day; an anthology of good-humored verse; selected, with an introduction by Ogden Nash. Lippincott 1953 177p illus $5.95 (3-6) 821.08

1 English poetry—Collections 2 American poetry—Collections

ISBN 0-397-30244-4

Illustrated by Rose Shirvanian

"Mr. Nash's name and the humorous line drawings give immediately the impression that this is composed entirely of humorous verse, but that is not the case. Lewis Carroll, Edward Lear, Hilaire Belloc and other less-known nonsense writers are here; but so also are William Blake, Walter de la Mare, Sara Teasdale, Emily Dickinson. Included are a goodly number of poems not available in other anthologies for children." Horn Bk

"The arrangement of the anthology is, as Ogden Nash suggests, rather 'helterskelter' although there are six sections under such headings as 'Has anybody seen my mouse?' 'Blum, blum, blum' and 'Dog in the meadow.' But the gaiety and inconsequence of the compiler's selection has the unmistakable quality of good humour which is so contagious." Ontario Library Rev

Includes an index of titles and first lines

The Oxford Book of children's verse; chosen and ed. with notes, by Iona and Peter Opie. Oxford 1973 xxxi, 407p illus $10 821.08

1 English poetry—Collections 2 American poetry—Collections

ISBN 0-19-812140-7

Arranged chronologically, these 332 selections from British and American children's poetry include works by such poets as Chaucer, Charles and Mary Lamb, Kipling, Farjeon, Milne, Eliot and Nash. Poets still living are not included

This "volume serves as a solid base for a logical

The Oxford Book of children's verse—*Cont.*
presentation of the historical development of children's verse. . . . Although few child readers will find the collection especially exciting because of the clear connections of the verses with the historical periods that produced them, scholars at last have an intelligent, comprehensive anthology of verse for children or about children that clearly demonstrate changing attitudes and values. An excellent chronological collection that should be in every library." Choice

Includes sources and biographical notes and indexes of authors, first lines and familiar titles

Parker, Elinor
(ed.) 100 more story poems; illus. by Peter Spier. Crowell 1960 374p illus $5.50 (6-7)   821.08
1 English poetry—Collections 2 American poetry—Collections
ISBN 0-690-59690-1
Companion volume to: 100 story poems, listed below
"The collection is well rounded, containing favorites like 'The Jumblies,' 'The Listeners,' 'The Vision of Sir Launfal' and a wide representation of poets such as Poe, Yeats, Thackeray, and Browning and a good portion of English and Scottish ballads. The section on Christmastide is noteworthy, being devoted almost exclusively to lovely poems about the Christ Child." Library J

Includes indexes of authors, titles, and first lines

(ed.) 100 poems about people; illus. by Ismar David. Crowell 1955 234p illus $5 (6-7)   821.08
1 English poetry—Collections 2 American poetry—Collections
ISBN 0-690-59744-4
This volume "is entirely made up of poems that are also character sketches. . . . The collection will serve to introduce young readers to the work of many fine poets, including some whose work is not included in anthologies often enough." Pub W

Separate author, title, and first line indexes

(ed.) 100 story poems; illus. by Henry C. Pitz. Crowell 1951 499p illus $5.95 (6-7)   821.08
1 English poetry—Collections 2 American poetry—Collections
ISBN 0-690-59815-7
Covers English and American poetry from the old ballads of Robin Hood to Robert Nathan's 'Dunkirk.' There is something here for every taste and mood: poems about history, the sea, animals, people; poems of romance, chivalry, and magic; humorous poems and pure nonsense. Indexes of authors, titles and first lines
"They are mostly old favorites well tested in schools; we find few surprises. But there is always some one who has missed them, and some one who will like them more when now seen in a new place, the title will lure both teachers and children . . . through junior high." N Y Her Trib Bks

Read, Herbert
(ed.) This way, delight; a book of poetry for the young; illus. by Juliet Kepes. Pantheon Bks. 1956 155p illus $3.50, lib. bdg. $5.69 (5-7)   821.08
1 English poetry—Collections 2 American poetry—Collections
ISBN 0-394-91741-3; 0-394-81741-9
"The distinguished poet and writer has compiled an anthology of some one hundred and twenty-five poems chosen from among great writers and each can be understood within the range of children's experience." Commonweal
"Imaginatively illustrated, it is rounded out with

the essay 'What is poetry,' which points to 'deep delight' as the best introduction to the world of poetry." L.C. Children & Poetry
The table of contents is at the back of the book, preceding the indices of first lines and authors

Reed, Gwendolyn
(comp.) Bird songs; drawings by Gabriele Margules. Atheneum Pubs. 1969 64p illus lib. bdg. $5.50 (5-7)   821.08
1 Birds—Poetry 2 English poetry—Collections 3 American poetry—Collections
ISBN 0-689-30004-2
"This compilation of 81 poems describes and pays tribute to such feathered protagonists as the robin, blue jay, woodpecker, swallow, heron and so on. The book is divided into 13 areas, such as types of birds, cages, and birds in winter and summer. About 50 very different poets are represented including Longfellow, Keats, Frost, Sandburg, Dickinson, Williams, and Roethke. . . . There is an author-title index." Sch Library J
"Not only is the quality of the drawing carefully fitted to the accompanying poem, so that both drawing and poem enrich one another, but the page spreads that result seem as airy as the bird world the poems deal with." N Y Times Bk Rev

Sechrist, Elizabeth Hough
(ed.) One thousand poems for children; based on the selections of Roger Ingpen; selected and arranged by Elizabeth Hough Sechrist; with decorative drawings by Henry C. Pitz. Macrae Smith Co. 1946 601p illus $9.75   821.08
1 English poetry—Collections 2 American poetry—Collections
ISBN 0-8255-8146-X
First published 1903 with Roger Ingpen as the compiler
Part I includes selections, grouped by subject for children from nursery age to sixth grade; part II, for seventh to tenth grades. . . . [There are] decorated end papers and black and white drawings. Indexes of authors, first lines and titles." Bookmark

(comp.) Poems for red letter days; illus. by Guy Fry. Macrae Smith Co. 1951 349p illus lib. bdg. $5.97   821.08
1 Holidays—Poetry 2 English poetry—Collections 3 American poetry—Collections
ISBN 0-8255-8155-9
"A poetry anthology ranging from Shakespeare to Edgar Guest and provided with good indexes [of authors, titles, first lines] and the happy arrangement by season, holiday, and to-be-celebrated-in-the-schools weeks should by all means be recommended. This one is further enhanced by an attractive format." Library J

Stevenson, Burton Egbert
(comp.) The home book of verse for young folks; selected and arranged by Burton Egbert Stevenson; decorations by Willy Pogány. [Rev. and enl. ed] Holt 1958 xxii, 676p $6   821.08
1 English poetry—Collections 2 American poetry—Collections
ISBN 0-03-032645-1
First published 1915
A poetry anthology divided into the following sections: In the nursery, The duty of children, Rhymes of childhood, Just nonsense, Fairyland, The glad evangel, This wonderful world, Stories in rhyme, My country, The happy warrior, Life lessons, A garland of gold
"A delightful collection including old favorites and

Stevenson, Burton Egbert—*Continued*
new poems for children of all ages. . . . Indexes of authors, titles and first lines. Twelve decorated pages and end-papers." Booklist

Thompson, Blanche Jennings
(ed.) All the Silver pennies; combining Silver pennies and More Silver pennies. Decorations by Ursula Arndt. Macmillan (N Y) 1967 224p illus $4.95 (3-6)
821.08
1 English poetry—Collections 2 American poetry—Collections
This is a reissue in one volume of two anthologies of modern verse for children Silver pennies (1925) and More Silver pennies (1938)
"Time-tested poems for children, organized into Part I for the young child and Part II for older children. Includes an introduction, notes for individual poems, and author, title, and first-line indexes." Hodges. Bks for Elem Sch Libraries

Tripp, Wallace
(comp.) A great big ugly man came up and tied his horse to me; a book of nonsense verse; [comp. and] illus. by Wallace Tripp. Little 1973 46p illus $5.95 (k-3)
821.08
1 Nonsense verses
ISBN 0-316-85280-5
This book is "a case of an imaginative illustrator taking a new look at some old words—nursery rhymes, oral chants, verse and occasional doggerel, and coming up with some zany interpretations. Assorted animals and humans frolic through the pages in a lively series of 41 bits of verse spanning several centuries. . . . About half the verses are nursery rhymes; the rest run to oral verse, some limericks and one parody." N Y Times Bk Rev

Tudor, Tasha
(comp.) Wings from the wind; an anthology of poems selected and illus. by Tasha Tudor. Lippincott 1964 119p illus $4.95, lib. bdg. $3.79 (3-6) 821.08
1 English poetry—Collections 2 American poetry—Collections
ISBN 0-397-30790-X; 0-397-30789-6
"Mother Goose, Wordsworth, Longfellow, Mary Webb, Shakespeare, Robert Frost are among those represented [in this collection of 65 poems]. Each poem is embellished with soft black-and-white illustrations. . . . Each section has a full-page color plate. This is a handsome book." Sch Library J

Untermeyer, Louis
(ed.) The Golden Treasury of poetry; selected and with a commentary by Louis Untermeyer; illus. by Joan Walsh Anglund. Golden Press 1959 324p illus $7.95, lib. bdg. $6.95
821.08
1 English poetry—Collections 2 American poetry—Collections
ISBN 0-307-16852-2; 0-307-60852-2
"Mr. Untermeyer has collected here [in twelve categories] over 400 poems to enjoy, ranging from Chaucer to Ogden Nash, and including the familiar and the unfamiliar, nonsense lyrics, limericks, and a fine selection of ballads. Brief comments on particular poems, poets, forms of poetry, or subjects are unobtrusive and interesting. The illustrations, on every page, give the book such a lively appearance that confirmed haters of poetry will be irresistibly drawn into reading." Horn Bk
Separate indexes of authors, titles, and first lines

(ed.) Rainbow in the sky; collected and ed. by Louis Untermeyer; illus. by Reginald Birch. Harcourt 1935 xxvii, 498p illus $9.50 (k-4)
821.08

1 English poetry—Collections 2 American poetry—Collections 3 Nursery rhymes
ISBN 0-15-265477-1
"More than five hundred poems from Mother Goose to modern times are included in this anthology for younger children. Mr. Birch's drawings in black and white are lively and . . . amusing." N Y Pub Library
"This is a grand, large collection that is a necessity for the young child's library." Sat Rev
Author, title and first line indexes

(ed.) This singing world; an anthology of modern poetry for young people, collected and ed. by Louis Untermeyer; illus. by Florence Wyman Ivins. Harcourt 1923 xxi, 445p illus $9.50 (4-7) 821.08
1 English poetry—Collections 2 American poetry—Collections
ISBN 0-15-286041-X
"Three hundred twenty-one poems of forty-nine English and American writers, chosen for their appeal to readers from 9 to 16 years of age, and likely to please adults as well. Selection excellent, relatively unfamiliar, and unusually rich in humor. Author, title and first line indexes." N Y State Lib
"The drawings, while turning it into a gift book of genuine value, have not blinded the publishers to the necessity of giving it a durable but very attractive outward form." Bookman's Manual

822 English drama

Aiken, Joan
The mooncusser's daughter; a play for children; illus. by Arvis Stewart; music by John Sebastian Brown. Viking [1974 c1973] 95p illus music lib. bdg. $5.95 (5-7) 822
1 Lighthouses—Drama 2 Buried treasure—Drama
ISBN 0-670-48795-3
First published 1973 in England
Characters: 7 men, 2 women and extras
"This supernatural drama is based on the remorse of Saul, keeper of Sabertooth Light, who has given up his career as a mooncusser, a shipwrecker. Saul and his blind wife live in the lighthouse from which he has banished his daughter, Sympathy, for fear that the curse blighting his life will fall upon her. But she shows up as a pawn for a ruthless boss figure and his henchmen. The gang is bent on invading the cavern under Saul's stronghold, to grab a treasure that will enable them to rule the world." Pub W
"All of this may sound impossible, and it certainly seems to call for professional production, with all its special effects. But Joan Aiken has a flair, and the nonsensical pastiche has some broadly comic scenes, along with some parodies of Shakespeare's songs that are very funny for those who recognize them." Chicago. Children's Bk Center

Langstaff, John
Saint George and the dragon; a mummer's play; with woodcuts by David Gentleman. Atheneum Pubs. 1973 47p illus music lib. bdg. $4.95 (4-6) 822
1 Christmas plays 2 Folk drama
ISBN 0-689-30421-8
"A Margaret K. McElderry book"
This dramatic production version of an old folk play includes music of the traditional songs, instructions for performing the sword dance, stage directions, and costume suggestions
The play "offers an original approach to the traditional holiday pageantry. This version with glowing woodcuts is meant to be performed, not just read.

Langstaff, John—*Continued*

There's everything to delight both audience and young actors: a dragon, a comic hobby horse, dancers, a noble knight, and a magical fool. The mixture of ritual and good-natured buffoonery makes this ancient mummer's play very appealing." Christian Sci Monitor

Miller, Katherine

Saint George; a Christmas mummers' play; illus. by Wallace Tripp. Houghton 1967 48p illus $3.95 (5-7)
822

1 Christmas plays 2 Folk drama
ISBN 0-395-06944-0

This folk play "is compiled from old English plays and dances; the language has been modernized . . . . Notes on the history and production of . . . [mummers'] plays are included." Sch Library J

This "will be enjoyable either for reading as a story or for performance by children. The stage directions which tie the lines together give continuity to a tale full of horseplay . . . . Spirited illustrations enlarge the buffoonery." Horn Bk

"The script and stage directions are given together, with production notes at the end of the book." Sutherland. The Best in Children's Bks

822.3   William Shakespeare

Shakespeare, William

Seeds of time (Selections from Shakespeare) Comp. by Bernice Grohskopf; drawings by Kelly Oechsli. Atheneum Pubs. 1963 59p illus $3.25, lib. bdg. $3.07 (5-7)
822.3

ISBN 0-689-20122-2; 0-689-20121-4

"Brief, simple examples of lyric poetry selected from the plays of Shakespeare, but quite complete within themselves. A beautifully designed book, pleasing to both eye and ear." Top of the News

Index of sources: p58-59

When daisies pied, and violets blue; songs from Shakespeare; illus. by Mary Chalmers. Coward, McCann & Geoghegan 1974 unp illus $5.95 (2-5)
822.3

ISBN 0-698-20286-4

"Comprising eight songs and one excerpted speech from Shakespeare's plays, this dainty book is just the ticket for introducing youngsters to the bard. The musical, lighthearted verses which describe the changing of the seasons and of life, the magic of dreams, etc. are enhanced by delicately wrought and whimsically detailed pastel watercolors. Explanatory notes by C. Walter Hodges at the end (although they make reference to nonexistent page numbers), provide an intelligent and humorous postscript to this imaginative assemblage." Sch Library J

Shakespeare's England, by the editors of Horizon Magazine, in consultation with Louis B. Wright; illus. with paintings, drawings, and engravings of the period. Am. Heritage [distributed by Harper] 1964 153p illus maps $5.95, lib. bdg. $6.89 (6-7)
822.3

1 Shakespeare, William—Contemporary England 2 Theater—Great Britain 3 Great Britain—History—Tudors, 1485-1603
ISBN 0-06-022590-4; 0-06-02291-2

"A Horizon Caravel book"

A portrayal of Shakespeare as a man of his time against the background of England under Elizabeth I and James I

"A book that should enthrall the student of English history as much as it does the reader interested in the theatre. The illustrations [many from European sources] are handsome, varied, and carefully placed and captioned. . . . It gives, especially, interesting material about touring companies, patronage, literary criticism, and the intrigue and competition in the world of Elizabethan actors and playwrights." Chicago. Children's Bk Center

Further reference: p151

828   English miscellany

Farjeon, Eleanor

The new book of days; illus. by Philip Gough and M. W. Hawes. Walck, H.Z. 1961 400p illus lib. bdg. $6.50 (5-7)
828

1 Calendars
ISBN 0-8098-2348-9

First published 1941 in England

This is a "collection of poems and short pieces of prose, arranged to provide something for each day of the year. Here, in addition to verses by the author, are such things as proverb tales, seasonal bits about nature and customs, historical oddities about people and incidents, and explanations of word meanings." Booklist

"We do not see how anyone can help but be fascinated and stimulated. . . . This is a book to be read straight through, or dipped into by those who love the lively byways of knowledge." N Y Her Trib Bks

Greenaway, Kate

The Kate Greenaway treasury; introduction by Ruth Hill Viguers; an anthology of the illustrations and writings of Kate Greenaway; ed. and selected by Edward Ernest, assisted by Patricia Tracy Lowe. World Pub. 1967 319p illus $10.95
828

ISBN 0-529-00313-9

This collection contains the complete text and pictures for A Apple pie, The Pied Piper of Hamelin, by Robert Browning, A day in a child's life, by M.B. Foster, and the Alphabet, with selections from Mother Goose, Little Ann, and others. A biography of Kate Greenaway, a selection of her letters to and from John Ruskin excerpts from Anne Carroll Moore's A century of Kate Greenaway and a bibliography are included

"A valuable insight into the life and work of a truly creative artist whose vision of childhood was translated into gay and tender picture books." Library J

Milne, A. A.

The Christopher Robin story book. . . . Decorations by Ernest H. Shepard. Dutton [1966 c1957] 171p illus $4.95 (k-3)
828

ISBN 0-525-27933-4

A reissue in new format of the title first published 1929

"Introduced and selected by the author from When we were very young; Now we are six; Winnie-the-Pooh; The house at Pooh Corner." Title page

"You will find here a collection of verses and stories, mostly about a little boy called Christopher Robin." Author's note

Descriptions of the titles listed above can be found entered separately. Winnie-the-Pooh and The house at Pooh Corner are entered under Fiction, while the other two titles are entered in class 821

841   French poetry

Gasztold, Carmen Bernos de
Prayers from the Ark; tr. from the French and with foreword and epilogue by Rumer Godden; illus. by Jean Primrose. Viking 1962 71p illus $5.95, pa $1.25   841
1 Animals—Poetry
ISBN 0-670-57177-6; 0-670-00258-5
First published as two smaller books, 1947 and 1955, in France
A collection of 27 poems "addressed to their creator by animals large and small: the cock, the cat, the ox, the little pig, the lark, and others." L.C. Children & Poetry

873   Latin epic poetry

Church, Alfred J.
The Aeneid for boys and girls; retold by Alfred J. Church; illus by Eugene Karlin; afterword by Clifton Fadiman. Macmillan (N Y) 1962 172p illus $4.95 (6-7)   873
1 Virgil—Adaptations 2 Aeneas
"The Macmillan classics"
"This is the story of the sack of Troy and of the wanderings of King Aeneas until he establishes a new kingdom in Italy." Bks for Boys & Girls
"A simple and dignified prose rendering of the Aeneid. The monologues and conversations are translated almost literally, and the whole version keeps close to the original in spirit and atmosphere. There are . . . attractive illustrations in delicate colors, and the binding is artistic and serviceable." Booklist

883   Classical Greek epic poetry

Church, Alfred J.
The Iliad and the Odyssey of Homer; retold by Alfred J. Church; illus. by Eugene Karlin; afterword by Clifton Fadiman. Macmillan (N Y) 1964 277p illus $4.95 (6-7)   883
1 Homer—Adaptations 2 Trojan War 3 Ulysses
"The Macmillan classics"
This is a combined edition of two books: The Iliad for boys and girls, and The Odyssey for boys and girls, first published 1907 and 1906, respectively
The Iliad retells the story of the Trojan War, while The Odyssey recounts the adventures of Odysseus on his voyage homeward
These classic retellings "are in simple, dignified prose with memorable phrases, inspiring to the imagination of children lucky enough to have them as an introduction to the great heroes and the immortals of Olympus." Four to Fourteen

Picard, Barbara Leonie
The Iliad of Homer; retold by Barbara Leonie Picard; illus. by Joan Kiddell-Monroe. Walck, H.Z. 1960 201p illus $5.75 (6-7)   883
1 Homer—Adaptations 2 Trojan War
"Relates the incidents which took place in the ninth year of the Trojan War, centering around Achilles' quarrel with Agamemnon and the death of Patrocius. Includes a prologue and an epilogue and a list of names, with identifications." Hodges. Bks for Elem Sch Libraries

891.7   Russian literature

Morton, Miriam
(ed.) A harvest of Russian children's literature; ed. with introduction and commentary, by Miriam Morton; foreword by Ruth Hill Viguers. Univ. of Calif. Press 1967 474p illus $16.50, pa $5.95   891.7
1 Russian literature—Collections
ISBN 0-520-00886-3; 0-520-01745-5
This is "a superb anthology for any collection, useful for a number of diverse purposes and, better still, a source of pleasure in its variety, scope, and quality. All of the material included is in print in Russia today; the selections range from classic writers like Tolstoy and Gorky to contemporary authors, some of whose work has already been published in English— Chukovsky and Sholokhov, for example. The book's contents are divided both by age groups and by genre or type of literature; the illustrations are also from Russian children's books. Many of the selections are preceded by notes about the author. The editor has provided a long, thoughtful, and informative introduction. Separate author and title indexes are appended." Sutherland. The Best in Children's Bks

(ed.) The moon is like a silver sickle; a celebration of poetry by Russian children; collected and tr. by Miriam Morton; illus. by Eros Keith. Simon & Schuster 1972 93p illus $4.95 (4-7)   891.7
1 Russian poetry—Collections 2 Children as authors
ISBN 0-671-65198-6
Ninety-two poems, selected and "translated from poetry composed by young Russians, bring glimpses into sentiments, expressions, and experiences of children in a foreign land. Both boys and girls from the ages of four to fifteen wrote poems which are about themselves and the world around them." Top of the News
"Many of the poems are charming; however, some have been damaged by the attempt to preserve the rhyme in translation. Dreamy, delicate monochrome illustrations add much to the book's appeal." Sch Library J

892   Literature from Babylonia

Feagles, Anita
He who saw everything; the epic of Gilgamesh; retold by Anita Feagles. With an afterword about the origins of the epic by Cyrus H. Gordon; illus. with sculptures by Xavier González. Young Scott Bks. 1966 63p illus map lib. bdg. $5.50 (4-6)   892
1 Gilgamesh
ISBN 0-201-09215-8
This is a retelling of the "3000-year-old epic of the ancient Sumerian king who met and conquered his enemy, his fear of death." Pub W
"This is the first account of the legend written specifically for children, and it moves along at a good pace. . . . Handsome reproductions of plaster friezes and striking paper sculptures illustrate the text." Sch Library J

895   Literature of the Chinese and Japanese

Lewis, Richard
(ed.) The moment of wonder; a collection of Chinese and Japanese poetry; illus. with paintings by Chinese and Japanese masters. Dial Press 1964 138p illus $5.95 (4-7)   895

Lewis, Richard—*Continued*

1 Chinese poetry—Collections 2 Japanese poetry—Collections 3 Nature in poetry
ISBN 0-8037-5788-3

"Some of the poems were written nearly 2,000 years ago and some as recently as the twentieth century; all are concerned with nature, the seasons, or the 'ages of man'. . . . Illustrated with black-and-white reproductions." Booklist

"The compiler has written a perceptive preface to the book and brief introductions to each grouping of poems. . . . A book beautiful in appearance and in content, bringing together samplings of the work of many poets who 'felt a deep and lasting companionship with nature and life.' " Horn Bk

Author index: p133-34

895.6   Japanese poetry

Baron, Virginia Olsen

(ed.) The seasons of time; tanka poetry of ancient Japan; illus. by Yasuhide Kobashi. Dial Press 1968 63p illus $4.95 (6-7)   895.6

1 Japanese poetry—Collections 2 Nature in poetry
ISBN 0-8037-7785-X

This anthology opens with poems about spring, then moves "into summer, autumn and winter. Tanka poetry, which the introduction translates as 'short song,' is an ancient form. Most of the poems here were first collected between 759 and 905 [A.D.]." Pub W

The poems "together with interpretive wash-and-ink drawings in black and white comprise a book that is distinctive in design as well as in pictorial and poetic content. . . . An understanding of the poems is greatly aided by the editor's brief introduction describing the source and traditional symbolism of the poems and tanka." Booklist

Behn, Harry

(comp.) Cricket songs; Japanese haiku; tr. by Harry Behn; with pictures selected from Sesshu and other Japanese masters. Harcourt 1964 unp illus $3.95 (4-7)   895.6

1 Haiku 2 Japanese poetry—Collections 3 Nature in poetry
ISBN 0-15-220890-9

"A collection of Japanese 'haiku'—nonrhyming, three-line, seventeen-syllable nature poems suggesting the seasons of the year—selected and translated by an American poet. The 'haiku' presented here speak of chirping frogs, the moon, rain, fog, a sleeping butterfly, cicadas buzzing in the sun, and other aspects of nature." Booklist

"A small, exquisite book . . . perfect for reading aloud or to inspire creative writing of poetry." Hodges. Bks for Elem Sch Libraries

(comp.) More Cricket songs; Japanese haiku; tr. by Harry Behn; illus. with pictures by Japanese masters. Harcourt 1971 64p illus $4.50 (4-7)   895.6

1 Haiku 2 Japanese poetry—Collections 3 Nature in poetry
ISBN 0-15-255440-8

Companion volume to: Cricket songs, entered above

"The haiku here are drawn from the work of twenty-nine poets, the selections varied in mood and subject, deceptively simple in their miniature perfection, and translated with that sensitivity and authority that indicate the poet's vision." Chicago. Children's Bk Center

Cassedy, Sylvia

(comp.) Birds, frogs, and moonlight; haiku tr. by Sylvia Cassedy and Kunihiro Suetake; illus. by Vo-Dinh; calligraphy by Koson Okamura. Doubleday 1967 47p illus lib. bdg. $4.95 (3-6)   895.6

1 Haiku 2 Japanese poetry—Collections 3 Nature in poetry
ISBN 0-385-08315-7

Twenty "haiku celebrate the child's experiences with animals. Pictures and calligraphy inform the reader that writing and slippers in Japan are different but poems inform the readers that kittens, birds, spiders, frogs, and feelings are delightfully the same." Reading Ladders for Human Relations. 5th edition

Lewis, Richard

(ed.) In a spring garden; pictures by Ezra Jack Keats. Dial Press 1965 unp illus lib. bdg. $4.58 (k-3)   895.6

1 Haiku 2 Japanese poetry—Collections 3 Nature in poetry
ISBN 0-8037-4025-5

An "introductory collection of twenty-eight haiku which follow a day in spring from a red morning sky to the passing of a giant firefly." Children's Bks Too Good to Miss

"The universal quality of childhood is exemplified by the haiku, e.g. 'Just simply alive/Both of us, I/And the poppy' is complemented by the brilliant collage and water color illustrations. This beautiful, creative blend of poetry and illustrations is most welcome to the poetry collection for young children." Sch Library J

897   Literatures of North American aboriginal languages

Belting, Natalia

(comp.) Our fathers had powerful songs; illus. by Laszlo Kubinyi. Dutton 1974 unp illus map $4.95 (3-6)   897

1 Indian poetry—Collections
ISBN 0-525-36485-4

"Selected and translated into English, poems from one Canadian Indian and several American Indian tribes are illustrated by softly drawn, imaginative pictures in black and white. Like other Indian poetry, these reflect a closeness to and reverence for nature and a quiet joy in the dignity of men and the power of the gods. The collection comprises nine poems, one each from the Apache, Cochiti, Diegueno, Kwakiutl, Luiseno, Mandan, Navaho, Papago, and Wintu cultures." Chicago. Children's Bk Center

"An interesting addition to poetry shelves as well as to North American Indian collections. . . . The poetry expresses an understated intensity." Sch Library J

Bierhorst, John

(ed.) In the trail of the wind; American Indian poems and ritual orations. Farrar, Straus 1971 201p illus $4.95 (6-7)   897

1 Indian poetry—Collections 2 Indians—Poetry
ISBN 0-374-33640-7

This "collection of poetry, taken from the oral literature of more than 30 tribes of Indians of North, Central, and South America and the Eskimos, is arranged topically under such headings as The beginning, Of rain and birth, The words of war, and Death.

Bierhorst, John—*Continued*
. . . Background information on certain aspects of
Indian thought and the problems of translation are
discussed in the introduction. Appended are notes on
each poem including translator and source; a glossary
of tribes, cultures, and languages; and suggestions for
further reading." Booklist
"A fascinating book to read, and to reread. . . . Its
illustrations, selected from period engravings, makes
it a distinguished book to look at as well." Pub W

Gerez, Toni de
(comp.) 2-rabbit, 7-wind; poems from ancient Mexico; retold from Nahuatl texts. Viking 1971 56p illus
$4.75 (5-7)   897
   1 Aztec poetry—Collections
   ISBN 0-670-73687-2
From the codices of the Nahuatl-speaking peoples
of ancient Mexico comes this "ensemble of pieces
[which] reflects the great deity and the many deities
of these ancients and their sages' graphic ponderings
on life, death, nature, art, wisdom, and their content
and meaning." Booklist
This volume "would be enticing just as a piece of
bookmaking. The russet design motifs . . . are beautifully placed on the handsome pages. The selections
—poignant or dramatic, often tender or lyric, always
lovely—are fragments of songs and poems of the
Nahuatl. They are to be read, the author's note states,
'as parts of one long poem, a poem that does not begin
anywhere and does not end anywhere.' " Pub W

Houston, James
(ed.) Songs of the dream people; chants and images
from the Indians and Eskimos of North America. Ed.
and illus. by James Houston. Atheneum Pubs. 1972
83p illus lib. bdg. $5.95 (4-7)   897
   1 Indian poetry—Collections 2 Indians of North
   America—Poetry
   ISBN 0-689-30306-8
"A Margaret K. McElderry book"
This book contains "Indian and Eskimo songs and
chants gathered from many North American tribes."
Booklist
"The verses, many short and haiku-like, are rich
with the magic of words and ritual. . . . Distinctive,
two-color drawings of Eskimo and Indian artifacts,
labeled with tribal designations, illuminate the text. A
Foreword notes the significance of dreams and the
employment of secret terms in the songs." Horn Bk
   Suggestions for further reading: p[86]

Jones, Hettie
(comp.) The trees stand shining; poetry of the
North American Indians; paintings by Robert Andrew
Parker. Dial Press 1971 unp illus $4.95, lib. bdg.
$4.58 (3-6)   897
   1 Indian poetry—Collections 2 Indians of North
   America—Poetry
   ISBN 0-8037-9083-X; 0-8037-9084-8
"The poems are grouped by subject, with sources
given, most of them reflecting the love and respect for
natural things that are part of the great heritage of the
Indian cultures of North America; they were originally songs, many of them brief fragments that seem
almost chants or lamentations." Chicago. Children's
Bk Center
"Fourteen large full-color paintings are provided
for this handsome picture book. . . . Some are like rich
impressionistic backdrops and illuminate the intense,
haikulike word images. . . . Others portray animal or
human figures against sweeping brush strokes of
color." Horn Bk

Lewis, Richard
(ed.) I breathe a new song; poems of the Eskimo;
illus. by Oonark; with an introduction by Edmund
Carpenter. Simon & Schuster 1971 128p illus lib. bdg.
$5.95 (4-7)   897
   1 Eskimo poetry—Collections
   ISBN 0-671-65170-6
A representative collection of Eskimo poetry from
the journals of Arctic expeditions and other sources.
Most of the pieces are anonymous but are identified
by Eskimo group or geographical origin. The
introduction by anthropologist Edmund Carpenter
describes the people, Eskimo beliefs, and their ways
of forming poetry
"Illustrations that resemble the stick figures of cave
paintings complement the directness and simplicity of
the lovely poems. . . . The poems reflect a closeness
to nature, and a concern with the aspects of life that
loom large in a primitive culture, and the love poems
are enchanting." Chicago. Children's Bk Center
   Bibliography: p126-28

900   GEOGRAPHY AND HISTORY

901   Philosophy and theory of general history

Morgan, Edmund S.
So what about history? Atheneum Pubs. 1969 95p
illus maps lib. bdg. $5.95 (4-6)   901
   1 History—Philosophy
   ISBN 0-689-20663-1
By means of text and "photographs, prints, and
reproductions, Morgan elucidates his thesis that history is not only a record of man's past but also a means
of understanding the ways and ideas of man today. In
addition, he points out the importance of man's
curiosity about himself as a motivating force in historical research." Booklist
"Lively style and fresh perspective make this
stimulating and unorthodox approach to history (it is
not a history book) provocative." Sutherland. The
Best in Children's Bks

901.9   Civilization

Foster, Genevieve
Birthdays of freedom; from early man to July 4,
1776. Scribner 1973 128p illus maps $6.95, lib. bdg.
$6.95 (6-7)   901.9
   1 Civilization—History
   ISBN 0-684-13496-9
Originally published separately in two volumes,
1952 and 1957 respectively. Book I: The ancient
world; Book II: From the fall of Rome to July 4, 1776
Includes information on the early Egyptians,
democracy in Athens, the Magna Carta, and other
high points or setbacks in the struggle for freedom

909.08   World history— Modern, 1450/1500-

Foster, Genevieve
The world of William Penn; illus. by the author.
Scribner 1973 192p illus maps $5.95 (5-7)   909.08
   1 Seventeenth century 2 Penn, William
   ISBN 0-684-13188-9
The author looks at the whole world as it existed during the time of William Penn, and how it affected the direction of his life
"The clear textual treatment brings to life the backgrounds and activities of the second half of the seventeenth and the first quarter of the eighteenth century—in the arts and sciences, and in war and peace. Portraits, scenes, diagrams, and pictorial maps clarify and enliven the text. The broad compass of the book permits paths to cross, as when William Penn meets with Peter the Great. An enlightened approach to the study of world history." Horn Bk

Year of Columbus, 1492. Scribner 1969 64p illus maps lib. bdg. $5.95 (3-6)   909.08
   1 Fifteenth century 2 Columbus, Christopher 3 America—Discovery and exploration
   ISBN 0-684-12695-8
This book, illustrated by the author, gives "younger children a world-wide perspective on historic events. About half of the . . . book is devoted to Columbus and half to the concurrent activities of Copernicus, Leonardo da Vinci, and Michelangelo and events in Ethiopia, China, Japan, Peru, and Mexico." Booklist
The author writes "in a manner calculated to whet the reading appetites of middle graders. . . . Illustrations are plentiful, and include carefully researched maps and charts. Wider in scope than most books bearing on the subject for this age group." Sch Library J

Year of the Pilgrims, 1620. Scribner 1969 64p illus maps lib. bdg. $5.95 (3-6)   909.08
   1 Seventeenth century 2 Pilgrim Fathers 3 U.S.—History—Colonial period
   ISBN 0-684-12626-5
This book, illustrated by the author, "describes the plight of the Puritans in England, their life in Holland, and the establishment of the Plymouth Colony in America. The account also covers the work of Grotius, Shakespeare, Rembrandt, Harvey, and Galileo and events in Africa's Kingdom of Benin, India, China, and Japan." Booklist
"The text is written simply, but is not oversimplified; maps, diagrams, and pictures accompany it. The book is good for either reference or pleasure reading and will therefore have . . . wide appeal." Sch Library J

909.7   World history— 1700-1799

Foster, Genevieve
Year of independence, 1776. Scribner 1970 64p illus maps lib. bdg. $5.95 (3-6)   909.7
   1 Eighteenth century 2 U.S. Declaration of Independence
   ISBN 0-684-12689-3
"This book consists of three parts. First, the author describes political events in the United States from 1776 to 1783. Parts two and three present some of the artistic and scientific developments in other parts of the world during the same period." Commonweal
"Copiously illustrated with [the author's] two-color pictures and maps." Booklist

909.81   World history— 1800-1899

Foster, Genevieve
Year of Lincoln, 1861. Scribner 1970 64p illus maps lib. bdg. $5.95 (3-6)   909.81
   1 Nineteenth century 2 Lincoln, Abraham, President U.S. 3 U.S.—History—Civil War
   ISBN 0-684-20823-7
"The author uses 1861 and the start of the American Civil War as her base and gives a brief historical perspective during that period of Lincoln, Darwin, Mark Twain, Dickens, Frederick Douglass, Queen Victoria, Empress Tzu Hsi, and Prince (later Emperor) Mutsuhito, who followed up Commodore Perry's introduction of Western culture to Japan with 'enlightened' economic reform." Horn Bk
The survey "moves from 1830 to 1865. . . . Useful but not unusual in the coverage of American history; the second half of the book has some interesting material, but each section seems isolated. An index is appended." Chicago. Children's Bk Center

910   General geography

Arnold, Pauline
How we named our states, by Pauline Arnold and Percival White. Criterion Bks. [1966 c1965] 192p illus maps $5.50 (5-7)   910
   1 Names, Geographical—U.S. 2 U.S.—History
   ISBN 0-200-71911-4
The authors trace the reasons for the names of the states and their capitals, often including historical anecdotes through which the panorama of America's early history emerges
"There are interesting bits of historical information and, although the book doesn't have reference use, it is useful for the information it gives and enjoyable for browsing. An index is appended." Chicago. Children's Bk Center

Buehr, Walter
The Portuguese explorers. Putnam 1966 95p illus maps lib. bdg. $4.79 (4-6)   910
   1 Discoveries (in geography) 2 Explorers 3 Henry the Navigator, Prince of Portugal
   ISBN 0-399-60518-5
This book covers "early exploration and Portugal's domination of the seas in the fifteenth century. The thrill of discovery is . . . depicted through the voyages of the great explorers Bartolomeo Diaz, and Vasco da Gama, among others. Much of the book is devoted to Prince Henry the Navigator and his many contributions to the science of navigation." Sch Library J
"Useful supplementary material which illuminates the aspirations and problems of Renaissance explorers." Booklist

Chubb, Thomas Caldecot
Prince Henry the Navigator and the highways of the sea. Viking 1970 160p maps $4.95 (6-7)   910

Chubb, Thomas Caldecot—*Continued*
1 Discoveries (in geography) 2 Henry the Navigator, Prince of Portugal
ISBN 0-670-57623-9
An "account of Prince Henry of Portugal who had a far-reaching influence on navigation and exploration without ever sailing a ship. Incidents from the life of the fifteenth-century prince are related, but the emphasis is on his achievements in stimulating exploration, gathering knowledge about the world, and revolutionizing navigation." Booklist
Prince Henry's "captains appear in lively detail, with exciting and amusing excerpts from the journals. The methods of navigation, ship building, and the cartographic innovations which made the 15th-century Portuguese 'geographic explosion' possible are described easily as part of the narrative, so as to make the technical details understandable." Sci Bks
Suggestions for further reading: p155-56

Fletcher, Christine
100 keys: names across the land. Abingdon 1973 288p illus $5.95 (6-7) 910
1 Names, Geographical—U.S. 2 U.S.—History
ISBN 0-687-29077-5
The names included were chosen for originality and because they reflect political, social and religious ideas which altered the course of American history. Each of the names is related to leading personalities of the past or to the character and national background of the early settlers
"The brief stories associated with the names of 100 towns in the United States (two from each state) make interesting reading. However, this book's reference value is doubtful: the essay form precludes picking out facts at a glance." Sch Library J

Lands and peoples. Grolier 7v illus maps set $150 (5-7) 910
1 Geography
Originally published 1929-30. Periodically revised
Contents for 1972 edition: v 1 Africa; v2 Asia, Australia, New Zealand, Oceania; v3-4 Europe; v5 North America; v6 South and Central America; v7 The world: facts and figures; Index
"Taking the continents as the unifying theme, Volumes I-VI give a good overview (history, geography, culture, and economics) of each continent followed by a more careful study of each country. Organization of material is both attractive and practical. Volume VII, an encyclopedia, contains the index, general statistics, topics such as: language, religion, forms of government, monetary system, etc. The cumulative reading list of 2,000 books plus audiovisual materials provided in Volume VII might be better placed according to country." Choice [Review of the 1972 edition]
For a fuller review see: The Booklist, February 1, 1973

Webster's New geographical dictionary. Merriam maps $14.95 910
1 Geography—Dictionaries 2 Gazetteers
First published 1949 with title: Webster's Geographical dictionary. Periodically revised
This dictionary includes "some 47,000 geographical names from biblical times, ancient Greece and Rome, medieval Europe, and today's world. Entries provide gazetteer-type information, geographical features, monuments, and a brief history. Pronunciation is marked and cross references are given for alternative spellings. There are 217 inset maps included in the text. Additional features include a list of geographical terms, signs and symbols, and information on maps and map projections." Wynar. Guide to Ref Bks for Sch Media Centers [Review of the 1972 edition]

"A very useful, standard ready reference tool." Cur Ref Bks [Review of the 1972 edition]

Worldmark Encyclopedia of the nations; editor and publisher: Moshe Y. Sachs. Worldmark Press [distributed by Harper] 5v illus maps set $69.95 910
1 Geography—Encyclopedias 2 World history—Encyclopedias 3 United Nations 4 World politics
ISBN 0-87900-006-6
First published 1960 in one volume under the editorship of Benjamin A. Cohen. Periodically revised to bring material up to date
This five-volume set contains "factual and statistical information on 146 countries of the world exhibited in uniform format under such rubrics as topography, population, public finance, language, and ethnic composition, etc. Country articles appear in volumes 2-5 arranged geographically by continent. Volume 1 is devoted to the United Nations and its affiliated agencies. Illustrations, maps. No indexes." ALA Ref Bks for Small and Medium Sized Libraries [Review of the 1971 edition]
"The one-stop quick reference treatment offered by Worldmark will continue to be attractive to students and teachers." Wynar. Guide to Ref Bks for Sch Media Centers [Review of the 1971 edition]

910.1 General geography— Indexes

National Geographic Magazine
Handy key to your "National Geographics," subject and picture locater. Underhill, C.S. pa $3.50 910.1
1 National Geographic Magazine—Indexes 2 Pictures—Indexes
Biennial. First published 1954. Since 1962, all issues have been cumulative from 1915
Compiler: 1954- C. S. Underhill
An index to subjects and pictures, including art work, maps and other illustrations, of the National Geographic magazines. Arrangement is alphabetical citing issues, though not specific page references, published in the preceding year. "The arrangement of citations under headings and subheadings is seldom alphabetical. Under certain headings the order is geographical, from north to south, from the Western Hemisphere to the Eastern; under others, such as historical, it is chronological; under others, like Aviation or Birds, it is by types, which may be combined with the other methods. In short, related subjects will usually be found in close proximity, even if the relationship is not stated. As with any reference tool, it takes a little familiarity to use it best. The basic treatment of the 'Geographic' is by region. References here are usually to entire articles. In other headings such as Industry or Sports, citations are usually to parts of articles only and may require some searching in the issues named." Foreword [to the 1974 edition]

910.4 Accounts of travel

Graham, Robin Lee
The boy who sailed around the world alone, by Robin Lee Graham with Derek L. T. Gill; editor: Vera R. Webster; art director: Frances Giannoni. Golden Press 1973 140p illus maps $5.95 (5-7) 910.4
1 Voyages around the world
ISBN 0-307-16510-8
Robin Graham is a Californian who set out on a solo

Graham, Robin Lee—*Continued*
round-the-world voyage in 1967 on a 24-foot sloop.
This book recounts that journey which lasted nearly
five years
"The writing reveals Robin as a modest, wholly
likable boy. Illustrated with color photos from various
sources, including the National Geographic Society."
Pub W

Heyerdahl, Thor
Kon-Tiki; a special Rand McNally color edition for
young people. Rand McNally 1960 165p illus maps pa
$4.95 (4-7)   910.4
1 Kon-Tiki Expedition, 1947 2 Pacific Ocean 3 Ethnology—Polynesia
ISBN 0-528-81865-1
Adapted from the author's: Kon-Tiki; across the
Pacific by raft, published 1948 in Norway, 1950 in the
U.S.
An account of the author's adventures as he sailed
across the Pacific from Peru to Polynesia on a primitive raft attempting to establish the route of the pre-
Inca Indians
"The text has been cut moderately to eliminate
portions merely obstacles to young readers. The
book's size and typography seem perfect for a young-
ster's hands and eyes." Chicago Sunday Trib

McClung, Robert M.
Treasures in the sea. Natl. Geographic Soc. 1972
29p illus map (k-3)   910.4
1 Buried treasure 2 Skin diving
ISBN 0-87044-122-1
Obtainable only as part of a set for $6.95 with:
Dinosaurs, by Kathryn Jackson, class 568; Dogs working for people, by Joanna Foster, class 636.7; and Lion
cubs, by the National Geographic Society, class 599
"Books for young explorers"
Prepared by the Special Publications Division of
the National Geographic Society
Following a description of the sinking of a Spanish
treasure ship and the struggles of pirates for booty,
this book describes how modern divers search for
sunken treasure and the living treasure of the sea life
they encounter
"Here are excellent color photos to complement the
text. . . . A lovely introductory book." Appraisal

Murphy, Barbara Beasley
Thor Heyerdahl and the reed boat Ra [by] Barbara
Beasley Murphy and Norman Baker; foreword by
Thor Heyerdahl. Lippincott 1974 64p illus map $4.95
(4-7)   910.4
1 Ra (Boat) 2 Voyages and travels
ISBN 0-397-31503-1
"Convinced that the similarity between some cultural aspects of life in the ancient Middle East and
among ancient Indians of the New World meant some
communication, Heyerdahl had a papyrus boat built
that duplicated those pictured in Egyptian carvings.
He proposed to sail to America, and he used the trip
also as an opportunity to demonstrate that men from
different cultures could live in amity. The first voyage
was unsuccessful, the second brought the Ra triumphantly into Barbados; the details of the provision, the
accidents and dangers, the way the crew lived and
coped with emergencies is engrossing." Chicago.
Children's Bk Center
"The author's ability to transport the reader into the
feeling of 'being there' should appeal to the reader.
The many photographs taken along the way highlight
this book, and help make this an interesting, informative, current historical event." Best Sellers

Stockton, Frank R.
Buccaneers & pirates of our coasts. Macmillan (N Y)
1967 248p illus $5.95, pa 95¢ (5-7)   910.4
1 Pirates
First published 1898
Here are true accounts of such sea-going scoun-
drels, who plundered North America from the sixteenth through the nineteenth century, as Jean
Lafitte, Henry Morgan, Blackbeard, Captain Kidd,
and others

Villiers, Alan
Men, ships, and the sea, by Alan Villiers and other
adventurers on the sea. New ed. Natl. Geographic
Soc. 1973 436p illus maps (The Story of man lib) $7.95
(6-7)   910.4
1 Ships—History 2 Voyages and travels 3 Seafaring
life
ISBN 0-87044-018-7
A reissue with minor revisions of the 1962 edition
The articles are divided into the following topics:
Man learns to sail; He discovers new worlds; He turns
oceans into highways; He perfects his ships; He employs the power of steam; Man sails again for pleasure
There are "magnificent illustrations in color, black
and white, and monochrome that begin with pictorial
endpapers and continue on almost every
page. . . . There are lists of maritime museums and
of historic ships still to be seen. The selection, of
necessity, is episodic, but it is very good." Library J

Whipple, Addison Beecher Colvin
Famous pirates of the New World; illus. by Robert
Pious. Random House 1958 184p illus maps lib. bdg.
$4.39 (5-7)   910.4
1 Pirates
ISBN 0-394-90535-0
"World Landmark books"
"Blackbeard, Captain Flood, Dixey Bull, women
pirates who wore men's clothes, prayer-saying pirates
out to bring order out of lawlessness and chaos, pirates
who retired and lived their lives out as respectable
citizens are all here. Planks are walked, ships are
sunk, treasures are buried and dug up." Christian Sci
Monitor

912   Atlases

The First book atlas, by the editors and cartographers
of Hammond Incorporated. 3d ed. Watts, F. 1973
96p illus maps lib. bdg. $3.90 (3-6)   912
1 Atlases
ISBN 0-531-00473-2
First published 1960 under firm's earlier name:
C.S. Hammond and Company, Inc.
This atlas "should appeal to the elementary school
child because of its clear maps, simple text, and convenient size. Its area-emphasis reflects the interests
of children , . . inset maps for larger cities and for
products are included for most areas, as are statistics
for area and population. Place names are indexed by
page number and not by their location on individual
maps. A table of facts about the fifty states gives the
capital, popular name, area, and population of each."
Cur Ref Bks [Review of 1968 edition]

Goode's World atlas. Rand McNally illus maps
$12.95   912
1 Atlases 2 Geography, Commercial—Maps
ISBN 0-528-83020-1
All editions, from the first in 1922 to 1949, published with title: Goode's School atlas. Through the
eighth edition compiled by John Paul Goode. 9th

Goode's World atlas—*Continued*
through 13th editions edited by Edward B. Espenshade, Jr. 14th edition edited by Edward B. Espenshade, Jr. and Joel L. Morrison. Periodically revised
"A long time favorite and standard work in schools and educational material centers. One of the best atlas values available and certainly the best inexpensive small atlas for home use. More a true atlas than most works. . . . Very well balanced, includes a wealth of statistical information on climate, soils, resources, industries, population, etc. Especially useful are the maps of cities and their environs. Maps are clear, easily read, usually attractive, beautifully reproduced, with excellent relief features. This atlas is on practically all approved lists." General World Atlases in Print
Includes a glossary

Hammond Citation world atlas. Hammond illus maps $12.95   912
1 Atlases 2 Geography
ISBN 0-8437-1233-3
Periodically revised to bring material up-to-date
Each section concerning a state or country has an index that lists the cities in that area, the population, the map coordinates, and for the United States ZIP code numbers are given. Topographic maps which indicate valleys and mountains of each section are given along with resource area maps indicating dominant land use, minerals and manufacturing assets of the area. Inset maps of major cities are included plus the national flags for foreign countries

Hammond's Illustrated atlas for young America; full color maps and up-to-date facts with new concepts about our physical and political world. Hammond illus. maps $4.50 (4-7)   912
1 Atlases 2 Geography
ISBN 0-8437-1040-3
Published 1956-1965 by the firm under its earlier name: C.S. Hammond and Company, Inc.
Periodically revised to bring material up to date
"A complete guide to map reading, supplemented by useful and interesting geographic and historical sketches covering the world of yesterday, today—and what we can expect tomorrow." Christian Sci Monitor

National Geographic Atlas of the world. Natl. Geographic Soc. illus maps $23.90   912
1 Atlases
ISBN 0-87044-137-X
First published 1963, periodically revised to keep it up to date. Editor-in-chief: Melville Bell Grosvenor
Maps and text of this atlas "treat the world by geographic regions. Each region is discussed first as a unit, followed by individual vignettes of the political divisions that make it up. . . . Statistical digests follow the country summaries. . . . The digest for each country gives its population, in latest figures from the most authoritative source. . . . Here are facts to answer a multitude of queries: The religion and racial background of a nation's people. What the climate is, what industries and natural resources exist. The population—within city limits— of the country's largest city, with other major cities listed after it according to size. And an address to write to for travel or other information from an agency of the country itself." Introduction to fourth edition

Rand McNally Cosmopolitan world atlas. Rand McNally illus maps $24.95   912
1 Atlases
ISBN 0-528-83071-6
First published 1949. Periodically revised. 1965-1967 volumes appeared with title: Rand McNally New Cosmopolitan world atlas

"Map types include physical, political, metropolitan area, and oceanographic. Cartographic information is as . . . complete as practicable. All the maps are well executed, pleasing to the eye, and uncluttered, thus lending themselves to facile reading. . . . There are also lavishly illustrated, informative articles on the atmosphere, geology, and the ocean world. A superior general atlas, with exceptionally comprehensive coverage." Library J [Review of the 1971 edition]

Rhodes, Dorothy
How to read a city map; photography and cartography by Aerial Surveying and Engineering Co. Elk Grove Press 1967 46p illus lib. bdg. $6 (1-4)   912
1 Maps
ISBN 0-516-07517-9
This "elementary introduction to map reading uses matched pairs of aerial photographs and line maps to show how streets, expressways, railroads, parks, buildings, and other features are represented on maps by symbols. Each of 20 common map symbols including compass point signs and scale of miles is illustrated and explained." Booklist
"One knows how many people grow up foreign to maps, and how much they lose. Here is an attractive effort to bring about a change." Scientific Am
Glossary: p46

The World book atlas. Field Enterprises illus maps apply to publisher for price   912
1 Atlases
First published 1963. Frequently revised
"Map types include general reference, historic, physiographic and thematic (i.e., demographic, economic, political, social, etc.) Arrangement is by continent or major geographical region with separate section on the United States, Canada, and the moon. Many graphs and attractive color photos combine effectively with the text to complement the maps (most of which were adapted from Rand McNally's Cosmo series, long popular with school teachers). Population figures for major cities are shown along with a pronouncing gazetteer. Well-constructed, though far from comprehensive." American Ref Bks Annual, 1972 [Review of the 1970 edition]
List of abbreviations and glossary included
For a fuller review see: The Booklist and Subscription Books Bulletin, January 15, 1965

913   Geography of the ancient world

Aylesworth, Thomas G.
(ed.) Mysteries from the past; stories of scientific detection from Nature and Science magazine. Natural Hist. Press 1971 114p illus maps $4.95, lib. bdg. $5.70 (6-7)   913
1 Archeology 2 Anthropology
ISBN 0-385-06796-8; 0-385-06798-4
"Published for the American Museum of Natural History"
Selected from Nature and Science magazine, these articles tell of studies that were carried out to discover the solutions to some scientific mysteries of antiquity. Was there a lost continent of Atlantis? How were the Easter Island stone statues erected? What happened to the Mayas? These are some of the problems discussed
"Archeology buffs and those just beginning to read in this area will find the subjects familiar, although all their origins are not definitely established. The chap-

Aylesworth, Thomas G.—*Continued*
ters are short though adequately comprehensive and, in some instances, arouse enough interest and enthusiasm to make the reader investigate further." Appraisal

Baumann, Hans
The caves of the great hunters. Newly illus. and rev. ed. Pantheon Bks. 1962 183p illus maps lib. bdg. $6.59 (5-7)   913
1 Lascaux Cave, France 2 Art, Primitive 3 Man, Prehistoric
ISBN 0-394-91006-0
Originally published 1953 in Germany
"The story of the discovery and paintings of the prehistoric caves of Europe, many of which were found by children." The AAAS Sci Bk List for Children. 3d edition
"Children will read this book as a good adventure story and will get at the same time a lively introduction to art and archeology." Sat Rev

Clymer, Eleanor
The second greatest invention; search for the first farmers; illus. by Lili Réthi. Holt 1969 117p illus map lib. bdg. $3.59 (5-7)   913
1 Man, Prehistoric 2 Agriculture—History 3 Archeology
ISBN 0-03-072390-6
"Tools were the first great invention that made it possible for primitive men to survive; the second greatest invention was the planned food production that led to settled communities, diversification of function, and the consequent beginnings of civilization. In a crisp, matter-of-fact examination of archeological findings, the author moves further and further backward in time, following the scientific evidence of early farming. The illustrations and index add to the book's usefulness, but more appealing is the element of suspense in the true and exciting pursuit of knowledge about the agricultural communities of primitive men." Sat Rev

Cohen, Daniel
Ancient monuments and how they were built; drawings by Judith Gwyn Brown. McGraw 1971 96p illus lib. bdg. $4.72 (6-7)   913
1 Civilization, Ancient 2 Architecture, Ancient 3 Monuments
ISBN 0-07-011567-2
The author discusses probable methods used in the construction of seven of the world's ancient monuments—The Tower of Babel; the pyramids; Stonehenge; the Nazca drawings in Peru; Sacsahuaman, the Inca fortress at Cuzco; the Easter Island statues; and Zimbabwe, the ruined stone city in southern Africa
"The book's value is in its treatment of the lesser known monuments and in its brevity which make it a possible reference source. An index and carefully selected bibliography are included." Appraisal

Dickinson, Alice
The first book of stone age man; pictures by Lorence Bjorklund. Watts, F. 1962 82p illus lib. bdg. $3.90 (4-7)   913
1 Man, Prehistoric 2 Stone age
ISBN 0-531-00643-3
The book "traces the development of man from our earliest record of him—Zinjanthropus—to 'Homo sapiens,' and the beginning of recorded history. Follows his increasing intelligence and use of tools and metals, and the physical changes which took place over a period of about a million years." The AAAS Sci Bk List for Children

"Arrangement is chronological, with a few introductory pages in which the author attempts to show the great age of the earth itself, how man has learned of its development and has come to inquire into his own pre-history. . . . The book is readable, well illustrated, up to date; and seems based on sound scholarship." Sch Library J
Other books to read: p78

Freeman, Mae Blacker
Finding out about the past; illus. with photographs. Random House 1967 79p illus $2.95, lib. bdg. $3.87 (3-5)   913
1 Archeology
ISBN 0-394-80144-X; 0-394-90144-4
"Gateway books"
"The author gives a step-by-step description of the work of archaeologists, expanded to show the development of early civilizations through the discovery of the Dead Sea Scrolls, Swiss lake houses, Lascaux Cave, Machu Picchu, Pompeii and others." Bruno. Bks for Sch Libraries, 1968
"A welcome addition to the social studies curriculum. . . . A topical index and encompassing table of contents augment the excellent text. A good beginning book that will prepare young children for the many books on archaeology which start at slightly higher grade levels." Sch Library J

Hall, Jennie
Buried cities. Rev. under the editorship of Lily Poritz; introduction by Katharine Taylor. Macmillan (N Y) 1964 116p illus lib. bdg. $4.95 (5-7)   913
1 Excavations (Archeology) 2 Cities and towns, Ruined, extinct, etc.
First published 1922
"The book contains a description of daily life in four buried cities: Pompeii, Herculaneum, Olympia, and Mycenae, with major emphasis on Pompeii. A chapter on the discovery of each site and the digging by archeologists is preceded by a simple story in the sections on Pompeii and Olympia; Mycenae is revealed through a fictionalized account of Schliemann's excavation, and a brief history of the discovery of Herculaneum. . . . [is included]. The revised edition is without condescension and reads more smoothly than the original. Many excellent new photographs and illustrations are now interspersed through the text." Library J

913.32   Geography of Egypt
to 640 A.D.

Cottrell, Leonard
Land of the Pharaohs; illus. by Richard M. Powers. Collins 1960 127p illus map lib. bdg. $5.91 (6-7)
913.32
1 Egypt—Antiquities 2 Tutenkhamun, King of Egypt
ISBN 0-529-03612-6
"A vivid picture of a significant period in the history of ancient Egypt emerges from this richly detailed book. Prefaced and concluded with descriptions of the investigations that have given us the knowldge of the period, the body of the text deals with the Egyptian scene at the time of Tutankhamen's reign. The black and white illustrations (based on ornamentation found in the tomb of the Pharoah) are stylized and handsome. The author has quoted several passages from scrolls of inscriptions; the fact that these are still pertinent and humorous make the Egyptians of three

Cottrell, Leonard—*Continued*
thousand years ago seem the more real." Chicago. Children's Bk Center
Books for further reading: p124. Index and glossary: p125

Robinson, Charles Alexander
The first book of ancient Egypt, by Charles Alexander Robinson, Jr. Pictures by Lili Réthi. Watts, F. 1961 61p illus map lib. bdg. $3.90 (4-7)   913.32
1 Egypt—Antiquities 2 Egypt—Civilization
ISBN 0-531-00462-7
The author "gives an outline of Egyptian history from its beginning to its fall, 1085 B.C., showing Egyptian daily life, religion, science and art. The book is unusually well illustrated with pencil drawings in colour." Ontario Library Rev

Van Duyn, Janet
The Egyptians; pharaohs and craftsmen; illus. in black and white and full color. McGraw [1971] 176p illus maps (Early culture ser) lib. bdg. $7.71 (6-7)   913.32
1 Egypt—Civilization 2 Egypt—Antiquities
ISBN 0-07-067036-6
The author describes life in ancient Egypt and the legacy of Egyptian civilization as revealed through archeological discoveries
Suggested reading: p172-73

913.35 Geography of Mesopotamia and Iranian Plateau to 642 A.D.

Baumann, Hans
In the land of Ur; the discovery of ancient Mesopotamia; tr. by Stella Humphries. Pantheon Bks. 1969 166p illus map lib. bdg. $6.29 (6-7)   913.35
1 Mesopotamia—Antiquities 2 Mesopotamia—Civilization
ISBN 0-394-90807-4
Original German edition, 1968
This "introduction to the early history of the 'land between the two rivers,' Mesopotamia, recounts the archaeological discoveries of the ruins of ziggurats and palaces and whole cities long buried under the shifting sands. . . . There are also: a glossary of the words, places, and people; a list of the more famous explorers of Mesopotamia; a chronological listing of the major excavations; a chronological table with the names of the kings; and a map of the area." Best Sellers
It "is necessarily a fragmentary account. Still, it is somewhat redeemed. . . .by Mr. Baumann's apt use of quotations from the cuneiform records, so many of which were found in the Assyrian Library of Ashurbanipal, and by the similarly apt choice of color photos and line drawings." NY Times Bk Rev

Collins, Robert
The Medes and Persians; conquerors and diplomats; illus. in black and white and full color. McGraw [1972] 176p illus maps (Early culture ser) lib. bdg. $7.71 (6-7)   913.35
1 Iran—Antiquities 2 Iran—Civilization
ISBN 0-07-011813-2
The Persians and their forerunners the Medes have often been characterized as blood-thirsty villains. The author, using recent archeological finds and language breakthroughs, presents their achievements, failures and contributions to civilization by exposing the reader to their art, culture, customs and ways of life in both war and peace
Suggested reading: p172

Gregor, Arthur S.
How the world's first cities began; illus. by W. T. Mars. Dutton 1967 64p illus map lib. bdg. $5.50 (4-6)   913.35
1 Mesopotamia—Civilization 2 Cities and towns—History
ISBN 0-525-32417-8
In this book which focuses on the Mesopotamian civilization, the author unfolds the story of the long and gradual development of the first cities. Here also is the story of the emergence of civilization
"The illustrations are adequate; the book is written in an easy, conversational style." Chicago. Children's Bk Center

Lansing, Elizabeth
The Sumerians; inventors and builders; illus. in black and white and full color. McGraw [1971] 176p illus map (Early culture ser) lib. bdg. $7.71 (6-7)   913.35
1 Sumerians
ISBN 0-07-036357-9
The book presents "the panorama of Sumerian civilization, and its technological and aesthetic contribution . . . uncovered by archaeologists only in this century after over four thousand years of silence." Introduction
"Handsomely illustrated with photographs, many in full color, that show the artifacts, art objects, and architecture of the Sumerians, this study of their culture is written competently, in a straightforward but informal style. . . . The high gloss of the pages is a weakness of an otherwise excellent survey. A reading list and a relative index are appended." Chicago. Children's Bk Center

Neurath, Marie
They lived like this in ancient Mesopotamia. Artist: Evelyn Worboys. Watts, F. [1965 c1964] 32p illus map lib. bdg. $3.90 (3-5)   913.35
1 Mesopotamia—Civilization 2 Sumerians
ISBN 0-531-01383-9
First published 1964 in England
A book "about the Assyrian, Babylonian, and Sumerian cultures, in a continuous text with illustrations that capture the feeling of the original art and artifacts on which they are based. The text begins abruptly with an awkward first page that would be clearer were there a map; there is a map on the last page. This is, however, a minor weakness in an otherwise competent description of life in the land between the two rivers, of the houses, transportation, religion, the development of cuneiform writing, and of the number system." Chicago. Children's Bk Center

Robinson, Charles Alexander
The first book of ancient Mesopotamia and Persia, by Charles Alexander Robinson, Jr. Illus. with maps and photographs. Watts, F. 1962 61p illus maps lib. bdg. $3.90 (4-7)   913.35
1 Mesopotamia—Civilization
ISBN 0-531-00465-1
This is "an introduction to the earliest civilization—Sumeria, Babylonia, Assyria, and Persia—in readable text." Hodges. Bks for Elem Sch Libraries
"Photographs of architectural discoveries enhance the inherent fascination of the study." Horn Bk

Weisgard, Leonard
The beginnings of cities; re-creation in pictures and text of Mesopotamian life from farming to early city building. Coward-McCann 1968 61p illus maps (Life long ago) lib. bdg. $4.69 (6-7)   913.35

Weisgard, Leonard—*Continued*

1 Mesopotamia—Antiquities 2 Cities and towns, Ruined, extinct, etc.
ISBN 0-698-30022-X

The author conjectures that communal living in the Tigris-Euphrates Valley sparked trade and therefore record keeping, the alphabet, taxation, and transportation. There is information on Sumerian religion and many drawings of artifacts

913.362   Geography of British Isles to 5th century A.D.

Pittenger, W. Norman

Early Britain: the Celts, Romans, and Anglo-Saxons; illus. by Errol le Cain. Watts, F. 1972 76p illus maps lib. bdg. $3.90 (5-7)   913.362

1 Great Britain—Antiquities
ISBN 0-531-00742-1

"A First book"

The author discusses the influence of the Celts, Romans, and Anglo-Saxons on the history, culture, religion, and way of life of early Britain

A selected bibliography: p71

913.37   Geography of Italian peninsula and adjacent territories to 476 A.D.

Robinson, Charles Alexander

The first book of ancient Rome [by] Charles Alexander Robinson, Jr. [Rev. ed] Watts, F. [1965 c1964] 66p illus maps lib. bdg. $3.90 (5-7)   913.37

1 Rome—History 2 Rome—Civilization
ISBN 0-531-00466-X

First published 1959

Contents: The founding of Rome; The Roman Republic; Hannibal; Trouble in the State; Daily life in Rome; Julius Caesar; Cicero; Augustus and the Roman Empire; Literature and art in the Augustan Age; After Augustus; Constantine and Christianity; Rome's legacy; Words inherited from the Romans

"Keeping in mind that this is a 'first' book, with no pretensions of being comprehensive, much ground is covered in brief span. . . . This fills a definite need on this lower grade level." Library J

913.38   Geography of Greece to 323 A.D.

Boyer, Sophia A.

Gifts from the Greeks; alpha to omega, by Sophia A. Boyer and Winifred Lubell. Rand McNally 1970 144p illus maps $5.95, lib. bdg. $5.79 (6-7) 913.38

1 Civilization, Greek 2 Greece—Antiquities
ISBN 0-528-82132-6; 0-528-80501-0

"An unusual presentation of the many facets of life in ancient Greece. Twenty-four separate sections of the book are arranged to follow the order of the letters of the Greek alphabet, each letter being the initial of a Greek word which becomes the springboard for the ensuing discussion. Despite the unusual arrangement of topics—such as 'Athletes, Geometry, Democracy,

Crete, The Lyre, Philosophy'—the whole range of Hellenic experience is explored simply, accurately, and significantly. Most of the illustrations, found on at least every other page, 'were redrawn from paintings on ancient Greek pottery,' and there are also some excellent photographs, especially of sculpture. Many of the illustrations reveal activities of everyday life, and all of the illustrations give the book an unusual feeling of verve." Horn Bk

For further reading: p136-37

Fenton, Sophia Harvati

Greece; a book to begin on; illus. by Joseph Low. Holt 1969 unp illus map $3.50, lib. bdg. $3.27 (1-4)   913.38

1 Greece 2 Civilization, Greek
ISBN 0-03-072425-2; 0-03-072430-9

This study of Greece, which emphasizes the ancient period, includes information about Greek history, geography, society, government, religion, and culture

Robinson, Charles Alexander

The first book of ancient Greece, by Charles Alexander Robinson, Jr. Pictures by Lili Réthi. Watts, F. 1960 61p illus maps lib. bdg. $3.90 (5-7) 913.38

1 Civilization, Greek 2 Greece—Antiquities
ISBN 0-531-00465-3

"Robinson points out succinctly contributions of his ancient subject to life today, its role as creator 'of what we call Western civilization.' His survey of mythology, historical events, daily life, art, drama, and philosophy is brief, but of interest and value for first reading on the subject. Maps, index, lively and informative two-color sketches, and a glossary of words inherited from the Greeks [are included]." Horn Bk

Rockwell, Anne

Temple on a hill; the building of the Parthenon. Atheneum Pubs. 1969 108p illus maps $5.95 (4-7)   913.38

1 Athens. Parthenon 2 Civilization, Greek
ISBN 0-689-20619-4

"The book deals not only with the actual building of the Parthenon but envisions its construction as a fitting climax to the rise and development of a humanistic Athens during and after the Persian invasion of Greece; due weight is given to the personalities of Themistocles, Pericles, and Phidias. Atlhough the text makes use of material from Herodotus and Thucydides, the style of the narrative is direct and vigorous, and meets the requirements of the architectural subject by a detailed use of traditional architectural terminology. Full respect is paid to the use of the optical devices embodied in the Parthenon and acknowledgment is made of the mathematical basis of its proportions. The line drawings, diagrams, and maps are explanatory rather than decorative, and the author relies essentially on her words to evoke the Panathenaic Procession or to explain the present location of most of the Parthenon sculptures." Horn Bk

Van Duyn, Janet

The Greeks; their legacy; illus. in black and white and full color. McGraw [1972] 192p illus maps (Early culture ser) lib. bdg. $7.71 (6-7)   913.38

1 Civilization, Greek 2 Greece—Antiquities

The author traces the cultural heritage of ancient Greece, including the growth of democracy, the evolution of the theatre, the beginnings of scientific and philosophical investigation, and the start of the Olympic games

Suggested reading: p187-88

914.1 Geography of Scotland

Sasek, M.
This is Edinburgh. Macmillan (N Y) 1961 59p illus $5.95 (3-6)   914.1
1 Edinburgh—Description
The author/illustrator "has caught the greyness of the city, the misty, romantic aura surrounding Castle Rock and the bustle of Princes Street perfectly. He seems to have enjoyed painting an enormous variety of tartans, and they give the book a special charm." Pub W

914.15 Geography of Ireland

O'Brien, Elinor
The land and people of Ireland. Rev. ed. Lippincott 1972 159p illus map (Portraits of the nations ser) $5.95 (5-7)   914.15
1 Ireland
ISBN 0-397-31299-7
First published 1953
This is an introduction to the history, geography, culture and people of Ireland

Sasek, M.
This is Ireland. Macmillan (N Y) [1965 c1964] 59p illus map $4.95 (3-6)   914.15
1 Ireland
First published 1964 in England
In this pictorial tour of Ireland, the author-artist describes the country's history, geography, cathedrals, colleges and universities, landmarks of Irish history and civilization, and people. "Shamrocks, shillelaghs and sheep, bathed in all-pervading green and accompanied by harps, jaunting carts and a leprecaun or two, enliven this gay, bright and pleasantly conventional book." Bk Week
The text "consists chiefly of brief captions (a phrase, a sentence, or at most a few paragraphs) for utterly charming [watercolor] pictures. The book has a little less cohesion than do the books about individual cities, but it does convey atmosphere and give information. . . . It is delightful for browsing." Chicago. Children's Bk Center

914.2 Geography of the British Isles

Branley, Franklyn M.
The mystery of Stonehenge; illus. by Victor G. Ambrus. Crowell 1969 51p illus maps $4.50, lib. bdg. $5.25 (4-7)   914.2
1 Stonehenge
ISBN 0-690-57046-5; 0-690-57047-3
"How long did men toil to build the still-impressive ring of massive stones on the Salisbury plain? How did they do it, and what was it for? Scientists can only conjecture, save for the time of building, now determined by carbon-14 dating to have been approximately 1800 B.C. The author discusses the various theories about the ways in which primitive men might have made the stone pillars, brought them to the site, and erected them. He describes the tentative answers as to the reason for its existence: the possibility that it had religious significance or was used for astronomical observation. Fascinating material in a lucid, measured book, the handsome illustrations and diagrams making vivid the massive effort that went into the building of Stonehenge." Chicago. Children's Bk Center

Duggan, Alfred
Growing up with the Norman Conquest; illus. by C. Walter Hodges. Pantheon Bks. [1966 c1965] 217p illus $3.95, lib. bdg. $5.69 (6-7)   914.2
1 England—Social life and customs 2 Great Britain—History—Norman period, 1066-1154
ISBN 0-394-81206-9; 0-394-91206-3
First published 1965 in England
This book describes the daily life of children during the reign of William the Conquer/or at various economic levels "in a Norman castle, a Saxon hall, a London house, an abbey, a peasant village. Food, clothing, recreation, education, and daily work routines are all shown . . . also, the growing complexity of the lives of these people, as language, law, and age-old custom felt the breath of change." Christian Sci Monitor
Mr. Duggan's writing displays "delightful wit, and the easy familiarity with detail that is born only of deep knowledge." Chicago. Children's Bk Center

Gidal, Sonia
My village in England [by] Sonia and Tim Gidal. Pantheon Bks. 1963 83p illus maps $3.50, lib. bdg. $5.67 (4-6)   914.2
1 England—Social life and customs
ISBN 0-394-81902-0; 0-394-91902-5
Maps by Anne Marie Jauss
"Written as though told by the boy, this narrative description of the daily lives of Nicholas Lansbury, his sister, and parents in the village of Temple Grafton in Warwickshire County presents a good picture of the English home and village, the surrounding countryside, and nearby historical landmarks. The many photographs are excellent and the text is fairly animated despite the use of the present tense in its narration." Booklist
Glossary: p81

Hinds, Lorna
Looking at Great Britain. Lippincott 1973 64p illus maps (Looking at other countries) $5.95 (4-6)   914.2
1 Great Britain
ISBN 0-397-31335-7
This is an introduction to the history, geography, people, customs, and industries of Great Britain
"The attractive format—photographs, half in color, appear on every page—is the outstanding feature of this supplemental book. The pictures are well synchronized with the text which combines geography with a short travelogue on England, Wales, and Scotland. . . . British terms are used in the text; however, there is no glossary to explain 'firth,' 'moor,' etc." Sch Library J

Kirtland, G. B.
One day in Elizabethan England; drawings by Jerome Snyder. . . . Harcourt 1962 38p illus $3.95 (2-5)   914.2
1 England—Social life and customs
ISBN 0-15-258368-8
"The place: England. The time: 1590. The characters: you." Title page
"Elizabethan words and phrases are woven into a light-hearted picture of two children in a Manor House, during the reign of Elizabeth I. The book describes their rising, breakfast, lessons, play and the preparations for the arrival of the queen herself on a Royal Progress. Amusing line drawings." Ontario Library Rev
Includes a glossary

Sasek, M.

This is historic Britain. Macmillan Pub. Co. 1974 60p illus map lib. bdg. $6.95 (3-6)   914.2

1 Great Britain—Description and travel 2 Great Britain—History

ISBN 0-02-778200-X

In pictures and text, the author/illustrator presents a tour of famous and historic places, buildings and monuments in England, Wales and Scotland, with brief comments on the events and personalities associated with these sites

"The book can serve as an adjunct to a historical unit of the curriculum, but the primary appeal is visual: carefully detailed and accurate paintings in restrained color of the period architecture found in castles, cathedrals, and historic buildings." Chicago. Children's Bk Center

Streatfeild, Noel

The Thames; London's river; illus. by Kurt Wiese; maps by Fred Kliem. Garrard 1964 96p illus map (Rivers of the world) lib. bdg. $3.68 (4-6)   914.2

1 Thames River 2 London—Description

ISBN 0-8116-6362-0

"Describes the Thames from its source, and how it becomes a great river by the time it empties into the North Sea. Its history includes peoples, buildings and river traffic." Sch Library J

"A book that gives a great deal of specific detail and that has some vivid passages of writing, but is weakened by the loose organization of material and by digressions into ancillary subject matter. . . . Interesting but spotty." Chicago. Children's Bk Center

Street, Alicia

The land and people of England. Rev. ed. Lippincott 1969 155p illus map (Portraits of the nations ser) $5.95 (5-7)   914.2

1 England—Description and travel

ISBN 0-397-31373-X

First published 1946 with title: The land of the English people

The book discusses England's history, geographical area, social life and customs, natural resources, agriculture and industry

914.21   Geography of London

Sasek, M.

This is London. Macmillan (N Y) 1959 60p illus $4.95 (3-6)   914.21

1 London—Description

This picture travel book "describes in sprightly text and handsome, vividly colored illustrations [by the author] the delights of London. [Sasek] has included such points of interest as St. Paul's Cathedral and the British Museum, but he has given almost equal importance to such everyday sights as the mail boxes and Smith's bookstalls. He has not neglected any of the things with special appeal for the young, the various kinds of guards' uniforms, for example, and the double decker busses." Pub W

914.3   Geography of Germany

Fles, Barthold

East Germany. Watts, F. 1973 64p illus maps lib. bdg. $3.45 (5-7)   914.3

1 Germany (Democratic Republic)

ISBN 0-531-00807-X

"A First book"

Illustrated with photographs

"After a brief summary of events, post World War II, that led to the growth of the GDR (Communist German Democratic Republic), the author . . . traces 'political, industrial, social, and cultural development of East Germany.' The Berlin Wall, labor troubles, rebuilding industries and homes, commodity shortages, educational restructuring, cultural changes based on a government-centered atmosphere rather than on individual-oriented goals [are all described]." Best Sellers

Bibliography: p62

Gidal, Sonia

My village in Germany [by] Sonia and Tim Gidal. Pantheon Bks. 1964 85p illus maps $3.95, lib. bdg. $5.67 (4-6)   914.3

1 Germany (Federal Republic)—Social life and customs

ISBN 0-394-81901-2; 0-394-91901-7

Black and white photographs illustrate the daily life and activities of Markus and Robert, young apprentice masons, who "live in the beautiful village of Mittenwald high in the Bavarian Alps. While Markus aspires to become a mountain guide, Robert wants above all to attend the local violin-making school for which Mittenwald has been famous throughout the world since the seventeenth century. . . . [In this account, they] enjoy the prankish spring festival of Crazy Thursday." p 1

Glossary: p83

Kirby, George

Looking at Germany. Lippincott 1972 64p illus maps (Looking at other countries) $5.95, lib. bdg. $5.79 (4-6)   914.3

1 Germany (Federal Republic)

ISBN 0-397-31338-1; 0-397-31337-3

This "account of West Germany covers the people, their language, types of food and drink, geography and landmarks, characteristics of different regions, etc." Sch Library J

"Useful mainly for its attractive and interesting details." Minnesota

Lobsenz, Norman M.

The first book of West Germany. Rev. ed. Illus. with photographs. Watts, F. 1972 90p illus map lib. bdg. $3.90 (4-7)   914.3

1 Germany (Federal Republic)

ISBN 0-531-00668-9

First published 1959

Contents: The land and its history; The people and their cities; Highways and byways; Going to school in West Germany; Sports and games; Fun and festivals; Germany today; A few famous Germans; Simple German words and phrases; The Länder of the Federal Republic of Germany

Wohlrabe, Raymond A.

The land and people of Germany, by Raymond A. Wohlrabe and Werner E. Krusch. Rev. ed. Lippincott 1972 159p illus map (Portraits of the nations ser) $5.95 (5-7)   914.3

1 Germany

ISBN 0-397-31261-X

First published 1957

This introduction to Germany, past and present, describes the history, geography, economy, culture and people of the Federal Republic of Germany as well as the German Democratic Republic

914.36 Geography of Austria

Wohlrabe, Raymond A.
The land and people of Austria, by Raymond A. Wohlrabe and Werner E. Krusch. Rev. ed. Lippincott 1972 159p illus map (Portraits of the nations ser) lib. bdg. $5.95 (5-7)   914.36
1 Austria
ISBN 0-397-31395-0
First published 1956
An introduction to the people, history, geography, and culture of the European country known for its famous composers and scenic beauty, particularly the Alps, and the Danube region

914.37 Geography of Czechoslovakia

Hall, Elvajean
The land and people of Czechoslovakia. [Rev] Lippincott [1972 c1966] 154p illus map (Portraits of the nations ser) $5.95 (5-7)   914.37
1 Czechoslovak Republic
ISBN 0-397-31601-1
First published 1966
This "account describes the geographic features and complex history of Czechoslovakia and the varied cultural heritage of the people. The book also describes the formation of the nation following World War I, the tragic events leading to and during the German occupation of the country under Hitler, the establishment of a communist government after World War II, and the effect of communism on present-day Czechoslovakian life and customs." Booklist [Review of the 1966 edition]

914.38 Geography of Poland

Brandys, Marian
Poland; photographs by Wieslaw Prazuch. Doubleday 1974 156p illus maps $4.95, lib. bdg. $5.70 (6-7)   914.38
1 Poland
ISBN 0-385-07200-7; 0-385-02273-5
A survey of the geography and history of Poland, describing its cities, the people's resistance to foreign invaders, and the country's post war industrial development

Kelly, Eric Philbrook
The land and people of Poland. Rev. by Dragos D. Kostich. Rev. ed. Lippincott 1972 143p illus map (Portraits of the nations ser) $5.95 (5-7)   914.38
1 Poland
ISBN 0-397-31313-6
First published 1943 with title: The land of the Polish people
This book covers Poland's history, the cities of Krakow and Warsaw as they were before the past war and as they are today, people of the past and the present, folklore, and social life and customs. Includes keys to pronunciation

914.39 Geography of Hungary

Dormandy, Clara
Hungary in pictures. Sterling 1974 64p illus maps (Visual geography ser) lib. bdg. $3.39, pa $1.75 (5-7)   914.39
1 Hungary
ISBN 0-8069-1128-X; 0-8069-1129-8
First published 1970
Supplemented with photographs, the book offers a look at the past and present of the Hungarian people, their culture and way of life

Gidal, Sonia
My village in Hungary. Pantheon Bks. 1974 86p illus maps lib. bdg. $5.67 (3-6)   914.39
1 Hungary—Social life and customs
ISBN 0-394-92127-5
"Zoltán Sardi, a Hungarian farmer's son, describes his family, village, and country. Gidal follows him to school, to the commune where he is researching a homework assignment, and to the homes of friends. An excellent addition to the series, this boasts exceptional black-and-white photographs, a glossary of Hungarian words used, and maps of Hungary as well as Zoltán's village." Sch Library J

914.4 Geography of France

Bragdon, Lillian J.
The land and people of France. Rev. ed. Lippincott 1972 157p illus map (Portraits of the nations ser) lib. bdg. $5.95 (5-7)   914.4
1 France
ISBN 0-397-31190-7
First published 1939 with title: The land of Joan of Arc
The author describes the geography of France from the metropolitan centers to the famous resort areas and provinces. Also provided is a discussion of France's complex history

Church, R. J. Harrison
Looking at France. Lippincott 1970 64p illus (Looking at other countries) $5.95 (4-6)   914.4
1 France
ISBN 0-397-31135-4
"The book contains a good deal of interesting information for young students of France and its customs. French cities, famous historical monuments, and the characteristics of different rural areas are systematically and on the whole effectively described. Endpaper maps of major thoroughfares and products are a bonus." Library J

Sasek, M.
This is Paris. Macmillan (N Y) 1959 60p illus $3.95 (3-6)   914.4
1 Paris—Description
Illustrated by the author, this picture book presents "a potpourri of Parisian landmarks and life. The famous and the commonplace, the old and the new are all mixed together in that exciting jumble in which they present themselves to the actual visitor: the Eiffel Tower, subways, bistros, street merchants, cats, lampposts, much more." Library J

914.5   Geography of Italy

Epstein, Sam
The first book of Italy. Rev. ed. by Sam and Beryl
Epstein; illus. with photographs. Watts, F. 1972 90p
illus map lib. bdg. $3.90 (4-7)   914.5
    1 Italy
    ISBN 0-531-00562-3
    First published 1958
    The book provides a "description of the religion,
art, education, crafts, living conditions, and politics of
the Italian people, with geographical and historical
facts interwoven throughout." Sch Library J

Martin, Rupert
Looking at Italy. Lippincott [1967 c1966] 64p illus
maps (Looking at other countries) $5.95 (4-6) 914.5
    1 Italy
    ISBN 0-397-30966-X
    First published 1966 in England
    The "text covers the country, people, cities, moun-
tains and lakes, harbors, education, art, music and
history. Maps on end papers." Bruno. Bks for Sch
Libraries, 1968
    The book is "enhanced by numerous fine photo-
graphs many of which are in color." Booklist

Sasek, M.
This is Rome. Macmillan (N Y) 1960 60p illus $5.95
(3-6)   914.5
    1 Rome (City)—Description
    The author-artist provides a "panoramic view of
Rome with many interesting close-ups of her people,
buildings, and great art." Library J
    This volume "is oversize and is filled with beautiful
and humorous paintings of both famous landmarks
and typical local touches. It is informational, it is
evocative and nostalgic." Chicago. Children's Bk
Center

This is Venice. Macmillan (N Y) 1961 56p illus $4.95
(3-6)   914.5
    1 Venice—Description
    "Mr. Sasek's text combines history, description,
special tips to travelers, and statistics—such as the
dimensions of a gondola. His illustrations . . . are the
key to the city, and take one up and down the waterways and alleyways, showing the pigeons, palaces and
piazzas." N Y Times Bk Rev
    "The romantic background of Venice, both histori-
cal and present-day, naturally makes this . . . an
especially fascinating volume. His paintings have
their usual brilliance and flavor and, accompanied by
humorous text, ensure a wide range of interest again."
Horn Bk

Winwar, Frances
The land and people of Italy. Rev. ed. Lippincott
1972 159p illus map (Portraits of the nations ser) $5.95
(5-7)   914.5
    1 Italy
    ISBN 0-397-31300-4
    First published 1951 with title: The land of the
Italian people
    This survey of Italian geography, culture and his-
tory offers information on the Renaissance, industry,
literature, art, and notable Italians, including Marco
Polo, Columbus, Michelangelo, and Mussolini

914.6   Geography of Spain

Goldston, Robert
Spain. Watts, F. 1972 88p illus maps lib. bdg. $3.90
(4-7)   914.6
    1 Spain
    ISBN 0-531-00781-2
    "A First book"
    The author describes the geography, history,
industry, people, culture and projected future of
Spain
    He "emphasizes the many changes which have
taken place in Spain and tells how the tourist boom has
influenced the country's economy in recent years.
Well illustrated with black-and-white photographs
and three maps." Booklist

Loder, Dorothy
The land and people of Spain. Rev. ed. Lippincott
1972 157p illus map (Portraits of the nations ser) lib.
bdg. $5.95 (5-7)   914.6
    1 Spain
    ISBN 0-397-31396-6
    First published 1955
    This book describes the history and civilization of
Spain, with accounts of its foreign domination, influences, religion, and political conflicts from the times
of the Romans, through the Moors and Napoleon to
the Civil War and contemporary factions. Places of
note are described, and attention is given to the country's commerce, industry and natural resources, and
the life of the people
    "An especially interesting aspect of the account is
the introduction of outstanding writers and artists,
with a discussion of how their work reflects the section
of the country in which each lived or the temper of the
times in which each one worked." Chicago. Children's Bk Center [Review of the 1955 edition]

Martin, Rupert
Looking at Spain. Lippincott [1970 c1969] 64p illus
(Looking at other countries) $5.95 (4-6)   914.6
    1 Spain
    ISBN 0-397-31137-0
    First copyright 1969
    The author describes cities, churches, shrines,
agriculture, climate, geography, and the way of life of
the Spanish people
    The book "might be described as an attractively
produced junior travel guide. It includes some paragraphs on the bullfight." Times (London) Literary
Sup
    Maps on lining-papers

914.7   Geography of Eastern Europe. Russia

Morton, Miriam
Pleasures and palaces; the after-school activities of
Russian children. Atheneum Pubs. 1972 136p illus
map $5.25 (4-7)   914.7
    1 Children in Russia
    ISBN 0-689-30057-3
    This is an account of the activity circles or kruzhki,
sponsored by the Young Pioneers to help Soviet children decide on future careers. These meetings are
held in pioneer palaces, hence the title, and serve as
an after-school activity for children to enjoy

Morton, Miriam—*Continued*
"Motivated Soviet students are described in the various career activities that are offered—not unlike the current emphasis on career education courses in the United States. An interesting aspect is the apparent lack of stereotyped sex roles in career orientation." Notable Children's Trade Bks (Social Studies)

Nazaroff, Alexander
The land and people of Russia. [Rev] Lippincott [1972 c1966] 190p illus maps (Portraits of the nations ser) $5.95, lib. bdg. $5.95 (5-7)   914.7
1 Russia
ISBN 0-397-30706-3; 0-397-31207-5
First published 1944 with title: The land of the Russian people
A survey of Russia's history from the earliest times through rule by the czars and emperors to the present Soviets. It describes also the country's vast and varied terrain, including Siberia, Moscow, Leningrad and western Russia

Picture map geography of the USSR; illus by Thomas R. Funderburk. Lippincott 1969 165p illus maps $4.95, lib. bdg. $5.19 (4-6)   914.7
1 Russia
ISBN 0-397-31096-X; 0-397-31097-8
"After a brief general summary of Russian geography, history, and political organization, Nazaroff describes the physical features, climate, resources, economy, and ethnic character of different areas of European and Asian Russia. Terse in treatment but comprehensive in coverage and illustrated with regional maps showing products, physical features, and location of major cities." Booklist

Rice, Tamara Talbot
Finding out about the early Russians; introduction by Harrison E. Salisbury. Lothrop [1964 c1962] 168p illus maps $4.75 (6-7)   914.7
1 Russia—Antiquities 2 Russia—Civilization
ISBN 0-688-41233-5
First published 1963 in England. Line drawings by Margaret Scott, maps by Ursula Suess
"Russian history from 3000 B.C. to the time of Peter the Great is surveyed with special attention to the Russian influence on world art, architecture, and religion. Maps and numerous photographs and paintings illustrate the text." Hodges. Bks for Elem Sch Libraries

Snyder, Louis L.
The first book of the Soviet Union. Rev. ed. Watts, F. 1972 84p illus map lib. bdg. $3.90 (5-7)   914.7
1 Russia
ISBN 0-531-00638-7
First published 1959
The author traces the history of the Soviet Union from czarist rule through the revolution of 1917 to the modern Communist state. Also detailed are the stages in Soviet space exploration. Facts about geography, education, and activities of the people complete this presentation

914.71   Geography of Finland

Berry, Erick
The land and people of Finland. Rev. ed. Lippincott 1972 159p illus map (Portraits of the nations ser) $5.95 (5-7)   914.71
1 Finland
ISBN 0-397-31255-5

First published 1959
An introduction to the history, geography, social conditions and people of Finland

914.8   Geography of Scandinavia

Carter, Samuel
Vikings bold: their voyages & adventures, by Samuel Carter III; illus. by Ted Burwell. Crowell 1972 195p illus maps $4.50 (5-7)   914.8
1 Northmen
ISBN 0-690-86191-5
The author describes the life of the Vikings on land and sea, including their advanced form of democracy, their great leaders, their military triumphs and rare defeats, and their westward journeys which brought them to Iceland, Greenland, and eventually the coast of North America
Selected further reading: p189-90

Rich, Louise Dickinson
The first book of the Vikings; pictures by Lili Réthi. Watts, F. 1962 66p illus map lib. bdg. $3.90 (4-6)   914.8
1 Northmen
ISBN 0-531-00660-3
Here is "the life of the Vikings at home and abroad: their democratic organization, laws, games, their ships, their love of the sea and the feeling of brotherhood expressed in their sagas, all told in a manner that stirs the imagination and conveys the author's own interest in her subject. Illustrations are black-and-white pen drawings, and are useful for school projects." Ontario Library Rev
"Much more information about the Vikings than is usually found in books for elementary schools. . . . No bibliography, unfortunately." Horn Bk

914.81   Geography of Norway

Ashby, Gwynneth
Looking at Norway. Lippincott 1967 63p illus (Looking at other countries) lib. bdg. $5.79 (4-6)   914.81
1 Norway
ISBN 0-397-30964-3
The author describes many aspects of Norwegian life: the land and cities; the people, their lives and entertainment; traditional festivals; transport, farming, and industry. The book includes a brief outline of Norwegian history
"The many illustrations, half of them in color, are fine, and the endpapers provide a clear map and a box of up-to-date statistics." Sch Library J

Hall, Elvajean
The land and people of Norway. Rev. ed. Lippincott 1973 159p illus map (Portraits of the nations ser) $6.95 (5-7)   914.81
1 Norway
ISBN 0-397-31408-6
First published 1963
This is a survey of the history, geography, social life and customs, and the politics and government of Norway. The author also describes Norway's status as an industrial nation and as a participant in international trade

914.85   Geography of Sweden

Arbman, Maj
Looking at Sweden. Lippincott 1971 64p illus
(Looking at other countries) lib. bdg. $5.79 (4-6)
914.85
1 Sweden
ISBN 0-397-31363-2
"The book gives a fairly revealing if sketchy view of
Sweden describing the people and their homes, the
country's history, cities and regions, industry, education, and recreation." Booklist
"The attractive format (with half of the many photographs in color) will appeal to younger children for
browsing. . . . The book is indexed, and has guides to
pronunciation and place names." Sch Library J
Map on lining-papers

Merrick, Helen Hynson
Sweden; illus. with photographs. Watts, F. 1971
87p illus maps lib. bdg. $3.90 (4-6)   914.85
1 Sweden
ISBN 0-531-00751-0
"A First book"
"This concise, factual introduction to Sweden
. . . covers such aspects as the country's geography,
climate, history, resources, industry, holidays,
people, education, and housing. Swedes of note in the
arts, sciences, international relations, and other fields
are mentioned briefly." Booklist

914.89   Geography of Denmark

Rutland, Jonathan
Looking at Denmark. Lippincott 1968 64p illus
(Looking at other countries) $5.95, lib. bdg. $5.79
(4-6)   914.89
1 Denmark
ISBN 0-397-31035-8; 0-397-31036-6
In this book about Denmark, the world's oldest
kingdom, the author describes in text and pictures the
country and its people, agricultural practices, the fishing industry, and its educational and social system
While the text is confusing at times and overburdened with place-names, libraries serving elementary
schools may find this a helpful addition to books on
foreign countries for its splendid photographs in color
and in black and white and for its succinct . . . information on Danish agriculture, fishing, schools, and
home life." Booklist
Maps on lining-papers

Wohlrabe, Raymond A.
The land and people of Denmark, by Raymond A.
Wohlrabe and Werner E. Krusch. Rev. ed. Lippin-
cott 1972 160p illus map (Portraits of the nations ser)
$5.95 (5-7)   914.89
1 Denmark
ISBN 0-397-31296-2
First published 1961
"This profile of Denmark traces its history from
prehistoric times to the present, takes the reader on a
tour of the country, discusses the art, music, litera-
ture and men of science, and describes life, customs,
agriculture, and industry in present-day Denmark.
. . . Illustrated with a few photographs and a map."
Booklist
"Naturally there is a chapter on Hans Christian
Andersen. This is a worthwhile addition to any li-
brary." Best Sellers

914.91   Geography of Iceland

Berry, Erick
The land and people of Iceland. Rev. ed. Lippincott
1972 158p illus map (Portraits of the nations ser) $5.95
(5-7)   914.91
1 Iceland
ISBN 0-397-31401-9
First published 1959
This is an introduction to Iceland, describing the
history, geography, economy, culture and people of
the island republic

914.92   Geography of the Netherlands

Barnouw, Adriaan J.
The land and people of Holland, by Adriaan J.
Barnouw and Raymond A. Wohlrabe. Rev. ed. Lip-
pincott 1972 159p illus map (Portraits of the nations
ser) $5.95 (5-7)   914.92
1 Netherlands
ISBN 0-397-31254-7
First published 1961
This is an introduction to the history, geography,
people and culture of Holland

Cohn, Angelo
The first book of the Netherlands. Rev. ed. Illus.
with photographs. Watts, F. 1971 80p illus map lib.
bdg. $3.90 (4-6)   914.92
1 Netherlands
ISBN 0-531-00593-3
First published 1962
The author explains the important role geography
has played in the history and development of the
Netherlands. Information about the government,
cities, industry, culture and unique qualities of the
country is included
Other books to read: p77

914.93   Geography of Belgium

Loder, Dorothy
The land and people of Belgium. Rev. ed. Lippincott 1973 143p illus maps (Portraits of the nations ser)
$6.95 (5-7)   914.93
1 Belgium
ISBN 0-397-31462-0
First published 1957
The author surveys Belgium's history and cities, as
well as the ways of life of the Flemish-speaking people
and the Walloons, or French-speaking people

914.95   Geography of Greece

Gianakoulis, Theodore
The land and people of Greece. [Rev] Lippincott
[1972 c1965] 160p illus map (Portraits of the nations
ser) $5.95 (5-7)   914.95
1 Greece, Modern 2 Greece
ISBN 0-397-31523-6
First published 1952
Against a detailed background of Greek history

Gianakoulis, Theodore—*Continued*
from earliest to modern times, this book surveys
Greece's physical geography, culture, government,
and social and economic conditions

Noel-Baker, Francis
Looking at Greece. Lippincott [1968 c1967] 64p
illus (Looking at other countries) $5.95, lib. bdg.
$5.79 (4-6)   914.95
1 Greece, Modern
ISBN 0-397-31033-1; 0-397-31034-X
First published 1967 in England
"An attractive book with photos (many colored) of
ancient and modern Greece. Topics briefly discussed
are: the country, people, homes, villages, cities,
island, education, churches, traditions, festivals,
farming, industries and history." Bruno. Bks for Sch
Libraries, 1968
Map on lining-papers

Sasek, M.
This is Greece. Macmillan (N Y) 1966 60p illus maps
$4.95 (4-6)   914.95
1 Greece, Modern 2 Greece—Antiquities
Illustrated by the author, this is an introduction to
the Mediterranean country through a tour of ancient
landmarks and modern everyday scenes
"Though the layout is sometimes confusing, the
poster pictures of ancient and modern Greece have a
pleasing sense of vista, and the reader leaves the book
with a definite idea of the country and its significance." N Y Times Bk Rev

914.96   Geography of the Balkan peninsula

Kostich, Dragos D.
The land and people of the Balkans; Albania, Bulgaria, Yugoslavia. Rev. ed. Lippincott 1973 159p illus
map (Portraits of the nations ser) $6.95, lib. bdg. $5.95
(5-7)   914.96
1 Balkan peninsula
ISBN 0-397-31398-5; 0-397-31397-7
First published 1962
An introduction to the geography, history, politics,
social life and culture of the Balkan area which contains the three modern nations of Albania, Bulgaria
and Yugoslavia

914.97   Geography of Yugoslavia

Feuerlicht, Roberta Strauss
Zhivko of Yugoslavia; photographs by Herbert A.
Feuerlicht. Messner 1971 64p illus maps $3.95, lib.
bdg. $3.79 (3-6)   914.97
1 Yugoslavia—Social life and customs 2 Skopje,
Yugoslavia—Earthquake, 1963
ISBN 0-671-32455-1; 0-671-32456-X
The book describes the culture of the Yugoslavian
people. By focusing on the life of one child's family,
this text is concerned both with the family and with
the town and the country in which they live. The
writing is direct and matter-of-fact, the description of
Zhivko's activities interspersed with information
about the earthquake that almost demolished the
town (Skopje, capital of Macedonia) and the holiday
ceremonies in memory of that day. There is some

material about Tito and about Yugoslavian history and
government, a bit about education, and so on, but
most of the text discusses such homely things as Zhivko's chores and Baba's cooking. . . . A pronunciation
guide is appended." Sutherland. The Best in Children's Bks

Rothkopf, Carol Z.
Yugoslavia; illus. with photographs. Watts, F. 1971
66p illus map lib. bdg. $3.90 (5-7)   914.97
1 Yugoslavia
ISBN 0-531-00738-3
"A First book"
Map by George Buctel
The author "describes present-day Yugoslavia as a
leader in the Third World of independent nations
which are uncommitted to either the West or the
East. She discusses the autonomous, communist government's accomplishments in building a unified
nation of people with diverse languages, religions,
and cultural backgrounds and comments briefly on
the country's prospects for the future. Numerous
photographs illustrate the text." Booklist

914.977   Geography of Bulgaria

McLellan, Jill
Bulgaria in pictures. Sterling 1973 64p illus map
(Visual geography ser) lib. bdg. $3.39, pa $1.75
(5-7)   914.977
1 Bulgaria
ISBN 0-8069-1130-1; 0-8069-1131-X
First published 1970
The book, accompanied by black and white photographs, gives information on Bulgaria's history, government, geography, economy, and the Bulgarians
themselves

914.98   Geography of Romania

Hale, Julian
The land and people of Romania. Lippincott 1972
143p illus map (Portraits of the nations ser) $5.95
(5-7)   914.98
1 Rumania
ISBN 0-397-31288-1
The book provides a brief survey of the history,
geography, economic and social life of the people of
Romania

915   Geography of Asia

Walsh, Richard J.
Adventures and discoveries of Marco Polo; illus. by
Cyrus Le Roy Baldridge. Random House 1953 183p
illus lib. bdg. $4.39 (5-7)   915
1 East—Description and travel 2 Polo, Marco
ISBN 0-394-90503-2
"World Landmark books"
"Basing his account on the Marsden edition of
Marco Polo's own book, the author has chosen picturesque details that would be of particular interest to
young readers. Its usefulness is augmented by the
simple style and large print which make it easily
understood. . . . Description of Kublai Khan and his
court are noteworthy. The author states in his
foreword that no quotation or conversation has been
invented by him." Ontario Library Rev

915.1   Geography of China

Gray, Noel

Looking at China. Lippincott [1975 c1974] 64p illus maps (Looking at other countries) $5.95 (4-6)   915.1
1 China (People's Republic of China, 1949-   )
ISBN 0-397-31584-8)
"A concise, lively, and colorful look at modern-day mainland China. Gray covers history, geography, industry, science, and transportation but concentrates on the seven major cities and the daily lives of the people. The arrangement is sometimes illogical . . . and Gray glosses over the negative aspects of Chinese life. . . . However, the text reads smoothly and numerous color photographs provide a clear, well-balanced picture of Chinese life." Sch Library J

Hsiao, Ellen

A Chinese year; written and illus. by Ellen Hsiao. Pub. by Evans, M.&Co. and distributed in association with Lippincott 1970 64p illus $3.95 (3-5)   915.1
1 China—Social life and customs
ISBN 0-87131-095-3
"A Two worlds book"
"Born in China, the author describes her year in a small town; she and her family had come for grandmother's funeral, and it had been decided that two children should be left there for a time to comfort the grandfather. The text is simply written, its continuity broken by topical headings; despite the episodic structure, the book has an easy, conversational flow. The details of family rites and funeral observances, of New Year festivity and school games, of learning to use an abacus and sing her first English song are told by Ai-lan (Ellen) with unpretentious directness. The illustrations include decorative cut paper designs (a Chinese folk art) and drawings in black and white." Chicago. Children's Bk Center
Chinese words in this book: p63-64

Rau, Margaret

Our world: the People's Republic of China; illus. with photographs. Messner [1974 c1973] 128p illus map $7.25, lib. bdg. $6.64 (6-7)   915.1
1 China (People's Republic of China, 1949-   )
ISBN 0-671-32639-2; 0-671-32640-6
"The first half of the book is a capsule history emphasizing recent times, the development of Communism and the contributions of Mao Tsetung. The remainder describes China as it is today—education, industry, and agriculture—and ends with a few questions about the future." Best Sellers
"A brisk and objective overview. . . . Rau deals competently with historical material and discusses internal politics and international relations lucidly. Such topics are covered in many other books about China, however; what is less usual is the coverage (at this reading level, particularly) of the contemporary scene." Chicago. Children's Bk Center

Sasek, M.

This is Hong Kong. Macmillan (N Y) 1965 60p illus maps lib. bdg. $5.95 (3-6)   915.1
1 Hongkong
In this pictorial tour of the exotic British Crown Colony, the author-illustrator describes Hong Kong's geography, transportation, harbors, cities, peoples, homes, religions, farm and factory products, and language
Here "the astounding beauty and variety of Hong Kong are captured in brilliant scenic spreads. Concise, lively text." Horn Bk

Sidel, Ruth

Revolutionary China: people, politics, and ping-pong. Delacorte Press 1974 178p illus map $5.95, lib. bdg. $5.57 (6-7)   915.1
1 China (People's Republic of China, 1949-   )
ISBN 0-440-07410-X; 0-440-07394-4
The author, who visited China in 1971-1972, gives a brief history of China from early times to the end of the cultural Revolution. She then discusses Communist China today: the communes, social and economic achievements and conditions, education and language reform, life in Peking and other major cities, and China's renewed importance in world affairs
This book is "largely informational rather than interpretive. . . . Still, Sidel is careful to present lifestyles of the Chinese on their own terms, fairly and favorably comparing them to prerevolutionary days." Booklist
Bibliography: p173-74

Spencer, Cornelia

The Yangtze, China's river highway; illus. by Kurt Wiese; maps by Fred Kliem. Garrard 1963 96p illus maps (Rivers of the world) lib. bdg. $3.68 (4-6)   915.1
1 Yangtze River 2 China
ISBN 0-8116-6357-4
"Straightforward account of one of the world's important rivers whose basin supports one-tenth of the human race. Emphasis on modern times with some details about modern flood control projects." Asia. A Guide to Bks for Children

915.19   Geography of Korea

Gurney, Gene

North & South Korea, by Gene and Clare Gurney. Watts, F. 1973 87p illus map lib. bdg. $3.45 (5-7)   915.19
1 Korea
ISBN 0-531-00804-5
"A First book"
The authors discuss the history, geography, customs, industries and cities of one of the oldest countries in the world, now divided by war and political philosophy
"A concise history of North and South Korea . . . albeit from a pro-South Korean point of view." Sch Library J

Mathews, William H.

Korea—North & South—in pictures. Sterling 1975 64p illus map (Visual geography ser) lib. bdg. $3.39, pa $1.75 (5-7)   915.19
1 Korea
ISBN 0-8069-1105-0; 0-8069-1104-2
First published 1968 with title: Korea in pictures
Along with photographs, the text gives insight into the history, economy, customs, art, and daily life of the Korean people

Solberg, S. E.

The land and people of Korea. Rev. ed. Lippincott 1973 159p illus maps (Portraits of the nations ser) $6.95 (5-7)   915.19
1 Korea
ISBN 0-397-31405-1
First published 1966
"The first part of the book highlights the major conflict of Korea's long, turbulent history including the causes of the late Korean War and the present, unsolved problems of unification. The latter part of

Solberg, S. E.—*Continued*
the book discusses Korean art, literature, education, and religion and describes the daily life and customs of the people and the planting and harvesting of rice, and contrasts village and city life in South Korea." Booklist [Review of the 1966 edition]
"A very good book for its coverage and the detailed and extensive historical section." Chicago. Children's Bk Center [Review of the 1966 edition]

915.2   Geography of Japan

Ashby, Gwynneth
Looking at Japan. Lippincott 1969 63p illus (Looking at other countries) $5.95, lib. bdg. $5.79 (4-6)
915.2
1 Japan
ISBN 0-397-31086-2; 0-397-31087-0
The text describes many aspects of Japanese life— the people, their customs, the history, geography, culture and industry
"A pithy text illustrated with excellent photographs, many in color." Keating. Building Bridges of Understanding Between Cultures
Maps on lining-papers

Boardman, Gwenn R.
Living in Tokyo. Nelson 1970 128p illus maps (Living around the world) $4.95, lib. bdg. $4.65 (5-7)
915.2
1 Tokyo—Description
ISBN 0-8407-7128-2; 0-8407-7129-0
The author describes life in modern day Tokyo, with its unique blend of old and new, where department stores stand beside historic castles, and women in kimonos can be seen riding the world's fastest train
This account "is supplemented by more than 60 photographs, which considerably help the text." Best Sellers

Vaughan, Josephine Budd
The land and people of Japan. Rev. ed. Lippincott 1972 158p illus map (Portraits of the nations ser) $5.95 (5-7)
915.2
1 Japan
ISBN 0-397-31301-2
First published 1952
This introduction to Japan describes its history, geography, people and culture

Yashima, Taro
The village tree. Viking 1953 34p illus $4.95, pa $1.25 (k-3)
915.2
1 Children in Japan 2 Japan
ISBN 0-670-05072-5; 0-670-74697-5
A "beautiful interpretation in poetic prose and picture of the author's childhood portrayed as he recalls the fun he enjoyed with other boys by the river where a great tree still stretches its branches. The brief text and full-color sketches illustrate, in an atmosphere of great peace and happiness, the kind of tree-play, diving and underwater fun that boys anywhere might invent." Horn Bk

915.3   Geography of Arabian Peninsula. Bedouins

Gordon, Eugene
Saudi Arabia in pictures. Sterling 1975 64p illus map (Visual geography ser) lib. bdg. $3.39, pa $1.75 (5-7)
915.3

1 Saudi Arabia
ISBN 0-8069-1169-7; 0-8069-1168-9
First published 1973
This book records the economic and social changes this nation has undergone along with the history, customs, government and life style of the people. Black and white photographs supplement the text

Hoyt, Olga
The Bedouins; illus. with photographs. Lothrop 1969 128p illus map lib. bdg. $4.59 (4-6)   915.3
1 Bedouins
ISBN 0-688-51074-4
"The hardships of the Bedouins' nomadic existence and their rich cultural heritage are stressed in this interesting, informative text, enhanced by many good black-and-white photographs. In a clear, concise style, using many Arabic names and terms, the author depicts daily tribal life, and thoroughly discusses: food, shelter, religion, customs, and desert wildlife and warfare. The Bedouins' historic beginnings and their future are briefly touched upon." Sch Library J

915.4   Geography of India

Bergman Sucksdorff, Astrid
Chendru: the boy and the tiger; English version by William Sansom. Harcourt 1960 [c1959] unp illus $6.50 (3-6)   915.4
1 India—Social life and customs 2 Muria 3 Tigers
ISBN 0-15-216431-6
First published 1959 in France
Illustrated with photographs by the author
Colored photographs and text tell the story of Chendru, a young boy of India, and his pet tiger. This book also pictures the everyday life and activities of the Murias, a primitive tribe living in the jungle village of Gahr-Bengal, India
"Excellent for social studies in that it shows India is not all maharajahs, precious jewels, and Taj Mahals!" Library J

Tooni, the elephant boy. Harcourt 1971 unp illus $5.95 (1-5)   915.4
1 Children in India 2 Assam 3 Elephants
ISBN 0-15-289426-8
This is a "photographic account of Tooni's life in a village near the Kaziranga Game Sanctuary in Assam, India. His father is a mahout (elephant driver) and Tooni wants to be a mahout, too. . . . [Given is a] picture of daily routines in the home, at school and especially in the game sanctuary." Library J
"The story of [the boys's] daily life and the appealing color photographs [by the author] make a most successful book. . . . This is a book to broaden young horizons and to delight readers of any age." Pub W

Bothwell, Jean
The first book of India. Rev. ed. Illus. with photographs. Watts, F. 1971 81p illus map lib. bdg. $3.90 (4-7)   915.4
1 India
ISBN 0-531-00559-3
First published 1966
Map by Walter Hortens
"An introduction to India with adequate coverage of all topics except religion, about which very little is mentioned. Discussed are geography and climate, history and government, the economy, and village life. Many of the black-and-white photos show works of art . . . those sections which treat language, arts, and the caste system, are especially thorough." Sch Library J
Glossary: p75-76. Other books to read: p77

Riwkin-Brick, Anna

Salima lives in Kashmir; photographs by Anna Riwkin-Brick; story by Vera Forsberg. Macmillan (N Y) 1971 unp illus lib. bdg. $4.50 (2-4)   915.4

1 Children in Kashmir 2 Kashmir—Social life and customs

Original Swedish edition, 1970

Nine-year-old Salima and her family live on a boat in Kashmir. This story, illustrated with photographs, tells of Salima's desire to attend school in order to learn to read and write

"The scenes of the countryside, of the town of Srinagar, and of the activities of Salima's family convey an accurate and revealing picture of life in Kashmir." Booklist

Shetty, Sharat

A Hindu boyhood; illus. by Mehlli Gobhai. Pub. by Evans, M. & Co. and distributed in association with Lippincott [1971 c1970] 59p illus map $3.95 (3-5)   915.4

1 Children in India 2 India—Social life and customs
ISBN 0-87131-096-1

"The first-person narrative is comprised of a series of short episodes embodying the daily life, the customs, and the beliefs of the people of the village. . . . The story has vitality and is enjoyable as well as enlightening. The two-color drawings by an illustrator also born in India add flavor to the book." Booklist

Kannada and Hindi words in this book: p57-58

Weingarten, Violet

The Ganges; sacred river of India; map by Henri Fluchere. Garrard 1969 96p illus map (Rivers of the world) lib. bdg. $3.68 (4-6)   915.4

1 India 2 Ganges River
ISBN 0-8116-6372-8

This is the "story of the 1500 mile long Ganges River. Includes the religion, industry, language, caste, and political developments of the people." Minnesota

"The text is clear, concise and accurate. . . . The black and white photographs are good." Sch Library J

915.49   Geography of Pakistan, Bangladesh, Ceylon and Nepal

Lang, Robert

The land and people of Pakistan. Rev. ed. Lippincott 1974 159p illus map (Portraits of the nations ser) lib. bdg. $4.95 (6-7)   915.49

1 Pakistan
ISBN 0-397-31551-1

First published 1968

Partial contents: The land of the great river Indus; Ancient cities and Buddhist ruins; Muslims and Moghuls; British rule and the struggle for independence; Pakistan becomes a nation; An historic city: Lahore; Life in a mud-walled village in the Punjab; Feasts, fasts, and festivals; Troubled Kashmir

"Well written and readable, this portrait of Pakistan . . . [includes the] changes caused by the recent civil war and separation of East Pakistan (Bangladesh). Lang has also included material on the emerging role of women and changes in education. The complicated history is well explained as are social customs. A thoughtful appraisal of how Pakistan will fare in the future concludes this overview which has many excellent new photographs." Sch Library J

Larsen, Peter

Boy of Nepal [by] Peter and Elaine Larsen; illus. with photographs by Peter Larsen. Dodd 1970 59p illus map lib. bdg. $4.50 (3-5)   915.49

1 Children in Nepal 2 Nepal—Social life and customs
ISBN 0-396-06063-3

This book shows the everyday life of a boy of Kathmandu. There are pictures and descriptions of his home, his family, and of many aspects of Nepalese life, including Hindu religious festivals

"There is no pretense in the text—it is simply the story of a young boy's life in Nepal—and what a fascinating life it is. The photographs not only are good, but they also enrich and extend the text." Pub W

Lauré, Jason

Joi Bangla! The children of Bangladesh [by] Jason Lauré with Ettagale Lauré; photographs by Jason Lauré. Farrar, Straus 1974 153p illus map $6.95 (5-7)   915.49

1 Children in Bangladesh 2 Bangladesh
ISBN 0-374-33780-2

A year after the war which established Bangladesh as a country, the authors interviewed "a cross-section of the children of Bangladesh. One is a Bihari whose family's wealth and business were commandeered by the authorities; another is an orphan of eleven who serves as foster mother to the many children of a teacher; a third is a country boy who came to Dacca and earns a meagre living as a rickshaw wallah . . . and all of them, living in a country with a literacy rate of less than 20%, an abysmally low standard of living, corruption, inflation, and little food, are tough and resilient—the hope of a nation that lost most of its potential leadership in a mass extermination of intellectuals during a bitter war. Very occasionally, Lauré wanders from the interviews to discourse about customs or to provide background; for the most part, the text consists of descriptions of the children, their reports of wartime experiences and their present situations, and their hopes—or fears—for the future." Chicago. Children's Bk Center

"History told in terms of kings, dictators, soldiers, governments, or geography means little to children. But tell it in terms of everyday suffering to children their own age . . . and all young people will sit still and listen. . . . A moving, valuable report." Best Sellers

Glossary: p153-[54]

Wilber, Donald N.

The land and people of Ceylon. Rev. ed. Lippincott 1972 156p illus map (Portraits of the nations ser) $5.95, lib. bdg. $5.95 (5-7)   915.49

1 Ceylon
ISBN 0-397-31399-3; 0-397-31400-0

This introduction to the island nation of Ceylon discusses its history and geography, as well as its industries, its political life, and the customs of its people

915.5   Geography of Iran

Hinckley, Helen

The land and people of Iran. [Rev] Lippincott [1973 c1964] 160p illus maps (Portraits of the nations ser) $5.95 (5-7)   915.5

1 Iran
ISBN 0-397-31202-4

First published 1964

"The nation's history is extensively covered, show-

Hinckley, Helen—*Continued*

ing the background for current religious and social practices. Hinckley discusses nomadic herders, village farmers, and city dwellers and explains how modernizing forces are slowly changing their lives." Sch Library J

Lengyel, Emil

Iran; illus. with photographs. Watts, F. 1972 85p illus map lib. bdg. $3.90 (5-7)   915.5

1 Iran
ISBN 0-531-00760-X
"A First book"

In this "introduction to Iran today and yesterday the author shows how the oil-rich nation has survived throughout history and is presently struggling to educate its people to a more modern life. He also surveys the area's geography and resources, city and village life, nomadic tribes, religion, foods, dress, customs, and literature and art." Booklist

The book "is excellent for topic work, being easy to follow and read, concise, up to date, well illustrated and well indexed." Jr Bkshelf

915.6 Geography of the Middle East

Caldwell, John C.

Let's visit the Middle East. [Rev] Day 1972 96p illus lib. bdg. $3.96 (5-7)   915.6

1 Near East
ISBN 0-381-99883-5
First published 1958

The author describes the complex area of the Middle East and shows why this region is important today. He give information about the history, economic conditions, and political problems of Egypt, Israel, Lebanon, Syria, Jordan, Saudi Arabia, Yemen, Kuwait, Aden, Iraq and Iran

915.61 Geography of Turkey

Spencer, William

The land and people of Turkey. Rev. ed. Lippincott 1972 158p illus map (Portraits of the nations ser) $5.95 (5-7)   915.61

1 Turkey
First published 1958

An introduction to the history, social conditions and geography of Turkey as the author guides the reader through modern Ankara, Asia Minor, the cities of the Hittites and the Turkish riviera, ending in Istanbul

915.691 Geography of Syria

Copeland, Paul W.

The land and people of Syria. [Rev] Lippincott [1972 c1964] 160p illus map (Portraits of the nations ser) $5.95 (5-7)   915.691

1 Syria
ISBN 0-397-31537-6
First published 1964

This book "explores Syria's location, its strange customs, and her people who are Arabs of Semitic stock, all of which give to this country in the Near East an aura of fantasy and the enchantment of Aladdin and

his magic lamp. Paul Copeland explains Muslim holy days and holidays, famous old towns where early Christians had built monastic retreat houses, and the various types of architecture. Pictures of every phase of Syria's culture show great diversity of development. Short index." Best Sellers

The book "is simple enough for a child of 11 to get an excellent idea of the nation and its people, yet so comprehensive that we wish we had read it before we visited the country." Bk Week

915.692 Geography of Lebanon

Winder, Viola H.

The land and people of Lebanon. [Rev] Lippincott [1973 c1965] 159p illus maps (Portraits of the nations ser) $5.95 (5-7)   915.692

1 Lebanon
ISBN 0-397-31407-8

This book describes the history, economic resources, government and social and cultural aspects of the land once known as Phoenicia

915.694 Geography of Israel

Edwardson, Cordelia

Miriam lives in a kibbutz; photography by Anna Riwkin-Brick. Lothrop [1971 c1969] 46p illus $4.95, lib. bdg. $4.59 (1-4)   915.694

1 Children in Israel 2 Israel—Social life and customs
ISBN 0-688-41365-X; 0-688-51365-4

Original Swedish edition, 1969. This translation first published 1970 in England

Newly arrived from Morocco, five-year-old Miriam is faced with a new way of life on an Israeli kibbutz. In text and photographs, this story tells how Miriam, helped by her new friend Daniel, discovers that life on a kibbutz can be fun

Hoffman, Gail

The land and people of Israel. Rev. ed. Lippincott 1972 159p illus map (Portraits of the nations ser) $5.95 (5-7)   915.694

1 Israel
ISBN 0-397-31258-X
First published 1950

Here is an introduction to Israel, emphasizing the people, their way of life, and the modern problems and progress of this ancient land

Kubie, Nora Benjamin

Israel. rev. ed. Watts, F. 1975 88p illus maps lib. bdg. $3.90 (4-7)   915.694

1 Israel 2 Jews—History
ISBN 0-531-00563-1
"A First book"

First published 1953 with title: The first book of Israel

An introduction to the modern state. The author discusses the social, political and cultural institutions as well as daily life in Israel. She also discusses the Palestinian movement and the Yom Kippur War

"It is valuable and informative so long as one remembers that it presents only one side of the matter." Christian Sci Monitor [Review of 1968 edition]

Rutland, Jonathan

Looking at Israel; illus. with 95 photographs by the author. Lippincott 1970 64p illus (Looking at other countries) $5.95 (4-6)   915.694

Rutland, Jonathan—*Continued*
1 Israel
ISBN 0-397-31375-6
This survey of Israel since its establishment as a state in 1948 discusses its history, social life and customs, industry and agriculture, religion and education, and its most famous cities and geographical areas
Maps on lining-papers

915.695   Geography of Jordan

Poole, Frederick King
Jordan. Watts, F. 1974 65p illus map lib. bdg. $3.45 (5-7)   915.695
1 Jordan
ISBN 0-531-00818-5
"A First book"
"This presentation acknowledges the strife that has ripped much of Jordan's recent history, but analysis is peripheral and the thrust of the book is toward describing the geographical and cultural factors that shape the country. Poole introduces the people, mainly the Bedouin of the east, along with the role they have come to play in the national military, and the displaced Palestinians of the west, who form nearly 40 percent of the population and who opposed Hussein in the 1970 civil war. A perspective on the Moslem tradition of Hashemite rule, personified by King Hussein, and on today's Jordan, its progress, and its future round out this introductory survey." Booklist
Books for further reading: p62

915.7   Geography of Siberia

Lengyel, Emil
Siberia. Watts, F. 1974 65p illus map lib. bdg. $3.45 (5-7)   915.7
1 Siberia
ISBN 0-531-00821-5
"A First book"
This book surveys Siberia's weather, geography, natural resources, cities, population, religion, history, industries and future, as well as the Trans-Siberian Railroad
"A concise, accurate overview." Sch Library J
Books for further reading: p63

915.81   Geography of Afghanistan

Clifford, Mary Louise
The land and people of Afghanistan. Rev. ed. Lippincott 1973 159p illus maps (Portraits of the nations ser) $5.95 (5-7)   915.81
1 Afghanistan
ISBN 0-397-31461-2
First published 1962
The author describes the history, geography, culture and people of this central Asian nation, adding sections on recent political, economic, educational and social reforms

915.9   Geography of Southeast Asia

Poole, Frederick King
Southeast Asia. Rev. ed. Watts, F. [1973 c1972] 90p illus map $3.90 (5-7)   915.9
1 Asia, Southeastern
ISBN 0-531-00801-0
"A First book"
Title page date: 1972
First published 1968
The author describes the people, history, geography, politics and civilization of the ten nations of Southeast Asia—Thailand, North and South Vietnam, Cambodia, Laos, Burma, Malaysia, Singapore, Indonesia and the Philippines

915.93   Geography of Thailand

Poole, Frederick King
Thailand; illus. with photographs. Watts, F. 1973 73p illus map lib. bdg. $3.90 (5-7)   915.93
1 Thailand
ISBN 0-531-00791-X
"A First book"
The author surveys Thailand's geography, history, people, culture, religion and political situation
"An informative and well-written narrative. . . . Unfortuantely, the black-and-white photographs are unclear, often dark, and sometimes do not coincide with the text: however, the information on . . . Thailand compensates for the poor format." Sch Library J

915.95   Geography of Malaysia and Singapore

Poole, Frederick King
Malaysia & Singapore. Watts, F. 1975 59p illus map lib. bdg. $3.90 (5-7)   915.95
1 Malaysia 2 Singapore
ISBN 0-531-02778-3
"A First book"
"This competently written description of two adjacent Asian nations covers their geography, natural resources, racial and cultural composition, recent history, and modern social and economic advancements. The writing is clear, and black-and-white photographs are additionally informative. Suggested titles for further reading are appended." Booklist

915.96   Geography of Cambodia

Chandler, David P.
The land and people of Cambodia. Lippincott 1972 158p illus map (Portraits of the nations ser) $5.95 (5-7)   915.96
1 Cambodia
ISBN 0-397-31321-7
The author "describes with clarity the geography, people, history, economy, and religion of Cambodia. He also profiles Prince Norodom Sihanouk and traces the course of events during his rule and the causes of recent unrest in the country." Booklist

915.97   Geography of Vietnam

Buell, Hal
Viet Nam; land of many dragons; illus. with photographs. Dodd 1968 142p illus maps lib. bdg. $4.50 (5-7)   915.97
1 Vietnam
ISBN 0-396-06466-3
"In text and picture the author attempts to trace the history of Viet Nam for young readers. In such a short work the text is sketchy, but adequate for the purpose of the volume. The pictures are well done and they are sure to keep the attention of the young reader as he delves into the background of the country and the present complicated situation of the war and American intervention." Best Sellers

915.98   Geography of Indonesia

Poole, Frederick King
Indonesia; illus. with photographs. Watts, F. 1971 66p illus maps lib. bdg. $3.90 (4-7)   915.98
1 Indonesia
ISBN 0-531-00735-9
"A First book"
"An accurate, concise survey of Indonesia's historical, social and political development. Of particular importance is the material on local and national governmental administration, with a detailed outline of the country's struggle against Dutch domination, its shaky independence, and Sukarno's overthrow. . . . The photographs here are well chosen and illustrative while the text is interesting and informative." Sch Library J

Smith, Datus C.
The land and people of Indonesia, by Datus C. Smith, Jr. [Rev] Lippincott [1972 c1968] 158p illus map $5.95 (5-7)   915.98
1 Indonesia
ISBN 0-397-21533-3
First published 1961
"The author surveys Indonesia's geography, natural resources, religions, languages, education, arts, the people and their way of life. He also details the country's complex history as it emerged from colonial status to independence

915.99   Geography of the Philippine Islands

Poole, Frederick King
The Philippines; illus. with photographs. Watts, F. 1971 90p illus map $3.90 (5-7)   915.99
1 Philippine Islands
ISBN 0-531-00739-1
"A First book"
The author considers the geographic characteristics of the Philippine Islands, the varied ethnic and cultural heritage of the inhabitants and the country's current social, political and economic problems

916   Geography of Africa

Bernheim, Marc
In Africa [by] Marc & Evelyne Bernheim. Atheneum Pubs. 1973 unp illus $6.95 (k-3)   916

1 Africa
ISBN 0-689-30315-7
"A Margaret K. McElderry book"
"A picture book of ninety-one highly effective photographs has sequences that illustrate varied types of African houses, costumes, occupations, and activities in the forest, on the desert, or on the coast. From these well-reproduced pictures, aspects of geography and culture are made vivid—so lively are the people and scenes of action. Captions provide simple but adequate identifications in a word, a phrase, or a short sentence." Horn Bk

Murphy, E. Jefferson
Understanding Africa; illus. by Louise E. Jefferson. Crowell 1969 209p illus maps $5.95 (6-7)   916
1 Africa
ISBN 0-690-84452-2
A "survey of Africa presenting facts about its history, geography, resources, population, culture, and government. It emphasizes the area south of the Sahara with its complex social structure and multiplicity of nations and languages. A well-designed, beautifully illustrated book with full index and bibliography." Top of the News
"Present problems are duly represented, but there is also a wealth of material that makes the reader appreciate the increasing importance and potential of this emerging, so-called 'black' continent. This is rewarding reading material." Best Sellers

Pine, Tillie S.
The Africans knew, by Tillie S. Pine and Joseph Levine; pictures by Ann Grifalconi. McGraw 1967 28p illus lib. bdg. $4.72 (1-4)   916
1 Africa 2 Science—Experiments
ISBN 0-07-050076-2
"The authors describe things the Africans knew how to do long ago, tell how the same ideas are used today, and suggest ways the reader can experiment with these ideas. . . . The illustrations supplement the text well. This book . . . is useful for the elementary presentation of scientific ideas, for the suggested activities and as an aid to elementary understanding of another culture." Sch Library J

916.1   Geography of North Africa

Carpenter, Allan
Tunisia, by Allan Carpenter and Bechir Chourou; consulting editor: Ivor G. Wilks. Childrens Press 1973 94p illus maps (Enchantment of Africa) lib. bdg. $6.60 (4-7)   916.1
1 Tunisia
ISBN 0-516-04590-3
The authors survey Tunisia's geography, history, government, resources, people and cultures, industries and major cities
Handy reference section: p90-91

Copeland, Paul W.
The land and people of Libya. [Rev] Lippincott [1972 c1967] 158p illus map (Portraits of the nations ser) $5.95 (5-7)   916.1
1 Libya
ISBN 0-397-31532-5
1 First published 1967
Libya's history dates back to 8000 B.C. The author explores the country's customs, its people, and industries. The reader is also introduced to the physical characteristics of the land
"An enjoyable informational book, this survey of Libya is well organized and competently written." Sutherland. The Best in Children's Bks

Lollar, Coleman

Tunisia in pictures. Sterling 1973 64p illus maps (Visual geography ser) lib. bdg. $3.39, pa $1.75 (5-7)   916.1

1 Tunisia

ISBN 0-8069-1159-X; 0-8069-1158-1

First published 1972

The people, history, political structure and geography of Tunisia are surveyed from its beginnings as ancient Carthage up to the present times

Spencer, William

The land and people of Tunisia. [Rev] Lippincott [1972 c1967] 160p illus map (Portraits of the nations ser) $5.95 (5-7)   916.1

1 Tunisia

ISBN 0-397-31600-3

First published 1967

The historic city of Tunis, formerly Carthage, for centuries provided access to the African wilds. This book discusses the heritage of the people of Tunisia as it was effected by the geography of the country

"Illustrated with photographs. A specialist on Middle Eastern affairs writes cogently of this 'land of mild contrasts.' " Horn Bk [Review of the 1969 edition]

916.2   Geography of Egypt

Lengyel, Emil

Modern Egypt. Watts, F. 1973 87p illus map lib. bdg. $3.90 (5-7)   916.2

1 Egypt

ISBN 0-531-00788-X

"A First book"

The author surveys Egypt's geography, history, cities, religions, culture, and political situation

Books for further reading: p83

Mahmoud, Zaki Naguib

The land and people of Egypt. Rev. ed. Lippincott 1972 159p illus map (Portraits of the nations ser) $5.95 (5-7)   916.2

1 Egypt

ISBN 0-397-31259-8

First published 1959

"Describes the geography of Egypt and its effect on the character of the people and traces the history and the social, economic, and political development of the country." Booklist

The Egyptian author presents the material "clearly and concisely. . . . Good format, index, table of contents, first-class photographs, good map." Library J

Mirepoix, Camille

Egypt in pictures. Sterling 1974 64p illus maps (Visual geography ser) lib. bdg. $3.39, pa $1.75 (5-7)   916.2

1 Egypt

ISBN 0-8069-1157-3; 0-8069-1156-5

First published 1973

This book traces the development of this country from its ancient beginnings up to its present involvement in world affairs

916.3   Geography of Ethiopia

Englebert, Victor

Camera on Africa; the world of an Ethiopian boy. Harcourt 1970 87p illus $5.50 (3-5)   916.3

1 Children in Ethiopia   2 Ethiopia—Social life and customs

ISBN 0-15-214068-9

"Curriculum-related books"

"Photographs and accompanying text describe life in the remote Ethiopian mountain village of Lalibela, famous for its ancient, rock-carved churches. Attention centers on the activities of a twelve-year-old school boy, home for Christmas holidays, who helps with household chores, visits relatives, plays with his friends, and takes part in the traditional village Christmas and Epiphany celebrations. Of value mainly as supplementary material for social studies." Booklist

Perl, Lila

Ethiopia; land of the lion; illus. with 67 photographs. Morrow 1972 160p illus map $5.95, lib. bdg. $5.11 (5-7)   916.3

1 Ethiopia

ISBN 0-688-20033-8; 0-688-30033-2

The author "clearly and accurately surveys Ethiopia's geography, history, races, religions, [education] economy, culture, and daily life through an interesting, understandable text and varied photographs. Controversial topics . . . are treated objectively; an extensive glossary and bibliography facilitate research." Sch Library J

Riwkin-Brick, Anna

Gennet lives in Ethiopia; photographs: Anna Riwkin-Brick; text: Vera Forsberg. Macmillan (N Y) 1968 unp illus (Children of the world bks) $3.95 (2-4)   916.3

1 Children in Ethiopia   2 Ethiopia—Social life and customs

Original Swedish edition, 1967

"When Gennet's baby brother is bitten by a poisonous snake, she must go for help, as there is no one else at home. Her journey enables the author to present an interesting and accurate picture of family life in this African country." Sch Library J

916.4   Geography of Morocco

Sheridan, Noel

Morocco in pictures. Sterling 1974 64p illus maps (Visual geography ser) lib. bdg. $3.39, pa $1.75 (5-7)   916.4

1 Morocco

ISBN 0-8069-1087-9; 0-8069-1086-0

First published 1967

The book provides an overview of a country with contrasting scenes such as busy market places and remote villages, snow-capped mountains and parched oases. A close-up of unusual customs and traditions is given along with the history. Social and economic life of the people is also covered

Spencer, William

The land and people of Morocco. Rev. ed. Lippincott 1973 160p illus map (Portraits of the nations ser) $5.95 (5-7)   916.4

1 Morocco

ISBN 0-397-31481-7

First published 1965

An introduction to the geography, people, history, social life, and cities of the North African country which is separated from Europe by the strait of Gilbraltar

916.5   Geography of Algeria

Spencer, William
The land and people of Algeria. Lippincott 1969
156p illus map (Portraits of the nations ser) $5.95, lib.
bdg. $5.95 (5-7)   916.5
1 Algeria
ISBN 0-397-31080-3; 0-397-31081-1
"Politics and economics rather than daily life and
culture are the focus of attention in the account which
also points out the important role of youth in solving
the contemporary problems of a country in which 47
percent of the population is under 19 years of age."
Booklist

916.6   Geography of West Africa

Bernheim, Marc
The drums speak; the story of Kofi, a boy of West
Africa [by] Marc & Evelyne Bernheim. Harcourt
[1972 c1971] unp illus $6.50 (3-5)   916.6
1 Children in West Africa 2 Africa, West
ISBN 0-15-224233-3
"A brief story in a large format about a West African
village boy. By passing an exam, Kofi wins the chance
to become the first of his village to go to high school;
then, by conquering his fear of heights and climbing a
coconut tree in the coming-of-age ceremony, he wins
the chief's endorsement of him as eventual successor." Sch Library J
"Brilliant, large, color photographs give importance to a slender volume with a forced sociological
narrative. The rich tones of printed costumes and
jungle verdure are remarkably sharp in detail; the
boy's activities in the cocoa grove, in canoe-building,
and with animals are vivid." Horn Bk

Carpenter, Allan
Sierra Leone, by Allan Carpenter and Susan L.
Eckert. Consulting editor: John Rowe. Childrens
Press 1974 93p illus map (Enchantment of Africa) lib.
bdg. $6.60 (4-7)   916.6
1 Sierra Leone
ISBN 0-516-04583-0
This is an introductory survey of the history, geog-
raphy, government, resources, major cities, culture
and people of this small West African country

Clifford, Mary Louise
The land and people of Sierra Leone. Lippincott
1974 159p illus maps (Portraits of the nations ser)
$5.95 (5-7)   916.6
1 Sierra Leone
ISBN 0-397-31490-6
The author discusses the geography, history,
economy, government, culture and people of this
West African country
"Clifford provides a straightforward overview of
the West African nation that in the eighteenth century
was viewed as a refuge for freed slaves from the U.S.
and continental Europe. Description of historical and
political events outweighs social and cultural examination, but this still works well as useful introductory
fare." Booklist

Englebert, Victor
The goats of Agadez. Harcourt 1973 48p illus $5.50
(1-3)   916.6
1 Africa, West 2 Goats
ISBN 0-15-231118-1
The author-photographer depicts the daily life of

Agadez, a town at the edge of the Sahara Desert, with
emphasis on the goats who roam freely through the
streets and houses

Gordon, Eugene
Senegal in pictures; photographs by the author.
Sterling 1974 64p illus maps (Visual geography ser)
lib. bdg. $3.39, pa $1.75 (5-7)   916.6
1 Senegal
ISBN 0-8069-1185-9; 0-8069-1184-0
Illustrated with many black and white photographs,
this book gives information on the history, land,
people, government, and economy of Senegal

Perl, Lila
Ghana and Ivory Coast: spotlight on West Africa;
illus. with 74 photographs. Morrow 1975 160p illus
maps $5.95, lib. bdg. $5.11 (6-7)   916.6
1 Ghana 2 Ivory Coast
ISBN 0-688-21833-4; 0-688-31833-9
"In this personalized survey of two key West African nations Perl strikes a nice balance between
examining the past and present as well as the social
and political. Early tribal migrations and colonial history are clearly related to each country's current
status, including both its accomplishments and its
unsolved problems. . . . Informative and well illustrated with many of the author's own photographs."
Booklist
Bibliography: p155-56

Watson, Jane
The Niger: Africa's river of mystery. Maps by Henri
Fluchere. Garrard 1971 96p illus maps (Rivers of the
world) lib. bdg. $3.68 (4-6)   916.6
1 Niger River
ISBN 0-8116-6374-4
The text "traces the history of the Niger River from
the time of the Mali and Songhai empires to the
present. The author describes the efforts of such
European explorers as Mungo Park and Richard
Lander to map the course of the river from its source
to the sea, discusses briefly the period of European
colonization of the region, and concludes with a look
at present-day life along the river." Booklist

916.66   Geography of Liberia

Carpenter, Allan
Liberia; by Allan Carpenter and Harrison Owen;
consulting editor: John Rowe. Childrens Press 1974
93p illus maps (Enchantment of Africa) lib. bdg. $6
(4-7)   916.66
1 Liberia
ISBN 0-516-04570-9
This survey describes Liberia's geography, children, history, government, education, population,
natural resources, economy, and several tourist
attractions
Handy reference section: p90-91

Clifford, Mary Louise
The land and people of Liberia. Lippincott 1971
160p illus map (Portraits of the nations ser) $5.95
(5-7)   916.66
1 Liberia
ISBN 0-397-31168-0
"Clifford traces the growth and development of
Africa's first independent, self-governing republic
from its founding in 1822 as a home for free black
Americans to the present. She discusses the background and character of the people and relationships

Clifford, Mary Louise—*Continued*
between indigenous tribesmen and immigrant settlers, describes the country's geography, natural resources, and governmental and economic structure, and assesses the Liberians' past accomplishments and future prospects in a crisp, detailed account illustrated with photographs." Booklist

916.67   Geography of Ghana

Bleeker, Sonia
The Ashanti of Ghana; illus. by Edith G. Singer. Morrow 1966 160p illus map lib. bdg. $4.59 (4-7)
916.67
1 Ashantis 2 Ghana
ISBN 0-688-31052-4
The author "describes, in a semifictionized style, the culture, daily life, customs and government of the Ashanti, a tribal group living in the central region of the land now called Ghana. Of particular interest is the account of their religion based on ancestor worship. The last three chapters trace the history of the Ashanti from the time when the Europeans established a profitable gold and slave trade with the West Coast natives, up to the present, when Ghana has become an independent nation. The material is well presented and will be useful in the classroom as well as for general reading. There are detailed and informative line drawings, and an excellent index." Sch Library J

Sale, J. Kirk
The land and people of Ghana. Rev. ed. Lippincott 1972 159p illus map (Portraits of the nations ser) $5.95 (5-7)
916.67
1 Ghana
ISBN 0-397-31298-9
First published 1963
This introduction to Ghana, the first Black African country to achieve independence in the twentieth century, describes its history, social and cultural life, geography and economy

Sutherland, Efua
Playtime in Africa; photographs by Willis E. Bell. Atheneum Pubs. 1962 56p illus lib. bdg. $4.95 (1-4)
916.67
1 Children in Ghana 2 Games
ISBN 0-689-20589-9
First published in Ghana
A book of rhythmic text "and photographs about children [of Ghana] at play. They make things out of old boxes and tin cans, play marbles, hide-and-seek, and hopscotch and jump rope, pretty much as children do everywhere." Pub W
"There is great variation of activities in the photographs, with lively action in some and the capturing of a quiet mood in others. The great value of the book lies in the picture it will give our own children of the African children." Chicago. Children's Bk Center

916.69   Geography of Nigeria

Forman, Brenda
The land and people of Nigeria, by Brenda Forman and Harrison Forman. [Rev] Lippincott [1972 c1964] 160p illus map (Portraits of the nations ser) $5.95 (5-7)
916.69
1 Nigeria
ISBN 0-397-31205-9

First published 1964
This book introduces the history; religion; political, social, and economic conditions; and regions of the African land that became an independent nation in 1960

Jenness, Aylette
Along the Niger River; an African way of life; text and photographs by Aylette Jenness. Crowell 1974 135p illus map $6.95 (5-7)   916.69
1 Nigeria—Social life and customs
ISBN 0-690-00514-8
The author describes life in the town of Yelwa, Nigeria—its inhabitants, their customs, their culture, and their adaptations to western technology
"This is not just a travelogue: the book is sympathetic, thoughtful, and objective. Well-written, well-organized, and informative, it gives historical background for a discussion of the life styles of tribes that are fishers or herders or farmers or town dwellers, commenting perceptively on cultural integration, mores, and patterns of individual and group life. A bibliography and a relative index are appended." Chicago. Children's Bk Center

916.7   Geography of Central and East Africa

Bleeker, Sonia
The Masai; herders of East Africa; illus. by Kisa N. Sasaki. Morrow 1963 155p illus maps lib. bdg. $4.59 (4-7)
916.7
1 Masai
ISBN 0-688-31460-0
This is a "description of the history, customs, ceremonies, religion, and daily life of the nomadic Masai herders of eastern Africa. Included is a vivid account of the training of boys for warfare and girls for homemaking. . . . Very little information exists for children on this group." Sch Library J
"Here is a concise, scholarly, yet thoroughly interesting and enjoyable narrative of the Masai. . . . [It] should capture the interest of most young readers by its style and sketches." Best Sellers

The Pygmies; Africans of the Congo forest; illus. by Edith G. Singer. Morrow 1968 143p illus map lib. bdg. $4.59 (4-7)   916.7
1 Pygmies
ISBN 0-688-31462-7
"An excellent study of the diminutive Pygmy tribe, a formerly great nation shrouded in legend and mystery, now dwelling in the jungles of Central Africa. Dealing with the everyday lives of the Mbuti Pygmies, Miss Bleeker describes in detail their religion, history, family structure, hunting techniques, and manhood rites. The accompanying black-and-white drawings lack detail and realism." Sch Library J
"The text conveys the author's admiration for as well as her knowledge of the tribe." Horn Bk

Carpenter, Allan
Burundi, by Allan Carpenter and Matthew Maginnis; consulting editor: John Rowe. Childrens Press 1973 93p illus maps (Enchantment of Africa) lib. bdg. $6.60 (4-7)   916.7
1 Burundi
ISBN 0-516-04554-7
The authors survey Burundi's geography, history, government, resources, people and cultures, economic conditions, industries, and current problems
Handy reference section: p90-91

Carpenter, Allan—*Continued*
Rwanda, by Allan Carpenter and Matthew Maginnis; consulting editor: Ethel M. Albert. Childrens Press 1973 94p illus maps (Enchantment of Africa) lib. bdg. $6.60 (4-7)   916.7
   1 Rwanda
   ISBN 0-516-04581-4
This is a description of the "densely populated, landlocked country in equatorial Africa west of Uganda and Tanzania. Formerly a protectorate of Belgium, the nation gained independence in 1962. Well illustrated with photographs and maps, this good introduction to Rwanda's history, geography, government, peoples, and customs should be useful in school and public libraries." Sch Library J
Handy reference section: p90-91

Kaula, Edna Mason
The Bantu Africans; illus. with photographs. Watts, F. 1968 90p illus map lib. bdg. $3.90 (4-7)   916.7
   1 Bantus
   ISBN 0-531-00478-3
"Although Bantu is a language, it has come to mean the group of people living in Central and South Africa. This book traces the history of these people as they grew in number and became different tribes and nations. It charts the Bantus' struggles for independence and self rule. [Includes] an index, guide to the pronunciation of Bantu terms, photos, and map of the area." Bruno. Bks for Sch Libraries, 1968

Perl, Lila
East Africa; Kenya, Tanzania, Uganda; illus. with 58 photographs. Morrow 1973 160p illus map lib. bdg. $5.11 (4-7)   916.7
   1 Africa, East
   ISBN 0-688-30088-X
This book offers background on the geography, people and history of East Africa. The first chapter looks at the area as a whole and the following chapters examine individual present-day conditions of Tanzania, Uganda, and Kenya
Bibliography: p154-55

916.75   Geography of Congo Republic (Zaire)

Carpenter, Allan
Zaire, by Allan Carpenter and Matthew Maginnis; consulting editor: John Rowe. Childrens Press [1974 c1973] 93p illus maps (Enchantment of Africa) lib. bdg. $6.60 (4-7)   916.75
   1 Zaire
   ISBN 0-516-04593-8
An introduction to the land and people of Zaïre, formerly known as the Congo, discussing its geography, history, government, natural resources and major cities
Handy reference section: p90-91

Crane, Louise
The land and people of the Congo. Lippincott 1971 143p illus map (Portraits of the nations ser) $5.95 (5-7)   916.75
   1 Zaire
   ISBN 0-397-31172-9
"After reviewing the history of the area from its discovery by Europeans to the rule of President Mobutu, [the author] discusses the government, people, religion, education, industry, and other aspects of present-day life in the African nation." Booklist

McKown, Robin
The Congo: river of mystery; illus. by Tom Feelings. McGraw 1968 144p illus $5.50, lib. bdg. $5.72 (6-7)   916.75
   1 Congo River 2 Zaire
   ISBN 0-07-045360-8; 0-07-045361-6
The 2,716 mile long Congo river has played a fundamental part in the history and economy of Zaire. The author uses the description of life along the river as a connecting element in this discussion of the land and people of this former Belgian territory
"Famous people involved with the area are depicted unsentimentally: the greed and cruelty of Leopold II are shown, Stanley is unglamorized, Brazzi is portrayed sympathetically for his unselfish humanity. The account of post-independence confusion is, on the whole, well handled; Lumumba emerges as a heroic martyr. The many handsome, clearly labeled illustrations . . . enliven and extend the text." Sch Library J

916.76   Geography of Kenya

Carpenter, Allan
Kenya, by Allan Carpenter and Milan De Lany; consulting editor: David Rubadiri. Childrens Press 1973 96p illus maps (Enchantment of Africa) lib. bdg. $6.60 (4-7)   916.76
   1 Kenya
   ISBN 0-516-04566-0
A survey of Kenya's geography, history, economy, natural resources, culture, people, and attractions
Handy reference section: p92-93

Uganda, by Allan Carpenter and James Hughes; consulting editor: John Rowe. Children Press 1973 94p illus maps (Enchantment of Africa) lib. bdg. $6.60 (4-7)   916.76
   1 Uganda
   ISBN 0-516-04591-1
The authors survey Uganda's geography, history, government, resources, people, cultures, industries and economy
"The 1971 political crisis precipitated by General Amin's seizure of the government is mentioned but not discussed in enough detail for readers to comprehend its impact on Uganda's future. However, the book is well illustrated . . . and, since there is little else available on Uganda, librarians will find this a useful addition to African studies collections." Sch Library J
Handy reference section: p90-91

916.78   Geography of Tanzania

Carpenter, Allan
Tanzania, by Allan Carpenter and James W. Hughes; consulting editor: John Rowe. Childrens Press [1974 c1973] 95p illus maps (Enchantment of Africa) lib. bdg. $6.60 (4-7)   916.78
   1 Tanzania
   ISBN 0-516-04588-1
An introduction to the land and people of Tanzania, discussing its geography, history, politics and natural resources
Handy reference section: p92-93

Kaula, Edna Mason
The land and people of Tanzania. Lippincott 1972 139p illus map (Portraits of the nations ser) $6.95 (5-7)   916.78

Kaula, Edna Mason—*Continued*

1 Tanzania
ISBN 0-397-31544-9
An "account of the growth of and the progress being made in Tanzania since independence in 1964. Kaula briefly but adequately covers geography, the people, and history and outlines the rise of President Nyerere and the Tanganyika African National Union (the TANU party). The rest of the book treats the effects on the people of government programs to improve agriculture, education, medicine, transportation, industry, and urban conditions. Accompanied by good black-and-white photographs, this provides new material which will be valuable where African studies are taught." Sch Library J

916.8   Geography of South Africa

Bleeker, Sonia
The Zulu of South Africa; cattlemen, farmers, and warriors; illus. by Kisa N. Sasaki. Morrow 1970 160p illus maps lib. bdg. $4.59 (4-7)   916.8
1 Zulus
ISBN 0-688-21451-7
An "account of the Zulu people, this book includes a historical narrative; a full picture of Zulu customs concerning daily life, marriage, and cattle raising; and a description of life in modern South Africa. The author uses fictional characters in episodes to tell about customs, but she tells the life of historically known leaders as well. This is a sympathetic study of the Zulu told without polemic. Line drawings illustrate many parts of the book showing details of life and custom that are difficult to comprehend without pictures." Sci Bks
"Dependably comprehensive and authentic. . . . The material is well-organized, the writing straightforward and objective." Chicago. Children's Bk Center

Carpenter, Allan
Botswana, by Allan Carpenter and Tom Balow; consulting editor: Ronald Cohen. Childrens Press 1973 94p illus maps (Enchantment of Africa) lib. bdg. $6.60 (4-7)   916.8
1 Botswana
ISBN 0-516-04553-9
A survey of the geography, history, government, economy, natural resources, people, culture, and attractions of this African nation
Handy reference section: p90-91

Paton, Alan
The land and people of South Africa. Rev. ed. Lippincott 1972 159p illus map (Portraits of the nations ser) $5.95 (5-7)   916.8
1 Africa, South
ISBN 0-397-31302-0
First published 1955
This book introduces the land, people, industries, history, customs, natural resources, government, and racial problems of the southernmost country on the African continent

Perkins, Carol Morse
"I saw you from afar;" a visit to the Bushmen of the Kalahari Desert [by] Carol Morse Perkins and Marlin Perkins. Atheneum Pubs. 1965 56p illus lib. bdg. $4.95 (3-6)   916.8

1 Bushmen 2 Kalahari Desert
ISBN 0-689-30011-5
"The authors describe the people of a desert Bushman tribe; the photographic illustrations are very good, the writing style has a matter-of-fact simplicity, and the attitude is sympathetic without being sentimental or patronizing. There is little fictionalization and little intrusion of the experiences of the authors; the text discusses the cultural patterns of the Kalahari Bushmen, their adaptations to the desert environment, and their grace and courtesy as a people." Chicago. Children's Bk Center
Maps on lining-papers

916.89   Geography of Zambia

Carpenter, Allan
Zambia, by Allan Carpenter and Lynn Ragin; consulting editor: John Rowe. Childrens Press 1973 94p illus maps (Enchantment of Africa) lib. bdg. $6.60 (4-7)   916.89
1 Zambia
ISBN 0-516-04594-6
A survey of the geography, history, government, economy, natural resources, culture, people, and attractions of this south-central African nation
Handy reference section: p90-91

Dresang, Eliza T.
The land and people of Zambia. Lippincott 1975 159p illus maps (Portraits of the nations ser) $5.95 (5-7)   916.89
1 Zambia
ISBN 0-397-31561-9
"The history, geography, and natural resources of Zambia, formerly Northern Rhodesia, are related to its current politics, goals, achievements, and life styles. The author's admiration for the government's efforts to capitalize on their natural resources, especially copper, is tempered by the criticism of the abuses of political and economic power which resulted in the nationalization of industries, political oppression, and preferential treatment of native Zambians. Information on efforts to encourage nationalism over tribalism, cultural activities, sports, holidays, city life, copper mining and production rounds out the coverage along with fine photos and maps." Sch Library J

916.9   Geography of the Malagasy Republic

Carpenter, Allan
Malagasy Republic (Madagascar), by Allan Carpenter and Matthew Maginnis; consulting editor: John Rowe. Childrens Press 1972 93p illus maps (Enchantment of Africa) lib. bdg. $6.60 (4-7) 916.9
1 Madagascar
ISBN 0-516-04575-X
An introduction to the history, geography, industry, natural resources, people, social life and customs of the African island republic of Madagascar
Handy reference section: p90-91

917 Geography of North America

Coy, Harold
Man comes to America; illus. by Leslie Morrill.
Little 1973 150p illus $5.95 (6-7)   917
1 America—Antiquities 2 Man, Prehistoric 3
Indians of North America—Origin
ISBN 0-316-15906-9
"After distinguishing man from other animals, Coy
relates how he adjusted to his harsh existence (cold,
need to hunt for food, etc.). He then progresses to
early man's arrival in North America via a land bridge
which formerly connected Siberia and Alaska. The
final half of the text is devoted to a projection of what
life was like for these early Americans, including
plants and animals they might have found." Sch Library J
"The book provides a sound, broad-brush account
of man in the New World." Sci Bks
Further reading: p139-50

Lauber, Patricia
Who discovered America? Settlers and explorers of
the New World before the time of Columbus; illus.
with photographs, prints, and maps. Random House
1970 128p illus maps lib. bdg. $6.29 (4-7)   917
1 America—Antiquities 2 America—Discovery and
exploration
ISBN 0-394-91855-X
The author gives an "account of the known and
speculative evidence in the New World's beginnings
and re-beginnings, discoveries and rediscoveries. . . .
A long-view examination of human and animal migrations and development during and after the Ice Age
flows . . . into a discussion of pre-Columbian outside
influences and their possible origins." N Y Times Bk
Rev
Selected bibliography: p124-25

May, Julian
Before the Indians; illus. by Symeon Shimin. Holiday House 1969 unp illus map lib. bdg. $5.95 (2-4)
                                                   917
1 North America—Antiquities 2 Man, Prehistoric
ISBN 0-8234-0005-0
An account of "the world of prehistoric America as
far back as that of the Paleo-Indians, who inhabited
our continent forty thousand years ago. The brief
text—easy for young readers—and the picture
details, which amplify the story of how archeologists
derive their knowledge, make an inviting introduction to early cultures—from those of the Ancient
Hunters and Big Game Hunters to the Old Desert
Culture people, Archaic people, and the Burial
Mound people." Horn Bk
"Although primarily chronological, this is a rather
haphazard presentation of facts. . . . The text is continuous, the pages not numbered, and there is no
index. The writing is direct and simple, so that the
book is good for browsing or as an introduction either
to archeology or to a study of American Indians."
Chicago. Children's Bk Center

Scheele, William E.
The earliest Americans; written and illus. by William E. Scheele. Collins 1963 58p illus map lib. bdg.
$4.51 (5-7)   917
1 North America—Antiquities 2 Man, Prehistoric
3 Indians of North America—Antiquities
ISBN 0-529-03747-5
"Briefly and authoritatively [the author] explores
clues, discoveries, and theories related to Folsom
man [of what is now New Mexico], Sandia man, and

the Tule Springs culture, basing his discussion on the
most up-to-date archaeological research. [There are]
many meaningful drawings." Booklist

917.1 Geography of Canada

Ross, Frances Aileen
The land and people of Canada; foreword by
A. R. M. Lower. [Rev. ed] Lippincott 1964 128p illus
maps (Portraits of the nations ser) $5.95 (5-7) 917.1
1 Canada
ISBN 0-397-31567-8
First published 1947
The author traces the political and social history of
our neighbor to the north
She "is objective about relations between this country and Canada but does not analyze them deeply. The
friction between French and British factions is described. . . . The historical and political coverage is
detailed and comprehensive; there is no discussion of
cultural aspects of Canadian life." Chicago. Children's Bk Center

917.127 Geography of Manitoba

Kurelek, William
A prairie boy's summer; paintings and story by
William Kurelek. Houghton 1975 unp illus $7.95
(3-5)   917.127
1 Children in Canada 2 Farm life—Canada
3 Summer
ISBN 0-395-20280-9
A companion volume to the author's: A prairie boy's
winter, entered below
This book shows "many details of the artist's life
when he was a boy growing up on a farm in western
Canada. . . . Summer brought a great variety of
experiences, including such regular, homely chores as
milking and such demanding ones as driving the tractor that pulled the huge mowing machines. There was
also the fun of skinny dipping, the excitement of great
thunderstorms that swept across the prairie, and the
drudgery of 'stooking,' when grain had to be bundled
by hand during wet spells." Horn Bk
"It is, of course, the pictures by this distinguished
Canadian artist that give the book its distinction; each
full-color page glows with life and vigor, and the
paintings have both a felicity of small details and a
remarkable evocation of the breadth and sweep of the
Manitoba prairie." Chicago. Children's Bk Center

A prairie boy's winter; paintings and story by William Kurelek. Houghton 1973 unp illus $5.95 (3-5)
                                                 917.127
1 Children in Canada 2 Farm life—Canada
3 Winter
ISBN 0-395-17708-1
Based on his own experiences, the author depicts
the rigors and pleasures of boyhood winters on a
Manitoba farm in the 1930's including hauling hay,
playing hockey, and surviving a blizzard
"Kurelek's 20 full-page paintings combine a child's
directness of expression with a technique subtle
enough to make absolute distinctions in tone and texture between newly fallen snow and the waterlogged
blanket of slush that characterizes the landscape of
early spring. He captures the color of cold, the weight
of a late autumn sky heavy with pending precipitation." N Y Times Bk Rev

917.2   Geography of Mexico

Epstein, Sam
The first book of Mexico, by Sam and Beryl Epstein; illus. with photographs. Rev. ed. Watts, F. 1967 88p illus map lib. bdg. $3.90 (4-7)   917.2
1 Mexico
ISBN 0-531-00583-6
First published 1955
"The reader tours Mexican towns and cities, visits a Mexican school, takes part in games and festivals, and learns the highlights of Mexican history. Illustrated with photographs." Hodges. Bks for Elem Sch Libraries

Grant, Clara Louise
Mexico, land of the plumed serpent, by Clara Louise Grant and Jane Werner Watson. Garrard 1968 111p illus maps lib. bdg. $4.38 (3-5)   917.2
1 Mexico
ISBN 0-8116-6859-2
"Living in today's world"
Illustrated by Ernesto Alvarez and others
This "account of the history and geography of Mejico from the time of the Mayas to the present combines legends and stories with straightforward factual material. The variety is appealing and sustains interest throughout the book even for older slow readers." Sch Library J

Kirtland, G. B.
One day in Aztec Mexico; drawings by Jerome Snyder. Harcourt 1963 40p illus $4.50, lib. bdg. $3.95 (2-5)   917.2
1 Aztecs
ISBN 0-15-258381-5; 0-15-258383-1
A story in the form of a dialogue between a brother and sister, set in the Aztec civilization of the year 1510. There is a glossary of Aztec words used in the text
The story "begins with the rising sun and skillfully suggests sun-worship. Aztec customs, pleasant and otherwise, are woven through the narrative—including their method of human sacrifice, which the boy and girl discuss—and here again the author is skillfull. . . . Jerome Snyder's illustrations are as effective and amusing as ever." Sat Rev

Neurath, Marie
They lived like this in ancient Mexico; artist: John Ellis. Watts, F. 1971 32p illus map lib. bdg. $3.90 (4-6)   917.2
1 Mexico—Antiquities
ISBN 0-531-01395-2
Concentrating on the period of history predating both the Inca and Aztec civilizations, the author studies the products of these ancient Mexican craftsmen, their buildings, their writing of numbers and words, and their pictures
"The author has done a good job with the help of abundant illustrations, most of which are copied from ancient codicils. The technique of using the aboriginal drawings as illustrations of the daily life of the ancient Mexicans is excellent. . . . The treatment is accurate, and the author has also been careful not to burden the juvenile reader with a lot of strange names which would make comprehension more difficult. There is also a successful attempt to relate ancient Mexican life to cultural universals such as food, dress, family life, etc., in such a way that the reader can contrast these with his own situation. Young readers should find the volume both instructive and entertaining." Sci Bks

917.28   Geography of Central America

Markun, Patricia Maloney
The first book of Central America and Panama. Rev. ed. Illus. with photographs. Watts, F. 1972 85p illus map lib. bdg. $3.90 (5-7)   917.28
1 Central America
ISBN 0-531-00497-X
A general introduction to the geography, history, principal industry, and way of life of Central America accompanies a description of each of its seven countries

917.281   Geography of Guatemala

Carpenter, Allan
Guatemala. Consulting editor: Luis E. Rivera. Childrens Press 1971 93p illus maps (Enchantment of Central America) lib. bdg. $6.60 (4-6)   917.281
1 Guatemala
ISBN 0-516-04517-2
A survey of the history, geography, natural resources, and life and customs of the people of Guatemala
Handy reference section: p90-93

917.282   Geography of British Honduras

Carpenter, Allan
British Honduras, by Allan Carpenter and Tom Balow. Childrens Press 1971 95p illus maps (Enchantment of Central America) lib. bdg. $6.60 (4-6)   917.282
1 British Honduras
ISBN 0-516-04518-0
A survey of the history, geography, natural resources, and life and customs of the people of British Honduras
Handy reference section: p91-92

917.283   Geography of Honduras

Carpenter, Allan
Honduras, by Allan Carpenter and Tom Balow. Consulting editor: María Weddle de Jiménez. Childrens Press 1971 95p illus maps (Enchantment of Central America) lib. bdg. $6.60 (4-6)   917.283
1 Honduras
ISBN 0-516-04521-0
A survey of the history, geography, natural resources, and life and customs of the people of Honduras
Handy reference section: p89-91

917.284 Geography of El Salvador

Carpenter, Allan
El Salvador, by Allan Carpenter and Eloise Baker.
Consulting editor: Hernany Miranda. Childrens
Press 1971 95p illus maps (Enchantment of Central
America) lib. bdg. $6.60 (4-6)   917.284
1 Salvador
ISBN 0-516-04516-4
A survey of the history, geography, natural
resources, and life and customs of the people of El
Salvador
Includes a handy reference section

Haverstock, Nathan A.
El Salvador in pictures, by Nathan A. Haverstock
and John P. Hoover. Sterling 1974 64p illus map
(Visual geography ser) lib. bdg. $3.39, pa $1.75
(5-7)   917.284
1 Salvador
ISBN 0-8069-1181-6; 0-8069-1180-8
An introduction to the country of El Salvador along
with a description of the land, people, government,
economy and history

917.285 Geography of Nicaragua

Carpenter, Allan
Nicaragua, by Allan Carpenter and Tom Balow.
Childrens Press 1971 95p illus maps (Enchantment of
Central America) lib. bdg. $6.60 (4-6)   917.285
1 Nicaragua
ISBN 0-516-04519-9
A survey of the history, geography, natural
resources, and life and customs of the people of
Nicaragua
Handy reference section: p90-93

917.286 Geography of Costa Rica

Carpenter, Allan
Costa Rica. Consulting editor: Guillermo Segreda.
Childrens Press 1971 96p illus maps (Enchantment of
Central America) lib. bdg. $6.60 (4-6)   917.286
1 Costa Rica
ISBN 0-516-04515-6
A survey of the history, geography, natural
resources, and life and customs of the people of Costa
Rica
Handy reference section: p90-93

917.29 Geography of the West Indies

Sherlock, Philip
The land and people of the West Indies. Lippincott
1967 172p illus map (Portraits of the nations ser) $5.95
(5-7)   917.29

1 West Indies
ISBN 0-397-30956-2
This is an overview of the history and way of life in
this area. Despite a similarity in agriculture, climate
and physical contour, these islands vary remarkably in
culture, language, nationality, and government

917.291 Geography of Cuba

Ortiz, Victoria
The land and people of Cuba. Lippincott 1973 157p
illus map (Portraits of the nations ser) $5.95 (5-7)
917.291

1 Cuba
ISBN 0-397-31382-9
"Following the history and struggle of the Cuban
people to shed all foreign shackles, this is a well-
written document which expresses compassion for
Cuba and her centuries of suffering. Including much
interesting information about climate, diet, labor, and
history, [the author] makes a clear statement against
any foreign intervention, and her picture of present-
day Cuba is pro-Castro. Far from a weak pawn of the
Soviet Union, Cuba is presented as a country of men
and women who finally are able to reap some reward
from their labors. There is also a chapter on the feminist movement in Cuba, and the epilogue attempts to
foresee Socialist Cuba's role in the world community." Sch Library J

917.295 Geography of Puerto Rico

Buckley, Peter
I am from Puerto Rico; illus. with photographs.
Simon & Schuster 1971 127p illus map $4.95 (4-6)
917.295

1 Puerto Rico—Social life and customs
ISBN 0-671-65164-1
This is the actual story of Federico Ramirez, a
twelve-year-old boy who has moved from New York
City to a small village in Puerto Rico. There his greatest fear is the ocean, or rather, the sharks and other
dangerous fish. This story tells how he overcomes this
fear with the aid of a young fisherman
The book is "illustrated with photographs which are
well correlated with the text. Useful supplementary
material for social studies units on Puerto Rico."
Booklist

Colorado, Antonio J.
The first book of Puerto Rico. Rev. ed. Illus. with
photographs. Watts, F. 1972 75p illus map lib. bdg.
$3.90 (5-7)   917.295
1 Puerto Rico
ISBN 0-531-00617-4
First published 1965
This book discusses Puerto Rico's history, geography, economics, politics, people, cities and towns,
education, art, sports, historic buildings, and the capital city of San Juan
Some Puerto Rican words: p69-71

Kurtis, Arlene Harris
Puerto Ricans; from island to mainland; illus. with
photographs. Messner 1969 96p illus maps $3.95, lib.
bdg. $3.64 (4-7)   917.295
1 Puerto Rico 2 Puerto Ricans in the U.S.
ISBN 0-671-32084-X; 0-671-32085-8

Kurtis, Arlene Harris—*Continued*

This is both a social and historical account of Puerto Rico in which the author attempts to convey the life, hopes and aspirations of the Puerto Rican people on their island and in the cities of the United States mainland

It is "a simply written, comprehensive survey of Puerto Ricans, dry but informative. . . . The historical background is ample and interesting, and the analyses of present-day problems briskly competent. The author is candid about inadequacies and hopeful about the future." Chicago. Children's Bk Center

Pronunciation guide and glossary: p87-91

917.3   Geography of the U.S.

Bergere, Thea

The homes of the Presidents; illus. by Richard Bergere. Dodd 1962 94p illus $3.95 (5-7)   917.3

1 U.S.—Historic houses, etc. 2 Presidents—U.S.
ISBN 0-306-04726-2

A collection of "drawings of the birthplaces of the presidents and of the considerably more elaborate establishments that they occupied in later life. The book includes President Kennedy's summer home at Hyannisport, Mass. There are also several views of the White House and . . . [biographical sketches] of the Presidents." Pub W

Goetz, Delia

State capital cities; illus. with 92 photographs. Morrow 1971 159p illus lib. bdg. $4.81 (4-6)   917.3

1 Capitals (Cities) 2 Cities and towns—U.S.
ISBN 0-688-31955-6

This book consists of "brief sketches of each of the state capitals and Washington, D. C., covering the founding of the city, the derivation of the name, the design of the capitol building, and some of the activities presently carried on there." Sch Library J

Loeper, John J.

Going to school in 1776; illus. with old woodcuts. Atheneum Pubs. 1973 79p illus $5.95 (3-6)   917.3

1 U.S.—Social life and customs 2 Education—U.S.—History 3 Children in the U.S.
ISBN 0-689-30089-1

The author tells what it was like to be a child and to go to school in America in 1776. He describes children's dress, schools, teachers, school books, lessons, discipline and after-school recreation

Bibliography: p[83-84]

Melbo, Irving Robert

Our country's national parks. Centennial ed. By Irving Robert Melbo with the assistance of Robert Irving Melbo. Bobbs 1973 2v illus ea $7.50 (5-7)   917.3

1 National parks and reserves—U.S.
ISBN v1 0-672-51825-2; v2 0-672-51826-0
First published 1941

In this story of our national parks, each one is described in a separate chapter with information on history, terrain, flora and fauna, climate, and outstanding features

National Geographic Society

America's historylands; touring our landmarks of liberty. New ed. The Society 1967 576p illus maps (World in color lib) $9.95   917.3

1 U.S.—Description and travel 2 U.S.—Historic houses, etc. 3 U.S.—History
First published 1962

A report on hundreds of national historic sites, state parks, battlefields, towns, homes, and restorations in the United States with an explanation of their historic significance

"Signed articles by American writers and historians closely integrated with colorful illustrations and maps give readers of all ages a sense of participation in the events as they occur." Booklist

The new America's wonderlands; our national parks. The Society 1975 464p illus (World in color lib) $9.95   917.3

1 National parks and reserves—U.S. 2 Natural monuments—U.S.
ISBN 0-87044-004-7

First published 1959 with title: America's wonderlands

Illustrated with many color photographs, this book describes 78 national parks and natural monuments of the United States. Some of the areas are described in personal narratives; others are described more briefly

Contents: The Rocky Mountains; The Great plateau; The Southwest; The golden West; The Pacific Northwest; The East; Alaska, Hawaii, Virgin Islands

Folded map in end-paper pocket

Ross, Frank

Stories of the states; a reference guide to the fifty states and the U.S. territories, by Frank Ross, Jr. Illus. by Lee J. Ames. Crowell 1969 327p illus maps $6.95 (4-6)   917.3

1 United States
ISBN 0-690-77849-X

"Basic information plus a map and brief history of exploration and settlement, statehood, and current status is given for each state." Pub W

"An objective, extremely useful encyclopedia supplement and reference source, particularly for school libraries." Sch Library J

Sloane, Eric

ABC book of early Americana; a sketchbook of antiquities and American firsts. Doubleday 1963 unp illus $4.95, lib. bdg. $5.70 (4-7)   917.3

1 U.S.—Social life and customs—Colonial period 2 Alphabet books
ISBN 0-385-04663-4; 0-385-05169-7

Pencil sketches accompany descriptions of early American objects from the almanack, hex sign, and johnny-cake to the niddy noddy, quill pen, and zig-zag fence. Includes a section on the alphabet

"Mr. Sloane has hand-lettered his alphabet and the names of articles so that his pages are not only informative but extremely pleasant to look at. Particularly engaging is the artist's admiration for the work of skilled craftsmen." Bk Week

Tunis, Edwin

The tavern at the ferry; illus. by the author. Crowell 1973 109p illus $7.95 (5-7)   917.3

1 U.S.—Social life and customs—Colonial period
ISBN 0-690-00099-5

"Tracing the development of the taverns and ferry-crossings along the Pennsylvania and New Jersey sides of the Delaware River, [the author] perforce traces the growth of transportation of commerce, and —finally—of rebellion in the colonies. . . . The main characters in the story are the family and descendants of Henry Baker, a Quaker who came to the New World in 1684 and settled in what became Makefield Township, Bucks County, Pennsylvania. The account of how the Baker house became first a convenient place for the occasional wayfarer to get help in crossing the river, then an 'ordinary,' or ordinary household, whose master sold food and drink, and finally a full-fledged tavern is intermittently inter-

Tunis, Edwin—*Continued*
rupted by chapters of a more general nature: Expansion, Enterprise and Taverns in Country and Town. . . . The final section describes Washington's crossing of the Delaware and the battle of Trenton, events which make an appropriately grand finale for a book on ferry crossings." Horn Bk

This book "is profusely illustrated with pictures that give, in their meticulous detail, authoritative information about clothing, buildings, weapons, vehicles, and other artifacts of the period. . . . Useful for social studies, fascinating for the history buff or the reader interested in Americana, well organized and written, this is a handsome book." Chicago. Children's Bk Center

917.4 Geography of North-eastern states. New England

McGovern, Ann
If you lived in Colonial times; pictures by Brinton Turkle. Four Winds [1966 c1964] 79p illus map $4.95 (2-4)   917.4
1 U.S.—Social life and customs—Colonial period 2 Children in the U.S. 3 New England
ISBN 0-590-17015-5
This account of life in colonial New England tells what it was like to be a girl or boy in those days. It describes food, houses, clothing, schooling, manners, games, means of communication, and occupations
"A book that gives a great deal of information and is nicely appropriate to the capability of the beginning reader: short topics, simple style, large print; the illustrations are plentiful, attractive, and often humorous." Sutherland. The Best in Children's Bks

Stearns, Monroe
The story of New England; illus. with prints and paintings by Paul Revere, John Singleton Copley, Gilbert Stuart, Winslow Homer, and many other New England artists, as well as maps and photographs. Random House 1967 179p illus maps $4.95, lib. bdg. $5.99 (5-7)   917.4
1 New England
ISBN 0-394-81894-6; 0-394-91894-0
"Landmark giant"
This account of New England, beginning with its earliest days, explores both the religious and civic traditions of the people and the events which shaped the history of the region
"Profusely illustrated. . . . The text is written with easy informality, its only weakness being the comparatively scanty treatment of twentieth century events. A useful book, however, and an interesting one. Appended are a list of some important dates, a list of suggested readings . . . and an index." Chicago. Children's Bk Center

917.47 Geography of New York. New York (City)

Sasek, M.
This is New York. Macmillan (N Y) 1960 60p illus lib. bdg. $5.95 (3-6)   917.47
1 New York (City)—Description
Beginning with the purchase of Manhattan Island from the Indians in 1626, the author-artist presents

the pageant of New York City and its skyscrapers, subways, boats, bridges, parks, and people
"An impressionistic tour of New York City in brief text and the author's gay, colorful pictures." Hodges. Bks for Elem Sch Libraries

Young, Bernice Elizabeth
Harlem: the story of a changing community; illus. with photographs and drawings. Messner 1972 64p illus maps lib. bdg. $4.29 (3-6)   917.47
1 Harlem, New York (City)
ISBN 0-671-32519-1
"An easy-to-read capsule history of Harlem describing its evolution: from countryside, to fashionable neighborhood, to America's most notorious ghetto. Engravings from early days as well as contemporary photos speak with more meaning and force than the words. . . . An excellent book for increasing social awareness, especially in well-off white classrooms." Pub W

917.53 Geography of Washington, D.C.

Sasek, M.
This is Washington, D.C. Macmillan (N Y) 1969 60p illus maps $4.95 (3-6)   917.53
1 Washington, D.C.—Description
The reader is taken on a guided tour of Washington, D.C. and is shown the interesting places in the nation's capital. Historical facts and views of the national government at work are also included
"The chief lure, as always, is in [the author-artist's] illustrations. The buildings are drawn with photographic precision, and the page layout and use of color are skilled." Sat Rev

917.55 Geography of Virginia

Gurney, Gene
Monticello, by Gene and Clare Gurney; with special photography by Harold Wise and drawings and maps by Dan Dagle. Watts, F. 1966 74p illus maps lib. bdg. $3.90 (5-7)   917.55
1 Monticello, Va. 2 Jefferson, Thomas, President U.S.
ISBN 0-531-00585-2
"Both accurate and interesting historical information is given on Thomas Jefferson's famous mountaintop plantation near Charlottesville, Virginia. The drawings of the interior of the house and of Jefferson's possessions are very well done. The photographs are clear, in most cases, but do not show up the unusual features of Monticello to advantage." Sch Library J
"A good supplement for study about or interest in Jefferson and Southern colonial life." Horn Bk

917.64 Geography of Texas

Sasek, M.
This is Texas. Macmillan (N Y) 1967 60p illus map lib. bdg. $5.95 (3-6)   917.64
1 Texas—Description and travel
The author-illustrator gives his "impressions of such diversities as grain elevators in the Panhandle, prairie dogs in Lubbock . . . the King Ranch and such

Sasek, M.—*Continued*
modern attractions as the Houston Astrodome . . .
[and] Dallas's Neiman-Marcus Specialty Store." N Y
Times Bk Rev

"An entertaining and fun-poking hodgepodge of
places and faces, bits of historical information,
oddities, and statistics." Sat Rev

917.7   Geography of North Central states

Naden, Corinne J.
The Mississippi; America's great river system.
Watts, F. 1974 65p illus maps lib. bdg. $3.90 (4-7)
917.7

1 Mississippi River
ISBN 0-531-00819-3
"A First book"
This book describes the Mississippi's route through
the heartland of America; its exploration; its importance in the history of our country and its economic
importance; its floods and what's being done to control them; its romantic steamboat period, documented by Mark Twain and others; and the major
cities that have grown up on its banks

"Facts and statistics are interwoven with many colorful stories about the role of the Mississippi River in
America's development. Many photographs and
drawings enhance the text. The bibliography, glossary, index and maps make this book a valuable reference aid." Cath Library World

Solomon, Louis
The Mississippi; America's mainstream; illus. with
photographs and line drawings. McGraw 1971 128p
illus $5.50, lib. bdg. $5.72 (5-7)   917.7
1 Mississippi River
ISBN 0-07-059627-1; 0-07-059628-X
The author traces the history of the Mississippi
River from the conquistadors' exploration to its
present polluted state
Bibliography: p126

917.71   Geography of Ohio

Renick, Marion
Ohio. Coward-McCann 1970 123p illus maps
(States of the nation) lib. bdg. $5.99 (5-7)   917.71
1 Ohio
ISBN 0-698-30267-2
"In a clear narrative style, this book explores what
makes Ohio 'tick' through historical, economic and
contemporary points of view. Sounding more like a
travelogue than a social studies text, the book covers
areas of high interest for children: e.g., the state fair,
archaeological findings, transportation, the Teenage
Hall of Fame, festivals, resorts, sports, arts and crafts,
education, colleges, and natural resources." Library J

917.8   Geography of Western states. Cowboys

Cowboys and cattle country, by the editors of American Heritage, The Magazine of History; narrative
by Don Ward; in consultation with J. C. Dykes.
Am. Heritage [distributed by Harper] 1961 153p
illus map $5.95, lib. bdg. $6.89 (5-7)   917.8

1 Cowboys 2 The West—History
ISBN 0-06-026345-8; 0-06-026365-2
"American Heritage Junior library"
"With handsome prints, photographs and colorful
reproductions of paintings by Charles Russell,
Frederic Remington and others, the authentic life of
the American cowboy from the 'vaquero' to the television gunfighter is told in a lively style with scholarly
accuracy that destroys a number of popular myths.
. . . This book will make a definite contribution to any
library's American history collection and yet will have
a wide range of general reading appeal. Excellent list
of further readings." Sch Library J

Malone, John Williams
An album of the American cowboy; illus. with
photographs. Watts, F. 1971 89p illus maps lib. bdg.
$4.90 (4-7)   917.8
1 Cowboys 2 The West—History
ISBN 0-531-01512-2
"The selection of black-and-white photographs and
reproductions in this sturdy, attractive album stresses
the difficulties, hazards and loneliness of cowboy life.
. . . The brief, factual text suitably develops and
amplifies the illustrations. Chapters deal with different phases of the cowboy's work (e.g., herding and
driving cattle from the prairie range to the railheads,
etc.), the development of the cattle industry, the
Western boom towns, and the legends of violence. In
all, this well-balanced volume offers a fresh approach
to the cowboy scene and a fine stock of illustrations."
Sch Library J
Glossary: p86-87

Rounds, Glen
The cowboy trade; written and illus. by Glen
Rounds. Holiday House 1972 95p illus $5.95 (4-7)
917.8
1 Cowboys 2 The West—History
ISBN 0-8234-0206-1
A "picture of how cowboys lived and worked in the
Old West, carefully pointing out that the demanding,
monotonous, and frequently unpleasant life that cowboys actually led bears little resemblance to what is
portrayed on television and in the movies. Enlivened
by frequent humor in both the text and the drawings,
the book covers such topics as the cowboy's duties,
equipment, dress, behavior in town, and life during
the winter." Booklist
"Narrated with zest and affection, the book offers
an honest, incisive look at the life style of the American cowboy. . . . Unpretentious but interpretive
sketches reflect the gusto of the text." Horn Bk

The treeless plains; written and illus. by Glen
Rounds. Holiday House 1967 95p illus $5.95 (4-6)
917.8
1 Frontier and pioneer life—The West 2 Sod
houses
ISBN 0-8234-0122-7
A "lively but fully authentic account of sod houses
of early settlers on the Great Plains. Full of wry
humor as it tells of their peculiar housekeeping problems, fun and 'fraid holes.' Line drawings add greatly
to the immediacy and realism of this memorable
book." Bruno. Bks for Sch Libraries, 1968

Veglahn, Nancy
Getting to know the Missouri River; illus. by William K. Plummer. Coward, McCann & Geoghegan
1972 71p illus maps lib. bdg. $3.97 (3-5)   917.8
1 Missouri River
ISBN 0-698-30445-4

Veglahn, Nancy—*Continued*

This book describes the geography and history of the Missouri River and the prominent personalities associated with it, including explorers Lewis and Clark, fur trader Manuel Lisa, Kenneth Mackenzie (known as "King of the Missouri"), Prince Maximilian of Germany, steamboat pilot Joseph La Barge and poet John Neihardt. It also tells of attempts to tame the river and harness its waterpower

917.803 The West—Encyclopedias and dictionaries

Grant, Bruce

The cowboy encyclopedia; the old and the new West from the open range to the dude ranch; illus. by Jackie & Fiore Mastri; cover by Clark Bronson. Rand McNally 1951 160p illus maps pa $1.50 (3-6)

917.803

1 The West—Dictionaries 2 Cowboys—Dictionaries 3 English language—Provincialisms
ISBN 0-528-87710-0

A "dictionary of western and cowboy terms containing about 600 entries and 200 line drawings on the old and the new west. . . . Useful for slow readers at any level." Los Angeles. Sch Libraries

Bibliography: p[161-62]

917.87 Geography of Wyoming

Kirk, Ruth

Yellowstone; the first national park; photographs by Ruth and Louis Kirk. Atheneum Pubs. 1974 103p illus maps $6.95 (5-7) 917.87

1 Yellowstone National Park
ISBN 0-689-50006-8

"A Margaret K. McElderry book"

The author describes the plant and animal life of the park, as well as its famous geysers. She also discusses wildlife policies, and provides a travel guide for those planning to visit Yellowstone

"The book is well organized and has excellent graphic support. The writing style is readable and interesting." Sci and Children

917.94 Geography of California

Sasek, M.

This is San Francisco. Macmillan (N Y) 1962 60p illus $5.95 (3-6) 917.94

1 San Francisco—Description

The author-artist presents his views of San Francisco including such sights as the Golden Gate Bridge, Stow Lake, the zoo's koala bears, Chinatown, the cable cars, Union Square with its underground garage, and a machine that washes your money

"The casual text, the format, and the humor in both text and delightful illustrations give the flavor and individual quality of the city rather than giving information of a guidebook variety." Chicago. Children's Bk Center

917.97 Geography of Washington (State)

Kirk, Ruth

The oldest man in America; an adventure in archaeology; foreword by Roald Fryxell and Richard Daugherty; with photographs by Ruth and Louis Kirk. Harcourt 1970 95p illus map $5.75 (5-7)

917.97

1 Excavations (Archeology)—Washington (State) 2 Man, Prehistoric
ISBN 0-15-257830-7

"Thirty people lived and died at Marmes Rock shelter over a period of some 10,000 years. The record of these earliest Americans, their tools, their cooking, their ages and the manner of their deaths were found in the recent excavation at the Marmes site in eastern Washington. Ruth Kirk has recounted the discovery of the oldest, reliably documented evidence of human life in America." Sci Bks

"The details of the dig and of further finds are fascinating, particularly because the archeological volunteers who quickly rallied to search for other traces (which were, indeed, found) were fighting against time. The site was threatened by a projected reservoir for which a dam was being constructed. The combination of suspense in the outcome and of the detailed description of meticulous scientific work is dramatic, the matter-of-fact writing style leaving the stage clear for the exciting facts." Sutherland. The Best in Children's Bks

917.98 Geography of Alaska

Stefansson, Evelyn

Here is Alaska. New rev. ed. Scribner 1973 178p illus maps lib. bdg. $6.95 (6-7) 917.98

1 Alaska
ISBN 0-684-13253-2

First published 1943

"The book explores all aspects of Alaskan life, agricultural and urban, geographic and historical, and industrial; it discusses the Eskimos, the Indians, the oil rush and the struggle between industrialists and environmentalists. Useful, well-organized and well-written." Chicago Children's Bk Center

918 Geography of South America

Carter, William E.

The first book of South America. Rev. ed. Watts, F. 1972 90p illus map lib. bdg. $3.90 (4-6) 918

1 South America
ISBN 0-531-00636-0

First published 1961

"The author first considers the continent as a whole, then briefly describes each country's history, geography, and people." Hodges. Bks for Elem Sch Libraries

918.1   Geography of Brazil

Brown, Rose
The land and people of Brazil; rev. by Leslie F. Warren. Rev. ed. Lippincott 1972 158p illus map (Portraits of the nations ser) $6.95 (5-7)   918.1
1 Brazil
ISBN 0-397-31342-X
First published 1946
This introduction to Brazil covers its history and geography as well as the customs and occupations of its people

Kendall, Sarita
Looking at Brazil. Lippincott [1975 c1974] 64p illus maps (Looking at other countries) $5.95 (4-6) 918.1
1 Brazil
ISBN 0-397-31527-9
First published 1974 in England
"Excellent photographs and maps detail the sharp contrasts in the economy, geography, and climate of this South American nation. [The author] clearly explains why, despite its vast size and rich natural resources, Brazil is still relatively poor and backward. She pulls no punches in relating the hardships and poverty that have resulted from government mismanagement (e.g., native Indians and immigrants endure poor education, unemployment, disease, and substandard living conditions) and explains why plans for the new capital city of Brasilia have failed. [This is] an objective, well-illustrated account." Sch Library J

Sheppard, Sally
The first book of Brazil. Rev. ed. Illus. with photographs. Watts, F. 1972 87p illus maps lib. bdg. $3.90 (4-6)   918.1
1 Brazil
ISBN 0-531-00488-0
First published 1962
Contents: The land; A pioneer nation; Brazil's history; The people; Brazil's music and art; Coffee galore; A variety of products; The rubber boom—and its end; Some cities of Brazil; The capital moves west; Carnival; Religious and national holidays; A glimpse into a wilderness; Summing up

Sperry, Armstrong
The Amazon, river sea of Brazil. Garrard 1961 96p illus maps (Rivers of the world) lib. bdg. $3.48 (4-6)   918.1
1 Amazon River 2 Brazil
ISBN 0-8116-6351-5
The book "gives a colorful picture of the Amazon River, its exploration and the human, animal, and plant life in the surrounding area." Booklist
Modern efforts to control the river are emphasized. It is illustrated with photographs, old prints, and engravings

918.2   Geography of Argentina

Hall, Elvajean
The land and people of Argentina. Rev. ed. Lippincott 1972 159p illus map (Portraits of the nations ser) $6.95 (5-7)   918.2
1 Argentine Republic
ISBN 0-397-31257-1
First published 1960
In this introduction to Argentina, the author surveys its history and the varied life of its peoples, past and present

918.3   Geography of Chile

Carpenter, Allan
Chile. Childrens Press 1969 95p illus maps (Enchantment of South America) $6.60 (4-6)   918.3
1 Chile
ISBN 0-516-04505-9
The author presents a picture of Chile and her people, concentrating on the Araucanian Indians whose ancestors resisted the Spanish invaders. The contrasts of Chile's topography, from frozen wastes to sun-soaked northern regions, as well as her success in foreign trade despite the lack of natural harbors is explored

918.4   Geography of Bolivia

Carpenter, Allan
Bolivia, by Allan Carpenter with Jean Currens Lyon. Consulting editor: Alicia Flix de Taendler. Childrens Press 1970 95p illus maps (Enchantment of South America) lib. bdg. $6.60 (4-6)   918.4
1 Bolivia
ISBN 0-516-04503-2
In this book about Bolivia, "ancient and modern history are covered, as are geography, natural resources, economy, politics, religion, culture and recreation. . . . [Included also is] a chapter on life in that country as it is lived today by children from several levels of society." Library J

Warren, Leslie F.
The land and people of Bolivia. Lippincott 1974 156p illus map (Portraits of the nations ser) $5.95 (5-7)   918.4
1 Bolivia
ISBN 0-397-31578-3
The book provides a survey of the history, geography, major cities, natural resources, and social customs of Bolivia

918.5   Geography of Peru

Bowen, J. David
The land and people of Peru. Rev. ed. Lippincott 1973 158p illus map (Portraits of the nations ser) $6.95 (5-7)   918.5
1 Peru
ISBN 0-397-31483-3
First published 1963
An introduction to the geography, history, culture, social life and economic conditions of this South American republic

Carpenter, Allan
Peru. Consulting editor: Carlos Panizo. Childrens Press 1970 95p illus maps (Enchantment of South America) lib. bdg. $6.60 (4-6)   918.5
1 Peru
ISBN 0-516-04509-1
"Ancient and modern history are covered, as are geography, natural resources, economy, politics, religion, culture and recreation. . . . Events and situations showing the current relationship between the United States and its Latin American neighbors are included, such as Rockefeller's 1969 trip and Nixon's Latin American policies." Library J

918.61   Geography of Colombia

Carpenter, Allan
Colombia, by Allan Carpenter with Jean Currens
Lyon. Childrens Press 1969 95p illus maps (Enchant-
ment of South America) lib. bdg. $6.60 (4-6) 918.61
1 Colombia
ISBN 0-516-04506-7
The authors concentrate on a political history of
Colombia, describing its relations to other countries
on the continent, its revolutions, and other factors
which have influenced the state of affairs

Landry, Lionel
The land and people of Colombia. Lippincott 1970
159p illus maps (Portraits of the nations ser) $5.95, lib.
bdg. $5.95 (5-7)   918.61
1 Colombia
ISBN 0-397-31131-1; 0-397-31132-X
This survey of the geography, history, natural
resources, culture, religion and industries of Colombia focuses on its progress on the social and economic
fronts
"While Landry's own ideal of moderation in pursuit
of progress occasionally intrudes on his account of the
republic's political history and government practices,
the book benefits from his direct contact with the
people. An intelligently organized . . . report."
Booklist

918.62   Geography of Panama

Carpenter, Allan
Panama. Consulting editor: Dídimo Ríos. Chil-
drens Press 1971 96p illus maps (Enchantment of
Central America) lib. bdg. $6 (4-6)   918.62
1 Panama
ISBN 0-516-04520-2
A survey of the history, geography, natural
resources, and life and customs of the people of
Panama
Includes a handy reference section

918.66   Geography of Ecuador

Carpenter, Allan
Ecuador, by Allan Carpenter and Tom Balow. Childrens Press 1969 95p illus maps (Enchantment of
South America) lib. bdg. $6.60 (4-6)   918.66
1 Ecuador
ISBN 0-516-04507-5
In this description of Ecuador's political and geographical aspects, the author covers the topography,
the mixture of the country's population, which
includes mestizos, Chalos Indians, Blacks and
Ecuadorians of Spanish descent. Includes also a brief
account of its natural resources, industry and agriculture

918.7   Geography of Venezuela

Carpenter, Allan
Venezuela, by Allan Carpenter and Enno R. Haan.
Consulting editor: John McCaul. Childrens Press
1970 95p illus maps (Enchantment of South America)
lib. bdg. $6.60 (4-6)   918.7

1 Venezuela
ISBN 0-516-04511-3
In this "history and travel book for young readers
. . . ancient and modern history are covered, as are
geography, natural resources, economy, politics,
religion, culture and recreation. . . . [There is] a
chapter on life in [Venezuela] as it is lived today by
children from several levels of society. Events and
situations showing the current relationship between
the United States and its Latin American neighbors
are included." Library J

918.8   Geography of the Guianas

Carpenter, Allan
French Guiana. Consulting editor: Gérald Brody.
Childrens Press 1970 illus maps (Enchantment of
South America) lib. bdg. $6.60 (4-6)   918.8
1 French Guiana
ISBN 0-516-04512-1
A survey of the history, geography, natural
resources, and life and customs of French Guiana
Handy reference section: p89-92

918.92   Geography of Paraguay

Carpenter, Allan
Paraguay, by Allan Carpenter with Tom Balow.
Consulting editor: Ruben I. Alvarenga. Childrens
Press 1970 93p illus maps (Enchantment of South
America) lib. bdg. $6.60 (4-6)   918.92
1 Paraguay
ISBN 0-516-04510-5
This book contains information on the geography,
history, government, economics, and everyday life
and customs of the country

918.95   Geography of Uruguay

Carpenter, Allan
Uruguay, by Allan Carpenter with Jean Currens
Lyon. Childrens Press 1969 95p illus maps (Enchantment of South America) lib. bdg. $6.60 (4-6) 918.95
1 Uruguay
ISBN 0-516-04514-8
The authors describe Uruguay's past and present,
its people, geography and culture. Located on the
south eastern shore of South America, this small
republic holds a prominent position in commerce and
tourism for the region

Dobler, Lavinia
The land and people of Uruguay. Rev. ed. Lippincott 1972 160p illus map (Portraits of the nations ser)
$5.95 (5-7)   918.95
1 Uruguay
ISBN 0-397-31391-8
First published 1965
The author discusses the history, geography, government, economy, people and customs of the
smallest country in South America

919   Geography of Pacific Ocean islands

Captain Cook and the South Pacific, by the editors of Horizon Magazine. Author: Oliver Warner; consultant: J. C. Beaglehole. Am. Heritage [distributed by Harper] 1963 153p illus maps $5.95, lib. bdg. $6.89 (6-7)   919
1 Islands of the Pacific 2 Discoveries (in geography) 3 Cook, James
ISBN 0-06-026355-5; 0-06-026356-3
"A Horizon Caravel book"
"The great and popular explorer is revealed as zealous, determined, precise, cool. For him, exploration was a quest based on intelligence, and discipline was an art rooted in planning. . . . [The book includes a] section dealing with the impact of Cook's discoveries on Western civilization, especially on the arts." Horn Bk
"Technical aspects and the scientific procedures of the day are explained. But more than that the young reader is given a fair picture of the personality of Cook. . . . The book is replete with the usual handsome illustrations." Best Sellers
Further reference: p151

May, Charles Paul
Oceania: Polynesia, Melanesia, Micronesia. Nelson 1973 224p illus map (World neighbors) $6.95, lib. bdg. $6.75 (5-7)   919
1 Islands of the Pacific
ISBN 0-8407-7068-5; 0-8407-7069-3
"An overall view of the islands of the Pacific Ocean which includes their possible origins, the sources of plants, animals, and insects, and the coming of human inhabitants as well as their history and present development. The author devotes considerable space to a description of everyday life covering clothing, food, sports, education, handicrafts, religion, dances, crops, and business and mentions foreign artists and writers who have used the South Seas as subject material." Booklist
"The many photographs accompanying the text aid understanding, and this will be a useful supplementary title where courses are given in world geography and the culture of other lands." Sch Library J
Other books of interest: p217-18

919.31   Geography of New Zealand

Kaula, Edna Mason
The land and people of New Zealand. [Rev] Lippincott [1972 c1964] 160p illus maps (Portraits of the nations ser) $5.95 (5-7)   919.31
1 New Zealand
ISBN 0-397-30748-9
First published 1964
A "short history, from 14th-century Polynesian settlement to the present decade. Interwoven are descriptions of the natural scene, social life, economics and politics, also the spectacular scenery, strange wildlife, the remarkable Maoris and their past and present relationships to the white settlers." Sch Library J [Review of the 1964 edition]
"Photographs, engravings, and maps enhance this book." Best Sellers [Review of the 1964 edition]

919.4   Geography of Australia

Blunden, Godfrey
The land and people of Australia. Rev. ed. Lippincott 1972 144p illus map (Portraits of the nations ser) $5.95 (5-7)   919.4
1 Australia
ISBN 0-397-31256-3
First published 1954
The author discusses the geographical and geological history of the continent of Australia with its aboriginal tribes and flora and fauna before examining the country's government, language, customs and developed cities and states

Sasek, M.
This is Australia. Macmillan (N Y) [1971 c1970] 60p illus map $4.95 (3-6)   919.4
1 Australia
First published 1970 in England
Illustrated by the author, "the book focuses on major cities, historical sites and new architecture, and on the plants and animals that are so intriguing to non-Australians, giving tangentially some impressions of the atmosphere and character of the country." Chicago. Children's Bk Center
"This is another informative and diverting pictorial introduction to a region. The architectural precision of the street scenes and buildings is impressive, and the humor of the text (more captions than running commentary) is reflected in the witty touches of caricature in the drawings of people." Sat Rev

919.6   Geography of Polynesia

Cavanna, Betty
The first book of Fiji; illus. with photographs. Watts, F. 1969 66p illus map lib. bdg. $3.90 (4-6)   919.6
1 Fiji Islands
ISBN 0-531-00530-5
The author provides a brief summary of the geography and history of the one hundred and six inhabited Fiji Islands. The islanders are discussed in terms of their social and economic problems, racial background, language, customs, food and dress

Pine, Tillie S.
The Polynesians knew, by Tillie S. Pine and Joseph Levine; pictures by Marilyn Hirsh. McGraw 1974 unp illus map lib. bdg. $4.72 (4-6)   919.6
1 Polynesia 2 Science—Experiments
ISBN 0-07-050090-8
This book tells how the early Polynesians mastered navigation, printing, and the manufacture of many useful objects. The authors present simple experiments so that the reader can explore modern-day applications of the same principles
Among the projects "included are boat construction and navigation, weaving, fire-making, cooking, lamp-making, carving, music and the use of coconuts. On each page are simple two-color drawings of the Polynesians and the project and its relationship to our culture. . . . The projects are intended to demonstrate, at an attainable level of understanding for children in middle grades, scientific principles which are known and used by peoples all over the world." Sci Bks

919.69   Geography of Hawaii

Floethe, Louise Lee
The islands of Hawaii; with pictures by Richard Floethe. Scribner 1964 unp illus map lib. bdg. $5.95 (2-4)   919.69
1 Hawaii
ISBN 0-684-12822-5
This is "a modest introduction to the fiftieth state, with pastel illustrations that have informative detail. The simple, continuous text has a quiet conversational quality as it comments on volcanic origin, crops, the local foods, recreation and holidays, and—above all—the diversity of peoples and the harmony in which they live." Chicago. Children's Bk Center

919.8   Geography of the Arctic Islands and Antarctica

Dukert, Joseph M.
This is Antarctica. New and rev. Coward, McCann & Geoghegan [1972 c1971] 192p illus maps lib. bdg. $5.49 (6-7)   919.8
1 Antarctic regions
ISBN 0-698-30364-4
First published 1965
The history of Antarctic exploration and descriptions of current conditions are presented as well as projections into Antarctica's future, including control of the effects of earthquakes, climate and pollution; ties with space travel; robot stations linked with satellites and involvement with world commerce

Goetz, Delia
The Arctic tundra; illus. by Louis Darling. Morrow 1958 62p illus map lib. bdg. $4.32 (3-5)   919.8
1 Arctic regions 2 Eskimos 3 Natural history—Arctic regions
ISBN 0-688-31049-4
"Animal and plant life, the changes of season and the life and customs of Eskimos and Lapps are subjects of this generously illustrated book." Pub W
"Illustrations of Arctic flora and fauna are excellent. Both the text and the illustrations capture the feeling of brooding space and silence in a remote land." Chicago. Children's Bk Center

Harrington, Lyn
The polar regions; earth's frontiers. Nelson 1973 192p illus maps (World neighbors) $5.95, lib. bdg. $5.80 (5-7)   919.8
1 Polar regions
ISBN 0-8407-6338-7; 0-8407-6339-5
The author describes the geography, history, resources and people of the polar regions. She also discusses the changes that are occurring and their effects on the regions
"Valuable for its scope, which is broader both geographically and topically than most books on the subject and illustrated with black-and-white photographs and maps. A chronology and suggestions for further reading are included." Booklist

Icenhower, Joseph B.
The first book of the Antarctic. Rev. ed. Illus. with photographs. Watts, F. 1971 66p illus maps lib. bdg. $3.90 (4-6)   919.8

1 Antarctic regions
ISBN 0-531-00468-6
First published 1956
The author describes the climate, terrain, animal life, transportation, and scientific value of the region
"The small size of the book and its brief, concise explanations would make it useful for students' reports." Sch Library J

Liversidge, Douglas
Arctic exploration; illus. with photographs. Watts, F. 1970 88p illus map lib. bdg. $3.90 (5-7)   919.8
1 Arctic regions 2 Scientific expeditions
ISBN 0-531-00711-1
"A First book"
The author "describes some of the expeditions which have made the greatest contributions to the exploration of the Arctic. Starting with the discovery of the Norwegian coast by Pytheas in about 325 B.C., the book chronologically treats other explorations made in the Arctic up to and including the voyage of the U. S. oil tanker Manhattan in September, 1969." The AAAS Sci Bk List for Children

The first book of the Arctic; illus. with photographs. Watts, F. 1967 74p illus map lib. bdg. $3.90 (4-7)   919.8
1 Arctic regions
ISBN 0-531-00472-4
"The first half of the book is a concise survey of the geography, wildlife, ard ethnic origins and life of Eskimos and Indians. The latter half discusses the advent of the white man placing major emphasis on the current military, industrial, and scientific developments in the area by Russia, America, and Canada." Booklist
"The book's strength lies in the sections on the present-day importance and economy of the Arctic." Sch Library J

Lord, Walter
Peary to the Pole; illus. with 27 photographs. Harper 1963 141p illus map $4.79 (5-7)   919.8
1 North Pole 2 Peary, Robert Edwin
ISBN 0-06-024001-6
"A Breakthrough book"
This is the "story of Robert E. Peary's heroic conquest of the North Pole on April 6, 1909, after six attempts and twenty-two years of longing and hope. . . . Peary is portrayed with his good points and his weaknesses, his courage is contrasted with his blunt manner and tactless ways. It is interesting to note that Peary chose Matthew Henson, a Negro, for his final assault on the Pole because of his skill as a sledge driver and his facility in handling Eskimos. Some of the details of the sordid fight with Dr. Frederick A. Cook, who claimed to have reached the Pole one year ahead of Peary are brought out." Best Sellers
"Peary's own photographs are informatively captioned to give added reality." Sch Library J

Scarf, Maggie
Antarctica: exploring the frozen continent; illus. with photographs and maps. Random House 1970 82p illus maps $3.50, lib. bdg. $4.39 (3-6)   919.8
1 Antarctic regions
ISBN 0-394-80799-5; 0-394-90799-X
"The story of the discovery and exploration of a continent which is dedicated as a base station for scientific studies introduces the young reader to geographic and meteorological information in a pleasant, informal manner. The continent is described as a huge natural laboratory, ideal for the study of weather, gravity, and the upper atmosphere of the earth." The AAAS Sci Bk List for Children

920   BIOGRAPHY

Books of biography are arranged as follows: 1 Biographical collections (920) 2 Biographies of individuals arranged alphabetically by names of biographees (92)

920   Collective biography

Asimov, Isaac
Breakthroughs in science; illus. by Karoly and Szanto. Houghton 1960 [c1959] 197p illus $4.95 (5-7)   920
1 Scientists 2 Science
ISBN 0-395-06561-5
"These essays first appeared in Senior Scholastic." Verso of title page
Here are thirty "biographies of people famous for their contributions toward progress in knowledge. The discoverers here cited worked chiefly in the biological or physical sciences; although they are described quite briefly, their important contribution is given in a crisp and lively report." Chicago. Children's Bk Center
"Such a nontechnical book as this, with well organized and understandable presentations of many basic discoveries, permits the reader to grasp the central ideas and significances involved in each." Chicago Sunday Trib

Benét, Laura
Famous poets for young people. Dodd 1964 160p illus (Famous biographies for young people) $4.50 (5-7)   920
1 Poets, English 2 Poets, American
ISBN 0-396-04941-9
"This collection includes [26] biographical sketches of British and American poets of the 19th and 20th centuries who have written poetry that appeals to young children." Sch Library J
"The biographies are quite brief, in most cases just about three or four pages with a selection of poetry which will entice the young reader. Photographs of several poets are included. The book is well indexed." Best Sellers

Famous storytellers for young people. Dodd 1968 159p illus (Famous biographies for young people) $3.95 (5-7)   920
1 Authors
ISBN 0-396-05667-9
Included are biographies of twenty-three authors whose works are among the best-loved of children's stories, plus excerpts from their works. Among the storytellers considered are the Grimm brothers, Hans Christian Andersen, Dinah Maria Mulock, Kenneth Grahame, Margaret Sidney, William Thackeray, Howard Pyle, and E. Nesbit

Burt, Olive W.
Black women of valor; illus. by Paul Frame. Messner 1974 96p illus $6.25, lib. bdg. $5.79 (4-7)   920
1 Woman—Biography 2 Negroes—Biography
ISBN 0-671-32699-8; 0-671-32700-3
"Written in a vivid, easy-to-read style, this deals with the careers of four little-known Black women. Included are Juliette Derricotte (1897-1931) who tried to achieve racial harmony through working with the YWCA; Maggie Mitchell Walker (1867-1934), this country's only Black female bank president in the late 1920's; Ida Wells Barnett (1862-1931), a journalist responsible for many articles about discrimination and the first book-length study of lynching; and Septima Poinsette Clark (1898-   ), an educator who worked to improve conditions for Black students and teachers in South Carolina as well as to bring about innovations in adult basic education. A list of 62 successful Black women and a good index are provided." Sch Library J

Negroes in the early West; illus. by Lorence F. Bjorklund. Messner 1969 96p illus lib. bdg. $4.29 (4-6)   920
1 Negroes—Biography 2 Frontier and pioneer life—The West
ISBN 0-671-32146-3
Biographies of Negro soldiers, explorers, businessmen, cowboys and mountain men who contributed to the development of the West. A chapter on Negro women pioneers is also included
"Although somewhat pedestrian in treatment, the book provides useful material on the role played by several little-known Negroes in the westward expansion of the U.S. Appropriately illustrated with fine drawings." Booklist
Suggestions for further reading: p91-92

Captains of industry, by the editors of American Heritage, The Magazine of History. Author: Bernard A. Weisberger; consultant: Allan Nevins. Am. Heritage [distributed by Harper] 1966 153p illus $5.95, lib. bdg. $6.89 (5-7)   920
1 Capitalists and financiers 2 U.S.—Industries
ISBN 0-06-026378-4; 0-06-026379-2
"American Heritage Junior library"
"Brief biographies of ten industrial giants of the late nineteenth and early twentieth centuries, emphasizing their personalities and accomplishments and touching lightly on their personal lives. Excellent contemporary photographs and prints and a list for further reading." Hodges. Bks for Elem Sch Libraries

Chittenden, Elizabeth F.
Profiles in black and white; stories of men and women who fought against slavery; illus. with photographs and engravings. Scribner 1973 182p illus $5.95 (5-7)   920
1 Abolitionists 2 Negroes—Biography
ISBN 0-684-13387-3
"A well-written, interesting portrayal of the sometimes unsuccessful but nonetheless courageous efforts of lesser-known individuals to improve the lot of Black Americans before and after the Civil War. [Among the 12 persons] covered are: Theodore Parker, an activist minister; Elijah Lovejoy, a crusading newspaper editor; P.B.S. Pinchback, a Black politician endeavoring to work within the system; and educators like Prudence Crandall, Charlotte Forten, and Sarah Dickey, who extended educational opportunities for Blacks. Despite frequent fictionizing of feelings and dialogue, this collection can serve as a useful introduction to more detailed and scholarly accounts of abolitionist and civil rights activists. Most other books on the topic in this grade range focus on the more famous historical figures." Sch Library J
Bibliography: p176-79

Cone, Molly
The Ringling brothers; illus. by James and Ruth McCrea. Crowell 1971 40p illus (Crowell biographies) $4.50, lib. bdg. $5.25, pa $1.25 (2-4)   920
1 Ringling Brothers 2 Circus—Biography
ISBN 0-690-70287-6; 0-690-70288-4; 0-690-70289-2
"An entertaining account of how five brothers were captivated by the circus and eventually owned the 'Greatest Show on Earth.' " Chicago
"The style is simple, the print large, and the subject is alluring." Sat Rev

Cottler, Joseph

Heroes of civilization, by Joseph Cottler and Haym Jaffe. Rev. ed. Little 1969 393p $7.50 (6-7)   920

1 Scientists 2 Explorers
ISBN 0-316-15790-2
First published 1931
This book contains "biographies of thirty-five scientists in the fields of exploration, pure science, invention, biology and medicine." The AAAS Sci Bk List for Children

More Heroes of civilization, by Joseph Cottler and Haym Jaffe. Little 1969 274p $5.95 (6-7)   920

1 Scientists 2 Explorers
ISBN 0-316-15791-0
A companion volume to Heroes of civilization, entered above, this collection contains over twenty biographies of scientists, inventors and explorers and describes the adventures and extraordinary achievements of each. "Among the individuals included are Edmund Hillary, Charles Babbage, Robert Goddard, Margaret Mead, Carl Linnaeus, Theodor Schwann, Karl Gauss, Heinrich Hertz, and Enrico Fermi. Two chapters deal more briefly with the men who conquered polio and pioneers in electronics." Booklist

Coy, Harold

Presidents. Watts, F. illus $3.90, pa $1.25 (4-6)   920

1 Presidents—U.S.
ISBN 0-531-00615-8; 0-531-02316-8
"A First book"
First published 1952 with title: The first book of Presidents. Periodically revised to keep material up to date
"A discussion of the Presidency—the qualifications and duties required by the office; the process of election; the President's salary, household, and social life; the Cabinet; and the traditional two-party system—is followed by brief biographical sketches of each U.S. President." Sch Library J

Daugherty, Sonia

Ten brave men; makers of the American way. With drawings by James Daugherty. Lippincott 1951 152p illus $5.25 (5-7)   920

1 U.S.—Biography
ISBN 0-397-30197-9
"The dramatic story of ten American heroes at a time of crisis in their lives and in the life of our country and how each nobly met the crisis so that it influenced the destiny of America. . . . [This book] will give new meaning to major historical events and to America's struggle for freedom. James Daugherty's illustrations are noteworthy." Library J

Ten brave women. With drawings by James Daugherty. Lippincott 1953 147p illus $4.95, lib. bdg. $4.79 (5-7)   920

1 Women in the U.S.—Biography
ISBN 0-397-30255-X; 0-397-31443-4
"Significant incidents in the lives of ten women, from Anne Hutchinson to Eleanor Roosevelt, highlighting their influence on the development of American ideals." Hodges. Bks for Elem Sch Libraries

Davis, Burke

Heroes of the American Revolution; illus. with photographs, prints, and maps. Random House 1971 146p illus maps $4.95, lib. bdg. $5.99 (5-7)   920

1 U.S.—History—Revolution—Biography
ISBN 0-394-82152-1; 0-394-92152-6
"An adequate treatment of eleven men who contributed in various ways to the success of our War of Independence. In a few pages one meets first the major war-related activity of the men and then a brief general biography. The book is copiously illustrated with copies of famous paintings of the men and events. An index increases its reference value." Best Sellers
"Davis's book is vividly written, has judicious and relevant quotes from the sources, contains wholesome good humor—and a properly highminded appraisal of Washington himself." N Y Times Bk Rev

Epstein, Sam

Baseball Hall of Fame: stories of champions, by Sam and Beryl Epstein; illus. by Ken Wagner. Garrard 1965 96p illus (Garrard Sports lib) lib. bdg. $3.58 (3-5)   920

1 Baseball—Biography 2 Cooperstown, N.Y. National Baseball Hall of Fame and Museum
ISBN 0-8116-6650-6
"Every player named to the Hall of Fame has his own story. In this book you will find five of them, the stories of the five men who first earned baseball's greatest honor." p7
Includes Honus Wagner, Christy Mathewson, Ty Cobb, Walter Johnson, Babe Ruth

Feerick, John D.

The Vice-Presidents of the United States, by John D. and Emalie P. Feerick; illus. with engravings and photographs. Rev. ed. Watts, F. 1973 91p illus lib. bdg. $3.90 (4-6)   920

1 Vice-Presidents—U.S.
ISBN 0-531-00659-X
"A First book"
First published 1967
"Brief, factual descriptions of the office and duties of the Vice-President are coupled with interesting sketches of the life of each man who has held that office from John Adams to Spiro Agnew." Sch Library J

Fisher, Aileen

We Alcotts. . . . [By] Aileen Fisher & Olive Rabe; decorations by Ellen Raskin. Atheneum Pubs. 1968 278p front lib. bdg. $5.25 (5-7)   920

1 Alcott family
ISBN 0-689-20613-5
"The story of Louisa M. Alcott's family as seen through the eyes of 'Marmee,' mother of Little Women." Title page
"In a deceptively simple style, the wife of Bronson Alcott and the mother of Louisa May recounts the joys and vicissitudes of her married life, and the moral and literary developments of her most famous daughter. 'Much of the dialogue incorporates sentences, words, and phrases from the writings of the Alcotts, Ralph Waldo Emerson, Henry Thoreau, and others.'" Horn Bk
"Because of the nature and scope of both Abba May's and Bronson's interests and activities, the book offers illuminating sidelights on many of the controversial issues of the times in addition to giving a lively picture of the poverty-stricken but emotionally fulfilling and mentally stimulating home life which exerted a profound influence on Louisa May Alcott. A bibliography is included." Booklist

Gridley, Marion E.

American Indian women. Hawthorn Bks. 1974 178p illus $5.95 (5-7)   920

1 Indians of North America—Biography 2 Women in the U.S.—Biography
ISBN 0-8015-0234-9
"Well-selected biographies of 19 estimable American Indian women (not all full-blooded), some famous and others whose achievements have gone unnoticed.

Gridley, Marion E.—*Continued*
The lives of these women range over a 300-year period from the 17th Century Queen Wetamoo of the Wampanoags, who helped the Pilgrims, to the 20th Century Tallchief sisters, prima ballerinas, and Elaine Ramos of the Tlingits tribe, the vice-president of Sheldon Jackson College in Alaska. . . . [Others] include peace-makers, an artist, a medical worker, a guide, a potter, and an educator. Gridley corrects misconceptions about the role and status of Indian women among their own people, e.g. that they were submissive, and about customs pertaining to them. . . . An eight-page photo insert, an index, and a useable, updated bibliography complete the coverage."
Sch Library J

Gurney, Gene
Flying aces of World War I; illus. with photographs. Random House 1965 185p illus map $2.95, lib. bdg. $4.27 (4-7)   920
1 European War, 1914-1918—Aerial operations 2 Air pilots
ISBN 0-394-80560-7; 0-394-90560-1
"World Landmark books"
"Recounts the exploits of the famed Flying Aces of World War I, who, in their frail single-seated planes, made aviation history. American, British, French, and German fliers are included, with a list of 58 high-scoring pilots." Hodges. Bks for Elem Sch Libraries

Hayden, Robert C.
Eight Black American inventors. Addison-Wesley 1972 142p illus lib. bdg. $5.50 (6-7)   920
1 Inventors 2 Negroes—Biography
ISBN 0-201-02823-9
"An Addisonian Press book"
This book "is a useful addition to the biographies of black Americans of the nineteenth and early twentieth centuries [including G. A. Morgan, F. M. Jones, L. H. Latimer, and G. T. Woods]. The men selected all invented devices or machines which markedly improved industrial processes. Brief descriptions of their lives and accomplishments, emphasizing their outstanding intelligence, aptitude, and persistence in the face of definite discrimination, bring their contributions to the reader's attention in a sincere but uninspired manner. Illustrations of inventions as drawn by their creators add interest to the text as do photographs of the inventors." Appraisal

Seven Black American scientists. Addison-Wesley 1970 172p illus lib. bdg. $5.50 (6-7)   920
1 Scientists 2 Negroes—Biography
ISBN 0-201-02828-X
"An Addisonian Press book"
The seven biographical sketches presented here "are representative rather than exhaustive: Charles Drew, Dr. Daniel Hall Williams, Benjamin Banneker, Charles H. Turner, Ernest E. Just, Matthew Henson, George W. Carver. The contribution of each to his scientific field is described without technical jargon, and the question of racial barriers is treated without bias or emotion." Sci Bks
Glossary: p163-65

Hirsch, S. Carl
Guardians of tomorrow; pioneers in ecology; illus. by William Steinel. Viking 1971 192p illus lib. bdg. $5.95 (6-7)   920
1 Naturalists 2 Ecology—Biography 3 Conservation of natural resources
ISBN 0-670-35646-8
"The philosophy and accomplishments of seven men and one woman who were concerned with protecting the natural resources and environment of the U.S. are presented in an account which is useful for both its brief biographical information on the early ecologists and its history of the conservation movement. Included are Thoreau, Marsh, Olmsted, Muir, Pinchot, Norris, Leopold, and Carson. Hirsch concludes the account with an examination of the challenges facing today's guardians of the environment."
Booklist
Suggestions for further reading: p179-82

Hughes, Langston
Famous American Negroes. Dodd 1954 147p illus (Famous biographies for young people) $3.95 (5-7)   920
1 Negroes—Biography 2 U.S.—Biography
ISBN 0-396-03561-2
"Well-written biographical sketches of 17 outstanding Negroes. . . . Photographs are poorly reproduced." Booklist
Contents: Phillis Wheatley; Richard Allen; Ira Aldridge; Frederick Douglass; Harriet Tubman; Booker T. Washington; Daniel Hale Williams; Henry Ossawa Tanner; George Washington Carver; Robert S. Abbott; Paul Laurence Dunbar; W. C. Handy; Charles C. Spaulding; A. Philip Randolph; Ralph Bunche; Marian Anderson; Jackie Robinson

Famous Negro heroes of America; illus. by Gerald McCann. Dodd 1958 202p illus (Famous biographies for young people) $3.95 (5-7)   920
1 Negroes—Biography 2 U.S.—Biography
ISBN 0-396-04072-1
"In interesting biographical sketches, Hughes tells of contributions sixteen Negroes have made to America. Some of the personalities included are warriors, pioneers, abolitionists, and seamen, such as Estaban, credited with the discovery of what is now Arizona; Crispus Attucks, first to die for American independence; Jean Baptiste Pointe du Sable, founder of Chicago; and Ida B. Wells, crusader. Spans a period from the founding of the nation through World War II. The author includes figures not found in his 'Famous American Negroes' [entered above]." We Build Together

Famous Negro music makers; illus. with photographs. Dodd 1955 179p illus (Famous biographies for young people) $4.50 (5-7)   920
1 Negro musicians 2 Music, American
ISBN 0-396-03766-6
"Short biographies of seventeen outstanding Negro musicians, including James A. Bland, Dean Dixon, Bill Robinson, 'Leadbelly,' William Grant Still, Fisk Jubilee Singers, Bert Williams, Jelly Roll Morton, Roland Hayes, Bessie Smith, Duke Ellington, Ethel Waters, Louis Armstrong, Marian Anderson, Bennie Benjamin, Mahalia Jackson, and Lena Horne." We Build Together

Hume, Ruth Fox
Great men of medicine; illus. by Robert Frankenberg. Random House 1961 192p illus lib. bdg. $4.27 (4-6)   920
1 Medicine—Biography
ISBN 0-394-90549-0
"World Landmark books"
This book "is based in part on 'Great Men of Medicine' (1947) and 'Milestones of Medicine' (1950)." Verso of title page
The book gives "biographical sketches of 10 of the leading figures in the history of medicine, including Vesalius, Paré, Koch, Morton, Laënnec and Pasteur. . . . [It] concludes with a brief note on medical research and the future." The AAAS Sci Bk List for Children

Hume, Ruth Fox—*Continued*

The "illustrations are most appropriate and expressive; the text, accurate and factual, yet interesting and fascinating. The latter has been achieved by the generous use of dialogue, real and imaginary. An excellent Bibliography includes at least one other authoritative work on each of the great men mentioned. . . . The Index will make the book useful for reference work." Best Sellers

Johnston, Johanna

The Indians and the strangers; illus. with woodcuts by Rocco Negri. Dodd 1972 109p illus lib. bdg. $4.95 (2-5)   920

1 Indians of North America—Biography
ISBN 0-396-06610-0

"Not full biographies, but short sketches that describe the confrontations between some major figures in American Indian history and the white men with whom they warred or planned for peace, this gives an excellent overview of the remorseless manipulation and persecution of Indians. It does so particularly effectively because the text, very simply written, is so restrained and objective, including some instances of amicable relationships; it is in the mounting evidence that the impact is made. The stories are chronologically arranged." Chicago. Children's Bk Center

A special bravery; illus. by Ann Grifalconi. Dodd 1967 94p illus $3.75, lib. bdg. $4.50 (2-5)   920

1 Negroes—Biography 2 U.S.—Biography
ISBN 0-396-05608-3; 0-396-05609-1

"The lives of 15 American Negroes from Crispus Attucks to Martin Luther King, Jr. are presented briefly in a book designed and written for easy reading. . . . Printed in short lines that give the appearance of blank verse, almost every biographical sketch is accompanied by a full-page action drawing of the subject." Booklist

"Miss Johnston's own special bravery is in her frank, didactic treatment of prejudice and discrimination." N Y Times Bk Rev

Jones, Hettie

Big star fallin' mama; five women in Black music. Viking 1974 150p illus $5.95 (6-7)   920

1 Negro musicians 2 Women as musicians 3 Singers 4 Blues (Songs, etc.)
ISBN 0-670-16408-9

"Ma Rainey, Bessie Smith, Mahalia Jackson, Billie Holiday, and Aretha Franklin are portrayed in their life situations: on the stage, in theatres, at night clubs, performing at special shows, playing and singing ragtime, recording and/or singing at Gospel gatherings. Hettie Jones gives an insight into black music from the 1920's to 1967. She tries to preserve the cultural value of black music which tends to be the basis for our rock music—of the 1970's. Blues, jazz, ragtime, spirituals, rock music—each has its distinctive way of conveying to the reader the feelings of these black women." Best Sellers

The biographies "are written with candor and sensitivity, objective in viewpoint and vigorous in style." Chicago. Children's Bk Center

Bibliography: p137-38. Discography: p139-40

Kane, Joseph Nathan

Facts about the Presidents; a compilation of biographical and historical data. 3d ed. Wilson, H. W. 1974 407p illus $15   920

1 Presidents—U.S.
ISBN 0-8242-0538-3

First published 1959

"This dictionary is divided into two sections. The first contains a chapter for each President from Washington through Nixon. In statistical form, it concisely presents the family histories, elections, congressional sessions, vice-presidents and cabinets, and highlights in their lives. The second section is a tabulation of comparative data concerning the Presidents. The extensive information included and the index make this a valuable tool. The third edition incorporates two new sections: an alphabetical list of Presidential and Vice-Presidential candidates and a chronological list of the State of the Union messages." Peterson. Ref Bks for Elem and Jr High Sch Libraries. 2d edition

An eleven page supplement to the third edition covering events from January 1974-April 1975 is included with each order

Kennedy, John F.

Profiles in courage. Young readers Memorial ed; abridged; special memorial foreword by Robert F. Kennedy; illus. by Emil Weiss. Harper 1964 illus $4.95, lib. bdg. $4.79 (5-7)   920

1 Statesmen, American 2 Courage 3 U.S.—Politics and government
ISBN 0-06-023125-4; 0-06-023126-2

Original edition published 1956, awarded the Pulitzer Prize, 1957. Young readers' edition first published 1961

"Except for a few deletions which have been made for narrative pace, the author's words appear here as he originally wrote them." Publisher's note

This series of profiles of Americans who took courageous stands at crucial moments in public life includes John Quincy Adams, Daniel Webster, Thomas Hart Benton, Sam Houston, Edmund G. Ross, Lucius Q. C. Lamar, George Norris, Robert A. Taft, and others

"Mr. Kennedy has largely eliminated the political overtones from this abridgement and treated [the figures] . . . with considerable talent to interest children. Many school librarians will find it highly readable and worth recommending to the reluctant 7th-grader as well as to the inquiring fifth grader. Recommended for wide purchase." Library J

Libby, Bill

Baseball's greatest sluggers; illus. with photographs. Random House 1973 153p illus (Major league lib) $2.50, lib. bdg. $3.77 (5-7)   920

1 Baseball—Biography
ISBN 0-394-82538-1; 0-394-92538-6

This book features "Babe Ruth, Jimmy Foxx, Ted Williams, Willie Mays, and Hank Aaron. All of these men, except possibly Foxx, have been picked clean by writers, but Libby manages to introduce new material for each. Batting and slugging averages are made more palatable by the addition of plentiful commentary on personalities. There are also fresh photographs of these stars." Sch Library J

Lorimer, Lawrence T.

(ed.) Breaking in; nine first-person accounts about becoming an athlete; comp. and ed. by Lawrence T. Lorimer; illus. with photographs. Random House 1974 198p illus $2.95, lib. bdg. $4.59 (5-7)   920

1 Athletes 2 Sports—Biography
ISBN 0-394-82653-1; 0-394-92653-6

Nine athletes—Mickey Mantle; Spencer Haywood; Dave Meggyesy; Althea Gibson; Rube Marquard; Don Schollander; Jackie Robinson; Ted Green; and actor Anthony Quinn (who was once a boxer)—describe their experiences during their early careers

The author's "tokenism in including only one woman athlete is disappointing, but the book's attempt to view firsthand the real world of the athlete is welcome." Booklist

McConnell, Jane

Presidents of the United States; the story of their lives, closely interwoven with the vast political and economic changes of the nation [by] Jane and Burt McConnell. Portraits by Constance Joan Naar. Crowell illus $6.95   920

1 Presidents—U.S.

ISBN 0-690-65282-8

First published 1951 and periodically updated

For each of the Presidents presented here, the authors supply a picture of the boyhood and family life of the future chief executive as well as an account of his achievements in office. A pen and ink portrait of the subject heads each chapter

Includes bibliography

McNeer, May

Armed with courage, by May McNeer and Lynd Ward. Abingdon 1957 112p illus $6.95 (4-6)   920

1 Biography 2 Courage

ISBN 0-687-01740-8

Illustrated by Lynd Ward

This book contains "biographical sketches of seven great humanitarians: Gandhi, Schweitzer, Nightingale, Grenfell, Carver, Addams, and Father Damien." Adventuring with Bks. 2d edition

"The biographies are vividly written and with the attractive format and illustrations make this a good book for school and public libraries, personal ownership and Sunday schools." Horn Bk

Give me freedom; drawings by Lynd Ward. Abingdon 1964 128p illus $4.95 (5-7)   920

1 U.S.—Biography 2 Liberty

ISBN 0-687-14740-9

Brief biographies of seven Americans who have been concerned with freedom for themselves and others

Contents: To freedom's shore: William Penn; Voice of the Revolution: Thomas Paine; I take my stand: Elijah Parish Lovejoy; As good as a boy: Elizabeth Cady Stanton; The shoes of happiness: Edwin Markham; The whole world in His hands: Marian Anderson; A game called "X": Albert Einstein

"Each biography is a vigorous absorbing story, and the strong black-and-white illustrations decorating almost every page combine with the narratives to make rousing reading." Christian Sci Monitor

Nathan, Dorothy

Women of courage; illus. by Carolyn Cather. Random House 1964 188p illus $2.95, pa 75¢ (4-6) 920

1 Women in the U.S.—Biography

ISBN 0-394-80407-4; 0-394-82186-6

"Landmark books"

This book contains short biographies of Susan B. Anthony, Jane Addams, Mary McLeod Bethune, Amelia Earhart and Margaret Mead

"Although the choice of subjects seems random and although much of the material is familiar, the biographies should serve to encourage a reader's interest in full-length biographies." Chicago. Children's Bk Center

Bibliography: p178-81

Newlon, Clarke

Famous Mexican-Americans; foreword by Uvaldo H. Palomares; illus. wlth photographs. Dodd 1972 187p illus (Famous biographies for young people) $4.50 (6-7)   920

1 Mexicans in the U.S.—Biography

ISBN 0-396-06489-2

These 20 biographical sketches of Mexican-Americans who have attained success and acclaim

include: educator Henry Ramirez; golfer Lee Trevino; labor leader Cesar Chavez; actors Anthony Quinn and Ricardo Montalban; Senator Joseph Montoya; singers Trini Lopez and Vikki Carr

"These brief, vigorous biographical sketches are written in an informal style that is punctuated only occasionally by banalities. The foreword . . . gives some historical background and discusses the derivation of the word 'Chicano.' . . . This collective biography should be welcomed by both Anglos and Chicanos." Sat Rev

Source material: p181

Ojigbo, A. Okion

(comp.) Young and Black in Africa; comp. with introductory notes by A. Okion Ojigbo. Random House 1971 107p illus $3.95, lib. bdg. $4.99, pa $1.50 (6-7)   920

1 Africa—Biography 2 Autobiographies

ISBN 0-394-82304-4; 0-394-92304-9; 0-394-70802-4

A collection of eight autobiographical writings by young Africans. "The earliest selection is from Olaudah Equiano's autobiography and describes his being kidnapped and sold into slavery in 1756 at the age of eleven. Others recall the cultural shock encountered by a young man leaving his village for the city, a young South African's experiences with racism, and a Nigerian student's mixed reactions to the U.S." Booklist

"We see the painful questions young people must raise in order to map out a sensible route to personal and national liberation. And it is both vital and significant, for it is the African, not the safari expert or the sundowner or the know-nothing scholar, who speaks to us." N Y Times Bk Rev

Bibliography: p107

Posell, Elsa Z.

American composers; illus. with photographs. Houghton 1963 183p illus (5-7)   920

1 Composers, American 2 Music, American

ISBN 0-395-07035-X

The "life stories of 29 old favorites like Stephen Foster and newer young composers like Menotti and Norman Dello Joio, is a readable collection for young people interested in music. Excellent photographs of the composers accompany the text which includes much personal detail and less musical criticism." Cur Ref Bks

Russian composers; illus. with photographs. Houghton 1967 181p illus $4.25 (5-7)   920

1 Composers, Russian 2 Music, Russian

ISBN 0-395-07034-1

"Brief biographies of 17 composers arranged chronologically from Glinka to Shostakovich describe each composer's family background, education, personality, and musical works. Separate discussions of music under the czars and under the Soviets stress the importance of the fine arts throughout Russian history and the privileges accorded talented musicians and composers since the Revolution. . . . Illustrated with full-page portraits of the composers." Booklist

"The biographies are necessarily brief, consisting of fact after fact presented at almost breathtaking speed." Christian Sci Monitor

Suggested reading on Russian music and musicians: p[182]

Rollins, Charlemae

Famous American Negro poets. Dodd 1965 95p illus (Famous biographies for young people) $3.95 (5-7)   920

1 Negro authors—2 Poets, American

ISBN 0-396-05129-4

This is a "collective biography of a dozen Negro

Rollins, Charlemae—*Continued*

poets, with the material chronologically arranged and with a section of portraits (some drawings, some photographs) inserted. . . . Each of the biographical sketches is a few pages long, gives some facts about the subject's personal life and more about his writing, and quotes a poem or poems. A bibliography of books by the poets or anthologies in which their works appear is included." Chicago. Children's Bk Center
"The book is useful for reference as well as for enjoyable reading." Wis Library Bul

Famous Negro entertainers of stage, screen, and TV. Dodd 1967 122p illus (Famous biographies for young people) $3.95 (5-7)   920
  1 Entertainers 2 Negroes—Biography
  ISBN 0-396-05503-6
"Biographical sketches of 16 Negro entertainers in various fields of the performing arts. Included are Ira Aldridge, Marian Anderson, Louis Armstrong, Josephine Baker, Harry Belafonte, Nat 'King' Cole, Sammy Davis, Jr., 'Duke' Ellington, Lena Horne, Eartha Kitt, Sidney Poitier, Leontyne Price, Paul Robeson, Bill 'Bojangles' Robinson, 'Bert' Williams, and Thomas 'Fats' Waller. Extremely brief and strictly utilitarian. Illustrated with photographs." Booklist

They showed the way; forty American Negro leaders. Crowell 1964 165p $3.95 (5-7)   920
  1 Negroes—Biography 2 U.S.—Biography
  ISBN 0-690-81612-X
The forty "brief biographical sketches represent a great variety of occupations and professions in which Negroes have made a great contribution to American life." Adventuring With Bks. 2d edition
"Although the individual factual accounts are almost too brief . . . the book is worthwhile because it contains a number of persons not found in other collective biographies." Booklist

Ross, Nancy Wilson

Heroines of the early West; illus. by Paul Galdone. Random House 1960 182p illus lib. bdg. $4.39 (4-6)
920
  1 Women in the West—Biography 2 Frontier and pioneer life
  ISBN 0-394-90391-9
"Landmark books"
"The material in this book first appeared, in somewhat different form, in 'Westward the Women' by Nancy Wilson Ross (1944)." Verso of title page
"Accounts obviously taken from original sources (although not documented) of the hardships of dangers of pioneer life courageously endured by five intrepid women: Sacajawea, Narcissa Whitman, Mary Walker . . . Sister Loyola . . . and Abigail Scott Duniway (who pioneered for women's rights). Introductory chapter generalizes on pioneer women and their importance in history. Particularly useful in the Northwest but of general interest to libraries everywhere." Library J

Ross, Pat

(ed.) Young and female; turning points in the lives of eight American women: personal accounts comp. with introductory notes by Pat Ross. Random House 1972 107p illus $3.95, lib. bdg. $4.99, pa $1.50 (6-7)   920
  1 Women in the U.S.—Biography 2 Autobiographies
  ISBN 0-394-82392-3; 0-394-92392-8; 0-394-70808-3
"Excerpts from the autobiographies of Shirley MacLaine, Shirley Chisholm, Dorothy Day, Emily Hahn, Margaret Sanger, Althea Gibson, Edna Ferber, and Margaret Bourke-White make a pertinent, stimulat-

ing contribution to an understanding of the problems and challenges women face in a male-dominated society." Pub W
"For girls seeking alternatives to the roles of cheerleader and homemaker, the book offers the inspiration of individuals who were able to make their own, widely differing lives. Interested readers will probably want to go beyond these brief excerpts to the full autobiographies from which they are taken." Bk World
  Bibliography: p107

Smaridge, Norah

Famous author-illustrators for young people; illus. with photographs. Dodd 1973 159p illus (Famous biographies for young people) $3.95 (5-7)   920
  1 Authors 2 Illustrators 3 Children's literature—History and criticism
  ISBN 0-396-06831-6
This book contains biographies of 16 American and 3 English author-illustrators of children's books, including Edward Lear, Kate Greenaway, Beatrix Potter, Maurice Sendak and Lois Lenski

Steele, William O.

Westward adventure; the true stories of six pioneers; maps by Kathleen Voute. Harcourt 1962 188p maps $5.95 (5-7)   920
  1 Adventure and adventurers 2 Frontier and pioneer life
  ISBN 0-15-294999-2
"Utilizing little-known sources, the author tells the true stories of six people—an Indian trader, a writer, a farmer's wife, an explorer, a colonizer, and a Moravian brother—who ventured into the American wilderness west and south of the 13 colonies during the eighteenth century. Recounting the experience of each he shows the reasons for their hazardous journeys, depicts their characters and personalities, and vivifies life on the frontier." Booklist
  Bibliography: p185-88

Sterling, Philip

Four took freedom; the lives of Harriet Tubman, Frederick Douglass, Robert Smalls, and Blanche K. Bruce [by] Philip Sterling and Rayford Logan; illus. by Charles White. Doubleday 1967 116p illus $3.75, pa $1.45 (5-6)   920
  1 Negroes—Biography 2 U.S.—Biography
  ISBN 0-385-04569-7; 0-385-03844-5
"Zenith books"
"Succinct accounts of the lives of four American blacks and their escape from slavery. The drama, pathos, and great excitement of these biographies will cause children to be interested in learning more about Harriet Tubman, Frederick Douglass, Robert Small, and Blanche K. Bruce. Well-selected and well-told incidents from these lives give the reader an understanding of some social issues facing us today." Reading Ladders

The quiet rebels; four Puerto Rican leaders; José Celso Barbosa, Luis Muñoz Rivera, José de Diego [and] Luis Muñoz Marín, by Philip Sterling and Maria Brau; illus. by Tracy Sugarman. Doubleday 1968 118p illus map $3.95, pa $1.45 (5-6)   920
  1 Puerto Rico—Biography
  ISBN 0-385-06312-1; 0-385-06313-X
"Zenith books"
"This offers brief life sketches of four Puerto Rican leaders whose activities contributed to the political and social development of the island during the past 100 years. Factual material, occasionally limited, is accompanied by fictional dialogue and emphasis on devotion to cause, loyalty to country, and strength to persevere for justice and self-determination. . . . The

Sterling, Philip—*Continued*
overall appeal of the book is enhanced by vigorous and attractive illustrations, sturdy binding and excellent typeset." Library J

Sullivan, George
Queens of the court; illus. with photographs. Dodd 1974 111p illus lib. bdg. $4.95 (5-7)　　920
1 Tennis—Biography 2 Women—Biography
ISBN 0-396-06973-8
The author profiles the lives and careers of six stars in women's professional tennis—Billie Jean King, Chris Evert, Margaret Court, Evonne Goolagong, Rosemary Casals, and Virginia Wade
Glossary: p107-08

Wood, James Playsted
The people of Concord; drawings by Richard Cuffari. Seabury 1970 152p illus $6.95 (6-7)　　920
1 Concord, Mass.—Biography
ISBN 0-8164-3056-X
A "vibrant portrait of Concord, Massachusetts—its quiet history, its great events, and its gifted people. Unfolding almost as a recollection, this socio-cultural history covers the facts and feelings of Concord from the Puritan influx to its present day, concentrating on Indian-colonial relations, the American Revolution and abolitionist activities." Best Sellers
Bibliography: p147-48

920.01　Biography—Indexes

Ireland, Norma Olin
Index to women of the world, from ancient to modern times: biographies and portraits. Faxon 1970 xxcviii, 573p (Useful reference ser.) $16　　920.01
1 Woman—Biography—Indexes
"Includes references to about 13,000 women, whose biographies, and, in some cases portraits, appear in 945 collective biographies; Current Biography, 1940-68; New Yorker's Profiles, 1925-68; Time's 'Cover stories,' 1924-68; and Bulletin of Bibliography's special features on librarians and authors. Most encyclopedias, biographical dictionaries, and other reference books have been omitted. Books for younger readers have been included to make the book more useful to small libraries and schools. Since birth dates, nationality, and vocation are given for each, this index serves as a source for brief identification as well as for sources of further information. Its emphasis on pioneer women will be of interest in school libraries. It is also a good source for women authors, who make up more than thirteen percent of the entries. A lengthy introduction traces women's contributions through the ages, in religion, fine arts, literature, and other fields." Cur Ref Bks

Nicholsen, Margaret E.
People in books; a selective guide to biographical literature arranged by vocations and other fields of reader interest. Wilson, H.W. 1969 498p $14
920.01
1 Biography—Indexes 2 Biography—Bibliography
ISBN 0-8242-0394-1
This reference tool designed for libraries serving children, young adults and adults "has a main section arranged by vocation or activity, a country-century appendix which indexes by country and by century the persons whose biographies are listed in the main section, a second appendix listing alphabetically by author books of an autobiographical nature, and an index listing all those persons about whom a book or part of a collective biography is included in the main section." Preface

Silverman, Judith
(comp.) An index to young readers' collective biographies; elementary and junior high-school level. Bowker 1970 282p illus $14.95　　920.01
1 Biography—Indexes 2 Biography—Bibliography
ISBN 0-8352-0741-2
This is "a guide to short biographies of approximately 4,600 persons of many nations, periods, and occupations in 471 collective biographies. The main section is the alphabetic listing of the biographees; other sections are a subject listing of the biographees, an index of the subject headings, and a listing of indexed books by title. A key to symbols for titles indexed and a list of the publishers are also included." Booklist

920.03　Biography—Dictionaries

Current biography yearbook. Wilson, H.W. illus
920.03
1 Biography—Dictionaries
Annual. First published 1940 with title: Current biography
Also issued monthly except August at a subscription price of $14 per year. Earlier yearbooks are obtainable: 1940-1943 ea $24; 1944-45 ea $20; 1946- ea $15
Each volume presents articles on the life and work of people in the news—in national and international affairs, the sciences, the arts, labor, and industry. Sources of information for the articles are newspapers, magazines, books, and, in most cases, the biographees themselves. The heading of each article includes the pronunciation of the name if it is unusual, date of birth, occupation, and address. Source references are given at the end of each article. Brief obituary notices, with a reference to the New York Times obituary, are given for persons whose biographies have previously appeared in current biography. Each yearbook contains an index by profession, a necrology, and a cumulated index up to a 10 year period

De Montreville Doris
(ed.) Third book of junior authors; ed. by Doris de Montreville and Donna Hill. Wilson, H.W. 1972 320p illus (The Authors ser) $12　　920.03
1 Authors—Dictionaries 2 Illustrators—Dictionaries 3 Children's literature—Bio-bibliography
ISBN 0-8242-0408-5
Companion volume to: Junior book of authors, second edition (1951) edited by Stanley Kunitz and Howard Haycraft and More junior authors (1963) edited by Muriel Fuller, both entered below
Contains 255 sketches, both biographical and autobiographical, with 249 portraits, of authors and illustrators of books for children and young people. New to this volume in the series are the lists of selected works and of biographical references. An index of authors and illustrators is included which covers this volume and, in addition, its two predecessors

Fuller, Muriel
(ed.) More junior authors. Wilson, H.W. 1963 235p illus (The Authors ser) $10　　920.03
1 Authors—Dictionaries 2 Illustrators—Dictionaries 3 Children's literature—Bio-bibliography
ISBN 0-8242-0036-5
"This work is designed to be a companion volume to 'The Junior Book of Authors' [listed below]. . . . [It] includes biographical or autobiographical sketches [arranged alphabetically] of 268 authors and illus-

Fuller, Muriel—_Continued_

trators of books for children and young people. The great majority are authors and illustrators who have become prominent since the publication of the second edition of 'The Junior Book of Authors.' " Preface

"Selected from a preliminary list of almost 1,200 names, by a distinguished group of librarians working with children and young people in school and public libraries, the sketches represent only the most familiar and popular names. Photographs of many of the writers accompany the well-written accounts which should appeal to young people because of their personal flavor. Only partial lists of works by, and none about, the authors are given." Cur Ref Bks

Kunitz, Stanley J.

(ed.) The junior books of authors. 2d ed. rev. Ed. by Stanley J. Kunitz and Howard Haycraft; illus with 232 photographs and drawings. Wilson, H.W. 1951 309p illus (The Authors ser) $10   920.03

1 Authors—Dictionaries 2 Illustrators—Dictionaries 3 Children's literature—Bio-bibliography

ISBN 0-8242-0028-4

"First published in 1934, this contains 289 biographical [or autobiographical] sketches of authors and illustrators of children's books. . . . Many people using the book will, of course miss some favorite authors, even though the selection was carefully made by a large committee of librarians and other specialists in children's books; but all will agree that this is an indispensable reference tool for schools and libraries." Horn Bk

Each account gives birth date, death date—if subject is deceased, author's background, mention of his work, and a photograph or drawing

Something about the author; facts and pictures about contemporary authors and illustrators of books for young people. Gale Res. v 1-7 ea $25, v8 $22.50
920.03

1 Authors—Dictionaries 2 Illustrators—Dictionaries 3 Children's literature—Bio-bibliography

ISBN v1 0-8103-0050-8; v2 0-8103-0052-4; v3 0-8103-0054-4; v4 0-8103-0056-7; v5 0-8103-0058-3; v6 0-8103-0060-5; v7 0-8103-0062-1; v8 0-8103-0064-8

Editor 1971-   Anne Commire

First published 1971

An alphabetically arranged guide to authors who are writing for young people today. Many of the articles were drawn partly from Contemporary authors

Each entry includes "such personal information as age, place of birth, parents, marital status, children, education, politics, religion, home address, address of agent, career, awards, honors, and a complete bibliography of the writings or illustrating done by the subject, with references to work in progress. . . . 'Sidelights' is a statement written by the biographee especially for this volume explaining his creative philosophy and sources of inspiration. This generally reveals much about his personality. . . . Almost every biography is accompanied by a large, distinct photograph of the biographee and illustrations from one of his books. . . . ['Biographical Sources'] cites references to magazine articles, books, and even newspaper accounts for additional material on each of the authors. . . . 'Something About the Author' will be useful not only to boys and girls needing information on authors and their lives, but also to students of children's literature, authors and would-be authors, librarians, and teachers." Booklist

Ward, Martha E.

Authors of books for young people. 2d ed. by Martha E. Ward and Dorothy A. Marquardt. Scarecrow 1971 579p $17   920.03

1 Authors—Dictionaries 2 Children's literature—Bio-bibliography

ISBN 0-8108-0404-2

This volume contains "brief biographical entries for some 2,100 writers of juvenile books. . . . The entries, arranged alphabetically by name, give dates, profession, place of birth, education and degrees, family and residence, career, interests, and a partial list of writings. The entries vary in fullness. . . . [The book] identifies publisher and year for each title listed and provides cross references for pseudonyms. . . . The Preface indicates three factors for inclusion. The biographies were taken from an 'author file' compiled in the Children's Department of the Free Public Library of Quincy, Illinois. Secondly, 'a contemporary author whose biography proved difficult to locate was given preference' over a well-known author. Thirdly, all Newbery and Caldecott winners are included." Am Ref Bks Annual, 1972

Illustrators of books for young people. 2d ed. by Martha E. Ward and Dorothy A. Marquardt. Scarecrow 1975 223p $8   920.03

1 Illustrators—Dictionaries

ISBN 0-8108-0819-6

First published 1970

This book provides brief biographical information for 750 illustrators of books for children. References to works where additional information about an illustrator can be found follow many of the entries. A list of Caldecott Medal winners and a title index have been provided

Webster's Biographical dictionary; a dictionary of names of noteworthy persons with pronunciations and concise biographies. Merriam $12.95   920.03

1 Biography—Dictionaries

William Allan Neilson, editor in chief

First published 1943 and frequently reprinted with slight revisions

"Forty thousand people of historical importance from all countries . . . are given brief concise factual treatment. The work treats fully persons prominent in all fields except sports, motion pictures, contemporary theater, and radio, entries for which were cut to the minimum. Syllabication and pronunciation is given for surnames. American and British subjects receive the fullest treatment. . . . 'Webster's' has lost much of its value as a contemporary source, because of the slight revisions since the first 1943 edition." Booklist [Review of the 1972 edition]

The entries "vary from a few lines to a full page. Concise and clearly written, the sketches are unsigned but considered trustworthy and adequate. Liberal cross references aid the user in locating information. Also included are tables of popes, American government officials, and rulers of various countries." Peterson. Ref Bks for Elem and Jr High Sch Libraries [Review of the 1968 edition]

92   Individual biography

Lives of individuals are arranged alphabetically under the names of the persons written about

A number of subjects have been added to the titles in this section to help in curriculum work. It is not necessarily recommended that these subjects be used in the card catalog

Aaron, Henry Louis

Hirshberg, Al. The up-to-date biography of Henry Aaron; quiet superstar. Putnam 1974 189p illus (Putnam Sports shelf) lib. bdg. $4.97 (5-7)   92

1 Baseball—Biography 2 Negro athletes
ISBN 0-399-60915-6
First published 1969 with title: Henry Aaron: quiet superstar
Spine has original title
This biography of Hank Aaron describes his boyhood days in Mobile, Alabama, his family, and his baseball career, including Aaron's record-breaking 715th home run

Young, B. E. The picture story of Hank Aaron; illus. with photographs. Messner 1974 62p illus lib. bdg. $4.79, pa $1.95 (3-5)   92

1 Baseball—Biography
ISBN 0-671-32672-4; 0-671-32671-6
This biography "gives some information about Aaron's childhood, the early prowess that earned a berth with a sandlot team, and the years with the Indianapolis Clowns and minor league teams before he joined the Milwaukee Braves. The pace of Young's description of Aaron's career broadens at the close of the book, moving from homer to homer (rather than from one highlight or seasonal statistic to another) as the record-breaker draws closer." Chicago. Children's Bk Center
The book "contains all that a young reader will find relevant and the action pictures are truly professional and well chosen." Pub W

Adams, Abigail (Smith)

Peterson, Helen Stone. Abigail Adams: "Dear Partner"; illus. by Betty Fraser. Garrard 1967 80p illus lib. bdg. $3.40 (2-5)   92

1 Presidents—U.S.—Wives
ISBN 0-8116-6299-3
"A Discovery book"
This is the story of the wife of the second President of the United States and the mother of the sixth President, who, herself, played an important role in early American history
"Simple, well-chosen words make this little girl from the past real. Everyday incidents lend believability to important historical events making them more understandable to the young reader." Bruno. Bks for Sch Libraries, 1968

Adams, Samuel

Fritz, Jean. Why don't you get a horse, Sam Adams? Illus. by Trina Schart Hyman. Coward, McCann & Geoghegan 1974 47p illus $5.95 (3-5) 92

1 U.S.—History—Colonial period
ISBN 0-698-20292-9
Sam Adams "wears his soles thin treading the cobblestones and wharves of Boston while agitating against the King. Although reasonable in most respects—he knows when to hold his rebellious tongue and when to unleash it—Sam stubbornly refuses to ride a horse. Despite goading from cousin John Adams and an 'unheroic' escape from the Redcoats via horse drawn carriage, Sam persists in his pedestrian preferences until an appeal to his patriotism finally convinces him to get a horse." Sch Library J
"Hyman's seemingly effortless, deft lines and the engaging drollery reflected in her details amply extend Fritz' bridled humor. An afterword attests to the historical facts behind the amusing perspective, and the novel approach . . . works well to raise this above the crowd of Bicentennial-related publications." Booklist

Addams, Jane

Judson, Clara Ingram. City neighbor; the story of Jane Addams; illus. by Ralph Ray. Scribner 1951 130p illus lib. bdg. $5.95 (4-6)   92

1 Hull House, Chicago
ISBN 0-684-12650-8
"The story of the amazing Jane Addams is largely the story of Hull House, the settlement house she founded in Chicago in 1889, which was to have such an impact on the American city. During her forty-five years there, she brought about countless legal reforms in the fields of health and child labor, showing how one person with a vision can prevail against great odds." Moorachian. What is a City?
"Mrs. Judson has used Miss Addams' own writings in letters, articles and books, newspapers, magazine articles, reports and other documents; and her own acquaintance with Miss Addams. [This biography] is told in fiction form with conversation because as the author says 'it seems to make her story more vivid. . . . But nothing herein is fiction in the sense that an incident is imagined.' " Wis Library Bul

Keller, Gail Faithfull. Jane Addams; illus. by Frank Aloise. Crowell 1971 41p illus (Crowell biographies) $4.50, lib. bdg. $5.25 (1-3)   92

1 Hull House, Chicago
ISBN 0-690-45791-X; 0-690-45792-8
In 1889 Jane Addams founded Hull House, a settlement house in a poor section of Chicago. It became a center for community activity where people of all ages and nationalities came seeking advice, recreation, meals and company. The author depicts the forty-five-year career of this pioneer in social work who in 1931 was awarded the Nobel Peace Prize

Alcott, Louisa May

Papashvily, Helen Waite. Louisa May Alcott; illus. by Bea Holmes. Houghton 1965 183p illus lib. bdg. $2.95 (4-6)   92

1 Authors, American 2 Alcott family
ISBN 0-395-07254-9
"North star books"
This biography of Little Women's author reveals "how she managed to rise from poverty through teaching herself to be one of America's best-selling writers, and how she carried, as part of her willing load, the entire dependent family." p5

Alexander the Great

Gunther, John. Alexander the Great; illus. by Isa Barnett. Random House 1953 183p illus lib. bdg. $4.27 (5-7)   92

1 Kings and rulers
ISBN 0-394-90502-4
"World Landmark books"
"John Gunther skips an eon or two to tell the story of the first of the world's great conquerors. . . . From his boyhood days as the son of Philip, King of Macedon, to his death in Asia and the breakup of his empire, Alexander led a life filled with excitement and danger. A man of great strength and ability, he had one fatal weakness which this biography, to its credit, does not overlook." N Y Times Bk Rev
Map on lining-papers

Allen, Ethan

Brown, Slater. Ethan Allen and the Green Mountain Boys; illus. by William Moyers. Random House 1956 184p illus map lib. bdg. $4.27 (5-7)   92

1 U.S.—History—Revolution—Biography 2 Green Mountain Boys
ISBN 0-394-90366-8
"Landmark books"
As a young man Ethan Allen championed the cause

Allen, Ethan—*Continued*

of his fellow Vermonters when the governor of New York tried to impose on them the ancient feudal system of landowning. This led to the formation of the Green Mountain Boys who, under Ethan's leadership, captured Fort Ticonderoga from the British in the Revolutionary War. These and other events in the life of this great American are related in this biography

"A simply written, perceptive account. . . . Allen emerges as a vigorous character, not always a wise leader, but a dedicated man whose basic motives were honest and worth while, and who was not afraid to fight against any odds for what he thought was right." Chicago. Children's Bk Center

Holbrook, Stewart Hall. America's Ethan Allen; pictures by Lynd Ward. Houghton 1949 95p illus $4.50, lib. bdg. $3.90 (5-7) 92

1 U.S.—History—Revolution—Biography 2 Green Mountain Boys
ISBN 0-395-06820-7; 0-395-06821-5

This is the story of a great and fearless American figure, Ethan Allen, hero of Fort Ticonderoga and one of the first men who saw America's destiny and rebelled against authority from England

"Told with spirit and pace, this story of the Green Mountain Boys and the founding of Vermont gives fresh interest to a segment of American history. The illustrations in full color accentuate the stature of the hero and evoke the rugged frontier." N Y Pub Library

Anderson, Marian

Newman, Shirlee P. Marian Anderson: lady from Philadelphia. Westminster Press 1966 175p illus $5.50 (5-7) 92

1 Singers 2 Negro musicians
ISBN 0-664-32370-7

"From early childhood Marian Anderson embraced music for which she had great talent; she endured indignities and succeeded somewhat in alleviating prejudices by her regal appearance and ladylike conduct. In . . . [this biography] Miss Newman traces the life of this great singer from her high school days . . . to her final concert at Carnegie Hall." Best Sellers

"A warm, readable biography about a great black artist and humanitarian which shows her struggle to achieve." NYPL. The Black Experience in Children's Bks

Selected bibliography: p163-65

Tobias, Tobi. Marian Anderson; illus. by Symeon Shimin. Crowell 1972 40p illus (A Crowell biography) $4.50, lib. bdg. $5.25 (2-4) 92

1 Singers 2 Negro musicians
ISBN 0-690-51846-3; 0-690-51847-X

"Beautifully illustrated with the soft and gentle faces that are [the illustrator's] distinctive style, a biography of the great singer is simply written, dispassionate in tone, and balanced in treatment. The text describes the now-familiar (but never before so competently written for very young readers) story of the small girl in Philadelphia whose big, golden voice was so appreciated by the members of her church that they financed her first professional training. The rest is musical history." Chicago. Children's Bk Center

Anthony, Susan Brownell

Noble, Iris. Susan B. Anthony. Messner 1975 189p $5.95, lib. bdg. $5.29 (5-7) 92

1 Woman—Civil rights
ISBN 0-671-32714-3; 0-671-32715-1

This is a biography of the nineteenth century crusader for women's rights who also contributed her talents to the antislavery movement

Bibliography: p181-82

Peterson, Helen Stone. Susan B. Anthony, pioneer in woman's rights; illus. by Paul Frame. Garrard 1971 96p illus (Americans all) lib. bdg. $3.58 (3-5) 92

1 Woman—Civil rights
ISBN 0-8116-4570-3

"This sympathetic biography covers the career of Susan B. Anthony from age 12 until her death, with emphasis on her involvement with women's rights and brief mention of her work for black emancipation. Miss Anthony is not presented as a superwoman, nor does the author make comparisons between her and like-minded ladies today. There is too much fictionized dialogue and attributed emotion in the childhood section, but the account of her later life is more accurate and the writing is clear and generally factual throughout. [It is] illustrated with photographs, engravings, and less effective two-color pen-and-ink sketches." Library J

Armstrong, Louis

Cornell, Jean Gay. Louis Armstrong, Ambassador Satchmo; illus. by Victor Mays. Garrard 1972 96p illus (Americans all) lib. bdg. $3.58 (4-6) 92

1 Negro musicians
ISBN 0-8116-4576-2

This is the story of Louis Armstrong, who began his musical career on New Orleans street corners and later became a world-famous jazz trumpeter and ambassador of good will

Audubon, John James

Kieran, Margaret. John James Audubon, by Margaret and John Kieran; illus. by Christine Price. Random House 1954 182p illus lib. bdg. $4.27 (4-6) 92

1 Ornithologists 2 Painters, American
ISBN 0-394-90348-X

"Landmark books"

An account of the American artist's efforts to achieve perfection in his paintings of birds

"To their life of Audubon, John and Margaret Kieran have brought a sensitive appreciation of the artist's monumental achievements and an understanding of the urge which forced him on to perfection despite failures, poverty and bad luck. They have also done full justice to the charming and long-suffering Lucy Audubon." N Y Times Bk Rev

Balboa, Vasco Núñez de

Syme, Ronald. Balboa, finder of the Pacific; illus. by William Stobbs. Morrow 1956 92p illus map lib. bdg. $4.32 (4-6) 92

1 Explorers 2 Discoveries (in geography)
ISBN 0-688-31061-3

"A vigorous, forceful biography of Balboa, with the emphasis on the years he spent in the New World. Although history books seldom mention more than Balboa's trek across the Isthmus of Panama and rest his fame entirely on the fact that he was the first white man to view the Pacific, he actually played an important role in the exploration and early settlement of America, and this role is given full treatment by Syme. The rugged illustrations give added force and vigor to the text." Chicago. Children's Bk Center

Banneker, Benjamin

Lewis, Claude. Benjamin Banneker: the man who saved Washington; illus. by Ernest T. Crichlow. McGraw 1970 127p illus (McGraw-Hill Black legacy) lib. bdg. $4.72 (5-7) 92

1 Mathematicians 2 Negroes—Biography
ISBN 0-07-037539-9

Banneker, Benjamin—*Continued*

"A Rutledge book"

"A well-researched narrative biography brings to life an eighteenth-century Afro-American scientist who played an important role in the planning and surveying of the nation's capital city. Lewis' account ably reveals the full range of talents and accomplishments of this little-known black man who was internationally famous in the scientific circles of his day. The account which also discusses Banneker's interest in government and his efforts in behalf of equal rights is documented with excerpts from his writings and correspondence. The introductions to two of his published almanacs are appended." Booklist

Bibliography: p126-27

Barton, Clara Harlowe

Boylston, Helen Dore. Clara Barton, founder of the American Red Cross; illus. by Paula Hutchison. Random House 1955 182p illus lib. bdg. $4.27 (4-7)
                                                        92

1 Nurses and nursing 2 Red Cross. United States. American National Red Cross

ISBN 0-394-90358-7

"Landmark books"

The story of the shy young school teacher who started the first public school in New Jersey and whose Civil War nursing service grew into the foundation of the American Red Cross with its peacetime as well as wartime services

"An interesting and well-paced . . . biography of Clara Barton, emphasizing her work as an army nurse during the Civil War rather than her work as the founder of the American Red Cross." Chicago. Children's Bk Center

Grant, Matthew G. Clara Barton; Red Cross pioneer; illus. by John Keely. [Creative Educ. Soc. distributed by Childrens Press] 1974 31p illus (Gallery of great Americans ser. Women of America) lib. bdg. $4.95 (3-4)   92

1 Nurses and nursing 2 Red Cross. United States. American National Red Cross

ISBN 0-87191-306-2

This is "a brief, easy-to-read account of the 'angel of the battlefields.' Beginning with Clara Barton's professional nursing experience at age 11 and her early experience as a teacher, [the author] follows her career as one of the first women to hold a government office job, her work nursing soldiers during the Civil War, and her later organization of the American Red Cross. . . . [This] biography presents an adequate introduction for beginning readers." Sch Library J

Beard, Daniel Carter

Blassingame, Wyatt. Dan Beard, scoutmaster of America; illus. by Dom Lupo. Garrard [1972] 80p illus lib. bdg. $3.68 (3-5)   92

1 Boy Scouts 2 Naturalists

ISBN 0-8116-6754-5

This is the story of Daniel Carter Beard, the writer, artist, and naturalist whose love of young people and of nature led him to start a boys' club called the Sons of Daniel Boone. He later helped Sir Robert Baden-Powell to organize the Boy Scouts of America

Beckwourth, James Pierson

Felton, Harold W. Jim Beckwourth, Negro mountain man; illus. with photographs, prints of the period, and maps. Dodd 1966 173p illus maps $4.50 (5-7)   92

1 Frontier and pioneer life—The West 2 Crow Indians 3 Negroes—Biography

ISBN 0-396-05378-5

"Jim Beckwourth leaves his blacksmith apprentice-ship in St. Louis to go into the wilderness. There he becomes one of the best hunters, trappers, and guides among the mountain men. He also learns the dangers and hardships of life among Indians and wild animals. Finally Jim is named chief of the Crows, whom he guides wisely for many years." Reading Ladders for Human Relations. 5th edition

"Information has been culled from old accounts, one of which was dictated but not written by the biographee. The reproductions are clearly printed on glossy paper." Library J

Selected bibliography: p169-70

Place, Marian T. Mountain man; the life of Jim Beckwourth; illus. by Paul Williams. Crowell-Collier Press 1970 120p illus lib. bdg. $3.95 (4-7)   92

1 Frontier and pioneer life—The West 2 Crow Indians 3 Negroes—Biography

Jim Beckwourth was the son of a Virginia planter and a Negro slave. He later became chief of the Crow Indians. "This exciting biography depicts the adventures of the famous black fur trader who helped to blaze a trail to the West." N Y Pub Library. The Black Experience in Children's Bks

Selected bibliography: p117

Bell, Alexander Graham

Shippen, Katherine B. Mr. Bell invents the telephone; illus. by Richard Floethe. Random House 1952 183p illus lib. bdg. $4.39 (4-7)   92

1 Inventors 2 Telephone

ISBN 0-394-90330-7

"Landmark books"

"Bell's work with the deaf, his invention of the telephone, and his difficulties in getting it accepted are the highlights of a readable biography." Hodges. Bks for Elem Sch Libraries

Bernstein, Leonard

Cone, Molly. Leonard Bernstein; illus. by Robert Galster. Crowell 1970 30p illus (Crowell biographies) $4.50, lib. bdg. $5.25, pa $1.25 (3-5)   92

1 Conductors (Music) 2 Composers, American

ISBN 0-690-48785-1; 0-690-48786-X; 0-690-00209-2

This biography tells the story of Leonard Bernstein's life, from the time he was ten and received an old piano from his Aunt Clara to his adult success as composer and conductor

"The warm, off-beat illustrations, many in blue and gold, are done in a flat, child-like style and are most appropriate to the story." Sch Library J

Berry, Martha McChesney

Myers, Elisabeth P. Angel of Appalachia: Martha Berry. Messner 1968 191p lib. bdg. $4.29 (5-7)   92

1 Berry Schools, Mount Berry, Ga. 2 Educators

ISBN 0-671-32599-X

"This is the biography of a woman who saw the need for education for the children of the mountain folk. Born into wealth and accustomed to luxury, she gave everything she possessed to make possible opportunities for a better life for those children. Despite opposition from her family and friends, she dedicated her life to her schools. Her philosophy was that children needed both study and work." Best Sellers

Bibliography: p187-88

Phelan, Mary Kay. Martha Berry; illus. by Charles W. Walker. Crowell 1972 41p illus (A Crowell biography) $4.50, lib. bdg. $5.25 (2-4)   92

1 Berry Schools, Mount Berry, Ga. 2 Educators

ISBN 0-690-52112-X; 0-690-52113-8

This is the story of a Georgia plantation owner's daughter whose desire to help the poor children in the

Berry, Martha McChesney—*Continued*
Appalachian Mountains near her home led to the establishment of Sunday schools which evolved into innovative boarding schools combining work and study. Today a high school, Berry Academy, and Berry College remain as testaments to her work
The story "is told in a straightforward manner with little fictionalization." Sch Library J

Bethune, Mary (McLeod)
Carruth, Ella Kaiser. She wanted to read; the story of Mary McLeod Bethune; illus. by Herbert McClure. Abingdon 1966 80p illus $2.95 (4-6)   92
1 Educators 2 Negroes—Biography
ISBN 0-687-38353-6
"Mary McLeod Bethune grew up on a cotton plantation in South Carolina. The first person in her family to learn to read and write, Mary dedicated her life to helping black children get an education. Fighting the Ku Klux Klan and overcoming other hardships, she started many schools, becoming a college president and a civic leader." Reading Ladders for Human Relations. 5th ed.
Bethune's personality and work "are sketched in a simple biography, useful for slow readers in the upper grades." Hodges. Bks for Elem Sch Libraries

Radford, Ruby L. Mary McLeod Bethune; illus. by Lydia Rosier. Putnam 1973 61p illus (A See and read Beginning to read biography) lib. bdg. $3.96 (2-4)
          92
1 Educators 2 Negroes—Biography
ISBN 0-399-60811-7
The life story of a Black woman who founded and directed a school for Black girls and a hospital for Black people in Florida. Later, she served under President Franklin Roosevelt in the National Youth Administration
Key words: p[62]

Blackwell, Elizabeth
Clapp, Patricia. Dr Elizabeth; the story of the first woman doctor. Lothrop 1974 156p $4.95, lib. bdg. $4.59 (4-7)   92
1 Women as physicians
ISBN 0-688-40052-3; 0-688-50052-8
An "account written in journal form as though by its subject. The author has kept close to important realities in relating Blackwell's struggles to open the medical profession to women in 1847 and to raise its educational and hygienic standards." Booklist
"By writing in first person, Ms. Clapp helps the reader live through the many highs and lows of Dr. Blackwell's life. Although the book does have the power to create deep interest and feeling within the reader, the theme of rights for women is almost overdone." Cath Library World

Bolívar, Simón
Syme, Ronald. Bolívar, the liberator; illus. by William Stobbs. Morrow 1968 190p illus maps $4.95 (4-7)   92
1 Statesmen, Venezuelan 2 South America—History
ISBN 0-688-21113-5
"There could be no more dramatic a story than Bolívar's—the gilded youth whose extravagant gambling shocked Paris, whose hauteur offended the Spanish Prince, whose Venezuelan fortune was lost forever when young Simón decided to put into practice the revolutionary ideas he had been acquiring. South America was under the Spanish thumb, and at first Simón Bolívar was just another hothead whose ragged army failed miserably. But he learned, he fought, and he won; born a multimillionaire and at one time president of five countries, he died a pauper, maligned by his enemies and exiled from his home. His biography is written succinctly and smoothly, with no trace of adulation but with an objective approach both to Bolívar's limitations and errors and to the political immaturity of his countrymen. A very brief bibliography is appended." Sutherland. The Best in Children's Bks

Bonheur, Rosa
Price, Olive. Rosa Bonheur, painter of animals; illus. by Cary. Garrard 1972 144p illus lib. bdg. $3.94 (4-6)   92
1 Painters, French
ISBN 0-8116-4515-0
The author describes her subject's special love of nature and animals, which, combined with the talent for painting inherited from her artist-father, established Rosa Bonheur as a much acclaimed artist of the nineteenth century. The French art world and her many famous fellow painters provide a backdrop for the story of the first woman to win the Legion of Honor medal

Boone, Daniel
Averill, Esther. Daniel Boone; illus. by Feodor Rojankovsky. Harper 1945 56p illus maps lib. bdg. $5.89 (3-6)   92
1 Frontier and pioneer life
ISBN 0-06-020181-9
A life of Daniel Boone, relating his adventures as a hunter and scout, his capture and adoption by the Cherokee Indians, and his escape from them to warn Boonesborough of the attack planned by the Indians
"Miss Averill quotes freely from Boone's own words. Her book has drama and strength." N Y Her Trib Bks

Daugherty, James. Daniel Boone; with original lithographs in color by the author. Viking 1939 94p illus lib. bdg. $7.95 (5-7)   92
1 Frontier and pioneer life
ISBN 0-670-25589-0
Awarded the Newbery Medal, 1940
A biography of the semi-legendary frontier pioneer who played an important role in the expansion of early America
The saga of Daniel Boone "and of the wilderness he loved is recounted in singing prose. . . . The rhythmic, sculptured quality of the author-artist's brown-and-green lithographs sustains the sweep of the text." Coughlan. Creating Independence, 1763-1789
Maps on lining-papers

Boone, Rebecca (Bryan)
DeGering, Etta. Wilderness wife; the story of Rebecca Bryan Boone; illus. by Ursula Koering. McKay 1966 xx, 138p illus map $3.95, lib. bdg. $3.59 (5-7)   92
1 Boone, Daniel 2 Frontier and pioneer life
ISBN 0-679-20248-X; 0-679-25175-8
"A carefully researched episodic narrative account of the life of Daniel Boone's wife recreates in telling detail the challenges and hardships of managing a household on the early wilderness frontier and evinces the strength and endurance of the courageous woman who faced the adversities of pioneer living with cheerful willingness for love of her 'traipsin' man.'" Booklist
Selected bibliography: p135-38

Bowie, James
Garst, Shannon. James Bowie and his famous knife. Messner 1955 192p lib. bdg. $3.79 (5-7)   92
1 Frontier and pioneer life 2 The West—History
ISBN 0-671-32527-2

Bowie, James—*Continued*

"James Bowie, a headstrong, fearless boy, grew up in the wild Teche country of Louisiana, pushed west with the widening frontier to the plains of Texas, and was, at last, doomed to die a hero at the Alamo. Little is known of his youth, but Shannon Garst, delving into the pages of contemporary records, creates a life of persistent excitement quite probable for this intrepid frontiersman." Sat Rev

Bibliography: p184-87

Bradford, William

Jacobs, W. J. William Bradford of Plymouth Colony; illus. with authentic prints, documents, and maps. Watts, F. 1974 57p illus maps (A Visual biography) lib. bdg. $4.33 (4-6)   92

1 Massachusetts—History—Colonial period 2 Pilgrim Fathers
ISBN 0-531-02724-4

"Original maps and drawings by William K. Plummer." Verso of title page

This biography of the first governor of the Plymouth Colony examines the idealistic motives and practical capabilities of the Pilgrims that made the colony an early model of self-government at work

A note on sources: p53

Braille, Louis

Davidson, Margaret. Louis Braille; the boy who invented books for the blind; illus. by Janet Compere. Hastings House [1972 c1971] 80p illus $4.95 (3-5)   92

1 Blind—Education
ISBN 0-8038-4281-3

First published 1971 by Scholastic Book Services in a paperback edition

"The little French boy was only three when he blinded himself in his father's workshop. . . . By the age of 12, he had begun devising his raised-dot system. Sightless students were enormously excited by his invention, but Louis had a hard time convincing administrators of its value. Fortunately, before his death at age 43, he saw his Braille win acceptance. Children will be intrigued by the 'feelable' alphabet and will enjoy this warm biography." Pub W

Neimark, Anne E. Touch of light; the story of Louis Braille; illus. by Robert Parker. Harcourt 1970 186p illus $5.95 (4-7)   92

1 Blind—Education
ISBN 0-15-289605-8

This book "traces Braille's life and accomplishment from the age of three when he was blinded by an accident and conveys his obsession to learn to read and to make books available to the blind." Booklist

The author "tells Louis Braille's story with simplicity—it is a touching and compassionate story, in no way melodramatic—but all the way through it remains a dramatic story." Pub W

Bibliography: p185-86

Bridger, James

Garst, Shannon. Jim Bridger, greatest of the mountain men; illus. by William Moyers. Houghton 1952 242p illus $5.95 (4-7)   92

1 Frontier and pioneer life 2 The West—History
ISBN 0-395-06778-2

A fictionalized biography of the fur trader and scout who joined Ashley's fur trapping expedition in 1822. He remained in the Rocky Mountain region thereafter and became famous as a mountain man

Bibliography: p239-42. Map on lining-papers

Bridgman, Laura Dewey

Hunter, Edith Fisher. Child of the silent night; illus. by Bea Holmes. Houghton 1963 124p illus $4.95 (3-5)   92

1 Blind—Education 2 Deaf—Education
ISBN 0-395-06835-5

"Biographies of persons who have overcome physical handicaps can often reassure and inspire. This is the story of Laura Bridgman, a blind-deaf child whose successful attempts at communication paved the way for Helen Keller." Cincinnati

Brontë, Charlotte

Vipont, Elfrida. Weaver of dreams; the girlhood of Charlotte Brontë. Walck, H.Z. 1966 182p $5 (5-7)   92

1 Brontë family 2 Authors, English
ISBN 0-8098-3063-9

"The austere, often sad childhood, which the talented Brontë children transformed with their powers of imagination into a realm of fantasied delight is seen here through Charlotte's eyes." Minnesota

This account "establishes the subtle relationships among the [Brontë] children and lets the reader partake of the feast of moor and imagination that nourished Charlotte, Emily, Anne and Branwell." N Y Times Bk Rev

Some books suggested for further reading: p[183]

Bunche, Ralph Johnson

Haskins, Jim. Ralph Bunche: a most reluctant hero. Hawthorn Bks. 1974 134p illus $6.95 (6-7)   92

1 United Nations 2 Negroes—Biography 3 Diplomats

This is a biography of the diplomat who achieved international fame for his work with the United Nations. The author "doesn't shout praises but, instead, compellingly shows evidence of Bunche's greatness by describing his activities, quoting his speeches, and relating anecdotes which show the man in action. Beginning with Bunche's childhood, this relates how he rose above poverty and discrimination to become an outstanding student and athlete, a Harvard Ph.D. in political science, the first Black American to hold an important state department position and winner of the Nobel Peace Prize (awarded to him in 1950 for negotiating peace between the Israelis and Arabs). The material is well chosen and presented, integrating Bunche's life with the political and social movements of his day." Sch Library J

Bibliography: p127-30

Cabot, John

Kurtz, Henry Ira. John and Sebastian Cabot; illus. with authentic prints and maps. Watts, F. 1973 58p illus maps (A Visual biography) lib. bdg. $4.90 (4-6)   92

1 Cabot, Sebastian 2 Explorers 3 America—Discovery and exploration
ISBN 0-531-00970-X

John Cabot was responsible for the British claims in North America, but he is often overshadowed by his son Sebastian. This book highlights the importance of John Cabot's accomplishments and paints a picture of the commercial trade interests of Venice and England that set him on his way

"Based on accurate and extensive research in which sources are noted, Kurtz does an excellent job of showing how events in the East affected Europe. . . . The clear and interesting text is accompanied by black-and-white illustrations as well as contemporary prints and maps which provide a wealth of detail about life at sea." Sch Library J

Cabot, John—*Continued*

Syme, Ronald. John Cabot and his son Sebastian; illus. by William Stobbs. Morrow 1972 96p illus map lib. bdg. $4.32 (3-5)   92

1 Cabot, Sebastian 2 Explorers 3 America—Discovery and exploration

ISBN 0-688-31816-9

"This briskly written account traces what is known of the life of John Cabot and his explorations of the coast of North America. In the final section, Syme focuses on John Cabot's boastful son, Sebastian, pointing out that Sebastian's many confusing and contradictory claims make it difficult to ascertain the truth about his activities. Illustrated with numerous black-and-white drawings and a map showing the route of John Cabot's two voyages." Booklist

Cabot, Sebastian

Kurtz, Henry Ira. John and Sebastian Cabot. See entry under Cabot, John   92

Syme, Ronald. John Cabot and his son Sebastian. See entry under Cabot, John   92

Caesar, Caius Julius

Caesar, by the editors of Horizon Magazine. Author: Irwin Isenberg; consultant: Richard M. Haywood. . . . Am. Heritage [distributed by Harper] 1964 151p illus maps lib. bdg. $6.89 (6-7)   92

1 Roman emperors 2 Rome—History—Republic, 510-30 B.C.

ISBN 0-06-022771-0

"A Horizon Caravel book"

"Illustrated with sculpture, mosaics, and artifacts of the period." Title page

"This book brings together the facts and myths of Caesar's life with pertinent art, documents, and photographs and reconstructions of significant sites." Foreword

"The pictures, as always in these books, will be useful especially to young students of history, and, in this case, Latin." Sat Rev

Further reference: p151

Campanella, Roy

Schoor, Gene. Roy Campanella: man of courage. Putnam 1959 1959 190p lib. bdg. $4.97 (4-7)   92

1 Baseball—Biography 2 Negro athletes

ISBN 0-399-60550-9

This is "the story of the career of the Dodger catcher and of his courage and skill as a ballplayer, his pioneering role as a Negro in major league baseball, and the spirit he showed in facing up to the paralysis which resulted from an automobile accident." Pub W

Carnegie, Andrew

Shippen, Katherine B. Andrew Carnegie and the age of steel; illus. with photographs and with drawings by Ernest Kurt Barth. Random House 1958 183p illus lib. bdg. $4.39 (4-7)   92

1 Capitalists and financiers 2 Steel industry and trade

ISBN 0-394-90380-3

"Landmark books"

"The poor Scottish boy who rose to be a steel magnate and one of the world's great philanthropists is the subject of a sympathetic biography. A success story emphasizing the importance of ambition and hard work and including much information about the development of the steel industry." Hodges. Bks for Elem Sch Libraries

Carson, Christopher

Bell, Margaret E. Kit Carson: mountain man; illus. by Harry Daugherty. Morrow 1952 71p illus lib. bdg. $4.32 (4-7)   92

1 Frontier and pioneer life 2 The West—History

ISBN 0-688-31483-X

An "account of the indomitable frontiersman, beginning with his first trip as a herder with a wagon train at the age of sixteen and following his adventurous life and career as trapper, guide, and Indian fighter." Wis Lib Bul

"The author succeeds in conveying in clear, simple prose the character of the [man]. . . . The narrative of the painful march to the Far West is excellent, and the many dramatic pencil sketches complement the text." Library J

Carson, Rachel Louise

Latham, Jean Lee. Rachel Carson: who loved the sea; illus. by Victor Mays. Garrard 1973 80p illus lib. bdg. $3.40 (3-5)   92

1 Biologists

ISBN 0-8116-6312-4

"A Discovery book"

"This short career-biography tells about scientist Rachel Carson's girlhood and . . . explains the difficulties of entering a field dominated by men. Because her knowledge of marine biology was coupled with an ability to write well, she was assigned to prepare scripts for a radio program, 'Romance under the Waters;' these articles became the nucleus for her notable books about the sea." Sch Library J

"The personal material tends to be superficial, so that the reader learns how Rachel Carson took care of young relatives rather than what sort of person she was; however, the book does give the most pertinent facts about a subject who is important because of what she accomplished, and it touches on the topical issue of pollution." Chicago. Children's Bk Center

Sterling, Philip. Sea and earth; the life of Rachel Carson; illus. with photographs. Crowell 1970 213p illus (Women of America) $4.95 (6-7)   92

1 Biologists

ISBN 0-690-72288-5

In this account of the marine biologist, author and conservationist, Sterling tells of Miss Carson's "childhood, young womanhood, the years of work and the later years of success marred by sickness. The smear campaign against her is described . . . [her] fight against it, and her . . . vindication." Christian Sci Monitor

This "biography is objective in tone, smoothly and seriously written, and thoroughly documented with an impressive list of sources." Sat Rev

Cartier, Jacques

Syme, Ronald. Cartier, finder of the St Lawrence; illus. by William Stobbs. Morrow 1958 95p illus map lib. bdg. $4.32 (4-6)   92

1 Explorers 2 America—Discovery and exploration 3 St Lawrence River

ISBN 0-688-31146-6

"An account of the French explorer's voyages to the New World in search of a waterway to the Pacific Ocean, his meetings with Indians and the building of two forts on the St. Lawrence River." Pub W

"A map shows the routes of Cartier's first two voyages (the later ones are only briefly covered in the text) while doublespread and other black-and-white drawings reconstruct realistically scenes of the voyaging, meetings with Indians, and wilderness life." Horn Bk

Carver, George Washington
Aliki. A weed is a flower: the life of George Washington Carver; written and illus. by Aliki. Prentice-Hall 1965 unp illus lib. bdg. $4.95, pa 95¢ (k-3)   92
1 Scientists 2 Negroes—Biography
ISBN 0-13-947861-2; 0-13-947879-5
A read-aloud picturebook biography which "gives a fairly balanced picture of Dr. Carver as a person and of his research and teaching. The illustrations are most attractive in their composition and use of color." We Build Together

Catlin, George
Rockwell, Anne. Paintbrush & peacepipe: the story of George Catlin. Atheneum Pubs. 1971 86p illus lib. bdg. $5.25 (4-6)   92
1 Painters, American
ISBN 0-689-20686-0
"A simply told biography of George Catlin and the beginnings of his interest in the American Indians which led him to interest others in their way of life and to make countless paintings of them. Illustrations are based on the drawings of Catlin and the simple lines convey the spirit of the text which shows his deep appreciation for our early native Americans." Top of the News

Cavell, Edith Louisa
De Leeuw, Adèle. Edith Cavell: nurse, spy, heroine; illus. by Charles Brey. Putnam 1968 95p illus (Spies of the world) lib. bdg. $4.29 (5-7)   92
1 Nurses and nursing 2 European War, 1914-1918—Belgium
ISBN 0-399-60146-5
This is a biography of Edith Cavell, known for establishing the nursing profession in Belgium and for her brave activities during World War I. Because she helped all people, regardless of nationality, her wartime activities were considered clandestine and she was shot as a spy

Chamberlain, Wilton Norman
Rudeen, Kenneth. Wilt Chamberlain; illus. by Frank Mullins. Crowell 1970 32p illus (Crowell biographies) $4.50, lib. bdg. $5.25, pa $1.45 (2-5)   92
1 Basketball—Biography 2 Negro athletes
ISBN 0-690-89458-9; 0-690-89459-7; 0-690-89460-0
This biography "describes Wilt's boyhood, the difficulties of growing up both black and extra-tall, and the young athlete's prowess and progress at school, at college, with the Harlem Globetrotters, and . . . with the Lakers. Then to his nightclub in his beloved Harlem, and his present prosperity." Christian Sci Monitor
This book has "good, easy reading type and . . . [is] most attractively designed and illustrated. . . . [The story emphasizes] the dedication and hard work necessary for black Americans to make their way [and] should fill an immediate need." Commonweal

Champlain, Samuel de
Jacobs, W. J. Samuel de Champlain; illus. with authentic prints, documents, and maps. Watts, F. 1974 58p illus maps (A Visual biography) lib. bdg. $4.33 (4-6)   92
1 Explorers 2 Canada—History—To 1763 (New France)
ISBN 0-531-01275-1
"Original maps by William K. Plummer." Verso of title page
Biography of the French explorer who founded Quebec City and Montreal and was responsible for the exploration and settlement of Canada in the 1600's

Includes some photographs and "reproductions of Champlain's own drawings." Booklist
A note on sources: p55

Syme, Ronald. Champlain of the St Lawrence; illus. by William Stobbs. Morrow 1952 189p illus $4.95 (4-6)   92
1 Explorers 2 America—Discovery and exploration
ISBN 0-688-21158-5
When young Samuel de Champlain first left France in the year 1582 to sail across the North Atlantic in a small, ill-provisioned schooner, he hoped he might see the newly discovered great river beyond the Newfoundland fishing banks. It was only after long years of struggle against the brutal northern winter, the hostile Iroquois, and the inertia of his own countrymen that Champlain really established New France and opened up the vast interior of North America to Europeans
"Mr. Syme writes briskly, evocatively, recreating both the personality of the man and the rugged life in the silent forests of seventeenth-century Canada and New England." N Y Times Bk Rev

Chapman, John
Aliki. The story of Johnny Appleseed; written and illus. by Aliki. Prentice-Hall 1963 unp illus lib. bdg. $4.95, pa 95¢ (k-3)   92
1 Frontier and pioneer life
ISBN 0-13-850800-3; 0-13-850818-6
This is a picture-story of "Johnny Appleseed, the New Englander who wandered through the Middle West in the early days distributing seeds of apple trees for planting, and remaining to share his love for wild creatures, pioneer folk, and nature." Christian Sci Monitor

Charles, Ray
Mathis, Sharon Bell. Ray Charles; illus. by George Ford. Crowell 1973 31p illus (A Crowell biography) $4.50, lib. bdg. $5.25 (2-5)   92
1 Negro musicians 2 Singers
ISBN 0-690-67065-6; 0-690-67066-4
This is a biography of the popular Black singer who overcame his blindness to achieve renown in the music world
"Enhanced by Ford's two-color charcoal drawings, this will broaden Black biography collections." Sch Library J

Chavez, César Estrada
Franchere, Ruth. Cesar Chavez; illus. by Earl Thollander. Crowell 1970 42p illus (Crowell biographies) $4.50, lib. bdg. $5.25, pa $1.25 (2-5)   92
1 Migrant labor 2 Mexicans in the U.S.
ISBN 0-690-18383-6; 0-690-18384-4; 0-690-18385-2
Coming from a Mexican-American family of migrant workers, César Chavez has experienced first hand the miserable conditions under which the migrant worker lives and works. This is a biography of Chavez—unionizer of the grape pickers of California and leader of a nationwide grape boycott to get decent wages for migrant workers
"The type is large, and the illustrations, line drawings with orange and gold overlays, give a feeling for the vast, dry setting. In spite of its picture-book format, this could be useful with older, reluctant readers." Sch Library J

Churchill, Sir Winston Leonard Spencer
Reynolds, Quentin. Winston Churchill; illus. with photographs. Random House 1963 183p illus maps lib. bdg. $4.39 (4-7)   92
1 Statesmen, British 2 Great Britain—History—20th century
ISBN 0-394-90556-3

Churchull, Sir Winston Leonard Spencer
—*Continued*
"World Landmark books"
"The many facets of Sir Winston's personality and
career are brought out in a smoothly written biog-
raphy, ending with his resignation as prime minister
in 1955. Photographs include pictures of his funeral."
Hodges. Bks for Elem Sch Libraries
Other books of interest: p178-79

Clark, George Rogers
De Leeuw, Adèle. George Rogers Clark: frontier
fighter; illus. by Russ Hoover. Garrard 1967 80p
lib. bdg. $3.40 (2-4)   92
1 Soldiers—U.S. 2 U.S.—History—Revolution
ISBN 0-8116-6298-5
"A Discovery book"
When the American Revolution began, this famous
young Indian fighter was determined to help his country win independence. How he captured English forts
and contributed to the expansion of the United States
is told in this biography

Clemens, Samuel Langhorne
Daugherty, Charles Michael. Samuel Clemens;
illus. by Kurt Werth. Crowell 1970 41p illus (A
Crowell biography) $4.50, lib. bdg. $5.25 (2-4)   92
1 Authors, American
ISBN 0-690-71850-0; 0-690-71851-9
This biography of Samuel Clemens, better known
as Mark Twain, describes his early childhood and days
as an apprentice printer in Missouri. It depicts his
adventures as a steamboat pilot on the Mississippi
River and his life in the mining camps of Nevada. It
concludes with his rise from a position as a journalist
with the Virginia City "Enterprise," a Nevada paper,
to world-wide renown as a writer, humorist, and
lecturer
"A crisp, easy-reading narrative biography, illustrated with lively drawings in color or black and white
on every page." Booklist

McKown, Robin. Mark Twain; novelist, humorist,
satirist, grassroots historian and America's unpaid
goodwill ambassador at large. McGraw 1974 160p
front lib. bdg. $5.72 (6-7)   92
1 Authors, American
ISBN 0-07-045368-3
"McKown carefully weaves anecdotes and descriptive snatches by and about Twain into a colorful biography that entertains and informs. The result is a clear
portrait of the man against a blurred setting of fact and
fiction, which is fun but perhaps frustrating to readers
who may wish to distill the reality out of it all.
Weighted more toward visualizing Twain through his
life and work than analyzing his writings in depth, this
is . . . solid biographical fare." Booklist
Includes bibliographies and index

McNeer, May. America's Mark Twain; with illus.
by Lynd Ward. Houghton 1962 159p illus lib. bdg.
$6.95 (5-7)   92
1 Authors, American
ISBN 0-395-19842-9
This book tells about Mark Twain's life of adventure
on the Mississippi River, his success as a humorist, his
escapades that entertained America and most of
Europe, and the tragedies that befell him in later life
"This version is a joy to read and to look at. . . . The
Wards have worked together with genuine affection
and respect for their subject—and for their readers.
As a supplement to Mark Twain's life, they have
added at the end of each chapter a sort of preview of
the particular book which was related to that part of
his life. These little previews, each consisting of sev-

eral pages with text and pictures illustrating sample
episodes, are designed to interest the reader in
exploring the books themselves." Horn Bk

Clemente, Roberto Walker
Hano, Arnold. Roberto Clemente: batting king.
[Rev. ed] Putnam 1973 190p (Putnam Sports shelf)
lib. bdg. $4.97 (5-7)   92
1 Baseball—Biography
ISBN 0-399-60865-6
First published 1968
A biography of the baseball star who died in a plane
crash in 1972 while aiding earthquake victims in
Nicaragua. He became a hero in his native Puerto
Rico because of his baseball prowess and in his last
season became only the eleventh man in major league
history to get 3,000 hits
"Hano's opinions of players, managers, and execu-
tives are at times negative, and he's even slightly
critical of some of Clemente's attitudes. This candid-
ness plus a bit of Pittsburgh Pirate history and references to the tempo of the times are what make this
biography much more readable than usual." Sch Library J

Rudeen, Kenneth. Roberto Clemente; illus. by
Frank Mullins. Crowell 1974 32p illus (A Crowell
biography) $3.95, lib. bdg. $4.70 (2-4)   92
1 Baseball—Biography
ISBN 0-690-00315-3; 0-690-00322-6
A biography of the Puerto Rican who began to train
himself as a baseball player in his youth, became an
outstanding member of the Pittsburgh Pirates
baseball club, and died tragically in a plane crash
while on a good will mission to earthquake-damaged
Nicaragua
The book is "simply written, straightforward in
tone, and well-organized." Chicago. Children's Bk
Center

Cochise, Apache chief
Wyatt, Edgar. Cochise, Apache warrior and states-
man; illus. by Allan Houser. McGraw 1953 192p illus
lib. bdg. $4.72 (5-7)   92
1 Apache Indians—Biography 2 Southwest, New—
History
ISBN 0-07-072157-2
"Whittlesey House publications"
"Both sides of the Indian problem are shown in a
thought-provoking biography of the Apache chief who
tried to live in peace with the white man but was
forced into war by dishonorable dealings." Hodges.
Bks for Elem Sch Libraries
"An attractive book with lively drawings by the
Indian artist Allan Houser heighten interest for
readers." Library J
Guide to Indian and Spanish words: p186-90.
Sources: p191-92

Cody, William Frederick
Aulaire, Ingri d'. Buffalo Bill, by Ingri & Edgar
Parin d'Aulaire. Doubleday 1952 unp illus lib. bdg.
$5.95 (1-4)   92
1 Frontier and pioneer life 2 The West—History
ISBN 0-385-07605-3
Youngsters "will be enthusiastic about this recreation of the life of one of their heroes. Beginning
with his boyhood in Kansas Territory and his friendship with the Kickapoo Indians, the biography
authentically pictures the outstanding events of his
long and exciting life against the background of our
western frontier. The illustrations, in the d'Aulaire
manner, are bright and filled with interesting
details." Library J
"The text is factual, with no talking down, and the

Cody, William Frederick—*Continued*
many big pictures a pleasant introduction to the old
west." N Y Her Trib Bks
Map on lining-papers

Columbus, Christopher
Aulaire, Ingri d'. Columbus [by] Ingri & Edgar
Parin d'Aulaire. Doubleday 1955 56p illus lib. bdg.
$5.95 (1-4)   92
1 Explorers 2 America—Discovery and exploration
ISBN 0-385-07606-1
"This is an account of Columbus' four voyages to the
New World. . . . The authors have a lively enthusiasm
for their subject, and have imbued this biography
with the excitement of exploring the unknown; and
they have successfully brought to life the restless
ambitious spirit, which sent Columbus out into the
'trackless waste of the sea.' The illustrations are striking full-page lithographs, some in colour and some in
black and white, and imaginative marginal drawings."
Ontario Library Rev
This book "is perhaps better suited to a child who
has already heard the story and who has begun to want
more information. . . . The portrait of the aging,
disappointed man who 'wanted too much and so did
not get enough' in no way detracts from the reader's
sense of his greatness. Rather it adds to our understanding." N Y Times Bk Rev

Dalgliesh, Alice. The Columbus story; pictures by
Leo Politi. Scribner 1955 unp illus lib. bdg. $6.95
(k-3)   92
1 Explorers 2 America—Discovery and exploration
ISBN 0-684-13179-X
"The story of Columbus told with simple dignity for
young readers or listeners. The bare facts of Columbus's early life and first voyage are presented in brief
text and colorful, distinctive illustrations to give the
child a first acquaintance with the subject, without the
introduction of legendary materials that frequently
lead to misunderstandings." Chicago. Children's Bk
Center
"Use of the Admiral's own words and handsome
colored illustrations add authenticity and vitality."
Hodges. Bks for Elem Sch Libraries

Sperry, Armstrong. The voyages of Christopher
Columbus; written and illus. by Armstrong Sperry.
Random House 1950 186p illus lib. bdg. $4.39 (5-7)
                                                       92
1 Explorers 2 America—Discovery and exploration
ISBN 0-394-90301-3
"Landmark books"
An account of the four voyages of Columbus, relat-
ing the oft-told incidents as well as the seldom-heard
accounts of his sea voyages, the mutinies of his crews,
and land colonization
"Mr. Sperry brings all his feeling for the sea and his
ability to tell a brisk adventure story to his tale of
Columbus; his hero is appealingly real and his fine
pictures a moving dramatic unit." N Y Her Trib Bks

Syme, Ronald. Columbus, finder of the New
World; illus. by William Stobbs. Morrow 1952 70p
illus maps lib. bdg. $4.32 (4-6)   92
1 Explorers 2 America—Discovery and exploration
ISBN 0-688-31179-2
Here is the story of a brave man and his four famous
voyages of discovery, a man whose faith in his own
vision triumphed over mutiny, hostile natives, and
physical suffering
"It is a pictorial record as well as a text. The story is
told in a direct, simple wording with clear continuity."
Sat Rev

Cook, James
Syme, Ronald. Captain Cook, Pacific explorer;
illus. by William Stobbs. Morrow 1960 96p illus map
lib. bdg. $4.32 (4-6)   92
1 Explorers 2 Discoveries (in geography)
ISBN 0-688-31140-7
A biography of the youth and career of James Cook,
world-famous explorer, who traveled around the
world and accurately charted areas of New Zealand
and Australia that no one had ever mapped before.
Under his command, Cook's crew survived attacks by
Maori warriors, imprisonment on a coral pinnacle of
the Great Barrier Reef, and deadly tropical diseases
"The information included has been well selected
for this age group. Easy to read, colorfully written,
and narrative flows smoothly. Forceful illustrations."
Library J

Cortés, Hernando
Jacobs, W. J. Hernando Cortes; illus. with authentic prints, documents, and maps. Watts, F. 1974 58p
illus maps (A Visual biography) lib. bdg. $4.90 (4-6)
                                                       92
1 Explorers 2 Mexico—History
ISBN 0-531-00974-2
"A brief but vivid record of the epic battles led by
Hernando Cortes in 1519-21 that destroyed the Mexican Aztec civilization. The text has been carefully
researched and two events—the defeat of 'La Noche
Triste' and the battle at Atumbo—are especially well
detailed. Illustrated with fascinating prints and
maps." Sch Library J

Syme, Ronald. Cortés of Mexico; illus. by William
Stobbs. Morrow 1951 191p illus lib. bdg. $4.59
(4-6)   92
1 Explorers 2 Mexico—History
ISBN 0-688-31188-1
"A fast-paced and authentic account of Cortés' con-
quest of Mexico, attributing the destruction of the
Aztec civilization to the men under Cortés, rather
than to the explorer himself." Hodges. Bks for Elem
Sch Libraries
"Mr. Stobbs' drawings add richness and reality to
Mr. Syme's colorful biography." N Y Times Bk Rev

Craft, Ellen
Freedman, Florence B. Two tickets to freedom; the
true story of Ellen and William Craft, fugitive slaves.
See entry under Craft, William   92

Craft, William
Freedman, Florence B. Two tickets to freedom; the
true story of Ellen and William Craft, fugitive slaves;
illus. by Ezra Jack Keats. Simon & Schuster 1971 96p
illus lib. bdg. $5.95 (4-6)   92
1 Craft, Ellen 2 Slavery in the U.S. 3 Negroes—
Biography
ISBN 0-671-65169-2
Using contemporary newspaper articles, journals
and William Craft's own narrative, the author
recounts the escape of William and Ellen Craft from
their slave owners in Macon, Georgia in 1842
"The story is not well known, so children may need
some introduction to it. But once begun, it is hard to
put down. . . . Ezra Jack Keats' charcoal drawings
effectively decorate the text. An excellent selection
for history buffs and those who enjoy warm human
interest stories." Sch Library J
Sources: p96

Crazy Horse, Oglala Indian

Meadowcroft, Enid La Monte. Crazy Horse, Sioux warrior; illus. by Cary. Garrard 1965 80p illus lib. bdg. $3.40 (2-5) 92

1 Oglala Indians—Biography
ISBN 0-8116-6600-X

"This life of the great Sioux warrior [of the Oglala tribe] tells not only of the white men's injustices but also of the unreasoning warfare of the Indians among themselves." Adventuring With Bks

"A sympathetic and interesting account. . . . The illustrations, by Cary, are excellent." N Y Times Bk Rev

Crockett, David

Holbrook, Stewart. Davy Crockett; illus. by Ernest Richardson. Random House 1955 179p illus $2.95, lib. bdg. $4.27 (5-7) 92

1 Frontier and pioneer life 2 The West—History
ISBN 0-394-80357-4; 0-394-90357-9

"Landmark books"

"The half-legendary hero of the Alamo appears larger than life in a story interweaving fact and tall tale. Covers Crockett's life as a frontiersman, politician, and soldier and includes a list of Crockett memorials." Hodges. Bks for Elem Sch Libraries

Custer, George Armstrong

Reynolds, Quentin. Custer's last stand; illus. by Frederick T. Chapman. Random House 1951 185p illus $2.95, lib. bdg. $4.39 (5-7) 92

1 Generals 2 Little Big Horn, Battle of the, 1876
ISBN 0-394-80320-5; 0-394-90320-X

"Landmark books"

"The life story of the famous U.S. cavalry officer—boyhood, preparation for and training at West Point, Civil War experiences, Indian fighting, and the disastrous battle at Little Big Horn. The courageous, headstrong soldier is animatedly portrayed in this exciting and well-written book." Booklist

"The realistic portrayal of the relations between the Indians and white men make this an important addition to the books on the making of America." Library J

Darwin, Charles Robert

Gallant, Roy A. Charles Darwin: the making of a scientist. Doubleday 1972 172p illus maps $4.95, lib. bdg. $5.70 (4-7) 92

1 Naturalists 2 Evolution
ISBN 0-385-02109-7; 0-385-06086-6

The author "presents a very readable biography of Charles Darwin, drawing on Darwin's own 'Recollections' for his childhood and youth and on 'The voyage of the Beagle' for his experiences as a naturalist sailing around the world. Smoothly integrating the carefully selected excerpts into his summary of events . . . [the author] not only portrays the scientist's personality but also explains the theories of catastrophism and creationism, shows how Darwin gradually came to discard such theories, and describes the furor raised by his publication of 'The origin of species.'" Booklist

Dickinson, Emily

Barth, Edna. I'm nobody! Who are you? The story of Emily Dickinson; drawings by Richard Cuffari. Seabury 1971 128p illus $6.95 (5-7) 92

1 Poets, American
ISBN 0-8164-3029-2

This is "a very good biography that begins with the nine-year-old Emily, smoothly incorporates passages of her writing within the context of the text, and includes selected poems at the conclusion of the biographical material. The writing style is direct and informal, all of the dialogue based on research, and the tone is objective. A bibliography, a list of sources, an index of poems by first lines, and a general index are appended." Sutherland. The Best in Children's Bks

Disney, Walt

Montgomery, Elizabeth Rider. Walt Disney: master of make-believe; illus. by Vic Mays. Garrard 1971 96p illus (Americans all) lib. bdg. $3.58 (3-5) 92

1 Moving pictures—Biography 2 Moving picture cartoons
ISBN 0-8116-4568-1

This "interesting, simply written narrative biography . . . covers Disney's life from his harsh, unhappy childhood to his death in 1966. [The author] relates some of the problems Disney encountered during his early years in Hollywood, describes the origin of Mickey Mouse and other well-known Disney cartoon characters, and tells how Disney's dream of a clean imaginative amusement park led to the development of Disneyland." Booklist

Douglass, Frederick

Bontemps, Arna. Frederick Douglass: slave-fighter-freeman; illus. by Harper Johnson. Knopf 1959 177p illus lib. bdg. $4.99 (4-7) 92

1 Abolitionists 2 Negroes—Biography
ISBN 0-394-91168-7

Frederick Douglass was born a slave. When he got his hard-won freedom, he dedicated his life to the cause of freedom for all men. From a lowly slave boy, he forged ahead to become a great statesman, newsman, orator, and writer. The path was rough but the goal worth winning

"Mr. Bontemps has used great restraint in this account of the sufferings of those early years, but even so this is an exciting story of struggle against almost insurmountable odds, and of the triumph of human greatness. Direct style, large type and good illustrations make this an appealing book." Horn Bk

Graves, Charles P. Frederick Douglass; illus. by Joel Snyder. Putnam 1970 64p illus (A See and read Beginning to read biography) lib. bdg. $3.96 (2-4) 92

1 Abolitionists 2 Negroes—Biography
ISBN 0-399-60187-2

This is "a well-written biography of Frederick Douglass which covers his life as a child, slave, freeman and abolitionist." N Y Pub Library. The Black Experience in Children's Bks

Key words: p62

Patterson, Lillie. Frederick Douglass: freedom fighter; illus. by Gray Morrow. Garrard 1965 80p illus lib. bdg. $3.40 (4-6) 92

1 Abolitionists 2 Negroes—Biography
ISBN 0-8116-6285-3

"A Discovery book"

"The institution of slavery, abolitionist activities, and the operation of the Underground Railroad are explained in terms children can grasp. Grim incidents are balanced with anecdotes about white friends. [It is] a biography for all young readers." Keating. Building Bridges of Understanding Between Cultures

Drake, Sir Francis

Latham, Jean Lee. Drake: the man they called a pirate; illus. by Frederick T. Chapman. Harper 1960 278p illus lib. bdg. $5.79 (5-7) 92

1 Adventure and adventurers
ISBN 0-06-023701-5

"A full biography which reads like historical fiction as it covers its hero's voyages from the precocious age of ten through his one-man war on Spain in the Caribbean and around the world, to the climax of his career

Drake, Sir Francis—*Continued*

vanquishing the Armada. . . . A clear account of Drake's genius as a mariner." Horn Bk

"The action at sea is vividly described, and the Elizabethan background lends drama; Drake himself is a strong character. The book concludes with the conquest of the Invincible Armada, a fitting climax to the long years of Drake's remorseless enmity toward Spain." Chicago. Children's Bk Center

Syme, Ronald. Francis Drake, sailor of the unknown seas; illus. by William Stobbs. Morrow 1961 96p illus map lib. bdg. $4.32 (4-6)   92
1 Adventure and adventurers
ISBN 0-688-31311-6

This biography "highlights Sir Francis Drake's career from his boyhood through his voyage of circumnavigation to his part in the defeat of the Spanish Armada. Colorful and readable; large print, vigorous drawings." Bks for Children, 1960-1965

Drew, Charles Richard

Bertol, Roland. Charles Drew; illus. by Jo Polseno. Crowell 1970 31p illus (Crowell biographies) $4.50, lib. bdg. $5.25 (3-5)   92
1 Physicians 2 Negroes—Biography
ISBN 0-690-18597-9; 0-690-18598-7

This is "a fictionized biography of the Negro doctor who discovered how to make blood transfusions and how to preserve blood. . . . [The author] traces Drew's life: his childhood desire to be a jockey, the discrimination he encountered while an athlete at Amherst College, his blood research at McGill University, and the controversy he generated during World War II when he insisted that black and white blood could be used interchangeably in transfusions." Sch Library J

"The account also contains some interesting sidelights on scientific research. Designed for young readers, the book is printed in large type with pictures on almost every page." Booklist

Du Bois, William Edward Burghardt

Hamilton, Virginia. W.E.B. Du Bois; a biography. Illus. with photographs. Crowell 1972 218p illus $6.95 (6-7)   92
1 Negroes—Biography
ISBN 0-690-87256-9

This is an account of the life and career of W.E.B. Du Bois who "struggled for ninety-five years as educator, writer, intellectual, and poet against prejudice and fear. . . . [The author describes Du Bois'] life from his birth in 1868 as a free man in Great Barrington, Massachusetts, to his death in 1963 in Ghana, a Ghanian citizen. . . . The book is an affirmation of Du Bois' life, and a fascinating historical document of the Black Movement in America." Horn Bk

This "work is meticulously annotated, comprehensive, and generally objective—too detailed for preteens, perhaps, but extremely good for slightly older readers." Christian Sci Monitor
Bibliography: p204-08

Dunbar, Paul Laurence

Schultz, Pearle Henriksen. Paul Laurence Dunbar: Black poet laureate; illus. by William Hutchinson. Garrard 1974 143p illus lib. bdg. $3.58 (4-7)   92
1 Poets, American 2 Negroes—Biography
ISBN 0-8116-4516-9

The author shows "what it was like for Dunbar to grow up in the Midwest of the late 1800's, and a good selection of photographs from the period are included. Although some dialogue is fictionalized, there is also a healthy sampling of Dunbar's better-known dialect poems, which have particular appeal to children, as well as verse in his classical style." Sch Library J

Earhart, Amelia

Mann, Peggy. Amelia Earhart: first lady of flight; illus. by Kiyo Komoda. Coward-McCann 1970 126p illus lib. bdg. $3.99 (3-5)   92
1 Women in aeronautics
ISBN 0-698-30008-4

This is "a fictionalized biography of Amelia Earhart which stresses her personal courage and her belief that women should have the same opportunities to develop and use their abilities as men. The book covers Earhart's tomboy childhood, her growing preoccupation with airplanes, her record-breaking flights, and her ill-fated attempt to fly around the world." Booklist

Edison, Thomas Alva

Cousins, Margaret. The story of Thomas Alva Edison; illus. with photographs and map. Random House 1965 175p illus map lib. bdg. $4.27 (4-6)   92
1 Inventors
ISBN 0-394-90410-9
"Landmark books"

"A readable biography of one of America's greatest inventors, with emphasis on his part in the development of the phonograph, the incandescent light, and motion pictures." Hodges. Bks for Elem Sch Libraries
Includes bibliography

North, Sterling. Young Thomas Edison; illus. with photographs, decorations, diagrams, and maps by William Barss. Houghton 1958 182p illus maps $2.95 (5-7)   92
1 Inventors
ISBN 0-395-07252-2
"North star books"

"A biography of Thomas A. Edison, stressing his inventions and the fact that his life was fruitful despite many vicissitudes and disappointments." Pub W

"A well-written, authentic biography which reveals the human qualities of the inventor as well as his genius." Booklist

Einstein, Albert

Beckhard, Arthur J. Albert Einstein; illus. by Charles Beck. Putnam 1959 126p illus lib. bdg. $4.97 (4-7)   92
1 Physicists 2 Nuclear physics
ISBN 0-399-60011-6

"The life of the great mathematician and physicist, presented with accuracy and warmth. Einstein is portrayed as a great humanitarian as well as a brilliant scientist. His basic theories [in nuclear physics] are explained in general terms." The AAAS Sci Book List for Children

Ericsson, John

Latham, Jean Lee. Man of the Monitor; the story of John Ericsson; pictures by Leonard Everett Fisher. Harper 1962 231p illus lib. bdg. $5.79 (5-7)   92
1 U.S.—History—Civil War—Naval operations 2 Monitor (Ironclad)
ISBN 0-06-023711-2

The author "presents a lively sketch of John Ericsson, Swedish-born engineer and inventor . . . best remembered for designing and supervising the construction of the 'Monitor.' She takes up his story in a somewhat sentimental vein when he is nine and his family is on the verge of ruin. About half the book covers his life from child genius in Sweden to modest success in England; the remaining part describes his frustrated early days in America to final triumph at the close of the Civil War. . . . Miss Latham's story moves at a good pace, uncluttered by dates and details. Its main difficulty is with the dialogue, which seems to

Ericsson, John—*Continued*
fall short in its attempt to reach the young teenager because of its artificiality." Best Sellers

This book "has value not only as a biography but also as a good book of the Civil War period." Chicago. Children's Bk Center

Farragut, David Glasgow
Latham, Jean Lee. Anchor's aweigh; the story of David Glasgow Farragut; illus. by Eros Keith. Harper 1968 273p maps $4.50, lib. bdg. $5.79 (5-7)   92
1 U.S.—History—Civil War—Biography 2 U.S.—History, Naval
ISBN 0-06-023702-3; 0-06-023703-1
"David Glasgow Farragut, whose 'Damn the torpedoes!' will long be remembered, was the naval hero, who won a victory at Mobile Bay that broke the power of the South. Jean Lee Latham has written an exciting and fast-paced story of a man who began his career as midshipman before he was ten years old and rose to the rank of Admiral." Pub W

Feelings, Tom
Black pilgrimage. Lothrop 1972 72p illus $6.95, lib. bdg. $5.81 (5-7)   92
1 Negroes—Biography 2 Illustrators
ISBN 0-688-41630-6; 0-688-51630-0
This Black "children's book illustrator describes his life and work, particularly his decision to leave the United States and live in Africa. Tom Feelings grew up in Bedford-Stuyvesant, served in the army, and went to art school. He drew and painted the life he knew, but it was not until he worked for a time in Ghana that Feelings saw how much the oppression suffered by his people was evident in his pictures. [His illustrations supplement the text throughout]." Sat Rev
"His statement is honest, often bitter, and always sensitive, particularly interesting for the insight his own work gave Tom Feelings into the attitudes of black Americans after he had been in Africa and returned. The illustrations, some in color and some in black and white, are stunning." Sutherland. The Best in Children's Bks

Field, Cyrus West
Latham, Jean Lee. Young man in a hurry; the story of Cyrus W. Field; pictures by Victor Mays. Harper 1958 238p illus lib. bdg. $5.79 (5-7)   92
1 Cables, Submarine
ISBN 0-06-023756-2
"Field's work in laying the Atlantic cable in 1858 is the focus of a biography emphasizing the energy, enthusiasm, and hard work which made the achievement possible." Hodges. Bks for Elem Sch Library
"The story is powerfully written, and intensely exciting. The solving of the numerous apparently unsolvable problems involved in the manufacture and laying of thousands of miles of cable becomes spellbinding." Horn Bk

Forten, Charlotte L.
Douty, Esther M. Charlotte Forten: free Black teacher. Garrard 1971 144p illus lib. bdg. $3.94 (4-6)   92
1 Teachers 2 Negroes—Biography
ISBN 0-8116-4512-6
"A simply-written narrative biography of Charlotte Forten, granddaughter of the Negro businessman and abolitionist James Forten. Many quotations from a journal kept by Charlotte Forten are incorporated into the account. It focuses on her childhood in Philadelphia, her education in Salem, Massachusetts, and on her experiences, in her twenties, as a teacher among the freed slaves on the Carolina Sea Islands

during the Civil War." Reading Ladders for Human Relations. 5th edition

Longsworth, Polly. I, Charlotte Forten, Black and free. Crowell 1970 248p $4.95 (6-7)   92
1 Teachers 2 Negroes—Biography
ISBN 0-690-42869-3
"Civil war movements and black-American history form the major part of the account, its framework based on a journal kept by the granddaughter of James Forten, well-to-do black sailmaker of Philadelphia. More intimate and lively portions of the writing . . . describe Charlotte's teen-age life in Salem, Massachusetts, where she came in 1854 to study and then to teach. . . . Charlotte seemed always to meet the great leaders, both black and white. . . . Case histories of individual slaves and eyewitness accounts of historic meetings and trials further enrich the biographical history." Horn Bk
Bibliography: p234-37

Forten, James
Johnston, Brenda A. Between the devil and the sea; the life of James Forten; illus. by Don Miller. Harcourt 1974 125p illus $6.75 (4-6)   92
1 Negroes—Biography
ISBN 0-15-206965-8
A "fictionalized biography of the free black Philadelphian who served as powder boy on the 'Royal Lewis' during the Revolutionary War, lived for a time in England, and returned to his native city to become a wealthy businessman and a tireless worker in the black cause." Chicago. Children's Bk Center
"This portrait is notable for its forthright discussion of the new nation's anti-Black sentiments." Sch Library J
Suggested readings: p125

Francis of Assisi, Saint
Jewett, Sophie. God's troubadour; the story of Saint Francis of Assisi; with paintings by Giotto. [3d ed] Crowell 1957 115p illus $4.50 (4-6)   92
1 Saints
ISBN 0-690-33260-2
First published 1910
"An informal biography charmingly describing the simple and austere life of St. Francis of Assisi and telling of his love for all created things." Right Bk for the Right Child
"Harmoniously illustrated with reproductions of the Giotto frescoes which portray the life of Saint Francis." Booklist

Franklin, Benjamin
Aulaire, Ingri d'. Benjamin Franklin [by] Ingri & Edgar Parin d'Aulaire. Doubleday 1950 48p illus $5.95, lib. bdg. $6.70 (2-4)   92
1 Statesmen, American 2 Authors, American
ISBN 0-385-07219-8; 0-385-07603-7
"There is vigour and simplicity in the telling of this story of Benjamin Franklin for young children, and wisdom in the choice of incidents from his varied and active career [from printer and inventor to author and statesman]. The full-page lithographs in colour and in sepia are effectively designed and not only portray Franklin's story but give an expansive picture of the time. The marginal drawings, which include Poor Richard's sayings add to the general attractiveness of the book as well as providing further details of the life and customs of pre-revolutionary America." Ontario Library Rev

Daugherty, James. Poor Richard; illus. with lithographs in two colors by the author. Viking 1941 158p illus lib. bdg. $6.95 (6-7)   92

Franklin, Benjamin—_Continued_

1 Statesmen, American 2 Authors, American
ISBN 0-670-56450-8

This biography "reveals Franklin's interest in people, his inventive genius, and his tireless efforts in behalf of his country. The author has been unusually successful in portraying Franklin's contributions to the American people." Library J

"James Daugherty's fine portrait of Benjamin Franklin, delightfully illustrated by the author, brings that wise and lovable great man right into our midst and gives us an insight into the 'many rooms in that luminous mind.'" Horn Bk

Freeman, Elizabeth

Felton, Harold W. Mumbet: the story of Elizabeth Freeman; illus. by Donn Albright. Dodd 1970 63p illus lib. bdg. $4.50 (4-6)   92

1 Negroes—Biography 2 Slavery in the U.S.
ISBN 0-396-06558-9

This "fictionalized biography of the first slave to achieve freedom through the courts portrays Elizabeth Freeman as a quiet woman heroically determined to force a literal interpretation of the Massachusetts constitution's provision that all men are created equal. In his introduction Felton cites some of the few sources of information about Mrs. Freeman before telling her story, which . . . makes interesting reading." Booklist

Frémont, John Charles

Syme, Ronald. John Charles Frémont; the last American explorer; illus. by Richard Cuffari. Morrow 1974 190p illus map $4.95, lib. bdg. $4.59 (5-7) 92

1 Explorers 2 The West—Discovery and exploration
ISBN 0-688-20120-2; 0-688-30120-7

The explorer and pathfinder whose expeditions into the American West made viable a route for travelers to Oregon and California is the subject of this biography

This writing "is generally clear, and nicely done black-and-white line drawings illustrate prominent persons or scenes mentioned in the text." Sch Library J

Bibliography: p189-90

Fulton, Robert

Judson, Clara Ingram. Boat builder; the story of Robert Fulton; illus. by Armstrong Sperry. Scribner 1940 121p illus lib. bdg. $5.95 (4-6)   92

1 Inventors 2 Steamboats
ISBN 0-684-13469-1

"The first half deals with the inventor's boyhood, beginning with his first day of school at the age of eight, and is more fictionized than the latter half. The story of the 'Clermont's' voyage is told in detail. Fulton's interest in submarines and torpedoes is attributed . . . to a desire 'to make weapons so powerful that war and piracy would be impossible.' . . . There is some sentimentality, but it is, on the whole, a very usable and simple biography. Excellent format." Library J

Gama, Vasco da

Syme, Ronald. Vasco da Gama; sailor toward the sunrise; illus. by William Stobbs. Morrow 1959 95p illus map lib. bdg. $4.32 (4-6)   92

1 Explorers
ISBN 0-688-31588-7

The author "gives a straightforward but compelling account of the Portuguese navigator who discovered the sea-route to India. He describes Vasco da Gama's voyage around Cape Horn, recounts his experiences in east Africa and in India, and portrays him as an honest and fearless but violent-tempered, ruthless man who brought new wealth to Portugal but also made countless enemies for his country. Forceful illustrations in black and white." Booklist

Garibaldi, Giuseppe

Syme, R. Garibaldi; the man who made a nation; illus. by William Stobbs. Morrow 1967 190p illus map $4.95 (5-7)   92

1 Statesmen, Italian 2 Italy—History—1815-1915
ISBN 0-688-21326-X

An account of Garibaldi's "military accomplishment in freeing and uniting Italy by capturing 'the imagination and enthusiasm of the masses' in the mid-nineteenth century." Horn Bk

"The life of Garibaldi is well presented in this dramatic occasionally fictionized account. . . . [Included is] a bibliography although there is no index." Sch Library J

Gautama Buddha

Serage, Nancy. The prince who gave up a throne; a story of the Buddha; illus. by Kazue Mizumura. Crowell 1966 62p illus $3.95 (4-6)   92

1 Buddha and Buddhism
ISBN 0-690-65566-5

"Historical fact and legend are interwoven in a simple retelling of the real and mystical experiences which reveal the intense religious faith and great human compassion of Prince Siddhartha who became the Buddha. Basing her interpretation on authentic sources but changing the emphasis of the story 'from a desire to escape pain to a desire to find eternal joy,' the author presents the life and precepts of the founder of Buddhism with sensitivity and understanding. Black-and-white drawings reflect the Oriental origin of the story." Booklist

Gehrig, Lou

Graham, Frank, 1893- Lou Gehrig, a quiet hero. Putnam 1942 250p illus (Putnam Sports shelf) lib. bdg. $4.97 (5-7)   92

1 Baseball—Biography
ISBN 0-399-60431-6

The story of Lou Gehrig is the story of one who not only was a great ball player but, by the very pattern of his life, became a symbol of courage and decency and kindness to millions who were not interested in baseball

"A sports columnist's tribute, this is more than a story of his career as a baseball star: it is the life story of 'a quiet hero.' . . . The closing scenes of this career, whose poignancy would be unbearable were it overplayed, are presented so quietly that all their dignity is revealed. There are many interesting photographs." N Y Her Trib Bks

Luce, Willard. Lou Gehrig: iron man of baseball, by Willard and Celia Luce; illus. by Dom Lupo. Garrard 1970 95p illus (Americans all) lib. bdg. $3.58 (3-5)   92

1 Baseball—Biography
ISBN 0-8116-4559-2

"The life and playing career of one of the game's great sentimental favorites are carefully and appealingly portrayed. . . . Its simplified but absorbing style should make it attractive to fourth and even third grade readers, and the excitement and honest emotions captured will sustain the interest of fifth and sixth graders who have problems in reading." Sch Library J

Geronimo, Apache chief

Syme, Ronald. Geronimo, the fighting Apache; illus. by Ben F. Stahl. Morrow 1975 95p illus map $4.95, lib. bdg. $4.59 (3-5)   92

1 Apache Indians—Biography
ISBN 0-688-22013-4; 0-688-32013-9
"This biography spans the Apache chieftain's life from childhood until death, emphasizing his battles against the 'White Eyes.' " Sch Library J
Bibliography: p95

Wilson, Charles Morrow. Geronimo. Dillon Press 1973 74p illus map lib. bdg. $4.95 (5-7)   92

1 Apache Indians—Biography
ISBN 0-87518-059-0
Cover title: Geronimo: the story of an American Indian
In this biography of the Apache chief "the author shows Geronimo to be a superior military strategist and defender of his people, but does not neglect the personal side of Geronimo as a husband, father, and beloved tribal member. The successful incorporation of both aspects of his personality allows a depth that happily avoids the mundane depictions so common to his genre." Booklist

Wyatt, Edgar. Geronimo, the last Apache war chief; illus. by Allan Houser. McGraw 1952 188p illus lib. bdg. $4.72 (4-6)   92

1 Apache Indians—Biography
ISBN 0-07-072154-8
"Whittlesey House publications"
"Geronimo was the last great war chief of the Apache Indians. He was born in 1829 in Arizona and lived to be 90 years old. During his lifetime he brought terror and death to many Americans and Mexicans. How he came to hate the white men, why he was hunted for years before he gave up, is [the story told here.]" Pub W
"Children will read about him because of the excitement and adventure in his story; but they cannot help getting from it also a better understanding of the Indian problem." Horn Bk
Guide to pronunciation of Indian names: p183-86.
Sources: p187-88

Giotto di Bondone

Rockwell, Anne. The boy who drew sheep; illus. with photographs. Atheneum Pubs. 1973 37p illus lib. bdg. $4.50 (3-5)   92

1 Painters, Italian
ISBN 0-689-30097-2
Combining facts and legends, the author tells what is known of the life of Giotto, the Italian painter who was the first to put a feeling of reality into his paintings
"The narrative begins with the famous legend of the little boy who scratched pictures of sheep on meadow stones while he tended his father's flock, and captured the attention of Cimabue from Florence. The book emphasizes the grown artist's skill in painting murals of scenes from the life of Saint Francis (in the church at Assisi) and the succeeding works." Horn Bk

Grieg, Edvard Hagerup

Kyle, Elisabeth. Song of the waterfall; the story of Edvard and Nina Grieg. Holt 1970 233p lib. bdg. $4.50 (5-7)   92

1 Grieg, Nina (Hagerup) 2 Composers, Norwegian
ISBN 0-03-089509-X
"A fictionalized, lively, nontechnical but informative biography of the Norwegian composer, Edvard Grieg. The author chronicles Grieg's boyhood as the lazy but gifted son of a musician and a merchant, and as the darling of Hanna, the housekeeper who introduced Edvard to traditional Norwegian tunes;

his student days in Germany; his marriage to his cousin, Nina; and his development and slow acceptance as an important Norwegian nationalist composer." Sch Library J

Hamer, Fannie Lou

Jordan, June. Fannie Lou Hamer; illus. by Albert Williams. Crowell 1972 39p illus (A Crowell biography) $4.50, lib. bdg. $5.25 (2-4)   92

1 Negroes—Biography 2 Negroes—Civil rights
ISBN 0-690-28893-X; 0-690-28894-8
Fannie Lou Hamer "had worked in the cotton fields since she was six-years-old. Her independence and impatience with racial hatred encouraged her to be among the first to sign up during voter registration drives in the summer of 1962. She lived through violence to tell her story to the American public, became active in the fight for political reform and established the Freedom Farm Cooperative, a self-help project to provide food for poor families." Elem English
"Using a starkly simple prose style, the author has achieved maximum effect with a minimum of detail. She creates for younger readers a true people's heroine in a chronicle of the triumph of one woman's confidence in herself and in her race." Horn Bk

Hammarskjöld, Dag

Richards, Norman. Dag Hammarskjöld. Childrens Press 1968 95p illus (People of destiny: a humanities ser) lib. bdg. $5.25 (6-7)   92

1 United Nations 2 Statesmen
ISBN 0-516-02629-1
A biography of the man whose tact and leadership made the United Nations, for the first time, an effective force for peace in the world
Bibliography: p92

Handy, William Christopher

Montgomery, Elizabeth Rider. William C. Handy: father of the blues; illus. by David Hodges. Garrard 1968 95p illus (Americans all) lib. bdg. $3.58 (3-4)
                                                                    92

1 Negro musicians 2 Blues (Songs, etc.)
ISBN 0-8116-4551-7
"An interesting and authentic account of the great originator of Negro blues. The biography starts with Handy as a 12-year-old boy and continues through his life realistically depicting the biases, prejudices, and problems he encountered." Adventuring With Bks. 2d edition

Henry, Patrick

Campion, Nardi Reeder. Patrick Henry, firebrand of the Revolution; illus. by Victor Mays. Little 1961 261p illus $6.95 (5-7)   92

1 Statesmen, American 2 U.S.—History—Colonial period—Biography
ISBN 0-316-12765-5
"Lawyer, soldier, legislator, five times governor of Virginia, the greatest orator of his times . . . Patrick Henry had 'a consummate knowledge of the human heart, which directed his eloquence and enabled him to gain a popularity with the people at large perhaps never equaled.' His easy friendliness, ability to enjoy life fully, and pleasure in his family, along with his deep convictions regarding the dignity and rights of man and the excitement of his power with words make Patrick Henry a hero especially congenial to young people. This is a vivid presentation of that hero, of the times, and of the great men who made possible a new country and a new government." Horn Bk
"This competent and well-documented biography presents a three-dimensional portrait of its somewhat

Henry, Patrick—*Continued*

flamboyant protagonist. Virtues are stressed, but shortcomings are acknowledged." Sat Rev

Bibliography of principal sources: p253

Henson, Matthew Alexander

Ripley, Sheldon N. Matthew Henson: Arctic hero; illus. by E. Harper Johnson. Houghton 1966 191p illus maps $4.36 (4-6)   92

1 Explorers 2 Negroes—Biography 3 North Pole

ISBN 0-395-01736-X

"Piper books"

An account of the Negro explorer who went to sea as a young boy, and later was the only American with Admiral Peary on the Arctic team that reached the North Pole in 1909

Eskimo words and names: p191

Hickok, James Butler

Holbrook, Stewart. Wild Bill Hickok tames the West; illus. by Ernest Richardson. Random House 1952 179p illus lib. bdg. $4.27 (4-6)   92

1 Frontier and pioneer life 2 The West—History

ISBN 0-394-90325-0

"Landmark books"

An account of "the man who was a member of the Underground Railroad, a Union spy during the Civil War, a stage driver and plainsman, and finally, one of the greatest single forces in the bringing of order to the lawless western frontier." Pub W

"A readable [biography]. . . . The author justifies Hickok's many slayings in terms of the lack of laws and legally appointed law enforcement offices and of the general code of the period in which Hickok lived." Chicago. Children's Bk Center

Bibliography: p179

Homer, Winslow

Hyman, Linda. Winslow Homer: America's old master. Doubleday 1973 95p illus $4.95, lib. bdg. $5.70 (5-7)   92

1 Artists, American

ISBN 0-385-03488-1; 0-385-07823-4

Illustrated with black and white and color reproductions of Winslow Homer's paintings

The author "traces Homer's life and work from his early years as an apprentice in a print shop, through the years he spent as an illustrator during the Civil War, up to the end of his life as a well-known and successful painter of the sea and other aspects of nature and wildlife." Best Sellers

"The generous sampling of pictures enables the reader to observe for himself the sensitive qualities of the artist which the author so deftly describes." Babbling Bookworm

Houdini, Harry

Kendall, Lace. Houdini: master of escape. Macrae Smith Co. 1960 187p front $6.25 (6-7)   92

1 Magic

ISBN 0-8255-5075-0

"A biography of the man who began his career as a magician at the age of nine and by hard work, self-mastery, and unswerving purpose rose to fame as the greatest escape artist of all time." Bks for Children, 1960-1965

Howe, Samuel Gridley

Meltzer, Milton. A light in the dark; the life of Samuel Gridley Howe. Crowell 1964 239p $3.95 (6-7)   92

1 Physicians 2 Physically handicapped

ISBN 0-690-49165-4

"The life of the Boston doctor who established the Perkins Institute for the Blind is vividly delineated against a background of nineteenth-century New England social conditions. This account of his pioneer work with the blind, the deaf, the feebleminded, and the delinquent makes inspiring reading." Hodges. Bks for Elem Sch Libraries

"An excellent biography, candid in tone, written in a style that is informal yet dignified, and particularly lively because Samuel Howe was involved in so many great causes, controversial issues, and new programs." Chicago. Children's Bk Center

Bibliography: p228-31

Hudson, Henry

Syme, Ronald. Henry Hudson; illus. by William Stobbs. Morrow 1955 190p illus lib. bdg. $4.59 (4-6)   92

1 Explorers 2 Discoveries (in geography) 3 America—Discovery and exploration

ISBN 0-688-31384-1

A narrative reconstruction of the four voyages of the English explorer in search of the northwest passageway to the East

"In terse, vivid style, the author draws a realistic picture of Hudson, with all his strengths and weaknesses, and brings to life an often neglected figure in American exploration. Stobbs' vigorous drawings add to the appeal of the subject." Chicago. Children's Bk Center

Map on lining-papers

Hughes, Langston

Myers, Elisabeth P. Langston Hughes: poet of his people; illus. by Russell Hoover. Garrard 1970 144p illus (Creative people in the arts and sciences ser) lib. bdg. $3.94 (4-6)   92

1 Poets, American 2 Negro authors

ISBN 0-8116-4507-X

"Poet, novelist, playwright and lyricist—Langston Hughes was all these. From his earliest childhood days as a writer, he believed he could write best from his own experience. It was this belief that led him to become, for over thirty years, one of black America's loudest and most illustrious spokesmen. Here is an uncomplicated, sympathetic yet factual account of Hughes' life that devotes equal space to his early years and career. . . . A combination of good black-and-white photos and adequate drawings enhance the text, which is also indexed." Sch Library J

Walker, Alice. Langston Hughes, American poet; illus. by Don Miller. Crowell 1974 33p illus (A Crowell biography) $3.95, lib. bdg. $4.70 (2-4)   92

1 Poets, American 2 Negro authors

ISBN 0-690-00218-1; 0-690-00219-X

In this biography of the beloved Black writer, the author traces Langston Hughes' childhood in Kansas, the discovery of his poems by Vachel Lindsay, his later fame as a writer, and his efforts to bring his work directly to the people

The author "includes a candid assessment of the poet's bitter, biased father that is not usually found in books about Hughes written for children. The illustrations are adequate, the biography as substantial as one for the primary grades reader can be." Chicago. Children's Bk Center

Hutchinson, Anne (Marbury)

Faber, Doris. A colony leader: Anne Hutchinson. Illus. by Frank Vaughn. Garrard 1970 64p illus map (Colony leaders) lib. bdg. $3.40 (4-6)   92

1 U.S.—History—Colonial period

ISBN 0-8116-4654-8

A biography of the woman who was banished from the Massachusetts Bay Colony for disagreeing with the prevailing religious practices

Ishi

Kroeber, Theodora. Ishi; last of his tribe. Drawings by Ruth Robbins. Parnassus Press 1964 209p illus maps $5.95, lib. bdg. $5.88 (5-7)   92

1 Yana Indians

ISBN 0-87466-049-1; 0-87466-018-1

"The true story of a California Yahi Indian who survives the invasion by the white man, while the rest of his tribe die off." A L A Notable Bks, 1964

Written "with a grave simplicity . . . utterly right for the subject. The cultural details are quite unobtrusive: they are simply there, an evidence of the author's knowledge and empathy." Chicago. Children's Bk Center

Glossary of Yahi words: p[211]

Jackson, Jesse

Halliburton, Warren. The picture life of Jesse Jackson; William Loren Katz, consulting editor. Watts, F. 1972 47p illus lib. bdg. $3.90 (1-3)   92

1 Negroes—Civil rights 2 Negroes—Biography

ISBN 0-531-00986-6

A biography of the Black minister who is a leader in the civil rights movement

"The effective use of pictures shows Jackson at school receiving honors, with his family, and with national dignitaries, but even more powerful are the photos which spotlight tensions, hatred, and squalor. Halliburton's clear writing style binds these pictures into a satisfactory whole." Sch Library J

Jackson, Mahalia

Cornell, Jean Gay. Mahalia Jackson: queen of gospel song; illus. by Victor Mays. Garrard 1974 96p illus (Americans all) lib. bdg. $3.58 (4-6)   92

1 Singers 2 Negro musicians

ISBN 0-8116-4581-9

The book "covers all the events in the life of Mahalia Jackson from her beginnings as a washerwoman in New Orleans through her moving to Chicago and the gradual steps in a career that ended with her death in 1972. In addition to Victor Mays's exuberant drawings, the book features photographs of Ms. Jackson, taken during her performances at home and abroad." Pub W

Jackson, Jesse. Make a joyful noise unto the Lord! The life of Mahalia Jackson, queen of gospel singers (5-7)   92

1 Singers 2 Negro musicians

Some editions are:

Crowell $5.50 (ISBN 0-690-43344-1)

Hall, G.K.&Co. $8.95 Large print book (ISBN 0-8161-6254-9)

First published 1974 by Crowell

"An often moving portrait of 'Sister Haley.' From choir girl in New Orleans to world-renowned artist, she never let European music destroy her Afro-American roots. . . . Parallel to the story of her rise to fame are the accounts of major developments in the civil rights movements of the 1950's and 1960's and her increasing support of them up to her death in 1972." Horn Bk

Bibliography included in Acknowledgments

Jackson, Thomas Jonathan

Daniels, Jonathan. Stonewall Jackson; illus. by William Moyers. Random House 1959 183p illus maps lib. bdg. $4.27 (5-7)   92

1 Generals 2 U.S.—History—Civil War—Biography

ISBN 0-394-90386-2

"Landmark books"

"The early life, teaching career, and military exploits of a great soldier are recounted by a Southern writer, with Jackson's famous Valley Campaign described in detail." Hodges. Bks for Elem Sch Libraries

"Mr. Daniels is a specialist on problems of this region, and he handles the grim theme with sincerity. Flashes of humor and a few well-chosen poems relieve the tension in the detailed account of battle maneuvers of the Southern campaign in the Shenandoah Valley." Library J

Jefferson, Thomas, President U.S.

Barrett, Marvin. Meet Thomas Jefferson; illus. by Angelo Torres. Random House 1967 86p illus map $2.50, lib. bdg. $3.77 (2-4)   92

1 Presidents—U.S. 2 U.S.—History—1783-1809—Biography

ISBN 0-394-80067-2; 0-394-90067-7

"Step-up books"

This book describes the man who was a friend to the Indians and to the British governors. He wrote the Declaration of Independence, and as third President of the United States, purchased Louisiana and doubled his country's size without any bloodshed

Jemison, Mary

Gardner, Jeanne LeMonnier. Mary Jemison: Seneca captive; illus. by Robert Parker. Harcourt 1966 128p illus map $5.50 (4-6)   92

1 Indians of North America—Captivities 2 Seneca Indians

ISBN 0-15-252190-9

This book encompasses "the years from Mary Jemison's capture by Indians in 1758 to her death in 1833. . . . The account describes Mary's gradual change in attitude from hatred and distrust of the Indians to understanding and acceptance of their culture and way of life." Booklist

This "biography focuses on the close family relationships and the culture of the Senecas. . . . Useful as background for a study of the French and Indian wars and to show how the culture of the Indians changed with the encroachment of the white man and his civilization." Sch Library J

Bibliography: p127-28

Lenski, Lois. Indian captive; the story of Mary Jemison; written and illus. by Lois Lenski. Lippincott 1941 269p illus $7.95, lib. bdg. $5.93 (5-7)   92

1 Indians of North America—Captivities 2 Seneca Indians

ISBN 0-397-30072-7; 0-397-30076-X

First published by Stokes

The story of Mary Jemison, a white child of Scotch-Irish parentage, captured by the Indians in 1758, and taken from her Pennsylvania home to a Seneca village in New York State. . . . This story is based on records and recounts for young readers her experiences in the early years of her captivity

"The ways of living followed by the Seneca Indians in the Eighteenth Century have been carefully studied as background for this book and the drawings are not only attractive, but exact and authentic." Horn Bk

Bibliography: p[273]. Map on lining-papers

Joan of Arc, Saint

Fisher, Aileen. Jeanne d'Arc; illus. by Ati Forberg. Crowell 1970 52p illus $4.50, lib. bdg. $5.25 (3-5)   92

1 Saints 2 France—History—House of Valois, 1328-1589

ISBN 0-690-45827-4; 0-690-45828-2

"Joan—the religious, patriotic, courageous and, at times, astute tomboy—materializes here, fresh, vibrant and believable, from her 15th-Century world. . . . The skillful writing combines acceptable conver-

Joan of Arc, Saint—*Continued*
sation and good narrative which includes enough
information on the era and the war to draw readers
into the ranks of the French, cheering for Joan. Sixteen full-page illustrations, many flooded with warm
colors, expand the story and strongly individualize
Joan and her countrymen." Sch Library J

Johnson, James Weldon
Egypt, Ophelia Settle. James Weldon Johnson;
illus. by Moneta Barnett. Crowell 1974 40p illus (A
Crowell biography) $3.95, lib. bdg. $4.70 (2-4)   92
1 Authors, American 2 Negroes—Biography
ISBN 0-690-00214-9; 0-690-00215-7
"This biography of James Weldon Johnson covers
his aptness in writing music and poetry, in starting the
first United States daily Negro newspaper, in public
speaking, education, law, and diplomacy during a
crucial period in Negro History." Children's Bk Rev
Serv
"The text is simply written, most of it devoted to
Johnson's childhood and the early part of his career,
but it touches on his major contributions and it avoids
the adulatory tone that would be so easy to adopt with
a subject so deserving." Chicago. Children's Bk
Center

Felton, Harold W. James Weldon Johnson; illus. by
Charles Shaw. Dodd 1971 91p illus $3.75, lib. bdg.
$4.50 (4-6)   92
1 Authors, American 2 Negroes—Biography
ISBN 0-396-06274-1; 0-396-06275-X
"James Weldon Johnson was a versatile man of
many talents: teacher, editor, a founder and secretary
of the NAACP, American consul and writer of the
Negro National Hymn, 'Lift Ev'ry Voice and Sing.'
This straightforward account of a man who 'fought for
equality for his people and for all people' will be of
particular interest to those seeking recommended
titles on black achievement in America. Words and
piano-guitar arrangement of his song are included."
Pub W

Joliet, Louis
Syme, Ronald. Marquette and Joliet. See entry
under Marquette, Jacques   92

Jones, John Paul
Sperry, Armstrong. John Paul Jones, fighting
sailor; written and illus. by Armstrong Sperry. Random House 1953 180p illus lib. bdg. $4.39 (4-6) 92
1 U.S. Navy—Biography 2 Seamen
ISBN 0-394-90339-0
"Landmark books"
This is "a zestful fictionized account of the sea
battles and exploits of the Scottish-born naval hero
who fought his best when the odds were hopelessly
against him. The book actually begins in 1773 with the
mutiny of the 'Betsy's' crew and John Paul Jones'
flight to America, and ends in 1779 with his triumph in
the battle of the 'Bon Homme Richard' with the
'Serapis.' " Booklist
"There is neither padding nor rambling narrative to
get in the way of important events, and the result is a
clear and inspiring picture of a great naval hero."
Horn Bk

Syme, Ronald. Captain John Paul Jones: America's
fighting seaman; illus. by William Stobbs. Morrow
1968 94p illus maps $5.25, lib. bdg. $4.64 (3-5) 92
1 U.S. Navy—Biography 2 Seamen
ISBN 0-688-21141-0; 0-688-31141-5
"The weaknesses as well as the strengths of the
dashing Revolutionary War naval hero are revealed in
a brief but enlightening account of his personal prob-

lems and daring sea exploits while serving with the
British navy and the newly formed Colonial American
navy. Documented with quotations from contemporary sources and containing maps and numerous
black-and-white illustrations, the book provides interesting sidelights on the period as well as a well-
balanced biography of the man." Booklist
"The book depicts Jones as a complex figure, brave,
yet conceited and ruthless." Sch Library J
Bibliography: p[95]

Joseph, Nez Percé chief
Davis, Russell. Chief Joseph; war chief of the Nez
Percé, by Russell Davis and Brent Ashabranner.
McGraw 1962 190p illus map lib. bdg. $4.72 (5-7)
92
1 Nez Percé Indians 2 Indians of North America—
Wars
ISBN 0-07-015926-2
A "biography of the Indian leader who wanted
peace but instead became the greatest fighting chief
of the Nez Perce. His slogan was 'Whenever white
man treats Indians as they treat each other, then we
shall have no more wars.' " Adventuring With Bks. 2d
edition
"It would be easy to turn so much grief into sentimentality, so much action into mere blood and thunder. With restraint, the authors avoid both pitfalls.
They vary the pace with interesting Indian lore." N Y
Times Bk Rev

Juárez, Benito Pablo, President Mexico
Syme, Ronald. Juárez: the founder of modern Mexico; illus. by Richard Cuffari. Morrow 1972 191p illus
map $4.95, lib. bdg. $4.59 (5-7)   92
1 Mexico—Presidents 2 Mexico—History
ISBN 0-688-21769-9; 0-688-31769-3
In this biography of the Mexican leader, the author
"sketches the youth of Juarez very briefly and
emphasizes his dedication to improving the lot of the
peasants. Quoting frequently from primary sources
Syme tells how Juarez began his climb to power in the
state legislature at the age of twenty-eight and
describes his accomplishments as governor of Oaxaca,
his leadership of the Liberal Party during a civil war,
his opposition to Maximilian, and his years as President of Mexico." Booklist
"The political ferment of the time and Juárez's life
are colorfully treated. Syme's interpretation is objective and accurate, and he carefully points out Juárez's
weaknesses as well as his strengths." Sch Library J
Bibliography: p191

Keller, Helen Adams
Peare, Catherine Owens. The Helen Keller story.
Crowell 1959 183p illus $4.50 (5-7)   92
1 Blind—Education 2 Deaf—Education
ISBN 0-690-37520-4
This is a "biography of Helen Keller, the child who
was deaf and blind, and therefore mute, who became,
with the loving, intelligent guidance of Anne Sullivan
Macy, a graduate of Radcliffe College, a most potent
force in coordinating the work with the blind as both
writer and lecturer and an outstanding woman of the
world." Bookmark
Selected bibliography: p176-79

Kemble, Frances Anne
Scott, John Anthony. Fanny Kemble's America;
illus. with photographs. Crowell 1973 146p illus map
(Women of America) $4.95 (5-7)   92
1 Abolitionists 2 Actors and actresses
ISBN 0-690-28911-1
This biography of the English actress who came to

Kemble, Frances Anne—*Continued*
America in 1832 highlights her interest and involvement in the anti-slavery movement
Bibliography: p138-40

Kennedy, John Fitzgerald, President U.S.
Four days: the historical record of the death of President Kennedy; comp. by United Press International and American Heritage Magazine. Am. Heritage 1964 143p illus $2.95   92
1 Presidents—U.S.—Assassination
ISBN 0-671-26870-8
A "commemorative book with a day-by-day account of the assassination and funeral of President Kennedy. Also, with 116 photographs in black and white and 15 in color." Pub W
"With an introduction by Bruce Catton. . . . Included are eulogies, the resolutions of Congress, comments from the world press, and other memorabilia of the tragedy." Sch Library J

Wood, James Playsted. The life and words of John F. Kennedy, by James Playsted Wood and the editors of Country Beautiful Magazine. Published by Country Beautiful Foundation; distributed by Doubleday 1964 80p illus $1.98 (3-7)   92
1 Presidents—U.S.
ISBN 0-385-03294-3
This "is a collection of some of the best Kennedy photographs, a generous sampling of his speeches and writings, and a narrative of his life that is straightforward and moving. . . . This book bends over backward to avoid sentimentalizing Kennedy's death; instead it brings to life his character and his ideas." N Y Times Bk Rev

King, Billie Jean
Burchard, Marshall. Sports hero: Billie Jean King, by Marshall and Sue Burchard. Putnam 1975 93p illus (The Sports hero biographies) lib. bdg. $4.69 (2-4)
                                                                  92
1 Tennis—Biography
ISBN 0-399-60907-5
"Using an easy-to-read format with large print and a liberal sprinkling of photographs (inexplicably interrupted by several stilted pencil sketches), the Burchards lightly chronicle Billie Jean King's rise from a beginning tennis player in Long Beach, California, to a high-ranking professional. Also included are King's activities toward equalizing the sport by demanding top money prizes for women contenders and advocating that the major amateur tournaments be opened to pro competitors." Booklist
Glossary: p[94-95]

King, Martin Luther
Clayton, Ed. Martin Luther King: the peaceful warrior; illus. by David Hodges. 3d ed. Prentice-Hall 1968 95p illus lib. bdg. $4.50 (5-7)   92
1 Negroes—Civil rights 2 Negroes—Biography
ISBN 0-13-559765-X
First published 1964
Biography of the Negro leader who tried to achieve equality for his race through nonviolent methods
"An amazing amount of drama and material is packed into this short, clear, moving biography." Commonweal

De Kay, James T. Meet Martin Luther King, Jr. Illus. with photographs and drawings by Ted Burwell. Random House 1969 89p illus $2.50, lib. bdg. $3.77 (2-5)   92
1 Negroes—Civil rights 2 Negroes—Biography
ISBN 0-394-80055-9; 0-394-90055-3

"Step-up books"
"The major concern of this useful biography for reluctant readers is with Dr. King's philosophy of civil disobedience and with his leadership of the civil rights movement. The writing is simple, clear and objective though pedestrian. The print is large and readable; the photographs are good and give the book a sense of immediacy." Library J

Young, Margaret B. The picture life of Martin Luther King, Jr. Illus. with photographs. Watts, F. 1968 45p illus lib. bdg. $3.90 (k-3)   92
1 Negroes—Civil rights 2 Negroes—Biography
ISBN 0-531-00981-5
"A very good selection of photographs accompanies a very simple but quite adequate outline of Martin Luther King's life, the book having been published before his assassination. The vocabulary is simple, the print large, and the writing style straightforward." Chicago. Children's Bk Center

Lafitte, Jean
Tallant, Robert. Pirate Lafitte and the Battle of New Orleans; illus. by John Chase. Random House 1951 186p illus lib. bdg. $4.39 (5-7)   92
1 Pirates 2 New Orleans, Battle of, 1815
ISBN 0-394-90319-6
"Landmark books"
A biography of the slave smuggler and privateer who, because of his aid to the Americans in the battle of New Orleans, was acclaimed a patriot
"A carefully written, exciting account of a mysterious and controversial figure. His bold undertakings are evaluated in the light of the customs of the times and places in which he lived. Emphasis is on background material and events in his career that explain why he was on the American side in the Battle of New Orleans. . . . Excellent format." Library J
Map on lining-papers

La Guardia, Fiorello Henry
Kaufman, Mervyn. Fiorello La Guardia; illus. by Gene Szafran. Crowell 1972 32p illus (A Crowell biography) lib. bdg. $4.50 (2-4)   92
1 New York (City)—Politics and government
ISBN 0-690-29817-X
"Although sedately written, this biography of La Guardia does give a warm, sympathetic picture of the lively and beloved former mayor of New York City. A fighter for the oppressed, a man of honesty and courage, La Guardia is a fascinating person, and his story is interesting also because of the picture it gives of the political scene in New York. The book gives balanced treatment to his personal life and his career, emphasizing his years in office but giving adequate attention to his childhood and youth." Sutherland. The Best in Children's Bks

La Salle, Robert Cavelier, sieur de
Syme, R. La Salle of the Mississippi; illus. by William Stobbs. Morrow 1953 184p illus lib. bdg. $4.95 (4-7)   92
1 Explorers 2 America—Discovery and exploration
ISBN 0-688-21591-2
An account of the French navigator and colonizer. It describes his first voyages, efforts to find sites for settlement and trade, the founding of Quebec, experiences with the Indians and finally his death at the hands of a treacherous follower
"Gives a picture which is authentic in its interpretation of La Salle's character, and dramatic in the telling of his accomplishments." Ontario Library Rev
Map on lining-papers

Lawrence, Thomas Edward

MacLean, Alistair. Lawrence of Arabia; illus. by Gil Walker. Random House 1962 177p illus maps lib. bdg. $4.27 (6-7)   92

1 European War, 1914-1918—Near East
ISBN 0-394-90552-0
"World Landmark books"

This book "deals almost entirely with Lawrence's exploits as leader of the Arabs in their rebellion against the Turks during World War I. . . . The book ends, not with Lawrence's death in 1935, but in 1922 when at last he had seen his Arab friends freed in part from foreign rule." Chicago Sunday Trib

"This is no attempt to write a complete biography, or even to try to give any idea of Lawrence's complex character. Rather it is a war story and a very good one, based on Lawrence's own writings and on writings about him. . . . It is a stirring story of desert warfare with fine glimpses of the young Lawrence." N Y Her Trib Bks

Other [adult] books about T. E. Lawrence: p173

Lee, Robert Edward

Commager, Henry Steele. America's Robert E. Lee [by] Henry Steele Commager & Lynd Ward. Houghton 1951 111p illus $4.25, lib. bdg. $3.73 (5-7)   92

1 Generals 2 U.S.—History—Civil War—Biography
ISBN 0-395-06707-3; 0-395-06708-1

An account of the great Confederate general's life and military career from his childhood to the surrender at Appomattox

"The progress of the war is described vividly and impartially. There could be no more moving account of a surrender than the one on the closing pages taken from a Union officer's diary." Chicago Sunday Trib

"The illustrations, in color and black and white, half page, full page, and double page, are superb. Mr. Ward has caught the spirit as well as the substance of events and of the people." Sat Rev

Leif Ericsson

Aulaire, Ingri d'. Leif the Lucky, by Ingri & Edgar Parin d'Aulaire. Doubleday [1965 c1941] 61p illus $4.50, lib. bdg. $5.25 (2-4)   92

1 Explorers 2 Northmen 3 America—Discovery and exploration
ISBN 0-385-07366-6; 0-385-07628-2

A reissue of the book first published 1941

The story of Leif the Lucky, as a boy and as a man, and the Viking discoveries in Greenland and America, are told here for young readers

The lithograph "illustrations have the wealth of detail which appeals to younger boys and girls and yet there is a sweep of colour which is dramatic in the extreme. The incidents in his life which are related here are selected with discrimination; the narrative is direct and simple. Combined with [the] pictures it conveys a sense of the impulse behind these early voyages, a vivid impression of the countries visited and of the vigour and hardihood of the men themselves." Ontario Library Rev

Grant, Matthew G. Leif Ericson; explorer of Vinland; illus. by Dick Brude. [Creative Educ. Soc. distributed by Childrens Press] 1974 29p illus map (Gallery of great Americans ser. Explorers of America) lib. bdg. $4.95 (1-3)   92

1 Explorers 2 America—Discovery and exploration
ISBN 0-87191-278-3

This life story of the Norse explorer describes his journeys and discoveries

"The large type, picture-book format is attractive; the illustrations are pleasant although undistinguished; and a simple map charting the route of four Viking explorers is helpful." Sch Library J

Janeway, Elizabeth. The Vikings; illus. by Henry C. Pitz. Random House 1951 175p illus lib. bdg. $4.27 (4-6)   92

1 Explorers 2 Eric the Red 3 Northmen 4 America—Discovery and exploration
ISBN 0-394-90312-9
"Landmark books"

The story of Eric the Red and his son Leif the Lucky in Iceland, Greenland and Vinland

For this readable history, the author has partially "chosen the medium of fiction to tell her story, but in the interest of historical accuracy she has explained, in her foreword, which parts of her story are fact and which are fiction." N Y Times Bk Rev

Liliuokalani, Queen of the Hawaiian Islands

Wilson, Hazel. Last queen of Hawaii: Liliuokalani; illus. by W. T. Mars. Knopf 1963 176p illus lib. bdg. $4.99 (4-6)   92

1 Hawaii—Kings and rulers 2 Queens
ISBN 0-394-91315-9

The move from monarchy to territorial status of "the Hawaiian Islands is the background for Liliuokalani's life story. Includes a pronouncing glossary of Hawaiian words." Hodges. Bks for Elem Sch Library

Lincoln, Abraham, President U.S.

Aulaire, Ingri d'. Abraham Lincoln, by Ingri & Edgar Parin d'Aulaire. Doubleday 1957 unp illus $5.95, lib. bdg. $6.70 (2-4)   92

1 Presidents—U.S.
ISBN 0-385-07669-X; 0-385-07674-6
Awarded the Caldecott Medal, 1940
First published 1939

"The story devotes itself more to pioneer phases than to darker scenes of Lincoln's later life, and it closes before he has started for Ford's Theater." N Y Her Trib Bks

Presented "in a brief, direct, semiwhimsical text and in notable lithographic drawings by the authors, some of which have soft rich color, others being reproduced in black and white. The illustrations, detailed and faithful to the atmosphere of the various settings are both tender and humorous in their interpretation. . . . A distinguished piece of bookmaking." Bookmark
Map on lining-papers

Foster, Genevieve. Abraham Lincoln. Scribner 1950 111p illus maps (An Initial biography) lib. bdg. $5.95 (3-6)   92

1 Presidents—U.S. 2 U.S.—History—Civil War—Biography
ISBN 0-684-13159-5

A biography which covers the outstanding periods and events in Lincoln's life

"Dramatically and simply told, historically accurate and illustrated [by the author] with double spreads and simple page pictures in green and brown." Wis Library Bul

"Here again is the prose style that makes easy reading for younger children, and the sense of humanity which reaches and satisfies older readers. Many a biography three times as long reveals less truth and understanding of Lincoln." N Y Times Bk Rev

Lincoln, Abraham, President U.S.—*Continued*

McGovern, Ann. If you grew up with Abraham Lincoln; pictures by Brinton Turkle. Four Winds 1966 79p illus lib. bdg. $3.89 (2-4)   92

1 Presidents—U.S. 2 Middle West—Social life and customs

ISBN 0-590-07017-7

The author gives "facts about how Abe Lincoln (and other boys) dressed, what his chores were, what his frontier cabin was like. The text moves from the Kentucky frontier to New Salem, then to Springfield; thus the author has an . . . opportunity to describe country life, the small town, and the larger town." Sutherland. The Best in Children's Bks

"Humor is evident in the illustrations. A picture-appendix shows important changes during Lincoln's lifetime." Adventuring With Bks. 2d edition

McNeer, May. America's Abraham Lincoln; illus. by Lynd Ward. Houghton 1957 119p illus $4, lib. bdg. $3.57 (5-7)   92

1 Presidents—U.S. 2 U.S.—History—Civil War—Biography

ISBN 0-395-06916-5; 0-395-06917-3

"This is not merely a recounting of the events of his life but a really perceptive picture of the man himself. . . . One can trace his development from the boy who, in spite of his love of fun, is already a serious thinker to the man whose strength and determination are softened by compassion, particularly as he visits the soldiers on the battlefield or in the hospitals." Horn Bk

"This biography is outstanding for its simple, yet dignified, language and, though comparatively short, the background and important events of Lincoln's life are made very real. Beautiful illustrations in color and black and white by Lynd Ward are perfectly suited to the story and in themselves tell a memorable tale." Library J

Phelan, Mary Kay. Mr Lincoln's inaugural journey; drawings by Richard Cuffari. Crowell 1972 211p illus map $4.50 (5-7)   92

1 Presidents—U.S. 2 U.S.—History—Civil War—Biography

ISBN 0-690-54562-6

"A detailed, carefully documented account of Abraham Lincoln's departure from Springfield and his journey to Washington to take the oath of office as President. The trip, a rambling tour through seven states, is given immediacy by the use of present tense and is given suspense by the foreknowledge of an assassination plot uncovered by the Pinkerton agency and kept secret even from Lincoln until he was close to the Baltimore engagement during which the plotters hoped to kill him." Chicago. Children's Bk Center

"Based on firsthand sources the story includes no imagined conversations and is skillfully written and suspenseful." Booklist

Bibliography: p199-203

Lombardi, Vincent Thomas

Schoor, Gene. Football's greatest coach: Vince Lombardi. Doubleday 1974 204p illus $4.95, lib. bdg. $5.70 (6-7)   92

1 Football coaching

ISBN 0-385-08513-1; 0-385-07335-6

The author "traces Lombardi's early days on Brooklyn's sand lots, at Fordham where he was scholar and athlete, coaching at a high-school, being an assistant at West Point, with the New York Giants, and championship years as head coach at Green Bay." Sch Library J

"With a competent, fast-paced writing style, Schoor relates Lombardi's experience and character to his greatness as a coach. The considerable amount of dialog is unforced, and game action, which also takes up a fair share of the book, is well focused. Illustrated with black-and-white photographs." Booklist

Love, Nat

Felton, Harold W. Nat Love, Negro cowboy; illus. by David Hodges. Dodd 1969 93p illus $3.95, lib. bdg. $4.50 (4-6)   92

1 Cowboys 2 The West—History 3 Negroes—Biography

ISBN 0-396-05899-X; 0-396-05900-7

This book relates the adventures of Nat Love, a Negro hero of the Wild West who became a cowboy at fifteen and was known as Deadwood Dick, a cowboy who could shoot a running buffalo at 200 yards

The author has written "a book that is not a full biography but that gives a vivid picture of the Old West. . . . Nat Love wrote an autobiography on which these anecdotes are based. The stories are full of action, written in a brisk style that is rather heavily sprinkled with dialogue." Chicago. Children's Bk Center

Low, Juliette Gordon

Radford, Ruby L. Juliette Low: Girl Scout founder; illus. by Vic Dowd. Garrard 1965 80p illus lib. bdg. $3.68 (3-5)   92

1 Girl Scouts of the United States of America

ISBN 0-8116-6751-0

This book traces the life of Juliette "Daisy" Gordon Low, the founder of the Girl Scouts. Her dedication to the ideals and promise of the scouting movement in America is highlighted as is her active support of scouting and guiding as a worldwide service organization

MacArthur, Douglas

Archer, Jules. Front-line general, Douglas MacArthur. Messner 1963 191p $3.50, lib. bdg. $4.79 (5-7)   92

1 Generals 2 U.S.—History, Military

ISBN 0-671-69425-1; 0-671-32602-3

The story of a man whose "career spanned half a century of patriotic service at home and abroad on the decisive battlefields of three wars and in the days of peace. Douglas MacArthur, an outstanding West Point man, made soldiering his career and rose from second lieutenant to five star general." p 1

"Although [the author] writes enthusiastically of MacArthur's courage, intelligence, dedication and military genius, he also discusses his passion for showmanship, aloofness and vanity. The result is a superior juvenile biography, better than most available 'adult' studies of the General." N Y Times Bk Rev

Bibliography: p184-85

Mackenzie, Sir Alexander

Syme, Ronald. Alexander Mackenzie, Canadian explorer; illus. by William Stobbs. Morrow 1964 96p illus map $5.25, lib. bdg. $4.64 (3-5)   92

1 Explorers 2 Discoveries (in geography) 3 Canada—Exploring expeditions

ISBN 0-688-21010-4; 0-688-31010-9

An "account of the voyages of discovery of the young Scotsman who was sent to take charge of the Northwest Fur Company at Fort Chipewyan in 1788. The hardships, disappointments, and reverses of his struggle to reach the Pacific along the Mackenzie and Peace Rivers through the rugged mountains and forests of western Canada are [described]. . . . Excerpts from Mackenzie's journals add interest and authenticity. His stubborn, canny Scottish character comes through the text, and William Stobbs' vigorous illustrations give some idea of the forbidding terrain." Sch Library J

Macy, Anne (Sullivan)

Brown, Marion Marsh. The silent storm [by] Marion Marsh Brown [and] Ruth Crone; illus. by Fritz Kredel. Abingdon 1963 250p illus $4.95 (5-7)   92

1 Teachers 2 Blind—Education 3 Deaf—Education 4 Keller, Helen Adams

ISBN 0-687-38453-2

This biography of Annie Sullivan reveals that "the famous teacher of Helen Keller had a grim childhood scarred with anger, fear, and partial blindness. This book flashes back to those early years as Annie travels to the Keller's household and then tells of the valiant efforts that led to a Radcliffe degree for Helen and marriage for Annie." Pub W

"The characters of both Annie Sullivan and Helen Keller are vividly life-like and the [somewhat fictionalized] dialogue has a wonderful naturalness about it." Best Sellers

Malone, Mary. Annie Sullivan; illus. by Lydia Rosier. Putnam 1971 61p illus (A See and read Beginning to read biography) lib. bdg. $3.96 (2-4)   92

1 Teachers 2 Blind—Education 3 Deaf—Education 4 Keller, Helen Adams

ISBN 0-399-60031-0

The story "begins when ten-year-old Annie Sullivan arrives with her little brother at the Massachusetts state poor house. The last two-thirds of the book treat her association with Helen Keller, but still it is Annie's—not Helen's—story." Elementary English

Illustrated by "simple sepia and turquoise line drawings in cross-hatch style that convey the appearance of blind eyes without making them look grotesque. . . . It is forthright, honest and factual." Sch Library J

Key words: p[62]

Magellan, Ferdinand

Israel, Charles E. Five ships west; the story of Magellan; illus. with prints and maps. Macmillan (N Y) 1966 154p illus maps $5.95 (4-6)   92

1 Explorers 2 Voyages around the world 3 Discoveries (in geography)

"Following a brief resume of Magellan's early life the author focuses on events relating to Magellan's proposed voyage to the Molucca Islands which led to the first circumnavigation of the globe. His graphic detailed narrative of the varied problems Magellan had to overcome in securing financial support, in equipping and manning his ships, and during his voyage gives a realistic picture of the man and his times. Illustrated with contemporary prints and maps." Booklist

Syme, Ronald. Magellan, first around the world; illus. by William Stobbs. Morrow 1953 71p illus maps lib. bdg. $4.32 (4-6)   92

1 Explorers 2 Voyages around the world 3 Discoveries (in geography)

ISBN 0-688-31594-1

An "account of Magellan's voyages and discoveries from the time back in 1504 when he set out as an ordinary seaman with Vasco da Gama's fleet." Christian Sci Monitor

"Striking storytelling illustrations, including six doublespreads, are an important part of the book's portrayal of history." Horn Bk

Malcolm X

Adoff, Arnold. Malcolm X; illus. by John Wilson. Crowell 1970 41p illus (Crowell biographies) $4.50, lib. bdg. $5.25, pa $1.25 (2-5)   92

1 Negroes—Biography

ISBN 0-690-51413-1; 0-690-51414-X; 0-690-51415-8

"This short forthright biography vividly outlines the events, both tragic and rewarding, which influenced the life and thought of Malcolm X from childhood to death and clearly evinces his significance as a black leader. The account describes the adverse effects of Malcolm's bitter childhood experiences, the changes which began during his incarceration in the Norfolk Prison Colony, his association with the Black Muslims and his later break with them, and the hostility of both black and white groups toward his Organization of Afro-American Unity." Booklist

"Deceptively simple text and illustrations help to produce the picture of a vigorous character, without sensationalism." Top of the News

Marquette, Jacques

Kjelgaard, Jim. Explorations of Père Marquette; illus. by Stephen J. Voorhies. Random House 1951 181p illus maps lib. bdg. $4.27 (4-6)   92

1 Joliet, Louis 2 Mississippi River 3 Explorers 4 America—Discovery and exploration

ISBN 0-394-90317-X

"Landmark books"

A simply told account of the Jesuit priest and Louis Joliet, who opened the Great Lakes and Mississippi regions. The information is based on Père Marquette's journals

"In addition to being a good story of a real hero, this addition to the 'Landmark' series will be useful for supplementary reading on exploration." Library J

Syme, Ronald. Marquette and Joliet; voyagers on the Mississippi; illus. by William Stobbs. Morrow 1974 95p illus map $4.50, lib. bdg. $4.14 (3-5)   92

1 Joliet, Louis 2 Mississippi River 3 Explorers 4 America—Discovery and exploration

ISBN 0-688-20105-9; 0-688-30105-3

This dual biography of the French Jesuit, Jacques Marquette, and the Quebec-born fur trader, Louis Joliet, tells of the explorers' historic 2500 mile canoe voyage which resulted in the first charting of the Mississippi River

"Clear and useful as introductory reading for elementary history assignments." Booklist

Bibliography: p[96]

Marshall, Thurgood

Fenderson, Lewis H. Thurgood Marshall: fighter for justice; illus. by Dave Hodges. McGraw 1969 127p illus (Black legacy bks) lib. bdg. $4.72 (4-6)   92

1 Judges 2 Negroes—Biography

ISBN 0-07-020410-1

"A Rutledge book"

"This is a gripping account of the determination of this grandson of slaves to make the Thirteenth, Fourteenth and Fifteenth Amendments meaningful. It is the true story of the life of a once-struggling Baltimore lawyer with road signs showing how his zest for equality led him to the highest judicial bench in the land . . . and at the same time pried open doors of opportunity for black Americans in many fields—doors closed for generations." Foreword

"An inspiring biography which should be of special interest to those seeking Black History material at the upper-elementary level. . . . Early chapters establish the importance of judging people on individual merits, and pressing for social reform through litigation. The description of Justice Marshall's preparation for a brief connected with a suit against a law school gives an excellent review of court action regarding civil rights." Keating. Building Bridges of Understanding Between Cultures

Martin de Porres, Saint

Bishop, Claire Huchet. Martin de Porres, hero; illus. by Jean Charlot. Houghton 1954 120p illus $4.25, pa 95¢ (5-7)   92

1 Saints 2 Negroes—Biography
ISBN 0-395-06634-4; 0-395-17704-9

"Martin de Porres, a Negro-Spanish child born in poverty and subject to prejudice and mistreatment, devoted his life to work with the underprivileged in sixteenth-century Peru. An inspiring story of dedication and self-sacrifice." Hodges. Bks for Elem Sch Libraries

Mayo, Charles Horace

Goodsell, Jane. The Mayo brothers; illus. by Louis S. Glanzman. Crowell 1972 41p illus (A Crowell biography) $4.50, lib. bdg. $5.25, pa $1.25 (2-4)   92

1 Mayo, William James 2 Physicians
ISBN 0-690-52750-0; 0-690-52751-9; 0-690-00639-X

In boyhood, both William and Charles Mayo helped their doctor-father in his office and often went with him when he visited his sick patients. When they became old enough each in turn went to medical school. This biography tells the story of their lives and careers bound up with the development of the now world-famous Mayo Clinic from a small hospital opened by their father in Rochester, Minnesota, in 1889

"This is an interesting biography of the Mayo brothers and their achievement in the world of medicine, written in an easy style—interesting to the young child, as it points out facts which he can readily understand and relate to, and in no way appears to be teaching him. At the same time there is a great deal of information imparted." Appraisal

Mays, Willie Howard

Einstein, Charles. Willie Mays: coast to coast Giant. Putnam 1963 191p illus lib. bdg. $4.97 (5-7)   92

1 Baseball—Biography 2 Negro athletes
ISBN 0-399-60673-4

"A fast-paced story of Willie Mays's baseball career." Hodges. Bks for Elem Sch Libraries

Schoor, Gene. Willie Mays, modest champion. Putnam 1960 187p lib. bdg. $4.97 (4-6)   92

1 Baseball—Biography 2 Negro athletes
ISBN 0-399-60674-2

A biography of the Giant outfielder who made baseball history at an early age by his batting, speed and agility and became one of the most popular figures in the sport because of his good-natured modesty and eagerness to help his team mates

The book "will intrigue the aficionado who is a little less concerned with background and motivation and likes his biography straight." N Y Her Trib Bks

Sullivan, George. Willie Mays; illus. by David Brown. Putnam 1973 64p illus (A See and read Beginning to read biography) lib. bdg. $3.96 (1-3)   92

1 Baseball—Biography 2 Negro athletes
ISBN 0-399-60824-9

Childhood anecdotes and career highlights round out this presentation of the life story of baseball star Willie Mays

Meir, Golda

Dobrin, Arnold. A life for Israel; the story of Golda Meir; illus. with photographs. Dial Press 1974 98p illus $4.95, lib. bdg. $4.58 (4-6)   92

1 Israel—History
ISBN 0-8037-4816-7; 0-8037-4817-5

"Golda's life makes a story inherently inspiring and fast-paced; this brief, forthright report, together with early and recent black-and-white photographs, lets her light shine through without neglecting some of the shadows over her personal life as work took precedence over family. There is some tendency to misrepresent the Middle Eastern conflict in giving Golda her due, and the bias is of course purely Zionist." Booklist

Miller, Bertha E. (Mahony)

Ross, Eulalie Steinmetz. The spirited life: Bertha Mahony Miller and children's books. Selected bibliography, comp. by Virginia Haviland. Horn Bk. 1973 274p illus $12   92

1 Children's literature—History and criticism
ISBN 0-87675-057-9

This is "a stately, detailed, and sometimes nostalgic trip into early crusading for children's literature. Bertha Mahony Miller's intense creative energy, her feminine independence and her optimistic sense of wonder are highlighted throughout the account of her childhood, her founding of the successful Bookshop for Boys and Girls in Boston, the launching and long, fruitful editorship of 'The Horn Book,' and her contribution to publications on children's literature. Her close association with such pioneers in the field as Alice Jordan and Anne Carroll Moore and her enormous correspondence, including exchanges with Beatrix Potter, will bring contemporary professionals in touch with earlier developments. [The] comprehensive bibliography points to directions for further pursuit of the subject." Booklist

Morgan, Sir Henry

Syme, Ronald. Sir Henry Morgan: buccaneer; illus. by William Stobbs. Morrow 1965 96p illus map lib. bdg. $4.59 (4-6)   92

1 Pirates
ISBN 0-688-31599-2

This is a "fictionalized biography of the colorful, sixteenth century buccaneer, not a full biography but a description of Morgan's career as an adult. As a young man who had come to Barbados from Wales, Henry Morgan was one of the volunteers who . . . wrested Jamaica from Spain. Some of the buccaneer's subsequent ploys and adventures were on behalf of England and some were simply piratical maraudings on behalf of Morgan. . . . A brief bibliography of sources is appended." Chicago. Children's Bk Center

"The controversial, swaggering, fierce-looking pirate-patriot is well depicted in the drawings, which also include broader scenes of action. Set in large print with wide leading for comfortable reading, the book has the full color of undiluted narrative with all the good words necessary." Horn Bk

Mozart, Johann Chrysostom Wolfgang Amadeus

Wheeler, Opal. Mozart, the wonder boy [by] Opal Wheeler & Sybil Deucher; illus. by Mary Greenwalt. Dutton [1968 c1941] 127p illus maps music $4.50 (4-6)   92

1 Composers, Austrian
ISBN 0-525-35304-6

First published 1934. This book is a reprint of the 1941 edition, with title: New enlarged edition of Mozart, the wonder boy

The book covers Mozart's childhood, musical development, and personality

"It is a delightful little book for children, especially those who are musically inclined and should increase their love for music." Springf'd Republican

Includes a supplement of 35 pages of Mozart's music

Muir, John

Dines, Glen. John Muir; written and illus. by Glen Dines. Putnam 1974 64p illus (A See and read biography) lib. bdg. $3.96 (2-4)   92

1 Naturalists

ISBN 0-399-60880-X

"Emigrating from Scotland to America as a young boy, John Muir became interested in the country's natural history and later travelled on foot to California. There, impressed with the untouched beauty of the Yosemite Valley, he formulated his philosophy of life in harmony with nature. Through great determination and perseverance he was able to ensure the area's preservation. Dines' beginning-to-read version of·Muir's life, enhanced by illustrations in gray and green wash, is a good introduction to this hero of conservation for very young children." Sch Library J

Graves, Charles P. John Muir; illus. by Robert Levering. Crowell 1973 33p illus (A Crowell biography) $4.50, lib. bdg. $5.25 (2-4)   92

1 Naturalists

ISBN 0-690-46412-6; 0-690-46413-4

The author's "simple narrative relates the major events of Muir's life from his boyhood in Scotland through his last losing battle to save the Hetch Hetchy Valley from destruction and his subsequent death in 1914. Some of the dramatic moments first told by Muir in his books are recalled, such as his exploration of the treacherous Alaskan glaciers with the dog Stickeen. The text is accompanied by colorful illustrations which convey both the ruggedness of the man and the country which he explored and fought to preserve." Because of Muir's insistence that 'everything is hitched to everything else' and his life of action in support of this belief, young children will find this biography both exciting and informative." Appraisal

Silverberg, Robert. John Muir; prophet among the glaciers. Putnam 1972 255p front (Lives to remember) lib. bdg. $4.97 (6-7)   92

1 Naturalists

ISBN 0-399-60714-5

This is a biography of writer and naturalist John Muir. Born in Scotland and brought to America at eleven, Muir spent much of his life exploring wilderness areas and studying wildlife, climate and geology

Muir "is here portrayed vividly as a heroic figure who was, nevertheless, a misfit in his own time. . . . This book provides a good introduction to the turn-of-the-century conservation movement, a movement which greatly strengthened the national park system and led to the creation of the Sierra Club." Sci Bks

Bibliography: p250-51

Nightingale, Florence

Harmelink, Barbara. Florence Nightingale; founder of modern nursing. Watts, F. 1969 116p illus map (Immortals of history) lib. bdg. $4.90 (5-7)   92

1 Nurses and nursing

ISBN 0-531-00911-4

This is the biography of Florence Nightingale who defied the wishes of her wealthy family and devoted her life to bettering the nursing profession

Some writings of Florence Nightingale: p111-12. Suggestions for further reading: p113

Ortiz, Juan

Steele, William O. The wilderness tattoo; a narrative of Juan Ortiz; illus. with old prints. Harcourt 1972 184p illus map lib. bdg. $5.95 (5-7)   92

1 Indians of North America—Captivities 2 Soto, Hernando de

ISBN 0-15-297325-7

When Pánfilo de Narváez sailed from Spain in 1527 to explore Florida, seventeen-year-old Juan Ortiz was a member of his expedition. One year later, he was captured by Indians on the shores of Tampa Bay. This is an account of his life with the Indians and of his later participation in Hernando de Soto's expedition through what became the southeastern United States

"A well-written and researched narrative biography interlaced with 'interludes' giving historical background and enhanced by an eight-page section of appropriate prints and woodcuts." Booklist

Selected bibliography: p183-84

Osceola, Seminole Chief

Alderman, Clifford Lindsey. Osceola and the Seminole wars. Messner 1973 189p $5.25, lib. bdg. $4.79 (5-7)   92

1 Seminole Indians—Biography 2 Seminole War, 2d, 1835-1842

ISBN 0-671-32625-2; 0-671-32626-0

"The transfer of Florida from Spain to the U.S. began a concentrated effort to move the Seminoles from their home. During the 1820s and 1830s strong Seminole resistance resulted from the brilliant leadership of the Indians' war chief Osceola as well as from their superior knowledge of the swamps. This skillful history tells not only of an exceptional individual but also of his people and the defense of their land." Booklist

"Both the white man's and the Indian's sides are objectively set forth. . . . The account is factual, interesting, and well written. An outstanding bibliography, a reading list with critical annotations, and an index are included." Sch Library J

McNeer, May. War chief of the Seminoles; illus. by Lynd Ward. Random House 1954 180p illus map lib. bdg. $4.27 (4-6)   92

1 Seminole Indians—Biography 2 Seminole War, 2d, 1835-1842

ISBN 0-394-90350-1

"Landmark books"

During the second Seminole War the war whoop of Osceola, chief of the Seminoles, was often heard in the swamps of Florida. Osceola led his people in their fight against the settlers who wanted the Indians' land. Skirmishes at last burst into war. In spite of Osceola's skillful leadership he was finally captured by the U.S. Army and later died in prison

The author, "a descendant of Dr. Weedon, who attended the Indian warrior in prison, writes with sympathy but without sentimentality of Osceola's tragic resistance to the greed and treachery of the white men." N Y Times Bk Rev

Owens, Jesse

The Jesse Owens story, by Jesse Owens with Paul G. Neimark. Putnam 1970 109p (Putnam Sports shelf) lib. bdg. $4.97 (5-7)   92

1 Track athletics—Biography 2 Negro athletes

ISBN 0-399-60315-8

A "first-person account of Owens' life, from a sharecropper farm in Alabama and the slums of Cleveland to a position as Ambassador of Sport for President Eisenhower. Between these times he became one of the greatest sprinters ever to compete in national and Olympic events. He relates with honest pride and sincerity his winning of four gold medals under the furious gaze of Hitler in the 1936 Olympics in Berlin. Especially moving is the account of the friendship he established at those games with the German broad-

Owens, Jesse—*Continued*
jump champion, Luz Long. The narration is fast-paced, sincere, sometimes emotionally charged, but never melodramatic." Sch Library J

Kaufman, Mervyn. Jesse Owens; illus. by Larry Johnson. Crowell 1973 33p illus (A Crowell biography) $4.50, lib. bdg. $5.25 (2-4)   92
1 Track athletics—Biography 2 Negro athletes
ISBN 0-690-45934-3; 0-690-45935-1
This is a biography of Jesse Owens, the Black athlete who won four gold medals in the 1936 Olympic Games in Germany and has struggled since then to promote brotherhood and equality for all people
"Written in direct and simple style, [this book] gives good coverage of [Owens'] career and an adequate balance of personal information." Chicago. Children's Bk Center

Paige, Leroy
Rubin, Robert. Satchel Paige; all-time baseball great. Putnam 1974 157p (Putnam Sports shelf) lib. bdg. $4.97 (5-7)   92
1 Baseball—Biography 2 Negro athletes
ISBN 0-399-60876-1
This is a biography of the man considered by many to be one of the greatest pitchers in baseball history. Barred from the major leagues by racial barriers for much of his career, Paige dominated Black baseball for nearly three decades. At 42 he became the oldest rookie in the major leagues, where he continued his career for another 8 years
This "frank portrayal of Satchel Paige's career and personal life is bound to be of great interest to young readers." Sch Library J

Parks, Gordon
Harnan, Terry. Gordon Parks: Black photographer and film maker; illus. by Russell Hoover. Garrard 1972 96p illus (Americans all) lib. bdg. $3.58 (3-6)   92
1 Photographers 2 Negroes—Biography
ISBN 0-8116-4572-X
This is "a biography that begins in Parks' fifteenth year, with the death of his mother and his subsequent move to St. Paul to live with a married sister. His brother-in-law threw the young man out, and from there on Gordon Parks made it on his own, working as a waiter and in the C.C.C. before he became interested in photography. The book has only a little information (but enough) about Parks' personal life, and it is candid about the prejudice he encountered." Chicago. Children's Bk Center

Parks, Rosa Lee
Greenfield, Eloise. Rosa Parks; illus. by Eric Marlow. Crowell 1973 32p illus (A Crowell biography) $4.50, lib. bdg. $5.25 (2-4)   92
1 Negroes—Civil rights 2 Negroes—Biography 3 Discrimination in public accommodations
ISBN 0-690-71210-3; 0-690-71211-1
"Effective balance between dialogue and narrative relates facts about Rosa Parks' life and about segregated southern society. The engaging text, illustrated with expressive line drawings, builds quickly to the climax—the Montgomery, Alabama bus boycott precipitated by the arrest and jailing of Rosa Parks who refused to give up her bus seat to a white rider. This is a valuable addition for elementary school and public libraries needing supplementary material on the Civil Rights Movement." Sch Library J

Penn, William
Aliki. Story of William Penn; written and illus. by Aliki. Prentice-Hall 1964 unp illus lib. bdg. $5.95 (k-2)   92
1 Friends, Society of 2 Pennsylvania—History
ISBN 0-13-850446-6
"This picture-story of Penn's adult life, emphasizing his belief in brotherly love, introduces Penn to young children." Hodges. Bks for Elem Sch Libraries
"Aliki's charming illustrations are done in soft, warm colors and have a pleasant and appropriate hint of the American primitive style in the way they are done." Pub W

Pizarro, Francisco, marqués
Syme, Ronald. Francisco Pizarro, finder of Peru; illus. by William Stobbs. Morrow 1963 96p illus lib. bdg. $4.64 (4-6)   92
1 Explorers 2 America—Discovery and exploration
ISBN 0-688-31313-2
The story of how Francisco Pizarro, along with Diego de Almagro and their small band of threadbare companions, overcame stormy seas, battled Indians, tropical jungles, starvation and disease before reaching Peru, the legendary Land of Gold
The author "contrasts the penniless but doughty adventurer who in the early 1500's risked his life again and again . . . with the successful explorer made cruel and greedy by his enormous wealth. . . . It is good to be reminded that explorers were not always as virtuous as schoolbooks indicate." N Y Times Bk Rev

Pocahontas
Aulaire, Ingri d'. Pocahontas, by Ingri & Edgar Parin d'Aulaire. Doubleday 1946 unp illus $4.95, lib. bdg. $5.70 (2-4)   92
1 Indians of North America—Biography
ISBN 0-385-07454-9; 0-385-07650-9
With "simplicity and dignity, the . . . authors have told the story of Pocahontas and Captain John Smith, bringing in the romantic and courageous elements as well as authentic historical fact. The lithographs are colourful, primitive in design and picture the story of Pocahontas from her childhood to her reception as a princess in England." Ontario Library Rev

Bulla, Clyde Robert. Pocahontas and the strangers; illus. by Peter Burchard. Crowell 1971 180p illus $4.50, lib. bdg. $5.25 (3-5)   92
1 Indians of North America—Biography
ISBN 0-690-62904-4
"The familiar story of the Indian princess who married John Rolfe is told very simply here, with more detail than is usually provided for middle grades readers; for example, the incident in which Pocahontas saves John Smith's life is given background and added credibility by the descriptions of her secret watching of the white men and by her discussions with an older woman about Indian law that permitted the claiming of a prisoner. The story gets off to a slow start with an episode perhaps intended as symbolic, in which Pocahontas sets free an eagle that has been caught in a snare, but it moves briskly enough thereafter and gives a balanced and objective picture of the motivations and actions of the Indians and the white men." Sutherland. The Best in Children's Bks

Polo, Marco
Buehr, Walter. The world of Marco Polo; written and illus. by Walter Buehr. Putnam 1961 91p illus map lib. bdg. $4.79 (4-6)   92
1 Voyages and travels 2 Explorers
ISBN 0-399-60687-4

Polo, Marco—*Continued*

"A concise, factual description of the travels of Marco Polo, his father Nicolo, and his uncle Maffeo. Sufficiently detailed to re-create vividly the thirteenth-century world in which they traveled, the strange sights they saw, the people they encountered, and the adventures experienced. Of particular interest is the view of life in the country and court of Kublai Khan. Illustrated with colored drawings." Booklist

Marco Polo's adventures in China, by the editors of Horizon Magazine. Author: Milton Rugoff; consultant: L. Carrington Goodrich. . . . Am. Heritage [distributed by Harper] 1964 153p illus maps $5.95, lib. bdg. $6.89 (5-7)   92
   1 China—Social life and customs 2 Voyages and travels 3 Explorers
   ISBN 0-06-024959-5; 0-06-024960-9
"A Horizon Caravel book"
"Illustrated with paintings, maps, and illuminations, many of the period." Title page
The author describes Marco Polo's four-year overland journey to China and the seventeen years he spent in the service of Kublai Khan
"A competently written account . . . the restrained prose sets off admirably the exotic and romantic facts. The book gives very good background material about the known world of the thirteenth century. Illustrations in this volume are reproductions of Oriental and Occidental scenes, or artifacts, or maps not necessarily associated with Marco Polo but typical of the period, or of places; there are many examples of Venetian art, for example." Chicago. Children's Bk Center
   Further reference: p151

Potter, Beatrix

Aldis, Dorothy. Nothing is impossible; the story of Beatrix Potter; drawings by Richard Cuffari. Atheneum Pubs. 1969 156p illus lib. bdg. $5.50 (4-6)   92
   1 Authors, English
   ISBN 0-689-20618-6
"Adhering to fact with regard to characters and incidents but using imagined conversations, Aldis . . . re-creates Beatrix Potter's life focusing on her lonely but not unhappy Victorian childhood and young womanhood and showing how her genius developed." Booklist
"The narrative makes use of extracts from Beatrix Potter's letters and journal. . . . The simple style makes available to the middle reader the events in the life of Beatrix Potter and at the same time conveys the atmosphere of her life with her parents and her enchantment with nature and with country life. The pencil drawings are in keeping with the unglamorized events of the story and wisely avoid any suggestion of Beatrix Potter's own style." Horn Bk
   A list of Beatrix Potter's books: p155-56

Letters to children. Harvard College Lib. and Walker & Co. [1967 c1966] 48p illus $3   92
   1 Authors, English
   ISBN 0-8027-6042-2
"Reproduced for the first time in facsimile here are nine letters written by Beatrix Potter to her young friends, Noel, Eric and Freda Moore in the late 1890's. The origins of some of the stories which Miss Potter eventually published are clearly visible in the letters and the enchanting drawings which the letters hold. . . . For ease in reading aloud, the letters have also been transcribed in type." Pub W

Raleigh, Sir Walter

Syme, Ronald. Walter Raleigh; illus. by William Stobbs. Morrow 1962 96p illus lib. bdg. $4.32 (3-6)
                                                    92

1 Great Britain—History—Tudors, 1485-1603
   ISBN 0-688-31595-X
This biography "shows that the many-talented Raleigh served his queen well in spite of his faults and helped to push back the boundaries of the sixteenth-century world. A well-written and vigorously illustrated story of an adventurous life." Hodges. Bks for Elem Sch Libraries

Revere, Paul

Fritz, Jean. And then what happened, Paul Revere? Pictures by Margot Tomes. Coward, McCann & Geoghegan 1973 45p illus $5.95 (2-4) 92
   1 U.S.—History—Revolution—Biography
   ISBN 0-698-20274-0
This "description of Paul Revere's ride to Lexington is funny, fast-paced, and historically accurate; it is given added interest by the establishment of Revere's character: busy, bustling, versatile, and patriotic, a man who loved people and excitement. The account of his ride is preceded by a description of his life and the political situation in Boston, and it concludes with Revere's adventures after reaching Lexington." Chicago. Children's Bk Center
This "slightly unfamiliar and entertaining version of [Revere's] 'Big Ride' is documented in the informal and readable notes at the end of the book. The light-hearted humor in the illustrations—like that in the writing—proves that historical accuracy need not be solemn." Horn Bk

Kelly, Regina Z. Paul Revere: colonial craftsman; illus. by Harvey Kidder. Houghton 1963 188p illus maps $4.36, pa $2.44 (3-6)   92
   1 U.S.—History—Revolution—Biography
   ISBN 0-395-01718-1; 0-395-01719-X
"Piper books"
"An easy-to-read, animated biography which, though fictionalized, follows faithfully the known facts about the life of the silversmith and patriot. Attractive illustrations." Booklist

Richards, Linda Ann Judson

Collins, David R. Linda Richards: first American trained nurse; illus. by Cary. Garrard 1973 80p illus lib. bdg. $3.40 (3-6)   92
   1 Nurses and nursing 2 Education of women
   ISBN 0-8116-6312-2
"A Discovery book"
"This interesting biography of Linda Richards . . . America's first graduate nurse, covers her childhood, her struggle to obtain adequate education, and her work to set up training programs for women in this country as well as in Japan where she lived for five years. The emphasis is on the difficulties that serious, capable women of that era encountered in entering the medical field." Sch Library J

Richter, Hans Peter

I was there; tr. from the German by Edite Kroll. Holt 1972 204p lib. bdg. $4.95 (6-7)   92
   1 National socialism 2 Youth—Germany 3 Germany—Social conditions
   ISBN 0-03-088372-5
Original German edition, 1962
"This narrative recreates the atmosphere of Nazi Germany, the day-to-day life and attitudes, from a young boy's perspective." Chicago
"It is the author's intent to explore the diversity of reasons which compelled youngsters to join the Hitler youth movement and to delineate the extent to which that movement both dictated and reflected the life style of the Third Reich. Historical events are frequently handled as staccato preludes to the personal agonies they induced." Horn Bk

Robeson, Paul

Hamilton, Virginia. Paul Robeson; the life and times of a free Black man; illus. with photographs. Harper 1974 217p illus $6.95, lib. bdg. $6.79 (6-7)

92

1 Negroes—Biography
ISBN 0-06-022188-7; 0-06-022189-5

This is a "portrait of the cosmopolitan black performer whose social sympathies left him a casualty of the anticommunist fever that swept America in the 1950s. Hamilton . . . examines the successes that led Robeson to perceive the biting contradiction between his resounding European acceptance and the guarded, racially shadowed treatment he experienced as a performer in the U.S. . . . The people of Russia . . . welcomed him openly when he performed there. His politicization gradually followed as he saw that discriminatory treatment applied to economic classes as well as minority groups, and his articulate identification with third-world peoples eventually led to career-damaging clashes with the House Un-American Activities Committee." Booklist

"Drawing information from an impressive list of sources, [the author] painstakingly tells the story of Robeson's life: his academic, athletic, musical, and theatrical accomplishments, and his long struggle—not for personal success but for the freedom of his people and their right to decent, dignified lives. . . . Virginia Hamilton deals objectively and skillfully with the tangled complexities of Robeson's beliefs and with the American political climate of the Cold War period. . . . An important book for readers of all ages." Horn Bk

Bibliography: p205-09

Robinson, John Roosevelt

Breakthrough to the big league; the story of Jackie Robinson, by Jackie Robinson and Alfred Duckett; illus. with 21 photographs. Harper 1965 178p lib. bdg. $4.79 (4-7)

92

1 Baseball—Biography 2 Negro athletes
ISBN 0-06-025046-1

"A Breakthrough book"

"Jackie Robinson describes his impoverished childhood and early racial degradation, a stay at a college in Los Angeles where he began a career in sports, and even greater racial problems when he became the first Negro in the major leagues. The chatty text becomes vivid because it is so clearly drawn from Robinson's own speech. As a plain-speaking, highly personal sharing of experience, the book is a forceful picture of the challenge of crossing barriers." Reading Ladders for Human Relations. 5th edition

Rudeen, Kenneth. Jackie Robinson; illus. by Richard Cuffari. Crowell 1971 40p illus (A Crowell biography) $4.50, lib. bdg. $5.25, pa $1.25 (2-4) 92

1 Baseball—Biography 2 Negro athletes
ISBN 0-690-45649-2; 0-690-45650-6; 0-690-00208-4

"A very good biography for young readers, with balanced treatment of Robinson's childhood, his years as a college athlete, and his career in professional baseball. The writing is matter-of-fact, brisk, and candid. . . . The problems Robinson encountered as the first black player in major league baseball are [also] described." Chicago. Children's Bk Center

Roosevelt, Eleanor (Roosevelt)

Goodsell, Jane. Eleanor Roosevelt; illus. by Wendell Minor. Crowell 1970 38p illus (A Crowell biography) $4.50, lib. bdg. $5.25, pa $1.25 (2-4) 92

1 Presidents—U.S.—Wives
ISBN 0-690-25625-6; 0-690-25626-4; 0-690-25627-2

Once a shy and awkward young girl, Eleanor Roosevelt grew up to become the wife of the thirty-

second President of the United States. This biography pictures her as a child, as a wife and mother, as a First Lady helping the underprivileged of all nations and, in her later years, as a worker for the cause of making a better world for all people

Roosevelt, Franklin Delano, President U.S.

Franklin Delano Roosevelt, by the editors of American Heritage, The Magazine of History. Author: Wilson Sullivan; consultant: Frank Freidel. Am. Heritage [distributed by Harper] 1970 153p illus $5.95, lib. bdg. $6.89 (5-7)

92

1 Presidents—U.S. 2 U.S.—History—1933-1945
ISBN 0-06-026086-6; 0-06-026087-4

"American Heritage Junior library"

"This volume recounts the life of the man who was president of the United States for 13 years, elected to a fourth term in 1944, when the nation was at war in Europe and in the South Pacific. He had been active in politics (after a splendid early life) before the August of 1921 when he was struck down by infantile paralysis. But his indomitable will and the devoted affection of his wife Eleanor helped him to recover enough to reenter public life as Governor of New York and later as President. Illustrated with many photographs and reproductions of contemporary cartoons." Best Sellers

Johnson, Gerald W. Franklin D. Roosevelt; portrait of a great man; illus. with 30 photographs; decorations by Leonard Everett Fisher. Morrow 1967 192p illus $5.50, lib. bdg. $4.81 (5-7) 92

1 Presidents—U.S.
ISBN 0-688-21314-6; 0-688-31314-0

"In this book no attempt will be made to tell the whole story. Much of it does not help us to understand Roosevelt, for usually he did what he had to do, what any other man in his high office would have had to do. But there were a few instances in which the kind of man he was decided the kind of thing he did, and those events are the ones I have tried to select for this biography." Author's note

The author's "thesis is that Roosevelt was just another bright and capable young man in politics until his illness, and that the crippling effects of polio brought out the courage and determination that made him a statesman. Perhaps the most interesting aspect of the book is in the picture it gives of the political struggles of the beginner." Sat Rev

Wise, William. Franklin Delano Roosevelt; illus. by Paul Frame. Putnam 1967 63p illus (A See and read Beginning to read biography) lib. bdg. $3.96 (2-4)

92

1 Presidents—U.S.
ISBN 0-399-60185-6

A "biography that is a satisfactory introduction to a U.S. president. The courage of Franklin Roosevelt in overcoming his illness is stressed. The many illustrations add to comprehension." Bruno. Bks for Sch Libraries, 1968

Key words: p[64]

Rose, Edward, fl. 1811-1834

Felton, Harold W. Edward Rose: Negro trail blazer; illus. with photographs, prints of the period, and maps. Dodd 1967 111p illus maps $4.50 (5-7)

92

1 Negroes—Biography 2 Crow Indians
ISBN 0-396-05597-4

Rose, the nineteenth-century Black hunter and trapper, figured prominently in American westward expansion. This biography features "a series of events reflecting the vivid personality of Edward Rose, trapper, guide, interpreter and leader of the Crow

Rose, Edward—*Continued*

Indians." N Y Pub Library. The Black Experience in Children's Bks

Selected bibliography: p106-08

Rose, Pete

Rubin, Bob. Pete Rose; illus. with photographs. Random House 1975 152p illus (Major league lib) $2.50, lib. bdg. $3.69 (5-7)   92

1 Baseball—Biography
ISBN 0-394-83026-1; 0-394-93026-6

Key moments in the career of Cincinnati Reds star outfielder, Pete Rose, are highlighted in this biography

Sacagawea

Voight, Virginia Frances. Sacajawea; illus. by Erica Merkling. Putnam 1967 63p illus (A See and read Beginning to read biography) lib. bdg. $3.96 (2-4)   92

1 Shoshoni Indians 2 Lewis and Clark Expedition
ISBN 0-60553-3

An "account of the famous Shoshone princess who guided the Lewis and Clark expedition to the Pacific Ocean in 1805." Adventuring with Bks. 2d edition

"Sacajawea's life is described in surprising detail for a brief text. Charboneau, her French husband, members of the Lewis and Clark expedition, the black servant, York, and little Pompe are all mentioned. A fine biography of a distinguished Indian woman." Keating. Building Bridges of Understanding Between Cultures

Sanger, Margaret (Higgins)

Lader, Lawrence. Margaret Sanger: pioneer of birth control [by] Lawrence Lader [and] Milton Meltzer; illus. with photographs. Crowell 1969 174p illus (Women of America) $4.95 (6-7)   92

1 Birth control
ISBN 0-690-51934-6

"Margaret Sanger realized the need for birth control in the early 1900's. She fought the laws and established birth-control clinics, having travelled abroad to locate effective birth control methods. The authors tell the story of her struggle and eventual success." The AAAS Sci Bk List for Children

This biography "provides straightforward, explicit information about the birth control methods available at various points in history. This makes the whole story of Margaret Sanger's crusades much more understandable. . . . [The authors] also use quotes from Mrs. Sanger . . . to convey why she worked so hard and sacrificed her personal happiness for the movement she created." Library J

Bibliography: p164-66

Schweitzer, Albert

Montgomery, Elizabeth Rider. Albert Schweitzer, great humanitarian; illus. by William Hutchinson. Garrard 1971 144p illus lib. bdg. $3.94 (4-6)   92

1 Missionaries 2 Physicians
ISBN 0-8116-4510-X

This is the story of "how this unique man gave up his comfortable life as minister and musician to study medicine and fulfill his dream of serving mankind." LC. Children's Bks, 1968

Serra, Junípero

Politi, Leo. The mission bell. Scribner 1953 unp illus lib. bdg. $5.95 (2-5)   92

1 Missionaries 2 California—History
ISBN 0-684-12877-2

The author "tells here of Father Junipero Serra—his difficult journey from Old Mexico to California, the building of the first mission settlement and, above

all, Father Serra's interest in the Indians and his unwavering faith and endurance in the face of adversity." Booklist

Mr. Politi's "almost-reverent style of writing is well suited to his subject . . . and the [author's] pictures are very much alive. I was particularly conscious of all the movement in them. . . . The author has given the story added interest for children by using as one of his main characters the small Indian boy who accompanied Father Serra from Old Mexico and led the mule that carried the mission bell." Horn Bk

Singer, Isaac Bashevis

A day of pleasure; stories of a boy growing up in Warsaw; with photographs by Roman Vishniac. Farrar, Straus 1969 227p illus $4.50 (4-7)   92

1 Jews in Warsaw
ISBN 0-374-31749-6

Translated from the original Yiddish. Fourteen of these episodes previously appeared in somewhat different form in the author's book: In my father's court

An autobiographical collection of stories in which the author writes of his boyhood, as a rabbi's son, in Warsaw, from 1908 to 1918

The stories "present a well-rounded picture of Jewish ghetto life—religion, schooling, family life, friendships, relationships with neighbors, and the richness of the Jewish experience." Wolfe. About 100 Bks

Sitting Bull, Dakota Chief

O'Connor, Richard. Sitting Bull: war chief of the Sioux; illus. by Eric von Schmidt. McGraw 1968 144p illus lib. bdg. $4.72 (4-6)   92

1 Indians of North America—Wars
ISBN 0-07-047582-2

"A thought-provoking account of the white man's treatment of the Indians and of a great Sioux chief whose overriding concern was the welfare of his people. Realizing that with the encroachment of the white man the free-roaming life of the Plains Indians was coming to an end, Sitting Bull believed he could help his people most through diplomacy and courage. This attractive, enjoyable detailed biography treats Sitting Bull as a poet, diplomat, and man of mercy, as well as a man of war." Library J

"The treachery of the white Americans as depicted here is beyond belief. One feels that it must be possible to say something in their favour, but the author does not say it. Nevertheless he gives a fascinating account of Sitting Bull and his world." Times (London) Literary Sup

Smith, John

Syme, Ronald. John Smith of Virginia; illus. by William Stobbs. Morrow 1954 192p illus $4.95 (5-7)   92

1 U.S.—History—Colonial period—Biography
ISBN 0-688-21597-1

This biography emphasizes John Smith's leadership of the struggling English colonists in seventeenth century Virginia. It tells of his legendary rescue by Pocahontas, and also his work as explorer and map maker

"It makes good reading for those who like quick blood-and-thunder action. At the same time it gives a real impression of the early colony at Jamestown. William Stobbs' drawings as usual add strength to the historical picture." Horn Bk

Map on lining-papers

Soto, Hernando de

Syme, Ronald. De Soto, finder of the Mississippi; illus. by William Stobbs. Morrow 1957 96p illus map lib. bdg. $4.32 (4-6)   92

1 Explorers 2 Mississippi River
ISBN 0-688-31224-1

Soto, Hernando de—*Continued*

A story of Hernando de Soto's great adventures in the New World. He and his followers were the first Europeans to see the Mississippi. With Pizarro he made the journey to Peru; he also led his own expedition through Florida

"The story, one of almost constant hardship, is well told, and its attractive illustrations will help interest younger readers. Older slow readers, or those who want a quick review, will also find it useful." Horn Bk

Squanto, Wampanoag Indian

Bulla, Clyde Robert. Squanto, friend of the Pilgrims; illus. by Peter Burchard. Crowell 1954 106p illus $4.50, lib. bdg. $5.25 (2-4)   92

1 Indians of North America—Biography
ISBN 0-690-76642-4; 0-690-76643-2

The "story of a Pawtuxet Indian boy who made friends with some early English voyagers to the new world, went back to England with them for a visit and returned to these shores in time to welcome the Pilgrims." Pub W

"A highly fictionalized account. . . . The author gives no authority for his version of Squanto's first meeting with white men and it is not one of the more generally accepted versions. Aside from this point the book gives an interestingly new and different approach to the subject of the first settlement in New England." Chicago. Children's Bk Center

Stanton, Elizabeth (Cady)

Faber, Doris. Oh, Lizzie! The life of Elizabeth Cady Stanton. Lothrop 1972 159p illus $5.95, lib. bdg. $5.11 (5-7)   92

1 Woman—Suffrage
ISBN 0-688-41405-2; 0-688-51405-7

The author "tells how Elizabeth Cady became interested in women's rights as a young girl visiting her father's law office, where she observed the unfairness of the law toward women. Picturing Elizabeth as enthusiastic and energetic, with a keen mind and good writing and speaking ability, Faber describes her life as the wife of reformer Henry B. Stanton and mother of seven children and her tireless work, largely with her friend Susan B. Anthony, for legislation for women's rights." Booklist

"Effortlessly, the book reveals how the struggle for women's rights grew naturally alongside two other 19th-century crusades: abolitionism and temperance. The reader comes to understand the uphill battle of Mrs. Stanton and her colleagues to convince not only male legislators but members of their own sex that all men—and women—are created equal. It is a timely, sound, and entertaining work." Bk World

Suggestions for further reading: p155-56

Tallchief, Mari

Tobias, Tobi. Maria Tallchief; illus. by Michael Hampshire. Crowell 1970 32p illus (A Crowell biography) $4.50, lib. bdg. $5.25 (2-4)   92

1 Ballet—Biography 2 Indians of North America—Biography
ISBN 0-690-51828-5; 0-690-51829-3

"Elizabeth Marie Tallchief's father was Osage, her mother Scots-Irish, and the family well able to afford both dancing and piano lessons for their daughters. But when the family moved to California, a ballet teacher said that Betty Marie had been taught wrong and would have to start over. At seventeen she came to New York, joining the Ballet Russe company, where her dancing earned her solo parts. Wed to the choreographer George Ballanchine, she rose to prima ballerina; after divorce, she remarried. At the age of forty-one, America's most famous ballet dancer retired to devote herself to her daughter and husband. The writing style is dry, simple, and factual but the

ethnic and cultural appeals are strong and the soft, almost photographic illustrations are most attractive." Chicago. Children's Bk Center

Tchaikovsky, Peter Ilyich

Wheeler, Opal. Peter Tschaikowsky and the Nutcracker ballet; illus. by Christine Price. Dutton 1959 95p illus music $4.50 (3-6)   92

1 Composers, Russian
ISBN 0-525-36950-3

This is "a story-biography for younger children telling of Tchaikovsky's early life and education, his travels, and his most famous compositions. Piano arrangements for some of his best-known works are included." Hodges. Bks for Elem Sch Libraries

There are "many excellent illustrations in black and white." Library J

Thorpe, James Francis

Fall, Thomas. Jim Thorpe; illus. by John Gretzer. Crowell 1970 33p illus (A Crowell biography) $4.50, lib. bdg. $5.25, pa $1.25 (2-5)   92

1 Athletes 2 Indians of North America—Biography
ISBN 0-690-46217-4; 0-690-46218-2; 0-690-46219-0

From his boyhood at Indian boarding schools in Oklahoma Territory to his reward of a gold medal for the decathlon in the 1912 Olympic Games, this biography examines the abilities of Jim Thorpe, one of the world's finest all-around athletes

This biography has "social relevance. . . . Jim Thorpe, lonely and often troubled as a boy, endured hardships common to Indians in the Oklahoma Territory. The author portrays convincingly how, out of his early experience came the skills which later made him famous." N Y Times Bk Rev

Toussaint Louverture, Pierre Dominique

Syme, Ronald. Toussaint: the Black liberator; illus. by William Stobbs. Morrow 1971 191p illus map $4.95, lib. bdg. $4.59 (5-7)   92

1 Haiti—History 2 Negroes—Biography
ISBN 0-688-21806-7; 0-688-31806-1

Born a slave in 1743, Toussaint, the man who started the island of Haiti on the path toward freedom, did not become free himself until 1777. In this biography, the author traces Toussaint's career from his humble beginnings as a plantation overseer to his tragic end in a French prison

"Objective in tone, candid in approach, and written with authoritative informality, Syme's biography of the Haitian leader is both informative and interesting reading." Chicago. Children's Bk Center

Bibliography: p[192]

Truth, Sojourner

Ortiz, Victoria. Sojourner Truth, a self-made woman. Lippincott 1974 157p illus $5.50 (6-7)   92

1 Abolitionists 2 Negroes—Biography
ISBN 0-397-31504-X

"Sojourner Truth's metamorphosis from a properly behaved slave to a determined, self-possessed fighter for human rights begins at the age of thirty when she simply walks off after her New York State master breaches his promise of freedom to her. After an unsettling association with an unorthodox religious group and her subsequent itinerant preaching, she finds her way to Northampton, a utopian community in Massachusetts where she has her first contact with future abolitionist leaders—including Frederick Douglass and William Lloyd Garrison—and embraces the cause herself. Her later adoption of the women's rights struggle comes as a natural consequence of the tenor of the times and her associations." Booklist

The author's "emphasis is on the historical context in which the anti-slavery and feminist movements came into being, and she explores the politics of 19th-

Truth, Sojourner—*Continued*
century America with depth and complexity. Her Sojourner Truth is less a vivid personality and a presence than she is a spokesman and generator of ideas in a fierce, continuing struggle. . . . This book is a welcome addition to a growing literature of self-discovery by women and blacks." N Y Times Bk Rev

Tubman, Harriet (Ross)
Epstein, Sam. Harriet Tubman: guide to freedom, by Sam and Beryl Epstein; illus. by Paul Frame. Garrard 1968 96p illus (Americans all) lib. bdg. $3.58 (3-5)   92
1 Negroes—Biography 2 Slavery in the U.S. 3 Underground railroad
ISBN 0-8116-4550-9
This is "an episodic narrative biography of the heroic slave who freed and helped hundreds of her fellow Negroes. Illustrated with two-color drawings and photographs, the brief account is easy to read and inspiring." Booklist

McGovern, Ann. Runaway slave; the story of Harriet Tubman; pictures by R. M. Powers. Four Winds 1965 unp illus $4.95 (2-4)   92
1 Negroes—Biography 2 Slavery in the U.S. 3 Underground railroad
ISBN 0-590-17004-4
This biography of Harriet Tubman, the escaped slave who led hundreds of people to freedom via the Underground railroad, presents the highlights of her life from childhood to her death
Harriet Tubman's story "is told interestingly and simply." Adventuring with Bks. 2d edition

Sterling, Dorothy. Freedom train: the story of Harriet Tubman; illus. by Ernest Crichlow. Doubleday 1954 191p illus $3.95, lib. bdg. $4.70 (5-7)   92
1 Negroes—Biography 2 Slavery in the U.S. 3 Underground railroad
ISBN 0-385-07301-0; 0-385-07111-6
This is "an excellent portrait of Harriet Tubman, the resourceful and fearless escaped slave who led over 300 Negroes out of bondage. Beginning with her miserable existence as a slave field hand and her own escape, this engrossing account follows Harriet Tubman's hazardous adventures and almost incredible feats as she shuttled up and down the land transporting parties of fugitive slaves to freedom, her amazing war activities as nurse, scout, and spy for the Union army, and her last years working for the advancement of her race." Booklist
Includes bibliography

Velázquez, Diego Rodríguez de Silva y
Ripley, Elizabeth. Velazquez; a biography. Lippincott 1965 72p illus $3.75, lib. bdg. $3.39 (6-7)   92
1 Painters, Spanish
ISBN 0-397-30851-5; 0-397-30852-3
In this account, the "discussion accompanies thirty-four reproductions in black and white of Velazquez's paintings, relating them to different periods in the artist's life. First come his strong, brilliant peasant portraits, then his portraits of Philip IV and the royal family, the court dwarves, Pope Innocent X, and the artist's assistant Juan de Pareja." Horn Bk
"This biography is not detailed, but there is enough information to get to know the personality and work of the painter." Best Sellers

Verne, Jules
Born, Franz. Jules Verne; the man who invented the future; tr. from the German by Juliana Biro; illus. by Peter P. Plasencia. Prentice-Hall 1964 102p illus lib. bdg. $4.95 (5-7)   92

1 Authors, French
ISBN 0-13-512228-7
Original German edition published 1960
"Two-thirds of the book reviews plots or exciting events of Verne's outstanding novels and relates them to later real-life expeditions, discoveries and inventions. Only one chapter concentrates on Verne's life, providing the background of childhood and early struggles before fame touched him." N Y Times Bk Rev
"Juliana Biro's translation of this book from the German makes a swift, absorbing biography. Verne's fertile imagination, his scientific accuracy, and his careful documentation and research set good standards for children. The fact that some of his fantastic ideas of so long ago have now come true will make this book very much alive to young readers . . . steeped in events of the space age." Christian Sci Monitor

Verrazano, Giovanni da
Syme, Ronald. Verrazano: explorer of the Atlantic Coast; illus. by William Stobbs. Morrow 1973 95p illus map $4.75, lib. bdg. $4.32 (4-6)   92
1 Explorers 2 America—Discovery and exploration
ISBN 0-688-21771-0; 0-688-31771-5
A "biography of the Florentine explorer who sailed up the coast of North America searching for a passage to the Pacific in 1524. Sent by the French king, Verrazano was hunting a trade route; his hopes, based on erroneous information about the continent, were not fulfilled but he did find New York Bay and was treated with great courtesy by the Indians of the region." Chicago. Children's Bk Center
"Excerpts from his journal, including some vivid descriptions of Indians, add interest to this readable book and Stobbs's strong, black-and-white illustrations capture the spirit of the text." Sch Library J
Bibliography: p[96]

Vespucci, Amerigo
Syme, R. Amerigo Vespucci, scientist and sailor; illus. by William Stobbs. Morrow 1969 94p illus maps lib. bdg. $4.32 (3-5)   92
1 Explorers 2 America—Discovery and exploration
ISBN 0-688-31020-6
This biography tells about the life and accomplishments of Amerigo Vespucci, who is best known for giving his name to America
"A sympathetic, well written, well researched, minimally fictionized account of Vespucci's life and contributions to navigation and cartography, as well as a glimpse at the general history of the late 15th Century. . . . An attractive format, large, clear print pleasing to the eye, and very well executed black-and-white illustrations enhance the text." Sch Library J
Bibliography: p[95]

Washington, Booker Taliaferro
Graham, Shirley. Booker T. Washington: educator of hand, head, and heart; frontispiece and jacket by Donald W. Lambo. Messner 1955 192p front lib. bdg. $5.29 (5-7)   92
1 Educators 2 Negroes—Biography 3 Tuskegee Institute
ISBN 0-671-32562-0
"A sympathetic story of the slave who overcame tremendous difficulties to establish the Tuskegee Normal and Industrial School for the education of his people." Hodges. Bks for Elem Sch Libraries
Bibliography: p185

Washington, George, President U.S.
Aulaire, Ingri d'. George Washington, by Ingri & Edgar Parin d'Aulaire. Doubleday 1936 unp illus $5.95, lib. bdg. $6.70 (2-4)   92
1 Presidents—U.S.
ISBN 0-385-07306-2; 0-385-07611-8

Washington, George, President U.S.—*Continued*

"Using their usual technique of lithographing on stone the d'Aulaire's have done a gay, stylized picture book in five colors showing Washington's life. Familiar incidents have been chosen. The most appealing small animals find their way into many of the pictures. The text is a simple recounting of his life." Booklist

"The D'Aulaires have given our newest generation material for true and joyous hero-worship." N Y Her Trib Bks

McNeer, May. The story of George Washington; pictures by Lynd Ward. Abingdon 1973 40p illus $4.95 (k-3)　　　　92
　　1 Presidents—U.S.
　　ISBN 0-687-39685-9
"A biographical story for young children which refrains from distorting by oversimplification. There is a combination of facts which can be documented and opinions which are clearly identified as such. Short enough to read aloud at one time to young children." New Bks for Young Readers
　　Glossary: p38-40

North, Sterling. George Washington, frontier colonel; illus. by Lee Ames. Random House 1957 184p illus maps lib. bdg. $4.39 (4-6)　　　　92
　　1 Presidents—U.S.
　　ISBN 0-394-90371-4
　　"Landmark books"
"This is not a complete biography but a portrayal of George Washington's early life, the years which prepared him for future achievements. Quoting liberally from Washington's journals and letters the direct, factual account covers his life from childhood to his arrival in New York City to become the first President of the U.S., but is largely concerned with his frontier experiences during the French and Indian War. More mature in tone than most biographies of Washington for children." Booklist

Washington, Martha (Dandridge) Custis

Vance, Marguerite. Martha, daughter of Virginia; the story of Martha Washington; illus. by Nedda Walker. Dutton 1947 190p illus $5.95 (4-6)　　　92
　　1 Presidents—U.S.—Wives
　　ISBN 0-525-34653-8
A biography of Martha Washington from her eleventh year until she became the first First Lady of the United States

"Martha Washington's life is here presented pleasantly for children of the middle age group, with emphasis about equally divided between childhood and adult years. . . . Soft drawings add charm to the book." Horn Bk

West, Benjamin

Henry, Marguerite. Benjamin West and his cat Grimalkin, by Marguerite Henry and Wesley Dennis. Bobbs 1947 147p illus $4.95 (4-6)　　　92
　　1 Painters, American 2 Cats 3 Friends, Society of
　　ISBN 0-672-50220-8
"As a small boy, Quaker-born Benjamin West, known as the 'father of American painting,' wanted so much to paint that he made his own brushes from his cat's tail, made his colors from earth and clay, and used boards for paper. This is a well-written story, touched with humor and tenderness, of Benjamin's boyhood at his father's inn near Philadelphia, of his early experiences and training in painting, and of his adventures with his remarkable cat, Grimalkin." Booklist

"The happy way in which Benjamin West's biography is combined with a real cat story gives this book

an unusually friendly appeal. . . . A delightful picture of American Quaker life before the Revolution. . . . [Drawings] are admirably suited to it." Horn Bk

Wheatley, Phillis

Fuller, Miriam Morris. Phillis Wheatley, America's first Black poetess; illus. by Victor Mays. Garrard 1971 94p illus (Americans all) lib. bdg. $3.58 (3-6)
　　　　　　　　　　　　　　　　　　92
　　1 Poets, American 2 Negro authors
　　ISBN 0-8116-4569-X
This book traces the life of one of America's first Black poets from her sale as a child slave to her death as a freedwoman in 1784

Whitman, Marcus

Place, Marian T. Marcus and Narcissa Whitman, Oregon pioneers; illus. by Gerald McCann. Garrard 1967 80p illus lib. bdg. $3.40 (2-5)　　　92
　　1 Whitman, Narcissa (Prentiss) 2 Frontier and pioneer life 3 Missionaries
　　ISBN 0-8116-6302-7
　　"A Discovery book"
This adventurous and courageous couple traveled west, hoping to bring Christianity and civilization to the Indians in Oregon. Although they experienced many disappointments, they found their lives as missionaries very rewarding

Wilder, Laura Ingalls

West from home; letters of Laura Ingalls Wilder to Almanzo Wilder, San Francisco, 1915. Ed. by Roger Lea MacBride. Historical setting by Margot Patterson Doss. Harper 1974 124p illus $4.95, lib. bdg. $4.79 (6-7)　　　　　　　　　　　　　　　　　92
　　1 San Francisco—Description 2 Authors, American 3 Letters
　　ISBN 0-06-024110-1; 0-06-024111-X
This collection is "edited from letters sent to her beloved husband while Laura spent two months in late 1915 visiting their daughter and immersing herself in the sights of bustling San Francisco and the exciting Panama-Pacific Exposition. Wilder readers of all ages will lose themselves in this trip—the adults with nostalgia and wholesome pleasure, the youth with wonder and awe over the sights vividly described in her inimitable combination of homespun literary and journalistic styles." Children's Bk Rev Serv

"One of the most noteworthy aspects of her letters is that they reveal her budding interest in writing. . . . The book is prefaced with two competent essays that provide historical background." Horn Bk

Wright, Orville

Graves, Charles P. The Wright brothers; illus. by Fermin Rocker. Putnam 1973 62p illus (A See and read Beginning to read biography) lib. bdg. $3.96 (2-4)　　　　　　　　　　　　　　　　92
　　1 Wright, Wilbur 2 Aeronautics—History
　　ISBN 0-399-60790-0
The author "traces the brothers' lives from their childhood in the Midwest, through their interest in bicycles, automobiles, and gliders, to their invention of the first successful airplane. . . . Fermin Rocker's illustrations adequately complement the clear text." Sch Library J
　　Key words: p62

Reynolds, Quentin. The Wright brothers; pioneers of American aviation; illus. by Jacob Landau. Random House 1950 183p illus lib. bdg. $4.39 (3-6)　　　92
　　1 Wright, Wilbur 2 Aeronautics—History
　　ISBN 0-394-90310-2
　　"Landmark books"

Wright, Orville—*Continued*

This is the story of how these two Americans—who made their living running a bicycle shop—invented, built, and flew the first airplane

Readers "will eagerly seize upon this book which portrays simply but vividly the story of two boys who flew the first heavier-than-air machine. Very well written, with excellent characterizations, good print, wide margins, and delightful illustrations." Library J

929.4   Personal names

Lambert, Eloise

Our names; where they came from and what they mean, by Eloise Lambert and Mario Pei. Lothrop 1960 192p lib. bdg. $4.59   929.4

1 Names, Personal
ISBN 0-688-51378-6

The authors present "little-known facts about first, last, and brand names." Sat Rev

"The study is rather inclusive and mature in approach and treatment for young readers but offers much fascinating information for the interested." Booklist

Shankle, George Earlie

American nicknames; their origin and significance. 2d ed. Wilson, H.W. 1955 524p $12   929.4

1 Nicknames 2 Names, Personal—U.S. 3 Names, Geographical—U.S.
ISBN 0-8242-0004-7

First published 1937

"More than 4000 nicknames, belonging to famous Americans, cities and states, political organizations, and military regiments, arranged in dictionary form with cross references, with sources given in footnotes." Booklist

"What makes the book so authoritative is the citation to sources of information, which cover newspapers, biographical directories, interviews, and other varied sources. . . . It should be remembered that not only persons and places but things and events are included, e.g. William Jennings Bryan's 'Grape-juice Diplomacy,' or Harvard's 'Great Butter Rebellion'. . . . Because of Mr. Shankle's interesting style, this makes good reading as well as good reference." Cur Ref Bks

929.9   Flags

Crouthers, David D.

Flags of American history; flag illustrations by Nicholas Zarrelli. Hammond 1973 93p illus (Profile ser) $4.50, lib. bdg. $4.39 (6-7)   929.9

1 Flags—U.S.
ISBN 0-8437-3080-3; 0-8437-3965-7

First published 1962

Eighty-nine flags which figured in American history are pictured in this book. The author identifies the importance of the flags in our nation's history

Eggenberger, David

Flags of the U.S.A. Enl. ed. Crowell 1964 222p illus $7.95 (6-7)   929.9

1 Flags—U.S.
ISBN 0-690-30491-9

First published 1959

"Describing first the flags of the countries that colonized the New World, the author traces the history of the flags in our country up to the evolution of the fifty-star flag of the United States today. Many drawings are included in addition to the color plates illustrating national, naval, army, and regimental flags as well as the national flag as it evolved. The text is solid with information about the flags themselves and about the historical background to which they are related. . . . Chief use of the book will probably be as a reference source, especially since the closing section is a compilation of facts about the flag code and tradition, and since the index is thorough." Chicago. Children's Bk Center

Freeman, Mae Blacker

Stars and stripes; the story of the American flag; illus. by Lorence Bjorklund. Random House 1964 57p illus music lib. bdg. $3.87 (2-5)   929.9

1 Flags—U.S.
ISBN 0-394-90134-7

Here is the story of the first American flag, how it changed as the United States grew, and events in which the flag played an important part. Also included are rules about the flag; the Pledge of Allegiance; words and melody for "The Star-Spangled Banner"; how flags are made; dates when each of the 50 states joined the Union

"The blue-printed text with red topic headings is appropriate for the subject, but a bit distracting; illustrations are good." Chicago. Children's Bk Center

Parrish, Thomas

The American flag; illus. with photographs, prints and drawings. Simon & Schuster 1973 101p illus lib. bdg. $5.95 (4-7)   929.9

1 Flags—U.S.
ISBN 0-671-65204-4

"This well-written account traces the evolution of the present-day flag from its British origins. Beginning with the historic placing of the American flag on the moon in 1969, Parrish interestingly describes the incidents and legends related to the changes in our flag. The idea that the flag does not stand for American perfection but rather represents our highest goals is carefully pointed out. The illustrations and photographs are well placed in the clear text." Sch Library J

Flag talk: Important words and their meanings: p96-99

Pedersen, Christian Fogd

The international flag book in color; color plates: Wilhelm Petersen; editor of the English language edition: John Bedells. Morrow 1971 237p illus $5.95   929.9

1 Flags
ISBN 0-688-01883-1

Translated by Frederick and Christine Crowley

Original Danish edition, 1970

Supersedes Preben Kannik's: The flag book, first published 1957 by Barrows

National, state, naval and mercantile flags in use today, currently recognized official flags, and national coats of arms are illustrated by 853 colored reproductions arranged geographically and keyed to an explanatory text at the end of the book. Rules for the display of the American flag are included

"The information is accurate and up-to-date, the colors are surprisingly good for so inexpensive a book, relative dimensions are given for many flags, and special terminology is explained in a glossary." Library J

930-999 HISTORY

930 The ancient world to ca. 500 A.D.

Unstead, R. J.
  Looking at ancient history. Macmillan (N Y) [1960] 112p illus maps $5.95 (4-6) 930
  1 History, Ancient 2 Civilization, Ancient
  First published 1959 in England
  "A history of the ancient world—Egypt, Mesopotamia, Greece, and Rome—presented in brief text and many drawings and photographs. While it is mainly a social history, other aspects such as political events and outstanding men of the times are not neglected; a separate chapter is devoted to Alexander the Great. The wide spacing between paragraphs and the topical arrangement of the text give the book the appearance of an outline. Packed with information and easy to read." Booklist

932 Egypt to 640 A.D.

Meadowcroft, Enid La Monte
  The gift of the river; a history of ancient Egypt; introduction by Kirk Meadowcroft; illus. adapted from Egyptian sources by Katharine Dewey. Crowell 1937 235p illus $4.50 (3-5) 932
  1 Egypt—History
  ISBN 0-690-33047-2
  A history of ancient Egypt "which is unusually successful in its presentation and its selection of facts. Based on an understanding of what will appeal to young readers, the author's sketches of rulers from 3400 B.C. to 609 B.C., the descriptions of customs, inventions and contributions of this first civilized country, can not fail to hold a child's interest or to give him a zest for further information." N Y Libraries
  "Quotations from original sources and illustrations from Egyptian material increase the effectiveness of the book." Wis Library Bul

Payne, Elizabeth
  The Pharaohs of ancient Egypt; illus. with photographs. Random House 1964 191p illus maps lib. bdg. $4.39 (5-7) 932
  1 Egypt—Kings and rulers 2 Egypt—History
  ISBN 0-394-90559-8
  "The entire history of the Pharaohs is covered in this . . . account which begins with the discovery and deciphering of the Rosetta Stone—the key to knowledge of ancient Egypt. Early chapters deal with the unification of the country under Menes (shortly before 3200 B.C.). . . . Later chapters depict the reigns of queen Hatshepsut, Thutmose III, and Akhnaton. A closing chapter deals with Rameses II and the aftermath. The author is particularly lucid in describing the character of the Pharaohs; their foibles and faults. The book has good photographs, two excellent maps, a selected bibliography and is indexed." Sci Bks

Pharaohs of Egypt, by the editors of Horizon Magazine. Author: Jacquetta Hawkes; consultant: Bernard V. Bothmer. . . . Am. Heritage [distributed by Harper] 1965 153p illus maps lib. bdg. $6.89 (6-7) 932
  1 Egypt—History 2 Egypt—Kings and rulers
  ISBN 0-06-022241-7
  "A Horizon Caravel book"
  "Illustrated with reliefs, sculptures, wall paintings, and monuments of ancient Egypt." Title page

"The reigning kings are treated in historical perspective—from the unification of Upper and Lower Egypt by Narmer (the legendary Menes) in 3100 B.C. to the closing days of the New Kingdom. Special treatment is given to Zoser, who with his vizier Imhotep, raised the first pyramid, to Cheops and Chephren, to Mentuhotep II, Tuthmosis I, Amenhotep III, and the brilliant Akhenaten. . . . The volume is well written, exceptionally well illustrated (black-and-white and color), has two good maps, an index, and a suggested reading list." Sci Bks

937 Rome to 476 A.D.

Brooks, Polly Schoyer
  When the world was Rome, 753 B.C. to A.D. 476, by Polly Schoyer Brooks and Nancy Zinsser Walworth. Lippincott 1972 235p illus maps $7.95 (6-7) 937
  1 Rome—History
  ISBN 0-397-31214-8
  "A history of Rome is told . . . with emphasis on leaders and battles, intrigue and succession." Chicago. Children's Bk Center
  "The emphasis is on political and military events. . . . Illustrated with many photographic reproductions; an extensive bibliography of ancient and modern sources, including books especially recommended for young readers, is appended." Booklist

Erdoes, Richard
  A picture history of ancient Rome. Macmillan (N Y) [1967] 60p illus $4.95 (4-6) 937
  1 Rome—History
  This is a picture book with brief text describing how the Roman Empire was founded, grew and fell, with stories of its rulers, peoples, and wars." Library J
  "This colorful and highly condensed story of the rise and fall of the Roman kingdom, then republic, and finally empire, is a rather uneven account, but the numerous illustrations, done with a practiced hand, are imaginative and lively." N Y Times Bk Rev

938 Greece to 323 A.D.

Coolidge, Olivia
  The golden days of Greece; illus. by Enrico Arno. Crowell 1968 211p illus $5.50 (4-6) 938
  1 Greece—History 2 Civilization, Greek
  ISBN 0-690-33473-7
  "Highlights of Greek history combined with anecdotes depicting the exploits of gods and men and accounts describing the lives and accomplishments of Greek philosophers, artists, poets, and playwrights provide a lively, illuminating introduction to ancient Greek civilization." Booklist
  "The author draws parallels with contemporary situations and events and gives special attention to the everyday life of ancient Athenian and Spartan boys. The black-and-white Greek-style illustrations are unusually good and there is a useful glossary." Sch Library J
  "It is largely through the lives and exploits of notable personalities that the author presents her skillfully unified view of ancient Greece. Although the style is instructive and at times almost condescending the book provides a valuable basis for further study." Horn Bk

940.1   Europe—Middle Ages, 476-1453

Black, Irma Simonton

Castle, abbey and town; how people lived in the Middle Ages; illus. by W. T. Mars. Holiday House 1963 101p illus $4.95 (3-6)   940.1

1 Middle Ages 2 Civilization, Medieval

ISBN 0-8234-0023-9

"A factual introductory chapter in each of the three sections—castle, abbey, and town—is followed by a narrative written to include as many illustrative details as possible. The training of a knight, position of women, adventures of a crusader, duties of a copyist monk, and life of the serf and bourgeois are . . . described." Booklist

"Attractively illustrated, the book was checked by an expert." Sat Rev

Boardman, Fon W.

Castles, by Fon W. Boardman, Jr. Walck, H. Z. 1957 104p illus $5 (5-7)   940.1

1 Castles 2 Middle Ages

ISBN 0-8098-3015-9

First published by Oxford

The author presents a selection of tales of medieval chivalry and romance as a basis for the understanding of the feudal system and the importance of castles. Diagrams of the castles as they were originally constructed contrast with the accompanying photographs of the fortresses as they look today

"An accurate and careful study of castles from the first 'motte-and-bailey' built by William the Conqueror to the gradual disuse of the battlemented buildings. . . . An excellent book for either school or public library." Massachusetts Dept of Educ Library Lists

Glossary: p7-8

Buehr, Walter

Chivalry and the mailed knight; written and illus. by Walter Buehr. Putnam 1963 93p illus maps lib. bdg. $4.79 (3-6)   940.1

1 Knights and knighthood

ISBN 0-399-60094-9

The author "notes the varied forces that produced the medieval system and shows the place of the knight in that society. He describes the knight's training and his responsibilities in peace and war, traces the development of castles and weapons and shows the way in which the longbow, crossbow and firearms affected the use of armor and the domination of the knight in warfare. The rise of such military orders as the Knights Templar and the Knights of Malta is told." N Y Times Bk Rev

The crusaders. Putnam 1959 96p illus lib. bdg. $5.39 (5-7)   940.1

1 Crusades

ISBN 0-399-60113-9

"A book that concentrates on the First Crusade at the close of the eleventh century. The author discusses the background of European feudal structure and the motivations of the Crusaders, describing the four armies that marched to Jerusalem and telling in detail the battles of Nicaea, Antioch, and Jerusalem. The last fifteen pages of the book survey briefly other Crusades, especially the ill-fated Children's Crusade. Mr. Buehr is candid in his description of the behavior of the marchers, which was not always exemplary. . . . The omission of a map is regrettable." Chicago. Children's Bk Center

"The futility of war and invasion are apparent. . . . Well written." Library J

Knights and castles, and feudal life. Putnam 1957 72p illus lib. bdg. $4.79 (4-7)   940.1

1 Knights and knighthood 2 Castles

ISBN 0-399-60341-7

"This book describes many aspects of life in feudal times, does not over-romanticize the glamour of knights and castles and shows something of the hard life led by peasants. It covers the daily life and household tasks in a castle as well as its layout and the ways by which it was defended against attack. It shows the different classes of society in the feudal system, the training of a knight, his arms and armour and describes a tourney and a typical siege." Ontario Library Rev

Uden, Grant

A dictionary of chivalry; illus. by Pauline Baynes. Crowell [1969 c1968] 352p illus $11.95 (6-7) 940.1

1 Chivalry—Encyclopedias 2 Knights and knighthood—Encyclopedias 3 Civilization, Medieval

ISBN 0-690-23815-0

"A handsome, lively, and informative reference book on the Age of Chivalry. The alphabetically arranged entries range in length from one sentence to several paragraphs and cover such topics as people, events, places, accoutrements, clothing, and weapons, at times incorporating quotations from literature and early chronicles. Sharply drawn illustrations, some in full color, border each page of easy-to-read single-column type. Numerous cross-references throughout the text and an appended subject index add to the usefulness of the book." Booklist

Unstead, R. J.

Living in a castle; illus. by Victor Ambrus. Addison-Wesley 1971 43p illus (The 'Living in' ser) lib. bdg. $4.95 (4-6)   940.1

1 Feudalism

ISBN 0-201-08495-3

A fictional account of daily life in a feudal castle in southern England in the year 1250. The author describes the various occupants of the castle and their traditional duties, and details the events of a single day, from the business problems of the lord and his steward to the menu of the evening meal. Included also is an analysis of the architectural plan of the castle

940.3   World War I, 1914-1918

Leckie, Robert

The story of World War I. . . . Random House 1965 189p illus maps $4.95, lib. bdg. $7.99 (5-7)
940.3

1 European War, 1914-1918

ISBN 0-394-81693-5; 0-394-91693-X

"Landmark giant"

Companion volume to the author's: The story of World War II, class 940.53

"Adapted for young readers from The American Heritage History of World War I by the editors of American Heritage with narrative by S. L. A. Marshall." Title page

A "vivid account of the horrifying loss of life and official bungling of World War I illustrated with contemporary drawings and photographs." Ontario Library Rev

"A general coverage of World War I from its causes to the final victories and defeats. Well illustrated. This serves as a good introduction to the period." Wis Library Bul

Snyder, Louis L.
The first book of World War I; maps by Leonard Derwinski. Watts, F. 1958 94p illus maps lib. bdg. $3.90, pa $1.25 (5-7)   940.3
    1 European War, 1914-1918
    ISBN 0-531-00675-1; 0-531-02318-4
    Companion volume to the author's: The first book of World War II, class 940.53
    "An interesting and informative overview of the first World War. The author has, by presenting the events that set the stage for the conflict and by making clear the relationship between the harsh treaty of World War I and the inevitability of World War II, given more than a record of one war. The book shows as well the confusion and complication of political and economic relationships between countries." Chicago. Children's Bk Center
    "Like the other volume this is profusely illustrated with well-chosen photographs." Booklist
    World War I words: p94

940.4   World War I, 1914-1918 (Military conduct of the war)

Bowen, Robert Sidney
They flew to glory: the story of the Lafayette Flying Corps; illus. by Bernard Case. Lothrop 1965 160p illus $4.95 (4-6)   940.4
    1 France. Army. Lafayette Flying Corps 2 European War, 1914-1918—Aerial operations
    ISBN 0-688-40991-1
    "An action-filled account of the American fighter pilots who flew for France during the early years of World War I, describing planes, methods of combat, and exploits of individual fliers." Hodges. Bks for Elem Sch Libraries
    For further reading: p157

940.53   World War II, 1939-1945

Leckie, Robert
The story of World War II; illus. with photographs & maps. Random House 1964 193p illus maps $4.95, lib. bdg. $5.99 (5-7)   940.53
    1 World War, 1939-1945
    ISBN 0-394-80295-0; 0-394-90295-5
    "Landmark giant"
    Companion volume to the author's: The story of World War I, class 940.3
    "Designed for 'reading' rather than reference. This account . . . gives more space to the war in the Pacific than other areas. The struggle in Finland, in Norway and the Balkans; the fall of France; the Battle of Britain: the campaigns in North Africa and Italy; all these are described in readable but not overly dramatised chapters which would give the young reader a fair picture of the events of those days." Toronto

Snyder, Louis L.
The first book of World War II. Watts, F. 1958 94p illus maps lib. bdg. $3.90, pa $1.25 (5-7)   940.53
    1 World War, 1939-1945
    ISBN 0-531-00676-X; 0-531-02319-2
    Companion volume to the author's: The first book of World War I, class 940.3

"Here in brief are causes, occasion, the 'phony' war, Dunkirk, 'Hitler master of Europe' after the fall of France, and the Battle of Britain. Then the various theaters of war are mentioned, the Balkans, North Africa, and the Pacific after the Japanese attack on Pearl Harbor. Finally there is the closing in on the Germans in Europe and the A-Bomb victory over Japan. Some suggestions of the problems of peace are made with hope for victory over war itself." N Y Her Trib Bks
    "The writing is lively, maps are good, and the book [is] . . . profusely illustrated with photographs." Chicago. Children's Bk Center
    World War II words: p93

940.54   World War II, 1939-1945 (Military conduct of the war)

Bliven, Bruce
The story of D-Day; June 6, 1944; illus. by Albert Orbaan. Random House 1956 180p illus map $2.95, lib. bdg. $4.27 (5-7)   940.54
    1 Normandy, Attack on, 1944
    ISBN 0-394-80362-0; 0-394-90362-5
    "Landmark books"
    An account of the planning and resources of the Allied invasion of Normandy which was the turning point of the Second World War, and of the brave men who implemented it
    "A brief, dramatic account . . . recommended for reluctant older readers." Hodges. Bks for Elem Sch Libraries

Carter, Hodding
The Commandos of World War II; illus. with photographs and maps. Random House 1966 168p illus maps $2.95, lib. bdg. $4.27 (5-7)   940.54
    1 Great Britain. Combined Operations Command 2 World War, 1939-1945
    ISBN 0-394-80561-5; 0-394-90561-X
    "World Landmark books"
    "The Commandos (first formed to hit Germany through France in World War II) were highly skilled as a hit-and-run force of guerilla fighters, specializing in speed and surprise. Based on actual British war records, the origin, training, and operations of these skilled volunteer soldiers are reported in a straightforward narrative. A brief picture of their wartime activity in England and elsewhere is given along with character portrayals of a few of the leaders. The author achieves dramatic impact as he portrays the heroism and the dangers endured by this group. The illustrations enhance and clarify the text." Sch Library J
    Bibliography: p161-62

Conroy, Robert
The Battle of Bataan; America's greatest defeat. Macmillan (N Y) 1969 85p illus maps (Macmillan Battle bks) $4.95 (5-7)   940.54
    1 World War, 1939-1945—Philippine Islands
    The author describes the unsuccessful struggle of American and Filipino troops to defend Bataan against Japanese invasion in 1942
    In this book "the reader is told frankly that the past behavior of the United States in the Philippines had failed to win the affection of the people; and American military bungling, if not detailed, is clearly suggested. . . . By and large, [the author] succeeds in evoking the agony of America's greatest military defeat." N Y Times Bk Rev
    For further reading: p81

Hough, Richard

The Battle of Britain; the triumph of R.A.F. fighter pilots. Macmillan (N Y) 1971 88p illus maps $4.50 (5-7)   940.54

1 Britain, Battle of, 1940 2 World War, 1939-1945—Aerial operations

An account of the Luftwaffe's air invasion of England and the struggle of the Royal Air Force to bring about the defeat of the Germans in the Battle of Britain

"Hough's book is a well-written, well-organized account of the battle. While never neglecting the human interest aspect, Hough concentrates on presenting readers with a very clear picture of why the Battle of Britain was important, and why and how it was won by the British and lost by Germany. . . . The photographs are plentiful and well selected." Library J

For further reading: p86

Reiss, Johanna

The upstairs room (4-7)   940.54

1 World War, 1939-1945—Jews 2 Netherlands—History—German occupation, 1940-1945 3 Jews in the Netherlands

Some editions are:

Crowell $4.50 (ISBN 0-690-85127-8)

Hall, G.K.&Co. $7.95 Large print book (ISBN 0-8161-6119-4)

First published 1972 by Crowell

"The author recalls her experiences as a Jewish child hiding from the Germans occupying her native Holland during World War II. When German pressure on Dutch Jews is stepped up ten-year-old Annie and her twenty-year-old sister Sini, separated from their father and eldest sister who hide elsewhere and from their mother dying in a hospital, are taken in by a Dutch farmer, his wife, and mother who hide the girls in an upstairs room of the farm house." Booklist

In relating her true experiences "the author has skillfully captured, in a first person narrative, the tone, impressions, and expressions of the eight-year-old girl telling the story. Excellent characterization of real people reinforces a stirring and absorbing story which is filled with moments that are tense, frightening, sad, and humorous but never melodramatic. It is a story that is timeless though it is set in a specific period in history." Top of the News

Reynolds, Quentin

The Battle of Britain; illus. by Clayton Knight. Random House 1953 182p illus lib. bdg. $4.27 (6-7)   940.54

1 Britain, Battle of, 1940 2 World War, 1939-1945—Personal narratives

ISBN 0-394-90510-5

"World Landmark books"

"An account of the 83 days it took to defeat the German Luftwaffe's air invasion of England told very simply by a newspaper correspondent who was there to observe it. Because of the successful transmittal of British understatement, the book provides an objective appraisal of the action without an emotional involvement on the part of the reader." Booklist

Shirer, William L.

The sinking of the Bismarck; illus. with photographs & maps. Random House 1962 178p illus maps $2.95, lib. bdg. $4.39 (5-7)   940.54

1 Bismarck (Battleship) 2 World War, 1939-1945—Naval operations

ISBN 0-394-80551-8; 0-394-90551-2

"World landmark books"

A "reconstruction of the sinking of the German battleship 'Bismarck' by Great Britain in 1941. The suspenseful account begins with the British Admiralty's receipt of a report that the 'Bismarck' had been sighted heading for the North Atlantic, follows the more than 2,000-mile chase of the elusive ship through heavy seas, and closes with the cornering and sinking of the battleship." Booklist

"Maps help make even clearer this unforgettable story of courage and dogged determination." N Y Her Trib Bks

A note on sources: p171-72

Taylor, Theodore

Air raid—Pearl Harbor! The story of December 7, 1941; illus. by W. T. Mars. Crowell 1971 185p illus maps $4.50 (5-7)   940.54

1 Pearl Harbor, Attack on, 1941

ISBN 0-690-05373-8

"Well-documented and written with all the suspense of a mystery story, this is a detailed account of the events that led up to the disaster of Pearl Harbor. The story is told both from the American and the Japanese viewpoints, with all of the errors in planning, the gaps in communication, the secrecy of tactics and strategy; the text moves from the flurries of activity in Washington, the veiled manoeuvres of the fleet that had sailed from Japan in November, to the pre-Christmas relaxation of Pearl Harbor, the diplomatic backing and filling gaining impetus as December 7 approaches." Sutherland. The Best in Children's Bks

Bibliography: p177-78

Tregaskis, Richard

John F. Kennedy and PT-109. Random House 1962 192p illus $2.95, lib. bdg. $4.39 (5-7)   940.54

1 Kennedy, John Fitzgerald, President U.S. 2 PT-109 (Boat)

ISBN 0-394-80399-X; 0-394-90399-4

"Landmark books"

"A good book about operations in the Solomon Islands during World War II, with the story of Kennedy's shipwreck while in command of Torpedo Patrol-109. The material is dramatic, some of the battle scenes are vividly described, and there is no adulatory note in any of the author's references to Lt. Kennedy." Chicago. Children's Bk Center

"The book is best through the graphic descriptions of the disaster when PT-109 was struck by the Japanese destroyer and the excitement surrounding the efforts of Kennedy to save his crew. . . . Young readers will find this an attractive and inspiring offering." Best Sellers

942   British Isles

Unstead, R. J.

The story of Britain; illus. by Victor Ambrus. Nelson 1970 328p illus $6.95 (4-7)   942

1 Great Britain—History 2 Great Britain—Kings and rulers

ISBN 0-8407-6082-5

First published 1969 in England

"In short crisp chapters dramatically illustrated with black-and-white and full-color drawings, Unstead presents a well-synthesized, panoramic view of British history from the Stone Age to World War II. While major attention is given to kings, barons, bishops, and statesmen who were the decision makers, due attention is paid to the role of commoners, explorers and adventurers, and outstanding writers, inventors, and social reformers. A lively, instructive account for general reading or for reference." Booklist

942.02 British Isles— Norman period, 1066-1154

Hodges, C. Walter
The Norman Conquest; written and illus. by C. Walter Hodges. Coward, McCann & Geoghegan 1966 32p illus lib. bdg. $4.99 (4-7)   942.02
  1 Hastings, Battle of, 1066 2 William I, the Conqueror, King of England
  ISBN 0-698-30260-5
  Companion volume to: Magna Carta, class 942.03
This is "a stunningly illustrated book that describes the events of the Norman Conquest, first giving some general background and an account of the state of affairs immediately preceding William's victory. The text is crisply informational; the pictures are unusual in being both beautiful and highly informative." Chicago. Children's Bk Center

942.03 British Isles— House of Plantagenet, 1154-1399

Hodges, C. Walter
Magna Carta; written and illus. by C. Walter Hodges. Coward-McCann 1966 32p illus map lib. bdg. $4.29 (4-7)   942.03
  1 Magna Carta 2 Great Britain—History
  ISBN 0-698-30227-3
  Companion volume to: The Norman Conquest, class 942.02
"After a description of the hierarchy of power in Norman England, the author traces briefly the state of affairs during the reigns of Stephen, Matilda, Henry, Richard, and then John—whose mercenary oppression led to a revolt of the barons and to the signing of the Magna Carta at Runnymede." Chicago. Children's Bk Center
"Mr. Hodges is careful to point out the dangers of over-simplification, showing that King John was no worse than many of his barons. The book's chief excuse, of course, is the pictures, in glorious imaginative colour, which may teach quite as well as the text." Times (London) Literary Sup

947 Eastern Europe. Russia

Hall, Elvajean
The Volga: lifeline of Russia; illus. by Emil Weiss. Rand McNally 1965 112p illus maps lib. bdg. $3.69 (5-7)   947
  1 Volga River 2 Russia—History
  ISBN 0-8382-0917-3
In this volume, "the history, geography, life, and industry along the Volga River are . . . described in a . . . background picture of Russia—without discussion of politics or international relations. Following the several chapters on Russian history, an informal picture of travel and vacation cruising on the river presents modern conditions, with anecdotes, a few folk tales, and the 'Song of the Volga Boatmen." Horn Bk
"Mr. Weiss's drawings—marvellously precise and

picturesque in detail—admirably complement Miss Hall's words." N Y Times Bk Rev
  Bibliography: p104-05

948 Scandinavia

Buehr, Walter
The Viking explorers. Putnam 1967 91p illus maps lib. bdg. $4.79 (3-6)   948
  1 Northmen
  ISBN 0-399-60654-8
Illustrated by the author, this is "a discursive account of Viking pillage, trade, conquest, and colonization interspersed with enlightening details about Viking seamanship, life and customs. Similar in coverage to Rich's 'The first book of the Vikings' [entered in class 914.8] . . . but more casual in treatment, the book reveals the form and extent of Scandinavian penetration in the Western Hemisphere from the ninth to the thirteenth century." Booklist

The Vikings, by the editors of Horizon Magazine. Author: Frank R. Donovan; consultant: Sir Thomas D. Kendrick. Illus. with drawings, illuminations, carvings, and maps, many of the period. Am. Heritage [distributed by Harper] 1964 153p illus maps $5.95 (6-7)   948
  1 Northmen
  ISBN 0-06-021715-4
  "A Horizon Caravel book"
This is an account of the Scandinavians of 800-1100 A.D. who raided and plundered, then settled the lands of Europe, and also discovered Greenland
This volume is "interesting in its subject matter. It is a book for young people who want information rather than exciting tales, for it intentionally plays down the glamorous and dramatic concept of great sea rovers from the North." Pub W
It is "one of the most useful volumes of this series. . . . Stunning illustrations." Toronto
  Further reference: p151

956.1 Turkey

Constantinople: city on the Golden Horn, by the editors of Horizon Magazine. Author: David Jacobs; consultant: Cyril A. Mango. Am. Heritage [distributed by Harper] 1969 153p illus maps $5.95, lib. bdg. $6.89 (6-7)   956.1
  1 Istanbul—History
  ISBN 0-06-022798-2; 0-06-022799-0
  "A Horizon Caravel book"
The author "traces the history of Constantinople from its founding by Greek settlers in the seventh century B.C. to the 1920's, with major emphasis on the period during which it became, successively, the capital of the East Roman, the Byzantine, and the Ottoman Turk Empires. He describes the personalities and events that dominated the city's development, discusses Constantinople's role as a bridge between Eastern and Western culture, and comments on the sack of Constantinople by Crusaders in 1204 and its conquest by Turks in 1453. The text, maps, contemporary art and modern photographs ably portray the city's historic importance and rich, diverse heritage." Booklist
  Further reading: p149

959.704   Vietnam— Independence, 1949-

Lifton, Betty Jean

Children of Vietnam [by] Betty Jean Lifton and Thomas C. Fox. Illus. with photographs by Thomas C. Fox. Atheneum Pubs. 1972 111p illus map $5.50 (6-7)   959.704

1 Vietnamese Conflict, 1961- —Children
ISBN 0-689-30056-5

"A moving portrayal of the anguish suffered by the young victims of the war. Interviews with the children are interspersed with songs, poetry, prose, and photographs." Chicago

"The book ends with a sad account of the My Lai tragedy by some of the young survivors. In no other book on Vietnam is the plight of these children so personally and movingly depicted." Sch Library J

962   Countries of the Nile

Building the Suez Canal, by the editors of Horizon Magazine. Author: S. C. Burchell; consultant: Charles Issawi. . . . Am. Heritage [distributed by Harper] 1966 153p illus maps $5.95, lib. bdg. $6.89 (6-7)   962

1 Suez Canal 2 Lesseps, Ferdinand Marie, vicomte de
ISBN 0-06-020915-1; 0-06-020916-4

"A Horizon Caravel book"

"The history of the Suez Canal and its builder, Ferdinand de Lesseps, with many contemporary photographs, drawings, diagrams, maps and etchings." Title page

There are several chapters covering the political and financial negotiations of European and Mid-East governments, regarding the canal, as well as information on the Suez Crisis of 1956

Further reading: p151

Naden, Corinne J.

The Nile River; illus. with photographs. Watts, F. 1972 79p illus map lib. bdg. $3.90 (4-6)   962

1 Nile River 2 Nile Valley
ISBN 0-531-00774-X

"A First book"

Map by Walter Hortens

This is a history of the Blue and White Nile and of the civilizations that have flourished in the Nile Valley. Also covered are the many explorers and adventurers who searched for the river's source

967   Central Africa

Lauber, Patricia

The Congo; river into Central Africa; illus. by Ted Schroeder; maps by Fred Kliem. Garrard 1964 96p illus maps (Rivers of the world) lib. bdg. $3.68 (4-6)   967

1 Congo River 2 Africa, Central
ISBN 0-8116-6358-2

This is "a simply written account of the explorations of the Congo and the Nile and a description of countries and peoples along their banks." Hodges. Bks for Elem Sch Libraries

967.5   Congo Republic (Zaïre)

McKown, Robin

The Republic of Zaïre (formerly the Democratic Republic of the Congo) Illus. with prints and photographs. Watts, F. 1972 88p illus map lib. bdg. $3.90 (4-6)   967.5

1 Zaïre—History
ISBN 0-531-00770-7

"A First book"

An "introduction to the African Republic of Zaire, formerly the Democratic Republic of the Congo and, before that, the Belgian Congo. As background the author describes the land and its many tribes and traces the exploration and colonization of the country. . . . [She includes a] summary of events during the chaotic years after independence, and although she discusses the deficiencies of the present-day neocolonialism, she is hopeful about the future of the country. Illustrated with black-and-white photographs; bibliography appended." Booklist

970.1   Indians of North America

Baldwin, Gordon C.

How Indians really lived. Putnam 1967 223p illus maps (A Science survey bk) lib. bdg. $4.89 (5-7)   970.1

1 Indians of North America
ISBN 0-399-60268-2

"Generally concentrating on major tribes, but including many of the smaller ones as well, [the author] presents a detailed and easily comprehensible picture of how the Indians lived and thought, with a great deal of specific information about types and construction of homes, gathering and preparation of food, also clothing, cosmetics, and hairstyles, social units and kinship structures, recreation, politics, warfare, and religion. . . . The writing is smooth and consistently interesting, and the book never gets bogged down in details. The photographs—mostly of museum exhibits and 19th century location shots— are adequate but not distinguished." Sch Library J

Bibliography: p216-17. Glossary: p218-20

Bleeker, Sonia

The Eskimo; Arctic hunters and trappers; illus by Patricia Boodell. Morrow 1959 160p illus map lib. bdg $4.59 (4-6)   970.1

1 Arctic regions 2 Eskimos
ISBN 0-688-31275-6

"The rigorous Arctic climate plays an integral part in the Eskimo's way of life and outlook and the author gives . . . [a] picture of these sturdy and independent people, their homes, methods of hunting and fishing, crafts, games and folk lore. Well indexed." Ontario Library rev

"As authentic, well-organized information is always in demand, this [book] . . . will be welcomed by school and public librarians. Packed with details . . . it also reads well because of the author's straightforward and uncondescending style." Horn Bk

Bringle, Mary

Eskimos. Watts, F. 1973 87p illus map lib. bdg. $3.90 (5-6)   970.1

1 Eskimos
ISBN 0-531-00785-5

Bringle, Mary—*Continued*
"A First book"
"A good overview of the Eskimo way of life, giving facts about theories of migration and diffusion, is limited by the sparsity of coverage about contemporary life, although there are periodic references . . . to today's changes; a few pages at the close are devoted to this subject. The text, capably written and illustrated by clear photographs, discusses the ecology of the Arctic. Eskimo homes and clothing, customs and hunting techniques, and—very briefly—aspects of Eskimo arts and religion." Chicago. Children's Bk Center
Bibliography: p83

Grant, Bruce
American Indians, yesterday and today; a profusely illustrated encyclopedia of the American Indian; illus. by Lorence F. Bjorklund. Rev. ed. Dutton 1960 352p illus $8.95   970.1
1 Indians of North America
ISBN 0-525-25541-9
First published 1958
This is "an alphabetically arranged resource book giving information about Indian tribes, customs, beliefs, tools, food, homes, leaders, garments, games, animals, important events in Indian history, and Indians words in the American language. Easy to read and filled with black and white drawings, the book is extremely useful for elementary children. . . . Appendixes include a bibliography, a list of museums, Indian population on reservations, and an Indian family tree." Peterson. Ref Bks for Elem and Jr High Sch Libraries

Gridley, Marion E.
Indian tribes of America; illus. by Lone Wolf. Hubbard Press 1973 63p illus lib. bdg. $4.95 (4-6) 970.1
1 Indians of North America
The author discusses the major Indian tribes of the Northeast, Southeast, Plains, and Northwest coast, emphasizing the unique life style of each group

Hofsinde, Robert
The Indian and his horse; written and illus. by Robert Hofsinde (Gray-Wolf) Morrow 1960 96p illus lib. bdg. $4.32 (4-6)   970.1
1 Indians of North America 2 Horses
ISBN 0-688-31421-X
"Mr. Hofsinde discusses the coming of the horse and the first uses of the animal; the catching, raiding, trading and training of horses; and the breeds of horses used by Indians. He describes the buffalo horse, the war horse, and the medicine horse; he traces the development of increasingly complex equipment: he closes with a brief description of the horse by contemporary American Indians." Chicago. Children's Bk Center
The author "investigates [his subject] thoroughly and presents his findings simply and well." N Y Her Trib Bks

The Indian's secret world; written and illus. by Robert Hofsinde (Gray-Wolf) Morrow 1955 94p illus lib. bdg. $5.49 (5-7)   970.1
1 Indians of North America—Social life and customs 2 Indians of North America—Religion and mythology
ISBN 0-688-31612-3
Each chapter deals with some aspect of the culture of the North American Indian. Described through the experiences of individual Indians are the social or religious significance of such things as the making of a medicine pipe, the winning of a war bonnet, the painting of a new tepee, the decoration of a ceremonial mask and its use in healing ceremonies

The book "will be useful in developing an understanding among modern youngsters of the ways in which cultural mores develop. The illustrations help explain the text and add beauty to the book." Chicago. Children's Bk Center

La Farge, Oliver
The American Indian. Special ed. for young readers. Golden Press 1960 213p illus maps $6.95 (5-7)   970.1
1 Indians of North America
ISBN 0-307-17846-3
Based on the author's: A pictorial history of the American Indian, this young people's edition is "illustrated with color photographs, contemporary paintings, prints, and specially commissioned paintings by André Durenceau." Preceding title page
This is an account of how the American Indians arrived from Asia, their daily lives and rituals, their tribes and leaders, and, finally, how the Indians live today
It is "comprehensive in scope, detailed in treatment profusely illustrated. . . . The writing style is compact, serious, and a bit dry; the book is not dull, however, because of the diversity and drama of the material itself and because of the variety and the beauty of the illustrations." Chicago. Children's Bk Center

McNeer, May
The American Indian story; with lithographs by Lynd Ward. Ariel Bks. 1963 95p illus $5.95 (5-7)   970.1
1 Indians of North America
ISBN 0-374-30264-2
"This is not a single, continuous account; it consists of short narratives about important incidents [customs] and individuals which, together, comprise a colorful introduction to the history and life of the North American Indian from earliest times to the present." Booklist
"There are superb lithographs by Lynd Ward which epitomize all the beauty, terror and tragedy of the American Indian. For the artistry of these stupendous illustrations alone, this book should be purchased." Sch Library J

Marriott, Alice
Indians on horseback; drawings by Margaret Lefranc. Crowell [1968 c1948] 136p illus $4.95 (4-6)   970.1
1 Indians of North America
ISBN 0-690-43768-4
Reprint of a book first published 1948
Contents: Who the Plains Indians are; What the Great Plains are; When the white men came; One man's life on the plains; How the tribes governed themselves; The Sun Dance ceremony; Indian doctors and medicines; A Plains Indian cookbook; How the Plains Indians made things; What the Plains Indians are doing now; Bibliography
"The author, an experienced ethnologist who has lived with descendants of the original inhabitants of this area, writes about her subject with sympathetic understanding." Sat Rev

Pine, Tillie S.
The Eskimos knew, by Tillie S. Pine and Joseph Levine; illus. by Ezra Jack Keats. McGraw 1962 32p illus lib. bdg. $4.72 (1-4)   970.1
1 Eskimos 2 Science—Experiments
ISBN 0-07-050053-3
"Whitlesey House publications"
"This useful activity book for young children describes how Eskimos solved such problems as protecting their eyes from glare, getting fresh water from

Pine, Tillie S.—*Continued*
the sea, and using snow to build their houses. The principles involved are applied to today's world and accompanied by easy experiments." Bks for Elem Sch Libraries

The Indians knew; pictures by Ezra Jack Keats. McGraw 1957 31p illus $4.72 (1-3)   970.1
1 Indians of North America 2 Science
ISBN 0-07-050031-2
First published by Whittlesey House
"An excellent book for handicrafts and activities. Describes what Indians knew and contributed to society and then compares and teaches by suggesting that what they knew is reflected in everyday things that children can make or do themselves." Cane. Selected Media About the American Indian for Young Children

Stuart, Gene S.
Three little Indians; paintings by Louis S. Glanzman. Natl. Geographic Soc. 1974 31p illus (k-3)
970.1
1 Cheyenne Indians 2 Creek Indians 3 Nootka Indians
ISBN 0-87044-157-4
Obtainable only as part of a set for $6.95 with: Cats: little tigers in your house, by Linda McCarter Bridge, class 636.8; Creepy crawly things, by the National Geographic Society, class 598.1; and Spiders, by Lillian Bason, class 595
"Books for young explorers"
Prepared by the Special Publications Division of the National Geographic Society
This book tells of the life of a Cheyenne boy, a Creek girl and a Nootka boy. The locale of the tribes, the clothes, food and housing each used, their special skills and tribal traditions are described through the lives of the young Indians
"Contains oversimplified prose; also, it fails to give certain essential facts about the Cheyenne, Creek, and Nootka tribes of North America. It may be worth purchasing, however, since both text and full-color paintings are accurate and informative." Booklist

Yellow Robe, Rosebud
An album of the American Indian, by Rosebud Yellow Robe (Lacotawin). Watts, F. 1969 87p illus map lib. bdg. $4.90 (4-6)   970.1
1 Indians of North America
ISBN 0-531-01506-8
"Paintings, drawings, and photographs, accompanied by a brief text, serve to illustrate various facets of American Indian cultures and history from past to present." Byler. Indian Authors for Young Readers
Glossary: p86-87

970.3   Specific North American Indian tribes

Bealer, Alex W.
Only the names remain; the Cherokees and the Trail of Tears; illus. by William Sauts Bock. Little 1972 88p illus $5.95 (4-6)   970.3
1 Cherokee Indians
ISBN 0-316-08520-0
The author describes "the rise of the Cherokee Nation, with its written language, constitution, and republican form of government, and its tragic betrayal in the 1830s." Chicago
"The author's narrative style, which is dramatic and

immediate, is intensified by the illustrator's meticulous and evocative black-and-white illustrations. A helpful index is appended." Horn Bk

Beck, Barbara L.
The first book of the ancient Maya; pictures by Page Cary. Watts, F. 1965 87p illus maps lib. bdg. $3.90 (5-7)   970.3
1 Mayas
ISBN 0-531-00464-3
The history of the Mayas, traced through their destruction by the Spaniards in the sixteenth century, incorporates information on their social, religious, and artistic life
"Many illustrations show the art, temples, plans of cities, artifacts, and writing. This introductory book packs a great many facts concisely into its few pages." Library J
"This treatment of the subject is particularly good for the coverage of some of the lesser-known cities and stunningly beautiful buildings. An index is appended." Chicago. Children's Bk Center

The first book of the Aztecs; pictures by Page Cary. Watts, F. 1966 72p illus maps lib. bdg. $3.90 (4-6)
970.3
1 Aztecs
ISBN 0-531-00476-7
"This introductory account succinctly highlights the historical background, daily life, religious and social structure, and major achievements of the Aztec nation and explains the probable cause of its overwhelming defeat by the Spaniards in 1521. Numerous detailed drawings, some reproduced from native codices, authentically depict Aztecan architecture, customs, and life." Booklist

Bleeker, Sonia
The Apache Indians; raiders of the Southwest; illus. by Althea Karr. Morrow 1951 157p illus map lib. bdg. $4.59 (4-6)   970.3
1 Apache Indians
ISBN 0-688-31046-X
"Most of the book is given over to the customs of the Apaches, their home life, sports and contests, religious ceremonies, [and] crafts." Wis Library Bul
"The author's method is purely informative but in aiming at a younger audience she cleverly turns her descriptions into living incident. Many sketches offer authentic details." N Y Her Trib Bks

The Aztec; Indians of Mexico; illus. by Kisa Sasaki. Morrow 1963 160p illus maps lib. bdg. $4.59 (4-6)
970.3
1 Aztecs
ISBN 0-688-31057-5
A history of the Aztec Empire in Mexico before conquest by the Spaniards and a discussion of the Aztec civilization. A final chapter discusses the Aztecs living today
"Another volume in the anthropologist-author's excellent series of books about Indian tribes and cultural patterns. The writing is sedate, the material colorful; illustrations give information about architectural detail, clothing, and ceremonial occasions. . . . An index is appended." Chicago. Children's Bk Center

The Cherokee; Indians of the mountains; illus. by Althea Karr. Morrow 1952 159p illus maps lib. bdg. $4.59 (4-7)   970.3
1 Cherokee Indians
ISBN 0-688-31160-1
An account of the Cherokee who lived in the mountains of southeastern America—their "life, customs,

Bleeker, Sonia—*Continued*
and beliefs before the coming of the white man, the leader Sequoya's development of a written language, the uniting of the Cherokee Nation, the enforced march into exile, and mention of present-day life. Good reading as well as useful supplementary material; well illustrated." Booklist

Included is a chapter on their famous ball game, lacrosse

The Chippewa Indians; rice gatherers of the Great Lakes; illus. by Patricia Boodell. Morrow 1955 157p illus map lib. bdg. $4.59 (4-6) 970.3

1 Chippewa Indians
ISBN 0-688-31167-9
"Through the activities of one family, the author pictures the Chippewa way of life, their homes, food, games, customs, legends and ceremonies. As wild rice formed the staple item in the Chippewa diet, its growth, harvesting, and use are described in some detail. . . . The author presents accurate information in a well-planned text." Ontario Library Rev

The "last chapter on plight of the Chippewa today, presented in sympathetic, honest tone, includes map of reservations. Black-and-white line drawings by Patricia Boodell show culture accurately." Library J

The Crow Indians; hunters of the northern plains; illus. by Althea Karr. Morrow 1953 156p illus maps lib. bdg. $4.95 (4-6) 970.3

1 Crow Indians
ISBN 0-688-21202-6
An account of the Crow Indians from their wandering buffalo hunting existence before the white man came to their present day reservation life. It describes, among other things, various uses made of the buffalo, organization of the buffalo hunts after the introduction of the horse, dress, customs and legends of these Indians

The author "combines exciting action with many facts about an Indian tribe. She uses material of fairly adult tone, but writes in an easy reading style." N Y Her Trib Bks

The Delaware Indians; eastern fishermen and farmers; illus. by Patricia Boodell. Morrow 1953 160p illus map lib. bdg. $4.59 (4-6) 970.3

1 Delaware Indians
ISBN 0-688-31230-6
The fishing, clamming, hunting, and canoeing of these Indians, who lived near the Atlantic Ocean and along the Delaware River, are described. The tribe's typical habits and customs, legends and ceremonies, are presented through the eyes of one particular family and its children

"Useful and readable. . . . The history of the tribe from 1683 to the present is given in two final chapters." Cur Ref Bks

Horsemen of the western plateaus; the Nez Perce Indians; illus. by Patricia Boodell. Morrow 1957 157p illus map lib. bdg. $4.59 (4-6) 970.3

1 Nez Percé Indians
ISBN 0-688-31403-1
As in many of the other books about Indians by this author "the style is semi-fictionalized, with the everyday life, customs, beliefs, and activities shown through the experiences of a typical member of the tribe, usually a young man. In this volume the emphasis is on the period in the life of the Nez Perce Indians, after they had acquired horses from the white man and up to the time when their land began to be overrun by gold-miners. The last chapter sums up Chief Joseph's life, the final forcing of the tribe on to a

reservation, and a brief look at the Nez Perce of today. The illustrations are attractive." Chicago. Children's Bk Center

Indians of the longhouse; the story of the Iroquois; illus. by Althea Karr. Morrow 1950 160p illus maps lib. bdg. $4.59 (4-6) 970.3

1 Iroquois Indians
ISBN 0-688-31453-8
"A concisely written account. . . . Describes, through the four seasons, the various aspects of village life—farming and hunting, food, clothing, tools, weapons, festivals, ceremonies. A final chapter discusses the Iroquois since the early 1600's. Many drawings add interest and value to a book which will be especially useful as supplementary reading." Booklist

The Maya; Indians of Central America; illus. by Kisa Sasaki. Morrow 1961 160p illus map lib. bdg. $4.59 (4-6) 970.3

1 Mayas
ISBN 0-688-31461-9
"A first chapter gives background information about the location of Mayan peoples, describes the most important facts about the culture, and mentions some of the archeological exploration in the area. The major part of the book is devoted to a detailed report on the early life of the Mayan Indians: religion, recreation, clothing, mores, etc. The last chapter gives an historical overview of the Maya and of their subjugation by Spanish explorers. The appended index indicates illustrations by use of an asterisk; illustrations are like the text, detailed and informative." Chicago. Children's Bk Center

The Navajo; herders, weavers, and silversmiths; illus. by Patricia Boodell. Morrow 1958 159p illus map lib. bdg. $4.59 (4-6) 970.3

1 Navaho Indians
ISBN 0-688-31456-2
"Through an interesting narrative about a thirteen-year-old boy and his family, [this book] describes life on a modern reservation, Navaho customs, beliefs, special ceremonies, sand painting, and silversmithing. A final chapter considers briefly the history and present status of the Navaho." Booklist

"Although the narrative presentation is simple, it is convincing and conveys the dignity and sensitivity of these people. It is a sympathetic picture of the modern Indian's plight." Sat Rev

The Pueblo Indians; farmers of the Rio Grande; illus. by Patricia Boodell. Morrow 1955 155p illus map lib. bdg. $4.59 (4-6) 970.3

1 Pueblo Indians
ISBN 0-688-31454-6
"The life and customs of the Pueblo Indians in the times before the Spanish conquest, described in the careful and sympathetic manner of . . . this author. She pictures their farming methods, hunting, trading, crafts and ceremonies. In the last two chapters, she tells briefly of the coming of the Spaniards, and of their influence as seen in Pueblo customs today." Ontario Library Rev

"Slight story woven into the descriptions and traditional legends adds interest. Black-and-white line drawings by Patricia Boodell illustrate the dress and artifacts accurately. . . . Index, list, and map of the chief pueblos of the Rio Grande." Library J

The Seminole Indians; illus. by Althea Karr. Morrow 1954 156p illus map $4.95 (4-6) 970.3

1 Seminole Indians 2 Osceola, Seminole chief
ISBN 0-688-21455-X
An account of the past and present life of the Seminole Indians. The events of the early chapters

Bleeker, Sonia—*Continued*

are seen through the eyes of Little Owl, who later became the famous chief, Osceola. The tragic history of the Seminole Wars is followed by an account of the forced removal of thousands of Seminole from Florida to lands beyond the Mississippi

This book follows the author's "usual, intelligent pattern, alternating facts with story in a way that has proved very appealing to readers. . . . Large type, many informative line cuts, a pleasant small size." N Y Her Trib Bks

The Sioux Indians; hunters and warriors of the plains; illus. by Kisa Sasaki. Morrow 1962 160p illus maps lib. bdg. $4.59 (4-6)   970.3

1 Dakota Indians

ISBN 0-688-31457-0

In a straightforward style the author "deals with the life, customs, and beliefs of the Sioux Indians from the time of their migration to the Great Plains in the middle 1700's through their last battle with the U.S. Army in 1890. The book also touches upon the life of the Siouan people today and their immediate problems." Booklist

"There has been plenty of writing on this very subject, but the compact presentation here should make the book a favorite for schools and libraries. . . . There is enough on the early history of [the] Sioux and their present situation to give the picture depth. The illustrations are factual and interesting." N Y Times Bk Rev

Clark, Ann Nolan

Circle of seasons; illus. by W. T. Mars. Farrar, Straus 1970 113p illus $4.95 (5-7)   970.3

1 Pueblo Indians—Social life and customs 2 Rites and ceremonies

ISBN 0-374-31287-7

"A Bell book"

"In a book on Pueblo Indian ceremonial customs drawn mainly from the Tewa people, [the author] describes the special rituals, games, dances, and other activities which mark the observance of seasonal changes and particular days throughout the year. She discusses the background and meaning as well as the outward form of these ceremonies which combine both Indian and Christian traditions. . . . The detailed account, based on the author's firsthand knowledge and deep appreciation of the Indian way of life, gives remarkable insight into the Pueblos' attitude toward time and their close relationship with nature." Booklist

In my mother's house; illus. by Velino Herrera. Viking 1951 56p illus lib. bdg. $5.95 (1-4)   970.3

1 Tewa Indians

ISBN 0-670-39593-5

First published 1941

The story of the day-to-day life of the Tewa Indians of Tesuque pueblo near Santa Fe

"Indian children helped make the book, helped write the short sentences. . . . Illustrations by Velino Herrera add distinction; he uses tribal designs in addition to numerous drawings in black and white and lovely soft color, all illustrating Tewa Indian life." Library J

"The more one weighs relative importance of text and pictures the more one realizes that, while there have been other pictures as beautiful, it would be hard to find use of words—call it poetry or prose as you prefer—carrying a beautiful meaning more clearly to a young mind: what life means to a primitive community, close to earth and sky." N Y Her Trib Bks

Elting, Mary

The Hopi way; illus. by Louis Mofsie. Evans, M.&Co. distributed in association with Lippincott 1969 63p illus $3.95 (2-4)   970.3

1 Hopi Indians

ISBN 0-87131-097-X

This story "tells how Louis Mofsie, a Hopi Indian who was born and raised in New York City, spends a summer in his ancestral Hopi village in Arizona." Cooperative Children's Bk Center. Materials on Indians of North Am

"While the matter-of-fact style tends to make the book more informational than entertaining, Mofsie's account of what it meant to him to share in daily activities and celebration with his Hopi relatives and . . . [the] clear, simple drawings of events effectively interpret the Hopi way of life for young readers." Booklist

Hopi words in this book: p63

Erdoes, Richard

The Pueblo Indians; with illus. and photographs by the author. Funk [1969 c1967] 128p illus map (The Young Reader's Indian lib) $5.95 (5-7)   970.3

1 Pueblo Indians

ISBN 0-308-80044-3

These Indians "live in villages, many of them on tops of mesas, or 'table mountains' in the desert country of Arizona and New Mexico. [The author] briefly relates the history of these Indians and shows a real sympathy to their ideals and customs, which they are pridefully striving to preserve in spite of the incursions of modern commercialism. The book is well illustrated and should be a popular and properly informative book for the school library." Best Sellers

Suggested reading: p125

Floethe, Louise Lee

The Indian and his pueblo; with pictures by Richard Floethe. Scribner 1960 unp illus lib. bdg. $5.95 (1-3)   970.3

1 Pueblo Indians

ISBN 0-684-12397-5

"In this brief picture-book account of the life of the [New Mexican] Pueblo Indians, from the building of the pueblo to ceremonial dances, both the old ways and the new are described. . . . Each page of straightforward factual text is faced by a full-page drawing pleasing in design and color. Large print." Booklist

Goble, Paul

Lone Bull's horse raid [by] Paul and Dorothy Goble; pictures by Paul Goble. Bradbury Press 1973 unp illus $7.95 (3-6)   970.3

1 Dakota Indians

ISBN 0-87888-059-3

"This story tells of Lone Bull's first horse raid and the battle it led to, which enabled Lone Bull to stand before his people as a warrior. In addition to factual material about how an Indian horseraiding party operated, insight is provided into the values and culture of a society that idealized the warrior." Sch Library J

"Based on the art of the Plains Indians, the detailed panoramic spreads and smaller scenes of horsemen and tipis are full of rhythmic design and driving movement." Horn Bk

Includes bibliography

Kirk, Ruth

Hunters of the whale; an adventure in Northwest Coast archaeology, by Ruth Kirk with Richard D. Daugherty; photographs by Ruth and Louis Kirk. Morrow 1974 160p illus maps $5.95, lib. bdg. $5.11 (6-7)   970.3

1 Ozette Indian Village 2 Makah Indians—Antiquities

ISBN 0-688-20109-1; 0-688-30109-6

This is a description of "the natives of the Makah

Kirk, Ruth—*Continued*
Indian village of Ozette, Washington, as they strive to dig up and preserve records of their past. With the help of archaeologist, Richard Daugherty, and a crew of 25 college students from across the country, the Indians unearthed, preserved and catalogued over 20,000 artifacts, some as old as 6000 years." Babbling Bookworm

"The text and the photographs offer all the excitement and suspense of a superior detective story which should appeal to all readers, whether or not they are interested in archeology, anthropology and related subjects." Pub W

Price, Christine
Heirs of the ancient Maya; a portrait of the Lacandon Indians; photographs by Gertrude Duby Blom. Scribner 1972 64p illus map lib. bdg. $5.95 (5-7)
970.3
1 Lacandon Indians
ISBN 0-684-12811-X
The Lacandon Indians, descendants of the Mayas, live mostly in two settlements in the Mexican state of Chiapas—near Lake Nahá and on the banks of the Lacanhá River—where they preserve a way of life little affected by modern influences. This introduction to their life and culture focuses on the Nahá settlement

A "beautifully produced book. . . . The text is lyrical and appreciative, but carefully wrought and controlled. Taken as a whole, the book is a highly successful verbal and visual essay in which beauty and humanity are commingled." Horn Bk

Reit, Seymour
Child of the Navajos; photographs by Paul Conklin. Dodd 1971 64p illus lib. bdg. $4.50 (2-4) 970.3
1 Navaho Indians
ISBN 0-396-06414-0
This is the story of Jerry Begay, a nine-year-old Navajo boy living on the tribe's reservation in Arizona. The reader follows Jerry through his third-grade school activities, sees him at home helping with family chores, and joins him in exploring Black Mesa, the harsh terrain that is his home

Steiner, Stan
The Tiguas; the lost tribe of city Indians. Crowell-Collier Press 1972 90p illus lib. bdg. $4.95 (4-7)
970.3
1 Tigua Indians
This is the story of an Indian tribe thought to be extinct, but secretly living in El Paso, Texas, since 1682, preserving their ancient ways in a modern city

"The lively text, though simple, includes enough Indian words to challenge interested students. The black-and-white photographs showing housing, people at work, the cemetery, the church, etc. reinforce the account, which will be useful where the history of minority groups is taught." Sch Library J

Wood, Nancy
Hollering sun; photographs by Myron Wood. Simon & Schuster 1972 unp illus lib. bdg. $4.95 (4-7)
970.3
1 Taos Indians
ISBN 0-671-65192-7
"An effective evocation in text and photographs of the Indian way of looking at life as reflected in the thought of the Taos Indians collected by the author over a 10-year period and written down as poems, aphorisms, and sayings. The introduction gives a historical sketch of the Taos Indians; the main text

encompasses legend, superstition, philosophy of life, and veneration of nature; and the handsome photographs picture the Indian community, the countryside, and its wildlife." Booklist

"This is both a history of the Indians of the Taos Pueblo and a compilation of their poetic legends and beliefs. . . . The material is divided into 'The Legends,' 'The Village,' and 'Nature,' but there is an awareness of—and respect for—nature in all its forms that pervades all of the text." Chicago. Children's Bk Center

970.4 Indians in specific places

Baylor, Byrd
When clay sings; illus. by Tom Bahti. Scribner 1972 unp illus lib. bdg. $5.95 (1-4) 970.4
1 Indians of North America—Art 2 Indians of North America—Southwest, New 3 Pottery
ISBN 0-684-12807-1
By putting together pieces of pottery, the reader can reconstruct what the Indian way of life might have been like in the times when the pottery was made

"Every piece of clay, Indian parents tell children who find shards, should be treated with respect, since it was a part of somebody's life. They even say it has its own small voice and sings in its own way.' The pages, handsome in earth colors and black and white, show designs derived from prehistoric Indian pottery of the Southwest, and the text consists of what the children of today imagine about the four cultures (Anasazi, Mogollon, Hohokam, and Mimres) from which the clay pottery came. The book is dignified in format, the illustrations and text beautifully united, and the text both reveals the richness of the ancient cultures and hints, to the reader, the ways in which one learns about prehistory from artifacts." Chicago. Children's Bk Center

Bleeker, Sonia
The mission Indians of California; illus. by Althea Karr. Morrow 1956 142p illus map lib. bdg. $4.32 (4-6) 970.4
1 Indians of North America—California 2 Indians of North America—Missions
ISBN 0-688-31459-7
"Through the experiences of Little Singer, the reader sees the [California] Indians as they lived before the coming of the Spanish, and the effects on their lives of the establishment of the missions. No attempt is made to gloss over the injustices suffered by the Indians at the hands of the Spanish soldiers and priests." Chicago. Children's Bk Center

"Although the narrative framework becomes artificial . . . the information presented is of value." Booklist

The sea hunters; Indians of the Northwest Coast; illus. by Althea Karr. Morrow 1951 159p illus map $4.95 (4-6) 970.4
1 Indians of North America—Northwest, Pacific
ISBN 0-688-21458-4
"A useful and interesting account of the history of Indian tribes on the Pacific coast, in Alaska and in Canada, and a description of their lives today." Sutherland. History in Children's Bks

"An authentic record told with intimate details, a sense of family life and of the balance between work and play." Sat Rev

Ehrlich, Amy

Wounded Knee: an Indian history of the American West; adapted for young readers by Amy Ehrlich from Dee Brown's Bury my heart at Wounded Knee. Holt 1974 202p illus maps $6.95 (6-7)   970.4

1 Indians of North America—The West 2 Indians of North America—Wars 3 The West—History
ISBN 0-03-091559-7

This book traces the plight of the Navaho, Apache, Cheyenne and Sioux Indians in their struggles against the white man in the West between 1860 and 1890. It recounts battles and their causes, participants, and consequences during this era

"Basically a condensation of Brown's best seller. . . . Some chapters have been deleted, others condensed, and in some instances sentence structure and language have been simplified. The editing is good, and this version is interesting, readable, and smooth." Sch Library J

Bibliography: p193-96

Erdoes, Richard

The sun dance people; the Plains Indians, their past and present; written and photographed by Richard Erdoes. Knopf 1972 218p illus map $4.95, lib. bdg. $5.99 (5-7)   970.4

1 Indians of North America—Great Plains
ISBN 0-394-82316-8; 0-394-92316-2

In this book the lives of the Plains Indians are examined in both historical and contemporary contexts. The author describes the era when the Indians lived in tepees, hunted buffalo, counted coups, and fought against the U.S. Cavalry. He then tells of today's Indian, living on reservations in tarpaper shacks, trying to farm infertile land, having their children taken to government boarding schools, and dealing with the U.S. Bureau of Indian Affairs

"The book is well done, and filled with . . . fascinating information. . . . [It] is liberally illustrated with reproductions of old prints and paintings and photographs by the author. . . . Erdoes's versions [of some of the battles] are not the same as those in most textbooks. Chivington and Custer both wear the black hats of the villain, and high time." N Y Times Bk Rev

Farquhar, Margaret C.

The Indians of Mexico; a book to begin on; illus. by Mel Klapholz. Holt 1967 unp illus lib. bdg. $3.27 (2-4)   970.4

1 Indians of Mexico
ISBN 0-03-062470-3

"After identifying the first Mexican Indians as explorers who migrated southward during the ice age, a simply written book describes the Olmecs, the Toltecs, and, in some detail, the Aztecs, whose civilization ended with the coming of Cortes." Booklist

The book "reveals adequate research. The story, as the author tells it, is both entertaining and educational. The illustrations are attractive and accurate." Sci Bks

Le Sueur, Meridel

The mound builders. Watts, F. 1974 62p illus maps lib. bdg. $3.90 (4-7)   970.4

1 Mounds and mound builders 2 Indians of North America—Antiquities
ISBN 0-531-02717-1

"A First book"

"While the text makes references to other mounds and mound settlements, it focuses on those of North America, particularly the Adena, Poverty Point, Hopewell, and Mississippi structures." Chicago. Children's Bk Center

This book is "generously illustrated with photographs of the actual sites and diagrams locating

the remains of these prehistoric Indian cultures. . . . Although the author lucidly outlines the rise and fall of the mound 'cultures,' unfortunately she refrains from speculating on the origins and meanings of the intriguing artifacts and ornaments found in the mounds. As a result, readers will learn a lot about the structures but little about the people who built them." Sch Library J

Bibliography: p57

Marcus, Rebecca B.

The first book of the cliff dwellers; illus. with photographs; drawings by Julio Granda. Watts, F. 1968 90p illus map lib. bdg. $3.90 (4-7)   970.4

1 Cliff dwellers and cliff dwellings 2 Southwest, New—History 3 Mesa Verde National Park
ISBN 0-531-00501-1

"In this book [the author] tells the story of how the cliff dwellings of the Southwest were discovered by cowboys in the 1880's and how anthropologists solved the mystery of the construction and the people of these communities." Wis Library Bul

The book also "covers scientific speculation about that ancient culture, how its people conducted their daily lives, when and why they vanished. All of this is well documented with photographs." N Y Times Bk Rev

The cliff dwellings are now part of Mesa Verde National Park

Rounds, Glen

Buffalo harvest; written and illus. by Glen Rounds. Holiday House 1952 141p illus $3.95 (4-6)   970.4

1 Indians of North America—Great Plains 2 Bison
ISBN 0-8234-0016-6

This book tells "the story of the Indians of the Plains when they hunted the great herds of buffalo in the autumn. It is a detailed account showing how the buffalo were the sole harvest of the tribes, how they were food and shelter, clothing, utensils—everything that the Indians needed to sustain life." Sat Rev

"This lively, authentic chapter from our western past, expertly related, must also be prized for its strong, good-humored drawings." N Y Times Bk Rev

Scheele, William E.

The mound builders; written and illus. by William E. Scheele. Collins 1960 60p illus maps lib. bdg. $4.91 (4-7)   970.4

1 Hopewell culture 2 Mounds and mound builders 3 Ohio—Antiquities
ISBN 0-529-03581-2

The author discusses "the prehistoric mound builders, specifically the Indians of the Ohio River valley known as the Hopewell Indians who built mounds as burial chambers for their tribal leaders. Briefly and lucidly he discusses mound builders in general and archaeological methods employed in the search for and interpretation of evidence and describes the mounds and the culture of the Hopewell people as reconstructed by archaeologists." Booklist

971   Canada

McNeer, May

The Canadian story; with lithographs by Lynd Ward. Ariel Bks. 1958 96p illus map $5.95 (5-7) 971

1 Canada—History 2 Canada—Biography
ISBN 0-374-31023-8

"Handsomely illustrated [in black and white and four color lithographs] and excitingly written, this is an impressive book. Each brief chapter describes an explorer, a scientist, a typical Canadian or a period of

McNeer May—*Continued*

conflict. In this topical treatment of Canadian history, the author has been able to choose colorful instances and dramatic incidents; the reader is thereby given a broad picture of the new land that gives a historical panorama without the stolidity of textbook approach." Chicago. Children's Bk Center

972 Mexico

McNeer, May

The Mexican story; with lithographs by Lynd Ward. Ariel Bks. 1953 96p illus $5.95 (5-7)   972

1 Mexico—History 2 Mexico—Biography
ISBN 0-374-34950-9

"A skillfully condensed history from Mayan days to the present discusses not only the famous conquistadors, reformers and revolutionists, but the obscure and unhonored Mexicans, too. Short fictional chapters interpolated among many headed with celebrated names interpret everyday life: poverty, fiesta and market activity as shared by young people. Lynd Ward's brilliant full-page lithographs and numerous smaller drawings have great dramatic atmosphere and, like the text, reflect familiarity with subject and scene." Horn Bk

973 United States

Boorstin, Daniel J.

The Landmark history of the American people; illus. with prints and photographs. Random House 1968-1970 2v illus ea $5.95, lib. bdg. $5.99 (6-7)   973

1 U.S.—History
"Landmark giant"

Contents: v1 From Plymouth to Appomattox (ISBN 0-394-81259-X; 0-394-91259-4); v2 From Appomattox to the moon (ISBN 0-394-80290-X; 0-394-90290-4)

The first volume is "a facile and lively account, glib and chatty, which attempts to capture the essence of the American spirit from the first immigrant colonists to the Northerners and Southerners of the Civil War era. . . . The discussion of the Civil War is unusually interesting, as considerable attention is devoted to the workings of the Southern psyche, and the inflammatory writings of stubborn abolitionists get a resounding slap on the propaganda. Spotty in coverage, touching where the author's fancy lights, this [is an] engaging and informative book, with its excellent collection of old photographs, prints, and sketches." Sch Library J

The second volume "deviates from the usual compilations of facts and dates and discusses the people who influenced patterns of change, the American Go-Getters, Boorstin calls them. These were the energetic, ambitious, and inventive people who had come from many lands and who built the economy, made reforms, contributed to progress by their inventions, organized the farmers, built ever faster means of communication. The emphasis is on movements, regional patterns, national policies, and changing labor conditions rather than on political or military minutiae. Stimulating in its approach, informally written, and acutely perceptive." Chicago. Children's Bk Center

Commager, Henry Steele

The first book of American history; pictures by Leonard Everett Fisher. Watts, F. 1957 62p illus lib. bdg. $3.90, pa $1.25 (4-6)   973

1 U.S.—History
ISBN 0-531-00458-9; 0-531-02305-2

A "readable overview of United States history from early colonial days to the present time. Because of the brevity of the text the author has had to resort to some rather sweeping generalizations, but he has, for the most part, avoided misleading oversimplifications. The text will probably have more meaning for readers with some familiarity with the subject than for younger readers who are approaching American history for the first time." Chicago. Children's Bk Center

Grant, Bruce

Famous American trails; map and line drawings by Lorence Bjorklund. Rand McNally 1971 95p illus maps $4.95, lib. bdg. $4.79 (5-7)   973

1 U.S.—History
ISBN 0-528-32241-1; 0-528-80172-4

"Companion volume to Bern Keating's: Famous American explorers

An "account of 12 trails blazed across the continent by American Indians and early explorers, settlers, and cowboys." Sch Library J

"Bruce Grant's text, in clear, good type-size and Lorence Bjorklund's drawings (supplemented by color reproductions of works by Bingham, Russell, Remington, etc.) give an exciting and informative picture of America before the six-lane highways." Pub W

Hays, Wilma Pitchford

(ed.) Freedom. . . . Coward-McCann 1958 56p illus lib. bdg. $4.99 (4-6)   973

1 U.S.—History—Sources
ISBN 0-698-30093-9

"Reproductions of 26 significant documents, from The Declaration of Independence through the United Nations Charter; with a brief historical background of each." Subtitle

"Though of wide general interest, this will be especially valuable in history classes." Sat Rev

Johnson, Gerald W.

America grows up; a history for Peter; illus. by Leonard Everett Fisher. Morrow 1960 223p illus $6.50 (5-7)   973

1 U.S.—History
ISBN 0-688-21015-5

Second book in a trilogy, begun in: America is born

"This has a sweep, a scope, and a fresh approach that make it a joy to read. Mr. Johnson is both objective and sensitive; he explores the larger issues of United States history and the forces that move toward events. . . . The book begins with the formation of the thirteen colonies into one union of states, and ends with the United States about to engage in World War I. Again, in this volume the illustrations by Mr. Fisher are dramatic and powerful. An excellent and comprehensive index is appended." Chicago. Children's Bk Center

Followed by: America moves forward

America is born; a history for Peter; illus. by Leonard Everett Fisher. Morrow 1959 254p illus $6.50 (5-7)   973

1 U.S.—History
ISBN 0-688-21071-1

The first title of a "three-volume history of the U.S., this covers the period from Columbus' discovery of America through the Revolution to the Constitutional Convention of 1787. . . . [The] person-to-person style and the keenness and remarkable clarity with which the author explores and evaluates motives, causes, and effects make this a meaningful and excit-

Johnson, Gerald W.—*Continued*
ing book. Illustrated with many bold, dramatic drawings." Booklist
  Followed by: America grows up

  America moves forward; a history for Peter; illus.
by Leonard Everett Fisher. Morrow 1960 256p illus
$6.50 (5-7)   973
  1 U.S.—History
  ISBN 0-688-21018-X
  Third volume of the trilogy begun in: America is
born, and America grows up
  This book covers the crucial period, from 1917 to
the Eisenhower administration, that included the
League of Nations, the United Nations and two world
wars
  "Simple, fresh and exciting enough for a child to
read with pleasure yet heartily recommended for his
elders, it is filled with [the author's] strongly expressed opinions presented candidly but fairly." N Y
Her Tri Bks

Lawson, Robert
  Watchwords of liberty; a pageant of American quotations. New ed. with text and illus. by Robert Lawson. Little 1957 115p illus $5.95 (3-6)   973
  1 U.S.—History 2 Quotations
  ISBN 0-316-51742-9
  First published 1943
  Here are the words of great Americans in war and in
peace—more than fifty of the famous quotations
which highlight memorable moments in American
history from the time of the Pilgrims
  "Intended to give youngsters . . . a more vivid
sense of the great hours in our history, but a great
many grownups will enjoy and profit by it also."
Springf'd Republican
  "Illustrated with full page drawings in black and
white." Cleveland

Leckie, Robert
  Great American battles; illus. with maps, prints and
photographs. Random House 1968 177p illus maps
$4.95, lib. bdg. $5.99 (5-7)   973
  1 Battles 2 U.S.—History, Military
  ISBN 0-394-80297-7; 0-394-90297-1
  "Landmark giant"
  "America at war is skillfully mirrored in historically
accurate narrative and dramatic fictionized dialogue.
The author describes 11 battles from nine wars,
beginning with Wolfe and Montcalm at Quebec and
concluding with MacArthur at Pusan-Inchon, and
carefully details the immediate and long-range significance of each. Readers will enjoy the character studies
of such men as George Washington, Robert E. Lee,
Phil Sheridan, and Dwight Eisenhower, and will find
interesting the numerous maps, photographs, and
drawings depicting the evolution of military dress."
Sch Library J

Meadowcroft, Enid La Monte
  Land of the free; illus. by Lee J. Ames. Crowell
1961 151p illus maps $5.95 (3-5)   973
  1 U.S.—History
  ISBN 0-690-48454-2
  A history of our country from 1492 to the present.
The author "has recounted major events, brought
them to life through her warm prose and choice of
incidents, not cluttered with too much detail. Short
chapters, simple sentences and vocabulary, and Lee
J. Ames's many action-filled line drawings will entice
the reluctant reader as well as the less experienced
independent reader. Bibliography. Excellent index.
Clear, well-spaced print." Library J

Miller, Donald L.
  An album of Black Americans in the Armed Forces.
Watts, F. 1969 72p illus lib. bdg. $4.90 (3-6)   973
  1 Negro soldiers 2 U.S.—History, Military
  ISBN 0-531-01510-6
  The author notes "the accomplishments and disap-
pointments of black Americans in the armed forces
from colonial times to Vietnam." N Y Pub Library.
The Black Experience in Children's Bks
  Glossary: p71-72

Morris, Richard B.
  (ed.) Voices from America's past; ed. by Richard B.
Morris and James Woodress. Dutton 1963 3v illus ea
$4.95, set $12.95   973
  1 U.S.—History—Sources 2 American literature—
Collections
  v1 ISBN 0-525-42094-0; v2 0-525-42095-9; v3 0-
525-42096-7; set 0-525-42097-5
  Contents: v1 The colonies and the new nation; v2
Backwoods democracy to world power; v3 The twentieth century
  "The story of America, as told by those who were
there, the eyewitnesses and the participants. The
documents . . . consist of diaries, letters, biographies, memoirs, essays, and narratives—the raw
material of history. . . . We have sometimes—in
documents written in the seventeenth century—
modernized the spelling and punctuation. . . . We
have used complete selections wherever possible, but
occasionally space limitations have made cuts necessary in the original documents. Such cuts are marked
by spaced periods." Preface [to volume 1]
  "The form of the books is less austere than Commager's well-known 'Documents of American history.'
[The book has] . . . clear distinctions in type and
paragraphing, between introductory material and the
sources." Bk Week
  Each book includes: Notes on sources

Shapiro, Irwin
  The Golden Book of America; stories from our
country's past. Adapted for young readers by Irwin
Shapiro. With a foreword by Bruce Catton. Golden
Press 1957 216p illus maps $6.95, lib. bdg. $5.95, pa
$3.95 (5-7)   973
  1 U.S.—History 2 U.S.—Civilization
  ISBN 0-307-16833-6; 0-307-60833-6; 0-307-15998-1
  First published by Simon and Schuster
  A collection of stories adapted from articles in the
American Heritage magazine, and illustrated with 300
paintings in full color. The paintings are from old
prints and photographs, valentines, posters, book
jackets, etc. The sketches trace American life from
days of discovery to the beginning of World War I
  "Though episodic in the extreme this book could be
most useful in schools as the authentic pictures can be
studied and interpreted by both the able readers and
their weaker fellows while their alluring appearance
may arouse interest among the apathetic." N Y Her
Trib Bks

973.1   U.S.—Discovery and
exploration to 1607

Buehr, Walter
  The French explorers in America; written and illus.
by Walter Buehr. Putnam 1961 93p illus lib. bdg.
$4.79 (4-6)   973.1
  1 America—Discovery and exploration 2 Explorers
3 French in North America
  ISBN 0-399-60189-9

Buehr, Walter—*Continued*

The author "briefly describes the explorations of such men as Cartier, Champlain, and La Salle and discusses their influence on the settlement of America. Illustrated with maps and drawings." Hodges. Bks for Elem Sch Libraries

The Spanish conquistadores in North America; written and illus. by Walter Buehr. Putnam 1962 96p illus maps lib. bdg. $4.79 (4-7) 973.1

1 America—Discovery and exploration 2 Explorers 3 Spaniards in North America
ISBN 0-399-60595-9

Companion volume to: The French explorers

"The experiences, problems, and accomplishments of the Spanish conquistadores, particularly Cortes, who played an important role in the exploration and colonization of North America are described briefly." Booklist

"A succinct, impartial account of the Spanish explorations and a good general survey of the period. . . . Illustrations in black and white backed with brown are both informative and decorative." Sch Library J

Campbell, Elizabeth A.

The carving on the tree; illus. by William Bock. Little 1968 88p illus $5.95 (3-5) 973.1

1 Roanoke Island—History 2 America—Discovery and exploration
ISBN 0-316-12564-4

An "account of the brief life of the lost colony of Roanoke. The story offers vivid portraits of men such as Governor John White, who tried to get expeditions organized to save the small colony, and Simon Fernando, the captain who left the colonists on Roanoke Island against their own wishes." Adventuring with Bks. 2d edition

"Although the size of type and format of the book are suitable for a younger reader, events have not been over-simplified. The story is powerful and moving and should be read more than once. Effective illustration in gold, black, and white." Horn Bk

Dalgliesh, Alice

America begins; the story of the finding of the New World. With pictures by Lois Maloy. Rev. ed. Scribner 1958 64p illus maps lib. bdg. $5.95 (3-5) 973.1

1 America—Discovery and exploration
ISBN 0-684-13455-1

First published 1938

This book is designed to give young readers a connected view of the discoveries and explorations which led to the settlement of the New World. The narratives are brief. The stories of Leif the Lucky, Columbus, Marco Polo, Vasco da Gama, Ponce de Leon, Balboa, Magellan, Cartier, Coronado, Drake, and Champlain, are told, with some explanation of conditions before and after the white men came

"The chapters are written concisely and simply, but with color and the touch of drama which transforms history into a subject of living interest." N Y Times Bk Rev

Discoverers of the New World, by the editors of American Heritage, The Magazine of History; narrative by Josef Berger in consultation with Lawrence C. Wroth. Am. Heritage [distributed by Harper] 1960 153p illus maps $5.95, lib. bdg. $6.89 (5-7) 973.1

1 America—Discovery and exploration 2 Explorers
ISBN 0-06-020485-0; 0-06-020486-9

"American Heritage Junior library"

"Illustrated with maps, paintings, prints, and drawings of the period." Half title page

"Three hundred years of exploration by daring men of many countries, all seeking a short route to the Indies, are depicted with an authenticity we have come to expect in the series. Tales of accomplishment and avarice, of the familiar as well as lesser-known adventures unfold in smooth sequence. Illustrations, many in color, include reproductions of rare manuscript maps, paintings, prints, etc., from national museums. Useful in curriculum for both elementary and junior high, but fascinating reading for everyone." Library J

For further reading [and] Bibliography: p151

Duvoisin, Roger

And there was America; written and illus. by Roger Duvoisin. Knopf 1938 75p illus lib. bdg. $5.99 (3-5) 973.1

1 America—Discovery and exploration 2 U.S.—History
ISBN 0-394-90910-0

A narrative for young readers relating the early discoveries and settlements of North America made by peoples of many lands. It includes stories of Leif Ericsson, Columbus, Ponce de Leon, Hudson, the Pilgrims, Roger Williams, and others

"This account of finding America . . . is full of signs and wonders and yet of facts which give a true picture of this great adventure. The brilliant, glowing, illustrations and the short sentences add to the dramatic appeal and bring the story to the level of the young child's interest." Wis Library Bul

Golding, Morton J.

The mystery of the Vikings in America. Lippincott 1973 159p illus maps $5.95 (6-7) 973.1

1 America—Discovery and exploration 2 Northmen
ISBN 0-397-31247-4

The author discusses the various controversies concerning the Vikings. He also covers their background and way of life, their unique ships, and the navigational expertise which enabled them to explore and settle Viking Iceland, Greenland, and finally Vinland (i.e. America)

"Well illustrated with medieval and specially drawn maps of Viking explorations, this is both an excellent introduction to a fascinating part of European and American history and a wonderful tool in helping a young student understand historical problems. Author Golding is scrupulous in presenting both sides of all possible disputed questions—and with the Vikings there are many—asking the young reader to decide which evidence is strongest. He also adds intelligent bibliography notes for further research. Good pictures and outline drawings of Viking boats, implements, etc. A beautiful book." Best Sellers

Hirsch, S. Carl

Mapmakers of America; from the age of discovery to the space era; illus. by William Steinel. Viking 1970 175p illus maps $4.95 (5-7) 973.1

1 America—Discovery and exploration 2 Map drawing
ISBN 0-670-45439-7

This is a "story of mapping explorers from the time of Coronado's search for Cibola to the present. The author gives more than an account of the travels and hardships of the mapmakers. He discusses the initial needs for the maps and the effects that the finished maps had on the development of the country. A considerable amount of technical information about surveying and cartography is introduced in a way that does not interfere with the sense of adventure that the reader enjoys throughout." Sci Bks

Suggestions for further reading: p167-68

Lacy, Dan
The lost colony. Watts, F. 1972 87p illus maps lib.
bdg. $3.90 (5-7)   973.1
1 Roanoke Island—History 2 America—Discovery
and exploration
ISBN 0-531-00761-8
"A First book"
"Enhanced by many reproductions of contemporary engravings and other illustrations this is a brisk
account of the efforts sparked by Sir Walter Raleigh to
establish a colony in the 1580s on the island of
Roanoke off what is now North Carolina. The author
gives background information on the period,
Raleigh's position at the English court, and the first
abortive colony which alienated the formerly friendly
Indians. He describes the establishment of the colony
in which Virginia Dare was born and speculates on the
fate of the colonists, concluding with a brief look at the
site of the colony today." Booklist

973.2   U.S.—Colonial period, 1607-1775

Alderman, Clifford Lindsey
The story of the thirteen colonies; illus. by Leonard
Everett Fisher. Random House 1966 187p illus $2.95,
lib. bdg. $4.27 (5-7)   973.2
1 U.S.—History—Colonial period
ISBN 0-394-80415-5; 0-394-90415-X
"Landmark books"
The author "describes the events leading up to the
establishment of the colonies, including the lives and
characters of the men most important in each colony's
history." Library J
"Mr. Alderman writes smoothly, and the book will
(hopefully) stimulate young Americans to discover
more about the lively, complex world that existed
here before 1776." N Y Times Bk Rev
Bibliography: p176-80

Hall-Quest, Olga W.
How the Pilgrims came to Plymouth; illus. by
James MacDonald. Dutton 1946 115p illus map $4.95
(4-6)   973.2
1 Pilgrim Fathers 2 Mayflower (Ship) 3 U.S.—
History—Colonial period
ISBN 0-525-32388-0
The "story of the Separatists from the time they
first planned to leave England in 1607, through their
stay in Holland, to late in 1620 when as Pilgrims they
established their settlement in the new world." Library J
"Though, as the phrase goes, 'it reads like a story,' it
sticks closely to facts and brings out a sense of the
spirit of that memorable enterprise. . . . The voyage
is convincingly real." Weekly Bk Rev

Rich, Louise Dickinson
King Philip's War, 1675-76; the New England
Indians fight the colonists; illus. with photographs.
Watts, F. 1972 64p illus map lib. bdg. $3.90 (5-7)
973.2
1 Philip, King (Metacomet) Sachem of Wam-
panoags 2 King Philip's War, 1675-1676
ISBN 0-531-02453-9
"A Focus book"
In 1675, after a series of aggravations, the Indians of
the New England region, under the leadership of the
Wampanoag chieftain, King Philip, attacked the col-
onists
"This thorough, objective and interesting account
puts the complex factors that ignited the rebellion into

perspective and defines its social, historical and political significance." Sch Library J
A selected bibliography: p61

973.3   U.S.—Revolution and confederation, 1775-1789

The Battle of Yorktown, by the editors of American
Heritage, The Magazine of History; author: Thomas
J. Fleming; consultant: Francis S. Ronalds. Am.
Heritage [distributed by Harper] 1968 153p illus
maps $5.95, lib. bdg. $6.89 (6-7)   973.3
1 Yorktown, Va.—Siege, 1781
ISBN 0-06-020129-0; 0-06-020130-4
"The American Heritage Junior library"
This book traces the "military and diplomatic planning and strategy used by Washington and the French
allies to defeat Lord Cornwallis at Yorktown during
the American Revolution." Pub W
"A carefully, researched account replete with verbal and pictorial documentation. . . . Numerous quotations recording personal experiences of officers and
soldiers add color and vitality to the chronicle of historic events." Booklist
Further reference: p149

Bliven, Bruce
The American Revolution, 1760-1783; illus. by
Albert Orbaan. Random House 1958 182p illus maps
$2.95 (5-7)   973.3
1 U.S.—History—Revolution
ISBN 0-394-80383-3
"Landmark books"
An "overview of the causes, battles, and results of
the Revolution." Hodges. Bks for Elem Sch Libraries
"This very readable account . . . may well serve as
introductory material for a more detailed
study. . . . Events are viewed within the larger
framework of European history. [Illustrated with]
drawings and a section of infrequently seen photographs." Library J

Colby, Jean Poindexter
Lexington and Concord, 1775: what really happened; illus. with photographs by Barbara Cooney
[and] old prints and maps. Hastings House 1975 128p
illus maps lib. bdg. $7.95 (5-7)   973.3
1 Lexington, Battle of, 1775 2 Concord, Battle of,
1775 3 U.S.—History—Revolution
ISBN 0-8038-4292-9
The author provides an account of the events "at
Lexington and Concord in 1775 and also a record of
the sources behind the account. . . . In addition, the
book includes a summary of events leading to the war,
an annotated list of prominent men on both sides,
[and] a tour of Lexington and Concord." N Y Times Bk
Rev
"The volume does not include any unusual information or historical material not easily available
elsewhere; but the writing is brisk and light, and the
book has been enhanced with prolific illustrations,
which show everything from quaint drawings of cows
grazing on Boston Common to present-day photographs of historic buildings." Horn Bk
Bibliography: p122-25

Commager, Henry Steele
The great Declaration; a book for young Americans;
written and ed. by Henry Steele Commager. Drawings by Donald Bolognese. Bobbs 1958 112p illus
$4.50 (6-7)   973.3
1 U.S. Declaration of Independence
ISBN 0-672-50301-8

Commager, Henry Steele—*Continued*
"A distinguished historian, using excerpts from official documents, letters, and diaries, skillfully weaves together the story of the Declaration of Independence, explaining how it came into being and describing the men who discussed, debated, and finally drafted it. The text is complemented with pen sketches and reproductions of contemporary paintings and woodcuts." Wis Library Bul
"The narrative passages by the author (through which the quoted material is unified) are as moving and vivid as the proclamations and letters themselves." Chicago. Children's Bk Center
Bibliography included in Notes: p109-10

Dalgliesh, Alice
The Fourth of July story; illus. by Marie Nonnast. Scribner 1956 unp illus lib. bdg. $6.95, pa 95¢ (2-4) 973.3
1 Fourth of July 2 U.S. Declaration of Independence
ISBN 0-684-13164-1; 0-684-13035-1
The author tells "of the events that led up to the decision of the colonies to break with England, of the actual writing of the Declaration of Independence, and of its reception by the people of the colonies." Chicago. Children's Bk Center
"For the sake of clarity [the author] has deliberately chosen not to indicate the exact chronology of the signing of the Declaration. . . . [An account] notable for its compactness, its readability and its sense of history in the making." N Y Times Bk Rev
"The many full-page colored illustrations will help the young child to understand the meaning of this, one of the most colorful and dramatic of our American holidays." Sat Rev

Dickinson, Alice
The Boston Massacre, March 5, 1770; a colonial street fight erupts into violence; illus. with contemporary prints and maps. Watts, F. 1968 66p illus maps lib. bdg. $3.90, pa $1.25 (5-7) 973.3
1 Boston Massacre, 1770
ISBN 0-531-00996-3; 0-531-02326-5
"A Focus book"
"Examining British economic and political policies which aroused the anger of New England Colonists, the author explains the underlying causes and significance of the Boston Massacre. She gives a vivid, detailed description of the event and the subsequent trial of the British soldiers who were defended by Josiah Quincy and John Adams. Objective and factual in treatment, the book provides serviceable supplementary information on American history." Booklist
Bibliography: p63

Fisher, Leonard Everett
Two if by sea; written and illus. by Leonard Everett Fisher. Random House 1970 64p illus map $3.95, lib. bdg. $4.79 (5-7) 973.3
1 U.S.—History—Revolution 2 Revere, Paul
ISBN 0-394-80483-X; 0-394-90483-4
"The strong lines and dramatic contrast of dark blue and white illustrations are an attractive complement to the tension of the minutely described events of the evening of April 18, 1775. The book is in four sections, each giving an exact account, historically based and with some background information, of the actions of four men during two eventful hours of that night: Joseph Warren, who sent the message to Revere; Paul Revere, the young man who lit the signal lanterns, Robert Newman; and the commanding general of the British forces, Thomas Gage." Sutherland. The Best in Children's Bks
This is "an excellent example of how to build upon

and retain the essential nature of a widely known folk tale while sneaking up on the young reader with a variety of 'true facts.' The heroes remain heroes but far more real for having worries and foibles of their own; and the text, integrated nicely with pictures and a map, is a model of accuracy." N Y Times Bk Rev

Lomask, Milton
The first American Revolution. Farrar, Straus 1974 280p maps $6.95 (6-7) 973.3
1 U.S.—History—Revolution
ISBN 0-374-32337-2
This is an "account of all of the ramifications concerned with the American Revolution—the military, political, economic and social. The book is divided into three sections—the revolution, the war and the peace " Children's Bk Rev Serv
"This book about the turbulent years from 1763-1784 steers a clear course between over-romanticizing and over-denigrating the American Revolution. The author admits that the Revolution was not fought against royal tyranny and also counters Beardian arguments that it was mainly fought for economic reasons; he points to the propagandistic nature of the Declaration of Independence as well as to the sincerity of some of the colonists' actions. And he accurately records a number of points much confused by legend." Horn Bk
Bibliography: p267-71

Mason, F. Van Wyck
The winter at Valley Forge; illus. by Harper Johnson. Random House 1953 180p illus lib. bdg. $4.39 (5-7) 973.3
1 U.S.—History—Revolution 2 Valley Forge, Pa.—History
ISBN 0-394-90333-1
"Landmark books"
"The six long months of hunger, killing cold, and disease, the heartaches and despair suffered by General Washington's 'ragtag and bobtail' army in the winter encampment at Valley Forge are vividly reconstructed in this semi-factual, semi-narrative account." Booklist

Phelan, Mary Kay
Four days in Philadelphia, 1776; illus. by Charles Walker. Crowell 1967 189p illus $4.50, lib. bdg. $5.25 (5-7) 973.3
1 U.S. Declaration of Independence
ISBN 0-690-31485-X
The author reconstructs "the four July days of debate that preceded the adoption of the Declaration of Independence by the Continental Congress. . . . [She 'cuts'] from actor to actor—Thomas Jefferson, John Adams and many less familiar signers. Using original journals and letters, she describes what each man was like, his thoughts and problems, how he behaved from hour to hour in the taverns, lodgings, and meeting halls of Philadelphia." Bk World
Bibliography: p179-83

Midnight alarm; the story of Paul Revere's ride; illus. by Leonard Weisgard. Crowell 1968 131p illus maps $4.50, lib. bdg. $5.25 (3-6) 973.3
1 Revere, Paul 2 U.S.—History—Revolution
ISBN 0-690-53638-0
"A vivid present-tense narrative evokes the uneasy atmosphere of a city occupied by enemy troops and reconstructs the preparations for and details of Paul Revere's dramatic ride to warn Lexington patriots of a British attack." Booklist
"The historic ride is presented in a straightforward manner. . . . Satisfactory as curriculum-oriented background in history and supplementary informa-

Phelan, Mary Kay—*Continued*

tion to accompany Longfellow's poem [entered in class 811]." Sch Library J
Bibliography: p121-23

The story of the Boston Tea Party; drawings by Frank Aloise. Crowell 1973 113p illus $4.95 (4-6)
973.3
1 Boston Tea Party, 1773
ISBN 0-690-77653-5
This is "a detailed treatment of the causes and events of the Boston Tea Party on December 16, 1773. Phelan describes the town meetings and secret sessions in Boston, Whigs versus Tories, and the influence of such colonists as Sam Adams, John Hancock, and Paul Revere. The participants are pictured not as fanatics but as patriots who tried to find a peaceful way to resolve the issue of unfair taxation and turned to the tea party raid only as a last resort. Written in the present-tense, the mood of the period is evoked with striking immediacy. Frank Aloise's line drawings recreate the incidents with an exciting, on-the-spot quality. Quotations are documented, conversations have not been fictionalized, and an index and lengthy bibliography are included. For reference or read in its entirety, this is an important addition to accounts of the Revolutionary War period." Sch Library J

Taylor, Theodore

Rebellion town, Williamsburg, 1776; drawings by Richard Cuffari. Crowell 1973 212p illus $4.50 (5-7)
973.3
1 U.S.—History—Revolution—Causes 2 Virginia—History—Colonial period
ISBN 0-690-00019-7
Emphasizing events in Williamsburg, Virginia, this account of the colonial independence movement begins with Patrick Henry's speech in 1763 against the British Crown
"While the text is not cohesive, there are some moments of drama and a vivid picture of Patrick Henry as he develops from a rustic figure with a gift for oratory to a seasoned legislator who becomes the first governor of the state of Virginia. The book also makes clear how much of our Declaration of Independence (and other, similar documents in other countries) was based on the work of George Mason, whose Declaration of Rights for the Virginia colony was adapted by Thomas Jefferson." Chicago. Children's Bk Center
Bibliography: p202-05

973.4   U.S.—Constitutional period, 1789-1809

Lacy, Dan

The Lewis and Clark Expedition, 1804-06; the journey that opened the American Northwest. Watts, F. 1974 89p illus maps lib. bdg. $3.90 (5-7)   973.4
1 Lewis and Clark Expedition 2 Lewis, Meriwether 3 Clark, William, 1770-1838
ISBN 0-531-01048-1
"A Focus book"
This is an account of the expedition sent by President Jefferson to explore the newly acquired Louisiana Territory. It provided much scientific and geographic information and helped open the West to settlers and trade
Bibliography: p87

Morris, Richard B.

The first book of the founding of the Republic; illus. by Leonard Everett Fisher. Watts, F. 1968 64p illus lib. bdg. $3.90, pa $1.25 (4-6)   973.4
1 U.S.—History—1783-1809
ISBN 0-531-02313-3
A noted historian presents a simple, objective account of the years in early "America, highlighting the political leaders of the time, their opinions, agreements, and disagreements. Washington, Hamilton, Jefferson, Jay, and John Adams are discussed with their strengths and weaknesses. . . . The full page black-and-white scratchboard illustrations are strong and attractive." Sch Library J

Neuberger, Richard L.

The Lewis and Clark Expedition; illus. by Winold Reiss. Random House 1951 180p illus map lib. bdg. $4.39 (4-7)   973.4
1 Lewis and Clark Expedition 2 Lewis, Meriwether 3 Clark, William, 1770-1838
ISBN 0-394-90315-3
"Landmark books"
"This brisk retelling of a much chronicled event makes the 33 men and their amazing undertaking seem very real." Booklist
"The last chapter telling what happened later to the leaders is a satisfactory conclusion, leaving no loose ends. References to contemporary figures should lead to further reading. Format is excellent and double-page spread map showing the route is easy to follow and clarifies the material." Library J

Tallant, Robert

The Louisiana Purchase; illus. by Warren Chappell. Random House 1952 183p illus lib. bdg. $4.39 (5-7)   973.4
1 Louisiana Purchase 2 U.S.—History—1783-1809
ISBN 0-394-90324-2
"Landmark books"
The book "reviews the world situation which influenced Napoleon to sell the vast Louisiana territory to the United States and describes the negotiations which preceded the sale." Hodges. Bks for Elem Sch Libraries
"Altogether this makes a colorful and exciting chapter in American history." Library J

973.5   U.S.—Early 19th century, 1809-1845

Morris, Richard B.

The first book of the War of 1812; illus. by Leonard Everett Fisher. Watts, F. 1961 64p illus maps lib. bdg. $3.90 (4-6)   973.5
1 U.S.—History—War of 1812
ISBN 0-531-00662-X
This is an account of America's second war with England caused mostly by the British impressment of American seamen. The War of 1812 gave America her national anthem and such heroes as Captain Perry who turned seeming defeat into victory at the Battle of Lake Erie, and Andrew Jackson and his Kentucky riflemen who played a leading role in the American victory at the Battle of New Orleans
It is "a lucid account. . . . Illustrated with effective black-and-white drawings and several campaign maps." Booklist

973.6 U.S.—Middle 19th century, 1845-1861

Baker, Betty
The Pig War; pictures by Robert Lopshire. Harper 1969 64p illus map (An I can read History bk) $2.95, lib. bdg. $3.79 (k-2) 973.6
1 U.S.—History—1815-1861 2 Northwest, Pacific—History
ISBN 0-06-020332-3
It is the year 1859, and on a tiny island between the United States and British Canada, "a war almost begins when British pigs raid an American garden. All ends well when the islanders unite to get rid of the soldiers of both sides." Minnesota

973.7 Administration of Abraham Lincoln, 1861-1865 (Civil War)

Davis, Burke
Appomattox; closing struggle of the Civil War; ed. by Walter Lord; illus. with 29 Civil War photographs and drawings. Harper 1963 167p illus maps $5.79 (6-7) 973.7
1 Appomattox Campaign, 1865
ISBN 0-06-021401-5
"A Breakthrough book"
Based on the author's Gray Fox: Robert E. Lee and the Civil War, published 1956 by Rinehart
This is an "account of the few days before, during and after the surrender of Lee to Grant at the home of Maj. Wilmer McLean on Palm Sunday, 1865." America
Contemporary photographs of people and places are captioned in an informative and incisive way." Toronto Boys and Girls House

Duel of the ironclads; in pictures, by Fred Freeman. Editor and designer: Charles Mikolaycak; text by Carole Kismaric. Time-Life Bks. 1969 51p illus map $3.95 (4-7) 973.7
1 Merrimac (Frigate) 2 Monitor (Ironclad) 3 U.S.—History—Civil War—Naval operations
ISBN 0-8094-0950-X
"The dramatic battle between the 'Monitor' and the 'Merrimac' is recounted through vivid pictures on nearly every page. The concise narrative traces the month-by-month building of these new ironclad ships and climaxes with the actual battle—an unplanned confrontation in Hampton Roads, Virginia, on March 9, 1862. An excellent summary of the results (neither side won) and significance of the battle concludes the book." Sch Library J

Ironclads of the Civil War, by the editors of American Heritage, The Magazine of History. Author: Frank R. Donovan; consultant: Bruce Catton. Am. Heritage [distributed by Harper] 1964 153p illus maps $5.95, lib. bdg. $6.89 (6-7) 973.7
1 Merrimac (Frigate) 2 Monitor (Ironclad) 3 U.S.—History—Civil War—Naval operations
ISBN 0-06-021706-5; 0-06-021705-7
"American Heritage Junior library"
This "graphic reconstruction of the brief era of the ironclad vessel describes the building and develop-

ment of the armored ships and gives detailed accounts of the battles in which they engaged. The numerous sketches, photographs, paintings, and maps give a sense of immediacy to this period of naval history." Booklist
For further reading: p151

973.8 U.S.—Later 19th century, 1865-1901

Goble, Paul
Red Hawk's account of Custer's last battle; the Battle of the Little Bighorn, 25 June 1876 [by] Paul and Dorothy Goble. Pantheon Bks. [1970 c1969] 59p illus map $4.95, lib. bdg. $6.29 (4-7) 973.8
1 Little Big Horn, Battle of the, 1876 2 Custer, George Armstrong 3 Dakota Indians 4 Cheyenne Indians
ISBN 0-394-80158-X; 0-394-90158-4
First published 1969 in England
"Drawing from the accounts of actual Indian warriors who participated in the Battle of the Little Big Horn, the authors have created the character Red Hawk, a young Oglala Sioux, to tell the Indian version of Custer's Last Stand. Red Hawk's moving account of the warriors' efforts to fend off the attacking horse soldiers is contrasted and accentuated by the cold, factual passages, drawn from military records, which detail the movements of the cavalry." Sch Library J
"The illustrations, filled with drama, movement and occasional moments of stilness, are based on the work of Plains Indians of the period." New Statesman
Bibliography: p[62-63]

974.4 Massachusetts

Beck, Barbara L.
The Pilgrims of Plymouth; illus. with photographs. Watts, F. 1972 89p illus map lib. bdg. $3.90 (5-7) 974.4
1 Pilgrim Fathers 2 Massachusetts—History—Colonial period
ISBN 0-531-00776-6
"A First book"
This book traces the story of the Pilgrims and Plymouth Colony from the early days in Scrooby and the years in Holland until Plymouth joined with the Massachusetts Bay Colony in 1691. It treats their economy, relationship with the Indians, daily life and customs, government, law and religion
A selected bibliography: p84

Daugherty, James
The landing of the Pilgrims; written and illus. by James Daugherty. Random House 1950 186p illus lib. bdg. $4.27 (5-7) 974.4
1 Pilgrim Fathers 2 Massachusetts—History—Colonial period 3 Bradford, William
ISBN 0-394-90302-1
Only slightly fictionized, this is the story of William Bradford based on his own writings. Beginning with the young Will's decision to join the Separatists in Scrooby, England, the narrative tells of the travels of the Pilgrims to Holland and then to the New World, and of their adventures and hardships during the early years of their life there
"Humor enters into the story . . . dry, delightful humor. . . . [The account] is curiously timely." Sat Rev

Dickinson, Alice

The Colony of Massachusetts. Watts, F. 1975 87p
illus maps lib. bdg. $3.90 (5-7)   974.4
   1 Pilgrim Fathers 2 Massachusetts—History—
Colonial period
   ISBN 0-531-02775-9
   "A First book"
   The author "details the founding of Plymouth Colony, the life of the Puritans, and their outspoken
differences with England that finally culminated in
the American Revolution. [She] also points out the
much needed help and friendship which the Indians
gave the Puritans during their lean years." Sch Library J
   Bibliography: p83-84

Smith, E. Brooks

   (ed.) Pilgrim courage; from a firsthand account by
William Bradford, Governor of Plymouth Col-
ony. . . . Adapted and ed. by E. Brooks Smith [and]
Robert Meredith and illus. by Leonard Everett
Fisher. Little 1962 108p illus maps $4.95 (5-7)
                               974.4
   1 Pilgrim Fathers 2 Massachusetts—History—
Colonial period
   ISBN 0-316-80045-7
   "Selected episodes from his original history of
Plimoth Plantation and passages from the journals of
William Bradford and Edward Winslow." Title page
   "The selections have been judiciously abridged and
edited, with early syntax untangled, archaic words
modernized, and bracketed statements covering
omissions supplied to give continuity." Horn Bk

Weisgard, Leonard

   The Plymouth Thanksgiving; written and illus. by
Leonard Weisgard. Doubleday 1967 unp illus $4.50,
lib. bdg. $5.25 (3-5)   974.4
   1 Pilgrim Fathers 2 Massachusetts—History—
Colonial period
   ISBN 0-385-07312-7; 0-385-08297-5
   "The text is based on events cited in William Bradford's diary and the dates used are those of the old-
style calendar; a list of the Mayflower's passengers is
included. The story of the first Thanksgiving is told in
a businesslike, crisp style and includes the usual
essentials of religious persecution, pilgrimage, the
death of half the small company in that first grim
winter, the help of the Indians, the harvest and the
rejoicing, and the praise to God." Chicago. Children's
Bk Center
   "Comprehensive [and] carefully researched.
. . . The many illustrations (some in color, and some
in black and white) are handsome indeed, adding
informational details to those given by the text." Sat
Rev

974.5   Rhode Island

Webb, Robert N.

   The Colony of Rhode Island; illus. with contemporary prints and maps. Watts, F. 1972 89p illus map lib.
bdg. $3.90 (5-7)   974.5
   1 Rhode Island—History
   ISBN 0-531-00778-2
   "A First book"
   "Covers the period from the arrival of the first
settler, a recluse who is not credited with founding
the colony, through 1790 when Rhode Island became
a state after holding out for two years. There are also
sections on historical sights in modern Rhode Island, a
chronology, a selective bibliography and an index."
Sch Library J

974.6   Connecticut

Johnston, Johanna

   The Connecticut colony. Crowell-Collier Press
1969 136p illus maps $5.95 (5-7)   974.6
   1 Connecticut—History
   "A Forge of freedom book"
   "A crisp, straightforward account traces the exploration, settlement, and growth of the Connecticut
colony from the early seventeenth century to the
signing of the Declaration of Independence. Johnston
highlights significant historical events and personages, describes the daily life and character of the
settlers, and comments on Connecticut's distinctive
contribution to the development of a truly democratic
form of government. Illustrated with old prints and a
map and includes a chronology and tourist data on
historic places." Booklist
   Bibliography: p127

974.7   New York

The Erie Canal, by the editors of American Heritage,
The Magazine of History. Author: Ralph K. Andrist;
consultant: Carter Goodrich. Am. Heritage [distri-
buted by Harper] 1964 153p illus maps $5.95, lib.
bdg. $6.89 (5-7)   974.7
   1 Erie Canal
   ISBN 0-06-020100-2; 0-06-020101-0
   "American Heritage Junior library"
   "The problems in constructing the Erie Canal and
the place in United States history of the short-lived
canal era are made vivid with primitive paintings,
early photographs and brisk text." Horn Bk
   "A close historical and geographical examination. . . . The young readers will enjoy the story and
the usual good illustrations." Best Sellers
   For further reading: p149

Hults, Dorothy Niebrugge

   New Amsterdam days and ways; the Dutch settlers
of New York; illus. by Jane Niebrugge. Harcourt 1963
224p illus map $5.95 (4-7)   974.7
   1 New York (City)—History 2 Dutch in New York
(City)—Social life and customs
   ISBN 0-15-257030-6
   "This book tells how the Dutch founded the colony
of New Netherland in the New World and made their
capital city New Amsterdam and how New Amsterdam became New York City. But, in particular, this
book tells how the Dutch people lived in the days of
Peter Stuyvesant, when New Amsterdam was flourishing." Introduction
   "The early settlers come alive in this well-
researched account. . . . Detailed black-and-white
illustrations help to enliven the text. Appendices list
important dates, places where Dutch houses may be
seen today and extensive bibliographies." Sch Library J

974.8   Pennsylvania

Lengyel, Emil

   The Colony of Pennsylvania; illus. with contemporary prints and photographs. Watts, F. 1974 86p illus
maps lib. bdg. $3.90 (5-7)   974.8
   1 Pennsylvania—History
   ISBN 0-531-02721-X
   "A First book"

Lengyel, Emil—*Continued*
"This history of the Pennsylvania colony focuses on William Penn's founding of his 'holy experiment' and also discusses the Quakers, the Indians, and Benjamin Franklin's part in the Revolution. The events are portrayed clearly and accurately." Sch Library J
For further reading: p81-82

Milhous, Katherine
Through these arches; the story of Independence Hall. Lippincott 1964 96p illus $5.45 (5-7)   974.8
1 Philadelphia. Independence Hall 2 U.S.—History—Colonial period
ISBN 0-397-30785-3
Illustrated by the author
The reader is taken on a visit to Philadelphia's Independence Hall as it is today, while the author recounts the history and events it has seen
"While it is a picture book in form, with color on many of its ninety-six pages, it is not for young children, but excellent as a family book in which even adults may find interesting facts." Sat Rev

Miller, Natalie
The story of the Liberty Bell; illus. by Betsy Warren. Childrens Press 1965 30p illus lib. bdg. $5.70 (2-4)   974.8
1 Liberty Bell 2 Philadelphia—History
ISBN 0-516-04622-5
"Cornerstones of freedom"
In 1752 the Liberty Bell was first cast for the Pennsylvania State House in Philadelphia. Gradually the bell became a symbol of America's fight for independence. The author tells how Philadelphia's inhabitants gathered when the bell rang to discuss tax laws and freedom

974.9   New Jersey

Naden, Corinne J.
The Colony of New Jersey. Watts, F. 1974 80p illus maps lib. bdg. $3.90 (4-7)   974.9
1 New Jersey—History
ISBN 0-531-02722-8
"A First book"
"This illustrated account of the New Jersey colony concentrates on its founding, rule under royal government, and role in the American Revolution and the Constitutional Convention. Though well organized and objective, the treatment is oversimplified on occasion." Sch Library J
Books for further reading: p75

975.5   Virginia

Davis, Burke
Getting to know Jamestown; illus. by Tran Mawicke. Coward, McCann & Geoghegan 1971 72p illus maps lib. bdg. $3.97 (4-6)   975.5
1 Jamestown, Va.—History
ISBN 0-698-30130-7
The author presents the story of Jamestown, the first English colony to survive in the American wilderness, from its founding in 1607 to its destruction by fire in 1698
"The book is short, with adequate, descriptive illustrations on almost every page; the treatment is simplified but broad and complete. A chart of important dates is a helpful feature." Sch Library J

Lacy, Dan
The Colony of Virginia. Watts, F. 1973 85p illus lib. bdg. $3.90 (6-7)   975.5
1 Virginia—History—Colonial period
ISBN 0-531-00784-7
"A First book"
"A simple, well-written, compact history of colonial Virginia, from the establishment of Jamestown to the ratification of the Constitution [in 1788]. The format is attractive and the illustrations appropriate." Sch Library J
Books for further reading: p81

975.6   North Carolina

Lacy, Dan
The Colony of North Carolina; illus. with photographs and contemporary prints. Watts, F. 1975 86p illus maps lib. bdg. $3.90 (5-7)   975.6
1 North Carolina—History
ISBN 0-531-00830-4
"A First book"
The book traces the history of North Carolina from its founding in 1587 as the Lost Colony on Roanoke Island to the ratification of its constitution in 1789
For further reading: p81

975.8   Georgia

Vaughan, Harold Cecil
The Colony of Georgia. Watts, F. 1975 88p illus maps lib. bdg. $3.90 (4-7)   975.8
1 Georgia—History
ISBN 0-531-02774-0
"A First book"
The author "traces the history of the 13th colony from De Soto's search for gold in 1540 to the end of the Revolutionary War. Vaughan also ascribes proper importance to James Oglethorpe who founded the colony as a refuge for the poor, debtors, etc." Sch Library J
Bibliography: p83

977   North central states

Ault, Phil
These are the Great Lakes; illus. with photographs and a map. Dodd 1972 174p illus map $5.95 (5-7)   977
1 Great Lakes
ISBN 0-396-06607-0
A description of the Great Lakes area and 350 years of its history: from Indians and French explorers, steamboats and the growth of cities to the locks at Sault Ste Marie, water pollution, the St Lawrence Seaway, and atomic power plants
Bibliography: p171-72

977.3   Illinois

Phelan, Mary Kay
The story of the great Chicago fire, 1871; illus. by William Plummer. Crowell 1971 191p illus map $4.95 (5-7)   977.3

1 Chicago—Fire, 1871
ISBN 0-690-77671-3

This is an account of the famous Chicago fire of October 1871 which raged through the city for thirty hours leaving an area one mile wide and five miles long in ashes. It is also the story of how outstanding businessmen and ordinary citizens of Chicago joined forces to rebuild their city

"Regional or general interest in the Chicago fire . . . may be served by this book. Events are presented with a sense of their importance, and, in some cases, human interest; background of the city before the fire is fairly well handled. The book is written in the present tense, evidently in an effort to add drama or immediacy." Sch Library J

Bibliography: p180-84

978 Western states

Adams, Samuel Hopkins
The Santa Fe Trail; illus. by Lee J. Ames. Random House 1951 181p illus lib. bdg. $4.27 (5-7)   978
1 Sante Fé Trail 2 The West—History
ISBN 0-394-90313-7
"Landmark books"

"Partially fictionized account of the daring men, Spaniards first and later Americans, who laid the trail which opened up and developed the great Southwest. In particular it follows Captain William Becknell's wagon expedition, the first to make the journey, recounting succinctly and engrossingly, the hardships, discipline problems, and narrow escapes encountered on the trail. Throughout, the author . . . points to savagery by the whites matching that of the Indians." Booklist

Dorian, Edith
Trails West and men who made them [by] Edith Dorian & W. N. Wilson. McGraw 1955 92p illus maps lib. bdg. $4.72 (4-7)   978
1 The West—Discovery and exploration 2 Frontier and pioneer life
ISBN 0-07-017641-8
"Whittlesey House publications"

The author's "treatment of discovery and expansion across the American continent centers colorfully on famous roads and trails and on many trail-blazing pioneers who created history by making them. Most of these names will be familiar to western-minded children. With an easy command of detail she recreates activity on the trails to make the whole something of real interest." Horn Bk

Rounds, Glen
The prairie schooners. Holiday House 1968 95p illus map $5.95 (4-6)   978
1 Overland journeys to the Pacific 2 Oregon Trail
ISBN 0-8234-0088-3

Illustrated by the author, this book tells what it was like to make the grueling trek west from the Missouri River during the years of the Oregon migration between 1843 and 1868

"By vivid description and focus on minor incidents, the author recreates the lumbering prairie schooner and its occupants. Will be valuable for 'Northwest' history study and for entertaining reading." Bruno. Bks for Sch Libraries, 1968

"Lit with humor and gusto, both in the succinct prose and simple sketches." Horn Bk

978.7 Wyoming

Goble, Paul
Brave Eagle's account of the Fetterman Fight, 21 December 1866 [by] Paul and Dorothy Goble; illus. by Paul Goble. Pantheon Bks. 1972 58p illus maps $4.50, lib. bdg. $6.29 (5-7)   978.7
1 Fetterman Fight, 1866 2 Red Cloud, Sioux chief 3 Cheyenne Indians
ISBN 0-394-82314-1; 0-394-92314-6
Title on spine: The Fetterman Fight

"In 1866 the Federal Government attempted to secure land for a passageway through Sioux and Cheyenne territory in Montana and Wyoming [which] . . . threatened to disturb Indian hunting grounds. Although the U.S. Army attempted to protect the trail, the Indians constantly attacked the troops; finally, in an engagement called the Fetterman Fight, Captain Fetterman and his entire company were killed by Red Cloud and other Indian chiefs determined to protect their land." Horn Bk

"There is an illustration on almost every page, often a double spread, and the figures of Indians and ponies, cavalry men and foot soldiers are complete in minute detail, with action in every line. . . . The book concludes with the Fetterman battle, but it is so matter-of-factly told that it is not likely to bring on nightmares." N Y Times Bk Rev

Includes bibliographies

978.9 New Mexico

Folsom, Franklin
Red power on the Rio Grande; the native American revolution of 1680. Introduction by Alfonso Ortiz; jacket and symbol illus. by J. D. Roybal. Follett 1973 144p illus $5.95, lib. bdg. $5.97 (5-7)   978.9
1 Pueblo Revolt, 1680 2 Pueblo Indians
ISBN 0-695-80374-3; 0-695-40374-5

This is an "account of the Pueblo Native American uprising of 1680 against Spanish control in the Southwest, which was one of the few Indian victories in the history of white-Indian contact in America. Superbly organized by Popé and other Pueblo leaders, the rebellion represented the efforts of a people humiliated, oppressed, and exploited by the ruling class." Sch Library J

"The author presents the Indian's view of the battle for repossession of the American Southwest. Only the records of Spanish conquerors remain, painting the Indian in the colors of 'savage.' Franklin Folsom has attempted to end this neglect of an intricately planned and successfully executed revolution. The reader, quite sensibly, is on the side of the Red Man. . . . Additional tabulated information enriches an already excellent book." Best Sellers

Sources: p137-40

979.4 California

Chester, Michael
Forts of old California. Consultant: B. Ziebold; illus. by Steele Savage. Putnam [1967 c1966] 95p illus (Sagas of California) lib. bdg. $4.86 (5-7)   979.4
1 California—History 2 Fortification
ISBN 0-399-60181-3

"Information about California forts built by the Spanish, French, English, Russians and Americans and about the adventures of the early leaders. It is

Chester, Michael—*Continued*
written in an interesting manner with illustrations well-suited to the text. Index, bibliography and California chronology, 1769-1858, completes the text." Bruno. Bks for Sch Libraries, 1968

979.7 Columbia River

Holbrook, Stewart H.
The Columbia River; illus. by Paul Laune. Holt 1965 89p illus map lib. bdg. $3.27 (4-7) 979.7
1 Columbia River 2 Northwest, Pacific—History
ISBN 0-03-050995-5
"Along the Columbia River a great deal of history has been crowded into the relatively short span of years since the Lewis and Clark explorations in 1805. The river's role in the development of the Northwest is dramatic, and the parts played by the varied, colorful personalities—explorers, traders, loggers, fishermen, missionaries, outlaws, and empire builders—make a story sometimes tragic, often exciting." Horn Bk

Latham, Jean Lee
The Columbia; powerhouse of North America; map by Fred Kliem. Garrard 1967 96p illus map (Rivers of the world) lib. bdg. $3.68 (4-7) 979.7
1 Columbia River
ISBN 0-8116-6367-1
"The author reviews the stories of the discovery of the Columbia River by both America and Britain, describes the early fur-trading activities, chronicles the Indian problems, reports on surveys of the river, and tells of the modern power and irrigation projects." Sci Bks

980.3 Specific South American Indian tribes

Baumann, Hans
Gold and gods of Peru; tr. by Stella Humphries. Pantheon Bks. 1963 218p illus map lib. bdg. $6.29 (6-7) 980.3
1 Incas 2 Peru—Antiquities
ISBN 0-394-91198-9
Original German edition 1963
The "world of Inca Indians and of their mysterious mountain city of Machu Picchu has been recreated in the . . . detailed story of the everyday life of the people who lived in Peru during ancient times." Chicago. Children's Bk Center
Black and white sketches and colored plates show many Inca relics
Glossary: p202-13

Beals, Carleton
The incredible Incas; yesterday and today; illus. with photographs by Marianne Greenwood. Abelard-Schuman [1974 c1973] 191p illus $6.95 (5-7) 980.3
1 Incas
ISBN 0-200-71901-7
This is "a factually accurate account of the history of the Inca people. [There is] detailed information of everyday life. Information is interjected by tales and anecdotes of the people and relevant comments on change from past days of Inca supremacy to the position of the people today." New Bks for Young Readers
Bibliography: p179-80

Beck, Barbara L.
The first book of the Incas; pictures by Page Cary. Watts. F. 1966 78p illus maps lib. bdg. $3.90 (4-7) 980.3
1 Incas
ISBN 0-531-00558-5
"A serious and informative text, the plentiful illustrations giving many details of buildings, costumes, and artifacts. The author describes the pre-Inca cultures, the early history of the highland people whose record begins in approximately 1250 A.D., and the years of the great Inca empire, from the advent of the first strong ruler—Pachacuti—in 1438 to the time of the Spanish conquest in 1532. The book gives, in addition to the historical material, many facts about daily life, religion, mores, medicine, class and caste, engineering, et cetera. A list of rulers and of important dates and an index are appended." Chicago. Children's Bk Center

Bleeker, Sonia
The Inca; Indians of the Andes; illus. by Patricia Boodell. Morrow 1960 157p illus map lib. bdg. $4.59 (4-6) 980.3
1 Incas
ISBN 0-688-31417-1
"Beginning with an account of the probable dawn of the Inca power and prestige and their advanced form of government at the time of the Spanish conquest, the author continues with a description of their amazing road and bridge systems and of the people and animals who travelled on them. Other chapters describe home life, education, farming, crafts, beliefs and ceremonies of the Incas, with a concluding chapter on their ultimate destruction by the Spaniards." Ontario Library Rev
"The material is carefully organized and appropriately presented for young readers. Finely detailed black-and-white illustrations are in keeping with the simplicity of the author's style and purpose." Sat Rev
Recommended books about the Inca: p[159]

Glubok, Shirley
The fall of the Incas; designed by Gerard Nook. Macmillan (N Y) 1967 112p illus $5.95 (5-7) 980.3
1 Incas 2 Peru—History
"Abridged and adapted from 'Relation of the discovery and conquest of the kingdoms of Peru' by Pedro Pizarro . . . and from 'Royal commentaries of the Incas' by the Inca, Garcilaso de la Vega." Verso of title page
This is "a history of the Spanish conquest in Peru in the sixteenth century, unusual because it has been adapted from two contemporary documents. . . . [It is] not a full or balanced account, but that is not the purpose of the book, which is to give the reader the drama and immediacy of an eye-witness account and the colorful details of royal lineage. The illustrations are most appropriately chosen; they are ingenious and awkward pictures by an Indian who lived in Peru after the conquest. The pictures are effective and the format handsome." Chicago. Children's Bk Center

Pine, Tillie S.
The Incas knew, by Tillie S. Pine and Joseph Levine; pictures by Ann Grifalconi. McGraw 1968 32p illus lib. bdg. $4.72 (1-4) 980.3
1 Incas 2 Science—Experiments
ISBN 0-07-050078-9
This book describes the accomplishments of the ancient Incas of South America. It tells how they performed such activities as constructing suspension bridges and underground irrigation systems, building stone houses without cement and making maps. It also provides experiments for the reader to perform to

Pine, Tillie S.—*Continued*

enable him to understand how the Incas used what they knew in their everyday living

"Adult guidance will be necessary for younger children." Sci Bks

985 Peru

Glubok, Shirley

The art of ancient Peru; designed by Gerard Nook; special photography by Alfred H. Tamarin. Harper 1966 41p illus $4.50, lib. bdg. $5.89 (4-7)   985

1 Peru—Antiquities 2 Indians of South America—Art 3 Indians of South America—Peru

ISBN 0-06-022043-0; 0-06-022044-9

The art works pictures cover a 2,000 year span, from the very earliest cultures to the Chimu and Inca Empires, and the Spanish conquest. There are examples of pottery, textiles, metalwork, wood and stone work, and monuments

"The writing is simple and lucid, with professional authoritativeness but without technical terminology. The illustrations of art objects are stunning. . . . The text concentrates on the objects pictured, but in describing their uses or the ways in which they were made, also gives facts about their cultural matrix." Chicago. Children's Bk Center

998 Arctic islands and Antarctica

Owen, Russell

The conquest of the North and South Poles; adventures of the Peary and Byrd Expeditions; illus. by Lynd Ward. Random House 1952 181p illus maps lib. bdg. $4.39 (4-6)   998

1 North Pole 2 South Pole 3 Peary, Robert Edwin 4 Byrd, Richard Evelyn

ISBN 0-394-90327-7

"Landmark books"

The book is divided into two parts. The first describes the hardships of Peary's attempts to reach the North Pole between 1891 and 1909. The second deals with the first Byrd Antarctic Expedition, 1928-1930, with special emphasis on its scientific findings

"Readers will be entranced with this tale of brave adventure in our own century. Excellent drawings . . . add to the charm of this book." Chicago Sunday Trib

FICTION

A number of subjects have been added to the books in this section to help in curriculum work. It is not necessarily recommended that these subjects be used in the card catalog

Adams, Richard

Watership Down. Macmillan Pub. Co. [1974 c1972] 429p maps $6.95 (5-7)   Fic

1 Rabbits—Stories 2 Allegories

ISBN 0-02-700030-3

First published 1972 in England

"A small number of male rabbits, frightened by the imminent destruction of their warren, embark upon a hazardous exodus across the English downs in search of a new home. . . . These refugees are constantly beset by dangers and temptations, but fortunately they share among them the qualities of bravery, endurance and resourcefulness required for survival. In the course of their wanderings, these rabbits learn to care for each other, learn to work together. In time they find another warren, but the new community, lacking female company, faces the prospect of extinction. The search for female rabbits draws our heroes to a distant rabbit fortress ruled by a Fascist general of military genius. In two great battles our friends' outnumbered troops must prove their cleverness and courage." Newsweek

"An adventure tale about rabbits that has overtones of social comment, distinctive characterization, an intricate but sturdy plot, and a wonderfully flowing style. . . . The descriptions of the Berkshire countryside are poetic, but the most enthralling aspect of the story is surely the magnitude of the rabbit world, with its cultural patterns, tradition, folklore, language, and vigor." Chicago. Children's Bk Center

Lapine glossary: p427-29

Aiken, Joan

Black hearts in Battersea; illus. by Robin Jacques. Doubleday 1964 240p illus lib. bdg. $4.50 (5-7) Fic

1 Great Britain—Fiction

ISBN 0-385-07781-5

"Fifteen-year-old Simon comes to Victorian London to join a friend at art school. The rendezvous is delayed until Simon's search has led him to become entangled in discovering a Hanoverian plot against the good King James. In the course of his adventures Simon plays chess with the Duke of Battersea, takes Cockney Dido to a carnival, restores a painting, wins a scholarship, finds a sister, takes a balloon ride, outwits hungry wolves, and is kidnapped and dumped on an island." Sch Library J

"Like 'The Wolves of Willoughby Chase' [listed below] (in which Simon and Sophie are introduced) the new story, which moves from plotting against the king to kidnaping and shipwreck, and eventually to escape by balloon, is written with so much verve and ingenuity and presents such a variety of characters—typed though they are—that it keeps the reader fascinated and amused." Horn Bk

"There is a good deal of English slang which may make it rather slow going for some young readers but offsetting this, in part, is a strong element of mystery and danger." Pub W

Midnight is a place. Viking 1974 287p $6.95 (5-7) Fic

1 Great Britain—Fiction

ISBN 0-670-47483-5

"A boy and girl, Lucas Bell and Anna-Marie Murgatroyd, are homeless and penniless when Midnight Court burns to the ground. They had been living with a guardian, Mr. Randolph, who had won the estate and the town mill through chicanery from Mr. Murgatroyd. The children's only friend, their tutor, is Mr. Oakapple, who is burned badly and has to be hospitalized after the blaze which kills Randolph. The children earn their living at dangerous jobs but are lucky to find Lady Murgatroyd, the girl's grandmother." Pub W

"With her customary vivacity and inventiveness, the author has created another novel steeped in nineteenth-century literary traditions and devices. . . . The melodrama, which manages to avoid even a hint of sentimentality, never flags as it goes from incident to incident and reaches a happy ending." Horn Bk

Aiken, Joan—*Continued*

The whispering mountain; illus. by Frank Bozzo. Doubleday 1969 237p illus $4.95, lib. bdg. $5.70 (5-7)   Fic

1 Wales—Fiction

ISBN 0-385-06597-3; 0-385-04811-4

Set in a small Welsh town, this story centers on the theft and recovery of the fabled Golden Harp of Teirtu

"Joan Aiken has zestfully essayed a double parody of a Welsh legend and a picaresque tale, and succeeded beyond reasonable expectation. . . . [Her] sure touch enables her to dip occasionally into excesses of invented patois and broad character burlesque. The story, moreover, is richly diverse and extremely funny." Sat Rev

Glossary of Welsh words: p235-36. Map on lining-papers

The wolves of Willoughby Chase; illus. by Pat Marriott. Doubleday [1963 c1962] 168p illus $3.95, lib. bdg. $4.70 (5-7)   Fic

1 Great Britain—Fiction

ISBN 0-385-03594-2; 0-385-06398-9

First published 1962 in England

"Set in a country house in nineteenth-century England and related in the style of a Victorian melodrama, this story follows the adventures of two little cousins who are left in the care of an evil governess. The children are chased by wolves, and their parents are lost at sea. The wicked Miss Slighcarp sends them to an orphanage from which they escape and travel four hundred miles to London with their friend Simon and his geese. With the help of the family lawyer and the police constables from Bow Street Miss Slighcarp and her accomplice are outwitted." N Y Times Bk Rev

"The title is musical and intriguing; the story, an excellent spoof on Victorian books, will make adults laugh. . . . Young readers will probably take it seriously as an adventure story and not know it is tongue-in-cheek; a family might have a good time reading it aloud." Sat Rev

Alcott, Louisa May

Eight cousins (5-7)   Fic

1 New England—Fiction 2 Family—Fiction

Some editions are:

Grosset (Louisa May Alcott lib) $3.95 (ISBN 0-448-02359-8)

Little $5.95 Illustrated by Hattie Longstreet Price (ISBN 0-316-03091-0)

Set in New England, here are the "scrapes, mischief and fun of one girl and her seven boy cousins." Pittsburgh

"Filled with exciting and valorous action, humor, and truth the fantasy is completely convincing and has some of the appeal of the Narnia books." Booklist

Little women; or, Meg, Jo, Beth and Amy (5-7)   Fic

1 New England—Fiction 2 Family—Fiction

Some editions are:

Collins $8.95 Illustrated by Tasha Tudor (ISBN 0-529-00529-8) lib. bdg. $8.71 (ISBN 0-529-00530-1)

Crowell $5.95 Illustrated by Barbara Cooney (ISBN 0-690-50017-3)

Dutton (Children's illustrated classics) $4.50 Illustrated by S. Van Abbe (ISBN 0-525-33911-6)

Grosset (Louisa May Alcott lib) $3.95 Illustrated by Louis Jambor (ISBN 0-448-02364-4) (Illustrated junior lib) $3.95 (ISBN 0-448-05818-9)

Little $7.95 Centennial edition Illustrated by Jessie Wilcox (ISBN 0-316-03090-2) $5.95 (ISBN 0-316-03095-3)

Macmillan (N Y) (The Macmillan classics) $4.95, pa $1.50 Illustrated by Betty Fraser; afterword by Clifton Fadiman

First published 1868

The story of the New England home life of the four March sisters. Each "little woman's" personality differs: Jo's quick temper and restless desire for the freedom of a boy's life; Meg's hatred of poverty and her longing for pretty clothes; Amy's all-engulfing self-interest; and gentle Beth's love of home and family

The tale is "related with sympathy, humour, and sincerity. This lively, natural narrative of family experience is as well-loved today as when it first appeared." Bks for Boys & Girls. 3d edition

Followed by: Little men

An old-fashioned Thanksgiving; illus. by Holly Johnson. Lippincott 1974 73p illus $4.95 (3-5)   Fic

1 Thanksgiving Day—Stories

ISBN 0-397-31515-5

Text first published 1871 as part of the author's Aunt Jo's scrapbag

The author "tells of a critical day in the life of the Bassetts, a New Hampshire farm family. Parents and children are preparing for the great feast when word comes that Mrs. Bassett's mother is at death's door. When pa and ma have departed, the children take hold and begin cooking the dinner themselves. A day of adventures and misadventures results in jollity as the parents return home with good news that grandma is fine; the report of her illness was a false alarm." Pub W

"An old-fashioned story, replete with high moral tone and sentiment but tempered by homely warmth and Alcott's distinctive lawks-a-mussy humor. . . . Several recipes are included at the back of the book." Chicago. Children's Bk Center

Aleksin, Anatolii

A late-born child; tr. [from the Russian] by Maria Polushkin; illus. by Charles Robinson. World Pub. 1971 75p illus lib. bdg. $4.89 (5-7)   Fic

1 Family—Fiction 2 Russia—Fiction

ISBN 0-529-00732-0

Twelve-year-old Lenny's parents, who waited sixteen years for him to be born, love him very much. But they also protect him from family problems, and as Lenny sees it, from life itself. This story tells how the lively, Russian boy, remedies the situation

"Although a young male chauvinist, Lenny is still a lovable, vulnerable character whose good intentions bring unfortunate results. There are distinctly Russian overtones in this story written by a contemporary writer in the Soviet Union, but the experiences and emotions are universal." Horn Bk

Alexander, Lloyd

The black cauldron. Holt 1965 224p map lib. bdg. $4.95 (4-7)   Fic

1 Fairy tales

ISBN 0-03-089687-8

Sequel to: The book of three

"In this second of five fantasies set in the imaginary land of Prydain, Taran and his companions vow to destroy the Black Cauldron, source of power of Arawn, the Lord of the Land of Death. The forces of good battle evil in a tale of high adventure blending fantasy, realism, and humor." Hodges. Bks for Elem Sch Libraries

"Heroism, sacrifice and symbolic struggle give this a legendary flavor and make it memorable reading." Cincinnati

Followed by: The castle of Llyr

The book of three. Holt 1964 217p map lib. bdg. $3.59 (4-7)   Fic

1 Fairy tales

ISBN 0-03-048645-9

Alexander, Lloyd—*Continued*

"The first of five books about the mythical land of Prydain finds Taran, an assistant pig keeper, fighting with Prince Gwydion against the evil which threatens the kingdom. Elements of Welsh mythology are incorporated in a stirring tale, told in literate style and teeming with unusual characters." Hodges. Bks for Elem Sch Libraries

"Related in a simple, direct style, this fast-paced tale of high adventure has a well-balanced blend of fantasy, realism, and humor. Although the Welsh Mabinogion is the inspiration for the story and some of the characters, the incidents, mood, and characterization are more reminiscent of Tolkien's trilogy." Sch Library J

Followed by: The black cauldron

The castle of Llyr. Holt 1966 201p map lib. bdg. $3.67 (4-7)   Fic

1 Fairy tales

ISBN 0-03-057610-5

Sequel to: The black cauldron

"This is the third of a chronicle following 'The Book of Three' and 'The Black Cauldron.' Here Princess Eilonwy of Llyr, a true enchantress, is kidnapped and delivered to a wicked witch who wants to steal her secrets. To rescue Eilonwy come an assistant pig keeper who loves her, a bumbling prince, and other energetic characters." Sch Library J

"Although this third book showing the growth of Taran, the young Assistant Pig-Keeper, toward noble manhood may not reach the powerful heights of 'The Black Cauldron,' it has its own strong identity. Children can enjoy it without having to read the other books, but they will most certainly want the others once they have entered Prydain." Horn Bk

Followed by: Taran Wanderer

The cat who wished to be a man. Dutton 1973 107p $5.50 (4-6)   Fic

1 Cats—Stories 2 Fairy tales

ISBN 0-525-27545-2

"When his cat Lionel begged to be turned into a man for just a little while, the old magician relented, but exacted a promise that Lionel would return home without delay. Alas, neither foresaw that Lionel (a Billy Budd among thieves) would fall in love, would resent and fight against injustice, would rid the town of Brightford of its mercenary mayor. Nor did they know that the magician's spell-making would break down and Lionel remain a man." Chicago. Children's Bk Center

This is "a comic and ebullient fantasy; just right for reading aloud." Horn Bk

The four donkeys; illus. by Lester Abrams. Holt 1972 unp illus lib. bdg. $5.95 (2-4)   Fic

ISBN 0-03-089516-2

"Narrated in the style of a folktale [this] is the story of a lanky shoemaker, a rotund baker, and a dwarfish tailor (and a real donkey) who are delayed by controversy and misfortune on the way to a fair. Though they arrive too late to attend the fair, these human 'donkeys' have grown wiser by their journey's end." Top of the News

"Elaborate pen-and-ink and watercolor illustrations, full of humorous details, are reminiscent of medieval manuscripts, with lovely borders and illuminated letters. A difficult vocabulary will limit this book to better readers, but its dry wit will appeal to a certain group of young listeners." Booklist

The High King. Holt 1968 285p map lib. bdg. $5.95 (4-7)   Fic

1 Fairy tales

ISBN 0-03-089504-9

Concluding title in the chronicles of Prydain which include: The book of three, The black cauldron, The castle of Llyr, and Taran Wanderer

In this final volume Taran, the assistant pig-keeper "becomes High King of Prydain, Princess Eilonwy becomes his queen, the predictions of Taran's wizard guardian Dallben are fulfilled, and the forces of black magic led by Arawn, Lord of Annuvin, Land of the Dead, are vanquished forever." Sch Library J

"For those who have learned to love the land of Prydain, reading this last volume in the cycle will be a bittersweet experience. . . . The fantasy has the depth and richness of a medieval tapestry, infinitely detailed and imaginative." Sat Rev

The marvelous misadventures of Sebastian; grand extravaganza, including a performance by the entire cast of the Gallimaufry-Theatricus. Dutton 1970 204p $6.50 (4-7)   Fic

1 Adventure and adventurers—Fiction 2 Musicians—Fiction

ISBN 0-525-34739-9

National Book Award, 1970

"Steeped in an eighteenth century atmosphere, the fanciful story of a young musician who, having lost his position because of the harshness of the Royal Treasurer of Hamelin-Loring, goes off to seek his fortune. Sebastian meets a princess in disguise and devotes himself to saving her from a fate worse than death; he is aided by a mysteriously omniscient people's hero; he acquires a perceptive cat, becomes a clown, is given a violin with magical powers; he is imprisoned and saves his own life and the throne of the princess by playing the violin until the villainous Regent dances to his death." Sutherland. The Best in Children's Bks

The book "is all very eloquent, action-packed and ridiculous; but hybrids are the author's special talent. His prose is a disarming mixture of Regency grandeur and Medieval robustness. His plot uses and discards a dozen clichés of children's books without batting an eye. Most important, he knows how to write character in a way that can touch the heart." N Y Times Bk Rev

Taran Wanderer. Holt 1967 256p map lib. bdg. $5.95 (4-7)   Fic

1 Fairy tales

ISBN 0-03-089732-7

Sequel to: The castle of Llyr

"Taran, who has grown from a small Assistant Pig Keeper to a young man in love with a princess, goes off to find his identity. With no clue to his place of birth or parentage, Taran must ask for help where he can get it, and he is forced to meet an array of unsavory characters as well as some good, old friends. He doesn't learn who his parents were, but Taran learns something even more important: it doesn't matter who your parents are, but what sort of person you are." Chicago. Children's Bk Center

The author's "triumph is that while his plots follow a slashing heroic pattern, his quest is into the subtleties of manhood itself." N Y Times Bk Rev

Followed by: The High King

The truthful harp; illus. by Evaline Ness. Holt 1967 unp illus lib. bdg. $3.27, pa $1.45 (2-4)   Fic

1 Harp—Fiction 2 Fairy tales

ISBN 0-03-065635-4; 0-03-086618-9

This is a tale about king Fflewddur Fflam who yearned to be a wandering bard but failed his examination before the High Council of Bards. But the Chief Bard took pity on Fflewddur and presented him with a very special harp. Through his many adventures with the instrument, Fflewddur came to realize the truth about himself

This is "an enchanting picture book fan-

Alexander, Lloyd—*Continued*

tasy. . . . The illustrations match the humour and spirit of the tale in delightful colours of mulberry and green." Ontario Library Rev

The wizard in the tree; illus. by Laszlo Kubinyi. Dutton 1975 137p illus $7.50 (4-6)   **Fic**

1 Fairy tales
ISBN 0-525-43128-4

"When an overworked, orphaned servant girl with a firm faith in magic releases a displaced, crotchety enchanter from his centuries-long imprisonment in an oak, the impact on an eighteenth-century rural English village is at once chaotic and comic. Mallory, a determined, self-reliant female, is an apt choice as foil for acid-tongued Arbican whose wit is sharper than his wizardry, for he is out of practice because of long confinement. Arbican intends only to transport himself to Vale Innis, the Land of Heart's Desire, to which his peers have long since journeyed. But his inability to control his magical powers inevitably brings him and Mallory into confrontation with the villainous Squire Scrupnor. . . . The meticulously detailed, black-and-white illustrations effectively complement the story through their resemblance to eighteenth-century engravings." Horn Bk

Anckarsvärd, Karin

Madcap mystery; tr. from the Swedish by Annabelle MacMillan; illus. by Paul Galdone. Harcourt [1962 c1957] 189p illus $5.95, pa 75¢ (5-7) Fic

1 Sweden—Fiction 2 School stories 3 Mystery and detective stories
ISBN 0-15-250175-4; 0-15-655108-X
Sequel to: The robber ghost
Originally published 1957 in Sweden

Swedish Michael and Cecilia are "concerned with a mystery involving a series of thefts believed to be committed by teen-agers and with the deleterious effect of a bold, alluring, and sophisticated new girl on the camaraderie of their classmates and on their own longstanding friendship." Booklist

"The style—possibly due, or in part due, to translation—is faintly stilted, and in one classroom sequence there is a rather unsympathetic depiction of a teacher. Otherwise, the author has given an excellent picture of an adolescent group and the shifting relationships within it." Chicago. Children's Bk Center

The mysterious schoolmaster; tr. from the Swedish by Annabelle MacMillan; illus. by Paul Galdone. Harcourt 1959 190p illus $5.50, pa 75¢ (5-7)   **Fic**

1 Sweden—Fiction 2 Mystery and detective stories 3 Teachers—Fiction
ISBN 0-15-256527-2; 0-15-663971-8
First published 1955 in Sweden

"Two [Swedish] youngsters in secondary school, Cecilia and Michael, stumble upon the fact that there is something very peculiar about the new physics teacher. By the time the teacher and his accomplice have been caught in their plan to map fortifications, Cecilia and Michael have been involved in dangerous incidents, but have been instrumental in foiling espionage in a manner that is dashing, foolhardy, and not completely believable." Chicago. Children's Bk Center

"This far-better-than-average mystery story . . . has dramatic incidents, a continuously fast pace, and novelty of background. . . . The Swedish school life will strike American children as being interestingly like their own." Horn Bk

Followed by: The robber ghost

The robber ghost; tr. from the Swedish by Annabelle MacMillan; illus. by Paul Galdone. Harcourt 1961 188p illus $6.50, pa 75¢ (5-7)   **Fic**

1 Sweden—Fiction 2 Mystery and detective stories
ISBN 0-15-267804-2; 0-15-678350-9
Sequel to: The mysterious schoolmaster
Originally published 1955 in Sweden

Set in a suburb of Stockholm. "Investigating an eerie moving light in Nordvik Castle, said to be haunted, Michael and Cecilia solve the mystery of the ghostly apparition they have seen and in so doing stumble on the money recently stolen from the post office and discover the reason for the odd behavior of Bertil, the unpopular, arrogant new boy." Booklist

Followed by: Madcap mystery

Andersen, Hans Christian

The emperor's new clothes (2-5)   **Fic**

1 Fairy tales
Some editions are:
Addison-Wesley $5.95 With pictures by Monika Laimgruber (ISBN 0-201-00195-0)
Harcourt $5.50 Translated and illustrated by Erik Blegvad (ISBN 0-15-225918-X)
Houghton lib. bdg. $5.95 Designed and illustrated by Virginia Lee Burton (ISBN 0-395-06556-9)

A tale about the vain emperor whose only concern was his wardrobe. It tells of the clever rascals who pocketed the money given them to weave beautiful cloth for the emperor but did not weave any, his flattering courtiers who dared not voice their own opinions, and the child who pointed out the deceit as the emperor paraded proudly with nothing on

This favorite fairy tale "is really a gentle satire, but as usual, Andersen does not let the satire spoil the story. One thing which adds interest is the fact that it was a little boy who not only saw the truth but spoke it; a little child led them. Though this may be the point of most interest to children, to the adult the emperor's reaction to the child's revelation is a never-ending source of glee." Johnson, E. Anthology of Children's Lit

Hans Christian Andersen's The fir tree; illus. by Nancy Ekholm Burkert. Harper 1970 34p illus $4.95, lib. bdg. $4.79 (2-5)   **Fic**

1 Christmas stories 2 Fairy tales
ISBN 0-06-020077-4; 0-06-020078-2

This translation of the fairy tale is by H. W. Dulcken

Surrounded by the beauties of the forest, the little fir tree was unhappy and longed for its moment of glory. It came one Christmas Eve but it was neither what the tree expected nor wanted

"The delicacy and meticulousness of the illustrative details of this edition, beautiful in soft colors or in black and white, should please old fans and the felicity of mood should attract new ones." Chicago. Children's Bk Center

The little match girl; illus. by Blair Lent. Houghton 1968 43p illus lib. bdg. $6.95 (2-5)   **Fic**

1 Fairy tales
ISBN 0-395-21625-7

This is the "touching story of the lonely, shivering child who sees visions in the flames of the matches she cannot sell, and whose last vision is the loving grandmother who is dead and who comes to take the child. The illustrations are tremendously effective, the tiny figure lost and lorn against towering grey buildings and driving snow; even the glorious warmth and comfort of the hallucinations are pictured in muted tones." Sutherland. The Best in Children's Bks

Andersen, Hans Christian—*Continued*

The nightingale (3-5)   Fic
1 Nightingales—Stories 2 Fairy tales
Some editions are:
Harvey House $6, lib. bdg. $4.89 Illustrated by Anne
Marie Jauss. Has title: The nightingale and the
emperor (ISBN 0-8178-4581-X; 0-8178-4582-8)
Harper $5.95, lib. bdg. $5.45 Translated by Eva Le
Gallienne; designed and illustrated by Nancy
Ekholm Burkert. Has title: Hans Christian
Andersen's The nightingale (ISBN 0-06-023780-5;
0-06-023781-3)
Pantheon Bks. $2.95 Drawings and design by Bill
Sokol. Has title: The emperor and the nightingale
(ISBN 0-394-00133-7)
This is the "story of the Emperor's nightingale"
which entertained him with exquisite song. Replaced
by a gorgeous jewel-encrusted artificial bird, the
nightingale is banished from the empire, only to
return later to save the Emperor from sure death."
Pub W
"It is good to have this great storytelling favorite,
one of Andersen's most famous satires, all to itself."
Horn Bk

The Snow Queen (4-6)   Fic
1 Fairy tales
Some editions are:
Atheneum Pubs. $6.95 Translated by R. P. Keigwin;
drawings by June Atkin Corwin (ISBN 0-689-30018-
2)
Scribner lib. bdg. $5.95 With illustrations by Marcia
Brown (ISBN 0-684-12611-7)
The classic story of young Kay's capture by the
Snow Queen, and of his friend Gerda who rescues
him

The steadfast tin soldier (1-4)   Fic
1 Toys—Fiction 2 Fairy tales
Some editions are:
Atheneum Pubs. $4.95 With pictures by Monika
Laimgruber (ISBN 0-689-20661-5)
Scribner lib. bdg. $5.95 Translated by M. R. James;
illustrated by Marcia Brown (ISBN 0-684-12507-2)
A favorite among Hans Christian Andersen's
stories, this tells of the adventures of a tin soldier, and
his love for a little toy dancer

Thumbelina; tr. by R. P. Keigwin; illus. by
Adrienne Adams. Scribner [1961] unp illus lib. bdg.
$6.95 (1-4)   Fic
1 Fairy tales
ISBN 0-684-12705-9
Here is "Andersen's story . . . in an excellent translation. Stolen by a frog and befriended by a field
mouse, [a little girl only one inch high] finally flies
with a swallow to the land of sun, flowers, and fairies.
Many dainty illustrations with gemlike colors illustrate the text. This fantasy picture book will delight
young listeners." Adventuring with Bks, 2d edition
"Here we find the feminine counterpart of Tom
Thumb. . . . In this story we see how deftly Andersen
intermingles fantasy with folklore. He has taken the
theme of an old tale and touched it with the magic of
imagination." Johnson, E. Anthology of Children's
Lit

The ugly duckling (1-4)   Fic
1 Swans—Stories 2 Fairy tales
Some editions are:
Abelard-Schuman lib. bdg. $5.95 Adapted from the
story by Hans Christian Andersen. German transla-
tion edited by Phyllis Hoffman; pictures by Josef
Palacek (ISBN 0-200-71739-1)
Macmillan (N Y) $3.95 Illustrated by Johannes
Larsen; translated by R. P. Keigwin

Scribner lib. bdg. $5.95, pa 95¢ Translated by R. P.
Keigwin; illustrated by Adrienne Adams (ISBN 0-
684-12646-X; 0-684-13037-8)
A story about an ugly "duckling" who led an
unhappy life until he grew into a beautiful swan

The wild swans; tr. by M. R. James; illus. by Marcia
Brown. Scribner [1963] 80p illus lib. bdg. $5.95
(3-6)   Fic
1 Fairy tales
ISBN 0-684-12978-7
Text from Hans Andersen's: Forty-two stories,
published 1959 by A. S. Barnes
This is "the tale of the princess seeking to break the
spell that turned her 11 brothers into swans." Booklist
"The softness of swans-down, the steady sound of
surf, the solitude of a great wood, the elegance of a
King's palace, the purity of heart of a gentle princess—all these qualities have been caught to perfection in Marcia Brown's gray and rose pictures." Pub W

Anderson, C. W.

The blind Connemara. Macmillan (N Y) 1971 80p
illus $4.95, pa 95¢ (3-5)   Fic
1 Horses—Stories
The "plot involves Rhonda, a youngster who loves
horses but cannot afford one, and the horse who needs
the love and patience only she can give him. Rhonda
proves that even a supposedly worthless blind pony
will respond to affection and careful training." Library J
"Although the outcome may be anticipated early in
the book by most readers, it will probably satisfy all
who dote on horse stories. The soft black and white
illustrations are attractive, and the message of kindness to animals is worthy." Chicago. Children's Bk
Center

High courage. Macmillan (N Y) 1941 124p illus
$4.95 (5-7)   Fic
1 Horses—Stories
Patsy, young owner and trainer of Bobcat, bribed
him with carrots until he became a powerful, fast
horse. But Holley, the Black groom, was suspicious of
him. The day came, however, when even Holley
agreed that Bobcat was "somebody"
"The many action pictures are in Mr. Anderson's
moving manner; respect and admiration for a noble
horse gets into his drawings as much as into his
words." N Y Her Trib Bks

A pony for Linda. Macmillan (N Y) 1971 unp illus
$4.50 (1-3)   Fic
1 Ponies—Stories
Children "who love horses—and others, as well—
will find great charm in this picture storybook of a
small rider and her new pony. Linda, who grew up to
her father's promise that she should have a pony when
she was seven, found joy still greater when she met
another little girl with a pony. Each now had a friend
and could happily share a prize at the horseshow. The
lithograph drawings are superb, fully expressing Linda's devotion to Daisy." Horn Bk

Anderson, Lonzo

Ponies of Mykillengi; illus. by Adrienne Adams.
Scribner 1966 unp illus $5.95 (2-4)   Fic
1 Ponies—Stories 2 Iceland—Fiction
ISBN 0-684-20722-2
"Egli and her brother, Rauf, who live on a remote
farm in Iceland, go off with their ponies and are
caught in a severe snowstorm that has been preceded
by an earthquake. Alone and frightened, the children
must not only find their way home, but they must care
for the foal that is born during the storm. Doggedly

Anderson, Lonzo—*Continued*

fighting fear and fatigue, they at last reach the warmth and security of the family circle." Sat Rev

In this story the "use of the present tense destroys rather than emphasizes the sense of immediacy. The birth of a foal, however, in the midst of the blizzard is described with quiet effectiveness. The beautiful illustrations convey the isolation of the farm in winter, the darkness of the stormy night, the joy of returning home better than the text does." Horn Bk

Armer, Laura Adams

Waterless Mountain; illus. by Sidney Armer and Laura Adams Armer. McKay 1931 212p illus $6.95, lib. bdg. $6.50 (5-7)   Fic

1 Navaho Indians—Fiction 2 Arizona—Fiction
ISBN 0-679-20233-1; 0-679-25164-2

A reprint of the title first published by Longmans, Green and Company

Awarded the Newbery Medal, 1932

This is "an unusual story of Navaho Indian life as seen through the eyes of Younger Brother, who learns the songs of the medicine men and makes new songs for himself. The customs and tribal beliefs are skillfully woven into the narrative. The author is noted for her copies of sand paintings." Pittsburgh

"Written with sympathy and understanding, it reveals the mysticism and love of beauty which is innate in the Indian of the highest type. All children who like poetry and who care for the Indian will enjoy it. The illustrations in aquatone by the author and Sidney Armer reflect the beauty of the story and its setting in the deserts and canyons of northern Arizona." Cleveland

Armstrong, William H.

Sounder; illus. by James Barkley. Harper 1969 116p illus $4.95, lib. bdg. $4.79, pa $1.25 (5-7) Fic

1 Dogs—Stories 2 Negroes—Fiction 3 Poverty—Fiction
ISBN 0-06-020143-6; 0-06-020144-4; 0-06-440020-4

Awarded the Newbery Medal, 1969

Set in the Southland, at one level this "is the story of the coon dog, Sounder, and his devotion to his master. It is also a story of humans: the father, a black sharecropper, who must steal to feed his children, the timid mother fighting for survival, and the son who grows to maturity through his father's prison term and the devotion of Sounder." Best Sellers

"There is an epic quality in the deeply moving, long-ago story of cruelty, loneliness, and silent suffering. The power of the writing lies in its combination of subtlety and strength. Four characters are unforgettable: the mother, with her inscrutable fortitude and dignity; the crushed and beaten father; the indomitable boy; and the 'human animal,' Sounder." Horn Bk

Arnold, Elliott

A kind of secret weapon. Scribner 1969 191p lib. bdg. $5.95 (6-7)   Fic

1 World War, 1939-1945—Fiction 2 Denmark—Fiction
ISBN 0-684-12699-0

It is the winter of 1943 in Nazi-occupied Denmark, and Peter Andersen discovers that his parents are engaged in the Danish Resistance and are putting out an underground paper. He becomes involved in helping his parents and learns a great deal about loyalty, patriotism, love and sacrifice

"Hate, frustration, and resentment are depicted honestly, without sentimentalization. . . . Peter matures believably under stress and through tragic situations, and his story is appealing and thought-provoking reading." Library J

Arthur, Ruth M.

A candle in her room; illus. by Margery Gill. Atheneum Pubs. 212p illus $5.95, pa 95¢ (5-7) Fic

1 Dolls—Fiction
ISBN 0-689-30012-3; 0-689-70315-5

"An old house in Wales and a malevolent witch doll, Dido, dominate this story of three generations of the Mansell girls, all of whom come under Dido's spell. Excellent characterization, strong sense of place, and a haunting story of lives lived in an atmosphere of mystery and evil." Hodges. Bks for Elem Sch Libraries

Arundel, Jocelyn

Simba of the White Mane; illus. by Wesley Dennis. McGraw 1958 127p illus lib. bdg. $4.72 (5-7)   Fic

1 Lions—Stories 2 Africa—Fiction 3 Wildlife—Conservation—Fiction
ISBN 0-07-002366-2

"Whittlesey House publications"

"A new version of the Androcles tale in which Toki, a small African boy risks his life and defies Mr. Pike, the hunter, in order to save Simba the lion. Toki decides that he would rather work with the game warden than with hunters, since it often takes more courage to save wild animals than it does to kill them." Library J

"The attitudes and interrelations of [the] game warden, pompous white hunter, and African are revealing and credible. Sketches of Simba and other wild creatures are the kind children will turn back to for another look." Horn Bk

Atwater, Richard

Mr Popper's penguins, by Richard and Florence Atwater; illus. by Robert Lawson. Little 1938 138p illus $5.95 (3-5)   Fic

1 Penguins—Stories
ISBN 0-316-05842-4

When Mr Popper, a mild little painter and decorator with a taste for books and movies on polar explorations, was presented with a penguin, he named it Captain Cook. Mr Popper and his family exerted themselves to make the new pet happy, but the poor bird grew so lonely that they appealed to an aquarium and got another penguin named Greta. From that moment on life was changed for the Popper family

"To the depiction of the penguins in all conceivable moods Robert Lawson [the] artist has brought not only his skill but his individual humor, and his portrayal of the wistful Mr. Popper is memorable." N Y Times Bk Rev

"Here is a find, a book not only funny, but universally funny. Children will cherish it; so will anybody with a love of joy." N Y Her Trib Bks

Aulaire, Ingri d'

Children of the Northlights; by Ingri & Edgar Parin d'Aulaire. Viking 1935 unp illus lib. bdg. $6.50 (2-4)   Fic

1 Lapland—Fiction
ISBN 0-670-21741-7

"A notable picture story book which spans a year in the life of Lise and Lasse, two little children of Lapland. It is the result of the D'Aulaires' long journey by boat and sled into the north of Norway, and contains much interesting information concerning the customs of the Lapps." Booklist

"A distinguished book full of color, fun and the charm of ways that are just different enough to be fascinating." Horn Bk

The magic meadow [by] Ingri and Edgar Parin d'Aulaire. Doubleday 1958 55p illus $3.95 (2-4) Fic

Aulaire, Ingri d'—*Continued*

1 Switzerland—Fiction

ISBN 0-385-07760-2

Peterli and his old grandfather live on a farm high in the Swiss Alps where Peterli herds the cows and goats in a lovely 'magic' valley and Grandfather makes fine cheeses. Peterli's dream of finding treasure in the magic meadow to ease Grandfather's life comes true when a big hotel is built in the meadow bringing tourists and work for Peterli." Booklist

"The history and the charm of the rugged Swiss people are shown in several folk tales and the legend of William Tell. There is rich detail in the colorful illustrations." Adventuring with Bks. 2d edition

Babbitt, Natalie

Goody Hall; story and pictures by Natalie Babbitt. Farrar, Straus 1971 176p illus $4.50 (4-6)   Fic

1 Mystery and detective stories

ISBN 0-374-32745-9

In this Gothic mystery "Hercules Feltwright, a would-be actor, comes to a magnificent house—Goody Hall—to tutor the young master, Willet Goody. The boy soon announces his firm conviction that his father is not dead and interred in the family tomb. In trying to find an answer for Willet, Hercules' way is marked by chilling events, including a gypsy seance on a rainy night and a thrilling descent into Mr. Goody's burial vault." Wis Library Bul

"Lightened by humor and colored by suspense, the story whirls its delightfully just-short-of-burlesqued characters in a triumphant gavotte of melodrama." Sat Rev

Kneeknock Rise; story and pictures by Natalie Babbitt. Farrar, Straus 1970 117p illus $4.95 (3-5)   Fic

1 Allegories

ISBN 0-374-34257-1

"It was firmly understood by all those who lived near the Mammoth Mountains that any peculiar circumstance was due to the malevolent influence of a mysterious creature on the bleak and rocky heights of Kneeknock Rise. Egan, visiting Uncle Anson in the little village at the foot of the terrible cliff, hears the strange wail of the Megrimum during a storm. Taunted by his cousin Ada, he climbs up, and finds that the Megrimum's 'voice' is caused by a hot spring in a cave, but when he tries to explain this to the villagers, they will have none of it." Sat Rev

"An enchanting tale imbued with a folk flavor, enlivened with piquant imagery and satiric wit, and enhanced by an inviting format and amusing black-and-white drawings." Booklist

The search for delicious. Farrar, Straus 1969 167p illus $4.95 (5-7)   Fic

ISBN 0-374-36534-2

"An Ariel book"

The Prime Minister is compiling a dictionary and when no one at court can agree on the meaning of delicious, the King sends his twelve-year-old messenger to poll the country

"The characters' names fit their roles. The theme, foolish arguments can lead to great conflict, may not be clear to all children who will enjoy this fantasy." Best Sellers

Bacon, Martha

Sophia Scrooby preserved; illus. by David Omar White. Little 1968 227p illus $5.95 (5-7)   Fic

1 Slavery in the U.S.—Fiction 2 Negroes—Fiction

ISBN 0-316-07508-6

"An Atlantic Monthly Press book"

"Born in 1768, the small daughter of an African chieftain is taken into slavery and lives with a Connecticut family that fosters her natural bent for education

and musical training. Sophia and the Scroobys are separated, and she falls into the clutches of pirates, is the captive of a voodoo queen, the companion to an English lady of means, and a performer at Drury Lane before her reunion with the Scroobys in Canada." Sutherland. The Best in Children's Bks

"Martha Bacon has a lively style and when she is sure of her scene, writes with wit and perception. . . . But her story is too thin: the themes obtrude." N Y Times Bk Rev

Bailey, Carolyn Sherwin

Finnegan II, his nine lives; illus. by Kate Seredy. Viking 1953 95p illus lib. bdg. $4.95 (4-6)   Fic

1 Cats—Stories

ISBN 0-670-31508-7

Finnegan II was warned by the policeman who fished him out of the sewer that a cat has only nine lives and he'd better watch his step. This is the story of one year when Finnegan II lost one life after another, but happily, when the ninth life was gone, Finnegan II was still alive to remark "Who said only nine lives? I don't believe it!"

"Both the beautifully told story and Kate Seredy's fine, equally understanding illustrations give Finnie a distinct and memorable personality." Chicago Sunday Tribune

Miss Hickory; with lithographs by Ruth Gannett. Viking 1946 120p illus lib. bdg. $4.95, pa 85¢ (3-5)   Fic

1 Dolls—Fiction 2 New Hampshire—Fiction

ISBN 0-670-47940-3; 0-670-05006-7

Awarded the Newbery Medal, 1947

"With her hickory nut head glued to a body made of an apple-wood twig, Miss Hickory may have seemed to be merely a country doll—but actually, she was a real person, who had all sorts of exciting adventures after Great-Granny Brown closed her New Hampshire home for the winter." Bookmark

"Fascinating and harmonious lithographs adorn this imaginative and delightful story. . . . A refreshingly original story, full of the love of the countryside and its outdoor residents. There is a lovely Christmas chapter in the book." Horn Bk

Baker, Betty

Walk the world's rim. Harper 1965 168p illus map $4.95, lib. bdg. $4.79, pa $1.25 (5-7)   Fic

1 Estévan—Fiction 2 Núñez Cabeza de Vaca, Alvar—Fiction 3 America—Discovery and exploration—Fiction

ISBN 0-06-020380-3; 0-06-020381-1; 0-06-440026-3

Chakho, an Indian boy, travels from Texas to Mexico City with the Negro slave Esteban, Cabeza de Vaca, and two other Spanish explorers in the 16th century

"Told against an authentic background, the story has much to say about freedom and human dignity." Hodges. Bks for Elem Sch Libraries

"The book is written with an economy of construction that enhances the richness of its emotional impact." Chicago. Children's Bk Center

Bibliography: p169

Baker, Charlotte

Cockleburr Quarters; illus. by Robert Owens. Prentice-Hall 1972 176p illus $4.95 (4-6)   Fic

1 Dogs—Stories 2 Negroes—Fiction

ISBN 0-13-139485-1

A story about Dolph, a Black boy, and his friends who find a homeless dog and her eight puppies. To Dolph and his sister, the puppies are the beginning of a new awareness

Baker, Charlotte—*Continued*

"Although weakened by an all-problems-solved pat ending, the story of the black neighborhood community of Cockleburr Quarters is lively and believable, permeated with the belief in humane treatment for animals. . . . The dialogue is realistic, the home setting one in which it is accepted that there is an 'uncle' in the house, that two of Dolph's sisters have illegitimate babies, and that one of them goes off with Uncle, leaving her child for her mother to bring up, but this is emphasized less than the industry and ambition of other members of the family." Chicago. Children's Bk Center

Baker, Margaret J.

Home from the hill; illus. by W. T. Mars. Farrar, Straus [1969 c1968] 166p illus $3.95 (5-7) Fic

1 Family—Fiction 2 England—Fiction 3 Runaways—Fiction

ISBN 0-374-33300-9

First published 1968 in England

"Homesick and impatient when their family is forced by circumstances to be temporarily split up, Jennet and Tiffany who are in the Children's Home and their brothers Daniel and Stoker in foster homes bicycle off to find a place where the family can all be together again. The adventures of the four runaway English children in eluding the police and carrying on their search and their encounters with kind, helpful people are lightly narrated in a fairly plausible, satisfying story." Booklist

Ball, Zachary

Bristle Face. Holiday House 1962 206p $5.95 (5-7) Fic

1 Dogs—Stories 2 Mississippi—Fiction

ISBN 0-8234-0013-1

"In the fox-hunting back country of Mississippi in 1900, fourteen-year-old orphaned Jase Landers and his newly adopted dog Bristle Face are befriended by Lute Swank, a lazy but kind and understanding storekeeper. Told by Jase, the perceptive narrative tells how the turtle-chasing dog develops into a keen-nosed trail dog, how Lute wins the Widow Jarkey and his campaign for sheriff, and how Jase finds a permanent home. . . . The local idiom in the dialog may cause some reading difficulty but it adds much to the atmosphere of the tale." Booklist

"As Jase tells the story, quoting all the pithy comments of Lute, his friends and the widow Jarkey, it is side-splittingly funny . . . and exciting, poignant and satisfying with tragedy tempered by hope. . . . An excellent tale of the enduring friendship of a boy and a dog." N Y Her Trib Bks

Followed by: Sputters

Sputters. Holiday House 1963 220p front $5.95 (5-7) Fic

1 Dogs—Stories 2 Mississippi—Fiction

ISBN 0-8234-0109-X

Sequel to: Bristle Face

"Orphaned Jase, fourteen, acquires a new dog, Sputters, helps the new sheriff catch some moonshiners, sees Lute and the widow Pansy married at last and their adoption of him become a reality, is saddened by the death of his friend Emory, and inherits the old man's pack of foxhounds. Enriched by convincing regional speech, colorful if occasionally exaggerated characters, and robustly humorous situations, this first-person narrative is sometimes poignant, sometimes hilariously funny, but always warm and human." Booklist

Barret, Leighton

The adventures of Don Quixote de la Mancha; adapted from the Motteux translation by Leighton Barret, and illus. with drawings by Warren Chappell. Knopf 1960 307p illus $3.50, lib. bdg. $5.69 (5-7) Fic

1 Spain—Fiction

ISBN 0-394-80892-4; 0-394-90892-9

Adapted for younger readers

Original Spanish edition published in two parts, 1605 and 1615

"Treats of the pleasant manner of the knighting of that famous gentleman, Don Quixote, of the dreadful and never-to-be imagined adventure of the windmills, of the extraordinary battle he waged with what he took to be a giant, and of divers other rare and notable adventures and strange enchantments which befell this valorous and witty knight-errant." Pittsburgh

"A flavorful version of the addled knight's adventures, amusingly illustrated." Hodges. Bks for Elem Sch Libraries

Barrie, J. M.

Peter Pan (3-5) Fic

1 Fairy tales

Some editions are:

Grosset (Thrushwood Bks) $2.95 (ISBN 0-448-02525-6) Has subtitle: The story of Peter and Wendy

Scribner lib. bdg. $5.95, pa $2.95 Illustrated by Nora S. Unwin (ISBN 0-684-13214-1; 0-684-71707-7)

First published 1911 by Scribner with title: Peter and Wendy

This is the story of "how Wendy, John, and Michael flew with Peter Pan, the boy who never grows up, to adventures in the Never-Never Land with pirates, redskins, and the fairy Tinker Bell. [It is] in Barrie's inimitable style, pleasing the child with delightful absurdities and the adult with good-humored satire." Right Book for the Right Child

Barth, Edna

The day Luis was lost; illus. by Lilian Obligado. Little 1971 58p illus $4.50 (3-5) Fic

1 Puerto Ricans in the U.S.—Fiction

ISBN 0-316-08247-3

"Luis had come from Puerto Rico only six weeks before, so he couldn't speak English very well. On the day his older sister was ill and couldn't take him to school, he was sure he could get there alone—and he might have, if a burst main hadn't taken him out of his way. Taken to the police station, Luis found there was a communication gap. Why did they talk so fast? (Why, the policemen ask each other, does the boy talk so fast?) By chance, Luis looked out the window, and there was his school! The story is adequately told and realistic, but slight in plot. The incidents give it some vitality, however, and the lively illustrations and large print make it visually appealing." Chicago. Children's Bk Center

Bartos-Hoppner, B.

Avalanche dog; tr. by Anthea Bell. Walck, H.Z. 1967 [c1966] 159p $4.50 (5-7) Fic

1 Dogs—Stories 2 Alps—Fiction

ISBN 0-8098-3064-1

Original German edition published 1964; this translation first published 1966 in England

In this adventure story "one of a group of young men from an Alpine village describes some of the group's rescue operations, the problems in training and tracking, and the importance of the ability, stamina, and temperament of the German Shepherd

Bartos-Hoppner, B.—*Continued*

dogs. Since his own well-trained dog has been injured, Lofty is training a new dog, Aladdin; when the rescue call comes, Aladdin proves to be as good a tracker as any dog on the team. The dramatic situation has great appeal, and the appeal is added to by the suspense, pace, and style of a skilled writer of adventure stories." Chicago. Children's Bk Center

Baudouy, Michel-Aimé

Old One-Toe; tr. by Marie Ponsot; illus. by Johannes Troyer. Harcourt 1959 190p illus $5.75 (5-7) Fic

1 Foxes—Stories
ISBN 0-15-257780-7

First published 1957 in France

A "story set in the woods and fields around an old mill house where four children from Paris are visiting their aunt. The central characters are One-Toe, a cunning, marauding red fox tracked by hunters and championed by the children, the boy Piet, who discovers the joy in learning the ways of the forest creatures, particularly One-Toe, and the Commandant, an elderly and skillful hunter who shares his love and knowledge of the forest with Piet and matches wits with One-Toe." Booklist

"Superb characterization of children and adults, and of two special dogs. A prose style that is freshly poetic and evocative heightens feelings, relationships, and unusual scenes, and make the book (a French prize-winner) one worth sharing aloud." Horn Bk

Baum, Betty

Patricia crosses town; illus. by Nancy Grossman. Knopf 1965 178p illus lib. bdg. $5.39 (4-6) Fic

1 Negroes—Fiction 2 Segregation in education—Fiction
ISBN 0-394-91482-1

"Twelve-year-old Patricia is one of the first New York children to be bussed across town to integrate an all-white school. Impulsive and mischievous, she is suspicious of all white children and afraid of being rejected. Her teacher in the new school uses her interests in puppetry and acting to help her gain confidence; these interests also lead to her friendship with Sarah, who overcomes Pat's distrust. Sarah and another white girl later come across town to show their affection for Pat and put on their interracial puppet show to celebrate Pat's father's return from the hospital." We Build Together

"The problems of integration and human relationships in general are met head-on." Adventuring with Bks. 2d edition

Baum, L. Frank

The Wizard of Oz (3-6) Fic

1 Fairy tales
Some editions are:

Childrens Press (Fun-to-read classics) lib. bdg. $5.25 Illustrated by Brigitte Bryan. (ISBN 0-516-04246-7)

Grosset (Illustrated junior lib) $3.95 Illustrated by Evelyn Copelman; adapted from the famous pictures by W. W. Denslow (ISBN-0-448-05826-X (Deluxe ed) $5.95 (ISBN 0-448-06026-4) (Companion lib) $1.50 (ISBN 0-448-05470-1) (Grow-up bk ser) $1.95 (ISBN 0-448-02138-2)

Macmillan (N Y) (The Macmillan classics) $3.95 Illustrated by W. W. Denslow

Random House $2.50, lib. bdg. $3.79 Edited by Allen Chaffer (ISBN 0-394-80689-1; 0-394-90689-6)

First published 1900 with title: The wonderful Wizard of Oz

Here are the adventures of Dorothy who, in her dreams, escapes from her bed in Kansas to visit the Emerald City and to meet the wonderful Wizard of Oz, the Scarecrow, the Tin Woodman, and the Cowardly Lion

Bawden, Nina

Carrie's war. Lippincott 1973 159p illus $5.95 (4-7) Fic

1 Wales—Fiction 2 World War, 1939-1945—Fiction
ISBN 0-397-31450-7

"Carrie, recently widowed, takes her children to the small Welsh mining town where she and her younger brother, Nick, had been evacuated during World War II. Carrie is tormented by her mistaken belief that she caused a fire at the time which may have killed people she loved. For the most part, the story revolves around Carrie and Nick's days spent in the home of rigid, strict Mr. Evans and his kindly sister, their friendship with Hepzibah Green, who may have been a witch, and Albert Sandwich, another evacuee." Library J

"The pace and the dialogue and the characterisation all add up to a whole which could be read with interest and pleasure by any age, and in which the lessons are implied, delicately in the behaviour and relationships of the principal actors, never rammed home. . . . Beautifully told, perceptive, tough and at the same time tender, this is the sort of book from which I believe children learn about other people and about themselves." New Statesman

A handful of thieves. Lippincott 1967 189p $4.50 (4-6) Fic

1 Mystery and detective stories
ISBN 0-397-30950-3

This story concerns the efforts of Fred, a thirteen-year-old English boy, "and four friends to track down a confidence trickster and bring him to justice. . . . Mr. Gribble [Fred's grandmother's lodger] skips town, leaving his rent unpaid and making off with the savings Gran kept in her teapot. Since Gran, out of foolish pride, refuses to go to the police, the children decide they must try to capture the scoundrel." Bk World

"Miss Bawden rightly makes no concessions toward the argument that it is all right to do to others what they did to you, while she keeps an even balance between tough-minded independence and family warmth and security." Christian Science Monitor

The peppermint pig; frontispiece by Charles Lilly. Lippincott 1975 191p front $5.95 (5-7) Fic

1 Pigs—Stories 2 Family—Fiction 3 Great Britain—Fiction
ISBN 0-397-31618-6

"Just after the turn of the century, the Greengrass family left their comfortable London home because of financial problems and settled in a Norfolk country town. Father was going off to try his fortune in America, so Mother and the four children would be dependent upon the good grace and the generosity of two relatives, the schoolmistresses Aunt Sarah and Aunt Harriet. The story unfolds from the viewpoint of nine-year-old Poll, the youngest and naughtiest of the children, who frequently locks horns with her brother Theo. . . . Into their lives comes Johnnie, a remarkable runt pig who grows into a beloved family pet. . . . Representing a departure for the author, the story is historical rather than contemporary, subtle rather than mysterious; and its plot is more relaxed than suspenseful. Time and setting come sharply through the writing, which is typically graceful, witty, clear, and fluid." Horn Bk

The runaway summer. Lippincott 1969 185p $4.75 (4-6) Fic

ISBN 0-397-31102-8

This is "the story of two children's efforts to hide a Kenyan boy who, they believe, has entered England illegally. . . . The feeling that her parents do not

Bawden, Nina—*Continued*

want her has made [eleven-year-old Mary] cherish her unhappiness so stubbornly that she will not respond to the kindness of her aunt and her grandfather, with whom she has come to live. Her discovery of Krishna Patel and her determination to save him from the authorities lead her to seek help from a neighbor boy, Simon. He is just the friend Mary needs, and she begins to emerge from her unpleasant shell." Horn Bk

The author "writes so well. Not for her the adult-oriented view of the child. She is there with the child describing the adults—and filling the pages with action. This being a Nina Bawden book, the ending is both happy and realistic." Christian Science Monitor

Squib. Lippincott 1971 143p $4.50, pa $1.95 (4-6)   Fic

1 Cruelty to children—Fiction
ISBN 0-397-31509-0; 0-397-31231-8

When Kate Pollack, nearly twelve, first saw Squib, a small, pale, lonely looking child, in the park, she was sure he must be her long-lost little brother. This is the story of how Kate and her friends risked the perils of the woods, the Old People's Home, and the sinister caravan site in their efforts to find out who Squib really was

"The children's attempt to rescue Squib from a situation they don't quite understand but know is wrong, somehow, provides a dramatic and satisfying ending. The relationships among the children, and the family situation of each, are drawn with perception and warmth, and the story is written with just-bearable suspense." Chicago. Children's Bk Center

Three on the run; illus. by Wendy Worth. Lippincott 1965 224p illus $4.75, lib. bdg. $3.59 (4-6) Fic

1 Mystery and detective stories 2 Africans in Great Britain—Fiction
ISBN 0-397-30836-1; 0-397-30835-3

First published 1964 in England with title: On the run

"The action takes place in England and revolves around three . . . characters. Young Ben, recently arrived in London from Kenya, . . . speaks Swahili and takes African Thomas Okapi completely by surprise by addressing Thomas in this African language when the boys meet. Pluckily, resourceful Lil rounds out the trio. Children will understand Ben's distress at the prospects of gaining a step-mother, and Lil's desire to stay out of the clutches of well-meaning welfare officers. Thomas has a more unique problem. His uncle is trying to kidnap him as part of political maneuvers involving the unstable government of a new African nation. How these three extraordinary fictitious children meet each other and outwit adults pursuing Thomas will keep readers involved from start to finish." Keating. Building Bridges of Understanding Between Cultures

The witch's daughter. Lippincott 1966 181p $4.95 (4-7)   Fic

1 Blind—Fiction 2 Scotland—Fiction
ISBN 0-397-30922-8

This story, set on the Scottish island of Skua, involves "much more than the capture of jewel thieves. Perdita, a lonely orphan, is rejected by the other children because of her unusual power to see into the future. Through the arrival of a blind girl, Janey, and Janey's brother Tim, Perdita comes to realize that her powers are not a sign of witchcraft, but a special talent." Reading Ladders. 5th edition

"A credible suspense story, with a likeable and resourceful cast. A plausible plot, superior dialogue and an appropriate setting also work into a dramatization." N Y Times Bk Rev

Baylor, Byrd

Coyote cry; drawings by Symeon Shimin. Lothrop 1972 unp illus lib. bdg. $4.59 (2-4)   Fic

1 Coyotes—Stories 2 Southwest, New—Fiction
ISBN 0-688-51624-6

This is "a brief but poignant story of Antonio—a little boy in the Southwest to whom Coyote means enemy—and an old shepherd, who explains that even Coyote must stay alive. When a female coyote steals one of the sheepdog's pups, the pup is recovered; but later, surprisingly, the coyote returns to touch noses with the puppy; and Antonio admits, 'Maybe Coyote is not my enemy.' The illustrator's art, not essentially different from that of his previous picture books, is appropriate to the subject of this book and to its poetic treatment." Horn Bk

Beatty, Patricia

Hail Columbia; illus. by Liz Dauber. Morrow 1970 251p illus $6.50 (5-7)   Fic

1 Woman—Civil rights—Fiction 2 Oregon—Fiction
ISBN 0-688-21371-5

"After an absence of 19 years, Louisa's Aunt Columbia returns to Astoria, Oregon in 1893 for a year's visit. She is not the 'sainted maiden aunt' the family expected but an active suffragette accompanied by her two children. Neither Captain Baines, Louisa's vociferous, autocratic father, nor the town can abide emancipated women so the year that follows is one of upheaval and surprises as spirited, civic-minded Aunt Columbia embarks on one cause after another, doing good and winning friends and supporters. Narrated by thirteen-year-old Louisa, this zestful story with a memorable and likable adult heroine is fast-paced and eventful." Booklist

How many miles to sundown; frontispiece by Robert Quackenbush. Morrow 1974 222p front $5.95, lib. bdg. $5.11 (5-7)   Fic

1 Southwest, New—Fiction
ISBN 0-688-20102-4; 0-688-30102-9

This story "introduces thirteen-year-old Beulah Land (Beeler) Quiney, who demonstrates . . . that 'nineteenth-century Texas women were every bit as strong as their men.' The saga begins when Nate Graber, searching for his missing father, accepts help from eleven-year-old Leo Quiney. . . . Leo had helped himself to Beeler's horse, and the determined young woman set forth after her property with her pet steer Travis. In spite of the boys' protestations against her joining them, the duo becomes a trio—trekking through Texas, New Mexico, and Arizona Territories in search of Mr. Graber. In the course of the search, Beeler conclusively proves that she is the equal of any Quiney man." Horn Bk

"Humorous and suspenseful episodes throughout the story will be enjoyed by the many children who love tales of the Old West. Girls especially will enjoy meeting Beeler . . . who won't let Nate, Leo or any other male put her down." Cath Library World

A long way to Whiskey Creek; frontispiece by Franz Altschuler. Morrow 1971 224p front lib. bdg. $5.49 (5-7)   Fic

1 Texas—Fiction
ISBN 0-688-31427-9

"From Cottonwood, it was four hundred miles to Whiskey Creek, but there wasn't anybody else who could go—so thirteen-year-old Parker set off on the grim errand of bringing back his brother's body. He'd suggested to Nate Graber, an orphan, that he go along for company even though Nate was a Yankee who liked, of all things, to read books. The story is set in Texas in 1879, and it shows both the lingering hostility

Beatty, Patricia—*Continued*

between opposing factions and the easy violence of a frontier country." Sutherland. The Best in Children's Bks

"Despite the problems caused by personal differences in temperament and attitude and by officious and unscrupulous adults, the boys determinedly stick to their errand, learn to respect one another, make new friends, and, with the help of an aging outlaw, successfully complete their mission." Booklist

The Nickel-Plated Beauty; illus. by Liz Dauber. Morrow 1964 255p illus lib. bdg. $5.11 (5-7)   Fic

1 Stoves—Fiction 2 Washington (Territory)—Fiction 3 Family—Fiction

ISBN 0-688-31425-2

Set in "Washington Territory in 1886. The Kimball children join forces to earn money for a new stove, the Nickel-plated Beauty, as a surprise Christmas present for their mother." Hodges. Bks for Elem Sch Libraries

"As Hester describes their struggles, however, each effort of the determined little band, each setback, is interesting reading as part of a warm family story. The period details are excellently chosen; cuspidors, tight corsets, damp red flannel used as rouge, even the smells of the general store, all add conviction to this picture of an older day." Bk Week

O the Red Rose Tree; illus. by Liz Dauber. Morrow 1972 222p illus lib. bdg. $5.11 (5-7)   Fic

1 Coverlets—Fiction 2 Washington (State)—Fiction

ISBN 0-688-21429-0

"The story follows the adventures of four thirteen-year-old girls as they attempt the impossible in trying to find seven different shades of red colorfast material so an old woman can make the quilt of her dreams called 'O the Red Rose Tree.' " Booklist

"However exaggerated and fortuitous the circumstances, the background and details have the ring of truth, since they are based on the author's family records and on her research in Oregon history." Horn Bk

Sources included in Author's note: p219-22

Red rock over the river; frontispiece by Robert Quackenbush. Morrow 1973 253p front $6.50, lib. bdg. $5.49 (5-7)   Fic

1 Southwest, New—Fiction

ISBN 0-688-20065-6; 0-688-30065-0

The story is set in the Arizona Territory of 1881. "Dorcas Fox, 13-year-old daughter of an army lieutenant, moves in with her brother, Charlie, at Fort Yuma. . . . Though Dorcas narrates the story, Hattie Lou Mercer, a half-Pima Indian, is the main character. She is a mysterious, fascinating 14-year-old who enlivens the Fox home when she becomes their housekeeper. . . . Tension is created when the two girls write letters for prisoners in the notorious Arizona Territorial Prison and when Johnny Short, Hattie's tubercular half-brother, escapes from the prison." Sch Library J

"The social attitudes, popular superstitions, prison conditions, and harsh realities of frontier living in the Southwest Territory during the post-Civil War period are brought to life by the author's skillful integration of historical detail with a rousing mystery-adventure." Horn Bk

Beckman, Gunnel

The girl without a name; tr. from the Swedish by Anne Parker; illus. by Borghild Rud. Harcourt 1970 153p illus $5.50 (4-6)   Fic

1 Sweden—Fiction 2 Iranians in Sweden—Fiction

ISBN 0-15-230980-2

Original Swedish edition, 1967

"Nine-year-old Sara of Stockholm has happy times with the Iranian girl next door but sometimes she tires of always having to be kind and to remember not to question Gunilla about her life in Iran. Gunilla lost her entire family in an earthquake and since then has terrible nightmares and cannot or will not remember anything of the past, not even her name. One day Sara becomes impatient with Gunilla and lashes out at her, a shocking action which opens the way to Gunilla's recovery. Girls will enjoy the warm friendship between the two, the mystery surrounding Gunilla's past, and the psychological problem which, though complex for this age level, is satisfactorily explained." Booklist

Behn, Harry

The two uncles of Pablo; illus. by Mel Silverman. Harcourt 1959 96p illus $4.95 (4-7)   Fic

1 Uncles—Fiction 2 Mexico—Fiction

ISBN 0-15-292306-3

"The wisdom, understanding and sympathy of one little Mexican boy help to show the fallacy in the lives of two grown men. Uncle Silvan is lazy, untruthful and unreliable although basically kind. Uncle Pico, a poet, but sad and lonely, has sought happiness in seclusion and self-centeredness. An outstanding story, beautifully told, that will be read by the more perceptive child and enjoyed in family reading groups." Bookmark

"Rather than seeming incredible, Pablo's shrewd observations and movements for the good of his uncles seem motivated by a natural inner strength and nobility. Beautifully illustrated with stone-lithograph drawings." Horn Bk

Bellairs, John

The house with a clock in its walls; pictures by Edward Gorey. Dial Press 1973 179p illus $5.95, lib. bdg. $5.47 (5-7)   Fic

1 Witchcraft—Fiction

In 1948, Lewis, a ten-year-old orphan, goes to New Zebedee, Michigan with his warlock Uncle Jonathan, who lives in a big mysterious house and practices white magic. Together with their neighbor, Mrs Zimmerman, a witch, they search to find a clock that is programmed to end the world and has been hidden in the walls of the house by the evil Isaac Izard

"Bellairs's story and Edward Gorey's pictures are satisfyingly frightening." Pub W

Benary-Isbert, Margot

The Ark; tr. by Richard and Clara Winston. Harcourt 1953 246p $6.50 (5-7)   Fic

1 Germany—Fiction 2 Family—Fiction

ISBN 0-15-203901-5

Original German edition, 1948

"The Lechow family, after nine months of moving from refugee camp to refugee camp following World War II, finally settles in Western Germany. The happiness of being together means so much to the family that the oldest boy, Matthias, does work which he dislikes until he and Margret, his sister, find satisfactory employment on a farm and are able to make a home for the family in an old street car. There is a climate of warmth and tenderness within the family which encompasses their lonely landlady, and a small playmate who proceeds to make his home with them." Reading Ladders. 2d edition

"This rare and perceptive book, reflecting something of the author's own experience contains much of importance to reach the hearts and mind of young Americans. [Written] with an acute awareness of the effect of war on children and adolescents; with a consciousness of homely details that interest them; and with a wonderful depth of feeling for country things." Horn Bk

Benary-Isbert, Margot—*Continued*

Blue mystery; tr. from the German by Richard and Clara Winston; illus. by Enrico Arno. Harcourt 1957 190p illus $5.95, pa 75¢ (5-7)　　　　　Fic

1 Germany—Fiction 2 Plants—Stories 3 Mystery and detective stories

ISBN 0-15-209092-4; 0-15-613225-7

"An ancient German town in the Thuringian mountains, famous for its fine nursery gardens, is the unusual setting for this story. Annegret's father has developed a new deep blue gloxinia, a source of great pride and responsibility to the household. In mysterious circumstances, one flower-pot disappears, and the clues point to a member of the nursery staff. Suspicion rests on the stubborn boy apprentice, Fridolin, and Annegret's determination to prove his innocence forms the focal point of the plot. . . . The daily adventures of Annegret, her family and her friends, not forgetting her beloved dog, provide entertaining reading." Ontario Library Rev

The wicked enchantment; illus. by Enrico Arno; tr. from the German by Richard and Clara Winston. Harcourt 1955 181p illus $5.50 (5-7)　　　　Fic

1 Germany—Fiction 2 Fairy tales

ISBN 0-15-296423-1

Life in the old cathedral town of Vogelsang, Germany had gone on peacefully for many years but suddenly strange and disturbing things began to happen. A story of the present day interwoven with an ancient legend of a wicked tyrant and an evil enchantment culminates at Easter under the full moon

"With all its wealth of detail the story is clearly told and its very real human relations balance its magic. The pages glow with such colorful imagery that even the distinguished, fanciful drawings cannot match the words. It is a rare book to stimulate the wits of bright children besides stirring their hearts. It will be savored by families who read aloud and will live long in their minds." N Y Her Trib Bks

Benchley, Nathaniel

Feldman Fieldmouse; a fable. Drawings by Hilary Knight. Harper 1971 96p illus lib. bdg. $4.43, pa 95¢ (3-5)　　　　　Fic

1 Mice—Stories

ISBN 0-06-020484-2; 0-06-440032-8

Fendall Fieldmouse is befriended by Lonny, a boy who knows how to talk to mice. As a pet, Fendall leads a lazy, contented life. This story tells what happens when Fendall's uncle, Feldman Fieldmouse, appears to take over his nephew's education

"A engaging fanciful tale. . . . The style is delightful, the animal characters amusing, and the dialogue witty." Chicago. Children's Bk Center

Bennett, Anna Elizabeth

Little witch; illus by Helen Stone. Lippincott 1953 127p illus $5.95 (3-5)　　　　　Fic

1 Witchcraft—Fiction

ISBN 0-397-30240-1

"Miniken Snickasee was the daughter of a witch. She could ride on a broom; she could brew magic spells; she didn't have to go to school at all; and yet she wasn't happy. She wanted to be just an ordinary child. In a fresh and imaginative story, full of humor, Miss Bennett tells what happened when Miniken stole away from her mother and set out for school all by herself. Helen Stone's pictures of the 'little witch' and her adventures are exactly right too. Fun to read aloud to both boys and girls in October—or in any other month." Horn Bk

Berends, Polly Berrien

The case of the elevator duck; illus. by James K. Washburn. Random House 1973 54p illus lib. bdg. $5.99 (3-5)　　　　　Fic

1 Ducks—Stories 2 Apartment houses—Fiction 3 Mystery and detective stories

ISBN 0-394-92115-1

Gilbert finds a lost duck in the elevator of his apartment building, and must do some secret detective work to find its owner, since no pets are allowed in the housing project

A "light mystery for beginning readers. The action is humorously illustrated by Washburn's line sketches; and Berends' first-person, short-sentence story is personable, plausible, and useful for librarians needing simple, satisfying material for their easy mystery shelves." Booklist

Berna, Paul

The horse without a head; illus. by Richard Kennedy; tr. from the French by John Buchanan-Brown. Pantheon Bks. 1958 180p illus lib. bdg. $4.79 (4-7)　　　　　Fic

1 France—Fiction 2 Mystery and detective stories

ISBN 0-394-91255-1

First published 1955 in France. This translation first published 1957 in England with title: A hundred million francs

"A derelict neighborhood near Paris is the colorful setting for a . . . story of a gang of children who find mystery and adventure through their headless, iron-wheeled, wooden horse." Top of the News

"While the plot [involving a group of thieves] is rather far-fetched . . . the book is eminently readable: fast-paced, humorous and appealing in the presentation of the children who are colorful, individual and consistent." Chicago. Children's Bk Center

Bianco, Margery Williams

The little wooden doll; with pictures by Pamela Bianco. Macmillan (N Y) 1925 65p illus lib. bdg. $3.50 (2-4)　　　　　Fic

1 Dolls—Fiction

"Little library"

"An old-fashioned wooden doll has spent many days in the attic with only the mice and the spiders for company. But they are good friends and, with their aid, she becomes the treasure of a poor little girl. The drawings [in color and black and white] were done by the author's daughter when she was a little girl." Providence

It is "a slight but tender little story." Bookshelf

Binns, Archie

Sea pup; illus. by Robert Candy. Hawthorn Bks. 1954 215p illus $3.95 (4-7)　　　　　Fic

1 Seals (Animals)—Stories 2 Puget Sound—Fiction

ISBN 0-696-78500-5

A reprint of the title first published 1954 by Duell

When thirteen-year-old Clint who lives in a remote region of the Puget Bay country "finds an orphaned seal pup and makes a pet of it, in spite of his parents' warnings of trouble ahead, seal and boy become inseparable companions. . . . When 'Buster' stands between Clint and the education he needs to become an oceanographer, his parents leave the decision to Clint. This story of outdoor adventures and a boy with a strong scientific bent, gives also a heart-warming picture of close family relationships." Children's Bks Too Good to Miss

"Interesting information about marine life in Puget Sound is skillfully interwoven." Hodges. Bks for Elem Sch Libraries

Bishop, Claire Huchet

Pancakes—Paris; illus. by Georges Schreiber. Viking 1947 62p illus lib. bdg. $4.95 (3-5)   **Fic**

1 World War, 1939-1945—Fiction 2 Paris—Fiction

ISBN 0-670-53782-9

"Charles, a French boy whose father is a prisoner of war and whose mother goes out to work, looks after his small sister. Two American soldiers give him a box of pancake flour, but he cannot read the directions until finally the American Embassy comes to the rescue. This is a story of post-war Paris, of its lack of food, fuel and clothing, and of its hardships for children." Ontario Library Rev

"The courage, gaiety, and tenderness in the story are reflected in the illustrations." Booklist

Twenty and ten; as told by Janet Joly; illus. by William Pène du Bois. Viking 1952 76p illus lib. bdg. $4.95 (4-7)   **Fic**

1 World War, 1939-1945—Fiction 2 France—Fiction

ISBN 0-670-73407-1

During the Occupation, twenty French children were taken to a refuge in the mountains by a wise Sister. To their school came Jewish refugee children who had to be hidden from the Nazis. This is a tale of how the Sister and the children connive to hide their guests and outwit the Nazis

"Teachers should use this story with a degree of caution, recognizing that some Jewish or Gentile children, or their parents, may resent falsification of religious identity, and not give the author credit for her effort to show that a sense of belonging is a significant motivation for all children." Reading Ladders

"There are real emotion, humor, and courage in this vividly told story—all qualities that were a part of life during the occupation." Sat Rev

Blegvad, Lenore

The great hamster hunt, by Lenore and Erik Blegvad. Harcourt 1969 32p illus $5.50 (1-3)   **Fic**

1 Hamsters—Stories

ISBN 0-15-232500-X

Illustrated by Erik Blegvad

Nicholas wanted to own a hamster but his mother refused all his requests. When his friend Tony went away, Nicholas was allowed to look after Tony's hamster. But the day before Tony was expected to return, the hamster escaped. The search taught Nicholas and his family a great deal about hamsters and Nicholas was at last allowed to have a hamster of his own

"The perky drawings add to the pleasure of a realistic and satisfying story that is written with grace and humor." Sat Rev

Moon-watch summer; with illus. by Erik Blegvad. Harcourt 1972 62p illus $4.75 (3-5)   **Fic**

1 Farm life—Fiction 2 Apollo project—Fiction

ISBN 0-15-255350-9

Adam resents being sent, together with his younger sister, to spend the summer on his grandmother's farm without a TV to watch the Apollo 11 moon walk. This story tells how Adam gradually learns that larger values must sometimes take precedence over personal disappointments

"This is a convincing depiction of a child's deepening sense of values, a plea for conservation, and a hint that life can be lived without a television set. The story is written with deft simplicity, and the illustrations are small, precise, and graceful." Chicago. Children's Bk Center

Blue, Rose

Grandma didn't wave back; illus. by Ted Lewin. Watts, F. 1972 62p illus lib. bdg. $4.90 (3-5)   **Fic**

1 Grandmothers—Fiction 2 Old age—Fiction

ISBN 0-531-02557-8

A ten-year-old girl learns to accept the fact that her grandmother is growing senile and must be sent to a nursing home

"The problems of senility and its effect on the family, especially children, are treated with warmth and understanding. The soft gray-and-white illustrations are excellent and add much to the appealing book." Sch Library J

A month of Sundays; illus. by Ted Lewin. Watts, F. 1972 59p illus lib. bdg. $4.90 (3-5)   **Fic**

1 Divorce—Fiction 2 New York (City)—Fiction

ISBN 0-531-02037-1

"This story gives a credible portrayal of a ten-year-old boy's reaction to his parents' divorce. Unhappy over the divorce and at having to leave his friends, school, and home in the suburbs, Jeffrey finds it difficult at first to make friends in the city, misses his father, and discovers that having a working mother is not always easy for either of them. Time, new friends, and a conversation with his father about their activities together on Sundays help Jeffrey to adjust to and accept his new life." Booklist

"Adequately written, sensible and realistic in its evaluation of adjustment to change, casually interracial, the story has an added asset its positive attitude toward change from suburban to urban life." Chicago. Children's Bk Center

A quiet place; pictures by Tom Feelings. Watts, F. 1969 57p illus lib. bdg. $4.33 (3-5)   **Fic**

1 Foster home care—Fiction 2 Libraries—Fiction 3 Negroes—Fiction

ISBN 0-531-01773-7

"A tender story describing the feelings of a nine-year-old Negro boy who is heartbroken because the library he loves will be closed. Matthew had lived in two foster homes and an institution before finding security and warm family relationships in the Walters home. Much as he loves his foster family, his quiet retreat in the neighborhood library means so much to the boy that he cannot understand why the library must close." Keating. Building Bridges of Understanding between Cultures

"Although episodic rather than fully plotted, this story . . . [is] significant for [its] portrayal of universal childhood concerns in a ghetto setting." Booklist

Blume, Judy

Are you there God? It's me, Margaret. Bradbury Press 1970 149p $5.95 (5-7)   **Fic**

1 Adolescence—Fiction 2 Religions—Fiction

ISBN 0-87888-022-4

"A perceptive story about the emotional, physical, and spiritual ups and downs experienced by 12-year-old Margaret, child of a Jewish-Protestant union." Adventuring with Bks. 2d edition

"The writing style is lively, the concerns natural, and the problems are treated with both humor and sympathy, but the story is intense in its emphasis on the four girls' absorption in, and discussion of, menstruation and brassieres." Chicago. Children's Bk Center

It's not the end of the world. Bradbury Press 1972 169p $5.95 (4-6)   **Fic**

1 Divorce—Fiction

ISBN 0-87888-042-9

Unwilling to adjust to her parents' impending divorce, twelve-year-old Karen Newman attempts a last ditch effort at arranging a reconciliation. This story tells how her scheme goes awry when an unplanned confrontation between her parents sharply illuminates for Karen the reality of the situation

"Eventually Karen comes to accept her parents'

Blume, Judy—*Continued*

divorce and recognizes that it is not the end of the world for any of them. A believable first-person story with good characterization, particularly of twelve-year-old Karen, and realistic treatment of the situation." Booklist

Otherwise known as Sheila the Great. Dutton 1972 118p lib. bdg. $5.95 (4-6)   Fic

1 Fear—Fiction
ISBN 0-525-36455-2

Ten-year-old Sheila is secretly afraid of dogs, spiders, bees, ghosts and the dark. When she and her family leave New York for their summer home, she has to face up to her problems

"An unusual and merry treatment of the fears of a young girl. . . . This is a truly appealing book in which the author makes her points without a single preachy word." Pub W

Tales of a fourth grade nothing; illus. by Roy Doty. Dutton 1972 120p illus $5.95, pa 95¢ (3-6)   Fic

1 Brothers—Fiction 2 Family—Fiction
ISBN 0-525-40720-0; 0-525-45012-2

This story describes the trials and tribulations of nine-year-old Peter Hatcher who is saddled with a pesky two-year-old brother named Fudge who is constantly creating trouble, messing things up, and monopolizing their parents' attention. Things come to a climax when Fudge gets at Peter's pet turtle

"Illustrations that are reminiscent of the cartoons of Gluyas Williams capture the humor. . . . The episode structure makes the book a good choice for reading aloud." Sat Rev

Then again, maybe I won't; a novel. Bradbury Press 1971 164p $6.95 (5-7)   Fic

1 Adolescence—Fiction
ISBN 0-87888-035-6

"Thirteen-year-old Tony is not as thrilled as his parents are when the family's finances improve and they move to affluent suburbia. The 'nice' boy next door (of whom Tony's mother heartily approves) proves to be an inveterate shoplifter. Tony is, in fact, bothered by the eagerness of his parents to live up to their surroundings. He's also just discovered how he reacts to sexual provocation—and he worries about that, too. . . . Deftly handled, Tony's dilemma is really that he has become mature enough to see the conflicts and imperfections in his own life and in those around him, and he is sensitive enough to accept compromise." Chicago. Children's Bk Center

Bodecker, N. M.

The Mushroom Center disaster; pictures by Erik Blegvad. Atheneum Pubs. 1974 48p illus $4.25 (2-4)   Fic

1 Insects—Stories 2 Ecology—Fiction
ISBN 0-689-30424-2
"A Margaret K. McElderry book"

"An assortment of insects living in a quaint and tidy community of mushroom houses becomes the victim of littering humans. Under the guidance of an enterprising beetle, the little village recycles a huge pile of refuse into usable items." Booklist

"The finely detailed, black-and-white drawings in a small (7'' x 6'') format extend the expressiveness of this imaginative nature fantasy." Sch Library J

Bond, Michael

A bear called Paddington; with drawings by Peggy Fortnum. Houghton 1960 [c1958] 128p illus $4.95 (2-5)   Fic

1 Bears—Stories 2 Great Britain—Fiction
ISBN 0-395-06636-0
First published 1958 in England

"Mr. and Mrs. Brown first met Paddington on a railway platform in London. Noticing the sign on his neck reading 'Please look after this bear. Thank you,' they decided to do just that. From there on home was never the same though the Brown children were delighted." Pub W

"Listeners devoted to another small bear will most certainly like him, although he is no Pooh. . . . Peggy Fortnum's pen-and-ink sketches present a winsome little bear in bewitching poses and costume. Fun for reading aloud to devotees of this style of fantasy." Horn Bk

Several other books about Paddington are also available from Houghton: More about Paddington $5.95 (ISBN 0-395-06640-9); Paddington abroad $4.95 (ISBN 0-395-14331-4); Paddington at large $4.95 (ISBN 0-395-06641-7); Paddington at work $3.75 (ISBN 0-395-06637-9); Paddington goes to town $4.95 (ISBN 0-395-06635-2); Paddington helps out $4.95 (ISBN 0-395-06639-5); Paddington marches on $4.95 (ISBN 0-395-06642-5); Paddington on top $4.95 (ISBN 0-395-21897-7); Paddington takes the air $3.95 (ISBN 0-395-10909-4); Paddington takes to TV $4.95 (ISBN 0-395-19881-X)

The tales of Olga da Polga; illus. by Hans Helweg. Macmillan (N Y) [1973 c1971] 113p illus $4.95 (3-5)   Fic

1 Guinea pigs—Stories
First published 1971 in England

The adventures of Olga da Polga, a vain and talented guinea pig, as she leaves the pet shop to enter the world of the Sawdust People (guinea pigs' name for humans)

"The book will delight . . . [children] who like to imagine that their pets have their own lives and personalities. The style is easy and the characters flow from the author's pen, but he sketches his animal friends with a much surer stroke than the humans." Jr. Bookshelf

Bonham, Frank

The friends of the Loony Lake monster. Dutton 1972 135p $6.95 (4-6)   Fic

1 Dinosaurs—Stories 2 Ranch life—Fiction 3 Oregon—Fiction
ISBN 0-525-30205-0

On a sheep ranch in Oregon, Gussie discovers the huge egg of a dinosaur thought to be long extinct. When the animal hatches, she secretly takes care of it and finally convinces everyone that the dinosaur is harmless

"The fanciful and the realistic are nicely blended in a tale with good characterization and a briskly-paced plot; it's a deft story with an active heroine who should receive the Fem. Lib. seal of approval, and it is also a plea for conservation." Chicago. Children's Bk Center

Mystery of the fat cat; illus. by Alvin Smith. Dutton 1968 160p illus $4.95 (5-7)   Fic

1 Boys' clubs—Fiction 2 Mystery and detective stories
ISBN 0-525-35588-X

"A cat who inherited a fortune, Buzzer Atkins, is the center of attention in this action-filled adventure. The Boys Club is to receive the remainder of the inheritance when Buzzer dies, and many suspect that the cat thought to be Buzzer is an imposter. Boys Club members [who are mostly Black and Mexican-Americans] take drastic measures to secure the inheritance and save their club. Ralphie, a mentally retarded boy, provides the information needed to solve the mystery. Peer-group pressures, conflicts,

Bonham, Frank—_Continued_

and rivalry figure in the plot. Dialogue patterns fit the life-styles of the characters, although they may seem a bit startling to sheltered children from affluent neighborhoods." Keating. Building Bridges of Understanding Between Cultures

"Their unraveling of the mystery is believable and exciting. The characters are lively, the dialogue natural, and the inclusion of a backward child as a sympathetic—and contributing—character adds to the book's appeal." Chicago. Children's Bk Center

Bontemps, Arna

The fast Sooner hound, by Arna Bontemps and Jack Conroy; illus. by Virginia Lee Burton. Houghton 1942 28p illus lib. bdg. $4.95 (2-5)   Fic

1 Dogs—Stories
ISBN 0-395-06638-7

A "tall tale of railroad days in the far west." Horn Bk

"He would sooner run than eat and so got his name, and was he fast! As he could not be parted from his master, a railroad fireman, and could not ride in the cab, he ran beside the train. In a race with the Cannon Ball, a crack train, of course he won in spite of a detour to play with a rabbit. The excitement and hilarity of the race are the climax of a fresh picture book." Bookmark

The "drawings have a beautiful rhythm and a fine sense of motion. . . . The countryside is made vivid in beautiful greens and browns, and the locomotives convey the thrill and excitement which real locomotives have for children." N Y Times Bk Rev

Lonesome boy; illus. by Feliks Topolski. Houghton 1955 28p illus $4.50, lib. bdg. $3.90 (5-7)   Fic

1 Negroes—Fiction 2 Friendship—Fiction
ISBN 0-395-06644-1; 0-395-06645-X

Picture story book about a little Negro boy who only wanted to play his trumpet, and what happened to him

"There is a lyrical and human feeling in this book. Grandpa's advice to Bubber proves to be more insightful and helpful about contemporary issues than it was considered when the story was first published. Bubber learns the hard way that compensatory behavior leaves one with funny friends." Adventuring with Bks. 2d edition

Boston, L. M.

The children of Green Knowe; with illus. by Peter Boston. Harcourt 1955 157p illus $5.50 (4-6)   Fic

1 Fairy tales 2 Great Britain—Fiction
ISBN 0-15-217147-9

First published 1954 in England

"In the big ancestral house at Green Knowe [in England] to which a little boy comes to stay with his great-grandmother, hangs a portrait of three children who generations before had grown up there. As Tolly uses their room and playthings and listens to Granny's stories about them, the children become as real to him as they are to his great-grandmother—so real that Tolly thinks he hears and sees them. A special book for the imaginative child, in which mood predominates and fantasy and realism are skillfully blended; not the least of the book's charm is the rapport that exists between the lonely little boy and the understanding old woman who lives with her memories." Booklist

Several other books about Green Knowe are also available from Harcourt: An enemy at Green Knowe $5.50 (ISBN 0-15-225970-8); The river at Green Knowe $5.50, pa $1.45 (ISBN 0-15-267446-2) (0-15-66701-0); A stranger at Green Knowe $5.50 (ISBN 0-15-281752-2); Treasure of Green Knowe $5.75 (ISBN 0-15-2899790-0)

Bradbury, Bianca

The loner; illus. by John Gretzer. Houghton 1970 140p illus $3.95 (5-7)   Fic

1 Brothers—Fiction 2 Boats and boating—Fiction
ISBN 0-395-06655-7

"His older brother Mal got along with everybody, always was sure of himself, seemed to be a natural at any sport he tried. No wonder twelve-year-old Jay resented Mal. Jay didn't really need money, but he was delighted when he got a job as a dockboy at the summer resort. Nobody missed him, since he was always alone anyway, and Jay kept his work a secret. As he gained confidence and made new friends through his job at the marina, Jay began to realize that Mal wasn't so bad." Chicago. Children's Bk Center

"The plot development is smooth and believable, the depiction of relationships perceptive, and the dialogue easy and natural." Sat Rev

Two on an island; illus. by Robert MacLean. Houghton 1965 139p illus $4.95 (4-6)   Fic

1 Survival (after airplane accidents, shipwrecks, etc.)—Fiction 2 Maine—Fiction
ISBN 0-395-06651-4

"Two children are marooned on a tiny island just off shore from a large city on the Atlantic Coast. Hunger, thirst, exposure, fright, and courage are all ingredients of a three-day ordeal during which Trudy and Jeff learn much about themselves and each other." Reading Ladders. 5th edition

"The plausible framework for this unusual test of endurance has more than mere detail of dealing with [hardship]. . . . Miss Bradbury skillfully develops the heightened clash of different personalities." Horn Bk

Bragdon, Elspeth

There is a tide; illus. by Lilian Obligado. Viking 1964 192p illus lib. bdg. $4.95 (6-7)   Fic

1 Problem children—Fiction 2 Maine—Fiction
ISBN 0-670-69849-0

"Nat Weston tells the story of his experiences in an island community in Maine. Fifteen, motherless, and feeling that his father is a stranger, Nat has been shunted from school to school—and expelled from all of them. As he makes friends on the island and begins to feel security, Nat realizes that his father, too, had felt lonely; the boy, as he begins to think and act a man, awakens in his father a new feeling of response." Chicago. Children's Bk Center

"Strikingly real in island atmosphere. . . . Exceedingly well written, fresh, and genuine, it possesses the kind of introspection that enhances a book for thoughtful readers as well as some dramatic moments to satisfy the action-minded." Horn Bk

Brenner, Barbara

A year in the life of Rosie Bernard; illus. by Joan Sandin. Harper 1971 179p illus $3.95, lib. bdg. $4.79 (4-6)   Fic

1 Family—Fiction 2 Brooklyn—Fiction
ISBN 0-06-020656-X; 0-06-020657-8

Motherless, Rosie Bernard comes to Brooklyn in 1932 to live with her three cousins, two aunts, two uncles and grandparents while her actor-father travels. How she adjusts to her new life, wrestles with the problem of being half Jewish and half Christian, as well as winning a bout with pneumonia is portrayed

"When Daddy appears with a fiancee, Rosie runs away, but she is too sensible and pliant to maintain her resentment long, and her year ends with acceptance of the new situation. The story has an easy flow and humor, a delightful protagonist, and an understanding portrayal of an only child learning to love and be loved by her grandparents." Sutherland. The Best in Children's Bks

Brink, Carol Ryrie

Andy Buckram's tin men; illus. by W. T. Mars. Viking 1966 192p illus lib. bdg. $4.95 (4-6)   Fic

1 Robots—Fiction

ISBN 0-670-12467-2

"Andy, a highly inventive boy of twelve, builds a robot, but he doesn't think much of Campbell (named for the soup cans out of which he is largely composed) and builds another. Then a girl-robot; finally, a fourth and last tin man, this one able to row a boat. A sudden flood separates Andy and a friend of his and a baby cousin (each of the three separately) from their families, and they land on a deserted island with the four robots, who have come (more or less) alive after having been electrified by lightning." Chicago. Children's Bk Center

"Mrs. Brink writes with a kind of cheerful understatement, comfortably and sparely. . . . The shift from the plausible to the fantastic is deft and lighthearted. Andy's behavior is beautifully illustrative of children's aesthetic criteria, for the behavior of characters in fantasy. The proper question here is not 'How could robots come to life?' but 'How would you act if you were marooned on an island in a flood with four friendly, but unpredictable, tin men?'" Christian Science Monitor

The bad times of Irma Baumlein; pictures by Trina Schart Hyman. Macmillan (N Y) 1972 134p illus $5.95, pa $1.25 (4-6)   Fic

1 Dolls—Fiction 2 Truthfulness and falsehood—Fiction

"Irma's bad times begin when she tries to impress her classmates in a new school by claiming to own the biggest doll in the world. When she's asked to exhibit it at the school fair, she panics and 'borrows' a dummy from her family's store." Pub W

"The characterization is adequate, the plot farfetched here and there, but the story has plenty of action, humor, and the perennial appeal of a protagonist in a predicament with which readers can identify." Chicago. Children's Bk Center

Caddie Woodlawn; illus. by Trina Schart Hyman. [New ed] Macmillan Pub. Co. 1973 275p illus $6.95, pa $1.25 (4-6)   Fic

1 Frontier and pioneer life—Fiction 2 Wisconsin—Fiction

ISBN 0-02-713670-1

Awarded the Newbery Medal, 1936

First published 1935

Caddie Woodlawn was eleven in 1864. Because she was frail, she had been allowed to grow up a tomboy. Her capacity for adventure was practically limitless, and there was plenty of adventure on the Wisconsin frontier in those days. The story covers one year of life on the pioneer farm, closing with the news that Mr Woodlawn had inherited an estate in England, and the unanimous decision of the family to stay in Wisconsin. Based upon the reminiscences of the author's grandmother

The typeface "is eminently clear and readable, and the illustrations in black and white . . . are attractive and expressive." Wis Library Bul

Winter cottage; drawings by Fermin Rocker. Macmillan (N Y) 1968 178p illus $4.95, pa $1.25 (4-6)   Fic

1 Wisconsin—Fiction 2 Family—Fiction

First copyrighted 1939-1940

"Thirteen-year-old Minty Sparkes is intensely aware of the hardships which the Depression has placed on her dreamer father and younger sister. She becomes the acting leader of the family as first they decide to move into a vacant summer cottage and then include Joe, a runaway, in their plans. The chance of a new home rather than the constantly changing rented room gives Minty a new-found sense of responsibility and pride which the whole family shares. In an effort to win the money to pay rent for their 'borrowed' cottage, the children plot together to discover Pop's secret recipe for pancakes in order to enter a contest." Reading Ladders. 5th edition

"This book shows the author's ability to tell a good story, imbue her tale with a sense of time and place, and develop strong and believable characterizations. . . . Minty, the older girl, troubled by the need for a more conventional and secure life, emerges as the clear-headed, lovable heroine." Sch Library J

Brock, Betty

No flying in the house; illus. by Wallace Tripp. Harper 1970 139p illus $4.95, lib. bdg. $4.79 (3-5)   Fic

ISBN 0-06-020642-X; 0-06-020643-8

Mrs Vancourt, a rich dowager, befriends a 3x3 inch talking dog named Gloria and her three year old child companion, Annabel Tippens. This is the story of how Annabel solves the mystery of her own origins and stumbles upon some secrets about Mrs Vancourt

"Here is a delicious fantasy in the old-school tradition; it has everything: the cross old lady, the fat and friendly cook, the mysterious child, the more mysterious cat, the long-lost son. . . . With empathetic drawings by Wallace Tripp. The resulting book is sure to be one of the undisputed charmers of the year." Pub W

Brooks, Walter R.

Freddy, the detective; with illus. by Kurt Wiese. Knopf 1932 263p illus lib. bdg. $4.99 (3-5)   Fic

1 Domestic animals—Stories 2 Mystery and detective stories

ISBN 0-394-90827-9

This is a story about the animals on Mr Bean's farm. Freddy, the pig, sets up in business as a detective, after reading the stories of Sherlock Holmes. He then solves a number of very mysterious cases

"This book will be great fun for all who have not outgrown the gift of fitting becoming personalities to our animal friends." N Y Her Trib Bks

Buchwald, Emilie

Gildaen; the heroic adventures of a most unusual rabbit; illus. by Barbara Flynn. Harcourt 1973 189p illus $5.50 (4-6)   Fic

1 Rabbits—Stories

ISBN 0-15-230800-8

"A mettlesome rabbit sets out with an enchantress who has lost her memory to save a young king under the evil spell of a sorcerer. The two are loyally supported by an exiled huntsman and a girl with access to the palace, but after Evonna the enchantress discovers her identity and the extent of her powers, the salvation of king, friends, and country depends on her wisdom and, ultimately, Gildaen's courage." Booklist

"After several adventures that are dangerous and in which Gildaen proves that he is indeed heroic, the sorcerer is thwarted. . . . As for the adventurous rabbit, he decides that home is best—if he can periodically visit his companions—and he fares very well as a returning hero with tall tales to tell. The writing has pace and color, the plot is fresh and imaginative although it uses the traditional fairy tale devices, and the story is sparked with humor." Chicago. Children's Bk Center

Buck, Pearl S.

The big wave; illus. with prints by Hiroshige and Hokusai. Day [1973 c1948] 78p illus $5.95 (4-7) Fic

1 Japan—Fiction

ISBN 0-381-99923-8

Buck, Pearl S.—*Continued*

A reissue of the volume first published 1948

"The Japanese boys, Kino, son of a mountainside farmer, and Jiya, son of a fisherman, are only friends until the day a tidal wave sweeps away Jiya's family and village, and Jiya is alone. Kino's family helps Jiya through his grief, and the boys grow up as brothers. The lure of the sea is stronger for Jiya, and when grown, he returns to build again on the ocean's shore." Reading Ladders. 5th edition

"A gem of a story telling something about the eternal truths of life and death—and helping us to understand the Japanese heart." Asia

Matthew, Mark, Luke and John; illus. by Mamoru Funai. Day [1967 c1966] 80p illus lib. bdg. $4.95 (4-6)   Fic

1   Illegitimacy—Fiction   2   Adoption—Fiction 3 Korea—Fiction

ISBN 0-381-99914-9

"Matthew, no more than a boy himself, finds himself the father figure for three younger boys (Mark, Luke, and John). The bond that ties these homeless boys together is their being half American and half Korean, rejected by Korean society and abandoned by their Korean mothers. Matthew's unselfish devotion to his adopted orphans leads to a satisfying ending." Reading Ladders. 5th edition

"A book that treats with dignity and sympathy the problem of the illegitimate war baby, a problem here compounded by the fact that the four boys are spurned because their fathers were American soldiers." Sutherland. The Best in Children's Bks

Budd, Lillian

Tekla's Easter; pictures by Genia. Rand McNally 1962 unp illus lib. bdg. $3.79 (2-4)   Fic

1 Easter—Stories 2 Sweden—Fiction

ISBN 0-528-80381-6

"A charming story of Easter customs in Sweden, with illustrations that are distinguished, gay, and perfectly appropriate for the text. Tekla, age eight, makes straw witches for the auction that is always held just before Easter to benefit the school lunch program. On Easter Eve she dresses as a witch; on Easter Sunday she rides from her island on the church boat to the mainland service; the family celebrates at home in traditional fashion; the writing style is good although not distinguished; the details of Swedish custom are interesting in both text and illustration; the story has just enough about Tekla as a person—especially in her feelings toward her little sister—to make it the story of a little girl rather than the story of Easter only." Chicago. Children's Bk Center

Buff, Mary

The apple and the arrow, by Mary and Conrad Buff. Houghton 1951 74p illus lib. bdg. $6.95 (3-6)   Fic

1 Tell, William—Fiction 2 Switzerland—Fiction

ISBN 0-395-06669-7

Illustrated by Conrad Buff

"In this retelling of an old legend the spotlight is thrown on 11-year-old Walter Tell who so confidently awaited the outcome of his father's skill with the bow and arrow. The revolt of the Swiss mountaineers against Austrian tyranny at the dawn of 1291 is a story to thrill children. Though now completely discredited, it is the sort of thing which makes history interesting. Writing and illustrating are done with a vigor which makes the book impressive." Pittsburgh

Magic maize, by Mary and Conrad Buff. Houghton 1953 76p illus $4, lib. bdg. $3.57 (3-6)   Fic

1 Corn—Stories 2 Mayas—Fiction 3 Guatamala—Fiction

ISBN 0-395-06665-4; 0-395-06666-2

"An Indian boy of Guatemala becomes friends with the 'gringos' who have developed a new kind of maize and who are doing research in the Mayan ruins. As he learns to trust the foreigners, so too, but reluctantly, does his father who has clung to the ancient religion and customs of his [Mayan] forefathers." Pub W

"The story is conventional, but the pictures [by Conrad Buff] have great value. They will give the children a vivid sense of Central American Guatemala and its people." Sat Rev

Bulla, Clyde Robert

Eagle Feather; illus. by Tom Two Arrows. Crowell 1953 87p illus $4.50, lib. bdg. $5.25 (2-4)   Fic

1 Navaho Indians—Fiction

ISBN 0-690-24880-6; 0-690-24881-4

"Navaho Indian life today is sympathetically depicted in the story of a boy who must decide whether or not to go to the white man's school. Words and music of three Indian songs and illustrations by an Indian artist add to the book's effectiveness." Hodges. Bks for Elem Sch Libraries

John Billington, friend of Squanto; illus. by Peter Burchard. Crowell 1956 88p illus $4.50, lib. bdg. $5.25 (2-4)   Fic

1 Billington, John—Fiction 2 Squanto, Wampanoag Indian—Fiction 3 Pilgrim Fathers—Fiction

ISBN 0-690-46253-0; 0-690-46254-9

"A story of the beginnings of the Plymouth colony. Here young John is captured, and is released when Squanto intercedes with the tribe; later, the same Cape Cod tribe makes overtures of friendship to the Plymouth colony at their feast of Thanksgiving." Sutherland. History in Children's Bks

"Peter Burchard's black-and-white pictures and the clean, open format complete a splendid book for beginning or slow readers." N Y Times Bk Rev

Map on lining-papers

Open the door and see all the people; illus. by Wendy Watson. Crowell 1972 69p illus $3.95, lib. bdg. $4.70 (2-4)   Fic

1 Dolls—Fiction

ISBN 0-690-60045-3; 0-690-60046-1

"A widowed mother and her two daughters, seven-year-old Jo Ann and six-year-old Teeny, move to the city to make a fresh start after losing all their possessions in a fire and are faced with adjusting to a new way of life with very little money. The girls, especially Teeny, who mourn the loss of their dolls more than anything are delighted to discover Toy House where they can borrow dolls and even adopt one for keeps if they prove they will give it a good home." Booklist

"This is a moving story, with real people and, strangely enough, it is Mama who is the most appealing and interesting. The illustrations are also sensitive and revealing." Pub W

Viking adventure; illus. by Douglas Gorsline. Crowell 1963 117p illus $4.95, lib. bdg. $5.70 (3-5)   Fic

1 Northmen—Fiction

ISBN 0-690-86014-5; 0-690-86015-3

"Once again Mr. Bulla writes a good story, with strong plot interest, which is also very easy to read. This one will be particularly welcome because its subject is perennially interesting to younger readers. . . . [The story] tells of young Sigurd and his rigorous training in strength and courage under the firm but affectionate guidance of his father. This training is put to severe test during a long voyage in a great Viking ship to Wineland [America]. The tale and its telling are mature enough to hold the interest of older boys who find reading difficult." Horn Bk

Bulla, Clyde Robert—*Continued*

White Bird; illus. by Leonard Weisgard. Crowell 1966 79p illus $6.50, lib. bdg. $7.25 (4-6)   Fic
1 Crows—Stories 2 Tennessee—Fiction
ISBN 0-690-88499-0; 0-690-88500-8

Nineteenth-century Tennessee is the setting for this "story of a boy rescued from a flood as a baby and reared along by [Luke] a bachelor whose ways reflect the harshness of time and place. The boy's search for a white crow stolen by travelers leads him to a different world outside and to an understanding of Luke. Strong characterizations and theme are enhanced by . . . format and illustration." Top of the News

Burch, Robert

D.J.'s worst enemy; illus. by Emil Weiss. Viking 1965 142p illus lib. bdg. $5.95 (4-6)   Fic
1 Farm life—Fiction 2 Georgia—Fiction
ISBN 0-670-27456-9

A first-person story. "In the peach county of Georgia, D. J. Madison lives the joys of boyhood with his sidekick, Nutty, and the neighboring Castor boys. He teases his younger brother, Renfroe, and his older sister, Clara May, until they share a secret and he feels left out. The reformation which occurs leads to D. J.'s greater appreciation of his family." Wis Lib Bul

Hut School and the wartime home-front heroes; illus. by Ronald Himler. Viking 1974 140p illus lib. bdg. $5.95 (4-6)   Fic
1 School stories 2 World War, 1939-1945—Fiction 3 Georgia—Fiction
ISBN 0-670-38901-3

This story describes the reactions of Kate Coleman and her sixth grade Georgia classmates during World War II as they learn more about the war, its sorrows and its effects on their lives

"The appeal of the book is in the authenticity of the period detail and the growing understanding of the children of what war means. There are plenty of lively incidents, a few characters who seem overdrawn . . . while most of the children are convincing, and some local (Georgia) color." Chicago. Children's Bk Center

Queenie Peavy; illus. by Jerry Lazare. Viking 1966 159p illus lib. bdg. $5.95 (5-7)   Fic
1 Parent and child—Fiction 2 Georgia—Fiction
ISBN 0-670-58422-3

"Defiant, independent and intelligent, 13-year-old Queenie idolized her father who was in jail and was neglected by her mother who had to work all the time. Growing up in the 1930's in Georgia, Queenie eventually understands her father's real character, herself and her relationships to those about her." Wis Lib Bul

"There is no straining here to formulate a story about a problem child. On the surface the account is as dispassionate as a case study, but considerably more convincing, and Queenie is so real that the reader becomes deeply involved in everything that concerns her." Horn Bk

Renfroe's Christmas; illus. by Rocco Negri. Viking 1968 59p illus $3.50, pa 75¢ (3-5)   Fic
1 Christmas stories 2 Georgia—Fiction
ISBN 0-670-59466-0; 0-670-05060-1

"A gracefully written story of Christmas in rural northern Georgia. Eight-year-old Renfroe is uncomfortably aware that he is selfish. After half-hearted, self-conscious attempts to remedy that situation, he suddenly and spontaneously gives away 'the finest thing I've ever owned'—his new Mickey Mouse watch—to a retarded boy because it has made him smile. This understated story with its excellent

characterizations has year-round as well as holiday appeal." Sch Library J

"Nothing sentimental clouds the story of his taking this situation to heart . . . for Renfroe is real, as is everyone in his story. . . . The rural regional quality of the story is strong, the details of church pageant and party are relayed with humor, and the conversations abound in briskness and poignancy." Horn Bk

Skinny; illus. by Don Sibley. Viking 1964 127p illus lib. bdg. $5.95 (4-6)   Fic
1 Hotels, motels, etc.—Fiction 2 Orphans and orphans' homes—Fiction 3 Georgia—Fiction
ISBN 0-670-64999-6

"A sociable 12-year-old orphan boy, taken in by the proprietor of a small town hotel in Georgia, wins the affection of everyone through his sincerity and innocently humorous outlook on life." Bks on Exhibit

Burchard, Peter

Bimby. Coward-McCann 1968 91p illus map $5.95 (4-6)   Fic
1 Slavery in the U.S.—Fiction 2 Negroes—Fiction 3 Georgia—Fiction
ISBN 0-698-20012-8

Set on the Georgia coast shortly before the Civil War, this is the "story of one crucial day in the life of a young American slave—the day in which he decides to risk his life to reach freedom." Best Bks of the year, 1968

"Simply written and illustrated by the author 'Bimby' is a moving tribute to the human spirit and a valuable insight into a past that still haunts us." N Y Times Bk Rev

Jed; the story of a Yankee soldier and a Southern boy; drawings by the author. Coward-McCann 1960 94p illus $5.95 (5-7)   Fic
1 U.S.—History—Civil War—Fiction
ISBN 0-698-20071-3

"The brief encounter of the young Union soldier, Jed, and a Yankee-hating Mississippi boy with a broken leg after the Battle of Shiloh does not change Jed's belief in the Union cause but gives him momentary relief from the ugliness of war." Wis Lib Bul

"The book is quite different from the usual 'war' story for children—to read it is to experience life." Horn Bk

Burnett, Frances Hodgson

A little princess (4-6)   Fic
1 School stories 2 Great Britain—Fiction
Some editions are:
Lippincott $7.95, lib. bdg. $5.93 Pictures by Tasha Tudor (ISBN 0-397-30693-8; 0-397-31339-X)
Platt (A Platt & Munk Cricket bk) $3.95 Illustrated by Steward Sherwood (ISBN 0-8228-2648-8)
Scribner (Illustrated classics ser) pa $3.95 Being the whole story of Sara Crewe, now told for the first time; with illustrations in colors by Ethel Franklin Betts (ISBN 0-684-13811-5)

First American edition published 1892 by Scribner in shorter form with title: Sara Crewe

The story of Sara Crewe, "a persecuted little drudge, to whom a good fairy comes in the person of a rich Indian gentleman, bringing her a fortune." Baker. A Guide to the Best Fiction

"For three generations Mrs. Burnett has lured little girls . . . to slip into the person of Sara Crewe with her 'queer old-fashioned thoughtfulness' and try as she does to act as a princess despite the malicious people who surround her. The story is inevitably adorned with sentimental curlicues but the reader will hardly notice them since the story itself is such a satisfying one." Pub W

Burnett, Frances Hodgson—*Continued*

The secret garden; pictures by Tasha Tudor. Lippincott 1962 256p illus $6.50 (4-6)   Fic

ISBN 0-397-30632-6

First published 1909 by Stokes

"Neglected by his father because of his mother's death at his birth, Colin lives the life of a spoilt and incurable invalid until on the arrival of an orphaned cousin, the two children secretly combine to restore his mother's locked garden and Colin to health and his father's affection." Four to Fourteen

"A most attractive edition in every respect—format, binding, paper, print, and above all, the numerous appealing illustrations in color and in black and white." Booklist

Byars, Betsy

After the Goat Man; illus. by Ronald Himler. Viking 1974 126p illus lib. bdg. $5.95 (5-7)   Fic

ISBN 0-670-10908-8

Figgy's "grandfather, the town's oddball nicknamed the Goat Man, has barricaded himself with his shotgun in their old cabin in a last ditch attempt to halt the wrecking crew from flattening their home for a superhighway. In a crisis which develops when they set out to talk the old man away from the cabin, Ada, Figgy, [overweight] Harold and the Goat Man become linked by their mutual caring, generosity and gentleness." N Y Times Bk Rev

"The restrained plot, developed through spare, unsentimental prose, effectively and clearly delineates the need to recognize individual dignity and the pangs of adolescence. A compassionate and artistic treatment of human problems." Horn Bk

The 18th emergency; illus. by Robert Grossman. Viking 1973 126p illus lib. bdg. $5.95 (4-6)   Fic

1 Fear—Fiction

ISBN 0-670-29055-6

"You can tell quite a bit about a boy when his nickname is 'Mouse.' And when Mouse incites the vengefulness of the school's bully, you know he is petrified with apprehension. Mouse's friend Ezzie has survival plans for emergency situations (being bitten by a tarantula, or being threatened by an octopus) but none for Imminent Beating by Large Boy. Most of the story is concerned with Mouse's fear of this eighteenth emergency, his efforts to avoid it, his feeble attempts to get adult sympathy; when he comes to the inevitable, Mouse surprises himself by his stalwart acceptance of the fight." Chicago. Children's Bk Center

"For its skillful portrayal of the loneliness of fear as well as a boy's emotional battle with himself—his frantic thoughts, his fantasies of escape, his gradual awakening to the way things are as against the way he wishes they were—'The 18th Emergency' weighs in . . . as a bantam champion." N Y Times Bk Rev

The house of wings; illus. by Daniel Schwartz. Viking 1972 142p illus lib. bdg. $4.95 (4-6)   Fic

1 Cranes (Birds)—Stories 2 Grandfathers—Fiction

ISBN 0-670-38025-3

"A young boy reeling from the pain of temporary parental abandonment forges a relationship with an eccentric grandfather whom he despises. In attempting to rescue and mend a wounded crane, they come to respect each other for what they are, and as men." Bk World

This story "has an unsentimental and potent message about wildlife and draws a telling portrait of a human relationship. Save for the brief appearance of the parents, Sammy and his grandfather are the only characters. The book's spare construction makes it strong." Sat Rev

The midnight fox; illus. by Ann Grifalconi. Viking 1968 157p illus lib. bdg. $5.95 (4-6)   Fic

1 Foxes—Stories

ISBN 0-670-47473-8

"City-bred Tommy hates the idea of spending the summer on Aunt Millie's farm while his parents bicycle through Europe. Once he is there, however, a black fox shatters his conviction that he and animals share a mutual antipathy; fascinated, he stalks and watches the wild creature for two months—until it steals some of Aunt Millie's poultry and has to be hunted down." Booklist

"What distinguishes the story from many others on the same theme is the simplicity and beauty of the writing and the depth of the characterization." Horn Bk

The summer of the swans; illus. by Ted CoConis. Viking 1970 142p illus lib. bdg. $4.95 (5-7)   Fic

1 Slow learning children—Fiction 2 Brothers and sisters—Fiction

ISBN 0-670-68190-3

Awarded the Newbery Medal, 1970

"The thoughts and feelings of a young girl troubled by a sense of inner discontent which she cannot explain are tellingly portrayed in the story of two summer days in the life of fourteen-year-old Sara Godfrey. Sara is jolted out of her self-pitying absorption with her own inadequacies by the disappearance of her ten-year-old retarded brother who gets lost while trying to find the swans he had previously seen on a nearby lake. Her agonizing, albeit ultimately successful, search for Charlie and the reactions of others to this traumatic event help Sara gain a new perspective on herself and life." Booklist

"Seldom are the pain of adolescence and the tragedy of mental retardation presented as sensitively and as unpretentiously as in the story of Sara and Charlie. . . . [This is] a subtly told story, echoing the spoken and unspoken thoughts of young people." Horn Bk

Trouble River; illus. by Rocco Negri. Viking 1969 158p illus lib. bdg. $5.95 (4-6)   Fic

1 Frontier and pioneer life—Fiction 2 Rivers—Fiction

ISBN 0-670-73257-5

Dewey Martin and his grandmother must make their way down the Trouble River on a home-made raft to escape the danger of hostile Indians. They find the raft hard to navigate on the river, but they persevere and eventually reach Hunter City and safety

"A philosophy of not giving up amid hardships and a sense of real love and family solidarity predominate." Reading Ladders. 5th edition

Calhoun, Mary

High wind for Kansas; illus. by W. T. Mars. Morrow 1965 45p illus $5.50 (2-4)   Fic

1 Frontier and pioneer life—Fiction 2 Carriages and carts—Fiction

ISBN 0-688-21757-5

"Several men in the history of America's western migration built [prairie schooners or] windwagons. This story is based in part on an incident in Westport, Missouri, involving a man called 'Windwagon Thomas.' " p5

"The line-and-wash pictures have the proper gusto for the story's boisterous action." Horn Bk

Katie John; pictures by Paul Frame. Harper 1960 134p illus lib. bdg. $4.43, pa $1.25 (4-6)   Fic

1 Houses—Fiction

ISBN 0-06-020951-8; 0-06-440028-X

"When the Tuckers inherited an old house in a Missouri town, they decided to live in it until they

Calhoun, Mary—*Continued*

could get it ready to sell. Ten-year-old Katie John was gloomy at the prospect—until she made a new friend, helped to solve a mystery, and learned to love the house." Hodges. Bks for Elem Sch Libraries

A "story with a likable heroine, lively doings, and a credible ending." Booklist

Cameron, Eleanor

The court of the stone children. Dutton 1973 191p $7.25 (5-7)   Fic

1 Museums—Fiction 2 Mystery and detective stories

ISBN 0-525-28350-1

In a San Francisco museum of French art and furniture, Nina encounters the ghost of Dominique, a girl who lived in the nineteenth-century. Spurred on by the appearance of the ghost, Nina sets out to untangle a murder mystery which has remained unsolved since Napoleon's day

"A nice concoction of mystery, fantasy, and realism adroitly blended in a contemporary story. . . . The characters are interesting, the plot threads nicely integrated." Chicago. Children's Bk center

A room made of windows; illus. by Trina Schart Hyman. Little 1971 271p illus $6.95 (5-7)   Fic

ISBN 0-316-12523-7

"An Atlantic Monthly Press book"

"This is the tale of Julia, an aspiring young author, who is highly intelligent but emotionally immature. Although she revels in the satisfactions of good friends and progress in her writing, she is troubled by her mother's desire to remarry, the death of a much-loved elderly friend, and problems of those around her." Wis Lib Bul

"The portrayal and interaction of interesting and diverse characters are given unity and meaning by the genius of a fine storyteller." Top of the News

A spell is cast; illus. by Beth and Joe Krush. Little 1964 271p illus $5.95 (5-7)   Fic

1 California—Fiction 2 Mystery and detective stories

ISBN 0-316-12533-4

"An Atlantic Monthly Press book"

"Cory Winterslow, troubled because she has never been adopted by the actress with whom she lives, goes to California to visit her grandmother and uncle. Here she finds mystery and aloofness instead of the warmth she had hoped for, but eventually her problems are worked out, and she at last 'belongs.' " Hodges. Bks for Elem Sch Libraries

"From its opening the story is absorbing and real. Here is creative storytelling at its best: style, plot, characterizations, atmosphere, and flavor give importance and intensity to what might have been, in less skillful hands, just another story of an appealing child longing for a home." Horn Bk

The terrible churnadryne; illus. by Beth and Joe Krush. Little 1959 125p illus $5.95 (4-6)   Fic

1 California—Fiction 2 Mystery and detective stories

ISBN 0-316-12535-0

"An Atlantic Monthly Press book"

"Tom and Jennifer see a huge and mysterious monster roaming about in the fog and mist in a California coastal town. Few people believe them, but they eventually organize to trap the monster." Adventuring with Bks. 2d edition

"The story skirts the edge of fantasy while it tells [of events] with humor and good characterization. . . . A different kind of mystery with a great deal of atmosphere." Horn Bk

Time and Mr Bass; a Mushroom Planet book; illus. by Fred Meise. Little 1967 247p illus $5.95 (4-6)
                                                            Fic

1 Science fiction

ISBN 0-316-12536-9

"An Atlantic Monthly Press book"

In this science fiction story, Chuck and David come to the aid of Mr Bass who is attempting to translate the ancient Thirteenth Scroll. This scroll holds the secret to the evil power that has hounded the Mycetians, or spore people, for centuries

"Here is original, fast-moving fantasy with the added strength and significance of the conflict between good and evil." Sch Library J

Carew, Jan

The third gift; illus. by Leo and Diane Dillon. Little 1974 32p illus $5.95 (3-5)   Fic

1 Africa—Fiction

ISBN 0-316-12847-3

Set in Africa in the far past and drawing on folkloric themes, this tale "has a rich, poetic quality that is echoed in the brilliant colors and intricate patterns of the handsome illustrations. A prophet who had led his people from famine to a land of plenty decrees that when he dies, the tribe's young men must climb the Nameless Mountain, and that he who climbs the highest shall bring a gift to his people. Three times in the tribe's history, a gift is brought to the people; first they are given the gift of work, then the gift of beauty, then the gift of fantasy, of imagination and faith. 'So,' the story ends, 'with the gifts of Work and Beauty and Imagination, the Jubas became poets and bards and creators, and they live at the foot of Nameless Mountain to this day.' The writing style is rather grave and ornate, not as direct as most traditional folklore is, which may limit its appeal to some readers and be an added attraction for those who enjoy poetic prose." Chicago. Children's Bk Center

Carlson, Natalie Savage

Ann Aurelia and Dorothy; pictures by Dale Payson. Harper 1968 130p illus $4.95, lib. bdg. $4.79 (4-6)
                                                            Fic

1 Foster home care—Fiction 2 Negroes—Fiction

ISBN 0-06-020958-5; 0-06-020959-3

"Ann Aurelia, living in a foster home because her mother has remarried and can't have her, makes friends with Dorothy, another fifth grader with whom she shares pranks and good times. When her mother reappears, Ann must decide whether to stay with her foster mother or rejoin her real one." Bruno. Bks for Sch Libraries, 1968

The author "isn't peddling any clichés like 'poor, oppressed white girl finds love and comfort and goodness in black home.' All the people in this story . . . black and white, are normal, decent people. The black girl is no miracle of maturity. If she is the natural leader of the two, this is because she knows the district better and for the moment has the more stable background. And what is exceptionally well-realized is the girls' enjoyment of each other. This is no forced friendship for the sake of a 'mixed' story." Christian Sci Monitor

Befana's gift; drawings by Robert Quackenbush. Harper 1969 86p illus lib. bdg. $4.79 (3-5)   Fic

1 Rome (City)—Fiction 2 Christmas stories

ISBN 0-06-020965-8

"A Christmas story set in contemporary Rome. Only old Cesare, of all the carriage drivers, had no male progeny about whom he could boast; much as he doted upon his granddaughter Gemma, the old man was only half-joking when he asked an old woman who

Carlson, Natalie Savage—*Continued*
resembled Befana (the gift-giver in Italian Christmas tradition) to bring him a grandson. A shepherd lad from the Abruzzi, Davide, is wandering about the city; Cesare and Gemma bring him home. Gemma becomes jealous and sees to it that Davide leaves, then is repentant; she runs into the same old woman, who helps her find Davide and restore him to the bosom of his second family." Chicago. Children's Bk Center

"The author captures and communicates the spirit of people and place; her Romans with their simple dignity, self-reliance, and awareness of an ancient heritage are full of warmth and appeal in a setting of colorful, characteristic Christmas and New Year's celebrations." Horn Bk

The half sisters; pictures by Thomas di Grazia. Harper 1970 163p illus $3.95, lib. bdg. $4.79, pa $1.25 (4-6)   Fic
1 Family—Fiction 2 Maryland—Fiction
ISBN 0-06-021003-6; 0-06-021004-4; 0-06-440017-4
"Luvena Savage longs to be accepted as 'one of the girls.' Luvvy finally achieves her desire by winning the respect of the older girls. This spirited, satisfying story of family life and growing up in Maryland in 1915 was drawn from the author's own childhood." Reading Ladders. 5th edition

"The mood of the story is warm and quiet, although Luvvy is a forceful character. The book is permeated with family love, the writing is smooth, the pace sustained, and the dialogue natural." Sutherland. The Best in Children's Bks

The happy orpheline; pictures by Garth Williams. Harper 1957 96p illus lib. bdg. $4.43 (2-4)   Fic
1 Orphans and orphans' homes—Fiction 2 France —Fiction
ISBN 0-06-021007-9
"Twenty orphan girls dread adoption because it will mean separation. One gets lost and involved in adventures with the 'queen of France' who threatens to adopt her. Enough French words to spark the interest of a beginning French student." Sch Library J

Three other books about the orphelines are also available from Harper: A brother for the orphelines; illus. by Garth Williams lib. bdg. $4.79 (ISBN 0-06-020961-5) A pet for the orphelines; illus. by Fermin Rocker $4.95, lib. bdg. $4.79 (ISBN 0-021055-9; 0-06-021056-7) The orphelines in the enchanted castle; illus. by Adriana Saviozzi lib. bdg. $4.79 (ISBN 0-06-021046-X)

Carr, Mary Jane
Children of the covered wagon; a story of the old Oregon Trail; illus. by Bob Kuhn. Crowell 1957 [c1943] 318p illus $5.95 (4-6)   Fic
1 Oregon Trail—Fiction 2 Overland journeys to the Pacific—Fiction
ISBN 0-690-18987-7
First published 1934 with illustrations by Esther Brann
Recounts the dangers and experiences of a covered wagon trip from Missouri to the Willamette Valley, Oregon, in 1844. The story is told from the viewpoint of young Jerry Stephen who, with his cousin Jim and small Myra Dean, the doctor's daughter, went thru their share of the perils of the journey bravely
"The thrills and hardships . . . are well depicted. . . . There is heroism and humor in the telling." Wis Lib Bul

Carroll, Lewis
Alice's adventures in Wonderland (4-7)   Fic

1 Fairy tales
Some editions are:
Collins (Standard classic ed) $4.95 (ISBN 0-00-421450-1)
Crowell $10. Illustrated by Moritz Kennel (ISBN 0-690-00984-4)
Crown (Centennial ed) $7.95, pa $3.95 Illustrated by Ralph Steadman; prepared by the committee of the Lewis Carroll Society (ISBN 0-517-50857-5; 0-517-50838-3)
Random House $2.50, lib. bdg. $3.79 With the John Tenniel illustrations colored by Fritz Kredel (ISBN 0-394-80627-1; 0-394-90627-6)
Viking $6.95 Illustrated by Arthur Rackham; with a proem by Austin Dobson (ISBN 0-670-11277-1)
Watts, F. lib. bdg. $7.95. With forty-two illustrations by John Tenniel. Large type edition complete and unabridged. A Keith Jennison book (ISBN 0-531-00152-0)
"First told in 1862 to the little Liddell girls. Written out for Alice Liddell, published, and first copy given to her in 1865." Arnold
"A rabbit who took a watch out of his waistcoat pocket seemed well-worth following to Alice so she hurried after him across the field, down the rabbit hole, and into a series of adventures with a group of famous and most unusual characters." Let's Read Together
This fantasy "is one of the most quoted books in the English language. Every child should be introduced to Alice, though its appeal will not be universal." Adventuring With Bks. 2d edition

Alice's adventures in Wonderland, and Through the looking glass (4-7)   Fic
1 Fairy tales
Some editions are:
Collins (Rainbow classics) $3.50, lib bdg $3.91 Illustrated by John Tenniel; introduction by May Lamberton Becker (ISBN 0-529-05031-5; 0-529-05032-3)
Dutton (Children's illustrated classics) $3.95 With original engravings by John Tenniel of which 8 have been redrawn in colour by Diane Stanley (ISBN 0-525-25400-5)
Dutton (Everyman's lib) $3.95, pa $1.50 Actual illustrations by the author. Prefatory note by Roger Lancelyn Green (ISBN 0-460-00836-6; 0-460-01836-1)
Grosset (Illustrated junior lib) $3.95 Illustrated by John Tenniel. Has title: Alice in Wonderland and Through the Looking Glass (ISBN 0-448-05804-9)
Macmillan (N Y) (The Macmillan classics) lib. bdg. $4.95, pa $1.25 With illustrations by John Tenniel. Afterword by Clifton Fadiman
Oxford (Oxford English Novels) $11.25 With illustrations by John Tenniel. Edited with an introduction by Roger Lancelyn Green. Has title: Alice's adventure in Wonderland; & Through the looking glass and what Alice found there. (ISBN 0-19-255341-0)
An omnibus edition of the two titles listed above and below

Through the looking glass, and what Alice found there (4-7)   Fic
1 Fairy tales
Some editions are:
Potter, C.N. $7.95, pa $4.95. Illustrated by Ralph Steadman
St Martins $5.50. Reprint of the children's edition published in 1927. Illustrated by Sir John Tenniel First published 1872
Follows: Alice in Wonderland, and contains the famous: The Walrus and the Carpenter, and Jabberwocky poems

Carroll, Ruth

Beanie, by Ruth and Latrobe Carroll. Walck, H.Z. 1953 unp illus lib. bdg. $4.95 (1-4)   Fic

1 Dogs—Stories 2 Great Smoky Mountains—Fiction

ISBN 0-8098-2001-3

First published by Oxford; illustrated by the authors

A picture story book about a little six-year-old living in the Great Smoky Mountains. Beanie went for a walk in the woods on his birthday, with his new puppy and his toy gun. What happened when he met a bear and lost his puppy is related

"The pictures in gray-green are unusually effective in bringing out the atomosphere of the mountain country. They are so full of action that little children can read Beanie's story even without the text." Horn Bk

Followed by: Tough Enough

Tough Enough, by Ruth and Latrobe Carroll. Walck, H.Z. 1954 unp illus lib. bdg. $4.95 (2-4) Fic

1 Dogs—Stories 2 Great Smoky Mountains—Fiction

ISBN 0-8098-2004-8

Sequel to: Beanie

First published by Oxford

"Beanie Tatum, his Great Smoky Mountain family, and his dog Tough Enough come to life in an affectionately humorous story with realistic illustrations by Ruth Carroll." Hodges. Bks. for Elem Sch Libraries

Catherall, Arthur

Last horse on the sands; illus. by David Farris. Lothrop [1973 c1972] 128p illus $4.95, lib. bdg. $4.59 (4-6)   Fic

1 Rescue work—Fiction 2 Great Britain—Fiction

ISBN 0-688-40049-5; 0-688-50049-8

First published 1972 in England

A brother and sister in an English seaside village risk their lives and that of an old cart horse as they try to rescue victims of a plane crash before the tide comes in

The author "utilizes good plot development and well-built tension. . . . [He] makes the unusual events plausible and develops unrelenting suspense as disaster piles upon disaster. The book authentically reflects the way crises happen and presents a believable picture of the courage, as well as the foolishness, of the protagonists." Library J

Prisoners in the snow; drawings by Victor Ambrus. Lothrop 1967 128p illus lib. bdg. $4.59 (3-5)   Fic

1 Rescue work—Fiction 2 Disasters—Fiction 3 Austria—Fiction

ISBN 0-688-51081-7

"Trapped in their undamaged Austrian farm house by an avalanche caused by a plane crash, two children and their lame grandfather risk life and limb to rescue the pilot, who is buried against the collapsing roof of their shed. Their clever use of the things at hand and their persistence make this both a rousing adventure story and lesson on the value of clear thinking." Bruno. Bks for Sch Libraries, 1968

Caudill, Rebecca

A certain small shepherd; with illus. by William Pène Du Bois. Holt 1965 48p illus lib. bdg. $5.95, pa $1.45 (4-6)   Fic

1 Physically handicapped children—Fiction 2 Appalachian Mountains—Fiction 3 Christmas stories

ISBN 0-03-089755-6; 0-03-08010-7

The author tells of "the singleminded enthusiasm of [Jamie], a little mute boy, who is given the part of one of the shepherds in a church celebration. . . . The pageant never takes place as a blizzard immobilizes the poor mountain community where the child lives, but the small shepherd is so deeply committed to his part that he acts it out impulsively [and speaks] when a baby is born to a family of travelers, caught by the storm and obliged to take refuge in the church." Bk Week

"There is a terrible poignancy in the episodes . . . of the cruel sting of laughter from other children over Jamie's grunts as he counts for hide-and-seek: of Jamie's knowing the answers in school but not being able to utter them. . . . [A story] that renews and revitalizes the meaning of love and joy." N Y Times Bk Rev

Did you carry the flag today, Charley? Illus. by Nancy Grossman. Holt 1966 94p illus $3.50, lib. bdg. $5.95, pa $1.45 (2-4)   Fic

1 Appalachian Mountains—Fiction 2 School stories

ISBN 0-03-055620-1; 0-03-089753-X; 0-03-086620-0

"A really delightful, tender story of exuberantly curious, five-year-old Charley who is just beginning to attend school in the Appalachian Mountains. No one expects it to happen, but somehow, independent little Charley does manage to receive the highest honor in school, being chosen to 'carry the flag' for having been the most helpful." Wis Lib Bul

"This is a realistic and low-keyed story with good dialogue, although Charley seems precocious, and excellent classroom scenes." Chicago. Children's Bk Center

"A very fine book and a very funny one enhanced by wry pencil drawings." Sch Library J

The far-off land; drawings by Brinton Turkle. Viking 1964 287p map lib. bdg. $4.95 (6-7)   Fic

1 Frontier and pioneer life—Fiction

ISBN 0-670-30774-2

"Reunited with her frontiersman brother after 14 years, Ketty Petrie travels with him, his family, and a handful of neighbors on a flatboat from Fort Patrick Henry to the French Lick. The dangerous journey gives sixteen-year-old Ketty, raised by pacifist Moravians, an insight into the beliefs and ways of those who rely on the power of the gun. A deeply moving story, strong in characterization, which does not minimize the cruelties and hardships of frontier life. Written mostly in vernacular dialog." Booklist

Glossary of German words and phrases: p8

Tree of freedom; illus. by Dorothy Bayley Morse. Viking 1949 279p illus lib. bdg. $5.95 (6-7)   Fic

1 Frontier and pioneer life—Fiction 2 Kentucky—Fiction

ISBN 0-670-72807-1

"Neither thirteen-year-old Stephanie nor her brother Noel saw eye to eye with Pappy when in 1780 he moved the family from North Carolina to Kentucky hoping to leave the Revolution behind. Stephanie, as well as Noel, wanted desperately to serve her country in its fight for freedom. Her chance came when Pappy went away on a mission and Noel went off to war, for it was she who took care of family and land against threats of Indian raids and land grabbers." Booklist

"A real pioneer book. . . . Stephanie plants and nurtures the 'tree of freedom,' an apple tree that symbolizes the tie with the past and the new way of life." Wis Lib Bul

Cavanna, Betty

Petey; illus. by Beth and Joe Krush. Westminster Press 1973 144p illus $4.95 (4-7)   Fic

1 Great Danes—Stories

ISBN 0-664-32532-7

"Petey, an intelligent but inept Great Dane belonging to Ernest Bodman, provides the focus for Ernest's

Cavanna, Betty—*Continued*

first-person account of life for a big dog in a little housing development. Because of his size Petey is alternately used and abused for neighborhood needs, and although Ernest knows his dog's capabilities better than anyone else, he can't forsee the turns of fate that exploit Petey's weak spots concerning such things as gunshots, cats, small dogs, and veterinary visits. . . . Ernest's boyish practical appraisals of the assorted situation comedies lend an easy humor with a scope that can encompass more than dog lovers." Booklist

Chaffin, Lillie D.

John Henry McCoy; illus. by Emanuel Schongut. Macmillan (N Y) 1971 169p illus $4.95 (4-6)   Fic

1 Kentucky—Fiction 2 Poverty—Fiction

This is the story of a Southern Appalachian family that moved around in search of jobs, and particularly it is the story of John Henry McCoy who wants to go all year to the same school, to have a real friend, and to own a dog. With the aid of his granny, who shares his need to belong somewhere, an ingenious plan is worked out to achieve their dream

"The pace of the story is sedate, but it suits the resigned, day-to-day existence of the McCoys; the characters ring true, and the book gives a good picture of the plight of the Southern Appalachian worker without being a treatise in disguise. Not a story filled with excitement, this has a depth and tenderness that are appealing." Chicago. Children's Bk Center

Christopher, John

The city of gold and lead. Macmillan (N Y) 1967 185p $4.95 (5-7)   Fic

1 Science fiction

Sequel to: The White Mountains

"Massive gold walls and a high crystal dome surround the City of the Tripods where Earth's alien Masters live. Within, the oppressive, poisonous atmosphere soon kills each fresh group of human slaves despite the masks they wear. Two young athletes from an underground society of free people masquerade as slaves and discover the plan with which the Masters intend to destroy humans and make Earth safe for their race to colonize." Moorachian. What is a City?

"For the young science fiction fan who likes to read about the same characters but eschews the patterned banality of most series books, here's a very good sequel" Sat Rev

Followed by: The pool of fire

The pool of fire. Macmillan (N Y) 1968 178p $5.95 (5-7)   Fic

1 Science fiction

In this final volume of the trilogy begun with "The White Mountains" and "The city of gold and lead," Will and a handful of free men of the world must foil the Masters' Plan for world domination. The Masters' Plan is to turn the earth's atmosphere into choking green fog, the only air which the fearsome invaders can breathe naturally

"It doesn't matter whether or not one has read the earlier books of this trilogy, each stands by itself and each tells a good straight yarn." Christian Sci Monitor

The White Mountains. Macmillan (N Y) 1967 184p $4.95, pa $1.25 (5-7)   Fic

1 Science fiction

"The world of the future is ruled by huge and powerful machine-creatures, the Tripods, who control mankind by implanting metal caps in their skulls when they reach the age of fourteen. Three boys

[Will, Henry, and Beanpole] . . . see that the people about them are mindless conformists [and] decide to flee to the White Mountains (Switzerland), where there is a colony of free men. Their journey is hazardous, bringing them at one time into an almost medieval French household and another into the ruins of a deserted and crumbling Paris." Sat Rev

"A remarkable story . . . it belongs to the school of science-fiction which puts philosophy before technology and is not afraid of telling an exciting story." Times (London) Lit Sup

Followed by: The city of gold and lead

Wild Jack. Macmillan Pub. Co. 1974 147p $5.95 (5-7)   Fic

1 Science fiction

ISBN 0-02-718300-9

The first book in a projected trilogy

The author's "23rd-Century world is divided into two parts: civilization (ultra-urbanized, mechanized, and stratified by class) and the Outlands (simple living, respect for all people, etc.). After Clive, son of a controversial government leader, and two other young men are imprisoned for various 'crimes' against civilization, the three escape to the Outlands. Led by a former city person—'Wild Jack'—the so-called 'savages' of the Outlands turn out to be humane and friendly. . . . The characters are not well developed and the dialogue is stiff and stilted, but the story is swiftly paced and adventure fans will probably enjoy this simplistic world where there is little difficulty understanding where virtue and vice lie." Sch Library J

Christopher, Matt

Catch that pass! Illus. by Harvey Kidder. Little 1969 130p illus $4.50 (3-5)   Fic

1 Football—Fiction

ISBN 0-316-13932-7

Jim, a linebacker for the Vulcans, froze everytime he had the football and the opposing team came flying at him. This is the story of how Jim gained confidence and conquered his fear of being tackled, with the help of a physically handicapped friend's example

The kid who only hit homers; illus. by Harvey Kidder. Little 1972 151p illus $4.95 (3-5)   Fic

1 Baseball—Fiction

ISBN 0-316-13918-1

Sylvester looks like a poor prospect for the Redbirds baseball team until the mysterious Mr George Baruth gives him special talent. This story tells how Sylvester handles his new fame and what happens to Sylvester's baseball ability when Mr Baruth goes away, as he said he would have to

"Presumably Sylvester's ability to hit homers will leave him after Mr. Baruth's departure, but this easy-to-read book will still make a hit with fans." Sch Library J

Look who's playing first base; illus. by Harvey Kidder. Little 1971 131p illus $4.50 (3-5)   Fic

1 Baseball—Fiction 2 Russians in the U.S.—Fiction

ISBN 0-316-13933-5

"Yuri Dotzen, whose family had come from Russia the year before, has had no baseball experience, but Mike is sure he can fill in at first base. Yuri's play is full of errors, but he develops fast as a hitter; not fast enough to keep Don, the catcher, from taunting him and threatening to quit. Don calls Yuri a communist and Yuri explains that his parents had decided to leave Russia to get away from communism. Don quits, then returns to apologize and take his old position." Chicago. Children's Bk Center

Christopher, Matt—*Continued*

The team that couldn't lose; illus. by Foster Caddell. Little 1967 133p illus $4.50 (3-5)   Fic

1 Baseball—Fiction
ISBN 0-316-13916-5

"On the first day of practice, the Cayugans certainly looked like losers. As they won game after game, they realized it was because of the new plays that had been sent to the coach in the mail. Excitement and mystery are packed into this story of an inexperienced team learning to have faith in itself." Bruno. Bks for Sch Libraries, 1968

Clapp, Patricia

Constance; a story of early Plymouth. Lothrop 1968 255p map lib. bdg. $5.11 (5-7)   Fic

1 Pilgrim Fathers—Fiction 2 Massachusetts—History—Colonial period—Fiction
ISBN 0-688-51127-9

The imaginary "journal kept by Constance Hopkins, daughter of Stephen Hopkins and ancestress of Patricia Clapp. Constance began jotting down her impressions and intimate thoughts at the age of fifteen on the eve of the 'Mayflower's' arrival and continued up to the day of her wedding five years later. With disarming candor, quick wit, and sprightliness she tells of her despair at leaving London, the discomforts of the voyage, her instant hatred of the wilderness and fear of the native savages, her gradual awareness of growing up during the agonies of the dreadful Sickness and the famine, her new understanding of her stepmother, her awareness of the political and economic issues of the settlement, her friends and flirtations, her often immodest impulses, and her narrow escape from marrying the wrong man." Horn Bk

"The characters come alive, the writing style is excellent, and the historical background is smoothly integrated." Chicago. Children's Bk Center

Jane-Emily. Lothrop 1969 160p lib. bdg. $4.81 (5-7)   Fic

1 Ghost stories

"While visiting her grandmother, young Jane finds a crystal ball which reflects the image of Emily, a dead girl. Jane is soon possessed by the ghost of Emily, and the events which follow are chilling." Cincinnati

"Well written and with a convincing strong Gothic strain, the story is spellbinding, building up to an exciting climax." Horn Bk

Clark, Ann Nolan

Blue Canyon horse; illus. by Allan Houser. Viking 1954 54p illus lib. bdg. $4.95 (2-4)   Fic

1 Horses—Stories 2 Indians of North America—Fiction 3 Utah—Fiction
ISBN 0-670-17456-4

One night a young mare fled from her Utah canyon pasture and the Indian boy who loved her and took care of her—clattering up the stony trail, across the mesa, to run with the wild herd. But when the canyon field was green again, she came back with her colt, drawn by a loyalty deeper than her longing to be free

"A poetic story, written with sensitive understanding of the bond which can exist between a boy and an animal." Secondary Educ Board

"It should be read aloud—and children will want it more than once. Obviously both the author and the Indian artist love the country of the canyon and the mesa." Horn Bk

Hoofprint on the wind; illus. by Robert Andrew Parker. Viking 1972 128p illus lib. bdg. $5.50 (5-7)   Fic

1 Ireland—Fiction 2 Horses—Stories
ISBN 0-670-37874-7

"Patcheen's two eldest brothers and his father have been lost at sea as have so many of the men of their sparse and barren island [of western Ireland]. His brother Sean and his grandmother refuse to believe that Patcheen has seen a beautiful Connemara horse running wild on the island; his gentle mother half believes it. From one of the older men, the boy learns that the horse had belonged to his father and was his to sell, but when a breeder comes and offers to buy the horse, Patcheen can not give it up. The story is rich in dialect, but it is occasionally obtrusive." Chicago. Children's Bk Center

"Survival and affection for the family vie for prominence in the book. Use this book to provide a feeling for people who are close to the land." Notable Children's Trade Bks (Social Studies)

Little Navajo Bluebird; illus. by Paul Lantz. Viking 1943 143p illus lib. bdg. $4.95 (3-5)   Fic

1 Navaho Indians—Fiction
ISBN 0-670-43235-0

Little Bluebird, a Navajo girl, "who has seen how Big Brother had returned from School with only scorn for the life of his mother's hogan, is determined that she will never let them send her to school. But from Uncle's young wife and Sister Hobah, she learns that School may have much to teach her that will make life healthier and happier without taking away any of the old customs that she loves." Wis Lib Bul

"The quiet beauty of the Navajo country is fully realized in both the pictures and text of this sensitive story." N Y Pub Library

Magic money; illus. by Leo Politi. Viking 1950 121p illus $3.50 (3-5)   Fic

1 Costa Rica—Fiction
ISBN 0-670-44916-4

Story of Tony who lived in Costa Rica. He wanted very much to earn enough money so he could realize a Secret: he wanted to buy oxen for his beloved grandfather. The story is of Tony's efforts to earn money and the lessons he learned on the way to success

"The characters are warmer and better drawn than in most books of this type. . . . The setting . . . is portrayed with all Leo Politi's striking sense of colour and design and adds a rich background to the story." Ontario Library Rev

Secret of the Andes; with drawings by Jean Charlot. Viking 1952 130p illus $5.95 (4-7)   Fic

1 Incas—Fiction 2 Peru—Fiction
ISBN 0-670-62975-8

Awarded the Newbery Medal, 1953

"A young South American Indian boy searches for his destiny, eventually realizing that he wants to be a llama herder just as he has been trained to do. Interwoven into the story is the history of the Spanish conquerors and the value of continuing the ancient Incan traditions." Reading Ladders. 5th edition

It is a "rarely beautiful and subtle story. . . . Perceptive young readers will respond to the beauty of the telling, with mysticism in Incan songs and vivid description of wild and unvisited grandeur in the high Andes. It has a distinguished format, with richly toned lithograph frontispiece, end papers and jacket." Horn Bk

Clark, Mavis Thorpe

The min-min. Macmillan (N Y) 1969 216p $5.95 (5-7)   Fic

1 Runaways—Fiction 2 Australia—Fiction
First published 1967 in England

"In this novel set in Australia, Reg has vandalized the schoolhouse, so the 'coppers' will surely send him away; his sister, Sylvie, is trapped by unending household tasks, helped not at all by an ailing mother and

Clark, Mavis Thorpe—*Continued*
drinking father. Like the aborigines' min-min, an elusive light which beckons but remains unreachable, Sylvie's dream of further education seems futile. So the two run away deep into the Australian outback. . . . Their destination is the sheep-station of Gulla Tank and the sympathetic ear of a friend, Mrs. Tucker." N Y Times Bk Rev

"A story of adolescent growth and family relationships with preceptive characterization and a novel locale." Horn Bk

Clarke, Pauline
The return of the Twelves; illus. by Bernarda Bryson. Coward-McCann [1963 c1962] 251p illus $7.95 (4-7) Fic

1 Toys—Fiction 2 Great Britain—Fiction
ISBN 0-698-20117-5

First published 1962 in England with title: The Twelve and the genii

"Twelve wooden soldiers come to life and, aided by three present-day children, return to their former home, the Brontë Museum at Haworth." Hodges. Bks for Elem Sch Libraries

"Throughout the book are long and lively scenes that exploit the past and present ploys and personalities of the twelve. Smoothly knit, humorous, and highly original, the book gives in addition a perceptive portrayal of Max and the other members of the family. Winner of the Carnegie Medal in 1962, the book will surely appeal to many older readers who can appreciate the author's literary skill and who can enjoy the allusive references to the Brontes." Chicago. Children's Bk Center

Cleary, Beverly
Beezus and Ramona; illus. by Louis Darling. Morrow 1955 159p illus $5.50; lib. bdg. $4.81; pa $1.50 (3-5) Fic

ISBN 0-688-21076-7; 0-688-31076-1; 0-688-25078-8

"Ramona Quimby, the strong-willed four-year-old who has spiced previous episodes of this gay series, now has a whole book in which to try the patience of well-behaved big sister Beezus. Wearing the rabbit ears she constructed at nursery school, Ramona moves purposefully through her world, leaving destruction and distraction in her wake. This is a very funny book; its situations are credible, and it has a perceptive handling of family relationships that is unfortunately rare in easily read books." Horn Bk

"Young readers who have small brothers and sisters will understand Beezus' perplexity about her relationship with four-year-old Ramona and will be interested in the conclusion that you don't have to love them all the time." Wis Library Bul

Followed by: Ramona the pest

Ellen Tebbits; illus. by Louis Darling. Morrow 1951 160p illus $5.50, lib. bdg. $4.81 (3-5) Fic

1 School stories
ISBN 0-688-21264-6; 0-688-31264-0

"Ellen Tebbits is eight years old, takes ballet lessons, wears bands on her teeth, and has a secret—she wears woolen underwear. But she finds a friend in Austine, a new girl in school, who also wears woolen underwear. They have the usual troubles that beset 'best friends' in grade school plus some that are unusual." Pittsburgh

"Their experiences in the third grade are comical and very appealing to children in the middle grades." Hodges. Bks for Elem Sch Libraries

Henry Huggins; illus. by Louis Darling. Morrow 1950 155p illus $5.50, lib. bdg. $4.81, pa $1.50 (3-5) Fic

ISBN 0-688-21385-5; 0-688-31385-X; 0-688-25385-7

"Henry Huggins is a typical small boy who, quite innocently, gets himself into all sorts of predicaments—often with the very apt thought, 'Won't Mom be surprised.' There is not a dull moment but some hilariously funny ones in the telling of Henry's adventures at home and at school." Booklist

Four other books about Henry Huggins are also available from Morrow: Henry and Beezus $5.50, lib. bdg. $4.81, pa $1.50 (ISBN 0-688-21383-9; 0-688-31383-3; 0-688-25383-0) Henry and Ribsy $5.50, lib. bdg. $4.81, pa $1.50 (ISBN 0-688-21382-0; 0-688-31382-5; 0-688-25382-2) Henry and the paper route $5.50, lib. bdg. $4.81, pa $1.50 (ISBN 0-688-21380-4; 0-688-31380-9; 0-688-25380-6) Henry and the clubhouse $5.50, lib. bdg. $4.81, pa $1.50 (ISBN 0-688-21381-2; 0-688-31381-7; 0-688-25381-4)

Mitch and Amy; illus. by George Porter. Morrow 1967 222p illus $5.50; lib. bdg. $4.81 (3-5) Fic

1 Twins—Fiction 2 School stories
ISBN 0-688-21688-9; 0-688-31688-3

"The twins Mitch and Amy are in the fourth grade. Mitch is plagued by a bully and by reading difficulties, Amy struggles with multiplication tables, and their patient mother mediates their squabbles." Sch Library J

"The writing style and dialogue, the familial and peer group relationships, the motivations and characterizations all have the ring of truth. Written with ease and vitality, lightened with humor, the story is perhaps most appealing because it is clear that the author respects children." Chicago. Children's Bk Center

The mouse and the motorcycle; illus. by Louis Darling. Morrow 1965 158p illus $5.50; lib. bdg. $4.81 (3-5) Fic

1 Mice—Stories
ISBN 0-688-21698-6; 0-688-31698-0

"A fantasy about Ralph, a mouse, who learns to ride a toy motorcycle and goes on wild rides through the corridors of the hotel where he lives. Keith, the boy to whom the motorcycle belongs, becomes fast friends with Ralph and defends him when danger threatens." Hodges. Bks for Elem Sch Libraries

"The author shows much insight into the thoughts of children. She carries the reader into an imaginative world that contains many realistic emotions." Wis Lib Bul

Followed by: Runaway Ralph

Otis Spofford, illus. by Louis Darling. Morrow 1953 191p illus $5.50, lib. bdg. $4.81 (3-5) Fic

1 School stories
ISBN 0-688-21720-6; 0-688-31720-0

"Otis, a mischievous, fun loving boy, is always getting in and out of trouble. His mother, a dancing teacher, is busy earning their living and often leaves Otis on his own. This book tells of several episodes in Otis's life—from his sneaking vitamins to a white rat to 'disprove' a diet experiment, to getting his final 'come-uppance' when a trick on Ellen Tebbits backfires." Reading Ladders. 5th edition

"This writer has her elementary school down pat, and manages to report her growing boys, teachers, and P.T.A. meetings so that parents chuckle and boys laugh out loud." N Y Her Trib Bks

Ribsy; illus. by Louis Darling. Morrow 1964 192p illus $5.50, lib. bdg. $4.81 (3-5) Fic

1 Dogs—Stories
ISBN 0-688-21662-5; 0-688-31662-X

"Henry Huggins' dog, Ribsy, wanders away, can't find his way home, and has a series of adventures

Cleary, Beverly—*Continued*

before he is found. Mrs. Cleary's style is—as always—refreshing; the characters are real, the dialogue is lively, the humor is unquenchable. The emphasis here is on Ribsy rather than his owner; the story is therefore episodic, with some sequences that are ridiculous—but hilariously ridiculous." Chicago. Children's Bk Center

Runaway Ralph; illus. by Louis Darling. Morrow 1970 175p illus $5.50, lib. bdg. $4.81 (3-5)   Fic

1 Mice—Stories

ISBN 0-688-21701-X; 0-688-31701-4

Sequel to: The mouse and the motorcycle

"Ralph, resident mouse at the Mountain View Inn, has found that he could communicate with any human beings sensible enough to understand that to make a toy motorcycle real you have only to say, 'Pb-pb-b-b-b!' Tired of giving rides to his little cousins, Ralph decides to run away, and goes zooming off. He is caught by a homesick camper who is suspected of having stolen a watch. Ralph, who knows that the thief was a cat, makes a deal with the camper—a boy intelligent enough to go 'Pb-pb-b-b-b!'—and thus achieves freedom. The combination of reality and fantasy is deft, the depiction of camp life delightfully wry, and the saga of Ralph's adventures a musine triumph." Sat Rev

Socks; illus. by Beatrice Darwin. Morrow 1973 156p illus $5.50; lib. bdg. $4.81 (3-5)   Fic

1 Cat—Stories 2 Infants—Fiction

ISBN 0-688-20067-2; 0-688-30067-7

"The Brickers' kitten, Socks, is jealous when they bring a baby home from the hospital. How he copes with this rivalry makes an amusing story true to cat nature." Cleveland Pub Library

"Not being child-centered, this may have a smaller audience than earlier Cleary books, but it is written with the same easy grace, the same felicitous humor and sharply observant eye." Chicago. Children's Bk Center

Cleaver, Vera

Ellen Grae [by] Vera and Bill Cleaver; illus. by Ellen Raskin. Lippincott 1967 89p illus $4.75 (4-6)   Fic

1 Truthfulness and falsehood—Fiction 2 Mentally handicapped—Fiction

ISBN 0-397-30938-4

"Eleven-year-old Ellen Grae is an imaginative and original girl and an inventor of tall tales. She is also the only one in whom simple-minded Ira confides the horrible facts of an attempted euthanasia, of death by rattlesnake venom, and the burial of his parents in a nearby swamp. Caught in the responsibility of knowing, she is confronted with the realities of conformity and life as it is; she must choose between asserting her own integrity or resigning to the status quo. Her choice may confuse some; to others it may appear as a comment upon adult values and their effect upon the young." Wis Lib Bul

Followed by: Lady Ellen Grae

Grover [by] Vera and Bill Cleaver; illus. by Frederic Marvin. Lippincott 1970 125p illus $4.50 (4-6)   Fic

1 Death—Fiction

ISBN 0-397-31118-4

Companion volume to the authors': Ellen Grae, and: Lady Ellen Grae

Ten-year-old Grover "goes through an agonizing period of adjustment beginning with his mother's sudden departure to the hospital and ending with his eventual acceptance of her death. The strain is increased by adult attempts to 'protect' him from the truth during her illness and by his father's withdrawal into grief after her suicide." Booklist

Although the elements of the story "may sound grim, there's nothing depressing about this book—it seems very real, with its most deeply touching or dramatic moments heightened by superbly comic incidents or dialogue." Sch Library J

Me too [by] Vera and Bill Cleaver. Lippincott 1973 158p $6.95 (5-7)   Fic

1 Mentally handicapped children—Fiction 2 Twins—Fiction

ISBN 0-397-31485-X

"The story concerns two girls, twins, 12 years old. Lydia is bright and intelligent; Lorna is an exceptional child with a mental age of about 5. During the summer in which the father deserts the family, Lydia takes on the care and education of Lornie. Her dream is that she will make Lornie so much like herself that no one will be able to tell the difference." N Y Times Bk Rev

"The contrast between the twins is dramatic, the interplay fascinating, and the Lydia's efforts and self-searching moving. But her failure is neither pathetic nor sad; for she has grown during her trials and frustrations, has learned to accept the reality of her father's desertion, and has come to an understanding of the 'exceptional' status of her sister." Horn Bk

Where the lilies bloom [by] Vera & Bill Cleaver; illus. by Jim Spanfeller. Lippincott 1969 174p illus $4.95 (5-7)   Fic

1 Orphans and orphans' homes—Fiction 2 Appalachian Mountains—Fiction

ISBN 0-397-31111-7

"Mary Call Luther [is] fourteen years old and made of granite. When her sharecropper father dies, Mary Call becomes head of the household, responsible for a boy of ten and a retarded, gentle older sister. Mary and her brother secretly bury their father so they can retain their home; tenaciously she fights to keep the family afloat by selling medicinal plants and to keep them together by fending off [Kiser Pease, their landlord], who wants to marry her sister." Sat Rev

"The setting is fascinating, the characterization good, and the style of the first-person story distinctive." Chicago. Children's Bk Center

Clewes, Dorothy

Guide Dog; illus. by Peter Burchard. Coward-McCann 1965 159p illus lib. bdg. $4.19 (5-7)   Fic

1 Blind—Fiction 2 Guide dogs—Stories 3 Great Britain—Fiction

ISBN 0-698-30183-8

The story of a teenage "boy's sudden blindness and his rebellion against being helped. Gradually he becomes reconciled and agrees to accept the help of a Guide Dog." Sch Library J

Roley "is no saint; he has to fight through a lot of bitterness and resentment." Pub W

Clifford, Eth

The year of the three-legged deer; illus. by Richard Cuffari. Houghton 1972 164p illus $4.95 (4-7)   Fic

1 Frontier and pioneer life—Fiction 2 Delaware Indians—Fiction 3 Prejudices and antipathies—Fiction 4 Indiana—Fiction

ISBN 0-395-13724-1

Callous and inhumane acts by white men against the Delaware Indians in Indiana during the early 19th century bring anguish and separation to Jesse Benton, his Indian wife and their two children

"Authentic in background and compelling despite its awkward flashback technique, a thought-provoking dramatization of the evils of prejudice." Booklist

Clifton, Lucille

All us come cross the water. Holt 1973 unp illus $4.95 (2-4)   **Fic**

1 Negroes—Fiction

ISBN 0-03-089262-7

" 'I got this teacher name Miss Wills,' Ujamaa begins, 'This day she come asking everybody to tell where they people come from.' But Ujamaa doesn't respond; first of all, he doesn't answer to 'Jim' when Miss Wills uses that name. He is disturbed. Africa is a continent, not a country: where does he come from? He learns from his grandmother that his people are Whydah and Ashanti, but is not satisfied until an elderly friend explains that 'We one people, Ujamaa . . . All us crossed the water.' He proudly announces to Miss Wills, 'My name is Ujamaa and that means Unity and that's where I'm from.' . . . The story highlights a concern for identity and emphasizes black pride; it is capably written and beautifully illustrated. Both the vocabulary and the concepts seem better suited to the independent reader than the 'K-4' group suggested by the publisher." Chicago. Children's Bk Center

Clymer, Eleanor

The big pile of dirt; illus. by Robert Shore. Holt 1968 unp illus lib. bdg. $3.95 (2-5)   **Fic**

1 Playgrounds—Fiction 2 New York (City)—Fiction

ISBN 0-03-089506-5

"Children in an old building, harassed by adult tenants, take proud, creative possession of a dirt-pile on an adjacent vacant lot. When the visiting Mayor would disrupt this satisfying state of affairs, the tenants surprisingly rally to the support of the protesting children." Moorachian. What is a city?

"It's a simply told, almost wistful story that makes no issue of poverty but presents a milieu familiar to many urban children." Sat Rev

How I went shopping and what I got; illus. by Trina Schart Hyman. Holt 1972 33p illus lib. bdg. $4.95 (4-6)   **Fic**

1 Family—Fiction 2 Shopping—Fiction

ISBN 0-03-088365-2

"Debbie, who is twelve, feels that her family is taking advantage of her. When she goes shopping with some slightly older friends, she temporarily loses her little sister but gains an understanding about familial love." Chicago

"The dialogue is convincing, and Hyman's expressive, realistic illustrations add to the satisfying whole." Sch Library J

Luke was there; illus. by Diane de Groat. Holt 1973 74p illus lib. bdg. $4.95 (3-6)   **Fic**

1 Runaways—Fiction 2 New York (City)—Fiction

ISBN 0-03-011161-7

Set in New York City, this is the story of Julius and his brother Danny, who "are committed to a children's shelter where Luke, a young Black conscientious objector, becomes the focus of Julius' respect and affection. When Luke must leave to serve his military time in a federal hospital, Julius reacts to his departure by running away . . . but he can't run from heartache or fast enough to avoid the danger and treachery that awaits on New York City's streets." Sch Library J

"Told in the first person, the story shows credible and moving insight concerning a child's response to difficult problems. Brown-and-white drawings effectively interpret both the personalities and the city scenes." Horn Bk

Me and the Eggman; illus. by David K. Stone. Dutton 1972 56p illus $4.95 (3-6)   **Fic**

1 Farm life—Fiction

ISBN 0-525-34775-5

"Running away from responsibilities at home, Donald finds himself involved in even greater ones with an old, lonely farmer." N Y Pub Library Children's Bks & Recordings, 1972

"Neither the relationship between the man and the boy nor the picture given of farm life moves beyond the boundaries of realism, and the story is told convincingly as a first-person narrative." Chicago. Children's Bk Center

My brother Stevie. Holt 1967 76p front lib. bdg. $3.50 (4-6)   **Fic**

1 Brothers and sisters—Fiction 2 Teachers—Fiction

ISBN 0-03-089508-1

Annie Jenner, a twelve-year-old living with her harsh but well-meaning grandmother, is overwhelmed by the responsibility of caring for her difficult younger brother, Stevie. When she is befriended by an understanding teacher, however, she gains new strength to cope with her dilemma

"Miss Clymer opens a world which many youthful readers may have little contact with. She depicts it skillfully and sympathetically, so that Annie, Stevie, and their grandmother emerge as vivid personalities. And if that pretty and kindly school teacher, Miss Stover who sets everything right, may seem a little too good to be true, at least she's the kind of teacher every slum child (and some non-slum children, too) dreams of coming across some day. This is a warm and sentimental, as well as an adventuresome, little book." Bk Week

The spider, the cave and the pottery bowl; illus. by Ingrid Fetz. Atheneum Pubs. 1971 66p illus lib. bdg. $4.95 (3-5)   **Fic**

1 Hopi Indians—Fiction 2 Pottery—Fiction

ISBN 0-689-20655-0

A "story of a young Hopi Indian girl who, with her brother, goes back to the mesa to help her elderly grandmother for the summer. The simple plot revolves around an ancient clay bowl: its legend; its accidental breakage by Johnny; and the discovery of some fine clay in an old cave where Johnny hides—clay with which to make a replica of the original bowl." Sch Library J

"The story line is simple, but woven around it are the traditions of the mesa people; simply told, the story is particularly effective because it takes for granted the advantages of Kate's two cultures: she is irritated when a white tourist is patronizing, but her pride of heritage is not shaken." Chicago. Children's Bk Center

Coatsworth, Elizabeth

Away goes Sally; pictures by Helen Sewell. Macmillan (N Y) 1934 122p illus $4.95 (4-6)   **Fic**

1 New England—Fiction

The author tells "How, long ago, Sally, her three aunts, and two uncles moved from Massachusetts to Maine and how one of those uncles devised a way in which Aunt Deborah could accompany them and still not break her vow to stay in her own house." Booklist

"This charming story of a little girl transported from Massachusetts to Maine in a little house on runners, drawn by twelve strong oxen, is refreshingly different from other tales of 1800. The short poems between chapters, and Helen Sewell's interpretive illustrations make it one of the distinctive books." N Y Pub Library

Coatsworth, Elizabeth—*Continued*

Bess and the Sphinx; illus. by Bernice Loewenstein. Macmillan (N Y) 1967 88p illus $4.50 (3-5)
Fic

1 Egypt—Fiction

This story, recounted in verse and poems and drawn from the author's own experiences, tells of the trip young Bess takes to Egypt with her family at the turn of the century. "Bess had one mortifying experience after another. . . . But when the family went to see the Sphinx timid Bess felt she had a friend. . . . Then Bess found a clay figure of Osiris in the sand, and felt it was a gift of the Sphinx, a protective charm she had discovered alone. A gentle, touching story in itself, the book is doubly interesting because it is Miss Coatsworth's first narrative of her own childhood." Sutherland. The Best in Children's Bks

The Cat and the Captain; illus. by Bernice Loewenstein. [New ed.] Macmillan Pub. Co. 1974 56p illus $4.95 (2-4)
Fic

First published 1927

1 Cats—Stories 2 Seamen—Fiction

"The Cat, who lives with a sailing man, is appreciated by his master but not by the housekeeper; the Cat remembers when he was at sea and his Captain saved him from a watery death at the hands of an irascible Mate. The Cat detects the Mate hidden in a closet, wakes the Captain and leads him to the would-be robber, and finally wins the approbation of the housekeeper. Not a startling plot, but it's adequately carried along by a few amusing incidents; the Cat never exceeds believable feline behavior, and the writing style is deft." Chicago. Children's Bk Center

The cat who went to heaven; illus. by Lynd Ward. Macmillan (N Y) 1958 62p illus $4.95, pa 95¢ (4-7)
Fic

1 Cats—Stories 2 Japan—Fiction

First published 1930. The 1958 edition is a reprint with new illustrations of the book which won the Newbery Medal award in 1931

"Watched by his little cat, Good Fortune, a Japanese artist paints a picture of the Buddha receiving homage from the animals. By tradition the cat should not be among them, but the artist risks his reputation by adding Good Fortune and is vindicated by a miracle." Hodges. Bks for Elem Sch Libraries

"Into this lovely and imaginative story the author has put something of the serenity and beauty of the East and of the gentleness of a religion that has a place even for the humblest of living creatures." N Y Times Bk Rev

The princess and the lion; illus. by Evaline Ness. Pantheon Bks. 1963 77p illus lib. bdg. $4.79 (4-6)
Fic

1 Ethiopia—Fiction

ISBN 0-394-91520-8

"Basing her tale on accounts of the Abyssinian Prison of Princes of 200 years ago, Mrs. Coatsworth tells how the princess Mariam, thinking her brother had no chance of being chosen heir to the throne, plotted his escape from the prison on almost inaccessible Mount Wachni. Her plans are completely upset when the old king suddenly proclaims Michael his heir, and Mariam [accompanied by the palace lion] then undertakes a most dangerous and arduous journey from the palace at Gondar to bring this news to her brother to prevent his attempted escape which would almost certainly end in his death." Sch Library J

"With its basis in historical fact, this simple tale. . . . has charm, novelty, and an endearing lion. Striking double-spread illustrations." Booklist

The sod house; illus. by Manning de V. Lee. Macmillan (N Y) 1954 64p illus $3.50 (2-4)
Fic

1 Frontier and pioneer life—Fiction 2 Germans in Kansas—Fiction 3 Kansas—Fiction

"A German immigrant family from Boston joins the Northerners settling in Kansas to help keep the state free. Their determination to maintain their beliefs is tested by their pro-slavery neighbors, and rewarded when they are joined by other Northern families." Minnesota

"Large print, easy-to-read text, and suitable illustrations in black and white." Library J

Cohen, Barbara

The carp in the bathtub; illus. by Joan Halpern. Lothrop 1972 48p illus $4.95, lib. bdg. $4.59 (2-4)
Fic

1 Jews in New York (City)—Fiction 2 Carp—Stories 3 New York (City)—Fiction

ISBN 0-688-41627-6; 0-688-51627-0

Set in New York City. "Leah and Harry have made friends of Joe, the appealing carp their mother has swimming in the bathtub, awaiting its execution on the Feast of Seder. Joe will make marvelous 'gefilte' fish but the children are determined to save him. They sneak him into the tub of a neighbor, but alas; his change of scene is only a reprieve, not a pardon. A delightfully warm book with pictures equally appealing." Pub W

Thank you, Jackie Robinson; drawings by Richard Cuffari. Lothrop 1974 125p illus $4.50, lib. bdg. $4.14 (4-6)
Fic

1 Robinson, John Roosevelt—Fiction 2 Baseball—Fiction 3 Friendship—Fiction

ISBN 0-688-41580-6; 0-688-51580-0

"Fatherless, Sam had never seen a baseball game until he met Davy. Davy was sixty, black, and the cook in Sam's mother's restaurant. Sam describes the trips to Ebbets Field with Davy, and sometimes with Davy's daughter and son-in-law; he is casual and candid about their discussions of race and the problems created when they travel together to other ball parks. The book ends on a poignant note, with Davy in the hospital after a heart attack and Sam bringing him a baseball (procured after considerable effort) signed by Jackie Robinson." Chicago. Children's Bk Center

"Cohen's characters have unusual depth and her story succeeds as a warm, understanding consideration of friendship and, finally, death." Booklist

Collier, James Lincoln

My brother Sam is dead, by James Lincoln Collier and Christopher Collier. Four Winds 1974 216p maps $6.50 (6-7)
Fic

1 U.S.—History—Revolution—Fiction

ISBN 0-590-07339-7

To Tim Meeker, in the Tory village of Redding Ridge, Connecticut, the rebellion against England was an event that had nothing to do with him. Then his older brother Sam joined the Minutemen. The story shows how Sam's decision affected his family and what happened when the town became caught up in the Revolution

"A fast-moving tale of adventure and tragedy. The complex factors which influenced the political choices of everyday citizens and soldiers are skillfully developed and add significantly to the book's strength." Babbling Bookworm

Collodi, Carlo

The adventures of Pinocchio (3-6) Fic

1 Puppets and puppet plays—Fiction 2 Fairy tales

Some editions are:

Children's Press (Fun to read classics ser) lib. bdg. $5.25 Translated by Joseph Walder; illustrated by William Dempster. Has title: Pinocchio (ISBN 0-516-04233-5)

Dutton (The Children's illustrated classics) $4.50 Illustrated by Charles Folkard. Has title: Pinocchio: The story of a puppet (ISBN 0-525-37092-7)

Grosset (Illustrated junior library) $3.95 (ISBN 0-448-05801-4), $5.95 deluxe edition (ISBN 0-448-06001-9)

Macmillan (N Y) $9.95 Translated by Carol della Chiesa; illustrated by Attilio Mussino

Macmillan (N Y) (The Macmillan classics) $5.25 Illustrated by Naiad Einsel; afterword by Clifton Fadiman

An Italian classic for children, written late in the 19th century

"When Geppetto discovered a piece of wood which talked, he carved it into a marionette and named him Pinocchio. Although he is a wooden boy, Pinocchio has a lively and nimble mind and an ardent curiosity which lead to unexpected and extraordinary results. A lighthearted and original fantasy in which children can identify themselves with Pinocchio and grasp the simple and practical morality which underlies the story." Bks for Boys and Girls

Colver, Anne

The wayfarer's tree, by Anne Colver and Stewart Graff. Dutton 1973 103p $4.50 (5-7) Fic

1 Thoreau, Henry David—Fiction 2 Massachusetts—Fiction

ISBN 0-525-42290-0

"During a year spent in Concord, a lad has rich experiences, new friends, and Henry Thoreau as a tutor." Children's Bks of the year, 1973

Cone, Molly

Annie, Annie; illus. by Marvin Friedman. Houghton 1969 112p illus $4.95 (5-7) Fic

ISBN 0-395-06705-7

Annie's parents allow her to make all her own decisions. She misunderstands their policy, feels that they don't really care about her, and rebels by taking a live-in job with the Sigbys, where there are rules for everything. All Annie has to do is what she's told and she loves it—at first, that is

Mishmash; illus. by Leonard Shortall. Houghton 1962 114p illus $4.95 (3-5) Fic

1 Dogs—Stories

ISBN 0-395-06711-1

The dog Mishmash moved like a cyclone into Pete's heart, his family's new house, the neighbor's gardens and life was never the same again! Pete, who was new in town, found that suddenly good old Mish had introduced him to practically everybody. But Pete had to solve the problem of troublesome Mish; also the problem of what to give his teacher

"Sprightly and enjoyable [the book's] charm [is] enhanced by Leonard Shortall's lively pictures." N Y Her Trib Bks

The other side of the fence; illus. by John Gretzer. Houghton 1967 117p illus $3.75 (4-7) Fic

1 Prejudices and antipathies—Fiction 2 Negroes—Fiction 3 Race problems—Fiction

ISBN 0-395-06713-8

"Joey visited his aunt every summer, enjoying the familiarity of Pearl Street. . . . Joey was surprised when Aunt Liz said a house was empty—when Joey could see that somebody had just moved in. It soon became clear to Joey that the neighbors had decided to ignore the existence of the newcomers because they were Negro; uncomfortably, Joey made a few feeble attempts to defend the newcomers—even more uncomfortably, he kept quiet when he found nobody to agree with him. Torn between his desire to be accepted by his own circle of friends and the inner conviction that they were wrong, Joey rebelled when a spiteful neighbor painted his side of the fence white and the Foster's side black. The small victory Joey achieves is that Aunt Liz invites Mrs. Foster in for a cup of coffee." Sutherland. The Best in Children's Bks

"This book makes its point in an entertaining manner, providing a good basis for constructive discussion in religious education classes and schoolrooms. Plot and characters are developed with wit and realism." Keating. Building Bridges of Understanding Between Cultures

A promise is a promise; illus. by John Gretzer. Houghton 1964 153p illus $5.95 (5-7) Fic

1 Jews in the U.S.—Fiction

ISBN 0-395-06703-0

"Ruthy Morgen develops a self-conscious attitude because she is Jewish. The neighborhood homes celebrating Christmas, the invitation to a party at the church, and the hidden feelings she holds about her brother's Bar Mitzvah all naturally intensify her desire to be like everyone else. The descriptions of Ruthy's perceptive inner thoughts and of exchanges with her gentile friend Sandra about religion, rituals, and customs contribute to her growing pride in her own heritage." Reading Ladders. 5th edition

Conford, Ellen

Dreams of Victory; illus. by Gail Rockwell. Little 1973 121p illus $5.95 (4-6) Fic

ISBN 0-316-15294-3

"Victory Benneker couldn't dance; she couldn't skate; she got only six votes in an election for class president; and she was a miserable failure in an unimportant role in the class play. Despite the optimistic name her mother had given her, nothing came out to her satisfaction. But Vicky had a wonderful safeguard. She could daydream. And so fertile was her imagination that she became—in turn—the first woman President, winner of the Miss Galaxy Beauty Contest, recipient of an Oscar for her acting." Horn Bk

"The fiasco episodes are ruefully funny, the classroom scenes amusing, and the conversations between Vicky and her parents especially deft; while the focus is on the situation rather than the plot, there is enough action in the catalog of small failures to sustain interest, and many children can empathize with Vicky as a character." Chicago. Children's Bk Center

Felicia the critic; illus. by Arvis Stewart. Little 1973 145p illus $5.95 (4-6) Fic

1 Criticism—Fiction

ISBN 0-316-15295-1

"When her negative communications meet with looks of loathing, Felicia, mostly undaunted and with good intentions, embarks on a career as a constructive critic, hoping that she will be valued for her talent. She systematizes her job by compiling lists of suggestions for the local traffic cop, her children's-book-author aunt, and a restaurant owner, to name a few. Felicia's audacity continues to be regarded with coldness by her family, her friends, and many of her victims. Nevertheless, she is so often on target that some people find themselves taking up her advice in spite of themselves." Booklist

"Fresh, entertaining, and percipient. . . . It all adds up to a deft, sympathetic portrait of a real child—a loner aware of the obtuseness and supercritical responses of other people." Horn Bk

Conford, Ellen—*Continued*

Me and the terrible two; illus. by Charles Carroll. Little 1974 117p illus $4.95 (3-6)　　Fic

1 Friendship—Fiction

ISBN 0-316-15303-6

"Dorrie, a sixth-grader . . . not only loses her best friend when the family next door moves to Australia, but must be plagued by the new incumbents—a pair of zany, prankish, totally self-sufficient, identical-twin boys. Dorrie, predictably, not only manages to survive, but ultimately settles into a three-way friendship with her tormentors." Horn Bk

"A witty, brisk and altogether effective story." Pub W

Coolidge, Olivia

Come by here; illus. by Milton Johnson. Houghton 1970 239p illus $5.95 (5-7)　　Fic

1 Orphans and orphans' homes—Fiction 2 Negroes—Fiction

ISBN 0-395-10912-4

Minty Lou's warm, secure world is shattered when her parents are accidentally killed. She becomes an unwelcomed burden in homes where both money and hope are in short supply. Set in Baltimore in 1900 this book is based on an actual life story of a Black girl who struggled to regain the security she once had known

"Minty Lou's is not a cheering story, but it should be read, not only for its insights into black history but for its realistic depiction of conditions which too often apply, in some measure, to human beings of any color." Sch Library J

Cooper, Susan

The dark is rising; illus. by Alan E. Cober. Atheneum Pubs. 1973 216p illus $7.50 (5-7)　　Fic

1 Good and evil—Fiction 2 Fantastic fiction 3 Great Britain—Fiction

ISBN 0-689-30317-3

"A Margaret K. McElderry book"

This book continues the battle between dark and light begun in Over sea, under stone, entered below

"On his 11th birthday, Will Stanton discovers that he is one of the Old Ones—those who have special powers and primary roles in the battle [between light and dark]. With the power of the dark on the rise during the 12 days of Christmas, Will receives training and must pass several tests, continuing to exist normally but leading an extra life outside of Time. The climax comes on Twelfth Night, and the life of Will's sister is in the balance." Sch Library J

"The fantastic style is virile and, for all its paraphernalia, spare. Susan Cooper's vocabulary is athletic; the complications are dense. Her book seems to have been prepared for a special small age group: those who can read with fluency and attention, but who haven't yet been afflicted by adolescent cynicism." N Y Times Bk Rev

Followed by: Greenwitch

Dawn of fear; illus. by Margery Gill. Harcourt 1970 157p illus map $5.95 (5-7)　　Fic

1 Great Britain—Fiction 2 World War, 1939-1945—Fiction

ISBN 0-15-266201-4

During World War II, three English boys' fearless unconcern with the enemy planes that flew daily on their way to bomb London, gradually underwent a change as the night raids grew more severe. This is the story of how, through the destruction—not by bombs—of the secret camp they were building, the boys came face-to-face with grown-up hatred, and then they knew the meaning of fear

"The characterization [is] deft and the dialogue natural [and] the relationship between the boys and a young man who is about to enter the Merchant Navy [is] particularly perceptive." Sutherland. The Best in Children's Bks

Greenwitch; frontispiece by Michael Heslop. Atheneum Pubs. 1974 147p front $5.50 (5-7)　　Fic

1 Good and evil—Fiction 2 Fantastic fiction 3 Great Britain—Fiction

ISBN 0-689-30426-9

"A Margaret K. McElderry book"

Sequel to: The dark is rising

While trying to recover a stolen grail, Simon, Jane and Barney, who are visiting their uncle in Cornwall, get involved with the Greenwitch and the forces of evil known as the Dark

"The marvelously sustained pace of the story skillfully modulates from the reality of everyday life through superstition and folklore to confrontation with the numinous." Horn Bk

Over sea, under stone; illus. by Margery Gill. Harcourt [1966 c1965] 252p illus $6.25 (5-7)　　Fic

1 Good and evil—Fiction 2 Fantastic fiction 3 Great Britain—Fiction

ISBN 0-15-259034-X

First published 1965 in England

"Three children—Barney, Jane, and Simon—spending a summer holiday in a seaside village in Cornwall find a crumbling parchment map in an attic. Unwittingly they have stumbled upon the clues to a long-sought relic of Arthurian days, a relic which is not merely of antiquarian interest but which also holds some secret source of strength and goodness. Protected and aided by enigmatic, scholarly Great-Uncle Merry, the children struggle to decipher the clues and plot their quest, until at last, against a . . . gay holiday background, the ancient battle of good against evil is fought once more." Horn Bk

"This is one of the best mysteries we have had in some time. The air of mysticism and the allegorical quality of the continual contest between good and evil add much value to a fine plot, setting, and characterization." Library J

Followed by: The dark is rising

Corbett, Scott

The baseball trick; illus. by Paul Galdone. Little 1965 105p illus $4.95 (3-5)　　Fic

1 Baseball—Fiction 2 Dogs—Stories

ISBN 0-316-15708-2

"An Atlantic Monthly Press book"

"With the help of his pal Kerby and his Feats o' Magic chemical set, Fenton at last hits a home run and wins the baseball game against unfair competition. [It is a] humorous blend of fantasy and realism, with real-life boys, lively dialogue, and a very funny dog." Hodges. Bks for Elem Sch Libraries

The hairy horror trick; illus. by Paul Galdone. Little 1969 101p illus $4.95 (3-5)　　Fic

1 Halloween—Stories

Kerby and Fenton attempt to persuade Kerby's cousin Gay to remain quiet about their secret Feats O'Magic chemistry set by mixing a potion that unexpectedly grows hair on their faces and makes Kerby's dog Waldo hairless

"Mr. Corbett is again in good form, and so is his competent illustrator, Paul Galdone. Their book does not try to be a literary masterpiece, but it is certainly a rollicking good farce." Christian Sci Monitor

The lemonade trick; illus. by Paul Galdone. Little 1960 103p illus $4.95 (3-5)　　Fic

ISBN 0-316-15694-9

"An Atlantic Monthly Press book"

A brew from his magic chemistry set changes Kerby

Corbett, Scott—*Continued*

into a perfect gentleman; unfortunately, it has the opposite effect on good boys

"An ingenious bit of magic has been mixed by [the author] and dashingly illustrated . . . to please eight-year-old readers . . . and even some a bit older who like a fairly simple story that doesn't take too long to read." N Y Her Trib Bks

Corbin, William

Golden mare; illus. by Pers Crowell. Coward-McCann 1955 122p illus $5.95 (4-6)   Fic

1 Horses—Stories

ISBN 0-698-20054-3

A "story of a handicapped boy whose affection for an old mare brings him to a complete realization of his unique capabilities." Cincinnati

"This is an unusual horse story, sensitive without being sentimental, and so simply written that many fourth-graders will join older children in reading it." Horn Bk

Smoke. Coward-McCann 1967 253p $6.95 (4-6)   Fic

1 Dogs—Stories 2 Stepchildren—Fiction 3 Oregon—Fiction

ISBN 0-698-20131-0

Fourteen year old Chris secretly nurses a stray German shepherd which he found in the woods around his Oregon ranch. When the animal's condition worsens, the boy must overcome his resentment of his new stepfather and seek his help

Corcoran, Barbara

A dance to still music; illus. by Charles Robinson. Atheneum Pubs. 1974 180p illus $6.95 (5-7)   Fic

1 Deaf—Fiction 2 Florida—Fiction

ISBN 0-689-30406-4

"As fourteen-year-old Margaret struggles to cope with deafness caused by a recent illness, her misery is compounded by the loneliness of strange surroundings; for her mother has moved from Maine to Florida in search of a better job. When her mother decides to marry, Margaret knows that she will be sent away to a special school. . . . Flight back to Maine and the security of her grandfather's house seem the only solution, but she never actually leaves Florida. In her efforts to help a Key West fawn that is hit by a truck, she is joined by a middle-aged woman, Josie, who accepts Margaret's deafness and self-imposed silence without surprise or comment and takes the girl and the wounded deer to the refuge of her small houseboat at the edge of the Gulf. Matter-of-fact Josie . . . not only helps return the fawn to health but also helps Margaret come to terms with her deafness and family relationships." Horn Bk

"The major characters are convincing, especially the protagonist and her mother—not a bad woman, but lacking in understanding." Chicago. Children's Bk Center

The long journey; illus. by Charles Robinson. Atheneum Pubs. 1970 187p illus lib. bdg. $5.50, pa $1.25 (4-7)   Fic

1 Montana—Fiction

ISBN 0-689-20596-1; 0-689-70404-6

"Grandfather, with whom orphaned [thirteen-year-old] Laurie has lived from the age of three in an abandoned mining town, is going blind and because he fears hospitals and orphanages Laurie must ride horseback across the state of Montana to fetch Uncle Arthur. Since everything Laurie knows of the outside world is secondhand, the things she sees and the people she encounters on her eventful journey are new experiences—some frightening, some astonishing, some rewarding. Though in retrospect the story

as a whole strains credibility, Laurie is a believable character holding the reader's interest and concern from beginning to end of the enjoyable narrative." Booklist

Sasha, my friend; drawings by Richard L. Shell. Atheneum Pubs. 1969 203p illus $5.95, pa 95¢ (5-7)   Fic

1 Wolves—Stories 2 Montana—Fiction

ISBN 0-689-20582-1; 0-689-70358-9

"After her mother's death teen-age Hallie and her father move from Los Angeles to northwestern Montana for his health. Living in a trailer on a Christmas tree farm and isolated from school, Hallie is homesick, desolate, and unprepared for wilderness living but, as she learns to cope, acquires an orphaned wolf cub for company, and experiences the friendship and helpfulness of neighbors, she begins to regard the place as home." Booklist

"The themes are not new to children's books: a girl's painful adjustment to wilderness living and a fierce attachment to an unconventional pet. But the author, who lives in Montana by preference, writes with conviction as she tells an absorbing story set against the austere beauty of her adopted state." Horn Bk

Courlander, Harold

The Son of the Leopard; woodcuts by Rocco Negri. Crown 1974 55p illus $5.95 (4-6)   Fic

1 Africa, North—Fiction

ISBN 0-517-51191-6

"Saddled with the sins of his infamous forebear, the reincarnated 'Son of the Leopard' fights back as soldier of fortune but finds salvation through misfortune." Sch Library J

"Courlander proves himself . . . a master storyteller and Negri's woodcuts are brilliant accompaniments to a compelling legend." Pub W

Coutant, Helen

First snow; pictures by Vo-Dinh. Knopf 1974 30p illus $4.50, lib. bdg. $4.99 (2-4)   Fic

1 Death—Fiction 2 Vietnamese in the U.S.—Fiction

ISBN 0-394-82831-3; 0-394-92831-8

This is the "story of a Vietnamese family's first winter in New England. The excitement and happiness of the impending first snow is mingled with the uncertainty and sadness of Grandmother's dying. Young Lien soon sees dying as a natural process: a change—just as in the life of a snowflake." Children's Bk Rev Serv

"So 'that' was dying, something disappeared and in its place came something else! This is the Buddhist view, the oneness of life and death. . . . The story has a quiet serenity and delivers effectively its message of the continuity of the life-death cycle." Chicago. Children's Bk Center

Crayder, Dorothy

She, the adventuress; illus. by Velma Ilsey. Atheneum Pubs. 1973 188p illus $5.95 (5-7)   Fic

1 Ocean travel—Fiction

ISBN 0-689-30082-4

"Since pre-teen Maggie has to travel alone from Iowa to Italy, she decides to pretend it's a glamorous adventure. But the shipboard stowaway, an international art thief, and a man from Interpol are no daydream." Chicago

"Reduced to simple plot summary, the story would sound contrived and heavily dependent on an unlikely combination of possible occurrences, but it succeeds admirably as an entertainment because of the adolescent heroine's believable reactions and the evocation of the momentous minutiae of shipboard existence." Horn Bk

Cresswell, Helen

The night watchmen; illus. by Gareth Floyd. Macmillan (N Y) [1970 c1969] 122p illus $4.95 (4-6) Fic

1 Tramps—Fiction 2 Great Britain—Fiction 3 Fantastic fiction

First published 1969 in England

"A young boy's boredom vanishes when he meets a pair of tramps and helps them in their elaborate ruse to remain 'do-as-you-pleasers' in a modern world." Children's Bks 1970

"This hilarious, disturbing, sometimes frightening excursion to the borderline of reality is no more 'for children' than the bitter irony of Gulliver is for adults. . . . In her ear for dialogue, her feeling for place and her delight in the craft of living, Miss Cresswell is here the unquestionable master of her fine and characteristic art." Times (London) Lit Sup

Up the pier; illus. by Gareth Floyd. Macmillan (N Y) [1972 c1971] 144p illus $4.95 (4-6) Fic

1 Wales—Fiction 2 Fantastic fiction

First published 1971 in England

"Ten-year-old Carrie becomes involved with an invisible family that has been transported forward in time from 1921." Chicago

"Highly successful as a time-fantasy, it skillfully weaves together the interaction of a lonely little girl, a deserted summer resort, and the possessive dreams of an old man." Horn Bk

Cretan, Gladys Yessayan

All except Sammy; illus. by Symeon Shimin. Little 1966 42p illus $3.95 (2-5) Fic

ISBN 0-316-16086-5

"An Atlantic Monthly Press book"

"Each member of Sammy's family played an instrument, and well, except Sammy, who had to answer that he played baseball—but he could join in their circle after his discovery of talent in another art." Children's Bks 1966

"The illustrations are marvelous for their ability to portray distinctive characters." Minnesota

Ctvrtek, Václav

The little chalk man; illus. by Muriel Batherman; tr. from the Czech. Knopf 1970 81p illus lib. bdg. $5.69 (2-4) Fic

ISBN 0-394-90489-3

Original Czech edition, 1961. Translated by Ivo and Atya Havlu

Confined to the wall on which he was drawn, a little chalk man must combat an evil blue line with the only weapon he has—the truth

Cunningham, Julia

Burnish me bright; pictures by Don Freeman. Pantheon Bks. 1970 78p illus $3.95, lib. bdg. $4.79 (4-6) Fic

1 Physically handicapped children—Fiction 2 Pantomimes—Fiction 3 France—Fiction

ISBN 0-394-80851-7; 0-394-90851-1

A mute orphan boy's "friendship with a dying mime helps him to learn a skill which incidentally strengthens the inner resources he needs for survival and for his relationships with others." Top of the News

"Two underlying themes—the perils of being different and death—are handled with poignant directness." Adventuring With Bks. 2d edition

Dorp dead; illus. by James Spanfeller. Pantheon Bks. 1965 88p illus $3.50, lib. bdg. $4.79 (5-7) Fic

1 Orphans and orphans' homes—Fiction

ISBN 0-394-81089-9; 0-394-91089-3

"In this highly symbolic story orphan Gilly Ground

describes his deliberately lonely life. He shuns friendships, disguises his intelligence, is glad to leave the orphanage to be the solitary apprentice of Kobalt the laddermaker. The security of Kobalt's routine soon becomes stifling, however, and Gilly discovers that he is, in fact, to become a prisoner. Helped by the dog Mash, with whom he has shared affection, Gilly escapes to the promise of freedom." Reading Ladders. 5th edition

"In fine clean line James Spanfeller's illustrations bring out the sensitive character of a frightened child who awakens from an ugly dream to a smiling world." N Y Times Bk Rev

Curry, Jane Louise

Beneath the hill; illus. by Imero Gobbato. Harcourt 1967 255p illus map $5.95 (4-7) Fic

1 Good and evil—Fiction 2 Pennsylvania—Fiction 3 Fantastic fiction

ISBN 0-15-206600-4

"The age-old conflict between good and evil is the underlying theme of a modern American fantasy that blends ancient Celtic legendary lore with the devastating effects of strip coal mining in western Pennsylvania. A treasure hunt devised by Miggle Arthur to impress her visiting cousins leads to the children's involvement with Welsh elfin folk who accidentally emigrated to America centuries ago and whose secret cavern home is now being threatened by evil forces unearthed by the strip mining. How the children help the little people find a way to return to their ancestral home of Tir na'nOg and also save the countryside from further despoilment is told in an involved but skillfully plotted tale full of mystery and magic." Booklist

The daybreakers; illus. by Charles Robinson. Harcourt 1970 191p illus $5.95 (4-7) Fic

1 Negroes—Fiction 2 West Virginia—Fiction 3 Fantastic fiction

ISBN 0-15-222853-5

In a milltown in West Virginia "two black children and one white . . . achieve the impossible: they live in two worlds, in the ugly milltown and in an ancient, beautiful world they discover for themselves. They are able to live in both reality and fantasy, because their story is told by a writer who is magnificently at ease in both worlds." Pub W

The ice ghosts mystery. Atheneum Pubs. 1972 215p $5.95 (4-7) Fic

1 Austria—Fiction 2 Mystery and detective stories

ISBN 0-689-30302-5

"A Margaret K. McElderry book"

"The mystery is threefold. First, Mrs. Bird and her three children attempt to learn whether Professor Bird, a California seismologist, is missing or dead after his disappearance during a ski trip in Austria. Secondly, they try to find an explanation for the ghosts who keep superstitious people away from a vast mountain cave. Finally, they ferret out the origin of elusive, illegal underground detonations that cause earthquakes and avalanches. The complex plot is ingeniously woven and sustained in a beautifully vivid setting." Horn Bk

Dahl, Roald

James and the giant peach; a children's story; illus. by Nancy Ekholm Burkert. Knopf 1961 118p illus $4.95, lib. bdg. $5.99 (4-6) Fic

1 Peach—Stories

ISBN 0-394-81282-4; 0-394-91282-9

After the death of his parents, little James is forced to live with Aunt Sponge and Aunt Spike, two cruel old harpies. A magic potion causes the growing of a giant-sized peach on a puny peach tree. James sneaks

Dahl, Roald—*Continued*

inside the peach and finds a new world of insects. With his new family, James heads for many adventures

"A 'juicy' fantasy, 'dripping' with humor and imagination." Commonweal

Dahlstedt, Marden

The terrible wave; illus. by Charles Robinson. Coward, McCann & Geoghegan 1972 125p illus $5.95 (4-6)   Fic

1 Johnstown, Pa.—Flood, 1889—Fiction
ISBN 0-698-20188-4

"An exciting and often terrifying story of the disasters that struck Johnstown, Pennsylvania, in wake of the great flood of 1889. When the dam bursts, Megan Maxwell is the rather spoiled daughter of an affluent family. She is swept from her house onto a floating mattress and joined in the raging waters by Brian O'Meara. What follows is an account of the young people's experiences, helping other refugees and trying to find their families. Through her encounters with others—some heroic, some selfish—Megan grows as a human being. The novel is well structured and deeply engrossing." Pub W

Dalgliesh, Alice

The bears on Hemlock Mountain; illus. by Helen Sewell. Scribner 1952 unp illus lib. bdg. $5.95, pa 95¢ (1-4)   Fic

1 Bears—Stories
ISBN 0-684-12654-0; 0-684-12786-5

"This is the story of a little boy sent by his mother to borrow an iron pot from an aunt who lived on the other side of Hemlock Mountain—really only a hill. Jonathan's mother did not believe that there were bears on Hemlock Mountain but Jonathan did. . . . The two-color, somewhat stylized illustrations seem right for the story." Booklist

"Jonathan's adventure is a tall tale passed down in Pennsylvania, which might have happened to a pioneer boy almost anywhere. Full of suspense and humor, it will make good reading aloud for small boys of today." N Y Her Trib Bks

The courage of Sarah Noble; illus. by Leonard Weisgard. Scribner 1954 52p illus lib. bdg. $5.95, pa 95¢ (2-4)   Fic

1 Frontier and pioneer life—Fiction 2 Indians of North America—Fiction 2 Connecticut—Fiction
ISBN 0-684-12795-4; 0-684-12632-X

"Here is a remarkable book for younger readers—a true pioneer adventure, written for easy reading but without any sacrifice of literary quality or depth of feeling. . . . Sarah, though only eight, was her father's companion on a grueling and dangerous journey to build a new home in the Connecticut wilderness of 1707, and she succeeded well in following her mother's advice to 'keep up your courage, Sarah Noble.' When, however, the log house was finished and her father was leaving her with the Indians while he went back alone to get the rest of the family, Sarah, who had been very brave, confessed that she had lost her courage. To this her father made the discerning and heartening reply, 'To be afraid, and to be brave is the best courage of all.' " Horn Bk

"Based on a true incident in Connecticut history— the founding of New Milford—this story is one to be long remembered for its beautiful simplicity and dignity. Leonard Weisgard's pictures add just the right sense of background." N Y Times Bk Rev

Daringer, Helen F.

Adopted Jane; illus. by Kate Seredy. Harcourt 1947 225p illus $6.25 (4-6)   Fic

1 Orphans and orphans' homes—Fiction
ISBN 0-15-201395-4

Jane was a plain little girl with beautiful eyes and a large fund of integrity. Ever since she could remember Jane had lived in an orphanage, and she longed for a family and a dog of her own. There came a summer when she had the blissful experience of having two visits to real homes, and at the end she has acquired both a home and a dog. The time of the story is about 1900

"This is a refreshing story, told skilfully and with a flair for creating amusing and interesting people. Kate Seredy's drawings make the period around 1900. But wherever and whenever Jane lived, she would be well worth knowing." Sat Rev

Day, Véronique

Landslide! Tr. from the French by Margaret Morgan; illus. by Margot Tomes. Coward-McCann [1964 c1963] 158p illus $5.95 (4-7)   Fic

1 Disasters—Fiction 2 Survival (after airplane accidents, shipwrecks, etc.)—Fiction 3 France— Fiction
ISBN 0-698-20076-4

Original French edition published 1958; first English translation published 1961 in England; the included illustrations copyright 1963

Five French "children, on vacation in the mountains, are trapped inside a lonely cottage by a landslide. While they are asleep, earth covers the roof and windows of the house, cutting them off from the outside world. . . . Twelve precious days of their Christmas vacation are gone before Laurent, the oldest boy and the one in charge of the party invents a way of sending out signals for help." About this book

"The rescue is dramatic but not unrealistic; in fact, none of the episodes in the story is unrealistic, although some of the things that the children do are based on knowledge or skills that seem a bit artificial." Chicago. Children's Bk Center

De Angeli, Marguerite

Bright April. Doubleday 1946 86p illus $4.95, lib. bdg. $5.70 (3-5)   Fic

1 Negroes—Fiction 2 Girl Scouts—Fiction 3 U.S.- Race relations—Fiction
ISBN 0-385-07238-4; 0-385-06247-8

Story of a bright little Negro girl, whose home life was so happy that her first knowledge of racial intolerance came on her tenth birthday, when a little white girl refused to sit beside her at a Brownie party. Her intelligent parents help her to make the needed adjustments

"Amid the tumult and tensions of racial strain, Mrs. de Angeli's story of April stands out with refreshing serenity and wisdom. . . . Once again, in this story of Germantown, Mrs. de Angeli presents a special cultural group with sincerity and kindly appreciation and more of her colorful pictures." Horn Bk

"One of the first acceptable books showing life in a middle-class black home." NYPL. The Black Experience in Children's Bks

The door in the wall. Doubleday [1964 c1949] 120p illus $4.95, lib. bdg. $5.70, pa 95¢ (4-6)   Fic

1 Physically handicapped—Fiction 2 Great Britain—History—Plantagenets, 1154-1399—Fiction
ISBN 0-385-07283-X; 0-385-05743-1; 0-385-07909-5

Awarded the Newbery Medal, 1950

First published 1949

"Thirteenth-century England with its castles and churches and traveling folk is evident in the adventures of Robin, crippled son in a noble family. Wartime conditions and the great London plague combine to take Robin away from his castle home. He meets Brother Luke who teaches him wood carving; he falls

De Angeli, Marguerite—*Continued*
in with the minstrel, John-in-the-Wynd, who journeys with him from London through Oxford and farther north to rejoin his parents and serve his King." Horn Bk
"An enthralling and inspiring tale of triumph over handicap. [The author-artist's] unusually beautiful illustrations, full of authentic detail, combine with the text to make life in England during the Middle Ages come alive." N Y Times Bk Rev

Elin's Amerika. Doubleday 1941 unp illus $3.50 (4-6)   Fic
1 Swedes in the U.S.—Fiction 2 Delaware—Fiction 3 U.S.—History—Colonial period—Fiction
ISBN 0-385-07287-2
Elin came to America in 1643 with the first Swedish people who settled in Delaware. Her attempts to help her mother at home, her adventures with Indians, friendly and otherwise, her share in pioneer activities and in the celebrations dating back to the homeland, are all told
"A sense of Swedish festival is given by the [author's] water colors which illustrate an account of early days of colonization along the 'De La Ware.' " N Y Pub Lib
Map on lining-papers

Thee, Hannah! Doubleday 1940 unp illus $5.95, lib. bdg. $6.70 (3-5)   Fic
1 Friends, Society of—Fiction 2 Philadelphia—Fiction
ISBN 0-385-07525-1; 0-385-06130-7
The scene is Philadelphia, some time before the Civil War. Hannah, the youngest member of a large Quaker family, had a hankering after frills and pretty clothes, and her pursuit of them often called forth an admonitory, 'Thee, Hannah!' On the night when her plain Quaker bonnet led her to help an escaping Negro slave Hannah learned at last the meaning of the Quaker garb
"Hannah and the other children are very real and, in addition to the [author's] lovely pictures that follow the story, the street cries of old Philadelphia are effectively introduced and illustrated at the beginning of each chapter." Library J
"To an exceptional degree, the pictures, end papers, and story seem all of a piece to make a harmonious book." N Y Pub Library

Yonie Wondernose; for three little Wondernoses, Nina, David and Kiki. Doubleday 1944 unp illus $4.95, lib. bdg. $5.70 (1-4)   Fic
1 Farm life—Fiction 2 Pennsylvania Dutch—Fiction 3 Mennonites—Fiction
ISBN 0-385-07573-1; 0-385-07662-2
"Because he is curious and must know about everything, seven-year-old Yonie is called Wondernose. Pop goes away leaving Yonie in charge of the farm with the admonition to remember he is the man of the house and not to be a Wondernose. The story and pictures of how the little [Amish] boy wins his father's approval have both charm and reality." Booklist
"The story develops in many of the manners and customs of the Pennsylvania Dutch, showing their independence and strength of character. The pictures are pleasant lithographs in the familiar style of Marguerite de Angeli." Ontario Library Rev

Degens, T.
Transport 7-41-R. Viking 1974 171p $5.95 (6-7)   Fic
1 World War, 1939-1945—Fiction 2 Refugees—Fiction
ISBN 0-670-72429-7
A thirteen-year-old girl describes her trip to Cologne from the Russian sector of occupied Germany as she travels aboard a refugee transport. Her relationships with other passengers in the boxcar bring her into contact with a wide range of human behavior from intense greed and pettiness to loyalty and staunch idealism
"A powerful and unforgettable novel, taut and dramatic, which succeeds both as a suspense-filled adventure tale and as an evocative study of the psychological and emotional effects of war on its most innocent victims—children." Horn Bk

DeJong, Meindert
Along came a dog; pictures by Maurice Sendak. Harper 1958 172p illus $4.95, lib. bdg. $4.79 (4-6)   Fic
1 Dogs—Stories 2 Chickens—Stories
ISBN 0-06-021420-1; 0-06-021421-4
"The friendship of a timid, lonely dog and a little red hen who lost her toes in a frost is the subject. . . . The dog, repeatedly driven away by the farmer, keeps returning—to hide in the barn, to struggle to keep alive, and to protect the little hen from the rest of the barnyard flock and from greedy hawks." Chicago Sunday Tribune
It is "a very moving story, full of suspense. Like all [the author's] books, it is distinguished for the quality of its writing and for the way in which he is able to interpret the thoughts and feelings not only of human beings but also of animals and even the members of the henyard. Mr. Sendak's drawings are so closely in sympathy with the story that it seems impossible to imagine the one without the other." Horn Bk

Far out the long canal; pictures by Nancy Grossman. Harper 1964 231p illus $3.95, lib. bdg. $5.43 (4-6)   Fic
1 Skating—Fiction 2 Netherlands—Fiction
ISBN 0-06-021465-1; 0-06-021466-X
"Moonta is nine; because of an earlier illness and because there has been no good ice for several winters, Moonta cannot skate. Every child in town can skate. . . . His struggles to succeed, his embarrassment when he fails at first, and the alternate teasing and stout comfort he gets from friends and family are described with sympathetic realism. The picture of the small [Dutch] community, madly skating . . . has the charm and the color of a canvas." Chicago. Children's Bk Center

A horse came running; illus. by Paul Sagsoorian. Macmillan (N Y) 1970 147p illus $5.95, pa $1.25 (4-6)   Fic
1 Horses—Stories 2 Tornadoes—Fiction
A boy, Mark, "his two beloved horses (which he fears he may lose), and an old neighbor [Mr Sayers] together face the havoc surrounding them after a tornado twists through their farms." Commonweal
"The story consists of more than mere happenings; it is made up of deeply felt experiences. Mark's birthday, his love for the two horses, and his responses to Mr. and Mrs. Sayers and to his unobtrusively understanding mother are so melded in his emotional world that the fact that neither locale nor decade is mentioned becomes immaterial. The pencil sketches suggest the vigor and the simplicity of the story." Horn Bk

The house of sixty fathers; pictures by Maurice Sendak. Harper 1956 189p illus lib. bdg. $4.79 (4-6)   Fic
1 China—Fiction 2 World War, 1939-1945—Fiction
ISBN 0-06-021481-3
"A vividly realistic story of China during the early days of the Japanese invasion. Tien Pao, a small

DeJong, Meindert—*Continued*

Chinese boy, and his family fled inland on a sampan when the Japanese attacked their coastal village, but Tien Pao was separated from his parents during a storm and swept back down the river on the sampan. . . . Once again the author has shown his ability to paint starkly realistic word pictures that give the reader the full impact of the terror, pain, hunger and finally the joy that Tien Pao knew during his search for his family." Chicago. Children's Bk Center

"The hero is a very engaging character, the kind who makes young readers feel sure that they, too, would be brave and clever if left to their own devices in a situation like this." Pub W

Hurry home, Candy; pictures by Maurice Sendak. Harper 1953 244p illus $4.95, lib. bdg. $4.79, pa $1.50 (4-6)   Fic

1 Dogs—Stories
ISBN 0-06-021485-6; 0-06-021486-4; 0-06-440025-5

The story of a lonely little lost dog, who survives several terrifying experiences, and finally is taken into a good home

"Perceptive readers will recognize the deeper significance of the story and find its beauty of expression a rewarding reading experience." Horn Bk

Journey from Peppermint Street; pictures by Emily Arnold McCully. Harper 1968 242p illus $5.95, lib. bdg. $5.43 (4-6)   Fic

1 Netherlands—Fiction
ISBN 0-06-021488-0; 0-06-021489-9

"Siebren's first journey away from his Dutch village by the sea begins with small incidents, exciting only for a boy who has had to spend all his free time at home caring for a troublesome baby brother. By the end of three days, however, he has caught a gigantic pike in the marsh, survived a tornado, and discovered a secret passageway in the ancient monastery where his aunt lives. Through these adventures Siebren has also learned to love and understand his gruff old grandfather, his deaf-and-dumb uncle, and his courageous little aunt." Booklist

It is "beautifully written, with vivid characterization. . . . The relationships between Siebren and the members of his family are particularly good; they have a universality that is compelling." Chicago. Children's Bk Center

Puppy summer; pictures by Anita Lobel. Harper 1966 98p illus lib. bdg. $5.49 (4-6)   Fic

1 Dogs—Stories 2 Farm life—Fiction
ISBN 0-06-021540-2

"A small brother and sister are spending the summer at their grandparents' farm; they are told they may have a puppy, and they find it difficult to decide which of three pups to choose. Grandma, who hasn't been enthusiastic at all, is captivated, too, and she agrees to take all three. The rest of the story describes the children's caring for their pets—or shirking the job—and their acceptance of the fact that things won't be quite the same next summer. Quietly written, with a gentle affection that permeates the story, both an affection for the puppies and a sympathetic and quite charming relationship between the children and their grandparents." Sutherland. The Best in Children's Bks

Shadrach; pictures by Maurice Sendak. Harper 1953 182p illus lib. bdg. $4.79 (1-4)   Fic

1 Rabbits—Stories 2 Netherlands—Fiction
ISBN 0-06-021546-1

"Based on the author's own childhood in the Netherlands, it tells of Davie's great joy when his grandfather promises him a real rabbit; of the almost unbearably long week of waiting for the rabbit to come; and to the happiness—and worry—of having something alive all his own." Horn Bk

"A rare understanding of childhood emotions makes this poignant story of a small boy's anticipation of and devotion to a pet rabbit a memorable reading experience for both children and their parents. [There are] sensitive pen-and-ink drawings by Maurice Sendak." Cincinnati

The wheel on the school; pictures by Maurice Sendak. Harper 1954 298p illus $5.95, lib. bdg. $5.79, pa $1.50 (4-6)   Fic

1 Storks—Stories 2 School stories 3 Netherlands—Fiction
ISBN 0-06-021585-2; 0-06-021586-0; 0-06-44021-2
Awarded the Newbery Medal, 1955

"Long ago, there had been storks on the roofs of the Dutch village of Shora, but when the storm came and the great waves sent salt spray flying over the dikes, the storks had gone away and never returned. The six school children of Shora are determined that the storks shall come back. Their enthusiasm arouses the whole village, and the story of the coming of the storks is a tale of faith and ingenuity, and even of physical endurance and courage when the great storms and crashing seas threaten their plans." Ontario Library Rev

"This unusual tale is told with much lively, colloquial children's talk, and plenty of humor. . . . Few writers of today offer this sort of realism to the young, with its insight that stimulates imagination and its clear, beauty, like that of a Vermeer painting." N Y Her Trib Bks

"It is difficult to imagine drawings more in time with the text than these unforgettable ones by Maurice Sendak." N Y Times Bk Rev

De La Mare, Walter

Mr Bumps and his monkey; illus. by Dorothy P. Lathrop. Winston 1942 69p illus lib. bdg. $3.59 (4-6)   Fic

1 Monkeys—Stories
ISBN 0-03-035370-X

This is the story of a sailor by the name of John Bumps and Jasper, a monkey that came from Africa. Dressed in striped trousers, waistcoat, and high hat, Jasper learns to speak English and becomes the toast of the theater

"A lovely quality of eerie tenderness pervades this story. . . . The illustrations are an affirmation of the mood and appeal of the text." N Y Pub Lib

Desbarats, Peter

Gabrielle and Selena; pictures by Nancy Grossman. Harcourt 1968 unp illus $5.50, pa 95¢ (2-4)   Fic

ISBN 0-15-230514-9; 0-15-634080-1

"Gabrielle and Selena decide to exchange identities and homes but are outsmarted by their parents who convince them both that they would really rather be themselves." Chicago

"Charming illustrations done in warm sepia reveal the fact that Gabrielle is white and Selena is a Negro." Bruno. Bks for Sch Libraries, 1968

Dickens, Charles

A Christmas carol in prose (4-7)   Fic

1 Christmas stories 2 Ghost stories 3 Great Britain—Fiction
Some editions are:

Lippincott $5.50 Illustrated by Arthur Rackham (ISBN 0-397-00033-2) Has title: A Christmas carol

Macmillan Pub Co. (The Macmillan classics) $3.95 Illustrated by John Groth. Afterword by Clifton Fadiman

Watts, F. lib. bdg. $7.95 Large type edition complete and unabridged. A Keith Jennison book (ISBN 0-531-00175-X) Has title: A Christmas carol

Dickens, Charles—*Continued*

Written in 1843

"This Christmas story of nineteenth century England has delighted young and old for generations. In it, a miser, Scrooge, through a series of dreams, finds the true Christmas spirit. . . . The story ends with the much-quoted cry of Tiny Tim, the cripple son of Bob Cratchit, whom Scrooge now aids: 'God bless us, every one!' " Haydn. Thesaurus of Bk Digests

"There is perhaps no story in English literature better known . . . or one that carries a more potent appeal to the Christmas sentiment." Springf'd Republican

The magic fishbone (3-5)   Fic

1 Fairy tales

Some editions are:

Harvey House $6, lib. bdg. $4.89 Illustrated by Faith Jaques (ISBN 0-8178-4611-5; 0-8178-4612-3)

Vanguard $4.95 Illustrated by Louis Slobodkin (ISBN 0-8149-0296-0)

Warne $4.95 Illustrated by F. D. Bedford (ISBN 0-7232-0319-9)

Taken from: A holiday romance, first published 1868

This is a "delightful story of the Princess Alicia and her eighteen brothers and sisters whose 'ages varied from seven years to six months'; and of the Fairy Grandmarina and the wish granted by the magic fishbone." Horn Bk

"This little masterpiece bubbles with fun and humor and is especially recommended for the storyteller." Library J

Dickinson, Peter

The Devil's children. Little 1970 188p $5.95. (5-7)   Fic

1 Fantastic fiction 2 Great Britain—Fiction

ISBN 0-316-18421-7

Sequel to: Heartsease

"An Atlantic Monthly Press book"

This book "describes the beginning of the inexplicable changes in England when people suddenly turn against machines. Separated from her parents in the madding confusion, twelve-year-old Nicky Gore forms a mutual assistance pact with a group of Sikhs who are unaffected by the changes but are now looked upon by the native population as the devil's children because of their alien ways. Nicky helps them barter their iron-working skills for food until they win acceptance by saving English villagers from marauding armored robbers." Booklist

"The whole concept is imaginative, the details consistent, and the characters solidly drawn, and the book is fast-paced, well written, and subtle in its message of brotherhood." Sat Rev

The gift. Little [1974 c1973] 188p $5.95 (5-7) Fic

1 Clairvoyance—Fiction

ISBN 0-316-18427-6

"An Atlantic Monthly Press book"

"Davy Price has inherited The Gift of clairvoyance from a legendary Welsh ancestor. Sometimes entertaining (at church Davy tunes into the sex fantasies of parishioners) and sometimes embarrassing (he unintentionally eavesdrops on the millionaire pipedreams of his down-and-out father), the gift becomes a terrifying burden when Davy's mind is flooded with the mad imaginings of a half-wit [named Wolf] out to destroy the Prices. From Wolf's distorted visions . . . Davy discovers and helps foil a robbery scheme involving his father." Library J

"The author has avoided sensationalism by consistently retaining the perspective of his adolescent protagonist both in dialogue and in narration. Superb touches of humor, contrasting sharply with the gravity of the situations, give depth to the characterizations and balance to the structure without destroying the feeling of thrill and suspense." Horn Bk

Heartsease. Little 1969 223p illus $5.95 (5-7) Fic

1 Fantastic fiction 2 Great Britain—Fiction

ISBN 0-316-18420-9

Sequel to: The weathermonger

"An Atlantic Monthly Press book"

"In a fantasy taking place in England 'now, or soon,' four young people rescue a foreign young man stoned by the witch-hunting villagers. Spurred by fitful memories of five years ago (before 'The Changes' made everyone think machines were evil, and those who used them, witches to be killed), and helped by the 'witch's' mechanical know-how, they recondition a tugboat, the Heartsease, and flee to still-modern Ireland." Library J

This book "scores very high marks for sheer storytelling, narrative which is packed full of suspense and pace and in which the action springs from the clash of personalities and the stress of circumstance. It is more than a very good yarn. The scene-painting is masterly, discreet and economical and always consistent. Some of the characters are types or ciphers, but Margaret, the central figure, is finely conceived." Times (London) Lit Sup

Followed by: The devil's children

The weathermonger. Little 1969 216p $5.95 (5-7)   Fic

1 Fantastic fiction 2 Great Britain—Fiction

ISBN 0-316-18419-5

"An Atlantic Monthly Press book"

First published 1968 in England

The people of the British Isles have been catapulted by the Changes back into the Middle Ages. Left to drown as witches, Geoffrey the weathermonger and his sister Sally, with the help of their twentieth century knowledge, escape but suffer many trials before the country returns to normal

"An engrossing suspensefully plotted yarn." Booklist

Followed by: Heartsease

Dillon, Eilís

A family of foxes; illus by Vic Donahue. Funk [1965 c1964] 119p illus $3.25 (5-7)   Fic

1 Foxes—Stories 2 Ireland—Fiction

ISBN 0-308-80005-2

First published 1964 in England

"Set on the Irish island of Inishowman, this is the story of four boys and their careful guarding of silver foxes rescued from the sea. The animals had been shipped to the Zoo at Dublin, and the boys reported their find, but by the time the foxes were picked up, the boys had had a long, hard job hiding them and feeding them. It was necessary to hide the beasts because the island population hated and hunted the local red foxes." Chicago. Children's Bk Center

It is a "tender animal story and a memorable re-creation of an island world shaped by isolation, superstition, and ceaseless economic struggle." Library J

The seals; illus. by Richard Kennedy. Funk [1969 c1968] 127p illus $4.50 (5-7)   Fic

1 Ireland—Fiction 2 Sea stories

ISBN 0-308-80063-X

First published 1968 in England

Warfare between Irish independence fighters and the Black and Tans in 1920 forms the background of this tale. "Young Pat Conneeley, two of his friends, and his grandfather sail a small boat across seven miles of storm-tossed sea from their offshore island to the west coast of Ireland to aid in the rescue of Pat's Uncle Roddy whose life is endangered by the English forces." Booklist

Dillon, Eilis—_Continued_

The telling of the story "is done in Eilis Dillon's inimitable Irish style. As always, her setting is vivid, her characters alive and colorful, and her action compelling." Bk World

Dixon, Paige

Lion on the mountain; illus. by J. H. Breslow. Atheneum Pubs. 1972 118p illus $4.95 (5-7)   Fic

1 Hunting—Fiction
ISBN 0-689-30050-6

Animal-loving Jamie and his father, who hunt only for the meat they need, become unwilling guides for a Hemingway-inspired city hunter who kills for the pleasure of killing and to obtain trophies. When he is asked to track a rare mountain lion to obtain photographs, Jamie is almost certain that the man intends to kill it

"A fast-paced outdoor adventure which explores man's relationship with nature." Minnesota

Dodge, Mary Mapes

Hans Brinker; or, The silver skates (4-7)   Fic

1 Skating—Fiction 2 Netherlands—Fiction
Some editions are:
Childrens Press lib. bdg. $5.25 Illustrated by Dennis A. Dierks. Complete and unabridged (ISBN 0-516-04248-3)
Collins (Rainbow classics) $3.50, lib. bdg. $3.91 Illustrated by Hilda van Stockum; with an introduction by May Lamberton Becker (ISBN 0-529-05025-0; 0-529-05026-9
Dutton (The Children's illustrated classics) $3.95 Illustrated with 8 colour plates and drawings in the text by Hans Baumhauer (ISBN 0-525-31424-5)
Grosset (Illustrated junior lib) lib. bdg. $3.95, pa $1.50 Illustrated by Cyrus Leroy Baldridge. Has subtitle: A story of life in Holland (ISBN 0-448-05811-1; 0-448-05462-0)
Scribner (The Scribner Illustrated classics) $10, pa $3.95 with drawings and decorations by George Wharton Edwards (ISBN 0-684-20800-8; 0-684-13812-3)
First published 1865

"All the strange fascination of Holland, its great flapping windmills, its canals, its dykes, its waterroads, its customs and traditions, are unfolded in the domestic tale of Hans and Gretel and the winning of the silver skates." Toronto

Du Bois, William Pène

The Alligator Case; story and pictures by William Pène Du Bois. Harper 1965 63p illus lib. bdg. $4.79 (3-5)   Fic

1 Circus—Fiction 2 Mystery and detective stories
ISBN 0-06-021746-4

"This is the tallish tale of three dastardly thieves who use a small-town circus as cover for their crime. Using an amazing series of disguises, the boy detective tenaciously follows clues, suspecting that the criminals have used alligator costumes to merge with those of the performers. (The cashier, of course, is a real alligator.) The author has immense fun with plot and word-plays." Chicago. Children's Bk Center

Call me Bandicoot. Harper 1970 63p illus $4.95, lib. bdg. $4.79 (5-7)   Fic

ISBN 0-06-024697-9; 0-06-024698-7
Illustrated by the author

This book "tells of a fast-talking young genius (who has the look of a miser) and of the two people he encounters who end up buying him food and giving him money." Pub W

The giant; story and pictures by William Pène Du Bois. Viking 1954 124p illus lib. bdg. $5.95 (4-7)   Fic

1 Giants—Fiction
ISBN 0-670-33856-7

A "story of a young boy of giant proportions who is being hidden away in a town in middle Europe. The boy has spent his life in hiding in various parts of Europe, but eventually he finds a town where the people neither fear him nor ridicule him, and he settles down there to live happily. The account of how the author discovered the giant, and helped to bring him out into the open is told." Chicago. Children's Bk Center

"El Muchacho is a one-dimensional figure, a useful peg upon which to hang a lesson in kindliness and tolerance. However, the description and illustrations of a boy's playroom, in which the electric trains, menagerie and toy soldiers are life-size, and of the many unusual arrangements which had to be made for this outsize boy, are entertaining." Ontario Library Rev

This "has all the necessities of good fantasy—warmth, humor, a spice of mystery and a wealth of factual detail. . . . Illustrations are delightful." N Y Times Bk Rev

The 3 policemen; or, Young Bottsford of Farbe Island. Viking 1960 95p illus lib. bdg. $5.95 (3-6)   Fic

1 Mystery and detective stories
ISBN 0-670-70912-3
First published 1938

This detective story is "about the three policemen and clever Young Bottsford who solve the mystery of the stolen fishing nets on the fabulous island of Farbe. . . . New illustrations in color and in black and white." Booklist

"One of Du Bois' funniest tales of high-handed humor and intrigue. Give it to mystery readers for widening their reading world." Bookmark

The twenty-one balloons; written and illus. by William Pène Du Bois. Viking 1947 179p illus $5.95 (5-7)   Fic

1 Balloons—Fiction
ISBN 0-670-73441-1
Awarded the Newbery Medal, 1948

"Professor Sherman set off on a flight across the Pacific in a giant balloon, but three weeks later the headlines read 'Professor Sherman in wrong ocean with too many balloons.' This book is concerned with the professor's explanation of this phenomenon. His account of his one stopover on the island of Krakatoa which blew up with barely a minute to spare to allow time for his escape, is the highlight of this hilarious narrative." Ontario Library Rev

"There is a twinkling humor underneath every word of the story that leaves the reader wondering. . . . The drawings are in keeping with the period and show great strength and originality. An exciting book that will be claimed by every member of the family." Sat Rev

Durham, John

Me and Arch and the Pest; illus. by Ingrid Fetz. Four Winds 1970 96p illus lib. bdg. $5.95 (3-5) Fic

1 Dogs—Stories 2 Negroes—Fiction
ISBN 0-590-07148-3

"Bit, who tells the story, is white; Arch is black. The story of their adoption of a large dog and taking on a poorly-paid job to support Pest is capped by an exciting (if not wholly believable) sequence in which they and a wounded policeman are pitted against a gang of dog-nappers. The appeal of the book is in the natural

Durham, John—*Continued*

dialogue, the warm relationships, and the candid and casual way in which Bit and Arch discuss natural speech versus schoolroom language, the difficulties of parental attitudes toward pets, and their own color difference. The illustrations are realistic, deft, and attractive." Chicago. Children's Bk Center

Du Soe, Robert C.

Three without fear; illus. by Ralph Ray, Jr. Longmans 1947 185p illus map lib. bdg. $3.59 (5-7)   Fic

  1 Baja California—Fiction 2 Survival (after airplane accidents, shipwrecks, etc.)—Fiction

  ISBN 0-679-25149-9

"A Robinson Crusoe story of an American boy, shipwrecked on the coast of Baja California, and two orphaned Indian children who together live on the country as they make their way to Santo Tomas. Perseverance, ingenuity and resourcefulness of the three make a thrilling story." Wis Lib Bul

Eager, Edward

Half magic; drawings by N. M. Bodecker. Harcourt 1954 217p illus $5.95, pa 75¢ (4-6)   Fic

  ISBN 0-15-233078-X; 0-15-637990-2

"Three sisters, a brother and a widowed mother made up the family. Jane, the eldest, found a magic charm [an ancient coin] which granted half of any wish; after finding that out, and barring accidents, the children wished for twice as much as they wanted. The charm made for a week of adventures including Katharine's defeat of Sir Launcelot in a thoroughly unfair tourney and ending with mother's acquisition of a new husband amid a burst of what Mark called 'love blah.'" N Y Times Bk Rev

"The chief effect of such a book is humor, arising from the ridiculous yet logical situations. . . . [It is] a book whose total contribution is one of fun and relaxation." Sat Rev

Followed by: Magic by the lake

Magic by the lake; illus. by N. M. Bodecker. Harcourt 1957 183p illus $5.95 (4-6)   Fic

  ISBN 0-15-250441-9

Sequel to: Half magic

Further adventures of Mark, Katharine, Jane and Martha. This time their magic comes from a lake, near which they are spending the summer

"It is still better than average fantasy, and its humor will make it popular even with children who usually prefer realism." Horn Bk

Magic or not? Illus. by N. M. Bodecker. Harcourt 1959 190p illus $5.95 (4-6)   Fic

  ISBN 0-15-251157-1

The story "concerns a well which 'could' be a magic wishing well and a group of children who are led by its magic, if it is magic, into a series of adventures and misadventures stemming from wishes to do good turns to others." Booklist

"Everything that happens just could be coincidence—the reader, along with the children, will have to decide for himself. In any event, a real mystery develops. Characters and events are fresh and lively, for although unmistakably an Eager book, it is not written to formula." Horn Bk

Seven-day magic; illus. by N. M. Bodecker. Harcourt 1962 156p illus $5.50, lib. bdg. $4.95 (4-6) Fic

  ISBN 0-15-272919-4; 0-15-272918-6

"A sophisticated fantasy in which five children find a magic book that describes themselves, and realize that they can create their own magic by wishing with the book. In one episode . . . they disrupt a telecast by silencing all the cast except for one member of a male quartet. The children are lively and a bit preco-

cious. . . . [The book has] humor, and some fresh and imaginative situations." Chicago. Children's Bk Center

Edmonds, Walter D.

Beaver valley; illus. by Leslie Morrill. Little 1971 70p illus map lib. bdg. $5.50 (4-6)   Fic

  1 Beavers—Stories 2 Mice—Stories

  ISBN 0-316-21164-8

"At first Skeet, a young deer mouse, is excited by the activities of the beavers that settle in his valley, despite his grandfather's warning that the beavers will change the valley to suit themselves regardless of the effect on anyone else. What happens to Skeet and the other animals as the rising water from the beavers' dams forces them from their homes is told in a briskly written nature story in which the similarities between the actions of the beavers and those of man are subtly pointed out." Booklist

Cadmus Henry; illus. by Manning de V. Lee. Dodd 1949 137p illus $3.95 (5-7)   Fic

  1 Balloons—Fiction 2 U.S.—History—Civil War—Fiction

  ISBN 0-396-03067-X

"The part which reconnaissance balloons played in the Civil War is shown through the experiences of a Confederate soldier. Excitement is added when young Henry's balloon goes out of control and drifts back and forth over the Union and Confederate lines." Hodges. Bks for Elem Sch Libraries

The matchlock gun; illus. by Paul Lantz. Dodd 1941 50p illus lib. bdg. $5.50 (4-6)   Fic

  1 New York (State)—Fiction 2 U.S.—History—French and Indian War, 1755-1763—Fiction

  ISBN 0-396-06369-1

  Awarded the Newbery Medal, 1942

"New York State during the French and Indian War is the setting for this story of a boy's courage and resourcefulness. In his father's absence, ten-year-old Edward Alstine helps his mother fight off an Indian attack by firing an old Spanish musket." Hodges. Bks for Elem Sch Libraries

"As literature, this story for ten-year-olds ranks with anything Mr. Edmonds has written for adults. The words are within their vocabulary—save for a few Dutch phrases they will find interesting—and though the tale is one of suspense, mounting terror and a climax of heroism what happens is no more than many a ten-year-old in our early history went through." N Y Her Trib Bks

"The dramatic telling of a tragic incident in the life of a colonial family . . . is heightened by lithographs of unusual quality. An authentic story." N Y Pub Library

Edwards, Sally

When the world's on fire; illus. by Richard Lebenson. Coward, McCann & Geoghegan 1972 125p illus $5.95 (4-6)   Fic

  1 U.S.—History—Revolution—Fiction 2 Negroes—Fiction 3 South Carolina—Fiction

  ISBN 0-698-20172-8

Set during the Revolutionary War in Charleston, South Carolina, this is the story of Annie, a young Black slave. She is the only person who can set off an explosion which will destroy the 5,000 pounds of ammunition stored in the British barracks

"Told from the viewpoint of the small frightened girl more interested in her brother's fate [he has been captured by the British] than the cause of patriotism, the third-person story has a certain realism and sense of the period. The black-and-white illustrations are appropriate to the mood and action of the story." Booklist

Ellis, Ella Thorp

Celebrate the morning. Atheneum Pubs. 1972 177p $6.25 (6-7)   Fic

1 Mental illness—Fiction 2 Parent and child—Fiction 3 California—Fiction

ISBN 0-689-30051-4

"Fourteen-year-old April and her mother live on welfare in a small house at the edge of a California town. Secure in her mother's love and sharing her joie de vivre April knows her mother is different from other people but is unaware that she is schizophrenic until she has been committed. The discomforting sight of her mother among other mentally ill persons in an institution and the fear that she, too, could be locked up keep April away from the hospital until, with the help of the widower next door who loves them both, she gradually comes to terms with herself and her mother's illness." Booklist

"The author deals sensitively with the relationship between fourteen-year-old April and her divorced mother. . . . Minor incidents and situations are described in an understated manner, and although without a complicated plot, the story rests on an honest portrayal of a likeable heroine's dilemmas." Horn Bk

Roam the wild country; drawings by Bret Schlesinger. Atheneum Pubs. 1967 212p illus $4.25, lib. bdg. $4.08, pa 95¢ (5-7)   Fic

1 Horses—Stories 2 Argentine Republic—Fiction

ISBN 0-689-20095-1; 0-689-20097-8; 0-689-70310-4

"A story of excitement, suspense and personal courage set in Northern Argentina on a ranch where fine horses are broken and trained. Prolonged drought makes it necessary to take the horses over the Andes mountains to greener pastures. The head trainer, his nephew and the two ranch owner's sons make this trip in spite of storms, difficult terrain, poisonous snakes and wild animals." Bruno. Bks for School Libraries, 1968

"In spite of all the wild happenings, the story is told simply and lucidly." Library J

Glossary: p211-12

Ellis, Mel

Caribou Crossing; a novel. Holt 1971 183p map lib. bdg. $4.95 (5-7)   Fic

1 Canada—Fiction

ISBN 0-03-089729-7

Two boys' dream of a fishing lodge in the Canadian wilderness comes true at the expense of the same natural wonders they sought to share with others

"Despite touches of melodrama the story is authentic in its depiction of the outdoors and strong in its plea for conservation." Booklist

Embry, Margaret

The blue-nosed witch; pictures by Carl Rose. Holiday House 1956 [c1955] 45p illus $3.95 (1-4)   Fic

1 Witches—Fiction 2 Halloween—Stories

ISBN 0-8234-0011-5

Blanche, a real witch, though a young one, had a nose that glowed a marvelous blue in the dark. One Halloween, cruising on her broom with black cat, Brockett, she found a band of children and joined them on their trick-or-treat forage

Engebrecht, P. A.

Under the haystack. Nelson 1973 124p $5.95 (5-7)   Fic

1 Sisters—Fiction 2 Farm life—Fiction

ISBN 0-8407-6296-8

Abandoned by her mother and stepfather, thirteen-year-old Sandy accepts full responsibility for her two younger sisters and their small run-down farm. Fac-

ing crises, big and small, she emerges with a new understanding of life's problems

"The story has moments that are tender, but it is most effective in its depiction of the endless routine of work on a poor farm, the impact coming from the very weight of trivia. The characterization is good; Sandy is a sturdy, courageous, and believable heroine, and her struggle for survival is balanced by her growing interest in a boy, her increasing awareness of physical changes in herself, and her friendship with a neighbor who is well aware that the three girls are alone, and offers both her help and her sympathy." Chicago. Children's Bk Center

Enright, Elizabeth

Gone-Away Lake; illus. by Beth and Joe Krush. Harcourt 1957 192p illus $6.50, pa $1.35 (4-6)   Fic

ISBN 0-15-231646-9; 0-15-636460-3

"Portia, going on eleven and her six-year-old brother, Foster, spend the summer holidays with their cousin Julian who is twelve and 'crazy about Nature.' On an exploring and 'collecting' excursion, Portia and Julian leave the woods behind and discover a reed-covered swamp into which they pursue a rare butterfly. Suddenly, across the swamp, they see a row of once elegant summer homes half in ruins on the distant edge. How the houses came to be there, their history and mystery, fills the children's holidays with excitement and delight. The enterprising out-of-doors, interested-in-everything children are warmly and lightly drawn, but the characters of Mrs. Cheever, who rejoices in the name of Minnehaha, and of her brother Pindar come alive as the authentic original inhabitants of the ruined mansions in the days of their splendour. This is a day-dreaming kind of story, with a wish fulfillment ending, but it is as pleasant a holiday book to read as the summer breezes, the bird songs, the flowers of the woods and dogs were pleasant to the children of the story." Ontario Library Rev

Followed by: Return to Gone-Away

Return to Gone-Away; illus. by Beth and Joe Krush. Harcourt 1961 191p illus $5.95, pa $1.15 (4-6)   Fic

ISBN 0-15-266372-X; 0-15-676900-X

Sequel to: Gone-Away Lake

The Blake family "have bought the old house, the Villa Caprice, which the children had discovered at the end of the previous wonderful summer. The problems and jobs of making the fascinating old house habitable, and the mystery of a treasure believed to be concealed in it make a summer of so much fun and excitement that the children cannot bear to have it end. Readers will be just as reluctant to finish the story." Horn Bk

"Although the book contains less true adventures than 'Gone-Away Lake' and leans somewhat too heavily on catalogues of all the findings in the old mansion, even these details are in fine contrast to the kind of world where too many houses are exactly like other houses, and people are as exactly like other people as they can make themselves. Here all is individualized, and told with Miss Enright's good-humored knowledge of human beings, especially children." N Y Times Bk Rev

The Saturdays; written and illus. by Elizabeth Enright. Holt 1941 175p illus lib. bdg. $4.95 (4-6)   Fic

1 Family—Fiction

ISBN 0-03-089690-8

"There were four children, a father, a maid, a janitor, and a dog in the Melendy household. The oldest child was Mona, then came a brother of twelve, a sister ten and over, and little Oliver, aged six. Their

Enright, Elizabeth—*Continued*

playroom on the top floor always seemed to afford enough amusement until they got the bright idea of pooling their allowance and each having a Saturday for their individual and special amusement. . . . [This story describes] what each child did on these successive Saturdays and how they eventually decide Saturdays together are more fun." Sch Library J

Two additional titles about the Melendy's are available from Holt: The Four-Story Mistake, $3.50, lib. bdg. $3.27 (ISBN 0-03-032830-6; 0-03-035765-9) and Then there were five, $3.95, lib. bdg. $3.59 (ISBN 0-03-032835-7; 0-03-035755-1). All three stories are available in an omnibus volume with title: The Melendy family $4.95 (ISBN 0-03-032840-3)

Tatsinda; pictures by Irene Haas. Harcourt 1963 80p illus $6.95 (3-5)   Fic

1 Fairy tales
ISBN 0-15-284276-4

"In the land of Tatrajan, the graceful timtik, the shy timbertock—all the animals—had fur as white as snow. And all the people of the kingdom had cool greenish-blue eyes and 'glittering white hair.' All, that is, except the golden-haired, brown-eyed girl, Tatsinda, who was therefore an object of pity." Pub W

"A beautifully conceived fairy tale with illustrations that have an appropriate charm. . . . All of the traditional elements are here: the wise woman and her magic, the bird who is cast out by a spell, the maiden who weaves a net for her release. Fine writing." Chicago. Children's Bk Center

Thimble summer; written and illus. by Elizabeth Enright. Holt 1938 124p illus $4.95; lib. bdg. $4.59 (4-6)   Fic

1 Farm life—Fiction 2 Wisconsin—Fiction
ISBN 0-03-032815-2; 0-03-035255-X
Awarded the Newbery Medal, 1939

"A story of life on a Wisconsin farm, filled with experiences and incidents of the present day. . . . Garnet believes that most of the happiness and good luck of the summer came from the thimble she found in the dry creek bed." Wis Library Bul

"There is swift keen characterization, natural conversation, and almost inspired selection of incident and detail, and rare humor and skill in the telling. Bright full-page illustrations in color, line drawings and lovely end papers will make it attractive to the girls from nine to twelve who will find Garnet Linden and her experiences absorbing." Library J

Zeee; pictures by Irene Haas. Harcourt 1965 46p illus $5.50 (2-4)   Fic

1 Fairy tales
ISBN 0-15-299955-8

This story tells of what happens when "clumsy human beings keep ruining the tiny homes set up by peppery little Zeee, a bumblebee-sized fairy." Top of the News

"Deliciously illustrated and deftly told, this fairy tale has overtones of humor and of allegory that are lightly evident." Chicago. Children's Bk Center

Erickson, Russell E.

A toad for Tuesday; pictures by Lawrence Di Fiori. Lothrop 1974 63p illus $4.25, lib. bdg. $3.94 (2-4)   Fic

1 Frogs—Stories 2 Owls—Stories 3 Mice—Stories 4 Friendship—Fiction
ISBN 0-688-41569-5; 0-688-51569-X

"Warton and Morton, toad brothers, are enjoying Morton's delicious beetle brittle and Warton decides to take some to an elderly aunt despite the wintry weather. He makes skis and sets off, stopping to rescue a mouse who tells him that there is a dangerous owl in the wood. And Warton is indeed caught by the owl, who says he will save this tasty morsel until Tuesday, his birthday. By that time Warton has so endeared himself to the owl by his friendly ways that plans have changed—but Warton doesn't know it. He escapes with the help of a troop of skiing mice, relatives of the one he'd saved, and they go off to safety, but risk their lives to rescue the owl from a fox." Chicago. Children's Bk Center

The book "stresses friendship, caring for and helping others without motivational self-gain. . . . Real feelings are expressed in this story. Fine illustrations." Children's Bk Rev Serv

Erwin, Betty K.

Behind the magic line; illus. by Julia Iltis. Little 1969 178p illus $4.95 (4-6)   Fic

1 Negroes—Fiction 2 Family—Fiction
ISBN 0-316-24945-9

"The story of a large Negro family, tight-knit and loving, poor and hard-working. Dozie, the oldest girl, is the protagonist, and when she meets elderly Uncle Samuel Dan, she is half-convinced that he is a magician who can solve her problems and open new doors for her. Uncle Samuel Dan does help, but it is really her father who brings a change; he has been working in another city and returns to move the family out west." Chicago. Children's Bk Center

"A feeling of unapologetic optimism pervades the story of a huge family grappling with its problems in a midwestern ghetto." Horn Bk

Go to the room of the eyes; illus. by Irene Burns. Little 1969 180p illus $5.95 (4-6)   Fic

1 Seattle—Fiction 2 Mystery and detective stories
ISBN 0-316-24946-7

The Evans family, with their six children "move into an old mansion on Seattle's Capitol Hill and immediately become involved in tracking down clues in a treasure hunt left by children who lived in the house 30 years before." Booklist

"It includes themes other than the mystery (an interracial friendship, adjustment to a new school) and . . . the writing style is adequate, with some humor and with realistic family relationships." Chicago. Children's Bk Center

Estes, Eleanor

The coat-hanger Christmas tree; illus. by Susanne Suba. Atheneum Pubs. 1973 77p illus $5.95 (4-6)   Fic

1 Christmas stories 2 Brooklyn—Fiction
ISBN 0-689-30416-1
"A Margaret K. McElderry book"

"Brooklyn Heights at Christmastime is aglow with lights, except in the home of Marianna and Kenny. Their mother refuses to let the children have a tree. . . . Marianna and Kenny devise plots to persuade their mother into changing her mind but she remains intransigent. Finally, Marianna constructs the coat-hanger Christmas tree, which delights the mother—an artsy-craftsy type." Pub W

"The plot isn't strong, but the characterization is convincing, and the story is appealing . . . gentle, cozy, realistic, achieving a sense of family life and home atmosphere that frame and permeate the small events of the action." Chicago. Children's Bk Center

Ginger Pye. Harcourt 1951 250p illus $6.95, pa $2.15 (4-6)   Fic

1 Dogs—Stories
ISBN 0-15-230930-6; 0-15-634750-4
Awarded the Newbery Medal, 1952

The Pyes lived in the little New England town of Cranbury. There was Mr. Pye, a famous ornithologist, his pretty young wife, their two children Jerry

Estes, Eleanor—*Continued*

and Rachel, and Gracie the cat. Later there was the dog Ginger. The story is about the loss of Ginger, and his return to his beloved family, through the cleverness of Uncle Benny, aged three

"Not many writers can give us the mind and heart of a child as Eleanor Estes can. . . . [She] has illustrated [the book] with her own drawings—vivid, amusing sketches that point up and confirm the atmosphere of the story. It is a book to read and reread." Sat Rev

Followed by: Pinky Pye

The hundred dresses; illus. by Louis Slobodkin. Harcourt 1944 80p illus $5.95, pa $1.50 (4-6)   Fic

ISBN 0-15-237374-8; 0-15-642350-2

"The 100 dresses are just dream dresses, pictures Wanda Petronski has drawn, but she describes them in self-defense as she appears daily in the same faded blue dress. Not until Wanda, snubbed and unhappy, moves away leaving her pictures at school for an art contest, do her classmates realize their cruelty." Bks for Deaf Children

"Written with great simplicity it reveals, in a measure, the pathos of human relationships and the suffering of those who are different. Mr. Slobodkin's water-colors interpret the mood of the story and fulfill the quality of the text." N Y Pub Library

The middle Moffat; illus. by Louis Slobodkin. Harcourt 1942 317p illus $5.95 (4-6)   Fic

ISBN 0-15-253663-9

Sequel to: The Moffats

"Janey Moffat, aged ten, considers herself a very mysterious person, though no one except the Oldest Inhabitant recognizes her special quality." Hodges. Bks for Elem Sch Libraries

"That grown-ups will enjoy the humor of this book does not detract from its suitability for children, for the situations are reasonable and entertaining from their point of view as well. . . . The episode of the Middle Bear is the best of them all. The black and white line drawings of Louis Slobodkin contribute to the reader's complete enjoyment." Wis Library Bul

The Moffats; illus. by Louis Slobodkin. Harcourt 1941 290p illus $6.50, pa $1.95 (4-6)   Fic

ISBN 0-15-255095-X; 0-15-661850-8

"The story of a family, not poverty-stricken but just poor, never strikes a false note: no sentimentality. . . . There are four young Moffats, from five and a half to fifteen, and Mama. Mostly we see things through the eyes of nine-year-old Janey, and her viewpoint is seldom commonplace. . . . The author has succeeded in conveying the large significance of small events in children's lives." Library J

Followed by: The middle Moffat

Pinky Pye; illus. by Edward Ardizzone. Harcourt 1958 192p illus $5.95 (4-6)   Fic

ISBN 0-15-262076-1

Sequel to: Ginger Pye

"Another story about the Pye family who, with cat and dog and four-year-old Uncle Benny, go to Fire Island for a summer of bird watching. The family acquires a new member: a small black kitten who can use the typewriter. . . . The book has the same spontaneity, humor and sincerity as other books by Estes." Chicago. Children's Bk Center

"Edward Ardizzone, though clothing the family in a vaguely British fashion, catches the spirit of every scene marvelously." N Y Her Trib Bks

The witch family; illus. by Edward Ardizzone. Harcourt 1960 186p illus $6.50, pa $1.45 (1-4)   Fic

1 Witches—Fiction 2 Halloween—Stories

ISBN 0-15-298571-9; 0-15-697645-5

"The Old Witch, the Little Witch Girl and Witch Baby are all the creations of crayons wielded by Amy and Clarissa, two little girls almost seven who sit drawing at home in Washington. As their imaginations run riot, the witches take on an independent life of their own, and the two groups mix and mingle in a series of adventures that reach a climax on Halloween. Ardizzone's pictures add the perfect illustration to a book full of wonderful fun." Library J

Certain "to give pleasure "to children who are not afraid of venturing beyond vocabulary levels, who enjoy play with words, and who like their reality and fantasy mixed; and especially if it is read aloud by adults who are able 'to give themselves up' to the childlike nonsense and fancy of the story." Horn Bk

Farley, Walter

The Black Stallion; illus. by Keith Ward. Random House 1941 275p illus $3.95, lib. bdg. $5.97, pa 95¢ (4-7)   Fic

1 Horses—Stories

ISBN 0-394-80601-8; 0-394-90601-2; 0-394-82194-7

A boy and a wild black stallion, the only survivors from a shipwreck, live for a time on an uninhabited island, and somehow manage to exist until they are rescued. Back in the United States the boy and a retired jockey tame the horse and race him to the entire satisfaction of all concerned

Farmer, Penelope

Charlotte sometimes; pictures by Chris Connor. Harcourt 1969 192p illus $5.50 (5-7)   Fic

1 School stories 2 Fantastic fiction

"A newcomer to boarding school finds that she has somehow been shifted back to the days of World War I; not always, but sometimes she becomes Clare instead of Charlotte, living with a younger sister at the same school. Slowly Charlotte realizes that she and Clare are changing places and that her life as Charlotte is being lived by Clare on the days she herself is in the past. Trapped by a mishap in Clare's time, Charlotte must scheme to get back to the present. . . . The boarding school setting and the period details are quite convincing, and the suspense is maintained even when the mechanics of the mystery are explained." Chicago. Children's Bk Center

The summer birds; illus. by James J. Spanfeller. Harcourt 1962 155p illus $4.95 (4-6)   Fic

1 Fairy tales

ISBN 0-15-282485-5

This is "a fantasy unusual in sustained mood and quiet style. Two sisters meet a strange boy who teaches them to fly; one by one, all the children in school are taught and they spend the summer secretly enjoying the joy of flight. Until the end of the summer, the children do not learn who the strange boy is, and when they find out, he must leave them and they lose their ability to fly." Chicago. Children's Bk Center

Faulkner, Georgene

Melindy's medal, by Georgene Faulkner and John Becker; illus. by E. C. Fax. Messner 1945 172p illus $3.50, lib. bdg. $4.79 (3-5)   Fic

1 Courage—Fiction 2 Negroes—Fiction

ISBN 0-671-32327-X; 0-671-32057-2

Melindy had only one fault—she was a girl. All the men in Melindy's family had won medals for bravery in war. Then came a day when being eight years old, Black, and a girl, did not hold Melindy back from

Faulkner, Georgene—*Continued*

saving the lives of all the children in her school, and she, too, won a medal

This is "an unusual story glowing with tenderness and mirth." N Y Times Bk Rev

Fenton, Edward

Duffy's Rocks. Dutton 1974 198p $5.95 (6-7) Fic

1 Pittsburgh—Fiction 2 Grandmothers—Fiction

ISBN 0-525-28940-2

"At age 13, Timothy Brennan has one deep need: to escape from dreary Duffy's Rocks, a suburb of Pittsburgh, and find his absconding father. He lives with his old Gran and, though he is favored by the rich Lachlan family, the boy is disillusioned when he finds they have no real interest in helping the poor. Timothy runs away to New York in search of his father and learns more hurtful facts about faithless Bart Brennan. Going home, he finds his grandmother dying but she leaves him her hopes and blessings, the strength he needs to live with his insular, hidebound aunt and uncle." Pub W

"Although Timothy's final disillusionment, which sent him back to his dying grandmother, may seem a bit pat, the author has given skillful and pertinent utterance to the elements in the background of the boy's life. . . . The contrast between Timothy's grandmother, with her old-fashioned Irish virtues, and Timothy's aunt, with her brashness and vulgarity, is admirably as well as humorously delineated. And Timothy himself is constantly sensitive to the interesting diversity of ethnic strains in a large American city." Horn Bk

A matter of miracles. Holt 1967 239p illus map lib. bdg. $3.97 (4-7) Fic

1 Puppets and puppet plays—Fiction 2 Sicily—Fiction

ISBN 0-03-064055-5

"On the Day of the Dead in poverty-filled Sicily, 13-year-old Gino knows that only a miracle will bring the gift his crippled little sister expects. He is frustrated and helpless because of his fatherless family's poverty, his own youth, and his concern for his family. But a miracle does happen when Gino finds his identity as an apprentice puppeteer, discovering that life itself is a miracle. A host of intriguing characters, a true evocation of the Sicilian people and their land, and the picture of puppeteering make an interesting novel." Wis Library Bul

Field, Rachel

Calico bush; engravings on wood by Allen Lewis. Macmillan (N Y) 1931 213p illus $4.95 (4-7) Fic

1 Frontier and pioneer life—Fiction 2 U.S.—History—French and Indian War, 1755-1763—Fiction 3 Maine—Fiction

This is the story of Marguerite, called Maggie, a brave little French girl 'bound out' to a family of American pioneers in the days of the French and Indian War

"Colonial Maine in its days of first settlement is the background for this story. The hardships of pioneer life and the dangers from hostile Indians make it a very exciting tale of adventure." Wis Library Bul

Hitty: her first hundred years; with illus. by Dorothy P. Lathrop. Macmillan (N Y) 1929 207p illus $4.95 Fic

1 Dolls—Fiction

Awarded the Newbery Medal, 1930

"Hitty, a doll of real character carved from a block of mountain ash, writes the story of her eventful life from the security of an antique-shop window which she shares with Theobold, a rather over-bearing cat. Her career, begun in a quiet Maine village, is crowded with adventures and she gives lively doll's-eye glimpses of the widely differing places and people that she encounters during her hundred years, and of the manners and modes of her times. The illustrations by Dorothy P. Lathrop are the happiest extension of the text. Will be enjoyed by both grown-ups and children." Cleveland

It is the author's "careful yet unlabored re-creation of the [1800's] period that adds to the value of the book and heightens the effect of Miss Field's keen characterization." N Y Her Trib Bks

Fife, Dale

Ride the crooked wind; illus. by Richard Cuffari. Coward, McCann & Geoghegan 1973 95p illus $5.95 (4-6) Fic

1 Paiute Indians—Fiction

ISBN 0-698-20249-X

"A well-built story centered around a Paiute boy who clings to the old Indian ways in spite of pressure to yield to white influences. Sent to boarding school when his grandmother is hospitalized, Po resists his new guardian, a bachelor uncle who has reconciled the Indian with the white world. In the end, Po's stubbornness subsides and he agrees to 'Ride the Crooked Wind' by living his life one day at a time. The culture conflict is deftly handled." Sch Library J

Who's in charge of Lincoln? Illus. by Paul Galdone. Coward-McCann 1965 61p illus lib. bdg. $4.49 (2-4) Fic

1 Negroes—Fiction 2 Washington, D.C.—Fiction

ISBN 0-698-30406-3

"A resourceful little New York boy thwarts some bank robbers, goes by train to Washington, D.C., visits his namesake's Memorial statue, and returns safely, with no one realizing that he has had an extraordinary experience. It happens when his mother goes to the hospital for a new baby and he is left alone despite careful plans. This is a funny, believable story about an engaging Negro child whose security is firmly based on warm family relationships." Moorachian. What is a City?

Finlayson, Ann

Rebecca's war; illus. by Sherry Streeter. Warne 1972 280p illus map $4.95 (5-7) Fic

1 U.S.—History—Revolution—Fiction 2 Philadelphia—Fiction

ISBN 0-7232-6090-7

While her father and brothers are fighting the British, fourteen-year-old Rebecca Ransome is left in charge of the family house and her small brother and sister. This story, set in Philadelphia during the American Revolution, tells of Rebecca's resourcefulness in helping the rebel cause in the face of enemy occupation of the city and even her own house

"While Rebecca at times seems larger than life, her courage is infused with enough humor and recklessness to make her a believable and likeable heroine." Sch Library J

Fisher, Dorothy Canfield

Understood Betsy; illus. by Martha Alexander. [Rev. ed] Holt 1972 211p illus lib. bdg. $5.50 (4-6) Fic

1 Country life—Fiction 2 Vermont—Fiction

ISBN 0-03-088364-4

First published 1917. This edition has been newly illustrated

"Elizabeth Ann, who has been too much 'understood' and coddled by an over-conscientious aunt, is suddenly set down on a Vermont farm in a simple, wholesome environment which changes the nervous self-conscious child into a strong, self-reliant little individual." Cleveland

Fisher, Leonard Everett

The death of Evening Star; the diary of a young New England whaler; written and illus. by Leonard Everett Fisher. Doubleday 1972 125p illus $4.95 (5-7)   Fic

1 Sea stories 2 Whaling—Fiction

ISBN 0-385-07649-5

New England whaling of the 1840's is observed through the secret diary kept by a young cabin boy throughout the ill-fated voyage of the whaler Evening Star. The boy's story is revealed in this fictionalized account by a narrator who mysteriously acquires the rain-soaked diary on a stormy night in the not so distant past

"The whaling jargon is accurate; the handsome black-and-white scratchboard illustrations are detailed and graphic; but the author's research has produced more than a historical documentary. . . . Rather, by judicious use of the story-within-a-story technique, he adds further dimension to his tale by suggesting a sense of the past, the possible influence of supernatural forces, and the conflict between good and evil. . . . An engrossing combination of social history and the occult." Horn Bk

The warlock of Westfall; written and illus. by Leonard Everett Fisher. Doubleday 1974 119p illus $4.95, lib. bdg. $5.70 (5-7)   Fic

1 Witchcraft—Fiction 2 Massachusetts—History—Colonial period—Fiction

ISBN 0-385-07125-6; 0-385-04476-3

In seventeenth-century Massachusetts "a senile old man invents a family out of loneliness, and at night he puts markers on their imaginery graves. When some cocky boys spy on him and tell the townspeople, witchcraft hysteria and tragedy result." Chicago

"Somber yet dramatic, the stark black and white illustrations in Fisher's distinctive style are particularly well suited to the taut and brooding atmosphere evoked in this tale of witch-hunting in colonial America. . . . Both the mood of the times and the physical atmosphere are skillfully evoked in a stirring and convincing story." Chicago. Children's Bk Center

Fitzgerald, John D.

The Great Brain; illus. by Mercer Mayer. Dial Press 1967 175p illus $5.95, lib. bdg. $5.47 (4-7)   Fic

1 Utah—Fiction

ISBN 0-8037-3074-8; 0-8037-3076-4

"The Great Brain was Tom Dennis ('T.D.') Fitzgerald, age ten, of Adenville, Utah; the time, 1896. . . . This autobiographical yarn is spun by his brother John Dennis ('J.D.'), age seven . . . who can tell stories about himself and his family with enough tall-tale exaggeration to catch the imagination." Horn Bk

Other books about the Great Brain are available from Dial Press: More adventures of the Great Brain $5.95, lib. bdg. $5.47 (ISBN 0-8037-5819-7; 0-8037-5821-9); The Great Brain at the academy $5.95, lib. bdg. $5.47 (ISBN 0-8037-3039-X; 0-8037-3040-3); The Great Brain reforms $5.95, lib. bdg. $5.47 (ISBN 0-8037-3067-5; 0-8037-3068-3); Return of the Great Brain $5.95, lib. bdg. $5.47 (ISBN 0-8037-6403-6; 0-8037-7413-3); The Great Brain does it again $5.95, lib. bdg. $5.47 (ISBN 0-8037-5065-X; 0-8037-5066-8)

Fitzhugh, Louise

Harriet the spy; written and illus. by Louise Fitzhugh. Harper 1964 298p illus $5.95, lib. bdg. $5.79 (4-7)   Fic

1 School stories

ISBN 0-06-021910-6; 0-06-021911-4

Also available in a large type edition $7.50 ISBN 0-06-021912-2

"A marvelous and terrifying child, Harriet. An imaginative and intelligent sixth grader, she has two preoccupations: she writes and she spies. Harriet writes honestly and caustically her opinions of her peers and of adults, and she spies in an organized and industrious way. When her classmates find Harriet's notebook, war ensues and Harriet finds she is an outcast. Having just been separated from the one adult with whom she was in rapport, Harriet becomes very upset and is taken to a psychiatrist. His suggestions are sensible, and Harriet, too bright to be anything but bored at home, goes back to school and a more constructive channeling of her rampaging abilities." Chicago. Children's Bk Center

"Children will love everything about the book and probably accept without question the rather too neatly contrived happy ending and the remote, ineffectual parents. Their elders will admire the book's vigor and originality and the essential truth of the children's thoughts and actions." Bk Week

The long secret; written and illus. by Louise Fitzhugh. Harper 1965 275p illus map $5.95, lib. bdg. $5.49 (4-7)   Fic

1 Long Island—Fiction

ISBN 0-06-021410-4; 0-06-021411-2

Further adventures of eleven-year-old Harriet M. Welsch, heroine of: Harriet the spy. Investigating a mysterious series of anonymous notes warning various members of the small Long Island beach community to mend their ways, Harriet learns that her summer friend, Beth Ellen Hansen, is the culprit

Nobody's family is going to change. Farrar, Straus 1974 221p illus $5.95 (5-7)   Fic

1 Family—Fiction 2 Negroes—Fiction

ISBN 0-374-35539-8

"The Sheridan family is Black, middle class (the maid is White), with two children. Emma is eleven, fat and with two overwhelming concerns: eating and becoming a lawyer. William is seven and his main concern is to become a dancer like his uncle. Mr. Sheridan is a lawyer and has no use for female lawyers or male dancers. Emma thinks that she has found a way out of her difficulties when she joins 'the children's army,' a group dedicated to the non-existent rights of children." Children's Bk Rev Serv

"Beneath the surface layer of plot and of characters that suggest stereotypes but take on a life of their own is a probe of the intense, destructive Sheridan family relationships. Emma, from whose viewpoint the story is told, comes to confront her father's distaste and indifference toward her as a person and to perceive her mother's determination to ignore the unpleasant undercurrents in their family. With surprising but believable acumen she figures out that she herself must change . . . that her parents are not going to transform their attitudes. . . . The only shaky ground is the difficulty of a white author's depicting a black family accurately and intimately." Booklist

Flack, Marjorie

Walter the lazy mouse; illus. by Cyndy Szekeres. Doubleday 1963 95p illus $4.50, lib. bdg. $5.25, pa 75¢ (2-4)   Fic

1 Mice—Stories 2 Frogs—Stories

ISBN 0-385-02772-9; 0-385-03771-6; 0-385-01078-8

A reissue of a title first published 1937

Walter, a mouse, was so lazy he never went anywhere on time. His seven brothers and sisters, father and mother were accustomed to seeing him so rarely that they moved one day and forgot to tell him. That's when Walter's adventure began. While searching for his family he met three very backward frogs, whom he tried to teach, so that there just wasn't time to be lazy

This is a "whimsical . . . classic. The unforgettable

Flack, Marjorie—*Continued*
scenes of Walter's ingenious mouse house and games of real live leap frog are captured in [new] illustrations." Growing Up With Bks

Fleischman, Sid
By the Great Horn Spoon! Illus. by Eric von Schmidt. Little 1963 193p illus $5.95 (4-6)   Fic
  1 California—Gold discoveries—Fiction
  ISBN 0-316-28577-3
  "An Atlantic Monthly Press book"
  "Jack and his aunt's butler, Praiseworthy, stow away on a ship bound for California. Here are their adventures aboard ship and in the Gold Rush of '49." Pub W
  "This whimsical situation-adventure promises only fun. . . . Pen-and-ink drawings." Chicago Sch J

  Chancy and the grand rascal; illus. by Eric von Schmidt. Little 1966 179p illus $5.95 (4-6)   Fic
  1 Middle West—Fiction
  ISBN 0-316-28575-7
  "An Atlantic Monthly Press book"
  "A young boy sets out to find his brothers and sisters, separated by the death of their parents in the Civil War, and meets a 'Grand Rascal' who leads him through many adventures in the battle of wits and colorful tall-talking." Bruno. Bks for School Libraries, 1968
  "This is one of those rare children's books where language and story are one. It is a world of hyperbole and homely detail, an ebullient, frontier, Bunyanesque world, coarse, new and incurably optimistic." Christian Sci Monitor

  The ghost in the noonday sun; illus. by Warren Chappell. Little 1965 173p illus $5.95 (4-6)   Fic
  1 Pirates—Fiction 2 Buried treasure—Fiction
  ISBN 0-316-28576-5
  "An Atlantic Monthly Press book"
  "A real pirate story unfolds when twelve-year-old Oliver Finch is shanghaied aboard the 'Bloody Molly' and made to search for buried treasure—all because the villainous captain thinks that a boy born at the stroke of midnight ought to have the power to see the ghost of Gentleman Jack dancing on the treasure that fills his grave. Told with humor, color, and plenty of salty language." Wis Library Bul

  The ghost on Saturday night; illus. by Eric von Schmidt. Little 1974 57p illus $3.95 (3-5)   Fic
  1 Robbers and outlaws—Fiction
  ISBN 0-316-28583-8
  "Opie makes a career of guiding folk through dense fog [in a California town] and saves up the coins he earns to buy a saddle; his great-aunt Etta will buy him a horse to go with it when he has done his share of the purchase. So the boy is disappointed when a visitor, Professor Pepper, gives him two tickets to a ghost-raising instead of a nickel. Opie and his aunt go to the performance at which Crookneck John, a long-dead bandit, is supposed to appear. But the Professor and his henchman use the act as a coverup for a bank robbery, a theft that's thwarted by the resourcefulness of our boy, Opie." Pub W
  "The short scenario, illustrated with figures as overstated and caricatured as those in the text, is filled with the same kind of hyperbole, piquant phrasing, and bravura that have made the author's other books so delightful and so much fun to read." Horn Bk

  Jingo Django; illus. by Eric von Schmidt. Little 1971 172p illus $5.95 (4-6)   Fic
  1 Orphans and orphans' homes—Fiction 2 Buried treasure—Fiction
  ISBN 0-316-28580-3

"An Atlantic Monthly Press book"
  "Jingo Hawks, of Mrs. Daggatt's Beneficent Orphan House in Boston, is hired out to General Dirty-Face Jim Scurlock as a chimney sweep. A mysterious Mr. Peacock 'buys' Jingo and, financed by Peacock's highly saleable artistic talent, they set out on a treasure hunt pursued by Daggatt and Scurlock. Hilarious scenes follow involving highwaymen, gypsies and a block of ice which becomes a rapidly melting life raft. Readers are clued in early to the fact that Mr. Peacock is really Jingo's father and that his mother was a beautiful gypsy girl who died when Jingo (Django is his gypsy name) was little." Sch Library J
  "The story is a vitally told, just-plain-fun tale to read. The broadly farcical caricaturing of the line drawings perfectly complements the burlesque mood of the story." Horn Bk

  Mr Mysterious & Company; illus. by Eric von Schmidt. Little 1962 151p illus $5.95 (4-6)   Fic
  1 Magic—Fiction 2 Overland journeys to the Pacific—Fiction
  ISBN 0-316-28578-1
  "An Atlantic Monthly Press book"
  "An engaging story of a traveling magic show during the 1880's in which Pa is Mr. Mysterious and the whole family performs. A sound philosophy of good will and common sense underlies their sheer, happy bravado as they play the frontier towns westward to California." Chicago

Flora, James
Grandpa's farm; 4 tall tales; story & pictures by James Flora. Harcourt 1965 unp illus $6.95 (1-4)
                                                                  Fic
  ISBN 0-15-232340-6
  Grandpa, the farmer, spins four "wildly preposterous tales. . . . He tells of the great wind of '34 that blew him a fine blue barn; of Grandma's cow salve that could make anything grow, from cows' tails to cornstalks; of the miraculous productions of little Hatchy Hen; and of the terrible winter when conversation froze in the air and remained unheard until summer." Horn Bk

Fox, Paula
Blowfish live in the sea. Bradbury Press 1970 116p $6.95 (6-7)   Fic
  ISBN 0-87888-024-0
  To twelve-year-old Carrie, her older half-brother Ben is the most important person alive. This story tells of their search for Ben's real father whose only link with his son has been a stuffed blowfish—a present he gave to Ben as a small boy
  "If this most perceptive book falls into the hands of adult readers, its message will be clear—that specific environments of body and spirit are needed for us to be ourselves. But Miss Fox presents the idea in such a subtle manner that younger readers may miss it, though still enjoying a wonderful story." Best Sellers

  How many miles to Babylon? A novel; illus. by Paul Giovanopoulos. White 1967 117p illus lib. bdg. $5.95 (4-6)   Fic
  1 Brooklyn—Fiction 2 Negroes—Fiction
  ISBN 0-87250-415-8
  Ten-year-old James Douglas, a Negro boy who lives in Brooklyn, knows his mother is in the hospital but fantasizes that she has gone to Africa, home of his ancestors. He runs away from his aunts to find his mother. After a harrowing encounter with three dog thieves, he returns home to find his mother back in their room
  "Against the background, suggested rather than described, Jimmy is a small bewildered victim of an

Fox, Paula—*Continued*

almost overwhelming situation. . . . [The story] is far more important for young people who have no knowledge of Negro ghettos than it is for children to whom the setting may be all too familiar." Horn Bk

Maurice's room; pictures by Ingrid Fetz. Macmillan (N Y) 1966 63p illus $4.95, pa 95¢ (3-5) Fic

1 Collectors and collecting—Fiction

"As a 'collector,' Maurice has a problem in his small room keeping things in order. His problem is solved when his family moves to the country where he will have a barn to keep his treasures." Rdng Ladders. 5th edition

"An absolutely enchanting book, written in low key, with deadpan humor, and with marvelously real people. . . . The writing style is deft, the illustrations engaging." Sutherland. The Best in Children's Bks

Portrait of Ivan; illus. by Saul Lambert. Bradbury Press 1969 131p illus $5.95 (4-7) Fic

1 Parent and child—Fiction

ISBN 0-87888-015-1

"Ivan is a lonely, motherless boy whose home life with a busy father who travels a lot and a friendly sympathetic Haitian housekeeper is comfortable but circumscribed. Getting to know artist Matt Mustazza and Miss Manderby who reads to him while he sits for his portrait and joining them on a trip to Florida not only enlarge Ivan's horizon but awaken him to new awareness of himself as a person. The quiet, introspective story is notable for its sensitive and discerning interpretations of a young boy's thoughts, feelings, and reactions to people, places, and situations." Booklist

The slave dancer; a novel. With illus. by Eros Keith. Bradbury Press 1973 176p illus $6.95 (6-7) Fic

1 Slave trade—Fiction 2 Sea stories

ISBN 0-87888-062-3

Awarded the Newbery Medal, 1974

Set in 1840, this "is the story of fourteen-year-old Jessie, impressed into service on a slave ship so that he can play his fife. To his horror, Jessie discovers that he is a slave dancer, his piping meant to keep the wretched black captives jigging in order to maintain their health—the motive mercenary rather than humanitarian. Jessie and a slave his age escape after a shipwreck and are taken in by a black man who sends each of them safely on his way—but this is after a four-month voyage on which Jessie has learned the horrors of the slave trade and the depravity and avarice of the crew." Chicago. Children's Bk Center

"Hunger and thirst, hazardous voyaging under sail, a degraded crew's callousness, calculated torture, and greed are not minimized but have the veracity of the retelling in a journal. Jessie is a fully realized figure, whose perceptions and agonies are presented in depth." Horn Bk

The stone-faced boy; illus. by Donald A. Mackay. Bradbury Press 1968 106p illus $5.95 (4-6) Fic

1 New England—Fiction

ISBN 0-87888-000-3

"The story is a perceptive character study of a lonely, timid middle child in a family of five self-possessed, individualistic children. To save himself from teasing by classmates and siblings, Gus Oliver has learned to mask his feelings so well that he has lost all ability to show emotion. Even the startling and unexpected arrival of an eccentric, outspoken great-aunt appears to leave Gus unmoved but the night his sister inveigles him into going out in the dark and the cold to rescue a stray dog, he gains a new-found confidence in himself." Booklist

"The plot is simple, and the lively characters embody the obstacles that Gus learns to contend with. A quiet story, told simply and sensitively, but for a perceptive sympathetic reader. The pencil drawings subtly capture the rustic background and the feelings of the boy around whom the story revolves." Horn Bk

Franchere, Ruth

Willa; decorations by Leonard Weisgard. Crowell 1958 169p illus $5.95 (6-7) Fic

1 Cather, Willa Sibert—Fiction 2 Frontier and pioneer life—Fiction 3 Nebraska—Fiction

ISBN 0-690-89138-5

This is "an episodic, extremely romantic biography of Willa Cather from the time when her family moved to Nebraska, when she was a child of about 10, to her graduation from high school. Much of its effectiveness comes from the reader's knowledge of Miss Cather's novels, knowledge which few if any 10 or 12 year olds can possibly have. However, the book does give a very clear picture of life in the Nebraska that Willa Cather knew so well, and it tells a pleasant enough story about an extraordinary little girl." Pub W

Sources: p168-69

Freuchen, Pipaluk

Eskimo boy; tr. from the Danish; illus. by Ingrid Vang Nyman. Lothrop 1951 96p illus $4.75 (4-6) Fic

1 Eskimos—Fiction 2 Greenland—Fiction

ISBN 0-688-41329-3

"While the family is on a hunting expedition on a barren island, Ivik's father is killed. The inexperienced small boy must fill his father's place in providing for the family. Helplessly isolated and near starvation they experience real suffering until with grim courage Ivik kills a polar bear. This boy suffers deep humiliation from being unprepared by age or skills to carry the responsibilities of manhood in a primitive culture." Rdng Ladders

Friedman, Frieda

Ellen and the gang; illus. by Jacqueline Tomes. Morrow 1963 191p illus lib. bdg. $4.81 (4-6) Fic

1 Juvenile delinquency—Fiction 2 New York (City)—Fiction

ISBN 0-688-31263-2

"During a dull summer, innocent twelve-year-old Ellen Ward associates with a group of delinquents who use her to cover their shoplifting. When they are apprehended, Ellen feels that she is disgraced forever, but she recovers her self-respect and wins community approbation for her work with small children on the project playground." Moorachian. What is a City?

"A good urban story, with excellent human relations. . . . The final episode seems a bit overdrawn, not beyond the bounds of credibility, but a bit elaborate." Chicago. Children's Bk Center

Friis-Baastad, Babbis

Don't take Teddy; tr. from the Norwegian by Lise Somme McKinnon. Scribner 1967 218p lib. bdg. $6.95 (5-7) Fic

1 Mentally handicapped children—Fiction 2 Norway—Fiction

ISBN 0-684-13213-3

Original Norwegian edition, 1965

Mildred L. Batchelder Award, 1969

"Thirteen-year-old Mikkel, in addition to the problems of any boy his age, bears an extra burden. His 15-year-old brother Teddy is severely retarded, and has been kept at home, despite the strain his presence puts on normal family living. Mikkel feels strongly protective towards Teddy and when Teddy accidentally injures another boy, Mikkel feels they must run

Friis-Baastad, Babbis—*Continued*
away before Teddy is institutionalized by the authorities." Sch Library J

"This is quite a remarkable book, because the author teaches a lesson without preaching. In Mikkel's love for his brother there is a realistic embarrassment but no shame; there is a realistic range of reactions from people he meets, and a realistic acceptance of the limits of the educability of the retarded." Sat Rev

Fritz, Jean
Brady; illus. by Lynd Ward. Coward-McCann 1960 223p illus $6.95 (4-7)   Fic
1 Slavery in the U.S.—Fiction 2 Underground railroad—Fiction 3 Pennsylvania—Fiction
ISBN 0-698-20014-4

"In 1836, after Brady, a Pennsylvania preacher's son, discovered [an Underground Railroad] station near his family's farm and knew his father did not trust him with that secret, he wished he had never heard of slavery because it had got him into such trouble; but in a time of great need he was able to prove that he was becoming a man. The writing of this story is unhurried and vivid. Brady is entirely believable—both he and his father are drawn with particular skill—and the incidents of controversy centered in Abolitionism and church division are made exciting. The background of farm and family activity has colorful period flavor." Horn Bk

The cabin faced west; illus. by Feodor Rojankovsky. Coward-McCann 1958 124p illus $5.95 (3-6)   Fic
1 Scott, Ann (Hamilton)—Fiction 2 Frontier and pioneer life—Fiction 3 Pennsylvania—Fiction
ISBN 0-698-20016-0

"Ann is unhappy when her family moves from Gettysburg to the Pennsylvania frontier, but she soon finds friends and begins to see that there is much to enjoy about her new home—including a visit from General Washington." Hodges. Bks for Elem Sch Libraries

"Ann is a very real little heroine, demure and appealing in Mr. Rojankovsky's pencil sketches." N Y Her Trib Bks

Early thunder; illus. by Lynd Ward. Coward, McCann & Geoghegan 1967 255p illus $6.95 (6-7)   Fic
1 U.S.—History—Colonial period—Fiction 2 Salem, Mass.—Fiction
ISBN 0-698-20036-5

"The political conflict in Salem, Mass., 1774-75, is realized in the agony of David, the 14-year-old son of a Tory doctor, who struggles to determine where his own allegiance lies." Coughlan. Creating Independence, 1763-1789

"The period details and the historical background are excellent, both in themselves and in the easy way they are incorporated into the story. The characters are believable, but are less interesting as people than as examples of people's attitudes. The plot, based on some facts . . . is less interesting in itself than it is as a means of showing the general pattern and movement of events and morale." Chicago. Children's Bk Center
Map on lining-papers

George Washington's breakfast; Paul Galdone drew the pictures. Coward-McCann 1969 unp illus lib. bdg. $4.99 (2-4)   Fic
1 Washington, George, President U.S.—Fiction
ISBN 0-698-30099-8
George W. Allen "was named for George Washington and he had the same birthday. It made him feel almost related. So related he wanted to know everything he could about George Washington. . . . [He especially wanted to] know what George Washington ate for breakfast. He got his grandmother to promise she'd cook George Washington's breakfast if he found out what it was, and he was going to find out—no matter what." About the Book

"Paul Galdone's red, white, and blue illustrations don't equal many of his earlier ones, but they are appropriate to the story and, like it, are not overstated. Younger and reluctant readers may enjoy this, as it offers a painless way of picking up information." Sch Library J

Gage, Wilson
Big blue island; pictures by Glen Rounds. World Pub. 1964 120p illus $4.95 (4-6)   Fic
1 Tennessee—Fiction
ISBN 0-529-03773-4

"Deserted by his shiftless father, orphaned by the death of his mother, eleven-year-old Darrell is sent from his sordid surroundings in Detroit to his only relative, a cantankerous old great-uncle living in a shack on a lonely island in the middle of a Tennessee river. The boy is vindictive, confused, and sullen; cut off from the shabby excitement of big city life, he longs for a little money so that he can run away. The island, a game reserve, is the home of some big blue herons, and on these creatures he focuses his resentment, for he is terrified and maddened by their strength and haughty independence. Yet it is also the great birds who draw Darrell into eventual acceptance of a new life, new friends, and new values embodied in the proud, free-spirited old man living in perfect communion with nature. The author's deep conviction and honest, dispassionate writing give intense realism to both characters and story." Horn Bk

The ghost of Five Owl Farm; illus. by Paul Galdone. Collins 1966 127p illus lib. bdg. $4.91 (4-6)   Fic
1 Twins—Fiction 2 Mystery and detective stories
ISBN 0-529-03889-7

"Ted, who has a rather scornful opinion of his ten-year-old twin cousins, is disgusted to discover they are arriving for a visit during his spring vacation. A scheme to keep them busy investigating planted clues indicating mysterious activity around the barn takes an unexpected turn when the twins convince Ted that there really are weird things going on in the old barn at night. The story gains originality and freshness through the deft blending of eeriness and humor with delightful characters [and] . . . bits of nature lore." Booklist

Mike's toads; illus. by Glen Rounds. World Pub. 1970 93p illus $4.50, lib. bdg. $4.91 (3-5)   Fic
1 Frogs—Stories
ISBN 0-529-00683-9; 0-529-00684-7

"Mike knew from experience that it wasn't wise to proffer other people's help without consulting them, but he had thoughtlessly done it again. A friend of his brother's had asked if David would care for his pet toads while he was away. Of course he would, Mike said—but he'd forgotten that David was going to camp, and he himself was saddled with the responsibility. His small catastrophes are entertaining, and the story—written in an easy, natural style—incorporates information unobtrusively." Chicago. Children's Bk Center

Gannett, Ruth Stiles
The dragons of Blueland; illus. by Ruth Chrisman Gannett. Random House 1951 87p illus lib. bdg. $4.79 (1-4)   Fic
1 Dragons—Stories 2 Fairy tales
ISBN 0-394-91092-3

Gannett, Ruth Stiles—*Continued*

Sequel to: Elmer and the dragon

"The baby dragon had just left Elmer Elevator safe in Nevergreen City and was looking forward to joining his family in the mountains of Blueland beyond the Awful Desert when he discovered an expedition of men trying to capture the dragons. He returned to get Elmer's help and together they devise an ingenious scheme to outwit the hunters." Wis Library Bul

"Especially enchanting are the dragon family, each of the fifteen members with a different design and personality. . . . For fairy-tale enthusiasts." Library J

Elmer and the dragon; illus. by Ruth Chrisman Gannett. Random House 1950 86p illus lib. bdg. $4.79 (1-4) Fic

1 Dragons—Stories 2 Fairy tales 3 Canaries—Stories

ISBN 0-394-91120-2

Sequel to: My father's dragon

"This story continues the tale of Elmer's adventures begun in 'My father's dragon.' A storm forces Elmer and the baby dragon down in the middle of the ocean on an island inhabited by escaped canaries, where they cure King Cam and his subjects, all sick with curiosity." Wis Library Bul

"A fresh and original plot, delightfully logical non-sense appealing characters and irrepressible humor." N Y Times Bk Rev

Followed by: The dragons of Blueland

My father's dragon; illus. by Ruth Chrisman Gannett. Random House 1948 86p illus maps $2.95, lib. bdg. $4.99 (1-4) Fic

1 Dragons—Stories 2 Fairy tales 3 Animals—Stories

ISBN 0-394-81438-X; 0-394-91438-4

This is a combination of fantasy, sense, and non-sense. It describes the adventures of a small boy, Elmer Elevator, who befriended an old alley cat and in return heard the story of the captive baby dragon on Wild Island. Right away Elmer decided to free the dragon. The tale of Elmer's voyage to Tangerina and his arrival on Wild Island, his encounters with various wild animals, and his subsequent rescue of the dragon follows

"This is without question, the funniest book that we have seen for a month of Sundays. It is also an exciting adventure story that will please small boys and girls, and their elders, from Maine to Florida and from Canada to Mexico. As a book to share with children it is a treasure, and story-tellers will read it with a solemn joy, hearing in imagination the delighted chuckles of their listeners." Sat Rev

Followed by: Elmer and the dragon

Gardam, Jane

A few fair days; illus. by Peggy Fortnum. Macmillan (N Y) [1972 c1971] 148p illus $4.95 (4-7) Fic

1 Great Britain—Fiction

First published 1971 in England

The author writes nine vignettes of Lucy's days growing up in Yorkshire before World War II with her best friend Mary Fell and her younger brother Jake

"The pictures and the text are an inspired combination; like the author, Peggy Fortnum conveys a world of detail about people and places in a few controlled and vivid lines." Pub W

Garfield, James B.

Follow my Leader; illus. by Robert Greiner. Viking 1957 191p illus lib. bdg. $5.95 (4-7) Fic

1 Blind—Fiction 2 Guide dogs—Stories

ISBN 0-670-32332-2

"An 11-year-old blind boy gradually resumes his

normal life with the aid of loyal friends and his guide dog, Leader." Hodges. Bks for Elem Sch Libraries

Garfield, Leon

Mister Corbett's ghost; illus. by Alan E. Cober. Pantheon Bks. 1968 87p illus lib. bdg. $4.99 (5-7) Fic

1 Ghost stories 2 London—Fiction

ISBN 0-394-91601-8

In this story set in London, "young Benjamin Partridge is apprentice to a harsh, relentless apothecary. On a black and windy New Year's Eve—when he should have been merrymaking at home—Benjamin is sent to deliver some medicine to a mysterious, black-clothed customer. In fury and despair the boy sets forth, willing the death of his detested master with every step he trudges. But long before the night is over, his . . . errand has turned into an . . . adventure with the Devil himself." Horn Bk

"Garfield's writing is always evocative, his dialogue period-perfect, and his characters vivid." Chicago. Children's Bk Center

Smith; illus. by Antony Maitland. Pantheon Bks. 1967 $3.95, lib. bdg. $5.19 (5-7) Fic

1 Juvenile delinquency—Fiction 2 London—Fiction

ISBN 0-394-81641-2; 0-394-91641-7

"A 12-year-old pickpocket pursued by other thieves, leads a swift-paced descent into 18th century London's underground peopled with timeless personalities cleverly self-revealed through dialogue passages that echo Dickens." Best Bks for Children, 1968

Garfield, Nancy

The Tuesday elephant; illus. by Tom Feelings. Crowell 1968 unp illus $4.50, lib. bdg. $5.25 (2-4) Fic

1 Elephants—Stories 2 Kenya—Fiction

ISBN 0-690-83884-0; 0-690-83885-9

"The little boys introduced in this picture book belong to the Kamba tribe of Kenya. Gideon tames a baby elephant, then shares his secret with his younger brother, Peter. After a season of happy adventures, the elephant disappears just before the annual village elephant hunt. A lonely jungle vigil is rewarded when the elephant, now full grown, returns to see Gideon before joining the herd. A tender story, beautifully illustrated." Keating. Building Bridges of Understanding Between Cultures

Garner, Alan

The moon of Gomrath. Walck, H.Z. 1967 [c1963] 184p lib. bdg. $5.50 (5-7) Fic

1 Good and evil—Fiction 2 Fantastic fiction

ISBN 0-8098-2395-0

First published 1963

"Moon magic was about, working through forces like the evil Brollachan that had no shape but took the shape of others, and the Morrigan, a shape-shifting witch. They had been awakened after many centuries by the power of a bracelet worn by a young girl of the 20th century. In a stirring climax, Susan and the dwarfs and elves battle against these evil ones whose power fades as the moon waxes." Sch Library J

"At times overpoweringly rich in its use of British folklore and mythology. . . . Although the beginning of the book is somewhat in touch with the everyday world of Cheshire, the tenseness & the suspense of the events end in a burst of glory. . . . For the very unusual reader." Horn Bk

Includes bibliography

Garnett, Eve

The family from One End Street, and some of their adventures; written and illus. by Eve Garnett. Vanguard 1960 208p illus $4.95 (4-7)   Fic

1 Great Britain—Fiction 2 Family—Fiction
ISBN 0-8149-0302-9

A reprint of a book first published 1937 in England and 1939 in the United States

Mr Ruggles, a dustman, and Mrs Ruggles, a washerwoman, and their seven children lived on One End Street in Otwell-on-the-Ouse. This large, gay family had many adventures—at a baby show, at the cinema and with a green silk petticoat

"Carnegie Medal winner in England for the best children's book of its year . . . this story of the Ruggles children, the baby and their parents, has long been a favorite with British children." Pub W

Map on lining-papers

Gates, Doris

Blue willow; illus. by Paul Lantz. Viking 1940 172p illus lib. bdg. $5.95, pa 95¢ (4-7)   Fic

1 Migrant labor—Fiction 2 California—Fiction
ISBN 0-670-17557-9; 0-670-05030-X

"Janey was so tired of always moving on to another place so that Father would have work. She longed for a home, friends and school-days like the other children had. Her only possession was a blue willow plate, which she prized above everything in the world. Then she met Lupe and knew what it was to have a friend, and after many adventures in which the blue willow plate played no small part, Janey learned at last what it was to have a settled home, as well." Ontario Library Rev

"This book may be used to considered the differences between the family patterns of old stock Americans and those of Mexican-Americans, and also the poignant longing for security that grows out of the disorganized family life of many migratory workers." Rdng Ladders

The Cat and Mrs Cary; illus. by Peggy Bacon. Viking 1962 216p illus $3.50 (4-6)   Fic

1 Cats—Stories 2 Mystery and detective stories
ISBN 0-670-20645-8

A "story in which realistic and fanciful elements are combined with a light and successful hand. Widowed Mrs. Cary has just bought an old house in a seacoast town, and she is not in the least prepared to acquire a cat that talks (but not to anybody else) or Brad, a convalescent nephew of twelve. All of them become involved in solving the mystery of local parakeet-smuggling. . . . The cat is delightful: suspicious, sophisticated, sarcastic." Chicago. Children's Bk Center

"The pleasure of the story is mostly in the quality of the writing and in the amusing characters. Only Peggy Bacon could have drawn that redoubtable character The Cat." Sat Rev

Gauch, Patricia Lee

This time, Tempe Wick? Illus. by Margot Tomes. Coward, McCann & Geoghegan 1974 43p illus $5.95 (2-5)   Fic

1 U.S.—History—Revolution—Fiction 2 Wick, Temperance—Fiction
ISBN 0-698-20300-3

Based on a Revolutionary War legend about a real girl, this story tells how Tempe Wick helped feed and clothe the thousands of American soldiers who spent the winters of 1780 and 1781 in Jockey Hollow, New Jersey. When the soldiers mutinied, Tempe had to use her wits and courage to prevent two of them from stealing her horse

"The book presents a realistic and humane view of the war and of the people who fought it. . . .The

writing is the perfect vehicle for the illustrations—in the artist's inimitable style—which capture the down-to-earth, unpretentious, and humorous quality of the storytelling." Horn Bk

Gault, William Campbell

Stubborn Sam. Dutton 1969 158p $5.50 (5-7) Fic

1 Baseball—Fiction
ISBN 0-525-40433-3

"From childhood Sam Bogosian has wanted to play baseball for a living so after college he signs with the New York Titans and becomes catcher for a Class-A team in the Florida State League. Told informally by Sam himself the fast-paced story follows Sam's move up in baseball to the major leagues and a starting position with the Titans. Including plenty of realistic playing field action and natural dialog this will have wide appeal among baseball enthusiasts." Booklist

George, Jean Craighead

Coyote in Manhattan; illus. by John Kaufmann. Crowell 1968 203p illus map $4.50 (4-7)   Fic

1 Coyotes—Stories 2 New York (City)—Fiction
ISBN 0-690-21969-5

"Those living on 109th Street in New York come from all over the world and prize freedom above all else. In this imaginative and deeply moving story, these people quietly and effectively support the efforts of Tako, a coyote, [who had been set free by a rebellious girl], for survival and freedom against those who wish him captured and killed. Throughout the fast-moving narrative one sees clearly the concerns of the young and their similarity to nature's creatures, as they attempt to find a liveable world in the demanding complexity of city life." Rdng Ladders. 5th edition

Julie of the wolves; pictures by John Schoenherr (6-7)   Fic

1 Eskimos—Fiction 2 Wolves—Stories 3 Arctic regions—Fiction
Some editions are:
Hall, G.K.&Co. lib. bdg. $6.95 Large print edition (ISBN 0-8161-6102-X)
Harper $4.95, lib. bdg. $4.79, pa $1.25 (ISBN 0-06-02193-2; 0-06-021944-0; 0-06-440058-1)
Awarded the Newbery Medal, 1973
First published 1972 by Harper

"Lost in the Alaskan wilderness thirteen-year-old Miyax [Julie in English] an Eskimo girl, is gradually accepted by a pack of Arctic wolves that she comes to love." Booklist

"The superb narration includes authentic descriptions and details of the Eskimo way-of-life and of Eskimo rituals. . . . The story graphically pictures the seasonal changes of the vast trackless tundra and reveals Miyax's awakening to the falseness of the white man's world. Through the eyes of Julie, who survives for months in the wilderness with the wolves, the author lovingly describes the wildlife: the golden plover, the snow buntings, the snowshoe rabbits, as well as the wolves. She evokes in full measure the terrors of losing directions and facing storms in abysmal temperatures. The whole book has a rare, intense reality which the artist enhances beautifully with animated drawings." Horn Bk

My side of the mountain; written and illus. by Jean George. Dutton 1959 178p illus $6.95, pa $1.95 (5-7)   Fic

1 Outdoor life—Fiction 2 Catskill Mountains—Fiction 3 Nature—Fiction
ISBN 0-525-35530-8; 0-525-45030-0

"A New York City boy determines to run away from home and to live alone and be completely self-sufficient. This, his diary, tells about his adventures during the year he spent in the Catskills—his struggle

George, Jean Craighead—*Continued*
for survival, his dependence on nature, his animal friends, and his ultimate realization that he needs human companionship." Pub W

"The book is all the more convincing for the excellence of style, the subtlety of humor, aptness of phrases, and touches of poetry. Sam's descriptions . . . have the fascination of detail that children appreciate in 'Robinson Crusoe.' Sam's own personality emerges clearly. . . . This book brings a great deal to children; emphasis on the rewards of courage and determination and an abundance of scientific knowledge, certainly, but, far more important, unforgettable experiences in the heart of nature." Horn Bk

"The black-and-white drawings of the things Sam made—fish hooks, animal snares, willow whistles—and how he did things—cooked and ate and washed and slept—should prove useful perhaps even a challenge to boy and girl scouts alike." Best Sellers

Who really killed Cock Robin? An ecological mystery. Dutton 1971 149p map lib. bdg. $4.95 (4-6)
Fic

1 Ecology—Fiction
ISBN 0-525-42700-7
"The residents of Saddleboro were ecology conscious, and none more so than the mayor, whose particular pride was the robins nesting in a hat on his front porch. Nevertheless, despite the carefulness of its citizens, the town is subject to some undetected pollutant, for one day the father robin is found dead. Young Tony Isidoro, assisted by his friend Mary Alice, decides to investigate the cause." Sat Rev

"A great deal of sound ecological information is presented, and the story is timely and entertaining. Above all, the message is clear: 'The Earth is one ecosystem.' " Horn Bk

George, John
Dipper of Copper Creek, by John George and Jean George; illus. by Jean George. Dutton 1956 183p illus (American woodland tales) $4.50 (4-6)
Fic

1 Birds—Stories 2 Colorado—Fiction 3 Rocky Mountains—Fiction
ISBN 0-525-28724-8
Set in the Colorado Rockies, this book "stirs interest in animals and prospecting as well as in the dippers [or ouzels] which are the chief characters. Few birds are as remarkable as the unique dippers, who walk on the bottoms of streams and sometimes nest behind waterfalls. The effect of heavy rains in the high mountains provides much danger and suspense. The principal human character, Doug, grows up visibly at the same time as the dipper nestlings." Chicago Sunday Trib

"Much of the writing is sheer poetry while conveying accurate nature lore. Jean George's charming wash drawings are in perfect keeping with the spirit of the book, which any nature lover will enjoy." Christian Sci Monitor

Godden, Rumer
The dolls' house; illus. by Tasha Tudor. Viking 1962 136p illus lib. bdg. $5.95, pa 95¢ (2-4)
Fic

1 Dollhouses—Fiction 2 Dolls—Fiction
ISBN 0-670-27767-3; 0-670-05048-2
First published 1947 in England, 1948 in the United States

Adventures of a brave little hundred-year-old Dutch farthing doll, her family, their Victorian dollhouse home and the two little English girls to whom they all belonged. Tottie's great adventure was when she went to the exhibition, Dolls thru the ages, and was singled out for notice by The Queen who opened the exhibition

"Each doll has a firmly drawn, recognizably true character; the children think and behave convincingly; only the grown-ups are remote and Olympian, as grown-ups must be. The story is enthralling, and complete in every detail. . . . This is an exceptionally good book." Spectator

Home is the sailor; illus. by Jean Primrose. Viking 1964 128p illus $3.50 (4-6)
Fic

1 Dolls—Fiction 2 Wales—Fiction
ISBN 0-670-37700-7
The scene of this doll story "is a seaport town in Wales; the characters are a large dollhouse family, the children to whom the dollhouse belongs, and a French boy and his fellows at the Sea School; the plot concerns the loss—through adventure or misadventure—and the return of the three male members of the doll household." Booklist

"The characters, human and doll, are alive, the atmosphere of the seacoast village vivid, and . . . the book has more than one level of interest and meaning. The drama of human life is somehow sharpened when seen through these stories of dolls. . . . A beautiful, enchanting book." Horn Bk

Impunity Jane; the story of a pocket doll; illus. by Adrienne Adams. Viking 1954 47p illus lib. bdg. $4.95 (2-4)
Fic

1 Dolls—Fiction
ISBN 0-670-39429-7
A story about Jane, a 4-inch "pocket doll" neglected by four generations of little girls, who finally finds happiness with a 7-year-old boy who steals her from his cousin. He and his friends use Jane as a model to fly their "rocket ships," sail their boats and live in their toy houses

"Rumer Godden brings to her writing not only careful craftsmanship but that quality so essential to good children's books, yet so rare, the sharp memory of childhood and the things of childhood. The illustrations are in such harmony they seem to have grown with the story." Sat Rev

Little Plum; with drawings by Jean Primrose. Viking 1963 97p illus $3.50 (3-5)
Fic

1 Dolls—Fiction
ISBN 0-670-43322-5
Sequel to: Miss Happiness and Miss Flower
"A feud begins between harum-scarum Belinda and Gem Tiffany Jones, the little girl who moved into the elegant house next door. To the distress of the two Japanese dolls, Miss Happiness and Miss Flower, Gem's Japanese doll child, Little Plum, becomes caught up in this unseemly affair." Pub W

"An enthralling tale with a satisfying ending. Illustrations in soft, hazy colors have a mistily vague Japanese quality." Christian Sci Monitor

Mouse house; illus. by Adrienne Adams. Viking 1957 63p illus $5.95, pa $1.50 (2-4)
Fic

1 Mice—Stories
ISBN 0-670-49147-0; 0-670-05012-1
"Upstairs in Mary's room was Mouse House, a little jewelry box in the shape of a furnished house inhabited by two cloth mice; down in the cellar lived a family of real mice crowded into a broken flower pot with not an eighth of an inch to spare. The enchanting story tells how, through the adventures of Bonnie, the little mouse that was crowded out of the nest and found her way upstairs, Mouse House became the comfortable new home of a family of real mice." Booklist

"Rumer Godden offers both quality in her writing and delightful fantasy in her story pattern. Children will be captivated by the illustrations so perfectly suited in every smallest detail to this Mouse family story." Top of the News

Graham, Lorenz B.

I, Momolu; illus. by John Biggers. Crowell 1966
226p illus $4.95 (5-7)   Fic

1 Liberia—Fiction
ISBN 0-690-43200-3

"Fourteen year old Momolu, a member of the Kew-pessie tribe of Liberia, goes from deep bush country to the bustling modern city of Cape Roberts with his father who must settle a dispute. For the first time in his life he sees what Westerners are familiar with: trucks, radios, planes and books. On their canoe trip and stay in the city, Momulu learns much about the world, himself and the meaning of his father's question, 'Does strength make good?' Illustrated with drawings of great strength." Africa

"Growing understanding between father and son and the impact of industrialization on tribal customs are interesting aspects of the story." Hodges. Bks for Elem Sch Libraries

Grahame, Kenneth

The reluctant dragon; illus. by Ernest H. Shepard. Holiday House 1953 [c1938] unp illus lib. bdg. $3.50 (3-5)   Fic

1 Dragons—Stories 2 Fairy tales
ISBN 0-8234-0093-X

A reissue of the 1938 book which is a chapter from: Dream days

A story of the boy who made friends with a dragon and arranged a match for him with St George

"When considered for its excellent bookmaking and for its enduring humor and charm heightened by the Ernest Shepard illustrations, it is a title for every child's library. And a good many adults, if they do not already know him, will be delighted with this delectable dragon who had a kind heart. . . . The book belongs wherever it finds a kindred spirit." Library J

The wind in the willows (4-6)   Fic

1 Animals—Stories
Some editions are:
Scribner (Golden anniversary edition) $7.95, pa $2.45
Illustrated in color and black and white by Ernest H. Shepard (ISBN 0-684-20838-5; 0-684-71788-3)
World Pub $7.50, lib. bdg. $8.91 Illustrated by Tasha Tudor (ISBN 0-529-00119-5; 0-529-00120-9)
First published 1908 by Scribner

"The simple joys of life—Water Rat's pleasure in messing about in boats. Toad's enthusiasm for caravans and motor cars, the embracing light and warmth of kindly Badger's home, the brave boyish impulse that sent Mole into the winter wildwood—are expressed in terms of the familiar and universal values that lie close to the human heart, yet placed in a world where instinct is the predominating factor. Humour, perception, and poetic feeling are written into a story which is an imaginative springboard for any reader." Bks for Boys & Girls

This "is equally suited for reading aloud. The dignified discourse of the animals is even funnier when it's spoken. And the exquisite descriptions of the woods and riverbanks take on fresh color and depth. Although many children will not start this book by themselves, almost every youngster gets a glow of pleasure from listening." A Parent's Guide to Children's Reading

Gray, Elizabeth Janet

Adam of the road; illus. by Robert Lawson. Viking 1942 317p illus $7.50, pa $1.50 (5-7)   Fic

1 Great Britain—Fiction 2 Middle Ages—Fiction 3 Minstrels—Fiction
ISBN 0-670-10435-3; 0-670-05080-6
Awarded the Newbery Medal, 1943

Tale of a minstrel and his son Adam, who wandered through southeastern England in the thirteenth cen-

tury. Adam's adventures in search of his lost dog and his beloved father led him from St Alban's Abbey to London, and thence to Winchester, back to London, and then to Oxford where the three were at last reunited

"Without display of erudition, the framework of history is sound and the sense of place as strong as if written on the spot. The appearance of this book, from type to Mr. Lawson's many drawings, is so right it falls upon the eye like music on the ear." N Y Her Trib Bks

Map on lining-papers

Greene, Bette

Philip Hall likes me. I reckon maybe. Pictures by Charles Lilly. Dial Press 1974 135p illus $4.95, lib. bdg. $4.58 (4-6)   Fic

1 Friendship—Fiction 2 Negroes—Fiction 3 Arkansas—Fiction
ISBN 0-8037-6098-1; 0-8037-6096-5

This "story tells of a year in the life of a bright and lively black girl whose only real problems resulted from her infatuation with the boy from the next farm. . . . The book . . . deals chiefly with Beth's minor trials and triumphs: She tracks down a pair of turkey thieves, discovers that she is allergic to dogs, embarks on a vegetable-selling business venture, rescues Philip when he injures his leg on a mountaintop, and, finally, wins first prize in a calf-raising contest." Horn Bk

"The action is sustained; the narration, in first person Black dialect, is good or bad, depending on your linguistic stance; the illustrations are excellent black-and-white pencil sketches. This is a pleasant, undemanding little tale, good for a rainy afternoon." Rdng Teacher

Summer of my German soldier. Dial Press 1973 230p $4.95 (6-7)   Fic

1 World War, 1939-1945—Fiction 2 Prisoners of war—Fiction
ISBN 0-8037-8321-3

"Patty Bergen, daughter of the shopkeeper in Jenkinsville, Arkansas, is a lonely, misunderstood 12-year-old during a crucial summer. When German prisoners of war are encamped outside the town, at the height of World War II hostilities, Patty secretly makes friends with Anton and helps him hide out when he escapes. The FBI track down the prisoner and shoot him dead; Patty's family are vilified as 'Jew-Nazis' and forced to give up their home and business. Patty, too young to be tried for treason, goes to a reform school." Pub W

"Patty's story . . . is more than a mirror of reality. It offers no panaceas for loneliness, no easy solutions for problems; and this verisimilitude extends to the depiction of the minor characters as well. Although they seem types at first, they become individuals because of the particular details Patty chooses to recall. . . . A moving first novel, unforgettable because of the genuine emotion it evokes." Horn Bk

Greene, Constance C.

The ears of Louis; illus. by Nola Langner. Viking 1974 90p illus lib. bdg. $5.95 (4-6)   Fic

1 Prejudices and antipathies—Fiction
ISBN 0-670-28718-0

His big ears are Louis' special problem, but the support of an elderly neighbor and an unexpected talent help the small boy handle the teasing and bullying of his classmates

"This has none of the gritty kind of realism used so often in today's 'character molding' books. Rather, its strength lies in a low-key approach, complete with unique but understated characters and a great deal of

Greene, Constance C.—*Continued*
humor and empathy. The black-and-white drawings,
of which there are few, charmingly reflect the story."
Booklist

A girl called Al; illus. by Byron Barton. Viking 1969
127p illus $4.95, pa 95¢ (5-7)   Fic
 1 Friendship—Fiction
 ISBN 0-670-34153-3; 0-670-05050-4
"Told in the first person in a disarmingly casual,
amusing style, the story deals with a few months in the
lives of the two seventh-grade girls. The narrator
(never actually named) is a forthright, good-humored
child whose family life is stable and secure. Her best
friend Al (short for Alexandra), whose parents are
divorced, lives in an apartment down the hall with her
busy, distracted working mother. Al—a bright, over-
fat girl—proudly tries to be a 'non-conformist' to hide
the hurt and loneliness. Their unconventional friendship with Mr Richards, an elderly ex-bartender who
works as assistant superintendent of the building,
draws the girls together." Horn Bk
"Both the pre-teen protagonists and the minor performers—sketched with admirable economy—are
accurately and affectionately drawn." N Y Times Bk
Rev

Isabelle the itch; illus. by Emily A. McCully. Viking 1973 126p illus lib. bdg. $5.95 (4-6)   Fic
 ISBN 0-670-40177-3
Isabelle, a hyperactive fifth grader, spends a great
deal of time getting nowhere, until she realizes that
she must channel her energy in order to reach her
goals, which include taking over her brother's paper
route and winning the fifty-yard dash at school
"A refreshing book in many ways: it's good clean fun
with no redeeming social value; the ten-year-old
heroine is in perpetual motion, running, fighting, and
talking, while her father bakes bread on Saturdays—
both break a mold without being 'counter-culture.'
Isabelle's mother is an honestly normal blend of
impatience and loving warmth. None of the children
are brooding introverts but react to each other with
natural spontaneity ranging from mean teasing to
kindness. Low-key and somewhat episodic . . . this is
fun to read alone or aloud." Booklist

Leo the lioness. Viking 1970 118p lib. bdg. $4.95
(6-7)   Fic
 ISBN 0-670-42456-0
"Thirteen can be a very bad age, especially when
your sister is fifteen, attractive to boys, and the owner
of a bikini. Tibb consoles herself by remembering that
she is a Leo, which she firmly believes is the best sign
in the zodiac. Leos are strong and steadfast and practically everything good. The year brings disappointments: the babysitter whom she still reveres marries
out of necessity, Tibb's best friend becomes boy-
crazy, and the moods of her sister are a real burden."
Sat Rev
"Not an unusual theme, the adolescent girl who
grows into a more mature person, but is handled
unusually well here. The writing is convincingly that
of a teen-ager, the problems are universal and imbued
with a humor that does not lessen their importance,
the dialogue is excellent and the relationships are
drawn with sympathetic understanding." Sutherland.
The Best in Children's Bks

The unmaking of Rabbit. Viking 1972 125p lib. bdg.
$4.50 (5-7)   Fic
 ISBN 0-670-74136-1
"Paul has been shunted off to live with his
grandmother in a small town because his flighty and
divorced mother is living it up in New York and can't
be tied down by her 11-year-old son. Known as Rabbit
because his ears stick out, the boy is miserable, living

in the hope that his mother will get the promised
bigger apartment with room for him. A crisis arises
when some of his classmates involve Paul in breaking
and entering; he goes along, for a while, because he
yearns to be accepted but surprises the bullies and
himself by changing his mind in time. There is a
bittersweet resolution as Paul realizes that a future
with his mother is a pipe-dream but a hint of future
happiness as he makes a new friend. A solid plot and
well-defined characterizations." Pub W

Greenfield, Eloise
Sister; drawings by Moneta Barnett. Crowell 1974
83p illus $4.95 (4-7)   Fic
 1 Family—Fiction 2 Negroes—Fiction
 ISBN 0-690-00497-4
A 13-year-old Black girl whose father is dead
watches her 16-year-old sister drifting away from her
and her mother and fears she may fall into the same
self-destructive behavior herself. While waiting for
her sister's return home, she leafs through her diary,
reliving both happy and unhappy experiences while
gradually recognizing her own individuality
"The book is strong . . . strong in perception, in its
sensitivity, in its realism." Chicago. Children's Bk
Center

Gripe, Maria
The glassblower's children; with drawings by
Harald Gripe; tr. from the Swedish by Sheila La
Farge. Delacorte Press 1973 170p illus $4.95, lib.
bdg. $4.58 (4-6)   Fic
 1 Fairy tales
 ISBN 0-440-03051-X; 0-440-03065-X
 Original Swedish edition 1964
This is a "story about the kidnapping of a glassblower's two children by a wealthy lord who hopes to
alleviate his wife's ennui by giving her something she
does not already have. Once added to her collection,
however, the children pall on her quickly, and a sinister governess takes over their care, terrifying both the
children and everyone in the castle before the good
wizard Flutter Mildweather comes to the rescue along
with her raven Wise Wit." Booklist
"Set in the Gothic mood, the tale of the struggle
between the sisters is a saga of good and evil. Style,
mood, and tempo are adroitly integrated, and the
illustrations—reminiscent of Leonard Everett
Fisher's scratch-board work—effectively support the
story." Chicago. Children's Bk Center

Hugo; with drawings by Harald Gripe; tr. from the
Swedish by Paul Britten Austen. Delacorte Press
1970 153p illus $4.95, lib. bdg. $4.58 (3-5)   Fic
 1 Friendship—Fiction 2 School stories 3 Sweden—
 Fiction
 ISBN 0-440-03927-4; 0-440-03928-2
 "A Seymour Lawrence book"
 Original Swedish edition, 1966
This volume completes the trilogy begun with:
Josephine, and Hugo and Josephine
Hugo always behaves in a totally independent and
direct manner, whether he is reacting to school regulations or to the death of his mother. Together with his
friend Josephine he engages in ingenious schemes to
earn money. When a strange, aloof girl, whose icy
manner is resented by her classmates, appears, Hugo
and Josephine recognize her loneliness and help her

Hugo and Josephine; with drawings by Harald
Gripe; tr. from the Swedish by Paul Britten Austin.
Delacorte Press 1969 168p illus $4.95, lib. bdg. $4.58
(3-5)   Fic
 1 Friendship—Fiction 2 School stories 3 Sweden—
 Fiction
 ISBN 0-440-03929-0; 0-440-03930-4

Gripe, Maria—_Continued_
"A Seymour Lawrence book"
Original Swedish edition, 1962
Sequel to: Josephine
"Josephine hated her real name so much that she refused to answer to it in school, where her classmates teased her and the teacher tried to smooth over an awkward situation; but it was Hugo who defended her and became her staunch friend. Hugo, very much his own man, is the most convincing example of self-possession to come along in many years of childrens' books, and the quiet, episodic story of his and Josephine's friendship has an innocent charm. There's a Swedish flavor, but the appeal is universal, with thanks to the translator who preserved the artless, direct style of the author." Sat Rev
Followed by: Hugo

Josephine; with drawings by Harald Gripe; tr. from the Swedish by Paul Britten Austin. Delacorte Press 1970 132p illus $4.95 (3-5)   Fic
1 Family—Fiction 2 Sweden—Fiction
ISBN 0-440-04283-6; 0-440-04284-4
"A Seymour Lawrence book"
Original Swedish edition, 1961
Six year old "Josephine's story is simultaneously the account of a small Swedish girl's misadventures . . . and an exemplification of the universality of childhood experience. It is difficult to be the youngest of the family—especially when one's brothers and sisters are old enough to be uncles and aunts. And when one possesses the kind of imagination which transforms a bearded gardener into Old Man God and the local gossip into a witch, the problem is compounded. Fortunately, Josephine's father, the village vicar, understands a child's confusion when faced with the complexity of adult behavior and abstractions. His tender resolution of her problems and questions shows the wisdom of one capable of comprehending the child's world view." Horn Bk
Followed by: Hugo and Josephine

The night daddy; with drawings by Harald Gripe; tr. from the Swedish by Gerry Bothmer. Delacorte Press 1971 150p illus $4.95, lib. bdg. $4.58 (4-6)
Fic
1 Baby sitters—Fiction
ISBN 0-440-06390-6; 0-440-06391-4
"A Seymour Lawrence book"
Original Swedish edition, 1968
This story deals with "the developing friendship between an adult and a child. . . . The night daddy, a young writer hired as babysitter for precocious, fatherless Julia, [and Julia herself] describe their relationship in a series of alternating journal entries." Pub W
"The story has a direct, ingenuous style and a warmth and affection that are truly touching." Sat Rev

Guillot, René
Grishka and the bear; tr. by Gwen Marsh; illus. by Joan Kiddell-Monroe. Criterion Bks. 1959 115p illus $4.95 (5-7)   Fic
1 Bears—Stories 2 Siberia—Fiction
ISBN 0-200-00000-4
"A Criterion Book for young people"
Original French edition published 1958
"Grishka, outcast son of a great bear hunter, rescues a bear cub which is brought up with great care and ceremony by the village and, secretly, in a more practical way by Grishka. When the time comes for the bear to be sacrificed as the village ritual demands, Grishka escapes with him to the forest where both live with the wild boars. . . . Story of a beautiful friendship with good atmosphere and picture of life on the taigu-tundra edge of Siberia." Library J

Haar, Jaap ter
Boris; tr. from the Dutch by Martha Mearns; illus. by Rien Poortvliet. Delacorte Press [1970 c1969] 152p illus $4.50, lib. bdg. $4.17 (5-7)   Fic
1 Leningrad—Siege, 1941-1944—Fiction
ISBN 0-440-00747-X; 0-440-00748-8
"A Seymour Lawrence book"
Original Dutch edition, 1966. This translation first published 1969 in England
"The siege of Leningrad is vividly depicted in a moving, grimly realistic story of a twelve-year-old Russian boy who learns to forgive during the hostilities of war. Foraging for buried potatoes in No-man's-land, Boris and his friend Nadia are captured by a group of German soldiers who share their food with the starving children and risk their own lives to return Boris and Nadia safely to the Russian lines." Booklist

Hale, Lucretia P.
The complete Peterkin papers; with the original illus. Introduction by Nancy Hale. Houghton 1960 302p illus $5.95 (5-7)   Fic
1 Family—Fiction
ISBN 0-395-06792-8
The first of the Peterkin papers appeared in: Our Young Folks, in 1867 and continued in its successor: Saint Nicholas, until 1879. First published in book form 1880. This is the first one volume edition of the tales. Included are four stories that have not been in print since the 1886 edition, and the complete text of: The last of the Peterkins
"Such a resourceful and ingenuous family as the Peterkins is seldom beheld. Undaunted by the little difficulties of everyday life, they meet every crisis with spirit [and the help of the Lady from Philadelphia]. Like all good nonsense stories, it is told with a very straight face." Bks for Boys & Girls. 3d edition
"Here are all that gaiety and absurdity—the absurdity of the familiar and the commonplace that give these stories their special character." N Y Times Bk Rev

Hall, Lynn
Riff, remember. Follett 1973 107p $4.95, lib. bdg. $5.97 (4-7)   Fic
1 Dogs—Stories
ISBN 0-695-80413-8; 0-695-40413-X
"Riff's life changes dramatically after his first owner's death; from a luxurious, well-regulated household, the elegant borzoi is transplanted into the rough world of a hunting camp, where he becomes the special pet of a gentle young boy who is also something of a misfit. When the boy is killed in a hunting accident, Riff proves himself by tracking down the man who is responsible, and thus wins the love of the boy's father." Booklist

Hamilton, Virginia
The house of Dies Drear; illus. by Eros Keith. Macmillan (N Y) 1968 246p $5.95, pa $1.25 (5-7)
Fic
1 Negroes—Fiction 2 Ohio—Fiction 3 Mystery and detective stories
Thirteen year old Thomas Small moves with his family from North Carolina to a house in Ohio which is reputed to be haunted because of its connection with run-away slaves and murders of the past. In his search to answer the secrets of the past, Thomas also finds a deeper sense of his own connection with that past
"The answer to the mystery comes in a startling dramatic dénouement that is pure theater. This is gifted writing; the characterization is unforgettable, the plot imbued with mounting tension. It is in a way irrelevant that the principals are black, for the haunting story and the author's craftsmanship are para-

Hamilton, Virginia—*Continued*
mount, but, in a deeper sense, that this kind of book has been written about Negroes is of tremendous importance. Not a problem novel, [this] is memorable literature that gives dignity to black heritage." Sat Rev

M. C. Higgins, the great. Macmillan Pub. Co. 1974 278p $6.95 (6-7)   Fic
1 Negroes—Fiction 2 Family—Fiction 3 Appalachian region—Fiction
ISBN 0-02-742480-4
Awarded the Newbery Medal, 1975
"M. C. is a thirteen-year-old black boy who lives with his close-knit family in the rolling hills near the Ohio River. Within two days he is confronted with experiences involving two strangers which make him examine his past and his future: his feelings for the hill country and his dreams about the world beyond, and his relationship with his family and his own desires." Babbling Bookworm
"All of the characters have vitality and credibility as well as a unique quality that makes them unforgettable. . . . Visual images are strong and vivid; and many passages are poetic in their beauty. . . . All of the themes are handled contrapuntally to create a memorable picture of a young boy's growing awareness of himself and of his surroundings." Horn Bk

Zeely; illus. by Symeon Shimin. Macmillan (N Y) 1967 122p illus $5.95, pa $1.25 (4-7)   Fic
1 Negroes—Fiction
"A Negro girl learns to distinguish between fantasy and reality when she finally meets the majestic woman she has imagined to be a Watusi princess." Notable Children's Bks 1967
"A carefully constructed mood narrative with a little bit of mystery and a great deal of understanding for girls going through the hero-worshiping phase." Wis Library Bul

Hámori, László
Dangerous journey; tr. from the Swedish by Annabelle MacMillan; illus. by W.T. Mars. Harcourt 1962 190p illus $5.50, pa 65¢ (5-7)   Fic
1 Refugees, Hungarian—Fiction
ISBN 0-15-22179 Harcourt 1962 190p illus $5.50, pa 65¢ (5-7)   Fic
1 Refugees, Hungarian—Fiction
ISBN 0-15-221790-8; 0-15-023821-7
Original Swedish edition, 1959
During the Russian occupation of Hungary, twelve-year-old Latsi and his friend Pishta flee from Budapest in a freight car. This is only the beginning of a dangerous journey for Latsi who seeks freedom and hopes to join his parents who had fled earlier to Sweden
"In addition to his youth and inexperience [Latsi] has the problems of refugees everywhere with language barriers, unscrupulous 'helpers,' red tape homesickness and confusion. . . . Enlightening reading for American boys and girls." Pub W

Hamre, Leif
Operation Arctic; tr. from the Norwegian by Dag Ryen. Atheneum Pubs. 1973 154p $4.95 (6-7)   Fic
1 Arctic regions—Fiction 2 Rescue work—Fiction
ISBN 0-689-30418-8
"A Margaret K. McElderry book"
Original Norwegian language edition published 1971
"Three children, stowaways on a Norwegian air force plane, trying to reach their father, end up by error alone on a desolate arctic island. The eldest helps the younger twins survive in a trapper's cabin, but the dangers of wild storms and shifting ice, as well as a fear of not being found, are constant. A dramatic

story of adventures and heroism." New Bks for Young Readers

Harris, Rosemary
The bright and morning star. Macmillan (N Y) 1972 254p $4.95 (5-7)   Fic
1 Deaf—Fiction 2 Egypt—Fiction
Sequel to: The shadow on the sun
The affairs of Reuben, Prince of Canaan, "are once more interwoven with those of the Royal House of Kemi (Egypt). When Thamar, Reuben's wife, sees a great star shining over Kemi, she takes it as a sign that she must take her afflicted [deaf-mute] son Sadhi there to be cured." Horn Bk
"The use of psychological techniques in treating the sick boy is as practical as the talking cat Cefalu is fanciful. The intriguing setting, strong characters and humor make for a charming and vital story." Sat Rev

The moon in the cloud. Macmillan (N Y) [1970 c1968] 182p $5.95 (5-7)   Fic
1 Noah's Ark—Fiction 2 Egypt—Fiction
First published 1968 in England
"Reuben and Thamar are a young couple who live in a tent near Noah and his family, and it is Reuben who goes to Egypt to hunt for the animals needed to make up Noah's quota. Ham is supposed to go, but he is lazy and besides, he has his eye on pretty Thamar, so he promises Reuben passage on the Ark if he returns with a cat and two lions. Most of the story is concerned with Reuben's adventures: his captivity, his friendship with the Lord of Two Lands, and his escape into the desert. The cat Cefalu, which Reuben has brought from home, has some adventures of his own, events on which Cefalu makes caustic and frequent comments." Chicago. Children's Bk Center
"The style is simple, crisp, and direct; precise in imagery; and unabashedly frank and humorous. . . . The characters are richly varied. . . . Subjecting both the myth-making faculty of the ancient world and the foibles of human—and animal—nature to an implacable scrutiny, the book successfully blends fantasy with comedy." Horn Bk
Followed by: The shadow on the sun

The shadow on the sun. Macmillan (N Y) 1970 198p $4.95 (5-7)   Fic
1 Egypt—Fiction
Sequel to: The moon in the cloud
Returning to Egypt after the flood, "Reuben, his lovely wife Thamar, and their animals help smooth out the troubled romance between young King Merenkere and Meri-Mekhmet, the beautiful astute daughter of the court chamberlain, who scorns the king for wooing her in disguise since he is officially married and has a harem of 93 foreign princesses besides. Later, when Meri-Mekhmet is kidnapped by a barbaric prince, Reuben journeys to the distant land of Punt to rescue her." Sat Rev
"The plot has flamboyant embroidery, but the sophistication of humor and writing style, the half-invented background of the land of Punt and the colorful Egyptian setting, the vigorous characterization and dialogue make this as diverting as its predecessor." Sutherland. The Best in Children's Bks
Followed by: The bright and morning star

Hauff, Wilhelm
Dwarf Long-Nose; tr. by Doris Orgel; illus. by Maurice Sendak. Random House 1960 60p illus lib. bdg. $5.19 (3-5)   Fic
1 Fairy tales
ISBN 0-394-91100-8
"Jacob, the shoemaker's son, was 'herb-enchanted' by an Evil fairy and turned into a dwarf with a

Hauff, Wilhelm—*Continued*

hunched back and a long nose but with amazing culinary skill. Unrecognized by the parents and turned from his home, he became successful as a chef in the kitchen of the Duke's palace until, aided by a goose, also under an enchantment, he found the herb that could give him back his true form." Horn Bk

This "fairy tale, well loved in Germany, is illustrated with many drawings which capture to perfection the qualities of enchantment and earthiness present in the story." Booklist

Haugaard, Erik Christian

Orphans of the wind; illus. by Milton Johnson. Houghton 1966 186p illus $3.50 (6-7)   Fic

1 Sea stories 2 U.S.—History—Civil War—Fiction

"At twelve, Jim is signed on as deckboy for the Civil War blockade runner 'Four Winds' by his selfish uncle. Leaving Bristol and sailing to Charleston, his life is changed by the people he meets and the things that happen. Many crewmen are concerned about slavery and question the ship's cargo of guns and powder. When the ship is burned Jim and three of his fellow crewmen row to shore. In order to travel North to join what they feel is the right cause, they travel with the Confederate Army. Their feelings as men in battle as well as their desire to do the right thing are well described." Rdng Ladders. 5th edition

Hawkinson, Lucy

Dance, dance, Amy-Chan! Story and pictures by Lucy Hawkinson. Whitman, A. 1964 unp illus $3.95 (1-4)   Fic

1 Japanese in the U.S.—Fiction 2 Family—Fiction

ISBN 0-8075-1451-9

"During Amy's and her younger sister Susie's visit to their Japanese grandparents in the city, they learn Japanese customs and make preparations to participate in a Japanese street dance. Amy misses the first dance while looking for lost, scared Susie. The children discover that basic similarities in family relationships and interdependence exist among all peoples." Rdng Ladders. 5th edition

Hays, Wilma Pitchford

Christmas on the Mayflower; illus. by Roger Duvoisin. Coward-McCann 1956 unp illus lib. bdg. $4.49 (3-5)   Fic

1 Pilgrim Fathers—Fiction 2 Christmas stories

ISBN 0-698-30043-2

"The author tells of the events of Christmas week as seen through the eyes of young Giles Hopkins. The big event of the week, to Giles, was getting to go ashore. Even though the expedition meant cold, hard work, it was a relief to be on solid ground after months at sea. Giles did not, however, forget his sister or the other women and children on the Mayflower, and managed to gather some evergreens for decorations and to contrive some simple toys for the younger children. A simply told story that will convey to younger readers something of the courage and faith of these first settlers." Chicago. Children's Bk Center

For ma and pa; on the Oregon Trail, 1844; illus. by Peter Burchard. Coward, McCann & Geoghegan 1972 63p illus map lib. bdg. $4.49 (4-7)   Fic

1 Sager family—Fiction 2 Oregon Trail—Fiction

ISBN 0-698-30425-X

A fictionalized account "of how the seven Sager children continued on to Oregon after their parents died on the trip westward. Gives a picture of the hardships faced by pioneers." Notable Children's Trade Bks (Social Studies)

Pilgrim Thanksgiving; illus. by Leonard Weisgard. Coward-McCann 1955 unp illus lib. bdg. $4.49 (3-5)   Fic

1 Thanksgiving Day—Stories 2 Pilgrim Fathers—Fiction

ISBN 0-698-30281-8

"Damaris Hopkins finds that the best thing about the first Thanksgiving feast is making friends with the dreaded Indians." Hodges. Bks for Elem Sch Libraries

"The true meaning of Thanksgiving is here brought out in an authentic and personal narrative of a real Pilgrim family, and in the beautiful saffron, brown and black illustrations." N Y Times Bk Rev

Haywood, Carolyn

Away went the balloons; written and illus. by Carolyn Haywood. Morrow 1973 189p illus $5.95, lib. bdg. $5.11 (2-4)   Fic

1 Balloons—Fiction

ISBN 0-688-20095-8; 0-688-30095-2

"It's Balloon Day at Blue Bell School. All the students release their balloons, containing their names and addresses, and a request for a letter from the finder. Each chapter in the book is a short story about the adventures of a particular balloon and the stories can be read separately or as a continued novel. One balloon winds up in a children's hospital (to the delight of a small patient); others land at a circus, on a sailboat and other wildly different places. The episodes are brisk and often surprising; the author's style is pleasant and easy for beginners to handle." Pub W

"B" is for Betsy; written and illus. by Carolyn Haywood. Harcourt 1939 159p illus $5.95, pa $1.35 (2-4)   Fic

1 School stories

ISBN 0-15-204975-4; 0-15-611695-2

"The first day of school is a momentous one. For Betsy it would have been nearly overwhelming but for the comforting knowledge of the presence of Koala bear in her schoolbag and the new friendship with Ellen. A simple, direct story of a six-year-old girl's first year in school; the incidents chosen are the commonplace ones which loom large in a child's life. . . . Appealing black-and-white illustrations; large type, well leaded." Booklist

Several other books about Betsy are also available. The following titles are published by Harcourt: Back to school with Betsy $5.95, pa $1.15 (ISBN 0-15-205512-6; 0-15-610200-5) Betsy and Billy $5.95 (ISBN 0-15-206765-5) Betsy and the boys $5.95 (ISBN 0-15-206944-5) All other titles in this series are published by Morrow: Betsy and Mr Kilpatrick $6.50, lib. bdg. $5.49 (ISBN 0-688-21085-6; 0-688-31085-0); Betsy and the circus, lib. bdg. $5.81 (ISBN 0-688-31086-9); Betsy's busy summer $6.50, lib. bdg. $5.49 (ISBN 0-688-21087-2; 0-688-31087-7); Betsy's little Star, lib. bdg. $5.49 (ISBN 0-688-31088-5); Betsy's winterhouse, lib. bdg. $5.49 (ISBN 0-688-31090-7); Merry Christmas from Betsy $6.50, lib. bdg. $5.49 (ISBN 0-688-21695-1; 0-688-31695-6); Snowbound with Betsy $6.50, lib. bdg. $5.49 (ISBN 0-688-21684-6, 0-688-31684-0)

Here's a Penny; written and illus. by Carolyn Haywood. Harcourt 1944 158p illus $5.95, pa 60¢ (2-4)   Fic

1 Adoption—Fiction

ISBN 0-15-233794-6; 0-15-640062-6

This is a "story of a little boy nicknamed Penny, of his year in first grade, his search for a pet kitten, and other adventures. . . . That Penny is an adopted child may give it a special appeal for children in like situation." Wis Library Bul

Haywood, Carolyn—*Continued*

"A friendly human book, in which [the author] writes of children with quiet humor and thorough understanding. The many drawings by the author have a lively action." N Y Times Bk Rev

Two additional stories about Penny are available. Published by Harcourt: Penny and Peter $6.95 (ISBN 0-15-260465-0) Published by Morrow: Penny goes to camp $6.50 (ISBN 0-688-21728-1)

Little Eddie; written and illus. by Carolyn Haywood. Morrow 1947 160p illus lib. bdg. $5.11 (2-4)   Fic

ISBN 0-688-31682-4

Seven-year-old Eddie Wilson is a little boy who knows what he wants and goes after it. Collecting—stray animals and junk—is his favorite activity. His projects, which sometimes inconvenience his parents are graphically told. Betsy and some of the other playmates reappear here

Eddie Wilson's adventures are continued in the following books, also published by Morrow: Annie Pat and Eddie $6.50, lib. bdg. $5.49 (ISBN 0-688-21045-7; 0-688-31045-1); Eddie and Gardenia, lib. bdg. $5.49 (ISBN 0-688-31255-1); Eddie and his big deals, lib. bdg. $5.49 (ISBN 0-688-31251-9); Eddie and Louella $6.50, lib. bdg. $5.49 (ISBN 0-688-21254-9; 0-688-31254-3); Eddie and the fire engine $6.50, lib. bdg. $5.49 (ISBN 0-688-21252-2; 0-688-31252-7); Eddie makes music $6.50 (ISBN 0-688-21256-5); Eddie, the dog holder, lib. bdg. $5.49 (ISBN 0-688-31253-5); Eddie's green thumb, lib. bdg. $5.49 (ISBN 0-688-31257-8); Eddie's happenings $6.50, lib. bdg. $5.49 (ISBN 0-688-21258-1; 0-688-31258-6); Eddie's pay dirt, lib. bdg. $5.49 (ISBN 0-688-31259-4); Eddie's valuable property $6.50, lib. bdg. $5.49 (ISBN 0-688-22014-2; 0-688-32014-7); Ever-ready Eddie $6.50, lib. bdg. $5.49 (ISBN 0-688-21277-8; 0-688-31277-2)

Taffy and Melissa Molasses; written and illus. by Carolyn Haywood. Morrow 1969 190p illus lib. bdg. $5.11 (2-4)   Fic

ISBN 0-688-31690-5

In this book, "Taffy, Melissa, and their friend, Jonathan . . . have a summer of fun and misadventure in spite of Taffy's prediction that 'nufin' ever happens. The style of country living is portrayed well enough for children with town or city backgrounds to settle into the mood of the story easily. As usual, Miss Haywood has faithfully captured the spirit of youngsters in her characters' conversation, humor and behavior; and her writing is so well suited to the reading level of her audience." Sch Library J

Henry, Marguerite

Black Gold; illus. by Wesley Dennis. Rand McNally 1957 172p illus $4.95, lib. bdg. $4.97, pa $1.50 (4-6)   Fic

1 Black Gold (Race horse)—Stories 2 Horse racing—Fiction

ISBN   0-528-82130-X;   0-528-80160-0;   0-528-87688-0

The story "of a black stallion, [a Kentucky Derby winner] whose splendid turf record put him in the front rank of champions. Black Gold's courage and will to win were strengthened by the faith which two people, his trainer and his rider held in him. Marguerite Henry tells their story with conviction, and with a sympathetic knowledge of horses and the people who care for them. Black and white illustrations by Wesley Dennis are full of action." Ontario Library Rev

Brighty of the Grand Canyon; illus. by Wesley Dennis. Rand McNally 1953 222p illus map $4.95, lib. bdg. $4.79, pa $1.50 (4-7)   Fic

1 Donkeys—Stories 2 Grand Canyon—Fiction

ISBN 0-528-82150-4; 0-528-80163-5; 0-528-87689-9

Drawn from a real-life incident, this is the story of "Brighty, the shaggy little burro who roamed the canyons of the Colorado River [and] had a will of his own. He liked the old prospector and Uncle Jim and he helped solve a mystery, but chiefly he was the freedom loving burro." Chicago

"Only those who are unfamiliar with the West would say it is too packed with drama to be true. And the author's understanding warmth for all of God's creatures still shines through her superb ability as a story teller making this a vivid tale." Christian Sci Monitor

"The book is decorated on nearly every page with drawings of the canyon, of Brighty in various moods, his human companions and the wild animals of the area." N Y Times Bk Rev

Gaudenzia, pride of the Palio; illus. by Lynd Ward. Rand McNally 1960 237p illus $4.95, lib. bdg. $3.97 (4-7)   Fic

1 Horse racing—Fiction 2 Siena. Palio—Fiction 3 Terni, Giorgio—Fiction 4 Gaudenzia (Race horse)—Stories

ISBN 0-528-82030-3; 0-528-82258-6

The author "weaves together two careers, that of the famous half-Arabian horse Gaudenzia . . . and her rider, the Tuscan farm boy Giorgio who trained and rode her to victory in the Palio race, although this great ex-carthorse was afflicted with both a nervous tic and a damaged cartilage. The account is, of course, inherently exciting, full of the yearnings, worries, and problems of a competition 'more battle than race.' . . . Lavishly illustrated in rich color and in black and white." Horn Bk

Justin Morgan had a horse; illus. by Wesley Dennis. Rand McNally 1954 169p illus $4.95, lib. bdg. $4.97, pa $1.50 (4-7)   Fic

1 Morgan horse—Stories 2 Vermont—Fiction

ISBN 0-528-82255-1; 0-528-80173-2; 0-528-87682-1

An expanded version of the book first published 1945 by Wilcox & Follett

Story of the brave little Vermont work horse from which came the famous American breed of Morgan horses. Justin Morgan first owned the horse, but it was the boy Joel Goss who loved "Little Bub", later called "Justin Morgan", followed him thru his career, rescued him from a cruel master, and finally had the pleasure of having him ridden by James Monroe when he was President of the United States

A horse story "in a book that is rich in human values—the sort of book that makes you proud and sometimes brings a lump to your throat." Bk Week

Books consulted: p[174-75]

King of the Wind; illus. by Wesley Dennis. Rand McNally 1948 172p illus $4.95, lib. bdg. $4.97, pa $1.95 (4-7)   Fic

1 Horses—Stories

ISBN 0-528-82265-9; 0-528-80174-0; 0-528-87686-4

Awarded the Newbery Medal, 1949

"A beautiful, sympathetic story of the famous [horse] . . . and the little mute Arabian stable boy who accompanies him on his journey across the seas to France and England. The lad's fierce devotion to his horse and his great faith and loyalty are skillfully woven into an enthralling tale which children will long remember. The moving quality of the writing is reflected in the handsome illustrations." Wis Library Bul

Books consulted: p[174]

Henry, Marguerite—*Continued*

Misty of Chincoteague; illus. by Wesley Dennis. Rand McNally 1947 173p illus $4.95, lib. bdg. $4.97, pa $1.95 (4-7)   Fic

1 Ponies—Stories 2 Chincoteague Island—Fiction 3 Assateague Island—Fiction

ISBN 0-528-82315-9; 0-528-80175-9; 0-528-87685-6

"Each year the wild ponies of Assateague, a small island in Chesapeake Bay, are driven to the neighboring island of Chincoteague to be sold as children's pets. This is the story of one pony, Misty, and the two Chincoteague children who owned her. The atmosphere of the islands and an understanding of the freedom-loving ponies pervade the story and illustrations." Hodges. Bks for Elem Sch Libraries

Two other books about the ponies of Chincoteague Island are available from Rand McNally: Sea Star, orphan of Chincoteague $4.95, lib. bdg. $4.97, pa $1.50 (ISBN 0-528-82370-0; 0-528-80178-3; 0-528-87687-2);·Stormy, Misty's foal $4.95, lib. bdg. $4.97, pa $1.95 (ISBN 0-528-82083-4; 0-528-80157-0; 0-528-87690-2)

Mustang, wild spirit of the West; illus. by Robert Lougheed. Rand McNally 1966 222p illus $3.95, lib. bdg. $3.79, pa $1.95 (5-7)   Fic

1 Johnston, Annie (Bronn)—Fiction 2 Mustang—Stories

ISBN   0-528-82327-2;   0-528-80176-7;   0-528-87683-X

The "story of how Wild Horse Annie Johnston successfully led the recent fight to save the mustangs from virtual extinction. Tells of her lifelong fight, first in Nevada and then on a national level, against the cruel practices of mustangers who hunt their prey in planes and trucks." Adventuring with Bks. 2d edition

White stallion of Lipizza; illus. by Wesley Dennis. Rand McNally 1964 116p illus $4.95, lib. bdg. $4.79 (5-7)   Fic

1 Lippizaner horse—Stories 2 Vienna. Spanish Riding School—Fiction 3 Horsemanship—Fiction

ISBN 0-528-82041-9; 0-528-80154-6

The "story of a young boy and his [Lipizzaner] show stallion in the Spanish Court Riding School of Vienna. The book [also] relates factual history of horsemanship and a rider's devotion to the art of classical riding." Pub W

"The book seems over-extended, however, with many incidents that do not contribute to the story line; the writing style is pedestrian, the authenticity of detail about the horses giving the book its chief value." Chicago. Children's Bk Center

Henry, O.

The ransom of Red Chief; illus. by Paul Frame. Hawthorn Bks. 1970 unp illus lib. bdg. $3.95 (4-6)
Fic

1 Kidnapping—Fiction

ISBN 0-8015-6240-6

The "story about two kidnappers who, driven to distraction by their mischievous hostage, finally pay his father to take him off their hands. . . . Its humor and irony, combined with its brief length, should make it useful as well for reluctant readers. . . . Paul Frame's sepia illustrations provide humor and capture the atmosphere of the times (early 1900's)." Sch Library J

Hicks, Clifford

Alvin's secret code; illus. by Bill Sokol. Holt 1963 159p illus lib. bdg. $4.95 (4-6)   Fic

1 Cryptography—Fiction

ISBN 0-03-089736-X

"Alvin Fernald, the Magnificent Brain, becomes a cryptographer and as Secret Agent K 21-½ solves the mystery of the buried treasure. An appendix gives entertaining information about codes and ciphers, along with samples and problems." Hodges. Bks for Elem Sch Libraries

Hightower, Florence

Dark horse of Woodfield; illus. by Joshua Tolford. Houghton 1962 233p illus $5.95 (5-7)   Fic

1 Horses—Stories 2 Massachusetts—Fiction

ISBN 0-395-06812-6

During the Depression of the 1930's, the Armistead family of Wolverton, Massachusetts, had a little money and a few horses left in their once famous stable. Maggie Armistead, thirteen, worked with her ten-year-old brother, Bugsy, a butterfly expert, to get enough money to buy back Aunt Cinny's horse. Maggie also entered an essay contest, hoping to win the entry fee in the horse show for her mare, Stardust

"This humorous story involves characters who have distinct roles. Though it is basically a horse story, good family relations, some mystery, and a love story are also interwoven in the plot." Adventuring with Bks. 2d edition

The ghost of Follonsbee's Folly; illus. by Ati Forberg. Houghton 1958 218p illus $5.95 (5-7)   Fic

1 Mystery and detective stories

ISBN 0-395-06814-2

"Follonsbee's Folly, an old house of pre-Civil War vintage in the country, is the new home of the Stackpole family, individuals all, and their Negro housekeeper, Angela, who rules them with a firm but loving hand. The mansion's intriguing history unearthed by Elsie, twelve, and the identity of the vagabond young Negro man with whom Tom, eleven, secretly spends idyllic days on the river, provide the mystery for this thoroughly enjoyable story." Booklist

It is "above standard mystery fare, and both boys, and girls will find it very funny." Horn Bk

Hildick, Edmond W.

Manhattan is missing; illus. by Jan Palmer. Doubleday 1969 239p illus $4.95, lib. bdg. $5.70 (4-6) Fic

1 Siamese cat—Stories 2 New York (City)—Fiction 3 British in the U.S.—Fiction

ISBN 0-385-02776-1; 0-385-03095-9

"An English family sublets a New York apartment and assumes responsibility for Manhattan, the owner's precious Siamese cat. But Manhattan is kidnapped and held for ransom. In tracking down the culprit, the children, with the help of new American friends, learn something of Central Park, the subway, and other aspects of New York City." Moorachian. What is a City?

"This is a lively, very funny story. Mr Hildick's keen awareness of human nature, his good ear for conversation, and his obvious enjoyment of his subject make for delightful reading." Bk World

Hodges, Margaret

The hatching of Joshua Cobb; illus. by W. T. Mars. Farrar, Straus 1967 135p illus $3.75 (4-6)   Fic

1 Camps—Fiction

ISBN 0-374-32871-4

"An Ariel book"

An unathletic boy surprises himself by having fun at summer camp despite an unsympathetic cabin counselor

"Pleasantly low-keyed and smoothly written." Sutherland. The Best in Children's Bks

The making of Joshua Cobb; illus. by W. T. Mars. Farrar, Straus 1971 169p illus lib. bdg. $4.50 (5-7)
Fic

Hodges, Margaret—*Continued*

1 School stories

ISBN 0-374-34737-9

"An Ariel book"

The author tells the story of a boy's first year in a boarding school. After a year filled with hard work, ups and downs, and all kinds of learning, twelve-year-old Josh Cobb began to feel that he belonged at Oakley

"The pattern of school life, the relationships between teachers and pupils, the pranks and ploys of the boys, all have a touch of Mr. Chips-milieu-American-style, and the episodic structure is firmly based on good characterization and on Joshua's growing acceptance of—and being accepted by—the school community. This has good humor, in both meanings of the term." Chicago. Children's Bk Center

Hoff, Syd

Irving and me. Harper 1967 226p $4.95, lib. bdg. $4.79 (5-7)   Fic

1 Jews in the U.S.—Fiction 2 Florida—Fiction

ISBN 0-06-022498-3; 0-06-022499-1

"Poor Artie, he wanted to live in Brooklyn forever, but a thirteen-year-old has little choice. His parents wanted to move to Florida, and that was how Artie met Irving. He had a few problems: girls, bullies, the youth director of the Community Center, and no dog; and his life was not eased by the determined companionship of Irving, a boy with a real flair for doing the wrong thing. Once Artie resigned himself to the fact that his girl had given her heart to another, and decided to keep a stray dog, he was willing to admit that Florida wasn't so bad. The story has a zestful, zany, sometimes sophisticated humor; told by Artie, it is spontaneous and colloquial; and it is refreshingly casual about being Jewish and about being an only child." Sutherland. The Best in Children's Bks

Holling, Holling Clancy

Minn of the Mississippi; written and illus. by Holling Clancy Holling. Houghton 1951 85p illus maps lib. bdg. $4.07 (4-6)   Fic

1 Turtles—Stories 2 Mississippi River—Fiction

ISBN 0-395-06823-1

Minn of the Mississippi is a tough snapping turtle. The story of the Mississippi River is here told in text and pictures as Minn is carried from the Minnesota headwaters of the Mississippi to the Gulf of Mexico. The time required in Minn's life is twenty-five years but the story reaches back into history to make the tale complete

"In telling the story of Minn, a snapping turtle, the author touches on the geography, history, geology and climate of the Mississippi River. . . . Illustrated with full page pictures in color and many marginal pencil drawings." Los Angeles. Sch Libraries

Paddle-to-the-sea; written and illus. by Holling Clancy Holling. Houghton 1941 unp illus map lib. bdg. $6.95 (4-6)   Fic

1 Great Lakes—Fiction

ISBN 0-395-15082-5

A toy canoe with a seated Indian figure is launched in Lake Nipigon by the Indian boy who carved it and in four years travels thru all the Great Lakes and the St Lawrence River to the Atlantic. An interesting picture of the shore life of the lakes and the river with striking full page pictures in bright colors and marginal pencil drawings

"The canoe's journey is used to show the flow of currents and of traffic, and each occurrence is made to seem plausible. . . . There are also diagrams of a sawmill, a freighter, the canal locks at the Soo, and Niagara Falls." Library J

"This is geography of the best kind made vivid by the power of imagination." Horn Bk

Seabird; written and illus. by Holling Clancy Holling. Houghton 1948 58p illus $6.95 (4-6)   Fic

1 Whaling—Fiction 2 Sea stories

ISBN 0-395-06829-0

Seabird is an ivory gull carved by Ezra Brown when he was just a boy while on a whaler in 1832. It brought luck and good sailing to him and to his descendants on all the seven seas, and through many years of thrilling sea adventures

"Through four generations of seamen Seabird saw the whaler give way to the clipper, the clipper yield to steam, the airplane succeed both. The subject takes the reader over the globe and provides room for imagination to aid history in vitalizing the period. The beauty of the illustrations [full-page color pictures and decorative sketches] gives the book distinction." Horn Bk

Tree in the trail; written and illus. by Holling Clancy Holling. Houghton 1942 unp illus map lib. bdg. $6.95 (4-7)   Fic

1 Trees—Stories 2 Sante Fé Trail—Fiction

ISBN 0-395-18228-X

"The story of a cottonwood growing beside the Santa Fe trail. A young Indian boy nourished and tended it as a sapling. The tree brought good luck to his tribe and came to be looked on as a medicine tree. To the white traders who followed, it was the post office tree, a place for leaving messages. Cottonwoods don't live forever, and in time the ox-yoke made from its wood is left to carry on the story." Wis Library Bul

"The care with which this [book] is documented by pictures gives it exceptional usefulness. Besides the large color plates, every important detail in the story appears in small pencil studies on the wide margins of facing pages." N Y Her Trib Bks

Holm, Anne

North to freedom; tr. from the Danish by L. W. Kingsland. Harcourt 1965 190p $5.95 (6-7)   Fic

1 Refugees—Fiction

ISBN 0-15-257550-2

First published 1963 in Denmark. Winner of the 1963 Gyldendal Prize for the best Scandinavian children's book

Twelve-year-old "David, a prisoner of war, is given a chance to escape and is told only to make his way to Denmark. Distrusting human beings, he makes his way silently from Eastern Europe and on the journey regains his faith in mankind." Rdng Ladders. 5th edition

"The writing style is good, the psychological insight into David's changing reactions is perceptive: as the boy meets people, he slowly loses the suspicion and hostility engendered by his past life. . . . The story is somewhat weakened by the pat ending." Chicago. Children's Bk Center

Holman, Felice

Slake's limbo. Scribner 1974 117p $5.95 (6-7) Fic

1 Runaways—Fiction 2 Subways—Fiction 3 New York (City)—Fiction

ISBN 0-684-13926-X

Aremis Slake, at the age of thirteen, takes to the New York City subways as a refuge from an abusive home life and oppressive school system

"The economically told chronicle of Slake's adventures is more than a survival saga; it is also an eloquent study of poverty, of fear, and finally of hope." Horn Bk

Houston, James

Akavak; an Eskimo journey; written and illus. by James Houston. Harcourt 1968 75p illus $5.50, lib. bdg. $4.95 (4-6)   Fic

1 Eskimos—Fiction

ISBN 0-15-201729-1; 0-15-201730-5

Houston, James—*Continued*

The Eskimo "Akavak and his grandfather set out on a long and difficult journey because the old man feels he is nearing the end of his life and has promised to see his brother before he dies. When their cache of food is stolen by a bear, they are forced to go into the mountains; the journey becomes a struggle for survival against cold and hunger. The story of their terrible time, of Akavak's battle with the musk ox, and of the last wild-sled ride down the mountain makes exciting reading." Horn Bk

"Stark and dramatic, Houston's black and white pictures reflect remarkably the elemental and violent quality of the setting, the frozen isolation of the Far North. . . . The style has rugged simplicity and a cadence that are eminently suitable for the setting and theme." Chicago. Children's Bk Center

Eagle mask; a West Coast Indian tale; written and illus. by James Houston. Harcourt 1966 63p illus $5.50, lib. bdg. $5.50 (3-5)   Fic
1 Indians of North America—Fiction
ISBN 0-15-224444-1; 0-15-224445-X
"On the north Pacific coast, where giant cedars look down upon a little village, the Indian prince Skemshan approaches manhood. With a boyhood friend, he spends three days fasting in the cold forest: later he joins the men for his first terrifying battle with a killer whale. Finally Skemshan is honored at a great midwinter festivity." Horn Bk

The author's "quiet writing has a simplicity that is eminently appropriate for the rich and dignified living patterns of the Eagle clan." Sat Rev

Ghost paddle; a northwest coast Indian tale; written and illus. by James Houston. Harcourt 1972 55p illus $5.50 (4-6)   Fic
1 Indians of North America—Fiction
ISBN 0-15-230760-5
"In a tale of the Northwest Canadian Indian, the author tells of an island clan tired of warfare with the Inland River people and determined to make a peace-seeking expedition to these Indians. Two canoes set forth, led by brave young Hooits and his father, the famous chieftain Wasco, who has carved for his son a 'ghost' paddle with magical powers. Hooits wields this implement against a gigantic slave of the Inland Warriors, defeats the giant, and thus secures an opportunity to talk about deceptions of the past and make the way clear to the resumption of friendship." Horn Bk

The author's "writing, like his illustrations, has a stark and dramatic simplicity that is eminently right for the dignity of the Indian peoples he describes. . . . The story is so deftly imbued with the spirit and the cultural details of Hooits' people that the incorporation seems effortless, and the theme has a pertinence for today." Chicago. Children's Bk Center

The white archer; an Eskimo legend; written and illus. by James Houston. Harcourt 1967 95p illus $6.25 (4-6)   Fic
1 Eskimos—Fiction
ISBN 0-15-295851-7
"A desire for revenge consumed the heart of the young Eskimo, Kungo, and it was only after months of preparation for an act of revenge that he found he could not kill those who destroyed his village." Cincinnati

This "story of an Eskimo boy's personal triumph over hatred reflects the author's knowledge and appreciation of Eskimo character and culture." Notable Children's Bks of 1967

Wolf run; a Caribou Eskimo tale; written and illus. by James Houston. Harcourt 1971 52p illus $5.75 (4-6)   Fic

1 Eskimos—Fiction 2 Arctic regions—Fiction
ISBN 0-15-299104-2
His father having died the summer before, thirteen-year-old Punik must leave his family's camp on a last desperate hunt for food when the migrating caribou herds which they count on each spring fail to appear. His grandfather and the women are left behind to invoke—by chants and drumming—the magic that would bring the caribou—a magic Punik could not believe in

"In Punik's thoughts and memories, the way of life of his people is revealed, their admiration and affection for each other, and the strength of their unwavering belief in the interrelationships of man and animal. This belief is stronger than the hostile environment and brings the story to a dramatic and deeply satisfying climax. Strong black-and-white drawings increase the intensity of the experience." Horn Bk

Hunt, Irene

Across five Aprils; jacket and endsheets by Albert John Pucci. Follett 1964 223p map $4.95, lib. bdg. $4.98 (6-7)   Fic
1 U.S.—History—Civil War—Fiction 2 Farm life—Fiction 3 Illinois—Fiction
ISBN 0-695-80100-7; 0-695-40100-9
"It was April 1861 when the Civil War became a reality for the Creighton family on their farm in southern Illinois. One by one the war pulled the able-bodied men away leaving only the youngest, Jethro, to keep the farm going. This great war that ran across five Aprils is here chronicled by means of what happened to the various members of Jethro's family." Pub W

"In handling her characters the author is particularly skillful. . . . Young readers will appreciate this story more for its warmth of character study than for the action involved, although there is action and the reader is made anxious to see how the family finally makes out at the end of the war." Best Sellers

No promises in the wind. Follett 1970 249p $4.95, lib. bdg. $4.98 (6-7)   Fic
1 Depressions—Fiction
ISBN 0-695-80065-5; 0-695-40065-7
This novel "opens in October 1932 in a near-slum Chicago neighborhood. Young Josh Grondowski can take no more of his unemployed father's overbearing behavior, and he leaves home with his little brother and his best friend. Through the Depression's darkest winter they hitchhike, ride freights, hook up with a carnival and a trucker. They are turned out and taken in, cheated and befriended. The brothers must bear their best friend's death and their own deprivation and illness before they reach home again, Josh having gained some understanding of himself and his father." N Y Times Bk Rev

The telling of the story "is delicate, feminine, tender; but it clearly shows how hundreds of children and thousands of adults lived in the '30s. For any well-fed reader romantically inclined towards poverty—here's a harsh antidote." Christian Sci Monitor

Hunter, Kristin

Boss cat; illus. by Harold Franklin. Scribner 1971 58p illus lib. bdg. $5.95 (2-5)   Fic
1 Cats—Stories 2 Negroes—Fiction
ISBN 0-684-12491-2
When Pharaoh, a black cat, moves into the Tanner household, he's welcomed by everyone but Mrs Tanner. This story tells how Mr Tanner finds a way to help Pharaoh make friends with her

"Dialog is natural and characters and family relationships lifelike in a good-humored, winning story of a proud-to-be-black family." Booklist

Hunter, Mollie

The haunted mountain; a story of suspense; illus. by Laszlo Kubinyi. Harper 1972 125p illus lib. bdg. $4.79, pa 95¢ (5-7) Fic

1 Scotland—Fiction 2 Fantastic fiction
ISBN 0-06-022667-6; 0-06-440041-7

"MacAllister defies tradition and plows the Goodman's Croft, a small portion of land that all Scottish Highlanders once set aside for the sidhe, the small shadowy people who have an ancient magic at their command. Although MacAllister wins his initial confrontations with the angered sidhe, they eventually capture and enslave him; only the courage and loyalty of his son saves MacAllister from certain death." Booklist

"Written in bleak, spare prose [this novel] makes good use of its highland setting, where such things seem more possible anyhow, even down to the local names given to certain lakes and mountains. It all happens at no particular time in the past, and has the atmosphere of a real legend. That it is in fact an original work is a tribute to the sustained imagination that went into the gripping mini-epic." New Statesman

The kelpie's pearls; illus. by Joseph Cellini. Funk [1966 c1964] 112p illus $3.25 (4-6) Fic

1 Fairy tales 2 Scotland—Fiction
ISBN 0-308-80030-3

First published 1964 in England

"A kelpie who can change into a black horse with flaming eyes, the Loch Ness monster, a good witch . . . and Tirnan-Og (the land of eternal youth) are woven into [this] . . . fantasy. Morag MacLeod, a lonely old woman, befriends a kelpie and Torquil, a boy who understands animals so well he can almost talk to them, but she makes an enemy of wicked Alasdair, the trapper, because she will not help him steal the kelpie treasure horde of pearls." Sch Library J

"This is so enchantingly told in the gentle dialect of the Highlands that it is a spellbinder from first to last. Read it aloud—in school, home or library." Horn Bk

A sound of chariots (5-7) Fic

1 Death—Fiction 2 Scotland—Fiction
Some editions are:
Hall, G.K.&Co. lib. bdg. $8.95 Large print book (ISBN 0-8161-6148-8)
Harper $4.95, lib. bdg. $4.79 (ISBN 0-06-022668-4; 0-06-022669-2)

First published 1972 by Harper

This is a story set in post World War I Scotland. Bridie McShane's happy early childhood is interrupted by the death of her beloved father whose favorite child she was. Her sorrow colors her life as she matures, leading her to morbid reflections on time and death which she finally learns to deal with through her desire to write poetry

"The characterization of Bridie is strikingly realistic, and the story—gay and lively in the first part, more somber yet still vital in the second—is a departure from the author's usual suspenseful fare." Booklist

The stronghold. Harper 1974 259p $5.95, lib. bdg. $5.79 (6-7) Fic

1 Druids and Druidism—Fiction 2 Scotland—Fiction
ISBN 0-06-022653-6; 0-06-022654-4

Set during the days when Druids were the priests in Scotland and the Romans raided the Scottish coasts for slaves, this is the story of Coll, a youth crippled as a result of such a raid, who designs fortresses to turn back the Roman invaders

The author "takes an enormous leap back in time, to the origins of the brochs—mysterious circular Bronze Age fortresses found only in the Highlands and islands of Scotland. . . . The force of Druidical magic, and the mercilessness of tribal ritual, are effectively shown without sadistic over-emphasis on detail. And the story of Coll's generation coming of age entwines neatly with the building of the first broch and the rejection of an ambitious traitor. This . . . is a good book well-written, original and convincing." Christian Sci Monitor

The walking stones; a story of suspense; illus. by Trina Schart Hyman. Harper 1970 143p illus lib. bdg. $4.79, pa $1.25 (5-7) Fic

1 Scotland—Fiction 2 Fantastic fiction
ISBN 0-06-022664-1; 0-06-440034-4

"Circles of huge standing stones are familiar in Celtic countries, but it is seldom that anyone expects them to move. The stones in young Donald's highland glen were due to walk down to the river for a centennial ceremony very soon after the completion of a dam that would drown the glen. The Bodach, an old man with mystical powers, was determined to delay the flooding until after the stones had walked. He succeeded, with the help of Donald, who would one day inherit the Bodach's powers." America

This is "a smooth blending of realism and fantasy, a story that reflects Celtic folklore. . . . The story has pace and suspense, and the writing has an authentic cadence that adds to the flavor of the Scottish setting." Chicago. Children's Bk Center

Irving, Washington

Rip Van Winkle; with drawings by Arthur Rackham. Lippincott 1967 64p illus $8.95 Fic

1 New York (State)—Fiction 2 Dutch in the U.S.—Fiction
ISBN 0-397-30981-3

First appeared 1819-1820 in Irving's: The sketch book of Geoffrey Crayon, Gent.

"Rip Van Winkle was a lazy, good-natured ne'er-do-well. He had an impatient wife who scolded constantly. On one of his hunting trips Rip met an odd crew of Dutchmen in the forests of the Catskill Mountains. They were playing nine-pins. Rip was ordered to serve them liquor, of which he also drank. As a result, he fell into a sleep which lasted twenty years. . . .The story emphasizes changes in American political life during the twenty years he slept." World Bk

Ish-Kishor, Sulamith

A boy of old Prague; drawings by Ben Shahn. Pantheon Bks. 1963 90p illus lib. bdg. $5.69 (5-7) Fic

1 Jews in Bohemia—Fiction 2 Prague—Fiction
ISBN 0-394-90978-X

"Tomás, a peasant boy, lives on the domains of the young Bohemian lord near the city of Prague in the sixteenth century, experiencing the harsh life of the serf and sharing the Christians' superstitious hatred of the Jews. As part payment of a debt he is given by his lord to an old Jew of the ghetto to be his bond servant. The succinct, sharply felt first-person narrative describes sensitively and with realism Tomás' reaction to the first kindness and respect he has ever known and the effect on him of witnessing a pogrom instigated by his once-admired lord." Booklist

"Important in subject, dramatic in incident, and sensitive in characterization, it is highly recommended. Ben Shahn's deft character sketches and darkly atmospheric ghetto scenes add enormously to the effectiveness of the book." Horn Bk

Ish-Kishor, Sulamith—_Continued_
The Master of Miracle; a new novel of the Golem; pictures by Arnold Lobel. Harper 1971 108p illus $3.95, lib. bdg. $3.79 (5-7) Fic
1 Golem—Fiction 2 Jews in Bohemia—Fiction 3 Prague—Fiction
ISBN 0-06-026088-2
This "beautifully written fantasy based on the Jewish golem legend is set in the 16th century Prague ghetto. . . . Gideon, a lonely orphan of uncertain parentage, is entrusted with controlling the golem, a huge clay humanoid fashioned by 'the master of miracle,' the venerated High Priest of Prague, in order to save the ghetto population from a pogrom. In his excitement, Gideon forgets to deactivate the golem when the task is completed and so faces punishment. The background is skillfully done and Gideon is a well-developed character." Rdng Ladders. 5th edition

Iterson, S. R. van
Pulga; tr. from the Dutch by Alexander and Alison Gode. Morrow 1971 240p map lib. bdg. $4.97 (5-7) Fic
1 Colombia—Fiction
ISBN 0-688-31796-0
Mildred L. Batchelder Award, 1973
Original Dutch edition 1967
This book was "chosen as the best children's book of 1967 in Holland. . . . In one incident Pulga is responsible for saving the life of a kidnapped boy; the wealthy father wants to make a substantial show of gratitude—but Pulga has gone on his way by then, so there is no pat ending. The style is competent, with only an occasional indication that the story has been translated; the structure is tight, the characters not deeply drawn but wholly convincing." Sutherland. The Best in Children's Bks
"From a ragged street urchin in Colombia, accepting whatever fate brings, to a truck driver's helper, journeying up and down the coast of South America, [15-year-old] Pulga finds his life broadened with the discovery of self-respect and usefulness." Pub W

Jackson, Jacqueline
Missing Melinda, by C. Gibbs and O. Gibbs; illus. by Irene Burns. Little 1967 142p illus $4.95 (4-6) Fic
1 Dolls—Fiction 2 Mystery and detective stories
ISBN 0-316-45478-8
Ophelia and Cordelia Gibbs, "twin daughters of a literary scholar, solve the theft of a valuable antique doll and collaborate on this narrative report of the case." Booklist
"Exciting, modern; with much data on old dolls, many Shakespearean tags, and a lot of casual mentioning of juvenile book characters." America

The taste of spruce gum; illus. by Lillian Obligado. Little 1966 212p illus $5.95 (5-7) Fic
1 Vermont—Fiction 2 Stepchildren—Fiction
ISBN 0-316-45476-1
"Libby and her mother return to Vermont after Libby's father's death. Libby, recently left nearly hairless from a serious illness, self-consciously meets her father's family whom she has never known. Adjusting to a stepfather proves difficult, especially in the extremely rough environment of a logging camp." Rdng Ladders. 5th edition
"The story is never overdone as the whole family determines to make a success of their new life." Wis Library Bul

Janeway, Elizabeth
Ivanov Seven; pictures by Eros Keith. Harper 1967 176p illus lib. bdg. $4.79 (5-7) Fic

1 Russia. Army—Fiction
ISBN 0-06-022808-3
Stepan Mgaloblishvili "bombards neighbors in his mountain village with uncomfortable questions until Tushin recruits him for the [Czar's] military. . . . Asked to obey an obviously foolish order, he refuses. The penalty is death, but even the officer who gave the order thinks it unwise; the solution is to 'reassign' the rebel to his home in the mountains. On the way, Stepan and his old friend Tushin make their fortune, arriving in style." Sch Library J
"This comic novel is moving and thought-provoking." Commonweal

Jansson, Tove
The exploits of Moominpappa; described by himself. Set down and illus. by Tove Jansson. Tr. by Thomas Warburton. Walck, H.Z. 1966 156p illus $4.50 (4-6) Fic
ISBN 0-8098-2387-X
Original Swedish edition published 1950; this translation first published 1952 in England
"The Moomin world has, in its characters, the same sort of set of individualists that are in the Milne books; the plot is more complicated and the writing—especially the dialogue—far more sophisticated. Although older readers may enjoy subtler references that the younger ones miss, there is enough humor even at the simplest level to amuse any age. . . . Moominpappa, writing the Memoirs that are obviously going to make him famous, reads them aloud to Moomintroll, Snufkin, and Sniff; they are enthralled at hearing about the deeds of their three fathers and the ridiculous adventures of the oddly assorted crew of the 'Oshun Oxtra.' (The Muddler had been asked to paint the boat's name, 'The Ocean Orchestra' in marine blue.)" Sutherland. The Best in Children's Bks

Finn family Moomintroll; written and illus. by Tove Jansson; tr. by Elizabeth Portch. Walck, H.Z. 1965 [c1958] 170p illus map $4.50 (4-6) Fic
ISBN 0-8098-2385-3
First published in Swedish. This translation first published 1950 in England, and 1951 in the United States with title: The happy Moomins
Unexpected and disturbing events occur in Moominvalley when Moomintroll and his friends Sniff and Snufkin find a hobgoblin's hat and take it home to Moominmamma and Moominpappa

Moominpappa at sea; written and illus. by Tove Jansson; tr. by Kingsley Hart. Walck, H.Z. 1967 [c1966] 192p illus $4.50 (4-6) Fic
1 Islands—Fiction 2 Ocean—Fiction
ISBN 0-8098-2397-7
Originally written in Swedish. This translation first published 1966 in England
In this story about the Moomins, a family of small gnome-like creatures, Moominpappa "sees his family's life as disturbingly safe and fixed and plans to move to an island. . . . 'That's where we're going to live, and lead a wonderful life, full of troubles.' [Moominmamma] explains. . . . The island proves strange and temperamental; why is the lighthouse abandoned? Who is the silent fisherman? . . . Moomintroll is secretly kind to the awful, freezing Groke; secretly longs for a word from the heartless sea-horses; shrewd Little My [the Moomins precocious adopted child] sees all but doesn't waste words." Times (London) Lit Sup
"The sea, awesome, mysterious and changeable, permeates the story and Miss Jansson renders its lonely beauty with inspired assurance. . . . Despite the emphasis on the adults and their struggle to come

Jansson, Tove—*Continued*

to terms with a new way of life ultimately it is Moomintroll whose compassion miraculously warms the Groke and brings an end to the restless hostility of the island." Bk Week

Jarrell, Randall

The animal family; decorations by Maurice Sendak. Pantheon Bks. 1965 179p illus $3.50, lib. bdg. $5.69 (4-7)   Fic

1 Animals—Stories

ISBN 0-394-81043-0; 0-394-91043-5

A "tale about a lonely hunter who acquires an amazing family. One by one, he takes into his log cabin by the sea a mermaid, a bear cub, a lynx, and a small boy washed ashore from a shipwreck. The arrival and adjustment of each new member to this extraordinary family circle are sensitively related with touches of humor and wisdom." Booklist

"Simple enough to read aloud to children too young to read the book by themselves, the story is probably best suited to the sensitive reader who can appreciate the perceptive writing." Chicago. Children's Bk Center

The bat-poet; pictures by Maurice Sendak. Macmillan (N Y) 1964 42p illus $3.95 (2-4)   Fic

1 Bats—Stories 2 Poets—Fiction

The bat-poet, a little brown bat, "opened his eyes to the daytime and began to see the world in another light. . . . He made up poems about the daytime world's sights and sounds, and recited them to the unappreciative ears of his fellow bats and then hunted around for more receptive listeners, (other small animals and birds in his environment). Hidden in his 'discourse' are explanations of iambic pentameter and iambic trimeter." Toronto

"Fortunately, the book does not come right out and baldly make its points about poetry, one, two, three. But like a good poem, it uses words, to make the reader think and feel the ideas, rather than just hear them. A lovely book, perfectly illustrated—one well worth a child's attention and affection." Pub W

Jewett, Sarah Orne

A white heron; a story of Maine; illus. by Barbara Cooney. Crowell 1963 34p illus $3.95, lib. bdg. $4.70 (4-6)   Fic

1 Herons—Stories 2 Maine—Fiction

ISBN 0-690-88570-9; 0-690-88571-7

A story first written in 1886 and taken from the author's collection of short stories: The country of the pointed firs, and other stories

"The white heron was rare but no more so than visitors at the lonely cabin shared by Sylvy and her grandmother. The visitor who came had great charm, but Sylvy could not bring herself to lead him to the white heron's nest." Pub W

"Barbara Cooney has slightly abridged the story and has illustrated it with some of her finest pictures, matching her own art to the serene beauty of the story, its characters, and its setting." Horn Bk

Johnson, Annabel

The grizzly, by Annabel and Edgar Johnson; pictures by Gilbert Riswold. Harper 1964 160p illus $4.95, lib. bdg. $4.79, pa $1.25 (5-7)   Fic

1 Bears—Stories 2 Outdoor life—Fiction 3 Parent and child—Fiction

ISBN 0-06-022870-9; 0-06-022871-7; 0-06-440036-0

"Eleven-year-old David, living with his divorced mother, is doubtful about going on a camping trip with his father. When a grizzly injures the father and disables the truck, David surprises both himself and his father by his resourcefulness." Hodges. Bks for Elem Sch Libraries

"Through a fine balance of descriptive detail and dialogue between the characters, the authors offer much insight into human relationships, especially those between father and son." Adventuring with Bks. 2d edition

Johnson, Elizabeth

Break a magic circle; illus. by Trina Schart Hyman. Little 1971 70p illus $4.50, lib. bdg. $5.10 (3-5) Fic

1 Hudson Valley—Fiction

ISBN 0-316-46939-4; 0-316-46938-6

"An invisible boy, a strange little man, and a perfectly ordinary brother and sister are the chief characters in this modern tale of magic and enchantment. Robert had been perfectly normal until he broke a mushroom circle in the woods and incurred the fury of the strange little man who then made him invisible. He knew he had to restore the circle before he could become visible again and sought help from Tilly and David who believed in him even though they could not see him. The story is lively and funny and even slightly scary when it turns out that the little man is one of the company of Henry Hudson's 'Half Moon,' which makes its ghostly rounds every twenty years." Horn Bk

Johnston, Norma

Glory in the flower. Atheneum Pubs. 1974 198p lib. bdg. $6.95 (6-7)   Fic

ISBN 0-689-30140-5

Sequel to: The keeping days

In her journal of 1901, fourteen-year-old Tish Sterling records her "trials and tears" of growing up in the Bronx. She copes with her energetic family, the lead role in "Romeo and Juliet" and the complexities of friendship

"The outstanding feature here is the total picture it offers of one girl's life—at home, at school, at church, with her girl friends and with her boyfriend. . . . [The book is] in refreshing contrast to the many juvenile novels with contemporary settings that overdirect all characters to a single social or emotional problem. Offering the interaction of many vivid characters of all ages and tracing attractively serious Tish's growth from self-concern to mature consideration for others, this will assuredly satisfy adolescents in search of a long read." Library J

The keeping days. Atheneum Pubs. 1973 233p $5.95 (5-7)   Fic

1 Family—Fiction

ISBN 0-689-30110-3

Tish Sterling graduated from grammar school in Yonkers, New York in 1900. That year her father lost his job; her mother was pregnant again; and her brother Ben was growing away from his family and his old beliefs. In this story of family life the author describes how Tish faced these and other problems

"Nostalgic but not sentimental, flavored generously with romance, the novel captures the anxieties of adolescence with its naïveté and awareness." Horn Bk

Followed by: Glory in the flower

Jones, Elizabeth Orton

Big Susan. Macmillan (N Y) 1947 82p illus $3.95 (1-4)   Fic

1 Dolls—Fiction 2 Dollhouses—Fiction 3 Christmas stories

The story and pictures portray the daily life in a little girl's doll house. The Doll family were very fond of Big Susan, and so on Christmas Eve when all toys come alive Mr and Mrs Doll, their six celluloid children, the cook and the nurse tidied up the house, and the new doll baby looked enchanting in her little bed. Big Susan had the surprise of her life

Jones, Elizabeth Orton—*Continued*

"The author has modelled her attractive drawings on dolls she treasured when she was a child." New Yorker

Twig. Macmillan (N Y) 1942 152p illus $5.95 (3-5)   Fic

1 Fairy tales

Illustrated by the author

"Four floors down from Twig's apartment there was a tiny back yard, and there Twig has adventures with a little elf, a fairy queen, and a family of sparrows." ALA. CSD. Selected Lists of Children's Bks and Recordings

"A story full of fun and magic and make-believe. . . . Twig is warmhearted, human and loveable and, like many children in real life, can be practical and wide-eyed with wonder at the same time. Miss Jones writes with freshness and originality. There is genuine humor in her story and events follow one another with a delightful unexpectedness." N Y Times Bk Rev

Jones, Weyman

Edge of two worlds; illus. by J. C. Kocsis. Dial Press 1968 143p illus $5.95 (5-7)   Fic

1 Sequoya, Cherokee Indian—Fiction 2 Texas—Fiction

ISBN 0-440-2211-7

Based on incidents in the life of Sequoyah, creator of the Cherokee's written language. "This is a story of a young Missouri boy and an old Cherokee Indian [Sequoyah] who face a long and difficult journey across the plains together; first as enemies, then as comrades in peril." Pub W

"The writing is taut and sustained and will especially be enjoyed by better readers." Wis Library Bul

Justus, May

A new home for Billy; illus. by Joan Balfour Payne. Hastings House 1966 55p illus $4.95 (2-4)   Fic

1 Negroes—Fiction 2 Race problems—Fiction

ISBN 0-8038-5002-6

"Six-year-old Billy Allen and his parents want to move from their cramped apartment in the city to a little house in the suburbs. While house hunting with his father, Billy hears a man tell his father he will not rent to little Billy. He has been raised in an integrated setting and cannot understand why this man would be silly enough to like or dislike people by their color. Billy's new neighbors prove there are people who judge the person, not the skin color." Rdng Ladders. 5th edition

"The plot is simple and well constructed; characters are believable; situations are realistic and accurate." Adventuring with Bks. 2d edition

Kästner, Erich

Emil and the detectives; a story for children; tr. by May Massee; illus. by Walter Trier. Doubleday 1930 224p illus $4.95, lib. bdg. $5.70 (4-6)   Fic

1 Berlin—Fiction 2 Mystery and detective stories

ISBN 0-385-07289-9; 0-385-06142-0

Also available in a German language edition from Holt for $4.65 (ISBN 0-03-015650-5)

Original German edition published 1928 in Switzerland

On his way to Berlin to visit his grandmother, Emil fell asleep and had his money stolen by the man who shared his compartment. Although he came from the country Emil was not stupid, and he determined to get that money back. He followed the man, met the boy with the auto horn, who summoned his friends, and among them all they caught a very clever thief

"The satisfying adventure will please young readers while many older ones will delight in the revealing glimpse of boyhood in a book refreshingly objective rather than analytic." Booklist

Lisa and Lottie; illus. by Victoria de Larrea; tr. by Cyrus Brooks. Knopf 1969 136p illus lib. bdg. $5.69 (4-6)   Fic

1 Twins—Fiction

ISBN 0-394-91374-4

Original German edition, 1949. This translation first published 1950 in England

"When Lisa (of Vienna) sees Lottie (of Munich) alight from the summer camp bus, she feels as if she has just looked into a mirror. The two start comparing backgrounds: Lisa's father has no wife, and once hid a portrait of a lady from his daughter; Lottie's mother has never spoken of the girl's father. When the girls discover they are the same age and have the same birthdays, they rapidly conclude that they are twins. An exchange plan is formed for Lisa and Lottie to trade homes in the hope of reuniting their parents." Sch Library J

"The writing is ebullient and sophisticated, more than compensating for the plot." Chicago. Children's Bk Center

The little man; pictures by Rick Schreiter; tr. from the German by James Kirkup. Knopf 1966 183p illus lib. bdg. $5.49 (4-6)   Fic

1 Circus—Fiction 2 Fairy tales

ISBN 0-394-91402-3

Mildred L. Batchelder Award, 1968

Original German edition published 1963 in Switzerland

"Maxie, who is two inches tall, has been left an orphan by the tiny parents who came from a Bohemian village of tiny people. A protégé of the famous conjuror, Professor Hokus von Pokus, Maxie becomes a famous circus and television star; among his ancillary activities, he rescues himself from his own kidnapping." Chicago. Children's Bk Center

"It is also a story that almost stands up and begs to be read out loud, for it is rich with the ingredient that warrants calling it a 'good' children's book; its appeal is both to the adult who reads it and the child who listens to it." Pub W

Kendall, Carol

The Gammage Cup; illus. by Erik Blegvad. Harcourt 1959 221p illus maps $6.50, pa $1.45 (4-6) Fic

1 Fairy tales

ISBN 0-15-230572-6; 0-15-634277-4

"In the Land between the Mountains live a lost people, the Minnipins, who faithfully preserve their ancient customs until challenged by a few nonconformists. When they are attacked by an enemy race, it is the banished rebels who save the Minnipins from destruction." Hodges. Bks for Elem Sch Libraries

"This highly creative fantasy [offers] . . . an almost inexhaustible variety of reading pleasures: plot surprises, humor, fascinating characters, richness of ideas, and delight in words. . . . The story, generous in length, rises to a wonderfully dramatic climax in the final out-and-out battle." Horn Bk

The Whisper of Glocken; illus. by Imero Gobbato. Harcourt 1965 256p illus $5.95 (4-6)   Fic

1 Fairy tales

ISBN 0-15-295697-2

Another fantasy about the Minnipins, or Small Ones who dwell in the Land Between the Mountains. In the year of Gammage 885, the Watercress River floods its valley. Among the fleeing villagers are Gam Lutie, Crustabread, Silky, Scumble, and Glocken. They set out on a quest that makes the Watercress Valley safe again and restores an ancient treasure to its people

Kendall, Carol—*Continued*

"The story, told with many delightful plays on words, is good fantasy and well-paced adventure." Horn Bk

Kerr, Judith

When Hitler stole Pink Rabbit; illus. by the author. Coward, McCann & Geoghegan [1972 c1971] 191p illus $5.95 (4-7)   Fic

1 Refugees, Jewish—Fiction
ISBN 0-698-20182-5
First published 1971 in England

"Anna, aged nine, finds that her family suddenly has to leave Berlin for Switzerland because the Nazis have won an election. In packing, she has to choose between two stuffed animals—an old beloved pink rabbit and a new dog. She chooses the dog, assuming that their exile will be temporary. Only gradually as her family moves from Switzerland to France to England in search of a meagre living does she realise that she will never return to Germany and that she will never see the rabbit again." Economist

"This tale of a refugee family is based on the author's childhood experiences and, although anti-Semitism in Germany and financial depression everywhere are a somber backdrop, the book is warm and cozy, filled with the small, homely details of events that are important in a child's life." Sat Rev

Key, Alexander

Escape to Witch Mountain; illus. by Leon B. Wisdom, Jr. Westminster Press 1968 172p illus $5.50 (5-7)   Fic

1 Science fiction
ISBN 0-664-32417-7

Orphaned "Tony and his sister Tia, who is mute to others but able to communicate with him . . . [are] menaced by a thug with a custody order. They flee to the town shown on their map, which is located deep in the Great Smokies. Closely pursued, their need for sanctuary prompts them to piece together out of deeply repressed memories the story of a trip . . . from a disintegrating planet to a carefully prepared new home on earth." Sch Library J

The forgotten door. Westminster Press 1965 126p $4.75 (6-7)   Fic

1 Science fiction
ISBN 0-664-32342-1

"A strange child falls—from another planet—through a doorway onto a Southern Appalachian landing place. People, both evil in intent and good, wonder at Jon's differences: his mind reading, his capacity to communicate with animals, his ability to make his feet 'light' so that he can move as quickly as a deer. A rock hound and his family, who run a gem shop for tourists, accept the boy. Defending him against suspicious neighbors, they come under the spell of Jon's revelation of another way of life." Horn Bk

"Call it adventure, mystery, or science fiction, this deceptively simple story is tension-packed, thought-provoking, and oddly disturbing." Library J

Kingman, Lee

The year of the raccoon. Houghton 1966 246p front $4.25 (6-7)   Fic

1 Raccoons—Stories
ISBN 0-395-06865-7

"Fifteen-year-old Joey, the middle son in a brilliant family, considers himself a disappointment to his parents. A pet raccoon helps to tide him over a difficult period in which he proves himself a person of worth and importance." Hodges. Bks for Elem Sch Libraries

This book "is perhaps closer to everyday reality,

less an idealized, isolated instance than most child-animal stories. Its hero . . . is also a lover of nature and a keen-eyed observer of the world around him. But he is more accident-prone, more boy, less a wish fulfillment figure." Bk Week

"The many-faceted story has humor, excellent characterization, and problems that build up to a dramatic but convincing climax." Horn Bk

Kipling, Rudyard

How the leopard got his spots; illus. by Leonard Weisgard. Walker & Co. [1973 c1972] unp illus $4.95, lib. bdg. $4.85 (1-4)   Fic

1 Leopards—Stories
ISBN 0-8027-6111-9; 0-8027-6112-7
First published 1972 in England

"Kipling's tale from the 'Just so stories' telling how the Ethiopian and the leopard changed color is strikingly illustrated by Weisgard's paintings, which project the atmosphere of hot plains or shadowy forest with a skillful contrast of colors." Booklist

How the rhinoceros got his skin; illus. by Leonard Weisgard. Walker & Co. 1974 unp illus $4.95, lib. bdg. $4.85 (2-4)   Fic

1 Rhinoceros—Stories
ISBN 0-8027-6149-6; 0-8027-6150-X

"This is about a Parsee whose freshly baked cake is eaten by a Rhinoceros. For revenge the Parsee puts itchy cake crumbs inside the Rhino's skin while the beast is bathing. The animal rubs its hide so much that its skin falls into the folds that are the trademark of the rhino." Sch Library J

"The soft, slightly stylized plane figures of Weisgard's Parsee and Rhinoceros go well with Kipling's quaint, witty text." Booklist

Kjelgaard, Jim

Big Red. . . . Illus. by Bob Kuhn [New ed] Holiday House 1956 [c1945] 254p illus $5.95 (4-7)   Fic

1 Dogs—Stories 2 Outdoor life—Fiction
ISBN 0-8234-0007-7
First published 1945

"The story of a champion Irish setter and a trapper's son who grew up together, roaming the wilderness." Title page

Together they conquered blizzards and varmints, and eventually tracked down Old Majesty, the great outlaw bear. In the process boy and dog grew to real maturity, and found a place for themselves

"A tale which paints the stern life of the Wintapi wilderness in strong, clear strokes." N Y Times Bk Rev

Followed by: Irish Red, son of Big Red

Fire-hunter; illus. by Ralph Ray. Holiday House 1951 217p illus $4.95 (4-7)   Fic

1 Man, Prehistoric—Fiction
ISBN 0-8234-0034-4

"A dramatic story of the days when men lived in wandering tribes and were not much better off than the animals they hunted. The story concerns Hawk, the chief spearmaker, and Willow, a young girl of the tribe, both of whom were abandoned and left to die. Hawk had more ability than some of his tribesmen to observe what went on around him and use what he saw, with the result that he and Willow not only survived but even found new and better ways of living and hunting. The story is authentic as far as the sequence of happenings is known but time has been telescoped to fit the needs of the story. The writing is excellent and the story one that will hold the interest of all readers." Chicago. Children's Bk Center

Kjelgaard, Jim—*Continued*

Swamp cat; illus. by Edward Shenton. Dodd 1957
175p illus $4.50 (5-7)   Fic
1 Cats—Stories 2 Outdoor life—Fiction
3 Louisiana—Fiction
ISBN 0-396-03982-0
A sixteen-year-old boy's attempt to stock a
[Louisiana] swamp with muskrats is aided by a little
half-wild cat he saves and befriends. The cat responds
to the boy's kindness, and in turn saves his life
"As with all the author's books, there is a feel and
smell of the wilderness, and an identification on the
part of the reader with the boy's success in wresting a
livelihood from uncompromising nature." Best
Sellers

Knight, Eric

Lassie come-home (4-7)   Fic
1 Dogs—Stories 2 Great Britain—Fiction
Some editions are:
Holt lib. bdg. $4.59 Illustrated by Don Bolognese
(ISBN 0-03-080228-8)
Watts, F. lib. bdg. $6.95 Large type edition. Illus-
trated by Cyrus LeRoy Baldridge. A Keith Jennison
book (ISBN 0-531-00219-5)
First published 1940
Story of a prize collie belonging to a Yorkshire boy
from a humble home. When the family went on the
dole, Lassie was sold to a wealthy man and taken
hundreds of miles away to Scotland. But Lassie had
still kept her loyalty to a boy in England. She escaped
from the kennels in Scotland and after gruelling hardships, made her way back to her first home

Konigsburg, E. L.

About the B'nai Bagels; written & illus. by E. L.
Konigsburg. Atheneum Pubs. 1969 172p illus lib.
bdg. $5.50, pa 95¢ (4-6)   Fic
1 Jews in the U.S.—Fiction 2 Little league baseball—Fiction
ISBN 0-689-20631-3; 0-689-70348-1
"A warm and humorous story of a Jewish Little
League team. Twelve-year-old Mark Setzer has problems: his mother is manager of the team; his brother is
coach. This makes some sticky situations and 'over-
laps' in his life. And he has worries about losing his
best friend. Mark matures, having to make some difficult decisions on his own." Rdng Ladders. 5th
edition
"Continuing to explore aspects of suburban life, the
author has written a Little League baseball story,
featuring, as chief character, a delightful example of
that increasingly familiar literary heroine, the Jewish
Mother. . . . Penetrating characterization emerge by
implication; and the author's unfailing humor and her
deep understanding of human nature are as notice-
able as ever." Horn Bk

From the mixed-up files of Mrs Basil E. Frankweiler; written and illus. by E. L. Konigsburg.
Atheneum Pubs. 1967 162p illus $6.95, pa $1.50
(4-7)   Fic
1 New York. Metropolitan Museum of Art—Fiction
ISBN 0-689-20586-4; 0-689-70308-X
Awarded the Newbery Medal, 1968
"Claudia, feeling misunderstood at home, takes her
younger brother and runs away to New York where
she sets up housekeeping in the Metropolitan
Museum of Art, making ingenious arrangements for
sleeping, bathing, and laundering. She and James also
look for clues to the authenticity of an alleged Michelangelo statue, the true story of which is locked in the
files of Mrs Frankweiler, its former owner. Claudia's
progress toward maturity is also a unique introduction
to the Metropolitan Museum." Moorachian. What is a
City?

"An exceptional story, notable for superlative writing, fresh humor, an original theme, clear-eyed
understanding of children, and two young protagonists whom readers will find funny, real and unforgettable." Bk World

Jennifer, Hecate, Macbeth, William McKinley,
and me, Elizabeth; written and illus. by E. L. Konigsburg. Atheneum Pubs. 1967 117p illus lib. bdg. $5.95,
pa 95¢ (4-6)   Fic
1 Negroes—Fiction 2 School stories
ISBN 0-689-30007-7; 0-689-70296-5
"Jennifer, who claims to be a witch, at first over-
whelms and dominates her new classmate Elizabeth,
who is convinced by coincidences that Jennifer really
has magic powers. Elizabeth's gradual self assertion
leads to a fight and real friendship. Incidental and
inconspicuously woven in is the fact that Jennifer is
Negro and Elizabeth is white." Bruno. Bks for Sch
Libraries, 1968
"A brilliant engrossing, funny, sad, and touching
book. . . . Mrs. Konigsburg draws children as they are,
rather than as adults would like them to be. Jennifer is
not at all polite; Elizabeth is not above lying to her
elders; and the one child thought perfect by 'every
grown-up in the whole U. S. of A.' is known by
Elizabeth for what she really is: two faced and mean.
. . . All in all, Mrs. Konigsburg has stirred realism and
humor into a triumphant brew." Bk Week

A proud taste for scarlet and miniver; written and
illus. by E. L. Konigsburg. Atheneum Pubs. 1973
201p illus map $6.95 (5-7)   Fic
1 Eleanor of Aquitaine, consort of Henry II—
Fiction
ISBN 0-689-30111-1
This is an historical novel about the 12th century
queen, Eleanor of Aquitaine, wife of kings of France
and England and mother of King Richard the Lion
Heart and King John. Impatiently awaiting the arrival
of her second husband, King Henry II, in heaven, she
recalls her life with the aid of some contemporaries
The author "has succeeded in making history
amusing as well as interesting. . . . The characterization is superb—not only of Eleanor, who dominates
the Tales, but of aesthetic Abbot Suger, who was
responsible for the invention of Gothic architecture,
and of William the Marshal, who always backed the
winning Plantagenet. . . . The black-and-white drawings are skillfully as well as appropriately modeled
upon medieval manuscript illuminations and add
their share of joy to the book." Horn Bk

Krumgold, Joseph

. . . and now Miguel; illus. by Jean Charlot. Crowell
1953 245p illus $5.50 (6-7)   Fic
1 Shepherds—Fiction 2 Sheep—Stories 3 New
Mexico—Fiction
ISBN 0-690-09118-4
Awarded the Newberry Medal, 1954
"A memorable and deeply moving story of a family
of New Mexican sheepherders, in which Miguel,
neither child nor man, tells of his great longing to
accompany men and sheep to summer pasture, and
expresses his need to be recognized as a maturing
individual. Harmonious illustrations." Cincinnati
The "seasonal life of the shepherds is realistically
and sensitively drawn. Nevertheless the book's appeal
is likely to be limited because of the introspective
character that the author has given to Miguel and
because of the stylized form in which the tale is told."
Ontario Library Rev

Henry 3; drawings by Alvin Smith. Atheneum
Pubs. 1967 268p illus lib. bdg. $5.95 (5-7)   Fic
ISBN 0-689-30010-7

Krumgold, Joseph—*Continued*

"Every time the family moved, Henry had found himself an outcast [because of his high I.Q.]; now they had reached the top, and he hoped that Fletch, who had discovered his secret, wouldn't tell. 'The top' was [Crestview], an upperclass New York suburb, just the right setting for a successful young executive, and for the first time Henry 3 was part of a group. Until the bomb shelter, that is. Directed by the company president to install it, Mr. Lovering did, and thereby aroused a deep hostility in his neighbors. Strangely enough, it was the misfit and loner, Fletcher, who proved to be Henry's one real friend when trouble came, and through him Henry learned to shed the strictures of conformity." Sat Rev

"Despite the underlying concern with social issues and moral values, this is a warm and engaging story about a special boy, his friends and, most of all, his parents." Bk World

Onion John; illus. by Symeon Shimin. Crowell 1959 248p illus $4.95 (5-7)   Fic
ISBN 0-690-59957-9
Awarded the Newbery Medal, 1960

The story, "at once humorous and compassionate, of Andy Rusch, twelve, and European-born Onion John, the town's odd-jobs man and vegetable peddler who lives in a stone hut and frequents the dump. Andy . . . tells of their wonderful friendship and of how he and his father, as well as Onion John, are affected when the Rotary Club, at his father's instigation, attempts to transform Onion John's way of life." Booklist

"This is certainly one of the distinguished books of our time with all the literary finesse and perceptiveness of 'Miguel' and stronger story appeal. The problems it deals with are basic: how understanding can we be of the bits of alien culture and superstition an immigrant clings to? . . . How does a 12-year-old boy meet his father on a man-to-man basis after a conscientious struggle inside? . . . The writing has dignity and strength. There is conflict, drama, and excellent character portrayal. There should be more of this kind of realism in children's books." Library J

Krüss, James

My great-grandfather and I. . . . Tr. from the German by Edelgard von Heydekampf Brühl. Atheneum Pubs. 1964 245p illus $4.50, lib. bdg. $4.13 (3-6)
     Fic

ISBN 0-689-20212-1; 0-689-20214-8
First published 1960 in Germany

"Useful and amusing occurrences and inspirations from the Lobster Shack on Helgoland told to the 'Leathery Lisbeth' and embellished with verses from my great-grandfather and me, carefully put on paper for children of all ages by James Krüss and garnished with more than 200 pictures by Jochen Bartsch." Title page

A boy and his great-grandfather spin stories and rhymes, mostly about words and language

This "is the perfect book to read aloud in family groups for the humor of the conversations begs to be shared. Once adults and children discover together the fun of these rhyming games, they will want to try composing some for themselves. The translation must have been a challenge, yet Mr Brühl has done an excellent job catching the full humor and lilt of the language of the original German." N Y Times Bk Rev

"An utterly original, creative book. . . . Delightful drawings add to the piquant flavor." Horn Bk

Kumin, Maxine

Joey and the birthday present [by] Maxine Kumin [and] Anne Sexton; illus. by Evaline Ness. McGraw 1971 unp illus $4.95, lib. bdg. $4.72 (3-5)   Fic

1 Mice—Stories
ISBN 0-07-035634-3; 0-07-035635-1

Joey was a field mouse who lived in a deserted farmhouse. When a family moved in for the summer he discovered the little boy had a pet, a white mouse named Prince. Joey made friends with Prince and all summer long each night Joey let Prince out of his cage and they played happily together

"Beguiling four-color illustrations complement the gently told story." Booklist

Lagerlöf, Selma

The wonderful adventures of Nils; tr. from the Swedish by Velma Swanston Howard; illus. by H. Baumhauer. Pantheon Bks. 1947 539p illus lib. bdg. $7.19 (4-6)   Fic

1 Fairy tales 2 Sweden—Fiction
ISBN 0-394-91832-0

An abridged edition of the English translation published in two volumes with titles: The wonderful adventures of Nils (1907) and Further adventures of Nils (1911)

"Nils (as Thumbietot), astride the grey goose and flying always several gooselengths behind the others, becomes acquainted with Sweden, its mountains and valleys, its birds and animals, its customs and folklore." Bks for Boys and Girls

"The classic story appears [here] with a rich abundance of the most satisfying pictures it has ever had." Horn Bk

Table of pronunciation: p[541]. Map on lining-papers

Lamorisse, Albert

The red balloon. Doubleday 1957 [c1956] unp illus $5.95, lib. bdg. $6.70 (1-4)   Fic

1 Balloons—Fiction 2 Paris—Fiction
ISBN 0-385-00343-9; 0-385-08289-4
Original French edition published 1956

"The chief feature of this book is the stunning photographs, many in color, which were taken during the filming of the French movie of the same name. A little French schoolboy Pascal catches a red balloon which turns out to be magic. The streets of Paris form a backdrop for a charming story and superb photographs. . . . The photographs will interest any age." Library J

Lampman, Evelyn Sibley

The shy stegosaurus of Cricket Creek; illus. by Hubert Buel. Doubleday 1955 218p illus $4.95 (5-7)   Fic

1 Dinosaurs—Stories
ISBN 0-385-07490-5

Joan and Joey Brown and their widowed mother were trying to make a go of a newly acquired ranch but were having a hard time until Joan and Joey found a real dinosaur, genus stegosaurus, who proved to be a loyal friend

"To an adult it is far-fetched imagining, but Mrs. Lampman's vigorous, humorous style makes it good reading nevertheless. There are delightful line cuts." N Y Her Trib Bks

Langton, Jane

The boyhood of Grace Jones; pictures by Emily Arnold McCully. Harper 1972 210p illus $4.95, lib. bdg. $4.79, pa $1.50 (5-7)   Fic

ISBN 0-06-023686-8; 0-06-023687-6; 0-06-440065-4

"Wrapped up in dreams of adventure and success inspired by the boy hero of her favorite book, [junior high school student, Grace Jones] pays little heed to the admonitions of concerned adults or friends about her tomboyish ways. She meets life with zest and neither the inevitable instances of defeat and disillusionment nor the increasing awareness of her femi-

Langton, Jane—*Continued*

ninity which brings about changes in attitude keep her from developing her own personality in her own way." Booklist

"The author has done more than skim the surface of early adolescence; she has plumbed the wellsprings of memory, has created individual, three-dimensional human beings, and written a wise and wonderfully entertaining book." Horn Bk

Her Majesty, Grace Jones; formerly The majesty of Grace; pictures by Emily Arnold McCully. Harper [1974 c1961] 189p illus $4.79, pa $1.25 (4-7)   **Fic**

1 Depressions—Fiction

ISBN 0-06-023691-1; 0-06-440027-1

Reissue of a title first published 1961, with illustrations by the author, under title: The majesty of Grace

"The story of the Jones family during the Depression, particularly of Grace who, a plain, ordinary girl with six faults, imagines herself the rightful heir to the British throne. During the worrisome, penny-pinching time when Pop is jobless and family treasures, including the car Petunia, are converted into cash, Grace finds it hard to believe that prosperity is just around the corner and writes to her 'real' father, King George, for help. She finally realizes that her escape into pretense is not only foolish but selfish and is relieved to learn that she has virtues that offset her faults." Booklist [Review of 1961 edition]

Lattimore, Eleanor Frances

Little Pear; the story of a little Chinese boy; written and illus. by Eleanor Frances Lattimore. Harcourt 1931 144p illus $5.95, pa 75¢ (1-4)   **Fic**

1 China—Fiction

ISBN 0-15-246682-7; 0-15-652799-5

Little Pear is a solemn-looking, but very mischievous five-year-old Chinese boy. His adventurous nature leads him into many mishaps. He resolves to be good after his antics cause him to fall into the river, an adventure from which he must be rescued

"Simple as it is, this little story has charm and a natural, childlike quality which will endear it to the six and seven-year-olds who are beginning to read to themselves. They will get from it also a picture of how Chinese children live, their toys, their food and their clothes." N Y Her Trib Bks

Lauritzen, Jonreed

The ordeal of the young hunter; with illus. by Hoke Denetsosie. Little 1954 246p illus $4.95 (6-7)   **Fic**

1 Arizona—Fiction 2 Navaho Indians—Fiction

ISBN 0-316-51640-6

"A penetrating story of a young [Navaho] Indian boy's maturing and of his growing understanding of the values of his own culture and of that of the white man. Twelve-year-old Jadih lives with his family on a sheep farm near Flagstaff, Arizona. . . . How he proves his courage, both by killing a cougar and by participating in the annual Powwow at Flagstaff, is told with discernment and . . . real understanding." Chicago. Children's Bk Center

Lawson, Robert

Ben and me; a new and astonishing life of Benjamin Franklin, as written by his good mouse Amos; lately discovered, ed. & illus. by Robert Lawson. Little 1939 113p illus $5.95 (5-7)   **Fic**

1 Franklin, Benjamin—Fiction 2 Mice—Stories

ISBN 0-316-51732-1

This "diary" of Amos the mouse provides a mouse-eye view of the major incidents in Ben Franklin's life

"How Amos, a poor church mouse, oldest son of a large family, went forth into the world to make his living, and established himself in Benjamin Franklin's old fur cap, 'a rough frontier-cabin type of residence,'

and made himself indispensable to Ben with his advice and information, and incidentally let himself in for some very strange experiences is related here in a merry compound of fact and fancy." Bookmark

"The sophisticated and clever story is illustrated by even more sophisticated and clever line drawings." Roundabout of Bks

Mr Revere and I. . . . Set down and embellished with numerous drawings by Robert Lawson. Little 1953 152p illus $5.95 (5-7)   **Fic**

1 Revere, Paul—Fiction 2 Horses—Stories 3 U.S.—History—Revolution—Fiction

ISBN 0-316-51739-9

"Being an account of certain episodes in the career of Paul Revere, Esq., as recently revealed by his horse, Scheherazade, late pride of His Royal Majesty's 14th Regiment of Foot." Subtitle

"A delightful tale which is perfect for reading aloud to the whole family. The make-up is excellent, illustrations are wonderful, and the reader will get a very interesting picture of the American Revolution." Library J

Rabbit Hill. Viking 1944 127p illus lib. bdg. $5.95 (3-6)   **Fic**

1 Animals—Stories

ISBN 0-670-58675-7

Awarded the Newbery Medal, 1945

"The small animals living at Rabbit Hill were excited and concerned about the new folks who were moving into the Big House. Shiftless folk without a garden meant hard times for the animals, planting folks meant good times. The story centres around the Rabbit family—Father, a southern gentleman from Kentucky; Mother, a born worrier; little Georgie, their son, and the pride and joy of the whole community; and the gruff old rabbit, Uncle Analdos." Ontario Library Rev

"Robert Lawson, because he loves the Connecticut country and the little animals of field and wood and looks at them with the eye of an artist, a poet and a child, has created for the boy and girl, indeed for the sensitive reader of any age, a whole, fresh, lively, amusing world." N Y Times Bk Rev

Followed by: The tough winter

The tough winter. Viking 1954 128p illus lib. bdg. $5.95 (3-6)   **Fic**

1 Animals—Stories

ISBN 0-670-72208-1

Sequel to: Rabbit Hill

"The 'Folks' are planning to be away for the winter and have left the house and grounds in the hands of a caretaker and his wife. The caretaker turns out to be a sour man who owns a mean, badly-trained dog, and between them they make life miserable for the small animals. To add to the animals' troubles the winter is an unusually severe one, and only Georgie, Willie, and Father Rabbit are able to stay on the hill throughout the winter months. In the end, of course, the Folks return, the small animals come back to their favorite haunts, and all is well again." Chicago. Children's Bk Center

"The many pictures are from Mr. Lawson in top form, giving us the animals with realism plus his own superb action and humor, and the country scene with striking beauty. The friendliness and courtesy of the familiar creatures and their trust in their Folks and need for them gives younger boys and girls that same sense of kindness and of a special animal world that pervaded 'Rabbit Hill.' " N Y Her Trib Bks

Le Guin, Ursula K.

The farthest shore; illus. by Gail Garraty. Atheneum Pubs. 1972 223p map $6.95 (6-7)   **Fic**

Le Guin, Ursula K.—*Continued*
1 Fantastic fiction
ISBN 0-689-30054-9
Sequel to: The Tombs of Atuan
This book continues "the story of Ged and introduces a new hero, Arren, the young prince who travels with the Archmage Ged on his last perilous mission. The writing has, as the concept has, a majestic intricacy; to appreciate it the reader must enjoy ornate language, the grave discussion of life and death and love and courage, and the tongue-rolling exotic names of a legendary land. In traveling together to the far reaches of Earthsea, Ged and Arren seek the evil spirit who is choking the land, taking the mystic powers from the mages and dragonlords. Using all of his magic in one heroic effort, Ged seals the breach through which potency is being drained and gives up his life in the effort." Chicago. Children's Bk Center

The Tombs of Atuan; illus. by Gail Garraty. Atheneum Pubs. 1971 163p maps lib. bdg. $6.50 (6-7)   Fic
1 Fantastic fiction
ISBN 0-689-20680-1
Sequel to: A wizard of Earthsea
"At the age of five, Arha (or Tenar as she was then called) is taken from her home and consecrated as the High Priestess serving the Nameless Ones, the powers of earth and darkness. Thereafter, her life is spent in the barren Place of the Tombs of Atuan with the other priestesses. In the dark, subterranean Labyrinth of the Tombs, familiar only to her, Arha finds the wizard Ged who is looking for the missing half of the powerful Ring of Erreth-Akbe. Ged forces Arha to decide if he is to live or die and to choose for herself whether to continue to serve the Dark Ones or to escape from her bondage to evil." Sch Library J
"The author has created a successful high fantasy which may be read on a number of levels. But the storytelling is so good and the narrative pace so swift that a young reader may have to think twice before realizing that the adventures that befell Tenar [Arha] were really the experiences that marked the growth of her personality." Horn Bk
Followed by: The farthest shore

A wizard of Earthsea; drawings by Ruth Robbins. Parnassus Press 1968 205p maps $6.50, lib. bdg. $5.97 (6-7)   Fic
1 Fantastic fiction
ISBN 0-87466-057-2; 0-87466-032-7
"An imaginary archipelago is the setting for . . . [this] fantasy about a talented but proud, overzealous student of wizardry. In a willful misuse of his limited powers, the novice wizard unleashes a shadowy, malevolent creature that endangers his life and the world of Earthsea. To atone for his misdeed, Ged goes on a perilous journey through the island kingdom to find the baleful beast and destroy its evil influence." Booklist
A "powerful fantasy-allegory. Though set as prose, the rhythms of the language are truly and consistently poetical." Rdng Ladders. 5th edition
Followed by: The Tombs of Atuan

L'Engle, Madeleine
A wind in the door. Farrar, Straus 1973 211p lib. bdg. $4.95 (6-7)   Fic
1 Fantastic fiction
ISBN 0-374-38443-6
"The protagonists of 'A Wrinkle in Time' [entered below] are embroiled in a new fantasy. . . . The precocious young Charles Wallace is not in good health, and Meg worries, trying to block her thoughts so that Charles Wallace won't be able to read her mind. The 'dragons' he claims to have seen prove to be

a cherubim who appears with a giant Master out of space and time. With Meg's friend Calvin and the school principal, the two unearthly creatures and Meg go on a mission to save Charles Wallace, a mission in which they become infinitesimally small and live inside the boy, in which shadowy duplicates of the principal fight to be recognized as the real Mr. Jenkins, in which they all fight the Echthroi, the spirits of evil, etc." Chicago. Children's Bk Center
"L'Engle mixes classical theology, contemporary family life, and futuristic science fiction to make a completely convincing tale that should put under its spell both readers familiar with the Murrys and those meeting them for the first time. It isn't any advance on Miss L'Engle's earlier work . . . but the formula works as well a second time as it did the first, which is, after all, no small accomplishment." N Y Times Bk Rev

A wrinkle in time. Farrar, Straus 1962 211p $4.50 (6-7)   Fic
1 Fantastic fiction 2 Family—Fiction
ISBN 0-374-38613-7
Awarded the Newbery Medal, 1963
"A brother and sister, together with a friend, go in search of their scientist father who was lost while engaged in secret work for the government on the tesseract problem. A tesseract is a wrinkle in time. The father is a prisoner on a forbidding planet, and after awesome and terrifying experiences, he is rescued, and the little group returns safely to Earth and home." Children's Bks Too Good to Miss
"Truth would make one add that the book has a generous sprinkling of aphoristic quotations in at least seven languages, and that it considers quite seriously the philosophic problems of good and evil." Library J
"It makes unusual demands on the imagination and consequently gives great rewards." Horn Bk
Followed by: A wind in the door

Lenski, Lois
Prairie school. Lippincott 1951 196p illus map $6.95, lib. bdg. $5.19 (4-6)   Fic
1 South Dakota—Fiction 2 School stories 3 Blizzards—Fiction
ISBN 0-397-30194-4; 0-397-30201-0
A story of children who gallop to school on horseback, across the windswept South Dakota plains. Miss Martin is "Teacher," beloved by Darrell and Delores and their schoolmates. The action centers on what follows when a great blizzard sweeps down and isolates the schoolhouse
"The Great Blizzard of 1949 is the setting for this school story which is valuable in showing boys and girls the problems of going to school in the wheat growing prairie country." Pittsburgh
The story is "supplemented by [the author's] drawings which bring the homely setting to life and emphasize the hardy, endearing qualities of the prairie people." N Y Times Bk Rev

Shoo-fly girl. Lippincott 1963 176p illus map $6.95 (4-6)   Fic
1 Amish—Fiction 2 Pennsylvania—Fiction
ISBN 0-397-31607-0
"Suzanna, Pennsylvania-Amish girl nicknamed Shoo-Fly, lives a confined, controlled life, yet a happy one. Curiosity about the non-Amish 'English' neighbors leads her to question, 'Why do we wear bonnets?' 'Why do we wear black aprons?' The answer is that it has always been done this way and the Amish do not change. One gets a vivid glimpse into the inner life of the 'Plain People,' a religious sect who live close to the teaching of the Bible." Rdng Ladders. 5th edition

Lenski, Lois—Continued

Strawberry girl; written and illus. by Lois Lenski. Lippincott 1945 193p illus $5.95 (4-6)   Fic

1 Florida—Fiction

ISBN 0-397-30109-X

Awarded the Newbery Medal, 1946

"A strong sense of place pervades this story of Birdie Boyer, a little Cracker girl who helps her Florida family to raise strawberries and to cope with the shiftless Slaters next door." Hodges. Bks for Elem Sch Libraries

"An authentic regional tale told with humor and vigor." Children's Bks Too Good to Miss

Le Sueur, Meridel

The river road; a story of Abraham Lincoln; illus. by Aldren A. Watson. Knopf 1954 175p illus $2.75, lib. bdg. $5.39 (5-7)   Fic

1 Lincoln, Abraham, President U.S.—Fiction

ISBN 0-394-81551-3; 0-394-91551-8

"A few months in the life of 18-year-old Abe Lincoln during which he seeks an answer for his loneliness and uncertainty in a trip down the Mississippi by raft. The things he sees and experiences along the way help to lay the foundation for his later greatness." Pub W

Lincoln's "place in his small community as a popular storyteller, his preparation for the journey, and the trip itself when he first sees slavery in action—all are convincingly pictured. It is a short story, but a very vivid one with parts which have almost the rhythm of an old folksong." Horn Bk

Levitin, Sonia

Journey to America; illus. by Charles Robinson. Atheneum Pubs. 1970 150p illus lib. bdg. $4.25 (4-7)   Fic

1 Refugees, Jewish—Fiction

ISBN 0-689-20665-8

"A fictionalized account of a young Jewish girl, Lisa, who with her mother and two sisters escape from Hitler's Germany to Switzerland and finally to America where they are reunited with their father. A story of great courage and fortitude." Top of the News

"The first-person narrative reflects the middle girl's experience with a crumbling world in which friends and families are scattered or killed, hunger and illness threaten, and people show unexpected cruelty or kindness. Commendably, neither issues nor ideals intrude on the reader abstractly, but emerge naturally from the human condition portrayed in the story." Booklist

Roanoke; a novel of the lost colony; illus. by John Gretzer. Atheneum Pubs. 1973 213p illus maps $7.95 (6-7)   Fic

1 Roanoke Island—Fiction 2 Virginia—History— Colonial period—Fiction

ISBN 0-689-30114-6

"A strong narrative about a young man in the late 16th century. Then Roanoke Island, off the coast of what is now North Carolina, harbored a small group of English colonists. Their leader John White sailed back to England for supplies and when he returned to the island three years later he could find no living trace of the settlers. Within this true setting the author vividly describes young William, his adjustments to the New World and its unfamiliar problems. William's relationship with the Indians is handled with great sensitivity. The older reader will be absorbed in William's self-conscious search for his purpose and goal in life and the growing contrast between his attitudes and the other settlers." Babbling Bookworm

Lewis, C. S.

The lion, the witch and the wardrobe; a story for children; illus. by Pauline Baynes. Macmillan (N Y) 1950 154p illus $4.95, pa $1.25 (4-7)   Fic

1 Fairy tales

"Four English children walk through the wardrobe in a strange home they are visiting and enter the cold, wintry land of Narnia, which is suffering under the spell of the White Witch. They are guided to the noble lion Aslan and loyally aid him in freeing Narnia and its inhabitants from their unhappy fate." Children's Bks Too Good To Miss

The following other books about the land of Narnia are also available from Macmillan: Prince Caspian $5.95, pa $1.25; The voyage of the Dawn Treader $4.95, pa $1.25; The silver chair $4.95, pa $1.25; The horse and his boy $4.95, pa $1.25; The magician's nephew $4.95, pa $1.25; The last battle $5.95, pa $1.25

Lewis, Elizabeth Foreman

Young Fu of the upper Yangtze; illus. by Ed Young; introduction by Pearl S. Buck. [Rev. ed] Holt 1973 267p illus $5.95 (5-7)   Fic

1 China—Fiction

ISBN 0-03-007471-1

First published 1932. Awarded the Newbery Medal, 1933

Set in China in the 1920's, this story describes the adventures of Young Fu, a country boy, who goes with his widowed mother to live in the city of Chungking, and is apprenticed to a master coppersmith

"This handsome fortieth-anniversary edition . . . has subtle pen-and-ink drawings, a brief historical introduction by Pearl Buck, and concluding background notes enlarged to contrast facts about old and new China." Booklist

Glossary of Chinese words: p253-55

Lexau, Joan M.

Archimedes takes a bath; illus. by Salvatore Murdocca. Crowell 1969 56p illus $3.95, lib. bdg. $4.70 (3-5)   Fic

1 Archimedes—Fiction

ISBN 0-690-09899-5; 0-690-09900-2

Archimedes had to decide whether the king's crown was pure gold or whether the crownmaker had cheated by putting in silver. Young Xanthius had to see to it that Archimedes remembered to eat and bathe every day, and this was difficult because the latter was so preoccupied. However, when Archimedes was forced to bathe, he made a very important discovery

This is "a sprightly story that very deftly weaves into the fictional matrix some scientific facts. . . . The almost-cartoon style illustrations are admirably suitable for the sophisticated nonsense of the tale. A brief epilogue gives some facts about the life and work of Archimedes, pointing out which characters in the story are fictional." Chicago. Children's Bk Center

Striped ice cream; illus. by John Wilson. Lippincott 1968 95p illus $4.95 (2-4)   Fic

1 Birthdays—Fiction 2 Negroes—Fiction

ISBN 0-397-31046-3

"Mama had refused to go on welfare. She worked in a button factory and tried to augment a scanty income by outside cleaning. The older children helped with housework and odd jobs, but Becky, the youngest, feared that with Mama worrying about new school shoes for five children she might not have chicken-spaghetti and striped ice cream (vanilla, strawberry and chocolate) for her eighth birthday." Bk World

"Despite the upright tone and somber notes of realism that creep in, Miss Lexau has achieved an

Lexau, Joan M.—*Continued*

exceedingly warm and satisfying story of a [Negro] city family that is true to childhood." N Y Times Bk Rev

Lifton, Betty Jean

The cock and the ghost cat; illus. by Fuku Akino. Atheneum Pubs. 1965 32p illus lib. bdg. $5.25 (2-4)   Fic

1 Roosters—Stories 2 Fairy tales 3 Japan—Fiction
ISBN 0-689-30039-5

"Koko, a beautiful red cock, lives with Gembei, an elderly Japanese farmer, and every morning crows loudly to awaken the village. When a ghost cat in disguise tries to kill Gembei, Koko sacrifices his own life to save his master's." Wis Library Bul

"A dramatic and poignant tale based on a Japanese legend. . . . Strong illustrations in the style of Japanese brush painting." LC. Children's Bks. 1965

The dwarf pine tree; illus. by Fuku Akino. Atheneum Pubs. 1963 37p illus lib. bdg. $3.87 (2-4)   Fic

1 Pine—Stories 2 Japan—Fiction 3 Fairy tales
ISBN 0-689-20238-5; 0-689-20239-3

"The youngest in a forest of pine trees longed to become a dwarf tree, beautiful enough to make the princess well again. His sacrifice cost him intense pain and his life—but not before his purpose was achieved." Cincinnati

A "legend of the forest pine which through selflessness attained rare and beneficent beauty. Perfect harmony of poetic language and artistic illustration." Top of the News

The one-legged ghost; illus. by Fuku Akino. Atheneum Pubs. 1968 unp illus lib. bdg. $5.95 (2-4)   Fic

1 Japan—Fiction
ISBN 0-689-30019-0

In this Japanese folktale, "a mysterious creature with a round body, one bamboo leg, oiled paper skin, and 40 wooden bones comes flying into a Japanese village from the other side of the mountain. The puzzled villagers proclaim the apparition a god and build it a mountain-top shrine. The pictures shortly reveal to readers that the ghost is really an umbrella, but not until the end of the tale does a little boy discover its usefulness in keeping off the rain." Booklist

"Fresh and imaginative, the story is told in bland style with sly humor; the illustrations, chiefly black and white, combined strong lines and delicate shadings to charming effect." Sat Rev

Linde, Gunnel

The white stone; tr. from the Swedish by Richard and Clara Winston; illus. by Imero Gobbato. Harcourt 1966 185p illus $4.50 (4-7)   Fic

ISBN 0-15-295910-6

Original Swedish edition, 1964

This is "a rather extraordinary story of two children—both of them loners—and their private escape-world of offbeat adventure. Fia lived with her pretty widowed mother, a piano teacher, in an apartment at the back of the Judge's house. To her small-town, provincial schoolmates she was 'Fia-plink-plonk' Peters; to the Judge's shrewish housekeeper (the aproned witch) she was an unmitigated nuisance. Across the street was the boy Hampus, an orphan, living in sordidness and poverty with his uncle and a big, quarreling family. A smooth, round stone became for the children a symbol of mutual triumph as each in turn claimed the stone after completing a difficult—and often outrageous—escapade. Befriended by the wise and realistic Judge, the children began to see

their problems resolved and the world in proper perspective. Characterizations are vivid full-length portraits, often humorous, always convincing." Horn Bk

Lindgren, Astrid

Christmas in Noisy Village, by Astrid Lindgren and Ilon Wikland; tr. by Florence Lamborn. Viking 1964 30p illus lib. bdg. $6.50 (1-4)   Fic

1 Christmas stories 2 Sweden—Fiction
ISBN 0-670-22106-6

Original Swedish edition 1963

"A little girl old enough to help with the preparations and young enough to enjoy fully every aspect of Christmas tells of the joyful time the seven children of Noisy Village have for three days before Christmas and then on Christmas Day itself." Horn Bk

"The charming pictures showing the seven children happily engaged in such activities as baking cookies, cutting and decorating trees, eating Christmas Eve supper, and going to church are delectably detailed in full color. An irresistible book for the Christmas season." Booklist

Mischievous Meg; pictures by Janina Domanska; tr. by Gerry Bothmer. Viking 1962 139p illus lib. bdg. $3.50 (3-6)   Fic

1 Sweden—Fiction
ISBN 0-670-47806-7

Original Swedish edition, 1960

"Meg, 'almost ten,' lives happily with her parents and small sister Betsy in a big house by a river in Sweden. She wants to be a good girl, but an impulsive, excitement loving nature often interferes." Chicago Sunday Trib

"The story has interesting details about Swedish holiday traditions as well as giving a good picture of Sweden today." Chicago. Children's Bk Center

Pippi in the South Seas; tr. by Gerry Bothmer; illus. by Louis S. Glanzman. Viking 1959 126p illus lib. bdg. $3.50, pa 95¢ (3-6)   Fic

ISBN 0-670-55711-0; 0-670-05037-7

Original Swedish edition 1957; first English edition, translated by Marianne Turner published 1957 in England

Pippi "goes to the South Seas to visit her sea-captain father and . . . her young friends, Tommy and Anika, from next door are allowed to go along. So is Pippi's horse, which she is . . . able to carry with one arm. Pippi's tongue is as caustic as ever, her remarks to adults as shocking (and as close to what many children would often like to say). She can pull a shark out of the ocean, squeeze its sharp nose and tell it to go home. She can outthink the craftiest villain. The particular m xture of realism and magic in these stories is unique." Horn Bk

Pippi Longstocking; tr. from the Swedish by Florence Lamborn; illus. by Louis S. Glanzman. Viking 1950 158p illus lib. bdg. $3.95, pa 95¢ (3-6)   Fic

1 Sweden—Fiction
ISBN 0-670-55745-5; 0-670-05019-9

Original Swedish edition, 1945

Nine-year-old Pippi is a little Swedish girl who "lives alone with her horse and monkey, and foils all attempts of police, schools, and polite neighbors to make her conform to the accepted social pattern. Her wild doings are shared by a very 'nice,' normal little boy and girl who live next door. Her rare conversation includes tall tales of her life in many lands, with her father, a ship's captain. Sometimes Pippi admits she invents, but her hoards of gifts and of gold pieces are real. . . . It is ably, vivaciously translated by Florence Lamborn, and most amusingly illustrated." N Y Her Trib Bks

"Pippi's fantastic stories and humorous escapades

Lindgren, Astrid—*Continued*
exemplify many of the frustrations of normal children. They will, therefore, delight young readers."
N Y Times Bk Rev

Lindquist, Jennie D.
The golden name day; pictures by Garth Williams. Harper 1955 247p illus lib. bdg. $5.79, pa $1.50 (3-5)   Fic
  1 Swedes in the U.S.—Fiction 2 Country life—Fiction 3 New England—Fiction
  ISBN 0-06-023881-X; 0-06-440024-7
"A summer with Swedish friends on a New England farm was full of delights for nine-year-old Nancy, except for one thing—the Swedish calendar did not include her name day. When a way was found to allow her to share the Swedish custom of celebrating a name day, all was perfect." Hodges. Bks for Elem Sch Libraries
Followed by: The little silver house

Lippincott, Joseph Wharton
The Wahoo bobcat; illus. by Paul Bransom. Lippincott 1950 207p illus $6.25 (5-7)   Fic
  1 Lynx—Stories 2 Florida—Fiction
  ISBN 0-397-30198-7
"A great bobcat roamed the swamps of Florida and was hunted by all except Sammy, a boy who became his friend and protector. A dramatic story with vivid background and colorful characters, useful to encourage conservation." Hodges. Bks for Elem Sch Libraries

Wilderness champion; the story of a great hound (5-7)   Fic
  1 Dogs—Stories 2 Canada—Fiction
  Some editions are:
Grosset $2.95 (ISBN 0-448-02191-9)
Lippincott $5.95, lib. bdg. $4.82 Illustrated by Paul Bransom (ISBN 0-397-30099-9; 0-397-31320-9)
  First published 1944 by Lippincott
"On the way to his ranger cabin in the Alberta mountains, Johnny loses his favorite pup, Reddy, and this exciting, colorful story tells how Reddy becomes the running mate of King, an old black wolf, how he returns to Johnny, wins fame as a hunter and then goes back to stay with King, his 'first loyalty,' until the old wolf's death." Bookmark
The author's "style is forthright, unpretentious, but he can make you remember the wilderness and the suspense of the chase, the savagery of titanic battles, almost as clearly as if you had seen them first hand." N Y Times Bk Rev

Little, Jean
Kate. Harper 1971 162p $4.95, lib. bdg. $5.79, pa $1.25 (4-6)   Fic
  1 Jews—Fiction 2 Friendship—Fiction
  ISBN 0-06-023913-1; 0-06-023914-X; 0-06-440037-9
  Sequel to: Look through my window
Emily's character sketch of her best friend seems almost perfect, but she does not mention that Kate is half Jewish because it does not seem a real part of her character. Kate's image of herself changes during the following year as she gains new insight into relationships with her family, her friends and her Jewish heritage
"A convincing as well as entertaining story, in which a realistic plot is laced with humor and brisk dialog." Pub W

Look through my window; pictures by Joan Sandin. Harper 1970 258p illus lib. bdg. $5.79, pa $1.25 (4-6)   Fic
  1 Family—Fiction 2 Friendship—Fiction
  ISBN 0-06-023924-7; 0-06-440010-7
Emily's very predictable life as an only child suddenly changes when her family moves into an eighteen-room house and her cousins—those wild Sutherland kids—come to stay with them. She discovers that life in a big family can be rewarding if sometimes exasperating and after meeting Kate she discovers both the hurts and the joys of true friendship
"The small but absorbing crises of family life are described with vitality, and the book is garlanded with Emily's and Kate's rapt discussions of books and their candid exploration of what it means to be Jewish (as Kate is)." Sat Rev
Followed by: Kate

Mine for keeps; with illus. by Lewis Parker. Little 1962 186p illus $5.95 (4-6)   Fic
  1 Cerebral palsy—Fiction 2 Physically handicapped—Fiction
  ISBN 0-316-52793-9
"Sarah Jane Copeland, home from a cerebral palsy center, is unhappy not to get the pampering she had expected from her parents. In caring for a timid puppy and helping a sick boy, Sarah Jane forgets her self-pity and begins to lead a normal life. An interesting story with insight into the problems of rehabilitating the handicapped." Hodges. Bks for Elem Sch Libraries
"One of the most valuable aspects of the book is in the depiction of Sally's family; they are real people, who try to help, but who make mistakes and lose their tempers." Chicago. Children's Bk Center

One to grow on; illus. by Jerry Lazare. Little 1969 140p illus $4.95 (4-6)   Fic
  1 Family—Fiction
  ISBN 0-316-52796-3
This story "focuses on a twelve-year-old middle child who, wanting attention, lies to such an extent that her family distrusts her. Through a hurtful experience with a schoolmate, Lisa, who is a malicious liar, and the help of a discerning and sympathetic godmother who gives her a vacation away from her family, Janie comes to understand her own problem and Lisa's and is able to be herself and to accept Lisa as she is." Booklist
"The story flows easily, and the characterization and relationships are especially vivid in the depiction of shifting allegiance in Janie's circle of friends and in the warm realistic family scenes." Sat Rev

Take wing; illus. by Jerry Lazare. Little 1968 176p illus $5.95 (4-6)   Fic
  1 Slow learning children—Fiction
  ISBN 0-316-52795-5
"Although her parents refuse to admit it, Laurel knows that there's something wrong with her younger brother. When her mother is hospitalized, Laurel's aunt comes to take over the household—and the family is forced to acknowledge the fact that seven-year-old James is retarded." Library J
"The author has written an absorbing story that is a thoroughly realistic treatment of a too common situation in which parents ignore reality to the detriment of the whole family. Recommended reading for parents and teachers as well as for young people." Horn Bk

Lively, Penelope
The ghost of Thomas Kempe; illus. by Antony Maitland. Dutton 1973 186p illus $6.50 (4-6)   Fic
  1 Great Britain—Fiction 2 Ghost stories
  ISBN 0-525-30495-9
"Workmen getting an English cottage ready for its new tenants break an old bottle and let loose the spirit of Thomas Kempe, a sorcerer whose mortal remains have been buried since 1639. Thus begin the persecu-

Lively, Penelope—*Continued*

tions and perils of young James Harrison, a prankish boy who moves into the house and is blamed for the high jinks of the ghost. Aware that he can't convince his pragmatic parents that the house is haunted and that he is not to blame for the tricks played when the vicar comes to call, as well as other disasters, Jim seeks out an exorcist." Pub W

"Although the British vocabulary and spelling may seem strange at times to middle graders, they are sure to enjoy this exciting and involving tale of the supernatural." Sch Library J

Lofting, Hugh

Doctor Dolittle; a treasury. Lippincott 1967 246p illus $5.95 (4-6)   Fic
1 Animals—Stories
ISBN 0-397-30937-6
Compiled by Olga Fricker

"Adventures from eight Doctor Dolittle books, with many illustrations, some never before published. Each story is complete in itself, with continuity provided by the Doctor and his animals. Especially recommended for reading aloud." Hodges. Bks for Elem Sch Libraries

Children "can still discover the humane and unfrenzied pleasures of life with the world's most winning polyglot." Newsweek

Lord, Beman

Mystery guest at left end; pictures by Arnold Spilka. Walck, H.Z. 1964 62p illus lib. bdg. $4.95 (2-5)   Fic
1 Football—Fiction
ISBN 0-8098-2030-7

Amusing things begin to happen when two members of the Packers football team allow their 'cousin George'—a girl—to play left end

Quarterback's aim; pictures by Arnold Spilka. Walck, H.Z. 1960 60p illus lib. bdg. $4.95, pa 75¢ (2-5)   Fic
1 Football—Fiction
ISBN 0-8098-2013-7; 0-8098-2904-5

"Alan wanted to play football, but he only weighed fifty-two pounds. No matter how many malteds and bananas he ate, his weight did not improve. But he had another asset, which finally won him his desire

"Easy-to-read, but still brisk and funny with lively pictures to match." Horn Bk

Shrimp's soccer goal; pictures by Harold Berson. Walck, H.Z. 1970 62p illus lib. bdg. $4.95 (2-5) Fic
1 Soccer—Fiction
ISBN 0-8098-2070-6

"Shrimp and his friends adjust to the fact that the new teacher is a soccer fan. Shrimp, who had been looking forward to playing football with Mr. Allen, the teacher who left, was not enchanted, but Miss Taylor was enthusiastic and knowledgeable, and her fervor sparked not only the team of boys and girls but also their cheering classmates." Sutherland. The Best in Children's Bks

"The description of soccer is smoothly incorporated, the balance of game sequences and other interests is sensible, and the prowess of the new team believably moderate. Lively drawings add to the attraction of a good story." Sat Rev

Lovelace, Maud Hart

Betsy-Tacy; illus. by Lois Lenski. Crowell 1940 112p illus $3.95, lib. bdg. $4.70 (2-4)   Fic

1 Friendship—Fiction 2 Minnesota—Fiction
ISBN 0-690-13804-0; 0-690-13805-9

"Betsy and Tacy (short for Anastacia) were two little five-year-olds, such inseparable friends that they were regarded almost as one person. This is the story of their friendship in a little Minnesota town in the early 1900's

The author "has written a story about two very natural, very appealing little girls. More than this, she has written a story of real literary merit as well as one with good story interest." Library J

Followed by: Betsy-Tacy and Tib

The Valentine Box; illus. by Ingrid Fetz. Crowell 1966 unp illus $3.95, lib. bdg. $4.70 (2-4)   Fic
1 Valentine's Day—Stories 2 Negroes—Fiction
3 School stories
ISBN 0-690-85659-8; 0-690-85660-1

The author "gives an excellent portrayal of how a little girl feels in a new neighborhood and a new school, when she has not been there long enough to get acquainted before Valentine's Day. The fact that Janice is a Negro child (only in the realistic pencil illustrations is the reader so informed) is beside the point. . . . At school there is a Valentine Box, and Janice wonders if she will receive any cards. It is a snowy day, and on the way back to school after lunch Janice helps a classmate rescue her valentines from a gusty wind. This makes for a happy and natural ending." Sch Library J

McCloskey, Robert

Centerburg tales. Viking 1951 190p illus lib. bdg. $6.95 (4-7)   Fic
ISBN 0-670-20977-5
Sequel to: Homer Price

"The small-town characters of 'Homer Price,' . . . reappear in this story, as funny as ever and still telling tall tales. The author's lively drawings add to the fun." Hodges. Bks for Elem Sch Libraries

"The actual incidents of the story are not completely original, but the characters are so believable, the situations so hilarious, that you feel you have discovered something new." Ontario Library Rev

Homer Price. Viking 1943 149p illus lib. bdg. $5.95, pa 95¢ (4-7)   Fic
ISBN 0-670-37729-5; 0-670-05074-1

Six blithe stories about the adventures of an American boy, Middlewestern variety. Homer is a poker-faced youth to whom almost anything might happen, and usually does. Sometimes he is catching burglars with the aid of his pet skunk, Aroma, or making nonstop doughnuts in his uncle's lunchroom; again he is discovering the Super-Duper, comic strip hero, has feet of clay

"This boy is a real boy, thinking out loud and living out these rich and hilarious dilemmas with solemn and devastating humor." Horn Bk

Followed by: Centerburg tales

MacDonald, Betty

Mrs Piggle-Wiggle; illus. by Hilary Knight. Lippincott 1957 118p illus $4.95 (2-4)   Fic
ISBN 0-397-30380-7

Chapters follow "the amazing versatility of Mrs Piggle-Wiggle who loves children good or bad, who never scolds but who has positive cures for 'Answer-Backers,' 'Never-Want-To-Go-To-Bedders,' and other children with special problems." Bks for Deaf Children

Macdonald, George

At the back of the North Wind (4-6)   Fic
1 Fairy tales
Some editions are:
Dutton (The Children's illustrated classics) $4.50
With 8 colour plates and line drawings by E. H.
Shepard (ISBN 0-525-25997-X)
Macmillan (N Y) (The Macmillan classics) lib. bdg.
$4.95 With illustrations by Harvey Dinnerstein.
Afterword by Clifton Fadiman
First published 1871. Appeared first in: Good
Words for the Young, a children's magazine
"There is a rare quality in Macdonald's lovely fairy
tales which relates spiritual ideals with the everyday
things of life. This one tells of Diamond, the little son
of a coachman, and his friendship with the North
Wind who appears to him in various guises." Bks for
Boys & Girls

The light princess (3-6)   Fic
1 Fairy tales
Some editions are:
Crowell $5.95, lib. bdg. $6.70 Illustrated by William
Pène du Bois (ISBN 0-690-49307-X; 0-690-49308-8)
Farrar, Straus (An Ariel book) lib. bdg. $3.95 With
pictures by Maurice Sendak (ISBN 0-374-34455-8)
First published 1893 by Putnam as a story in: The
light princess, and other fairy tales
"The problems of the princess who had been de-
prived, as an infant, of her gravity and whose life hung
in the balance when she grew up." Sutherland. The
Best In Children's Bks
"Having no gravity and no weight, the little princess is always in danger of floating away. The Du Bois
pictures give her personality if not weight." Adventuring with Bks. 2d edition

The princess and the goblin (3-6)   Fic
1 Fairy tales
Some editions are:
Dutton (Children's illustrated classics) $4.50 Illus-
trated by Charles Folkard (ISBN 0-525-37771-9)
Macmillan (N Y) (New Children's classics) lib. bdg.
$4.95 Illustrated by Nora S. Unwin
First published 1872
"Living in a great house on the side of a mountain in
a country where hideous spiteful goblins inhabit the
dark caverns below the mines, little Princess Irene
and Curdie the miner's son have many strange adventures. . . . To adults Macdonald's stories have an
allegorical significance, to each succeeding generation of children they are wonderful fairytale adventures." Four to Fourteen

McGinley, Phyllis

The most wonderful doll in the world; with drawings by Helen Stone. Lippincott 1950 unp illus $3.95
(1-4)   Fic
1 Dolls—Fiction
ISBN 0-397-31525-2
Angela, the most wonderful doll in the world,
existed only in the imagination of Dulcy, who had lost
Angela the same day she had received her. But each
time Dulcy told the story of her loss she added some
new details of the glories that were Angela's
"The difference between reality and the dream is
the motive of this beguiling story. The illustrations
add charm of mood and color." N Y Pub Library

The plain princess; with pictures by Helen Stone.
Lippincott 1945 62p illus $6.95 (2-4)   Fic
1 Fairy tales
ISBN 0-397-30107-3
"Rich and spoiled Princess Esmeralda has everything her heart desires except good looks. In this
charming, whimsical fairy tale sensible Dame Goodwit, knowing how to change 'a Plain Young Lady into a
Beautiful Young Lady,' takes Esmeralda to live in her
shabby but cheerful, busy cottage where, during
months of work and play with Dame Goodwit's five
lovely daughters, the Princess, little by little, acquires
a down-tilted nose, a dimply smile and a twinkle in her
eye." Bookmark
"Charm, wit and common sense are deftly combined in this endearing story. The gaiety of the text is
sustained in the illustrations." N Y Pub Library

McGraw, Eloise Jarvis

The golden goblet. Coward-McCann 1961 248p lib.
bdg. $5.97 (5-7)   Fic
1 Goldsmithing—Fiction 2 Egypt—Fiction
ISBN 0-698-30534-5
"Though Ranofer dreams of being a goldsmith, he is
apprenticed as a stonecutter to his cruel half brother.
When he proves that his brother is a tomb robber,
Ranofer is free to follow his dream. Exciting story,
vivid characterization, and excellent recreation of
ancient Egypt." Hodges. Bks for Elem Sch Libraries

Mara, daughter of the Nile. Coward-McCann 1953
279p $6.95 (5-7)   Fic
1 Egypt—Fiction
ISBN 0-698-20087-X
Set in ancient Egypt, when the court was torn by a
rivalry between Queen Hatshepsut and her young
half-brother, this novel concerns the dangerous and
romantic role played by Mara, a slave girl, on both
sides of the royal intrigue
"The book contains many details about Egyptian
life. The characters are solid flesh and blood beneath
their ancient costumes and the vigor of their thoughts,
emotions and actions lend an appeal beyond that of
historical fiction. This is a good full bodied story." N Y
Times Bk Rev

Moccasin trail. Coward-McCann 1952 247p $6.75
(5-7)   Fic
1 Crow Indians—Fiction 2 Frontier and pioneer
life—Fiction 3 Oregon—Fiction
ISBN 0-698-20092-6
Runaway ten-year-old Jim Keath, trapping for
beaver in the vast wild country beyond the Missouri
River, is left for dead after a grizzly's attack. Found
and adopted by Crow Indians, he grows up knowing
only the Indian's wandering restless life. A mysterious
letter, signed by a brother he has not seen in nine
years, points a new trail—to Oregon and reunion with
a family he has all but forgotten
"This distinguished and unusual pioneer and Indian
tale concerns the inner conflicts of Jim Keath in his
attempt to return to the white man's way of living after
he had spent six years with Crow Indians." Minnesota

MacGregor, Ellen

Miss Pickerell goes to Mars; illus. by Paul Galdone.
McGraw 1951 128p illus $3.95, lib. bdg. $4.72 (4-6)
          Fic
1 Space flight to Mars—Fiction 2 Science fiction
ISBN 0-07-044560-5; 0-07-044559-1
"Whittlesey House publications"
When Miss Pickerell returned from her month's
vacation she was very surprised to find someone had
been living in her house and that a large rocket ship
was in her pasture. How Miss Pickerell took off with
the rocket ship crew, and what she found on Mars are
told here
"This mixture of humor and scientific fact will
please nine to eleven year olds, with its many funny

MacGregor, Ellen—*Continued*

pictures and large type. Miss Pickerell is a happily drawn character, a most welcome intruder into the cold world of interstellar space." N Y Her Trib Bks

The following books about Miss Pickerell are also available from McGraw: Miss Pickerell and the Geiger counter $4.95, lib. bdg. $4.72 (ISBN 0-07-044561-3; 0-07-044554-0); Miss Pickerell and the weather satellite $4.95, lib. bdg. $4.72 (ISBN 0-07-044569-9; 0-07-044570-2); Miss Pickerell goes on a dig lib. bdg. $4.72 (ISBN 0-07-044574-5); Miss Pickerell goes to the Arctic lib. bdg. $4.72 (ISBN 0-07-044564-8); Miss Pickerell goes undersea $4.95, lib. bdg. $4.72 (ISBN 0-07-044562-1; 0-07-044558-3); Miss Pickerell harvests the sea $4.95, lib. bdg. $4.95 (ISBN 0-07-044571-0; 0-07;044572-9); Miss Pickerell meets Mr H. U. M. $4.95, lib. bdg. $4.72 (ISBN 0-07-044577-X; 0-07-044578-8); Miss Pickerell on the moon $4.95, lib. bdg. $4.72 (ISBN 0-07-044552-4; 0-07-044551-6)

MacKellar, William

A very small miracle; illus. by W. T. Mars. Crown 1969 120p illus $3.95 (4-6)   Fic

1 Orphans and orphans' homes—Fiction 2 Scotland—Fiction

ISBN 0-571-502496

"Young books from Crown"

Set in Scotland, this story "centers on the friendship which develops between an orphaned boy, grieving over the death of his deceased father's old sheep dog, and an embittered recluse who, scorned as a drunkard and unbeliever by the villagers and Jamie's stern guardian, lovingly cares for numerous wild creatures in his isolated cottage. Concerned about Murdo MacMunn's seeming lack of faith, Jamie Cameron prays for God to bring him, Jamie, a puppy for Christmas to prove to his friend that miracles can happen as well as to fill the void left by the death of old Rab." Booklist

Macken, Walter

The flight of the Doves. Macmillan (N Y) 1968 200p lib. bdg. $5.95, pa 95¢ (4-6)   Fic

1 Runaways—Fiction 2 Ireland—Fiction

"Orphaned Finn and his younger sister Derval, brutally mistreated by Uncle Toby, their legal guardian, run away from their English home. Concentrating upon a vague memory of a visit long ago to Granny O'Flaherty in the west of Ireland, Finn carefully plots their escape. Walking, hiding, begging rides, sometimes sustained by beneficent strangers, or hindered by unscrupulous ones, the children—a brave and believable pair—cross the Irish sea and begin their journey toward freedom." Horn Bk

"The sights and sounds of Ireland are in this book, the seedy streets and the pinched urban existence as well as the blue mountains in the distance. The impetus, however, lies in the characters of Finn and Derval. They shine out like two good little deeds in a naughty world." N Y Times Bk Rev

McKillip, Patricia A.

The house on Parchment Street; drawings by Charles Robinson. Atheneum Pubs. 1973 190p illus $5.95 (5-7)   Fic

1 Ghost stories 2 Great Britain—Fiction

ISBN 0-689-30090-5

"An American teenager comes to England for a month's stay with relatives. Carol finds her cousin Bruce hostile and she herself is ill-at-ease; however, when Bruce realizes that Carol too has seen the cellar ghosts that intrigue him, he changes his attitude. The

ghosts—a beckoning girl who speaks, and a man who fades into the wall, cannot be seen by adults. The mystery of the ghosts' behavior is ferreted out, and they are appeased and vanish after some detective work by the cousins." Chicago. Children's Bk Center

This is "a thoroughly satisfying tale of mystery and secret adventure, much wider in appeal than the usual ghost story." Sch Library J

McMeekin, Isabel McLennan

Journey cake; illus. by Nicholas Panesis. Messner 1942 231p illus $3.95 (5-7)   Fic

1 Wilderness Road—Fiction 2 Negroes—Fiction 3 Chapman, John—Fiction

ISBN 0-671-74380-5

In 1793, Gordon Shadrow had gone West to Kentucky to make a new home for his wife and children who were to follow him in the spring. The wife died suddenly, leaving the six children in the care of Juba, a freed slave. Despite strong opposition of the town elders, Juba led her charges on the long trek until they were reunited with their father. Johnny Appleseed appears in the story

"Freshness, authenticity and fine characterization mark this account of a journey along the Wilderness Road to Kentucky in the 1790's." N Y Pub Library

McNeer, May

Stranger in the pines; illus. by Lynd Ward. Houghton 1971 248p illus $4.95 (5-7)   Fic

1 Runaways—Fiction 2 New Jersey—Fiction

ISBN 0-395-12367-4

"Set in the ore bogs and pine barrens of southern New Jersey in the 1830s, the story traces the flight of an embittered fifteen-year-old orphaned boy who falsely assumes he killed his master in escaping from a hated, enforced apprenticeship. Burdened by his sense of guilt and fearful of recapture, Adam Quinn keeps moving from one job to another until he finds a new purpose in life working with a black herb-doctor and his wife and gains the courage to face up to his problems." Booklist

"The text is full of perceptive social and religious comments via the dialogue and deeds of the characters; it shows different faiths and races . . . working together for a common goal in crisis. The plot is skillfully woven, and outcomes fortunately are not always predictable. And, the settings are varied even though they cover only a relatively small geographical area, providing a background of contrasting customs and communities." Sch Library J

McNeill, Janet

The battle of St George Without; illus by Mary Russon. Little [1968 c1966] 188p illus $5.95 (5-7)   Fic

1 Great Britain—Fiction

ISBN 0-316-56294-7

First published 1966 in England

Once Dove Square "had been an exclusive residential neighborhood, but now the old houses were cut up into small apartments, and the local population, which tended to be poor, was mixed in every way. At the center of the square proper was the church of St George Without, long closed. Its roof was being stripped by thieves until a group of neighborhood children tenaciously and quietly foiled them." Sat Rev

"The writing style has resilience and humor, and the author gives a lively and varied picture of the urban neighborhood in which, amongst the transient people, live those who remember the old days." Chicago. Children's Bk Center

Followed by: Goodbye, Dove Square

McNeill, Janet—*Continued*

Goodbye, Dove Square; illus. by Mary Russon. Little 1969 196p illus $5.95 (5-7)   Fic

1 Great Britain—Fiction

ISBN 0-316-56290-4

Sequel to: The battle of St George Without

The book is "set two years later, when the Dove Square residents have all left the area, cleared for renewal. Matt Mudge discovers that an old man still lives there, hiding in the basement of a deserted house. Matt, determined to protect old Mr. Frick, tries to fend off an inquisitive and unpleasant salesman whose motives he suspects. He discovers that the man had once hidden some money in the old house and is sure that Mr. Frick knows where it is." Sutherland. The Best in Children's Bks

"It is not necessary to have read the first book . . . to enjoy the second. . . . [The children are] drawn into a terrifying and wholly believable adventure with an ex-convict, and it is a tribute to Miss McNeill's art that much as we—and Matt—hate and fear this man, we are also filled with compassion for him. At the book's end the children are learning to let go, both to Dove Square, and to their own childhood." Bk World

McSwigan, Marie

Snow treasure; illus. by Mary Reardon. Dutton 1942 178p illus $5.95 (4-6)   Fic

1 World War, 1939-1945—Fiction 2 Norway—Fiction

ISBN 0-525-39556-3

Set in the early days of the Nazi occupation, this is the story of how a group of Norwegian children managed to get blocks of gold out of Norway by fastening them to their sleds and coasting through the German camps

"A dramatic reconstruction of an actual happening. . . . Well written and superior to previous books about the war in that the actions of the children are planned and controlled by their elders. Striking black and white illustrations." Booklist

Madian, Jon

Beautiful junk; a story of the Watts Towers; with photographs by Barbara and Lou Jacobs, Jr. Little 1968 44p illus $4.95 (2-5)   Fic

1 Los Angeles. Simon Rodia Towers—Fiction 2 Rodia, Simon—Fiction

ISBN 0-316-54352-7

"An old man and two black boys posed for the photographs that help tell the story about the famous Watts Towers in Los Angeles built by Simon Rodia. The text describes how Charlie and a friend learn that broken bottles, tiles, odd lengths of pipe, and other discards can be used to create things of beauty. An old man whom they taunted becomes a friend. The story helps channel negative attitudes and destructive actions into constructive directions." Keating. Building Bridges of Understanding Between Cultures

"The sensitive photography of the real towers is extremely impressive." Rdng Ladders. 5th edition

Mann, Peggy

My dad lives in a downtown hotel; illus. by Richard Cuffari. Doubleday 1973 92p illus $4.50, lib. bdg. $5.25 (3-5)   Fic

1 Divorce—Fiction

ISBN 0-385-07080-2; 0-385-08784-5

This is the story of 10-year-old Joey and his reactions and gradual adjustment to his parents' divorce

"A realistic story of a child's reaction to his parents' separation. . . . The ending is hopeful: Joey's mother spends more time with him, and his father is relaxed and able to spend at least a day with him each week. Cuffari's sensitive, full-page, black-and-white illus-

trations help to create an accurate portrayal of a troubled middle-class family." Sch Library J

The street of the flower boxes; illus. by Peter Burchard. Coward-McCann 1966 71p illus lib. bdg. $4.49 (3-5)   Fic

1 Puerto Ricans in New York (City)—Fiction 2 New York (City)—Fiction 3 Flowers—Stories

ISBN 0-698-30341-5

"Everybody watched the remodeling of the old house and the planting of the window boxes which changed the whole aspect of the drab [New York City] street. Then a gang of boys uprooted the flowers. The new tenants, recognizing Carlos as a leader, enlisted his aid in caring for their next plantings and gradually a new spirit of pride spread all along the street. A convincing story tells how a good example can improve a neighborhood." Moorachian. What is a City?

Mason, Miriam E.

Caroline and her kettle named Maud; with illus. by Kathleen Voute. Macmillan (N Y) 1951 134p illus $3.95 (2-4)   Fic

1 Frontier and pioneer life—Fiction 2 Michigan—Fiction 3 Kettles—Fiction

Caroline was "going on eight" when her family moved to frontier Michigan. She had hoped for a gun for a farewell present, but instead she was given a shiny copper kettle. To add to her woe Old Witch, the cow Caroline hated, went along. But in the wilds of Michigan Caroline's kettle and Old Witch proved just as useful as the gun she did not possess

In large print for "early readers, this offers a very real small girl, plenty of action, and a good honest look at pioneer America." N Y Her Trib Bks

Mathis, Sharon Bell

Sidewalk story; illus. by Leo Carty. Viking 1971 71p illus lib. bdg. $5.95 (3-5)   Fic

1 Friendship—Fiction 2 Negroes—Fiction

ISBN 0-670-64377-7

"An affecting easy-to-read story of a persistent little black girl to whom friendship means caring and helping a friend in trouble. Upset because her best friend Tanya and her family are being evicted and their belongings piled on the sidewalk and frustrated by her own mother's unwillingness to become involved, Lilly Etta phones first the police and then the newspaper for help and in the night creeps out to cover the things with sheets and blankets—and herself—to protect them from the wind and rain. Enhanced by several sensitive double-spread paintings in black and white." Booklist

Mayne, William

Earthfasts. Dutton [1967 c1966] 154p lib. bdg. $5.95 (5-7)   Fic

1 Fantastic fiction 2 Great Britain—Fiction

ISBN 0-525-29008-7

First published 1966 in England

Two twentieth century English boys become involved in unusual adventures when "an eighteenth-century English drummer boy returns to earth carrying a candle which causes the past to become confused with the present and sets off a series of fantastic events involving King Arthur, a boggart, and other legendary characters. For the imaginative reader with sufficient background to appreciate the historical allusions." Hodges. Bks for Elem Sch Libraries

There is an "overuse of old English, and even some Latin, that no average young reader could know without more explanation than is offered. But the flavor of the word is there, if not the meaning, and the bone-chilling adventure is what's really important." N Y Times Bk Rev

Mazer, Harry

Snow bound. Delacorte Press 1973 146p $5.95 (5-7)   Fic

1 Wilderness survival—Fiction

ISBN 0-440-08087-8

"Tony, a pampered only son among four children, steals his mother's car and tears off toward Canada. During a severe snowstorm, he picks up Cindy, a subdued girl who has trouble making friends. After wrecking the car far from the main highway, Cindy and Tony spend 11 perilous days together. It is fascinating to watch them slowly shed their stereotyped boy-girl camouflage, as they discover that interdependence is their only chance for survival." Ms. Gazette

Meader, Stephen W.

Boy with a pack; illus by Edward Shenton. Harcourt 1939 297p illus $5.95 (5-7)   Fic

1 Frontier and pioneer life—Fiction 2 U.S.—History—1815-1861—Fiction

ISBN 0-15-211240-5

"Bill Crawford, 17, sets out from New Hampshire in 1837 to peddle 'Yankee notions' throughout Vermont, New York, Pennsylvania, and Ohio." Hodges. Bks for Elem Sch Libraries

"The story, involving horse thieves in Vermont, canalboat life in New York, and forwarding slaves by the Underground Railroad in Ohio, is continuously readable." New Yorker

"Edward Shenton's drawings are interesting and descriptive, and the end papers show a map of the hero's journey." N Y Times Bk Rev

Red Horse Hill; illus. by Lee Townsend. Harcourt 1930 244p illus $6.95 (5-7)   Fic

1 Horses—Stories 2 New Hampshire—Fiction

ISBN 0-15-266193-X

After his father's death Bud faced the problem of earning a living and found it difficult, until he went to live with the Masons on their New Hampshire farm. In time the lucky winning of a cutter race and the finding of an old will, enabled Bud to look forward to a college education and to setting up a fine dairy herd in partnership with Mr Mason

The author "knows the life of a New Hampshire farming community in the day of oxen and horses. He knows how much horses have meant in that life—workhorses, roadhorses, and racehorses, and he has put it into such a story as will warm the . . . heart of [anyone] . . . who likes horseracing." N Y Her Trib Bks

Meadowcroft, Enid La Monte

By secret railway; illus. by Henry C. Pitz. Crowell 1948 275p illus $4.95 (4-7)   Fic

1 Underground railroad—Fiction 2 U.S.—History—1815-1861—Fiction

ISBN 0-690-16431-9

"Jim, a freed slave boy whose freedom depends on the certificate he keeps in his pocket, seeks shelter with David Morgan, a friendly white boy, in Chicago, 1860. The Morgans take in a boarder, who betrays Jim and kidnaps him in order to get the reward for runaway slaves. Then David sets out to find Jim and set him on his way to Canada by the Underground Railroad. The latter, nineteenth-century Chicago, and Lincoln's election campaign form the historical background." We Build Together

"Not only a stirring adventure story but a fine account of a loyal friendship. Good format and excellent illustrations by Henry Pitz." Library J

The first year; illus. by Grace Paull. Crowell 1946 153p illus $4.95 (4-6)   Fic

1 Pilgrim Fathers—Fiction 2 U.S.—History—Colonial period—Fiction

ISBN 0-690-30349-1

First published 1937 with illustrations by Frank E. Phares

A retelling of the story of life on the Mayflower, and of the Pilgrims in Plymouth during their first year. The Hopkins children: Giles, Constance, Damaris, and Oceanus, who was born on the Mayflower, are the central characters

"Told as simply and directly as if by word of mouth, but with more than the usual amount of accuracy and significant detail than such versions generally include." N Y Times Bk Rev

Includes bibliography

Menotti, Gian Carlo

Gian-Carlo Menotti's Amahl and the night visitors. This narrative adaptation by Frances Frost preserves the exact dialogue of the opera; illus. by Roger Duvoisin. McGraw 1952 86p illus $4.95, lib. bdg. $4.72 (4-7)   Fic

1 Christmas stories

ISBN 0-07-041489-0; 0-07-041484-X

"Whittlesey House publications"

The story of a crippled shepherd boy who entertained the Wise Men on their way to Bethlehem, of the simple gift he gave them for the Christ Child, and of the miraculous gift he received in return

"The wonder and mystery of Christmas are felt anew in the poetically human tale. The illustrations in color and black and white complement the spirit of the text." N Y Pub Library

Merrill, Jean

The Pushcart War; with illus. by Ronni Solbert. Young Scott Bks 1964 222p illus lib. bdg. $4.95 (5-7)   Fic

1 New York (City)—Fiction 2 Trucks—Fiction

ISBN 0-201-09313-8

"By 1976 arrogant, mammoth trucks threaten to crowd people, small cars, pushcarts, and peddlers off the streets of New York. When a truck contemptuously runs down a pushcart, the peddlers rebel and wage a guerrilla war against the trucks, using a primitive, but effective, secret weapon. Funny, dramatic, tongue-in-cheek satire on the sheer bigness which is overwhelming urban life but which is here, for once, defeated by the little people who 'are' the city." Moorachian. What is a City?

The superlative horse; illus. by Ronni Solbert. Young Scott Bks. 1961 79p illus lib. bdg. $4.95 (4-6)   Fic

1 Horses—Stories 2 China—Fiction

ISBN 0-201-09357-9

"This story was suggested by a Taoist tale in the Book of Lieh Tzu, c. 350 B.C. The illustrations were suggested by scenes in the frescoes of the Tun-huang caves in Western China." Half-title page

"The son of a lowly fuel hawker wins the post of High Groom after proving his ability to distinguish between the superior and the inferior in horses. Because his talent has wider application, he later becomes the Chief Minister too." Asia: a Guide to Bks for Children

"An unusual story about ancient China . . . illustrated beautifully in appropriate technique that resembles the art of early China. . . . Although the writing style has a quiet dignity, it does not lack momentum and seems particularly well suited to the period and place." Chicago. Children's Bk Center

Merrill, Jean—*Continued*
The toothpaste millionaire; prepared by the Bank Street College of Education. Houghton [1974 c1972] 90p illus lib. bdg. $5.95 (4-6)   Fic
> 1 Business—Fiction
> ISBN 0-395-18511-4
> First copyright 1972
> Illustrated by Jan Palmer

"The teller of the tale is a classmate of brilliantly inventive sixth-grade Rufus Mayflower, who 'doesn't seem to mind that I'm white and he's black.' Rufus makes and markets an extraordinarily inexpensive toothpaste—which still sells at a low price even when stockholders, promotion, and all the necessary apparatus of a growing business introduce expenses." Horn Bk

The story "is laden rather heavily with arithmetic and business details, but rises above it. . . . The illustrations are engaging, the style is light, the project interesting (with more than a few swipes taken at advertising and business practices in our society) and Rufus a believable genius." Chicago. Children's Bk Center

Miles, Miska
Annie and the Old One; illus. by Peter Parnall. Little 1971 44p illus $5.95 (1-4)   Fic
> 1 Navaho Indians—Fiction 2 Death—Fiction
> ISBN 0-316-57117-2
> "An Atlantic Monthly Press book"

"Annie, a young Navajo girl, struggles with the realization that her grandmother, the Old One, must die. Slowly and painfully, she accepts the fact that she cannot change the cyclic rhythms of the earth to which the Old One has been so sensitively attuned." Wis Library Bul

This is "a poignant, understated, rather brave story of a very real child, set against a background of Navajo traditions and contemporary Indian life. Fine expressive drawings match the simplicity of the story." Horn Bk

Eddie's bear; illus. by John Schoenherr. Little 1970 43p illus lib. bdg. $3.95 (1-4)   Fic
> 1 Bears—Stories
> ISBN 0-316-56967-4
> "An Atlantic Monthly Press book"

"A face-to-face encounter in the forest between a boy and a brown bear causes Eddie to comment that the bear 'seemed almost friendly.' However, when the tawny-colored brother of Eddie's bear crumples the fender of the truck and breaks into the cabin, the brown bear is blamed, captured, branded as an enemy of man, and transported into the wilderness." Booklist

"It looks like a picture book, but the story itself seems geared to older children, and even some of them might find the vocabulary (placidly, pungent, carrion, luxurious) too difficult. Realistic, uncluttered, and impressive illustrations, in black, brown and gold, are the book's best feature." Library J

Hoagie's rifle-gun; illus. by John Schoenherr. Little 1970 40p illus $5.95 (1-4)   Fic
> 1 Appalachian region—Fiction 2 Hunting—Fiction
> ISBN 0-316-57014-1
> "An Atlantic Monthly Press book"

"There are only potatoes left in the garden patch, and Pa is out of work; so Hoagie, who never misses, takes one bullet and the rifle-gun and goes out with his brother Ira to look for meat. Old Bob, an old mountain cat and almost friend, is hunting for his supper, too. Rabbits are hard to find in the barren hills; and when the bobcat gets a rabbit, Hoagie is bitterly angry. Ira sobs as Hoagie aims to shoot Old Bob. At the last instant, Hoagie knows he does not want to kill the cat; he misses. The stark prose bares Hoagie's desperation and records the mounting tension of his hatred until it is resolved in the knowledge that the cat shares a kinship with his family in their struggle for survival. The terse language and the rugged black-and-white drawings convey the staunch independence and spiritual strength of the mountain people." Horn Bk

Mississippi possum; illus. by John Schoenherr. Little 1965 41p illus $3.95 (2-4)   Fic
> 1 Opossums—Stories 2 Negroes—Fiction
> ISBN 0-316-57116-4
> "An Atlantic Monthly Press book"

"The beautiful format and the vivid woodcuts match a significant story, perfectly told. A fearful young possum, who must leave his hollow log for higher ground when the Mississippi floods its banks, creeps into the tent of a family of other refugees and sleeps beside the children. The country Negro family is indigenous to the river banks as is the possum himself. The story is a fine picture of a close-knit family with room in their hearts for a scared little wild creature." Adventuring with Bks. 2d edition

Nobody's cat; illus. by John Schoenherr. Little 1969 43p illus $4.95 (2-4)   Fic
> 1 Cats—Stories
> ISBN 0-316-56969-0
> "An Atlantic Monthly Press book"

"Here are city sights and sounds from the point of view of a tough, resourceful alley cat. Independent rather than homeless, he survives because he knows the ways of the city. Striking, full-page illustrations show him responding to many challenges and encounters, including a brief stay at a school where he accepts attention but does not sacrifice his independence. This convincing, sensitive presentation is written and illustrated with fidelity to the nature of the cat." Moorachian. What is a City?

Otter in the cove; illus. by John Schoenherr. Little 1974 47p illus $5.25 (3-5)   Fic
> 1 Sea otters—Stories
> ISBN 0-316-56970-4
> "An Atlantic Monthly Press book"

"Maggie, whose father is an abalone fisherman, knows that she must tell him that otters (voracious eaters) are in their cove, but the small herd is so entertaining and one of them seems so tame that she is heartbroken when her father says he must kill them. Maggie takes her father's gun and shoots over the otters' heads to frighten them off; she is roundly scolded for using a gun, but her action has made her father realize how important the creatures are to her (he already knows his action would be illegal) and he spares the otters, to Maggie's joy." Chicago. Children's Bk Center

"Although the story borders on melodrama, the simple but vivid prose is complemented by subtly shaded brown ink drawings that expressively mirror Maggie's moods in the changing storminess and calm of nature." Sch Library J

Milhous, Katherine
Appolonia's valentine. Scribner 1954 unp illus lib. bdg. $5.95 (2-5)   Fic
> 1 Pennsylvania Dutch—Fiction 2 Valentine's Day —Stories
> ISBN 0-684-92306-8

In a one-room school in Pennsylvania the teacher showed the children how to make cut-out valentines to be sent as "tokens of love and friendship" to their friends. This story tells how Appolonia who wasn't good with scissors succeeded in making the valentine chosen to be sent to a little French boy

Milhous, Katherine—*Continued*

"The story is delightful and the [author's] illustrations—some of them of valentines—are perfect in color and in design." Horn Bk

Milne, A. A.

The house at Pooh Corner; with decorations, by Ernest H. Shepard. Dutton [1961 c1928] 180p illus $3.95, lib. bdg. $3.91, pa $1.25 (1-4)   Fic

1 Teddy bears—Fiction 2 Animals—Stories

ISBN 0-525-32302-3; 0-525-32303-1; 0-525-45002-5

Sequel to: Winnie-the-Pooh

First published 1928

"Concerned with the adventures and misadventures of Christopher Robin and those quaint small beasties, the astute and poetical Pooh, the melancholy Jaques, Eeyore, the bouncy Tigger, Piglet, Rabbit, Kanga, Roo, and W O L, the burlesque tragic fall of the house of Owl, the mysterious fog in the Hundred Acre Wood, the diverting conversations and recreations of the storied Forest around Pooh Corner, and comedy of errors, the building of a new house for Eeyore." Sat Rev

"It is hard to tell what Pooh Bear and his friends would have been without the able assistance of Ernest H. Shepard to see them and picture them so cleverly. . . . They are, and should be, classics." N Y Times Bk Rev

The Pooh story book; with decorations and illus. in full color by E. H. Shepard. Dutton 1965 77p illus $4.95 (1-4)   Fic

1 Teddy bears—Fiction 2 Animals—Stories

ISBN 0-525-37546-5

Excerpts from: The house at Pooh Corner and Winnie-the-Pooh

Contents: In which a house is built at Pooh Corner for Eeyore; In which Piglet is entirely surrounded by water; In which Pooh invents a new game and Eeyore joins in

This compilation is "illustrated with new pictures by Mr Shepard very much like those drawings he did for the original Milne editions. An attractive book with some pictures in color." Sch Library J

Winnie-the-Pooh; with decorations by Ernest H. Shepard. Dutton [1961 c1926] 161p illus $3.95 (1-4)   Fic

1 Teddy bears—Fiction 2 Animals—Stories

ISBN 0-525-43035-0

First published 1926

" 'Winnie-the-Pooh' is a joy; full of solemn idiocies and the sort of jokes one weeps over helplessly, not even knowing why they are so funny, and with it all the real wit and tenderness which alone could create such a priceless little masterpiece. [Toy] Kanga and baby Roo, Piglet, and above all Pooh and Christopher Robin himself, are characters no one can afford to miss. . . . The drawings by E. H. Shepard which accompany the story are thoroughly delightful." Sat Rev

Map on lining-papers

Followed by: The house at Pooh Corner

The world of Pooh; the complete Winnie-the-Pooh and The house at Pooh Corner; with decorations and new illus. in full color by E. H. Shepard. Dutton 1957 314p illus $7.50 (1-4)   Fic

1 Teddy bears—Fiction 2 Animals—Stories

ISBN 0-525-43320-1

"Despite the fact that separate volumes are usually preferable, many libraries will want this pleasing combination volume." Booklist

Molarsky, Osmond

Song of the empty bottles; illus. by Tom Feelings. Walck, H.Z. 1968 unp illus music $4.95 (2-4)   Fic

1 Negroes—Fiction 2 Music—Fiction

ISBN 0-8098-1142-1

"A music-loving little boy collects bottles and newspapers to earn money for a guitar. Encouraged by Mr Andrews, leader of weekly singing sessions at Neighborhood House, Thaddeus composes a jaunty little song about his collecting experiences. Words and music are given at the end of the book and might stimulate some children to add verses of their own. Realistic pictures show Thaddeus, a Negro child, in the city he knows." Moorachian. What is a City?

"The story line is slim indeed, but the theme is clear—that a folk song comes out of homely activities and yearnings. The pictures establish the mood and the background." Horn Bk

Monjo, F. N.

The Jezebel wolf; illus. by John Schoenherr. Simon & Schuster 1971 47p illus $4.50 (3-5)   Fic

1 Putnam, Israel—Fiction 2 Wolves—Stories

ISBN 0-671-65191-9

"Thi fictionalized account of a true incident in the life of Israel Putnam, the 'Old Put' of the Revolutionary War, is narrated in a natural, conversational style, chiefly as a reminiscence. Putnam's younger son had never heard the story of the wolf his father had killed, and he gets the full details in several installments. The wolf having ravaged the local livestock, was hunted over many miles, and finally trapped and killed in her lair. The author's note explains that, whereas wolves were a menace in colonial times, they are not so now, and every effort should be made to prevent their extinction. The illustrations are stunning, and the tale is told with a storyteller's flair." Sat Rev

King George's head was made of lead; illus. by Margot Tomes. Coward, McCann & Geoghegan 1974 47p illus $5.95 (2-4)   Fic

1 U.S.—History—Revolution—Fiction 2 George III, King of Great Britain—Fiction

ISBN 0-698-20298-8

Events leading to the outbreak of the American Revolution are told "by a statue of King George III which was sent to the colonies in 1770. The figure was toppled by irate patriots; its body was used to make ammunition for the Revolutionary Cause." Pub W

"Bold illustrations in gold, orange, and rust and the use of cartoon bubbles to enclose dialogue underscore the rollicking wit of the text." Sch Library J

Me and Willie and Pa; the story of Abraham Lincoln and his son Tad; illus. by Douglas Gorsline. Simon & Schuster 1973 94p illus $6.95 (3-5)   Fic

1 Lincoln family—Fiction 2 Lincoln, Thomas, 1853-1871—Fiction 3 U.S.—History—Civil War—Fiction

ISBN 0-671-65211-7

"By casting Tad Lincoln as the narrator of the story, the author presents a child's eye view of Lincoln's presidency. Many familiar Lincoln anecdotes are included, yet Tad's innocent observations reveal details about the presidential household normally glossed over: Mrs. Lincoln's extravagances, her hot-tempered jealousy of other women, her interest in spiritualism following the tragic death of her son Willie. And Tad's own problems—his speech defect, his feelings as a student—are also incorporated into a narrative which is honest and poignant and somewhat . . . subdued in tone." Horn Bk

"Illustrations which look like old photographs provide excellent portraits of the Lincolns; the people who were close to them; and other figures of the war

Monjo, F. N.—*Continued*

years. An outstanding [fictionalized] biography that is also a good introduction to the Civil War." Sch Library J

Poor Richard in France; pictures by Brinton Turkle. Holt 1973 58p illus lib. bdg. $4.95 (2-4) Fic
1 Franklin, Benjamin—Fiction
ISBN 0-03-088598-1
Using historical facts, this is the fictional reconstruction of Benjamin Franklin's mission to Paris as supposedly recounted by his seven-year-old grandson
"The drawings are authentic in detail and attractive; the text is historically accurate and lively. . . . Seven-year-old Benny's comments are lively and humorous, and in a perfectly natural way they give a good bit of information about Franklin and about the rebellion against the British." Chicago. Children's Bk Center

Moore, Lilian

The snake that went to school; illus. by Mary Stevens. Random House 1957 114p illus lib. bdg. $4.39 (2-4) Fic
1 Snakes—Stories
ISBN 0-394-90101-0
"Hank Jenkins returned from summer camp with a new pet, a hog-nosed snake much to the delight of his younger brother and the dismay of his mother. When she refused to allow him to keep it at home, he solved the problem by presenting it to the science museum at school. There it caused mixed reactions on the part of teachers and students alike, but was finally accepted." Chicago. Children's Bk Center

Morey, Walt

Deep trouble. Dutton 1971 214p $5.95 (5-7) Fic
1 Skin diving—Fiction 2 Alaska—Fiction
ISBN 0-525-28620-9
After his father's death, eighteen-year-old Joey assumes the support of his family. This story tells of Joey's struggle to convince the Alaskan cannery superintendents that he is capable of doing a good job diving the salmon traps
"The story is told in brisk, easy style with natural dialogue; the characterization is not deep, but the characters are believable and the family relationships well depicted." Chicago. Children's Bk Center

Gentle Ben; illus. by John Schoenherr. Dutton 1965 191p illus $5.95 (5-7) Fic
1 Bears—Stories 2 Alaska—Fiction
ISBN 0-525-30429-0
Set in Alaska before statehood, this is the story of 13-year-old Mark Anderson who befriends a huge brown bear which has been chained in a shed since it was a cub. Finally Mark's father buys the bear, but Orca City's inhabitants eventually insist that the animal, named Ben, be shipped to an uninhabited island. However, the friendship of Mark and Ben endures
The author "has written a vivid chronicle of Alaska, its people and places, challenges and beauties. Told with a simplicity and dignity which befits its characters, human and animal, [it] is a memorable reading experience." Sch Library J

Morgan, Alison

A boy called Fish; illus. by Joan Sandin. Harper 1973 201p illus $4.95, lib. bdg. $5.79 (5-7) Fic
1 Dogs—Stories 2 Wales—Fiction
ISBN 0-06-024351-1; 0-06-024352-X
First published 1971 in England
A Welsh boy nicknamed Fish who lives unhappily with his father and stepmother adopts an abandoned mongrel dog. When the animal is suspected of killing sheep, the boy's father immediately orders it destroyed and Fish runs away with it. The story tells

of his adventures with his friend Jimmy, who sets out during a snowstorm to bring him supplies
"Although the background of the narrative is Welsh farm country, it sets up no barrier to enjoyment by American readers; and the characterization and narration are those of a first-rate story teller." Horn Bk

Morrow, Elizabeth

The painted pig; a Mexican picture book; pictures by René d'Harnoncourt. Knopf 1930 32p illus lib. bdg. $5.99 (1-4) Fic
1 Mexico—Fiction
ISBN 0-394-90745-0
Pita and her little brother Pedro lived in Mexico. Pita had the most fascinating painted China pig, with roses on the back and a tiny rosebud on his tail. The story tells what happened when Pedro wanted that pig or one just like it
It is "a circumstantial story for children a little older than those of picture book age, thus giving to the book a wide range of appeal." N Y Her Trib Bks
Here is "a picture book that children will enjoy for its brilliant colors and gayety, and grownups for its charming introduction to a foreign art. The unusual illustrations . . . [show some of the artist's] collection of Mexican toys in Mexico City." Springf'd Republican

Muehl, Lois

The hidden year of Devlin Bates; illus. by John Martinez. Holiday House 1967 138p illus $3.75 (4-6) Fic
ISBN 0-8234-0045-X
"A very convincing portrait of a 'loner' whose nonconformity and poor achievement at school cause friction and conflict between him and his parents. His gradual acceptance of responsibility and decision to 'make the first move' toward mutual understanding is believable and satisfying. Very well written and timely with excellent characterization and dialogue." Bruno. Bks for Sch Libraries, 1968

Mulock, Dinah Maria

The little lame prince; illus. by Jon Nielsen; introduction by May Lamberton Becker. Collins [1975 c1974] 135p illus $3.50, lib. bdg. $3.91 (4-6) Fic
1 Fairy tales 2 Physically handicapped children—Fiction
ISBN 0-529-05036-6; 0-529-05037-4
"Rainbow classics"
First published 1893; in this edition 1946
"He was the most beautiful prince that ever was born—but he was very unfortunate, and, but for his fairy godmother, would hardly have known the happiness that came to him with his magic cloak. No small child can afford not to know Prince Dolor." Bks for Boys & Girls

Murphy, Robert

Wild geese calling; illus. by John Kaufmann. Dutton 1966 96p illus map $3.75 (4-6) Fic
1 Geese—Stories
ISBN 0-525-42781-3
"A fictionalized story about a pair of Canada Geese begins on their wintering grounds in the Aransas National Wildlife Refuge in Texas, then goes on to describe their northward migration, the nesting and rearing of a brood, and their southward migration in the fall. The relation between a farm boy and a wounded male that later recovers heightens interest." The AAAS Science Bk List for Children
"Information on geese and other birds is handled in good literary style. Bird enthusiasts and conservationists will enjoy this." Sch Library J

Murray, Michele

Nellie Cameron; drawings by Leonora E. Prince. Seabury 1971 185p illus $6.95 (4-6) Fic

1 Reading—Fiction 2 Negroes—Fiction 3 Family—Fiction

ISBN 0-8164-3049-7

"Sometimes a child in a big family can feel she has no place. Nellie was nine, she felt lost in the shuffle, and she was miserably conscious of the fact that she couldn't learn to read. Sent to the school reading clinic, Nellie was both apprehensive and hopeful. Much of the story is devoted to Nellie's progress with a sympathetic teacher, but the book is balanced by family scenes and is perceptive in describing the relationships within the family." Sutherland. The Best in Children's Bks

"The teacher-child relationship has warmth and vitality, and the school sequences are balanced by sharply realistic scenes picturing a black family at home and Nellie's visits with a friend who has moved away." Sat Rev

Neufeld, John

Edgar Allan. Phillips 1968 95p $5.95 (5-7) Fic

1 Race problems—Fiction 2 Family—Fiction

ISBN 0-87599-149-1

Set in a southern California town and "narrated by Michael the twelve-year-old son in Rev. Fickett's family, this records the arrival and adoption of a tiny Negro boy [Edgar Allan] into the well-to-do white family. Mary Nell, the eldest, is . . . bitterly opposed to this manifestation of her parents' sense of righteousness. . . . Nevertheless, Edgar Allan becomes a happy alert child and member of the family until he is enrolled in nursery school. Anger and disapproval from schoolmates and church members, threatening phone calls and division of the once close family circle are the result. After much soul-searching by the members of the Fickett family, they realize that their community is not yet mature enough to accept this source of conflict in its midst." Best Sellers

"There is no melodrama [here], no stunning climax: people of good will have made a gesture and have not been strong enough to withstand pressure. The story is told with thoughtful simplicity, and the reactions and interactions of the family members are perceptive and convincingly drawn." Sat Rev

Neville, Emily Cheney

Berries Goodman. Harper 1965 178p $5.50, lib. bdg. $5.11, pa $1.50 (5-7) Fic

1 Jewish question—Fiction 2 Jews in the U.S.—Fiction

ISBN 0-06-024380-5; 0-06-024384-8; 0-06-440072-7

When his family moves from New York City to the suburbs, Berries Goodman feels uprooted and lonely—an outsider—until he meets another outsider in his class, Sidney Fine. Sidney is Jewish. The situation that develops after Sidney suffers a near-fatal accident forces Berries to recognize the power of prejudice. He does not understand the reason for it; all he understands is that he has lost his best friend

"The book is told in appropriate teen idiom by Berries six years later when he and Sidney find each other again. Far more than a 'problem' story, this is a wonderful chunk of life with good family feeling, outstanding characters and rare understanding." Sch Library J

The Seventeenth-Street gang; pictures by Emily McCully. Harper 1966 148p illus map $4.95, lib. bdg. $4.79, pa $1.25 (5-7) Fic

1 New York (City)—Fiction

ISBN 0-06-024394-5; 0-06-024395-3; 0-06-440019-0

"Minnow dominates a group of boys and girls of mixed ages and backgrounds living in a heterogeneous

New York neighborhood. When a new boy moves into the area, she takes the lead in plans to ostracize him. Discovering that the boy, Hollis, is not bad, other members of the Seventeenth-Street Gang are less eager to go along with Minnow, and they end by putting group pressure on her so that Hollis is accepted." Sat Rev

"Both as a group and as individuals, the children are drawn with devastating clarity. . . . One of the most striking things the author does is to reflect, with percipient fidelity, the double behavior patterns children display as they move from the circle of their peers to the relationships with adults—particularly with parents." Chicago. Children's Bk Center

Nichols, Ruth

A walk out of the world; illus. by Trina Schart Hyman. Harcourt 1969 192p illus $5.95 (4-6) Fic

1 Fantastic fiction

ISBN 0-15-294514-8

"A walk in a forest on an eerie day leads Judith and Tobit into another world, where they find that Judith . . . is the one who must right an ancient wrong. It's been 500 years since a usurper seized the throne in the White City and sent the queen and her family into exile; a restlessness in the earth hints the time is near for his comeuppance." Bk World

"The writing is disciplined and beautiful; the story exciting and triumphant; there is a youthfulness about it that gives it unusual quality. That the moving between the two worlds [fantasy and reality] is accomplished not with the ease of most fantasies but with deep sorrow seems to stem from the intuition of a young writer." Horn Bk

Nordstrom, Ursula

The secret language; pictures by Mary Chalmers. Harper 1960 167p illus $3.95, lib. bdg. $3.79, pa $1.25 (3-5) Fic

1 School stories

ISBN 0-06-024575-1; 0-06-024576-X; 0-06-440022-0

Also available in a large type edition for $7.50 (ISBN 0-06-024577-8)

A "story about two eight-year-old girls at boarding school. None of the experiences that Vicky and Martha have are unusual; none dramatic; yet all of the details of their year make absorbing reading. Vicky is homesick and Martha is a rebel; as they adjust to each other and as they adapt themselves to the pattern of school life, both girls find satisfactions and both grow up a little. The writing style has a gentle humor, a warm understanding, and an easy narrative flow that seems effortless." Chicago. Children's Bk Center

Norris, Gunilla B.

The good morrow; drawings by Charles Robinson. Atheneum Pubs. 1969 92p illus lib. bdg. $5.25 (4-6) Fic

1 Camps—Fiction 2 Negroes—Fiction

ISBN 0-689-20670-4

This "is the tale of a black girl's first experience away from the city, when she goes to summer camp. Josie has not wanted to go to camp in the first place, and her homesickness increases when she finds herself being picked on by an unhappy fellow camper. That her nemesis is a white girl intensifies Josie's fears of being hated because she's 'different,' but she ultimately discovers that Nancy's enmity has nothing to do with skin color." Bk World

"Written with compassion and understanding of the fears and insecurity that can haunt children, regardless of background, this should spark readers' interest and hold it all the way." Sch Library J

Norris, Gunilla B.—_Continued_
Green and something else; illus. by Charles Robinson. Simon & Schuster 1971 48p illus $3.95 (3-5)
Fic
1 Fear—Fiction 2 Mice—Stories
ISBN 0-671-65174-9
"Thinking about the tawny-colored mouse that he longs for comforts Green when he is frightened, and many things frighten Green. He discovers an unexpected courage in himself, however, when his efforts to buy the mouse and make a cage for it require him to face a growling dog, the teasing of older boys, and an eerie deserted house at twilight. A short, credible story which portrays Green's fears with sympathy." Booklist

Norton, Mary
Bed-knob and broomstick; illus. by Erik Blegvad. Harcourt 1957 189p illus $5.50, pa $1.65 (3-5) Fic
1 Fairy tales
ISBN 0-15-206228-9; 0-15-611500-X
A combined edition of: The magic bed-knob, first published 1943 by Putnam and Bonfires and broomsticks, originally published only in England
"In the first book, Carey, Charles, and Paul Wilson, visiting their aunt one summer, meet the very proper Miss Price, who is somewhat embarrassed when the children discover that she is studying to become a witch. Modest as she is about her prowess, Miss Price does succeed in giving to a bed-knob the power of transporting passengers. After some exciting adventures, the children return to London. Two years and one book later, they read an ad inserted by Miss Price for summer boarders. They convince Mrs. Wilson to send them to Miss Price and are dismayed to find that she has given up witchcraft. Urging one last ploy, they negotiate a trip to the past; from the 17th century they return with a necromancer who eventually takes Miss Price back to his own time as his wife. While there is one unpleasant note in text and illustration of Negroid cannibals, the story has the same quiet humor and calm acceptance of the fantastic as does 'The Borrowers' . . . [listed below]." Chicago. Children's Bk Center

The Borrowers; illus. by Beth and Joe Krush. Harcourt 1953 180p illus $5.50, pa $1.50 (3-6) Fic
1 Fairy tales
ISBN 0-15-209987-5; 0-15-613600-7
First published 1952 in England
A "fascinating fantasy about a tiny family that lived beneath the kitchen floor of an old English country house and 'borrowed' from the larger human residents to fill their modest needs. Their sudden discovery by a small boy visitor almost proves to be their undoing. The imaginative details about the activities of the miniature people have tremendous appeal for children." Children's Bks Too Good to Miss
Four additional titles about the Borrowers are available from Harcourt: The Borrowers afield $5.95, pa $1.50 (ISBN 0-15-210166-7; 0-15-613601-5) The Borrowers afloat $5.50, pa $1.35 (ISBN 0-15-210345-7; 0-15-613603-1) The Borrowers aloft $5.50, pa $1.35 (ISBN 0-15-210524-7; 0-15-613604-X) Poor Stainless $4.95 (ISBN 0-15-263221-2) The Borrowers and the first three titles listed above are available in an omnibus volume with title: The complete adventures of the Borrowers $9.50, pa $5.95 (ISBN 0-15-219850-4; 0-15-613605-8)

O'Brien, Robert C.
Mrs Frisby and the rats of NIMH; illus. by Zena Bernstein. Atheneum Pubs. 1971 223p illus lib. bdg. $6.25, pa $1.95 (4-7) Fic
1 Mice—Stories 2 Rats—Stories
ISBN 0-689-20651-8; 0-689-70413-5

Awarded the Newbery Medal, 1971
"Mrs. Frisby, a widowed mouse, is directed by an owl to consult with the rats that live under the rosebush about her problem of moving her sick son from the family's endangered home. Upon entering the rats' quarters, Mrs. Frisby discovers to her astonishment that the rats are not ordinary rodents, but highly intelligent creatures that escaped from an NIMH laboratory after being taught to read. How the rats help Mrs. Frisby and she, in turn, helps them from being captured, is told in a thoroughly enjoyable animal fantasy." Booklist
"The story is fresh and ingenious, the style witty, and the plot both hilarious and convincing." Sat Rev

O'Dell, Scott
Island of the Blue Dolphins (5-7) Fic
1 Wilderness survival—Fiction 2 San Nicolas Island, Calif.—Fiction 3 Indians of North America—Fiction
Some editions are:
Hall, G. K. & Co. $7.95 Large print edition (ISBN 0-8161-6170-4)
Houghton $4.95 (ISBN 0-395-06962-9)
First published 1960 by Houghton
Awarded the Newbery Medal, 1961
"Years of research must have gone into this book to turn historical fact into so moving and lasting an experience." Horn Bk
"Because her brother had missed the ship that was taking their tribe to the mainland, Karana, a young Indian girl, remains with him. After her brother's death she lives alone for eighteen years on this wildly beautiful, treeless island off the coast of California. The struggle for survival is told in grim, realistic detail, alleviated by Karana's ability to find some comfort, beauty, and a measure of happiness in her solitary life. Based on the few facts known about an actual experience, the story is told with stark simplicity beautifully fitted to such a deeply moving experience." Children's Bks Too Good to Miss

The King's fifth; decorations and maps by Samuel Bryant. Houghton 1966 264p maps $5.95 (6-7) Fic
1 Estévan—Fiction 2 Mexico—History—Fiction
ISBN 0-395-06963-7
"Writing at night in his cell between sessions of his 20-day trial for withholding the King's Fifth or royal share of treasure, Estéban de Sandoval, young cartographer with Coronado, recalls all that happened on the hazardous, inglorious journey he made with Captain Mendoza and five others to the Seven Cities of Cibola to find gold. The low-keyed, powerful writing and the first-person narration, which skillfully interweaves Estéban's chronicle of the past with his report of the on-going trial, give a strong sense of reality and immediacy to this compelling, deeply felt story of a boy who, almost too late, comes to realize the awful cost of the lust for gold in honor and human life." ALA Bks for Children, 1966-67

Sing down the moon. Houghton 1970 137p $3.95 (5-7) Fic
1 Navaho Indians—Fiction
ISBN 0-395-10919-1
A "story based on the white and Navajo conflict of the Civil War period. The United States Government, provoked by the raiding of some Navajos, appointed Kit Carson to drive them out of their traditional home place, the Canyon de Chelly in Arizona. The story is told in the first person by a young Navajo girl who is kidnapped and enslaved by Spaniards, then rescued by her husband-to-be. She and her clan are forced out of the Canyon by white soldiers (who burned their peach trees, killed their sheep and

O'Dell, Scott—Continued

destroyed their hogans) and are marched 400 miles, under tragic hardships, to Fort Sumner where they are to make a new life." Library J

"There is a poetic sonority of style, a sense of identification, and a note of indomitable courage and stoicism that is touching and impressive." Sat Rev

Orgel, Doris

Next door to Xanadu; a novel; pictures by Dale Payson. Harper 1969 160p illus lib. bdg. $4.79 (4-6)   Fic

1 Friendship—Fiction 2 Brooklyn—Fiction
ISBN 0-06-024610-3

"Patricia Malone is going to be ten years old soon, but she still has no special friend. Her two great wishes are that she find a friend and that she be thin so that Bill Wexler and Charlie Kriefer won't call her Fatsy Patsy any more. One day when Patricia comes home from school she finds that a family has moved in next door with a girl her own age. Friendship with Dorothy begins to change Patricia's life." Rdng Ladders. 5th edition

"There is no major action in the story, but the realistic and perceptive events and relationships are touched with humor and told in a style that is convincingly that of a girl of ten." Sutherland. The Best in Children's Bks

Ormondroyd, Edward

Time at the top; illus. by Peggie Bach. Parnassus Press 1963 176p illus $5.50 (5-7)   Fic

1 Fantastic fiction
ISBN 0-87466-029-7

"The elevator in her apartment house traveled past the top floor one day, and carried Susan Shaw to a Victorian mansion that had stood on the same site in 1881. With Robert and Victoria Walker, Susan unearthed a buried hoard of gold and rescued Mrs. Walker from a fortune hunter. This appealing combination of mystery and fantasy contrasts noisy, hectic, twentieth century city life with quiet, leisurely country life in the same area a hundred years previously, and ends with an original surprise." Moorachian. What is a City?

"The plot is sturdy and well-paced, the writing style lively and easy; the conversation is especially good, with some of the adult characters being etched with mild acidity in some monologues." Chicago. Children's Bk Center

Otis, James

Toby Tyler; or, Ten weeks with a circus. Harper 1923 251p front lib. bdg. $3.79 (4-6)   Fic

1 Circus—Fiction 2 Monkeys—Stories
ISBN 0-06-024616-2
First published 1880

"Little Toby ran away from home with the lemonade man to join the circus, and then worked very hard to run away from the circus and go home again. In the meantime he had made several good friends, including the Living Skeleton and Mr. Stubbs, the monkey." Bks for Boys & Girls

Ottley, Reginald

Boy alone; illus. by Clyde Pearson. Harcourt [1966 c1965] 191p illus $5.95 (5-7)   Fic

1 Ranch life—Fiction 2 Dogs—Stories
3 Australia—Fiction
ISBN 0-15-210682-0

First published 1965 in England with title: By the sandhills of Yamboorah

"On an isolated cattle ranch in Australia a nameless boy works as a 'wood and water joey.' His aloneness, his longing for a dog to call his own, and his relationships with other workers on the ranch are understandingly depicted." Hodges. Bks for Elem Sch Libraries

This book "conveys powerfully the feel of Australia and the feeling of adolescence." Times (London) Lit Sup

Followed by: The roan colt

The roan colt; illus. by David Parry. Harcourt [1967 c1966] 159p illus $5.50 (5-7)   Fic

1 Ranch life—Fiction 2 Horses—Stories
3 Australia—Fiction
ISBN 0-15-267700-3

Sequel to: Boy alone

First published 1966 in England with title: The roan colt of Yamboorah

The young hero of this story, "a 'wood and water joey' at an Australian cattle-station, becomes attached to a roan colt which must be shot. With two Aborigine girls he resolves to hide it until Kanga, the native animal expert, returns—and will, perhaps, be allowed to spend the time necessary to correct the colt's defective hoof. One of the vicious bush fires of Australia's central country reveals their secret." N Y Times Bk R

"The vast distances of Australia, the atmosphere of a cattle station, the kind of people who work on it are magnificently evoked in [this book]." Christian Sci Monitor

Paradis, Marjorie

Mr De Luca's horse; drawings by Judith Brown. Atheneum Pubs. 1962 167p illus lib. bdg. $3.48 (4-7)   Fic

1 Horses—Stories 2 New York (City)—Fiction
ISBN 0-8382-0532-1

Set in New York City. "Brett shares a studio apartment with his father, an art teacher at his school, during his mother's convalescence away from home. The companionship of father and son is warm and happy. Brett has a friendly relationship, too, with a junkman, whose ancient horse he admires and aims to buy—if he can earn and save sufficient money (Brett also plans to buy an electric beater as a home-coming gift for his mother). Economic setbacks and accidents increase suspense and emotional involvement up to the happy conclusion. Outstanding for characterization." Horn Bk

Parish, Helen Rand

Estebanico. Viking 1974 128p map $5.95 (5-7) Fic

1 Estévan—Fiction 2 Mexico—History—Fiction
ISBN 0-670-29814-X

"Estebanico's report to Charles V, King of Spain, starts with his birth in Africa and concludes shortly before he departs on the expedition to the Seven Cities of Cibola where he lost his life. Emphasis is on the journey from Florida to Mexico City when Estebanico, along with his master Don Andrés Dorantes, Cabeza de Vaca, and Captain Castille covered territory never before explored by Europeans." Sch Library J

"The writing is appropriately stylized, the author's theories intriguing, and the tale grim and exciting." Booklist

Peake, Katy

The Indian heart of Carrie Hodges; illus. by Thomas B. Allen. Viking 1972 125p illus lib. bdg. $4.95 (4-7)   Fic

1 Animals—Stories
ISBN 0-670-39788-1

"Young Carrie's unusual sensitivity to animals and affinity for the land enchanted the taciturn lion hunter, Foster Grant. He brought her a puppy and began taking her on long rides into the hills sharing with her his vast knowledge of animals and Indian lore. Carrie's growing competence in tracking and observing wildlife and her solitary quest for her own Indian spirit animal are encouraged by parents who

Peake, Katy—*Continued*

exhibit much warmth and understanding for their unique daughter." Elementary English

"In a well-written story that effectively conveys a feeling for nature and a sense of Indian mysticism the portrayal of Carrie is particularly sensitive." Booklist

Pearce, Philippa

The squirrel wife; design & illus. [by] Derek Collard. Crowell [1972] c1971 61p illus $4.50, lib. bdg. $5.25 (2-4)   Fic

1 Fairy tales

ISBN 0-690-76678-5; 0-690-76679-3

First published 1971 in England

"One stormy night Jack the swineherd 'goes out and saves a 'green man' whom a tree has crushed nearly to death. In return, the 'green people,' fairy rulers of the forest, give Jack a ring with which he wins the love of a marvelous, mysterious being, part forest creature, part woman: the squirrel wife. Then his elder brother, enraged by Jack's happiness, connives to have Jack thrown in jail. And there he stays till the squirrel wife, at great cost, sets him free." N Y Times Bk Rev

"The artist-designer has embellished the story fittingly. His intricate linocuts are printed with rich overlays of dark wood colors. Both pictures and text are printed on beige paper in the same brown ink as the borders of intertwining vines and leaves. Extraordinary lettering-designs emphasize an occasional important sentence, word, or phrase. A combination of the arts has produced an exceptional book." Horn Bk

Tom's midnight garden; illus. by Susan Einzig. Lippincott 1959 [c1958] 229p illus $5.25 (4-7)   Fic

1 Fantastic fiction

ISBN 0-397-30475-1

First published 1958 in England, where it was awarded the Carnegie Medal as the outstanding English children's book of that year

"Tom would rather have stayed home at the risk of catching measles from his brother than spend the holidays with his unimaginative uncle and aunt in their pokey flat with its chilling and unwelcome atmosphere. But one night, when the old grandfather clock struck thirteen, and Tom crept downstairs to investigate, he discovered a wonderful garden with well laid out flower beds and, best of all, very climbable trees. In daylight the garden vanished and only in his nocturnal visits did he find it waiting for him. Here he met Hatty, a little girl of the late Victorian era. The secret of his garden and his passage back into time continued to puzzle Tom, until he and Hatty found a clue in the grandfather clock. In the end Tom was able to provide his own theory of Time." Ontario

"The author claims as her readers those of '9 up': rightly so, for this brilliant fantasy on the theme of time has a quality capable of capturing all ages. . . . A work of the greatest distinction." New Statesman

Peck, Robert Newton

Soup; illus. by Charles C. Gehm. Knopf 1974 96p illus $4.95, lib. bdg. $5.49 (5-7)   Fic

1 Friendship—Fiction 2 Vermont—Fiction

ISBN 0-394-92700-1; 0-394-82700-7

"Peck strings together a series of . . . autobiographical recollections centered around boyhood good times with his friend Soup. . . . Peck tells of their throwing apples from sticks and inevitably breaking a window, rolling down a hill inside a barrel, or sneaking a smoke from cornsilk 'tobacco' in an acorn pipe. Neighborhood characters add color to the tellings. Janice Riker, the only person Soup is afraid of, is expert at captive and torture games; Aunt Carrie constantly wishes thrashings on Peck, but we are treated to her comic downfall as a trussed-up captive in a downpour." Booklist

"Rural Vermont during the 1920's is the setting for this nostalgic account. . . . In a laconic and wryly humorous style, the author relates the activities of the mischievous twosome. . . . The black-and-white pencil drawings, artistically executed in the manner of Norman Rockwell, reflect the understated story." Library J

Perl, Lila

That crazy April. Seabury 1974 188p front $5.95 (5-7)   Fic

1 Family—Fiction 2 Women's Liberation Movement—Fiction

ISBN 0-8164-3117-5

"Eleven-year-old Cress Richardson is caught in an identity crisis between her ardent 'women's rights' mother and her 'male chauvinistic' teacher and friends. . . . While she is working it out, her beautiful model friend, Monique, gets Cress a job in a department store bridal show as a 'boy' page. Further complications in Cress' dilemma arise when her brilliant and beloved cousin, Xandra, decides to quit college to get married, much to Cress' mother's disapproval." Babbling Bookworm

"One of the best feminist stories to appear so far. . . . Although her mother wants to make a crusading issue out of Cress's exclusion from metal-working club, Cress is adamantly non-crusading. The gamut of feminist issues is dealt with, often humorously, but with clarity and suspense. Not at all didactic, the story has humor, tension, sound character development, and a loving but liberated family." Children's Bk Rev Serv

Phipson, Joan

The boundary riders; illus. by Margaret Horder. Harcourt [1963 c1962] 189p illus $3.50 (5-7)   Fic

1 Australia—Fiction

ISBN 0-15-210681-2

First published 1962 in England

"Three young Australians, two boys and a girl, set out to spend a week checking the ranch's fence where it runs through a stretch of rugged foothills. All goes well until they do some unscheduled exploring and become hopelessly lost." Pub W

"It is a story of courage and suspense with well-drawn characters and vivid description of the countryside." Wis Library Bul

The family conspiracy; illus. by Margaret Horder. Harcourt [1964 c1962] 224p illus $5.95, pa 65¢ (5-7)   Fic

1 Australia—Fiction 2 Family—Fiction

ISBN 0-15-227110-4; 0-15-630150-4

First published 1962 in England

"The resourceful children in this Australian [Barker] family conspire to earn money themselves when they believe there are no family funds to pay for their mother's necessary operation. Mrs Barker is a believable character who demonstrates the firm and selfless nature of many a mother." Cincinnati

Followed by: Threat to the Barkers

Good luck to the rider; illus. by Margaret Horder. Harcourt 1968 186p illus $4.75 (5-7)   Fic

1 Ranch life—Fiction 2 Horses—Stories 3 Australia—Fiction

ISBN 0-15-231706-6

First published 1953 in England

"Barbara, a frail twelve-year-old Australian girl, feels that she must be as good a horseback rider as her older sister. Barbara finds a colt in the woods whose mother has been killed and decides to raise the colt herself. Through her love for this colt, Barbara overcomes her own weakness." Rdng Ladders. 5th edition

"The story is distinguished by good characterization

Phipson, Joan—*Continued*
and vividly drawn scenes of Australian boarding-school and ranch life." Booklist

The way home. Atheneum Pubs 1973 184p lib. bdg. $5.50 (5-7) Fic
1 Australia—Fiction 2 Fantastic fiction
ISBN 0-689-30322-X
"A Margaret K. McElderry book"
"Lost in the Australian wilderness after their car is overturned by a flash flood, three young people struggle to survive. Escaping from a brush fire, they find themselves moving through different time periods from the prehistoric past into the future. . . . The locale is convincingly evoked, characterization is good, and the transition from the present to the past and future is smoothly done." Sch Library J

[Politzer, Anie]
My journals and sketchbooks [by] Robinson Crusoe. Harcourt 1974 78p illus map $5.95 (4-7) Fic
1 Survival (after airplane accidents, shipwrecks, etc.)—Fiction
ISBN 0-15-267836-0
Text by Anie Politzer. Drawings by Michel Politzer
Original French edition published 1972
Based on Daniel Defoe's novel Robinson Crusoe, this work is presented as a newly-discovered journal and sketchbook in which the "real" Robinson Crusoe describes his experiences after being shipwrecked and the items he constructed in order to survive
"The drawings are handsome, meticulously detailed and spirited; we feel the artist, Michel Politzer, deserves special credit. The reader is given graphic examples of the animal and plant life of Crusoe's island, of how he learned to make baskets and tools, of his home and ingenious ways of coping with his lonely, exiled years." Pub W

Pope, Elizabeth Marie
The Perilous Gard; illus. by Richard Cuffari. Houghton 1974 280p illus $5.95 (6-7) Fic
1 Great Britain—Fiction 2 Druids and Druidism—Fiction *other Bk (Rev Sherwood Ring Way)*
ISBN 0-395-18512-2
"Kate Sutton, lady-in-waiting to Princess Elizabeth, is exiled because her . . . sister, Alicia, has dispatched a critical letter to Queen Mary Tudor. Sent to Perilous Gard, an old castle in Derbyshire surrounded by many odd legends, Kate meets Randal, an old half-witted minstrel; Sir Geoffrey Heron, master of the castle; and Sir Geoffrey's younger brother Christopher. Through clues in Randal's songs, Kate stumbles on the secret of the castle: it is the last stronghold of the Fairy Folk (or People of the Hill). Discovering his long-believed dead niece is held by the Fairies as their next sacrifice, Christopher exchanges himself for the child and Kate, witnessing the agreement, is also taken captive.'" Sch Library J
"Pope blends a scholar's knowledge of Tudor England with a liberating dash of fantasy. . . . [Her story] borders on the ridiculous, but [she] has crafted all these complicated ingredients into an exciting adventure. Never suggesting that her Fairy Folk are anything more than human, she makes the fanatic priestesses completely credible. And Kate—brave, down to earth, self-effacing—is a noble foil to the fantastic doings above and below ground. But best of all is the author's use of old English ballads and riddle songs as keys that unlock the mystery of the Gard." Christian Sci Monitor

Potter, Beatrix
The tale of the faithful dove; illus. by Marie Angel. 2d ed. Warne 1970 unp illus lib. bdg. $2.50 (2-4) Fic

1 Pigeons—Stories
ISBN 0-7232-1336-4
Written in 1907. First published 1956
"A gentle story of a little pigeon who was chased into a chimney by a hawk. An unillustrated, posthumous manuscript by the author which is illustrated [by Marie Angel] and printed in the style and format of the other Potter books." Best Bks for Children, 1972

Wag-by-Wall; with decorations by J. J. Lankes. Horn Bk. 1944 unp illus $2 (3-5) Fic
ISBN 0-87675-076-5
This book "tells of Sally Benson, who lived by herself in a little thatched cottage with one handsome piece of furniture, the clock Wag-by-Wall, left her by her grandfather, and her singing kettle. This homely tale flows as quietly and serenely as Sally's life in the little cottage with the ticking clock and the kettle's song." N Y Times Bk Rev
"The delicate woodcut illustrations are completely in keeping with the story. It is a distinguished little book and one that has enduring value." Sat Rev

Rankin, Louise
Daughter of the mountains; illus. by Kurt Wiese. Viking 1948 191p illus lib. bdg. $4.95 (4-7) Fic
1 India—Fiction 2 Tibet—Fiction
ISBN 0-670-25787-7
Story of a Tibetan girl who makes a long journey from her wild mountain home to the coast of India to try to find her dog who has been stolen. Description of the country and an air of mystery and suppressed excitement are evident throughout the book
"Intimate knowledge of the country enabled Miss Rankin to make not only the people and the monastery real, but the very pass itself with its twists and sharp descents, its rocks and forests. It is a beautiful and inspiring book with pictures that fit in every respect." Horn Bk

Raskin, Ellen
Figgs & phantoms. Dutton 1974 152p illus $5.95 (5-7) Fic
1 Family—Fiction
ISBN 0-525-29680-8
Illustrated by the author
"This concerns Mona Lisa Newton, fat and frustrated member of the Figg Newton family in the town of Pineapple. Of the Figg Newton family, which includes ex-variety show stars Truman the Human Pretzel and uncles Romulus and Remus, Mona loves only Uncle Florence Italy Figg—a book dealer who dreams of dying and going to Capri, the Figg fantasy heaven. When Florence dies, Mona embarks on a clue-solving search for Capri, takes a wild mind trip, and returns a wiser and happier person." Booklist
"It's a mad, mad, mad, mad book. . . . Yeasty style and high humor should appeal to all readers except those who like their fiction served up with sobriety." Chicago. Children's Bk Center

The mysterious disappearance of Leon (I mean Noel). Dutton 1971 149p illus $5.50, pa 95¢ (4-7) Fic
1 New York (City)—Fiction 2 Mystery and detective stories
ISBN 0-525-35540-5; 0-525-45010-6
"Wed at the age of five to a seven-year-old husband (it solved a business difficulty for their two families), the very young Mrs. Leon Carillon immediately loses her spouse, who is sent off to boarding school. This is the hilarious account of her search for Leon, aided by adopted twins, when she is older. With clever clues to stimulate the reader's participation, the story is a bouquet of wordplay garnished with jokes, sly pokes

Raskin, Ellen—*Continued*

at our society, daft characters, and soupçon of slapstick. Fresh and funny, it's the kind of book that passes from child to child." Sat Rev

The author "has ingeniously incorporated a word puzzle, a game about names and turns of mind and phrase in her first full-length novel (a mystery). The result is a highly original romp into comedy and absurdity in both text and illustrations." Pub W

The tattooed potato and other clues. Dutton 1975 170p $7.50 (5-7)   Fic

1 Mystery and detective stories
ISBN 0-525-40805-3

"The book consists of mini-mysteries within a larger suspense story and stars a teenaged girl who suffers from her name, Dickory Dock. Her life is altogether unsatisfactory, since she lives with her selfish brother and his wife in a grubby flat. But Dickory, an art student, lands a post as apprentice to an eccentric Greenwich Village artist, Garson. Then the fun begins as artist and assistant are called upon by the police for help in solving a number of crimes." Pub W

Rawlings, Marjorie Kinnan

The secret river; illus. by Leonard Weisgard. Scribner 1955 unp illus lib. bdg. $5.95, pa 95¢ (1-4)   Fic

1 Florida—Fiction
ISBN 0-684-13119-6; 0-684-12636-2

"When hard times come to the Florida forest, a small girl sets out with her dog to find the secret river where there are reported to be quantities of fish. She finds the river, catches a large string of fish, and returns home. Her father sells the fish to the people of the community, who regain their strength once they have eaten a good meal and are again able to work and bring prosperity back to the forest. The little girl searches for, but never again finds the secret river." Chicago. Children's Bk Center

"A strange, haunting tale which lends itself to different interpretations, according to age and temperament. . . . Certainly this is not a story for realists who demand a definite answer, but for the imaginative it will have an indefinable quality of wonder." N Y Times Bk Rev

Rich, Louise Dickinson

Three of a kind; illus. by William M. Hutchinson. Watts, F. 1970 151p illus lib. bdg. $4.90 (4-6) Fic

1 Foster home care—Fiction 2 Problem children—Fiction 3 Maine—Fiction
ISBN 0-531-01837-7

Until eleven-year-old Sally, an orphan and ward of the state, came under the foster care of the Coopers in Maine, she had never really known a good home. But the arrival of Benjie, the Coopers' silent and withdrawn grandson, marred her happiness as their attention centered upon him. Gradually, as Sally learned to care about Benjie, she and a homeless kitten played important parts in bringing about his emergence into the real world

"The way in which each of the characters reacts to Benjie, and the way in which the child begins to react, slowly at first and then in a rush, are logical; the characters are vibrantly real and the total picture of the island community balanced and sympathetic." Chicago. Children's Bk Center

Richter, Hans Peter

Friedrich; tr. from the German by Edite Kroll. Holt 1970 149p lib. bdg. $4.50 (5-7)   Fic

1 Jews in Germany—Fiction 2 Germany—Fiction
ISBN 0-03-012721-1
Mildred L. Batchelder Award, 1972
Original German edition, 1961

In Germany in 1929 two-4-year-old boys, one a Jew named Friedrich, become friends. History envelops them, and through a series of tragic events the reader sees how this friendship is affected. The story ends with Friedrich's death in 1942 during an air raid

"The tragedy and terror suffered by German Jews are made more vivid by the simplicity and candor of a child's viewpoint and by the focus on one small, obscure family." Sat Rev

"Episodes are closely correlated with actual events, laws, decrees, and regulations which are listed in a chronology." Booklist

Rinkoff, Barbara

Member of the gang; illus. by Harold James. Crown 1968 127p illus $3.50 (4-7)   Fic

1 Juvenile delinquency—Fiction 2 Negroes—Fiction
ISBN 0-517-50117-1

In this story set in a Black urban slum, "Leroy was a leader, an important guy and Woodie wanted to be in his gang. Other kids played hookey and got away with it, so Woodie agreed to be the front man for a store robbery. When one of the gang was knifed in a fight, Woodie stayed with him and was picked up by the police, tried, and put on probation. Although the probation officer was black also, he was authority and Woodie resisted his arguments at first. Gradually Mr. Henry made Woodie see that there was no future in being tough, that his parents were right about getting an education, that being a member of the gang meant only trouble." Sutherland. The Best in Children's Bks

"An honest and realistic treatment of boys seeking easy prestige and of their handling by the understanding personnel representing authority." Rdng Ladders. 5th edition

Ritchie, Barbara

Ramón makes a trade; Los cambios de Ramón; illus. by Earl Thollander. Parnassus Press 1959 48p illus $4.95, lib. bdg. $4.77 (3-5)   Fic

1 Mexico—Fiction 2 Markets—Fiction 3 Bilingual books—Spanish-English
ISBN 0-87466-053-X; 0-87466-022-X

"With only one pottery bowl to trade for a parakeet and cage which are worth several such bowls resourceful Ramón makes not one but a series of trades until he is able to obtain the coveted bird and cage. His adventures in the Mexican market place are well told and are illustrated with brightly colored, flavorsome drawings. The Spanish translation, which is considerably more difficult than the English text, appears on the bottom half of each page. Appended are seven pages of 'useful expressions,' with their English equivalents, taken from the story." Booklist

"Self-reliance, ingenuity, self-discipline, family pride, love, and hard work are stressed. An outstanding story which helps develop an interest in Mexican culture as it improves language skills." Keating. Building Bridges of Understanding Between Cultures

Robbins, Ruth

The Emperor and the drummer boy; illus. by Nicolas Sidjakov. Parnassus Press 1962 unp illus map $4.95, lib. bdg. $4.98 (3-5)   Fic

1 Napoleon I, Emperor of the French—Fiction
ISBN 0-87466-043-2; 0-87466-011-4

Also available in a French language edition for $4.95

"Two drummer boys, Jean and Armand, demonstrate their loyalty and courage in this exciting story focused on Napoleon's visit to Boulogne in 1804." Adventuring With Bks. 2d edition

An "extraordinary book, harmonious in every aspect. . . . Mr. Sidjakov's use of many lines is most

Robbins, Ruth—*Continued*
suitable in the pictures of ships and rigging and stunning in those of stormy seas. Red and blue are added most effectively." Horn Bk

Roberts, Charles G. D.
Red Fox; illus. by John Schoenherr; introduction by David McCord. Houghton 1972 187p illus $4.95 (4-7)   Fic
1 Foxes—Stories 2 Canada—Fiction
ISBN 0-395-13735-7
First published 1905 by Page with illustrations by Charles Livingston Bull
"Here is a biography of a superbly clever fox in Eastern Canada, from his birth to his masterpiece of trickery which saves his life for the last time." Appraisal
"Children today will find this account of the wily fox and his relationships with the other animals in the New Brunswick woods both moving and informative. The dramatic story, one of the best of its type, is supported by striking black-and-white pen-and-ink drawings by John Schoenherr and there is also an excellent introduction by David McCord." Sch Library J

Robertson, Keith
Henry Reed, Inc. Illus. by Robert McCloskey. Viking 1958 239p illus lib. bdg. $5.95 (5-7)   Fic
ISBN 0-670-36796-6
"Henry Reed, on vacation from the American School in Naples, keeps a record of his research into the American free-enterprise system, to be used as a school report on his return. With a neighbor, Midge Glass, he starts a business in pure and applied research, which results in some very free and widely enterprising experiences, all recorded deadpan in his journal. Very funny and original escapades." Hodges. Bks for Elem Sch Libraries
Three additional titles about Henry Reed are available from Viking: Henry Reed's journey, lib. bdg. $5.95 (ISBN 0-670-36854-7); Henry Reed's babysitting service, lib. bdg. $5.95 (ISBN 0-670-36825-3); Henry Reed's big show, lib. bdg. $5.50 (ISBN 0-670-36839-3)

In search of a sandhill crane; illus. by Richard Cuffari. Viking 1973 201p illus lib. bdg. $5.95 (5-7) Fic
1 Wilderness areas—Fiction 2 Cranes (Birds)—Stories 3 Michigan—Fiction
ISBN 0-670-39662-1
"Fifteen-year-old Link Keller did not believe that any place could be so lonely and isolated as his Aunt Harriet's cabin on Michigan's Upper Peninsula, but he knew that to be polite he had to endure two weeks cheerfully. Besides he had promised to take some photographs of a sandhill crane for his uncle in New York. In the occasional company of a Chippewa Indian, Link gradually develops an interest in the wilderness and with a little encouragement from his aunt has some exciting and amusing experiences." Booklist
"While there is a small element of suspense in Link's search for the sandhill crane, the story as a whole is quiet and contained, its strength in the economy of structure, the convincing characterization, the wealth of natural lore, and the evocation of the setting of the beautiful North Woods." Chicago. Children's Bk Center

Robinson, Barbara
The best Christmas pageant ever; pictures by Judith Gwyn Brown. Harper 1972 80p illus $3.95, lib. bdg. $4.43 (4-6)   Fic
1 Christmas stories 2 Pageants—Fiction
ISBN 0-06-025043-7; 0-06-025044-5
In this story the Herdmans, "absolutely the worst kids in the history of the world," discover the meaning of Christmas when they bully their way into the leading roles of the local church nativity play
"Although there is a touch of sentiment at the end (Imogene has tears in her eyes, the Wise Men produce not the usual gift but the Christmas ham that had been in their charity basket) the story otherwise romps through the festive preparations with comic relish, and if the Herdmans are so gauche as to seem exaggerated, they are still enjoyable, as are the not-so-subtle pokes at pageant-planning in general." Chicago. Children's Bk Center

Robinson, Joan G.
Charley; illus. by Prudence Seward. Coward-McCann [1970 c1969] 251p illus map $5.95 (4-6) Fic
1 Runaways—Fiction 2 Great Britain—Fiction
ISBN 0-698-20021-7
First published 1969 in England
Feeling unwanted by the aunt with whom she is staying during her parents' absence, an English girl runs "away, camping out in the open and baffling the good people of the nearby village. . . . Taken in by a motherly woman after she has reached the end of her resources, Charley is discovered and scolded by Aunt Emm, but she realizes for the first time how constricted a life her aunt leads and finds that she can pity the friendless, lonely woman." Sutherland. The Best in Children's Bks
"Although there are hints that [Charley's] ordeal may have given her a measure of awareness and maturity, the ending of the story is completely unsentimental. Charley returns home with Aunt Emm—quite unregenerate, a wonderfully real and convincing child." Horn Bk

Robinson, Tom
Trigger John's son; illus. by Robert McCloskey. Viking 1949 284p illus $3.50 (5-7)   Fic
1 Orphans and orphans' homes 2 Pennsylvania—Fiction
ISBN 0-670-73042-4
First published 1934
"Tom, a lively orphan adopted by a childless couple [in a Pennsylvania town] joins the Goosetown Gang and engineers some hilarious escapades." Hodges. Bks for Elem Sch Libraries
"The humor and liveliness of [McCloskey's] drawing of Trigger and the Goosetown gang must be reminiscent of his own boyhood." Horn Bk

Robinson, Veronica
David in silence; illus. by Victor Ambrus. Lippincott 1966 [c1965] 126p illus $6.50, lib. bdg. $3.39 (4-6)   Fic
1 Deaf—Fiction
ISBN 0-397-30867-1; 0-397-31371-3
First published 1965 in England
"The story is set in a small English town, where the neighborhood children are interested but uncomfortable with the new boy, David. David has always been deaf, and his older brother tries to explain to Michael, who is David's age and has made friendly overtures, what the problems of communication are. David is chased by a gang of boys playing a game, gets lost and frightened in an abandoned tunnel, and finds Michael and safety. At the close of the story there has been some change in the attitude of the other boys, but nothing melodramatic or unrealistic." Chicago. Children's Bk Center
"As a documentary study [this book] is excellent, precisely yet imaginatively conveying the difficulty of crossing that baffling wall over which the deaf regard

Robinson, Veronica—Continued

the land of sound, the ordinary hearing crowd regard the deaf. . . . The splendid chapters of climax (the lost boy's journey) compellingly lift the story out of the merely informational field." Times (London) Lit Sup

Rockwell, Thomas

How to eat fried worms; pictures by Emily McCully. Watts, F. 1973 115p illus lib. bdg. $5.95 (3-6)   Fic

1 Worms—Stories

ISBN 0-531-02631-0

"The stakes are high when Alan bets $50 that his friend Billy can't eat 15 worms (one per day). . . . Billy's mother, instead of upchucking, comes to her son's aid by devising gourmet recipes like Alsatian Smothered Worm. Alan wants to win as desperately as Billy, who is itching to buy a used minibike, and few holds are barred in the contest." Sch Library J

"A hilarious story that will revolt and delight bumptious, unreachable, intermediate-grade boys and any other less particular mortals that read or listen to it. . . . The characters and their families and activities are natural to a T, and this juxtaposed against the uncommon plot, makes for some colorful, original writing in a much-needed comic vein." Booklist

Rodgers, Mary

A billion for Boris. Harper 1974 211p $4.95, lib. bdg. $4.79, pa $1.50 (4-7)   Fic

1 Clairvoyance—Fiction

ISBN 0-06-025047-X; 0-06-025054-2; 0-06-44075-1

"An Ursula Nordstrom book"

Further adventures of Annabel Andrews, who first appeared in: Freaky Friday

When her younger brother fixes a hopelessly broken television set, fourteen-year-old Annabel Andrews discovers that the set broadcasts the following day's news. Annabel, her brother, and her boyfriend disagree on how to deal with their newfound clairvoyant powers

"This jubilant work is an engaging story and also a barometer of adolescent emotions and needs—real and imagined." Pub W

Freaky Friday. Harper 1972 145p $4.95, lib. bdg. $4.79 (4-7)   Fic

1 Mothers—Fiction

ISBN 0-06-025048-8; 0-06-025049-6

" 'When I woke up this morning, I found I'd turned into my mother.' So begins the most bizarre day in the life of 13-year-old Annabel Andrews, who discovers one Friday morning she has taken on her mother's physical characteristics while retaining her own personality. Readers will giggle in anticipation as Annabel plunges madly from one disaster to another trying to cope with various adult situations." Pub W

"There's nothing didactic here; the story bubbles along in fine style as Annabel sees herself as others see her (a more complimentary set of attitudes than she might have anticipated) and adjusts to the rigors of her mother's problems and the inevitable complications of changed roles. A fresh, imaginative, and entertaining story." Chicago. Children's Bk Center

Rounds, Glen

The blind colt; written & illus. by Glen Rounds. Holiday House 1960 unp illus $5.95 (4-6)   Fic

1 Ponies—Stories 2 South Dakota—Fiction

ISBN 0-8234-0010-7

First published 1941

Set in the South Dakota Badlands, this is the story of a pony colt that was born blind. It tells of his experiences growing up with a mustang band, and of his eventual adoption and training by ten-year-old Whitey

"The story has stood the test of time and is well worth continued replacement. The courage of the horse in spite of his handicap, the feeling of apprehension throughout the story lest Whitey have to give up the colt, the authentic feeling of cowboy life pervading all the stories of this author have just as much impact on the present-day reader as they did when the book first appeared." Library J

Followed by: Stolen pony

Stolen pony; written and illus. by Glen Rounds. Holiday House 1969 unp illus $5.95 (4-6)   Fic

1 Ponies—Stories 2 Dogs—Stories 3 South Dakota—Fiction

ISBN 0-8234-0110-3

First published 1949

Continues the story begun in the author's The blind colt. When the pony was stolen from the ranch, the dog who had guarded him followed. The thieves turned the pony loose when they discovered he was blind, and together the two animals made their way back to the ranch thru almost incredible hardships

"This is a fine, simple story, with unsentimental truth about animals and humans. Mr. Rounds' sketches are as free and moving as his story." N Y Times Bk Rev

Whitey & the wild horse. Holiday House 1958 90p illus $3.95 (4-6)   Fic

1 Horses—Stories 2 Ranch life—Fiction

ISBN 0-8234-0138-3

"Young ranch hand Whitey [who appeared in The blind colt] and his cousin Josie are considering the possibility of catching and taming a wild horse when they discover an injured and very wild horse trapped in a pothole. . . . How they care for and tame the horse and, with Uncle Torwal's help, protect their claim of ownership are pleasurably recounted." Booklist

"With economy of words and distinctive black-and-white drawings Mr. Rounds tells a tale of the real West for young readers." Sat Rev

Rugh, Belle D.

Crystal Mountain; illus. by Ernest H. Shepard. Houghton 1955 208p illus $4.95 (4-6)   Fic

1 Americans in Lebanon—Fiction 2 Mystery and detective stories 3 Lebanon—Fiction

ISBN 0-395-07083-X

"Four American boys living in Lebanon learn the language and grow to love the people of the country. The wild, beautiful mountains are their playground, and presently they discover an oddly built, empty house which fascinates them. A tomboy English girl proves a worthy companion and helps them rescue a mistreated pup, reform a brat of an American boy, and eventually solve the mystery of the deserted house." Children's Bks Too Good to Miss

"Based on the author's experiences in Lebanon is this delightful adventure story . . . in the tradition of E. Nesbit. . . . Warm family life; story is interesting and well told; good characterizations. Appeal to good and unusual readers. Good illustrations in black and white." Library J

"The book also has value for intercultural relations." Wis Library Bul

Rutgers van der Loeff, Anna

Avalanche! Illus. by Gustav Schrotter. Morrow 1958 [c1957] 219p illus $5.95 (6-7)   Fic

1 Switzerland—Fiction 2 Disasters—Fiction

ISBN 0-688-21055-4

Original Dutch edition published 1955. Published 1957 in England

"Story of a Swiss boy's experience when he, the people of his village, and a group of war orphans from

Rutgers van der Loeff, Anna—*Continued*
an international Children's Village are caught in an avalanche." Pub W

"The author has written with great understanding of the effect that tension and tragedy have on human beings and their relationships with each other. Awarded the prize for the best children's book [of the year, when it was first] published in Holland." Chicago. Children's Bk Center

Sachs, Marilyn
Amy and Laura; illus. by Tracy Sugarman. Doubleday 1966 189p illus lib. bdg. $5.70 (4-6)   Fic
1 Sisters—Fiction
ISBN 0-385-06984-7

Two "sisters face the family problem of a convalescent mother as well as their own individual problems at school." LC. Children's Bks. 1966

"Natural conversations and a lively pace well within the grasp of average readers assure popular reception of a story that is as realistic as it is readable." Horn Bk

Marv; illus. by Louis Glanzman. Doubleday 1970 160p illus lib. bdg. $5.70 (4-6)   Fic
1 Brothers and sisters—Fiction
ISBN 0-385-00009-X

This is the "story of a boy who is considered a failure by his much admired older sister. Marv is a daydreamer, a doodler, and a prolific builder, marvelously inventive but impractical. He dreams of such elaborate schemes as automating the butcher's shop and kidnapping Hitler, and he builds revolving doors that lead nowhere and other useless contraptions. No matter how he tries Marv cannot, in the eyes of his brilliant sister, create anything of benefit to anyone. Marv does not change but his ill-fated attempts to impress his sister keep the reader's fullest sympathies with the well-meaning dreamer." Booklist

A pocket full of seeds; illus. by Ben Stahl. Doubleday 1973 137p illus $4.95, lib. bdg. $5.70 (5-7)   Fic
1 World War, 1939-1945—Fiction 2 France—Fiction 3 Jews in France—Fiction
ISBN 0-385-06091-2; 0-385-06092-0

"Nicole Nieman is eight when she leaves the foster home in which she and her small sister have been living, and rejoins the parents who had not until then been able to afford a home big enough for four. Self-assured and rather self-satisfied, Nicole is baffled by the hostility of some of her classmates, a hostility that presages the persecution that French Jews suffered during World War II. When her parents are taken by the Nazis, Nicole goes to her foster parents; since it is unsafe there, she goes to school, where the teacher, who Nicole has disliked, shows unexpected compassion and takes Nicole in as a boarding pupil. A touching story, realistic in the way Nicole adjusts to the drastic changes of war and changes from a blithe eight-year-old to a mature adolescent. Style and characterization are deft, and the atmosphere of the place and period are convincingly recreated." Chicago. Children's Bk Center

The truth about Mary Rose; illus. by Louis Glanzman. Doubleday 1973 159p illus $4.95, lib. bdg. $5.70 (4-7)   Fic
1 Family—Fiction
ISBN 0-385-09448-5; 0-385-09449-3

"Fans of 'Veronica Ganz' will be pleased to learn that Sach's highly individual heroine now has children of her own, one of whom narrates this story. Eleven-year-old Mary Rose Ramirez is named for her aunt, Veronica's sister, who was killed in a fire at age 11. The central question: was Mary Rose Ganz an angelic child who died a heroine (as grandmother says)? Was

she the selfish, bitchy terror that Uncle Stanley remembers? Or was she a 'poor, little thing' as Veronica remembers? The question arises when Mary Rose's artist father wins a competition that lands him a job in New York, and the family moves to Veronica's mother's house in the Bronx." Sch Library J

"Woven through and around the story of Mary Rose is a rich and perceptive picture of the intricacies of family relationships, a picture peopled with vivid characters. Particularly telling: the obdurately prejudiced grandmother." Chicago. Children's Bk Center

Veronica Ganz; illus. by Louis Glanzman. Doubleday 1968 156p illus lib. bdg. $5.70 (4-7)   Fic
ISBN 0-385-01436-8

"At thirteen Veronica, the bully of her school in the Bronx, hasn't got a friend. Afraid of being made fun of because she's so big, she has long since beaten (boys) or slapped (girls) her classmates into subservience. (She also enjoys making sport of teachers and a librarian.) Then a new boy arrives. Although small, Peter is smart and he side-steps Veronica's persistent attempts to pulverize him. At last the big girl and the undersized boy have a confrontation, which brings some pleasant surprises for the belligerent Veronica." Bk World

Followed by: Peter and Veronica

Saint-Exupéry, Antoine de
The little prince; written and drawn by Antoine de Saint-Exupéry; tr. from the French by Katherine Woods. Harcourt 1943 91p illus $5.95, pa $1.25 Fic
ISBN 0-15-246503-0; 0-15-652820-7

Also available in French language edition for $6.95 (ISBN 0-15-243818-1) lib. bdg. $6.95 (ISBN 0-15-243819-X) pa 95¢ (ISBN 0-15-650300-X); German pa $1.65 (ISBN 0-15-625285-6); Spanish pa $1.35 (ISBN 0-15-628450-2)

"A flier has [a] forced landing in the Sahara. He is met by the little Prince of Asteroid B612. The Prince tells the flier of his experiences on many planets with men, flowers, and animals." Library J

"Only time and use will determine whether adults or children will enjoy this book more, or whether both will enjoy it equally. A great many children will treasure it without necessarily grasping its full significance." Booklist

Salten, Felix
Bambi (4-6)   Fic
1 Deer—Stories
Some editions are:
Grosset (Thrushwood bks) $2.99, lib. bdg. $2.69 Illustrated by Kurt Wiese (ISBN 0-448-02518-3; 0-448-03202-3)
Simon & Schuster $5.95 Illustrated by Barbara Cooney. Has subtitle: A life in the woods (ISBN 0-671-65136-6)

Original German edition published 1923. First American edition published 1928 by Simon & Schuster

"Bambi is a young deer, growing up in a forest, at first a curious child playing about his mother in glade and meadow, conversing with grasshoppers, squirrels and his own little cousins, Faline and Gobo." N Y Libraries.

"Felix Salten's story of deer life in the woods that fringe the Danube is neither sentimental nor used to point a moral. It derives its dramatic value, legitimately, from the animals' fear and terror of their historic enemy—man. . . . In his absorption with details the author has brought his whole forest to life, yet these details are selected with a poet's intuition for delicacy of effect." N Y Her Trib Bks

Sauer, Julia

Fog magic. Viking 1943 107p illus lib. bdg. $5.95
(4-6)   Fic
1 Nova Scotia—Fiction 2 Fantastic fiction
ISBN 0-670-32303-9
Delicately beautiful story of a little Nova Scotian
girl, whose love of the fog brought her happy adventures in a village lost for a hundred years. On her
twelfth birthday, Greta made her last visit to Blue
Cove and brought back her one tangible evidence of
her dream village—a grey kitten
The author "has written a choice story, bringing the
past into the present imagination, inspired by love of
place. It is a beautiful book, too, with decorations by
Lynd Ward." Horn Bk

The light at Tern Rock; illus. by Georges Schreiber.
Viking 1951 62p illus lib. bdg. $3.50 (3-5)   Fic
1 Christmas stories 2 Lighthouses—Fiction
ISBN 0-670-32303-9
Originally published in: The Horn Book, with title:
The light at Christmas
"The isolation and beauty of Tern Rock in text and
pictures does something to the reader as well as young
Ronnie who learns that Christmas is in your heart. It is
an unusual and unforgettable Christmas story of
learning truly to give." Wis Library Bul

Savery, Constance

The Reb and the Redcoats; illus. by Vera Bock.
McKay 1961 241p illus lib. bdg. $4.19 (5-7)   Fic
1 U.S.—History—Revolution—Fiction 2 Great
Britain—Fiction
ISBN 0-679-25117-0
First published by Longmans
This is a story about the "Revolutionary War as
seen, at long distance, by a family of English children
whose father is fighting in America. In their comfort-
able English home is billeted a prisoner of war from
Virginia who at 15 is already a major with a formidable
record of escape. He charms the household, espe-
cially the children, but keeps them on the alert." N Y
Times Bk Rev

Sawyer, Ruth

Roller skates; illus. by Valenti Angelo. Viking 1936
186p illus $6.95 (4-6)   Fic
1 New York (City)—Fiction
ISBN 0-670-60310-4
Awarded the Newbery Medal, 1937
"For one never-to-be-forgotten year Lucinda
Wyman (ten years old) was free to explore New York
on roller skates. She made friends with Patrick Gilligan and his hansom cab, with Policeman M'Gonegal,
with the fruit vendor, Vittore Coppicco and his son
Tony, and with many others. All Lucinda's adventures
are true and happened to the author herself as is borne
out by the occasional pages of Lucinda's diary which
are a part of the story." Horn Bk

This way to Christmas; with illus. in colors by
Maginel Wright Barney. Harper 1952 175p illus lib.
bdg. $5.89 (3-5)   Fic
1 Christmas stories
ISBN 0-06-025212-X
First published 1916
This is "a delightful book of real Christmas stories
told to a little boy stranded in a lonesome spot up in
northern New York. A locked-out fairy from Ireland
suggests that he visit his neighbors and from each
comes a tale." Booklist

Schoenherr, John

The barn; written and illus. by John Schoenherr.
Little 1968 40p illus $3.95 (2-4)   Fic

1 Skunks—Stories 2 Animals—Stories
ISBN 0-316-77420-0
"An Atlantic Monthly Press book"
"Strong pictures in black and white combine
meticulously realistic drawings of animals with delicate background details. The drama of the illustrations is tempered by the quiet writing, which
describes the predatory excursions of a hungry skunk,
himself preyed upon by an owl who must feed three
owlets. Low-keyed, the text is less a story than a
revealing vignette of the constant struggle for survival
in the animal world." Sutherland. The Best in Children's Bks

Selden, George

The cricket in Times Square; illus. by Garth Williams. Farrar, Straus 1960 151p illus $5.95 (3-6) Fic
1 Cats—Stories 2 Crickets—Stories 3 Mice—
Stories 4 New York (City)—Fiction
ISBN 0-374-31650-3
"An Ariel book"
"A touch of magic comes to Times Square subway
station with Chester, a cricket from rural Connecticut. He is introduced to the distinctive character of
city life by three friends: Mario Bellini, whose parents
operate a newsstand; Tucker, a glib Broadway mouse;
and Harry, a sagacious cat. Chester saves the Bellinis'
business by giving concerts from the newsstand,
bringing to rushing commuters moments of beauty
and repose. This modern fantasy shows that, in New
York, anything can happen." Moorachian. What is a
City?

The genie of Sutton Place. Farrar, Straus 1973 175p
$5.95 (4-7)   Fic
ISBN 0-374-32527-8
Adapted from the television play written by the
author and Kenneth Heuer
"A large brown genie is evoked by a boy in trouble,
in a sophisticated but somewhat low-comedy story set
in New York City. Tim's father has just died, and he is
not enthralled to hear that he must live with his
wealthy Aunt Lucy in Sutton Place. Tim prefers the
comfortable milieu of Greenwich Village and the
companionship of his friend Madame Sosostris—
Antiques and Seances. The crux of the problem: Aunt
Lucy is allergic to dogs. The genie turns Tim's dog into
a man, one that Aunt Lucy finds not unattractive, and
there's a French farce atmosphere as the uncomfortable dog repeatedly makes woofy noises and is nearly
discovered. There's also a romance between Aunt
Lucy's intellectual maid and the genie, who happily
becomes mortal at the end of the story. There's a good
bit of wit in the writing, exaggeration of characters,
overstimulated plot albeit original in concept."
Chicago. Children's Bk Center

Harry Cat's pet puppy; illus. by Garth Williams.
Farrar, Straus 1974 167p illus $5.95 (3-6)   Fic
1 Animals—Stories 2 New York (City)—Fiction
ISBN 0-374-32856-0
Harry Cat and Tucker Mouse, characters from The
cricket in Times Square, "live in a drainpipe in a
Manhattan subway station, a cozy home into which
compassionate Harry brings a helpless, homeless
puppy. Fussy Tucker is frantic because the intruder is
a messy burden but, like Harry, he soon falls under
the baby's spell. Harry and Tucker care for the puppy
but find, to their dismay, that their hearty feeding of
the dog fattens him so he can't get through the drain.
The two friends realize that their formidable task now
is to find a good home for the 'child.' And they do, to
the delight not only of children who can read on their
own but to adults who'll relish the opportunity to
share the story with non-readers." Pub W
"As usual, Selden's animal characters are delightfully human, and scenes in which they interact are

Selden, George—*Continued*

filled with wit and a reassuring sense of psychological order. Garth Williams' familiar line drawings are as warm and funny as ever." Booklist

Tucker's countryside; illus. by Garth Williams. Farrar, Straus 1969 166p illus map $4.50 (3-6)   Fic

1 Animals—Stories 2 Connecticut—Fiction
ISBN 0-374-37854-1
"An Ariel book"

Here are the further adventures of Chester Cricket, Harry Cat, and Tucker Mouse, the three heroes who first appeared in: The cricket in Times Square. When John Robin arrives in the Times Square subway station where Tucker and Harry live, with a message that Chester urgently needs them in Connecticut, they take the perilous journey. The country is a happy revelation to the city-bred friends, but they also find many problems there

"Several engaging new animal characters are added to the story, along with some determined, right-minded children, who unwittingly help the small creatures trick the materialistic grown-ups into preserving their natural sanctuary. A charming, though not extraordinary pastoral fantasy, with a strong plea for conservation. Beautifully illustrated." Horn Bk

Sendak, Maurice

Higglety pigglety pop! or, There must be more to life; story and pictures by Maurice Sendak. Harper 1967 69p illus $4.95, lib. bdg. $5.49 (2-4)   Fic

1 Dogs—Stories
ISBN 0-06-025487-4; 0-06-025488-2

In this modern fairy tale "Jennie, the Sealyham terrier, leaves home because 'there must be more to life than having everything.' When she applies for a job as the leading lady of the World Mother Goose Theater, she discovers that what she lacks is experience. What follows are her adventures and her gaining of experience; finally Jennie becomes the leading lady of the play." Wis Library Bul

"The story has elements of tenderness and humor; it also has . . . typically macabre Sendak touches. . . . The illustrations are beautiful, amusing, and distinctive." Sutherland. The Best in Children's Bks

Seredy, Kate

The Good Master; written and illus. by Kate Seredy. Viking 1935 210p illus $4 (4-6)   Fic

1 Farm life—Fiction 2 Hungary—Fiction
ISBN 0-670-34592-X

Into this story of Jancsi, a ten-year-old Hungarian farm boy and his little hoyden of a cousin Kate from Budapest, is woven a description of Hungarian farm life, fairs, festivals, and folk tales. Under the tutelage of Jancsi's kind father, called by the neighbors, The Good Master, Kate calms down and becomes a more docile young person

"The steady warm understanding of the wise father, the Good Master, is a shining quality throughout." Horn Bk
Map on lining-papers
Followed by: The singing tree

The singing tree; written and illus. by Kate Seredy. Viking 1939 247p illus $6.95 (4-6)   Fic

1 Farm life—Fiction 2 Hungary—Fiction 3 European War, 1914-1918—Fiction
ISBN 0-670-64700-4

The setting of this sequel to The Good Master is the same ranch in Hungary four years later, during the First World War. Jancsi's kind father has gone to the war, leaving the young master in charge of the farm, which becomes a refuge for relatives, Russian prisoners and German war orphans

It is "a sincere and thoughtful tale, stressing the values of happier racial relations and of doing one's best in all circumstances. Beautifully illustrated by the author." Bookmark

The white stag; written and illus. by Kate Seredy. Viking 1937 94p illus $6.95 (4-6)   Fic

1 Hungary—Fiction
ISBN 0-670-76375-6
Awarded the Newbery Medal, 1938

"Striking illustrations interpret this hero tale of the legendary founding of Hungary, when a white stag and a red eagle led the people to their promised land." Hodges. Bks for Elem Sch Libraries

Serraillier, Ian

The silver sword; illus. by C. Walter Hodges. Phillips [1959 c1956] 187p illus $5.95 (5-7)   Fic

1 World War, 1939-1945—Fiction 2 Refugees, Polish—Fiction
ISBN 0-87599-104-1

First published 1956 in England, and 1959 in the United States by Criterion Books

"Three Polish children struggle to find their parents after the family becomes separated following the Nazi invasion in 1940. In late August, 1945, they reach their goal in Switzerland, after wanderings and 'ordeals before which the bravest spirit might quail.' For over two-and-a-half years the two girls are without Edek, their brother and lifeline who was imprisoned for smuggling food. Jan, a homeless boy who met their father while he was searching for them, becomes the fourth in the group, a talisman figure like the silver sword he treasures, now aiding, now endangering them with his unpredictable exploits and irrepressible love of animals. Jan remains—with Ruth, the eldest—the most memorable and sympathetic character, and his charm lingers long after the book is closed. English critics said this book is 'touched with greatness.' A powerful story-idea transcends unexceptional writing, and there is no tinge of condemnation of any nation involved." Horn Bk

Sewell, Anna

Black Beauty (4-6)   Fic

1 Horses—Stories 2 Great Britain—Fiction
Some editions are:
Collins (Rainbow classics) $2.95, lib. bdg. $3.91 Illustrated by Wesley Dennis. Introduction by May Lamberton Becker. Has subtitle: The autobiography of a horse (ISBN 0-529-04775-6; 0-529-04776-4)
Grosset (Illustrated junior library) $3.95 Illustrated by Fritz Eichenberg (ISBN 0-448-06007-8)
Macmillan (N Y) (The Macmillan classics) $3.95 Illustrated by John Groth. Afterword by Clifton Fadiman
Watts, F. lib. bdg. $7.95 Pictures by Charles Mozley. Large type edition complete and unabridged. A Keith Jennison book (ISBN 0-531-00163-6)
First published 1877

"As Black Beauty, a fine horse, goes from one master to another, readers learn the story of his life in nineteenth century England." Gateways to Readable Bks

The book has "enjoyed tremendous popularity for many years. Some children wept over Beauty's sufferings. . . . 'Black Beauty' was written as a protest against the tight checkrein and other more serious cruelties to horses. It relates, in the first person, a good story. . . . Black Beauty, while presumably a real horse, thinks and talks out of horse character. He is humanly sensitive to the social and moral tone of the people with whom he lives." Arbuthnot. Children & Bks. 3d edition

Sharmat, Marjorie Weinman

Getting something on Maggie Marmelstein; pictures by Ben Shecter. Harper 1971 101p illus $3.95, lib. bdg. $4.43, pa 95¢ (3-5)   Fic

ISBN 0-06-025551-X; 0-06-025552-8; 0-06-440038-7

"Crisply told by Thad Smith, this story of boy/girl rivalry involves the trouble that develops when Tad calls Maggie Marmelstein a mouse. She retaliates by threatening to tell that she has seen him helping her mother cook. His desperate search for something on Maggie leads to his discovery that she writes mushy fan letters to movie stars. Rehearsals for a dramatization of 'The Frog Prince' provide an entertaining backdrop for their competition, the means of ending it, and much of the humor in the well-executed story." Sch Library J

"Simple black-and-white illustrations provide a natural extension of the text which combines genuine character and plot development with amusing dialog." Pub W

Sharp, Margery

Miss Bianca; with illus. by Garth Williams. Little 1962 152p illus $6.95 (3-6)   Fic

1 Mice—Stories
ISBN 0-316-78310-2
Sequel to: The rescuers

"Miss Bianca is a charming and sophisticated white mouse, who, with her sturdy ally, Bernard, leads the Mouse Prisoners' Aid Society to the rescue of a little girl held prisoner by a wicked Grand Duchess. Well-sustained fantasy with mouse personalities engagingly depicted in story and illustrations." Hodges. Bks for Elem Sch Libraries

The rescuers; with illus. by Garth Williams. Little 1959 149p illus $6.95 (3-6)   Fic

1 Mice—Stories
ISBN 0-316-78314-5

This is "a story featuring animals. The Prisoners' Aid Society of mice want to free a Norwegian poet held captive in the Black Castle in a barbarous country. The difficulties and intrigues of the sleek, sophisticated spy and her helpers who are chosen for the task by the Society, and their eventual triumph, provide the adventure and suspense in this liberally illustrated tale." Pub W

"Many line drawings in the artist's best style, giving individuality to a great number of small animals, make this volume look like a children's book; the text, which is a 'heroic tale' in talking-animal fantasy, has no audience limitations. . . . Delightful family fare, with some humorous allusions and overtones to enrich the story for older listeners and, for all, the most charming deft details of characterization, scene, and incident." Horn Bk

Followed by: Miss Bianca

Shepard, Ray Anthony

Sneakers (4-6)   Fic

1 Race problems—Fiction 2 Football—Fiction
Some editions are:
Dutton $4.50 (ISBN 0-525-39510-5)
Hall, G.K.&Co. lib. bdg. $5.95 Large print edition (ISBN 0-8161-6127-5)

"An eighth grade [Black] football player feels he desperately needs new sneakers to play in the championship game, and gets into trouble acquiring them. The relationship between Chuck and his mother and the situation and feelings of suburban whites and bussed-in blacks are treated realistically and with understanding." New Bks for Young Readers

Shotwell, Louisa R.

Magdalena; illus. by Lilian Obligado. Viking 1971 124p illus lib. bdg. $5.95 (5-7)   Fic

1 Puerto Ricans in New York (City)—Fiction
2 Brooklyn—Fiction
ISBN 0-670-44799-4

"Magdalena hates her long, disgustingly prim braids, but to Nani, Magdalena's grandmother, braids are the proper way for a Puerto Rican girl to wear her hair, even in Brooklyn. Although Nani does not seem to understand why Magdalena, with the encouragement of her classmate Spook Gonzalez and eccentric Miss Lilley, has her braids cut off, she shows considerable insight into Spook's strange behavior and Miss Lilley's problems and eventually even learns to accept Magdalena's short hair. The relationships between Magdalena and the other children and Magdalena and her grandmother are well portrayed in this warm, gently humorous story." Booklist

Roosevelt Grady; illus. by Peter Burchard. Collins 1963 151p illus $4.95, lib. bdg. $5.91 (4-6)   Fic

1 Migrant labor—Fiction 2 Negroes—Fiction
ISBN 0-529-03780-7; 0-529-03781-5

The story of Roosevelt Grady, "a boy in a lively Negro family, migrant crop-workers of the Eastern seaboard, and his problems moving from one school to another and trying to make friends." Pub W

"Written with candor and simplicity, a convincing story that has good characterization and a setting described with sympathy but no sentimentality. There is no reference in the text to the fact that the characters are Negro; this is shown in the illustrations. Several of the characters have names like Pearly Ann, Bethalene, Lulubelle, Princess Anne; this seems unfortunate, since it may type the characters for readers who are not aware that this is a custom of a regional and economic level rather than a racial idiosyncrasy." Chicago. Children's Bk Center

Singer, Isaac Bashevis

The fearsome inn; tr. by the author and Elizabeth Shub; illus. by Nonny Hogrogian. Scribner 1967 unp illus $5.95 (4-6)   Fic

1 Witchcraft—Fiction 2 Poland—Fiction 3 Jews—Fiction
ISBN 0-684-20943-8

"Three beautiful girls are imprisoned in a remote [Polish] inn as servants to the witch Doboshova and Lapitut, half man, half devil. When three young men arrive at the inn, Doboshova and Lapitut contrive to bewitch them, but one of the three, a student of the cabala, is too clever for the evil ones and drives them back to the 'wastes of the netherworld.' . . . The six young people settle amicably who will marry whom, each couple then following the path for which they are best suited. . . . [The author] has used the pattern of folklore and the devices of Jewish traditional tales to tell an original fairy story rich in atmosphere. The wonderful illustrations in full color flow with the story, contributing greatly to the feeling and giving individual personality to each character. Combining romance and fearsomeness the book is beautiful, distinguished, and wholly satisfying." Horn Bk

The fools of Chelm and their history; pictures by Uri Shulevitz; tr. by the author and Elizabeth Shub. Farrar, Straus 1973 57p illus $4.95 (3-6)   Fic

1 Jews—Fiction
ISBN 0-374-32444-1

The "town of Chelm is just like every place else, only worse, as numerous shortages, foolish citizens, and inept leaders combine to make life thoroughly miserable. . . . Singer mocks the 'advantages'—such as war, crime, and revolution—that civilization brings to Chelm, as the leadership changes but never

Singer, Isaac Bashevis—*Continued*

improves, passing from Gronam Ox to Bunem Pok-raka to Feitel Thief and, finally, to the women of the town." Booklist

"Drawing loosely—very loosely—on [Jewish] Chelm legendry, the author satirizes government, politics, and human foibles in a story that should have different meanings to readers of different ages but that emerges for all readers as a smooth, humorous narrative—an amusing story, well-told. The pen-and-ink illustrations embellish the text, adding droll touches of their own." Horn Bk

Sleigh, Barbara

Carbonel, the King of the Cats; illus. by V. H. Drummond. Bobbs 1957 [c1955] 253p illus $3.25 (4-6)   Fic

1 Cats—Stories 2 Witches—Fiction 3 Fairy tales
ISBN 0-672-50241-0

First published 1955 in England with title: Carbonel

Rosemary, a little English girl, bought a second-hand broom so she could help her mother. All innocence Rosemary found that the broom was a witch's broom, and the black cat that went with it, was bewitched. This little fantasy describes Rosemary's attempts, along with her friend John, to free the enchanted cat

"Crammed with fun and thrills. It's a highly diverting fantasy, told exactly as though it all 'could' happen." Chicago Sunday Tribune

Slobodkin, Louis

The space ship under the apple tree. Macmillan (N Y) 1952 114p illus $5.95, pa $1.25 (3-5)   Fic

1 Science fiction
Illustrated by the author

"An ordinary summer vacation turns into high adventure when Eddie tracks what looks like a falling star to the old apple tree and finds a strange little man standing upside down on one of the branches." Bks for Deaf Children

"An entertaining blend of Boy Scout activities, pseudo science, and country fun." Hodges. Bks for Elem Sch Libraries

Followed by: The space ship returns to the apple tree

Slote, Alfred

Hang tough, Paul Mather. Lippincott 1973 156p $5.95 (4-7)   Fic

1 Leukemia—Fiction 2 Little league baseball—Fiction
ISBN 0-397-31451-5

"When Paul begins his story, he is in the hospital and talking to his doctor. Very deftly the author makes it clear that Paul's prime interest in life is baseball; he's been a star [pitcher] on two Little League teams, and has just moved to town. Paul's retrospective account is without sentimentality or self-pity, but the tragic fact is that he has leukemia and knows it. He has, against orders, seized a chance to play baseball and it has exhausted him. There are some baseball scenes, but these are balanced by the family sequences and the conversations between Paul and Dr. Kinsella. Both the doctor-patient relationship and the bond between Paul and his younger brother are beautifully developed, and the story of Paul's candor and courage is convincing, sad but never morbid, in a book that has depth and integrity." Chicago. Children's Bk Center

Jake. Lippincott 1971 155p $3.95, pa $1.95 (4-6)   Fic

1 Little league baseball—Fiction 2 Negroes—Fiction
ISBN 0-397-31414-0; 0-397-31327-6

"An above-average sports story with a well-developed plot, nonstereotyped characterizations, and fast-paced baseball action. Jake is a self-reliant eleven-year-old [black boy] who lives with his young rock musician uncle, comes and goes when he wants, and virtually runs his Little League team, the Print-Alls. Jake's difficulties begin when the league president warns that the Print-Alls will be disbanded unless they have a male coach at each game and Jake's principal threatens to send him to a foster home. Both problems are eventually solved, but not without further complications for Jake and the team." Booklist

My father, the coach. Lippincott 1972 157p $4.50 (4-6)   Fic

1 Little league baseball—Fiction
ISBN 0-397-31413-2

Eleven-year-old "Ezell Corkins and his friends have been yearning to get into a [baseball little] league, but they are taken aback when Mr. Corkins announces he has arranged it—with himself as coach. He doesn't know anything about coaching, but one of the boys does. . . . The team the boys most want to beat is the one sponsored by the bank and coached by its vice-president, Gardner. And Mr. Corkins hates Gardner, who patronizingly makes it clear each day that Willie Corkins is only a parking lot attendant." Chicago. Children's Bk Center

"The characters are well drawn, and the book effectively deals with small town factions and the pressures exerted by leading citizens on those not considered social equals. It also touches on the ways adults maneuver kids, especially in sports." Sch Library J

Tony and me. Lippincott 1974 156p $5.50 (4-6)
                                                         Fic

1 Little league baseball—Fiction 2 Friendship—Fiction 3 Juvenile delinquency—Fiction
ISBN 0-397-31507-4

"Star athlete Tony befriends Bill, a lonely new boy in town, and gives hope to their Little League baseball team, until a shoplifting incident [involving Tony] creates tough problems in conflicting loyalties." Children's Bks 1974

Smith, Doris Buchanan

A taste of blackberries; illus. by Charles Robinson. Crowell 1973 58p illus $3.95, lib. bdg. $4.70 (3-6)
                                                         Fic

1 Death—Fiction 2 Friendship—Fiction
ISBN 0-690-80511-X; 0-690-80512-8

A "portrayal of the death of a close friend. While gathering Japanese beetles to help a neighbor, Jamie is stung by a bee and falls screaming and writhing to the ground. His best friend (never named) disgustedly stalks off, only to find later that Jamie is dead of the bee sting. The boy feels guilty because he thought Jamie was clowning and didn't try to help. The boy is very withdrawn the week of the funeral, but comes to grips with the tragedy and learns to manage his grief." Sch Library J

"A difficult and sensitive subject, treated with taste and honesty, is woven into a moving story about a believable little boy. The black-and-white illustrations are honest, effective, and sensitive." Horn Bk

Tough Chauncey; frontispiece by Michael Eagle. Morrow 1974 222p front map $5.95, lib. bdg. $5.11 (5-7)   Fic

1 Runaways—Fiction 2 Family—Fiction
ISBN 0-688-20112-1; 0-688-30112-6

Abused by his grandfather and neglected by his mother, "tough" thirteen-year-old Chauncey decides

Smith, Doris Buchanan—*Continued*

running away is the only solution to changing his life until a friend shows him an alternative

"Sensitive to the feelings of a young adolescent desperately searching for stability and love, Doris Smith has created a vivid character that will capture young readers." Cath Library World

Smith, Emma

No way of telling. Atheneum Pubs. 1972 256p map $5.50 (5-7)   Fic

1 Blizzards—Fiction 2 Mystery and detective stories 3 Wales—Fiction

ISBN 0-689-30311-4

"A Margaret K. McElderry book"

One winter evening during a blizzard a stranger bursts into the Welsh farmhouse where Amy Bowen and her grandmother live, and leaves after taking some provisions. When two other men who claim to be policemen come searching for the first man, Amy's grandmother is suspicious about them. The Bowens, who begin aiding the fugitive, find themselves facing great danger

"What a pleasant change it makes to come upon a solid book in which plot and characters and scenic background are developed leisurely and suspense extended until it is almost forgotten. . . . The landscape and the weather are significantly intertwined, as is the past as well as the future of family affairs. The book is full of excitement and interest, and very well written indeed." Jr Bookshelf

Snedeker, Caroline Dale

Downright Dencey; with illus. by Maginel Wright Barney. Doubleday 1927 314p illus $3.95 (4-6) Fic

1 Nantucket—Fiction 2 Friends, Society of—Fiction

ISBN 0-385-07284-8

Set in the early 19th century, this story "is redolent with the atmosphere of time and place. In it a determined little Quaker girl keeps her promise made as an atonement and teaches the little waif Jetsam to read. Charming end papers and illustrations." Booklist

Sneve, Virginia Driving Hawk

Jimmy Yellow Hawk; illus. by Oren Lyons. Holiday House 1972 76p illus lib. bdg. $4.95 (3-5)   Fic

1 Dakota Indians—Fiction

ISBN 0-8234-0197-9

"He was tired of being called Little Jim. After all, he was ten now. . . . In the past, Sioux boys had earned a new name through some brave deed, but what could a boy do today? After a near-disaster with a skunk, Little Jim succeeded in his determined trapping, caught a mink, and was thrilled to hear his father say, 'My son, Jimmy, trapped it!' . . . [The strength of the story] lies in the picture it gives of a contemporary Indian family that has adjusted to ranch life, and has accepted the benefits of white civilization but given up neither their participation nor their pride in their Indian heritage. The book was awarded the Council on Interracial Books' 1971 award for the best book by an American Indian author." Chicago. Children's Bk Center

Glossary of Sioux words: p9

Snyder, Zilpha Keatley

Black and blue magic; drawings by Gene Holtan. Atheneum Pubs. 1966 186p illus lib. bdg. $5.95, pa 95¢ (4-6)   Fic

1 San Francisco—Fiction 2 Fantastic fiction

ISBN 0-689-30075-1; 0-689-70313-9

"A very likable boy, Harry Houdini Marco, is the central figure in this funny, modern fantasy. Harry and his mother run a boarding house in a decaying

section of San Francisco. They cannot afford a vacation; and since most of his friends have moved, Harry anticipates a dull summer. But a gift of wings from mysterious Mr. Mazzeeck, a temporary boarder who deals in charms, changes Harry's summer into a highly entertaining one with an 'angel's' view of the city." Moorachian. What is a City?

The changeling; illus. by Alton Raible. Atheneum Pubs. 1970 220p illus lib. bdg. $5.95, pa 95¢ (4-7)   Fic

1 Friendship—Fiction

ISBN 0-689-20610-0; 0-689-70351-1

Martha was a shy seven-year-old when she met Ivy, the daughter of a disreputable, vagabond family. This story, told partly in flashbacks, tells about their "long friendship in which Ivy, wildly imaginative and firmly insisting she was a changeling, led in fanciful play—interspersed with some mischief. A natural dancer, Ivy was given the lead in a junior high play, and a jealous competitor made it appear that Ivy was the perpetrator of an act of vandalism. Although Martha's brother confessed that he and two others had been the culprits, Ivy left town. Only when she was a high school sophomore did Martha learn that Ivy was dancing in New York, and she became sharply aware that her own poise and popularity were due in large measure to the salubrious influence of Ivy's personality." Sutherland. The Best in Children's Bks

"Though the finale is weak, the story is distinguished by its vivid characterization and sensitive writing." Sat Rev

The Egypt game; drawings by Alton Raible. Atheneum Pubs. 1967 215p illus lib. bdg. $6.95, pa $1.95 (4-7)   Fic

ISBN 0-689-30006-9; 0-689-70297-3

"Six children of different ethnic backgrounds secretly play a game invented by a white girl and a Negro girl who are fascinated by their own imaginations and by ancient Egypt. The Egypt game helps solve one girl's personal problems and it leads to the capture of a mentally ill murderer who attacks one of the girls." Wis Library Bul

"This may prove to be one of the controversial books of the decade: it is strong in characterization, the dialogue is superb, the plot is original, and the sequences in which the children are engaged in sustained imaginative play are fascinating, and often very funny. On the other hand, the murder scare and the taciturn, gloomy Professor seem grim notes. In this story, the fact that the children are white, Negro, and Oriental seems not a device but a natural consequence of grouping in a heterogeneous community. [This] is a distinguished book." Sat Rev

The headless cupid; illus. by Alton Raible. Atheneum Pubs. 1971 203p illus $4.95, pa $1.95 (4-7)   Fic

1 Occult sciences—Fiction

ISBN 0-689-20687-9; 0-689-70414-3

"Amanda the 12-year-old daughter of their new stepmother, proclaims herself an expert in the occult and puts the Stanley children, 11-year-old David and his three younger siblings, through an initiation, a series of ritual ordeals, and a seance. The children learn that in 1896 their house had been the scene of poltergeist activity which culminated in the beheading of a carved cupid figure on the stairway. Thereafter it seems that the poltergeist has returned, but David proves that the manifestations are being caused by Amanda. However, in a final plot twist, the cupid's head is recovered through a genuine ESP experience. This is believable fiction—with a touch of fantasy—supported throughout by solid, three-dimensional characterizations." Sch Library J

Snyder, Zilpha Keatley—_Continued_

The truth about Stone Hollow; illus. by Alton Raible. Atheneum Pubs. 1974 211p illus $6.95 (4-7) Fic

1 Supernatural—Fiction 2 California—Fiction

ISBN 0-689-30147-2

"In 1938, at Taylor Springs, California, Amy Polonski becomes friend and defender of an English boy, Jason Fitzmaurice, who is an odd-man-out in her sixth-grade class. Together they visit the supposedly haunted Stone Hollow, which their classmates slavishly avoid. There they sense the presence of ghostly shapes. . . . A small piece of stone [Jason] gives to Amy enables her to bring something magical to view in her attic at home. But the story consists of more than discoveries and wonderings. A clear picture emerges of the smug little town riddled with religious prejudices and family differences." Horn Bk

"Convincing characters and dialogue impart strength to an atmospheric fantasy." Top of the News

The velvet room; drawings by Alton Raible. Atheneum Pubs. 1965 216p illus lib. bdg. $4.75 (4-6) Fic

1 California—Fiction 2 Migrant labor—Fiction 3 Depressions—Fiction

ISBN 0-689-30040-9

"Beset by the problems of growing up [in California during the Depression] in a migrant worker's family, Robin finds refuge from the real world in a deserted mansion with a book-lined room and a mysterious past." Adventuring With Bks, 2d edition

"Robin's character has far more facets than the usual sensitive child of fiction who needs a private place for dreaming. She is normally selfish and has a tough resilience behind her sensitivity. Her brothers and sisters are real children too. The reader, however, remembers not the realism of the rather stark tale of a migratory worker's family, but the magical aura through which an imaginative child sees the world. Illustrations characteristic of the artist reflect atmosphere and mood." Horn Bk

The witches of Worm; illus. by Alton Raible. Atheneum Pubs. 1972 183p illus $6.25 (4-7) Fic

1 Witchcraft—Fiction 2 Cats—Stories

ISBN 0-689-30066-2

Jessica, the neglected child of a swinging divorcee, "finds a deserted, new-born kitten which she calls 'Worm' since it is virtually hairless and blind. When this Worm turns—daily becoming more dominant over its mistress—Jessica is convinced she is in the grip of a hellish force that makes her play harmful tricks on her mother and on her few friends." Pub W

"This is a haunting story of the power of mind and ritual, as well as of misunderstanding, anger, loneliness and friendship. It is written with humor, pace, a sure feeling for conversation and a warm understanding of human nature." Commonweal

Sorensen, Virginia

Plain girl; illus. by Charles Geer. Harcourt 1955 151p illus $5.95, pa 75¢ (4-6) Fic

1 Amish—Fiction 2 School stories

ISBN 0-15-262434-1; 0-15-672020-5

"Ten-year-old Esther, an Amish girl, is thoroughly enjoying school after the authorities force her father to send her there. Although she still loves the ways of the Plain People, she begins to understand why her brother Dan has run away from the strict home discipline. Although Esther is confused by marked social differences, she learns to think for herself and stands her ground with gentle firmness." Rdng Ladders. 5th edition

"Developing her theme tactfully, her characters

perceptively, the author reaches into the heart of Amish life. . . . Readers will leave this engrossing tale with appreciation and understanding of the tradition, ideals and problems of the Amish." N Y Times Bk Rev

Southall, Ivan

Hills End. Macmillan Pub. Co. [1974 c1962] 215p $5.95 (6-7) Fic

1 Australia—Fiction

ISBN 0-02-786120-1

First published 1962 in Australia. This is a reissue of the first American edition published 1963 by St Martins

"Few ever missed the annual picnic of Hills End. This year, because of a fabricated tale of prehistoric drawings, seven children are not going. Instead they find themselves climbing up to the caves high above the town, led by their teacher, Miss Godwin, who had planned to explore alone. These events, however, combine to save the lives of the people of Hills End when a sudden, violent storm threatens to devastate the town, maroon their families, and trap the children in the caves." Rdng Ladders. 5th edition

"Australian adventure with a difference. . . . In plot, a cross between 'Robinson Crusoe' and a happy-ending 'Lord of the Flies.' The background and touches of dialect set the scene adequately. . . . The handling of pace and incident is excellent." Library J

Sperry, Armstrong

Call it courage; illus. by the author. Macmillan (N Y) 1940 95p illus lib. bdg. $4.95, pa 95¢ (5-7) Fic

1 Polynesia—Fiction

Awarded the Newbery Medal, 1941

"Because he fears the ocean, a Polynesian boy is scorned by his people and must redeem himself by an act of courage. His lone journey to a sacred island and the dangers he faces there earn him the name Mafatu, 'Stout Heart.' Dramatic illustrations add atmosphere and mystery." Hodges. Bks for Elem Sch Libraries

Storm canvas; written and illus. by Armstrong Sperry. Holt 1944 301p illus lib. bdg. $3.59 (6-7) Fic

1 U.S.—History—War of 1812—Fiction 2 Sea stories

ISBN 0-03-043145-X

"A tale of the blockade runners of the war of 1812, and of the Thunderbolt and her courageous commander Thomas Blythe in particular. The story is told through the adventures of Jason Cobb, a Connecticut Yankee who has the sea in his blood, and it is full of the joys of sea life, of stirring naval encounters, and glimpses of such picturesque figures as Henry Christophe, Haiti's exotic ruler." Ontario Library Rev

"Armstrong Sperry writes with knowledge of the sea and his pictures add their salty tang to the exciting story." Horn Bk

Seagoing glossary: p295-301

Spykman, E. C.

Terrible, horrible Edie. Harcourt 1960 224p $5.95, pa 75¢ (5-7) Fic

ISBN 0-15-284788-X; 0-15-627650-X

"Edie, the youngest of the Cares children, first met in 'A Lemon and a Star' and again in 'Wild Angel,' has now become ten years old. . . . Her activities during their summer (still early in the century) at the shore, while their parents travel abroad, swing from hazardous sailing and some burglar detection to quieter periods of craving excitement, and explosive ones when adult control seems unjust." Horn Bk

Spyri, Johanna
Heidi (4-6)   Fic
1 Alps—Fiction 2 Switzerland—Fiction
Some editions are:
Collins (Rainbow classics) $2.95, lib. bdg. $3.91 Illus-
trated by Leonard Weisgard; introduction by May
Lamberton Becker (ISBN 0-529-04779-9; 0-529-
04780-2)
Grosset lib. bdg. $3.95 (ISBN 0-448-06012-4)
Macmillan (N Y) (The Macmillan classics) $4.95 After-
word by Clifton Fadiman; illustrated by Greta
Elgaard
Scribner (Scribner Illustrated classics) $10 Illustrated
by Jessie Wilcox Smith (ISBN 0-684-20946-2)
Watts, F. lib. bdg. $7.95 Pictures by Charles Mozley.
Large type edition complete and unabridged. A
Keith Jennison book (ISBN 0-531-00200-4)
First published 1880
"The story of Heidi is the story of the greatness of
her affection for her pet goats, for Peter and her
grandfather, and for her mountain home. Permeating
the whole tale is the play of sunshine and shadow on
the slopes of the jagged peaks of the great, glittering,
snow-capped mountains of Heidi's [Swiss] Alpine
home. A book which finds a responsive chord in every
young heart." Toronto

Steele, Mary Q.
Journey outside; woodcuts by Rocco Negri. Viking
1969 143p illus $4.50 (5-7)   Fic
ISBN 0-670-40952-9
"For all of his life, Dilar had unquestioningly
accepted what Grandfather had said: the Raft People
were searching, as they drifted down the dark underground river, for a Better Place. Now suspecting that
they were simply circling, the boy leaped to a ledge of
the cave and made his way to the strange world of
grass and sunshine. In his quest for help for his own
people, Dilar stays for a time in each of several cultures, each known to the other but isolated from
them." Chicago. Children's Bk Center
"This allegory is an exciting enough quest to please
a reader who enjoys action. On a deeper level the
book dramatizes man's basic desire to know himself."
Wis Library Bul

Steele, William O.
Flaming arrows; illus. by Paul Galdone. Harcourt
1957 178p illus $5.95, pa $1.15 (4-6)   Fic
1 Frontier and pioneer life—Fiction 2 Chick-
amauga Indians—Fiction 3 Tennessee—Fiction
ISBN 0-15-228424-9; 0-15-631550-5
"Warned that the Chickamaugas were on the war-
path Chad Rabun and his family along with other
Cumberland settlers fled to the fort. Bitter feeling
arose when Mrs. Logan and her children, under suspicion because the father was a white renegade,
sought refuge with them. During the three days of
forting up, days of terror, dissension, thirst, and wear-
iness, Chad learned lessons he was not likely to
forget—about courage, hating and being hated, thinking things through, and condemning someone for the
misdeeds of another." Booklist
The author's "crisp dialogue, authentic background
and furious action—plus the excellent message that
not always is father-like-son—makes this story a
choice item for the young readers' library." N Y Times
Bk Rev

The perilous road; illus. by Paul Galdone. Harcourt
1958 191p illus $6.25, pa 75¢ (5-7)   Fic
1 U.S.—History—Civil War—Fiction 2 Tennessee—Fiction
ISBN 0-15-260644-0; 0-15-671696-8
"Ten-year-old Chris, enraged when the Yankees
raid his father's farm and baffled when his older

brother joins the Northern Army, tries to aid the
Confederacy in every possible way. Only when his
spy report threatens his brother's life and he himself is
caught in a cavalry raid does he realize the meaning of
his father's words, 'war is the worst thing that can
happen to folks.' " Library J
"Mr. Steele makes the tensions and excitements of
the Brothers' War very real, and the customs of the
mountain people, the speech and setting are well
integrated into the narrative." N Y Times Bk Rev

Wilderness journey; illus. by Paul Galdone. Harcourt 1953 209p illus $5.95 (4-6)   Fic
1 Frontier and pioneer life—Fiction
ISBN 0-15-297318-4
A "lively picture of frontier days in the story of a boy
who journeys over the Wilderness Trail to the French
Salt Lick in the company of a Long Hunter. Small for
his age and as 'unhandy as all git,' ten-year-old Flan
agreed with the general opinion that he was not much
account. On the dangerous trek through the wilderness Flan discovered that size was often less important than quick wit and endurance and that what
mattered most was knowing you could do what you
had to do." Booklist

Winter danger; illus. by Paul Galdone. Harcourt
1954 183p illus $5.95 (4-6)   Fic
1 Frontier and pioneer life—Fiction 2 Tennessee—
Fiction
ISBN 0-15-298034-2
A story of Caje, an 11-year-old, and his efforts to
adjust to a Tennessee frontier village after a freer life
in the woods with his father. Jared, a wanderer and
hunter, leaves his son to make adjustments with kinfolk, rather than settle down himself. The time is
about 1780
It is "distinguished not only for its clear evocation of
the sense of physical danger, of hunger and cold but
also because Mr. Steele makes us feel deeply the
emotions of a boy who is fiercely independent but
wants to belong." N Y Times Bk Rev

Steig, William
Dominic; story and pictures by William Steig. Farrar, Straus 1972 145p illus $5.95 (4-6)   Fic
1 Dogs—Stories
ISBN 0-374-31822-0
Dominic, a gregarious dog, sets out on the high
road one day, going no place in particular, but moving
along to find whatever he can. And that turns out to be
plenty, including an invalid pig who leaves Dominic
his fortune; a variety of friends and adventures; and
even—in the end—his life's companion
"A singular blend of naïveté and sophistication,
comic commentary and philosophizing, the narrative
handles situation clichés with humor and flair—
perhaps because of the author's felicitous turn of
phrase, his verbal cartooning, and his integration of
text and illustrations. A chivalrous and optimistic
tribute to gallantry and romance." Horn Bk

The real thief; story and pictures by William Steig.
Farrar, Straus 1973 58p illus lib. bdg. $4.95 (2-5)
                                                    Fic
1 Animals—Stories
ISBN 0-374-36217-3
"Proud of his job as guard to the Royal Treasury,
loyal to his king (Basil the bear) Gawain the goose is
baffled by the repeated theft of gold and jewels from
the massive building to which only Gawain and Basil
have keys. He is heartsick when the king dismisses
him publicly and calls him a disgrace to the kingdom.
Sentenced to prison, the goose flies off to isolation.
The true thief, a mouse, is penitent and decides that
he will go on stealing so that the king will know

Steig, William—_Continued_

Gawain is innocent; still suffering guilt, he takes back the loot piece by piece, searches for Gawain, and confesses. They decide to keep it secret, but Gawain goes back to accept royal apologies and greater status than before." Chicago. Children's Bk Center

"For young readers or listeners, it's an involving story with animal characters displaying more real emotions than many supposedly human characters. Steig's gray line-and-wash drawings provide a charming accompaniment to a wholly winning story." Sch Library J

Stephens, Mary Jo

Witch of the Cumberlands; illus. by Arvis Stewart. Houghton 1974 243p illus $4.95 (5-7)   Fic

1 Mystery and detective stories 2 Kentucky—Fiction

ISBN 0-395-18509-2

Miss Birdie, an elderly woman in the Cumberland Mountains of Kentucky, tells fortunes, prepares herbal remedies and believes in communication with the dead. She has waited 40 years to learn the truth behind a mine disaster during which her fiancé, a union organizer, disappeared. The three MacGregor children, who have come to live in her house, help unravel the mystery

"Frank about the evils of strip mining and flavored with Kentucky Mountain folklore, the story has an authentic Cumberland setting. . . . The book is a mélange, barely supported by the strong scenes and characters; but it has a sense of atmosphere. Child readers will probably find the occult aspect most entrancing." Horn Bk

Steptoe, John

Train ride. Harper 1971 unp illus $3.95, lib. bdg. $4.79 (3-6)   Fic

1 New York (City)—Fiction 2 Negroes—Fiction

ISBN 0-06-025773-3; 0-06-025774-1

Illustrated by the author

"Having boasted about his familiarity with New York City transport, Charlie can hardly refuse when some of his friends suggest going to Times Square. The boys enjoy the sights, see more white people than they ever did in Brooklyn, enjoy the brightness and the penny arcade. Their money gone, they wheedle free rides and get home to the beatings they had realized were coming. Next day, they decide they won't go again—but it was worth it. . . . The illustrations are stunning, vibrant with color and effective in composition. The story has an all-boy quality: contempt for girls, the relish of a ploy, the fellowship and resourcefulness that emerge particularly when children function as a group. The writing style is adequate, livened only by the cadence of black idiom, a fact that will make the book welcome to some and anathema to others." Chicago. Children's Bk Center

Sterling, Dorothy

Mary Jane; illus. by Ernest Crichlow. Doubleday 1959 214p illus $4.95, lib. bdg. $5.70 (5-7)   Fic

1 Segregation in education—Fiction 2 Negroes—Fiction 3 School stories

ISBN 0-385-07797-1; 0-385-06250-8

The "story of a Negro girl's experiences in a newly-integrated [junior] high school. . . . [The author] describes her heroine's surprise at the treatment she receives and the ways in which she gradually wins over the white students who had opposed her." Pub W

"Sensibly and sensitively written, this is a realistic story of school integration. . . . The author has a sure knowledge of children and schools. Excellent illustrations and charming bookjacket by Ernest Crichlow (a Negro artist) add appeal." Library J

Stevenson, William

The bushbabies; illus. by Victor Ambrus. Houghton 1965 278p illus map $5.95 (4-7)   Fic

1 Kenya—Fiction

ISBN 0-395-07116-X

"Jackie, the daughter of an English game warden, discovers she has lost the permit necessary to take her pet tarsier or bushbaby out of Africa. Enlisting the help of Tembo, an African headman, she leaves the ship to return her pet to his native Kenya. A hazardous and suspenseful journey follows." Wis Library Bul

This is "a most unusual story, both in the setting and in the beautifully built-up relationship between two people disparate in age, sex, race, and station." Chicago. Children's Bk Center

Stewart, Mary

The little broomstick; illus. by Shirley Hughes. Morrow 1972 [c1971] 192p illus $5.95, lib. bdg. $5.11 (3-6)   Fic

1 Witches—Fiction 2 Great Britain—Fiction

ISBN 0-688-21507-6; 0-688-31507-0

First published 1971 in England

"Ten-year-old Mary is bored and lonely during her holiday at her great-aunt's house in Shropshire, England, until she befriends a black cat, discovers a rare flower in the woods, and accidentally rubs the handle of a small birch broomstick with the flower. The broom springs to life, carrying Mary and her cat to a mysterious school for witches where the cat is borrowed for transformation experiments and Mary has to become a practitioner of magic and spells to rescue him." Booklist

Stockton, Frank R.

The Bee-man of Orn; pictures by Maurice Sendak. Holt 1964 44p illus lib. bdg. $3.27, pa $1.65 (4-6)   Fic

1 Fairy tales

ISBN 0-03-044810-7; 0-03-080114-1

First published 1887 by Scribner in: The Bee-man of Orn, and other fanciful tales

"Completely content, living a simple and busy life with his omnipresent bees, the Bee-Man becomes perturbed when a Junior Sorcerer informs him that he has undoubtedly been transformed from some other sort of being. What kind of being that is, he is not qualified to say—so the Bee-Man sets out to find his previous incarnation." Chicago. Children's Bk Center

"Perfect for reading aloud and can raise the literary standard of books shared in the classroom." Horn Bk

The story "has been illustrated to perfection. . . . A delightful and imaginative piece of bookmaking." Pub W

The Griffin and the Minor Canon; with illus. by Maurice Sendak. Holt 1963 55p illus lib. bdg. $3.27, pa $1.65 (3-5)   Fic

1 Griffins—Stories 2 Fairy tales

ISBN 0-03-035825-6; 0-03-086626-X

A story from the author's: Fanciful tales, first published 1894 by Scribner

"The townspeople are terrified when a griffin arrives to view his stone likeness over the great door of the church. They are even more alarmed when he develops a great fondness and admiration for both the sculpture and the minor canon and gives no indication of leaving the town before his seasonal meal." Sch Library J

"The fine flow of language . . . will please those who read aloud to children as well as the children themselves; and on their own the fairy-tale ages will be drawn naturally to this fully illustrated book. Sendak's carefully detailed gothic sketches and his prefacing words reveal his work to have been a labor of love." Horn Bk

Stolz, Mary

The bully of Barkham Street; pictures by Leonard Shortall. Harper 1963 194p illus lib. bdg. $4.79 (4-6)   Fic

1 Dogs—Stories

ISBN 0-06-025821-7

Also available in a large print edition for $7.50 (ISBN 0-06-025823-3)

"Fatso" Martin, "the bully who tormented Edward Frost in 'A dog on Barkham Street' is brought back in a story which retells events of the earlier book—the fights, the loss of Martin's dog, the disgrace at the school assembly, and other incidents—strictly from Martin's point of view. No longer is Martin simply big, mean, and hateful; here he is seen as insecure, rejected, and misunderstood." Booklist

"Characters, family relationships, peer group intricacies, and quiet humor [are] as effectively meshed as they were in the first book. . . . [The reader] can not only see the other side of the picture through Martin's eyes, but . . . [also the] ingenuity of a literary craftsman." Chicago. Children's Bk Center

A dog on Barkham Street; pictures by Leonard Shortall. Harper 1960 184p illus $4.50, lib. bdg. $3.99 (4-6)   Fic

1 Dogs—Stories

ISBN 0-06-025840-3; 0-06-025841-1

"Fifth-grader Edward Frost has two seemingly insurmountable problems—to rid himself of the constant tormenting by the bully who lives next door and to convince his parents that he is responsible enough to have a dog. It is the coming of his irresponsible vagabond uncle with a beautiful young collie that precipitates the solution of Edward's problems." Booklist

"Simple, everyday events and very familiar people make up this story, but there is nothing ordinary about the way those ingredients are assembled. . . . This author has a remarkable ability to get inside her characters, whether they are young boys, adolescent girls, parents or hobos, and the result in this book is a reading experience as sharp as reality." Horn Bk

The edge of next year. Harper 1974 195p $5.95, lib. bdg. $5.79 (6-7)   Fic

1 Death—Fiction 2 Alcoholism—Fiction

ISBN 0-06-025857-8; 0-06-025858-6

"Orin and Vic Woodward are in the family car when they have a bad accident. Their mother is killed. The author conveys the feelings of Orin after his mother's death. This . . . [fourteen-year-old] boy takes on himself the housework, the care of his brother, Vic, and constantly worries about his father. The father is trying to 'drown his sorrow' by drinking. Orin and his family are portrayed in a painful situation. Finally, the father joins A. A. (Alcoholics Anonymous) and Orin feels that there is hope and a future in their lives." Best Sellers

"All of the members of the family are skillfully individualized; the commonplace details of everyday living jostle with sensitive transcriptions of the changes of the seasons; and Orin's experiences strike the reader as accurate and truly felt." Horn Bk

The noonday friends. Harper 1965 182p illus lib. bdg. $4.79 (4-6)   Fic

1 Domestic relations—Fiction 2 New York (City)—Fiction 3 School stories

ISBN 0-06-025946-9

Illustrated by Louis S. Glanzman

"Franny hated qualifying for a free school lunch ticket, never having enough to wear, having to hurry home to care for her little brother; but nothing seemed to bother her twin brother Jim. Their father had trouble keeping a job, their mother had to work,

and Franny's home duties meant that the desired friendship with a classmate became largely a noonday affair shared over lunch. This memorable story of children in Greenwich Village illustrates their reactions to problems, families, and each other." Moorachian. What is a City?

This is "a realistic story of the family relationship and school life of a little girl in a lower middle-class urban family." Univ. of Chicago. Reading

A wonderful, terrible time; pictures by Louis S. Glanzman. Harper 1967 182p illus $4.50, lib. bdg. $4.79 (4-6)   Fic

1 Camps—Fiction 2 Negroes—Fiction 3 New York (City)—Fiction

ISBN 0-06-026063-7; 0-06-026064-5

"Sue Ellen and Mady are enjoying a comfortable summer with doll parties, walks through the dimestore, and cooling half hours at the open fire hydrant when they receive the unexpected gift of two weeks away at camp." Booklist

"A good book as a camp story or as a picture of friendship values, but the most striking aspect is the fact that both at home and at camp, the girls are in a racially mixed community where integration is not The Issue of the book. Mady and Sue Ellen are both Negro; while this is a fact that enters naturally into the dialogue, it is a minor fact compared to the importance of personalities and familial relationships." Chicago. Children's Bk Center

Streatfeild, Noel

Ballet shoes; illus. by Richard Floethe. Random House 1937 249p illus $2.95, lib. bdg. $5.39 (4-6)   Fic

1 Ballet—Fiction 2 Theater—Fiction 3 London—Fiction

ISBN 0-394-80875-4; 0-394-90875-9

First published 1936 in England

Three little girls attend the Children's Academy of Dancing in London to train for the professional stage. . . . Petrova prefers the mechanics of automobiles and airplanes, but Pauline becomes a promising young actress and Posy shows great skill as a dancer

"The author has made real a section of life too often distorted by fiction. By pointing out some of the things which make up stage magic, she has done a real service to the theater for its young audience." N Y Her Trib Bks

The family at Caldicott Place; illus. by Betty Maxey. Random House [1968 c1967] 177p illus $3.95, lib. bdg. $5.39 (4-6)   Fic

1 Family—Fiction 2 Great Britain—Fiction

ISBN 0-394-81189-5; 0-394-91189-X

First published 1967 in England with title: Caldicott Place

"Their father's automobile accident and long psychological withdrawal force the Johnstone family to cope with a series of personal and financial problems. The biggest adjustment involves taking in several wealthy children as boarders on the run-down country estate willed to the youngest Johnstone boy by the woman whose car almost killed his father." Booklist

"Here is an English family coping with personal disaster in the best possible chin-up fashion. As romantic as a valentine, the story avoids base sentimentality because of the author's light, graceful style and her signal ability to create characters that come alive." Sat Rev

Thursday's child; illus. by Peggy Fortnum. Random House [1971 c1970] 275p illus $4.50, lib. bdg. $5.39 (4-7)   Fic

Streatfeild, Noel—_Continued_

1 Orphans and orphans' homes—Fiction 2 Great Britain—Fiction
ISBN 0-394-82096-7; 0-394-92096-1
First published 1970 in England

Ten-year-old Margaret Thursday, an "orphan of turn-of-the-century England refuses to be subdued by anybody—or anything. For openers, she becomes the first runaway from St. Luke's orphanage [taking two little orphan boys with her;] the first girl to work as a 'legger' on the canals; and as the story ends she has started a career as actress (playing Little Lord Fauntleroy) . . . with a repertory theater group." Best Sellers

"Although the setting and situations are in the turn-of-the-century tradition of 'orphan stories,' the heroine is a remarkably contemporary character whose final decision to remain independent of her would-be benefactors is logical and consistent with a fully realized personality. A fresh and sprightly addition to a perennially popular genre." Horn Bk

Street, James H.

Good-bye, my Lady. Lippincott 1954 222p $7.95 (5-7)   Fic

1 Dogs—Stories 2 Mississippi—Fiction
ISBN 0-397-00049-9

"Skeeter, a swamp boy who lives with his Uncle Jess in Mississippi, finds a rare breed of hunting dog lost in the swamps, trains it, and grows to love it. Through his own desire to keep the dog, he comes to see and understand the hidden desires in the lives of those around him. With the help of his uncle, he decides that he must return Lady to her rightful owner. Thus he crosses the first hurdle in the maturing process and the search for values." Rdng Ladders

Stuart, Jesse

The beatinest boy; illus. by Robert Henneberger. McGraw 1953 110p illus lib. bdg. $4.72 (4-6)   Fic

1 Mountain life—Southern States—Fiction 2 Kentucky—Fiction 3 Grandmothers—Fiction
ISBN 0-07-062303-1

"Whittlesey House publications"

Davy lives with his grandmother in her Kentucky mountain home. His efforts to earn the money to buy her a special Christmas gift are described

"A warm hearted story. . . . Simplicity and directness of style communicate the author's love of people and of nature." Bookmark

"The illustrations are unusual—strong black-and-white drawings that reproduce the atmosphere of the Cumberland Mountains." Sat Rev

Suhl, Yuri

Uncle Misha's partisans. Four Winds 1973 211p lib. bdg. $5.95 (5-7)   Fic

1 World War, 1939-1945—Fiction 2 Jews in the Ukraine—Fiction 3 Ukraine—Fiction
ISBN 0-590-07295-1

"The exploits of a twelve-year-old Ukrainian boy, Motele, are modeled from an actual group of resistance fighters during the Second World War. Orphaned by the Nazis, Motele is harbored in the forest of the partisans. As he joins their perilous missions, his skill in playing the violin causes him to be sent on a dangerous assignment which involves striking a blow at the Nazis and thus avenging the death of his family." Top of the News

"Richly detailed, convincing, and consistently told from a twelve-year-old's point of view, the account has immediacy, poignancy, strong character interest, and suspense." Horn Bk

Sutcliff, Rosemary

The witch's brat; illus. by Richard Lebenson. Walck, H.Z. 1970 143p illus $5.50 (5-7)   Fic

1 Great Britain—Fiction 2 Physically handicapped children—Fiction
ISBN 0-8098-3095-7

Lovel, aged 11 and misshapen, was stoned and had to leave his native home a week after his grandmother's death because the villagers thought her to have been a witch and he 'the witch's brat.' He found refuge at a Benedictine Abbey. Lovel became well and used to good advantage his skills in growing physic herbs and caring for the ill. Later Lovel joins Rahere, jongleur to King Henry I turned monk, in the founding of St. Bartholomew's Hospital near London. Twelfth Century England is accurately depicted." Wis Library Bul

The book "gives glimpses into the various strata of feudal society: the harsh law of the manor, the orderly, disciplined regimen of the monastery, the teeming city with its hopeless poor, the craftsmen and builders with their own complex structure of skills and rewards. The writing is vivid and the characters alive." Horn Bk

Swayne, Sam

Great-grandfather in the honey tree; written and illus. by Sam and Zoa Swayne. Viking 1949 53p illus lib. bdg. $3.95 (2-4)   Fic

ISBN 0-670-34932-1

This story tells how great-grandfather went out to net some geese and came home with a barrel of honey, a bear, a fish, a partridge, a deer and seven wild turkeys, as well as the net of geese

"This book absolutely crackles with action and humor. It leaves a grown-up breathless with laughter and envy." Sat Rev

Tapley, Caroline

John come down the backstay; illus. by Richard Cuffari. Atheneum Pubs. 1974 182p illus maps lib. bdg. $6.25 (6-7)   Fic

1 Arctic regions—Fiction 2 Fox (Steam yacht)—Fiction
ISBN 0-689-30149-9

"In 1845, Sir John Franklin set sail to complete the exploration of the arctic Northwest Passage. He never returned; 12 years and over 40 search expeditions later, Captain Franklin's wife financed the journey of the sailing ship 'Fox.' This historical novel, a diary of the fictional character John Micklethwaite, youngest crew member, is based on a report of the 'Fox's' captain, published after his return to England in 1859." Booklist

"The tensions developed in the ship's close quarters are fully delineated, as are the measures used to relieve boredom—storytelling, formal lessons conducted by the chief officers, and occasional celebrations. Giving added interest to what might seem to be just another well-spun adventure yarn, several forces underlie the narrative—the interplay of personalities, contrasts in social attitude, the psychology of stress. Although the principal characters are not as fully developed as they might be in a conventionally plotted novel, they are more than types. . . . The black-and-white drawings appropriately reflect the awesome loneliness of the Arctic landscape. A listing of the ship's company and a glossary are appended." Horn Bk

Taylor, Sydney

All-of-a-kind family; illus. by Helen John. Follett 1951 192p illus $4.95, lib. bdg. $4.98 (4-6)   Fic

1 Jews in New York (City)—Fiction 2 New York (City)—Fiction
ISBN 0-695-80280-1; 0-695-40280-3

Taylor, Sydney—*Continued*

Received the Charles W. Follett award, 1951

"Five little Jewish girls grow up in New York's lower East side in a happy home atmosphere before the first World War." Pittsburgh

"A genuine and delightful picture of a Jewish family . . . with an understanding mother and father, rich in kindness and fun though poor in money. The important part the public library played in the lives of these children is happily evident; and the Jewish holiday celebrations are particularly well described." Horn Bk

Three additional titles about this family are available from Follett: More all-of-a-kind family $4.95, lib. bdg. $4.98 (ISBN 0-695-85880-7; 0-695-45880-9); All-of-a-kind family uptown $4.95, lib. bdg. $4.98 (ISBN 0-695-80285-2; 0-695-40285-4); All-of-a-kind family downtown $4.95, lib. bdg. $4.98 (ISBN 0-695-80308-5; 0-695-40308-7)

Taylor, Theodore

The cay. Doubleday 1969 137p $5.95, lib. bdg. $6.70 (5-7) Fic

1 World War, 1939-1945—Fiction 2 Caribbean area —Fiction 3 Survival (after airplane accidents, shipwrecks, etc.)—Fiction

ISBN 0-385-07906-0; 0-385-08152-9

"Phillip, a resident of the war-torn Caribbean island of Curacao, is forced to leave his home. As he is being evacuated, the ship on which he is being transported is sunk. With only an old West Indian man as a companion and guide, he ekes out a precarious existence on a tiny island. Burdened with blindness, caused by a head injury around the time of the shipwreck, the boy grows in understanding and maturity as he faces ever increasing challenges." Wis Library Bul

"World War II provides the background for this sensitive tale of two survivors of a torpedoed ship, a blind white boy and a black seaman. . . . An absorbing story about the color of friendship and human dignity." Top of the News

Teetoncey; illus. by Richard Cuffari. Doubleday 1974 153p illus $4.50, lib. bdg. $5.25 (6-7) Fic

1 Amnesia—Fiction 2 North Carolina—Fiction

ISBN 0-385-09584-8; 0-385-09587-2

This first novel in a projected Hatteras Banks trilogy is about eleven-year-old Ben O'Neal, who lives "with his mother on the Outer Banks of North Carolina in 1898. After a storm, he rescues a young girl, victim of a shipwreck, who is washed up on the beach. The girl eventually recovers physically but remains [amnesiac] mute and unresponsive. In the process of helping Teetoncey recover, Ben comes to terms with his manhood, his mother, and his image of his dead father." Children's Bk Rev Serv

"The novel is rich with details of local geography, history, and folklore; but they are kept subordinate to the presentation of the dramatic tension between [Ben and his mother] and to the unfolding of Ben's growing awareness of his feelings for Teetoncey. Although the story is sympathetically and realistically told from the boy's point of view, the best-realized character in the book is the boy's mother." Horn Bk

Terris, Susan

The drowning boy. Doubleday 1972 189p $4.50, lib. bdg. $5.25 (6-7) Fic

1 Problem children—Fiction 2 Family—Fiction

ISBN 0-385-03981-6; 0-385-04050-4

This novel deals with a critical two-month period in the life of a twelve-year-old boy; a period in which he finds the demands of his family, especially his sister and father unbearable; a period in which he is frustrated by not being able to cure an autistic child he has befriended

"Characterizations are convincing and the well-written story is engrossing and moving." Booklist

Thiele, Colin

Blue Fin; pictures by Roger Haldane. Harper 1974 243p illus $4.95, lib. bdg. $4.79, pa $1.50 (6-7) Fic

1 Sea stories 2 Fisheries—Fiction

ISBN 0-06-026104-8; 0-06-026105-6; 0-06-440077-8

First published 1969 in Australia

" 'Blue Fin' is Snook Pascoe's father's tuna fishing boat, but the hero of the book . . . is homely, ungainly, and shy Snook himself, who, although blamed and disparaged as a jinx by his scornful father, saves both of their lives when a disaster hits their boat." Babbling Bookworm

"A gripping good story, masterfully woven around a trite theme, is made exciting by vivid words, clear characterization, beautiful language, sound information, and an unusual revelation of outcome of incidents often before completion of events creating the climax. About Australian off-shore tuna fishing, the wealth of information may deter an immature or casual reader, but once begun, the story itself takes over and the information becomes incidental." Children's Bk Rev Serv

Thrasher, Crystal

The dark didn't catch me. Atheneum Pubs. 1975 182p $6.50 (5-7) Fic

1 Indiana—Fiction 2 Depressions—Fiction 3 Family—Fiction

ISBN 0-689-50025-4

"A Margaret K. McElderry book"

"Seely, second of four children, describes her family's move into the southern Indiana hills where her father mistakenly counts on finding work. Her twelfth year was a time of personal, family, and school developments, all reported with frank detail. Domestic relationships twisted by pain and hardship, deaths, and economic austerity are not softened but are related as a slice of life." Horn Bk

This "is by no means a sentimental remembrance. It is a tough, funny, tragic, splendid first novel filled with vivid characters." N Y Times Bk Rev

Thurber, James

The great Quillow; illus. by Doris Lee. Harcourt 1944 54p illus $6.50, pa $1.95 (3-5) Fic

1 Fairy tales

ISBN 0-15-232541-7; 0-15-6360-15-636490-5

"He was called the Great Quillow in derision, for he was only the village toy maker and so regarded by the truly important people, the baker, the butcher, the tailor and others, as a person of little consequence. But when the giant Hunder appears on the scene, threatening to wipe out the village, it is the ingenious toy maker who gets the better of him." Wis Library Bul

"It is the old folk-theme—as old as the Panchatantra—of intelligence and courage against brute force. Mr. Thurber has brought to it grace and humor and a phrasing that is an unending delight. The drawings are a delight, too. It is a book for everyone." Sat Rev

Many moons; illus. by Louis Slobodkin. Harcourt 1943 unp illus $5.95, pa $1.65 (1-4) Fic

1 Fairy tales

ISBN 0-15-251873-8; 0-15-656980-9

Awarded the Caldecott Medal, 1944

This is "the story of a little princess who fell ill of a surfeit of raspberry tarts and would get well only if she could have the moon. The solving of this baffling court problem, how to get the moon, results in an original and entertaining picture-storybook." Booklist

"Louis Slobodkin's pictures float on the pages in four colors; black and white cannot represent them.

Thurber, James—*Continued*

They are the substance of dreams . . . the long thoughts little children, and some adults wise as they, have about life." N Y Her Trib Bks

The 13 clocks; illus. by Mark [sic!] Simont. Simon & Schuster 1950 124p illus $6.95 (6-7)   Fic
1 Fairy tales
ISBN 0-671-72100-3

This is "a fairy tale not for [younger] children about a duke, so cold and cruel that time has frozen around him, who has imprisoned a beautiful princess in his castle, and about a prince who rescues her by performing a seemingly impossible task." New Yorker

"Mr. Thurber has done it again, though I don't know just what it is he has done this time—a fairy tale, a comment on human cruelty and human sweetness or a spell, an incantation compounded of poetry and logic and wit." N Y Her Trib Bks

The white deer; drawings by the author and Don Freeman. Harcourt 1945 115p illus $6.50, pa $1.75 (6-7)   Fic
1 Deer—Stories 2 Fairy tales
ISBN 0-15-196119-0; 0-15-696264-0

This is a fantasy written in the guise of a fairy tale, with three princes, an enchanted princess, and a happy outcome

"A serene and beautiful fantasy. . . . Considering the eerie flight of Thurber's average imaginings, this fairy story is a comparative still-life of beauty and grace. Prose runs back and forth into poetry, and irony is subdued to the gentlest breath of mockery. The book is really written for children and Thurber's dealings with candor and innocence are always on the basis of grave, beautiful simplicity." N Y Times Bk Rev

Titus, Eve

Basil of Baker Street; illus. by Paul Galdone. McGraw 1958 96p illus lib. bdg. $4.72 (3-5)   Fic
1 Mice—Stories 2 Mystery and detective stories 3 Doyle, Sir Arthur Conan—Parodies, travesties, etc.
ISBN 0-07-064907-3

"Whittlesey House publications"

"Basil of Baker Street is the Sherlock Holmes of the mouse world, having studied scientific sleuthing at the feet of the famous English detective. Here in an entertaining, delightfully illustrated story Basil's assistant, Dr. Dawson, tells how the great Basil solves a baffling kidnapping case, restores the children to their parents, and brings the dangerous kidnappers to justice. Acquaintance with Sherlock Holmes and Dr. Watson is not essential to the enjoyment of this small-scale detective story." Booklist

Tolkien, J. R. R.

The hobbit; or, There and back again; illus. by the author. Houghton 1938 310p illus $5.95 (4-7)   Fic
1 Fairy tales
ISBN 0-395-07122-4

First published 1937 in England

A tale of the adventures of Bilbo Baggins, the hobbit, in a land inhabited by dwarfs, elves, goblins, dragons, and humans—although the last named play only a small part in the story. Bilbo's adventures begin when he is persuaded to join a band of dwarfs, led by Gandalf, the Wizard, who are off on an expedition to recover the treasure stolen by Smaug, the Dragon, and hidden in the depths of the Lonely Mountain

"The background of the story is full of authentic bits of mythology and magic and the book has the rare quality of style. It is written with a quiet humor and the logical detail in which children take delight. Nine- and ten-year-olds who discovered the book in the English edition have greeted it with keen enthusiasm, but this is a book with no age limits." Horn Bk

Maps on lining-papers

Townsend, John Rowe

Pirate's Island. Lippincott 1968 159p map $4.50, lib. bdg. $4.43 (5-7)   Fic
1 Great Britain—Fiction
ISBN 0-397-31044-7; 0-397-31425-6

"Gordon Dobbs, overprotected, fat, and timid, was a natural butt for tormenting by the young toughs in a northern English industrial city. His only friend was Sheila, a waif with a superb imagination, who drew Gordon into a quest for pirate treasure on the mucky Midwell River, a make-believe which turned into a frightening reality." Moorachian. What is a City?

"In the author's setting of rat-ravaged alleys, where policemen and rent collectors travel in pairs for safety; in his characters, who can curse and brawl and beat children; in his picture of poverty, which creates numb, blank-eyed mothers and sickly little ones, Townsend brings the dimensions of reality to children's books." N Y Times Bk Rev

Trouble in the jungle; (originally Gumble's Yard); illus. by W. T. Mars. Lippincott 1969 158p illus map $4.50, lib. bdg. $3.59 (5-7)   Fic
1 Great Britain—Fiction
ISBN 0-397-31108-7; 0-397-31109-5

First published 1961 with title: Gumble's Yard

"Set in Cobchester slums referred to as the Jungle, the story includes several characters who appeared in the author's Pirate's Island. . . . Abandoned by irresponsible Uncle Walter and his common-law wife, orphaned thirteen-year-old Kevin and his twelve-year-old sister Sandra, with Uncle Walter's two small motherless children, take up residence in a supposedly deserted area of the slum which turns out to be the headquarters for a gang of smugglers." Booklist

"The milieu is deftly established, the characterization and dialogue are good, and the plot has pace and suspense." Chicago. Children's Bk Center

Travers, P. L.

Mary Poppins; illus. by Mary Shepard. Harcourt 1962 206p illus $5.95 (4-6)   Fic
1 Fairy tales
ISBN 0-15-252410-X

First published 1934

"Here are related the remarkable things that transpired during the time Mary Poppins served as nursemaid for the [British] Banks family. This astonishing person blew in with an east wind and stayed as she had agreed until it changed, and after that, life was never the same for Jane and Michael. Delightful nonsense that defies an age boundary of appreciation. Amusing line drawings." Booklist

"The Poppins books are extremely British, with cooks, gardeners, maids, nanas, nurseries, and teas. . . . But children who like these books like them enormously and wear them to shreds with reareadings." Children and Bks

Treffinger, Carolyn

Li Lun, lad of courage; illus. by Kurt Wiese. Abingdon 1947 93p illus $4.95 (4-6)   Fic
1 China—Fiction
ISBN 0-687-21693-1

"Ten year old Li Lun's fear of the sea was so great that he defied his father and refused to go on his man-making voyage. The task that his father sets him to raise seven times seven grains of rice on the top of the nearby mountain tests his courage as he conquers rain, rats and drought as well as loneliness." Wis Library Bul

Treffinger, Carolyn—*Continued*
"Effectively written and attractively illustrated, this is a moving tale of courage which will have universal appeal." Booklist

Tregarthen, Enys
The doll who came alive; ed. by Elizabeth Yates; illus. by Nora S. Unwin. Day 1972 75p illus $4.95 (3-5)   Fic
1 Dolls—Fiction 2 Fairy tales
ISBN 0-381-99683-2
First published 1942
These are the adventures of a young English girl named Jyd with her wooden Dutch doll named Jane that comes to life because it is loved so much
"Very romantic and somewhat moralistic, the story's appeal—in addition to the ever-entrancing lure of dolls for some children—is in the unusual setting and in the vigorous imagination of Jyd." Chicago. Children's Bk Center

Treviño, Elizabeth Borton de
Nacar, the white deer; illus. by Enrico Arno. Farrar, Straus 1963 149p illus $3.95 (5-7)   Fic
1 Deer—Stories 2 Mexico—Fiction
ISBN 0-374-35478-2
"A Bell book"
In 17th century Mexico, Lalo, a mute herder, is entrusted with the care of a sickly white deer destined to be a present from Mexico to the King of Spain. When the animal becomes strong enough to be shipped to Spain, Lalo accompanies him to the royal court where the boy faces a crisis
"The style of writing is deliberate and ornate. . . . The themes of compassion for animals [and] of piety [are] both heavily stressed." Chicago. Children's Bk Center

Tudor, Tasha
Becky's Christmas; written and illus. by Tasha Tudor. Viking 1961 45p illus lib. bdg. $5.95 (3-5)
                                                                Fic
1 Christmas stories
ISBN 0-670-15425-3
"Tells of the exciting preparations for and the wonderful celebration of Christmas in Becky's farm home where the Christmas season began early in December, gifts were homemade, and the whole family had a part in the traditional baking, decorating, and other festive activities. An aura of anticipation and joy and a sense of family sharing shine through both the story and the pleasing drawings in color and black and white." Booklist

Tunis, John R.
Silence over Dunkerque. Morrow 1962 215p lib. bdg. $5.81 (6-7)   Fic
1 Dunkirk, France, Battle of, 1940—Fiction
ISBN 0-688-31760-X
"During the confusion of evacuating British troops from Dunkerque in 1940, Sergeant Williams and one of his men are left behind. The suspenseful story of the sergeant's rescue by a young French girl and his eventual reunion with his family is quietly recounted in a tense and moving story." Hodges. Bks for Elem Sch Libraries

Turkle, Brinton
The fiddler of High Lonesome; written and illus. by Brinton Turkle. Viking 1968 44p illus $3.50 (3-6)
                                                                Fic
1 Mountain life—Southern States—Fiction
ISBN 0-670-31170-7
"The crude Fogle clan accepts their young kinfolk Bochamp, only because they can't resist the way he plays the fiddle. Although Bochamp can't stand the way the Fogles kill the animals, he agrees to stay with them because he's lonely. But one evening, after showing the Fogles how he can magically make the animals dance, Bochamp realizes for good that he can't possibly accept these people as his own. Both story and illustrations have a haunting beauty of their own; both are distinguished in this regional southern mountain tale. The text is written in the relaxed vernacular of those areas, and to this reviewer this seems most appropriate." Wis Library Bul

Mooncoin Castle; or, Skulduggery rewarded. Viking 1970 141p illus lib. bdg. $4.95 (4-6)   Fic
1 Fantastic fiction 2 Ireland—Fiction
ISBN 0-670-48790-2
"Jeremy, head of the Jackdaw family, called a meeting of the Jackdaws to make war on the humans because they were about to demolish a historic Irish castle so Mr Crotty could build a shopping center. Patrick de Lucy, a ghost, and Maude Muldoon, a pseudo-witch, try saving the castle but it is Patrick that finally finds the magic formula." Wis Library Bul
"The fantastical story is full of humor. . . . Turkle's numerous illustrations evoke the setting and add to the merriment; his scenes are heavily shaded and moody, his people deftly drawn and very lively." Sch Library J

Uchida, Yoshiko
Journey to Topaz; a story of the Japanese-American evacuation; illus. by Donald Carrick. Scribner 1971 149p illus lib. bdg. $5.95 (4-7)   Fic
1 Japanese in the U.S.—Fiction 2 Concentration camps—Fiction
ISBN 0-684-12497-1
This is the story of eleven-year-old Yuki, her eighteen-year-old brother and her mother, who were uprooted, evacuated and interned in Topaz, the War Relocation Center in Utah during World War II
"This tragic herding of innocent people is described with dignity and a sorrowful sense of injustice that never becomes bitter." Sat Rev

The promised year; illus. by William M. Hutchinson. Harcourt 1959 192p illus $6.50 (4-6)   Fic
1 California—Fiction 2 Japanese in California—Fiction 3 Cats—Stories 4 Flower gardening—Fiction
ISBN 0-15-263866-0
"Story of a 10-year-old girl who comes from Japan to California to spend a year with her aunt and uncle. Because her uncle has no use for her cat Tama, to which he is allergic, and seems stern and interested only in his carnation-growing business, Keiko thinks he does not like her and even blames him for Tama's disappearance. It is by her actions when her aunt is in the hospital and the carnation crop is imperiled by smog that Keiko and Uncle Henry come to understand and love each other." Booklist
"Adjustment to the life of a Japanese-American household and to an American community, interesting sidelights on the carnation industry, unusually real characters—all these are part of a story that only someone completely at home in the two cultures could have written with so much humor and verve." Horn Bk
Glossary: p191. Pronunciation of proper names: p191-92

Samurai of Gold Hill; illus. by Ati Forberg. Scribner 1972 119p illus lib. bdg. $5.95 (4-7)   Fic
1 California—Fiction 2 Japanese in California—Fiction
ISBN 0-684-12955-8
Based on historical fact, this is the story of a young

Uchida, Yoshiko—*Continued*

boy, Koichi, and his samurai father who were among the first Japanese immigrants to the U.S. in 1869 when they came with the hope of establishing a tea and silkworm farm in the California hills

"The story of the group's high hopes for the future and their gradual disillusionment and failure as a result of natural catastrophes, prejudices, and villainy comprises a moving narrative of courage and patience in the face of adversity. Author's note on the factual background of the story and a glossary are included." Booklist

Sumi & the goat & the Tokyo Express; pictures by Kazue Mizumura. Scribner 1969 unp illus $5.95 (1-4)   Fic

1 Goats—Stories 2 Railroads—Fiction 3 Japan—Fiction
ISBN 0-684-20967-5

"Miki, a goat, grazing on the tracks, stops the Tokyo Express in Sumi's village, and the whole school tours the train." Shargel. We Can Change It

"The soft, expressive, Oriental-type water-colored drawings reflect the warm humor and the very human qualities of the story, which will appeal to young independent readers and make a good read-aloud." Sch Library J

Sumi's prize; pictures by Kazue Mizumura. Scribner 1964 unp illus lib. bdg. $5.95 (1-4)   Fic

1 Kites—Fiction 2 Japan—Fiction
ISBN 0-684-13157-9

"Since Sumi always wanted to win a prize, she enters the village kite contest on New Year's Day. She is sure she has won until the mayor's top hat is caught by the wind and her butterfly kite crashes as she tries to rescue the hat. Sumi's special prize helps make up for the disaster." Rdng Ldders 5th edition

"A simple and delightful story set in modern Japan. The lively pictures that accompany it are in red and gray." Pub W

Underwood, Betty

The tamarack tree; illus. by Bea Holmes. Houghton 1971 230p illus $5.95 (6-7)   Fic

1 Philleo, Prudence (Crandall)—Fiction 2 Discrimination in education—Fiction 3 Connecticut—Fiction
ISBN 0-395-12761-0

"The appalling restrictions on women in 1833 and the struggle of Prudence Crandall to operate her school for 'young ladies of color' are highlighted in a tale of a white orphan girl who is determined to go to college." Children's Bks, 1971

"A credible story with good characterization and a realistic portrayal of the attitudes toward women and Negroes in the 1830's." Booklist

Unnerstad, Edith

Little O; illus. by Louis Slobodkin. Macmillan (N Y) 1957 150p illus $4.50 (2-5)   Fic

1 Sweden—Fiction
Translated from the Swedish by Inger Boye

"Little O is the nickname of the youngest member of the family first introduced to children in the author's 'The Saucepan Journey.' She is not yet old enough to go to school but spends her days happily finding adventures for herself and getting into all sorts of amusing scrapes usually because she is trying to help somebody else. . . . [The book] will hold the interest of the reader as well as of the young listener." Horn Bk

The spettecake holiday; illus. by Iben Clante. Macmillan (N Y) 1958 211p illus lib. bdg. $4.95 (4-6)   Fic

1 Farm life—Fiction 2 Sweden—Fiction
Translated from the Swedish by Inger Boye

"When young Pelle-Goran's mother was taken off to the hospital, the boy went to stay with his grandmother on Stubba Farm after promising to bring the doctor a spettecake if he made Pelle-Goran's mother well again. His holiday on the farm brought new adventure and friends, and his grandmother sent him home with the finest spettecake ever, for the doctor." Pub W

"The author has a fine philosophy and understanding of children, and the translator, Inger Boye, imparts a feeling for the country with her sometimes too literal wording. Winner of the Nils Holgersson award which is similar to our Newbery award." Library J

Vance, Marguerite

While shepherds watched; illus. by Nedda Walker. Dutton 1946 48p illus $3.75 (1-4)   Fic

1 Jesus Christ—Nativity—Fiction 2 Donkeys—Stories
ISBN 00-525-42610-8

"Young son of a Bethlehem shepherd, Obed loved the little donkey Cephus and was saddened that he was too old to be of service. And then it was Christmas time and the great miracle took place. Cephus was chosen to carry the Baby Jesus and that same night Obed slept out in the fields and learned of the wonders that the shepherds witnessed." Horn Bk

"A charming and well-conceived retelling of the story of the Nativity." Commonweal

Van Stockum, Hilda

The winged watchman; written and illus. by Hilda Van Stockum. Farrar, Straus 1962 204p illus map lib. bdg. $5.95 (4-7)   Fic

1 World War, 1939-1945—Fiction 2 Netherlands—Fiction
ISBN 0-374-38448-7

"A Bell book"

A "story about a Dutch family in the time of German occupation during the last war. The winged watchman is a windmill, one of those used by the Dutch underground to send messages by positioning the vanes of the mill. The two boys of the Verhagen family become involved in the resistance movement, and their parents help Dirk Jan and Joris conceal a British flyer. Excellent family relationships, and good pace in plot development. The Verhagen family is impressive in its courage, patriotism, and calm faith, but it is the whole Dutch people who are the heroes of this moving book." Chicago. Children's Bk Center

Vestly, Anne-Cath.

Hello, Aurora; tr. from the Norwegian by Eileen Amos; United States ed. adapted by Jane Fairfax; illus. by Leonard Kessler. Crowell 1974 135p illus $4.95 (3-5)   Fic

1 Family—Fiction 2 Norway—Fiction
ISBN 0-690-00513-X

Original Norwegian edition 1966; this translation first published in 1973 in England with title: Hallo, Aurora!

"Aurora, her baby brother, and her parents are very happy with their lifestyle—Father stays home to watch the kids and work on his doctorate while Mother is a lawyer. The neighbors, however, cannot believe that Mother isn't overbearing and selfish and that Father isn't a Mr. Milquetoast." Children's Bk Rev Serv

The story "would be interesting from the feminist viewpoint alone, but it has much, much more to offer readers: it is written in a smooth, casually deft, and lightly humorous style, it has good characterization and warm family relationships, and it gives a sym-

Vestly, Anne-Cath.—*Continued*

pathetic picture of the child who has just moved and is adjusting to other children and their life-styles." Chicago. Children's Bk Center

Wagner, Jane

J. T. With pictures by Gordon Parks, Jr. Van Nostrand-Reinhold 1969 63p illus $5.95 (3-6)   **Fic**

1 Cats—Stories 2 Harlem, New York (City)—Fiction

ISBN 0-442-29152-3

"J. T., a constant worry to his anxious mother since his father has left, is running from neighborhood toughs [who are] after the radio he has stolen, when he finds a badly wounded one-eyed alley cat. Secretly and ingeniously J. T. builds a shelter for the cat in an abandoned stove and feeds and nurses it until it is killed by a car. His brief association with the cat and the resultant understanding of the adults in his life are sharply felt." Booklist

Walker, David

Big Ben; illus. by Victor Ambrus. Houghton 1969 134p $5.95 (3-5)   **Fic**

1 Dogs—Stories

ISBN 0-395-07167-4

An automobile accident on the highway that ran past the Bruce farm was responsible for the fact that Big Ben, a bumbling St Bernard pup, became the Bruces' dog. However, although Big Ben was gentle, a bad-tempered neighboring farmer and his miserable dog caused him and his young owners, Tim and Jinny Bruce many problems

"With simplicity, [the author] tells a good story featuring very real people and a very lovable dog." Sch Library J

Walter, Mildred Pitts

Lillie of Watts; a birthday discovery; illus. by Leonora E. Prince. Ward Ritchie Press 1969 61p illus lib. bdg. $3.95, pa $1.95 (3-5)   **Fic**

1 Birthdays—Fiction 2 Family—Fiction 3 Negroes—Fiction 4 Los Angeles—Fiction

ISBN 0-378-68073-0; 0-378-68072-2

This "story of a few days in the life of an eleven-year-old girl has interest because it is set in Watts and because it puts into perspective the problems of a ghetto child. That her home is overcrowded, her mother works for a white woman, and she has only one good set of clothes are only factors in Lillie's life, although they affect her. Her concerns, on her birthday weekend, are getting along with her sisters, overcoming her fears, and wanting to please her mother and her teacher." Sat Rev

"A low-keyed story with strong illustrations, a weak story line and an interesting setting. . . . Appeal is vested in the very ordinariness of Lillie's day-to-day life." Chicago. Children's Bk Center

Warburg, Sandol Stoddard

On the way home; illus. by Dan Stolpe. Houghton 1973 137p illus $4.95 (5-7)   **Fic**

1 Bears—Stories 2 Fairy tales

ISBN 0-395-17510-0

"This mythic tale will be perceived as an absorbing adventure fantasy by young children and as a symbolic quest by older readers. Awakening in the frozen North, Boy and Bear wander to the Southlands in search of Home. After frightening adventures in an enchanted castle and battles with the evil and hideous Monkey King, the two find refuge in a friendly village of the South. However, Boy's quest for the meaning of truth, dreams, and reality carries him away from the town, leaving readers to wonder about the hope

for his future. Stolpe's imaginative black-and-white spot drawings add to the book's charm and point up the mysterious elements." Sch Library J

Ward, Lynd

The silver pony; a story in pictures. Houghton 1973 174p illus $7.95 (2-4)   **Fic**

1 Horses—Stories 2 Stories without words

ISBN 0-395-14753-0

"Eighty pictures in shades of gray, black, and white tell the story of a lonely farm boy whose dreams of his adventures on a winged horse become confused with reality. One night the boy leans out his window fantasizing that the horse is carrying him to the moon; but the dream turns into a nightmare as rockets and missiles fill the air around them, then explode, killing the horse and sending the boy hurtling through space—really out the window to his own yard below. The boy recovers physically and, with the help of his parents, doctor, and a real colt, emotionally. This is a complex story subtly conveyed without words—a unique experience for readers and nonreaders alike." Booklist

Weik, Mary Hays

The Jazz Man; woodcuts by Ann Grifalconi. Atheneum Pubs. 1966 42p illus lib. bdg. $4.95 (3-5) Fic

1 Jazz music—Fiction 2 Negroes—Fiction 3 Harlem, New York (City)—Fiction

ISBN 0-689-30021-2

"Lame and lonely, isolated because he lives on the top floor of a large Harlem building, young Zeke finds comfort and pleasure listening to the jazz pianist in a neighboring apartment. But his mother, defeated by poverty, leaves home. Then his father disappears and, finally, even the jazz man moves away. For a brief time, Zeke is truly abandoned." Moorachian. What is a City?

"Illustrated with expressive woodcuts, an honest picture of a child with real problems." Notable Children's Bks, 1966

White, Anne H.

Junket, the dog who liked everything "just so"; illus. by Robert McCloskey. Viking 1955 183p illus lib. bdg. $4.95, pa 75¢ (4-6)   **Fic**

1 Dogs—Stories 2 Farm life—Fiction

ISBN 0-670-41090-X; 0-670-05028-8

"Junket is an independent airdale, with a strong will of his own and a determination to have everything 'just so.' Thus when his owners sell the farm and disperse all its animals, Junket immediately sets about teaching the new owners (a city family with no knowledge or appreciation of farm life) how a farm should be run. How he succeeds in getting the other animals back and in refuting Mr. McDonegal's 'Positively no animals' verdict makes a very funny story, true to both human and dog nature. McCloskey's illustrations are a perfect complement to the text." Chicago. Children's Bk Center

White, E. B.

Charlotte's web; pictures by Garth Williams. Harper 1952 184p illus $4.95, lib. bdg. $4.79, pa $1.25 (3-6)   **Fic**

1 Pigs—Stories 2 Spiders—Stories

ISBN 0-06-026385-5; 0-06-026386-3; 0-06-440055-2

The story of a little girl who could talk to animals, but especially the story of the pig, Wilbur, and his friendship with Charlotte, the spider, who could not only talk but write as well

"Illustrated with amusing sketches . . . [this] story is a fable for adults as well as children and can be recommended to older children and parents as an amusing story and a gentle essay on friendship." Library J

White, E. B.—*Continued*

Stuart Little; illus. by Garth Williams. Harper 1945 131p illus $4.95, lib. bdg. $4.79, pa $1.25 (3-6) Fic

1 Mice—Stories

ISBN 0-06-026395-4; 0-06-026396-2; 0-06-440056-5

Into a normal American family there was born a second son whom everybody noticed was no bigger than a mouse. It was no time at all until everybody knew that he was a mouse. This is the story of the life and adventures of this unusual person, named Stuart by his parents

"Although 'Stuart Little' may be listed as a children's book, and children will undoubtedly be the excuse for getting it into the house, it is for all ages, all shapes and sizes of readers who like the light fantastic tone." Sat Rev

The trumpet of the swan; pictures by Edward Frascino. Harper 1970 210p illus $4.95, lib. bdg. $4.79, pa $1.25 (4-6) Fic

1 Swans—Stories

ISBN 0-06-026397-0; 0-06-026398-9; 0-06-440048-4

"The focus of this book is Louis, a trumpeter swan who was born mute. Unable to court a lovely swan, Serena, Louis is saved from a lonely fate by his father, who steals a trumpet so that his son may communicate better. Because he is talented and resourceful, Louis is able to earn enough money as a professional musician to pay for the instrument, and most importantly, to win Serena." Wis Library Bul

The author "deftly blends true birdlore with fanciful adventures in a witty, captivating fantasy." Booklist

Wibberley, Leonard

Flint's Island. Farrar, Straus 1972 165p map $4.95 (6-7) Fic

1 Pirates—Fiction 2 Buried treasure—Fiction

ISBN 0-374-32331-3

This story, inspired by Robert Louis Stevenson's Treasure Island, reintroduces the cunning pirate Long John Silver. The New England trading ship Jane stops at Flint's Island where Long John has been marooned. The pirate gains control of the ship by treachery when he promises the captain and crew shares in the treasure still remaining on the island

"Scrupulous attention to details of rig and sailing will make the book a favorite with sailing enthusiasts, and the exciting, well-constructed plot and surprise ending will hold the attention of most young readers." Library J

Wiberg, Harald

Christmas at the Tomten's farm; written and illus. by Harald Wiberg. Coward-McCann 1968 unp illus lib. bdg. $4.49 (2-4) Fic

1 Sweden—Fiction 2 Christmas stories

ISBN 0-698-30044-0

Originally printed in Sweden

"A pictorial description of the preparations for and celebration of an old-fashioned Christmas on a Swedish farm. . . . Following the details of each day's family festivities is a depiction of the tomten, an old dwarf who guards the farm animals, on his nightly rounds." Booklist

"A beautiful picture book evokes Christmas in Sweden at the turn of the century. The dark austerity of a Scandinavian winter is dramatically depicted by black ink sketches on gray paper, brightened only with touches of white." Horn Bk

Wier, Ester

The loner; illus. by Christine Price. McKay 1963 153p illus $4.95, lib. bdg. $4.50 (5-7) Fic

1 Shepherds—Fiction 2 Migrant labor—Fiction 3 Montana—Fiction

ISBN 0-679-20097-5; 0-679-25185-5

"A juvenile migratory worker, who knows neither his name nor his age, searches for identity. . . . After his only friend is killed by a farm machine, the rootless waif winds up with a Montana sheep herder, a lonely old woman. Living with her, he adjusts, painfully at first, to a new life, earns the name David, slays his Goliath (a grizzly bear) and best of all, overcomes his self-doubt." N Y Times Bk Rev

"Unusually well developed characterization of both people and animals. The shocking death . . . is realistically but not morbidly treated. Many values for a young adolescent, especially one who is himself a 'loner' or who has sustained a sudden personal tragedy. A sensitive [tale]." Sch Library J

Wiggin, Kate Douglas

The Birds' Christmas Carol; illus. by Jessie Gillespie. Memorial ed. Houghton 1941 84p illus $6.95 (3-5) Fic

1 Christmas stories

ISBN 0-395-07204-2

"How Carol Bird made a merry Christmas for the 'Ruggleses in the rear.'" Prentice and Power

A well-known Christmas story, first published 1888, which has both humor and pathos. Nearly every page of this edition is illustrated in color or in black and white

Wilder, Laura Ingalls

Little house in the big woods; illus. by Garth Williams. Newly illustrated, uniform ed. Harper 1953 237p illus $5.95, lib. bdg. $5.79, pa $1.50 (4-6) Fic

1 Frontier and pioneer life—Fiction 2 Wisconsin—Fiction

ISBN 0-06-026430-6; 0-06-026431-4; 0-06-440001-8

Also available in a large type edition for $7.50 (ISBN 0-06-026432-2)

First published 1932

This book, the first in a series, "has a refreshingly genuine and lifelike quality. . . . [and takes place] on the edge of the Big Woods of Wisconsin. . . . The story of Laura, and Mary and their parents, who lived in a log cabin, miles from neighbors and a settlement, is full of incidents and accounts of daily doings that boys and girls will enjoy." N Y Times Bk Rev

Eight additional titles in this series are also available from Harper: Little house on the prairie $5.95, lib. bdg. $5.79, pa $1.50 (ISBN 0-06-026445-4; 0-06-026446-2; 0-06-440002-6); Farmer boy $5.95, lib. bdg. $5.79, pa $1.50 (ISBN 0-06-026425-X; 0-06-026421-7; 0-06-440003-4); On the banks of Plum Creek $5.95, lib. bdg. $5.79, pa $1.50 (ISBN 0-06-026470-5; 0-06-026471-3; 0-06-440004-2); By the shores of Silver Lake $5.95, lib. bdg. $5.79, pa $1.50 (ISBN 0-06-026416-0; 0-06-026417-9; 0-06-440005-0); The long winter $5.95, lib. bdg. $5.79, pa $1.50 (ISBN 0-06-026460-8; 0-06-026461-6; 0-06-440006-9); Little town on the prairie $5.95, lib. bdg. $5.79, pa $1.50 (ISBN 0-06-026450-9; 0-06-026451-9; 0-06-440007-7); These happy golden years $5.95, lib. bdg. $5.79, pa $1.50 (ISBN 0-06-026480-2; 0-06-026481-0; 0-06-440008-5); The first four years $5.95, lib. bdg. $5.79, pa $1.50 (ISBN 0-06-026426-8; 0-06-026427-6; 0-06-440031-X)

Willard, Barbara

The Richleighs of Tantamount; illus. by C. Walter Hodges. Harcourt [1967 c1966] 189p illus $5.50 (4-7) Fic

1 Great Britain—Fiction

ISBN 0-15-266750-4

First published 1966 in England

"Four properly brought-up English children of a wealthy [Cornish coast] Victorian household . . . [are

Willard, Barbara—*Continued*

left] to shift for themselves. Their joy in the first freedom they have ever known, their companionship with two helpful children of different background, and their discovery of Tantamount's dark secret make a memorable story strong in atmosphere, characterization, and suspense." Booklist

Williams, Jay

Danny Dunn and the homework machine; by Jay Williams and Raymond Abrashkin; illus. by Ezra Jack Keats. McGraw 1958 141p illus $4.95, lib. bdg. $4.72 (3-6)   Fic

1 Computers—Fiction
ISBN 0-07-070519-4; 0-07-070520-8

"Whittlesey House publications"

"Professor Bullfinch leaves Danny in charge of his miniature automatic computer while he goes to Washington. Danny and two friends work out a scheme using the computer to do their homework. Complications develop when a jealous boy tells their teacher and sabotages the machine." Library J

"Amusing and ingenious." Hodges. Bks for Elem Sch Libraries

Several other titles about Danny Dunn are available from McGraw

Petronella; with pictures by Friso Henstra. Parents Mag. Press 1973 unp illus $4.95, lib. bdg. $4.59 (2-4)   Fic

1 Fairy tales
ISBN 0-8193-0636-3; 0-8193-0637-1

Princess Petronella sets out to rescue a prince from the house of an enchanter. She proves herself brave, kind and talented, as well as beautiful, while accomplishing three tasks which have been set for her. When she discovers that the lazy prince does not want to be rescued she enchants the enchanter

"A story with appeal for both boys and girls, the language is 'today.' ('You're not much of a prince,' she said grimly. 'But you're the best I can do.') The adventure moves along with magical fun, enhanced by sophisticated, thought provoking and endlessly interpretive drawings." Babbling Bookworm

The practical princess; illus. by Friso Henstra. Parents Mag. Press 1969 unp illus $4.95, lib. bdg. $4.59 (2-4)   Fic

1 Fairy tales
ISBN 0-8193-0233-3; 0-8193-0234-1

"Blessed by one of her fairy godmothers with common sense, the lovely Princess Bedelia solves her problems in forthright fashion by using her mind and taking action. Princesses are supposed to be fed to dragons? Bedelia arranges for an explosion. Princesses are supposed to be rescued, when imprisoned by disgruntled elderly suitors in a tower, by a cavalier? Bedelia has to work out her own escape plan—which she does by letting down the long, flowing locks of her young swain's beard." Chicago. Children's Bk Center

"Though some words in the text may require explanation for the youngest audience (snob, geographical, salamander, boundary), this delightful story is an excellent choice for readalouds and story hour programs. Today's children will relish the exploits of the gutsy, independent, and practical Bedelia, and find this spoof uncommonly good." Library J

Map on lining-papers

Williams, Margery

The velveteen rabbit; or, How toys become real; with illus. by William Nicholson. Doubleday 1926 33p illus $3.95, lib. bdg. $4.70 (2-4)   Fic

1 Toys—Fiction 2 Rabbits—Stories 3 Fairy tales
ISBN 0-385-07725-4; 0-385-07748-3

First published 1922 by Doran

"About the adventures of a rabbit, velveteen at first, and finally, through the agency of the 'Fairy of old toys,' a real rabbit, of whom we catch a last glimpse in William Nicholson's lifelike pictures as he twinkles off into a real wood." Bks for Boys and Girls

Winterfeld, Henry

Castaways in Lilliput; tr. from the German by Kyrill Schabert; illus. by William M. Hutchinson. Harcourt 1960 [c1958] 188p illus $5.95 (4-6)   Fic

1 Fantastic fiction
ISBN 0-15-214820-5

Original German edition 1958

"A drifting raft brings three children to an island visible only in a mirage—it is the land of Lilliput, surrounded by a 'layer of air which makes it vanish.' The two boys and a girl . . . meet miniature people speaking English taught by the giant Gulliver who had visited their land 250 years ago. Innocently terrifying them into flight, the three young giants manage, through discovery of a streamlined train, to get to a town and convince the residents that they are harmless." Horn Bk

"A lively and ingenious book, well-written, and with the perennial appeal of the combination of the familiar and fantastic." Chicago. Children's Bk Center

Detectives in togas. Tr. from the German by Richard and Clara Winston. Illus. by Charlotte Kleinert. Harcourt 1956 205p illus $5.95, pa $1.45 (5-7)   Fic

1 Mystery and detective stories 2 Rome—Fiction
ISBN 0-15-223412-8; 0-15-625315-1

"A rollicking mystery story set in ancient Rome. A group of school boys become involved in the mystery when one of their members is accused of having defaced the wall of a temple by scrawling the words 'Caius is a dumbell' on it in red paint. The other boys rally round to save him and in proving his innocence uncover a political plot. . . . The solving of the mystery is well-handled and plausible." Chicago. Children's Bk Center

"The author's merry style and his ability to draw flesh-and-blood boys and the amusing line drawings of Charlotte Kleinert make this an attractive volume." Sat Rev

Mystery of the Roman ransom; tr. from the German by Edith McCormick; illus. by Fritz Biermann. Harcourt 1971 186p illus $5.50 (5-7)   Fic

1 Rome—Fiction 2 Mystery and detective stories
ISBN 0-15-256612-0

Seven schoolboys of ancient Rome become "involved in an assassination plot. The trouble starts when the boys (all sons of Roman senators) purchase a newly-captured slave, a young Gaul who is carrying a secret message from the governor of the German provinces. This message, when deciphered by the boys, orders the murder of a Roman senator who just happens to be the father of the ringleader. The group decides to deliver the message to the unknown assassins as arranged, hoping thereby to discover who the villains are. Predictably, everything goes wrong, and the boys find themselves fighting all sorts of enemies, from a one-eyed gladiator to a lion from the Circus Maximus. The boys' brash behavior and their ridiculous, anachronistic conversations are full of wry humor that should give special pleasure to those who enjoy literate fun." Sch Library J

Winthrop, Elizabeth

Walking away; pictures by Noëlle Masséna. Harper 1973 218p illus $4.95, lib. bdg. $5.11 (5-7)   Fic

Winthrop, Elizabeth—*Continued*

1 Grandfathers—Fiction 2 Friendship—Fiction
3 Farm life—Fiction
ISBN 0-06-026533-7; 0-06-026534-5

"Emily looks forward each year to spending the
summer at her grandparents' farm. This time, the
vacation will be super because Nina, Emily's best
friend in the city, will also be a guest. But the sweet
times turn sour, as Nina is gradually revealed as a
shallow, troublemaking girl. She causes a wide rift
between Emily and her beloved grandfather, a situation which can be only partially resolved. The crises
which many young people have to face are honestly
and forcefully presented in this interesting novel."
Pub W

"The descriptions of daily life, realistic dialogue
and well-defined characters make this a good read for
pre-teens." Library J

Wojciechowska, Maia

Shadow of a bull; drawings by Alvin Smith.
Atheneum Pubs. 1964 165p illus $5.95, pa $1.25
(6-7)   Fic

1 Bullfights—Fiction 2 Spain—Fiction
ISBN 0-689-30042-5; 0-689-70298-1

Awarded the Newbery Medal, 1965

"Manolo was the son of the great bullfighter Juan
Olivar. Ever since his father's death the town of
Arcangel [Spain] has waited for [the time] when
Manolo would be twelve and face his first bull. From
the time he was nine and felt in his heart that he was a
coward, Manolo worked and prayed that he might at
least face this moment with honor, knowing it could
well bring his death." Pub W

"In spare, economical prose [the author] makes one
feel, see, smell the heat, endure the hot Andalusian
sun and shows one the sand and glare of the bullring.
Above all, she lifts the veil and gives glimpses of the
terrible loneliness in the soul of a boy. Perhaps the
ending was ever so slightly contrived. But the whole is
so good it does not detract from an eloquent, moving
book [of a boy's maturing], superbly illustrated." N Y
Times Bk Rev

Glossary of bullfighting terms: p157-65

Wormser, Richard

The black mustanger; illus. by Don Bolognese.
Morrow 1971 190p illus $5.95, lib. bdg. $5.11 (5-7)
           Fic

1 Horses—Stories 2 The West—Fiction
ISBN 0-688-21104-6; 0-688-31104-0

In post-Civil War days the Riker family moved from
Tennessee to Texas where they hoped to escape from
the problems and hatreds of the past. But they found
life just as difficult there and it was not until Mesteño
Will, a half Negro-half Apache mustanger appeared
that things began to improve

"The setting is colorful, the construction of the
story taut and economical, the plot well-paced and
convincing." Sutherland. The Best in Children's Bks

Wrightson, Patricia

Down to earth; illus. by Margaret Horder. Harcourt 1965 222p illus $5.95 (5-7)   Fic

1 Australia—Fiction 2 Science fiction
ISBN 0-15-224179-5

A story set in Sydney, Australia. "When George
and his friends discover a young boy living in a
deserted house, they find it difficult to accept his
story that he is from outer space. Later, they find it
more difficult to protect him from the Child Welfare
officials and others who are becoming too interested
in him." Sch Library J

"The book will lend itself well to book-talks, and its

audience should be among those who think they do
not like fantasy, as well as among the readers who
enjoy all unusual books." Horn Bk

A racecourse for Andy; illus. by Margaret Horder.
Harcourt 1968 156p illus $4.95 (5-7)   Fic

1 Australia—Fiction 2 Mentally handicapped children—Fiction 3 Horse racing—Fiction
ISBN 0-15-265080-6

Sydney, Australia is the setting of this story about
"mentally retarded Andy [who] 'buys' the local race-
track from a bottlepicker. Convinced that he is the
owner, no amount of logic can persuade Andy that he
isn't." Sch Library J

"This outstanding story . . . has no aura of sentimentality, no obtrusive message; it is poignant just
because of the simple acceptance of Andy by both
adults and children. They do not tolerate him, they
like and protect him. A distinguished book." Sat Rev

Wuorio, Eva-Lis

Save Alice! Holt 1968 165p map lib. bdg. $3.59
(5-7)   Fic

1 Mystery and detective stories 2 Spain—Fiction
3 Cockatoos—Stories
ISBN 0-03-072275-6

"English twins—brother and sister, an American
boy, and a young man in the role of temporary tutor
are en route across France and Spain to the twins'
home on Ibiza. Driving in an ancient Dodge . . . they
have just passed through Spanish customs when suddenly an old lady, all in black, thrusts a huge cockatoo
in a cage into the rumble seat with the two boys and
whispers the command, 'Save Alice!' From then on,
the journey turns into a chase and a plot to outwit
some suspicious characters who seem bent on stealing
Alice. . . . The people are well enough characterized
to make events convincing, and the story keeps moving with a great deal of humor as well as with suspense, chiefly because Alice, the cockatoo, is such an
extraordinary personality. The greatest charm of the
story, however, which children are bound to feel, is
the Spanish background." Horn Bk

To fight in silence. Holt 1973 216p map lib. bdg.
$5.95 (5-7)   Fic

1 World War, 1939-1945—Fiction 2 Jews—Fiction
3 Denmark—Fiction
ISBN 0-03-080241-5

This is the "story of a large Danish family during
World War II. Gorm Jensen's sons and daughters
have married into Danish, Norwegian, and German-
Jewish families and during the war those not imprisoned or in hiding work with the underground or manage to escape and join their country's fighting forces
abroad. The author is principally concerned with
Thor, who is twelve in 1939, too young to enlist and
resentful that adults at first think him too immature to
be trusted in the underground. Thor's character
development during the war is natural and gratifying." Booklist

"The pace is fast and exciting, the characters well-
defined, the setting vividly evoked." Chicago. Children's Bk Center

Wyss, Johann David

The Swiss family Robinson (5-7)   Fic

1 Survival (after airplane accidents, shipwrecks,
etc.)—Fiction

Some editions are:

Collins (Rainbow classics) $2.95, lib. bdg. $3.91
Edited by William H. G. Kingston; illustrations by
Jeanne Edwards; introduction by May Lamberton
Becker (ISBN 0-529-04785-3; 0-529-04786-1)

Grosset $3.95 Edited by W. H. Kingston; Illustrated
by Lynd Ward (ISBN 0-448-05822-7)

Wyss, Johann David—_Continued_

Originally published 1813 in Switzerland

Tale of a Swiss family shipwrecked on a desert island, and of their adventures there

"The very improbability of this tale makes it delightful. 'They did sail in the tubs,' says the Spectator, 'and train zebras and ostriches for riding, and grow pines and apples in the same garden,' and why shouldn't they?" Olcott

Yashima, Taro

The golden footprints [by] Taro Yashima and Hatoju Muku; illus. by Taro Yashima. World Pub. 1960 50p illus lib. bdg. $4.91 (3-6)　　　　Fic

1 Foxes—Stories 2 Japan—Fiction

"A young Japanese boy conspires with a pair of foxes to feed their captive baby and eventually saves it from destruction by his father. A sensitive story for reading aloud." Hodges. Bks for Elem Sch Libraries

"There is artistry in every line of this translation . . . and the delicate mood is sustained by the shadowy brown and black pictures. . . . This story of devotion has a touching mingling of realism and Mysticism. A beautiful, unusual tale." N Y Her Trib Bks

Yates, Elizabeth

Carolina's courage; illus. by Nora S. Unwin. Dutton 1964 94p illus $5.95 (3-5)　　　　Fic

1 Frontier and pioneer life—Fiction 2 Dolls—Fiction

ISBN 0-525-27480-4

"Carolina, her family, and her beloved china doll Lydia-Lou leave their New Hampshire home and make a long journey in an ox-drawn covered wagon to their new home in the Nebraska wilderness. Carolina proves that she is a real pioneer when she makes the costly sacrifice of trading her Lydia-Lou for the wagon train's safe passage through Indian country. A warm, sensitive story of a close-knit family whose mutual love and steadfast courage enable them to face the sorrows, the hardships, and the dangers of pioneer life." Booklist

"The authoritative writing is that of a poet. . . . Illustrations are as rich and simple as these innocent [characters'] lives." N Y Times Bk Rev

Yolen, Jane

The boy who had wings; pictures in wax-crayon by Helga Aichinger. Crowell 1974 unp illus $5.50, lib. bdg. $6.25 (3-5)　　　　Fic

1 Greece—Fiction

ISBN 0-690-15899-8; 0-690-15900-5

"Cast in the general style of a legend, the story tells of Aetos, a Greek boy who was born with a pair of soft, 'golden-white' wings. His family was uneasy and ashamed, and his mother made him a black goat-hair cape to cover his shoulders, admonishing him never to show his wings. Forgotten and lonely, Aetos played by himself. . . . Not until his father was lost in a mountain storm did Aetos discover the great joy of flying; for when he set forth in search of his father, the icy mountain winds tore the cape from his shoulders and the great golden wings were freed. But after the rescue of his father, the beautiful wings, frozen by the bitter cold, dropped from his shoulders." Horn Bk

"An original tale with allegorical overtones distinguished by dazzling art work. . . . The simple story is set off to best advantage by the impressive full-page wax-crayon paintings. Aichinger achieves myriad effects and textures—from sea foam to a spinner's yarn—to convey a timeless Aegean scene." Sch Library J

The seventh mandarin; pictures by Ed Young. Seabury 1970 unp illus $6.95 (2-4)　　　　Fic

1 Kites—Fiction 2 Kings and rulers—Fiction

ISBN 0-8164-3060-8

"One of the tasks of the seven mandarins who guarded their king, long ago in an eastern land, was to fly the huge dragon kite while the monarch slept—for the king's soul was safe only when the royal kite flew. But the seventh and youngest mandarin learned, one night when a fierce wind blew the kite down, that there was no truth in the superstition. . . . Looking for the fallen kite, he had to leave the palace confines [for the first time] and so saw the misery of the people. So the good king discovered the harsh reality of life outside; the palace walls came down, and the land knew a peace and plenty it had never had." Sutherland. The Best in Children's Bks

"The illustrations are stunning: large, sweeping paintings, subtly colored and beautifully composed." Sat Rev

The wizard of Washington Square; illus. by Ray Cruz. World Pub. 1969 126p illus lib. bdg. $5.71 (3-5)　　　　Fic

1 Greenwich Village, New York (City)—Fiction

ISBN 0-529-00706-1

"The wizard of Washington Square is a second class magician who has trouble remembering his incantations and is therefore stationed in America (where no one but babies believe in magic) instead of in the home territory of Europe. This enjoyable fantasy also includes the classic ingredients of a boy, a girl, and a dog whom the wizard accidentally changes into a statue. The statue is snatched by an unethical interior decorator, a chase ensues. . . . Much fun is poked at 'happenings,' petitions, tourists, policemen, the white alligators that inhabit New York sewers, and the general life in Greenwich Village." Sch Library J

"As much fun as a white rabbit popping out of a magician's hat is this sprightly tale. . . . Young readers would do well to tag along." Pub W

Young, Miriam

Christy and the cat jail; illus. by Pat Grant Porter. Lothrop 1972 92p illus $4.95, lib. bdg. $4.59 (3-5)　　　　Fic

1 Cats—Stories

ISBN 0-688-21834-2; 0-688-31834-7

"Ever since a cat had killed her parakeet, Christy hated cats, and now she had decided she was going to set up a cat jail, hoping to catch the black cat she had seen kill a baby rabbit. She did catch Patches, and gradually discovered that her concern and amusement were growing; by the time Patches had a litter, Christy really loved her cat—but its owner came and took Patches and the kittens. Christy had also been adjusting to the arrival of a baby sister, and had just begun to appreciate 'her' . . . when her happiness was completed by having Patches' owner offer her the pick of the litter." Chicago. Children's Bk Center

"Pat Porter's realistic black-and-white illustrations of Christy and her cat add to the story which should win the interest of young readers." Sch Library J

Zei, Alki

Petros' war; tr. from the Greek by Edward Fenton. Dutton 1972 236p $5.95 (5-7)　　　　Fic

1 World War, 1939-1945—Fiction 2 Greece, Modern—Fiction

ISBN 0-525-36962-7

Mildred L. Batchelder Award, 1974

Original Greek edition, 1971

When World War II came to Greece, 10-year-old Petros found his dreams of heroism shattered by the grim reality of endurance under the Fascist occupation. He painted slogans on walls for the Resistance but when his best friend was shot in an Athens

Zei, Alki—*Continued*

demonstration he realized that there would be no liberation for the dead

"Here are pleasure and sorrow, courage and cowardice, grandeur and pettiness, all shown with a Chaucerian humour, through the lively family and friends of one sublimely ordinary boy. . . . This is a book which every child should read." Times (London) Lit Sup

Wildcat under glass; tr. from the Greek by Edward Fenton. Holt 1968 177p maps lib. bdg. $4.50 (5-7)
                                                                    Fic

1 Greece, Modern—Fiction
ISBN 0-03-089512-X
Mildred L. Batchelder Award, 1970
First published 1963 in Greece

"A dramatic picture of the impact of dictatorship on an ordinary Greek family and their small community in the 1930's. Melita discovers that her beloved cousin Niko, a freedom-fighter, must hide for his life and that her sister Myrto has joined the Fascist youth legion at school." Bruno. Bks for School Libraries, 1968

"A superbly told story, translated by one who knows the land and the language so well that the writing lacks any feeling of translation. . . . The writing is rich in characterization, convincing in its incidents, and totally rewarding for the reader in its vivid theme of the meaning of freedom and democracy." Horn Bk

Zimnik, Reiner

The bear and the people; written and illus. by Reiner Zimnik; tr. from the German by Nina Ignatowicz. Harper 1971 78p illus lib. bdg. $3.79 (3-6)
                                                                    Fic

1 Bears—Stories
ISBN 0-06-026818-2
Original German edition, 1956

"A bear and his master travel round the fairs of Central Europe, the man a juggler and the bear dancing. Rivals threaten, using the arts of the devil (chief being the bare-breasted dancing of their women) but with the help of God are defeated. The years pass, the coming of the motor drives the devoted pair off the highways, and eventually the man dies. After further mishaps and adventures the bear finally achieves happiness in a life half wild, half tamed." Jr Bookshelf

"A beautiful, unusual, deceptively simple tale. . . . Pen-and-ink illustrations are in harmony with the text and children of almost any age should be caught up in this deeply moving story." Library J

The crane; tr. from the German by Nina Ignatowicz and F. N. Monjo. Harper 1970 92p illus $3.50, lib. bdg. $3.27 (4-6)
                                                                    Fic

1 Cranes, derricks, etc.—Fiction
ISBN 0-06-026819-0; 0-06-026820-4
Original German edition, 1956

This "is the tale of a craneman who loved his machine, was always happy and had an unexpected knack for handing out justice. War comes but it scarcely involves him—he never comes down to earth. The breaking of the dams and the flooding of the land doesn't depress him. Safely marooned above the waters he befriends an eagle, keeps his girders rust-free and signals to passing ships. Only at the right moment, when peace returns and progress demands change, does he leave his crane." Christian Sci Monitor

"Every page has a line drawing of some kind. Most are both sketchy and inventively witty. . . . This is a very moral story . . . but the wittiness of the [author's] drawings also pervades the text. . . . A book for a thoughtful child." Times (London) Lit Sup

S C   STORY COLLECTIONS

Books in this class contain both collections of short stories by one author and collections by more than one author. Folklore is in class 398 and its subdivisions. General literature collections are in class 808.8

Alcott, Louisa May

Glimpses of Louisa; a centennial sampling of the best short stories; selected with an introduction and editor's notes by Cornelia Meigs. Little 1968 222p $6.50 (5-7)
                                                                    S C

1 Short stories
ISBN 0-316-03100-3

"Issued in honor of the centennial of the publication of 'Little Women,' this is an excellent selection of 10 stories, each accompanied by a paragraph by Miss Meigs giving background on composition and publication. All have been chosen from . . . volumes of short stories published during the author's lifetime. The subjects range from Indian captives, the plight of Civil War soldiers and European travels to a Polish boy who was the main inspiration for the character of Laurie in 'Little Women.' Louisa May Alcott may have written in the last century, but the appeal of these stories about poor girls, rich girls, a boy facing a wildcat alone spiced with innocent romance is perennial." Sch Library J

Alden, Raymond M.

Why the chimes rang, and other stories; with illus. by Evelyn Copelman. Bobbs 1945 146p illus $4.95 (3-5)
                                                                    S C

1 Fairy tales
ISBN 0-672-50581-9
First published 1908

A collection of eleven "unusually successful modern fairy tales each with its allegory and not too obtrusive moral." N Y State Lib

Alexander, Lloyd

The foundling, and other tales of Prydain; pictures by Margot Zemach. Holt 1973 87p illus lib. bdg. $5.95 (4-6)
                                                                    S C

1 Fairy tales 2 Short stories
ISBN 0-03-007431-2

This book contains six short tales which "tell of events in mythical Prydain before the birth of Taran, key character in the five books of the Prydain cycle [entered in Fiction]." Horn Bk

"The stories are written with vivid grace and humor . . . echoed in the soft, deft black and white Zemach drawings." Chicago. Children's Bk Center

Andersen, Hans Christian

Andersen's Fairy tales; illus. by Lawrence Beall Smith; afterword by Clifton Fadiman. Macmillan (N Y) 1963 542p illus $4.95 (3-6)
                                                                    S C

1 Fairy tales

"The Macmillan classics"

"The text of the Andersen tales is based on the Hurd and Houghton edition of 'Andersen's Stories and Tales' and 'Andersen's Wonder Stories' (Boston, 1871, 1872), on the translations of Mrs. E. V. Lucas and Mrs. H. B. Paull, and on the Signe Toksvig edition, Macmillan, 1953. These translations have been especially edited and revised for this edition." Verso of title page

A collection of fifty-three of the author's tales

Andersen, Hans Christian—*Continued*

The complete fairy tales and stories; tr. from the Danish by Erik Christian Haugaard; foreword by Virginia Haviland. Doubleday 1974 xxiv, 1101p $15, lib. bdg. $15.75 (4-7)   S C

1 Fairy tales

ISBN 0-385-01901-7; 0-385-05867-5

This translation "follows the text and the order of the stories in the Danish edition of 1874 which Andersen edited." Foreword

"In its completeness this collection of Andersen's 156 stories reveals his genius for preserving human character and folk culture. Haugaard's translation is eloquent, elegantly formal and aesthetically sensitive to fine gradations of tone and color, which doubtless belong to the original as well. These qualities will make the volume a lasting fireside reader while the tales plus the author's preface and notes on his stories will serve the Andersen student admirably." Booklist

"Not all of the fairy tales will appeal to young readers, and many of the stories were intended for adults. In addition the lack of illustrations and the length of the book make it more of a resource book . . . than a children's anthology." Sch Library J

Hans Andersen's Fairy tales; tr. by L. W. Kingland; illus. by Ernest H. Shepard. Walck, H.Z. 1962 [c1961] 327p illus $5.50 (3-6)   S C

1 Fairy tales

ISBN 0-8098-2354-3

First published 1961 in England

This selection of thirty-two stories consists of an "assortment of familiar tales such as Thumbelina and the Little Mermaid and lesser known tales such as The Old House and Willie Winky." Chicago Sunday Tribune

"An edition that is attractively illustrated; most of the pictures are small and charming black-and-white drawings, and some few are full page illustrations, delicately colored." Chicago. Children's Bk Center

It's perfectly true, and other stories; tr. from the Danish by Paul Leyssac; illus. by Richard Bennett. Harcourt 1938 305p illus $6.95 (4-7)   S C

1 Fairy tales

ISBN 0-15-239343-9

"A new translation of twenty-eight stories by a Dutch actor who has been telling them from the platform and over the radio for some time. The translation is easy and stresses the conversational tone and ordinary salty language in which Andersen desired to cast his tales." Booklist

Seven tales; tr. from the Danish by Eva Le Gallienne; pictures by Maurice Sendak. Harper 1959 127p illus $5.95, lib. bdg. $5.89 (2-5)   S C

1 Fairy tales

ISBN 0-06-023790-2; 0-06-023791-0

"Translator and artist show understanding and appreciation of Andersen's poignant stories. Charming illustrations, large print, and open page invite independent reading." Hodges. Bks for Elem Sch Libraries

Association for Childhood Education International

Told under spacious skies; regional stories about American children; selected by the Literature Committee of the Association for Childhood Education International; illus. by William Moyers. Macmillan (N Y) 1952 329p illus $4.75 (3-6)   S C

1 Short stories 2 Storytelling—Collections

"The Umbrella books"

"A collection of twenty-seven regional stories of the United States. . . . Includes short stories as well as selections from books by recognized children's

authors, such as Elizabeth Coatsworth, Elizabeth Enright, Marjorie Kinnan Rawlings, Lois Lenski, and others. Good format: illustrated in black and white." Library J

Told under the blue umbrella; read-aloud stories in the here-and-now; selected by the Literature Committee of the Association for Childhood Education International; illus. by Marguerite Davis. Macmillan Pub. Co. 1961 161p illus $5.95 (k-4)   S C

1 Short stories 2 Storytelling—Collections

"The Umbrella books"

First published 1933. Copyright renewed 1961

"Thirty-eight imaginative and realistic stories for young children, arranged by age levels." Hodges. Bks for Elem Sch Libraries

"The selection has been carefully made and teachers and mothers will find this book useful. The illustrations by Marguerite Davis are pleasing and childlike." N Y Times Bk Rev

Told under the city umbrella; selected by the Literature Committee of the Association for Childhood Education International; illus. by Lisl Weil. Macmillan (N Y) 1972 306p illus $5.95 (3-6)   S C

1 Short stories

"This compilation contains excerpts from 17 books by Paula Fox, Rose Blue, George Selden, E. B. White, Yoshiko Uchida, Mary Stolz, and Emily Neville, among others. The selections are varied in mood and background but consistent in carrying out the committee's desire to give the feel of urban life and suggest the multifaceted nature of city living." Booklist

"While it would be preferable to assume that a reading of excerpts would lead children to read the books in their entirety, this is still an excellent culling of good books." Chicago. Children's Bk Center

Told under the magic umbrella; modern tales of fancy and humor; selected by the Literature Committee of the Association for Childhood Education International; illus. by Elizabeth Orton Jones. Macmillan Pub. Co. 1939 242p illus $5.95 (k-4)   S C

1 Fairy tales 2 Short stories 3 Storytelling—Collections

"The Umbrella books"

"This volume is devoted to 33 modern fanciful tales, arranged from the more elementary ones on, the majority appealing to the imaginative interests of children in the second, third and fourth grades. There is Marjorie Flack's nursery story, 'Ask Mr. Bear'; Emma L. Brock's 'Gingham Lena,' about 'the smudgy, carefree adventurous rag doll'; Caroline D. Emerson's 'Merry-go-round and the Griggses' an irresistible humorous tale, Edith Rickert's 'Bojabi tree,' an adapted folk tale, and others by Margery Bianco, Carl Sandburg, Eleanor Farjeon, Clare Leighton and so on." Bookmark

Told under the Stars and Stripes; stories of all of America's children; stories selected by the Literature Committee of the Association for Childhood Education International; illus. by Nedda Walker. Macmillan (N Y) 1945 346p illus lib. bdg. $4.25 (3-6)   S C

1 Short stories 2 Storytelling—Collections 3 Minorities—Fiction

"The Umbrella books"

A "collection of 27 stories about minority groups—racial, religious, and national—living in America. A few of the stories were written especially for this book, but for the most part they are chapters from the books of well-known authors." Booklist

Authors' choice; stories chosen by Gillian Avery [and others]. . . . Illus. by Krystyna Turska. Crowell [1971 c1970] 216p illus $6.95 (5-7)   S C

1 Short stories
ISBN 0-690-11141-X
First published 1970 in England

"Seventeen of the most distinguished British writers for children have each chosen their favorite stories for inclusion in an anthology that ranges from Tove Jansson and Hans Christian Andersen to Katherine Mansfield and Ray Bradbury. Most of the selections are by children's authors and each is preceded by a word of praise by its selector. Brief notes about contributors and selectors of choice are appended." Sutherland. The Best in Children's Bks

Authors' choice 2; stories chosen by Joan Aiken [and others]. Illus. by Krystyna Turska. Crowell [1974 c1973] 246p illus $7.95 (5-7)   S C

1 Short stories
ISBN 0-690-00313-7
First published 1973 in England
Companion volume to: Authors' choice

In this collection of favorite stories chosen by eighteen modern authors, selections range from Damon Runyon's A piece of pie to Oscar Wilde's The Happy Prince

Averill, Esther

Jenny and the Cat Club; a collection of favorite stories about Jenny Linsky; written and illus. by Esther Averill. Harper 1973 5v in 1 illus $4.95, lib. bdg. $4.43 (k-2)   S C

1 Cats—Stories
ISBN 0-06-020222-X; 0-06-020223-8
Includes the following previously published titles, all of which are available separately: The Cat Club (1944); Jenny's first party (1948); When Jenny lost her scarf (1951); Jenny's adopted brothers (1952) entered in Easy books; How the brothers joined the Cat Club (1953)

These stories tell "about Jenny Linsky, the little black cat who overcame her shyness and joined that organization of the elite of feline society, the Cat Club. The gentle heroine and the ingenious dialogue are as charming as ever, and Jenny's small adventures have a timeless appeal." Chicago. Children's Bk Center

Babbitt, Natalie

The Devil's storybook; stories and pictures by Natalie Babbitt. Farrar, Straus 1974 101p illus $4.95 (4-6)   S C

1 Devil—Fiction 2 Short stories
ISBN 0-374-31770-4
Ten "stories about the machinations of the Devil to increase the population of his realm. He is not always successful and, despite his clever ruses, meets frustration as often as his intended victims do." Horn Bk

"Twists of plot within traditional themes and a briskly witty style distinguish this book, illustrated amusingly with black-and-white line drawings." Booklist

Carlson, Natalie Savage

The talking cat, and other stories of French Canada; retold by Natalie Savage Carlson; pictures by Roger Duvoisin. Harper 1952 87p illus lib. bdg. $4.79 (3-6)   S C

1 Short stories 2 French Canadians—Fiction
ISBN 0-06-021081-8
"These seven once-in-another-time tales of French Canada were told first by the author's great-great uncle, . . . handed down in her family and now retold

in an enchanting manner that will appeal to today's storytellers." Wis Library Bul

"They are not, I am glad to say, written in dialect. Easy for the children to read themselves and perfect for the story hour." Horn Bk

Child Study Association of America

Round about the city; stories you can read to yourself; selected by the Child Study Association of America; illus. by Harper Johnson. Crowell 1966 116p illus $3.75 (2-4)   S C

1 Short stories 2 Cities and towns—Fiction
ISBN 0-690-71317-7
Contents: Wake up, city, by A. Tresselt; Hurray for Bobo, by J. Savage; Saturday surprise, by J. Fritz; Nobody listens to Andrew, by E. Guilfoile; Olaf reads, by J. Lexau; How to find a friend, by S. Asheron; Show and tell, by P. Martin; Betsy and Ellen go to market, by C. Haywood; A tulip for Tony, by M. Moskin; Meet Miki Takino, by H. Copeland

"Varied short stories of proven popularity deal with children from diverse backgrounds and their everyday doings in streets and playgrounds, at the market or the library. They are proffered as good read-aloud or storytelling material." Moorachian. What is a City?

Chrisman, Arthur Bowie

Shen of the sea; Chinese stories for children; illus. by Else Hasselriis. Dutton [1968 c1953] 221p illus $6.50 (5-7)   S C

1 China—Fiction 2 Fairy tales
ISBN 0-525-39244-0
First published 1925; copyright renewed 1953
Awarded the Newbery Medal, 1926
Here are "original tales of China told with humor and illustrated with distinctive silhouettes. [These] stories reveal Chinese philosophy and way of life." Asia. A Guide to Bks for Children

The stories' "charm lies in the brisk directness of the telling and in the very serious face with which Mr Chrisman conceals his bubbling glee over the utterly subversive conduct of his characters." Boston Transcript

De La Mare, Walter

The magic jacket; illus. by Paul Kennedy. Knopf 1962 277p illus $3.25, lib. bdg. $4.99 (5-7)   S C

1 Short stories
ISBN 0-394-81388-X; 0-394-91388-4
There is a touch of the supernatural in this "collection of ten short stories beautifully told. The collection has variety, the illustrations are in appropriate mood, the writing is of superb and distinctive literary quality." Chicago. Children's Bk Center

A penny a day; illus. by Paul Kennedy. Knopf 1960 209p illus lib. bdg. $4.99 (3-6)   S C

1 Fairy tales
ISBN 0-394-91493-7
Collection of six fairy tales, reprints from other books, most of them now out of print

" 'Only the rarest kind of best in anything is good enough for the young.' This was the guiding principle in all the writing Walter de la Mare did for children. It is clearly demonstrated in this collection of wondrous fairy tales." Cincinnati

Doyle, Sir Arthur Conan

The boys' Sherlock Holmes. New and enl. ed. A selection from the works of A. Conan Doyle arranged with introduction by Howard Haycraft. Harper 1961 524p illus map $7.95, lib. bdg. $7.49 (6-7)   S C

1 Mystery and detective stories 2 Short stories
ISBN 0-06-021736-7; 0-06-021735-9
First published 1936

Doyle, Sir Arthur Conan—*Continued*

This book contains three full-length novels: A study in scarlet; The sign of the four; The hound of the Baskervilles; a new selection of six short stories; and a sketch of Dr Joseph Bell, the man upon whom Sherlock Holmes is modeled

"The whole book is an admirable introduction to the subject for any reader—boy or man—who is fortunate enough to be reading these tales for the first time." Chicago Sunday Trib

Tales of Sherlock Holmes; illus. by H. Dinnerstein; afterword by Clifton Fadiman. Macmillan (N Y) 1963 608p illus $5.95 (6-7)   S C
1 Mystery and detective stories 2 Short stories
"The Macmillan classics"
This book includes three complete novels: A study in scarlet; The sign of the four; The hound of the Baskervilles, and seven short stories

Farjeon, Eleanor

The little bookroom; Eleanor Farjeon's short stories for children, chosen by herself; illus. by Edward Ardizzone. Walck, H.Z. 1956 [c1955] 302p illus $7 (1-4)   S C
1 Short stories 2 Fairy tales
ISBN 0-8098-2323-3
Received the Hans Christian Andersen award, 1956
First published 1955 by Oxford
"Fantasy, realism, humor, and wisdom are to be found in this collection of 27 delightful stories selected by the author from her own writings and characterized by her inventiveness and her charm and beauty of expression. The book takes its title from a dusty little room crammed with a motley assortment of overflow books in which the author browsed as a child. A book to be savored and treasured; a perfect choice for reading aloud. Harmonious illustrations." Booklist

Martin Pippin in the apple orchard; illus. by Richard Kennedy. Lippincott [1961 c1949] 305p illus $5.95 (2-4)   S C
1 Fairy tales
ISBN 0-397-30571-0
First published 1921 in England. The 1961 edition is a reprint of the 1922 Stokes edition with new illustrations
"Martin Pippin, himself a part of an unfolding fairy tale in the background, bribes with stories the six milkmaids who guard the farmer's daughter." Bks for Boys and Girls
Words and music to the song: "The Spring Green Lady": p300-05

Hamilton, Virginia

The time-ago tales of Jahdu; illus. by Nonny Hogrogian. Macmillan (N Y) 1969 61p illus $4.95 (3-5)
                                                 S C
1 Short stories
"In her 'tight little room in a fine, good place called Harlem' Mama Luka, takes care of Lee Edward after school until his mother comes home from work, telling him stories about Jahdu. In Mama Luka's tales, Jahdu discovers that he has a magic power that can banish Nightmare from the daylight: Jahdu conquers the giant Trouble with his cleverness; Jahdu makes mischief, and in the last tale, Jahdu becomes himself." Horn Bk
"Attractively illustrated and written in the easy natural mode of everyday speech, this would be an appealing choice for all collections." Wis Library Bul

Hardendorff, Jeanne B.

Witches, wit, and a werewolf; retold by Jeanne B. Hardendorff; illus. by Laszlo Kubinyi. Lippincott 1971 124p illus $4.95, pa $1.95 (5-7)   S C
1 Short stories
ISBN 0-397-31542-2; 0-397-31251-2
In this collection of humorous and scary stories, the author retells fifteen folk, ghost and witchcraft tales from Maupassant, Wiggin, Aesop and others. Three tales by Bierce, Dickens and Richard Hughes are also included
"Several of the stories may require adult interpretation of such terms as corpse candle . . . but there is enough variety in the selections to interest both readers and storytellers." Booklist

Harter, Walter

Osceola's head, and other American ghost stories; illus. by Neil Waldman. Prentice-Hall 1974 71p illus $4.95 (4-6)   S C
1 Ghost stories 2 U.S.—History—Fiction
ISBN 0-13-642991-2
"A description of witches, poltergeists, and warlocks introduces ten ghost stories based on incidents in American history. The stories are short, interesting to read, and feature ghosts from various eras—for example, 'The Ghost at Valley Forge' visited George Washington; 'The Actor Who Wouldn't Stay Dead' concerns the ghost of John Wilkes Booth; and 'Osceola's Head' is about the spirit of the Indian leader. Neil Waldman's gray-and-white sketches of the ghostly characters complement these stories about the preternatural." Sch Library J

Hitchcock, Alfred

(comp.) Alfred Hitchcock's Supernatural tales of terror and suspense; illus. by Robert Shore. Random House 1973 172p illus $3.95, lib. bdg. $5.67 (5-7)
                                                 S C
1 Horror stories 2 Short stories
ISBN 0-394-82676-0; 0-394-92676-5
Contents: The triumph of death, by H. R. Wakefield; The strange valley, by T. V. Olsen; The Christmas spirit, by D. B. Bennett; The bronze door, by R. Chandler; Slip stream, by S. Hodgson; The quest for "Blank Claveringi," by P. Highsmith; Miss Pinkerton's apocalypse, by M. Spark; The reunion after three hundred years, by A. Tolstoy; The attic express, by A. Hamilton; The pram, by A. W. Bennett; Mr Ash's studio, by H. R. Wakefield
The eleven stories included here "have been taken from adult collections and compiled for children." Booklist

Hoke, Helen

(ed.) Spooks, spooks, spooks; illus. by W. R. Lohse. . . .Watts, F. 1966 213p illus lib. bdg. $4.95 (4-6)
                                                 S C
1 Ghost stories 2 Short stories
ISBN 0-531-01797-4
"Beasties and bogles; creatures and creepies; Ghoulies and ghosties; Shades and spectres; Spooks and spirits; Witches and weirdies—a whole closetful of supernatural spellbinders." Title page
"High literary quality gives distinction and unity to this fine collection of stories and poems. . . . Included are such masters of the art of mystification as Walter de la Mare, Seumas MacManus, L. M. Boston, Elizabeth Coatsworth, Madeleine L'Engle, Ian Serraillier, Sorche Nic Leodhas, and Richard Chase. A few of the selections are excerpts from full-length novels." Sch Library J

Housman, Laurence

The rat-catcher's daughter; a collection of stories; selected and with an afterword by Ellin Greene; illus. by Julia Noonan. Atheneum Pubs. 1974 169p illus $5.95 (4-7)   S C

1 Fairy tales

ISBN 0-689-30420-X

"A Margaret K. McElderry book"

"Here are [twelve tales of] princesses both sweet and selfish, magic toys, crafty gnomes, brave boys and foolhardy ones, and . . . an appreciation of old age and death as part of nature. Not all of these tales are from the English tradition—one is Oriental, one American Indian." Pub W

"With their lovely imagery, their lilting use of language, their skillful twists of plot, these tales, drawn from a number of Housman's collections now out of print, are a delight to read or tell. Beautifully illustrated by Julia Noonan's sensitive pencil drawings." Babbling Bookworm

Ireson, Barbara

(comp.) Haunting tales; ed. by Barbara Ireson; illus. by Freda Woolf. Dutton [1974 c1973] 279p illus $6.95 (5-7)   S C

1 Ghost stories 2 Short stories

ISBN 0-525-31533-0

First published 1973 in England

Contents: Huw, by G. Palmer; The man who didn't believe in ghosts, by S. Nic Leodhas; Hans and his master, by R. Manning-Sanders; The haunted trailer, by R. Arthur; The magic shop, by H. G. Wells; John Charrington's wedding, by E. Nesbit; The ghostly earl, by R. Chetwynd-Hayes; Through the veil, by Sir A. C. Doyle; The doll's ghost, by M. Crawford; A long day without water, by J. Aiken; The demon king, by J. B. Priestley; Faithful Jenny Dove, by E. Farjeon; The twilight road, by H. F. Brinsmead; Fiddler, play fast, play faster, by R. Sawyer; Uncle Einar, by R. Bradbury; The ghost ship, by R. Middleton; Jimmy takes vanishing lessons, by W. R. Brooks; The crossways, by L. P. Hartley; Master ghost and I, by B. Softly

"Avoiding obvious sensationalism in the selection, editor Ireson has culled a fairly refined group of alternately spine-tingling, bittersweet, and tongue-in-cheek writings that involve ghosts and an occasional sorcerer, devil, or supernatural being. A sturdy volume, mixing classics and modern works." Booklist

Irving, Washington

Rip Van Winkle, The legend of Sleepy Hollow, and other tales; illus. by Roberta Carter Clark. Grosset 1967 158p illus $1.50 (4-6)   S C

1 Short stories

ISBN 0-448-05482-5

"Companion library"

Other tales included in this collection are: The spectre bridegroom and The Moor's legacy

Johnson, Sally Patrick

(ed.) The Princesses; sixteen stories about princesses; with biographical notes on each author; pictures by Beni Montresor. Harper 1962 318p illus $4.95, lib. bdg. $5.89 (4-6)   S C

1 Fairy tales 2 Short stories

ISBN 0-06-023040-1; 0-06-023041-X

"Of all these stories, which are literary rather than traditional fairy tales, only the first, Andersen's 'The Princess on the Pea,' will be very familiar to children. The other stories [are] by Mary de Morgan, Somerset Maugham, Walter de la Mare, Eleanor Farjeon, Ruth Sawyer, Rudyard Kipling, and others (no author has more than one story here)." Horn Bk

In this "handsome book . . . the selection has been

most judicious. . . . A good book for any collection, for a story-telling source, or for reading aloud." Chicago. Children's Bk Center

Kipling, Rudyard

The jungle book (4-7)   S C

1 Animals—Stories 2 India—Fiction 3 Short stories

Some editions are:

Doubleday $4.95, lib. bdg. $5.70 Illustrated by Philip Hays (ISBN 0-385-06133-1; 0-385-05392-4)

Grosset (Illustrated junior library) $3.95 Illustrated by Fritz Eichenberg (ISBN 0-448-05814-6)

First published 1894

These are stories of India and "the jungle life of Mowgli who was adopted by the wolf pack and taught the laws of the jungle by Bagheera the panther and Baloo the bear. Also unconnected stories of such animal personalities as Rikki Tikki the mongoose and Kotic the white seal." Toronto

The jungle books (4-7)   S C

1 Animals—Stories 2 India—Fiction 3 Short Stories

Some editions are:

Doubleday $4.95, lib. bdg. $5.70 Revised edition. With illustrations by Aldren Watson, foreword by Nelson Doubleday (ISBN 0-385-06133-1; 0-385-05392-4)

Macmillan (N Y) (The Macmillan classics) $4.95 Illustrations by Robert Shore; afterword by Clifton Fadiman

Watts, F. lib. bdg. $7.95 Large type edition complete and unabridged, with illus. by J. L. Kipling, W. H. Drake, and P. Frenzeny. A Keith Jennison book (ISBN 0-531-00210-1)

A collection of fifteen animal stories first published 1894 and 1895

The central figure in the stories is the human, Mowgli, brought up in the jungle by Mother Wolf

Just so stories (3-6)   S C

1 Animals—Stories 2 India—Fiction 3 Short stories

Some editions are:

Doubleday $3.50 Black and white illustrations throughout by the author (ISBN 0-385-07351-8)

Doubleday $4.95, lib. bdg. $5.70 Pictures by Joseph M. Gleason (ISBN 0-385-07352-6; 0-385-07110-8)

Doubleday $8.95, lib. bdg. $9.70 (Anniversary edition) Illustrated by Etienne Delessert; foreword by Nelson Doubleday (ISBN 0-385-07225-2; 0-385-07443-3)

Watts, F. lib. bdg. $7.95 Large type edition complete and unabridged. Illustrated by the author. A Keith Jennison book. Has subtitle: For little children (ISBN 0-531-00211-X)

The book consists of twelve animal fables

"While Kipling's original and humorous elucidation of how the elephant got his trunk and the leopard his spots are barely believable, he has nevertheless drawn animal characteristics and habits 'just so.' First published in 1902." Bks for Boys & Girls. 3d edition

The second jungle book; with illus. by J. Lockwood Kipling. Doubleday 1946 [c1895] 238p illus $4.50, lib. bdg. $5.25 (4-7)   S C

1 Animals—Stories 2 India—Fiction 3 Short stories

ISBN 0-385-07483-2; 0-385-08708-X

First published 1895

"Stories of animal life in the East Indian forest, where the animals talk together and tell the secrets of the jungle." Pittsburgh

The animals in these eight tales "are not men in hides and on all fours discussing human problems. Kipling's genius represents them thinking and behaving, each according to his own peculiar beastly

Kipling, Rudyard—_Continued_
habit and experience, with such dramatic skill that one is almost forced to believe that he has intimately dwelt among them." Keller's Reader's Digest of Bks

Leach, Maria
The thing at the foot of the bed, and other scary tales; illus. by Kurt Werth. Collins 1959 126p illus $5.91 (3-6)   S C
  1 Ghost stories 2 Short stories
  ISBN 0-529-03545-6
  This is an eerie collection of twenty-three short tales and two poems which includes funny stories and scary ones, and shivery witch stories; also a section entitled "Do's and don'ts about ghosts"
  "There is also information about legends and folklore concerning ghosts. A very amusing book, it is also a well-illustrated attractive package." Pub W
  Includes: Author's notes and bibliography

Levoy, Myron
The witch of Fourth Street, and other stories; pictures by Gabriel Lisowski. Harper 1972 110p illus $4.95, lib. bdg. $4.79, pa $1.25 (4-7)   S C
  1 New York (City)—Fiction 2 Short stories
  ISBN 0-06-023795-3; 0-06-023796-1
  "The eight stories [set on the Lower East Side of New York in the 1920's] tell about a group of neighbors, young and old: little Cathy Dunn, terrified of the old woman who sold pencils at the corner; the old-clothesman and his horse called Socrates; Vincent DeMarco, whose father longed for a set of electric trains; Mrs. Dunn, with her kitchen hencoop and fire-escape farm; and Aaron Kandel, whose grandmother on her sixtieth birthday expunged the bitter childhood memory of a Russian pogrom. Tales and characters are highly original, sometimes humorous, sometimes poignant, and often profound. The art of the short story is not always one that children recognize; one would serve the book well by introducing it, or better still, reading it aloud. The soft drawings are exactly right." Horn Bk

Nesbit, E.
The complete book of dragons; illus. by Erik Blegvad. Macmillan (N Y) [1973 c1972] 198p illus $5.95 (3-6)   S C
  1 Dragons—Stories 2 Fairy tales
  Eight of these stories were first published in book form in 1901 with title: The book of dragons; the story, Last of the dragons, was first published 1925 in: Five of us—and Madeline. This collection first published 1972 in England
  "This collection of dragon stories is scary, exciting, altogether delightful. The book should give hours of pleasure to readers with sturdy nerves." Pub W

Pearce, Philippa
What the neighbors did, and other stories; illus. by Faith Jaques. Crowell [1973 c1972] 130p illus $4.50, lib. bdg. $5.25 (4-6)   S C
  1 Short stories
  ISBN 0-690-87932-6; 0-690-87933-4
  First published 1972 in England
  This is a collection of stories about "the environmental experiences and the domestic adventures of children living in a present-day English village. The fly that woke Charlie in the middle of the night leads into the story of a midnight snack; old Jim finds a way of proving to young Jim that his own grandfather had been seven feet tall; against his better judgment, Pat takes Lucy, the little girl next door, with him on his free Saturday afternoon to the open country." Horn Bk
  "Each of these eight short stories is beautifully

written and thought-provoking. The author narrates with humor, sadness, and a strong sense of adventure the relationships between children and the adult world around them." Top of the News

Picard, Barbara Leonie
The faun and the woodcutter's daughter; illus. by Charles Stewart. Criterion Bks. 1964 255p illus $3.95 (4-7)   S C
  1 Fairy tales
  ISBN 0-200-71999-8
  First published 1951 in England
  "Fourteen original allegorical fairy tales. . . . Although the central theme, the triumph of love and selfless courage, dominates all the stories, each one is remarkably different from the others. They are written in the smooth prose of the traditional tale and would be delightful for reading aloud. As stories for telling they will have a wide audience." Horn Bk

Poe, Edgar Allan
Tales of terror and fantasy; ten stories from "Tales of mystery and imagination," chosen and ed. by Roger Lancelyn Green; with colour plate and line drawings by Arthur Rackham. Dutton [1972 c1971] 150p illus $6.95 (6-7)   S C
  1 Mystery and detective stories 2 Short stories
  ISBN 0-525-40750-2
  "Children's illustrated classics"
  First published 1971 in England
  Ten of the most chilling of the author's tales are included in this collection

Proysen, Alf
Little old Mrs Pepperpot, and other stories; illus. by Bjorn Berg. Obolensky [1960 c1959] 95p illus $4.95 (1-3)   S C
  1 Fairy tales 2 Short stories
  ISBN 0-8392-3021-4
  "An Astor book"
  Originally published in Norway. This translation by Marianne Helweg first published in England 1959
  A collection of twelve fanciful tales, five of "which deal with Mrs. Pepperpot, an old lady who occasionally changes into a tiny doll-like creature so small that she can ride around on a pet cat." Pub W

Ritchie, Alice
The treasure of Li-Po; with illus. by T. Ritchie. Harcourt 1949 154p illus $4.50 (3-6)   S C
  1 China—Fiction 2 Fairy tales
  ISBN 0-15-290158-2
  "While the six charming tales in this book are not traditional, they have an authentic Chinese flavor and the quality of the true fairy tale. The title story has to do with a humble basket-maker and his generosity, and into the others, enter such characters as a faithful lantern-bearer, a fox's child who becomes human, and a devoted son who travels through strange lands to the country of sleep to find a cure for his ailing father. The illustrations by T. Ritchie are drawn with humor and repose." Horn Bk

Sandburg, Carl
Rootabaga stories; illus. and decorations by Maud and Miska Petersham. Harcourt 1936 2v in 1 illus $7.95 (5-7)   S C
  1 Fairy tales
  ISBN 0-15-29057-3
  This edition contains: Rootabaga stories (1922) and Rootabaga pigeons (1923) reprinted in one volume. They are also available in a two volume paperback edition for $1.50 ea (ISBN 0-15-678900-0, v2 0-15-678901-9)
  "A collection of unique nonsense stories combining

Sandburg, Carl—*Continued*

the realism of the American middle West with a great deal of fancy and symbolism. A certain amount of repetition and the use of mouth-filling words create a rhythm and a singing quality which make the stories particularly suitable for reading aloud." Right Bk for the Right Child

Shepard, Ray Anthony

Conjure tales, by Charles W. Chesnutt; retold by Ray Anthony Shepard; illus. by John Ross and Clare Romano. Dutton 1973 99p illus $5.50 (5-7) S C

1 Occult sciences—Fiction 2 Slavery in the U.S.—Fiction 3 Short stories
ISBN 0-525-28140-1

Retold from Chesnutt's: The conjure woman. The seven stories in this collection are about North Carolina slaves and their experiences with voodoo and conjuring

"Some of the tales are very funny; most of them are touched with hurt and acrimony. Although the storytelling is direct and the supernatural subject matter tempting and timely, none but a sensitive reader will detect the real strength of the book—its subtle irony. For behind the conventional simplicity of the slaves, one may perceive the essential human tragedy and waste." Horn Bk

Silverberg, Barbara

(ed.) Phoenix feathers; a collection of mythical monsters; illus. with old prints. Dutton 1973 206p illus $6.50 (6-7) S C

1 Animals, Mythical—Stories 2 Short stories
ISBN 0-525-36985-6

Short stories included are: The Griffin and the Minor Canon, by F. R. Stockton; The Kraken, by F. Englehardt; Chinese puzzle, by J. Wyndham; The reluctant dragon, by K. Grahame; The ancient last, by H. Lehrman; The Silkenswift, by T. Sturgeon; The second voyage of Sinbad the Seaman; Bird in the hand, by L. Niven; The egg, by E. Nesbit

In this collection of stories about mythical creatures "brief primary source selections, alternating with the editor's explanatory notes, precede each section of modern fiction on a given creature. . . . The reader will need some knowledge of mythological beasts to enjoy much of the humor and implication in the stories, all of which are written on a more or less adult level. Suggestions for further reading are appended." Booklist

Simon, Solomon

The wise men of Helm and their merry tales; illus. by Lillian Fischel. Behrman 1945 135p illus $4.50 (4-7) S C

1 Jews in Poland—Fiction 2 Poland—Fiction 3 Short stories
ISBN 0-87441-125-4

Originally published 1942 in Yiddish. Translated by Ben Bengal and David Simon

An "attractively designed [book] which relates the misadventures of the [Jewish] people who lived in the town of Helm deep in the forests of Poland. While all the world looked upon them as fools, the Helmites believed themselves wondrously wise. The foolishness of Helm was fabulous only because 'foolish things were always happening to them.' Rich in humor, folklore quality—and in the underlying truths of life." Booklist

Sobol, Donald J.

Encyclopedia Brown, boy detective; illus. by Leonard Shortall. Nelson 1963 88p illus $4.95 (3-5) S C

1 Mystery and detective stories
ISBN 0-8407-7200-9

"Leroy Brown earns his nickname by applying his encyclopedic learning to community mysteries. The reader is asked to anticipate solutions before checking them in the back of the book." Adventuring With Bks. 2d edition

"The answers are logical; some are tricky, but there are no trick questions, and readers who like puzzles should enjoy the . . . challenge. The episodes are lightly humorous, brief, and simply written." Chicago. Children's Bk Center

Several other titles about Encyclopedia Brown are available from Nelson

Sutcliff, Rosemary

Heather, oak, and olive; three stories; illus. by Victor Ambrus. Dutton 1972 120p illus $5.95 (5-7) S C

1 Civilization, Ancient—Fiction 2 Short stories
ISBN 0-525-31599-3

Stories first published separately in England

"Three tales of ancient times, each different in setting and all compelling, are told by a master storyteller who is also an excellent historian. The period details are vivid but do not overburden the stories, the structure is deft and sturdy, the characters strong. . . . The black and white illustrations, handsome in themselves, echo the dignity and the romanticism of Rosemary Sutcliff's writing." Chicago. Children's Bk Center

Tolstoy, Leo

Twenty-two Russian tales for young children; selected, tr. and with an afterword by Miriam Morton; illus. by Eros Keith. Simon & Schuster 1969 57p illus lib. bdg. $4.50 (3-5) S C

1 Short stories
ISBN 0-671-65073-4

These moral tales, fairy tales, "fables, fantasies and animal stories by Leo Tolstoy, with illustrations by Eros Keith (which lend a certain air of simplicity and grace), make this book a delightful reading experience." Pub W

"These stories were written and then translated in a style that will allow them to be enjoyed orally or silently." Rdng Ladders. 5th edition

Wilde, Oscar

The Happy Prince, and other stories; illus. with four colour plates and line drawings in the text by Peggy Fortnum. Dutton 1968 154p illus $6.95 (3-6) S C

1 Fairy tales
ISBN 0-525-31396-6

"Children's illustrated classics"

A combined edition, first published 1952 in England, of The Happy Prince, and other stories (1888) and A house of pomegranates (1891)

Yolen, Jane

The girl who cried flowers, and other tales; illus. by David Palladini. Crowell 1974 55p illus $5.95, lib. bdg. $6.70 (4-6) S C

1 Short stories 2 Fairy tales
ISBN 0-690-00216-5; 0-690-00217-3

"The five stories are original but have a flavor of long ago. Each is memorable and stays with you. The unifying factor in this book is the ability of the protagonist in each story to do something very unusual. Naturally, the special trait offers disadvantages as well as advantages. Included are a boy who can stare everyone down, a girl whose tears are flower petals, and a girl who has an obsession to know the future. Each tale can be listened to (or read) for several purposes; each can be attended to on several levels. The plots themselves are good, as each individual copes

Yolen, Jane—*Continued*

with the straits caused by his or her trait. In addition, each story offers symbolic discussion about something very important in life. . . . Finally, there is the beauty of Yolen's language, which instantly sucks you into the story and glues you there." Rdng Teacher

(ed.) Zoo 2000; twelve stories of science fiction and fantasy beasts; comp. and introduced by Jane Yolen. Seabury 1973 224p $7.95 (5-7) S C

1 Animals, Mythical—Stories 2 Science fiction 3 Short stories
ISBN 0-8164-3103-5

Contents: Zoo 2000, by R. Curtis; The hurkle is a happy beast, by T. Sturgeon; The deep range, by A. C. Clarke; There is a wolf in my time machine, by L. Niven; Apple, by J. Baxter; Interview with a lemming, by J. Thurber; All cats are gray, by A. Norton; The mouse, by H. Fast; The island of the endangered, by D. Ferguson; Country doctor, by W. Morrison; The day of the dragon, by G. Endore; The king of beasts, by P. J. Farmer

"In a thoughtful introduction to the stories, Jane Yolen points out that whereas our ancestors used beast tales to explain the world's beginnings, science fiction uses them as a warning." Chicago. Children's Bk Center

E EASY BOOKS

This section consists mostly of fiction books which would interest children from pre-school through second grade. For the most part, those easy books which have a definite nonfiction subject content are classified with other nonfiction books. Easy books listed here include:

1 All picture books whether fiction or nonfiction which the young child can use independently

2 Fiction books with very little text, widely spaced or scattered, with large print, and with vocabulary suitable for children with reading levels of grades 1-2

3 Picture storybooks with a larger amount of text to be used primarily by or with children in preschool through grade 2

Adams, Adrienne

A woggle of witches. Scribner 1971 unp illus lib. bdg. $6.95 E

1 Witches—Fiction 2 Halloween—Stories
ISBN 0-684-12506-4

Illustrated by the author, here are the adventures of a woggle of witches on Halloween night as they wake up the forest to feast on bat stew, circle the moon on their brooms, and descend on a corn field only to be frightened away by a group of trick-or-treaters

"This book is just right for storytelling to preschool and primary groups: the minimal text is greatly expanded by lovely, dusky double-page spreads which humorously highlight the airborne antics." Sch Library J

Adoff, Arnold

Black is brown is tan; pictures by Emily Arnold McCully. Harper 1973 31p illus $4.95, lib. bdg. $5.11 E

1 Family—Fiction 2 Stories in rhyme
ISBN 0-06-020083-9; 0-06-020084-7

This story in rhyme describes "a warm, racially-mixed family who reads, cuts wood, plays, and eats together." Booklist

"The illustrations appear rough, and the text reads better if done aloud. Although this title is not the best,

it deals fairly with the subject and serves as an important beginning in the field of easy books for children about different kinds of families." Children's Bk Rev Serv

MA nDA LA; pictures by Emily McCully. Harper 1971 unp illus $3.95, lib. bdg. $4.43 E

ISBN 0-06-020085-5; 0-06-020086-3

The text of this chant celebrating an African family's cultivation and harvest of a corn crop "consists entirely of syllables from the word mandala, the name of a Hindu or Buddhist symbol of the universe, rearranged to tell a simple story in which MA stands for mother, DA for father, LA for singing, and HA for laughing, RA for cheering, NA for sighing, and AH for feeling good." Booklist

"It must be read aloud to get the full effect of a child's blithe crooning, it must be seen for the full effect of the dark figures . . . against the colors of the tropical foliage. Not suitable for group use, but right for reading aloud to an individual child." Chicago. Children's Bk Center

Adshead, Gladys L.

Brownies—hush! With pictures by Elizabeth Orton Jones. Walck, H.Z. 1938 unp illus lib. bdg. $4.50, pa $1.50 E

1 Fairy tales
ISBN 0-8098-1003-4; 0-8098-1808-6
First published by Oxford

"The playful Brownies help an old couple with their work, but run away when seen and rewarded with new clothes." Hodges. Bks for Elem Sch Libraries

"The prose is such as to be read aloud with gusto." N Y Times Bk Rev

"The drawings in three colors, brown, white, and red . . . suit the text and add to the charm of the book." Booklist

Brownies—it's Christmas! With pictures by Velma Ilsley. Walck, H.Z. 1955 unp illus lib. bdg. $4.50, pa $1.35 E

1 Christmas stories 2 Fairy tales
ISBN 0-8098-1041-7; 0-8098-2913-4
First published by Oxford

"When the Brownies trim a Christmas tree for Grandmother and Grandfather they are rewarded with their own tiny tree, a gift from the old couple." Chicago

"The easy-to-read, gay text is hand-lettered in manuscript style. . . . It is printed in green with touches of Christmas red." N Y Her Trib Bks .

Alexander, Lloyd

The king's fountain; illus. by Ezra Jack Keats. Dutton 1971 unp illus $6.95 E

ISBN 0-525-33240-5

A "king decides to build a fountain in his garden for 'the glory of his name.' Unfortunately for the city, it would eliminate the water supply. A poor man tries to find someone with wisdom, courage and persuasive speech to point out to the king the disastrous consequences of the plan. Everyone lets him down. . . . The despairing poor man realizes he must go himself." N Y Times Bk Rev

"Stunningly beautiful full-page paintings, among the artists' finest, greatly expand this short, trenchant parable. . . . Keats's acrylics on canvas effectively evoke the Near Eastern setting; Alexander's theme—that the buck must stop with Everyman, that each person's conscience must form a continuum with constructive action—has obvious relevance for readers of any time or place." Library J

Alexander, Martha

And my mean old mother will be sorry, blackboard bear; story and pictures by Martha Alexander. Dial Press 1972 unp illus $4.95, lib. bdg. $4.58   E

1 Bears—Stories

ISBN 0-8037-0592-1; 0-8037-0593-X

Sequel to: Blackboard bear

A little boy, angry with his mother, runs away to live in the woods with his imaginary companion, blackboard bear

The story "parallels fantasies experienced by children who would also like to make someone sorry, and will be recognized and enjoyed for its pertinence and humor." Horn Bk

Blackboard bear; story and pictures by Martha Alexander. Dial Press 1969 unp illus $4.95, lib. bdg. $4.58   E

1 Bears—Stories

ISBN 0-8037-0651-0; 0-8037-0652-9

This small, "sparely worded, fantastical picture-book stars a little boy who is spurned when he attempts to play with the bigger boys. Told to go play with his teddy bear, he defiantly tosses teddy out the window and, on his blackboard, draws a big bear, which then steps right down to become his friend and playmate. . . . The softly-hued illustrations will carry the story for sensitive, imaginative children, and capture childhood feelings of solitude and revenge." Sch Library J

Followed by: And my mean old mother will be sorry, blackboard bear

Bobo's dream. Dial Press 1970 unp illus $4.95, lib. bdg. $4.58   E

1 Dogs—Stories 2 Negroes—Fiction 3 Stories without words

This story without words tells "how a black boy and his dachshund feel about each other. Boy and dog settle under a shady tree to enjoy a book, a bone, and companionship. A large dog tries to steal the dachshund's bone, but the boy retrieves the bone. The grateful dog dreams of daring exploits in which he comes to the rescue of his master." Keating. Building Bridges of Understanding Between Cultures

"Unpretentious three-color drawings, childlike and humorous, show that might does not make right." Horn Bk

I'll protect you from the jungle beasts. Dial Press 1973 unp illus $4.95, lib. bdg. $4.58   E

1 Teddy bears—Fiction

ISBN 0-8037-4308-4; 0-8037-4309-2

"A little boy walking through the lonesome, scarey woods of his mind assures his teddy bear of protection until he himself becomes frightened by the night noise; his teddy bear then grows big enough to hold him and find the way home to their snuggly bed, where the boy awakens next morning to find the stuffed toy shrunk back to normal size." Booklist

"Most children will recognize the feeling of gaining security from a loved object, but some listeners may not understand at the start that the action is imagined by the child." Chicago. Children's Bk Center

No ducks in "our" bathtub; story and pictures by Martha Alexander. Dial Press 1973 unp illus $4.95, lib. bdg. $4.58   E

1 Pets—Stories

ISBN 0-8037-6239-9; 0-8037-6217-8

"Poor David has a mother who's a 'mean old crab. She will allow no bugs in their apartment, no pigeons, no ducks in the bathtub. But David finds fish eggs to bring home and they are acceptable; when they hatch, the boy will have pets. David and his family go on vacation and Mr. Garfunkel and other friends care for

the 'fish' in their absence, with stunning results. David comes home to find he's the owner of . . . [103] frogs." Pub W

"A genuinely amusing book for even the youngest preschooler. . . . The simple drawings in orange, brown, and black stress each nuance of the childlike story." Horn Bk

Nobody asked me if I wanted a baby sister; story and pictures by Martha Alexander. Dial Press 1971 unp illus $4.95, lib. bdg. $4.58   E

1 Brothers and sisters—Fiction 2 Infants—Fiction

ISBN 0-8037-6401-4; 0-8037-6402-2

"Jealous of the fuss made over his baby sister, Oliver bundles Bonnie into his wagon and, wheeling her around the neighborhood, tries to give her away. He changes his mind, however, and decides to keep her when the baby, unhappy at being held by strangers, cries until he takes her." Booklist

"Not a brand-new theme, but pictures and text together make a charming variation, the precise little drawings affectionate and humorous, the writing ingenuous and direct." Chicago. Children's Bk Center

Out! Out! Out! Dial Press 1968 unp illus $4.95, lib. bdg. $4.58   E

1 Pigeons—Stories 2 Stories without words

ISBN 0-8037-6663-7; 0-8037-6665-3

"When a pigeon flies through the open window into the kitchen a hullabaloo ensues as the mother, aided by a deliveryman and the janitor, pursues the pigeon from room to room, from cupboard to fireplace. Watching with obvious delight are two small children one of whom succeeds in getting rid of the pigeon when the adults fail. All of this is told without words." Booklist

The softly shaded line drawings make the household confusion easy and pleasant to follow." Sch Library J

Sabrina; story and pictures by Martha Alexander. Dial Press 1971 unp illus $4.95, lib. bdg. $4.58   E

1 Names, Personal—Fiction

ISBN 0-8037-7547-4; 0-8037-7546-6

"Sabrina had never thought that her name was the least peculiar until the day she started nursery school. Then mistaking the other children's whispered admiration for scorn, she tried to escape from her name and become a Lisa or a Susan—until she realized that she actually had an enviable 'princess' name. . . . Diminutive boys and girls, busy with nursery-school activities, are shown on clean, uncluttered, small-sized pages." Horn Bk

The story grandmother told; story and pictures by Martha Alexander. Dial Press 1969 unp illus $4.95, lib. bdg. $4.58   E

1 Balloons—Fiction 2 Negroes—Fiction

ISBN 0-8037-8299-3; 0-8037-8300-0

"Lisa begs Gramma for a story, and says she'd like the one about Ivan and Lisa and the green humming cat . . . the one in which Lisa buys a green cat-shaped balloon which unfortunately breaks (picture of Ivan, the real cat, smugly smiling at the clawed balloon which has been taking all attention away from him) . . . and, having told the whole story, Lisa sits in happy anticipation as Gramma obligingly prepares to tell it. The routine is a familiar one, the story (and the story within it) are at just the right level for the very young read-aloud audience, and the illustrations add to the book's appeal with a bright-eyed brown child and a cat whose expressions range from malevolent to angelic." Sutherland. The Best in Children's Bks

Alexander, Martha—*Continued*

We never get to do anything; story and pictures by Martha Alexander. Dial Press 1970 unp illus $4.95, lib. bdg. $4.58   E

ISBN 0-8037-9415-0; 0-8037-9416-9

The ingredients of this story are a "small boy, large dog, busy mother, hot summer day. Adam wants to go swimming, but his mother is hanging out laundry. He disappears, is hauled back and tied to the clothesline. 'We never get to do anything,' Adam grumbles, as he slips out of his sunsuit and hares off 'au natural.' He looks enviously at a dog under a hydrant, at birds in a fountain, at an overflowing drainpipe. Then—o joy! Rain falls, Adam shoves his empty sand box under the drain, and on the last page he is blissfully relaxing in a do-it-yourself pool." Sat Rev

"The text is slight but more than adequate, since the pictures almost tell the story. The tidy, brisk little drawings have affection and humor; the ending is sheer triumph." Chicago. Children's Bk Center

Aliki

June 7! Macmillan (N Y) 1972 unp illus lib. bdg. $4.95   E

1 Family—Fiction 2 Birthdays—Fiction

Illustrated by the author

"On that memorable date, the doorbell rings at the home of the narrator; she lives with her mother and father and her brother. In come her mother's parents and her father's parents and their son and daughter-in-law, and so on until the house is bursting with people, all related in a variety of bewildering degrees. These are all identified as the story progresses to its climax, when everybody sings 'Happy Birthday' to the narrator. An engaging story and pictures and a painless way of learning how to keep track of relationships." Pub W

All the pretty horses [illus. by] Susan Jeffers. Macmillan Pub. Co. 1974 unp illus $6.95   E

1 Lullabies

ISBN 0-02-747680-4

"Tucked in at night under her flowered quilt, a small girl dreams of horses. The words are those of the familiar lullaby, the pictures imaginative drawings, softly colored, of the child riding and playing with her dream horses among the flowers of the quilt, now huge." Chicago. Children's Bk Center

"Susan Jeffers has taken a simple lullaby and transformed it into a truly striking picture book which will hold and captivate children—especially those who love horses. . . . Even if there were no text this title would be a must simply for its beautiful art. Highly recommended." Cath Library World

Anderson, C. W.

Billy and Blaze. Macmillan (N Y) 1962 [c1936] 48p illus lib. bdg. $4.95   E

1 Ponies—Stories

"The Billy and Blaze books"

First published 1936. Reissued 1962 in a new format

A picture-story book about Billy, "a little boy who loved horses more than anything else in the world," and his pony Blaze. There is a picture for each sentence of text

"The book has the convincing quality of actual experience, for the artist-author understands horses and knows how to make them come to life on the printed page." N Y Times Bk Rev

Anderson, Lonzo

The day the hurricane happened; illus. by Ann Grifalconi. Scribner 1974 39p illus $5.95   E

1 Hurricanes—Fiction 2 Virgin Islands of the U.S.—Fiction

ISBN 0-684-13495-0

Set on St John, in the Virgin Islands, this is the story of a family coping with a hurricane. "Two small children, Eldra and Albie, tell their father of the strange flags (warning flags) they have seen on a flagpole. Father, a constable, goes off to warn others while Grandfather tells the children and their mother what to do. Their house is destroyed, so—during the lull of the storm's eye—each ties himself to a tree to wait out the buffeting of the hurricane." Chicago. Children's Bk Center

"Family solidarity and a by-product of information on hurricanes make this interesting, even adventuresome material for the beginning-to-read group. Grifalconi's broad watercolors capture the tension engendered by the storm and its aftermath." Booklist

Izzard; illus. by Adrienne Adams. Scribner 1973 unp illus lib. bdg. $5.95   E

1 Lizards—Stories 2 Virgin Islands of the U.S.—Fiction

ISBN 0-684-13247-8

"Jamie of St. John in the Virgin Islands finds a lizard egg and it hatches in his hand. The little anole thinks that he's her mother! But, the time comes when Izzard realizes she's really a lizard, and Jamie learns with difficulty to let her go, physically and emotionally." Babbling Bookworm

This is "not an unusual boy-animal plot, but [it is] given freshness here by the fact that the pet is unusual, the telling is deft, and the illustrations are handsome in the carefree detail with which they are drawn." Chicago. Children's Bk Center

Mr Biddle and the birds; illus. by Adrienne Adams. Scribner 1971 unp illus lib. bdg. $5.95   E

1 Flight—Fiction 2 Birds—Stories

ISBN 0-684-12315-0

"Mr. Biddle decides it would be fun to fly. He designs a flying boat and enlists the aid of four feathered friends to carry his 'chair-in-the-air.' But things don't work too well the first time since the four birds want to fly in different directions." Sch Library J

The "story is told with admirable economy, and the illustrations are large and clear with details of costume and setting reflecting an eighteenth-century atmosphere. A welcome addition to the picture-book story hour and great fun for today's space-age children." Horn Bk

Two hundred rabbits [by] Lonzo Anderson and Adrienne Adams. Viking 1968 32p illus $4.50, pa 95¢   E

1 Fairy tales 2 Rabbits—Stories

ISBN 0-670-73640-6; 0-670-05051-2

The unidentified narrator of this folkbased tale describes "the humble lad who yearns to participate in the Festival Day in the palace of the king of Jamais. Kind and cheerful but inept, the boy is given a magic whistle by a mysterious old woman. When he blows it, 199 rabbits appear and, in serried ranks, march with him to the palace gates. The king is enchanted until he sees that the last row doesn't come out even, but the day is saved by the commentator." Sat Rev

Adrienne Adams' "beautiful soft color pictures create a complete admirable medieval world with a traditional fairy story plot of the poor boy making good at the king's court. . . . Along with the loveliness of the pictures there's fun too in the boy's struggle to find something to entertain the king." Bk World

Anno, Mitsumasa

Anno's alphabet; an adventure in imagination. Crowell [1975 c1974] unp illus $6.95, lib. bdg. $7.70   E

1 Alphabet books

ISBN 0-690-00540-7; 0-690-00541-5

Anno, Mitsumasa—*Continued*

The artist "has produced another exercise in optical delusion featuring more of his technical virtuosity and visual witticisms. Each alphabetic character is cleanly painted as though fashioned of wood; but a searching look reveals the subtle deception which turns the realistic letters into three-dimensional surrealistic forms. Lines and textures are sharply communicated, but shapes are convoluted, angled, or inverted to produce an uncanny effect of motion. Facing each letter is an object, appropriately chosen but unconventionally illustrated; while the page borders are embellished with intertwining pen-and-ink drawings that conceal pictures of plants, animals, and objects, most of which are identified at the end of the book." Horn Bk

Topsy-turvies; pictures to stretch the imagination. Weatherhill [distributed by Lippincott] 1970 27p illus $4.50   E

1 Puzzles
ISBN 0-8348-2004-8

This book consists of illustrations featuring the activities of some elves. Each picture "features little men with pointed hats in unlikely situations involving matching staircases that don't, level platforms that aren't, walls and ceilings that are floors, and mazes that turn upside down." Library J

"In a constant flow of motion through the ensuing pages, the elves march or run or dive—may even rest—but are never static figures. Both in their faces and in their bodies they express individual and very human moods; tired, mischievous, or speculative, they are always alive. Although younger children may not be able to discover the 'real' solutions to the puzzles the elves demonstrate, they will be captivated by the little figures as they progress through their elaborately conceived world of building blocks, bottles, and playing cards. Older children, too, will be fascinated by the sophisticated perspective puzzles presented in sharply detailed line and watercolor drawings subtly vibrant with color." Horn Bk

Upside-downers; more pictures to stretch the imagination. Weatherhill [distributed by Lippincott] 1971 27p illus $4.50   E

1 Puzzles
ISBN 0-8348-2005-6

Original Japanese edition, 1969

"Awakened from their sleep, the kings' own soldiers in the land of playing cards resume their age-old quarreling over what is up and what is down until an old king with a new idea proclaims that since the world is round, up and down are all in the point of view. The reader is encouraged to examine the picture book from various angles both by the many optical illusions in the gaily colored illustrations and by the fact that part of the text is printed upside down." Booklist

"In a companion volume to Topsy-Turvies [entered above] the artist performs further feats of optical ingenuity with the same joyous dexterity that characterized the earlier book. . . . A kind of mad logic runs through the book." Horn Bk

Ardizzone, Edward

Little Tim and the brave sea captain. [2d ed. completely redrawn and with additional text]. Walck, H.Z. 1955 unp illus lib. bdg. $5.95   E

1 Sea stories
ISBN 0-8098-1042-5

First published 1936 by Oxford

The story "tells how Tim stowed away on a ship, learned to be useful, and showed his courage when the ship was wrecked." Horn Bk

"The pictures [by the author] are rapid wash drawings full of swing, salt and slap, the sea scenes especially good, full of action." N Y Her Trib Bks

Tim all alone. Walck, H.Z. 1957 unp illus lib. bdg. $5.95   E

ISBN 0-8098-1048-4
First published by Oxford

"One day Tim arrived at his home by the sea after a long holiday to find the house locked and shuttered. A notice pinned to the door said. 'Gone away. House to let.' Surprised and upset, Tim set out to search for his parents. First he joined the crew of a small coastal steamer which called at all the little ports, where he could inquire for his parents. His varied adventures included an escape from an orphanage and a shipwreck, before he was eventually reunited with his family." Ontario Library Rev

"Mr Ardizzone puts just about everything into this story, but he tells it all with that disarming matter-of-factness which makes you believe it happened exactly like that. There are plenty of illustrations, done in the relaxed, humorous Ardizzone style." N Y Times Bk Rev

Tim in danger. Walck, H.Z. 1953 unp illus lib. bdg. $5.95   E

1 Sea stories
ISBN 0-8098-1032-8
First published by Oxford

"Another episode in the life of Tim in which his brother Ginger leaves home to go to sea, and Tim and his sister Charlotte go to find him. To pursue the search they join up with the crew of another ship, finally meet Ginger, and all return home. Well written and illustrated in color wash by the author." Library J

Tim to the lighthouse. Walck, H.Z. 1968 unp illus $5.95   E

1 Lighthouses—Fiction
ISBN 0-8098-1133-2

"In this voyage, brave Tim with his friend Captain McFee, accompanied by two stowaways, go over stormy waters to rescue a lighthouse keeper and to foil the schemes of evil men." Pub W

"The charming illustrations, some in black and white, others in soft colors, feature cartoon blurbs; the large print enhances the visual appeal and utility of the book. Good for read alouds and enjoyable material for young independent readers." Sch Library J

Tim's last voyage. Walck, H.Z. [1973 c1972] unp illus lib. bdg. $5.95   E

1 Sea stories
ISBN 0-8098-1200-2
First published 1972 in England

Two boys, Tim and Ginger "sign on as deck hands for a three-day voyage on the steamer 'Arabella.' A storm wrecks the 'Arabella' on the sands not far from Tim's house. After Tim and the crew are rescued by lifeboatmen, Tim's mother extracts a promise that he will not go to sea again until he is grown up." Sch Library J

"This understated tale of improbable happenings is enhanced by richly appealing pictures [by the author]. . . . The subtle humor of this book makes it well worth reading; much of it appears in the balloon speeches of the crew on the doomed ship." Pub W

Aruego, Jose

Look what I can do. Scribner 1971 unp illus lib. bdg. $5.95   E

1 Water buffalo—Stories
ISBN 0-684-12493-9

"The story of two carabaos who get carried away trying to outdo each other and almost come to a sad end." Booklist

"There are just fifteen words in this story . . . whose valuable message should be intelligible to the

Aruego, Jose—*Continued*
young non-reader. . . . Sprightly, cartoon-like drawings [by the author] are the focal point." Bk World

Aulaire, Ingri d'
Animals everywhere, by Ingri and Edgar Parin d'Aulaire. Doubleday 1954 unp illus $4.50, lib. bdg. $5.25, pa 95¢   E
  1 Animals—Pictorial works
  ISBN 0-385-07216-3; 0-385-07703-3; 0-385-08128-6
This book introduces very young children to animals from the tropics to the arctic regions. The authors picture animals in their natural habitats
"The generous doublespread pictures in color provide hours of entertainment for a small child. The brief text when read aloud will give him the fun of hunting for each animal mentioned, and he will surely want to imitate the cries the authors have so thoughtfully included." Horn Bk

Don't count your chicks [by] Ingri & Edgar Parin d'Aulaire. Doubleday 1943 unp illus $5.95, pa 95¢   E
  1 Chickens—Stories 2 Farm life—Fiction
  ISBN 0-385-07282-1; 0-385-05233-2
The story "tells of the laughable schemes of the old woman who counted too much on her eggs before they were hatched and found herself left with only her little red house, her dog and cat, and her cock and hen." Ontario Library Rev
"A humorous story illustrated [by the authors] with large lithographs showing colorful country scenes." Hodges. Bks for Elem Sch Libraries

Ola, by Ingri & Edgar Parin d'Aulaire. Doubleday 1932 unp illus $3.95, lib. bdg. $4.70   E
  1 Norway—Fiction
  ISBN 0-385-09104-4; 0-385-07670-3
The adventures of Ola, a little Norwegian boy, who went out on his skis one wintry day. He got lost in a snowdrift and was dug out by Per [the] peddler with whom he went to visit the Lapps, then a fishing village on the coast, and finally the bird rocks where he collected down from the birds' nest
"A beautiful and entirely childlike large picture book of Norway which is authentic in spirit and in every detail. The artists have provided an appealing story as accompaniment to lithographic drawings in full color and in black and white which record the adventures of Ola and serve also as a pictorial background for future reading of Norse literature." N Y Pub Library

Averill, Esther
The fire cat; story and pictures by Esther Averill. Harper 1960 63p illus $2.95, lib. bdg. $3.79   E
  1 Cats—Stories 2 Fire departments—Fiction
  ISBN 0-06-020195-9; 0-06-020196-7
"An I can read book"
"A story in three parts for beginning independent readers. Pickles, a spotted cat, wanted to do big things: he didn't want to live in the home of Mrs. Goodkind, and he spent his time chasing small cats. One day he was rescued, when treed, by the Fire Department. He stayed at the firehouse and learned to slide down the pole and help with the hose. The Chief had a hat made for Pickles and he became the departmental Fire Cat. The writing pace is sedate but steady, the humor is in the situation rather than in the narration. A pleasant story, and one that younger children will enjoy having read aloud." Chicago. Children's Bk Center

Jenny's adopted brothers; written and illus. by Esther Averill. Harper 1952 32p illus lib. bdg. $3.79   E

  1 Cats—Stories
  ISBN 0-06-020231-9
"Compassion turns to jealousy when Jenny [the little black cat] sees Edward and Checkers, two homeless cats she brought home for adoption, ensconced on Captain Tinker's knees. But Jenny's true character shines forth when, on a rainy night, she searches for and brings back the two brothers her selfishness had driven out." Booklist
"A delight to read aloud. The many little pictures exactly match it, amusing and naive, yet masterfully cat-like." N Y Her Trib Bks

Ayer, Jacqueline
Little Silk. Harcourt 1970 unp illus $6.50   E
  1 Dolls—Fiction 2 Hongkong—Fiction
  ISBN 0-15-247450-1
Once beautiful, but now faded and worn, Miss Silk, a beautiful padded doll, lives with the Shu family on a hillside in Hong Kong. This is the story of how Miss Silk is lost in a busy marketplace, found by an old man and taken to a place of peace and happiness
"A gentle and endearing story in a picture book with detailed four-color drawings [by the author] evocative of the Hong Kong setting." Booklist

Nu Dang and his kite. Harcourt 1959 unp illus $6.50, pa $1.25   E
  1 Kites—Fiction 2 Thailand—Fiction
  ISBN 0-15-257601-0; 0-15-667800-4
"The story of Nu Dang, a small Siamese boy who had an unusual kite which was his dearest possession. One day the kite floated away and Nu Dang hunted everywhere for it, finally finding it when he had given up and gone home. The text is simple and affords, as Nu Dang searches, opportunity for information about Siam. The illustrations [by the author] also are informative and are striking in their unusual use of color, although they may confuse the smaller child who cannot identify the many unfamiliar details." Chicago. Children's Bk Center

A wish for Little Sister. Harcourt 1960 unp illus $6.50   E
  1 Thailand—Fiction
  ISBN 0-15-298213-2
Illustrated by the author
"A mynah bird tells little sister on her birthday that a wish will be granted her at twilight. All day long she seeks a suitable, sensible, usable wish asking advice of her relatives and friends, all hard at work spinning and weaving the precious silk of Bangkok, famous all over the world. She receives only gay impractical suggestions, which she visualizes and discards. . . . Finally all by herself she thinks of the perfect 'little-sister-wish,' and to her great delight . . . her simple happy wish is granted." N Y Her Trib Bks
"An attractive [colorful] picture book. . . . Welcome addition to the growing number of authentic books picturing the East." Library J

Balet, Jan
The fence; a Mexican tale; story and pictures by Jan Balet. Delacorte Press 1969 unp illus $4.95, lib. bdg. $4.58   E
  1 Mexico—Fiction
  ISBN 0-440-02556-7; 0-440-02559-1
"A Seymour Lawrence book"
Originally published in Germany
"A poor family is taken to court by the rich family next door for stealing the smell of their food. At the trial the poor man slyly steps outside the door and jingles some coins in a hat whereupon the judge decrees that if money is owing for the smells, suitable payment has been made. As told here the amusing tale is set in Mexico and is illustrated in Balet's distinc-

Balet, Jan—*Continued*

tive style in striking, brilliantly colored pictures that delightfully detail the Mexican scene." Booklist

The gift; a Portuguese Christmas tale; story and pictures by Jan Balet. Delacorte Press 1967 unp illus lib. bdg. $5.47   E

1 Christmas stories 2 Portugal—Fiction
ISBN 0-440-02906-6
"A Seymour Lawrence book"
Original German edition published 1966

This "is the quiet story of little Joanjo, who wonders the reason for the gifts and festivities he sees being prepared. Joanjo follows the procession to the Christ Child, and presents his own gifts: the sunshine, moonbeams, and starlight treasured in his heart. The author's bright, stylized illustration depict Portuguese folk art carvings; Joanjo is portrayed in black-and-white line drawings as he wanders among the colorful crèche figures. The text, a stiff translation from the German, does not reflect the vitality of the pictures." Sch Library J

Joanjo; a Portuguese tale; story and pictures by Jan Balet. Delacorte Press 1967 unp illus $4.95, lib. bdg. $4.58   E

1 Portugal—Fiction
ISBN 0-440-04236-4; 0-440-04233-X
"A Seymour Lawrence book"
Original German edition published 1965

"Joanjo, living in a fishing village by the sea, decides he is tired of the taste and smell of the everyday diet of fish in this Portuguese village. Traditionally the men in his family were all fishermen, but this small boy falls asleep and vividly dreams of another life." Rdng Ladders. 5th edition

"The story line isn't strong, but the illustrations are delightful in this dreams-of-glory picture book." Sat Rev

Balian, Lorna

Humbug witch. Abingdon 1965 unp illus $3.95 E

1 Witches—Fiction
ISBN 0-687-18023-6

Illustrations by the author accompany this story of "a little witch and her unsuccessful attempts at witchcraft. One evening she wearily takes off piece after piece of comical attire—the last of which proves to be a mask, revealing a hilarious little girl underneath! Too good to miss." Adventuring With Bks, 2d edition

Where in the world is Henry? [Story and pictures by Lorna Balian] Bradbury Press 1972 unp illus $4.95   E

1 Dogs—Stories
ISBN 0-87888-049-6

"When last seen, Henry was hiding: under the quilt, on the bed, in the bedroom, in this house, on this street, and so on until the universe is pinpointed. And when hiding Henry is found as last, he turns out to be a dog who is not allowed on the bed, in the bedroom." Pub W

"Although the general theme (finding someone lost) is a familiar one, youngsters should enjoy this journey of discovery. . . . With its judicious use of red and appealingly open format, this title would be an attractive addition to the read-aloud shelf." Wis Library Bul

Barrett, Judi

Animals should definitely not wear clothing; written by Judi Barrett and drawn by Ron Barrett. Atheneum Pubs. 1970 unp illus lib. bdg. $5.95, pa $1.25   E

1 Animals
ISBN 0-689-20592-9; 0-689-70412-7

"The pitfalls of clothing for animals are humorously described in this unusual picture book. A minimum of words in oversized letters illuminate pictures such as a snake slithering out of his trousers or a walrus in a sopping wet sports jacket." Wis Library Bul

Benjamin's 365 birthdays; written by Judi Barrett and drawn by Ron Barrett. Atheneum Pubs 1974 unp illus $6.50   E

1 Birthdays—Fiction
ISBN 0-689-30130-8

"Benjamin loves birthdays so much that the thought of waiting a whole year after his ninth till his next one makes him weep and then inspires him to rewrap his presents, one each day, and go on to wrap everything in his house." Booklist

Benjamin's "solution to prolonging pleasure will amuse preschoolers familiar with post-party blues. . . . The theme is familiar, but its execution both in text and humorously detailed illustrations is fresh and spontaneous." Horn Bk

Baylor, Byrd

Everybody needs a rock; with pictures by Peter Parnall. Scribner 1974 unp illus $5.95   E

1 Rocks
ISBN 0-684-13899-9

The free verse of this book speaks "to the spiritual-sensual affinity that can spring up between a living being and an inanimate object, specifically in this case, a rock. Not just any rock, Baylor is careful to note, but 'a special rock that you find yourself and keep as long as you can—maybe forever.' To this end she unaffectedly sets out her own 10 rules for discovering that special rock." Booklist

"Parnall's striking pictures combine mysticism and a splendid sense of dignity. The lines of his drawings (which combine black-and-white with earthen shades) soar and suggest rather than depict the text, a quality which enhances Ms. Baylor's inspired and economical message." Pub W

Beim, Lorraine

Two is a team, by Lorraine and Jerrold Beim; pictures by Ernest Crichlow. Harcourt 1945 unp illus $6.50, pa $1.25   E

1 Negroes—Fiction 2 Friendship—Fiction
ISBN 0-15-291948-1; 0-15-692050-6

"Ted, a Negro boy, and Paul, a white boy, are the same age and the same size. They play happily together until they quarrel over making a scooter. After trying to work alone, they run into still more trouble and discover that only through cooperation in work and play can they clear up their difficulties. This story shows the twosome—the group in which the six-year-old is best able to function." Rdng Ladders

"The significance of the book lies in the naturalness with which the two friends play together, color being of no importance whatsoever to them. Illustrated [with lithographs] by a Negro artist." Booklist

Belpré, Pura

Santiago; illus. by Symeon Shimin. Warne 1969 31p illus lib. bdg. $4.95   E

1 Puerto Ricans in New York (City)—Fiction
2 Chickens—Stories
ISBN 0-7232-6019-2

Selina, Santiago's pet hen had been left behind in Puerto Rico when the family had moved to New York, yet Santiago talked about her incessantly. Everyone believed him except Ernie whom he wanted to impress most. But one day Santiago had an opportunity to convince Ernie

"The story is not strong, but it is modest, and realistic, and the illustrations are lovely, those of the two

Belpré, Pura—*Continued*

boys (Ernie is black) being especially sensitive in the capture of fleeting moods." Chicago. Children's Bk Center

Bemelmans, Ludwig

Madeline; story & pictures by Ludwig Bemelmans. Viking 1939 unp illus lib. bdg. $5.95, pa $1.25   E

1 Paris—Fiction 2 Stories in rhyme

ISBN 0-670-44580-0; 0-670-05023-7

First published by Simon & Schuster

"Madeline is a nonconformist in a regimented world—a Paris convent school. This rhymed story tells how she made an adventure out of having appendicitis." Hodges. Bks for Elem Sch Libraries

"The illustrations are in Ludwig Bemelmans' characteristic technique. There are eight pages and end papers in color of familiar Paris scenes with the other pictures in yellow, black, and white. . . . It will appeal to children of any age as well as to adults." Library J

Madeline and the bad hat; written and illus. by Ludwig Bemelmans. Viking 1956 54p illus lib. bdg. $5.95, pa $1.50   E

1 Paris—Fiction 2 Stories in rhyme

ISBN 0-670-44614-9; 0-670-05001-6

Another picture story book about the little French girl, Madeline, who lived in a school in Paris with eleven other little girls 'in two straight lines.' The bad hat was the mischievous son of the Spanish ambassador who lived next door

"Blithe as ever, Mr. Bemelmans tells it all in the familiar rhythms and unexpected rhymes that children love. The pictures of Paris, the school, the little girls and Pepito are just as funny and handsome as you'd expect." N Y Times Bk Rev

Madeline and the gypsies. Viking 1959 56p illus $5.95, pa $1.50   E

1 Gypsies—Fiction 2 Circus—Fiction 3 France—Fiction 4 Stories in rhyme

ISBN 0-670-44682-3; 0-670-05081-4

"Stuck in a ferris wheel, Madeline [one of the 'twelve little girls in two straight lines'] and Pepito are left behind by mistake at a gypsy carnival. They become part of the troupe and travel about France in a gypsy caravan until at last Miss Clavel finds them. The combination of circus-like background with scenes of actual places, such as Chartres, Deauville, and Avignon makes these typically Bemelmans pictures gayer, livelier, and more full of interest than ever, but the verse seems inexcusably limp." Horn Bk

Madeline in London. Viking 1961 56p illus lib. bdg. $5.95, pa $1.50   E

1 Horses—Stories 2 London—Fiction 3 Stories in rhyme

ISBN 0-670-44648-3; 0-670-05071-7

"Madeline and her school mates [fly to London] for a birthday visit with Pepito, lonesome son of the Spanish ambassador. [This] is a full verse report of that trip, including what happens when a retired guard's horse answers the trumpet's summons with Pepito and Madeline aboard." N Y Times Bk Rev

"The text is bland in tone and nonsensical in message, a combination that is happily complemented by the lively and colorful illustrations. The rhyming is occasionally jarring, especially when the book is read aloud, but this is of minor import in a story rife with tongue-in-cheek exaggeration." Chicago. Children's Bk Center

Madeline's rescue; story and pictures by Ludwig Bemelmans. Viking 1953 56p illus lib. bdg. $5.95, pa $1.50

1 Dogs—Stories 2 Paris—Fiction 3 Stories in rhyme

ISBN 0-670-44716-1; 0-670-05076-8

Awarded the Caldecott Medal, 1954

Another picture-story book with rhymed text about little Madeline in Paris. This time she falls into the Seine and is rescued by "a dog that kept its head." The dog, named Genevieve, was promptly adopted by the boarding school mistress and her twelve pupils. When Genevieve was turned out by snobbish trustees the little girls were inconsolable, until Genevieve solved their problem

"This sort of tale will amuse and delight children. For grown-ups, the joy will be in the Bemelmans views of Paris, eight elegant full-color plates, and enchanting end papers." N Y Her Trib Bks

Benchley, Nathaniel

The deep dives of Stanley Whale, pictures by Mischa Richter. Harper 1973 31p illus lib. bdg. $4.79   E

1 Whales—Stories

ISBN 0-06-020464-8

"Stanley is only about as big as an automobile, small for a whale, too little to dive beneath the light-green water, past the blue and the purple to the black. But he does, and is scared out of his wits by a huge white creature. . . . [It turns out to be his] mild-mannered Uncle Moby who likes everyone—except people. When people (whalers) appear, they harpoon old Moby but he is rescued by the bravery and ingenuity of his little nephew." Pub W

"The story is told with light-hearted humor, and the crayon wash illustrations on every page contribute to the playful tone." Sch Library J

A ghost named Fred; pictures by Ben Shecter. Harper 1968 unp illus (An I can read mystery) $2.95, lib. bdg. $3.79   E

1 Ghost stories

ISBN 0-06-020473-7; 0-06-020474-5

"George, an imaginative child used to playing alone, went into an empty house to get out of the rain; there he met an absent-minded ghost named Fred, who knew there was a treasure but had forgotten where. Only when Fred opened an umbrella for George's homeward journey did the treasure materialize." Chicago. Children's Bk Center

"More humorous than scary . . . this is a pleasing and acceptable ghost story for beginning readers." Booklist

Oscar Otter; illus. by Arnold Lobel. Harper 1966 64p illus $2.95 lib. bdg. $3.79   E

1 Otters—Stories 2 Animals—Stories

ISBN 0-06-020471-0; 0-06-020472-9

"An I can read book"

Oscar the Otter disobeys his father and "builds a slide to the top of the mountain, only to have a procession of ridiculous predators land in a heap at the bottom of it." Wis Library Bul

"A merry book for the beginning independent reader, the illustrations having humor." Chicago. Children's Bk Center

Sam the Minuteman; pictures by Arnold Lobel. Harper 1969 62p illus (An I can read history bk) $2.95, lib. bdg. $3.79   E

1 Lexington, Battle of, 1775—Fiction

ISBN 0-06-020479-6; 0-06-020480-X

In this book about the Minutemen and the "Lobster Backs," the British soldiers, the author describes what it must have been like for a young boy to fight in the Battle of Lexington, which marked the beginning of the American Revolution

"The story, told from a boy's viewpoint, conveys a

Benchley, Nathaniel—*Continued*

sense of immediacy. . . . Excellent drawings faithfully re-create the people, the time, and the place;
[set] against soft pencil-gray and mustard brown [are]
the scarlet-coated British troops." Horn Bk

The several tricks of Edgar Dolphin; pictures by
Mamoru Funai. Harper 1970 60p illus $2.95, lib. bdg.
$3.79   E

1 Dolphins—Stories
ISBN 0-06-020467-2; 0-06-020468-0

"An I can read book"

Young Edgar Dolphin was very clever. He could
jump straight up, and he could even chase ships. One
day, against his mother's advice, he swam over to a
strange-looking ship. Before he knew it, he was
hauled aboard in a net. Then Edgar was able to show
his human shipmates just how smart he really was

"The three-color drawings amplify the entertainment." Horn Bk

Small Wolf; pictures by Joan Sandin. Harper 1972
64p illus (An I can read history bk) $2.95, lib. bdg.
$3.79   E

1 Indians of North America—Fiction 2 U.S.—
History—Colonial period—Fiction
ISBN 0-06-020491-5; 0-06-020492-3

"Small Wolf is astonished at the white-faced people
and their strange animals that he sees on a hunting trip
to Manhattan Island, but his father tells him that the
white men are all right if left alone. Small Wolf and his
people soon learn, however, that the white men have
different ideas about owning land than they do, and as
the white men move farther inland, the Indians are
forced to move 'again. And again. And again. And
again.' " Booklist

"Simply written but not stilted, the book has
dramatic and humanitarian interest as well as historical use, and the illustrations have the same dramatic
simplicity." Chicago. Children's Bk Center

The strange disappearance of Arthur Cluck; pictures by Arnold Lobel. Harper 1967 64p illus (An I can
read mystery) $2.95, lib. bdg. $3.79   E

1 Owls—Stories 2 Chickens—Stories
ISBN 0-06-020477-X; 0-06-020478-8

"Arthur's mother, the hen, questioned all animals
when Arthur is found missing. Only the barn owl
located Arthur in a crate of baby chicks." Bruno. Bks
for Sch Libraries, 1968

"Not much of a mystery but entertaining." Sch
Library J

Bennett, Rainey

The secret hiding place; written and illus. by
Rainey Bennett. Collins 1960 unp illus lib. bdg.
$5.21   E

1 Hippopotamus—Stories
ISBN 0-529-03540-5

"Little Hippo, the pet of the herd, is tired of always
being petted and fussed over. He searches for a place
where he can be alone but then is afraid. All ends well
when he finds a secret hiding place where he can be
alone but 'not too alone.' " Rdng Ladders. 5th edition

"Small children who are themselves 'pet of the
herd' will understand Little Hippo. . . . The delightfully expressive pictures carry the story along almost
without the need of text." Top of the News

Berenstain, Stan

The bears' almanac. . . . By Stan and Jan Berenstain. Beginner Bks. 1973 64p illus $3.94, lib. bdg.
$4.99   E

1 Seasons—Fiction 2 Bears—Stories 3 Stories in
rhyme
ISBN 0-394-82693-0; 0-394-92693-5

"I can read it all by myself"

"A year in bear country . . . holidays, seasons,
weather, actual facts about snow, wind, rain, thunder,
lightning, the sun, the moon . . . and lots more." Title
page

Illustrated by the authors, this series of rhymed
verses offers a bear family's observations on the
seasons

"Each section concludes with a list of the various
objects and activities typical of that season. Every
page is filled with amusing pictures of the familiar
Berenstain bears, which non-readers as well as readers will find funny." Sch Library J

Bears on wheels, by Stan and Jan Berenstain. Random House 1969 unp illus $2.95, lib. bdg. $3.37 E

1 Counting books 2 Bears—Stories
ISBN 0-394-80967-X; 0-394-90967-4

"A Bright & early book"

The authors' illustrations are used with numbers in
this counting book which tells the story of a small bear
who goes out for a ride on one small wheel. As the bear
rides on, traffic and unwanted passengers accumulate

Berson, Harold

Balarin's goat; story and pictures by Harold Berson.
Crown 1972 unp illus lib. bdg. $3.95   E

1 Goats—Stories
ISBN 0-517-50105-8

"To his goat Fleurette, Balarin gives hugs and
flower wreaths and the finest delicacies, but to his
wife Marinette, he shows only bad temper. At last
Marinette rebels and answers Balarin's snarl with a
baa. She puts Fleurette in the bed and spends the
night in the goat house, while Balarin dreams that his
wife has really turned into a goat. Awakened by a lick
from Fleurette, he rushes out and begs Marinette to
return, promising to be kind, patient, and cheerful.
The author's modest drawings invest the homely
threesome, drawn from an old folktale, with ironic
humor." Booklist

Henry Possum; story and pictures by Harold Berson. Crown 1973 unp illus lib. bdg. $4.95   E

1 Opossums—Stories
ISBN 0-517-50297-6

"Rather than pay attention to his mother's instructions on playing dead, Henry is much more interested
in humming and watching butterflies. When he is
separated from his mother, Henry is given a flute by a
magpie and learns to play a variety of styles on his
travels. The appearance of a sly gray fox startles
Henry into lying perfectly still, tricking the fox and
making his mother very proud. Berson's brisk colored
line drawings make the book a visually pleasing
experience." Top of the News

Beskow, Elsa

Pelle's new suit; picture book by Elsa Beskow; tr.
by Marion Letcher Woodburn. Harper 1929 unp illus
$5.95, lib. bdg. $6.89   E

1 Sweden—Fiction
ISBN 0-06-020495-8; 0-06-020496-6

"Charming pictures tell the story of how Pelle
earned his new suit. He is shown raking hay, bringing
in wood, feeding pigs, going on errands and at the
same time, each process in the making of the suit is
followed, beginning with the shearing of the lamb.
The coloring of the pictures (which show both Swedish peasant house interiors and out-of-door scenes) is
quite lovely." N Y Libraries

Binzen, Bill

Miguel's Mountain. Coward-McCann 1968 unp
illus lib. bdg. $4.69   E

1 New York (City)—Fiction
ISBN 0-698-30034-3

Binzen, Bill—*Continued*

This is "the story of a small boy and his friends who, used to the flat space of the city, were enchanted by the huge pile of earth left by a steamshovel. When Miguel heard that the 'mountain' was to be moved, he wrote the mayor; a man came out to see Miguel and tell him that the mountain could stay, so all the children held a parade of triumph and the mound was called 'Miguel's Mountain.' " Chicago. Children's Bk Center

"The photographs taken by the author-artist in New York City's Tompkins Park capture the vigor with which big city children seize upon whatever their environment affords their imaginations and increase the book's value as a realistic image of life among urban children." Library J

Birnbaum, A.

Green Eyes; story and pictures by A. Birnbaum. Golden Press 1973 c1953 unp illus $2.95, lib. bdg. $4.45   E

1 Cats—Stories
ISBN 0-307-13761-9; 0-307-60182-X
First published 1953 by Capitol Pub. Co.

"Told in the first person, this picture storybook . . . gives the high spots in the first year of a cat—from the time he first climbs out of his box to explore to the time when he is quite willing to curl up in his snug box by the fire on a cold winter's night." Library J

The story "is simple enough for the smallest child. The pictures are subtle and amusing enough to charm adults." Pub W

Bishop, Claire Huchet

The five Chinese brothers, by Claire Huchet Bishop and Kurt Wiese. Coward-McCann 1938 unp illus $4.95, lib. bdg. $4.29   E

1 Fairy tales
ISBN 0-698-20044-6; 0-698-30089-0

"Each of five identical Chinese brothers has a special talent which he uses to save the lives of all." Hodges. Bks for Elem Sch Libraries

"The cleverness of . . . [the five brothers who find their] similarity a great help in outwitting the executioner is described in a picture-story book which has the flavor of a folk tale, and the repetition and rhythm that appeal to little children. Kurt Wiese's gaily exaggerated illustrations in black and yellow capture the blithe quality of the story. Excellent for storytelling." N Y Libraries

The man who lost his head; illus. by Robert McCloskey. Viking 1942 unp illus lib. bdg. $4.95, pa $1.25   E

ISBN 0-670-45349-8; 0-670-05094-6

"A man without a head tries several substitutes but finds none satisfactory. Droll illustrations match the absurdity of the story." Hodges. Bks for Elem Sch Libraries

The truffle pig, by Claire Huchet Bishop and Kurt Wiese. Coward, McCann & Geoghegan 1971 48p illus lib. bdg. $4.49   E

1 Pigs—Stories 2 France—Fiction
ISBN 0-698-30378-4
"A Break-of-day book"

"If they bought a piglet, Pierre's parents decided, they could fatten it up and have delicious sausages. So they saved their pennies and bought Marcel, of whom Pierre became so fond that he didn't want his pet killed. They ran away, and it was then that Pierre discovered that Marcel could detect truffles. Home they went to announce the glad news and to start a new way of life—and the story ends with Marcel receiving a medal in a nationwide Truffle-Pig Con-

test, fortune for the family, and for Marcel a blue-tiled pool in his sty." Sutherland. The Best in Children's Bks

"Kurt Wiese's two-color and black-and-white drawings add a Gallic touch to a diverting easy-to-read story." Booklist

Twenty-two bears; illus. by Kurt Wiese. Viking 1964 31p illus lib. bdg. $4.95   E

1 Counting books 2 Bears—Stories
ISBN 0-670-73507-8

"This picture book describes the antics of a large family of bears in the wild woods of Wyoming." Library J

"Kurt Wiese's bears have individuality and lively humor. His sure, soft line is a lasting pleasure." Commonweal

Blue, Rose

I am here: yo estoy aqui; pictures by Moneta Barnett. Watts. F. 1971 unp illus lib. bdg. $4.33   E

1 Puerto Ricans in the U.S.—Fiction 2 School stories
ISBN 0-531-01943-8

"Luz, who speaks no English, is lonely and frightened in kindergarten, until a Spanish speaking aide and her teacher help her to understand how to exchange words with the other children." Rdng Ladders. 5th edition

This is "a warm and agreeable story of a minority child, illustrated with unpretentious, expressive two-color drawings on every page." Booklist

Bolognese, Don

A new day. Delacorte Press 1970 unp illus $4.95, lib. bdg. $4.58 (k-3)   E

1 Christmas stories 2 Southwest, New—Fiction
ISBN 0-440-06375-2; 0-440-06378-7
Illustrated by the author

"The Nativity story is translated in this book into a modern setting with migrant workers in the Southwest substituted for the Holy family." Pub W

"The beautiful paintings strengthen the parallel of this contemporary interpretation of the Christmas legend." Adventuring With Bks. 2d edition

Bonsall, Crosby

And I mean it, Stanley. Harper 1974 32p illus $2.50, lib. bdg. $2.92   E

ISBN 0-06-020567-9; 0-06-020568-7
"An Early I can read book"

This story "depicts a small scamp playing with neighborhood discards near a high board fence. As she constructs a junkyard sculpture, she conducts a one-sided conversation with the invisible Stanley, who is presumably behind the fence. Although she insists over and over 'I don't want to play with you,' it's a classic case of protesting too much. When Stanley finally makes his grand entrance, he surprises readers as well as the scruffy heroine." Library J

"A childlike and genuinely humorous creation, the book is also a positive portrayal of a girl in a non-stereotyped role." Horn Bk

The case of the cat's meow. Harper 1965 64p illus (An I can read mystery) $2.95, lib. bdg. $3.79   E

1 Cats—Stories
ISBN 0-06-020560-1; 0-06-020561-X

"A small boy's slightly older friends laugh at him when he tries to convince them that his cat, Mildred, is so special that someone may steal her. But, when Mildred disappears mysteriously, they help him search for her. When she is found, they share her kittens." We Build Together

A "humorous story for the beginning reader, attractively illustrated [by the author] and suitable for read-

Bonsall, Crosby—*Continued*

ing aloud to younger children. . . . The illustrations show boys of assorted sizes, shapes, and colors; the dialogue is really childlike, and Snitch's devotion to his perfectly ordinary cat is captivating." Chicago. Children's Bk Center

The case of the dumb bells. Harper 1966 64p illus (An I can read mystery) $3.79, lib. bdg. $3.43   E

ISBN 0-06-020623-3; 0-06-020624-1

This is "an easy-to-read mystery about the problems which develop when Skinny mistakenly connects the boys' clubhouse telephone to his friend's doorbell wires." Hodges. Bks for Elem Sch Libraries

"The illustrations [by the author] show the . . . [boys] in various poses of despair or triumph. . . . The writing is a vast improvement over Dick and Jane; although the print is large, the sentences short, and the vocabulary repetitive, there is no sense of halting contrivance. Both text and illustrations use, just slightly, exaggeration to stress humorous aspects." Chicago. Children's Bk Center

The case of the hungry stranger. Harper 1963 64p illus (An I can read mystery) $3.79, lib. bdg. $3.43   E

ISBN 0-06-020570-9; 0-06-020571-7

Also available in a Spanish language edition (ISBN 0-06-020574-1) lib. bdg. $3.79

Illustrated by the author

"Wizard, Skinny, Tubby, and Snitch are four sturdy little boys who share a no-girls-allowed clubhouse, Wizard pronounces himself a private eye, and soon Mrs Meech, the lady next door, commissions him to discover who has stolen her blueberry pie. One scarcely resents the vocabulary limitations, for the author has combined real humor, suspense and even definite characterization." Horn Bk

The case of the scaredy cats. Harper 1971 64p illus (An I can read mystery) $2.95, lib. bdg. $3.79   E

ISBN 0-06-020565-2; 0-06-020566-0

Illustrated by the author

"Although the sign on the clubhouse door clearly states 'No Girls,' six girls venture in. The boys retaliate by adding signs: 'Alice eats hay,' 'Annie is a scaredy cat,' 'Gertie cant spel,' and the war is on. Routed out of their clubhouse, the boys return to help hunt for the littlest girl, Annie, who has disappeared." Sat Rev

"A slight, pleasant story with an interracial cast." Chicago. Children's Bk Center

The day I had to play with my sister. Harper 1972 32p illus $2.50, lib. bdg. $2.92   E

1 Brothers and sisters—Fiction

ISBN 0-06-020575-X; 0-06-020576-8

"An early I can read book"

Illustrated by the author, this story tells of an impatient boy who tries to teach his younger sister to play hide and seek

"The extremely simple text, written from the boy's point of view, is one with which children can readily identify. Pastel illustrations on every page add touches of humor to the text, which is divided into chapters. The realistic atmosphere makes Bonsall's book an excellent addition to the very early reading shelves." Sch Library J

Mine's the best. Harper 1973 32p illus $2.50, lib. bdg. $3.43   E

ISBN 0-06-020577-6; 0-06-020578-4

"An Early I can read book"

"Two boys meet by the seashore and create a fracas over whose inflated rubber sea monster is the 'best'— they are identical. During the arguments about whose

is bigger, has more spots, can be ridden more easily and so forth, the toys take such a pummeling that they deflate. This signals the appearance of a little girl; her toy is still new and whole, clearly 'the best.' " Pub W

"The humorous illustrations [by the author] add immeasurably to the simple text, which even earliest readers can enjoy." Sch Library J

Piggle. Harper 1973 64p illus $2.95, lib. bdg. $3.79   E

1 Games—Fiction 2 Animals—Stories

ISBN 0-06-020579-2; 0-06-020580-6

"An I can read book"

"Rebuffed by his four sisters—Lolly, Molly, Polly, and Dolly—who are playing Pin the Tail, Homer goes in search of someone who will play a game with him. . . . Homer and Bear play Piggle, a fascinating word game; and soon Homer's four sisters, Rabbit, and Duck are also playing. Only Pig, after whom the game was named, can't understand how to play it." Horn Bk

"Piquant pictures [by the author] of children and animals add zest to a playful story for beginning independent readers. . . . Light-hearted and nicely gauged for the primary audience, the story is, despite the easy vocabulary, not too stilted—as many books for beginning readers are—to read aloud to preschool children." Chicago. Children's Bk Center

Tell me some more; pictures by Fritz Siebel. Harper 1961 64p illus $2.95, lib. bdg. $3.79   E

1 Libraries—Fiction

ISBN 0-06-020600-4; 0-06-020601-2

"An I can read book"

"A fresh and original introduction to the public library, a special place where one can hold an elephant, pat a lion on the nose, tickle a seal, and do all sorts of unusual things. At least that's what Andrew told Tim, and Tim always answered 'Tell me some more.' The artist has caught the small boys' delight in books." Chicago

"Highly original and full of fun. . . . Humorous sketches in which the children appear in black line only, although bright color is added for backgrounds and animals." Horn Bk

Borack, Barbara

Grandpa; pictures by Ben Shecter. Harper 1967 32p illus $4.95, lib. bdg. $4.43   E

1 Grandfathers—Fiction

ISBN 0-06-020627-6; 0-06-020628-4

"A charming monologue by a small girl, the tender and humorous illustrations reflecting the mood of the text. Marilyn describes her grandfather (who is all grandfathers) and their relationship and it is lovely all the way." Chicago. Children's Bk Center

Bourne, Miriam Anne

Raccoons are for loving; illus. by Marian Morton. Random House 1968 44p illus lib. bdg. $5.19   E

1 Raccoons—Stories 2 Negroes—Fiction

ISBN 0-394-91556-9

"Josephine, an urban Negro child, loved hearing her grandmother tell stories of her own childhood on a South Carolina farm, especially about when she held a wild raccoon in her arms, and heard the animal whisper, 'You got any loving for me?' When Josephine's school class went on a field trip to the country and she was allowed to hold a tame raccoon. As she petted him she was sure she heard the whisper, 'Josie, you got any loving for me?' This simple, incidental story with pictures in warm color successfully projects the affinity between children and animals and will be a useful addition to most library collections." Sch Library J

Brenner, Barbara

The five pennies; illus. by Erik Blegvad. Knopf 1964 unp illus lib. bdg. $4.69, pa 95¢   E

1 Pets—Stories

ISBN 0-394-91163-6; 0-394-82739-2

"A Read alone book"

"Nicky puts five shiny new pennies in his pocket and goes out to buy a pet. . . . [He] finds pets not within his reach, and buys other things, but has a surprise—and a pet—in the end." Sat Rev

"For beginning independent readers, a brief story written with direct simplicity and illustrated with charming three-color drawings. The story contains some basic arithmetic, but it is unobtrusively introduced." Chicago. Children's Bk Center

Brian Wildsmith's The twelve days of Christmas. Watts, F. 1972 unp illus $3.95, lib. bdg. $4.95 E

1 Carols

ISBN 0-531-01555-6; 0-531-01554-8

"The text of the traditional English Christmas song surrounded by [Wildsmith's] small but clear drawings in black and white appears on the lefthand page opposite full-page, stylized paintings in glowing colors. Oversize in format and distinctive in presentation, the book will be especially useful for story hour showing and for display." Booklist

Briggs, Raymond

Father Christmas. Coward, McCann & Geoghegan 1973 unp illus $4.95   E

1 Santa Claus—Fiction

ISBN 0-698-20272-4

Illustrated by the author in cartoon format, this book "portrays Christmas Eve as Santa sees it. Dreaming of tropic weather, he grumbles his way through the preparations for a long, cold night of work: feeding the animals, loading the sleigh, packing a snack. He grumbles at chimneys, catches cold, wearily distributes gifts, and rides home to a steaming bath and a solitary Christmas dinner." Chicago. Children's Bk Center

"A Christmas book with tremendous appeal for a wide age range: very young children will enjoy the homely, intimate details of this individualistic Santa . . . older ones will appreciate the gently satirical humor in his reluctance to go to work and his gruff, monosyllabic comments throughout. . . . Each small picture is precisely detailed, convincingly well-drawn, and alive with action, the longer and larger frames—including some full-page spreads—offer a lot of visual contrast in size, color, and content." Booklist

Jim and the beanstalk; written and illus. by Raymond Briggs. Coward-McCann 1970 unp illus $5.50, lib. bdg. $5.29   E

1 Fairy tales

ISBN 0-698-20072-1; 0-698-30203-6

"A sprightly sequel to the original tale, illustrated alternately in black and white and in melting color. Jim sees a tall plant outside his window, an invitation to climbing. He goes up, meets a sad and aging giant who complains that some boy once came up and robbed his father. Ruthfully, Jim arranges to improve the giant's lot by getting him false teeth and spectacles. The delighted giant, now able to read the poetry he had missed . . . suggests Jim cut down the beanstalk (now that he can chew again) lest he be tempted to endulge once more in fried boys on toast. Silly and engaging, the story is enhanced by the humorous details of the illustrations." Sutherland. The Best in Children's Bks

Bright, Robert

Georgie. Doubleday 1944 unp illus $4.95, lib. bdg. $5.70, pa 95¢   E

1 Ghost stories

ISBN 0-385-07307-0; 0-385-07612-6; 0-385-08030-1

"Georgie is an extremely personable little ghost who lives with the Whittakers and haunts their house. Trouble begins for Georgie when he feels it necessary to find another house to haunt. Every house already has a ghost. The friendliness of little Georgie and the [author's] just pleasantly spooky-looking pictures make this the perfect Halloween picture storybook for little children." Booklist

My red umbrella. Morrow 1959 unp illus lib. bdg. $4.14   E

1 Umbrellas and parasols—Fiction

ISBN 0-688-31619-0

Also available in a Spanish language edition (ISBN 0-666-31788-X) lib. bdg. $4.32

"A good read-aloud story for very young listeners, about a little girl whose red umbrella grew to accommodate all the creatures who sought shelter under it. Cheerful colored pictures by the author." Hodges. Bks for Elem Sch Libraries

Brooke, L. Leslie

Johnny Crow's garden; a picture book drawn by L. Leslie Brooke. Warne 1903 unp illus $4.95   E

1 Animals—Stories 2 Stories in rhyme

ISBN 0-7232-0567-1

"The animal friends who come to Johnny Crow's garden are amazing personalities, introduced to little children in a simple and memorable fashion through a nonsense rhyme with its perfect, accompanying illustrations." Bks for Boys and Girls

Johnny Crow's new garden; drawn by L. Leslie Brooke. Warne 1935 unp illus $4.95   E

1 Animals—Stories 2 Stories in rhyme

ISBN 0-7232-0568-X

"Here are pictured the adventures of Johnny Crow that ensued when he extended his garden plot and welcomed to it new friends. One of the pleasantest features is that many of the old acquaintances appear—the lion and the bear, to say nothing of Johnny Crow himself. Will in no way replace 'Johnny Crow's garden,' [entered above] as it simply continues the familiar story. Told in irregular rime and engaging, humorous pictures." Booklist

Johnny Crow's party; another picture book drawn by L. Leslie Brooke. Warne 1907 unp illus $4.95 E

1 Animals—Stories 2 Stories in rhyme

ISBN 0-7232-0566-3

"Leslie Brooke's understanding of children, his interest in detail and his kindly sense of humour give his excellent drawings and watercolours great importance in a small child's library." Four to Fourteen

Brown, Marcia

All butterflies; an ABC, cut by Marcia Brown. Scribner 1974 unp illus $5.95   E

1 Alphabet books

ISBN 0-684-13771-2

"Handsome woodcuts in muted colors show creatures of all kinds in realistic or fanciful situations; save for a few pictures in which they would be inappropriate (the Arctic, the ocean depths) butterflies of varied shapes and colors appear on all the pages. Each of the double-page spreads uses words for two letters of the alphabet: 'All Butterflies, Cat Dance, Elephant Fly? Giraffes High.' Some of the pictures have a grave serenity, others are vigorous or humorous. Moderately useful as an alphabet book, graphically delightful." Chicago. Children's Book Center

Brown, Marcia—*Continued*

Felice. Scribner 1958 unp illus lib. bdg. $6.95 E

1 Cats—Stories 2 Venice—Fiction
ISBN 0-684-13163-3

"Through the square of Venice wanders Felice, a striped cat, searching for food and fighting with other stray cats for every morsel. Young Gino, whose father operates a gondola, adopts Felice with interesting results. Vivid drawings [by the author] of canals, graceful gondolas, high houses, and old ladies feeding the cats capture the unique quality which is Venice." Moorachian. What is a City?

How, Hippo! Scribner 1969 unp illus $6.95, pa 95¢   E

1 Hippopotamus—Stories
ISBN 0-684-12543-9; 0-684-13036-X

Little Hippo had stayed close to his mother ever since the night he was born. This story, illustrated by the author, tells what happened to him the very first time he wandered too far away from his mother

The woodcuts, which "are primarily in shades of blue, green, and pink, capture the various expressions of the hippo pair and the mean crocodile." Sch Library J

The little carousel. Scribner 1946 unp illus lib. bdg. $5.95   E

1 Merry-go-round—Fiction 2 New York (City)—Fiction
ISBN 0-684-12314-2

This is a picture-story about a lonely little boy who lived in Sullivan Street in New York City. On a day when he was feeling very sad a gay little carousel invaded the street, but Anthony had no money. And then, while he was looking longingly at the other children riding the animals, a miracle happened. He earned a ride all by himself

"The author-artist has pictured in words and drawings, full of action and color, the activities of a city street in Greenwich village. Anthony's ride on the carousel, drawn by a black and white horse with red harness and brass studs, provides the climax." Wis Library Bul

Peter Piper's alphabet. . . . Scribner 1959 unp illus lib. bdg. $5.95   E

1 Alphabet books 2 Nonsense verses
ISBN 0-684-13128-5

A new version of some old rhymes originally published in England, 1813

"Peter Piper's practical principles of plain and perfect pronunciation [with] manifold manifestations made by Marcia Brown." Title page

"It is no small feat of both imagination and artistic skill to illustrate nonsense, but Marcia Brown has, as usual, proved equal to the challenge. Each rhyme has received individual treatment in brilliant colors and hilarious drawings." Horn Bk

Brown, Margaret Wise

A child's good night book; illus. by Jean Charlot. Young Scott Bks. 1950 unp illus lib. bdg. $4.50 E
ISBN 0-201-09155-0

As an invitation to sleepiness the author writes of birds and animals, sailboats, automobiles and little children as they settle down for the night

The brief text is accompanied by full-page softly colored lithographs

Country noisy book; with illus. by Leonard Weisgard. Harper 1940 unp illus lib. bdg. $4.79, pa $1.95   E

1 Sounds—Fiction 2 Dogs—Stories
ISBN 0-06-020811-2; 0-06-443002-2

Picture story book for very small children, describing a little dog's trip to the country and all the noises he heard on the way and after he arrived

"Children love this story because they can join in it, making appropriate noises for all the sounds that Muffin hears." New Repub

Goodnight moon; pictures by Clement Hurd. Harper 1947 unp illus $3.95, lib. bdg. $3.79   E

1 Rabbits—Stories 2 Stories in rhyme
ISBN 0-06-020705-1; 0-06-020706-X
Written in rhymed verse

"The coming of night is shown in pictures which change from bright to dark as a small rabbit says good night to the familiar things in his nest." Hodges. Bks for Elem Sch Libraries

"A clever goodnight book in which pages are progressively darker as the leaves are turned. There are many objects to identify and children enjoy picking out familiar words." Bks for Deaf Children

Indoor noisy book; pictures by Leonard Weisgard. Harper 1942 unp illus lib. bdg. $4.79, pa $1.95   E

1 Sounds—Fiction 2 Dogs—Stories
ISBN 0-06-020821-X; 0-06-443003-0
First published by W. R. Scott

A simple little picture-story book about the dog Muffin and all the noises he heard—and some perhaps he didn't hear?—the day he had to stay in the house because he had a cold

The runaway bunny; pictures by Clement Hurd. Harper 1972 c1942 unp illus $3.95, lib. bdg. $3.79
                                                            E

1 Rabbits—Stories
ISBN 0-06-020765-5; 0-06-020766-3

Reissue, with some illustrations redrawn, of the title first published 1942

"Within a framework of mutual love, a bunny tells his mother how he will run away and she answers his challenge by indicating how she will catch him." Sch Library J

"The text has the simplicity of a folk tale and the illustrations are black and white or double page drawings in startling colour effects to illustrate the more imaginative parts of the theory." Ontario Library Rev

Wait till the moon is full; pictures by Garth Williams. Harper 1948 unp illus $4.95, lib. bdg. $4.79
                                                            E

1 Raccoons—Stories
ISBN 0-06-020800-7; 0-06-020801-5

"The mystery and wonder of nighttime is presented here in a way to sharpen the awareness of the very young child and to dispel any fears of it which the more timorous may have. . . . This is very slight, but the words, the rhythm and the mood have a great deal of charm and humor, which is matched by Garth Williams' pictures of a cozy, well-furnished raccoon home and the moonlit world waiting outside." N Y Times Bk Rev

Wheel on the chimney, by Margaret Wise Brown and Tibor Gergely. Lippincott 1954 unp illus $7.95
                                                            E

1 Storks—Stories
ISBN 0-397-30288-6

"First there was one stork, then there were two. They built their nest on a wheel on the chimney of a little Hungarian house, thus promising good luck to the family. This annual ritual inspired Gergely's tracing of the stork's migration from their summer European habitat to their winter sojourn in Africa." Sec Ed Brd

"The simple text tells of the ways of storks and of the hazards of their long flight south, while the illustrations [by Tibor Gergely] in strong contrasting col-

Brown, Margaret Wise—*Continued*
ours show much of the beauty and interest of the seas
and continents the great birds cross in their journey."
Ontario Library Rev

Brown, Palmer
Something for Christmas. Harper 1958 32p illus
$2.95   E
    1 Mice—Stories 2 Christmas stories
    ISBN 0-06-020910-0
"A small mouse wants to give a very special present
to a very special person—his mother. He finds that
the best gift of all is love. A tender story reflecting the
true spirit of Christmas and illustrated with endearing
pictures by the author." Hodges. Bks for Elem Sch
Libraries

Brunhoff, Jean de
The story of Babar, the little elephant; tr. from the
French by Merle S. Haas. Random House 1933 47p
illus $2.50, lib. bdg. $3.79   E
    1 Elephants—Stories
    ISBN 0-394-80575-5; 0-394-90575-X
    Original French edition published 1931
"Babar runs away from the jungle and goes to live
with an old lady in Paris, where he adapts quickly to
French amenities. Later he returns to the jungle and
becomes king. Much of the charm of the story is
contributed by the author's gay pictures." Hodges.
Bks for Elem Sch Libraries

Buckley, Helen E.
Grandfather and I; pictures by Paul Galdone. Lothrop 1959 unp illus lib. bdg. $4.97   E
    1 Grandfathers—Fiction
    ISBN 0-688-51211-9
"Unlike mothers, fathers, brothers, sisters, cars
and buses, Grandfather does not hurry but has time to
play with the little boy, walk slowly with him, sit and
rock, sing and talk as long as they wish." Wis Library
Bul
"The repetitive text, the uncluttered colored pictures, and the amusing surprise ending will please
young children." Booklist

Grandmother and I; pictures by Paul Galdone. Lo-
thrup 1961 unp illus lib. bdg. $4.97   E
    1 Grandmothers—Fiction
    ISBN 0-688-51204-6
    Companion volume to: Grandfather and I
"Brief text and full-page pictures in bright colors
show how just right Grandmother's lap is for many
things: for sitting and thinking; for when you have
measles, or when lightning flashes, or 'when you don't
want to do anything but sit in the big chair, and rock
back and forth, and back and forth.'" Horn Bk
"The illustrations are pleasant, realistic and sympathetic but not sentimental." Chicago. Children's Bk
Center

Budney, Blossom
A kiss is round; verses. Pictures by Vladimir Bobri.
Lothrop 1954 unp illus lib. bdg. $5.11   E
    1 Size and shape
    ISBN 0-688-51177-5
A picture book intended to teach the concept of
roundness, with the aid of brief verses
"This is a book to stimulate and sharpen a child's
perception of forms, but first of all it is great fun. It is
good to look at, for Bobri has illustrated it with an
originality to match the author's. His color is bright,
but soft, his line is witty and his humor genial." N Y
Times Bk Rev

Bulla, Clyde Robert
The poppy seeds; illus. by Jean Charlot. Crowell
1955 unp illus $4.50, lib. bdg. $5.25   E
    1 Mexico—Fiction
    ISBN 0-690-64856-1; 0-690-64857-X
A little [Mexican] Indian boy, given a present of
some poppy seeds, plants them thruout the village.
The only seeds that survive the drought are those
spilled beside the stream where the child had met
rebuff, but the coming of the flowers brought happiness to all—the bitter old man, the trusting child, and
the whole village at last given access to good water
"This gentle story is told with color and drama, yet
in simple language. The Charlot pictures . . . are
superb." N Y Her Trib Bks

The valentine cat; illus. by Leonard Weisgard.
Crowell 1959 unp illus $5.95, lib. bdg. $6.70   E
    1 Cats—Stories 2 Valentine's Day—Stories
    ISBN 0-690-85730-6; 0-690-85731-4
"A Valentine picture-story fantasy of a little black
cat with a heart-shaped marking on his head, who is
befriended by a young, discouraged artist, stolen by
an evil chimney sweep, and finally rescued by a princess." Wis Library Bul
"A happy, satisfying story . . . is made extra-
specially worthwhile with big, handsome pictures full
of color and design." Christian Sci Monitor

Burch, Robert
Joey's cat; illus. by Don Freeman. Viking 1969 unp
illus lib. bdg. $4.95, pa 75¢   E
    1 Cats—Stories 2 Negroes—Fiction
    ISBN 0-670-40789-5; 0-670-05063-6
"Joey's cat had had her kittens in a carton at the top
of a pile of crates in the garage, and there was little
chance that they would be allowed in the house. His
mother didn't like pets. When Joey and his father
brought the kittens in after they had been threatened
by an opossum, Mother said they absolutely could not
stay—but she looked at the four tiny creatures and
capitulated. An uncomplicated plot and Don
Freeman's brisk illustrations showing a middle-class
Negro family add to the appeal of the subject for the
very young." Sat Rev

Burningham, John
John Burningham's ABC. Bobbs [1967 c1964] unp
illus $4.95   E
    1 Alphabet books
    ISBN 0-672-50196-1
    First published 1964 in England
"This is an ABC, pure and simple, handsome and
devoid of special gimmicks. The initial letters and the
words they accompany face full-page, colorful, varied
illustrations which range from striking, uncluttered
pictures of single objects (apple, sun) to multi-figured
depictions of plurals (pigs) and collectives (jungle) for
viewers to linger over. An excellent sampler of this
artist's work and a good source of visual satisfaction for
the preschoolers." Library J

Mr Gumpy's outing. Holt [1971 c1970] unp illus lib.
bdg. $5.95   E
    1 Animal—Stories
    ISBN 0-03-089733-5
    First published 1970 in England
"Mr. Gumpy is about to go off for a boat ride and is
asked by two children, a rabbit, a cat, a dog, and other
animals if they may come. To each Mr. Gumpy says
yes, if—if the children don't squabble, if the rabbit
won't hop, if the cat won't chase the rabbit or the dog
tease the cat, and so on. Of course each does exactly
what Mr. Gumpy forbade, the boat tips over, and they
all slog home for tea in friendly fashion." Sutherland.
The Best in Children's Bks

Burningham, John—*Continued*
"The illustrations, skillfully drawn cross-hatched brown ink drawings alternating with full-page impressionistic paintings dominantly in muted greens and browns, are outstanding for their very expressive animals and numerous warm, humorous touches. . . . And, the simple, cumulative text and easy, natural attitudes of Gumpy and company are sure to please the picture-book audience." Sch Library J

Seasons. Bobbs [1971 c1969] unp illus $5.95   E
1 Seasons—Pictorial works
ISBN 0-672-50928-8
First published 1969 in England
In this large "almost cumulative picture book, strikingly beautiful, full-color pages depicting the seasons of the year are made doubly fascinating by the sometimes humorous antics of the cartooned people and creatures who romp across them." Library J

Burton, Virginia Lee
Katy and the big snow; story and pictures by Virginia Lee Burton. Houghton 1943 32p illus lib. bdg. $5.95, pa 95¢   E
1 Tractors—Fiction
ISBN 0-395-18155-0; 0-395-18562-9
"Katy is a crawler tractor who saves the city when it is snowed in by a blizzard. Though personified, Katy is presented accurately in the author's colored illustrations." Hodges. Bks for Elem Sch Libraries
"Anyone who has ever watched a small boy's intense interest in one of these monsters of iron and steel that roll the roads or plow the fields will rejoice that this artist and author has made it possible for children to follow the fortunes of Katy." N Y Times Bk Rev

The little house; story and pictures by Virginia Lee Burton. Houghton 1942 40p illus lib. bdg. $6.95 E
1 Houses—Fiction
ISBN 0-395-06678-6
Awarded the Caldecott Medal, 1943
"The little house was very happy as she sat on the quiet hillside watching the changing seasons. As the years passed, however, tall buildings grew up around her, and the noise of city traffic disturbed her. She became sad and lonely until one day someone who understood her need for twinkling stars overhead and dancing apple blossoms moved her back to just the right little hill." Children's Bks Too Good To Miss
"This story is important in showing changes in a neighborhood and in telling what happens as cities grow larger and swallow up more and more fields and orchards." Rdng Ladders
"An original and charming picture book. . . . The colors are clear and beautiful and effectively suggest day and night in both country and city, and the aspects of the seasons." N Y Times Bk Rev

Maybelle, the cable car. Houghton 1952 42p illus lib. bdg. $4.23   E
1 Street railroads—Fiction 2 San Francisco—Fiction
ISBN 0-395-06679-4
Illustrated by the author
"Maybelle lived happily in San Francisco until the City Fathers decided the cable cars must go because they were out of date and too slow. . . . Some people agreed with the City Fathers but others, who loved Maybelle and her sisters, formed the Citizens' Committee to Save the Cable Cars and 'got busy with posters, parades and publicity.' All the excitement and suspense of those anxious times live within these pages. The artist, without drawing faces on Bill and Maybelle, has nevertheless succeeded in giving even them exactly the right expression to suit the mood of

the moment. And the Citizens are not just a group of people; each tiny figure has individuality." Horn Bk

Mike Mulligan and his steam shovel; story and pictures by Virginia Lee Burton. Houghton 1939 unp illus lib. bdg. $5.95   E
1 Steam shovels—Fiction
ISBN 0-395-06681-6
"This is fun both in its text and gay crayon drawings. Mike Mulligan remains faithful to his steam shovel, Mary Anne, against the threat of the new gas and Diesel-engine contraptions and digs his way to a surprising and happy ending." New Yorker

Byars, Betsy
Go and hush the baby; illus. by Emily A. McCully. Viking 1971 unp illus lib. bdg. $4.95   E
1 Infants—Fiction
ISBN 0-670-34270-X
"Just as he is about to leave the house, bat in hand, Will is asked by his mother to pacify the baby. He performs and the baby smiles, but as soon as Will leaves the crying resumes. Play a game, mother suggests. Finally Will launches on a story that quiets the baby and so intrigues the storyteller that he is surprised when he loses his audience to a nursing bottle. 'Well, I have to play this game of baseball anyway.' he announces as he goes off." Chicago. Children's Bk Center
"A charming little picture book, told with simplicity and illustrated with appealing two-color drawings." Booklist

Caines, Jeannette Franklin
Abby; pictures by Steven Kellogg. Harper 1973 32p illus $3.95, lib. bdg. $3.79   E
1 Adoption—Fiction 2 Brothers and sisters—Fiction 3 Negroes—Fiction
ISBN 0-06-020921-6; 0-06-020922-4
Abby, an adopted pre-schooler, "loves to look at her baby book, even more, to listen to stories told by her mother and by her brother, Kevin, about the day she became part of the family. . . . A crisis arises when Kevin announces he can't be bothered with her because she's a girl. But the clouds roll by when big brother says he was only fooling and that he loves her. In fact, he will even take her to school with him and feature Abby at show-and-tell time." Pub W
This "story of a warm and loving black family living in a city apartment could be used to introduce the subject of adoption. . . . Shaded drawings showing the family at home perfectly complement the story: there's a shaggy dog underfoot, a child's picture of a monster on the wall, an overstuffed chair with sagging springs, and a mom wearing slacks and glasses who gives big hugs to her very believable kids." Sch Library J

Cameron, Polly
"I can't" said the ant; a second book of nonsense; words and pictures by Polly Cameron. Coward-McCann 1961 unp illus lib. bdg. $3.99   E
1 Nonsense verses
ISBN 0-698-30197-8
"Nonsense rhymes tell how the ants, the spiders, and the kitchen utensils help to put poor broken Miss Teapot back on the shelf. Each helper is shown in an amusing picture." Hodges. Bks for Elem Sch Libraries
"Fun with rhyming, and an unobtrusive moral that dates back to [Robert] Bruce and the spider." Sat Rev

The cat who thought he was a tiger; written and illus. by Polly Cameron. Coward-McCann 1965 unp illus lib. bdg. $3.99   E

Cameron, Polly—*Continued*

1 Cats—Stories
ISBN 0-698-30039-4
"A whimsical tale about a tiger-like kitten who runs away to the circus. At the circus he meets a real tiger and returns happily home to his cat family. Modern tawny and black illustrations add interest to the book." Bookmark

Carle, Eric

All about Arthur (an absolutely absurd ape). Watts, F. 1974 unp illus $5.95   E
1 Alphabet books 2 Animals—Stories
ISBN 0-531-02662-0
Illustrated by the author
In this alphabet book, Arthur the ape feels lonely, so he travels from Baltimore to Yonkers making friends that range from a bashful bear to a zither-playing yak
"A combination of photographic and woodcut techniques is used to illustrate an alphabet book . . . that should amuse children because of the appeal of absurdity. There's no liaison, simply a cataloging, but the combined appeals of interesting pages, each of which has a large photograph of a letter from a signboard, nonsense, and animals should be attractive as well as instructive to the audience for alphabet books." Chicago. Children's Bk Center

Do you want to be my friend? Crowell 1971 unp illus $4.95, lib. bdg. $5.70   E
1 Mice—Stories 2 Stories without words
ISBN 0-690-24276-X; 0-690-24277-8
"The only text is the title question at the start and a shy 'Yes' at the close. The pictures do the rest, as the hopeful mouse overtakes one large creature after another. With each encounter, the mouse sees (on the right-hand page) an interesting tail. Turn the page, and there is a huge lion, or a malevolent fox, or a peacock, and then, at last another wee mouse." Sat Rev
"Good material for discussion and guessing games. . . . The pictures tell an amusing story and they are good to look at as well." Times (London) Lit Sup

Have you seen my cat? Watts, F. [1973] unp illus lib. bdg. $5.95   E
1 Cats—Stories
ISBN 0-531-02552-7
While searching for his cat, a small boy gets "to various parts of the world where he is introduced to different members of the feline family. The boy finds a lion, a bobcat, a tiger, a cheetah, a jaguar and a Persian cat. But only when he returns home does he find his own missing pet and the babies she has had while he was away." Pub W
The author-illustrator's "vividly colored collage illustrations [are] effective against the clean, blank background. . . . All of the members of the cat family that are shown are identified on the endpapers, so that the book has some usefulness as well as being attractive and having game appeal." Chicago. Children's Bk Center

1, 2, 3 to the zoo. Collins 1968 unp illus $5.95, lib. bdg. $5.91   E
1 Counting books
ISBN 0-529-00479-8; 0-529-00480-1
Illustrated by the author
After a lone elephant on a flatcar, for number one, this counting book gives groups of "animals in ascending numbers on their way to the zoo in open box cars." N Y Times Bk Rev
"Superb paintings of animals, bold, lively, handsome, spreading over big double-spread pages.

. . . This is a book to grow with its owner. The tiny mouse lurking in every picture may remain invisible to the smallest reader and, as the title implies, the book is waiting to teach the art of counting." Christian Sci Monitor

The rooster who set out to see the world. Watts, F. 1972 unp illus lib. bdg. $5.95   E
1 Counting books 2 Animals—Stories
ISBN 0-531-02042-8
"A rooster who wants to see the world entices two cats, three frogs, four turtles, and five fishes to accompany him. But when night falls with no provisions for food or shelter, the morale of the traveling companions deteriorates dramatically, and five, four, three, two, they abandon their leader to his own devices. Not surprisingly, the rooster goes back home—to dream about a trip around the world." Horn Bk
"The pictures are fetching and colourful, and organized so as to show how the different numbers relate to one another." Times (London) Lit Sup

The very hungry caterpillar. Collins 1970 unp illus $4.95, lib. bdg. $4.89   E
1 Caterpillars—Stories
ISBN 0-529-00775-4; 0-529-00776-2
Illustrated by the author
"This caterpillar is so hungry he eats right through the pictures on the pages of the book—and after leaving many holes emerges as a beautiful butterfly on the last page." Best Bks for Children, 1972

Carrick, Carol

Lost in the storm; pictures by Donald Carrick. Seabury 1974 unp illus $5.95   E
1 Islands—Fiction 2 Dogs—Stories
ISBN 0-8164-3124-8
"A Clarion book"
A "story of a young boy who temporarily loses his dog. On a chilly, cloudy October Saturday Christopher and his dog Bodger ferry to an offshore island to visit Gray, a school friend. The boys become absorbed in their play, unmindful of Bodger's disappearance even when a storm drives them indoors. Christopher's sudden realization of the dog's absence fills him with dismay, and Bodger's reappearance the next day is an occasion of glowing, good feeling." Booklist
"Soft, misty watercolors picture the children set against the rain-soaked, windswept island landscape." Horn Bk

Sleep out [by] Carol and Donald Carrick. Seabury 1973 unp illus $6.95   E
1 Camping—Fiction
ISBN 0-8164-3094-2
Illustrated by Donald Carrick
"Christopher, a city boy, gets a sleeping bag for his birthday, a canteen for water, and a flashlight. His father promises that they will sleep out when they go to the family cottage for the summer. When they get there, Christopher insists on taking his gear deep into the woods, alone, without even his faithful dog. He has an uneasy time but sticks it out—through rain, an encounter with a porcupine, and other excitement. The pictures are lovely and the writing is pleasant." Pub W

Carroll, Ruth

What Whiskers did. Walck, H.Z. 1965 unp illus $4.95   E
1 Dogs—Stories 2 Rabbits—Stories 3 Stories without words
ISBN 0-8098-1108-1
First published 1932 by Macmillan (N Y)
"Action pictures without text encourage children to

Carroll, Ruth—*Continued*

tell the story of a runaway puppy befriended by a rabbit family." Hodges. Bks for Elem Sch Libraries

"The illustrations [by the author] carry the action perfectly, and plenty of it there is from cover to cover." Sat Rev

Caudill, Rebecca

Contrary Jenkins, by Rebecca Caudill and James Ayars; illus. by Glen Rounds. Holt 1969 unp illus lib. bdg. $5.50, pa 95¢   E

1 Tennessee—Fiction

ISBN 0-03-015046-9; 0-03-080106-0

"In the tradition of the Tennessee tale come the exploits of one of the most stubborn individuals that anyone could possibly want to meet. As soon as a person said 'yes,' Contrary Jenkins would say 'no.' Several episodes in this hill character's life are recounted in appropriate dialect." Wis Library Bul

"Vigorous, comic illustrations capture the obdurate bravado of Ebenezer Jenkins, called Contrary, in a charming tale for the readaloud audience. . . . His various adventures are hilarious, and the writing style has the true storyteller's cadence and rhythm." Chicago. Children's Bk Center

A pocketful of cricket; illus. by Evaline Ness. Holt 1964 unp illus lib. bdg. $5.95, pa $1.65   E

1 Crickets—Stories 2 Farm life—Fiction

ISBN 0-03-089752-1; 0-03-086619-7

"A six-year-old Kentucky farm boy on his way home with the cows one afternoon catches a cricket, makes a pet and friend of it, and on the first day of school takes it along in his pocket. Happily the teacher understands about friends and instead of putting Cricket out lets Jay introduce Cricket in the first 'Show and tell.' " Booklist

"A perceptive nature story with distinctively designed pictures of farm life. Excellent for reading aloud." Hodges. Bks for Elem Sch Libraries

Chalmers, Mary

Be good, Harry; story and pictures by Mary Chalmers. Harper 1967 32p illus lib. bdg. $3.43   E

1 Cats—Stories 2 Baby sitters—Fiction

ISBN 0-06-021173-4

Mother cat "is going to visit a sick friend, and Harry is taken over to stay with Mrs. Brewster, an elderly cat. Fortified by a wagon full of toys, Harry sobs briefly and accepts the status quo; the status quo consists of being fed cookies, being cuddled and read to, and having Mrs. Brewster soothe her visitor with praise and appreciative laughter." Chicago. Children's Bk Center

The charm of this book "rests in the completely childlike text and the modest format with expressive soft-pencil drawings of kitten, mother cat, and neighboring babysitter . . . As a happily recognizable experience, this little story makes pleasant sharing with an individual preschool child or two." Horn Bk

Charlip, Remy

Harlequin and the gift of many colors, by Remy Charlip & Burton Supree; design & paintings by Remy Charlip. Parents Mag. Press 1973 unp illus $4.95, lib. bdg. $4.59   E

1 Harlequin—Fiction 2 Costume—Fiction 3 Festivals—Fiction

ISBN 0-8193-0494-8; 0-8193-0495-6

This story describes how the traditional Harlequin patchwork costume originated—when Harlequin's friends gave him pieces of their costumes so that he might have something to wear at a Carnival

"This is illustrated in soft, soft colors, the first scenes of a small boy alone in his room a dramatic contrast to later pages, swirling with the action of a festival. . . . The writing style is subdued, but the story has enough conflict-resolution and the perennial appeal of a granted wish to compensate." Chicago. Children's Bk Center

Chenery, Janet

The toad hunt; pictures by Ben Shecter. Harper 1967 64p illus (A Science I can read bk) $2.95, lib. bdg. $3.79   E

1 Amphibians—Stories

ISBN 0-06-021262-4; 0-06-021263-2

"While hunting for a toad, Teddy and Peter find a turtle, salamander, polliwogs and frogs." Best Bks for Children, 1968

"This story, though it is not likely to keep readers glued to their chairs, is pleasantly told. Several of Ben Shecter's illustrations are particularly amusing." N Y Times Bk Rev

Chönz, Selina

A bell for Ursli; illus. by Alois Carigiet. Walck, H.Z. 1966 unp illus $8.50   E

1 Switzerland—Fiction 2 Stories in rhyme

ISBN 0-8098-1034-4

Originally published 1946 in Switzerland. First English language edition published 1950 by Oxford

The story, told in verse form, of Ursli, who lives in a tiny village in the Engadine Mountains. He is a helpful small boy, assisting his father to look after the animals and helping his mother in the kitchen, and his adventure when the spring festival comes round is the action of the tale

"Beautiful water colors distinguish this picture book of life in the mountains of Switzerland. . . . Preserves the same beauty of design and format of the original." N Y Pub Library

Clark, Margery

The poppy seed cakes; illus. by Maud and Miska Petersham. Doubleday 1924 unp illus $4.95, lib. bdg. $5.70   E

1 Russia—Fiction

ISBN 0-385-07457-3; 0-385-03834-8

"Auntie Katushka came from the old country with a bag full of presents, a featherbed, a shawl and five pounds of poppy seeds. She came to visit Andrewshek who was four years old. The story tells about the fun and pranks of Andrewshek and his little friend Erminka." St Louis Monthly Bul

"A nursery book of some novelty, beautifully decorated; dog, ducks, goat, and red-topped boots enter into its simple but sprightly annals. We have seen few books for [young] children . . . that are more thoroughly artistic in appearance, pictorially vivid, or jollier in simple narrative. The setting is, of course, Russian—which, however, lends the book a flavor of its own." Sat Rev

Cleary, Beverly

The real hole; pictures by Mary Stevens. Morrow 1960 unp illus lib. bdg. $5.11   E

ISBN 0-688-31655-7

Four-year-old "Jimmy's twin sister liked to pretend things but Jimmy liked real things. If he played with hammer and nails he wanted them to be real grown-up hammer and nails, and when he dug a hole he wanted to use a real shovel and dig a real grown-up hole. This is the story, illustrated with likable drawings in color and in black and white, of the hole that four-year-old Jimmy dug and the satisfying use to which it was put." Booklist

Coatsworth, Elizabeth

Under the green willow; etchings by Janina Domanska. Macmillan (N Y) 1971 unp illus $4.50 E

Coatsworth, Elizabeth—*Continued*
1 Fresh-water animals
The sun describes a place where ducks, ducklings, turtles, trout, catfish, and eels all come together to wait for crumbs
"A little book of graphic distinction, which a child will appreciate even if only on a subconscious level. The words have the imagery of a brief poem. . . . On each page an etching, stylized in pattern, conveys an astonishing sense of movement: the water, fluid; the creatures, in rhythmic motions trying to outdo each other in the competition for crumbs. The etchings are printed, like the words, in a dark olive-green, and each has come through the press with three overlays (in brush-and-ink and pencil: yellow, light green, and bright yellow-green—a totally happy, sunny result." Horn Bk

Cohen, Miriam
Best friends; pictures by Lillian Hoban. Macmillan (N Y) 1971 unp illus $3.95, pa 95¢   E
1 Friendship—Fiction 2 School stories
At the beginning of the school day Jim is almost sure that Paul is his best friend, but as the day goes by he begins to have his doubts. How at the end of the day the two boys know they are best friends is related in this story
"The light touch, good style, and realistic treatment make a pleasant tale out of an experience with which most children can identify." Sutherland. The Best in Children's Bks

Will I have a friend? Pictures by Lillian Hoban. Macmillan (N Y) 1967 illus $4.95, pa $1.25   E
1 School stories
"As Jim approaches nursery school, his chief concern is whether he will have a friend there. For most of his first day he moves around on the edge of things, until someone speaks to him, and they play together. Colored wash drawings show pleasantly recognizable toys, equipment, and activities of a typical nursery school." Moorachian. What is a City?
"The setting is an urban neighborhood, the children a racially mixed group, and the story—simply told—should encourage the child anticipating the start of school." Sat Rev

Conford, Ellen
Impossible, possum; illus. by Rosemary Wells. Little 1971 32p illus $4.95   E
1 Opossums—Stories
ISBN 0-316-15297-8
"All possums hang by their tails—all except Randolph, a young possum with an embarrassing problem. But clever sister Geraldine comes up with a solution to dispel Randolph's fears and to give him confidence in himself." Pub W
"Droll illustrations add to the humor of the easily read story." Booklist

Coombs, Patricia
Dorrie and the amazing magic elixir. Lothrop 1974 unp illus $4.75, lib. bdg. $4.32   E
1 Witches—Fiction
ISBN 0-688-41640-3; 0-688-51640-8
"While her mother gathers moon herbs, Dorrie is to tend a magic elixir that makes things 'hex-proof, spell-proof, potion-proof.' When there is a knock at the door, Dorrie assumes it is her helper, Mr. Obs, but a greenish mist—the Green Wizard—gets into the secret room and turns Dorrie and Mr. Obs into toads. All ends satisfactorily after some excitement and fun. The drawings with touches of soft color are appealing, and the story has enough magic to keep Dorrie fans happily absorbed." Sch Library J

Dorrie and the birthday eggs. Lothrop 1971 unp illus $4.75, lib. bdg. $4.32   E
1 Witches—Fiction 2 Birthdays—Fiction
ISBN 0-688-30000-6; 0-688-35000-3
Little witch Dorrie and her cat Gink decide to help Cook bake Big Witch's birthday cake by getting eggs from the Egg Witch. But Thinnever Vetch was lurking in the forest, waiting for an opportunity to make mischief for Dorrie, the Big Witch, Cook, and the Egg Witch. It is Dorrie who finally outwits her
"An agreeable story with equally likable black-and-white drawings accented with color." Booklist

Dorrie and the Blue Witch; written and illus. by Patricia Coombs. Lothrop 1964 37p illus lib. bdg. $4.32   E
1 Witches—Fiction
ISBN 0-688-51189-9
Dorrie, an untidy little witch, "is called on by a nasty Blue Witch; she shrinks the visitor and puts her in a bottle; when [her mother] the Big Witch returns, she says the Blue Witch is Mildred [the Bad Witch] and she banishes her. Dorrie wins a prize for Witch-Catching." Chicago. Children's Bk Center

Dorrie and the goblin. Lothrop 1972 unp illus $4.75, lib. bdg. $4.32   E
1 Witches—Fiction
ISBN 0-688-41315-3; 0-688-51315-8
"In her latest adventure, Dorrie the little witch finds a Goblin in the laundry basket. Although Cook protests that 'A little Goblin is "BIG TROUBLE," ' Dorrie promises to take care of him until Big Witch's Tea and Magic Show. Goblin-sitting proves quite a job. . . . The plentiful action will delight Dorrie fans, and the story is a good read-aloud, especially before Halloween." Sch Library J

Cooney, Barbara
Chanticleer and the fox, by Geoffrey Chaucer; adapted and illus. by Barbara Cooney. Crowell 1958 unp illus $4.50, lib. bdg. $5.25   E
1 Fables 2 Foxes—Stories 3 Roosters—Stories
ISBN 0-690-18561-8; 0-690-18562-6
Awarded the Caldecott Medal, 1959
"Adaptation of the 'Nun's Priest's Tale' from the Canterbury Tales." Verso of title page
"The familiar fable of the vain cock and the shrewd fox from Chaucer's 'Canterbury tales' has been skillfully adapted for children and presented in picture-book form. The excellent storytelling, the beautiful pictures with their rich, sparkling colors and authentically detailed, medieval background, and the clean-looking, handsomely designed format make this a truly distinguished book." Booklist
"This handsome picture book with its rather lengthy text will be excellent for reading aloud to children." Library J

Credle, Ellis
Down, down the mountain. Nelson 1961 unp illus $4.95, lib. bdg. $4.75   E
1 Mountain life—Southern States—Fiction 2 Blue Ridge Mountains—Fiction
ISBN 0-8407-6020-5; 0-8407-6021-3
First published 1934
The story of Hetty and her brother Hank who lived in a log cabin in the Blue Ridge mountain country. They longed for new creaky shoes and the only way to get them seemed to be to raise a crop of turnips and sell them. This they did and the very next day after their trip to town to sell their turnips, they wore their beautiful new squeaky shoes to church
"The drawings [by the author] have zest and humor and a sympathetic understanding of the mountain

Credle, Ellis—*Continued*

country; they are attractively reproduced in two colors, and the result is a genuinely American picture book with freshness, strength and imagination." N Y Times Bk Rev

Monkey see, monkey do; a folktale retold by Ellis Credle. Nelson 1968 unp illus $3.50, lib. bdg. $3.55   E

1 Monkeys—Stories
ISBN 0-8407-6056-6; 0-8407-6057-4

The Cullifer "family's life [in the Carolina lowlands] is gloomy and sedate till sea-going Uncle Bill presents his young nephew Chub with a monkey who sees and does what the family does, but in a manner that results in one ruckus after another. Monk is given back to Uncle Bill, only to be reclaimed by the Cullifers who miss the zest he adds to their life. Realistic black and green illustrations [by the author] on cream paper help make this action-packed story an attractive purchase—good for read-alouds, and not too difficult for beginning independent readers." Sch Library J

Crews, Donald

We read: A to Z. Harper 1967 26 (i.e. 52)p illus lib. bdg. $5.49   E

1 Alphabet books
ISBN 0-06-021372-8

"An indispensable book that will provide days of fun for children. Instead of the conventional approach to the alphabet, the author has combined the letters and the illustrations with definite concepts that a child can see and use. The format is good, the print excellent, and the use of colors unusual and very appealing to a child's imagination." Bruno. Bks for Sch Libraries, 1968

Damjan, Mischa

Atuk; pictures by Gian Casty. Pantheon Bks. [1966 1964] unp illus lib. bdg. $6.69   E

1 Eskimos—Fiction
ISBN 0-394-91129-6

Original German edition published 1964 in Switzerland. This translation published 1965 in England

"A picture book story with a mystical quality, eloquently illustrated. . . . When Atuk is five, he is given a husky puppy, Taruk. The Eskimo boy and his dog become devoted companions. A wolf kills Taruk, and the boy vows revenge. For many years Atuk prepares himself to hunt down the killer wolf. In the end, he learns that love is more powerful than hatred." Keating. Building Bridges of Understanding Between Cultures

Dana, Doris

The elephant and his secret; based on a fable by Gabriela Mistral; in Spanish and English; illus. by Antonio Frasconi. Atheneum Pubs. 1974 unp illus $5.25   E

1 Elephants—Stories 2 Fables 3 Bilingual books—Spanish-English
ISBN 0-689-30430-7

"A Margaret K McElderry book"

This story "concerns a time, long ago, when the elephant did not yet exist but yearned to be the biggest creature on earth. He covers himself with the shadow of a mountain which gives him his great, gray shape and the fable goes on to tell how he got his tusks and his comparatively small eyes." Pub W

"The well-designed title page, the uncrowded bilingual text, and the nine doublespread woodcuts in effective black, white, orange, and purple are a graphic delight. The text is . . . embellished with poetic details." Horn Bk

Daugherty, James

Andy and the lion. Viking 1938 unp illus lib. bdg. $4.95, pa $1.25   E

1 Lions—Stories
ISBN 0-670-12433-8; 0-670-05033-4

A modern picture story of Androcles and the lion in which Andy, who read a book about lions, was almost immediately plunged into action. The next day he met a circus lion with a thorn in his paw. Andy removed the horn and earned the lion's undying gratitude

"This is a tall tale for little children. It is typically American in its setting and its fun. . . . "[Daugherty's] large full page illustrations are in yellow, black and white and the brief, hand-lettered text on the opposite page is clear and readable." Library J

Davis, Alice Vaught

Timothy Turtle; illus. by Guy Brown Wiser. Harcourt 1940 unp illus $5.95, pa $1.35   E

1 Turtles—Stories 2 Animals—Stories
ISBN 0-15-288368-1; 0-15-690450-0

"The comic predicament of a turtle who falls on his back and cannot turn over is ingeniously solved by his animal friends. A colorful picture story for little children." Cleveland

Dawson, Rosemary

A walk in the city, by Rosemary and Richard Dawson. Viking 1950 39p illus lib. bdg. $4.95   E

1 New York (City)—Fiction 2 Stories in rhyme
ISBN 0-670-74909-5

"A gay picture book in which the sights a little boy notices on a walk with his mother are described in rhymes and detailed illustrations in bright colors on alternate pages. Reds, greens and yellows prevail in . . . [Richard Dawson's] pictures. All the really important events are stored in memory to tell his father about at night. [New York] City children will recognize much that is familiar here." Horn Bk

Delton, Judy

Two good friends; pictures by Giulio Maestro. Crown 1974 32p illus lib. bdg. $4.50   E

1 Friendship—Fiction 2 Bears—Stories 3 Ducks—Stories
ISBN 0-517-51401-X

"Duck and Bear have different ways of keeping house, but each sees the virtues of the other's ways, and each knows that friendship means toleration of differences. Duck is a tidy housekeeper, but no cook; Bear is a dab hand at baking, but creates havoc in the kitchen." Chicago. Children's Bk Center

"The charming crayon-like pictures and the equally attractive text blend into a book that is outstanding. A good choice for reading aloud but also an excellent book for the novice reader. Without moralizing, the story shows the wisdom of sharing talents." Children's Bk Rev Serv

Dennis, Wesley

Flip; story and pictures by Wesley Dennis. Viking 1941 unp illus $2.75   E

1 Horses—Stories
ISBN 0-670-31876-0

"To be able to jump the brook in the pasture was Flip's greatest desire. One day, dreaming he had beautiful silvery wings, the little colt jumped high and wide around the farm. Upon awakening, believing he still had wings, Flip cleared the brook with the greatest of ease. A picture book to delight children with an eye for horses." Booklist

This book "contains some of the most enchanting sketches of a colt ever put on paper. . . . Whether on the ground or in the air, Flip is a delight to the eye." Boston Transcript

De Paola, Tomie

Andy (that's my name). Prentice-Hall 1973 unp illus
lib. bdg. $4.95   E

1 Word games—Fiction
ISBN 0-13-036731-1

"A group of costumed children spurn the advances
of a smaller boy who comes on the scene pulling a
wagon with large letters: A. N. D. Y. They seize on this,
and remove the last two, add another letter, and make
'can,' then 'fan,' and by shifting letters, words like
'hand' and 'dandy.' Finally Andy tumbles everything
off and moves away with the original letters, murmur-
ing that he may be little but he's important." Chicago.
Children's Bk Center

"The text (all in the form of conversation balloons) is
humorously extended by Tomie de Paola's soft, expressive, pastel wash illustrations. . . . 'Andy' should
meet the need for preschool material on human relationships (sharing) as well as on spelling and word
composition." Sch Library J

"Charlie needs a cloak." Story and pictures by
Tomie de Paola. Prentice-Hall [1974 c1973] unp illus
$4.95   E

ISBN 0-13-128355-3

"Charlie the shepherd, a black faced sheep, and a
filching mouse combine skills and pranks to create a
beautiful new red cloak. The facts of clothmaking are
amusingly presented." Brooklyn Public Library. Art
Bks for Children

Nana Upstairs & Nana Downstairs; story and pictures by Tomie de Paola. Putnam 1973 unp illus
$5.95   E

1 Grandmothers—Fiction 2 Death—Fiction
ISBN 0-399-20300-1

"A tender, unpretentious story describing four-
year-old Tommy's Sunday visits with his
grandmother, Nana Downstairs, and his invalid great-
grandmother, Nana Upstairs. When Nana Upstairs is
tied into her chair so she won't fall out, Tommy
demands to be tied also, and the two sit side by side
companionably eating candy and discussing the Little
People. Then Tommy experiences his first contact
with death when Mother tells him simply and honestly that Nana Upstairs has died, comforting him first
when he grasps her absence, and again in the middle
of the night. De Paola's illustrations in pink and beige
softly complement the text." Booklist

Watch out for the chicken feet in your soup; story
and pictures by Tomie de Paola. Prentice-Hall 1974
unp illus $4.95   E

1 Grandmothers—Fiction
ISBN 0-13-945782-8

"Joey brings his friend Eugene over to visit his Old
World Italian grandmother and through Eugene's
eyes gains a new appreciation of his grandmother."
Children's Bk Rev Serv

"Nice in itself, and attractively illustrated, the
story's bonus is that it can help a child adjust to the
ideas that there's nothing wrong (far from it) with
people who have a foreign accent and that differences
(in manners, in food, in home decoration) are interesting rather than peculiar." Chicago. Children's Bk
Center

De Regniers, Beatrice Schenk

A little house of your own; drawings by Irene Haas.
Harcourt 1954 unp illus $4.50   E

ISBN 0-15-245787-9

"This is a delightful book by an author who obviously understands children well and has observed
them very carefully. Her descriptions of little
'houses,' the places to which one can retire for a few
moments of peace and privacy will instantly strike a

chord in little boys and girls and give them a few new
ideas as well. Among these make believe 'houses' are,
for example, the space under the dining room table
and a corner, behind a large chair. . . . The illustrations are perfectly matched to the text." Pub W

May I bring a friend? Illus. by Beni Montresor.
Atheneum Pubs. 1964 unp illus $5.95, pa $1.25   E

1 Animals—Stories
ISBN 0-689-20615-1; 0-689-70405-4
Awarded the Caldecott Medal, 1965

"Each time the little boy in this picture book is
invited to take tea or dine with the King and Queen,
he brings along a somewhat difficult animal friend.
Their Highnesses always cope and are wonderfully
rewarded in the end." Pub W

"The pictures are simpler, with a more direct story
quality, than some of Montresor's previous
work. . . . The technique, particularly of the more
elaborate illustrations, is interesting. The pictures,
suggesting the kind of sketches made for stage scenery, have an unusual texture and a three dimensional
quality." Toronto

"Rich color and profuse embellishment adorn an
opulent setting. Absurdities and contrasts are so
imaginatively combined in a hilarious comedy of manners that the merriment can be enjoyed on several
levels." Horn Bk

The shadow book; photographs by Isabel Gordon.
Harcourt 1960 unp illus $5.95   E

1 Shades and shadows
ISBN 0-15-272991-7

A "picture book which traces a day in the life of a
child from the time he wakes in the morning to see
shadows on his bedroom wall until the time when the
shadows lengthen as evening comes. It is illustrated
with photographs of children and their shadows."
Pub W

"This beautiful book . . . has the validity of a fine
poem on a small but exciting topic." Sat Rev

Snow party; illus. by Reiner Zimnik. Pantheon Bks.
1959 unp lib. bdg. $4.79   E

ISBN 0-394-91647-6

"A lonely little old woman gets her wish to have a
party when dozens of people stop in out of the snow
and a snowbound bakery truck provides refreshments." Hodges. Bks for Elem Sch Libraries

Was it a good trade? Drawings by Irene Haas.
Harcourt 1956 unp illus $3.95   E

1 Nonsense verses
ISBN 0-15-294812-0

"Nonsense rhymes built on the pattern of the traditional swapping song. There is humor in the items
involved in each trade and in the illustrations of each."
Chicago. Children's Bk Center

Devlin, Wende

How Fletcher was hatched, by Wende and Harry
Devlin. Parents Mag. Press 1969 unp illus $4.95, lib.
bdg. $4.59   E

1 Dogs—Stories
ISBN 0-8193-0247-3; 0-8193-0248-1

"An amusing story with a rural setting that quietly
indicates understanding of emotions strongly felt by
the young: friendship and affection, seeming loss of
friendship and consequent loneliness, joy and relief
when affection is verified after all. Young Alexandra
becomes interested in tiny, fluffy, yellow chicks, and
her large, doting hound dog Fletcher feels forgotten,
neglected, and unloved. Fletcher mournfully shuffles
away to his faithful friends, Beaver and Otter, who
cleverly build an egg around him, thereby enabling

Devlin, Wende—*Continued*

him to hatch spectacularly in front of Alexandra. The story culminates with Fletcher's realization that he was loved all along, and for just being himself. . . . The theme is an old one, the telling here freshly humorous. The full-color illustrations [by Harry Devlin], large and cartoon-like, echo the warm tone and happy outcome of the story." Sch Library J

Dolbier, Maurice

Torten's Christmas secret; illus by Robert Henneberger. Little 1951 61p illus lib. bdg. $5.95 E

1 Christmas stories 2 Fairy tales
ISBN 0-316-18914-6

"An imaginative tale of the things that happened at the North Pole when [Santa], the gnome, Torten, and his good friend Drusus, the polar bear, set out to do something about the bad children whose stockings might not be filled at Christmas. [There is] the liveliness of the story and of the many colored pictures. . . . Storytellers and the children themselves will welcome it." Horn Bk

Domanska, Janina

What do you see? Pictures by Janina Domanska. Macmillan Pub. Co. 1974 unp illus lib. bdg. $6.95 E

1 Animals—Stories 2 Stories in rhyme
ISBN 0-02-732830-9

The frog, the fly, the bat and the fern all see the world differently, but it takes the soaring lark to show them that they are all correct

he author-illustrator "uses what appears to be scratch painting and collage technique to create a most inviting, imaginative world. With each turn of the page, the reader is delighted by a new creation of color and contrast. The body shapes are anatomically correct but filled with designs and colors that challenge the imagination of the reader. The visual intensity of these illustrations makes the book appealing to even very young children. It would also be effective to read to early and pre-readers. The text uses simple language, with much repetition and rhyming. The print is large. It would be fairly easy for youngsters to begin to recognize some of the words and begin to 'read' the story themselves." Rdng Teacher

Du Bois, William Pène

Bear Circus. Viking 1971 48p illus $4.95 E

1 Koalas—Stories 2 Circus—Fiction
ISBN 0-670-15073-8

A companion volume to: Bear party, entered below

The bears lose "their food supply (the leaves of the gum trees) to a horde of grasshoppers, but some kindly kangaroos appear and carry the bears to new territory. To show their gratitude, the slow-moving koalas spend seven long years mounting a great circus; but the first performance is scarcely ended when the grasshoppers return and the kangaroos must effect a second mass rescue." Horn Bk

"This tale of friendship-extraordinary is delightful nonsense sedately told, with [the author-illustrator's] pictures as amusing as they are lovely. . . . A completely engaging joyous book." Sat Rev

Bear party. Viking [1963 c1951] 48p illus lib. bdg. $4.95 E

1 Koalas—Stories
ISBN 0-670-15124-6

A reissue of the title first published 1951

This is "the story of the angry bears of Koala Park whose good will and good sense were restored by a masked costume ball. . . . [The author-illustrator's] colored pictures of the Koala bears in costumes are gay and charming and the book as a whole quite irresistible." Booklist

Lion. Viking 1956 36p illus lib. bdg. $5.95 E

1 Lions—Stories
ISBN 0-670-42950-3

"Artist Foreman of the Animal Factory thought of a fine name for a new animal—'Lion'—but he was out of practice and found it exceedingly difficult to draw an animal as majestic as the name. After much trial and error and embarrassment . . . he arrived, somewhat by accident, at the lion as we know him, and greeted him with a happy roar, which he gave to the King of Beasts himself." Ontario Library Rev

"Any age will enjoy the humor and invention of the tale. The [author's] illustrations are stunning. It is an altogether well designed and fully-realized book." Sat Rev

Otto at sea; the adventures of Otto. [Rev ed] Viking 1958 37p illus lib. bdg. $5.95 E

1 Dogs—Stories
ISBN 0-670-529990-0

First published 1936

"After receiving 22 medals for brave adventures in 18 different countries, Otto, a giant dog, and his master, Duke, set out on a goodwill tour to America. It turns out that they don't leave adventure behind." Pub W

"The text is hardly more than a series of captions. . . . But who needs more of a story when there are so many fascinating, exquisitely drawn details to look at?" N Y Her Trib Bks

Duvoisin, Roger

A for the Ark. Lothrop 1952 unp illus lib. bdg. $4.59 E

1 Noah's Ark 2 Alphabet books
ISBN 0-688-50985-1

God commanded Noah to take two of every kind of animal into the Ark, so he went straight through the alphabet to be sure to include them all! This is the introduction to Roger Duvoisin's presentation of the Old Testament story of the flood

"In a brilliant charming, colorful book, rather nonsensical as to drawings [made by the author] very realistic in its dramatic, simple text, Mr. Duvoisin plays on a familiar theme in a new way." N Y Her Trib Bks

The house of four seasons. Lothrop 1956 unp illus lib. bdg. $5.49 E

1 Color—Fiction 2 House painting—Fiction
ISBN 0-688-51191-0

"When each member of the family wanted to paint a new house to harmonize with a different season, Father mixed his paints into a color that pleased everybody. Duvoisin's illustrations skillfully extend the pleasant story into a lesson in color combinations." Hodges. Bks for Elem Sch Libraries

Lonely Veronica; written and illus. by Roger Duvoisin. Knopf 1963 unp illus lib. bdg. $5.99 E

1 Hippopotamus—Stories
ISBN 0-394-91364-7

"When men and machines invade her jungle swamp and the other hippopotamuses leave because the good old days are gone, Veronica remains to see what the good new days will bring. They bring Veronica to America, as the pet of a building crew, where she has a most unsettling adventure in a skyscraper under construction." Booklist

"Nice details in exposition; text and illustrations have a light humor and a lively quality that is very pleasant." Chicago. Children's Bk Center

Our Veronica goes to Petunia's farm; written and illus. by Roger Duvoisin. Knopf 1962 unp illus lib. bdg. $5.99, pa 95¢ E

Duvoisin, Roger—*Continued*

1 Hippopotamus—Stories 2 Domestic animals—
Stories
ISBN 0-394-91469-4; 0-394-82737-6
Veronica, the hippopotamus "arrives at a farm
where she expects to find everything just right. The
farm animals, however, meet her with animosity. She
is a stranger, different from them, and therefore, does
not belong on their farm. Veronica's reaction brings a
change of heart, however, and she finally is accepted
as one of them. Delightful and symbolic. Abundantly
illustrated with author's bright, appealing pictures."
Sch Library J

Petunia; written and illus. by Roger Duvoisin.
Knopf 1950 unp illus lib. bdg. $5.99, pa $1.25   E

1 Geese—Stories
ISBN 0-394-90865-1; 0-394-82617-5
" 'He, who owns a book and loves them is wise' is
the premise that Petunia, the silly goose, begins with.
After the many errors that Petunia causes—the kind
children love, she decides that 'It is not enough to
carry wisdom under my wing. I must put it in my mind
and heart. And to do that I must learn to read.' " Wis
Library Bul
"The story may be a little forced but it is full of
amusing incidents and conversation, and the pictures
are spirited and gay." Horn Bk

Petunia, I love you; written and illus. by Roger
Duvoisin. Knopf 1965 unp illus lib. bdg. $5.99   E

1 Geese—Stories 2 Raccoons—Stories
ISBN 0-394-90870-8
"Raccoon, looking at Petunia, the goose, sees a
wonderful feast, so he invites her for a walk, planning
by guile to forestall any danger from her powerful
wings. When Petunia continually saves Raccoon from
the results of the backfiring of his wily schemes, he is
forced to give up his wicked plans, to thank Petunia,
and to swear to be her truest friend forever." Horn Bk
This book "won't give [its readers] any goose pimples, just . . . amusement. Mr. Duvoisin's pictures
are, as always, richly colored and full of action."
Christian Sci Monitor

Petunia's Christmas; written and illus. by Roger
Duvoisin. Knopf 1952 unp illus lib. bdg. $5.99   E

1 Geese—Stories 2 Christmas stories
ISBN 0-394-90868-6
Petunia is here again in a Christmas story. "A
romance develops when Petunia rescues Charles, a
handsome gander earmarked for the farmer's Christmas dinner." Hodges. Bks for Elem Sch Libraries

Veronica; written and illus. by Roger Duvoisin.
Knopf 1961 unp illus lib. bdg. $5.99, pa 95¢   E

1 Hippopotamus—Stories
ISBN 0-394-91792-8; 0-394-82616-7
"Longing to be different, a hippopotamus named
Veronica left the herd where nobody noticed her and
walked until she reached a city. There she was not just
different, she was gloriously conspicuous, so conspicuous in fact that she ended in jail. Veronica's
misadventures in the city and her return to the mud-
bank and the acclaim of the herd are recounted in a
diverting picture book illustrated with laughable
drawings in color and in black and white." Booklist

Veronica and the birthday present. Knopf 1971 unp
illus lib. bdg. $5.99   E

1 Hippopotamus—Stories 2 Cats—Stories
ISBN 0-394-92282-4
Illustrated by the author
When Farmer Pumpkin's hippopotamus, Veronica,
and Farmer Applegreen's kitten, Candy become the

best of friends, both farms are thrown into turmoil
over this inseparable pair

Eastman, P. D.

Are you my mother? Written and illus. by P. D.
Eastman. Beginner Bks. 1960 63p illus $2.95 lib. bdg.
$3.69   E

1 Birds—Stories
ISBN 0-394-80018-4; 0-394-90018-9
Also available in a bilingual Spanish-English edition
for $3.50, lib. bdg. $4.99 (ISBN 0-394-81596-3; 0-394-
91596-8) and in a bilingual French-English edition for
$2.95, lib. bdg. $3.99 (ISBN 0-394-80174-1; 0-394-
90174-6)
"A small bird falls from his nest and searches for his
mother. He asks a kitten, a hen, a dog, a cow, a boat,
[and] a plane . . . 'Are you my mother?' Repetition of
words and phrases and funny pictures are just right for
beginning readers." Chicago

Eichenberg, Fritz

Ape in a cape; an alphabet of odd animals. Harcourt
1952 unp illus $6.95, pa $1.35   E

1 Animals—Pictorial works 2 Alphabet books
ISBN 0-15-203722-5; 0-15-607830-9
"Each letter of the alphabet from A for ape to Z for
zoo is represented by a full-page picture of an animal
with a brief nonsense rhyme caption explaining it. For
example: mouse in a blouse, pig in a wig, toad on the
road, whale in a gale." Pub W
"The skill of a craftsman distinguishes this picture
book illustrated [by the author] with bold and lively
drawings printed in three colors." N Y Pub Library

Dancing in the moon; counting rhymes. Harcourt
1955 20p illus $5.95, pa $1.85   E

1 Animals—Pictorial works 2 Counting books
ISBN 0-15-221443-7; 0-15-623811-X
This book "introduces numbers up to twenty, from
'1 raccoon dancing in the moon' to '20 fishes juggling
dishes.' The three-color wonderfully detailed and
humorous drawings [by the author] show gay and
serious animals and birds who can be examined with
fun again and again. . . . And the irresistible rhyming
lines are likely to be chanted over and over." Horn Bk

Elkin, Benjamin

Gillespie and the guards; illus. by James
Daugherty. Viking 1956 62p illus $3.75   E
ISBN 0-670-34083-9
"An amusing variation on an old folk theme. The
king has three guards with eyesight so good that
nothing can be put over on them. A reward is offered
to anyone who can fool them, and it is claimed by
young Gillespie after he has left the palace each day
with a wagon loaded with leaves, sand, rocks and
other junk. He is, of course, taking a different wagon
from the palace each day. When this is disclosed,
Gillespie wins the award and the guards become less
pompous. Daugherty's illustrations are a perfect complement to the text." Chicago. Children's Bk Center
"A tale that's fun to read and perfect for the story
hour. . . . The story and the vigorous, jolly pictures
that tell how he did it will delight children from four
or five on." Horn Bk

How the tsar drinks tea; pictures by Anita Lobel.
Parents Mag. Press 1971 unp illus $4.95, lib. bdg.
$4.59   E

1 Russia—Fiction
ISBN 0-8193-0455-7; 0-8193-0456-5
"As Petya prepares tea in his newly found brass
samovar, he sings happily, 'Steam away, my samovar.
Petya the peasant is like the tsar.' The tsar is amused
when he hears of Petya's boast and directs the peasant
to observe the elegance and ceremony that accom-

Elkin, Benjamin—*Continued*

pany his tea drinking in the palace. In the end, however, the truth of Petya's words is proven. . . . Droll illustrations in rich colors reflect the spirit and humor of the story." Booklist

The loudest noise in the world; illus. by James Daugherty. Viking 1954 64p illus lib. bdg. $5.95 E
1 Noise—Fiction
ISBN 0-670-44170-8

Prince Hulla-Baloo of Hub-Bub, the noisiest city in the world, asked his father for the loudest noise in the world for his sixth birthday present. His kind father made elaborate arrangements to give him his wish. But the plan involving millions of people went wrong; with the result that Prince Hulla-Baloo had the most beautiful birthday present of his whole life

"Not only the children will laugh long and loud over this delightfully absurd story. Their elders, too, will chuckle over it and over James Daugherty's vigorous, robust drawings." Sat Rev

Ellentuck, Shan

A sunflower as big as the sun. Doubleday 1968 unp illus lib. bdg. $5.70 E
1 Sunflowers—Fiction 2 Russia—Fiction
ISBN 0-385-01106-7

"Uncle Vanya plants a seed and boasts about how fast it grows—and so it does. He brags that it is as high as his knee—and so it is. Every time he carries on, the flower grows. It blots out the sun, and the townspeople beg Uncle Vanya to stop lest the world come to an end. When he finally tells the truth, the sun shines, the flowers revive, and the people celebrate with a party to end all parties." Sat Rev

"This is an excellently told and substantial tale set in an old Russian village. . . . The [author-illustrator's] pictures have a familiar Russian peasant credibility." Bk World

Emberley, Ed

Klippity klop. Little 1974 unp illus $4.95 E
ISBN 0-316-23607-1

Illustrated by the author, this story follows Prince Krispin and his horse, Dumpling, as they set out in search of adventure, meet a dragon, and return to the security of the castle

"This light diversion is jauntily line-sketched on sepia-toned paper, and the result is an artful, clean-looking book." Booklist

The wing on a flea; a book about shapes; written and illus. by Ed Emberley. Little 1961 48p illus $5.50 E
1 Size and shape
ISBN 0-316-23600-4

"Gay rhymes and lively green-and-blue drawings show children how to identify triangles, circles, and rectangles in the everyday objects around them. Though some of the examples are a little far-fetched, this should prove effective in nudging boys and girls toward more intelligent observation." Library J

Ets, Marie Hall

Gilberto and the Wind. . . . Viking 1963 32p illus lib. bdg. $4.95, pa 95¢ E
1 Winds—Fiction
ISBN 0-670-34025-1; 0-670-05021-0

"I am Gilberto and this is the story of me and the Wind." Title page

"A little Mexican boy thinks aloud about all the things his playmate the wind does with him, for him, and against him. The wind calls him to play, floats his balloon, refuses to fly his kite, blows his soap bubbles into the air, races with him, and rests with him under a tree." Sch Library J

"In brown, black, and white against soft gray pages, this author-artist has caught in a very appealing book . . . the emotions and attitudes of childhood." Horn Bk

In the forest; story and pictures by Marie Hall Ets. Viking 1944 unp illus lib. bdg. $4.50, pa 75¢ E
1 Animals—Stories
ISBN 0-670-39687-7; 0-670-05032-6

"A delightful, oblong book, with an amusing black and white picture to each page and a sentence or two about a very small boy with a new horn and paper hat who goes for a walk in a great big forest. Along with him go a wild lion, two elephant babies, two brown bears, three kangaroos, two little monkeys, a stork and a rabbit, making quite a parade. But strangely enough, when Dad comes hunting for him and he opens his eyes, there are no animals at all!" Bookmark

"An imaginative story. . . . [The pictures] have a suggestion of Leslie Brooke about them." Booklist

Just me; written and illus. by Marie Hall Ets. Viking 1965 32p illus $2.50, pa 75¢ E
1 Animals—Stories
ISBN 0-670-41109-4; 0-670-05044-X

"A little boy plays a game commonly enjoyed by small children for its imaginative as well as muscular demands. He goes from one animal to another, mimicking its ambulation, moving 'just like' it. When there is a chance to take a boat ride with Dad, the game ends abruptly, and another kind of imitation begins—emulation of father." Horn Bk

"Strong, simply designed illustrations and brief, rhythmic text." LC. Children's Bks, 1965

Mr T. W. Anthony Woo; the story of a cat and a dog and a mouse. Viking 1951 54p illus lib. bdg. $3.95 E
1 Animals—Stories
ISBN 0-670-49347-3

"The cat, Meola, the dog, Rodigo, and a little gray mouse whose name was Mr. T. W. Anthony Woo, all lived together with the little old cobbler of Shooshko. Rodigo liked to chase Meola and Meola was always bothering Mr T. W. Anthony Woo. 'Please!' said the cobbler. 'I must get on with my work. Can we never have peace?' But peace did not come. Instead, the cobbler's interfering but well-meaning sister came to set the house aright, and with her was Pollyandrew, a talkative and tiresome parrot. The tale of how the animals extricated themselves from this undesirable situation without losing their animal traits, is told." Ontario Library Rev

"This original story has the heartiness and the coziness of a folktale. . . . Its special qualities are emphasized by Mrs. Ets' noteworthy illustrations—robust black and white drawings on paper batik." N Y Times Bk Rev

Nine days to Christmas, by Marie Hall Ets and Aurora Labastida; illus. by Marie Hall Ets. Viking 1959 48p illus lib. bdg. $5.95 E
1 Mexico—Fiction 2 Christmas stories
ISBN 0-670-51350-4
Awarded the Caldecott Medal, 1960

This "is the story of Ceci, a little girl of Mexico City, just five, and now old enough to have her own posada, the gay parties held on the nine days preceding Christmas. She may also choose her own piñata. . . . The pictures capture all the gaiety, excitement and anticipation preparatory to the Christmas season. With simple lines, a few colors, and a soft gray background that deepens in intensity as the day comes to a close, Marie Ets has caught the brilliant richness of color, the movement and vibrant life that are so much a part of this handsome city." Top of the News

Ets, Marie Hall—*Continued*
Play with me; story and pictures by Marie Hall Ets.
Viking 1955 31p illus lib. bdg. $4.95, pa 95¢   E
1 Animals—Stories
ISBN 0-670-55977-6; 0-670-05003-2
On a sunny morning in the meadow an excited little
girl tries to catch the meadow creatures and play with
them. But, one by one, they all run away. Finally,
when she learns to sit quietly and wait, there is a
happy ending
The "pictures done in muted tones of brown, gray
and yellow . . . accurately reflect the little girl's
rapidly changing moods of eagerness, bafflement, disappointment and final happiness." N Y Times Bk Rev
"Simplicity of text and freshness of drawing make
this idea fare for the very youngest." Library J

Falls, Charles Buckles
The A B C book. Doubleday 1923 unp illus $4.95,
lib. bdg. $5.70, pa 95¢   E
1 Animals—Pictorial works 2 Alphabet books
ISBN 0-385-07663-0; 0-385-07698-3; 0-385-08097-2
" 'A is for Antelope, Z is for Zebra.' An animal A B C
with fine decorative wood blocks in colour illustrating
each animal." Bks for Boys & Girls

Farber, Norma
Where's Gomer? Illus. by William Pène du Bois.
Dutton 1974 unp illus $6.95   E
1 Noah's Ark—Fiction 2 Stories in rhyme
ISBN 0-525-42590-X
This story in rhyme "deals with a 'missing person' in
the complement of Noah's Ark. Noah's grandson
Gomer misses embarkation, and the ship sails without
him. Consternation reigns, but all is resolved happily
by the end of the story." Rdng Teacher
"The poem obviously provided pure inspiration for
the creativity of the illustrator. The joyous full-color
paintings show a menagerie of splendid animals, along
with Noah's numerous family, all properly dressed as
for an Edwardian sailing party." Horn Bk

Farley, Walter
Little Black, a pony; illus. by James Schucker.
Beginner Bks. 1961 60p illus $2.95, lib. bdg. $3.69
        E
1 Ponies—Stories 2 Horses—Stories
ISBN 0-394-80021-4; 0-394-90021-9
The story of a boy, a horse named Big Red, and
Little Black, a pony who wishes he were big

Fatio, Louise
The happy lion; pictures by Roger Duvoisin.
McGraw 1954 unp illus $4.95, lib. bdg. $4.72   E
1 Lions—Stories 2 France—Fiction
ISBN 0-07-020045-9; 0-07-020044-0
"Whittlesey House publications"
"A lion in a zoo in France is everybody's favorite—
until he escapes. Then his only friend is a little boy
who leads him back to his cage." Hodges. Bks for
Elem Sch Libraries
"Children will chuckle over a little boy's success in
settling a problem that perplexed all the grownups."
Horn Bk
"A merry nonsense story, whose pictures have cap-
tured an air of irresponsible gaiety." Ontario Library
Rev

The happy lion in Africa; pictures by Roger
Duvoisin. McGraw 1955 30p illus $4.95, lib. bdg.
$4.72   E
1 Lions—Stories 2 Africa—Fiction
ISBN 0-07-020046-7; 0-07-020043-2
"This is an account of the Happy Lion's adventures
in Africa, where he is scared by the wild animals and

longs for his comfortable home in the zoo." Pub W
"More bright nonsense about The Happy Li-
on. . . . Effective spreads in three colors alternating
with black and white enhance the story's gaiety and
atmosphere." Horn Bk

The three happy lions; pictures by Roger Duvoisin.
McGraw 1959 32p illus lib. bdg. $4.72   E
1 Lions—Stories 2 France—Fiction
ISBN 0-07-020050-5
"Whittlesey House publications"
"The happy lion and his happy lioness were concerned about the future of their cub François. . . .
After François had failed successively as a household
pet [because he was too large] and the circus performer [because he was gentle] he was returned to the
zoo where he had decided long ago what he really
wanted to do. . . . Like its predecessors, this nonsense
story has spontaneity and charm with a decided
French flavour [and some vocabulary]. The story
thread is stronger and more unified than in the other
books about the happy lion, the illustrations are as
irresistible." Ontario Library Rev

Feelings, Muriel
Jambo means hello; Swahili alphabet book; pictures
by Tom Feelings. Dial Press 1974 unp illus map
$5.95, lib. bdg. $5.47   E
1 Swahili language 2 Alphabet books 3 Africa, East
ISBN 0-8037-4346-7; 0-8037-4350-5
Companion volume to: Moja means one
This book "gives a word for each letter of the
alphabet (the Swahili alphabet has 24 letters) save for
'q' and 'x', and a sentence or two provides additional
information. A double-page spread of soft black and
white drawings illustrates each word; for example: 'V,
vyombo are utensils (vee-oam-bow). A craftsman
makes utensils for the village. Carved wooden bowls
and ladles and pitchers made from gourds are useful
and decorative objects for the home.' The picture
shows such a craftsman making one object and surrounded by others. The text gives a considerable
amount of information about traditional East African
life as well as some acquaintance with the language
that is used by approximately 45 million people."
Chicago. Children's Bk Center
"An introduction explains the prevalence of Swahili
in Africa and notes the 24-letter alphabet. Words like
'arusi' meaning wedding, 'baba' meaning father, or
'chakula' meaning food are coupled with a sentence or
two imparting information on their meaning in terms
of African culture." Booklist

Moja means one; Swahili counting book; pictures
by Tom Feelings. Dial Press 1971 unp illus $4.95, lib.
bdg. $4.58   E
1 Counting books 2 Africa, East 3 Swahili language
ISBN 0-8037-5776-X; 0-8037-5777-8
The book "uses double-page spreads for each
number, one to ten, with beautiful illustrations that
depict aspects of East African culture as well as numbers of objects in relation to the various numbers."
Pub W
"A short introduction explaining the importance of
Swahili and providing a map of the areas in which it is
spoken expands the book's use beyond the preschool
level of the text into the first three school grades." Sch
Library J

Zamani goes to market; illus. by Tom Feelings.
Seabury 1970 unp illus $5.95   E
1 Africa, East—Fiction
ISBN 0-8164-3078-0
"Zamani, an East African boy, accompanies his
father to market for the first time and decides to spend

611

Feelings, Muriel—*Continued*

the shilling his father gives him on a necklace for his mother." Adventuring With Bks. 2d edition

"A harmonious and unified picture storybook. The soft browns and golds of the pencil drawings convey a gentle, pleasant atmosphere of African village life, with its spirit of family closeness." Horn Bk

Fenton, Edward

Fierce John; a story. Illus. by William Pène du Bois. Holt [1969 c1959] 59p illus lib. bdg. $3.27   E
   ISBN 0-03-072925-4

A reissue of the title first published 1959 by Doubleday

"This is the story of a little boy's daylong masquerade as the fierce, roaring lion he has seen at the zoo. John's family amiably goes along with the jape which puts John on the spot when he is ready to return to humanity." N Y Times Bk Rev

"Never has the game of pretend been more engagingly portrayed than in this enchanting picture book by an author and artist who have combined their special gifts of imagination and humor to create a captivating small boy." Chicago Sunday Trib

Fife, Dale

Adam's A B C; illus. by Don Robertson. Coward, McCann & Geoghegan 1971 unp illus lib. bdg. $4.49   E
   1 Alphabet books 2 Cities and towns—Fiction 3 Negroes—Fiction
   ISBN 0-698-30002-5

"An alphabet book that describes a day in a black child's life begins with Adam and his friends Arthur and Albert, moves on to little BROTHER, the storm CLOUDS in the morning sky, and ends with Adam's YAWN as he goes to bed to snore, 'Zzzz. . . .' The stress is on blackness: black children, black cloud, black-spotted dog, elephant made of ebony, and so on, to the day that ends with black tire tracks and dark umbrellas. Not outstanding as an alphabet book, but welcome because of the orientation and the urban setting." Sat Rev

Fisher, Aileen

Going barefoot; illus. by Adrienne Adams. Crowell 1960 unp illus $4.50, lib. bdg. $5.25   E
   1 Animals—Stories 2 Stories in rhyme
   ISBN 0-690-33331-5; 0-690-33332-3

A picture book of poetry "describing the joys of going barefoot and a child's envy of the many little animals and birds who are not required to wear shoes." Pub W

The "spontaneous rhyming text and pleasing drawings in color and in black and white create a happy mood of anticipation and discovery." Booklist

I like weather; illus. by Janina Domanska. Crowell 1963 unp illus $4.95, lib. bdg. $5.70   E
   1 Seasons—Fiction 2 Weather—Fiction 3 Stories in rhyme
   ISBN 0-690-43129-5; 0-690-43130-9

A story in verse about a boy and his dog who seek the pleasures of the four seasons of the year with their different kinds of weather

In the middle of the night; illus. by Adrienne Adams. Crowell 1965 unp illus $4.50, lib. bdg. $5.25   E
   1 Stories in rhyme
   ISBN 0-690-53496-5; 0-690-53497-3

"A nocturnal walk as a birthday present delights a little girl who discovers for the first time the beauty and magic of a country night. Illustrations evoke the mood and combine with the gentle verses to reassure

the small child about nighttime." Hodges. Bks for Elem Sch Libraries

Listen, rabbit; illus. by Symeon Shimin. Crowell 1964 unp illus $5.95, lib. bdg. $6.95   E
   1 Rabbits—Stories 2 Stories in rhyme
   ISBN 0-690-49591-9; 0-690-49592-7

"This enchanting picture-poetry book tells a happy story of a small boy as he tries to make friends with a rabbit through the four seasons and satisfyingly at the end discovers '. . . and five baby rabbits/to watch grow up!' Illustrated with lovely Symeon Shimin drawings, it will be a delight for the picture book hour as well as for family sharing." Wis Library Bul

We went looking; pictures by Marie Angel. Crowell 1968 25p illus $4.95, lib. bdg. $5.75   E
   1 Animals—Stories 2 Stories in rhyme
   ISBN 0-690-87150-3; 0-690-87151-1

"A longish, lilting nature poem in which a slow perambulation through the wilds affords glimpses of no sought-for badger but of many other animals. The poetry's quiet mood is matched by the delicate details and subdued tones of the small, precise pictures. Each illustration has a brief line of text above and another below, the whole effectively framed by wide, restful space. The lack of plot or action may limit the book's appeal to those children who enjoy the elegant, pressed-flower charm of the pictures or the rhythm of the verse." Chicago. Children's Bk Center

Where does everyone go? Illus. by Adrienne Adams. Crowell 1961 unp illus $3.95, lib. bdg. $4.70   E
   1 Autumn 2 Stories in rhyme
   ISBN 0-690-88215-7; 0-690-88216-5

"A picture book in rhyme answering children's questions about what happens to small creatures when winter approaches. A good seasonal book for the youngest, enhanced by sensitive illustrations in fall colors." Hodges. Bks for Elem Sch Libraries

Flack, Marjorie

Angus and the ducks; told and pictured by Marjorie Flack. Doubleday 1930 unp illus $4.50, lib. bdg. $5.25, pa 95¢   E
   1 Dogs—Stories 2 Ducks—Stories
   ISBN 0-385-07213-9; 0-385-07600-2; 0-385-01026-5

A "picture book describing the amusing experiences of Angus, a Scotch terrier puppy, when curiosity led him to slip under the hedge." Cleveland

This book "stands out for good and sufficient reasons. It is good to look at, it is delightful to read aloud, it is a convenient size for small hands to hold, and above all it has an inner and outer harmony." N Y Her Trib Bks

Ask Mr Bear. Macmillan (N Y) 1932 unp illus $3.95, pa $1.25   E
   1 Animals—Stories 2 Birthdays—Fiction

Danny did not know what to give his mother for a birthday present, so he set out to ask various animals—the hen, the duck, the goose, the lamb, the cow and others, but he met with very little success until he met Mr Bear

This "will have a strong appeal to very young children because of its repetition, its use of the most familiar animals, its gay pictures and the cumulative effect of the story." N Y Times Bk Rev

The boats on the river; pictures by Jay Hyde Barnum. Viking 1946 31p illus lib. bdg. $6.95   E
   1 Ships
   ISBN 0-670-17725-3

"From the giant ocean liner down to the tiny rowboat, they are all shown here as they travel up or down

Flack, Marjorie—*Continued*

the great river, flowing from the mountains to the sea. Full of drama and bright color the pictures will please children of different ages. . . . The prose . . . [has a] quiet rhythm." Horn Bk

The story about Ping, by Marjorie Flack and Kurt Wiese. Viking 1933 unp illus lib. bdg. $4.50, pa 95¢
E

1 Ducks—Stories 2 China—Fiction
ISBN 0-670-67223-8; 0-670-05041-5
The story of Ping, a duck who lived on a house-boat in the Yangtze River

"An irresistible picture book with so much atmosphere and kindly humor that its readers of any age will unconsciously add to their understanding and appreciation of a far distant country. . . . Few books for little children have the genuinely artistic quality of this one." N Y Times Bk Rev

"Colorful illustrations by Kurt Wiese and a humorous text make this a good animal story and a delightful introduction to Chinese life." Children's Bks Too Good to Miss

Flory, Jane

We'll have a friend for lunch; pictures by Carolyn Croll. Houghton 1974 32p illus lib. bdg. $5.95 E

1 Cats—Stories
ISBN 0-395-18448-7
"Peaches is one of a group of cats who gather daily to hang around the fish store, boast about the birds they have caught, and 'talk tough' to compensate for being coddled at home. Peaches is the only cat who's never caught a bird, so she gets a book on birds and forms a birdwatcher's club. The goal is knowledge that will bring bird-catching skill—but by the time Peaches and her friends have watched some baby robins hatch and grow, they've lost their predatory interest." Chicago. Children's Bk Center

"It's hard to convey the humor, warmth and originality of this charming book, which owes its success to the estimable story-telling skills of the author and their perfect visualization by the artist." Pub W

Foster, Doris Van Liew

A pocketful of seasons; illus. by Talivaldis Stubis. Lothrop [1961] unp illus lib. bdg. $5.11 E

1 Seasons—Fiction
ISBN 0-688-51600-9
"The changing seasons bring different reactions to a farmer and a little boy. Illustrations effectively show changing moods and colors." Hodges. Bks for Elem Sch Libraries

Fox, Paula

Good Ethan; pictures by Arnold Lobel. Bradbury Press 1973 unp illus $4.95 E

ISBN 0-87888-057-7
"When Ethan's ball rolls across the street after his mother just told him he must not walk across, Ethan must rely on his own cleverness to get it back." New Bks for Young Readers

"Words and pictures are wonderfully balanced in a book which could have come straight out of the literal—yet endlessly imaginative—mind of a small child." Horn Bk

Françoise

The big rain. Scribner 1961 unp illus lib. bdg. $5.95 E

1 Domestic animals—Stories 2 Floods—Fiction 3 France—Fiction
ISBN 0-684-12400-9
"When the river rises and spreads over the farm the

little French girl Jeanne-Marie leads her grandmother and the animals to safety, signals rescuers from the roof, and, after the flood recedes, helps clean the mud from the village houses." Booklist

"The preschool group who would willingly share Jeanne-Marie's exciting danger, will become absorbed in the [author-illustrator's] pictures of busy animals and dramatic weather which give life to every page." Horn Bk

Jeanne-Marie at the fair. Scribner 1959 unp illus lib. bdg. $5.95 E

1 Fairs—Fiction 2 Sheep—Stories 3 France—Fiction
ISBN 0-684-92297-5
"Before Jeanne-Marie goes off with her father to the fair on the scooter, she ties her pet sheep Patapon to a tree in the garden. While Jeanne-Marie is enjoying all the sights and pleasures of the fair, the merry-go-round, the orangeade and the lucky spin, Patapon breaks loose and follows the road her mistress took. Patapon too has adventures in the big fairground before she finds Jeanne-Marie. Then they all return home tired and happy." Ontario

The author-illustrator's "gay and stylized illustrations (alternately in many colors and in pink, black, and white) enhance another ingenuous story about [the little French girl] Jeanne-Marie. . . . Just enough suspense for small listeners, and the perennial appeal of familiar characters." Chicago. Children's Bk Center

Jeanne-Marie counts her sheep. Scribner 1951 unp illus lib. bdg. $5.95, pa 95¢ E

1 Counting books 2 Sheep—Stories
ISBN 0-684-13175-7; 0-684-13034-3
"A little French girl counts the number of lambs her sheep may have and plans what she will buy with the money from their wool. . . . Designed to help the child . . . in learning his numbers." Pub W

"Another gay, colorful, and delightful picture book by a famous author-illustrator. . . . A natural for the nursery group." Library J

Noël for Jeanne-Marie. Scribner 1953 unp illus lib. bdg. $5.95 E

1 Christmas stories 2 Sheep—Stories 3 France—Fiction
ISBN 0-684-13165-X
Christmas is coming and Jeanne-Marie tells her sheep Patapon all about it. The picture story reveals what Jeanne-Marie did about Patapon's share in Christmas

"The colour and design of the pictures of the little crèche figures, the 'santons,' set the tone of the illustrations for the whole book, which gives a light-hearted and warm feeling of the Christmas season in the south of France." Ontario Library Rev

Springtime for Jeanne-Marie. Scribner 1955 unp illus lib. bdg. $5.95, pa 95¢ E

1 Sheep—Stories 2 Ducks—Stories 3 France—Fiction
ISBN 0-684-12719-9; 0-684-12633-8
In this "book about the little French girl and her two pets, the white duck Madelon swims away and is lost. In their search for her, Jeanne-Marie and Patapon, the little white sheep, find another friend as well." Library J

"Charming details of the French countryside are pictured with the author-illustrator's characteristic style. She makes good use of pastels, emphasized by rich browns and heavy black outlines." Chicago. Children's Bk Center

Freeman, Don

Corduroy; story and pictures by Don Freeman.
Viking 1968 32p illus lib. bdg. $4.95   E
1 Teddy bears—Fiction 2 Negroes—Fiction
ISBN 0-670-24133-4
"A winning, completely childlike picture book in
which a stuffed bear waiting hopefully in a toy department finds a home with a little Negro girl who wants
Corduroy so much that, when her mother refuses to
buy him, she comes back the next day with her own
money. Endearing, brightly colored pictures together
with the text affectionately recount Corduroy's
adventures in the big store one night as he hunts for a
button missing from his overalls and his happiness at
being taken home to live with Lisa." Booklist
"The art and story are direct and just right for the
very young who like bears and escalators." Bk World

Dandelion; story and pictures by Don Freeman.
Viking 1964 48p illus lib. bdg. $4.95, pa 95¢   E
1 Lions—Stories
ISBN 0-670-25532-7; 0-670-05004-0
"Dandelion, properly invited by note to Jennifer
Giraffe's tea-and-taffy party, pays no heed to the
words, 'Come as you are.' At his regular haircut
appointment he allows Lou Kangaroo and helper to do
him up properly, according to the new fashions for
lions. But pride goeth before a fall—and it is not
surprising that Jennifer's tall door is closed on the
unrecognizable stranger; nor that after being restored
by a heavy rainfall to something nearer his usual state,
he makes the party, after all. Mr. Freeman cleverly
depicts an assortment of personalities in his many
animal characters. The party scenes and the barber
shop are wonderfully amusing." Horn Bk

Fly high, fly low. Viking 1957 58p illus lib. bdg.
$5.95, pa $1.50   E
1 Pigeons—Stories 2 San Francisco—Fiction
ISBN 0-670-32218-0; 0-670-05068-7
"An enchanting story about a pigeon that made its
home in the letter "B" of a neon sign, high on a San
Francisco hill. There is terrific suspense when the
sign is torn down before the hero and his mate nest in
another sign over a bakery." Pub W
"The illustrations are almost breathtaking in their
color and sweep as they give a bird's eye view of San
Francisco." Chicago. Children's Bk Center

Norman the doorman. Viking 1959 64p illus lib.
bdg. $5.95, pa $1.50   E
1 Mice—Stories 2 Museums—Fiction
ISBN 0-670-51515-9; 0-670-05022-9
"Norman, the mouse doorman at the basement of
the museum, wins an award with a 'sculpture' made
from mousetrap parts. Full-color lithographs by the
author are as full of fun as the imaginative text."
Hodges. Bks for Elem Sch Libraries

Freschet, Berniece

The old bullfrog; illus. by Roger Duvoisin. Scribner
1968 unp illus $5.95, pa 95¢   E
1 Frogs—Stories 2 Herons—Stories
ISBN 0-684-13935-9; 0-684-13033-5
"A wise old bullfrog squats on a rock at the edge of
the pool. The hungry heron moves slowly and silently
toward the frog. His sharp beak opens and strikes
downward, but the old bullfrog plops into the water
and swims away. This simple story exploring the idea
of the survival of the fittest (or the wisest) is told
effectively with a minimum of words." Library J
"The illustrations are very handsome, the artist
using collage with restraint and color with profusion."
Chicago. Children's Bk Center

The web in the grass; illus. by Roger Duvoisin.
Scribner 1972 unp illus lib. bdg. $5.95   E
1 Spiders—Stories
ISBN 0-684-12956-6
This is the story of a little spider as she carries on
her daily activities—spinning a web to trap insects for
food, hiding from her enemies, and forming a sac
where she lays her eggs which soon hatch into hundreds of spiderlings
"This book is delightful because it presents spiders
as neutral animals who have specific life functions,
but who are inherently neither good nor bad. The life
cycle of the spider is presented in story form with
excellent color drawings." AAAS Science Booklist for
Children

Friskey, Margaret

Chicken Little, count-to-ten; pictures by Katherine
Evans. Childrens Press 1946 unp illus lib. bdg.
$5.25   E
1 Counting books 2 Chickens—Stories 3 Animals—
Stories
ISBN 0-516-03431-6
"Chicken Little's quest for a drink of water adds up
to a delightful counting book in which he meets one
cow, two elephants, three camels—finally ten scary
foxes." Bks for Deaf Children

Fujikawa, Gyo

A to Z picture book. Grosset 1974 unp illus $4.95,
lib. bdg. $4.99   E
1 Alphabet books
ISBN 0-448-11741-X; 0-448-13205-2
"You could travel far and never find as thoroughly
satisfying an alphabet book as Ms. Fujikawa's. Her
pictures (some in color and some in black-and-white)
are utterly captivating whether they feature her
endearing children, animals or things. The drawings
are precise and delicate and for each letter she presents not a measly one or two examples but a flock of
them: 'E' features edelweiss, Emma cleaning her
ears, elephant, Eskimo, Edward is eating, eggs, eye,
elf—all with appropriate action. A bonus follows some
letters, verses which the artist has created to express a
child's reactions to various experiences." Pub W

Gaeddert, LouAnn

Noisy Nancy Norris; illus. by Gioia Fiammenghi.
Doubleday 1965 63p illus lib. bdg. $3.95, pa 75¢ E
1 Apartment houses—Fiction 2 Cities and towns—
Fiction
ISBN 0-385-04749-5; 0-385-08812-4
"Nancy loved to bang, jump, rattle, run, shout and
laugh. She never kept still until the landlady
threatened eviction, and then she became such a sad,
quiet little girl that the landlady baked her some
favorite cookies and asked her please to make just a
little noise." Moorachian. What is a City?
This is "an unpretentious, thoroughly engaging picture-story book. The diverting colored illustrations
are most expressive." Booklist

Gág, Wanda

The A B C bunny; hand lettered by Howard Gág.
Coward-McCann 1933 unp illus $5.95, lib. bdg.
$4.69   E
1 Rabbits—Stories 2 Alphabet books 3 Stories in
rhyme
ISBN 0-698-20000-4; 0-698-30000-9
An alphabet book which tells in verse and pictures
the story of a little rabbit's adventures. The verse has
been set to music by the author's sister
"The book has the freshness of invention, and the
drawings, the beauty, humor and originality characteristic of this artist's work. The illustrations are original lithographs. N Y Times Bk Rev
Music on endpapers

Gág, Wanda—*Continued*

The funny thing. Coward-McCann 1929 unp illus lib. bdg. $3.99   E

ISBN 0-698-30097-1

"Once there was a funny thing, an 'animal' who ate dolls, but Bobo soon taught him to eat jum-jills so that his tail grew so long he had to sit on the top of a mountain and curl it around the sides. A nonsense picture-book." Pittsburgh

"Original plot, colorful words, and enticing black-and-white illustrations [by the author] make this a perennial favorite." Adventuring With Bks. 2d edition

Millions of cats. Coward-McCann 1928 unp illus $4.95, lib. bdg. $3.99   E

1 Cats—Stories

ISBN 0-698-20091-8; 0-698-30236-2

"An unusual story-picture book [illustrated by the author] about a very old man and very old woman who wanted one little cat and who found themselves with 'millions and billions and trillions of cats.' " St Louis

It is "a perennial favorite among children and takes a place of its own, both for the originality and strength of its pictures and the living folktale quality of its text." N Y Her Trib Bks

Snippy and Snappy. Coward-McCann 1931 unp illus lib. bdg. $3.99   E

1 Mice—Stories

ISBN 0-698-30319-9

This story tells how Snippy, and Snappy, two little field mice, ventured forth one day in search of cheese, and were rescued by their father just as they were about to investigate a mouse trap

"The text is fuller than in 'Millions of cats' [entered above]. . . . The drawings have Wanda Gág's distinctive power, sweep and rhythm." N Y Libraries

Garelick, May

Down to the beach; illus. by Barbara Cooney. [Four Winds] 1973 unp illus $5.95, lib. bdg. $5.92   E

1 Seashore

This is a description of a day at the beach: watching the activities of boats, seabirds and fishermen; swimming and playing in the sand; searching for seashells, listening to waves, and observing the tides; watching lighted buoys and listening to foghorns at night

"No plot, no dramatic action, but there's plenty of activity, plenty of variation, and lovely pictures to look at." Chicago. Children's Bk Center

Where does the butterfly go when it rains; with pictures by Leonard Weisgard. Young Scott Bks. 1961 unp illus lib. bdg. $4.95   E

1 Animals—Habits and behavior 2 Rain and rainfall

ISBN 0-201-09401-0

"Pictures of flowers and animals . . . adorn this simple picture book which shows children how various creatures protect themselves from the rain. The question about the butterfly however, is never answered." Pub W

"The soft blue misty pictures and the lilting poetic style create a mood of mystery and a real appreciation of nature. Excellent for discussion and pondering." Adventuring With Bks. 2d edition

Garrett, Helen

Angelo, the naughty one; pictures by Leo Politi. Viking 1944 40p illus lib. bdg. $5.95, pa 95¢   E

1 Mexico—Fiction

ISBN 0-670-12568-7; 0-670-05047-4

"Angelo the naughty one was so named because he was afraid of water and hated baths. Amusing text and charming pictures tell what happened to the little Mexican boy the day of his sister's wedding when,

refusing to take a bath, he ran off to the soldiers at the fort. A colorful picture book with a Mexican village background." Booklist

Gauch, Patricia Lee

Aaron and the Green Mountain Boys; pictures by Margot Tomes. Coward, McCann & Geoghegan 1972 62p illus lib. bdg. $4.69   E

1 Vermont—History—Fiction 2 U.S.—History—Revolution—Fiction

ISBN 0-698-30423-3

"A Break-of-day book"

"Based on a true Revolutionary War incident, this simply written, attractively illustrated story has action, excitement, and a very believable nine-year-old central character. When the Redcoats capture Fort Ticonderoga and head toward Bennington, Vermont, where supplies are stored, Aaron longs to deliver messages to the general or ride with his father and the Green Mountain Boys, but he is relegated to staying home and helping his grandfather bake bread for the army. Not until his father and the Green Mountain Boys arrive home exhausted and hungry from a long march does Aaron recognize the importance of bread to the war effort." Booklist

George, Jean

The hole in the tree; story and pictures by Jean George. Dutton 1957 unp illus $4.50   E

1 Ecology 2 Animals

"A clever little nature book that beginning readers can probably manage by themselves and one that younger children will find fascinating. In it Miss George describes a hole in a tree, tells how it was made and discusses the various insects, birds and animals [and children] that use it as a refuge or as a storage place." Pub W

Ginsburg, Mirra

The chick and the duckling; tr. [and adapted] from the Russian of V. Suteyev; pictures by Jose & Ariane Aruego. Macmillan (N Y) 1972 unp illus $5.95   E

1 Ducks—Stories 2 Chicken—Stories

"The adventures of a duckling who is a leader and a chick who follows suit. When the chick decides that an aquatic life is not for him, this brief selection for reading aloud comes to a humorous conclusion." Wis Library Bul

"The sunny simplicity of the illustrations is just right for a slight but engaging text, and they add a note of humor that is a nice foil for the bland directness of the story. . . . Easy enough to be read by a beginning reader, but too right (by length, subject, and level of concept) for the lap audience not to be directed primarily at them." Chicago. Children's Bk Center

Mushroom in the rain; adapted from the Russian of V. Suteyev; pictures by Jose Aruego & Ariane Dewey. Macmillan Pub. Co. 1974 unp illus lib. bdg. $4.95   E

1 Animals—Stories 2 Mushrooms—Stories

ISBN 0-02-736240-X

An ant, a butterfly, a mouse, a sparrow and a rabbit take shelter under a mushroom during a rainstorm. The other animals convince a fox who is hunting the rabbit that the rabbit couldn't possibly fit under a mushroom with all of them, and they themselves don't know how it was possible until a wise frog explains

"An intriguing variation on a somewhat familiar theme springs to life with irresistible pictures; subdued and rain-drenched at first, they fairly burst—after the storm—into a riot of joyous colors." Horn Bk

Ginsburg, Mirra—*Continued*

Three kittens; tr. [and adapted] from the Russian of V. Suteyev; pictures by Giulio Maestro. Crown 1973 unp illus lib. bdg. $4.95   E

1 Cats—Stories

ISBN 0-517-50328-X

Three kittens "chase a mouse into flour and all turn white, chase a toad through an old stovepipe and all turn black, dive into a pond after fish and come home as before: black, gray, white." Top of the News

"Economically told with a maximum of nine words on a page, this is a charming story. . . . The simple, expressive pictures in soft yellow and beige match the playful mood of the story." Sch Library J

Goodall, John S.

The adventures of Paddy Pork. Harcourt 1968 unp illus $4.75   E

1 Pigs—Stories 2 Stories without words

ISBN 0-15-201589-2

"While his mother is shopping, Paddy darts away to find a traveling circus that had caught his eye. The amusing story depicts how Paddy becomes lost in the woods and nearly [becomes] a wolf's dinner, his disastrous attempts to join the bears' act when he does find the circus, and his eventual happy reunion with his mother." Sch Library J

"There is no text to this picture book; detailed black-and-white drawings tell the whole story. . . . The insertion of half-width pages between the full-width pages gives the delightful effect of opening doors, peering around corners, and uncovering surprises." Booklist

The ballooning adventures of Paddy Pork. Harcourt 1969 unp illus $4.75   E

1 Pigs—Stories 2 Balloons—Fiction 3 Stories without words

ISBN 0-15-205693-9

"This is a story in pictures, each page alternating with a half-page, so that there is a partial change of scene with each turn of the half-page. Paddy, sailing along in his balloon, spies a pig about to be eaten by gorillas and rescues her; they are threatened by storms, monsters of the sea, and land creatures, but emerge unscathed and are greeted by welcoming throngs on their return." Chicago. Children's Bk Center

"As in the previous book, the cleverly interpolated half-pages accelerate the action. Without text the series of exploits leaves nothing unclear; the ink drawings abound in animated detail, fully characterizing both the endearing pigs and the grosser creatures. There is more real storytelling in this book than in many a picture book with a text." Horn Bk

Jacko. Harcourt 1972 c1971 unp illus $4.75   E

1 Monkeys—Stories 2 Stories without words

ISBN 0-15-239493-1

First published 1971 in England

"An exciting wordless picture book in which an organ grinder's monkey escapes and is reunited with his jungle parents." N Y Pub Library. Children's Bks & Recordings, 1972

"Artful half-pages hide part of what's happening, to be revealed when the 'reader' lifts them." Pub W

Paddy's evening out. Atheneum Pubs. 1973 unp illus $4.25   E

1 Pigs—Stories 2 Theater—Fiction 3 Stories without words

ISBN 0-689-30412-9

"A Margaret K. McElderry book"

"Paddy Pork makes a return appearance in another comfortably small picture book. The wordless drama

unfolds as a show within a show: When Paddy's lady friend drops her fan from her box seat at the theatre, Paddy gallantly tries to catch it and plunges over the rail into the orchestra pit below. Pandemonium follows, as poor Paddy—in the classic low comedy tradition—flounders about onstage and off and finally, as the comic hero, brings down the house." Horn Bk

"A very successful story without words in . . . small (5″x7″) format with alternating half pages which partially change the previous picture's action. . . . Taking their cue from the red velvet theater curtains, the tempera illustrations are in deep, rich colors. Small groups or individual children will be delighted as Paddy's predicament worsens with each turned page." Sch Library J

Shrewbettina's birthday. Harcourt 1971 c1970 unp illus $3.50   E

1 Shrews—Stories 2 Mice—Stories 3 Birthdays—Fiction 4 Stories without words

ISBN 0-15-274080-5

First published 1970 in England

"As Shrewbettina goes marketing for her birthday party, her purse is snatched by a thief. A dashing young friend apprehends the villain and restores her money; and the day ends happily with a gala evening of feasting and dancing." Horn Bk

"John Goodall has used half-page insertions between the pages to add an extra bit of action to a story without text. The Victorian dress and the English village setting give a quaint and pastoral flavor to the story. . . . Soft, sentimental drawings have a pastel charm, telling the tale very clearly." Chicago. Children's Bk Center

Goudey, Alice E.

The day we saw the sun come up; illus. by Adrienne Adams. Scribner 1961 unp illus lib. bdg. $5.95   E

1 Sun

ISBN 0-684-12365-7

"Two children rise before dawn and see the sun come up for the first time in their lives . . . then they note, through the day how their shadows change as the sun moves. At dusk their mother explains night and day, and the movement of the earth. The prose is simple and childlike, the explanations are lucid and accurate, yet there is a lyric quality to the writing. The illustrations are soft in color and quality, the scenes at sunrise and sunset are especially lovely, with delicate nuances of tone." Chicago. Children's Bk Center

"This little book edges toward the thin lines that divide poetry from science and entertainment from instruction. Beginning as a summer holiday romp, complete with picnic lunch, the story gradually turns an analytical eye toward the sun overhead." Christian Sci Monitor

Graham, Al

Timothy Turtle; pictures by Tony Palazzo. Viking 1946 unp illus lib. bdg. $4.95, pa 85¢   E

1 Turtles—Stories 2 Stories in rhyme

ISBN 0-670-71579-4; 0-670-05035-0

First published by Robert Welch Publishing Company

"Irresistible verse destined to be sung and shouted all over the house, and pictures full of fun and laughter tell what happened when Timothy Turtle decided to be an adventurer. Took-a-look Lake and the business firm of Turtle and Drake, with Timothy climbing the hill near by, belong among the favorite picture books in every household of children. The verse is exceedingly clever and musical as well as amusing and the drawings are both funny and knowledgeable." Horn Bk

Map on end papers

Graham, Margaret Bloy

Be nice to spiders. Harper 1967 unp illus $3.95, lib. bdg. $4.43
E

1 Spiders—Stories 2 Animals—Stories 3 Zoological gardens—Fiction
ISBN 0-06-022072-4; 0-06-022073-2

"The story of Helen, Billy's pet spider, who weaves her webs in the local zoo and thus helps keep the flies off the backs of the animals. The title comes from an order issued by the zoo superintendent to his cleaning staff to leave spider webs alone." Christian Sci Monitor

The "slight humor and fitting cartoon illustrations [by the author] will appeal to young children." Bruno Bks for School Libraries, 1968

Benjy's dog house. Harper 1973 unp illus $4.50, lib. bdg. $4.43
E

1 Dogs—Stories
ISBN 0-06-022083-X; 0-06-022084-8
Illustrated by the author

"Benjy is cozy and happy with his human family until the father decides the dog is too big to sleep with Jimmy and Linda and builds a doghouse, outside. Benjy is miserable and lonely; he cuts out to find a better place to sleep. . . . [He] at last finds a friendly baker who lets him spend the night. Benjy leads a double life, for a while, playing with Linda and Jimmy during the day and sleeping at the baker's at night. But an unexpected development reveals the situation to his owners and the father relents." Pub W

"Benjy is a particularly amiable animal character, and there is just enough in his story (both in the length and in the conflict resolution) for the read-aloud audience, which can also enjoy the happy and credible ending and the light but perky humor of the pictures." Chicago. Children's Bk Center

Gramatky, Hardie

Hercules; the story of an old-fashioned fire engine; written and illus. by Hardie Gramatky. Putnam 1940 unp illus lib. bdg. $4.97
E

1 Fire engines—Fiction
ISBN 0-399-60240-2
"A dramatic picture storybook in brilliant colors in which [Hercules] the old horse-drawn fire engine becomes a hero and saves the City Hall. Children will delight in the gusto and fun." N Y Pub Library

Little Toot; pictures and story by Hardie Gramatky. Putnam 1939 unp illus $5.95, lib. bdg. $4.97
E

1 Tugboats—Fiction
ISBN 0-399-20144-0; 0-399-60422-7
Story and pictures describe the early career of a saucy little tug-boat too pleased with himself to do any real work until one day when he found himself out on the ocean in a storm. Then Little Toot earned the right to be called a hero

The illustrations are "mobile, exciting affairs in nautical blues and greens and stormy blacks, painted in a dashing offhand manner which exactly matches the bravado of Little Toot." N Y Times Bk Rev

"Mr. Gramatky tells his story with humor and enjoyment, giving, too, a genuine sense of the water front in both pictures and story." Horn Bk

Grant, Sandy

Hey, look at me! A city ABC; photographed by Larry Mulvehill. Bradbury Press 1973 unp illus $5.95
E

1 Alphabet books 2 Cities and towns—Fiction
ISBN 0-87888-060-7
"A book of action photographs shows city children at work and play, and also functions as an alphabet book. . . . Each page has the action word, the letter

in upper and lower cases, and a large picture, sometimes two or three in sequence." Chicago. Children's Bk Center

"All activities depicted are significantly familiar to small children while the majority of the clear black-and-white photographs show motion scenes peculiar to the city and use children as their subjects. There are direct, uncomplicated spatial relationships between the words, the photographs, and the pages on which they are placed." Booklist

Greenaway, Kate

A Apple pie. Warne n.d. unp illus $4.95
E

1 Alphabet books
ISBN 0-7232-0590-6
A reprint of the Greenaway A B C book, with the original illustrations in color, which first appeared in 1886, published by Routledge and Sons

A picture "book in which little girls in quaint frilled dresses with flowing sashes, and little boys in long breeches, merrily demolish A—apple pie." Toronto

Greenfield, Eloise

She come bringing me that little baby girl; illus. by John Steptoe. Lippincott 1974 unp illus $5.95
E

1 Brothers and sisters—Fiction 2 Infants—Fiction 3 Negroes—Fiction
ISBN 0-397-31586-4
"For Kevin, who had wanted a baby brother, the arrival of his pink-shawled baby sister proved a bitter disappointment. Not only was she the wrong sex, she also cried too much, had too many wrinkles to look new, and most provoking of all she occupied everyone's attention. How he changed his opinion about his sister is developed in a sensitive first-person text, complemented and extended by the poignant, darkly brilliant, three-color illustrations. A familiar situation handled with rare charm, culminating in a visual and verbal paean to familial love." Horn Bk

Gretz, Susanna

Teddy bears 1 to 10; written and illus. by Susanna Gretz. Follett 1969 unp illus $4.95, lib. bdg. $4.98
E

1 Counting books
ISBN 0-695-88460-3; 0-695-48460-5
This book is "simple, and childlike. Each pair of pages has a readily evocative phrase and a teddy-bear picture, beginning with 'I teddy bear' and the furry toy pictured on the opposite page. And then, '2 old teddy bears,' '3 dirty old teddy bears,' '4 teddy bears in the wash.' A restful, unpretentious counting book in soft warm colors." Horn Bk

Grifalconi, Ann

City rhythms. Bobbs [1966 c1965] unp illus $4.95
E

1 Negroes—Fiction 2 New York (City)—Fiction
ISBN 0-672-50253-4
Illustrated by the author
"A handsomely illustrated book about the exciting sounds of . . . [New York City] on a hot summer day. Jimmy, a little Negro boy, suddenly becomes aware of the sounds of the subway, the market place, the pigeons on the roof, and the many other rhythms of the things about him as he listens intently. A delightful combination of text and pictures which will appeal to the small child's sense of wonder and imagination." We Build Together

Grossman, Barney

Black means . . . by Barney Grossman with Gladys Groom and the pupils of P.S. 150, The Bronx, New York; illus. by Charles Bible. Hill & Wang 1970 unp illus $4.95
E

1 Black—Fiction
ISBN 0-8090-3037-3

Grossman, Barney—*Continued*

"The pejorative uses of the word 'black' have persisted so long that they have been built into the language with resulting damage to the self image of some black people. In an effort to overcome this, the authors, teachers and pupils in a Bronx public school re-evaluate the word and come up with some beautiful new meanings." Wolfe. About 100 Bks

"The series of pictures that bear such captions are attractive, strong and realistic. Some of the captions have vigor and validity, but the level of concept is erratic." Chicago. Children's Bk Center

Guilfoile, Elizabeth

Nobody listens to Andrew; illus. by Mary Stevens. Follett 1957 27p illus lib. bdg. $2.97   E

ISBN 0-695-46345-4

"A Follett Beginning-to-read book"

"Andrew tries to tell each member of his family and a neighbor what he saw in his bed but each one is too busy to . . . [listen]. Only when Andrew screams out that he saw a bear, do they pay attention." Chicago. Children's Bk Center

Gurney, Nancy

The king, the mice and the cheese, by Nancy and Eric Gurney. Beginner Bks. 1965 63p illus $2.95, lib. bdg. $3.69   E

1 Mice—Stories 2 Animals—Stories

ISBN 0-394-80039-7; 0-394-90039-1

"I can read it all myself"

Also available in a bilingual Spanish-English edition, lib. bdg. $3.99 (ISBN 0-394-91600-X and in a bilingual French-English edition for $3.50, lib. bdg. $4.99 (ISBN 0-394-80173-3; 0-394-90173-8)

The king loves to eat cheese, but unfortunately so do the mice. When the royal food supply is raided by the mice, the king calls on his wise men and on the animals of the kingdom for a solution to the problem

Hader, Berta

The big snow, by Berta and Elmer Hader. Macmillan (N Y) 1948 unp illus $5.95, pa $1.25   E

1 Animals

Awarded the Caldecott Medal, 1949

This book shows "the birds and animals which come for the food put out by an old couple after a big snow." Hodges. Bks for Elem Sch Libraries

"There is no real story but children will enjoy the animals' busy preparation for winter and the book catches some of the excitement of the first snowfall." Christian Sci Monitor

"Both the coloured and black and white pictures are descriptive. . . . They carry through the feeling of the story in a dignified and enjoyable way." Ontario Library Rev

Handforth, Thomas

Mei Li. Doubleday 1938 unp illus $4.95, lib. bdg. $5.70, pa 95¢   E

1 China—Fiction 2 Fairs—Fiction

ISBN 0-385-07401-8; 0-385-07639-8; 0-385-08155-3

Awarded the Caldecott Medal, 1939

The story "tells of Mei Li, a little girl of North China, and her day at the Fair in the town and of her part in all the doings along with her brother San Yu, his kitten Igo and her thrush, until at the end of a long day she goes riding home on a camel just in time to greet the Kitchen God at midnight on New Year's Eve." Horn Bk

"This gay, brief story, with its really wonderful big black and white drawings, illustrated by [the author] will give children a wealth of clear, simple impressions of traditional Chinese life. . . . [It is an] original and artistic picture book." Sat Rev

Hawes, Judy

The goats who killed the leopard; a story of Ethiopia; illus. by Ric Estrada. Crowell 1970 48p illus (Stories from many lands) $3.75, lib. bdg. $4.50   E

1 Ethiopia—Fiction

ISBN 0-690-33224-6; 0-690-33225-4

Abebe, a young shepherd in Ethiopia, must decide between the old magic of the medicine man and the new medicine when two of his sheep become ill and threaten the whole flock. Abebe's determination, and a traditional folktale, convince his father that the new ways can help his people

Hawkinson, John

The old stump; story and pictures by John Hawkinson. Whitman, A. 1965 unp illus $3.75   E

1 Animals

ISBN 0-8075-5969-5

An old tree stump which is the home for a family of mice is visited by little creatures from the forest

"Here is a truly lovely picture book [which] . . . may well serve as a first nature book for the picture book age." Library J

Hawkinson, Lucy

Picture book farm; illus. by Robert Pippenger. Childrens Press 1971 unp illus lib. bdg. $5.25   E

1 Farm life 2 Animals

ISBN 0-516-03463-4

Examines the variety of animals which appear in an illustration of farm life

Hazen, Barbara Shook

The gorilla did it; illus. by Ray Cruz. Atheneum Pubs. 1974 unp illus $6.95   E

1 Gorillas—Stories

ISBN 0-689-30138-3

"An imaginary ape interrupts the boy's nap, and together they make a wreck of his room, to his mother's annoyance. She can hardly believe him when he lays the blame on a gorilla she can't see." Sat Rev

"The absolute pitch of familiarity in the dialog and line drawings, which contrast the huge, innocent-but-destructive gorilla in blue with everything unimagined in black and white, makes a picture book humorously tuned into a child's fantasy friend without making fun of it. The child could pass for boy or girl, and the mommy is archetypal: plenty of room for identification here." Booklist

Where do bears sleep? Illus. by Ian E. Staunton. Addison-Wesley 1970 42p illus lib. bdg. $5.95   E

1 Sleep—Poetry

ISBN 0-201-02801-8

"A charming 'good-night' picture book tells where different animals take their rest and, at the end, where a child sleeps." Booklist

"The print is large, with the animal's name in a contrasting color, so that the book is visually dramatic as well as informative." Sat Rev

Heide, Florence Parry

Sound of sunshine, sound of rain; pictures by Kenneth Longtemps. Parents Mag. Press 1970 unp illus $4.95, lib. bdg. $4.59   E

1 Negroes—Fiction 2 Blind—Fiction

ISBN 0-8193-0422-0; 0-8193-0423-9

"A blind boy's experiences in discovering his world—including 'color'—are captured in sensitive text and brilliant pictures." NY Pub Library. The Black Experience in Children's Bks

Heilbroner, Joan

The happy birthday present; pictures by Mary Chalmers. Harper 1962 illus $2.95, lib. bdg. $3.79

E

ISBN 0-06-022270-0

"An I can read book"

"Two small brothers with limited funds went shopping for a birthday present for mother. Stores where they tried to find something within their budget kept giving them tidbits, until they were finally able to construct a most unusual gift." Chicago Sunday Tribune

"Their excursions are realistic. Davy's behavior is entertaining, and the conversation captures remarkably the ingenious childlike attitude." Chicago. Children's Bk Center

Heyward, Du Bose

The country bunny and the little gold shoes, as told to Jenifer; pictures by Marjorie Flack. Houghton 1939 unp illus lib. bdg. $5.95, pa $1.25

E

1 Rabbits—Stories 2 Easter—Stories

ISBN 0-395-15990-3; 0-395-18557-2

This is an Easter story for young readers which grew out of a story the author has told and retold to his young daughter. It is of the little country rabbit who wanted to become one of the five Easter bunnies, and how she managed to realize her ambition

"It is really imaginative and well written. It ought to be read to little children. . . . The colored pictures are just right too." New Yorker

Hill, Elizabeth Starr

Evan's corner; illus. by Nancy Grossman. Holt 1967 unp illus lib. bdg. $5.95, pa $1.45

E

1 Negroes—Fiction 2 Apartment houses—Fiction

ISBN 0-03-059835-4; 0-03-080123-0

"Creating a haven in a corner of [his family's] . . . crowded apartment brought real satisfaction to Evan only after he shared his talent for decoration with brother Adam." Top of the News

"Despite the author's purposeful earnestness, an appealing little boy emerges in the simple, sensitive storytelling. Abundant illustrations—done in soft water colors—present vivid, warmly sympathetic views of Evan and his life at home and in the city's restless, kaleidoscopic streets." Horn Bk

Hitte, Kathryn

Mexicali soup; written by Kathryn Hitte and William D. Hayes; pictures by Anne Rockwell. Parents Mag. Press 1970 unp illus $4.95, lib. bdg. $4.59 E

1 Cookery, Mexican—Fiction

ISBN 0-8193-0402-6; 0-8193-0403-4

"Now that they had moved to the city, Mama looked forward to her shopping. The grocery stores had the best of everything—the potatoes, celery, peppers, tomatoes, garlic, and onions for the Mexicali soup that her family all said was the best soup in the world. But—as she shops, Mama meets one after another of her children, and each has learned that in the city one doesn't eat this or that for some reason. They persuade her to leave out various ingredients. Mama comes to a slow boil, and teaches them a lesson. Gathered at the table, anticipating the best soup in the world, they are served 'soup' with no onions, garlic, tomatoes, etc. A subtle lesson in over-adapting to the Joneses, and a good picture of a cheery Chicano family, not often placed in an urban setting." Sutherland. The Best in Children's Bks

Hoban, Lillian

Arthur's Christmas cookies; words and pictures by Lillian Hoban. Harper 1972 63p illus $2.95, lib. bdg. $3.79

E

1 Christmas stories 2 Chimpanzees—Stories 3 Baking—Fiction

ISBN 0-06-022367-7; 0-06-022368-5

"An I can read book"

When Arthur decides to make Christmas cookies for his parents, a "disastrous mistake in the ingredients makes the cookies inedible but the story ends happily when Arthur turns them into holiday decorations." Pub W

The characters are chimpanzees but "are endearingly like human children. Their conversation is realistically childlike, as are their actions. The Christmas setting is appealing, the plot has problem, conflict, and solution yet is not too complex for the beginning independent reader, and the simplicity and humor make the book an appropriate one for reading aloud to preschool children also." Chicago. Children's Bk Center

Arthur's Honey Bear; story and pictures by Lillian Hoban. Harper 1974 62p illus $2.95, lib. bdg. $3.43

E

1 Chimpanzees—Stories 2 Teddy bears—Fiction

ISBN 0-06-022369-3; 0-06-022370-7

"An I can read book"

Arthur, a chimpanzee-child, is growing up. "Although he won't admit it, he is relieved when no one buys the ragged Honey Bear at his personal spring-cleaning rummage sale. He finally—and grudgingly—sells Honey Bear to his little sister, but later makes the happy discovery that he is now Honey Bear's uncle and can once again openly lavish warmth on his toy." Booklist

The "dialogue is pricelessly childlike, with Arthur's ambivalance felt but never stated, and the expressively humorous watercolors are perfect for playing up Arthur's predicament." Library J

The sugar snow spring; words and pictures by Lillian Hoban. Harper 1973 39p illus $3.95, lib. bdg. $3.79

E

1 Mice—Stories

ISBN 0-06-022333-2; 0-06-022334-0

"Everett Mouse didn't come back from a food-hunting expedition, so son Oscar must try to get grain and straw for the expected new baby's bed. When things look their grimmest, an Easter Rabbit rescues and reunites the family." Chicago

"Pale blue, green, and yellow drawings complement the appealing story which will be enjoyed by young animal lovers." Sch Library J

Hoban, Russell

A baby sister for Frances; pictures by Lillian Hoban. Harper 1964 unp illus $3.95, lib. bdg. $3.79, pa $1.95

E

1 Badgers—Stories 2 Infants—Fiction

ISBN 0-06-02233-5; 0-06-022336-7; 0-06-443006-5

Frances, the badger "has a baby sister who, in Frances' opinion, gets more than her share of parental attention. One evening after supper Frances packs her knapsack and runs away—to a place under the dining room table which is cozy, near the cooky supply, and close enough to hear her parents talk about missing her. The author's tender treatment of a familiar situation will delight and profit, both children and parents in homes with new babies." Booklist

The illustrations echo "the gentle humor and the warmth of the story." Chicago. Children's Bk Center

A bargain for Frances; pictures by Lillian Hoban. Harper 1970 62p illus $2.95, lib. bdg. $3.79

E

1 Badgers—Stories 2 Friendship—Fiction

ISBN 0-06-022329-4; 0-06-022330-8

"An I can read book"

"The story centers around friendship and trust, as

Hoban, Russell—*Continued*

Frances is tricked into buying her friend Thelma's plastic tea set with the red flowers instead of the china set that she's been saving for. Even though Thelma has insisted on 'no backsies' (a significant clue for any child), the story ends happily with a more sophisticated Frances, the proud possessor of Thelma's new china tea set." Horn Bk

"The writing is blithe and natural, the situation familiar, the development satisfying. The book can be used for reading aloud as well as for independent readers, and the humor of the story obviates any hint of preaching." Chicago. Children's Bk Center

Bedtime for Frances; illus. by Garth Williams. Harper 1960 unp illus $3.95, lib. bdg. $3.79, pa $1.95   E

1 Badgers—Stories

ISBN 0-06-022350-2; 0-06-022351-0; 0-06-443005-7

"A little badger with a lively imagination comes up with one scheme after another to put off going to sleep but father badger proves himself as smart as his daughter." Bookmark

"Nothing at all unusual in this story—but Mr. Williams was inspired to make Frances a small round appealing badger, with kindly badger parents, although badgers are not mentioned in the text. The soft humorous pictures of these lovable animals in human predicaments are delightful." Horn Bk

Best friends for Frances; pictures by Lillian Hoban. Harper 1969 31p illus $3.95, lib. bdg. $3.79, pa $1.95   E

1 Badgers—Stories 2 Friendship—Fiction

ISBN 0-06-022327-8; 0-06-022328-6; 0-06-443008-1

"Miffed because her friend Albert will not let her join a boys' ball game, Frances strikes back. She packs a . . . picnic lunch, well aware that Albert will notice, permits her forlorn younger sister, Gloria, to join the party and marches off bearing a sign that says, 'Best Friends Outing—No Boys.' Albert pleads, Frances condescends, and they have a gourmet bash followed by baseball for three." Sat Rev

"Text and pictures are full of the humor and the homely details of family life that characterize the stories of Frances the Badger and make them beloved by both children and adults." Horn Bk

A birthday for Frances; pictures by Lillian Hoban. Harper 1968 31p illus $3.95, lib. bdg. $3.79, pa $1.95   E

1 Badgers—Stories 2 Birthdays—Fiction

ISBN 0-06-022338-3; 0-06-022339-1; 0-06-443007-3

"Jealous Frances turns her back on the preparations for little sister Gloria's birthday party, managing to make herself feel left out. Mother Badger wisely waits for Frances to think of buying a present with her own allowance, and Father Badger gently offers to take care of the gift candy after half of it disappears. At the party, however, Frances' generosity comes to the fore, and she and Gloria exchange words of goodwill." Booklist

"The illustrations are a charming accompaniment to a story that has humor, affection, and the appeal of a familiar situation." Chicago. Children's Bk Center

Bread and jam for Frances; pictures by Lillian Hoban. Harper 1964 31p illus $3.95   E

1 Badgers—Stories

ISBN 0-06-022359-6; 0-06-022360-X

A "tale of how Frances, a badger child, comes to recognize that a varied diet has more interest than her temporarily permissive feast of bread and jam." Children's Bks. 1964

"The diverting picture-book story makes its point

for fussy-eaters—and their parents—gently, amusingly, and most effectively." Booklist

Emmet Otter's Jug-Band Christmas; pictures by Lillian Hoban. Parents Mag. Press 1971 unp illus $4.95, lib. bdg. $4.59   E

1 Otters—Stories 2 Christmas stories

ISBN 0-8193-0404-2; 0-8193-0405-0

A "story of a poor Otter family, young Emmet and his widowed mother, and of their determination to give each other a very special present for Christmas. Although their plans don't quite turn out as expected, they are rewarded with something more special than any present." Pub W

"A warm, unsentimental story with expressive, old-fashioned colored illustrations." Booklist

Harvey's hideout; pictures by Lillian Hoban. Parents Mag. Press 1969 unp illus $4.95, lib. bdg. $4.59   E

1 Muskrats—Stories

ISBN 0-8193-0237-6; 0-8193-0238-4

"Mildred Muskrat calls Harvey a selfish, inconsiderate, stupid no-good little brother and Harvey says she is a loud-mouthed, bossy, mean, and rotten big sister. Each goes off supposedly to a happy meeting with friends; in reality Harvey's secret club has a membership of one and Mildred's only party guest is her doll." Booklist

"The author reveals his remarkable understanding of the psychology of the young child and his ear for children's conversation. The full-color illustrations are appealing but a trifle lush and over-pretty. . . . Children will identify with Harvey and Mildred and will appreciate the humorous way in which they solve their problems." Horn Bk

How Tom beat Captain Najork and his hired sportsmen; illus. by Quentin Blake. Atheneum Pubs. 1974 unp illus $6.95   E

ISBN 0-689-30441-2

Tom's aunt, Miss Fidget Wonkham-Strong, disapproves of his constant fooling around and calls in Captain Najork and his hired sportsmen to teach Tom a lesson. But Tom beats them at their own games

"The story and Quentin Blake's pictures are a combination of originality and hilarity, from start to quirky close." Pub W

The little Brute family; pictures by Lillian Hoban. Macmillan (N Y) 1966 unp illus $4.50, pa $1.25   E

"A family of five disagreeable Brutes and their unpleasant home life are happily transformed when Baby Brute brings home a little lost good feeling which he finds wandering around in a field of daisies. The beguiling story and pictures present a lesson in human relationships which is both funny and meaningful to small children." Booklist

The Mole family's Christmas; pictures by Lillian Hoban. Parents Mag. Press 1969 unp illus $4.95, lib. bdg. $4.59   E

1 Moles (Animals)—Stories 2 Christmas stories

ISBN 0-8193-0293-7; 0-8193-0294-5

"An amusing story of a mole family who, through the efforts of their enterprising son, receive the gift of a telescope from the fat man in the red suit which enables them to see the stars. Engaging illustrations add to the charm and appeal of the book." Booklist

Nothing to do; pictures by Lillian Hoban. Harper 1964 32p illus lib. bdg. $3.79   E

1 Opossums—Stories

ISBN 0-06-022390-1

"Walter Possum, like most other young children, can never think of anything to do until his father gives

Hoban, Russell—*Continued*

him a magic something-to-do stone. A useful lesson is lightly veiled in this slight but pleasing story that second-graders can read for themselves." Sch Library J

"Walter Possum and his little sister Charlotte have those human qualities that make the behavior of Frances the badger child so engaging and self-reflecting for young listeners." Horn Bk

The sorely trying day; pictures by Lillian Hoban. Harper 1964 unp illus lib. bdg. $4.43   E

1 Family—Fiction

ISBN 0-06-022421-5

"Poor, weary father, after 'a sorely trying day,' came home to a commotion of brawling children, misbehaving pets, and a distraught mother. One by one the guilty characters repented, confessed, and submitted to a week's punishment . . . and peace and contentment were restored." Horn Bk

A "burlesque of the Victorian moral tale. . . . Delightfully illustrated." Chicago. Children's Bk Center

Hoban, Tana

Circles, triangles and squares. Macmillan Pub. Co. 1974 unp illus lib. bdg. $4.95   E

1 Size and shape

ISBN 0-02-744830-4

"There is no division of the material into sections and no text here, simply a series of photographs in which the three most familiar geometric forms occur. Often more than one shape appears in the photograph." Chicago. Children's Bk Center

"An imaginative exercise for the development of visual awareness." Horn Bk

Count and see. Macmillan (N Y) 1972 unp illus lib. bdg. $5.95, pa 95¢   E

1 Counting books

"A counting book that moves from 1 to 15, then—in tens—to 50, and then to 100. The left hand pages are black, with large numerals and the number-word in white, and with large white dots to corroborate the counting. The right hand pages are clear photographs in black and white, all objects that are easy to recognize: 4 children, 8 windows, 12 eggs in a carton, 15 cookies on a baking sheet, 40 peanuts, 100 peas in their pods, ten per pod." Chicago. Children's Bk Center

"The texture of the photographs, the vivid capturing of small objects, and the graphic excellence of its design make the book outstanding in comparison with the many dismal, unattractive counting books in print." Horn Bk

Look again! Macmillan (N Y) 1971 unp illus $5.95   E

1 Nature photography

"This captivating book of photographs invites the reader to look once through a two-inch cut-out square at a pattern or portion of something larger. On the next page, the complete picture of the object is revealed. On the verso of the second page is another view of the object. And so, as each set is displayed, one is impelled to look again and again and again. This unusual and exciting book is one that should not be missed." Wis Library Bul

Over, under & through, and other spatial concepts. Macmillan (N Y) 1973 unp illus lib. bdg. $4.95   E

In brief text and photographs, the author depicts several spatial concepts—over, under, through, on, in, around, across, between, beside, below, against, and behind

"Children who are confused by these concepts may need help understanding that many of the pictures illustrate more than one concept. However, both the photographs and the format, with the words printed large on broad yellow bands at the beginning of each section, are uncluttered and appealing." Booklist

Push pull, empty full; a book of opposites. Macmillan (N Y) 1972 unp illus $4.95, pa $1.25   E

1 English language—Synonyms and antonyms

Brief text and black and white photographs illustrate fifteen pairs of opposites—push pull, empty full, wet dry, in out, up down, thick thin, whole broken, front back, big little, first last, many few, heavy light, together apart, left right, and day night

"Most of the meanings are immediately apparent from the pictures although some children may have difficulty with thick (elephants) and thin (flamingos)." Booklist

Shapes and things. Macmillan (N Y) 1970 unp illus lib. bdg. $4.95   E

1 Esthetics

This book, without text, contains photograms—photographs made without a camera by placing an object in direct contact with light-sensitive photographic paper. The author's purpose is to introduce new ways of seeing and to present the understated beauty of pure shape

"It is a book through which a small child may wish to browse, alone or with a friend to share the pleasure of recognizing simple things by their shapes. . . . The objects, white on black, are almost wholly in silhouette, although there are hints of shadow. Some of the pages are almost blunt: a single apple. Some are arranged in patterns on a theme: tools, sewing things, kitchen utensils. Very attractive, useful for discussion, good for stirring perceptual acuteness." Sat Rev

Where is it? Macmillan Pub. Co. 1974 unp illus lib. bdg. $4.95   E

1 Rabbits—Stories 2 Easter—Stories 3 Stories in rhyme

ISBN 0-02-744070-2

In this story in rhyme, illustrated with photographs, a rabbit searches for its own Easter basket full of garden vegetables

The author's "photography here is outstanding. . . . The type is large and the scanning lines short while some end words rhyme—all factors considered helpful to the decoding practice of the youngest readers as well as older reluctants." Library J

Hoberman, Mary Ann

All my shoes come in twos, by Mary Ann and Norman Hoberman. Little 1957 40p illus $4.95   E

1 Shoes and shoe industry 2 Stories in rhyme

ISBN 0-316-36728-1

"A story in rhyme tells about all kinds of shoes and uses the idea of two over and over again." Hardgrove. Math Library—Elem and Jr High Sch

Hoff, Syd

Danny and the dinosaur; story and pictures by Syd Hoff. Harper 1958 64p illus $2.95, lib. bdg. $3.79   E

1 Dinosaurs—Stories

ISBN 0-06-022465-7; 0-06-022466-5

Also available in a Spanish language edition lib. bdg. $3.79 (ISBN 0-06-022469-X)

"An I can read book"

The story is "about an amiable dinosaur who leaves his home in the museum to stroll about town and play with Danny, a small boy who loves dinosaurs. The dinosaur talks (of course) to Danny's friends and plays games with them, visits the zoo, goes to a baseball

Hoff, Syd—*Continued*

game and enjoys, with a beatific smile, an ice cream cone." Chicago. Children's Bk Center

"The bold, humorous, colored pictures convey the imaginative story of the wonderful day the dinosaur steps out of the museum to play with Danny [and share his exploits around town]. Because of the simple vocabulary and sentence structure, first-graders can actually read this story." Library J

My Aunt Rosie; story and pictures by Syd Hoff. Harper 1972 32p illus $3.50, lib. bdg. $3.79   E

1 Family—Fiction
ISBN 0-06-022503-3; 0-06-022504-1

Sherman does not enjoy seeing his aunt because she makes a fuss over him. But when he misses a visit, he realizes how much she means to him

The "pictures are a delightful accompaniment to this slight but warm and enjoyable story." Pub W

Stanley; story and pictures by Syd Hoff. Harper 1962 64p illus $2.95, lib. bdg. $3.79   E

1 Cave dwellers—Fiction
ISBN 0-06-022535-1; 0-06-022536-X

"An I can read book"

Stanley is "a caveman 'sport' ahead of his time (and perhaps ours) who wishes to live at peace with his neighbors, paint cave pictures, be kind to animals and cultivate his garden. This problem creature is unacceptable to his fellows until he invents a house to live in and calls caves 'old fashioned.' " N Y Her Trib Bks

Thunderhoof; story and pictures by Syd Hoff. Harper 1971 32p illus $2.50, lib. bdg. $3.43   E

"An Early I can read book"
1 Horses—Stories
ISBN 0-06-022559-9; 0-06-022560-2

The story of how Thunderhoof, the last great horse to run wild out West, is at last tamed

"The bold-lined humor of illustrations with a story to match will hold its own between TV and could-be." Sch Library J

When will it snow? Pictures by Mary Chalmers. Harper 1971 unp illus $3.50, lib. bdg. $3.79   E

1 Winter—Fiction
ISBN 0-06-022553-X; 0-06-022554-8

"A child just old enough to remember the fun of playing in the snow asks his mother, now that it is winter, when the snow will come. 'Soon,' she tells him, but it isn't soon enough. Bears go into hibernation, the winds are cold and it rains, people put up Christmas decorations—and the sled waits. One night as the boy is going to bed, his mother says, 'Now,' and the story closes with a delighted child looking out at the whirling snowflakes. The small-scale, softly colored illustrations are attractive, the text written simply, the story slight and low-keyed." Chicago. Children's Bk Center

Hoffman, Phyllis

Steffie and me; pictures by Emily Arnold McCully. Harper 1970 32p illus lib. bdg. $3.79   E

1 Friendship—Fiction 2 Negroes—Fiction
ISBN 0-06-022564-5

"The everyday activities of a lovely little white girl with her best friend, Steffie, a black child, are narrated in first person in a sprightly picture book. The narrator's comments on finger paint 'It tastes delicious and it makes your teeth green,' on her brother, 'My brother wants to be a lawyer and a garbage collector,' and on a classmate 'Stephanie and I are going to marry him' have an uncontrived humor. The three-color illustrations capture the humor and spirit of the book." Booklist

Hogrogian, Nonny

Apples. Macmillan (N Y) 1972 unp illus $4.95   E

1 Stories without words

A "picture book without words, the plot slight but clear. Two children and some animals cross, in turn, a green and sunny landscape, discarding their apple cores. One by one, apple trees spring up until the pages are filled with trees bearing ripe fruit. . . . In the end the apple vendor (who was seen at the beginning) is picking apples and filling his cart." Chicago. Children's Bk Center

"The tender greens and blues make a charming background for the steady progression of characters that move with the rhythm of a piece of music. One must not look too closely for a story line because the story is not so important as is the experience of viewing the book." Horn Bk

Holl, Adelaide

The rain puddle; pictures by Roger Duvoisin. Lothrop 1965 unp illus lib. bdg. $4.81   E

1 Domestic animals—Stories
ISBN 0-688-51096-5

"Each of the silly barnyard animals sees his reflection in a rain puddle and thinks that one of his own kind is drowning. When the sun dries up the puddle, the animals are relieved, thinking that everyone has been saved. An absurd, repetitive story with a folktale quality in style and illustrations, suitable for the story hour." Hodges. Bks for Elem Sch Libraries

The remarkable egg; illus. by Roger Duvoisin. Lothrop 1968 unp illus lib. bdg. $4.59   E

1 Birds—Stories 2 Eggs—Fiction
ISBN 0-688-51090-6

"A slight text affords opportunity for some very pleasant pictures of birds, some accurate enough to be used for identification; a few facts about the birds and their nests emerge from the frail fictional framework. Coot finds a large red egg in her nest; she asks other birds if it belongs to them; Robin, Catbird, Meadow lark, Mourning dove, Cowbird, Oriole, Cardinal, Hummingbird and Owl all discuss the matter with the coot. A boy retrieves his red ball from the nest. Commenting on what a funny creature that was, the coot settles down happily to lay her eggs." Chicago. Children's Bk Center

Holland, Marion

A big ball of string; written and illus. by Marion Holland. Beginner Bks. 1958 64p illus $2.95, lib. bdg. $3.69   E

1 Stories in rhyme
ISBN 0-394-80005-2; 0-394-90005-7

"For beginning readers"

This is a rhymed story of a child who dreams about the things he would do if he had a big ball of string—and what he does when he gets it! Only 212 different words are used in this book

Holland, Viki

We are having a baby; photographs by the author. Scribner 1972 unp illus lib. bdg. $5.95   E

1 Brothers and sisters—Fiction 2 Infants—Fiction
ISBN 0-684-12809-8

"A warm, gently reassuring photo-story narrated by four-year-old Dana chronicles her reactions to the birth of her brother from her curiosity about the baby before he is born to her moments of jealousy, uncertainty, and pride after Mother and the baby return home from the hospital. Except for a rather superfluous dream sequence, the photographs of Dana, her parents, the hospital, and the baby seem completely natural. No pictures of the actual birth are included though one lovely photograph shows Dana's mother

Holland, Viki—*Continued*
breast-feeding the baby while Dana watches intently at her shoulder." Booklist

Hosie's alphabet; pictures by Leonard Baskin; words by Hosea, Tobias & Lisa Baskin. Viking 1972 unp illus lib. bdg. $5.95   E
1 Alphabet books 2 Animals—Pictorial works
ISBN 0-670-37958-1
Hosie was three when he asked his father to draw this alphabet for him. He, his mother and his brother have chosen such unusual phrases as: G, a ghastly, garrulous gargoyle, to go along with the pictures
"A stunning book that is definitely not the pedantic and traditional alphabet book. The ear will enjoy the unusual tongue-tantalizing words and the eye will delight in the beauty and variety of illustrations. The graphic design in the painting and in the printing is dramatic and in complete harmony with the short text consisting of words that, though they are out of the ordinary and not in the day to day vocabulary of small children, will tickle their senses and pique their curiosity." Top of the News

Hurd, Edith Thacher
Come and have fun; pictures by Clement Hurd. Harper 1962 32p illus lib. bdg. $3.43   E
1 Cats—Stories 2 Mice—Stories 3 Stories in rhyme
ISBN 0-06-022681-1
"An Early I can read book"
In this story the sly cat invited the mouse to come out of his house but the mouse was careful. He would not leave his house at the cat's urging either to have fun, to sit in the sun, or for any other reason. However, when the mouse could no longer see the cat, he felt secure enough to leave his house. And then, a merry chase was on

Johnny Lion's bad day; pictures by Clement Hurd. Harper 1970 64p illus $2.95, lib. bdg. $3.79   E
1 Lions—Stories
ISBN 0-06-022707-9; 0-06-022708-7
"An I can read book"
"While forced to stay in bed and be dosed with red medicine, Johnny Lion has two terrifying nightmares. In the first, he is menaced by a huge, big-eyed owl and, in the second, by an oversize red rabbit but is saved from both by opportune, resounding 'kerchews.' His recovery is marked by a pleasant dream in which he is a big, big lion with an enormous roar that scares even Mother and Father Lion." Booklist
"There are very funny, simple illustrations in beige and pink." Sch Library J

Johnny Lion's book; pictures by Clement Hurd. Harper 1965 63p illus lib. bdg. $3.79   E
1 Lions—Stories
ISBN 0-06-022706-0
"An I can read book"
"A small lion, told to stay home and read his new book while his parents are out hunting, reads about another small lion. Less dutiful than the reader, the lion cub in the book wanders off and is later put to bed early. Johnny Lion pretends to his parents that he has strayed, but quickly informs them that he has really stayed home and read his book." Chicago. Children's Bk Center
The "book-within-a-book technique is admirably handled, though it may be a bit sophisticated for the youngest readers without some guidance. More experienced readers . . . will enjoy the gay pictures and understand the central idea that adventures in a book are almost as exciting and interesting as real ones." N Y Times Bk Rev

Johnny Lion's rubber boots; pictures by Clement Hurd. Harper 1972 63p illus $2.95, lib. bdg. $3.79   E
1 Lions—Stories
ISBN 0-06-022709-5; 0-06-022710-9
"An I can read book"
"Forced by the rain and his lack of rubber boots to stay inside the house, Johnny Lion plays with blocks, paints, and boxes and creates several 'awful messes' which his mother makes him clean up. Fortunately, just as Johnny Lion is becoming totally bored, Father Lion comes home with a pair of red rubber boots and Johnny Lion happily goes outside to play in the puddles and the rain." Booklist
"This good story with humorous pictures is truly easy to read and is another successful portrayal of the moods of young children." Sch Library J

Last one home is a green pig; pictures by Clement Hurd. Harper 1959 63p illus $2.95, lib. bdg. $3.79   E
1 Ducks—Stories 2 Monkeys—Stories
ISBN 0-06-022715-X; 0-06-022716-8
"An I can read book"
"A duck and a monkey use many ingenious means of transportation when they race each other home." Hodges. Bks for Elem Sch Libraries
An "excellent use of green and tan watercolor wash and bold black figures on white background plus well spaced type make a most attractive format." Library J

No funny business; pictures by Clement Hurd. Harper 1962 62p illus $2.95, lib. bdg. $3.79   E
1 Cats—Stories
ISBN 0-06-022725-7; 0-06-022726-5
"An I can read book"
"Father decides to take the family on a picnic but Carl, their talking pet cat, refuses to go. Hurriedly preparing for the picnic the family forgets that Carl likes to be coaxed and before they leave Carl is told to watch the house and is warned that there is to be 'no funny business—no fooling around.' Carl settles down to sleep and dreams that he goes on the picnic and is the instigator of many kinds of 'funny business.' " Booklist
"Almost all of this text—and the entire story-within-in-the-story—is what Carl the cat dreamed. . . . The imagined conversation will seem very funny to the beginning reader, and the pictures of Carl wonderfully full of life and personality." Horn Bk

Hutchins, Pat
Changes, changes. Macmillan (N Y) 1971 unp illus lib. bdg. $4.95, pa 95¢   E
1 Toys—Fiction 2 Dolls—Fiction 3 Stories without words
"Bright colored building blocks and wooden dolls create their own adventures and solve their own problems as they progress from house to fire engine, to barge, to truck, to locomotive, and back home." Top of the News
"Another book for the very young child who delights in 'reading' by himself, the lack of text amply compensated for by the bright, bold pictures and the imaginative use of blocks and two stiff little dolls." Chicago. Children's Bk Center

Clocks and more clocks. Macmillan (N Y) 1970 unp illus $4.95, pa 95¢   E
1 Clocks and watches—Fiction
"A quaint old gentleman, Mr. Higgins, in a neat little cutaway house, is shown in simple drawings with elaborate detail. To check his grandfather clock, he buys another; there is a discrepancy, so he buys a third and a fourth. Still they disagree. He calls in a specialist, who goes from clock to clock, watch in hand, and

Hutchins, Pat—*Continued*

pronounces them all correct. Mr. Higgins promptly buys a watch . . . 'And since he bought his watch all his clocks have been right,' the story ends. Children who are ready—or just beginning—to tell time will enjoy the fact that Mr. Higgins never sees the very obvious answer. Simply told, nicely conceived." Sutherland. The Best in Children's Bks

Good-night, Owl! Macmillan (N Y) 1972 unp illus lib. bdg. $4.95, pa $1.25　　　　　　　　E

1 Owls—Stories

Illustrated by the author

Owl takes revenge on the birds and the animals who have not let him sleep during the day

"The ending is perky, the pictures funny, and the simplicity and repetition of pattern in the text are encouraging for the pre-reader." Chicago. Children's Bk Center

Rosie's walk. Macmillan (N Y) 1968 unp illus lib. bdg. $4.95　　　　　　　　　　　　　E

1 Chickens—Stories 2 Foxes—Stories

"In this diverting picture book only 33 words are used to guide the way through the [author-illustrator's] doublespread stylized pictures aglow with sunshiny colors, and even those few words are not actually needed. Rosie the hen goes for a walk around the farm and gets home in time for dinner, completely unaware that a fox has been hot on her heels every step of the way. The viewer knows, however, and is not only held in suspense but tickled by the ways in which the fox is foiled at every turn by the unwitting hen. A perfect choice for the youngest." Booklist

The silver Christmas tree. Macmillan Pub. Co. 1974 unp illus lib. bdg. $5.95　　　　　　E

1 Squirrels—Stories 2 Animals—Stories 3 Christmas stories

ISBN 0-02-745920-7

Illustrated by the author

"Squirrel has decorated his tree for the season and is delighted when a silver star appears at its top. But the next day it's gone. Squirrel visits Duck, Mouse, Rabbit, Fox—all his friends—and finds them furtive. But it turns out that they're just hiding the presents they have for him, not his star. At the end of the festivities, Squirrel offers his gift, the decorated tree, to which an unexpected snowfall gives just the right touch. (P.S. The star is back too.)" Pub W

"There's a pattern in the writing that enables children to enjoy anticipation, and the story affords small listeners an opportunity to feel the satisfaction of superior knowledge. Brief, but the elements of problem and solution are here, and the book has the triple appeals of animal characters, Christmas setting, and a wish granted; the illustrations are stylized, colorful, and deft." Chicago. Children's Bk Center

The surprise party. Macmillan (N Y) 1969 unp illus lib. bdg. $4.50, pa 95¢　　　　　　　E

1 Animals—Stories

Illustrated by the author

Rabbit whispers to Owl, "I'm having a party tomorrow. It's a surprise." But Owl passes the news along to Squirrel as "Rabbit is hoeing the parsley tomorrow. It's a surprise." And by the time the word has spread to each of Rabbit's friends, there are conflicting opinions as to what Rabbit is really planning to do

"Full-page, ultra-cheerful pictures in yellow, orange, and green carry this story." Sch Library J

Titch. Macmillan (N Y) 1971 unp illus lib. bdg. $5.95, pa 95¢　　　　　　　　　　　　E

1 Brothers and sisters—Fiction

"How does it feel to be the youngest child in the family? To have an older brother and sister who lead a more exciting life? . . . [The author] has, with a minimum of well-chosen words and bright, engaging illustrations, triumphantly related the story of a small boy who surpasses his brother and sister with one simple action." Pub W

"The amazing growth of Titch's tiny seed, planted as his share of a family project, is a satisfying conclusion to the story as well as a logical symbol of human potentiality for the many small persons who will sympathize with his position and delight in his success. Imaginative realism for preschoolers which is reassuring, but never condescending." Horn Bk

The wind blew. Macmillan Pub. Co. 1974 unp illus lib. bdg. $4.95　　　　　　　　　　E

1 Winds—Fiction 2 Stories in rhyme

ISBN 0-02-745910-1

"Full-color paintings illustrate a rhymed cumulative text depicting the frantic efforts of unwary pedestrians to recover possessions snatched away by a mischievous and unpredictable wind. . . . Although the brief text is a pleasant, rhythmic accompaniment to the pictures, the story can be 'read' from the doublespread illustrations. A humorous and imaginative treatment of a familiar situation." Horn Bk

Ipcar, Dahlov

Brown Cow Farm; a counting book. Doubleday 1959 unp illus lib. bdg. $4.95　　　　　　E

1 Domestic animals 2 Counting books

ISBN 0-385-07856-0

This is "a counting book for young children describing the animals at Brown Cow Farm. The first half of the book shows the animals from the one horse to the ten cows, sheltering in the big brown barn during the winter. But when spring comes, the baby animals are born, the horse has one colt, each of the three cats has ten kittens, the ten wild geese hatch ten little goslings each, until on the final pages when all the farm animals and their offspring are shown, there are over five hundred animals to count. The text is simple and in a few sentences pinpoints effectively the characteristics of the different animals, and helps the children identify them. The [author's] illustrations, mainly in brown and green, are full of life and variety, and in spite of the necessary repetitions, are never monotonous." Ontario Library Rev

Iwasaki, Chihiro

The birthday wish. McGraw 1974 c1972 unp illus $4.95　　　　　　　　　　　　　　　　E

1 Birthdays—Fiction

ISBN 0-07-032072-1; 0-07-032073-X

First published 1972 in Japan

Illustrated by the author, this story depicts Allison's predicament on the day before her fifth birthday. In her excitement, she accidentally makes her own birthday wish for snow on Judy's birthday cake. But Allison's wish comes true and Judy bears no ill feelings. Out of fairness and happiness, Allison gives Judy a chance to make a wish on her birthday cake

"The artistic layout, heavy, textured paper, and beautiful watercolors result in a quality book." Babbling Bookworm

Will you be my friend. McGraw [1974] c1970 unp illus $4.95, lib. bdg. $4.72　　　　　　E

1 Friendship—Fiction

ISBN 0-07-032076-4; 0-07-032077-2

Original Japanese edition, 1970. British publication, 1972 with title: Neighbours

"Allison tries in vain to make friends with the rude new boy next door. When she stops trying so hard, he asks her to be his friend. The slight text conveys well

Iwasaki, Chihiro—*Continued*

the situation of both having and being a new child in the neighborhood. Iwasaki's delicate paintings express the shyness of the children in the pastel tones and textured paper." Children's Bk Rev Serv

Janice

Little Bear's Christmas; pictures by Mariana. Lothrop 1964 unp illus lib. bdg. $4.14   E

1 Bears—Stories 2 Christmas stories
ISBN 0-688-51076-0

"Little Bear wakes from hibernation early and sees snow; he joins children skating, hears about Christmas, and writes Santa Claus. He helps Santa, then returns home to find friends, presents, a tree, and a jar of honey in every stocking he had hung; then he goes back to bed to sleep until spring." Chicago. Children's Bk Center

"A number of teddybear-like little creatures have become endearing book heroes. This one in his Santa Claus suit—in full-color Christmas-card style of painting (alternating with black and white)—has the utmost of sweet innocence. . . . It is a book elders will delight in sharing with the very youngest." Horn Bk

Little Bear's Thanksgiving; illus. by Mariana. Lothrop 1967 unp illus lib. bdg. $4.14   E

1 Bears—Stories 2 Thanksgiving Day—Stories
ISBN 0-688-51078-7

"Appealing, winsome Little Bear gets invited to Thanksgiving dinner by his great friend Goldie, and it falls to his forest friends not only to explain the holiday but also to get him there on time." Adventuring With Bks. 2d edition

"Although not outstanding or particularly original, this is, nonetheless, an engaging holiday story for young listeners and independent readers in first and second grades." Booklist

Johnson, Crockett

Harold and the purple crayon. Harper 1955 unp illus $2.95, lib. bdg. $3.43   E

ISBN 0-06-022935-7; 0-06-022936-5
Illustrated by the author

This story describes the "fantasy of a small boy who decides to go for a walk one night. He uses his purple crayon to draw all the things necessary for a successful walk—a moon, a path, houses, the ocean, a boat, a mountain, a balloon, and finally his own room again. Imaginative children (the book is not for the literal-minded child, or adult) can appreciate Harold's adventures, and they may even be tempted to imitate his drawings on the nearest flat surface. . . . Nursery school teachers and parents should find this a book that is fun to use with children to stimulate them in their own imaginative adventures." Chicago. Children's Bk Center

A picture for Harold's room; a purple crayon adventure. Harper 1960 64p illus $2.95, lib. bdg. $3.43   E

ISBN 0-06-023005-3; 0-06-023006-1
"An I can read book"

When Harold starts to draw a picture for his room and then steps into it, his travels begin. He wades through an ocean, narrowly escapes being bumped by a high-flying jet and sees a large daisy—all of which he has drawn with his purple crayon. He then discovers that he is smaller than some objects and larger than others

The author-artist "suggests as an alternative title: 'A first glance at perspective.' . . . One is always amazed by Crockett Johnson's cleverness." Library J

Johnson, Elizabeth

All in free but Janey; illus. by Trina Schart Hyman. Little 1968 31p illus lib. bdg. $3.95   E

ISBN 0-316-46729-4

"Janey, playing Hide and Seek with her friends, sees pictures in the clouds while she is hiding; when she is It, she imagines gnomes and pixies under the porch. While imaginative Janey is absorbed in her fancies, the other children get in free. Not very good at hiding or seeking, the story concludes, 'but she was very good at finding fleecy castles in the clouds and goblin faces in the dark.' " Chicago. Children's Bk Center

"Lacy, delicate leaf prints are spattered over solid lines and color just as Janey's fantasies overlay the solid world of house and garden, tree and telegraph pole. Sharp eyes can discern the laughing faces of hiding children." Horn Bk

Joslin, Sesyle

Baby Elephant and the secret wishes; pictures by Leonard Weisgard. Harcourt 1962 unp illus $4.50   E

1 Elephants—Stories 2 Christmas stories
ISBN 0-15-205156-2

In this story Baby Elephant "manages to get his adoring family to wish secretly for the very Christmas presents he is able to produce for them." N Y Her Trib Bks

"Pleasantly illustrated, gently humorous, and most engaging in the way the adults converse with their child." Chicago. Children' Bk Center

Brave Baby Elephant; pictures by Leonard Weisgard. Harcourt 1960 unp illus $4.95   E

1 Elephants—Stories
ISBN 0-15-211598-6

The author "tells a story of a baby elephant who makes all kinds of preparations for a journey which turns out to be simply a trip upstairs at bedtime." Pub W

"Small children will be beguiled by the stylized colored pictures and by the suspense engendered as Baby Elephant readies himself . . . for his big adventure, the nature of which is not revealed until the end of the story. The animals are tenderly humanized in both the story and illustrations." Booklist

Kahl, Virginia

The Duchess bakes a cake; written and illus. by Virginia Kahl. Scribner 1955 unp illus lib. bdg. $5.95, pa 95¢   E

1 Cake—Fiction 2 Stories in rhyme
ISBN 0-684-12313-4; 0-684-12635-4

"The Duchess lived happily with her Duke and thirteen daughters until one day she became bored and decided to bake a 'lovely light luscious delectable cake.' It was light, all right—so light that it rose almost to the sky and took the Duchess up with it. After vainly trying to bring her down with cannon shot and arrows, the people gave up and decided she would simply have to remain on top of the cake. Then the baby Gunhilde began crying for her supper—and there was the solution." Chicago. Children's Bk Center

"A fine nonsense story, told in lively rhymes and illustrated with bright pictures." Hodges. Bks for Elem Sch Libraries

How do you hide a monster? Scribner 1971 unp illus lib. bdg. $5.95   E

1 Sea monsters—Stories 2 Stories in rhyme
ISBN 0-684-12318-5

Illustrated by the author and written in rhymed verse, this is a story about Phinney, a friendly sea

Kahl, Virginia—*Continued*

serpent, who almost lost his life when he was mistaken for a frightful monster

"Offers spontaneous, amusing rhymes in an original plot." Horn Bk

Kantrowitz, Mildred

I wonder if Herbie's home yet; pictures by Tony De Luna. Parents Mag. Press 1971 unp illus $4.95, lib. bdg. $4.59   E

1 Friendship—Fiction

ISBN 0-8193-0465-4; 0-8193-0466-2

"The first-person narration is terse and authentically childlike. Each page of text is followed by a page of illustrations, in most cases a cartoon-type sequence of from two to eight pictures, depicting the immediately preceding text. The appealing, big-headed little boys underline this low-keyed but so true story about the seriousness with which children take their friendships." Library J

Kay, Helen

One mitten Lewis; illus. by Kurt Werth. Lothrop 1955 unp illus lib. bdg. $5.11   E

ISBN 0-688-51082-5

Lewis was the losingest little boy in town—and mostly he lost mittens. Not both mittens, of course, never a pair of them—Oh no, only one! This little story explains the solution adopted by Lewis' mother

"Entertaining could-be-true story. . . . Surprise ending." Bks for Deaf Children

Keats, Ezra Jack

Apt. 3. Macmillan (N Y) 1971 unp illus $5.95   E

1 Cities and towns—Fiction 2 Blind—Fiction

Set in a dingy tenement house, this book describes "the encounter of two young and lonely boys with a blind musician whose beautiful music helps them learn that communication is possible through ways other than words." Wolfe. About 100 Bks

"The subtle colors of Keats's paintings and his restrained use of detail to establish atmosphere make Apt. 3 a pleasure to look at, but it is less a story than a situation picture book." Sat Rev

Dreams. Macmillan Pub. Co. 1974 unp illus $5.95   E

1 Cities and towns—Fiction

ISBN 0-02-749610-4

A "city story of a Puerto Rican boy Roberto whose paper mouse saves Archie's cat from a dog in the night when everyone else is dreaming." Children's Bk Rev Serv

"Keats captures in brilliant oranges, blues, reds, and greens the sense of a hot, steamy summer night in a densely packed big city. Children will love this book, and it will provide them with opportunity after opportunity for recounting their own experiences with the shadow world that reigns at night." Rdng Teacher

Goggles! Macmillan (N Y) 1969 unp illus $5.50, pa $1.25   E

1 Negroes—Fiction

Illustrated by the author

"Peter finds a pair of motorcycle goggles glassless but impressive, and shows them off to an admiring younger boy. Some big boys come along and demand the goggles, Peter's dog races off with them, and Peter—with small Archie in tow—outwits the gang and retrieves his loot." Sat Rev

"The illustrations are lovely: big, clear, colorful pictures with a city background, excellent for using with a group. The story is slight but realistic; a situation encountered by most small boys should evoke the pleasure of recognition and the added pleasure of vicarious triumph." Chicago. Children's Bk Center

Hi, cat! Macmillan (N Y) 1970 unp illus $6.50, pa $1.25   E

1 Negroes—Fiction 2 Cats—Stories

Illustrated by the author

"On his way to meet Peter, Archie passes a stray cat, and says, casually, 'Hi, cat!' Dressed in a paper bag, Archie is clowning away for the benefit of Peter and other friends when the cat scrambles into his costume. The bag bursts, Peter's dog gives enthusiastic chase, the cat disappears. That night, while Archie tells his mother that the cat liked him, the cat, visible to the reader but not to Archie, sits expectantly on the doorstep. The modest action has the appeal of everyday things, an urban background, and a clownish humor, which are given vitality by the colorful collage-and-paint pictures of bright brown faces." Sat Rev

Jennie's hat. Harper 1966 unp illus $5.95, lib. bdg. $5.79   E

1 Hats—Fiction

ISBN 0-06-023113-0; 0-06-023114-9

"Jennie is counting on a new hat from her aunt—and dreaming of its beauty. A very plain hat comes, and after unsuccessful attempts to make herself a hat, Jennie goes to church in the drab one. In the interval she has fed her friends the birds, and they save the day by flying down and trimming the hat for her." Sat Rev

This fantasy "has a sense of freshness, of spring, about it. Attractive, colorful pictures [by the author] make most telling use of collage." Christian Sci Monitor

A letter to Amy. Harper 1968 unp illus $4.95, lib. bdg. $4.79   E

1 Negroes—Fiction 2 Birthdays—Fiction

ISBN 0-06-023108-4; 0-06-023109-2

"Peter is planning a birthday party that at the moment is an 'all-boy' party. When he expresses a desire to invite another friend, Amy, he is encouraged to do so by his mother; however, he isn't quite sure the fellows will understand his wanting a girl at the party. Peter begins to build some personal values of his own when he makes a decision, sticks by it, and is very pleased that he did." Rdng Ladders.

"A master of ingenious collages, the [author-] artist has made brilliant, variegated pictures showing a yellow-slicked boy against a background of angry skies, sodden buildings, and rain-drenched pavements." Horn Bk

My dog is lost! By Ezra Jack Keats and Pat Cherr; illus. by the authors. Crowell 1960 40p illus $3.95, lib. bdg. $4.70   E

1 Puerto Ricans in New York (City)—Fiction 2 New York (City)—Fiction 3 Dogs—Stories

ISBN 0-690-56691-3; 0-690-56692-1

"Juanito was sad and lonely. He had just arrived in New York from Puerto Rico, could speak only Spanish, and had lost his dog. When the children he met could not understand him, sign language worked effectively. Juanito not only found his shaggy, bow-legged red dog, he also made many friends and visited many sections of New York. A bilingual picture book introduces a beginning Spanish vocabulary." Moorachian. What is a City?

Pet show! Macmillan (N Y) 1972 unp illus $4.95, pa $1.25   E

1 Pets—Stories 2 Negroes—Fiction

Illustrated by the author

The children of the neighborhood are prepared for

Keats, Ezra Jack—*Continued*

the pet show, but Archie's pet cat vanishes at the crucial moment. However, his ingenuity in substituting another pet is amply rewarded

This "is a warm, funny story. . . . [The illustrations] are vividly coloured and full of the kind of incidental detail children love to pick out when picture books are being read to them." Times (London) Lit Sup

Peter's chair. Harper 1967 unp illus $4.95, lib. bdg. $4.79   E

1 Negroes—Fiction 2 Brothers and sisters—Fiction
ISBN 0-06-023111-4; 0-06-023112-2

Peter, no longer an only child, finds it difficult to adjust to his new role as big brother. "It's Peter's high chair, and it is his crib, too, being painted pink. Dispirited and jealous, Peter rescues his little chair and other belongings—like his own baby picture—and plans to run away (but not very far). When he finds that he is too big to fit into the chair, Peter realizes that he has superior status and is able to make the magnanimous gesture of offering to paint the chair pink." Children's Bk Center

"With artful artlessness, this very simple story of sibling dethronement suggests the behavior patterns of the resentful child but does so with an amused affection that robs the book of either minatory or purposive message. . . . The deft and colorful collage pictures [by the author] show an engaging little brown face intent upon preserving—if not enhancing—his role." Sat Rev

The snowy day. Viking 1962 31p illus lib. bdg. $4.95, pa 95¢   E

1 Negroes—Fiction 2 Snow—Fiction
ISBN 0-670-65400-0; 0-670-05061-X
Awarded the Caldecott Medal, 1963

A small "boy's ecstatic enjoyment of snow in the city is shown in vibrant pictures. Peter listens to the snow crunch under his feet, makes the first tracks in a clean patch of snow, makes angels and a snowman. At night in his warm bed he thinks over his adventures, and in the morning wakens to the promise of another lovely snowy day." Moorachian. What is a City?

"It is refreshing to have a natural story in which only the illustrations show that Peter is a Negro child." Library J

A mood "picture book which is outstanding for [the author-illustrator's] adroit use of vivid colors and interesting 'cutpaper' shapes. . . . These [are] bold drawings. This is a perfect book for the nursery school age as well as for those in kindergarten and first grade." Pub W

Whistle for Willie. Viking 1964 33p illus lib. bdg. $4.95, pa 95¢   E

1 Negroes—Fiction
ISBN 0-670-76240-7; 0-670-05016-4

Peter "wants to learn to whistle so he can call his dog to him quickly as other people do. While trying to whistle he engages in various antics such as spinning around until he is dizzy, walking inside a huge carton, pretending to be his father, etc. Finally, he assumes just the right position of his lips and does produce a whistle." Sch Library J

"Using the same technique [of painting and collage] as he did in 'The Snowy Day' [entered above] with no less originality and somewhat more universality Mr. Keats again gives eloquent expression to a child's solitary play. . . . Vividly colored, exquisitely simple, his spacious environment is a place of texture, shape, and belonging." Horn Bk

Keith, Eros

Rrra-ah; story and pictures by Eros Keith. Bradbury Press 1969 unp illus $6.95   E

1 Frogs—Stories
ISBN 0-87888-032-1

"Written from a toad's viewpoint, this story describes his experiences and horror at being captured and taken home by some children. Their mother eventually orders his release because he is always jumping around the house, and Rrra-ah is happy to return to nature." Adventuring With Bks 2d edition

"Young children will delight in following Rrra-ah's lively leaps toward freedom in the fresh, gay illustrations of this amusing picture book." Booklist

Kellogg, Steven

Can I keep him? Story and pictures by Steven Kellogg. Dial Press 1971 unp illus $4.95, lib. bdg. $4.58   E

1 Pets—Stories
ISBN 0-8037-0988-9; 0-8037-0989-7

"Lonely Arnold wants a playmate but his mother objects to every one he suggests—grandma is allergic to cat fur, bears have a disagreeable odor, pythons shed their skins which clog the vacuum cleaner, and so on." Booklist

"Finely detailed pictures of Arnold's real and imagined pets and an amusing, cumulative storyline." Library J

The mystery of the missing red mitten; story and pictures by Steven Kellogg. Dial Press 1974 unp illus $3.95, lib. bdg. $3.69   E

ISBN 0-8037-6195-3; 0-8037-6194-5

"Annie loses a red mitten and sets out to search for it with her dog, Oscar. She fantasizes about the mitten's possible fate (e.g., 'Do you think that the mouse and his family are using my mitten for a sleeping bag?') and imagines planting her remaining mitten and reaping a multitude from the resultant mitten tree. Annie's search ends when what appears to be the heart of a snowman is revealed to be the missing mitten." Library J

"Kellogg's imagination extends from a clever story to captivating black-and-white drawings with accents of red. His use of a bubble to show the little girl's thoughts is perfect. And this is a perfect book for a winter day." Babbling Bookworm

Kepes, Juliet

Lady Bird, quickly. Little 1964 47p illus $4.50 E

1 Ladybugs—Stories 2 Insects—Stories
ISBN 0-316-48952-2

"An Atlantic Monthly Press book"

"All the insects pass the word along to Lady Bird when her house seems to be on fire. In this variation of the old nursery rhyme, 'Lady Bug, Lady Bug, fly away home,' the house is not on fire but is filled with fireflies. The author's pictures of insects, each kind on a different color of paper, are simple and pleasing." Hodges. Bks for Elem Sch Libraries

Kessler, Leonard

Here comes the strikeout. Harper 1965 64p illus (A Sports I can read bk) $2.95, lib. bdg. $3.79   E

1 Baseball—Fiction 2 Negroes—Fiction
ISBN 0-06-023155-6; 0-06-023156-4

Also available in a Spanish language edition, lib. bdg. $3.79. (ISBN 0-06-023154-8)

"A delightful book for beginning independent readers, the engaging illustrations showing Willie, the friend and mentor of the strikeout king (Bobby, a white boy), to be Negro. Bobby, in despair, because his batting is weak, tries Willie's lucky hat. No luck! Then Willie coaches Bobby, who practices and practices and finally gets a hit—no instant success, but a

Kessler, Leonard—*Continued*
combination of hard work and encouragement from
Willie. The home attitude is good, too." We Build
Together

Kick, pass, and run. Harper 1966 64p illus (A Sports
I can read bk) $2.95, lib. bdg. $3.79   E
  1 Football—Fiction
  ISBN 0-06-023159-9; 0-06-023160-2
  "Football rules and terms are tackled in easy-to-
read, easy-to-remember terms and reinforced by the
illustrated glossary that follows the comic story of
animal teams imitating the Giants and the Jets." Best
Bks for Children, 1968
  "May [also] appeal to the older reluctant reader."
Hodges. Bks for Elem Sch Libraries

Last one in is a rotten egg. Harper 1969 64p illus (A
Sports I can read bk) $2.95, lib. bdg. $3.79   E
  1 Swimming—Fiction 2 Negroes—Fiction
  ISBN 0-06-023157-2; 0-06-023158-0
  Illustrated by the author
  Because Freddy can't swim, he must stay in the
shallow water while his friends have fun diving and
racing. Support from his mother and from his friends
Bobby and Willy, and lessons from Tom the lifeguard
enable Freddy to overcome his fear of the water

On your mark, get set, go! The first all-animal
Olympics. Harper 1972 63p illus (A Sports I can read
bk) $2.95, lib. bdg. $3.79   E
  1 Animals—Stories
  ISBN 0-06-023152-1; 0-06-023153-X
  Illustrated by the author
  This story depicts "the antics of an owl, a frog, cat,
dog, duck, turtle, rabbit, three birds, a family of ants,
a spider, and a worm who organize and carry out their
own version of the Olympics." Booklist
  "The mildly humorous plot is well built and
matched by the author's simple, amusing color drawings. It's not the type of book most young sports
enthusiasts are demanding, but it's still a worthwhile
purchase." Sch Library J

Kingman, Lee
Peter's long walk; pictures by Barbara Cooney.
Doubleday 1953 47p illus lib. bdg. $5.70   E
  ISBN 0-385-07747-5
  A story of five year old Peter's adventures as he
takes a long walk in search of playmates
  "Small children anxiously waiting to go to school
will enjoy his experiences, told with repetition and
rhythm that makes good reading aloud. Barbara
Cooney's pictures emphasize the feeling of spring, a
small boy's experiences, and the countryside." Wis
Library Bul

Klein, Norma
Girls can be anything; illus. by Roy Doty. Dutton
1973 unp illus $5.50, pa $1.95   E
  1 Woman—Employment—Fiction
  ISBN 0-525-30662-5; 0-525-45029-7
  "Marina and Adam are best friends but the little girl
rebels at always performing traditional female roles in
their games. She has to be a nurse while Adam plays
doctor, stewardess while he pilots a jet, and first lady
when he's president. With the encouragement of her
parents, Marina convinces Adam that she too could be
a doctor (after all, her own aunt is a famous surgeon), a
pilot and even, some day, president." Pub W
  "The cartoon-like illustrations in red, white, and
blue make the point with a smile, and the dialog could
be heard anywhere around the block." Booklist

Knight, Hilary
Where's Wallace? Story and panoramas by Hilary
Knight. Harper 1964 40p illus $5.95, lib. bdg.
$5.43   E
  1 Orangutans—Stories
  ISBN 0-06-023170-X; 0-06-023171-8
  "A kindly zookeeper cooperates with Wallace, a
little orangutan who likes to explore the city occasionally. Detailed color spreads invite readers and listeners to find Wallace in unlikely places." Hodges. Bks
for Elem Sch Libraries

Knotts, Howard
The winter cat; story and pictures by Howard
Knotts. Harper 1972 32p illus $3.50, lib. bdg.
$3.79   E
  1 Cats—Stories 2 Winter—Fiction
  ISBN 0-06-023166-1; 0-06-023167-X
  "A winsome, wild gray cat is homeless and nameless
but enjoying his freedom until he sees a strange new
sight: snow. Though he grows daily colder and more
hungry, he still refuses the neighborhood children's
offers of food and friendship. They leave him scraps of
food and, after a while, he begins to trust them. At
last, the children coax him into their house and
'Homer' gets a name and a home after all." Pub W
  "Illustrations of small, precise figures in black,
white, and grey convey the snow-wrapped stillness of
winter in a simply written book that has a sedate and
gentle text." Chicago. Children's Bk Center

Koch, Dorothy
I play at the beach; illus. by Feodor Rojankovsky.
Holiday House 1955 unp illus lib. bdg. $4.95   E
  1 Seashore—Fiction
  ISBN 0-8234-0057-3
  A little girl's experiences during a day at the beach
told in blank verse
  "The glowing pictures convey with vividness the
warmth of sun and sand and the coolness of the water
and ocean breezes." Booklist

Krasilovsky, Phyllis
The cow who fell in the canal; illus. by Peter Spier.
Doubleday 1957 unp illus $4.50, pa $1.25   E
  1 Cows—Stories 2 Netherlands—Fiction
  ISBN 0-385-07585-5; 0-385-08096-4
  Picture story book about Hendrika, a fat cow living
in Holland. Hendrika loved her master and was usually content to eat a great deal and produce rich
creamy milk. But sometimes she got bored. But after
she fell into the canal and floated down to the distant
city on a raft she was never bored again, because she
had so much to think about
  The artist's "watercolor illustrations are remarkable
for details lovingly recalled, panoramic scenes of town
and country, and colors as fresh and clean as a newly
scrubbed Dutch floor." Cincinnati

The man who didn't wash his dishes; illus. by Barbara Cooney. Doubleday 1950 unp illus $4.50, lib.
bdg. $5.20   E
  ISBN 0-385-07735-1; 0-385-06353-9
  "When there were so many dirty dishes that there
was no place to sit, the man set them out for the rain to
wash, but thereafter he washed his dishes right after
each meal." ALA Children's Service Division.
Selected Lists of Children's Bks and Recordings

Kraus, Robert
Leo the late bloomer; pictures by Jose Aruego.
Windmill Bks. [distributed by Abelard-Schuman]
1971 unp illus lib. bdg. $5.95   E
  1 Tigers—Stories
  ISBN 0-87807-043-5

Kraus, Robert—*Continued*

"Leo is a small, sad-eyed creature, who looks more tigerish than leonine in orange with gray-blue stripes. Everybody writes and reads but Leo. He's just a late bloomer, mother assures father. Father watches and worries. 'A watched bloomer doesn't bloom,' says Leo's mother. Father stops watching, but he peeks. No bloom. Spring comes, and 'one day, in his own good time,' Leo blooms. He reads! He writes! He eats neatly! And he speaks a whole sentence: 'I made it!' Artfully bland, sunny, and reassuring for other late bloomers, the book is illustrated with beguiling pictures." Sat Rev

Milton the early riser; pictures by Jose & Ariane Aruego. Windmill Bks. and Dutton 1972 unp illus lib. bdg. $5.95 E
1 Pandas—Stories
ISBN 0-525-61000-6
When Milton, a young panda bear, wakes up early he can't find anyone to play with so he has to watch television, dance, sing, do tricks, and jump up and down by himself until, by the time others awake, he is exhausted and ready to sleep

"The simple text generates just enough fantasy and gaiety to give the artists an outlet for their all-pervading humor: The scenes of animals sleeping and being buffeted by the wind are ablaze with color and detail, but are always controlled and precise." Horn Bk

Owliver; pictures by Jose Aruego & Ariane Dewey. Windmill Bks. and Dutton 1974 unp illus lib. bdg. $6.95 E
1 Owls—Stories
ISBN 0-525-61526-1
Owliver is "a young owl who loves to act, much to the joy of his mother and the discomfiture of his father, who hopefully gives him doctor and lawyer toys (which Owliver uses to put on a play) with no more chance than readers of guessing what his son will really turn out to be." Booklist

"This is an entertaining spoof on parental guidance with top-notch illustrations." Library J

Whose mouse are you? Pictures by Jose Aruego. Macmillan (N Y) 1970 unp illus lib. bdg. $5.95, pa $1.25 E
1 Mice—Stories 2 Stories in rhyme
In this story in rhyme, "a little mouse feeling unloved and therefore hostile toward members of his family mentally places each in a hazardous situation, heroically rescues them, and so restores himself in their affection." Booklist

"Bold drawings in pink and grey add sparkle to this simple question-and-answer text." Children's Bks, 1970

Krauss, Ruth

The birthday party; pictures by Maurice Sendak. Harper 1957 unp illus lib. bdg. $3.79 E
1 Birthdays—Fiction
ISBN 0-06-023330-3
"David had been everywhere—to the beach, to the woods, to the corner alone. But he had never been to a birthday party. One day he came in and found the house seemingly deserted, but, when he walked into the dining room, there was everyone waiting to surprise him with a birthday party..A happy combination of simple text and amusing drawings to delight the young child." Eakin. Good Bks for Children

The growing story; pictures by Phyllis Rowand. Harper 1947 unp illus $3.95, lib. bdg. $4.43 E
1 Growth
ISBN 0-06-023380-X; 0-06-023381-8

"A little boy watches the things around him growing all spring and summer and is delighted when the time comes to put on winter clothes again to discover that he has grown, too. A picture book with delightful four color illustrations by Phyllis Rowand that has as its underlying concept the child's interest in the processes of growth." Wis Library Bul

A hole is to dig; a first book of first definitions; pictures by Maurice Sendak. Harper 1952 unp illus $2.95, lib. bdg. $3.40 E
ISBN 0-06-023406-7
Humorous, unexpected definitions of things and actions which have a place in the child's world. Samples: A hole is to plant a flower; A hole is to sit in; A mountain is to climb to the top; Dishes are to do; A nose is to blow; Steps are to sit on

"A revelation to grown-ups as to children's impressions, this could also be the basis of a wonderful game of questions and answers which would set children thinking. Maurice Sendak has illustrated it with drawings bouncing with action and good humor." N Y Times Bk Rev

A very special house; pictures by Maurice Sendak. Harper 1953 unp illus $4.95, lib. bdg. $4.79 E
ISBN 0-06-023455-5; 0-06-023456-3
"The little boy of this story knows just what a Very Special House should be. It would have a bed to bounce on, a table 'very special where to put your feet feet feet' and it would be a place to bring any friends—a lion, a giant, some monkeys. Best of all, it would always suggest 'MORE MORE MORE'; 'NOBODY ever says stop stop stop.' " Horn Bk

Kroeber, Theodora

A green Christmas; illus. by John Larrecq. Parnassus Press 1967 unp illus lib. bdg. $4.38 E
1 Christmas stories
ISBN 0-87466-047-5
"A prose poem and full-color pictures tell of a Christmas many years ago when two small children, new in California, learn that Santa Claus will find children even where there is no snow." Booklist

Includes "illustrations that are notable for the outdoor scenes, although all of the pictures are attractive. . . . The quiet story will appeal to some children, but it is limited by the slight plot, especially for the child who does not believe in Santa Claus." Chicago. Children's Bk Center

Krüss, James

3x3: three by three; a picture book for all children who can count to three. Pictures by Eva Johanna Rubin; English text by Geoffrey Strachan. Macmillan (N Y) 1965 unp illus $4.75, pa $1.25 E
Original German edition published 1963
In this book animals and hunters march "smartly across the page. Three cocks crow, three cats dance, three mice look on; foxes chase chickens, cats chase mice, dogs chase foxes, and so on." Times (London) Lit Sup

"Eva J. Rubin's pictures in pseudo-old-fashioned technique scamper across the pages, adding hilarity to an already 'three times' cheery book." America

Kumin, Maxine W.

The beach before breakfast, illus. by Leonard Weisgard. Putnam 1964 46p illus lib. bdg. $4.97 E
1 Seashore—Fiction
ISBN 0-399-60048-5
"The reader, as 'you,' and an adult friend, as 'I,' explore a beach during early morning. We squat and peer, looking for squirt holes, rake up shells and quahogs, and observe the minnows and the gulls.

Kumin, Maxine W.—*Continued*

Finally we return to the beachside cottage to decide whether breakfast is to be clams or pancakes." p 1

"Lovely illustrations in color and black and white. . . . While this is a mood piece, its person-to-person approach . . . [should] hold the interest of many children." Booklist

La Farge, Phyllis

Joanna runs away; with pictures by Trina Schart Hyman. Holt 1973 55p illus $4.95   E

1 Horses—Stories 2 Brooklyn—Fiction
ISBN 0-03-091306-3

This is a "story about a lonely apartment house child who loves animals. Every day Joanna meets the vegetable peddler's clopping horse on its rounds; but, one day, Joanna hides in the wagon, overcome by her wish to fulfill a dream of living with Costanza [the horse] in a green meadow." Horn Bk

"A pleasant story that quietly makes its point about being needed. . . . The pencil-and-sepia-tone drawings accurately portray the interracial Brooklyn neighborhood and add humor and realism to the text, from the flies buzzing around the horse to the wrinkles in Joanna's tights." Sch Library J

Lasker, Joe

He's my brother; story and illus. by Joe Lasker. Whitman, A. 1974 unp illus lib. bdg. $4.25   E

1 Slow learning children—Fiction
ISBN 0-8075-3218-5

A young boy describes the various experiences his slow learning younger brother has at home and in school

"Written for youngest readers, this is humorously illustrated in alternating watercolor and black-and-white spreads. Young children will sympathize with Jamie's story even though they may not realize that the boy suffers from learning disabilities or an 'invisible handicap' as described in the author's note addressed to parents at the end of the book." Sch Library J

Lathrop, Dorothy P.

Who goes there? Macmillan (N Y) 1963 unp illus lib. bdg. $4.95   E

1 Animals—Stories
First published 1935

Two little children decide to give the animals a picnic. They carry apples, carrots, nuts and grain to a little clearing in the woods, tie the larger offerings on a hemlock tree, and scatter the grain as an invitation. Then the snow comes. The animals accept the invitation with glee and in pictures and text the story of their picnic is told

"Dorothy Lathrop has seen these little creatures as an artist, as a naturalist and as one who loves animals in the same way that children do. . . . The two first pages, with their exquisite reproductions of tiny-footprints, serve at the same time as an entrancing table of contents and an elfin guide to the woods." N Y Times Bk Rev

Lawrence, James

Binky brothers and the Fearless Four; pictures by Leonard Kessler. Harper 1970 64p illus (An I can read mystery) $2.95, lib. bdg. $3.79   E

1 Mystery and detective stories
ISBN 0-06-02360-0; 0-06-023761-9

Companion volume to: Binky brothers, detectives

Dinky Binky once again proves that you don't have to be big to be smart, when he solves the mysterious troubles of the Fearless Four's snow fort

"The bright, simple and humorous illustrations by Leonard Kessler are a strong point in the book." Sch Library J

Binky brothers, detectives; pictures by Leonard Kessler. Harper 1968 60p illus (An I can read mystery) $2.95, lib. bdg. $3.79   E

1 Mystery and detective stories
ISBN 0-06-023758-9; 0-06-023759-7

"Although the detective business in which he and his older brother Pinky are engaged was his idea, Dinky is treated as a helper, not a partner, until he solves the mystery of the missing catcher's mitt and outsmarts Pinky as well. An agreeable story with amusing illustrations." Booklist

Leaf, Munro

Noodle; pictures by Ludwig Bemelmans. Four Winds [1969 c1937] unp illus $4.95, lib. bdg. $4.46   E

1 Dachshunds—Stories
ISBN 0-590-17139-9; 0-590-01739-4
First published 1937 by Stokes

Humorous pictures and text describe the search of Noodle, the dachshund, for a shape better adapted than his own for digging. He ends by deciding that even a dachshund's shape has its advantages

The story of Ferdinand; illus. by Robert Lawson. Viking 1936 unp illus lib. bdg. $4.50, pa 95¢   E

1 Bulls—Stories 2 Bullfights—Fiction 3 Spain—Fiction
ISBN 0-670-67424-9; 0-670-05014-8

"Ferdinand was a peace-loving little bull who preferred smelling flowers to making a reputation for himself in the bull ring. His story is told irresistibly in pictures and few words." Wis Library Bul

"The drawings picture not only Ferdinand but Spanish scenes and characters as well." N Y Libraries

Wee Gillis; illus. by Robert Lawson. Viking 1938 unp illus lib. bdg. $4.95, pa 95¢   E

1 Scotland—Fiction
ISBN 0-670-75608-3; 0-670-05009-1

"Faced with two loyalties—to live in the Highlands and stalk stags with his father's people, or go down into the Lowlands and raise long-haired cows with his mother's people—Wee Gillis solves the problem in his sturdy Scottish way." Booklist

This "is not quite so subtle a fable as Ferdinand's but perhaps an even better story to read aloud." Sat Rev

"The drawings of Robert Lawson combine beauty and humor with a reality that makes the reader feel he has taken a trip to Scotland. With its gay plaid cover, beautifully reproduced illustrations and fine design, this is a distinguished volume." N Y Times Bk Rev

Lear, Edward

Whizz! Pictures by Janina Domanska. Macmillan (N Y) 1973 unp illus lib. bdg. $4.95   E

1 Limericks

"The merry nonsense of six of . . . Lear's familiar limericks has been matched with drawings as delightfully wacky as the verse. . . . Each new character coming into view joins those already moving across the bridge in a succession of doublespreads, until all are present—when the structure suddenly collapses in a surprising debacle. The action takes place against a backdrop composed of stylized hills, rectangular fields, and neat row houses, whose windows gradually fill with cheering spectators. The inventive humor of the minidrama adds a new dimension to the distinguished body of the artist's work. An exuberant and joyous expression." Horn Bk

Lenski, Lois

I like winter. Walck, H.Z. 1950 unp illus music lib.
bdg. $3.95   E

1 Winter—Poetry
ISBN 0-8098-1024-7
First published by Oxford
"There is no story, but the rhyming couplets tell of
winter fun. Simple music to which the rhymes may be
sung is given at the beginning." Ontario Library Rev

In this gay book, illustrated by the author in blues,
reds, and greens, "there are snowmen, skates, sleds
and, of course, Christmas." Horn Bk

The little family; a little book. Doubleday 1932 unp
illus $1.95, lib. bdg. $2.70   E

1 Family—Fiction
ISBN 0-385-07379-8; 0-385-07629-0
This small book, with very brief text and many
simple pictures by the author, about a little family
busy doing everyday things will appeal to young
children

Now it's fall. Walck, H. Z. 1948 unp illus lib. bdg.
$3.95   E

1 Autumn—Poetry
ISBN 0-8098-1018-2
First published by Oxford
Illustrated by the author
"Bright fall colors accent verses telling the fun of
gathering nuts, raking leaves, and Halloween."
Hodges. Bks for Elem Sch Libraries

Papa Small. Walck, H.Z. 1951 unp illus lib. bdg.
$4.25   E

1 Family—Fiction
ISBN 0-8098-1029-8
First published by Oxford
Also available in a bilingual Spanish-English edition
for $4.95 (ISBN 0-8098-1075-1) and an initial teaching
alphabet edition, lib. bdg. $3.50 (ISBN 0-8098-1120-
0)
For very small readers, this picture-story book
recounts the day by day doings of the Small family
from Monday's washing to Sunday's church going and
afternoon drive
"The toy-like figures, the use of one bright color,
the clear arrangement of details, the humor, all prove
this [author-artist's] mastery of appeal to the seeing
eyes of the nursery age." N Y Her Trib Bks

Spring is here. Walck, H.Z. 1945 unp illus $4.50
    E

1 Spring—Poetry
ISBN 0-8098-1014-X
First published by Oxford
"Calligraphy by Hilda Scott"
The song of a child's spring—birds, rabbits and
budding flowers—hop-scotch, sailing kites, hoops
and swings
"A gay small picture book for very young children
[illustrated by the author]. Each page has a brightly
colored picture of springtime scenes and activities
with a verse to accompany it." Library J

Levitin, Sonia

Who owns the moon? Illus. by John Larrecq. Parnassus Press 1973 unp illus $4.95, lib. bdg. $4.77 E

1 Moon—Fiction
ISBN 0-87466-066-1; 0-87466-005-X
This is the story of three argumentative farmers,
each of whom claims to own the moon, and of how the
wise teacher in the valley resolves their quarrel
"The simple story basically provides a background
for the illustrations, which portray boldly-shaped,
blustering men, furrowed and cultivated fields, and
beautiful night skies dominated by lunar light. Bright

yellow and blue endpapers depicting the moon in
different stages, the varied layout of pictures and text,
and the composition of each illustration to fill an arch-
shaped form enhance the physical appearance of the
book; the rustic tones and the earthiness of the illustrations convey the comic, peasant coarseness of the
story." Horn Bk

Lewis, Thomas P.

Hill of fire; pictures by Joan Sandin. Harper 1971
63p illus (An I can read history bk) $2.95, lib. bdg.
$3.79   E

1 Mexico—Fiction 2 Paricutin (Volcano)—Fiction
ISBN 0-06-023803-8; 0-06-023804-6
"The hill of fire is Paricutin and the story . . . is
about the way this volcanic eruption changes the lives
of the people who lived near it, in particular the man
in whose field the hill of fire began." Top of the News
"Here is basically a human story, sympathetically
and expressively illustrated with simple lines and
warm colors, that will give readers understanding of a
people, as well as a good story based on fact." Sch
Library J

Lexau, Joan M.

Benjie; illus. by Don Bolognese. Dial Press 1964
unp illus $4.95, lib. bdg. $4.58   E

1 Negroes—Fiction 2 Bashfulness—Fiction
ISBN 0-8037-0537-9; 0-8037-0536-0
"Benjie, a small Negro boy who lives with his
grandmother in a one-room city apartment, is so painfully shy that he cannot talk to anyone, even the
neighbors. But when Granny loses a favorite earring,
he tries to find it, and in doing so, overcomes his
shyness. The loving relationship between the child
and his grandmother gives warmth and credibility to a
charming, picture book." Moorachian. What is a City?
Followed by: Benjie on his own

Benjie on his own; illus. by Don Bolognese. Dial
Press 1970 unp illus $4.95, lib. bdg. $4.58   E

1 Negroes—Fiction 2 Bashfulness—Fiction
ISBN 0-8037-0712-6; 0-8037-0713-4
"Benjie is worried when Granny doesn't meet him
after school. Older boys intimidate him as he tries to
find his way home. When he finally does reach his
apartment, he discovers that Granny is sick. Benjie
brushes fear aside and seeks the aid of neighbors and
the police." Keating. Building Bridges of Understanding Between Cultures
"This is a charming story, well-developed, with
good characterization, full of suspense, and beautifully written. The illustrations enhance the telling of
the story, a good sequel to the first book about Benjie
[entered above]." Rdng Ladders. 5th edition

Emily and the klunky baby and the next-door dog;
pictures by Martha Alexander. Dial Press 1972 unp
illus $4.95, lib. bdg. $4.58   E

1 Divorce—Fiction
ISBN 0-8037-2309-1; 0-8037-2310-5
On a sunny winter day, when her divorced mother
is too preoccupied with tax forms to notice the little
girl, frustrated Emily decides to run away. She takes
her baby brother and her sled, but has to contend with
the next-door dog and getting lost which complicates
her resolution to reach Daddy
"Joan Lexau has captured the lonely puzzled, angry
feelings of a little girl in crisis. . . . This book may be
almost too real in its treatment of a whole family's
frustration. The mother looks absolutely frazzled and
the house seems cold, as if the heat had been turned
back." Christian Sci Monitor

Lexau, Joan M.—*Continued*

The homework caper; pictures by Syd Hoff. Harper 1966 64p illus (An I can read mystery) lib. bdg. $3.79 **E**

1 Mystery and detective stories
ISBN 0-06-023856-9

"The strange disappearance of Bill's missing arithmetic homework is resolved through true detective methods." Best Bks for Children, 1968

I should have stayed in bed; pictures by Syd Hoff. Harper 1965 48p illus lib. bdg. $3.79 **E**

1 Negroes—Fiction
ISBN 0-06-023861-5

"Sam awakens late and from then on everything goes wrong—at home and school. Told with a gay simplicity in the first person, this will appeal to beginning readers because it is a familiar situation told entertainingly. The pictures are the only indication that Sam and others in his class are Negroes." We Build Together

Me day; pictures by Robert Weaver. Dial Press 1971 unp illus $4.95, lib. bdg. $4.58 **E**

1 Birthdays—Fiction 2 Negroes—Fiction
ISBN 0-8037-5572-4; 0-8037-5573-2

"What begins as a particularly good day for Rafer quickly turns into disappointment when there is no birthday letter from his father. But then a mysterious errand to the local store reveals a surprise that turns an ordinary birthday into a very special 'me day.'" Pub W

"Lifting the book out of the ordinary as a portrayal of a black family are the positive tone, lack of moralizing, and the heads-up attitude of the family members as they cope with the problems of a broken home. . . . The cadence of black speech is effectively incorporated in the natural-sounding dialogue, and softly shaded black-and-white illustrations skillfully depict facial expressions and reinforce the mood of the text." Sch Library J

Olaf reads; illus. by Harvey Weiss. Dial Press 1961 53p illus $4.95, lib. bdg. $4.58 **E**

1 Reading—Fiction
ISBN 0-440-6559-4

Three stories showing how "Olaf, a self-possessed little boy, interprets signs, when he first learns to read, strictly in his own way." Pub W

"Olaf's reading mistakes [are] both hilarious and instructive." Sat Rev

The rooftop mystery; pictures by Syd Hoff. Harper 1968 64p illus (An I can read mystery) $2.95, lib. bdg. $3.79 **E**

1 Mystery and detective stories 2 Negroes—Fiction
ISBN 0-06-023864-X; 0-06-023865-8

"Sam and Albert are helping Sam's family move to another home within walking distance; unfortunately Sam finds any distance too long in which he can be seen in public carrying his sister's large, conspicuous doll." Sutherland. The Best in Children's Bks

"A humorous mystery for beginning readers that features a Negro boy, Sam, and his well-intentioned friends, Albert and Amy Lou. . . . Comical illustrations add chuckles." Keating. Building Bridges of Understanding Between Cultures

Lindgren, Astrid

Christmas in the stable; pictures by Harald Wiberg. Coward-McCann 1962 unp illus lib. bdg. $5.39 **E**

1 Christmas stories
ISBN 0-698-30042-4

A "tender telling of the Christmas story by a Swedish mother to her small child, who visualizes the birth of Jesus as happening now on a farm like their own." Wis Library Bul

"Beautiful paintings of the Swedish countryside interpret the . . . story." N Y Pub Library

The Tomten; adapted by Astrid Lindgren from a poem by Viktor Rydberg; illus. by Harald Wiberg. Coward-McCann 1961 unp illus $6.50, lib. bdg. $5.39 **E**

1 Winter—Fiction 2 Fairy tales
ISBN 0-698-20147-7; 0-698-30370-9

"Snowy farm pictures and warm scenes inside barn, sheds, and house show the Tomten, a little Swedish troll, going quietly about to the animals on cold winter nights comforting them with the promise that spring will come. The text was adapted from a nineteenth-century poem by Viktor Rydberg, and the pictures are by an outstanding Swedish painter of animals and nature. An unusual and beautiful picture book." Horn Bk

The Tomten and the fox; adapted by Astrid Lindgren from a poem by Karl-Erik Forsslund; illus. by Harald Wiberg. Coward-McCann 1966 unp illus lib. bdg. $5.39 **E**

1 Foxes—Stories 2 Winter—Fiction 3 Fairy tales
ISBN 0-698-30371-7

A story taken from an old Swedish poem

"Inside, the family celebrates around a candlelit tree before going to bed. Outside, the snow glistens in the moonlight, and Reynard the fox creeps toward the hen house. But Tomten [the troll] guardian of all life on the farm, admonishes Reynard, satisfies his hunger with a bowl of porridge, and sends him back to his den in the forest just as the morning star brightens the sky." Horn Bk

This picture book "is set at Christmastime, although it is not a Christmas story. The text is slight, but it is gently appealing. . . . The illustrations are quite lovely: soft in technique, subdued in color and mood, perfectly catching the feeling of the hushed and blue-white quiet of the countryside on a snowy night." Chicago. Children's Bk Center

Lionni, Leo

Alexander the the wind-up mouse. Pantheon Bks. [1970] c1969 unp illus $4.95, lib. bdg. $5.99, pa $1.25 **E**

1 Mice—Stories
ISBN 0-394-80914-9; 0-394-90914-3; 0-394-82911-5

Illustrated by the author "Alexander wants to be a wind-up mouse like Willie, who is the little girl's favorite toy. A magic lizard can change him, but then he learns that Willie's key is broken and decides to turn Willie into a real mouse like himself." Adventuring With Bks. 2d edition

"The illustrations employ the same imaginative collage techniques [as the author's Frederick entered below]—less subtly perhaps, but with even richer and more spectacular effects. Tissue-paper, marbleized and patterned papers, newspaper, Japanese rice paper are some of the surfaces used to provide a brilliant background for the endearing little grey mouse who looks a lot like Frederick but has a personality all his own." Sch Library J

The biggest house in the world. Pantheon Bks. 1968 unp illus $4.95, lib. bdg. $5.99 **E**

1 Snails—Stories
ISBN 0-394-80944-0; 0-394-90944-5

"In this picture book [illustrated by the author] a small snail has a very large wish. He wants the largest house in the world. But by telling the youngster a story, his wise father helps him to see the impracticality of being encased in a magnificent monstrosity too big to move." Bk Week

Lionni, Leo—*Continued*

"In the style of fine picture books, the illustrations extend the story so the reader experiences both the wonder and excitement of watching the enormous shell grow, and later the relief and joy of the small snail as he explores his own world. The translucent color of the pictures and the simplicity of the text make a perfect combination." Bk World

Fish is fish. Pantheon Bks. 1970 unp illus $4.95, lib. bdg. $5.99, pa 95¢   E
1 Fishes—Stories 2 Frogs—Stories
ISBN 0-394-80440-6; 0-394-90440-0; 0-394-82799-6
Illustrated by the author
The frog tells the fish all about the world above the sea. The fish, however, can only visualize it in terms of fish-people, fish-birds and fish-cows
"The story is slight but pleasantly and simply told, the illustrations are page-filling, deft, colorful, and amusing." Chicago. Children's Bk Center

Frederick. Pantheon Bks. 1967 unp illus $4.95, lib. bdg. $5.99   E
1 Mice—Stories
ISBN 0-394-81040-6; 0-394-91040-0
"While other mice are gathering food for the winter, Frederick seems to daydream the summer away. When dreary winter comes, it is Frederick the poet-mouse who warms his friends and cheers them with his words." Wis Library Bul
"This captivating book is about a field mouse, but it sings a hymn of praise to poets in a gentle story that is illustrated [by the author] with gaiety and charm. The mice are plump little creatures with round, wondering eyes and the backgrounds of the pages echo in soft tones the appropriate colors of the seasons Frederick enjoys." Sat Rev

Inch by inch. Obolensky 1960 unp illus $4.95   E
1 Worms—Stories 2 Birds—Stories
ISBN 0-8392-3010-9
Also available in a French language edition (ISBN 0-8392-3028-1) and a Spanish language edition (ISBN 0-8392-3030-3) for $4.95 each
"An Astor book"
Illustrated by the author, this is a "small tale about an inchworm who liked to measure the robin's tail, the flamingo's neck, the whole of a hummingbird but not a nightingale's song." Christian Sci Monitor
"This is a book to look at again and again. The semi-abstract forms are sharply defined, clean and strong, the colors subtle and glowing, and the grassy world of the inchworm is a special place of enchantment." N Y Times Bk Rev

Little blue and little yellow; a story for Pippo and Ann and other children. Obolensky 1959 unp ullus $4.95   E
1 Color—Fiction
ISBN 0-8392-3018-4
"An Astor book"
The author uses "splashes of color and abstract forms to tell the story of little blue and his friend little yellow who hugged and hugged each other until they were green—and unrecognizable to their parents." Booklist
"So well are the dots handled on the pages that little blue and little yellow and their parents seem to have real personalities. It should inspire interesting color play and is a very original picture book by an artist." N Y Her Trib Books

Swimmy. Pantheon Bks. 1963 unp illus $4.95, lib. bdg. $5.99   E
1 Fishes—Stories
ISBN 0-394-81713-3; 0-394-91713-8
Also available in a French language edition for

$3.50 (ISBN 0-394-81715-X) and a Spanish language edition, $3.50 (ISBN 0-394-81709-5) lib. bdg. $5.69 (ISBN 0-394-91709-X)
"Swimmy, an insignificant fish escapes when a whole school of small fish are swallowed by a larger one. As he swims away from danger he meets many wonderful, colourful creatures and later saves another school of fish from the jaws of the enemy." Ontario Library Rev
"To illustrate his clever, but very brief story, Leo Lionni has made a book of astonishingly beautiful pictures, full of undulating, watery nuances of shape, pattern, and color." Horn Bk

Tico and the golden wings. Pantheon Bks. 1964 unp illus $4.95, lib. bdg. $5.99 pa $1.25   E
1 Birds—Stories
ISBN 0-394-81749-4; 0-394-91749-4; 0-394-83078-4
"A picture book with richly detailed illustrations [by the author] stylized in adaptation of the ornate richness of Indian Art, and—with few exceptions—restrained in the use of space. The pictures have a dignity achieved by dark, plummy colors. . . . The text describes the longing of a small wingless bird for the power of flight; granted a pair of golden wings, Tico gave away his golden feathers, one by one, to help humans. Each feather was replaced by one black one, and when Tico had all-black wings, he found that the other birds, who had mocked him when he was beautiful but different, now accepted him as one of them." Chicago. Children's Bk Center

Livermore, Elaine

Find the cat; written and illus. by Elaine Livermore. Houghton 1973 46p illus lib. bdg. $3.95   E
1 Cats—Stories 2 Dogs—Stories
ISBN 0-395-14756-5
"Cat and dog fight over a bone and dog wins. When dog is napping, though, cat retrieves the prize and hides it. Waking up, dog tries in vain—for most of the story—to find the elusive feline and his treat. The pictures are designed as bewildering mazes in which the cat is hidden and the child reader is invited to help dog find the artful pest." Pub W
"Children who like the challenge of a puzzle will enjoy pouring over the author's squiggly yellow and black line drawings in an effort to help the dog locate the cat which has hidden the bone." Booklist

Lobel, Anita

The troll music; story and pictures by Anita Lobel. Harper 1966 unp illus lib. bdg. $4.43   E
1 Musicians—Fiction 2 Fairy tales
ISBN 0-06-023930-1
"This beautifully illustrated story involves a group of travelling musicians who played lovely music until a mischievous troll cast a spell over them while they were sleeping; then only animal sounds come from their instruments. The people run them out, but the animals like their music. Together the musicians and animals work out a plan to charm the troll, but it takes Mrs. Troll to set him straight." Bruno. Bks for Sch Libraries, 1968

Lobel, Arnold

Frog and Toad are friends. Harper 1970 64p illus $2.95, lib. bdg. $3.79   E
1 Frogs—Stories
ISBN 0-06-023957-3; 0-06-023958-1
"An I can read book"
Here are five stories, illustrated by the author, which recount the adventures of two best friends—Toad and Frog. The stories are: Spring; The story; A lost button; A swim; The letter
"Five very short stories in a direct and ingenuous style, appealing because of their ease and the familiar-

Lobel, Arnold—*Continued*

ity of the situations, translated into animal terms. The mild humor that permeates the tales . . . adds to the value of some of the concepts obliquely presented (differences in shape and size in 'A Lost Button'; time concepts in 'Spring') and the give-and-take of a fast friendship is gently affectionate." Chicago. Children's Bk Center

Followed by: Frog and Toad together

Frog and Toad together. Harper 1972 64p illus $2.95, lib. bdg. $3.79   E

1 Frogs—Stories
ISBN 0-06-023959-X; 0-06-023960-3
Sequel to: Frog and Toad are friends
"An I can read book"
"Each of the five stories demonstrates the enduring quality of the two animals' friendship whether they are sitting and doing nothing due to the loss of Toad's list of things to do that day, growing gardens, exercising will power, testing their courage, or dreaming of grandeur." Booklist
"Lobel draws with both precision and ease on almost every one of these old-fashioned-looking pages. Whether Frog's country cottages or Toad's dreams of grandeur, the pictures make them real. And Lobel's words are full of insight into the concerns of small children. The book is a delight—and a bargain." Bk World

Mouse tales. Harper 1972 61p illus $2.95, lib. bdg. $3.79   E

1 Mice—Stories
ISBN 0-06-023941-7; 0-06-023942-5
"An I can read book"
Papa Mouse tells seven bedtime stories, one for each of his sons
Contents: The wishing well; Clouds; Very tall mouse and very short mouse; The mouse and the winds; The journey; The odd mouse; The bath
"The illustrations [by the author] have soft colors and precise, lively little drawings of the imaginative and humorous events in the stories. The themes are familiar to children: cloud shapes, wishing, a tall and a short friend who observe—and greet—natural phenomena on a walk, taking a bath, et cetera." Chicago. Children's Bk Center

On the day Peter Stuyvesant sailed into town. Harper 1971 unp illus $4.95, lib. bdg. $5.79   E

1 Stuyvesant, Peter—Fiction 2 New York (City)—History—Fiction 3 Stories in rhyme
ISBN 0-06-023971-9; 0-06-023972-7
Illustrated by the author, this is the "story of Peter Stuyvesant who, arriving in New Amsterdam in 1647, found the whole dirty place a total disgrace, and angrily set the Dutchmen to work transforming the village into a pleasant place in which to live." Booklist
"The illustrations, many framed like Dutch tiles, are done in yellow and blue and have a rhythm and humor that complement the verses exactly. The double-page spread at the end of the book—showing the future of Peter's tidy city—provides an unexpected shock of recognition." Horn Bk

Small pig; story and pictures by Arnold Lobel. Harper 1969 63p illus $2.95, lib. bdg. $3.79   E

1 Pigs—Stories
ISBN 0-06-023931-X; 0-06-023932-8
"An I can read book"
This "is the story of a pig who, finding the clean farm unbearable, runs away to look for mud—and ends up stuck in cement. His facial expressions alone are worth the price of the book; the illustrations, in blue, green, and gold, are a perfect complement to

the story. Humor, adventure, and short, simple sentences provide a real treat for beginning readers." Sch Library J

Lord, Beman

Our new baby's ABC; pictures by Velma Ilsley. Walck, H.Z. 1964 unp illus $4   E

1 Alphabet books 2 Infants
ISBN 0-8098-1100-6
"A pleasant combination of alphabet book and constructive approach to the new baby. A small brother and sister are pictured, surveying the baby with rather cheerful complacency. . . . The text should be useful for learning the alphabet also, because it uses as examples such familar objects. The illustrations are not outstanding, but they augment the mood of the text particularly in showing the inclusive affection of parents and grandparents." Chicago. Children's Bk Center

Lord, John Vernon

The giant jam sandwich; story and pictures by John Vernon Lord; with verses by Janet Burroway. Houghton 1973 [c1972] 32p illus lib. bdg. $6.95   E

1 Wasps—Stories 2 Stories in rhyme
ISBN 0-395-16033-2
First published 1972 in England
This is a story in rhymed verse "about the citizens of Itching Down, who, attacked by four million wasps, make a giant jam sandwich to attract and trap the insects. With dump truck, spades, and hoes the people spread butter and strawberry jam across an enormous slice of bread; then, when the wasps settle, they drop the other slice from five helicopters and a flying tractor." Booklist
"Highly amusing in the details of John Vernon Lord's illustrations. . . . The figures are deliciously grotesque their expressions wickedly accurate and the colours cheerfully vivid." Jr Bookshelf

Lowrey, Janette Sebring

Six silver spoons; pictures by Robert Quackenbush. Harper 1971 63p illus (An I can read history bk) $2.95, lib. bdg. $3.79   E

1 U.S.—History—Revolution—Fiction
ISBN 0-06-024036-9; 0-06-024037-7
This is the "story of two Colonial children who, on the eve of the Revolution, are attempting to get their Revere silver spoons through the British lines to their mother for her birthday." Pub W
"The credible plot and effectively portrayed setting make this an excellent historical story for beginning readers. Illustrated with colored drawings on almost every page." Booklist

Lund, Doris Herold

You ought to see Herbert's house; pictures by Steven Kellogg. Watts, F. 1973 unp illus lib. bdg. $4.90   E

1 Houses—Fiction
ISBN 0-531-02595-0
"Herbert comes to visit Roger, who lives in a house just like all the others on his block, and tells his friend that he lives in a castle with a moat, a drawbridge and flags flying from its turrets. Herbert explains further that his mother doesn't mind snakes. . . . Roger is impressed and Herbert goes home—to a house just like Roger's—and confides in his mother his worry that he might have exaggerated a little. When Roger comes to visit, all is well, because Herbert can offer a real chocolate cake and a tent to sleep outside in, where they can pretend they live almost anywhere. The pictures, contrasting imaginary and real scenes, are most ingratiating. The story is well organized and convincing." Pub W

Lundgren, Max

Matt's grandfather; pictures by Fibben Hald; tr. by Ann Pyk. Putnam 1972 unp illus $5.95   E
  1 Grandfathers—Fiction 2 Old age—Fiction
ISBN 0-399-20257-9
Original Swedish edition, 1970
"This story describes a child's adjustment to a grandparent who is in a nursing home and is senile. . . . It is Grandfather's eighty-fifth birthday, and Matt has been told that his grandfather is almost like a baby—but he finds that Grandfather has his own way of keeping in touch with reality, and that it is a way that a small child can understand and feel empathetic about. The story . . . is gentle and affectionate, told with grace and simplicity. A very good introduction to the concept of the changes that come with old age." Chicago. Children's Bk Center

McClintock, Mike

A fly went by; illus. by Fritz Siebel. Beginner Bks. 1958 unp illus $2.95, lib. bdg. $3.69   E
  1 Animals—Stories 2 Stories in rhyme
ISBN 0-394-80003-6; 0-394-90003-0
In rhymed verse the author describes an exciting chase that involves a fly, a cat, a dog, a sheep and all sorts of fetching and familiar animals. Only 177 different words are used

Stop that ball! Illus. by Fritz Siebel. Beginner Bks. 1958 62p illus $2.95, lib. bdg. $3.69   E
  1 Stories in rhyme
ISBN 0-394-80010-9; 0-394-90010-3
"When a small boy hits a red ball it flies off on some amazing adventures." ALA Children's Service Division. Selected Lists of Children's Bks and Recordings
"Longer than most first-grade stories, this has enough action in both rhyming text and realistic pictures to make good readers keep their eye on the ball all the way." N Y Times Bk Rev

What have I got? Pictures by Leonard Kessler. Harper 1961 32p illus lib. bdg. $3.43   E
  1 Stories in rhyme
ISBN 0-06-024141-1
"An Early I can read book"
"The rhyming text describes the objects a boy has in his pocket, then tells of what can be done, in one's imagination, with those objects." Chicago. Children's Bk Center

McCloskey, Robert

Blueberries for Sal. Viking 1948 54p illus lib. bdg. $4.95, pa 95¢   E
  1 Bears—Stories 2 Maine—Fiction
ISBN 0-670-17591-9; 0-670-05002-4
"The author-artist tells what happens on a summer day in Maine when a little girl and a bear cub, wandering away from their blueberry-picking mothers, each mistakes the other's mother for its own. The Maine hill-side and meadows are real and lovely, the quiet humor is entirely childlike, and there is just exactly the right amount of suspense for small children." Wis Library Bul

Burt Dow, deep-water man; a tale of the sea in the classic tradition. Viking 1963 61p illus lib. bdg. $5.95   E
  1 Whales—Stories 2 Sea stories
ISBN 0-670-19748-3
The "adventure of an old Maine fisherman, who puts to sea in a leaky dory accompanied by his giggling pet gull and who almost meets disaster in the belly of a huge whale." Atlantic
"The enchanting scenes of Burt Dow making off with his multi-colored dory into the wild, purple sea and meeting pink-mouthed whales really needs no

text at all. It's a deep water voyage into art." Christian Sci Monitor

Lentil. Viking 1940 unp illus lib. bdg. $5.95, pa 95¢   E
  1 Mouth organ—Fiction 2 Ohio—Fiction
ISBN 0-670-42357-2; 0-670-05090-3
Picture-story book about a small boy who could not sing, but who could work wonders on a simple harmonica, especially on the day when the great Colonel Carter returned to his home town
"Big, vigorous, amusing pictures [by the author] in black-and-white, with an Ohio small-town background." New Yorker

Make way for ducklings. Viking 1941 unp illus lib. bdg. $5.95, pa 95¢   E
  1 Ducks—Stories 2 Boston—Fiction
ISBN 0-670-45149-5; 0-670-05017-2
Awarded the Caldecott Medal, 1942
"A family of baby ducks was born on the Charles River near Boston. When they were old enough to follow, Mother Duck, with some help from a friendly policeman, trailed them through Boston traffic to the pond in the Public Garden. . . . This large picture book . . . is both picturesque and amusing." Bookmark
"In a series of large lithographs [the author-illustrator] reveals his instinct for the beauty of wild life and that of the city [of Boston] and a sure knowledge of ducks and their ways. . . . There are some very beautiful drawings in this book." Horn Bk

One morning in Maine. Viking 1952 64p illus lib. bdg. $5.95, pa 95¢   E
  1 Maine—Fiction
ISBN 0-670-52627-4; 0-670-05053-9
The events of this "story—Sal's discovery of her first loose tooth, the loss of the tooth while digging clams, the consequent wish on a gull's feather, and the wish come true—occur in the course of one morning in Maine. The lovely Maine seacoast scenes and the doings of Sal with her family and friends are drawn [by the author] with enticing detail in beautiful, big double-spread lithographs printed in dark blue." Booklist

Time of wonder. Viking 1957 63p illus lib. bdg. $6.95   E
  1 Maine—Description and travel
ISBN 0-670-71512-3
Awarded the Caldecott Medal, 1958
"A summer on an island in Maine is described through the simple everyday experiences of children, but also reveals the author's deep awareness of an attachment to all the shifting moods of season and weather, and the salty, downright character of the New England people. Written in rhythmic style and occasionally rhyme, this is a fine example of illustrating and writing." Top of the News
Robert McCloskey "has succeeded in transferring his love for the island to the printed page and as you listen to his words and look at his pictures you feel that every day and every season is a 'time of wonder.' This is entirely different from any book he has done before, and he has made it a thing of great beauty." Horn Bk

MacDonald, Golden

The little island; with illus. by Leonard Weisgard. Doubleday 1946 unp illus $5.95, lib. bdg. $6.70, pa $1.25   E
  1 Islands
ISBN 0-385-07381-X; 0-385-07631-2; 0-385-087050-5
Awarded the Caldecott Medal, 1947
"In some of his most brilliant and exciting pictures

MacDonald, Golden—*Continued*

Leonard Wiesgard shows the changes that the seasons [and storms, day and night] bring to a little island out in the ocean. The rhythmic story tells of the kitten who came ashore from a sailboat and found out the secret of being an island from a wise and talkative fish." Horn Bk

"Superbly beautiful pictures fill 20 full pages, their rich color flowing off the page to make them seem as unhampered as the sky. This is a book to sharpen the senses and expand one's personal horizons." Bk Week

Red light, green light; illus. by Leonard Weisgard. Doubleday 1944 unp illus $4.95, lib. bdg. $5.70, pa 95¢   E
1 Traffic regulations
ISBN 0-385-07466-2; 0-385-07651-7; 0-385-05364-9
"The Red Light says they can't go, the Green Light says they can, as the truck and the jeep, the horse, the boy and dog, the cat and mouse go through the day, obeying signals. Even when all things are asleep, the Red Light and Green Light wink good night. Echoing the rhythm of the text are the striking oblong book's bold vivid [lithograph] drawings in sepia, red and green." Bookmark

McGinley, Phyllis

All around the town; illus. by Helen Stone. Lippincott 1948 unp illus lib. bdg. $3.93   E
1 New York (City) 2 Alphabet books
ISBN 0-397-30142-1
An ABC book "in rhyme about 'The gay things, the stray things that city children see.' From A for Aeroplane to Z for Zoo, and touching upon such items as E for Escalator, J for Jaywalker, N for Next-door Neighbors and T for Taxicab." Moorachian, What is a City?
"For each letter of the alphabet there is a double-page picture, rich in color and beautiful in design. . . . The city is New York." N Y Libraries

MacGregor, Ellen

Theodore Turtle; pictures by Paul Galdone. McGraw 1955 32p illus lib. bdg. $4.72   E
1 Turtles—Stories
ISBN 0-07-044567-2
"Whittlesey House publications"
"The story of turtle with a one-track mind. Theodore just wanted to go down town, but he couldn't seem to get ready. Every time he found one thing he needed, he mislaid another! The highly detailed drawings are cheerful in yellow and red and help make this especially nice for reading to young children." Horn Bk

McPhail, David

The bear's toothache; written and illus. by David McPhail. Little 1972 31p illus lib. bdg. $5.95   E
1 Bears—Stories 2 Teeth—Fiction
ISBN 0-316-56312-9
"An Atlantic Monthly Press book"
"In this delightful fantasy, a small boy receives a nocturnal visit from a bear with a sore tooth. Pulling on the tooth doesn't work, eating fails to loosen it, and hitting it with a pillow breaks a lamp and wakes up father. The boy's cowboy rope is securely fastened to tooth and bedpost and, as the bear jumps out the window, the tooth finally pops out. The grateful bear then gives it to the boy to put under his pillow. The simple text is accompanied by full-page pastel pictures which are filled with action and detail and are superbly suited to this imaginative bedtime tale." Sch Library J

Mann, Peggy

That new baby; illus. by Susanne Suba. Coward, McCann [1968 c1967] unp illus lib. bdg. $3.86   E

1 Infants—Fiction 2 Sisters—Fiction
ISBN 0-698-30252-4
This story concerns Jenny, an only child, and her experiences in adjusting to her mother's pregnancy and the arrival of a baby sister
Jenny "eventually comes to realize that for Mommy and Daddy the baby is more work, but for her the baby is 'extra fun.'" Rdng Ladders. 5th edition

Mari, Iela

The chicken and the egg, by Iela and Enzo Mari. Pantheon Bks. [1970] c1969 unp illus lib. bdg. $4.79   E
1 Chickens 2 Stories without words
ISBN 0-394-90858-9
Original Italian edition published 1969
"A book without words. The pictures, colorful and captivating, tell the story of the chicken life cycle, and they are bound to get the child to talk about them. . . . [The book] encourages the child to supply the words himself. The book will intrigue and excite most youngsters (and even some not-so-youngsters as well)." The AAAS Science Bk List for Children

Marshall, James, 1942-

George and Martha; written and illus. by James Marshall. Houghton 1972 46p illus lib. bdg. $4.95, pa 95¢   E
1 Hippopotamus—Stories 2 Friendship—Fiction
ISBN 0-395-16619-5; 0-395-19972-7
In these five short episodes which include a misunderstanding about split pea soup, invasion of privacy and a crisis over a missing tooth, two not very delicate hippopotamuses reveal various aspects of friendship
"The pale pictures of these creatures and their adventures—in yellows, pinks, greens, and grays—capture the directness and humor of the stories." Horn Bk

George and Martha encore. Houghton 1973 46p illus lib. bdg. $4.95   E
1 Hippopotamus—Stories 2 Friendship—Fiction
ISBN 0-395-17512-7
Illustrated by the author
In these five short episodes the two hippopotamus friends are involved with "a dance recital, a French lesson, an Indian disguise, a frolic on the beach, and planting in the garden." Top of the News
"There is genial good humor in the juxtaposition of the absurd and the delicate, and the understated costumes on the stolid, grey figures are witty and winning." Horn Bk

What's the matter with Carruthers? A bedtime story; written and illus. by James Marshall. Houghton 1972 32p illus lib. bdg. $4.95   E
1 Bears—Stories 2 Friendship—Fiction
ISBN 0-395-13895-7
When Carruthers the bear becomes very contrary, his friends Emily and Eugene begin to worry and try to make him happy, until they finally realize that Carruthers has forgotten about his winter nap
"An amusing picture book of just the right length and consistency for bedtime. . . . The color illustrations are original and very funny, especially the animals' expressions." Booklist

Willis. Houghton 1974 46p illus $5.95   E
1 Animals—Stories
ISBN 0-395-19494-6
Illustrated by the author
Willis, a crocodile, would be very happy on the beach, if he only had 29 cents to buy sunglasses. His friends—Bird, Snake and Lobster—finally think of a way to get the money for Willis' glasses
"Readers will get many chortles from the antics of

Marshall, James—*Continued*

this mild-mannered menagerie; the illustrations in blue, green, black, and lobster, are a·carefree rendering of the text." Booklist

Yummers! Houghton 1973 30p illus lib. bdg. $5.95   E

1 Weight control—Fiction 2 Pigs—Stories 3 Turtles—Stories

ISBN 0-395-14757-3

Illustrated by the author

Worried about her weight, Emily Pig "jumps rope; her friend Eugene [Turtle] suggests a walk as better exercise, but the walk is interrupted by a series of snacks. Emily, who has said 'Yummers,' to everything, finally has a tummy ache. She thinks it must have been due to all the walking, and agrees with Eugene when he suggests that she stay in bed and eat plenty of good food." Chicago. Children's Bk Center

"Corpulent, amiable Emily moves with monumental charm in the humorous, bright pastel pictures." Horn Bk

Martin, Patricia Miles

The little brown hen; illus. by Harper Johnson. Crowell 1960 23p illus $4.50, lib. bdg. $5.25   E

1 Negroes—Fiction 2 Chickens—Stories

ISBN 0-690-49733-4; 0-690-49734-2

"A Negro boy's search for his missing brown hen and his desire to give his mother some ducks for her birthday come to a happy conclusion when he finds the little brown hen in the woods brooding a nestful of ducklings." Booklist

"An attractive picture-book story about black Americans in a rural setting." Keating. Building Bridges of Understanding Between Cultures

The rice bowl pet; illus. by Ezra Jack Keats. Crowell 1962 unp illus $5.50, lib. bdg. $6.25   E

1 Chinese in the U.S.—Fiction 2 Pets—Stories 3 San Francisco—Fiction

ISBN 0-690-69968-9; 0-690-69969-7

A picture-story book with a "background of San Francisco, especially of Chinatown and Fisherman's Wharf. The story is about Ah Jim's efforts to find a pet which is small enough to fit into his rice bowl (his mother's stipulation) and yet which is alive and warm and pleasant to hold (his own requirements)." Horn Bk

"An appealing story that points up, without preaching, courtesy and consideration for others." N Y Times Bk Rev

Massey, Jeanne

The littlest witch; illus. by Adrienne Adams. Knopf 1959 unp illus $2.75, lib. bdg. $4.99   E

1 Witches—Fiction 2 Halloween—Stories

ISBN 0-394-80734-0; 0-394-90734-5

"The littlest witch did not enjoy playing the usual Hallowe'en pranks so she lost her chance to fly to the moon. She was very lonely until she found that there was a place for her in the Witches' Circle after all. While the pictures for this gentle, amusing story do justice to the good little witch, they are also full of Hallowe'en atmosphere, and witches on broomsticks sweep across the sky." Horn Bk

Matsuno, Masako

A pair of red clogs; illus. by Kazue Mizumura. Collins unp illus lib. bdg. $4.91   E

1 Japan—Fiction

ISBN 0-529-03636-3

A Japanese "grandmother, preparing to send a pair of red lacquer clogs to her young granddaughter, reminisces about her own childhood. She remembers the red clogs she cracked playing a weather-telling

game and how she tried to make them very dirty so her mother would buy her a new pair. The voice of her own conscience and her mother's loving kindness so shamed her that she knew she would never trick her mother again. Charming family story with rich Oriental flavor, warm sympathy, and gentle humor." Library J

Matthiesen, Thomas

ABC; an alphabet book. Photographs in color by Thomas Matthiesen. Platt 1966 unp illus $2.95   E

1 Alphabet books

ISBN 0-8228-1050-6

"Familiar objects—shoes, a clock, a balloon—represent the 26 letters of the alphabet." Hodges. Bks for Elem Sch Libraries

"The forthright, three-dimensional photography is colorful in more than the literal sense. Each letter is given in upper and lower case, and the simplest things used to illustrate them are photographed with great imagination. You can hear a child's questions and sense his concentration as he pores over these pictures." Bk Week

Things to see; a child's world of familiar objects. Photographs in color by Thomas Matthiesen. Platt 1966 unp illus $2.95   E

ISBN 0-8228-1051-4

"A compilation of color photographs, each full page and each faced by a page that has a few lines of text and—in heavy type face—the name of the pictured object. The arrangement is random; the pictures are excellent both in the choices of subjects and in the quality of reproduction. The text verges on cuteness here and there, but is for the most part rather simple, almost naive in style; the short sentences and large print could be read by beginning readers, but probably won't be because of the format." Chicago. Children's Bk Center

Mayer, Mercer

A boy, a dog, a frog and a friend; a new book by Mercer and Marianna Mayer. Dial Press 1971 unp illus $2.95, lib. bdg. $2.96   E

1 Fishing—Fiction 2 Animals—Stories 3 Stories without words

ISBN 0-8037-0754-1; 0-8037-0755-X

"A boy, his dog and, secondarily, a frog go fishing and meet with what appears to be an enemy—a turtle. After nipping the dog's paw and then his tail and pulling him into the water, the turtle plays dead. A funeral procession is forming of the now saddened boy, dog and frog when suddenly the turtle flips himself over. All is joy and the enemy becomes a friend." Library J

"This is a delightful little picture book that can be read by everybody, even little kids who can't read, because it doesn't have any writing to read. . . . It tells a warm and charming story." N Y Times Bk Rev

A boy, a dog, and a frog. Dial Press 1967 unp illus $2.95, lib. bdg. $2.96   E

1 Frogs—Stories 2 Stories without words

ISBN 0-8037-0763-0; 0-8037-0767-3

"Without the need of a single word, humorous, very engaging pictures [by the author] tell the story of a little boy who sets forth with his dog and a net on a summer day to catch an enterprising and personable frog. Even very young preschoolers will 'read' the tiny book with the greatest satisfaction and pleasure." Horn Bk

Bubble bubble. Parents Mag. Press 1973 unp illus $4.95, lib. bdg. $4.59   E

1 Stories without words

ISBN 0-8193-0630-4; 0-8193-0631-2

Mayer, Mercer—*Continued*

"A wordless picture book about a boy who buys a magic bubble maker and discovers he can create all kinds of shapes and monsters. The expressions generated by the bubble monsters attest to Mayer's consummate artistic skill." Top of the News

Frog goes to dinner. Dial Press 1974 unp illus $2.95, lib. bdg. $2.96   E

1 Frogs—Stories 2 Stories without words
ISBN 0-8037-3386-0; 0-8037-3381-X

"Frog slips into the boy's pocket as he prepares to go off to an elegant restaurant with his parents, and once there he wreaks havoc as he hops into a musician's instrument, leaps into a dowager's salad, and takes a dive into a man's cocktail. The ride home is a picture of gloomy disgrace—but once inside their own bedroom, boy and frog dissolve into whoops of joy." Chicago. Children's Bk Center

"Although similar in format and style to the earlier wordless picture books in the series, this story is less subtle than its predecessors—closer to farce than to comedy. But Frog, who has been endowed by his creator with infinite charm, continues to be irresistibly funny." Horn Bk

Frog on his own. Dial Press 1973 unp illus $2.95, lib. bdg. $2.96   E

1 Frogs—Stories 2 Stories without words
ISBN 0-8037-2701-1; 0-8037-2695-3

"Another amusing wordless picture book about that happy foursome of frog, dog, turtle, and boy. Here they set off for a jaunt in a public park and frog is separated from his friends. At first he scampers happily about, but he soon finds that people do not take kindly to such friendly overtures as sharing a carriage with a baby or emerging from an inviting picnic basket. Chased by a cat, frog is rescued by his friends and is carried off in the arms of his boy. The story line is crystal clear, and the pictures have a blithe quality that is engaging." Chicago. Children's Bk Center

Frog, where are you? Dial Press 1969 unp illus $2.95, lib. bdg. $2.96   E

1 Frogs—Stories 2 Dogs—Stories 3 Stories without words
ISBN 0-8037-2737-2; 0-8037-2732-1

In this story without words, illustrated by the author, a "boy and his dog search for their missing frog friend. After tangling with a nest of hornets, an owl, and other woodland creatures, they find the frog—with a large family of offspring." Booklist

"There are no words in this beguiling little book, and none are needed; it is easy for children to follow the action and to appreciate the antic progress of the hero. The drawings are very funny, especially one in which a companionable dog who has stuck his head irretrievably in the empty frog-jar peers hopefully about for the lost one." Sat Rev

Merriam, Eve

Boys & girls, girls & boys; pictures by Harriet Sherman. Holt 1972 unp illus lib. bdg. $4.59, pa $1.65   E

ISBN 0-03-091979-7; 0-03-005716-7

A "multi-ethnic group of children play together unrestricted by sex role stereotyping." Shargel. We Can Change It

Milhous, Katherine

The egg tree; story and pictures by Katherine Milhous. Scribner 1950 unp illus lib. bdg. $5.95   E

1 Pennsylvania Dutch—Fiction 2 Easter—Stories
3 Egg decoration—Fiction
ISBN 0-684-12716-4

Awarded the Caldecott Medal, 1951

"A seasonal book with the illustrations and 'things to do' aspect of more value than the actual story. A group of children taking part in a Pennsylvania Dutch Easter have an Easter egg hunt and learn how to decorate eggs and hang them on an Easter egg tree. The full page coloured illustrations are Pennsylvania Dutch in character and the smaller ones are decorative Easter egg designs." Ontario Library Rev

There "are lovely illustrations and decorations . . . plus directions for making an egg tree." N Y Times Bk Rev

Miller, Edna

Mousekin's family; story and pictures by Edna Miller. Prentice-Hall 1969 unp illus lib. bdg. $5.95, pa 95¢   E

1 Mice—Stories
ISBN 0-13-604462-X; 0-13-604157-4

A whitefoot mouse, "Mousekin finds a small relative, or thinks she has, a confusion that creates the story." Pub W

"The pictures, accurate in detail and softly colored, complement a text which, though it offers some natural history information and the chance for discussion of family children relationships, will be appreciated basically as a light, pleasant little story." Sch Library J

Minarik, Else Holmelund

Father Bear comes home; pictures by Maurice Sendak. Harper 1959 62p illus $2.95, lib. bdg. $3.79 E

1 Bears—Stories 2 Animals—Stories
ISBN 0-06-024230-2; 0-06-024231-0

"An I can read book"

These adventures of Little Bear and his animal friends tell of his fishing trip with Owl, and of Father Bear's homecoming

"An engaging book for beginning readers and for the adults who may read it to younger children. The guileful ingenuousness of Little Bear emerges with art from the simple vocabulary, and the illustrations are a delight. Little Bear's struggles to end the hiccups form an especially amusing episode." Chicago. Children's Bk Center

A kiss for Little Bear; pictures by Maurice Sendak. Harper 1968 32p illus $2.95, lib. bdg. $3.79   E

1 Bears—Stories 2 Animals—Stories
ISBN 0-06-024298-1; 0-06-024299-X

"An I can read book"

Little Bear draws a picture of a wild thing and sends the "picture to his grandmother who sends a kiss back to him, relayed to him by an animal pony express [via] a hen, a cat, a frog, and a skunk." Pub W

"Little Bear is a creature of love and joy and he spreads it around in this enchanting story. The illustrations are incredibly alive and expressive. This is a good easy reader, the vocabulary is simple but vivid and the story is well constructed." Commonweal

Little Bear; pictures by Maurice Sendak. Harper 1957 63p illus $2.95, lib. bdg. $3.79   E

1 Bears—Stories
ISBN 0-06-024240-X; 0-06-024241-8

Also available in a Spanish language edition, lib. bdg. $3.79 (ISBN 0-06-024244-2)

"An I can read book"

Four episodes "about Little Bear, a charming creature who will delight young readers [and listeners] as he persuades his mother to make him a winter outfit—only to discover his fur coat is all he needs; makes himself some birthday soup—and then is surprised with a birthday cake; takes an imaginary trip to the moon, and finally goes happily off to sleep as his mother tells him a story about 'Little Bear.'" Chicago. Children's Bk Center

Minarik, Else Holmelund—*Continued*

The pictures "depict all the warmth of feeling and the special companionship that exists between a small child and his mother." Pub W

Little Bear's friend; pictures by Maurice Sendak. Harper 1960 unp illus $2.95, lib. bdg. $3.79   E

1 Bears—Stories 2 Animals—Stories
ISBN 0-06-02455-8; 0-06-024256-6

"After playing all summer with his human friend, Emily, Little Bear is sad when she must go back to school, until Father Bear shows him a way to keep in touch with her." Hodges. Bks for Elem Sch Libraries

"Told and pictured with . . . tenderness, charm, and childlike simplicity." Booklist

Little Bear's visit; pictures by Maurice Sendak. Harper 1960 unp illus $2.95, lib. bdg. $3.79   E

1 Bears—Stories 2 Grandparents—Fiction
ISBN 0-06-024265-5; 0-06-024266-3

"On a wonderful day with his grandparents, Little Bear hears a story about his mother when she was a little girl, has lots of good things to eat, and plays games, until he falls asleep." Hodges. Bks for Elem Sch Libraries

"Among other delights of these stories are the relationships between Little Bear and his family, and the gentle, understanding humor that seems to come so naturally both to author and artist." Sat Rev

Mizumura, Kazue

If I built a village. Crowell 1971 unp illus $4.50, lib. bdg. $5.25   E

ISBN 0-690-42903-7; 0-690-42904-5

"A child playing with building blocks muses about what he would have in his world if he built a village, a town, or a city." Booklist

"An entirely childlike book with a simple but poetic statement on ecology. . . . The [author] illustrator's bright, energetic designs of leaping rabbits and trout, owls, mice, geese, and moles—all in their respective habitats—are pictured in alternating black and white, and sunny full-color wash-spreads. The theme is effectively expressed without becoming burdensome for the small child." Horn Bk

If I were a mother . . . Crowell [1968] unp illus $4.50, lib. bdg. $5.25   E

1 Mothers—Fiction 2 Animals—Stories
ISBN 0-690-42916-9; 0-690-42917-7

Illustrated by the author

"A little girl dreams of being a mother—in terms of the mothers she knows. She thinks of the mother cat keeping her kittens neat and clean, the bear teaching her cubs what and how to eat (not all sweets), and the mare letting her foal stand on his own feet as soon as he is ready. At last she decides that of all the mothers she knows, she would most want to be like her own." Booklist

"A combination of simplicity and sentimentality with colorful wash drawings." Bruno. Bks for Sch Libraries, 1968

The way of an ant. Crowell 1970 unp illus $3.95, lib. bdg. $4.75   E

1 Ants—Stories
ISBN 0-690-87044-2; 0-690-87045-0

"An ant wants to climb to the sky—to the highest point that he can reach. He first tries a tall blade of grass, then moves on to a dandelion, rose, sunflower, apple tree, etc. Each time he reaches a pinnacle, he spots some point higher, hurries down to the ground, and begins a new climb. Finally, old, proud of his past accomplishments, but unable to climb anymore, he realizes that 'As long as he kept on climbing, The blue sky grew higher and higher.'" Library J

"The visual lesson of the value of striving depicts a sunnily beautiful, growing world; the alternating black-and-white and predominantly green-and-yellow pictures on tall pages are striking." Horn Bk

Monjo, F. N.

The drinking gourd; pictures by Fred Brenner. Harper 1970 62p illus (An I can read history bk) $2.95, lib. bdg. $3.79   E

1 Underground railroad—Fiction
ISBN 0-06-024329-5; 0-06-024330-9

Set in New England in the decade before the Civil War. For mischievous behavior in church, Tommy is sent home to his room, but wanders instead into the barn. There he discovers that his father is helping runaway slaves escape to Canada

"The simplicity of dialogue and exposition, the level of concepts, and the length of the story [makes] it most suitable for the primary grades reader. The illustrations are deftly representational, the whole a fine addition to the needed body of historical books for the very young." Chicago. Children's Bk Center

Indian summer; pictures by Anita Lobel. Harper 1968 62p illus (An I can read history bk) lib. bdg. $3.79   E

1 Frontier and pioneer life—Fiction 2 Indians of North America—Fiction
ISBN 0-06-024328-7

"Using a controlled vocabulary, the book recounts how the children of a Kentucky pioneer family help to avert destruction by attacking Indians. . . . This tale relates the less than cordial relations that existed between the Indians and many early white settlers." Wis Library Bul

"Vigorous illustrations in black and white or muted colors add to the appeal of a frontier story for the primary grades reader. . . . The story seems a bit stretched, and the small glimpse of Indian characters verges on stereo-typical. The incident is not unusual, but it is both typical of the dangers of pioneer life and a simple enough episode for the beginning reader." Chicago. Children's Bk Center

The one bad thing about father; pictures by Rocco Negri. Harper 1970 62p illus (An I can read history bk) $2.95, lib. bdg. $3.79   E

1 Roosevelt family—Fiction 2 Roosevelt, Theodore, President U.S.—Fiction
ISBN 0-06-024333-3; 0-06-024334-1

The author ascribes this childhood diary to Quentin Roosevelt, youngest son of President Theodore Roosevelt. It is a fictitious memoir of family life at the White House and at the summer home at Oyster Bay, New York which provides glimpses into the history of the period as well as the vigorous activities of our twenty-sixth President

"This is harder than many books in the series, with more sophisticated humor; but it's a very amusing account of life in the White House from a child's viewpoint. Rocco Negri's pen-and-ink drawings in color are a fine, funny complement to the text." Sch Library J

Moore, Lilian

Little Raccoon and the thing in the pool; pictures by Gioia Fiammenghi. McGraw 1963 44p illus lib. bdg. $4.72   E

1 Raccoons—Stories
ISBN 0-07-042892-1

"Whittlesey House publications"

"Little Raccoon meets several animal friends on the way to the pool to catch crayfish for supper. He is apprehensive on the first trip without his mother and becomes frightened of his reflection in the water. After several unsuccessful attempts, he succeeds in

Moore, Lilian—*Continued*

overcoming his fear and brings home the crayfish. Children will enjoy the humor of Little Raccoon's fear of his own reflection." Sch Library J

Morrow, Suzanne Stark

Inatuk's friend; illus. by Ellen Raskin. Little 1968 48p illus $3.95   E

1 Eskimos—Fiction 2 Alaska—Fiction

ISBN 0-316-58397-9

"An Atlantic Monthly Press book"

The story of an Alaskan Eskimo boy who must leave his best friend behind when his family moves into the city, and how an unexpected substitute friend materializes

"Reinforcing the sparse style, the splendid illustrations add power and drama by their sharp contrasts of color and form." Adventuring With Bks. 2d edition

Munari, Bruno

ABC. Collins. 1960 unp illus $4.95, lib. bdg. $4.91   E

1 Alphabet books

ISBN 0-529-03620-7; 0-529-03621-5

Title on spine: Bruno Munari's ABC

Illustrated by the author, the pictures "are handsome and original, but every object is clear and simple enough for even a very small child to identify. The objects are familiar ones, and there are two or more words, adjectives as well as nouns for many of the letters. For example, 'U' is represented by an umbrella that is up and 'L' by a long leaf and a little leaf." Pub W

"With clean lines and brilliant full-color work, Bruno Munari's 'ABC' is at once unconventional, yet childlike, modern, yet timeless. A bold and refreshing kind of ABC book, its great simplicity almost conceals its art." Library J

The circus in the mist. World Pub. [1969 c1968] unp illus $5.95 lib. bdg. $5.71   E

1 Circus

ISBN 0-529-00756-8; 0-529-00757-6

Originally published 1968 in Italy

"Ingeniously using semitranslucent pages, pages of different colors, peepholes, and design to good effect a well-known Italian artist and designer has created a unique and diverting picture book with surprises on every page. There is no real story line but interest is captured and sustained by changing mood and pace as the viewer is led through fog-dimmed city streets, into the brightness, movement, and excitement of a circus, and then home again across a misty park. While the book may seem too experimental and gimmicky to many adults, children will undoubtedly find it great fun." Booklist

Myrick, Mildred

The Secret Three; drawings by Arnold Lobel. Harper 1963 64p illus $2.95, lib. bdg. $3.79   E

1 Clubs—Fiction 2 Ciphers—Fiction 2 Seashore—Fiction

ISBN 0-06-024355-4; 0-06-024356-2

"An I can read book"

"Three boys, two on the mainland and one on an island lighthouse, exchange messages in a bottle carried by the tide. They organize a club with a secret code, handshake, and name. On a trip to the island the boys explore the lighthouse and camp out overnight." Sch Library J

"The cryptography is elementary enough for the age of the readers, and should delight girls as well as boys. The illustrations are charming." Chicago. Children's Bk Center

Ness, Evaline

Do you have the time, Lydia? Written and illus. by Evaline Ness. Dutton 1971 unp illus $5.50, pa $1.25   E

1 Brothers and sisters—Fiction

ISBN 0-525-28790-6; 0-525-45024-6

Spanish language edition available for $6.95 (ISBN 0-525-41325-1)

Lydia, who lived with her family on a tropical island, was always so busy painting pictures, reading books, hammering nails, sewing clothes, and baking cakes that she never had time to finish anything. But it wasn't until she disappointed her younger brother that she finally learned the true significance of time

"Many familiar details drawn from daily child life contribute to the believability of the characters and situations. . . . The personalities of the children emerge from the expressive ink drawings shaded with pencil and highlighted in sunny shades of pink, orange, and yellow." Sch Library J

Exactly alike; written and illus. by Evaline Ness. Scribner 1964 unp illus lib. bdg. $5.95   E

ISBN 0-684-12403-3

"Elizabeth had four freckled brothers who looked exactly alike and who constantly teased her. She never knew which brother was teasing, or what his name was. In the end she found out how to distinguish between her brothers, and how to keep their names straight. . . . The story ends happily with Elizabeth hugging all four brothers at once." Sat Rev

"Lonely Elizabeth and the amusing little boys are clearly characterized in the beautiful strong illustrations in red, blue, olive, and black against a gray background. The story will probably be appreciated most by six- and seven-year-olds; but all ages . . . will enjoy the pictures." Horn Bk

The girl and the goatherd; or, This and that and thus and so; written and illus. by Evaline Ness. Dutton 1970 unp illus $4.25, lib. bdg. $4.21   E

1 Fairy tales

ISBN 0-525-30657-9; 0-525-30658-7

A story "about a girl who was ugly, 'got uglier as she got older, and when it came time for her to marry, no man except the goatherd would look at her.' . . . The heroine turns him down and thinks of 'nought else except to be beautiful.' . . . Girl meets witch and gains heart's desire only to find that flawless beauty provides cold comfort. A patient goatherd ultimately wins a wiser girl." N Y Times Bk Rev

"The picture-book story with striking three color illustrations follows a traditional folk tale pattern and is written in lilting prose that makes for easy telling and effective reading aloud." Booklist

Josefina February; written and illus. by Evaline Ness. Scribner 1963 unp illus lib. bdg. $5.95   E

1 Donkeys—Stories 2 Haiti—Fiction

ISBN 0-684-12404-1

"Josefina lived alone with her grandfather, Mr. February [in Haiti]; she wanted to give her grandfather a pair of real leather shoes for his birthday, but her day was disrupted when a baby burro wandered over. Josefina loved the burro on sight, but she gave him up in a trade for the shoes. That night Mr. February told her that the man who had the burro needed help with his responsibilities . . . the door opened, and in wobbled the burro." Chicago. Children's Bk Center

"The color harmonies from orange through dull greenish tan to black against bands of pale lavender are unusual and beautiful and the patterns of the wood cuts such that you come back to admire them again and again. . . . For the sake of the children we are

Ness, Evaline—*Continued*

especially happy that a distinguished picture book has what is exceedingly difficult to find, a story they can delight in." N Y Her Trib Bks

Sam, Bangs & Moonshine, written and illus. by Evaline Ness. Holt 1966 unp illus lib. bdg. $5.95, pa $1.45   E

ISBN 0-03-12716-5; 0-03-08011-7

Awarded the Caldecott Medal, 1967

"Motherless Samantha (called Sam), living on an island, had the lonely child's predilection for day-dreams: her mother was not dead—but a mermaid, and Sam had at home not only Bangs, her wise old cat (who could talk),.but a fierce lion and a baby kangaroo! Her practical fisherman-father was worried '. . . for a change, talk 'Real' not 'Moonshine.' 'Moonshine' spells trouble.' Not until her wildly exaggerated 'Moonshine' talk sent her only friend [Thomas] with her beloved cat to near destruction did Sam realize the grown-up difference between true imagination and uncontrolled flights of fancy." Horn Bk

"In this unusually creative story the fantasy in which many, many children indulge is presented in a realistic and sympathetic context. The illustrations in ink and pale color wash (mustard, grayish-aqua) have a touching realism, too. This is an outstanding book and one that no library will want to miss." Sch Library J

Newberry, Claire Turlay

The kittens' ABC; verse and pictures by Clare Turlay Newberry. New ed. completely redrawn. Harper [1965 c1946] unp illus $5.95, lib. bdg. $5.79   E

1 Cats—Poetry 2 Alphabet books

ISBN 0-06-024450-X; 0-06-024451-8

A reissue of the title published 1946

Each letter of the alphabet is represented by a picture of a kitten or cat, accompanied by a brief verse

The illustrations of "the animals are so appealingly furry that small children will want to pat and stroke them. This is a book to share with children for the pleasure of the pictures and the mildly amusing verse rather than for its alphabet instruction." Booklist

Marshmallow; story and pictures by Clare Turlay Newberry. Harper 1942 unp illus $5.95, lib. bdg. $5.79   E

1 Rabbits—Stories 2 Cats—Stories

ISBN 0-06-024460-7; 0-06-024461-5

"A little white bunny, looking as soft as a marshmallow, comes to live in the house with a pampered bachelor cat who at first does not know whether or not to accept so strange a thing. But before long the big black cat and the little white bunny are such friends that, cuddled up together, asleep, and playing, they give the artist an excuse for some of her best work." Bookmark

It is a delightful combination of beauty, understanding of children and animals and droll humor." N Y Times Bk Rev

Mittens; story and pictures by Clare Turlay Newberry. Harper 1936 28p illus lib. bdg. $4.79   E

1 Cats—Stories

ISBN 0-06-024471-2

"There is an irresistible charm about kittens which is caught in the story and pictures of Mittens. Bought at the market for six-year-old Richard, he was christened Mittens because of the six toes on each front paw. A kitten itself could hardly look more kittenish than the illustrations by the author." Wis Library Bul

There is an audience "for picture-books so true to this difficult subject, and a little child will find the story might have been told about his own kitten." N Y Her Trib Bks

Newell, Hope

The little old woman who used her head; pictures by Margaret Ruse. Nelson 1935 63p illus $4.95   E

ISBN 0-84-07-6328-X

Here are ten short episodes about an old woman who solved her many problems by an ingenious and amusing manner of using her head

"Sufficiently simple for children of eight to read and useful for story telling and reading aloud to younger children. Amusing illustration." Booklist

Nodset, Joan L.

Come here, cat; pictures by Steven Kellogg. Harper 1973 unp illus $3.50, lib. bdg. $3.27   E

1 Cats—Stories

ISBN 0-06-024557-3; 0-06-024558-1

"A young girl chases a cat through the halls, up the stairs to the roof of her apartment house, and back down again coaxing and cajoling it to be her friend." Elementary English

"The ingenuousness of the girl . . . [is] well served by the artist's line drawings in shades of brown and orange on tan. Having appropriately simplified his style to picture a simple story, he squanders his inventive ingenuity in occasional corners only and sets up a happy contrast between the single-minded little girl and the bustling, exuberant urban community in which she lives." Horn Bk

Go away, dog; pictures by Crosby Bonsall. Harper 1963 unp illus $2.50, lib. bdg. $3.79   E

1 Dogs—Stories

ISBN 0-06-024555-7; 0-06-024556-5

"In a brief volume with expressive pictures touched with red, an important, complete tale develops as a little boy who doesn't like dogs becomes irresistibly drawn to an importunate puppy brimming with playfulness and affection. The drawings captivate as fully as do the words each so rightly expressing the feelings of boy and dog." Horn Bk

Who took the farmer's [hat]? Pictures by Fritz Siebel. Harper 1963 unp illus lib. bdg. $4.79   E

1 Animals—Stories

ISBN 0-06-024566-2

"Away flew the farmer's hat. In his search for it he found that his hat could be many things to many animals including, most permanently, a bird's nest." Pub W

Oakley, Graham

The church mouse. Atheneum Pubs. 1972 unp illus $7.95   E

1 Mice—Stories

ISBN 0-689-30058-1

Illustrated by the author

"Arthur, the church mouse, had a happy and peaceful life. . . . However, Arthur was lonely, so he invited the town mice to live with him and they made a pact with the parson—a weekly cheesefest in return for odd jobs. All went well until Sampson, [the church cat] dreaming, chased some mice and disrupted a service. The congregation was irate, the parson sadly announced a general eviction. The situation was saved when the combined efforts of Sampson and the mice foiled a burglar, and they all were invited to stay on." Chicago. Children's Bk Center

"Full-color paintings with an abundance of activity and detail contribute much to the telling of the story. . . . Very British allusions give the fulsome text a certain sophistication; but the action and the clever illustrations are wholly childlike in their fun." Horn Bk

Ormondroyd, Edward

Broderick; illus. by John Larrecq. Parnassus Press 1969 unp illus $4.50, lib. bdg. $4.38   E
1 Mice—Stories 2 Surfing—Fiction
ISBN 0-87466-041-6; 0-87466-009-2
"A young mouse with a fondness for chewing the covers of books becomes an avid reader through the accidental discovery of a book about mice. Inspired by the exploits of such literary mouse personalities as Anatole and Miss Bianca, Broderick determines to make his own mark in the world and by diligent practice wins fame and fortune as a surfer. The author and the illustrator . . . have created a very real and endearing mouse hero to delight small children." Booklist
"This gay story is told with a straight face in polished style, the illustrations matching the deftness and humor of the writing. Appended is a brief list of other books about famous mice." Chicago. Children's Bk Center

Theodore; illus. by John M. Larrecq. Parnassus Press 1966 unp illus $4.25, lib. bdg. $4.11   E
1 Teddy bears—Fiction
ISBN 0-87466-056-4; 0-87466-028-9
"Because Lucy was careless, her poor bear Theodore got mixed up with the clothes in the laundry basket and was taken to the self-service laundry. When he emerged he was so clean that Lucy did not recognize him. But a friendly dog and two disputing cats remedied that situation, and Lucy and Theodore were happily reunited. The simple story, engaging line drawings washed with blue and yellow, and the well-designed format make a book for the youngest children that is all of a piece—unpretentious and charming." Horn Bk
Followed by: Theodore's rival

Theodore's rival; illus. by John Larrecq. Parnassus Press 1971 unp illus $4.25, lib. bdg. $4.11   E
1 Teddy bears—Fiction
ISBN 0-87466-035-1; 0-87466-001-7
Sequel to: Theodore
"Dismayed and annoyed when Lucy received a black-and-white bear for her birthday, Theodore was later pleased when Benjamin, the new bear, fell out of the carriage at the supermarket and was lost. But when Lucy began to cry for her lost toy, he became uneasy; and after he heard that Benjamin was a panda, not a teddy bear, he went into action and engineered Benjamin's rescue with great resourcefulness. The book presents settings and situations within the everyday experience of very young children. The humor is delightful, and story-telling illustrations in cheerful blue and yellow add lively details to the birthday-party and the supermarket scenes." Horn Bk

Over in the meadow; illus. by Ezra Jack Keats. Four Winds [1972 c1971] unp illus $5.95, lib. bdg. $5.62   E
1 Animals 2 Counting books
ISBN 0-590-17197-6; 0-590-07197-1
Text based on the original version by Olive A. Wadsworth. This counting rhyme tells about the animals in the meadow and their young, describing where they live, what noises they make, and what their favorite activities are
"Children can enjoy both the counting and the animals, whose prompt obedience is more cheery compliance than a lesson. ('Buzz!' said the mother. 'We buzz,' said the five. So they buzzed and they hummed, near the snug beehive.') The illustrations are colorful and lively, and the little creatures are easy to see for the counting." Sat Rev

Oxenbury, Helen

Helen Oxenbury's ABC of things. Watts, F. [1972 c1971] unp illus lib. bdg. $4.95   E
1 Alphabet books
ISBN 0-531-02020-7
Illustrated by the author
First published 1971 in England
"This simple and delightfully silly book presents humorous pictures and amusing word choices for every letter of the alphabet. The pastel illustrations show a fish bringing flowers to a frog, a pig and pelican posed on a pier, and a bedraggled father holding a baby, badger, and bear, while a bird bedecks his cap. Often drawn from entertaining perspectives—an overhead view of umbrellas shows only feet sticking out from underneath—the illustrations combine charming creatures and situations. A refreshing, unpretentious book." Horn Bk

Numbers of things. Watts, F. 1968 unp illus lib. bdg. $4.90   E
1 Counting books
ISBN 0-531-01751-6
This is "a tall counting book from England, the shape used to great advantage for the contrasting facing pages. In heavy, clear type on one page, each on a separate line, '1, ONE, one, lion' and on the facing page, filling the long space, a mildly dolorous and quite amiable lion. The pictures [by the author] are imaginative and intricately handsome, with humorous details that give an added fillip." Chicago. Children's Bk Center

Pig tale. Morrow 1973 unp illus $5.50, lib. bdg. $4.81   E
1 Pigs—Stories 2 Stories in rhyme
ISBN 0-688-20092-3; 0-688-30092-8
Illustrated by the author
This is the "story of what happened to two little pigs who are discontented with their simple life. They suddenly find themselves overburdened with the luxurious life they thought they wanted and, in the end, choose the carefree, simple life that they had to begin with." Top of the News
"A unified, hilarious picture book with crisp, concise verses and absurd, full-color illustrations that emphasize the blithe innocence of the massive porkers." Horn Bk

Parish, Peggy

Amelia Bedelia; pictures by Fritz Siebel. Harper 1963 unp illus $2.95, lib. bdg. $3.43   E
ISBN 0-06-024640-5; 0-06-024641-3
"Amelia Bedelia is a maid whose talent for interpreting instructions literally results in comical situations, such as dressing the chicken in fine clothes." Hodges. Bks for Elem Sch Libraries

Ootah's lucky day; pictures by Mamoru Funai. Harper 1970 63p illus $2.95, lib. bdg. $3.79   E
1 Eskimos—Fiction
ISBN 0-06-024669-3; 0-06-024670-7
"An I can read book"
"An eskimo boy is left all alone, with no food or heat, because he is too young to go hunting with the men. Off Ootah goes, alone, and kills a walrus, has an encounter with a polar bear and takes the walrus home to the village." Sch Library J

Parkin, Rex

The red carpet; story and pictures by Rex Parkin. Macmillan (N Y) 1948 unp illus $4.95, pa $1.25   E
1 Carpets—Fiction 2 Stories in rhyme
A tale in rhyme and colorful pictures about a runaway carpet. When it was rolled out of the hotel to receive a visiting duke, it rolled on and on, down the

Parkin, Rex—*Continued*
street, along the highway and over the country roads, bringing excitement wherever it went

Parnall, Peter
The mountain; written and illus. by Peter Parnall. Doubleday 1971 unp illus $4.50, lib.bdg. $5.25   E
1 Natural resources—U.S. 2 Pollution
ISBN 0-385-05800-4; 0-385-02605-6
This "picture book on the ecology theme . . . tells of a mountain in the West on which flowers grow and animals live. It is a beautiful place which some people want to preserve, so the mountain is made into a national park. But then trees are cut down, roads are built, tourists flock, etc. Refuse grows but the flowers don't and the animals can't." Sch Library J
"An unusually good book on preserving ecological balance, lucid enough in its message to be understood by preschool children, sophisticated enough in its treatment to be appreciated by the reader in primary grades. The illustrations are spare in composition and beautifully detailed." Chicago. Children's Bk Center

Paterson, A. B.
Waltzing Matilda; poem. Illus. by Desmond Digby. Holt [1972 c1970] unp illus lib. bdg. $5.95
    E
ISBN 0-03-088370-9
First published 1970 in Australia
A picture book version of the Australian song, the title of which refers "to the bundle, or swag, which a tramp uses to carry his personal possessions. The interpretation of the song given here tells of a swagman who steals a sheep (jumbuck) and in an attempt to escape the police, drowns in a water hole." Pub W
"The familiar words of the song, 'Waltzing Matilda,' were written years ago to the tune of an old English marching song; here they are illustrated with charming paintings in a picture book version . . . designated [in Australia] as the picture book of the year." Chicago. Children's Bk Center
Includes a glossary

Payne, Emmy
Katy No-Pocket; pictures by H. A. Rey. Houghton 1944 unp illus lib. bdg. $5.95, pa $1.25   E
1 Kangaroos—Stories 2 Animals—Stories
ISBN 0-395-06996-3; 0-395-13717-9
Katy Kangaroo was most unfortunately unprovided with a pocket in which to carry her son Freddy. She asked other animals with no pockets how they carried their children but none seemed satisfactory. Finally a wise old owl advised her to try to find a pocket in the City, and so off she went and in the City she found just what she and Freddy needed

Peet, Bill
The whingdingdilly; written and illus. by Bill Peet. Houghton 1970 60p illus $4.95, lib. bdg. $4.23   E
1 Dogs—Stories 2 Witches—Fiction
ISBN 0-395-0699-8; 0-395-07000-7
"Scamp, the dog, wants to be a horse, but a well-meaning witch turns him into a Whingdingdilly with the hump of a camel, zebra's tail, giraffe's neck, elephant's front legs and ears, rhinoceros' nose, and reindeer's horns." Adventuring With Bks. 2d edition

Peppé, Rodney
Circus numbers; a counting book. Delacorte Press 1969 unp illus $5.95, lib. bdg. $5.47   E
1 Counting books
ISBN 0-440-01288-0; 0-440-01289-9
In this book readers encounter 1 ringmaster, 2 horses etc. up to 10 clowns, 20 doves and then "100

elephants, divided according to units of 10 (9 to a cage drawn by the 10th). . . . Sets of bright blue stars are sprinkled through the book, providing a second chance to count each number. Minimum text in large, clear upper- and lower-case type together with the impact of the [author's] jolly, poster-like illustrations set a smart tempo." Sch Library J

Odd one out. Viking 1974 unp illus lib. bdg. $5.95, pa $1.25   E
1 Puzzles
ISBN 0-670-52029-2; 0-670-05097-0
Illustrated by the author
"A little boy, Peter, experiences the ordinary adventures of eating breakfast, walking through the garden, riding the bus to school, and learning his lessons. After school he visits the zoo and the toy shop, and his uncle and aunt on the farm." Rdng Teacher
"In each colorful spread Peppé has purposely inserted a mistake that lends puzzle-solving appeal and tickles a child's budding sense of absurdity. Providing a base for the trick are precisely designed collage and gouache illustrations filled with funny details of a little boy's action-packed day." Booklist

Perrine, Mary
Salt Boy; illus. by Leonard Weisgard. Houghton 1968 31p illus $3.75, lib. bdg. $3.40, pa 95¢   E
1 Navaho Indians—Fiction
ISBN 0-395-07029-5; 0-395-07030-9; 0-395-17450-3
"Little Salt Boy's job is to take care of his mother's sheep; his greatest wish, however, is to learn to rope the black horse. During a sudden storm, Salt Boy's courage and tenderness earn his father's respect and the coming true of his own wish." Wis Library Bul
"This quiet, powerful story of a Navajo child's experience, enhanced with sensitive drawings, shows cultural values that few of our children have an opportunity to see." Adventuring With Bks. 2d edition

Piatti, Celestino
Celestino Piatti's Animal ABC; English text by Jon Reid. Atheneum Pubs. 1966 [c1965] unp illus $4.95
    E
1 Animals 2 Alphabet books
ISBN 0-689-20335-7
First published 1965 in Switzerland
This alphabet book shows "animals from alligator to zebra, with a witty four-line rhyme for each." Hodges. Bks for Elem Sch Libraries
In this "brilliantly handsome alphabet book . . . the artist has made remarkable expressionistic pictures full of contrasting colors and startling patterns, shapes, and textures. . . . The book is full of controlled humor and fantasy." Horn Bk

The happy owls. Atheneum Pubs. 1964 [c1963] unp illus $5.95   E
1 Owls—Stories
ISBN 0-689-20337-3
First published 1963 in Switzerland
A picture book illustrated by the author. "Originally a Dutch story, this version has been translated from the German." Top of the News
"The other fowl, always quarreling, ask the two happy owls how they live together so peacefully. The owls describe their contentment in the phenomena of the seasons, but the other birds cannot understand this and they go back to living and squabbling as before." Chicago. Children's Bk Center
"Beautiful designs and rich colours carry the mood and narrative of . . . [this legendary tale] through the four seasons of the year." Toronto

Piper, Watty

The little engine that could; retold [from The pony engine, by Mabel C. Bragg]. Illus. by George & Doris Hauman. [Silver anniversary ed] Platt 1954 unp illus $1.95, lib. bdg. $2.39   E

1 Locomotives—Fiction

First published 1930

"Star books for children"

"When a train carrying good things to children breaks down, the little blue engine proves his courage and determination. The rhythmic, repetitive text encourages children to help tell the story." Hodges. Bks for Elem Sch Libraries

Politi, Leo

Juanita. Scribner 1948 unp illus music lib. bdg. $5.95   E

1 Mexicans in the U.S.—Fiction 2 Easter—Stories 3 Los Angeles—Fiction

ISBN 0-684-12658-3

"It is at Easter that the Blessing of the Animals takes place at the Mission Church in Los Angeles. Juanita [a little Mexican girl] lives on Olvera Street near by and she looks happily forward to her share in the parade. The pictures [by the author] in soft colors have a warmth and tenderness that bring out the happiness of the little Mexican faces as they lead their pets of many kinds to the good parish priest." Horn Bk

"The words and music of several Mexican songs are included." Pub W

Mieko. Golden Gate Junior Bks. 1969 unp illus $6.60   E

1 Japanese in the U.S.—Fiction 2 Los Angeles—Fiction

ISBN 0-516-08728-2

Illustrated by the author

"Mieko is a Japanese-American girl living in Los Angeles whose dream is to please her parents by becoming queen of the Nisei Week festival. Though working very hard to live up to her name, which means beautiful, graceful, girl, she learns that it will be many years before she is old enough to be queen. Her . . . parents then assure her that to them she is already a queen." Library J

"The illustrations contrast the serene beauty of the Japanese home with the bustling life of Little Tokyo and the excitement of the festival." Horn Bk

Moy Moy. Scribner 1960 unp illus lib. bdg. $6.95   E

1 Chinese in the U.S.—Fiction 2 New Year—Stories 3 Los Angeles—Fiction

ISBN 0-684-13178-1

Illustrated by the author

"Moy Moy, who lives on Chanking Street in Los Angeles, experiences the first Chinese New Year she is old enough to appreciate. Through her wondering eyes, in simple words, and pictures reminiscent of Chinese lacquer work, are depicted the children's lion dance, the dragon parade, firecrackers, goodies, toys—all the brilliant splendor of the festival." Moorachian. What is a City?

Pedro, the angel of Olvera Street. Scribner 1946 unp illus music lib. bdg. $5.95   E

1 Mexicans in the U.S.—Fiction 2 Los Angeles—Fiction 2 Christmas stories

ISBN 0-684-12628-1

Also available in a Spanish language edition, lib. bdg. $5.95 (ISBN 0-684-13804-2)

"Beguiling both in text and in the pictures with their soft, rich colors, this is the story of Mexican Olvera Street, little and lost in the heart of the great city of Los Angeles, but loved by young Pedro because of the shops and good Mexican foods, the music, the friendly people and the artisans at work at their interesting crafts. How Pedro, who sings like an angel, is chosen at Christmas-time to lead La Posada is a happy introduction to a traditional Mexican custom. The words and music of two carols are included." Bookmark

Rosa. Scribner 1963 unp illus lib. bdg. $5.95   E

1 Mexico—Fiction

ISBN 0-684-12653-2

"Rosa, a little Mexican girl, yearns for a baby doll that she see in the toy shop each day on her way to school. It seems beyond all hope, but then Christmas brings something even better, a real baby sister." Pub W

"Richly applied earth colors and sober greens lit with sudden bursts of pinks and purples, oranges and blues—just to open 'Rosa' is to be instantaneously carried back into the special Latin-American world this author-artist's books are opening up for the [young]. . . . Huge double-spread pictures have a Gauguin air about them. They are full of tiny scenes that tell more about everyday in Mexico than many words." Christian Sci Monitor

Song of the swallows. Scribner 1949 unp illus music lib. bdg. $5.95, pa 95¢   E

1 Swallows—Stories 2 California—Fiction

ISBN 0-684-92309-2; 0-684-12780-6

Awarded the Caldecott Medal, 1950

"The swallows always appeared at the old Mission of Capistrano on St Joseph's Day and Juan who lived nearby wondered how they could tell that from all others. This tender poetic story of the coming of springtime is touched by the kindliness of the good Fathers of the Mission as a little boy knew it. Lovely pictures [by the author] in soft colors bring out the charm of the southern California landscape and the melody of the swallow song adds to the feeling of Spring." Horn Bk

"There are three double-page paintings of the mission. . . . Two songs are given in full, with the music." Sat Rev

Pomerantz, Charlotte

The piggy in the puddle; pictures by James Marshall. Macmillan Pub. Co. 1974 unp illus $4.95   E

1 Pigs—Stories 2 Stories in rhyme

ISBN 0-02-774900-2

"The squishy-squashy, mooshy-sqooshy, oofy-poofy joy of mud is celebrated in this rhythmic tale of a small pig that scorns soap and refuses to leave her puddle. Her pleasure is infectious and finally mother, father, and brother join her in 'the very merry middle' of the 'muddy little puddle.' " Booklist

"The soft pastel drawings add just the right touch to the humorous bedtime story which demands to be read aloud." Children's Bk Rev Serv

Potter, Beatrix

The pie and the patty-pan. Warne 76p illus lib. bdg. $2.50   E

1 Cats—Stories 2 Dogs—Stories

ISBN 0-7232-0608-2

Illustrated by the author

First published 1905 with title: A tale of the pie and the patty-pan

"Ribby, a pussy cat, invites a little dog named Duchess to tea." Bks for Boys and Girls

The roly-poly pudding. Warne 76p illus lib. bdg. $2.50   E

1 Cats—Stories

ISBN 0-7232-0607-4

First published 1908

Potter, Beatrix—_Continued_
Present English edition published under title: The tale of Samuel Whiskers
Illustrated by the author, this is "an adventure of Tom Kitten's in which Samuel Whiskers, his wife, Anna Maria, and a rolling pin, take a prominent part." Bks for Boys and Girls

The sly old cat; written and illus. by Beatrix Potter. Warne [1972 c1971] 34p illus lib. bdg. $2.50   E
1 Cats—Stories 2 Rats—Stories
ISBN 0-7232-1420-4
"Written in 1906, this is the tale of "an unusual tea party at [Cat's house in] which a rat saves himself from being the dessert." N Y Pub Library. Children's Bks & Recordings, 1972
"Appearing now for the first time, the book is simple, slight, and ingenious, but amiable in its good-versus-evil appeal." Sat Rev

The story of Miss Moppet. Warne 34p illus lib. bdg. $2.50   E
1 Cats—Stories 2 Mice—Stories
ISBN 0-7232-0635-X
Illustrated by the author
First published 1906
Miss Moppet is a kitten who uses her wiles to capture a curious mouse. But her trickery amounts to naught when she herself is outwitted

The tailor of Gloucester. Warne 60p illus lib. bdg. $2.50   E
1 Tailors—Fiction 2 Mice—Stories 3 Christmas stories
ISBN 0-7232-0594-9
Also available in a French language edition for $2.50 (ISBN 0-7232-0658-9)
First published 1903
"The cat Simpkin looked after his master when he was ill, but it was the nimble-fingered mice who used snippets of cherry-coloured twist and so finished the embroidered waist coat for the worried tailor. A Christmas-time story set in old Gloucester." Four to Fourteen
"A readaloud classic in polished style, perfectly complemented by the author's exquisite watercolor illustrations." Hodges. Bks for Elem Sch Libraries

The tale of Benjamin Bunny. Warne 60p illus lib. bdg. $2.50   E
1 Rabbits—Stories
ISBN 0-7232-0595-7
Also available in a French language edition for $2.50 (ISBN 0-7232-0651-1)
First published 1904
"Benjamin and his cousin Peter pay dearly for their exciting adventure in Mr. McGregor's garden." Hodges. Bks for Elem Sch Libraries
"All of Beatrix Potter's books are illustrated by herself with exquisite miniature water colours of an excellent story telling quality." Bks for Boys and Girls

The tale of Jemima Puddle-duck. Warne 60p illus lib. bdg. $2.50   E
1 Ducks—Stories
ISBN 0-7232-0600-7
Also available in a French language edition (ISBN 0-7232-0653-8) and a Latin language edition (ISBN 0-7232-0649-X) for $2.50 each
Illustrated by the author
First published 1908
"Jemima Puddle-duck's obstinate determination to hatch her own eggs, makes a story of suspense and sly humor." Bks for Boys and Girls

The tale of Mr Jeremy Fisher. Warne 60p illus lib. bdg. $2.50   E

1 Frogs—Stories
ISBN 0-7232-0598-1
Also available in a French language edition for $2.50 (ISBN 0-7232-0656-2)
Illustrated by the author
First published 1906
Mr Jeremy Fisher, a frog, encounters some problems when he goes fishing
The author's "paintings of lily pads and green marshes are cool and lovely." Bks for Boys and Girls

The tale of Mr Tod. Warne 93p illus lib. bdg. $2.50   E
1 Foxes—Stories 2 Badgers—Stories 3 Rabbits—Stories
ISBN 0-7232-0628-7
First published 1912
Illustrated by the author
Two woodland villains, Mr Tod, the fox, and Tommy Brock, the badger, come to blows when Tommy becomes a squatter in Mr Tod's vacant house. The melee enables Benjamin Bunny and Peter Rabbit to rescue the baby bunnies the badger had kidnapped

The tale of Mrs Tiggy-Winkle. Warne 60p illus lib. bdg. $2.50   E
1 Hedgehogs—Stories
ISBN 0-7232-0597-3
Also available in a French language edition for $2.50 (ISBN 0-7232-0652-X)
Illustrated by the author
First published 1905
"Little Lucy loses her pocket-handkin, and finds Mrs. Tiggy-Winkle, a hedgehog washer-woman." Bks for Boys and Girls

The tale of Mrs Tittlemouse. Warne 60p illus lib. bdg. $2.50   E
1 Mice—Stories
ISBN 0-7232-0602-3
First published 1910
The now classic story of Mrs Tittlemouse, a very tidy, particular woodmouse, illustrated with the author's delicate water colors

The tale of Peter Rabbit. Warne 60p illus lib. bdg. $2.50   E
1 Rabbits—Stories
ISBN 0-7232-0592-2
Also available in the following foreign language editions: French (ISBN 0-7232-0650-3); Italian (ISBN 0-7232-0670-8); Latin (ISBN 0-7232-0648-1); Spanish (ISBN 0-7232-0671-6) for $2.50 each
First published 1903
All about the famous rabbit family consisting of Flopsy, Mopsy, Cotton-tail and especially Peter Rabbit who disobeys Mother Rabbit's admonishment not to go into Mr McGregor's garden
"Distinctive writing and a strong appeal to a small child's sense of justice and his sympathies make this an outstanding story. The water color illustrations [by the author] add charm to the narrative by their simplicity of detail and delicacy of color." Children's Bks Too Good to Miss

The tale of Pigling Bland. Warne 94p illus lib. bdg. $2.50   E
1 Pigs—Stories
ISBN 0-7232-0606-6
Illustrated by the author
First published 1913

Potter, Beatrix—*Continued*

"Pigling's story ends happily with a perfectly lovely little black Berkshire pig called Pigwig." Bks for Boys and Girls

The tale of Squirrel Nutkin. Warne 60p illus lib. bdg. $2.50   E

  1 Squirrels—Stories
  ISBN 0-7232-0593-0
Also available in a French language edition for $2.50 (ISBN 0-7232-0654-6)
Illustrated by the author
First published 1903
Each day the squirrels gather nuts, Nutkin propounds a riddle to Mr Brown, the owl, until impertinent Nutkin, over-estimating Mr Brown's patience, gets his due

The tale of the flopsy bunnies. Warne 60p illus lib. bdg. $2.50   E

  1 Rabbits—Stories
  ISBN 0-7232-0601-5
Also available in a French language edition for $2.50 (ISBN 0-7232-0655-4)
Illustrated by the author
First published 1909
"The second generation of the Peter Rabbit family has a narrow escape in Mr. McGregor's garden." Bks for Boys and Girls

The tale of Tom Kitten. Warne 60p illus lib. bdg. $2.50   E

  1 Cats—Stories
  ISBN 0-7232-0599-X
Also available in a French language edition for $2.50 (ISBN 0-7232-0657-0)
Illustrated by the author
First published 1907
Tom Kitten and his sisters Moppet and Mittens undo the careful scrubbing and dressing their mother, Mrs. Tabitha Twitchet, has subjected them to in anticipation of company

The tale of Tuppenny; illus. by Marie Angel. Warne [1973 c1971] 39p illus lib. bdg. $2.95   E

  1 Guinea pigs—Stories
  ISBN 0-7232-6097-4
Text written 1903. This version first published 1971 in England in Leslie Linder's: A history of the writings of Beatrix Potter, including unpublished work
"In a town inhabited by guinea pigs, a quack medication was touted, guaranteed to grow hair. . . . After using several bottles of this, poor Tuppenny began to grow hair—but at a fantastic rate. The surprised concocter, beleaguered, vanished; Tuppenny had to spend all his time getting his hair cut until he finally gave up and joined a circus as Tuppenny the Hairy Guinea Pig." Chicago. Children's Bk Center

The tale of two bad mice. Warne 60p illus lib. bdg. $2.50   E

  1 Mice—Stories
  ISBN 0-7232-0596-5
Illustrated by the author
First published 1904
"Two mischievous little mice pilfer a doll's house to equip their own. They are caught and finally make amends for what they have done. Perfectly charming illustrations and a most enticing tale." Adventuring With Bks. 2d edition

Preston, Edna Mitchell

Pop Corn & Ma Goodness; illus. by Robert Andrew Parker. Viking 1969 unp illus lib. bdg. $5.95, pa $1.25   E

  ISBN 0-670-56499-0; 0-670-05070-9

"Vigorous illustrations in soft water color tones face pages that describe the blitzkrieg love and the married life of Pop Corn and Ma Goodness, in a rhyming text in folk style. The two meet head-on, literally, when 'The rain it starts coming a-drippitty droppetty/ The lane it gets slippitty slippitty sloppetty / Old Ma goes a-flying-aflippitty floppetty / Old Pop takes a header a-dippitty doppetty / They meet—oh their heads crack a-bippitty boppetty / All doon the hill.' With similar rhyming nonsense words, the two are wed, raise a family, make them a farm and build them a house, etc. The final pages cumulate all the nonsense words. There is some humor in the writing, and the rhythm has appeal, but the folksy-colloquial language almost obscures the story, which could serve as a singing game for children." Chicago. Children's Bk Center

Squawk to the moon, Little Goose; illus. by Barbara Cooney. Viking 1974 unp illus lib. bdg. $5.95   E

  1 Geese—Stories 2 Moon—Fiction
  ISBN 0-670-66609-2
This is the "story of a gosling that is both silly and resourceful. . . . Tucked in for the night, Little Goose steals out for a night ramble; she sees the moon covered by a cloud and wakes the farmer with her squawking; it happens again when she sees the moon reflected in the pond and decides it has fallen. When she's caught by a fox, Little Goose squawks, but the disgruntled farmer won't get up a third time. However, Little Goose uses her wits and outfoxes the fox, going home to a maternal spank and cuddle." Chicago. Children's Bk Center
"Ms. Cooney has infused her watercolor illustrations with so much personality, drollery and beauty that fortunate owners of this book will find themselves gazing at the pictures again and again, finding new aspects at which to marvel each time. And Ms. Preston's fable is equally enchanting." Pub W

Quackenbush, Robert

Go tell Aunt Rhody; starring the old gray goose who is a living legend in her own lifetime and the greatest American since the American eagle. Lippincott 1973 unp illus music $4.95   E

  1 Geese—Stories 2 Folk songs—U.S.
  ISBN 0-397-31459-0
Illustrated by the author
"A combination puzzle, picture and song book. The verses are based on the death of the old gray goose [of the American folk song], the one 'Aunt Rhody' is planning to use to make a feather bed and other things. Some of the brain teasers here will be over the heads of the littlest readers but it's a book that can be enjoyed, over and over, with the help of older friends." Pub W

Radlauer, Ruth Shaw

What can you do with a box? Illus. by Jay Rivkin. Childrens Press 1973 unp illus lib. bdg. $6   E

  1 Boxes
  ISBN 0-516-07623-X
"Spells out ways to play with various kinds of boxes. Most children will have already discovered the obvious suggestions on their own ('You can get under a big box so no one can see you'), and the most novel idea demonstrates how to make a garden in an egg carton. Black-and-white drawings supplement the limited text." Sch Library J

Rand, Ann

Sparkle and spin; a book about words, by Ann & Paul Rand. Harcourt 1957 unp illus $5.95   E

  1 Vocabulary
  ISBN 0-15-277459-9
The authors "deal with the abstract concept of

Rand, Ann—*Continued*

words—what they stand for, how they sound, how they are used as a means of communication. Some of the ideas, both in the text and pictures, will require adult interpretation but on the whole the presentation is as childlike as it is fresh and imaginative." Booklist

"Both in the concepts in the text and in the brilliance of design and illustration, the author-artist team has produced a refreshingly original book." Wis Library Bul

Raskin, Ellen

And it rained. Atheneum Pubs. 1969 unp illus lib. bdg. $5.95   E

1 Rain and rainfall—Fiction 2 Animals—Stories
ISBN 0-689-20587-2
Illustrated by the author
"Ellen Raskin presents the pig, the parrot, the potto, and an all-star cast of characters in And it rained." Title page
A tale of what happens "when a group of animals are frustrated in their attempts to have a proper four o'clock tea." Wis Library Bul
"The wisdom contained in this deceptively simple story may be lost on some small children, but all youngsters will be charmed by the [author's] finely detailed pictures, which alternate yellow and blue backgrounds with the green foregrounds. In the backgrounds, among exotic trees, other animals—which are identified at the back of the book—frolic. A fun, witty achievement." Sch Library J

Franklin Stein. Atheneum Pubs. 1972 unp illus $5.25, pa $1.50   E

ISBN 0-689-30035-2; 0-689-70417-8
Illustrated by the author
Friendless Franklin Stein creates a creature named Fred out of mops, a potato masher, his father's tie, and other objects. Almost everyone considers Fred monstrous until he is awarded first prize at the pet show. Then everyone echoes the judge's praise except one girl who genuinely appreciates Fred and his creator
"The pure-white pages of the book are a perfect background for the clear blues and greens coloring the drawings; in practically each picture Fred appears in blatant red. The illustrations are rich with impossible details that are only hinted at in the text; and if the youngest of readers or viewers fails to catch the implied irony (the inconsistency of human reactions and opinions), he can, at least, give himself unreservedly to the exuberance of the slapstick." Horn Bk

Ghost in a four-room apartment. Atheneum Pubs. 1969 unp illus $3.75, lib. bdg. $4.81   E

1 Ghost stories
ISBN 0-689-20353-5; 0-689-20354-3
This story, illustrated by the author, is about a poltergeist who haunts a four-room apartment and creates havoc there. The narrative is divided between the ghost, who recounts his activities, and a narrator who describes in verse the members of the haunted family and their relatives
"The illustrations are a series of stained-glass showcases for Miss Raskin's considerable talents. Bright blocks of colorfully detailed line drawings exploit the hilarity of bewildered guests trying to dodge objects flying about everywhere." N Y Times Bk Rev

Nothing ever happens on my block. Atheneum Pubs. 1966 unp illus lib. bdg. $5.95   E

ISBN 0-689-20588-0
Illustrated by the author
"Chester Filbert, the personification of the 'grass is greener,' sits on the curb longing to see fierce lions, monsters, or other fantastic sights. Meanwhile he misses all the fantastic events, including robberies

and fires transpiring around him. Much of the fun is in combing the [author's] illustrations for all the things Chester is missing." Minnesota
"In all fairness to Chester all those thefts and parachute jumps never happened on my block either. This in no way detracts from the inventive excellence of the book, which is a delight." N Y Times Bk Rev

Spectacles. Atheneum Pubs. 1968 unp illus lib. bdg. $5.23, pa 95¢   E

1 Eyeglasses—Fiction
ISBN 0-689-20352-7; 0-689-70317-1
Illustrated by the author
Even though nearsighted "Iris swears that there's a fire-breathing dragon at the door, a giant pygmy nuthatch on the lawn, a chestnut mare in the parlor, her readers will see, by flipping the page each time, that it's only Great-aunt Fanny, her friend Chester, and the baby sitter respectively. Iris detests specs but gets them, anyway." Sch Library J
"Laughable picture book, conceived and illustrated with imagination and humor. May be useful with children resisting needed glasses." Booklist

Who, said Sue, said whoo? Atheneum Pubs. 1973 unp illus $5.95   E

1 Animals—Stories 2 Stories in rhyme
ISBN 0-689-30096-4
Illustrated by the author, this "cumulative rhyming tongue-twister with a surprise ending . . . will provide both aural and visual fun for children. Driving her car through a jungle of fantastical vegetation, Sue collects a menagerie of beasts by asking which one is making whatever noise she hears. Her car quickly unloads, however, when the one animal she has not been able to identify throughout the book finally appears—a skunk, who drives away with a chimpanzee unable to smell because of a cold. The brightly colored pictures, splashed liberally with lime green, are nicely nonsensical." Booklist

Reiss, John J.

Colors; a book by John J. Reiss. Bradbury Press 1969 unp illus $6.95   E

1 Color
ISBN 0-87888-008-9
Things to eat and wear and animals to chase appear in this introduction to the primary and secondary colors
"The simplest of formats and a sophisticated use of color and design combine to make a big and beautiful first book for the child learning to distinguish colors. The text consists entirely of the names of colors and the names of objects pictured. . . . The shades are vibrant, the layout stunning." Sat Rev

Numbers; a book. Bradbury Press 1971 unp illus $6.95   E

1 Counting books
ISBN 0-87888-029-1
"This is a big, brilliantly colored picture book which first counts from one to ten and then by tens to one hundred and ends with the number one thousand (raindrops). It enumerates such things as shoes, starfish arms, baseball players, kites, radishes, crayons, beads, gumballs, and centipede legs. The colorful pages and clear drawings invite viewer participation both in identifying objects and counting them." Booklist

Shapes; a book. Bradbury Press 1974 unp illus $5.95   E

1 Size and shape
ISBN 0-87888-053-4
"Absolutely luscious in its spectrum of vivid colors . . . [this book presents] examples of such shapes as

Reiss, John J.—*Continued*

oval, circle, triangle, rectangle, and square. Reiss carries it a bit farther, showing how squares form a cube, or circles a sphere, and he tosses in a few more complex shapes at the close of the book to intrigue the audience: a hexagon, an octagon, a pentagon. Examples of each shape are included; for rectangles, for example, there are doors, wooden planks, and sticks of gum. Animals cavort among the shapes, adding interest to the visual appeal and the clearly presented concepts." Chicago. Children's Bk Center

Rey, H. A.

Cecily G. and the 9 monkeys. Houghton 1942 31p illus lib. bdg. $4.95   E

1 Giraffes—Stories 2 Monkeys—Stories
ISBN 0-395-18430-4

A nonsense book describing in prose and picture the adventures of a lonely giraffe, and some homeless little monkeys

"Mr. Rey's big, colored pictures of Cecily Giraffe are unexpected and laughable, and it's remarkable to how many surprising uses his nine young monkeys can put one obliging giraffe." N Y Libraries

Curious George. Houghton 1941 unp illus lib. bdg. $4.95   E

1 Monkeys—Stories
ISBN 0-395-15993-8

Also available in a Spanish language edition: lib. bdg. $6.95 (ISBN 0-395-17075-3)

Illustrated by the author

Colored picture book, with simple text, describing the adventures of a curious small monkey, and the difficulties he had in getting used to city life, before he went to live in the zoo

"The bright lithographs in red, yellow, and blue, are gay and lighthearted, following the story closely with the same speed and animated humour." Ontario Library Rev

Curious George learns the alphabet. Houghton 1963 72p illus lib. bdg. $4.50, pa $1.95   E

1 Monkeys—Stories 2 Alphabet books
ISBN 0-395-16031-6; 0-395-18559-9

"The man in the yellow hat decides to teach George [the monkey] how to read: an alphabet book that uses a visual device in which each letter is incorporated into the drawing itself. . . . The text is interrupted pleasantly here and there by a bit of narrative about George's prowess or his ploys." Chicago. Children's Bk Center

"The text is both informative and amusing. Children will love George and the [author's] highly entertaining illustrations every bit as much as [George's] previous adventures. A delightful way to meet the alphabet." Sch Library J

Curious George rides a bike. Houghton 1952 45p illus lib. bdg. $5.95   E

1 Monkeys—Stories 2 Bicycles and bicycling—Fiction
ISBN 0-395-16964-X

"To his great delight, George is presented with a small bike; agrees to help a boy with his paper route; and is, again, because of his curiosity, led into a fascinating adventure. Troubles he has, to be sure, but the adventure ends in a blaze of glory with George performing in a circus and gallantly rescuing a frightened baby bear." Horn Bk

His escapades "are fast and funny enough to keep any youngster happy once he has glimpsed Mr. Rey's comic pictures." N Y Times Bk Rev

Curious George takes a job. Houghton 1947 47p illus lib. bdg. $5.95   E

1 Monkeys—Stories
ISBN 0-395-15086-8

"Once again George's curiosity gets him into trouble, this time when he escapes from the zoo and starts out to find his friend, the man who had brought him from Africa. The monkey's escapades furnish riotous fun and the big city background in the colorful and amusing pictures [by the author] is worthy of note." Booklist

Rey, Margret

Curious George flies a kite; pictures by H. A. Rey. Houghton 1958 80p illus lib. bdg. $4.95   E

1 Monkeys—Stories
ISBN 0-395-16965-8

"Another appealing story about the small and determined monkey who gets into, and out of, one predicament after another. Gay pictures and simple text show George playing with a baby rabbit, going fishing and flying a kite. . . . This is an addition to materials for beginning readers, and action is more slow-moving than is usual for Curious George because of the attention to vocabulary—resulting in quite a long story for the beginning reader. Not a read-aloud book." Chicago. Children's Bk Center

Curious George goes to the hospital, by Margret & H. A. Rey in collaboration with the Children's Hospital Medical Center. Houghton 1966 48p illus lib. bdg. $5.95   E

1 Monkeys—Stories 2 Hospitals—Fiction
ISBN 0-395-18158-7

"When George goes to the hospital to have a piece of jigsaw puzzle removed from his stomach, he behaves very well until the last day, when curiosity again gets him into trouble." Hodges. Bks for Elem Sch Libraries

"As a book that prepares the child for the hospital this new 'Curious George' is one of the best. . . . There is truth and realism in the text as well as in the illustrations. George is apprehensive, tearful and uncomfortable. The book doesn't make going to the hospital a joyous thing, but its honesty will help dispel some of the fears and mysteries." N Y Times Bk Rev

Ricciuti, Edward R.

Donald and the fish that walked; pictures by Syd Hoff. Harper 1974 62p illus (A Science I can read bk) $2.95, lib. bdg. $3.43   E

1 Catfishes
ISBN 0-06-024997-8; 0-06-024998-6

"No one believes Donald's story of a fish that walks until a news story cites the growing numbers of walking catfish in the south of Florida. A brief ecology lesson takes form as a neighborhood scientist explains to Donald and his friends where the catfish come from and why they pose a threat to the area's ecological balance." Booklist

"The sprightly conversational text, accompanied by Syd Hoff's typical cartoons, is both instructive and fun." Library J

Rojankovsky, Feodor

Animals on the farm. Knopf 1967 unp illus lib. bdg. $4.99   E

1 Domestic animals
ISBN 0-394-91875-4

Illustrated by the author

This picture book identifies 19 farm animals, including goats, cats, horses, donkeys, cows, pigs, sheep, rabbits, and turkeys

They are lovingly pictured with life and warmth and humor." LC. Children's Bks. 1967

Rounds, Glen

The day the circus came to Lone Tree. Holiday House 1973 unp illus lib. bdg. $4.95   E

1 Circus—Fiction 2 The West—Fiction

ISBN 0-8234-0232-0

Illustrated by the author, this story tells of a circus' first and last visit to Lone Tree, a western cow town. The enthusiastic audience takes the lady lion tamer's act too seriously and goes to her rescue when she appears to be in danger. The result is total bedlam

"The descriptions and pictures of the cowboys trying to rope elephants, kangaroos, and tigers using their best rodeo style are the funniest part of the book. Written with the homey humor that characterizes Rounds' stories of the West, this will be a good yarn for story hour." Sch Library J

Once we had a horse. Holiday House 1971 unp illus $3.95   E

1 Horses—Stories

ISBN 0-8234-0193-6

Illustrated by the author, this story tells of "two determined children [who] spend one summer learning to mount and stay mounted on a patient old cow pony." Pub W

"Economy of words and humorous drawings in black and white . . . [make this] a delightful little picture book for young horse fanciers." Top of the News

Russ, Lavinia

Alec's sand castle; pictures by James Stevenson. Harper 1972 30p illus $4.95, lib. bdg. $4.79   E

1 Seashore—Fiction

ISBN 0-06-025150-6; 0-06-025151-4

"When Alec's parents and his aunt and uncle take over building his sand castle, Alec wanders off to build another of his own. He builds the biggest, most magnificent, and versatile castle his imagination can create." Booklist

"Sly humor and bright illustrations point up the merits of fantasy over fact." Pub W

Sandburg, Carl

The wedding procession of the Rag Doll and the Broom Handle and who was in it; pictures by Harriet Pincus. Harcourt [1967 c1950] unp illus $6.50   E

1 Dolls—Fiction 2 Marriage customs and rites—Fiction

ISBN 0-15-294930-5

A picture book version of a tale from: Rootabaga stories, first published 1922 and recopyrighted 1950

"A splendid procession at the rag doll's wedding is led by the nuptial pair, who are followed by limp and lumpy fun babies. Dolled up in birthday-party colors and quaintly modern costumes, they parade in a line—laughing, licking, tickling, wiggling, chuzzling, snozzling, clear to the "last of all," the staggering Sleepy heads." Horn Bk

"Small children (and the parents who read it with them) will be very grateful, as they giggle over this antic picture book story, that no one told Harriet Pincus that Carl Sandburg . . . [was] high man on the Legend In His Time totem pole. . . . For she has illustrated this story . . . not with the solemn reverence due the work of a Living Legend, but with the earthy exuberance that Sandburg had when he wrote it, way back in 1922." Pub W

Sandburg, Helga

Joel and the wild goose; illus. by Thomas Daly. Dial Press 1963 unp illus $4.95, lib. bdg. $4.58   E

1 Geese—Stories

ISBN 0-8037-4237-1; 0-8037-4238-X

"A lonely little farm boy who longs for something of his own finds a wild goose wounded by hunters and takes it home. Through the winter Joel cares for the goose and in the spring, though he loves it dearly, he lets it fly away knowing that memory of the wild bird will remain with him always." Booklist

"The simple, oft-told story is distinctive here for the individuality of little Joel, who was always telling himself riddles, and for the background of the farm and its animals. The illustrations in muted colors and the design of the book are reminiscent of the lovely Swedish picture books so familiar in the United States in the early part of this century before American picture books began appearing in quantity. In fact, the flavor of the book is a pleasant amalgam of Sweden and America." Horn Bk

Sauer, Julia L.

Mike's house; illus. by Don Freeman. Viking 1954 31p illus lib. bdg. $3.50, pa 85¢   E

1 Libraries—Fiction 2 Snow—Fiction

ISBN 0-670-47573-4; 0-670-05034-2

"Because 'Mike Mulligan' is his favorite book, four-year-old Robert loves the public library—'Mike's House'—and never misses a story hour there. One day he gets lost in a snowstorm and is helped by many kindly people before arriving at the library." Hodges. Bks for Elem Sch Libraries

"The humor and understanding of the text are perfectly complemented by Don Freeman's vigorous illustrations." N Y Times Bk Rev

Scarry, Richard

Richard Scarry's ABC word book. Random House 1971 61p illus $4.50, lib. bdg. $5.69   E

1 Alphabet books

ISBN 0-394-82339-7; 0-394-92339-1

Illustrated by the author, this is a "picture book full of animal characters who introduce the letters of the alphabet. In addition [the author] shows how letters are used to form words and names by means of rhymes [tongue twisters] and short stories." Pub W

Scheer, Julian

Rain makes applesauce [by] Julian Scheer & Marvin Bileck. Holiday House 1964 unp illus $5.95   E

ISBN 0-8234-0091-3

Illustrated by Marvin Bileck

"A book of original nonsense, illustrated with intricate drawings. Small children love the refrains, 'Rain makes applesauce' and 'You're just talking silly talk.' and enjoy the fantastic details in the pictures." Hodges. Bks for Elem Sch Libraries

Schick, Eleanor

Peggy's new brother. Macmillan (N Y) 1970 unp illus $4.50   E

1 Infants—Fiction

The author's "clean-lined and simply-drawn pictures show a small girl and a pregnant mother; grandmother's appearance heralds the arrival of the new baby. Peggy, who has had the usual doubts about the value of babies versus that of cats, finds that her new brother is a scene-stealer. Disgruntled but anxious to participate, Peggy tries to help but finds that she is not deft enough; but—only Peggy can make the baby laugh when he is cranky. Not innovative, but so natural and realistic a picture book that it can be very effective in preparing the small child for a new baby." Chicago. Children's Bk Center

Schlein, Miriam

Fast is not a ladybug; a book about fast and slow things; illus. by Leonard Kessler. Young Scott Bks. 1953 unp illus lib. bdg. $3.95   E

1 Speed

ISBN 0-201-09181-X

A book about slow things and fast things and the

Schlein, Miriam—*Continued*

relations between fast and faster, slow and slower—a
ladybug, a little boy running, a fire engine, a train on a
track, a cloud on a lazy day, and a seed slowly growing

Heavy is a hippopotamus; pictures by Leonard Kessler. Young Scott Bks. 1954 unp illus lib. bdg.
$3.95   E
1 Weights and measures
ISBN 0-201-09217-4
Ounces, pounds, tons—what do they mean? In this
elementary book the author develops an understanding of weights and measures by showing different
ways of thinking about heaviness or lightness in relation to some familiar objects
The author "is ably assisted by illustrator Leonard
Kessler, who can make something as prosaic as a
weighing machine almost as funny and attractive as a
very heavy hippopotamus." N Y Times Bk Rev

The rabbit's world; illus. by Peter Parnall. Four
Winds 1973 unp illus $4.95   E
1 Rabbits—Stories
ISBN 0-590-17210-7
"The snowshoe rabbit's first months of life are
narrated in a lyrical story. Little Snowshoe Rabbit
cannot refrain from asking his mother about the
strange new world. She urges him to let his senses
develop at their own pace, then to use them to discover and possess the objects of his curiosity. He
finally arrives at an understanding that the world is his
to keep if he would but use it to his advantage and
retain that wisdom which only anthropomorphized
animals seem to have. The writing is sophisticated but
contains a smattering of baby talk. Wide, white spaces
and fine line drawings depict a purified yet delicately
detailed form of the natural world." Booklist

Shapes; pictures by Sam Berman. Addison-Wesley
1952 unp illus lib. bdg. $3.95   E
1 Size and shape
ISBN 0-201-09343-X
"Young Scott books"
"Familiar objects help develop geometric concepts
of round, square, line, straight line, curve, long, and
tall." Hardgrove. Math Library—Elem and Jr High
Sch
"This is a brilliant little book which will help to train
a youngster's eye and make him sharply aware of form
and design." N Y Times Bk Rev

Schmiderer, Dorothy

The alphabeast book; an abecedarium. Holt 1971
unp illus $3.95, pa $1.25   E
1 Alphabet books
ISBN 0-03-088344-X; 0-03-091950-9
Illustrated by the author
"A unique presentation of the alphabet. By simple
transformation of the shapes of the letters, with four
illustrations per letter in red, white, and blue, the
letters of the alphabet emerge into animals." Top of
the News
"This is gay and simple, a catalyst for interest in
form as well as in the letters of the alphabet."
Chicago. Children's Bk Center

Schweitzer, Byrd Baylor

Amigo; illus. by Garth Williams. Macmillan (N Y)
1963 41p illus $5.95, pa 95¢   E
1 Mexico—Fiction 2 Prairie-dogs—Stories 3
Stories in rhyme
"This story in verse about a little Mexican boy who
longs for a dog, but is satisfied by making friends with
a prairie dog, is a charming one, told with sympathetic
understanding and pictures in soft desert colors. The
amusing and touching feature of it is that boy and

prairie dog think they are taming each other. 'Now /
Francisco thought / 'I've tamed me a prairie dog. He's
my greatest joy.' / And / Amigo thought / 'Mine is the
best pet. I've tamed me a boy.' " Sat Rev

Scott, Ann Herbert

Big Cowboy Western; pictures by Richard W.
Lewis. Lothrop 1965 unp illus lib. bdg. $4.59   E
1 Negroes—Fiction 2 Cities and towns—Fiction
ISBN 0-688-51199-6
"Martin receives a cowboy outfit for his fifth birthday and immediately becomes Big Cowboy Western.
But he is a city child living in a housing project; and his
play is never quite real until Mr. Arrico, the fruit and
vegetable man, shares his old horse with Martin.
Lively, natural illustrations show a Negro child and
his family against the background of a large housing
project." Moorachian. What is a City?

Segal, Lore

All the way home; pictures by James Marshall.
Farrar, Straus 1973 unp illus $4.95   E
ISBN 0-374-30215-4
"When mother takes Juliet and baby George to the
park, Juliet falls down and cries. Finding this enjoyable, she proposes to keep it up although mother
threatens an immediate return home. Juliet bawls,
the baby grins, and the procession is joined by a
barking dog, a meowing cat, and a squawking bird.
The group keeps walking around the block until Juliet
stops crying, because the doorman refuses to let the
family in until there is quiet." Chicago. Children's Bk
Center
"The cumulative nonsense of the slight but amusing
text is interpreted in droll, nonsentimental illustrations, executed in pen and ink and in green, yellow,
and red watercolors." Horn Bk

Tell me a Mitzi; pictures by Harriet Pincus. Farrar,
Straus 1970 unp illus $4.95   E
1 Family—Fiction
ISBN 0-374-37392-2
The author injects an element of fantasy into these
three stories of family life, the first of which deals with
Mitzi's safari to grandma's and grandpa's house, the
second with a confrontation with the common cold,
and the third with her brother Jacob's encounter with
a Presidential motorcade
"The illustrations, while they do not boast attractive
children, are full of vitality and humor, the busy
urban neighborhood and homely people having a rueful charm." Sutherland. The Best in Children's Bks

Sendak, Maurice

Chicken soup with rice; a book of months. Harper
1962 30p illus lib. bdg. $3.79   E
1 Months—Fiction
ISBN 0-06-025535-6
Originally published in smaller format as volume
two of the "Nutshell library"
Pictures and verse illustrate the delight of eating
chicken soup with rice in every season of the year

In the night kitchen. Harper 1970 unp illus $5.95,
lib. bdg. $5.79   E
ISBN 0-06-25489-0; 0-06-025490-4
"In a highly original dream fantasy a small boy falls
through the dark, out of his clothes, and into the
bright night kitchen where he is stirred into the cake
batter and almost baked, jumps into the bread dough,
kneads and shapes it into an airplane, and flies up over
the top of the Milky Way to get milk for the bakers."
Booklist
The author-illustrator "abandons his recent subtle,
evocative black-and-white echoes of the 19th-
Century English illustrators for a bold, graphic style

Sendak, Maurice—*Continued*
that evokes a more recent past—the comic books and movies of his own childhood in the 1930's. Both story and pictures combine the timeless themes of childhood fantasy with concrete images of food products (favorite pop art subjects) and the wild illogic of the animated cartoons familiar to today's children through TV." Sch Library J

Where the wild things are; story and pictures by Maurice Sendak. Harper 1963 unp illus $4.95, lib. bdg. $5.11   E
    ISBN 0-06-025520-X; 0-06-025521-8
Awarded the Caldecott Medal, 1964
"A tale of very few words about Max, sent to his room for cavorting around in his wolf suit, who dreamed of going where the wild things are, to rule them and share their rumpus. Then a longing to be 'where someone loved him best of all' swept over him." Bk Week
"This vibrant picture book in luminous, understated full color has proved utterly engrossing to children with whom it has been shared. . . . A sincere, perceptive contribution which bears repeated examination." Horn Bk

Serraillier, Ian
Suppose you met a witch; illus. by Ed Emberley. Little 1973 unp illus $4.95   E
    1 Witches—Fiction 2 Stories in rhyme
    ISBN 0-316-78125-8
Told in verse, this is the story of Roland and Miranda who, "popped and tied into the sack of an evil crone, are whisked off to her traditional candy house, there to be devoured. But the resourceful children outwit the hag as enchanted readers will find to their satisfaction. . . . [The illustrator] has created an unsurpassably horrible witch but his scenes of violence are tempered by gentle scenes of swans on a lake and a rose garden as the hero and heroine take on other guises to escape their captor." Pub W

Seuss, Dr
And to think that I saw it on Mulberry Street. Vanguard 1937 unp illus $3.50   E
    1 Nonsense verses
    ISBN 0-8149-0387-8
"A rollicking nonsense story in verse true to a child's imagination. In a small boy's mind a plain horse and cart on Mulberry Street gradually grow into a circus bandwagon drawn by an elephant and two spirited giraffes." N Y Libraries
"A fresh, inspiring picture-story book [illustrated by the author] in bright colors. . . . As convincing to a child as to the psychologist in quest of a book with an appeal to the child's imagination." Horn Bk

Bartholomew and the oobleck; written and illus. by Dr Seuss. Random House 1949 unp illus $3.95, lib. bdg. $4.99   E
    ISBN 0-394-80075-3; 0-394-90075-8
"More perfect nonsense from the kingdom of Didd with King Derwin, dissatisfied with only rain, sunshine, fog and snow, ordering the royal magicians to produce oobleck. The greenish, sticky stuff was almost disastrous and it is Bartholomew Cubbins who rescues the kingdom." Wis Library Bul

The cat in the hat. Random House 1957 61p illus $2.95, lib. bdg. $3.69   E
    1 Cats—Stories 2 Nonsense verses
    ISBN 0-394-80001-X; 0-394-90001-4
Also available in a bilingual Spanish-English edition for $3.50, lib. bdg. $4.99 (ISBN 0-394-81626-9; 0-394-91626-3) and a bilingual French-English edition lib. bdg. $4.99 (ISBN 0-394-90171-1)

A nonsense story in verse illustrated by the author about an unusual cat and his tricks which he displayed for the children one rainy day
"Using simple vocabulary and verse form, the author, with fertile imagination, has produced a beginning reader that avoids the usual dullness of limited vocabulary and frequent word repetition." Top of the News

The cat in the hat comes back! Beginner Bks. 1958 61p illus $2.95, lib. bdg. $3.69   E
    1 Cats—Stories 2 Nonsense verses
    ISBN 0-394-80002-8; 0-394-90002-2
"A top-notch sequel to 'The Cat in the Hat,' providing delightful fare for beginning readers. Using only 252 different words, the cat comes back and wreaks havoc in the house of Sally and the teller of the story. But, of course, all is eventually put right." Library J

The 500 hats of Bartholomew Cubbins. Vanguard 1938 unp illus $3.50   E
    1 Hats—Fiction
    ISBN 0-8149-0388-6
"A read-aloud story telling what happened to Bartholomew Cubbins when he couldn't take his hat off before the King." Hodges. Bks for Elem Sch Libraries
"It is a lovely bit of tomfoolery which keeps up the suspense and surprise until the last page, and of the same ingenious and humorous imagination are the author's black and white illustrations in which a red cap and then an infinite number of red caps titillate the eye." N Y Times Bk Rev

Horton hatches the egg. Random House 1940 unp illus $3.95, lib. bdg. $4.99   E
    1 Elephants—Stories 2 Nonsense verses
    ISBN 0-394-80077-X; 0-394-90077-4
"Left in charge of a bird's egg, Horton the elephant [faithful one hundred per cent] guards it through so many trials that his final triumph is most gratifying. Rollicking verse and the illustrations make Horton an endearing figure." Let's Read Together
"A moral is a new thing to find in a Dr. Seuss book, but it doesn't interfere much with the hilarity with which he juggles an elephant up a tree. . . . Neither young nor old are going to quibble with the fantastic comedy of his pictures." N Y Times Bk Rev

Horton hears a Who! Random House 1954 unp illus $3.95, lib. bdg. $4.99   E
    1 Elephants—Stories 2 Nonsense verses
    ISBN 0-394-80078-8; 0-394-90078-2
"The verses are full of the usual lively, informal language and amazing rhymes that have delighted such a world-wide audience in the good 'doctor's' other books. The story, with its moral, does not match the gayety of some of the older books. But the pictures are as wildly original and funny as ever." N Y Her Trib Bks

How the Grinch stole Christmas. Random House 1957 unp illus $3.95, lib. bdg. $4.99   E
    1 Christmas stories 2 Nonsense verses
    ISBN 0-394-80079-6; 0-394-90079-0
"The Grinch lived on a mountain where it was able to ignore the people of the valley except at Christmas time when it had to endure the sound of their singing. One year it decided to steal all the presents so there would be no Christmas, but much to its amazement discovered that people did not need presents to enjoy Christmas. It thereupon reformed, returned the presents and joined in the festivities." Chicago. Children's Bk Center

Seuss, Dr—*Continued*

If I ran the circus. Random House 1956 unp illus
$3.95, lib. bdg. $4.99   E
1 Circus—Fiction 2 Nonsense verses
ISBN 0-394-80080-X; 0-394-90080-4
The author-illustrator "presents the fabulous Circus McGurkus with its highly imaginative young owner, Morris McGurk and its intrepid performer, Sneelock, behind whose store the circus is to be housed. There are the expected number of strange creatures with nonsensical names, but the real humor lies in the situations, and especially those involving Mr. Sneelock. There is fun for the entire family here." Chicago. Children's Bk Center

If I ran the zoo. Random House 1950 unp illus
$3.95, lib. bdg. $4.99   E
1 Zoological gardens—Fiction 2 Nonsense verses
ISBN 0-394-80081-8; 0-394-90081-2
"This rhyming tale [illustrated by the author] of young Gerald McGrew who thought of all sorts of unusual animals he'd have in a zoo is Dr. Seuss at his best. It will be a treasure for the storyteller if she learns the verses by heart and holds the book up so that the children may see the pictures of the ten-footed lion, the hen 'who roosts in another hen's top-knot,' the bustard 'who only eats custard with sauce made of mustard' and all the others." Horn Bk
"As you turn the pages, the imaginings get wilder and funnier, the rhymes more hilarious. There will be no age limits for this book, because families will be forced to share rereading and quotation, for a long, long time." N Y Her Trib Bks

McElligot's pool; written and illus. by Dr Seuss.
Random House 1947 unp illus $3.95, lib. bdg.
$4.99   E
1 Fishing—Fiction 2 Nonsense verses
ISBN 0-394-80083-4; 0-394-90083-9
"In spite of warnings that there are no fish in McElligot's Pool, a boy continues to fish and to imagine the rare and wonderful denizens of the deep which he just 'might' catch." Hodges. Bks for Elem Sch Libraries
"Prepare to chuckle under water for you'll be meeting the weirdest, wildest, funniest citizens of the deep which imagination can conjure." Chicago Sun Bk Week

Shapiro, Irwin

Twice upon a time; illus. by Adrienne Adams.
Scribner 1973 unp illus $5.95   E
1 Kings and rulers—Fiction
ISBN 0-684-13358-X
"Rambling Richard, a story writer, travels to the city of Gig-Gib where the populace suffers under a ruler who demands twice as much of everything. They labor to build higher mountains and dig deeper ditches only to have each day's work undone by natural forces. When the king orders Rambling Richard to tell a story that begins 'Twice upon a time,' the latter refuses and succeeds in ridiculing the king's greed by suggesting Gig-Gib needs two monarchs." Sch Library J
"The telling is succinct and well-balanced; the pictures, lively with medieval detail, complement the text, though their reproduction sometimes lacks sharpness." Horn Bk

Shapp, Martha

Let's find out what's big and what's small, by Martha and Charles Shapp; pictures by Carol Nicklaus. Rev. full color ed. Watts, F. 1975 40p illus lib. bdg. $4.90   E
1 Size and shape
ISBN 0-531-00106-7
First published 1959, illustrated by Vana Earle

With less than a 100 word vocabulary, this book "emphasizes that 'big' and 'small' are relative." Sch Library J

Sharmat, Marjorie Weinman

Gladys told me to meet her here; pictures by Edward Frascino. Harper 1970 31p illus lib. bdg. $4.79   E
1 Friendship—Fiction
ISBN 0-06-025550-1
"Not for worlds would Irving have let Gladys know, when she finally showed up, what he had been going through. The style is gently doleful, as Irving's stream-of-consciousness envisions all the dire reasons why Gladys is late meeting him at the zoo and as he indulges himself alternately in daydreams of his best friend suffering and memories of her staunch loyalty. Amusingly illustrated, this is a story as enjoyable for the adult reader-aloud as it is for the young listener." Sutherland. The Best in Children's Bks

Goodnight, Andrew; goodnight, Craig. Pictures by Mary Chalmers. Harper 1969 32p illus $4.50, lib. bdg. $4.79   E
1 Sleep—Fiction 2 Brothers—Fiction
ISBN 0-06-025547-1; 0-06-025548-X
A "picture book of special interest to small boys describes the bedtime antics of two brothers. Andrew refuses to settle down to sleep until he obtains from his older brother Craig a promise to play ball with him the next day." Booklist
"The pale, demure illustrations have a note of humor, and the young listener should relish the fun and the typical bedtime pranks." Sat Rev

Morris Brookside, a dog; illus. by Ronald Himler. Holiday House 1973 unp illus lib. bdg. $3.95   E
1 Dogs—Stories
ISBN 0-8234-0225-8
Morris, a stray dog, finds a home with the elderly Brooksides. They treat him as one of the family and even try to find some canine friends for him, but Morris passes up their choices in favor of a dirty, bedraggled female
"This is that oddity, a successful child's story with no children in it; the quiet humor, the appealing characters, and the bland, ingenuous style are echoed in the attractive illustrations." Chicago. Children's Bk Center

Nate the Great; illus. by Marc Simont. Coward, McCann & Geoghegan 1972 60p illus lib. bdg. $4.69   E
1 Mystery and detective stories
ISBN 0-698-30444-6
"A Break-of-day book"
Nate the Great, a junior detective who has found missing balloons, books, slippers, chickens and even a goldfish, is now in search of a painting of a dog by Annie, the girl down the street
"The illustrations capture the exaggerated, tongue-in-cheek humor of the story." Booklist

Showers, Paul

The listening walk; illus. by Aliki. Crowell 1961 unp illus $4.50, lib. bdg. $5.25   E
1 Sounds
ISBN 0-690-49662-1; 0-690-49663-X
"Let's-read-and-find-out-books"
In pictures and text this book shows many of the sights and sounds a boy may see on a walk down the street and through the park. Among them are such sounds as those of his father's shoes on the sidewalk, a power lawn mower, the brakes of a car stopping quickly, a jet plane flying over the park, ducks quack-

Showers, Paul—*Continued*

ing, and pigeons flying down to be fed by people in the park

Shub, Elizabeth

Uncle Harry [by] Gerlinde Schneider; pictures by Lilo Fromm; adapted from the German by Elizabeth Shub. Macmillan (N Y) 1972 unp illus $3.95   E

1 Cats—Stories

Original German edition, 1971

"Uncle Harry hates cats but is stuck with a kitten he rescues from drowning. After days of trying to give it away—to children who already have cats, to the pound where there is no more room, to the grocer who already has a good mouser—Uncle Harry finally finds a taker. But, surprise: he finds he loves the minx after all, and keeps her." Pub W

This book "should appeal to the very young, intriguing illustrations." Children's Bks of the Year, 1972

Shulevitz, Uri

Dawn; words and pictures by Uri Shulevitz. Farrar, Straus 1974 unp illus $5.95   E

ISBN 0-374-31707-0

"Drawn from a Chinese poem, the spare text tells of an old man and his grandson asleep by the shore of a mountain lake. With the approach of daylight, the watercolor illustrations, which start out small, dark, and blurred, slowly become more focused and detailed: the moon casts a soft glow; a breeze riffles the water; mists rise. As the old man and the boy push out on to the lake in their boat, a hint of color suffuses the scene; and finally, in a visual tour-de-force, the sun rises over the mountain and they are bathed in full color." Sch Library J

"The purity of the hues, well-produced on ample spreads, the subtle graphic development from scene to scene, and the sharply focused simplicity of the few words make this a true art experience." Horn Bk

One Monday morning. Scribner 1967 unp illus lib. bdg. $5.95, pa 95¢   E

ISBN 0-684-13195-1; 0-684-12781-4

Illustrated by the author

" 'One Monday morning, the king, the queen, and the little prince came to visit me. But I wasn't home. . . .' So goes the daydream of a small child in a drab tenement. As the week progresses, the royal entourage, in the panoply of playing card figures, increases. Their pageantry blots out the grey background while commonplace activities play counterpoint to the fantasy theme." Moorachian. What is a City?

"Humor, dignity, imagination, and a remarkable interplay between text and illustration make . . . [this] a beautiful book that is easy and fun to read. . . . Children will be able to identify, understand, and enjoy both worlds of [the book's] imaginative child." Wis Library Bul

Rain, rain, rivers; words and pictures by Uri Shulevitz. Farrar, Straus 1969 unp illus $4.95   E

1 Rain and rainfall—Fiction

ISBN 0-374-36171-1

"In her attic room a little girl hears the rain. Outside her window the gutters are rain-swollen, the rain beats down on the city streets and the few scurrying people, cold and wet. The rain pours into country streams, the brooks feed the rivers, the rain-lashed rivers pour into the frothing sea. Only at the end is there a change of mood, as a pale, watery sun shines on delightful puddles and the joyful children reappear. The little girl feels the urgent freshening and sees her tiny potted plant begin to grow." Chicago. Children's Bk Center

"Even more distinguished than his earlier Cal-

decott winning book, [The Fool of the World and the flying ship, by Arthur Ransome entered in class 398.2] is this lovely buoyant hymn to the wonders of rain on cities, mountains, meadows, and sea. This lovely book brings a renewal of life and spirit—even as the rain itself." Commonweal

Sivulich, Sandra Stroner

I'm going on a bear hunt; illus. by Glen Rounds. Dutton 1973 unp illus $5.50   E

ISBN 0-525-32535-2

This is "a new version of an old tale about the adventures of a little boy pretending to go on a bear hunt. Appropriate gestures are indicated in brown print for the storyteller, who demonstrates the boy's climbing, sliding, swimming, rowing, walking, crawling, finding the bear and then reversing the whole process double time." Booklist

"The illustrations are engaging; however, the storyteller will achieve better results by using the story without the book, for freedom of the hands is needed to direct action, and it is the type of story which lends itself to enlarging or changing at will." Sch Library J

Skorpen, Liesel Moak

Old Arthur; pictures by Wallace Tripp. Harper 1972 46p illus $3.95, lib. bdg. $4.43   E

1 Dogs—Stories

ISBN 0-06-025714-8; 0-06-025715-6

This is the story of a special friendship which develops between a young boy and an old dog who is forced to leave a farm when he can no longer work effectively

"Sweet but not saccharine, both the story and illustrations offer young readers a quiet blend of reality and security." Booklist

Slobodkin, Louis

Excuse me! Certainly! Vanguard 1959 unp illus $4.95   E

1 Courtesy—Fiction 2 Stories in rhyme

ISBN 0-8149-0403-3

Companion volume to: Thank you—you're welcome

"A picture book in rhyme tells how 'Willie White who was not polite' learned better manners. Amusing illustrations by the author." Hodges. Bks for Elem Sch Libraries

Thank you—you're welcome. Vanguard 1957 unp illus $4.95   E

1 Courtesy—Fiction 2 Stories in rhyme

ISBN 0-8149-0404-1

Illustrated by the author, this is the "story of Jimmy who was happy and good and always said 'Thank-you' whenever he should—until the day he was sad because he, too, wanted to say 'You're welcome.' Having learned how one earns the right to say this, Jimmy is good again and the story ends happily." Secondary Educ Brd

Slobodkina, Esphyr

Caps for sale; a tale of a peddler, some monkeys & their monkey business; told and illus. by Esphyr Slobodkina. Young Scott Bks. 1947 unp illus lib. bdg. $3.95   E

1 Monkeys—Stories 2 Peddlers and peddling—Fiction

ISBN 0-201-09147-X

A picture book story which "provides hilarious confusion. A cap peddler takes a nap under a tree. When he wakes up, his caps have disappeared. He looks up in the tree and sees countless monkeys, each wearing a cap and grinning." A Parent's Guide To Children's Rdng

Solbert, Ronni

I wrote my name on the wall; text and photographs by Ronni Solbert. Little 1971 unp illus $5.95   E

1 New York (City)

ISBN 0-316-80350-2

"Within the confines of a few New York City blocks, Ronni Solbert shows through expressive photographs and poetic prose the innermost feelings of children. The diversity of racial mixtures in our country is evidenced by the black, Puerto Rican, Oriental and white youngsters who find beauty and humor in an unlikely environment." Wis Library Bul

The book "is a graphic juxtaposition of faces and words that might have seemed ugly but are truly beautiful. What begins as ordinary speech ends as blank verse." Christian Sci Monitor

Solot, Mary Lynn

100 hamburgers; the getting thin book; Paul Galdone drew the pictures. Lothrop 1972 unp illus $4.95   E

1 Weight control—Fiction

ISBN 0-688-41247-5

"If it is possible for the fat child to approach the subject of his fatness cheerfully, he can with this little book. It is written in the first person: the little boy soliloquizing on the woes of being fat; his pleasure in eating; and then, his understanding and acceptance of the doctor's advice about getting thin. The accompanying pictures illustrate the mood splendidly; the information and advice given is sound but not too severe, and the tone is always sympathetic." Appraisal

Sonneborn, Ruth A.

Friday night is Papa night; illus. by Emily A. McCully. Viking 1970 unp illus lib. bdg. $3.95   E

1 Puerto Ricans in the U.S.—Fiction

ISBN 0-670-32938-X

Because Pedro's father is unable to come home during the week, each Friday night is a special occasion. One evening Papa doesn't come, and the children are brokenhearted. But when a weary Papa finally does arrive in the middle of the night, with Popsicles and presents for everyone, they all agree it is time for a celebration

"The structure is slight, but the story conveys a real feeling of family love, echoed in the illustrations of an attractive Puerto Rican family." Chicago. Children's Bk Center

Spier, Peter

Crash! Bang! Boom! Doubleday 1972 unp illus $5.95, lib. bdg. $6.70   E

1 Sounds

ISBN 0-385-06780-1; 0-385-02496-7

"In a colorful cacophony of precise sound . . . [the author-illustrator] sets out to capture visually the audible quality of inanimate objects: the BLUBBA-LUBBA-LUBBA of a pot of boiling potatoes and the PFF PFF PFF of a bicycle tire being pumped up. Clean white pages are filled with detailed, bright-colored pictures of objects grouped according to use, relationship, or activity." Horn Bk

Fast-slow, high-low; a book of opposites. Doubleday 1972 unp illus $5.95, lib. bdg. $6.70   E

ISBN 0-385-06781-X; 0-385-02876-8

"Pages filled with delightful drawings, in pairs, that illustrate objects or concepts like fast or slow, young or old, over or under, heavy or light, dark or light, and so on. There is no print on the pages save the headings. The book may require adult interpretation in many instances, since some of the pictures may need translations. . . . Useful for development of awareness of differences, yet limited by the subtlety of some examples, the book is not the best choice for learning

opposites but it is probably the most attractive." Chicago. Children's Bk Center

Gobble, growl, grunt. Doubleday 1971 unp illus $5.95, lib. bdg. $6.70   E

1 Animals—Pictorial works 2 Animal communication

ISBN 0-385-06779-8; 0-385-00681-0

"Over 600 animals parade across double-page spreads, identified by name and the sound each animal makes. There is no need for any other text; the illustrations speak for themselves in a humorous and lighthearted fashion." Pub W

"Children who enjoy pictures of animals will have hours of fun poring over the lively illustrations while parents can use the book with young children to identify animals and their sounds." Booklist

Steig, William

Amos & Boris. Farrar, Straus 1971 unp illus $5.50   E

1 Mice—Stories 2 Whales—Stories

ISBN 0-374-30278-2

Illustrated by the author, this story "has two heroes, Amos the mouse and Boris the whale, 'a devoted pair of friends with nothing at all in common, except good hearts and a willingness to help their fellow mammal.' And help each other they do indeed, in a most uncommmon way." Pub W

"The water-color paintings deftly convey changing qualities of light—day and night, sunshine and rain—and a realistic flowing and heaving of seawater. . . . [The] genuine story builds its atmosphere and mood with freshness, compassion, and child interest, and is enhanced by the illustrations." Horn Bk

Farmer Palmer's wagon ride; story and pictures by William Steig. Farrar, Straus 1974 unp illus $5.95   E

1 Pigs—Stories 2 Donkeys—Stories

ISBN 0-374-32288-0

Farmer Palmer, a pig and his hired hand Ebenezer, an ass, manage an unusually hazardous trip home from the market by putting to use the presents they had bought for the family

"The text, longer than that of most picture books, boasts some captivating and original onomatopoeia, lending itself to reading aloud. Full-color illustrations add action, expression, and countryside colors appropriate to the story." Booklist

Sylvester and the magic pebble. Windmill Bks. [distributed by] Simon & Schuster 1969 unp illus $6.95, lib. bdg. $5.70   E

1 Donkeys—Stories

ISBN 0-671-66511-1; 0-671-66512-X

Awarded the Caldecott Medal, 1969

"Sylvester the young donkey was a pebble collector; one day he found a flaming red stone, shiny and round—and quite unaccountably able to grant wishes. Overjoyed, Sylvester was planning to share his magic with his family when 'a mean, hungry lion' appeared. Startled and panicky, Sylvester wished himself transformed into a rock. In vain his grieving parents searched for their beloved child; all the worried animals took up the hunt. Then, after months of sorrow and mourning, poor Sylvester was fortuitously but logically restored. A remarkable atmosphere of childlike innocence pervades the book; [the author's] beautiful pictures in full, natural color show daily and seasonal changes in the lush countryside and greatly extend the kindly humor and the warm, unselfconscious tenderness." Horn Bk

Steptoe, John

Stevie. Harper 1969 unp illus $4.95, lib. bdg. $4.79 E

1 Negroes—Fiction

ISBN 0-06-025763-6; 0-06-025764-4

Illustrated by the author

A small Black boy, Robert "tells the story of the intruder, Stevie, who comes to stay at his house because both parents are working. Stevie is a pest. He tags along after Robert, he messes up toys, he wants everything he sees. Worst of all, 'my momma never said nothin' to him.' But Robert is an only child, and after Stevie goes, the house is still. He remembers the games they played, the way Stevie looked up to him." Sat Rev

"While characters in this picture-story are black, the theme of childhood jealousy and rivalry for Mother's attention is universal. The story evokes a warm response and the bold pastel paintings are notable." Top of the News

Stevenson, James

The bear who had no place to go. Harper 1972 47p illus lib. bdg. $4.79 E

1 Bears—Stories 2 Friendship—Fiction

ISBN 0-06-025781-4

"Ralph, a bicycle-riding circus bear, finds his act suddenly replaced by a seal. . . . Lonely and disoriented without the familiar circus environment, Ralph tries unsuccessfully to find a new home. Just before despair overtakes him, Ralph meets a rat named Frank, who introduces him to a more rewarding woodland habitation. Ralph is an endearing bear and this story of friendship is brilliantly illustrated [by the author] with shaded black-and-white drawings." Pub W

Stolz, Mary

Emmett's pig; pictures by Garth Williams. Harper 1959 61p illus $2.95, lib. bdg. $3.79 E

1 Pigs—Stories

ISBN 0-06-025855-1; 0-06-025856-X

"An I can read book"

"Although Emmett lives in a city apartment and is surrounded by toy pigs, pictures and books about pigs, his great desire for a real live pig is finally granted as a birthday present—a pig to be his own, but to be boarded on a farm outside the city." Wis Library Bul

This book is "far above the average in both interest and illustration." Bookmark

Suhl, Yuri

Simon Boom gives a wedding; illus. by Margot Zemach. Four Winds 1972 unp illus $6.95, lib. bdg. $6.72 E

ISBN 0-590-17209-3; 0-590-07209-9

"No illustrator but Margot Zemach could create such whimsical illustrations to match this funny, preposterous tale about braggart Simon Boom, who always had to buy the best, even if 'sometimes the best happens to be a size too short, or too long, or absurdly out of season.' When Simon's daughter is to be married, he is determined to serve only the best food at the wedding party—and the incredulous wedding guests are astounded when only pure spring water is served." Pub W

Surany, Anico

Ride the cold wind; pictures by Leonard Everett Fisher. Putnam 1964 unp illus lib. bdg. $5.39 E

1 Peru—Fiction 2 Fishing—Fiction

ISBN 0-399-60535-5

"To prove that he is big enough to be a fisherman like his father a little Peruvian llama herder tries, with his sister's help, to catch the great elusive fish, El Rayo de Oro. Losing his catch—and very nearly his life—Paco finally understands that fishing is a man's work. . . . [This] picture-book story is illustrated with striking pictures compatible in color and design with the Peruvian background." Booklist

Swift, Hildegarde H.

The little red lighthouse and the great gray bridge, by Hildegarde H. Swift and Lynd Ward. Harcourt 1942 unp illus $5.50, pa $1.45 E

1 Lighthouses—Fiction 2 George Washington Bridge—Fiction

ISBN 0-15-247040-9; 0-15-652840-1

"After the great beacon atop the . . . George Washington Bridge was installed, the little red lighthouse feared he would no longer be useful; but when an emergency arose, the little lighthouse proved that he was still important." Hodges. Bks for Elem Sch Libraries

"The story is written with imagination and a gift for bringing alive this little lighthouse and its troubles. . . . [Lynd Ward's] illustrations have some distinction and one in particular, the fog creeping over the river clutching at the river boats, has atmosphere, rhythm and good colour." Ontario Library Rev

Taylor, Mark

Henry the explorer; illus. by Graham Booth. Atheneum Pubs. 1966 unp illus $6.95 E

ISBN 0-689-20627-5

"One morning after breakfast Henry packed his explorer's kit and, with his dog, set out to explore the world. By nightfall he had made several important discoveries—including the fact that he was far from home and unsure of the way. Henry's safe return ahead of the search party and his anticipation of his next exploring expedition climax . . . [a] mildly suspenseful picture-book story." Booklist

"This appealing picture-tale adventure has a storyteller's concise narrative that should make it one of those books which stand up under repeated sharing." Horn Bk

Thayer, Jane

The puppy who wanted a boy; illus. by Seymour Fleishman. Morrow 1958 47p illus lib. bdg. $4.59 E

1 Dogs—Stories 2 Christmas stories

ISBN 0-688-31631-X

"The one thing Petey [a puppy] wanted for Christmas was a boy, but his mother simply couldn't find one. She offered Petey a rabbit or a canary, but he still wanted a boy, so he trotted off to see if any dogs would give their boys away. The dogs he asked were very rude, and Petey was discouraged and tired by the time he reached the orphan home. The happy ending for Petey was that he got fifty boys for Christmas." Chicago. Children's Bk Center

"The reversal of the boy-wants-dog-for-Christmas plot will delight pre-school children. . . . Pictures on every page are coordinated exactly to the text." Library J

Quiet on account of dinosaur; pictures by Seymour Fleishman. Morrow 1964 unp illus lib. bdg. $4.59 E

1 Dinosaurs—Stories

ISBN 0-688-31632-8

"In this fanciful tale, Mary Ann's interests in prehistoric animals lead her to discover a real live dinosaur. Dandy the dinosaur is as friendly as a puppy and everyone loves him, but Mary Ann discovers that the hustle, bustle, and noise of our world and time are just too much for him. With the cooperation of all the people in the world, the story ends with a happy

Thayer, Jane—*Continued*
dinosaur and a new, very famous scientist—Mary
Ann." Rdng Ladders. 5th edition

Thomas, Ianthe
Walk home tired, Billy Jenkins; pictures by Thomas
di Grazia. Harper 1974 unp illus $4.95, lib. bdg.
$4.79   E
    1 Negroes—Fiction
    ISBN 0-06-026108-0; 0-06-026109-9
Nina, a young Black girl, walks home pretending
that she is being transported by a silver sailboat, a
plane, and a train. City blocks seem to fly by as she
and her skeptical little friend Billy Jenkins take imaginary flight
    The illustrator's "antique brown-and-white city
street scenes have an air-brushed, dreamland atmosphere out of which the expressive features of the girl
and boy emerge like familiar faces in a crowd. A brief,
gratifying journey through one beguiling girl's imagination." Booklist

Titus, Eve
Anatole; pictures by Paul Galdone. McGraw 1956
32p illus $4.95, lib. bdg. $4.72   E
    1 Mice—Stories 2 France—Fiction
    ISBN 0-07-064906-5; 0-07-064908-1
    "Whittlesey House publications"
    "Anatole is a French mouse who was made quite
unhappy one day by hearing some people saying rude
and unpleasant things about mice. He resolved never
to go hunting for food in a house again, and turned his
attention to the Duval Cheese Factory. There he
spent every evening tasting the cheeses and leaving
notes on them, rating them as to quality and indicating
where improvements could be made. The owners
were delighted and made him their official taster."
Chicago. Children's Bk Center
    "A very original story. . . . Anatole [is] wearing a
beret at a rakish angle, and Paul Galdone's pictures of
the typically French town in which he lives are gay
and lively." Pub W

Anatole and the cat; pictures by Paul Galdone.
McGraw 1957 32p illus $4.95, lib. bdg. $4.72   E
    1 Mice—Stories 2 Cats—Stories 2 France—Fiction
    ISBN 0-07-064909-X; 0-07-064910-3
    "Whittlesey House publications"
    "The French mouse Anatole runs into [cat] diffi-
culty at the factory where he is Cheese Taster. He
very cleverly and courageously works out a solution to
his problem and once again becomes the most honored, respected mouse in all France—and the bravest." Top of the News
    The book features "merry pictures in color and
black and white." Bookmark

Anatole and the piano; pictures by Paul Galdone.
McGraw 1966 32p illus lib. bdg. $4.72   E
    1 Mice—Stories 2 Pianos—Fiction 3 France—
    Fiction
    ISBN 0-07-064892-1
A "captivating story about Anatole, cheese-taster
extraordinary, Parisian pianist, Mouse Magnifique.
Only one piano in Paris worthy of Anatole's talents,
and that one is a museum-piece miniature; not only
does Anatole receive the piano as a gift (because he
has done a noble deed that benefits orphans and
delights music lovers) but he has a concerto named in
his honor. Tongue firmly in cheek, Eve Titus has
again produced a blandly ridiculous, engaging tale."
Sutherland. The Best in Children's Bks

Anatole and the thirty thieves; illus. by Paul Galdone. McGraw 1969 32p illus $4.95, lib. bdg.
$4.72   E

    1 Mice—Stories 2 Mystery and detective stories
    3 France—Fiction
    ISBN 0-07-064887-5; 0-07-064888-3
Upon returning from a brief vacation, Anatole
learns of the robbery in M'sieu Duval's cheese factory. Being a "mouse of action," Anatole loses no time
in seeking a solution to the mystery
    "Bracing as ever, the tongue-in-cheek tall tale is
illustrated in a light, humorous vein that echoes the
bravura of the writing." Sat Rev

Anatole and the toyshop; pictures by Paul Galdone.
McGraw 1970 36p illus $4.95, lib. bdg. $4.72   E
    1 Mice—Stories 2 France—Fiction
    ISBN 0-07-064885-9; 0-07-064886-7
    "With ingenuity and great risk to himself Anatole
rescues his wife and six children held captive by a
toyshop owner and forced to ride their bicycles in the
shop window to attract customers." Booklist

Anatole over Paris; pictures by Paul Galdone.
McGraw 1961 32p illus $4.95, lib. bdg. $4.72   E
    1 Mice—Stories 2 Kites—Fiction 3 Paris—Fiction
    ISBN 0-07-065001-2; 0-07-065000-4
    "Whittlesey House publications"
    "Another entertaining story about that entertaining
mouse, Anatole; delightful illustrations in clear colors
echo the insouciance of the story and give the Parisian
background. Anatole, always the kind father, is
repairing a huge kite for his six little ones; a gust of
wind carries them all off on the kite and it is only
because Anatole is brave, resourceful, and intrepid
that all his dear ones once again reach French soil."
Chicago. Children's Bk Center

Tobias, Tobi
A day off; pictures by Ray Cruz. Putnam 1973 unp
illus lib. bdg. $4.97   E
    1 Sick—Fiction
    ISBN 0-399-60762-5
    "A book that should bring a recognition-reflex
gleam to the eyes of its audience. . . . It isn't a story
with a plot, but a situation expanded and relished in
just the way children daydream extravagantly. Once a
year, the speaker (a wily young male) says, how nice to
be sick. Just a little sick, sick enough to be fussed over
but not restricted to bed, sick enough to have lunch on
a tray but not too sick to join the hamburger-eaters at
the dinner table, sick enough . . . and so on."
Chicago. Children's Bk Center
    "Most of the fun and interest happens in the pic-
tures with their flat, bright reds and yellows; the
inventive juxtaposition of patterns (checks, plaids,
dots, flowers, etc.) and shapes; and the chunky, funny
people, especially the star of the story who usually
manages to look a little sicker when there is someone
watching him." Sch Library J

Tresselt, Alvin
Autumn harvest; illus. by Roger Duvoisin. Lothrop
1951 unp illus lib. bdg. $4.59   E
    1 Autumn
    ISBN 0-688-51155-4
The author and artist "describe in bright, appropriately colored pictures and rhythmic text, the
changes that take place in the countryside in the season between late summer and Thanksgiving."
Booklist
    "There is a subtle interplay between text and pic-
tures, which makes one sharply aware of the mellow
light of Indian summer, the sharpness of first frost,
the smell of bonfires. In a few instances the borders
surrounding the pages of text distract the eye from the
facing illustrations, but as a whole this book is lovely to
look at and to listen to." N Y Times Bk Rev

Tresselt, Alvin—*Continued*

Bonnie Bess the weathervane horse; with illus. by Erik Blegvad. Parents Mag. Press 1970 unp illus $4.95, lib. bdg. $4.59　　　　E

1 Vanes—Fiction

ISBN 0-8193-0374-7; 0-8193-0375-5

A reissue with new water color illustrations of the title first published 1949 by Lothrop

Atop the red barn stands Bonnie Bess, the "familiar weathervane horse that had been there for a hundred years or more. The farm is abandoned, the barn collapses under a snowfall and the weathervane horse is rescued in the spring by a junk dealer. Later, a customer sees Bonnie Bess and says, 'That's just the weathervane for my barn,' and Bess returns to her old home. The artist dresses the story with interesting detail for second- and third-grade readers and younger listeners." Sch Library J

The dead tree; illus. by Charles Robinson. Parents Mag. Press 1972 unp illus $4.95, lib. bdg. $4.59 E

1 Oak

ISBN 0-8193-0563-4; 0-8193-0564-2

The author gives a poetic description of the life cycle of an oak tree noting what lives on it, in it and the many things dependent upon it through the oak's stages of growth, decay and eventual return to the soil

"The regeneration of life in nature is beautifully celebrated in this picture book, in which the accuracy of observation is enriched by perceptive interpretation. The text is set against lovely watercolor illustrations, each doublespread depicting some aspect of the changing life of the tree." Horn Bk

Follow the wind; pictures by Roger Duvoisin. Lothrop 1950 unp illus lib. bdg. $4.81　　　　E

1 Winds

ISBN 0-688-51156-2

"Rhythmic text and pictures in splashy colors tell about the wind that blew for days and days, dancing with the dandelions, tossing the kite, blowing off hats, turning the windmill, sometimes a gale, now a breeze, until finally it quietly rocked itself to sleep." Booklist

"Excellent not only as a picture book but also for use in the younger children's nature classes." Horn Bk

"Hi, Mister Robin!" Pictures by Roger Duvoisin. Lothrop 1950 unp illus lib. bdg. $4.81　　　　E

1 Spring

ISBN 0-688-51168-6

After a "little boy who is tired of winter sees the first robin, he watches the changes in the landscape from bare branches to blossoms on the peach tree. Then, he is told, the spring has come." Horn Bk

"This very tenuous little story, of watching and waiting is retold with an enrichment of 'looking' in the big color pictures. Mr. Duvoisin combines a love of the atmospheric with ability to make details clear and dramatic for the child. . . . For anyone, not in the country, the pages offer fields, brooks, trees and the drama of a cold world changing to the warmth of spring." N Y Her Trib Bks

Hide and seek fog; illus. by Roger Duvoisin. Lothrop 1965 unp illus $5.50　　　　E

1 Fog

ISBN 0-688-41169-X

"This is not a plotted story but rather a mood picture book . . . describing a fog which rolls in from the sea to veil an Atlantic seacoast village for three days. The beautiful paintings, most of them doublespreads, and the brief, poetic text sensitively and effectively evoke the atmosphere of 'the worst fog in twenty years' and depict the reactions of children and grown-ups to it." Booklist

I saw the sea come in; illus. by Roger Duvoisin. Lothrop 1954 unp illus lib. bdg. $4.81　　　　E

1 Seashore

ISBN 0-688-51167-8

"The colors in this pleasing picture book are as fresh as the early morning in which the little boy went down to the sea with his pail, his shovel, and his sea-captain's cap. Pictures and words convey the thrill of being the first on the white beach, the joy of poking about and discovering treasures, and the changing moods of sea and morning as minute by minute the new tide creeps up the sandy shore." Booklist

Rain drop splash; pictures by Leonard Weisgard. Lothrop 1946 unp illus $5.50, lib. bdg. $4.81　　E

1 Rain and rainfall

ISBN 0-688-41165-7; 0-688-51165-1

"The brief, poetic text follows the falling raindrops as they form first a puddle and then a pond, spilling over into a brook, tumbling into a lake, overflowing into a river until, just before the sun comes out, the river flows into the sea." Bookmark

"Striking pictures in tones of yellow and brown . . . describe a rainstorm in terms a small child can understand." Booklist

White snow, bright snow; illus. by Roger Duvoisin. Lothrop 1947 33p illus $4.95, lib bdg. $4.59　　E

1 Snow

ISBN 0-688-41161-4; 0-688-51161-9

Awarded the Caldecott Medal, 1948

"The approach of the first snowfall of winter is forecast by the postman, the policeman, the farmer, and the rabbit—all friends of the young child. The description of winter activities and the changes brought about by the coming of spring are told in rhythmic prose that is not only beautiful and vivid but also childlike in its simplicity. . . . Clear-colored pictures add to the charm of this book." Children's Bks Too Good To Miss

The world in the candy egg; illus. by Roger Duvoisin. Lothrop 1967 unp illus lib. bdg. $4.81 E

1 Easter—Stories

ISBN 0-688-51160-0

"Each of the toys in a toyshop peeks into a spun-sugar Easter egg and sees the things that please him most, and a little girl sees the whole 'magic world, little world, made for a child's delight.' " Hodges. Bks for Elem Sch Libraries

"The magical world of a candy egg comes alive in this gentle picture book-fantasy. . . . The text, combining prose and poetry, and the lovely springtime color illustrations make an appealing book." Sch Library J

Tudor, Tasha

The dolls' Christmas. Walck, H.Z. 1950 unp illus $4.95, pa $1.95　　　　E

1 Dolls—Fiction 2 Christmas stories

ISBN 0-8098-1026-3; 0-8098-2912-6

First published by Oxford

A story of two very old dolls, the little girl they lived with, their very own doll house, and the dolls' Christmas dinner party

"Tasha Tudor's exquisite pictures . . . will be enjoyed by sensitive little girls who love beauty and imagery." Christian Sci Monitor

1 is one. Walck, H.Z. 1956 unp illus $4.95　　E

1 Counting books

ISBN 0-8098-1047-6

First published by Oxford

"The author-artist has with characteristic charming quaintness written and illustrated a counting book. Delicately tinted, decoratively bordered pictures and

Tudor, Tasha—*Continued*

rhyming lines of text count from one to twenty. The fact that some of the objects are pictured too indistinctly for easy counting should not lessen the over-all enjoyment of the book." Booklist

Turkle, Brinton

The adventures of Obadiah. Viking 1972 unp illus lib. bdg. $5.95   E

1 Friends, Society of—Fiction 2 Nantucket, Mass. —Fiction

ISBN 0-670-10614-3

Sequel to: Thy friend, Obadiah

"Obadiah, who lived in Nantucket hundreds of years ago, had a character flaw not uncommon today: He frequently told falsehoods. Unlike the boy who cried 'Wolf,' the redhaired little Quaker has a real adventure that is wilder than his fancies and which is quickly proven true to his family." Wis Library Bul

"Readers can share the complacent satisfaction that any child would feel in such a circumstance, and the whole book is gay and affectionate in tone. A lively tale, delightful pictures [by the author]." Chicago. Children's Bk Center

Obadiah the Bold; story and pictures by Brinton Turkle. Viking 1965 unp illus lib. bdg. $4.95, pa 85¢
E

1 Friends, Society of—Fiction 2 Nantucket, Mass. —Fiction

ISBN 0-670-52001-2; 0-670-05018-8

"This story, with its setting in Nantucket about one hundred years ago, shows young Obadiah in the midst of a happy Quaker family. Brothers will tease, however, and when Obadiah wants to 'play pirate' (in hopes of someday being one), he is not spared a little fright. An understanding father helps his son think about following in the footsteps of another kind of seafarer, his grandfather, Captain Obadiah Starbuck." Rdng Ladders. 5th edition

The story "is told in clear, clean prose; its pictures, bright with color and humor, reflect the story's mood with a mirror's exactness." Pub W

Followed by: Thy friend Obadiah

Thy friend, Obadiah; written and illus. by Brinton Turkle. Viking 1969 unp illus $3.95, pa 95¢   E

1 Gulls—Stories 2 Friends, Society of—Fiction 3 Nantucket, Mass.—Fiction

ISBN 0-670-71229-9; 0-670-05062-8

Sequel to: Obadiah the Bold

"Obadiah is irritated by a sea gull that follows him—until the day he helps the bird when something is tangled in its beak; then his feeling changes. And that is how Obadiah discovers that one way to feel friendly is to do something for another." Sutherland. The Best in Children's Bks

"The old-fashioned costumes in this engaging story are authentically detailed; the faces are bright with humor and affection, and the cheery firelight of the interior scenes are an effective contrast to those of the cold gray wintry streets." Sat Rev

Followed by: The Adventures of Obadiah

Turner, Nancy Byrd

When it rained cats and dogs; pictures by Tibor Gergely. Lippincott 1956 [c1946] unp illus lib. bdg. $3.79   E

1 Stories in rhyme

ISBN 0-397-30354-8

A reissue of a title first published 1946

"A picture book which will provide fun for children who like cats and dogs and one which may help them to identify different breeds. The story, written in rhyming couplets, tells what happens on the 'remarkable day of great renown when cats and dogs rained

down, and the pages are filled with amusing pictures." Booklist

Tworkov, Jack

The camel who took a walk; pictures by Roger Duvoisin. Dutton 1951 unp illus $5.95, pa $1.25   E

1 Camels—Stories

ISBN 0-525-27393-X; 0-525-45021-1

First published by Aladdin

A nonsense picture-story book about a beautiful young camel who took an early morning walk, about a terrible tiger that planned to pounce on her, and the plans of the monkey, the squirrel, and the bird—all of which came to naught

"Excitement rises to a surprise ending, which will be a relief to young children and a merry joke to slightly older ones. . . . The pictures are full of imagination and humor." N Y Times Bk Rev

Uchida, Yoshiko

The forever Christmas tree; illus. by Kazue Mizumura. Scribner 1963 unp illus lib. bdg. $4.95   E

1 Christmas stories 2 Japan—Fiction

ISBN 0-684-12704-0

"No one had ever had a Christmas tree in a little village in the high hills of Japan, but, when Takashi's sister told him what she had learned about such trees, he wanted one more than anything. This is an unusual story which shows how the contagious spirit of Christmas enables children to bring happiness to an old man." Sch Library J

A simple childlike "story with unusual freshness and charm. Quiet in its two colors when compared with other Christmas books." Pub W

Udry, Janice May

Let's be enemies; pictures by Maurice Sendak. Harper 1961 unp illus $2.95, lib. bdg. $3.79   E

1 Friendship—Fiction

ISBN 0-06-026130-7; 0-06-026131-5

"John, annoyed because James is entirely too bossy, decides that he no longer wants him for a friend and goes to tell him so. Instead of becoming enemies, they agree that it would be more fun to go skating. An artless little treatise on childhood friendships, with illustrations that exactly suit the story." Hodges. Bks for Elem Sch Libraries

Mary Jo's grandmother; illus. by Eleanor Mill. Whitman, A. 1970 unp illus lib. bdg. $4.25   E

1 Negroes—Fiction 2 Grandmothers—Fiction

ISBN 0-8075-4984-3

"Mary Jo, who is staying alone with Grandmother after the family goes back to the city, copes with the crisis of finding Grandmother with a hurt leg during a severe snowstorm in the country." Church & Synagogue Library Assn.

"Despite the crisis situation, this is a placid book, its emphasis on the relationships in a pleasant, middle class black family, the appeal of a visit to grandmother universal. Although the country setting is shown as attractive in both the text and the illustrations, the book does not condemn (as often happens) or unfavorable contrast city living." Sutherland. The Best in Children's Bks

The Moon Jumpers; pictures by Maurice Sendak. Harper 1959 unp illus $4.95, lib. bdg. $4.79   E

ISBN 0-06-026145-4; 0-06-026146-3

"Here is a child's exhilaration and enchantment with the liveliness of summer nights, with the magic of moonlight and the downy warmth of the night wind. The goldfish play with the moonfish in the lily pond, the fireflies come from the woods, and a giant moth flies by on his search for moon flowers. At this time the call of 'Children, oh, children' from the

Udry, Janice May—*Continued*

house is meaningless, for there are no children present, only Moon Jumpers." Lutheran Educ

"There are black-and-white drawings and brief text in between double-page spreads in full luminous color. The pictures are the kind that children can enter directly 'into' and feel . . . the exhilaration of just being alive and full of motion." Horn Bk

What Mary Jo shared; pictures: Eleanor Mill. Whitman, A. 1966 unp illus lib. bdg. $4.25   E

1 School stories 2 Negroes—Fiction

ISBN 0-8075-8842-3

"Whenever Mary Jo [a little Black girl] selected something to 'show and tell', her classmates had already chosen it. Finally she brought a very special person to share with the class—her [~~physician~~] *teacher* father." NY Pub Library. The Black Experience in Children's Bks

"The writing is smooth and natural, and the illustrations, done in soft colors and black and white, are charming." We Build Together   *color*

Ueno, Noriko

Elephant buttons. Harper 1973 unp illus $3.50, lib. bdg. $3.79   E

1 Stories without words

ISBN 0-06-026160-9; 0-06-026161-7

In this wordless picture book, "a huge stuffed elephant pops the buttons running across his middle, and a horse jumps out. The horse has buttons too, and the result is an imaginative menagerie in ever-decreasing size." Chicago

"The softly shaded pencil drawings are childlike and charming, and each animal has a distinct personality." Horn Bk

Ungerer, Tomi

Crictor. Harper 1958 32p illus $4.95, lib. bdg. $4.79   E

1 Snakes—Stories

ISBN 0-06-026180-3; 0-06-026181-1

"An entertaining bit of nonsense about the boa constrictor that was sent to Madame Bodot, who lived and taught school in a little French town. She called the snake Crictor and he became a great pet, learned, debonair and brave. The boys used him for a slide and the girls for a jump-rope. When Crictor captured a burglar by coiling around him until the police came, he was awarded impressive tokens of esteem and affection of the townspeople. Engaging line drawings [by the author] echo the restrained and elegant absurdities of the text." Chicago. Children's Bk Center

One, two, where's my shoe? Harper 1964 unp illus lib. bdg. $4.79   E

ISBN 0-06-026241-9

A picture puzzle book concealing "pumps, oxfords, boots, mocassins! Find them in the shoulders, snouts, beards, and beaks of a virtually textless shape-identification book, where familiar forms hide in bold, vividly colored pictures [by the author]." Horn Bk

Snail, where are you? Harper 1962 unp illus lib. bdg. $5.79   E

ISBN 0-06-026261-3

Illustrated by the author, this is "a book that is almost entirely pictures. The text consists of just eleven words. The shape of a snail, introduced on the first page, is repeated in all the other pictures. Small children will enjoy finding the snail shape in pictures of such different objects as waves, a violin and a birthday party 'blower.' " Pub W

Viorst, Judith

Alexander and the terrible, horrible, no good, very bad day; illus. by Ray Cruz. Atheneum Pubs. 1972 unp illus $6.95   E

ISBN 0-689-30072-7

The author "describes the plight of a boy for whom everything goes wrong from the moment he steps out of bed and discovers he has gum stuck in his hair to return to bed that night when he has to wear his hated railroad-train pajamas and the cat decides to sleep with one of his brothers instead of with him. His mother consoles him by remarking that some days are like that." Booklist

"The humor and truthfulness of the text combined with Ray Cruz's expressive black-and-white illustrations should make this story a favorite." Wis Library Bul

My mama says there aren't zombies, ghosts, vampires, creatures, demons, monsters, fiends, goblins, or things; drawings by Kay Chorao. Atheneum Pubs. 1973 unp illus $5.95   E

1 Monsters—Fiction 2 Mothers—Fiction

ISBN 0-689-30102-2

This book deals humorously with the childhood sense of being threatened by "imaginary monsters and a mother's reassurances that they don't exist. While wanting to believe his mother, Nick is also aware that she often makes mistakes . . . like the time she made Nick wear his boots on a sunny day." Sch Library J

"Ms. Chorao's drawings accent the spirit of Ms. Viorst's latest set piece, an amiable expression of human experiences." Pub W

The tenth good thing about Barney; illus. by Erick Blegvad. Atheneum Pubs. 1971 25p illus $5.95, pa $1.25   E

1 Death—Fiction 2 Cats—Stories

ISBN 0-689-20688-7; 0-689-70416-X

"A little boy saddened by the death of his cat thinks of nine good things to say about Barney to say at his funeral. Later his father helps him discover a tenth good thing: Barney is in the ground helping grow flowers and trees and grass and 'that's a pretty nice job for a cat.' " Booklist

"The author succinctly and honestly handles both the emotions stemming from the loss of a beloved pet and the questions about the finality of death which naturally arise in such a situation. . . . An unusually good book that handles a difficult subject straightforwardly and with no trace of the macabre." Horn Bk

Waber, Bernard

An anteater named Arthur. Houghton 1967 46p illus lib. bdg. $6.95   E

1 Anteaters—Stories

ISBN 0-395-20336-8

Illustrated by the author

"Although Arthur is an anteater, he embodies the exasperating, if lovable, ways of all little boys from the moment he declines the red ants his mother offers him for breakfast, wanting brown ones instead, until he dashes back to the house to kiss his mother goodby before going off to school." Bruno. Bks for Sch Libraries, 1968

"Children and mothers will recognize themselves in this book, which casually pokes fun at the way things are but also suggests, in the easy and good-humored relationship that exists between mother and son . . . that they really aren't so bad." New Yorker

A firefly named Torchy. Houghton 1970 29p illus lib. bdg. $5.95   E

1 Fireflies—Stories

ISBN 0-395-18656-0

Waber, Bernard—*Continued*

"So zealous was Torchy in his light-producing activities that he greatly upset many nocturnal animals with his blazing show. After a refreshing evening flashing among the many lights of a city, however, the firefly returns home, tired, happy and still twinkling." Wis Library Bul

"This daft little tale has a modicum of message and a maximum of fun. The pert writing is outshone by the brilliant arabesques of color and movement in the [author's] illustrations." Sat Rev

The house on East 88th Street. Houghton 1962 48p illus lib. bdg. $5.95, pa $1.95   E
1 Crocodiles—Stories 2 New York (City)—Fiction
ISBN 0-395-18157-7; 0-395-19970-0
"In an amusing fantasy, Mr. and Mrs. Joseph F. Primm and their young son Joshua move into a new home in New York City and discover a crocodile in the bathtub. The illustrations [by the author] detail the wrought iron railings, the graceful doorway with its fanlight, the sweeping staircase, elaborate fireplaces, and ornate chandeliers, characteristic of a comfortable old brownstone dwelling." Moorachian. What is a City?

Ira sleeps over. Houghton 1972 48p illus lib. bdg. $5.95, pa $1.25   E
ISBN 0-395-13893-0; 0-395-20503-4
"A small boy's joy in being asked to spend the night with a friend who lives next door is unrestrained until his sister raises the question of whether or not he should take his teddy bear. Torn between fear of being considered babyish and fear of what it may be like to sleep without his bear, Ira has a hard time deciding what to do. His dilemma is resolved happily, however, when he discovers that his friend Reggie also has a nighttime bear companion. An appealing picture book which depicts common childhood qualms with empathy and humor in brief text and colorful illustrations [by the author]." Booklist

Lyle finds his mother. Houghton 1974 47p illus lib. bdg. $5.95   E
1 Crocodiles—Stories
ISBN 0-395-19489-X
Illustrated by the author
"Lyle accepts the impoverished Signor Valenti's offer to go back into show business on the promise of being reunited with his crocodile mother. After a time on the stage, the two trek through foreign jungles where Lyle does find her, and she is just charming and talented as her son. All three return to Lyle's human family and happily celebrate." Booklist
"Pictures in greens, oranges, and yellows are splashed onto each page in Mr. Waber's original style." Babbling Bookworm

Lyle, Lyle, crocodile. Houghton 1965 48p illus lib. bdg. $6.95, pa $1.25   E
1 Crocodiles—Stories 2 New York (City)—Fiction
ISBN 0-395-16995-X; 0-395-13720-9
"The benign and amiable crocodile who lives a life of incongruous contentment in the Primms' Victorian home becomes the center of controversy when he frightens a neighbor's cat. Poor Lyle is taken downtown where his day's activities—frolicking in the park, skating at Rockefeller Center, browsing in antique shops, and finally creating a commotion in a department store—make hilarious picture-book sequences but fail to help him out of his difficulties. Only Lyle's great heroism in a middle-of-the-night fire establishes him as a desirable citizen and restores neighborhood harmony." Horn Bk
"Lively illustrations [by the author] match this colorful and amusing story." Christian Sci Monitor

Several other titles about Lyle are available from Houghton

You look ridiculous, said the rhinoceros to the hippopotamus. Houghton 1966 32p illus lib. bdg. $5.95   E
1 Hippopotamus—Stories 2 Animals—Stories
ISBN 0-395-07156-9
"The title of the rollicking tale suggests perfectly the nature of the fun. It develops freshly from the fable motif of a discontented animal who at length learns to leave well enough alone. Bold, free drawings [by the author] extend the humor of the words in picturing the self-deprecating hippo, whose dream showed her a ridiculous image of her remodeled self, equipped with the various unique appendages of her jungle associates. She will go on being 'just what she is—a big, fat, wonderful hippopotamus.' " Horn Bk

Wahl, Jan

The woman with the eggs, by Hans Christian Andersen; adapted by Jan Wahl; pictures by Ray Cruz. Crown 1974 unp illus lib. bdg. $5.95   E
ISBN 0-517-515873
Adapted from a poem by Hans Christian Andersen originally published in a Danish periodical in 1836
A foolish woman sets off to market with a basket of eggs on her head and begins dreaming of the riches they will bring her. Her dreams grow grander and grander until she gives a toss of her head and smashes the eggs on the ground
This "adaptation, with its economical narrative and unobtrusive rhyme suggesting the original poetic source, will . . . lend itself admirably to picture-book presentation as well as to independent reading." Horn Bk

Ward, Lynd

The biggest bear. Houghton 1952 84p illus lib. bdg. $5.95, pa $1.25   E
1 Bears—Stories
ISBN 0-395-07182-8; 0-395-15024-8
Awarded the Caldecott Medal, 1953
"Johnny Orchard never did acquire the bearskin for which he boldly went hunting. Instead, he brought home a cuddly bear cub, which grew in size and appetite to mammoth proportions and worried his family and neighbors half to death!" Children's Bks Too Good to Miss
"A perfect collaboration between Lynd Ward, distinguished artist, and Lynd Ward, writer, this first story written for small children has everything they will love—imagination, humor, excitement, and beautiful and dramatic full-page illustrations." Chicago Sunday Trib

Watson, Clyde

Tom Fox and the apple pie; illus. by Wendy Watson. Crowell 1972 unp illus $3.95, lib. bdg. $4.70   E
1 Foxes—Stories
ISBN 0-690-82783-0; 0-690-82784-9
Tom Fox was the laziest, greediest, sweetest and youngest of all the Fox children. Unable to resist the apple pie sold at the Fair, he dashed off before finishing his chores. How he gets the apple pie and what he does with it is told here

Watson, Nancy Dingman

The birthday goat; pictures by Wendy Watson. Crowell 1974 unp illus $5.95, lib. bdg. $6.69   E
1 Goats—Stories
ISBN 0-690-00145-2; 0-690-00146-0
"Warned of a kidnapper at loose, yet wanting to celebrate Paulette's birthday, the goat family, includ-

Watson, Nancy Dingman—*Continued*
ing baby Souci, sets off for the carnival, where the mean Pig abducts Souci. Eventually, after seizing the kidnapper, visiting Pickpocket Place (where napped babes are auctioned), and consulting a hesitatingly inept policeman, baby Souci turns up. She had hidden from the mean Pig under Mother's hat." Rdng Teacher
"In cartoon strip style, a series of lively pictures almost tell the tale of an exciting day by themselves, each frame filled with color, action and humor. There is also dialogue (in balloons) and it is amusing dialogue to read aloud. . . . This is humor at the child's level, it's a good picture of family affection, and it has the carnival background for added interest." Chicago. Children's Bk Center

Sugar on snow; illus. by Aldren A. Watson. Viking 1964 43p illus lib. bdg. $4.95   E
1 Maple sugar—Fiction
ISBN 0-670-68123-7
"Cammie, whose birthday comes at maple-sugaring time, awaits the day with more than the usual degree of anticipation; if the sap is right and if it snows she will have a sugar-on-snow party." Booklist
"Throughout this slightly bucolic story there's a good presentation of the maple-sugaring process from tree-tapping through boiling the sap to dribbling the hot syrup over packed snow for the waxy, chewy candy treat. Nancy Watson has some nice descriptive phrases . . . and Aldren Watson's clear, frosty-blue illustrations convey the feel of late winter's feeble breath." N Y Times Bk Rev

Welber, Robert
The winter picnic; pictures by Deborah Ray. Pantheon Bks. 1970 unp illus lib. bdg. $4.79   E
1 Winter—Fiction
ISBN 0-394-90444-3
"A small boy who is unconvinced that one must wait for summer to have a picnic, makes some dishes out of snow, fixes and carries out a lunch of peanut-butter-and-jelly sandwiches, potato chips, and lemonade, and prevails upon his busy mother to have a picnic with him in the snow. A winning picture book with a simple, natural story and paintings in bright colors against snow-white backgrounds." Booklist

Wells, Rosemary
Benjamin & Tulip. Dial Press 1973 unp illus $4.95, lib. bdg. $4.58   E
1 Raccoons—Stories
ISBN 0-8037-1808-X; 0-8037-2057-2
"This is the story of two raccoons with a problem: Tulip wants to fight Benjamin, but Benjamin isn't the fighting type. However, enough is enough, and Benjamin gets . . . [even] when he and his huge watermelon accidentally fall from a tree and land right smack on top of Tulip." Babbling Bookworm
"The brief text, interpreted in delicately amusing pastel and pen-and-ink drawings [by the author] is appropriate to the size of the book, comfortably scaled for small hands." Horn Bk

Noisy Nora; story and pictures by Rosemary Wells. Dial Press 1973 unp illus $4.95, lib. bdg. $4.58   E
1 Mice—Stories
ISBN 0-8037-6638-6; 0-8037-6639-4
Little Nora, tired of being ignored, tries to gain her family's attention by being noisy. When this doesn't work Nora disappears but returns when she is sure she has been missed
"A small book with rhymed verses and anthropomorphic mice has been illustrated with buoyant pastel drawings that add humorous details to the story. . . . The universal emotion of a child's feeling

slighted because of its siblings has been given life in a simple book." Horn Bk

Wenning, Elisabeth
The Christmas mouse; drawings by Barbara Remington. Holt 1959 unp illus music lib. bdg. $5.95   E
1 Silent night (Carol)—Fiction 2 Mice—Stories 3 Christmas stories
ISBN 0-03-015066-3
"Based on fact, this is the story of composition of 'Silent night' by Father Joseph Mohr and Organist Franz Gruber of Oberndorf, Austria on Christmas Eve, 1818, told from the viewpoint of the mouse that lived in the Church of St. Nicholas. It was because Kaspar Kleinmaus had chewed holes in the organ bellows that the carol was played for the first time, at Midnight Mass, on a guitar instead of on the church organ." Booklist
The pictures "are very handsome, done in pale, unusual shades of the traditional Christmas red and green. Music and words (in both German and English) for the familiar hymn are included in the book." Pub W

Wildsmith, Brian
ABC. Watts, F. [1963 c1962] unp illus lib. bdg. $4.95   E
1 Alphabet books
ISBN 0-531-01525-4
First published 1962 in England
Illustrated by the author
An alphabet book "printed in Austria [illustrates] . . . animals and objects, identifying each on a facing page in capital and lower case letters, setting off the first letter with special emphasis." N Y Times Bk Rev
"Bold, original pictures drawn in the individual style of an artist provide an excellent beginning for a child's education. Children should have a variety of books with this sort of picture, pictures that are paintings and not merely illustrations." N Y Her Trib Bks

Brian Wildsmith's Birds. Watts, F. 1967 unp illus lib. bdg. $4.95   E
1 Birds—Pictorial works
ISBN 0-531-01526-2
"Mr. Wildsmith has tied a series of pictures of birds . . . to their group names: a watch of nightingales, a nye of pheasants, a congregation of plover, et cetera. There is no other text." Sat Rev
"Birds—how well the subject lends itself to this artist's exquisite use of color! . . . The child will have fun with the terms while absorbing truly beautiful illustrations." Horn Bk
"An exceptional picture book that is original in concept and distinguished in illustration." Booklist

Brian Wildsmith's Circus. Watts, F. 1970 unp illus lib. bdg. $4.95   E
1 Circus—Pictorial works
ISBN 0-531-01541-6
"Enclosed between a notice that the circus is coming to town and an announcement of its move to the next place is a series of pictures with no text. In double-page spreads Brian Wildsmith has painted vibrant, beautiful illustrations of animals and acrobats, clowns, and jugglers, birds on a seesaw, and the full panoply of a circus parade. The pictures have action and humor and . . . are remarkable for the quality of the colors." Sat Rev

Brian Wildsmith's Fishes. Watts, F. 1968 unp illus lib. bdg. $4.95   E
1 Fishes—Pictorial works
ISBN 0-531-01528-9
The author explains in his foreword the origins of

Wildsmith, Brian—*Continued*
the various names that have been given to groups of fishes by fishermen, zoologists and poets. The main part of the book consists of illustrations of fishes, including a flock of dolphins, a hover of trout, a flotilla of swordfish

"The colors are no less magnificent, though the page designs perhaps less striking, than in the artist's earlier zoological sequences—and the total richness is still a reward. To the fortunate small child who may have peered at the near-fantasies of the aquarium, these creatures may seem no more bizarre: the 'herd' of rainbow-wrapped sea horses, the 'hover' of radiantly spotted trout, the 'flotilla' of spearheaded swordfish, the 'stream' of iridescent minnows." Horn Bk

Brian Wildsmith's 1, 2, 3's. Watts, F. 1965 unp illus lib. bdg. $5.95　　　　　　　　　　　　E
1 Counting books
ISBN 0-531-01527-0
"Taking the basic shapes—the rectangle, the triangle, and the circle—Wildsmith relates them to numbers. The geometric shapes illustrate the numbers one through ten. The higher the number the more complex the figure becomes—7 makes a house; 8 a man; 10 a locomotive. The author's intent is to help children appreciate the role of these three shapes in building more complex figures." Wis Library Bul

The author-illustrator gives "a kaleidescopic presentation of counting for the beginner. . . . The closing pages contain exercises for picking out designated shapes. Although it may not be possible to predict the importance of the book as an introduction to mathematics, it can stand alone as an introduction to form and color." Horn Bk

Brian Wildsmith's Puzzles. Watts, F. 1971 c1970 unp illus lib. bdg. $4.95　　　　　　　　　　E
1 Puzzles
ISBN 0-531-01550-5
First published 1970 in England
Illustrated by the author
"The puzzles range from pictures in which there are hidden details to those that require comparison or deduction to find the answer." Chicago. Children's Bk Center

"Brilliant colors that almost leap from the page are often used as clues to very simple puzzles that can help sharpen a child's powers of observation while he enjoys the fun of finding answers." Sat Rev

Brian Wildsmith's Wild animals. Watts, F. 1967 unp illus lib. bdg. $4.95　　　　　　　　　　E
1 Mammals—Pictorial works
ISBN 0-531-01530-0
Illustrated by the author
"A pride of lions, a lepe of leopards, a skulk of foxes, and a cete of badgers are among the cleverly captured groups of wild beasts that stalk the vivid, glowing pages of this fascinating picture book. A splendid, eyecatching . . . volume." Booklist

The lazy bear. Watts, F. 1974 c1973 unp illus lib. bdg. $5.95　　　　　　　　　　　　　E
1 Bears—Stories 2 Animals—Stories
ISBN 0-531-01559-9
First published 1973 in England
Illustrated by the author
"A bear who enjoys many glorious rides down a hill on a wagon hates the work of hauling it back up. So he invites some friends to ride with him and fiercely asks them to push him back to the top. Eventually they rebel; and the lazy bear has to do all the pushing himself until he realizes how selfish he has been. The pages are filled with the brilliant color that is the artist's hallmark. Handsome animals—set against

detailed backgrounds—make each page an exciting visual experience; while the bear, with his heart-shaped face, is a charming creature." Horn Bk

"The effect on youngest listeners is unlikely to be an instant commitment to sharing, but, as usual, Wildsmith's pictures show and share well for group use." Library J

The little wood duck. Watts, F. 1973 [c1972] unp illus lib. bdg. $5.95　　　　　　　　　E
1 Ducks—Stories
ISBN 0-531-02593-4
First published 1972 in England
"Unlike his brothers and sisters, the youngest duckling couldn't swim properly but only in circles, because one of his feet was larger than the other. This peculiarity brought him nothing but scolding and teasing, until the day he saved the others by swimming round and round in front of a fox who was waiting to pounce upon them. Giddy from watching, the fox collapsed, and the little wood ducks raced for safety." Horn Bk

"Mr Wildsmith illustrates his brief narrative with all the gorgeous colour and minute attention to detail that we have come to expect of him." Times (London) Lit Sup

The owl and the woodpecker. Watts, F. [1972 c1971] unp illus lib. bdg. $5.95　　　　　　E
1 Owls—Stories 2 Woodpeckers—Stories
ISBN 0-531-01553-X
First published 1971 in England
Illustrated by the author, this story is about the dispute between a woodpecker who liked to sleep all night and work all day and a neighboring owl who liked to sleep during the day and stay up at night

"The glowing watercolor and crayon illustrations present striking designs in contrasting colors which will delight children. The large type and simple vocabulary will enable beginning readers to handle this independently." Sch Library J

Will
Finders keepers, by Will and Nicolas. Harcourt 1951 unp illus $5.95, pa $1.35　　　　　E
1 Dogs—Stories
ISBN 0-15-227529-0; 0-15-630950-5
Awarded the Caldecott Medal, 1952
"Nap and Winkle, two dogs, find a bone while digging. Says Nap, 'I saw it first.' Says Winkle, 'I touched it first.' In turn they ask a farmer, a goat, an apprentice barber and a big dog. 'Whose bone is it, Nap's or mine?' When the big dog starts away with that bone, Nap and Winkle fight the big dog to regain their prize—and then both chew away at it together. Story and pictures will appeal to children." Pittsburgh

"There is a touch of folk-lore or the fable in this story. . . . The illustrations [by Nicolas] have many humorous touches and achieve a highly dramatic effect by the artist's use of red, gold and black." Ontario Library Rev

Williams, Barbara
Albert's toothache; illus. by Kay Chorao. Dutton 1974 unp illus $4.95　　　　　　　　　　E
1 Turtles—Stories
ISBN 0-525-25368-8
This is the "story of a small turtle, toothless as are all of his kind, who takes to his bed with an announced toothache. His mother worries; his father thunders incredulous impatience; his siblings cast scorn. So it goes until grandmother investigates and discovers 'where' he has a toothache." Library J

"The humor of the concise dialogue and of the stylized repetitions of the narrative is carefully reflected in the sepia-line and half-tone drawings that

Williams, Barbara—_Continued_
reveal the anthropomorphically domestic life of the turtles." Horn Bk

Williams, Garth
The chicken book. Delacorte Press 1970 31p illus $5.95, lib. bdg. $5.47   E
1 Counting books
ISBN 0-440-01202-3; 0-440-01203-1
"An attractive picture book for the very young, originally published in 1946 by Howell, Soskind." Booklist
"Their no-nonsense mother informs five hungry chicks that the way to a full gizzard is through arduous scratching. This old, brief counting rhyme is greatly expanded by [the author's] bright, full-page, beautifully drawn, very funny pictures." Library J

Wiseman, Bernard
Little new kangaroo; pictures by Robert Lopshire. Macmillan Pub. Co. 1973 unp illus lib. bdg. $4.95   E
1 Kangaroos—Stories 2 Stories in rhyme
The little kangaroo "generously provides transportation for his friends in Mama's pocket—though Mama is weary by the time they arrive at their destination. After the day's outing, Mama Kangaroo drops each guest off at his own home and all the travelers are ready for sleep. The simple, rhyming text is appropriate for youngest readers, but they might need help with the Australian animals' names, e.g., platypus and bandicoot. Besides giving youngsters an adequate idea of the unfamiliar animals, Robert Lopshire's humorous, cluttered illustrations are delightful to view." Sch Library J

Wondriska, William
The stop. Holt 1972 30p illus $5.95   E
1 Monument Valley—Fiction 2 Navaho Indians—Fiction
ISBN 0-03-005651-9
"Full-color paintings [by the author] depict the same scene of sandstone buttes in Monument Valley at different times of the day and night, as a young Indian is left to guard a sick pony while his older brother goes for help." Chicago

Yashima, Mitsu
Momo's kitten, by Mitsu and Taro Yashima. Viking 1961 33p illus $3.50   E
1 Cats—Stories
ISBN 0-670-48480-6
Illustrated by Taro Yashima
"A picture book with a text of simplicity and charm. Momo finds a miserable stray kitten, brings it home and cares for it; the cat has a litter of five and Momo is sad that the kittens must be given away; she makes a birth certificate for each departing kitten and is solaced by the fact that her cat is expecting again. Supplemented by the illustrations, the facts of life are presented with candor and the story gives a very nice example of tender loving care of pets. The book has additional value in the unusual presentation it gives of the feeling that life is continuing." Chicago. Children's Bk Center

Yashima, Taro
Crow Boy. Viking 1955 37p illus lib. bdg. $5.95, pa $1.25   E
1 School stories 2 Japan—Fiction
ISBN 0-670-24931-9; 0-670-05024-5
"A young boy from the mountain area of Japan goes to school in a nearby village, where he is taunted by his classmates and feels rejected and isolated. Finally an understanding teacher helps the boy gain acceptance. The other students recognize how wrong they

have been and nickname him 'Crow Boy' because he can imitate the crow's calls with such perfection." Adventuring With Bks. 2d edition
"A moving story interpreted by the author's distinctive illustrations, valuable for human relations and for its picture of Japanese school life." Hodges. Bks for Elem Sch Libraries

Seashore story. Viking 1967 unp illus $4.95   E
1 Japan—Fiction 2 Folklore—Japan
ISBN 0-670-62710-0
An ancient Japanese tale "with a Rip Van Winkle motif is told to young ballet-school campers on a Japanese beach. This mysterious tale of Urashima . . . follows the adventures of a fisherman who is carried on a turtle's back to a palace under the sea, where he becomes unconscious of time. On his return home, he is suddenly transformed into an old man." Horn Bk
"The author's misty illustrations have the same haunting quality as the story." Hodges. Bks for Elem Sch Libraries

Umbrella. Viking 1958 30p illus lib. bdg. $4.95, pa $1.25   E
1 Umbrellas and parasols—Fiction
ISBN 0-670-73858-1; 0-670-05031-8
Illustrated by the author
"Momo, given an umbrella and a pair of red boots on her third birthday, is overjoyed when at last it rains and she can wear her new rain togs." Hodges. Bks for Elem Sch Libraries
In this simple tale, young children "will be carried along by their identification with the actions of this very real little girl. . . . The beauty of the book makes this worth while." Horn Bk

Yeoman, John
Mouse trouble; pictures by Quentin Blake. Macmillan (N Y) [1973] c1972 unp illus $4.95, pa $1.25   E
1 Mice—Stories 2 Cats—Stories
First published 1972 in England
"A horde of frisky mice inhabiting an old mill outwit the disagreeable miller by joining forces with a great hungry cat he has brought in to exterminate them." Top of the News
"Dozens of winsome little creatures disport themselves with purpose and glee over the colorful pages of a brisk and breezy picture-story of cat-and-mouse slapstick." Horn Bk

Yezback, Steven A.
Pumpkinseeds; illus. by Mozelle Thompson. Bobbs 1969 unp illus $4.50   E
1 Negroes—Fiction
ISBN 0-672-50437-5
After breakfast, David uses the nickel his mother has left him to buy some pumpkinseeds. The lonely little Black boy offers to share them with everyone he meets

Yolen, Jane
The bird of time; illus. by Mercer Mayer. Crowell 1971 unp illus $4.50, lib. bdg. $5.25   E
1 Fairy tales 2 Time—Fiction
ISBN 0-690-14425-3; 0-690-14426-1
"Rich, glowing full-page illustrations, in tempera style, depict 16th century peasant life in Flanders, in a story, written in the tradition of a classic folktale, focusing on the ageless confrontation between good and evil. Pieter, the miller's son, is given a gift, the bird of time, which he uses wisely to rescue a princess from a greedy giant. A stunning book, both to read and to look at." Pub W

Yolen, Jane—_Continued_

The girl who loved the wind; pictures by Ed Young. Crowell 1972 unp illus $4.50, lib. bdg. $5.25   E

ISBN 0-690-33100-2; 0-690-33101-0

"Wanting his beautiful daughter Danina to have no unhappiness in her life, her father—a wealthy Eastern merchant of long ago—builds a house walled on three sides and open to the sea on the fourth. Danina grows up surrounded by kindness, supplied with flowers and music, and she knows only smiles and happiness until she hears the wind moaning its description of the world outside and its mixture of pleasure and sorrow. Troubled and restless, Danina spreads her cape and sails off on the wind, over the sea, to learn what goes on in the 'ever-changing world.' " Chicago. Children's Bk Center

"The striking illustrations, combining watercolor and collage, are stylized and oriental. The story unfolds at a measured pace, with a subtly implied message that life must be a mixture of happiness and sadness." Booklist

Zacharias, Thomas

But where is the green parrot? A picture book by Thomas and Wanda Zacharias. Delacorte Press 1968 unp illus $4.95, lib. bdg. $4.58   E

1 Parrots—Stories

ISBN 0-440-00141-2; 0-440-00872-7

"A Seymour Lawrence book"

Originally published 1965 in Germany

Illustrated by Wanda Zacharias

"This picture book is an amusing game rather than a story. A green parrot is to be found somewhere in each of nine full-color double-spreads, more carefully hidden in some than in others. The illustrations showing among other things a toy chest, a house, a train, and a garden are large, clearly drawn, and pleasingly detailed while the text merely describes the scene and asks the question: But where is the green parrot?" Booklist

Zemach, Harve

The judge; an untrue tale; with pictures by Margot Zemach. Farrar, Straus 1969 unp illus $4.50   E

1 Nonsense verses 2 Stories in rhyme

ISBN 0-374-33960-0

"An engaging and humorous nonsense story, told in rhyme and illustrated with raffish deftness. Enthroned on his bench, a curmudgeon of a judge hears a prisoner plead that he didn't know that what he did was against the law, but that he had seen a horrible beast. 'This man has told an untrue tale. Throw him in jail!' Each additional prisoner adds to the story; each infuriates the judge." Sutherland. Best in Children's Bks

"In a perfect, wordless conclusion, a splendidly ludicrous monster is pictured devouring the doubting magistrate, while the five freed prisoners walk happily away. The illustrations, featuring absurd, somewhat Hogarthian caricatures, make a comic, thoroughly unified picture book." Horn Bk

Mommy, buy me a china doll; adapted from an Ozark children's song. Illus. by Margot Zemach. Follett 1966 32p illus lib. bdg. $5.95   E

1 Folk songs—Ozark Mountains

ISBN 0-374-35005-1

A "picture book version of the cumulative folk song that has the appeals of repetition, of a chain of mildly nonsensical actions, and of a warmly satisfying ending. Eliza Lou's request for a china doll leads to proposals that it be bought with Daddy's feather bed, so Daddy would have to sleep in the horsey's bed, and the horsey would have to sleep in Sister's bed, and so on, and so on. Each page of print is faced by a full-

page illustration in color, humorous in mood." Chicago. Children's Bk Center

Zion, Gene

Dear garbage man; pictures by Margaret Bloy Graham. Harper 1957 unp illus $4.95, lib. bdg. $4.79   E

1 Refuse and refuse disposal—Fiction

ISBN 0-06-026840-9; 0-06-026841-7

"One family's trash is another family's treasure, or so thought the new garbage man who couldn't bear to throw anything into the grinder. Stan's gigantic junk swap is hilarious. Pictures and text poke fun at human nature, while they show the workings of the sanitation department of a bustling metropolis." Moorachian. What is a City?

Harry by the sea; pictures by Margaret Bloy Graham. Harper 1965 unp illus $4.95, lib. bdg. $4.79   E

1 Dogs—Stories 2 Seashore—Fiction

ISBN 0-06-026855-7; 0-06-026856-5

Sequel to: No roses for Harry!

"Harry, a friendly little dog on a visit to the seashore with his family, creates havoc on the beach when a wave covers him with seaweed and makes him look like a sea monster. A farcical story supported by very funny illustrations." Hodges. Bks for Elem Sch Libraries

Harry the dirty dog; pictures by Margaret Bloy Graham. Harper 1956 unp illus $3.95, lib. bdg. $4.79   E

1 Dogs—Stories

ISBN 0-06-026865-4; 0-06-026866-2

"A runaway dog becomes so dirty his family almost doesn't recognize him. Harry's flight from scrubbing brush and bath water takes him on a tour of the city. Road repairs, railroad yards, construction sites, and coal deliveries contribute to his grimy appearance and show aspects of city life that contrast with the tidy suburb that is 'home.' " Moorachian. What is a City?

"Harry's fun and troubles are told simply, and the drawings are full of action and humor. The combination will have great appeal for the very young." Horn Bk

Followed by: No roses for Harry!

No roses for Harry! Pictures by Margaret Bloy Graham. Harper 1958 unp illus $4.95, lib. bdg. $4.79   E

1 Dogs—Stories

ISBN 0-06-026890-5; 0-06-026891-3

Sequel to: Harry the dirty dog

Harry the dog is the not-too-happy recipient of a sweater, hand knitted by Grandma. And what a sweater it is, with its pattern of full-blown roses. He tried vainly to lose the gaudy object but someone always brought it back. While Harry didn't like his sweater, he never expected a bird to solve all his problems

"The final disposition is so logical and the result so ludicrous that gales of laughter will accompany the reading of this book." Sat Rev

Followed by: Harry by the sea

The plant sitter; pictures by Margaret Bloy Graham. Harper 1959 unp illus $4.95, lib. bdg. $4.79   E

1 Plants—Stories

ISBN 0-06-026900-6; 0-06-026901-4

"Tommy's father and mother were surprised when their house became filled with plants, and Tommy explained that he was caring for the plants for all the neighbors who had gone on vacation. Tommy enjoyed

Zion, Gene—*Continued*

having the house crowded with plants, but his father was rather irritated. The plants had such good care that they became overgrown, so Tommy found out about trimming them and making cuttings. When the neighbors came home, they were very pleased with Tommy's work." Chicago. Children's Bk Center

"Wonderful fun, and a bit of science, too, for the kindergarten age, with . . . blue, green, and yellow drawings giving bright impressions of luxurious plant life." Horn Bk

Zolotow, Charlotte

Do you know what I'll do? Pictures by Garth Williams. Harper 1958 unp illus $4.95, lib. bdg. $4.79   E

ISBN 0-06-026930-8; 0-06-026940-5

"A small girl expresses her love for her baby brother by telling him what she will do. When she goes to the movies, she will remember the song and sing it to him; when the wind blows, she will catch him some in a bottle and cool the house; when it snows, she'll build him a snowman; when he has nightmares she'll blow them away." Chicago. Children's Bk Center

"Good bedtime reading for the nursery age with Garth Williams' sensitively drawn pictures and the simple, tender story." Wis Library Bul

A father like that; pictures by Ben Shecter. Harper 1971 unp illus $3.50, lib. bdg. $3.79   E

1 Fathers—Fiction
ISBN 0-06-026949-9; 0-06-026950-2

"A small boy, left fatherless at a very young age, imagines what it would be like to have a father and what the two of them would do together in the course of a day." Rdng Ladders. 5th edition

"The wistful catalog of perfection is lightened by humor, and the soliloquy catches both a child's way of thinking and his way of expressing his thoughts." Chicago. Children's Bk Center

The hating book; pictures by Ben Shecter. Harper 1969 32p illus $3.95, lib. bdg. $3.79   E

1 Friendship—Fiction
ISBN 0-06-026923-5; 0-06-026924-3

"A little girl tells of several instances of being rebuffed by her friend, ending with the comment, 'I hated my friend.' Finally, at the urging of her mother, she goes to see the friend and asks her why she's been so 'rotten.' The answer is that 'Sue said Jane said you said I looked like a freak.' The actual remark had been that she looked 'neat.' The point of the book is clear as the two friends make plans to play together the following day." Rdng Ladders. 5th edition

If it weren't for you; pictures by Ben Shecter. Harper 1966 32p illus $4.95, lib. bdg. $4.79   E

1 Brothers
ISBN 0-06-026942-1; 0-06-026943-X

"A child ruefully lists the joys of life with no small brother. 'I could watch any program I wanted . . . and I could cry without anyone knowing . . . and my paintbrushes would never be mashed. . . .' The end isn't sugar-coated, but there is an admission that all is not gloom. The illustrations are engaging; the text needs no plot, since it will probably awaken Instant Recognition Reflexes on every page. A percipient and charming book." Sutherland. The Best in Children's Bks

Mr Rabbit and the lovely present; pictures by Maurice Sendak. Harper 1961 unp illus $3.95, lib. bdg. $3.79   E

1 Birthdays—Fiction 2 Color—Fiction 3 Rabbits—Stories
ISBN 0-06-026945-6; 0-06-026946-4

"A serious little girl and a tall, otherworldly white rabbit converse about a present for her mother. ' "But what?" said the little girl. "Yes, what?" said Mr. Rabbit.' It requires a day of searching—for red, yellow, green, and blue, all things the mother likes, to make a basket of fruit for the present." Horn Bk

"The quiet story, told in dialogue, is illustrated in richly colored pictures which exactly fit the fanciful mood." Hodges. Bks for Elem Sch Libraries

My friend John; pictures by Ben Shecter. Harper 1968 32p illus $3.95, lib. bdg. $3.79   E

1 Friendship—Fiction
ISBN 0-06-026947-2; 0-06-026948-0

A picture book "of two small boys who are best friends, carrying on their routine activities. Particularly interesting is the author's implication that the minor differences which exist between the two are not a deterrent to the formation of a valid friendship." Sch Library J

"The drawings in this warm and engaging picture book are uncluttered, expressive, and altogether likable." Booklist

My grandson Lew; pictures by William Pène du Bois. Harper 1974 30p illus $4.95, lib. bdg. $4.79   E

1 Death—Fiction 2 Grandfathers—Fiction
ISBN 0-06-026961-8; 0-06-026962-6

"An Ursula Nordstrom book"

"Warm, rich, and beautiful, a comforting consideration of death. Lew, now six, awakes and remembers back to when he was two and his grandfather came to him in the night when he called. . . . Lew recounts the images he has retained and then his mother tells of her remembrances, concluding, 'We will remember him together and neither of us will be so lonely as we would be if we had to remember him alone.' Pène du Bois' finely washed illustrations exude a serenity and understanding perfectly in tune with the story." Booklist

The quarreling book; pictures by Arnold Lobel. Harper 1963 unp illus $3.95, lib. bdg. $3.79   E

ISBN 0-06-026975-8; 0-06-026976-6

"Father forgets to kiss Mother goodbye when starting to work one morning, so Mother is unhappy and becomes cross with Jonathan James who takes out his feelings on his sister, and the chain continues until reversed by the dog who thinks being shoved off the bed is just a game and lots of fun. The sequence, then starts in happy reverse until at five, with the rain ending, Mr. James comes home and kisses Mrs. James." Sch Library J

It is "a worthwhile book which clearly demonstrates the far-reaching effects one's actions have on others. Even the youngest child will grasp its lesson easily. The illustrations are whimsical, detailed and expressive." N Y Times Bk Rev

The summer night; pictures by Ben Shecter. Harper 1974 unp illus $4.95, lib. bdg. $4.79   E

1 Parent and child—Fiction
ISBN 0-06-026959-6; 0-06-026960-X

"An Ursula Nordstrom book"

Text first published 1958 by Lothrop with title: The night when mother was away

"A pleasant variation on the usual bedtime story, this is entirely a father-child interaction in which an adult extends himself in timely patience with his little girl's reluctance to spend a beautiful evening sleeping. The classic requests for a glass of water, apple, and open window lead on to a long story, piano-playing, a walk beside the night-becalmed pond, and a warm-milk-with-bread-and-butter snack—after which bed is finally welcome. The loving mood is

Zolotow, Charlotte—*Continued*
reflected in graphite-shaded drawings washed with
blue and pink." Booklist

A tiger called Thomas; pictures by Kurt Werth.
Lothrop 1963 unp illus lib. bdg. $4.59 E
1 Halloween—Stories
ISBN 0-688-51623-8
"Fall colors and fanciful costumes make this Halloween story attractive to children. Shy Thomas, new
to the neighborhood, goes out in his tiger suit and
finds that he already has many friends." Hodges. Bks
for Elem Sch Libraries

William's doll; pictures by William Pène du Bois.
Harper 1972 30p illus $4.95, lib. bdg. $4.79 E
1 Dolls—Fiction
ISBN 0-06-027047-0; 0-06-027048-9
When little William asks for a doll, the other boys
scorn him and his father tries to interest him in conventional boys' playthings such as a basketball and a
train. His sympathetic grandmother buys him the
doll, explaining his need to have it to love and care for
so that he can practice being a father
"Very, very special. The strong, yet delicate pictures . . . convey a gentleness of spirit and longing
most effectively, as William pantomimes his craving."
N Y Times Bk Rev

PART 2

AUTHOR, TITLE, SUBJECT AND ANALYTICAL INDEX

AUTHOR, TITLE, SUBJECT, AND ANALYTICAL INDEX

This Index to the books in the Classified Catalog includes author, title, subject and analytical entries, arranged in one alphabet. Added entries for illustrators and joint authors are also included.

References in the Index are to Dewey Decimal Classification number in Part 1, not to pages in this Catalog. These numbers are printed in boldface type.

A title entry is provided for each book unless the title of the book and its subject heading are similar. In that case, only the subject heading is given.

Analytical entries are introduced by the word *In* or the phrase *See also pages in the following book.* These give (1) the page numbers in the book where the material is to be found (2) grading (3) the classification number of the book.

For further directions for the use of this Index, see page viii.

AAAS. See American Association for the Advancement of Science

A Apple pie. Greenaway, K.   **E**
  also in Greenaway, K. The Kate Greenaway treasury p228-48   **828**

A for the Ark. Duvoisin, R.   **E**

ABC. Matthiesen, T.   **E**

ABC. Munari, B.   **E**

ABC. Wildsmith, B.   **E**

The A B C book. Falls, C. B.   **E**

ABC book of early Americana. Sloane, E.   **917.3**

ABC books. See Alphabet books

The A B C bunny. Gág, W.   **E**
—Same
  In Arbuthnot, M. H. comp. The Arbuthnot Anthology of children's literature p63   **808.8**
  In Arbuthnot, M. H. comp. Time for poetry p104   **821.08**

ABC, John Burningham's. Burningham, J.   **E**

ABC of ecology. Milgrom, H.   **614.7**

ABC of things, Helen Oxenbury's. Oxenbury, H.   **E**

ABC word book, Richard Scarry's. Scarry, R.   **E**

The ABC'S of origami. Sarasas, C.   **736**

ABC'S of space. Asimov, I.   **629.403**

A.D. 123: Rome builds a wall. Sutcliffe, R.
  In Arbuthnot, M. H. comp. The Arbuthnot Anthology of children's literature p738-42   **808.8**

AECT. See Association for Educational Communications and Technology

ALA Rules for filing catalog cards   **025.3**

APC. See All People's Congress

A to Z picture book. Fujikawa, G.   **E**

Aardema, Verna
  Behind the back of the mountain (4-6)   **398.2**
  Contents: Little hen eagle; The trick on the trek; Tshinyama's heavenly maidens; How Blue Crane taught Jackal to fly; The winning of Kwelanga; Sebgugugu the glutton; This for that; Tusi and the great beast; Saso and Gogwana the witch; The house in the middle of the road

  The Sloogeh Dog and the stolen aroma

  In Arbuthnot, M. H. comp. The Arbuthnot Anthology of children's literature p323-25   **808.8**
  In Arbuthnot, M. H. comp. Time for old magic p200-02   **398.2**
  Tales from the story hat (3-6)   **398.2**
  Contents: Tricksy Rabbit Wikki, the weaver; The Sloogeh Dog and the stolen aroma; Madame Giraffe; Monkeys in the sausage tree; Nansii and the eagle; How Dog outwitted Leopard; Koi and the kola nuts; The prince who wanted the moon

Aardvark

Poetry

Nash, O. The cruise of the Aardvark (3-5)   **811**

Aaron, Hank. See Aaron, Henry Louis

Aaron, Henry Louis
  Hirshberg, A. The up-to-date biography of Henry Aaron (5-7)   **92**
  Young, B. E. The picture story of Hank Aaron (3-5)   **92**

  See also pages in the following books:

  Libby, B. Baseball's greatest sluggers p121-48 (5-7)   **920**
  Sullivan, G. Baseball's art of hitting p107-15 (5-7)   **796.357**

Aaron and the Green Mountain Boys. Gauch, P. L.   **E**

Aaron's gift. Levoy, M.
  In Levoy, M. The witch of Fourth Street, and other stories p84-98   **S C**

Abacus
  Dilson, J. The abacus: a pocket computer (5-7)   **513.028**

Abbé, S. Van. See Van Abbé, S.

Abbott, Jacob
  See pages in the following books:

  Andrews, S. ed. The Hewins lectures, 1947-1962 p129-49   **028.5**
  Haviland, V. ed. Yankee Doodle's literary sampler of prose, poetry, & pictures p89-92   **028.5**
  Jordan, A. M. from Rollo to Tom Sawyer, and other papers p72-81   **028.5**

Admiral Graf Spee (Battleship)
See pages in the following book:
Carpenter, A. Uruguay p8-10 (4-6)   **918.95**

Adobe Christmas. Peterson, M. N.
In Kamerman, S. E. ed. A treasury of
Christmas plays p254-62   **812.08**

Adoff, Arnold
Black is brown is tan   **E**
(ed.) I am the darker brother (5-7)   **811.08**
Malcolm X (2-5)   **92**
MA nDA LA   **E**
(comp.) My Black me (4-7)   **811.08**

Adolescence
LeShan, E. You and your feelings (6-7) **155.5**
    Fiction
Blume, J. Are you there God? It's me Margaret (5-7)   **Fic**
Blume, J. Then again, maybe I won't (5-7)   **Fic**

Adopted Jane. Daringer, H. F.   **Fic**

Adoption
See also Foster home care
    Fiction
Buck, P. S. Matthew, Mark, Luke and John (4-6)   **Fic**
Caines, J. F. Abby   **E**
Haywood, C. Here's a Penny (2-4)   **Fic**

Adriatic Sea
See pages in the following book:
Kostich, D. D. The land and people of the
Balkans p35-46 (5-7)   **914.96**

Adshead, Gladys L.
Brownies—hush!   **E**
Brownies—it's Christmas!   **E**
(comp.) An inheritance of poetry (5-7) **821.08**

Advanced junior dictionary, Thorndike-Barnhart   **423**

Advent
See pages in the following book:
Ickis, M. The book of festivals and holidays
the world over p127-34   **394.2**
See also Christmas

The **Advent** wreath. Luckhardt, M. C.
In Luckhardt, M. C. ed. Christmas comes
once more p48-61   **394.2**

Adventure. Camp Fire Girls, Inc.   **369.47**

Adventure and adventurers
Latham, J. L. Drake: the man they called a
pirate [biography of Sir Francis Drake]
(5-7)   **92**
Steele, W. O. Westward adventure (5-7) **920**
Syme, R. Francis Drake, sailor of the unknown seas (4-6)   **92**
See also Discoveries (in geography); Explorers; Frontier and pioneer life; Sea
stories; Voyages and travels
    Fiction
Alexander, L. The marvelous misadventures
of Sebastian (4-7)   **Fic**
    Poetry
Cole, W. ed. Rough men, tough men (5-7)
    821.08

The **adventure** book of weather. See Milgrom,
H. Understanding weather   **551.6**

Adventure of Nera
The Adventures of Nera
In Garner, A. ed. A cavalcade of goblins
p92-97   **398.2**

The **adventure** of the Blue Carbuncle. Doyle,
Sir A. C.
In Doyle, Sir A. C. The boy's Sherlock
Holmes p335-55   **S C**
In Doyle, Sir A. C. Tales of Sherlock
Holmes p259-80   **S C**

The **adventure** of the speckled band. Doyle, Sir
A. C.
In Doyle, Sir A. C. The boy's Sherlock
Holmes p213-39   **S C**
In Doyle, Sir A. C. Tales of Sherlock
Holmes p326-54   **S C**

The **Adventure** of three little rabbits
In Ward, W. ed. Stories to dramatize p25-27   **372.6**

Adventures and discoveries of Marco Polo.
Walsh, R. J.   **915**

Adventures in paper modelling. Payne, G. C.
    745.54

Adventures in the wilderness   **500.9**

The **adventures** of a thistle. Andersen, H. C.
In Andersen, H. C. The complete fairy
tales and stories p967-70   **S C**

The **adventures** of Billy MacDaniel. Manning-
Sanders, R.
In Manning-Sanders, R. A choice of magic
p191-99   **398.2**

The **Adventures** of Bona and Nello
In Baker, A. comp. The golden lynx, and
other tales p101-10   **398.2**

Adventures of Bradamante
Green, R. L. Bradamante and the wizard
In Green, R. L. ed. A cavalcade of magicians p84-94   **808.8**

The **adventures** of Ciad. MacManus, S.
In MacManus, S. Hibernian nights p60-73
    398.2

The **adventures** of Don Quixote de la Mancha.
Barret, L.   **Fic**

The **adventures** of Little Peachling. Redesdale,
Lord
In Fairy tales from many lands p84-86
    398.2
See also Momotaro

The **adventures** of Magboloto. Sechrist, E. H.
In Sechrist, E. H. Once in the first times
p67-75   **398.2**

The **Adventures** of Nera
In Garner, A. ed. A cavalcade of goblins
p92-97   **398.2**

The **adventures** of Obadiah. Turkle, B.   **E**

The **adventures** of Paddy Pork. Goodall, J. S.
    E

Adventures of Peronnik
Souvestre, E. The Castle of Kerglas
In Green, R. L. ed. A cavalcade of magicians p161-78   **808.8**

The **adventures** of Pinocchio. Collodi, C. **Fic**

The **adventures** of Pinocchio; excerpt. Collodi, C.
In Arbuthnot, M. H. comp. The Arbuthnot
Anthology of children's literature
p496-98   **808.8**

Aglauros
> *See pages in the following book:*
Gates, D. The warrior goddess: Athena p18-23 (4-7)   **292**

Agle, Nan Hayden
Maple Street; excerpt
> *In* Association for Childhood Education International. Told under the city umbrella p81-102   **S C**

Agree, Rose H.
(ed.) How to eat a poem & other morsels (3-5)   **821.08**

Agricultural chemistry
> *See pages in the following book:*
Freeman, I. M. The science of chemistry p91-100 (5-7)   **540**
> *See also* Soils

Agricultural laborers. See Migrant labor; Peasantry

Agricultural pests
> *See also* Fungi; Insects, Injurious and beneficial; Weeds

Biological control
> *See* Pest control—Biological control

Agricultural products. See Farm produce

Agriculture
Buehr, W. Food from farm to home (4-6) **631**
Floethe, L. L. Farming around the world (2-4)   **631**
Hays, W. P. Foods the Indians gave us (5-7)   **641.3**
Lavine, S. A. Indian corn and other gifts (4-7)   **641.3**
Raskin, E. World food (5-7)   **338.1**
> *See also pages in the following book:*
Duffey, E. Conservation of nature p19-29 (6-7)   **333.7**
> > *See also* Botany, Economic; Dairying; Domestic animals; Organiculture; Pastures; also names of agricultural products, e.g. Corn; and headings beginning with the words Agricultural and Farm

Afghanistan
> *See pages in the following book:*
Clifford, M. L. The land and people of Afghanistan p139-56 (5-7)   **915.81**

Cambodia
> *See pages in the following book:*
Chandler, D. P. The land and people of Cambodia p92-105 (5-7)   **915.96**

Canada
> *See pages in the following book:*
Ross, F. A. The land and people of Canada p8-11, 113-15 (5-7)   **917.1**

Ceylon
> *See pages in the following book:*
Wilber, D. N. The land and people of Ceylon p91-94, 137-41 (5-7)   **915.49**

China (People's Republic of China, 1949)
> *See pages in the following book:*
Rau, M. Our world: the People's Republic of China p99-107 (6-7)   **915.1**

Denmark
> *See pages in the following book:*
Wohlrabe, R. A. The land and people of Denmark p145-48 (5-7)   **914.89**

Egypt
> *See pages in the following book:*
Mahmoud, Z. N. The land and people of Egypt p117-27 (5-7)   **916.2**

Ghana
> *See pages in the following book:*
Sale, J. K. The land and people of Ghana p21-26 (5-7)   **916.67**

Great Britain
> *See pages in the following book:*
Street, A. The land and people of England p57-65 (5-7)   **914.2**

History
Clymer, E. The second greatest invention (5-7)   **913**
> *See also pages in the following book:*
Gregor, A. S. Man's mark on the land p10-20 (4-7)   **301.31**

Indonesia
> *See pages in the following book:*
Smith, D. C. The land and people of Indonesia p60-69, 110-14 (5-7)   **915.98**

Ireland
> *See pages in the following book:*
O'Brien, E. The land and people of Ireland p15-17, 85-86 (5-7)   **914.15**

Italy
> *See pages in the following book:*
Epstein, S. The first book of Italy p11-16 (4-7)   **914.5**

Japan
> *See pages in the following book:*
Vaughan, J. B. The land and people of Japan p19-26 (5-7)   **915.2**

Liberia
> *See pages in the following book:*
Clifford, M. L. The land and people of Liberia p130-34 (5-7)   **916.66**

Morocco
> *See pages in the following book:*
Spencer, W. The land and people of Morocco p16-19 (5-7)   **916.4**

Nigeria
> *See pages in the following books:*
Forman, B. The land and people of Nigeria p113-21 (5-7)   **916.69**
Jenness, A. Along the Niger River p18-28 (5-7)   **916.69**

North America
> *See pages in the following book:*
Meyer, R. Festivals U.S.A. & Canada p 1-11   **394.2**

Norway
> *See pages in the following book:*
Hall, E. The land and people of Norway p98-108 (5-7)   **914.81**

Agriculture—*Continued*

Rumania

See pages in the following book:

Hale, J. The land and people of Romania p14-16, 132-33 (5-7)   914.98

Rwanda

See pages in the following book:

Carpenter, A. Rwanda p70-77 (4-7)   916.7

Uruguay

See pages in the following book:

Dobler, L. The land and people of Uruguay p82-88 (5-7)   918.95

West Indies

See pages in the following book:

Sherlock, P. The land and people of the West Indies p30-42 (5-7)   917.29

Zaire

See pages in the following book:

Crane, L. The land and people of the Congo p96-99 (5-7)   916.75

Agrippa von Nettesheim, Heinrich Cornelius

See pages in the following book:

Aylesworth, T. G. The alchemists: magic into science p85-91 (6-7)   540.1

Agronomy. See Agriculture

Ah-dunno Ben. Jagendorf, M. A.

In Jagendorf, M. A. Folk stories of the South p216-18   398.2

Ah Mee's invention. Chrisman, A. B.

In Chrisman, A. B. Shen of the sea p17-28   S C

Ah Tcha the sleeper. Chrisman, A. B.

In Chrisman, A. B. Shen of the sea p146-57   S C

In Gruenberg, S. M. ed. Favorite stories old and new p388-93   808.8

In Harper, W. comp. Ghosts and goblins p141-49   394.2

In Hoke, H. ed. Witches, witches, witches p5-14   808.8

In Johnson, E. ed. Anthology of children's literature p310-13   808.8

A-hunting we will go (Folk song)

Catch a little fox (k-2)   784.4

Oh, a-hunting we will go (k-2)   784.4

Aichinger, Helga

The shepherd (k-3)   232.9

(illus.) Bolliger, M. Noah and the rainbow   221.9

(illus.) Bulla, C. R. Jonah and the great fish   221.9

(illus.) Yolen, J. The boy who had wings   Fic

Aida; adaptation. Bulla, C. R.

In Bulla, C. R. Stories of favorite operas p159-67   782.1

Aiken, Conrad

Cats and bats and things with wings (k-4)   811

Aiken, Joan

All you've ever wanted

In Authors' choice p149-58   S C

Black hearts in Battersea (5-7)   Fic

A long day without water

In Ireson, B. comp. Haunting tales p132-55   S C

Midnight is a place (5-7)   Fic

The mooncusser's daughter (5-7)   822

The whispering mountain (5-7)   Fic

The wolves of Willoughby Chase (5-7)   Fic

Authors' choice 2. See Authors' choice 2   S C

About

See pages in the following book:

Townsend, J. R. A sense of story p17-23   028.5

Aili's quilt. Jagendorf, M. A.

In Jagendorf, M. A. Noodlehead stories from around the world p196-201   398.2

The **Ailpein** bird, the stolen princess, and the brave knight. Nic Leodhas, S.

In Nic Leodhas, S. Heather and broom p15-33   398.2

Ainu

Carpenter, F. People from the sky (4-6) 398.2

Air

Adler, I. Air (3-5)   551.5

Rosenfeld, S. Science experiments with air (5-7)   507.2

See also pages in the following books:

Barr, G. Show time for young scientists p50-64 (5-7)   793.8

Gardner, M. Science puzzlers p101-09 (6-7)   507.2

Wyler, R. The first book of science experiments p9-31 (4-6)   507.2

Wyler, R. Prove it! p25-40 (1-3)   507.2

See also Atmosphere

Pollution

Elliott, S. M. Our dirty air (3-5)   614.7

Shuttlesworth, D. E. Clean air—sparkling water (3-6)   614.7

Stevens, L. A. How a law is made (5-7)   328.73

Tannenbaum, B. Clean air (3-5)   614.7

See also pages in the following books:

Berger, M. The National Weather Service p75-81 (4-7)   551.6

Miles, B. Save the earth! p33-53 (4-7) 301.31

Air conditioning

See pages in the following book:

Harman, C. A skyscraper goes up p106-12 (5-7)   690

Air defenses. See Radar defense networks

Air engines. See Heat engines

Air lines

See pages in the following books:

Berger, M. Those amazing computers! p44-53 (5-7)   001.6

Dukert, J. M. This is Antarctica p104-21 (6-7)   919.8

Air navigation. See Navigation (Aeronautics)

Air pilots

Gurney, G. Flying aces of World War I (4-7)   920

See also Women in aeronautics

Air planes. See Airplanes

Air pollution. See Air—Pollution

Air ports. See Airports

Air raid—Pearl Harbor! Taylor, T.   940.54

Air routes. See Airways

Alaska
Stefansson, E. Here is Alaska (6-7)   **917.98**
Earthquake, 1964
See pages in the following book:
Lauber, P. Earthquakes p3-9, 71-72 (4-6)
551.2

Fiction
Morey, W. Deep trouble (5-7)   **Fic**
Morey, W. Gentle Ben (5-7)   **Fic**
Morrow, S. S. Inatuk's friend   **E**
Natural history
See Natural history—Alaska

The **Albahaca** plant. Belpré, P.
In Belpré, P. The tiger and the rabbit, and
and other tales p89-94   **398.2**

Albania. See Balkan peninsula

Albatrosses
Fisher, H. I. Wonders of the world of the
albatross (4-7)   **598.2**

Alberto and the monsters. Sechrist, E. H.
In Sechrist, E. H. Once in the first times
p204-13   **398.2**

Alberts, Edith
(illus.) Marks, M. K. Op-tricks   **702.8**

Albert's toothache. Williams, B.   **E**

Albertus, Magnus, Saint, Bp. of Ratisbon
See pages in the following book:
Aylesworth, T. G. The alchemists: magic into
science p64-73 (6-7)   **540.1**

Albright, Donn
(illus.) Felton, H. W. Mumbet: the story of
Elizabeth Freeman   **92**

An **album** of Black Americans in the Armed
Forces. Miller, D. L.   **973**

Album of dinosaurs. McGowen, T.   **568**

Album of dogs. Henry, M.   **636.7**

Album of horses. Henry, M.   **636.1**

Album of North American animals. Dugdale, V.
591.9

Album of North American birds. Dugdale, V.
598.2

Album of prehistoric animals. McGowen, T.
569

An **album** of the American cowboy. Malone,
J. M.   **917.8**

An **album** of the American Indian. Yellow
Robe, R.   **970.1**

An **album** of the Irish Americans. Murphy, E.
301.45

An **album** of the Italian-American. LaGumina,
S. J.   **301.45**

An **album** of women in American history. Ingraham, C. R.   **301.41**

Alcestis
See pages in the following book:
Gates, D. The golden god: Apollo p55-76
(4-7)   **292**

The **alchemists:** magic into science. Aylesworth,
T. G.   **540.1**

Alchemy
Aylesworth, T. G. The alchemists: magic into
science (6-7)   **540.1**

See also pages in the following book:
Helfman, E. S. Signs & symbols of the sun
p123-28 (5-7)   **398**

Alcohol
See pages in the following book:
Gorodetzky, C. W. What you should know
about drugs p77-89 (5-7)   **613.8**

Alcohol and youth
See pages in the following book:
LeShan, E. You and your feelings p95-102
(6-7)   **155.5**

Alcoholics. See Alcoholism

Alcoholism
See pages in the following book:
Hyde, M. O. ed. Mind drugs p60-71 (5-7)
613.8

Fiction
Stolz, M. The edge of next year (6-7)   **Fic**

Alcorn, John
(illus.) Winn, M. ed. The fireside book of
children's songs   **784.6**

Alcott, Amos Bronson
See pages in the following book:
Wood, J. P. The people of Concord p69-77
(6-7)   **920**

Alcott, Louisa May
Eight cousins (5-7)   **Fic**
Glimpses of Louisa (5-7)   **S C**
Contents: Onawandah; An ivy spray and ladies'
slippers; My Red Cap; Poppies and wheat; Kate's
choice; Tessa's surprises; Mountain laurel and maiden-
hair; Corny's catamount; Water lilies; Laurie
Little women (5-7)   **Fic**
Little women; dramatization. See Howard,
V. Happy holidays for Little women
Little women; dramatization. See Morley,
O. J. Little women
A Merry Christmas
In Association for Childhood Education In-
ternational. Told under the Christ-
mas tree p138-52   **808.8**
An old-fashioned Thanksgiving (3-5)   **Fic**
—Same
In A St Nicholas anthology p5-16   **810.8**
Playing Pilgrims
In Martignoni, M. E. ed. The illustrated
treasury of children's literature p484-
90   **808.8**
"The witch's curse"
In Hope-Simpson, J. ed. A cavalcade of
witches p114-23   **808.8**
About
Papashvily, H. W. Louisa May Alcott (4-6) **92**
See also pages in the following books:
Egoff, S. ed. Only connect p286-90   **028.5**
Haviland, V. ed. Children and literature p64-
70   **028.5**
Johnson, E. ed. Anthology of children's lit-
erature p1074-82   **808.8**

Alcott family
Fisher, A. We Alcotts (5-7)   **920**
Papashvily, H. W. Louisa May Alcott (4-6)
92

See also pages in the following book:
Arbuthnot, M. H. comp. The Arbuthnot Anthology of children's literature p810-14
808.8

Alden, Raymond MacDonald
The boy who discovered the spring
  In Sechrist, E. H. ed. It's time for Easter
    p176-83   394.2
The boy who found the king
  In Luckhardt, M. C. ed. Christmas comes
    once more p72-84   394.2
Dragon's treasure
  In Hoke, H. comp. Dragons, dragons,
    dragons p211-19   398.2
The ghosts of Forefathers' Hill
  In Harper, W. comp. Ghosts and goblins
    p110-21   394.2
In the Great Walled Country
  In Association for Childhood Education In-
    ternational. Told under the Christ-
    mas tree p31-39   808.8
  In Luckhardt, M. C. ed. Christmas comes
    once more p148-53   394.2
Why the chimes rang, and other stories (3-5)
                                                  S C

Contents: Why the chimes rang; Knights of the silver
shield; Boy who discovered the spring; Brook of the
king's garden; Hunt for the beautiful; Boy who went
out of the world; Palace made by music; Forest full
of friends; Bag of smiles; Castle under the sea; In the
Great Walled Country

Alderman, Clifford Lindsey
Osceola and the Seminole wars (5-7)   92
The story of the thirteen colonies (5-7) 973.2

Aldis, Dorothy
All together (k-3)   811
Nothing is impossible; the story of Beatrix
  Potter (4-6)   92
William and Jane
  In Association for Childhood Education In-
    ternational. Told under the blue um-
    brella p125-33   S C
  In Gruenberg, S. M. ed. Favorite stories
    old and new p23-28   808.8

Aldridge, Ira Frederick
  See pages in the following books:
Hughes, L. Famous American Negroes p19-
  21 (5-7)   920
Rollins, C. Famous Negro entertainers of
  stage, screen, and TV p21-24 (5-7)   920
Rollins, C. H. They showed the way p6-11
  (5-7)   920

Aldrin, Edwin Eugene
  See pages in the following book:
Branley, F. M. Pieces of another world p 1-11
  (5-7)   552

Alec's sand castle. Russ, L.   E

Alegría, Ricardo E.
The three wishes (4-6)   398.2

Contents: The animal musicians; The three brothers
and the marvelous things; The bird of seven colors;
Juan Bobo, the sow, and the chicks; The woodman's
daughter and the lion; The ant in search of her leg;
The rabbit and the tiger; Death's godchild; Perez and
Martina; The chili plant; The plumage of the owl;
Lazy Peter and the three-cornered hat; Juan Bobo and
the caldron; The three wishes; The young girl and the
devil; The troubadour and the devil; The witch's skin;
The Castle of No Return; Juanito and the princess; The
singing sack; Lazy Peter and the king; Juan Bobo and
the princess who answered riddles; Count Crow and
the princess

Aleksin, Anatolii
A late-born child (5-7)   Fic

Alenoushka and her brother. Ransome, A.
  In Ransome, A. Old Peter's Russian tales
    p231-41   398.2

Aleppo, Syria
  See pages in the following book:
Copeland, P. W. The land and people of
  Syria p103-11 (5-7)   915.691

Aleutian Islands
  See pages in the following book:
Stefansson, E. Here is Alaska p127-35 (6-7)
                                               917.98

Alexander the Great
Gunther, J. Alexander the Great (5-7)   92
  See also pages in the following books:
Collins, R. The Medes and Persians p158-66
  (6-7)   913.35
Coolidge, O. The golden days of Greece
  p178-95 (4-6)   938
Mahmoud, Z. N. The land and people of
  Egypt p21-23, 34-35 (5-7)   916.2
Unstead, R. J. Looking at ancient history p74-
  78 (4-6)   930
Van Duyn, J. The Greeks p167-86 (6-7)
                                               913.38

Alexander, John E.
(illus.) Matthews, W. H. The story of the
  earth   551

Alexander, Lloyd
The black cauldron (4-7)   Fic
The book of three (4-7)   Fic
The book of three; excerpt
  In Arbuthnot, M. H. comp. The Arbuthnot
    Anthology of children's literature
    p514-18   808.8
The castle of Llyr (4-7)   Fic
The cat who wished to be a man (4-6)   Fic
The foundling, and other tales of Prydain
  (4-6)   S C

Contents: The foundling; The stone; The true enchanter; The rascal crow; The sword; The smith, the
weaver, and the harper

The four donkeys (2-4)   Fic
Gurgi
  In Arbuthnot, M. H. comp. The Arbuthnot
    Anthology of children's literature
    p514-18   808.8
Gwystyl
  In Johnson, E. ed. Anthology of children's
    literature p687-90   808.8
The High King (4-7)   Fic
The king's fountain   E
The marvelous misadventures of Sebastian
  (4-7)   Fic
Newbery Medal acceptance paper
  In Kingman, L. ed. Newbery and Calde-
    cott Medal books: 1966-1975 p48-52
                                               028.5
Taran Wanderer (4-7)   Fic
The truthful harp (2-4)   Fic
The wizard in the tree (4-6)   Fic

About
  See pages in the following book:
Kingman, L. ed. Newbery and Caldecott
  Medal books: 1966-1975 p53-55   028.5

Alexander, Martha
And my mean old mother will be sorry, black-
  board bear   E
Blackboard bear   E
Bobo's dream   E
I'll protect you from the jungle beasts   E
No ducks in "our" bathtub   E

Alexander, Martha—*Continued*
Nobody asked me if I wanted a baby sister E
Out! Out! Out! E
Sabrina E
The story grandmother told E
We never get to do anything E
(illus.) Fisher, D. C. Understood Betsy Fic
(illus.) Lexau, J. M. Emily and the klunky baby and the next-door dog E

Alexander and the terrible, horrible, no good, very bad day. Viorst, J. E

Alexander and the wind-up mouse. Lionni, L. E

Alexandria, Egypt
See pages in the following book:
Mahmoud, Z. N. The land and people of Egypt p34-38, 102-06 (5-7) 916.2

Algae
Kavaler, L. The wonders of algae (5-7) 589
See also pages in the following books:
Cooper, E. K. Science on the shores and banks p46-47, 153-65 (5-7) 574.92
Hutchins, R. E. Plants without leaves p11-35 (5-7) 586
Silverstein, A. A world in a drop of water p25-30 (3-5) 576
Zim, H. S. Seashores p18-35 (5-7) 574.92

Alger, Leclaire. See Nic Leodhas, Sorche

Algeria
Spencer, W. The land and people of Algeria (5-7) 916.5

Algonquian Indians. See Chippewa Indians

Ali Baba and the forty thieves
Ali Baba
In Rackham, A. comp. Arthur Rackham Fairy book p206-22 398.2
In Untermeyer, B. ed. The Golden Treasury of children's literature p366-76 808.8
The forty thieves
In Lang, A. ed. Arabian nights p48-59 398.2
In Lang, A. ed. The blue fairy book p242-50 398.2
Story of Ali Baba and the forty thieves
In Wiggin, K. D. ed. The Arabian nights p229-63 398.2

Ali Cogia, merchant of Bagdad
In Lang, A. ed. Arabian nights p232-43 398.2

Alice in Puzzleland. Fisher, A.
In Fisher, A. United Nations plays and programs p61-70 812

Alice in Wonderland. See Carroll, L. Alice's adventures in Wonderland Fic

Alice's adventures in Wonderland. Carroll, L. Fic
also in Carroll, L. Alice's adventures in Wonderland, and Through the looking glass Fic
also in Darrell, M. ed. Once upon a time p71-138 808.8

Alice's adventures in Wonderland; excerpt. Carroll, L.
In Arbuthnot, M. H. comp. The Arbuthnot Anthology of children's literature p531-35 808.8

In Johnson, E. ed. Anthology of children's literature p632-39 808.8

Alice's adventures in Wonderland; puppet play. Mahlmann, L.
In Mahlmann, L. Puppet plays for young players p135-48 791.5

Alice's adventures in Wonderland, and Through the looking glass. Carroll, L. Fic

Alice's godmother. De La Mare, W.
In De La Mare, W. The magic jacket p89-120 S C

Aliki
The eggs (k-3) 398.2
Fossils tell of long ago (1-3) 560
Green grass and white milk (2-4) 637
June 7! E
The long lost coelacanth: and other living fossils (1-3) 597
My five senses (k-2) 612
My visit to the dinosaurs (k-3) 568
The story of Johnny Appleseed [biography of John Chapman] (k-3) 92
Story of William Penn (k-2) 92
Three gold pieces (k-2) 398.2
A weed is a flower: the life of George Washington Carver (k-3) 92
(illus.) Gans, R. Birds at night 598.2
(illus.) Go tell Aunt Rhody (Folk song) Go tell Aunt Rhody 784.4
(illus.) Hautzig, E. At home 410
(illus.) Hawes, J. Bees and beelines 595.7
(illus.) Heilbroner, J. This is the house where Jack lives 398.8
(illus.) Showers, P. The listening walk E
(illus.) Srivastava, J. J. Weighing & balancing 389

Alkema, Chester Jay
Creative paper crafts in color (3-7) 745.54
Greeting cards you can make (4-7) 745.59
Monster masks 745.59
Puppet-making (5-7) 745.59

All aboard! Elting, M. 385.09

All about Arthur (an absolutely absurd ape). Carle, E. E

All about cats. Burger, C. 636.8

All about Jewish holidays and customs. Epstein, M. 296.4

All about light and radiation. See Freeman, I. M. Light and radiation 535

All about mothers. Boiko, C.
In Boiko, C. Children's plays for creative actors p315-21 812

All about rabbits as pets. Cooper, K. 636.08

All about the planet earth. See Lauber, P. This restless earth 551

All-around-the-house art and craft book. Wirtenberg, P. Z. 745.5

All around the town. McGinley, P. E

All because of a pair of shoes. Simon, S.
In Simon, S. The wise men of Helm and their merry tales p89-102 S C

All butterflies. Brown, M. E

All cats are gray. Norton, A.
In Yolen, J. ed. Zoo 2000 p105-17 S C

All day long. McCord, D. 811

All except Sammy. Cretan, G. Y. Fic

All Fools' Day. See April Fools' Day

Alligator. Shaw E.   **598.1**

The **alligator** and the jackal. Haviland, V.
  In Haviland, V. Favorite fairy tales told in
    India p53-62   **398.2**
    See also Little jackal and the alligator

The **Alligator** Case. Du Bois, W. P.   **Fic**

Alligators
  George, J. C. The moon of the alligators (3-5)
    598.1
  Ricciuti, E. R. The American alligator (5-7)
    598.1
  Shaw, E. Alligator (1-2)   **598.1**
  Zim, H. S. Alligators and crocodiles (4-6)
    598.1

  See also pages in the following books:

  Conant, R. A field guide to reptiles and am-
    phibians of Eastern and Central North
    America p34-36   **598.1**
  Huntington, H. E. Let's look at reptiles p50-
    57 (4-6)   **598.1**
  McCoy, J. J. Nature sleuths p81-93 (5-7) **639**

Alligators and crocodiles. Zim, H. S.   **598.1**

Allingham, William
  See pages in the following book:
  Benét, L. Famous poets for young people
    p36-39 (5-7)   **920**

Allstrom, Elizabeth
  The lights of Christmas
    In Luckhardt, M. C. ed. Christmas comes
      once more p131-37   **394.2**

Allusions
  Brewer's Dictionary of phrase and fable **803**

Almanacs
  Information please almanac   **317.3**
  The Official Associated Press Almanac **317.3**
  The World almanac and book of facts **317.3**

Almedingen, E. M.
  Volkh's journey to the East
    In Colwell, E. ed. A second storyteller's
      choice p46-56   **372.6**

The **almond** tree. Grimm, J.
  In Grimm, J. Household stories p186-94
    398.2

  See also Juniper tree

Almost an ambush. Henderson, Le G.
  In Gruenberg, S. M. ed. Favorite stories
    old and new p189-97   **808.8**

Aloise, Frank
  (illus.) Axon, G. V. Let's go to a stock ex-
    change   **332.6**
  (illus.) Keller, G. F. Jane Addams   **92**
  (illus.) Kohn, B. Secret codes and ciphers
    652.8
  (illus.) Phelan, M. K. The story of the Boston
    Tea Party   **973.3**

Along came a dog. DeJong, M.   **Fic**

Along came a dog; excerpt. DeJong, M.
  In Arbuthnot, M. H. comp. The Arbuthnot
    Anthology of children's literature
    p644-46   **808.8**

Along sandy trails. Clark, A. N.   **500.9**

Along the Niger River. Jenness, A.   **916.69**

Along the seashore. Buck, M. W.   **574.92**

The **alphabeast** book. Schmiderer, D.   **E**

Alphabet
  See pages in the following book:
  Neal, H. E. Communication p39-49 (5-7)
    001.54
  See also Writing

  History
  Dugan, W. How our alphabet grew (4-6) **411**

Alphabet. Greenaway, K.
  In Greenaway, K. The Kate Greenaway
    treasury p220-27   **828**

Alphabet books
  Anno, M. Anno's alphabet   **E**
  Asimov, I. ABC's of space (2-5)   **629.403**
  Brown, M. All butterflies   **E**
  Brown, M. Peter Piper's alphabet   **E**
  Burningham, J. John Burningham's ABC **E**
  Carle, E. All about Arthur (an absolutely ab-
    surd ape)   **E**
  Charlip, R. Handtalk   **419**
  Clifton, L. The Black B C's (k-2)   **301.45**
  Crews, D. We read: A to Z   **E**
  Duvoisin, R. A for the Ark   **E**
  Eichenberg, F. Ape in a cape   **E**
  Falls, C. B. The A B C book   **E**
  Feelings, M. Jambo means hello   **E**
  Fife, D. Adam's A B C   **E**
  Fujikawa, G. A to Z picture book   **E**
  Gág, W. The A B C bunny   **E**
  Grant, S. Hey, look at me!   **E**
  Greenaway, K. A Apple pie   **E**
  Hoberman, M. A. Nuts to you & nuts to me
    (k-2)   **811**
  Hosie's alphabet   **E**
  Lord, B. Our new baby's ABC   **E**
  McGinley, P. All around the town   **E**
  Matthiesen, T. ABC   **E**
  Miles, M. Apricot ABC (k-3)   **811**
  Milgrom, H. ABC of ecology (k-2)   **614.7**
  Munari, B. ABC   **E**
  Newberry, C. T. The kittens' ABC   **E**
  Oxenbury, H. Helen Oxenbury's ABC of
    things   **E**
  Piatti, C. Celestino Piatti's Animal ABC **E**
  Rey, H. A. Curious George learns the alpha-
    bet   **E**
  Sarasas, C. The ABC's of origami (4-6) **736**
  Scarry, R. Richard Scarry's ABC word book
    E
  Schmiderer, D. The alphabeast book   **E**
  Sloane, E. ABC book of early Americana (4-7)
    917.3
  Wildsmith, B. ABC   **E**

Alphabets. See Lettering

Alphege
  In Lang, A. ed. The yellow fairy book
    p119-25   **398.2**

The **alphorn.** Duvoisin, R.
  In Duvoisin, R. The three sneezes, and
    other Swiss tales p218-22   **398.2**

Alps
  Hürlimann, B. Barry (k-3)   **636.7**

  Fiction
  Bartos-Hoppner, B. Avalanche dog (5-7) **Fic**
  Spyri, J. Heidi (4-6)   **Fic**

Alston, Eugenia
  Growing up chimpanzee (2-4)   **599**

Altogether! Heave; play. Carlson, B. W.
　In Carlson, B. W. The right play for you
　　p128-32　　　　　　　　　　　　　792
Alvarado's leap. Campbell, C.
　In Campbell, C. Star Mountain, and other
　　legends of Mexico p33-36　　　398.2
Alvin (Bathyscaphe)
　See pages in the following book:
Berger, M. Oceanography lab p48-57 (4-6)
　　　　　　　　　　　　　　　　551.4
Alvin's secret code. Hicks, C.　　　　Fic
Always room for one more. Nic Leodhas, S.
　　　　　　　　　　　　　　　　784.4
Amadan Mor and the Gruagach of the castle of
　gold
Nic Leodhas, S. The tale of the lay of the
　　Amadhain Mhor
　In Nic Leodhas, S. By loch and by lin p15-
　　29　　　　　　　　　　　　　398.2
Amahl and the night visitors, Gian-Carlo Men-
　otti's. Menotti, G. C.　　　　　Fic
Amapola and the butterfly. Belpré, P.
　In Belpré, P. Once in Puerto Rico p29-33
　　　　　　　　　　　　　　　　398.2
Amateur theatricals
　Carlson, B. W. Act it out (3-7)　　792
　Carlson, B. W. Play a part (3-6)　　792
　Carlson, B. W. The right play for you (4-7)
　　　　　　　　　　　　　　　　792
　Smith, M. R. Plays & how to put them on
　　(4-7)　　　　　　　　　　　　792
　Smith, M. R. ed. 7 plays & how to produce
　　them (4-7)　　　　　　　　　　792
　　See also Charades; Drama in education;
　　One-act plays; Shadow pantomimes and
　　plays
The amazing animals of North America.
　Wise, W.　　　　　　　　　　　599
Amazing Life Games Company
　Good cents (4-7)　　　　　　　　658
The amazing seeds. Hutchins, R. E.　　582
The amazing stethoscope. Marks, G.　610.28
Amazon River
　Sperry, A. The Amazon, river sea of Brazil
　　(4-6)　　　　　　　　　　　918.1
　See also pages in the following book:
Bowen, J. D. The land and people of Peru
　　p113-20 (5-7)　　　　　　　918.5
The Amazon, river sea of Brazil. Sperry, A.
　　　　　　　　　　　　　　　918.1
The ambassador from Chi. Courlander, H.
　In Courlander, H. The tiger's whisker, and
　　other tales and legends from Asia and
　　the Pacific p43-45　　　　　398.2
Ambrus, Victor G.
　The three poor tailors (k-2)　　　398.2
　(illus.) Branley, F. M. The mystery of Stone-
　　henge　　　　　　　　　　　914.2
　(illus.) Catherall, A. Prisoners in the snow Fic
　(illus.) Farjeon, E. ed. A cavalcade of kings
　　　　　　　　　　　　　　　808.8
　(illus.) Farjeon, E. ed. A cavalcade of queens
　　　　　　　　　　　　　　　808.8
　(illus.) Green, R. L. ed. A cavalcade of magi-
　　cians　　　　　　　　　　　808.8
　(illus.) Robinson, V. David in silence　Fic

　(illus.) Stevenson, W. The bushbabies　　Fic
　(illus.) Sutcliff, R. Heather, oak, and olive S C
　(illus.) Unstead, R. J. Living in a castle 940.1
　(illus.) Unstead, R. J. The story of Britain 942
　(illus.) Walker, D. Big Ben　　　　Fic
Amelia Bedelia. Parish, P.　　　　　E
Amenhetep IV, King of Egypt
　See pages in the following books:
Payne, E. The Pharaohs of ancient Egypt
　　p129-63 (5-7)　　　　　　　　932
Van Duyn, J. The Egyptians p127-38 (6-7)
　　　　　　　　　　　　　　913.32
Amenhotep. See Amenhetep IV, King of Egypt
America
　See also North America
Antiquities
Coy, H. Man comes to America (6-7)　917
Lauber, P. Who discovered America? (4-7)
　　　　　　　　　　　　　　　917

Discovery and exploration
Adventures in the wilderness (6-7)　500.9
Aulaire, I. d'. Columbus (1-4)　　　　92
Aulaire, I. d'. Leif the Lucky (2-4)　　92
Buehr, W. The French explorers in America
　(4-6)　　　　　　　　　　　973.1
Buehr, W. The Spanish conquistadores in
　North America (4-7)　　　　　973.1
Campbell, E. A. The carving on the tree (3-5)
　　　　　　　　　　　　　　　973.1
Dalgliesh, A. America begins (3-5)　973.1
Dalgliesh, A. The Columbus story (k-3) 973.1
Discoverers of the New World (5-7)　973.1
Duvoisin, R. And there was America (3-5)
　　　　　　　　　　　　　　　973.1
Foster, G. Year of Columbus, 1492 (3-6)
　　　　　　　　　　　　　　909.08
Golding, M. J. The mystery of the Vikings in
　America (6-7)　　　　　　　973.1
Grant, M. G. Leif Ericson (1-3)　　　92
Hirsch, S. C. Mapmakers of America (5-7)
　　　　　　　　　　　　　　　973.1
Janeway, E. The Vikings [biography of Leif
　Ericsson] (4-6)　　　　　　　　92
Kjelgaard, J. Explorations of Père Marquette
　(4-6)　　　　　　　　　　　　92
Kurtz, H. I. John and Sebastian Cabot (4-6)
　　　　　　　　　　　　　　　　92
Lacy, D. The lost colony (5-7)　　973.1
Lauber, P. Who discovered America? (4-7)
　　　　　　　　　　　　　　　917
Schiller, B. The Vinlanders' saga (4-6)　398.2
Sperry, A. The voyages of Christopher Co-
　lumbus (5-7)　　　　　　　　　92
Syme, R. Amerigo Vespucci, scientist and
　sailor (3-5)　　　　　　　　　　92
Syme, R. Cartier, finder of the St Lawrence
　(4-6)　　　　　　　　　　　　92
Syme, R. Champlain of the St Lawrence
　(4-6)　　　　　　　　　　　　92
Syme, R. Columbus, finder of the New World
　(4-6)　　　　　　　　　　　　92
Syme, R. Francisco Pizarro, finder of Peru
　(4-6)　　　　　　　　　　　　92
Syme, R. Henry Hudson (4-6)　　　92
Syme, R. John Cabot and his son Sebastian
　(3-5)　　　　　　　　　　　　92
Syme, R. La Salle of the Mississippi (4-7) 92
Syme, R. Marquette and Joliet (3-5)　92

American music. See Music, American

American names. See Names, Personal—United States

American National Red Cross. See Red Cross. United States. American National Red Cross

American national songs. See National songs, American

American newspapers

History

See pages in the following book:

Neal, H. E. Communication p99-115 (5-7) **001.54**

American nicknames. Shankle, G. E. **929.4**

American painters. See Painters, American

American paintings. See Paintings, American

American periodicals

Indexes

Abridged Readers' guide to periodical literature **051**

Subject index to children's magazines **051**

American poetry **811**

Collections

Adoff, A. ed. I am the darker brother (5-7) **811.08**

Adshead, G. L. comp. An inheritance of poetry (5-7) **821.08**

Agree, R. H. ed. How to eat a poem & other morsels (3-5) **821.08**

Allen, T. ed. The whispering wind (6-7) **811.08**

Arbuthnot, M. H. comp. Time for poetry **821.08**

Association for Childhood Education International. Sung under the silver umbrella (k-2) **821.08**

Baron, V. O. ed. Here I am! (4-7) **811.08**

Benét, W. R. comp. Poems for youth (6-7) **811.08**

Bogan, L. comp. The golden journey (4-7) **821.08**

Bontemps, A. comp. Golden slippers (5-7) **811.08**

Brewton, J. E. comp. Gaily we parade (3-6) **821.08**

Brewton, S. comp. Birthday candles burning bright (4-7) **821.08**

Brewton, S. comp. Laughable limericks (4-7) **821.08**

Brewton, S. comp. My tang's tungled and other ridiculous situations (3-6) **821.08**

Brewton, S. comp. Shrieks at midnight (4-7) **821.08**

Brewton, S. comp. Sing a song of seasons (3-7) **821.08**

Cole, W. comp. The birds and the beasts were there (5-7) **821.08**

Cole, W. comp. A book of animal poems (5-7) **821.08**

Cole, W. ed. A book of nature poems (5-7) **821.08**

Cole, W. comp. Humorous poetry for children (5-7) **821.08**

Cole, W. ed. Oh, how silly! (3-6) **821.08**

Cole, W. comp. Oh, that's ridiculous! (3-6) **821.08**

Cole, W. comp. Oh, what nonsense! (3-6) **821.08**

Cole, W. comp. Poems for seasons and celebrations (5-7) **821.08**

Cole, W. comp. The poet's tales (6-7) **821.08**

Cole, W. ed. Rough men, tough men (5-7) **821.08**

Colum, P. ed. Roofs of gold (6-7) **821.08**

De La Mare, W. ed. Come hither **821.08**

Dunning, S. comp. Reflections on a gift of watermelon pickle . . . and other modern verse (6-7) **811.08**

Geismer, B. P. comp. Very young verses (k-1) **821.08**

Grahame, K. comp. The Cambridge Book of poetry for children **821.08**

Hannum, S. comp. Lean out of the window (4-7) **821.08**

Henry, R. comp. My American heritage (4-7) **810.8**

Hine, A. ed. This land is mine (6-7) **811.08**

Hopkins, L. B. comp. Me! (k-2) **811.08**

Huffard, G. T. comp. My poetry book (5-7) **821.08**

Larrick, N. comp. Green is like a meadow of grass (k-4) **811.08**

Larrick, N. comp. I heard a scream in the street (5-7) **811.08**

Larrick, N. ed. On city streets (5-7) **811.08**

Larrick, N. ed. Piper, pipe that song again! (2-5) **821.08**

Livingston, M. C. ed. Listen, children, listen (k-4) **821.08**

McFarland, W. ed. For a child (k-3) **821.08**

Nash, O. ed. The moon is shining bright as day (3-6) **821.08**

The Oxford Book of children's verse **821.08**

Parker, E. ed. 100 more story poems (6-7) **821.08**

Parker, E. ed. 100 poems about people (6-7) **821.08**

Parker, E. ed. 100 story poems (6-7) **821.08**

Read, H. ed. This way, delight (5-7) **821.08**

Reed, G. comp. Bird songs (5-7) **821.08**

Sechrist, E. H. ed. One thousand poems for children **821.08**

Sechrist, E. H. comp. Poems for red letter days **821.08**

Stevenson, B. E. comp. The home book of verse for young folks **821.08**

Thompson, B. J. ed. All the Silver pennies (3-6) **821.08**

Tudor, T. comp. Wings from the wind (3-6) **821.08**

Untermeyer, L. ed. The Golden Treasury of poetry **821.08**

Untermeyer, L. ed. Rainbow in the sky (k-4) **821.08**

Untermeyer, L. ed. This singing world (4-7) **821.08**

Weiss, R. K. comp. A paper zoo (1-4) **811.08**

See also Negro poetry—Collections

American poets. See Poets, American

American pottery. See Pottery, American

American Red Cross. See Red Cross. United States. American National Red Cross

American Revolution. See United States—History—Revolution

The **American** Revolution, 1760-1783. Bliven, B. **973.3**

The **American** riddle book. Withers, C. comp. **398.6**

Ander's new cap—*Continued*

Carlson, B. W. The one and only cap
In Carlson, B. W. Let's pretend it happened to you p89-98   **792**

Andersen, Benny E.

Let's start a puppet theatre (4-7)   **791.5**

Andersen, Hans Christian

Andersen's Fairy tales (3-6)   **S C**

Contents: The Rose Elf; The drop of water; Thumbelina; The ugly duckling; Great Claus and Little Claus; The princess and the pea; Little Ida's flowers; The tinderbox; The wild swans; The emperor's new clothes; The darning needle; Peiter, Peter, and Peer; The greenies; The storks; The girl who trod on a loaf; The Elder-Tree Mother; The steadfast tin soldier; The shepherdess and the chimney sweep; Aunty; The butterfly; Pen and inkstand; The Snow Queen; The swineherd; The flying trunk; Sunshine stories; The Garden of Paradise; The toad; The old street lamp; The swans' nest; The snow man; The red shoes; The neck of the bottle; The nightingale; The ice maiden; The little match girl; The little mermaid; The Marsh King's daughter; The traveling companion; Booby Hans; The windmill; In the duck yard; The fir tree; The false collar; The comet; The leapfrog; Good-for-nothing; The days of the week; What the old man does is always right; What one can invent; "It's quite true!"; The beetle; The strange galoshes; Ole Shut-Eye

The angel
In Martignoni, M. E. ed. The illustrated treasury of children's literature p255-56   **808.8**

Blockhead Hans
In Lang, A. ed. The yellow fairy book p313-18   **398.2**

The complete fairy tales and stories (4-7) **S C**

Contents: The tinderbox; Little Claus and Big Claus; The princess and the pea; Little Ida's flowers; Inchelina; The naughty boy; The traveling companion; The little mermaid; The emperor's new clothes; The magic galoshes; The daisy; The steadfast tin soldier; The wild swans; The garden of Eden; The flying trunk; The storks; The bronze pig; The pact of friendship; A rose from Homer's grave; The sandman; The rose elf; The swineherd; The buckwheat; The angel; The nightingale; The sweethearts; The ugly duckling; The pine tree; The Snow Queen; Mother Elderberry; The darning needle; The bell; Grandmother; The hill of the elves; The red shoes; The jumping competition; The shepherdess and the chimney sweep; Holger the Dane; The little match girl; From the ramparts of the citadel; From a window in Vartov; The old street lamp; The neighbors; Little Tuck; The shadow; The old house; A drop of water; A happy family; The story of a mother; The collar; The flax; The bird Phoenix; A story; The silent album; The old gravestone; There is a difference; The world's most beautiful rose; The year's story; On the last day; It is perfectly true; The swan's nest; A happy disposition; Grief; Everything in its right place; The pixy and the grocer; The millennium; Under the willow tree; Five peas from the same pod; A leaf from heaven; She was no good; The last pearl; The two maidens; The uttermost parts of the sea; The piggy bank; Ib and little Christina; Clod Hans; The thorny path; The servant; The bottle; The philosopher's stone; How to cook soup upon a sausage pin; The pepperman's nightcap; "Something"; The old oak tree's last dream; The talisman; The bog king's daughter; The winners; The bell deep; The evil king; What the wind told about Valdemar Daae and his daughters; The girl who stepped on bread; The watchman of the tower; Anne Lisbeth; Children's prattle; A string of pearls; The pen and the inkwell; The dead child; The cock and the weathercock; "Lovely"; A story from the dunes; The puppeteer; The two brothers; The old church bell; The twelve passengers; The dung beetle; What father does is always right; The snowman; In the duckyard; The muse of the twentieth century; The ice maiden; The butterfly; Psyche; The snail and the rosebush; "The will-o'-the-wisps are in town," said the bog witch; The windmill; The silver shilling; The Bishop of Borglum Cloister and his kinsmen; In the children's room; The golden treasure; How the storm changed the signs; The teapot; The songbird of the people; The little green ones; The pixy and the gardener's wife; Peiter, Peter, and Peer; Hidden but not forgotten; The janitor's son; Moving day; The snow-

drop; Auntie; The toad; Godfather's picture book; The rags; The two islands; Who was the happiest; The wood nymph; The family of Hen-Grethe; The adventures of a thistle; A question of imagination; Luck can be found in a stick; The comet; The days of the week; The sunshine's story; Great-grandfather; The candles; The most incredible; What the whole family said; "Dance, dance, dolly mine"; "It is you the fable is about"; The great sea serpent; The gardener and his master; The professor and the flea; The story old Johanna told; The front door key; The cripple; Auntie Toothache

The emperor's new clothes (2-5)   **Fic**
—Same
In Arbuthnot, M. H. comp. The Arbuthnot Anthology of children's literature p565-68   **808.8**
In Authors' choice p63-70   **S C**
In Gruenberg, S. M. ed. Favorite stories old and new p317-21   **808.8**
In Haviland, V. comp. The fairy tale treasury p174-79   **398.2**
In Johnson, E. ed. Anthology of children's literature p726-28   **808.8**
In Martignoni, M. E. ed. The illustrated treasury of children's literature p229-32   **808.8**
In Rackham, A. comp. Arthur Rackham Fairy book p240-45   **398.2**
In Untermeyer, B. ed. The Golden Treasury of children's literature p214-19   **808.8**
In Ward, W. ed. Stories to dramatize p210-14   **372.6**

The fir tree
In Cavanah, F. ed. Holiday roundup p304-10   **394.2**
In Dalgliesh, A. comp. Christmas p6-18   **394.2**
In Harper, W. comp. Merry Christmas to you p194-207   **394.2**
In Martignoni, M. E. ed. The illustrated treasury of children's literature p206-11   **808.8**
In Parents' Magazine's Christmas holiday book p224-31   **394.2**
In Sechrist, E. H. ed. It's time for Christmas p229-37   **394.2**
In Tudor, T. ed. Take joy! p14-22   **394.2**

Five peas in the pod
In Harper, W. comp. Easter chimes p64-68   **394.2**
In Johnson, E. ed. Anthology of children's literature p700-02   **808.8**

Hans Andersen's Fairy tales (3-6)   **S C**

Contents: The tinder-box; Little Claus and Big Claus; The princess and the pea; Little Ida's flowers; Thumbelina; The little mermaid; The emperor's new clothes; The daisy; The steadfast tin-soldier; The wild swans; The flying trunk; The storks; Willy Winky; The swineherd; The buckwheat; The angel; The nightingale; The sweethearts; The ugly duckling; The fir-tree; The Snow Queen; Eldermother; The darning-needle; The red shoes; The shepherdess and the chimney-sweep; The little match-girl; The old street lamp; The old house; The shirt collar; The goblin at the provision-dealer's; What the old man does is always right; The tea-pot

Hans Christian Andersen's The fir tree (2-5)   **Fic**

How to tell a real princess
In Fenner, P. R. comp. Princesses & peasant boys p29-32   **398.2**

How to tell a true princess
In Lang, A. ed. The yellow fairy book p254-55   **398.2**

Andersen, Hans Christian—_Continued_
It's perfectly true, and other stories (4-7) **S C**

Contents: It's perfectly true; Thousands of years from now; Old house; The butterfly; Little mermaid; Shepherdess and the chimney-sweep; Ugly duckling; Tinder-box; Story of a mother; Shirt collar; Happy family; Little match-girl; Steadfast tin soldier; Princess on the pea; Red shoes; Emperor's new clothes; Darning needle; The nightingale; Snow Queen; The jumpers; The shadow; The swineherd; Little Claus and Big Claus; Fir tree; Top and the ball; Thumbelina; Numskull Jack; Wild Swans

The leaping match
> _In_ Untermeyer, B. ed. The Golden Treasury of children's literature p528-29
> **808.8**

The little match girl (2-5) **Fic**
—Same
> _In_ Martignoni, M. E. ed. The illustrated treasury of children's literature p172-74 **808.8**

The loveliest rose in the world
> _In_ Harper, W. comp. Easter chimes p129-33 **394.2**
> _In_ Sechrist, E. H. ed. It's time for Easter p198-201 **394.2**

The nightingale (3-5) **Fic**
—Same
> _In_ Colwell, E. ed. A storyteller's choice p174-84 **372.6**
> _In_ Farjeon, E. ed. A cavalcade of kings p16-30 **808.8**
> _In_ Johnson, E. ed. Anthology of children's literature p721-26 **808.8**
> _In_ Lang, A. ed. The yellow fairy book p291-300 **398.2**
> _In_ Sechrist, E. H. ed. It's time for story hour p249-58 **372.6**
> _In_ Shedlock, M. L. The art of the storyteller p243-58 **372.6**

Of the Snow Queen's palace
> _In_ Harper, W. comp. Easter chimes p224-31 **394.2**

Olé Luköië, the dustman
> _In_ Association for Childhood Education International. Told under the green umbrella p 1-4 **398.2**

The princess and the pea
> _In_ Martignoni, M. E. ed. The illustrated treasury of children's literature p212 **808.8**
> _In_ Rackham, A. comp. Arthur Rackham Fairy book p140-42 **398.2**

The princess and the pea; puppet play. See Mahlmann, L. The princess and the pea

The princess and the peas
> _In_ Opie, I. ed. The classic fairy tales p217 **398.2**

The princess on the pea
> _In_ Johnson, S. P. ed. The Princesses p2-7 **S C**
> _In_ Shedlock, M. L. The art of the storyteller p259-60 **372.6**

The real princess
> _In_ Arbuthnot, M. H. comp. The Arbuthnot Anthology of children's literature p504-06 **808.8**
> _In_ Haviland, V. comp. The fairy tale treasury p170-73 **398.2**
> _In_ Johnson, E. ed. Anthology of children's literature p700 **808.8**

Seven tales (2-5) **S C**

Contents: The fir tree; The princess and the pea; Happy family; The ugly duckling; The darning needle; It's absolutely true; The steadfast tin soldier

The Snow Queen (4-6) **Fic**

The steadfast tin soldier (1-4) **Fic**
—Same
> _In_ Arbuthnot, M. H. comp. The Arbuthnot Anthology of children's literature p501-04 **808.8**
> _In_ Gruenberg, S. M. ed. Favorite stories old and new p314-17 **808.8**
> _In_ Johnson, E. ed. Anthology of children's literature p715-17 **808.8**
> _In_ Lang, A. ed. The yellow fairy book p308-12 **398.2**
> _In_ Martignoni, M. E. ed. The illustrated treasury of children's literature p199-202 **808.8**

A story about a darning-needle
> _In_ Lang, A. ed. The yellow fairy book p319-21 **398.2**

The story of Big Klaus and Little Klaus
> _In_ Lang, A. ed. The yellow fairy book p225-36 **398.2**

Story of the Emperor's new clothes
> _In_ Lang, A. ed. The yellow fairy book p21-25 **398.2**

The swineherd
> _In_ Johnson, E. ed. Anthology of children's literature p733-36 **808.8**
> _In_ Lang, A. ed. The yellow fairy book p249-53 **398.2**
> _In_ Opie, I. ed. The classic fairy tales p232-35 **398.2**
> _In_ Sechrist, E. H. ed. It's time for story hour p222-27 **372.6**
> _In_ Shedlock, M. L. The art of the storyteller p235-42 **372.6**

Thumbelina (1-4) **Fic**
—Same
> _In_ Lang, A. ed. The yellow fairy book p279-90 **398.2**
> _In_ Untermeyer, B. ed. The Golden Treasury of children's literature p193-203 **808.8**

Thumbelisa
> _In_ Johnson, E. ed. Anthology of children's literature p702-07 **808.8**

The tinder box
> _In_ Johnson, E. ed. Anthology of children's literature p718-21 **808.8**
> _In_ Lang, A. ed. The yellow fairy book p265-73 **398.2**
> _In_ Manning-Sanders, R. ed. A book of magical beasts p49-60 **398.2**
> _In_ Martignoni, M. E. ed. The illustrated treasury of children's literature p194-99 **808.8**
> _In_ Opie, I. ed. The classic fairy tales p207-15 **398.2**

The tinderbox; puppet play. See Mahlmann, L. The tinderbox

Tommelise
> _In_ Opie, I. ed. The classic fairy tales p221-29 **398.2**

The ugly duckling (1-4) **Fic**
—Same
> _In_ Gruenberg, S. M. ed. Favorite stories old and new p276-81 **808.8**
> _In_ Haviland, V. comp. The fairy tale treasury p180-91 **398.2**
> _In_ Johnson, E. ed. Anthology of children's literature p728-33 **808.8**

Animals—Habits and behavior—*Continued*

Berrill, J. Wonders of the woods and desert at night (4-6) **591.5**

Branley, F. M. Big tracks, little tracks (k-2) **591.5**

Buck, M. W. Small pets from woods and fields (4-7) **639**

Buck, M. W. Where they go in winter (3-6) **591.5**

Cohen, D. Night animals (4-6) **591.5**

Cohen, D. Watchers in the wild (6-7) **591.5**

Conklin, G. I caught a lizard (k-3) **639**

Earle, O. L. Paws, hoofs, and flippers (5-7) **599**

Earle, O. L. Scavengers (3-5) **591.5**

Feldman, A. The inflated dormouse (6-7) **591.5**

Freedman, R. Animal instincts (5-7) **156**

Freschet, B. Year on Muskrat Marsh (3-5) **591.5**

Garelick, M. Where does the butterfly go when it rains **E**

Goldstein, P. Animals and plants that trap (4-7) **574.5**

Hopf, A. L. Misunderstood animals (4-7) **591.5**

Hutchins, R. E. How animals survive (3-6) **591.5**

Hyde, M. O. Animal clocks and compasses (5-7) **591.5**

Kirn, A. Let's look at more tracks (k-3) **591.5**

Kirn, A. Let's look at tracks (k-3) **591.5**

Mason, G. F. Animal baggage (4-7) **591.5**

Mason, G. F. Animal habits (4-7) **591.5**

Mason, G. F. Animal tracks (4-7) **591.5**

Mason, G. F. Animal weapons (4-7) **591.4**

Murie, O. J. A field guide to animal tracks **591.5**

Ricciuti, E. R. Shelf pets (5-7) **639**

Rounds, G. Wildlife at your doorstep (4-7) **591.5**

Selsam, M. E. Animals as parents (5-7) **591.5**

Selsam, M. E. How animals live together (5-7) **591.5**

Selsam, M. E. How animals tell time (4-7) **591.5**

Shuttlesworth, D. E. Animals that frighten people (5-7) **591.5**

Silverstein, A. Metamorphosis: the magic change (4-6) **591.3**

Webster, D. Track watching (4-7) **591.5**

Zim, H. S. Armored animals (3-5) **591.5**

See also pages in the following books:

The Doubleday Nature encyclopedia p104-33 (3-6) **500.9**

Peattie, D. C. The rainbow book of nature p181-237 (5-7) **574**

Silverstein, A. Sleep and dreams p33-52 (6-7) **154.6**

Sterling, D. Fall is here! p75-86 (4-6) **500.9**

See also Animal communication; Animal intelligence; Animal locomotion; Animals—Hibernation; Animals—Migration; Camouflage (Biology); Nature study; Tracking and trailing

Hibernation

Sarasy, P. Winter-sleepers (3-5) **591.5**

See also pages in the following book:

Silverstein, A. Sleep and dreams p134-47 (6-7) **154.6**

Infancy

Schwartz, E. When animals are babies (k-3) **591**

Selsam, M. E. All kinds of babies (k-3) **591**

Selsam, M. E. When an animal grows (k-3) **591**

Shannon, T. New at the zoo (5-7) **590.74**

Ylla. Animal babies (k-3) **591**

Kenya

See pages in the following book:

Carpenter, A. Kenya p49-54 (4-7) **916.76**

Language

See Animal communication

Legends

See Animals—Stories

Migration

Berrill, J. Wonders of animal migration (5-7) **591.5**

Frisch, O. von. Animal migration **591.5**

Hyde, M. O. Animal clocks and compasses (5-7) **591.5**

Laycock, G. Wild travelers (5-7) **591.5**

May, J. How the animals came to North America (2-4) **591.5**

See also pages in the following books:

Sterling, D. Fall is here! p67-74 (4-6) **500.9**

Wellman, A. Africa's animals p37-44 (6-7) **591.9**

See also Birds—Migration

Movements

See Animal locomotion

New Zealand

See pages in the following book:

Kaula, E. M. The land and people of New Zealand p99-111 (5-7) **919.31**

North America

Dugdale, V. Album of North American animals (4-7) **591.9**

Mason, G. F. The wildlife of North America (5-7) **639**

May, J. How the animals came to North America (2-4) **591.5**

Wise, W. The amazing animals of North America (1-3) **599**

Pictorial works

Aulaire, I. d'. Animals everywhere **E**

Eichenberg, F. Ape in a cape **E**

Eichenberg, F. Dancing in the moon **E**

Falls, C. B. The A B C book **E**

Hosie's alphabet **E**

Spier, P. Gobble, growl, grunt **E**

Ylla. Animal babies (k-3) **591**

Ylla. Whose eye am I? (k-3) **591**

See also Animal painting and illustration

Poetry

Aiken, C. Cats and bats and things with wings (k-4) **811**

Belloc, H. The bad child's book of beasts (1-4) **821**

Belloc, H. More beasts for worse children (1-4) **821**

Brewton, J. E. comp. Under the tent of the sky (3-7) **808.81**

Cole, W. comp. The birds and the beasts were there (5-7) **821.08**

Animals—Poetry—Continued

Cole, W. comp. A book of animal poems (5-7) **821.08**

Cole, W. ed. I went to the animal fair (k-3) **808.81**

De Regniers, B. S. It does not say meow, and other animal riddle rhymes (k-1) **793.7**

Eaton, A. T. comp. The animals' Christmas (4-7) **394.2**

Fisher, A. Do bears have mothers, too? (k-2) **811**

Fisher, A. Feathered ones and furry (k-3) **811**

Gasztold, C. B. de. Prayers from the Ark **841**

Hoberman, M. A. A little book of little beasts (k-3) **811**

Lear, E. Edward Lear's The Scroobious Pip (2-6) **821**

Mizumura, K. If I were a cricket (k-2) **811**

Nash, O. The cruise of the Aardvark (3-5) **811**

Prelutsky, J. A gopher in the garden, and other animal poems (2-5) **811**

Weiss, R. K. comp. A paper zoo (1-4) **811.08**

See also pages in the following books:

Arbuthnot, M. H. comp. The Arbuthnot Anthology of children's literature p34-49 **808.8**

Association for Childhood Education International. Sung under the silver umbrella p59-74 (k-2) **821.08**

Ferris, H. ed. Favorite poems, old and new p153-79 (4-6) **808.81**

Field, R. Poems p63-72 (2-5) **811**

Geismer, B. P. comp. Very young verses p 1-42 (k-1) **821.08**

Huffard, G. T. comp. My poetry book p184-210 (5-7) **821.08**

Larrick, N. ed. Piping down the valleys wild p105-26, 139-60 **808.81**

McEwen, C. S. comp. Away we go! p52-62 (k-3) **808.81**

Parker, E. ed. 100 more story poems p307-43 (6-7) **821.08**

Parker, E. ed. 100 story poems p413-37 (6-7) **821.08**

Sechrist, E. H. ed. One thousand poems for children p105-24, 403-34 **821.08**

Untermeyer, L. ed. The Golden Treasury of poetry, p27-81 **821.08**

Untermeyer, L. ed. Rainbow in the sky p229-48 (k-4) **821.08**

Research

See pages in the following book:

Berger, M. Animal hospital p96-104 (4-7) **636.089**

Songs and music

Yolen, J. ed. The fireside song book of birds and beasts **784.4**

South America

Shuttlesworth, D. E. The wildlife of South America (5-7) **591.9**

Stories

Aardema, V. Tales from the story hat (3-6) **398.2**

Arnott, K. Animal folk tales around the world (4-6) **398.2**

Belpré, P. Dance of the animals (k-3) **398.2**

Benchley, N. Oscar Otter **E**

Bible. Selections. Animals of the Bible (1-4) **220.8**

Bloch, M. H. ed. Ukrainian folk tales (4-6) **398.2**

Bonsall, C. Piggle **E**

Brooke, L. L. Johnny Crow's garden **E**

Brooke, L. L. Johnny Crow's new garden **E**

Brooke, L. L. Johnny Crow's party **E**

Brown, M. The neighbors (k-2) **398.2**

Brown, M. W. Brer Rabbit (3-5) **398.2**

Burningham, J. Mr Gumpy's outing **E**

Carle, E. All about Arthur (an absolutely absurd ape) **E**

Carle, E. The rooster who set out to see the world **E**

Courlander, H. Terrapin's pot of sense (4-6) **398.2**

Curry, J. L. Down from the lonely mountain (3-5) **398.2**

Davis, A. V. Timothy Turtle **E**

Davis, R. Padre Porko, the gentlemanly pig (4-6) **398.2**

De La Mare, W. ed. Animal stories **398.2**

De Regniers, B. S. May I bring a friend? **E**

DeRoin, N. ed. Jataka tales (3-5) **398.2**

Domanska, J. What do you see? **E**

Eaton, A. T. comp. The animals' Christmas (4-7) **394.2**

Ets, M. H. In the forest **E**

Ets, M. H. Just me **E**

Ets, M. H. Mr T. W. Anthony Woo **E**

Ets, M. H. Play with me **E**

Fisher, A. Going barefoot **E**

Fisher, A. We went looking **E**

Flack, M. Ask Mr Bear **E**

Fournier, C. The coconut thieves (k-3) **398.2**

Friskey, M. Chicken Little, count-to-ten **E**

Galdone, P. Henny Penny (k-2) **398.2**

Gannett, R. S. My father's dragon (1-4) **Fic**

Gillham, C. E. Beyond the Clapping Mountains (3-6) **398.2**

Ginsburg, M. Mushroom in the rain **E**

Graham, M. B. Be nice to spiders **E**

Grahame, K. The wind in the willows (4-6) **Fic**

Grimm, J. The Bremen town musicians (k-3) **398.2**

Grimm, J. The traveling musicians (k-3) **398.2**

Gurney, N. The king, the mice and the cheese **E**

Hutchins, P. The silver Christmas tree **E**

Hutchins, P. The surprise party **E**

Jarrell, R. The animal family (4-7) **Fic**

Kessler, L. On your mark, get set, go! **E**

Kipling, R. The jungle book (4-7) **S C**

Kipling, R. The jungle books (4-7) **S C**

Kipling, R. Just so stories (3-6) **S C**

Kipling, R. The second jungle book (4-7) **S C**

Lathrop, D. P. Who goes there? **E**

Lawson, R. Rabbit Hill (3-6) **Fic**

Lawson, R. The tough winter (3-6) **Fic**

Leach, M. How the people sang the mountains up (3-6) **398.2**

Lester, J. The knee-high man, and other tales (k-3) **398.2**

Lofting, H. Doctor Dolittle (4-6) **Fic**

McClintock, M. A fly went by **E**

McGovern, A. Too much noise (k-3) **398.2**

Manning-Sanders, R. ed. A book of magical beasts (3-6) **398.2**

Marshall, J. Willis **E**

Mayer, M. A boy, a dog, a frog and a friend **E**

Ann Aurelia and Dorothy. Carlson, N. S.   **Fic**

Anne Boleyn. Leach, M.
In Leach, M. Whistle in the graveyard
p22-23   **398.2**

Anne Lisbeth. Andersen, H. C.
In Andersen, H. C. The complete fairy
tales and stories p620-29   **S C**

Annie and the Old One. Miles, M.   **Fic**

Annie, Annie. Cone, M.   **Fic**

Annie Pat and Eddie. Haywood, C. See note
under Haywood, C. Little Eddie   **Fic**

Anniversaries. See Holidays

Anniversary. Sangster, M. E.
In Sechrist, E. H. ed. It's time for Christmas p204-13   **394.2**

Annixter, Jane
Sea otter (5-7)   **599**

Annixter, Paul
(jt. auth.) Annixter, J. Sea otter   **599**

Anno, Mitsumasa
Anno's alphabet   **E**
Topsy-turvies   **E**
Upside-downers   **E**

Annuals. See Almanacs; Calendars

Annulment of marriage. See Divorce

Another way; play. Carlson, B. W.
In Carlson, B. W. Play a part p151-56 **792**

Another way to weigh an elephant. Blumen-
geld, L.
In Burack, A. S. ed. Popular plays for classroom reading p94-99   **808.82**

Ansige Karamba, the glutton. Courlander, H.
In Courlander, H. The cow-tail switch, and
other West African stories p119-27
398.2

Ant. See Ants

The ant and the tower to God. Davis, R.
In Davis, R. The lion's whiskers p132-35
398.2

The ant in search of her leg. Alegría, R. E.
In Alegría, R. E. The three wishes p40-43
398.2

An ant is born. Doering, H.   **595.7**

Ant lions
See pages in the following books:
Goldstein, P. Animals and plants that trap
p20-28 (4-7)   **574.5**
Villiard, P. Insects as pets p57-63 (5-7) **595.7**

The ant, the lamb, the cricket, and the mouse.
Brenner, A.
In Brenner, A. The boy who could do anything, & other Mexican folk tales
p25-26   **398.2**

Antar the hero. Tietjens, E.
In Hazeltine, A. I. ed. Hero tales from
many lands p333-46   **398.2**

Antarctic regions
Dukert, J. M. This is Antarctica (6-7)   **919.8**
Icenhower, J. B. The first book of the Antarc-
tic (4-6)   **919.8**
Scarf, M. Antarctica: exploring the frozen
continent (3-6)   **919.8**

See also pages in the following book:
Harrington, L. The polar regions p143-81
(5-7)   **919.8**
See also South Pole

Antarctica: exploring the frozen continent.
Scarf, M.   **919.8**

An anteater named Arthur. Waber, B.   **E**

Anteaters
Stories
Waber, B. An anteater named Arthur   **E**

The antelope skin. Courlander, H.
In Courlander, H. Olode the hunter, and
other tales from Nigeria p29-31 **398.2**

Antelope's mother: the woman in the moon.
Courlander, H.
In Courlander, H. Olode the hunter, and
other tales from Nigeria p72-76 **398.2**

Anthology of children's literature. Johnson, E.
ed.   **808.8**

Anthology of children's literature, The Arbuthnot. Arbuthnot, M. H. comp.   **808.8**

Anthony, Susan Brownell
Noble, I. Susan B. Anthony (5-7)   **92**
Peterson, H. S. Susan B. Anthony, pioneer in
woman's rights (3-5)   **92**
See also pages in the following books:
Daugherty, S. Ten brave women p108-22
(5-7)   **920**
Faber, D. Oh, Lizzie! The life of Elizabeth
Cady Stanton p89-95 (5-7)   **92**
Nathan, D. Women of courage p3-39 (4-6)
920
Sechrist, E. H. Women's rights p16-25 (5-7)
324.73

Anthony the trumpeter; short story. Carmer, C.
In Carmer, C. comp. America sings p68-73
784.4

Anthracite coal. See Coal

Anthropology
Aylesworth, T. G. ed. Mysteries from the
past (6-7)   **913**
McKern, S. S. The many faces of man (5-7)
572

Antibiotics
See pages in the following book:
Selsam, M. E. Plants that heal p82-88 (4-6)
581.6
See also names of specific antibiotics,
e.g. Penicillin

Antiquities. See Archeology; Indians of North
America—Antiquities; Man—Origin and an-
tiquity; Man, Prehistoric; and names of
countries, cities, etc. with the subdivision
Antiquities, e.g. Greece—Antiquities; Easter
Island—Antiquities

Antisemitism. See Jewish question

Antonacci, Robert J.
Physical fitness for young champions (5-7)
613.7
Track and field for young champions (4-7)
796.4

Antonescu, Ion
See pages in the following book:
Hale, H. The land and people of Romania
p88-92 (5-7)   **914.98**

Arms of our fighting men. Colby, C. B.   623.4

Armstrong, Louis
Cornell, J. G. Louis Armstrong, Ambassador Satchmo (4-6)   92

See also pages in the following books:

Hughes, L. Famous Negro music makers p115-23 (5-7)   920
Rollins, C. Famous Negro entertainers of stage, screen, and TV p33-37 (5-7)   920

Armstrong, Neil A.
See pages in the following book:
Branley, F. M. Pieces of another world p 1-11 (5-7)   552

Armstrong, William H.
Newbery Medal acceptance paper
In Kingman, L. ed. Newbery and Caldecott Medal books: 1966-1975 p58-61   028.5
Sounder (5-7)   Fic

About

See pages in the following book:
Kingman, L. ed. Newbery and Caldecott Medal books: 1966-1975 p62-65   028.5

Arnason, Jón
The man whale
In Brown, M. ed. A cavalcade of sea legends p54-60   808.8

Arndt, Ursula
(illus.) Barth, E. Hearts, cupids, and red roses   394.2
(illus.) Barth, E. Holly, reindeer, and colored lights   394.2
(illus.) Barth, E. Lilies, rabbits, and painted eggs   394.2
(illus.) Barth, E. Witches, pumpkins, and grinning ghosts   394.2
(illus.) Cantwell, M. St Patrick's Day   394.2
(illus.) Thompson, B. J. ed. All the Silver pennies   821.08

Arno, Enrico
(illus.) Benary-Isbert, M. Blue mystery   Fic
(illus.) Benary-Isbert, M. The wicked enchantment   Fic
(illus.) Charosh, M. Straight lines, parallel lines, perpendicular lines   516
(illus.) Cole, W. ed. Rough men, tough men   821.08
(illus.) Coolidge, O. The golden days of Greece   938
(illus.) Courlander, H. The hat-shaking dance, and other tales from the Gold Coast   398.2
(illus.) Courlander, H. The king's drum, and other African stories   398.2
(illus.) Courlander, H. Olode the hunter, and other tales from Nigeria   398.2
(illus.) Courlander, H. People of the short blue corn (5-7)   398.2
(illus.) Courlander, H. The tiger's whisker, and other tales and legends from Asia and the Pacific   398.2
(illus.) Curry, J. L. Down from the lonely mountain   398.2
(illus.) Ross, E. S. ed. The lost half-hour   372.6
(illus.) Trevino, E. B. de. Nacar, the white deer   Fic
(illus.) Urquhart, D. I. The airplane and how it works   629.133

Arnold, Adelaide Wilson
Storm on the mountain
In Association for Childhood Education International. Told under the Stars and Stripes p295-314   S C

Arnold, E. W.
Make him smile
In Burack, A. S. ed. One hundred plays for children p 1-9   808.82

Arnold, Elliott
A kind of secret weapon (6-7)   Fic

Arnold, Emma J.
The story of the sphinx
In A St Nicholas anthology p175-78   810.8

Arnold, Pauline
How we named our states (5-7)   910

Arnott, Kathleen
African myths and legends (4-7)   398.2
Contents: Why the dog is the friend of man; The man who learned the language of the animals; Tortoise and the lizard; The rubber man; Tortoise and the baboon; Spider and the lion; Thunder and Lightning; Why the crab has no head, or, How the first river was made; A test of skill; The tale of the Superman; Why the bushfowl calls at dawn and why flies buzz; Spider and Squirrel; Unanana and the elephant; Spider's web; The magic horns; Snake magic; Hare and the corn bins; What the squirrel saw; Hare and the Hyena; The calabash children; The blacksmith's dilemma; The magic drum; Why the sun and the moon live in the sky; The monkey's heart; The children who lived in a tree-house; Why the bat flies at night; Tug of war; The discontented fish; Hallabau's jealousy; Goto, king of the land and the water; The singing drum and the mysterious pumpkin; The snake chief; Fereyel and Debbo Engal the witch

Animal folk tales around the world (4-6)   398.2
Contents: The buffalo, the coyote and the peace pipe; The fox and the sheepskin jacket; The magic pony; The Chief of the Water Snakes; The Hyena's horns; The battle of the birds; The big black bear; The heron and the turtle; The Rajah of the Fishes; The thieving dragon; The tale of the dog's skin; The lizard and the cockatoo; The fox, the fish and the bear; Why Siberian birds migrate in winter; Why you find spiders in banana bunches; The sad tale of the crabs; The seal bride; How the birds got their coloured feathers; The hare and the lioness; The three animal servants; The dragons of Peking; One little pig and ten wolves; The five little foxes and the tiger; The seven foals; Why the hawk is the hen's enemy; The mouse-deer and the crocodiles; The butterfly wager; The snake prince; The crow and the sparrow's eggs; How the fox saved the horse's life; The slaying of the Sea Serpent; The lion and the turtle; How the pelican babies were saved; Spider feeds his family; The little bull calf; Why rabbits have short tails; The fox and the gulls; The golden fish; Elephant and Giraffe go farming

Fereyel and Debbo Engal the witch
In Hope-Simpson, J. ed. A cavalcade of witches p156-67   808.8

Around the world-by way of America. Howard, V.
In Howard, V. The complete book of children's theater p494-505   812

Around the world in 80 dishes. Van der Linde, P.   641.5

Arrow. See Bow and arrow

Arrow to the sun. McDermott, G.   398.2

Art
Chase, A. E. Looking at art (6-7)   701
Grigson, G. Shapes and stories (5-7)   701
See also pages in the following book:
Childcraft: the how and why library v13   031
See also Animals in art; Architecture; Children in literature and art; Collage;

Art industries and trade—United States—*Cont.*
See also pages in the following book:
Downer, M. The story of design p141-79 (6-7)
745.4

Art metalwork
See pages in the following book:
Price, C. Made in West Africa p32-41 (5-7)
709.6

See also Jewelry

The art of Africa. Glubok, S. 709.6
The art of America from Jackson to Lincoln. Glubok, S. 709.73
The art of America in the early twentieth century. Glubok, S. 709.73
The art of America in the gilded age. Glubok, S. 709.01
The art of ancient Egypt. Glubok, S. 709.32
The art of ancient Greece. Glubok, S. 709.38
The art of ancient Mexico. Glubok, S. 709.01
The art of ancient Peru. Glubok, S. 985
The art of ancient Rome. Glubok, S. 709.37
The art of China. Glubok, S. 709.51
The art of colonial America. Glubok, S. 709.73
The art of India. Glubok, S. 709.54
The art of Japan. Glubok, S. 709.52
The art of lands in the Bible. Glubok, S. 709.01
The art of the Eskimo. Glubok, S. 709.98
The art of the Etruscans. Glubok, S. 709.37
The art of the new American nation. Glubok, S. 709.73
The art of the North American Indian. Glubok, S. 709.01
The art of the Northwest coast Indians. Glubok, S. 709.01
The art of the Old West. Glubok, S. 709.73
The art of the Southwest Indians. Glubok, S. 709.01
The art of the Spanish in the United States and Puerto Rico. Glubok, S. 709.73
The art of the story-teller. Shedlock, M. L. 372.6

Artemis
See pages in the following book:
Gates, D. The golden god: Apollo p58-60 (4-7) 292

Arthur, King
Bulfinch, T. Bulfinch's Mythology 291
Hieatt, C. The Joy of the Court (4-7) 398.2
Hieatt, C. The knight of the cart (4-7) 398.2
Hieatt, C. Sir Gawain and the Green Knight (4-6) 398.2
MacLeod, M. The book of King Arthur and his noble knights (5-7) 398.2
Picard, B. L. Stories of King Arthur and his Knights (5-7) 398.2
Robbins, R. Taliesin and King Arthur (3-5) 398.2

See also pages in the following books:
Hazeltine, A. I. ed. Hero tales from many lands p100-18 (5-7) 398.2
Johnson, E. ed. Anthology of children's literature p503-09 808.8
Martignoni, M. E. ed. The illustrated treasury of children's literature p497-502 808.8

Shedlock, M. L. The art of the story-teller p173-78 372.6

Arthur, Robert
The haunted trailer
In Ireson, B. comp. Haunting tales p40-62
S C

Arthur, Ruth M.
A candle in her room (5-7) Fic

Arthur in the cave. Thomas, W. J.
In Shedlock, M. L. The art of the story-teller p173-78 372.6

Arthur Rackham Fairy book. Rackham, A. comp. 398.2

Arthurian romances. See Arthur, King

Arthur's Christmas cookies. Hoban, L. E
Arthur's Honey Bear. Hoban, L. E
Arthur's sword; play. Smith, M. R.
In Smith, M. R. Plays &—how to put them on p35-43 792

The artificial earthquake. Sechrist, E. H.
In Sechrist, E. H. Once in the first times p91-93 398.2

Artificial satellites
Branley, F. M. A book of satellites for you (1-3) 629.43
Branley, F. M. Rockets and satellites (1-3) 629.4
Coombs, C. Spacetrack (5-7) 629.43
See also Space stations
Models
Ross, F. Model satellites and spacecraft (5-7) 629.4

Artificial satellites in telecommunication
See pages in the following book:
Neal, H. E. Communication p171-78 (5-7) 001.54

Artigas, José Gervasio
See pages in the following book:
Dobler, L. The land and people of Uruguay p33-46 (5-7) 918.95

Artistic anatomy. See Anatomy, Artistic
Artists. See Children as artists; Illustrators; Negro artists; Painters, American; Potters

Artists, American
Hyman, L. Winslow Homer: America's old master (5-7) 92

Artists, Negro. See Negro artists

Artists' materials
Sattler, H. R. Recipes for art and craft materials (4-7) 745.5

The arts
See pages in the following books:
Berger, M. Those amazing computers! p168-74 (5-7) 001.6
Neal, H. E. Communication p162-70 (5-7) 001.54
Bibliography
See pages in the following book:
National Council of Teachers of English. Adventuring with books p331-44 028.52

The arts, American
See pages in the following book:
Jackson, F. The Black man in America [v6] p38-70 (6-7) 301.45

Arts, Fine. See Art

Arts, Graphic. See Graphic arts

The arts, Icelandic

See pages in the following book:

Berry, E. The land and people of Iceland p122-31 (5-7)   **914.91**

The arts, Nigerian

See pages in the following book:

Forman, B. The land and people of Nigeria p85-96 (5-7)   **916.69**

The arts, Spanish

See pages in the following book:

Loder, D. The land and people of Spain p66-72 (5-7)   **914.6**

Arts, Useful. See Technology

Arts and crafts

D'Amato, J. African crafts for you to make (4-7)   **745.5**

    See also Basket making; Beadwork; Bookbinding; Design, Decorative; Folk art; Handicraft; Jewelry; Leather work; Modeling; Needlework; Pottery; Weaving; Wood carving

Arts and crafts you can eat. Cobb, V.   **745.5**

Artzybasheff, Boris

Seven Simeons (3-6)   **398.2**

—Same

    In Johnson, E. ed. Anthology of children's literature p244-51   **808.8**

(illus.) Young, E. The wonder smith and his son   **398.2**

Aruego, Ariane

(jt. auth.) Aruego, J. A crocodile's tale **398.2**

(illus.) Ginsburg, M. The chick and the duckling   **E**

(illus.) Kraus, R. Milton the early riser   **E**

    For other works by this illustrator see Dewey, Ariane

Aruego, Jose

A crocodile's tale (k-3)   **398.2**

Look what I can do   **E**

Symbiosis (1-3)   **591.5**

(illus.) Ginsburg, M. The chick and the duckling   **E**

(illus.) Ginsburg, M. How the sun was brought back to the sky   **398.2**

(illus.) Ginsburg, M. Mushroom in the rain **E**

(illus.) Kraus, R. Leo the late bloomer   **E**

(illus.) Kraus, R. Milton the early riser   **E**

(illus.) Kraus, R. Owliver   **E**

(illus.) Kraus, R. Whose mouse are you?   **E**

Arundel, Jocelyn

Little Stripe (2-4)   **599**

Simba of the White Mane (5-7)   **Fic**

The wildlife of Africa (5-7)   **591.9**

As Hai Low kept house. Chrisman, A. B.

    In Chrisman, A. B. Shen of the sea p208-21   **S C**

As I went over the water. See Sendak, M.

Hector Protector, and As I went over the water   **398.8**

As long as this. Leach, M.

    In Leach, M. The thing at the foot of the bed, and other scary tales p44-45   **S C**

"As long as we can." Gates, D.

    In Association for Childhood Education

International. Told under spacious skies p302-12   **S C**

Asbjørnsen, Peter Christen

Boots and his brothers

    In Arbuthnot, M. H. comp. Time for old magic p120-22   **398.2**

    In Association for Childhood Education International. Told under the green umbrella p146-55   **398.2**

    In Johnson, E. ed. Anthology of children's literature p293-95   **808.8**

Buttercup

    In Fenner, P. R. comp. Giants & witches and a dragon or two p108-14 **398.2**

The cat on the Dovrefell

    In Johnson, E. ed. Anthology of children's literature p307   **808.8**

The cormorants of Udröst

    In Brown, M. ed. A cavalcade of sea legends p87-94   **808.8**

East o' the sun and west o' the moon

    In Arbuthnot, M. H. comp. The Arbuthnot Anthology of children's literature p252-57   **808.8**

    In Arbuthnot, M. H. comp. Time for old magic p135-40   **398.2**

    In Johnson, E. ed. Anthology of children's literature p300-05   **808.8**

    In Lang, A. ed. The blue fairy book p19-29   **398.2**

East of the sun and west of the moon, and other tales (5-7)   **398.2**

Contents: East of the sun and west of the moon; The three billy goats Gruff; The husband who was to mind the house; The lad who went to the North Wind; The princess on the Glass Hill; The giant who had no heart in his body; The blue belt; The three princesses of Whiteland; Soria Moria Castle; The three princesses in the blue mountain; The widow's son; The cat on the Dovrefell

Farmer Weatherbeard

    In Lang, A. ed. The red fairy book p294-302   **398.2**

The giant who had no heart in his body

    In Fenner, P. R. comp. Giants & witches and a dragon or two p39-49   **398.2**

    In Mayne, W. ed. William Mayne's Book of giants p108-18   **398.2**

Gudbrand on the hill-side

    In Arbuthnot, M. H. comp. The Arbuthnot Anthology of children's literature p244-46   **808.8**

    In Arbuthnot, M. H. comp. Time for old magic p127-29   **398.2**

    In Johnson, E. ed. Anthology of children's literature p291-93   **808.8**

The husband who was to mind the house

    In Arbuthnot, M. H. comp. The Arbuthnot Anthology of children's literature p246-47   **808.8**

    In Arbuthnot, M. H. comp. Time for old magic p129-30   **398.2**

    In Martignoni, M. E. ed. The illustrated treasury of children's literature p161-62   **808.8**

Kari Woodengown

    In Lang, A. ed. The red fairy book p189-201   **398.2**

The lad who went to the North Wind

    In Arbuthnot, M. H. comp. Time for old magic p119-20   **398.2**

    In Johnson, E. ed. Anthology of children's literature p305-07   **808.8**

Asbjørnsen, Peter Christen—*Continued*

Little Freddy with his fiddle

In Arbuthnot, M. H. comp. The Arbuthnot Anthology of children's literature p249-52   **808.8**

In Arbuthnot, M. H. comp. Time for old magic p132-35   **398.2**

The master-maid

In Lang, A. ed. The blue fairy book p120-35   **398.2**

The master thief

In Lang, A. ed. The red fairy book p67-81   **398.2**

Norwegian folk tales (4-7)   **398.2**

Contents: The boys who met the Trolls in the Hedal woods; The seventh father of the house; The parson and the sexton; The Ash Lad who made the princess say, "You're a liar"; Taper-Tom who made the princess laugh; The charcoal burner; The three princesses in the Mountain-in-the-Blue; The golden bird; The Squire's bride; Little Freddie with his fiddle; Soria Moria Castle; The princess who always had to have the last word; The Ash Lad who had an eating match with the Troll; The companion; Butterball; The ram and the pig who went into the woods to live by themselves; The fox as shepherd; The mill that grinds at the bottom of the sea; The old woman against the sea; The Hare who had been married; The House Mouse and the Country Mouse; The Bear and the Fox who made a bet; Squire Per; The key in the distaff; The boy with the beer keg; The Cock and the Fox; Not driving and not riding; The golden castle that hung in the air; White-Bear-King-Valemon; "Good day, fellow!" "Axe handle!"; The Tabby who was such a glutton; The Devil and the bailiff; The Ash Lad and the good helpers; Gudbrand of the Hillside; The twelve wild ducks

The pancake

In Arbuthnot, M. H. comp. The Arbuthnot Anthology of children's literature p238-39   **808.8**

In Arbuthnot, M. H. comp. Time for old magic p116-17   **398.2**

In Johnson, E. ed. Anthology of children's literature p288-89   **808.8**

Princess on the glass hill

In Arbuthnot, M. H. comp. The Arbuthnot Anthology of children's literature p240-44   **808.8**

In Arbuthnot, M. H. comp. Time for old magic p123-27   **398.2**

In Association for Childhood Education International. Told under the green umbrella p122-38   **398.2**

In Johnson, E. ed. Anthology of children's literature p295-300   **808.8**

In Lang, A. ed. The blue fairy book p332-41   **398.2**

The princess whom nobody could silence

In Dobbs, R. ed. Once upon a time p110-17   **372.6**

The ram and the pig who went into the woods

In Johnson, E. ed. Anthology of children's literature p289-91   **808.8**

Soria Moria Castle

In Lang, A. ed. The red fairy book p30-41   **398.2**

The squire's bride (1-4)   **398.2**

The three Billy Goats Gruff (k-3)   **398.2**

—Same

In Arbuthnot, M. H. comp. The Arbuthnot Anthology of children's literature p237-38   **808.8**

In Arbuthnot, M. H. comp. Time for old magic p115-16   **398.2**

In Haviland, V. comp. The fairy tale treasury p56-57   **398.2**

In Johnson, E. ed. Anthology of children's literature p287-88   **808.8**

In Ross, L. Puppet shows using poems and stories p156-59   **791.55**

Why the bear is stumpy-tailed

In Arbuthnot, M. H. comp. Time for old magic p117-18   **398.2**

In Martignoni, M. E. ed. The illustrated treasury of children's literature p89-90   **808.8**

Why the sea is salt

In Brown, M. ed. A cavalcade of sea legends p158-64   **808.8**

In Lang, A. ed. The blue fairy book p136-40   **398.2**

Aulaire, I. d'. East of the sun and west of the moon   **398.2**

Haviland, V. Favorite fairy tales told in Norway (2-5)   **398.2**

Undset, S. ed. True and untrue, and other Norse tales   **398.2**

Asbrand, Karin

China comes to you

In Burack, A. S. ed. One hundred plays for children p10-18   **808.82**

The crystal flask

In Burack, A. S. ed. One hundred plays for children p570-76   **808.82**

Friendly as can be

In Kamerman, S. E. ed. Little plays for little players p143-46   **812.08**

Little hero of Holland

In Burack, A. S. ed. One hundred plays for children p577-86   **808.82**

What's a penny?

In Burack, A. S. ed. One hundred plays for children p19-22   **808.82**

Aschenputtel. Grimm, J.

In Grimm, J. Household stories p118-25   **398.2**

See also Cinderella

The **Ash Lad and the good helpers.** Asbjørnsen, P. C.

In Asbjørnsen, P. C. Norwegian folk tales p170-77   **398.2**

See also Ashiepattle and his goodly crew

The **Ash Lad who had an eating match with the Troll.** Asbjørnsen, P. C.

In Asbjørnsen, P. C. Norwegian folk tales p81-83   **398.2**

See also Ashiepattle who ate with the troll for a wager

The **Ash Lad who made the princess say, "You're a liar."** Asbjørnsen, P. C.

In Asbjørnsen, P. C. Norwegian folk tales p17-19   **398.2**

See also Ashiepattle who made the princess tell the truth at last

Ashabranner, Brent

(jt. auth.) Davis, R. Chief Joseph: war chief of the Nez Percé   **92**

(jt. auth.) Davis, R. The lion's whiskers   **398.2**

Ashanti folklore. See Folklore, Ashanti

The **Ashanti of Ghana.** Bleeker, S.   **916.67**

Aspinwall, Alicia
A quick-running squash
In Harper, W. comp. The harvest feast
p175-81 **394.2**

The Ass in the lion's skin
In Jacobs, J. ed. Indian fairy tales p150-51
398.2

The Ass, the table, and the stick
In De La Mare, W. ed. Animal stories
p144-48 **398.2**
In Jacobs, J. ed. English folk and fairy tales
p215-19 **398.2**
See also Table, the ass, and the stick

Assam
Bergman Sucksdorff, A. Tooni, the elephant
boy (1-5) **915.4**

Assassination. See Presidents—United States—
Assassination

Assateague Island

Fiction
Henry, M. Misty of Chincoteague (4-7) **Fic**

Assembly, Right of. See Freedom of assembly

Asses and mules. See Donkeys; Mules

Assipattle and the giant sea serpent. Haviland, V.
In Haviland, V. Favorite fairy tales told in
Scotland p71-92 **398.2**

Association for Childhood Education International
Bibliography: books for children **028.52**
Good and inexpensive books for children
028.52
Sung under the silver umbrella (k-2) **821.08**
Told under spacious skies (3-6) **S C**
Told under the blue umbrella (1-4) **S C**
Told under the Christmas tree (3-6) **808.8**
Told under the city umbrella (3-6) **S C**
Told under the green umbrella (1-4) **398.2**
Told under the magic umbrella (k-4) **S C**
Told under the Stars and Stripes (3-6) **S C**
Childhood Education: a journal for teachers,
administrators, church-school workers, li-
brarians, pediatricians. See Childhood Edu-
cation: a journal for teachers, admini-
strators, church-school workers, librarians,
pediatricians **370.5**

**Association for Educational Communications
and Technology**
Audio Visual Instruction. See Audio Visual In-
struction **371.3305**
Media programs: district and school. See
Media programs: district and school **371.33**

Assyria
See pages in the following book:
Robinson, C. A. The first book of ancient
Mesopotamia and Persia p36-43 (4-7)
913.35

Assyro-Babylonian inscriptions. See Cuneiform
inscriptions

Asteroids. See Planets, Minor

The asteroids. Nourse, A. E. **523.4**

Astrology
Aylesworth, T. G. Astrology and foretelling
the future (5-7) **133.3**

Astrology and foretelling the future. Aylesworth,
T. G. **133.3**

Astronautics
Americans in space (5-7) **629.4**
See also Artificial satellites; Navigation
(Astronautics); Outer space; Space flight;
Space flight to the moon; Space stations

Dictionaries
Asimov, I. ABC's of space (2-5) **629.403**

Astronauts
See pages in the following book:
Americans in space p64-85 (5-7) **629.4**

Astronavigation. See Navigation (Astronautics)

Astronomy
Gallant, R. A. Exploring the universe (5-7)
523
Zim, H. S. Stars (5-7) **523**
Zim, H. S. The universe (4-6) **523.1**
See also pages in the following book:
Boy Scouts of America. Fieldbook p512-29
369.43
See also Eclipses, Solar; Moon; Outer
space; Planets; Planets, Minor; Seasons;
Solar system; Space sciences; Stars; Sun;
Tides

Atlases
See Stars—Atlases

At home. Hautzig, E. **410**

At old Trinity. Moore, A. C.
In Luckhardt, M. C. ed. Christmas comes
once more p14-15 **394.2**

At school a hundred years ago. Repplier, A.
In A St Nicholas anthology p64-67 **810.8**

At the back of the North Wind. Macdonald, G.
Fic

At the castle gate. Lowell, J. R.
In Luckhardt, M. C. ed. Christmas comes
once more p97-103 **394.2**

At the center of the world. Baker, B. **398.2**

At the grandfather's. Spyri, J.
In Arbuthnot, M. H. comp. The Arbuthnot
Anthology of children's literature
p708-12 **808.8**

Atabalipa. See Atahuallpa

Atahuallpa
See pages in the following book:
Bleeker, S. The Inca p131-37 (4-6) **980.3**

Atalanta. Miles, B.
In Free to be . . . you and me p128-35
810.8

Atatürk, Kamâl, President Turkey
See pages in the following book:
Spencer, W. The land and people of Turkey
p61-75 (5-7) **915.61**

Atene, Ann
(illus.) Cooper, L. Fun with French **448**
(illus.) Cooper, L. Fun with Italian **458**
(illus.) Cooper, L. Fun with Spanish **468**
(illus.) Cooper, L. More Fun with Spanish **468**

Athena
Gates, D. The warrior goddess: Athena (4-7)
292

Athens
See pages in the following book:
Unstead, R. J. Looking at ancient history p59-
72 (4-6) **930**

Audio-visual education

Media programs: district and school 371.33

See also Audio-visual materials

Bibliography

Taggart, D. T. A guide to sources in educational media and technology 016.3713

Directories

Audio visual market place 371.33

Periodicals

Audio Visual Instruction 371.3305

Media & Methods 371.3305

Audio Visual Instruction 371.3305

Audio visual market place 371.33

Audio-visual materials

Hicks, W. Developing multi-media libraries 025.17

Media programs: district and school 371.33

See also pages in the following books:

Gillespie, J. T. Creating a school media program p197-221 027.8

Larrick, N. A parent's guide to children's reading p147-64, 388-402 028.5

See also Moving pictures; Phonograph records

Bibliography

American Library Association. Library Service to the Disadvantaged Child Committee. I read, you read, we read 028.5

The Black experience in children's audio-visual materials 016.3014

Greene, E. ed. A multimedia approach to children's literature 028.52

Perkins, F. L. Book and non-book media 016.028

Cataloging

See Cataloging—Audio-visual materials

Catalogs

The Elementary school library collection 011

McDaniel, R. ed. Resources for learning 016.3713

National Information Center for Educational Media. [NICEM Indexes to nonbook media] 016.3713

Periodicals

Previews 016.3713

Reviews

Previews 016.3713

Audio-visual materials centers. See Instructional materials centers

Audubon, John James

The birds of America 598.2

About

Kieran, M. John James Audubon (4-6) 92

See also pages in the following book:

Johnson, E. ed. Anthology of children's literature p1059-61 808.8

Augustus, Emperor of Rome

See pages in the following books:

Brooks, P. S. When the world was Rome, 753 B.C. to A.D. 476 p117-49 (6-7) 937

Robinson, C. A. The first book of ancient Rome p37-40 (5-7) 913.37

Augustus goes south. Le Grand

In Martignoni, M. E. ed. The illustrated

treasury of children's literature p338-42 808.8

Aulaire, Edgar Parin d'

Caldecott Medal acceptance paper

In Miller, B. M. ed. Caldecott Medal books: 1938-1957 p49-54 028.5

(jt. auth.) Aulaire, I. d'. Abraham Lincoln 92

(jt. auth.) Aulaire, I. d'. Animals everywhere E

(jt. auth.) Aulaire, I. d'. Benjamin Franklin 92

(jt. auth.) Aulaire, I. d'. Buffalo Bill [biography of William Frederick Cody] 92

(jt. auth.) Aulaire, I. d'. Children of the Northlights Fic

(jt. auth.) Aulaire, I. d'. Columbus 92

(jt. auth.) Aulaire, I. d'. D'Aulaires' Trolls 398.2

(jt. auth.) Aulaire, I. d'. Don't count your chicks E

(jt. auth.) Aulaire, I. d'. East of the sun and west of the moon 398.2

(jt. auth.) Aulaire, I. d'. George Washington 92

(jt. auth.) Aulaire, I. d'. Ingri and Edgar Parin d'Aulaire's Book of Greek myths 292

(jt. auth.) Aulaire, I. d'. Leif the Lucky [biography of Leif Ericsson] 92

(jt. auth.) Aulaire, I. d'. The magic meadow Fic

(jt. auth.) Aulaire, I. d'. Norse gods and giants 293

(jt. auth.) Aulaire, I. d'. Ola E

(jt. auth.) Aulaire, I. d'. Pocahontas 92

About

See pages in the following book:

Miller, B. M. ed. Caldecott Medal books: 1938-1957 p55-62 028.5

Aulaire, Ingri d'

Abraham Lincoln (2-4) 92

Animals everywhere E

Benjamin Franklin (2-4) 92

Buffalo Bill [biography of William Frederick Cody] (1-4) 92

Caldecott Medal acceptance paper

In Miller, B. M. ed. Caldecott Medal books: 1938-1957 p45-49 028.5

Children of the Northlights (2-4) Fic

Columbus (1-4) 92

D'Aulaires' Trolls (3-6) 398.2

Don't count your chicks E

East of the sun and west of the moon (3-6) 398.2

Contents: Herding the king's hares; The ship that went as well by land as by sea; The quern that stands and grinds at the bottom of the sea; The maid on the glass mountain; The widow's son; Lord Per; Soria Moria Castle; Per, Paal, and Espen Cinderlad; Cinderlad and the troll's seven silver ducks; The Big Bird Dan; Kari Woodenskirt; Why the Bear is stumpy-tailed; East of the Sun and West of the Moon; The three princesses in the mountain of blue; The three bushy billy goats; Tatterhood; Dapplegrim; Gudbrand on the Hillside; The hen trips in the mountain; The three aunts; Doll in the grass

George Washington (2-4) 92

Ingri and Edgar Parin d'Aulaire's Book of Greek myths (3-6) 292

Leif the Lucky [biography of Leif Ericsson] (2-4) 92

The magic meadow (2-4) Fic

Norse gods and giants (4-6) 293

Ola E

Aulaire, Ingri d'—*Continued*
Pocahontas (2-4)   **92**
Three aunts
In Martignoni, M. E. ed. The illustrated
treasury of children's literature p243-
45   **808.8**

About
See pages in the following book:
Miller, B. M. ed. Caldecott Medal books:
1938-1957 p55-62   **028.5**

The **auld** cailleach's curse. Nic Leodhas, S.
In Nic Leodhas, S. Twelve great black
cats, and other eerie Scottish tales
p71-87   **398.2**

Aulnoy, comtesse d'
The Blue Bird
In Lang, A. ed. The green fairy book p 1-
26   **398.2**
Felicia and the pot of pinks
In Lang, A. ed. The blue fairy book p148-
56   **398.2**
The friendly frog
In Perrault, C. Perrault's Complete fairy
tales p135-62   **398.2**
The golden branch
In Lang, A. ed. The red fairy book p220-
37   **398.2**
Graciosa and Percinet
In Lang, A. ed. The red fairy book p158-
74   **398.2**
The little good mouse
In Lang, A. ed. The red fairy book p146-
57   **398.2**
Princess Mayblossom
In Lang, A. ed. The red fairy book p13-29
                                398.2
Princess Rosette
In Lang, A. ed. The red fairy book p89-
103   **398.2**
In Perrault, C. Perrault's Complete fairy
tales p163-84   **398.2**
The story of Pretty Goldilocks
In Lang, A. ed. The blue fairy book p193-
205   **398.2**
The White Cat
In Arbuthnot, M. H. comp. The Arbuth-
not Anthology of children's litera-
ture p224-31   **808.8**
In Arbuthnot, M. H. comp. Time for old
magic p102-09   **398.2**
In Colwell, E. ed. A storyteller's choice
p133-41   **372.6**
In Lang, A. ed. The blue fairy book p157-
73   **398.2**
The White Cat, and other old French fairy
tales (3-6)   **398.2**
Contents: The White Cat; Graciosa and Percinet;
The pot of carnations; Prince Sprite; The good little
mouse
The wonderful sheep
In Lang, A. ed. The blue fairy book p214-
30   **398.2**
The yellow dwarf
In Lang, A. ed. The blue fairy book p30-
50   **398.2**
In Opie, I. ed. The classic fairy tales p68-
80   **398.2**

**Aulnoy, Marie Catherine (Jumelle de Berneville)
comtesse d'. See Aulnoy, Comtesse d'**

Ault, Phil
These are the Great Lakes (5-7)   **977**
Wonders of the mosquito world (5-7) **595.7**

Ault, Roz
Parents' Nursery School. Kids are natural
cooks   **641.5**

Aunt Beast. L'Engle, M.
In Arbuthnot, M. H. comp. The Arbuthnot
Anthology of children's literature
p595-99   **808.8**

Aunt Tilly. Leach, M.
In Leach, M. The thing at the foot of the
bed, and other scary tales p73-74 **S C**

Auntie. Andersen, H. C.
In Andersen, H. C. The complete fairy tales
and stories p890-95   **S C**
See also Aunty

Auntie Toothache. Andersen, H. C.
In Andersen, H. C. The complete fairy tales
and stories p1058-67   **S C**

The aunts. Roy, C.
In Roy, C. The serpent and the sun p110-
19   **398.2**

Aunty
Andersen, H. C. Auntie
In Andersen, H. C. The complete fairy tales
and stories p890-95   **S C**
Andersen, H. C. Aunty
In Andersen, H. C. Andersen's Fairy tales
p137-42   **S C**

Austen, Jane
History of England
In Authors' choice p41-52   **S C**

Austin, Mary
The search for Jean Baptiste
In A St Nicholas anthology p27-30 **810.8**

Australia
Blunden, G. The land and people of Australia
(5-7)   **919.4**
Sasek, M. This is Australia (3-6)   **919.4**
Fiction
Clark, M. T. The min-min (5-7)   **Fic**
Ottley, R. Boy alone (5-7)   **Fic**
Ottley, R. The roan colt (5-7)   **Fic**
Phipson, J. The boundary riders (5-7) **Fic**
Phipson, J. The family conspiracy (5-7) **Fic**
Phipson, J. Good luck to the rider (5-7) **Fic**
Phipson, J. The way home (5-7)   **Fic**
Southall, I. Hills End (6-7)   **Fic**
Wrightson, P. Down to earth (5-7)   **Fic**
Wrightson, P. A racecourse for Andy (5-7) **Fic**

Australian aborigines
See pages in the following book:
Blunden, G. The land and people of Australia
p58-69 (5-7)   **919.4**

Australian literature
See pages in the following book:
Blunden, G. The land and people of Australia
p122-33 (5-7)   **919.4**

Austria
Wohlrabe, R. A. The land and people of
Austria (5-7)   **914.36**
Fiction
Catherall, A. Prisoners in the snow (3-5) **Fic**
Curry, J. L. The ice ghosts mystery (4-7) **Fic**

Austria—Continued

Industries

See pages in the following book:

Wohlrabe, R. A. The land and people of Austria p127-37 (5-7)   **914.36**

Austrian composers. See Composers, Austrian

Authors

Benét, L. Famous storytellers for young people (5-7)   **920**

Hoffman, M. ed. Authors and illustrators of children's books   **028.5**

Kingman, L. ed. Newbery and Caldecott Medal books: 1956-1965   **028.5**

Kingman, L. ed. Newbery and Caldecott Medal books: 1966-1975   **028.5**

Miller, B. M. ed. Newbery Medal books: 1922-1955   **028.5**

Smaridge, N. Famous author-illustrators for young people (5-7)   **920**

See also pages in the following books:

Bechtel, L. S. Books in search of children p63-138   **028.5**

Johnson, E. ed. Anthology of children's literature p1217-64   **808.8**

   See also Children as authors; Negro authors; also classes of writers, e.g. Poets; and names of individual authors

Dictionaries

De Montreville, D. ed. Third book of junior authors   **920.03**

Fuller, M. ed. More junior authors   **920.03**

Kunitz, S. J. ed. The junior book of authors   **920.03**

Something about the author   **920.03**

Ward, M. E. Authors of books for young people   **920.03**

Authors, American

Aulaire, I. d'. Benjamin Franklin (2-4)   **92**

Daugherty, C. M. Samuel Clemens (2-4)   **92**

Daugherty, J. Poor Richard [biography of Benjamin Franklin] (6-7)   **92**

Egypt, O. S. James Weldon Johnson (2-4)   **92**

Felton, H. W. James Weldon Johnson (4-6) **92**

McKown, R. Mark Twain [biography of Samuel Langhorne Clemens] (6-7)   **92**

McNeer, M. America's Mark Twain [biography of Samuel Langhorne Clemens] (5-7)   **92**

Papashvily, H. W. Louisa May Alcott (4-6) **92**

Wilder, L. I. West from home (6-7)   **92**

See also pages in the following book:

MacCann, D. The child's first books p95-106   **741.64**

Authors, English

Aldis, D. Nothing is impossible; the story of Beatrix Potter (4-6)   **92**

Potter, B. Letters to children   **92**

Vipont, E. Weaver of dreams; the girlhood of Charlotte Brontë (5-7)   **92**

Authors, French

Born, F. Jules Verne (5-7)   **92**

Authors, Negro. See Negro authors

Authors and illustrators of children's books. Hoffman, M. ed.   **028.5**

Authors' choice   **S C**

Authors' choice 2   **S C**

Authors of books for young people. Ward, M. E.   **920.03**

Autobiographies

Ojigbo, A. O. comp. Young and Black in Africa (6-7)   **920**

Ross, P. ed. Young and female (6-7)   **920**

Autobiography of a horse. See Sewell, A. Black Beauty   **Fic**

Automatic computers. See Computers

Automatic teaching. See Teaching machines

Automobile industry and trade

Harris, L. Behind the scenes in a car factory (4-6)   **629.22**

Automobile racing

Cooke, D. C. Racing cars that made history (5-7)   **796.7**

Jackson, R. B. Road racing, U.S.A. (4-7)   **796.7**

See also pages in the following book:

The Junior illustrated encyclopedia of sports p 1-30 (5-7)   **796.03**

   See also New York to Paris Race, 1908

History

Stevenson, P. The greatest days of racing (5-7)   **796.7**

Automobile trucks. See Trucks

Automobiles

Barris, G. Famous custom & show cars (6-7)   **629.22**

Bendick, J. The first book of automobiles (3-5)   **629.22**

Cooke, D. C. Racing cars that made history (5-7)   **796.7**

Corbett, S. What makes a car go? (3-6)   **629.22**

Lawrie, R. Under the hood (4-6)   **629.28**

See also pages in the following books:

McLeod, S. How will we move all the people? p57-78 (6-7)   **380.5**

Pringle, L. Recycling resources p69-79 (6-7)   **604.6**

   See also Dune buggies; Sports cars; Trucks

Design and construction

Harris, L. Behind the scenes in a car factory (4-6)   **629.22**

Lent, H. B. The X cars (5-7)   **629.22**

Stambler, I. Unusual automobiles of today and tomorrow (6-7)   **629.22**

Stevenson, P. The Buffy-Porson (4-6)   **688.6**

History

Bergere, T. Automobiles of yesteryear (4-7)   **629.22**

Jackson, R. B. Classic cars (5-7)   **629.22**

Lent, H. B. Car of the year (5-7)   **629.22**

See also pages in the following book:

Jackson, R. B. Waves, wheels and wings p36-49 (4-6)   **380.5074**

Models

Weiss, H. Model cars and trucks and how to build them (4-7)   **629.22**

Pictorial works

Bergere, T. Automobiles of yesteryear (4-7)   **629.22**

Bailey, Margery—*Continued*
The brownie in the house
In Association for Childhood Education International. Told under the magic umbrella p172-79 **S C**

Baird, Evelyn
(illus.) Hanley, H. Fun with needlepoint **746.4**

Baisden, Leo B.
(jt. auth.) Mott, C. Children's book on how to use books and libraries **028.7**

Baja California

Fiction

Du Soe, R. C. Three without fear (5-7) **Fic**

Bakacs, George
(illus.) Silverstein, A. Cells: building blocks of life **574.8**
(illus.) Silverstein, A. The respiratory system **574.1**

Baker, Augusta
(comp.) The golden lynx, and other tales (3-6) **398.2**
The horned woman
In Hoke, H. ed. Witches, witches, witches p 1-4 **808.8**
(comp.) The talking tree (3-6) **398.2**
The Black experience in children's books. See The Black experience in children's books **016.3014**

Baker, Betty
At the center of the world (4-6) **398.2**
Contents: Earth magician; Coyote drowns the world; The killing pot; The monster eagle; The killing of Eetoi; The first war
The Pig War (k-2) **973.6**
Walk the world's rim (5-7) **Fic**

Baker, Charlotte
The bottle
In Association for Childhood Education International. Told under spacious skies p295-301 **S C**
Cockleburr Quarters (4-6) **Fic**

Baker, Eloise
(jt. auth.) Carpenter, A. El Salvador **917.284**

Baker, Francis Noel- See Noel-Baker, Francis

Baker, Henry
See pages in the following book:
Tunis, E. The tavern at the ferry p 1-8, 11-14 (5-7) **917.3**

Baker, Jeffrey J. W.
The vital process: photosynthesis (4-7) **581**

Baker, Josephine
See pages in the following book:
Rollins, C. Famous Negro entertainers of stage, screen, and TV p39-43 (5-7) **920**

Baker, Laura Nelson
The friendly beasts (Carol). The friendly beasts **783.6**

Baker, Margaret
The lost merbaby
In Association for Childhood Education International. Told under the magic umbrella p133-44 **S C**
Rhyming ink
In Gruenberg, S. M. ed. Favorite stories old and new p478-83 **808.8**

Tomson's Halloween
In Harper, W. comp. Ghosts and goblins p124-40 **394.2**
A week of Sundays
In Gruenberg, S. M. ed. Favorite stories old and new p359-63 **808.8**

Baker, Margaret J.
Home from the hill (5-7) **Fic**

Baker, Michael
(illus.) Doherty, C. H. Tunnels **624**

Baker, Norman
(jt. auth.) Murphy, B. B. Thor Heyerdahl and the reed boat Ra **910.4**

Baker, Richard
(jt. comp.) Keller, C. comp. The star spangled banana, and other revolutionary riddles **793.7**

Baker, Robert H.
(jt. auth.) Zim, H. S. Stars **523**

Baker, Samm Sinclair
The indoor and outdoor grow-it book (1-6) **635**

Baker's daughter
Bianco, M. W. The baker's daughter
In Sechrist, E. H. ed. It's time for story hour p29-35 **372.6**
Williams-Ellis, A. The baker's daughter
In Williams-Ellis, A. Fairy tales from the British Isles p103-05 **398.2**

A baker's dozen. Davis, M. G. ed. **372.6**

The baker's neighbor. Thane, E.
In Kamerman, S. E. ed. Dramatized folk tales of the world p471-80 **812.08**

The Baker's new coat. Self, M. C.
In Sechrist, E. H. ed. It's time for story hour p51-59 **372.6**

Baking

See pages in the following books:
Girl Scouts of the United States of America. Cooking out-of-doors p99-122 (4-7) **641.5**
Girl Scouts of the United States of America. Girl Scout cookbook p108-39 (4-7) **641.5**
See also Bread; Cake; Cookies

Fiction

Hoban, L. Arthur's Christmas cookies **E**
The baking contest. Simon, S.
In Kamerman, S. E. ed. Fifty plays for junior actors p554-63 **812.08**

Balance of nature. See Ecology

Balarin's goat. Berson, H. **E**

Balaton lake
The tale of the Balaton
In Baker, A. comp. The talking tree p191-98 **398.2**

Balboa, Vasco Núñez de
Syme, R. Balboa, finder of the Pacific (4-6) **92**

Balch, Glenn
The book of horses (4-7) **636.1**

Bald eagle
Turner, J. F. The magnificent bald eagle (4-6) **598.2**

Baldur and the mistletoe
Baldur the bright
In Garner, A. ed. A cavalcade of goblins p201-08 **398.2**

Baldur the bright
In Garner, A. ed. A cavalcade of goblins
p201-08   398.2

Baldwin, Clara
Seed for Thanksgiving
In Luckhardt, M. C. comp. Thanksgiving
p339-45   394.2

Baldwin, Gordon C.
How Indians really lived (5-7)   970.1

Baldwin, James
A cause of war
In Hazeltine, A. I. ed. Hero tales from
many lands p13-25   398.2
Cornelia's jewels
In Cavanah, F. ed. Holiday roundup p142-
44   394.2
Fafnir, the dragon
In Johnson, E. ed. Anthology of children's
literature p528-32   808.8
A Roland for an Oliver
In Hazeltine, A. I. ed. Hero tales from
many lands p220-34   398.2
The story of Roland (6-7)   398.2
The story of Siegfried (6-7)   398.2
The story of William Tell
In Ward, W. ed. Stories to dramatize
p199-200   372.6
The wise people of Gotham
In Ward, W. ed. Stories to dramatize
p154-57   372.6
A young prince named Siegfried
In Hazeltine, A. I. ed. Hero tales from
many lands p253-68   398.2

Balestrino, Philip
Hot as an ice cube (k-3)   536
The skeleton inside you (1-3)   611

Balet, Jan
The fence   E
The gift   E
Joanjo   E

Balian, Lorna
Humbug witch   E
Where in the world is Henry?   E

Balkan peninsula
Kostich, D. D. The land and people of the
Balkans (5-7)   914.96

Ball, Albert
See pages in the following book:
Gurney, G. Flying aces of World War I p40-
56 (4-7)   920

Ball, Zachary
Bristle Face (5-7)   Fic
Sputters (5-7)   Fic

Ball games. See names of games, e.g. Baseball;
Soccer

Ballads
See pages in the following book:
Parker, E. ed. 100 more story poems p85-144
(6-7)   821.08
See also Folk songs

Ballads, American
Emrich, D. comp. American folk poetry: an
anthology   811.08
Sandburg, C. ed. The American songbag   784.7

Ballads, English
Malcolmson, A. ed. Song of Robin Hood (5-7)   398.2

Ballads, Scottish
Langstaff, J. Frog went a-courtin' (k-3)   784.4
Nic Leodhas, S. By loch and by lin (4-7)   398.2

Ballads and boots
In Gunterman, B. L. ed. Castles in Spain,
and other enchantments p247-50   398.2

Ballet
Draper, N. Ballet for beginners (5-7)   792.8
Freeman, M. Fun with ballet (4-7)   792.8
Mara, T. First steps in ballet (4-7)   792.8
Streatfeild, N. A young person's guide to
ballet (6-7)   792.8
See also pages in the following book:
Wohlrabe, R. A. The land and people of
Denmark p126-36 (5-7)   914.89

Biography
Tobias, T. Maria Tallchief (2-4)   92

Fiction
Streatfeild, N. Ballet shoes (4-6)   Fic

Ballet. Brock, E. L.
In Gruenberg, S. M. ed. Favorite stories
old and new p63-68   808.8

Ballet for beginners. Draper, N.   792.7

Ballet shoes. Streatfeild, N.   Fic

Ballets
Stories, plots, etc.
Chappell, W. The Nutcracker (2-5)   792.8
Chappell, W. The Sleeping Beauty (1-4)   792.8
Untermeyer, L. Tales from the ballet (4-6)   792.8

Un **ballo** in maschera; adaptation. Bulla, C. R.
In Bulla, C. R. More Stories of favorite
operas p85-98   782.1

The **ballooning** adventures of Paddy Pork.
Goodall, J. S.   E

Balloons
Burchard, P. Balloons (3-6)   629.133
Stone, A. H. Take a balloon (3-6)   530.72
See also pages in the following book:
Wyler, R. What happens if . . ? p4-13 (2-4)   507.2

Fiction
Alexander, M. The story grandmother told   E
Du Bois, W. P. Twenty-one balloons (5-7)   Fic
Edmonds, W. D. Cadmus Henry (5-7)   Fic
Goodall, J. S. The ballooning adventures of
Paddy Pork   E
Haywood, C. Away went the balloons (2-4)   Fic
Lamorisse, A. The red balloon (1-4)   Fic

History
See pages in the following book:
Arbuthnot, M. H. comp. The Arbuthnot An-
thology of children's literature p879-80   808.8

Balloons, Dirigible. See Airships

Ballyutility's Christmas tree. McNeill, J.
In Reeves, J. comp. The Christmas book
p78-85   394.2

Barr, June
Cinderella
In Kamerman, S. E. ed. Little plays for
little players p240-48   **812.08**
The lion and the mouse
In Kamerman, S. E. ed. Little plays for
little players p249-54   **812.08**
A present for mother
In Burack, A. S. ed. One hundred plays for
children p336-40   **808.82**
In Kamerman, S. E. ed. Little plays for
little players p67-71   **812.08**
A white Christmas
In Kamerman, S. E. ed. A treasury of
Christmas plays p367-71   **812.08**

The **barrel** bung. Wahlenberg, A.
In Olenius, E. comp. Great Swedish fairy
tales p29-37   **398.2**

The **barrel**-organ. Farjeon, E.
In Farjeon, E. The little bookroom p116-19   **S C**

Barrer-Russell, Gertrude
(illus.) Feagles, A. Autun and the bear   **398.2**

Barret, Leighton
The adventures of Don Quixote de la Mancha
(5-7)   **Fic**

Barrett, Alan
(illus.) Pearce, P. Beauty and the beast   **398.2**

Barrett, Judi
Animals should definitely not wear clothing   **E**
Benjamin's 365 birthdays   **E**

Barrett, Marvin
Meet Thomas Jefferson (2-4)   **92**

Barrett, Ron
(illus.) Barrett, J. Animals should definitely
not wear clothing   **E**
(illus.) Barrett, J. Benjamin's 365 birthdays **E**

Barrie, J. M.
Lock-out time
In Untermeyer, B. ed. The Golden Trea-
sury of children's literature p426-35   **808.8**
Peter Pan (3-5)   **Fic**
Peter Pan; excerpt
In Untermeyer, B. ed. The Golden Trea-
sury of children's literature p406-15   **808.8**
Peter Pan in Kensington Gardens
In Darrell, M. ed. Once upon a time p249-
96   **808.8**
The thrush's nest
In Untermeyer, B. ed. The Golden Trea-
sury of children's literature p416-25   **808.8**

Barris, George
Famous custom & show cars (6-7)   **629.22**

Barron, John N.
(illus.) Van Rensselaer, A. Fun with magic   **793.8**

Barrows. See Mounds and mound builders

Barry, James E.
(illus.) Rosenfeld, S. Science experiments with
air   **507.2**
(illus.) Rosenfeld, S. The story of coins   **737.4**

Barry, Katharina
(illus.) Joslin, S. Spaghetti for breakfast   **458**
(illus.) Joslin, S. There is a bull on my balcony   **468**

Barry. Hürlimann, B.   **636.7**

Bars and restaurants. See Restaurants, bars, etc.

Barss, William
(illus.) Asimov, I. More Words of science   **503**
(illus.) Asimov, I. Words from the myths   **292**
(illus.) Asimov, I. Words of science, and the
history behind them   **503**
(illus.) North, S. Young Thomas Edison   **92**

The **bartered** bride; adaptation. Bulla, C. R.
In Bulla, C. R. More Stories of favorite
operas p159-68   **782.1**

Barth, Edna
The day Luis was lost (3-5)   **Fic**
Hearts, cupids, and red roses (3-6)   **394.2**
Holly, reindeer, and colored lights (3-6)   **394.2**
I'm nobody! Who are you? The story of
Emily Dickinson (5-7)   **92**
Jack-o'-lantern (2-4)   **398.2**
Lilies, rabbits, and painted eggs (3-6)   **394.2**
Witches, pumpkins, and grinning ghosts (3-6)   **394.2**

Barth, Ernest Kurt
(illus.) Freeman, M. B. Do you know about
water?   **553**
(illus.) Shippen, K. B. Andrew Carnegie and
the age of steel   **92**

Bartholomew and the oobleck. Seuss, Dr   **E**

Bartlett, John
(comp.) Familiar quotations   **808.88**

Bartlett, Robert Merrill
Thanksgiving Day (1-3)   **394.2**

Bartlett, Susan
Books (3-5)   **686**

Barton, Byron
(illus.) Greene, C. C. A girl called Al   **Fic**
(illus.) Simon, S. The paper airplane book   **629.133**

Barton, Clara Harlowe
Boylston, H. D. Clara Barton, founder of the
American Red Cross (4-7)   **92**
Grant, M. G. Clara Barton (3-4)   **92**
See also pages in the following book:
Rothkopf, C. Z. The Red Cross (4-6)   **361.7**

Bartos-Hoppner, B.
Avalanche dog (5-7)   **Fic**

Bartram, Robert
(illus.) Helfman, H. Fun with your fingers   **745.5**
(illus.) Helfman, H. Tricks with your fingers   **793.8**

Baruch, Dorothy
Big Fellow's first job
In Gruenberg, S. M. ed. Favorite stories old
and new p78-82   **808.8**
Building
In Association for Childhood Education In-
ternational. Told under the blue um-
brella p7-8   **S C**
Express wagon
In Association for Childhood Education In-
ternational. Told under the blue um-
brella p8-9   **S C**
In the grass
In Association for Childhood Education In-
ternational. Told under the blue um-
brella p10-11   **S C**

Baruch, Dorothy—*Continued*
A visit to the farm
In Association for Childhood Education International. Told under the blue umbrella p75-79   **S C**

Baseball
Brewster, B. Baseball (3-5)   **796.357**
Kalb, J. How to play baseball better than you did last season (4-6)   **796.357**
Sports Illustrated Baseball (5-7)   **796.357**
Sullivan, G. Baseball's art of hitting (5-7)   **796.357**
Sullivan, G. Pitchers and pitching (5-7)   **796.357**

See also pages in the following books:
The Junior illustrated encyclopedia of sports p31-147 (5-7)   **796.03**
Keith, H. Sports and games p20-55 (5-7)   **796**
   See also Little league baseball; Softball

Biography
Einstein, C. Willie Mays: coast to coast Giant (5-7)   **92**
Epstein, S. Baseball Hall of Fame: stories of champions (3-5)   **920**
Graham, F. Lou Gehrig, a quiet hero (5-7)   **92**
Hano, A. Roberto Clemente: batting king (5-7)   **92**
Hirshberg, A. The up-to-date biography of Henry Aaron (5-7)   **92**
Libby, B. Baseball's greatest sluggers (5-7)   **920**
Luce, W. Lou Gehrig: iron man of baseball (3-5)   **92**
Robinson, J. R. Breakthrough to the big league (4-7)   **92**
Rubin, B. Pete Rose (5-7)   **92**
Rubin, R. Satchel Paige (5-7)   **92**
Rudeen, K. Jackie Robinson (2-4)   **92**
Rudeen, K. Roberto Clemente (2-4)   **92**
Rudeen, K. Wilt Chamberlain (2-5)   **92**
Schoor, G. Roy Campanella: man of courage (4-7)   **92**
Schoor, G. Willie Mays, modest champion (4-6)   **92**
Sullivan, G. Willie Mays (1-3)   **92**
Young, B. E. The picture story of Hank Aaron (3-5)   **92**

Dictionaries
Archibald, J. Baseball talk for beginners (4-7)   **796.357**

Encyclopedias
Turkin, H. The official encyclopedia of baseball   **796.357**

Fiction
Christopher, M. The kid who only hit homers (3-5)   **Fic**
Christopher, M. Look who's playing first base (3-5)   **Fic**
Christopher, M. The team that couldn't lose (3-5)   **Fic**
Cohen, B. Thank you, Jackie Robinson (4-6)   **Fic**
Corbett, S. The baseball trick (3-5)   **Fic**
Gault, W. C. Stubborn Sam (5-7)   **Fic**
Kessler, L. Here comes the strikeout   **E**

History
Rosenburg, J. M. The story of baseball (6-7)   **796.357**

Poetry
Thayer, E. L. Casey at the bat (4-7)   **811**
Baseball Hall of Fame. See Cooperstown, N.Y. National Baseball Hall of Fame and Museum
Baseball Hall of Fame: stories of champions. Epstein, S.   **920**
Baseball talk for beginners. Archibald, J.   **796.357**
The **baseball trick.** Corbett, S.   **Fic**
Baseball's art of hitting. Sullivan, G.   **796.357**
Baseball's greatest sluggers. Libby, B.   **920**
Bash Tchelik
In Garner, A. ed. A cavalcade of goblins p63-75   **398.2**
Bashfulness

Fiction
Lexau, J. M. Benjie   **E**
Lexau, J. M. Benjie on his own   **E**
Basic basketball strategy. Knosher, H.   **796.32**
Basil of Baker Street. Titus, E.   **Fic**
A **basket for Thanksgiving.** Bailey, C. S.
In Harper, W. comp. The harvest feast p137-47   **394.2**
Basket making
See also pages in the following book:
Hofsinde, R. Indian arts p48-54 (4-6)   **709.01**
Basketball
Kaplan, A. Basketball: how to improve your technique (5-7)   **796.32**
Knosher, H. Basic basketball strategy (4-7)   **796.32**
Monroe, E. The basketball skill book (4-7)   **796.32**

See also pages in the following books:
The Junior illustrated encyclopedia of sports p149-96 (5-7)   **796.03**
Keith, H. Sports and games p56-89 (5-7)   **796**

Dictionaries
Liss, H. Basketball talk for beginners (4-7)   **796.32**

Basketball: how to improve your technique. Kaplan, A.   **796.32**
The **basketball skill book.** Monroe, E.   **796.32**
Basketball talk for beginners. Liss, H.   **796.32**
Baskets in a little cart. Manning-Sanders, R.
In Manning-Sanders, R. A book of dragons p95-102   **398.2**
Baskin, Hosea
Hosie's alphabet. See Hosie's alphabet   **E**
Baskin, Leonard
(illus.) Hosie's alphabet   **E**
Bason, Lillian
Spiders (k-3)   **595**
Bastianelo. Haviland, V.
In Haviland, V. Favorite fairy tales told in Italy p55-66   **398.2**
Bat. See Bats
The **bat.** Tolstoy, L.
In Tolstoy, L. Twenty-two Russian tales for young children p44   **S C**
The **bat-poet.** Jarrell, R.   **Fic**
Bataan, The battle of. Conroy, R.   **940.54**

Baum, Betty
Patricia crosses town (4-6)   **Fic**
Baum, L. Frank
Discovery of Oz, the Terrible
  In Martignoni, M. E. ed. The illustrated
    treasury of children's literature p289-
    93   **808.8**
Dorothy meets the Wizard
  In Untermeyer, B. ed. The Golden Trea-
    sury of children's literature p256-70
    808.8
The Wizard of Oz (3-6)   **Fic**
The Wizard of Oz; dramatization. See
  Schwartz, L. S. The Wizard of Oz
The Wizard of Oz; puppet play. See Mahl-
  mann, L. The Wizard of Oz
About
See pages in the following books:
Benét, L. Famous storytellers for young peo-
  ple p113-17 (5-7)   **920**
Egoff, S. ed. Only connect p156-69   **028.5**
Baum, Willi
(illus.) Fletcher, A. M. Fishes dangerous to
  man   **597**
Baumann, Hans
The caves of the great hunters (5-7)   **913**
Gold and gods of Peru (6-7)   **980.3**
In the land of Ur (6-7)   **913.35**
The stolen fire (4-6)   **398.2**
  Contents: Staver and Vassilissa; Dobrynya at the
Saracens' Mount; Urismag; George in the realm of
darkness; Tardanak; Kara Khan's daughter; The her-
ald of war; Big Kihuo and Little Kihuo; Nana Miriam;
Mbega the kigego; The leopard; The stolen fire; Etana's
flight to Heaven; Muchukunda and Krishna; Kutune
Shirka and the golden otter; Isanagi and Isanami;
Kesar of Ling and the giant of the north; Girrowin;
The Prince of the House of Liu; Prince Five-Weapons;
One-Two-Man and Stoneshirt; The flute player; Smok-
ing Star; Vitziton and the first quarrel; The seven
deeds of Onkoito; Norwan; After the great fire
Baumhauer, Hans
(illus.) Dodge, M. M. Hans Brinker   **Fic**
(illus.) Lagerlof, S. The wonderful adventures
  of Nils   **Fic**
Bawden, Nina
Carrie's war (4-7)   **Fic**
A handful of thieves (4-6)   **Fic**
The peppermint pig (5-7)   **Fic**
The runaway summer (4-6)   **Fic**
Squib (4-6)   **Fic**
Three on the run (4-6)   **Fic**
The witch's daughter (4-7)   **Fic**
Baxter, John
Apple
  In Yolen, J. ed. Zoo 2000 p83-98   **S C**
Bay, J. C.
Hatch, M. C. 13 Danish tales   **398.2**
Bayeux tapestry
Denny, N. The Bayeux tapestry (5-7) **746.3**
Baylor, Byrd
Before you came this way (1-4)   **709.01**
Coyote cry (2-4)   **Fic**
Everybody needs a rock   **E**
Sometimes I dance mountains (k-3)   **793.3**
They put on masks (1-4)   **391**
When clay sings (1-4)   **970.4**
Bayne, Julia Taft
The show in the White House attic
  In Cavanah, F. ed. Holiday roundup p28-
    33   **394.2**

Baynes, Pauline
(illus.) Hieatt, C. The Joy of the Court **398.2**
(illus.) Lewis, C. S. The lion, the witch and
  the wardrobe   **Fic**
(illus.) Opie, I. comp. A family book of
  nursery rhymes   **398.8**
(illus.) Tolkein, J. R. R. The adventures of
  Tom Bombadil, and other verses from The
  Red Book   **821**
(illus.) Uden, G. A dictionary of chivalry
    940.1
(illus.) Williams-Ellis, A. Fairy tales from the
  British Isles   **398.2**
Bayong of the lazy woman
Skipper, M. Lazy Tok
  In Colwell, E. ed. A storyteller's choice
    p169-73   **372.6**
Be a frog, a bird, or a tree. Carr, R.   **613.7**
Be a smart shopper. Gay, K.   **640.73**
Be a winner in football. Coombs, C.   **796.33**
Be a winner in ice hockey. Coombs, C. **796.9**
Be a winner in tennis. Coombs, C.   **796.34**
Be good, Harry. Chalmers, M.   **E**
Be nice to spiders. Graham, M. B.   **E**
Beach, Marcia Moray
On the fence
  In Kamerman, S. E. ed. Fifty plays for
    junior actors p19-34   **812.08**
The beach before breakfast. Kumin, M. W. **E**
The beachcomber's book. Kohn, B.   **745.5**
Beaches. See Seashore
Beacon, Robert
(jt. comp.) Ward, P. L. comp. The school
  media center   **027.8**
Bead craft. Donna, N.   **746.5**
The beaded moccasins. Bennett, R.
  In Bennett, R. Creative plays and programs
    for holidays p202-09   **812**
Beadwork
Donna, N. Bead craft (5-7)   **746.5**
Hofsinde, R. Indian beadwork (5-7)   **746.5**
See also pages in the following books:
D'Amato, J. American Indian craft inspira-
  tions p14-34 (5-7)   **745.5**
Hunt, W. B. The complete book of Indian
  crafts and lore p58-64 (4-7)   **745.5**
Beaks, Birds and their. Earle, O. L.   **598.2**
Beale Street folks. Jagendorf, M. A.
  In Jagendorf, M. A. Folk stories of the
    South p260-65   **398.2**
Bealer, Alex W.
Only the names remain (4-6)   **970.3**
Bealmear, J. H.
The covetous councilman
  In Kamerman, S. E. ed. Dramatized folk
    tales of the world p504-13   **812.08**
Beals, Carleton
The incredible Incas (5-7)   **980.3**
The beam. Grimm, J.
  In Grimm, J. The complete Grimm's Fairy
    tales p645   **398.2**
Beam of straw
Grimm, J. The beam
  In Grimm, J. The complete Grimm's Fairy
    tales p645   **398.2**

The **Bear's** son
  In Ginsburg, M. ed. The Kaha bird p109-30   **398.2**

The **bear's** toothache. McPhail, D.   **E**

Bearskin
  Grimm, J. Bearskin
    In Grimm, J. The complete Grimm's Fairy tales p467-72   **398.2**
    In Grimm, J. The juniper tree, and other tales from Grimm v2 p217-27   **398.2**
  Pyle, H. Bearskin
    In Pyle, H. The wonder clock p 1-14 **398.2**

Beastly boys and ghastly girls. Cole, W. comp.   **808.81**

Beasts. See Animals

The **beasts** of never. McHargue, G.   **398**

The **beatinest** boy. Stuart, J.   **Fic**

Beatty, John
  Copyist
    In Arbuthnot, M. H. comp. The Arbuthnot Anthology of children's literature p742-45   **808.8**

Beatty, Patricia
  Hail Columbia (5-7)   **Fic**
  How many miles to sundown (5-7)   **Fic**
  A long way to Whiskey Creek (5-7)   **Fic**
  The Nickel-Plated Beauty (5-7)   **Fic**
  O the Red Rose Tree (5-7)   **Fic**
  Red rock over the river (5-7)   **Fic**

Beaumont, Marie Le Prince de. See Le Prince de Beaumont, Marie

Beautiful junk. Madian, J.   **Fic**

Beautiful Lady. Wells, R.
  In Eaton, A. T. comp. The animals' Christmas p 37-39   **394.2**

Beauty. See Esthetics

Beauty, Personal
  See pages in the following book:
  Post, E. The Emily Post Book of etiquette for young people p49-62 (5-7)   **395**

The **Beauty** and her gallant. Manning-Sanders, R.
  In Manning-Sanders, R. A book of ghosts & goblins p101-02   **398.2**

Beauty and the beast
  Beauty and the beast
    In Rackham, A. comp. Arthur Rackham Fairy book p49-65   **398.2**
  Berger, T. The beauty & the beast
    In Berger, T. Black fairy tales p55-67 **398.2**
  Haviland, V. Beauty and the beast
    In Haviland, V. Favorite fairy tales told in France p38-59   **398.2**
  Le Prince de Beaumont, M. Beauty and the beast
    In Opie, I. ed. The classic fairy tales p139-50   **398.2**
    In Perrault, C. Perrault's Complete fairy tales p115-34   **398.2**
  Pearce, P. Beauty and the beast   **398.2**
  Villeneuve, Madame de. Beauty and the beast
    In Arbuthnot, M. H. comp. The Arbuthnot Anthology of children's literature p216-24   **808.8**
    In Arbuthnot, M. H. comp. Time for old magic p93-102   **398.2**

In Johnson, E. ed. Anthology of children's literature p173-81   **808.8**
In Lang, A. ed. The blue fairy book p100-19   **398.2**

Beauty and the beast; puppet play. Jagendorf, M.
  In Jagendorf, M. Penny puppets, penny theatre, and penny plays p157-67   **791.5**

Beauty and the horns. Fillmore, P.
  In Fillmore, P. The laughing prince p27-50   **398.2**

The **beauty** of birth. Portal, C.   **612.6**

Beauty of form and beauty of mind
  Andersen, H. C. "Lovely"
    In Andersen, H. C. The complete fairy tales and stories p650-56   **S C**

The **beauty** of the Lily. Olcott, F. J.
  In Harper, W. comp. Easter chimes p39-43   **394.2**

Beaver, Tony
  See pages in the following books:
  Carmer, C. comp. America sings p140-44 (5-7)   **784.4**
  Malcolmson, A. Yankee Doodle's cousins p109-14 (4-7)   **398.2**

The **beaver** pond. Tresselt, A.   **574.92**

Beaver valley. Edmonds, W. D.   **Fic**

Beavers
  Eberle, I. Beavers live here (1-3)   **599**
  Hurd, E. T. The mother beaver (k-2)   **599**
  Tresselt, A. The beaver pond (k-3)   **574.92**
  See also pages in the following books:
  Cartwright, S. Animal homes p34-42 (1-3)   **591.5**
  Mason, G. F. Animal homes p52-57 (4-7)   **591.5**
  Shuttlesworth, D. E. The story of rodents p67-76 (4-6)   **599**

Stories
  Edmonds, W. D. Beaver valley (4-6)   **Fic**

Beavers live here. Eberle, I.   **599**

Because of a tree. Milne, L. J.   **582**

Bechdolt, Jack
  Paul Revere rides again
    In Cavanah, F. ed. Holiday roundup p126-31   **394.2**

Bechstein, Ludwig
  Wiesner, W. Hansel and Gretel: a shadow puppet picture book   **791.5**

Bechtel, Louise Seaman
  Books in search of children   **028.5**

Bechuanaland. See Botswana

Beck, Barbara L.
  The first book of fruits (4-6)   **634**
  The first book of the ancient Maya (5-7)   **970.3**
  The first book of the Aztecs (4-6)   **970.3**
  The first book of the Incas (4-7)   **980.3**
  The Pilgrims of Plymouth (5-7)   **974.4**
  Vegetables (4-6)   **581.6**

Beck, Charles
  (illus.) Beckhard, A. J. Albert Einstein   **92**

Beck, Margaret V.
  Library skills   **028.7**

Bell, Thelma Harrington
Black Face
  In Gruenberg, S. M. ed. Favorite stories old
    and new p169-76   **808.8**
Snow (3-6)   **551.5**
Bell, Willis E.
(illus.) Sutherland, E. Playtime in Africa
                                             916.67
The **bell.** Andersen, H. C.
  In Andersen, H. C. The complete fairy tales
    and stories p275-79   **S C**
The **bell** deep. Andersen, H. C.
  In Andersen, H. C. The complete fairy tales
    and stories p588-91   **S C**
A **bell** for Ursli. Chönz, S.   **E**
The **bell** ringer of Pinsk. Kelly, E. P.
  In Harper, W. comp. Merry Christmas to
    you p68-86   **394.2**
  In Johnson, L. S. ed. Christmas stories
    round the world p61-71   **394.2**
Bella, Ahmed Ben, President Algeria. See Ben
  Bella, Ahmed, President Algeria
Bellah, Melanie
The blue toadstool
  In Kamerman, S. E. ed. Little plays for
    little players p147-52   **812.08**
Bellairs, John
The house with a clock in its walls (5-7) **Fic**
Bellamy, Charles
  See pages in the following book:
Whipple, A. B. C. Famous pirates of the
    New World p128-30 (5-7)   **910.4**
Bealleau Wood, Battle of, 1918
  See pages in the following book:
Leckie, R. Great American battles p101-16
    (5-7)   **973**
Bellerophon
Turska, K. Pegasus (2-4)   **292**
  See also pages in the following book:
Gates, D. The warrior goddess: Athena p50-
    61 (4-7)   **292**
Bellerophontes. See Bellerophon
Belloc, Hilaire
The bad child's book of beasts (1-4)   **821**
More beasts for worse children (1-4)   **821**
About
  See pages in the following book:
Benét, L. Famous poets for young people
    p91-97 (5-7)   **920**
Bells
Yolen, J. Ring out! (5-7)   **789**
Poetry
  See pages in the following book:
Yolen, J. Ring out! p113-22 (5-7)   **789**
Bells and grass. De La Mare, W.   **821**
Belmont antics. Jagendorf, M. A.
  In Jagendorf, M. A. Noodlehead stories
    from around the world p229-33
                                             398.2
Belpré, Pura
Dance of the animals (k-3)   **398.2**
Once in Puerto Rico (3-6)   **398.2**
Contents: The land of brave men; The legend of
the Royal Palm; Guaní; The legend of the humming-
bird; Amapola and the butterfly; Iviahoca; Yuisa and

Pedro Mexias; The legend of the Ceiba of Ponce; The
little blue light; The chapel on Cristo Street; The cistern of San Cristobal; The Rogativa; The miracle of
Hormigueros; Pedro Animala and the carrao bird; The
stone dog; The parrot who wouldn't say Cataño; Pablo
and the pirate's ghost

Oté (1-4)   **398.2**
Perez and Martina (1-4)   **398.2**
Santiago   **E**
The Three Magi
  In Eaton, A. T. comp. The animals' Christ-
    mas p62-71   **394.2**
The tiger and the rabbit, and other tales (4-6)
                                             398.2
Contents: The tiger and the rabbit; Nangato; The
earrings; The bed; The Jurga; The wolf, the fox, and
the jug of honey; Juan Bobo; La Hormiguita; The
shepherd and the princess; Señor Billy Goat; Casi
Lampu'a Lentemué; The gluttonous wife; The Alba-
haca plant; The dance of the animals; The Three
Magi; The cat, the mountain goat, and the fox; The
three petitions; The three figs

New York. Public Library. Libros en español
                                             028.52
Belting, Natalia
Calendar moon (4-7)   **398.2**
Christmas folk (2-5)   **394.2**
(comp.) Our fathers had powerful songs (3-6)
                                             897
The stars are silver reindeer (4-7)   **398.2**
The sun is a golden earring (4-7)   **398.2**
Whirlwind is a ghost dancing (3-6)   **398.2**
Bemelmans, Ludwig
Caldecott Medal acceptance paper
  In Miller, B. M. ed. Caldecott Medal
    books: 1938-1957 p255-59   **028.5**
Christmas Eve in the Tyrol
  In Association for Childhood Education In-
    ternational. Told under the Christmas
    tree p200-05   **808.8**
The golden basket
  In Martignoni, M. E. ed. The illustrated
    treasury of children's literature p252-
    54   **808.8**
Madeline   **E**
Madeline and the bad hat   **E**
Madeline and the gypsies   **E**
Madeline in London   **E**
Madeline's rescue   **E**
(illus.) Leaf, M. Noodle   **E**
About
  See pages in the following books:
Hoffman, M. ed. Authors and illustrators of
    children's books p6-18   **028.5**
Miller, B. M. ed. Caldecott Medal books:
    1938-1957 p260-65   **028.5**
Smaridge, N. Famous author-illustrators for
    young people p70-77 (5-7)   **920**
Ben and me. Lawson, R.   **Fic**
Ben and me; excerpt. Lawson, R.
  In Arbuthnot, M. H. comp. The Arbuthnot
    Anthology of children's literature
    p571-73   **808.8**
Benagh, Christine L. See Fletcher, Christine
Benary-Isbert, Margot
The Ark (5-7)   **Fic**
Blue mystery (5-7)   **Fic**
Spring
  In Johnson, E. ed. Anthology of children's
    literature p885-89   **808.8**
The wicked enchantment (5-7)   **Fic**

Ben Bella, Ahmed, President Algeria
See pages in the following book:
Spencer, W. The land and people of Algeria
p92-95 (5-7)   **916.5**

Benchley, Nathaniel
The deep dives of Stanley Whale   **E**
Feldman Fieldmouse (3-5)   **Fic**
A ghost named Fred   **E**
Oscar Otter   **E**
Sam the Minuteman   **E**
The several tricks of Edgar Dolphin   **E**
Small Wolf   **E**
The strange disappearance of Arthur Cluck
    E

Bendick, Jeanne
Adaptation (2-4)   **574.5**
Electronics for young people (5-7)   **621.381**
The first book of automobiles (3-5)   **629.22**
The first book of time (4-6)   **529**
How to make a cloud (1-3)   **551.5**
The human senses (3-5)   **612**
Living things (3-5)   **574**
Mathematics illustrated dictionary (4-7) **510.3**
Measuring (3-5)   **389**
Motion and gravity (3-5)   **531**
Names, sets and numbers (2-5)   **511**
Observation (2-4)   **153.7**
The shape of the earth (4-6)   **551**
Shapes (2-4)   **516**
Space and time (2-4)   **530.1**
Take a number (4-6)   **513**
What to do (5-7)   **395**
Why can't I? (1-4)   **591.5**
Why things work (2-4)   **531**
(illus.) Blough, G. O. Bird watchers and bird
feeders   **598.2**
(illus.) Brewster, B. Baseball   **796.357**

Bendick, Karen
(illus.) Bendick, J. Why things work   **531**

Beneath the hill. Curry, J. L.   **Fic**

Benedict, Lois Trimble
Thanksgiving in Old Jerusalem
In Luckhardt, M. C. comp. Thanksgiving
p199-208   **394.2**

Benes, Edvard, President Czechoslovak Republic
See pages in the following book:
Hall, E. The land and people of Czechoslovakia p105-10 (5-7)   **914.37**

Benét, Laura
Famous poets for young people (5-7)   **920**
Famous storytellers for young people (5-7)
    920

Benét, Rosemary
A book of Americans (5-7)   **811**
About
See pages in the following book:
Benét, L. Famous poets for young people
p129-34 (5-7)   **920**

Benét, Stephen Vincent
(jt. auth.) Benét, R. A book of Americans **811**
About
See pages in the following book:
Benét, L. Famous poets for young people
p129-34 (5-7)   **920**

Benet, Sula
(jt. comp.) Withers, C. comp. The American

riddle book   **398.6**
(jt. comp.) Withers, C. comp. Riddles of many
lands   **398.6**

Benét, William Rose
(comp.) Poems for youth (6-7)   **811.08**
(ed.) The Reader's encyclopedia. See The
Reader's encyclopedia   **803**

Benevolent frog
Aulnoy, Mme d'. The friendly frog
In Perrault, C. Perrault's Complete fairy
tales p135-62   **398.2**

Benghazi, Libya
See pages in the following book:
Copeland, P. W. The land and people of
Libya p94-102 (5-7)   **916.1**

Ben-Gurion, David
See pages in the following book:
Hoffman, G. The land and people of Israel
p110-16 (5-7)   **915.694**

Benito the faithful. Sechrist, E. H.
In Sechrist, E. H. ed. It's time for story
hour p213-21   **372.6**
In Sechrist, E. H. Once in the first times
p156-67   **398.2**

Benjamin, Bennie
See pages in the following book:
Hughes, L. Famous Negro music makers
p133-38 (5-7)   **920**

Benjamin & Tulip. Wells, R.   **E**

Benjamin West and his cat Grimalkin. Henry, M.   **92**

Benjamin's 365 birthdays. Barrett, J.   **E**

Benjie. Lexau, J. M.   **E**

Benjie on his own. Lexau, J. M.   **E**

Benjie's hat. Hunt, M. L.
In Association for Childhood Education International. Told under the Stars and
Stripes p71-82   **S C**

Benjy's dog house. Graham, M. B.   **E**

Bennett, A. W.
The pram
In Hitchcock, A. comp. Alfred Hitchcock's
Supernatural tales of terror and suspense p146-55   **S C**

Bennett, Anna Elizabeth
Little witch (3-5)   **Fic**
Witch wood
In Hoke, H. ed. Spooks, spooks, spooks
p13-20   **S C**

Bennett, Dorothy B.
The Christmas spirit
In Hitchcock, A. comp. Alfred Hitchcock's
Supernatural tales of terror and suspense p30-37   **S C**

Bennett, Helen Cott
Rumpelstiltskin
In Burack, A. S. ed. One hundred plays
for children p587-95   **808.82**
Sleeping Beauty
In Burack, A. S. ed. One hundred plays for
children p596-604   **808.82**

Bennett, Rainey
The secret hiding place   **E**

Bennett, Richard
(illus.) Andersen, H. C. It's perfectly true, and
other stories   **S C**

Better softball for boys and girls. Sullivan, G.
796.357

Better swimming and diving for boys and girls.
Sullivan, G. 797.2

Better table tennis for boys and girls. Sullivan, G. 796.34

Better tennis for boys and girls. Hopman, H.
796.34

Betts, Ethel Franklin
(illus.) Burnett, F. H. A little princess   **Fic**

Between sea and sky. Boyesen, H. H.
In A St Nicholas anthology p148-58 810.8

Between the devil and the sea; the life of James
Forten. Johnston, B. A. 92

Bevans, Michael H.
(illus.) Kieran, J. An introduction to trees **582**

Beverages
See pages in the following books:
Better Homes and Gardens Junior cook book
p10-17 (4-7) **641.5**
Camp Fire Girls Mother daughter cookbook
p173-82 (4-7) **641.5**
Ellison, V. H. The Pooh get-well book p21-
32 (2-5) **790.19**
Girl Scouts of the United States of America.
Girl Scout cookbook p31-35 (4-7) **641.5**

Bewley, Sheila
(illus.) Sheffield, M. Where do babies come
from? **612.6**

Beyond the Clapping Mountains. Gillham, C. E.
398.2

Bhimsa, the dancing bear; excerpt. Weston, C.
In Ward, W. ed. Stories to dramatize p183-
87 **372.6**

Bialik, Kayyim Nahman
The bee
In Hardendorff, J. B. ed. Just one more
p150-58 **372.6**

Bianco, Margery Williams
The apple tree
In Harper, W. comp. Easter chimes p135-
49 **394.2**
In Sechrist, E. H. ed. It's time for Easter
p209-20 **394.2**
The baker's daughter
In Sechrist, E. H. ed. It's time for story
hour p29-35 **372.6**
How toys become real
In Martignoni, M. E. ed. The illustrated
treasury of children's literature p368-
70 **808.8**
The hurdy-gurdy man
In Colwell, E. ed. A storyteller's choice
p158-68 **372.6**
In Ward, W. ed. Stories to dramatize p169-
76 **372.6**
The little guest
In Sechrist, E. H. ed. It's time for Christ-
mas p243-50 **394.2**
The little wooden doll (2-4) **Fic**
Mr A and Mr P
In Gruenberg, S. M. ed. Favorite stories
old and new p495-99 **808.8**
The Saddler's Horse
In Association for Childhood Education In-
ternational. Told under the magic
umbrella p119-26 **S C**

(jt. auth.) Bowman, J. C. Tales from a Fin-
nish tupa **398.2**
For another title by this author see
Williams, Margery

Bianco, Pamela
(illus.) Bianco, M. W. The little wooden doll
Fic

Bible, Charles
(illus.) Giovanni, N. Spin a soft Black song
811

Bible
The Holy Bible [King James Bible] **220.5**
The Holy Bible [Rev. standard. Reference ed]
220.5

Bible. Selections
Animals of the Bible (1-4) **220.8**
Bible selections
In Johnson, E. ed. Anthology of children's
literature p569-83 **808.8**
A first Bible (4-7) **220.5**
Small rain (k-3) **220.5**
Wings of the morning (1-4) **220.5**

Bible (as subject)
See pages in the following book:
The World's great religions. Special edition
for young readers p139-43, 163-69 (5-7)
291

Animals
See Bible—Natural history

Biography
Northcott, C. People of the Bible (5-7) **220.9**

Birds
See Bible—Natural history

Dictionaries
Northcott, C. Bible encyclopedia for children
(5-7) **220.3**
Young readers dictionary of the Bible **220.3**

Flowers
See Bible—Natural history

Geography
See pages in the following book:
Farb, P. The land, wildlife, and peoples of
the Bible p 1-13 (5-7) **220.8**

Natural history
Bible. Selections. Animals of the Bible (1-4)
220.8
Farb, P. The land, wildlife, and peoples of
the Bible (5-7) **220.8**

Plants
See Bible—Natural history

Stories
Gwynne, J. H. The rainbow book of Bible
stories (4-7) **220.9**
Jones, M. A. Bible stories for children (3-6)
220.9
Northcott, C. People of the Bible (5-7) **220.9**
Peale, N. V. Bible stories (5-7) **220.9**
Turner, P. Brian Wildsmith's Illustrated Bible
stories (2-6) **220.9**
See also pages in the following book:
Gruenberg, S. M. ed. Favorite stories old and
new p425-47 **808.8**

Zoology
See Bible—Natural history

The **big** day. Budney, B.
 In Gruenberg, S. M. comp. Let's hear a
  story p34-37   **808.8**

The **Big** Dipper. Branley, F. M. **523.8**

Big feet of the Empress Tu Chin. Carpenter, F.
 In Carpenter, F. Tales of a Chinese grandmother p81-88   **398.2**

Big Fellow's first job. Baruch, D. W.
 In Gruenberg, S. M. ed. Favorite stories
  old and new p78-82   **808.8**

Big-Foot Wallace. See Wallace, William Alexander Anderson

Big Fraid and Little Fraid. Leach, M.
 In Leach, M. The thing at the foot of
  the bed, and other scary tales p27-29   **S C**

Big Jack and Little Jack
 In Chase, R. ed. The Jack tales p67-75
            398.2

Big Kihuo and Little Kihuo. Baumann, H.
 In Baumann, H. The stolen fire p46-52
            398.2

Big mudhole. Credle, E.
 In Credle, E. Tall tales from the high hills,
  and other stories p9-15   **398.2**

Big Paul Bunyan. Thane, E.
 In Kamerman, S. E. ed. Dramatized folk
  tales of the world p514-25 **812.08**

The **big** pile of dirt. Clymer, E.   **Fic**

The **big** rain. Françoise   **E**

Big Red. Kjelgaard, J.   **Fic**

The **big** shoo. Boiko, C.
 In Boiko, C. Children's plays for creative
  actors p45-54   **812**

Big Sixteen. Jagendorf, M. A.
 In Jagendorf, M. A. Folk stories of the
  South p247-49   **398.2**

The **big** snow. Hader, B.   **E**

Big star fallin' mama. Jones, H. **920**

Big Susan. Jones, E. O.   **Fic**

Big talk. Schlein, M.
 In Gruenberg, S. M. comp. Let's hear a
  story p42-43   **808.8**

Big tracks, little tracks. Branley, F. M. **591.5**

Big tree. Buff, M.   **582**

Big tree. Hardy, M.
 In Association for Childhood Education
  International. Told under the blue
  umbrella p134-39   **S C**

The **big** wave. Buck, P. S.   **Fic**

Bigelow, Edward
 (illus.) Hurd, E. T. Come with me to nursery
  school   **372.21**

Bigfoot. See Sasquatch

Bigger and smaller. Froman, R. **513**

Biggers, John
 (illus.) Graham, L. B. I, Momolu **Fic**

The **biggest** bear. Ward, L.   **E**

The **biggest** house in the world. Lionni, L. **E**

Biggs, Louise
 The key to understanding
  In Kamerman, S. E. ed. Fifty plays for
   junior actors p35-44   **812.08**

Bigham, Madge
 Why the ivy is always green
  In Sechrist, E. H. ed. It's time for Easter
   p184-88   **394.2**

The **bighorn** sheep. Hiser, I. S. **599**

Bike-ways (101 things to do with a bike).
 Frankel, L.   **796.6**

Bikes. Henkel, S. C.   **629.22**

Bileck, Marvin
 (jt. auth.) Scheer, J. Rain makes applesauce
            E

Bilingual books
Bibliography
See pages in the following book:
National Council of Teachers of English. Adventuring with books p345-47 **028.52**

French-English
Brunhoff, L. de. Babar's French lessons (1-3)
            448
Colyer, P. comp. I can read French (2-4) **448**
Eastman, P. D. Are you my mother? **E**
Gurney, N. The king, the mice and the
 cheese   **E**
The House that Jack built (1-4) **398.8**
Joslin, S. There is a dragon in my bed (3-6)
            448
Mother Goose. Rimes de la Mère Oie. Mother
 Goose rhymes (3-5)   **398.8**
Rockwell, A. ed. Savez-vous planter les
 choux? and other French songs (3-6) **784.4**
Seuss, Dr. The cat in the hat   **E**

Italian-English
Joslin, S. Spaghetti for breakfast (3-6) **458**

Spanish-English
Brunhoff, L. de. Babar's Spanish lessons
 (1-3)   **468**
Dana, D. The elephant and his secret **E**
Du Bois, W. P. The hare and the tortoise &
 The tortoise and the hare (1-4) **398.2**
Eastman, P. D. Are you my mother? **E**
Gurney, N. The king, the mice and the cheese
            E
Hubp, L. B. ed. ¿Qué será? What can it be?
 (3-6)   **398.6**
Joslin, S. There is a bull on my balcony
 (2-5)   **468**
Lenski, L. Papa Small   **E**
Mi diccionario ilustrado   **463**
Ritchie, B. Ramón makes a trade (3-5) **Fic**
Seuss, Dr. The cat in the hat   **E**
The Snow and the sun (1-4) **398.8**
Yurchenco, H. ed. A fiesta of folk songs from
 Spain and Latin America (2-6) **784.7**

Bill is with me now. Leach, M.
 In Leach, M. Whistle in the graveyard p66-67   **398.2**

Bill of Rights. See United States. Constitution—Amendments

Billboards. See signs and signboards

Billington, Elizabeth T.
 Understanding ecology (5-7) **574.5**

Billington, John
Fiction
Bulla, C. R. John Billington, friend of
 Squanto (2-4)   **Fic**

A **billion** for Boris. Rodgers, M.   **Fic**

Billy and Blaze. Anderson, C. W.   **E**

Billy Beg and the bull
Billy Beg and his bull
  In Hutchinson, V. S. ed. Chimney corner
    fairytales p167-83   **398.2**
Haviland, V. Billy Beg and the bull
  In Haviland, V. Favorite fairy tales told in
    Ireland p39-60   **398.2**
MacManus, S. Billy Beg and the bull
  In Fenner, P. R. comp. Giants & witches
    and a dragon or two p64-78   **398.2**
  In Johnson, E. ed. Anthology of children's
    literature p210-14   **808.8**
  In Ross, E. S. ed. The lost half-hour p137-
    51   **372.6**

Billy Boy (Folk song)
Billy Boy (k-3)   **784.4**

The **billy** goat and the king. Lang, A.
  In Farjeon, E. ed. A cavalcade of queens
    p63-68   **808.8**

The **Billy** goat and the sheep
  In Bloch, M. H. ed. Ukrainian folk tales
    p19-23   **398.2**

Billy the kid. Untermeyer, L.
  In Untermeyer, L. Tales from the ballet
    p20-23   **792.8**

Bilyk, Ivan. See Rudchenko, Ivan

Bimby. Burchard, P.   **Fic**

Binding of books. See Bookbinding

Binky brothers and the Fearless Four. Lawrence, J.   **E**

Binky brothers, detectives. Lawrence, J.   **E**

Binnorie
  In Jacobs, J. ed. English folk and fairy tales
    p43-47   **398.2**

Binns, Archie
Sea pup (4-7)   **Fic**

Binstock, Ruth Atlas
Bobby's best Hanukkah
  In Association for Childhood Education In-
    ternational. Told under the Christmas
    tree p241-53   **808.8**

Binzen, Bill
Miguel's Mountain   **E**

Bio-bibliography. See Authors; names of general
subjects with the subdivision Bio-bibliography, e.g. American literature—Bio-bibliography

Biogeography. See Geographical distribution of
animals and plants

Biographical dictionary, Webster's   **920.03**

Biography
McNeer, M. Armed with courage (4-6)   **920**
Sechrist, E. H. It's time for brotherhood (5-7)
                   301.11
See also pages in the following books:
Arbuthnot, M. H. comp. The Arbuthnot An-
  thology of children's literature p776-852
                   808.8
Johnson, E. ed. Anthology of children's litera-
  ture p1043-99   **808.8**
    See also names of classes of persons
    (e.g. Authors); names of countries, cities,
    etc. and special subjects with the subdivi-
    sion Biography (e.g. United States—Biogra-

phy; Woman—Biography); and names of
persons for biographies of individuals
Bibliography
Kerr, L. J. comp. Who's where in books
                   016.92
Metzner, S. World history in juvenile books
                   016.9
Nicholsen, M. E. People in books   **920.01**
Silverman, J. comp. An index to young read-
  ers' collective biographies   **920.01**
See also pages in the following books:
Feminists on Children's Media. Little Miss
  Muffet fights back p37-53   **028.52**
National Council of Teachers of English. Ad-
  venturing with books p196-218   **028.52**
Dictionaries
Current biography yearbook   **920.03**
Webster's Biographical dictionary   **920.03**
Indexes
Kerr, L. J. comp. Who's where in books
                   016.92
Nicholsen, M. E. People in books   **920.01**
Silverman, J. comp. An index to young read-
  ers' collective biographies   **920.01**
United States
See United States—Biography

Biography of a leaf. Davis, B.   **581**

Biography of a rhino. Hopf, A. L.   **599**

Biography of an atom. Bronowski, J.   **541**

Biological clocks. See Periodicity

Biological control of pests. See Pest control—
Biological control

Biologists
Latham, J. L. Rachel Carson: who loved the
  sea (3-5)   **92**
Sterling, P. Sea and earth; the life of Rachel
  Carson (6-7)   **92**

Biology
Bendick, J. Living things (3-5)   **574**
Peattie, D. C. The rainbow book of nature
  (5-7)   **574**
Selsam, M. E. Is this a baby dinosaur? (k-3)
                   574
    See also Adaptation (Biology); Anatomy;
  Botany; Cells; Embryology; Evolution;
  Freshwater biology; Genetics; Life (Biol-
  ogy; Marine biology; Microbiology; Natu-
  ral history; Physiology; Reproduction; Zo-
  ology
Ecology
See Ecology

Biology, Economic. See Zoology, Economic

Biology, Marine. See Marine biology

Biology as a profession
  See pages in the following book:
Berger, M. Oceanography lab p63-70 (4-6)
                   551.4

Bioluminescence
Harris, L. D. Flash (1-3)   **595.7**

Birch, Cyril
A shiver of ghosts
  In Mayne, W. ed. Ghosts p168-83   **820.8**

Birch, Reginald
(illus.) Untermeyer, L. ed. Rainbow in the sky
                   821.08

Birch trees of Temiskamingue. Hooke, H. M.
In Hooke, H. M. Thunder in the mountains
p111-22 **398.2**

Bird. See Birds

Bird feeders and shelters you can make. Pettit,
T. S. **745.59**

Bird houses
Pettit, T. S. Bird feeders and shelters you can
make (3-6) **745.59**

Bird in the hand. Niven, L.
In Silverberg, B. ed. Phoenix feathers p151-
76 **S C**

Bird in the linden tree. Pyle, H.
In Pyle, H. Pepper & salt p82-95 **398.2**

Bird of popular song
Andersen, H. C. The songbird of the people
In Andersen, H. C. The complete fairy tales
and stories p847-50 **S C**

The **bird** of seven colors. Alegría, R. E.
In Alegría, R. E. The three wishes p25-30
398.2

Bird of the Golden Land. O'Faolain, E.
In O'Faolain, E. Irish sagas and folktales
p219-31 **398.2**

The **bird** of time. Yolen, J. **E**

The **bird** Phoenix. Andersen, H. C.
In Andersen, H. C. The complete fairy tales
and stories p374-75 **S C**

Bird song
Gans, R. Bird talk (k-3) **598.2**
See also pages in the following books:
Mason, G. F. Animal sounds p10-47 (4-7)
591.5
Selsam, M. E. The language of animals p41-
58 (5-7) **591.5**

Bird songs. Reed, G. comp. **821.08**

Bird talk. Gans, R. **598.2**

The **bird** that would not stay dead. Carpenter, F.
In Carpenter, F. African wonder tales
p179-86 **398.2**

The **Bird**, the mouse, and the sausage
In Ginsburg, M. ed. The lazies p46-48
398.2
See also Mouse, the bird, and the sausage

Bird watchers and bird feeders. Blough, G. O.
598.2

Bird watching. See Birds

The **bird** who spoke three times. Sawyer, R.
In Sawyer, R. The way of the storyteller
p297-304 **372.6**

Birdbanding
See pages in the following books:
Blough, G. O. Bird watchers and bird feeders
p31-37 (1-3) **598.2**
Laycock, G. Wild travelers p91-92 (5-7) **591.5**

Birds
Anderson, J. M. The changing world of birds
(6-7) **598.2**
Blough, G. O. Bird watchers and bird feeders
(1-3) **598.2**
Earle, O. L. Birds and their beaks (3-6) **598.2**
Earle, O. L. Birds and their nests (3-6) **598.2**
Gans, R. Birds at night (k-2) **598.2**
Gans, R. Birds eat and eat and eat (k-2) **598.2**

George, J. C. The moon of the winter bird
(3-5) **598.2**
Hudson, R. G. Nature's nursery: baby birds
(4-7) **598.2**
Kaufmann, J. Birds in flight (5-7) **598.2**
Peterson, R. T. How to know the birds **598.2**
Selsam, M. E. A first look at birds (1-3) **598.2**
Selsam, M. E. Tony's birds (k-2) **598.2**
Zim, H. S. Birds **598.2**

See also pages in the following books:
Batten, M. The tropical forest p86-96 (5-7)
574.5
Berrill, J. Wonders of animal migration p7-35
(5-7) **591.5**
Boy Scouts of America. Fieldbook p448-63
369.43
Brown, V. How to make a miniature zoo
p165-84 (5-7) **579**
Buck, M. W. Small pets from woods and
fields p66-70 (4-7) **639**
Buck, M. W. Where they go in winter p43-
56 (3-6) **591.5**
Chrystie, F. N. Pets p126-38 (4-7) **636.08**
Cooper, E. K. Science in your own back yard
p133-47 (5-7) **500.9**
The Doubleday Nature encyclopedia p62-71
(3-6) **500.9**
Earle, O. L. Scavengers p34-[63] (3-5) **591.5**
Ellison, V. H. The Pooh get-well book p46-
52 (2-5) **790.1**
Hyde, M. O. Animal clocks and compasses
p36-55 (5-7) **591.5**
Mason, G. F. Animal baggage p18-21, 84-91
(4-7) **591.5**
Mason, G. F. Animal tools p54-63 (4-7) **591.4**
Mason, G. F. The wildlife of North America
p39-52 (5-7) **639**
Parker, B. M. The new Golden Treasury of
natural history p168-201 (5-7) **500.9**
Pringle, L. P. ed. Discovering the outdoors
p18-23 (4-7) **574**
Rounds, G. Wildlife at your doorstep p25-35
(4-7) **591.5**
Sarasy, P. Winter-sleepers p36-39 (3-5) **591.5**
Selsam, M. E. How animals live together
p24-38 (5-7) **591.5**
Shuttlesworth, D. E. Animals that frighten
people p102-09 (5-7) **591.5**
Silverstein, A. Animal invaders p13-32 (4-7)
591.5
Sterling, D. Fall is here! p40-66 (4-6) **500.9**
Zim, H. S. Seashores p147-53 (5-7) **574.92**
See also Birds of prey; Cage birds;
State birds; Water birds; and names of
birds, e.g. Sparrows

Antarctic regions
See pages in the following book:
Icenhower, J. B. The first book of the Antarc-
tic p58-63 (4-6) **919.8**

Banding
See Birdbanding

Eggs and nests
Earle, O. L. Birds and their nests (3-6) **598.2**
Gans, R. It's nesting time (k-2) **598.2**
Vevers, G. Birds and their nests (1-4) **598.2**

See also pages in the following books:
Hudson, R. G. Nature's nursery: baby birds
p105-35 (4-7) **598.2**

Birds—Eggs and nests—*Continued*

Mason, G. F. Animal habits p76-85 (4-7)
591.5

Villiard, P. Birds as pets p101-06 (5-7) 636.6

Everglades National Park

See pages in the following book:

National Geographic Society. The new America's wonderlands p338-51   917.3

Flight

See Flight

Iceland

See pages in the following book:

Berry, E. The land and people of Iceland p83-87 (5-7)   914.91

Marking

See Birdbanding

Migration

Kaufmann, J. Robins fly north, robins fly south (3-5)   598.2

Laycock, G. Wild travelers (5-7)   591.5

See also pages in the following book:

Frisch, O. von. Animal migration p57-74 (6-7)   591.5

New Zealand

See pages in the following book:

Day, B. Life on a lost continent p15-38, 50-66, 79-101 (5-7)   500.9

North America

Audubon, J. J. The birds of America   598.2

Dugdale, V. Album of North American birds (4-6)   598.2

Kieran, J. An introduction to birds   598.2

National Geographic Society. Song and garden birds of North America   598.2

Peterson, R. T. A field guide to the birds
598.2

Pictorial works

Audubon, J. J. The birds of America   598.2

National Geographic Society. Song and garden birds of North America   598.2

Wildsmith, B. Brian Wildsmith's Birds   E

Poetry

Fisher, A. Feathered ones and furry (k-3)
811

Lear, E. The pelican chorus (k-3)   821

Reed, G. comp. Bird songs (5-7)   821.08

See also pages in the following books:

Brewton, J. E. comp. Under the tent of the sky p83-95 (3-7)   808.81

Cole, W. comp. A book of animal poems p9-64 (5-7)   821.08

Ferris, H. ed. Favorite poems, old and new p279-97 (4-6)   808.81

Huffard, G. T. comp. My poetry book p212-42 (5-7)   821.08

Larrick, N. ed. Piping down the valleys wild p127-38   808.81

Sechrist, E. H. ed. One thousand poems for children p105-17, 403-34   821.08

Untermeyer, L. ed. The Golden Treasury of poetry p58-67   821.08

Untermeyer, L. ed. Rainbow in the sky p217-29 (k-4)   821.08

Protection

Stoutenburg, A. A vanishing thunder (5-7)
598.2

See also pages in the following book:

McCoy, J. J. Nature sleuths p65-80, 94-110 (5-7)   639

Song

See Bird song

South America

See pages in the following book:

Shuttlesworth, D. E. The wildlife of South America p57-66 (5-7)   591.9

Stories

Anderson, L. Mr Biddle and the birds   E

Eastman, P. D. Are you my mother?   E

George, J. L. Dipper of Copper Creek (4-6)
Fic

Holl, A. The remarkable egg   E

Lionni, L. Inch by inch   E

Lionni, L. Tico and the golden wings   E

United States

See pages in the following book:

Clement, R. C. Hammond Nature atlas of America p140-75   500.9

Uruguay

See pages in the following book:

Dobler, L. The land and people of Uruguay p20-25 (5-7)   918.95

The West

Peterson, R. T. A field guide to Western birds   598.2

Birds, Aquatic. *See* Water birds

Birds, Extinct

Stoutenburg, A. A vanishing thunder (5-7)
598.2

Birds, Rare. *See* Rare birds

The **birds** and the beasts were there. Cole, W.
821.08

Birds and their beaks. Earle, O. L.   598.2

Birds and their nests. Earle, O. L.   598.2

Birds and their nests. Vevers, G.   598.2

Birds as pets. Villiard, P.   636.6

Birds at night. Gans, R.   598.2

The **Birds'** Christmas Carol. Wiggin, K. D.   **Fic**

The **Birds'** Christmas Carol; play. Olfson, L.
In Kamerman, S. E. ed. A treasury of Christmas plays p483-95   812.08

Birds eat and eat and eat. Gans, R.   598.2

Birds' eggs. *See* Birds—Eggs and nests

Birds, frogs, and moonlight. Cassedy, S. comp.
895.6

Birds in flight. Kaufmann, J.   598.2

Birds' nests. *See* Birds—Eggs and nests

The **birds** of America. Audubon, J. J.   598.2

Birds of prey

Hogner, D. C. Birds of prey (4-6)   598.2

See also names of birds of prey, e.g. Eagles

Birmingham, Lloyd

(illus.) Keen, M. L. How it works   600

(illus.) Milgrom, H. Understanding weather
551.6

The **black** thing. L'Engle, M.
  In Hoke, H. ed. Spooks, spooks, spooks
    p63-80   **S C**

Black within and red without. Morrison, L.
  comp.   **398.6**

Black women of valor. Burt, O. W.   **920**

Blackbeard. See Teach, Edward

Blackbeard's treasure. Leach, M.
  In Leach, M. Whistle in the graveyard
    p45-46   **398.2**

The **blackbird's** song. Picard, B. L.
  In Picard, B. L. The faun and the wood-
    cutter's daughter p193-205   **S C**

Blackboard bear. Alexander, M.   **E**

Blackburn, G. Meredith
  (jt. comp.) Brewton, J. E. comp. Index to
    poetry for children and young people,
    1964-1969   **808.81**
  (jt. comp.) Brewton, S. comp. My tang's
    tungled and other ridiculous situations
                                              821.08

Blackfoot Indians. See Siksika Indians

Blackmail
  In DeRoin, N. ed. Jataka tales p16-19
                                              398.2

Blacks (United States) See Negroes

The **blacksmith** and the devil. Manning-San-
  ders, R.
  In Manning-Sanders, R. A book of devils
    and demons p76-86   **398.2**
  See also Smith and the devil

The **Blacksmith** they were afraid to receive in
  hell
  In Undset, S. ed. True and untrue, and
    other Norse tales p137-46   **398.2**
  See also Smith and the devil

The **blacksmiths.** Courlander, H.
  In Courlander, H. The piece of fire, and
    other Haitian tales p84-88   **398.2**

The **blacksmith's** dilemma. Arnott, K.
  In Arnott, K. African myths and legends
    p119-23   **398.2**

Blacksmith's wife of Yarrowfoot
  Olcott, F. J. The witch's shoes
  In Harper, W. comp. Ghosts and goblins
    p192-94   **394.2**
  In Hoke, H. ed. Witches, witches, witches
    p219-20   **808.8**

The **Blackstairs** Mountains. Manning-Sanders, R.
  In Manning-Sanders, R. A book of witches
    p123-27   **398.2**

Blackwell, Elizabeth
  Clapp, P. Dr Elizabeth (4-7)   **92**
    Poetry
  See pages in the following book:
  Merriam, E. Independent voices p11-18 (5-7)
                                              811

Blackwood, Algernon
  Transition
  In Mayne, W. ed. Ghosts p26-32   **820.8**

Blackwood, Lord Basil. See B. T. B.

Bladderworts
  See pages in the following book:
  Goldstein, P. Animals and plants that trap
    p85-96 (4-7)   **574.5**

Blaine, Betty Gray
  The rosy-cheeked ghost
  In Kamerman, S. E. ed. Fifty plays for
    junior actors p45-53   **812.08**

Blaine, Mahlon
  (illus.) Gunterman, B. L. ed. Castles in Spain,
    and other enchantments   **398.2**

Blaisell, Elinore
  (illus.) De La Mare, W. Rhymes and verses
                                              821

Blake, Quentin
  (illus.) Hoban, R. How Tom beat Captain
    Najork and his hired sportsmen   **E**
  (illus.) Rees, E. Riddles, riddles everywhere
                                              398.6
  (illus.) Yeoman, J. Mouse trouble   **E**

Blake, William
  See pages in the following book:
  Benét, L. Famous poets for young people
    p14-16 (5-7)   **920**

Blanche's high-flying Halloween. Embry, M.
  In Hoke, H. ed. Witches, witches, witches
    p45-55   **808.8**

Blanck, Jacob
  Peter Parley to Penrod   **020.75**

Bland, Edith (Nesbit)
  See pages in the following books:
  Benét, L. Famous storytellers for young peo-
    ple p124-29 (5-7)   **920**
  Horn Book Reflections on children's books
    and reading p211-17   **028.5**
  Townsend, J. R. Written for children p102-
    06   **028.5**
    For titles by this author see Nesbit, E.

Bland, James A.
  See pages in the following book:
  Hughes, L. Famous Negro music makers
    p29-34 (5-7)   **920**

Bland, Joellen
  Oliver Twist
  In Burack, A. S. ed. Popular plays for
    classroom reading p266-83   **808.82**

Blanton, Catherine
  The dulce man
  In Burack, A. S. ed. One hundred plays
    for children p23-30   **808.82**

Blass, Jacqueline
  (illus.) Weber, A. Elizabeth gets well   **362.1**

Blassingame, Wyatt
  Dan Beard, scoutmaster of America (3-5)   **92**
  Story of the Boy Scouts (4-7)   **369.43**

Blaze. McClung, R. M.   **599**

Blechman, R. O.
  (illus.) Kohn, B. What a funny thing to say!
                                              422

Bleeker, Sonia
  The Apache Indians (4-6)   **970.3**
  The Ashanti of Ghana (4-7)   **916.67**
  The Aztec (4-6)   **970.3**
  The Cherokee (4-7)   **970.3**
  The Chippewa Indians (4-6)   **970.3**
  The Crow Indians (4-6)   **970.3**
  The Delaware Indians (4-6)   **970.3**
  The Eskimo (4-6)   **970.1**
  Horsemen of the western plateaus (4-6)
                                              970.3
  The Inca (4-6)   **980.3**

Bleeker, Sonia—Continued

Indians of the longhouse (4-6)	**970.3**
The Masai (4-7)	**916.7**
The Maya (4-6)	**970.3**
The mission Indians of California (4-6)	**970.4**
The Navajo (4-6)	**970.3**
The Pueblo Indians (4-6)	**970.3**
The Pygmies (4-7)	**916.7**
The sea hunters (4-6)	**970.4**
The Seminole Indians (4-6)	**970.3**
The Sioux Indians (4-6)	**970.3**
The Zulu of South Africa (4-7)	**916.8**

Blegvad, Erik

(illus.) Andersen, H. C. The emperor's new clothes **Fic**
(jt. auth.) Blegvad, L. The great hamster hunt **Fic**
(illus.) Blegvad, L. comp. Mittens for kittens, and other rhymes about cats **398.8**
(illus.) Blegvad, L. Moon-watch summer **Fic**
(illus.) Bodecker, N. M. The Mushroom Center disaster **Fic**
(illus.) Brenner, B. The five pennies **E**
(illus.) Kendall, C. The Gammage Cup **Fic**
(illus.) Nesbit, E. The complete book of dragons (3-6) **S C**
(illus.) Norton, M. Bed-knob and broomstick **Fic**
(illus.) Selsam, M. E. Plenty of fish **639**
(illus.) Tresselt, A. Bonnie Bess the weathervane horse **E**
(illus.) Viorst, J. The tenth good thing about Barney **E**

Blegvad, Lenore

The great hamster hunt (1-3) **Fic**
(comp.) Mittens for kittens, and other rhymes about cats (k-1) **398.8**
Moon-watch summer (3-5) **Fic**

Blériot, Louis

See pages in the following book:

Ross, F. Historic plane models p47-51 (5-7) **629.133**

Bless this day. Vipont, E. comp. **242**

The blessing of the tree; puppet play. Adair, M. W.

In Adair, M. W. Folk puppet plays for the social studies p37-40 **791.5**

Bley, Edgar S.

The best singing games for children of all ages **796.1**

Blind

Putnam, P. The triumph of the Seeing Eye (5-7) **636.7**

Education

Brown, M. M. The silent storm [biography of Anne Sullivan Macy] (5-7) **92**
Davidson, M. Louis Braille (3-5) **92**
Hunter, E. F. Child of the silent night [biography of Laura Dewey Bridgman] (3-5) **92**
Malone, M. Annie Sullivan [biography of Anne Sullivan Macy] (2-4) **92**
Neimark, A. E. Touch of light; the story of Louis Braille (4-7) **92**
Peare, C. O. The Helen Keller story (5-7) **92**

Fiction

Bawden, N. The witch's daughter (4-7) **Fic**
Clewes, D. Guide Dog (5-7) **Fic**
Garfield, J. B. Follow my Leader (4-7) **Fic**

Heide, F. P. Sound of sunshine, sound of rain **E**
Keats, E. J. Apt. 3 **E**

Rehabilitation

See Blind—Education

Blind, Books for the

Bibliography

For younger readers: braille and talking books **028.52**

Blind, Dogs for the. See Guide dogs

The **Blind** Baba-Abdalla

In Lang, A. ed. Arabian nights p223-31 **398.2**

The **blind** colt. Rounds, G. **Fic**
The **blind** Connemara. Anderson, C. W. **Fic**
The **Blind** man and the deaf man

In Baker, A. comp. The golden lynx, and other tales p78-88 **398.2**

The **blind** man, the deaf man, and the donkey. Haviland, V.

In Haviland, V. Favorite fairy tales told in India p35-52 **398.2**

The **blind** men and the elephant. Quigley, L. **398.2**

The **blind** mouse. Kim, S.

In Kim, S. The story bag p83-85 **398.2**

Blinded giant

In Jacobs, J. ed. More English folk and fairy tales p92-93 **398.2**

Blishen, Edward

(comp.) Oxford Book of poetry for children (4-7) **821.08**

Bliven, Bruce

The American Revolution, 1760-1783 (5-7) **973.3**

The story of D-Day: June 6, 1944 (5-7) **940.54**

Blizzard of '98. Credle, E.

In Credle, E. Tall tales from the high hills, and other stories p40-42 **398.2**

Blizzards

Fiction

Lenski, L. Prairie school (4-6) **Fic**
Smith, E. No way of telling (5-7) **Fic**

Bloch, Lucienne

(illus.) Hurd, E. T. Sandpipers **598.2**
(illus.) Hurd, E. T. Starfish **593**

Bloch, Marie Halun

Ivanko and the dragon (k-3) **398.2**
(ed.) Ukrainian folk tales (4-6) **398.2**

Block printing. See Linoleum block printing; Wood engraving

The **block** tower. Lindsay, M.

In Association for Childhood Education International. Told under the blue umbrella p20-22 **S C**

Blockhead Hans. Andersen, H. C.

In Lang, A. ed. The yellow fairy book p313-18 **398.2**

See also Hans Clodhopper

Blom, Gertrude Duby

(illus.) Price, C. Heirs of the ancient Maya **970.3**

Blood

Showers, P. A drop of blood (1-3) **612**
Zim, H. S. Blood (4-6) **612**

Blood—*Continued*

Circulation

Heintze, C. The priceless pump: the human heart (6-7)   **612**

Showers, P. Hear your heart (k-3)   **612**

Simon, S. About your heart (2-4)   **612**

The **blood**-drawing ghost. Hardendorff, J. B.
In Hardendorff, J. B. Witches, wit, and a werewolf p107-17   **S C**

Bloody handprints on the wall. Harter, W.
In Harter, W. Osceola's head, and other American ghost stories p13-17   **S C**

Blough, Glenn O.
Bird watchers and bird feeders (1-3)   **598.2**

Blow, Michael
Men of science and invention. See Men of science and invention   **609**

Blowfish live in the sea. Fox, P.   **Fic**

Blue, Rose
Grandma didn't wave back (3-5)   **Fic**
I am here: yo estoy aqui   **E**
A month of Sundays (3-5)   **Fic**
A quiet place (3-5)   **Fic**
A quiet place; excerpt
In Association for Childhood Education International. Told under the city umbrella p14-24   **S C**

Blue Beard. Perrault, C.
In Lang, A. ed. The blue fairy book p290-95   **398.2**
In Opie, I. ed. The classic fairy tales p106-09   **398.2**
In Perrault, C. Famous fairy tales p41-58   **398.2**
In Perrault, C. Perrault's Complete fairy tales p78-88   **398.2**
In Rackham, A. comp. Arthur Rackham Fairy book p143-52   **398.2**
In Untermeyer, B. ed. The Golden Treasury of children's literature p106-16 **808.8**
See also Bluebeard

The **blue** belt. Asbjörnsen, P. C.
In Asbjörnsen, P. C. East of the sun and west of the moon, and other tales p53-71   **398.2**

The **Blue** Bird. Aulnoy, Mme. d'
In Lang, A. ed. The green fairy book p 1-26   **398.2**

The **Blue** Bird wish. Camp Fire Girls, Inc.   **369.47**

Blue Canyon horse. Clark, A. N.   **Fic**

The **blue**-eyed pussy. Mathiesen, E.
In Gruenberg, S. M. ed. Favorite stories old and new p152-55   **808.8**

The **blue** fairy book. Lang, A. ed.   **398.2**

Blue fin. Thiele, C.   **Fic**

The **Blue** lake
In Baker, A. comp. The talking tree p138-78   **398.2**

Blue light
Grimm, J. The blue light
In Grimm, J. The complete Grimm's Fairy tales p530-34   **398.2**
In Grimm, J. Grimms' Fairy tales; illus. by F. Kredel p208-13   **398.2**
See also Tinder box

Blue men of the Minch. MacKenzie, D. A.
In Brown, M. ed. A cavalcade of sea legends p145-50   **808.8**

The **Blue** Mountains
In Lang, A. ed. The yellow fairy book p256-64   **398.2**

Blue mystery. Benary-Isbert, M.   **Fic**

The **blue**-nosed witch. Embry, M.   **Fic**

Blue Ridge Mountains

Fiction
Credle, E. Down, down the mountain   **E**

The **blue** rose. Baring, M.
In Shedlock, M. L. The art of the story-teller p204-12   **372.6**

Blue silver. Sandburg, C.
In Gruenberg, S. M. ed. Favorite stories old and new p234-35   **808.8**
In Sandburg, C. Rootabaga stories v2 p215-18   **S C**
In Sandburg, C. The Sandburg treasury p159-60   **818**

The **blue** toadstool. Bellah, M.
In Kamerman, S. E. ed. Little plays for little players p147-52   **812.08**

The **blue** umbrella. Tippett, J.
In Association for Childhood Education International. Told under the blue umbrella p 1-6   **S C**

Blue whale. Cook, J. J.   **599**

The **blue** whale. Mizumura, K.   **599**

Blue willow. Gates, D.   **Fic**

Bluebeard
De La Mare, W. Bluebeard
In De La Mare, W. Tales told again p131-41   **398.2**
Perrault, C. Blue Beard
In Lang, A. ed. The blue fairy book p290-95   **398.2**
In Opie, I. ed. The classic fairy tales p106-09   **398.2**
In Perrault, C. Famous fairy tales p41-58   **398.2**
In Perrault, C. Perrault's Complete fairy tales p78-88   **398.2**
In Rackham, A. comp. Arthur Rackham Fairy book p143-52   **398.2**
In Untermeyer, B. ed. The Golden Treasury of children's literature p106-16   **808.8**

Bluebeard. Untermeyer, L.
In Untermeyer, L. Tales from the ballet p42-46   **792.8**

Blueberries for Sal. McCloskey, R.   **E**

Blueprints for better reading. Cleary, F. D.   **028.5**

Blues (Songs, etc.)
Jones, H. Big star fallin' mama (6-7)   **920**
Montgomery, E. R. William C. Handy: father of the blues (3-4)   **92**

Blum, Burt
(illus.) Cross, L. Kitchen crafts   **745.5**

Blume, Judy
Are you there God? It's me, Margaret (5-7)   **Fic**
It's not the end of the world (4-6)   **Fic**

Boggs, Ralph Steele—*Continued*
The tinker and the ghost
In Johnson, E. ed. Anthology of children's
literature p236-38 **808.8**

Bogle, Kate Cutler
(jt. auth.) Cutler, K. N. Crafts for Christmas
745.59

The **bogles** from the Howff. Nic Leodhas, S.
In Nic Leodhas, S. Heather and broom
p113-28 **398.2**

Bogotá
See pages in the following book:
Carpenter, A. Colombia p79-81 (4-6) **918.61**

Bogs. See Marshes

La **Boheme**; adaptation. Bulla, C. R.
In Bulla, C. R. Stories of favorite operas
p211-19 **782.1**

Bohemia

Folklore
See Folklore—Bohemia

Bohlen, Marie Nonnast
(illus.) Wong, H. H. My ladybug **595.7**

Bohr, Niels Henrik David
See pages in the following book:
Cottler, J. More Heroes of civilization p244-
51 (6-7) **920**

Boiko, Claire
All hands on deck
In Burack, A. S. ed. Popular plays for
classroom reading p206-17 **808.82**
Children's plays for creative actors (3-7) **812**
Contents: Small crimson parasol; Peter, Peter, Peter;
Anywhere and everywhere; The wonderful circus of
words; The big shoo; Spaceship Santa Maria; Penny
wise; Scaredy cat; The wayward witch; The runaway
bookmobile; The insatiable dragon; Meet the pilgrims;
The Christmas revel; Star bright; Mother Goose's
Christmas surprise; A clean sweep; The marvelous
Time Machine; Young Abe's destiny; The "T" party;
Cupivac; A tale of two drummers; The exterior decorator; Lion to lamb; Cinder-Riley; The snowman who
overstayed; All hands on deck; The crocus who couldn't
bloom; Sun up; The punctuation proclamation; Terrible Terry's surprise; Trouble in Tree-Land; All about
mothers; Operation litterbug; The Franklin reversal;
All points West

Cinder-Riley
In Kamerman, S. E. ed. Fifty plays for
junior actors p54-63 **812.08**
Lady Moon and the thief
In Kamerman, S. E. ed. Dramatized folk
tales of the world p23-31 **812.08**
Pepe and the cornfield bandit
In Kamerman, S. E. ed. Dramatized folk
tales of the world p324-33 **812.08**
Take me to your Marshal
In Burack, A. S. ed. Popular plays for
classroom reading p22-31 **808.82**

Boillot, Georges
See pages in the following book:
Stevenson, P. The greatest days of racing
p19-33 (5-7) **796.7**

Bois, William Pène du. See Du Bois, William
Pène

The **Bojabi** tree. Rickert, E.
In Association for Childhood Education
International. Told under the magic
umbrella p101-12 **S C**

The **bold** heroes of Hungry Hill. MacManus, S.
In MacManus, S. The bold heroes of
Hungry Hill, and other Irish folk
tales p3-18 **398.2**
In MacManus, S. Hibernian nights p212-
23 **398.2**

The **bold** heroes of Hungry Hill, and other
Irish folk tales. MacManus, S. **398.2**

The **bold** Mixtec. Campbell, C.
In Campbell, C. Star Mountain, and
other legends of Mexico p25-28
398.2

Bolian, Polly
(illus.) Marks, G. The amazing stethoscope
610.28

Bolívar, Simón
Syme, R. Bolívar, the liberator (4-7) **92**

Bolivia
Carpenter, A. Bolivia (4-6) **918.4**
Warren, L. F. The land and people of Bolivia
(5-7) **918.4**
See also pages in the following book:
Carter, W. E. The first book of South Amer-
ica p36-41 (4-6) **918**

Bolliger, Max
Joseph (4-6) **221.9**
Noah and the rainbow (k-3) **221.9**

Bolognese, Don
A new day (k-3) **E**
(illus.) Balestrino, P. The skeleton inside you
611
(illus.) Commager, H. S. The great Declaration **973.3**
(illus.) Gates, D. The warrior goddess:
Athena **292**
(illus.) George, J. C. All upon a sidewalk
595.7
(illus.) George, J. C. All upon a stone **595.7**
(illus.) Hardendorff, J. B. ed. Just one more
372.6
(illus.) Knight, E. Lassie come-home **Fic**
(illus.) Lexau, J. M. Benjie **E**
(illus.) Lexau, J. M. Benjie on his own **E**
(illus.) Palmer, R. Dragons, unicorns, and
other magical beasts **398.2**
(illus.) Smith, M. R. Plays &—how to put
them on **792**
(illus.) Wormser, R. The black mustanger **Fic**

Bolton, Ivy
The golden egg
In Harper, W. comp. Easter chimes p195-
207 **394.2**

Bomar, Cora Paul
Guide to the development of educational media selection centers **021**

Bomba, the Brave. Carpenter, F.
In Carpenter, F. African wonder tales
p169-78 **398.2**

Bombers
Cooke, D. C. Famous U.S. Air Force bombers (5-7) **623.74**

Bona and Nello, The Adventures of. See The
adventures of Bona and Nello

Bond, Michael
A bear called Paddington (2-5) **Fic**
Christmas
In Reeves, J. comp. The Christmas book
p153-66 **394.2**

Boston, L. M.—*Continued*

The children of Green Knowe; excerpt

  In Arbuthnot, M. H. comp. The Arbuthnot Anthology of children's literature p535-39   **808.8**

  In Johnson, E. ed. Anthology of children's literature p657-60   **808.8**

Demon at Green Knowe

  In Hoke, H. ed. Spooks, spooks, spooks p178-205   **S C**

An enemy at Green Knowe. See note under Boston, L. M. The children of Green Knowe   **Fic**

The river at Green Knowe. See note under Boston, L. M. The children of Green Knowe   **Fic**

A stranger at Green Knowe. See note under Boston, L. M. The children of Green Knowe   **Fic**

Tolly's new home

  In Arbuthnot, M. H. comp. The Arbuthnot Anthology of children's literature p535-39   **808.8**

Treasure of Green Knowe. See note under Boston, L. M. The children of Green Knowe   **Fic**

About

See pages in the following book:

Townsend, J. R. A sense of story p28-34   **028.5**

Boston, Lucy Maria. See Boston, L. M.

Boston, Peter

  (illus.) Boston, L. M. The children of Green Knowe   **Fic**

Boston

Fiction

McCloskey, R. Make way for ducklings   **E**

Boston. Children's Hospital Medical Center

What to do when "there's nothing to do"   **790**

Boston. Committee of Correspondence

See pages in the following book:

Phelan, M. K. The story of the Boston Tea Party p53-57, 69-84 (4-6)   **973.3**

Boston Massacre, 1770

Dickinson, A. The Boston Massacre, March 5, 1770 (5-7)   **973.3**

Boston Post Road

See pages in the following book:

Grant, B. Famous American trails p9-16 (5-7)   **973**

Boston Tea Party, 1773

Phelan, M. K. The story of the Boston Tea Party (4-6)   **973.3**

Botany

Dowden, A. O. T. Look at a flower (6-7) **582**

Selsam, M. E. Bulbs, corms, and such (2-5)   **584**

See also pages in the following book:

Cooper, E. K. Science in your own back yard p68-99 (5-7)   **500.9**

    See also Flower gardening; Fruit; Leaves; Plants; Seeds; Shrubs; Trees; Vegetables; Weeds

Anatomy

Zim, H. S. What's inside of plants? (2-4) **581**

See also pages in the following book:

Selsam, M. E. How to grow house plants p10-14 (4-7)   **635.9**

Ecology

Selsam, M. E. Birth of a forest (4-6)   **581.5**

Wright, R. H. What good is a weed? (4-6)   **581.5**

See also pages in the following book:

Batten, M. The tropical forest p18-27 (5-7)   **574.5**

Experiments

Rahn, J. E. Grocery store botany (3-5) **581.6**

Rahn, J. E. Seeing what plants do (3-5)   **581.072**

Selsam, M. E. Play with plants (3-6)   **581.072**

Botany, Economic

Rahn, J. E. Grocery store botany (3-5) **581.6**

Schaeffer, E. Dandelion, pokeweed, and goosefoot (4-7)   **581.6**

  See also Cotton; Grain; Grasses; Plants, Edible; Weeds

Botany, Fossil. See Plants, Fossil

Botany, Medical

Schaeffer, E. Dandelion, pokeweed, and goosefoot (4-7)   **581.6**

Selsam, M. E. Plants that heal (4-6) **581.6**

Botany of the Bible. See Bible—Natural history

Both ends of the leash. Unkelbach, K.   **636.7**

Bothwell, Jean

The first book of India (4-7)   **915.4**

Botswana

Carpenter, A. Botswana (4-7)   **916.8**

Böttger, Johann Friedrich

See pages in the following book:

Aylesworth, T. G. The alchemists: magic into science p103-08 (6-7)   **540.1**

Böttiger, Johann Friedrich. See Böttger, Johann Friedrich

The bottle. Andersen, H. C.

  In Andersen, H. C. The complete fairy tales and stories p492-500   **S C**

  See also Bottle neck

The bottle. Baker, C.

  In Association for Childhood Education International. Told under spacious skies p295-301   **S C**

Bottle Hill. Manning-Sanders, R.

  In Manning-Sanders, R. A choice of magic p54-62   **398.2**

Bottle neck

Andersen, H. C. The bottle

  In Andersen, H. C. The complete fairy tales and stories p492-500   **S C**

Andersen, H. C. The neck of the bottle

  In Andersen, H. C. Andersen's Fairy tales p251-61   **S C**

Bouki and Ti Bef. Courlander, H.

  In Courlander, H. The piece of fire, and other Haitian tales p94-96   **398.2**

Bouki buys a burro. Courlander, H.

  In Courlander, H. The piece of fire, and other Haitian tales p55-57   **398.2**

Bouki cuts wood. Courlander, H.
  In Courlander, H. The piece of fire, and
    other Haitian tales p76-80   398.2
Bouki gets whee-ai. Courlander, H.
  In Courlander, H. The piece of fire, and
    other Haitian tales p20-22   398.2
Bouki rents a horse. Courlander, H.
  In Courlander, H. The piece of fire, and
    other Haitian tales p25-28   398.2
  See also Uncle Boqui rents a horse
Bouki's glasses. Courlander, H.
  In Courlander, H. The piece of fire, and
    other Haitian tales p89-90   398.2
Boumedienne, Houari, President Algeria
  See pages in the following book:
Spencer, W. The land and people of Algeria
    p111-16 (5-7)   916.5
The **boundary** riders. Phipson, J.   Fic
Bourbon, House of
  See pages in the following book:
Loder, D. The land and people of Spain
    p77-85 (5-7)   914.6
Bourguiba, Habib, President Tunisia
  See pages in the following book:
Spencer, W. The land and people of Tu-
    nisia p103-20 (5-7)   916.1
Bourhill, E. J.
Berger, T. Black fairy tales   398.2
Bourke-White, Margaret
  See pages in the following book:
Ross, P. ed. Young and female p91-104 (6-7)
                                       920
Bourne, Miriam Anne
Raccoons are for loving   E
Boutwell, Edna
"Kate Douglas Wiggin—The Lady with the
    Golden Key"
  In Andrews, S. ed. The Hewins lectures,
    1947-1962 p297-319   028.5
Bova, Ben
The weather changes man (5-7)   551.6
Bow and arrow
  See pages in the following book:
Bleeker, S. The Apache Indians p92-96 (4-6)
                                       970.3
  See also Archery
The **bow**, the deer, and the talking bird. Bren-
    ner, A.
  In Brenner, A. The boy who could do any-
    thing, & other Mexican folk tales
    p98-103   398.2
A **bow** to Thanksgiving. Bailey, C. S.
  In Luckhardt, M. C. comp. Thanksgiving
    p163-74   394.2
Bowden, Charlotte Edmands
(illus.) Foley, D. J. Christmas the world over
                                       394.2
Bowditch, Nathaniel
  See pages in the following book:
Hirsch, S. C. On course! p87-93 (5-7) 623.89
Bowed instruments. See Stringed instruments
Bowen, J. David
The land and people of Peru (5-7)   918.5

Bowen, Robert Sidney
They flew to glory: the story of the Lafayette
    Flying Corps (4-6)   940.4
Bowen, Vernon
Trials of Ting Ling
  In Child Study Association of America.
    Castles and dragons p79-95   398.2
Bowie, James
Garst, S. James Bowie and his famous knife
    (5-7)   92
Bowleg Bill
Felton, H. W. Bowleg Bill, seagoing cow-
    puncher (5-7)   398.2
Bowling
Dolan, E. F. The complete beginner's guide
    to bowling (5-7)   794.6
  See also pages in the following books:
The Junior illustrated encyclopedia of sports
    p197-230 (5-7)   796.03
Keith, H. Sports and games p91-107 (5-7)
                                       796
Dictionaries
Liss, H. Bowling talk for beginners (4-7)
                                       794.6
Bowling talk for beginners. Liss, H.   794.6
Bowman, James Cloyd
Hidden Laiva
  In Arbuthnot, M. H. comp. Time for old
    magic p143-47   398.2
  In Johnson, E. ed. Anthology of children's
    literature p282-86   808.8
The pig-headed wife
  In Arbuthnot, M. H. comp. The Arbuth-
    not Anthology of children's literature
    p261-62   808.8
Slue-foot Sue dodges the moon
  In Johnson, E. ed. Anthology of children's
    literature p351-56   808.8
Tales from a Finnish tupa (5-7)   398.2
  Contents: Ship that sailed by land and sea; Men of
the wallet; Mouse bride; Vaino and the swan princess;
Hidden Laiva; Antti and the wizard's prophecy; Lippo
and Tapio; Wooing of Seppo Ilmarinen; Jurma and
the sea god; Timo and the Princess Vendla; Severi and
Vappu; Ei-Niin-Mita, or No-So-What; Girl who sought
her nine brothers; Two pine cones; Kalle and the
wood grouse; Niilo and the wizard; Urho and Marja;
Mielikki and her nine sons; Leppä Pölkky and the blue
cross; Liisa and the prince; Pig-headed wife; Finland's
greatest fisherman; Stupid Peikko; Wise men of Hol-
mola; Pekka and the rogues; End of the world; Mouse
that turned tailor; The feast; Farmers three; Stupid
wolf; Wily fox; Song of the fox; Wolf and the fox;
Fox as a judge; Rooster and the hen; Why the squirrel
lives in trees; Vain bear; Wisdom of the rabbit; Fox
and the rabbit; Stupid bear; Song of the wolf; Bear
goes fishing; Rabbit's self-respect

Timo and the Princess Vendla
  In Arbuthnot, M. H. comp. The Arbuth-
    not Anthology of children's litera-
    ture p262-64   808.8
  In Fenner, P. R. comp. Princesses & peas-
    ant boys p148-53   398.2
Bowman, Phila B.
The Christmas tree
  In Harper, W. comp. Merry Christmas to
    you p38-43   394.2
The Easter Bunnies and the Lily
  In Harper, W. comp. Easter chimes p189-
    94   394.2
A **box** on the ear. Manning-Sanders, R.
  In Manning-Sanders, R. A book of ghosts
    & goblins p9-13   398.2

The **box** with something pretty in it
In Hardendorff, J. B. ed. Just one more
p26-27 **372.6**

Boxes
Radlauer, R. S. What can you do with a
box? **E**

Boxing
See pages in the following books:
The Junior illustrated encyclopedia of sports
p231-70 (5-7) **796.03**
Keith, H. Sports and games p108-44 (5-7)
796

A **boy**, a dog, a frog and a friend. Mayer, M. **E**

A **boy**, a dog, and a frog. Mayer, M. **E**

Boy alone. Ottley, R. **Fic**

Boy alone; excerpt. Ottley, R.
In Arbuthnot, M. H. comp. The Arbuthnot Anthology of children's literature
p725-29 **808.8**

The **boy** and the cloth. Courlander, H.
In Courlander, H. The tiger's whisker, and
other tales and legends from Asia
and the Pacific p80-82 **398.2**

The **boy** and the leopard. Walker, B. K.
In Walker, B. K. The dancing palm tree,
and other Nigerian folktales p84-93
398.2

The **boy** and the trolls, or the adventure. Sten-
ström, W.
In Olenius, E. comp. Great Swedish fairy
tales p203-20 **398.2**

The **boy** and the water-sprite. Haviland, V.
In Haviland, V. Favorite fairy tales told
in Sweden p3-13 **398.2**

The **Boy** and the wolves
In Lang, A. ed. The yellow fairy book
p138-40 **398.2**

Boy Blue the crab-catcher. Lamming, G.
In McDowell, R. E. ed. Third World
voices for children p66-71 **398.2**

A **boy** called Fish. Morgan, A. **Fic**

The **boy** drummer of Vincennes. Carmer, C.
811

The **Boy** in Nazareth. King, E. E.
In Sechrist, E. H. ed. It's time for Christmas p198-203 **394.2**

The **boy** Jody. Rawlings, M. K.
In Association for Childhood Education
International. Told under spacious
skies p136-52 **S C**

The **boy** knight of Reims; excerpt. Lownsbery, E.
In Ward, W. ed. Stories to dramatize p214-
18 **372.6**

Boy-man
McDermott, G. Arrow to the sun (1-3) **398.2**

Boy meets girl; play. Stone, P.
In Free to be . . . you and me p24-31 **810.8**

A **boy** named John; excerpt. Cournos, J.
In Association for Childhood Education
International. Told under the Stars
and Stripes p257-69 **S C**

A **boy** of Galatia. Scoville, S.
In A St Nicholas anthology p243-53 **810.8**

The **boy** of Nazareth; puppet play. Jagendorf, M.
In Jagendorf, M. Penny puppets, penny
theatre, and penny plays p173-81
791.5

Boy of Nepal. Larsen, P. **915.49**

A **boy** of old Prague. Ish-Kishor, S. **Fic**

The **boy** on a broomstick. Masefield, J.
In Hope-Simpson, J. ed. A cavalcade of
witches p78-82 **808.8**

The **boy** Pu-nia and the king of the sharks.
Colum, P.
In Colum, P. The Stone of Victory, and
other tales of Padraic Colum p44-49
398.2

Boy Scouts
Blassingame, W. Dan Beard, scoutmaster of
America (3-5) **92**
Handbooks, manuals, etc.
Boy Scouts of America. Bear Cub Scout book
(3-4) **369.43**
Boy Scouts of America. Scout handbook (5-7)
369.43
Boy Scouts of America. Webelos Scout book
(4-5) **369.43**
Boy Scouts of America. Wolf Cub Scout book
(2-3) **369.43**
History
Blassingame, W. Story of the Boy Scouts (4-7)
369.43

Boy Scouts of America
Bear Cub Scout book (3-4) **369.43**
Fieldbook **369.43**
Reading **028.5**
Scout handbook (5-7) **369.43**
Webelos Scout book (4-5) **369.43**
Wolf Cub Scout book (2-3) **369.43**

A **boy** tells the story of being caught in a storm.
Tolstoy, L.
In Tolstoy, L. Twenty-two Russian tales
for young children p18-19 **S C**

The **boy** who beat the Devil. Brenner, A.
In Brenner, A. The boy who could do anything, & other Mexican folk tales
p92-97 **398.2**

The **boy** who became a reindeer. Melzack, R.
In Melzack, R. The day Tuk became a
hunter & other Eskimo stories p41-
48 **398.2**

The **boy** who could do anything, & other Mexican folk tales. Brenner, A. **398.2**

The **boy** who could not tell a lie. Very, A.
In Kamerman, S. E. ed. Little plays for
little players p42-46 **812.08**

Boy who cried "Wolf"
Evans, K. The boy who cried wolf **398.2**
Wolf! Wolf!
In The Tall book of nursery tales p74-76
398.2

The **boy** who crossed the great water and returned. Courlander, H.
In Courlander, H. People of the short blue
corn p63-81 **398.2**

Boy who discovered the spring. Alden, R. M.
In Alden, R. M. Why the chimes rang, and
other stories p30-40 **S C**
In Sechrist, E. H. ed. It's time for Easter
p176-83 **394.2**

Brewton, John E.—*Continued*
(jt. comp.) Brewton, S. comp. Shrieks at midnight   **821.08**
(jt. comp.) Brewton, S. comp. Sing a song of seasons   **821.08**

Brewton, Sara
(comp.) Birthday candles burning bright (4-7)   **821.08**
(comp.) Bridled with rainbows (3-7)   **808.81**
(comp.) Christmas bells are ringing (4-7)   **808.81**
(comp.) Laughable limericks (4-7)   **821.08**
(comp.) My tang's tungled and other ridiculous situations (3-6)   **821.08**
(comp.) Shrieks at midnight (4-7)   **821.08**
(comp.) Sing a song of seasons (3-7)   **821.08**
(jt. comp.) Brewton, J. E. comp. Index to children's poetry   **808.81**
(jt. comp.) Brewton, J. E. comp. Index to children's poetry; first supplement   **808.81**
(jt. comp.) Brewton, J. E. comp. Index to children's poetry; second supplement   **808.81**
(jt. comp.) Brewton, J. E. comp. Index to poetry for children and young people, 1964-1969   **808.81**

Brey, Charles
(illus.) De Leeuw, A. Edith Cavell: nurse, spy, heroine   **92**

Briar Rose. Grimm, J.
In Darrell, M. ed. Once upon a time p51-54   **808.8**
In Grimm, J. Grimms' Fairy tales; illus. by F. Kredel p101-06   **398.2**
In Hutchinson, V. S. ed. Chimney corner fairy tales p65-70   **398.2**
See also Sleeping beauty

Brick, Anna Riwkin- See Riwkin-Brick, Anna

The **bridal** chamber of Silver Springs. Jagendorf, M. A.
In Jagendorf, M. A. Folk stories of the South p82-86   **398.2**

Bridal customs. See Marriage customs and rites

The **bridal** ghost dinner. Jagendorf, M. A.
In Jagendorf, M. A. Folk stories of the South p135-37   **398.2**

The **bride** who melted away. Carpenter, F.
In Carpenter, F. African wonder tales p161-68   **398.2**

The **bride** who out talked the water kelpie. Nic Leodhas, S.
In Arbuthnot, M. H. comp. The Arbuthnot Anthology of children's literature p166-70   **808.8**
In Nic Leodhas, S. Thistle and thyme p82-97   **398.2**

The **bridegroom's** shopping. Kim, S.
In Kim, S. The story bag p44-50   **398.2**

Bridge, Linda McCarter
Cats: little tigers in your house (k-3)   **636.8**

A **bridge** of children's books. Lepman, J. **028.5**

The **Bridge** of St Cloud
In Courlander, H. ed. Ride with the sun p173-77   **398.2**

The **bridge** to Killybog Fair. Watts, F. B.
In Kamerman, S. E. ed. Dramatized folk tales of the world p227-38   **812.08**

Bridger, James
Garst, S. Jim Bridger, greatest of the mountain men (4-7)   **92**

Bridges, William
Zoo careers (6-7)   **590.74**

Bridges
Peet, C. The first book of bridges (4-7)   **624.2**

Bridgman, Laura Dewey
Hunter, E. F. Child of the silent night (3-5)   **92**

Bridled with rainbows. Brewton, S. comp.   **808.81**

Bridwell, Norman
(illus.) Bethell, J. How to care for your dog   **636.7**

Brier Rose. Grimm, J.
In Grimm, J. About wise men and simpletons p23-27   **398.2**
See also Sleeping beauty

Briggs, Raymond
Father Christmas   **E**
Fee fi fo fum (k-1)   **398.8**
Jim and the beanstalk   **E**
(illus.) Duggan, A. The castle book   **728.8**
(illus.) Haviland, V. comp. The fairy tale treasury   **398.2**
(illus.) Manning-Sanders, R. ed. A book of magical beasts   **398.2**
(illus.) Manning-Sanders, R. ed. Festivals   **394.2**
(illus.) Mayne, W. ed. William Mayne's Book of giants   **398.2**
(illus.) Mother Goose. The Mother Goose treasury   **398.8**
(illus.) Reeves, J. comp. The Christmas book   **394.2**

Bright, Robert
Georgie   **E**
My red umbrella   **E**

The **bright** and morning star. Harris, R.   **Fic**

Bright April. De Angeli, M.   **Fic**

The **bright** sun brings it to light. Grimm, J.
In Grimm, J. The complete Grimm's Fairy tales p528-29   **398.2**

Brighty of the Grand Canyon. Henry, M.   **Fic**

Brindze, Ruth
Hurricanes (5-7)   **551.5**
The rise and fall of the seas (4-7)   **551.4**
The sea (5-7)   **333.9**
The story of our calendar (4-7)   **529**
The story of the totem pole (4-7)   **299**

Bring me a light. Manning-Sanders, R.
In Manning-Sanders, R. A book of ghosts & goblins p25-29   **398.2**

Bringing in the spring. Yates, E.
In Sechrist, E. H. ed. It's time for Easter p202-08   **394.2**

Bringing up puppies. Levin, J. W.   **636.7**

Bringle, Mary
Eskimos (5-6)   **970.1**

Brink, Carol Ryrie
Andy Buckram's tin men (4-6)   **Fic**
The bad times of Irma Baumlein (4-6)   **Fic**
Breeches and clogs
In Johnson, E. ed. Anthology of children's literature p791-95   **808.8**
Caddie Woodlawn (4-6)   **Fic**

Bronson, Wilfrid S.
Beetles (4-7) **595.7**
Dogs (3-7) **636.7**

Brontë, Charlotte
Vipont, E. Weaver of dreams (5-7) **92**

Brontë family
Vipont, E. Weaver of dreams; the girlhood of Charlotte Brontë (5-7) **92**

Bronx Zoo. See New York (City) Zoological Park

Bronze boar
Andersen, H. C. The bronze pig
In Andersen, H. C. The complete fairy tales and stories p156-66 **S C**

The **bronze door.** Chandler, R.
In Hitchcock, A. comp. Alfred Hitchcock's Supernatural tales of terror and suspense p38-67 **S C**

The **bronze pig.** Andersen, H. C.
In Andersen, H. C. The complete fairy tales and stories p156-66 **S C**

The **Bronze ring**
In Lang, A. ed. The blue fairy book p 1-11 **398.2**

Bronzeville boys and girls. Brooks, G. **811**

The **brook.** Carrick, C. **574.92**

Brook in the king's garden. Alden, R. M.
In Alden, R. M. Why the chimes rang, and other stories p41-52 **S C**

Brooke, L. Leslie
Johnny Crow's garden **E**
—Same
In Johnson, E. ed. Anthology of children's literature p75-76 **808.8**
Johnny Crow's new garden **E**
Johnny Crow's party **E**
(illus.) Grimm, J. The house in the wood, and other fairy stories **398.2**
(illus.) Lear, E. Nonsense songs **821**
(illus.) Lear, E. The pelican chorus & other nonsense verses **821**
About
See pages in the following book:
A Horn Book Sampler on children's books and reading p60-69, 224-27 **028.5**

Brooke, Leonard Leslie. See Brooke, L. Leslie

Brooke, Leslie. See Brooke, L. Leslie

Brooklyn
Fiction
Brenner, B. A year in the life of Rosie Bernard (4-6) **Fic**
Estes, E. The coat-hanger Christmas tree (4-6) **Fic**
Fox, P. How many miles to Babylon? (4-6) **Fic**
La Farge, P. Joanna runs away **E**
Orgel, D. Next door to Xanadu (4-6) **Fic**
Shotwell, L. R. Magdalena (5-7) **Fic**

Brooks, Anita
The picture book of grains (4-6) **633**

Brooks, Gwendolyn
Bronzeville boys and girls (2-5) **811**
About
See pages in the following book:
Rollins, C. Famous American Negro poets p87-91 (5-7) **920**

Brooks, Noah
President Lincoln reprieves a turkey
In Cavanah, F. ed. Holiday roundup p34-37 **394.2**

Brooks, Polly Schoyer
When the world was Rome, 753 B.C. to A.D. 476 (6-7) **937**

Brooks, Walter R.
Freddy, the detective (3-5) **Fic**
Henry and his dog Henry
In Gruenberg, S. M. ed. Favorite stories old and new p257-63 **808.8**
Jimmy takes vanishing lessons
In Ireson, B. comp. Haunting tales p235-45 **S C**

Brooks, William
(illus.) Kay, E. Let's find out about the hospital **362.1**

Broom and brush industry
See pages in the following book:
Fisher, L. E. The homemakers p29-35 (4-7) **680**

Broom market day. Molloy, L. L.
In Burack, A. S. ed. One hundred plays for children p656-65 **808.82**

Broome, Dora
The moon of gobbags
In Mayne, W. ed. William Mayne's Book of giants p170-76 **398.2**

Brooms and brushes. See Broom and brush industry

Broomsticks. De La Mare, W.
In De La Mare, W. The magic jacket p249-77 **S C**

The **broth** of Christkindli. Leuser, E.
In Burack, A. S. ed. Christmas plays for young actors p136-42 **812.08**

Brother and sister. Grimm, J.
In Grimm, J. The complete Grimm's Fairy tales p67-73 **398.2**
In Grimm, J. Household stories p65-71 **398.2**
In Grimm, J. The juniper tree, and other tales from Grimm v 1 p42-54 **398.2**
In Johnson, E. ed. Anthology of children's literature p130-33 **808.8**
In Lang, A. ed. The red fairy book p82-88 **398.2**

Brother Annancy fools Brother Fire
In Carter, D. S. ed. Greedy Mariani, and other folktales of the Antilles p68-72 **398.2**

Brother Breeze and the pear tree. Sherlock, P. M.
In Sherlock, P. M. Anansi, the spider man p13-19 **398.2**

A **brother** for the orphelines. Carlson, N. S. See Carlson, N. S. The happy orpheline **Fic**

Brother Gaily. Grimm, J.
In Grimm, J. The juniper tree, and other tales from Grimm v 1 p129-49 **398.2**
See also Brother Lustig

Brother Lustig
Grimm, J. Brother Gaily
In Grimm, J. The juniper tree, and other tales from Grimm v 1 p129-49 **398.2**

The **Brownie** o' Ferne-Den. Haviland, V.
 In Haviland, V. Favorite fairy tales told in
  Scotland p49-58   **398.2**

Brownies—hush! Adshead, G. L.   **E**

Brownies—it's Christmas! Adshead, G. L. **E**

Browning, Colleen
 (illus.) Graham, L. Every man heart lay down
            232.9

Browning, Robert
 The Pied Piper of Hamelin (3-7) **821**
 —Same
  In Arbuthnot, M. H. comp. The Arbuthnot
   Anthology of children's literature
   p16-19   **808.8**
  In Arbuthnot, M. H. comp. Time for
   poetry p28-31   **821.08**
  In Greenaway, K. The Kate Greenaway
   treasury p255-300   **828**
  In Martignoni, M. E. ed. The illustrated
   treasury of children's literature p401-
   08   **808.8**
 The Pied Piper of Hamelin; dramatization.
  See Kennedy, L. The Pied Piper of Ham-
  elin

Bruce, Blanche Kelso
 See pages in the following book:
 Sterling, P. Four took freedom p98-111 (5-6)
            920

Bruce, Margery
 The half-chick
  In Dobbs, R. ed. Once upon a time p8-14
           372.6

Bruce-Brown, David L.
 See pages in the following book:
 Stevenson, P. The greatest days of racing
  p21-26 (5-7)   **796.7**

Brude, Dick
 (illus.) Grant, M. G. Leif Ericson **92**

Bruges
 See pages in the following book:
 Loder, D. The land and people of Belgium
  p102-08 (5-7)   **914.93**

Bruin and Reynard partners
 Bowman, J. C. Farmers three
  In Bowman, J. C. Tales from a Finnish
   tupa p247-48   **398.2**

Brunhoff, Jean de
 The story of Babar, the little elephant **E**
 —Same
  In Martignoni, M. E. ed. The illustrated
   treasury of children's literature p316-
   18   **808.8**
     About
 See pages in the following book:
 Egoff, S. ed. Only connect p176-82 **028.5**

Brunhoff, Laurent de
 Babar's French lessons (1-3) **448**
 Babar's Spanish lessons (1-3) **468**

Brush, Warren D.
 (jt. auth.) Collingwood, G. H. Knowing your
  trees   **582**

Brussel-Smith, B.
 (illus.) Weart, E. L. The royal game **794.1**

Brussels
 See pages in the following book:
 Loder, D. The land and people of Belgium
  p120-30 (5-7)   **914.93**

Brustlein, Janice. See Janice

Bryan, Ashley
 Walk together children   **784.7**
 (illus.) Tagore, R. Moon, for what do you
  wait?   **821**

Bryan, Brigitte
 (illus.) Baum, L. F. The Wizard of Oz **Fic**
 (illus.) Graham, G. B. The beggar in the
  blanket, & other Vietnamese tales **398.2**

Bryan, Catherine
 Why the burro lives with the man
  In Johnson, E. ed. Anthology of children's
   literature p357-59   **808.8**

Bryan, Dorothy
 Pixie, Dixie, Trixie, and Nixie: the four little
  puppies who grow up and find happy
  homes
  In Gruenberg, S. M. comp. Let's hear a
   story p112-17   **808.8**

Bryant, Samuel
 (illus.) O'Dell, S. The King's fifth **Fic**

Bryant, Sarah Cone
 The cat and the parrot
  In Johnson, E. ed. Anthology of children's
   literature p318-19   **808.8**
  In Ross, E. S. ed. The lost half-hour p101-
   05   **372.6**
  In Sechrist, E. H. ed. It's time for story
   hour p81-84   **372.6**
 The Gingerbread Boy
  In Haviland, V. comp. The fairy tale trea-
   sury p7-11   **398.2**
 How Brother Rabbit fooled the whale and
  the elephant
  In Sechrist, E. H. ed. It's time for story
   hour p132-35   **372.6**
 The little jackal and the alligator
  In Sechrist, E. H. ed. It's time for story
   hour p121-25   **372.6**
 The little pink rose
  In Ward, W. ed. Stories to dramatize
   p46-47   **372.6**
 The little red hen and the grain of wheat
  In Haviland, V. comp. The fairy tale trea-
   sury p32-35   **398.2**
 The story of Epaminondas and his auntie
  In Colwell, E. ed. A second storyteller's
   choice p35-38   **372.6**
 The sun and the wind
  In Haviland, V. comp. The fairy tale trea-
   sury p100-01   **398.2**

Bryant, William Cullen
 The boys of my boyhood
  In A St Nicholas anthology p169-74 **810.8**

Bryce Canyon National Park
 See pages in the following book:
 Melbo, I. R. Our country's national parks
  v 1 p231-41 (5-7)   **917.3**

Brydon, Margaret Wylie
 The dreadful dragon
  In Kamerman, S. E. ed. Fifty plays for
   junior actors p64-85 **812.08**

Bryson, Bernarda
Gilgamesh (5-7)   **398.2**
The monster Humbaba
   In Arbuthnot, M. H. comp. The Arbuthnot
     Anthology of children's literature
     p455-58   **808.8**
   In Arbuthnot, M. H. comp. Time for old
     magic p319-22   **398.2**
(illus.) Belting, N. Calendar moon   **398.2**
(illus.) Belting, N. M. The sun is a golden
   earring   **398.2**
(illus.) Clarke, P. The return of the Twelves
   Fic

Buba, Joy
(illus.) Zim, H. S. Frogs and toads   **597**
(illus.) Zim, H. S. Goldfish   **639**

Bubble bubble. Mayer, M.   **E**

Bubley, Esther
(illus.) Selsam, M. E. How kittens grow **636.8**
(illus.) Selsam, M. E. How puppies grow
   636.7

Bubo, the great horned owl. George, J. L. 598.2

Buccaneers. See Pirates

Buccaneers & pirates of our coasts. Stockton,
F. R.   **910.4**

Buchanan-Brown, John
(illus.) Berne, P. The horse without a head **Fic**

Bucharest
   See pages in the following book:
Hale, J. The land and people of Romania
   p36-41, 48-52 (5-7)   **914.98**

Buchwald, Emilie
Gildaen (4-6)   **Fic**

Buck, Alan Michael
Deirdre
   In Hazeltine, A. I. ed. Hero tales from
     many lands p174-83   **398.2**

Buck, Margaret Waring
Along the seashore (3-6)   **574.92**
Pets from the pond (4-7)   **639**
Small pets from woods and fields (4-7)   **639**
Where they go in winter (3-6)   **591.5**

Buck, Pearl S.
The big wave (4-7)   **Fic**
Matthew, Mark, Luke and John (4-6)   **Fic**

Buckley, Helen E.
Grandfather and I   **E**
Grandmother and I   **E**

Buckley, Peter
I am from Puerto Rico (4-6)   **917.295**

Buckmaster, Henrietta
Flight to freedom (5-7)   **326**

Buckwheat
Andersen, H. The buckwheat
   In Andersen, H. C. The complete fairy
     tales and stories p198-99   **S C**
   In Andersen, H. Hans Andersen's Fairy
     tales p165-67   **S C**

Budbill, David
Christmas tree farm (k-2)   **634.9**

Budd, Lillian
Tekla's Easter (2-4)   **Fic**

Buddha and Buddhism
Serage, N. The prince who gave up a throne
   [biography of Gautama Buddha] (4-6)   **92**

   See also pages in the following books:
Chandler, D. P. The land and people of Cam-
   bodia p106-20 (5-7)   **915.96**
Fitch, F. M. Their search for God p111-55
   (4-7)   **291**
Kettelkamp, L. Religions, East and West p37-
   45 (5-7)   **291**
Poole, F. K. Thailand p29-33 (5-7)   **915.93**
Seeger, E. Eastern religions p57-102 (6-7)
   291
Vaughan, J. B. The land and people of Japan
   p54-61 (5-7)   **915.2**
Wilber, D. N. The land and people of Ceylon
   p132-35 (5-7)   **915.49**
Wolcott, L. Religions around the world p53-
   69, 89-105 (5-7)   **291**
The World's great religions. Special edition
   for young readers p35-56 (5-7)   **291**

Budgerigars
Zim, H. S. Parrakeets (4-7)   **636.6**
   See also pages in the following book:
Stevens, C. Your first pet p65-80 (2-4) **636.08**

Budget, Personal. See Finance, Personal

Budlong, Ware T.
Performing plants (5-7)   **581**

Budney, Blossom
The big day
   In Gruenberg, S. M. comp. Let's hear a
     story p34-37   **808.8**
A kiss is round   **E**

Budulinek
Fillmore, P. Budulinek
   In Arbuthnot, M. H. comp. The Arbuthnot
     Anthology of children's literature
     p277-80   **808.8**
   In Arbuthnot, M. H. comp. Time for old
     magic p160-63   **398.2**
   In Haviland, V. comp. The fairy tale trea-
     sury p692-99   **398.2**
   In Johnson, E. ed. Anthology of children's
     literature p263-65   **808.8**
   In Ross, E. S. ed. The lost half-hour p128-
     36   **372.6**

Buechler, James
Stone soup
   In Kamerman, S. E. ed. Dramatized folk
     tales of the world p381-87   **812.08**

Buehr, Walter
Chivalry and the mailed knight (3-6)   **940.1**
Cloth from fiber to fabric (5-7)   **677**
The crusaders (5-7)   **940.1**
Food from farm to home (4-6)   **631**
The French explorers in America (4-6)   **973.1**
Knights and castles, and feudal life (4-7)
   940.1
The magic of paper (4-7)   **676**
The marvel of glass (5-7)   **666**
The Portuguese explorers (4-6)   **910**
Salt, sugar, and spice (3-6)   **664**
The Spanish conquistadores in North Amer-
   ica (4-7)   **973.1**
Storm warning (3-6)   **551.5**
The Viking explorers (3-6)   **948**
The world of Marco Polo (4-6)   **92**

Buel, Hubert
(illus.) Lampman, E. S. The shy stegosaurus
   of Cricket Creek   **Fic**

Buell, Hal
Viet Nam (5-7)   **915.97**

Buenos Aires
    See pages in the following book:
Hall, E. The land and people of Argentina
    p9-12, 38-46 (5-7)   **918.2**
Buff, Conrad
    (jt. auth.) Buff, M. The apple and the arrow
        Fic
    (jt. auth.) Buff, M. Big tree   **582**
    (jt. auth.) Buff, M. Dash & Dart   **599**
    (jt. auth.) Buff, M. Elf owl   **591.5**
    (jt. auth.) Buff, H. Magic maize   **Fic**
Buff, Mary
    The apple and the arrow (3-6)   **Fic**
    Big tree (5-7)   **582**
    Catching wild horses
        In Association for Childhood Education International. Told under spacious skies
        p271-86   **S C**
    Dash & Dart (k-3)   **599**
    Elf owl (1-4)   **591.5**
    Magic maize (3-6)   **Fic**
Buffalo, American. See Bison
Buffalo Bill. See Cody, William Frederick
Buffalo harvest. Rounds, G.   **970.4**
Buffalo hunting. Roosevelt, T.
    In A St Nicholas anthology p137-45 **810.8**
The **buffalo**, the coyote and the peace pipe.
    Arnott, K.
    In Arnott, K. Animal folk tales around the
        world p 1-5   **398.2**
Buffaloes
    See pages in the following book:
Raskin, E. World food p61-67 (5-7)   **338.1**
    See also Water buffalo
The **Buffy-Porson.** Stevenson, P.   **688.6**
The **bug clan.** Hutchins, R. E.   **595.7**
The **bug club book.** Conklin, G.   **595.7**
Bugs. See Insects
Buh Fox's number nine shoes. Courlander, H.
    In Courlander, H. Terrapin's pot of sense
        p37-40   **398.2**
Buh Mouse testifies. Courlander, H.
    In Courlander, H. Terrapin's pot of sense
        p53-56   **398.2**
Buh Rabbit and the king. Courlander, H.
    In Courlander, H. Terrapin's pot of sense
        p60-64   **398.2**
Buh Rabbit's big eat. Courlander, H.
    In Courlander, H. Terrapin's pot of sense
        p33-36   **398.2**
Buh Rabbit's graveyard. Courlander, H.
    In Courlander, H. Terrapin's pot of sense
        p57-59   **398.2**
Buh Rabbit's human weakness. Courlander, H.
    In Courlander, H. Terrapin's pot of sense
        p31-32   **398.2**
Buh Rabbit's tail. Courlander, H.
    In Courlander, H. Terrapin's pot of sense
        p41-45   **398.2**
Buh Rabbit's tight necktie. Courlander, H.
    In Courlander, H. Terrapin's pot of sense
        p21-33   **398.2**
The **builder** of the wall. Roberts, H.
    In Kamerman, S. E. ed. Dramatized folk
        tales of the world p422-34   **812.08**

Building
    Harman, C. A skyscraper goes up (5-7)   **690**
    Tannenbaum, B. High rises (3-6)   **690**
    See also Architecture; Roofs
Building. Baruch, D.
    In Association for Childhood Education International. Told under the blue umbrella p7-8   **S C**
Building bridges of understanding between cultures. Keating, C. M.   **028.52**
Building materials. See Cement; Concrete
Building of Balor's dune. Young, E.
    In Young, E. The wonder smith and his
        son p115-28   **398.2**
Building the Suez Canal   **962**
Building with cardboard. Lidstone, J.   **745.54**
Building with wire. Lidstone, J.   **745.56**
Building wrecking. Colby, J. P.   **690**
The **buildings** of ancient Egypt. Leacroft, H.   **722**
The **buildings** of ancient Greece. Leacroft, H.   **722**
The **buildings** of ancient man. Leacroft, H. **722**
The **buildings** of ancient Rome. Leacroft, H.   **722**
Bukolla
    In Courlander, H. ed. Ride with the sun
        p194-96   **398.2**
Bulbs
    Selsam, M. E. Bulbs, corms, and such (2-5)   **584**
    See also pages in the following books:
Abell, E. Flower gardening p35-38 (5-7)   **635.9**
Fenten, D. X. Indoor gardening p40-44 (4-7)   **635.9**
Fenten, D. X. Plants for pots p52-61 (4-7)   **635.9**
Selsam, M. E. How to grow house plants p80-84 (4-7)   **635.9**
Bulbs, corms, and such. Selsam, M. E.   **584**
Bulfinch, Thomas
    The age of chivalry
        In Bulfinch, T. Bulfinch's Mythology **291**
    The age of fable
        In Bulfinch, T. Bulfinch's Mythology **291**
    Baucis and Philemon
        In Martignoni, M. E. ed. The illustrated treasury of children's literature p508   **808.8**
    A book of myths (5-7)   **292**
    Bulfinch's Mythology (6-7)   **291**
    Legends of Charlemagne
        In Bulfinch, T. Bulfinch's Mythology **291**
Bulgaria
    McLellan, J. Bulgaria in pictures (5-7)   **914.977**
    See also Balkan peninsula
Bulgaria in pictures. McLellan, J.   **914.977**
Bull, Dixey
    See pages in the following book:
Whipple, A. B. C. Famous pirates of the New World p109-11 (5-7)   **910.4**
The **bull** didn't have a chance. Jagendorf, M. A.
    In Jagendorf, M. A. Folk stories of the
        South p42-43   **398.2**

Caldecott Medal books

Aulaire, I. d' and Aulaire, E. P. d'. See Aulaire, I. d'. Abraham Lincoln (1940) **92**

Bemelmans, L. See Bemelmans, L. Madeline's rescue (1954) **E**

Brown, M. See Brown, M. Once a mouse (1962) **398.2**

Brown, M. See Perrault, C. Cinderella (1955) **398.2**

Burton, V. L. See Burton, V. L. The little house (1943) **E**

Cooney, B. See Cooney, B. Chanticleer and the fox (1959) **E**

Duvoisin, R. See Tresselt, A. White snow (1948) **E**

Emberley, E. See Emberley, B. Drummer Hoff (1968) **398.8**

Ets, M. H. See Ets, M. H. Nine days to Christmas (1960) **E**

Hader, B. See Hader, B. The big snow (1949) **E**

Haley, G. E. See Haley, G. E. A story, a story (1970) **398.2**

Handforth, T. See Handforth, T. Mei Li (1939) **E**

Hogrogian, N. See Hogrogian, N. One fine day (1971) **398.2**

Hogrogian, N. See Nic Leodhas, S. Always room for one more (1966) **784.4**

Jones, E. O. See Field, R. Prayer for a child (1945) **242**

Keats, E. J. See Keats, E. J. The snowy day (1963) **E**

Lathrop, D. P. See Bible. Selections. Animals of the Bible (1938) **220.8**

Lent, B. See Mosel, A. The funny little woman (1972) **398.2**

McCloskey, R. See McCloskey, R. Make way for ducklings (1942) **E**

McCloskey, R. See McCloskey, R. Time of wonder (1958) **E**

McDermott, G. See McDermott, G. Arrow to the sun (1974) **398.2**

Milhous, K. See Milhous, K. The egg tree (1951) **E**

Montresor, B. See De Regniers, B. S. May I bring a friend? (1965) **E**

Ness, E. See Ness, E. Sam, Bangs & Moonshine (1967) **E**

Nicolas. See Will. Finders keepers (1952) **E**

Petersham, Maud and Petersham, Miska. See Petersham, M. comp. The rooster crows (1946) **398.8**

Politi, L. See Politi, L. Song of the swallows (1950) **E**

Rojankovsky, F. See Langstaff, J. Frog went a-courtin' (1956) **784.4**

Sendak, M. See Sendak, M. Where the wild things are (1964) **E**

Shulevitz, U. See Ransome, A. The Fool of the World and the flying ship (1969) **398.2**

Sidjakov, N. See Robbins, R. Baboushka and the three kings (1961) **398.2**

Steig, W. See Steig, W. Sylvester and the magic pebble (1969) **E**

Thurber, J. See Thurber, J. Many moons (1944) **Fic**

Ward, L. See Ward, L. The biggest bear (1953) **E**

Weisgard, L. See MacDonald, G. The little island (1947) **E**

Zemach, M. See Zemach, H. Duffy and the devil (1974) **398.2**

Caldecott Medal books (as subject)

Kingman, L. ed. Newbery and Caldecott Medal books: 1956-1965 **028.5**

Kingman, L. ed. Newbery and Caldecott Medal books: 1966-1975 **028.5**

Miller, B. M. ed. Caldecott Medal books: 1938-1957 **028.5**

See also pages in the following books:

Haviland, V. ed. Children and literature p416-35 **028.5**

MacCann, D. The child's first books p115-20 **741.64**

Caldecott Medal books: 1938-1957. Miller, B. M. ed. **028.5**

Caldicott Place. See Streatfeild, N. The family at Caldicott Place **Fic**

Caldwell, Erskine

Molly Cottontail

In Untermeyer, B. ed. The Golden Treasury of children's literature p50-55 **808.8**

Caldwell, John C.

Let's visit the Middle East (5-7) **915.6**

Caleb Thorne's day. Coatsworth, E.

In Hoke, H. ed. Spooks, spooks, spooks p116-27 **S C**

The calendar. Adler, I. **529**

Calendar moon. Belting, N. **398.2**

Calendars

Adler, I. The calendar (3-5) **529**

Brindze, R. The story of our calendar (4-7) **529**

Farjeon, E. The new book of days (5-7) **828**

Zarchy, H. Wheel of time (6-7) **529**

See also pages in the following books:

Adler, I. Time in your life p35-42 (5-7) **529**

Sechrist, E. H. Red letter days p231-42 **394.2**

Calhoun, Mary

High wind for Kansas (2-4) **Fic**

Katie John (4-6) **Fic**

Calico bush. Field, R. **Fic**

Calico bush; excerpt. Field, R.

In Arbuthnot, M. H. comp. The Arbuthnot Anthology of children's literature p745-48 **808.8**

California

Fiction

Cameron, E. A spell is cast (5-7) **Fic**

Cameron, E. The terrible churnadryne (4-6) **Fic**

Ellis, E. T. Celebrate the morning (6-7) **Fic**

Gates, D. Blue willow (4-7) **Fic**

Politi, L. Song of the swallows **E**

Snyder, Z. K. The truth about Stone Hollow (4-7) **Fic**

Snyder, Z. K. The velvet room (4-6) **Fic**

Uchida, Y. The promised year (4-6) **Fic**

Uchida, Y. Samurai of Gold Hill (4-7) **Fic**

Gold discoveries—Fiction

Fleischman, S. By the Great Horn Spoon! (4-6) **Fic**

History

Chester, M. Forts of old California (5-7) **979.4**

Campbell, Camilla

The morning maker

In Kamerman, S. E. ed. Little plays for little players p266-69   812.08

Star Mountain, and other legends of Mexico (4-5)   398.2

Hummingbird and eagle; Star Mountain; Moon-God of the Mayas; Sleeping woman of the snows; The bold Mixtec; The two trees of sadness; Alvarado's leap; Our Lady of Guadalupe; The ghost of Marina; Our Lady of the Remedies; City of Angels; El niño de la Panelita; Street of the Deer; China Poblana; Street of the Green Cross; The princess of the lake; The sad song of Carlota; The morning-maker; El Pájaro-cu; 'Mano Coyote

Campbell, Elizabeth A.

The carving on the tree (3-5)   973.1

Nails to nickels (3-5)   737.4

Campbell, J. F.

The battle of the birds

In Fairy tales from many lands p15-27   398.2

Campbell, Josephine E.

Pink roses for Christmas

In Burack, A. S. ed. Christmas plays for young actors p3-12   812.08

Camping

Paul, A. Kids camping (4-6)   796.54

See also pages in the following books:

Boy Scouts of America. Fieldbook p32-65   369.43

Frankel, L. Bike-ways (101 things to do with a bike) p68-80 (4-6)   796.6

Fiction

Carrick, C. Sleep out   E

Campion, Nardi Reeder

Patrick Henry, firebrand of the Revolution (5-7)   92

Camps

Fiction

Hodges, M. The hatching of Joshua Cobb (4-6)   Fic

Norris, G. B. The good morrow (4-6)   Fic

Stolz, M. A wonderful, terrible time (4-6) Fic

Can I keep him? Kellogg, S.   E

Canada

Ross, F. A. The land and people of Canada (5-7)   917.1

See also pages in the following book:

Discoverers of the New World p112-25 (5-7)   973.1

Agriculture

See Agriculture—Canada

Biography

McNeer, M. The Canadian story (5-7)   971

Biography—Bibliography

See pages in the following book:

Egoff, S. The republic of childhood p204-38   028.5

Discovery and exploration

See America—Discovery and exploration

Festivals

See Festivals—Canada

Fiction

Ellis, M. Caribou Crossing (5-7)   Fic

Lippincott, J. W. Wilderness champion (5-7)   Fic

Roberts, C. G. D. Red Fox (4-7)   Fic

Folklore

See Folklore—Canada

History

McNeer, M. The Canadian story (5-7)   971

History—To 1763 (New France)

Jacobs, W. Samuel de Champlain (4-6)   92

History—1763-1791

See pages in the following book:

Lomask, M. The first American Revolution p127-32, 170-75 (6-7)   973.3

History—Bibliography

See pages in the following book:

Egoff, S. The republic of childhood p204-38   028.5

Legends

See Legends—Canada

Social life and customs

See pages in the following book:

Sechrist, E. H. ed. Christmas everywhere p36-43   394.2

Canadian literature

History and criticism

Egoff, S. The republic of childhood   028.5

Periodicals

In Review   028.505

Canadian poetry

Collections

Downie, M. A. comp. The wind has wings (5-7)   811.08

The Canadian story. McNeer, M.   971

Canals

History

Boardman, F. W. Canals (5-7)   386

Franchere, R. Westward by canal (5-7)   386

Canaries

See pages in the following books:

Chrystie, F. N. Pets p60-68 (4-7)   636.08

Villiard, P. Birds as pets p39-74 (5-7)   636.6

Stories

Gannett, R. S. Elmer and the dragon (1-4) Fic

Candies, cookies, cakes. Paul, A.   641.8

A candle in her room. Arthur, R. M.   Fic

Candle-light stories. Hutchinson, V. S. ed. 398.2

Candles

See pages in the following books:

Cross, L. Kitchen crafts p80-87 (3-7)   745.5

Fisher, L. E. The homemakers p11-21 (4-7)   680

Pettit, F. H. How to make whirligigs and whimmy diddles, and other American folkcraft objects p158-73 (5-7)   745.5

The candles. Andersen, H. C.

In Andersen, H. C. The complete fairy tales and stories p992-94   S C

Candles at midnight. Kelsey, A. G.

In Harper, W. comp. Easter chimes p26-38   394.2

In Sechrist, E. H. ed. It's time for Easter p189-97   394.2

Candles for Christmas. Howard H. L.
In Kamerman, S. E. ed. A treasury of
Christmas plays p372-75 **812.08**

Candles, radishes and garlic. Simon, S.
In Simon, S. The wise men of Helm and
their merry tales p103-18 **S C**

Candy, Robert
(illus.) Binns, A. Sea pup **Fic**
(illus.) Waters, B. Salt-water aquariums **639**

Candy. See Confectionery

Candy canes. Spamer, C.
In Burack, A. S. ed. Christmas plays for
young actors p219-22 **812.08**

Canfield, Dorothy. See Fisher, Dorothy Canfield

Cannetella. Manning-Sanders, R.
In Manning-Sanders, R. A book of wizards
p118-[27] **398.2**

The cannibal and his sweet singing bird. Carpenter, F.
In Carpenter, F. African wonder tales
p195-203 **398.2**

The cannibal who ate too fast. Holladay, V.
In Holladay, V. Bantu tales p24-25 **398.2**

The cannibal's drum. Holladay, V.
In Holladay, V. Bantu tales p38-41 **398.2**

The canoe in the rapids. Carlson, N. S.
In Arbuthnot, M. H. comp. The Arbuthnot
Anthology of children's literature
p362-65 **808.8**
In Carlson, N. S. The talking cat and other
stories of French Canada p54-65 **S C**
In Johnson, E. ed. Anthology of children's
literature p335-38 **808.8**

Canoes and canoeing
See pages in the following books:
Bleeker, S. The Chippewa Indians p37-42
(4-6) **970.3**
Bleeker, S. The sea hunters p60-66 (4-6)
970.4

Can't rest. Leach, M.
In Leach, M. Whistle in the graveyard
p43-44 **398.2**

Canton, China

Description
See pages in the following book:
Sidel, R. Revolutionary China: people, poli-
tics, and ping-pong p131-40 (6-7) **915.1**

Cantwell, Mary
St Patrick's Day (1-3) **394.2**

Canvas embroidery
Hanley, H. Fun with needlepoint (5-7) **746.4**
Lightbody, D. M. Introducing needlepoint
(5-7) **746.4**

Canyonlands National Park
See pages in the following books:
Melbo, I. R. Our country's national parks
v 1 p285-303 (5-7) **917.3**
National Geographic Society. The new Amer-
ica's wonderlands p142-53 **917.3**

Cap o' rushes
Cap o' Rushes
In Jacobs, J. ed. English folk and fairy
tales p51-56 **398.2**
Williams-Ellis, A. Cap o' Rushes
In Williams-Ellis, A. Fairy tales from the
British Isles p117-23 **398.2**

The Cap that mother made
In Gruenberg, S. M. ed. Favorite stories old
and new p68-71 **808.8**
See also Ander's new cap

Capell, Loretta Camp
The first Christmas tree
In Kamerman, S. E. ed. A treasury of
Christmas plays p279-87 **812.08**

Capitalists and financiers
Captains of industry (5-7) **920**
Shippen, K. B. Andrew Carnegie and the age
of steel (4-7) **92**

Capitals (Cities)
Goetz, D. State capital cities (4-6) **917.3**

Capitol Reef National Park
See pages in the following book:
Melbo, I. R. Our country's national parks
v 1 p304-16 (5-7) **917.3**

Caps for sale. Slobodkina, E. **E**

Captain Cook and the South Pacific **919**

Captain Cook, Pacific explorer. Syme, R. **92**

Captain John Paul Jones: America's fighting seaman. Syme, R. **92**

Captain Kidd. See Kidd, William

Captain Murderer. Dickens, C.
In Hardendorff, J. B. Witches, wit, and a
werewolf p97-101 **S C**

Captains of industry (5-7) **920**

Car of the year, 1895-1970. Lent, H. B. **629.22**

Carabao. See Water buffalo

Caracciola, Rudolf
See pages in the following book:
Stevenson, P. The greatest days of racing p86-
99 (5-7) **796.7**

Caras, Roger
The bizarre animals **591**
A zoo in your room (4-7) **636.08**

The caravan. Sawyer, R.
In Tudor, T. ed. Take joy! p43-46 **394.2**

Caraway, James
(illus.) Shuttlesworth, D. The Doubleday
First guide to rocks **552**

Carbon
Bronowski, J. Biography of an atom (4-7) **541**
See also pages in the following book:
Freeman, I. M. The science of chemistry p37-
44 (5-7) **540**

Carbonel, the King of the Cats. Sleigh, B. **Fic**

Card catalogs. See Library catalogs

Card tricks
See pages in the following books:
Leeming, J. Fun with magic p40-52 (4-7)
793.8
Leeming, J. More Fun with magic p20-30
(4-7) **793.8**
Severn, B. Bill Severn's Big book of magic
p16-31 (6-7) **793.8**

Cardboard, Building with. Lidstone, J. **745.54**

Cardboard crafting. Granit, I. **745.54**

Cardiac diseases. See Heart—Diseases

Cardinals (Birds)
McClung, R. M. Redbird (2-4) **598.2**

Cards. See Fortune telling

Carpenter, Frances—*Continued*

and the honeybees; A dream of the Sphinx; The monkeys and the little red hats; The girl who lived with the gazelles; The battle between the birds and the beasts; Strange men with tails; The two rascals; Pemba and the python and the friendly rat; Polo, the snake-girl; Omar's big life; The young hunter and the JuJu man; The Jinni's magic flute; The proud camel and the rude monkey; The bride who melted away; Bomba, the Brave; The bird that would not stay dead; The six horsemen; The cannibal and his sweet singing bird; The enchanted tortoise

The daughter of Dragon King

In Hoke, H. comp. Dragons, dragons, dragons p43-50   **398.2**

People from the sky (4-6)   **398.2**

Contents: People from the sky; A-e-oina, the demon, and the tattle-tale dog; Animals from heaven; "Goodby, dear little Bear God"; The hungry time; Yoshitsuni, brave warrior from Japan; The Old Man on the mountain; The frog's tattoo; The mad dancers of Upopou-shi; The one-eyed monster; Fox magic; Pan'ambe and Pen'ambe; The bats of Ru-pe-shi-pe; The Golden Mare; The flying sword; Two terrible fish; The "Little People"

Sinterklaas Eve

In Johnson, L. S. ed. Christmas stories round the world p47-52   **394.2**

Tales of a Chinese grandmother (5-7)   **398.2**

Contents: Inside the bright red gate; How Pan Ku made the world; Sister in the sun; Gentle Gwan Yin; God that lived in the kitchen; Guardians of the gate; Painted eyebrow; Ting Lan and the lamb; Daughter of the dragon king; Big feet of the Empress Tu Chin; Grateful fox fairy; Lady with the horse's head; King of the monkeys; Two dutiful sons; Poet and the peony princess; First emperor's magic whip; Wonderful pear tree; How the eight old ones crossed the sea; White snake; Prince Chu Ti's city; Ko-Ai's lost shoe; Spinning maid and the cowherd; Lost star princess; Mandarin and the butterflies; Heng O, the moon lady; Cheng's fighting cricket; Maid in the mirror; Miss Lin, the sea goddess; Simple Seng and the parrot; Old Old One's birthday

The **carpenter** bee. Hutchins, R. E.   **595.7**

Carpenter, Ralph

(illus.) Shaw, E. Octopus   **594**

Carpentry

See also Cabinet work

Tools

Adkins, J. Toolchest (5-7)   **621.9**

Carpet bag rule. See Reconstruction

The **carpet** of Solomon. Ish-Kishor, S.   **398.2**

Carpets

Fiction

Parkin, R. The red carpet   **E**

Carr, Mary Jane

Children of the covered wagon (4-6)   **Fic**

Carr, Rachel

Be a frog, a bird, or a tree (1-4)   **613.7**

Carr, Vikki

See pages in the following book:

Newlon, C. Famous Mexican-Americans p108-15 (6-7)   **920**

Carriages and carts

Fiction

Calhoun, M. High wind for Kansas (2-4)   **Fic**

Carrick, Carol

The brook (k-2)   **574.92**

Lost in the storm   **E**

The pond (k-2)   **574.92**

Sleep out   **E**

Swamp spring (k-3)   **574**

Carrick, Donald

(illus.) Budbill, D. Christmas tree farm **634.9**

(jt. auth.) Carrick, C. The brook   **574.92**

(illus.) Carrick, C. Lost in the storm   **E**

(jt. auth.) Carrick, C. The pond   **574.92**

(jt. auth.) Carrick, C. Sleep out   **E**

(jt. auth.) Carrick, C. Swamp spring   **574**

(illus.) Freschet, B. Bear mouse   **599**

(illus.) Freschet, B. Turtle pond   **598.1**

(illus.) Uchida, Y. Journey to Topaz (4-7) **Fic**

Carrick, Valéry

Mr Samson Cat

In Johnson, E. ed. Anthology of children's literature p259-61   **808.8**

Carrie-Barry-Annie. Fyleman, R.

In Gruenberg, S. M. ed. Favorite stories old and new p240-44   **808.8**

Carrie's war. Bawden, N.   **Fic**

Carroll, Charles

(illus.) Conford, E. Me and the terrible two   **Fic**

Carroll, David

Make your own chess set (5-7)   **745.59**

Carroll, Gladys Hasty

Merry, merry, merry

In Burack, A. S. ed. One hundred plays for children p492-506   **808.82**

Carroll, Latrobe

(jt. auth.) Carroll, R. Beanie   **Fic**

(jt. auth.) Carroll, R. Tough Enough   **Fic**

Carroll, Lewis

Alice's adventures in Wonderland (4-7) **Fic**

also in Carroll, L. Alice's adventures in Wonderland, and Through the looking glass   **Fic**

also in Darrell, M. ed. Once upon a time p71-138   **808.8**

Alice's adventures in Wonderland; excerpt

In Arbuthnot, M. H. comp. The Arbuthnot Anthology of children's literature p531-35   **808.8**

Alice's adventures in Wonderland; excerpts

In Johnson, E. ed. Anthology of children's literature p632-39   **808.8**

In Martignoni, M. E. ed. The illustrated treasury of children's literature p294-301   **808.8**

Alice's adventures in Wonderland; puppet play. See Mahlmann, L. Alice's adventures in Wonderland

Alice's adventures in Wonderland, and Through the looking glass (4-7)   **Fic**

Down the rabbit hole

In Johnson, E. ed. Anthology of children's literature p632-35   **808.8**

In Martignoni, M. E. ed. The illustrated treasury of children's literature p294-97   **808.8**

The hunting of the snark (3-6)   **821**

A mad tea-party

In Arbuthnot, M. H. comp. The Arbuthnot Anthology of children's literature p532-35   **808.8**

In Untermeyer, B. ed. The Golden Treasury of children's literature p517-21   **808.8**

The pool of tears

In Martignoni, M. E. ed. The illustrated treasury of children's literature p298-301   **808.8**

Carroll, Lewis—*Continued*
Queen Alice
In Farjeon, E. ed. A cavalcade of queens p222-32   **808.8**
The rabbit sends in a little Bill
In Johnson, E. ed. Anthology of children's literature p635-39   **808.8**
Through the looking glass, and what Alice found there (4-7)   **Fic**
also in Carroll, L. Alice's adventures in Wonderland, and Through the looking glass   **Fic**
Tweedledum and Tweedledee
In Untermeyer, B. ed. The Golden Treasury of children's literature p508-16   **808.8**
The walrus and the carpenter (3-6)   **821**
For material about this author see Dodgson, Charles Lutwidge

Carroll, Pamela
(illus.) Knight, D. C. Thirty-two moons **523.9**

Carroll, Ruth
Beanie (1-4)   **Fic**
Tough Enough (2-4)   **Fic**
What Whiskers did   **E**

Carroll, Sidney B.
You be the judge (4-7)   **347**

The **carrot** and other root vegetables. Selsam, M. E.   **635**

A **carrot** for a nose. Gladstone, M. J.   **745**

Carruth, Ella Kaiser
She wanted to read; the story of Mary McLeod Bethune (4-6)   **92**

Cars (Automobiles) See Automobiles

Cars, trucks and trains. Swallow, S.   **380.5**

Carson, Christopher
Bell, M. E. Kit Carson: mountain man (4-7)   **92**
See also pages in the following books:
Bleeker, S. The Navajo p138-42 (4-6)   **970.3**
Dorian, E. Trails West and men who made them p59-61 (4-7)   **978**

Carson, Kit. See Carson, Christopher

Carson, Rachel L.
The sea around us. A special edition for young readers; adapted by Anne Terry White (6-7)   **551.4**
About
Latham, J. L. Rachel Carson: who loved the sea (3-5)   **92**
Sterling, P. Sea and earth (6-7)   **92**
See also pages in the following book:
Hirsch, S. C. Guardians of tomorrow p154-65 (6-7)   **920**

Carter, Dorothy Sharp
The first flute
In Arbuthnot, M. H. comp. The Arbuthnot Anthology of children's literature p409-11   **808.8**
(ed.) Greedy Mariani, and other folktales of the Antilles (3-7)   **398.2**
Contents: How the moonfish came to be; How the clever doctor tricked death; Why dog lost his voice; Why misery remains in the world; How El Bizarrón fooled the Devil; Brer Rabbit's trickery; The goat and the tiger; Compae Rabbit's ride; The tortoise who flew to heaven; Rabbit's long ears; Brother Annancy fools Brother Fire; Man-crow; Snake the postman; Wheeler; Malice, Bouki and Momplaisir; Greedy Mariani; The

three fairies; Juan Bobo; The shepherd and the princess; The miser who received his due
The three fairies
In Arbuthnot, M. H. comp. The Arbuthnot Anthology of children's literature p403-04   **808.8**

Carter, Helene
(illus.) Brindze, R. The story of our calendar   **529**

Carter, Hodding
The Commandos of World War II (5-7)   **940.54**

Carter, Samuel
Vikings bold: their voyages & adventures (5-7)   **914.8**

Carter, William E.
The first book of South America (4-6)   **918**

Carthage
See pages in the following books:
Brooks, P. S. When the world was Rome, 753 B.C. to A.D. 476 p27-33 (6-7)   **937**
Spencer, W. The land and people of Tunisia p32-40 (5-7)   **916.1**

Carthy, John
Animal camouflage (3-5)   **591.5**

Cartier, Jacques
Syme, R. Cartier, finder of the St Lawrence (4-6)   **92**
See also pages in the following book:
Discoverers of the New World p112-16 (5-7)   **973.1**

Cartledge, T. M.
(jt. ed.) Shaw, M. ed. National anthems of the world   **784.7**

The **cartman's** stories. Spellman, J. W.
In Arbuthnot, M. H. comp. The Arbuthnot Anthology of children's literature p351-53   **808.8**
In Arbuthnot, M. H. comp. Time for old magic p230-31   **398.2**

Cartography. See Map drawing; Maps

Carton crafts, Kitchen. Sattler, H. R.   **745.54**

Cartoons and caricatures
Emberley, E. Ed Emberley's Drawing book of faces (3-6)   **743**
See also pages in the following books:
Holme, B. Drawings to live with p141-56   **741.9**
Illustrators of children's books: 1744-1945 p197-214   **741.64**
See also Comic books, strips, etc.

Carts. See Carriages and carts

Cartwright, Sally
Animal homes (1-3)   **591.5**
The tide (1-3)   **525**

Carty, Leo
(illus.) Mathis, S. B. Sidewalk story   **Fic**

Carver, George Washington
Aliki. A weed is a flower (k-3)   **92**
See also pages in the following books:
Asimov, I. Breakthroughs in science p172-76 (5-7)   **920**
Hayden, R. C. Seven Black American scientists p142-60 (6-7)   **920**
Hughes, L. Famous American Negroes p69-76 (5-7)   **920**

Carver, George Washington—*Continued*
Johnston, J. A special bravery p55-59 (2-5)
 920
McNeer, M. Armed with courage p39-54 (4-6)
 920
Rollins, C. H. They showed the way p39-42
 (5-7) **920**

Carving, Wood. See Wood carving

The **carving** on the tree. Campbell, E. A. **973.1**

Cary
 (illus.) Collins, D. R. Linda Richards: first
 American trained nurse **92**
 (illus.) Meadowcroft, E. L. Crazy Horse,
 Sioux warrior **92**
 (illus.) Price, O. Rosa Bonheur, painter of
 animals **92**

Cary, Louis F. See Cary

Cary, Page
 (illus.) Beck, B. L. The first book of fruits **634**
 (illus.) Beck, B. L. The first book of the ancient Maya **970.3**
 (illus.) Beck, B. L. The first book of the
 Aztecs **970.3**
 (illus.) Beck, B. L. The first book of the Incas
 980.3
 (illus.) Beck, B. L. Vegetables **581.6**

Casals, Rosemary
 See pages in the following book:
 Sullivan, G. Queens of the court p84-91 (5-7)
 920

Case, Bernard
 (illus.) Bowen, R. S. They flew to glory: the
 story of the Lafayette Flying Corps (4-6)
 940.4

A **case** of identity. Doyle, Sir A. C.
 In Doyle, Sir A. C. Tales of Sherlock
 Holmes p307-25 **S C**

The **case** of the cat's meow. Bonsall, C. **E**

The **case** of the dumb bells. Bonsall, C. **E**

The **case** of the elevator duck. Berends, P. B.
 Fic

The **case** of the hungry stranger. Bonsall, C. **E**

The **case** of the missing masterpiece. Huff, B. T.
 In Burack, A. S. ed. Popular plays for
 classroom reading p173-88 **808.82**

The **case** of the scaredy cats. Bonsall, C. **E**

Casey at the bat. Thayer, E. L. **811**
 —Same
 In Henry, R. comp. My American heritage
 p88-90 **810.8**

Casey joins the circus. Dobias, D. F.
 In Gruenberg, S. M. ed. Favorite stories
 old and new p159-64 **808.8**

Casey Jones (Folk song)
 Casey Jones (2-4) **784.4**

Casey Jones and Locomotive No. 638. Shapiro, I.
 In Shapiro, I. Heroes in American folklore
 p7-57 **398.2**

Casi Lampu'a Lentemué. Belpré, P.
 In Belpré, P. The tiger and the rabbit, and
 other tales p75-82 **398.2**

The **cask** of Amontillado. Poe, E. A.
 In Poe, E. A. Tales of terror and fantasy
 p37-44 **S C**

Casperl. Bunner, H. C.
 In Child Study Association of America.
 Castles and dragons p227-41 **398.2**

Cassedy, Sylvia
 (comp.) Birds, frogs, and moonlight (3-6)
 895.6
 (comp.) Moon-uncle, moon-uncle (k-3) **398.8**

Cassell, Lili
 (illus.) Withers, C. comp. Riddles of many
 lands **398.6**

Cassell, Sylvia
 Indoor games and activities (3-7) **793**

Cassell, Sylvia S.
 (illus.) Cassell, S. Indoor games and activities
 793

Casserley, Anne
 The three apples
 In Association for Childhood Education International. Told under the magic
 umbrella p95-100 **S C**

Casserole cooking fun. McDonald, B. G. **641.8**

Castagnetta, Grace
 Malcolmson, A. ed. Song of Robin Hood
 398.2

Castaways. See Survival (after airplane accidents, shipwrecks, etc.)

Castaways in Lilliput. Winterfeld, H. **Fic**

Caste
 See pages in the following books:
 Bothwell, J. The first book of India p28-34
 (4-7) **915.4**
 Wilber, D. N. The land and people of Ceylon
 p76-79 (5-7) **915.49**

Castle, abbey and town. Black, I. S. **940.1**

The **castle** book. Duggan, A. **728.8**

The **Castle** of Bim. Stockton, F. R.
 In A St Nicholas anthology p117-29 **810.8**

The **Castle** of Kerglas. Souvestre, E.
 In Green, R. L. ed. A cavalcade of magicians p161-78 **808.8**

The **castle** of Llyr. Alexander, L. **Fic**

The **Castle** of No Return. Alegría, R. E.
 In Alegría, R. E. The three wishes p90-99
 398.2

Castle under the sea. Alden, R. M.
 In Alden, R. M. Why the chimes rang, and
 other stories p123-35 **S C**

Castles
 Adkins, J. The art and industry of sandcastles
 (4-7) **728.8**
 Boardman, F. W. (5-7) **940.1**
 Buehr, W. Knights and castles, and feudal
 life (4-7) **940.1**
 Duggan, A. The castle book (4-7) **728.8**
 Unstead, R. J. British castles (5-7) **728.8**
 See also pages in the following book:
 Buehr, W. Chivalry and the mailed knight
 p16-28 (3-6) **940.1**

Castles and dragons. Child Study Association
 of America **398.2**

Castles in Spain, and other enchantments. Gunterman, B. L. **398.2**

Castro, Fidel
 See pages in the following book:
 Ortiz, V. The land and people of Cuba p77-
 83 (5-7) **917.291**

Casty, Gian
Damjan, M. Atuk   **E**

Cat. See Cats

A cat and a broom. Sleigh, B.
In Hope-Simpson, J. ed. A cavalcade of witches p133-42   **808.8**

Cat and Dog. Sherlock, P.
In Sherlock, P. West Indian folk-tales p93-96   **398.2**

The Cat and Mrs Cary. Gates, D.   **Fic**

The cat and mouse in partnership. See Cat and the mouse in partnership

Cat and mouse keep house. Grimm, J.
In Grimm, J. Tales from Grimm p27-38   **398.2**
    See also Cat and the mouse in partnership

The cat and mouse who shared a house. Hurlimann, R.   **398.2**
    See also Cat and mouse in partnership

The Cat and the Captain. Coatsworth, E.   **Fic**

The cat and the chanticleer
In Bloch, M. H. ed. Ukrainian folk tales p11-18   **398.2**

Cat and the dream man. Finger, C.
In Finger, C. Tales from silver lands p197-225   **398.2**

The cat and the fox. Grimm, J.
In Grimm, J. More Tales from Grimm p61-62   **398.2**
    See also Fox and the cat

The Cat and the mouse
In De La Mare, W. ed. Animal stories p40-41   **398.2**
In Hutchinson, V. S. ed. Fireside stories p31-33   **398.2**
In Jacobs, J. ed. English folk and fairy tales p197-98   **398.2**

The cat and the mouse, and other Spanish tales. De La Iglesia, M. E.   **398.2**

Cat and the mouse in partnership
All gone
In De La Mare, W. ed. Animal stories p59-69   **398.2**
The cat and the mouse in partnership
In Lang, A. ed. The yellow fairy book p 1-13   **398.2**
Grimm, J. Cat and mouse in partnership
In Grimm, J. The complete Grimm's Fairy tales p21-23   **398.2**
In Grimm, J. Grimms' Fairy tales; illus. by F. Kredel p76-79   **398.2**
In Grimm, J. Household stories p37-39   **398.2**
Grimm, J. Cat and mouse keep house
In Grimm, J. Tales from Grimm p27-38   **398.2**
Haviland, V. The cat and mouse in partnership
In Haviland, V. Favorite fairy tales told in Germany p32-40   **398.2**
Hurlimann, R. The cat and mouse who shared a house   **398.2**

Cat and the parrot
Bryant, S. C. The cat and the parrot
In Johnson, E. ed. Anthology of children's literature p318-19   **808.8**

In Ross, E. S. ed. The lost half-hour p101-05   **372.6**
In Sechrist, E. H. ed. It's time for story hour p81-84   **372.6**
Haviland, V. The cat and the parrot
In Haviland, V. Favorite fairy tales told in India p27-34   **398.2**

The cat and the sparrows. Hardendorff, J. B.
In Hardendorff, J. B. ed. Just one more p78-81   **372.6**

The cat book. Besser, M.   **636.8**

The cat book. Daly, K. N.   **636.8**

The cat came back. Ipcar, D.   **784.4**

The Cat Club. Averill, E.
In Averill, E. Jenny and the Cat Club **S C**

A cat comes to Helm. Simon, S.
In Simon, S. The wise men of Helm and their merry tales p119-26   **S C**

The cat in the hat. Seuss, Dr   **E**

The Cat in the hat Beginner book dictionary   **423**

The Cat in the hat Beginner book dictionary in French. See The Cat in the hat Beginner book dictionary   **423**

The Cat in the hat Beginner book dictionary in Spanish. See The Cat in the hat Beginner book dictionary   **423**

The cat in the hat comes back! Seuss, Dr   **E**

Cat Inspector. Jagendorf, M. A.
In Jagendorf, M. A. New England beanpot p226-30   **398.2**

A cat is a cat is a cat. Vo-Dinh
In Vo-Dinh. The toad is the Emperor's uncle p123-28   **398.2**

A cat may look at a king. Thomas, E.
In Farjeon, E. ed. A cavalcade of kings p169-70   **808.8**

Cat 'n mouse
In Chase, R. ed. The Jack tales p127-34   **398.2**

The cat on the Dovrefell. Asbjörnsen, P. C.
In Asbjörnsen, P. C. East of the sun and west of the moon, and other tales p118-20   **398.2**
In Johnson, E. ed. Anthology of children's literature p307   **808.8**
    See also Bear and skrattel

Cat-skin
In De La Mare, W. ed. Animal stories p297-306   **398.2**

The cat that walked by himself. Kipling, R.
In Kipling, R. Just so stories (Doubleday) p197-224   **S C**
In Kipling, R. Just so stories (Doubleday. Anniv. ed.) p89-99   **S C**
In Kipling, R. Just so stories (Watts, F.) p197-221   **S C**

The cat, the dog, and death. Courlander, H.
In Courlander, H. The piece of fire, and other Haitian tales p24-36   **398.2**

The cat, the mountain goat, and the fox. Belpré, P.
In Belpré, P. The tiger and the rabbit, and other tales p113-17   **398.2**

The **cat** who became head-forester. Ransome, A.

 In Ransome, A. Old Peter's Russian tales p106-19   **398.2**

  See also Fox and the cat

The **cat** who thought he was a tiger. Cameron, P.   **E**

The **cat** who went to heaven. Coatsworth, E.   **Fic**

The **cat** who wished to be a man. Alexander, L.   **Fic**

Catalog cards, ALA Rules for filing. Abridged   **025.3**

Cataloging

 Akers, S. G. Simple library cataloging   **025.3**

 Anglo-American cataloging rules   **025.3**

 Piercy, E. J. Commonsense cataloging   **025.3**

  See also Subject headings

    Audio-visual materials

 Weihs, J. R. Nonbook materials   **025.3**

Catalogs. See subjects with the subdivision Catalogs, e.g. Moving pictures—Catalogs

Catalogs, Classified

 Books for children, 1960-1965   **011**

 The Elementary school library collection **011**

 Junior high school library catalog   **011**

Catalogs, Subject

 Subject guide to Children's books in print   **015**

  See also Subject headings

Catalogs, Systematic. See Catalogs, Classified

Cataloguing. See Cataloging

Catch a cricket. Stevens, C.   **595.7**

Catch a little fox. A-hunting we will go (Folk song)   **784.4**

Catch that pass! Christopher, M.   **Fic**

Catching wild horses. Buff, M.

 In Association for Childhood Education International. Told under spacious skies p271-86   **S C**

Caterpillars

 Conklin, G. I like caterpillars (k-3)   **595.7**

 Hutchins, R. E. Scaly wings (2-4)   **595.7**

 McClung, R. M. Caterpillars and how they live (2-4)   **595.7**

 Selsam, M. E. Terry and the caterpillars (k-2)   **595.7**

 Sterling, D. Caterpillars (3-6)   **595.7**

 See also pages in the following books:

 Anderson, M. J. Exploring the insect world p71-76 (5-7)   **595.7**

 Sterling, D. Insects and the homes they build p15-21 (5-7)   **595.7**

  See also Butterflies; Moths

    Stories

 Carle, E. The very hungry caterpillar   **E**

Caterpillars and how they live. McClung, R. M.   **595.7**

Catfishes

 Ricciuti, E. R. Donald and the fish that walked   **E**

 See also pages in the following book:

 Silverstein, A. Animal invaders p72-77 (4-7)   **591.5**

Catharine of Aragon, consort of Henry VIII, King of England

 See pages in the following book:

 Aymar, B. Laws and trials that created history p24-31 (6-7)   **345.7**

Cathedral: the story of its construction. Macaulay, D.   **726**

Cathedrals

 Grant, N. Cathedrals (4-6)   **726**

 Macaulay, D. Cathedral: the story of its construction (4-7)   **726**

  See also Architecture, Gothic

Cather, Katherine Dunlap

 The Easter eggs

 In Harper, W. comp. Easter chimes p173-86   **394.2**

Cather, Willa Sibert

    Fiction

 Franchere, R. Willa (6-7)   **Fic**

Catherall, Arthur

 Last horse on the sands (4-6)   **Fic**

 Prisoners in the snow (3-5)   **Fic**

Catholic Church

 See pages in the following book:

 Hall, E. The land and people of Argentina p47-50, 132-34 (5-7)   **918.2**

  See also Saints

Cathon, Laura E.

 Stories to tell to children. See Stories to tell to children   **028.52**

Catlin, George

 Rockwell, A. Paintbrush & peacepipe (4-6)   **92**

Cats

 Besser, M. The cat book (4-6)   **636.8**

 Bridge, L. M. Cats: little tigers in your house (k-3)   **636.8**

 Burger, C. All about cats (5-7)   **636.8**

 Daly, K. N. The cat book (k-2)   **636.8**

 Fichter, G. S. Cats (5-7)   **599**

 Henry, M. Benjamin West and his cat Grimalkin (4-6)   **92**

 Rockwell, J. Cats and kittens (4-7)   **636.8**

 Selsam, M. E. How kittens grow (k-2)   **636.8**

 Stevens, C. The birth of Sunset's kittens (k-4)   **636.8**

 Unkelbach, K. Tiger up a tree (1-4)   **636.8**

 See also pages in the following books:

 Chrystie, F. N. Pets p26-39 (4-7)   **636.08**

 Fenton, C. L. Animals that help us p93-103 (4-6)   **636**

 Stevens, C. Your first pet p83-93 (2-4) **636.08**

  See also Siamese cat

    Poetry

 Blegvad, L. comp. Mittens for kittens, and other rhymes about cats (k-1)   **398.8**

 Fisher, A. My cat has eyes of sapphire blue (2-4)   **811**

 Newberry, C. T. The kittens' ABC   **E**

 See also pages in the following book:

 Cole, W. comp. A book of animal poems p81-94 (5-7)   **821.08**

    Stories

 Alexander, L. The cat who wished to be a man (4-6)   **Fic**

 Averill, E. The fire cat   **E**

Censorship
See pages in the following book:
Issues in children's book selection p43-72
028.5
See also Free speech; also subjects with the subdivision Censorship, e.g. Libraries—Censorship
Periodicals
Newsletter on Intellectual Freedom **323.44**
Center for Understanding Media
Rice, S. ed. Films kids like **016.3713**
Centerburg tales. McCloskey, R. **Fic**
Central America
Markun, P. M. The first book of Central America and Panama (5-7) **917.28**
See also names of individual countries in Central America, e.g. Honduras
Central Asia. See Asia, Central
Central city/spread city. Schwartz, A. **301.34**
Central heating and how it works. Urquhart, D. I. **697**
Central Pacific Railroad
Latham, F. B. The transcontinental railroad, 1862-69 (5-7) **385.09**
Ceramic industries. See Clay industries; Glass manufacture
Ceramic materials. See Clay
Ceramics. See Pottery
Ceramics. Weiss, H. **738.1**
Cereals. See Grain
Cerebral palsy
Fiction
Little, J. Mine for keeps (4-6) **Fic**
Ceremonies. See Rites and ceremonies
Cerf, Bennett
Bennett Cerf's Book of animal riddles (k-3)
793.7
Bennett Cerf's Book of riddles (k-2) **793.7**
A certain small shepherd. Caudill, R. **Fic**
Certainty. See Probabilities
Cervantes, Miguel de
The adventures of Don Quixote de la Mancha; adaptation. See Barret, L. The adventures of Don Quixote de la Mancha
Don Quixote de la Mancha; dramatization. See Howard, V. Don Quixote saves the day
Cervasio, Thomas
Shuttlesworth, D. E. Litter—the ugly enemy
614.7
Cesarino and the dragon. Waters, G. W.
In Fairy tales from many lands p66-76
398.2
Ceylon
Wilber, D. N. The land and people of Ceylon (5-7) **915.49**
Agriculture
See Agriculture—Ceylon
Education
See Education—Ceylon
Ceylon sillies. Jagendorf, M. A.
In Jagendorf, M. A. Noodlehead stories from around the world p72-74 **398.2**

Chaco Canyon National Monument
See pages in the following book:
National Geographic Society. The new America's wonderlands p208-15 **917.3**
Chafetz, Henry
Thunderbird, and other stories (4-6) **398.2**
Contents: Thunderbird; The tale of Bat; The peace pipe
Chaffin, Lillie D.
Coal: energy and crisis (3-5) **553**
John Henry McCoy (4-6) **Fic**
Chaka, Zulu chief
See pages in the following book:
Bleeker, S. The Zulu of South Africa p102-36 (4-7) **916.8**
Chalmers, Mary
Be good, Harry **E**
(illus.) Heilbroner, J. The happy birthday present **E**
(illus.) Hoff, S. When will it snow? **E**
(illus.) Nordstrom, U. The secret language **Fic**
(illus.) Shakespeare, W. When daisies pied, and violets blue **822.3**
(illus.) Sharmat, M. Goodnight, Andrew **E**
Chalmers, Patrick R.
The little pagan faun
In Association for Childhood Education International. Told under the Christmas tree p82-86 **808.8**
In Colwell, E. ed. A storyteller's choice p144-48 **372.6**
In Eaton, A. T. comp. The animals' Christmas p52-59 **394.2**
Chaloner, Gwen
The bookworm
In Kamerman, S. E. ed. Fifty plays for junior actors p108-17 **812.08**
The court of King Arithmetic
In Kamerman, S. E. ed. Fifty plays for junior actors p118-27 **812.08**
Chamberlain, B. H.
The silly jelly-fish
In Farjeon, E. ed. A cavalcade of queens p158-62 **808.8**
Chamberlain, Wilton Norman
Rudeen, K. Wilt Chamberlain (2-5) **92**
Chameleons
Hess, L. The remarkable chameleon (3-5)
598.1
The **champion.** Courlander, H.
In Courlander, H. Terrapin's pot of sense p69-73 **398.2**
The **champion** spearsman. Thompson, V. L.
In Thompson, V. L. Hawaiian tales of heroes and champions p58-65 **398.2**
The **championship** of Ireland. Sutcliff, R.
In Arbuthnot, M. H. comp. The Arbuthnot Anthology of children's literature p465-71 **808.8**
In Arbuthnot, M. H. comp. Time for old magic p329-35 **398.2**
Champlain, Samuel de
Jacobs, W. Samuel de Champlain (4-6) **92**
Syme, R. Champlain of the St Lawrence (4-6)
92

Charlemagne
Baldwin, J. The story of Roland (6-7) **398.2**
        Romances
Bulfinch, T. Bulfinch's Mythology (6-7) **291**
See also pages in the following book:
White, A. T. The Golden Treasury of myths
  and legends p82-101 (5-7) **292**

**Charles V, Emperor of the Holy Roman Em-
pire**
See pages in the following book:
Loder, D. The land and people of Spain
  p50-54 (5-7) **914.6**

Charles I, King of Great Britain
See pages in the following book:
Aymar, B. Laws and trials that created his-
  tory p42-53 (6-7) **345.7**

Charles, Ray
Mathis, S. B. Ray Charles (2-5) **92**

Charles Legoun and his friend. Courlander, H.
In Courlander, H. The piece of fire, and
  other Haitian tales p91-92 **398.2**

Charley. Robinson, J. G. **Fic**

The **Charlie** Brown dictionary. Schulz, C. M.
423

"**Charlie** needs a cloak." De Paola, T. **E**

Charlie rides in the engine of a real train.
Hill, H.
In Association for Childhood Education
  International. Told under the blue
  umbrella p89-96 **S C**
In Gruenberg, S. M. ed. Favorite stories
  old and new p88-91 **808.8**

Charlip, Remy
Handtalk **419**
Harlequin and the gift of many colors **E**

Charlot, Jean
(illus.) Bishop, C. H. Martin de Porres, hero
92
(illus.) Brenner, A. The boy who could do
  anything, & other Mexican folk tales **398.2**
(illus.) Brown, M. W. A child's good night
  book **E**
(illus.) Bulla, C. R. The poppy seeds **E**
(illus.) Clark, A. N. Secret of the Andes **Fic**
(illus.) Krumgold, J. . . . and now Miguel **Fic**

Charlotte. White, E. B.
In Arbuthnot, M. H. comp. The Arbuthnot Anthology of children's literature p479-81 **808.8**

Charlotte sometimes. Farmer, P. **Fic**

Charlotte sometimes; excerpt. Farmer, P.
In Arbuthnot, M. H. comp. The Arbuthnot Anthology of children's literature p562-65 **808.8**

Charlotte's web. White, E. B. **Fic**

Charlotte's web; excerpt. White, E. B.
In Arbuthnot, M. H. comp. The Arbuthnot Anthology of children's literature p479-81 **808.8**

The **charmed** ring. Knowles, J. H.
In Jacobs, J. ed. Indian fairy tales p90-99
398.2

Charms
Cohen, D. Curses, hexes, & spells (5-7) **133.4**

Charney, Beth
(illus.) Camp Fire Girls, Inc. Adventure
369.47

Charosh, Mannis
The ellipse (2-4) **516**
Mathematical games for one or two (1-4)
793.7
Number ideas through pictures (2-4) **513**
Straight lines, parallel lines, perpendicular
  lines (2-4) **516**

Chartography. See Map making; Maps

Charts. See Maps

Chase, Alice Elizabeth
Looking at art (6-7) **701**

Chase, John
(illus.) Tallant, R. Pirate Lafitte and the Battle of New Orleans **92**

Chase, Richard
(ed.) Grandfather tales (4-7) **398.2**
Jack and the three sillies (k-3) **398.2**
(ed.) The Jack tales (4-6) **398.2**
Sop doll!
In Hoke, H. ed. Spooks, spooks, spooks
  p141-46 **S C**
(ed.) Billy Boy (Folk song) Billy Boy **784.4**

Chase, Sara Hannum
Diamonds (4-7) **553**

Chastain, Madye Lee
(illus.) Courlander, H. The cow-tail switch,
  and other West African stories **398.2**

Chateaux. See Castles

Chaucer, Geoffrey
The franklin's tale; adaptation. See Farjeon,
  E. The franklin's tale
Nun's priest's tale; adaptation. See Cooney,
  B. Chanticleer and the fox **E**

Chavez, César Estrada
Franchere, R. Cesar Chavez (2-5) **92**
See also pages in the following books:
Katz, W. L. Modern America, 1957 to the
  present p17-18, 28-29 (5-7) **301.45**
Newlon, C. Famous Mexican-Americans p50-
  69 (6-7) **920**

"**Checking-in**" at the museum. Konigsburg,
E. L.
In Arbuthnot, M. H. comp. The Arbuthnot Anthology of children's literature
  p655-60 **808.8**

Cheerful temper
Andersen, H. C. A happy disposition
In Andersen, H. C. The complete fairy
  tales and stories p410-13 **S C**

Cheese
See pages in the following book:
Meyer, C. Milk, butter, and cheese p55-72
  (5-7) **641.3**

Cheese, peas, and chocolate pudding. Van Wit-
sen, B.
In Gruenberg, S. M. comp. Let's hear a
  story p82-86 **808.8**
In Sechrist, E. H. ed. It's time for story
  hour p43-45 **372.6**

Cheetahs
Adamson, J. Pippa (1-4) **599**

Children's books suggested as holiday gifts. See New York. Public Library. Children's books and recordings suggested as holiday gifts **028.52**

Children's books too good to miss **028.52**

Children's classics. Jordan, A. M. **028.52**

Children's Crusade, 1212
See pages in the following book:
Buehr, W. The crusaders p83-94 (5-7) **940.1**

Children's games. Untermeyer, L.
In Untermeyer, L. Tales from the ballet p41 **792.8**

Children's games from many lands. Millen, N. comp. **796.1**

Children's games in street and playgrounds. Opie, I. **796.1**

Children's libraries. See Libraries, Children's; School libraries

Children's library service. Burke, J. G. ed. **027.62**

Children's literature
Broderick, D. M. An introduction to children's work in public libraries **027.62**
Hill, J. Children are people **027.62**
Jacobs, L. B. ed. Using literature with young children **028.5**
Sayers, F. C. Summoned by books **028.5**
See also pages in the following book:
Arbuthnot, M. H. comp. The Arbuthnot Anthology of children's literature p901-83 **808.8**
See also Picture books for children; Storytelling

Addresses and essays
Andrews, S. ed. The Hewins lectures, 1947-1962 **028.5**
Bechtel, L. S. Books in search of children **028.5**

Bibliography
American Library Association. Children's Services Division. Book Evaluation Committee. Notable children's books **028.52**
American Library Association. Children's Services Division. Book Reevaluation Committee. Notable children's books, 1940-1959 **028.52**
Association for Childhood Education International. Bibliography: books for children **028.52**
Association for Childhood Education International. Good and inexpensive books for children **028.52**
Bauer, C. F. Getting it together with books **028.5**
Blanck, J. Peter Parley to Penrod **020.75**
Books for children, 1960-1965 **011**
Child Study Association of America/Wel-Met. Children's Book Committee. Children's books of the year **028.52**
Children's books **028.52**
Children's books: awards and prizes **016.807**
Children's books in print **015**
Children's books too good to miss **028.52**
The Chinese in children's books **016.3014**
Egoff, S. The republic of childhood **028.5**
The Elementary school library collection **011**

Field, C. W. ed. Subject collections in children's literature **028.52**
Greene, E. ed. A multimedia approach to children's literature **028.52**
Greene, E. comp. Stories **028.52**
Griffin, L. comp. Multi-ethnic books for young children **028.52**
Haviland, V. ed. Children's books of international interest **028.52**
Johnson, E. ed. Anthology of children's literature **808.8**
Jordan, A. M. Children's classics **028.52**
Keating, C. M. Building bridges of understanding between cultures **028.52**
Kujoth, J. S. Best-selling children's books **028.52**
Larrick, N. A parent's guide to children's reading **028.5**
Let's read together **028.52**
Moore, A. C. My roads to childhood **028.5**
National Council of Teachers of English. Adventuring with books **028.52**
New York. Public Library. Children's books and recordings suggested as holiday gifts **028.52**
New York. Public Library. Libros en español **028.52**
Palmer, J. R. Read for your life **028.52**
Reading ladders for human relations **016.301**
Rollins, C. ed. We build together **028.52**
Rosenbach, A. S. W. Early American children's books **020.75**
Stories to tell to children **028.52**
Subject guide to Children's books in print **015**
Welch, D. A. A bibliography of American children's books printed prior to 1821 **028.52**
Withrow, D. E. Gateways to readable books **028.52**
See also pages in the following book:
Arbuthnot, M. H. comp. The Arbuthnot Anthology of children's literature p985-1063 **808.8**

Bio-bibliography
De Montreville, D. ed. Third book of junior authors **920.03**
Fuller, M. ed. More junior authors **920.03**
Kunitz, S. J. ed. The junior book of authors **920.03**
Something about the author **920.03**
Ward, M. E. Authors of books for young people **920.03**

Collections
McGuffey, W. H. Old favorites from the McGuffey readers, 1836-1936 **028.5**

Discography
New York. Public Library. Children's books and recordings suggested as holiday gifts **028.52**

Examinations, questions, etc.
Harshaw, R. In what book? **793.7**

History and criticism
Arbuthnot, M. H. Children and books **028.5**
Broderick, D. M. Image of the Black in children's fiction **028.5**
Cameron, E. The green and burning tree **028.5**

The **Chinese** dragons. Green, R. L.
    In Green, R. L. ed. A cavalcade of dragons
        p161-64 **808.8**

A **Chinese** fairy tale. Housman, L.
    In Colwell, E. ed. A storyteller's choice
        p36-44 **372.6**
    In Davis, M. G. ed. A baker's dozen p135-
        51 **372.6**
    In Housman, L. The rat-catcher's daughter
        p130-41 **S C**

The **Chinese** helped build America. Dowdell, D.
        301.45

The **Chinese** in America. Jones, C. **301.45**

The **Chinese** in America. Sung, B. L. **301.45**

The **Chinese** in children's books **016.3014**

Chinese in New York (City)
    Reit, S. Rice cakes and paper dragons (3-5)
        301.45

Chinese in the United States
    Dowdell, D. The Chinese helped build
        America (4-7) **301.45**
    Jones, C. The Chinese in America (5-7) **301.45**
    Sung, B. L. The Chinese in America (5-7)
        301.45

    See also pages in the following books:

    Katz, W. L. Modern America, 1957 to the
        present p36-37, 55-58 (5-7) **301.45**
    Latham, F. B. The transcontinental railroad,
        1862-69 p37-47 (5-7) **385.09**
    Sechrist, E. H. It's time for brotherhood p144-
        49 (5-7) **301.11**

Fiction

Martin, P. M. The rice bowl pet **E**
Politi, L. Moy Moy **E**

Chinese language
    Wiese, K. You can write Chinese **495.1**
    See also pages in the following book:
    Sidel, R. Revolutionary China: people, poli-
        tics, and ping-pong p91-98 (6-7) **915.1**

Chinese literature

Bibliography

The Chinese in children's books **016.3014**

Chinese Mother Goose rhymes. Wyndham, R.
    ed. **398.8**

Chinese poetry
    Wyndham, R. ed. Chinese Mother Goose
        rhymes (k-2) **398.8**
    See also pages in the following book:
    Koch, K. comp. Rose, where did you get that
        red? p305-11 **808.81**

Collections

Lewis, R. ed. The moment of wonder (4-7)
        895

Chinese puzzle. Wyndham, J.
    In Silverberg, B. ed. Phoenix feathers p56-
        80 **S C**

A **Chinese** Rip Van Winkle. Chandler, A. C.
    In Burack, A. S. ed. One hundred plays for
        children p37-44 **808.82**

A **Chinese** year. Hsiao, E. **915.1**

A **chipmunk** lives here. Eberle, I. **599**

Chipmunks
    Eberle, I. A chipmunk lives here (k-3) **599**
    Tunis, E. Chipmunks on the doorstep (5-7)
        599

Chipmunks on the doorstep. Tunis, E. **599**

Chipmunk's stripes
    Hardendorff, J. B. How the chipmunk came
        to be
    In Hardendorff, J. B. ed. Just one more
        p42-43 **372.6**

Chippewa Indians
    Bleeker, S. The Chippewa Indians (4-6) **970.3**
    See also pages in the following books:
    Hofsinde, R. Indian costumes p61-71 (3-6)
        391
    Hofsinde, R. The Indian medicine man p69-
        83 (4-7) **398**
    Hofsinde, R. Indian warriors and their weap-
        ons p9-26 (3-6) **739.7**
    Hofsinde, R. Indians at home p12-24 (4-7)
        728

Legends
    See pages in the following book:
    Bleeker, S. The Chippewa Indians p118-22
        (4-6) **970.3**

Music
    Bierhorst, J. comp. Songs of the Chippewa
        (3-6) **781.7**

Chisholm, James R.
    A prince is where you find him
    In Kamerman, S. E. ed. Fifty plays for
        junior actors p128-35 **812.08**

Chisholm, Shirley (St Hill)
    See pages in the following books:
    Arbuthnot, M. H. comp. The Arbuthnot An-
        thology of children's literature p848-52
        808.8
    Ross, P. ed. Young and female p15-24 (6-7)
        920

Chisholm Trail
    See pages in the following books:
    Dorian, E. Trails West and men who made
        them p81-89 (4-7) **978**
    Grant, B. Famous American trails p74-81
        (5-7) **973**

Chittenden, Elizabeth F.
    Profiles in black and white (5-7) **920**

Chivalry
    Bulfinch, T. Bulfinch's Mythology (6-7) **291**
    See also pages in the following book:
    Arbuthnot, M. H. comp. The Arbuthnot An-
        thology of children's literature p866-67
        808.8
    See also Arthur, King; Civilization,
        Medieval; Crusades; Feudalism; Knights
        and knighthood

Encyclopedias
    Uden, G. A dictionary of chivalry (6-7) **940.1**

Chivalry and the mailed knight. Buehr, W.
        940.1

Chocolate
    Smaridge, N. The world of chocolate (4-6)
        641.3

    See also pages in the following books:

    Hays, W. P. Foods the Indians gave us p48-
        55 (5-7) **641.3**
    Sullivan, G. How do they grow it? p15-24
        (5-7) **631.5**
    See also Cocoa

Chocolate-tree. See Cacao

Choice of books. See Book selection; Books and reading; Books and reading—Best books

A **choice** of magic. Manning-Sanders, R. **398.2**

Chollick, Jay
(illus.) MacManus, S. The bold heroes of Hungry Hill, and other Irish folk tales **398.2**

Chönz, Selina
A bell for Ursli **E**

Choo Choo: the story of a little engine who ran away. Burton, V. L.
In Gruenberg, S. M. comp. Let's hear a story p88-96 **808.8**

Chop-Chin and the golden dragon; play
In Smith, M. R. ed. 7 plays & how to produce them p113-31 **792**

Chop-sticks. Chrisman, A. B.
In Chrisman, A. B. Shen of the sea p58-69 **S C**

Choral speaking
See pages in the following book:
Jacobs, L. B. ed. Using literature with young children p25-29 **028.5**

Chorao, Kay
(illus.) Viorst, J. My mama says there aren't any zombies, ghosts, vampires, creatures, demons, monsters, fiends, goblins, or things **E**
(illus.) Williams, B. Albert's toothache **E**

Choreography. See Ballet

The **chosen** one. Duvall, L. M.
In Kamerman, S. E. ed. A treasury of Christmas plays p313-29 **812.08**

Chourou, Bechir
(jt. auth.) Carpenter, A. Tunisia **916.1**

Chrestien de Troyes
Erec and Enid; adaptation. See Hieatt, C. The Joy of the Court **398.2**

Chrisman, Arthur Bowie
Ah Tcha the sleeper
In Gruenberg, S. M. ed. Favorite stories old and new p388-93 **808.8**
In Harper, W. comp. Ghosts and goblins p141-49 **394.2**
In Hoke, H. ed. Witches, witches, witches p5-14 **808.8**
In Johnson, E. ed. Anthology of children's literature p310-13 **808.8**
Pies of a princess
In Fenner, P. R. comp. Giants & witches and a dragon or two p178-88 **398.2**
Shen of the sea (5-7) **S C**
Contents: Ah Mee's invention; Shen of the sea; How wise were the old men; Chop-sticks; Buy a father; Four generals; The Rain King's daughter; Many wives; That lazy Ah Fun; The Moon Maiden; Ah Tcha the sleeper; I wish it would rain; High as Han Hsin; Contrary Chueh Chun; Pies of the princess; As Hai Low kept house

About
See pages in the following book:
Miller, B. M. ed. Newbery Medal books: 1922-1955 p40-43 **028.5**

Christ. See Jesus Christ

Christ-child
Harrison, E. The legend of the Christ child

In Harper, W. comp. Merry Christmas to you p87-93 **394.2**

The **Christ** child. Bible. New Testament. Selections **232.9**

The **Christ** child and St Christopher. Woolsey, J.
In Sechrist, E. H. ed. It's time for Christmas p54-57 **394.2**

The **christening** in the village. Ransome, A
In Ransome, A. Old Peter's Russian tales p316-34 **398.2**

Christensen, Gardell D.
(illus.) Zim, H. S. Monkeys **599**

Christian, Samuel T.
(jt. auth.) Gorodetzky, C. W. What you should know about drugs **613.8**

Christian art and symbolism
Daves, M. Young readers book of Christian symbolism (4-6) **246**
See also pages in the following book:
Helfman, E. S. Signs & symbols of the sun p60-73 (5-7) **398**

Christian biography. See Missionaries; Pilgrim Fathers; Saints

Christian names. See Names, Personal

Christian symbolism. See Christian art and symbolism

Christian Unity
See pages in the following book:
Sechrist, E. H. It's time for brotherhood p25-39 (5-7) **301.11**

Christianity
See pages in the following books:
Crane, L. The land and people of the Congo p22-25, 74-81 (5-7) **916.75**
Hall, E. The land and people of Argentina p47-50, 132-34 (5-7) **918.2**
Kettelkamp, L. Religions, East and West p78-91 (5-7) **291**
Kostich, D. D. The land and people of the Balkans p49-54 (5-7) **914.96**
Mahmoud, Z. N. The land and people of Egypt p34-41 (5-7) **916.2**
O'Brien, E. The land and people of Ireland p41-48 (5-7) **914.15**
Spencer, W. The land and people of Tunisia p42-45 (5-7) **916.1**
Winder, V. H. The land and people of Lebanon p43-46 (5-7) **915.692**
Wolcott, L. Religions around the world p129-57 (5-7) **291**
The World's great religions. Special edition for young readers p119-88 (5-7) **291**
See also God

Christiansen, Reidar Thorwald
Flying with witches
In Hope-Simpson, J. ed. A cavalcade of witches p82-84 **808.8**

Christie, Frances N.
Pets (4-7) **636.08**

Christie and the growing hand. Green, K.
In Green, K. Leprechaun tales p74-84 **398.2**

La **Christine** comes. Lenski, L.
In Lenski, L. Lois Lenski's Christmas stories p105-13 **394.2**

Churchward, James
See pages in the following book:
Kettelkamp, L. Religions, East and West
p116-20 (5-7)   **291**

Chwast, Seymour
(illus.) Merriam, E. Finding a poem (6-7) **811**
(illus.) Mother Goose. Rimes de la Mère Oie.
Mother Goose rhymes   **398.8**

Ciad, Adventures of. See Adventures of Ciad

Cianciolo, Patricia Jean
(ed.) National Council of Teachers of English.
Picture Book Committee. Picture books for
children   **028.52**

Ciardi, John
I met a man (1-3)   **811**
The man who sang the sillies (2-5)   **811**
The reason for the pelican (1-4)   **811**
Someone could win a polar bear (2-5)   **811**
You read to me, I'll read to you (1-4)   **811**

Cibola
See pages in the following book:
Discoverers of the New World p94-103 (5-7)
     973.1

Cicada
See pages in the following book:
Hutchins, R. E. The bug clan p51-61 (5-7)
     595.7

El Cid Campeador
See pages in the following books:
Hazeltine, A. I. ed. Hero tales from many
lands p235-51 (5-7)   **398.2**
Johnson, E. ed. Anthology of children's lit-
erature p539-43   **808.8**

Cider
See pages in the following book:
Fisher, L. E. The homemakers p37-44 (4-7)
     680

Cinch bug
See pages in the following book:
Hutchins, R. E. The bug clan p22-24 (5-7)
     595.7

Cincinnati. Public Library
Books for mentally retarded children. See
Books for mentally retarded children
     028.52

Cinder-Riley. Boiko, C.
In Boiko, C. Children's plays for creative
actors p239-48   **812**
In Kamerman, S. E. ed. Fifty plays for
junior actors p54-63   **812.08**

Cinder wagon. Reeves, K.
In Association for Childhood Education
International. Told under the blue
umbrella p11-13   **S C**

Cinderella
    Cinderella
In Association for Childhood Education
International. Told under the green
umbrella p113-21   **398.2**
In Baker, A. comp. The talking tree p25-
32   **398.2**
In Gruenberg, S. M. ed. Favorite stories
old and new p281-86   **808.8**
In Hutchinson, V. S. ed. Chimney corner
stories p137-49   **398.2**

Colum, P. The girl who sat by the ashes
     398.2

De La Mare, W. Ashputtel
In Child Study Association of America.
Castles and dragons p109-25   **398.2**
In De La Mare, W. ed. Animal stories
p285-95   **398.2**

De La Mare, W. Cinderella and the glass
slipper
In De La Mare, W. Tales told again p44-
60   **398.2**
In Johnson, E. ed. Anthology of children's
literature p162-68   **808.8**

Evans, C. S. Cinderella   **398.2**

Grimm, J. Aschenputtel
In Grimm, J. Household stories p118-25
     398.2

Grimm, J. Cinderella
In Grimm, J. The complete Grimm's Fairy
tales p121-28   **398.2**
In Grimm, J. Grimms' Fairy tales; illus.
by F. Kredel p155-65   **398.2**
In Grimm, J. Tales from Grimm p101-22
     398.2
In Martignoni, M. E. ed. The illustrated
treasury of children's literature p232-
36   **808.8**

Perrault, C. Cinderella   **398.2**
—Same
In Arbuthnot, M. H. comp. The Arbuth-
not Anthology of children's literature
p210-13   **808.8**
In Arbuthnot, M. H. comp. Time for old
magic p87-90   **398.2**
In Haviland, V. comp. The fairy tale trea-
sury p138-45   **398.2**
In Lang, A. ed. The blue fairy book p64-
71   **398.2**
In Perrault, C. Famous fairy tales p135-
60   **398.2**
In Perrault, C. Perrault's Complete fairy
tales p58-70   **398.2**
In Rackham, A. comp. Arthur Rackham
Fairy book p223-32   **398.2**
In Untermeyer, B. ed. The Golden Trea-
sury of children's literature p65-75
     808.8
In Ward, W. ed. Stories to dramatize
p129-34   **372.6**

Perrault, C. Cinderilla
In Opie, I. ed. The classic fairy tales
p123-27   **398.2**
See also Ashpet; Liisa and the prince;
The pumpkin child; Tattercoats; Vasilisa
the beauty

Cinderella; adaptation. Montresor, B.   **782.1**

Cinderella; play. Barr, J.
In Kamerman, S. E. ed. Little plays for
little players p240-48   **812.08**

Cinderella; play. D'Arcy, A.
In Burack, A. S. ed. One hundred plays
for children p633-42   **808.82**

Cinderella; play. Thane, A.
In Thane, A. Plays from famous stories
and fairy tales p430-49   **812**

**Cinderella and the glass slipper. De La
Mare, W.**
In De La Mare, W. Tales told again p44-
60   **398.2**

Cinderella and the glass slipper—*Continued*
In Johnson, E. ed. Anthology of children's literature p162-68　　**808.8**
See also Cinderella

Cinderella of New Hampshire. Jagendorf, M. A.
In Jagendorf, M. A. New England bean-pot p37-45　　**398.2**

Cinderilla. Perrault, C.
In Opie, I. ed. The classic fairy tales p123-27　　**398.2**
See also Cinderella

Cinderlad and the troll's seven silver ducks. Aulaire, I. d'
In Aulaire, I. d'. East of the sun and west of the moon p100-07　　**398.2**

Cinema. See Moving pictures

Cinnamon
See pages in the following book:
Cooper, E. K. And everything nice p37-41 (3-5)　　**641.3**

Cinque, Joseph
See pages in the following book:
Rollins, C. H. They showed the way p43-45 (5-7)　　**920**

Ciphers
Gardner, M. Codes, ciphers and secret writing (5-7)　　**652.8**
Kohn, B. Secret codes and ciphers (4-7)　　**652.8**
Peterson, J. How to write codes and send secret messages (2-4)　　**652.8**
Rothman, J. Secrets with ciphers and codes (3-7)　　**652.8**
Fiction
Myrick, M. The Secret Three　　**E**

Circe's palace. Hawthorne, N.
In Farjeon, E. ed. A cavalcade of queens p72-108　　**808.8**

Circle of seasons. Clark, A. N.　　**970.3**

Circles. Sitomer, M.　　**516**

Circles, triangles and squares. Hoban, T.　　**E**

A **circlet** of oak leaves. Sutcliff, R.
In Sutcliff, R. Heather, oak, and olive p29-74　　**S C**

Circumnavigation. See Voyages around the world

Circus
De Regniers, B. S. Circus (k-3)　　**791.3**
Great days of the circus (5-7)　　**791.3**
Munari, B. The circus in the mist　　**E**
Biography
Cone, M. The Ringling brothers (2-4)　　**920**
Fiction
Bemelmans, L. Madeline and the gypsies　**E**
Du Bois, W. P. The Alligator Case (3-5)　**Fic**
Du Bois, W. P. Bear Circus　　**E**
Kästner, E. The little man (4-6)　　**Fic**
Otis, J. Toby Tyler (4-6)　　**Fic**
Rounds, G. The day the circus came to Lone Tree　　**E**
Seuss, Dr. If I ran the circus　　**E**
Pictorial works
Wildsmith, B. Brian Wildsmith's Circus　**E**

Poetry
Prelutsky, J. Circus (k-3)　　**811**
See also pages in the following book:
Brewton, J. E. comp. Under the tent of the sky p3-12 (3-7)　　**808.81**

Circus. Prelutsky, J.　　**811**

Circus, Brian Wildsmith's. Wildsmith, B.　**E**

The **circus** in the mist. Munari, B.　　**E**

Circus numbers. Peppé, R.　　**E**

The **cistern** of San Cristobal. Belpré, P.
In Belpré, P. Once in Puerto Rico p64-65　　**398.2**

Citation world atlas, Hammond　　**912**

Cities and towns
Busch, P. S. Exploring as you walk in the city (1-4)　　**500.9**
Corcos, L. The city book (k-2)　　**301.34**
Tresselt, A. It's time now! (k-2)　　**525**
See also Markets; Parks; Villages; and names of individual cities and towns

Brazil
See pages in the following book:
Sheppard, S. The first book of Brazil p43-67 (4-6)　　**918.1**

Fiction
Child Study Association of America. Round about the city (2-4)　　**S C**
Fife, D. Adam's A B C　　**E**
Gaeddert, L. Noisy Nancy Norris　　**E**
Grant, S. Hey, look at me!　　**E**
Keats, E. J. Apt. 3　　**E**
Keats, E. J. Dreams　　**E**
Scott, A. H. Big Cowboy Western　　**E**

History
Gregor, A. S. How the world's first cities began (4-6)　　**913.35**

Netherlands
See pages in the following book:
Barnouw, A. J. The land and people of Holland p38-45 (5-7)　　**914.92**

Poetry
Larrick, N. comp. I heard a scream in the street (5-7)　　**811.08**
Larrick, N. ed. On city streets (5-7)　　**811.08**
Lenski, L. City poems (k-3)　　**811**
Moore, L. I thought I heard the city (3-6)　　**811**

United States
Goetz, D. State capital cities (4-6)　　**917.3**
Howell, R. R. A crack in the pavement (2-4)　　**500.9**
See also pages in the following book:
Naden, C. J. The Mississippi p45-58 (4-7)　　**917.7**

Cities and towns, Ruined, extinct, etc.
Hall, J. Buried cities (5-7)　　**913**
Weisgard, L. The beginnings of cities (6-7)　　**913.35**

City. Macaulay, D.　　**711**

The **city** book. Corcos, L.　　**301.34**

City leaves, city trees. Gallob, E.　　**582**

City life. See Cities and towns

City mouse and the country mouse
In The Tall book of nursery tales p12-15
         398.2
The city mouse and the country mouse. Bennett, R.
In Bennett, R. Creative plays and programs for holidays p178-85 812
City neighbor; the story of Jane Addams. Judson, C. I. 92
City of Angels. Campbell, C.
In Campbell, C. Star Mountain, and other legends of Mexico p49-52 398.2
The city of gold and lead. Christopher, J.
City planning
Rome
Macaulay, D. City (4-7) 711
City poems. Lenski, L. 811
City rhythms. Grifalconi, A. E
City rocks, city blocks, and the moon. Gallob, E.
         552
City traffic
Tannenbaum, B. City traffic (3-5) 388.4
City transit. See Local transit
Ciulla, A. J.
Papa was a riot
In Cavanah, F. ed. Holiday roundup p176-81 394.2
Civil engineering
Macaulay, D. City (4-7) 711
  See also Bridges; Canals; Dams; Highway engineering; Roads; Tunnels; Water supply
Civil liberty. See Liberty
Civil rights
Fisher, A. Human Rights Day (1-3) **394.2**
Kohn, B. The spirit and the letter (5-7) **323.4**
Wise, W. American freedom and the Bill of Rights (2-4) **323.4**
  See also Liberty; also names of groups of people with the subdivision Civil rights, e.g. Negroes—Civil rights
Civil rights demonstrations. See Negroes—Civil rights
Civil War
United States
See United States—History—Civil War
Civilization
  See also Acculturation; Anthropology; Archeology; Inventions; Religions; Social problems; also names of countries with the subdivision Civilization, e.g. Egypt—Civilization
Bibliography
See pages in the following book:
National Council of Teachers of English. Adventuring with books p259-66 **028.52**
History
Foster, G. Birthdays of freedom (6-7) **901.9**
Rome
See Rome—Civilization
Civilization, Ancient
Cohen, D. Ancient monuments and how they were built (6-7) 913
Glubok, S. The art of lands in the Bible (4-7)
         709.01

Leacroft, H. The buildings of ancient man (5-7) 722
Unstead, R. J. Looking at ancient history (4-6) 930
Fiction
Sutcliff, R. Heather, oak, and olive (5-7) **S C**
Civilization, Arab
Price, C. The story of Moslem art (6-7)
         709.56
Civilization, Egyptian. See Egypt—Civilization
Civilization, Greek
Boyer, S. A. Gifts from the Greeks (6-7)
         913.38
Coolidge, O. The golden days of Greece (4-6)
         938
Fenton, S. H. Greece (1-4) **913.38**
Glubok, S. The art of ancient Greece (4-7)
         709.38
Leacroft, H. The buildings of ancient Greece (5-7) 722
Robinson, C. A. The first book of ancient Greece (5-7) **913.38**
Rockwell, A. Temple on a hill (4-7) **913.38**
VanDuyn, J. The Greeks (6-7) **913.38**
Civilization, Medieval
Black, I. S. Castle, abbey and town (3-6)
         940.1
Uden, G. A dictionary of chivalry (6-7) **940.1**
See also pages in the following book:
Arbuthnot, M. H. comp. The Arbuthnot Anthology of children's literature p864-67
         808.8
  See also Art, Medieval; Chivalry; Feudalism; Renaissance
Civilization, Sumerian. See Sumerians
Cizik, Milka
(illus.) Rappaport, U. The story of the Dead Sea scrolls 229
Clairvoyance
Kettelkamp, L. Sixth sense (5-7) **133.8**
  See also Extrasensory perception; Fortune telling
Fiction
Dickinson, P. The gift (5-7) **Fic**
Rodgers, M. A billion for Boris (4-7) **Fic**
Clans and clan system. See Tartans
Clante, Iben
(illus.) Unnerstad, E. The spettecake holiday
         Fic
Clapp, Patricia
Constance (5-7) **Fic**
The Do-Nothing Frog
In Burack, A. S. ed. One hundred plays for children p353-60 **808.82**
Dr Elizabeth [biography of Elizabeth Blackwell] (4-7) 92
Jane-Emily (5-7) **Fic**
The magic bookshelf
In Kamerman, S. E. ed. Fifty plays for junior actors p136-50 **812.08**
Clark, Ann Nolan
Along sandy trails (2-5) **500.9**
Blue Canyon horse (2-4) **Fic**
Circle of seasons (5-7) **970.3**
The hogan
In Association for Childhood Education International. Told under spacious skies p287-94 **S C**

Clark, Ann Nolan—*Continued*

Hoofprint on the wind (5-7) **Fic**

In my mother's house (1-4) **970.3**

Little Navajo Bluebird (3-5) **Fic**

Little Von-Dos-Smai

In Association for Childhood Education International. Told under the Stars and Stripes p31-46 **S C**

Magic money (3-5) **Fic**

Newbery Medal acceptance paper

In Miller, B. M. ed. Newbery Medal books: 1922-1955 p396-404 **028.5**

Secret of the Andes (4-7) **Fic**

The Trading Post

In Gruenberg, S. M. ed. Favorite stories old and new p104-09 **808.8**

About

See pages in the following books:

Hoffman, M. ed. Authors and illustrators of children's books p62-69 **028.5**

Miller, B. M. ed. Newbery Medal books: 1922-1955 p390-95 **028.5**

Clark, David Allen

(ed.) Jokes, puns, and riddles (4-6) **817.08**

Clark, Elizabeth

The story of Brother Johannick and his silver bell

In Colwell, E. ed. A second storyteller's choice p39-45 **372.6**

Clark, Fletcher

(illus.) Jagendorf, M. Penny puppets, penny theatre, and penny plays **791.5**

Clark, George Rogers

De Leeuw, A. George Rogers Clark: frontier fighter (2-4) **92**

See also pages in the following book:

Davis, B. Heroes of the American Revolution p89-100 (5-7) **920**

Clark, Margery

Erminka and the crate of chickens

In Martignoni, M. E. ed. The illustrated treasury of children's literature p51-52 **398.2**

The picnic basket

In Association for Childhood Education International. Told under the blue umbrella p62-65 **S C**

The poppy seed cakes **E**

The poppy-seed cakes; excerpt

In Association for Childhood Education International. Told under the blue umbrella p58-65 **S C**

In Gruenberg, S. M. ed. Favorite stories old and new p59-62 **808.8**

The tea party

In Association for Childhood Education International. Told under the blue umbrella p66-69 **S C**

Clark, Mary E. and Quigley, Margery Chosey.
See Clark, Margery

Clark, Mavis Thorpe

The min-min (5-7) **Fic**

Clark, Roberta Carter

(illus.) Irving, W. Rip Van Winkle, The legend of Sleepy Hollow, and other tales **S C**

Clark, Septima Poinsette

See pages in the following book:

Burt, O. W. Black women of valor p71-88 (4-7) **920**

Clark, William, 1770-1838

Lacy, D. The Lewis and Clark Expedition, 1804-06 (5-7) **973.4**

Neuberger, R. L. The Lewis and Clark Expedition (4-7) **973.4**

Clarke, Arthur C.

The deep range

In Yolen, J. ed. Zoo 2000 p39-54 **S C**

Into space (5-7) **629.4**

Rescue

In Arbuthnot, M. H. comp. The Arbuthnot Anthology of children's literature p588-91 **808.8**

Clarke, Pauline

The four genii

In Johnson, E. ed. Anthology of children's literature p666-69 **808.8**

The patriarch

In Arbuthnot, M. H. comp. The Arbuthnot Anthology of children's literature p498-501 **808.8**

The return of the Twelves (4-7) **Fic**

The return of the Twelves; excerpt

In Arbuthnot, M. H. comp. The Arbuthnot Anthology of children's literature p498-501 **808.8**

Clarry, Siriol

(illus.) Hornby, J. Clowns through the ages **791.3**

Classed catalogs. See Catalogs, Classified

Classes (Mathematics) See Set theory

Classic cars. Jackson, R. B. **629.22**

The classic fairy tales. Opie, I. ed. **398.2**

Classical antiquities. See Art, Greek; Art, Roman; Greece—Antiquities; Mythology, Classical

Classical art. See Art, Greek; Art, Roman

Classical mythology. See Mythology, Classical

Classification

Books

See Classification, Dewey Decimal

Classification, Dewey Decimal

Beck, M. V. Library skills bk. 2 **028.7**

Dewey, M. Abridged Dewey Decimal classification and relative index **025.4**

Classified catalogs. See Catalogs, Classified

Claus and his wonderful staff. Pyle, H.

In Pyle, H. Pepper & salt p14-27 **398.2**

Clay

Seidelman, J. Creating with clay (4-7) **731.4**

See also Modeling

Clay-dough play-dough. Chernoff, G. T. **731.4**

Clay industries

See pages in the following book:

Tunis, E. Colonial craftsmen and the beginnings of American industry p119-22 (5-7) **680**

See also Pottery

Clay manikin

Jameson, C. The clay pot boy **398.2**

Coatsworth, Elizabeth—*Continued*

Give my love to Boston

In Luckhardt, M. C. comp. Thanksgiving p255-65   **394.2**

The new cabin boy

In Johnson, E. ed. Anthology of children's literature p836-39   **808.8**

The princess and the lion (4-6)   **Fic**

The return

In Association for Childhood Education International. Told under spacious skies p 1-20   **S C**

The sod house (2-4)   **Fic**

Story of Wang Li

In Child Study Association of America. Castles and dragons p211-25   **398.2**

Under the green willow   **E**

The wisdom of Solomon

In Gruenberg, S. M. ed. Favorite stories old and new p357-59   **808.8**

Witch girl

In Hoke, H. ed. Spooks, spooks, spooks p206-13   **S C**

About

See pages in the following books:

Hoffman, M. ed. Authors and illustrators of children's books p84-107   **028.5**

Miller, B. M. ed. Newbery Medal books: 1922-1955 p94-98   **028.5**

Cobb, Ty. See Cobb, Tyrus Raymond

Cobb, Tyrus Raymond

See pages in the following book:

Epstein, S. Baseball Hall of Fame: stories of champions p44-61 (3-5)   **920**

Cobb, Vicki

Arts and crafts you can eat (4-7)   **745.5**

How the doctor knows you're fine (2-4)   **616**

Science experiments you can eat (5-7)   **507.2**

Cobbler Kopytko and Drake Kwak. Borski, L. M.

In Borski, L. M. The jolly tailor, and other fairy tales p117-33   **398.2**

The **cobbler's** tale. Jones, E. O.

In Association for Childhood Education International. Told under the magic umbrella p27-29   **S C**

Cober, Alan E.

(illus.) Cooper, S. The dark is rising   **Fic**

(illus.) Garfield, L. Mister Corbett's ghost   **Fic**

Coblentz, Catherine Cate

Andrew Brewster's own secret

In Luckhardt, M. C. comp. Thanksgiving p65-73   **394.2**

Leyden's day of thanksgiving

In Luckhardt, M. C. comp. Thanksgiving p74-83   **394.2**

Martin and Abraham Lincoln: excerpt

In Arbuthnot, M. H. comp. The Arbuthnot Anthology of children's literature p756-61   **808.8**

The secret in the Brewsters' attic in Leyden

In Luckhardt, M. C. comp. Thanksgiving p59-64   **394.2**

Cochise, Apache chief

Wyatt, E. Cochise, Apache warrior and statesman (5-7)   **92**

See also pages in the following book:

Ehrlich, A. Wounded Knee: an Indian history of the American West p19-35 (6-7)   **970.4**

Cochrane, Louise

Shadow puppets in color (2-5)   **791.5**

Puppet plays included are: Moon Dragon; Karagiosis and the dragon; The story of Rama and Sita

Tabletop theatres (4-6)   **791.5**

Cock-a-doodle-doo! Cock-a-doodle-dandy! Kapp, P.   **784.6**

The **cock** and the dragon. Green, R. L.

In Green, R. L. ed. A cavalcade of dragons p157-60   **808.8**

The **Cock** and the Fox. Asbjørnsen, P. C.

In Asbjørnsen, P. C. Norwegian folk tales p135-36   **398.2**

The **cock** and the ghost cat. Lifton, B. J.   **Fic**

The **cock** and the sparrow-hawk. Sechrist, E. H.

In Sechrist, E. H. Once in the first times p25-27   **398.2**

The **cock** and the weathercock. Andersen, H. C.

In Andersen, H. C. The complete fairy tales and stories p647-49   **S C**

Cock, the mouse, and the little red hen

Cock, the mouse, and the little red hen

In Hutchinson, V. S. ed. Chimney corner stories p79-88   **398.2**

Lefèvre, F. The cock, the mouse, and the little red hen

In Arbuthnot, M. H. comp. The Arbuthnot Anthology of children's literature p155-57   **808.8**

In Arbuthnot, M. H. comp. Time for old magic p10-12   **398.2**

See also Little red hen

Cockatoos

Stories

Wuorio, E. L. Save Alice! (5-7)   **Fic**

Cocklebur

See pages in the following book:

Wright, R. H. What good is a weed? p44-52 (4-6)   **581.5**

Cockleburr Quarters. Baker, C.   **Fic**

Cockroaches

Cole, J. Cockroaches (3-6)   **595.7**

Pringle, L. Cockroaches: here, there, and everywhere (k-3)   **595.7**

Stories

Belpré, P. Perez and Martina (1-4)   **398.2**

Cockroaches: here, there, and everywhere. Pringle, L.   **595.7**

Cocoa

See pages in the following book:

Cooper, E. K. And everything nice p14-23 (3-5)   **641.3**

See also Chocolate

CoConis, Constantinos

(illus.) Gates, D. The golden god: Apollo   **292**

CoConis, Ted

(illus.) Byars, B. The summer of the swans   **Fic**

The **coconut** thieves. Fournier, C.   **398.2**

Cocoons. See Butterflies; Caterpillars; Moths

Code names. See Ciphers

The **code** of life. Silverstein, A.   **575.1**

Codes, ciphers and secret writing. Gardner, M.   **652.8**

Cole, William—*Continued*
(ed.) I went to the animal fair (k-3)   **808.81**
(ed.) Oh, how silly! (3-6)   **821.08**
(comp.) Oh, that's ridiculous! (3-6)   **821.08**
(comp.) Oh, what nonsense! (3-6)   **821.08**
(ed.) Pick me up (4-7)   **808.81**
(comp.) Poems for seasons and celebrations
       (5-7)   **821.08**
(comp.) Poems of magic and spells (4-7)
                                            821.08
(comp.) The poet's tales (6-7)   **821.08**
(ed.) Rough men, tough men (5-7)   **821.08**

Coleman, Henry
(jt. ed.) Shaw, M. ed. National anthems of
       the world   **784.7**

Coleridge, Samuel Taylor
The rime of the ancient mariner (6-7)   **821**

Collage
Weiss, H. Collage and construction (4-7)
                                            745.59

See also pages in the following book:
Comins, J. Art from found objects p69-94
       (5-7)   **745.5**

Collage and construction. Weiss, H.   **745.59**

The **collar**. Andersen, H. C.
    In Andersen, H. C. The complete fairy
       tales and stories p366-68   **S C**
    See also Shirt collar

Collard, Derek
(illus.) Pearce, P. The squirrel wife   **Fic**

Collect, print and paint from nature. Hawkinson, J.   **751.4**

Collecting cocoons. Hussey, L. J.   **595.7**

Collecting small fossils. Hussey, L. J. **560**

Collecting stamps. Villiard, P.   **769**

Collections of literature. See Short stories; and
    names of literatures and literary forms with
    the subdivision Collections, e.g. Russian
    literature—Collections; Poetry—Collections

Collections of objects. See Collectors and collecting; and names of objects collected
    with the subdivision Collectors and collecting, e.g. Postage stamps—Collectors and
    collecting

Collective settlements

China
(People's Republic of China, 1949-   )
    See pages in the following book:
Sidel, R. Revolutionary China: people, politics, and ping-pong p3-12, 59-78 (6-7)
                                            915.1

Israel
    See pages in the following books:
Dobrin, A. A life for Israel; the story of
    Golda Meir p30-37 (4-6)   **92**
Hoffman, G. The land and people of Israel
    p65-78 (5-7)   **915.694**

Collectors and collecting
    See also Book collecting; also names of
    objects with the subdivision Collectors and
    collecting, e.g. Postage stamps—Collectors
    and collecting; and names of natural specimens with the subdivision Collection and
    preservation, e.g. Shells—Collection and
    preservation

Fiction
Fox, P. Maurice's room (3-5)   **Fic**
The **collector's** book of children's books.
    Quayle, E.   **020.75**

College and school drama
    Collections—Periodicals
Plays, the Drama Magazine for Young People
                                            808.82

Collier, Christopher
(jt. auth.) Collier, J. L. My brother Sam is
    dead   **Fic**

Collier, James Lincoln
My brother Sam is dead (6-7)   **Fic**

Collier's encyclopedia   **031**

Collier's encyclopedia yearbook. See Collier's
    encyclopedia   **031**

Collingwood, G. H.
Knowing your trees   **582**

Collins, David R.
Linda Richards: first American trained nurse
    (3-6)   **92**

Collins, Patricia
(illus.) Baker, J. J. W. The vital process:
    photosynthesis   **581**

Collins, Peter
    See pages in the following book:
Stevenson, P. The greatest days of racing
    p121-40 (5-7)   **796.7**

Collins, Robert
The Medes and Persians (6-7)   **913.35**

Collodi, Carlo
The adventures of Pinocchio (3-6)   **Fic**
The adventures of Pinocchio; criticism
    In Haviland, V. ed. Children and literature
       p71-77   **028.5**
The adventures of Pinocchio; puppet play.
    See Mahlmann, L. Pinocchio
Pinocchio's ears become like those of a
    donkey
    In Arbuthnot, M. H. comp. The Arbuthnot
       Anthology of children's literature
       p496-98   **808.8**
Pinocchio's first pranks
    In Johnson, E. ed. Anthology of children's
       literature p631-32   **808.8**
Pinocchio's nose grows longer
    In Martignoni, M. E. ed. The illustrated
       treasury of children's literature p309-
       11   **808.8**
A stick of wood that talked
    In Untermeyer, B. ed. The Golden Treasury of children's literature p229-34
                                            808.8

Coloma, Louis de
Perez the Mouse
    In Harper, W. comp. Merry Christmas to
       you p230-40   **394.2**

Colombia
Carpenter, A. Colombia (4-6)   **918.61**
Landry, L. The land and people of Colombia
    (5-7)   **918.61**

    See also pages in the following book:
Carter, W. E. The first book of South
    America p18-23 (4-6)   **918**

Fiction
Iterson, S. R. van. Pulga (5-7)   **Fic**

The **Columbia**. Latham, J. L.   **979.7**

Columbia River
Holbrook, S. H. The Columbia River (4-7)
                                          979.7
Latham, J. L. The Columbia (4-7)   **979.7**

Columbus, Christopher
Aulaire, I. d'. Columbus (1-4)   **92**
Dalgliesh, A. The Columbus story (k-3) **92**
Foster, G. Year of Columbus, 1492 (3-6)
                                       909.08
Sperry, A. The voyages of Christopher Co-
   lumbus (5-7)   **92**
Syme, R. Columbus, finder of the New World
   (4-6)   **92**
   See also pages in the following books:
Brindze, R. Hurricanes p29-36 (5-7) **551.5**
Discoverers of the New World p18-33 (5-7)
                                       973.1
Johnson, E. ed. Anthology of children's lit-
   erature p1047-49   **808.8**
Winwar, F. The land and people of Italy
   p65-70 (5-7)   **914.5**

Columbus Day
   See pages in the following books:
Araki, C. Origami in the classroom: Book I
   p10-16 (4-7)   **736**
Sechrist, E. H. Red letter days p156-63 **394.2**
Drama
   See pages in the following books:
Fisher, A. Holiday programs for boys and
   girls p3-25 (4-7)   **812**
Kamerman, S. E. ed. Little plays for little
   players p79-85 (1-6)   **812.08**
Poetry
   See pages in the following book:
Sechrist, E. H. comp. Poems for red letter
   days p179-83   **821.08**
Columbus, finder of the New World. Syme, R.
                                         92

Columbus sails the sea. Barbee, L.
   In Burack, A. S. ed. One hundred plays
      for children p375-81   **808.82**

The **Columbus** story. Dalgliesh, A.   **92**

Colver, Anne
The wayfarer's tree (5-7)   **Fic**

Colwell, Eileen
Round about and long ago (3-6)   **398.2**
  Contents: The wizard of Alderley Edge; The enchanted fisherman; The Devil's bridge; The wizard of
Long Sleddale; The cuckoo of Borrowdale; The enchanted princess; The fairies of Midridge; The mysterious traveller; The fish and the ring; The tailor and the
fairies; The boggart and the farmer; The pedlar of
Swaffham; The giant of the fens; Brother Mike; The
green children; The king and the witch; The little
man in green; The farmer and the cheeses; Jack But-
termilk; The little red hairy man; The giant and the
Wrekin; Jack and the white cap; The great bell of
Bosham; The piglet and the fairy; The dragon of
Shervage Wood; The pixy visitors; Bob o' the Carn;
Skillywidden
  (ed.) A second storyteller's choice   **372.6**
  (ed.) A storyteller's choice   **372.6**

Colyer, Penrose
(comp.) I can read French (2-4)   **448**

The **comb**, the flute and the spinning wheel.
  Manning-Sanders, R.
  In Manning-Sanders, R. A book of mer-
    maids p66-72   **398.2**

Combustion
  See pages in the following book:
Rosenfeld, S. Science experiments with air
  p67-75 (5-7)   **507.2**
Come along! Caudill, R.   **811**
Come and have fun. Hurd, E. T.   **E**
Come and laugh with Bobby Gum. Jagendorf,
  M. A.
  In Jagendorf, M. A. Folk stories of the
    South p242-44   **398.2**
Come by here. Coolidge, O.   **Fic**
Come Christmas. Farjeon, E.
  In Farjeon, E. Eleanor Farjeon's Poems for
    children p197-229   **821**
Come here, cat. Nødset, J. L.   **E**
Come hither. De La Mare, W. ed.   **821.08**
Come with me to nursery school. Hurd, E. T.
                                         372.21

The **comet.** Andersen, H. C.
  In Andersen, H. C. Andersen's Fairy tales
    p454-58   **S C**
  In Andersen, H. C. The complete fairy
    tales and stories p978-81   **S C**

Comets
  See pages in the following book:
Branley, F. M. Comets, meteoroids, and as-
  teroids p61-76 (6-7)   **523.2**
Comets, meteoroids, and asteroids. Bran-
  ley, F. M.   **523.2**
Comic books, strips, etc.
Schulz, C. M. The Snoopy festival (4-7) **741.5**
Comic strips. See Comic books, strips, etc.
The **coming** of Arthur. Malory, Sir T.
  In Hazeltine, A. I. ed. Hero tales from
    many lands p101-18   **398.2**
The **Coming** of Asin
  In Courlander, H. ed. Ride with the sun
    p206-12   **398.2**
The **Coming** of Finn
  In Baker, A. comp. The talking tree p52-
    62   **398.2**
The **coming** of Max. St Clair, M. H.
  In Gruenberg, S. M. ed. Favorite stories
    old and new p149-52   **808.8**
The **coming** of the Prince. McGowan, J.
  In Kamerman, S. E. ed. A treasury of
    Christmas plays p439-49   **812.08**
The **coming** of the Spaniards. Sechrist, E. H.
  In Sechrist, E. H. Once in the first times
    p107-09   **398.2**
Coming of the yams. Courlander, H.
  In Courlander, H. The hat-shaking dance,
    and other tales from the Gold Coast
    p96-100   **398.2**

Comins, Jeremy
Art from found objects (5-7)   **745.5**
Latin American crafts, and their cultural
  backgrounds (4-7)   **745.5**

Commager, Henry Steele
America's Robert E. Lee (5-7)   **92**
The first book of American history (4-6) **973**
The great Constitution (6-7)   **342.2**
The great Declaration (6-7)   **973.3**
The great Proclamation (6-7)   **326**

The **Commandos** of World War II. Carter, H. **940.54**

Commencements

Drama

See pages in the following book:

Fisher, A. Holiday programs for boys and girls p340-49 (4-7) **812**

Commerce. See Transportation

Commercial aviation. See Aeronautics, Commercial

Commercial fishing. Zim, H. S. **639**

Commercial geography. See Geography, Commercial

Commercial products. See Manufactures

Commire, Anne
(ed.) Something about the author. See Something about the author **920.03**

Committee on Reading Ladders for Human Relations. See National Council of Teachers of English. Committee on Reading Ladders for Human Relations

Commonsense cataloging. Piercy, E. J. **025.3**

Communicable diseases. See Bacteriology; Germ theory of disease

Communication
Cahn, W. The story of writing (6-7) **411**
Rinkoff, B. Red light says stop! (1-3) **001.54**

See also pages in the following book:

Childcraft: the how and why library v12 **011**

See also Books and reading; Language and languages; Telecommunication

Bibliography

See pages in the following book:

National Council of Teachers of English. Adventuring with books p255-59 **028.52**

History

Adler, I. Communication (4-6) **301.16**
Neal, H. E. Communication (5-7) **001.54**

Communication. Adler, I. **301.16**

Communication. Neal, H. E. **001.54**

Communication among animals. See Animal communication

Communications relay satellites. See Artificial satellites in telecommunication

Communism

See pages in the following book:

Kostich, D. D. The land and people of the Balkans p99-121 (5-7) **914.96**

Czechoslovak Republic

See pages in the following book:

Hall, E. The land and people of Czechoslovakia p106-14, 146-50 (5-7) **914.37**

Indonesia

See pages in the following book:

Smith, D. C. The land and people of Indonesia p73-75, 139-43 (5-7) **915.98**

Rumania

See pages in the following book:

Hale, H. The land and people of Romania p92-101 (5-7) **914.98**

Community life
Pitt, V. Let's find out about the community (3-5) **301.34**

See also Cities and towns

Compae Rabbit's ride
In Carter, D. S. ed. Greedy Mariani, and other folktales of the Antilles p41-45 **398.2**

The **companion.** Asbjørnsen, P. C.
In Asbjørnsen, P. C. Norwegian folk tales p84-96 **398.2**

Companions of the forest. Macdonnell, A.
In Sechrist, E. H. ed. It's time for story hour p206-12 **372.6**

The **Company** you keep
In DeRoin, N. ed. Jataka tales p45-47 **398.2**

Comparative anatomy. See Anatomy, Comparative

Comparative physiology. See Physiology, Comparative

Comparative religion. See Religions

Compass
Branley, F. M. North, south, east, and west (1-3) **538**

See also pages in the following book:

Boy Scouts of America. Fieldbook p20-27 **369.43**

Compere, Janet
(illus.) Davidson, M. Louis Braille **92**

The **complete** adventures of the Borrowers. Norton, M. See note under Norton, M. The Borrowers **Fic**

The **complete** beginner's guide to bowling. Dolan, E. F. **794.6**

The **complete** book of children's theater. Howard, V. **812**

The **complete** book of dragons. Nesbit, E. **S C**

Complete book of horses and horsemanship, C. W. Anderson's. Anderson, C. W. **636.1**

The **complete** book of Indian crafts and lore. Hunt, W. B. **745.5**

The **complete** fairy tales and stories. Andersen, H. C. **S C**

Complete fairy tales, Perrault's. Perrault, C. **398.2**

The **complete** Grimm's Fairy tales. Grimm, J. **398.2**

The **complete** junior encyclopedia of transportation. Zehavi, A. M. ed. **380.503**

The **complete** nonsense book. Lear, E. **821**

The **complete** Peterkin papers. Hale, L. P. **Fic**

Complete version of Ye three blind mice. Ivimey, J. W. **398.8**

Composers, American
Cone, M. Leonard Bernstein (3-5) **92**
Posell, E. Z. American composers (5-7) **920**

Composers, Austrian
Wheeler, O. Mozart, the wonder boy (4-6) **92**

Composers, Norwegian
Kyle, E. Song of the waterfall; the story of Edvard and Nina Grieg (5-7) **92**

The **conjure** wives. Wickes, F. G.
  In Harper, W. comp. Ghosts and goblins
    p44-47   **394.2**
  In Hoke, H. ed. Spooks, spooks, spooks
    p157-60   **S C**
  In Sechrist, E. H. ed. It's time for story
    hour p176-79   **372.6**
  In Ward, W. ed. Stories to dramatize p157-
    59   **372.6**
The **conjurer's** revenge. Shepard, R. A.
  In Shepard, R. A. Conjure tales p15-25 **S C**
Conjuring. See Magic
Conklin, Gladys
  The bug club book (3-5)   **595.7**
  Elephants of Africa (2-4)   **599**
  I caught a lizard (k-3)   **639**
  I like butterflies (k-3)   **595.7**
  I like caterpillars (k-3)   **595.7**
  Insects build their homes (1-4)   **595.7**
  Little apes (k-3)   **599**
  Tarantula: the giant spider (1-3)   **595**
  When insects are babies (k-3)   **595.7**
Conklin, Paul
  (illus.) Reit, S. Child of the Navajos   **970.3**
Conly, Robert Leslie. See O'Brien, Robert C.
Connecticut

          Fiction
Dalgliesh, A. The courage of Sarah Noble
  (2-4)   **Fic**
Selden, G. Tucker's countryside (3-6)   **Fic**
Underwood, B. The tamarack tree (6-7)   **Fic**

          History
Johnston, J. The Connecticut colony (5-7)
          974.6
The **Connecticut** colony. Johnston, J.   **974.6**
Conn-Eda, Story of. See Story of Conn-Eda
Connemara donkey. Farjeon, E.
  In Farjeon, E. The little bookroom p184-
    203   **S C**
Connla and the fairy maiden
  In Arbuthnot, M. H. comp. The Arbuthnot
    Anthology of children's literature
    p180-81   **808.8**
  In Arbuthnot, M. H. comp. Time for old
    magic p41-42   **398.2**
Connolly, Jerome
  (illus.) Farb, P. Face of North America.
  Young readers' edition   **500.9**
Connor, Chris
  (illus.) Farmer, P. Charlotte sometimes   **Fic**
  (illus.) Farmer, P. Daedalus and Icarus   **292**
The **conquest** of the North and South Poles.
  Owen, R.   **998**
Conquistadors. See America—Discovery and ex-
  ploration
Conrad and the dragon. Harley, L. P.
  In Green, R. L. ed. A cavalcade of dragons
    p213-45   **808.8**
Conroy, Jack
  The Boomer fireman's fast Sooner hound
  In Arbuthnot, M. H. comp. The Arbuthnot
    Anthology of children's literature
    p378-79   **808.8**
  In Arbuthnot, M. H. comp. Time for old
    magic p254-55   **398.2**
  (jt. auth.) Bontemps, A. The fast Sooner
  hound   **Fic**

Conroy, Robert
  The Battle of Bataan (5-7)   **940.54**
Conservation of energy. See Force and energy
Conservation of forests. See Forests and forestry
Conservation of natural resources
  Asimov, I. Earth: our crowded spaceship
    (5-7)   **301.32**
  Duffey, E. Conservation of nature (6-7) **333.7**
  Hirsch, S. C. Guardians of tomorrow (6-7)
          920
  Hyde, M. O. For pollution fighters only (5-7)
          614.7
  Miles, B. Save the earth (4-7)   **301.31**
  Smith, F. C. The first book of conservation
    (4-7)   **333.7**
Conservation of nature. Duffey, E.   **333.7**
Conservation of the soil. See Soil conservation
Conservation of wildlife. See Wildlife—Conser-
  vation
Constance. Clapp, P.   **Fic**
Constantes and the Dhrako
  Haviland, V. Constantes and the dragon
  In Haviland, V. Favorite fairy tales told
    in Greece p3-19   **398.2**
  Manning-Sanders, R. Constantes and the
    dragon
  In Manning-Sanders, R. A book of dragons
    p9-19   **398.2**
  In Manning-Sanders, R. A choice of magic
    p235-45   **398.2**
Constantes and the dragon. See Constantes and
  the Dhrako
Constantine I, the Great
  See pages in the following book:
  Brooks, P. S. When the world was Rome, 753
    B.C. to A.D. 476 p199-223 (6-7)   **937**
Constantinople   **956.1**
Constellations. See Astronomy; Stars
Constitution
        United States
  See United States. Constitution
Constitutional Amendments
        United States
  See United States. Constitution—
  Amendments
The **constitutional** amendments. Katz, W. L.
          342.2
Constitutional history. See United States—Con-
  stitutional history
Constitutional law. See Civil rights
Construction. See Architecture; Building
Construction of roads. See Roads
Construction workers
  See pages in the following book:
  Colby, J. P. Building wrecking p41-50 (4-7)
          690
Consumer education
  Gay, K. Be a smart shopper (4-6)   **640.73**
  See also pages in the following book:
  Issues in children's book selection p125-35
          028.5
Consumer goods. See Manufactures

Consumer protection
See pages in the following books:
Arbuthnot, M. H. comp. The Arbuthnot Anthology of children's literature p886-90
808.8
Gay, K. Be a smart shopper p49-62 (4-6)
640.73

Consumers' guides. See Consumer education

Contaminated food. See Food contamination

Contamination of the environment. See Pollution

Contemporary art. See Art, Modern—20th century

The **contest.** Gates, D.
In Association for Childhood Education International. Told under the Stars and Stripes p122-35 **S C**

Continental drift
Branley, F. M. Shakes, quakes, and shifts: earth tectonics (5-7) 551.4
See also pages in the following book:
Lauber, P. Earthquakes p34-36, 41-44 (4-6)
551.2

Continents. See Continental drift

Contrary Chueh Chun. Chrisman, A. B.
In Chrisman, A. B. Shen of the sea p185-95 **S C**

Contrary Jenkins. Caudill, R. **E**

The **Contrary wife**
In Courlander, H. ed. Ride with the sun p159-62 398.2

The **contrary woman.** Courlander, H.
In Courlander, H. The fire on the mountain, and other Ethiopian stories p35-39 398.2

Contreras, Gerry
(illus.) Wiesenthal, E. Let's find out about rivers 551.4

Conundrums. See Riddles

Converse, Harriet Maxwell
Jones, H. Longhouse winter 398.2

Conveying machinery. See Hoisting machinery

Conwell, Mary K.
New York. Public Library. Libros en español
028.52

Cook, Fred J.
The rise of American political parties (5-7)
329

Cook, James, 1728-1779
Captain Cook and the South Pacific (6-7) 919
Syme, R. Captain Cook, Pacific explorer (4-6)
92
See also pages in the following books:
Cottler, J. Heroes of civilization p37-50 (6-7)
920
Kaula, E. M. The land and people of New Zealand p56-62 (5-7) 919.31

Cook, Jan
(illus.) Cook, J. J. Blue whale 599
(illus.) Cook, J. J. The nocturnal world of the lobster 595

Cook, Joseph J.
Blue whale (4-7) 599
The nightmare world of the shark (4-7) 597
The nocturnal world of the lobster (4-6) 595
Wonders of the pelican world (4-7) 598.2

The **cook** and the house goblin. Manning-Sanders, R.
In Manning-Sanders, R. A book of ghosts & goblins p30-37 398.2

Cook book for boys and girls, The Seabury. Moore, E. 641.5

Cook books. See Cookery

Cookbook for boys & girls, Betty Crocker's. Crocker, B. 641.5

A **cookbook for girls and boys.** Rombauer, I. S.
641.5

Cooke, Ann
Giraffes at home (1-3) 599

Cooke, David C.
Famous U.S. Air Force bombers (5-7) 623.74
Famous U.S. Navy fighter planes (5-7) 623.74
Inventions that made history (5-7) 609
Racing cars that made history (5-7) 796.7
The tribal people of Thailand (5-7) 301.2

Cooke, Flora J.
How the robin's breast became red
In Ward, W. ed. Stories to dramatize p77-78 372.6
The maid who defied Minerva
In Ward, W. ed. Stories to dramatize p119-21 372.6

Cookery
Better Homes and Gardens Junior cook book (4-7) 641.5
Borghese, A. The down to earth cookbook (4-6) 641.5
Camp Fire Girls Mother daughter cookbook (4-7) 641.5
Cavin, R. 1 pinch of sunshine, ½ cup of rain (4-6) 641.5
Cobb, V. Arts and crafts you can eat (4-7)
745.5
Cobb, V. Science experiments you can eat (5-7) 507.2
Cooper, T. T. Many hands cooking (4-7)
641.5
Crocker, B. Betty Crocker's Cookbook for boys & girls (3-7) 641.5
Ellison, V. H. The Pooh cook book (4-7)
641.5
Ellison, V. H. The Pooh party book (1-5)
793.2
Girl Scouts of the United States of America. Girl Scout cookbook (4-7) 641.5
Greene, E. comp. Clever cooks (3-6) 398.2
Hautzig, E. Cool cooking (2-5) 641.7
McDonald, B. G. Casserole cooking fun (4-6)
641.8
MacGregor, C. The storybook cookbook (3-6)
641.5
Meyer, C. Christmas crafts (5-7) 745.59
Meyer, C. Milk, butter, and cheese (5-7)
641.3
Moore, E. The Seabury Cook book for boys and girls (1-3) 641.5
Parents' Nursery School. Kids are natural cooks (3-6) 641.5
Paul, A. Kids cooking (3-6) 641.5
Perkins, W. L. The Fannie Farmer Junior cook book (5-7) 641.5
Rombauer, I. S. A cookbook for girls and boys (4-7) 641.5
Shapiro, R. A whole world of cooking (5-7)
641.5
Shapiro, R. Wide world cookbook (5-7) 641.5

Counting books—_Continued_

Francoise. Jeanne-Marie counts her sheep   E
Friskey, M. Chicken Little, count-to-ten   E
Gretz, S. Teddy bears 1 to 10   E
Hoban, T. Count and see   E
Ipcar, D. Brown Cow Farm   E
Langstaff, J. Over in the meadow (k-2) **784.4**
Over in the meadow   E
Oxenbury, H. Numbers of things   E
Peppé, R. Circus numbers   E
Reiss, J. J. Numbers   E
Tudor, T. 1 is one   E
Wildsmith, B. Brian Wildsmith's 1, 2, 3's E
Williams, G. The chicken book   E

The **counting** of the crocodiles. Courlander, H.
_In_ Courlander, H. The tiger's whisker, and
other tales and legends from Asia
and the Pacific p87-89   **398.2**

Country Beautiful
The Story of soil. See The Story of soil **631.4**
Wood, J. P. The life and words of John F.
Kennedy   **92**

The **country** bunny and the little gold shoes.
Heyward, D. B.   E

Country life
See also Outdoor life
Fiction
Fisher, D. C. Understood Betsy (4-6)   **Fic**
Lindquist, J. D. The golden name day (3-5)
Fic

Wisconsin
North, S. Little Rascal (3-5)   **599**
North, S. Rascal (5-7)   **599**

Country mouse and the town mouse
Asbjørnsen, P. C. The House Mouse and the
Country Mouse
_In_ Asbjørnsen, P. C. Norwegian folk tales
p116-19   **398.2**

Country noisy book. Brown, M. W.   E

The **country** of the mice. Hume, L. C.
_In_ Hume, L. C. Favorite children's stories
from China and Tibet p102-08 **398.2**

Courage
Kennedy, J. F. Profiles in courage. Young
readers Memorial edition, abridged (5-7)
920
McNeer, M. Armed with courage (4-6) **920**
See also Fear
Fiction
Faulkner, G. Melindy's medal (3-5)   **Fic**

The **courage** of Sarah Noble. Dalgliesh, A. **Fic**

The **Courage** Piece. Leuser, E.
_In_ Kamerman, S. E. ed. Fifty plays for
junior actors p280-92   **812.08**

Courlander, Harold
Anansi's hat-shaking dance
_In_ Arbuthnot, M. H. comp. The Arbuthnot
Anthology of children's literature
p321-23   **808.8**
_In_ Arbuthnot, M. H. comp. Time for old
magic p198-200   **398.2**
The cow-tail switch, and other West African
stories (4-6)   **398.2**
Contents: The cow-tail switch; Kaddo's wall; Talk;
One you don't see coming; Kassa, the strong one;
Anansi's fishing expedition; Younde goes to town; Sing-
ing tortoise; Time; Messenger to Maftam; Guinea Fowl

and Rabbit get justice; Anansi and Nothing go hunting
for wives; How Soko brought debt to Ashanti; Hungry
Spider and the turtle; Throw Mountains; Ansige Karamba, the glutton; Don't shake hands with everybody

The fire on the mountain
_In_ Arbuthnot, M. H. comp. The Arbuthnot
Anthology of children's literature
p312-14   **808.8**
_In_ Arbuthnot, M. H. comp. Time for old
magic p191-93   **398.2**
The fire on the mountain, and other Ethiopian stories (4-6)   **398.2**
Contents: The fire on the mountain; The donkey who
sinned; The woodcutter of Gura; The goats who killed
the leopard; The jackal's lawsuit; The contrary woman;
The messenger donkey; The hero of Adi Nifas; The
judgement of the wind; The goat well; Dinner with the
tota; Justice; The game board; How Abunawas was exiled; The marriage of the mouse; Tecle's goat; The
storyteller; Ojje Ben Onogh; The lion and the hare go
hunting; May it not happen; The farmer of Babbia;
Fire and water, truth and falsehood; The battle of
Eghal Shillet; The golden earth

The goat well
_In_ Colwell, E. ed. A second storyteller's
choice p97-102   **372.6**
_In_ Johnson, E. ed. Anthology of children's
literature p369-71   **808.8**
The hat-shaking dance, and other tales from
the Gold Coast (3-6)   **398.2**
Contents: All stories are Anansi's; Anansi, the oldest
of animals; Anansi's hat-shaking dance; Two feasts for
Anansi; Anansi plays dead; Liars' contest; Why wisdom
is found everywhere; Osebo's drum; Anansi and the
elephant go hunting; Planting party; Okraman's medicine; Anansi borrows money; Anansi's rescue from the
river; Anansi and the elephant exchange knocks; How
the lizard lost and regained his farm; Anansi steals the
palm wine; Elephant's tail; Porcupine's hoe; Sword
that fought by itself; Nyame's well; Coming of the
yams

The king's drum, and other African stories
(4-7)   **398.2**
Contents: The song of Gimmile; The chief of the
Gurensi; Three fast men; The King of Sedo; The fisherman; A song for the new chief; The search: who gets
the chief's daughter; The king's drum; The Sky God's
daughter; The wedding of the hawk; How poverty
was revealed to the king of Adja; Three sons of a
chief; The brave man of Golo; The feast; Frog's wives
make ndiba pudding; Two friends: how they parted;
The hunter and his talking leopard; The past and the
future; The elephant hunters; A father-in-law and his
son-in-law; The donkeys ask for justice; The lion's
share; Nawasi goes to war; Ruda, the quick thinker;
The giraffe hunters; The stone lute; Why the chameleon shakes his head; The hemp smoker and the hemp
grower; The message from the moon

The leopard's daughter
_In_ Tashjian, V. A. ed. With a deep sea
smile p56-60   **372.6**
Olode the hunter, and other tales from
Nigeria (4-6)   **398.2**
Contents: Olomu's bush rat; The man who looked
for death; Ekun and Opolo go looking for wives; The
lizard's lost meat; The antelope skin; Olode the hunter
becomes an oba; How Ijapa, who was short, became
long; Ijapa cries for his horse; Kigbo and the bush
spirits; The chief's knife; Why the lion, the vulture,
and the hyena do not live together; Ijapa and the oba
repair a roof; Sofo's escape from the leopard; How
Ologbon-Ori sought wisdom; Ijapa and Yanrinbo swear
an oath; Antelope's mother: the woman in the moon;
The oba asks for a mountain; The journey to Lagos;
Ijapa goes to the Osanyin shrine; Ijapa and the hot-
water test; Ogungbemi and the battle in the bush; The
quarrel between Ile and Orun; Ijapa demands corn
fufu; The wrestlers; How the people of Ife became
scattered; How Moremi saved the town of Ife; The
staff of Oranmiyan; The first woman to say "dim";
Why no one lends his beauty

People of the short blue corn (5-7)   **398.2**
Contents: How the people came from the Lower
World; Coyote helps decorate the night; Sikakokuh

Courlander, Harold—*Continued*

and the hunting dog; The beetle's hairpiece; Joshokiklay and the eagle; Mockingbird gives out the calls; The boy who crossed the great water and returned; Coyote and the crying song; Honwyma and the Bear Fathers of Tokoanave; Two friends, Coyote and bull snake, exchange visits; The foot racers of Payupki; Why the salt is far away; How the village of Pivanhonkapi perished; The sun callers; The journey to the Land of the Dead; Coyote's needle; How the Tewas came to First Mesa

The piece of fire, and other Haitian tales (4-6)
398.2

Contents: Merisler, stronger than the elephants; The chief of the well; Bouki gets whee-ai; Break Mountains; Bouki rents a horse; Pierre Jean's tortoise; The cat, the dog, and death; Sweet misery; The gun, the pot, and the hat; The lizard's big dance; Bouki buys a burro; Ticoumba and the President; Nananbouclou and the piece of fire; The fishermen; Who is the older; The voyage below the water; Bouki cuts wood; The donkey driver; The blacksmiths; Bouki's glasses; Charles Legoun and his friend; Bouki and Ti Bef; The king of the animals; Janot cooks for the Emperor; Jean Britisse, the champion; Waiting for a turkey

(ed.) Ride with the sun (4-7)   398.2

The search: who gets the chief's daughter
In Tashjian, V. A. ed. With a deep sea
smile p70-74   372.6

The Son of the Leopard (4-6)   Fic

Talk
In Gruenberg, S. M. ed. Favorite stories
old and new p354-57   808.8

Terrapin's pot of sense (4-6)   398.2

Contents: Waiting on salvation; Reform meeting; Rabbit, fox, and the rail fence; Buh Rabbit's tight necktie; Terrapin's pot of sense; Slow train to Arkansas; Buh Rabbit's human weakness; Buh Rabbit's big eat; Buh Fox's number nine shoes; Buh Rabbit's tail; The well; Rabbit scratches Buh Elephant's back; Buh Mouse testifies; Buh Rabbit's graveyard; Buh Rabbit and the king; Texas sandstorm; Hot times; The champion; The skull; Old Master and Okra; Do-all ax; King and Kuffie; Old Boss, John, and the mule; Crossing the river; Old Boss and George; Devil in church; Preacher and the Devil; What the preacher's talking about; Sharing the crops; Death and the old man; Moon's a woman

The tiger's tail
In Gruenberg, S. M. ed. Favorite stories
old and new p396-97   808.8

The tiger's whisker, and other tales and legends from Asia and the Pacific (4-6)
398.2

Contents: The scholar of Kosei; The tiger's whisker; The tiger's minister of state; the trial of the stone; The hidden treasure of Khin; The king who ate chaff; The musician of Tagaung; The rice puller of Chaohwa; The spear and shield of Huan-tan; The ambassador from Chi; The trial of the forest; The trial of Avichára-pura; The prince of the six weapons; The man from Kailasa; Krishna the cowherd; The scholars and the lion; The traveler and the nut tree; The debt; The boy and the cloth; The wrestler of Kyushu; The counting of the crocodiles; Abunuwas the trickster; The spotted rug; The philosophers of King Darius; Dinner for the monk; The well diggers; Guno and Koyo and the Kris; The learned men; The war of the plants; Maui the great; The great lizard of Nimple

Uncle Bouqui and Godfather Malice
In Arbuthnot, M. H. comp. The Arbuthnot Anthology of children's literature
p399-401   808.8
In Arbuthnot, M. H. comp. Time for old
magic p268-70   398.2

Cournos, John
A boy named John; excerpt
In Association for Childhood Education International. Told under the Stars and
Stripes p257-69   S C

Court, Margaret (Smith)
See pages in the following book:
Sullivan, G. Queens of the court p11-33 (5-7)
920

The **court** of King Arithmetic. Chaloner, G.
In Kamerman, S. E. ed. Fifty plays for
junior actors p118-27   812.08

The **court** of the stone children. Cameron, E.
Fic

Courtesy
See also Etiquette
Fiction
Slobodkin, L. Excuse me! Certainly!   E
Slobodkin, L. Thank you—you're welcome E

Courtis, Stuart A.
The Courtis-Watters Illustrated Golden dictionary for young readers. See The Courtis-Watters Illustrated Golden dictionary for young readers   423

The **Courtis**-Watters Illustrated Golden dictionary for young readers   423

Cousin Greylegs, the great red fox and Grandfather Mole. Pyle, L.
In Pyle, H. The wonder clock p77-88 398.2

Cousins, Margaret
The story of Thomas Alva Edison (4-6)   92

Coutant, Helen
First snow (2-4)   Fic

Coverlets
See pages in the following book:
Pettit, F. H. How to make whirligigs and whimmy diddles, and other American folkcraft objects p85-114 (5-7)   745.5
Fiction
Beatty, P. O the Red Rose Tree (5-7)   Fic

The **covetous** Councilman. Bealmear, J. H.
In Kamerman, S. E. ed. Dramatized folk
tales of the world p504-13   812.08

Cow. See Cows

The **cow** and the thread. Jagendorf, M. A.
In Jagendorf, M. A. Noodlehead stories
from around the world p68-72 398.2

Cow Bu-cola. Manning-Sanders, R.
In Manning-Sanders, R. A book of ogres
and trolls p75-79   398.2

Cow ghost
Du Bois, W. P. Elizabeth—the cow ghost
In Gruenberg, S. M. ed. Favorite stories
old and new p487-90   808.8

The **cow**-tail switch. Courlander, H.
In Courlander, H. The cow-tail switch,
and other West African stories p5-12
398.2

The **cow**-tail switch, and other West African
stories. Courlander, H.   398.2

Cow that cried. Brenner, A.
In Brenner, A. The boy who could do anything, & other Mexican folk tales
p108-13   398.2

The **cow** who fell in the canal. Krasilovsky, P.
E

Cowboy; excerpt. Santee, R.
In Anderson, C. W. ed. C. W. Anderson's
Favorite horse stories p165-75 808.8

The **cowboy** and the cook; puppet play. Jagendorf, M.
In Jagendorf, M. Penny puppets, penny theatre, and penny plays p99-107
791.5

The **cowboy** encyclopedia. Grant, B.   917.803

Cowboy jamboree: western songs & lore. Felton, H. W. ed.   784.4

The **cowboy** trade. Rounds, G.   917.8

Cowboys
Cowboys and cattle country (5-7)   917.8
Felton, H. W. Nat Love, Negro cowboy (4-6)
92
Malone, J. W. An album of the American cowboy (4-7)   917.8
Rounds, G. The cowboy trade (4-7)   917.8
Sackett, S. J. comp. Cowboys & the songs they sang (4-7)   784.6
See also pages in the following books:
Burt, O. W. The horse in America p128-36 (5-7)
636.109
Carpenter, A. Uruguay p60-62 (4-6)   918.95
Dobler, L. The land and people of Uruguay p104-10 (5-7)   918.95
Hall, E. The land and people of Argentina p90-105 (5-7)   918.2

Dictionaries
Grant, B. The cowboy encyclopedia (3-6)
917.803

Fiction
Felton, H. W. Bowleg Bill, seagoing cowpuncher (5-7)   398.2
Felton, H. W. New tall tales of Pecos Bill (5-7)   398.2
Felton, H. W. Pecos Bill and the mustang (k-3)   398.2
Felton, H. W. Pecos Bill, Texas cowpuncher (5-7)   398.2

Songs and music
Felton, H. W. ed. Cowboy jamboree: western songs & lore   784.4
Rounds, G. The Strawberry Roan (k-4)   784.6
Sackett, S. J. comp. Cowboys & the songs they sang (4-7)   784.6

Cowboys and cattle country   917.8

Cowboys & the songs they sang. Sackett, S. J. comp.   784.6

Cowell, Henry Dixon
See pages in the following book:
Posell, E. Z. American composers p22-27 (5-7)   920

Cows
Aliki. Green grass and white milk (2-4)   637
See also Dairying

Stories
Krasilovsky, P. The cow who fell in the canal   E

Cox, Charles
(illus.) Carlson, B. W. Funny-bone dramatics
812

Coy, Harold
The first book of Congress (6-7)   328.73
Man comes to America (6-7)   917
Presidents (4-6)   920

Coyote and Mole. Curry, J. L.
In Curry, J. L. Down from the lonely mountain p101-02   398.2

Coyote and the crying song. Courlander, H.
In Courlander, H. People of the short blue corn p82-85   398.2

The **coyote** and the fox. De Huff, E. W.
In Gruenberg, S. M. ed. Favorite stories old and new p338-40   808.8

Coyote conquers the Iya. Jones, H.
In Jones, H. Coyote tales p41-49   398.2

Coyote cry. Baylor, B.   Fic

Coyote drowns the world. Baker, B.
In Baker, B. At the center of the world p8-15   398.2

Coyote helps decorate the night. Courlander, H.
In Courlander, H. People of the short blue corn p25-26   398.2

Coyote in Manhattan. George, J. C.   Fic

Coyote loses his dinner. Jones, H.
In Jones, H. Coyote tales p15-21   398.2

Coyote rescues the ring-girl. Jones, H.
In Jones, H. Coyote tales p23-49   398.2

Coyote steals the fire
Hardendorff, J. B. How the coyote stole fire for the Klamaths
In Hardendorff, J. B. ed. Just one more p73-77   372.6

Coyote steals the summer. Jones, H.
In Jones, H. Coyote tales p 1-13   398.2

Coyote tales. Jones, H.   398.2

Coyotes
Fox, M. Sundance coyote (5-7)   599
See also pages in the following book:
Mason, G. F. Animal homes p13-17 (4-7)
591.5

Stories
Baylor, B. Coyote cry (2-4)   Fic
George, J. C. Coyote in Manhattan (4-7)   Fic
Hodges, M. The Fire Bringer (2-5)   398.2
Jones, H. Coyote tales (3-5)   398.2

Coyote's needle. Courlander, H.
In Courlander, H. People of the short blue corn p143-44   398.2

Coyote's new hairdo. Curry, J. L.
In Curry, J. L. Down from the lonely mountain p80-87   398.2

The **crab** and the crane. Babbitt, E. C.
In Babbitt, E. C. Jataka tales p84-89 398.2

The **Crab** and the monkey
In Sakade, F. ed. Japanese children's favorite stories p94-96   398.2

Crab grass. See Crabgrass

The **crab** that played with the sea. Kipling, R.
In Green, R. L. ed. A cavalcade of magicians p242-53   808.8
In Kipling, R. Just so stories (Doubleday) p171-96   S C
In Kipling, R. Just so stories (Doubleday. Anniv. ed.) p79-88   S C
In Kipling, R. Just so stories (Watts, F.) p171-93   S C

Crabgrass
See pages in the following book:
Wright, R. H. What good is a weed? p74-85 (4-6)   581.5

Crabs
Holling, H. C. Pagoo (4-7)   595
Zim, H. S. Crabs (3-5)   595

A crack in the pavement. Howell, R. R. **500.9**

Cradle songs. *See* Lullabies

The cradle that rocked by itself. Leach, M.
In Leach, M. The thing at the foot of the
bed, and other scary tales p75-76
S C

Craft, Ellen
Freedman, F. B. Two tickets to freedom; the
true story of Ellen and William Craft, fugitive slaves (4-6) **92**
See also pages in the following book:
Chittenden, E. F. Profiles in black and white
p68-87 (5-7) **920**

Craft, William
Freedman, F. B. Two tickets to freedom
(4-6) **92**
See also pages in the following book:
Chittenden, E. F. Profiles in black and white
p68-87 (5-7) **920**

The craft of sail. Adkins, J. **623.88**

Crafts. *See* Handicraft

Crafts for Christmas. Cutler, K. N. **745.59**

Craigie, William A.
Huldu-folk, nisses and sea-sprites
In Brown, M. ed. A cavalcade of sea leg-
ends p138-44 **808.8**
Mermen
In Brown, M. ed. A cavalcade of sea leg-
ends p30-34 **808.8**

Craik, Dinah Maria (Mulock)
See pages in the following book:
Benét, L. Famous storytellers for young peo-
ple p63-69 (5-7) **920**
For a title by this author see Mulock,
Dinah Maria

Crandall, Elizabeth L.
Dwight Eisenhower, hero
In Cavanah, F. ed. Holiday roundup p148-
53 **394.2**

Crandall, Prudence. *See* Philleo, Prudence
(Crandall)

Crane, Lois
The empty city
In Hazeltine, A. I. ed. Hero tales from
many lands p417-27 **398.2**

Crane, Louise
The land and people of the Congo (5-7)
916.75

Crane, T.
Clever peasant
In Dobbs, R. ed. Once upon a time p34-
37 **372.6**

Crane, Walter
(illus.) Grimm, J. Household stories **398.2**

The crane. Zimnik, R. **Fic**

Crane and the crab
Babbitt, E. C. The crab and the crane
In Babbitt, E. C. Jataka tales p84-89
398.2

The Crane and the fox
In Bloch, M. H. ed. Ukrainian folk tales
p36-38 **398.2**

The crane maiden. Matsutani, M. **398.2**

Cranes (Birds)
See also Whooping cranes

Stories
Byars, B. The house of wings (4-6) **Fic**
Matsutani, M. The crane maiden (k-3) **398.2**
Robertson, K. In search of a sandhill crane
(5-7) **Fic**
Yamaguchi, T. The golden crane (3-5) **398.2**

Cranes, whooping. *See* Whooping cranes

Cranes, derricks, etc.
Zim, H. S. Hoists, cranes, and derricks (3-6)
621.8
See also pages in the following book:
Harman, C. A skyscraper goes up p49-57
(5-7) **690**

Fiction
Zimnik, R. The crane (4-6) **Fic**

Crash! Bang! Boom! Spier, P. **E**

Cratchits' Christmas dinner. Dickens, C.
In Dalgliesh, A. comp. Christmas p205-11
394.2
In Tudor, T. ed. Take joy! p30-31 **394.2**

Crater Lake National Park
See pages in the following book:
Melbo, I. R. Our country's national parks
v2 p216-32 (5-7) **917.3**

Craven, Thomas
The rainbow book of art (5-7) **709**

Crawford, Ethan
See pages in the following book:
Carmer, C. comp. America sings p20-24
(5-7) **784.4**

Crawford, Marion
The doll's ghost
In Ireson, B. comp. Haunting tales p117-
31 **S C**

Crayder, Dorothy
She, the adventuress (5-7) **Fic**

Crayfish
Cook, J. J. The nocturnal world of the lobster (4-6) **595**

Crayon drawing. *See* Pastel drawing

Crazy Horse, Oglala Indian
Meadowcroft, E. L. Crazy Horse, Sioux warrior (2-5) **92**
See also pages in the following books:
Arbuthnot, M. H. comp. The Arbuthnot Anthology of children's literature p827-31
808.8
Johnston, J. The Indians and the strangers
p99-109 (2-5) **920**

Crazy Horse, Sioux warrior. Meadowcroft, E. L.
92

Creating a school media program. Gillespie,
J. T. **027.8**

Creating independence, 1763-1789. Coughlan,
M. ed. **016.9733**

Creating with clay. Seidelman, J. **731.4**

Creating with paint. Seidelman, J. E. **751.4**

Creating with papier-mache. Seidelman, J. E.
731.4

Creating with wood. Seidelman, J. E. **745.51**

Creation
Baker, B. At the center of the world (4-6)
398.2

Creation—*Continued*
See also Earth; Evolution; Geology; Mythology; Universe

Creation of man
Chandler, K. The creation of man
In Cavanah, F. ed. Holiday roundup p216-18 **394.2**
Sechrist, E. H. The creation of Man
In Sechrist, E. H. ed. It's time for story hour p142-45 **372.6**

The **creation** of the sun and the moon. Traven, B. **398.2**

The **creation** of the wolf. Maas, S.
In Maas, S. The moon painters, and other Estonian folk tales p56-59 **398.2**

Creative dramatics. Siks, G. B. **372.6**

Creative paper crafts in color. Alkema, C. J. **745.54**

Creative plays and programs for holidays. Bennett, R. **812**

Creative shellcraft. Cutler, K. N. **745.55**

The **creature** with no claws. Harris, J. C.
In A St Nicholas anthology p105-06 **810.8**

Credibility. See Truthfulness and falsehood

Credle, Ellis
Down, down the mountain **E**
—Same
In Sechrist, E. H. ed. It's time for story hour p14-22 **372.6**
Monkey see, monkey do **E**
The perambulatin' pumpkin
In Greene, E. comp. Clever cooks p137-42 **398.2**
The pudding that broke up the preaching
In Luckhardt, M. C. comp. Thanksgiving p267-72 **394.2**
Tall tales from the high hills, and other stories (4-7) **398.2**
Contents: Big mudhole; Perambulatin' pumpkin; Pudding that broke up the preaching; Bear and the wildcat; Tall turnip; Saved by a turkey; Blizzard of '98; Old Plott; Popcorn patch; Bear in the black hat; Short horse; How Pa learned to grow hot peppers; Fighting rams; Self-kicking machine; Lake that flew; Man who rode the bear; Surprise for the black bull; Voice in the jug; Goat that went to school; Janey's shoes

Creek Indians
Stuart, G. S. Three little Indians (k-3) **970.1**

Creepy crawly things. National Geographic Society **598.1**

Creoles
See pages in the following book:
Clifford, M. L. The land and people of Sierra Leone p110-21 (5-7) **916.6**

Crespi, Pachita
Gift of the earth
In Dalgliesh, A. comp. Christmas p225-36 **393.2**

Cresswell, Helen
The night watchmen (4-6) **Fic**
Up the pier (4-6) **Fic**
About
See pages in the following book:
Townsend, J. R. A sense of story p57-63 **028.5**

The **crested** curassow. Sherlock, P.
In Sherlock, P. West Indian folk-tales p13-20 **398.2**

Creston, Paul
See pages in the following book:
Posell, E. Z. American composers p30-34 (5-7) **920**

Crests. See Heraldry

Cretan, Gladys Yessayan
All except Sammy (2-5) **Fic**

Cretan mythology. See Mythology, Cretan

Crews, Donald
We read: A to Z **E**
(illus.) Branley, F. M. Eclipse **523.7**
(illus.) Dennis, J. R. Fractions are parts of things **513**
(illus.) Milgrom, H. ABC of ecology **614.7**

Crichlow, Ernest
(illus.) Beim, L. Two is a team **E**
(illus.) King, M. L. We shall live in peace: the teachings of Martin Luther King, Jr. **301.45**
(illus.) Lewis, C. Benjamin Banneker: the man who saved Washington **92**
(illus.) Sterling, D. Freedom train: the story of Harriet Tubman **92**
(illus.) Sterling, D. Mary Jane **Fic**

The **cricket** fight. Hume, L. C.
In Hume, L. C. Favorite children's stories from China and Tibet p33-38 **398.2**

Cricket in a thicket. Fisher, A. **811**

The **cricket** in Times Square. Selden, G. **Fic**

The **cricket** in Times Square; excerpt. Selden, G.
In Association for Childhood Education International. Told under the city umbrella p73-80 **S C**

Cricket songs. Behn, H. comp. **895.6**

Crickets
George, J. C. All upon a stone (1-3) **595.7**
Hogner, D. C. Grasshoppers and crickets (2-5) **595.7**
See also pages in the following books:
Ricciuti, E. R. Shelf pets p92-97 (5-7) **639**
Villiard, P. Insects as pets p101-06 (5-7) **595.7**
Stories
Caudill, R. A pocketful of cricket **E**
Selden, G. The cricket in Times Square (3-6) **Fic**

Crickety Cricket! Tippett, J. S. **811**

Crictor. Ungerer, T. **E**

Crime and criminals
See also Counterfeits and counterfeiting; Pirates; Trials
Identification
See pages in the following book:
Berger, M. Those amazing computers! p79-94 (5-7) **001.6**
See also Fingerprints

The **crimson** feather. Watts, F. B.
In Kamerman, S. E. ed. Fifty plays for junior actors p627-34 **812.08**

The **cripple**. Andersen, H. C.
In Andersen, H. C. The complete fairy tales and stories p1049-57 **S C**

Crippled children. See Physically handicapped children

Cripples. See Physically handicapped

A **critical** approach to children's literature. Chicago. University. Graduate Library School 028.5

A **critical** approach to children's literature. Smith, J. S. 028.5

A **critical** history of children's literature. Meigs, C. ed. 028.5

Criticism

See pages in the following book:

Haviland, V. ed. Children and literature p391-414 028.5

Fiction

Conford, E. Felicia the critic (4-6) **Fic**

The **Crochera**. MacManus, S.

In MacManus, S. The bold heroes of Hungry Hill, and other Irish folk tales p44-63 398.2

Crochet for beginners. Rubenstone, J. 746.4

Crocheting

Parker, X. L. A beginner's book of knitting and crocheting (5-7) 746.4

Rubenstone, J. Crochet for beginners (3-5) 746.4

See also pages in the following book:

Meyer, C. Yarn—the things it makes and how to make them p11-42 (4-7) 746.4

Crocker, Betty

Betty Crocker's Cookbook for boys & girls (3-7) 641.5

Freeman, L. M. Betty Crocker's Parties for children 793.2

Crockett, David

Holbrook, S. Davy Crockett (5-7) 92

See also pages in the following books:

Carmer, C. comp. America sings p100-05 (5-7) 784.4

Gruenberg, S. M. ed. Favorite stories old and new p398-402 808.8

Malcolmson, A. Yankee Doodle's cousins p149-55 (4-7) 398.2

Crockett, Davy. See Crockett, David

Crocodile and Hen. Lexau, J. M. 398.2

Crocodiles

Zim, H. S. Alligators and crocodiles (4-6) 598.1

See also pages in the following books:

Huntington, H. E. Let's look at reptiles p50-57 (4-6) 598.1

Shuttlesworth, D. E. Animals that frighten people p80-88 (5-7) 591.5

See also Alligators

Stories

Aruego, J. A crocodile's tale (k-3) 398.2

Galdone, P. The monkey and the crocodile (k-2) 398.2

Waber, B. The house on East 88th Street E

Waber, B. Lyle finds his mother E

Waber, B. Lyle, Lyle, crocodile E

A **crocodile's** tale. Aruego, J. 398.2

The **crocus** who couldn't bloom. Boiko, C.

In Boiko, C. Children's plays for creative actors p272-81 812

Croll, Carolyn

(illus.) Flory, J. We'll have a friend for lunch E

Crom Duv, the giant

Colum, P. The House of Crom Duv

In Colum, P. The King of Ireland's Son p211-53 398.2

Crone, Ruth

(jt. auth.) Brown, M. M. The silent storm [biography of Anne Sullivan Macy] 92

Crook, George

See pages in the following book:

Ehrlich, A. Wounded Knee: an Indian history of the American West p42-50, 145-52 (6-7) 970.4

Cropper, Bill

See pages in the following book:

Carmer, C. comp. America sings p132-37 (5-7) 784.4

Crops. See Farm produce

Crosby, Muriel

Reading ladders for human relations. See Reading ladders for human relations 016.301

Cross, Helen Reeder

Christmas without Kriss Kringle

In Johnson, L. S. ed. Christmas stories round the world p95-100 394.2

Cross, John

(jt. auth.) Cross, L. Kitchen crafts 745.5

Cross, Linda

Kitchen crafts (3-7) 745.5

Cross-country running. See Track athletics

The **cross** princess. MacLellan, E.

In Kamerman, S. E. ed. Fifty plays for junior actors p322-32 812.08

Cross your fingers, spit in your hat. Schwartz, A. comp. 398

Crossing the bridge. Leach, M.

In Leach, M. Whistle in the graveyard p75 398.2

Crossing the river. Courlander, H.

In Courlander, H. Terrapin's pot of sense p91-92 398.2

Crossley, B. Alice

(jt. auth.) Burack, A. S. ed. Popular plays for classroom reading 808.82

Crossroads to childhood. Moore, A. C.

In Moore, A. C. My roads to childhood p203-329 028.5

The **crossways**. Hartley, L. P.

In Ireson, B. comp. Haunting tales p246-55 **S C**

Crouthers, David D.

Flags of American history (6-7) 929.9

The **Crow**

In Lang, A. ed. The yellow fairy book p92-94 398.2

The **Crow** and the peacock

In Hardendorff, J. B. ed. Just one more p37-39 372.6

The **crow** and the sparrow's eggs. Arnott, K.

In Arnott, K. Animal folk tales around the world p174-78 398.2

The **crow** and the whale. Gillham, C. E.

In Gillham, C. E. Beyond the Clapping Mountains p51-67 398.2

Curie, Pierre
See pages in the following book:
Asimov, I. Breakthroughs in science p154-62 (5-7)   **920**

Curiosities and wonders
Guinness Book of world records   **032**
Soule, G. Surprising facts about our world and beyond (5-7)   **031**

Curious George. Rey, H. A.   **E**

Curious George flies a kite. Rey, M.   **E**

Curious George goes to the hospital. Rey, M.
                                            E

Curious George learns the alphabet. Rey, H. A.   **E**

Curious George rides a bike. Rey, H. A.   **E**

Curious George takes a job. Rey, H. A.   **E**

The curious raccoons. Hess, L.   **599**

The curious world of crystals. Sander, L.   **548**

Current biography yearbook   **920.03**

Curriculum materials centers. See Instructional materials centers

Curry, Jane Louise
Beneath the hill (4-7)   **Fic**
The daybreakers (4-7)   **Fic**
Down from the lonely mountain (3-5)   **398.2**
Contents: The beginning of the world and the making of California; The securing of light; The theft of Dawn; Cottontail and the Sun; The theft of fire; The rescue of fire; Coyote's new hairdo; The Witsduks; Coyote and Mole; Cottontail's song; The out-foxed fox; The Growing Rock
The ice ghosts mystery (4-7)   **Fic**

The curse of Lorenzo Dow. Jagendorf, M. A.
In Jagendorf, M. A. Folk stories of the South p105-07   **398.2**

The curse of Polyphemus. Peabody, J. P.
In Arbuthnot, M. H. comp. The Arbuthnot Anthology of children's literature p458-60   **808.8**
In Arbuthnot, M. H. comp. Time for old magic p322-24   **398.2**

Curses, hexes, & spells. Cohen, D.   **133.4**

Curtin, Jeremiah
The voyage of Cud
In Brown, M. ed. A cavalcade of sea legends p198-217   **808.8**

Curtis, Anna L.
The ghosts of the Mohawk
In Hoke, H. ed. Spooks, spooks, spooks p167-74   **S C**

Curtis, Richard
Zoo 2000
In Yolen, J. ed. Zoo 2000 p13-22   **S C**

Cushman, Alice B.
A nineteenth century plan for reading; The American Sunday School Movement
In Andrews, S. ed. The Hewins lectures, 1947-1962 p205-33   **028.5**

Custer, George Armstrong
Goble, P. Red Hawk's account of Custer's last battle (4-7)   **973.8**
Reynolds, Q. Custer's last stand (5-7)   **92**
See also pages in the following book:
Bleeker, S. The Sioux Indians p133-36 (4-6)
                                           970.3

Custer's last stand. Reynolds, Q.   **92**

Customs, Social. See Manners and customs; and names of ethnic groups and countries with the subdivision Social life and customs, e.g. Indians of North America—Social life and customs; China—Social life and customs

Cutler, Katherine N.
Crafts for Christmas (3-7)   **745.59**
Creative shellcraft (4-6)   **745.55**
From petals to pinecones (4-7)   **745.92**
Growing a garden, indoors or out (4-7) **635**

Cyaxares, King of Media
See pages in the following book:
Collins, R. The Medes and Persians p10-20 (6-7)   **913.35**

Cycles, Motor. See Motorcycles

Cycling. See Bicycles and bicycling; Motorcycles

Cyclones
See pages in the following book:
Weiss, M. E. Storms—from the inside out p63-74 (4-6)   **551.5**

Cyphers. See Cryptography

Cyrus the Great, King of Persia
See pages in the following book:
Collins, R. The Medes and Persians p34-48 (6-7)   **913.35**

Cytology. See Cells

Czechoslovak Republic
Hall, E. The land and people of Czechoslovakia (5-7)   **914.37**

Folklore
See Folklore—Czechoslovak Republic

Industries
See pages in the following book:
Hall, E. The land and people of Czechoslovakia p93-99 (5-7)   **914.37**

Religion
See pages in the following book:
Hall, E. The land people of Czechoslovakia p55-66 (5-7)   **914.37**

D

D Day. See Normandy, Attack on, 1944

DDT (Insecticide)
See pages in the following books:
McClung, R. M. Gypsy moth p40-53 (4-7)
                                           632
Silverstein, A. The chemicals we eat and drink p80-95 (4-7)   **664**

D.J.'s worst enemy. Burch, R.   **Fic**

DNA
Silverstein, A. The code of life (6-7)   **575.1**

Dachshunds

Stories
Leaf, M. Noodle   **E**

D'Adamo, Anthony
(illus.) Barker, A. Black on white and read all over   **686.2**

Daddy longlegs
Hawes, J. My daddy longlegs (1-3)   **595**

D'Amato, Janet—Continued
American Indian craft inspirations (5-7)
745.5
Colonial crafts for you to make (4-7)   745.5
Indian crafts (4-7)   745.5
(illus.) Ruchlis, H. Your changing earth   551
Dame Fortune and Don Money. Corson, H. W.
In Kamerman, S. E. ed. Dramatized folk
tales of the world p481-92   812.08
Dame Gudbrand
Asbjörnsen, P. C. Gudbrand on the hill-side
In Arbuthnot, M. H. comp. The Arbuth-
not Anthology of children's litera-
ture p244-46   808.8
In Arbuthnot, M. H. comp. Time for old
magic p127-29   398.2
In Asbjørnsen, P. C. Norwegian folk tales
p178-81   398.2
In Johnson, E. ed. Anthology of children's
literature p291-93   808.8
Aulaire, I. d'. Gudbrand on the Hillside
In Aulaire, I. d'. East of the sun and west
of the moon p202-06   398.2
Gudbrand on the hillside
In Undset, S. ed. True and untrue, and
other Norse tales p185-89   398.2
**Dame Wiggins of Lee and her seven wonder-
ful cats**
Dame Wiggins of Lee and her seven won-
derful cats
In Hutchinson, V. S. ed. Candle-light
stories p137-46   398.2
Damian and the dragon. Manning-Sanders, R.
In Hoke, H. comp. Dragons, dragons,
dragons p5-21   398.2
Damien, Father
See pages in the following books:
McNeer, M. Armed with courage p23-38
(4-6)   920
Sechrist, E. H. It's time for brotherhood
p62-67 (5-7)   301.11
Damien de Veuster, Joseph. See Damien,
Father
Damjan, Mischa
Atuk   E
Dams
Farb, P. The story of dams (5-7)   627
Damsel flies
Hutchins, R. E. The world of dragonflies and
damselflies (5-7)   595.7
Simon, H. Dragonflies (5-7)   595.7
See also Dragonflies
Dan McGirth and his gray goose mare. Jag-
endorf, M. A.
In Jagendorf, M. A. Folk stories of the
South p95-97   398.2
Dana, Doris
The elephant and his secret   E
Dance, dance, Amy-Chan! Hawkinson, L.   Fic
"Dance, dance, dolly mine!" Andersen, H. C.
In Andersen, H. C. The complete fairy
tales and stories p1002-03   S C
Dance music. See Jazz music
Dance of the animals. Belpré, P.   398.2
also in Belpré, P. The tiger and the rab-
bit, and other tales p97-103   398.2

A dance to still music. Corcoran, B.   Fic
Dancing
See also Ballet; Modern dance
Great Britain
See pages in the following book:
Fox, L. M. Costumes and customs of the
British Isles p31-37 (4-7)   391
North America
See pages in the following book:
Meyer, R. Festivals U.S.A. & Canada p44-
49   394.2
Dancing in the moon. Eichenberg, F.   E
The dancing kettle. Uchida, Y.
In Uchida, Y. The dancing kettle, and
other Japanese folk tales p3-10
398.2
See also Accomplished and lucky tea
kettle
The dancing kettle, and other Japanese folk
tales. Uchida, Y.   398.2
The dancing palm tree. Walker, B. K.
In Walker, B. K. The dancing palm tree,
and other Nigerian folktales p15-26
398.2
The dancing palm tree, and other Nigerian folk-
tales. Walker, B. K.   398.2
The dancing princesses. De La Mare, W.
In Colwell, E. ed. A second storyteller's
choice p85-96   372.6
In De La Mare, W. Tales told again p61-
73   398.2
In Johnson, S. P. ed. The Princesses p50-67
S C
See also Twelve dancing princesses
Dandelion. Freeman, D.   E
Dandelion, pokeweed, and goosefoot. Schaef-
fer, E.   581.6
Dandelions
See pages in the following book:
Wright, R. H. What good is a weed? p53-61
(4-6)   581.5
Dandelions don't bite. Adelson, L.   422
Danger! Norton, M.
In Arbuthnot, M. H. comp. The Arbuthnot
Anthology of children's literature
p510-12   808.8
The dangerous game. Miller, S.
In Burack, A. S. ed. Popular plays for class-
room reading p142-57   808.82
Dangerous journey. Hámori, L.   Fic
Daniels, Guy
(illus.) Portal, C. The beauty of birth   612.6
Daniels, Jonathan
Stonewall Jackson (5-7)   92
Danish literature
See pages in the following book:
Wohlrabe, R. A. The land and people of Den-
mark p112-19 (5-7)   914.89
Dan'l Boone
In Malcolmson, A. Yankee Doodle's cousins
p139-47   398.2
Danny and the dinosaur. Hoff, S.   E
Danny Dunn and the homework machine. Wil-
liams, J.   Fic

Danny Kaye, UNICEF ambassador. Singer, K.
  In Cavanah, F. ed. Holiday roundup p248-
  51   **394.2**
Danska, Herbert
  (illus.) Branley, F. J. Pieces of another world
                                                 552
  (illus.) Haviland, V. Favorite fairy tales told
  in Russia   **398.2**
Danube River
  See pages in the following books:
  Hale, J. The land and people of Romania
  p16-25 (5-7)   **914.98**
  Kostich, D. D. The land and people of the
  Balkans p15-20 (5-7)   **914.96**
Daphne (Nymph)
  See pages in the following book:
  Gates, D. The golden god: Apollo p24-28
  (4-7)   **292**
Dapplegrim
  Aulaire, I. d'. Dapplegrim
  In Aulaire, I. d'. East of the sun and west
    of the moon p188-201   **398.2**
  Dapplegrim
  In Undset, S. ed. True and untrue, and
    other Norse tales p83-96   **398.2**
  Dasent, G. W. Dapplegrim
  In Manning-Sanders, R. ed. A book of
    magical beasts p70-83   **398.2**
  Moe, J. Dapplegrim
  In Lang, A. ed. The red fairy book p246-
    56   **398.2**
Dar es Salaam, Tanzania
  Description
  See pages in the following book:
  Kaula, E. M. The land and people of Tan-
  zania p79-84 (5-7)   **916.78**
D'Arcy, Alice
  Cinderella
  In Burack, A. S. ed. One hundred plays for
    children p633-42   **808.82**
  Wonders of Storybook Land
  In Burack, A. S. ed. One hundred plays for
    children p412-22   **808.82**
Dare, Virginia
  See pages in the following book:
  Anderson, J. The haunting of America p57-
  63 (6-7)   **398.2**
The **dare**. Leach, M.
  In Leach, M. The thing at the foot of the
    bed, and other scary tales p37-39
                                                 S C
The **daring** of Yellow Doc. Jagendorf, M. A.
  In Jagendorf, M. A. Folk stories of the
    South p54-57   **398.2**
The **daring** venture. Luckhardt, M. C.
  In Luckhardt, M. C. comp. Thanksgiving
    p21-43   **394.2**
Daringer, Helen F.
  Adopted Jane (4-6)   **Fic**
  The departure
  In Luckhardt, M. C. comp. Thanksgiving
    p49-58   **394.2**
Darius I, King of Persia
  See pages in the following book:
  Collins, R. The Medes and Persians p80-94
  (6-7)   **913.35**

Dark Ages. See Middle Ages
The **dark** didn't catch me. Thrasher, C.   **Fic**
Dark horse of Woodsfield. Hightower, F.   **Fic**
The **dark** is rising. Cooper, S.   **Fic**
Darley, Felix Octavius Carr
  See pages in the following book:
  Haviland, V. ed. Yankee Doodle's literary
    sampler of prose, poetry, & pictures p168-
    84   **028.5**
Darling, Frances C.
  Susan Coolidge, 1835-1905
  In Andrews, S. ed. The Hewins lectures,
    1947-1962 p251-64   **028.5**
Darling, John
  See pages in the following books:
  Carmer, C. comp. America sings p44-49 (5-7)
                                                 784.4
  Malcolmson, A. Yankee Doodle's cousins
    p 1-10 (4-7)   **398.2**
Darling, Lois
  Before and after dinosaurs (5-7)   **568**
  Sixty million years of horses (4-7)   **636.109**
  Turtles (3-5)   **598.1**
  Worms (1-3)   **595**
Darling, Louis
  The gull's way (5-7)   **598.2**
  Kangaroos and other animals with pockets
    (4-6)   **599**
  (illus.) Cleary, B. Beezus and Ramona   **Fic**
  (illus.) Cleary, B. Ellen Tebbits   **Fic**
  (illus.) Cleary, B. Henry Huggins   **Fic**
  (illus.) Cleary, B. The mouse and the motor-
    cycle   **Fic**
  (illus.) Cleary, B. Otis Spofford   **Fic**
  (illus.) Cleary, B. Ribsy   **Fic**
  (illus.) Cleary, B. Runaway Ralph   **Fic**
  (jt. auth.) Darling, L. Before and after dino-
    saurs   **568**
  (jt. auth.) Darling, L. Sixty million years of
    horses   **636.109**
  (jt. auth.) Darling, L. Turtles   **598.1**
  (jt. auth.) Darling, L. Worms   **595**
  (illus.) Goetz, D. The Arctic tundra   **919.8**
  (illus.) Goetz, D. Deserts   **551.4**
  (illus.) Goetz, D. Mountains   **551.4**
  (illus.) Goetz, D. Swamps   **551.4**
Darning needle
  Andersen, H. C. The darning needle
  In Andersen, H. C. Andersen's Fairy tales
    p88-91   **S C**
  In Andersen, H. C. The complete fairy
    tales and stories p271-74   **S C**
  In Andersen, H. Hans Andersen's Fairy
    tales p266-69   **S C**
  In Andersen, H. C. It's perfectly true, and
    other stories p141-46   **S C**
  In Andersen, H. C. Seven tales p93-103
                                                 S C
  Andersen, H. C. A story about a darning-
    needle
  In Lang, A. ed. The yellow fairy book
    p319-21   **398.2**
Darrell, Margery
  (ed.) Once upon a time   **808.8**
Darrow, Whitney
  (illus.) Winn, M. ed. The fireside book of fun
    and game songs   **784.6**

David and Goliath
    In Ross, L. Puppet shows using poems
        and stories p181-88   791.5
David and Goliath. De Regniers, B. S. 221.9
    also in De Regniers, B. S. ed. The giant
        book p39-46   398.2
David and Goliath; play. Howard, V.
    In Howard, V. The complete book of chil-
        dren's theater p476-80   812
David and the big drum. Green, K.
    In Green, K. Leprechaun tales p107-17
                                     398.2
David and the second Lafayette. Davis, L. R.
    In Burack, A. S. ed. One hundred plays
        for children p312-23   808.82
David comes home. Schneider, N.
    In Association for Childhood Education
        International. Told under the Christ-
        mas tree p266-83   808.8
David he no fear. Graham, L.   221.9
David in silence. Robinson, V.   Fic
Davidson, Margaret
    Louis Braille (3-5)   92
Davies, Ruth Ann
    The school library media program 027.8
Da Vinci, Leonardo. See Leonardo da Vinci
Davis, Alice Vaught
    Timothy Turtle   E
Davis, Angela
    See pages in the following book:
    Aymar, B. Laws and trials that created his-
        tory p202-08 (6-7)   345.7
Davis, Benjamin Oliver, 1912-
    See pages in the following book:
    Hughes, L. Famous Negro heroes of Amer-
        ica p187-98 (5-7)   920
Davis, Burke
    Appomattox (6-7)   973.7
    Biography of a leaf (3-5)   581
    Getting to know Jamestown (4-6)   975.5
    Heroes of the American Revolution (5-7)
                                        920
Davis, Harriet (Ross) Tubman. See Tubman,
    Harriet (Ross)
Davis, Joseph A.
    Five hundred animals from A to Z (3-7)
                                     591.03
Davis, Katherine
    The Little Drummer Boy (Carol) The Little
        Drummer Boy   783.6
Davis, Lavinia R.
    Aboard the "Sweet Cecile"
    In Luckhardt, M. C. comp. Thanksgiving
        p329-38   394.2
    David and the second Lafayette
    In Burack, A. S. ed. One hundred plays
        for children p312-23   808.82
    Pinney's Easter hunt
    In Cavanah, F. ed. Holiday roundup p86-
        91   394.2
    In Harper, W. comp. Easter chimes p18-
        25   394.2
    Saint Patrick and the last snake
    In Cavanah, F. ed. Holiday roundup p64-
        66   394.2
    St Patrick and the last snake in Ireland;
        play

    In Kamerman, S. E. ed. Little plays for
        little players p47-52   812.08
    A turtle, a flute and the General's birthday
    In Kamerman, S. E. ed. Fifty plays for
        junior actors p167-77   812.08
Davis, Marguerite
    (illus.) Association for Childhood Education
        International. Told under the blue um-
        brella   S C
    (illus.) Richards, L. E. Tirra lirra   811
    (illus.) Rossetti, C. G. Sing-song   821
Davis, Marilyn Kornreich
    Music dictionary (6-7)   780.3
Davis, Mary Gould
    (ed.) A baker's dozen   372.6
    The enchanted cow
    In Harper, W. comp. Ghosts and goblins
        p60-66   394.2
    In Hoke, H. ed. Witches, witches, witches
        p37-44   808.8
    The truce of the wolf
    In Johnson, E. ed. Anthology of children's
        literature p590-94   808.8
    (jt. auth.) Boggs, R. S. Three golden oranges,
        and other Spanish folk tales   398.2
Davis, Richard H.
    Midsummer pirates
    In A St Nicholas anthology p305-15 810.8
Davis, Robert
    The general's horse
    In Johnson, E. ed. Anthology of children's
        literature p239-41   808.8
    The jokes of Single-Toe
    In Arbuthnot, M. H. comp. The Arbuth-
        not Anthology of children's literature
        p267-69   808.8
    In Arbuthnot, M. H. comp. Time for old
        magic p150-52   398.2
    Padre Porko, the gentlemanly pig (4-6) 398.2
    Contents: Padre Porko, the gentlemanly pig; The
    general's horse; Celestina's silver coffee-pot; Dog who
    talked; Bully learns a lesson; Money-bag of Neigh-
    bor Felix; Pablo's goose and the evil eye; White sister;
    Jokes of Single-Toe; New-moon meeting; The outlaw
Davis, Russell
    Chief Joseph; war chief of the Nez Percé
        (5-7)   92
    The lion's whiskers (5-7)   398.2
    Contents: The lion's whiskers; The snake in the
    bottle; The king's black curtain; The bob-tailed mon-
    key and the king's honey; The gold-lined donkey;
    Digit the Midget; To outleap a rabbit; The smiling
    innkeeper; Lion bones and the Gardula magicians;
    The lion's share; Know your own strength; The fight
    with Crazy man; Four good men; The brave prince;
    A most generous host; The wise judge; King Firdy
    the Just; The long walk; Live alone, die alone; Gift
    for the lazy; The ant and the tower to God; The
    peace between the leopard and the antelope; The un-
    grateful snake; How God helped Mammo; The prize;
    Saint Gabre Manfas and his animals; King Solomon
    and the Queen of Sheba; The gift and the giver; The
    three suitors; The man with a lion head in a can;
    The talkative turtle
Davis, Sammy
    See pages in the following book:
    Rollins, C. Famous Negro entertainers of
        stage, screen, and TV p57-62 (5-7)   920
Davy, Sir Humphry, bart.
    See pages in the following book:
    Cottler, J. Heroes of civilization p169-79
        (6-7)   920

Davy Crockett
In Malcolmson, A. Yankee Doodle's cousins p149-55   398.2

Davy Crockett. Gorham, M.
In Gruenberg, S. M. ed. Favorite stories old and new p398-402   808.8

Davy Crockett. Holbrook, S.   92

Dawn. Shulevitz, U.   E

Dawn of fear. Cooper, S.   Fic

Dawn-Strider. Yolen, J.
In Yolen, J. The girl who cried flowers, and other tales p13-22   S C

Dawson, Richard
(jt. auth.) Dawson, R. A walk in the city   E

Dawson, Rosemary
A walk in the city   E

Day, Beth
Life on a lost continent (5-7)   500.9
The secret world of the baby   612.6

Day, Dorothy
See pages in the following book:
Ross, P. ed. Young and female p25-36 (6-7)   920

Day, Véronique
Landslide! (4-7)   Fic

Day and night
Origin of day and night
In Hardendorff, J. B. ed. Just one more p22-23   372.6

The day I had to play with my sister. Bonsall, C.   E

A day in a child's life. Greenaway, K.
In Greenaway, K. The Kate Greenaway treasury p36-61   828

A day in the life of a sea otter. McDearmon, K.   599

The day is bright. Myrick, N.
In Burack, A. S. ed. One hundred plays for children p253-67   808.82

The day Luis was lost. Barth, E.   Fic

Day of destiny. Fisher, A.
In Fisher, A. Holiday programs for boys and girls p14-24   812

A day of pleasure. Singer, I. B.   92

The day of the dragon. Endore, G.
In Yolen, J. ed. Zoo 2000 p179-219   S C

The day of the scholars. MacManus, S.
In Macmanus, S. Hibernian nights p224-32   398.2

Day of work and no cheer. Lenski, L.
In Lenski, L. Lois Lenski's Christmas stories p3-15   394.2

A day off. Tobias, T.   E

The day the circus came to Lone Tree. Rounds, G.   E

The day the hurricane happened. Anderson, L.   E

The day the Moonmen landed. Rybak, R. K.
In Kamerman, S. E. ed. Fifty plays for junior actors p521-29   812.08

The day Tuk became a hunter. Melzack, R.
In Melzack, R. The day Tuk became a hunter & other Eskimo stories p13-20   398.2

The day Tuk became a hunter & other Eskimo stories. Melzack, R.   398.2

The day we saw the sun come up. Goudey, A. E.   E

Dayan, Moshe
See pages in the following book:
Hoffman, G. The land and people of Israel p122-25 (5-7)   915.694

The daybreakers. Curry, J. L.   Fic

Dayrell, Elphinstone
Why the sun and the moon live in the sky (k-2)   398.2

Days. See Birthdays; Fasts and feasts; Festivals; Holidays; and names of special days, e.g. Christmas

Days of the dinosaurs. See Jackson, K. Dinosaurs   568

The days of the week. Andersen, H. C.
In Andersen, H. C. Andersen's Fairy tales p469-71   S C
In Andersen, H. C. The complete fairy tales and stories p982-83   S C

De Knee-high man; short story. Carmer, C.
In Carmer, C. comp. America sings p156-61   784.4

The dead, Worship of. See Ancestor worship

The dead child. Andersen, H. C.
In Andersen, H. C. The complete fairy tales and stories p642-46   S C

Dead man. Leach, M.
In Leach, M. Whistle in the graveyard p111-12   398.2

Dead man who was alive. Brenner, A.
In Brenner, A. The boy who could do anything, & other Mexican folk tales p104-07   398.2

Dead Sea
See pages in the following book:
Hoffman, G. The land and people of Israel p26-29 (5-7)   915.694

Dead Sea scrolls
Palmer, G. Quest for the Dead Sea scrolls (5-7)   229
Rappaport, U. The story of the Dead Sea scrolls (5-7)   229

The dead tree. Tresselt, A.   E

The Dead wife
In Lang, A. ed. The yellow fairy book p149-51   398.2

Deaf
Levine, E. S. Lisa and her soundless world (1-3)   617.8

Education
Brown, M. M. The silent storm [biography of Anne Sullivan Macy] (5-7)   92
Hunter, E. F. Child of the silent night [biography of Laura Dewey Bridgman] (3-5)   92
Malone, M. Annie Sullivan [biography of Anne Sullivan Macy] (2-4)   92
Peare, C. O. The Helen Keller story (5-7)   92

Fiction
Corcoran, B. A dance to still music (5-7)   Fic
Harris, R. The bright and morning star (5-7)   Fic

Deaf—*Fiction*—*Continued*
Robinson, V. David in silence (4-6)   **Fic**
    Means of communication
Charlip, R. Handtalk   **419**

Deafness
Levine, E. S. Lisa and her soundless world (1-3)   **617.8**
   See also pages in the following book:
Adler, I. Your ears p30-45 (3-5)   **612**

Dean, Elizabeth
Printing: tool of freedom (4-6)   **686.2**

De Angeli, Marguerite
Bright April (3-5)   **Fic**
Christmas in the Gaspé
   In Association for Childhood Education International. Told under the Christmas tree p154-61   **808.8**
The Christmas spider
   In Cavanah, F. ed. Holiday roundup p325-26   **394.2**
   In Eaton, A. T. comp. The animals' Christmas p48-49   **394.2**
The costume party
   In Association for Childhood Education International. Told under the Stars and Stripes p136-49   **S C**
The door in the wall (4-6)   **Fic**
Elin's Amerika (4-6)   **Fic**
Fun with the calf
   In Martignoni, M. E. ed. The illustrated treasury of children's literature p312-16   **808.8**
The market
   In Association for Childhood Education International. Told under the Stars and Stripes p54-61   **S C**
Newbery Medal acceptance paper
   In Miller, B. M. ed. Newbery Medal books: 1922-1955 p342-52   **028.5**
Thee, Hannah! (3-5)   **Fic**
Yonie Wondernose (1-4)   **Fic**
(illus.) Grimm, J. The goose girl   **398.2**
(illus.) Mother Goose. Marguerite de Angeli's Book of nursery and Mother Goose rhymes   **398.8**

    About
   See pages in the following books:
Hoffman, M. ed. Authors and illustrators of children's books p108-14   **028.5**
Miller, B. M. ed. Newbery Medal books: 1922-1955 p337-41   **028.5**

Dear dragon. Joslin, S.   **808.6**

Dear garbage man. Zion, G.   **E**

Death
Zim, H. S. Life and death (4-7)   **393**
   See also pages in the following book:
LeShan, E. What makes me feel this way? p103-10 (3-6)   **152.4**
    Fiction
Cleaver, V. Grover (4-6)   **Fic**
Coutant, H. First snow (2-4)   **Fic**
De Paola, T. Nana Upstairs & Nana Downstairs   **E**
Hunter, M. A sound of chariots (5-7)   **Fic**
Miles, M. Annie and the Old One (1-4)   **Fic**
Smith, D. B. A taste of blackberries (3-6)   **Fic**
Stolz, M. The edge of next year (6-7)   **Fic**

Viorst, J. The tenth good thing about Barney   **E**
Zolotow, C. My grandson Lew   **E**

Death and the old man. Courlander, H.
   In Courlander, H. Terrapin's pot of sense p108-11   **398.2**

Death of Cuchullin. O'Faolain, E.
   In O'Faolain, E. Irish sagas and folktales p101-09   **398.2**

The death of Evening Star. Fisher, L. E.   **Fic**

The death of Koschei the Deathless. Ralston, W. R. S.
   In Lang, A. ed. The red fairy book p42-53   **398.2**

The death of the hen. Grimm, J.
   In Grimm, J. Household stories p12-13   **398.2**

The death of the little hen. Grimm, J.
   In Grimm, J. The complete Grimm's Fairy tales p365-67   **398.2**

The Death of the Sun-hero
   In Lang, A. ed. The yellow fairy book p213-15   **398.2**

Death Valley National Monument
   See pages in the following book:
National Geographic Society. The new America's wonderlands p254-59   **917.3**

Death's godchild. Alegría, R. E.
   In Alegría, R. E. The three wishes p51-55   **398.2**

Death's messengers. Grimm, J.
   In Grimm, J. The complete Grimm's Fairy tales p718-20   **398.2**

Debates and debating. See Parliamentary practice

De Beaumont, Madame Le Prince. See Le Prince de Beaumont, Marie

De Brunhoff, Jean. See Brunhoff, Jean de

De Brunhoff, Laurent. See Brunhoff, Laurent de

The debt. Courlander, H.
   In Courlander, H. The tiger's whisker, and other tales and legends from Asia and the Pacific p78-79   **398.2**

De Caylus, Comte. See Caylus, Comte de

December. Coatsworth, E.
   In Association for Childhood Education International. Told under the Christmas tree p120-30   **808.8**

De Champlain, Samuel. See Champlain, Samuel de

Decide for yourself
   In DeRoin, N. ed. Jataka tales p78-79   **398.2**

Decimal classification. See Classification, Decimal

Decimal classification and relative index, Abridged Dewey. Dewey, M.   **025.4**

Declaration of Independence. See United States. Declaration of Independence

De Coloma, Louis. See Coloma, Louis de

Decoration and ornament. See Design, Decorative; Flower arrangement; Gems; Holiday decorations; Illustration of books; Jewelry; Leatherwork; Lettering; Painting; Pottery; Sculpture; Wood carving

Decoration Day. See Memorial Day

Decorations, Holiday. See Holiday decorations

Decorative arts. See Design, Decorative

The **deep** dives of Stanley Whale. Benchley, N.   **E**

The **deep** range. Clarke, A. C.
In Yolen, J. ed. Zoo 2000 p39-54   **S C**

Deep-sea diving. See Skin diving

Deep sea technology. See Oceanography

Deep trouble. Morey, W.   **Fic**

Deer
Bergman Sucksdorff, A. The roe deer (3-6)
                                        599
Buff, M. Dash & Dart (k-3)   **599**
Eberle, I. Fawn in the woods (k-3)   **599**
Hurd, E. T. The mother deer (k-2)   **599**
See also Reindeer

Stories
Salten, F. Bambi (4-6)   **Fic**
Thurber, J. The white deer (6-7)   **Fic**
Trevino, E. B. de. Nacar, the white deer (5-7)
                                        Fic

The **Deer** and the jaguar share a house
In Courlander, H. ed. Ride with the sun
p198-201   **398.2**

The **deer** and the woodcutter. Kim, S.
In Kim, S. The story bag p86-98   **398.2**

Deer mice. See Mice

Deer of five colors. Uchida, Y.
In Uchida, Y. The magic listening cap p65-
71   **398.2**

The **deer**, the rabbit, and the toad. Kim, S.
In Kim, S. The story bag p31-33   **398.2**

Defense, Radar. See Radar defense networks

Defensive football. Anderson, D.   **796.33**

Defoe, Daniel
The ghost of Dorothy Dingley; adaptation.
See Mayne, W. T. The ghost of Dorothy
Dingley
Robinson Crusoe. See Politzer, A. My jour-
nals and sketchbooks   **Fic**
Robinson Crusoe on the desolate island
In Martignoni, M. E. ed. The illustrated
treasury of children's literature p429-
36   **808.8**

DeForest, Charlotte B.
The prancing pony (k-3)   **398.8**

De Garza, Patricia
Chicanos (4-6)   **301.45**

De Gasztold, Carmen Bernos. See Gasztold,
Carmen Bernos de

Degens, T.
Transport 7-41-R (6-7)   **Fic**

De Gerez, Toni. See Gerez, Toni de

DeGering, Etta
Wilderness wife; the story of Rebecca Bryan
Boone (5-7)   **92**

De Groat, Diane
(illus.) Clymer, E. Luke was there   **Fic**

De Hartog, Jan
The mermaid of Emmeloord
In Brown, M. ed. A cavalcade of sea
legends p5-20   **808.8**

De Huff, Elizabeth Willis
The coyote and the fox
In Gruenberg, S. M. ed. Favorite stories
old and new p338-40   **808.8**

Deirdre. Buck, A. M.
In Hazeltine, A. I. ed. Hero tales from
many lands p174-83   **398.2**

DeJong, Meindert
Along came a dog (4-6)   **Fic**
Along came a dog; excerpt
In Arbuthnot, M. H. comp. The Arbuthnot
Anthology of children's literature
p644-46   **808.8**
Far out the long canal (4-6)   **Fic**
A horse came running (4-6)   **Fic**
The house of sixty fathers (4-6)   **Fic**
Hurry home, Candy (4-6)   **Fic**
Journey from Peppermint Street (4-6) **Fic**
The little boss
In Arbuthnot, M. H. comp. The Arbuthnot
Anthology of children's literature
p644-46   **808.8**
The mighty ones (6-7)   **221.9**
Newbery Medal acceptance paper
In Miller, B. M. ed. Newbery Medal books:
1922-1955 p434-39   **028.5**
Puppy summer (4-6)   **Fic**
Shadrach (1-4)   **Fic**
The wheel on the school (4-6)   **Fic**
The wheel on the school; excerpt
In Johnson, E. ed. Anthology of children's
literature p779-87   **808.8**

About
See pages in the following books:
Haviland, V. ed. Children and literature
p160-68   **028.5**
Hoffman, M. ed. Authors and illustrators of
children's books p115-21   **028.5**
Miller, B. M. ed. Newbery Medal books:
1922-1955 p427-33   **028.5**
Townsend, J. R. A sense of story p68-74
                                      028.5

De Kay, James T.
Meet Martin Luther King, Jr. (2-5)   **92**

De La Fontaine, Jean. See La Fontaine, Jean de

De La Iglesia, Maria Elena
The cat and the mouse, and other Spanish
tales (2-4)   **398.2**

De La Mare, Walter
(ed.) Animal stories   **398.2**
Ashputtel
In Child Study Association of America.
Castles and dragons p109-25 **398.2**
In De La Mare, W. ed. Animal stories
p285-95   **398.2**
Bells and grass (3-7)   **821**
Cinderella and the glass slipper
In Johnson, E. ed. Anthology of children's
literature p162-68   **808.8**
Clever Grethel
In Greene, E. comp. Clever cooks p109-14
                                      398.2
(ed.) Come hither   **821.08**
The dancing princesses
In Colwell, E. ed. A second storyteller's
choice p85-96   **372.6**
In Johnson, S. P. ed. The Princesses p50-
67   **S C**
The hare and the hedgehog
In Johnson, E. ed. Anthology of children's
literature p202-04   **808.8**
The magic jacket (5-7)   **S C**

De La Mare, Walter—*Continued*
Contents: The magic jacket; The scarecrow; Maria-Fly; Alice's godmother; The old lion; Miss Jemima; The riddle; Lucy; Visitors; Broomsticks

Mr Bumps and his monkey (4-6)   **Fic**
Peacock Pie (4-7)   **821**
A penny a day (3-6)   **S C**
Contents: A penny a day; The three sleeping boys of Warwickshire; The lovely Myfanwy; The Dutch cheese; Dick and the beanstalk; The Lord Fish

Rhymes and verses (4-7)   **821**
The sleeping beauty
In Johnson, E. ed. Anthology of children's literature p168-73   **808.8**
Stories from the Bible (5-7)   **221.9**
Tales told again (4-7)   **398.2**
Contents: The hare and the hedgehog; Four brothers; The musicians; Dick Whittington; Cinderella and the glass slipper; Dancing princesses; Little Red Riding Hood; Jack and the beanstalk; The turnip; The wolf and the fox; Three sillies; Bluebeard; Snow-White; Twelve windows; Clever Grethel; Rumplestilskin; Sleeping Beauty; Molly Whuppie; Rapunzel

(ed.) Tom Tiddler's ground   **821.08**
Visitors
In Authors' choice 2 p75-87   **S C**

About
See pages in the following books:
Benét, L. Famous poets for young people p98-103 (5-7)   **920**
Horn Book Reflections on children's books and reading p265-70   **028.5**

De Lany, Milan
(jt. auth.) Carpenter, A. Kenya   **916.76**

De Larrea, Victoria
(illus.) Green, K. Leprechaun tales   **398.2**
(illus.) Kästner, E. Lisa and Lottie   **Fic**
(illus.) Tashjian, V. A. ed. Juba this and Juba that   **372.6**

Delaware

Fiction
De Angeli, M. Elin's Amerika (4-6)   **Fic**

Delaware Indians
Bleeker, S. The Delaware Indians (4-6) **970.3**

Fiction
Clifford, E. The year of the three-legged deer (4-7)   **Fic**

De Leeuw, Adèle
Edith Cavell: nurse, spy, heroine (5-7)   **92**
George Rogers Clark: frontier fighter (2-4) **92**
The Girl Scout story (2-5)   **369.463**

De Lesseps, Ferdinand Marie, vicomte. See Lesseps, Ferdinand Marie, vicomte de

Delessert, Etienne
(illus.) Kipling, R. Just so stories   **S C**

The **deliverers** of their country. Nesbit, E.
In Nesbit, E. The complete book of dragons p47-67   **S C**

Dello Joio, Norman
See pages in the following book:
Posell, E. Z. American composers p36-39 (5-7)   **920**

Delta Plan, Netherlands
See pages in the following book:
Cohn, A. The first book of the Netherlands p13-17 (4-6)   **914.92**

Delton, Judy
Two good friends   **E**

The **deluded** dragon. Manning-Sanders, R.
In Hoke, H. comp. Dragons, dragons, dragons p149-54   **398.2**

Deluge and how it came about, Story of the. See Story of the deluge and how it came about

Delulio, John
(illus.) Paul, A. Kids camping   **796.54**

De Luna, Tony
(illus.) Kantrowitz, M. I wonder if Herbie's home yet   **E**

Demeter
Farmer, P. The story of Persephone (3-5) **292**
Gates, D. Two queens of heaven: Aphrodite [and] Demeter (4-7)   **292**
Proddow, P. Demeter and Persephone (3-6)   **292**

Demeter and Persephone. Proddow, P.   **292**

Deming, Dorothy
First aid first
In Kamerman, S. E. ed. Little plays for little players p153-56   **812.08**
Grey ghosts
In Burack, A. S. ed. One hundred plays for children p45-52   **808.82**
Old man river
In Burack, A. S. ed. One hundred plays for children p53-60   **808.82**

Demolition workers. See Construction workers

Demon at Green Knowe. Boston, L. M.
In Hoke, H. ed. Spooks, spooks, spooks p178-205   **S C**

The **demon** king. Priestley, J. B.
In Ireson, B. comp. Haunting tales p156-73   **S C**

The **Demon** with the matted hair
In Jacobs, J. ed. Indian fairy tales p194-98   **398.2**

Demonology
See pages in the following book:
McHargue, G. The impossible people p74-104 (5-7)   **398**
See also Occult sciences

The **demon's** daughter. Manning-Sanders, R.
In Manning-Sanders, R. A book of devils and demons p15-29   **398.2**

Demon's mother-in-law
Boggs, R. S. Don Demonio's mother-in-law
In Boggs, R. S. Three golden oranges, and other Spanish folk tales p59-74   **398.2**

Demonstrations for Negro civil rights. See Negroes—Civil rights

De Montreville, Doris
(ed.) Third book of junior authors   **920.03**

De Morgan, Mary
The hair tree
In Farjeon, E. ed. A cavalcade of queens p166-206   **808.8**
The necklace of Princess Fiorimonde; dramatization. See Smith, M. R. The necklace of Princess Fiorimonde
A toy princess
In Johnson, S. P. ed. The Princesses p8-31   **S C**

Diamonds and toads
Perrault, C. Diamonds and toads
In Perrault, C. Famous fairy tales p117-24
398.2
Perrault, C. The fairies
In Perrault, C. Perrault's Complete fairy
tales p42-46   398.2
Perrault, C. The fairy
In Opie, I. ed. The classic fairy tales p100-
02   398.2
Perrault, C. Toads and diamonds
In Johnson, E. ed. Anthology of children's
literature p181-82   808.8
In Lang, A. ed. The blue fairy book p274-
77   398.2
In Rackham, A. comp. Arthur Rackham
Fairy book p196-98   398.2
Toads and diamonds
In Hutchinson, V. S. ed. Candle-light sto-
ries p93-100   398.2

Diana. See Artemis

Dias, Earl S.
Christmas spirit
In Kamerman, S. E. ed. A treasury of
Christmas plays p79-94   812.08

Diaz de Vivar, Rodrigo, called El Cid. See
El Cid Campeador

Di Bondone, Giotto. See Giotto di Bondone

Dick and the beanstalk. De La Mare, W.
In De La Mare, W. A penny a day p116-
64   S C

Dick o' the cow
Nic Leodhas, S. The tale of Dick o' the cow
In Nic Leodhas, S. By loch and by lin
p53-67   398.2

Dick Whittington and his cat
Brown, M. Dick Whittington and his cat
398.2
—Same
In Johnson, E. ed. Anthology of children's
literature p205-07   808.8
Carey, M. C. Dick Whittington
In Martignoni, M. E. ed. The illustrated
treasury of children's literature p223-
28   808.8
De La Mare, W. Dick Whittington
In De La Mare, W. Tales told again p33-
43   398.2
Dick Whittington
In Rackham, A. comp. Arthur Rackham
Fairy book p30-40   398.2
The History of Whittington
In Lang, A. ed. The blue fairy book p206-
13   398.2
Reeves, J. Dick Whittington and his cat
In Reeves, J. English fables and fairy sto-
ries p221-34   398.2
Whittington and his cat
In Arbuthnot, M. H. comp. Time for old
magic p25-29   398.2
In De La Mare, W. ed. Animal stories
p116-26   398.2
In Jacobs, J. ed. English folk and fairy
tales p174-85   398.2
Dick Whittington and his cat; play. Thane, A.
In Thane, A. Plays from famous stories
and fairy tales p414-29   812

Dickens, Charles
"Barkis is willing"
In Martignoni, M. E. ed. The illustrated
treasury of children's literature p437-
40   808.8
Bob Cratchit's Christmas
In Reeves, J. comp. The Christmas book
p108-13   394.2
Captain Murderer
In Hardendorff, J. B. Witches, wit, and
a werewolf p97-101   S C
A Christmas carol
In Darrell, M. ed. Once upon a time p171-
234   808.8
A Christmas carol; abridged
In Parents' Magazine's Christmas holiday
book p190-223   394.2
In Ward, W. ed. Stories to dramatize
p329-39   372.6
A Christmas carol; play. See Hackett, W. A.
A Christmas carol
A Christmas carol; play. See Olfson, L.
A Christmas carol
A Christmas carol in prose (4-7)   Fic
The Christmas spirit enters Scrooge
In Martignoni, M. E. ed. The illustrated
treasury of children's literature p453-
55   808.8
Christmas with the Cratchits
In Ross, L. Puppet shows using poems and
stories p168-76   791.5
Cratchits' Christmas dinner
In Dalgliesh, A. comp. Christmas p205-11
394.2
In Tudor, T. ed. Take joy! p30-31   394.2
The magic fishbone (3-5)   Fic
—Same
In Gruenberg, S. M. ed. Favorite stories
old and new p299-309   808.8
In Johnson, S. P. ed. The Princesses p76-
95   S C
In Sechrist, E. H. ed. It's time for story
hour p194-205   372.6
In Untermeyer, B. ed. The Golden Trea-
sury of children's literature p349-
54   808.8
The magic fishbone; play. See Peterson,
M. N. The magic fishbone
The magic fishbone; play. See Smith, M. R.
The magic fishbone
Mr Pickwick on the ice
In Reeves, J. comp. The Christmas book
p178-85   394.2
Oliver Twist; dramatization. See Bland, J.
Oliver Twist
Oliver Twist; dramatization. See Howard,
V. Oliver Twist asks for more
The White Ship
In Brown, M. ed. A cavalcade of sea leg-
ends p253-57   808.8

Dickey, Sarah
See pages in the following book:
Chittenden, E. F. Profiles in black and white
p125-41 (5-7)   920

Dickinson, Alice
The Boston Massacre, March 5, 1770 (5-7)
973.3
The Colony of Massachusetts (5-7)   974.4
The first book of stone age man (4-7)   913

Dinosaurs—*Continued*

Shuttlesworth, D. E. To find a dinosaur (5-7)
568

Zim, H. S. Dinosaurs (4-6) **568**

See also Reptiles, Fossil; Stegosaurus

Stories

Bonham, F. The friends of the Loony Lake monster (4-6) **Fic**

Hoff, S. Danny and the dinosaur **E**

Lampman, E. S. The shy stegosaurus of Cricket Creek (5-7) **Fic**

Thayer, J. Quiet on account of dinosaur **E**

Dinosaurs and their world. Pringle, L. **568**

Dionysos. See Dionysus

Dionysos and the pirates. Proddow, P. **292**

Dionysus

Proddow, P. Dionysos and the pirates (3-6)
292

See also pages in the following books:

Coolidge, O. The golden days of Greece p98-112 (4-6) **938**

Gates, D. Lord of the sky: Zeus p110-24 (4-7)
292

Diplomats

Haskins, J. Ralph Bunche: a most reluctant hero (6-7) **92**

Dipper of Copper Creek. George, J. L. **Fic**

Diptera. See Flies; Mosquitoes

Dirigible balloons. See Airships

Dirr, Adolf

The fisherman's son

In Manning-Sanders, R. ed. A book of magical beasts p39-44 **398.2**

The dirty shepherdess. Sébillot, P.

In Lang, A. ed. The green fairy book p180-85 **398.2**

Disabled. See Physically handicapped

Disadvantaged children. See Socially handicapped children

Disappearing energy. Shuttlesworth, D. E. **333.7**

Disasters

See also Earthquakes

Fiction

Catherall, A. Prisoners in the snow (3-5) **Fic**

Day, V. Landslide! (4-7) **Fic**

Rutgers van der Loeff, A. Avalanche! (6-7)
Fic

Discography. See Phonograph records; and subjects with the subdivision Discography, e.g. Children's literature—Discography

The discontented fish. Arnott, K.

In Arnott, K. African myths and legends p156-59 **398.2**

Discoverers. See Discoveries (in geography); Explorers

Discoverers of the New World (5-7) **973.1**

Discoveries (in geography)

Buehr, W. The Portuguese explorers (4-6)
910

Captain Cook and the South Pacific (6-7) **919**

Chubb, T. C. Prince Henry the Navigator and the highways of the sea (6-7) **910**

Israel, C. E. Five ships west; the story of Magellan (4-6) **92**

Syme, R. Alexander Mackenzie, Canadian explorer (3-5) **92**

Syme, R. Balboa, finder of the Pacific (4-6)
92

Syme, R. Captain Cook, Pacific explorer (4-6)
92

Syme, R. Henry Hudson (4-6) **92**

Syme, R. Magellan, first around the world (4-6) **92**

See also America—Discovery and exploration; Antarctic regions; Arctic regions; Explorers; Voyages and travels; also names of countries with the subdivision Description and travel, e.g. U.S.—Description and travel

Discoveries (in science) See Inventions; Science

Discoveries, Maritime. See Discoveries (in geography)

Discovering books and libraries. Cleary, F. D. **028.7**

Discovering design. Downer, M. **745.4**

Discovering nature indoors. Pringle, L. ed. **591**

Discovering the outdoors. Pringle, L. ed. **574**

Discovering what earthworms do. Simon, S. **595**

Discovering what frogs do. Simon, S. **597**

Discovering what gerbils do. Simon, S. **636.08**

Discovery. Camp Fire Girls, Inc. **369.47**

Discovery of Oz, the Terrible. Baum, L. F.

In Martignoni, M. E. ed. The illustrated treasury of children's literature p289-93 **808.8**

Discovery of salt. Wyndham, R.

In Wyndham, R. Tales the people tell in China p9-13 **398.2**

Discrimination

See pages in the following book:

Sung, B. L. The Chinese in America p90-96 (5-7) **301.45**

See also Civil rights; Minorities

Discrimination in education

See also Segregation in education

Fiction

Underwood, B. The tamarack tree (6-7) **Fic**

Discrimination in public accommodations

Greenfield, E. Rosa Parks (2-4) **92**

Discussion groups

See pages in the following book:

Arbuthnot, M. H. comp. The Arbuthnot Anthology of children's literature p958-65
808.8

Disease germs. See Bacteriology; Germ theory of disease

Diseases

See pages in the following book:

Berger, M. Enzymes in action p77-86 (6-7)
574.1

See also names of diseases, e.g. Ulcers

Diseases, Mental. See Mental illness

Diseases and pests. See Insects, Injurious and beneficial

Diseases of animals. See Veterinary medicine

Diseases of plants. See Plants—Diseases

Disney, Walt
Montgomery, E. R. Walt Disney: master of make-believe (3-5)　　92
See also pages in the following book:
Haviland, V. ed. Children and literature p116-25　　028.5

The **disowned** student. Kim, S.
In Kim, S. The story bag p166-71　398.2

Displaced persons. See Refugees; Refugees, Jewish

Disposal of refuse. See Refuse and refuse disposal

Disposal of waste. See Refuse and refuse disposal

Distribution of animals and plants. See Geographical distribution of animals and plants

The **Ditmars** tale of wonders. Grimm, J.
In Grimm, J. The complete Grimm's Fairy tales p662　　398.2

Dive to danger; puppet play. Cochrane, L.
In Cochrane, L. Tabletop theatres p45-48　　791.5

Dividing night. Lawson, R.
In Martignoni, M. E. ed. The illustrated treasury of children's literature p333-35　　808.8

Divination. See Fortune telling

Diving
Sullivan, G. Better swimming and diving for boys and girls (5-7)　　797.2
See also pages in the following book:
Keith, H. Sports and games p278-95 (5-7) 796

Diving, Skin. See Skin diving

Diving, Submarine. See Bathyscaphe; Skin diving

Diving birds. Ripper, C. L.　　598.2

Divorce
Gardner, R. The boys and girls book about divorce (4-7)　　301.42
Fiction
Blue, R. A month of Sundays (3-5)　**Fic**
Blume, J. It's not the end of the world (4-6)　**Fic**
Lexau, J. M. Emily and the klunky baby and the next-door dog　**E**
Mann, P. My dad lives in a downtown hotel (3-5)　**Fic**

Dix, Dorothea Lynde
See pages in the following book:
Daugherty, S. Ten brave women p80-94 (5-7)　　920

Dixie, the Knight of the Silver Spurs. Jagendorf, M. A.
In Jagendorf, M. A. Folk stories of the South p77-78　　398.2

Dixon, Dean
See pages in the following book:
Hughes, L. Famous Negro music makers p147-54 (5-7)　　920

Dixon, Paige
Lion on the mountain (5-7)　**Fic**
Silver Wolf (4-7)　　599
The young grizzly (4-7)　　599

Djakarta
See pages in the following book:
Smith, D. C. The land and people of Indonesia p45-52 (5-7)　　915.98

Djurklo, G.
The old woman and the tramp
In Sechrist, E. H. ed. It's time for story hour p126-31　　372.6
Twigmuntus, Cowbelliantus, Perchnosius
In Sechrist, E. H. ed. It's time for story hour p136-41　　372.6

Do-all ax. Courlander, H.
In Courlander, H. Terrapin's pot of sense p80-83　　398.2

Do bears have mothers, too? Fisher, A.　811

Do-it-in-a-day puppets for beginners. Adair, M. W.　　791.5

Do it yourself! Carlson, B. W.　　893

The **Do-Nothing** Frog. Clapp, P.
In Burack, A. S. ed. One hundred plays for children p353-60　　808.82

Do you have the time, Lydia? Ness, E.　**E**

Do you know? Jagendorf, M. A.
In Jagendorf, M. A. Noodlehead stories from around the world p37-39 398.2

Do you know about water? Freeman, M. B. 553

Do you know what I'll do? Zolotow, C.　**E**

Do you see what I see? Borten, H.　707

Do you want to be my friend? Carle, E.　**E**

Dobbs, Rose
The foolish dragon
In Dobbs, R. ed. Once upon a time p15-18　　372.6
Happy cure
In Dobbs, R. ed. Once upon a time p27-33　　372.6
No room (2-4)　　398.2
(ed.) Once upon a time　　372.6
The pine tree
In Dobbs, R. ed. Once upon a time p3-7　　372.6
Please all—please none
In Dobbs, R. ed. Once upon a time p38-41　　372.6
Stubborn sillies
In Dobbs, R. ed. Once upon a time p105-09　　372.6
Why cats always wash themselves after eating
In Dobbs, R. ed. Once upon a time p67-69　　372.6
The wise king and the little bee
In Dobbs, R. ed. Once upon a time p19-23　　372.6

Dobias, Dorothea F.
Casey joins the circus
In Gruenberg, S. M. ed. Favorite stories old and new p159-64　　808.8

Dobias, Frank
(illus.) Kelsey, A. G. Once the Hodja　398.2

Dobkin, Alexander
(illus.) Stevenson, R. L. A child's garden of verses　　821

Dobler, Lavinia
(ed.) The Dobler World directory of youth periodicals　　050

Dobler, Lavinia—*Continued*
The land and people of Uruguay (5-7) **918.95**
National holidays around the world (5-7)
394.2

The **Dobler** International list of periodicals for boys and girls. See Dobler, L. ed. The Dobler World directory of youth periodicals **050**

The **Dobler** World directory of youth periodicals. Dobler, L. ed. **050**

Dobrin, Arnold
Gerbils (3-6) **636.08**
A life for Israel; the story of Golda Meir (4-6) **92**

Dobrinya at the Saracens' Mount. Baumann, H.
In Baumann, H. The stolen fire p13-17
398.2

Dobry's Christmas. Shannon, M.
In Association for Childhood Education International. Told under the Christmas tree p207-16 **808.8**
In Harper, W. comp. Merry Christmas to you p208-15 **394.2**

Doctor and detective, too. Hatch, M. C.
In Hatch, M. C. 13 Danish tales p94-106
398.2

Doctor Dolittle. Lofting, H. **Fic**

Doctor Dolittle and the green canary; excerpts. Lofting, H.
In Lofting, H. Doctor Dolittle p207-22 **Fic**

Doctor Dolittle and the secret lake; excerpts. Lofting, H.
In Lofting, H. Doctor Dolittle p223-33
Fic

Doctor Dolittle learns animal language. Lofting, H.
In Untermeyer, B. ed. The Golden Treasury of children's literature p273-77
808.8

Doctor Dolittle's caravan; excerpts. Lofting, H.
In Lofting, H. Doctor Dolittle p193-205
Fic

Doctor Dolittle's circus; excerpts. Lofting, H.
In Lofting, H. Doctor Dolittle p19-76 **Fic**

Doctor Dolittle's post office; excerpts. Lofting, H.
In Lofting, H. Doctor Dolittle p181-92 **Fic**

Doctor Dolittle's Puddleby adventures; excerpts. Lofting, H.
In Lofting, H. Doctor Dolittle p207-22 **Fic**

Dr Elizabeth [biography of Elizabeth Blackwell]. Clapp, P. **92**

A **doctor** for Lucinda. Mantle, M.
In Kamerman, S. E. ed. Fifty plays for junior actors p344-54 **812.08**

A **doctor** in spite of himself; puppet play. Cochrane, L.
In Cochrane, L. Tabletop theatres p34-38
791.5

Doctor Know-all
Grimm, J. Doctor Knowall
In Grimm, J. The complete Grimm's Fairy tales p456-58 **398.2**
Grimm, J. Doctor Know-It-All
In Grimm, J. Tales from Grimm p77-86
398.2

See also Harisarman; and Juan Cigarron

Doctor Know All; play. Howard, H. L.
In Burack, A. S. ed. Popular plays for classroom reading p69-77 **808.82**

Doctor Manners. Hark, M.
In Kamerman, S. E. ed. Little plays for little players p179-87 **812.08**

Dr Seuss. See Seuss, Dr

Doctors. See Physicians

The **doctors.** Fisher, L. E. **610**

Dodge, Mary Mapes
Festival of Saint Nicholas
In Dalgliesh, A. comp. Christmas p159-67
394.2
Hans Brinker (4-7) **Fic**
Hans Brinker; play. See Thane, A. A gift for Hans Brinker

About

See pages in the following book:
Benét, L. Famous storytellers for young people p70-75 (5-7) **920**

Dodgson, Charles Lutwidge
See pages in the following books:
Benét, L. Famous poets for young people p49-57 (5-7) **920**
Haviland, V. ed. Children and literature p57-63 **028.5**
Horn Book Reflections on children's books and reading p286-90 **028.5**
Jan, I. On children's literature p60-64 **028.5**
Townsend, J. R. Written for children p94-150
028.5

For titles by this author see Carroll, Lewis

Dodo
See pages in the following book:
Shuttlesworth, D. E. Dodos and dinosaurs p11-18 (4-6) **568**

Dodos and dinosaurs. Shuttlesworth, D. E. **568**

Dodson, Bert
(illus.) Marcus, R. B. Fiesta time in Mexico
394.2

Doering, Harald
An ant is born (4-7) **595.7**
A bee is born (4-7) **595.7**

Dog. See Dogs

Dog and the sparrow
Dog and the sparrow
In De La Mare, W. ed. Animal stories p160-68 **398.2**
Grimm, J. The dog and the sparrow
In Grimm, J. The complete Grimm's Fairy tales p280-82 **398.2**
In Grimm, J. Household stories p244-47
398.2

Dog guides. See Guide dogs

A **dog** named Fireball. Kim, S.
In Kim, S. The story bag p23-30 **398.2**

A **dog** on Barkham Street. Stolz, M. **Fic**

A **dog** on Barkham Street; excerpt. Stolz, M.
In Arbuthnot, M. H. comp. The Arbuthnot Anthology of children's literature p670-73 **808.8**

Dog who talked. Davis, R.
In Davis, R. Padre Porko, the gentlemanly pig p47-72 **398.2**

The **Dog** who wanted to be a lion
In DeRoin, N. ed. Jataka tales p32-34
398.2

Dogs

Bethell, J. How to care for your dog (2-4)
636.7
Bronson, W. S. Dogs (3-7) **636.7**
Cole, J. My puppy is born (k-2) **636.7**
Foster, J. Dogs working for people (k-3) **636.7**
Henry, M. Album of dogs (3-6) **636.7**
Lauber, P. The story of dogs (3-5) **636.7**
Levin, J. W. Bringing up puppies (3-6) **636.7**
Sabin, F. Dogs of America (5-7) **636.7**
Selsam, M. E. How puppies grow (k-3) **636.7**
Unkelbach, K. Both ends of the leash (3-6)
636.7
Unkelbach, K. How to bring up your pet dog
(4-7) **636.7**
See also pages in the following books:
Chrystie, F. N. Pets p3-25 (4-7) **636.08**
Fenton, D. L. Animals that help us p10-21
(4-6) **636**
Stevens, C. Your first pet p95-109 (2-4)
636.08
See also classes of dogs, e.g. Guide
dogs; also names of specific breeds, e.g.
Dachshunds

Poetry
See pages in the following book:
Cole, W. comp. A book of animal poems p95-
118 (5-7) **821.08**

Stories
Alexander, M. Bobo's dream **E**
Armstrong, W. H. Sounder (5-7) **Fic**
Baker, C. Cockleburr Quarters (4-6) **Fic**
Balian, L. Where in the world is Henry? **E**
Ball, Z. Bristle Face (5-7) **Fic**
Ball, Z. Sputters (5-7) **Fic**
Bartos-Hoppner, B. Avalanche dog (5-7) **Fic**
Bemelmans, L. Madeline's rescue **E**
Bontemps, A. The fast Sooner hound (2-5) **Fic**
Brown, M. W. Country noisy book **E**
Brown, M. W. Indoor noisy book **E**
Carrick, C. Lost in the storm **E**
Carroll, R. Beanie (1-4) **Fic**
Carroll, R. Tough Enough (2-4) **Fic**
Carroll, R. What Whiskers did **E**
Cleary, B. Ribsy (3-5) **Fic**
Cone, M. Mishmash (3-5) **Fic**
Corbett, S. The baseball trick (3-5) **Fic**
Corbin, W. Smoke (4-6) **Fic**
DeJong, M. Along came a dog (4-6) **Fic**
DeJong, M. Hurry home, Candy (4-6) **Fic**
DeJong, M. Puppy summer (4-6) **Fic**
Devlin, H. How Fletcher was hatched **E**
Du Bois, W. P. Otto at sea **E**
Durham, J. Me and Arch and the Pest (3-5)
Fic
Estes, E. Ginger Pye (4-6) **Fic**
Flack, M. Angus and the ducks **E**
Graham, M. B. Benjy's dog house **E**
Hall, L. Riff, remember (4-7) **Fic**
Keats, E. J. My dog is lost! **E**
Kjelgaard, J. Big Red (4-7) **Fic**
Lippincott, J. W. Wilderness champion (5-7)
Fic
Livermore, E. Find the cat **E**
Mayer, M. Frog, where are you? **E**
Morgan, A. A boy called Fish (5-7) **Fic**
Nodset, J. L. Go away, dog **E**

Ottley, R. Boy alone (5-7) **Fic**
Peet, B. The whingdingdilly **E**
Potter, B. The pie and the patty-pan **E**
Rounds, G. Stolen pony (4-6) **Fic**
Sendak, M. Higglety pigglety pop! (2-4) **Fic**
Sharmat, M. W. Morris Brookside, a dog **E**
Skorpen, L. M. Old Arthur **E**
Steig, W. Dominic (4-6) **Fic**
Stolz, M. The bully of Barkham Street (4-6)
Fic
Stolz, M. A dog on Barkham Street (4-6) **Fic**
Street, J. H. Good-bye, my Lady (5-7) **Fic**
Thayer, J. The puppy who wanted a boy **E**
Walker, D. Big Ben (3-5) **Fic**
White, A. H. Junket, the dog who liked
everything "just so" (4-6) **Fic**
Will. Finders keepers **E**
Zion, G. Harry by the sea **E**
Zion, G. Harry the dirty dog **E**
Zion, G. No roses for Harry! **E**

Training
Broderick, D. M. Training a companion dog
(4-7) **636.7**
Unkelbach, K. Both ends of the leash (3-6)
636.7

Dogs for the blind. See Guide dogs

The **dog's** nose is cold. Sherlock, P.
In Sherlock, P. West Indian folk-tales p34-
38 **398.2**

Dogs of America. Sabin, F. **636.7**

Dogs working for people. Foster, J. **636.7**

Doherty, C. H.
Tunnels (6-7) **624**

Dolan, Edward F.
The complete beginner's guide to bowling
(5-7) **794.6**

Dolan, Tom
(illus.) Reid, G. K. Pond life **574.92**

Dolbier, Maurice
Half-pint Jinni
In Child Study Association of America.
Castles and dragons p 1-27 **398.2**
Torten's Christmas secret **E**

Doll. See Dolls

The **doll.** Manning-Sanders, R.
In Manning-Sanders, R. Gianni and the
ogre p67-75 **398.2**

Doll collecting. See Young, H. Here is your
hobby: doll collecting **745.59**

Doll in the grass
Aulaire, I. d'. Doll in the Grass
In Aulaire, I. d'. East of the sun and west
of the moon p222-24 **398.2**
Doll in the grass
In Hutchinson, V. S. ed. Candle-light stor-
ies p11-15 **398.2**

Doll making. See Dollmaking

The **doll** under the briar rosebush. Thorne-
Thomsen, G.
In Association for Childhood Education International. Told under the blue umbrella p109-13 **S C**

The **doll** who came alive. Tregarthen, E. **Fic**

Dollar watch and the five jack rabbits. Sandburg, C.
In Sandburg, C. Rootabaga stories v 1
p141-50 **S C**

Dollar watch and the five jack rabbits.—*Cont.*
  In Sandburg, C. The Sandburg treasury
    p57-61   **818**

Dollhouses
  See pages in the following book:
  Glubok, S. Dolls, dolls, dolls p48-57 (3-6)
                             688.7
              Fiction
  Godden, R. The dolls' house (2-4)   **Fic**
  Jones, E. O. Big Susan (1-4)   **Fic**

Dollmaking
  Heady, E. B. Make your own dolls (3-5)
                         745.59

  See also pages in the following book:
  Pettit, F. H. How to make whirligigs and
    whimmy diddles, and other American folk-
    craft objects p218-30, 254-78 (5-7) **745.5**

Dolls
  Glubok, S. Dolls, dolls, dolls (3-6)   **688.7**
  Young, H. Here is your hobby: doll collecting
    (5-7)   **745.59**
    See also Dollmaking
             Fiction
  Arthur, R. M. A candle in her room (5-7) **Fic**
  Ayer, J. Little Silk   **E**
  Bailey, C. S. Miss Hickory (3-5)   **Fic**
  Bianco, M. W. The little wooden doll (2-4)
                              Fic
  Brink, C. R. The bad times of Irma Baum-
    lein (4-6)   **Fic**
  Bulla, C. R. Open the door and see all the
    people (2-4)   **Fic**
  Field, R. Hitty: her first hundred years (4-7)
                              Fic
  Godden, R. The dolls' house (2-4)   **Fic**
  Godden, R. Home is the sailor (4-6)   **Fic**
  Godden, R. Impunity Jane (2-4)   **Fic**
  Godden, R. Little Plum (3-5)   **Fic**
  Hutchins, P. Changes, changes   **E**
  Jackson, J. Missing Melinda, by C. Gibbs and
    O. Gibbs (4-6)   **Fic**
  Jones, E. O. Big Susan (1-4)   **Fic**
  McGinley, P. The most wonderful doll in the
    world (1-4)   **Fic**
  Sandburg, C. The wedding procession of the
    Rag Doll and the Broom Handle and who
    was in it   **E**
  Tregarthen, E. The doll who came alive (3-5)
                              Fic
  Tudor, T. The dolls' Christmas   **E**
  Yates, E. Carolina's courage (3-5)   **Fic**
  Zolotow, C. William's doll   **E**

The **dolls'** Christmas. Tudor, T.   **E**
Dolls, dolls, dolls. Glubok, S.   **688.7**
The **doll's** ghost. Crawford, M.
  In Ireson, B. comp. Haunting tales p117-
    31   **S C**
The **dolls'** house. Godden, R.   **Fic**
The **doll's** house. Mansfield, K.
  In Authors' choice p 1-10   **S C**
Dolly saves the day. Miller, H. L.
  In Burack, A. S. ed. One hundred plays for
    children p838-47   **808.82**
Dolphins
  Moffett, M. Dolphins (4-6)   **599**
  See also pages in the following books:
  Arbuthnot, M. H. comp. The Arbuthnot An-

thology of children's literature p861-64
                             808.8
  Hoke, H. Whales p54-66 (4-7)   **599**
              Stories
  Benchley, N. The several tricks of Edgar
    Dolphin   **E**

Dom Pedro I, Emperor of Brazil. See Pedro I,
  Emperor of Brazil

Dom Pedro II, Emperor of Brazil. See Pedro II,
  Emperor of Brazil

Domanska, Janina
  Look, there is a turtle flying (k-2)   **398.2**
  The turnip (k-2)   **398.2**
  What do you see?   **E**
  (illus.) Coatsworth, E. Under the green wil-
    low   **E**
  (illus.) Fisher, A. I like weather   **E**
  (illus.) Fournier, C. The coconut thieves **398.2**
  (illus.) I saw a ship a-sailing. See I saw a ship
    a-sailing   **398.8**
  (illus.) If all the seas were one sea. See If
    all the seas were one sea   **398.8**
  (illus.) Lear, E. Whizz!   **E**
  (illus.) Lindgren, A. Mischievous Meg **Fic**
  (illus.) Little red hen. See Little red hen
    (Macmillan Pub. Co.)   **398.2**
  (illus.) Reck, A. K. Clocks tell the time **681**

Domestic animals
  Fenton, C. L. Animals that help us (4-6) **636**
  Ipcar, D. Brown Cow Farm   **E**
  Rojankovsky, F. Animals on the farm   **E**
  See also pages in the following books:
  Chrystie, F. N. Pets p159-88 (4-7) **636.08**
  Peattie, D. C. The rainbow book of nature
    p74-87 (5-7)   **574**
    See also Camels; Cats; Cows; Dogs;
    Goats; Horses; Livestock; Pets; Poultry;
    Reindeer; Sheep

              Diseases
  See Veterinary medicine
              Stories
  Brooks, W. R. Freddy, the detective (3-5) **Fic**
  Duvoisin, R. Our Veronica goes to Petunia's
    farm   **E**
  Françoise. The big rain   **E**
  Holl, A. The rain puddle   **E**

Domestic architecture. See Architecture, Domestic

Domestic relations
  See also Divorce; Family
              Fiction
  Stolz, M. The noonday friends (4-6)   **Fic**

Dominic. Steig, W.   **Fic**

Domjan, Joseph
  (illus.) Hardendorff, J. B. The little cock **398.2**

Don Carlos; adaptation. Bulla, C. R.
  In Bulla, C. R. More Stories of favorite
    operas p113-30   **782.1**

Dom Demonio's mother-in-law. Boggs, R. S.
  In Boggs, R. S. Three golden oranges, and
    other Spanish folk tales p59-74 **398.2**

Don Fernan and the orange princess
  In Gunterman, B. L. ed. Castles in Spain,
    and other enchantments p132-50
                             398.2

Don Giovanni; adaptation. Bulla, C. R.
In Bulla, C. R. Stories of favorite operas
p19-31   782.1

Don Pedro's Christmas. Kelly, E. P.
In Cavanah, F. ed. Holiday roundup p311-
16   394.2

Don Quixote de la Mancha, The adventures of.
Barret, L.   **Fic**

Don Quixote saves the day. Howard, V.
In Howard V. The complete book of children's theater p525-35   812

Donahue, Vic
(illus.) Dillion, E. A family of foxes   **Fic**

Donal from Donegal. MacManus, S.
In MacManus, S. The bold heroes of Hungry Hill, and other Irish folk tales
p64-82   398.2

Donal O'Ciaran from Connaught. MacManus, S.
In MacManus, S. The bold heroes of Hungry Hill, and other Irish folk tales
p120-37   398.2

Donal O'Donnell's Standing Army. Mac-
Manus, S.
In MacManus, S. Hibernian nights p240-
50   398.2

Donald and the fish that walked. Ricciuti, E. R.
E

Donehogawa. See Parker, Eli Samuel, Seneca
chief

The dong with a luminous nose. Lear, E. **821**

The Donkey
In De La Mare, W. ed. Animal stories
p203-11   398.2
In Grimm, J. The complete Grimm's Fairy
tales p632-35   398.2

Donkey and the salt
Brenner, A. Some impatient mule-drivers
In Brenner, A. The boy who could do anything, & other Mexican folk tales
p27-29   398.2

Donkey and the scholars. Jagendorf, M. A.
In Jagendorf, M. A. Noodlehead stories
from around the world p175-79
398.2

Donkey cabbage
The Donkey cabbage
In Lang, A. ed. The yellow fairy book
p42-49   398.2
Grimm, J. Donkey cabbages
In Grimm, J. The complete Grimm's Fairy
tales p551-58   398.2
Grimm, J. The salad
In Grimm, J. Grimms' Fairy tales; illus. by
F. Kredel p135-43   398.2
Manning-Sanders, R. The donkey lettuce
In Manning-Sanders, R. A book of witches
p72-82   398.2

The donkey driver. Courlander, H.
In Courlander, H. The piece of fire, and
other Haitian tales p81-83   398.2

The donkey egg. Kelsey, A. G.
In Kelsey, A. G. Once the Hodja p151-56
398.2

The donkey goes to market. Kelsey, A. G.
In Kelsey, A. G. Once the Hodja p63-70
398.2

The donkey lettuce. Manning-Sanders, R.
In Manning-Sanders, R. A book of witches
p72-82   398.2
See also Donkey cabbage

The donkey of Abdera. Jagendorf, M. A.
In Jagendorf, M. A. Noodlehead stories
from around the world p40-42 398.2

Donkey-skin. Perrault, C.
In Perrault, C. Perrault's Complete fairy
tales p92-99   398.2

The donkey, the table, and the stick. Reeves, J.
In Reeves, J. English fables and fairy
stories p195-210   398.2
See also Table, the ass, and the stick

The donkey who sinned. Courlander, H.
In Courlander, H. The fire on the mountain, and other Ethiopian stories p15-
17   398.2

Donkeys
See pages in the following books:
Fenton, C. L. Animals that help us p53-57
(4-6)   636
Henry, M. Album of horses p98-101 (4-7)
636.1

Stories

Henry, M. Brighty of the Grand Canyon (4-7)
Fic
Ness, E. Josefina February   **E**
Steig, W. Farmer Palmer's wagon ride **E**
Steig, W. Sylvester and the magic pebble **E**
Vance, M. While shepherds watched (1-4) **Fic**

Donkeys all. Jagendorf, M. A.
In Jagendorf, M. A. Noodlehead stories
from around the world p63-67 398.2

The donkeys ask for justice. Courlander, H.
In Courlander, H. The king's drum, and
other African stories p74-76   398.2

Donna, Natalie
Bead craft (5-7)   746.5
Peanut craft (4-7)   745.5

Donoghue, Steve
Donoghue up! Excerpts
In Anderson, C. W. ed. C. W. Anderson's
Favorite horse stories p67-80 808.8

Donoghue up! Excerpts. Donoghue, S.
In Anderson, C. W. ed. C. W. Anderson's
Favorite horse stories p67-80 808.8

Donovan, Frank R.
Ironclads of the Civil War. See Ironclads of
the Civil War   973.7
The Vikings. See The Vikings   948

Don't count your chicks. Aulaire, I. d'   **E**

Don't drop into my soup. Jagendorf, M. A.
In Jagendorf, M. A. Folk stories of the
South p10-12   398.2

Don't feel sorry for Paul. Wolf, B.   362.4

Don't marry two wives. Jagendorf, M. A.
In Jagendorf, M. A. Noodlehead stories
from around the world p24-29 398.2

Don't shake hands with everybody. Courlander, H.
In Courlander, H. The cow-tail switch, and
other West African stories p129-31
398.2

Don't take Teddy. Friis-Baastad, B.   **Fic**

Don't tell a soul; play. Carlson, B. W.
   In Carlson, B. W. The right play for you
     p147-57 **792**
Don't throw stones from not yours to yours
   In Courlander, H. ed. Ride with the sun
     p99-100 **398.2**
Don't try the same trick twice.
   In DeRoin, N. ed. Jataka tales p66-67
     398.2
Don't you turn back. Hughes, L. **811**
The **doom** of Soulis. Mayne, W.
   In Mayne, W. ed. Ghosts p107-17 **820.8**
The **door** in the wall. De Angeli, M. **Fic**
Door to door selling. See Peddlers and peddling
Doremus, Robert
   (illus.) De Leeuw, A. The Girl Scout story
     369.463
Dorian, Edith
   Animals that made U.S. history (5-7) **591.9**
   Trails West and men who made them (4-7)
     978
Dormandy, Clara
   Hungary in pictures (5-7) **914.39**
Dorn, Daniel
   (illus.) Johnson, H. L. From seed to jack-o'-
     lantern **635**
   (illus.) Johnson, H. L. Let's bake bread **641.8**
Dorothy meets the Wizard. Baum, L. F.
   In Untermeyer, B. ed. The Golden Treasury of children's literature p256-70
     808.8
Dorp dead. Cunningham, J. **Fic**
Dorrie and the amazing magic elixir. Coombs, P. **E**
Dorrie and the birthday eggs. Coombs, P. **E**
Dorrie and the Blue Witch. Coombs, P. **E**
Dorrie and the goblin. Coombs, P. **E**
Dorris, Sid
   (illus.) Coskey, E. Easter eggs for everyone
     745.59
Dot for short; excerpt. Friedman, F.
   In Association for Childhood Education International. Told under spacious skies p65-74 **S C**
Doty, Roy
   Puns, gags, quips and riddles (4-6) **793.7**
   (illus.) Blume, J. Tales of a fourth grade nothing **Fic**
   (illus.) Klein, N. Girls can be anything **E**
Dotzenko, Grisha
   (illus.) Luckhardt, M. C. ed. Christmas comes once more **394.2**
Double or quits. Sturton, H.
   In Sturton, H. Zomo, the Rabbit p77-88
     398.2
The **Doubleday** First guide to rocks. Shuttlesworth, D. **552**
The **Doubleday** Nature encyclopedia **500.9**
The **doughnuts.** McCloskey, R.
   In Arbuthnot, M. H. comp. The Arbuthnot Anthology of children's literature p687-91 **808.8**
   In Johnson, E. ed. Anthology of children's literature p816-21 **808.8**

Douglas, Emily Taft
   The birthday orchard
     In Cavanah, F. ed. Holiday roundup p110-17 **394.2**
   Johnnie Appleseed
     In Ward, W. ed. Stories to dramatize p207-10 **372.6**
Douglass, Frederick
   Bontemps, A. Frederick Douglass: slave-fighter-freeman (4-7) **92**
   Graves, C. P. Frederick Douglass (2-4) **92**
   Patterson, L. Frederick Douglass: freedom fighter (4-6) **92**
   See also pages in the following books:
   Hughes, L. Famous American Negroes p25-31 (5-7) **920**
   Hughes, L. Famous Negro heroes of America p77-100 (5-7) **920**
   Johnston, J. A special bravery p40-44 (2-5) **920**
   Rollins, C. H. They showed the way p46-52 (5-7) **920**
   Sterling, P. Four took freedom p34-65 (5-6) **920**

Poetry
   See pages in the following book:
   Merriam, E. Independent voices p19-30 (5-7)
     811
Douty, Esther M.
   Charlotte Forten: free Black teacher (4-6) **92**
   The U.N.'s Marian Anderson
     In Cavanah, F. ed. Holiday roundup p251-54 **394.2**
Doves. See Pigeons
Dowd, Vic
   (illus.) Radford, R. L. Juliette Low: Girl Scout founder **92**
Dowdell, Dorothy
   The Chinese helped build America (4-7)
     301.45
   The Japanese helped build America (4-7)
     301.45
Dowdell, Joseph
   (jt. auth.) Dowdell, D. The Chinese helped build America **301.45**
   (jt. auth.) Dowdell, D. The Japanese helped build America **301.45**
Dowden, Anne Ophelia T.
   Look at a flower (6-7) **582**
   Wild green things in the city (4-7) **582**
Down, down the mountain. Credle, E. **E**
   —Same
     In Sechrist, E. H. ed. It's time for story hour p14-22 **372.6**
Down from the hills. Lenski, L.
   In Association for Childhood Education International. Told under spacious skies p200-16 **S C**
Down from the lonely mountain. Curry, J. L.
     398.2
Down the rabbit hole. Carroll, L.
   In Martignoni, M. E. ed. The illustrated treasury of children's literature p294-97 **808.8**
Down the rabbit hole. Lanes, S. G. **028.5**

Down the well. Duvoisin, R.
   In Duvoisin, R. The three sneezes, and
      other Swiss tales p67-88   **398.2**

Down to earth. Wrightson, P.   **Fic**

Down to earth; excerpt. Wrightson, P.
   In Arbuthnot, M. H. comp. The Arbuthnot
      Anthology of children's literature
      p579-82   **808.8**

The **down** to earth cookbook. Borghese, A.
          641.5

Down to the beach. Garelick, M.   **E**

Downer, Marion
   Children in the world's art (4-7)   **704.94**
   Discovering design (5-7)   **745.4**
   Kites (4-7)   **796.1**
   Roofs over America (5-7)   **721**
   The story of design (6-7)   **745.4**

Downie, Mary Alice
   (comp.) The wind has wings (5-7)   **811.08**

Downright Dencey. Snedeker, C. D.   **Fic**

Doyle, Sir Arthur Conan
   The boy's Sherlock Holmes (6-7)   **S C**
   Short stories included are: The adventure of the
speckled band; Silver Blaze; The Red-headed League;
A scandal in Bohemia; The Musgrave ritual; The ad-
venture of the Blue Carbuncle
   The hound of the Baskervilles
     In Doyle, Sir A. C. The boy's Sherlock
      Holmes p357-524   **S C**
     In Doyle, Sir A. C. Tales of Sherlock
      Holmes p431-605   **S C**
   Sherlock Holmes and the Red-headed
     League; play. See Olfson, L. Sherlock
     Holmes and Red-headed League
   The sign of the four
     In Doyle, Sir A. C. The boy's Sherlock
      Holmes p91-209   **S C**
     In Doyle, Sir A. C. Tales of Sherlock
      Holmes p131-255   **S C**
   A study in scarlet
     In Doyle, Sir A. C. The boy's Sherlock
      Holmes p 1-82   **S C**
     In Doyle, Sir A. C. Tales of Sherlock
      Holmes p 1-129   **S C**
   Tales of Sherlock Holmes (6-7)   **S C**
   Includes the following short stories: The adventure
of the Blue Carbuncle; A scandal in Bohemia; A case
of identity; The adventure of the speckled band; Silver
Blaze; The Red-headed League; The Musgrave ritual
   Through the veil
     In Ireson, B. comp. Haunting tales p110-
      16   **S C**

        Parodies, travesties, etc.

   Titus, E. Basil of Baker Street (3-5)   **Fic**

The **dozen** from Lakerim. Hughes, R.
   In A St Nicholas anthology p322-30 **810.8**

The **Dozier** Brothers Band. Bontemps, A.
   In Association for Childhood Education
      International. Told under the Stars
      and Stripes p270-81   **S C**

Dragon and his grandmother
   The dragon and his grandmother
     In Fenner, P. R. comp. Giants & witches
      and a dragon or two p155-61 **398.2**
     In Lang, A. ed. The yellow fairy book p38-
      41   **398.2**
   Grimm, J. The Devil and his grandmother
     In Grimm, J. The complete Grimm's Fairy
      tales p563-66   **398.2**

   Grimm, J. The dragon and his grandmother
     In Grimm, J. Tales from Grimm p225-34
          398.2
   Grimm, J. The dragon's grandmother
     In Hoke, H. comp. Dragons, dragons,
      dragons p192-98   **398.2**
   Manning-Sanders, R. The dragon and his
     grandmother
     In Manning-Sanders, R. A book of dragons
      p79-86   **398.2**
   Sellar, M. The dragon and his grandmother
     In Green, R. L. ed. A cavalcade of dragons
      p120-24   **808.8**

Dragon and the prince
   Fillmore, P. Dragon's strength
     In Fillmore, P. The laughing prince p139-
      60   **398.2**
   Green, R. L. The prince and the dragon
     In Green, R. L. ed. A cavalcade of dragons
      p148-56   **808.8**
   Lang, A. The prince and the dragon
     In Hoke, H. comp. Dragons, dragons,
      dragons p129-38   **398.2**

The **dragon** and the stepmother. Manning-
   Sanders, R.
   In Hoke, H. comp. Dragons, dragons,
     dragons p22-28   **398.2**

The **dragon** at Hide-and-Seek. Chesterton, G. K.
   In Green, R. L. ed. A cavalcade of dragons
     p204-12   **808.8**

The **dragon** of an ordinary family. Mahy, M.
   In Hoke, H. comp. Dragons, dragons,
     dragons p139-44   **398.2**

The **dragon** of Rhodes. Westwood, J.
   In Hoke, H. comp. Dragons, dragons,
     dragons p145-48   **398.2**

The **dragon** of Shervage Wood. Colwell, E.
   In Colwell, E. Round about and long ago
     p110-13   **398.2**

Dragon of the North
   Green, R. L. The Dragon of the North
     In Green, R. L. ed. A cavalcade of dragons
      p125-32   **808.8**
   Kreutzwald, F. R. The Dragon of the North
     In Lang, A. ed. The yellow fairy book p9-
      20   **398.2**
   Lang, A. The Dragon of the North
     In Hoke, H. comp. Dragons, dragons,
      dragons p179-91   **398.2**

The **dragon** of the well. Manning-Sanders, R.
   In Manning-Sanders, R. A book of dragons
     p123-28   **398.2**

The **dragon** slayer. Grayl, D.
   In Hoke, H. comp. Dragons, dragons,
     dragons p95-108   **398.2**

The **dragon** tamers. Nesbit, E.
   In Nesbit, E. The complete book of dragons
     p95-117   **S C**

Dragonflies
   Hutchins, R. E. The world of dragonflies and
     damselflies (5-7)   **595.7**
   Simon, H. Dragonflies (5-7)   **595.7**
   See also pages in the following books:
   Anderson, Margaret J. Exploring the insect
     world p121-30 (5-7)   **595.7**
   Mason, G. F. Animal tools p79-84 (4-7)
          591.4

Dragonflies—*Continued*

Silverstein, A. Metamorphosis: the magic
change p26-33 (4-6) **591.3**
Teale, E. W. The junior book of insects p140-
48 (6-7) **595.7**
Villiard, P. Insects as pets p115-22 (5-7)
595.7

Dragons

See pages in the following book:

McHargue, G. The beasts of never p13-35
(5-7) **398**

Stories

Bloch, M. H. Ivanko and the dragon (k-3)
398.2
Gannett, R. S. The dragons of Blueland (1-4)
Fic
Gannett, R. S. Elmer and the dragon (1-4) **Fic**
Gannett, R. S. My father's dragon (1-4) **Fic**
Grahame, K. The reluctant dragon (3-5) **Fic**
Green, R. L. ed. A cavalcade of dragons (4-7)
808.8
Hoke, H. comp. Dragons, dragons, dragons
(4-7) **398.2**
Manning-Sanders, R. A book of dragons (3-6)
398.2
Nesbit, E. The complete book of dragons
(3-6) **S C**

Dragons? Vo-Dinh

In Vo-Dinh. The toad is the Emperor's
uncle p137-41 **398.2**

Dragons, dragons, dragons. Hoke, H. comp.
398.2

The **dragon's** grandmother. Grimm, J.

In Hoke, H. comp. Dragons, dragons,
dragons p192-98 **398.2**
See also Dragon and his grandmother

The **dragons** of Blueland. Gannett, R. S. **Fic**

The **dragons** of Peking. Arnott, K.

In Arnott, K. Animal folk tales around the
world p122-28 **398.2**

The **dragon's** rock. Spence, L.

In Hoke, H. comp. Dragons, dragons,
dragons p220-22 **398.2**

Dragon's strength. Fillmore, P.

In Fillmore, P. The laughing prince p139-
60 **398.2**
See also Dragon and the prince

The **dragon's** tail. Marks, J.

In Hoke, H. comp. Dragons, dragons,
dragons p109-28 **398.2**

Dragon's treasure. Alden, R. M.

In Hoke, H. comp. Dragons, dragons,
dragons p211-19 **398.2**

Dragons, unicorns, and other magical beasts.
Palmer, R. **398.2**

Drake, Sir Francis

Latham, J. L. Drake: the man they called a
pirate (5-7) **92**
Syme, R. Francis Drake, sailor of the unknown seas (4-6) **92**

Drake, W. H.

(illus.) Kipling, R. The jungle books **S C**

Drake: the man they called a pirate [biography
of Sir Francis Drake]. Latham J. L. **92**

Drakesbill and his friends

Drakestail

In Hutchinson, V. S. ed. Fireside stories
p51-64 **398.2**

In Johnson, E. ed. Anthology of children's
literature p159-62 **808.8**
In Untermeyer, B. ed. The Golden Treasury of children's literature p88-95
808.8

Haviland, V. Drakestail

In Haviland, V. Favorite fairy tales told in
France p76-91 **398.2**

Lang, A. Drakestail

In Martignoni, M. E. ed. The illustrated
treasury of children's literature p83-
88 **808.8**

Marelles, C. Drakestail

In Lang, A. ed. The red fairy book p202-07
398.2
In Manning-Sanders, R. ed. A book of
magical beasts p226-35 **398.2**

Drakestail. See Drakesbill and his friends

Drama

See also Acting; Ballet; One-act plays;
Opera; Puppets and puppet plays; Theater; also American drama; English drama;
etc.; and names of special subjects and
historical events with the subdivision
Drama, e.g. Holidays—Drama

Collections

Carlson, B. W. Play a part (3-6) **792**
Carlson, B. W. The right play for you (4-7)
792
Kamerman, S. E. ed. Dramatized folk tales
of the world (5-7) **812.08**
Smith, M. R. Plays & how to put them on
(4-7) **792**
Smith, M. R. ed. 7 plays & how to produce
them (4-7) **792**
See also American drama—Collections

Collections—Periodicals

Plays, the Drama Magazine for Young People
808.82

Indexes

Chicorel Theater index to plays for young
people in periodicals, anthologies, and col-
lections **808.82**
Play index, 1949-1952 **808.82**
Play index, 1953-1960 **808.82**
Play index, 1961-1967 **808.82**
Play index, 1968-1972 **808.82**

Drama in education

Siks, G. B. Creative dramatics **372.6**
Ward, W. ed. Stories to dramatize **372.6**

See also pages in the following book:

Arbuthnot, M. H. comp. The Arbuthnot Anthology of children's literature p965-71
808.8

Dramatic art. See Acting

Dramatized folk tales of the world. Kamerman,
S. E. ed. **812.08**

Draper, Nancy

Ballet for beginners (5-7) **792.8**

Drawing

Borten, H. A picture has a special look (k-3)
741.2
Campbell, A. Start to draw (k-3) **741**
Emberley, E. Ed Emberley's Drawing book:
make a world (2-6) **743**
Emberley, E. Ed Emberley's Drawing book
of animals (2-6) **743**

Drum
Price, C. Talking drums of Africa (2-5) 789
See also pages in the following book:
Hunt, W. B. The complete book of Indian crafts and lore p88-91 (4-7) 745.5

The **drummer.** Grimm, J.
In Grimm, J. The complete Grimm's Fairy tales p781-91 398.2

Drummer Hoff. Emberley, B. 398.8

Drummond, V. H.
(illus.) Sleigh, B. Carbonel, the King of the Cats Fic

Drums. See Drum

Drums. Sperry, A.
In Johnson, E. ed. Anthology of children's literature p843-46 808.8

Drums, rattles, and bells. Kettelkamp, L. 789
The **drums** speak. Bernheim, M. 916.6

Drunkeness. See Alcoholism

Druon, Maurice
In which Tistou has a bad dream and what happens as a result of it
In Arbuthnot, M. H. comp. The Arbuthnot Anthology of children's literature p513-14 808.8

Druses
See pages in the following book:
Winder, V. H. The land and people of Lebanon p55-57, 78-79 (5-7) 915.692

Druzes. See Druses

Dry-Bone and Anansi. Sherlock, P.
In Sherlock, P. West Indian folk-tales p77-85 398.2

Dryad
Andersen, H. C. The wood nymph
In Andersen, H. C. The complete fairy tales and stories p934-53 S C

Dublin
See pages in the following book:
O'Brien, E. The land and people of Ireland p128-38 (5-7) 914.15

DuBois, Graham
The humblest place
In Kamerman, S. E. ed. A treasury of Christmas plays p112-28 812.08
A room for a King
In Kamerman, S. E. ed. A treasury of Christmas plays p45-62 812.08

Du Bois, H. Graham
The perfect gift
In Burack, A. S. ed. Christmas plays for young actors p67-80 812.08

Du Bois, William Edward Burghardt
Hamilton, V. W. E. B. Du Bois (6-7) 92
See also pages in the following book:
Rollins, C. H. They showed me the way p55-58 (5-7) 920

Du Bois, William Pène
Airy-go-round
In Arbuthnot, M. H. comp. The Arbuthnot Anthology of children's literature p583-88 808.8
The Alligator Case (3-5) Fic
Bear Circus E
Bear party E

Call me Bandicoot (5-7) Fic
Elizabeth—the cow ghost Fic
In Gruenberg, S. M. ed. Favorite stories old and new p487-90 808.8
The giant (4-7) Fic
The hare and the tortoise & The tortoise and the hare (1-4) 398.2
Lion E
Newbery Medal acceptance paper
In Miller, B. M. ed. Newbery Medal books: 1922-1955 p309-17 028.5
Otto at sea E
The policemen (3-6) Fic
The twenty-one balloons (5-7) Fic
The twenty-one balloons; excerpt
In Arbuthnot, M. H. comp. The Arbuthnot Anthology of children's literature p583-88 808.8
(illus.) Bishop, C. H. Twenty and ten Fic
(illus.) Caudill, R. A certain small shepherd Fic
(illus.) Child Study Association of America. Castles and dragons 398.2
(illus.) Farber, N. Where's Gomer? E
(illus.) Fenton, E. Fierce John E
(illus.) Lear, E. The owl and the pussy-cat 821
(illus.) Macdonald, G. The light princess Fic
(illus.) The Three little pigs. See The Three little pigs 398.2
(illus.) Zolotow, C. My grandson Lew E
(illus.) Zolotow, C. William's doll E

About
See pages in the following book:
Miller, B. M. ed. Newbery Medal books: 1922-1955 p302-08 028.5

The **Duchess** bakes a cake. Kahl, V. E

Duckett, Alfred
(jt. auth.) Robinson, J. R. Breathrough to the big league 92

Ducks
See pages in the following book:
Laycock, G. Wild travelers p11-28 (5-7) 591.5

Stories
Berends, P. B. The case of the elevator duck (3-5) Fic
Delton, J. Two good friends E
Flack, M. Angus and the ducks E
Flack, M. The story about Ping E
Françoise. Springtime for Jeanne-Marie E
Ginsburg, M. The chick and the duckling E
Hurd, E. T. Last one home is a green pig E
McCloskey, R. Make way for ducklings E
Potter, B. The tale of Jemima Puddle-duck E
Wildsmith, B. The little wood duck E

Ductless glands. See Glands, Ductless

Dudley Pippin and the principal; short story. Ressner, P.
In Free to be . . . you and me p88-89 810.8

Duel of the ironclads 973.7

Duff, Annis
(jt. comp.) Adshead, G. L. comp. An inheritance of poetry 821.08

Duffey, Eric
Conservation of nature (6-7) 333.7

Duffy and the devil. Zemach, H. 398.2

Dutchman's Breeches
Carlson, B. W. A joke on Dutchman's Breeches
In Carlson. B. W. Let's pretend it happened to you p100-05   **792**

The **dutiful** daughter. Hodges, E. J.
In Hodges, E. J. Serendipity tales p138-74   **398.2**

Dutiful daughter. Pyle, K.
In Child Study Association of America. Castles and dragons p135-59   **398.2**

Dutton, Maude Barrows
The partridge and the crow
In Arbuthnot, M. H. comp. The Arbuthnot Anthology of children's literature p420   **808.8**
In Arbuthnot, M. H. comp. Time for old magic p284   **398.2**
The tyrant who became a just ruler
In Arbuthnot, M. H. comp. The Arbuthnot Anthology of children's literature p420-21   **808.8**
In Arbuthnot, M. H. comp. Time for old magic p284-85   **398.2**

Duvall, Lucille M.
The chosen one
In Kamerman, S. E. ed. A treasury of Christmas plays p313-29   **812.08**
Little Chip's Christmas tree
In Kamerman, S. E. ed. A treasury of Christmas plays p383-89   **812.08**
Valentine's Day
In Kamerman, S. E. ed. Fifty plays for junior actors p178-88   **812.08**

Duvoisin, Roger
A for the Ark   **E**
And there was America (3-5)   **973.1**
The bad joke that ended well
In Ward, W. ed. Stories to dramatize p150-52   **372.6**
Caldecott Medal acceptance paper
In Miller, B. M. ed. Caldecott Medal books: 1938-1957 p166-74   **028.5**
The house of four seasons   **E**
Lonely Veronica   **E**
Our Veronica goes to Petunia's farm   **E**
Petunia   **E**
Petunia, I love you   **E**
Petunia's Christmas   **E**
The three sneezes, and other Swiss tales (4-6)   **398.2**

Contents: The three sneezes; Green Pea John; Absent-minded farmer; Pig music; Bad joke that ended well; It all came out of an egg; Silly Jean; For lack of a thread; Wolf and the fox; Red-chicken; Private La Ramée; Down the well; Herdsman of Lona; Stubborn man; Herdsman's choice; Vaudai; Four towers of Vufflens; Hole of the Burgundians; For an oven full of bread; Bad old woman; Foolish folks; Grateful Bergmännlein; Baltzli; Hans Kuhschwanz; Flaxen thread; Fritz and Franz; Secret of the rock; Old Man of the Mountains; Haunted Alp; Vengeance of the dwarf; Knight with the stone heart; Schoch, d'Altschmidja spinnt Noch; The alphorn; How the robber band was tricked; "Brenggen" field; Wise Alois

Veronica   **E**
Veronica and the birthday present   **E**
(illus.) Carlson, N. S. The talking cat, and other stories of French Canada   **S C**
(illus.) Courlander, H. ed. Ride with the sun   **398.2**
(illus.) Fatio, L. The happy lion   **E**

(illus.) Fatio, L. The happy lion in Africa   **E**
(illus.) Fatio, L. The three happy lions   **E**
(illus.) Freschet, B. The old bullfrog   **E**
(illus.) Freschet, B. The web in the grass   **E**
(illus.) Haviland, V. Favorite fairy tales told in France   **398.2**
(illus.) Hays, W. P. Christmas on the Mayflower   **Fic**
(illus.) Holl, A. The rain puddle   **E**
(illus.) Holl, A. The remarkable egg   **E**
(illus.) Menotti, G. C. Gian-Carlo Menotti's Amahl and the night visitors   **Fic**
(illus.) Tresselt, A. Autumn harvest   **E**
(illus.) Tresselt, A. The beaver pond   **574.92**
(illus.) Tresselt, A. Follow the wind   **E**
(illus.) Tresselt, A. "Hi, Mister Robin!"   **E**
(illus.) Tresselt, A. Hide and seek fog   **E**
(illus.) Tresselt, A. I saw the sea come in   **E**
(illus.) Tresselt, A. It's time now!   **525**
(illus.) Tresselt, A. White snow, bright snow   **E**
(illus.) Tresselt, A. The world in the candy egg   **E**
(illus.) Tworkov, J. The camel who took a walk   **E**

About
See pages in the following books:
Hoffman, M. ed. Authors and illustrators of children's books p125-34   **028.5**
Miller, B. M. ed. Caldecott Medal books: 1938-1957 p175-83   **028.5**
Smaridge, N. Famous author-illustrators for young people p85-92 (5-7)   **920**

The **dwarf** and the cobbler's sons. Pulver, M. B.
In Harper, W. comp. Merry Christmas to you p94-101   **394.2**
In Ward, W. ed. Stories to dramatize p87-90   **372.6**

Dwarf Long Nose
In Greene, E. comp. Clever cooks p56-86   **398.2**

Dwarf Long-Nose. Hauff, W.   **Fic**

The **dwarf** pine tree. Lifton, B. J.   **Fic**

The **dwarf** with the long beard. Manning-Sanders, R.
In Manning-Sanders, R. A book of charms and changelings p40-50   **398.2**

Dwarf's daughter
Manning-Sanders, R. The daughter of the dwarf
In Manning-Sanders, R. Gianni and the ogre p108-18   **398.2**

The **dwarfs** of the anthill. Holladay, V.
In Holladay, V. Bantu tales p26-29   **398.2**

Dwellings. See Architecture, Domestic; Houses

Dwight Eisenhower, hero. Crandall, E. L.
In Cavanah, F. ed. Holiday roundup p148-53   **394.2**

Dyes and dyeing
Deyrup, A. Tie dyeing and batik (4-6) **746.6**
See also pages in the following book:
Papier mâché, dyeing & leatherwork p86-111 (3-7)   **745.5**

Dynamics. See Aerodynamics; Force and energy; Hydrodynamics; Matter; Motion, Physics

Dyspepsia. See Indigestion

E

ESP. See Extrasensory perception

Ea and Eo
    In Ginsburg, M. ed. The lazies p56-58
        398.2

Eager, Edward
    Half magic (4-6)   **Fic**
    Magic by the lake (4-6)   **Fic**
    Magic or not? (4-6)   **Fic**
    Seven-day magic (4-6)   **Fic**
    What happened to Katharine
    In Johnson, E. ed. Anthology of children's
        literature p669-80   808.8

The eagle. Tolstoy, L.
    In Tolstoy, L. Twenty-two Russian tales
        for young children p28-29   **S C**

Eagle Feather. Bulla, C. R.   **Fic**

Eagle mask. Houston, J.   **Fic**

Eagles
    Lavine, S. A. Wonders of the eagle world
        (4-7)   598.2

Ear
    Adler, I. Your ears (3-5)   612
    See also Hearing

The ear of corn. Grimm, J.
    In Grimm, J. The complete Grimm's Fairy
        tales p791-92   398.2

Earhart, Amelia
    Mann, P. Amelia Earhart: first lady of flight
        (3-5)   92
    See also pages in the following books:
    Nathan, D. Women of courage p117-46 (4-6)
        920
    Ross, F. Historic plane models p167-70 (5-7)
        629.133

Earl Gerald. Leach, M.
    In Leach, M. Whistle in the graveyard
        p20-21   398.2

Earl Mar's daughter
    Earl Mar's daughter
    In Jacob's, J. ed. English folk and fairy
        tales p166-70   398.2
    Nic Leodhas, S. The tale of the Earl of Mar's
        daughter
    In Nic Leodhas, S. By loch and by lin
        p43-52   398.2

Earle, Olive L.
    Birds and their beaks (3-6)   598.2
    Birds and their nests (3-6)   598.2
    Nuts (3-6)   582
    Paws, hoofs, and flippers (5-7)   599
    Peas, beans, and licorice (4-6)   583
    Pond and marsh plants (3-6)   581
    Praying mantis (2-4)   595.7
    The rose family (4-6)   583
    Scavengers (3-5)   591.5
    State birds and flowers   500.9
    State trees (4-7)   582

The earliest Americans. Scheele, W. E.   917

The earl's son of the sea. Hunt, B.
    In Brown, M. ed. A cavalcade of sea leg-
        ends p178-83   808.8

Early America, 1492-1812. Katz, W. L. 301.45

Early American children's books. Rosenbach,
    A. S. W.   020.75

Early American crafts. Colby, C. B.   680

Early Britain: the Celts, Romans, and Anglo-
    Saxons. Pittenger, W. N.   913.362

The early days of automobiles. Janeway, E.
        629.22

Early morn. Sandburg, C.
    In Sandburg, C. The Sandburg treasury
        p161-207   818

Early thunder. Fritz, J.   **Fic**

The earrings. Belpré, P.
    In Belpré, P. The tiger and the rabbit, and
        other tales p27-31   398.3
    See also Singing sack

The ears of Louis. Greene, C. C.   **Fic**

Earth
    Bendick, J. The shape of the earth (4-6) 551
    Branley, F. M. The beginning of the earth
        (1-3)   551
    Branley, F. M. The end of the world (5-7)
        525
    Ravielli, A. The world is round (2-5)   525
    Ruchlis, H. Your changing earth (2-4)   551
    See also pages in the following books:
    Branley, F. M. The nine planets p41-48 (6-7)
        523.4
    Gardner, M. Space puzzles: curious questions
        and answers about the solar system p11-
        19 (6-7)   523.2
    Knight, D. C. Thirty-two moons p15-29 (5-7)
        523.9
    See also Anarctic regions; Arctic regions;
        Atmosphere; Earthquakes; Geography; Ge-
        ology; Glacial epoch; Meteorology; Ocean;
        Oceanography; Universe

Earth, Effect of man on. See Man—Influence
    on nature

Earth gnome
    Grimm, J. The earth gnome
    In Grimm, J. More Tales from Grimm
        p171-87   398.2
    Grimm, J. The gnome
    In Grimm, J. The complete Grimm's Fairy
        tales p420-24   398.2

The earth is the Lord's. Plotz, H. comp. 808.81

Earth magician. Baker, B.
    In Baker, B. At the center of the world
        p 1-6   398.2

Earth: our crowded spaceship. Asimov, I.
        301.32

Earth satellites. See Artificial satellites

Earthenware. See Pottery

Earthfasts. Mayne, W.   **Fic**

Earthquakes
    Brown, B. W. Historical catastrophes: earth-
        quakes (5-7)   551.2
    Lauber, P. Earthquakes (4-6)   551.2
    Marcus, R. B. The first book of volcanoes
        & earthquakes (5-7)   551.2
    Matthews, W. H. The story of volcanoes and
        earthquakes (4-6)   551.2
    See also pages in the following books:
    Lauber, P. This restless earth p21-42 (5-7)
        551

Educational Film Library Association
Film evaluation guide   **016.3713**
Educational games for fun. Mulac, M. E. **372.1**
Educational media selection centers. Rowell, J.   **021**
Educational overhead transparencies, Index to. See Index to educational overhead transparencies
Educational records, Index to. See Index to educational records
Educational slide sets, Index to. See Index to educational slide sets
Educational video tapes, Index to. See Index to educational video tapes
Educators
Carruth, E. K. She wanted to read: the story of Mary McLeod Bethune (4-6)   **92**
Graham, S. Booker T. Washington: educator of hand, head, and heart (5-7)   **92**
Myers, E. P. Angel of Appalachia: Martha Berry (5-7)   **92**
Phelan, M. K. Martha Berry (2-4)   **92**
Radford, R. L. Mary McLeod Bethune (2-4)   **92**

See also Teachers

Educators guide to free films   **016.3713**
Edward cleans his room. Stolz, M.
In Arbuthnot, M. H. comp. The Arbuthnot Anthology of children's literature p670-73   **808.8**
Edward Frank and the friendly cow
In Garner, A. ed. A cavalcade of goblins p41   **398.2**
Edwards, George Wharton
(illus.) Dodge, M. M. Hans Brinker   **Fic**
Edwards, Jeanne
(illus.) Wyss, J. D. The Swiss family Robinson   **Fic**
Edwards, Margaret Dulles
A saga of the prairie
In Luckhardt, M. C. comp. Thanksgiving p245-52   **394.2**
Edwards, Sally
When the world's on fire (4-6)   **Fic**
Edwardson, Cordelia
Miriam lives in a kibbutz (1-4)   **915.694**
Ee-aw! Ee-aw! Haviland, V.
In Haviland, V. Favorite fairy tales told in Denmark p15-26   **398.2**
The **eel** and the porgy. Vo-Dinh
In Vo-Dinh. The toad is the Emperor's uncle p45-49   **398.2**
Eells, Elsie Spencer
Why the bananas belong to the monkey
In Dobbs, R. ed. Once upon a time p60-66   **372.6**
Eels

See pages in the following book:

Silverstein, A. Metamorphosis: the magic change p60-66 (4-6)   **591.3**
Eelworms. See Nematoda
The **egg.** Nesbitt, E.
In Silverberg, B. ed. Phoenix feathers p187-205   **S C**
Egg craft. Newsome, A. J.   **745.59**

Egg decoration
Coskey, E. Easter eggs for everyone (5-7)   **745.59**
Newsome, A. J. Egg craft (4-7)   **745.59**
See also pages in the following book:
Cross, L. Kitchen crafts p30-41 (3-7) **745.5**
Fiction
Milhous, K. The egg tree   **E**
Egg thoughts, and other Frances songs. Hoban, R.   **811**
Egg to chick. Selsam, M. E.   **574.3**
The **egg** tree. Milhous, K.   **E**
Eggenberger, David
Flags of the U.S.A. (6-7)   **929.9**
Eggs
Cosgrove, M. Eggs—and what happens inside them (3-6)   **574.3**
Flanagan, G. L. Window into an egg (4-6)   **574.3**
Milgrom, H. Egg-ventures (1-3)   **636.5**
Selsam, M. E. Egg to chick (k-3)   **574.3**
See also Birds—Eggs and nests
Fiction
Holl, A. The remarkable egg   **E**
The **eggs.** Aliki   **398.2**
Eggs—and what happens inside them. Cosgrove, M.   **574.3**
Eggshell craft
Pflug, B. Egg-speriment (1-3)   **745.5**
Egg-speriment. Pflug, B.   **745.5**
Egg-ventures. Milgrom, H.   **636.5**
Egoff, Sheila
(ed.) Only connect   **028.5**
The republic of childhood   **028.5**
Egypt, Ophelia Settle
James Weldon Johnson (2-4)   **92**
Egypt
Lengyel, E. Modern Egypt (5-7)   **916.2**
Mahmoud, Z. N. The land and people of Egypt (5-7)   **916.2**
Mirepoix, C. Egypt in pictures (5-7) **916.2**
See also pages in the following book:
Caldwell, J. C. Let's visit the Middle East p35-49 (5-7)   **915.6**

Agriculture
See Agriculture—Egypt
Antiquities
Cottrell, L. Land of the Pharaohs (6-7) **913.32**
Pace, M. M. Wrapped for eternity (5-7)   **393**
Robinson, C. A. The first book of ancient Egypt (4-7)   **913.32**
Van Duyn, J. The Egyptians (6-7)   **913.32**
See also pages in the following books:
Clymer, E. The second greatest invention p25-38 (5-7)   **913**
Helfman, E. S. Signs & symbols of the sun p21-31 (5-7)   **393**
McHargue, G. Mummies p33-55 (5-7)   **393**
Art
See Art, Egyptian
Civilization
Glubok, S. The art of ancient Egypt (4-7)   **709.32**

Egypt—Civilization—*Continued*
Leacroft, H. The buildings of ancient Egypt (5-7) **722**
Robinson, C. A. The first book of ancient Egypt (4-7) **913.32**
Van Duyn, J. The Egyptians (6-7) **913.32**

Commerce
See pages in the following book:
Van Duyn, J. The Egyptians p139-49 (6-7) **913.32**

Education
See also Education—Egypt

Fiction
Coatsworth, E. Bess and the Sphinx (3-5) **Fic**
Harris, R. The bright and morning star (5-7) **Fic**
Harris, R. The moon in the cloud (5-7) **Fic**
Harris, R. The shadow on the sun (5-7) **Fic**
McGraw, E. J. The golden goblet (5-7) **Fic**
McGraw, E. J. Mara, daughter of the Nile (5-7) **Fic**

History
Meadowcroft, E. L. The gift of the river (3-5) **932**
Payne, E. The Pharaohs of ancient Egypt (5-7) **932**
Pharaohs of Egypt (6-7) **932**
See also pages in the following book:
Unstead, R. J. Looking at ancient history p5-23 (4-6) **930**
See also Sinai Campaign, 1956

Industries
See pages in the following book:
Mahmoud, Z. N. The land and people of Egypt p128-34 (5-7) **916.2**

Kings and rulers
Payne, E. The Pharaohs of ancient Egypt (5-7) **932**
Pharaohs of Egypt (6-7) **932**

Religion
See pages in the following book:
Mahmond, Z. N. The land and people of Egypt p34-51 (5-7) **916.2**

Science
See Science—Egypt

The **Egypt** game. Snyder, Z. K. **Fic**

The **Egypt** game; excerpt. Snyder, Z. K.
In Arbuthnot, M. H. comp. The Arbuthnot Anthology of children's literature p691-95 **808.8**

Egypt in pictures. Mirepoix, C. **916.2**

Egyptian architecture. See Architecture, Egyptian

Egyptian art. See Art, Egyptian

Egyptian language
Scott, J. Hieroglyphs for fun (4-7) **411**

Egyptian mythology. See Mythology, Egyptian

The **Egyptians.** Van Duyn, J. **913.35**

Egyptology. See Egypt—Antiquities

Ehlert, Lois
(illus.) Charosh, M. Mathematical games for one or two **793.7**

Ehrenberg, Myron
(illus.) Sterling, D. Insects and the homes they build **595.7**

Ehret, Walter
The international book of Christmas carols **783.6**

Ehrlich, Amy
Wounded Knee: an Indian history of the American West (6-7) **970.4**

Ehrlich, Paul
See pages in the following book:
Asimov, I. Breakthroughs in science p137-44 (5-7) **920**

Eichenberg, Fritz
Ape in a cape **E**
Dancing in the moon **E**
(illus.) Davis, R. Padre Porko, the gentlemanly pig (4-6) **398.2**
(illus.) Dobbs, R. No room **398.2**
(illus.) Jagendorf, M. Tyll Ulenspiegel's merry pranks **398.2**
(illus). Johnson, E. ed. Anthology of children's literature **808.8**
(illus.) Kipling, R. The jungle book **S C**
(illus.) Sewell, A. Black Beauty **Fic**

Eichmann, Adolf
See pages in the following book:
Aymar, B. Laws and trials that created history p170-80 (6-7) **345.7**

Eight Black American inventors. Hayden, R. C. **920**

Eight cousins. Alcott, L. M. **Fic**

Eight-headed dragon. Uchida, Y.
In Uchida, Y. The dancing kettle, and other Japanese folk tales p27-33 **398.2**

Eight immortals
Carpenter, F. How the eight old ones crossed the sea
In Carpenter, F. Tales of a Chinese grandmother p150-58 **398.2**

8mm motion cartridges, Index to. See Index to 8mm motion cartridges

Eighteenth century
Foster, G. Year of independence, 1776 (3-6) **909.7**

The **18th emergency.** Byars, B. **Fic**

Eighty-one brothers
Haviland, V. The white hare and the crocodiles
In Haviland, V. Favorite fairy tales told in Japan p73-89 **398.2**
Olcott, F. J. The white hare of Inabi
In Gruenberg, S. M. ed. Favorite stories old and new p347-48 **808.8**

Eimerl, Sarel
Baboons (3-5) **599**
Gulls (3-5) **598.2**

Ei-Niin-Mita, or No-So-What. Bowman, J. C.
In Bowman, J. C. Tales from a Finnish tupa p105-15 **398.2**
See also Go I know not whither—fetch I know not what

Einsel, Naiad
(illus.) Collodi, C. The adventures of Pinocchio **Fic**

Einstein, Albert
Beckhard, A. J. Albert Einstein (4-7) **92**
See also pages in the following books:
Asimov, I. Breakthroughs in science p163-71 (5-7) **920**
Cottler, J. Heroes of civilization p193-204 (6-7) **920**
McNeer, M. Give me freedom p111-28 (5-7) **920**

Einstein, Charles
Willie Mays: coast to coast Giant (5-7) **92**

Einzig, Susan
(illus.) Pearce, A. P. Tom's midnight garden **Fic**

Eitzen, Allan
(illus.) Millen, N. comp. Children's games from many lands **796.1**
(illus.) O'Brien, T. C. Odds and evens **513**
(illus.) Urquhart, D. I. The refrigerator and how it works **621.5**

Ekun and Opolo go looking for wives. Courlander, H.
In Courlander, H. Olode the hunter, and other tales from Nigeria p19-23 **398.2**

El-hi textbooks in print **016.371**

El Salvador. See Salvador

El Salvador. Carpenter, A. **917.284**

El Salvador in pictures. Haverstock, N. A. **917.284**

Elbert, Virginie Fowler
Potterymaking (4-6) **738.1**

Elder-tree mother
Andersen, H. C. The Elder-Tree Mother
In Andersen, H. C. Andersen's Fairy tales p116-24 **S C**
Andersen, H. Eldermother
In Andersen, H. Hans Andersen's Fairy tales p256-65 **S C**
Andersen, H. C. Mother Elderberry
In Andersen, H. C. The complete fairy tales and stories p263-70 **S C**

Eldermother. Andersen, H.
In Andersen, H. Hans Andersen's Fairy tales p256-65 **S C**
See also Elder-tree mother

The **Elders** of Chelm & Genendel's key. Singer, I. B.
In Singer, I. B. When Shlemiel went to Warsaw & other stories p45-51 **398.2**

Eleanor of Aquitaine, consort of Henry II
Fiction
Konigsburg, E. L. A proud taste for scarlet and miniver (5-7) **Fic**

Election Day
Phelan, M. K. Election Day (1-3) **394.2**
Drama
See pages in the following book:
Fisher, A. Holiday programs for boys and girls p77-91 (4-7) **812**
Poetry
See pages in the following book:
Sechrist, E. H. comp. Poems for red letter days p200-03 **821.08**

Elections
United States
Lindop, E. The first book of elections (4-7) **324.73**
See also Presidents—United States—Election

Electoral college. See Presidents—United States—Election

Electric apparatus and appliances. See Burglar alarms; Electric motors

Electric automobiles. See Automobiles, Electric

Electric communication. See Telecommunication

Electric lighting
Corbett, S. What makes a light go on? (3-5) **612.32**

Electric machinery. See Electric motors

Electric motors
Renner, A. G. How to make and use electric motors (5-7) **621.46**

Electric power
See pages in the following books:
Men of science and invention p80-101 **609**
Shuttlesworth, D. E. Disappearing energy p14-19 (5-7) **333.7**

Electric waves
See pages in the following book:
Bendick, J. Electronics for young people p142-50 (5-7) **621.381**

Electricity
Feravolo, R. V. Junior science book of electricity (3-5) **537.072**
Stone, A. H. Turned on: a look at electricity (4-7) **537.072**
See also pages in the following books:
Barr, G. Show time for young scientists p36-49 (5-7) **793.8**
Mark, S. J. A physics lab of your own p107-39 (5-7) **530.72**
The Way things work. Special edition for young people p149-75 (6-7) **600**
Wilson, M. Seesaws to cosmic rays p51-58 (5-7) **530**
Wyler, R. The first book of science experiments p57-69 (4-6) **507.2**
See also Electrons; Lightning; Magnetism; Radioactivity; Telegraph; Telephone; X rays; also headings beginning with Electric and Electro

Electricity. Lawson, R.
In Arbuthnot, M. H. comp. The Arbuthnot Anthology of children's literature p571-73 **808.8**

Electromagnetism
See pages in the following books:
Barr, G. Show time for young scientists p29-36 (5-7) **793.8**
Mark, S. J. A physics lab of your own p153-70 (5-7) **530.72**

Electromagnets
Feravolo, R. V. Junior science book of magnets (3-5) **538**

Electron tubes. See Vacuum tubes

Electronic calculating machines. See Computers

Electronic circuits

See pages in the following book:

Bendick, J. Electronics for young people p81-84 (5-7)   **621.381**

Electronic computers. See Computers

Electronics

Bendick, J. Electronics for young people (5-7)   **621.381**

See also pages in the following book:

Wilson, M. Seesaws to cosmic rays p59-74 (5-7)   **530**

Electronics for boys and girls. See Bendick, J. Electronics for young people   **621.381**

Electronics for young people. Bendick, J.   **621.381**

Electrons

See pages in the following book:

Bendick, J. Electronics for young people p7-20 (5-7)   **621.381**

Elementary dictionary, Webster's New   **423**

Elementary English   **420.5**

Elementary English review. See Elementary English   **420.5**

Elementary school libraries. Lowrie, J. E.   **027.8**

The **Elementary** school library collection   **011**

Elena's ciambella. Upjohn, A. M.

In Harper, W. comp. Easter chimes p92-99   **394.2**

Elephant and Giraffe go farming. Arnott, K.

In Arnott, K. Animal folk tales around the world p241-52   **398.2**

The **elephant** and his secret. Dana, D.   **E**

Elephant buttons. Ueno, N.   **E**

The **elephant** Girly-Face. Babbitt, E. C.

In Babbitt, E. C. Jataka tales p52-57   **398.2**

The **elephant** hunters. Courlander, H.

In Courlander, H. The king's drum, and other African stories p68-70   **398.2**

Elephants

Bergman, Sucksdorff, A. Tooni, the elephant boy (1-5)   **915.4**

Conklin, G. Elephants of Africa (2-4)   **599**

Eberle, I. Elephants live here (1-3)   **599**

See also pages in the following books:

Earle, O. L. Paws, hoofs, and flippers p105-10 (5-7)   **599**

Fenton, C. L. Animals that help us p117-25 (4-6)   **636**

Wellman, A. Africa's animals p163-68 (6-7)   **591.9**

Stories

Brunhoff, J. de. The story of Babar, the little elephant   **E**

Dana, D. The elephant and his secret   **E**

Garfield, N. The Tuesday elephant (2-4)   **Fic**

Joslin, S. Baby Elephant and the secret wishes   **E**

Joslin, S. Brave Baby Elephant   **E**

Seuss, Dr. Horton hatches the egg   **E**

Seuss, Dr. Horton hears a Who!   **E**

The **elephant's** child. Kipling, R.

In Arbuthnot, M. H. comp. The Arbuth-

not Anthology of children's literature p484-87   **808.8**

In Gruenberg, S. M. ed. Favorite stories old and new p456-63   **808.8**

In Kipling, R. Just so stories (Doubleday) p63-84   **S C**

In Kipling, R. Just so stories (Doubleday. Anniv. ed.) p30-38   **S C**

In Kipling, R. Just so stories (Watts, F.) p63-81   **S C**

In Ross, E. S. ed. The lost half-hour p50-60   **372.6**

Elephants don't have manners. Klein, L.

In Gruenberg, S. M. comp. Let's hear a story p127-31   **808.8**

Elephants live here. Eberle, I.   **599**

Elephants of Africa. Conklin, G.   **599**

Elephant's tail. Courlander, H.

In Courlander, H. The hat-shaking dance, and other tales from the Gold Coast p80-85   **398.2**

Elf-hill

Andersen, H. C. The hill of the elves

In Andersen, H. C. The complete fairy tales and stories p282-88   **S C**

Elf of the rose

Andersen, H. C. The rose elf

In Andersen, H. C. Andersen's Fairy tales p 1-6   **S C**

In Andersen, H. C. The complete fairy tales and stories p188-92   **S C**

Elf owl. Buff, M.   **591.5**

Elfenbein, Josef A.

The ten-penny tragedy

In Burack, A. S. ed. Popular plays for classroom reading p78-93   **808.82**

Elgaard, Greta

(illus.) Spyri, J. Heidi   **Fic**

Elgin, Kathleen

The human body: the brain (3-5)   **612**

The human body: the digestive system (4-6)   **612**

The human body: the heart (3-5)   **612**

The human body: the muscles (3-6)   **612**

The human body: the skeleton (3-6)   **611**

The Mormons (4-7)   **289.3**

The Quakers (4-7)   **289.6**

Twenty-eight days (5-7)   **612.6**

(illus.) Selsam, M. E. How animals live together   **591.5**

(illus.) Selsam, M. E. How to grow house plants   **635.9**

(illus.) Selsam, M. E. The language of animals   **591.5**

(illus.) Selsam, M. E. Plants that heal   **581.6**

(illus.) Selsam, M. E. Underwater zoos   **639**

Elijah, the prophet

Shulevitz, U. The magician (k-2)   **398.2**

Elin's Amerika. De Angeli, M.   **Fic**

Elizabeth I, Queen of England

See pages in the following book:

Farjeon, E. ed. A cavalcade of queens p153-56 (4-7)   **808.8**

Fiction

See pages in the following book:

Farjeon, E. ed. A cavalcade of queens p134-52 (4-7)   **808.8**

Emotionally disturbed children. See Problem children

Emotions
LeShan, E. What makes me feel this way? (3-6) **152.4**
LeShan, E. You and your feelings (6-7) **155.5**

The **Emperor** and the drummer boy. Robbins, R. **Fic**

The **emperor** and the kite. Yolen, J. **398.2**

The **emperor** and the nightingale. See Andersen, H. C. The nightingale **Fic**

The **Emperor** of Lilliput. Swift, J.
In Martignoni, M. E. ed. The illustrated treasury of children's literature p491-96 **808.8**

The **emperor** penguins. Mizumura, K. **598.2**

Emperors. See Kings and rulers; Roman emperors; and names of emperors, e.g. Napoléon I, Emperor of the French

The **emperor's** magic bow. Robertson, D. L.
In Robertson, D. L. Fairy tales from Viet Nam p66-75 **398.2**

Emperor's new clothes
Andersen, H. C. The emperor's new clothes **Fic**
—Same
In Andersen, H. C. Andersen's Fairy tales p82-87 **S C**
In Andersen, H. C. The complete fairy tales and stories p77-81 **S C**
In Andersen, H. Hans Andersen's Fairy tales p86-92 **S C**
In Andersen, H. C. It's perfectly true, and other stories p133-40 **S C**
In Arbuthnot, M. H. comp. The Arbuthnot Anthology of children's literature p565-68 **808.8**
In Authors' choice p63-70 **S C**
In Gruenberg, S. M. ed. Favorite stories old and new p317-21 **808.8**
In Haviland, V. comp. The fairy tale treasury p174-79 **398.2**
In Johnson, E. ed. Anthology of children's literature p726-28 **808.8**
In Martignoni, M. E. ed. The illustrated treasury of children's literature p229-32 **808.8**
In Rackham, A. comp. Arthur Rackham Fairy book p240-45 **398.2**
In Untermeyer, B. ed. The Golden Treasury of children's literature p214-19 **808.8**
In Ward, W. ed. Stories to dramatize p210-14 **372.6**
Andersen, H. C. Story of the Emperor's new clothes
In Lang, A. ed. The yellow fairy book p21-25 **398.2**

The **Emperor's** new robes. Foley, M. A.
In Kamerman, S. E. ed. Fifty plays for junior actors p203-21 **812.08**

The **Emperor's** Nightingale. Thane, A.
In Thane, A. Plays from famous stories and fairy tales p319 **812**

Empty bowls. Fisher, A.
In Fisher, A. United Nations plays and programs p212-17 **812**

The **empty** city. Crane, L.
In Hazeltine, A. I. ed. Hero tales from many lands p417-27 **398.2**

The **empty** sea. Thompson, V. L.
In Thompson, V. L. Hawaiian tales of heroes and champions p93-102 **398.2**

Emrich, Duncan
(comp.) American folk poetry: an anthology **811.08**
(comp.) The hodgepodge book **398**
(ed.) The nonsense book of riddles, rhymes, tongue twisters, puzzles and jokes from American folklore (3-7) **398**

Emu and the crows
Parker, K. L. Dinewan the emu and Goomble-gubbon the turkey
In Johnson, E. ed. Anthology of children's literature p332-34 **808.8**

El Enano. Finger, C.
In Finger, C. Tales from silver lands p59-68 **398.2**

The **enchanted** buck. Berger, T.
In Berger, T. Black fairy tales p43-54 **398.2**

The **enchanted** canary. Deulin, C.
In Lang, A. ed. The red fairy book p257-73 **398.2**

The **enchanted** cave of Cesh Corran. Stephens, J.
In Stephens, J. Irish fairy tales p201-18 **398.2**

The **enchanted** cow. Davis, M. G.
In Harper, W. comp. Ghosts and goblins p60-66 **394.2**
In Hoke, H. ed. Witches, witches, witches p37-44 **808.8**

The **enchanted** fisherman. Colwell, E.
In Colwell, E. Round about and long ago p19-22 **398.2**

Enchanted grouse
Bowman, J. C. Kalle and the wood grouse
In Bowman, J. C. Tales from a Finnish tupa p129-40 **398.2**

Enchanted horse
The enchanted horse
In Lang, A. ed. Arabian nights p244-69 **398.2**
The story of the enchanted horse
In Untermeyer, B. ed. The Golden Treasury of children's literature p356-64 **808.8**

The **enchanted** mule. Haviland, V.
In Haviland, V. Favorite fairy tales told in Spain p70-87 **398.2**

Enchanted peafowl. Fillmore, P.
In Fillmore, P. The laughing prince p107-38 **398.2**

The **Enchanted** pig
In Lang, A. ed. The red fairy book p104-15 **398.2**

The **enchanted** prince. Manning-Sanders, R.
In Manning-Sanders, R. A book of princes and princesses p49-56 **398.2**
In Manning-Sanders, R. A choice of magic p183-90 **398.2**

The **enchanted** princess. Colwell, E.
In Colwell, E. Round about and long ago p34-39 **398.2**

The **enchanted** ring. Fénelon, F. de S. de la
Mothe
In Lang, A. ed. The green fairy book
p137-44   **398.2**

The **Enchanted** snake
In Lang, A. ed. The green fairy book
p186-93   **398.2**

The **enchanted** tortoise. Carpenter, F.
In Carpenter, F. African wonder tales
p205-13   **398.2**

The **enchanted** watch. Deulin, C.
In Lang, A. ed. The green fairy book p43-
47   **398.2**

The **enchanted** wine jug. Manning-Sanders, R.
In Manning-Sanders, R. A book of charms
and changelings p21-33 **398.2**
See also Why the dog and cat are
enemies

Enchantment of Gearoidh Iarla. O'Faolain, E.
In O'Faolain, E. Irish sagas and folk-tales
p232-34   **398.2**

Encyclopaedia Britannica
Britannica Junior encyclopaedia for boys and
girls. See Britannica Junior encyclopaedia
for boys and girls **031**

Encyclopedia and fact-index, Compton's **031**

Encyclopedia Brown, boy detective. Sobol,
D. J.   **S C**

The **encyclopedia** of sports. Menke, F. G.
    796.03

Encyclopedia of sports, The Junior illustrated.
See The Junior illustrated encyclopedia of
sports   **796.03**

Encyclopedia of transportation, The complete
junior. Zehavi, A. M. ed. **380.503**

Encyclopedias and dictionaries
Britannica Junior encyclopaedia for boys and
girls   **031**
Childcraft: the how and why library **031**
Collier's encyclopedia **031**
Compton's Encyclopedia and fact-index **031**
Guinness Book of world records **032**
Kane, J. N. Famous first facts **031**
The Lincoln library of essential information
    031
Merit students encyclopedia **031**
The New book of knowledge **031**
The World book encyclopedia **031**
See also names of languages and sub-
jects with the subdivision Dictionaries for
works with definitions of words, e.g. En-
glish language—Dictionaries; Biography—
Dictionaries; and subjects with the sub-
division Encyclopedias for facts presented
in condensed form, e.g. Mythology—En-
cyclopedias

Bibliography
General encyclopedias in print **016.03**
See also pages in the following book:
Larrick, N. A parent's guide to children's
reading p165-83 **028.5**

End of the world
Branley, F. M. The end of the world (5-7) **525**

End of the world. Bowman, J. C.
In Bowman, J. C. Tales from a Finnish
tupa p239-41   **398.2**

Endangered species. See Rare animals

The **endocrine** system. Silverstein, A. **612**

Endocrinology. See Glands, Ductless

Endore, Guy
The day of the dragon
In Yolen, J. ed. Zoo 2000 p179-219 **S C**

Endowed charities. See Endowments

Endowments
See pages in the following book:
Sechrist, E. H. It's time for brotherhood
p184-93 (5-7) **301.11**

Endurance, Physical. See Physical fitness

An **enemy** at Green Knowe. Boston, L. M. See
note under Boston, L. M. The children of
Green Knowe   **Fic**

Energy. See Force and energy

Energy. Adler, I.   **531**

Engebrecht, P. A.
Under the haystack (5-7) **Fic**

Engelhardt, Frederick
The Kraken
In Silverberg, B. ed. Phoenix feathers p27-
52   **S C**

Engineering. See Civil engineering

Engines
Limburg, P. R. Engines (5-7) **621.4**
Weiss, H. Motors and engines and how they
work (5-7)   **621.4**
See also Gas and oil engines; Steam
engines

England
See also Great Britain
Description and travel
Street, A. The land and people of England
(5-7)   **914.2**
Folklore
See Folklore—Great Britain
Legends
See Legends—Great Britain
Social life and customs
Duggan, A. Growing up with the Norman
Conquest (6-7) **914.2**
Gidal, S. My village in England (4-6) **914.2**
Kirtland, G. B. One day in Elizabethan En-
gland (2-5)   **914.2**

Englebert, Victor
Camera on Africa (3-5) **916.3**
The goats of Agadez (1-3) **916.6**

Englefield, Cicely
George and Angela
In Association for Childhood Education
International. Told under the magic
umbrella p50-54 **S C**

Engler, Larry
Making puppets come alive **791.5**

English art. See Art, British

English authors. See Authors, English

English ballads. See Ballads, English

English composition. See English language—
Composition and exercises

English poetry—Collections—*Continued*
Cole, W. comp. Oh, what nonsense! (3-6)
    821.08
Cole, W. comp. Poems for seasons and celebrations (5-7)   **821.08**
Cole, W. comp. Poems of magic and spells (4-7)   **821.08**
Cole, W. comp. The poet's tales (6-7) **821.08**
Cole, W. ed. Rough men, tough men (5-7)
    821.08
Colum, P. ed. Roofs of gold (6-7) **821.08**
De La Mare, W. ed. Come hither **821.08**
De La Mare, W. ed. Tom Tiddler's ground
    821.08
Geismer, B. P. comp. Very young verses (k-1)
    821.08
Grahame, K. comp. The Cambridge Book of poetry for children **821.08**
Hannum, S. comp. Lean out of the window (4-7)   **821.08**
Huffard, G. T. comp. My poetry book (5-7)
    821.08
Larrick, N. ed. Piper, pipe that song again! (2-5)   **821.08**
Livingston, M. C. ed. Listen, children, listen (k-4)   **821.08**
McFarland, W. ed. For a child (k-3) **821.08**
Nash, O. ed. The moon is shining bright as day (3-6)   **821.08**
The Oxford Book of children's verse **821.08**
Parker, E. ed. 100 more story poems (6-7)
    821.08
Parker, E. ed. 100 poems about people (6-7)
    821.08
Parker, E. ed. 100 story poems (6-7) **821.08**
Read, H. ed. This way, delight (5-7) **821.08**
Reed, G. comp. Bird songs (5-7) **821.08**
Sechrist, E. H. ed. One thousand poems for children **821.08**
Sechrist, E. H. comp. Poems for red letter days   **821.08**
Stevenson, B. E. comp. The home book of verse for young folks **821.08**
Thompson, B. J. ed. All the Silver pennies (3-6)   **821.08**
Tudor, T. comp. Wings from the wind (3-6)
    821.08
Untermeyer, L. ed. The Golden Treasury of poetry **821.08**
Untermeyer, L. ed. Rainbow in the sky (k-4)
    821.08
Untermeyer, L. ed. This singing world (4-7)
    821.08

Engraving. See Engravings; Gems; Lithography; Wood engraving

Engravings
    See pages in the following book:
Holme, B. Drawings to live with p95-107
    741.9

Engvick, William
  (ed.) Lullabies and night songs (k-3) **784.6**

Enigmas. See Curiosities and wonders

Enjoying opera. See Streatfeild, N. The first book of the opera **782.1**

Enoch Pratt Free Library, Baltimore
  Black is . . . **016.3014**

The **enormous** genie. Tashjian, V. A.
  In Tashjian, V. A. Three apples fell from heaven p23-30 **398.2**

Enright, Elizabeth
A Christmas tree for Lydia
  In Author's choice p111-21 **S C**
The Four-Story Mistake. See note under Enright, E. The Saturdays **Fic**
Gone-Away Lake (4-6) **Fic**
Gone-Away Lake; excerpt
  In Johnson, E. ed. Anthology of children's literature p826-30 **808.8**
The Melendy family. See note under Enright, E. The Saturdays **Fic**
Newbery Medal acceptance paper
  In Miller, B. M. ed. Newbery Medal books: 1922-1955 p172-75 **028.5**
Return to Gone-Away (4-6) **Fic**
Saturday five
  In Association for Childhood Education International. Told under spacious skies p75-87 **S C**
The Saturdays (4-6) **Fic**
Tatsinda (3-5) **Fic**
Then there were five. See note under Enright, E. The Saturdays **Fic**
Thimble summer (4-6) **Fic**
Zeee (2-4) **Fic**

About
  See pages in the following book:
Miller, B. M. ed. Newbery Medal books: 1922-1955 p168-71 **028.5**

Ensembles (Mathematics) See Set theory

Ensigns. See Flags

Enter Melanie—and Marshall. Snyder, Z. K.
  In Arbuthnot, M. H. comp. The Arbuthnot Anthology of children's literature p691-95 **808.8**

Entertainers
Rollins, C. Famous Negro entertainers of stage, screen and TV (5-7) **920**
  See also Actors and actresses; Clowns

Entertaining
  See pages in the following book:
Bailard, V. So you were elected! p121-58 (6-7) **367**
  See also Amusements; Etiquette; Games; Parties

Entertaining with number tricks. Barr, G. **793.7**

Entertainments. See Amusements; Christmas entertainments; Skits

Enthoven, Jacqueline
Stitchery for children **746.4**

Entomology. See Insects

Entomology, Economic. See Insects, Injurious and beneficial

Environment. See Adaptation (Biology); Ecology; Man—Influence of environment; Man—Influence on nature

Environment and pesticides. See Pesticides and the environment

Environmental policy. See Conservation of natural resources; Human ecology; Man—Influence on nature; Natural resources; Pollution

Environmental pollution. See Pollution

Enzymes
Berger, M. Enzymes in action (6-7) **574.1**

Enzymes in action. Berger, M. **574.1**

Escourido, Joseph
(illus.) Carpenter, F. African wonder tales
398.2

Esenwein, J. B.
The Woodman and the goblins
In Harper, W. comp. Ghosts and goblins
p49-56 394.2

Eshugbayi, Ezekiel A.
(jt. auth.) Courlander, H. Olode the hunter,
and other tales from Nigeria 398.2

The Eskimo. Bleeker, S. 970.1

Eskimo art. *See* Eskimos—Art

Eskimo boy. Freuchen, P. **Fic**

Eskimo folklore. *See* Folklore, Eskimo

Eskimo legends. *See* Legends, Eskimo

Eskimo poetry
Collections
Field, E. ed. Eskimo songs and stories (3-7)
398.2
Lewis, R. ed. I breathe a new song (4-7) **897**
See also pages in the following book:
Houston, J. ed. Songs of the dream people
p66-83 (4-7) 821.08

Eskimo songs and stories. Field, E. ed. 398.2

Eskimos
Bleeker, S. The Eskimo (4-6) 970.1
Bringle, M. Eskimos (5-6) 970.1
Goetz, D. The Arctic tundra (3-5) 919.8
Pine, T. S. The Eskimos knew (1-4) 970.1
See also pages in the following books:
Baldwin, G. C. How Indians really lived
p188-205 (5-7) 970.1
Coy, H. Man comes to America p91-108 (6-7)
917
Harrington, L. The polar regions p40-47 (5-7)
919.8
Hofsinde, R. Indian fishing and camping p59-
73 (3-6) 799.1
Liversidge, D. The first book of the Arctic
p19-24 (4-7) 919.8
Stefansson, E. Here is Alaska p29-72 (6-7)
917.98

Art
Glubok, S. The art of the Eskimo (4-7) 709.98
Bibliography
See pages in the following book:
Griffin, L. comp. Multi-ethnic books for
young children p4-21 028.52
Fiction
Damjan, M. Atuk **E**
Freuchen, P. Eskimo boy (4-6) **Fic**
George, J. C. Julie of the wolves (6-7) **Fic**
Houston, J. Akavak (4-6) **Fic**
Houston, J. The white archer (4-6) **Fic**
Houston, J. Wolf run (4-6) **Fic**
Morrow, S. S. Inatuk's friend **E**
Parish, P. Ootah's lucky day **E**
Folklore
See Folklore, Eskimo
Legends
See Legends, Eskimo
Poetry
See Eskimo poetry

Social life and customs
Glubok, S. The art of the Eskimo (4-7) **709.98**
See also pages in the following book:
Berry, E. Eating and cooking around the
world p9-17 (5-7) 641.3
The Eskimos knew. Pine, T. S. 970.1

Espenshade, Edward B.
(ed.) Goode's World atlas. *See* Goode's World
atlas 912

Esquemeling, John. *See* Exquemelin, Alexandre
Olivier

Esquimaux. *See* Eskimos

Essences and essential oils. *See* Flavoring essences

Essenes
See pages in the following book:
Kettelkamp, L. Religions, East and West p78-
82 (5-7) 291

Esteban. *See* Estévan

Estebanico. *See* Estévan

Estebanico. Parish, H. R. **Fic**

Estes, Eleanor
An afternoon with the oldest inhabitant
In Arbuthnot, M. H. comp. The Arbuthnot
Anthology of children's literature
p627-33 808.8
The coat-hanger Christmas tree (4-6) **Fic**
Ginger Pye (4-6) **Fic**
The hundred dresses (4-6) **Fic**
The middle bear
In Gruenberg, S. M. ed. Favorite stories
old and new p109-16 808.8
The middle Moffat (4-6) **Fic**
The middle Moffat; excerpt
In Arbuthnot, M. H. comp. The Arbuthnot
Anthology of children's literature
p627-33 808.8
The Moffats (4-6) **Fic**
Newbery Medal acceptance paper
In Miller, B. M. ed. Newbery Medal
books: 1922-1955 p379-87 028.5
Pinky Pye (4-6) **Fic**
Rufus M; excerpt
In Johnson, E. ed. Anthology of children's
literature p773-79 808.8
The witch family (1-4) **Fic**
About
See pages in the following books:
Miller, B. M. ed. Newbery Medal books:
1922-1955 p374-78 028.5
Sayers, F. C. Summoned by books p116-21
028.5
Townsend, J. R. A sense of story p79-85
028.5

Estévan
See pages in the following books:
Burt, O. W. Negroes in the early West p13-
21 (4-6) 920
Hughes, L. Famous Negro heroes of America
p11-20 (5-7) 920
Fiction
Baker, B. Walk the world's rim (5-7) **Fic**
O'Dell, S. The King's fifth (6-7) **Fic**
Parish, H. R. Estebanico (5-7) **Fic**

Estévanico. *See* Estévan

Esther, Queen of Persia
Cone, M. Purim (1-3)   296.4
Esthetics
Hoban, T. Shapes and things   E
  See also pages in the following book:
Van Duyn, J. The Greeks p85-106 (6-7)
          913.38
       See also Rhythm
Estimation. Linn, C. F.   513
Estonia
      Folklore
    See Folklore—Estonia
Estrada, Ric
(illus.) Hawes, J. The goats who killed the
   leopard   E
Estuaries
Pringle, L. Estuaries (4-6)   574.92
Etana's flight to Heaven. Baumann, H.
  In Baumann, H. The stolen fire p81-82
          398.2
Ethan Allen and the Green Mountain Boys.
   Brown, S.   92
Ethelred the Unready
    See pages in the following book:
Carter, S. Vikings bold: their voyages & ad-
   ventures p130-35 (5-7)   914.8
Ethics
Black, A. D. The first book of ethics (5-7) 170
Ethiopia
Perl, L. Ethiopia (5-7)   916.3
       Fiction
Coatsworth, E. The princess and the lion
   (4-6)   Fic
Hawes, J. The goats who killed the leopard E
       Folklore
    See Folklore—Ethiopia
       Religion
    See pages in the following book:
Perl, L. Ethiopia p61-83 (5-7)   916.3
    Social life and customs
Englebert, V. Camera on Africa (3-5)   916.3
Riwkin-Brick, A. Gennet lives in Ethiopia
   (2-4)   916.3
Ethiopian art. See Art, Ethiopian
Ethiopian-Italian War, 1935-1936. See Italo-
   Ethiopian War, 1935-1936
Ethiopian literature
    See pages in the following book:
Perl, L. Ethiopia p119-23 (5-7)   916.3
Ethiopian music. See Music, Ethiopian
Ethnic groups. See Minorities
Ethnology
    See also Acculturation; Anthropology;
   Archeology; Color of man; Costume; Folk-
   lore; Language and languages; Man, Pre-
   historic; Manners and customs; Race; To-
   tems and totemism; also names of races,
   tribes, and people, e.g. Negroes; and
   names of countries with the subdivision
   Social life and customs, e.g. United States
   —Social life and customs

       Polynesia
Heyerdahl, T. Kon-Tiki; edition for young
   people (4-7)   910.4
       Thailand
Cooke, D. C. The tribal people of Thailand
   (5-7)   301.2
Etiquette
Bendick, J. What to do (5-7)   395
Hoke, H. Etiquette (3-5)   395
Joslin, S. What do you do, dear? (k-3)   395
Joslin, S. What do you say, dear? (k-3)   395
Pitt, V. Let's find out about manners (2-4)
          395
Post, E. L. The Emily Post Book of etiquette
   for young people (5-7)   395
     See also Courtesy
Etruscan art. See Art, Etruscan
Ets, Marie Hall
Caldecott Medal acceptance paper
  In Kingman, L. ed. Newbery and Calde-
     cott Medal books: 1956-1965 p209-
     11   028.5
Gilberto and the Wind   E
In the forest   E
Just me   E
Mr T. W. Anthony Woo   E
Nine days to Christmas   E
Play with me   E
—Same
  In Johnson, E. ed. Anthology of children's
     literature p80-81   808.8
       About
    See pages in the following books:
Hoffman, M. ed. Authors and illustrators of
   children's books p141-48   028.5
Kingman, L. ed. Newbery and Caldecott
   Medal books: 1956-1965 p212-16   028.5
Smaridge, N. Famous author-illustrators for
   young people p62-69 (5-7)   920
Etymology. See English language—Etymology
Eudoxus
    See pages in the following book:
Diggins, J. E. String, straightedge, and
   shadow p126-34 (6-7)   516
Eui-hwan, Kim. See Kim, Eui-hwan
Eulenspiegel
Jagendorf, M. Tyll Ulenspiegel's merry pranks
   (4-6)   398.2
    See also pages in the following book:
Ward, W. ed. Stories to dramatize p176-81
          372.6
Europa
    See pages in the following book:
Gates, D. Lord of the sky: Zeus p43-50 (4-7)
          292
Europe
    Biography—Bibliography
Hotchkiss, J. European historical fiction and
   biography for children and young people
          016.8
       Festivals
  See Festivals—Europe
       Folklore
  See Folklore—Europe

Everybody needs a rock. Baylor, B.   **E**

Everything in its right place. Andersen, H. C.
In Andersen, H. C. The complete fairy tales and stories p416-23   **S C**

Everywhere Christmas. Very, A.
In Burack, A. S. ed. Christmas plays for young actors p187-96   **812.08**

Eve's various children. Grimm, J.
In Grimm, J. The complete Grimm's Fairy tales p734-36   **398.2**

Evil. See Good and evil

The **evil** king. Andersen, H. C.
In Andersen, H. C. The complete fairy tales and stories p592-94   **S C**

Evil spirits. See Demonology

Evolution
Cosgrove, M. Bone for bone (5-7)   **596**
Gallant, R. A. Charles Darwin: the making of a scientist (4-7)   **92**
May, J. How the animals came to North America (2-4)   **591.5**
See also Adaptation (Biology); Anatomy, Comparative; Biology; Color of animals; Color of man; Embryology; Heredity; Man—Origin and antiquity; Mendel's law

Ewbank, Constance
Insect zoo (4-7)   **595.7**

Ewing, Juliana Horatia
The hillman and the housewife
In Ward, W. ed. Stories to dramatize p102-03   **372.6**
The magician turned mischief-maker
In Green, R. L. ed. A cavalcade of magicians p200-05   **808.8**
The magician's gifts
In Green, R. L. ed. A cavalcade of magicians p190-99   **808.8**
Murdoch's Rath
In Sechrist, E. H. ed. It's time for story hour p180-86   **372.6**
The ogre courting
In Mayne, W. ed. William Mayne's Book of giants p161-69   **398.2**
Our field
In Authors' choice p159-70   **S C**
About
See pages in the following book:
Benét, L. Famous storytellers for young people p88-93 (5-7)   **920**

Exactly alike. Ness, E.   **E**

Excavations (Archeology)
Hall, J. Buried cities (5-7)   **913**
Washington (State)
Kirk, R. The oldest man in America (5-7)   **917.97**

Exchange of persons programs
See pages in the following book:
Sechrist, E. H. It's time for brotherhood p196-220 (5-7)   **301.11**

Excretion
Silverstein, A. The excretory system (4-6)   **574.1**

The **excretory** system. Silverstein, A.   **574.1**

Excuse me! Certainly! Slobodkin, L.   **E**

Executive ability. See Leadership

Exercise
Antonacci, R. J. Physical fitness for young champions (5-7)   **613.7**
Carr, R. Be a frog, a bird, or a tree (1-4)   **613.7**
Cheki Haney, E. Yoga for children (2-5)   **613.7**
Turner, A. K. Yoga for beginners (6-7)   **613.7**
See also Physical fitness

Exiles. See Refugees; Refugees, Jewish

Exotic fish as pets. Villiard, P.   **639**

Expeditions, Antarctic and Arctic. See Arctic regions

Experiments, Scientific. See Science—Experiments; and particular branches of science with subdivision Experiments, e.g. Chemistry—Experiments

Experiments in optical illusion. Beeler, N. F.   **535.072**

Experiments in the principles of space travel. Branley, F. M.   **629.4**

The **exploits** of Moominpappa. Jansson, T.   **Fic**

Exploration, Submarine. See Underwater exploration

Exploration, Underwater. See Underwater exploration

Explorations. See America—Discovery and exploration; Discoveries (in geography); Explorers

Explorations of Père Marquette. Kjelgaard, J.   **92**

Explorers
Aulaire, I. d'. Columbus (1-4)   **92**
Aulaire, I. d'. Leif the Lucky (2-4)   **92**
Buehr, W. The French explorers in America (4-6)   **973.1**
Buehr, W. The Portuguese explorers (4-6)   **910**
Buehr, W. The Spanish conquistadores in North America (4-7)   **973.1**
Buehr, W. The world of Marco Polo (4-6)   **92**
Cottler, J. Heroes of civilization (6-7)   **920**
Cottler, J. More Heroes of civilization (6-7)   **920**
Dalgliesh, A. The Columbus story (k-3)   **92**
Discoverers of the New World (5-7)   **973.1**
Grant, M. G. Leif Ericson (1-3)   **92**
Israel, C. E. Five ships west; the story of Magellan (4-6)   **92**
Jacobs, W. J. Hernando Cortes (4-6)   **92**
Jacobs, W. J. Samuel de Champlain (4-6)   **92**
Janeway, E. The Vikings [biography of Leif Ericsson] (4-6)   **92**
Kjelgaard, J. Explorations of Père Marquette (4-6)   **92**
Kurtz, H. I. John and Sebastian Cabot (4-6)   **92**
Marco Polo's adventures in China (5-7)   **92**
Ripley, S. N. Matthew Henson: Arctic hero (4-6)   **92**
Sperry, A. The voyages of Christopher Columbus (5-7)   **92**
Syme, R. Alexander Mackenzie, Canadian explorer (3-5)   **92**
Syme, R. Amerigo Vespucci, scientist and sailor (3-5)   **92**

Explorers—*Continued*

Syme, R. Balboa, finder of the Pacific (4-6) 92

Syme, R. Captain Cook, Pacific explorer (4-6) 92

Syme, R. Cartier, finder of the St Lawrence (4-6) 92

Syme, R. Champlain of the St Lawrence (4-6) 92

Syme, R. Columbus, finder of the New World (4-6) 92

Syme, R. Cortés of Mexico (4-6) 92

Syme, R. De Soto, finder of the Mississippi 92

Syme, R. Francisco Pizarro, finder of Peru (4-6) 92

Syme, R. Henry Hudson (4-6) 92

Syme, R. John Cabot and his son Sebastian (3-5) 92

Syme, R. John Charles Frémont (5-7) 92

Syme, R. La Salle of the Mississippi (4-7) 92

Syme, R. Magellan, first around the world (4-6) 92

Syme, R. Marquette and Joliet (3-5) 92

Syme, R. Vasco da Gama (4-6) 92

Syme, R. Verrazano: explorer of the Atlantic coast (4-6) 92

See also pages in the following book:

Hall, E. The land and people of Norway p40-51 (5-7) **914.81**

See also America—Discovery and exploration; Discoveries (in geography); Voyages and travels; also names of countries with the subdivision Description and travel, e.g. United States—Description and travel; and names of individual explorers

Explorers of the atom. Gallant, R. A. **539.7**

Exploring a coral reef. Burgess, R. F. **574.92**

Exploring as you walk in the city. Busch, P. S. **500.9**

Exploring as you walk in the meadow. Busch, P. S. **500.9**

Exploring expeditions. See names of expeditions, e.g. Lewis and Clark Expedition

Exploring the insect world. Andersen, M. J. **595.7**

Exploring the universe. Gallant, R. A. **523**

Exploring with a microscope. Simon, S. **578**

Express highways

See pages in the following book:

Tannenbaum, B. City traffic p30-39 (3-5) **388.4**

Express wagon. Baruch, D.
In Association for Childhood Education International. Told under the blue umbrella p8-9 **S C**

Expressways. See Express highways

Exquemelin, Alexandre Olivier

See pages in the following book:

Stockton, F. R. Buccaneers & pirates of our coasts p50-54 (5-7) **910.4**

The **exterior** decorator. Boiko, C.
In Boiko, C. Children's plays for creative actors p222-29 **812**

Extinct animals. See Rare animals; also names of extinct animals, e.g. Mastodon

Extinct cities. See Cities and towns, Ruined, extinct, etc.

Extinct plants. See Plants, Fossil

Extrasensory perception

Horwitz, E. L. The soothsayer's handbook: a guide to bad signs & good vibrations (5-7) **133.3**

Kettelkamp, L. Sixth sense (5-7) **133.8**

Extraterrestrial life. See Life on other planets

Eye

Adler, I. Your eyes (3-5) **612**

Schuman, B. N. The human eye (4-6) **612**

Showers, P. Look at your eyes (k-2) **612**

Ylla. Whose eye am I? (k-3) **591**

See also pages in the following book:

Kettelkamp, L. Tricks of eye and mind p17-28 (4-6) **535**

See also Vision

Eye winker, Tom Tinker, Chin chopper. Glazer, T. **796.1**

Eyeglasses

See also Lenses

Fiction

Raskin, E. Spectacles **E**

Eyre, Frank
British children's books in the twentieth century **028.5**

Ezra's Thanksgivin' out west. Field, E.
In Harper, W. comp. The harvest feast p226-38 **394.2**

F

FAO. See Food and Agriculture Organization of the United Nations

FLN. See National Liberation Front

Faber, Doris
A colony leader: Anne Hutchinson (4-6) **92**
Oh, Lizzie! The life of Elizabeth Cady Stanton (5-7) **92**
The perfect life (6-7) **289.8**

The **Faber** Book of nursery songs. See Mitchell, D. ed. Every child's book of nursery songs **784.6**

Fables

Babbitt, E. C. Jataka tales (1-3) **398.2**

Brown, M. Once a mouse (k-3) **398.2**

Cooney, B. Chanticleer and the fox **E**

Dana, D. The elephant and his secret **E**

De La Iglesia, M. E. The cat and the mouse, and other Spanish tales (2-4) **398.2**

DeRoin, N. ed. Jataka tales (3-5) **398.2**

Domanska, J. Look, there is a turtle flying (k-2) **398.2**

Du Bois, W. P. The hare and the tortoise & The tortoise and the hare (1-4) **398.2**

Evans, K. The boy who cried wolf (k-2) **398.2**

Gaer, J. The fables of India (5-7) **398.2**

Galdone, P. Androcles and the lion (k-3) **398.2**

Galdone, P. The monkey and the crocodile (k-2) **398.2**

Galdone, P. Three Aesop fox fables (k-3) **398.2**

Fairy tales—*Continued*

Lang, A. ed. The red fairy book (4-7) 398.2
Lang, A. ed. The yellow fairy book (4-7) 398.2
Lewis, C. S. The lion, the witch and the wardrobe (4-7) Fic
Lifton, B. J. The cock and the ghost cat (2-4) Fic
Lifton, B. J. The dwarf pine tree (2-4) Fic
Lindgren, A. The Tomten E
Lindgren, A. The Tomten and the fox E
Lobel, A. The troll music E
Macdonald, G. At the back of the North Wind (4-6) Fic
Macdonald, G. The light princess (3-6) Fic
Macdonald, G. The princess and the goblin (3-6) Fic
McGinley, P. The plain princess (2-4) Fic
MacManus, S. The bold heroes of Hungry Hill, and other Irish folk tales (5-7) 398.2
MacManus, S. Hibernian nights (4-7) 398.2
Manning-Sanders, R. A book of charms and changelings (3-6) 398.2
Manning-Sanders, R. A book of dragons (3-6) 398.2
Manning-Sanders, R. ed. A book of magical beasts (3-6) 398.2
Manning-Sanders, R. A book of mermaids (3-6) 398.2
Manning-Sanders, R. A book of ogres and trolls (3-6) 398.2
Manning-Sanders, R. A book of princes and princesses (3-6) 398.2
Manning-Sanders, R. A book of sorcerers and spells (3-6) 398.2
Manning-Sanders, R. A book of witches (3-6) 398.2
Manning-Sanders, R. A book of wizards (3-6) 398.2
Manning-Sanders, R. A choice of magic (3-6) 398.2
Manning-Sanders, R. Gianni and the ogre (4-6) 398.2
Mehdevi, A. S. Persian folk and fairy tales (4-6) 398.2
Mulock, D. M. The little lame prince (4-6) Fic
Nesbit, E. The complete book of dragons (3-6) S C
Ness, E. The girl and the goatherd E
Ness, E. Long, Broad & Quickeye (1-4) 398.2
Nic Leodhas, S. Heather and broom (4-7) 398.2
Nic Leodhas, S. Thistle and thyme (4-7) 398.2
Norton, M. Bed-knob and broomstick (3-5) Fic
Norton, M. The Borrowers (3-6) Fic
O'Faolain, E. Irish sagas and folk-tales (5-7) 398.2
Olenius, E. comp. Great Swedish fairy tales (4-7) 398.2
Opie, I. ed. The classic fairy tales 398.2
Pearce, P. Beauty and the beast (3-5) 398.2
Pearce, P. The squirrel wife (2-4) Fic
Perrault, C. Cinderella (k-3) 398.2
Perrault, C. Famous fairy tales (4-6) 398.2
Perrault, C. Perrault's Complete fairy tales (4-6) 398.2
Perrault, C. Puss in Boots (k-3) 398.2
Picard, B. L. The faun and the woodcutter's daughter (4-7) S C

Proysen, A. Little old Mrs Pepperpot, and other stories (1-3) S C
Pyle, H. King Stork (k-3) 398.2
Pyle, H. Pepper & salt (4-6) 398.2
Pyle, H. The wonder clock (4-6) 398.2
Rackham, A. comp. Arthur Rackham Fairy book (3-6) 398.2
Ransome, A. Old Peter's Russian tales (3-6) 398.2
Reeves, J. English fables and fairy stories (4-7) 398.2
Ritchie, A. The treasure of Li-Po (3-6) S C
Robertson, D. L. Fairy tales from Viet Nam (4-6) 398.2
Sakade, F. ed. Japanese children's favorite stories (2-4) 398.2
Sandburg, C. Rootabaga stories (5-7) S C
Schiller, B. The white rat's tale (k-3) 398.2
Sleigh, B. Carbonel, the King of the Cats (4-6) Fic
Stephens, J. Irish fairy tales (6-7) 398.2
Stockton, F. R. The Bee-man of Orn (4-6) Fic
Stockton, F. R. The Griffin and the Minor Canon (3-5) Fic
The Tall book of nursery tales (k-2) 398.2
The Three wishes (k-2) 398.2
Thurber, J. The great Quillow (3-5) Fic
Thurber, J. Many moons (1-4) Fic
Thurber, J. The 13 clocks (6-7) Fic
Thurber, J. The white deer (6-7) Fic
Tolkien, J. R. R. The hobbit (4-7) Fic
Tom Tit Tot (k-3) 398.2
Travers, P. L. Mary Poppins (4-6) Fic
Tregarthen, E. The doll who came alive (3-5) Fic
The Twelve dancing princesses (k-3) 398.2
Uchida, Y. The dancing kettle, and other Japanese folk tales (3-5) 398.2
Uchida, Y. The magic listening cap (3-5) 398.2
Undset, S. ed. True and untrue, and other Norse tales (4-7) 398.2
Warburg, S. S. On the way home (5-7) Fic
Wiesner, W. Hansel and Gretel: a shadow puppet picture book (1-4) 791.5
Wiggin, K. D. ed. The Arabian nights (5-7) 398.2
Wilde, O. The Happy Prince, and other stories (3-6) S C
Williams, J. Petronella (2-4) Fic
Williams, J. The practical princess (2-4) Fic
Williams, M. The velveteen rabbit (2-4) Fic
Williams-Ellis, A. Fairy tales from the British Isles (5-7) 398.2
Yolen, J. The bird of time E
Yolen, J. The girl who cried flowers, and other tales (4-6) S C
Zemach, H. Too much nose (k-3) 398.2

See also pages in the following books:

Arbuthnot, M. H. comp. The Arbuthnot Anthology of children's literature p148-413 808.8

Childcraft: the how and why library v2 031

Darrell, M. ed. Once upon a time p37-70 808.8

Johnson, E. ed. Anthology of children's literature p119-389 808.8

Tolstoy, L. Twenty-two Russian tales for young children p39-54 (3-5) S C
See also Folklore

Family—Fiction—*Continued*
Little, J. Look through my window (4-6) **Fic**
Murray, M. Nellie Cameron (4-6) **Fic**
Neufeld, J. Edgar Allan (5-7) **Fic**
Perl, L. That crazy April (5-7) **Fic**
Phipson, J. The family conspiracy (5-7) **Fic**
Raskin, E. Figgs & phantoms (5-7) **Fic**
Sachs, M. The truth about Mary Rose (4-7)
Fic
Segal, L. Tell me a Mitzi **E**
Smith, D. B. Tough Chauncey (5-7) **Fic**
Streatfeild, N. The family at Caldicott Place
(4-6) **Fic**
Terris, S. The drowning boy (6-7) **Fic**
Thrasher, C. The dark didn't catch me (5-7)
Fic
Vestly, A. C. Hello, Aurora (3-5) **Fic**
Walter, M. P. Lillie of Watts (3-5) **Fic**

Poetry
See pages in the following book:
Ferris, L. ed. Favorite poems, old and new
p29-57 (4-6) **808.81**
The **family** at Caldicott Place. Streatfeild, N.
Fic
A **family** book of nursery rhymes. Opie, I.
comp. **398.8**
The **family** conspiracy. Phipson, J. **Fic**
The **family** from One End Street, and some of
their adventures. Garnett, E. **Fic**
A **family** in space. Rittenhouse, C.
In Burack, A. S. ed. One hundred plays
for children p204-17 **808.82**
Family life and child development. Child Study
Association of America/Wel-Met. Book Re-
view Committee **016.3014**
Family life education. See Finance, Personal;
Human relations; Sex instruction
Family names. See Names, Personal
A **family** of foxes. Dillon, E. **Fic**
The **family** of Hen-Grethe. Andersen, H. C.
In Andersen, H. C. The complete fairy
tales and stories p954-66 **S C**
Family relations. See Domestic relations; Family
Famous American Negro poets. Rollins, C. **920**
Famous American Negroes. Hughes, L. **920**
Famous American trails. Grant, B. **973**
Famous author-illustrators for young people.
Smaridge, N. **920**
Famous custom & show cars. Barris, G. **629.22**
Famous fairy tales. Perrault, C. **398.2**
Famous first facts. Kane, J. N. **031**
Famous fossil finds. Holden, R. **560**
Famous French fairy tales. See Perrault, C.
Famous fairy tales **398.2**
Famous Mexican-Americans. Newlon, C. **920**
Famous Negro entertainers of stage, screen, and
TV. Rollins, C. **920**
Famous Negro heroes of America. Hughes, L.
920
Famous Negro music makers. Hughes, L. **920**
Famous pirates of the New World. Whipple,
A. B. C. **910.4**
Famous poets for young people. Benét, L. **920**

Famous storytellers for young people. Benét. L.
920
Famous U.S. Air Force bombers. Cooke, D. C.
623.74
Famous U.S. Navy fighter planes. Cooke, D. C.
623.74
Fancy dress. See Costume
Fancy free. Untermeyer, L.
In Untermeyer, L. Tales from ballet p88
792.8
The **Fannie** Farmer Junior cook book. Perkins,
W. L. **641.5**
Fanny Kemble's America. Scott, J. A. **92**
Fantastic fiction
Cooper, S. The dark is rising (5-7) **Fic**
Cooper, S. Greenwitch (5-7) **Fic**
Cooper, S. Over sea, under stone (5-7) **Fic**
Cresswell, H. The night watchmen (4-6) **Fic**
Cresswell, H. Up the pier (4-6) **Fic**
Curry, J. L. Beneath the hill (4-7) **Fic**
Curry, J. L. The daybreakers (4-7) **Fic**
Dickinson, P. The Devil's children (5-7) **Fic**
Dickinson, P. Heartsease (5-7) **Fic**
Dickinson, P. The weathermonger (5-7) **Fic**
Farmer, P. Charlotte sometimes (5-7) **Fic**
Garner, A. The moon of Gomrath (5-7) **Fic**
Hunter, M. The haunted mountain (5-7) **Fic**
Hunter, M. The walking stones (5-7) **Fic**
Le Guin, U. K. The farthest shore (6-7) **Fic**
Le Guin, U. K. The tombs of Atuan (6-7) **Fic**
Le Guin, U. K. A wizard of Earthsea (6-7)
Fic
L'Engle, M. A wind in the door (6-7) **Fic**
L'Engle, M. A wrinkle in time (6-7) **Fic**
Mayne, W. Earthfasts (3-5) **Fic**
Nichols, R. A walk out of the world (4-6) **Fic**
Ormondroyd, E. Time at the top (5-7) **Fic**
Pearce, A. P. Tom's midnight garden (4-7)
Fic
Phipson, J. The way home (5-7) **Fic**
Sauer, J. L. Fog magic (4-6) **Fic**
Snyder, Z. K. Black and blue magic (4-6) **Fic**
Turkle, B. Mooncoin Castle (4-6) **Fic**
Winterfeld, H. Castaways in Lilliput (4-6) **Fic**
See also pages in the following books:
Arbuthnot, M. H. comp. The Arbuthnot An-
thology of children's literature p476-599
808.8
Johnson, E. ed. Anthology of children's litera-
ture p607-750 **808.8**
See also Ghost stories; Science fiction

History and criticism
See pages in the following book:
Haviland, V. ed. Children and literature
p231-49 **028.5**
Far and few. McCord, D. **811**
The **far**-off land. Caudill, R. **Fic**
Far out the long canal. DeJong, M. **Fic**
Faraday, Michael
See pages in the following books:
Asimov, I. Breakthroughs in science p67-75
(5-7) **920**
Cottler, J. More Heroes of civilization p188-
97 (6-7) **920**

Farb, Peter
Face of North America. Young readers' edition. (6-7)   500.9
The land, wildlife, and peoples of the Bible (5-7)   220.8
The story of dams (5-7)   627

Farber, Norma
Where's Gomer?   E

Farjeon, Eleanor
Bertha Goldfoot
    In Colwell, E. ed. A second storyteller's choice p59-66   372.6
The birth of Simnel cake
    In Greene, E. comp. Clever cooks p130-33
                                                      398.2
(ed.) A cavalcade of kings (5-7)   808.8
(ed.) A cavalcade of queens (4-7)   808.8
Cherrystones
    In Farjeon, E. Then there were three p 9-61   821
The children's bells (3-6)   821
Come Christmas
    In Farjeon, E. Eleanor Farjeon's Poems for children p197-229   821
Eleanor Farjeon's Poems for children (3-5)
                                                        821
Elsie Piddock skips in her sleep
    In Association for Childhood Education International. Told under the magic umbrella p217-37   S C
    In Colwell, E. ed. A storyteller's choice p13-29   372.6
Faithful Jenny Dove
    In Ireson, B. comp. Haunting tales p174-94
                                                        S C
The franklin's tale
    In Green, R. L. ed. A cavalcade of magicians p95-105   808.8
The giant and the mite
    In Mayne, W. ed. William Mayne's Book of giants p211-15   398.2
The glass peacock
    In Authors' choice p139-47   S C
Joan's door
    In Farjeon, E. Eleanor Farjeon's Poems for children p155-95   821
The lady's room
    In Tashjian, V. A. ed. With a deep sea smile p82-85   372.6
The little bookroom (1-4)   S C
Contents: King and the corn; King's daughter cries for the moon; Young Kate; Flower without a name; The goldfish; Clumber Pup; Miracle of the poor island; Girl who kissed the peach-tree; Westwoods; The barrel-organ; Giant and the mite; Little dressmaker; Lady's room; Seventh princess; Leaving paradise; Little lady's roses; In those days; Connemara donkey; The Tims; Pennyworth; And I dance mine own child; The lovebirds; San Fairy Ann; Glass peacock; Kind farmer; Old Surly and the boy; Pannychis
Little Boy Pie
    In Gruenberg, S. M. ed. Favorite stories old and new p244-49   808.8
Martin Pippin in the apple orchard (2-4) S C
Contents: The King's barn; Young Gerard; The Mill of Dreams; Open Winkins; Proud Rosalind and the hart-royal; The imprisoned princess
The miracle of the Poor Island
    In Farjeon, E. ed. A cavalcade of queens p52-62   808.8
The mulberry bush
    In Farjeon, E. Then there were three p62-117   821

The new book of days (5-7)   828
Over the garden wall
    In Farjeon, E. Eleanor Farjeon's Poems for children p81-153   821
A prayer for little things (k-3)   242
The princess of China
    In Johnson, S. P. ed. The Princesses p68-75   S C
St Nicholas
    In Johnson, E. ed. Anthology of children's literature p594-97   808.8
Sing for your supper
    In Farjeon, E. Eleanor Farjeon's Poems for children p15-79   821
The starry floor
    In Farjeon, E. Then there were three p119-74   821
Then there were three (4-7)   821
Westwoods
    In Farjeon, E. ed. A cavalcade of kings p68-93   808.8

About
See pages in the following books:
Benét, L. Famous poets for young people p113-18 (5-7)   920
A Horn Book Sampler on children's books and reading p255-58   028.5
Sayers, F. C. Summoned by books p122-32
                                                      028.5

Farley, Walter
The Black Stallion (4-7)   Fic
Little Black, a pony   E

Farm animals. See Domestic animals; Livestock

Farm crops. See Farm produce

Farm life
Hawkinson, L. Picture book farm   E
Canada
Kurelek, W. A prairie boy's summer (3-5)
                                                  917.127
Kurelek, W. A prairie boy's winter (3-5)
                                                  917.127
Fiction
Aulaire, I. d'. Don't count your chicks   E
Blegvad, L. Moon-watch summer (3-5)   Fic
Burch, R. D.J.'s worst enemy (4-6)   Fic
Caudill, R. A pocketful of cricket   E
Clymer, E. Me and the Eggman (3-6)   Fic
De Angeli, M. Yonie Wondernose (1-4)   Fic
DeJong, M. Puppy summer (4-6)   Fic
Engebrecht, P. A. Under the haystack (5-7)
                                                        Fic
Enright, E. Thimble summer (4-6)   Fic
Hunt, I. Across five Aprils (6-7)   Fic
Seredy, K. The Good Master (4-6)   Fic
Seredy, K. The singing tree (4-6)   Fic
Unnerstad, E. The spettecake holiday (4-6)
                                                        Fic
White, A. H. Junket, the dog who liked everything "just so" (4-6)   Fic
Winthrop, E. Walking away (5-7)   Fic

Farm produce
Sullivan, G. How do they grow it? (5-7)
                                                      631.5

Farmer, Penelope
Charlotte sometimes (5-7)   Fic
Charlotte sometimes; excerpt

Fate of the children of Lir—*Continued*
O'Faolain, E. Children of Lir
In O'Faolain, E. Irish sagas and folktales
p27-39   398.2
Young, E. The children of Lir
In Johnson, E. ed. Anthology of children's
literature p224-29   808.8
Fate of the sons of Usnach. O'Faolain, E.
In O'Faolain, E. Irish sagas and folktales
p88-100   398.2
Father Bear comes home. Minarik, E. H.   E
Father Catfish. Vo-Dinh
In Vo-Dinh. The toad is the Emperor's
uncle p23-27   398.2
Father Christmas. Briggs, R.   E
Father Fox's pennyrhymes. Watson, C.   811
Father hits the jackpot. Garver, J.
In Kamerman, S. E. ed. Fifty plays for
junior actors p222-35   812.08
A **father-in-law** and his son-in-law. Cour-
lander, H.
In Courlander, H. The king's drum, and
other African stories p71-73   398.2
Father in the laundry room. Vestly, A. C.
In Arbuthnot, M. H. comp. The Arbuthnot
Anthology of children's literature
p701-05   808.8
A **father** like that. Zolotow, C.   E
Father of the family
Asbjørnsen, P. C. The seventh father of the
house
In Asbjørnsen, P. C. Norwegian folk tales
p13-14   398.2
Fathers
Fiction
Zolotow, C. A father like that   E
Father's Day
Poetry
See pages in the following book:
Sechrist, E. H. comp. Poems for red letter
days p151-54   821.08
Father's Day. Taber, G.
In Cavanah, F. ed. Holiday roundup p174-
76   394.2
The **father's legacy.** Kim, S.
In Kim, S. The story bag p186-98   398.2
Fatio, Louise
The happy lion   E
The happy lion in Africa   E
The three happy lions   E
Faulhaber, Martha
(jt. auth.) Hawkinson, J. Music and instru-
ments for children to make   781
(jt. auth.) Hawkinson, J. Rhythms, music and
instruments to make   781
Faulkner, Georgene
Melindy's medal (3-5)   Fic
The **faun** and the woodcutter's daughter. Picard,
B. L.   S C
The **faun** and the woodcutter's daughter; story.
Picard, B. L.
In Picard, B. L. The faun and the wood-
cutter's daughter p 7-25   S C
Fauna. See Animals

Faust; adaptation. Bulla, C. R.
In Bulla, C. R. Stories of favorite operas
p169-77   782.1
Favorite American songs, The fireside book of.
Boni, M. B. ed   784
Favorite children's stories from China and Tibet.
Hume, L. C.   398.2
Favorite fairy tales told in Czechoslovakia.
Haviland, V.   398.2
Favorite fairy tales told in Denmark. Havi-
land, V.   398.2
Favorite fairy tales told in France. Haviland, V.
398.2
Favorite fairy tales told in Germany. Havi-
land, V.   398.2
Favorite fairy tales told in Greece. Haviland, V.
398.2
Favorite fairy tales told in India. Haviland, V.
398.2
Favorite fairy tales told in Ireland. Haviland, V.
398.2
Favorite fairy tales told in Italy. Haviland, V.
398.2
Favorite fairy tales told in Japan. Haviland, V.
398.2
Favorite fairy tales told in Norway. Haviland, V.
398.2
Favorite fairy tales told in Poland. Haviland, V.
398.2
Favorite fairy tales told in Russia. Haviland, V.
398.2
Favorite fairy tales told in Scotland. Havi-
land, V.   398.2
Favorite fairy tales told in Spain. Haviland, V.
398.2
Favorite fairy tales told in Sweden. Haviland, V.
398.2
Favorite horse stories, C. W. Anderson's. Ander-
son, C. W. ed.   808.8
Favorite poems, old and new. Ferris, H. ed.
808.81
Favorite stories old and new. Gruenberg, S. M.
ed.   808.8
Fawcett, Margaret Georgia
The talking Christmas tree
In Kamerman, S. E. ed. A treasury of
Christmas plays p398-403   812.08
Fawn in the woods. Eberle, I.   599
Fax, E. C.
(illus.) Faulkner, G. Melindy's medal   Fic
Fax, Elton
(illus.) Aardema, V. Tales from the story hat
398.2
(illus.) Courlander, H. Terrapin's pot of sense
398.2
Fay, Maxine
Saving the old homestead
In Kamerman, S. E. ed. Fifty plays for
junior actors p189-202   812.08
Feagles, Anita
Autun and the bear (2-4)   398.2
He who saw everything (4-6)   892

Fear

Fiction

Blume, J. Otherwise known as Sheila the Great (4-6)　**Fic**

Byars, B. The 18th emergency (4-6)　**Fic**

Norris, G. B. Green and something else (3-5)　**Fic**

Fear. Hardendorff, J. B.

In Hardendorff, J. B. Witches, wit, and a werewolf p67-75　**S C**

Fearing the wind

In DeRoin, N. ed. Jataka tales p6-7 **398.2**

Fearless Emma. Jagendorf, M. A.

In Jagendorf, M. A. Folk stories of the South p4-9　**398.2**

Fearless Nancy Hart. Jagendorf, M. A.

In Jagendorf, M. A. Folk stories of the South p118-20　**398.2**

The **fearsome** inn. Singer, I. B.　**Fic**

Feaser, Daniel D.

(illus.) Peterson, H. L. Forts in America **623**

(illus.) Peterson, H. L. A history of body armor　**623.4**

(illus.) Peterson, H. L. A history of knives **683**

The **feast.** Bowman, J. C.

In Bowman, J. C. Tales from a Finnish tupa p245-46　**398.2**

The **feast.** Courlander, H.

In Courlander, H. The king's drum, and other African stories p56-57　**398.2**

Feast of lights. See Hanukkah (Feast of lights)

Feast of Thanksgiving. Behrens, J.　**812**

The **Feast** of the Thousand Lanterns. Huff, B. T.

In Kamerman, S. E. ed. Fifty plays for junior actors p271-79　**812.08**

Feather, Jean

One wish too many

In Kamerman, S. E. ed. Dramatized folk tales of the world p191-99　**812.08**

Quick-witted Jack

In Kamerman, S. E. ed. Dramatized folk tales of the world p400-12　**812.08**

Feathered ones and furry. Fisher, A.　**811**

Feathers

See pages in the following books:

Mason, G. F. Animal clothing p38-50 (4-7)　**591.4**

Mason, G. F. Animal tails p68-79 (4-7) **591.4**

Feboldson, Febold

See pages in the following book:

Malcolmson, A. Yankee Doodle's cousins p173-80 (4-7)　**398.2**

Fedelma the Enchanter's daughter. Colum, P.

In Colum, P. The King of Ireland's Son p2-50　**398.2**

Fedor and the fairy. Manning-Sanders, R.

In Manning-Sanders, R. A book of charms and changelings p56-61　**398.2**

Fee fi fo fum. Briggs, R.　**398.8**

Feeble-minded. See Mentally handicapped

Feeding the city. Tannenbaum, B.　**338.1**

The **feel** of things. Phillips, M. G.

In Association for Childhood Education International. Told under the blue umbrella p25-29　**S C**

Feeling. See Touch

Feelings, Muriel

Jambo means hello　**E**

Moja means one　**E**

Zamani goes to market　**E**

Feelings, Tom

Black pilgrimage (5-7)　**92**

(illus.) Blue, R. A quiet place　**Fic**

(illus.) Feelings, M. Jambo means hello　**E**

(illus.) Feelings, M. Moja means one　**E**

(illus.) Feelings, M. Zamani goes to market **E**

(illus.) Garfield, N. The Tuesday elephant **Fic**

(illus.) Heady, E. B. When the stones were soft　**398.2**

(illus.) Kerina, J. African crafts　**745.5**

(illus.) Lester, J. To be a slave　**326**

(illus.) McKown, R. The Congo: river of mystery　**916.75**

(illus.) Molarsky, O. Song of the empty bottles　**Fic**

Feelings. See Emotions

Feerick, Emalie P.

(jt. auth.) Feerick, J. D. The Vice-Presidents of the United States　**920**

Feerick, John D.

The Vice-Presidents of the United States (4-6)　**920**

Feet. See Foot

Feet for all. Kelsey, A. G.

In Kelsey, A. G. Once the Hodja p116-22　**398.2**

Feldman, Anne

The inflated dormouse (6-7)　**591.5**

Feldman Fieldmouse. Benchley, N.　**Fic**

Felice. Brown, M.　**E**

Felicia and the pot of pinks. Aulnoy, Madame la Comtesse d'

In Lang, A. ed. The blue fairy book p148-56　**398.2**

See also Fortunée

Felicia the critic. Conford, E.　**Fic**

Fellows, Muriel

The rabbit hunt

In Gruenberg, S. M. ed. Favorite stories old and new p44-46　**808.8**

Fell's United States coin book. Andrews, C. J.　**737.4**

Felt, Make it with. Newsome, A. J.　**745.5**

Felton, Harold W.

Bowleg Bill, seagoing cowpuncher (5-7)　**398.2**

(ed.) Cowboy jamboree: western songs & lore　**784.4**

Edward Rose: Negro trail blazer (5-7)　**92**

James Weldon Johnson (4-6)　**92**

Jim Beckwourth, Negro mountain man (5-7)　**92**

John Henry and his hammer (5-7)　**398.2**

Mike Fink, best of the keelboatmen (5-7)　**398.2**

Mumbet: the story of Elizabeth Freeman (4-6)　**92**

Nat Love, Negro cowboy (4-6)　**92**

New tall tales of Pecos Bill (5-7)　**398.2**

Pecos Bill and the mustang (k-3)　**398.2**

Pecos Bill, Texas cowpuncher (5-7)　**398.2**

Festivals—*Continued*

Brazil

See pages in the following book:

Sheppard, S. The first book of Brazil p67-73 (4-6)   **918.1**

Canada

Meyer, R. Festivals U.S.A. & Canada   **394.2**

Ceylon

See pages in the following book:

Wilber, D. N. The land and people of Ceylon p103-09 (5-7)   **915.49**

Europe

Epstein, S. European folk festivals (2-4)   **394.2**

Fiction

Charlip, R. Harlequin and the gift of many colors   **E**

Germany

See pages in the following book:

Lobsenz, N. M. The first book of West Germany p55-69 (4-7)   **914.3**

Japan

See pages in the following book:

Vaughan, J. B. The land and people of Japan p62-75 (5-7)   **915.2**

Jews

See Fasts and feasts—Judaism

Mexico

Marcus, R. B. Fiesta time in Mexico (4-6)   **394.2**

Peru

See pages in the following book:

Bleeker, S. The Inca p122-27 (4-6)   **980.3**

Syria

See pages in the following book:

Copeland, P. W. The land and people of Syria p47-53 (5-7)   **915.691**

United States

Meyer, R. Festivals U.S.A. & Canada   **394.2**

Festivals. Manning-Sanders, R. ed.   **394.2**

Festivals for you to celebrate. Purdy, S.   **394.2**

Festivals U.S.A. & Canada. Meyer, R.   **394.2**

Fetterman Fight, 1866

Goble, P. Brave Eagle's account of the Fetterman Fight, 21 December 1866 (5-7)   **978.7**

Fetz, Ingrid

(illus.) Brewton, S. comp. Laughable limericks   **821.08**

(illus.) Clymer, E. The spider, the cave and the pottery bowl   **Fic**

(illus.) Durham, J. Me and Arch and the Pest   **Fic**

(illus.) Fox, P. Maurice's room   **Fic**

(illus.) Lovelace, M. H. The Valentine Box   **Fic**

(illus.) Showers, P. Before you were a baby   **612.6**

Feudalism

Unstead, R. J. Living in a castle (4-6)   **940.1**

See also pages in the following books:

Arbuthnot, M. H. comp. The Arbuthnot Anthology of children's literature p864-66   **808.8**

Buehr, W. Knights and castles, and feudal life p7-25 (4-7)   **940.1**

Duggan, A. Growing up with the Norman Conquest p3-50 (6-7)   **914.2**

Feuerlicht, Herbert A.

(illus.) Feuerlicht, R. S. Zhivko of Yugoslavia   **914.97**

Feuerlicht, Roberta Strauss

Zhivko of Yugoslavia (3-6)   **914.97**

Fever

Berry, J. R. Why you feel hot, why you feel cold (2-4)   **612**

See also names of fevers, e.g. Malaria

A few fair days. Gardam, J.   **Fic**

Fey, James T.

Long, short, high, low, thin, wide (1-3)   **389**

Fez, Morocco

See pages in the following book:

Spencer, W. The land and people of Morocco p42-47, 120-31 (5-7)   **916.4**

Fiammenghi, Gioia

(illus.) Fisher, A. Skip around the year   **811**

(illus.) Froman, R. Bigger and smaller   **513**

(illus.) Gaeddert, L. Noisy Nancy Norris   **E**

(illus.) Moore, L. Little Raccoon and the thing in the pool   **E**

(illus.) Sherlock, Sir P. The iguana's tail **398.2**

Fibers

Adler, I. Fibers (3-6)   **677**

See also Cotton; Paper; Wool

Fichter, George S.

Cats (5-7)   **599**

Fiction

See also Fables; Fantastic fiction; Ghost stories; Historical fiction; Science fiction; Sea stories

Bibliography

Rosenberg, J. K. Young people's literature in series: fiction   **016.8**

See also pages in the following books:

Feminists on Children's Media. Little Miss Muffet fights back p18-37   **028.52**

National Council of Teachers of English. Adventuring with books p44-174   **028.52**

Fiction, Historical. *See* Historical fiction

Fictitious animals. *See* Animals, Mythical

Fiddivaw. Hatch, M. C.

In Hatch, M. C. More Danish tales p138-49   **398.2**

The fiddler going home. Manning-Sanders, R.

In Manning-Sanders, R. Gianni and the ogre p173-78   **398.2**

The Fiddler of Echternach

In Courlander, H. ed. Ride with the sun p169-72   **398.2**

The fiddler of High Lonesome. Turkle, B.   **Fic**

Fiddler, play fast, play faster. Sawyer, R.

In Ireson, B. comp. Haunting tales p203-10   **S C**

Fiddler's Rock. Jagendorf, M. A.

In Jagendorf, M. A. Folk stories of the South p236-39   **398.2**

Fidelio; adaptation. Bulla, C. R.

In Bulla, C. R. More Stories of favorite operas p17-29   **782.1**

Fidell, Estelle A.
(ed.) Play index, 1953-1960. See Play index, 1953-1960 **808.82**
(ed.) Play index, 1961-1967. See Play index, 1961-1967 **808.82**
(ed.) Play index, 1968-1972. See Play index, 1968-1972 **808.82**

Fiefs. See Feudalism

Field, Carolyn W.
(ed.) Subject collections in children's literature **028.52**

Field, Cyrus West
Latham, J. L. Young man in a hurry (5-7) **92**
Nathan, A. G. The first transatlantic cable (5-7) **621.382**

Field, Edward
(ed.) Eskimo songs and stories (3-7) **398.2**

Field, Elinor Whitney
Neighborhood stories by Mrs. A. D. T. Whitney
In Andrews, S. ed. The Hewins lectures, 1947-1962 p107-26 **028.5**
(ed.) Horn Book Reflections on children's books and reading. See Horn Book Reflections on children's books and reading **028.5**
(jt. ed.) Miller, B. M. ed. Caldecott Medal books: 1938-1957 **028.5**
(jt. ed.) Miller, B. M. ed. Newbery Medal books: 1922-1955 **028.5**

Field, Eugene
Barbara; play. See McGowan, J. The coming of the Prince
Ezra's Thanksgivin' out West
In Harper, W. comp. The harvest feast p226-38 **394.2**
The mouse and the moonbeam; abridged
In Harper, W. comp. Merry Christmas to you p185-93 **394.2**
Mouse that didn't believe in Christmas
In Association for Childhood Education International. Told under the Christmas tree p46-53 **808.8**
The mouse that didn't believe in Santa Claus
In Reeves, J. comp. The Christmas book p68-73 **394.2**
Poems of childhood (3-5) **811**
About
See pages in the following book:
Benét, L. Famous poets for young people p82-90 (5-7) **920**

Field, Rachel
All through the night; excerpt
In Association for Childhood Education International. Told under the Christmas tree p9-17 **808.8**
Calico bush (4-7) **Fic**
Calico bush; excerpt
In Arbuthnot, M. H. comp. The Arbuthnot Anthology of children's literature p745-48 **808.8**
Christmas in London
In Dalgliesh, A. comp. Christmas p189-204 **394.2**
In Tudor, T. ed. Take joy! p32-42 **394.2**
Hitty: her first hundred years (4-7) **Fic**
I go up in the world and am glad to come down again
In Johnson, E. ed. Anthology of children's literature p799-804 **808.8**

Newbery Medal acceptance paper
In Miller, B. M. ed. Newbery Medal books: 1922-1955 p86-88 **028.5**
Old Gally Mander
In Hoke, H. ed. Witches, witches, witches p15-18 **808.8**
Poems (2-5) **811**
Prayer for a child (k-3) **242**
Taxis and toadstools (2-5) **811**
Winter
In Arbuthnot, M. H. comp. The Arbuthnot Anthology of children's literature p745-48 **808.8**
Aulnoy, Comtesse d'. The White Cat, and other old French fairy tales **398.2**
About
See pages in the following books:
Andrews, S. ed. The Hewins lectures, 1947-1962 p343-75 **028.5**
Benét, L. Famous poets for young people p123-28 (5-7) **920**
Miller, B. M. ed. Newbery Medal books: 1922-1955 p76-85 **028.5**

The field; short story. Roiphe, A.
In Free to be . . . you and me p96-99 **810.8**

Field athletics. See Track athletics

Field book of common rocks and minerals. Loomis, F. B. **549**

Field book of insects of the United States and Canada. Lutz, F. E. **595.7**

A **field** guide to animal tracks. Murie, O. J. **591.5**

A **field** guide to reptiles and amphibians of Eastern and Central North America. Conant, R. **598.1**

A **field** guide to rocks and minerals. Pough, F. H. **549**

A **field** guide to the birds. Peterson, R. T. **598.2**

A **field** guide to the butterflies of North America, east of the Great Plains. Klots, A. B. **595.7**

A **field** guide to the mammals. Burt, W. H. **599**

A **field** guide to trees and shrubs. Petrides, G. A. **582**

A **field** guide to Western birds. Peterson, R. T. **598.2**

The **field** of Boliauns. Williams-Ellis, A.
In Williams-Ellis, A. Fairy tales from the British Isles p135-39 **398.2**

Fieldbook. Boy Scouts of America **369.43**

Fields, Mary
Burt, O. W. Negroes in the early West p85-90 (4-6) **920**

Fierce John. Fenton, E. **E**

The **fierce** yellow pumpkin. Brown, M. W.
In Gruenberg, S. M. ed. Favorite stories old and new p231-33 **808.8**

The **fiery** dragon. Nesbit, E.
In Green, R. L. ed. A cavalcade of dragons p185-202 **808.8**
In Nesbit, E. The complete book of dragons p119-40 **S C**

A **fiesta** of folk songs from Spain and Latin America. Yurchenco, H. ed. **784.7**

The first four years. Wilder, L. I. See note under Wilder, L. I. Little house in the big woods   **Fic**

First graces   **249**

First guide to rocks, The Doubleday. Shuttlesworth, D.   **552**

First humming bird
Belpré, P. The legend of the hummingbird
    In Belpré, P. Once in Puerto Rico p25-28   **398.2**

A first look at birds. Selsam, M. E.   **598.2**

A first look at psychology. Kohn, B.   **150**

The first men. May, J.   **573.2**

The first New England Christmas tree. Colbo, E. S.
    In Burack, A. S. ed. One hundred plays for children p507-17   **808.82**

The first New England dinner. Warren, M. R.
    In Harper, W. comp. The harvest feast p27-36   **394.2**

The first of May. Haviland, V.
    In Haviland, V. Favorite fairy tales told in Greece p71-81   **398.2**

The First old man and the hind
    In Lang, A. ed. Arabian nights p12-16   **398.2**

The first overland mail. Pinkerton, R.   **383**

First prayers   **242**

The first shlemiel. Singer, I. B.
    In Singer, I. B. Zlateh the goat, and other stories p55-65   **398.2**

First snow. Coutant, H.   **Fic**

The first spell. Lee, J.
    In Hoke, H. ed. Spooks, spooks, spooks p147-56   **S C**

First steps in ballet. Mara, T.   **792.8**

The first tale of Alabama. Jagendorf, M. A.
    In Jagendorf, M. A. Folk stories of the South p3-4   **398.2**

The first Thanksgiving. Barksdale, L.   **394.2**

The first tinsel. Carlson, B. W.
    In Carlson, B. W. Let's pretend it happened to you p44-52   **792**

The first transatlantic cable. Nathan, A. G.   **621.382**

The first war. Baker, B.
    In Baker, B. At the center of the world p43-49   **398.2**

The First woman
    In McDowell, R. E. ed. Third World voices for children p119-29   **398.2**

The first woman to say "dim". Courlander, H.
    In Courlander, H. Olode the hunter, and other tales from Nigeria p121-23   **398.2**

The first year. Meadowcroft, E. L.   **Fic**

Fischel, Lillian
(illus.) Simon, S. The wise men of Helm and their merry tales   **S C**

Fischer, Hans
Puss in Boots (k-2)   **398.2**
(illus.) Grimm, J. The traveling musicians   **398.2**

Fischstrom, Margot (Zemach)
    See pages in the following book:
Kingman, L. ed. Newbery and Caldecott Medal books: 1966-1975 p260-64   **028.5**
    For titles by this author see Zemach, Margot

Fish, Helen Dean
(comp.) Four & twenty blackbirds (k-3) **398.8**
(ed.) Bible. Selections. Animals of the Bible   **220.8**

Fish. See Fishes

Fish and the ring
Colwell, E. The fish and the ring
    In Colwell, E. Round about and long ago p46-50   **398.2**
Fish and the ring
    In Jacobs, J. ed. English folk and fairy tales p199-203   **398.2**
Reeves, J. The fish and the ring
    In Reeves, J. English fables and fairy stories p35-48   **398.2**

The fish angel. Levoy, M.
    In Levoy, M. The witch of Fourth Street, and other stories p75-83   **S C**

Fish as food. See Sea food

Fish culture
    See pages in the following book:
Raskin, E. World food p131-39 (5-7)   **338.1**

Fish friends. Stoutenburg, A.
    In Stoutenburg, A. American tall-tale animals p54-67   **398.2**

Fish hatcheries. See Fish culture

Fish in the forest. Corson, H. W.
    In Burack, A. S. ed. Popular plays for classroom reading p45-55   **808.82**
    In Kamerman, S. E. ed. Dramatized folk tales of the world p388-99   **812.08**

Fish is fish. Lionni, L.   **E**

The fish with the deep sea smile. Brown, M. W.
    In Gruenberg, S. M. ed. Favorite stories old and new p503-04   **808.8**

Fisher, Aileen
Angel in the looking-glass
    In Burack, A. S. ed. Christmas plays for young actors p125-35   **812.08**
Arbor Day (1-3)   **394.2**
Cricket in a thicket (k-3)   **811**
Do bears have mothers, too? (k-2)   **811**
Easter (1-3)   **394.2**
Feathered ones and furry (k-3)   **811**
Going barefoot   **E**
Holiday programs for boys and girls (4-7) **812**
Contains the following plays: The weaver's son; Day of destiny; Three and the dragon; A play without a name; Ghosts on guard; The voice of liberty; Once upon a time; Treasure hunt; Mother of Thanksgiving; Unexpected guests; Angel in the looking-glass; The merry Christmas Elf; Time out for Christmas; Christmas tree for Kitty; Abe's winkin' eye; New hearts for old; Hearts, tarts, and valentines; Washington marches on; On strike; Mother's Day off and on; Caves of the earth
Human Rights Day (1-3)   **394.2**
I like weather   **E**
In one door and out the other (1-3)   **811**
In the middle of the night   **E**
In the woods, in the meadow, in the sky (k-3)   **811**
Jeanne d'Arc [biography of Joan of Arc, Saint] (3-5)   **92**

The flail from heaven. Grimm, J.
In Grimm, J. The complete Grimm's Fairy
tales p514-15   **398.2**

Flaming arrows. Steele, W. O.   **Fic**

Flaming tales. Jagendorf, M. A.
In Jagendorf, M. A. The gypsies' fiddle,
and other gypsy tales p148-51 **398.2**

Flanagan, Geraldine Lux
Window into an egg (4-6)   **574.3**

Flanders

Legends

See Legends—Flanders

Flash. Harris, L. D.   **595.7**

Flash, crash, rumble, and roll. Branley, F. M.
    551.5

Flashes and flags. Coggins, J.   **384**

Flashlights
See pages in the following book:
Wyler, R. What happens if . . ? p22-39 (2-4)
    507.2

Flavoring essences
Cooper, E. K. And everything nice (3-5)
    641.3

The flax. Andersen, H. C.
In Andersen, H. C. The complete fairy
tales and stories p369-73   **S C**

Flax leavings
Grimm, J. The hurds
In Grimm, J. The complete Grimm's Fairy
tales p656-57   **398.2**
Grimm, J. Lucky scraps
In Grimm, J. More Tales from Grimm p59-
60   **398.2**

Flaxen thread. Duvoisin, R.
In Duvoisin, R. The three sneezes, and
other Swiss tales p167-77   **398.2**

The flea. Haviland, V.
In Haviland, V. Favorite fairy tales told
in Spain p3-17   **398.2**

The flea. Sawyer, R.
In Johnson, E. ed. Anthology of children's
literature p233-36   **808.8**

Fleabane
See pages in the following book:
Wright, R. H. What good is a weed? p98-109
(4-6)   **581.5**

Fleas
Cole, J. Fleas (3-6)   **595.7**

Fleischman, Albert Sidney. See Fleischman,
Sid

Fleischman, Sid
By the Great Horn Spoon! (4-6)   **Fic**
Chancy and the grand rascal (4-6)   **Fic**
The ghost in the noonday sun (4-6)   **Fic**
The ghost on Saturday night (3-5)   **Fic**
Jingo Django (4-6)   **Fic**
Mr Mysterious & Company (4-6)   **Fic**
Saved by a whisker
In Johnson, E. ed. Anthology of children's
literature p787-91   **808.8**

Fleishman, Seymour
(illus.) Carmer, C. The boy drummer of Vincennes   **811**
(illus.) Thayer, J. The puppy who wanted a
boy   **E**

(illus.) Thayer, J. Quiet on account of dinosaur   **E**

Fleming, Sir Alexander
See pages in the following books:
Cottler, J. More Heroes of civilization p156-
64 (6-7)   **920**
Hume, R. F. Great men of medicine p170-83
(4-6)   **920**

Fleming, Thomas J.
The Battle of Yorktown. See The Battle of
Yorktown   **973.3**

Flemish art. See Art, Flemish

Fles, Barthold
East Germany (5-7)   **914.3**

Fletcher, Alan Mark
Fishes dangerous to man (4-6)   **597**
Unusual aquarium fishes (5-7)   **597**

Fletcher, Charlie May. See Simon, Charlie May

Fletcher, Christine
100 keys: names across the land (6-7) **910**

Fleutiaux, Pierrette
Munari, B. From afar it is an island   **741.2**

Flexner, Stuart Berg
(ed.) The Random House Dictionary of the
English language. See The Random House
Dictionary of the English language   **423**

Flibber turns the table. Knight, L.
In Kamerman, S. E. ed. Little plays for
little players p53-60   **812.08**

Flies
See pages in the following books:
Mason, G. F. Animal tools p39-43 (4-7)
    591.4
Teale, E. W. The junior book of insects p210-
16 (6-7)   **595.7**
See also names of flies, e.g. Fruit flies

Flies
In Ginsburg, M. ed. The Kaha bird p140-
141   **398.2**

Flight
Corbett, S. What makes a plane fly? (3-6)
    629.132
Kaufmann, J. Birds in flight (5-7)   **598.2**
See also pages in the following books:
Urquhart, D. I. The airplane and how it
works p7-15 (3-5)   **629.133**
Yolen, J. World on a string p44-61 (5-7)
    629.133

Fiction

Anderson, L. Mr Biddle and the birds   **E**

Flight
Borski, L. M. The flight
In Borski, L. M. The jolly tailor, and other
fairy tales p134-39   **398.2**
The Flight
In Baker, A. comp. The golden lynx, and
other tales p131-34   **398.2**

The flight of the Doves. Macken, W.   **Fic**

The flight of the Lone Eagle. Foster, J. T.
    629.13

Flight to freedom. Buckmaster, H.   **326**

Flight to Mars. See Space flight to Mars

Flight to the Moon. See Space flight to the
moon

Flint's Island. Wibberley, L.   **Fic**

Folk songs—*Continued*

A-hunting we will go (Folk song) Oh, a-hunting we will go (k-2) **784.4**

Bley, E. S. The best singing games for children of all ages **796.1**

Boni, M. B. ed. Fireside book of folk songs **784.4**

Girl Scouts of the United States of America. Sing together (4-7) **784.6**

Ipcar, D. The cat came back (k-3) **784.4**

Langstaff, J. ed. Hi! Ho! The rattlin' bag (4-7) **784.4**

Price, C. One is God **291**

Winn, M. ed. The fireside book of children's songs **784.6**

Yolen, J. ed. The fireside song book of birds and beasts **784.4**

See also Ballads; Carols; National songs

Kentucky

Ritchie, J. Jean Ritchie's Swapping song book (4-6) **784.4**

Ozark Mountains

Zemach, H. Mommy, buy me a china doll E

United States

Billy Boy (Folk song) Billy Boy (k-3) **784.4**

Boni, M. B. ed. The fireside book of favorite American songs **784.7**

Carmer, C. comp. America sings (5-7) **784.4**

Casey Jones (Folk song) Casey Jones (2-4) **784.4**

Emrich, D. comp. American folk poetry: an anthology **811.08**

The Erie Canal (Folk song) The Erie Canal (k-4) **784.4**

Felton, H. W. ed. Cowboy jamboree: western songs & lore **784.4**

The fox (Folk song) The fox went out on a chilly night (k-3) **784.4**

Go tell Aunt Rhody (Folk song) Go tell Aunt Rhody (k-3) **784.4**

Landeck, B. comp. Songs to grow on **784.4**

Langstaff, J. Ol' Dan Tucker (1-4) **784.4**

Old MacDonald had a farm (k-2) **784.4**

One wide river to cross (Folk song) One wide river to cross (k-3) **784.4**

Quackenbush, R. Go tell Aunt Rhody E

Sandburg, C. ed. The American songbag **784.7**

Seeger, R. C. American folk songs for children in home, school and nursery school **784.4**

Seeger, R. C. comp. American folk songs for Christmas **784.4**

Seeger, R. C. comp. Animal folk songs for children **784.4**

Seeger, P. The foolish frog **784.4**

She'll be comin' round the mountain (Folk song) She'll be comin' round the mountain (k-3) **784.4**

Sweet Betsy from Pike (Folk song) Sweet Betsy from Pike (1-3) **784.4**

See also Folk songs—Appalachian Mountains; Folk songs—Kentucky

Folk songs, American. See Folk songs—United States

Folk songs, English

Ritchie, J. comp. From fair to fair: folk songs of the British Isles (4-7) **784.4**

Folk songs, French

Rockwell, A. ed. Savez-vous planter les choux? and other French songs (3-6) **784.4**

Folk songs, Mexican

Yurchenco, H. ed. A fiesta of folk songs from Spain and Latin America (2-6) **784.7**

Folk songs, Scottish

Nic Leodhas, S. Always room for one more (k-3) **784.4**

Folk songs, Spanish

Rockwell, A. ed. El toro pinto, and other songs in Spanish (1-6) **784.4**

Yurchenco, H. ed. A fiesta of folk songs from Spain and Latin America (2-6) **784.7**

Folk songs, Ugandan

Serwadda, W. M. Songs and stories from Uganda **784.4**

Folk stories of the South. Jagendorf, M. A. **398.2**

Folk tales. See Folklore

Folk toys around the world and how to make them. Joseph, J. **745.59**

Folkard, Charles

(illus.) Collodi, C. The adventures of Pinocchio **Fic**

(illus.) Macdonald, G. The princess and the goblin **Fic**

Folklore

Adair, M. W. Folk puppet plays for the social studies (2-5) **791.5**

Arbuthnot, M. H. comp. Time for old magic **398.2**

Arnott, K. Animal folk tales around the world (4-6) **398.2**

Association for Childhood Education International. Told under the green umbrella (1-4) **398.2**

Baker, A. comp. The golden lynx, and other tales (3-6) **398.2**

Baker, A. comp. The talking tree (3-6) **398.2**

Barth, E. Jack-o'-lantern (2-4) **398.2**

Baumann, H. The stolen fire (4-6) **398.2**

Carlson, B. W. Let's pretend it happened to you (k-3) **792**

Courlander, H. ed. Ride with the sun (4-7) **398.2**

De La Mare, W. ed. Animal stories **398.2**

De La Mare, W. Tales told again (4-7) **398.2**

De Regniers, B. S. ed. The giant book (4-6) **398.2**

De Regniers, B. S. Red Riding Hood (1-3) **398.2**

Dobbs, R. No room (2-4) **398.2**

Elkin, B. Six foolish fishermen (1-3) **398.2**

Fairy tales from many lands (4-6) **398.2**

Fenner, P. R. comp. Giants & witches and a dragon or two (4-6) **398.2**

Fenner, P. R. comp. Princesses & peasant boys (3-6) **398.2**

Galdone, P. The gingerbread boy (k-2) **398.2**

Galdone, P. Henny Penny (k-2) **398.2**

Garner, A. ed. A cavalcade of goblins (4-7) **398.2**

Greene, E. comp. Clever cooks (3-6) **398.2**

Hardendorff, J. B. ed. Just one more (3-6) **372.6**

Harper, W. The Gunniwolf (k-1) **398.2**

Folklore—*Continued*

Hazeltine, A. I. ed. Hero tales from many lands (5-7) 398.2

Helfman, E. S. Signs & symbols of the sun (5-7) 398

Hutchinson, V. S. ed. Candle-light stories (2-4) 398.2

Hutchinson, V. S. ed. Chimney corner fairy tales (3-5) 398.2

Hutchinson, V. S. ed. Chimney corner stories (2-4) 398.2

Hutchinson, V. S. ed. Fireside stories (2-4) 398.2

Jagendorf, M. A. Noodlehead stories from around the world (4-6) 398.2

Lang, A. ed. The blue fairy book (4-6) 398.2

Lang, A. ed. The green fairy book (4-6) 398.2

Lang, A. ed. The red fairy book (4-7) 398.2

Lang, A. ed. The yellow fairy book (4-7) 398.2

Leach, M. How the people sang the mountains up (3-6) 398.2

Leach, M. Noodles, nitwits, and numbskulls (4-7) 398.6

Leach, M. Riddle me, riddle me, ree (3-6) 398.6

Leach, M. Whistle in the graveyard (4-6) 398.2

Little red hen; illus. by J. Domanska (k-1) 398.2

The Little red hen; illus. by P. Galdone (k-1) 398.2

McDowell, R. E. ed. Third World voices for children (4-7) 398.2

McGovern, A. Too much noise (k-3) 398.2

McHargue, G. The impossible people (5-7) 398

Manning-Sanders, R. A book of charms and changelings (3-6) 398.2

Manning-Sanders, R. A book of devils and demons (3-6) 398.2

Manning-Sanders, R. A book of dragons (3-6) 398.2

Manning-Sanders, R. A book of ghosts & goblins (3-6) 398.2

Manning-Sanders, R. ed. A book of magical beasts (3-6) 398.2

Manning-Sanders, R. A book of mermaids (3-6) 398.2

Manning-Sanders, R. A book of ogres and trolls (3-6) 398.2

Manning-Sanders, R. A book of princes and princesses (3-6) 398.2

Manning-Sanders, R. A book of sorcerers and spells (3-6) 398.2

Manning-Sanders, R. A book of witches (3-6) 398.2

Manning-Sanders, R. A book of wizards (3-6) 398.2

Manning-Sanders, R. A choice of magic (3-6) 398.2

The Old woman and her pig (k-2) 398.2

Opie, I. Children's games in street and playground 796.1

Palmer, R. Dragons, unicorns, and other magical beasts (4-6) 398.2

Pyle, H. Pepper & salt (4-6) 398.2

Pyle, H. The wonder clock (4-6) 398.2

Rackham, A. comp. Arthur Rackham Fairy book (3-6) 398.2

Rees, E. Riddles, riddles everywhere (3-6) 398.6

The Renowned history of Little Red Riding Hood (k-3) 398.2

Sawyer, R. Journey cake, ho! (k-2) 398.2

The Tall book of nursery tales (k-2) 398.2

The Three bears (k-1) 398.2

The Three wishes (k-2) 398.2

Withers, C. ed. I saw a rocket walk a mile (3-6) 398.2

Withers, C. A world of nonsense (4-7) 398.2

Zemach, M. The three sillies (k-3) 398.2

See also pages in the following books:

Arbuthnot, M. H. comp. The Arbuthnot Anthology of children's literature p148-413 808.8

Childcraft: the how and why library v2 031

Jan, I. On children's literature p30-41 028.5

Johnson, E. ed. Anthology of children's literature p117-389 808.8

Tashjian, V. A. ed. With a deep sea smile p41-92 372.6

See also Charms; Devil; Dragons; Fables; Fairy tales; Folk songs; Ghosts; Halloween; Legends; Mythology; Nursery rhymes; Plant lore; Proverbs; Sagas; Superstition; Witchcraft

Africa

Aardema, V. Tales from the story hat (3-6) 398.2

Arnott, K. African myths and legends (4-7) 398.2

Carpenter, F. African wonder tales (3-6) 398.2

Courlander, H. The king's drum, and other African stories (4-7) 398.2

Fournier, C. The coconut thieves (k-3) 398.2

Haley, G. E. A story, a story (k-3) 398.2

Robinson, A. Singing tales of Africa (3-5) 398.2

Rockwell, A. When the drum sang (k-3) 398.2

See also pages in the following books:

Bleeker, S. The Masai p118-23 (4-7) 916.7

Bleeker, S. The Zulu of South Africa p22-25 (4-7) 916.8

Withers, C. ed. I saw a rocket walk a mile p135-46 (3-6) 398.2

See also Folklore with geographic subdivisions of specific African nations, e.g. Folklore—Ghana

Africa—Bibliography

See pages in the following book:

Issues in children's book selection p136-41 028.5

Africa, East

Heady, E. B. When the stones were soft (4-6) 398.2

Africa, Southern

Aardema, V. Behind the back of the mountain (4-6) 398.2

Berger, T. Black fairy tales (4-7) 398.2

Africa, West

Arkhurst, J. C. The adventures of Spider (2-5) 398.2

Courlander, H. The cow-tail switch, and other West African stories (4-6) 398.2

Folklore—Germany—*Continued*

Grimm, J. Little Red Riding Hood (k-3)
398.2

Grimm, J. More Tales from Grimm (4-6)
398.2

Grimm, J. Rapunzel (1-4)   398.2

Grimm, J. Rumpelstiltskin; illus. by J. Ayer (k-3)   398.2

Grimm, J. Rumpelstiltskin; illus. by W. Stobbs (k-3)   398.2

Grimm, J. The seven ravens (k-3)   398.2

Grimm, J. The shoemaker and the elves (k-3)
398.2

Grimm, J. Snow White and Rose Red (1-3)
398.2

Grimm, J. Snow-White and the seven dwarfs; illus. by N. E. Burkert (k-3)   398.2

Grimm, J. Snow White and the seven dwarfs; illus. by W. Gág (1-4)   398.2

Grimm, J. Tales from Grimm (4-6)   398.2

Grimm, J. Three gay tales from Grimm (2-5)
398.2

Grimm, J. Tom Thumb (k-3)   398.2

Grimm, J. The traveling musicians (k-3) 398.2

Grimm, J. The wolf and the seven little kids (k-3)   398.2

Haviland, V. Favorite fairy tales told in Germany (2-5)   398.2

Hurlimann, R. The cat and mouse who shared a house (k-3)   398.2

Ghana

Appiah, P. Ananse the spider (4-7)   398.2

Courlander, H. The hat-shaking dance, and other tales from the Gold Coast (3-6)
398.2

McDermott, G. Anansi the spider (k-3) 398.2

Great Britain

Colwell, E. Round about and long ago (3-6)
398.2

Galdone, P. The three little pigs (k-2) 398.2

Godden, R. The old woman who lived in a vinegar bottle (k-3)   398.2

Jacobs, J. ed. English folk and fairy tales (4-6)   398.2

Jacobs, J. Hereafterthis (k-3)   398.2

Jacobs, J. Jack the Giant-Killer (k-3)   398.2

Jacobs, J. Johnny-cake (k-3)   398.2

Jacobs, J. ed. More English folk and fairy tales (4-6)   398.2

Opie, I. The lore and language of schoolchildren   398

Reeves, J. English fables and fairy stories (4-7)   398.2

The Three little pigs (k-1)   398.2

Tom Tit Tot (k-3)   398.2

Williams-Ellis, A. Fairy tales from the British Isles (5-7)   398.2

Zemach, H. Duffy and the devil (k-3) 398.2

Greece, Modern

Aliki. The eggs (k-3)   398.2

Aliki. Three gold pieces (k-2)   398.2

Haviland, V. Favorite fairy tales told in Greece (2-5)   398.2

Haiti

Courlander, H. The piece of fire, and other Haitian tales (4-6)   398.2

Hawaii

Thompson, V. L. Hawaiian myths of earth, sea, and sky (3-6)   398.2

Thompson, V. L. Hawaiian tales of heroes and champions (4-6)   398.2

History and criticism

See pages in the following books:

Egoff, S. The republic of childhood p56-94
028.5

Haviland, V. ed. Children and literature p206-12   028.5

Hungary

Ambrus, V. G. The three poor tailors (k-2)
398.2

Hardendorff, J. B. The little cock (1-4) 398.2

Indexes

Index to fairy tales, myths and legends 398.2

Index to fairy tales, myths and legends, supplement   398.2

Index to fairy tales, myths and legends, second supplement   398.2

Index to fairy tales, 1949-1972   398.2

India

Babbitt, E. C. Jataka tales (1-3)   398.2

Brown, M. Once a mouse (k-3)   398.2

Gaer, J. The fables of India (5-7)   398.2

Galdone, P. The monkey and the crocodile (k-2)   398.2

Haviland, V. Favorite fairy tales told in India (2-5)   398.2

Jacobs, J. ed. Indian fairy tales (4-6)   398.2

Price, C. The valiant chattee-maker (k-3)
398.2

Quigley, L. The blind men and the elephant (k-3)   398.2

Iran

See Folklore—Persia

Ireland

Colum, P. The King of Ireland's Son (5-7)
398.2

Colum, P. The Stone of Victory, and other tales of Padraic Colum (3-5)   398.2

Green, K. Leprechaun tales (3-5)   398.2

Haviland, V. Favorite fairy tales told in Ireland (2-5)   398.2

Jacobs, J. Munachar & Manachar (k-3) 398.2

MacManus, S. The bold heroes of Hungry Hill, and other Irish folk tales (5-7) 398.2

MacManus, S. Hibernian nights (4-7) 398.2

O'Faolain, E. Irish sagas and folk-tales (5-7)
398.2

Stephens, J. Irish fairy tales (6-7)   398.2

Young, E. The wonder smith and his son (5-7)   398.2

Italy

Haviland, V. Favorite fairy tales told in Italy (2-5)   398.2

Rockwell, A. Befana (1-3)   398.2

Zemach, H. Too much nose (k-3)   398.2

Jamaica

Sherlock, P. M. Anansi, the spider man (4-6)
398.2

Japan

Carpenter, F. People from the sky (4-6) 398.2

Haviland, V. Favorite fairy tales told in Japan (2-5)   398.2

Hodges, M. The wave (3-5)   398.2

Kijima, H. Little white hen (k-2)   398.2

McDermott, G. The stonecutter (k-3) 398.2

Mosel, A. The funny little woman (k-2) 398.2

Folklore—*Continued*
South America
Finger, C. Tales from silver lands (5-7) **398.2**

Southern States
Chase, R. ed. Grandfather tales (4-7) **398.2**
Chase, R. ed. The Jack tales (4-6) **398.2**
Jagendorf, M. A. Folk stories of the South (4-7) **398.2**

Spain
Boggs, R. S. Three golden oranges, and other Spanish folk tales (5-7) **398.2**
Davis, R. Padre Porko, the gentlemanly pig (4-6) **398.2**
De La Iglesia, M. E. The cat and the mouse, and other Spanish tales (2-4) **398.2**
Gunterman, B. L. ed. Castles in Spain, and other enchantments (4-6) **398.2**
Haviland, V. Favorite fairy tales told in Spain (2-5) **398.2**

Sweden
Haviland, V. Favorite fairy tales told in Sweden (2-5) **398.2**
Olenius, E. comp. Great Swedish fairy tales (4-7) **398.2**

Switzerland
Duvoisin, R. The three sneezes, and other Swiss tales (4-6) **398.2**

Tibet
Hume, L. C. Favorite children's stories from China and Tibet (3-6) **398.2**

Uganda
Serwadda, W. M. Songs and stories from Uganda **784.4**

Ukraine
Bloch, M. H. Ivanko and the dragon (k-3) **398.2**
Bloch, M. H. ed. Ukrainian folk tales (4-6) **398.2**
Tresselt, A. The mitten (k-2) **398.2**

United States
Chase, R. Jack and the three sillies (k-3) **398.2**
Credle, E. Tall tales from the high hills, and other stories (4-7) **398.2**
Emrich, D. comp. The hodgepodge book **398**
Emrich, D. ed. The nonsense book of riddles, rhymes, tongue twisters, puzzles and jokes from American folklore (3-7) **398**
Petersham, M. comp. The rooster crows (k-2) **398.8**
Schwartz, A. Whoppers (4-7) **398.2**
Stoutenburg, A. American tall-tale animals (4-6) **398.2**
Withers, C. comp. A rocket in my pocket (3-6) **398**
See also pages in the following book:
Withers, C. ed. I saw a rocket walk a mile p17-47 (3-6) **398.2**
See also Folklore, Negro

Vietnam
Graham, G. B. The beggar in the blanket, & other Vietnamese tales (2-5) **398.2**
Robertson, D. L. Fairy tales from Viet Nam (4-6) **398.2**
Vo-Dinh. The toad is the Emperor's uncle (4-6) **398.2**

West Indies
Carter, D. S. ed. Greedy Mariani, and other folk tales of the Antilles (3-7) **398.2**
Sherlock, Sir P. The iguana's tail (3-5) **398.2**
Sherlock, Sir P. West Indian folk-tales (4-6) **398.2**

Yugoslavia
Fillmore, P. The laughing prince (4-6) **398.2**

Zaïre
Holladay, V. Bantu tales (4-6) **398.2**
McDermott, G. The magic tree (k-3) **398.2**

Folklore, Ashanti
Appiah, P. Ananse the spider (4-7) **398.2**
Courlander, H. The cow-tail switch, and other West African stories (4-6) **398.2**
Courlander, H. The hat-shaking dance, and other tales from the Gold Coast (3-6) **398.2**
McDermott, G. Anansi the spider (k-3) **398.2**

Folklore, Bantu
Holladay, V. Bantu tales (4-6) **398.2**

Folklore, Celtic
Jacobs, J. Hudden and Dudden and Donald O'Neary (k-4) **398.2**

Folklore, Eskimo
Field, E. ed. Eskimo songs and stories (3-7) **398.2**
Gillham, C. E. Beyond the Clapping Mountains (3-6) **398.2**
Ginsburg, M. The proud maiden, Tungak, and the Sun (1-3) **398.2**
Melzack, R. The day Tuk became a hunter & other Eskimo stories (3-6) **398.2**
See also pages in the following book:
Egoff, S. The republic of childhood p20-55 **028.5**

Folklore, Friesian
Spicer, D. G. The owl's nest (4-6) **398.2**

Folklore, Gaelic
O'Faolain, E. Irish sagas and folk-tales (5-7) **398.2**
Young, E. The wonder smith and his son (5-7) **398.2**

Folklore, Gypsy
Jagendorf, M. A. The gypsies' fiddle, and other gypsy tales (5-7) **398.2**

Folklore, Hausa
Sturton, H. Zomo, the Rabbit (4-6) **398.2**

Folklore, Indian
Marriott, A. American Indian mythology **398.2**
See also pages in the following books:
Bleeker, S. The Navajo p68-72 (4-6) **970.3**
Egoff, S. The republic of childhood p20-55 **028.5**
See also Indians of Mexico—Legends; Indians of North America—Legends; Indians of South America—Legends; also names of tribes and linguistic families with subdivision Legends, e.g. Crow Indians—Legends

Bibliography
Folklore of the North American Indians **016.398**

Folklore, Jewish
Hirsh, M. Could anything be worse? (k-3) **398.2**

The **foolish** frog. Seeger, P.   **784.4**

Foolish goat mother
Noel, S. Foolish mother goat
In Hardendorff, J. B. ed. Just one more
p30-33   **372.6**

Foolish lad. Hatch, M. C.
In Hatch, M. C. 13 Danish tales p37-45
398.2

The **foolish lion and the silly rooster.** Jagendorf, M. A.
In Jagendorf, M. A. Noodlehead stories
from around the world p89-92 **398.2**

The **foolish man.** Tashjian, V.
In Arbuthnot, M. H. comp. The Arbuthnot
Anthology of children's literature
p283-85   **808.8**
In Arbuthnot, M. H. comp. Time for old
magic p166-68   **398.2**
In Tashjian, V. A. Once there was and was
not p3-10   **398.2**

Foolish milkmaid
In The Tall book of nursery tales p23-24
398.2

Foolish mother goat. Noel, S.
In Hardendorff, J. B. ed. Just one more
p30-33   **372.6**

The **"Foolish People".** Jagendorf, M. A.
In Jagendorf, M. A. Noodlehead stories
from around the world p271-73
398.2

The **Foolish, timid little hare**
In Gruenberg, S. M. ed. Favorite stories
old and new p341-43   **808.8**
See also Timid hare

The **Foolish, timid rabbit**
In Babbitt, E. C. Jataka tales p39-43 **398.2**
In Hutchinson, V. S. ed. Fireside stories
p43-47   **398.2**
See also Timid hare

The **foolish wife and her three foolish daugh-
ters.** Haviland, V.
In Haviland, V. Favorite fairy tales told in
Greece p29-37   **398.2**

Fools' bells ring in every town. Jagendorf,
M. A.
In Jagendorf, M. A. Noodlehead stories
from around the world p164-72
398.2

The **fools of Chelm and their history.** Singer,
I. B.   **Fic**

Fool's paradise. Singer, I. B.
In Singer, I. B. Zlateh the goat, and other
stories p5-16   **398.2**

Foot
Mason, G. F. Animal feet (4-7)   **591.4**

The **foot racers of Payupki.** Courlander, H.
In Courlander, H. People of the short
blue corn p101-14   **398.2**

Football
Anderson, D. Defensive football (3-6) **796.33**
Coombs, C. Be a winner in football (5-7)
796.33
Jackson, C. P. How to play better football
(4-7)   **796.33**
Young, A. S. Black champions of the grid-

iron: O. J. Simpson and Leroy Keyes (5-7)
796.33

See also pages in the following books:
The Junior illustrated encyclopedia of sports
p271-381 (5-7)   **796.03**
Keith, H. Sports and games p145-86 (5-7)
796

See also Soccer
Dictionaries
Liss, H. Football talk for beginners (4-7)
796.33

Fiction
Christopher, M. Catch that pass! (3-5)   **Fic**
Kessler, L. Kick, pass, and run   **E**
Lord, B. Mystery guest at left end (2-5) **Fic**
Lord, B. Quarterback's aim (2-5)   **Fic**
Shepard, R. A. Sneakers (4-6)   **Fic**

Football coaching
Schoor, G. Football's greatest coach: Vince
Lombardi (6-7)   **92**

Football talk for beginners. Liss, H.   **796.33**

Football's greatest coach: Vince Lombardi.
Schoor, G.   **92**

Foote, John Taintor
The look of eagles
In Anderson, C. W. ed. C. W. Anderson's
Favorite horse stories p93-118 **808.8**
Ole man Sanford
In Anderson, C. W. ed. C. W. Anderson's
Favorite horse stories p81-92 **808.8**

For a child. McFarland, W. ed.   **821.08**

For an oven full of bread. Duvoisin, R.
In Duvoisin, R. The three sneezes, and
other Swiss tales p126-29   **398.2**

For lack of a thread. Duvoisin, R.
In Duvoisin, R. The three sneezes, and
other Swiss tales p44-47   **398.2**

For ma and pa. Hays, W. P.   **Fic**

For me to say. McCord, D.   **811**

For pollution fighters only. Hyde, M. O. **614.7**

For soldiers everywhere; play. Carlson, B. W.
In Carlson, B. W. The right play for you
p142-45   **792**

For younger readers: braille and talking books
028.52

Forage plants. See Grasses; Pastures; also names
of specific forage plants, e.g. Corn

Forberg, Ati
(illus.) Fisher, A. Easter   **394.2**
(illus.) Fisher, A. Jeanne d'Arc [biography
of Joan of Arc, Saint]   **92**
(illus.) Hightower, F. The ghost of Follonsbee's Folly   **Fic**
(illus.) Tomaino, S. F. Persephone: bringer of
spring   **292**
(illus.) Uchida, Y. Samurai of Gold Hill **Fic**

Forbes, Esther
Newbery Medal acceptance paper
In Miller, B. M. ed. Newbery Medal
books: 1922-1955 p248-54   **028.5**
Salt-water tea
In Johnson, E. ed. Anthology of children's
literature p877-82   **808.8**

Forbes, Esther—*Continued*
"That a man can stand up"
In Arbuthnot, M. H. comp. The Arbuthnot Anthology of children's literature p748-53 **808.8**

About

See pages in the following book:
Miller, B. M. ed. Newbery Medal books: 1922-1955 p245-47 **028.5**

Forbes, Kathryn
Mama and the graduation present
In Cavanah, F. ed. Holiday roundup p134-37 **394.2**

Forbidden room
Grimm, J. Fitcher's bird
In Grimm, J. The complete Grimm's Fairy tales p216-20 **398.2**
Grimm, J. Fitcher's feathered bird
In Grimm, J. The juniper tree, and other tales from Grimm v 1 p71-79 **398.2**

Force and energy
Adler, I. Energy (3-5) **531**
Bendick, J. Why things work (2-4) **531**
Shuttlesworth, D. E. Disappearing energy (5-7) **333.7**
See also pages in the following book:
The Way things work. Special edition for young people p59-85 (6-7) **600**
See also Mechanics; Motion

Ford, George
(illus.) Mathis, S. B. Ray Charles **92**

Ford, H. J.
(illus.) Lang, A. ed. The blue fairy book **398.2**
(illus.) Lang, A. ed. The green fairy book **398.2**
(illus.) Lang, A. ed. The red fairy book **398.2**
(illus.) Lang, A. ed. The yellow fairy book **398.2**

Ford, Henry, 1863-1947
See pages in the following book:
Captains of industry p127-45 (5-7) **920**

Fording the river in a copper cauldron. Jagendorf, M. A.
In Jagendorf, M. A. The gypsies' fiddle, and other gypsy tales p170-76 **398.2**

Forecasting, Weather. See Weather forecasting

Foreign population. See names of countries with the subdivision Immigration and emigration, e.g. Liberia—Immigration and emigration; and names of countries, cities, etc. with the subdivision Foreign population, e.g. United States—Foreign population

Foreigners. See names of countries, cities, etc. with the subdivision Foreign population, e.g. United States—Foreign population; also Italians in the United States; and similar subjects

Forenames. See Names, Personal

Forest bride
Bowman, J. C. Mouse bride
In Bowman, J. C. Tales from a Finnish tupa p25-33 **398.2**
Fillmore, P. The forest bride
In Fenner, P. R. comp. Princesses & peasant boys p103-14 **398.2**

Forest conservation. See Forests and forestry

Forest full of friends. Alden, R. M.
In Alden, R. M. Why the chimes rang, and other stories p92-105 **S C**

Forest influences
See pages in the following book:
Kirk, R. Yellowstone ▫38-48 (5-7) **917.87**
See also Botany—Ecology; Flood control; Forests and forestry; Rain and rainfall

Forest reserves. See Forest and forestry

Forester, C. S.
Horatio enjoys his punishment
In Untermeyer, B. ed. The Golden Treasury of children's literature p32-39 **808.8**
Poo-Poo brings the dragon home
In Untermeyer, B. ed. The Golden Treasury of children's literature p29-31 **808.8**
Poo-Poo finds a dragon
In Untermeyer, B. ed. The Golden Treasury of children's literature p25-28 **808.8**

Forestry. See Forests and forestry

Forests and climate. See Forest influences

Forests and forestry
Atwood, A. The kingdom of the forest (4-6) **574.5**
Pringle, L. Into the woods (5-7) **574.5**
Selsam, M. E. Birth of a forest (4-6) **581.5**
See also pages in the following books:
Duffey, E. Conservation of nature p19-29 (6-7) **333.7**
Holbrook, S. H. The Columbia River p25-31 (4-7) **979.7**
Hungerford, H. R. Ecology p43-50 (5-7) **574.5**
Peattie, D. The rainbow book of nature p88-96 (5-7) **574**
Pringle, L. P. ed. Discovering the outdoors p51-87 (4-7) **574**
Riedman, S. R. Trees alive p102-24 (5-7) **582**
See also Lumber and lumbering; Trees

New Zealand

See pages in the following book:
Kaula, E. M. The land and people of New Zealand p116-22 (5-7) **919.31**

North America

See pages in the following book:
Meyer, R. Festivals U.S.A. & Canada p124-31 **394.2**

The **forever** Christmas tree. Uchida, Y. **E**

Forgotten books of the American nursery. Halsey, R. V. **028.5**

The **forgotten** door. Key, A. **Fic**

Forman, Brenda
The land and people of Nigeria (5-7) **916.69**

Forman, Harrison
(jt. auth.) Forman, B. The land and people of Nigeria **916.69**

The **former** time. Snedeker, C. D.
In Johnson, E. ed. Anthology of children's literature p839-43 **808.8**

Forsberg, Vera
Riwkin-Brick, A. Salima lives in Kashmir **915.4**

Fourteen songs from When we were very young.
Fraser-Simson, H.
In Fraser-Simson, H. The Pooh song book
p111-48 **784.6**
Fourth of July
Dalgliesh, A. The Fourth of July story (2-4)
973.3
Phelan, M. K. The Fourth of July (1-3) **394.2**
See also pages in the following book:
Sechrist, E. H. Red letter days p147-55 **394.2**
Poetry
See pages in the following book:
Sechrist, E. H. comp. Poems for red letter
days p157-63 **821.08**
The **Fourth** of July story. Dalgliesh, A. **973.3**
Fowke, Edith
(comp.) Sally go round the sun **796.1**
Fowler, H. Waller
Kites (4-7) **796.1**
Fox, Catherine. See Fox, Katherine
Fox, Damally U.
The littlest month
In Kamerman, S. E. ed. Little plays for
little players p157-61 **812.08**
Fox, Kate. See Fox, Katherine
Fox, Katherine
See pages in the following book:
Cohen, D. In search of ghosts p76-86 (6-7)
133
Fox, Lilla M.
Costumes and customs of the British Isles
(4-7) **391**
Folk costume of Southern Europe (4-7)
391.09
Folk costume of Western Europe (4-7) **391.09**
Fox, Margaret
See pages in the following book:
Cohen, D. In search of ghosts p76-86 (6-7)
133
Fox, Michael
Sundance coyote (5-7) **599**
The wolf (3-6) **599**
Fox, Paula
Blowfish live in the sea (6-7) **Fic**
Good Ethan **E**
How many miles to Babylon? (4-6) **Fic**
How many miles to Babylon? excerpt
In Arbuthnot, M. H. comp. The Arbuthnot
Anthology of children's literature
p633-38 **808.8**
Maurice's room (3-5) **Fic**
Maurice's room; excerpt
In Association for Childhood Education In-
ternational. Told under the city um-
brella p 1-6 **S C**
Newbery Medal acceptance paper
In Kingman, L. ed. Newbery and Caldecott
Medal books: 1966-1975 p116-22
028.5
Portrait of Ivan (4-7) **Fic**
The slave dancer (6-7) **Fic**
The stone-faced boy (4-6) **Fic**
Trapped by the gang
In Arbuthnot, M. H. comp. The Arbuthnot
Anthology of children's literature
p633-38 **808.8**

About
See pages in the following books:
Kingman, L. ed. Newbery and Caldecott
Medal books: 1966-1975 p123-25 **028.5**
Townsend, J. R. A sense of story p89-94 **028.5**
Fox, Thomas C.
(illus.) Lifton, B. J. Children of Vietnam
959.704
The **fox** (Folk song)
The fox went out on a chilly night (k-3) **784.4**
Fox (Steam yacht)
Fiction
Tapley, C. John come down the backstay (6-7)
Fic
Fox and the badger
In Ginsburg, M. comp. One trick too many
p14-16 **398.2**
The **fox and the bear.** Uchida, Y.
In Sechrist, E. H. ed. It's time for story
hour p111-16 **372.6**
In Uchida, Y. The magic listening cap
p103-11 **398.2**
See also Why the bear has a stumpy tail
Fox and the cat
Grimm, J. The cat and the fox
In Grimm, J. More tales from Grimm p61-
62 **398.2**
Grimm, J. The fox and the cat
In Grimm, J. The complete Grimm's Fairy
tales p354-55 **398.2**
Ransome, A. The cat who became head-
forester
In Ransome, A. Old Peter's Russian tales
p106-19 **398.2**
Fox and the crane
The crane and the fox
In Bloch, M. H. ed. Ukrainian folk tales
p36-38 **398.2**
Fox and the Crow
Bowman, J. C. Wily fox
In Bowman, J. C. Tales from a Finnish
tupa p255-56 **398.2**
Fox and the crow
In The Tall book of nursery tales p77-78
398.2
Fox and the geese
Fox and the geese
In De La Mare, W. ed. Animal stories
p78-79 **398.2**
Grimm, J. The fox and the geese
In Grimm, J. The complete Grimm's Fairy
tales p393-94 **398.2**
See also Stupid wolf
The **fox and the gulls.** Arnott, K.
In Arnott, K. Animal folk tales around the
world p224-30 **398.2**
The **fox and the horse.** Grimm, J.
In Grimm, J. The complete Grimm's Fairy
tales p595-96 **398.2**
The **Fox and the lion**
In Ginsburg, M. comp. One trick too many
p9 **398.2**
Fox and the peasant
Bowman, J. C. Finland's greatest fisherman
In Bowman, J. C. Tales from a Finnish
tupa p205-06 **398.2**

The **Fox** and the quail
  In Ginsburg, M. comp. One trick too many
    p31-37   398.2
Fox and the rabbit. Bowman, J. C.
  In Bowman, J. C. Tales from a Finnish
    tupa p254   398.2
Fox and the sculpin
  Gillham, C. E. The sculpin and the fox
  In Gillham, C. E. Beyond the Clapping
    Mountains p117-20   398.2
The **fox** and the sheepskin jacket. Arnott, K.
  In Arnott, K. Animal folk tales around the
    world p6-13   398.2
The **Fox** and the wolf
  In Baker, A. comp. The talking tree p71-
    76   398.2
Fox as a judge. Bowman, J. C.
  In Bowman, J. C. Tales from a Finnish
    tupa p264-65   398.2
Fox as herdsboy
  Asbjørnsen, P. C. The fox as shepherd
  In Asbjørnsen, P. C. Norwegian folk tales
    p106-07   398.2
  The **Fox** as herdsman
  In Undset, S. ed. True and untrue, and
    other Norse tales p182-83   398.2
Fox as partner
  Bowman, J. C. Farmers three
  In Bowman, J. C. Tales from a Finnish
    tupa p247-48   398.2
The **fox** as shepherd. Asbjørnsen, P. C.
  In Asbjørnsen, P. C. Norwegian folk tales
    p106-07   398.2
  See also Fox as herdsboy
Fox family
  See pages in the following book:
  Cohen, D. In search of ghosts p68-86 (6-7)
                                           133
The **fox** in the hole. Jagendorf, M. A.
  In Jagendorf, M. A. Noodlehead stories
    from around the world p45-47 398.2
Fox magic. Carpenter, F.
  In Carpenter, F. People from the sky p71-
    75   398.2
The **fox** outwits the tiger. Hume, L. C.
  In Hume, L. C. Favorite children's stories
    from China and Tibet p67-68 398.2
Fox sings
  Bowman, J. C. Song of the fox
  In Bowman, J. C. Tales from a Finnish
    tupa p258-59   398.2
Fox, the bear, and the poor farmer
  The farmer, the bear, and the fox
  In Bloch, M. H. ed. Ukrainian folk tales
    p64-67   398.2
The **fox**, the fish and the bear. Arnott, K.
  In Arnott, K. Animal folk tales around the
    world p79-82   398.2
The **fox**, the hare, and the toad have an argu-
    ment. Hume, L. C.
  In Hume, L. C. Favorite children's stories
    from China and Tibet p23-26 398.2
The **fox** turns a somersault. Hume, L. C.
  In Hume, L. C. Favorite children's stories
    from China and Tibet p99-101 398.2
The **fox** went out on a chilly night. The fox
  (Folk song)   784.4

Fox without a tail
  Hogrogian, N. One fine day   398.2
Foxes
  George, J. C. The moon of the fox pups (3-5)
                                           599
  Hess, L. Foxes in the woodshed (2-4)   599
  Ripper, C. L. Foxes and wolves (3-5)   599
    Stories
  Baudouy, M. A. Old One-Toe (5-7)   Fic
  Byars, B. The midnight fox (4-6)   Fic
  Cooney, B. Chanticleer and the fox   E
  Dillon, E. A family of foxes (5-7)   Fic
  Galdone, P. Three Aesop fox fables (k-3)
                                          398.2
  Ginsburg, M. comp. One trick too many (1-3)
                                          398.2
  Hogrogian, N. One fine day   398.2
  Hutchins, P. Rosie's walk   E
  Lindgren, A. The Tomten and the fox   E
  Potter, B. The tale of Mr Tod   E
  Roberts, C. G. D. Red Fox (4-7)   Fic
  Watson, C. Tom Fox and the apple pie   E
  Yashima, T. The golden footprints (3-6) Fic
Foxes and wolves. Ripper, C. L.   599
Foxes in the woodshed. Hess, L.   599
The **fox's** daughter. Ritchie, A.
  In Arbuthnot, M. H. comp. The Arbuthnot
    Anthology of children's literature
    p331-33   808.8
  In Arbuthnot, M. H. comp. Time for old
    magic p206-08   398.2
  In Ritchie, A. The treasure of Li-Po p65-
    74   S C
The **fox's** foxy tail. Tolstoy, L.
  In Tolstoy, L. Twenty-two Russian tales
    for young children p45-46   S C
The **fox's** wedding. Redesdale, Lord
  In Fairy tales from many lands p87-88
                                          398.2
Foxx, James Emory
  See pages in the following book:
  Libby, B. Baseball's greatest sluggers p38-63
    (5-7)   920
Fracé, Charles
  (illus.) Fox, M. The wolf   599
Fractions are parts of things. Dennis, J. R. 513
Fragolette
  Manning-Sanders, R. Prunella
  In Manning-Sanders, R. A book of witches
    p62-71   398.2
Frame, Jean
  How to give a party (4-6)   793.2
Frame, Paul
  (illus.) Burt, O. W. Black women of valor 920
  (illus.) Calhoun, M. Katie John   Fic
  (illus.) Cohen, D. How did life get there?
                                         574.5
  (illus.) Epstein, S. Harriet Tubman: guide to
    freedom   92
  (jt. auth.) Frame, J. How to give a party 793.2
  (illus.) Henry, O. The ransom of Red Chief
                                          Fic
  (illus.) Limburg, P. R. The story of corn 633
  (illus.) Peterson, H. S. Susan B. Anthony,
    pioneer in woman's rights   92
  (illus.) Thayer, E. L. Casey at the bat 811
  (illus.) Toye, C. Soccer   796.33

Frame, Paul—*Continued*
(illus.) Unkelbach, K. Tiger up a tree (1-4)
636.8
(illus.) Wise, W. Franklin Delano Roosevelt
92

France
Bragdon, L. J. The land and people of France (5-7)
914.4
Church, R. J. H. Looking at France (4-6)
914.4

Army. Lafayette Flying Corps
Bowen, R. S. They flew to glory: the story of the Lafayette Flying Corps (4-6) 940.4

Fiction
Bemelmans, L. Madeline and the gypsies E
Berna, P. The horse without a head (4-7)
Fic
Bishop, C. H. The truffle pig   E
Bishop, C. H. Twenty and ten (4-7)   Fic
Carlson, N. S. The happy orpheline (2-4) Fic
Cunningham, J. Burnish me bright (4-6) Fic
Day, V. Landslide! (4-7)   Fic
Fatio, L. The happy lion   E
Fatio, L. The three happy lions   E
Françoise. The big rain   E
Françoise. Jeanne-Marie at the fair   E
Françoise. Noël for Jeanne-Marie   E
Françoise. Springtime for Jeanne-Marie E
Sachs, M. A pocket full of seeds (5-7) Fic
Titus, E. Anatole   E
Titus, E. Anatole and the cat   E
Titus, E. Anatole and the piano   E
Titus, E. Anatole and the thirty thieves E
Titus, E. Anatole and the toyshop   E

Folklore
See Folklore—France

History—To 1328
See pages in the following book:
Carter, S. Vikings bold: their voyages & adventures p55-71 (5-7)   914.8

History—House of Valois, 1328-1589
Fisher, A. Jeanne d'Arc [biography of Joan of Arc, Saint] (3-5)
92

Legends
See Legends—France

Social life and customs
See pages in the following book:
Sechrist, E. H. ed. Christmas everywhere p107-10   394.2

Franchere, Ruth
Cesar Chavez (2-5)   92
Westward by canal (5-7)   386
Willa (6-7)   Fic

Francis Drake, sailor of the unknown seas. Syme, R.   92

Francis I, King of France
See pages in the following book:
Bragdon, L. J. The land and people of France p52-56 (5-7)   914.4

Francis of Assisi, Saint
Jewett, S. God's troubadour (4-6)   92
See also pages in the following book:
Johnson, E. ed. Anthology of children's literature p590-94   808.8

Francisco Pizarro, finder of Peru. Syme, R. 92

Françoise
The big rain   E
Jeanne-Marie at the fair   E
Jeanne-Marie counts her sheep   E
Noël for Jeanne-Marie   E
Springtime for Jeanne-Marie   E

Frankel, Godfrey
(jt. auth.) Frankel, L. Bike-ways (101 things to do with a bike)   796.6

Frankel, Lillian
Bike-ways (101 things to do with a bike) (4-6)
796.6

Frankenberg, Robert
(illus.) Hume, R. F. Great men of medicine
920
(illus.) Mowat, F. Owls in the family 636.6

Franklin, Aretha
See pages in the following book:
Jones, H. Big star fallin' mama p118-36 (6-7)
920

Franklin, Benjamin
Aulaire, I. d'. Benjamin Franklin (2-4)   92
Daugherty, J. Poor Richard (6-7)   92
See also pages in the following books:
Arbuthnot, M. H. comp. The Arbuthnot Anthology of children's literature p787-90
808.8
Daugherty, S. Ten brave men p97-110 (5-7)
920
Davis, B. Heroes of the American Revolution p64-78 (5-7)   920
Lengyel, E. The Colony of Pennsylvania p62-71 (5-7)   974.8

Fiction
Lawson, R. Ben and me (5-7)   Fic
Monjo, F. N. Poor Richard in France (2-4)
Fic

Poetry
See pages in the following book:
Merriam, E. Independent voices p 1-10 (5-7)
811

Franklin, Harold
(illus.) Hunter, K. Boss cat   Fic

The Franklin reversal. Boiko, C.
In Boiko, C. Children's plays for creative actors p329-40   812

Franklin Stein. Raskin, E.   E

The Franklin Watts Concise guide to babysitting. Saunders, R.   649

The franklin's tale. Farjeon, E.
In Green, R. L. ed. A cavalcade of magicians p95-105   808.8

Frascino, Edward
(illus.) Sharmat, M. W. Gladys told me to meet her here   E
(illus.) White, E. B. The trumpet of the swan
Fic

Frasconi, Antonio
See and say (3-7)   410
(illus.) Dana, D. The elephant and his secret
E
The House that Jack built. See The House that Jack built   398.8
The Snow and the sun. See The Snow and the sun   398.8
(illus.) Whitman, W. Overhead the sun 811

Freetown, Sierra Leone

Description

See pages in the following book:

Clifford, M. L. The land and people of Sierra Leone p43-63, 110-17 (5-7) **916.6**

Freeways. See Express highways

Freezers. See Refrigeration and refrigerating machinery

Freight and freightage

Behrens, J. Train cargo (3-5) **385**

Der Freischütz; adaptation. Bulla, C. R.
In Bulla, C. R. More stories of favorite operas p30-44 **782.1**

Frémont, John Charles

Syme, R. John Charles Frémont (5-7) **92**

See also pages in the following book:

Hirsch, S. C. Mapmakers of America p121-31 (5-7) **973.1**

French, Allen

Grettir becomes an outlaw
In Hazeltine, A. I. ed. Hero tales from many lands p279-95 **398.2**

Njal, the lawyer
In Hazeltine, A. I. ed. Hero tales from many lands p297-304 **398.2**

French architecture. See Architecture, French

French art. See Art, French

French authors. See Authors, French

French Canadians

Fiction

Carlson, N. S. The talking cat, and other stories of French Canada (3-6) **S C**

The **French doll's surprise.** Bennett, R.
In Bennett, R. Creative plays and programs for holidays p363-66 **812**

The **French explorers in America.** Buehr, W. **973.1**

French folk songs. See Folk songs, French

French Guiana

Carpenter, A. French Guiana (4-6) **918.8**

French in Algeria

See pages in the following book:

Spencer, W. The land and people of Algeria p64-81 (5-7) **916.5**

French in North America

Buehr, W. The French explorers in America (4-6) **973.1**

French language

Cooper, L. Fun with French (4-7) **448**

See also Bilingual books—French-English; French language editions

Dictionaries

Fonteneau, M. Mon premier Larousse en couleurs **443**

French language editions

The Cat in the hat Beginner book dictionary **423**

Lionni, L. Inch by inch **E**

Lionni, L. Swimmy **E**

Potter, B. The tailor of Gloucester **E**

Potter, B. The tale of Benjamin Bunny **E**

Potter, B. The tale of Jemima Puddle-duck **E**

Potter, B. The tale of Mr Jeremy Fisher **E**

Potter, B. The tale of Mrs Tiggy-Winkle **E**

Potter, B. The tale of Peter Rabbit **E**

Potter, B. The tale of Squirrel Nutkin **E**

Potter, B. The tale of the flopsy bunnies **E**

Potter, B. The tale of Tom Kitten **E**

Robbins, R. The Emperor and the drummer boy **Fic**

Saint Exupéry, A. de. The little prince **Fic**

French painters. See Painters, French

French poetry **841**

Frenzeny, P.

(illus.) Kipling, R. The jungle books **S C**

Freschet, Berniece

Bear mouse (2-4) **599**

The old bullfrog **E**

The owl and the prairie dog (k-4) **598.2**

Skunk baby (2-4) **599**

Turtle pond (k-3) **598.1**

The web in the grass **E**

Year on Muskrat Marsh (3-5) **591.5**

A fresco for UNESCO. Fisher, A.
In Fisher, A. United Nations plays and programs p199-202 **812**

Fresh. Pearce, P.
In Pearce, P. What the neighbors did, and other stories p45-59 **S C**

Fresh-water animals

Coatsworth, E. Under the green willow **E**

Reid, G. K. Pond life (6-7) **574.92**

See also pages in the following book:

Shuttlesworth, D. E. The wildlife of South America p67-77 (5-7) **591.9**

See also Aquariums; Marine animals; also names of individual fresh-water animals, e.g. Beavers

Fresh-water biology

Buck, M. W. Pets from the pond (4-7) **639**

Carrick, C. The brook (k-2) **574.92**

Carrick, C. The pond (k-2) **574.92**

Kane, H. B. The tale of a pond (4-7) **574.92**

Tresselt, A. The beaver pond (k-3) **574.92**

See also pages in the following books:

Hungerford, H. R. Ecology p30-42 (5-7) **574.5**

Pringle, L. P. ed. Discovering the outdoors p89-110 (4-7) **574**

See also Aquariums; Fresh-water animals; Fresh-water plants; Marine biology

Fresh-water plants

Earle, O. L. Pond and marsh plants (3-6) **581**

Reid, G. K. Pond life (6-7) **574.92**

See also pages in the following books:

Buck, M. W. Pets from the pond p14-21 (4-7) **639**

Cooper, E. K. Science on the shores and banks p165-72 (5-7) **574.92**

Pels, G. The care of water pets p44-48 (4-6) **639**

See also Aquariums; Marine plants

Freshman, Esther

The heavenly jam
In Luckhardt, M. C. comp. Thanksgiving p311-17 **394.2**

Freshman, Shelley

(illus.) Branley, F. M. Sunshine makes the seasons **525**

(illus.) Srivastava, J. J. Area **516**

Freuchen, Pipaluk

Eskimo boy (4-6) **Fic**

Freudenberger, Helen L.
Jack and Jill
In Burack, A. S. ed. One hundred plays for children p649-55 **808.82**

Freund, Rudolf
(illus.) Peattie, D. C. The rainbow book of nature **574**
(illus.) Zim, H. S. Flowers **582**

Friar Bacon and the brazen head
Williams-Ellis, A. The head of brass
In Williams-Ellis, A. Fairy tales from the British Isles p186-95 **398.2**

Friction

See pages in the following book:

Bendick, J. Motion and gravity p30-39 (3-5) **531**

The **Friday** foursome packs a box. Barbee, L.
In Burack, A. S. ed. Christmas plays for young actors p172-82 **812.08**

Friday night is Papa night. Sonneborn, R. A. **E**

Friedman, Frieda
Dot for short; excerpt
In Association for Childhood Education International. Told under spacious skies p65-74 **S C**
Ellen and the gang (4-6) **Fic**

Friedman, Marvin
(illus.) Cone, M. Annie, Annie **Fic**

Friedrich. Richter, H. P. **Fic**

The **friendly** animals. Petrovitch, W. M.
In Manning-Sanders, R. ed. A book of magical beasts p164-76 **398.2**

Friendly as can be. Asbrand, K.
In Kamerman, S. E. ed. Little plays for little players p143-46 **812.08**

The **friendly** beasts (Carol)
The friendly beasts (k-3) **783.6**

The **friendly** frog. Aulnoy, Mme d'
In Perrault, C. Perrault's Complete fairy tales p135-62 **398.2**

Friends, Society of
Aliki. Story of William Penn (k-2) **92**
Elgin, K. The Quakers (4-7) **289.6**
Henry, M. Benjamin West and his cat Grimalkin (4-6) **92**

See also pages in the following books:

Lengyel, E. The Colony of Pennsylvania p48-55 (5-7) **974.8**
Tunis, E. The tavern at the ferry p 1-10 (5-7) **917.3**

Fiction

De Angeli, M. Thee, Hannah! (3-5) **Fic**
Snedeker, C. D. Downright Dencey (4-6) **Fic**
Turkle, B. The adventures of Obadiah **E**
Turkle, B. Obadiah the Bold **E**
Turkle, B. Thy friend, Obadiah **E**

Friends and neighbors
In DeRoin, N. ed. Jataka tales p22-26 **398.2**

The **friends** of the Loony Lake monster. Bonham, F. **Fic**

Friendship

See pages in the following book:

LeShan, E. You and your feelings p60-74 (6-7) **155.5**

Fiction

Beim, L. Two is a team **E**
Bontemps, A. W. Lonesome boy (5-7) **Fic**
Cohen, B. Thank you, Jackie Robinson (4-6) **Fic**
Cohen, M. Best friends **E**
Conford, E. Me and the terrible two (3-6) **Fic**
Delton, J. Two good friends **E**
Erickson, R. E. A toad for Tuesday (2-4) **Fic**
Green, B. Philip Hall likes me. I reckon maybe (4-6) **Fic**
Green, C. C. A girl called Al (5-7) **Fic**
Gripe, M. Hugo **Fic**
Gripe, M. Hugo and Josephine (3-5) **Fic**
Hoban, R. A bargain for Frances **E**
Hoban, R. Best friends for Frances **E**
Hoffman, P. Steffie and me **E**
Iwasaki, C. Will you be my friend **E**
Kantrowitz, M. I wonder if Herbie's home yet **E**
Little, J. Kate (4-6) **Fic**
Little, J. Look through my window (4-6) **Fic**
Lovelace, M. H. Betsy-Tacy (2-4) **Fic**
Marshall, J. George and Martha **E**
Marshall, J. George and Martha encore **E**
Marshall, J. What's the matter with Carruthers? **E**
Mathis, S. B. Sidewalk story (3-5) **Fic**
Orgel, D. Next door to Xanadu (4-6) **Fic**
Peck, R. N. Soup (5-7) **Fic**
Sharmat, M. W. Gladys told me to meet her here **E**
Slote, A. Tony and me (4-6) **Fic**
Smith, D. B. A taste of blackberries (3-6) **Fic**
Snyder, Z. K. The changeling (4-7) **Fic**
Stevenson, J. The bear who had no place to go **E**
Udry, J. M. Let's be enemies **E**
Winthrop, E. Walking away (5-7) **Fic**
Zolotow, C. The hating book **E**
Zolotow, C. My friend John **E**

Friesian folklore. See Folklore, Friesian

Friis-Baastad, Babbis
Don't take Teddy (5-7) **Fic**

Frisch, Karl von

See pages in the following book:

Ipsen, D. C. What does a bee see? p32-40 (5-7) **595.7**

Frisch, Otto von
Animal migration (6-7) **591.5**

Friskey, Margaret
Chicken Little, count-to-ten **E**

Frithiof's journey to the Orkneys. Hatch, A.
In Hazeltine, A. I. ed. Hero tales from many lands p306-14 **398.2**

Fritz, Jean
And then what happened, Paul Revere? (2-4) **92**
Brady (4-7) **Fic**
The cabin faced west (3-6) **Fic**
Early thunder (6-7) **Fic**
George Washington's breakfast (2-4) **Fic**
He believed in the West
In Cavanah, F. ed. Holiday roundup p55-60 **394.2**
Saturday surprise
In Child Study Association of America. Round about the city p16-28 **S C**
Why don't you get a horse, Sam Adams? (3-5) **92**

Fritz and Franz. Duvoisin, R.
In Duvoisin, R. The three sneezes, and
other Swiss tales p178-84   **398.2**

Frog
Alleyne, L. The frog
In Manning-Sanders, R. ed. A book of
magical beasts p142-47   **398.2**
Borski, L. M. The frog
In Borski, L. M. The jolly tailor, and other
fairy tales p140-56   **398.2**
Manning-Sanders, R. The frog
In Manning-Sanders, R. A book of princes
and princesses p84-96   **398.2**
In Manning-Sanders, R. A choice of magic
p26-38   **398.2**

The **frog** and the moon. Holladay, V.
In Holladay, V. Bantu tales p83-86   **398.2**

The **frog** and the snake. Rouse, W. H. D.
In Hardendorff, J. B. ed. Just one more
p17-18   **372.6**

The **frog** and the stork. Tashjian, V. A.
In Tashjian, V. A. Three apples fell from
heaven p41-46   **398.2**

Frog and Toad are friends. Lobel, A.   **E**

Frog and Toad together. Lobel, A.   **E**

Frog goes to dinner. Mayer, M.   **E**

A **frog** he would a-wooing go; adaptation. See
Langstaff, J. Frog went a-courtin'   **784.4**

The **frog-king.** Grimm, J.
In Arbuthnot, M. H. comp. Time for old
magic p55-56   **398.2**
In Grimm, J. The complete Grimm's Fairy
tales p17-20   **398.2**
In Grimm, J. The juniper tree, and other
tales from Grimm v2 p169-77   **398.2**
See also Frog prince

Frog on his own. Mayer, M.   **E**

Frog prince
The Frog prince
In Hutchinson, V. S. ed. Fireside stories
p143-50   **398.2**
Grimm, J. The frog-king
In Arbuthnot, M. H. comp. Time for old
magic p55-56   **398.2**
Grimm, J. The frog-king, or Iron Henry
In Grimm, J. The complete Grimm's Fairy
tales p17-20   **398.2**
In Grimm, J. The juniper tree, and other
tales from Grimm v2 p169-77   **398.2**
Grimm, J. The frog prince
In Darrell, M. ed. Once upon a time p43-
46   **808.8**
In Grimm, J. Grimms' Fairy tales; illus. by
F. Kredel p86-90   **398.2**
In Grimm, J. Household stories p32-36
398.2
In Grimm, J. Tales from Grimm p179-90
398.2
In Gruenberg, S. M. ed. Favorite stories
old and new p295-98   **808.8**
In Haviland, V. comp. The fairy tale trea-
sury p114-17   **398.2**
In Opie, I. ed. The classic fairy tales p185-
87   **398.2**
Haviland, V. The frog prince
In Haviland, V. Favorite fairy tales told in
Germany p3-12   **398.2**

The **Frog** Prince; puppet play. Mahlmann, L.
In Mahlmann, L. Puppet plays for young
players p9-21   **791.5**

Frog travelers
The two frogs
In Shedlock, M. L. The art of the story-
teller p213-15   **372.6**

Frog went a-courtin'. Langstaff, J.   **784.4**

Frog, where are you? Mayer, M.   **E**

Froghoppers
See pages in the following book:
Hutchins, R. E. The bug clan p17-20 (5-7)
595.7

Frogs
Hawes, J. What I like about toads (k-3)   **597**
Hawes, J. Why frogs are wet (k-3)   **597**
Ommanney, F. D. Frogs, toads & newts (4-6)
597
Simon, S. Discovering what frogs do (2-4)
591.5
Zim, H. S. Frogs and toads (2-5)   **597**
See also pages in the following books:
Buck, M. W. Pets from the pond p44-51 (4-7)
639
Conant, R. A field guide to reptiles and
amphibians of Eastern and Central North
America p297-350   **598.1**
Cooper, E. K. Science on the shores and
banks p119-29 (5-7)   **574.92**
Mason, G. F. Animal sounds p54-58 (4-7)
591.5
Pels, G. The care of water pets p27-30 (4-6)
639
Ricciuti, E. R. Shelf pets p13-27 (5-7)   **639**
Selsam, M. E. The language of animals p33-
40 (5-7)   **591.5**
Silverstein, A. Metamorphosis: the magic
change p34-42 (4-6)   **591.3**
Zappler, G. Amphibians as pets p44-50, 59-72
(5-7)   **639**

Stories
Erickson, R. E. A toad for Tuesday (2-4)   **Fic**
Flack, M. Walter the lazy mouse (2-4)   **Fic**
Freschet, B. The old bullfrog   **E**
Gage, W. Mike's toads (3-5)   **Fic**
Keith, E. Rrra-ah   **E**
Lionni, L. Fish is fish   **E**
Lobel, A. Frog and Toad are friends   **E**
Lobel, A. Frog and Toad together   **E**
Mayer, M. A boy, a dog, and a frog   **E**
Mayer, M. Frog goes to dinner   **E**
Mayer, M. Frog on his own   **E**
Mayer, M. Frog, where are you?   **E**
Potter, B. The tale of Mr Jeremy Fisher   **E**

Frogs and toads. Zim, H. S.   **597**

Frogs of Windham Town. Jagendorf, M. A.
In Jagendorf, M. A. New England bean-
pot p202-05   **398.2**

The **frog's** tattoo. Carpenter, F.
In Carpenter, F. People from the sky p55-
60   **398.2**

Frogs, toads & newts. Ommanney, F. D.   **597**

Frog's wives make ndiba pudding. Courlander, H.
In Courlander, H. The king's drum, and
other African stories p58-59   **398.2**

From a window in Vartov. Andersen, H. C.
  In Andersen, H. C. The complete fairy
    tales and stories p311-12   S C

From afar it is an island. Munari, B.   741.2

From Appomattox to the moon. Boorstin, D. J.
  In Boorstin, D. J. The Landmark history
    of the American people v2   973

From childhood to childhood. Karl, J.   028.5

From fair to fair: folk songs of the British Isles.
  Ritchie, J. comp.   784.4

From idea into house. Myller, R.   728

From one cell to many cells. Zappler, G.   574.8

From petals to pinecones. Cutler, K. N.   745.92

From Plymouth to Appomattox. Boorstin, D. J.
  In Boorstin, D. J. The Landmark history
    of the American people v 1   793

From primer to pleasure in reading. Thwaite,
  M. F.   028.5

From Rollo to Tom Sawyer, and other papers.
  Jordan, A. M.   028.5

From seed to jack-o'-lantern. Johnson, H. L.
    635

From the loom of the dead. Hardendorff, J. B.
  In Hardendorff, J. B. Witches, wit, and a
    werewolf p13-21   S C

From the mixed-up files of Mrs Basil E. Frankweiler. Konigsburg, E. L.   Fic

From the mixed-up files of Mrs Basil E. Frank-
  weiler; excerpt. Konigsburg, E. L.
  In Arbuthnot, M. H. comp. The Arbuth-
    not Anthology of children's litera-
    ture p655-60   808.8
  In Johnson, E. ed. Anthology of children's
    literature p810-16   808.8

From the progressive era to the great depression, 1900-1929. Katz, W. L.   301.45

From the ramparts of the citadel. Andersen,
  H. C.
  In Andersen, H. C. The complete fairy
    tales and stories p309-10   S C

From the Turtle to the Nautilus. Hoyt, E. P.
    623.82

From tiger to Anansi. Sherlock, P. M.
  In Haviland, V. comp. The fairy tale trea-
    sury p86-91   398.2
  In Johnson, E. ed. Anthology of children's
    literature p367-69   808.8
  In Sherlock, P. M. Anansi, the spider man
    p3-12   398.2
    See also Anansi the spider-man

From trails to superhighways. Paradis, A. A.
    625.7

Froman, Robert
  Bigger and smaller (1-3)   513
  Mushrooms and molds (1-3)   589
  Rubber bands, baseballs and doughnuts (2-4)
    514

Fromm, Lilo
  (illus.) Shub, E. Uncle Harry   E

Frondizi, Arturo
  See pages in the following book:
  Hall, E. The land and people of Argentina
    p144-48 (5-7)   918.2

The front door key. Andersen, H. C.
  In Andersen, H. C. The complete fairy
    tales and stories p1039-48   S C

Front-line general, Douglas MacArthur. Archer, J.   92

Frontier and pioneer life
  Aliki. The story of Johnny Appleseed [biog-
    raphy of John Chapman] (k-3)   92
  Aulaire, I. d'. Buffalo Bill [biography of Wil-
    liam Frederick Cody] (1-4)   92
  Averill, E. Daniel Boone (3-6)   92
  Bell, M. E. Kit Carson: mountain man (4-7)
    92
  Daugherty, J. Daniel Boone (5-7)   92
  DeGering, E. Wilderness wife; the story of
    Rebecca Bryan Boone (5-7)   92
  Dorian, E. Trails West and men who made
    them (4-7)   978
  Garst, S. James Bowie and his famous knife
    (5-7)   92
  Garst, S. Jim Bridger, greatest of the moun-
    tain men (4-7)   92
  Holbrook, S. Davy Crockett (5-7)   92
  Holbrook, S. Wild Bill Hickok tames the
    West (4-6)   92
  Parish, P. Let's be early settlers with Daniel
    Boone (2-5)   745.5
  Place, M. T. Marcus and Narcissa Whitman,
    Oregon pioneers (2-5)   92
  Ross, N. W. Heroines of the early West
    (4-6)   920
  Steele, W. O. Westward adventure (5-7) 920

  See also pages in the following book:
  Burt, O. W. The horse in America p77-84
    (5-7)   636.109
    See also Cowboys; Indians of North
    America—Captivities; Overland journeys to
    the Pacific

Fiction
  Brink, C. R. Caddie Woodlawn (4-6)   Fic
  Byars, B. Trouble River (4-6)   Fic
  Calhoun, M. High wind for Kansas (2-4) Fic
  Caudill, R. The far-off land (6-7)   Fic
  Caudill, R. Tree of freedom (6-7)   Fic
  Clifford, E. The year of the three-legged
    deer (4-7)   Fic
  Coatsworth, E. The sod house (2-4)   Fic
  Dalgliesh, A. The courage of Sarah Noble
    (2-4)   Fic
  Field, R. Calico bush (4-7)   Fic
  Franchere, R. Willa (6-7)   Fic
  Fritz, J. The cabin faced west (3-6)   Fic
  McGraw, E. J. Moccasin trail (5-7)   Fic
  Mason, M. E. Caroline and her kettle named
    Maud (2-4)   Fic
  Meader, S. W. Boy with a pack (5-7)   Fic
  Monjo, F. N. Indian summer   E
  Steele, W. O. Flaming arrows (4-6)   Fic
  Steele, W. O. Wilderness journey (4-6) Fic
  Steele, W. O. Winter danger (4-6)   Fic
  Wilder, L. I. Little house in the big woods
    (4-6)   Fic
  Yates, E. Carolina's courage (3-5)   Fic

The West
  Burt, O. W. Negroes in the early West (4-6)
    920
  Felton, H. W. Jim Beckwourth, Negro moun-
    tain man (5-7)   92

Frontier and pioneer life—The West—Continued
Levenson, D. Women of the West (4-7) **301.41**

Place, M. T. Mountain man; the life of Jim Beckwourth (4-7) **92**

Rounds, G. The treeless plains (4-6) **917.8**

Frost, A. B.
(illus.) Brown, M. W. Brer Rabbit **398.2**

Frost, Frances
Menotti, G. C. Gian-Carlo Menotti's Amahl and the night visitors **Fic**

Frost, Robert
You come too (5-7) **811**
About
See pages in the following book:
Benét, L. Famous poets for young people p145-47 (5-7) **920**

Frost. Ralston, W. R. S.
In Fairy tales from many lands p92-99 **398.2**

See also King Frost

Frost. Ransome, A.
In Ransome, A. Old Peter's Russian tales p54-69 **398.2**
In Reeves, J. comp. The Christmas book p142-52 **394.2**
See also King Frost

Fruit
Beck, B. L. The first book of fruits (4-6) **634**
Fenton, C. L. Fruits we eat (4-7) **634**
Guilcher, J. M. A fruit is born (4-7) **582**
Selsam, M. E. The apple and other fruits (3-5) **582**
See also pages in the following book:
Parker, B. M. The new Golden Treasury of natural history p310-19 (5-7) **500.9**

Fruit flies
See pages in the following book:
Villiard, P. Insects as pets p97-100 (5-7) **595.7**

A fruit is born. Guilcher, J. M. **582**

Fruit vegetables, The tomato and other. Selsam, M. E. **635**

Fruits of health. Hatch, M. C.
In Hatch, M. C. More Danish tales p105-18 **398.2**

Fruits we eat. Fenton, C. L. **634**

Frustration. See Emotions

Fry, Guy
(illus.) Sechrist, E. H. ed. It's time for Thanksgiving **394.2**
(illus.) Sechrist, E. H. comp. Poems for red letter days **821.08**

Fry, Rosalie Kingsmill
King of the Hares
In Child Study Association of America. Castles and dragons p29-39 **398.2**

Fry, Rosalind
(illus.) Showers, P. A baby starts to grow **612.6**
(illus.) Showers, P. Use your brain **612**

Fryatt, Norma R.
(ed.) A Horn Book Sampler on children's books and reading. See A Horn Book Sampler on children's books and reading **028.5**

Frye, Burton C.
(ed.) A St Nicholas anthology. See A St Nicholas anthology **810.8**

Fuel. See Coal; Heating

Fujikawa, Gyo
A to Z picture book **E**
(illus.) Stevenson, R. L. A child's garden of verses **821**

Fulahs
See pages in the following books:
Forman, B. The land and people of Nigeria p30-36 (5-7) **916.69**
Jenness, A. Along the Niger River p42-55 (5-7) **916.69**

Fulani. See Fulahs

Fulford, Deborah
(illus.) Ommanney, F. D. Frogs, toads & newts **597**

Fuller, Eunice
Gulliver in the giants' country; retold from Jonathan Swift's Gulliver in the giants' country
In De Regniers, B. S. ed. The giant book p136-58 **398.2**

Fuller, Miriam Morris
Phillis Wheatley, America's first Black poetess (3-6) **92**

Fuller, Muriel
(ed.) More junior authors **920.03**
(jt. ed.) Dobler, L. G. ed. The Dobler World directory of youth periodicals **050**

Fulton, Robert
Judson, C. I. Boat builder (4-6) **92**
See also pages in the following book:
Cottler, J. Heroes of civilization p217-27 (6-7) **920**

Fun and experiments with light. Freeman, M. **535.072**

Fun and game songs, The fireside book of. Winn, M. ed. **784.6**

Fun with ballet. Freeman, M. **792.8**

Fun with crewel embroidery. Wilson, E. **746.4**

Fun with French. Cooper, L. **448**

Fun with German. Cooper, L. **438**

Fun with Italian. Cooper, L. **458**

Fun with lines and curves. Ellison, E. C. **745.4**

Fun with magic. Leeming, J. **793.8**

Fun with magic. Van Rensselaer, A. **793.8**

Fun with naturecraft. Nagle, A. **745.5**

Fun with needlepoint. Hanley, H. **746.4**

Fun with pencil and paper. Leeming, J. **793.7**

Fun with puzzles. Leeming, J. **793.7**

Fun with Spanish. Cooper. L. **468**

Fun with Spanish, More. Cooper, L. **468**

Fun with the calf. De Angeli, M.
In Martignoni, M. E. ed. The illustrated treasury of children's literature p312-16 **808.8**

Fun with your fingers. Helfman, H. **745.5**

Funai, Mamoru
(illus.) Benchley, N. The several tricks of Edgar Dolphin **E**
(illus.) Buck, P. S. Matthew, Mark, Luke and John **Fic**

G

The **games** the Indians played. Lavine, S. A.
790

Games the world around. See Hunt, S. E.
Games and sports the world around **790**

The **Gammage** Cup. Kendall, C. **Fic**

Gammelyn, the dressmaker. Housman, L.
In Housman, L. The rat-catcher's daughter
p24-32 **S C**

Gandhi, Mohandas Karamchand
See pages in the following books:
McNeer, M. Armed with courage p83-98 (4-6)
920
Sechrist, E. H. It's time for brotherhood p78-
83 (5-7) **301.11**

The **Ganges**. Weingarten, V. **915.4**

Ganges River
Weingarten, V. The Ganges (4-6) **915.4**

Gangs. See Juvenile delinquency

The **gangster** in the back seat. Leach, M.
In Leach, M. The thing at the foot of the
bed, and other scary tales p77-79 **S C**

Gannet, Deborah (Sampson)
See pages in the following book:
Rollins, C. H. They showed the way p68-69
(5-7) **920**

Gannett, Ruth Chrisman
(illus.) Bailey, C. S. Miss Hickory **Fic**
(illus.) Gannett, R. S. The dragons of Blueland **Fic**
(illus.) Gannett, R. S. Elmer and the dragon
Fic
(illus.) Gannett, R. S. My father's dragon **Fic**
(illus.) Reyher, B. My mother is the most
beautiful woman in the world **398.2**

Gannett, Ruth Stiles
The dragons of Blueland (1-4) **Fic**
Elmer and the dragon (1-4) **Fic**
My father's dragon (1-4) **Fic**

Gans, Roma
Bird talk (k-3) **598.2**
Birds at night (k-2) **598.2**
Birds eat and eat and eat (k-2) **598.2**
Hummingbirds in the garden (1-3) **598.2**
Icebergs (1-3) **551.3**
It's nesting time (k-2) **598.2**
Millions and millions of crystals (2-4) **548**
Water for dinosaurs and you (1-3) **551.4**

Garbage. See Refuse and refuse disposal

Garcilasco de la Vega, el Inca
Glubok, S. The fall of the Incas **980.3**

Gardam, Jane
A few fair days (4-7) **Fic**

The **garden** of Eden. Andersen, H. C.
In Andersen, H. C. The complete fairy
tales and stories p132-44 **S C**
See also Garden of paradise

Garden of paradise
Andersen, H. C. The garden of Eden
In Andersen, H. C. The complete fairy
tales and stories p132-44 **S C**
Andersen, H. C. The Garden of Paradise
In Andersen, H. C. Andersen's Fairy tales
p204-19 **S C**

Garden pests. See Insects, Injurious and beneficial; Plants—Diseases

The **gardener** and his master. Andersen, H. C.
In Andersen, H. C. The complete fairy
tales and stories p1015-21 **S C**

Gardening
Baker, S. S. The indoor and outdoor grow-it
book (1-6) **635**
Cutler, K. N. Growing a garden, indoors or
out (4-7) **635**
See also Bulbs; Climbing plants; Insects,
Injurious and beneficial; Organiculture;
Vegetable gardening; Weeds

Gardening . . . naturally. Fenten, D. X. **635**

Gardens, Miniature
See pages in the following book:
Selsam, M. E. How to grow house plants
p19-21, 50-62 (4-7) **635.9**

Gardner, Herb
How I crossed the street for the first time
all by myself; short story
In Free to be . . . you and me p100-11
810.8

Gardner, Jeanne LeMonnier
Mary Jemison: Seneca captive (4-6) **92**

Gardner, Martin
Codes, ciphers and secret writing (5-7) **652.8**
Perplexing puzzles and tantalizing teasers
(4-7) **793.7**
Science puzzlers (6-7) **507.2**
Space puzzles: curious questions and answers
about the solar system (6-7) **523.2**

Gardner, Mercedes
King Midas
In Kamerman, S. E. ed. Dramatized folk
tales of the world p177-90 **812.08**

Gardner, Richard
The baboon (5-7) **599**
The boys and girls book about divorce (4-7)
301.42

Garefowl. See Great auk

Garelick, May
Down to the beach **E**
Look at the moon (k-3) **811**
Where does the butterfly go when it rains
E

Garfield, James B.
Follow my Leader (4-7) **Fic**

Garfield, Leon
Mister Corbett's ghost (5-7) **Fic**
Smith (5-7) **Fic**
About
See pages in the following book:
Townsend, J. R. A sense of story p97-104
028.5

Garfield, Nancy
The Tuesday elephant (2-4) **Fic**

Gargal, Berry
Katz, B. ed. Magazines for libraries **016.05**
Katz, B. ed. Magazines for libraries; supple-
ment **016.05**

Gargoyles, monsters and other beasts. Rieger, S. **731**

Garibaldi, Giuseppe
Syme, R. Garibaldi (5-7) **92**

Garment making. See Dressmaking

Garner, Alan
  (ed.) A cavalcade of goblins (4-7)   **398.2**
  The moon of Gomrath (5-7)   **Fic**

About
See pages in the following book:
Townsend, J. R. A sense of story p108-16
    028.5

Garnet, Henry Highland
See pages in the following book:
Rollins, C. H. They showed the way p70-71
  (5-7)   **920**

Garnett, Eve
  The family from One End Street, and some
    of their adventures (4-7)   **Fic**

Garraty, Gail
  (illus.) Le Guin, U. The farthest shore   **Fic**
  (illus.) Le Guin, U. K. The Tombs of Atuan
    Fic

Garrett, Helen
  Angelo, the naughty one   **E**

Garson, Eugenia
  (ed.) The Laura Ingalls Wilder songbook
  (3-7)   **784**

Garst, Doris Shannon. See Garst, Shannon

Garst, Shannon
  A battle for mastery
    In Association for Childhood Education
      International. Told under spacious
      skies p257-70   **S C**
  James Bowie and his famous knife (5-7) **92**
  Jim Bridger, greatest of the mountain men
    (4-7)   **92**

Garthwaite, Marion
  Jamie's ghost horse
    In Hoke, H. ed. Spooks, spooks, spooks
      p51-58   **S C**

Garver, Juliet
  Father hits the jackpot
    In Kamerman, S. E. ed. Fifty plays for
      junior actors p222-35   **812.08**
  A howling success
    In Burack, A. S. ed. Popular plays for
      classroom reading p56-88   **808.82**

Garza, Patricia de. See De Garza, Patricia

Gas and oil engines
  Corbett, S. What about the Wankel engine?
    (4-7)   **621.43**
  See also pages in the following books:
  Limburg, P. R. Engines p35-49 (5-7) **621.4**
  Men of science and invention p62-79 **609**
  The Way things work. Special edition for
    young people p87-147 (6-7)   **600**

Gas engines. See Gas and oil engines

Gases
  See pages in the following books:
  Arbuthnot, M. H. comp. The Arbuthnot An-
    thology of children's literature p892-94
      808.8
  Rosenfeld, S. Science experiments with air
    p41-57 (5-7)   **507.2**
    See also Pneumatics

Gask, Lilian
  The shepherd and the Dragon
    In Hoke, H. comp. Dragons, dragons,
      dragons p90-94   **398.2**

Gasoline engines. See Gas and oil engines

Gastronomy. See Cookery

Gasztold, Carmen Bernos de
  Prayers from the Ark   **841**

Gates, Dee
  (illus.) Fox, M. Sundance coyote   **599**

Gates, Doris
  "As long as we can"
    In Association for Childhood Education
      International. Told under spacious
      skies p302-12   **S C**
  Blue willow (4-7)   **Fic**
  The Cat and Mrs Cary (4-6)   **Fic**
  The contest
    In Association for Childhood Education
      International. Told under the Stars
      and Stripes p122-35   **S C**
  The golden god: Apollo (4-7)   **292**
  Lord of the sky: Zeus (4-7)   **292**
  The shack
    In Johnson, E. ed. Anthology of children's
      literature p804-10   **808.8**
  Two queens of heaven: Aphrodite [and]
    Demeter (4-7)   **292**
  The warrior goddess: Athena (4-7)   **292**

About
See pages in the following book:
Hoffman, M. ed. Authors and illustrators of
  children's books p157-64   **028.5**

Gates, Horatio
See pages in the following book:
Lomask, M. The first American Revolution
  p199-206 (6-7)   **973.3**

Gateways to readable books. Withrow, D. E.
    028.52

Gatheru, R. Mugo
See pages in the following book:
Ojigbo, A. O. comp. Young and Black in
  Africa p71-84 (6-7)   **920**

Gauch, Patricia Lee
  Aaron and the Green Mountain Boys   **E**
  This time, Tempe Wick? (2-5)   **Fic**

Gauchos. See Cowboys

Gaudenzia (Race horse)
Stories
Henry, M. Gaudenzia, pride of the Palio
  (4-7)   **Fic**

Gaudenzia, pride of the Palio. Henry, M. **Fic**

Gaughan, Phoebe
  (illus.) Camp Fire Girls Mother daughter
    cookbook   **641.5**

Gaughran, Bernard
  (jt. auth.) Katz, W. L. The constitutional
    amendments   **342.2**

Gault, Joe
  (illus.) Clemons, E. Shells are where you find
    them   **594**
  (illus.) Clemons, E. Tide pools & beaches
    574.92

Gault, William Campbell
  Stubborn Sam (5-7)   **Fic**

Gauss, Karl Friedrich
See pages in the following book:
Cottler, J. More Heroes of civilization p198-
  210 (6-7)   **920**

Gautama Buddha
Serage, N. The prince who gave up a throne (4-6)   92
See also pages in the following book:
Kettelkamp, L. Religions, East and West p37-45 (5-7)   291

Gaver, Mary V.
(ed.) The Elementary school library collection. See the Elementary school library collection   011

Gavett, Bruce
Skiing for beginners (4-7)   796.9

Gawain and the Grene Knight
Hieatt, C. Sir Gawain and the Green Knight   398.2

Gay, Kathlyn
Be a smart shopper (4-6)   640.73
The Germans helped build America (4-7)   301.45

Gay, Zhenya
The Shire colt
In Gruenberg, S. M. ed. Favorite stories old and new p176-82   808.8

Gay Goshawk
Haynes, D. K. The gay goshawk
In Authors' choice 2 p119-27   S C
Nic Leodhas, S. The gay goss-hawk
In Nic Leodhas, S. Heather and broom p61-67   398.2

Gazetteers
Webster's New geographical dictionary   910

Geber. See Jābir ibn Haiyān

Geckos
See pages in the following book:
Villiard, P. Reptiles as pets p159-66 (5-7)   639

Geddes, Sir Patrick
See pages in the following book:
Cottler, J. More Heroes of civilization p95-105 (6-7)   920

Geer, Charles
(illus.) Hoyt, E. P. From the Turtle to the Nautilus   623.82
(illus.) Sorensen, V. Plain girl   Fic

Geese
See pages in the following book:
Cohen, D. Watchers in the wild p72-83 (6-7)   591.5
Stories
Duvoisin, R. Petunia   E
Duvoisin, R. Petunia, I love you   E
Duvoisin, R. Petunia's Christmas   E
Murphy, R. Wild geese calling (4-6)   Fic
Preston, E. M. Sqawk to the moon, Little Goose   E
Quackenbush, R. Go tell Aunt Rhody   E
Sandburg, H. Joel and the wild goose   E
The geese and the golden chain. Manning-Sanders, R.
In Manning-Sanders, R. A book of mermaids p98-107   398.2

Gehm, Charles C.
(illus.) Peck, R. N. Soup   Fic

Gehr, Mary
(illus.) Podendorf, I. The true book of weeds and wild flowers   582

Gehrig, Lou
Graham, F. Lou Gehrig, a quiet hero (5-7)   92
Luce, W. Lou Gehrig: iron man of baseball (3-5)   92

Geisel, Theodor Seuss
See pages in the following books:
Egoff, S. ed. Only connect p316-22   028.5
Hoffman, M. ed. Authors and illustrators of children's books p165-71   028.5
Smaridge, N. Famous author-illustrators for young people p93-100 (5-7)   920
For works by this author see Seuss, Dr

Geismer, Barbara Peck
(comp.) Very young verses (k-1)   821.08

Gekiere, Madeleine
(illus.) Ciardi, J. The reason for the pelican   811

Gems
Heaps, W. A. Birthstones (5-7)   553
See also Jewelry; Precious stones

General encyclopedias in print   016.03

Generals
Archer, J. Front-line general, Douglas MacArthur (5-7)   92
Commager, H. S. America's Robert E. Lee (5-7)   92
Daniels, J. Stonewall Jackson (5-7)   92
Reynolds, Q. Custer's last stand (5-7)   92

The **general's** horse. Davis, R.
In Davis, R. Padre Porko, the gentlemanly pig p13-26   398.2
In Johnson, E. ed. Anthology of children's literature p239-41   808.8

Generation. See Reproduction

Generation gap. See Conflict of generations

Genes. See Heredity

Genetics
Silverstein, A. The code of life (6-7)   575.1
See also Adaptation (Biology); Evolution; Heredity; Reproduction

Genia
(illus.) Budd, L. Tekla's Easter   Fic

The **genie** of Sutton Place. Selden, G.   Fic

The **Genii** of the Hearth. Graham, G. B.
In Graham, G. B. The beggar in the blanket, & other Vietnamese tales p33-43   398.2

Gennet lives in Ethiopia. Riwkin-Brick, A.   916.3

Gentle Ben. Morey, W.   Fic

The **gentle** Cockatrice. Housman, L.
In Authors' choice 2 p 1-10   S C

Gentle folk, Tale of the. See Tale of the gentle folk

Gentle Gwan Yin. Carpenter, F.
In Carpenter, F. Tales of a Chinese grandmother p29-38   398.2

Gentleman, David
(illus.) Langstaff, J. Saint George and the dragon   822

Geographical atlases. See Atlases

Geographical dictionary, Webster's New   910

George and Martha encore. Marshall, J.　　**E**

George and the field glasses. Green, K.
In Green, K. Leprechaun tales p42-52
398.2

George in the realm of darkness. Baumann, H.
In Baumann, H. The stolen fire p26-28
398.2

George III, King of Great Britain
Fiction
Monjo, F. N. King George's head was made
of lead (2-4)　　**Fic**

**George Peabody College for Teachers, Nash-
ville, Tenn.** Free and inexpensive learning
materials　　**016.371**

George Rogers Clark: frontier fighter. De
Leeuw, A.　　**92**

George, Saint
See pages in the following book:
Johnson, E. ed. Anthology of children's liter-
ature p502-03　　**808.8**

George Washington Bridge
Fiction
Swift, H. H. The little red lighthouse and
the great gray bridge　　**E**

George Washington's breakfast. Fritz, J.　　**Fic**

Georgia
Fiction
Burch, R. D.J.'s worst enemy (4-6)　　**Fic**
Burch, R. Hut School and the wartime home-
front heroes (4-6)　　**Fic**
Burch, R. Queenie Peavy (5-7)　　**Fic**
Burch, R. Renfroe's Christmas (3-5)　　**Fic**
Burch, R. Skinny (4-6)　　**Fic**
Burchard, P. Bimby (4-6)　　**Fic**
History
Vaughan, H. C. The Colony of Georgia (4-7)
975.8

Georgie. Bright, R.　　**E**

Georgie finds a grandpa. Young, M.
In Gruenberg, S. M. comp. Let's hear a
story p97-101　　**808.8**

Georgy Piney-Woods Peddler. Jagendorf, M. A.
In Jagendorf, M. A. Folk stories of the
South p99-105　　**398.2**

Geoscience. See Geology

Gerbils
Dobrin, A. Gerbils (3-6)　　**636.08**
Simon, S. Discovering what gerbils do (2-5)
636.08

See also pages in the following book:
Stevens, C. Your first pet p7-17 (2-4) **636.08**

Gerbils, and other small pets. Shuttlesworth,
D. E.　　**636.08**

Gerez, Toni de
(comp.) 2-rabbit, 7-wind (5-7)　　**897**

Gergely, Tibor
(jt. auth.) Brown, M. W. Wheel on the chimney　　**E**
(illus.) Davis, J. A. Five hundred animals
from A to Z　　**591.03**
(illus.) Turner, N. B. When it rained cats and
dogs　　**E**

Germ theory of disease
See pages in the following books:
Asimov, I. How did we find out about germs?
p43-55 (5-7)　　**616.01**
Silverstein, A. Germfree life p15-20 (5-7) **576**

German language
Cooper, L. Fun with German (4-7)　　**438**
See also pages in the following book:
Wohlrabe, R. A. The land and people of
Germany p127-33 (5-7)　　**914.3**

German language editions
Kästner, E. Emil and the detectives　　**Fic**
Saint Exupéry, A. de. The little prince　　**Fic**

German literature
See pages in the following book:
Wohlrabe, R. A. The land and people of
Germany p127-33 (5-7)　　**914.3**

Germanic art. See Art, Germanic

Germanic legends. See Legends, Germanic

The Germans helped build America. Gay, K.
301.45

Germans in Kansas
Fiction
Coatsworth, E. The sod house (2-4)　　**Fic**

Germans in the United States
Gay, K. The Germans helped build America
(4-7)　　**301.45**

Germany
Wohlrabe, R. A. The land and people of
Germany (5-7)　　**914.3**
Fiction
Benary-Isbert, M. The Ark (5-7)　　**Fic**
Benary-Isbert, M. Blue mystery (5-7)　　**Fic**
Benary-Isbert, M. The wicked enchantment
(5-7)　　**Fic**
Richter, H. P. Friedrich (5-7)　　**Fic**
Folklore
See Folklore—Germany
Social conditions
Richter, H. P. I was there (6-7)　　**92**
Social life and customs
See pages in the following book:
Sechrist, E. H. ed. Christmas everywhere
p111-17　　**394.2**

Germany (Democratic Republic)
Fles, B. East Germany (5-7)　　**914.3**

Germany (Federal Republic)
Kirby, G. Looking at Germany (4-6)　　**914.3**
Lobsenz, N. M. The first book of West
Germany (4-7)　　**914.3**
Social life and customs
Gidal, S. My village in Germany (4-6)　　**914.3**

Germfree life. Silverstein, A.　　**576**

Germs. See Bacteriology; Germ theory of disease; Microorganisms

Geronimo, Apache chief
Syme, R. Geronimo, the fighting Apache (3-5)
92
Wilson, C. M. Geronimo (5-7)　　**92**
Wyatt, E. Geronimo, the last Apache war
chief (4-6)　　**92**

Giant of the Hills. Jagendorf, M. A.
In Jagendorf, M. A. New England beanpot p62-66   398.2

The **Giant** Okab. Mehdevi, A. S.
In Mehdevi, A. S. Persian folk and fairy tales p62-68   398.2

Giant panda
Grosvenor, D. K. Pandas (k-3)   599
Hiss, A. The giant panda book (3-5)   599
Martin, L. The giant panda (3-6)   599

The **giant** panda book. Hiss, A.   599

Giant Pears and Giant Cows
In De Regniers, B. S. ed. The giant book p174-75   398.2

The **giant** planets. Nourse, A. E.   523.4

Giant who had no heart
Asbjörnsen, P. C. The giant who had no heart in his body
In Asbjörnsen, P. C. East of the sun and west of the moon, and other tales p42-52   398.2
In Fenner, P. R. comp. Giants & witches and a dragon or two p39-49   398.2
In Mayne, W. ed. William Mayne's Book of giants p108-18   398.2
The Giant who had no heart in his body
In De Regniers, B. S. ed. The giant book p81-93   398.2
In Undset, S. ed. True and untrue, and other Norse tales p108-17   398.2

The **Giant** who rode on the ark
In De Regniers, B. S. ed. The giant book p131-34   398.2

The **giant** who stole a river, Rust, D.
In Mayne, W. ed. William Mayne's Book of giants p27-34   398.2

Giant with the golden hair
Grimm, J. The Devil and his three golden hairs
In Grimm, J. The juniper tree, and other tales from Grimm v 1 p80-93   398.2
Grimm, J. The Devil with the three golden hairs
In Grimm, J. The complete Grimm's Fairy tales p151-58   398.2
Grimm, J. Giant with the three golden hairs
In Grimm, J. Grimms' Fairy tales; illus. by F. Kredel p313-21   398.2
Haviland, V. The three golden hairs of Grandfather Know All
In Haviland, V. Favorite fairy tales told in Czechoslovakia p67-90   398.2

Giants
See pages in the following book:
McHargue, G. The impossible people p 1-26 (5-7)   398

Fiction
De Regniers, B. S. ed. The giant book (4-6)   398.2
Du Bois, W. P. The giant (4-7)   Fic
Mayne, W. ed. William Mayne's Book of giants (4-6)   398.2

The **Giants** and the herd-boy
In Lang, A. ed. The yellow fairy book p75-77   398.2

Giants & witches and a dragon or two. Fenner, P. R. comp.   398.2

The **giants** of Towednack. Williams-Ellis, A.
In Mayne, W. ed. William Mayne's Book of giants p138-47   398.2
In Williams-Ellis, A. Fairy tales from the British Isles p216-48   398.2

Gibbs, Tony
Sailing (5-7)   797.1

Gibran, Kahlil
See pages in the following book:
Winder, V. H. The land and people of Lebanon p148-51 (5-7)   915.692

Gibson, Althea
See pages in the following books:
Lorimer, L. T. ed. Breaking in p133-56 (5-7)   920
Ross, P. ed. Young and female p71-79 (6-7)   920

Gibson, John R.
(illus.) Sechrist, E. H. It's time for brotherhood   301.11

Gidal, Sonia
My village in England (4-6)   914.2
My village in Germany (4-6)   914.3
My village in Hungary (3-6)   914.39

Gidal, Tim
(jt. auth.) Gidal, S. My village in England   914.2
(jt. auth.) Gidal, S. My village in Germany   914.3

Giese, Al
(illus.) De Regniers, B. S. Circus   791.3

The **gift**. Balet, J.   E

The **gift**. Dickinson, P.   Fic

The **gift** and the giver. Davis, R.
In Davis, R. The lion's whiskers p172-77   398.2

A **gift** for Hans Brinker. Thane, A.
In Kamerman, S. E. ed. Dramatized folk tales of the world p200-11   812.08

Gift for the lazy. Davis, R.
In Davis, R. The lion's whiskers p130-32   398.2

A **gift** from Johnny Appleseed. Whittaker, H.
In Kamerman, S. E. ed. Dramatized folk tales of the world p537-48   812.08

The **gift** of Father Frost. Maas, S.
In Maas, S. The moon painters, and other Estonian folk tales p17-25   398.2

The **Gift** of fishes
In Gunterman, B. L. ed. Castles in Spain, and other enchantments p241-46   398.2

The **gift** of gold. Tashjian, V. A.
In Tashjian, V. A. Three apples fell from heaven p63-76   398.2

The **Gift** of St Nicholas
In Association for Childhood Education International. Told under the Christmas tree p54-61   808.8
In Malcolmson, A. Yankee Doodle's cousins p11-19   398.2

Gift of the earth. Crespi, P.
In Dalgliesh, A. comp. Christmas p225-36   393.2

The **gift** of the fairies. Very, A.
    In Kamerman, S. E. ed. Little plays for
      little players p9-13   **812.08**
The **gift** of The Hairy One. Thompson, V. L.
    In Thompson, V. L. Hawaiian myths of
      earth, sea, and sky p53-59   **398.2**
The **gift** of the magi. Henry, O.
    In Parents' Magazine's Christmas holiday
      book p258-63   **394.2**
    In Tudor, T. ed. Take joy! p47-51   **394.2**
The **gift** of the old pine tree. Simon, C. M.
    In Johnson, L. S. ed. Christmas stories
      round the world p33-38   **394.2**
The **gift** of the river. Meadowcroft, E. L. **932**
A **gift** of the unicorn. Wyndham, R.
    In Wyndham, R. Tales the people tell in
      China p34-37   **398.2**
A **gift** should be given. Whitehouse, E.
    In Luckhardt, M. C. ed. Christmas comes
      once more p86-94   **394.2**
A **gift** that came back. Kelsey, A. G.
    In Kelsey, A. G. Once the Hodja p46-53
      398.2
Gift wrapping
    See pages in the following book:
Hautzig, E. Let's make more presents p139-
43 (4-7)   **745.5**
Gifts
Cutler, K. N. Crafts for Christmas (3-7)
    745.59
Hautzig, E. Let's make more presents (4-7)
    745.5
Gifts for the first birthday. Sawyer, R.
    In Sechrist, E. H. ed. It's time for Christ-
      mas p194-97   **394.2**
Gifts for the harvest festival. Marson, U.
    In Luckhardt, M. C. comp. Thanksgiving
      p281-89   **394.2**
Gifts from the Greeks. Boyer, S. A. **913.38**
The **gifts** of the magician. Green, R. L.
    In Green, R. L. ed. A cavalcade of magi-
      cians p122-30   **808.8**
Gilbert, Ann (Taylor)
    See pages in the following book:
Benét, L. Famous poets for young people
    p17-19 (5-7)   **920**
Gilbert, Helen Earle
Mrs Mallaby's birthday
    In Ward, W. ed. Stories to dramatize p62-
      68   **372.6**
Gilbert, Nan
House of the singing windows
    In Association for Childhood Education In-
      ternational. Told under the Stars and
      Stripes p159-71   **S C**
The meaning of the word
    In Association for Childhood Education In-
      ternational. Told under spacious skies
      p217-29   **S C**
Gilbert, William P.
    (illus.) Sabin, F. Dogs of America   **636.7**
Gilberto and the Wind. Ets, M. H.   **E**
Gilbertson, Mildred Geiger. See Gilbert, Nan
Gilbreath, Alice Thompson
Beginning-to-read riddles and jokes (1-3)
    793.7

Making costumes for parties, plays, and holi-
    days (4-6)   **391**
Gildaen. Buchwald, E.   **Fic**
Gilded age, The art of America in the. Glu-
    bok, S.   **709.73**
Giles, H. A.
The stone monkey
    In Manning-Sanders, R. ed. A book of
      magical beasts p45-48   **398.2**
Gilgamesh
Bryson, B. Gilgamesh (5-7)   **398.2**
Feagles, A. He who saw everything (4-6) **892**
    See also pages in the following books:
Arbuthnot, M. H. comp. The Arbuthnot An-
    thology of children's literature p455-58
    808.8
Arbuthnot, M. H. comp. Time for old magic
    p319-22   **398.2**
Baumann, H. In the land of Ur p57-69 (6-7)
    913.35
Lansing, E. The Sumerians p157-71 (6-7)
    913.35
Gilkison, Grace
    (illus.) Association for Childhood Education
    International. Told under the green um-
    brella   **398.2**
Gill, Derek L. T.
Graham, R. L. The boy who sailed around
    the world alone   **910.4**
Gill, Margery
    (illus.) Arthur, R. M. A candle in her room
    Fic
    (illus.) Cooper, S. Dawn of fear   **Fic**
    (illus.) Cooper, S. Over sea, under stone **Fic**
    (illus.) De La Mare, W. ed. Tom Tiddler's
    ground   **821.08**
Gillen, Denver
    (illus.) Nathan, A. G. The first transatlantic
    cable   **621.382**
Gillespie, Jessie
    (illus.) Wiggin, K. D. The Birds' Christmas
    Carol   **Fic**
Gillespie, John T.
Creating a school media program   **027.8**
Introducing books   **028.1**
Juniorplots   **028.1**
Paperback books for young people **070.5025**
The young phenomenon: paperbacks in our
    schools   **027.8**
Gillespie and the guards. Elkin, B.   **E**
Gillham, Charles E.
Beyond the Clapping Mountains (3-6) **398.2**
    Contents: Mountains that clapped together; How
    the sea gulls learned to fly; Mr Crow takes a wife;
    How the little owl's name was changed; The crow and
    the whale; The mouse and the flea; How Mr Crane's
    eyes became blue; How the ptarmigans learned to fly;
    How the foxes became red; Mrs Longspur's second
    marriage; The sculpin and the fox; Mr Crow and the
    mussel; How the black turnstone came to nest near the
    sea
How the little owl's name was changed
    In Arbuthnot, M. H. comp. The Arbuthnot
      Anthology of children's literature
      p394-96   **808.8**
    In Arbuthnot, M. H. comp. Time for old
      magic p263-65   **398.2**
Mr Crow takes a wife
    In Johnson, E. ed. Anthology of children's
      literature p338-41   **808.8**

Gilmore, H. H.
Model boats for beginners (5-7)   **623.82**
Model submarines for beginners (5-7)   **623.82**

Gilstrap, Robert
Allah will provide
   In Arbuthnot, M. H. comp. The Arbuthnot
     Anthology of children's literature
     p310-12   **808.8**
   In Arbuthnot, M. H. comp. Time for old
     magic p189-91   **398.2**

Gimpel's golden broth. Simon, S.
   In Simon, S. The wise men of Helm and
     their merry tales p77-88   **S C**

Ginger

   See pages in the following book:

Cooper, E. K. And everything nice p60-63
(3-5)   **641.3**

Ginger Pye. Estes, E.   **Fic**

Gingerbread boy
Bryant, S. C. The Gingerbread Boy
   In Haviland, V. comp. The fairy tale trea-
     sury p7-11   **398.2**
Galdone, P. The gingerbread boy   **398.2**
Gingerbread boy
   In The Tall book of nursery tales p16-22
     398.2

   See also Bun; Johnny-cake; Pancake;
Wee bannock

Gingham Lena. Brock, E. L.
   In Association for Childhood Education In-
     ternational. Told under the magic
     umbrella p12-17   **S C**

Ginsburg, Mirra
The chick and the duckling   **E**
How the sun was brought back to the sky
(k-2)   **398.2**
(ed.) The Kaha bird (4-6)   **398.2**
   Contents: The golden bowl; Living water; Oskus-
Ool and his nine red horses; Torko-Chachak—the
Silken Tassel; Three daughters; Three Maidens; Two
tricksters; Maymunyak or the magic of the yellow
monkey; The wise Nasreddin; The clever wife; The
shepherd, the tiger, and the fox; The Kaha bird; The
bear's son; The fool; The jackal and the polecat; I
was in it; Flies; Tsap-Tsarap; A hundred lies
(ed.) The lazies (3-5)   **389.2**
   Contents: Sheidulla; Who will wash the pot; Easy
bread; Who will row next; Three knots; Two frogs;
The clever chief; The ox and the ass; The princess who
learned to work; Toast and honey; The bird, the
mouse, and the sausage; The lazy daughter; Ea and
Eo; Ayoga; The miller's sons
Mushroom in the rain   **E**
(comp.) One trick too many (1-3)   **398.2**
The proud maiden, Tungak, and the Sun
(1-3)   **398.2**
Three kittens   **E**

La Gioconda; adaptaion. Bulla, C. R.
   In Bulla, C. R. More stories of favorite
     operas p169-81   **782.1**

Giotto di Bondone
(illus.) Jewett, S. God's troubadour; the story
   of Saint Francis of Assisi   **92**

About
Rockwell, A. The boy who drew sheep (3-5)
   92

   See also pages in the following book:

Jacobs, D. Master painters of the Renaissance
p18-25 (6-7)   **759.5**

Giovanni, Nikki
Spin a soft Black song (k-3)   **811**

Giovanopoulos, Paul
(illus.) How many miles to Babylon?   **Fic**

Gipsies. See Gypsies

Gipsy and the dragon
Manning-Sanders, R. The deluded dragon
   In Hoke, H. comp. Dragons, dragons,
     dragons p149-54   **398.2**

The **giraffe** hunters. Courlander, H.
   In Courlander, H. The king's drum, and
     other African stories p90-94   **398.2**

Giraffes
Cooke, A. Giraffes at home (1-3)   **599**
MacClintock, D. A natural history of giraffes
(6-7)   **599**

   See also pages in the following book:

Wellman, A. Africa's animals p58-63 (6-7)
   591.9

Stories
Rey, H. A. Cecily G. and the 9 monkeys   **E**

Giraffes at home. Cooke, A.   **599**

The **girl** and the goatherd. Ness, E.   **E**

A **girl** called Al. Greene, C. C.   **Fic**

The **girl** in the basket. Manning-Sanders, R.
   In Manning-Sanders, R. A book of ogres
     and trolls p66-74   **398.2**
   See also Girl in the chest

Girl in the chest
Fillmore, P. Girl in the chest
   In Fillmore, P. The laughing prince p201-
     17   **398.2**
Manning-Sanders, R. The girl in the basket
   In Manning-Sanders, R. A book of ogres
     and trolls p66-74   **398.2**

Girl Scout cookbook. Girl Scouts of the United
States of America   **641.5**

The **Girl Scout** story. De Leeuw, A.   **369.463**

Girl Scouts

Fiction
De Angeli, M. Bright April (3-5)   **Fic**

Handbooks, manuals, etc.
Girl Scouts of the United States of America.
Brownie Girl Scout handbook (1-3) **369.463**
Girl Scouts of the United States of America.
Junior Girl Scout handbook (4-7) **369.463**

History
De Leeuw, A. The Girl Scout story (2-5)
   369.463

Girl Scouts of the United States of America
Brownie Girl Scout handbook (1-3) **369.463**
Cooking out-of-doors (4-7)   **641.5**
Girl Scout cookbook (4-7)   **641.5**
Junior Girl Scout handbook (4-7)   **369.463**
Sing together (4-7)   **784.6**
De Leeuw, A. The Girl Scout story (2-5)
   369.463
Radford, R. L. Juliette Low: Girl Scout
   founder (3-5)   **92**
World Association of Girl Guides and Girl
   Scouts. Trefoil round the world   **369.463**

The **Girl** who could think
   In Gruenberg, S. M. ed. Favorite stories
     old and new p349-52   **808.8**
   See also Lantern and the fan

The girl who cried flowers. Yolen, J.
 In Yolen, J. The girl who cried flowers, and other tales p 1-10   **S C**

The girl who cried flowers, and other tales. Yolen, J.   **S C**

Girl who kissed the peach-tree. Farjeon, E.
 In Farjeon, E. The little bookroom p83-90   **S C**

The girl who lived with the gazelles. Carpenter, F.
 In Carpenter, F. African wonder tales p77-85   **398.2**

The girl who loved the wind. Yolen, J.   **E**

The girl who picked strawberries. Manning-Sanders, R.
 In Manning-Sanders, R. A choice of magic p291-94   **398.2**

The girl who sat by the ashes. Colum, P. **398.2**
 See also Cinderella

Girl who sought her nine brothers. Bowman, J. C.
 In Bowman, J. C. Tales from a Finnish tupa p116-25   **398.2**

The girl who stepped on bread. Andersen, H. C.
 In Andersen, H. C. The complete fairy tales and stories p606-13   **S C**
 See also Girl who trod on the loaf

Girl who trod on the loaf
 Andersen, H. C. The girl who stepped on bread
 In Andersen, H. C. The complete fairy tales and stories p606-13   **S C**
 Andersen, H. C. The girl who trod on a loaf
 In Andersen, H. C. Andersen's Fairy tales p107-15   **S C**

The Girl who used her wits
 In Tashjian, V. A. ed. With a deep sea smile p64-69   **372.6**

Girl with the horse's head
 Carpenter, F. Lady with the horse's head
 In Carpenter, R. Tales of a Chinese grandmother p98-106   **398.2**

The girl without a name. Beckman, G.   **Fic**

The girl without hands. Grimm, J.
 In Grimm, J. The complete Grimm's Fairy tales p160-66   **398.2**

Girls

Poetry

Hopkins, L. B. comp. Girls can too! (k-3)   **811.08**

Girls are equal too. Carlson, D.   **301.41**

Girls can be anything. Klein, N.   **E**

Girls can too! Hopkins, L. B. comp.   **811.08**

Girrowin. Baumann, H.
 In Baumann, H. The stolen fire p105-07   **398.2**

Giselle. Untermeyer, L.
 In Untermeyer, L. Tales from the ballet p61-66   **792.8**

Gissing and the telephone. Morley, C.
 In Association for Childhood Education International. Told under the magic umbrella p79-85   **S C**

Githens, Elizabeth M.
 (illus.) Cooper, L. Fun with German   **438**

Giuanni and the giant
 In De Regniers, B. S. ed. The giant book p60-68   **398.2**

Giufá and the judge. Jagendorf, M. A.
 In Jagendorf, M. A. Noodlehead stories from around the world p173-74   **398.2**

Giusti, George
 (illus.) Sitomer, M. Circles   **516**

Give me a river; excerpt. Palmer, E.
 In Association for Childhood Education International. Told under the Stars and Stripes p150-58   **S C**

Give me freedom. McNeer, M.   **920**

Give my love to Boston. Coatsworth, E.
 In Luckhardt, M. C. comp. Thanksgiving p255-65   **394.2**

Glacial epoch
 May, J. They lived in the ice age (1-3) **551.7**
 See also pages in the following book:
 Matthews, W. H. The story of glaciers and the ice age p113-32 (5-7)   **551.3**

Glacier National Park
 See pages in the following books:
 Melbo, I. R. Our country's national parks v2 p110-33 (5-7)   **917.3**
 National Geographic Society. The new America's wonderlands p80-94   **917.3**

Glaciers
 Lockard, R. Glaciers (1-3)   **551.3**
 Matthews, W. H. The story of glaciers and the ice age (5-7)   **551.3**
 See also pages in the following book:
 Kirk, R. Yellowstone p14-19 (5-7)   **917.87**

The gladiator, the belle, and the good snowstorm. Jagendorf, M. A.
 In Jagendorf, M. A. Folk stories of the South p257-59   **398.2**

Gladstone, Gary
 Dune buggies (4-7)   **629.22**
 (illus.) Samson, J. Watching the new baby   **649**

Gladstone, M. J.
 A carrot for a nose (4-7)   **745**

Gladys told me to meet her here. Sharmat, M. W.   **E**

Glands
 See pages in the following book:
 Silverstein, A. The excretory system p34-38 (4-6)   **574.1**

Glands, Ductless
 Silverstein, A. The endocrine system (4-7)   **612**
 See also Hormones

Glanzman, Louis S.
 (illus.) Branley, F. M. Man in space to the moon   **629.45**
 (illus.) Goodsell, J. The Mayo brothers   **92**
 (illus.) Lindgren, A. Pippi in the South Seas   **Fic**
 (illus.) Lindgren, A. Pippi Longstocking   **Fic**
 (illus.) Sachs, M. The truth about Mary Rose   **Fic**
 (illus.) Sachs, M. Veronica Ganz   **Fic**
 (illus.) Stolz, M. The noonday friends   **Fic**

Glanzman, Louis S.—*Continued*
(illus.) Stolz, M. A wonderful, terrible time **Fic**
(illus.) Stuart, G. S. Three little Indians **970.1**

Glaser, Milton
(illus.) Aiken, C. Cats and bats and things with wings **811**

Glass
Buehr, W. The marvel of glass (5-7) **666**
Fisher, L. E. The glassmakers (4-7) **666**
See also pages in the following book:
Schwartz, J. It's fun to know why p43-59 (4-7) **507.2**

The Glass axe
In Lang, A. ed. The yellow fairy book p141-48 **398.2**

Glass blowing and working
See pages in the following book:
Tunis, E. Colonial craftsmen and the beginnings of American industry p136-41 (5-7) **680**

The glass coffin. Grimm, J.
In Grimm, J. The complete Grimm's Fairy tales p672-78 **398.2**
See also Crystal coffin

Glass manufacture
Buehr, W. The marvel of glass (5-7) **666**
Fisher, L. E. The glassmakers (4-7) **666**

The Glass mountain
In Lang, A. ed. The yellow fairy book p114-18 **398.2**

The glass peacock. Farjeon, E.
In Author's choice p139-47 **S C**
In Farjeon, E. The little bookroom p263-71 **S C**

Glass, stones & crown. Rockwell, A. **726**

The glassblower's children. Gripe, M. **Fic**

The glassmakers. Fisher, L. E. **666**

Glazer, Tom
Eye winker, Tom Tinker, chin chopper (k-3) **796.1**

Gleeson, Joseph M.
(illus.) Kipling, R. Just so stories **S C**

Gleit, Maria
Paul becomes a nipper in a mine
In Association for Childhood Education International. Told under spacious skies p105-14 **S C**

Gleitsmann, Hertha. See Gleit, Maria

Glen Canyon National Recreation Area
See pages in the following book:
National Geographic Society. The new America's wonderlands p131-39 **917.3**

Glenn, John Herschel
See pages in the following book:
Americans in space p102-25 (5-7) **629.4**

Glick, Carl
My song Yankee Doodle
In Association for Childhood Education International. Told under the Stars and Stripes p91-101 **S C**

Gliders (Aeronautics)
Halacy, D. Soaring (3-6) **797.5**
Kettelkamp, L. Gliders (3-6) **629.133**
Models
Kettelkamp, L. Gliders (3-6) **629.133**

Gliding and soaring
Halacy, D. Soaring (3-6) **797.5**

Glimpses of Louisa. Alcott, L. M. **S C**

Glinka, Mikhail Ivanovich
See pages in the following book:
Posell, E. Z. Russian composers p10-17 (5-7) **920**

Glooscap's beads. Hooke, H. M.
In Hooke, H. M. Thunder in the mountains p27-43 **398.2**

Glooskap
In Garner, A. ed. A cavalcade of goblins p210-12 **398.2**

Gloriana. Kipling, R.
In Farjeon, E. ed. A cavalcade of queens p134-52 **808.8**

The glorious whitewasher. Twain, M.
In Arbuthnot, M. H. comp. The Arbuthnot Anthology of children's literature p673-76 **808.8**
In Martignoni, M. E. ed. The illustrated treasury of children's literature p441-45 **808.8**

Glory in the flower. Johnston, N. **Fic**

Glossaries. See names of languages or subjects with subdivision Dictionaries, e.g. English language—Dictionaries; Mythology—Dictionaries

Gloucester boy; excerpt. Holberg, R. L.
In Association for Childhood Education International. Told under the Stars and Stripes p239-48 **S C**

Glow-worms. See Fireflies

Glubok, Shirley
The art of Africa (4-7) **709.6**
The art of America from Jackson to Lincoln (4-7) **709.73**
The art of America in the early twentieth century (4-7) **709.73**
The art of America in the gilded age (4-7) **709.73**
The art of ancient Egypt (4-7) **709.32**
The art of ancient Greece (4-7) **709.38**
The art of ancient Mexico (4-6) **709.01**
The art of ancient Peru (4-7) **985**
The art of ancient Rome (4-7) **709.37**
The art of China (4-7) **709.51**
The art of colonial America (4-7) **709.73**
The art of India (4-7) **709.54**
The art of Japan (4-7) **709.52**
The art of lands in the Bible (4-7) **709.01**
The art of the Eskimo (4-7) **709.98**
The art of the Etruscans (4-7) **709.37**
The art of the new American nation (4-7) **709.73**
The art of the North American Indian (3-6) **709.01**
The art of the Northwest coast Indians (4-7) **709.01**
The art of the Old West (4-7) **709.73**
The art of the Southwest Indians (4-7) **709.01**
The art of the Spanish in the United States and Puerto Rico (4-7) **709.73**
Dolls, dolls, dolls (3-6) **688.7**
The fall of the Incas (5-7) **980.3**
Knights in armor (4-7) **623.4**

Glue
See pages in the following book:
Sattler, H. R. Recipes for art and craft materials p23-27 (4-7) **745.5**

The **gluttonous** wife. Belpré, P.
In Belpré, P. The tiger and the rabbit, and other tales p85-86 **398.2**

The **gnome**. Grimm, J.
In Grimm, J. The complete Grimm's Fairy tales p420-24 **398.2**
See also Earth gnome

Gnomes. See Fairies

Go and hush the baby. Byars, B. **E**

Go away, dog. Nodset, J. L. **E**

Go I know not whither—fetch I know not what
Bowman, J. C. Ei-Niin-Mita, or No-So-What
In Bowman, J. C. Tales from a Finnish tupa p105-15 **398.2**
Manning-Sanders, R. Go I Know Not Whither and Fetch I Know Not What
In Manning-Sanders, R. A book of sorcerers and spells p9-23 **398.2**

Go tell Aunt Rhody (Folk song)
Go tell Aunt Rhody (k-3) **784.4**
Quackenbush, R. Go tell Aunt Rhody **E**

Go to the room of the eyes. Erwin, B. K. **Fic**

The **Goat** and the tiger
In Carter, D. S. ed. Greedy Mariani, and other folktales of the Antilles p35-40 **398.2**

Goat comes to the Christmas party. Evans, E. K.
In Association for Childhood Education International. Told under the Christmas tree p132-36 **808.8**
In Rollins, C. comp. Christmas gif' p45-50 **394.2**

Goat girl
Aulaire, I. d'. Tatterhood
In Aulaire, I. d'. East of the sun and west of the moon p179-87 **398.2**
Manning-Sanders, R. Tatterhood
In Manning-Sanders, R. A book of witches p94-103 **398.2**
In Manning-Sanders, R. A choice of magic p246-55 **398.2**

Goat that went to school. Credle, E.
In Credle, E. Tall tales from the high hills, and other stories p133-44 **398.2**

The **goat** well. Courlander, H.
In Colwell, E. ed. A second storyteller's choice p97-102 **372.6**
In Courlander, H. The fire on the mountain, and other Ethiopian stories p57-63 **398.2**
In Johnson, E. ed. Anthology of children's literature p369-71 **808.8**

Goatherd who won a princess. Boggs, R. S.
In Boggs, R. S. Three golden oranges, and other Spanish folk tales p109-16 **398.2**

Goats
Englebert, V. The goats of Agadez (1-3) **916.6**
See also pages in the following book:
Fenton, C. L. Animals that help us p32-37 (4-6) **636**

Stories
Asbjørnsen, P. C. The three Billy Goats Gruff (k-3) **398.2**
Berson, H. Balarin's goat **E**
Galdone, P. The three Billy Goats Gruff (k-1) **398.2**
Grimm, J. The wolf and the seven little kids (k-3) **398.2**
Uchida, Y. Sumi & the goat & the Tokyo Express (1-4) **Fic**
Watson, N. D. The birthday goat **E**

Goats in the turnip field
Poulsson, E. The three goats
In Association for Childhood Education International. Told under the green umbrella p78-80 **398.2**

The **goats** of Agadez. Englebert, V. **916.6**

The **goats** who killed the leopard. Courlander, H.
In Courlander, H. The fire on the mountain, and other Ethiopian stories p25-26 **398.2**

The **goats** who killed the leopard. Hawes, J. **E**

Gobbato, Imero
(illus.) Colum, P. The girl who sat by the ashes **398.2**
(illus.) Curry, J. L. Beneath the hill **Fic**
(illus.) Kendall, C. The Whisper of Glocken **Fic**
(illus.) Linde, G. The white stone **Fic**

Gobble, growl, grunt. Spier, P. **E**

Gobbleknoll
In Garner, A. ed. A cavalcade of goblins p 1-2 **398.2**

The **gobble-uns'll** git you ef you don't watch out! Riley, J. W. **811**

Gobborn Seer
Young, E. The wonder smith and his son (5-7) **398.2**
See also pages in the following books:
Jacobs, J. ed. More English folk and fairy tales p60-64 **398.2**
Johnson, E. ed. Anthology of children's literature p513-17 **808.8**

Gobhai, Mehlli
(illus.) Shetty, S. A Hindu boyhood **915.4**

Goble, Dorothy
(jt. auth.) Goble, P. Brave Eagle's account of the Fetterman Fight, 21 December 1866 **978.7**
(jt. auth.) Goble, P. Lone Bull's horse raid **970.3**
(jt. auth.) Goble, P. Red Hawk's account of Custer's last battle **973.8**

Goble, Paul
Brave Eagle's account of the Fetterman Fight, 21 December 1866 (5-7) **978.7**
Lone Bull's horse raid (3-6) **970.3**
Red Hawk's account of Custer's last battle (4-7) **973.8**

The **goblin** and the grocer. Grimm, J.
In Grimm, J. The house in the wood, and other fairy stories p36-45 **398.2**
See also Nis at the grocer's

The **goblin** at the provision-dealer's. Andersen, H.
In Andersen, H. Hans Andersen's Fairy tales p313-17   S C
See also Nis at the grocer's

The **goblin** of the pitcher. Malkus, A. S.
In Harper, W. comp. Ghosts and goblins p103-09   394.2

Goblin parade. Folmsbee, B.
In Burack, A. S. ed. One hundred plays for children p390-98   808.82

The **Goblin** spider
In Garner, A. ed. A cavalcade of goblins p78-81   398.2

Goblins. See Fairies

The **goblins.** Grimm, J.
In Grimm, J. The juniper tree, and other tales from Grimm v 1 p150-51 398.2
See also Changeling

The **goblins** at the bath house. Manning-Sanders, R.
In Manning-Sanders, R. A book of ghosts & goblins p14-20   398.2
In Manning-Sanders, R. A choice of magic p74-80   398.2

God
Fitch, F. M. A book about God (k-3)   231

God that lived in the kitchen. Carpenter, F.
In Carpenter, F. Tales of a Chinese grandmother p39-46   398.2

Goddard, Ragna Tischler
(illus.) Perl, L. The hamburger book   641.6

Goddard, Robert Hutchings
See pages in the following books:
Americans in space p29-51 (5-7)   629.4
Asimov, I. Breakthroughs in science p190-93 (5-7)   920
Cottler, J. More Heroes of civilization p68-80 (6-7)   920

Godden, Rumer
The dolls' house (2-4)   Fic
Home is the sailor (4-6)   Fic
Impunity Jane (2-4)   Fic
Impunity Jane; excerpt
In Johnson, E. ed. Anthology of children's literature p757-62   808.8
Little Plum (3-5)   Fic
Mouse house (2-4)   Fic
The mousewife
In Colwell, E. ed. A storyteller's choice p149-57   372.6
The old woman who lived in a vinegar bottle (k-3)   398.2

The **godfather.** Grimm, J.
In Grimm, J. The complete Grimm's Fairy tales p206-08   398.2

Godfather Death. Grimm, J.
In Grimm, J. The complete Grimm's Fairy tales p209-12   398.2
In Grimm, J. The juniper tree, and other tales from Grimm v2 p228-35 398.2

Godfather's picture book. Andersen, H. C.
In Andersen, H. C. The complete fairy tales and stories p903-24   S C

Godin, Amelia
The magician and his pupil
In Green, R. L. ed. A cavalcade of magicians p179-89   808.8

Gods
See pages in the following book:
Hamilton, E. Mythology p21-76   292
See also Mythology

God's food. Grimm, J.
In Grimm, J. The complete Grimm's Fairy tales p822   398.2

The **Gods** know
In Sechrist, E. H. ed. It's time for story hour p23-28   372.6

God's troubadour; the story of Saint Francis of Assisi. Jewett, S.   92

Goetz, Delia
The Arctic tundra (3-5)   919.8
Deserts (3-6)   551.4
Grasslands (3-6)   551.4
Lakes (3-5)   551.4
Mountains (3-6)   551.4
A piñata for Pepita
In Association for Childhood Education International. Told under the Stars and Stripes p47-53   S C
In Harper, W. comp. Merry Christmas to you p124-31   394.2
In Johnson, L. S. ed. Christmas stories round the world p41-45   394.2
Rivers (3-6)   551.4
State capital cities (4-6)   917.3
Swamps (3-6)   551.4

Goggles! Keats, E. J.   E

Gogh, Vincent van
See pages in the following book:
Craven, T. The rainbow book of art p215-17 (5-7)   709

Going a traveling. Grimm, J.
In Grimm, J. The complete Grimm's Fairy tales p630-31   398.2

Going barefoot. Fisher, A.   E

Going for a walk with a line. MacAgy, D.   709.04

Going into space. See Clarke, A. C. Into space   629.4

Going to school in 1776. Loeper, J. J.   917.3

Going to waste. Marshall, J.   614.7

Gold
See pages in the following book:
Bleeker, S. The Ashanti of Ghana p125-36 (4-7)   916.67
See also Gold mines and mining; Goldsmithing; Money

Gold. Manning-Sanders, R.
In Manning-Sanders, R. A book of wizards p40-46   398.2

Gold and gods of Peru. Baumann, H.   980.3

The **gold** bug. Poe, E. A.
In Poe, E. A. Tales of terror and fantasy p 1-36   S C

The **gold**-children. Grimm, J.
In Grimm, J. The complete Grimm's Fairy tales p388-93   398.2
See also Golden lads

Gold fish. See Goldfish

The **gold**-giving serpent
In Jacobs, J. ed. Indian fairy tales p112-14   398.2

Goose girl—*Continued*
—Same
In Arbuthnot, M. H. comp. Time for old
magic p78-81   398.2
In Grimm, J. The complete Grimm's Fairy
tales p404-11   398.2
In Grimm, J. Grimm's Fairy tales; illus.
by A. Rackham p32-38   398.2
In Grimm, J. Grimms' Fairy tales; illus.
by F. Kredel p67-75   398.2
In Grimm, J. Household stories p20-25
398.2
In Lang, A. ed. The blue fairy book
p266-73   398.2
The goose-girl at the well. Grimm, J.
In Grimm, J. The complete Grimm's Fairy
tales p725-34   398.2
Goose Hans. Grimm, J.
In Grimm, J. Three gay tales from Grimm
p51-63   398.2
See also Prudent Hans
Goose that laid the golden eggs
In The Tall book of nursery tales p120
398.2
Gooseberry Garden. Lenski, L.
In Association for Childhood Education
International. Told under the magic
umbrella p23-26   S C
The goosegirl. Grimm, J.
In Grimm, J. Grimm's Fairy tales; illus.
by A. Rackham p32-38   398.2
See also Goose girl
A gopher in the garden, and other animal
poems. Prelutsky, J.   811
Gorbaty, Norman
(illus.) Riedman, S. R. Hormones: how they
work   612
Gordon, Eugene
Saudi Arabia in pictures (5-7)   915.3
Senegal in pictures (5-7)   916.6
Gordon, Isabel
De Regniers, B. S. The shadow book   E
Gordon, Margaret
(illus.) Horder, M. On Christmas day 783.6
Gordon, Sol
Facts about sex for today's youth (6-7) 612.6
Gore, Harriet Margolis
What to do when there's no one but you (2-5)
614.8
Gore-Gorinskoe
Ransome, A. Little Master Misery
In Ransome, A. Old Peter's Russian tales
p184-205 (3-6)   398.2
Gorey, Edward
(illus.) Bellairs, J. The house with a clock in
its walls   Fic
(illus.) Ciardi, J. The man who sang the sillies   811
(illus.) Ciardi, J. Someone could win a polar
bear   811
(illus.) Ciardi, J. You read to me, I'll read to
you   811
(illus.) De Regniers, B. S. Red Riding Hood
398.2
(illus.) Lear, E. The dong with a luminous
nose   821
(illus.) Lear, E. The Jumblies   821

Gorgas, William Crawford
See pages in the following book:
Cottler, J. Heroes of civilization p337-50 (6-7)
920
The Gorgon's head. Serraillier, I.   292
Gorham, Michael
Davy Crockett
In Gruenberg, S. M. ed. Favorite stories
old and new p398-402   808.8
The gorilla did it. Hazen, B. S.   E
Gorilla gorilla. Fenner, C.   599
Gorillas
Fenner, C. Gorilla gorilla (1-4)   599
See also pages in the following books:
Cohen, D. Watchers in the wild p100-20
(6-7)   591.5
Hopf, A. L. Misunderstood animals p110-23
(4-7)   591.5
Shuttlesworth, D. E. The story of monkeys,
great apes, and small apes p17-27 (5-7)599
Shuttlesworth, D. E. Animals that frighten
people p41-50 (5-7)   591.5
Wellman, A. Africa's animals p146-50 (6-7)
591.9
Stories
Hazen, B. S. The gorilla did it   E
Gorodetzky, Charles W.
What you should know about drugs (5-7)
613.8
Gorsline, Douglas
(illus.) Bulla, C. R. Viking adventure   Fic
(illus.) Monjo, F. N. Me and Willie and Pa
Fic
Gosner, Kenneth
(illus.) Milne, L. J. Because of a tree   582
(illus.) Milne, L. When the tide goes far out
574.92
(illus.) Silverstein, A. The code of life   575.1
Gossip Wolf and the fox, Grimm, J.
In Grimm, J. The complete Grimm's Fairy
tales p353-54   398.2
Gotama Buddha. *See* Gautama Buddha
Gothic architecture. *See* Architecture, Gothic
Goto, king of the land and the water. Arnott, K.
In Arnott, K. African myths and legends
p167-78   398.2
Goudey, Alice E.
Butterfly time (1-3)   595.7
The day we saw the sun come up   E
Houses from the sea (k-3)   594
Gough, Philip
(illus.) Farjeon, E. The new book of days 828
Gould, Jean
Seven little seeds
In Kamerman, S. E. ed. Little plays for
little players p162-68   812.08
Thanksgiving is for everybody
In Kamerman, S. E. ed. Little plays for
little players p102-07   812.08
Goulo, Norton
See pages in the following book:
Posell, E. Z. American composers p64-67 (5-7)
920

Gourds
See pages in the following book:
Fenton, C. L. Plants we live on p100-06
581.6

The **gouty** giant. Howell, D. M. G.
In Mayne, W. ed. William Mayne's Book
of giants p63-70 **398.2**

Governors
Hoopes, R. What a state governor does (4-7)
353.9

Grabianski
(illus.) Peale, N. V. Bible stories **220.9**

Graboff, Abner
(illus.) David, E. Crystal magic **548**

Gracchus, Caius Sempronius
See pages in the following book:
Brooks, P. S. When the world was Rome, 753
B.C. to A.D. 476 p66-75 (6-7) **937**

Gracchus, Tiberius Sempronius
See pages in the following book:
Brooks, P. S. When the world was Rome, 753
B.C. to A.D. 476 p60-67 (6-7) **937**

Grace Sherwood, the woman none could scare.
Jagendorf, M. A.
In Jagendorf, M. A. Folk stories of the
South p312-14 **398.2**

Graciosa and Percinet. Aulnoy, Comtesse d'
In Aulnoy, Comtesse d'. The White Cat,
and other old French fairy tales
p33-66 **398.2**
In Lang, A. ed. The red fairy book p158-
74 **398.2**

Graduation. See Commencements

Graduation ball. Untermeyer, L.
In Untermeyer, L. Tales from the ballet
p24 **792.8**

Graf Spee (Battleship). See Admiral Graf Spee
(Battleship)

Graff, Stewart
(jt. auth.) Colver, A. The wayfarer's tree **Fic**

Graham, Al
Timothy Turtle **E**

Graham, Frank
Lou Gehrig, a quiet hero (5-7) **92**

Graham, Gail B.
The beggar in the blanket & other Vietna-
mese tales (2-5) **398.2**
Contents: The beggar in the blanket; The Kinh; The
Genii of the Hearth; The jeweled slipper; The magic
crystal; The shadow on the wall; The destiny of
Princess Tien Dung; The Silver River

Graham, Lorenz B.
David he no fear (1-4) **221.9**
Every man heart lay down (1-4) **232.9**
I, Momolu (5-7) **Fic**

Graham, Margaret Bloy
Be nice to spiders **E**
Benjy's dog house **E**
(illus.) Zion, G. Dear garbage man **E**
(illus.) Zion, G. Harry by the sea **E**
(illus.) Zion, G. Harry the dirty dog **F**
(illus.) Zion, G. No roses for Harry! **E**
(illus.) Zion, G. The plant sitter **E**

Graham, Robin Lee
The boy who sailed around the world alone
(5-7) **910.4**

Graham, Shirley
Booker T. Washington: educator of hand,
head, and heart (5-7) **92**

Grahame, Kenneth
(comp.) The Cambridge Book of poetry for
children **821.08**
Christmas underground
In Reeves, J. comp. The Christmas book
p46-54 **394.26**
Dulce domum
In Association for Childhood Education In-
ternational. Told under the Christmas
tree p62-80 **808.8**
In Eaton, A. T. comp. The animals' Christ-
mas p93-119 **394.2**
Its walls were as of jasper
In Authors' choice p193-206 **S C**
Mr Toad
In Martignoni, M. E. ed. The illustrated
treasury of children's literature p322-
29 **808.8**
Mr Toad's disguise
In Ward, W. ed. Stories to dramatize p194-
99 **372.6**
The open road
In Arbuthnot, M. H. comp. The Arbuthnot
Anthology of children's literature
p488-93 **808.8**
The reluctant dragon (3-5) **Fic**
—Same
In Silverberg, B. ed. Phoenix feathers
p81-107 **S C**
The reluctant dragon; play. See Smith, M. R.
The reluctant dragon
The reluctant dragon; puppet play. See Mahl-
mann, L. The reluctant dragon
The river bank
In Untermeyer, B. ed. The Golden Trea-
sury of children's literature p437-47
808.8
The wild wood
In Johnson, E. ed. Anthology of children's
literature p690-96 **808.8**
The wind in the willows (4-6) **Fic**
The wind in the willows; excerpt
In Arbuthnot, M. H. comp. The Arbuthnot
Anthology of children's literature
p487-93 **808.8**

About
See pages in the following books:
Benét, L. Famous storytellers for young peo-
ple p130-37 (5-7) **920**
Egoff, S. ed. Only connect p316-22 **028.5**
A Horn Book Sampler on children's books
and reading p50-54 **028.5**

Grain
Brooks, A. The picture book of grains (4-6)
633
Fenton, C. L. Plants we live on (4-6) **581.6**
See also names of cereal plants, e.g.
Corn

Gramatky, Hardie
Hercules **E**
Little Toot **E**
—Same
In Gruenberg, S. M. comp. Let's hear a
story p15-24 **808.8**
In Johnson, E. ed. Anthology of chil-
dren's literature p81-83 **808.8**

Gramatky, Hardie—*Continued*
About
See pages in the following book:
Hoffman, M. ed. Authors and illustrations of
children's books p172-79   **028.5**
Grammar. See English language—Grammar
The grammatical ghost. Hardendorff, J. B.
In Hardendorff, J. B. Witches, wit, and a
werewolf p76-84   **S C**
◄Grand, Pierre le. See Pierre le Grand
Grand Canyon
Fiction
Henry, M. Brighty of the Grand Canyon (4-7)
Fic
Grand Canyon National Park
See pages in the following books:
Melbo, I. R. Our country's national parks v 1
p205-30 (5-7)   **917.3**
National Geographic Society. The new Amer-
ica's wonderlands p96-109   **917.3**
Grand Coulee Dam
See pages in the following book:
Holbrook, S. H. The Columbia River p66-70
(4-7)   **979.7**
The **grand** old man of labor. Cottler, J.
In Cavanah, F. ed. Holiday roundup p198-
201   **394.2**
Grand opera. See Opera
Grand Teton National Park
See pages in the following books:
Melbo, I. R. Our country's national parks v2
p94-109 (5-7)   **917.3**
National Geographic Society. The new Amer-
ica's wonderlands p50-61   **917.3**
Granda, Julio
(illus.) Marcus, R. B. The first book of the
cliff dwellers (4-7)   **970.4**
Grandfather and I. Buckley, H. E.   **E**
Grandfather tales. Chase, R. ed.   **398.2**
Grandfathers
Fiction
Borack, B. Grandpa   **E**
Buckley, H. E. Grandfather and I   **E**
Byars, B. The house of wings (4-6)   **Fic**
Lundgren, M. Matt's grandfather   **E**
Winthrop, E. Walking away (5-7)   **Fic**
Zolotow, C. My grandson Lew   **E**
Grandma and the pampered boarder. Watts,
F. B.
In Burack, A. S. ed. One hundred plays for
children p95-105   **808.82**
Grandma didn't wave back. Blue, R.   **Fic**
Grandmother. Andersen, H. C.
In Andersen, H. C. The complete fairy
tales and stories p280-81   **S C**
Grandmother and I. Buckley, H. E.   **E**
The **grandmother** and the butternut squash.
Carlson, B. W.
In Carlson, B. W. Let's pretend it hap-
pened to you p59-65   **792**
Grandmothers
Fiction
Blue, R. Grandma didn't wave back (3-5) **Fic**
Buckley, H. E. Grandmother and I   **E**

De Paola, T. Nana Upstairs & Nana Down-
stairs   **E**
De Paola, T. Watch out for the chicken feet
in your soup   **E**
Fenton, E. Duffy's Rocks (6-7)   **Fic**
Stuart, J. The beatinest boy (4-6)   **Fic**
Udry, J. M. Mary Jo's grandmother   **E**
Grandmother's golden dish
Babbitt, E. C. The merchant of Seri
In Babbitt, E. C. Jataka tales p13-17 **398.2**
The Golden bowl
In Ginsburg, M. ed. The Kaha bird p13-20
398.2
Grandmother's tale. Singer, I. B.
In Singer, I. B. Zlateh the goat, and other
stories p21-23   **398.2**
Grandpa. Borack, B.   **E**
Grandpa Joe's brother. Leach, M.
In Leach, M. Whistle in the graveyard p64-
65   **398.2**
Grandparents
See also Grandfathers; Grandmothers
Fiction
Minarik, E. H. Little Bear's visit   **E**
Grandpa's farm. Flora, J.   **Fic**
Granér, Cyrus
The four big trolls and little Peter Pasture-
man
In Olenius, E. comp. Great Swedish fairy
tales p59-74   **398.2**
Granger, Edith
(ed.) Granger's Index to poetry. See
Granger's Index to poetry   **808.81**
Granger's Index to poetry   **808.81**
Granit, Inga
Cardboard crafting (5-7)   **745.54**
Granny Goodman's Christmas. Bennett, R.
In Kamerman, S. E. ed. A treasury of
Christmas plays p355-61   **812.08**
Granny's Blackie. Babbitt, E. C.
In Arbuthnot, M. H. comp. The Arbuthnot
Anthology of children's literature
p348-49   **808.8**
In Arbuthnot, M. H. comp. Time for old
magic p227-28   **398.2**
In Babbitt, E. C. Jataka tales p77-83 **398.2**
Grant, Bruce
American Indians, yesterday and today **970.1**
The cowboy encyclopedia (3-6)   **917.803**
Famous American trails (5-7)   **973**
Grant, Clara Louise
Mexico, land of the plumed serpent (3-5)
917.2
Grant, Joan
The Monster who grew small
In Colwell, E. ed. A storyteller's choice
p84-91   **372.6**
Grant, Leonard J.
(ed.) National Geographic Society. Wondrous
world of fishes   **597**
Grant, Matthew G.
Clara Barton (3-4)   **92**
Leif Ericson (1-3)   **92**
Grant, Neil
Cathedrals (4-6)   **726**
Grant, Sandy
Hey, look at me!   **E**

The gray wolf's haint. Shepard, R. A.
  In Shepard, R. A. Conjure tales p27-40
  S C

Grayfoot. Haviland, V.
  In Haviland, V. Favorite fairy tales told
    in Denmark p43-63   **398.2**
  See also Greyfoot

Grayl, Druid
  The dragon slayer
  In Hoke, H. comp. Dragons, dragons,
    dragons p95-108   **398.2**

Graylegs. Hatch, M. C.
  In Hatch, M. C. More Danish tales p3-21
                                   398.2

  See also Greyfoot

Grayson, Marion
  Let's do fingerplays (k-2)   **796.1**

Grazia, Thomas di. See Di Grazia, Thomas

Great American battles. Leckie, R.   **973**

Great auk
  See pages in the following books:
  Shuttlesworth, D. E. Dodos and dinosaurs
    p19-27 (4-6)   **568**
  Stoutenburg, A. A vanishing thunder p58-71
    (5-7)   **598.2**

The great-aunt. Ransome, A.
  In Hope-Simpson, J. ed. A cavalcade of
    witches p212-23   **808.8**

The **Great** Bear of Orange. Manning-Sanders, R.
  In Manning-Sanders, R. A book of sor-
    cerers and spells p56-64   **398.2**

Great bell
  Carpenter, F. Ko-Ai's lost shoe
  In Carpenter, F. Tales of a Chinese grand-
    mother p175-81   **398.2**

The **great** bell of Bosham. Colwell, E.
  In Colwell, E. Round about and long ago
    p105-07   **398.2**

A **great** bicycle book. Sarnoff, J.   **629.22**

The **great** big enormous turnip. Tolstoy, A.
                                   398.2

  See also Turnip

A **great** big ugly man came up and tied his
  horse to me. Tripp, W.   **821.08**

The **great** blackberry pick. Pearce, P.
  In Pearce, P. What the neighbors did, and
    other stories p91-105   **S C**

The **Great** Brain. Fitzgerald, J. D.   **Fic**

The **Great** Brain at the academy. Fitzgerald,
  J. D. See note under Fitzgerald, J. D.
  The Great Brain   **Fic**

The **Great** Brain does it again. Fitzgerald, J.
  D. See note under Fitzgerald, J. D. The
  Great Brain   **Fic**

The **Great** Brain reforms. Fitzgerald, J. D. See
  note under Fitzgerald, J. D. The Great
  Brain   **Fic**

Great Britain
  Hinds, L. Looking at Great Britain (4-6)
                                   914.2

Agriculture
  See Agriculture—Great Britain

Antiquities
  Pittenger, W. N. Early Britain: the Celts,
    Romans, and Anglo-Saxons (5-7)   **913.362**

Christmas
  See Christmas—Great Britain

Combined Operations Command
  Carter, H. The Commandos of World War
    II (5-7)   **940.54**

Dancing
  See Dancing—Great Britain

Description and travel
  Sasek, M. This is historic Britain (3-6) **914.2**

Education
  See Education—Great Britain

Fiction
  Aiken, J. Black hearts in Battersea (5-7) **Fic**
  Aiken, J. Midnight is a place (5-7)   **Fic**
  Aiken, J. The wolves of Willoughby Chase
    (5-7)   **Fic**
  Baker, M. J. Home from the hill (5-7)   **Fic**
  Bawden, N. The peppermint pig (5-7)   **Fic**
  Bond, M. A bear called Paddington (2-5)   **Fic**
  Boston, L. M. The children of Green Knowe
    (4-6)   **Fic**
  Burnett, F. H. A little princess (4-6)   **Fic**
  Catherall, A. Last horse on the sands (4-6)
                                   Fic
  Clarke, P. The return of the Twelves (4-7)
                                   Fic
  Clewes, D. Guide Dog (5-7)   **Fic**
  Cooper, S. The dark is rising (5-7)   **Fic**
  Cooper, S. Dawn of fear (5-7)   **Fic**
  Cooper, S. Greenwitch (5-7)   **Fic**
  Cooper, S. Over sea, under stone (5-7)   **Fic**
  Cresswell, H. The night watchmen (4-6)   **Fic**
  Dickens, C. A Christmas carol in prose (4-7)
                                   Fic
  Dickinson, P. The devil's children (5-7) **Fic**
  Dickinson, P. Heartsease (5-7)   **Fic**
  Dickinson, P. The weathermonger (5-7)   **Fic**
  Gardam, J. A few fair days (4-7)   **Fic**
  Garnett, E. The family from One End Street,
    and some of their adventures (4-7)   **Fic**
  Gray, E. J. Adam of the road (5-7)   **Fic**
  Lively, P. The ghost of Thomas Kempe (4-6)
                                   Fic
  McKillip, P. A. The house on Parchment
    Street (5-7)   **Fic**
  McNeill, J. The battle of St George Without
    (5-7)   **Fic**
  McNeill, J. Goodbye, Dove Square (5-7)   **Fic**
  Mayne, W. Earthfasts (3-5)   **Fic**
  Pope, E. M. The Perilous Gard (6-7)   **Fic**
  Robinson, J. G. Charley (4-6)   **Fic**
  Savery, C. The Reb and the Redcoats (5-7)
                                   Fic
  Sewell, A. Black beauty (4-6)   **Fic**
  Stewart, M. The little broomstick (3-6)   **Fic**
  Streatfeild, N. The family at Caldicott Place
    (4-6)   **Fic**
  Streatfeild, N. Thursday's child (4-7)   **Fic**
  Sutcliff, R. The witch's brat (5-7)   **Fic**
  Townsend, J. R. Pirate's Island (5-7)   **Fic**
  Townsend, J. R. Trouble in the jungle (5-7)
                                   Fic
  Willard, B. The Richleighs of Tantamount
    (4-7)   **Fic**

Great Britain—*Continued*

Folk songs

See Folk songs, English

Folklore

See Folklore—Great Britain

History

Hodges, C. W. Magna Carta (4-7)   **942.03**
Sasek, M. This is historic Britain (3-6) **914.2**
Unstead, R. J. The story of Britain (4-7) **942**

History—To 1066

See pages in the following book:

Carter, S. Vikings bold: their voyages & adventures p79-89 (5-7)   **914.8**

History—Norman period, 1066-1154

Duggan, A. Growing up with the Norman Conquest (6-7)   **914.2**

See also Hastings, Battle of, 1066

History—Plantagenets, 1154-1399—Fiction

De Angeli, M. The door in the wall (4-6) **Fic**

History—Tudors, 1485-1603

Shakespeare's England (6-7)   **822.3**
Syme, R. Walter Raleigh (3-6)   **92**

History—20th century

Reynolds, Q. Winston Churchill (4-7)   **92**

Industries

See pages in the following book:

Street, A. The land and people of England p115-20 (5-7)   **914.2**

Kings and rulers

Unstead, R. J. The story of Britain (4-7) **942**

Legends

See Legends—Great Britain

Social life and customs

Fox, L. M. Costumes and customs of the British Isles (4-7)   **391**

See also pages in the following book:

Sechrist, E. H. ed. Christmas everywhere p58-74   **394.2**

Theater

See Theater—Great Britain

Great Claus and Little Claus. Andersen, H. C.
In Andersen, H. C. Andersen's Fairy tales p33-45   **S C**
See also Little Claus and Big Claus

The **great** conjure-alligator-man of Florida. Jagendorf, M. A.
In Jagendorf, M. A. Folk stories of the South p67-69   **398.2**

The **great** Constitution. Commager, H. S. **342.2**

Great Danes

Stories

Cavanna, B. Petey (4-7)   **Fic**

Great days of the circus   **791.3**

The **great** Declaration. Commager, H. S. **973.3**

The **great** flood. Kim, S.
In Kim, S. The story bag p66-75   **398.2**

The **great** flood. Sechrist, E. H.
In Sechrist, E. H. Once in the first times p8-11   **398.2**

The **Great** Flood. Thompson, V. L.
In Thompson, V. L. Hawaiian tales of heroes and champions p86-92 **398.2**

Great-grandfather. Andersen, H. C.
In Andersen, H. C. The complete fairy tales and stories p987-91   **S C**

Great-grandfather in the honey tree. Swayne, S.   **Fic**

The **great** hamster hunt. Blegvad, L.   **Fic**

Great Head and the ten brothers
In Garner, A. ed. A calvacade of goblins p101-04   **398.2**

The **great** island fish. Burton, R.
In Brown, M. ed. A cavalcade of sea legends p50-53   **808.8**

Great Lakes

Ault, P. These are the Great Lakes (5-7) **977**

Fiction

Holling, H. C. Paddle-to-the-sea (4-6) **Fic**

The **great** lizard of Nimple. Courlander, H.
In Courlander, H. The tiger's whisker, and other tales and legends from Asia and the Pacific p140-43   **398.2**

Great men of medicine. Hume, R. F.   **920**

Great monsters of the movies. Edelson, E.   **791.43**

Great peace. Hooke, H. M.
In Hooke, H. M. Thunder in the mountains p93-98   **398.2**

Great Piast. Young, E.
In Young, E. The wonder smith and his son p189-90   **398.2**

The **great** Proclamation. Commager, H. S. **326**

The **great** Quillow. Thurber, J.   **Fic**

The **great** Quillow; play. Smith, M. R.
In Smith, M. R. Plays &—how to put them on p121-34   **792**

Great Roving Uhu. Thompson, V. L.
In Thompson, V. L. Hawaiian tales of heroes and champions p109-21 **398.2**

The **great** Samurai sword. Winther, B.
In Kamerman, S. E. ed. Dramatized folk tales of the world p306-16   **812.08**

The **great** sea serpent. Andersen, H. C.
In Andersen, H. C. The complete fairy tales and stories p1006-14   **S C**

Great Smoky Mountains

Fiction

Carroll, R. Beanie (1-4)   **Fic**
Carroll, R. Tough Enough (2-4)   **Fic**

Great Smoky Mountains National Park

See pages in the following book:

Melbo, I. R. Our country's national parks v 1 p136-55 (5-7)   **917.3**
National Geographic Society. The new America's wonderlands p356-63   **917.3**

Great Swedish fairy tales. Olenius, E. comp.   **398.2**

The **great** traveler of Chelm. Jagendorf, M. A.
In Jagendorf, M. A. Noodlehead stories from around the world p53-58 **398.2**

The **great** tug-of-war. Sturton, H.
In Arbuthnot, M. H. comp. The Arbuthnot Anthology of children's literature p318-21 **808.8**
In Arbuthnot, M. H. comp. Time for old magic p195-98 **398.2**
In Sturton, H. Zomo, the Rabbit p114-25 **398.2**
See also How the elephant and the whale were tricked

The **great** white bear. Lindsay, M.
In Harper, W. comp. Ghosts and goblins p201-04 **394.2**

The **greatest** among Serpents. Topsell, E.
In Silverberg, B. ed. Phoenix feathers p54-56 **S C**

The **greatest** days of racing. Stevenson, P. **796.7**

Greaves, Red Legs
See pages in the following book:
Whipple, A. B. C. Famous pirates of the New World p118-20 (5-7) **910.4**

Greece
Fenton, S. H. Greece (1-4) **913.38**
Gianakoulis, T. The land and people of Greece (5-7) **914.95**

Antiquities
Boyer, S. A. Gifts from the Greeks (6-7) **913.38**
Robinson, C. A. The first book of ancient Greece (5-7) **913.38**
Sasek, M. This is Greece (4-6) **914.95**
Van Duyn, J. The Greeks (6-7) **913.38**

Civilization
See Civilization, Greek

Fiction
Yolen, J. The boy who had wings (3-5) **Fic**

Folklore
See Folklore—Greece

History
Coolidge, O. The golden days of Greece (4-6) **938**
See also pages in the following book:
Unstead, R. J. Looking at ancient history p46-73 (4-6) **930**

History—Peloponnesian War, 431-404 B.C.
See pages in the following book:
Van Duyn, J. The Greeks p155-66 (6-7) **913.38**

Greece, Modern
Gianakoulis, T. The land and people of Greece (5-7) **914.95**
Noel-Baker, F. Looking at Greece (4-6) **914.95**
Sasek, M. This is Greece (4-6) **914.95**

Fiction
Zei, A. Petros' war (5-7) **Fic**
Zei, A. Wildcat under glass (5-7) **Fic**

Folklore
See Folklore—Greece, Modern

Greedy cat
Asbjørnsen, P. C. The Tabby who was such a glutton

In Asbjørnsen, P. C. Norwegian folk tales p161-67 **398.2**
See also Clay manikin

The **Greedy** crow
In DeRoin, N. ed. Jataka tales p62-65 **398.2**

Greedy Mariani
In Carter, D. S. ed. Greedy Mariani, and other folktales of the Antilles p99-105 **398.2**

Greedy Mariani, and other folktales of the Antilles. Carter, D. S. ed. **398.2**

The **greedy** red lobster. Simon, S.
In Simon, S. The wise men of Helm and their merry tales p29-34 **S C**

Greek architecture. See Architecture, Greek

Greek art. See Art, Greek

Greek civilization. See Civilization, Greek

Greek drama

History and criticism
See pages in the following book:
Van Duyn, J. The Greeks p121-35 (6-7) **913.38**

The **Greek** king and the physician Douban
In Lang, A. ed. Arabian nights p27-29 **398.2**

Greek mythology. See Mythology, Classical

Greek philosophers. See Philosophers, Greek

The **Greeks.** Van Duyn, J. **913.38**

The **Greeks** in America. Jones, J. C. **301.45**

Greeks in the United States
Jones, J. C. The Greeks in America (5-7) **301.45**

Green, Kathleen
Leprechaun tales (3-5) **398.2**
Contents: The leprechaun and the wheelbarrow; Terence the Tailor's jacket; The piper who could not play; George and the field glasses; The Salmon's revenge; The three brothers and treacle toffee; Christie and the growing hand; Malachi and Red Cap the Leprechaun; The Banshee's birthday treat; David and the big drum; The Hermit's cabbage patch

Green, Roger Lancelyn
A book of myths (5-7) **291**
(ed.) A cavalcade of dragons (4-7) **808.8**
Stories retold or adapted by Green are: The Dragon of the North; The master thief and the dragon; Stan Bolovan and the dragon; The prince and the dragon; The cock and the dragon; The Chinese dragons

(ed.) A cavalcade of magicians (4-7) **808.8**
Stories retold or adapted by Green are: Teta the magician; The magician from Corinth; The sorcerer's apprentice; Virgilius the sorcerer; Aladdin and the African magician; Merlin, the wizard of Britain; Bradamante and the wizard; The magician's horse; The gifts of the magician; The magician's pupil; The wizard king; The magician who had no heart

Green, Ted
See pages in the following book:
Lorimer, L. T. ed. Breaking in p157-72 (5-7) **920**

The **green** and burning tree. Cameron, E. **028.5**

Green and something else. Norris, G. B. **Fic**

The **green** bird. Manning-Sanders, R.
In Manning-Sanders, R. A book of ogres and trolls p80-90 **398.2**

Grimké, Archibald Henry

See pages in the following book:

Rollins, C. H. They showed the way p72-74
(5-7) **920**

Grimké, Charlotte Forten. See Forten, Charlotte L.

Grimké, Sarah Moore

See pages in the following books:

Chittenden, E. F. Profiles in black and white
p50-67 (5-7) **920**

Stevenson, J. Women's rights p36-40 (5-7)
324.73

Grimm, Jacob

About wise men and simpletons (3-6) **398.2**

Contents: About a fisherman and his wife; The wolf
and the seven kids; Brier Rose; The elves and the
shoemaker whose work they did; The elves ask a
servant girl to be godmother; The woman and the
changeling elf; Rapunzel; The golden goose; The white
dove; The queen bee; The three feathers; The water
of life; Rumpelstiltskin; The six swans; King Thrushbeard; Hansel and Gretel; The Bremen town musicians;
About the Brothers Grimm

Allerleirauh

In Lang, A. ed. The green fairy book p276-
81 **398.2**

The bear and the skrattel

In Mayne, W. ed. Ghosts p87-97 **820.8**

Brave little tailor

In Lang, A. ed. The blue fairy book p304-
12 **398.2**

In Martignoni, M. E. ed. The illustrated
treasury of children's literature p213-
18 **808.8**

The Bremen town musicians (k-3) **398.2**
—Same

In Haviland, V. comp. The fairy tale
treasury p110-13 **398.2**

In Johnson, E. ed. Anthology of children's
literature p128-30 **808.8**

In Martignoni, M. E. ed. The illustrated
treasury of children's literature p219-
20 **808.8**

The Bremen town musicians; play. See Roberts, W. The musicians of Bremen town

Briar Rose

In Darrell, M. ed. Once upon a time p51-
54 **808.8**

The brother and sister

In Johnson, E. ed. Anthology of children's
literature p130-33 **808.8**

In Lang, A. ed. The red fairy book p82-88
398.2

Cinderella

In Martignoni, M. E. ed. The illustrated
treasury of children's literature p232-
36 **808.8**

Clever Elsie

In Arbuthnot, M. H. comp. The Arbuthnot
Anthology of children's literature
p188-90 **808.8**

In Arbuthnot, M. H. comp. Time for old
magic p63-65 **398.2**

In Dobbs, R. ed. Once upon a time p96-
104 **372.6**

The complete Grimm's Fairy tales (4-7) **398.2**

Contents: The frog-king, or Iron Henry; Cat and
mouse in partnership; Our Lady's child; The story of
the youth who went forth to learn what fear was;
The wolf and the seven little kids; Faithful John; The
good bargain; The strange musician; The twelve bro-

thers; The pack of ragamuffins; Brother and sister;
Rapunzel; The three little men in the wood; The
three spinners; Hänsel and Gretel; The three snake-
leaves; The white snake; The straw, the coal, and the
bean; The fisherman and his wife; The valiant little
tailor; Cinderella; The riddle; The mouse, the bird, and
the sausage; Mother Holle; The seven ravens; Little
Red-Cap; The Bremen town-musicians; The singing
bone; The Devil with the three golden hairs; The
louse and the flea; The girl without hands; Clever
Hans; The three languages; Clever Elsie; The tailor
in heaven; The wishing-table, the gold-ass, and the
cudgel in the sack; Thumbling; The wedding of Mrs
Fox; The elves; The robber bridegroom; Herr Korbes;
The godfather; Frau Trude; Godfather death; Thumbling's travels; Fitcher's bird; The juniper tree; Old
sultan; The six swans; Little Briar-Rose; Fundevogel;
King Thrushbeard; Little Snow-White; The knapsack,
the hat, and the horn; Rumpelstiltskin; Sweetheart
Roland; The golden bird; The dog and the sparrow;
Frederick and Catherine; The two brothers; The little
peasant; The queen bee; The three feathers; The golden
goose; Allerleirauh; The hare's bride; The twelve
huntsmen; The thief and his master; Jorinda and Joringel; The three sons of fortune; How six men got on
in the world; The wolf and the man; The wolf and
the fox; Gossip Wolf and the fox; The fox and the cat;
The pink; Clever Gretel; The old man and his grandson; The water-nixie; The death of the little hen;
Brother Lustig; Gambling Hansel; Hans in luck; Hans
married; The gold-children; The fox and the geese;
The poor man and the rich man; The singing, soaring
lark; The goose-girl; The young giant; The gnome;
The king of the Golden Mountain; The raven; The
peasant's wise daughter; Old Hildebrand; The three
little birds; The water of life; Doctor Knowall; The
spirit in the bottle; The Devil's sooty brother; Bearskin;
The willow-wren and the bear; Sweet porridge; Wise
folks; Tales of the paddock; The poor miller's boy and
the cat; The two travelers; Hans the hedgehog; The
shroud; The Jew among thorns; The skillful huntsman;
The flail from heaven; The two king's children; The
cunning little tailor; The bright sun brings it to light;
The blue light; The willful child; The three army-
surgeons; The seven swabians; The three apprentices;
The king's son who feared nothing; Donkey cabbages; The old woman in the wood; The three
brothers; The Devil and his grandmother; Ferdinand
the faithful and Ferdinand the unfaithful; The iron
stove; The lazy spinner; The four skillful brothers;
One-eye, Two-eyes, and Three-eyes; Fair Katrinelje
and Pif-Paf-Poltrie; The fox and the horse; The shoes
that were danced to pieces; The six servants; The white
bride and the black bride; Iron Hans; The three black
princesses; Knoist and his three sons; The maid of
Brakel; My household; The lambkin and the little
fish; Simeli mountain; Going a traveling; The donkey;
The ungrateful son; The turnip; The old man made
young again; The Lord's animals and the Devil's;
The beam; The old beggar-woman; The three slug-
gards; The twelve idle servants; The shepherd boy;
The star money; The stolen farthings; Looking for a
bride; The hurds; The sparrow and his four children;
The story of Schlauraffen land; The Ditmars tale of
wonders; A riddling tale; Snow-White and Rose-Red;
The wise servant; The glass coffin; Lazy Harry; The
griffin; Strong Hans; The peasant in heaven; Lean Lisa;
The hut in the forest; Sharing joy and sorrow; The
willow-wren; The sole; The bittern and the hoopoe;
The owl; The moon; The duration of life; Death's messengers; Master Pfriem; The goose-girl at the well;
Eve's various children; The nixie of the mill-pond;
The little folks' presents; The giant and the tailor; The
nail; The poor boy in the grave; The true bride; The
hare and the hedgehog; The spindle, the shuttle, and
the needle; The peasant and the Devil; The crumbs
on the table; The sea-hare; The master-thief; The
drummer; The ear of corn; The grave-mound; Old
rinkrank; The crystal ball; Maid Maleen; The boots of
buffalo leather; The golden key; St Joseph in the forest; The twelve apostles; The rose; Poverty and
humility lead to heaven; God's food; The three green
twigs; Our Lady's little glass; The aged mother; The
heavenly wedding; The hazel-branch

The crystal coffin

In Lang, A. ed. The green fairy book p290-
95 **398.2**

The dragon's grandmother

In Hoke, H. comp. Dragons, dragons,
dragons p192-98 **398.2**

The elves and the shoemaker

Grimm, Jacob—*Continued*

In Arbuthnot, M. H. comp. The Arbuthnot Anthology of children's literature p199-200 **808.8**

In Arbuthnot, M. H. comp. Time for old magic p47-48 **398.2**

In Haviland, V. comp. The fairy tale treasury p118-21 **398.2**

In Johnson, E. ed. Anthology of children's literature p124-25 **808.8**

In Martignoni, M. E. ed. The illustrated treasury of children's literature p203-04 **808.8**

In Ward, W. ed. Stories to dramatize p49-50 **372.6**

The elves and the shoemaker; puppet play. See Mahlmann, L. The magic shoes

The fisherman and his wife

In Arbuthnot, M. H. comp. The Arbuthnot Anthology of children's literature p193-97 **808.8**

In Arbuthnot, M. H. comp. Time for old magic p68-72 **398.2**

In Association for Childhood Education International. Told under the green umbrella p88-100 **398.2**

In Johnson, E. ed. Anthology of children's literature p137-42 **808.8**

In Martignoni, M. E. ed. The illustrated treasury of children's literature p237-42 **398.2**

In Untermeyer, B. ed. The Golden Treasury of children's literature p187-92 **808.8**

The four clever brothers (k-3) **398.2**

The four musicians

In Arbuthnot, M. H. comp. The Arbuthnot Anthology of children's literature p200-02 **808.8**

In Arbuthnot, M. H. comp. Time for old magic p48-50 **398.2**

The frog-king

In Arbuthnot, M. H. comp. Time for old magic p55-56 **398.2**

The frog prince

In Darrell, M. ed. Once upon a time p43-46 **808.8**

In Gruenberg, S. M. ed. Favorite stories old and new p295-98 **808.8**

In Haviland, V. comp. The fairy tale treasury p114-17 **398.2**

In Opie, I. ed. The classic fairy tales p185-87 **398.2**

The Frog Prince; puppet play. See Mahlmann, L. The Frog Prince

The golden goose

In Haviland, V. comp. The fairy tale treasury p58-65 **398.2**

In Johnson, E. ed. Anthology of children's literature p126-28 **808.8**

In Lang, A. ed. The red fairy book p340-45 **398.2**

In Martignoni, M. E. ed. The illustrated treasury of children's literature p303-06 **808.8**

The golden lads

In Lang, A. ed. The green fairy book p311-18 **398.2**

The golden mermaid

In Lang, A. ed. The green fairy book p328-38 **398.2**

The goose girl (2-4) **398.2**

In Arbuthnot, M. H. comp. Time for old magic p78-81 **398.2**

In Lang, A. ed. The blue fairy book p266-73 **398.2**

Grimm's Fairy tales; illus. by A. Rackham (3-6) **398.2**

Contents: Snowdrop; The white snake; The golden goose; The three languages; The goose-girl; Rumpelstiltskin; The valiant tailor; The twelve dancing princesses; The mouse, the bird and the sausage; The queen bee; The robber bridegroom; Fundevogel; The King of the Golden Mountain; Jorinda and Joringel; Clever Elsa; Tom Thumb; Sweetheart Roland; The fisherman and his wife; The Bremen town musicians; The golden bird

Grimms' Fairy tales; illus. by F. Kredel (4-6) **398.2**

Contents: Twelve dancing princesses; Golden bird; Three spinning fairies; Three children of fortune; King Thrushbeard; Jorinda and Joringel; Wren and the bear; Twelve brothers; Mouse, the bird, and the sausage; Wolf and the seven goats; Thumbling the dwarf and Thumbling the giant; Sweetheart Roland; Goose girl; The cat and mouse in partnership; White snake; The frog prince; The pink; Queen bee; Briar Rose (Sleeping Beauty); Six swans; Fisherman and his wife; Rumpelstiltskin; Rapunzel; The salad; The Bremen town musicians; The raven; Cinderella; Snow-White and the seven dwarfs; The elves and the shoemaker; Water of life; Gallant tailor; Golden goose; The straw, the coal, and the bean; Fundevogel; Blue light; Karl Katz; The table, the ass, and the stick; Red Riding Hood; King of the Golden Mountain; Robber bridegroom; The turnip; Seven ravens; Tom Thumb; Clever Gretel; Six servants; Frederick and Catherine; Snow-White and Rose-Red; Four accomplished brothers; Giant with the three golden hairs; How six traveled through the world; Hansel and Gretel; Twelve huntsmen; Faithful John; Iron Hans; Lady and the lion

Hansel and Gretel (1-3) **398.2**

—Same

In Arbuthnot, M. H. comp. The Arbuthnot Anthology of children's literature p185-88 **808.8**

In Arbuthnot, M. H. comp. Time for old magic p57-60 **398.2**

In Darrell, M. ed. Once upon a time p59-65 **808.8**

In Fenner, P. R. comp. Giants & witches and a dragon or two p126-37 **398.2**

In Johnson, E. ed. Anthology of children's literature p133-37 **808.8**

In Lang, A. ed. The blue fairy book p251-58 **398.2**

In Martignoni, M. E. ed. The illustrated treasury of children's literature p178-83 **808.8**

In Opie, I. ed. The classic fairy tales p238-44 **398.2**

In Rackham, A. comp. Arthur Rackham Fairy book p269-77 **398.2**

In Untermeyer, B. ed. The Golden Treasury of children's literature p142-56 **808.8**

The house in the wood, and other fairy stories (3-5) **398.2**

Contents: The house in the wood; The brave little tailor; The goblin and the grocer; The Bremen town musicians; The table, the ass, and the cudgel; The old man in the bramble bush; The vagabonds; Red Jacket; The straw, the coal, and the bean; Snow-White and Rose-Red

Household stories (4-6) **398.2**

Contents: The rabbit's bride; Six soldiers of fortune; Clever Grethel; The death of the hen; Hans in luck; The goose girl; The raven; The frog prince; Cat & mouse in partnership; The wolf and the seven little goats; Faithful John; The wonderful musician; The twelve brothers; The vagabonds; The brother and sister; Rapunzel; The three little men in the wood; The three

Grimm, Jacob—*Continued*

spinsters; Hansel and Grethel; The white snake; The straw, the coal, and the bean; The fisherman and his wife; The gallant tailor; Aschenputtel; The mouse, the bird, and the sausage; Mother Hulda; Little Red Cap; The Bremen Town musicians; Prudent Hans; Clever Else; The table, the ass, and the stick; Tom Thumb; How Mrs Fox married again; The elves (I); The elves (II); The elves (III); The robber bridegroom; Mr Korbes; Tom Thumb's travels; The almond tree; Old Sultan; The six swans; The sleeping beauty; King Thrushbeard; Snow-White; The knapsack, the hat, and the horn; Rumpelstiltskin; Roland; The golden bird; The dog and the sparrow; Fred and Kate; The little farmer; The queen bee; The golden goose

The hut in the forest
> *In* Arbuthnot, M. H. comp. Time for old
> magic p52-54   **398.2**

The iron stove
> *In* Lang, ed. The yellow fairy book p32-
> 37   **398.2**

Jack my Hedgehog
> *In* Lang, A. ed. The green fairy book
> p304-10   **398.2**

Jorinde and Joringel
> *In* Lang, A. ed. The green fairy book
> p271-75   **398.2**

The juniper tree, and other tales from Grimm
(4-7)   **398.2**

Contents: v 1 The three feathers; Hans my hedge-hog; The story of one who set out to study fear; Brother and sister; Spindle, shuttle, and needle; The twelve huntsmen; Fitcher's feathered bird. The devil and his three golden hairs; The fisherman and his wife; The master thief; Brother Gaily; The goblins; Hansel and Gretel. v2 The frog king, or Iron Henry; The poor miller's boy and the little cat; Frederick and Katelizabeth; The golden bird; Bearskin; Godfather Death; Many-Fur; Rapunzel; Snow-White and the seven dwarfs; Rabbit's bride; The two journeymen; Ferdinand Faithful and Ferdinand Unfaithful; Mrs Gertrude; The juniper tree

King Thrushbeard (1-3)   **398.2**
The lady and lion
> *In* Darrell, M. ed. Once upon a time p38-
> 42   **808.8**

Little One-eye, Little Two-eyes, and Little Three-eyes
> *In* Lang, A. ed. The green fairy book
> p262-70   **398.2**

Little Red Riding Hood (k-3)   **398.2**
The marvelous musician
> *In* Lang, A. ed. The red fairy book p354-
> 56   **398.2**

More Tales from Grimm (4-6)   **398.2**

Contents: The golden key; The seven Swabians; The wolf and the fox; Mother Holle; The water nixie; The mouse, the bird, and the sausage; Thorn Rose, the sleeping beauty; The sweet porridge; The little shepherd boy; The twelve lazy servants; Lucky scraps; The cat and the fox; The soldier and his magic helpers; The good-for-nothings; The star dollars; A trip to Schlaraffenland; The three languages; The straw, the coal, and the bean; The wishing table, the gold donkey, and the cudgel-in-the-sack; The tailor who went to Heaven; Presents of the little folk; The three spinners; The six swans; The Queen Bee; The hedgehog and the rabbit; The earth gnome; The three lucky ones; The sorcerer's apprentice; Iron Hans; Jorinda and Joringel; The wolf and the seven little kids; The shoemaker and the elves

Mother Holle
> *In* Arbuthnot, M. H. comp. The Arbuth-
> not Anthology of children's litera-
> ture p202-04   **808.8**
> *In* Arbuthnot, M. H. comp. Time for old
> magic p50-52   **398.2**
> *In* Lang, A. ed. The red fairy book p303-
> 06   **398.2**

The musicians of Bremen
> *In* Ward, W. ed. Stories to dramatize p43-
> 46   **372.6**

Old Sultan
> *In* Untermeyer, B. ed. The Golden Trea-
> sury of children's literature p530-31
>   **808.8**

One-Eye, Two-Eyes, and Three-Eyes
> *In* Arbuthnot, M. H. comp. Time for old
> magic p74-78   **398.2**

The race between the hare and the hedgehog
> *In* Untermeyer, B. ed. The Golden Trea-
> sury of children's literature p403-05
>   **808.8**

Rapunzel (1-4)   **398.2**
—Same
> *In* Arbuthnot, M. H. comp. The Arbuth-
> not Anthology of children's literature
> p204-06   **808.8**
> *In* Arbuthnot, M. H. comp. Time for old
> magic p81-83   **398.2**
> *In* Darrell, M. ed. Once upon a time p47-
> 50   **808.8**
> *In* Hoke, H. ed. Witches, witches, witches
> p85-89   **808.8**
> *In* Johnson, E. ed. Anthology of children's
> literature p142-44   **808.8**
> *In* Lang, A. ed. The red fairy book p282-
> 85   **398.2**
> *In* Martignoni, M. E. ed. The illustrated
> treasury of children's literature p374-
> 75   **808.8**
> *In* Untermeyer, B. ed. The Golden Trea-
> sury of children's literature p181-86
>   **808.8**

Red Riding Hood
> *In* Darrell, M. ed. Once upon a time p55-
> 58   **808.8**
> *In* Martignoni, M. E. ed. The illustrated
> treasury of children's literature p175-
> 77   **808.8**

The riddle
> *In* Lang, A. ed. The green fairy book
> p300-03   **398.2**

Rumpelstiltskin (k-3)   **398.2**
—Same
> *In* Arbuthnot, M. H. comp. The Arbuth-
> not Anthology of children's literature
> p197-99   **808.8**
> *In* Arbuthnot, M. H. comp. Time for old
> magic p72-74   **398.2**
> *In* Haviland, V. comp. The fairy tale trea-
> sury p158-61   **398.2**
> *In* Johnson, E. ed. Anthology of children's
> literature p150-52   **808.8**
> *In* Lang, A. ed. The blue fairy book p96-
> 99   **398.2**
> *In* Martignoni, M. E. ed. The illustrated
> treasury of children's literature p204-
> 06   **808.8**
> *In* Opie, I. ed. The classic fairy tales
> p197-98   **398.2**
> *In* Untermeyer, B. ed. The Golden Trea-
> sury of children's literature p136-41
>   **808.8**
> *In* Ward, W. ed. Stories to dramatize p126-
> 29   **372.6**

The seven ravens (k-3)   **398.2**
—Same
> *In* Darrell, M. ed. Once upon a time p66-
> 70   **808.8**

Grimm, Jacob—*Continued*

The shoemaker and the elves (k-3) 398.2

The sleeping beauty

In Martignoni, M. E. ed. The illustrated treasury of children's literature p248-51 808.8

In Ward, W. ed. Stories to dramatize p135-37 372.6

Snow-drop

In Farjeon, E. ed. A cavalcade of queens p110-20 808.8

In Lang, A. ed. The red fairy book p329-39 398.2

In Opie, I. ed. The classic fairy tales p177-82 398.2

Snow-White

In Haviland, V. comp. The fairy tale treasury p128-37 398.2

Snow White and Rose Red (1-3) 398.2

—Same

In Arbuthnot, M. H. comp. Time for old magic p60-63 398.2

In Lang, A. ed. The blue fairy book p259-65 398.2

In Untermeyer, B. ed. The Golden Treasury of children's literature p170-80 808.8

Snow-White and the seven dwarfs (k-3) 398.2

—Same

In Arbuthnot, M. H. comp. The Arbuthnot Anthology of children's literature p190-93 808.8

In Arbuthnot, M. H. comp. Time for old magic p65-68 398.2

In Johnson, E. ed. Anthology of children's literature p144-50 808.8

In Martignoni, M. E. ed. The illustrated treasury of children's literature p265-67 808.8

In Untermeyer, B. ed. The Golden Treasury of children's literature p126-35 808.8

In Ward, W. ed. Stories to dramatize p137-43 372.6

Snow White and the seven dwarfs; puppet play. See Mahlmann, L. Snow White and the seven dwarfs

Spindle, shuttle, and needle

In Lang, A. ed. The green fairy book p286-89 398.2

The story of a clever tailor

In Lang, A. ed. The green fairy book p324-27 398.2

The story of the fisherman and his wife

In Lang, A. ed. The green fairy book p343-52 398.2

The tale of a youth who set out to learn what fear was

In Lang, A. ed. The blue fairy book p86-95 398.2

Tales from Grimm (4-6) 398.2

Contents: Hansel and Gretel; Cat and mouse keep house; Six servants; Spindle, shuttle, and needle; Doctor Know-It-All; The musicians of Bremen; Cinderella; Clever Elsie; Rapunzel; The fisherman and his wife; Three brothers; Lazy Heinz; The frog prince; Lean Liesl and Lanky Lenz; The dragon and his grandmother; Snow White and Rose Red

The three dogs

In Lang, A. ed. The green fairy book p360-66 398.2

The three dwarfs

In Lang, A. ed. The red fairy book p238-45 398.2

Three gay tales from Grimm (2-5) 398.2

Contents: The clever wife; The three feathers; Goose Hans

The three musicians

In Lang, A. ed. The green fairy book p353-59 398.2

The three snake-leaves

In Lang, A. ed. The green fairy book p296-99 398.2

Tom Thumb (k-3) 398.2

—Same

In Untermeyer, B. ed. The Golden Treasury of children's literature p157-69 808.8

The tom-tit and the bear

In Farjeon, E. ed. A cavalcade of kings p47-54 808.8

The traveling musicians (k-3) 398.2

Trusty John

In Lang, A. ed. The blue fairy book p296-303 398.2

The twelve brothers

In Lang, A. ed. The red fairy book p274-81 398.2

The twelve dancing princesses

In Fenner, P. R. comp. Princesses & peasant boys p57-63 398.2

In Opie, I. ed. The classic fairy tales p191-94 398.2

The twelve huntsmen

In Lang, A. ed. The green fairy book p282-85 398.2

The war of the wolf and the fox

In Lang, A. ed. The green fairy book p339-42 398.2

The white snake

In Lang, A. ed. The green fairy book p319-23 398.2

The wolf and the seven little kids (k-3) 398.2

—Same

In Arbuthnot, M. H. comp. Time for old magic p46-47 398.2

In Haviland, V. comp. The fairy tale treasury p16-21 398.2

In Johnson, E. ed. Anthology of children's literature p125-26 808.8

In Martignoni, M. E. ed. The illustrated treasury of children's literature p74-76 808.8

Galdone, P. Little Red Riding Hood 398.2

(jt. auth.) Grimm, W. Hansel and Gretel 782.1

Haviland, V. Favorite fairy tales told in Germany 398.2

Hurlimann, R. The cat and mouse who shared a house 398.2

Wiesner, W. Hansel and Gretel: a shadow puppet picture book 791.5

About

See pages in the following book:

Benét, L. Famous storytellers for young people p15-19 (5-7) 920

Grimm, William

Hansel and Gretel; adaptation (3-5) 782.1

(jt. auth.) Grimm, J. About wise men and simpletons 398.2

(jt. auth.) Grimm, J. The Bremen town musicians 398.2

Groth, John
(illus.) Dickens, C. A Christmas carol in prose
Fic
(illus.) Sewell, A. Black Beauty Fic
Ground effect machines. See Helicopters
Ground hogs. See Woodchucks
Group discussion. See Discussion groups
Grover. Cleaver, V. Fic
Groves-Raines, Antony
(illus.) Langstaff, J. comp. On Christmas day
in the morning 783.6
Growing a garden, indoors or out. Cutler, K. N.
635
Growing Point 028.505
The Growing Rock. Curry, J. L.
In Curry, J. L. Down from the lonely
mountain p121-26 398.2
The growing story. Krauss, R. E
Growing up. De Schweinitz, K. 612.6
Growing up chimpanzee. Alston, E. 599
Growing up with the Norman Conquest. Dug-
gan, A. 914.2
Growth
Krauss, R. The growing story E
Meeks, E. K. How new life begins (k-3) 574.1
Selsam, M. E. When an animal grows (k-3)
591
Silverstein, A. Metamorphosis: the magic
change (4-6) 591.3
See also pages in the following books:
Riedman, S. R. Hormones: how they work
p43-57 (6-7) 612
Silverstein, A. The endocrine system p14-18
(4-7) 612
Growth (Plants)
Lubell, W. Green is for growing (3-5) 581
Gruber, Franz Xaver
Pauli, H. Silent night (4-7) 783.6
Gruelle, Johnny
Raggedy Andy's smile
In Martignoni, M. E. ed. The illustrated
treasury of children's literature p365-
67 808.8
Gruenberg, Sidonie Matsner
(ed.) Favorite stories old and new 808.8
(comp.) Let's hear a story 808.8
The wonderful story of how you were born
(k-5) 612.6
Grumpy Timothy Crumb. Jagendorf, M. A.
In Jagendorf, M. A. New England bean-pot
p248-55 398.2
Grundtvig, Svend
The most obedient wife
In Arbuthnot, M. H. comp. The Arbuthnot
Anthology of children's literature
p232-35 808.8
In Arbuthnot, M. H. comp. Time for old
magic p112-15 398.2
Hatch, M. C. More Danish tales 398.2
Guadalupe Mountains National Park
See pages in the following book:
Melbo, I. R. Our country's national parks
v2 p329-41 (5-7) 917.3
Guaní. Belpré, P.
In Belpré, P. Once in Puerto Rico p18-24
398.2

Guardians of the gate. Carpenter, F.
In Carpenter, F. Tales of a Chinese grand-
mother p47-55 398.2
Guardians of tomorrow. Hirsch, S. C. 920
Guatemala
Carpenter, A. Guatemala (4-6) 917.281
See also pages in the following book:
Markun, P. M. The first book of Central
America and Panama p23-31 (5-7) 917.28
Fiction
Buff, M. Magic maize (3-6) Fic
Gubbaun Saor. See Gobborn Seer
Gubbaun Saor's feast. Young, E.
In Young, E. The wonder smith and his
son p157-69 398.2
Gudbrand on the hill-side. Asbjörnsen, P. C.
In Arbuthnot, M. H. comp. The Arbuthnot
Anthology of children's literature
p244-46 808.8
In Arbuthnot, M. H. comp. Time for old
magic p127-29 398.2
In Asbjørnsen, P. C. Norwegian folk tales
p178-81 398.2
In Aulaire, I. d'. East of the sun and west
of the moon p202-06 398.2
In Johnson, E. ed. Anthology of children's
literature p291-93 808.8
In Undset, S. ed. True and untrue, and
other Norse tales p185-89 398.2
Gudea, Patesi of Lagash
See pages in the following book:
Baumann, H. In the land of Ur p140-47 (6-7)
913.35
Guerber, H. A.
The myths of Greece & Rome 292
Guess what grasses do. Rinkoff, B. 633
Guess who! Jagendorf, M. A.
In Jagendorf, M. A. Folk stories of the
South p168-71 398.2
Guest, Lady Charlotte
Lludd and Llevelys
In Fairy tales from many lands p28-33
398.2
A guest for Halil. Kelsey, A. G.
In Kelsey, A. G. Once the Hodja p29-33
398.2
Guevara, Ché. See Guevara, Ernesto
Guevara, Ernesto
See pages in the following book:
Ortiz, V. The land and people of Cuba p83-
86 (5-7) 917.291
Guggenheim, Meyer
See pages in the following book:
Captains of industry p60-69 (5-7) 920
Guide and index
In Childcraft: the how and why library
v15 031
Guide Dog. Clewes, D. Fic
Guide dogs
Putnam, P. The triumph of the Seeing Eye
(5-7) 636.7
Rappaport, E. "Banner, forward!" (5-7)
636.7
Stories
Clewes, D. Guide Dog (5-7) Fic
Garfield, J. B. Follow my Leader (4-7) Fic

A guide for George Washington. Barbee, L.
In Burack, A. S. ed. One hundred plays for
children p297-311 **808.82**

Guide to reference books for school media centers. Wynar, C. L. **016**

A **guide** to sources in educational media and
technology. Taggart, D. T. **016.3713**

A **guide** to subjects & concepts in picture book
format. Yonkers, N. Y. Public Library.
Children's Services **028.52**

Guide to the development of educational media
selection centers. Bomar, C. P. **021**

A **guidebook** for teaching library skills. See
Beck, M. V. Library skills **028.7**

Guided missiles
Colby, C. B. Countdown (4-7) **623.4**

Guilcher, J. M.
A fern is born (5-7) **587**
A fruit is born (4-7) **582**
A tree is born (4-7) **582**

Guilds
See pages in the following book:
Loder, D. The land and people of Belgium
p105-08 (5-7) **914.93**

Guilfoile, Elizabeth
Nobody listens to Andrew **E**
—Same
In Child Study Association of America.
Round about the city p29-33 **S C**
Valentine's Day (3-4) **394.2**

Guillot, René
Grishka and the bear (5-7) **Fic**

Guilty stone
Courlander, H. The trial of the stone
In Courlander, H. The tiger's whisker, and
other tales and legends from Asia
and the Pacific p24-28 **398.2**

Guinea Fowl and Rabbit get justice. Courlander, H.
In Courlander, H. The cow-tail switch,
and other West African stories p87-
93 **398.2**

Guinea pigs
Silverstein, A. Guinea pigs (3-6) **636.08**
See also pages in the following book:
Stevens, C. Your first pet p39-47 (2-4) **636.08**
Stories
Bond, M. The tales of Olga da Polga (3-5) **Fic**
Potter, B. The tale of Tuppenny **E**

Guinness Book of world records **032**

Guleesh. Hyde, Dr D.
In Fairy tales from many lands p34-51 **398.2**

Gulliver in the giants' country; retold from
Jonathan Swift's Gulliver in the giants'
country. Fuller, E.
In De Regniers, B. S. ed. The giant book
p136-58 **398.2**

Gulliver wins his freedom. Howard, V.
In Howard, V. The complete book of children's theater p505-14 **812**

Gulls
Darling, L. The gull's way (5-7) **598.2**
Eimerl, S. Gulls (3-5) **598.2**

See also pages in the following book:
Cohen, D. Watchers in the wild p28-51 (6-7) **591.5**
Stories
Turkle, B. Thy friend, Obadiah **E**

The **gull's** way. Darling, L. **598.2**

Gumble's Yard. See Townsend, J. R. Trouble in
the jungle **Fic**

The **gun,** the pot, and the hat. Courlander, H.
In Courlander, H. The piece of fire, and
other Haitian tales p39-49 **398.2**

The **Gunniwolf.** Harper, W. **398.2**

Guno and Koyo and the Kris. Courlander, H.
In Courlander, H. The tiger's whisker, and
other tales and legends from Asia and
the Pacific p118-21 **398.2**

Guns. See Firearms

Gunterman, Bertha L.
(ed.) Castles in Spain, and other enchantments (4-6) **398.2**

Gunther, John
Alexander the Great (5-7) **92**

Guralnik, David B.
(ed.) Webster's New World dictionary for
young readers. See Webster's New World
dictionary for young readers **423**

Gurgi. Alexander, L.
In Arbuthnot, M. H. comp. The Arbuthnot
Anthology of children's literature
p514-18 **808.8**

Gurney, Clare
(jt. auth.) Gurney, G. Monticello (5-7) **917.55**
(jt. auth.) Gurney, G. North & South Korea **915.19**

Gurney, Eric
(jt. auth.) Gurney, N. The king, the mice and
the cheese **E**

Gurney, Gene
Flying aces of World War I (4-7) **920**
Monticello (5-7) **917.55**
North & South Korea (5-7) **915.19**

Gurney, Nancy
The king, the mice and the cheese **E**

Gutenberg, Johann
See pages in the following books:
Asimov, I. Breakthroughs in science p9-16
(5-7) **920**
Barker, A. Black on white and read all over
p16-23 (4-6) **686.2**
Cottler, J. Heroes of civilization p207-16 (6-7) **920**
Dean, E. Printing: tool of freedom p20-25
(4-6) **686.2**

Guthrie, Vee
(illus.) McDonald, B. G. Casserole cooking
fun **641.8**

Guyer, Carol
(illus.) Glubok, S. The art of India **709.54**

Guynemer, Georges Marie Ludovic
See pages in the following book:
Gurney, G. Flying aces of World War I p22-
39 (4-7) **920**

Gwynne, J. Harold
The rainbow book of Bible stories (4-7) **220.9**

Gwystyl. Alexander, L.
In Johnson, E. ed. Anthology of children's
literature p687-90   **808.8**

Gymnastics
See pages in the following book:
Morton, M. The making of champions p43-59
(5-7)   **796**

Gypsies

Fiction
Bemelmans, L. Madeline and the gypsies   **E**
The gypsies' fiddle. Jagendorf, M. A.
In Jagendorf, M. A. The gypsies' fiddle,
and other gypsy tales p102-06   **398.2**
The gypsies' fiddle, and other gypsy tales. Jag-
endorf, M. A.   **398.2**
The gypsy and the snake. Jagendorf, M. A.
In Jagendorf, M. A. The gypsies' fiddle,
and other gypsy tales p24-34   **398.2**
Gypsy folklore. *See* Folklore, Gypsy
The gypsy in the ghost house. Jagendorf, M. A.
In Jagendorf, M. A. The gypsies' fiddle,
and other gypsy tales p111-17 **398.2**
The Gypsy look. Heath, A. L.
In Kamerman, S. E. ed. Fifty plays for
junior actors p245-56   **812.08**
Gypsy moth. McClung, R. M.   **632**

H

Haan, Enno R.
(jt. auth.) Carpenter, A. Venezuela   **918.7**

Haar, Jaap ter
Boris (5-7)   **Fic**

Haas, Irene
(illus.) De Regniers, B. S. A little house of
your own   **E**
(illus.) De Regniers, B. S. Something special
   811
(illus.) De Regniers, B. S. Was it a good
trade?   **E**
(illus.) Enright, E. Tatsinda   **Fic**
(illus.) Enright, E. Zeee   **Fic**
(illus.) Joslin, S. Dear dragon   **808.6**
(illus.) Joslin, S. There is a dragon in my
bed   **448**

Habetrot and Scantlie Mab
In Jacobs, J. More English folk and
fairy tales p195-200   **398.2**

Habitations, Human. *See* Architecture, Domestic; Houses

Habitations of animals. *See* Animals—Habitations

Habits of animals. *See* Animals—Habits and
behavior

Habsburg, House of
See pages in the following book:
Wohlrabe, R. A. The land and people of
Austria p33-40 (5-7)   **914.36**

Hackett, Walter
A Christmas carol
In Burack, A. S. ed. Popular plays for
classroom reading p337-53   **808.82**

A Christmas carol; adapted for radio
In Burack, A. S. ed. Christmas plays for
young actors p277-93   **812.08**
A Christmas carol; adapted for the stage
In Burack, A. S. ed. Christmas plays for
young actors p255-76   **812.08**
Swans of Ballycastle
In Child Study Association of America.
Castles and dragons p259-89 **398.2**

The Haddam witches. Jagendorf, M. A.
In Hoke, H. ed. Witches, witches, witches
p187-91   **808.8**
In Jagendorf, M. A. New England bean-
pot p206-11   **398.2**

Hader, Berta
The big snow   **E**
Caldecott Medal acceptance paper
In Miller, B. M. ed. Caldecott Medal
books: 1938-1957 p185-91   **028.5**
About
See pages in the following books:
Hoffman, M. ed. Authors and illustrators of
children's books p180-85   **028.5**
Miller, B. M. ed. Caldecott Medal books:
1938-1957 p192-99   **028.5**

Hader, Elmer
(jt. auth.) Hader, B. Caldecott Medal acceptance paper
In Miller, B. M. ed. Caldecott Medal
books: 1938-1957 p185-91   **028.5**
(jt. auth.) Hader, B. The big snow   **E**
About
See pages in the following books:
Hoffman, M. ed. Authors and illustrators of
children's books p180-85   **028.5**
Miller, B. M. ed. Caldecott Medal books:
1938-1957 p192-99   **028.5**

Hafiz, the stone-cutter. Shedlock, M. L.
In Shedlock, M. L. The art of the story-
teller p179-82   **372.6**
See also Stone cutter

Hahn, Emily
See pages in the following book:
Ross, P. ed. Young and female p37-56 (6-7)
   920

Hahn, James
The metric system (5-7)   **389**
Plastics (5-7)   **668.4**

Hahn, Lynn
(jt. auth.) Hahn, J. The metric system (5-7)
   389
(jt. auth.) Hahn, J. Plastics   **668.4**

Haifa, Israel
See pages in the following book:
Hoffman, G. The land and people of Israel
p13-15, 141-45 (5-7)   **915.694**

Haiku
Atwood, A. Haiku: the mood of earth (5-7)
   811
Atwood, A. My own rhythm (5-7)   **811**
Behn, H. comp. Cricket songs (4-7)   **895.6**
Behn, H. comp. More Cricket songs (4-7)
   895.6
Cassedy, S. comp. Birds, frogs, and moon-
light (3-6)   **895.6**
Caudill, R. Come along! (1-4)   **811**
Lewis, R. ed. In a spring garden (k-3) **895.6**

Hall, May Emery
Hearts of oak
In Burack, A. S. ed. One hundred plays
for children p821-37 **808.82**

Hall, Mazie
The language shop
In Burack, A. S. ed. One hundred plays
for children p106-12 **808.82**
The trial of Billy Scott
In Burack, A. S. ed. One hundred plays
for children p113-21 **808.82**

Hall-Quest, Olga W.
How the Pilgrims came to Plymouth (4-6)
973.2

Hallabu's jealousy. Arnott, K.
In Arnott, K. African myths and legends
p160-66 **398.2**

Halliburton, Warren
The picture life of Jesse Jackson (1-3) **92**

Hallmarks. See Silversmithing

Hallo, Aurora. See Vestly, A. Hello, Aurora **Fic**

Halloween
Barth, E. Witches, pumpkins, and grinning
ghosts (3-6) **394.2**
Borten, H. Halloween (1-3) **394.2**
Cooper, P. Let's find out about Halloween
(k-2) **394.2**
McGovern, A. Squeals & squiggles & ghostly
giggles (2-5) **394.2**
Patterson, L. Halloween (3-4) **394.2**
See also pages in the following books:
Araki, C. Origami in the classroom: Book I
p18-27 (4-7) **736**
Cutler, K. N. From petals to pinecones p81-
84 (4-7) **745.92**
Purdy, S. Festivals for you to celebrate p23-
34 (4-7) **394.2**
Sechrist, E. H. Red letter days p164-74 **394.2**
Drama
See pages in the following books:
Fisher, A. Holiday programs for boys and
girls p58-75 (4-7) **812**
Kamerman, S. E. ed. Little plays for little
players p86-96 (1-6) **812.08**
Poetry
Hopkins, L. B. comp. Hey-how for Hallo-
ween! (2-4) **811.08**
See also pages in the following book:
Sechrist, E. H. comp. Poems for red letter
days p192-95 **821.08**
Stories
Adams, A. A woggle of witches **E**
Barth, E. Jack-o'-lantern (2-4) **398.2**
Corbett, S. The hairy horror trick (3-5) **Fic**
Embry, M. The blue-nosed witch (1-4) **Fic**
Estes, E. The witch family (1-4) **Fic**
Harper, W. comp. Ghosts and goblins **394.2**
Massey, J. The littlest witch **E**
Zolotow, C. A tiger called Thomas **E**

Hallowell, Priscilla
The long-nosed princess
In Johnson, S. P. ed. The Princesses p254-
306 **S C**

Hallucinations and illusions. See Ghosts; Magic;
Optical illusions

Halsey, Rosalie V.
Forgotten books of the American nursery
028.5

Hamberger, John
(illus.) Annixter, J. Sea otter **599**
(illus.) Cohen, D. Watchers in the wild **591.5**
(illus.) Eberle, I. Prairie dogs in prairie dog
town **599**
(illus.) Kohn, B. Raccoons **599**
(illus.) May, J. Wild turkeys **598.2**
(illus.) Rau, M. The penguin book **598.2**

The hamburger book. Perl, L. **641.6**

Hamer, Fannie Lou
Jordan, J. Fannie Lou Hamer (2-4) **92**

Hamilton, Alex
The attic express
In Hitchcock, A. comp. Alfred Hitchcock's
Supernatural tales of terror and sus-
pense p126-45 **S C**

Hamilton, Alexander
See pages in the following book:
Cook, F. J. The rise of American political
parties p 1-13 (5-7) **329**

Hamilton, Ann. See Scott, Ann (Hamilton)

Hamilton, Edith
Mythology **292**

Hamilton, Patricia
(illus.) Healey, F. Light and color **535**

Hamilton, Virginia
The house of Dies Drear (5-7) **Fic**
The house of Dies Drear; excerpt
In Arbuthnot, M. H. comp. The Arbuth-
not Anthology of children's literature
p646-55 **808.8**
M. C. Higgins, the great (6-7) **Fic**
Newbery Medal acceptance paper
In Kingman, L. ed. Newbery and Calde-
cott Medal books: 1966-1975 p129-
36 **028.5**
Paul Robeson (6-7) **92**
The time-ago tales of Jahdu (3-5) **S C**
Contents: How Jahdu found his power; How Jahdu
took care of trouble; How Young Owl and almost
everybody got tired of Jahdu; How Jahdu became
himself

W.E.B. Du Bois (6-7) **92**
Zeely (4-7) **Fic**
About
See pages in the following books:
Hoffman, M. ed. Authors and illustrators of
children's books p186-92 **028.5**
Kingman, L. ed. Newbery and Caldecott
Medal books: 1966-1975 p137-40 **028.5**

The Hamish Hamilton Book of dragons. See
Green, R. L. ed. A cavalcade of dragons
808.8

The Hamish Hamilton Book of giants. See
Mayne, W. ed. William Mayne's Book of
giants **398.2**

The Hamish Hamilton Book of goblins. See
Garner, A. ed. A cavalcade of goblins **398.2**

The Hamish Hamilton Book of kings and rulers.
See Farjeon, E. ed. A cavalcade of kings
808.8

The Hamish Hamilton Book of magical beasts.
See Manning-Sanders, R. ed. A book of
magical beasts **398.2**

The **Hamish** Hamilton Book of magicians. See Green, R. L. ed. A cavalcade of magicians
808.8

The **Hamish** Hamilton Book of queens. See Farjeon, E. ed. A cavalcade of queens
808.8

The **Hamish** Hamilton Book of sea legends. See Brown, M. ed. A cavalcade of sea legends
808.8

The **Hamish** Hamilton Book of witches. See Hope-Simpson, J. ed. A cavalcade of witches
808.8

Hammarskjöld, Dag
Richards, N. Dag Hammarskjöld (6-7)   **92**
See also pages in the following book:
Sechrist, E. H. It's time for brotherhood p237-42 (5-7)   **301.11**

Hammon, Jupiter
See pages in the following book:
Rollins, C. Famous American Negro poets p15-17 (5-7)   **920**

Hammond, Winifred G.
The riddle of seeds (3-5)   **582**
Sugar from farm to market (4-6)   **664**

Hammond Citation world atlas   **912**

Hammond Incorporated
The First book atlas. See The First book atlas   **912**

Hammond Nature atlas of America. Clement, R. C.   **500.9**

Hammond's Illustrated atlas for young America   **912**

Hámori, László
Dangerous journey (5-7)   **Fic**

Hampshire, Michael
(illus.) May, J. How we are born   **612.6**
(illus.) Tobias, T. Maria Tallchief   **92**

Hampson, Alfred Leete
(ed.) Dickinson, E. Poems for youth   **811**

Hampton, Blake
(illus.) Andry, A. C. How babies are made   **612.6**

Hamre, Leif
Operation Arctic (6-7)   **Fic**

Hamsters
Silverstein, A. Hamsters (4-7)   **636.08**
See also pages in the following books:
Ricciuti, E. R. Shelf pets p116-20 (5-7)   **639**
Stevens, C. Your first pet p19-29 (2-4)   **636.08**
Stories
Blegvad, L. The great hamster hunt (1-3)   **Fic**

Hancock, Sibyl
The grizzly bear (2-5)   **599**

Hand in hand we'll go. Burns, R.   **821**

Hand puppets. Ross, L.   **791.5**

Hand weaving. See Weaving

Handball
See pages in the following book:
Keith, H. Sports and games p214-26 (5-7)   **796**

Handbook of classical mythology, Crowell's. Tripp, E.   **292.03**

Handforth, Thomas
Caldecott Medal acceptance paper
In Miller, B. M. ed. Caldecott Medal books: 1938-1957 p23-27   **028.5**
Mei Li   **E**
About
See pages in the following book:
Miller, B. M. ed. Caldecott Medal books: 1938-1957 p28-43   **028.5**

A **handful** of thieves. Bawden, N.   **Fic**

A **handfull** of peas
In De Roin, N. ed. Jataka tales p20-21   **398.2**

Handicapped. See Physically handicapped

Handicapped children. See Mentally Handicapped children; Physically handicapped children; Socially handicapped children

Handicraft
Alkema, C. J. Greeting cards you can make (4-7)   **745.59**
Better Homes and Gardens Holiday decorations you can make   **745.59**
Carroll, D. Make your own chess set (5-7)   **745.59**
Chernoff, G. T. Clay-dough play-dough (1-4)   **731.4**
Cobb, V. Arts and crafts you can eat (4-7)   **745.5**
Comins, J. Art from found objects (5-7) **745.5**
Comins, J. Latin American crafts, and their cultural backgrounds (4-7)   **745.5**
Cross, L. Kitchen crafts (3-7)   **745.5**
Cutler, K. N. Crafts for Christmas (3-7)   **745.59**
Cutler, K. N. Creative shellcraft (4-6) **745.55**
Cutler, K. N. From petals to pinecones (4-7)   **745.92**
D'Amato, J. American Indian craft inspirations (5-7)   **745.5**
D'Amato, J. Colonial crafts for you to make (4-7)   **745.5**
D'Amato, J. Indian crafts (4-7)   **745.5**
Donna, N. Peanut craft (4-7)   **745.5**
Facklam, M. Corn-husk crafts   **745.5**
Hautzig, E. Let's make more presents (4-7)   **745.5**
Helfman, H. Fun with your fingers (3-5)   **745.5**
Hunt, W. B. The complete book of Indian crafts and lore (4-7)   **745.5**
Joseph, J. Folk toys around the world and how to make them (5-7)   **745.59**
Kerina, J. African crafts (4-7)   **745.5**
Kinney, J. 21 kinds of American folk art and how to make each one (5-7)   **745.5**
Kohn, B. The beachcomber's book (3-7) **745.5**
Lee, T. Things to do (3-6)   **745.5**
Lidstone, J. Building with wire (5-7) **745.56**
Lopshire, R. How to make flibbers, etc. (k-3)   **745.5**
Mandell, M. Make your own musical instruments (3-7)   **781.9**
Mason, B. S. The book of Indian-crafts and costumes (5-7)   **745.5**
Meyer, C. Christmas crafts (5-7)   **745.59**
Meyer, C. Yarn—the things it makes and how to make them (4-7)   **746.4**
Musselman, V. W. Learning about nature through crafts (5-7)   **574**

Handicraft—Continued

Nagle, A. Fun with naturecraft (3-6) **745.5**

Newsome, A. J. Make it with felt (4-7) **745.5**

Newsome, A. J. Spoolcraft (4-6) **745.5**

Papier mâché, dyeing & leatherwork (3-7) **745.5**

Parish, P. Let's be early settlers with Daniel Boone (2-5) **745.5**

Parish, P. Let's be Indians (2-5) **745.5**

Pettit, F. H. How to make whirligigs and whimmy diddles, and other American folkcraft objects (5-7) **745.5**

Pflug, B. Egg-speriment (1-3) **745.5**

Purdy, S. Festivals for you to celebrate (4-7) **394.2**

Purdy, S. Holiday cards for you to make (5-7) **745.59**

Purdy, S. G. Jewish holidays (4-7) **296.4**

Razzi, J. Bag of tricks! (k-3) **745.5**

Razzi, J. Easy does it! (k-3) **745.5**

Razzi, J. Simply fun (k-3) **745.5**

Rockwell, H. I did it (1-3) **745.5**

Seidelman, J. E. Creating with wood (4-7) **745.51**

Sommer, E. The bread dough craft book (3-6) **745.5**

Villiard, P. Jewelrymaking (4-7) **745.59**

Weiss, P. Balsa wood craft (3-7) **745.51**

Wirtenberg, P. Z. All-around-the-house art and craft book (4-7) **745.5**

Wiseman, A. Making things (5-7) **745.5**

Wright, L. A. Weathered wood craft (4-7) **745.51**

See also pages in the following books:

Cassell, S. Indoor games and activities p 1-22, 84-100 (3-7) **793**

Childcraft: the how and why library v11 **031**

Ellison, V. H. The Pooh get-well book p53-66 (2-5) **790.19**

See also names of crafts, e.g. Egg decoration

Equipment and supplies

Sattler, H. R. Recipes for art and craft materials (4-7) **745.5**

Handtalk. Charlip, R. **419**

Handville, Robert

(illus.) Gates, D. Lord of the sky: Zeus **292**

Handwriting. See Writing

Handy, William Christopher

Montgomery, E. R. William C. Handy: father of the blues (3-4) **92**

See also pages in the following books:

Hughes, L. Famous American Negroes p95-104 (5-7) **920**

Rollins, C. H. They showed the way p75-79 (5-7) **920**

Handy key to your "National Geographics." National Geographic Magazine **910.1**

Hane, Setsuko

(illus.) Kijima, H. Little white hen **398.2**

Haney, Erene Cheki. See Cheki Haney, Erene

Hang tough, Paul Mather. Slote, A. **Fic**

Hanley, Hope

Fun with needlepoint (5-7) **746.4**

Hannibal

See pages in the following book:

Brooks, P. S. When the world was Rome, 753 B.C. to A.D. 476 p29-51 **937**

Hannum, Sara

(comp.) Lean out of the window (4-7) **821.08**

Hano, Arnold

Roberto Clemente: batting king (5-7) **92**

Hans and his master. Manning-Sanders, R.

In Ireson, B. comp. Haunting tales p33-39 **S C**

In Manning-Sanders, R. A book of ghosts & goblins p55-61 **398.2**

In Manning-Sanders, R. A choice of magic p224-30 **398.2**

Hans Brinker. Dodge, M. M. **Fic**

Hans Clodhopper

Andersen, H. C. Blockhead Hans

In Lang, A. ed. The yellow fairy book p313-18 **398.2**

Andersen, H. C. Booby Hans

In Andersen, H. C. Andersen's Fairy tales p425-29 **S C**

Andersen, H. C. Clod Hans

In Andersen, H. C. The complete fairy tales and stories p479-82 **S C**

Andersen, H. C. Numbskull Jack

Andersen, H. C. It's perfectly true, and other stories p279-85 **S C**

Hans Hecklemann's luck. Pyle, H.

In Pyle, H. Pepper & salt p57-68 **398.2**

Hans Humdrum. Hatch, M. C.

In Hatch, M. C. 13 Danish tales p148-69 **398.2**

Hans in luck

Grimm, J. Hans in luck

In Grimm, J. The complete Grimm's Fairy tales p381-86 **398.2**

In Grimm, J. Household stories p14-19 **398.2**

Hans in luck

In Hutchinson, V. S. ed. Fireside stories p129-39 **398.2**

Hans Kuchwanz. Duvoisin, R.

In Duvoisin, R. The three sneezes, and other Swiss tales p162-66 **398.2**

Hans married. Grimm, J.

In Grimm, J. The complete Grimm's Fairy tales p387-88 **398.2**

Hans my hedgehog

Grimm, J. Hans my hedgehog

In Grimm, J. The juniper tree, and other tales from Grimm v 1 p11-22 **398.2**

Grimm, J. Hans the Hedgehog

In Grimm, J. The complete Grimm's Fairy tales p497-502 **398.2**

Hans who made the princess laugh

Asbjørnsen, P. C. Taper-Tom who made the princess laugh

In Asbjørnsen, P. C. Norwegian folk tales p20-24 **398.2**

Haviland, V. Taper Tom

In Haviland, V. Favorite fairy tales told in Norway p50-64 **398.2**

Thorne-Thomsen, G. Taper Tom

In Ward, W. ed. Stories to dramatize p105-09 **372.6**

Hans, who made the Princess laugh; play. Rowland, E.
In Burack, A. S. ed. One hundred plays for children p726-33 **808.82**

Hansel and Gretel. See Hansel and Grethel

Hänsel and Gretel; adaptation. Bulla, C. R.
In Bulla, C. R. More stories of favorite operas p230-39 **782.1**

Hansel and Gretel; play. Thane, A.
In Thane, A. Plays from famous stories and fairy tales p335-51 **812**

Hansel and Gretel: a shadow puppet picture book. Wiesner, W. **791.5**

Hansel and Grethel
—Same
Grimm, J. Hansel and Gretel **398.2**
In Grimm, J. About wise men and simpletons p99-107 **398.2**
In Grimm, J. The complete Grimm's Fairy tales p86-94 **398.2**
In Grimm, J. Grimms' Fairy tales; illus. by F. Kredel p330-40 **398.2**
In Grimm, J. The juniper tree, and other tales from Grimm v 1 p152-68 **398.2**
In Grimm, J. Tales from Grimm p3-26 **398.2**
In Johnson, E. ed. Anthology of children's literature p133-37 **808.8**
In Martignoni, M. E. ed. The illustrated treasury of children's literature p178-83 **808.8**
In Opie, I. ed. The classic fairy tales p238-44 **398.2**
In Untermeyer, B. ed. The Golden Treasury of children's literature p142-56 **808.8**

Grimm, J. Hansel and Grethel
In Darrell, M. ed. Once upon a time p59-65 **808.8**
In Fenner, P. R. comp. Giants & witches and a dragon or two p126-37 **398.2**
In Grimm, J. Household stories p85-92 **398.2**
In Rackham, A. comp. Arthur Rackham Fairy book p269-77 **398.2**
Grimm, J. Hansel and Grettel
In Arbuthnot, M. H. comp. The Arbuthnot Anthology of children's literature p185-88 **808.8**
In Arbuthnot, M. H. comp. Time for old magic p57-60 **398.2**
In Lang, A. ed. The blue fairy book p251-58 **398.2**
Grimm, W. Hansel and Gretel; adaptation **782.1**
Haviland, V. Hansel and Gretel
In Haviland, V. Favorite fairy tales told in Germany p51-71 **398.2**
Manning-Sanders, R. Hansel and Gretel
In Manning-Sanders, R. A book of witches p82-93 **398.2**
See also Two lost babes

Hansel and Grethel; play. Simonds, N.
In Burack, A. S. ed. One hundred plays for children p751-56 **808.82**

Hansel and Grettel. See Hansel and Grethel

Hanser, Richard
Jesus: what manner of man is this? (5-7) **232.9**

Hansi, L'Oncle
Christmas tree of good Saint Florentin
In Dalgliesh, A. comp. Christmas p3-5 **394.2**

Hanson, Howard Harold
See pages in the following book:
Posell, E. Z. American composers p82-85 (5-7) **920**

Hanukkah (Feast of Lights)
Simon, N. Hanukkah (1-4) **296.4**

Poetry
See pages in the following book:
Association for Childhood Education International. Told under the Christmas tree p237-96 (3-6) **808.8**

Stories
See pages in the following book:
Association for Childhood Education International. Told under the Christmas tree p237-96 **808.8**

Hanukkah at Valley Forge. Solis-Cohen, E.
In Cavanah, F. ed. Holiday roundup p296-99 **394.2**

The Hanukkah Santa Claus. Levoy, M.
In Levoy, M. The witch of Fourth Street, and other stories p99-110 **S C**

The happy birthday present. Heilbroner, J. **E**

Happy Boz'll. Williams-Ellis, A.
In Williams-Ellis, A. Fairy tales from the British Isles p32-33 **398.2**

Happy Christmas to all. Nolan, J. C.
In Burack, A. S. ed. Christmas plays for young actors p143-56 **812.08**
In Burack, A. S. ed. One hundred plays for children p540-50 **808.82**

A happy Christmas Tree. Brown, F. A.
In Association for Childhood Education International. Told under the magic umbrella p68-78 **S C**

Happy cure. Dobbs, R.
In Dobbs, R. ed. Once upon a time p27-33 **372.6**

Happy days. Price, C. **392**

A happy disposition. Andersen, H. C.
In Andersen, H. C. The complete fairy tales and stories p410-13 **S C**

A happy family. Andersen, H. C.
In Andersen, H. C. The complete fairy tales and stories p356-59 **S C**
In Andersen, H. C. It's perfectly true, and other stories p102-07 **S C**
In Andersen, H. C. Seven tales p51-61 **S C**

Happy holidays for Little women. Howard, V.
In Howard, V. The complete book of children's theater p469-76 **812**

The happy lion. Fatio, L. **E**

The happy lion in Africa. Fatio, L. **E**

Happy milkmaid. Brenner, A.
In Brenner, A. The boy who could do anything, & other Mexican folk tales p18-19 **398.2**

The happy Moomins. See Jansson, T. Finn family Moomintroll **Fic**

Happy nesting; puppet play. Carlson, B. W.
In Carlson, B. W. Play a part p46-50 **792**

The **happy** orpheline. Carlson, N. S.   **Fic**

The **happy** owls. Piatti, C.   **E**

The **happy** Prince. Wilde, O.
In Authors' choice 2 p149-59   **S C**
In Harper, W. comp. Merry Christmas to
    you p241-53   **394.2**
In Wilde, O. The Happy Prince, and other
    stories p 1-12   **S C**

The **Happy** Prince, and other stories. Wilde, O.
    S C

Happy returns. Housman, L.
In Housman, L. The rat-catcher's daugh-
    ter p143-52   **S C**

Happy Thanksgiving! Luckhardt, M. C.
In Luckhardt, M. C. comp. Thanksgiving
    p94-98   **394.2**

Harbin, E. O.
    Games of many nations   **793**

The **Harcourt** Brace School dictionary   **423**

Hardendorff, Jeanne B.
    (ed.) Just one more (3-6)   **372.6**
    Stories retold or adapted by Hardendorff are: Mana-
bush and the moose; The most frugal of men; The
shepherd boy who was wiser than the king; How the
chipmunk came to be; The parrot and the parson;
The tiger and the frog; How the frog came; The wise
old shepherd; The wily tortoise; How the coyote stole
fire for the Klamaths; The cat and the sparrows; The
man who ate his wives; The giant and the dwarf;
The monkey and the heron; The ghost who was afraid
of being bagged; The wolf and the blacksmith; The
story of Yukpachen; Yehl outwits Kanukh; How the
Devil was outsmarted by the man; How the Hodja
outwits the Shah Ali; Heavy Collar and the Ghost
Woman
    The little cock (1-4)   **398.2**
    Witches, wit, and a werewolf (5-7)   **S C**
    Stories retold by the author are: From the loom of
the dead; The witch in the stone boat; On the river;
Vengeance will come; The questioning ghost; Striking a corpse candle; The strangling woman; The little
toe bone; Fear; The grammatical ghost; The power
of St Tegla's Well; The witch at Fraddam; A werewolf or a thief? Rap! Rap! Rap; The blood-drawing
ghost

Hardy, Marjorie
    Big tree
In Association for Childhood Education
    International. Told under the blue
    umbrella p134-39   **S C**

Hardy, Thomas
    The thieves who couldn't help sneezing
In Reeves, J. comp. The Christmas book
    p34-42   **394.26**

Hardy Hardback. Williams-Ellis, A.
In Williams-Ellis, A. Fairy tales from the
    British Isles p124-31   **398.2**

Hardy Hardhead
In Chase, R. ed. The Jack tales p96-105
    398.2

Hare and the corn bins. Arnott, K.
In Arnott, K. African myths and legends
    p101-04   **398.2**

Hare and the hedgehog
De La Mare, W. The hare and the hedgehog
In De La Mare, W. ed. Animal stories
    p3-10   **398.2**
In De La Mare, W. Tales told again p9-14
    398.2
In Johnson, E. ed. Anthology of children's
    literature p202-04   **808.8**

Grimm, J. The hare and the hedgehog
In Grimm, J. The complete Grimm's Fairy
    tales p760-64   **398.2**
Grimm, J. The hedgehog and the rabbit
In Grimm, J. More Tales from Grimm
    p163-70   **398.2**
Grimm, J. The race between the hare and the
    hedgehog
In Untermeyer, B. ed. The Golden Trea-
    sury of children's literature p403-05
    808.8
The Hare and the hedgehog
In Hutchinson, V. S. ed. Fireside stories
    p67-73   **398.2**
The Race between Hare and Hedgehog
In Association for Childhood Education
    International. Told under the green
    umbrella p30-35   **398.2**

Hare and the Hyena. Arnott, K.
In Arnott, K. African myths and legends
    p108-11   **398.2**

The **hare** and the lioness. Arnott, K.
In Arnott, K. Animal folk tales around the
    world p104-11   **398.2**

The **hare** and the tiger. Vo-Dinh
In Vo-Dinh. The toad is the Emperor's
    uncle p57-64   **398.2**

The **Hare** and the tortoise   **398.2**

The **hare** and the tortoise. Wildsmith, B. **398.2**

The **hare** and the tortoise & The tortoise and
    the hare. Du Bois, W. P.   **398.2**

The **hare** and the tortoise; play. Bennett, R.
In Bennett, R. Creative plays and programs
    for holidays p186-92   **812**

Hare in the moon
    The Rabbit in the moon
In Sakade, F. ed. Japanese children's favor-
    ite stories p35-37   **398.2**
Shedlock, M. L. The true spirit of a festival
    day
In Shedlock, M. L. The art of the story-
    teller p225-28   **372.6**

The **hare** that ran away. Shedlock, M.
In Arbuthnot, M. H. comp. The Arbuthnot
    Anthology of children's literature
    p347-48   **808.8**
In Arbuthnot, M. H. comp. Time for old
    magic p226-27   **398.2**
In Davis, M. G. ed. A baker's dozen p21-
    26   **372.6**
    See also Timid hare

The **Hare**, the Lions, the Monkey and Hare's
    spotted blanket. Worthington, F.
In Colwell, E. ed. A second storyteller's
    choice p80-84   **372.6**

The **Hare** who had been married. Asbjørnsen,
    P. C.
In Asbjørnsen, P. C. Norwegian folk tales
    p115   **398.2**

Hares. See Rabbits

The **hare's** bride. Grimm, J.
In Grimm, J. The complete Grimm's Fairy
    tales p332-33   **398.2**
    See also Rabbit's bride

The **hare's** kidneys. Tashjian, V. A.
In Tashjian, V. A. Three apples fell from
    heaven p49-60   **398.2**

Harisarman
In Jacobs, J. ed. Indian fairy tales p85-89
398.2
See also Doctor Know-all

Hark, Mildred
Christmas party
In Kamerman, S. E. ed. Little plays for little players p117-24 **812.08**
The Christmas snowman
In Burack, A. S. ed. Christmas plays for young actors p95-112 **812.08**
Doctor Manners
In Kamerman, S. E. ed. Little plays for little players p179-87 **812.08**
The magic egg
In Burack, A. S. ed. One hundred plays for children p324-35 **808.82**
Merry Christmas, Crawfords!
In Kamerman, S. E. ed. A treasury of Christmas plays p21-44 **812.08**
Merry Christmas customs
In Kamerman, S. E. ed. A treasury of Christmas plays p376-82 **812.08**
Off the shelf
In Burack, A. S. ed. One hundred plays for children p423-32 **808.82**

Harlem, New York (City)
Young, B. E. Harlem: the story of a changing community (3-6) **917.47**

Fiction
Wagner, J. J. T. (3-6) **Fic**
Weik, M. H. The Jazz Man (3-5) **Fic**
Harlem: the story of a changing community. Young, B. E. **914.47**

Harlequin

Fiction
Charlip, R. Harlequin and the gift of many colors **E**
Harlequin and the gift of many colors. Charlip, R. **E**

Harman, Carter
A skyscraper goes up (5-7) **690**

Harmelink, Barbara
Florence Nightingale (5-7) **92**

Harmon, Seth
Pink petunia
In Harper, W. comp. Easter chimes p118-28 **394.2**

Harmonica, Mouth. See Mouth organ

Harnan, Terry
Gordon Parks: Black photographer and film maker (3-6) **92**

Harnoncourt, René d'
(illus.) Morrow, E. The painted pig **Fic**

Harold and the purple crayon. Johnson, C. **E**

Haroun-al-Raschid, Caliph of Bagdad
In Lang, A. ed. Arabian nights p220-22 **398.2**

Harp

Fiction
Alexander, L. The truthful harp (2-4) **Fic**

Harper, Frances Ellen (Watkins)
See pages in the following books:
Rollins, C. Famous American Negro poets p22-27 (5-7) **920**

Rollins, C. H. They showed the way p80-82 (5-7) **920**

Harper, Wilhelmina
(comp.) Easter chimes **394.2**
(comp.) Ghosts and goblins **394.2**
The Gunniwolf (k-1) **398.2**
(comp.) The harvest feast **394.2**
(comp.) Merry Christmas to you **394.2**

Harper's Round Table
See pages in the following book:
Haviland, V. ed. Yankee Doodle's literary sampler of prose, poetry, & pictures p437-45 **028.5**

Harper's Young People. See Harper's Round Table

The harps of Heaven. Babbitt, N.
In Babbitt, N. The Devil's storybook p21-35 **S C**

Harrah's Automobile Collection, Reno, Nev.
See pages in the following book:
Jackson, R. B. Waves, wheels and wings p36-49 (4-6) **380.5074**

Harriet and the promised land. Lawrence, J. **811**

Harriet changes her mind. Fitzhugh, L.
In Arbuthnot, M. H. comp. The Arbuthnot Anthology of children's literature p676-79 **808.8**

Harriet the spy. Fitzhugh, L. **Fic**
Harriet the spy; excerpt. Fitzhugh, L.
In Arbuthnot, M. H. comp. The Arbuthnot Anthology of children's literature p676-79 **808.8**

Harrington, Lyn
The polar regions (5-7) **919.8**

Harris, Christie
Once more upon a totem (4-7) **398.2**
Contents: The prince who was taken away by the salmon; Raven traveling; Ghost story

Harris, Isabel Sherwin
(illus.) Hussey, L. J. Collecting cocoons **595.7**

Harris, Joel Chandler
Brer Rabbit grossly deceives Brer Fox
In Untermeyer, B. ed. The Golden Treasury of children's literature p226-28 **808.8**
Brer Rabbit's astonishing prank
In Johnson, E. ed. Anthology of children's literature p343-45 **808.8**
The creature with no claws
In A St Nicholas anthology p105-06 **810.8**
How Brer Rabbit was too sharp for Brer Fox
In Untermeyer, B. ed. The Golden Treasury of children's literature p224-25 **808.8**
Old Mr Rabbit, he's a good fisherman
In Arbuthnot, M. H. comp. The Arbuthnot Anthology of children's literature p385-86 **808.8**
In Arbuthnot, M. H. comp. Time for old magic p258-59 **398.2**
The wonderful tar-baby
In Johnson, E. ed. Anthology of children's literature p341-43 **808.8**
The wonderful tar-baby story
In Arbuthnot, M. H. comp. The Arbuthnot Anthology of children's literature p383-84 **808.8**

Haviland, Virginia—_Continued_
Favorite fairy tales told in Germany (2-5)
398.2

Contents: The frog prince; The elves and the shoe-maker; Rapunzel; The cat and mouse in partnership; Rumpelstiltskin; Hansel and Gretel; The 'Bremen town musicians

Favorite fairy tales told in Greece (2-5)
398.2

Contents: Constantes and the dragon; The princess who loved her father like salt; The foolish wife and her three foolish daughters; The fairy wife; The wonder of Skoupa; Fairy gardens; The first of May; Fairy mother

Favorite fairy tales told in India (2-5) **398.2**

Contents: The valiant chattee-maker; The little jackals and the lion; The cat and the parrot; The blind man, the deaf man, and the donkey; The alligator and the jackal; Sir Buzz; The tiger, the Brahman, and the jackal; The Banyan Deer

Favorite fairy tales told in Ireland (2-5) **398.2**

Contents: The bee, the harp, the mouse, and the bum-clock; The old hag's long leather bag; Billy Beg and the bull; The widow's lazy daughter; Patrick O'Donnell and the leprechaun

Favorite fairy tales told in Italy (2-5) **398.2**

Contents: Cenerentola; The story of Bensurdatu; The stone in the cock's head; Bastianelo; The three goslings; The golden lion

Favorite fairy tales told in Japan (2-5) **398.2**

Contents: One-Inch Fellow; The good fortune kettle; The tongue-cut sparrow; Momotaro; The white hare and the crocodiles

Favorite fairy tales told in Norway (2-5) **398.2**

Contents: The Princess on the glass hill; Why the sea is salt; The three billy goats Gruff; Taper Tom; Why the bear is stumpy-tailed; The lad and the North Wind; Boots and the Troll

Favorite fairy tales told in Poland (2-5) **398.2**

Contents: About the hedgehog who became Prince; The jolly tailor who became King; Krencipal and Krencipalka; The lark, the wolf, and the fox; About Jan the Prince, Princess Wonderface, and the Flame-bird; The jester who fooled a king

Favorite fairy tales told in Russia (2-5) **398.2**

Contents: To your good health; Vasilisa the beautiful; Snegourka, the snow maiden; The straw ox; The flying ship

Favorite fairy tales told in Scotland (2-5)
398.2

Contents: The page boy and the silver goblet; The wee bannock; Peerifool; The Brownie o' Ferne-Den; The good housewife and her night labors; Assipattle and the giant sea serpent

Favorite fairy tales told in Spain (2-5) **398.2**

Contents: The flea; Four brothers who were both wise and foolish; The half-chick; The Carlanco; Juan Cigarron; The enchanted mule

Favorite fairy tales told in Sweden (2-5) **398.2**

Contents: The boy and the water-sprite; The old woman and the tramp; The lad and the fox; Pinkel; The old woman and the fish; Lars, my lad!

The good housewife and her night labors
_In_ Arbuthnot, M. H. comp. Time for old
magic p29-31 **398.2**
The old woman and the tramp
_In_ Arbuthnot, M. H. comp. Time for old
magic p140-42 **398.2**
One-Inch Fellow
_In_ Haviland, V. comp. The fairy tale trea-
sury p162-69 **398.2**
The travelogue storybook of the nineteenth
century
_In_ Andrews, S. ed. The Hewins lectures,
1947-1962 p25-63 **208.5**
The twelve months
_In_ Cavanah, F. ed. Holiday roundup p4-9
394.2

(ed.) Yankee Doodle's literary sampler of
prose, poetry, & pictures **028.5**
(comp.) Bechtel, L. S. Books in search of children **028.5**
(comp.) Children's books. See Children's
books **028.52**

Hawaii
Floethe, L. L. The islands of Hawaii (2-4)
919.69

Folklore
See Folklore—Hawaii

Kings and rulers
Wilson, H. Last queen of Hawaii: Liliuokalani (4-6) **92**

Legends
See Legends—Hawaii

Natural history
See Natural history—Hawaii

Social life and customs
See pages in the following book:
Berry, E. Eating and cooking around the
world p18-26 (5-7) **641.3**

Hawaii National Park
See pages in the following book:
Melbo, I. R. Our country's national parks
v2 p252-71 (5-7) **917.3**

Hawaii Volcanoes National Park. See Hawaii
National Park

Hawaiian Islands. See Hawaii

Hawaiian Islands National Wildlife Refuge
See pages in the following book:
Laycock, G. Wild animals, safe places p83-
123 (5-7) **639**

Hawaiian myths of earth, sea, and sky. Thompson, V. L. **398.2**

Hawaiian tales of heroes and champions.
Thompson, V. L. **398.2**

Hawes, Charles Boardman
See pages in the following book:
Miller, B. M. ed. Newbery Medal books:
1922-1955 p30-32 **028.5**

Hawes, Dorothea Cable
Newbery Medal acceptance paper
_In_ Miller, B. M. ed. Newbery Medal books:
1922-1955 p31-32 **028.5**

Hawes, Judy
Bees and beelines (k-2) **595.7**
Fireflies in the night (k-3) **595.7**
The goats who killed the leopard **E**
Ladybug, ladybug, fly away home (k-3) **595.7**
My daddy longlegs (1-3) **595**
Shrimps (1-3) **595**
What I like about toads (k-3) **597**
Why frogs are wet (k-3) **597**

Hawes, M. W.
(illus.) Farjeon, E. The new book of days **828**

The hawk and the wildcat. Sechrist, E. H.
_In_ Sechrist, E. H. Once in the first times
p54-56 **398.2**

Hawkes, Jacquetta
Pharaohs of Egypt. See Pharaohs of Egypt
932

Haywood, Carolyn—*Continued*
Eddie makes music. See note under Haywood, C. Little Eddie **Fic**
Eddie, the dog holder. See note under Haywood, C. Little Eddie **Fic**
Eddie's green thumb. See note under Haywood, C. Little Eddie **Fic**
Eddie's happenings. See note under Haywood, C. Little Eddie **Fic**
Eddie's pay dirt. See note under Haywood, C. Little Eddie **Fic**
Eddie's valuable property. See note under Haywood, C. Little Eddie **Fic**
Ever-ready Eddie. See note under Haywood, C. Little Eddie **Fic**
Here's a Penny (2-4) **Fic**
Little Eddie (2-4) **Fic**
Little Eddie goes to town
In Gruenberg, S. M. ed. Favorite stories old and new p29-36 **808.8**
Merry Christmas from Betsy. See note under Haywood, C. "B" is for Betsy **Fic**
Penny and Peter. See note under Haywood, C. Here's a Penny **Fic**
Penny goes to camp. See note under Haywood, C. Here's a Penny **Fic**
Primrose Day: excerpt
In Association for Childhood Education International. Told under the Stars and Stripes p13-30 **S C**
Snowbound with Betsy. See note under Haywood, C. "B" is for Betsy **Fic**
Taffy and Melissa Molasses (2-4) **Fic**
About
See pages in the following book:
Hoffman, M. ed. Authors and illustrators of children's books p193-96 **028.5**

Haywood, Spencer
See pages in the following book:
Lorimer, L. T. ed. Breaking in p23-44 (5-7) **920**

Hazard, Paul
Books, children & men **028.5**

The **hazel**-branch. Grimm, J.
In Grimm, J. The complete Grimm's Fairy tales p830 **398.2**

The **Hazel**-nut child
In Lang, A. ed. The yellow fairy book p222-24 **398.2**

Hazeltine, Alice I.
(ed.) Hero tales from many lands (5-7) **398.2**
(comp.) The year around (4-7) **808.81**

Hazen, Barbara Shook
The gorilla did it **E**
Where do bears sleep? **E**

He believed in the West. Fritz, J.
In Cavanah, F. ed. Holiday roundup p55-60 **394.2**

He is our guest, let's not see his mistakes. Patri, A.
In Gruenberg, S. M. ed. Favorite stories old and new p250-52 **808.8**

He who laughs last. McNeill, J.
In Mayne, W. ed. William Mayne's Book of giants p71-82 **398.2**

He who saw everything. Feagles, A. **892**

Head, Faye E.
A spouse for Susie Mouse
In Kamerman, S. E. ed. Dramatized folk tales of the world p317-23 **812.08**

The **head**. Leach, M.
In Leach, M. The thing at the foot of the bed, and other scary tales p63-64 **S C**

The **head** of brass. Williams-Ellis, A.
In Williams-Ellis, A. Fairy tales from the British Isles p186-95 **398.2**

The **headless** cupid. Snyder, Z. K. **Fic**

The **headless** horseman. Manning-Sanders, R.
In Manning-Sanders, R. A book of ghosts & goblins p80-86 **398.2**
See also The legend of Sleepy Hollow

Heady, Eleanor B.
Make your own dolls (3-5) **745.59**
Men of different colors
In Arbuthnot, M. H. comp. The Arbuthnot Anthology of children's literature p316-18 **808.8**
Son of the long one
In Arbuthnot, M. H. comp. The Arbuthnot Anthology of children's literature p314-16 **808.8**
In Arbuthnot, M. H. comp. Time for old magic p193-95 **398.2**
When the stones were soft (4-6) **398.2**
Contents: Mumbele and the goats; The Namashepani; The cattle egret; The rug maker; The pots that sang; Why dogs live with men; The little crow; Colored coats; The baobab tree; The sky people; Why the hyrax has no tail; The slient maiden; The rainbow; The trap; Why cats live with woman; Men of different colors

Heady, Harold F.
(illus.) Heady, E. B. Make your own dolls **745.59**

Healey, Frederick
Light and color (3-5) **535**

Health and safety education—multimedia, Index to. *See* Index to health and safety education—multimedia

Heaps, Willard A.
Birthstones (5-7) **553**

Hear your heart. Showers, P. **612**

Hearing
Adler, I. Your ears (3-5) **612**
See also pages in the following book:
Silverstein, A. The sense organs p27-35 (4-7) **612**
See also Deafness

Hearn, Lafcadio
The boy who drew cats
In Gruenberg, S. M. ed. Favorite stories old and new p373-76 **808.8**
In Untermeyer, B. ed. The Golden Treasury of children's literature p525-27 **808.8**
The old woman and her dumpling; adaptation. *See* Mosel, A. The funny little woman **398.2**
The tongue-cut sparrow
In Johnson, E. ed. Anthology of children's literature p314 **808.8**
Hodges, M. The wave **398.2**

Heart

Elgin, K. The human body: the heart (3-5) **612**

Heintze, C. The priceless pump: the human heart (6-7) **612**

Showers, P. Hear your heart (k-3) **612**

Simon, S. About your heart (2-4) **612**

Diseases

Heintze, C. The priceless pump: the human heart (6-7) **612**

Heart of ice. Caylus, Comte de

In Lang, A. ed. The green fairy book p106-36 **398.2**

Hearts, cupids, and red roses. Barth, E. **394.2**

Hearts of oak. Hall, M. E.

In Burack, A. S. ed. One hundred plays for children p821-37 **808.82**

Hearts, tarts, and valentines. Fisher, A.

In Fisher, A. Holiday programs for boys and girls p250-60 **812**

Heartsease. Dickinson, P. **Fic**

Heat

Adler, I. Heat and its uses (4-6) **536**

Adler, I. Hot and cold (4-6) **536**

Balestrino, P. Hot as an ice cube (k-3) **536**

See also pages in the following book:

Mark, S. J. A physics lab of your own p43-63 (5-7) **530.72**

See also Combustion; Temperature

Heat and its uses. Adler, I. **536**

Heat engines

See pages in the following book:

Weiss, H. Motors and engines and how they work p42-50 (5-7) **621.4**

Heath, Anna Lenington

The Gypsy look

In Kamerman, S. E. ed. Fifty plays for junior actors p245-56 **812.08**

Much ado about ants

In Burack, A. S. ed. One hundred plays for children p127-34 **808.82**

Heather and broom. Nic Leodhas, S. **398.2**

Heather, oak, and olive. Sutcliff, R. **S C**

Heating

Urquhart, D. I. Central heating and how it works (3-6) **697**

The **heavenly** jam. Freshman, E.

In Luckhardt, M. C. comp. Thanksgiving p311-17 **394.2**

The **heavenly** wedding. Grimm, J.

In Grimm, J. The complete Grimm's Fairy tales p828-29 **398.2**

Heavy Collar and the Ghost Woman. Hardendorff, J. B.

In Hardendorff, J. B. ed. Just one more p139-49 **372.6**

Heavy is a hippopotamus. Schlein, M. **E**

Hebrew language

See pages in the following book:

Hoffman, G. The land and people of Israel p80-82, 90-93 (5-7) **915.694**

Hector Protector, and As I went over the water. Sendak, M. **398.8**

Hedderwick, Mairi

(illus.) Godden, R. The old woman who lived in a vinegar bottle **398.2**

The **hedgehog** and the rabbit. Grimm, J.

In Grimm, J. More Tales from Grimm p163-70 **398.2**

See also Hare and the hedgehog

The **hedgehog** who became a prince

In Baker, A. comp. The golden lynx, and other tales p119-22 **398.2**

See also Prince Hedgehog

Hedgehogs

Stories

Potter, B. The tale of Mrs Tiggy-Winkle **E**

Hedin, Don

(illus.) Carr, R. Be a frog, a bird, or a tree **613.7**

Hedley Kow

Jacobs, J. The Hedley Kow

In Jacobs, J. ed. More English folk and fairy tales p55-59 **398.2**

In Manning-Sanders, R. ed. A book of magical beasts p3-13 **398.2**

Palmer, R. The Hedley Kow

In Palmer, R. Dragons, unicorns, and other magical beasts p63-67 **398.2**

Heidbreder, M. Ann

(jt. auth.) Bomar, C. P. Guide to the development of educational media selection centers **021**

(jt. auth.) Rowell, J. Educational media selection centers **021**

Heide, Florence Parry

Sound of sunshine, sound of rain **E**

Heiderstadt, Dorothy

Indians for Thanksgiving

In Harper, W. comp. The harvest feast p50-63 **394.2**

In Sechrist, E. H. ed. It's time for Thanksgiving p60-69 **394.2**

Heidi. Spyri, J. **Fic**

Heidi; excerpt. Spyri, J.

In Arbuthnot, M. H. comp. The Arbuthnot Anthology of children's literature p708-12 **808.8**

Heidi; play. Thane, A.

In Thane, A. Plays from famous stories and fairy tales p315-34 **812**

The **heifer** hide

In Chase, R. ed. The Jack tales p161-71 **398.2**

Heilbroner, Joan

The happy birthday present **E**

This is the house where Jack lives (k-2) **398.8**

Heinlein, Robert

Space ship Bifrost

In Arbuthnot, M. H. comp. The Arbuthnot Anthology of children's literature p591-94 **808.8**

Heintze, Carl

The priceless pump: the human heart (6-7) **612**

Heir of Linne

Nic Leodhas, S. The tale of the heir of Linne

In Nic Leodhas, S. By loch and by lin p105-17 **398.2**

Henry, Marguerite—Continued
Justin Morgan had a horse; excerpts
  In Arbuthnot, M. H. comp. The Arbuthnot Anthology of children's literature p622-27   808.8
King of the Wind (4-7)   Fic
Misty of Chincoteague (4-7)   Fic
Mustang, wild spirit of the West (5-7) Fic
Newbery Medal acceptance paper
  In Miller, B. M. ed. Newbery Medal books: 1922-1955 p327-34   028.5
Pony Penning Day
  In Association for Childhood Education International. Told under spacious skies p128-35   S C
  In Gruenberg, S. M. ed. Favorite stories old and new p198-206   808.8
The pulling bee
  In Martignoni, M. E. ed. The illustrated treasury of children's literature p449-52   808.8
Sea Star, orphan of Chincoteague. See note under Henry, M. Misty of Chincoteague   Fic
Stormy, Misty's foal. See note under Henry, M. Misty of Chincoteague   Fic
White stallion of Lipizza (5-7)   Fic

About

See pages in the following books:

Hoffman, M. ed. Authors and illustrators of children's books p197-208   028.5
Miller, B. M. ed. Newbery Medal books: 1922-1955 p320-24   028.5

Henry, O.
The gift of the magi
  In Parents' Magazine's Christmas holiday book p258-63   394.2
  In Tudor, T. ed. Take joy! p47-51   394.2
The ransom of Red Chief (4-6)   Fic

Henry, Patrick
Campion, N. R. Patrick Henry, firebrand of the Revolution (5-7)   92

See also pages in the following books:

Arbuthnot, M. H. comp. The Arbuthnot Anthology of children's literature p799-806   808.8
Daugherty, S. Ten brave men p37-52 (5-7)   920
Taylor, T. Rebellion town, Williamsburg, 1776 p14-27 (5-7)   973.3

Henry, Ralph
(comp.) My American heritage (4-7)   810.8

Henry and Beezus. Cleary, B. See note under Cleary, B. Henry Huggins   Fic

Henry and his dog Henry. Brooks, W. R.
  In Gruenberg, S. M. ed. Favorite stories old and new p257-63   808.8

Henry and Ribsy. Cleary, B. See note under Cleary, B. Henry Huggins   Fic

Henry and the clubhouse. Cleary, B. See note under Cleary, B. Henry Huggins   Fic

Henry and the paper route. Cleary, B. See note under Cleary, B. Henry Huggins Fic

Henry Huggins. Cleary, B.   Fic

Henry VIII, King of England
  See pages in the following books:
Farjeon, E. ed. A cavalcade of kings p217-20 (5-7)   808.8
Street, A. The land and people of England p95-99 (5-7)   914.2
Henry Possum. Berson, H.   E
Henry Reed, Inc. Robertson, K.   Fic
Henry Reed's baby-sitting service. Robertson, K. See note under Robertson, K. Henry Reed, Inc.   Fic
Henry Reed's big show. Robertson, K. See note under Robertson, K. Henry Reed, Inc. Fic
Henry Reed's journey. Robertson, K. See note under Robertson, K. Henry Reed, Inc. Fic
Henry the Eighth. Marshall, A.
  In Farjeon, E. ed. A cavalcade of kings p217-20   808.8
Henry the explorer. Taylor, M.   E
Henry the Navigator, Prince of Portugal
Buehr, W. The Portuguese explorers (4-6)   910
Chubb, T. C. Prince Henry the Navigator and the highways of the sea (6-7)   910
Henry 3. Krumgold, J.   Fic
Hens. See Chickens
Henson, Matthew Alexander
Ripley, S. N. Matthew Henson: Arctic hero (4-6)   92

See also pages in the following books:

Hayden, R. C. Seven Black American scientists p116-41 (6-7)   920
Hughes, L. Famous Negro heroes of America p139-52 (5-7)   920
Johnston, J. A special bravery p60-64 (2-5)   920
Rollins, C. H. They showed the way p83-87 (5-7)   920

Henstra, Friso
(illus.) Williams, J. Petronella   Fic
(illus.) Williams, J. The practical princess Fic
Her Majesty, Grace Jones. Langton, J.   Fic
Her majesty's servants (The servants of the queen). Kipling, R.
  In Kipling, R. The jungle book (Doubleday) p183-209   E
  In Kipling, R. The jungle books (Doubleday) v2 p175-97   S C
  In Kipling, R. The jungle books (Macmillan N Y) p348-66   S C
  In Kipling, R. The jungle books (Watts, F.) v 1 p185-209   S C
Heracles. See Hercules
Heracles the strong. Serraillier, I.   292
Herakles. See Hercules
The herald of War. Baumann, H.
  In Baumann, H. The stolen fire p38-41 398.2
Heraldry
  See pages in the following book:
Buehr, W. Chivalry and the mailed knight p48-53 (3-6)   940.1
  See also Knights and knighthood
Herbage. See Grasses

Herbs, Medical. See Botany, Medical

Herculaneum
See pages in the following book:
Hall, J. Buried cities p49-57 (5-7)   913

Hercules
Newman, R. The twelve labors of Hercules (4-6)   292
Serraillier, I. Heracles the strong (4-6)   292
See also pages in the following books:
Aulaire, I. d'. Ingri and Edgar Parin d'Aulaire's Book of Greek myths p132-46 (3-6)   292
Colum, P. The Golden Fleece and the heroes who lived before Achilles p244-94 (5-7)   292
Gates, D. The golden god: Apollo p66-76 (4-7)   292
Gates, D. The warrior goddess: Athena p80-85 (4-7)   292
Johnson, E. ed. Anthology of children's literature p490-93   808.8

Hercules. Gramatky, H.   E

Hercules of Virginia. Jagendorf, M. A.
In Jagendorf, M. A. Folk stories of the South p297-301   398.2

Herd boy and the weaving maiden
Carpenter, F. Spinning maid and the cowherd
In Carpenter, F. Tales of a Chinese grandmother p182-89   398.2

Herda, H.
The Swan Princess
In Hoke, H. ed. Witches, witches, witches p176-86   808.8

Herding the king's hares. Aulaire, I. d'
In Aulaire, I. d'. East of the sun and west of the moon p15-26   398.2
In Undset, S. ed. True and untrue, and other Norse tales p161-72   398.2
See also Ashiepattle and the king's hares

Herdsman of Lona. Duvoisin, R.
In Duvoisin, R. The three sneezes, and other Swiss tales p89-93   398.2

Herdsman's choice. Duvoisin, R.
In Duvoisin, R. The three sneezes, and other Swiss tales p101-10   398.2

Here comes the strikeout. Kessler, L.   E

Here I am
In Camp Fire Girls, Inc. The Camp Fire Blue Bird Series bk.2   369.47

Here I am! Baron, V. O. ed.   811.08

Here is Alaska. Stefansson, E.   917.98

Here is your hobby: doll collecting. Young, H.   745.59

Here is your hobby: Indian dancing and costumes. Powers, W. K.   793.3

Here we go! Leach, M.
In Harper, W. comp. Ghosts and goblins p222-24   394.2
In Leach, M. The thing at the foot of the bed, and other scary tales p17-19 S C

Hereafterthis. Jacobs, J.   398.2
also in Jacobs, J. ed. More English folk and fairy tales p7-11   398.2

Heredity
Pomerantz, C. Why you look like you, whereas I tend to look like me (4-6)   575.1
See also pages in the following book:
Cole, J. Twins p43-51 (3-6)   612.6
See also DNA; Evolution; Mendel's law

Here's a Penny. Haywood, C.   Fic

Hermes
See pages in the following book:
Gates, D. The golden god: Apollo p29-42 (4-7)   292

Hermetic art and philosophy. See Alchemy

Hermit into scorpion. Roy, C.
In Roy, C. The serpent and the sun p30-35   398.2

The Hermit's cabbage patch. Green, K.
In Green, K. Leprechaun tales p118-27   398.2

Hermod and Hadvor
In Lang, A. ed. The yellow fairy book p301-07   398.2

Hernandez, Joseph
See pages in the following book:
Alderman, C. L. Osceola and the Seminole wars p152-61 (5-7)   92

The hero. Jagendorf, M. A.
In Jagendorf, M. A. Noodlehead stories from around the world p212-15 398.2

The hero of Adi Nifas. Courlander, H.
In Courlander, H. The fire on the mountain, and other Ethiopian stories p45-49   398.2

Hero tales from many lands. Hazeltine, A. L. ed.   398.2

Hero twins
Finger, C. Hero twins
In Finger, C. Tales from silver lands p69-78   398.2
Vukub-Cakix
In Garner, A. ed. A cavalcade of goblins p4-10   398.2

Heroes
See pages in the following book:
Johnson, E. ed. Anthology of children's literature p477-561   808.8
See also Courage; Explorers; Mythology; Saints

Heroes in American folklore. Shapiro, I. 398.2

Heroes of civilization. Cottler, J.   920

Heroes of the American Revolution. Davis, B.   920

Heroin
See pages in the following book:
Hyde, M. O. ed. Mind drugs p35-39, 84-98 (5-7)   613.8

The heroine of Wren. Colbo, E. S.
In Burack, A. S. ed. One hundred plays for children p813-20   808.82

Heroines. See Women in literature and art

Heroines of the early West. Ross, N. W. 920

Heroism. See Courage

The heron and the turtle. Arnott, K.
In Arnott, K. Animal folk tales around the world p49-58   398.2

History, Naval. See United States—History, Naval

A history of body armor. Peterson, H. L. 623.4

History of Codadad and his brothers
   In Wiggin, K. D. ed. The Arabian nights p264-89 **398.2**

History of England. Austen, J.
   In Authors' choice p41-52 **S C**

The History of Jack and the beanstalk
   In Opie, I. ed. The classic fairy tales p164-74 **398.2**
   See also Jack and the bean-stalk

The History of Jack the giant-killer
   In Opie, I. ed. The classic fairy tales p51-65 **398.2**
   See also Jack the giant-killer

The History of Jack the giant-killer
   In Lang, A. ed. The blue fairy book p374-79 **398.2**
   See also Jack the giant-killer

A history of knives. Peterson, H. L. **683**

History of the young king of the Black Isles
   In Wiggin, K. D. ed. The Arabian nights p67-80 **398.2**

The History of Tom Thumb
   In Haviland, V. The fairy tale treasury p72-77 **398.2**
   In Jacobs, J. ed. English folk and fairy tales p145-52 **398.2**
   In Johnson, E. ed. Anthology of children's literature p198-200 **808.8**
   In Martignoni, M. E. ed. The illustrated treasury of children's literature p184-86 **808.8**
   In Opie, I. ed. The classic fairy tales p33-46 **398.2**
   See also Tom Thumb

The History of Whittington
   In Lang, A. ed. The blue fairy book p206-13 **398.2**
   See also Dick Whittington and his cat

Hitchcock, Alfred
   (comp.) Alfred Hitchcock's Supernatural tales of terror and suspense (5-7) **S C**

Hitler, Adolf
   See pages in the following book:
   Hall, E. The land and people of Czechoslovakia p93-99 (5-7) **914.37**

Hitopadésa
   Brown, M. Once a mouse **398.2**
   Gaer, J. The fables of India p53-116 **398.2**

Hitte, Kathryn
   Mexicali soup **E**

Hittite mythology. See Mythology, Hittite

Hitty: her first hundred years. Field, R. **Fic**

Hnizdovsky, J.
   (illus.) Bloch, H. ed. Ukrainian folk tales **398.2**

Hoag, Edwin
   American houses: colonial, classic, and contemporary (6-7) **728**

Hoagie's rifle-gun. Miles, M. **Fic**

Hoban, Lillian
   Arthur's Christmas cookies **E**
   Arthur's Honey Bear **E**

The sugar snow spring **E**
   (illus.) Cohen, M. Best friends **E**
   (illus.) Cohen, M. Will I have a friend? **E**
   (illus.) Fisher, A. In one door and out the other **811**
   (illus.) Hoban, R. A baby sister for Frances **E**
   (illus.) Hoban, R. A bargain for Frances **E**
   (illus.) Hoban, R. Best friends for Frances **E**
   (illus.) Hoban, R. A birthday for Frances **E**
   (illus.) Hoban, R. Bread and jam for Frances **E**
   (illus.) Hoban, R. Egg thoughts, and other Frances songs **811**
   (illus.) Hoban, R. Emmet Otter's Jug-Band Christmas **E**
   (illus.) Hoban, R. Harvey's hideout **E**
   (illus.) Hoban, R. The little Brute family **E**
   (illus.) Hoban, R. The Mole family's Christmas **E**
   (illus.) Hoban, R. Nothing to do **E**
   (illus.) Hoban, R. The sorely trying day **E**

Hoban, Russell
   A baby sister for Frances **E**
   A bargain for Frances **E**
   Bedtime for Frances **E**
   Best friends for Frances **E**
   A birthday for Frances **E**
   Bread and jam for Frances **E**
   Egg thoughts, and other Frances songs (k-2) **811**
   Emmet Otter's Jug-Band Christmas **E**
   Harvey's hideout **E**
   How Tom beat Captain Najork and his hired sportsmen **E**
   The little Brute family **E**
   The Mole family's Christmas **E**
   Nothing to do **E**
   The sorely trying day **E**

Hoban, Tana
   Circles, triangles and squares **E**
   Count and see **E**
   Look again! **E**
   Over, under & through, and other spatial concepts **E**
   Push pull, empty full **E**
   Shapes and things **E**
   Where is it? **E**

Hobbies
   See also Handicraft; also names of hobbies

   Bibliography
   See pages in the following book:
   National Council of Teachers of English. Adventuring with books p326-30 **028.52**

The hobbit. Tolkien, J. R. R. **Fic**

The hobbit; excerpt. Tolkien, J. R. R.
   In Arbuthnot, M. H. comp. The Arbuthnot Anthology of children's literature p555-57 **808.8**

Hoberman, Mary Ann
   All my shoes comes in twos **E**
   A little book of little beasts (k-3) **811**
   Nuts to you & nuts to me (k-2) **811**

Hoberman, Norman
   (jt. auth.) Hoberman, M. A. All my shoes comes in twos **E**

A hobo adventure. Carlson, N. S.
 In Arbuthnot, M. H. comp. The Arbuthnot Anthology of children's literature p712-16   **808.8**

Hobson, Burton
Coins you can collect (4-7)   **737.4**

The Hobyahs
 In Fenner, P. R. comp. Giants & witches and a dragon or two p174-77   **398.2**
 In Jacobs, J. ed. More English folk and fairy tales p127-33   **398.2**
 In Tashjian, V. A. ed. Juba this and Juba that p51-54   **372.6**

Hockey
Coombs, C. Be a winner in ice hockey (5-7)   **796.9**

 See also pages in the following books:
The Junior illustrated encyclopedia of sports p451-98 (5-7)   **796.03**
Keith, H. Sports and games p227-42 (5-7) **796**

Terminology
Liss, H. Hockey talk for beginners (4-7) **796.9**

Hockey talk for beginners. Liss, H.   **796.9**

The **hodgepodge** book. Emrich, D. comp. **398**

Hodges, C. Walter
Magna Carta (4-7)   **942.03**
The Norman Conquest (4-7)   **942.02**
(illus.) Browning, R. The Pied Piper of Hamelin (Coward, McCann & Geoghegan) **821**
(illus.) Coleridge, S. T. The rime of the ancient mariner   **821**
(illus.) Duggan, A. Growing up with the Norman Conquest (6-7)   **914.2**
(illus.) Serraillier, I. The silver sword   **Fic**
(illus.) Willard, B. The Richleighs of Tantamount   **Fic**

Hodges, David
(illus.) Blassingame, W. Story of the Boy Scouts   **369.43**
(illus.) Clayton, E. Martin Luther King: the peaceful warrior   **92**
(illus.) Felton, H. W. Nat Love, Negro cowboy   **92**
(illus.) Fenderson, L. H. Thurgood Marshall: fighter for justice   **92**
(illus.) Montgomery, E. R. William C. Handy: father of the blues   **92**

Hodges, Elizabeth Jamison
Serendipity tales (4-7)   **398.2**
Contents: The magic muntr; The queen's care; The golden lion; The lost gift; The laughing statue; The flower faces; The dutiful daughter
The three princes of Serendip (4-7)   **398.2**

Hodges, Margaret
The Fire Bringer (2-5)   **398.2**
The hatching of Joshua Cobb (4-6)   **Fic**
The making of Joshua Cobb (5-7)   **Fic**
Persephone and the springtime (k-3)   **292**
The wave (3-5)   **398.2**
—Same
 In Arbuthnot, M. H. comp. Time for old magic p217-19   **398.2**

Hodgson, Richard
 See pages in the following book:
Cohen, D. In search of ghosts p120-27 (6-7)   **133**

Hodgson, Sheila
Slip stream
 In Hitchcock, A. comp. Alfred Hitchcock's Supernatural tales of terror and suspense p68-75   **S C**

The **Hodja** and the hens. Kelsey, A. G.
 In Kelsey, A. G. Once the Hodja p123-29   **398.2**

The **Hodja** preaches a sermon
 In Courlander, H. ed. Ride with the sun p82-84   **398.2**

Hoff, Carol
Kip and the red tractor
 In Association for Childhood Education International. Told under spacious skies p230-42   **S C**

Hoff, Syd
Danny and the dinosaur   **E**
Irving and me (5-7)   **Fic**
My Aunt Rosie   **E**
Stanley   **E**
Thunderhoof   **E**
When will it snow?   **E**
(illus.) Lexau, J. M. The homework caper   **E**
(illus.) Lexau, J. M. I should have stayed in bed   **E**
(illus.) Lexau, J. M. The rooftop mystery   **E**
(illus.) Ricciuti, E. R. Donald and the fish that walked   **E**

Hoffman, Gail
The land and people of Israel (5-7) **915.694**

Hoffman, Heinrich
The Crow-Biddy
 In Martignoni, M. E. ed. The illustrated treasury of children's literature p91   **808.8**

Hoffman, Miriam
(ed.) Authors and illustrators of children's books   **028.5**

Hoffman, Phyllis
Steffie and me   **E**

Hoffmann, Felix
(illus.) Grimm, J. The four clever brothers   **398.2**
(illus.) Grimm, J. King Thrushbeard   **398.2**
(illus.) Grimm, J. Rapunzel   **398.2**
(illus.) Grimm, J. The seven ravens   **398.2**
(illus.) Grimm, J. Tom Thumb   **398.2**
(illus.) Grimm, J. The wolf and the seven little kids   **398.2**
(illus.) Haviland, V. Favorite fairy tales told in Poland   **398.2**

Hoffmeister, Donald F.
(jt. auth.) Zim, H. S. Mammals   **599**

Hofmann, Charles
American Indians sing (5-7)   **784.7**

Hofsinde, Robert
The Indian and his horse (4-6)   **970.1**
Indians arts (4-6)   **709.01**
Indian beadwork (5-7)   **746.5**
Indian costumes (3-6)   **391**
Indian fishing and camping (3-6)   **799.1**
Indian games and crafts (4-7)   **790**
Indian hunting (3-6)   **799**
The Indian medicine man (4-7)   **398**
Indian music makers (3-7)   **781.7**
Indian picture writing (4-7)   **411**
Indian sign language (3-6)   **001.54**
Indian warriors and their weapons (3-6) **739.7**

Holland. See Netherlands

Hollering sun. Wood, N.   970.3

Holling, Holling Clancy
Minn of the Mississippi (4-6)   Fic
Paddle-to-the-sea (4-6)   Fic
Pagoo (4-7)   595
Seabird (4-6)   Fic
Tree in the trail (4-7)   Fic
About
See pages in the following book:
Hoffman, M. ed. Authors and illustrators of
children's books p209-16   028.5

Holling, Lucille Webster
(illus.) Holling, H. C. Pagoo   595

Hollingsworth, Leslie
Silent night
In Burack, A. S. ed. Christmas plays for
young actors p39-48   812.08

The **holly** hangs high. Barbee, L.
In Burack, A. S. ed. One hundred plays for
children p482-91   808.82

Holly, reindeer, and colored lights. Barth, E.
    394.2

Holm, Anne
North to freedom (6-7)   Fic
North to freedom; excerpt
In Johnson, E. ed. Anthology of children's
literature p889-98   808.8

Holman, Felice
Slake's limbo (6-7)   Fic

Holme, Bryan
Drawings to live with   741.9

Holmes, Bea
(illus.) Hunter, E. F. Child of the silent night
[biography of Laura Dewey Bridgman] 92
(illus.) Papashvily, H. W. Louisa May Alcott
    92
(illus.) Underwood, B. The tamarack tree Fic

Holmes, Ruth Vickery
Little Red Riding Hood
In Kamerman, S. E. ed. Little plays for
little players p277-84   812.08
The wise men of Gotham
In Burack, A. S. ed. One hundred plays for
children p675-85   808.82

Holtan, Gene
(illus.) Larrick, N. comp. The wheels of the
bus go round and round   784.6
(illus.) Snyder, Z. K. Black and blue magic
    Fic

The **Holy** Bible [King James Bible]. Bible 220.5

The **Holy** Bible [Rev. standard. Reference ed].
Bible   220.5

The **Holy** Family and the greedy woman. Woolsey, J.
In Sechrist, E. H. ed. It's time for Christmas p35-39   394.2

The **Holy** Night. Jüchen, A. von   232.9

The **Holy** Night. Lagerlöf, S.
In Eaton, A. T. comp. The animals' Christ-
mas p42-46   394.2
In Harper, W. comp. Merry Christmas to
you p33-37   394.2
In Tudor, T. ed. Take joy! p52-54   394.2

The **Holy** relic of Bannockburn. Nic Leodhas, S.
In Nic Leodhas, S. Gaelic ghosts p76-80
    398.2

Holy Week
See pages in the following book:
Ickis, M. The book of festivals and holidays
the world over p51-57   394.2
See also Easter

Holz, Loretta
Teach yourself stitchery (4-6)   746.4

Holzing, Herbert
(illus.) Baumann, H. The stolen fire   398.2

Homar, Lorenzo
(illus.) Alegría, R. E. The three wishes   398.2

Home
Hautzig, E. At home (k-3)   410

The **home** book of quotations. Stevenson, B. ed.
    808.88

The **home** book of verse for young folks. Stevenson, B. E. comp.   821.08

Home economics. See Consumer education;
Cookery; Food; Heating; Sewing

Home from the hill. Baker, M. J.   Fic

Home is the sailor. Godden, R.   Fic

Home life. See Family

The **homemakers.** Fisher, L. E.   680

Homer
Proddow, P. Demeter and Persephone   292
Proddow, P. Dionysos and the pirates   292
Adaptations
Church, A. J. The Iliad and the Odyssey of
Homer (6-7)   883
Picard, B. L. The Iliad of Homer (6-7)   883

Homer, Winslow
Hyman, L. Winslow Homer: America's old
master (5-7)   92

Homer Price. McCloskey, R.   Fic

Homer Price; excerpt. McCloskey, R.
In Arbuthnot, M. H. comp. The Arbuthnot
Anthology of children's literature
p687-91   808.8

Homeric hymn number seven. See Proddow, P.
Dionysos and the pirates   292

Homeric hymn number two. See Proddow, P.
Demeter and Persephone   292

Homes. See Houses

Homes (Institutions) See Orphans and orphans'
homes

The **homes** of the Presidents. Bergere, T. 917.3

The **homework** caper. Lexau, J. M.   E

Homing pigeons. Zim, H. S.   636.5

Honduras
Carpenter, A. Honduras (4-6)   917.283
See also pages in the following book:
Markun, P. M. The first book of Central
America and Panama p31-38 (5-7) 917.28

Honduras, British. See British Honduras

The **honest** ghost. Nic Leodhas, S.
In Nic Leodhas, S. Twelve great black
cats, and other eerie Scottish tales
p13-25   398.2

Honey. See Bees; Cookery—Honey

Horizon Magazine—*Continued*

Caesar. See Caesar   **92**

Captain Cook and the South Pacific. See Captain Cook and the South Pacific   **919**

Marco Polo's adventures in China. See Marco Polo's adventures in China   **92**

Pharaohs of Egypt. See Pharaohs of Egypt   **932**

Shakespeare's England. See Shakespeare's England   **822.3**

The Universe of Galileo and Newton. See The Universe of Galileo and Newton   **509**

The Vikings. See The Vikings   **948**

Hormel, Al

(illus.) Mulholland, J. Magic of the world   **793.8**

La Hormiguita. Belpré, P.

In Belpré, P. The tiger and the rabbit, and other tales p57-61   **398.2**

Hormones

Riedman, S. R. Hormones: how they work (6-7)   **612**

Silverstein, A. The endocrine system (4-7)   **612**

Hormones: how they work. Riedman, S. R. **612**

The Horn Book Magazine

Horn Book Reflections on children's books and reading. See Horn Book Reflections on children's books and reading   **028.5**

A Horn Book Sampler on children's books and reading. See A Horn Book Sampler on children's books and reading   **028.5**

Illustrators of children's books: 1744-1945. See Illustrators of children's books: 1744-1945   **741.64**

Illustrators of children's books: 1946-1956. See Illustrators of children's books: 1946-1956   **741.64**

Illustrators of children's books: 1957-1966. See Illustrators of children's books: 1957-1966   **741.64**

Jordan, A. M. Children's classics   **028.52**

Kingman, L. ed. Newbery and Caldecott Medal books: 1956-1965   **028.5**

Kingman, L. ed. Newbery and Caldecott Medal books: 1966-1975   **028.5**

Miller, B. M. ed. Caldecott Medal books: 1938-1957   **028.5**

Miller, B. M. ed. Newbery Medal books: 1922-1955   **028.5**

The Horn Book Magazine   **028.505**

Horn Book Reflections on children's books and reading   **028.5**

A Horn Book Sampler on children's books and reading   **028.5**

The horn of Roland. Williams, J.   **398.2**

Hornby, John

Clowns through the ages (3-5)   **791.3**

Horne, Esther Burnett

See pages in the following book:

Gridley, M. E. American Indian women p131-37 (5-7)   **920**

Horne, Lena

See pages in the following books:

Hughes, L. Famous Negro music makers p155-60 (5-7)   **920**

Rollins, C. Famous Negro entertainers of stage, screen, and TV p69-73 (5-7)   **920**

Horned goat. Borski, L. M.

In Borski, L. M. The jolly tailor, and other fairy tales p49-62   **398.2**

The Horned woman

In Baker, A. comp. The talking tree p48-51   **398.2**

In Hoke, H. ed. Witches, witches, witches p 1-4   **808.8**

Hornets

McClung, R. M. Bees, wasps, and hornets and how they live (3-6)   **595.7**

Hornyansky, Michael

The Golden Phoenix

In Colwell, E. ed. A second storyteller's choice p67-79   **372.6**

Horology. See Clocks and watches

Horoscope. See Astrology

Horror stories

Hitchcock, A. comp. Alfred Hitchcock's Supernatural tales of terror and suspense (5-7)   **S C**

Horse. See Horses

The horse and his boy. Lewis, C. S. See note under Lewis, C. S. The lion, the witch and the wardrobe   **Fic**

The horse and the eighteen bandits. Vo-Dinh

In Vo-Dinh. The toad is the Emperor's uncle p105-13   **398.2**

A horse came running. DeJong, M.   **Fic**

The horse-egg. Jagendorf, M. A.

In Jagendorf, M. A. Noodlehead stories from around the world p19-23 **398.2**

The horse family. Hogner, D. C.   **636.1**

The horse in America. Gay, O. W.   **636.109**

Horse racing

Anderson, C. W. Twenty gallant horses (5-7)   **798**

Fiction

Henry, M. Black Gold (4-6)   **Fic**

Henry, M. Gaudenzia, pride of the Palio (4-7)   **Fic**

Wrightson, P. A racecourse for Andy (5-7)   **Fic**

Horse stories. See Horses—Stories

Horse trading in Wichita Falls. Jagendorf, M. A.

In Jagendorf, M. A. Folk stories of the South p290-92   **398.2**

The horse who had his picture in the paper. McGinley, P.

In Gruenberg, S. M. ed. Favorite stories old and new p135-43   **808.8**

The horse who lived upstairs. McGinley, P.

In Martignoni, M. E. ed. The illustrated treasury of children's literature p345-46   **808.8**

The horse without a head. Berna, P.   **Fic**

The Horse without a master

In Courlander, H. ed. Ride with the sun p95-98   **398.2**

Horseback riding, Sports Illustrated.   **798**

The horsefly. Tashjian, V. A.

In Tashjian, V. A. Three apples fell from heaven p37-39   **398.2**

Hotchkiss, Jeanette
American historical fiction and biography for children and young people **016.813**
European historical fiction and biography for children and young people **016.8**

Hotels, motels, etc.
Fiction
Burch, R. Skinny (4-6) **Fic**

Houdini, Harry
Kendall, L. Houdini: master of escape (6-7) **92**

Hough, Charlotte
Angus
In Mayne, W. ed. William Mayne's Book of giants p55-62 **398.2**

Hough, Richard
The Battle of Britain (5-7) **940.54**

The hound of the Baskervilles. Doyle, Sir A. C.
In Doyle, Sir A. C. The boy's Sherlock Holmes p357-524 **S C**
In Doyle, Sir A. C. Tales of Sherlock Holmes p431-605 **S C**

The house at Pooh Corner. Milne, A. A. **Fic**
also in Milne, A. A. The world of Pooh p153-314 **Fic**

A house for the crocodile. Sturton, H.
In Sturton, H. Zomo, the Rabbit p100-13 **398.2**

The house in the middle of the road. Aardema, V.
In Aardema, V. Behind the back of the mountain p74-80 **398.2**

House in the wood
Grimm, J. The house in the wood
In Grimm, J. The house in the wood, and other fairy stories p 1-14 **398.2**
Grimm, J. The hut in the forest
In Arbuthnot, M. H. comp. Time for old magic p52-54 **398.2**
In Grimm, J. The complete Grimm's Fairy tales p698-704 **398.2**
Ransome, A. The hut in the forest
In Ransome, A. Old Peter's Russian tales p11-17 **398.2**

The house in the wood, and other fairy stories. Grimm, J. **398.2**

The house in the woods. Sechrist, E. H.
In Sechrist, E. H. Once in the first times p128-31 **398.2**

The House Mouse and the Country Mouse. Asbjørnsen, P. C.
In Asbjørnsen, P. C. Norwegian folk tales p116-19 **398.2**

House of Bourbon. See Bourbon, House of

The House of Crom Duv. Colum, P.
In Colum, P. The King of Ireland's Son p211-53 **398.2**

The house of Dies Drear. Hamilton, V. **Fic**

The house of Dies Drear; excerpt. Hamilton, V.
In Arbuthnot, M. H. comp. The Arbuthnot Anthology of children's literature p646-55 **808.8**

The house of four seasons. Duvoisin, R. **E**

A house of Pomegranates. See Wilde, O. The Happy Prince, and other stories **S C**

The house of sixty fathers. DeJong, M. **Fic**

House of the singing windows. Gilbert, N.
In Association for Childhood Education International. Told under the Stars and Stripes p159-71 **S C**

The house of wings. Byars, B. **Fic**

The house on East 88th Street. Waber, B. **E**

The house on Parchment Street. McKillip, P. A. **Fic**

House painting
Fiction
Duvoisin, R. The house of four seasons **E**

House plans. See Architecture, Domestic—Designs and plans

House plants
Baker, S. S. The indoor and outdoor grow-it book (1-6) **635**
Bulla, C. R. Flowerpot gardens (3-5) **635.9**
Cutler, K. N. Growing a garden, indoors or out (4-7) **635**
Fenten, D. X. Indoor gardening (4-7) **635.9**
Fenten, D. X. Plants for pots (4-7) **635.9**
Paul, A. Kids gardening (4-7) **635.9**
Selsam, M. E. How to grow house plants (4-7) **635.9**

House sparrows. McCoy, J. J. **598.2**

The house that hated war. Harter, W.
In Harter, W. Osceola's head, and other American ghost stories p31-37 **S C**

The House that Jack built **398.8**

House that Jack built; adaptation. See Heilbroner, J. This is the house where Jack lives **398.8**

The house that lacked a bogle. Nic Leodhas, S.
In Nic Leodhas, S. Gaelic ghosts p100-10 **398.2**

The house with a clock in its walls. Bellairs, J. (5-7) **Fic**

Household equipment and supplies
See pages in the following book:
The Way things work. Special edition for young people p235-54 (6-7) **600**

Household stories. Grimm, J. **398.2**

Houser, Allan
(illus.) Clark, A. N. Blue Canyon horse **Fic**
(illus.) Wyatt, E. Cochise, Apache warrior and statesman **92**
(illus.) Wyatt, E. Geronimo, the last Apache war chief **92**

Houses
Hofsinde, R. Indians at home (4-7) **728**
Myller, R. From idea into house (5-7) **728**
See also pages in the following books:
Hults, D. N. New Amsterdam days and ways p86-95 (4-7) **974.7**
Kirk, R. Hunters of the whale p149-54 (6-7) **970.3**

See also Apartment houses
Fiction
Burton, V. L. The little house **E**
Calhoun, M. Katie John (4-6) **Fic**
Lund, D. H. You ought to see Herbert's house **E**

Houses, Sod. See Sod houses

Houses from the sea. Goudey, A. E. **594**

Houses of animals. See Animals—Habitations

How the good gifts were used by two. Pyle, H.
　In Pyle, H. The wonder clock p121-33
　　　　　　　　　　　　　　　　398.2

How the great rocks grew. Fisher, A. B.
　In Fisher, A. B. Stories California Indians
　　told p88-95　　　　　　　　398.2

How the Grinch stole Christmas. Seuss, Dr　E

How the Gubbaun proved himself. Young, E.
　In Young, E. The wonder smith and his
　　son p31-41　　　　　　　　398.2

How the Gubbaun quarreled with Aunya and
　what came of it. Young, E.
　In Young, E. The wonder smith and his
　　son p87-94　　　　　　　　398.2

How the Gubbaun Saor got his son. Young, E.
　In Young, E. The wonder smith and his
　　son p45-48　　　　　　　　398.2

How the Gubbaun Saor got his trade. Young, E.
　In Young, E. The wonder smith and his
　　son p23-27　　　　　　　　398.2

How the Gubbaun Saor welcomed home his
　daughter. Young, E.
　In Young, E. The wonder smith and his
　　son p73-83　　　　　　　　398.2

How the Gubbaun Saor went into the country
　of the Ever-Young. Young, E.
　In Young, E. The wonder smith and his
　　son p173-87　　　　　　　398.2

How the Gubbaun tried his hand at match-
　making. Young, E.
　In Young, E. The wonder smith and his son
　　p51-57　　　　　　　　　　398.2

How the gypsy boy outsmarted death. Jagen-
　dorf, M. A.
　In Jagendorf, M. A. The gypsies' fiddle,
　　and other gypsy tales p129-33　398.2

How the Helmites bought a barrel of justice.
　Simon, S.
　In Simon, S. The wise men of Helm and
　　their merry tales p67-76　　　S C

How the Hodja outwits the Shah Ali. Harden-
　dorff, J. B.
　In Hardendorff, J. B. ed. Just one more
　　p135-38　　　　　　　　　372.6

How the hot ashes shovel helped Snoo Foo.
　Sandburg, C.
　In Sandburg, C. Rootabaga stories v 1
　　p105-08　　　　　　　　　S C
　In Sandburg, C. The Sandburg treasury
　　p45-46　　　　　　　　　818

How the kakok bird came to be. Sechrist, E. H.
　In Sechrist, E. H. Once in the first times
　　p22-24　　　　　　　　　398.2

How the leopard got his spots. Kipling, R.　Fic
　also in Kipling, R. Just so stories (Double-
　　day) p43-62　　　　　　　S C
　also in Kipling, R. Just so stories (Double-
　　day. Anniv. ed.) p23-29　　S C
　also in Kipling, R. Just so stories (Watts F.)
　　p43-59　　　　　　　　　S C

How the letter X got into the alphabet. Sand-
　burg, C.
　In Dobbs, R. ed. Once upon a time p70-73
　　　　　　　　　　　　　　　　372.6

How the lion rewarded the mouse's kindness.
　Appiah, P.
　In Appiah, P. Ananse the spider p89-93
　　　　　　　　　　　　　　　　398.2

How the little fox went after chaff
　In Bloch, M. H. ed. Ukrainian folk tales
　　p49-59　　　　　　　　　398.2

How the little owl's name was changed. Gill-
　ham, C.
　In Arbuthnot, M. H. comp. The Arbuthnot
　　Anthology of children's literature
　　p394-96　　　　　　　　　808.8
　In Arbuthnot, M. H. comp. Time for old
　　magic p263-65　　　　　　398.2
　In Gillham, C. E. Beyond the Clapping
　　Mountains p44-50　　　　398.2

How the lizard lost and regained his farm.
　Courlander, H.
　In Courlander, H. The hat-shaking dance,
　　and other tales from the Gold Coast
　　p70-76　　　　　　　　　398.2

How the lizards got their markings. Sechrist,
　E. H.
　In Sechrist, E. H. Once in the first times
　　p49-51　　　　　　　　　398.2

How the manx cat lost its tail
　In De La Mare, W. ed. Animal stories
　　p320-25　　　　　　　　398.2

How the Milky Way began. Evans, E. K.
　In Dobbs, R. Once upon a time p51-53
　　　　　　　　　　　　　　　　372.6

How the Milky Way came to be
　In McDowell, R. E. ed. Third World voices
　　for children p23-24　　　　398.2

How the millstones drowned. Simon, S.
　In Simon, S. The wise men of Helm and
　　their merry tales p23-28　　S C

How the monkey came to be. Sechrist, E. H.
　In Sechrist, E. H. Once in the first times
　　p37-38　　　　　　　　　398.2

How the moon and stars came to be. Sechrist,
　E. H.
　In Sechrist, E. H. Once in the first times
　　p12-13　　　　　　　　　398.2

How the moonfish came to be
　In Carter, D. S. ed. Greedy Mariani, and
　　other folktales of the Antilles p3-8
　　　　　　　　　　　　　　　　398.2

How the pelican babies were saved. Arnott, K.
　In Arnott, K. Animal folk tales around the
　　world p195-201　　　　　398.2

How the people came from the Lower World.
　Courlander, H.
　In Courlander, H. People of the short blue
　　corn p10-24　　　　　　　398.2

How the people of Ife became scattered. Cour-
　lander, H.
　In Courlander, H. Olode the hunter, and
　　other tales from Nigeria p110-12
　　　　　　　　　　　　　　　　398.2

How the people sang the mountains up.
　Leach, M.　　　　　　　　　398.2

How the pig got his snout. Appiah, P.
　In Appiah, P. Ananse the spider p39-45
　　　　　　　　　　　　　　　　398.2

How the Pilgrims built their towne in New
　England. Daugherty, J.
　In Luckhardt, M. C. comp. Thanksgiving
　　p99-103　　　　　　　　　394.2

How the Pilgrims came to Plymouth. Hall-
　Quest, O. W.　　　　　　　973.2

How the Potato Face Blind Man enjoyed himself on a fine spring morning. Sandburg, C.
In Sandburg, C. Rootabaga stories v 1 p45-51   **S C**
In Sandburg, C. The Sandburg treasury p25-26   **818**

How the princess's pride was broken. Pyle, H.
In Fenner, P. R. comp. Princesses & peasant boys p33-42   **398.2**
In Pyle, H. The wonder clock p267-78   **398.2**

How the ptarmigans learned to fly. Gillham, C. E.
In Gillham, C. E. Beyond the Clapping Mountains p86-98   **398.2**

How the Raja's son won the Princess Labam
In Jacobs, J. ed. Indian fairy tales p3-16   **398.2**

How the Raven brought light to the world. Melzack, R.
In Melzack, R. The day Tuk became a hunter & other Eskimo stories p51-58   **398.2**

How the rhinoceros got his skin. Kipling, R. **Fic**
In Kipling, R. Just so stories (Doubleday) p29-42   **S C**
In Kipling, R. Just so stories (Doubleday. Anniv. ed.) p19-22   **S C**
In Kipling, R. Just so stories (Watts, F.) p29-39   **S C**
In Martignoni, M. E. ed. The illustrated treasury of children's literature p336-37   **808.8**

How the robber band was tricked. Duvoisin, R.
In Duvoisin, R. The three sneezes, and other Swiss tales p223-29   **398.2**

How the robin's breast became red. Cooke, F. J.
In Ward, W. ed. Stories to dramatize p77-78   **372.6**

How the sea gulls learned to fly. Gillham, C. E.
In Gillham, C. E. Beyond the Clapping Mountains p17-30   **398.2**

How the singing water got to the tub. Mitchell, L. S.
In Gruenberg, S. M. ed. Favorite stories old and new p40-44   **808.8**

How the son of the Gubbaun met with good luck. Young, E.
In Young, E. The wonder smith and his son p61-69   **398.2**

How the son of the Gubbaun Saor talked with lords from a strange country. Young, E.
In Young, E. The wonder smith and his son p97-112   **398.2**

How the spark of fire was saved; puppet play. Adair, M. W.
In Adair, M. W. Folk puppet plays for the social studies p69-73   **791.5**

How the storm changed the signs. Andersen, H. C.
In Andersen, H. C. The complete fairy tales and stories p840-44   **S C**

How the sun was brought back to the sky. Ginsburg, M.   **398.2**

How the Swiss came to use the Alpine horn Duvoisin, R. The alphorn

In Duvoisin, R. The three sneezes, and other Swiss tales p218-22   **398.2**

How the Tewas came to First Mesa. Courlander, H.
In Courlander, H. People of the short blue corn p145-55   **398.2**

How the three wild Babylonian Baboons went away in the rain eating bread and butter. Sandburg, C.
In Sandburg, C. Rootabaga stories v2 p49-53   **S C**
In Sandburg, C. The Sandburg treasury p106-07   **818**

How the Thunder-Bird lost his courage. Hooke, H. M.
In Hooke, H. M. Thunder in the Mountains p45-55   **398.2**

How the tsar drinks tea. Elkin, B.   **E**

How the turtle saved his own life. Babbitt, E. C.
In Babbitt, E. C. Jataka tales p10-12 **398.2**

How the village of Pivanhonkapi perished. Courlander, H.
In Courlander, H. People of the short blue corn p119-25   **398.2**

How the whale got his throat. Kipling, R.
In Kipling, R. Just so stories (Doubleday) p 1-14   **S C**
In Kipling, R. Just so stories (Doubleday. Anniv. ed.) p9-14   **S C**
In Kipling, R. Just so stories (Watts, F.) p 1-12   **S C**
In Untermeyer, B. ed. The Golden Treasury of children's literature p8-11   **808.8**

How the wicked sons were duped. Knowles, J. H.
In Jacobs, J. ed. Indian fairy tales p221-22   **398.2**

How the world got wisdom. Arkhurst, J. C.
In Arkhurst, J. C. The adventures of Spider p50-58   **398.2**

How the world's first cities began. Gregor, A. S.   **913.35**

How they bring back the Village of Cream Puffs when the wind blows it away. Sandburg, C.
In Arbuthnot, M. H. comp. The Arbuthnot Anthology of children's literature p570-71   **808.8**
In Sandburg, C. Rootabaga stories v 1 p19-27   **S C**
In Sandburg, C. The Sandburg treasury p17-19   **818**

How they broke away to go to the Rootabaga country. Sandburg, C.
In Sandburg, C. Rootabaga stories v 1 p3-17   **S C**
In Sandburg, C. The Sandburg treasury p10-16   **818**

How they were all very busy. Lewis, C. S.
In Johnson, E. ed. Anthology of children's literature p660-66   **808.8**

How things work
In Childcraft: the how and why library v7   **031**

How Young Will Bradford made a great decision. Daugherty, J.
In Luckhardt, M. C. comp. Thanksgiving p45-48 **394.2**

Howard, Alan
(illus.) De La Mare, W. Tales told again **398.2**
(illus.) Mitchell, D. ed. Every child's book of nursery songs **784.6**

Howard, Helen Littler
Candles for Christmas
In Kamerman, S. E. ed. A treasury of Christmas plays p372-75 **812.08**
Christmas train
In Burack, A. S. ed. Christmas plays for young actors p215-18 **812.08**
Doctor Know All
In Burack, A. S. ed. Popular plays for classroom reading p69-77 **808.82**
I'll share my fare
In Burack, A. S. ed. One hundred plays for children p460-62 **808.82**
The little circus donkey
In Burack, A. S. ed. One hundred plays for children p140-43 **808.82**
The magic jack-o-lantern
In Burack, A. S. ed. One hundred plays for children p399-402 **808.82**
In Kamerman, S. E. Little plays for little players p85-89 **812.08**
Mother's gift
In Burack, A. S. ed. One hundred plays for children p341-44 **808.82**
Thanks to Sammy Scarecrow
In Burack, A. S. ed. One hundred plays for children p463-66 **808.82**
In Kamerman, S. E. ed. Little plays for little players p108-12 **812.08**

Howard, Richard E.
(illus.) Ickis, M. The book of festivals and holidays the world over **394.2**

Howard, Vernon
The complete book of children's theater (4-7) **812**

Plays included are: The treasure of Monte Cristo; Oliver Twist asks for more; Johnny Appleseed in danger; Sir Galahad and the maidens; Happy holidays for Little women; David and Goliath; The return of Rip Van Winkle; The strange tale of King Midas; Around the world-by way of America; Gulliver wins his freedom; The Swiss family Robinson—rescued; Don Quixote saves the day

Pantomimes, charades & skits (4-6) **792.3**

Howe, Julia (Ward)
See pages in the following books:
Browne, C. A. The story of our national ballads p182-91 (5-7) **784.7**
Daugherty, S. Ten brave women p95-107 (5-7) **920**

Howe, Samuel Gridley
Meltzer, M. A light in the dark (6-7) **92**

Howe, Stephen
(illus.) Zim, H. S. Sharks **597**

Howell, D. M. G.
The gouty giant
In Mayne, W. ed. William Mayne's Book of giants p63-70 **398.2**

Howell, Ruth Rea
A crack in the pavement (2-4) **500.9**

Howells, William Dean
Christmas every day
In A St Nicholas anthology p195-99 **810.8**
Christmas every day; play. See McGowan, J. Christmas every day

Howitt, Mary
A Christmas visit
In Reeves, J. comp. The Christmas book p129-37 **394.2**

A howling success. Garver, J.
In Burack, A. S. ed. Popular plays for classroom reading p56-88 **808.82**

Hoyt, Edwin P.
From the Turtle to the Nautilus (6-7) **623.82**

Hoyt, Olga
The Bedouins (4-6) **915.3**

Hsian. See Sian

Hsiao, Ellen
A Chinese year (3-5) **915.1**

Hubbard, Freeman
Great days of the circus. See Great days of the circus **791.3**

Hubbub on the bookshelf. Woster, A.
In Burack, A. S. ed. One hundred plays for children p439-54 **808.82**

Hubp, Loretta Burke
(ed.) ¿Qué será? What can it be? (3-6) **398.6**

Huck, Charlotte S.
Children's literature in the elementary school **028.5**

The Huckabuck family. Sandburg, C.
In Harper, W. comp. The harvest feast p240-46 **394.2**

The Huckabuck family and how they raised pop corn in Nebraska and quit and came back. Sandburg, C.
In Johnson, E. ed. Anthology of children's literature p623-25 **808.8**
In Sandburg, C. Rootabaga stories v2 p169-79 **S C**
In Sandburg, C. The Sandburg treasury p145-49 **818**

Hudden and Dudden and Donald O'Neary
Jacobs, J. Hudden and Dudden and Donald O'Neary **398.2**
MacManus, S. Nidden and Didden and Donal Beg O'Neary
In MacManus, S. Hibernian nights p141-47 **398.2**

Hudlow, Jean
Eric plants a garden (2-4) **635**

Hudson, Henry
Syme, R. Henry Hudson (4-6) **92**

Hudson, Robert G.
Nature's nursery: baby birds (4-7) **598.2**

Hudson Valley

Fiction

Johnson, E. Break a magic circle (3-5) **Fic**

Hudson's Bay Company
See pages in the following book:
Ross, F. A. The land and people of Canada p77-81 (5-7) **917.1**

Hume, Lotta Carswell—*Continued*
tower that reached from Earth to Heaven; The fox outwits the tiger; The story of the fairy boat; The tiger in court; The magic pancakes at the Footbridge Tavern; The King of the Mountain; The jackals and the tiger; The fox turns somersault; The country of the mice; How the deer lost his tail; The little hare's clever trick

Hume, Ruth Fox
Great men of medicine (4-6)   **920**

Hummingbird and eagle. Campbell, C.
In Campbell, C. Star Mountain, and other legends of Mexico p9-13   **398.2**

The **hummingbird** and the carabao. Sechrist, E. H.
In Sechrist, E. H. Once in the first times p43-46   **398.2**

Humming-bird and the flower. Finger, C.
In Finger, C. Tales from silver lands p43-47   **398.2**

Hummingbird of the South. Roy, C.
In Roy, C. The serpent and the sun p41-46   **398.2**

Hummingbirds
Gans, R. Hummingbirds in the garden (1-3)   **598.2**
Voight, V. F. Brave little hummingbird (2-4)   **598.2**

Hummingbirds in the garden. Gans, R.   **598.2**

Humor. See Wit and humor

Humorous pictures. See Cartoons and caricatures; Comic books, strips, etc.

Humorous poetry
Brewton, S. comp. My tang's tungled and other ridiculous situations (3-6)   **821.08**
Ciardi, J. Someone could win a polar bear (2-5)   **811**
Ciardi, J. You read to me, I'll read to you (1-4)   **811**
Cole, W. comp. The book of giggles (1-4)   **808.87**
Livingston, M. C. ed. What a wonderful bird the frog are (5-7)   **808.81**
Silverstein, S. Where the sidewalk ends (3-6)   **811**

See also pages in the following book:
Arbuthnot, M. H. The Arbuthnot Anthology of children's literature p70-85   **808.8**
See also Limericks; Nonsense verses

Humorous poetry for children. Cole, W. comp.   **821.08**

Humorous stories. See Wit and humor

Humperdinck, Engelbert
Grimm, W. Hansel and Gretel   **782.1**

Humphrey, Grace
The last Thursday in November
In Harper, W. comp. The harvest feast p247-55   **394.2**
The Pilgrim's Thanksgiving
In Cavanah, F. ed. Holiday roundup p282-85   **394.2**

The **hums** of Pooh. Fraser-Simson, H.
In Fraser-Simson, H. The Pooh song book p15-81   **784.6**

The **hunchback** and the miser. Spicer, D. G.
In Spicer, D. G. The owl's nest p86-105   **398.2**

The **hundred** dresses. Estes, E.   **Fic**

A **Hundred** lies
In Ginsburg, M. ed. The Kaha bird p151-59   **398.2**

A **hundred** million francs. See Berna, P. The horse without a head   **Fic**

Hungary
Dormandy, C. Hungary in pictures (5-7)   **914.39**

Fiction
Seredy, K. The Good Master (4-6)   **Fic**
Seredy, K. The singing tree (4-6)   **Fic**
Seredy, K. The white stag (4-6)   **Fic**

Folklore
See Folklore—Hungary

Social life and customs
Gidal, S. My village in Hungary (3-6) **914.39**

Hungary in pictures. Dormandy, C.   **914.39**

Hungerford, Harold R.
Ecology (5-7)   **574.5**

Hungry Hans
Keller, G. Hungry Hans
In Davis, M. G. ed. A baker's dozen p153-68   **372.6**
In Untermeyer, B. ed. The Golden Treasury of children's literature p487-93   **808.8**
Untermeyer, L. Hungry Hans
In Ward, W. ed. Stories to dramatize p243-49   **372.6**

The **hungry** old witch. Finger, C. J.
In Davis, M. G. ed. A baker's dozen p 1-19   **372.6**
In Fenner, P. R. comp. Giants & witches and a dragon or two p50-63   **398.2**
In Finger, C. Tales from silver lands p143-55   **398.2**
In Harper, W. comp. Ghosts and goblins p30-43   **394.2**
In Hoke, H. ed. Witches, witches, witches p90-100   **808.8**

Hungry sharks. Waters, J. F.   **597**

Hungry Spider and the turtle. Courlander, H.
In Courlander, H. The cow-tail switch, and other West African stories p107-12   **398.2**

The **hungry** time. Carpenter, F.
In Carpenter, F. People from the sky p33-40   **398.2**

The **Hungry** wolf
In Hutchinson, V. S. ed. Fireside stories p37-40   **398.2**

A **hungry** wolf. Hume, L. C.
In Hume, L. C. Favorite children's stories from China and Tibet p55-61 **398.2**

Hunt, B.
The earl's son of the sea
In Brown, M. ed. A cavalcade of sea legends p178-83   **808.8**

Hunt, Irene
Across five Aprils (6-7)   **Fic**
Newbery Medal acceptance paper
In Kingman, L. ed. Newbery and Caldecott Medal books: 1966-1975 p22-28   **028.5**
No promises in the wind (6-7)   **Fic**

Huw. Palmer, G.
In Ireson, B. comp. Haunting tales p11-24
S C

Huygens, Christiaan
See pages in the following book:
Cottler, J. Heroes of civilization p130-39 (6-7)
920

Hyde, Bruce G.
(jt. auth.) Hyde, M. O. Atoms today & tomorrow **539.7**

Hyde, Douglas
Guleesh
In Fairy tales from many lands p34-51
398.2

Hyde, Margaret O.
Animal clocks and compasses (5-7) **591.5**
Atoms today & tomorrow (6-7) **539.7**
For pollution fighters only (5-7) **614.7**
(ed.) Mind drugs (5-7) **613.8**
VD: the silent epidemic (5-7) **616.9**

Hyde, Mark Powell
The squires win golden spurs
In Hazeltine, A. I. ed. Hero tales from
many lands p204-18 **398.2**

Hydra
See pages in the following book:
Goldstein, P. Animals and plants that trap
p73-84 (4-7) **574.5**

Hydraulic engineering. See Hydrodynamics

Hydraulic structures. See Canals; Dams

Hydraulics. See Hydrodynamics; Water; Water
power

Hydrodynamics
Branley, F. M. Floating and sinking (1-3) **532**
Corbett, S. What makes a boat float? (3-5)
532
Kaufmann, J. Streamlined (2-4) **531**

Hydrofoil boats
See pages in the following book:
Hellman, H. Transportation in the world of
the future p130-45 (5-7) **380.5**

Hydrology. See Water

Hyenas
See pages in the following book:
Hopf. A. L. Misunderstood animals p93-103
(4-7) **591.5**

The Hyena's horns. Arnott, K.
In Arnott, K. Animal folk tales around the
world p31-37 **398.2**

Hygiene. See Beauty, Personal; Exercise; Gymnastics; Physiology; Sleep

Hyman, Linda
Winslow Homer: America's old master (5-7)
92

Hyman, Trina Schart
(illus.) Brink, C. R. The bad times of Irma
Baumlein **Fic**
(illus.) Brink, C. R. Caddie Woodlawn **Fic**
(illus.) Cameron, E. A room made of windows
Fic
(illus.) Carter, D. S. ed. Greedy Mariani, and
other folktales of the Antilles **398.2**
(illus.) Clymer, E. How I went shopping and
what I got **Fic**
(illus.) Fritz, J. Why don't you get a horse,
Sam Adams? **92**

(illus.) Gates, D. Two queens of heaven:
Aphrodite [and] Demeter **292**
(illus.) Greene, E. comp. Clever cooks **398.2**
(illus.) Haviland, V. Favorite fairy tales told
in Czechoslovakia **398.2**
(illus.) Hunter, M. The walking stones **Fic**
(illus.) Johnson, E. All in free but Janey **E**
(illus.) Johnson, E. Break a magic circle **Fic**
(illus.) La Farge, P. Joanna runs away **E**
(illus.) Livingston, M. C. ed. Listen, children,
listen **821.08**
(illus.) Meyer, C. The bread book **641.8**
(illus.) Nichols, R. A walk out of the world
Fic
(illus.) Pyle, H. King Stork **398.2**
(illus.) Sawyer, R. Joy to the world **394.2**

Hymenoptera. See Ants; Bees; Wasps

Hymns
See pages in the following books:
Boni, M. B. ed. Fireside book of folk songs
p278-97 **784.4**
Sechrist, E. H. ed. It's time for Easter p103-
37 (4-7) **394.2**
See also Carols; Religious poetry

Hyndman, Robert Utley. See Wyndham, Robert

I

ILO. See International Labor Organization

I am from Puerto Rico. Buckley, P. **917.295**

I am here: yo estoy aqui. Blue, R. **E**

I am the darker brother. Adoff, A. ed. **811.08**

I breathe a new song. Lewis, R. ed. **897**

I can do lots of things!
In Camp Fire Girls, Inc. The Camp Fire
Blue Bird Series bk. 3 **369.47**

I can fly! Brock, B.
In Arbuthnot, M. H. comp. The Arbuthnot
Anthology of children's literature
p523-26 **808.8**

I can read French. Colyer, P. **448**

"I can't" said the ant. Cameron, P. **E**

I caught a lizard. Conklin, G. **639**

I, Charlotte Forten, Black and free. Longsworth, P. **92**

I did it. Rockwell, H. **745.5**

I go up in the world and am glad to come down
again. Field, R. L.
In Johnson, E. ed. Anthology of children's
literature p799-804 **808.8**

I have a dream; abridged. King, M. L.
In Cavanah, F. ed. Holiday roundup p211-
12 **394.2**

I heard a scream in the street. Larrick, N.
comp. **811.08**

I know a newspaper reporter. Henriod, L. **070**

I know what I have learned
"To the Devil with the money!"
In Baker, A. comp. The talking tree p113-
17 **398.2**

I like butterflies. Conklin, G. **595.7**

I like caterpillars. Conklin, G. **595.7**

I like weather. Fisher, A. **E**

If you grew up with Abraham Lincoln. Mc-
Govern, A. **92**

If you had a wish? Finger, C. J.
In Association for Childhood Education International. Told under the magic
umbrella p189-96 **S C**

If you lived in Colonial times. McGovern, A.
917.4

If you were an ant. Brenner, B. **595.7**

Iger, Martin
(illus.) Stevens, C. Catch a cricket **595.7**

Iglesia, Maria Elena de la. See De La Iglesia,
Maria Elena

Igloos
See pages in the following books:
Bell, T. H. Snow p19-23 (3-6) **551.5**
Bleeker, S. The Eskimo p22-38 (4-6) **970.1**

The **iguana's** poison bag
In Courlander, H. ed. Ride with the sun
p20-24 **398.2**

The **iguana's** tail. Sherlock, Sir P. **398.2**

Iijima, Takeru
(jt. auth.) Levine, J. Understanding musical
instruments **781.9**

Ijapa and the hot-water test. Courlander, H.
In Courlander, H. Olode the hunter, and
other tales from Nigeria p90-95 **398.2**

Ijapa and the oba repair a roof. Courlander, H.
In Courlander, H. Olode the hunter, and
other tales from Nigeria p58-60
398.2

Ijapa and Yanrinbo swear an oath. Courlander, H.
In Courlander, H. Olode the hunter, and
other tales from Nigeria p69-71
398.2

Ijapa cries for his horse. Courlander, H.
In Courlander, H. Olode the hunter, and
other tales from Nigeria p40-44 **398.2**

Ijapa demands corn fufu. Courlander, H.
In Courlander, H. Olode the hunter, and
other tales from Nigeria p104-06
398.2

Ijapa goes to the Osanyin shrine. Courlander, H.
In Courlander, H. Olode the hunter, and
other tales from Nigeria p86-89
398.2

The **Iliad** and the Odyssey of Homer. Church,
A. J. **883**

The **Iliad** of Homer. Picard, B. L. **883**

I'll protect you from the jungle beasts. Alexander, M. **E**

I'll share my fare. Howard, H. L.
In Burack, A. S. ed. One hundred plays
for children p460-62 **808.82**

The **Ill-tempered** princess
In Gunterman, B. L. ed. Castles in Spain,
and other enchantments p46-60
398.2

Illinois
Fiction
Hunt, I. Across five Aprils (6-7) **Fic**

Illinois and Michigan Canal
See pages in the following book:
Franchere, R. Westward by canal p134-37
(5-7) **386**

Illiteracy. See Right to Read program

Illusions. See Optical illusions

Illustrated atlas for young America, Hammond's
912

Illustrated Bible stories, Brian Wildsmith's.
Turner, P. **220.9**

Illustrated chess for children. Kidder, H. **794.1**

Illustrated Golden dictionary for young readers,
The Courtis-Watters **423**

The **illustrated** treasury of children's literature.
Martignoni, M. E. ed. **808.8**

Illustration of books
The Children's Book Showcase **028.52**
Illustrators of children's books: 1744-1945
741.64
Illustrators of children's books: 1946-1956
741.64
Illustrators of children's books: 1957-1966
741.64

See also pages in the following books:
Arbuthnot, M. H. comp. The Arbuthnot An-
thology of children's literature p910-39
808.8
Egoff, S. ed. Only connect p347-83 **028.5**
Egoff, S. The republic of childhood p255-70
028.5
Haviland, V. ed. Children and literature
p169-201 **028.5**
Holme, B. Drawings to live with p109-23
741.9
Horn Book Reflections on children's books
and reading p73-93 **028.5**
A Horn Book Sampler on children's books
and reading p41-91 **028.5**
Johnson, E. ed. Anthology of children's lit-
erature p1171-81 **808.8**
Kingman, L. ed. Newbery and Caldecott
Medal books: 1966-1975 p276-89 **028.5**
Moore, A. C. My roads to childhood p127-34
028.5
Townsend, J. R. Written for children p142-
59 **028.5**

See also Caldecott Medal books; Drawing; Picture books for children

Illustrations. See subjects with the subdivision
Pictorial works, e.g., Animals—Pictorial
works

Illustrations, Humorous. See Cartoons and caricatures

Illustrators
Feelings, T. Black pilgrimage (5-7) **92**
Hoffman, M. ed. Authors and illustrators of
children's books **028.5**
Illustrators of children's books: 1744-1945
741.64
Illustrators of children's books: 1946-1956
741.64
Illustrators of children's books: 1957-1966
741.64
Kingman, L. ed. Newbery and Caldecott
Medal books: 1956-1965 **028.5**
Kingman, L. ed. Newbery and Caldecott
Medal books: 1966-1975 **028.5**

In the children's room. Andersen, H. C.
In Andersen, H. C. The complete fairy
tales and stories p827-31   S C
In the duck yard. Andersen, H. C.
In Andersen, H. C. Andersen's Fairy tales
p433-39   S C
In Andersen, H. C. The complete fairy
tales and stories p723-28   S C
In the Easter basket. Sechrist, E. H.
In Harper, W. comp. Easter chimes p246-
53   394.2
In the far south-west. Ritchie, A.
In Ritchie, A. The treasure of Li-Po p102-
41   S C
In the first times. Sechrist, E. H.
In Sechrist, E. H. Once in the first times
p11-12   398.2
In the forest. Ets, M. H.   E
In the grass. Baruch, D.
In Association for Childhood Education In-
ternational. Told under the blue um-
brella p10-11   S C
In the Great Walled Country. Alden, R. M.
In Alden, R. M. Why the chimes rang, and
other stories p136-46   S C
In Association for Childhood Education In-
ternational. Told under the Christ-
mas tree p31-39   808.8
In Luckhardt, M. C. ed. Christmas comes
once more p148-53   394.2
In the kingdom of the seals. MacKenzie, D. A.
In Brown, M. ed. A cavalcade of sea leg-
ends p23-29   808.8
In the Land of Souls
In Lang, A. ed. The yellow fairy book
p152-54   398.2
In the land of Ur. Baumann, H.   913.35
In the middle of the night. Fisher, A.   E
In the middle of the night. Pearce, P.
In Pearce, P. What the neighbors did, and
other stories p15-27   S C
In the night kitchen. Sendak, M.   E
In the nursery
Andersen, H. C. In the children's room
In Andersen, H. C. The complete fairy
tales and stories p827-31   S C
In the park. Hautzig, E.   410
In the pasture. Spyri, J.
In Johnson, E. ed. Anthology of children's
literature p767-73   808.8
In Martignoni, M. E. ed. The illustrated
treasury of children's literature p376-
82   808.8
In the trail of the wind. Bierhorst, J.   897
In the witch's house. Bennett, R.
In Bennett, R. Creative plays and programs
for holidays p123-29   812
In Kamerman, S. E. ed. Little plays for
little players p260-65   812.08
In the woods, in the meadow, in the sky.
Fisher, A.   811
In their own words. Meltzer, M. ed.   301.45
In those days. Farjeon, E.
In Farjeon, E. The little bookroom p179-83
S C
In what book? Harshaw, R.   793.7

In which Eeyore has a birthday and gets two
presents. Milne, A. A.
In Untermeyer, B. ed. The Golden Trea-
sury of children's literature p56-63
808.8
In which Eeyore loses a tail and Pooh finds one.
Milne, A. A.
In Martignoni, M. E. ed. The illustrated
treasury of children's literature p357-
59   808.8
In which Pooh goes visiting and gets into a tight
place. Milne, A. A.
In Arbuthnot, M. H. comp. The Arbuthnot
Anthology of children's literature
p494-96   808.8
In which Tistou has a bad dream and what hap-
pens as a result of it. Druon, M.
In Arbuthnot, M. H. comp. The Arbuthnot
Anthology of children's literature
p513-14   808.8
Inatuk's friend. Morrow, S. S.   E
The Inca. Bleeker, S.   980.3
Incas
Baumann, H. Gold and gods of Peru (6-7)
980.3
Beals, C. The incredible Incas (5-7)   980.3
Beck, B. L. The first book of the Incas (4-7)
980.3
Bleeker, S. The Inca (4-6)   980.3
Glubok, S. The fall of the Incas (5-7)   980.3
Pine, T. S. The Incas knew (1-4)   980.3
See also pages in the following books:
Bowen, J. D. The land and people of Peru
p54-70 (5-7)   918.5
Discoverers of the New World p77-81 (5-7)
973.1
Helfman, E. S. Signs & symbols of the sun
p91-97 (5-7)   398
Warren, L. F. The land and people of Bo-
livia p37-43 (5-7)   918.4
Fiction
Clark, A. N. Secret of the Andes (4-7)   Fic
Religion and mythology
See pages in the following book:
Bleeker, S. The Inca p110-29 (4-6)   980.3
The Incas knew. Pine, T. S.   980.3
Inch by inch. Lionni, L.   E
Inchelina. Andersen, H. C.
In Andersen, H. C. The complete fairy
tales and stories p29-37   S C
See also Thumbelina
Incineration. See Refuse and refuse disposal
The incredible Incas. Beals, C.   980.3
Independence Day. Wilder, L. I.
In Arbuthnot, M. H. comp. The Arbuthnot
Anthology of children's literature
p763-67   808.8
Independence Day (U.S.) See Fourth of July
Independence Hall, Philadelphia. See Phila-
delphia. Independence Hall
Independent voices. Merriam, E.   811
Index to Black history & studies—multimedia
In National Information Center for Educa-
tional Media. [NICEM Indexes to
nonbook media]   016.3713

It does not say meow, and other animal riddle
rhymes. De Regniers, B. S.   793.7

It doesn't always have to rhyme. Merriam, E.
811

It is perfectly true! Andersen, H. C.
In Andersen, H. C. The complete fairy
tales and stories p405-07   S C
See also It is quite true

It is quite true
Andersen, H. C. It is perfectly true!
In Andersen, H. C. The complete fairy
tales and stories p405-07   S C
Andersen, H. C. It's absolutely true
In Andersen, H. C. Seven tales p105-13
S C
Andersen, H. C. It's perfectly true
In Andersen, H. C. It's perfectly true, and
and other stories p 3-7   S C
Andersen, H. C. "It's quite true!"
In Andersen, H. C. Andersen's Fairy tales
p484-86   S C

"It is you the fable is about." Andersen, H. C.
In Andersen, H. C. The complete fairy
tales and stories p1004-05   S C

Italian architecture. See Architecture, Italian

Italian art. See Art, Italian

Italian language
Cooper, L. Fun with Italian (4-7)   458
See also Bilingual books—Italian-En-
glish

Italian language editions
Potter, B. The tale of Peter Rabbit   E

Italian literature
See pages in the following book:
Winwar, F. The land and people of Italy
p78-86 (5-7)   914.5

Italian painters. See Painters, Italian

Italian statesmen. See Statesmen, Italian

Italians in the United States
LaGumina, S. J. An album of the Italian-
American (4-7)   301.45

Italo-Ethiopian War, 1935-1936
See pages in the following book:
Perl, L. Ethiopia p144-47 (5-7)   916.3

Italy
Epstein, S. The first book of Italy (4-7) 914.5
Martin, R. Looking at Italy (4-6)   914.5
Winwar, F. The land and people of Italy
(5-7)   914.5

Fascism
See Fascism—Italy
Folklore
See Folklore—Italy
History—1815-1915
Syme, R. Garibaldi (5-7)   92
Industries
See pages in the following book:
Winwar, F. The land and people of Italy
p43-49 (5-7)   914.5
Painters
See Painters, Italian
Painting
See Painting, Italian

Social life and customs
See pages in the following book:
Sechrist, E. H. ed. Christmas everywhere
p126-36   394.2
Statesmen
See Statesmen, Italian

Iterson, S. R. van
Pulga (5-7)   Fic

It's a —; play. Carlson, B. W.
In Carlson, B. W. The right play for you
p94-96   792

It's absolutely true. Andersen, H. C.
In Andersen, H. C. Seven tales p105-13
S C
See also It is quite true

It's all about me
In Camp Fire Girls, Inc. The Camp Fire
Blue Bird Series bk. 1   369.47

It's all the fault of Adam. Walker, B. K.
In Walker, B. K. The dancing palm tree,
and other Nigerian folktales p65-71
398.2

It's fun to know why. Schwartz, J.   507.2

It's like this, Cat; excerpt. Neville, E.
In Association for Childhood Education
International. Told under the city
umbrella p255-74   S C

It's magic? Lopshire, R.   793.8

It's nesting time. Gans, R.   598.2

It's not the end of the world. Blume, J.   Fic

It's perfectly true. Andersen, H. C.
In Andersen, H. C. It's perfectly true, and
other stories p3-7   S C
See also It is quite true

It's perfectly true, and other stories. Andersen, H. C.   S C

"It's quite true!" Andersen, H. C.
In Andersen, H. C. Andersen's Fairy tales
p484-86   S C
See also It is quite true

It's raining said John Twaining. Bodecker, N. M.   398.8

It's time for brotherhood. Sechrist, E. H.
301.11

It's time for Christmas. Sechrist, E. H. ed.
394.2

It's time for Easter. Sechrist, E. H. ed.   394.2

It's time for story hour. Sechrist, E. H. ed.
372.6

It's time for Thanksgiving. Sechrist, E. H. ed.
394.2

It's time now! Tresselt, A.   525

Its walls were as of jasper. Grahame, K.
In Authors' choice p193-206   S C

Ivan and the gray wolf
Haviland, V. About Jan the Prince, Princess
Wonderface, and the Flamebird
In Haviland, V. Favorite fairy tales told
in Poland p55-81   398.2

Ivan IV, the Terrible, Czar of Russia
See pages in the following book:
Nazaroff, A. The land and people of Russia
p102-11 (5-7)   914.7

Jacobs, Leland B.
(ed.) Using literature with young children
028.5

Jacobs, Lou
Jumbo jets (5-7)   629.133
Space station '80 (5-7)   629.44
Wonders of an oceanarium (3-7)   591.92
(illus.) Madian, J. Beautiful junk   Fic

Jacobs, W. J.
Hernando Cortes (4-6)   92
Samuel de Champlain (4-6)   92
William Bradford of Plymouth Colony (4-6)
92

Jacobs, W. W.
The three sisters
In Mayne, W. ed. Ghosts p2-11   820.8

Jacomb-Hood, G. P.
(illus.) Lang, A. ed. The blue fairy book
398.2

Jacques, Robin
(illus.) Aiken, J. Black hearts in Battersea
Fic
(illus.) Langstaff, J. ed. Hi! Ho! The rattlin' bog   784.4
(illus.) Manning-Sanders, R. A book of charms and changelings   398.2
(illus.) Manning-Sanders, R. A book of devils and demons   398.2
(illus.) Manning-Sanders, R. A book of dragons   398.2
(illus.) Manning-Sanders, R. A book of ghosts & goblins   398.2
(illus.) Manning-Sanders, R. A book of mermaids   398.2
(illus.) Manning-Sanders, R. A book of ogres and trolls   398.2
(illus.) Manning-Sanders, R. A book of princes and princesses   398.2
(illus.) Manning-Sanders, R. A book of sorcerers and spells   398.2
(illus.) Manning-Sanders, R. A book of witches   398.2
(illus.) Manning-Sanders, R. A book of wizards   398.2
(illus.) Manning-Sanders, R. A choice of magic   398.2

Jaffe, Haym
(jt. auth.) Cottler, J. Heroes of civilization
920
(jt. auth.) Cottler, J. More Heroes of civilization   920

Jagendorf, M. A.
The burning ship
In Hoke, H. ed. Spooks, spooks, spooks p59-62   S C
Folk stories of the South (4-7)   398.2
Contents: The first tale of Alabama; Fearless Emma; Don't drop into my soup; Railroad Bill; The face in the courthouse window; How far is it to Jacob Cooper's; The battle of Bay Minette; The smartest one in the woods; False alarm; The Arkansas traveler; How red strawberries brought peace in the woods; The proud tale of David Dodd; The bull didn't have a chance; The sad-lovely end of Wilhelmina Inn; The judge and the baseball-pitching Indian chief; Sam Hudson the great; In Arkansas stick to bears: don't mess with swampland skeeters; The daring of Yellow Doc; A tale of steep-stair town; The colonel teaches the judge a lesson in good manners; The lost treasure; The great conjure-alligator-man of Florida; Nobody sees a mockingbird on Friday; The tale of Lura Lou; Dixie, the Knight of the Silver Spurs; Way deep down in the Okefenokee Swamps; The bridal chamber of Silver

Springs; Daddy Mention and Sourdough Gus; The song of the Cherokee rose; Dan McGirth and his gray goose mare; The tale of the Daughters of the Sun; Georgy Piney-Woods Peddler; The curse of Lorenzo Dow; Hoozah for fearless ladies and fearless deeds; Fearless Nancy Hart; The silver snake of Louisiana; Fairy web for Mr Durand's daughters; The life of Annie Christmas; Gray moss on green trees; The bridal ghost dinner; One pair of blue satin slippers and four clever maids; The silver bell of Chênière Caminada; Three great men at peace; The song in the sea; The living colors of the Twenty-first; The ghost wedding in Everhope; The ring around the tree; Tar wolf tale; Mike Hooter and the smart bears in Mississippi; The sad tale of the half-shaven head; Guess who; The savage birds of Bald Mountain; The white doe; The tale of the hairy toe; The revolution of the ladies of Edenton; Nollichucky Jack; Pirate Blackbeard's deep-sea end; The ways of the Lord; The man, the white steed, and the wondrous wood; The mystery of Theodosia Burr; Shake hands with a Yankee; The tragic tale of Fenwick Hall; Emily's famous meal; Chickens come home to roost; Ah-dunno Ben; The tale of Rebecca Motte; The perpetual motion in the sea; Young Sherman and the girl from Charleston; Kate, the Bell Witch; The best laugh is the last laugh; Fiddler's Rock; Trust not a new friend; Come and laugh with Bobby Gum; The ghost who wasn't a ghost; Big Sixteen; The ghost the whole town knew; The power of woman and the strength of man; The gladiator; the belle, and the good snowstorm; Beale Street folks; The Karankawa from the great gleaming oyster shells; How Joe became Snaky Joe; The white buffalo; The ghosts of Stampede Mesa; Only in Texas; Texas centipede coffee; Of Sam Bass; Horse trading in Wichita Falls; Lafitte's great treasure; Hercules of Virginia; All on a summer's day; The merry tale of Belle Boyd; Two foxes; The black ghost dog; Grace Sherwood, the woman none could scare; Thanks to Patrick Henry

Gray moss on green trees
In Arbuthnot, M. H. comp. The Arbuthnot Anthology of children's literature p392   808.8
The gypsies' fiddle, and other gypsy tales (5-7)   398.2
Contents: The silly fellow who sold his beard; The gypsy and the snake; The summer of the big snow; The peasant's strong wife; Saint Peter and his trombone; Noodlehead and the flying horse; The tale of the gypsy and his strange love; The gypsies' fiddle; The old gypsy and the good Lord; The gypsy in the ghost house; Traveling through the chimney; The silly men of Russia; How the gypsy boy outsmarted death; Fishing for pots in the pond; Prop for the tree; Flaming tales; The husband, the wife, and the Devil; How the cows flew across the sea; Fording the river in a copper cauldron

The Haddam witches
In Hoke, H. ed. Witches, witches, witches p187-91   808.8
In Arkansas stick to bears: don't mess with swampland skeeters
In Arbuthnot, M. H. comp. The Arbuthnot Anthology of children's literature p381-82   808.8
King clothes
In Arbuthnot, M. H. comp. The Arbuthnot Anthology of children's literature p272-73   808.8
In Arbuthnot, M. H. comp. Time for old magic p155-56   398.2
The king of the mountains
In Arbuthnot, M. H. comp. The Arbuthnot Anthology of children's literature p405-06   808.8
In Arbuthnot, M. H. comp. Time for old magic p271-72   398.2
Mike Hooter and the smart bears in Mississippi
In Arbuthnot, M. H. comp. The Arbuthnot Anthology of children's literature p380-81   808.8

Jagendorf, M. A.—*Continued*
New England bean-pot (5-7)   398.2

Contents: Young Paul; Skipper and the witch; Stubbornest man in Maine; Corsair of Spouting Horn; Smart woman of Kennebunkport; Tall Barney Beal; Cinderella of New Hampshire; Three times and out; Fairies in the White Mountains; Holding the bag; Giant of the Hills; Becky's garden; Old Ave Henry and the smart logger man; Lucky Rose Tuttle; Devil in the barrel; Green Mountain hero; Ride in the night; Tale of the tail of a bear; Well-Done-Peter-Parker; Strange adventure of the cowboy-sailor; Sacred horse with the silver mane; Jingling rhymes and jingling money; Magic in Marblehead; Lord of Massachusetts; Devil in the steeple; Merry tale of Merrymount; Sacred cod and the striped haddock; Tiny Perry; Smart husband and the smarter wife; Giant Kingfisher of Mount Riga; Wise men of Hebron; Bee man and the boundary man; Frogs of Windham Town; Haddam witches; Diamond Jim and Big Bill; Puffing Potter's powerful puff; Rich lady and the ring in the sea; Cat Inspector; Devil in red flannel; Mysteries of the sea; Old man Elias and the dancing sheriff; New way to cure old witch-hunting; Grumpy Timothy Crumb; Weaverwoman's monument; Little Annie and the whaler captain; Tale of Godfrey Malbone

Noodlehead stories from around the world (4-6)   398.2

Contents: The horse-egg; Don't marry two wives; The Noodlehead tiger; There are such people; Do you know; The donkey of Abdera; Barefoot in bed; The fox in the hole; The golden shoes; The great traveler of Chelm; Figs for gold, figs for folly; Donkeys all; The cow and the thread; Ceylon sillies; Like master, like servant; The sad victory; When Noodlehead marries Noodlehead; The foolish lion and the silly rooster; Who is who; Magic! Silly magic; The farmer's secret; The wisdom of the Lord; The costly feast; The flying fool; The wise men of Gotham; The brave men of Austwick; Knucklehead John; A sheep can only bleat; A new way to boil eggs; The needle crop of Sainte-Dodo; Bahhh; Tales from Tartari-Barbari; Peter's adventures; Faithful legs and lazy head; The man, the woman, and the fly; Fools' bells ring in every town; Giufá and the judge; Donkey and scholars; Silly Matt; The Schilda town hall; The stove and the town hall; The tailor from the sea; Aili's quilt; Kultani, the noodle gossip; The obedient servant; The hero; Luck for fools; Tandala and Pakala; Belmont antics; Lutonya; The tale of the men of Prach; Smartness for sale; The moon in the donkey; Not on the Lord's Day; The wolf in the sack; Juan Bobo; Noodlehead Pat; The sombreros of the men of Lagos; The "Foolish People"; Little head, big medicine; Sam'l Dany, Noodlehead; Noodlehead luck; John in the storeroom; Kibbe's shirt

Oversmart is bad luck
    In Arbuthnot, M. H. comp. The Arbuthnot Anthology of children's literature p408-09   808.8
Pancho Villa and the Devil
    In Arbuthnot, M. H. comp. The Arbuthnot Anthology of children's literature p413   808.8
Penny puppets, penny theatre, and penny plays (4-7)   791.5

Puppet plays included are: The boy of Nazareth; The winning of Wildcat Sue; The troubles of Old Mr MacGregor; In Rip Van Winkle's land; The cowboy and the cook; Rabbit rides Wolf; Ong's hat; Soldier's three; Beauty and the beast

The priceless cats
    In Johnson, E. ed. Anthology of children's literature p241-44   808.8
The sacred drum of Tepozteco
    In Arbuthnot, M. H. comp. The Arbuthnot Anthology of children's literature p411-13   808.8
Tyll Ulenspiegel
    In Ward, W. ed. Stories to dramatize p176-81   372.6
Tyll Ulenspiegel's merry pranks (4-6)   398.2
Who rules the roost?

In Arbuthnot, M. H. comp. The Arbuthnot Anthology of children's literature p401-03   808.8

Jagendorf, Moritz Adolf. See Jagendorf, M. A.

Jagr, Miloslav
(illus.) Seeger, P. The foolish frog   784.4

The **jaguar** and the crested curassow. Sherlock, P.
    In Sherlock, P. West Indian folk-tales p27-33   398.2

Jake. Slote, A.   Fic

Jal, Auguste
The flying Dutchman
    In Brown, M. ed. A cavalcade of sea legends p153-57   808.8

Jamaica

Folklore

See Folklore—Jamaica

Jambo means hello. Feelings, M.   E

Jambor, Louis
(illus.) Alcott, L. M. Little women (5-7)   Fic

James, Grace
The tea-kettle
    In Manning-Sanders, R. ed. A book of magical beasts p130-37   398.2

James, Harold
(illus.) Rinkoff, B. Member of the gang   Fic

James, Laurie
Camp Fire Girls, Inc. Adventure   369.47
Camp Fire Girls, Inc. The Blue Bird wish   369.47
Camp Fire Girls, Inc. Discovery   369.47

James, Will
Chapo—the faker
    In Anderson, C. W. ed. C. W. Anderson's Favorite horse stories p45-55   808.8
His first bronc
    In Gruenberg, S. M. ed. Favorite stories old and new p155-59   808.8
Sun up; excerpt
    In Anderson, C. W. ed. C. W. Anderson's Favorite horse stories p37-44   808.8

About

See pages in the following book:
Miller, B. M. ed. Newbery Medal books: 1922-1955 p47-48   028.5

James and the giant peach. Dahl, R.   Fic

James Bowie and his famous knife. Garst, S.   92

James the huntsman. Hatch, M. C.
    In Hatch, M. C. 13 Danish tales p3-15   398.2

Jameson, Cynthia
The clay pot boy (k-2)   398.2

Jameson, Helen D.
(illus.) Aldis, D. All together   811

Jamestown, Va.

History

Davis, B. Getting to know Jamestown (4-6)   975.5

Jamie Dawkin's drum. Harter, W.
    In Harter, W. Osceola's head, and other American ghost stories p19-23   S C

Jemison, Mary
Gardner, J. L. Mary Jemison: Seneca captive (4-6)   **92**
Lenski, L. Indian captive (5-7)   **92**

Jenkins, William A.
My second picture dictionary (2-4)   **423**
(jt. auth.) Greet, W. C. In other words   **423**
(jt. auth.) Greet, W. C. Junior thesaurus   **423**
(jt. auth.) Greet, W. C. My first picture dictionary   **423**

Jenkins' Ear, War of. See Anglo-Spanish War, 1739-1748

Jenks, Tudor
About flying-machines
   In A St Nicholas anthology p371-80   **810.8**

Jenner, Edward
   See pages in the following books:
Asimov, I. Breakthroughs in science p90-98 (5-7)   **920**
Cottler, J. Heroes of civilization p299-306 (6-7)   **920**
Hume, R. F. Great men of medicine p37-50 (4-6)   **920**

Jenness, Aylette
Along the Niger River (5-7)   **916.69**

Jennie's hat. Keats, E. J.   **E**

Jennifer, Hecate, Macbeth, William Mckinley, and me, Elizabeth. Konigsburg, E. L.   **Fic**

Jennings, Gary
The killer storms (5-7)   **551.5**

Jennison, Keith W.
(ed.) The Concise encyclopedia of sports. See The Concise encyclopedia of sports   **796.03**

Jenny and the Cat Club. Averill, E.   **S C**

Jenny-by-the-Day. Molloy, L. L.
   In Burack, A. S. ed. One hundred plays for children p666-74   **808.82**

Jenny Green Teeth. Leach, M.
   In Leach, M. Whistle in the graveyard p85   **398.2**

Jenny's adopted brothers. Averill, E.   **E**
   also in Averill, E. Jenny and the Cat Club   **S C**

Jenny's first party. Averill, E.
   In Averill, E. Jenny and the Cat Club   **S C**

Jensen, Stanley C.
North Pole confidential
   In Kamerman, S. E. ed. A treasury of Christmas plays p404-12   **812.08**

Jensen, Thea Bank- See Bank-Jensen, Thea

Jerome, Saint
   See pages in the following book:
Johnson, E. ed. Anthology of children's literature p588-90   **808.8**

Jerusalem
   See pages in the following book:
Hoffman, G. The land and people of Israel p44-48, 129-41 (5-7)   **915.694**

Jes' too lazy; play. Carlson, B. W.
   In Carlson, B. W. The right play for you p81-93   **792**

The Jesse Owens story. Owens, J.   **92**

The **jester who fooled a king.** Haviland, V.
   In Haviland, V. Favorite fairy tales told in Poland p82-90   **398.2**

Jesup, Thomas Sidney
   See pages in the following book:
Alderman, C. L. Osceola and the Seminole wars p127-64 (5-7)   **92**

Jesus Christ
Fisher, A. Easter (1-3)   **394.2**
   See also pages in the following books:
Farb, P. The land, wildlife, and peoples of the Bible p130-48 (5-7)   **220.8**
The World's great religions. Special edition for young readers p122-37 (5-7)   **291**
Biography
Bible. New Testament. Selections. The Christ child (k-3)   **232.9**
Hanser, R. Jesus: what manner of man is this? (5-7)   **232.9**
   See also Jesus Christ—Nativity
Birth
   See Jesus Christ—Nativity
Nativity
Aichinger, H. The shepherd (k-3)   **232.9**
Bible. New Testament. Selections. The Christmas story   **232.9**
Branley, F. M. The Christmas sky (3-6) **232.9**
Brown, M. W. Christmas in the barn (k-2)   **232.9**
Graham, L. Every man heart lay down (1-4)   **232.9**
Jüchen, A. von. The Holy Night (k-3)   **232.9**
Slaughter, J. comp. And it came to pass (k-4)   **783.6**

   See also pages in the following books:
Association for Childhood Education International. Told under the green umbrella p175-78 (1-4)   **398.2**
Parents' Magazine's Christmas holiday book p22-35   **394.2**
Ward, W. ed. Stories to dramatize p224-27   **372.6**

   See also Christmas
Nativity—Fiction
Vance, M. While shepherds watched (1-4) **Fic**
Nativity—Poetry
McGinley, P. A wreath of Christmas legends (5-7)   **811**

Jesus: what manner of man is this? Hanser, R.   **232.9**

Jet and rocket engines: how they work. Edmonds, I. G.   **621.43**

Jet planes
Jacobs, L. Jumbo jets (5-7)   **629.133**

Jet propulsion
Edmonds, I. G. Jet and rocket engines: how they work (5-7)   **621.43**

Jetport. Richards, N.   **629.136**

Jew among the thorns
Grimm, J. The Jew among thorns
   In Grimm, J. The complete Grimm's Fairy tales p503-08   **398.2**
Grimm, J. The old man in the bramble bush
   In Grimm, J. The house in the wood, and other fairy stories p81-94   **398.2**
   See also Little Fred and his fiddle

Johnny Crow's party. Brooke, L. L. E

Johnny Gloke
    In Jacobs, J. ed. More English folk and fairy tales p78-81 398.2
    In Reeves, J. English fables and fairy stories p23-34 398.2

Johnny Lion's bad day. Hurd, E. T. E

Johnny Lion's book. Hurd, E. T. E

Johnny Lion's rubber boots. Hurd, E. T. E

Johnny Littlejohn. Hurd, E. T.
    In Gruenberg, S. M. comp. Let's hear a story p118-25 808.8

Johnny Ping Wing. Phillips, E. C.
    In Gruenberg, S. M. ed. Favorite stories old and new p235-40 808.8

Johnny Reed's cat
    Knurre-Murre
    In De La Mare, W. ed. Animal stories p71-73 398.2
    Manning-Sanders, R. Knurremurre
    In Manning-Sanders, R. A choice of magic p49-53 398.2

Johnny's experiment. Tunis, J. R.
    In Association for Childhood Education International. Told under spacious skies p153-59 S C

Johnson, Andrew, President U.S.
    See pages in the following book:
    Aymar, B. Laws and trials that created history p74-83 (6-7) 345.7

Johnson, Annabel
    The grizzly (5-7) Fic

Johnson, Chester
    What makes a clock tick? (4-7) 681

Johnson, Crockett
    Harold and the purple crayon E
    A picture for Harold's room E

Johnson, E. Harper
    (illus.) Ripley, S. N. Matthew Henson: Arctic hero 92

Johnson, Edgar
    (jt. auth.) Johnson, A. The grizzly Fic

Johnson, Edna
    (ed.) Anthology of children's literature 808.8

Johnson, Elizabeth
    All in free but Janey E
    Break a magic circle (3-5) Fic

Johnson, Emily Pauline
    See pages in the following book:
    Gridley, M. E. American Indian women p67-73 (5-7) 920

Johnson, Fred
    Turtles and tortoises (1-3) 598.1

Johnson, Gerald W.
    America grows up (5-7) 973
    America is born (5-7) 973
    America moves forward (5-7) 973
    Franklin D. Roosevelt (5-7) 92

Johnson, Hannah Lyons
    From seed to jack-o'-lantern (1-3) 635
    Let's bake bread (2-5) 641.8

Johnson, Harper
    (illus.) Bontemps, A. Frederick Douglass: slave-fighter-freeman 92
    (illus.) Child Study Association of America. Round about the city S C

(illus.) Martin, P. M. The little brown hen E

(illus.) Mason, F. V. The winter at Valley Forge 973.3

Johnson, Henry
    See pages in the following books:
    Burt, O. W. Negroes in the early West p61-67 (4-6) 920
    Hughes, L. Famous Negro heroes of America p173-80 (5-7) 920

Johnson, Holly
    (illus.) Alcott, L. M. An old-fashioned Thanksgiving Fic

Johnson, James Weldon
    Egypt, O. S. James Weldon Johnson (2-4) 92
    Felton, H. W. James Weldon Johnson (4-6) 92
    See also pages in the following books:
    Rollins, C. Famous American Negro poets p28-37 (5-7) 920
    Rollins, C. They showed the way p88-90 (5-7) 920

Johnson, John E.
    (illus.) Withers, C. ed. I saw a rocket walk a mile 398.2
    (illus.) Withers, C. A world of nonsense 398.2

Johnson, Larry
    (illus.) Kaufman, M. Jesse Owens 92

Johnson, Lois S.
    (ed.) Christmas stories round the world (3-5) 394.2
    Following the New Year across the United States
    In Cavanah, F. ed. Holiday roundup 15-19 394.2

Johnson, Milton
    (illus.) Coolidge, O. Come by here Fic
    (illus.) Haugaard, E. C. Orphans of the wind Fic

Johnson, Pamela
    (illus.) Burkett, M. The year of the badger 599
    (illus.) Caras, R. A zoo in your room 636.08

Johnson, Pauline. See Johnson, Emily Pauline

Johnson, Sally Patrick
    (ed.) The Princesses (4-6) S C

Johnson, Walter Perry
    See pages in the following book:
    Epstein, S. Baseball Hall of Fame: stories of champions p62-77 (3-5) 920

Johnson, William Weber
    The story of sea otters (4-7) 599

Johnston, Annie (Brown)
    Fiction
    Henry, M. Mustang, wild spirit of the West (5-7) Fic

Johnston, Brenda A.
    Between the devil and the sea; the life of James Forten (4-6) 92

Johnston, Johanna
    The Connecticut colony (5-7) 974.6
    The Indians and the strangers (2-5) 920
    A special bravery (2-5) 920
    Together in America: the story of two races and one nation (5-7) 301.45

Johnston, Norma
    Glory in the flower (6-7) Fic
    The keeping days (5-7) Fic

The **jumping** competition. Andersen, H. C.
In Andersen, H. C. The complete fairy
tales and stories p295-96   **S C**
See also Leaping match

Jumping Jack and his friends. Proysen, A.
In Proysen, A. Little old Mrs Pepperpot,
and other stories p62-73   **S C**

June 7! Aliki   **E**

The **jungle.** Borten, H.   **500.9**

The **jungle** book. Kipling, R.   **S C**

The **jungle** books. Kipling, R.   **S C**

Jungles. See Tropics

The **junior** book of authors. Kunitz, S. J. ed.
   920.03

The **junior** book of insects. Teale, E. W. **595.7**

The **Junior** Bookshelf   **028.1**

Junior companion to music, The Oxford.
Scholes, P. A.   **780.3**

Junior cook book, Better Homes and Gardens
   641.5

Junior cook book, The Fannie Farmer. Perkins,
W. L.   **641.5**

Junior dictionary, Thorndike-Barnhart   **423**

Junior encyclopaedia for boys and girls, Britannica   **031**

Junior Girl Scout handbook. Girl Scouts of the
United States of America   **369.463**

Junior high school library catalog   **011**

The **Junior** illustrated encyclopedia of sports
   796.03

Junior karate. Kozuki, R.   **798.8**

Junior Libraries. See SLJ/School Library
Journal   **027.805**

Junior science book of electricity. Feravolo,
R. V.   **537.072**

Junior science book of magnets. Feravolo, R. V.
   538

Junior thesaurus. Greet, W. C.   **423**

Juniorplots. Gillespie, J.   **028.1**

Juniper tree
Grimm, J. The almond tree
In Grimm, J. Household stories p186-94
   398.2

Grimm, J. The juniper tree
In Grimm, J. The complete Grimm's Fairy
tales p220-29   **398.2**
In Grimm, J. The juniper tree, and other
tales from Grimm v2 p314-32 **398.2**
Juniper tree
In De La Mare, W. ed. Animal stories
p267-78   **398.2**
See also Rose-tree

The **juniper** tree, and other tales from Grimm.
Grimm, J.   **398.2**

Junket, the dog who liked everything "just so."
White, A. H.   **Fic**

Jupiter (Planet)
Asimov, I. Jupiter (6-7)   **523.4**
See also pages in the following books:
Branley, F. M. The nine planets p56-61 (6-7)
   523.4
Knight, D. C. Thirty-two moons p42-56 (5-7)
   523.9

Nourse, A. E. The giant planets p10-25 (5-7)
   523.4

Jupiter and the horse
In Hardendorff, J. B. ed. Just one more
p54-55   **372.6**

Jupo, Frank
The story of things (3-5)   **609**

The **Jurga.** Belpré, P.
In Belpré, P. The tiger and the rabbit,
and other tales p37-41   **398.2**

Jurma and the sea god. Bowman, J. C.
In Bowman, J. C. Tales from a Finnish
tupa p81-90   **398.2**

Just, Ernest Everett
See pages in the following book:
Hayden, R. C. Seven Black American scien-
tists p92-115 (6-7)   **920**

Just a box? Chernoff, G. T.   **745.54**

Just as strong; play. Carlson, B. W.
In Carlson, B. W. The right play for you
p71-77   **792**

Just me. Ets, M. H.   **E**

Just one more. Hardendorff, J. B. ed. **372.6**

Just so stories. Kipling, R.   **S C**

Justice. Courlander, H.
In Courlander, H. The fire on the mountain, and other Ethiopian stories p73-
76   **398.2**

Justice for all; play. Carlson, B. W.
In Carlson, B. W. Play a part p108-12 **792**

Justin Morgan had a horse. Henry, M.   **Fic**

Justin Morgan had a horse; excerpts. Henry, M.
In Arbuthnot, M. H. comp. The Arbuthnot
Anthology of children's literature
p622-27   **808.8**

Justus, May
A new home for Billy (2-4)   **Fic**

Juvenile delinquency
Fiction
Friedman, F. Ellen and the gang (4-6)   **Fic**
Garfield, L. Smith (5-7)   **Fic**
Rinkoff, B. Member of the gang (4-7)   **Fic**
Slote, A. Tony and me (4-6)   **Fic**

Juvenile literature. See Children's literature

The **Juvenile Miscellany (Periodical)**
See pages in the following book:
Jordan, A. M. From Rollo to Tom Sawyer,
and other papers p46-60   **028.5**

Juvenile reading. See Children's literature

K

Kaa's hunting. Kipling, R.
In Kipling, R. The jungle book (Doubleday) p35-72   **S C**
In Kipling, R. The jungle book (Grosset)
p43-94   **S C**
In Kipling, R. The jungle books (Doubleday) v 1 p31-64   **S C**
In Kipling, R. The jungle books (Macmillan N Y) p25-53   **S C**
In Kipling, R. The jungle books (Watts, F.)
v 1 p32-63   **S C**

Kelsey, Alice Geer—*Continued*
Three Fridays
In Johnson, E. ed Anthology of children's
literature p327-28   **808.8**
Too heavy
In Gruenberg, S. M. ed. Favorite stories
old and new p353-54   **808.8**

Kemal, Mustafa. See Atatürk, Kamâl, President
Turkey

Kemble, Frances Anne
Scott, J. A. Fanny Kemble's America (5-7) **92**

Kendall, Carol
The Gammage Cup (4-6)   **Fic**
A long night of terror
In Arbuthnot, M. H. comp. The Arbuthnot
Anthology of children's literature
p518-23   **808.8**
The Whisper of Glocken (4-6)   **Fic**
The Whisper of Glocken; excerpt
In Arbuthnot, M. H. comp. The Arbuthnot
Anthology of children's literature
p518-23   **808.8**

Kendall, Lace
Houdini: master of escape (6-7)   **92**

Kendall, Sarita
Looking at Brazil (4-6)   **918.1**

Kennedy, John Fitzgerald, President U.S.
Profiles in courage. Young readers Memorial
edition, abridged (5-7)   **920**
About
Four days: the historical record of the death
of President Kennedy   **92**
Tregaskis, R. John F. Kennedy and PT-109
(5-7)   **940.54**
Wood, J. P. The life and words of John F.
Kennedy (3-7)   **92**

Kennedy, Lucy
The Pied Piper of Hamelin; adapted from the
poem by R. B. Browning
In Burack, A. S. ed. One hundred plays for
children p686-700   **808.82**

Kennedy, Paul
(illus). De La Mare, W. The magic jacket **S C**
(illus.) De La Mare, W. A penny a day **S C**
(illus.) MacManus, S. Hibernian nights **398.2**
(illus.) Mehdevi, A. S. Persian folk and fairy
tales   **398.2**

Kennedy, Richard
(illus.) Dillon, E. The seals   **Fic**
(illus.) Farjeon, E. Martin Pippin in the apple
orchard   **S C**

Kennel, Moritz
(illus.) Carroll, L. Alice's adventures in Wonderland   **Fic**

Kennell, Ruth
Lisa's song
In Gruenberg, S. M. ed. Favorite stories
old and new p92-97   **808.8**

Kensington rune stone
See pages in the following book:
Golding, M. J. The mystery of the Vikings in
America p144-52 (6-7)   **973.1**

Kent, Rockwell
(illus.) Shephard, E. Paul Bunyan   **398.2**

Kentucky
Fiction
Caudill, R. Tree of freedom (6-7)   **Fic**

Chaffin, L. D. John Henry McCoy (4-6) **Fic**
Stephens, M. J. Witch of the Cumberlands
(5-7)   **Fic**
Stuart, J. The beatinest boy (4-6)   **Fic**
Folk songs
See Folks songs—Kentucky

Kenya
Carpenter, A. Kenya (4-7)   **916.76**
See also pages in the following book:
Perl, L. East Africa p117-40 (4-7)   **916.7**
Fiction
Garfield, N. The Tuesday elephant (2-4) **Fic**
Stevenson, W. The bushbabies (4-7)   **Fic**

Kenyatta, Jomo, President Kenya
See pages in the following books:
Aymar, B. Laws and trials that created his-
tory p161-69 (6-7)   **345.7**
Perl, L. East Africa p120-25 (4-7)   **916.7**

Kepes, Juliet
Lady Bird, quickly   **E**
(illus.) Read, H. ed. This way, delight **821.08**
(illus.) Smith, W. J. Laughing time   **811**

Keplik, the match man. Levoy, M.
In Levoy, M. The witch of Fourth Street,
and other stories p63-74   **S C**

Kerina, Jane
African crafts (4-7)   **745.5**

Kerkham, Roger
(illus.) Lidstone, J. Building with cardboard
    745.54
(illus.) Lidstone, J. Building with wire **745.56**
(illus.) Silverstein, A. Guinea pigs   **636.08**
(illus.) Silverstein, A. Rabbits   **599**

Kerr, Judith
When Hitler stole Pink Rabbit (4-7)   **Fic**

Kerr, Laura J.
(comp.) Who's where in books   **016.92**

Kesar of Ling and the giant of the north. Baumann, H.
In Baumann, H. The stolen fire p97-104
    398.2

Kessler, Leonard
Here comes the strikeout   **E**
Kick, pass, and run   **E**
Last one in is a rotten egg   **E**
On your mark, get set, go!   **E**
(illus.) Berger, M. The new water book **551.4**
(illus.) Branley, F. M. Big tracks, little tracks
    591.5
(illus.) Branley, F. M. A book of flying saucers
for you   **001.9**
(illus.) Branley, F. M. A book of moon rockets for you   **629.4**
(illus.) Branley, F. M. A book of outer space
for you   **523.1**
(illus.) Branley, F. M. A book of satellites for
you   **629.43**
(illus.) Branley, F. M. A book of stars for you
    523.8
(illus.) Charosh, M. The ellipse   **516**
(illus.) Jackson, C. P. How to play better football   **796.33**
(illus.) Knosher, H. Basic basketball strategy
    796.32
(illus.) Lawrence, J. Binky brothers   **E**
(illus.) Lawrence, J. Binky brothers and the
Fearless Four   **E**

Kigbo and the bush spirits. Courlander, H.
In Courlander, H. Olode the hunter, and
other tales from Nigeria p45-49
398.2

Kijima, Hajime
Little white hen (k-2) **398.2**

The Kildare pooka. Palmer, R.
In Palmer, R. Dragons, unicorns, and other
magical beasts p38-42 **398.2**

The killer storms. Jennings, G. **551.5**

Killing of Cabrakan. Finger, C.
In Finger, C. Tales from silver lands p92-
98 **398.2**

The killing of Eeetoi. Baker, B.
In Baker, B. At the center of the world
p33-42 **398.2**

The killing pot. Baker, B.
In Baker, B. At the center of the world
p16-24 **398.2**

Kim, Eui-Hwan
(illus.) Kim, S. The story bag **398.2**

Kim, So-Un
The story bag (4-7) **398.2**
Contents: The story bag; The man who planted
onions; Mountains and rivers; The pheasant, the dove,
and the magpie; A dog named Fireball; The deer, the
rabbit, and the toad; Mr Bedbug's feast; Why we have
earthquakes; The stupid noblewoman; The bridegroom's
shopping; The bad tiger; The three foolish brides; The
tiger and the rabbit; The great flood; The three little
girls; The blind mouse; The deer and the woodcutter;
The magic gem; The snake and the toad; The pheasant's bell; The green leaf; The grateful tiger; The
pumpkin seeds; The three princesses; The disowned
student; The signal flag; The magic hood; The
father's legacy; The tiger of Kumgan Mountains; The
silver spoon

Kimball, Edward
(illus.) Carr, R. Be a frog, a bird, or a tree
613.7

Kimball, Yeffe
(illus.) Brindze, R. The story of the totem pole
299

Kincaid, C. A.
Vashishta and the four queens
In Farjeon, E. ed. A cavalcade of queens
p45-49 **808.8**

Kind Brother, Mean Brother. Carlson, B. W.
In Carlson, B. W. Let's pretend it happened to you p72-79 **792**

Kind farmer. Farjeon, E.
In Farjeon, E. The little bookroom p272-
88 **S C**

Kind little Edmund. Nesbit, E.
In Nesbit, E. The complete book of dragons p141-61 **S C**

A kind of secret weapon. Arnold, E. **Fic**

Kindergarten

Periodicals

Childhood Education: a journal for teachers,
administrators, church-school workers, librarians, pediatricians **370.5**

The kindly ghost. Manning-Sanders, R.
In Manning-Sanders, R. A book of ghosts
& goblins p103-10 **398.2**

Kinetic art
Marks, M. K. Op-tricks (5-7) **702.8**

Kinetic sculpture. See Mobiles (Sculpture)

Kinetics. See Motion

King, Billie Jean
Burchard, M. Sports hero: Billie Jean King
(2-4) **92**
See also pages in the following book:
Sullivan, G. Queens of the court p34-53 (5-7)
920

King, Emilie E.
The Boy in Nazareth
In Sechrist, E. H. ed. It's time for Christ-
mas p198-203 **394.2**

King, Martin Luther
I have a dream; abridged
In Cavanah, F. ed. Holiday roundup p211-
12 **394.2**
We shall live in peace: the teachings of
Martin Luther King, Jr. (4-7) **301.45**

About

Clayton, E. Martin Luther King: the peace-
ful warrior (5-7) **92**
De Kay, J. T. Meet Martin Luther King, Jr.
(2-5) **92**
Young, M. B. The picture life of Martin
Luther King, Jr. (k-3) **92**
See also pages in the following book:
Johnston, J. A special bravery p86-92 (2-5)
920

King, Robin
(illus.) Hughes, L. The first book of rhythms
701

King, Walter
Little Snow White
In Kamerman, S. E. ed. Little plays for
little players p285-90 **812.08**

King Alfred and the cakes. Thane, A.
In Thane, A. Plays from famous stories and
fairy tales p143-52 **812**

King and Kuffie. Courlander, H.
In Courlander, H. Terrapin's pot of sense
p84-86 **398.2**

The king and the bee. Whitworth, V. P.
In Kamerman, S. E. ed. Dramatized folk
tales of the world p250-57 **812.08**

King and the corn. Farjeon, E.
In Farjeon, E. The little bookroom p 1-6
S C

The king and the humble hut. Tolstoy, L.
In Tolstoy, L. Twenty-two Russian tales
for young children p24-25 **S C**

The king and the merman. Leekley, T. D.
In Hoke, H. ed. Spooks, spooks, spooks
p 1-10 **S C**

The king and the nagas. Palmer, R.
In Palmer, R. Dragons, unicorns, and other
magical beasts p89-95 **398.2**

The King and the peasant
In Courlander, H. ed. Ride with the sun
p142-44 **398.2**

The king and the rain dwarfs. Roy, C.
In Roy, C. The serpent and the sun p59-65
398.2

The king and the ring. Walker, B. K.
In Walker, B. K. The dancing palm tree,
and other Nigerian folktales p43-50
398.2

Kip and the red tractor. Hoff, C.
  In Association for Childhood Education International. Told under spacious skies p230-42   **S C**

Kipling, J. Lockwood
  (illus.) Kipling, R. The jungle books   **S C**
  (illus.) Kipling, R. The second jungle book   **S C**

Kipling, Rudyard
  The butterfly that stamped
    In Farjeon, E. ed. A cavalcade of kings p225-36   **808.8**
  The crab that played with the sea
    In Green, R. L. ed. A cavalcade of magicians p242-53   **808.8**
  The elephant's child
    In Arbuthnot, M. H. comp. The Arbuthnot Anthology of children's literature p484-87   **808.8**
    In Gruenberg, S. M. ed. Favorite stories old and new p456-63   **808.8**
    In Ross, E. S. ed. The lost half-hour p50-60   **372.6**
  Gloriana
    In Farjeon, E. ed. A cavalcade of queens p134-52   **808.8**
  How Mowgli entered the wolf pack
    In Martignoni, M. E. ed. The illustrated treasury of children's literature p257-64   **808.8**
  How the camel got his hump
    In Johnson, E. ed. Anthology of children's literature p622-23   **808.8**
    In A St Nicholas anthology p3-4   **810.8**
  How the leopard got his spots (1-4)   **Fic**
  How the rhinoceros got his skin (2-4)   **Fic**
  —Same
    In Martignoni, M. E. ed. The illustrated treasury of children's literature p336-37   **808.8**
  How the whale got his throat
    In Untermeyer, B. ed. The Golden Treasury of children's literature p8-11   **808.8**
  The jungle book (4-7)   **S C**

Contents: Mowgli's brothers; Kaa's hunting; "Tiger! Tiger!"; The white seal; "Rikki-tikki-tavi"; Toomai of the elephants; Her Majesty's servants (The servants of the Queen)

  The jungle books (4-7)   **S C**

Contents: Mowgli's brothers; Kaa's hunting; How fear came; "Tiger! Tiger!"; The king's ankus; Letting in the jungle; Red Dog; The spring running; "Rikki-tikki-tavi"; The white seal; The miracle of Purun Bhagat; The undertakers; Quiquern; Toomai of the elephants; Her Majesty's servants

  Just so stories (3-6)   **S C**

Contents: How the whale got his throat; How the camel got his hump; How the rhinoceros got his skin; How the leopard got his spots; The elephant's child; The sing-song of Old Man Kangaroo; The beginning of the armadilloes; How the first letter was written; How the alphabet was made; The crab that played with the sea; The cat that walked by himself; The butterfly that stamped

  The Maltese Cat
    In Authors' choice p171-92   **S C**
  The miracle of Purun Bhagat
    In Authors' choice p123-38   **S C**
  The potted princess
    In Johnson, S. P. ed. The Princesses p118-31   **S C**

  The potted princess; play. See Smith, M. R. The potted princess
  The return of Imray
    In Mayne, W. ed. Ghosts p12-25   **820.8**
  Rikki-Tikki-Tavi
    In Untermeyer, B. ed. The Golden Treasury of children's literature p12-23   **808.8**
  The second jungle book (4-7)   **S C**

Contents: How fear came; Miracle of Purun Bhagat; Letting in the jungle; The undertakers; The King's ankus; Quiquern; Red Dog; The spring running

About

See pages in the following books:

Benét, L. Famous storytellers for young people p138-45   **920**
A St Nicholas anthology p84-87   **810.8**

Kirby, George
  Looking at Germany (4-6)   **914.3**

Kirby, Michael
  (jt. auth.) Scott, B. A. Skating for beginners   **796.9**

Kirk, Louis
  (illus.) Kirk, R. Desert life   **500.9**
  (illus.) Kirk, R. Hunters of the whale   **970.3**
  (illus.) Kirk, R. Yellowstone   **917.87**

Kirk, Ruth
  Desert life (k-3)   **500.9**
  Hunters of the whale (6-7)   **970.3**
  The oldest man in America (5-7)   **917.97**
  Yellowstone (5-7)   **917.87**

Kirkup, James
  The magic drum (3-5)   **398.2**

Kirkus Reviews   **028.1**

Kirn, Ann
  Let's look at more tracks (k-3)   **591.5**
  Let's look at tracks (k-3)   **591.5**

Kirtland, G. B.
  One day in Aztec Mexico (2-5)   **917.2**
  One day in Elizabethan England (2-5)   **914.2**

Kisander. Sherlock, P. M.
  In Sherlock, P. M. Anansi, the spider man p35-40   **398.2**

Kishor, Sulamith Ish- See Ish-Kishor, Sulamith

Kismaric, Carole
  Duel of the ironclads. See Duel of the ironclads   **973.7**

A **kiss** for Little Bear. Minarik, E. H.   **E**

A **kiss** is round. Budney, B.   **E**

Kiss Me. Sandburg, C.
  In Sandburg, C. Rootabaga stories v2 p207-13   **S C**
  In Sandburg, C. The Sandburg treasury p158-59   **818**

Kit Carson: mountain man. Bell, M. E.   **92**

Kitchen, Herminie B.
  (jt. auth.) Fenton, C. L. Animals that help us   **636**
  (jt. auth.) Fenton, C. L. Fruits we eat   **634**
  (jt. auth.) Fenton, C. L. Plants we live on   **581.6**

Kitchen carton crafts. Sattler, H. R.   **745.54**

Kitchen crafts. Cross, L.   **745.5**

Kitchen gardens. See Vegetable gardening

Kühn, Alfred
See pages in the following book:
Ipsen, D. C. What does a bee see? p38-52 (5-7)   **595.7**

Kuhn, Bob
(illus.) Carr, M. J. Children of the covered wagon   **Fic**
(illus.) Kjelgaard, J. Big Red   **Fic**

Kuhn, Doris Young
(jt. auth.) Huck, C. S. Children's literature in the elementary school   **028.5**

Kujoth, Jean Spealman
Best-selling children's books   **028.52**

Kultani, the noodle gossip. Jagendorf, M. A.
In Jagendorf, M. A. Noodlehead stories from around the world p202-06 **398.2**

Kumin, Maxine W.
The beach before breakfast   **E**
Joey and the birthday present (3-5)   **Fic**

Kumurchi's poultry farm. Sturton, H.
In Sturton, H. Zomo, the Rabbit p39-47   **398.2**

Kunitz, Stanley J.
(ed.) The junior book of authors   **920.03**

Kunos, Ignacz
The Black Dragon and the Red Dragon
In Hoke, H. comp. Dragons, dragons, dragons p76-85   **398.2**

Künstler, Mort
(illus.) Cole, J. Dinosaur story   **568**
(illus.) Johnston, J. Together in America: the story of two races and one nation   **301.45**

Kupferberg, Herbert
A rainbow of sound (4-7)   **781.9**

A kupua plays tricks. Thompson, V. L.
In Thompson, V. L. Hawaiian myths, of earth, sea, and sky p45-52   **398.2**

Kurage. Henderson, B. L. K.
In Hoke, H. comp. Dragons, dragons, dragons p63-75   **398.2**
See also Monkey and the jelly-fish

Kuratko the terrible
Fillmore, P. Kuratko the terrible
In Davis, M. G. ed. A baker's dozen p127-34   **372.6**
Haviland, V. Kuratko the terrible
In Haviland, V. Favorite fairy tales told in Czechoslovakia p21-33   **398.2**

Kurelek, William
Lumberjack (3-5)   **634.9**
A prairie boy's summer (3-5)   **917.127**
A prairie boy's winter (3-5)   **917.127**

Kurosaki, Yoshisuke
(illus.) Sakade, F. ed. Japanese children's favorite stories   **398.2**

Kurtis, Arlene Harris
The Jews helped build America (4-7) **301.45**
Puerto Ricans (4-7)   **917.295**

Kurtz, Henry Ira
John and Sebastian Cabot (4-6)   **92**

Kuskin, Karla
Any me I want to be (1-4)   **811**
(illus.) Winn, M. ed. What shall we do and Allee galloo!   **796.1**

Kutune Shirka and the golden otter. Baumann, H.
In Baumann, H. The stolen fire p87-92   **398.2**

Kwaku Ananse and the donkey. Appiah, P.
In Appiah, P. Ananse the spider p71-87   **398.2**

Kwaku Ananse and the greedy lion. Appiah, P.
In Appiah, P. Ananse the spider p27-37   **398.2**

Kwaku Ananse and the rain maker. Appiah, P.
In Appiah, P. Ananse the spider p113-21   **398.2**

Kwaku Ananse and the whipping cord. Appiah, P.
In Appiah, P. Ananse the spider p57-69   **398.2**

Kwangchow. See Canton, China

Kwitz, Mary DeBall
(illus.) Smith, F. C. The first book of conservation   **333.7**

Kyle, Anne D.
Easter lambs
In Harper, W. comp. Easter chimes p45-62   **394.2**

Kyle, Elisabeth
Song of the waterfall; the story of Edvard and Nina Grieg (5-7)   **92**

L

LJ/SLJ Previews. See Previews   **016.3713**

LMP. See Literary market place: LMP 070.5025

LSD. See Lysergic acid diethylamide

Labastida, Aurora
(jt. auth.) Ets, M. H. Nine days to Christmas   **E**

Labor, Migratory. See Migrant labor

Labor and laboring classes. See Guilds; Migrant labor; Occupations; Peasantry; Slavery; also names of classes of laborers, e.g. Construction workers

Labor Day
Marnell, J. Labor Day (1-3)   **394.2**

Laboratories, Space. See Space stations

Laboulaye, Edouard
Wiesner, W. Turnabout   **398.2**

A lac of rupees for a bit of advice. Knowles, J. H.
In Jacobs, J. ed. Indian fairy tales p103-11   **398.2**

Lacandon Indians
Price, C. Heirs of the ancient Maya (5-7)   **970.3**

Religion and mythology
See pages in the following book:
Price, C. Heirs of the ancient Maya p38-51 (5-7)   **970.3**

La Christine comes. Lenski, L.
In Lenski, L. Lois Lenski's Christmas stories p105-13   **394.2**

Lacotawin. See Yellow Robe, Rosebud

Lacy, Dan
The Colony of North Carolina (5-7) 975.6
The Colony of Virginia (6-7) 975.5
The Lewis and Clark Expedition, 1804-06 (5-7) 973.4
The lost colony (5-7) 973.1

The lad and the fox. Haviland, V.
In Haviland, V. Favorite fairy tales told in Sweden p30-32 398.2

The lad and the North Wind. Haviland, V.
In Haviland, V. Favorite fairy tales told in Norway p67-74 398.2
See also Lad who went to the north wind

The lad who stared everyone down. Yolen, J.
In Yolen, J. The girl who cried flowers, and other tales p37-44 S C

Lad who went to the north wind
Asbjørnsen, P. C. The lad who went to the North Wind
In Arbuthnot, M. H. comp. Time for old magic p119-20 398.2
In Asbjørnsen, P. C. East of the sun and west of the moon, and other tales p23-27 398.2
In Johnson, E. ed. Anthology of children's literature p305-07 808.8
Haviland, V. The lad and the North Wind
In Haviland, V. Favorite fairy tales told in Norway p67-74 398.2
The Lad who went to the North Wind
In Hutchinson, V. S. ed. Chimney corner fairy tales p19-24 398.2
Thorne-Thomsen, G. The lad who went to the North Wind
In Association for Childhood Education International. Told under the green umbrella p52-58 398.2
See also Jack and the northwest wind

Lad with the beer keg
Asbjørnsen, P. C. The boy with the beer keg
In Asbjørnsen, P. C. Norwegian folk tales p131-34 398.2
The Boy with the ale keg
In Undset, S. ed. True and untrue, and other Norse tales p132-36 398.2

Ladder Company 108. Beame, R. 363.3

Lader, Lawrence
Margaret Sanger: pioneer of birth control (6-7) 92

Ladies first; short story. Rodgers, M.
In Free to be . . . you and me p39-45 810.8

The lady and the lion. Grimm, J.
In Darrell, M. ed. Once upon a time p38-42 808.8
In Grimm, J. Grimms' Fairy tales; illus. by F. Kredel p366-73 398.2
See also Soaring lark

Lady-beetles. See Ladybugs

Lady Bird, quickly. Kepes, J. E

Lady birds. See Ladybugs

The Lady Dragonissa. Lang, A.
In Green, R. L. ed. A cavalcade of dragons p182-84 808.8

The lady in black. Yolen, J.
In Yolen, J. The wizard islands p10-19 551.4

Lady Moon and the thief. Boiko, C.
In Kamerman, S. E. ed. Dramatized folk tales of the world p23-31 812.08

The lady of Stavoren
In Courlander, H. ed. Ride with the sun p178-85 398.2

Lady of the lake
Williams-Ellis, A. The Lake lady
In Williams-Ellis, A. Fairy tales from the British Isles p255-62 398.2

Lady of the moon
Carpenter, F. Heng O, the moon lady
In Carpenter, F. Tales of a Chinese grandmother p206-16 398.2

The Lady of the Wood
In Garner, A. ed. A cavalcade of goblins p56-61 398.2

The lady who put salt in her coffee; play. Carlson, B. W.
In Carlson, B. W. The right play for you p40-44 792

The lady who put salt in her coffee; play. Lockwood, J.
In Smith, M. R. ed. 7 plays & how to produce them p7-21 792

Lady with the horse's head. Carpenter, F.
In Carpenter, F. Tales of a Chinese grandmother p98-106 398.2

Ladybirds. See Ladybugs.

Ladybug, ladybug, fly away home. Hawes, J. 595.7

Ladybugs
Hawes, J. Ladybug, ladybug, fly away home (k-3) 595.7
Wong, H. H. My ladybug (k-3) 595.7
Stories
Kepes, J. Lady Bird, quickly E

The lady's loaf-field. Nic Leodhas, S.
In Nic Leodhas, S. Gaelic ghosts p68-74 398.2

Lady's room. Farjeon, E.
In Farjeon, E. The little bookroom p138-41 S C
In Tashjian, V. A. ed. With a deep sea smile p82-85 372.6

Laënnec, René Théophile Hyacinthe
See pages in the following books:
Hume, R. F. Great men of medicine p51-66 (4-6) 920
Marks, G. The amazing stethoscope p23-24 (4-6) 610.28

La Farge, Oliver
The American Indian. Special edition for young readers (5-7) 970.1

La Farge, Phyllis
Joanna runs away E

Lafayette Flying Corps. See France. Army. Lafayette Flying Corps

Lafitte, Jean
Tallant, R. Pirate Lafitte and the Battle of New Orleans (5-7) 92
See also pages in the following books:
Malcolmson, A. Yankee Doodle's cousins p163-71 (4-7) 398.2
Stockton, F. R. Buccaneers & pirates of our coasts p212-22 (5-7) 910.4

Lafitte's great treasure. Jagendorf, M. A.
In Jagendorf, M. A. Folk stories of the
South p292-94 **398.2**

La Fleur, Marjorie
Little Duckling tries his voice
In Association for Childhood Education International. Told under the magic
umbrella p5-7 **S C**

La Fontaine
Fables of La Fontaine; selections
In Arbuthnot, M. H. comp. The Arbuthnot
Anthology of children's literature
p422-23 **808.8**
In Arbuthnot, M. H. comp. Time for old
magic p286-87 **398.2**
La Fontaine's Fables; selections
In Johnson, E. ed. Anthology of children's
literature p110-11 **808.8**
Wildsmith, B. The hare and the tortoise
398.2
Wildsmith, B. The lion and the rat **398.2**
Wildsmith, B. The miller, the boy and the
donkey **398.2**
Wildsmith, B. The North Wind and the Sun
398.2
Wildsmith, B. The rich man and the shoemaker **398.2**

La Fontaine, Jean de. See La Fontaine

La Fontaine's Fables. La Fontaine
In Johnson, E. ed. Anthology of children's
literature p110-11 **808.8**

Lagerlöf, Selma
The Holy Night
In Eaton, A. T. comp. The animals' Christmas p42-46 **394.2**
In Harper, W. comp. Merry Christmas to
you p33-37 **394.2**
In Tudor, T. ed. Take joy! p52-54 **394.2**
The legend of the Christmas rose
In Harper, W. comp. Merry Christmas to
you p155-77 **394.2**
The wonderful adventures of Nils (4-6) **Fic**

About
See pages in the following book:
Horn Book Reflections on children's books
and reading p282-85 **028.5**

Lagos, Nigeria
See pages in the following book:
Forman, B. The land and people of Nigeria
p146-51 (5-7) **916.69**

La Guardia, Fiorello Henry
Kaufman, M. Fiorello La Guardia (2-4) **92**

Poetry
See pages in the following book:
Merriam, E. Independent voices p67-79 (5-7)
811

LaGumina, Salvatore J.
An album of the Italian-American (4-7)
301.45

Lahore
See pages in the following book:
Lang, R. The land and people of Pakistan
p89-97 (6-7) **915.49**

Laidly worm of Spindleston
Jacobs, J. The laidly worm
In Green, R. L. ed. A cavalcade of dragons p103-08 **808.8**
Laidly Worm of Spindleston Heugh
In Jacobs, J. ed. English folk and fairy
tales p190-203 **398.2**
Williams-Ellis, A. The Laidly Worm of Spindleston Heugh
In Williams-Ellis, A. Fairy tales from the
British Isles p306-11 **398.2**
See also Lambton worm

La Iglesia, Maria Elena de. See De La Iglesia,
Maria Elena

Laimgruber, Monika
(illus.) Andersen, H. C. The emperor's new
clothes **Fic**
(illus.) Andersen, H. C. The steadfast tin
soldier **Fic**

Laird, Helene
(jt. auth.) Wright, W. W. The rainbow dictionary **423**

The **lairdie** with the heart of gold. Nic Leodhas, S.
In Nic Leodhas, S. Heather and broom
p45-59 **398.2**

The **laird's** lass and the gobha's son. Nic Leodhas, S.
In Nic Leodhas, S. Thistle and thyme
p17-38 **398.2**

Laite, Gordon
(illus.) Bulla, C. R. Joseph the dreamer **221.9**
(illus.) Daves, M. Young readers book of
Christian symbolism **246**
(illus.) Guilfoile, E. Valentine's Day **394.2**
(illus.) Hazeltine, A. I. ed. Hero tales from
many lands **398.2**

The **Lake** Lady. Williams-Ellis, A.
In Williams-Ellis, A. Fairy tales from the
British Isles p255-62 **398.2**

The **lake** maiden. Manning-Sanders, R.
In Manning-Sanders, R. A book of mermaids p114-21 **398.2**

Lake that flew. Credle, E.
In Credle, E. Tall tales from the high hills,
and other stories p96-99 **398.2**

Lake Victoria. See Victoria, Lake

Lakes
Goetz, D. Lakes (3-5) **551.4**
See also names of individual lakes, e.g.
Victoria, Lake

Lakmé; adaptation. Bulla, C. R.
In Bulla, C. R. More Stories of favorite
operas p182-91 **782.1**

Lamar, Lucius Quintus Cincinnatus
See pages in the following book:
Kennedy, J. F. Profiles in courage. Young
readers Memorial edition, abridged p103-
18 (5-7) **920**

La Mare, Walter de. See De La Mare, Walter

Lamb, Charles
A midsummer night's dream
In Darrell, M. ed. Once upon a time p147-
57 **808.8**
Romeo and Juliet
In Darrell, M. ed. Once upon a time p158-
69 **808.8**

Lamb, Charles—*Continued*
The taming of the shrew
In Darrell, M. ed. Once upon a time p140-
46   **808.8**

Lamb, Geoffrey
Mental magic tricks (5-7)   **793.8**

Lamb, Pompey
See pages in the following book:
Rollins, C. H. They showed the way p100-02
(5-7)   **920**

Lamb and the fish
Grimm, J. The lambkin and the little fish
In Grimm, J. The complete Grimm's Fairy
tales p625-27   **398.2**

Lamb that went to Fairyland. Fyleman, R.
In Association for Childhood Education
International. Told under the magic
umbrella p30-32   **S C**

Lambert, Clara
Theresa follows the crops
In Association for Childhood Education
International. Told under the Stars
and Stripes p83-90   **S C**

Lambert, Eloise
Our names   **929.4**

Lambert, Saul
(illus.) Fox, P. Portrait of Ivan   **Fic**

Lambie, Laurie Jo
(illus.) Adler, I. Integers: positive and negative   **513**
(illus.) Adler, I. Language and man   **401**

Lambikin
The Lambikin
In Hutchinson, V. S. ed. Candle-light
stories p3-8   **398.2**
Steel, F. A. The lambikin
In Jacobs, J. ed. Indian fairy tales p17-20
     398.2

The lambkin and the little fish. Grimm, J.
In Grimm, J. The complete Grimm's Fairy
tales p625-27   **398.2**

Lambo, Don
(illus.) Smaridge, N. The world of chocolate
     641.3

The Lambton worm. Jacobs, J.
In Green, R. L. ed. A cavalcade of dragons
p109-14   **808.8**
In Jacobs, J. ed. More English folk and
fairy tales p215-21   **398.2**
See also Laidly worm of Spindleston

The Lame dog
In Baker, A. comp. The talking tree p77-87
     398.2

Lame duck
In Hutchinson, V. S. ed. Candle-light
stories p117-22   **398.2**

The lame turkey. Kelsey, A. G.
In Luckhardt, M. C. comp. Thanksgiving
p274-80   **394.2**

The lame vixen. Wratislaw, H. H.
In Manning-Sanders, R. ed. A book of magical beasts p209-23   **398.2**

Lament of Cadieux. Hooke, H. M.
In Hooke, H. M. Thunder in the mountains
p199-209   **398.2**

Lamming, George
Boy Blue the crab-catcher
In McDowell, R. E. ed. Third World voices
for children p66-71   **398.2**

Lamorisse, Albert
The red balloon (1-4)   **Fic**

Lampman, Evelyn Sibley
The shy stegosaurus of Cricket Creek (5-7)
     Fic

Lampreys
See pages in the following book:
Ault, P. These are the Great Lakes p134-40
(5-7)   **977**

Lancelot
Hieatt, C. The knight of the cart (4-7) **398.2**

Land. See Agriculture; Farms; Feudalism

The land and people of Afghanistan. Clifford, M. L.   **915.81**

The land and people of Algeria. Spencer, M.
     916.5

The land and people of Argentina. Hall, E.
     918.2

The land and people of Australia. Blunden, G.
     919.4

The land and people of Austria. Wohlrabe, R. A.   **914.36**

The land and people of Belgium. Loder, D.
     914.93

The land and people of Bolivia. Warren, L. F.
     918.4

The land and people of Brazil. Brown, R. **918.1**

The land and people of Cambodia. Chandler, D. P.   **915.96**

The land and people of Canada. Ross, F. A.
     917.1

The land and people of Ceylon. Wilber, D. N.
     915.49

The land and people of Colombia. Landry, L.
     918.61

The land and people of Cuba. Ortiz, V. **917.291**

The land and people of Czechoslovakia. Hall, E.
     914.37

The land and people of Denmark. Wohlrabe, R. A.   **914.89**

The land and people of Egypt. Mahmoud, Z. N.
     916.2

The land and people of England. Street, A.
     914.2

The land and people of Finland. Berry, E.
     914.71

The land and people of France. Bragdon, L. J.
     914.4

The land and people of Germany. Wohlrabe, R. A.   **914.3**

The land and people of Ghana. Sale, J. K.
     916.67

The land and people of Greece. Gianakoulis, T.
     914.95

The land and people of Holland. Barnouw, A. J.
     914.92

The land and people of Iceland. Berry, E.
     914.91

The land and people of Indonesia. Smith, D. C.
     915.98

The **land** and people of Iran. Hinckley, H. 915.5

The **land** and people of Ireland. O'Brien, E. 914.15

The **land** and people of Israel. Hoffman, G. 915.694

The **land** and people of Italy. Winwar, F. 914.5

The **land** and people of Japan. Vaughan, J. B. 915.2

The **land** and people of Korea. Solberg, S. E. 915.19

The **land** and people of Lebanon. Winder, V. H. 915.692

The **land** and people of Liberia. Clifford, M. L. 916.66

The **land** and people of Libya. Copeland, P. W. 916.1

The **land** and people of Morocco. Spencer, W. 916.4

The **land** and people of New Zealand. Kaula, E. M. 919.31

The **land** and people of Nigeria. Forman, B. 916.69

The **land** and people of Norway. Hall, E. 914.81

The **land** and people of Pakistan. Lang, R. 915.49

The **land** and people of Peru. Bowen, J. D. 918.5

The **land** and people of Poland. Kelly, E. P. 914.38

The **land** and people of Romania. Hale, J. 914.98

The **land** and people of Russia. Nazaroff, A. 914.7

The **land** and people of Sierra Leone. Clifford, M. L. 916.6

The **land** and people of South Africa. Paton, A. 916.8

The **land** and people of Spain. Loder, D. 914.6

The **land** and people of Syria. Copeland, P. W. 915.691

The **land** and people of Tanzania. Kaula, E. M. 916.78

The **land** and people of the Balkans. Kostich, D. D. 914.96

The **land** and people of the Congo. Crane, L. 916.75

The **land** and people of the West Indies. Sherlock, P. 917.29

The **land** and people of Tunisia. Spencer, W. 916.1

The **land** and people of Turkey. Spencer, W. 915.61

The **land** and people of Uruguay. Dobler, L. 918.95

The **land** and people of Zambia. Dresang, E. T. 916.89

The **land** beneath the sea. May, J. 551.4

The **land** of brave men. Belpré, P.
In Belpré, P. Once in Puerto Rico p9-12 398.2

The **land** of Joan of Arc. See Bragdon, L. J. The land and people of France 914.4

The **land** of the English people. See Street, A. The land and people of England 914.2

Land of the free. Meadowcroft, E. L. 973

The **land** of the Italian people. See Winwar, F. The land and people of Italy 914.5

Land of the Pharaohs. Cottrell, L. 913.32

Land of the Pilgrims' pride. Lillie, A. M.
In Luckhardt, M. C. comp. Thanksgiving p176-88 394.2

The **land** of the Polish people. See Kelly, E. P. The land and people of Poland 914.38

The **land**, wildlife, and peoples of the Bible. Farb, P. 220.8

Landa, Peter
(illus.) Seidelman, J. E. Creating with paint 751.4

Landau, Jacob
(illus.) Lyons, J. H. Stories of our American patriotic songs 784.7
(illus.) Reynolds, Q. The Wright brothers 92

Landeck, Beatrice
(comp.) Songs to grow on 784.4

Landers Film Reviews 016.3713

The **landing** of the Pilgrims. Daugherty, J. 974.4

The **Landmark** history of the American people. Boorstin, D. J. 973

Landry, Lionel
The **land** and people of Colombia (5-7) 918.61

Lands and peoples 910

Landscape drawing
See pages in the following book:
Weiss, H. Pencil, pen and brush p35-43 (5-7) 741.2

Landslide! Day, V. Fic

Lane, Margaret
Rachel Field and her contribution to children's literature
In Andrews, S. ed. The Hewins lectures, 1947-1962 p343-75 028.5

Lanes, Selma G.
Down the rabbit hole 028.5

Lang, Andrew
(ed.) Arabian nights (5-7) 398.2
The billy goat and the king
In Farjeon, E. ed. A cavalcade of queens p63-68 808.8
(ed.) The blue fairy book (4-6) 398.2
The dragon of the north
In Hoke, H. comp. Dragons, dragons, dragons p179-91 398.2
Drakestail
In Martignoni, M. E. ed. The illustrated treasury of children's literature p83-88 808.8
(ed.) The green fairy book (4-6) 398.2
The half-chick
In Haviland, V. comp. The fairy tale treasury p66-71 398.2
In Lang, A. ed. The green fairy book p27-31 398.2
In Martignoni, M. E. ed. The illustrated treasury of children's literature p246-48 808.8
Jackal or tiger?
In Farjeon, E. ed. A cavalcade of queens p23-37 808.8

Lanyon, Ellen
(illus.) DeRoin, N. ed. Jataka tales   **398.2**
La Paz, Bolivia
See pages in the following book:
Warren, L. F. The land and people of Bolivia p21-32 (5-7)   **918.4**
Lapland

Fiction

Aulaire, I. d'. Children of the Northlights (2-4)   **Fic**

Social life and customs
See pages in the following book:
Berry, E. Eating and cooking around the world p30-35 (5-7)   **641.3**
Lapps
See pages in the following books:
Hall, E. The land and people of Norway p102-08 (5-7)   **914.81**
Harrington, L. The polar regions p29-36 (5-7)   **919.8**
Liversidge, D. The first book of the Arctic p12-15 (4-7)   **919.8**
Large print books
Carroll, L. Alice's adventures in Wonderland   **Fic**
Fitzhugh, L. Harriet the spy   **Fic**
Hamilton, E. Mythology   **292**
Hunter, M. A sound of chariots   **Fic**
Kipling, R. The jungle books   **S C**
Kipling, R. Just so stories   **S C**
Knight, E. Lassie come-home   **Fic**
Lang, A. ed. Arabian nights   **398.2**
Mother Goose. The large type Mother Goose   **398.8**
Nordstrom, U. The secret language   **Fic**
O'Dell, S. Island of the Blue Dolphins   **Fic**
Perrault, C. Famous fairy tales   **398.2**
Pyle, H. Some merry adventures of Robin Hood of great renown in Nottinghamshire   **398.2**
Reiss, J. The upstairs room   **940.54**
Sewell, A. Black Beauty   **Fic**
Shepard, R. A. Sneakers   **Fic**
Spyri, J. Heidi   **Fic**
Stolz, M. The bully of Barkham Street   **Fic**
Wilder, L. I. Little house in the big woods   **Fic**
Large type books. See Large print books
The **Large** type Mother Goose. Mother Goose   **398.8**
The **largest** sea monster in the world. Pontoppidan, E.
In Silverberg, B. ed. Phoenix feathers p25-27   **S C**
The **lark,** the wolf, and the fox. Haviland, V.
In Haviland, V. Favorite fairy tales told in Poland p39-54   **398.2**
Larousse en colores, Mi primer. Fonteneau, M.   **463**
Larousse en couleurs, Mon premier. Fonteneau, M.   **443**
Larousse Encyclopedia of mythology, New   **291.03**
Larrea, Victoria de. See De Larrea, Victoria
Larrecq, John
(illus.) Kroeber, T. A green Christmas   **E**

(illus.) Levitin, S. Who owns the moon?   **E**
(illus.) Ormondroyd, E. Broderick   **E**
(illus.) Ormondroyd, E. Theodore   **E**
(illus.) Ormondroyd, E. Theodore's rival   **E**
Larrick, Nancy
(comp.) Green is like a meadow of grass (k-4)   **811.08**
(comp.) I head a scream in the street (5-7)   **811.08**
(ed.) On city streets (5-7)   **811.08**
A parent's guide to children's reading   **028.5**
(ed.) Piper, pipe that song again! (2-5)   **821.08**
(ed.) Piping down the valleys wild   **808.81**
(comp.) Poetry for holidays (1-4)   **811.08**
(ed.) Room for me and a mountain lion (5-7)   **808.81**
(comp.) The wheels of the bus go round and round (1-4)   **784.6**
Lars, my lad! Haviland, V.
In Haviland, V. Favorite fairy tales told in Sweden p60-92   **398.2**
Larsen, Elaine
(jt. auth.) Larsen, P. Boy of Nepal   **915.49**
Larsen, Johannes
(illus.) Andersen, H. C. The ugly duckling   **Fic**
Larsen, Peter
Boy of Nepal (3-5)   **915.49**
The United Nations at work throughout the world (4-6)   **341.23**
Larson, Edith
The Christmas bug
In Kamerman, S. E. ed. A treasury of Christmas plays p95-111   **812.08**
Larson, Rodger
Young filmmakers (6-7)   **778.5**
La Rue, Mabel G.
The jack-o'-lantern
In Association for Childhood Education International. Told under the blue umbrella p69-74   **S C**
La Salle, Robert Cavelier, sieur de
Syme, R. La Salle of the Mississippi (4-7)   **92**
See also pages in the following book:
Discoverers of the New World p139-43 (5-7)   **973.1**
Lascaux Cave, France
Baumann, H. The caves of the great hunters (5-7)   **913**
Lasers
See pages in the following book:
Bendick, J. Electronics for young people p85-91 (5-7)   **621.381**
Lasker, Joe
He's my brother   **E**
Laski, Marghanita
The tower
In Authors' choice p53-62   **S C**
The **lass** and her good stout blackthorn stick. Nic Leodhas, S.
In Nic Leodhas, S. Twelve great black cats, and other eerie Scottish tales p147-60   **398.2**

Lawson, Robert—*Continued*

In Arbuthnot, M. H. comp. The Arbuthnot Anthology of children's literature p481-83   **808.8**

Robert Lawson, illustrator   **741.64**

The tough winter (3-6)   **Fic**

Watchwords of liberty (3-6)   **973**

Willie's bad night

In Arbuthnot, M. H. comp. The Arbuthnot Anthology of children's literature p481-83   **808.8**

(illus.) Atwater, R. Mr Popper's penguins **Fic**

(illus.) Brewton, J. E. comp. Gaily we parade   **821.08**

(illus.) Brewton, J. E. comp. Under the tent of the sky   **808.81**

(illus.) Fish, H. D. comp. Four & twenty blackbirds   **398.8**

(illus.) Gray, E. J. Adam of the road   **Fic**

(illus.) Leaf, M. The story of Ferdinand   **E**

(illus.) Leaf, M. Wee Gillis   **E**

About

See pages in the following books:

Hoffman, M. ed. Authors and illustrators of children's books p256-67   **028.5**

Miller, B. M. ed. Caldecott Medal books: 1938-1957 p75-78   **028.5**

Miller, B. M. ed. Newbery Medal books: 1922-1955 p258-60   **028.5**

Smaridge, N. Famous author-illustrators for young people p37-43 (5-7)   **920**

Lawson, Roberta Campbell

See pages in the following book:

Gridley, M. E. American Indian women p88-93 (5-7)   **920**

Lawyers. See Judges; Law as a profession

Laycock, George

The pelicans (3-6)   **598.2**

Wild animals, safe places (5-7)   **639**

Wild travelers (5-7)   **591.5**

Layout and typography. See Printing

Lazare, Jerry

(illus.) Burch, R. Queenie Peavy   **Fic**

(illus.) Little, J. One to grow on   **Fic**

(illus.) Little, J. Take wing   **Fic**

The lazies. Ginsburg, M. ed.   **398.2**

The lazy bear. Wildsmith, B.   **E**

The Lazy daughter

In Ginsburg, M. ed. The lazies p49-55   **398.2**

The lazy farmer. Prescott, J.

In Gruenberg, S. M. ed. Favorite stories old and new p394-95   **808.8**

Lazy Hans. Manning-Sanders, R.

In Manning-Sanders, R. A book of witches p27-37   **398.2**

See also Lazy Heinz

Lazy Harry. Grimm, J.

In Grimm, J. The complete Grimm's Fairy tales p678-81   **398.2**

See also Lazy Heinz

Lazy Heinz

Grimm, J. Lazy Harry

In Grimm, J. The complete Grimm's Fairy tales p678-81   **398.2**

Grimm, J. Lazy Heinz

In Grimm, J. Tales from Grimm p191-200   **398.2**

Manning-Sanders, R. Lazy Hans

In Manning-Sanders, R. A book of witches p27-37   **398.2**

Lazy Jack

Lazy Jack

In Jacobs, J. ed. English folk and fairy tales p159-61   **398.2**

In Sechrist, E. H. ed. It's time for story hour p94-96   **372.6**

In The Tall book of nursery tales p71-73   **398.2**

Steel, F. A. Lazy Jack

In Martignoni, M. E. ed. The illustrated treasury of children's literature p163-64   **808.8**

See also Jack and the king's girl

The lazy leprechaun; story. Taylor, J.

In Ross, L. Holiday puppets p70-72 **791.5**

The lazy man. Tashjian, V. A.

In Tashjian, V. A. Three apples fell from heaven p3-6   **398.2**

Lazy people, Tale of the. See Tale of the lazy people

Lazy Peter and the king. Alegría, R. E.

In Alegría, R. E. The three wishes p111-14   **398.2**

Lazy Peter and the three-cornered hat. Alegría, R. E.

In Alegría, R. E. The three wishes p66-73   **398.2**

The lazy spinner. Grimm, J.

In Grimm, J. The complete Grimm's Fairy tales p577-79   **398.2**

Lazy Tok. Skipper, M.

In Colwell, E. ed. A storyteller's choice p169-73   **372.6**

Leach, Maria

The ghostly hitchhiker

In Hoke, H. ed. Spooks, spooks, spooks p112-15   **S C**

Here we go!

In Harper, W. comp. Ghosts and goblins p222-24   **394.2**

How the people sang the mountains up (3-6)   **398.2**

Noodles, nitwits, and numskulls (4-7) **398.2**

Riddle me, riddle me, ree (3-6)   **398.6**

The thing at the foot of the bed, and other scary tales (3-6)   **S C**

Contents: The thing at the foot of the bed; Here we go; Ghost race; Wait till Martin comes; Big Fraid and Little Fraid; The lucky man; The golden arm; The dare; I'm in the room; No head; As long as this; The legs; Talk; Milk bottles; The head; The lovelorn pig; The ghostly hitchhiker; Aunt Tilly; The cradle that rocked by itself; The gangster in the back seat; Witch cat; Sop, doll; Singing bone

Whistle in the graveyard (4-6)   **398.2**

Contents: White House ghosts; Earl Gerald; Anne Boleyn; White ghosts; Skull race; Nobody here but you and me; What's the matter; Old Tom comes home; 'Tain't so; One handful; Can't rest; Blackbeard's treasure; The tired ghost; Cauld, cauld, forever cauld; The outside man; I'm coming up the stairs; The man on Morvan's Road; Staring at you; The sea captain at the door; Grandpa Joe's brother; Bill is with me now; Tony and his harp; Crossing the bridge; The ghostly spools; Tick, tick, tick; Pumpkin; Jenny Green Teeth; Baba Yaga; Nuinumma-Kwiten; Pot-Tilter; Willie Winkie; Raw Head and Bloody Bones; The black cat's eyes; How to become a witch; Next turn to the right; A breath of air; The ghost on Brass's Hill; Sunrise; Dead man

The **legend** of La Befana. Woolsey, J.
In Sechrist, E. H. ed. It's time for Christmas p33-35   394.26

A **Legend** of Knockmany
In De Regniers, B. S. ed. The giant book p109-24   398.2

The **Legend** of St Christopher
In Shedlock, M. L. The art of the storyteller p168-72   372.6

The **legend** of Saint Elizabeth. Sawyer, R.
In Sawyer, R. The way of the storyteller p307-15   372.6

Legend of Scar Face. Grinnell, G. B.
In Davis, M. G. ed. A baker's dozen p189-207   372.6

The **legend** of Sleepy Hollow. Irving, W.
In Irving, W. Rip Van Winkle, The legend of Sleepy Hollow, and other tales p45-98   S C

A **legend** of spring. Siks, G. B.
In Ward, W. ed. Stories to dramatize p112-15   372.6

The **legend** of the Black Madonna. Applegarth, M. T.
In Rollins, C. comp. Christmas gif' p36-44   394.2

The **legend** of the Ceiba of Ponce. Belpré, P.
In Belpré, P. Once in Puerto Rico p51-54   398.2

The **Legend** of the Chingolo bird
In Courlander, H. ed. Ride with the sun p213-14   398.2

The **legend** of the Christ child. Harrison, E.
In Harper, W. comp. Merry Christmas to you p87-93   394.2

The **legend** of the Christmas rose. Lagerlöf, S.
In Harper, W. comp. Merry Christmas to you p155-77   394.2

The **legend** of the Christmas rose. Leuser, E. D.
In Kamerman, S. E. ed. A treasury of Christmas plays p349-54   812.08

A **legend** of the first Christmas tree. Luckhardt, M. C.
In Luckhardt, M. C. ed. Christmas comes once more p110-18   394.2

Legend of the first Filipinos. Sechrist, E. H.
In Sechrist, E. H. Once in the first times p3-7   398.2

The **legend** of the hummingbird. Belpré, P.
In Belpré, P. Once in Puerto Rico p25-28   398.2

The **legend** of the Moor's legacy; adaptation. Irving, W.
In Ward, W. ed. Stories to dramatize p236-43   372.6

The **legend** of the Royal Palm. Belpré, P.
In Belpré, P. Once in Puerto Rico p13-17   398.2

Legend of the sleeping giant. Hooke, H. M.
In Hooke, H. M. Thunder in the mountains p101-10   398.2

The **legend** of the willow plate. Tresselt, A.   398.2

Legend of the wishing well. Hooke, H. M.
In Hooke, H. M. Thunder in the mountains p71-81   398.2

Legends
Belting, N. Calendar moon (4-7)   398.2
Belting, N. The stars are silver reindeer (4-7)   398.2
Belting, N. The sun is a golden earring (4-7)   398.2
Brown, M. ed. A cavalcade of sea legends (5-7)   808.8
Courlander, H. ed. Ride with the sun (4-7)   398.2
Hazeltine, A. I. ed. Hero tales from many lands (5-7)   398.2
Leach, M. How the people sang the mountains up (3-6)   398.2
Sawyer, R. Joy to the world (3-6)   394.2
White, A. T. The Golden Treasury of myths and legends (5-7)   292
See also pages in the following book:
Johnson, E. ed. Anthology of children's literature p477-561   808.8
    See also Fables; Fairy tales; Folklore; Mythology; Saints; and names of individual legendary characters, e.g. Robin Hood

Africa
Arnott, K. African myths and legends (4-7)   398.2
Bertol, R. Sundiata (4-7)   398.2

Canada
Hooke, H. M. Thunder in the mountains (5-7)   398.2

China
Tresselt, A. The legend of the willow plate (1-4)   398.2

England
See Legends—Great Britain

Flanders
Jagendorf, M. Tyll Ulenspiegel's merry pranks (4-6)   398.2

France
Baldwin, J. The story of Roland (6-7)   398.2
Cooney, B. The little juggler (3-6)   398.2
Williams, J. The horn of Roland (4-6)   398.2

Germany
Jagendorf, M. Tyll Ulenspiegel's merry pranks (4-6)   398.2

Great Britain
Brown, M. Dick Whittington and his cat (k-3)   398.2
Malcolmson, A. ed. Song of Robin Hood (5-7)   398.2
Pyle, H. The merry adventures of Robin Hood of great renown in Nottinghamshire (5-7)   398.2
Pyle, H. Some merry adventures of Robin Hood (5-7)   398.2
Serraillier, I. Beowulf the warrior (6-7)   398.2
    See also Arthur, King

Hawaii
Brown, M. Backbone of the king (5-7)   398.2

Indexes
Index to fairy tales, myths and legends   398.2
Index to fairy tales, myths and legends; supplement   398.2
Index to fairy tales, myths and legends; second supplement   398.2
Index to fairy tales, 1949-1972   398.2

Legends—*Continued*

Indians of North America

See Indians of North America—Legends

Israel

Elkin, B. The wisest man in the world (1-4)
398.2

Japan

Matsutani, M. The crane maiden (k-3) 398.2

Mexico

Campbell, C. Star Mountain, and other legends of Mexico (4-7)
398.2

Mongolia

Otsuka, Y. Suho and the white horse (1-4)
398.2

New England

Jagendorf, M. A. New England bean-pot (5-7)
398.2

Lent, B. John Tabor's ride (k-3)
398.2

Poland

See pages in the following book:

Kelly, E. P. The land and people of Poland
p21-28 (5-7)
914.38

Russia

Robbins, R. Baboushka and the three kings (1-4)
398.2

Southern States

Jagendorf, M. A. Folk stories of the South (4-7)
398.2

Spain

Gunterman, B. L. ed. Castles in Spain, and other enchantments (4-6)
398.2

Switzerland

Hürlimann, B. William Tell and his son (2-5)
398.2

Turkey

Kelsey, A. G. Once the Hodja (4-6)
398.2

United States

Anderson, J. The haunting of America (6-7)
398.2

Carmer, C. comp. America sings (5-7)
784.4

Felton, H. W. Bowleg Bill, seagoing cowpuncher (5-7)
398.2

Felton, H. W. John Henry and his hammer (5-7)
398.2

Felton, H. W. Mike Fink, best of the keelboatmen (5-7)
398.2

Felton, H. W. New tall tales of Pecos Bill (5-7)
398.2

Felton, H. W. Pecos Bill and the mustang (k-3)
398.2

Felton, H. W. Pecos Bill, Texas cowpuncher (5-7)
398.2

Keats, E. J. John Henry (k-3)
398.2

McCormick, D. J. Paul Bunyan swings his axe (4-6)
398.2

Malcolmson, A. Yankee Doodle's cousins (4-7)
398.2

Rounds, G. Ol' Paul, the mighty logger (3-6)
398.2

Shapiro, I. Heroes in American folklore (4-7)
398.2

Shephard, E. Paul Bunyan (5-7)
398.2

See also Legends—New England; Legends—Southern States

Wales

Robbins, R. Taliesin and King Arthur (3-5)
398.2

Legends, Celtic

Sutcliff, R. Tristan and Iseult (5-7)
398.2

Legends, Eskimo

Houston, J. Tiktak'liktak (4-6)
398.2

Melzack, R. The day Tuk became a hunter & other Eskimo stories (3-6)
398.2

Legends, Germanic

Baldwin, J. The story of Siegfried (6-7) 398.2

Legends, Indian. See Indians of Mexico—Legends; Indians of North America—Legends; Indians of South America—Legends; also names of individual tribes with subdivision Legends, e.g. Chippewa Indians—Legends

Legends, Jewish

Ish-Kishor, S. The carpet of Solomon (4-6)
398.2

Shulevitz, U. The magician (k-2)
398.2

Legends and stories of animals. See Animals—Stories; Fables; and names of animals with the subdivision Stories, e.g. Hippopotamus—Stories

Legends of Charlemagne. Bulfinch, T.
In Bulfinch, T. Bulfinch's Mythology   291

Legends of the flowers. Woolsey, J.
In Sechrist, E. H. ed. It's time for Christmas p43-48
394.2

Legends of the trees. Woolsey, J.
In Sechrist, E. H. ed. It's time for Christmas p49-53
394.2

Legends of the underground bells. Woolsey, J.
In Sechrist, E. H. ed. It's time for Christmas p42-43
394.2

Legerdemain. See Magic

Legislation

Stevens, L. A. How a law is made (5-7)
328.73

Weiss, A. E. Save the mustangs! (3-5) 328

Legislative bodies. See Parliamentary practice; also names of individual legislative bodies, e.g. United States. Congress

Le Grand

Augustus goes south
In Martignoni, M. E. ed. The illustrated treasury of children's literature p338-42
808.8

Le Grand, Pierre. See Pierre le Grand

The legs. Leach, M.
In Leach, M. The thing at the foot of the bed, and other scary tales p46-48 S C

Le Guin, Ursula K.

The farthest shore (6-7)   Fic
The Tombs of Atuan (6-7)   Fic
A wizard of Earthsea (6-7)   Fic

Legumes

Earle, O. L. Peas, beans, and licorice (4-6)
583

See also pages in the following book:

Fenton, C. L. Plants we live on p78-84 (4-6)
581.6

Lehman, John F.

Biskie the snowman
In Kamerman, S. E. ed. Little plays for little players p169-74
812.08

Light and shade. See Shades and shadows

The **light** at Tern Rock. Sauer, J. L.　　　**Fic**

A **light** in the dark; the life of Samuel Gridley Howe. Meltzer, M.　　　**92**

The **light** princess. Macdonald, G.　　　**Fic**
—Same
　　In Johnson, S. P. ed. The Princesses p190-233　　　**S C**

Light ships. See Lightships

Lightbody, Donna M.
　Introducing needlepoint (5-7)　　　**746.4**

Lighthouses
　Smith, A. Lighthouses (5-7)　　　**623.89**
　　　　　　Drama
　Aiken, J. The mooncusser's daughter (5-7)　　　**822**

　　　　　　Fiction
　Ardizzone, E. Tim to the lighthouse　　　**E**
　Sauer, J. L. The light at Tern Rock (3-5) **Fic**
　Swift, H. H. The little red lighthouse and the great gray bridge　　　**E**

Lighting. See Candles; Electric lighting

Lightning
　Branley, F. M. Flash, crash, rumble, and roll (k-3)　　　**551.5**
　　See also pages in the following book:
　Weiss, M. E. Storms—from the inside out p36-43 (4-6)　　　**551.5**

The **lights** of Christmas. Allstrom, E.
　　In Luckhardt, M. C. ed. Christmas comes once more p131-37　　　**394.2**

Lightships
　　See pages in the following book:
　Smith, A. Lighthouses p127-46 (5-7) **623.89**

Lignell, Lois
　(illus.) Bulla, C. R. A tree is a plant　　　**582**

Liisa and the prince. Bowman, J. C.
　　In Bowman, J. C. Tales from a Finnish tupa p187-98　　　**398.2**

Like master, like servant. Jagendorf, M. A.
　　In Jagendorf, M. A. Noodlehead stories from around the world p75-77 **398.2**

Like meat loves salt
　　In Chase, R. ed. Grandfather tales p124-29　　　**398.2**

Liley, Margaret
　(jt. auth.) Day, B. The secret world of the baby　　　**612.6**

Lilies, rabbits, and painted eggs. Barth, E.　　　**394.2**

Liliuokalani, Queen of the Hawaiian Islands
　Wilson, H. Last queen of Hawaii: Liliuokalani (4-6)　　　**92**

Lillie, Amy Morris
　Land of the Pilgrims' pride
　　In Luckhardt, M. C. comp. Thanksgiving p176-88　　　**394.2**

Lillie of Watts. Walter, M. P.　　　**Fic**

Li Lun, lad of courage. Treffinger, C.　　　**Fic**

Lilly, Charles
　(illus.) Greene, B. Philip Hall likes me. I reckon maybe　　　**Fic**

Lima
　　See pages in the following book:
　Bowen, J. D. The land and people of Peru p34-45 (5-7)　　　**918.5**

Limburg, Peter R.
　Engines (5-7)　　　**621.4**
　The story of corn (3-5)　　　**633**
　Watch out, it's poison ivy! (3-6)　　　**581.6**

Limericks
　Brewton, S. comp. Laughable limericks (4-7)　　　**821.08**
　Brewton, S. comp. My tang's tungled and other ridiculous situations (3-6)　　**821.08**
　Cole, W. comp. The book of giggles (1-4)　　　**808.87**
　Lear, E. Whizz!　　　**E**
　Love, K. comp. A little laughter (3-6) **821.08**
　　See also Nonsense verses

Lincoln, Abraham, President U.S.
　The Gettysburg Address
　　In Foster, G. Year of Lincoln, 1861 p28-29　　　**909.81**
　　　　　　About
　Aulaire, I. d'. Abraham Lincoln (2-4)　　**92**
　Commager, H. S. The great Proclamation (6-7)　　　**326**
　De Regniers, B. S. comp. The Abraham Lincoln joke book (4-6)　　　**817.08**
　Foster, G. Abraham Lincoln (3-6)　　**92**
　Foster, G. Year of Lincoln, 1861 (3-6)　　　**909.81**
　McGovern, A. If you grew up with Abraham Lincoln (2-4)　　　**92**
　McNeer, M. America's Abraham Lincoln (5-7)　　　**92**
　Phelan, M. K. Mr Lincoln's inaugural journey (5-7)　　　**92**
　　See also pages in the following books:
　Anderson, J. The haunting of America p40-48 (6-7)　　　**398.2**
　Arbuthnot, M. H. comp. The Arbuthnot Anthology of children's literature p806-09　　　**808.8**
　Daugherty, S. Ten brave men p140-52 (5-7)　　　**920**
　Johnson, E. ed. Anthology of children's literature p1065-71　　　**808.8**
　Sandburg, C. The Sandburg treasury p383-477 (5-7)　　　**818**
　　　　　　Fiction
　Le Sueur, M. The river road (5-7)　　　**Fic**
　　See also pages in the following books:
　Arbuthnot, M. H. comp. The Arbuthnot Anthology of children's literature p756-61　　　**808.8**
　Ward, W. ed. Stories to dramatize p265-70　　　**372.6**
　　　　　　Poetry
　　See pages in the following book:
　Sechrist, E. H. comp. Poems for red letter days p44-51　　　**821.08**

Lincoln, Tad. See Lincoln, Thomas, 1853-1871

Lincoln, Thomas, 1853-1871
　　　　　　Fiction
　Monjo, F. N. Me and Willie and Pa (3-5)　　　**Fic**

Lion bones and the Gardula magicians. Davis, R.
  In Davis, R. The lion's whiskers p70-72
      398.2

Lion cubs. National Geographic Society   **599**

The **lion**-hearted kitten. Bacon, P.
  In Gruenberg, S. M. ed. Favorite stories old and new p228-31   **808.8**
  In Martignoni, M. E. ed. The illustrated treasury of children's literature p371-72   **808.8**

The **Lion** hunt
  In Tashjian, V. A. ed. Juba this and Juba that p62-70   **372.6**

The **Lion**-makers
  In Dobbs, R. ed. Once upon a time p24-26   **372.6**

Lion on the mountain. Dixon, P.   **Fic**

The **lion**, the leopard, and the antelope. Holladay, V.
  In Holladay, V. Bantu tales p70-75 **398.2**

The **lion**, the witch and the wardrobe. Lewis, C. S.   **Fic**

The **lion**, the witch and the wardrobe; excerpt. Lewis, C. S.
  In Arbuthnot, M. H. comp. The Arbuthnot Anthology of children's literature p526-31   **808.8**

Lion to lamb. Boiko, C.
  In Boiko, C. Children's plays for creative actors p230-38   **812**

Lionni, Leo
  Alexander and the wind-up mouse   **E**
  The biggest house in the world   **E**
  Fish is fish   **E**
  Frederick   **E**
  Inch by inch   **E**
  Little blue and little yellow   **E**
  Swimmy   **E**
  Tico and the golden wings   **E**

About

See pages in the following books:

Hoffman, M. ed. Authors and illustrators of children's books p302-07   **028.5**
Smaridge, N. Famous author-illustrators for young people p101-05 (5-7)   **920**

Lions
  Adamson, J. Elsa (2-5)   **599**
  National Geographic Society. Lion cubs (k-3)   **599**

See also pages in the following book:

Paton, A. The land and people of South Africa p73-78 (5-7)   **916.8**

Stories

Arundel, J. Simba of the White Mane (5-7)   **Fic**
Daugherty, J. Andy and the lion   **E**
Du Bois, W. P. Lion   **E**
Fatio, L. The happy lion   **E**
Fatio, L. The happy lion in Africa   **E**
Fatio, L. The three happy lions   **E**
Freeman, D. Dandelion   **E**
Hurd, E. T. Johnny Lion's bad day   **E**
Hurd, E. T. Johnny Lion's book   **E**
Hurd, E. T. Johnny Lion's rubber boots **E**

Wildsmith, B. The lion and the rat (k-2)
      398.2

The **lion's** share. Courlander, H.
  In Courlander, H. The king's drum, and other African stories p78-79 **398.2**

The **lion's** share. Davis, R.
  In Davis, R. The lion's whiskers p77-80
      398.2

The **lion's** whiskers. Davis, R.   **398.2**

The **lion's** whiskers; short story. Davis, R.
  In Davis, R. The lion's whiskers p7-12
      398.2

Lipkind, William. See Will

Lipnick, Esther
  Angel of mercy
  In Kamerman, S. E. ed. Fifty plays for junior actors p302-12   **812.08**
  A son of liberty
  In Burack, A. S. ed. One hundred plays for children p828-37   **808.82**

Lippincott, Joseph Wharton
  The Wahoo bobcat (5-7)   **Fic**
  Wilderness champion (5-7)   **Fic**

Lippizaner horse

Stories

Henry, M. White stallion of Lipizza (5-7) **Fic**

Lippman, Peter
  (illus.) Cobb, V. Arts and crafts you can eat   **745.5**
  (illus.) Cobb, V. Science experiments you can eat   **507.2**

Lippo and Tapio. Bowman, J. C.
  In Bowman, J. C. Tales from a Finnish tupa p65-72   **398.2**

Liquids

See pages in the following book:

Wilson, M. Seesaws to cosmic rays p28-32 (5-7)   **530**
  See also Hydrodynamics

Lipuniushka. Tolstoy, L.
  In Tolstoy, L. Twenty-two Russian tales for young children p52-54   **S C**

Liquor problem. See Alcoholism

Lisa and her soundless world. Levine, E. S.
      617.8

Lisa and Lottie. Kastner, E.   **Fic**

Lisa's song. Kennell, R.
  In Gruenberg, S. M. ed. Favorite stories old and new p92-97   **808.8**

Lisowski, Gabriel
  (illus.) Levoy, M. The witch of Fourth Street, and other stories   **S C**

Liss, Howard
  Basketball talk for beginners (4-7)   **796.32**
  Bowling talk for beginners (4-7)   **794.6**
  Football talk for beginners (4-7)   **796.33**
  Hockey talk for beginners (4-7)   **796.9**
  UFOs, unidentified flying objects (4-6) **001.9**

List, Ely
  (ed.) Girl Scouts of the United States of America. Girl Scout cookbook   **641.5**

List, Ilka Katherine
  Questions and answers about seashore life (4-6)   **591.92**

List of subject headings, Sears   025.3

Listen! And help tell the story. Carlson, B. W.   372.6

Listen, children, listen. Livingston, M. C. ed.   821.08

Listen, rabbit. Fisher, A.   E

The listening walk. Showers, P.   E

Lister, Joseph Lister, 1st Baron

  See pages in the following books:

Cottler, J. Heroes of civilization p325-36 (6-7)   920

Hume, R. F. Great men of medicine p108-25 (4-6)   920

Literary awards. See Literary prizes; also names of awards, e.g. Caldecott Medal books

Literary criticism. See Criticism

Literary market place: LMP   070.5025

Literary prizes

  See pages in the following books:

Arbuthnot, M. H. comp. The Arbuthnot Anthology of children's literature p979-83   808.8

Haviland, V. ed. Children and literature p439-56   028.5

Johnson, E. ed. Anthology of children's literature p1182-85   808.8

  See also names of awards, e.g. Newbery Medal books

Bibliography

Children's books: awards and prizes **016.807**

Literature

  See also Children's literature; Drama; Fables; Fairy tales; Journalism; Legends; Negro literature; Poetry; Sagas; Wit and humor; Women in literature and art; also names of literatures, e.g. American literature

Bibliography

Rosenberg, J. K. Young people's literature in series: publishers' and non-fiction series   011

Biography

See Authors

Collections

Anderson, C. W. ed. C. W. Anderson's Favorite horse stories (5-7)   808.8

Arbuthnot, M. H. comp. The Arbuthnot Anthology of children's literature   808.8

Association for Childhood Education International. Told under the Christmas tree (3-6)   808.8

Darrell, M. ed. Once upon a time   808.8

Farjeon, E. ed. A cavalcade of kings (5-7)   808.8

Farjeon, E. ed. A cavalcade of queens (4-7)   808.8

Green, R. L. ed. A cavalcade of dragons (4-7)   808.8

Green, R. L. ed. A cavalcade of magicians (4-7)   808.8

Gruenberg, S. M. ed. Favorite stories old and new   808.8

Gruenberg, S. M. comp. Let's hear a story   808.8

Haviland, V. ed. Yankee Doodle's literary sampler of prose, poetry, & pictures **028.5**

Hoke, H. ed. Witches, witches, witches (5-7)   808.8

Hope-Simpson, J. ed. A cavalcade of witches (4-7)   808.8

Johnson, E. ed. Anthology of children's literature   808.8

Lewis, R. ed. Journeys (2-6)   808.88

Martignoni, M. E. ed. The illustrated treasury of children's literature   808.8

Pellowski, A. ed. Have you seen a comet?   808.88

Untermeyer, B. ed. The Golden Treasury of children's literature   808.8

Ward, W. ed. Stories to dramatize   372.6

Withers, C. ed. I saw a rocket walk a mile (3-6)   398.2

  See also pages in the following books:

Childcraft: the how and why library v2   031

Childcraft: the how and why library v3   031

    See also Quotations; Short stories; and names of literatures and literary forms with subdivision Collections; e.g. Russian literature—Collections; Poetry—Collections

Encyclopedias

Brewer's Dictionary of phrase and fable **803**

The Reader's encyclopedia   **803**

Evaluation

See Book reviews

History and criticism

See Criticism

Indexes

  See pages in the following book:

Childcraft: the how and why library v15   031

Prizes

  See Literary prizes; and names of prizes, e.g. Caldecott Medal books

Selections

See Literature—Collections

Stories, plots, etc.

Gillespie, J. Introducing books   028.1

Gillespie, J. Juniorplots   028.1

Literature by and about the American Indian. Stensland, A. L.   016.9701

Lithography

  See pages in the following book:

Barker, A. Black on white and read all over p42-53 (4-6)   686.2

History

Hirsch, S. C. Printing from a stone (6-7)   763

Litter—the ugly enemy. Shuttlesworth, D. E.   614.7

Litterbug convention; play. Carlson, B. W.

  In Carlson, B. W. The right play for you p97-100   792

Littering. See Refuse and refuse disposal

Little, Jean

Kate (4-6)   Fic

Look through my window (4-6)   Fic

Mine for keeps (4-6)   Fic

One to grow on (4-6)   Fic

The second day

The little circus donkey. Howard, H. L.
  In Burack, A. S. ed. One hundred plays for
    children p140-43   **808.82**

Little Claus and Big Claus
  Andersen, H. C. Great Claus and Little Claus
    In Andersen, H. C. Andersen's Fairy tales
      p33-45   **S C**
    In Andersen, H. C. The complete fairy
      tales and stories p8-19   **S C**
    In Andersen, H. Hans Andersen's Fairy
      tales p13-28   **S C**
    In Andersen, H. C. It's perfectly true, and
      other stories p230-45   **S C**
  Andersen, H. C. The story of Big Klaus and
    Little Klaus
    In Lang, A. ed. The yellow fairy book
      p225-36   **398.2**
    See also Heifer hide

The little cock. Hardendorff, J. B.   **398.2**
    See also Little rooster and the Turkish
  sultan

The little cowboy. Brown, M. W.
  In Gruenberg, S. M. ed. Favorite stories old
    and new p21-22   **808.8**

The little crow. Heady, E. B.
  In Heady, E. B. When the stones were soft
    p47-51   **398.2**

The little daughter of the Snow. Ransome, A.
  In Ransome, A. Old Peter's Russian tales
    p122-35   **398.2**
    See also Snowflake

Little Dog and Big Dog. Lindsay, M.
  In Association for Childhood Education In-
    ternational. Told under the magic
    umbrella p33-38   **S C**

Little dressmaker. Farjeon, E.
  In Farjeon, E. The little bookroom p125-37
      S C

The Little Drummer Boy (Carol)
  The Little Drummer Boy (k-2)   **783.6**

Little duck. Hatch, M. C.
  In Hatch, M. C. More Danish tales p33-48
      398.2

Little Duckling tries his voice. La Fleur, M.
  In Association for Childhood Education In-
    ternational. Told under the magic
    umbrella p5-7   **S C**

Little Eddie. Haywood, C.   **Fic**

Little Eddie goes to town. Haywood, C.
  In Gruenberg, S. M. ed. Favorite stories old
    and new p29-36   **808.8**

The little engine that could. Piper, W.   **E**

The little family. Lenski, L.   **E**

Little farmer
  Grimm, J. The little farmer
    In Grimm, J. Household stories p256-61
      398.2
  Grimm, J. The little peasant
    In Grimm, J. The complete Grimm's Fairy
      tales p311-16   **398.2**

Little Finger. Manning-Sanders, R.
  In Manning-Sanders, R. Gianni and the
    ogre p127-40   **398.2**

The little fisherman. Brown, M. W.
  In Gruenberg, S. M. comp. Let's hear a
    story p108-11   **808.8**

The little folks' presents. Grimm, J.
  In Grimm, J. The complete Grimm's Fairy
    tales p742-45   **398.2**
    See also Presents of the little folks

Little Fred and his fiddle
  Asbjørnsen, P. C. Little Freddy with his
    fiddle
    In Arbuthnot, M. H. comp. The Arbuthnot
      Anthology of children's literature
      p249-52   **808.8**
    In Arbuthnot, M. H. comp. Time for old
      magic p132-35   **398.2**
    In Asbjørnsen, P. C. Norwegian folk tales
      p61-66   **398.2**
  Little Frikk and his fiddle
    In Undset, S. ed. True and untrue, and
      other Norse tales p190-97   **398.2**

Little Frikk and his fiddle
  In Undset, S. ed. True and untrue, and
    other Norse tales p190-97   **398.2**
    See also Little Fred and his fiddle

Little Georgie sings a song. Lawson, R.
  In Johnson, E. ed. Anthology of children's
    literature p627-31   **808.8**

The little glass slipper. See Perrault, C. Cinderella   **398.2**

Little Goldenhood
  Marelles, C. The true history of Little Gol-
    den-hood
    In Lang, A. ed. The red fairy book p215-19
      398.2

The little good mouse. Aulnoy, Madame d'
  In Lang, A. ed. The red fairy book p146-57
      398.2
    See also Good little mouse

Little gray man. Hooke, H. M.
  In Hooke, H. M. Thunder in the moun-
    tains p135-48   **398.2**

The Little green fog
  In Lang, A. ed. The yellow fairy book p50-
    59   **398.2**

The little green ones. Andersen, H. C.
  In Andersen, H. C. The complete fairy
    tales and stories p851-52   **S C**
    See also Greenies

Little Gretchen and the wooden shoe. Harrison, E.
  In Harper, W. comp. Merry Christmas to
    you p111-23   **394.2**

The little guest. Bianco, M. W.
  In Sechrist, E. H. ed. It's time for Christ-
    mas p243-50   **394.2**

The little hare's clever trick. Hume, L. C.
  In Hume, L. C. Favorite children's stories
    from China and Tibet p115-19 **398.2**

Little head, big medicine. Jagendorf, M. A.
  In Jagendorf, M. A. Noodlehead stories
    from around the world p274-77 **398.2**

Little hen eagle. Aardema, V.
  In Aardema, V. Behind the back of the
    mountain p3-10   **398.2**

Little hero of Holland. Asbrand, K.
  In Burack, A. S. ed. One hundred plays for
    children p577-86   **808.82**

The little hill. Behn, H.   **811**

Little Hiram. Manning-Sanders, R.
  In Manning-Sanders, R. A choice of magic
    p200-15   **398.2**

Lobel, Arnold—*Continued*
(illus.) Benchley, N. The strange disappearance of Arthur Cluck   **E**
(illus.) Epstein, M. All about Jewish holidays   **296.4**
(illus.) Fox, P. Good Ethan   **E**
(illus.) Grimm, J. Hansel and Gretel   **398.2**
(illus.) Ish-Kishor, S. The Master of Miracle   **Fic**
(illus.) Jameson, C. The clay pot boy   **398.2**
(illus.) Morris, R. A. Seahorse   **597**
(illus.) Myrick, M. The Secret Three   **E**
(illus.) Parish, P. Dinosaur time   **568**
(illus.) Parish, P. Let's be early settlers with Daniel Boone   **745.5**
(illus.) Parish, P. Let's be Indians   **745.5**
(illus.) Prelutsky, J. Circus   **811**
(illus.) Selsam, M. E. Benny's animals, and how he put them in order   **591**
(illus.) Selsam, M. E. Greg's microscope   **578**
(illus). Selsam, M. E. Let's get turtles   **639**
(illus.) Selsam, M. E. Terry and the caterpillars   **595.7**
(illus.) Zolotow, C. The quarreling book   **E**
Lobo. Seton, E. T.
  In Authors' choice 2 p161-77   **S C**
Lobsenz, Norman M.
The first book of West Germany (4-7) **914.3**
Lobsters
Cook, J. J. The nocturnal world of the lobster (4-6)   **595**
Local transit
  See pages in the following books:
Hellman, H. Transportation in the world of the future p19-36 (5-7)   **380.5**
McLeod, S. How will we move all the people? p9-23 (6-7)   **380.5**
Localism. See English language—Provincialisms
Lochmaben harper
Nic Leodhas, S. The tale of the lay of the Lochmabern Harper
  In Nic Leodhas, S. By loch and by lin p31-42   **398.2**
Lockhard, Roget
Glaciers (1-3)   **551.3**
Lock-out time. Barrie, J. M.
  In Untermeyer, B. ed. The Golden Treasury of children's literature p426-35   **808.8**
Locks and keys
Kraske, R. Silent sentinels (5-7)   **683**
Lockwood, Julia
The lady who put salt in her coffee; play
  In Smith, M. R. ed. 7 plays & how to produce them p7-21   **792**
Lockwood, Myna
Macaroni: an American tune; excerpt
  In Association for Childhood Education International. Told under the Stars and Stripes p196-217   **S C**
Lockwood, Normand
  See pages in the following book:
Posell, E. Z. American composers p112-15 (5-7)   **920**
Locomotion. See Aeronautics; Animal locomotion; Automobiles; Boats and boating; Flight; Navigation; Transportation

Locomotives
    Fiction
Piper, W. The little engine that could   **E**
Locusts
Hogner, D. C. Grasshoppers and crickets (2-5)   **595.7**
  See also pages in the following books:
Ricciuti, E. R. Shelf pets p92-97 (5-7)   **639**
Villiard, P. Insects as pets p107-10 (5-7)   **595.7**
Loder, Dorothy
The land and people of Belgium (5-7) **914.93**
The land and people of Spain (5-7)   **914.6**
Lodewijk, T.
The Way things work. Special edition for young people. See The Way things work. Special edition for young people   **600**
Loeper, John J.
Going to school in 1776 (3-6)   **917.3**
Loewenstein, Bernice
(illus.) Coatsworth, E. Bess and the Sphinx   **Fic**
(illus.) Coatsworth, E. The Cat and the Captain   **Fic**
Lofting, Hugh
Doctor Dolittle (4-6)   **Fic**
Includes excerpts from the following books: The story of Doctor Dolittle; Doctor Dolittle's circus; The voyages of Doctor Dolittle; Doctor Dolittle's post office; Doctor Dolittle's caravan; Doctor Dolittle and the green canary; Doctor Dolittle and the secret lake; Doctor Dolittle's Puddleby adventures
Doctor Dolittle; criticism
  In MacCann, D. ed. The Black American in books for children: readings in racism p78-88   **028.5**
Doctor Dolittle learns animal language
  In Untermeyer, B. ed. The Golden Treasury of children's literature p273-77   **808.8**
Puddleby
  In Gruenberg, S. M. ed. Favorite stories old and new p226-28   **808.8**
The rarest animal of all
  In Johnson, E. ed. Anthology of children's literature p625-27   **808.8**
    About
  See pages in the following books:
Horn Book Reflections on children's books and reading p218-24   **028.5**
Miller, B. M. ed. Newbery Medal books: 1922-1955 p21-27   **028.5**
Log
Bowman, J. C. Leppä Pölkky and the blue cross
  In Bowman, J. C. Tales from a Finnish tupa p171-86   **398.2**
Logan, Rayford
(jt. auth.) Sterling, P. Four took freedom **920**
Loggerhead turtle. Scott, J. D.   **598.1**
Logging. See Lumber and lumbering
Logic. See Probabilities
Lohengrin; adaptation. Bulla, C. R.
  In Bull, C. R. Stories of favorite operas p79-89   **782.1**

"Loup-garou" in the woods. Carlson, N. S.
In Carlson, N. S. The talking cat, and
other stories of French Canada p77-
87   S C

The louse and the flea. Grimm, J.
In Grimm, J. The complete Grimm's Fairy
tales p158-60   398.2

Love, Katherine
(comp.) A little laughter (3-6)   821.08

Love, Nat
Felton, H. W. Nat Love, Negro cowboy (4-6)
92

Love
See pages in the following book:
LeShan, E. You and your feelings p75-94
(6-7)   155.5

The love crystal. Taylor, M.
In Arbuthnot, M. H. comp. The Arbuthnot
Anthology of children's literature
p344-46   808.8
In Arbuthnot, M. H. comp. Time for old
magic p221-23   398.2

Love poetry
Mizumura, K. If I were a cricket (k-2) 811

The lovebirds. Farjeon, E.
In Farjeon, E. The little bookroom p244-
47   S C

Lovejoy, Elijah Parish
See pages in the following books:
Chittenden, E. F. Profiles in black and white
p142-58 (5-7)   920
McNeer, M. Give me freedom p43-60 (5-7)
920

Lovelace, Maud Hart
Betsy-Tacy (2-4)   Fic
Queen of Summer
In Association for Childhood Education In-
ternational. Told under the Stars and
Stripes p102-14   S C
The Valentine Box (2-4)   Fic
The Valentine box; short story
In Cavanah, F. ed. Holiday roundup p41-
47   394.2

Loveliest rose in the world
Andersen, H. C. The loveliest rose in the
world
In Harper, W. comp. Easter chimes p129-
33   394.2
In Sechrist, E. H. ed. It's time for Easter
p198-201   394.2
Andersen, H. C. The world's most beautiful
rose
In Andersen, H. C. The complete fairy
tales and stories p390-92   S C

The lovelorn pig. Leach, M.
In Leach, M. The thing at the foot of the
bed, and other scary tales p65-67 S C

"Lovely." Andersen, H. C.
In Andersen, H. C. The complete fairy
tales and stories p650-56   S C

The lovely Myfanwy. De La Mare, W.
In De La Mare, W. A penny a day p64-
105   S C

Lovely wise hen. See Kijima, H. Little white
hen   398.2

Loving Laili
In Jacobs, J. ed. Indian fairy tales p51-65
398.2

Low, Edward
See pages in the following book:
Stockton, F. R. Buccaneers & pirates of our
coasts p202-11 (5-7)   910.4

Low, Joseph
(illus.) Bulla, C. R. More Stories of favorite
operas   782.1
(illus.) De La Iglesia, M. E. The cat and the
mouse, and other Spanish tales   398.2
(illus.) Fenton, S. H. Greece   913.38
(illus.) Goldin, A. Spider silk   595
(illus.) Hawes, J. Shrimps   595
(illus.) Longfellow, H. W. Paul Revere's ride
(Windmill Bks)   811
(illus.) Showers, P. Hear your heart 612
(illus.) Tresselt, A. The legend of the willow
plate   398.2
(illus.) Wright, W. W. The rainbow dictionary   423

Low, Juliette Gordon
Radford, R. L. Juliette Low: Girl Scout
founder (3-5)   92

Lowell, James Russell
At the castle gate
In Luckhardt, M. C. ed. Christmas comes
once more p97-103   394.2

Lowell, Percival
See pages in the following book:
Knight, D. C. The first book of Mars p62-69
(6-7)   523.4

Lowenheim, Alfred
(illus.) Gardner, R. The boys and girls book
about divorce   301.42

Lowenstein, Dyno
Graphs (5-7)   511

Lownsbery, Eloise
The boy knight of Reims; excerpt
In Ward, W. ed. Stories to dramatize p214-
18   372.6

Lowrey, Janette Sebring
Six silver spoons   E

Lowrie, Jean Elizabeth
Elementary school libraries   027.8

Loyalists, American. See American Loyalists

Loyola, Mary, Sister. See Vath, Mary Loyola,
Sister

Lubalin, Herb
(illus.) Mendoza, G. And I must hurry for sea
is coming in   811

Lubell, Cecil
Clothes tell a story (2-4)   391.09
(jt. auth.) Lubell, W. Green is for growing
581
(jt. auth.) Lubell, W. Picture signs & symbols
001.54

Lubell, Winifred
Green is for growing (3-5)   581
Picture signs & symbols (2-4)   001.54
(jt. auth.) Boyer, S. A. Gifts from the Greeks
913.28
(illus.) George, J. C. The moon of the mountain lions   599
(jt. auth.) Lubell, C. Clothes tell a story
391.09

Lubell, Winifred—*Continued*
(jt. auth.) Miller, I. P. The stitchery book
746.4
(illus.) Selsam, M. E. Birth of an island **551.4**
(illus.) Selsam, M. See through the sea **591.92**
(illus.) Sterling, D. Caterpillars **595.7**
(illus.) Sterling, D. Fall is here! **500.9**

Lucas the strong. Sechrist, E. H.
In Sechrist, E. H. Once in the first times
p196-204 **398.2**

Luce, Celia
(jt. auth.) Luce, W. Lou Gehrig: iron man of
baseball **92**

Luce, Willard
Lou Gehrig: iron man of baseball (3-5) **92**

Lucia Bride. Reel, A.
In Johnson, L. S. ed. Christmas stories
round the world p89-93 **394.2**

Lucia di Lammermoor; adaptation. Bulla, C. R.
In Bulla, C. R. Stories of favorite operas
p63-69 **782.1**

Lucian of Samothrace
Inside the monster
In Brown, M. ed. A cavalcade of sea leg-
ends p61-70 **808.8**

Luck can be found in a stick. Andersen, H. C.
In Andersen, H. C. The complete fairy
tales and stories p975-77 **S C**

Luck for fools. Jagendorf, M. A.
In Jagendorf, M. A. Noodlehead stories
from around the world p216-21 **398.2**

Luck may lie in a pin
Andersen, H. C. Luck can be found in a
stick
In Andersen, H. C. The complete fairy
tales and stories p975-77 **S C**

Luckhardt, Mildred Corell
The Advent wreath
In Luckhardt, M. C. ed. Christmas comes
once more p48-61 **394.2**
(ed.) Christmas comes once more (3-6) **394.2**
The daring venture
In Luckhardt, M. C. comp. Thanksgiving
p21-43 **394.2**
Happy Thanksgiving!
In Luckhardt, M. C. comp. Thanksgiving
p94-98 **394.2**
Harvest time the world around
In Luckhardt, M. C. comp. Thanksgiving
p319-26 **394.2**
A legend of the first Christmas tree
In Luckhardt, M. C. ed. Christmas comes
once more p110-18 **394.2**
Some North American Thanksgivings
In Luckhardt, M. C. comp. Thanksgiving
p132-48 **394.2**
(comp.) Thanksgiving (4-7) **394.2**

Lucky boy. Pearce, P.
In Pearce, P. What the neighbors did, and
other stories p107-123 **S C**

The lucky cook book for boys and girls. See
Moore, E. The Seabury Cook book for
boys and girls **641.5**

The lucky man. Leach, M.
In Leach, M. The thing at the foot of the
bed, and other scary tales p30 **S C**

Lucky Rose Tuttle. Jagendorf, M. A.
In Jagendorf, M. A. New England bean-
pot p79-83 **398.2**

Lucky scraps. Grimm, J.
In Grimm, J. More Tales from Grimm p59-
60 **398.2**
See also Flax leavings

Lucy. De La Mare, W.
In De La Mare, W. The magic jacket
p200-33 **S C**

Ludovici, L. J.
Origins of language (6-7) **401**

Ludovici, Raymonde
(illus.) Ludovici, L. J. Origins of language **401**

Ludwig, Helen
(illus.) Selsam, M. E. Play with seeds **582.072**

Lueders, Edward
(jt. comp.) Dunning, S. comp. Reflections on
a gift of watermelon pickle . . . and other
modern verse **811.08**

Lufbery, Raoul Gervais
See pages in the following book:
Gurney, G. Flying aces of World War I p77-
99 (4-7) **920**

Luke was there. Clymer, E. **Fic**

Lukiyanenko, Maia
Bloch, M. H. ed. Ukrainian folk tales **398.2**

The lull. Saki
In Authors' choice p23-30 **S C**

Lullabies
All the pretty horses **E**
Engvick, W. ed. Lullabies and night songs
(k-3) **784.6**
Yulya. Bears are sleeping (k-1) **784.6**
See also pages in the following books:
Association for Childhood Education Interna-
tional. Sung under the silver umbrella
p185-91 (k-2) **821.08**
Brewton, J. E. comp. Gaily we parade p187-
94 (3-6) **821.08**
Huffard, G. T. comp. My poetry book p108-
32 (5-7) **821.08**
Sechrist, E. H. ed. One thousand poems for
children p43-53 **821.08**
Untermeyer, L. ed. The Golden Treasury of
poetry p296-303 **821.08**
Untermeyer, L. ed. Rainbow in the sky p421-
33 (k-4) **821.08**
Untermeyer, L. ed. This singing world p341-
63 (4-7) **821.08**

Lullabies and night songs. Engvick, W. ed.
784.6

Lullaby. Bernhard, J. B.
In Association for Childhood Education International. Told under the Christmas tree p4-7 **808.8**

Lumber and lumbering
Kurelek, W. Lumberjack (3-5) **634.9**
Rich, L. D. The first book of lumbering (4-6)
634.9

Fiction
McCormick, D. J. Paul Bunyan swings his
axe (4-6) **398.2**
Rounds, G. Ol' Paul, the mighty logger (3-6)
398.2
Shephard, E. Paul Bunyan (5-7) **398.2**

Lumberjack. Kurelek, W.   634.9

Luminescence, Animal. See Bioluminescence

Lummis, Charles F.
Poh-hlaik, the cave boy
In A St Nicholas anthology p40-46   810.8

Lumumba, Patrice Emergy
See pages in the following books:
Crane, L. The land and people of the Congo
p41-50 (5-7)   916.75
McKown, R. The Republic of Zaïre p59-71
(4-6)   967.5

Luna. McClung, R. M.   595.7

Lunar bases
Bergaust, E. The next 50 years on the moon
(5-7)   629.45

Lunar eclipses. See Eclipses, Lunar

Lunar expeditions. See Space flight to the moon

Lunar petrology
Branley, F. M. Pieces of another world (5-7)
                                       552
Gallob, E. City rocks, city blocks, and the
moon (3-5)   552

Lunar probes
Branley, F. M. A book of moon rockets for
you (1-3)   629.4

Lund, Doris Herold
You ought to see Herbert's house   E

Lundgren, Max
Matt's grandfather   E

Lungs. See Respiration

Lupo, Dom
(illus.) Blassingame, W. Dan Beard, scoutmaster of America   92
(illus.) Luce, W. Lou Gehrig: iron man of
baseball   92
(illus.) Smith, P. Golf techniques: how to improve your game   796.352

Lurin, Larry
(illus.) Lewis, S. Making easy puppets 791.5

Lustig, Loretta
(illus.) Branley, F. M. Measure with metric
                                       389
(illus.) Morrison, L. comp. Best wishes, amen
                                    808.88
(illus.) Showers, P. Where does the garbage
go?   614.7

Lutonya. Jagendorf, M. A.
In Jagendorf, M. A. Noodlehead stories
from around the world p235-40 398.2

Lutz, Frank E.
Field book of insects of the United States
and Canada   595.7

Lyell, Sir Charles, 1st bart.
See pages in the following book:
Cottler, J. Heroes of civilization p359-76
(6-7)   920

Lying. See Truthfulness and falsehood

Lyle finds his mother. Waber, B.   E

Lyle, Lyle, crocodile. Waber, B.   E

Lynch, Brendan
(illus.) May, J. A new baby comes   612.6

Lynch, Don
(illus.) Hyde, M. O. For pollution fighters
only   614.7

Lynch, May
Finn McCool
In Kamerman, S. E. ed. Dramatized folk
tales of the world p218-26   812.08

Lynch, Patricia
See pages in the following book:
Horn Book Reflections on children's books
and reading p260-64   028.5

Lynx
Stories
Lippincott, J. W. The Wahoo bobcat (5-7)
                                       Fic

Lyon, Fred H.
(illus.) Beeler, N. F. Experiments in optical
illusion   535.072

Lyon, Jean Currens
Carpenter, A. Colombia   918.61
Carpenter, A. Uruguay   918.95

Lyon, Mary
See pages in the following book:
Daugherty, S. Ten brave women p63-79 (5-7)
                                       920

Lyons, John Henry
Stories of our American patriotic songs (4-7)
                                     784.7

Lyons, Oren
(illus.) Sneve, V. D. H. Jimmy Yellow Hawk
                                       Fic

Lysergic acid diethylamide
See pages in the following books:
Gorodetzky, C. W. What you should know
about drugs p44-57 (5-7)   613.8
Hyde, M. O. ed. Mind drugs p72-83 (5-7)
                                     613.8

M

M. C. Higgins, the great. Hamilton, V.   Fic

Ma Liang and his magic brush. Wyndham, R.
In Wyndham, R. Tales the people tell in
China p73-82   398.2

MA nDA LA. Adoff, A.   E

Maas, Julie
(illus.) Cooper, E. K. And everything nice
                                     641.3

Maas, Selve
The moon painters, and other Estonian folk
tales (4-6)   398.2
Contents: The moon painters; The gift of Father
Frost; The old traveler; The Wood of Tontla; The
birth of the River Emajogi; Tall Peter and Short
Peter; The creation of the wolf; The grateful prince;
The Rehepapp and Vanapagan; The goldspinners; The
wolf's food; The magic mirror; The clever peasant girl;
The water dwellers; The Northern Frog

The old traveler
In Arbuthnot, M. H. comp. The Arbuthnot
Anthology of children's literature
p285-87   808.8

Mabie, Hamilton Wright
Beowulf's fight with Grendel
In Johnson, E. ed. Anthology of children's
literature p497-502   808.8

Madian, Jon
Beautiful junk (2-5)   **Fic**

Madison, Dolley. See Madison, Dorothy (Payne) Todd

Madison, Dorothy (Payne) Todd
See pages in the following book:
Daugherty, S. Ten brave women p32-47 (5-7)   **920**

Madison, Steve
(illus.) Temko, F. Paper cutting   **736**

Madrid
See pages in the following book:
Loder, D. The land and people of Spain p103-10 (5-7)   **914.6**

Maestro, Giulio
(illus.) Branley, F. M. The beginning of the earth   **551**
(illus.) Charosh, M. Number ideas through pictures   **513**
(illus.) Cutler, K. N. Creative shellcraft   **745.55**
(illus.) Cutler, K. N. From petals to pinecones   **745.92**
(illus.) Delton, J. Two good friends   **E**
(illus.) Gans, R. Millions and millions of crystals   **548**
(illus.) Ginsburg, M. Three kittens   **E**
(illus.) Meyer, C. Milk, butter, and cheese   **641.3**
(illus.) Milgrom, H. Egg-ventures   **636.5**
(illus.) Riedman, S. R. Trees alive   **582**
(illus.) Sommer, E. The bread dough craft book   **745.5**

Maffia, Daniel
(illus.) Branley, F. M. Shakes, quakes, and shifts: earth tectonics   **551.4**

Magarac, Joe
See pages in the following books:
Carmer, C. comp. America sings p116-21 (5-7)   **784.4**
Malcolmson, A. Yankee Doodle's cousins p29-35 (4-7)   **398.2**
Shapiro, I. Heroes in American folklore p199-256 (4-7)   **398.2**

Magazines for libraries. Katz, B. ed.   **016.05**

Magazines for libraries; supplement. Katz, B. ed.   **016.05**

Magdalena. Shotwell, L. R.   **Fic**

Magdalena River, Colombia
See pages in the following book:
Landry, L. The land and people of Colombia p14-18 (5-7)   **918.61**

Magellan, Ferdinand
Syme, R. Magellan, first around the world (4-6)   **92**
See also pages in the following books:
Cottler, J. Heroes of civilization p26-36 (6-7)   **920**
Discoverers of the New World p53-63 (5-7)   **973.1**
Hall, E. The land and people of Argentina p68-72 (5-7)   **918.2**
Israel, C. E. Five ships west (4-6)   **92**

Magi
Branley, F. M. The Christmas sky (3-6) **232.9**

Magic
Helfman, H. Tricks with your fingers (3-6)   **793.8**
Kendall, L. Houdini: master of escape (6-7)   **92**
Kettelkamp, L. Magic made easy (4-7) **793.8**
Kettelkamp, L. Spooky magic (3-7)   **793.8**
Lamb, G. Mental magic tricks (5-7)   **793.8**
Leeming, J. Fun with magic (4-7)   **793.8**
Leeming, J. More Fun with magic (4-7) **793.8**
Lopshire, R. It's magic? (k-2)   **793.8**
McGovern, A. Squeals & squiggles & ghostly giggles (2-5)   **394.2**
Mulholland, J. Magic of the world (5-7)   **793.8**
Severn, B. Bill Severn's Big book of magic (6-7)   **793.8**
Severn, B. Magic across the table (5-7) **793.8**
Severn, B. Magic in your pockets (5-7) **793.8**
Van Rensselaer, A. Fun with magic (4-7)   **793.8**
White, L. B. So you want to be a magician? (5-7)   **793.8**
Wyler, R. Funny magic (1-3)   **793.8**
Wyler, R. Magic secrets (1-3)   **793.8**
Wyler, R. Spooky tricks (1-3)   **793.8**
See also Occult sciences; Tricks

Fiction
Fleischman, S. Mr Mysterious & Company (4-6)   **Fic**

Magic across the table. Severn, B.   **793.8**

The **magic** apples
In Baker, A. comp. The talking tree p118-22   **398.2**

Magic ball. Finger, C.
In Finger, C. Tales from silver lands p48-58   **398.2**
In Hoke, H. ed. Witches, witches, witches p56-64   **808.8**

The **magic** bed-knob. Norton, M.
In Norton, M. Bed-knob and broomstick p11-94   **Fic**

The **magic** belt. Manning-Sanders, R.
In Manning-Sanders, R. A book of princes and princesses p57-65   **398.2**

The **magic** bookshelf. Clapp, P.
In Kamerman, S. E. ed. Fifty plays for junior actors p136-50   **812.08**

The **magic** box. Peterson, M. N.
In Kamerman, S. E. ed. Dramatized folk tales of the world p265-77   **812.08**

The **magic** box. Sawyer, R.
In Sawyer, R. The way of the storyteller p219-25   **372.6**

The **magic** bridle. Manning-Sanders, R.
In Manning-Sanders, R. A book of charms and changelings p11-15   **398.2**

Magic by the lake. Eager, E.   **Fic**

Magic cap
Bowman, J. C. Pekka and the rogues
In Bowman, J. C. Tales from a Finnish tupa p231-36   **398.2**
Hart, J. The magic cap
In Sechrist, E. H. ed. It's time for story hour p117-20   **372.6**

Magnetism

Adler, I. Magnets (3-5)   **538**

See also pages in the following books:

Mark, S. J. A physics lab of your own p140-52 (5-7)   **530.72**

Stone, A. H. Turned on: a look at electricity (4-7)   **537.072**

Wyler, R. The first book of science experiments p57-69 (4-6)   **507.2**

    See also Compass; Electricity; Electromagnetism; Magnets

Magnets

Adler, I. Magnets (3-5)   **538**

Feravolo, R. V. Junior science book of magnets (3-5)   **538**

See also pages in the following books:

Renner, A. G. How to make and use electric motors p8-17 (5-7)   **621.46**

Wyler, R. Prove it! p53-64 (1-3)   **507.2**

The **magnificent** bald eagle. Turner, J. F.   **598.2**

The **Magpie** and her children

    In Hardendorff, J. B. ed. Just one more p15-16   **372.6**

The **magpie** with salt on her tail. Wahlenberg, A.

    In Olenius, E. comp. Great Swedish fairy tales p136-41   **398.2**

Magpie's nest

    In Jacobs, J. ed. English folk and fairy tales p204-06   **398.2**

Mahlmann, Lewis

Puppet plays for young players (4-7)   **791.5**

The plays included are: The magic mushrooms; The Frog Prince; The magic shoes; Why the sea is salt; The princess and the pea; Snow White and the seven dwarfs; Pinochio; The reluctant dragon; Jack and the beanstalk; The tinderbox; Alice's adventures in Wonderland; The Wizard of Oz

Mahmoud, Zaki Naguib

The land and people of Egypt (5-7)   **916.2**

Mahony, Bertha E.

(comp.) Illustrators of children's books: 1744-1945. See Illustrators of children's books: 1744-1945   **741.64**

(comp.) Illustrators of children's books: 1946-1956. See Illustrators of children's books: 1946-1956   **741.64**

(comp.) Illustrators of children's books: 1957-1966. See Illustrators of children's books: 1957-1966   **741.64**

    For other material compiled by this author see Miller, Bertha Mahony

Mahony, Elizabeth Winthrop. See Winthrop, Elizabeth

Mahy, Margaret

The dragon of an ordinary family

    In Hoke, H. comp. Dragons, dragons, dragons p139-44   **398.2**

Maid in the mirror. Carpenter, F.

    In Carpenter, F. Tales of a Chinese grandmother p226-34   **398.2**

Maid Maleen. Grimm, J.

    In Grimm, J. The complete Grimm's Fairy tales p801-07   **398.2**

The **Maid** of Brakel. Grimm. J.

    In Grimm, J. The complete Grimm's Fairy tales p623   **398.2**

The **maid** on the glass mountain. Aulaire, I. d'

    In Aulaire, I. d'. East of the sun and west of the moon p45-57   **398.2**

    See also Princess on the glass hill

The **maid** who defied Minerva. Cooke, F. J.

    In Ward, W. ed. Stories to dramatize p119-21   **372.6**

The **maiden** in the castle of rosy clouds. Östenson, H.

    In Olenius, E. comp. Great Swedish fairy tales p221-29   **398.2**

The **maiden** Suvarna. Manning-Sanders, R.

    In Manning-Sanders, R. A book of ghosts & goblins p95-99   **398.2**

The **maiden** with the black wooden bowl. Woolsey, J.

    In Sechrist, E. H. ed. It's time for story hour p160-63   **372.6**

Maiden without hands

Grimm, J. The girl without hands

    In Grimm, J. The complete Grimm's Fairy tales p160-66   **398.2**

Maiden's visit

Grimm, J. The elves ask a servant girl to be godmother

    In Grimm, J. About wise men and simpletons p33   **398.2**

Grimm, J. The elves: second story

    In Grimm, J. The complete Grimm's Fairy tales p199   **398.2**

    In Grimm, J. Household stories p173   **398.2**

Maidoff, Jules

(illus.) Yurchenco, H. ed. A fiesta of folk songs from Spain and Latin America   **784.7**

Mail-coach passengers

Andersen, H. C. The twelve passengers

    In Andersen, H. C. The complete fairy tales and stories p701-04   **S C**

Maine

Description and travel

McCloskey, R. Time of wonder   **E**

Fiction

Bradbury, B. Two on an island (4-6)   **Fic**

Bragdon, E. There is a tide (6-7)   **Fic**

Field, R. Calico bush (4-7)   **Fic**

Jewett, S. O. A white heron (4-6)   **Fic**

McCloskey, R. Blueberries for Sal   **E**

McCloskey, R. One morning in Maine   **E**

Rich, L. D. Three of a kind (4-6)   **Fic**

Mainguy, Marc

(illus.) Mendoza, G. Shadowplay   **791.5**

Maitland, Antony

(illus.) Garfield, L. Smith   **Fic**

(illus.) Lively, P. The ghost of Thomas Kempe   **Fic**

Maize. See Corn

The **majesty** of Grace. See Langton, J. Her Majesty, Grace Jones   **Fic**

Majka. Borski, L. M.

    In Borski, L. M. The jolly tailor, and other fairy tales p74-83   **398.2**

Makah Indians

Antiquities

Kirk, R. Hunters of the whale (6-7)   **970.3**

Make a joyful noise unto the Lord! The life of Mahalia Jackson, queen of gospel singers. Jackson, J.   **92**

The **man** who didn't wash his dishes. Krasilovsky, P.   **E**

The **man** who learned the language of the animals. Arnott, K.
In Arnott, K. African myths and legends p5-12   **398.2**

The **man** who looked for death. Courlander, H.
In Courlander, H. Olode the hunter, and other tales from Nigeria p15-18
398.2

The **man** who lost his head. Bishop, C. H.   **E**

The **man** who missed the Tay Bridge Train. Nic Leodhas, S.
In Nic Leodhas, S. Twelve great black cats, and other eerie Scottish tales p127-45   **398.2**

The **man** who planted onions. Kim, S.
In Kim, S. The story bag p11-16   **398.2**

Man who rode the bear. Credle, E.
In Credle, E. Tall tales from the high hills, and other stories p100-14   **398.2**

The **man** who sang the sillies. Ciardi, J.   **811**

The **man** who sold a ghost. Wyndham, R.
In Wyndham, R. Tales the people tell in China p48-51   **398.2**

Man who stayed too long. Brenner, A.
In Brenner, A. The boy who could do anything, & other Mexican folk tales p56-59   **398.2**

The **man** who stole a rope. Wyndham, R.
In Wyndham, R. Tales the people tell in China p38-39   **398.2**

Man who was going to mind the house
Asbjörnsen, P. C. The husband who was to mind the house
In Arbuthnot, M. H. comp. The Arbuthnot Anthology of children's literature p246-47   **808.8**
In Arbuthnot, M. H. comp. Time for old magic p129-30   **398.2**
In Asbjörnsen, P. C. East of the sun and west of the moon, and other tales p19-22   **398.2**
In Martignoni, M. E. ed. The illustrated treasury of children's literature p161-62   **808.8**
Gág, W. Gone is gone   **398.2**
—Same
In Haviland, V. comp. The fairy tale treasury p48-55   **398.2**
In Johnson, E. ed. Anthology of children's literature p152-55   **808.8**
Husband who was left to mind the house
In Hutchinson, V. S. ed. Candle-light stories p85-89   **398.2**
In Undset, S. ed. True and untrue, and other Norse tales p198-201   **398.2**
Wiesner, W. Turnabout   **398.2**

The **man** who would know magic. Wyndham, R.
In Wyndham, R. Tales the people tell in China p67-72   **398.2**

The **man** who wouldn't sell his pumpkin. Kelly, E. P.
In Johnson, E. ed. Anthology of children's literature p861-65   **808.8**

The **man** whose trade was tricks. Papashvily, G.
In Sechrist, E. H. ed. It's time for story hour p106-10   **372.6**

The **man** with a lion head in a can. Davis, R.
In Davis, R. The lion's whiskers p184-89
398.2

The **man** with the bag. Colum, P.
In Colum, P. The Stone of Victory, and other tales of Padraic Colum p76-84
398.2

Man with the wen
Uchida, Y. Old man with the bump
In Uchida, Y. The dancing kettle, and other Japanese folk tales p37-45
398.2

Manabush and the moose. Hardendorff, J. B.
In Hardendorff, J. B. ed. Just one more p24-25   **372.6**

Manawyddan son of the Boundless. Morris, K.
In Hazeltine, A. I. ed. Hero tales from many lands p149-59   **398.2**

Mancrow, bird of darkness. Sherlock, P.
In Sherlock, P. West Indian folk-tales p65-70   **398.2**

Mandala. See Adoff, A. MA nDA LA   **E**

Mandarin and the butterflies. Carpenter, F.
In Carpenter, F. Tales of a Chinese grandmother p198-205   **398.2**

Mandau Indians
See pages in the following book:
Hofsinde, R. Indians at home p48-56 (4-7)
728

Mandell, Muriel
Make your own musical instruments (3-7)
781.9

Manhattan is missing. Hildick, E. W.   **Fic**

Mann, Peggy
Amelia Earhart: first lady of flight (3-5)   **92**
My dad lives in a downtown hotel (3-5)   **Fic**
The street of the flower boxes (3-5)   **Fic**
The street of the flower boxes; excerpt
In Association for Childhood Education International. Told under the city umbrella p25-46   **S C**
That new baby   **E**

Manned space flight. See Astronauts; Outer space—Exploration; Space medicine; also names of projects, e.g. Skylab Project

Manners. See Courtesy; Etiquette

Manners and customs
Berry, E. Eating and cooking around the world (5-7)   **641.3**
See also pages in the following book:
Childcraft: the how and why library v9 **031**
See also Caste; Chivalry; Costume; Etiquette; Festivals; Funeral rites and ceremonies; Holidays; Marriage customs and rites; Rites and ceremonies; also names of ethnic groups and countries with the subdivision Social life and customs, e.g. Indians of North America—Social life and customs; China—Social life and customs

Mannikin Spanalong. Manning-Sanders, R.
In Manning-Sanders, R. A book of sorcerers and spells p33-36   **398.2**

Manufactures
See pages in the following book:
The Way things work. Special edition for
young people p255-73 (6-7)   **600**
    See also Machinery; also names of in-
dustries, e.g. Paper making and trade;
and names of countries with the subdivision Industries, e.g. Sweden—Industries

Manures. See Fertilizers and manures

Ms. found in a bottle. Poe, E. A.
    In Poe, E. A. Tales of terror and fantasy
p55-66   **S C**

The **many** faces of man. McKern, S. S.   **572**

Many-Fur. Grimm, J.
    In Grimm, J. The juniper tree, and other
tales from Grimm v2 p236-44   **398.2**
    See also Many-furred creature

Many-furred creature
Grimm, J. Allerleirauh
    In Grimm, J. The complete Grimm's Fairy
tales p326-31   **398.2**
    In Lang, A. ed. The green fairy book
p276-81   **398.2**
Grimm, J. Many-Fur
    In Grimm, J. The juniper tree, and other
tales from Grimm v2 p236-44   **398.2**

Many hands cooking. Cooper, T. T.   **641.5**

Many, many weddings in one corner house.
Sandburg, C.
    In Sandburg, C. Rootabaga stories v2 p19-
25   **S C**
    In Sandburg, C. The Sandburg treasury
p95-97   **818**

Many moons. Thurber, J.   **Fic**
—Same
    In Johnson, E. ed. Anthology of children's
literature p617-21   **808.8**
    In Johnson, S. P. ed. The Princesses p234-
49   **S C**

Many wives. Chrisman, A. B.
    In Chrisman, A. B. Shen of the sea p111-
21   **S C**

Mao, Tse-tung
    See pages in the following book:
Rau, M. Our world: the People's Republic
of China p29-33 (6-7)   **915.1**

Maoris
    See pages in the following book:
Kaula, E. M. The land and people of New
Zealand p78-85, 94-98 (5-7)   **919.31**

Map drawing
Brown, L. A. Map making (5-7)   **526**
Hirsch, S. C. Mapmakers of America (5-7)
          973.1
McFall, C. Maps mean adventure (5-7) **526**
Oliver, J. E. What we find when we look
at maps (3-5)   **526**

Map making. Brown, L. A.   **526**

Maple
Selsam, M. E. Maple tree (2-4)   **582**

Maple Street; excerpt. Agle, N. H.
    In Association for Childhood Education
International. Told under the city
umbrella p81-102   **S C**

Maple sugar
    See pages in the following book:
Lavine, S. A. Indian corn and other gifts
p29-36 (4-7)   **641.3**
    Fiction
Watson, N. D. Sugar on snow   **E**

Maple tree. Selsam, M. E.   **582**

Mapmakers of America. Hirsch, S. C.   **973.1**

Mapp, Frances
The ogre who built a bridge
    In Kamerman, S. E. ed. Dramatized folk
tales of the world p278-87   **812.08**

Maps
Brown, L. A. Map making (5-7)   **526**
McFall, C. Maps mean adventure (5-7) **526**
Oliver, J. E. What we find when we look
at maps (3-5)   **526**
Rhodes, D. How to read a city map (1-4)
          912

    See also pages in the following book:
Boy Scouts of America. Fieldbook p15-27
          369.43

    See also Atlases

Maps mean adventure. McFall, C.   **526**

Mara, Thalia
First steps in ballet (4-7)   **792.8**

Mara, daughter of the Nile. McGraw, E. J.
          Fic

Marais, Josef
Windbird and the Sun
    In Arbuthnot, M. H. comp. The Arbuth-
not Anthology of children's literature p326-29   **808.8**
    In Arbuthnot, M. H. comp. Time for old
magic p203-06   **398.2**

The **Marble** boy. Travers, P. L.
    In Johnson, E. ed. Anthology of children's
literature p639-48   **808.8**

March and the shepherd. Vittorini, D.
    In Arbuthnot, M. H. comp. The Arbuth-
not Anthology of children's literature p269-70   **808.8**
    In Arbuthnot, M. H. comp. Time for old
magic p152-53   **398.2**

Marco Polo's adventures in China   **92**

Marconi, Guglielmo, Marchese
    See pages in the following book:
Cottler, J. Heroes of civilization p260-64
(6-7)   **920**

Marcus, Judith
(jt. auth.) Marcus, R. B. Fiesta time in Mexico   **394.2**

Marcus, Rebecca B.
Fiesta time in Mexico (4-6)   **394.2**
The first book of the cliff dwellers (4-7)
          970.4
The first book of volcanoes & earthquakes
(5-7)   **551.2**

Marcus and Narcissa Whitman, Oregon pioneers. Place, M. T.   **92**

Marduk and the dragon. Mackenzie, D. A.
    In Hoke, H. comp. Dragons, dragons,
dragons p51-56   **398.2**

Mare, Walter de la. See De La Mare, Walter

Marelles, Charles
Drakestail
  In Lang, A. ed. The red fairy book p202-
  07   398.2
The ratcatcher
  In Lang, A. ed. The red fairy book p208-
  14   398.2
The true history of Little Golden-hood
  In Lang, A. ed. The red fairy book p215-
  19   398.2
Margai, Milton
  See pages in the following book:
Clifford, M. L. The land and people of
  Sierra Leone p78-88 (5-7)   916.6
Margrette. Manning-Sanders, R.
  In Manning-Sanders, R. A book of mer-
  maids p46-53   398.2
Marguerite de Angeli's Book of nursery and
  Mother Goose rhymes. Mother Goose 398.8
Margules, Gabriele
  (illus.) Reed, G. comp. Bird songs   821.08
Mari, Enzo
  (jt. auth.) Mari, I. The chicken and the egg
                                           E
Mari, Iela
  The chicken and the egg   E
Maria-Fly. De La Mare, W.
  In De La Mare, W. The magic jacket p72-
  88   S C
Maria sat on the fire. Brenner, A.
  In Brenner, A. The boy who could do any-
  thing, & other Mexican folk tales
  p129-32   398.2
Mariana
  (illus.) Janice. Little Bear's Christmas   E
  (illus.) Janice. Little Bear's Thanksgiving E
Maria's Christmas song. Meyer, E. P.
  In Johnson, L. S. ed. Christmas stories
  round the world p81-86   394.2
Mariette, Auguste Ferdinand François
  See pages in the following book:
Van Duyn, J. The Egyptians p68-74 (6-7)
                                       913.32
Marigold garden. Greenaway, K.   821
Marihuana
  See pages in the following books:
Gorodetzky, C. W. What you should know
  about drugs p30-43 (5-7)   613.8
Hyde, M. O. ed. Mind drugs p40-59 (5-7)
                                       613.8
Marijuana. See Marihuana
Marín, Luis Muñoz. See Muñoz Marín, Luis
Marine animals
  Fenton, C. L. In prehistoric seas (4-7) 560
  Goldin, A. The sunlit sea (1-3)   574.92
  Holling, H. C. Pagoo (4-7)   595
  Jacobs, L. Wonders of an oceanarium (3-7)
                                       591.92
  List, I. K. Questions and answers about sea-
  shore life (4-6)   591.92
  Selsam, M. See through the sea (2-4) 591.92
  Selsam, M. E. Underwater zoos (4-6) 639
  Waters, B. Salt-water aquariums (5-7) 639
  See also pages in the following books:
  Hyde, M. O. Animal clocks and compasses
  p12-21 (5-7)   591.5

Parker, B. M. The new Golden Treasury of
  natural history p72-91 (5-7)   500.9
Silverstein, A. The excretory system p46-53
  (4-6)   574.1
Silverstein, A. Metamorphosis: the magic
  change p46-66 (4-6)   591.3
  See also Corals; Fishes; Fresh-water
  animals
Marine aquariums
  Selsam, M. E. Underwater zoos (4-6) 639
  Waters, B. Salt-water aquariums (5-7) 639
  See also pages in the following books:
Pringle, L. ed. Discovering nature indoors
  p22-28 (5-7)   591
Simon, S. Science at work: projects in ocean-
  ography p57-64 (5-7)   551.4
Marine biology
  Buck, M. W. Along the seashore (3-6) 574.92
  Clemons, E. Tide pools & beaches (3-5)
                                       574.92
  Cooper, E. K. Science on the shores and
  banks (5-7)   574.92
  Kohn, B. The beachcomber's book (3-7)
                                       745.5
  Milne, L. When the tide goes far out (4-7)
                                       574.92
  Selsam, M. E. See along the shore (3-5)
                                       574.92
  Zim, H. S. Seashores (5-7)   574.92
  See also pages in the following books:
  Burgess, R. F. Exploring a coral reef p17-39
  (4-6)   574.92
  Pringle, L. This is a river p17-39 (4-6) 551.4
  Simon, S. Science at work: projects in ocean-
  ography p45-56 (5-7)   551.4
  Williams, J. Oceanography p47-59 (5-7)
                                       551.4
  See also Fresh-water biology; Marine
  animals; Marine ecology; Marine plants;
  Marine resources
Marine ecology
  Burgess, R. F. Exploring a coral reef (4-6)
                                       574.92
  See also pages in the following book:
  Johnson, W. W. The story of sea otters p76-
  87 (4-7)   599
Marine engineering
  Corbett, S. What makes a boat float? (3-5)
                                       532
Marine fauna. See Marine animals
Marine flora. See Marine plants
Marine geology. See Submarine geology
Marine mineral resources
  See pages in the following book:
  Brindze, R. The sea p55-61 (5-7)   333.9
Marine plants
  Goldin, A. The sunlit sea (1-3)   574.92
  List, I. K. Questions and answers about sea-
  shore life (4-6)   591.92
  See also Algae; Fresh-water plants
Marine resources
  Brindze, R. The sea (5-7)   333.9
  Fenten, D. X. Harvesting the sea (4-6) 333.9
  See also pages in the following book:
  Berger, M. Oceanography lab p66-70 (4-6)
                                       551.4
  See also Fisheries

Martin and Abraham Lincoln: excerpt. Coblentz, C. C.
In Arbuthnot, M. H. comp. The Arbuthnot Anthology of children's literature p756-61 **808.8**

Martin de Porres, Saint
Bishop, C. H. Martin de Porres, hero (5-7) **92**

Martin Pippin in the apple orchard. Farjeon, E. **S C**

Martinetti, Don
(illus.) Ehret, W. The international book of Christmas carols **783.6**

Martinez, John
(illus.) Holden, R. Famous fossil finds **560**
(illus.) Muehl, L. The hidden year of Devlin Bates **Fic**

Martínez, María Montoya
See pages in the following book:
Gridley, M. E. American Indian women p105-18 (5-7) **920**

Marv. Sachs, M. **Fic**

The marvel of glass. Buehr, W. **666**

The marvelous misadventures of Sebastian. Alexander, L. **Fic**

The marvelous musician. Grimm, J.
In Lang, A. ed. The red fairy book p354-56 **398.2**
See also Wonderful musician

The marvelous pear seed. Wyndham, R.
In Wyndham, R. Tales the people tell in China p20-24 **398.2**

The marvelous Time Machine. Boiko, C.
In Boiko, C. Children's plays for creative actors p173-84 **812**

Marvin, Frederic
(illus.) Cleaver, V. Grover **Fic**

Mary Beth
(jt. auth.) Charlip, R. Handtalk **419**

Mary Celeste (Brig)
See pages in the following book:
Cohen, D. Curses, hexes, & spells p60-68 (5-7) **133.4**

Mary, Mary, so contrary
Bowman, J. C. The pig-headed wife
In Arbuthnot, M. H. comp. The Arbuthnot Anthology of children's literature p261-62 **808.8**
In Bowman, J. C. Tales from a Finnish tupa p201-04 **398.2**

Mary Ellis has a birthday party. Newell, H.
In Association for Childhood Education International. Told under spacious skies p88-104 **S C**

Mary Jane. Sterling D. **Fic**

Mary Jo's grandmother. Udry, J. M. **E**

Mary Poppins. Travers, P. L. **Fic**

Marya Morevna
Ralston, W. R. S. The death of Koschei the Deathless
In Lang, A. ed. The red fairy book p42-53 **398.2**

Maryland
Fiction
Carlson, N. S. The half sisters (4-6) **Fic**

Masai
Bleeker, S. The Masai (4-7) **916.7**

Masaryk, Thomas Garrigue
See pages in the following book:
Hall, E. The land and people of Czechoslovakia p82-88 (5-7) **914.37**

Masefield, John
The boy on a broomstick
In Hope-Simpson, J. ed. A cavalcade of witches p78-82 **808.8**
The midnight folk
In Colwell, E. ed. A storyteller's choice p104-17 **372.6**

Masked prowler: the story of a raccoon. George, J. L. **599**

Masks and mask makers. Hunt, K. **391**

Masks (for the face)
Baylor, B. They put on masks (1-4) **391**
Hunt, K. Masks and mask makers (5-7) **391**
Lewis, S. Folding paper masks **736**

Masks (Sculpture)
Alkema, C. J. Monster masks **745.59**
See also pages in the following book:
Pettit, F. H. How to make whirligigs and whimmy diddles, and other American folkcraft objects p239-53 (5-7) **745.5**

Mason, Bernard S.
The book of Indian-crafts and costumes (5-7) **745.5**

Mason, F. Van Wyck
The winter at Valley Forge (5-7) **973.3**

Mason, George F.
Animal baggage (4-7) **591.5**
Animal clothing (4-7) **591.4**
Animal feet (4-7) **591.4**
Animal habits (4-7) **591.5**
Animal homes (4-7) **591.5**
Animal sounds (4-7) **591.5**
Animal tails (4-7) **591.4**
Animal teeth (4-7) **591.4**
Animal tools (4-7) **591.4**
Animal tracks (4-7) **591.5**
Animal vision (4-7) **591.4**
Animal weapons (4-7) **591.4**
The bear family (4-7) **599**
The wildlife of North America (5-7) **639**
(illus.) Shuttlesworth, D. E. The wildlife of South America **591.9**

Mason, Miriam E.
Caroline and her kettle named Maud (2-4) **Fic**

Masoy and the ape. Sechrist, E. H.
In Sechrist, E. H. Once in the first times p110-18 **398.2**

Mass communication. See Communication; Telecommunication

Mass media. See Moving pictures; Radio broadcasting; Television broadcasting

Massachusetts
Fiction
Colver, A. The wayfarer's tree (5-7) **Fic**
Hightower, F. Dark horse of Woodfield (5-7) **Fic**

History—Colonial period
Beck, B. L. The Pilgrims of Plymouth (5-7) **974.4**

Massachusetts—History—Continued

Daugherty, J. The landing of the Pilgrims (5-7) **974.4**

Dickinson, A. The Colony of Massachusetts (5-7) **974.4**

Jacobs, W. J. William Bradford of Plymouth Colony (4-6) **92**

Smith, E. B. ed. Pilgrim courage (5-7) **974.4**

Weisgard, L. The Plymouth Thanksgiving (3-5) **974.4**

History—Colonial period—Fiction

Clapp, P. Constance (5-7) **Fic**

Fisher, L. E. The warlock of Westfall (5-7) **Fic**

Massassoit, Wampanoag chief

See pages in the following book:

Johnston, J. The Indians and the strangers p29-33 (2-5) **920**

Masséna, Noëlle

(illus.) Winthrop, E. Walking away **Fic**

Massey, Jeanne

The littlest witch **E**

Massie, Kim

(illus.) Gavett, B. Skiing for beginners **796.9**

Masson, Elsie

The witch of Lok Island

In Harper, W. comp. Ghosts and goblins p176-91 **394.2**

In Hoke, H. ed. Witches, witches, witches p206-18 **808.8**

Masten, Helen Adams

Jordan, A. M. Children's classics **028.52**

Master and his pupil

Boggs, R. S. Black magic

In Boggs, R. S. Three golden oranges, and other Spanish folk tales p125-37 **398.2**

Godin, A. The magician and his pupil

In Green, R. L. ed. A cavalcade of magicians p179-89 **808.8**

Grimm, J. The sorcerer's apprentice

In Grimm, J. More Tales from Grimm p197-205 **398.2**

Master and his pupil

In Jacobs, J. ed. English folk and fairy tales p74-77 **398.2**

Williams-Ellis, A. The magician and his pupil

In Williams-Ellis, A. Fairy tales from the British Isles p181-85 **398.2**

See also Magician's pupil; Sorcerer's apprentice

The **master** and the servant. Tashjian, V. A.

In Johnson, E. ed. Anthology of children's literature p329-31 **808.8**

In Tashjian, V. A. Once there was and was not p29-38 **398.2**

The **master** cat. Perrault, C.

In Arbuthnot, M. H. comp. The Arbuthnot Anthology of children's literature p213-16 **808.8**

In Arbuthnot, M. H. comp. Time for old magic p90-92 **398.2**

In Lang, A. ed. The blue fairy book p141-47 **398.2**

In Opie, I. ed. The classic fairy tales p113-16 **398.2**

See also Puss in boots

Master ghost and I. Softly, B.

In Ireson, B. comp. Haunting tales p256-70 **S C**

Master Jacob. Pyle, H.

In Pyle, H. The wonder clock p161-74 **398.2**

Master James' nightmare. Shepard, R. A.

In Shepard, R. A. Conjure tales p43-58 **S C**

Master James' nightmare. Sutherland, Z.

In Arbuthnot, M. H. comp. The Arbuthnot Anthology of children's literature p386-91 **808.8**

Master-maid

Asbjørnsen, P. C. The master-maid

In Lang, A. ed. The blue fairy book p120-35 **398.2**

The Mastermaid

In Undset, S. ed. True and untrue, and other Norse tales p37-56 **398.2**

Master of all masters

In Arbuthnot, M. H. comp. The Arbuthnot Anthology of children's literature p157-58 **808.8**

In Arbuthnot, M. H. comp. Time for old magic p14-15 **398.2**

In Hutchinson, V. S. ed. Candle-light stories p19-21 **398.2**

In Jacobs, J. ed. English folk and fairy tales p230-31 **398.2**

In Johnson, E. ed. Anthology of children's literature p196 **808.8**

The **Master** of Miracle. Ish-Kishor, S. **Fic**

The **master** of the strait. Waite, H. E.

In Kamerman, S. E. ed. A treasury of Christmas plays p198-208 **812.08**

Master painters of the Renaissance. Jacobs, D. **759.5**

Master Pfriem. Grimm, J.

In Grimm, J. The complete Grimm's Fairy tales p720-24 **398.2**

Master thief

Asbjornsen, P. C. The master thief

In Lang, A. ed. The red fairy book p67-81 **398.2**

Grimm, J. The master-thief

In Grimm, J. The complete Grimm's Fairy tales p773-80 **398.2**

In Grimm, J. The juniper tree, and other tales from Grimm v 1 p113-28 **398.2**

In Undset, S. ed. True and untrue, and other Norse tales p213-32 **398.2**

See also Jack and the doctor's girl

The **master** thief and the dragon. Green, R. L.

In Green, R. L. ed. A cavalcade of dragons p133-37 **808.8**

The **Mastermaid**

In Undset, S. ed. True and untrue, and other Norse tales p37-56 **398.2**

See also Master-maid

Masters, Kelly Ray. See Ball, Zachary

The **Mastersingers** of Nuremberg; adaptation. Bulla, C. R.

In Bulla, C. R. Stories of favorite operas p101-13 **782.1**

Mastodon

See pages in the following book:

McHargue, G. Mummies p18-32 (5-7) **393**

Mastri, Fiore
(illus.) Grant, B. The cowboy encyclopedia
917.803

Mastri, Jackie
(illus.) Grant, B. The cowboy encyclopedia
917.803

The matchlock gun. Edmonds, W. D. **Fic**

Materia medica. See Anesthetics; Drugs; Poisons

Mathematical drawing. See Geometrical drawing

Mathematical games for one or two. Charosh, M.
793.7

Mathematical recreations
Adler, I. Magic house of numbers (6-7) 793.7
Barr, G. Entertaining with number tricks (5-7)
793.7
Charosh, M. Mathematical games for one or
two (1-4)   793.7
See also pages in the following book:
Mulac, M. E. Educational games for fun p 1-
47   372.1

Mathematical sets. See Set theory

Mathematicians
Lewis, C. Benjamin Banneker: the man who
saved Washington (5-7)   92

Mathematics
Bendick, J. Names, sets and numbers (2-5)
511
See also Arithmetic; Geometry; Me-
chanics; Mensuration; Number theory
Encyclopedias
Bendick, J. Mathematics illustrated dictio-
nary (4-7)   510.3

Mathematics illustrated dictionary. Bendick, J.   510.3

Mathews, William H.
Korea—North & South—in pictures (5-7)
915.19

Mathewson, Christopher
See pages in the following book:
Epstein, S. Baseball Hall of Fame: stories of
champions p24-43 (3-5)   920

Mathiesen, Egon
The blue-eyed pussy
In Gruenberg, S. M. ed. Favorite stories
old and new p152-55   808.8

Mathis, Sharon Bell
Ray Charles (2-5)   92
Sidewalk story (3-5)   **Fic**

Matilda, Princess of England, consort of Geoffrey, count of Anjou
Arbuthnot, M. H. comp. The Arbuthnot Anthology of children's literature p778-81
808.8

Matsuno, Masako
A pair of red clogs   **E**

Matsutani, Miyoko
The crane maiden (k-3)   398.2

Matter
Simon, S. Wet & dry (1-3)   530.4
See also pages in the following book:
Mark, S. J. A physics lab of your own p11-
42 (5-7)   530.72

A matter of brogues. Sawyer, R.
In Sawyer, R. The way of the storyteller
p259-70   372.6

A matter of miracles. Fenton, E.   **Fic**

Matternes, Jay H.
(illus.) Jackson, K. Dinosaurs   568

Matters of fact. Fisher, M.   028.52

Matterson, Elizabeth
(comp.) Games for the very young (k-1)
796.1

Matthew, Mark, Luke and John. Buck, P. S. **Fic**

Matthews, William H.
The earth's crust (5-7)   551
The story of glaciers and the ice age (5-7)
551.3
The story of the earth (5-7)   551
The story of volcanoes and earthquakes (4-6)
551.2

Matthiesen, Thomas
ABC   E
Things to see   E

Matt's grandfather. Lundgren, M.   E

Matulay, Laszlo
(illus.) Carlson, B. W. Act it out   792
(illus.) Carlson, B. W. Do it yourself! 793
(illus.) Hosford, D. By his own might 398.2

Matzeliger, Jan Ernest
See pages in the following books:
Hayden, R. C. Eight Black American inven-
tors p60-77 (6-7)   920
Rollins, C. H. They showed the way p93-96
(5-7)   920

Maud, consort of Henry V, Emperor of the
Holy Roman Empire. See Matilda, Princess of England, consort of Geoffrey, count
of Anjou

Maugham, W. Somerset
Princess September
In Johnson, S. P. ed. The Princesses p32-
49   **S C**

Maui captures the sun; puppet play.
Adair, M. W.
In Adair, M. W. Folk puppet plays for
the social studies p33-36   791.5

Maui the fire-bringer
In Courlander, H. ed. Ride with the sun
p14-19   398.2

Maui the great. Courlander, H.
In Courlander, H. The tiger's whisker,
and other tales and legends from
Asia and the Pacific p132-39   398.2

Maui traps Sun. Thompson, V. L.
In Thompson, V. L. Hawaiian myths, of
earth, sea, and sky p60-64   398.2

Maupassant, Guy de
On the river; adaptation. See Hardendorff,
J. B. On the river

Maurice's room. Fox, P.   **Fic**

Maurice's room; excerpt. Fox, P.
In Association for Childhood Education
International. Told under the city
umbrella p 1-6   **S C**

Maury, Jean West
(comp.) Bible. Selections. A first Bible 220.5

Meise, Fred
(illus.) Cameron, E. Time and Mr Bass **Fic**
Die **Meistersingen** von Nürnberg. See The
Mastersingers of Nuremberg
Melanesia
See pages in the following book:
May, C. P. Oceania: Polynesia, Melanesia,
Micronesia p97-115 (5-7)   **919**
Melbo, Irving Robert
Our country's national parks (5-7)   **917.3**
Melbo, Robert Irving
Melbo, I. R. Our country's national parks
917.3
Melcher, Frederic Gershom
See pages in the following book:
Miller, B. M. ed. Newbery Medal books:
1922-1955 p 1-5   **028.5**
Melchior, Hathaway Kale
Visit to the planets
In Kamerman, S. E. ed. Fifty plays for
junior actors p372-85   **812.08**
The **Melendy** family. Enright, E. See note under
Enright, E. The Saturdays   **Fic**
Melindy's medal. Faulkner, G.   **Fic**
Melisande. Nesbit, E.
In Johnson, S. P. ed. The Princesses p138-
63   **S C**
Meltzer, Milton
(ed.) In their own words (6-7)   **301.45**
A light in the dark; the life of Samuel Grid-
ley Howe (6-7)   **92**
(jt. auth.) Lader, L. Margaret Sanger: pioneer
of birth control   **92**
Melzack, Ronald
The day Tuk became a hunter & other
Eskimo stories (3-6)   **398.2**
The day Tuk became a hunter; The Owl and the
Raven; The Sedna legend; Netchillik and the bear;
The boy who became a reindeer; How the Raven
brought light to the world; The witch; Leealura and
Maleytato; The woman who raised a bear as her son;
The last of the thunderbirds
Member of the gang. Rinkoff, B.   **Fic**
Memorial Day
See pages in the following book:
Sechrist, E. H. Red letter days p124-30 **394.2**
Drama
See pages in the following book:
Fisher, A. Holiday programs for boys and
girls p336-37 (4-7)   **812**
Poetry
See pages in the following book:
Sechrist, E. H. comp. Poems for red letter
days p133-38   **821.08**
Memorial Day in the desert. Paine, R. D.
In Cavanah, F. ed. Holiday roundup p156-
62   **394.2**
Memories of Christmas. Thomas, D.
In Reeves, J. comp. The Christmas book
p168-76   **394.2**
Men of different colors. Heady, E. B.
In Arbuthnot, M. H. comp. The Arbuthnot
Anthology of children's literature
p316-18   **808.8**
In Heady, E. B. When the stones were soft
p91-94   **398.2**

Men of iron; excerpt. Pyle, H.
In Johnson, E. ed. Anthology of children's
literature p855-57   **808.8**
Men of science and invention (5-7)   **609**
Men of the wallet. Bowman, J. C.
In Bowman, J. C. Tales from a Finnish
tupa p12-24   **398.2**
Men, ships, and the sea. Villiers, A.   **910.4**
Menaseh's dream. Singer, I. B.
In Singer, I. B. When Shlemiel went to
Warsaw & other stories p83-96 **398.2**
Mende
See pages in the following book:
Clifford, M. L. The land and people of
Sierra Leone p122-29 (5-7)   **916.6**
Mendel, Gregor Johann
See pages in the following books:
Asimov, I. Breakthroughs in science p107-10
(5-7)   **920**
Cottler, J. Heroes of civilization p377-84 (6-7)
920
Mendeleev, Dmitrii Ivanovich
See pages in the following book:
Cottler, J. More Heroes of civilization p211-
22 (6-7)   **920**
Mendel's law
Pomerantz, C. Why you look like you, where-
as I tend to look like me (4-6)   **575.1**
Mendoza, George
And I must hurry for the sea is coming in
(3-6)   **811**
The digger wasp (2-5)   **595.7**
Shadowplay (3-6)   **791.5**
Mendoza, Pedro de
See pages in the following book:
Hall, E. The land and people of Argentina
p38-42 (5-7)   **918.2**
Menke, Frank G.
The encyclopedia of sports   **796.03**
Mennin, Peter
See pages in the following book:
Posell, E. Z. American composers p126-29
(5-7)   **920**
Mennonites
See also Amish
Fiction
De Angeli, M. Yonie Wondernose (1-4)   **Fic**
Menotti, Gian Carlo
Gian-Carlo Menotti's Amahl and the night
visitors (4-7)   **Fic**
The three kings arrive
In Martignoni, M. E. ed. The illustrated
treasury of children's literature p383-
85   **808.8**
About
See pages in the following book:
Posell, E. Z. American composers p132-36
(5-7)   **920**
Menstruation
Elgin, K. Twenty-eight days (5-7)   **612.6**
Mensuration
Bendick, J. Measuring (3-5)   **389**
Fey, J. T. Long, short, high, low, thin, wide
(1-3)   **389**

Mensuration—*Continued*
Froman, R. Bigger and smaller (1-3)   **513**
Gallant, R. A. Man the measurer (4-7)   **389**
Pine, T. S. Measurements and how we use them (2-4)   **389**
Srivastava, J. J. Area (2-3)   **516**
See also pages in the following book:
Moorman, T. How to make your science project scientific p41-48 (5-7)   **501**
See also Weights and measures

Mental illness
Fiction
Ellis, E. T. Celebrate the morning (6-7) **Fic**
Mental magic tricks. Lamb, G.   **793.8**
Mental philosophy. See Psychology

Mentally handicapped
See also Mental illness
Fiction
Cleaver, V. Ellen Grae (4-6)   **Fic**

Mentally handicapped children
See also Slow learning children
Fiction
Cleaver, V. Me too (5-7)   **Fic**
Friis-Baastad, B. Don't take Teddy (5-7) **Fic**
Wrightson, P. A racecourse for Andy (5-7)   **Fic**

Mentally handicapped children, Books for
Bibliography
Books for mentally retarded children   **028.52**
Mentally retarded children. See Mentally handicapped children

Menus
See pages in the following books:
Crocker, B. Betty Crocker's Cookbook for boys & girls p141-54 (3-7)   **641.5**
Freeman, L. M. Betty Crocker's Parties for children p153-66 (1-5)   **793.2**
Mercantile marine. See Merchant marine

Mercedes-Benz automobile
See pages in the following book:
Stevenson, P. The greatest days of racing p77-86, 92-97 (5-7)   **796.7**
The **Merchant** and the genie
In Lang, A. ed. Arabian nights p6-11 **398.2**

Merchant marine
Zim, H. S. Cargo ships (3-6)   **387.2**
The **merchant** of Seri. Babbitt, E. C.
In Babbitt, E. C. Jataka tales p13-17 **398.2**
See also Grandmother's golden dish
Mercury. See Hermes

Mercury (Planet)
See pages in the following book:
Branley, F. M. The nine planets p24-31 (6-7)   **523.4**

Mercury project
Americans in space (5-7)   **629.4**
Meredith, Robert
(jt. ed.) Smith, E. B. ed. Pilgrim courage   **974.4**

Mergenthaler, Ottmar
See pages in the following book:
Barker, A. Black on white and read all over p68-75 (4-6)   **686.2**

Merisier, stronger than the elephants. Courlander, H.
In Courlander, H. The piece of fire, and other Haitian tales p9-14   **398.2**
Merit students encyclopedia   **031**
Merit students year book. See Merit students encyclopedia   **031**
Merkling, Erica
(illus.) Voight, V. F. Sacajawea   **92**

Merlin
See pages in the following book:
Aylesworth, T. G. The alchemist: magic into science p13-17 (6-7)   **540.1**
Merlin plays minstrel; puppet play. Cochrane, L.
In Cochrane, L. Tabletop theatres p13-17   **791.5**
Merlin, the wizard of Britain. Green, R. L.
In Green, R. L. ed. A cavalcade of magicians p64-83   **808.8**
The **mermaid**. Jarrell, R.
In Johnson, E. ed. Anthology of children's literature p696-700   **808.8**
The **mermaid** of Emmeloord. De Hartog, J.
In Brown, M. ed. A cavalcade of sea legends p5-20   **808.8**

Mermaids
Manning-Sanders, R. A book of mermaids (3-6)   **398.2**
See also pages in the following book:
McHargue, G. The impossible people p146-57 (5-7)   **398**
Merman Rosmer. Manning-Sanders, R.
In Manning-Sanders, R. A book of mermaids p108-13   **398.2**
Mermen. Craigie, W. A.
In Brown, M. ed. A cavalcade of sea legends p30-34   **808.8**

Merriam, Eve
Boys & girls, girls & boys   **E**
Finding a poem (6-7)   **811**
Independent voices (5-7)   **811**
It doesn't always have to rhyme (4-7)   **811**
There is no rhyme for silver (2-5)   **811**

Merrick, Helen Hynson
Sweden (4-6)   **914.85**

Merrill, Jean
High, Wide and Handsome and their three tall tales (1-4)   **398.2**
The pea shooter campaign—phase I
In Arbuthnot, M. H. comp. The Arbuthnot Anthology of children's literature p573-76   **808.8**
The Pushcart War (5-7)   **Fic**
The Pushcart War; excerpt
In Arbuthnot, M. H. comp. The Arbuthnot Anthology of children's literature p573-76   **808.8**
Shan's lucky knife (3-5)   **398.2**
The superlative horse (4-6)   **Fic**
The toothpaste millionaire (4-6)   **Fic**

Merrimac (Frigate)
Duel of the ironclads (4-7)   **973.7**
Ironclads of the Civil War (6-7)   **973.7**

The **merry** adventures of Robin Hood of great renown in Nottinghamshire. Pyle, H.
398.2

A **Merry** Christmas. Alcott, L. M.
In Association for Childhood Education International. Told under the Christmas tree p138-52 **808.8**

Merry Christmas, Crawfords! Hark, M.
In Kamerman, S. E. ed. A treasury of Christmas plays p21-44 **812.08**

Merry Christmas customs. Hark, M.
In Kamerman, S. E. ed. A treasury of Christmas plays p376-82 **812.08**

The **Merry** Christmas Elf. Fisher, A.
In Fisher, A. Holiday programs for boys and girls p165-76 **812**

Merry Christmas from Betsy. Haywood, C.
See Note under Haywood, C. "B" is for Betsy **Fic**

Merry Christmas in Dakota. Havighurst, W.
In Association for Childhood Education International. Told under the Stars and Stripes p325-35 **S C**

Merry Christmas to you. Harper, W. comp.
394.2

Merry-go-round
See pages in the following book:
Gladstone, M. J. A carrot for a nose p54-63 (4-7) **745**

Fiction
Brown, M. The little carousel **E**
The **merry-go-round** and the Griggses. Emerson, C. D.
In Association for Childhood Education International. Told under the magic umbrella p18-22 **S C**
In Gruenberg, S. M. ed. Favorite stories old and new p466-69 **808.8**

Merry, merry, merry. Carroll, G. H.
In Burack, A. S. ed. One hundred plays for children p492-506 **808.82**

The **merry** tale of Belle Boyd. Jagendorf, M. A.
In Jagendorf, M. A. Folk stories of the South p304-06 **398.2**

Merry tale of Merrymount. Jagendorf, M. A.
In Jagendorf, M. A. New England beanpot p158-62 **398.2**

Merry Tyll and the three rogues. Thane, A.
In Kamerman, S. E. ed. Dramatized folk tales of the world p162-76 **812.08**

Merwin, Decie
(illus.) Brewton, S. comp. Christmas bells are ringing **808.81**

Meryman, Hope
(illus.) Gerson, M. J. Why the sky is far away **398.2**
(illus.) Les Tina, D. May Day **394.2**

Mesa Verde National Park
Marcus, R. B. The first book of the cliff dwellers (4-7) **970.4**
See also pages in the following books:
Melbo, I. R. Our country's national parks v2 p291-308 (5-7) **917.3**
National Geographic Society. The new America's wonderlands p216-28 **917.3**

Mesopotamia

Antiquities
Baumann, H. In the land of Ur (6-7) **913.35**
Weisgard, L. The beginnings of cities (6-7) **913.35**

Civilization
Baumann, H. In the land of Ur (6-7) **913.35**
Gregor, A. S. How the world's first cities began (4-6) **913.35**
Neurath, M. They lived like this in ancient Mesopotamia (3-5) **913.35**
Robinson, C. A. The first book of ancient Mesopotamia and Persia (4-7) **913.35**

Mesopotamian architecture. See Architecture, Mesopotamian

A **message** from Robin Hood. Colson, J. G.
In Kamerman, S. E. ed. Fifty plays for junior actors p151-66 **812.08**

The **message** from the moon. Courlander, H.
In Courlander, H. The king's drum, and other African stories p106-08 **398.2**

Messages from a sorcerer. Lively, P.
In Arbuthnot, M. H. comp. The Arbuthnot Anthology of children's literature p557-62 **808.8**

The **messenger** donkey. Courlander, H.
In Courlander, H. The fire on the mountain, and other Ethiopian stories p41-43 **398.2**

Messenger to Maftam. Courlander, H.
In Courlander, H. The cow-tail switch, and other West African stories p79-86 **398.2**

Messengers
Grimm, J. Death's messengers
In Grimm, J. The complete Grimm's Fairy tales p718-20 **398.2**

Metallurgy. See Metals

Metals
See pages in the following book:
Freeman, I. M. The science of chemistry p47-63 (5-7) **540**

Metals, Transmutation of. See Alchemy

Metalwork. See Coppersmithing; Ironwork; Jewelry; Silversmithing

Metamorphic rocks. See Rocks

Metamorphosis: the magic change. Silverstein, A. **591.3**

Metchinikoff, Elie. See Mechnikov, Il'íà Il'ich

Meteoric glass. See Tektite

Meteorites
See pages in the following book:
Branley, F. M. Comets, meteoroids, and asteroids p17-31 (6-7) **523.2**

Meteorology
Bendick, J. How to make a cloud (1-3) **551.5**
See also pages in the following book:
Boy Scouts of America. Fieldbook p502-11 **369.43**
See also Air; Atmosphere; Climate; Clouds; Fog; Hurricanes; Lightning; Rain and rainfall; Seasons; Snow; Solar radiation; Storms; Thunderstorms; Weather; Weather forecasting; Winds

Meyers, Michael K.
(illus.) Schuman, B. N. The human eye **612**

Mi diccionario ilustrado **463**

Mi primer Larousse en colores. Fonteneau, M.
463

Miasikovskiĭ, Nikolai
See pages in the following book:
Posell, E. Z. Russian composers p134-41
(5-7) **920**

Mice
Freschet, B. Bear mouse (2-4) **599**
Hess, L. Mouse and company (3-5) **599**
McClung, R. M. Whitefoot (1-4) **599**
Silverstein, A. Rats and mice (3-5) **599**
See also pages in the following books:
Mason, G. F. Animal homes p39-43 (4-7)
591.5
Pringle, L. ed. Discovering nature indoors
p105-19 (5-7) **591**
Shuttlesworth, D. E. The story of rodents
p13-24 (4-6) **599**
Stevens, C. Your first pet p31-37 (2-4) **636.08**

Poetry
Ivimey, J. W. Complete version of Ye three
blind mice (k-2) **398.8**

Stories
Belpré, P. Perez and Martina (1-4) **398.2**
Benchley, N. Feldman Fieldmouse (3-5) **Fic**
Brown, P. Something for Christmas **E**
Carle, E. Do you want to be my friend? **E**
Cleary, B. The mouse and the motorcycle
(3-5) **Fic**
Cleary, B. Runaway Ralph (3-5) **Fic**
Edmonds, W. D. Beaver valley (4-6) **Fic**
Erickson, R. E. A toad for Tuesday (2-4) **Fic**
Flack, M. Walter the lazy mouse (2-4) **Fic**
Freeman, D. Norman the doorman **E**
Gág, W. Snippy and Snappy **E**
Galdone, P. The town mouse and the country
mouse (k-2) **398.2**
Godden, R. Mouse house (2-4) **Fic**
Goodall, J. S. Shrewbettina's birthday **E**
Gurney, N. The king, the mice and the
cheese **E**
Hoban, L. The sugar snow spring **E**
Hurd, E. T. Come and have fun **E**
Hürlimann, R. The cat and mouse who
shared a house (k-3) **398.2**
Kraus, R. Whose mouse are you? **E**
Kumin, M. Joey and the birthday present
(3-5) **Fic**
Lawson, R. Ben and me (5-7) **Fic**
Lionni, L. Alexander and the wind-up mouse
E
Lionni, L. Frederick **E**
Lobel, A. Mouse tales **E**
Miller, E. Mousekin's family **E**
Norris, G. B. Green and something else (3-5)
Fic
Oakley, G. The church mouse **E**
O'Brien, R. C. Mrs Frisby and the rats of
NIMH (4-7) **Fic**
Ormondroyd, E. Broderick **E**
Potter, B. The story of Miss Moppet **E**
Potter, B. The tailor of Gloucester **E**
Potter, B. The tale of Mrs Tittlemouse **E**
Potter, B. The tale of two bad mice **E**

Selden, G. The cricket in Times Square (3-6)
Fic
Sharp, M. Miss Bianca (3-6) **Fic**
Sharp, M. The rescuers (3-6) **Fic**
Steig, W. Amos & Boris **E**
Titus, E. Anatole **E**
Titus, E. Anatole and the cat **E**
Titus, E. Anatole and the piano **E**
Titus, E. Anatole and the thirty thieves **E**
Titus, E. Anatole and the toyshop **E**
Titus, E. Anatole over Paris **E**
Titus, E. Basil of Baker Street (3-5) **Fic**
Wells, R. Noisy Nora **E**
Wenning, E. The Christmas mouse **E**
White, E. B. Stuart Little (3-6) **Fic**
Yeoman, J. Mouse trouble **E**

Mice and the cat
Belpré, P. Nangato
In Belpré, P. The tiger and the rabbit, and
other tales p21-25 **398.2**

The mice and the Christmas tree. Proysen, A.
In Proysen, A. Little old Mrs Pepperpot,
and other stories p78-86 **S C**

Mice, moose, and men. McClung, R. M. **574.5**

The mice that ate iron. Ryder, A. W.
In Arbuthnot, M. H. comp. The Arbuthnot
Anthology of children's literature
p421-22 **808.8**
In Arbuthnot, M. H. comp. Time for old
magic p285-86 **398.2**

Michael Scott and the demon. Nic Leodhas, S.
In Nic Leodhas, S. Thistle and thyme
p136-43 **398.2**

Michelangelo Buonarroti
See pages in the following books:
Craven, T. The rainbow book of art p82-89
(5-7) **709**
Jacobs, D. Master painters of the Renaissance
p78-89 (6-7) **759.5**
Winwar, F. The land and people of Italy p94-
99 (5-7) **914.5**

Michigan

Fiction
Mason, M. E. Caroline and her kettle named
Maud (2-4) **Fic**
Robertson, K. In search of a sandhill crane
(5-7) **Fic**

Micmac Indians

Legends
Toye, W. How summer came to Canada (k-3)
398.2

Microbes. See Bacteriology; Germ theory of
disease; Microorganisms

Microbes are something else. Stone, A. H.
576.072

Microbiology
Silverstein, A. A world in a drop of water
(3-5) **576**
See also Bacteriology; Microorganisms;
Microscope and microscopy

Experiments
Stone, A. H. Microbes are something else
(4-7) **576.072**
See also pages in the following book:
Lewis, L. Z. The first book of microbes p62-
71 (4-7) **576**

Microbiology—*Continued*

History

Asimov, I. How did we find out about germs? (5-7)   616.01

Research

Silverstein, A. Germfree life (5-7)   576

Micronesia

See pages in the following book:

May, C. P. Oceania: Polynesia, Melanesia, Micronesia p117-33 (5-7)   919

Microorganisms

Lewis, L. Z. The first book of microbes (4-7)   576

Silverstein, A. Germfree life (5-7)   576

Stone, A. H. Microbes are something else (4-7)   576.072

See also Amoeba; Bacteriology; Microbiology; Microscope and microscopy; Viruses

Microscope and microscopy

Selsam, M. E. Greg's microscope (1-3)   578

Simon, S. Exploring with a microscope (4-7)   578

See also pages in the following books:

Asimov, I. How did we find out about germs? p12-18 (5-7)   616.01

Pringle, L. ed. Discovering nature indoors p50-62 (5-7)   591

See also Microbiology

Microscopic analysis. See Microscope and microscopy

Microscopic organisms. See Microorganisms

Midas

See pages in the following books:

Farjeon, E. ed. A cavalcade of kings p113-32 (5-7)   808.8

Gruenberg, S. M. ed. Favorite stories old and new p408-10   808.8

Ward, W. ed. Stories to dramatize p159-63   372.6

Middle Ages

Black, I. S. Castle, abbey and town (3-6)   940.1

Boardman, F. W. Castles (5-7)   940.1

See also pages in the following books:

Copeland, P. W. The land and people of Libya p54-59 (5-7)   916.1

Mahmoud, Z. N. The land and people of Egypt p51-63 (5-7)   916.2

Spencer, W. The land and people of Tunisia p57-62, 66-70 (5-7)   916.1

Street, A. The land and people of England p84-93 (5-7)   914.2

Wohlrabe, R. A. The land and people of Austria p26-32 (5-7)   914.36

Wohlrabe, R. A. The land and people of Denmark p30-40 (5-7)   914.89

Wohlrabe, R. A. The land and people of Germany p24-30 (5-7)   914.3

See also Art, Medieval; Chivalry; Knights and knighthood; Renaissance

Fiction

Gray, E. J. Adam of the road (5-7)   Fic

History

See Civilization, Medieval; Crusades; Feudalism

The middle bear. Estes, E.

In Gruenberg, S. M. ed. Favorite stories old and new p109-16   808.8

Middle East. See Near East

The middle Moffat. Estes, E.   Fic

The middle Moffat; excerpt. Estes, E.

In Arbuthnot, M. H. comp. The Arbuthnot Anthology of children's literature p627-33   808.8

Middle West

Fiction

Fleischman, S. Chancy and the grand rascal (4-6)   Fic

Social life and customs

McGovern, A. If you grew up with Abraham Lincoln (2-4)   92

Middleton, Nellie Bly

A sackful of Thanksgiving

In Luckhardt, M. C. comp. Thanksgiving p303-10   394.2

Middleton, Richard

The ghost ship

In Ireson, B. comp. Haunting tales p221-34   S C

Midir and Etain, O'Faolain, E.

In O'Faolain, E. Irish sagas and folktales p23-26   398.2

Midnight alarm. Phelan, M. K.   973.3

Midnight burial. Hill, K.

In Burack, A. S. ed. One hundred plays for children p135-39   808.82

The midnight folk. Masefield, J.

In Colwell, E. ed. A storyteller's choice p104-17   372.6

The midnight fox. Byars, B.   Fic

The midnight fox; excerpt. Byars, B.

In Arbuthnot, M. H. comp. The Arbuthnot Anthology of children's literature p638-41   808.8

The midnight hunt. Williams-Ellis, A.

In Williams-Ellis, A. Fairy tales from the British Isles p302-05   398.2

Midnight is a place. Aiken, J.   Fic

The midnight rider, Paul Revere. Carmer, C.

In Cavanah, F. ed. Holiday roundup p122-25   394.2

A midsummer nights' dream. Lamb, C.

In Darrell, M. ed. Once upon a time p147-57   808.8

Midsummer pirates. Davis, R. H.

In A St Nicholas anthology p305-15 810.8

Mieko. Politi, L.   E

Mielikki and her nine sons. Bowman, J. C.

In Bowman, J. C. Tales from a Finnish tupa p161-70   398.2

Mier, Colin

(illus.) Colyer, P. I can read French   448

Mighty Mikko. Fillmore, P.

In Davis, M. G. ed. A baker's dozen p169-88   372.6

In Fenner, P. R. comp. Princesses & peasant boys p43-56   398.2

In Johnson, E. ed. Anthology of children's literature p278-82   808.8

The mighty ones. DeJong, M.   221.9

Mines and mineral resources—*Continued*

Bolivia

See pages in the following book:

Warren, L. F. The land and people of Bolivia p67-81 (5-7)   **918.4**

Colombia

See pages in the following book:

Landry, L. The land and people of Colombia p111-20 (5-7)   **918.61**

Liberia

See pages in the following book:

Clifford, M. L. The land and people of Liberia p102-07, 128-30 (5-7)   **916.66**

Sierra Leone

See pages in the following book:

Clifford, M. L. The land and people of Sierra Leone p137-43 (5-7)   **916.6**

Zaire

See pages in the following book:

Crane, L. The land and people of the Congo p36-37 (5-7)   **916.75**

Zambia

See pages in the following book:

Dresang, E. T. The land and people of Zambia p111-18 (5-7)   **916.89**

Mine's the best. Bonsall, C.   **E**

The miniature Darzis; play. Gregg, L.
In Smith, M. R. ed. 7 plays & how to produce them p43-60   **792**

Miniature gardens. *See* Gardens, Miniature

Miniature objects. *See* Dollhouses; Gardens, Miniature; Models and model making; Toys; and names of objects with the subdivision Models, e.g. Airplanes—Models

Minibikes and minicycles for beginners. Edmonds, I. G.   **629.22**

Minicycles for beginners, Minibikes and. Edmonds, I. G.   **629.22**

Mining. *See* Mines and mineral resources

Minks

See pages in the following book:

Paten, D. H. Weasels, otters, skunks, and their family p32-34, 64-66 (3-6)   **599**

The min-min. Clark, M. T.   **Fic**

Minn of the Mississippi. Holling, H. C.   **Fic**

Minnesota

Fiction

Lovelace, M. H. Betsy-Tacy (2-4)   **Fic**

Minnich, Harvey C.
(ed.) McGuffey, W. H. Old favorites from the McGuffey readers, 1836-1936   **028.5**

Minnikin. Moe, J.
In Lang, A. ed. The red fairy book p307-21   **398.2**

Minor, Margaret
His hero
In A St Nicholas anthology p31-35   **810.8**

Minor, Wendell
(illus.) Goodsell, J. Eleanor Roosevelt   **92**

Minorities
Katz, W. L. Early America, 1492-1812 (5-7)   **301.45**

Katz, W. L. From the progressive era to the great depression, 1900-1929 (5-7)   **301.45**

Katz, W. L. Modern America, 1957 to the present (5-7)   **301.45**

Katz, W. L. Reconstruction and national growth, 1865-1900 (5-7)   **301.45**

Katz, W. L. Slavery to Civil War, 1812-1865 (5-7)   **301.45**

Katz, W. L. Years of strife, 1929-1956 (5-7)   **301.45**

See also pages in the following book:

Sechrist, E. H. It's time for brotherhood p85-155 (5-7)   **301.11**

See also Discrimination; Nationalism; also names of races or peoples living within a country dominated by another nationality, e.g. Germans in the United States; and names of countries with the subdivision Race relations, e.g. United States—Race relations

Bibliography

Griffin, L. comp. Multi-ethnic books for young children   **028.52**

Keating, C. M. Building bridges of understanding between cultures   **028.52**

See also pages in the following book:

Withrow, D. E. Gateways to readable books p105-15   **028.52**

Fiction

Association for Childhood Education International. Told under the Stars and Stripes (3-6)   **S C**

Periodicals

Interracial Books for Children Bulletin   **028.505**

Poetry

Baron, V. O. ed. Here I am! (4-7)   **811.08**

Minorities in American history
Katz, W. L. Early America, 1492-1812   **301.45**

Katz, W. L. From the progressive era to the great depression, 1900-1929   **301.45**

Katz, W. L. Reconstruction and national growth, 1865-1900   **301.45**

Katz, W. L. Slavery to Civil War, 1812-1865   **301.45**

Katz, W. L. Years of strife, 1929-1956   **301.45**

Minos, King of Crete

See pages in the following book:

Gates, D. Lord of the sky: Zeus p61-66 (4-7)   **292**

Minotaur

See pages in the following book:

Gates, D. Lord of the sky: Zeus p79-92 (4-7)   **292**

Minstrel and the cobbler
Ballads and boots
In Gunterman, B. L. ed. Castles in Spain, and other enchantments p247-50   **398.2**

Minstrels

Fiction

Gray, E. J. Adam of the road (5-7)   **Fic**

Monkey see, monkey do. Credle, E.　　　**E**

Monkeys
Conklin, G. Little apes (k-3)　　　**599**
Goodall, J. S. Jacko　　　**E**
Shuttlesworth, D. E. The story of monkeys, great apes, and small apes (5-7)　　　**599**
Zim, H. S. Monkeys (3-6)　　　**599**
See also pages in the following books:
Batten, M. The tropical forest p103-16 (5-7)　　　**574.5**
Earle, O. L. Paws, hoofs, and flippers p168-74 (5-7)　　　**599**
Shuttlesworth, D. E. The wildlife of South America p42-46 (5-7)　　　**591.9**
See also Baboons

Stories
Credle, E. Monkey see, monkey do　　　**E**
De La Mare, W. Mr Bumps and his monkey (4-6)　　　**Fic**
Galdone, P. The monkey and the crocodile (k-2)　　　**398.2**
Hurd, E. T. Last one home is a green pig **E**
Otis, J. Toby Tyler (4-6)　　　**Fic**
Rey, H. A. Cecily G. and the 9 monkeys **E**
Rey, H. A. Curious George　　　**E**
Rey, M. Curious George flies a kite　　　**E**
Rey, M. Curious George goes to the hospital　　　**E**
Rey, H. A. Curious George learns the alphabet　　　**E**
Rey, H. A. Curious George rides a bike　　**E**
Rey, H. A. Curious George takes a job　　**E**
Slobodkina, E. Caps for sale　　　**E**
The **monkeys** and the little red hats. Carpenter, F.
In Carpenter, F. African wonder tales p71-75　　　**398.2**
The **monkeys'** feast. Holladay, V.
In Holladay, V. Bantu tales p76-77 **398.2**
The **monkey's** heart. Arnott, K.
In Arnott, K. African myths and legends p135-39　　　**398.2**
Monkeys in the sausage tree. Aardema, V.
In Aardema, V. Tales from the story hat p38-43　　　**398.2**
Monoprint. See Monotype (Engraving)
Monotype (Engraving)
See pages in the following book:
Rockwell, H. Printmaking p36-41 (4-6)　**760**
Monro, Gabriel
(illus.) Quayle, E. The collector's book of children's books　　　**020.75**
Monroe, Earl
The basketball skill book (4-7)　　　**796.32**
Monroe, Joan Kiddell- See Kiddell-Monroe, Joan
Monroe, Marion
My pictionary (k-1)　　　**423**
Monroe Doctrine
Vaughan, H. C. The Monroe Doctrine, 1823 (6-7)　　　**327.73**
The **Monroe** Doctrine, 1823. Vaughan, H. C.　　　**327.73**
Mons Tro. Manning-Sanders, R.
In Manning-Sanders, R. A choice of magic p148-65　　　**398.2**

Monsell, Helen A.
Paddy's Christmas
In Ward, W. ed. Stories to dramatize p83-85　　　**372.6**
Monsieur Santa Claus. Miller, H. L.
In Kamerman, S. E. ed. A treasury of Christmas plays p63-78　　**812.08**
The **monster** eagle. Baker, B.
In Baker, B. At the center of the world p25-32　　　**398.2**
The **monster** Humbaba. Bryson, B.
In Arbuthnot, M. H. comp. The Arbuthnot Anthology of children's literature p455-58　　　**808.8**
In Arbuthnot, M. H. comp. Time for old magic p319-22　　　**398.2**
Monster masks. Alkema, C. J.　　　**745.59**
The **monster** mo-o. Thompson, V. L.
In Thompson, V. L. Hawaiian myths, of earth, sea, and sky p65-69　　**398.2**
The **monster** we live on. Roy, C.
In Roy, C. The serpent and the sun p15-20　　　**398.2**
The **monster** who grew small. Grant, J.
In Colwell, E. ed. A storyteller's choice p84-91　　　**372.6**
Monsters
Edelson, E. Great monsters of the movies (4-6)　　　**791.43**
Rieger, S. Gargoyles, monsters and other beasts (1-5)　　　**731**
See also pages in the following book:
McHargue, G. The beasts of never p85-107 (5-7)　　　**398**
See also Giants

Fiction
Viorst, J. My mama says there aren't any zombies, ghosts, vampires, creatures, demons, monsters, fiends, goblins, or things **E**

Poetry
Riley, J. W. The Gobble-uns'll git you ef you don't watch out! (1-4)　　　**811**
Monsters on wheels. Ancona, G.　　　**621.8**
Montana

Fiction
Corcoran, B. The long journey (4-7)　　**Fic**
Corcoran, B. Sasha, my friend (5-7)　　**Fic**
Wier, E. The loner (5-7)　　　**Fic**
Montealegre, Marcelo
(illus.) Larson, R. Young filmmakers　**778.5**
Montevideo
See pages in the following book:
Dobler, L. The land and people of Uruguay p89-103 (5-7)　　　**918.95**
Montezuma II, Emperor of Mexico
See pages in the following book:
Buehr, W. The Spanish conquistadores in North America p46-56 (4-7)　　**973.1**
Montgomery, Elizabeth Rider
Albert Schweitzer, great humanitarian (4-6)　　　**92**
Walt Disney: master of make-believe (3-5) **92**
William C. Handy: father of the blues (3-4)　　　**92**

Montgomery, Ala.
Race relations
See pages in the following book:
Arbuthnot, M. H. comp. The Arbuthnot Anthology of children's literature p882-86
808.8

A month of Sundays. Blue, R.　**Fic**

Months
Belting, N. Calendar moon (4-7)　**398.2**
Fiction
Sendak, M. Chicken soup with rice　**E**
Poetry
Clifton, L. Everett Anderson's year (k-3) **811**
Updike, J. A child's calendar (k-3)　**811**

Monticello, Va.
Gurney, G. Monticello (5-7)　**917.55**

Montoya, Joseph Manuel
See pages in the following book:
Newlon, C. Famous Mexican-Americans p100-07 (6-7)　**920**

Montresor, Beni
Caldecott Medal acceptance paper
In Kingman, L. ed. Newbery and Caldecott Medal books: 1956-1965 p259-65　**028.5**
Cinderella; adaption (2-4)　**782.1**
(illus.) De Regniers, B. S. May I bring a friend?　**E**
(illus.) Johnson, S. P. ed. The Princesses **S C**
About
See pages in the following book:
Kingman, L. ed. Newbery and Caldecott Medal books: 1956-1965 p266-69　**028.5**

Monument Valley
Fiction
Wondriska, W. The stop　**E**

Monuments
Cohen, D. Ancient monuments and how they were built (6-7)　**913**
See also Pyramids; Tombs

Monuments, Natural. See Natural monuments

Moody, Ralph
Riders of the pony express (5-7)　**383**

Moominpappa at sea. Jansson, T.　**Fic**

Moon
Branley, F. M. The moon (6-7)　**523.3**
Branley, F. M. Pieces of another world　**552**
Shapp, M. Let's find out about the moon (1-3)　**523.3**
See also pages in the following books:
Clarke, A. C. Into space p86-94 (5-7)　**629.4**
Gardner, M. Space puzzles: curious questions and answers about the solar system p28-34 (6-7)　**523.2**
See also Tides
Fiction
Dayrell, E. Why the sun and the moon live in the sky (k-2)　**398.2**
Levitin, S. Who owns the moon?　**E**
Preston, E. M. Squawk to the moon, Little Goose　**E**
Traven, B. The creation of the sun and the moon (5-7)　**398.2**

Poetry
Garelick, M. Look at the moon (k-3)　**811**
The **moon.** Grimm, J.
In Grimm, J. The complete Grimm's Fairy tales p713-15　**398.2**
Moon, Voyages to. See Space flight to the moon
Moon bases. See Lunar bases
Moon Dragon; puppet play. Cochrane, L.
In Cochrane, L. Shadow puppets in color p18-25　**791.5**
Moon, for what do you wait? Tagore, R.　**821**
Moon-God of the Mayas. Campbell, C.
In Campbell, C. Star Mountain, and other legends of Mexico p17-20　**398.2**
The **moon** in the cloud. Harris, R.　**Fic**
The **moon** in the donkey. Jagendorf, M. A.
In Jagendorf, M. A. Noodlehead stories from around the world p249-52 **398.2**
The **moon** is like a silver sickle. Morton, M. ed.　**891.7**
The **moon** is shining bright as day. Nash, O. ed.　**821.08**
The **Moon** Jumpers. Udry, J. M.　**E**
The **Moon** Maiden. Chrisman, A. B.
In Chrisman, A. B. Shen of the sea p134-45　**S C**
The **moon** of gobbags. Broome, D.
In Mayne, W. ed. William Mayne's Book of giants p170-76　**398.2**
The **moon** of Gomrath. Garner, A.　**Fic**
The **moon** of the alligators. George, J. C.　**598.1**
The **moon** of the bears. George, J. C.　**599**
The **moon** of the chickarees. George, J. C. **599**
The **moon** of the fox pups. George, J. C.　**599**
The **moon** of the monarch butterflies. George, J. C.　**595.7**
The **moon** of the mountain lions. George, J. C.　**599**
The **moon** of the owls. George, J. C.　**598.2**
The **moon** of the salamanders. George, J. C. **597**
The **moon** of the wild pigs. George, J. C.　**599**
The **moon** of the winter bird. George, J. C.　**598.2**
The **moon** painters. Maas, S.
In Maas, S. The moon painters, and other Estonian folk tales p11-16　**398.2**
The **moon** painters, and other Estonian folk tales. Maas, S.　**398.2**
Moon rocks. See Lunar petrology
Moon-uncle, moon-uncle. Cassedy, S. comp.　**398.8**
Moon-watch summer. Blegvad, L.　**Fic**
Mooncoin Castle. Turkle, B.　**Fic**
The **mooncusser's** daughter. Aiken, J.　**822**
Moon's a woman. Courlander, H.
In Courlander, H. Terrapin's pot of sense p112-13　**398.2**
The **moon's** escape. Sechrist, E. H.
In Sechrist, E. H. Once in the first times p75-78　**398.2**

Morrison, Sean
The amoeba (3-6)   593
(illus.) Williams, J. The horn of Roland 398.2

Morrison, William
Country doctor
   In Yolen, J. ed. Zoo 2000 p145-78   S C

Morriss, James E.
(jt. auth.) Freedman, R. Animal instincts 156
(jt. auth.) Freedman, R. How animals learn
                 156

Morrow, Betty
Jewish holidays (2-5)   296.4
(jt. auth.) Selsam, M. See through the sea
             591.92

Morrow, Elizabeth
The painted pig (1-4)   Fic

Morrow, Gray
(illus.) Patterson, L. Frederick Douglass: freedom fighter   92

Morrow, Suzanne Stark
Inatuk's friend   E

Morse, Dorothy Bayley
(illus.) Caudill, R. Tree of freedom   Fic

Morse, Samuel Finley Breese
   See pages in the following book:
Cottler, J. Heroes of civilization p228-38
(6-7)   920

Morss, Corinthia
(illus.) Colby, J. P. Building wrecking   690

Mortality. See Death

Morton, Ferdinand Joseph
   See pages in the following book:
Hughes, L. Famous Negro music makers p63-
71 (5-7)   920

Morton, Jelly Roll. See Morton, Ferdinand
Joseph

Morton, Marian
(illus.) Bourne, M. A. Raccoons are for loving
                   E

Morton, Miriam
(ed.) A harvest of Russian children's literature   891.7
The making of champions (5-7)   796
(ed.) The moon is like a silver sickle (4-7)
            891.7
Pleasures and palaces (4-7)   914.7
(ed.) Tolstoy, L. Twenty-two Russian tales
for young children   S C

Morton, William Thomas Green
   See pages in the following book:
Hume, R. F. Great men of medicine p67-83
(4-6)   920

Morton-Sale, Isobel
(illus.) Farjeon, E. Then there were three 821

Morton-Sale, John
(illus.) Farjeon, E. Then there were three 821

Mortuary customs. See Funeral rites and ceremonies

Mosaics
   See pages in the following book:
Rockwell, H. I did it p9-17 (1-3)   745.5

Moscow
   See pages in the following book:
Nazaroff, A. The land and people of Russia
p27-47 (5-7)   914.7

Mosel, Arlene
The funny little woman (k-2)   398.2
Tikki Tikki Tembo (k-2)   398.2

Moses
   See pages in the following book:
Ward, W. ed. Stories to dramatize p116-19
            372.6

Moskin, Marietta
A tulip for Tony
   In Child Study Association of America.
      Round about the city p82-102   S C

Moslem art. See Art, Islamic

Moslemism. See Islam

Moslems. See Muslims

Mosques
   See pages in the following book:
Mahmoud, Z. N. The land and people of
Egypt p56-59 (5-7)   916.2

Mosquitoes
Ault, P. Wonders of the mosquito world (5-7)
            595.7
Ripper, C. L. Mosquitoes (3-5)   595.7
   See also pages in the following book:
Mason, G. F. Animal tools p44-48 (4-7)
            591.4

The moss-green princess. Berger, T.
   In Berger, T. Black fairy tales p3-14 398.2

Mosses
   See pages in the following book:
Hutchins, R. E. Plants without leaves p117-
38 (5-7)   586

The mossy rock. Manning-Sanders, R.
   In Manning-Sanders, R. A book of sorcer-
      ers and spells p122-25   398.2

The Most beautiful of all
   In DeRoin, N. ed. Jataka tales p43-44
            398.2

Most extraordinary thing
Andersen, H. C. The most incredible
   In Andersen, H. C. The complete fairy
      tales and stories p995-98   S C

The most frugal of men. Hardendorff, J. B.
   In Hardendorff, J. B. ed. Just one more
      p34-36   372.6

A most generous host. Davis, R.
   In Davis, R. The lion's whiskers p102-07
            398.2

The most incredible. Andersen, H. C.
   In Andersen, H. C. The complete fairy
      tales and stories p995-98   S C

The most magnificent cook of all. Olcott, F. J.
   In Sechrist, E. H. ed. It's time for story
      hour p85-90   372.6

The most obedient wife. Grundtvig, S.
   In Arbuthnot, M. H. comp. The Arbuthnot
      Anthology of children's literature
      p232-35   808.8
   In Arbuthnot, M. H. comp. Time for old
      magic p112-15   398.2

The most precious possession. Vittorini, D.
   In Arbuthnot, M. H. comp. The Arbuthnot
      Anthology of children's literature
      p271-72   808.8
   In Arbuthnot, M. H. comp. Time for old
      magic p154-55   398.2

Mother Sunday. Manning-Sanders, R.
In Manning-Sanders, R. Gianni and the
ogre p24-30   **398.2**

The **mother** whale. Hurd, E. T.   **599**

Mothers

Fiction

Mizumura, K. If I were a mother   **E**
Rodgers, M. Freaky Friday (4-7)   **Fic**
Viorst, J. My mama says there aren't any
zombies, ghosts, vampires, creatures, demons, monsters, fiends, goblins, or things **E**

Mother's Day

See pages in the following books:

Araki, C. Origami in the classroom: Book II
p32-36 (4-7)   **736**
Sechrist, E. H. Red letter days p118-23 **394.2**

Drama

See pages in the following books:

Fisher, A. Holiday programs for boys and
girls p321-34 (4-7)   **812**
Kamerman, S. E. ed. Little plays for little
players p67-78 (1-6)   **812.08**

Poetry

See pages in the following book:

Sechrist, E. H. comp. Poems for red letter
days p116-20   **821.08**

Mother's Day off and on. Fisher, A.
In Fisher, A. Holiday programs for boys
and girls p321-32   **812**

Mother's gift. Howard, H. L.
In Burack, A. S. ed. One hundred plays
for children p341-44   **808.82**

Mother's pet. Hatch, M. C.
In Hatch, M. C. 13 Danish tales p25-36
    398.2

Moths

Conklin, G. I like butterflies (k-3)   **595.7**
Hutchins, R. E. Scaly wings (2-4)   **595.7**
McClung, R. M. Gypsy moth (4-7)   **632**
McClung, R. M. Luna (2-4)   **595.7**
Mitchell, R. T. Butterflies and moths (4-7)
    595.7

See also pages in the following books:

Ewbank, C. Insect zoo p61-86 (4-7)   **595.7**
Silverstein, A. Metamorphosis: the magic
change p8-18 (4-6)   **591.3**
Sterling, D. Insects and the homes they build
p22-35 (5-7)   **595.7**
Teale, E. W. The junior book of insects p55-
71 (6-7)   **595.7**
Villiard, P. Insects as pets p64-83 (5-7) **595.7**
Zim, H. S. Insects p83-96 (4-7)   **595.7**
See also Butterflies; Caterpillars

Collection and preservation

Hussey, L. J. Collecting cocoons (4-6) **595.7**

Motion

Bendick, J. Motion and gravity (3-5)   **531**
See also pages in the following books:

Barr, G. Show time for young scientists p65-
77 (5-7)   **793.8**
Wilson, M. Seesaws to cosmic rays p15-26
(5-7)   **530**
See also Force and energy; Mechanics;
Speed

Motion and gravity. Bendick, J.   **531**

Motion pictures. See Moving pictures

Motor boats. See Motorboats

Motor cars. See Automobiles

Motor cycles. See Motorcycles

Motor trucks. See Trucks

Motorboats

Navarra, J. G. Safe motorboating for kids
(4-7)   **797.1**

Motorcycles

Edmonds, I. G. Minibikes and minicycles for
beginners (5-7)   **629.22**
Navarra, J. G. Wheels for kids (3-6)   **796.7**

Motors. See Electric motors; Engines

Motors and engines and how they work.
Weiss, H.   **621.4**

Mott, Carolyn

Children's book on how to use books and
libraries   **028.7**

Mott, Lucretia (Coffin)

Poetry

See pages in the following book:

Merriam, E. Independent voices p41-54 (5-7)
    811

The **mound** builders. Le Sueur, M.   **970.4**

The **mound** builders. Scheele, W. E.   **970.4**

Mounds and mound builders

Le Sueur, M. The mound builders (4-7) **970.4**
Scheele, W. E. The mound builders (4-7)
    970.4

Mount McKinley National Park

See pages in the following books:

Laycock, G. Wild animals, safe places p57-81
(5-7)   **639**
Melbo, I. R. Our country's national parks
v2 p175-96 (5-7)   **917.3**
National Geographic Society. The new
America's wonderlands p410-17   **917.3**

Mount Rainier National Park

See pages in the following books:

Melbo, I. R. Our country's national parks
v2 p233-51 (5-7)   **917.3**
National Geographic Society. The new
America's wonderlands p294-307   **917.3**

The **mountain.** Parnall, P.   **E**

Mountain born; excerpt. Yates, E.
In Association for Childhood Education
International. Told under spacious
skies p35-43   **S C**

Mountain laurel and maiden hair. Alcott, L. M.
In Alcott, L. M. Glimpses of Louisa p129-
59   **S C**

Mountain life

Southern States—Fiction

Credle, E. Down, down the mountain   **E**
Stuart, J. The beatinest boy (4-6)   **Fic**
Turkle, B. The fiddler of High Lonesome
(3-6)   **Fic**

Mountain lions. See Pumas

Mountain man; the life of Jim Beckwourth.
Place, M. T.   **92**

The **musicians** of Bremen Town. Roberts, W.
    In Kamerman, S. E. ed. Dramatized folk
      tales of the world p155-61   812.08

Musil, Rosemary G.
    The invisible dragon of Winn Sinn Tu
    In Kamerman, S. E. ed. Fifty plays for
      junior actors p386-406   812.08
    The Peach Tree Kingdom
    In Kamerman, S. E. ed. Dramatized folk
      tales of the world p288-305   812.08

Muskrats
    See pages in the following books:
    Mason, G. F. Animal homes p59-61 (4-7)
                            591.5
    Silverstein, A. Animal invaders p33-38 (4-7)
                            591.5

Stories
Hoban, R. Harvey's hideout   E

Muslimism. See Islam

Muslims
    See pages in the following book:
    Clifford, M. L. The land and people of Sierra
      Leone p128-34 (5-7)   916.6

Musorgskiĭ, Modest Petrovich
    See pages in the following book:
    Posell, E. Z. Russian composers p34-44 (5-7)
                            920

Musselman, Virginia W.
    Learning about nature through crafts (5-7)
                            574

Mussino, Attilio
    (illus.) Collodi, C. The adventures of Pinoc-
      chio   Fic

Mussolini, Benito
    See pages in the following book:
    Winwar, F. The land and people of Italy
      p143-47 (5-7)   914.5

Mussorgsky, Modest Petrovich. See Musorgskiĭ,
    Modest Petrovich

Mustang
    Ryden, H. The wild colt (2-4)   599
Stories
Henry, M. Mustang, wild spirit of the West
    (5-7)   Fic

Mustang, wild spirit of the West. Henry, M. **Fic**

Mustard
    See pages in the following book:
    Cooper, E. K. And everything nice p54-59
      (3-5)   641.3

Mutsmag
    In Chase, R. ed. Grandfather tales p40-51
                           398.2

My American heritage. Henry, R. comp. 810.8

My Aunt Rosie. Hoff, S.   E

My Black me. Adoff, A. comp.   811.08

My brother Sam is dead. Collier, J. L.   **Fic**

My brother Stevie. Clymer, E.   **Fic**

My cat has eyes of sapphire blue. Fisher, A. 811

My dad lives in a downtown hotel. Mann, P. **Fic**

My daddy longlegs. Hawes, J.   595

My doctor. Rockwell, H.   610.69

My dog is lost! Keats, E. J.   E

My father, the coach. Slote, A.   **Fic**

My father's dragon. Gannett, R. S.   **Fic**

My first picture dictionary. Greet, W. C.   423

My five senses. Aliki   612

My friend John. Zolotow, C.   E

My goldfish. Wong, H. H.   597

My grandson Lew. Zolotow, C.   E

My great-grandfather and I. Krüss, J.   **Fic**

My household. Grimm, J.
    In Grimm, J. The complete Grimm's Fairy
      tales p624   398.2

My journals and sketchbooks. Politzer, A. **Fic**

My ladybug. Wong, H. H.   595.7

My Lord Bag of Rice. Manning-Sanders, R.
    In Manning-Sanders, R. A book of dragons
      p38-42   398.2

My mama says there aren't zombies, ghosts,
    vampires, creatures, demons, monsters,
    fiends, goblins, or things. Viorst, J.   E

My mother is the most beautiful woman in the
    world. Reyher, B.   398.2
  —Same
    In Cavanah, F. ed. Holiday roundup p138-
      42   394.2

My own rhythm. Atwood, A.   811

My own self
    In Jacobs, J. ed. More English folk and
      fairy tales p16-19   398.2

My pictionary. Monroe, M.   423

My pictionary; bilingual edition. See Mi dic-
    cionario illustrado   463

My poetry book. Huffard, G. T. comp. 821.08

My puppy is born. Cole, J.   636.7

My Red Cap. Alcott, L. M.
    In Alcott, L. M. Glimpses of Louisa p43-60
                          S C

My red umbrella. Bright, R.   E

My roads to childhood. Moore, A. C.   028.5

My second picture dictionary. Jenkins, W. A.
                            423

My side of the mountain. George, J. C.   **Fic**

My side of the mountain; excerpt. George J.
    In Arbuthnot, M. H. comp. The Arbuthnot
      Anthology of children's literature
      p660-65   808.8

My song Yankee Doodle. Glick, C.
    In Association for Childhood Education
      International. Told under the Stars
      and Stripes p91-101   S C

My tang's tungled and other ridiculous situa-
    tions. Brewton, S. comp.   821.08

My treasure. Carlson, B. W.
    In Carlson, B. W. Funny-bone dramatics
      p60-64   812

My village in England. Gidal, S.   914.2

My village in Germany. Gidal, S.   914.3

My village in Hungary. Gidal, S.   914.39

My visit to the dinosaurs. Aliki   568

Myaskovsky, Nicholas. See Miaskovskiĭ, Nikolai

Mycenae
    See pages in the following book:
    Hall, J. Buried cities p101-16 (5-7)   913

N

Nacar, the white deer. Treviño, E. B. de **Fic**

Naden, Corinne J.
The Colony of New Jersey (4-7) 974.9
The Mississippi (4-7) 917.7
The Nile River (4-6) 962

Nagle, Avery
Fun with naturecraft (3-6) 745.5

Nagy, Al
(illus.) Branley, F. M. Rockets and satellites 629.4

Na-Ha the fighter. Finger, C.
In Finger, C. Tales from silver lands p35-42 398.2

The **nail.** Grimm, J.
In Grimm, J. The complete Grimm's Fairy tales p748-49 398.2

Nails and spikes
White, L. B. Investigating science with nails (4-7) 507.2

Nails to nickels. Campbell, E. 737.4

Nakuina, Moses K.
Brown, M. Backbone of the king 398.2

The **Namashepani.** Heady, E. B.
In Heady, E. B. When the stones were soft p21-26 398.2

Names
See pages in the following book:
Bendick, J. Names, sets and numbers p8-17 (2-5) 511

Names, Geographical
See also Gazetteers
United States
Arnold, P. How we named our states (5-7) 910
Fletcher, C. 100 keys: names across the land (6-7) 910
Shankle, G. E. American nicknames 929.4

Names, Personal
Lambert, E. Our names 929.4
Fiction
Alexander, M. Sabrina **E**
Mosel, A. Tikki Tikki Tembo (k-2) 398.2
United States
Shankle, G. E. American nicknames 929.4

Names and numbers. See Literary market place: LMP 070.5025

Names, sets and numbers. Bendick, J. 511

Namu. Fisher, R. M. 599

Nana Miriam. Baumann, H.
In Baumann, H. The stolen fire p53-57 398.2

Nana Upstairs & Nana Downstairs. De Paola, T. **E**

Nananbouclou and the piece of fire. Courlander, H.
In Courlander, H. The piece of fire, and other Haitian tales p62-63 398.2

Nangato. Belpré, P.
In Belpré, P. The tiger and the rabbit, and other tales p21-25 398.2

Nanka and Marianka make the big Christmas bread. Jones, E. O.
In Luckhardt, M. C. ed. Christmas comes once more p105-07 394.2

Nanny and Conn. MacManus, S.
In McManus, S. Hibernian nights p48-59 398.2

Nanny who wouldn't go home to supper
In Hutchinson, V. S. ed. Candle-light stories p51-54 398.2

Nansii and the eagle. Aardema, V.
In Aardema, V. Tales from the story hat p44-48 398.2

Nantucket, Mass.
Fiction
Snedeker, C. D. Downright Dencey (4-6) **Fic**
Turkle, B. The adventures of Obadiah **E**
Turkle, B. Obadiah the Bold **E**
Turkle, B. Thy friend, Obadiah **E**

Naomi-of-the-Inn. Waite, H. E.
In Burack, A. S. ed. Christmas plays for young actors p113-24 812.08

Napoleon, I, Emperor of the French
Fiction
Robbins, R. The Emperor and the drummer boy (3-5) **Fic**

Narcotic habit
Gorodetzky, C. W. What you should know about drugs (5-7) 613.8

Narcotics
See pages in the following book:
Gorodetzky, C. W. What you should know about drugs p16-29 (5-7) 613.8
See also names of specific narcotics, e.g. Heroin

Narcotics and youth. See Drugs and youth

Nariño, Antonio
See pages in the following book:
Landry, L. The land and people of Colombia p132-35 (5-7) 918.61

Nasca, Peru
Antiquities
See pages in the following book:
Cohen, D. Ancient monuments and how they were built p55-64 (6-7) 913

Nash, Ogden
The cruise of the Aardvark (3-5) 811
(ed.) The moon is shining bright as day (3-6) 821.08
Lear, E. Edward Lear's The Scroobious Pip 821

Nason, Thomas W.
(illus.) Frost, R. You come too 811

Nasr, al-dīn, khwājah
Kelsey, A. G. Once the Hodja (4-6) 398.2

See also pages in the following books:
Arbuthnot, M. H. comp. The Arbuthnot Anthology of children's literature p300-01 808.8
Arbuthnot, M. H. comp. Time for old magic p179-80 398.2

Nasser, Gamal Abdel, President United Arab Republic
See pages in the following books:
Lengyel, E. Modern Egypt p47-53 (5-7) 916.2
Mahmoud, Z. N. The land and people of Egypt p84-88 (5-7) 916.2

Natural history

The Doubleday Nature encyclopedia (3-6) **500.9**

Goetz, D. Deserts (3-6) **551.4**
Goetz, D. Grasslands (3-6) **551.4**
Goetz, D. Lakes (3-5) **551.4**
Goetz, D. Rivers (3-6) **551.4**
Goetz, D. Swamps (3-6) **551.4**
Kane, H. B. Four seasons in the woods (3-5) **500.9**
Kane, H. B. The tale of a meadow (4-6) **500.9**
Kane, H. B. The tale of a wood (4-6) **500.9**
Parker, B. M. The new Golden Treasury of natural history (5-7) **500.9**
Peattie, D. C. The rainbow book of nature (5-7) **574**
Sterling, D. Fall is here! (4-6) **500.9**
Ubell, E. The world of the living (3-5) **574**
  See also Aquariums; Biology; Botany; Fossils; Fresh-water biology; Geographical distribution of animals and plants; Geology; Marine biology; Mineralogy; Plant lore; Zoology

Alaska
See pages in the following book:
Adventures in the wilderness p108-27 (6-7) **500.9**

Arctic regions
Goetz, D. The Arctic tundra (3-5) **919.8**

Arizona
Clark, A. N. Along sandy trails (2-5) **500.9**

Australia
See pages in the following book:
Blunden, G. The land and people of Australia p37-57 (5-7) **919.4**

Encyclopedias
The Book of popular science **503**

Everglades, Fla.
Lauber, P. Everglades country (6-7) **574.5**

Galapagos Islands
Perry, R. The Galápagos Islands (5-7) **500.9**

Hawaii
See pages in the following book:
Adventures in the wilderness p128-47 (6-7) **500.9**

New Zealand
Day, B. Life on a lost continent (5-7) **500.9**

North America
Adventures in the wilderness (6-7) **500.9**
Farb, P. Face of North America. Young readers' edition (6-7) **500.9**

Outdoor books
See Nature study

United States
Clement, R. C. Hammond Nature atlas of America **500.9**

West Indies
See pages in the following book:
Sherlock, P. The land and people of the West Indies p143-51 (5-7) **917.29**

Natural history, Biblical. See Bible—Natural history

A natural history of giraffes. MacClintock, D. **599**

Natural law. See Civil rights

Natural monuments

United States
National Geographic Society. The new America's wonderlands **917.3**

Natural partnerships. Shuttlesworth, D. **574.5**

Natural resources
  See also Conservation of natural resources; Fisheries; Forests and forestry; Marine resources; Mines and mineral resources; Power resources; Soil conservation; Water resources development; Water supply

Arctic regions
See pages in the following book:
Harrington, L. The polar regions p97-119 (5-7) **919.8**

Botswana
See pages in the following book:
Carpenter, A. Botswana p55-59 (4-7) **916.8**

Burundi
See pages in the following book:
Carpenter, A. Burundi p57-61 (4-7) **916.7**

Great Britain
See pages in the following book:
Street, A. The land and people of England p68-75 (5-7) **914.2**

Kenya
See pages in the following book:
Carpenter, A. Kenya p49-57 (4-7) **916.76**

Liberia
See pages in the following books:
Carpenter, A. Liberia p71-76 (4-7) **916.66**
Clifford, M. L. The land and people of Liberia p125-38 (5-7) **916.66**

Libya
See pages in the following book:
Copeland, P. W. The land and people of Libya p138-53 (5-7) **916.1**

Madagascar
See pages in the following book:
Carpenter, A. Malagasy Republic (Madagascar) p73-79 (4-7) **916.9**

North America
Adventures in the wilderness (6-7) **500.9**

Rwanda
See pages in the following book:
Carpenter, A. Rwanda p55-58 (4-7) **916.7**

Uganda
See pages in the following book:
Carpenter, A. Uganda p53-57 (4-7) **916.76**

United States
Parnall, P. The mountain **E**

Natural selection. See Evolution

Naturalism in literature. See Realism in literature

Naturalists
Blassingame, W. Dan Beard, scoutmaster of America (3-5) **92**

Nematoda
See pages in the following book:
Goldstein, P. Animals and plants that trap
    p110-19 (4-7)   **574.5**

Nemeyer, Carol A.
(jt. auth.) Bomar, C. P. Guide to the de-
    velopment of educational media selection
    centers   **021**

Neo-Destour Party. See Destourian Socialist
    Party

Nepal

Social life and customs
Larsen, P. Boy of Nepal (3-5)   **915.49**

Neptune (Planet)
See pages in the following books:
Branley, F. M. The nine planets p73-76 (6-7)
                                                 523.4
Knight, D. C. Thirty-two moons p81-89 (5-7)
                                                 523.9

Nerman, Einar
Little Lisa
    In Martignoni, M. E. ed. The illustrated
        treasury of children's literature p282-
        84   **808.8**

Nerrink, old woman of the sea; puppet play.
    Adair, M. W.
    In Adair, M. W. Folk puppet plays for the
        social studies p74-77   **791.5**

Nerves. See Nervous system

Nervous system
Elgin, K. The human body: the brain (3-5)
                                                 612
Kalina, S. Your nerves and their messages
    (3-5)   **612**
Showers, P. Use your brain (1-3)   **612**
Silverstein, A. The nervous system (4-7)   **612**
Zim, H. S. Your brain and how it works (4-6)
                                                 612

See also pages in the following book:
Adler, O. Taste, touch and smell p6-9 (3-5)
                                                 612

Nesbit, E.
The complete book of dragons (3-6)   **S C**
Contents: The book of beasts; Uncle James; The
deliverers of their country; The ice dragon; The dragon
tamers; The fiery dragon; Kind little Edmund; The
Island of the Nine Whirlpools; The last of the dragons
The egg
    In Silverberg, B. ed. Phoenix feathers
        p187-205   **S C**
The fiery dragon
    In Green, R. L. ed. A cavalcade of dragons
        p185-202   **808.8**
John Charrington's wedding
    In Ireson, B. comp. Haunting tales p78-87
                                                 S C
The last of the dragons
    In Hoke, H. comp. Dragons, dragons,
        dragons p231-40   **398.2**
    In Manning-Sanders, R. ed. A book of
        magical beasts p14-25   **398.2**
Melisande
    In Johnson, S. P. ed. The Princesses p138-
        63   **S C**
The plush usurper
    In Farjeon, E. ed. A cavalcade of kings
        p94-112   **808.8**

The princess and the cat
    In Green, R. L. ed. A cavalcade of magi-
        cians p206-24   **808.8**
    For material about this author see
Bland, Edith (Nesbit)

Nesbitt, Elizabeth
A rightful heritage, 1890-1920
    In Meigs, C. ed. A critical history of
        children's literature p275-390   **028.5**

Nesbitt, Esta
(illus.) Belting, N. The stars are silver rein-
    deer   **398.2**

Nespojohn, Katherine V.
Worms (4-6)   **595**

Ness, Evaline
Caldecott Medal acceptance paper
    In Kingman, L. ed. Newbery and Calde-
        cott Medal books: 1966-1975 p186-
        91   **028.5**
Do you have the time, Lydia?   **E**
Exactly alike   **E**
The girl and the goatherd   **E**
Josefina February   **E**
Long, Broad & Quickeye (1-4)   **398.2**
Sam, Bangs & Moonshine   **E**
(illus.) Alexander, L. The truthful harp   **Fic**
(illus.) Black, A. D. The woman of the wood
    (k-3)   **398.2**
(illus.) Caudill, R. A pocketful of cricket   **E**
(illus.) Clifton, L. Everett Anderson's Christ-
    mas coming   **811**
(illus.) Clifton, L. Some of the days of Everett
    Anderson   **811**
(illus.) Coatsworth, E. The princess and the
    lion   **Fic**
(illus.) Haviland, V. Favorite fairy tales told
    in Italy   **398.2**
(illus.) Kumin, M. Joey and the birthday
    present   **Fic**
(illus.) Nic Leodhas, S. All in the morning
    early   **398.8**
(illus.) Nic Leodhas, S. Thistle and thyme
                                               398.2
(illus.) Old Mother Hubbard and her dog. See
    Old Mother Hubbard and her dog   **398.8**
(illus.) Tom Tit Tot. See Tom Tit Tot   **398.2**

About

See pages in the following book:
Kingman, L. ed. Newbery and Caldecott
    Medal books: 1966-1975 p192-98   **028.5**

Nests. See Birds—Eggs and nests

Netchillik and the bear. Melzack, R.
    In Melzack, R. The day Tuk became a
        hunter & other Eskimo stories p35-
        40   **398.2**

Netherlands
Barnouw, A. J. The land and people of Hol-
    land (5-7)   **914.92**
Cohn, A. The first book of the Netherlands
    (4-6)   **914.92**

Fiction
DeJong, M. Far out the long canal (4-6)   **Fic**
DeJong, M. Journey from Peppermint Street
    (4-6)   **Fic**
DeJong, M. Shadrach (1-4)   **Fic**
DeJong, M. The wheel on the school (4-6)   **Fic**
Dodge, M. M. Hans Brinker (4-7)   **Fic**

Netherlands—Fiction—*Continued*
Krasilovsky, P. The cow who fell in the canal
E
Van Stockum, H. The winged watchman (4-7)
Fic

History—German occupation, 1940-1945
Reiss, J. The upstairs room (4-7)   940.54

History, Naval
See pages in the following book:
Ward, R. T. Ships through history p83-99
(6-7)   387.2

Religion
See pages in the following book:
Barnouw, A. J. The land and people of Holland p53-57 (5-7)   914.92

Social life and customs
See pages in the following book:
Sechrist, E. H. ed. Christmas everywhere
p89-99   394.2
The nettle spinner. Deulin, C.
In Lang, A. ed. The red fairy book p286-
93   398.2

Nettles
See pages in the following book:
Wright, R. H. What good is a weed? p24-32
(4-6)   581.5

Neuberger, Richard L.
The Lewis and Clark Expedition (4-7) 973.4

Neufeld, John
Edgar Allan (5-7)   Fic

Neurath, Marie
They lived like this in ancient Mesopotamia
(3-5)   913.35
They lived like this in ancient Mexico (4-6)
917.2

Neurology. See Nervous system

Neuroptera. See Ant lions

Never kick a slipper at the moon. Sandburg, C.
In Sandburg, C. Rootabaga stories v 1
p185-88   S C
In Sandburg, C. The Sandburg treasury
p71-72   818

Never look a gift horse in the mouth.
Thomas, E.
In Farjeon, E. ed. A cavalcade of kings
p171-73   808.8

Never take no for an answer. Proysen, A.
In Proysen, A. Little old Mrs Pepperpot,
and other stories p87-90   S C

Neville, Emily Cheney
Berries Goodman (5-7)   Fic
It's like this, Cat; excerpt
In Association for Childhood Education International. Told under the city umbrella p255-74   S C
Newbery Medal acceptance paper
In Kingman, L. ed. Newbery and Caldecott
Medal books: 1956-1965 p131-36
028.5
The Seventeenth-Street gang (5-7)   Fic

About
See pages in the following book:
Kingman, L. ed. Newbery and Caldecott
Medal books: 1956-1965 p137-39   028.5

Nevins, Daniel
(illus.) Wyler, R. What happens if . . ? 507.2
The new America's wonderlands. National Geographic Society   917.3
New Amsterdam days and ways. Hults, D. N.
974.7
New at the zoo. Shannon, T.   590.74
A new baby comes. May, J.   612.6
The new book of days. Farjeon, E.   828
The New book of knowledge   031
The New book of knowledge annual. See The
New book of knowledge   031
The new cabin boy. Coatsworth, E.
In Johnson, E. ed. Anthology of children's
literature p836-39   808.8
A new day. Bolognese, D.   E
New Elementary dictionary, Webster's   423

New England
McGovern, A. If you lived in Colonial times
(2-4)   917.4
Stearns, M. The story of New England (5-7)
917.4

Fiction
Alcott, L. M. Eight cousins (5-7)   Fic
Alcott, L. M. Little women (5-7)   Fic
Coatsworth, E. Away goes Sally (4-6)   Fic
Fox, P. The stone-faced boy (4-6)   Fic
Lindquist, J. D. The golden name day (3-5)
Fic

Folklore
See Folklore—New England

Legends
See Legends—New England
New England bean-pot. Jagendorf, M. A. 398.2
New folks coming. Lawson, R.
In Gruenberg, S. M. ed. Favorite stories
old and new p206-14   808.8

New France

History
See Canada—History—To 1763 (New
France)
The new Golden Treasury of natural history.
Parker, B. M.   500.9

New Hampshire

Fiction
Bailey, C. S. Miss Hickory (3-5)   Fic
Meader, S. W. Red Horse Hill (5-7)   Fic
New hearts for old. Fisher, A.
In Fisher, A. Holiday programs for boys
and girls p237-49   812
A new home for Billy. Justus, M.   Fic
New international dictionary of the English
language; unabridged, Webster's Third 423

New Jersey

Fiction
McNeer, M. Stranger in the pines (5-7)   Fic

History
Naden, C. J. The Colony of New Jersey (4-7)
974.9

The New Junior illustrated encyclopedia of
sports. See The Junior illustrated encyclopedia of sports   796.03

New Larousse Encyclopedia of mythology
291.03

New Mexico

Fiction

Krumgold, J. . . . and now Miguel (6-7) **Fic**

New-moon meeting. Davis, R.
In Davis, R. Padre Porko, the gentlemanly
pig p169-80   398.2

New Orleans

See pages in the following book:

Naden, C. J. The Mississippi p45-49 (4-7)
917.7

New Orleans, Battle of, 1815

Tallant, R. Pirate Lafitte and the Battle of
New Orleans (5-7)   92

See also pages in the following book:

Lackie, R. Great American battles p30-45
(5-7)   973

A **new** pioneer. Fisher, D. C.
In Harper, W. comp. The harvest feast
p182-91   394.2
In Sechrist, E. H. ed. It's time for Thanksgiving p42-47   394.2

New Roads to childhood. Moore, A. C.
In Moore, A. C. My roads to childhood
p109-202   028.5

The **new** songs. Pratt, A. D.
In Association for Childhood Education International. Told under the blue umbrella p50-51   **S C**

New Southwest. See Southwest, New

New Students dictionary, Webster's   423

New tall tales of Pecos Bill. Felton, H. W.
398.2

The **new** water book. Berger, M.   551.4

A **new** way to boil eggs. Jagendorf, M. A.
In Jagendorf, M. A. Noodlehead stories
from around the world p130-32 398.2

New way to cure old witch-hunting. Jagendorf,
M. A.
In Jagendorf, M. A. New England bean-
pot p244-47   398.2

New world Bethlehem. Milhous, K.
In Dalgliesh, A. comp. Christmas p113-22
394.2

New World dictionary for young readers, Webster's   423

New world for Nellie. Emett, R.
In Martignoni, M. E. ed. The illustrated
treasury of children's literature p319-
21   808.8

The **new** world of paper. Eberle, I.   676

New Year

See pages in the following books:

Ickis, M. The book of festivals and holidays
the world over p 1-18   394.2

Sechrist, E. H. Red letter days p17-30 394.2

Drama

See pages in the following book:

Fisher, A. Holiday programs for boys and
girls p212-13 (4-7)   812

Poetry

See pages in the following book:

Sechrist, E. H. comp. Poems for red letter
days p27-33   821.08

Stories

Politi, L. Moy Moy   **E**

New York (City)

McGinley, P. All around the town   **E**

Solbert, R. I wrote my name on the wall **E**

See also pages in the following book:

Boorstin, D. J. The Landmark history of the
American people v 1 p27-33 (6-7)   973

Description

Sasek, M. This is New York (3-6)   **917.47**

Fiction

Binzen, B. Miguel's Mountain   **E**

Blue, R. A month of Sundays (3-5)   **Fic**

Brown, M. The little carousel   **E**

Clymer, E. The big pile of dirt (2-5) **Fic**

Clymer, E. Luke was there (3-6)   **Fic**

Cohen, B. The carp in the bathtub (2-4) **Fic**

Dawson, R. A walk in the city   **E**

Friedman, F. Ellen and the gang (4-6) **Fic**

George, J. C. Coyote in Manhattan (4-7) **Fic**

Grifalconi, A. City rhythms   **E**

Hildick, E. W. Manhattan is missing (4-6)
Fic

Holman, F. Slake's limbo (6-7)   **Fic**

Keats, E. J. My dog is lost!   **E**

Levoy, M. The witch of Fourth Street, and
other stories (4-7)   **S C**

Mann, P. The street of the flower boxes (3-5)
Fic

Merrill, J. The Pushcart War (5-7)   **Fic**

Neville, E. C. The Seventeenth-Street gang
(5-7)   **Fic**

Paradis, M. Mr De Luca's horse (4-7)   **Fic**

Raskin, E. The mysterious disappearance of
Leon (I mean Noel) (4-7)   **Fic**

Sawyer, R. Roller skates (4-6)   **Fic**

Selden, G. The cricket in Times Square (3-6)
Fic

Selden, G. Harry Cat's pet puppy (3-6) **Fic**

Steptoe, J. Train ride (3-6)   **Fic**

Stolz, M. The noonday friends (4-6)   **Fic**

Stolz, M. A wonderful, terrible time (4-6) **Fic**

Taylor, S. All-of-a-kind family (4-6) **Fic**

Waber, B. The house on East 88th Street **E**

Waber, B. Lyle, Lyle, crocodile   **E**

Fires and fire prevention

Beame, R. Ladder Company 108 (3-5) **363.3**

Government

See New York (City)—Politics and government

History

Hults, D. N. New Amsterdam days and ways
(4-7)   **974.7**

History—Fiction

Lobel, A. On the day Peter Stuyvesant sailed
into town   **E**

Politics and government

Kaufman, M. Fiorello La Guardia (2-4) **92**

Social life and customs

Hults, D. N. New Amsterdam days and ways
(4-7)   **974.7**

Zoological Park

Bridges, W. Zoo careers (6-7)   **590.74**

Nic Leodhas, Sorche—*Continued*

The bride who out talked the water kelpie
In Arbuthnot, M. H. comp. The Arbuthnot Anthology of children's literature p166-70   **808.8**
By loch and by lin (4-7)   **398.2**
Contents: The tale of the lay of the smithy; The tale of the lay of the Amadhain Mhor; The tale of the lay of the Lochmaben Harper; The tale of the Earl of Mar's daughter; The tale of Dick o' the cow; The tale of Bonnie Baby Livingston; The tale of lang Johnnie Mor; The tale of the famous flower of servingmen; The tale of the heir of Linne; The tale of the knight and the shepherd lass

The drowned bells of the abbey
In Brown, M. ed. A cavalcade of sea legends p131-37   **808.8**
Gaelic ghosts (4-7)   **398.2**
Contents: Sandy MacNeil and his dog; The giant bones; The gambling ghosts; The grateful old cailleach; The walking Boundary stone; The lady's loaf-field; The holy relic of Bannockburn; The man o' the clan; The old laird and his dogs; The house that lacked a bogle

The giant bones
In Mayne, W. ed. William Mayne's Book of giants p195-203   **398.2**
Heather and broom (4-7)   **398.2**
Contents: The Ailpein bird, the stolen princess, and the brave knight; The woman who flummoxed the fairies; The lairdie with the heart of gold; The gay goss-hawk; The lass that couldn't be frighted; The daughter of the King Ron; Spin, weave, wear; The bogles from the Howff

The man who didn't believe in ghosts
In Ireson, B. comp. Haunting tales p25-32   **S C**
Thistle and thyme (4-7)   **398.2**
Contents: The laird's lass and the gobha's son; St Cuddy and the gray geese; The stolen bairn and the Sidh; The lass who went out at the cry of dawn; The changeling and the fond young mother; The bride who out talked the water kelpie; The drowned bells of the abbey; The beekeeper and the bewitched hare; The fisherlad and the mermaid's ring; Michael Scott and the demon

Twelve great black cats, and other eerie Scottish tales (4-7)   **398.2**
Contents: Twelve great black cats and the red one; The honest ghost; The ghost of Hamish MacDonald, the fool of the family; The weeping lass at the dancing place; The flitting of the ghosts; The auld cailleach's curse; The shepherd who fought the March wind; The sea captain's wife; The man who missed the Tay Bridge Train; The lass and her good stout blackthorn stick

The woman who flummoxed the fairies
In Greene, E. comp. Clever cooks p13-24   **398.2**

Nicolas
(illus.) Will. Finders keepers   **E**
For other material by and about this illustrator see Mordvinoff, Nicolas

Nidden and Didden and Donal Beg O'Neary. MacManus, S.
In MacManus, S. Hibernian nights p141-47   **398.2**
See also Hudden and Dudden and Donald O'Neary

Niebrugge, Jane
(illus.) Hults, D. N. New Amsterdam days and ways   **974.7**

Nielsen, Jon
(illus.) Mulock, D. M. The little lame prince   **Fic**

The Niger: Africa's river of mystery. Watson, J.   **916.6**

Niger River
Watson, J. The Niger: Africa's river of mystery (4-6)   **916.6**

Nigeria
Forman, B. The land and people of Nigeria (5-7)   **916.69**

Agriculture
See Agriculture—Nigeria

Fisheries
See Fisheries—Nigeria

Folklore
See Folklore—Nigeria

Social life and customs
Jenness, A. Along the Niger River (5-7)   **916.69**

See also pages in the following book:
Berry, E. Eating and cooking around the world p63-69 (5-7)   **641.3**

Nigerian arts. See The arts, Nigerian

Night animals. Cohen, D.   **591.5**

The night before Christmas. Moore, C. C. **811**
—Same
In Martignoni, M. E. ed. The illustrated treasury of children's literature p144-45   **808.8**

The night daddy. Gripe, M.   **Fic**

Night people. Colby, C. B.   **331.7**

The night watchmen. Cresswell, H.   **Fic**

The night workers. Schwartz, A.   **331.7**

Nightingale, Florence
Harmelink, B. Florence Nightingale (5-7) **92**

See also pages in the following book:
McNeer, M. Armed with courage p7-22 (4-6)   **920**

The nightingale. Andersen, H. C.   **Fic**
—Same
In Andersen, H. C. Andersen's Fairy tales p262-72   **S C**
In Andersen, H. C. The complete fairy tales and stories p203-12   **S C**
In Andersen, H. Hans Andersen's Fairy tales p172-84   **S C**
In Andersen, H. C. It's perfectly true, and other stories p147-60   **S C**
In Colwell, E. ed. A storyteller's choice p174-84   **372.6**
In Farjeon, E. ed. A cavalcade of kings p16-30   **808.8**
In Johnson, E. ed. Anthology of children's literature p721-26   **808.8**
In Lang, A. ed. The yellow fairy book p291-300   **398.2**
In Sechrist, E. H. ed. It's time for story hour p249-58   **372.6**
In Shedlock, M. L. The art of the storyteller p243-58   **372.6**

The nightingale and the emperor. See Andersen, H. C. The nightingale   **Fic**

The Nightingale and the Rose. Wilde, O.
In Wilde, O. The Happy Prince, and other stories p13-20   **S C**

Nightingale in the mosque. Fillmore, P.
In Fillmore, P. The laughing prince p171-99   **398.2**

Nightingales

Stories

Andersen, H. C. The nightingale (3-5) **Fic**

The nightmare world of the shark. Cook, J. J.
597

Niilo and the wizard. Bowman, J. C.
In Bowman, J. C. Tales from a Finnish
tupa p141-46 **398.2**

Nile River

Naden, C. J. The Nile River (4-6) **962**

See also pages in the following books:

Mahoud, Z. N. The land and people of Egypt
p11-19 (5-7) **916.2**
Perl, L. East Africa p62-68 (4-7) **916.7**
Van Duyn, J. The Egyptians p21-31 (6-7)
913.32

Nile Valley

Naden, C. J. The Nile River (4-6) **962**

Nils in the forest. Manning-Sanders, R.
In Manning-Sanders, R. A book of ogres
and trolls p123-27 **398.2**

Nine cheers for Christmas. Wright, D. G.
In Kamerman, S. E. ed. A treasury of
Christmas plays p330-38 **812.08**

Nine days to Christmas. Ets, M. H. **E**

The nine doves. Manning-Sanders, R.
In Manning-Sanders, R. A book of dragons
p43-54 **398.2**
In Manning-Sanders, R. A choice of magic
p63-73 **398.2**

The Nine-headed giant
In De Regniers, B. S. ed. The giant book
p31-38 **398.2**

Nine pea-hens and the golden apples
Fillmore, P. Enchanted peafowl
In Fillmore, P. The laughing prince p107-
38 **398.2**

The nine planets. Branley, F. M. **523.4**

Nineteenth century
Foster, G. Year of Lincoln, 1861 (3-6) **909.81**

El Niño de la Panelita. Campbell, C.
In Campbell, C. Star Mountain, and other
legends of Mexico p53-54 **398.2**

Ninon
(illus.) McFarland, W. ed. For a child **821.08**

Niobe

See pages in the following book:

Gates, D. The golden god: Apollo p12-18
(4-7) **292**

Nis and the dame
Andersen, H. C. The pixy and the gardener's
wife
In Andersen, H. C. The complete fairy
tales and stories p853-56 **S C**

Nis at the grocer's
Andersen, H. The goblin at the provision-
dealer's
In Andersen, H. Hans Andersen's Fairy
tales p313-17 **S C**
Andersen, H. C. The pixy and the grocer
In Andersen, H. C. The complete fairy
tales and stories p424-27 **S C**
Grimm, J. The goblin and the grocer
In Grimm, J. The house in the wood, and
other fairy stories p36-45 **398.2**

Niven, Larry
Bird in the hand
In Silverberg, B. ed. Phoenix feathers p151-
76 **S C**
There is a wolf in my time machine
In Yolen, J. ed. Zoo 2000 p55-81 **S C**

Nivola, Claire A.
(illus.) Miles, B. Save the earth! **301.31**

Nix in the pond
Grimm, J. The nixie of the mill-pond
In Grimm, J. The complete Grimm's Fairy
tales p736-42 **398.2**
The Nixy
In Lang, A. ed. The yellow fairy book
p108-13 **398.2**

Nix Nought Nothing
In Jacobs, J. ed. English folk and fairy
tales p32-38 **398.2**

The nixie of the mill-pond. Grimm, J.
In Grimm, J. The complete Grimm's Fairy
tales p736-42 **398.2**
See also Nix in the pond

The Nixy
In Lang, A. ed. The yellow fairy book
p108-13 **398.2**
See also Nix in the pond

Njal, the lawyer. French, A.
In Hazeltine, A. I. ed. Hero tales from
many lands p297-304 **398.2**

Nkrumah, Kwame, President Ghana

See pages in the following book:

Sale, J. K. The land and people of Ghana
p91-120 (5-7) **916.67**

No-beard
In De La Mare, W. ed. Animal stories
p100-05 **398.2**

No braver soldier. Bierling, J. C. E.
In Burack, A. S. ed. One hundred plays for
children p803-12 **808.82**

No ducks in "our" bathtub. Alexander, M. **E**

No flying in the house. Brock, B. **Fic**

No flying in the house; excerpt. Brock, B.
In Arbuthnot, M. H. comp. The Arbuthnot
Anthology of children's literature
p523-26 **808.8**

No funny business. Hurd, E. T. **E**

No head. Leach, M.
In Leach, M. The thing at the foot of the
bed, and other scary tales p41-43 **S C**

No-mother land. Streacker, L.
In Kamerman, S. E. ed. Little plays for
little players p72-78 **812.08**

No one can fool a Helmite. Simon, S.
In Simon, S. The wise men of Helm and
their merry tales p17-22 **S C**

No promises in the wind. Hunt, I. **Fic**

No room. Dobbs, R. **398.2**

No room at the inn. Patterson, E. L.
In Burack, A. S. ed. Christmas plays for
young actors p13-23 **812.08**
In Burack, A. S. ed. One hundred plays
for children p551-59 **808.82**

No roses for Harry! Zion, G. **E**

No way of telling. Smith, E. **Fic**

Noah and the rainbow. Bolliger, M. **221.9**

O

Ocean—*Continued*

Selsam, M. See through the sea (2-4)   **591.92**

See also pages in the following books:

Bendick, J. The shape of the earth p56-60 (4-6)   **551**

Lauber, P. This restless earth p82-96 (5-7)   **551**

See also Icebergs; Oceanography; Seashore; Storms; Tides; also names of oceans and seas, e.g. Pacific Ocean

Economic aspects

See Marine resources

Fiction

Jansson, T. Moominpappa at sea (4-6)   **Fic**

Ocean cables. See Cables, Submarine

Ocean currents

Clemons, E. Waves, tides, and currents (4-6)   **551.4**

Ocean life. See Marine biology

Ocean mineral resources. See Marine mineral resources

Ocean travel

Fiction

Crayder, D. She, the adventuress (5-7)   **Fic**

Ocean waves

Clemons, E. Waves, tides, and currents (4-6)   **551.4**

Zim, H. S. Waves (3-5)   **551.4**

See also pages in the following books:

Carson, R. L. The sea around us. A special edition for young readers; adapted by Anne Terry White p89-105 (6-7)   **551.4**

Simon, S. Science at work: projects in oceanography p23-33 (5-7)   **551.4**

Oceanarium, Wonders of an. Jacobs, L.   **591.92**

Oceanariums. See Marine aquariums

Oceania. See Islands of the Pacific

Oceania: Polynesia, Melanesia, Micronesia. May, C. P.   **919**

Oceanographic Institute. Woods Hole, Mass. See Woods Hole, Mass. Oceanographic Institute

Oceanographic research. See Oceanography—Research

Oceanography

May, J. The land beneath the sea (3-5) **551.4**

Williams, J. Oceanography (5-7)   **551.4**

See also Marine biology; Marine resources; Ocean waves; Tides

Experiments

Simon, S. Science at work: projects in oceanography (5-7)   **551.4**

Research

Berger, M. Oceanography lab (4-6)   **551.4**

Brindze, R. The sea (5-7)   **333.9**

Oceanography as a profession

Berger, M. Oceanography lab (4-6)   **551.4**

Oceanography lab. Berger, M.   **551.4**

Oceanology. See Oceanography

O'Connell, Daniel

See pages in the following book:

O'Brien, E. The land and people of Ireland p82-85 (5-7)   **914.15**

O'Connor, Daniel

Peter's shadow

In Martignoni, M. E. ed. The illustrated treasury of children's literature p221-22   **808.8**

O'Connor, Frank

First confession

In Authors' choice p31-39   **S C**

O'Connor, Jerome J.

The telephone: how it works (5-7)   **621.385**

O'Connor, Richard

Sitting Bull: war chief of the Sioux (4-6) **92**

O'Connor, W. F.

The story of the stone lion

In Manning-Sanders, R. ed. A book of magical beasts p122-29   **398.2**

Octopus

Shaw, E. Octopus (1-2)   **594**

See also pages in the following book:

Hopf, A. L. Misunderstood animals p25-33 (4-7)   **591.5**

Oda and the snake. Manning-Sanders, R.

In Manning-Sanders, R. A book of sorcerers and spells p65-68   **398.2**

Odd one out. Peppé, R.   **E**

Oddities. See Curiosities and wonders

Odds and evens. O'Brien, T. C.   **513**

O'Dell, Scott

Island of the Blue Dolphins (5-7)   **Fic**

The King's fifth (6-7)   **Fic**

The King's fifth; excerpt

In Johnson, E. ed. Anthology of children's literature p882-84   **808.8**

Newbery Medal acceptance paper

In Kingman, L. ed. Newbery and Caldecott Medal books: 1956-1965 p99-104   **028.5**

Sing down the moon (5-7)   **Fic**

Sing down the moon; excerpt

In Arbuthnot, M. H. comp. The Arbuthnot Anthology of children's literature p767-69   **808.8**

About

See pages in the following books:

Hoffman, M. ed. Authors and illustrators of children's books p343-47   **028.5**

Kingman, L. ed. Newbery and Caldecott Medal books: 1956-1965 p105-08   **028.5**

Townsend, J. R. A sense of story p154-59   **028.5**

Odysseus. See Trojan War; Ulysses

Odysseus in the land of the giants. Colum, P.

In De Regniers, B. S. ed. The giant book p70-78   **398.2**

The **Odyssey** of Homer. Church, A. J.

In Church, A. J. The Iliad and the Odyssey of Homer   **883**

Oechsli, Kelly

(illus.) Larrick, N. comp. Green is like a meadow of grass   **811.08**

(illus.) Larrick, N. ed. Piper, pipe that song again!   **821.08**

(illus.) Larrick, N. comp. Poetry for holidays   **811.08**

(illus.) Shakespeare, W. Seeds of time **822.3**

Of course you can sew! Corrigan, B.   **646.4**

One trick too many. Ginsburg, M. comp.   398.2

One trick too many; story
   In Ginsburg, M. comp. One trick too many
     p17-20   398.2

One-Two-Man and Stoneshirt. Baumann, H.
   In Baumann, H. The stolen fire p122-26
                                                          398.2

1, 2, 3, to the zoo. Carle, E.   E

1, 2, 3's, Brian Wildsmith's. Wildsmith, B.   E

One, two, where's my shoe? Ungerer, T.   E

One wide river to cross (Folk song)
   One wide river to cross (k-3)   784.4

One wish too many. Feather, J.
   In Kamerman, S. E. ed. Dramatized folk
     tales of the world p191-99   812.08

One you don't see coming. Courlander, H.
   In Courlander, H. The cow-tail switch, and
     other West African stories p31-40
                                                          398.2

O'Neill, Mary
   Hailstones and halibut bones (k-4)   811

Ones that count. Moore, M. G.
   In Association for Childhood Education
     International. Told under spacious
     skies p160-69   S C

Ong's hat; puppet play. Jagendorf, M.
   In Penny puppets, penny theatre, and
     penny plays p127-34   791.5

Onion John. Krumgold, J.   Fic

Only a fair day's huntin'
   In Chase, R. ed. Grandfather tales p180-85
                                                          398.2

Only connect. Egoff, S. ed.   028.5

Only in Texas. Jagendorf, M. A.
   In Jagendorf, M. A. Folk stories of the
     South p281-83   398.2

Only the names remain. Bealer, A. W.   970.3

Ontario. Provincial Library Service
   In Review. See In Review   028.505

An Onteroa visitor. Wheeler, C.
   In A St Nicholas anthology p238-42   810.8

Onyshkewych, Zenowij
   (illus.) Freeman, I. M. The science of chem-
     istry   540

Oonark
   (illus.) Lewis, R. ed. I breathe a new song 897

Ootah's lucky day. Parish, P.   E

Opele-of-the-Long-Sleeps. Thompson, V. L.
   In Thompson, V. L. Hawaiian tales of
     heroes and champions p43-50   398.2

The open road. Grahame, K.
   In Arbuthnot, M. H. comp. The Arbuthnot
     Anthology of children's literature
     p488-93   808.8

Open the door and see all the people.
   Bulla, C. R.   Fic

Open Winkins. Farjeon, E.
   In Farjeon, E. Martin Pippin in the apple
     orchard p159-94   S C

Opera
   Streatfeild, N. The first book of the opera
     (4-7)   782.1

Operas
           Stories, plots, etc.
   Bulla, C. R. More Stories of favorite operas
     (5-7)   782.1
   Bulla, C. R. Stories of favorite operas (5-7)
                                                          782.1
   Grimm, W. Hansel and Gretel (3-5)   782.1
   Montresor, B. Cinderella (2-4)   782.1
   Updike, J. The Ring (4-7)   782.1

The operating room. Kay, E.   617

Operation Arctic. Hamre, L.   Fic

Operation litterbug. Boiko, C.
   In Boiko, C. Children's plays for creative
     actors p322-28   812

Operations Satellite; play. Carlson, B. W.
   In Carlson, B. W. Play a part p85-89 792

Opie, Iona
   Children's games in street and playground
                                                          796.1

   (ed.) The classic fairy tales   398.2
   (comp.) A family book of nursery rhymes
                                                          398.8
   The lore and language of schoolchildren 398
   Mother Goose. The Mother Goose treasury
                                                          398.8
   (ed.) The Oxford Book of children's verse.
     See The Oxford Book of Children's verse
                                                        821.08
   (ed.) The Oxford Dictionary of nursery
     rhymes. See The Oxford Dictionary of nur-
     sery rhymes   398.8
   (comp.) The Oxford Nursery rhyme book. See
     The Oxford Nursery rhyme book   398.8

Opie, Peter
   Mother Goose. The Mother Goose treasury
                                                          398.8
   (jt. auth.) Opie, I. Children's games in street
     and playground   796.1
   (jt. ed.) Opie, I. ed. The classic fairy tales
                                                          398.2
   (jt. comp.) Opie, I. comp. A family book of
     nursery rhymes   398.8
   (jt. auth.) Opie, I. The lore and language of
     schoolchildren   398
   (ed.) The Oxford Book of children's verse.
     See The Oxford Book of children's verse
                                                        821.08
   (ed.) The Oxford dictionary of nursery
     rhymes. See The Oxford Dictionary of
     nursery rhymes   398.8
   (ed.) The Oxford Nursery rhyme book. See
     The Oxford Nursery rhyme book   398.8

Opossum. Mizumura, K.   599

Opossums
   McClung, R. M. Possum (2-4)   599
   Mizumura, K. Opossum (k-2)   599
             Stories
   Berson, H. Henry Possum   E
   Conford, E. Impossible, possum   E
   Hoban, R. Nothing to do   E
   Miles, M. Mississippi possum (2-4)   Fic

Oppenheim, Joanne
   Have you seen roads? (k-2)   625.7

Oppenheimer, Lillian
   (jt. auth.) Lewis, S. Folding paper masks 736

Optical illusions
   Beeler, N. F. Experiments in optical illusion
     (5-7)   535.072

Painters, Flemish

See pages in the following book:

Craven, T. The rainbow book of art p115-24 (5-7)   **709**

Painters, French

Price, O. Rosa Bonheur, painter of animals (4-6)   **92**

Painters, German

See pages in the following book:

Craven, T. The rainbow book of art p146-57 (5-7)   **709**

Painters, Italian

Jacobs, D. Master painters of the Renaissance (6-7)   **759.5**

Rockwell, A. The boy who drew sheep [biography of Giotto di Bondone] (3-5)   **92**

Painters, Spanish

Ripley, E. Velasquez (6-7)   **92**

See also pages in the following book:

Craven, T. The rainbow book of art p158-71 (5-7)   **709**

Painters' materials. See Artists' materials

Painting

Chase, A. E. Looking at art (6-7)   **701**

Spilka, A. Paint all kinds of pictures (k-3) **751**

Weiss, H. Paint, brush and palette (5-7) **751**

    See also Color; Stencil work; Water color painting

Technique

Seidelman, J. E. Creating with paint (4-7)   **751.4**

Weiss, H. Paint, brush and palette (5-7) **751**

See also pages in the following book:

Downer, M. Discovering design p80-103 (5-7)   **745.4**

Painting, Colombian

See pages in the following book:

Landry, L. The land and people of Colombia p139-43 (5-7)   **918.61**

Painting, Danish

See pages in the following book:

Wohlrabe, R. A. The land and people of Denmark p127-31 (5-7)   **914.89**

Painting, Dutch

See pages in the following book:

Barnouw, A. J. The land and people of Holland p69-75, 121-26 (5-7)   **914.92**

Painting, Italian

Jacobs, D. Master painters of the Renaissance (6-7)   **759.5**

Painting, Spanish

See pages in the following book:

Goldston, R. Spain p54-56 (4-7)   **914.6**

Paintings, American

Jordan, J. Who look at me (6-7)   **811**

A pair of red clogs. Matsuno, M.   **E**

Paiute Indians

Fiction

Fife, D. Ride the crooked wind (4-6)   **Fic**

Legends

Hodges, M. The Fire Bringer (2-5)   **398.2**

El Pájaro-cú. Campbell, C.

In Campbell, C. Star Mountain, and other legends of Mexico p78-82   **398.2**

Pakistan

Lang, R. The land and people of Pakistan (6-7)   **915.49**

Palace in the rath. O'Faolain, E.

In O'Faolain, E. Irish sagas and folktales p200-04   **398.2**

Palace made by music. Alden, R. M.

In Alden, R. M. Why the chimes rang, and other stories p80-91   **S C**

Palace of the eagles

King Solomon's carpet

In Baker, A. comp. The talking tree p218-31   **398.2**

The **palace** of the seven little hills. Manning-Sanders, R.

In Manning-Sanders, R. A book of sorcerers and spells p45-55   **398.2**

Palaček, Josef

(illus.) Andersen, H. C. The ugly duckling **Fic**

Palazzo, Tony

(illus.) Bible. Selections. Wings of the morning   **220.5**

(illus.) Graham, A. Timothy Turtle   **E**

Paleobotany. See Plants, Fossil

Paleontology. See Fossils

Palestine

Description and travel

See pages in the following book:

Farb, P. The land, wildlife, and peoples of the Bible p149-59 (5-7)   **220.8**

History

See pages in the following book:

Savage, K. The story of the United Nations p133-51 (6-7)   **341.23**

Social life and customs

See pages in the following book:

Sechrist, E. H. ed. Christmas everywhere p178-86   **394.2**

A palindrome. Babbitt, N.

In Babbitt, N. The Devil's storybook p53-61   **S C**

Palio. See Siena. Palio

Palladini, David

(illus.) Branley, F. M. The end of the world   **525**

(illus.) Goode, R. People of the Ice Age   **573.2**

(illus.) Yolen, J. The girl who cried flowers, and other tales   **S C**

Palladino, Eusapia

See pages in the following book:

Cohen, D. In search of ghosts p104-14 (6-7)   **133**

Pallas, Dorothy Constance

(jt. auth) Fenton, C. L. Reptiles and their world   **598.1**

(jt. auth.) Fenton, C. L. Trees and their world   **582**

Palmer, Elizabeth
Give me a river; excerpt
In Association for Childhood Education
International. Told under the Stars
and Stripes p150-58 **S C**

Palmer, Geoffrey
Huw
In Ireson, B. comp. Haunting tales p11-
24 **S C**
Mungo
In Hoke, H. ed. Spooks, spooks, spooks
p21-33 **S C**
Quest for the Dead Sea scrolls (5-7) **229**

Palmer, Jan
(illus.) Hildick, E. W. Manhattan is missing **Fic**

Palmer, Joe H.
This was racing; excerpts
In Anderson, C. W. ed. C. W. Anderson's Favorite horse stories p15-23
808.8

Palmer, Julia Reed
Read for your life **028.52**

Palmer, Robin
Dragons, unicorns, and other magical beasts
(4-6) **398.2**

Contents: The bored tengu; The Kildare pooka; The
terrible-tempered dragon; The werewolf; The Hedley
Kow; Manstin, the rabbit; The story of Zal; The king
and the nagas

The same language
In Luckhardt, M. C. comp. Thanksgiving
p191-98 **394.2**
The terrible tempered dragon
In Hoke, H. comp. Dragons, dragons,
dragons p223-30 **398.2**
(comp.) Bible. Selections. Wings of the
morning **220.5**

Palsy, Cerebral. See Cerebral palsy

Pamphlets

Bibliography

George Peabody College for Teachers, Nashville, Tenn. Free and inexpensive learning materials **016.371**
Vertical file index **015**

Indexes

Vertical file index **015**

Pan American Day

See pages in the following book:

Sechrist, E. H. Red letter days p96-103
394.2

Pan (Deity)

See pages in the following book:

Gates, D. The golden god: Apollo p43-48
(4-7) **292**

Pán Kotsky
In Bloch, M. H. ed. Ukrainian folk tales
p24-27 **398.2**

Panama
Carpenter, A. Panama (4-6) **918.62**

See also pages in the following book:

Markun, P. M. The first book of Central
America and Panama p55-59 (5-7) **917.28**

Panama Canal
See pages in the following book:
Landry, L. The land and people of Colom-
bia p146-51 (5-7) **918.61**

Pan'ambe and Pen'ambe. Carpenter, F.
In Carpenter F. People from the sky
p76-80 **398.2**

Pancake
Asbjörnsen, P. C. The pancake
In Arbuthnot, M. H. comp. The Arbuth-
not Anthology of children's litera-
ture p238-39 **808.8**
In Arbuthnot, M. H. comp. Time for old
magic p116-17 **398.2**
In Johnson, E. ed. Anthology of chil-
dren's literature p288-89 **808.8**
The Pancake
In Hutchinson, V. S. ed. Chimney cor-
ner stories p19-24 **398.2**
Thorne-Thomsen, G. The pancake
In Association for Childhood Education In-
ternational. Told under the green
umbrella p10-15 **398.2**
See also Bun; Gingerbread boy; Johnny-
cake; Wee bannock

Pancakes and pies. Manning-Sanders, R.
In Manning-Sanders, R. A book of charms
and changelings p62-66 **398.2**

Pancakes—Paris. Bishop, C. H. **Fic**

Panchatantra
The Broken pot
In Jacobs, J. ed. Indian fairy tales p38-
39 **398.2**
Dutton, M. B. The partridge and the crow
In Arbuthnot, M. H. comp. The Arbuth-
not Anthology of children's litera-
ture p420 **808.8**
In Arbuthnot, M. H. comp. Time for old
magic p284 **398.2**
Dutton, M. B. The tyrant who became a
just ruler
In Arbuthnot, M. H. comp. The Arbuth-
not Anthology of children's litera-
ture p420-21 **808.8**
In Arbuthnot, M. H. comp. Time for old
magic p284-85 **398.2**
The Gold-giving serpent
In Jacobs, J. ed. Indian fairy tales p112-
14 **398.2**
Numskull and the rabbit
In Davis, M. G. ed. A baker's dozen p51-
62 **372.6**
In Johnson, E. ed. Anthology of children's
literature p315-18 **808.8**
The Panchatantra and Bidpai fables
In Johnson, E. ed. Anthology of chil-
dren's literature p103-06 **808.8**
Ryder, A. W. The mice that ate iron
In Arbuthnot, M. H. comp. The Arbuth-
not Anthology of children's litera-
ture p421-22 **808.8**
In Arbuthnot, M. H. comp. Time for old
magic p285-86 **398.2**

The **Panchatantra** and Bidpai fables
In Johnson, E. ed. Anthology of children's literature p103-06 **808.8**

Panchatantra; excerpts
In Gaer, J. The fables of India p11-49
398.2

Parker, Robert Andrew
(illus.) Clark, A. N. Hoofprint on the wind
　　Fic
(illus.) Cole, W. comp. A book of animal
　poems　　821.08
(illus.) Cole, W. ed. A book of nature poems
　　821.08
(illus.) Jones, H. comp. The trees stand shin-
　ing　　897
(illus.) Preston, E. M. Pop Corn & Ma Good-
　ness　　E

Parker, Theodore
　　See pages in the following book:
Chittenden, E. F. Profiles in black and white
　p88-106 (5-7)　　920

Parker, Xenia Ley
A beginner's book of knitting and crocheting
　(5-7)　　746.4

Parkhouse, Tony
(illus.) Hoke, H. Jokes and fun　　793.7

Parkin, Rex
The red carpet　　E

Parks, Gordon, 1912–
Harnan, T. Gordon Parks: Black photogra-
　pher and film maker (3-6)　　92

Parks, Gordon, 1935?–
(illus.) Wagner, J. J. T.　　Fic

Parks, Michael
(illus.) Jagendorf, M. A. Folk stories of the
　South　　398.2

Parks, Rosa Lee
Greenfield, E. Rosa Parks (2-4)　　92

Parks
Hautzig, E. In the park (k-3)　　410
　　See also National parks and reserves;
　　Zoological gardens

Parley, Peter. See Goodrich, Samuel Griswold

Parliamentary practice
Powers, D. G. The first book of how to run
　a meeting (5-7)　　060.4
Robert, H. M. Robert's Rules of order 060.4
　　See also pages in the following book:
Bailard, V. So you were elected! p21-85 (6-7)
　　367

Parnall, Peter
The mountain　　E
(illus.) Baylor, B. Everybody needs a rock　E
(illus.) Freschet, B. Year on Muskrat Marsh
　　591.5
(illus.) George, J. C. The moon of the wild
　pigs　　599
(illus.) Hoberman, M. A. A little book of little
　beasts　　811
(illus.) Hodges, M. The Fire Bringer　398.2
(illus.) Miles, M. Annie and the Old One　Fic
(illus.) Miles, M. Apricot ABC　　811
(illus.) Pringle, L. Twist, wiggle, and squirm
　　595
(illus.) Schlein, M. The rabbit's world　　E
(illus.) Yolen, J. ed. The fireside song book of
　birds and beasts　　784.4

Parnell's discovering nature. See The Double-
　day Nature encyclopedia　　500.9

Parrakeets. See Budgerigars

Parrakeets. Zim, H. S.　　636.6

Parrish, Anne
　　See pages in the following book:
A Horn Book Sampler on children's books and
　reading p4-7　　028.5

Parrish, Dillwyn
　　See pages in the following book:
A Horn Book Sampler on children's books and
　reading p4-7　　028.5

Parrish, George Dillwyn. See Parrish, Dillwyn

Parrish, Maxfield
(illus.) Field, E. Poems of childhood　　811
(illus.) Wiggin, K. D. ed. The Arabian nights
　　398.2

Parrish, Thomas
The American flag (4-7)　　929.9

The **parrot** and the parson. Hardendorff. J. B.
　In Hardendorff, J. B. ed. Just one more
　　p49-51　　372.6

The **Parrot** of Limo Verde
　In Baker, A. comp. The talking tree p179-
　　83　　398.2

Parrot that fed his parents
Shedlock, M. L. Filial piety
　In Shedlock, M. L. The art of the story-
　　teller p229-32　　372.6

The **parrot** who wouldn't say Cataño. Belpré, P.
　In Belpré, P. Once in Puerto Rico p85-90
　　398.2

Parrots

Stories

Zacharias, T. But where is the green parrot?
　　E

Parry, David
(illus.) Ottley, R. The roan colt　　Fic

Parry, Marian
(illus.) Ginsburg, M. ed. The lazies　　398.2

Parsifal; adaptation. Bulla, C. R.
　In Bulla, C. R. Stories of favorite operas
　　p115-27　　782.1

The **Parson** and the sexton
　In Asbjørnsen, P. C. Norwegian folk tales
　　p15-16　　398.2
　In Undset, S. ed. True and untrue, and
　　other Norse tales p233-35　　398.2

Parson Weems. See Weems, Mason Locke

Parsons, Margaret
Too much of a good thing
　In Kamerman, S. E. ed. Little plays for
　　little players p196-210　　812.08

Parthenon. See Athens. Parthenon

Parties
Ellison, V. H. The Pooh party book (1-5)
　　793.2
Frame, J. How to give a party (4-6)　793.2
Freeman, L. M. Betty Crocker's Parties for
　children (1-5)　　793.2
　　See also pages in the following book:
Girl Scouts of the United States of America.
　Girl scout cookbook p148-53 (4-7)　641.5

Parties, Political. See Political parties

Parties for children, Betty Crocker's. Freeman,
　L. M.　　793.2

A **penny** a day. De La Mare, W.   **S C**
A **penny** a day; short story. De La Mare, W.
    In De La Mare, W. A penny a day p3-31
       S C
A **penny** a look. Zemach, H.   **398.2**
Penny and Peter. Haywood, C. See note under
    Haywood, C. Here's a Penny   **Fic**
Penny goes to camp. Haywood, C. See note
    under Haywood, C. Here's a Penny   **Fic**
Penny puppets, penny theatre, and penny plays.
    Jagendorf, M.   **791.5**
Penny whistles. See Stevenson, R. L. A child's
    garden of verses   **821**
Penny wise. Boiko, C.
    In Boiko, C. Children's plays for creative
       actors p66-74   **812**
Pennyworth. Farjeon, E.
    In Farjeon, E. The little bookroom p208-
       15   **S C**
Penrod's story about Uncle John. Tarkington, B.
    In Martignoni, M. E. ed. The illustrated
       treasury of children's literature p470-
       74   **808.8**
People can't be made from iron
    In McDowell, R. E. ed. Third World
       voices for children p29-30   **398.2**
People from the sky. Carpenter, F.   **398.2**
People from the sky; story. Carpenter, F.
    In Carpenter, F. People from the sky p 1-8
       398.2
People in books. Nicholsen, M. E.   **920.01**
The **people** of Concord. Wood, J. P.   **920**
People of the Bible. Northcott, C.   **220.9**
People of the Heron and the Hummingbird.
    Roy, C.
    In Roy, C. The serpent and the sun p66-75
       398.2
People of the Ice Age. Goode, R.   **573.2**
People of the short blue corn. Courlander, H.
       398.2
Pepe and the cornfield bandit. Boiko, C.
    In Kamerman, S. E. ed. Dramatized folk
       tales of the world p324-33   **812.08**
Pepito. Manning-Sanders, R.
    In Manning-Sanders, R. A book of dragons
       p62-75   **398.2**
Peppé, Rodney
    Circus numbers   **E**
    Odd one out   **E**
    (illus.) Mother Goose. Hey riddle diddle!
       398.8
Pepper

    See pages in the following book:

    Sullivan, G. How do they grow it? p39-44
    (5-7)   **631.5**
Pepper (Spice)

    See pages in the following book:

    Cooper, E. K. And everything nice p30-36
    (3-5)   **641.3**
Pepper & salt. Pyle, H.   **398.2**
The **peppercorn** oxen. Manning-Sanders, R.
    In Manning-Sanders, R. A book of devils
       and demons p69-75   **398.2**

The **pepperman's** nightcap. Andersen, H. C.
    In Andersen, H. C. The complete fairy
       tales and stories p528-38   **S C**
The **peppermint** pig. Bawden, N.   **Fic**
Peppi. Manning-Sanders, R.
    In Manning-Sanders, R. A book of charms
       and changelings p85-97   **398.2**
Peppino. Manning-Sanders, R.
    In Manning-Sanders, R. Gianni and the
       ogre p179-92   **398.2**
Per, Paal, and Espen Cinderlad
    In Aulaire, I. d'. East of the sun and west
       of the moon p93-99   **398.2**
Perambulatin' pumpkin. Credle, E.
    In Credle, E. Tall tales from the high hills,
       and other stories p16-20   **398.2**
    In Greene, E. comp. Clever cooks p137-42
       398.2
The **perambulating** pie. Pyle, M. T.
    In Burack, A. S. ed. Christmas plays for
       young actors p81-94   **812.08**
Perception
    Bendick, J. Observation (2-4)   **153.7**
Percussion instruments
    Kettlekamp, L. Drums, rattles, and bells (4-7)
       789
Peretz, I. L.
    Shulevitz, U. The magician   **398.2**
Perez and Martina. Belpré, P.   **398.2**
    See also Perez the mouse
Perez and Martina. Alegría, R. E.
    In Alegría, R. E. The three wishes p56-58
       398.2

    See also Perez the mouse

Perez the mouse
    Alegría, R. E. Perez and Martina
    In Alegría, R. E. The three wishes p56-58
       398 2
    Belpré, P. Perez and Martina   **398.2**
    Coloma, Louis de. Perez the Mouse
    In Harper, W. comp. Merry Christmas to
       you p230-40   **394.2**
    See also Mistress Cockroach
The **perfect** gift. Du Bois, H. G.
    In Burack, A. S. ed. Christmas plays for
       young actors p67-80   **812.08**
The **perfect** life. Faber, D.   **289.8**
Perfection. Babbitt, N.
    In Babbitt, N. The Devil's storybook p73-
       77   **S C**
Performing arts. See art forms performed on
    stage or screen, e.g. Ballet
Performing plants. Budlong, W. T.   **581**
Pericles

    See pages in the following book:

    Coolidge, O. The golden days of Greece p70-
    80 (4-6)   **938**
The **Perilous** Gard. Pope, E. M.   **Fic**
The **perilous** road. Steele, W. O.   **Fic**
Periodical List Subcommittee. See American
    Library Association. Periodical List Sub-
    committee
Periodicals
    See also American periodicals; and
    general subjects with subdivision Periodi-
    cals, e.g. Children's literature—Periodicals

Perrault, Charles—*Continued*
Perrault's Complete fairy tales (4-6) **398.2**
The stories by Perrault are: The sleeping beauty in the wood; Puss in boots; Little Tom Thumb; The fairies; Ricky of the Tuft; Cinderella; Little Red Riding Hood; Blue Beard; The ridiculous wishes; Donkey-skin; Patient Griselda

Puss in Boots (k-3) **398.2**
—Same
In Haviland, V. comp. The fairy tale treasury p122-27 **398.2**
In Martignoni, M. E. ed. The illustrated treasury of children's literature p285-88 **808.8**
In Rackham, A. comp. Arthur Rackham Fairy book p233-39 **398.2**
In Untermeyer, B. ed. The Golden Treasury of children's literature p96-105 **808.8**

The sleeping beauty
In Fairy tales from many lands p52-65 **398.2**
In Rackham, A. comp. Arthur Rackham Fairy book p182-89 **398.2**
In Untermeyer, B. ed. The Golden Treasury of children's literature p76-87 **808.8**

The sleeping beauty in the wood
In Arbuthnot, M. H. comp. The Arbuthnot Anthology of children's literature p207-10 **808.8**
In Arbuthnot, M. H. comp. Time for old magic p84-87 **398.2**
In Lang, A. ed. The blue fairy book p54-63 **398.2**
In Opie, I. ed. The classic fairy tales p85-92 **398.2**

Toads and diamonds
In Johnson, E. ed. Anthology of children's literature p181-82 **808.8**
In Lang, A. ed. The blue fairy book p274-77 **398.2**
In Rackham, A. comp. Arthur Rackham Fairy book p196-98 **398.2**
Fischer, H. Puss in Boots **398.2**

Perrault's Complete fairy tales. Perrault, C. **398.2**

Perrifool
Haviland, V. Peerifool
In Haviland, V. Favorite fairy tales told in Scotland p25-48 **398.2**

Perrine, Mary
Salt Boy **E**

Perrott, Jennifer
(illus.) Meyer, C. Yarn—the things it makes and how to make them **746.4**

Perry, John
Zoos (4-6) **590.74**

Perry, Oliver Hazard

See pages in the following book:

Ault, P. These are the Great Lakes p73-81 (5-7) **977**

Perry, Roger
The Galápagos Islands (5-7) **500.9**

Persephone
Farmer, P. The story of Persephone (3-5) **292**
Hodges, M. Persephone and the springtime (k-3) **292**
Proddow, P. Demeter and Persephone (3-6) **292**

Tomaino, S. F. Persephone: bringer of spring (2-5) **292**

Persephone and the springtime. Hodges, M. **292**
Persephone: bringer of spring. Tomaino, S. F. **292**

Perseus

See pages in the following books:

Gates, D. The warrior goddess: Athena p24-50 (4-7) **292**
Hamilton, E. Mythology p197-208 **292**
Johnson, E. ed. Anthology of children's literature p486-90 **808.8**
Lang, A. ed. The blue fairy book p182-92 (4-6) **398.2**
Serraillier, I. The Gorgon's head (4-6) **292**

Persia

See also Iran

Folklore

See Folklore—Persia

Persia, The first book of ancient Mesopotamia and. Robinson, C. A. **913.35**
Persian folk and fairy tales. Mehdevi, A. S. **398.2**

Persian mythology. See Mythology, Persian
Personal finance. See Finance, Personal
Personal liberty. See Liberty
Personal names. See Names, Personal
Perspective

See pages in the following book:

Weiss, H. Pencil, pen and brush p44-45 (5-7) **741.2**

See also Drawing

Peru
Bowen, J. D. The land and people of Peru (5-7) **918.5**
Carpenter, A. Peru (4-6) **918.5**
See also pages in the following book:
Carter, W. E. The first book of South America p31-36 (4-6) **918**

Antiquities

Baumann, H. Gold and gods of Peru (6-7) **980.3**
Glubok, S. The art of ancient Peru (4-7) **985**

Education

See Education—Peru

Fiction

Clark, A. N. Secret of the Andes (4-7) **Fic**
Surany, A. Ride the cold wind **E**

History

Glubok, S. The fall of the Incas (5-7) **980.3**

Pessino, Catherine
(jt. auth.) Hussey, L. J. Collecting cocoons **595.7**
(jt. auth.) Hussey, L. J. Collecting small fossils **560**

Pest control
See also names of specific pests with the subdivision Control, e.g. Rats—Control

Biological control

Pringle, L. Pests and people (5-7) **632**
See also pages in the following book:
Fenten, D. X. Gardening . . . naturally p60-70 (4-7) **635**

Petersham, Miska—*Continued*
(illus.) Association for Childhood Education International. Told under the Christmas tree   **808.8**
(illus.) Bible. New Testament. Selections. The Christ child   **232.9**
(illus.) Clark, M. The poppy seed cakes   **E**
(jt. comp.) Petersham, M. comp. The rooster crows   **398.8**
(illus.) Sandburg, C. Rootabaga stories   **S C**

About

See pages in the following book:

Miller, B. M. ed. Caldecott Medal books: 1938-1957 p142-49   **028.5**

Peterson, Carolyn Sue
Reference books for elementary and junior high school libraries   **016**

Peterson, Harold L.
Forts in America (4-7)   **623**
A history of body armor (4-7)   **623.4**
A history of knives (4-7)   **683**

Peterson, Helen Stone
Abigail Adams: "Dear Partner" (2-5)   **92**
The making of the United States Constitution (4-6)   **342.2**
Susan B. Anthony, pioneer in woman's rights (3-5)   **92**

Peterson, John
How to write codes and send secret messages (2-4)   **652.8**

Peterson, Mary Nygaard
Abe buys a barrel
  In Kamerman, S. E. ed. Fifty plays for junior actors p460-70   **812.08**
Adobe Christmas
  In Kamerman, S. E. ed. A treasury of Christmas plays p254-62   **812.08**
The magic box
  In Kamerman, S. E. ed. Dramatized folk tales of the world p265-77   **812.08**
The magic fishbone
  In Kamerman, S. E. ed. Fifty plays for junior actors p471-80   **812.08**
Pedro and the burro
  In Kamerman, S. E. ed. Dramatized folk tales of the world p458-70   **812.08**
Simple Olaf
  In Kamerman, S. E. ed. Dramatized folk tales of the world p413-21   **812.08**

Peterson, Roger Tory
A field guide to the birds   **598.2**
A field guide to Western birds   **598.2**
How to know the birds   **598.2**
(illus.) Petrides, G. A. A field guide to trees and shrubs   **582**

Petey. Cavanna, B.   **Fic**

Petie, Haris
(illus.) Broderick, D. M. Training a companion dog   **636.7**
(illus.) Cohen, D. Night animals   **591.5**
(illus.) Keen, M. L. The world beneath our feet   **631.4**
(illus.) Limburg, P. R. Watch out, it's poison ivy!   **581.6**
(illus.) Nespojohn, K. V. Worms   **595**
(illus.) Unkelbach, K. Both ends of the leash   **636.7**

Petrides, George A.
A field guide to trees and shrubs   **582**

Petrie, Sir William Matthew Flinders
See pages in the following book:
Van Duyn, J. The Egyptians p74-78 (6-7)   **913.32**

Petrified Forest National Park
See pages in the following book:
Melbo, I. R. Our country's national parks v 1 p257-72 (5-7)   **917.3**

Petroleum
See pages in the following books:
Boorstin, D. J. The Landmark history of the American people v2 p8-15 (6-7)   **973**
Brindze, R. The sea p44-54 (5-7)   **333.9**
Freeman, I. M. The science of chemistry p29-35 (5-7)   **540**

Petroleum as fuel
See pages in the following book:
Shuttlesworth, D. E. Disappearing energy p41-49 (5-7)   **333.7**

Petroleum industry and trade
See pages in the following books:
Copeland, P. W. The land and people of Libya p144-53 (5-7)   **916.1**
Landry, L. The land and people of Colombia p113-20 (5-7)   **918.61**
Stefansson, E. Here is Alaska p5-18 (6-7)   **917.98**

Petroleum pollution of water
See pages in the following book:
Berger, M. Oceanography lab p90-97 (4-6)   **551.4**

Petrology
Fenton, C. L. Rocks and their stories (4-6)   **549**
  See also Crystallography; Geology; Lunar petrology; Mineralogy; Rocks; Stone

Petronella. Williams, J.   **Fic**

Petros' war. Zei, A.   **Fic**

Petros' war; excerpt. Zei, A.
  In Arbuthnot, M. H. comp. The Arbuthnot Anthology of children's literature p772-75   **808.8**

Petrouchka. Untermeyer, L.
  In Untermeyer, L. Tales from the ballet p36-39   **792.8**

Petrovitch, W. M.
The friendly animals
  In Manning-Sanders, R. ed. A book of magical beasts p164-76   **398.2**

Petry, Ann
Tituba of Salem Village; excerpt
  In Johnson, E. ed. Anthology of children's literature p873-77   **808.8**

Pets
Caras, R. A zoo in your room (4-7)   **636.08**
Chrystie, F. N. Pets (4-7)   **636.08**
Ricciuti, E. R. Shelf pets (5-7)   **639**
Shuttlesworth, D. E. Gerbils, and other small pets (3-6)   **636.08**
Stevens, C. Your first pet (2-4)   **636.08**
Villiard, P. Birds as pets (5-7)   **636.6**
Villiard, P. Insects as pets (5-7)   **595.7**
  See also pages in the following book:
Simon, H. Snakes p107-15 (5-7)   **598.1**
    See also Domestic animals; also names of animals, e.g. Cats

Philleo, Prudence (Crandall)—*Continued*
Fiction
Underwood, B. The tamarack tree (6-7)　**Fic**

Phillips, Ernestine
Aesop, man of fables
In Kamerman, S. E. ed. Fifty plays for junior actors p481-97　**812.08**

Phillips, Ethel Calvert
Johnny Ping Wing
In Gruenberg, S. M. ed. Favorite stories old and new p235-40　**808.8**
Wee Ann spends a penny
In Association for Childhood Education International. Told under the blue umbrella p80-86　**S C**

Phillips, Marguerite Kreger
Violets for Christmas
In Kamerman, S. E. ed. A treasury of Christmas plays p158-75　**812.08**

Phillips, Mary G.
The feel of things
In Association for Childhood Education International. Told under the blue umbrella p25-29　**S C**
Paddy's three pets
In Association for Childhood Education International. Told under the blue umbrella p43-48　**S C**

Phillips, Michael J.
(illus.) Slaughter, J. Horsemanship for beginners　**798**

Philology. See Language and languages

Philology, Comparative. See Language and languages

Philosophers, Greek

See pages in the following book:

Van Duyn, J. The Greeks p137-54 (6-7)　**913.38**

The philosophers of King Darius. Courlander, H.
In Courlander, H. The tiger's whisker, and other tales and legends from Asia and the Pacific p106-10　**398.2**

The philosopher's stone. Andersen, H. C.
In Andersen, H. C. The complete fairy tales and stories p501-15　**S C**

Philosophy, Moral. See Ethics

Phipson, Joan
The boundary riders (5-7)　**Fic**
The family conspiracy (5-7)　**Fic**
Good luck to the rider (5-7)　**Fic**
The way home (5-7)　**Fic**

Phoenician mythology. See Mythology, Phoenician

Phoenicians. See Phenicians

Phoenix feathers. Silverberg, B. ed.　**S C**

Phonograph records
Bibliography
New York Library Association. Children's and Young Adult Services Section. Recordings for children　**016.7899**

Photographers
Harnan, T. Gordon Parks: Black photographer and film maker (3-6)　**92**

Photography
Holland, V. How to photograph your world (3-5)　**770**
Noren, C. Photography: how to improve your technique (5-7)　**770.28**
Weiss, H. Lens and shutter (5-7)　**770.28**
See also pages in the following books:
Frankel, L. Bike-ways (101 things to do with a bike) p120-26 (4-6)　**796.6**
The Way things work. Special edition for young people p180-88, 192-201 (6-7)　**600**
See also Cameras; Moving picture photography; Nature photography

Moving pictures
See Moving picture photography

Photography: how to improve your technique. Noren, C.　**770.28**

Photography of animals. See Animals—Pictorial works

Photography of insects

See pages in the following book:

Teale, E. W. The junior book of insects p131-39 (6-7)　**595.7**

Photography of nature. See Nature photography

Photometry. See Color; Light; Optics

Photosynthesis
Baker, J. J. W. Photosynthesis (4-7)　**581**
See also pages in the following book:
Riedman, S. R. Trees alive p53-63 (5-7)　**582**

Phrygian mythology. See Mythology, Phrygian

Physical education and training. See Athletics; Exercise; Games; Gymnastics; Physical fitness; Sports; also names of kinds of exercises, e.g. Karate

Physical fitness
Antonacci, R. J. Physical fitness for young champions (5-7)　**613.7**
See also pages in the following book:
Boy Scouts of America. Fieldbook p190-205　**369.43**

Physical fitness for young champions. Antonacci, R. J.　**613.7**

Physical geography
See also Climate; Earth; Earthquakes; Glaciers; Icebergs; Lakes; Meteorology; Mountains; Ocean; Rivers; Tides; Volcanoes; Winds

North America
Farb, P. Face of North America. Young readers' edition (6-7)　**500.9**

Physical stamina. See Physical fitness

Physically handicapped
Meltzer, M. A light in the dark; the life of Samuel Gridley Howe (6-7)　**92**
See also pages in the following book:
Antonacci, R. J. Physical fitness for young champions p121-38 (5-7)　**613.7**
See also Blind; Deaf

Fiction
De Angeli, M. The door in the wall (4-6)　**Fic**
Little, J. Mine for keeps (4-6)　**Fic**

Physically handicapped children
Wolf, B. Don't feel sorry for Paul (3-6)　**362.4**

Physically handicapped children—*Continued*

Fiction

Caudill, R. A certain small shepherd (4-6) **Fic**
Cunningham, J. Burnish me bright (4-7) **Fic**
Mulock, D. M. The little lame prince (4-6) **Fic**
Sutcliff, R. The witch's brat (5-7) **Fic**

Physicians

Bertol, R. Charles Drew (3-5) **92**
Fisher, L. E. The doctors (4-7) **610**
Goodsell, J. The Mayo brothers (2-4) **92**
Meltzer, M. A light in the dark; the life of Samuel Gridley Howe (6-7) **92**
Montgomery, E. R. Albert Schweitzer, great humanitarian (4-6) **92**
Rockwell, H. My doctor (k-1) **610.69**

Physicists

Beckhard, A. J. Albert Einstein (4-7) **92**

Physics

Barr, G. Young scientist and sports (4-7) **796**
Wilson, M. Seesaws to cosmic rays (5-7) **530**
See also Electricity; Electronics; Gases; Gravitation; Light; Liquids; Magnetism; Matter; Mechanics; Nuclear physics; Pneumatics; Radiation; Relativity (Physics); Sound; Statics; Thermodynamics

Experiments

Branley, F. M. Experiments in the principles of space travel (5-7) **629.4**
Mark, S. J. A physics lab of your own (5-7) **530.72**
Stone, A. H. Take a balloon (3-6) **530.72**
A physics lab of your own. Mark, S. J. **530.72**
Physiological chemistry. See Cells; Digestion; Poisons; Vitamins

Physiology

Brenner, B. Bodies (k-2) **612**
Ravielli, A. Wonders of the human body (4-7) **611**
Silverstein, A. The excretory system (4-6) **574.1**
Silverstein, A. The skin (4-6) **574.1**
See also pages in the following books:
Childcraft: the how and why library v14 **031**
Gardner, M. Science puzzlers p23-27 (6-7) **507.2**
See also Anatomy; Blood; Bones; Cells; Digestion; Excretion; Growth; Muscles; Nervous system; Reproduction; Respiration; Senses and sensation; also names of organs, e.g. Heart

Physiology, Comparative

Silverstein, A. The muscular system (4-6) **574.1**

Pianos

Fiction

Titus, E. Anatole and the piano **E**

Piatti, Celestino

Celestino Piatti's Animal ABC **E**
The happy owls **E**
(illus.) Jüchen, A. von. The Holy Night **232.9**

Picard, Barbara Leonie

The faun and the woodcutter's daughter (4-7) **S C**

Contents: The faun and the woodcutter's daughter; Duke Roland's quest; The Corn Maiden; Malati and the prince; Clever Dick; The third witch; The three brothers and the black hen; The coral comb; Count

Alaric's lady; Tiger Lily and the dragon; The knight and the Naiad of the Lake; The blackbird's song; Count Bertrand; The white hound

The grey palfrey
In Arbuthnot, M. H. comp. Time for old magic p109-11 **398.2**
How Loki outwitted a giant
In Mayne, W. ed. William Mayne's Book of giants p35-41 **398.2**
The Iliad of Homer (6-7) **883**
The stones of Plouhinec
In Reeves, J. comp. The Christmas book p24-31 **394.2**
Stories of King Arthur and his knights (5-7) **398.2**
Three wishes
In Child Study Association of America. Castles and dragons p161-79 **398.2**

Piccola. Bennett, R.
In Bennett, R. Creative plays and programs for holidays p237-44 **812**

Pick me up. Cole, W. ed. **808.81**

Pickow, George

(illus.) Ritchie, J. comp. From fair to fair: folk songs of the British Isles **784.4**
(illus.) Ritchie, J. Jean Ritchie's Swapping song book **784.4**

Pickthall, Marjorie L. C.

The worker in sandalwood
In Sechrist, E. H. ed. It's time for Christmas p214-21 **394.2**

The picnic basket. Clark, M.
In Association for Childhood Education International. Told under the blue umbrella p62-65 **S C**

Picotte, Susan La Flesche

See pages in the following book:
Gridley, M. E. American Indian women p74-79 (5-7) **920**

Pictographs. See Picture writing

A **pictorial** history of the American Indian; adaptation. See La Farge, O. The American Indian. Special edition for young readers **970.1**

Pictorial works. See Pictures; and subjects with the subdivision Pictorial works, e.g. Animals—Pictorial works

Picture book farm. Hawkinson, L. **E**

The **picture** book of grains. Brooks, A. **633**

Picture book without pictures

Andersen, H. C. Godfather's picture book
In Andersen, H. C. The complete fairy tales and stories p903-24 **S C**

Picture books for children

MacCann, D. The child's first books **741.64**
See also pages in the following books:
A Horn Book Sampler on children's books and reading p219-33 **028.5**
Illustrators of children's books: 1946-1956 p2-12, 36-57 **741.64**
Johnson, E. ed. Anthology of children's literature p67-93 **808.8**
Kingman, L. ed. Newbery and Caldecott Medal books: 1966-1975 p276-89 **028.5**
Miller, B. M. ed. Caldecott Medal books: 1938-1957 p307-14 **028.5**
Smith, L. H. The unreluctant years p115-29 **028.5**

Pine, Tillie S.—*Continued*
The Polynesians knew (4-6)   **919.6**
Simple machines and how we use them (2-4)
    621.8

Pine

Stories

Lifton, B. J. The dwarf pine tree (2-4) **Fic**
The **pine** tree. Andersen, H. C.
    In Andersen, H. C. The complete fairy tales and stories p225-33   **S C**
      See also Fir tree
The **pine** tree. Dobbs, R.
    In Dobbs, R. ed. Once upon a time p3-7
    372.6

Pineapples

    See pages in the following books:

Hays, W. P. Foods the Indians gave us p40-47 (5-7)   **641.3**
Sullivan, G. How do they grow it? p89-97 (5-7)   **631.5**

Ping-pong

Sullivan, G. Better table tennis for boys and girls (5-7)   **796.34**
The **pink.** Grimm, J.
    In Grimm, J. The complete Grimm's Fairy tales p355-60   **398.2**
    In Grimm, J. Grimms' Fairy tales; illus. by F. Kredel p91-97   **398.2**
The **pink** china bonbon dish. Lenski, L.
    In Lenski, L. Lois Lenski's Christmas stories p35-52   **394.2**
Pink parasol. Miller, H. L.
    In Burack, A. S. ed. One hundred plays for children p361-74   **808.82**
Pink petunia. Harmon, S.
    In Harper, W. comp. Easter chimes p118-28   **394.2**
Pink roses for Christmas. Campbell, J. E.
    In Burack, A. S. ed. Christmas plays for young actors p3-12   **812.08**
Pinkel. Haviland, V.
    In Haviland, V. Favorite fairy tales told in Sweden p33-48   **398.2**
Pinkerton, Robert
The first overland mail (5-7)   **383**
Pinkney, Jerry
(illus.) Arkhurst, J. C. The adventures of Spider   **398.2**
Pinky Pye. Estes, E.   **Fic**
Pinney's Easter hunt. Davis, L. R.
    In Cavanah, F. ed. Holiday roundup p86-91   **394.2**
    In Harper, W. comp. Easter chimes p18-25   **394.2**
Pinocchio; puppet play. Mahlmann, L.
    In Mahlmann, L. Puppet plays for young players p79-94   **791.5**
Pinocchio goes to school. Thane, A.
    In Thane, A. Plays from famous stories and fairy tales p352-65   **812**
Pinocchio, The adventures of. Collodi, C.   **Fic**
Pinocchio's ears become like those of a donkey. Lorenzini, C.
    In Arbuthnot, M. H. comp. The Arbuthnot Anthology of children's literature p496-98   **808.8**

Pinocchio's first pranks. Collodi, C.
    In Johnson, E. ed. Anthology of children's literature p631-32   **808.8**
Pinocchio's nose grows longer. Collodi, C.
    In Martignoni, M. E. ed. The illustrated treasury of children's literature p309-11   **808.8**
Pinto Smalto. Greene, E.
    In Greene, E. comp. Clever cooks p90-99
    398.2
Pioneer life. See Frontier and pioneer life
Pious, Robert
(illus.) Whipple, A. B. C. Famous pirates of the New World   **910.4**
Pipe fitting. See Plumbing
Piper, Leonora E.

    See pages in the following book:

Cohen, D. In search of ghosts p118-30 (6-7)
    133
Piper, Watty
The little engine that could   **E**
Piper, pipe that song again! Larrick, N. ed.
    821.08
The **piper** who could not play. Green, K.
    In Green, K. Leprechaun tales p31-41
    398.2
Pipes and plumbing systems. Zim, H. S.   **696**
Piping down the valleys wild. Larrick, N. ed.
    808.81
Pippa. Adamson, J.   **599**
Pippenger, Robert
(illus.) Hawkinson, L. Picture book farm   **E**
Pippi in the South Seas. Lindgren, A.   **Fic**
Pippi Longstocking. Lindgren, A.   **Fic**
Piquet, Elise
(illus.) Zappler, G. From one cell to many cells   **574.8**
Pirate Blackbeard's deep-sea end. Jagendorf, M. A.
    In Jagendorf, M. A. Folk stories of the South p187-90   **398.2**
Pirate Jean Lafitte
    In Malcolmson, A. Yankee Doodle's cousins p163-71   **398.2**
Pirate Lafitte and the Battle of New Orleans. Tallant, R.   **92**
Pirates
Stockton, F. R. Buccaneers & pirates of our coasts (5-7)   **910.4**
Syme, R. Sir Henry Morgan: buccaneer (4-6)   **92**
Tallant, R. Pirate Lafitte and the Battle of New Orleans (5-7)   **92**
Whipple, A. B. C. Famous pirates of the New World (5-7)   **910.4**

Fiction

Fleischman, S. The ghost in the noonday sun (4-6)   **Fic**
Wibberley, L. Flint's Island (6-7)   **Fic**
Pirates; play. Carlson, B. W.
    In Carlson, B. W. Play a part p103-07   **792**
Pirate's Island. Townsend, J. R.   **Fic**

Po, Lee
The tortoise and the hare
In Du Bois, W. P. The hare and the tortoise & The tortoise and the hare p25-48 (1-4)   398.2

Pocahontas
Aulaire, I. d'. Pocahontas (2-4)   92
Bulla, C. R. Pocahontas and the strangers (3-5)   92

See also pages in the following book:

Gridley, M. E. American Indian women p22-29 (5-7)   920
Pocahontas and the strangers. Bulla, C. R. 92
Pocahontas, the tomboy princess. Roberts, H. M.
In Kamerman, S. E. ed. Fifty plays for junior actors p512-20   812.08
A pocket full of seeds. Sachs, M.   Fic
A pocketful of cricket. Caudill, R.   E
A pocketful of riddles. Wiesner, W.   793.7
A pocketful of seasons. Foster, D. V. L.   E
Podendorf, Illa
The true book of weeds and wild flowers (1-3)   582
Poe, Edgar Allan
Tales of terror and fantasy (6-7)   S C
Poems and rhymes
In Childcraft: the how and why library v 1   031
Poems for children, Eleanor Farjeon's. Farjeon, E.   821
Poems for red letter days. Sechrist, E. H. comp.   821.08
Poems for seasons and celebrations. Cole, W. comp.   821.08
Poems for youth. Benét, W. R. comp.   811.08
Poems for youth. Dickinson, E.   811
Poems of childhood. Field, E.   811
Poems of magic and spells. Cole, W.   821.08
Poet and the peony princess. Carpenter, F.
In Carpenter, F. Tales of a Chinese grandmother p124-33   398.2
Poetry

See pages in the following books:

Horn Book Reflections on children's books and reading p151-200   028.5
A Horn Book Sampler on children's books and reading p237-61   028.5
Jacobs, L. B. ed. Using literature with young children p20-24   023.5
Larrick, N. A parent's guide to children's reading p115-37   028.5
Read, H. ed. This way, delight p137-43 (5-7)   821.08
Sawyer, R. The way of the storyteller p187-99   372.6
Townsend, J. R. Written for children p131-41, 301-07   028.5
See also American poetry; Ballads; Children in poetry; English poetry; Hymns; Love poetry; Nature in poetry; Negro poetry; and general subjects, names of historical events and famous persons, with the subdivision Poetry, e.g. Animals

—Poetry; Revere, Paul—Poetry; United States—History—Revolution—Poetry
Bibliography
See pages in the following book:
National Council of Teachers of English. Adventuring with books p219-35   028.5
Collections
Adams, A. comp. Poetry of earth (3-6) 808.81
Brewton, J. E. comp. Under the tent of the sky (3-7)   808.81
Brewton, S. comp. Bridled with rainbows (3-7)   808.81
Cole, W. comp. Beastly boys and ghastly girls (5-7)   808.81
Cole, W. ed. I went to the animal fair (k-3)   808.81
Cole, W. ed. Pick me up (4-7)   808.81
Ferris, H. ed. Favorite poems, old and new (4-6)   808.81
Hazeltine, A. I. comp. The year around (4-7)   808.81
Koch, K. comp. Rose, where did you get that red?   808.81
Larrick, N. ed. Piping down the valleys wild   808.81
Larrick, N. ed. Room for me and a mountain lion (5-7)   808.81
Lewis, R. comp. Miracles   808.81
Lewis, R. ed. Out of the earth I sing (4-6)   808.81
Lewis, R. comp. The wind and the rain (3-6)   808.81
Livingston, M. C. ed. What a wonderful bird the frog are (5-7)   808.81
McEwen, C. S. comp. Away we go! (k-3)   808.81
Morrison, L. comp. Sprints and distances (5-7)   808.81
Parker, E. comp. The singing and the gold (6-7)   808.81
See also pages in the following books:
Arbuthnot, M. H. comp. The Arbuthnot Anthology of children's literature p2-145   808.8
Carlson, B. W. Listen! And help tell the story p79-98, 125-72   372.6
Childcraft: the how and why library v 1 031
Johnson, E. ed. Anthology of children's literature p907-1000   808.8
Tashjian, V. A. ed. With a deep sea smile p15-40   372.6
See also American poetry—Collections; Christmas poetry; English poetry—Collections; Nonsense verses; Patriotic poetry; Religious poetry; Russian poetry—Collections; Sea poetry; Songs; War poetry
Indexes
Brewton, J. E. comp. Index to children's poetry   808.81
Brewton, J. E. comp. Index to children's poetry; first supplement   808.81
Brewton, J. E. comp. Index to children's poetry; second supplement   808.81
Brewton, J. E. comp. Index to poetry for children and young people, 1964-1969   808.81
Granger's Index to poetry   808.81
Subject index to poetry for children and young people   808.81

Political science—Continued
Suffrage; World politics; also names of countries with the subhead Constitution, e.g. United States. Constitution; and names of countries with the subdivision Politics and government, e.g. United States—Politics and government

Politics. Markun, P. M.   **329**

Politics, Practical
Markun, P. M. Politics (4-6)   **329**

[Politzer, Anie]
My journals and sketchbooks (4-7)   **Fic**

Politzer, Michel
(illus.) Politzer, A. My journals and sketchbooks   **Fic**

Pollination. See Fertilization of plants

Pollution
Hyde, M. O. For pollution fighters only (5-7)   **614.7**
Leaf, M. Who cares? I do (k-2)   **614.7**
Miles, B. Save the earth! (4-7)   **301.31**
Milgrom, H. ABC of ecology (k-2)   **614.7**
Parnall, P. The mountain   **E**

See also pages in the following books:

Chaffin, L. D. Coal: energy and crisis p40-42 (3-5)   **553**
Duffey, E. Conservation of nature p81-93 (6-7)   **333.7**
Gregor, A. S. Man's mark on the land p78-90 (4-7)   **301.31**
    See also Air—Pollution; Pesticides and the environment; Water—Pollution

Pollution of air. See Air—Pollution

Pollution of water. See Water—Pollution

Polo, Marco
Buehr, W. The world of Marco Polo (4-6)   **92**
Marco Polo's adventures in China (5-7)   **92**
Walsh, R. J. Adventures and discoveries of Marco Polo (5-7)   **915**

See also pages in the following books:

Cottler, J. Heroes of civilization p3-13 (6-7)   **920**
Winwar, F. The land and people of Italy p61-65 (5-7)   **914.5**

Polo, the snake-girl. Carpenter, F.
In Carpenter, F. African wonder tales p121-27   **398.2**

Polseno, Jo
(illus.) Bertol, R. Charles Drew   **92**
(illus.) Gans, R. Bird talk   **598.2**

Poltergeists. See Ghosts

Polymers and polymerization. See Plastics

Polynesia
Pine, T. S. The Polynesians knew (4-6)   **919.6**

See also pages in the following book:

May, C. P. Oceania: Polynesia, Melanesia, Micronesia p73-95 (5-7)   **919**

Ethnology

See Ethnology—Polynesia

Fiction

Sperry, A. Call it courage (5-7)   **Fic**

Polynesian literature

Collections

See pages in the following book:

McDowell, R. E. ed. Third World voices for children p115-46 (4-7)   **398.2**

The **Polynesians** knew. Pine, T. S.   **919.6**

Pomerantz, Charlotte
The piggy in the puddle   **E**
Why you look like you, whereas I tend to look like me (4-6)   **575.1**

Pompeii

See pages in the following book:

Hall, J. Buried cities p2-46 (5-7)   **913**

Pompey. See Lamb, Pompey

Ponce de León, Juan

See pages in the following book:

Discoverers of the New World p64-69 (5-7)   **973.1**

The **pond.** Carrick, C.   **574.92**

Pond and marsh plants. Earle, O. L.   **581**

Pond life. Reid, G. K.   **574.92**

Ponds

See pages in the following book:

Peattie, D. C. The rainbow book of nature p58-66 (5-7)   **574**

Ponies
Brady, I. America's horses and ponies (5-7)   **636.1**
Hess, L. Shetland ponies (k-3)   **636.1**
Slaughter, J. Pony care (5-7)   **636.1**

See also pages in the following book:

Henry, M. Album of horses p86-97 (4-7)   **636.1**

Stories

Anderson, C. W. A pony for Linda (1-3)   **Fic**
Anderson, L. Ponies of Mykillengi (2-4)   **Fic**
Farley, W. Little Black, a pony   **E**
Henry, M. Misty of Chincoteague (4-7)   **Fic**
Rounds, G. The blind colt (4-6)   **Fic**
Rounds, G. Stolen pony (4-6)   **Fic**

Ponies of Mykillengi. Anderson, L.   **Fic**

Pontiac, Ottawa chief

See pages in the following book:

Johnston, J. The Indians and the strangers p51-58 (2-5)   **920**

Pontius Pilate. See Pilate, Pontius

Pontoppidan, Erich
The largest sea monster in the world
In Silverberg, B. ed. Phoenix feathers p25-27   **S C**

Pony care. Slaughter, J.   **636.1**

Pony express
Adams, S. H. The pony express (5-7)   **383**
Moody, R. Riders of the pony express (5-7)   **383**

See also pages in the following book:

Grant, B. Famous American trails p66-73 (5-7)   **973**

A **pony** for Linda. Anderson, C. W.   **Fic**

Pony Penning Day. Henry, M.
In Association for Childhood Education
International. Told under spacious
skies p128-35   S C
In Gruenberg, S. M. ed. Favorite stories
old and new p198-206   808.8

The pony tree. Brate, C.
In Association for Childhood Education
International. Told under the magic
umbrella p59-63   S C

The pony with a past. Bacon, P.
In Association for Childhood Education
International. Told under the blue
umbrella p97-100   S C

The Pooh cook book. Ellison, V. H.   641.5

The Pooh get-well book. Ellison, V. H.   790.19

Pooh goes visiting and gets into a tight place.
Milne, A. A.
In Gruenberg, S. M. ed. Favorite stories
old and new p451-55   808.8

The Pooh party book. Ellison, V. H.   793.2

The Pooh song book. Fraser-Simon, H.   784.6

The Pooh story book. Milne, A. A.   Fic

The pool of fire. Christopher, J.   Fic

The pool of tears. Carroll, L.
In Martignoni, M. E. ed. The illustrated
treasury of children's literature p298-
301   808.8

Poole, Frederick King
Indonesia (4-7)   915.98
Jordan (5-7)   915.695
Malaysia & Singapore (5-7)   915.95
The Philippines (5-7)   915.99
Southeast Asia (5-7)   915.9
Thailand (5-7)   915.93

Poole, Gray
(jt. auth.) Poole L. Insect-eating plants 581

Poole, Lynn
Insect-eating plants (3-6)   581

Poo-Poo brings the dragon home. Forester, C. S.
In Untermeyer, B. ed. The Golden Treasury of children's literature p29-31
    808.8

Poo-Poo finds a dragon. Forester, C. S.
In Untermeyer, B. ed. The Golden Treasury of children's literature p25-28
    808.8

The poor boy and the princess. Sechrist, E. H.
In Sechrist, E. H. Once in the first times
p168-73   398.2

The poor boy in the grave. Grimm, J.
In Grimm, J. The complete Grimm's Fairy
tales p749-52   398.2

The poor Count's Christmas. Stockton, F. R.
In Harper, W. comp. Merry Christmas to
you p44-54   394.2

The poor man and the rich man. Grimm, J.
In Grimm, J. The complete Grimm's Fairy
tales p394-98   398.2
See also Miller's boy and his cat

Poor miller's boy and the cat
In De La Mare, W. ed. Animal stories
p134-44   398.2

The poor miller's boy and the cat. Grimm, J.
In Grimm, J. The complete Grimm's Fairy
tales p482-85   398.2

The poor miller's boy and the little cat.
Grimm, J.
In Grimm, J. The juniper tree, and other
tales from Grimm v2 p178-86 398.2

Poor Richard [biography of Benjamin Frank-
lin]. Daugherty, J.   92

Poor Richard in France. Monjo, F. N.   Fic

Poor Sandy. Shepard, R. A.
In Shepard, R. A. Conjure tales p 1-12
    S C

Poor Stainless. Norton, M. See note under
Norton, M. The Borrowers   Fic

Poor widow bullfighter. Brenner, A.
In Brenner, A. The boy who could do anything, & other Mexican folk tales
p114-20   398.2

The Poor wolf
In Bloch, M. H. ed. Ukrainian folk tales
p28-35   398.2

Poortvliet, Rien
(illus.) Haar, J. ter. Boris   Fic

Pop Corn & Ma Goodness. Preston, E. M.   E

The pop-up books. Spamer, C.
In Kamerman, S. E. ed. Little plays for
little players p113-16   812.08

Popcorn patch. Credle, E.
In Credle, E. Tall tales from the high hills,
and other stories p53-54   398.2

Pope, Elizabeth Marie
The Perilous Gard (6-7)   Fic

Popé, Pueblo Indian
See pages in the following book:
Folsom, F. Red power on the Rio Grande
p59-91 (5-7)   978.9

Poppies and wheat. Alcott, L. M.
In Alcott, L. M. Glimpses of Louisa p61-
94   S C

The poppy seed cakes. Clark, M.   E

The poppy-seed cakes; excerpt. Clark, M.
In Association for Childhood Education
International. Told under the blue
umbrella p58-65   S C
In Gruenberg, S. M. ed. Favorite stories
old and new p59-62   808.8

The poppy seeds. Bulla, C. R.   E

Popular plays for classroom reading. Burack, A. S. ed.   808.82

Popularity
In DeRoin, N. ed. Jataka tales p48-50
    398.2

Population
Asimov, I. Earth: our crowded spaceship
(5-7)   301.32
McClung, R. M. Mice, moose, and men (4-7)
    574.5

See also pages in the following book:
Hyde, M. O. For pollution fighters only p98-
105 (5-7)   614.7

Population, Foreign. See names of countries
with the subdivision Immigration and emigration, e.g. United States—Immigration
and emigration; and names of countries

Proverbs

See pages in the following book:

Emrich, D. comp. The hodgepodge book
p192-99 **398**
See also Epigrams

Provincial Library Service. See Ontario. Provincial Library Service

Provincialism. See names of languages with the subdivision Provincialisms, e.g. English language—Provincialisms

Proysen, Alf
Little old Mrs Pepperpot, and other stories
(1-3) **S C**
Contents: Little old Mrs Pepperpot; Mrs Pepperpot and the mechanical doll; Mr Pepperpot buys macaroni; Queen of the Crows; Mrs Pepperpot at the bazaar; Mr Puffblow's hat; Miriam-from-America; Jumping Jack and his friends; The potato with big ideas; The mice and the Christmas tree; Never take no for an answer; Mr Learn-a-lot and the singing midges
Mrs Pepperpot at the bazaar
In Arbuthnot, M. H. comp. The Arbuthnot Anthology of children's literature p576-78 **808.8**

Prudent Hans
Grimm, J. Clever Hans
In Grimm, J. The complete Grimm's Fairy tales p166-68 **398.2**
Grimm, J. Goose Hans
In Grimm, J. Three gay tales from Grimm p51-63 **398.2**
Grimm, J. Prudent Hans
In Grimm, J. Household stories p140-44 **398.2**

Prunella. Manning-Sanders, R.
In Manning-Sanders, R. A book of witches p62-71 **398.2**

Psyche. Andersen, H. C.
In Andersen, H. C. The complete fairy tales and stories p785-95 **S C**

Psychical research
Cohen, D. In search of ghosts (6-7) **133**

See also pages in the following books:

Kettlekamp, L. Dreams p71-87 (5-7) **154.6**
Kettelkamp, L. Religions, East and West p108-14 (5-7) **291**
See also Clairvoyance; Dreams; Extrasensory perception; Ghosts; Spiritualism

Psychology
Kohn, B. A first look at psychology (4-6) **150**

See also pages in the following book:

Gardner, M. Science puzzlers p29-45 (6-7) **507.2**
See also Emotions; Perception; Psychical research; Senses and sensation

Psychology, Applied. See subjects with the subdivision Psychological aspects, e.g. Drugs—Psychological aspects

Psychology, Comparative. See Animal intelligence; Instinct

Psychology, Physiological. See Dreams; Emotions; Optical illusions; Pain; Senses and sensation; Sleep

Psychology—multimedia, Index to. See Index to psychology—multimedia

Psychoses. See Mental illness

Public accommodations, Discrimination in. See Discrimination in public accommodations

Public health. See Hospitals; Pollution; Refuse and refuse disposal; Water—Pollution; Water supply

Public lands. See National parks and reserves

Public Library Association
The Right to read and the Nation's libraries. See The Right to read and the Nation's libraries **027.6**

Public Library of Cincinnati and Hamilton County. See Cincinnati. Public Library

Public library service to children: foundation and development. Long, H. G. **027.62**

Public utilities. See Railroads; Telephone; Water supply

Publishers and publishing

See pages in the following book:

MacCann, D. ed. The Black American in books for children: readings in racism p156-203 **028.5**

Directories

Gillespie, J. T. Paperback books for young people **070.5025**
Literary market place: LMP **070.5025**

Periodicals

Publishers Weekly **070.505**
The **Publishers'** and Stationers' Weekly Trade Circular. See Publishers Weekly **070.505**
Publishers Weekly **070.505**

Publishing. See Publishers and publishing

The **pudding-bag string.** Bennett, R.
In Bennett, R. Creative plays and programs for holidays p262-68 **812**

The **pudding** that broke up the preaching. Credle, E.
In Credle, E. Tall tales from the high hills, and other stories p21-26 **398.2**
In Luckhardt, M. C. comp. Thanksgiving p267-72 **394.2**

Puddle: the real story of a baby hippo. Waring, R. A.
In Gruenberg, S. M. ed. Favorite stories old and new p146-48 **808.8**

Puddleby. Lofting, H.
In Gruenberg, S. M. ed. Favorite stories old and new p226-28 **808.8**

Puddocky
In Lang, A. ed. The green fairy book p222-28 **398.2**

Pudlo
(illus.) Field, E. ed. Eskimo songs and stories **398.2**

Pueblo Indians
Bleeker, S. The Pueblo Indians (4-6) **970.3**
Erdoes, R. The Pueblo Indians (5-7) **970.3**
Floethe, L. L. The Indian and his pueblo (1-3) **970.3**
Folsom, F. Red power on the Rio Grande (5-7) **978.9**

See also pages in the following books:

Hofsinde, R. Indian costumes p72-78 (3-6) **391**

Pythagoras

See pages in the following book:

Diggins, J. E. String, straightedge, and shadow p93-122 (6-7) **516**

Pytheas

See pages in the following book:

Hirsch, S. C. On course! p17-27 (5-7) **623.89**

Python

See pages in the following book:

Gates, D. The golden god: Apollo p19-23 (4-7) **292**

Q

Quackenbush, Robert

Go tell Aunt Rhody **E**

(illus.) Carlson, N. S. Befana's gift **Fic**

(illus.) Cooke, A. Giraffes at home **599**

(illus.) Lowrey, J. S. Six silver spoons **E**

(illus.) Old MacDonald had a farm. See Old MacDonald had a farm **784.4**

(illus.) Phelan, M. K. Election Day **394.2**

(illus.) She'll be comin' round the mountain (Folk song) She'll be comin' round the mountain **784.4**

(illus.) Yolen, J. The wizard islands **551.4**

The **quail.** Tolstoy, L.

In Tolstoy, L. Twenty-two Russian tales for young children p47-48 **S C**

Quakers. See Friends, Society of

The **Quakers.** Elgin, K. **289.6**

Quantum mechanics. See Quantum theory

Quantum theory

See pages in the following book:

Wilson, M. Seesaws to cosmic rays p75-87 (5-7) **530**

Qu'Appelle. Hooke, H. M.

In Hooke, H. M. Thunder in the mountains p123-31 **398.2**

The **quarrel.** Sherlock, P. M.

In Sherlock, P. M. Anansi, the spider man p105-12 **398.2**

The **quarrel** between Ile and Orun. Courlander, H.

In Courlander, H. Olode the hunter, and other tales from Nigeria p100-03 **398.2**

The **quarrel** of the quails. Babbitt, E. C.

In Babbitt, E. C. Jataka tales p30-33 **398.2**

The **quarreling** book. Zolotow, C. **E**

Quarries and quarrying. See Stone

Quarterback's aim. Lord, B. **Fic**

Quayle, Eric

The collector's book of children's books **020.75**

¿**Que será?** What can it be? Hubp, L. B. ed. **398.6**

Quebec Campaign, 1759

See pages in the following book:

Leckie, R. Great American battles p3-17 (5-7) **973**

The **queen.** Wahlenberg, A.

In Olenius, E. comp. Great Swedish fairy tales p230-38 **398.2**

Queen Alice. Carroll, L.

In Farjeon, E. ed. A cavalcade of queens p222-32 **808.8**

The **queen bee.** Grimm, J.

In De La Mare, W. ed. Animal stories p180-86 **398.2**

In Grimm, J. About wise men and simpletons p55-57 **398.2**

In Grimm, J. The complete Grimm's Fairy tales p317-19 **398.2**

In Grimm, J. Grimm's Fairy tales; illus. by A. Rackham p63-65 **398.2**

In Grimm, J. Grimms' Fairy tales; illus. by F. Kredel p98-100 **398.2**

In Grimm, J. Household stories p262-64 **398.2**

In Grimm, J. More tales from Grimm p155-62 **398.2**

In Hutchinson, V. S. ed. Candle-light stories p41-47 **398.2**

Queen Crane

In Baker, A. comp. The golden lynx, and other tales p46-53 **398.2**

Queen Esther saves her people; puppet play. Zeligs, D.

In Ross, L. Holiday puppets p98-101 **791.5**

Queen o' the tinkers. MacManus, S.

In Fenner, P. R. comp. Princesses & peasant boys p177-88 **398.2**

In MacManus, S. Hibernian nights p99-107 **398.**

Queen of heaven

Carpenter, F. Miss Lin, the sea goddess

In Carpenter, F. Tales of a Chinese grandmother p235-41 **398.2**

Queen of Summer. Lovelace, M. H.

In Association for Childhood Education International. Told under the Stars and Stripes p102-14 **S C**

Queen of the Crows. Proysen, A.

In Proysen, A. Little old Mrs Pepperpot, and other stories p33-41 **S C**

The **Queen of Underland.** Lewis, C. S.

In Hope-Simpson, J. ed. A cavalcade of witches p174-86 **808.8**

The **Queen** with the broken heart. Urban, C.

In Burack, A. S. ed. One hundred plays for children p288-91 **808.82**

In Kamerman, S. E. ed. Little plays for little players p26-30 **812.08**

Queenie Peavy. Burch, R. **Fic**

Queenie Peavy; excerpt. Burch, R.

In Arbuthnot, M. H. comp. The Arbuthnot Anthology of children's literature p666-69 **808.8**

Queens

Farjeon, E. ed. A cavalcade of queens (4-7) **808.8**

Wilson, H. Last queen of Hawaii: Liliuokalani (4-6) **92**

The **queen's care.** Hodges, E. J.

In Hodges, E. J. Serendipity tales p24-37 **398.2**

R

The **Rabbit** in the moon
  In Sakade, F. ed. Japanese children's favorite stories p35-37   **398.2**
  See also Hare in the moon
The **rabbit** prince. Berger, T.
  In Berger, T. Black fairy tales p91-105   **398.2**
Rabbit rides Wolf; puppet play. Jagendorf, M.
  In Penny puppets, penny theatre, and penny plays p113-21   **791.5**
Rabbit scratches Buh Elephant's back. Courlander, H.
  In Courlander, H. Terrapin's pot of sense p50-52   **398.2**
The **Rabbit** who crossed the sea
  In Sakade, F. ed. Japanese children's favorite stories p103-05   **398.2**
Rabbit who wanted to be a man. Brenner, A.
  In Brenner, A. The boy who could do anything, & other Mexican folk tales p73-78   **398.2**
Rabbits
  Cooper, K. All about rabbits as pets (3-6)   **636.08**
  Silverstein, A. Rabbits (4-7)   **599**
  See also pages in the following book:
  Silverstein, A. Animal invaders p53-63 (4-7)   **591.5**

Research
See pages in the following book:
Silverstein, A. Rabbits p78-89 (4-7)   **599**

Stories
Adams, R. Watership Down (5-7)   **Fic**
Anderson, L. Two hundred rabbits   **E**
Brown, M. W. Brer Rabbit (3-5)   **398.2**
Brown, M. W. Goodnight moon   **E**
Brown, M. W. The runaway bunny   **E**
Buchwald, E. Gildaen (4-6)   **Fic**
Carroll, R. What Whiskers did   **E**
DeJong, M. Shadrach (1-4)   **Fic**
Du Bois, W. P. The hare and the tortoise & The tortoise and the hare (1-4)   **398.2**
Fisher, A. Listen, rabbit   **E**
Gág, W. The A B C bunny   **E**
The Hare and the tortoise (k-3)   **398.2**
Heyward, D. B. The country bunny and the little gold shoes   **E**
Hoban, T. Where is it?   **E**
Newberry, C. T. Marshmallow   **E**
Potter, B. The tale of Benjamin Bunny   **E**
Potter, B. The tale of Mr Tod   **E**
Potter, B. The tale of Peter Rabbit   **E**
Potter, B. The tale of the flopsy bunnies   **E**
Schlein, M. The rabbit's world   **E**
Sturton, H. Zomo, the Rabbit (4-6)   **398.2**
Wildsmith, B. The hare and the tortoise (k-2)   **398.2**
Williams, M. The velveteen rabbit (2-4)   **Fic**
Zolotow, C. Mr Rabbit and the lovely present   **E**
Rabbit's bride
  Grimm, J. The hare's bride
  In Grimm, J. The complete Grimm's Fairy tales p332-33   **398.2**
  Grimm, J. The rabbit's bride
  In Grimm, J. Household stories p 1-2   **398.2**

In Grimm, J. The juniper tree, and other tales from Grimm v2 p275-77   **398.2**
Rabbits in literature
  See pages in the following book:
  Silverstein, A. Rabbits p146-53 (4-7)   **599**
Rabbit's long ears
  In Carter, D. S. ed. Greedy Mariani, and other folktales of the Antilles p62-67   **398.2**
Rabbit's self respect. Bowman, J. C.
  In Bowman, J. C. Tales from a Finnish tupa p266   **398.2**
Rabbits with wet eyes. Morley, C.
  In Association for Childhood Education International. Told under the blue umbrella p142-47   **S C**
The **rabbit's** world. Schlein, M.   **E**
Rabe, Olive
  (jt. auth.) Fisher, A. Human Rights Day   **394.2**
  (jt. auth.) Fisher, A. United Nations plays and programs   **812**
  (jt. auth.) Fisher, A. We Alcotts   **920**
Raccoons
  George, J. L. Masked prowler (4-6)   **599**
  Hess, L. The curious raccoons (3-5)   **599**
  Kohn, B. Raccoons (1-3)   **599**
  North, S. Little Rascal (3-5)   **599**
  North, S. Rascal (5-7)   **599**

Stories
Bourne, M. A. Raccoons are for loving   **E**
Brown, M. W. Wait till the moon is full   **E**
Duvoisin, R. Petunia, I love you   **E**
Kingman, L. The year of the raccoon (6-7)   **Fic**
Moore, L. Little Raccoon and the thing in the pool   **E**
Wells, R. Benjamin & Tulip   **E**
Raccoons are for loving. Bourne, M. A.   **E**
Race
  Cohen, R. The color of man (5-7)   **572**
  McKern, S. S. The many faces of man (5-7)   **572**
  May, J. Why people are different colors (2-4)   **572**
The **race.** Grinnell, G. B.
  In Hardendorff, J. B. ed. Just one more p82-84   **372.6**
Race awareness. *See* Prejudices and antipathies; Race problems
The **Race** between Hare and Hedgehog
  In Association for Childhood Education International. Told under the green umbrella p30-35   **398.2**
  See also Hare and the hedgehog
The **race** between the hare and the hedgehog. Grimm, J.
  In Untermeyer, B. ed. The Golden Treasury of children's literature p403-05   **808.8**
  See also Hare and the hedgehog
Race problems
  See also Acculturation; Intercultural education; also names of countries with the subdivision Race relations, e.g. United States—Race relations

Rats—*Continued*

Control

See pages in the following book:

Silverstein, A. Animal invaders p42-49 (4-7)
591.5

Stories

O'Brien, R. C. Mrs Frisby and the rats of NIMH (4-7)   Fic

Potter, B. The sly old cat   E

Wildsmith, B. The lion and the rat (k-2) 398.2

Rats and mice. Silverstein, A.   599

Rats and their son-in-law

Alleyne, L. The husband of the rat's daughter
In Manning-Sanders, R. ed. A book of magical beasts p160-63   398.2

Rattlers and rollers. Stoutenburg, A.
In Stoutenburg, A. American tall-tale animals p19-33   398.2

Rau, Margaret

Our world: the People's Republic of China (6-7)   915.1

The penguin book (4-6)   598.2

The raven. Grimm, J.
In Grimm, J. The complete Grimm's Fairy tales p431-36   398.2
In Grimm, J. Grimms' Fairy tales; illus. by F. Kredel p148-54   398.2
In Grimm, J. Household stories p26-31
398.2

Raven traveling. Harris, C.
In Harris, C. Once more upon a totem p67-146   398.2

The ravens build a bridge. Vo-Dinh
In Vo-Dinh. The toad is the Emperor's uncle p35-39   398.2

Raverat, Gwen

(illus.) Grahame, K. comp. The Cambridge Book of poetry for children   821.08

Ravielli, Anthony

Wonders of the human body (4-7)   611

The world is round (2-5)   525

(illus.) Cobb, V. How the doctor knows you're fine   616

(illus.) Gardner, M. Science puzzlers   507.2

Raw Head and Bloody Bones. Leach, M.
In Leach, M. Whistle in the graveyard p91
398.2

Rawlings, Marjorie Kinnan

The boy Jody
In Association for Childhood Education International. Told under spacious skies p136-52   S C

The secret river (1-4)   Fic

Rawlinson, Sir Henry Creswicke, 1st bart.

See pages in the following books:

Baumann, H. In the land of Ur p23-33 (6-7)
913.35

Cottler, J. Heroes of civilization p51-66 (6-7)
920

Ray, Deborah

(illus.) Welber, R. The winter picnic   E

Ray, Ralph

(illus.) Du Soe, R. C. Three without fear Fic

(illus.) Judson, C. I. City neighbor; the story of Jane Addams   92

(illus.) Kjelgaard, J. Fire-hunter   Fic

Rays (Fishes)

See pages in the following book:

Hopf, A. L. Misunderstood animals p34-39 (4-7)   591.5

Razzi, James

Bag of tricks! (k-3)   745.5

Easy does it! (k-3)   745.5

Simply fun! (k-3)   745.5

Read, Herbert

(ed.) This way, delight (5-7)   821.08

Read, Mary

See pages in the following books:

Stockton, F. R. Buccaneers & pirates of our coasts p194-98 (5-7)   910.4

Whipple, A. B. C. Famous pirates of the New World p134-37 (5-7)   910.4

Read about the brain. See Elgin, K. The human body: the brain   612

Read for your life. Palmer, J. R.   028.52

Readers

McGuffey, W. H. Old favorites from the McGuffey readers, 1836-1936   028.5
See also Primers

The Reader's encyclopedia   803

Readers' guide to periodical literature

How to use the Readers' guide to periodical literature   051

Readers' guide to periodical literature, Abridged   051

Reading

Cleary, F. D. Blueprints for better reading
028.5

See also pages in the following book:

Larrick, N. A parent's guide to children's reading p205-31   028.5

Fiction

Lexau, J. M. Olaf reads   E

Murray, M. Nellie Cameron (4-6)   Fic

Periodicals

The Reading Teacher   372.405

Remedial teaching—Bibliography

Withrow, D. E. Gateways to readable books
028.52

Study and teaching

See Reading

Reading. Boy Scouts of America   028.5

Reading interest. See Books and reading

Reading ladders for human relations   016.301

The Reading Teacher   372.405

Readings and recitations

See pages in the following books:

Arbuthnot, M. H. comp. The Arbuthnot Anthology of children's literature p944-55
808.8

Fisher, A. United Nations plays and programs p249-64   812

The real book of trains. See Elting, M. All aboard!   385.09

The real hole. Cleary, B.   E

The real Mother Goose. Mother Goose   398.8

Robertson, Dorothy Lewis
Fairy tales from Viet Nam (4-6) **398.2**
Contents: A story for Kiem; Chu Cuoi's trip to the moon; A flower to catch a thief; The princess of Mount Nam-Nhu; Why the monsoon comes each year; The emperor's magic bow; The farmer, the buffalo, and the tiger; The magic ruby; Three who couldn't be parted

Robertson, James
(illus.) Amazing Life Games Company. Good cents **658**

Robertson, Keith
Henry Reed, Inc. (5-7) **Fic**
Henry Reed's baby-sitting service. See note under Robertson, K. Henry Reed, Inc. **Fic**
Henry Reed's big show. See note under Robertson, K. Henry Reed, Inc. **Fic**
Henry Reed's journey. See note under Robertson, K. Henry Reed, Inc. **Fic**
In search of a sandhill crane (5-7) **Fic**

Robertson, Lilian
The runaway rocking horse
In Gruenberg, S. M. comp. Let's hear a story p74-81 **808.8**

Robeson, Paul
Hamilton, V. Paul Robeson (6-7) **92**

See also pages in the following book:
Rollins, C. Famous Negro entertainers of stage, screen, and TV p95-99 (5-7) **920**

Robin Hood
Malcolmson, A. ed. Song of Robin Hood (5-7) **398.2**
Pyle, H. The merry adventures of Robin Hood of great renown in Nottinghamshire (5-7) **398.2**
Pyle, H. Some merry adventures of Robin Hood (5-7) **398.2**

See also pages in the following books:
Arbuthnot, M. H. comp. The Arbuthnot Anthology of children's literature p460-65 **808.8**
Arbuthnot, M. H. comp. Time for old magic p324-29 **398.2**
Johnson, E. ed. Anthology of children's literature p509-12 **808.8**
Martignoni, M. E. ed. The illustrated treasury of children's literature p463-70 **808.8**
Ward, W. ed. Stories to dramatize p163-68 **372.6**

Robin Hood and Little John. Pyle, H.
In Johnson, E. ed. Anthology of children's literature p509-12 **808.8**

Robin Hood meets Little John; puppet play. Carlson, B. W.
In Carlson, B. W. Play a part p40-43 **792**

Robin Hood outwits the sheriff. Baher, C. W.
In Kamerman, S. E. ed. Dramatized folk tales of the world p61-78 **812.08**

Robin Hood turns butcher. Pyle, H.
In Martignoni, M. E. ed. The illustrated treasury of children's literature p463-70 **808.8**

Robin Hood's merry adventure with the miller. Pyle, H.
In Ward, W. ed. Stories to dramatize p163-68 **372.6**

Robins
Eberle, I. Robins on the window sill (k-2) **598.2**

Kaufmann, J. Robins fly north, robins fly south (3-5) **598.2**

Robin's Christmas song
Wee Robin's Christmas Day
In Association for Childhood Education International. Told under the green umbrella p162-64 **398.2**

Robins fly north, robins fly south. Kaufmann, J. **598.2**

Robins on the window sill. Eberle, I. **598.2**

Robinson, Adjai
Singing tales of Africa (3-5) **398.2**
Contents: Why the baboon has a shining seat; Why there is death in the world; The stepchild and the fruit trees; Ojumiri and the giant; Ayele and the flowers; "Leave it there!"; "Mother-in-Law, today is Shake-head Day!"

The stepchild and the fruit trees
In Arbuthnot, M. H. comp. The Arbuthnot Anthology of children's literature p329-30 **808.8**

Robinson, Barbara
The best Christmas pageant ever (4-6) **Fic**

Robinson, Bill, 1878-1949

See pages in the following books:
Hughes, L. Famous Negro music makers p45-62 (5-7) **920**
Rollins, C. Famous Negro entertainers of stage, screen, and TV p101-04 (5-7) **920**

Robinson, Charles
(illus.) Aleksin, A. A late-born child **Fic**
(illus.) Corcoran, B. A dance to still music **Fic**
(illus.) Corcoran, B. The long journey **Fic**
(illus.) Levitin, S. Journey to America **Fic**
(illus.) McKillip, P. A. The house on Parchment Street **Fic**
(illus.) Norris, G. B. The good morrow **Fic**
(illus.) Norris, G. B. Green and something else **Fic**
(illus.) Smith, D. B. A taste of blackberries **Fic**
(illus.) Tresselt, A. The dead tree **E**

Robinson, Charles Alexander
The first book of ancient Egypt (4-7) **913.32**
The first book of ancient Greece (5-7) **913.38**
The first book of ancient Mesopotamia and Persia (4-7) **913.35**
The first book of ancient Rome (5-7) **913.37**

Robinson, Harry Perry
On a mountain trail
In A St Nicholas anthology p107-11 **810.8**

Robinson, Jackie
Jackie Robinson's Little league baseball book (4-7) **796.357**
For material about this author see Robinson, John Roosevelt

Robinson, Jessie
(illus.) Leeming, J. Fun with magic **793.8**
(illus.) Leeming, J. Fun with pencil and paper **793.7**
(illus.) Leeming, J. Fun with puzzles **793.7**
(illus.) Leeming, J. More Fun with magic **793.8**
(illus.) Nagle, A. Fun with naturecraft **745.5**

Robinson, Joan G.
Charley (4-6) **Fic**

Robinson, John Roosevelt
Breakthrough to the big league (4-7) **92**

St Nicholas (Periodical) (as subject)

See pages in the following books:

Andrews, S. ed. The Hewins lectures, 1947-1962 p267-75 **028.5**

Haviland, V. ed. Yankee Doodle's literary sampler of prose, poetry, & pictures p393-436 **028.5**

Jordan, A. M. From Rollo to Tom Sawyer, and other papers p131-43 **028.5**

St Nicholas. Farjeon, E.

In Johnson, E. ed. Anthology of children's literature p594-97 **808.8**

St Nicholas. Sechrist, E. H.

In Sechrist, E. H. ed. It's time for Christmas p58-64 **394.2**

A St Nicholas anthology **810.8**

St Nicholas' Day

See pages in the following book:

Purdy, S. Festivals for you to celebrate p61-68 (4-7) **394.2**

St Nicholas in trouble. Timmermans, F.

In Harper, W. comp. Merry Christmas to you p216-29 **394.2**

St Nicholas just the same; play. Carlson, B. W.

In Carlson, B. W. The right play for you p54-59 **792**

Saint Patrick and the Hill of Tara. Colum, P.

In Colum, P. The Stone of Victory, and other tales of Padraic Colum p90-96 **398.2**

Saint Patrick and the last snake. Davis, L. R.

In Cavanah, F. ed. Holiday roundup p64-66 **394.2**

St Patrick and the last snake in Ireland. Davis, L. R.

In Kamerman, S. E. ed. Little plays for little players p47-52 **812.08**

Saint Patrick at Tara

Colum, P. Saint Patrick and the Hill of Tara

In Colum, P. The Stone of Victory, and other tales of Padraic Colum p90-96 **398.2**

St Patrick's Day

Cantwell, M. St Patrick's Day (1-3) **394.2**

Sechrist, E. H. Red letter days p57-66 **394.2**

Drama

See pages in the following books:

Fisher, A. Holiday programs for boys and girls p295-98 (4-7) **812**

Kamerman, S. E. ed. Little plays for little players p47-52 (1-6) **812.08**

Saint Peter and his trombone. Jagendorf, M. A.

In Jagendorf, M. A. The gypsies' fiddle, and other gypsy tales p47-51 **398.2**

St Valentine's Day. See Valentine's Day

St Valentine's Day. Bulla, C. R. **394.2**

Saints

Bishop, C. H. Martin de Porres, hero (5-7) **92**

Fisher, A. Jeanne d'Arc [biography of Joan of Arc, Saint] (3-5) **92**

Jewett, S. God's troubadour; the story of Saint Francis of Assisi (4-6) **92**

See also pages in the following book:

Johnson, E. ed. Anthology of children's literature p588-97 **808.8**

Poetry

See pages in the following book:

Farjeon, E. The children's bells p9-20 (3-6) **821**

Sakade, Florence

(ed.) Japanese children's favorite stories (2-4) **398.2**

Saki

The lull

In Authors' choice p23-30 **S C**

The salad. Grimm, J.

In Grimm, J. Grimms' Fairy tales; illus. by F. Kredel p135-43 **398.2**

See also Donkey cabbage

Salads

See pages in the following books:

Better Homes and Gardens Junior cook book p44-48 (4-7) **641.5**

Crocker, B. Betty Crocker's Cookbook for boys & girls p109-17 (3-7) **641.5**

Girl Scouts of the United States of America. Girl Scout cookbook p78-91 (4-7) **641.5**

Salamanders

George, J. C. The moon of the salamanders (3-5) **597**

Ommanney, F. D. Frogs, toads & newts (4-6) **597**

See also pages in the following books:

Buck, M. W. Pets from the pond p52-57 (4-7) **639**

Conant, R. A field guide to reptiles and amphibians of Eastern and Central North America p239-96 **598.1**

Ricciuti, E. R. Shelf pets p28-36 (5-7) **639**

Sale, J. Kirk

The land and people of Ghana (5-7) **916.67**

Salem, Peter

See pages in the following book:

Rollins, C. H. They showed the way p112-16 (5-7) **920**

Salem, Mass.

See pages in the following book:

Aymar, B. Laws and trials that created history p54-64 (6-7) **345.7**

Fiction

Fritz, J. Early thunder (5-7) **Fic**

Salima lives in Kashmir. Riwkin-Brick, A. **915.4**

Salisbury, Harrison E.

(illus.) Rice, T. T. Finding out about the early Russians **914.7**

Sally go round the sun. Fowke, E. comp. **796.1**

The Salmon's revenge. Green, K.

In Green, K. Leprechaun tales p53-62 **398.2**

Salt

Buehr, W. Salt, sugar, and spice (3-6) **664**

Goldin, A. Salt (1-3) **553**

See also pages in the following book:

Schwartz, J. It's fun to know why p85-93 (4-7) **507.2**

San Nicolas Island, Calif.
Fiction
O'Dell, S. Island of the Blue Dolphins (5-7)
Fic

Sanchez, Carlos
(illus.) Belpré, P. Perez and Martina 398.2

The **sand-carrier** crab. Vo-Dinh
In Vo-Dinh. The toad is the Emperor's uncle p89-97 398.2

Sand Creek, Battle of, 1864
See pages in the following book:
Ehrlich, A. Wounded Knee: an Indian history of the American West p64-75 (6-7)
970.4

Sand flat shadows. Sandburg, C.
In Sandburg, C. Rootabaga stories v 1 p191-292 S C
In Sandburg, C. The Sandburg treasury p72-77 818

Sandburg, Carl
Abe Lincoln grows up
In Sandburg, C. The Sandburg treasury p383-477 818
(ed.) The American songbag 784.7
And so he grew
In Cavanah, F. ed. Holiday roundup p22-27 394.2
Blue silver
In Gruenberg, S. M. ed. Favorite stories old and new p234-35 808.8
Early morn
In Sandburg, C. The Sandburg treasury p161-207 818
How the letter X got into the alphabet
In Dobbs, R. ed. Once upon a time p70-73 372.6
How they bring back the Village of Cream Puffs when the wind blows it away
In Arbuthnot, M. H. comp. The Arbuthnot Anthology of children's literature p570-71 808.8
How to tell corn fairies if you see 'em
In Association for Childhood Education International. Told under the magic umbrella p127-32 S C
The Huckabuck family
In Harper, W. comp. The harvest feast p240-46 394.2
The Huckabuck family and how they raised pop corn in Nebraska and quit and came back
In Johnson, E. ed. Anthology of children's literature p623-25 808.8
Prairie-town boy
In Sandburg, C. The Sandburg treasury p263-382 818
Rootabaga pigeons
In Sandburg, C. Rootabaga stories v2 S C
Rootabaga stories (5-7) S C

Contents: v 1 How they broke away to go to the Rootabaga Country; How they bring back the Village of Cream Puffs when the wind blows it away; How the five rusty rats helped find a new village; Potato Face Blind Man who lost the diamond rabbit on his gold accordion; How the Potato Face Blind Man enjoyed himself on a fine spring morning; Poker Face the Baboon and Hot Dog the Tiger; Toboggan-to-the-moon dream of the Potato Face Blind Man; How Gimme the Ax found out about the zigzag railroad and who made it zigzag; Story of Blixie Bimber and the power of the gold buckskin whincher; Story of Jason Squiff and why he had a popcorn hat, popcorn

mittens and popcorn shoes; Story of Rags Habakuk, the two blue rats, and the circus man who came with spot cash money; Wedding procession of the Rag Doll and the Broom Handle and who was in it; How the hot ashes shovel helped Snoo Foo; Three boys with jugs of molasses and secret ambitions; How Bimbo the Snip's thumb stuck to his nose when the wind changed; Two skyscrapers who decided to have a child; Dollar watch and the five jack rabbits; Wooden Indian and the Shaghorn Buffalo; White Horse Girl and the Blue Wind Boy; What six girls with balloons told the Gray Man on Horseback; How Henry Hagglyhoagly played the guitar with his mittens on; Never kick a slipper at the moon; Sand flat shadows; How to tell corn fairies if you see 'em; How the animals lost their tails and got them back traveling from Philadelphia to Medicine Hat

V2 Skyscraper to the moon and how the green rat with the rheumatism ran a thousand miles twice; Slipfoot and how he nearly always never gets what he goes after; Many, many weddings in one corner house; Shush, Shush, the big buff banty hen who laid an egg in the postmaster's hat; How Rag Bag Mammy kept her secret while the wind blew away the Village of Hat Pins; How six pigeons came back to Hatrack the Horse after many accidents and six telegrams; How the three wild Babylonian Baboons went away in the rain eating bread and butter; How six umbrellas took off their straw hats to show respect to the one big umbrella; How Bozo the Button Buster busted all his buttons when a mouse came; How Googler and Gaggler, the two Christmas babies came home with monkey wrenches; How Johnny the Wham sleeps in money all the time and Joe the Wimp shines and sees things; How Deep Red Roses goes back and forth between the clock and the looking glass; How Pink Peony sent Spuds, the ballplayer, up to pick four moons; How Dippy the Wisp and Slip Me Liz came in the Moonshine where the Potato Face Blind Man sat with his accordion; How Hot Balloons and his pigeon daughters crossed into the Rootabaga Country; How two sweetheart dippies sat in the moonlight on a lumber yard fence and heard about the sooners and boomers; Haystack cricket and how things are different up in the moon towns; Why the big ball game between Hot Grounders and the Grand Standers was a hot game; Huckabuck family and how they raised pop corn in Nebraska and quit and came back; Yang Yang and Hoo Hoo; How a skyscraper and a railroad train got picked up and carried away from Pig's Eve Valley far in the Pickax Mountains; Pig Wisps; Kiss Me; Blue silver

also in Sandburg, C. The Sandburg treasury p9-160 818
The Sandburg treasury (5-7) 818
The wedding procession of the Rag Doll and the Broom Handle and who was in it E
White Horse Girl and the Blue Wind Boy
In Davis, M. G. ed. A baker's dozen p41-49 372.6
In Sechrist, E. H. ed. It's time for story hour p60-63 372.6
Wind song (4-7) 811
also in Sandburg, C. The Sandburg treasury p209-61 818

About
See pages in the following book:
Benét, L. Famous poets for young people p148-51 (5-7) 920

Sandburg, Helga
Joel and the wild goose E
The **Sandburg** treasury. Sandburg, C. 818

Sandcastles, The art and industry of. Adkins, J. 728.8

Sander, Lenore
The curious world of crystals (4-7) 548

Sanderlin, Owenita
Follow the North Star
In Kamerman, S. E. ed. Little plays for little players p216-21 812.08

Sawyer, Ruth—*Continued*
Stories included are: The two lambs; This is the Christmas; The precious herbs of Christmas; What the Three Kings brought; San Froilan of the Wilderness; The miracle of Saint Cumgall

Newbery Medal acceptance paper
In Miller, B. M. ed. Newbery Medal books: 1922-1955 p153-56   **028.5**

The peddler of Ballaghadereen
In Arbuthnot, M. H. comp. The Arbuthnot Anthology of children's literature p181-84   **808.8**
In Arbuthnot, M. H. comp. Time for old magic p42-45   **398.2**

The princess and the vagabone
In Johnson, S. P. ed. The Princesses p164-83   **S C**

Roller skates (4-6)   **Fic**

The sack of truth
In Sechrist, E. H. ed. It's time for story hour p243-48   **372.6**

This way to Christmas (3-5)   **Fic**

The voyage of the wee red cap
In Association for Childhood Education International. Told under the Christmas tree p163-71   **808.8**
In Ward, W. ed. Stories to dramatize p219-24   **372.6**

The way of the storyteller   **372.6**
Stories included are: Wee Meg Barnileg and the fairies; The magic box; Señora, will you snip? Señora, will you sew; The peddler of Ballaghadereen; Where one is fed a hundred can dine; A matter of brogues; The juggler of Notre Dame; The deserted mine; The bird who spoke three times; The legend of Saint Elizabeth; The Princess and the vagabone

About

See pages in the following book:

Miller, B. M. ed. Newbery Medal books: 1922-1955 p149-52   **028.5**

Saxon, Gladys R.
Rosina's chickens
In Harper, W. comp. Easter chimes p153-61   **394.2**

Say, Allen
Once under the cherry blossom tree (1-3)   **398.2**

Sayers, Frances Clarke
Summoned by books   **028.5**
(jt. ed.) Johnson, E. ed. Anthology of children's literature   **808.8**

Sayings. See Epigrams; Proverbs; Quotations

Scagnetti, Jack
(jt. auth.) Barris, G. Famous custom & show cars   **629.22**

Scale-insects

See pages in the following book:

Hutchins, R. E. The bug clan p42-46 (5-7)   **595.7**

Scales (Fishes)

See pages in the following book:

Mason, G. F. Animal clothing p61-77 (4-7)   **591.4**

Scaly wings. Hutchins, R. E.   **595.7**

A scandal in Bohemia. Doyle, Sir A. C.
In Doyle, Sir A. C. The boys' Sherlock Holmes p291-314   **S C**
In Doyle, Sir A. C. Tales of Sherlock Holmes p281-306   **S C**

Scandinavia. See names of individual countries within Scandinavia, e.g. Sweden

Scandinavian mythology. See Mythology, Norse

Scandinavians. See Northmen

Scar Face
Grinnell, G. B. Legend of Scar Face
In Davis, M. G. ed. A baker's dozen p189-207   **372.6**

The scarecrow. De La Mare, W.
In De La Mare, W. The magic jacket p44-71   **S C**

The scarecrow and the witch. Bennett, R.
In Bennett, R. Creative plays and programs for holidays p112-22   **812**

Scaredy cat. Boiko, C.
In Bioko, C. Children's plays for creative actors p75-85   **812**

Scarf, Maggie
Antarctica: exploring the frozen continent (3-6)   **919.8**

Scarface; excerpt. Grinnell, G. B.
In Hazeltine, A. I. ed. Hero tales from many lands p448-59   **398.2**

The Scarlet Pimpernel. Leech, M. T.
In Burack, A. S. ed. Popular plays for classroom reading p300-24   **808.82**

Scarry, Richard
Richard Scarry's ABC word book   **E**

About

See pages in the following book:

Smaridge, N. Famous author-illustrators for young people p124-29 (5-7)   **920**

Scavengers. Earle, O. L.   **591.5**

Schachner, Erwin
(illus.) Dean, E. Printing: tool of freedom   **686.2**

Schackburg, Richard
Yankee Doodle (k-3)   **784.7**

Schaeffer, Elizabeth
Dandelion, pokeweed, and goosefoot (4-7)   **581.6**

Schaffert, Arthur
(illus.) Berger, M. Computers   **001.6**

Schaller, George B.
The tiger (4-7)   **599**

Scharl, Josef
(illus.) Grimm, J. The complete Grimm's Fairy tales   **398.2**

Schechter, Ilene R.
(ed.) Junior high school library catalog. See Junior high school library catalog   **011**

Schecter, Ben
(illus.) Chenery, J. The toad hunt   **E**

Scheele, William E.
The earliest Americans (5-7)   **917**
The mound builders (4-7)   **970.4**

Scheer, Julian
Rain makes applesauce   **E**

Scheffer, Victor B.
Little Calf (5-7)   **599**

Scheherazade
In Lang, A. ed. Arabian nights p 1-5 **398.2**

Scheherazade. Untermeyer, L.
In Untermeyer, L. Tales from ballet p85-87   **792.8**

Schrotter, Gustav
(illus.) Rutgers van der Loeff, A. Avalanche!
                                   Fic
(illus.) Zim, H. S. The universe   523.1

Schucker, James
(illus.) Farley, W. Little Black, a pony   E

Schule, Cliff
(illus.) Patterson, L. Christmas feasts and
    festivals   394.2

Schultz, Pearle Henriksen
Paul Laurence Dunbar: Black poet laureate
    (4-7)   92

Schulz, Charles M.
The Charlie Brown dictionary (k-3)   423
The Snoopy festival (4-7)   741.5

Schuman, Benjamin N.
The human eye (4-6)   612

Schuman, William Howard

     See pages in the following book:

Posell, E. Z. American composers p162-66
    (5-7)   920

Schwann, Theodor

     See pages in the following book:

Cottler, J. More Heroes of civilization p133-
    40 (6-7)   920

Schwartz, Alvin
Central city/spread city (5-7)   301.34
(comp.) Cross your fingers, spit in your hat
    (4-7)   398
The night workers (2-5)   331.7
(ed.) Tomfoolery (3-6)   398.6
(comp.) A twister of twists, a tangler of
    tongues (4-7)   808.88
Whoppers (4-7)   398.2
(ed.) Witcracks (4-7)   398.6

Schwartz, Beatrice
(illus.) Siegmeister, E. Invitation to music
                                   780.1

Schwartz, Charles
(jt. auth.) Schwartz, E. When animals are
    babies   591

Schwartz, Daniel
(illus.) Byars, B. The house of wings Fic

Schwartz, Elizabeth
When animals are babies (k-3)   591

Schwartz, Julius
It's fun to know why (4-7)   507.2

Schwartz, Lynne Sharon
The Wizard of Oz
    In Burack, A. S. ed. Popular plays for
      classroom reading p246-64   808.82
    In Kamerman, S. E. ed. Fifty plays for
      junior actors p530-53   812.08

Schwartz, Morton K.
All in favor
    In Burack, A. S. ed. One hundred plays
      for children p218-27   808.82
Twin cousins
    In Burack, A. S. ed. One hundred plays
      for children p228-36   808.82

Schweinitz, Karl de. See De Schweinitz, Karl

Schweitzer, Albert
Montgomery, E. R. Albert Schweitzer, great
    humanitarian (4-6)   92

     See also pages in the following books:

Johnson, E. ed. Anthology of children's lit-
    erature p1091-92   808.8
McNeer, M. Armed with courage p99-112
    (4-6)   920
Sechrist, E. H. It's time for brotherhood p68-
    75 (5-7)   301.11

Schweitzer, Byrd Baylor
Amigo   E
     For other titles by this author see
    Baylor, Byrd

Science
Asimov, I. Breakthroughs in science (5-7) 920
Pine, T. S. The Indians knew (1-3)   970.1
     See also pages in the following book:
Childcraft: the how and why library v4 031
     See also Astronomy; Biology; Botany;
    Chemistry; Crystallography; Fossils; Ge-
    ology; Mathematics; Meteorology; Min-
    eralogy; Natural history; Petrology; Phys-
    ics; Physiology; Space sciences; Zoology

                  Bibliography
     See pages in the following books:
National Council of Teachers of English.
    Adventuring with books p287-325 **028.52**
Withrow, D. E. Gateways to readable books
    p132-44   **028.52**
        Bibliography—Periodicals
Appraisal   **016.5**
Science Books & Films   **016.505**
                Denmark
     See pages in the following book:
Wohlrabe, R. A. The land and people of
    Denmark p137-44 (5-7)   **914.89**
                   Egypt
     See pages in the following book:
Van Duyn, J. The Egyptians p117-21 (6-7)
                                913.32
           Encyclopedias
The Book of popular science   **503**
           Exhibitions
     See pages in the following book:
Barr, G. Show time for young scientists p143-
    56 (5-7)   **793.8**
          Experiments
Barr, G. Show time for young scientists (5-7)
                                 793.8
Cobb, V. Science experiments you can eat
    (5-7)   **507.2**
Gardner, M. Science puzzlers (6-7) **507.2**
Milgrom, H. Adventures with a cardboard
    tube (k-2)   **507.2**
Milgrom, H. Adventures with a paper cup
    (k-2)   **507.2**
Milgrom, H. Adventures with a straw (k-2)
                                 507.2
Milgrom, H. Egg-ventures (1-3)   **636.5**
Pine, T. S. The Africans knew (1-4)   **916**
Pine, T. S. The Eskimos knew (1-4) **970.1**
Pine, T. S. The Incas knew (1-4)   **980.3**
Pine, T. S. The Polynesians knew (4-6) **919.6**
Rosenfeld, S. Science experiments with air
    (5-7)   **507.2**
Schneider, H. Science fun with a flashlight
    (1-4)   **535.072**
Schwartz, J. It's fun to know why (4-7) **507.2**

Seamanship. See Navigation

Seamen

Sperry, A. John Paul Jones, fighting sailor (4-6)   **92**

Syme, R. Captain John Paul Jones: America's fighting seaman (3-5)   **92**

    See also Merchant marine; Seafaring life; also names of countries with the subhead Navy, e.g. United States. Navy

Fiction

Coatsworth, E. The Cat and the Captain (2-4)   **Fic**

The search. Byars, B.

    In Arbuthnot, M. H. comp. The Arbuthnot Anthology of children's literature p638-41   **808.8**

The search for delicious. Babbitt, N.   **Fic**

The search for Jean Baptiste. Austin, M.

    In A St Nicholas anthology p27-30   **810.8**

The search for Sita; excerpt. Mukerji, D. G.

    In Hazeltine, A. I. ed. Hero tales from many lands p382-99   **398.2**

The search: who gets the chief's daughter. Courlander, H.

    In Courlander, H. The king's drum, and other African stories p28-31   **398.2**

    In Tashjian, V. A. ed. With a deep sea smile p70-74   **372.6**

Sears, Bill

(illus.) Baylor, B. Sometimes I dance mountains   **793.3**

Sears List of subject headings   **025.3**

Seashells. See Shells

Seashore

Buck, M. W. Along the seashore (3-6)   **574.92**

Garelick, M. Down to the beach   **E**

Kohn, B. The beachcomber's book (3-7) **745.5**

Selsam, M. E. See along the shore (3-5)   **574.92**

Tresselt, A. I saw the sea come in   **E**

Zim, H. S. Seashores (5-7)   **574.92**

    See also pages in the following book:

Peattie, D. C. The rainbow book of nature p97-109 (5-7)   **574**

Fiction

Koch, D. I play at the beach   **E**

Kumin, M. W. The beach before breakfast **E**

Myrick, M. The Secret Three   **E**

Russ, L. Alec's sand castle   **E**

Zion, G. Harry by the sea   **E**

Seashore story. Yashima, T.   **E**

Seashores. Zim, H. S.   **574.92**

The season for singing. Langstaff, J. comp.   **783.6**

Seasons

Branley, F. M. Sunshine makes the seasons (2-4)   **525**

Kane, H. B. Four seasons in the woods (3-5)   **500.9**

Polgreen, J. Sunlight and shadows (1-3) **525**

Tresselt, A. It's time now! (k-2)   **525**

    See also names of the seasons, e.g. Autumn

Drama

Bennett, R. Creative plays and programs for holidays (3-6)   **812**

    See also pages in the following book:

Fisher, A. Holiday programs for boys and girls p350-64 (4-7)   **812**

Fiction

Berenstain, S. The bears' almanac   **E**

Fisher, A. I like weather   **E**

Foster, D. V. L. A pocketful of seasons   **E**

Toye, W. How summer came to Canada (k-3)   **398.2**

Pictorial works

Burningham, J. Seasons   **E**

Poetry

Bennett, R. Creative plays and programs for holidays (3-6)   **812**

Brewton, S. comp. Sing a song of seasons (3-7)   **821.08**

Cole, W. comp. Poems for seasons and celebrations (5-7)   **821.08**

Hazeltine, A. I. comp. The year around (4-7)   **808.81**

    See also pages in the following books:

Association for Childhood Education International. Sung under the silver umbrella p157-68 (k-2)   **821.08**

Farjeon, E. The children's bells p109-203 (3-6)   **821**

Geismer, B. P. comp. Very young verses p112-48 (k-1)   **821.08**

Grahame, K. comp. The Cambridge Book of poetry for children p21-34   **821.08**

Huffard, G. T. comp. My poetry book p284-324 (5-7)   **821.08**

Larrick, N. ed. Piping down the valleys wild p79-90   **808.81**

McEwen, C. S. comp. Away we go! p32-50 (k-3)   **808.81**

Sechrist, E. H. ed. One thousand poems for children p361-78   **821.08**

Untermeyer, L. ed. The Golden Treasury of poetry p267-85   **821.08**

Untermeyer, L. ed. Rainbow in the sky p170-82 (k-4)   **821.08**

Seasons. Burningham, J.   **E**

Season's greetings. Miller, H. L.

    In Kamerman, S. E. ed. A treasury of Christmas plays p176-97   **812.08**

The seasons of time. Baron, V. O. ed.   **895.6**

Seattle

Fiction

Erwin, B. K. Go to the room of the eyes (4-6)   **Fic**

Seaweeds. See Algae

Sebgugugu the glutton. Aardema, V.

    In Aardema, V. Behind the back of the mountain p42-47   **398.2**

Sébillot, Paul

The dirty shepherdess

    In Lang, A. ed. The green fairy book p180-85   **398.2**

The Golden Blackbird

    In Lang, A. ed. The green fairy book p151-56   **398.2**

The snuff-box

    In Lang, A. ed. The green fairy book p145-50   **398.2**

See and say. Frasconi, A.   **410**

See through the sea. Selsam, M.   **591.92**

Seed for Thanksgiving. Baldwin, C.
  In Luckhardt, M. C. comp. Thanksgiving
    p339-45   **394.2**

The seed of liberty had taken root. Daugherty, J.
  In Luckhardt, M. C. comp. Thanksgiving
    p126-27   **394.2**

Seeds
  Carle, E. The tiny seed (k-3)   **582**
  Guilcher, J. M. A fruit is born (4-7)   **582**
  Hammond, W. G. The riddle of seeds (3-5)
    582
  Hutchins, R. E. The amazing seeds (5-7) **582**
  Jordan, H. J. How a seed grows (k-2)   **582**
  Jordan, H. J. Seeds by wind and water (k-2)
    582
  Rahn, J. E. How plants travel (4-6)   **582**
  Selsam, M. E. Play with seeds (3-6) **582.072**

  See also pages in the following books:

  Parker, B. M. The new Golden Treasury of
    natural history p340-47 (5-7)   **500.9**
  Villiard, P. Birds as pets p30-37 (5-7) **636.6**

Seeds by wind and water. Jordan, H. J.   **582**

Seeds of time. Shakespeare, W.   **822.3**

Seeger, Charles
  (jt. auth.) Seeger, P. The foolish frog   **784.4**

Seeger, Elizabeth
  Eastern religions (6-7)   **291**

Seeger, Pete
  The foolish frog   **784.4**

Seeger, Ruth Crawford
  American folk songs for children in home,
    school and nursery school   **784.4**
  (comp.) American folk songs for Christmas
    784.4
  (comp.) Animal folk songs for children **784.4**

Seeing eye dogs. See Guide dogs

Seeing Eye, Incorporated, Morristown, N.J.
  Putnam, P. The triumph of the Seeing Eye
    (5-7)   **636.7**

Seeing what plants do. Rahn, J. E.   **581.072**

Seely, Pauline A.
  (ed.) ALA Rules for filing catalog cards. See
    ALA Rules for filing catalog cards   **025.3**

Seer Gobborn. See Gobborn Seer

Seerko
  In Bloch, M. H. ed. Ukrainian folk tales
    p44-48   **398.2**

Seesaws to cosmic rays. Wilson, M.   **530**

Segal, Lore
  All the way home   **E**
  Tell me a Mitzi   **E**
  Grimm, J. The juniper tree, and other tales
    from Grimm   **398.2**

Segregation. See Discrimination; Minorities

Segregation in education

  See pages in the following books:

Jackson, F. The Black man in America [v6]
  p78-84 (6-7)   **301.45**
Young, M. B. The first book of American

Negroes p23-33 (4-7)   **301.45**
  See also Discrimination in education

    Fiction

Baum, B. Patricia crosses town (4-6)   **Fic**
Sterling, D. Mary Jane (5-7)   **Fic**

Segregation in public accommodations. See Discrimination in public accommodations

Ségur, Sophie (Rostopchine), comtesse de

  See pages in the following book:

Jan, I. On children's literature p118-21, 97-
  101   **028.5**

Seidelman, James E.
  Creating with clay (4-7)   **731.4**
  Creating with paint (4-7)   **751.4**
  Creating with papier-mache (4-6)   **731.4**
  Creating with wood (4-7)   **745.51**
  The rub book (1-3)   **741.2**

Seignobosc, Françoise. See Françoise

Seismography. See Earthquakes

Seismology. See Earthquakes

Selden, George
  The cricket in Times Square (3-6)   **Fic**
  The cricket in Times Square; excerpt
  In Association for Childhood Education
    International. Told under the city
    umbrella p73-80   **S C**
  The genie of Sutton Place (4-7)   **Fic**
  Harry Cat's pet puppy (3-6)   **Fic**
  Tucker's countryside (3-6)   **Fic**

Self, Margaret Cabell
  The Baker's new coat
  In Sechrist, E. H. ed. It's time for story
    hour p51-59   **372.6**

Self-defense. See Boxing; Karate

Self-kicking machine. Credle, E.
  In Credle, E. Tall tales from the high hills,
    and other stories p89-95   **398.2**

The Selfish Giant. Wilde, O.
  In Colwell, E. ed. A storyteller's choice
    p72-77   **372.6**
  In Harper, W. comp. Easter chimes p162-
    69   **394.2**
  In Mayne, W. ed. William Mayne's Book
    of giants p204-10   **398.2**
  In Ross, E. S. ed. The lost half-hour p120-
    27   **372.6**
  In Sechrist, E. H. ed. It's time for Easter
    p221-26   **394.2**
  In Untermeyer, B. ed. The Golden Treasury of children's literature p449-52
    808.8
  In Wilde, O. The Happy Prince, and other
    stories p21-26   **S C**

Sell, Violet
  (comp.) Subject index to poetry for children
    and young people. See Subject index to
    poetry for children and young people
    808.81

Sellar, May
  The dragon and his grandmother
  In Green, R. L. ed. A cavalcade of dragons
    p120-24   **808.8**

The seller of dreams. Beston, H.
  In Sechrist, E. H. ed. It's time for story
    hour p36-42   **372.6**

AUTHOR, TITLE, SUBJECT, AND ANALYTICAL INDEX
THIRTEENTH EDITION, 1976

Selormey, Francis

See pages in the following book:

Ojigbo, A. O. comp. Young and Black in Africa p31-45 (6-7)   920

Selsam, Millicent E.

All kinds of babies (k-3)   591

Animals as parents (5-7)   591.5

The apple and other fruits (3-5)   582

Benny's animals, and how he put them in order (1-3)   591

Birth of a forest (4-6)   581.5

Birth of an island (3-5)   551.4

Bulbs, corms, and such (2-5)   584

The carrot and other root vegetables (2-4)   635

Egg to chick (k-3)   574.3

A first look at birds (1-3)   598.2

Greg's microscope (1-3)   578

Hidden animals (k-3)   591.5

How animals live together (5-7)   591.5

How animals tell time (4-7)   591.5

How kittens grow (k-2)   636.8

How puppies grow (k-3)   636.7

How to grow house plants (4-7)   635.9

Is this a baby dinosaur? (k-3)   574

The language of animals (5-7)   591.5

Let's get turtles (1-3)   639

Maple tree (2-4)   582

Milkweed (2-4)   583

More potatoes! (1-3)   635

Peanut (2-4)   583

Plants that heal (4-6)   581.6

Play with plants (3-6)   581.072

Play with seeds (3-6)   582.072

Play with trees (3-5)   582.072

Plenty of fish (k-3)   639

Questions and answers about ants (2-5)   595.7

Questions and answers about horses (2-4)   636.1

See along the shore (3-5)   574.92

See through the sea (2-4)   591.92

Terry and the caterpillars (k-2)   595.7

The tomato and other fruit vegetables (2-4)   635

Tony's birds (k-2)   598.2

Underwater zoos (4-6)   639

Vegetables from stems and leaves (2-4)   635

When an animal grows (k-3)   591

(jt. auth.) Bronowski, J. Biography of an atom   541

(jt. auth.) Schaller, G. B. The tiger   599

Seminole Indians

Bleeker, S. The Seminole Indians (4-6)   970.3

See also pages in the following books:

Hofsinde, R. Indian costumes p79-85 (3-6)   391

Hofsinde, R. Indians at home p39-47 (4-7)   728

Biography

Alderman, C. L. Osceola and the Seminole wars (5-7)   92

McNeer, M. War chief of the Seminoles [biography of Osceola, Seminole chief] (4-6)   92

Seminole War, 2d, 1835-1842

Alderman, C. L. Osceola and the Seminole wars (5-7)   92

McNeer, M. War chief of the Seminoles [biography of Osceola, Seminole chief] (4-6)   92

Sendak, Maurice

Caldecott Medal acceptance paper

In Kingman, L. ed. Newbery and Caldecott Medal books: 1956-1965 p247-53   028.5

Chicken soup with rice   E

Hector Protector, and As I went over the water (k-1)   398.8

Higglety pigglety pop! (2-4)   Fic

In the night kitchen   E

Where the wild things are   E

(illus.) Andersen, H. C. Seven tales   S C

(illus.) DeJong, M. Along came a dog   Fic

(illus.) DeJong, M. The house of sixty fathers   Fic

(illus.) DeJong, M. Hurry home, Candy   Fic

(illus.) DeJong, M. Shadrach   Fic

(illus.) DeJong, M. The wheel on the school   Fic

(illus.) Engvick, W. ed. Lullabies and night songs   784.6

(illus.) Grimm, J. The juniper tree, and other tales from Grimm   398.2

(illus.) Hauff, W. Dwarf Long-Nose   Fic

(illus.) Jarrell, R. The animal family   Fic

(illus.) Jarrell, R. The bat-poet   Fic

(illus.) Joslin, S. What do you do, dear?   395

(illus.) Joslin, S. What do you say, dear?   395

(illus.) Krauss, R. The birthday party   E

(illus.) Krauss, R. A hole is to dig   E

(illus.) Krauss, R. A very special house   E

(illus.) Macdonald, G. The light princess   Fic

(illus.) Minarik, E. H. Father Bear comes home   E

(illus.) Minarik, E. H. A kiss for Little Bear   E

(illus.) Minarik, E. H. Little Bear   E

(illus.) Minarik, E. H. Little Bear's friend   E

(illus.) Minarik, E. H. Little Bear's visit   E

(illus.) Singer, I. B. Zlateh the goat, and other stories   398.2

(illus.) Stockton, F. R. The Bee-man of Orn   Fic

(illus.) Stockton, F. R. The Griffin and the Minor Canon   Fic

(illus.) Udry, J. M. Let's be enemies   E

(illus.) Udry, J. M. The Moon Jumpers   E

(illus.) Zolotow, C. Mr Rabbit and the lovely present   E

About

See pages in the following books:

Hoffman, M. ed. Authors and illustrators of children's books p364-77   028.5

Kingman, L. ed. Newbery and Caldecott Medal books: 1956-1965 p254-57   028.5

Smaridge, N. Famous author-illustrators for young people p138-45 (5-7)   920

Seneca Falls Convention

See pages in the following book:

Sechrist, E. H. Women's rights p45-50 (5-7)   324.73

Seneca Indians

Gardner, J. L. Mary Jemison: Seneca captive (4-6)   92

Lenski, L. Indian captive; the story of Mary Jemison (5-7)   92

Senegal

Gordon, E. Senegal in pictures (5-7)   916.6

Senegal in pictures. Gordon, E.   916.6

Shepherd's nosegay—Continued
Haviland, V. The shepherd's nosegay
In Haviland, V. Favorite fairy tales told in
Czechoslovakia p49-66　　**398.2**
See also Shepherd and the princess

The **Shepherd's** pie. Mincieli, R. L.
In Ross, L. Puppet shows using poems and
stories p159-62　　**791.5**

Shepherd's story of the bond of friendship
Andersen, H. C. The pact of friendship
In Andersen, H. C. The complete fairy
tales and stories p167-74　　**S C**

Sheppard, John
(illus.) Sechrist, E. H. Once in the first times
　　398.2

Sheppard, Sally
The first book of Brazil (4-6)　　**918.1**

Sheridan, Noel
Morocco in pictures (5-7)　　**916.4**

Sherlock, Sir Philip M.
Anansi, the spider man (4-6)　　**398.2**

Contents: Who was Anansi; From Tiger to Anansi;
Brother Breeze and the pear tree; Anansi and the Old
Hag; Anansi and Turtle and Pigeon; Kisander; Kling
Kling bird; Bandalee; Yung-Kyung-Pyung; Anansi and
the plantains; Anansi and the Fish Country; Ticky-
Picky Boom-Boom; Anansi and the alligator eggs;
Anansi and the crabs; The quarrel

Bandalee
In Arbuthnot, M. H. comp. The Arbuth-
not Anthology of children's literature
p396-99　　**808.8**
In Arbuthnot, M. H. comp. Time for old
magic p265-68　　**398.2**
From tiger to Anansi
In Haviland, V. comp. The fairy tale trea-
sury p86-91　　**398.2**
In Johnson, E. ed. Anthology of children's
literature p367-69　　**808.8**
The land and people of the West Indies (5-7)
　　917.29
The iguana's tail (3-5)　　**398.2**

Contents: The meeting; Green Parrot's story; Little
Capuchin Monkey's story; Brown Owl's story; Chimpanzee's story; Firefly's story; Armadillo's story

West Indian folk-tales (4-6)　　**398.2**

Contents: The Coomacka-Tree; The crested curassow; Irraweka, mischief-maker; The jaguar and the
crested curassow; The dog's nose is cold; The Warau
people discover the earth; Tiger story, Anansi story;
Tiger in the forest, Anansi in the web; Mancrow, bird
of darkness; Anansi and Snake the postman; Dry-Bone
and Anansi; How crab got a hard back; Cat and Dog;
Anansi and Candlefly; Anansi's old riding-horse; Why
women won't listen; Anansi hunts with Tiger; Work-
let-me-see; The Sea-Mammy; Born a monkey, live a
monkey; Mr Wheeler

Sherlock Holmes and the Red-headed League.
Olfson, L.
In Burack, A. S. ed. Popular plays for
classroom reading p232-45　　**808.82**

Sherman, Harriet
(illus.) Merriam, E. Boys & girls, girls & boys
　　E
(illus.) Pine, T. S. Measurements and how
we use them　　**389**
(illus.) Schneider, H. Science fun with a
flashlight　　**535.072**
(illus.) Whitney, D. C. Let's find out about
addition　　**513**

Sherwood, Merriam
The wedding of the Cid's daughters
In Hazeltine, A. I. ed. Hero tales from
many lands p236-51　　**398.2**

Sherwood, Stewart
(illus.) Burnett, F. H. A little princess　　**Fic**

Shetland ponies. Hess, L.　　**636.1**

Shetty, Sharat
A Hindu boyhood (3-5)　　**915.4**

Shields, Gerald R.
(jt. ed.) Burke, J. G. ed. Children's library
service　　**027.62**

Shillabeer, Mary
(illus.) Stevenson, R. L. A child's garden of
verses (Dutton)　　**821**

Shimin, Symeon
(illus.) Baylor, B. Coyote cry　　**Fic**
(illus.) Belpré, P. Santiago　　**E**
(illus.) Cretan, G. Y. All except Sammy　　**Fic**
(illus.) Fenner, C. Gorilla gorilla　　**599**
(illus.) Fisher, A. Listen, rabbit　　**E**
(illus.) Gruenberg, S. M. The wonderful story
of how you were born　　**612.6**
(illus.) Hamilton, V. Zeely　　**Fic**
(illus.) Krumgold, J. Onion John　　**Fic**
(illus.) May, J. Before the Indians　　**917**
(illus.) May, J. Why people are different
colors　　**572**
(illus.) Phelan, M. K. The Fourth of July
　　394.2
(illus.) Selsam, M. E. All kinds of babies　　**591**
(illus.) Simon, N. Hanukkah　　**296.4**
(illus.) Simon, N. Passover (1-3)　　**296.4**
(illus.) Tobias, T. Marian Anderson　　**92**

Shimmy shimmy coke-ca-pop! Langstaff, J.
　　796.1

Shining princess, The story of the. *See* The
story of the shining princess

Shinto
See pages in the following books:
Fitch, F. M. Their search for God p85-109
(4-7)　　**291**
Seeger, E. Eastern religions p157-96 (6-7)
　　291

Ship building. *See* Shipbuilding; Ships

Ship models. *See* Ships—Models

Ship models and how to build them. Weiss, H.
　　623.82

Ship that sailed by land and sea. Bowman, J. C.
In Bowman, J. C. Tales from a Finnish
tupa p 1-11　　**398.2**
See also Ashiepattle and his goodly
crew; Flying ship

The **ship that sailed on water and on land.**
Withers, C.
In Withers, C. A world of nonsense p9-17
　　398.2

The **ship that went as well by land as by sea.**
Aulaire, I. d'
In Aulaire, I. d'. East of the sun and west
of the moon p27-37　　**398.2**
See also Ashiepattle and his goodly
crew; Flying ship

The **shipbuilders.** Fisher, L. E.　　**623.82**

Shipbuilding
History
Fisher, L. E. The shipbuilders (4-7)　　**623.82**

Shrubs
Petrides, G. A. A field guide to trees and shrubs **582**

Shub, Elizabeth
Uncle Harry **E**

Shulevitz, Uri
Caldecott Medal acceptance paper
In Kingman, L. ed. Newbery and Caldecott Medal books: 1966-1975 p209-13 **028.5**
Dawn **E**
The magician (k-2) **398.2**
One Monday morning **E**
Rain, rain, rivers **E**
(illus.) Ish-Kishor, S. The carpet of Solomon **398.2**
(illus.) Ransome, A. The Fool of the World and the flying ship (k-3) **398.2**
(illus.) Singer, I. B. The fools of Chelm and their history **Fic**
(illus.) Soldier and Tsar in the forest. See Soldier and Tsar in the forest **398.2**

About
See pages in the following book:
Kingman, L. ed. Newbery and Caldecott Medal books: 1966-1975 p214-16 **028.5**

Shush Shush, the big buff banty hen who laid an egg in the postmaster's hat. Sandburg, C.
In Sandburg, C. Rootabaga stories v2 p27-30 **S C**
In Sandburg, C. The Sandburg treasury p97-98 **818**

Shut the door! Carlson, B. W.
In Carlson, B. W. Funny-bone dramatics p71-75 **812**

Shuttlesworth, Dorothy E.
All kinds of bees (4-6) **595.7**
Animal camouflage (4-7) **591.5**
Animals that frighten people (5-7) **591.5**
Clean air—sparkling water (3-6) **614.7**
Disappearing energy (5-7) **333.7**
Dodos and dinosaurs (4-6) **568**
The Doubleday First guide to rocks (2-3) **552**
Gerbils, and other small pets (3-6) **636.08**
Litter—the ugly enemy (3-5) **614.7**
Natural partnerships (5-7) **574.5**
The story of ants (4-7) **595.7**
The story of monkeys, great apes, and small apes (5-7) **599**
The story of rocks (5-7) **549**
The story of rodents (4-6) **599**
The story of spiders (4-6) **595**
To find a dinosaur (5-7) **568**
The wildlife of South America (5-7) **591.9**

The **shy** little horse. Brown, M. W.
In Martignoni, M. E. ed. The illustrated treasury of children's literature p301-03 **808.8**

The **shy** Prince. Spamer, C.
In Kamerman, S. E. ed. Little plays for little players p303-09 **812.08**

The **shy** stegosaurus of Cricket Creek. Lampman, E. S. **Fic**

Shyness. See Bashfulness

Siam. See Thailand

Siamese cat
Stories
Hildick, E. W. Manhattan is missing (4-6) **Fic**
Siamese fighting fish
See pages in the following book:
Pringle, L. ed. Discovering nature indoors p37-45 (5-7) **591**
Sian
Description
See pages in the following book:
Sidel, R. Revolutionary China: people, politics, and ping-pong p140-48 (6-7) **915.1**
Sibal, Joseph
(illus.) Wise, W. The amazing animals of North America **599**
Siberell, Anne
(illus.) Behrens, J. Feast of Thanksgiving **812**
Siberia
Lengyel, E. Siberia (5-7) **915.7**
See also pages in the following books:
Liversidge, D. The first book of the Arctic p9-12, 46-51 (4-7) **919.8**
Nazaroff, A. The land and people of Russia p9-26 (5-7) **914.7**
Fiction
Guillot, R. Grishka and the bear (5-7) **Fic**
Folklore
See Folklore—Siberia
Sibley, Don
(illus.) Burch, R. Skinny **Fic**
Sicily
See pages in the following book:
Winwar, F. The land and people of Italy p31-39 (5-7) **914.5**
Fiction
Fenton, E. A matter of miracles (4-7) **Fic**
Sick
Ellison, V. H. The Pooh get-well book (2-5) **790.19**
See also First aid; Hospitals
Fiction
Tobias, T. A day off **E**
Sickels, Evelyn R.
(jt. ed.) Johnson, E. ed. Anthology of children's literature **808.8**
Sickles, Noel
(illus.) McCoy, J. J. Nature sleuths **639**
Siddartha, Prince. See Gautama Buddha
Sidel, Ruth
Revolutionary China: people, politics, and ping-pong (6-7) **915.1**
Sidewalk story. Mathis, S. B. **Fic**
Sidjakov, Nicolas
Caldecott Medal acceptance paper
In Kingman, L. ed. Newbery and Caldecott Medal books: 1956-1965 p218-20 **028.5**
(illus.) The friendly beasts (Carol). The friendly beasts **783.6**
(illus.) Robbins, R. Baboushka and the three kings **398.2**
(illus.) Robbins, R. The Emperor and the drummer boy **Fic**

Sidjakov, Nicolas—*Continued*
About
See pages in the following book:
Kingman, L. ed. Newbery and Caldecott Medal books: 1956-1965 p221-24 **028.5**
Sidney, Margaret. See Lothrop, Harriet Mulford
Siebel, Fritz
(illus.) Bonsall, C. Tell me some more **E**
(illus.) McClintock, M. A fly went by **E**
(illus.) Nodset, J. L. Who took the farmer's [hat]? **E**
(illus.) Parish, P. Amelia Bedelia **E**
Siegel, Bertram M.
(jt. auth.) Stone, A. H. Take a balloon **530.72**
(jt. auth.) Stone, A. H. Turned on: a look at electricity **537.072**
Sieges. See Battles
Siegfried
Baldwin, J. The story of Siegfried (6-7) **398.2**
See also pages in the following books:
Hazeltine, A. I. ed. Hero tales from many lands p252-77 (5-7) **398.2**
Johnson, E. ed. Anthology of children's literature p523-32 **808.8**
Lang, A. ed. The red fairy book p357-67 **398.2**
Siegl, Helen
(illus.) Cole, W. comp. The birds and the beasts were there **821.08**
(illus.) Ginsburg, M. comp. One trick too many **398.2**
(illus.) Walker, B. K. The dancing palm tree, and other Nigerian folktales **398.2**
Siegmeister, Elie
Invitation to music (6-7) **780.1**
Siena. Palio
Fiction
Henry, M. Gaudenzia, pride of the Palio (4-7) **Fic**
Sierra Leone
Carpenter, A. Sierra Leone (4-7) **916.6**
Clifford, M. L. The land and people of Sierra Leone (5-7) **916.6**
Mines and mineral resources
See Mines and mineral resources—Sierra Leone
Sierra Leone People's Party
See pages in the following book:
Clifford, M. L. The land and people of Sierra Leone p80-93 (5-7) **916.6**
The sigakok bird. Sechrist, E. H.
In Sechrist, E. H. Once in the first times p24-25 **398.2**
Sight. See Vision
Sign boards. See Signs and signboards
Sign language. See Deaf—Means of communication; Indians of North America—Sign language
The sign of the four. Doyle, Sir A. C.
In Doyle, Sir A. C. The boy's Sherlock Holmes p91-209 **S C**
In Doyle, Sir A. C. Tales of Sherlock Holmes p131-255 **S C**
Sign painting. See Lettering

Signal **028.505**
The signal flag. Kim, S.
In Kim, S. The story bag p172-79 **398.2**
Signals and signaling
Coggins, J. Flashes and flags (5-7) **384**
Signs (Advertising) See Signs and signboards
Signs and signboards
See pages in the following book:
Gladstone, M. J. A carrot for a nose p30-43 (4-7) **745**
Signs and symbols
Barth, E. Hearts, cupids, and red roses (3-6) **394.2**
Barth, E. Holly, reindeer, and colored lights (3-6) **394.2**
Barth, E. Lilies, rabbits, and painted eggs (3-6) **394.2**
Barth, E. Witches, pumpkins, and grinning ghosts (3-6) **394.2**
Lubell, W. Picture signs & symbols (2-4) **001.54**
Rinkoff, B. Red light says stop! (1-3) **001.54**
See also Ciphers; Cryptography; Heraldry; Signals and signaling
Signs & symbols of the sun. Helfman, E. S. **398**
Sigurd. See Siegfried
Sigurd the king's son. Manning-Sanders, R.
In Manning-Sanders, R. A book of ogres and trolls p53-65 **398.2**
Sigurd's youth. Colum, P.
In Johnson, E. ed. Anthology of children's literature p523-28 **808.8**
Sihanouk Prince Norodom. See Norodom Sihanouk Varman, King of Cambodia
Sikakokuh and the hunting dog. Courlander, H.
In Courlander, H. People of the short blue corn p27-45 **398.2**
Siks, Geraldine Brain
Creative dramatics **372.6**
A legend of spring
In Ward, W. ed. Stories to dramatize p112-15 **372.6**
The peddler and his caps
In Ward, W. ed. Stories to dramatize p55-59 **372.6**
Siksika Indians
See pages in the following books:
Hofsinde, R. Indian costumes p21-32 (3-6) **391**
Hofsinde, R. Indian warriors and their weapons p57-67 (3-6) **739.7**
Silence over Dunkerque. Tunis, J. R. **Fic**
The silent album. Andersen, H. C.
In Andersen, H. C. The complete fairy tales and stories p381-82 **S C**
Silent Bianca. Yolen, J.
In Yolen, J. The girl who cried flowers, and other tales p46-55 **S C**
The silent maiden. Heady, E. B.
In Heady, E. B. When the stones were soft p72-76 **398.2**
Silent night (Carol)
Pauli, H. Silent night (4-7) **783.6**
Fiction
Wenning, E. The Christmas mouse **E**

Simont, Marc—*Continued*
Center. What to do when "there's nothing to do" **790**
(illus.) Chenery, J. Wolfie **595**
(illus.) McCord, D. Every time I climb a tree **811**
(illus.) Sharmat, M. W. Nate the Great **E**
(illus.) Thurber, J. The 13 clocks **Fic**
(illus.) Withers, C. comp. The American riddle book **398.6**

About

See pages in the following books:

Kingman, L. ed. Newbery and Caldecott Medal books: 1956-1965 p180-86 **028.5**
Miller, B. M. ed. Caldecott Medal books: 1938-1957 p300-06 **028.5**

Simple library cataloging. Akers, S. G. **025.3**

Simple machines and how to use them. Pine, T. S. **621.8**

Simple Olaf. Peterson, M. Y.
In Kamerman, S. E. ed. Dramatized folk tales of the world p413-21 **812.08**

Simple Seng and the parrot. Carpenter, F.
In Carpenter, F. Tales of a Chinese grandmother p242-51 **398.2**

Simpleton and his little black hen. Pyle, H.
In Pyle, H. The wonder clock p217-28 **398.2**

Simpleton Peter. Reeves, J.
In Reeves, J. English fables and fairy stories p103-14 **398.2**

Simpletons. Mehdevi, A. S.
In Mehdevi, A. S. Persian folk and fairy tales p33-43 **398.2**

Simply fun! Razzi, J. **745.5**

Simpson, Jean
(illus.) Gregor, A. S. Man's mark on the land **301.31**

Simpson, O. J. See Simpson, Orenthal James

Simpson, Orenthal James
Young, A. S. Black champions of the gridiron: O. J. Simpson and Leroy Keyes (5-7) **796.33**

Simunek, Kate
(illus.) Cochrane, L. Shadow puppets in color **791.5**
(illus.) Cochrane, L. Tabletop theatres **791.5**

Sinai Campaign, 1956

See pages in the following book:

Savage, K. The story of the United Nations p210-28 (6-7) **341.23**

Sinbad the sailor, Story of. See Story of Sinbad the sailor

Sing a song of seasons. Brewton, S. comp. **821.08**

Sing down the moon. O'Dell, S. **Fic**

Sing down the moon; excerpt. O'Dell, S.
In Arbuthnot, M. H. comp. The Arbuthnot Anthology of children's literature p767-69 **808.8**

Sing for your supper. Farjeon, E.
In Farjeon, E. Eleanor Farjeon's Poems for children p15-79 **821**

Sing-song. Rossetti, C. G. **821**

The sing-song of Old Man Kangaroo. Kipling, R.
In Kipling, R. Just so stories (Doubleday) p85-100 **S C**
In Kipling, R. Just so stories (Doubleday. Anniv. ed.) p39-43 **S C**
In Kipling, R. Just so stories (Watts, F.) p85-97 **S C**

Sing the songs of Christmas. Fisher, A.
In Kamerman, S. E. ed. A treasury of Christmas plays p222-40 **812.08**

Sing together. Girl Scouts of the United States of America **784.6**

Singapore
Poole, F. K. Malaysia & Singapore (5-7) **915.95**

Singer, Arthur B.
(illus.) Fichter, G. S. Cats **599**

Singer, Edith G.
(illus.) Bleeker, S. The Ashanti of Ghana **916.67**
(illus.) Bleeker, S. The Pygmies **916.7**

Singer, Isaac Bashevis
A day of pleasure (4-7) **92**
The Devil's trick
In Johnson, E. ed. Anthology of children's literature p274-75 **808.8**
The fearsome inn (4-6) **Fic**
The fools of Chelm and their history (3-6) **Fic**
Mazel and Shlimazel (2-5) **398.2**
When Shlemiel went to Warsaw & other stories (4-7) **398.2**
Contents: Shrewd Todie & Lyzer the Miser; Tsirtsur & Peziza; Rabbi Leib & the witch Cunegunde; The Elders of Chelm & Genendel's key; Shlemiel, the businessman; Utzel & his daughter Poverty; Menaseh's dream; When Shlemiel went to Warsaw

The wicked city (3-6) **221.9**
Zlateh the goat, and other stories (4-7) **398.2**
Contents: Fool's paradise; Grandmother's tale; The snow in Chelm; The mixed-up feet and the silly bridegroom; The first shlemiel; The Devil's trick; Zlateh the goat

Singer, Kurt
Danny Kaye, UNICEF ambassador
In Cavanah, F. ed. Holiday roundup p248-51 **394.2**

Singers
Cornell, J. G. Mahalia Jackson: queen of gospel song (4-6) **92**
Jackson, J. Make a joyful noise unto the Lord! The life of Mahalia Jackson, queen of gospel singers (5-7) **92**
Jones, H. Big star fallin' mama (6-7) **920**
Mathis, S. B. Ray Charles (2-5) **92**
Newman, S. P. Marian Anderson: lady from Philadelphia (5-7) **92**
Tobias, T. Marian Anderson (2-4) **92**

Singing
Kettelkamp, L. Song, speech, and ventriloquism (5-7) **808.5**

The singing and the gold. Parker, E. **808.81**

The singing bell. Spicer, D. G.
In Spicer, D. G. The owl's nest p41-55 **398.2**

The singing bone. Grimm, J.
In Grimm, J. The complete Grimm's Fairy tales p148-50 **398.2**

Snow White and the seven dwarfs—*Continued*
Snowdrop and the seven little dwarfs
In Hutchinson, V. S. ed. Chimney corner fairy tales p27-38   **398.2**

Snow White and the seven dwarfs; puppet play. Mahlmann, L.
In Mahlmann, L. Puppet plays for young players p65-78   **791.5**

Snowbound at Easter. Rowland, F. W.
In Harper, W. comp. Easter chimes p209-15   **394.2**

Snowbound with Betsy. Haywood, C. See note under Haywood, C. "B" is for Betsy   **Fic**

The snowdrop. Andersen. H. C.
In Andersen, H. C. The complete fairy tales and stories p886-89   **S C**

Snowdrop. Grimm, J.
In Grimm, J. Grimm's Fairy tales; illus. by A. Rackham p7-16   **398.2**
In Lang, A. ed. The red fairy book p329-39   **398.2**
See also Snow-White and the seven dwarfs

Snowdrop and the seven little dwarfs
In Hutchinson, V. S. ed. Chimney corner fairy tales p27-38   **398.2**
See also Snow-White and the seven dwarfs

Snowflake
Haviland, V. Snegourka, the snow maiden
In Haviland, V. Favorite fairy tales told in Russia p43-52   **398.2**
Ransome, A. The little daughter of the Snow
In Ransome, A. Old Peter's Russian tales p122-35   **398.2**
Shedlock, M. L. Snegourka
In Shedlock, M. L. The art of the story-teller p195-97   **372.6**
The Snow Maiden
In Gruenberg, S. M. ed. Favorite stories old and new p366-69   **808.8**

The snowman. Andersen, H. C.
In Andersen, H. C. The complete fairy tales and stories p718-22   **S C**
See also Snow man

The snowman who overstayed. Boiko, C.
In Boiko, C. Children's plays for creative actors p249-56   **812**

The snowman who played Santa. Bennett, R.
In Bennett, R. Creative plays and programs for holidays p278-82   **812**

The snowy day. Keats, E. J.   **E**

The snuff-box. Sébillot, P.
In Lang, A. ed. The green fairy book p145-50   **398.2**

Snyder, Jerome
(illus.) Cone, M. The Jewish New Year   **296.4**
(illus.) Kirtland, G. B. One day in Aztec Mexico   **917.2**
(illus.) Kirtland, G. B. One day in Elizabethan England   **914.2**

Snyder, Joel
(illus.) Graves, C. P. Frederick Douglass   **92**

Snyder, Louis L.
The first book of the Soviet Union (5-7) **914.7**
The first book of World War I (5-7)   **940.3**
The first book of World War II (5-7) **940.53**

Snyder, Zilpha Keatley
Black and blue magic (4-6)   **Fic**
The changeling (4-7)   **Fic**
The Egypt game (4-7)   **Fic**
The Egypt game; excerpt
In Arbuthnot, M. H. comp. The Arbuthnot Anthology of children's literature p691-95   **808.8**
Enter Melanie—and Marshall
In Arbuthnot, M. H. comp. The Arbuthnot Anthology of children's literature p691-95   **808.8**
The headless cupid (4-7)   **Fic**
The truth about Stone Hollow (4-7)   **Fic**
The velvet room (4-6)   **Fic**
The witches of Worm (4-7)   **Fic**

"So hallow'd and so gracious is the time—." Eaton, A. T.
In Eaton, A. T. comp. The animals' Christmas p16-21   **394.2**

So what about history? Morgan, E. S.   **901**

So you want to be a magician? White, L. B.   **793.8**

So you were elected! Bailard, V.   **367**

Soap

See pages in the following books:

Fisher, L. E. The homemakers p23-27 (4-7)   **680**
Schwartz, J. It's fun to know why p106-21 (4-7)   **507.2**

Soap box derbies
Radlauer, E. Soap box racing (1-4)   **796.6**

Soap box racing. Radlauer, E.   **796.6**

Soap, soap, soap
In Chase, R. ed. Grandfather tales p130-36   **398.2**

Soapweed. See Yucca

Soaring. Halacy, D.   **797.5**

Soaring flight. See Gliding and soaring

Soaring lark
Grimm, J. The lady and the lion
In Darrell, M. ed. Once upon a time **808.8**
In Grimm, J. Grimms' Fairy tales; illus. by F. Kredel p366-73   **398.2**
Grimm, J. The singing, soaring lark
In Grimm, J. The complete Grimm's Fairy tales p399-404   **398.2**

Sobol, Donald J.
Encyclopedia Brown, boy detective (3-5) **S C**

Soccer
Toye, C. Soccer (4-7)   **796.33**

See also pages in the following books:

Keith, H. Sports and games p243-65 (5-7) **796**
Morton, M. The making of champions p83-88 (5-7)   **796**

Fiction

Lord, B. Shrimp's soccer goal (2-5)   **Fic**

Social classes. See Caste

Social customs. See Manners and customs; and names of ethnic groups and countries with the subdivision Social life and customs, e.g. Indians of North America—Social life and customs; China—Social life and customs

Social ecology. See Human ecology

Social life and customs. See Manners and customs; and names of ethnic groups and countries with the subdivision Social life and customs, e.g. Indians of North America—Social life and customs; United States —Social life and customs

Social problems. See Discrimination; Divorce; Woman—Social conditions

Social psychology. See Human relations

Social service. See Social work

Social studies. See Geography

Social welfare. See Social work

Social work
Sechrist, E. H. It's time for brotherhood (5-7) **301.11**

Socially handicapped children
American Library Association. Library Service to the Disadvantaged Child Committee. I read, you read, we read **028.52**
See also pages in the following book:
Chicago. University. Graduate Library School. A critical approach to children's literature p32-45 **028.5**

Education
Palmer, J. R. Read for your life **028.52**

Socially handicapped children, Books for
Bibliography
Palmer, J. R. Read for your life **028.52**

Societies. See Clubs; Guilds

Society of Friends. See Friends, Society of

Socks. Cleary, B. **Fic**

Socrates
See pages in the following books:
Aymar, B. Laws and trials that created history p 1-11 (6-7) **345.7**
Coolidge, O. The golden days of Greece p113-27 (4-6) **938**
Giankoulis, T. The land and people of Greece p123-26 (5-7) **914.95**

The sod house. Coatsworth, E. **Fic**

Sod houses
Rounds, G. The treeless plains (4-6) **917.8**

Sodom
Singer, I. B. The wicked city (3-6) **221.9**

Sody sallyraytus
Sody saleratus
In Tashjian, V. A. ed. Juba this and Juba that p55-59 **372.6**
Sody Sallyraytus
In Chase, R. ed. Grandfather tales p75-80 **398.2**

Soe, Robert C. du. See Du Soe, Robert C.

Sofo's escape from the leopard. Courlander, H.
In Courlander, H. Olode the hunter, and other tales from Nigeria p61-64 **398.2**

Softball
Sullivan, G. Better softball for boys and girls (4-7) **796.357**
See also pages in the following book:
Keith, H. Sports and games p266-77 (5-7) **796**

Softly, Barbara
Master ghost and I
In Ireson, B. comp. Haunting tales p256-70 **S C**

Soil conservation
Keen, M. L. The world beneath our feet (4-6) **631.4**
See also Erosion

Soil erosion. See Erosion

Soil fertility. See Soils

Soils
Goldin, A. Where does your garden grow? (1-3)
Keen, M. L. The world beneath our feet (4-6) **631.4**
The Story of soil (4-6) **631.4**
See also pages in the following book:
Abell, E. Flower gardening p 1-15 (5-7) **635.9**
See also Fertilizers and manures

Sojo. Berry, E.
In Association for Childhood Education International. Told under the magic umbrella p39-49 **S C**

Sojourner Truth, a self-made woman. Ortiz, V. **92**

Sokol, Bill
(illus.) Andersen, H. C. The nightingale **Fic**
(illus.) Hicks, C. Alvin's secret code **Fic**

Solar eclipses. See Eclipses, Solar

Solar energy
See pages in the following book:
Shuttlesworth, D. E. Disappearing energy p68-74 (5-7) **333.7**

Solar heat. See Solar energy; Sun

Solar physics. See Sun

Solar radiation
Polgreen, J. Sunlight and shadows (1-3) **525**
See also pages in the following book:
Branley, F. M. Comets, meteoroids, and asteroids p84-96 (6-7) **523.2**

Solar system
Branley, F. M. Comets, meteoroids, and asteroids (6-7) **523.2**
Gardner, M. Space puzzles: curious questions and answers about the solar system (6-7) **523.2**
Knight, D. C. Thirty-two moons (5-7) **523.9**
See also Comets; Earth; Moon; Planets; Planets, Minor; Sun; also names of planets, e.g. Mars (Planet)

Solberg, S. E.
The land and people of Korea (5-7) **915.19**

Solbert, Ronni
I wrote my name on the wall **E**
(illus.) Brooks, G. Bronzeville boys and girls **811**
(illus.) Chafetz, H. Thunderbird, and other stories (4-6) **398.2**
(illus.) Haviland, V. Favorite fairy tales told in Sweden **398.2**
(illus.) Hoberman, M. A. Nuts to you & nuts to me **811**
(jt. auth.) Merrill, J. High, Wide and Handsome and their three tall tales **398.2**
(illus.) Merrill, J. The Pushcart War **Fic**
(illus.) Merrill, J. Shan's lucky knife **398.2**
(illus.) Merrill, J. The superlative horse **Fic**

The soldier and his magic helpers. Grimm, J.
  In Grimm, J. More Tales from Grimm p63-75   398.2
    See also How six men travelled through the wide world

The Soldier and the knapsack
  In Courlander, H. ed. Ride with the sun p145-53   398.2
    See also Knapsack

Soldier and Tsar in the forest   398.2

Soldier Jack
  In Chase, R. ed. The Jack tales p172-79   398.2

Soldier of the Revolution. Fisher, D. C.
  In Cavanah, F. ed. Holiday roundup p188-95   394.2

Soldiers
    See also Generals

        United States
De Leeuw, A. George Rogers Clark: frontier fighter (2-4)   92
    See also Negro soldiers

Soldier's soup
Brown, M. Stone soup   398.2
    See also Old woman and the tramp

Soldier's three; puppet play. Jagendorf, M.
  In Penny puppets, penny theatre, and penny plays p141-50   791.5

The sole. Grimm, J.
  In Grimm, J. The complete Grimm's Fairy tales p709   398.2

Solid geometry. See Geometry

Solis-Cohen, Emily
Hanukkah at Valley Forge
  In Cavanah, F. ed. Holiday roundup p296-99   394.2

Solomon, King of Israel
Elkin, B. The wisest man in the world (1-4)   398.2
Ish-Kishor, S. The carpet of Solomon (4-6)   398.2

    See also pages in the following book:
Gruenberg, S. M. ed. Favorite stories old and new p357-59   808.8

Solomon, Louis
The Mississippi (5-7)   917.7

Solot, Mary Lynn
100 hamburgers   E

The somberos of the men of Lagos. Jagendorf, M. A.
  In Jagendorf, M. A. Noodlehead stories from around the world p268-70   398.2

Some impatient mule-drivers. Brenner, A.
  In Brenner, A. The boy who could do anything, & other Mexican folk tales p27-29   398.2

Some merry adventures of Robin Hood of great renown in Nottinghamshire. Pyle, H. 398.2

Some North American Thanksgivings. Luckhardt, M. C.
  In Luckhardt, M. C. comp. Thanksgiving p132-48   394.2

Some of the days of Everett Anderson. Clifton, L.   811

Some white witchcraft. St Leger-Gordon, R. E.
  In Hope-Simpson, J. ed. A cavalcade of witches p88-90   808.8

Someone could win a polar bear. Ciardi, J. 811

"Something." Andersen, H. C.
  In Andersen, H. C. The complete fairy tales and stories p539-44   S C

Something about the author   920.03

Something for Christmas. Brown, P.   E

Something special. De Regniers, B. S.   811

Something wonderful. Manning-Sanders, R.
  In Manning-Sanders, R. A book of devils and demons p30-38   398.2

Sometimes I dance mountains. Baylor, B. 793.3

Sommer, Elyse
The bread dough craft book (3-6)   745.5

Son of Adam
  In Jacobs, J. ed. More English folk and fairy tales p118-19   398.2

A son of liberty. Lipnick, E.
  In Burack, A. S. ed. One hundred plays for children p828-37   808.82

The son of seven queens. Steel, F. A.
  In Jacobs, J. ed. Indian fairy tales p115-26   398.2

The son of strength. MacManus, S.
  In MacManus, S. Hibernian nights p 1-9   398.2

The Son of the hunter
  In Courlander, H. ed. Ride with the sun p120-27   398.2

The Son of the Leopard. Courlander, H.   Fic

Son of the long one. Heady, E. B.
  In Arbuthnot, M. H. comp. The Arbuthnot Anthology of children's literature p314-16   808.8
  In Arbuthnot, M. H. comp. Time for old magic p193-95   398.2

Song and garden birds of North America. National Geographic Society   598.2

A song for the new chief. Courlander, H.
  In Courlander, H. The king's drum, and other African stories p25-27   398.2

The song in the sea. Jagendorf, M. A.
  In Jagendorf, M. A. Folk stories of the South p149-50   398.2

The song of Gimmile. Courlander, H.
  In Courlander, H. The king's drum, and other African stories p9-12   398.2

The song of Hiawatha. Longfellow, H. W. 811

Song of Robin Hood. Malcolmson, A. ed. 398.2

The Song of Roland; excerpts
  In Johnson, E. ed. Anthology of children's literature p533-38   808.8

The song of the Cherokee rose. Jagendorf, M. A.
  In Jagendorf, M. A. Folk stories of the South p93-94   398.2

Song of the empty bottles. Molarsky, O.   Fic

Song of the fox. Bowman, J. C.
  In Bowman, J. C. Tales from a Finnish tupa p258-59   398.2

The **song** of the little donkey. Gall, A. C.
In Association for Childhood Education International. Told under the magic umbrella p145-53 **S C**

Song of the swallows. Politi, L. **E**

Song of the waterfall; the story of Edvard and Nina Grieg. Kyle, E. **92**

Song of the wolf. Bowman, J. C.
In Bowman, J. C. Tales from a Finnish tupa p260 **398.2**

Song, speech, and ventriloquism. Kettelkamp, L. **808.5**

The **songbird** of the people. Andersen, H. C.
In Andersen, H. C. The complete fairy tales and stories p847-50 **S C**

Songs
Boni, M. B. ed. Fireside book of folk songs **784.4**
Engvick, W. ed. Lullabies and night songs (k-3) **784.6**
Fraser-Simson, H. The Pooh song book (1-3) **784.6**
Girl Scouts of the United States of America. Sing together **784.6**
Kapp, P. Cock-a-doodle-doo! Cock-a-doodle-dandy! (k-2) **784.6**
Langstaff, J. Over in the meadow (k-2) **784.4**
Larrick, N. comp. The wheels of the bus go round and round (1-4) **784.6**
Mitchell, D. ed. Every child's book of nursery songs (k-3) **784.6**
Simon, H. W. ed. A treasury of Christmas songs and carols **783.6**
Winn, M. ed. The fireside book of children's songs **784.6**
Winn, M. ed. The fireside book of fun and game songs **784.6**
Winn, M. ed. What shall we do and Allee galloo! ((k-2) **796.1**
Yurchenco, H. ed. A fiesta of folk songs from Spain and Latin America (2-6) **784.7**

See also pages in the following book:

Tashjian, V. A. ed. With a deep sea smile p107-22 (k-3) **372.6**
See also Ballads; Carols; Folk songs; Hymns; Lullabies; National songs; also general subjects and names of classes of persons with the subdivision Songs and music, e.g. Cowboys—Songs and music; Thanksgiving Day—Songs and music; and names of individual songs

Songs, African
Robinson, A. Singing tales of Africa (3-5) **398.2**
See also Folk songs, Ugandan

Songs, American
Boni, M. B. ed. The fireside book of favorite American songs **784.7**
Garson, E. ed. The Laura Ingalls Wilder songbook (3-7) **784**
Sandburg, C. ed. The American songbag **784.7**
See also Folk songs—United States; National songs, American

Songs, English
London Bridge is falling down! (k-2) **784.4**

Songs, French. See Folk songs, French

Songs, National. See National songs

Songs and stories from Uganda. Serwadda, W. M. **784.4**

Songs of the Chippewa. Bierhorst, J. **781.7**

Songs of the dream people. Houston, J. ed. **897**

Songs to grow on. Landeck, B. **784.4**

Sonneborn, Ruth A.
Friday night is Papa night **E**

Soo Tan the tiger and the little green frog. Hume, L. C.
In Hume, L. C. Favorite children's stories from China and Tibet p9-14 **398.2**
See also Tiger and the frog

The **Sooner** hound and Flying-jib. Stoutenburg, A.
In Stoutenburg, A. American tall-tale animals p92-103 **398.2**

The **soothsayer's** handbook: a guide to bad signs & good vibrations. Horwitz, E. L. **133.3**

The **Soothsayer's** son
In Jacobs, J. ed. Indian fairy tales p70-84 **398.2**

Sootin, Harry
Easy experiments with water pollution (5-7) **614.7**

Sop doll!
In Chase, R. ed. The Jack tales p76-82 **398.2**
In Hoke, H. ed. Spooks, spooks, spooks p141-46 **S C**
In Leach, M. The thing at the foot of the bed, and other scary tales p95-98 **S C**

Sophia Scrooby preserved. Bacon, M. **Fic**

Sorcerer Kaldoon. Manning-Sanders, R.
In Manning-Sanders, R. A book of sorcerers and spells p99-111 **398.2**

Sorcerers and spells, A book of. Manning-Sanders, R. **398.2**

Sorcerer's apprentice
Gág, W. Sorcerer's apprentice
In Child Study Association of America. Castles and dragons p127-33 **398.2**
Green, R. L. The sorcerer's apprentice
In Green, R. L. ed. A cavalcade of magicians p19-24 **808.8**
Rostron, R. The sorcerer's apprentice
In Johnson, E. ed. Anthology of children's literature p155-57 **808.8**
In Ward, W. ed. Stories to dramatize p201-05 **372.6**
See also Master and his pupil

The **sorcerer's** apprentice. Grimm, J.
In Grimm, J. More Tales from Grimm p197-205 **398.2**
See also Master and his pupil

Sorcery. See Occult sciences; Witchcraft

The **sorely** trying day. Hoban, R. **E**

Sorensen, Virginia
Newbery Medal acceptance paper
In Kingman, L. ed. Newbery and Caldecott Medal books: 1956-1965 p34-42 **028.5**
Plain girl (4-6) **Fic**

Spider and the lion. Arnott, K.
In Arnott, K. African myths and legends
p25-31   398.2
Spider feeds his family. Arnott, K.
In Arnott, K. Animal folk tales around the
the world p202-09   398.2
The spider plant; excerpt. Speevack, Y.
In Association for Childhood Education In-
ternational. Told under the city um-
brella p194-203   S C
Spider silk. Goldin, A.   595
The spider, the cave and the pottery bowl.
Clymer, E.   Fic
The Spider weaver
In Sakade, F. ed. Japanese children's fa-
vorite stories p59-65   398.2
Spiders
Bason, L. Spiders (k-3)   595
Chenery, J. Wolfie (k-3)   595
Goldin, A. Spider silk (1-3)   595
Shuttlesworth, D. E. The story of spiders
(4-6)   595
See also pages in the following books:
Cooper, E. K. Science in your own back yard
p123-32 (5-7)   500.9
Goldstein, P. Animals and plants that trap
p46-64 (4-7)   574.5
Mason, G. F. Animal tools p73-78 (4-7) 591.4
Rhine, R. Life in a bucket of soil p60-72 (5-7)
                              592
Ricciuti, E. R. Shelf pets p75-79 (5-7)   639
Shuttlesworth, D. E. Animals that frighten
people p110-17 (5-7)   591.5
See also Tarantulas
Stories
Appiah, P. Ananse the spider (4-7)   398.2
Arkhurst, J. C. The adventures of Spider (2-5)
                             398.2
Courlander, H. The hat-shaking dance, and
other tales from the Gold Coast (3-6) 398.2
Freschet, B. The web in the grass   E
Graham, M. B. Be nice to spiders   E
Haley, G. E. A story, a story (k-3)   398.2
McDermott, G. Anansi the spider (k-3) 398.2
White, E. B. Charlotte's web (3-6)   Fic
Spider's web. Arnott, K.
In Arnott, K. African myths and legends
p74-77   398.2
Spier, Jo
(illus.) Morrison, L. comp. Black within and
red without   398.6
Spier, Peter
Crash! Bang! Boom!   E
Fast-slow, high-low   E
Gobble, growl, grunt   E
(illus.) And so my garden grows. See And so
my garden grows   398.8
(illus.) The Erie Canal (Folk song) The Erie
Canal   784.4
(illus.) The fox (Folk song) The fox went out
on a chilly night   784.4
(illus.) Key, F. S. The Star-Spangled Banner
(Doubleday)   784.7
(illus.) Krasilovsky, P. The cow who fell in
the canal   E
(illus.) London Bridge is falling down! See
London Bridge is falling down!   784.4
(illus.) Mother Goose. To market! To market!
                           398.8

(illus.) Parker, E. ed. 100 more story poems
                         821.08
Spilka, Arnold
Paint all kinds of pictures (k-3)   751
(illus.) Lord, B. Mystery guest at left end Fic
(illus.) Lord, B. Quarterback's aim   Fic
(illus.) Russell, S. P. Lines and shapes   516
Spin a soft Black song. Giovanni, N.   811
Spin, weave, wear. Nic Leodhas, S.
In Nic Leodhas, S. Heather and broom
p95-111   398.2
Spindle, shuttle, and needle. Grimm, J.
In Grimm, J. The complete Grimm's Fairy
tales p764-67   398.2
In Grimm, J. The juniper tree, and other
tales from Grimm v 1 p55-62   398.2
In Grimm, J. Tales from Grimm p65-76
                          398.2
In Lang, A. ed. The green fairy book p286-
89   398.2
Spinning maid and the cowherd. Carpenter, F.
In Carpenter, F. Tales of a Chinese grand-
mother p182-89   398.2
Spinning tops. Kettelkamp, L.   795
Spinning woman and the ghosts
Duvoisin, R. Schoch, d'Altschmidja spinnt
Noch
In Duvoisin, R. The three sneezes, and
other Swiss tales p214-17   398.2
The spirit and the letter. Kohn, B.   323.4
The spirit in the bottle. Grimm, J.
In Grimm, J. The complete Grimm's Fairy
tales p458-62   398.2
The spirit of Christmas. St Clair, R.
In Burack, A. S. ed. Christmas plays for
young actors p223-34   812.08
Spirit of St Louis (Airplane)
Dalgliesh, A. Ride on the wind (2-5) 629.13
Foster, J. T. The flight of the Lone Eagle
(5-7)   629.13
The spirit of the stone. Sechrist, E. H.
In Sechrist, E. H. Once in the first times
p98-104   398.2
The spirit of the willow tree saves family honor;
puppet play. Adair, M. W.
In Adair, M. W. Folk puppet plays for the
social studies p89-92   791.5
The spirit that lived in a tree. Shedlock, M. L.
In Johnson, E. ed. Anthology of children's
literature p106-07   808.8
The spirited life: Bertha Mahony Miller and
children's books. Ross, E. S.   92
Spiritism. See Spiritualism
Spirits. See Ghosts; Spiritualism; Witchcraft
Spiritualism
See pages in the following book:
Cohen, D. In search of ghosts p77-135 (6-7)
                         133
Spirituals, Negro. See Negro spirituals
Spirt, Diana L.
(jt. auth.) Gillespie, J. T. Creating a school
media program   027.8
(jt. auth.) Gillespie, J. T. Paperback books
for young people   070.5025
(jt. auth.) Gillespie, J. T. The young phenomenon: paperbacks in our schools 027.8

Spit Nolan. Naughton, B.
   In Authors' choice p101-10   **S C**
The **Spiteful** nanny goat
   In Bloch, M. H. ed. Ukrainian folk tales
     p39-43   **398.2**
Splendid gift. Angelo, V.
   In Eaton, A. T. comp. The animals' Christ-
     mas p24-33   **394.2**
Splicing. See Knots and splices
Spoodles: the puppy who learned. Black, I. S.
   In Gruenberg, S. M. comp. Let's hear a
     story p62-67   **808.8**
Spooks, spooks, spooks. Hoke, H. ed.   **S C**
Spooky magic. Kettelkamp, L.   **793.8**
The **Spooky** Thing. Steele, W. O.
   In Hoke, H. ed. Spooks, spooks, spooks
     p36-50   **S C**
Spooky tricks. Wyler, R.   **793.8**
Spoolcraft. Newsome, A. J.   **745.5**
Spooner, Malcolm
   (illus.) Merriam, E. It doesn't always have to
     rhyme   **811**
Sports
   Barr, G. Young scientist and sports (4-7)   **796**
   Hunt, S. E. Games and sports the world
     around   **790**
   Keith, H. Sports and games (5-7)   **796**
   Morton, M. The making of champions (5-7)
     796

   See also pages in the following books:
   Bancroft, J. H. Games p407-666   **790**
   Berger, M. Those amazing computers! p163-
     67 (5-7)   **001.6**
   Meyer, R. Festivals U.S.A. & Canada p198-
     215   **394.2**
      See also Aeronautical sports; Amuse-
   ments; Athletics; Games; Gymnastics;
   Olympic games; Outdoor life; also names
   of sports, e.g. Baseball

               Bibliography
   See pages in the following book:
   National Council of Teachers of English. Ad-
     venturing with books p326-30   **028.52**

               Biography
   Lorimer, L. T. ed. Breaking in (5-7)   **920**
     See also names of sports with subdi-
   vision Biography, e.g. Basketball—Biography

              Encyclopedias
The Concise encyclopedia of sports   **796.03**
The Junior illustrated encyclopedia of sports
   (5-7)   **796.03**
Menke, F. G. The encyclopedia of sports
     796.03

              Poetry
Morrison, L. comp. Sprints and distances
   (5-7)   **808.81**
Sports and games. Keith, H.   **796**
Sports cars
   Barris, G. Famous custom & show cars (6-7)
     629.22
Sports hero: Billie Jean King. Burchard, M.   **92**
Sports Illustrated Baseball (5-7)   **796.357**
Sports Illustrated Horseback riding (6-7)   **798**

The **spotted** rug. Courlander, H.
   In Courlander, H. The tiger's whisker, and
     other tales and legends from Asia
     and the Pacific p100-05   **398.2**
A **spouse** for Susie Mouse. Head, F. E.
   In Kamerman, S. E. ed. Dramatized folk
     tales of the world p317-23   **812.08**
Sprengel, Christian Konrad
   See pages in the following book:
   Ipsen, D. C. What does a bee see? p9-17
     (5-7)   **595.7**
Spring
   Carrick, C. Swamp spring (k-3)   **574**
   Tresselt, A. "Hi, Mister Robin!"   **E**

              Poetry
   Lenski, L. Spring is here   **E**
Spring. Benary-Isbert, M.
   In Johnson, E. ed. Anthology of children's
     literature p885-89   **808.8**
Spring in the forest. Ransome, A.
   In Ransome, A. Old Peter's Russian tales
     p120-21   **398.2**
Spring is here. Lenski, L.   **E**
The **spring** running. Kipling, R.
   In Kipling, R. The jungle books (Double-
     day) v 1 p223-50   **S C**
   In Kipling, R. The jungle books (Macmil-
     lan N Y) p184-207   **S C**
   In Kipling, R. The jungle books (Watts, F.)
     v2 p208-35   **S C**
   In Kipling, R. The second jungle book
     p208-35   **S C**
Springer, Harriett
   (illus.) Selsam, M. E. A first look at birds
     598.2
Springtail
   See pages in the following book:
   Rhine, R. Life in a bucket of soil p52-59 (5-7)
     592
Springtime for Jeanne-Marie. Françoise   **E**
Sprints and distances. Morrison, L.   **808.81**
Sputters. Ball, Z.   **Fic**
Spykman, E. C.
   Terrible, horrible Edie (5-7)   **Fic**
Spyri, Johanna
   At the grandfather's
     In Arbuthnot, M. H. comp. The Arbuthnot
       Anthology of children's literature
       p708-12   **808.8**
   Heidi (4-6)   **Fic**
   Heidi; excerpt
     In Arbuthnot, M. H. comp. The Arbuthnot
       Anthology of children's literature
       p708-12   **808.8**
   In the pasture
     In Johnson, E. ed. Anthology of children's
       literature p767-73   **808.8**
     In Martignoni, M. E. ed. The illustrated
       treasury of children's literature p376-
       82   **808.8**
Squanto, Wampanoag Indian
   Bulla, C. R. Squanto, friend of the Pilgrims
     (2-4)   **92**

   See also pages in the following book:
   Johnston, J. The Indians and the strangers
     p11-19 (2-5)   **920**

The **stone**. Alexander, L.
 In Alexander, L. The foundling, and other
  tales of Prydain p17-30 **S C**

Stone age
 Dickinson, A. The first book of stone age
  man (4-7) **913**
  See also Man, Prehistoric

Stone broth. See Old woman and the tramp;
 Soldier's soup

Stone cutter
 McDermott, G. The stonecutter (k-3) **398.2**
 Shedlock, M. L. Hafiz, the stone-cutter
 In Shedlock, M. L. The art of the story-
  teller p179-82 **372.6**
 Titus, E. The two stonecutters **398.2**

The **stone** dog. Belpré, P.
 In Belpré, P. Once in Puerto Rico p80-84
  398.2

The **stone**-faced boy. Fox, P. **Fic**

The **stone** in the cock's head. Haviland, V.
 In Haviland, V. Favorite fairy tales told in
  Italy p43-53 **398.2**

The **Stone** in the road
 In Ward, W. ed. Stories to dramatize p152-
  54 **372.6**

Stone lion
 O'Connor, W. F. The story of the stone lion
 In Manning-Sanders, R. ed. A book of mag-
  ical beasts p122-29 **398.2**
 Smedley, C. Stone lion
 In Davis, M. G. ed. A baker's dozen p63-79
  372.6

The **stone** lute. Courlander, H.
 In Courlander, H. The king's drum, and
  other African stories p95-97 **398.2**

Stone monkey
 Carpenter, F. King of the monkeys
 In Carpenter, F. Tales of a Chinese grand-
  mother p107-16 **398.2**
 Giles, H. A. The stone monkey
 In Manning-Sanders, R. ed. A book of mag-
  ical beasts p45-48 **398.2**

The **Stone** of Victory. Colum, P.
 In Colum, P. The Stone of Victory, and
  other tales of Padraic Colum p13-29
  398.2

The **Stone** of Victory, and other tales of Padraic
 Colum. Colum, P. **398.2**

The **stone** owl's nest. Spicer, D. G.
 In Spicer, D. G. The owl's nest p15-28
  398.2

Stone soup. Brown, M. **398.2**

  See also Old woman and the tramp

Stone soup; play. Buechler, J.
 In Kamerman, S. E. ed. Dramatized folk
  tales of the world p381-87 **812.08**

The **stonecutter.** McDermott, G. **398.2**
  See also Stone cutter

Stonehenge
 Branley, F. M. The mystery of Stonehenge
  (4-7) **914.2**

 See also pages in the following books:

 Aylesworth, T. G. ed. Mysteries from the past
  p 1-11 (6-7) **913**
 Cohen, D. Ancient monuments and how they
  were built p41-54 (6-7) **913**

 Leacroft, H. The buildings of ancient man
  p24-26 (5-7) **722**

Stones, Precious. See Precious stones

The **stones** of Plouhinec. Picard, B. L.
 In Reeves, J. comp. The Christmas book
  p24-31 **394.2**

Stonewall Jackson. Daniels, J. **92**

The **stop.** Wondriska, W. **E**

Stop that ball! McClintock, M. **E**

Stories. See Animals—Stories; Ballets—Stories,
 plots, etc.; Bible—Stories; Christmas stories;
 Easter—Stories; Fairy tales; Ghost stories;
 Legends; Mystery and detective stories;
 Operas—Stories, plots, etc.; School stories;
 Sea stories; Short stories; Stories in rhyme;
 Storytelling; and names of individual ani-
 mals, birds, flowers, fruits, trees, vegetables,
 and holidays with the subdivision Stories,
 e.g. Dogs—Stories

Stories. Green, E. comp. **028.52**

Stories and fables
 In Childcraft: the how and why library v2
  031

Stories California Indians told. Fisher, A. B.
  398.2

Stories from the Bible. De La Mare, W. **221.9**

Stories from the Bible. Tresselt, A. **221.9**

Stories in rhyme
 Adoff, A. Black is brown is tan **E**
 Bemelmans, L. Madeline **E**
 Bemelmans, L. Madeline and the bad hat **E**
 Bemelmans, L. Madeline and the gypsies **E**
 Bemelmans, L. Madeline in London **E**
 Bemelmans, L. Madeline's rescue **E**
 Berenstain, S. The bears' almanac **E**
 Brooke, L. L. Johnny Crow's garden **E**
 Brooke, L. L. Johnny Crow's new garden **E**
 Brooke, L. L. Johnny Crow's party **E**
 Brown, M. W. Goodnight moon **E**
 Chönz, S. A bell for Ursli **E**
 Dawson, R. A walk in the city **E**
 De Regniers, B. S. Red Riding Hood (1-3)
  398.2
 Domanska, J. What do you see? **E**
 Farber, N. Where's Gomer? **E**
 Fisher, A. Going barefoot **E**
 Fisher, A. I like weather **E**
 Fisher, A. In the middle of the night **E**
 Fisher, A. Listen, rabbit **E**
 Fisher, A. We went looking **E**
 Fisher, A. Where does everyone go? **E**
 Gág, W. The A B C bunny **E**
 Graham, A. Timothy Turtle **E**
 Hoban, T. Where is it? **E**
 Hoberman, M. A. All my shoes come in twos
  E
 Holland, M. A big ball of string **E**
 Hurd, E. T. Come and have fun **E**
 Hutchins, P. The wind blew **E**
 Kahl, V. The Duchess bakes a cake **E**
 Kahl, V. How do you hide a monster? **E**
 Kraus, R. Whose mouse are you? **E**
 Lobel, A. On the day Peter Stuyvesant sailed
  into town **E**
 Lord, J. V. The giant jam sandwich **E**
 McClintock, M. A fly went by **E**
 McClintock, M. Stop that ball! **E**
 McClintock, M. What have I got? **E**

The story of the sphinx. Arnold, E. J.
In A St Nicholas anthology p175-78 **810.8**
The story of the Statue of Liberty. Miller, N.
739
The story of the stone lion. O'Connor, W. F.
In Manning-Sanders, R. ed. A book of magical beasts p122-29 **398.2**
See also Stone lion
The Story of the three bears
In Arbuthnot, M. H. comp. The Arbuthnot Anthology of children's literature p150-52 **808.8**
In Arbuthnot, M. H. comp. Time for old magic p5-7 **398.2**
In De La Mare, W. ed. Animal stories p23-28 **398.2**
In Jacobs, J. ed. English folk and fairy tales p96-101 **398.2**
See also Three bears
The story of the three bears. Southey, R.
In Lang, A. ed. The green fairy book p234-37 **398.2**
In Opie, I. ed. The classic fairy tales p201-05 **398.2**
See also Three bears
The story of the three bears. Steel, F. A.
In Haviland, V. comp. The fairy tale treasury p36-43 **398.2**
In Johnson, E. ed. Anthology of children's literature p183-85 **808.8**
In Martignoni, M. E. ed. The illustrated treasury of children's literature p69-73 **398.2**
See also Three bears
The Story of the three little pigs
In Arbuthnot, M. H. comp. The Arbuthnot Anthology of children's literature p152-54 **808.8**
In Arbuthnot, M. H. comp. Time for old magic p7-9 **398.2**
In De La Mare, W. ed. Animal stories p16-19 **398.2**
In Haviland, V. comp. The fairy tale treasury p22-27 **398.2**
In Jacobs, J. ed. English folk and fairy tales p69-73 **398.2**
In Johnson, E. ed. Anthology of children's literature p185-86 **808.8**
In Martignoni, M. E. ed. The illustrated treasury of children's literature p80-82 **808.8**
See also Three little pigs
The story of the tortoise and the monkey. Hume, L. C.
In Hume, L. C. Favorite children's stories from China and Tibet p39-46 **398.2**
The story of the totem pole. Brindze, R. **299**
The story of the United Nations. Savage, K.
341.23
Story of the year
Andersen, H. C. The year's story
In Andersen, H. C. The complete fairy tales and stories p393-400 **S C**
The story of the youth who went forth to learn what fear was. Grimm, J.
In Grimm, J. The complete Grimm's Fairy tales p29-39 **398.2**
See also Youth who could not shiver and shake

The story of things. Jupo, F. **609**
The story of thirteen colonies. Alderman, C. L.
973.2
The story of Thomas Alva Edison. Cousins, M.
92
The story of Tom Thumb. Reeves, J.
In Reeves, J. English fables and fairy stories p63-70 **398.2**
See also Tom Thumb
The story of Tuan Mac Cairill. Stephens, J.
In Stephens, J. Irish fairy tales p4-32 **398.2**
The story of volcanoes and earthquakes. Matthews, W. H. **551.2**
Story of Wang Li. Coatsworth, E.
In Child Study Association of America. Castles and dragons p211-25 **398.2**
Story of William Penn. Aliki **92**
The story of William Tell. Baldwin, J.
In Ward, W. ed. Stories to dramatize p199-200 **372.6**
The story of World War I. Leckie, R. **940.3**
The story of World War II. Leckie, R. **940.53**
The story of writing. Cahn, W. **411**
Story of Ys
Colum, P. The lost city of Ys
In Colum, P. The Stone of Victory, and other tales of Padraic Colum p30-35 **398.2**
The story of Yukpachen. Hardendorff, J. B.
In Hardendorff, J. B. ed. Just one more p116-20 **372.6**
The story of Zal. Palmer, R.
In Palmer, R. Dragons, unicorns, and other magical beasts p79-86 **398.2**
See also Zal, the white-headed
The story old Johanna told. Andersen, H. C.
In Andersen, H. C. The complete fairy tales and stories p1026-38 **S C**
Story poems, new and old. See Cole, W. comp. The poet's tales **821.08**
The story without an end. Withers, C.
In Withers, C. A world of nonsense p101-03 **398.2**
The storybook cookbook. MacGregor, C. **641.5**
The storyteller. Courlander, H.
In Courlander, H. The fire on the mountain, and other Ethiopian stories p99-102 **398.2**
A storyteller's choice. Colwell, E. ed. **372.6**
Storytelling
Moore, V. Pre-school story hour **372.6**
Sawyer, R. The way of the storyteller **372.6**
Shedlock, M. L. The art of the story-teller **372.6**
Stories to tell to children **028.52**

See also pages in the following books:

Arbuthnot, M. H. comp. The Arbuthnot Anthology of children's literature p955-58 **808.8**
Horn Book Reflections on children's books and reading p293-41 **028.5**
Jacobs, L. B. ed. Using literature with young children p15-19 **028.5**
Johnson, E. ed. Anthology of children's literature p1141-47 **808.8**

Storytelling—*Continued*

Ross, E. S. ed. The lost half-hour p187-91
372.6

Sayers, F. C. Summoned by books p95-106
028.5

Bibliography

Greene, E. comp. Stories   028.52

Collections

Association for Childhood Education International. Told under spacious skies (3-6)
S C

Association for Childhood Education International. Told under the blue umbrella (k-4)   S C

Association for Childhood Education International. Told under the magic umbrella (k-4)   S C

Association for Childhood Education International. Told under the Stars and Stripes (3-6)   S C

Carlson, B. W. Listen! And help tell the story
372.6

Colwell, E. ed. A second storyteller's choice
372.6

Colwell, E. ed. A storyteller's choice   372.6

Davis, M. G. ed. A baker's dozen   372.6

Dobbs, R. ed. Once upon a time   372.6

Gruenberg, S. M. ed. Favorite stories old and new   808.8

Hardendorff, J. B. ed. Just one more (3-6)
372.6

Ross, E. S. ed. The lost half-hour   372.6

Sawyer, R. The way of the storyteller   372.6

Sechrist, E. H. ed. It's time for story hour
372.6

Shedlock, M. L. The art of the story-teller
372.6

Tashjian, V. A. ed. Juba this and Juba that
372.6

Tashjian, V. A. ed. With a deep sea smile
372.6

Stoutenburg, Adrien

American tall-tale animals (4-6)   398.2

Contents: Squonks, Whiffle-pooffles, and Gillygaloos; Rattlers and rollers; A bear as big as a cloud; Grizzlies, extra special; Fish friends; The hoss-mackerel and Bassoon Bobby; Big bucks and bullfrogs; The Sooner hound and Flying-jib; Old Sock and the swimming pits; Biters, hoppers, and feathered floppers

A vanishing thunder (5-7)   598.2
For another title by this author see Kendall, Lace

The stove and the town hall. Jagendorf, M. A.
In Jagendorf, M. A. Noodlehead stories from around the world p189-91 398.2

Stoves

Fiction

Beatty, P. The Nickel-Plated Beauty (5-7) Fic

Stowe, Harriet Elizabeth (Beecher)

See pages in the following book:

Haviland, V. ed. Yankee Doodle's literary sampler of prose, poetry, & pictures p192-96   028.5

Straight hair, curly hair. Goldin, A.   612

Straight lines, parallel lines, perpendicular lines. Charosh, M.   516

Strain, Frances Bruce

Being born (4-7)   612.6

Strains and stresses

See pages in the following book:

Tannenbaum, B. High rises p20-31 (3-6) **690**

Strang, Ruth

Withrow, D. E. Gateways to readable books
028.52

The strange adventure of Paddy O'Toole. Manning-Sanders, R.
In Manning-Sanders, R. A book of ghosts & goblins p68-73   398.2

Strange adventure of the cowboy-sailor. Jagendorf, M. A.
In Jagendorf, M. A. New England bean-pot p117-25   398.2

The strange disappearance of Arthur Cluck. Benchley, N.   **E**

The strange galoshes. Andersen, H. C.
In Andersen, H. C. Andersen's Fairy tales p497-527   S C
See also Goloshes of fortune

Strange godfather

Grimm, J. Godfather Death
In Grimm, J. The complete Grimm's Fairy tales p209-12   398.2
In Grimm, J. The juniper tree, and other tales from Grimm v2 p228-35 398.2
See also Soldier Jack

Strange men with tails. Carpenter, F.
In Carpenter, F. African wonder tales p93-101   398.2

The strange musician. Grimm, J.
In Grimm, J. The complete Grimm's Fairy tales p56-58   398.2
See also Wonderful musician

Strange plants and their ways. Hutchins, R. E.
581

A strange sled race. Thompson, V. L.
In Thompson, V. L. Hawaiian myths of earth, sea, and sky p28-32   398.2

The strange tale of King Midas. Howard, V.
In Howard, V. The complete book of children's theater p489-94   812

The strange valley. Olsen, T. V.
In Hitchcock, A. comp. Alfred Hitchcock's Supernatural tales of terror and suspense p20-29   S C

A stranger at Green Knowe. Boston, L. M. See note under Boston, L. M. The children of Green Knowe   **Fic**

Stranger in the pines. McNeer, M.   **Fic**

The strangling woman. Hardendorff, J. B.
In Hardendorff, J. B. Witches, wit, and a werewolf p53-58   S C

Strasburg Rail Road, Strasburg, Pa.

See pages in the following book:

Jackson, R. B. Waves, wheels and wings p25-35 (4-6)   380.5074

Stravinskiĭ, Igor Fedorovich

See pages in the following book:

Posell, E. Z. Russian composers p100-12 (5-7)
920

Stravinsky, Igor. See Stravinskiĭ, Igor Fedorovich

Swayne, Sam
Great-grandfather in the honey tree (2-4) **Fic**
Swayne, Zoa
(jt. auth.) Swayne, S. Great-grandfather in the honey tree **Fic**
Sweat, Lynn
(illus.) Hellman, H. The lever and the pulley **531**
(illus.) Parish, P. Costumes to make **391**
(illus.) Seidelman, J. E. Creating with wood **745.51**
(illus.) Seidelman, J. E. The rub book **741.2**
(illus.) Simon, S. Science at work: projects in oceanography **551.4**
(illus.) Simon, S. Science at work: projects in space science **500.5**
Sweden
Arbman, M. Looking at Sweden (4-6) **914.85**
Merrick, H. H. Sweden (4-6) **914.85**

Fiction
Anckarsvärd, K. Madcap mystery (5-7) **Fic**
Anckarsvärd, K. The mysterious schoolmaster (5-7) **Fic**
Anckarsvärd, K. The robber ghost (5-7) **Fic**
Beckman, G. The girl without a name (4-6) **Fic**
Beskow, L. Pelle's new suit **E**
Budd, L. Tekla's Easter (2-4) **Fic**
Gripe, M. Hugo (3-5) **Fic**
Gripe, M. Hugo and Josephine (3-5) **Fic**
Gripe, M. Josephine (3-5) **Fic**
Lagerlof, S. The wonderful adventures of Nils (4-6) **Fic**
Lindgren, A. Christmas in Noisy Village (1-4) **Fic**
Lindgren, A. Mischievous Meg (3-6) **Fic**
Lindgren, A. Pippi Longstocking (3-6) **Fic**
Unnerstad, E. Little O (2-5) **Fic**
Unnerstad, E. The spettecake holiday (4-6) **Fic**
Wiberg, H. Christmas at the Tomten's farm (2-4) **Fic**

Folklore
See Folklore—Sweden

Industries
See pages in the following book:
Arbman, M. Looking at Sweden p49-54 (4-6) **914.85**

Manufactures
See Sweden—Industries

Social life and customs
See pages in the following book:
Sechrist, E. H. ed. Christmas everywhere p82-88 **394.2**

Swedes in the United States

Fiction
De Angeli, M. Elin's Amerika (4-6) **Fic**
Lindquist, J. D. The golden name day (3-5) **Fic**

Sweet, Ozzie
(illus.) Scott, J. D. Loggerhead turtle **598.1**

Sweet Betsy From Pike (Folk song)
Sweet Betsy from Pike (1-3) **784.4**

Sweet infection. Mayne, W.
In Mayne, W. ed. Ghosts p33-49 **820.8**

Sweet misery. Courlander, H.
In Courlander, H. The piece of fire, and other Haitian tales p37-38 **398.2**
Sweet porridge. Grimm, J.
In Grimm, J. The complete Grimm's Fairy tales p475-76 **398.2**
In Grimm, J. More Tales from Grimm p43-46 **398.2**
Sweet tooth
In DeRoin, N. ed. Jataka tales p4-5 **398.2**
Sweetheart Roland. Grimm, J.
In Grimm, J. The complete Grimm's Fairy tales p268-71 **398.2**
In Grimm, J. Grimm's Fairy tales; illus. by A. Rackham p99-103 **398.2**
In Grimm, J. Grimms' Fairy tales; illus. by F. Kredel p62-66 **398.2**
See also Roland

The sweethearts. Andersen, H. C.
In Andersen, H. C. The complete fairy tales and stories p213-15 **S C**
In Andersen, H. Hans Andersen's Fairy tales p185-87 **S C**
See also Top and ball

Swift, Hildegarde Hoyt
The little red lighthouse and the great gray bridge **E**
North star shining (5-7) **301.45**

Swift, Jonathan
The Emperor of Lilliput
In Martignoni, M. E. ed. The illustrated treasury of children's literature p491-96 **808.8**
Gulliver in the giants' country; adaptation. See Fuller, E. Gulliver in the giants' country
Gulliver's travels; play. See Howard, V. Gulliver wins his freedom
A voyage to Brobdingnag
In Mayne, W. ed. William Mayne's Book of giants p177-94 **398.2**
A voyage to Lilliput; condensation
In Lang, A. ed. The blue fairy book p313-31 **398.2**

Swiftest runners
Andersen, H. C. The winners
In Andersen, H. C. The complete fairy tales and stories p585-87 **S C**

Swimming
Sullivan, G. Better swimming and diving for boys and girls (5-7) **797.2**
See also pages in the following books:
Boy Scouts of America. Fieldbook p206-17 **369.43**
The Junior illustrated encyclopedia of sports p519-52 (5-7) **796.03**
Keith, H. Sports and games p278-95 (5-7) **796**
Morton, M. The making of champions p60-67 (5-7) **796**
See also Diving

Fiction
Kessler, L. Last one in is a rotten egg **E**

Swimmy. Lionni, L. **E**

Swine. See Hogs

Tallant, Robert
The Louisiana Purchase (5-7)   **973.4**
Pirate Lafitte and the Battle of New Orleans (5-7)   **92**

Tallchief, Maria
Tobias, T. Maria Tallchief (2-4)   **92**

See also pages in the following book:

Gridley, M. E. American Indian women p138-53 (5-7)   **920**

Tallchief, Marjorie

See pages in the following book:

Gridley, M. E. American Indian women p138-53 (5-7)   **920**

Tallon, James
(illus.) Halacy, D. Soaring   **797.5**

Talmud
The princess and Rabbi Joshuah
In Johnson, S. P. ed. The Princesses p250-53   **S C**

The **tamarack** tree. Underwood, B.   **Fic**

Tamarin, Alfred H.
(illus.) Glubok, S. The art of Africa   **709.6**
(illus.) Glubok, S. The art of India   **709.54**
(illus.) Glubok, S. The art of Japan   **709.52**
(illus.) Glubok, S. The art of the Eskimo   **709.98**
(illus.) Glubok, S. The art of the Etruscans   **709.37**
(illus.) Glubok, S. The art of the Southwest Indians   **709.01**
(illus.) Glubok, S. The art of the Spanish in the United States and Puerto Rico   **709.73**
(illus.) Glubok, S. Dolls, dolls, dolls   **688.7**

Tamenend. See Tammany, Delaware chief

The **taming** of the shrew. Lamb, C.
In Darrell, M. ed. Once upon a time p140-46   **808.8**

Taming the colt. O'Hara, M.
In Martignoni, M. E. ed. The illustrated treasury of children's literature p456-62   **808.8**

Tamlane
Jacobs, J. Tamlane
In Harper, W. comp. Ghosts and goblins p90-94   **394.2**
In Jacobs, J. ed. More English folk and fairy tales p172-76   **398.2**
In Johnson, E. ed. Anthology of children's literature p200-01   **808.8**
Williams-Ellis, A. Tamlane
In Williams-Ellis, A. Fairy tales from the British Isles p263-71   **398.2**

Tammany, Delaware chief

See pages in the following books:

Bleeker, S. The Delaware Indians p123-35 (4-6)   **970.3**
Johnston, J. The Indians and the strangers p43-50 (2-5)   **920**

Tampere, Finland

See pages in the following book:

Berry, E. The land and people of Finland p98-103 (5-7)   **914.71**

Tandala and Pakala. Jagendorf, M. A.
In Jagendorf, M. A. Noodlehead stories from around the world p222-26 **398.2**

Tanglewood tales. Hawthorne, N.
In Hawthorne, N. A wonder-book, and Tanglewood tales p201-421   **292**

Tanks (Military science)
Colby, C. B. Arms of our fighting men (4-7)   **623.4**

Tannenbaum, Beulah
City traffic (3-5)   **388.4**
Clean air (3-5)   **614.7**
Feeding the city (2-4)   **338.1**
High rises (3-6)   **690**

Tanner, Henry Ossawa

See pages in the following books:

Hughes, L. Famous American Negroes p63-65 (5-7)   **920**
Rollins, C. H. They showed the way p121-25 (5-7)   **920**

The **tanners.** Fisher, L. E.   **675**

Tannhauser; adaptation. Bulla, C. R.
In Bulla, C. R. Stories of favorite operas p71-77   **782.1**

Tanning
Fisher, L. E. The tanners (4-7)   **675**

Tanzania
Carpenter, A. Tanzania (4-7)   **916.78**
Kaula, E. M. The land and people of Tanzania (5-7)   **916.78**

See also pages in the following book:

Perl, L. East Africa p73-91 (4-7)   **916.7**

Taoism

See pages in the following books:

Fitch, F. M. Their search for God p67-83 (4-7)   **291**
Kettelkamp, L. Religions, East and West p46-51 (5-7)   **291**
Seeger, E. Eastern religions p103-20 (6-7)   **291**

Taos Indians
Wood, N. Hollering sun (4-7)   **970.3**

Tape recorders. See Magnetic recorders and recording

Taper Tom. Haviland, V.
In Haviland, V. Favorite fairy tales told in Norway p50-64   **398.2**

Taper Tom. Thorne-Thomsen, G.
In Ward, W. ed. Stories to dramatize p105-09   **372.6**

Taper-Tom who made the princess laugh. Asbjørnsen, P. C.
In Asbjørnsen, P. C. Norwegian folk tales p20-24   **398.2**

Tapestry, Bayeux. See Bayeux tapestry

Tapley, Caroline
John come down the backstay (6-7)   **Fic**

Tar baby
Brer Rabbit and the tar baby
In Malcolmson, A. Yankee Doodle's cousins p79-83   **398.2**
Brown, M. W. The wonderful Tar-baby story
In Brown, M. W. Brer Rabbit p6-11 **398.2**
Harris, J. C. The wonderful tar-baby story
In Arbuthnot, M. H. comp. The Arbuthnot Anthology of children's literature p383-84   **808.8**

The **terrible** tempered dragon. Palmer, R.
In Hoke, H. comp. Dragons, dragons, dragons p223-30 **398.2**
In Palmer, R. Dragons, unicorns, and other magical beasts p46-54 **398.2**

Terrible Terry's surprise. Boiko, C.
In Boiko, C. Children's plays for creative actors p297-307 **812**

The **terrible** wave. Dahlstedt, M. **Fic**

Terris, Susan
The drowning boy (6-7) **Fic**

Terry and the caterpillars. Selsam, M. E. **595.7**

Tessa's surprises. Alcott, L. M.
In Alcott, L. M. Glimpses of Louisa p115-28 **S C**

The **test.** Tobey, L. C.
In Burack, A. S. ed. One hundred plays for children p766-76 **808.82**

A **test** for William Tell. Roberts, H.
In Kamerman, S. E. ed. Dramatized folk tales of the world p493-503 **812.08**

Test of a friendship. Walker, B. K.
In Walker, B. K. The dancing palm tree, and other Nigerian folktales p80-83 **398.2**

A **test** of skill. Arnott, K.
In Arnott, K. African myths and legends p40-42 **398.2**

Teta the magician. Green, R. L.
In Green, R. L. ed. A cavalcade of magicians p3-9 **808.8**

Teutli, the mountain that is alive. Brenner, A.
In Brenner, A. The boy who could do anything, & other Mexican folk tales p30-33 **398.2**

Tewa Indians
Clark, A. N. In my mother's house (1-4) **970.3**

Texas

Description and travel
Sasek, M. This is Texas (3-6) **917.64**

Fiction
Beatty, P. A long way to Whiskey Creek (5-7) **Fic**
Jones, W. Edge of two worlds (5-7) **Fic**

Texas centipede coffee. Jagendorf, M. A.
In Jagendorf, M. A. Folk stories of the South p284-86 **398.2**

Texas sandstorm. Courlander, H.
In Courlander, H. Terrapin's pot of sense p65-66 **398.2**

Textbooks

Bibliography
El-hi textbooks in print **016.371**
Textbooks in print, El-hi **016.371**

Textile chemistry. See Dyes and dyeing

Textile design
See pages in the following book:
Price, C. Made in West Africa p14-31 (5-7) **709.6**

Textile fabrics. See Textile industry and fabrics

Textile fibers. See Fibers

Textile industry and fabrics
Buehr, W. Cloth from fiber to fabric (5-7) **677**
See also pages in the following books:
Corrigan, B. Of course you can sew! p15-19 (5-7) **646.4**
Landry, L. The land and people of Colombia p121-26 (5-7) **918.61**
See also Dyes and dyeing; Weaving

Thacher, Mary M.
(illus.) Busch, P. S. Exploring as you walk in the city **500.9**
(illus.) Busch, P. S. Exploring as you walk in the meadow **500.9**
(illus.) Busch, P. S. A walk in the snow **500.9**

Thackeray, William Makepeace
See pages in the following book:
Benét, L. Famous storytellers for young people p28-34 (5-7) **920**

Thailand
Poole, F. K. Thailand (5-7) **915.93**
See also pages in the following book:
Poole, F. K. Southeast Asia p13-24 (5-7) **915.9**

Fiction
Ayer, J. Nu Dang and his kite **E**
Ayer, J. A wish for Little Sister **E**

Religion
See pages in the following book:
Cooke, D. C. The tribal people of Thailand p47-56 (5-7) **301.2**

Thales
See pages in the following book:
Diggins, J. E. String, straightedge, and shadow p62-91 (6-7) **516**

The **Thames.** Streatfeild, N. **914.2**

Thames River
Streatfeild, N. The Thames (4-6) **914.2**

Thampi, Parvathi
(jt. comp.) Cassedy, S. Moon-uncle, moon-uncle **398.8**

Thane, Adele
The baker's neighbor
In Kamerman, S. E. ed. Dramatized folk tales of the world p471-80 **812.08**
Big Paul Bunyan
In Kamerman, S. E. ed. Dramatized folk tales of the world p514-25 **812.08**
A gift for Hans Brinker
In Kamerman, S. E. ed. Dramatized folk tales of the world p200-11 **812.08**
The king who was bored
In Kamerman, S. E. ed. Dramatized folk tales of the world p334-45 **812.08**
Merry Tyll and the three rogues
In Kamerman, S. E. ed. Dramatized folk tales of the world p162-76 **812.08**
Plays from famous stories and fairy tales (4-6) **812**

Contents: The Emperor's Nightingale; The Pied Piper of Hamelin; Aladdin and his wonderful lamp; Rumpelstiltskin; Tom Sawyer, pirate; The elves and the shoemaker; Dummling and the golden goose; The three wishes; The saucy scarecrow; King Alfred and the cakes; The apple of contentment; The swine-herd; Rapunzel; The magic nutmeg-grater; Christmas every day; The twelve dancing princesses; Puss in Boots; The reluctant dragon; The little princess; The Sleeping Beauty; Heidi; Hansel and Gretel; Pinocchio goes to school; Jack and the magic beanstalk; Rip Van Winkle; The brave little tailor; Dick Whittington and his cat; Cinderella

The **Three** brothers and the giant
  In De Regniers, B. S. ed. The giant book
    p49-59   **398.2**
The **three** brothers and the marvelous things.
  Alegría, R. E.
  In Alegría, R. E. The three wishes p15-24
                                                   398.2
The **three** brothers and the treacle toffee.
  Green, K.
  In Green, K. Leprechaun tales p63-73
                                                   398.2
The **three** bushy billy goats. Aulaire, I. d'
  In Aulaire, I. d'. East of the sun and west
    of the moon p175-78   **398.2**
  See also Three billy goats gruff
3x3: three by three. Krüss, J.   **E**
Three chests
  Bowman, J. C. Jurma and the sea god
  In Bowman, J. C. Tales from a Finnish
    tupa p81-90   **398.2**
Three children of fortune
  In De La Mare, W. ed. Animal stories
    p128-33   **398.2**
  In Grimm, J. Grimms' Fairy tales; illus.
    by F. Kredel p23-26   **398.2**
  See also Fortune seekers
Three copecks
  Manning-Sanders, R. The good ogre
  In Manning-Sanders, R. A book of ogres
    and trolls p9-19   **398.2**
Three cows
  In Jacobs, J. ed. More English folk and
    fairy tales p89-91   **398.2**
Three daughters
  In Ginsburg, M. ed. The Kaha bird p53-
    54   **398.2**
Three dogs
  Grimm, J. The three dogs
  In Lang, A. ed. The green fairy book
    p360-66   **398.2**
  Manning-Sanders, R. The three dogs
  In Manning-Sanders, R. A book of drag-
    ons p114-22   **398.2**
The **three** dwarfs. Grimm, J.
  In Lang, A. ed. The red fairy book p238-
    45   **398.2**
  See also Three little men in the wood
The **three** elevators. Burgess, G.
  In Association for Childhood Education
    International. Told under the magic
    umbrella p64-67   **S C**
The **Three** fairies
  In Arbuthnot, M. H. comp. The Arbuth-
    not Anthology of children's litera-
    ture p403-04   **808.8**
  In Carter, D. S. ed. Greedy Mariani, and
    other folktales of the Antilles p106-
    11   **398.2**
Three fast men. Courlander, H.
  In Courlander, H. The king's drum, and
    other African stories p17-18   **398.2**
The **three** feathers. Grimm, J.
  In Grimm, J. About wise men and sim-
    pletons p58-61   **398.2**
  In Grimm, J. The complete Grimm's Fairy
    tales p319-22   **398.2**

In Grimm, J. The juniper tree, and other
    tales from Grimm v 1 p3-10   **398.2**
  In Grimm, J. Three gay tales from Grimm
    p29-48   **398.2**
  In Jacobs, J. ed. More English folk and
    fairy tales p37-42   **398.2**
The **three** figs. Belpré, P.
  In Belpré, P. The tiger and the rabbit,
    and other tales p123-27   **398.2**
The **three** foolish brides. Kim, S.
  In Kim, S. The story bag p56-57   **398.2**
Three Fridays. Kelsey, A. G.
  In Johnson, E. ed. Anthology of children's
    literature p327-28   **808.8**
  In Kelsey, A. G. Once the Hodja p21-28
                                                   398.2
Three gay tales from Grimm. Grimm, J. **398.2**
The **three** goats. Poulsson, E.
  In Association for Childhood Education
    International. Told under the green
    umbrella p78-80   **398.2**
Three gold pieces. Aliki   **398.2**
The **three** golden apples. Hawthorne, N.
  In Mayne, W. ed. William Mayne's Book of
    giants p 1-26   **398.2**
The **three** golden ducats. Spicer, D. G.
  In Spicer, D. G. The owl's nest p74-85
                                                   398.2
The **three** golden eggs. MacManus, S.
  In MacManus, S. Hibernian nights p25-35
                                                   398.2
The **three** golden hairs of Grandfather Know
  All. Haviland, V.
  In Haviland, V. Favorite fairy tales told in
    Czechoslovakia p67-90   **398.2**
  See also Giant with the golden hair
Three golden oranges. Boggs, R. S.
  In Boggs, R. S. Three golden oranges, and
    other Spanish folk tales p15-35 **398.2**
Three golden oranges, and other Spanish folk
  tales. Boggs, R. S.   **398.2**
The **three** goslings. Haviland, V.
  In Haviland, V. Favorite fairy tales told in
    Italy p67-77   **398.2**
Three great men at peace. Jagendorf, M. A.
  In Jagendorf, M. A. Folk stories of the
    South p143-45   **398.2**
The **three** green twigs. Grimm, J.
  In Grimm, J. The complete Grimm's Fairy
    tales p823-25   **398.2**
The **three** happy lions. Fatio, L.   **E**
Three heads of the well
  The King of Colchester's daughter
  In Opie, I. ed. The classic fairy tales p159-
    61   **398.2**
  Reeves, J. The well of the three heads
  In Reeves, J. English fables and fairy stories
    p115-26   **398.2**
  Three heads of the well
  In Jacobs, J. ed. English folk and fairy tales
    p232-37   **398.2**
The **three** Ivans. Manning-Sanders, R.
  In Manning-Sanders, R. A book of sorcerers
    and spells p69-90   **398.2**
Three jovial huntsmen. Jeffers, S.   **398.8**

The **tiger** catcher. McFarlan, E.
> *In* Kamerman, S. E. ed. Dramatized folk tales of the world p32-37   **812.08**

The **tiger** in court. Hume, L. C.
> *In* Hume, L. C. Favorite children's stories from China and Tibet p74-78 **398.2**

Tiger in the forest, Anansi in the web. Sherlock, P.
> *In* Sherlock, P. West Indian folk-tales p59-64   **398.2**

Tiger Lily and the dragon. Picard, B. L.
> *In* Picard, B. L. The faun and the woodcutter's daughter p159-78   **S C**

The **tiger** of Kumgan Mountains. Kim, S.
> *In* Kim, S. The story bag p199-214   **398.2**

Tiger story, Anansi story. Sherlock, P.
> *In* Sherlock, P. West Indian folk-tales p45-58   **398.2**

The **tiger**, the Brahman and the jackal. Steel, F. A.
> *In* Arbuthnot, M. H. comp. The Arbuthnot Anthology of children's literature p350-51   **808.8**
> *In* Arbuthnot, M. H. comp. Time for old magic p229-30   **398.2**
> *In* Haviland, V. Favorite fairy tales told in India p83-90   **398.2**
> *In* Jacobs, J. ed. Indian fairy tales p66-69   **398.2**
> *In* Johnson, E. ed. Anthology of children's literature p105-06   **808.8**
> *In* Ross, L. Puppet shows using poems and stories p139-44   **791.5**
> *See also* Brahmin, the tiger and the jackal

The **tiger**, the Brahman, and the jackal; play. Smith, G. V.
> *In* Kamerman, S. E. ed. Dramatized folk tales of the world p212-17   **812.08**

"**Tiger!** Tiger!" Kipling, R.
> *In* Kipling, R. The jungle book (Doubleday) p73-98   **E**
> *In* Kipling, R. The jungle book (Grosset) p95-130   **S C**
> *In* Kipling, R. The jungle books (Doubleday) v 1 p95-118   **S C**
> *In* Kipling, R. The jungle books (Macmillan N Y) p78-96   **S C**
> *In* Kipling, R. The jungle books (Watts, F.) v 1 p65-92   **S C**

Tiger up a tree. Unkelbach, K.   **636.8**

Tiger woman. Jewett, E. M.
> *In* Child Study Association of America. Castles and dragons p243-57 **398.2**

Tigers
Bergman Sucksdorff, A. Chendru: the boy and the tiger (3-6)   **915.4**
Schaller, G. B. The tiger (4-7)   **599**
> *See also pages in the following book:*

Shuttlesworth, D. E. Animals that frighten people p18-24 (5-7)   **591.5**

Stories
Kraus, R. Leo the late bloomer   **E**

The **tiger's** minister of state. Courlander, H.
> *In* Courlander, H. The tiger's whisker, and other tales and legends from Asia and the Pacific p20-23   **398.2**

The **tiger's** stripes. Vo-Dinh
> *In* Vo-Dinh. The toad is the Emperor's uncle p65-73   **398.2**

The **tiger's** tail. Courlander, H.
> *In* Gruenberg, S. M. ed. Favorite stories old and new p396-97   **808.8**

The **tiger's** whisker. Courlander, H.
> *In* Courlander, H. The tiger's whisker, and other tales and legends from Asia and the Pacific p16-19   **398.2**

The **tiger's** whisker, and other tales and legends from Asia and the Pacific. Courlander, H.   **398.2**

Tigger has breakfast. Milne, A. A.
> *In* Ward, W. ed. Stories to dramatize p69-76   **372.6**

Tigua Indians
Steiner, S. The Tiguas (4-7)   **970.3**

The **Tiguas**. Steiner, S.   **970.3**

Tijerina, Reies
> *See pages in the following book:*
Newlon, C. Famous Mexican-Americans p116-23 (6-7)   **920**

The **tikgi** birds. Sechrist, E. H.
> *In* Sechrist, E. H. Once in the first times p86-90   **398.2**

Tikki Tikki Tembo. Mosel, A.   **398.2**

Tikta'liktak. Houston, J.   **398.2**

Tillhagen, C. H.
(jt. auth.) Jagendorf, M. A. The gypsies' fiddle, and other gypsy tales   **398.2**

Tillin, Alma M.
(jt. auth.) Hicks, W. Developing multi-media libraries   **025.17**

Tim all alone. Ardizzone, E.   **E**

Tim in danger. Ardizzone, E.   **E**

Tim to the lighthouse. Ardizzone, E.   **E**

Timber. See Forests and forestry; Lumber and lumbering; Trees

Time
Adler, I. Time in your life (5-7)   **529**
Bendick, J. The first book of time (4-6)   **529**
Bradley, D. Time for you (4-6)   **529**
Selsam, M. E. How animals tell time (4-7)   **591.5**
Zarchy, H. Wheel of time (6-7)   **529**
> *See also* Calendars; Clocks and watches; Periodicity

Fiction
Yolen, J. The bird of time   **E**

Time. Courlander, H.
> *In* Courlander, H. The cow-tail switch, and other West African stories p73-77   **398.2**

The **time**-ago tales of Jahdu. Hamilton, V.   **S C**

Time and Mr Bass. Cameron, E.   **Fic**

Time at the top. Ormondroyd, E.   **Fic**

Time at the top; excerpt. Ormondroyd, E.
> *In* Arbuthnot, M. H. comp. The Arbuthnot Anthology of children's literature p545-53   **808.8**

Time for fairy tales, old and new. See Arbuthnot, M. H. comp. Time for old magic **398.2**

Time for old magic. Arbuthnot, M. H. comp.   **398.2**

Tokyo

Description

Boardman, G. R. Living in Tokyo (5-7) 915.2

Told again. See De La Mare, W. Tales told again 398.2

Told under spacious skies. Association for Childhood Education International **S C**

Told under the blue umbrella. Association for Childhood Education International **S C**

Told under the Christmas tree. Association for Childhood Education International 808.8

Told under the city umbrella. Association for Childhood Education International **S C**

Told under the green umbrella. Association for Childhood Education International 398.2

Told under the magic umbrella. Association for Childhood Education International **S C**

Told under the Stars and Stripes. Association for Childhood Education International **S C**

Tolford, Joshua
(illus.) Chase, R. Jack and the three sillies 398.2
(illus.) Hightower, F. Dark horse of Woodfield **Fic**

Tolkien, J. R. R.
The adventures of Tom Bombadil, and other verses from The Red Book (6-7) 821
The hobbit (4-7) **Fic**
The hobbit; excerpt
In Arbuthnot, M. H. comp. The Arbuthnot Anthology of children's literature p555-57 808.8
In Untermeyer, B. ed. The Golden Treasury of children's literature p463-86 808.8
The hobbit; another excerpt
In Johnson, E. ed. Anthology of children's literature p680-87 808.8
Riddles in the dark
In Johnson, E. ed. Anthology of children's literature p680-87 808.8
An unexpected party
In Arbuthnot, M. H. comp. The Arbuthnot Anthology of children's literature p555-57 808.8
In Untermeyer, B. ed. The Golden Treasury of children's literature p463-86 808.8

Tolly's new home. Boston, L. M.
In Arbuthnot, M. H. comp. The Arbuthnot Anthology of children's literature p535-39 808.8

Tolstoy, Alexei
The great big enormous turnip (k-2) 398.2
The reunion after three hundred years
In Hitchcock, A. comp. Alfred Hitchcock's Supernatural tales of terror and suspense p104-25 **S C**
The turnip
In Haviland, V. comp. The fairy tale treasury p44-47 398.2

Tolstoy, Leo
How much land does a man need? play. See Leech, M. T. How much land does a man need?

Twenty-two Russian tales for young children (3-5) **S C**
Contents: Philipok; The two friends; The old man and the apple tree; The trapped bird; A boy tells the story of being caught in a storm; Rusak's night frolic; The peasant and the horse; The king and the humble hut; The old grandfather and his little grandson; The eagle; The kitten; The watchman's dog; The jump; The dew on the grass; What the little mouse saw on her walk; The squirrel and the wolf; The hen and her chicks; The bat; The fox's foxy tail; The quail; The two brothers; Lipuniushka
Where love is, God is
In Colwell, E. ed. A storyteller's choice p185-99 372.6

Tom Bombadil, The adventures of. Tolkien, J. R. R. 821

Tom Fox and the apple pie. Watson, C. **E**

Tom Hickathrift
In Jacobs, J. ed. More English folk and fairy tales p46-54 398.2

Tom meets Becky. Twain, M.
In Johnson, E. ed. Anthology of children's literature p821-26 808.8

Tom Sawyer discovers a law of human action. Twain, M.
In Ward, W. ed. Stories to dramatize p145-49 372.6

Tom Sawyer, pirate. Thane, A.
In Burack, A. S. ed. Popular plays for classroom reading p325-36 808.82
In Thane, A. Plays from famous stories and fairy tales p77-89 812

Tom Thumb
The history of Tom Thumb
In Haviland, V. comp. The fairy tale treasury p72-77 398.2
In Jacobs, J. ed. English folk and fairy tales p145-52 398.2
In Johnson, E. ed. Anthology of children's literature p198-200 808.8
In Martignoni, M. E. ed. The illustrated treasury of children's literature p184-86 808.8
In Opie, I. ed. The classic fairy tales p33-46 398.2
Reeves, J. The story of Tom Thumb
In Reeves, J. English fables and fairy stories p63-70 398.2
See also Hop-o'-my-Thumb; One inch fellow; Thumbling

Tom Thumb. Grimm, J. 398.2
also in Grimm, J. Grimm's Fairy tales; illus. by A. Rackham p91-98 398.2
also in Grimm, J. Grimms' Fairy tales; illus. by F. Kredel p268-75 398.2
also in Grimm, J. Household stories p160-66 398.2
also in Untermeyer, B. ed. The Golden Treasury of children's literature p157-69 808.8
See also Thumbling

Tom Thumb's travels. Grimm, J.
In Grimm, J. Household stories p181-85 398.2
See also Thumbling

Tom Tichenor's puppets. Tichenor, T. 791.5

Tom Tiddler's ground. De La Mare, W. ed. 821.08

Turner, Charles Henry

See pages in the following book:

Hayden, R. C. Seven Black American scientists p68-91 (6-7)   **920**

Turner, John F.

The magnificent bald eagle (4-6)   **598.2**

Turner, Joseph Mallord William

See pages in the following book:

Craven, T. The rainbow book of art p184-87 (5-7)   **709**

Turner, Nancy Byrd

When it rained cats and dogs   **E**

Turner, Nat

See pages in the following book:

Rollins, C. H. They showed the way p132-37 (5-7)   **920**

Turner, Philip

Brian Wildsmith's Illustrated Bible stories (2-6)   **220.9**

Turner, Thyra

Christmas House

In Dalgliesh, A. comp. Christmas p123-34   **394.2**

Turning the tables. Fisher, A.

In Fisher, A. United Nations plays and programs p108-24   **812**

Turnip

De La Mare, W. The turnip

In De La Mare, W. Tales told again p107-18   **398.2**

Domanska, J. The turnip   **398.2**

Grimm, J. The turnip

In Grimm, J. The complete Grimm's Fairy tales p637-40   **398.2**

In Grimm, J. Grimms' Fairy tales; illus. by F. Kredel p260-63   **398.2**

Tolstoy, A. The great big enormous turnip   **398.2**

Tolstoy, A. The turnip

In Haviland, V. comp. The fairy tale treasury p44-47   **398.2**

Turnips

Stories

Domanska, J. The turnip (k-2)   **398.2**

Tolstoy, A. The great big enormous turnip (k-2)   **398.2**

Turska, Krystyna

Pegasus (2-4)   **292**

The woodcutter's duck (k-3)   **398.2**

(illus.) Authors' choice. See Authors' choice   **S C**

(illus.) Authors' choice 2. See Authors' choice 2   **S C**

(illus.) Brown, M. ed. A cavalcade of sea legends   **808.8**

(illus.) Garner, A. ed. A cavalcade of goblins   **398.2**

(illus.) Green, R. L. ed. A cavalcade of dragons   **808.8**

(illus.) Hope-Simpson, J. ed. A cavalcade of witches   **808.8**

A turtle, a flute and the General's birthday. Davis, L. R.

In Kamerman, S. E. ed. Fifty plays for junior actors p167-77   **812.08**

The **Turtle** and the monkey share a tree

In Courlander, H. ed. Ride with the sun p25-27   **398.2**

Turtle pond. Freschet, B.   **598.1**

The **turtle** who couldn't stop talking. Babbitt, E. C.

In Babbitt, E. C. Jataka tales p18-20 **398.2**

In Gruenberg, S. M. ed. Favorite stories old and new p222   **808.8**

See also Talkative tortoise

Turtles

Darling, L. Turtles (3-5)   **598.1**

Freschet, B. Turtle pond (k-3)   **598.1**

Goode, J. Turtles, tortoises, and terrapins (4-6)   **598.1**

Hoke, J. Turtles and their care (5-7)   **639**

Johnson, F. Turtles and tortoises (1-3) **598.1**

Scott, J. D. Loggerhead turtle (4-6)   **598.1**

Selsam, M. E. Let's get turtles (1-3)   **639**

Waters, J. F. Green turtle mysteries (1-3)   **598.1**

See also pages in the following books:

Buck, M. W. Pets from the pond p58-63 (4-7)   **639**

Conant, R. A field guide to reptiles and amphibians of Eastern and Central North America p37-81   **598.1**

Cooper, E. K. Science on the shores and banks p135-39 (5-7)   **574.92**

Huntington, H. E. Let's look at reptiles p58-85 (4-6)   **598.1**

Pels, G. The care of water pets p30-35 (4-6)   **639**

Perry, R. The Galápagos Islands p62-70 (5-7)   **500.9**

Ricciuti, E. R. Shelf pets p66-74 (5-7)   **639**

Villiard, P. Reptiles as pets p117-33 (5-7)   **639**

See also Snapping turtles

Stories

Davis, A. V. Timothy Turtle   **E**

Domanska, J. Look, there is a turtle flying (k-2)   **398.2**

Du Bois, W. P. The hare and the tortoise & The tortoise and the hare (1-4)   **398.2**

Graham, A. Timothy Turtle   **E**

The Hare and the tortoise (k-3)   **398.2**

Holling, H. C. Minn of the Mississippi (4-6)   **Fic**

MacGregor, E. Theodore Turtle   **E**

Marshall, J. Yummers!   **E**

Wildsmith, B. The hare and the tortoise (k-2)   **398.2**

Williams, B. Albert's toothache   **E**

Turtles and their care. Hoke, J.   **639**

Turtles and tortoises. Johnson, F.   **598.1**

Turtles, tortoises, and terrapins. Goode, J. **598.1**

Tusi and the great beast. Aardema, V.

In Aardema, V. Behind the back of the mountain p57-65   **398.2**

Tuskegee Institute

Graham, S. Booker T. Washington: educator of hand, head, and heart (5-7)   **92**

Tutankhamen. See Tutenkhamûn, King of Egypt

Tutankhaten. See Tutenkhamûn, King of Egypt

Ubell, Earl
The world of candle and color (4-6)   535
The world of the living (3-5)   574

Uchida, Yoshiko
The dancing kettle, and other Japanese folk
tales (3-5)   398.2
Contents: The dancing kettle; Urashima Taro and
the princess of the sea; Eight-headed dragon; Old
man with the bump; Rabbit and the crocodile; Jewels
of the sea; Princess of Light; Wedding of the mouse;
Momotaro: boy-of-the-peach; Piece of straw; Tongue-
cut sparrow; Princess and the fisherman; Old man of
the flowers; Isun Boshi, the one-inch lad
The forever Christmas tree   E
The fox and the bear
In Sechrist, E. H. ed. It's time for story
hour p111-16   372.6
Gold Hill at last
In Arbuthnot, M. H. comp. The Arbuthnot
Anthology of children's literature
p769-72   808.8
Journey to Topaz (4-7)   Fic
The magic listening cap (3-5)   398.2
Contents: The magic listening cap; Terrible leak;
The wrestling match of the two Buddhas; Magic mor-
tar; Tubmaker who flew to the sky; Three tests for the
prince; Deer of five colors; The golden axe; Mountain
witch and the peddler; The man who bought a dream;
Fox and the bear; Tiny god; Rice cake that rolled
away; Grateful stork
Momotaro: boy-of-the-peach
In Arbuthnot, M. H. comp. The Arbuthnot
Anthology of children's literature
p336-38   808.8
In Arbuthnot, M. H. comp. Time for old
magic p211-13   398.2
The promised year (4-6)   Fic
The promised year; excerpt
In Association for Childhood Education In-
ternational. Told under the city um-
brella p157-72   S C
Samurai of Gold Hill (4-7)   Fic
Samurai of Gold Hill; excerpt
In Arbuthnot, M. H. comp. The Arbuthnot
Anthology of children's literature
p769-72   808.8
Sumi & the goat & the Tokyo Express (1-4)
Fic
Sumi's prize (1-4)   Fic
Urashima Taro and the princess of the sea
In Arbuthnot, M. H. comp. The Arbuthnot
Anthology of children's literature
p338-42   808.8
In Arbuthnot, M. H. comp. Time for old
magic p213-17   398.2

Uden, Grant
The adventures of the Countess Jeanne
In Arbuthnot, M. H. comp. The Arbuthnot
Anthology of children's literature
p471-74   808.8
A dictionary of chivalry (6-7)   940.1

Udry, Janice May
Let's be enemies   E
Mary Jo's grandmother   E
The Moon Jumpers   E
What Mary Jo shared   E

Ueno, Noriko
Elephant buttons   E

Uganda
Carpenter, A. Uganda (4-7)   916.76
See also pages in the following book:
Perl, L. East Africa p94-116 (4-7)   916.7

Economic conditions
See pages in the following book:
Carpenter, A. Uganda p71-81 (4-7)   916.76
Folklore
See Folklore—Uganda
Ugandan folk songs. See Folk songs, Ugandan
The **ugly duckling.** Andersen, H. C.   Fic
also in Andersen, H. C. Andersen's Fairy
tales p22-32   S C
also in Andersen, H. C. The complete fairy
tales and stories p216-24   S C
also in Andersen, H. Hans Andersen's Fairy
tales p188-201   S C
also in Andersen, H. C. It's perfectly true,
and other stories p65-78   S C
also in Andersen, H. C. Seven tales p63-91
S C
also in Gruenberg, S. M. ed. Favorite
stories old and new p276-81   808.8
also in Haviland, V. comp. The fairy tale
treasury p180-91   398.2
also in Johnson, E. ed. Anthology of children's literature p728-33   808.8
also in Martignoni, M. E. ed. The illustrated treasury of children's literature p188-93   808.8
also in Rackham, A. comp. Arthur Rackham Fairy book p128-39   398.2
also in The Tall book of nursery tales p25-
35   398.2
also in Untermeyer, B. ed. The Golden
Treasury of children's literature
p204-13   808.8

Ukraine

Fiction
Suhl, Y. Uncle Misha's partisans (5-7)   Fic
Folklore
See Folklore—Ukraine
Ukrainian folk tales. Bloch, M. H. ed.   398.2

Ulcers
See pages in the following book:
Zim, H. S. Your stomach and digestive tract
p57-62 (3-6)   612

Ulenspiegel. See Eulenspiegel

Ullom, Judith C.
(comp.) Folklore of the North American Indians. See Folklore of the North American
Indians   016.398

Ulysses
Church, A. J. The Iliad and the Odyssey of
Homer (6-7)   883
See also pages in the following books:
Arbuthnot, M. H. comp. The Arbuthnot An-
thology of children's literature p458-60
808.8
Arbuthnot, M. H. comp. Time for old magic
p322-24   398.2
Asimov, I. Words from the myths p201-11
(6-7)   292
Farjeon, E. ed. A cavalcade of kings p133-
39 (5-7)   808.8
Farjeon, E. ed. A cavalcade of queens p72-
108 (4-7)   808.8
Hamilton, E. Mythology p291-318   292
Hazeltine, A. I. ed. Hero tales from many
lands p51-67 (5-7)   398.2
Johnson, E. ed. Anthology of children's literature p484-86   808.8

Villiard, Paul—*Continued*
  Insects as pets (5-7)   **595.7**
  Jewelrymaking (4-7)   **745.59**
  Reptiles as pets (5-7)   **639**
  Wild mammals as pets (5-7)   **639**

Villiers, Alan
  Men, ships, and the sea (6-7)   **910.4**

Vincent-the-Good and the electric train.
  Levoy, M.
    In Levoy, M. The witch of Fourth Street,
     and other stories p14-28   **S C**

Vinci, Leonardo da. See Leonardo da Vinci

Vines. See Climbing plants

Vineyards. See Grapes

Vining, Elizabeth (Gray) See Gray, Elizabeth
  Janet

The **Vinlanders' saga.** Schiller, B.   **398.2**

Violets for Christmas. Phillips, G. M.
  In Kamerman, S. E. ed. A treasury of
   Christmas plays p158-75   **812.08**

Viorst, Judith
  Alexander and the terrible, horrible, no good,
   very bad day   **E**
  My mama says there aren't zombies, ghosts,
   vampires, creatures, demons, monsters,
   fiends, goblins, or things   **E**
  The southpaw; short story
   In Free to be . . . you and me p71-75
     810.8
  The tenth good thing about Barney   **E**

Vipers. See Snakes

Vipont, Elfrida
  (comp.) Bless this day (2-5)   **242**
  Weaver of dreams; the girlhood of Charlotte
   Brontë (5-7)   **92**

Virgil

Adaptations
Church, A. J. The Aeneid for boys and girls
  (6-7)   **873**

Virgilius the sorcerer. Green, R. L.
  In Green, R. L. ed. A cavalcade of magicians p25-36   **808.8**

Virgin Islands National Park
  See pages in the following book:
Melbo, I. R. Our country's national parks v 1
  p189-202 (5-7)   **917.3**

Virgin Islands of the United States

Fiction
Anderson, L. The day the hurricane hap-
  pened   **E**
Anderson, L. Izzard   **E**

Virginia

History—Colonial period
Lacy, D. The Colony of Virginia (6-7)   **975.5**
Taylor, T. Rebellion town, Williamsburg,
  1776 (5-7)   **973.3**

History—Colonial period—Fiction
Levitin, S. Roanoke (6-7)   **Fic**

Virginia giant; short story. Carmer, C.
  In Carmer, C. comp. America sings p188-
  93   **784.4**

Viruses
  See pages in the following book:
Silverstein, A. Germfree life p27-31 (5-7)
    576

Vishniac, Roman
  (illus.) Singer, I. B. A day of pleasure   **92**

Vision
Adler, I. Your eyes (3-5)   **612**
Ipsen, D. C. What does a bee see? (5-7)
    595.7
Mason, G. F. Animal vision (4-7)   **591.4**
Schuman, B. N. The human eye (4-6)   **612**
  See also pages in the following book:
Silverstein, A. The sense organs p10-26 (4-7)
    612

  See also Blind; Eye; Optical illusions

The **vision of the silver bell.** Weathers, W.
  In Burack, A. S. ed. Christmas plays for
   young actors p235-44   **812.08**

A **visit from outer space;** puppet play. Ross, L.
  In Ross, L. Hand puppets p184-87   **791.5**

A **visit from St Nicholas.** Moore, C. C.
  In Arbuthnot, M. H. comp. The Arbuthnot Anthology of children's literature p120   **808.8**
  In Arbuthnot, M. H. comp. Time for
   poetry p193   **821.08**
  In Henry, R. comp. My American heritage p78-79   **810.8**
  In Ross, L. Puppet shows using poems and
   stories p82-86   **791.5**
   See also Moore, C. C. The night before Christmas   **811**

Visit of the Shepherds, a Nativity play. Lenski, L.
  In Lenski, L. Lois Lenski's Christmas
   stories p141-52   **394.2**

A **visit to the farm.** Baruch, D.
  In Association for Childhood Education
   International. Told under the blue
   umbrella p75-79   **S C**

Visit to the planets. Melchior, H. K.
  In Kamerman, S. E. ed. Fifty plays for
   junior actors p372-85   **812.08**

Visitors. De La Mare, W.
  In Authors' choice 2 p75-87   **S C**
  In De La Mare, W. The magic jacket
   p234-48   **S C**

Visitors' exchange programs. See Exchange of
  persons programs

Visitors for Nancy Hanks. Bennett, R.
  In Bennett, R. Creative plays and programs for holidays p13-28   **812**

Visual instruction. See Audio-visual education

The **vital process.** Baker, J. J. W.   **581**

Vitamins
Asimov, I. How did we find out about vitamins? (4-7)   **574.1**

Vittorini, Domenico
  March and the shepherd
   In Arbuthnot, M. H. comp. The Arbuthnot Anthology of children's literature p269-70   **808.8**
   In Arbuthnot, M. H. comp. Time for old
   magic p152-53   **398.2**

Vittorini, Domenico—*Continued*
The most precious possession
In Arbuthnot, M. H. comp. The Arbuthnot Anthology of children's literature p271-72 **808.8**
In Arbuthnot, M. H. comp. Time for old magic p154-55 **398.2**
The one-legged crane
In Greene, E. comp. Clever cooks p117-23 **398.2**

Vitziton and the first quarrel. Baumann, H.
In Baumann, H. The stolen fire p135-37 **398.2**

Vivar, Rodrigo Diaz de. See El Cid Campeador

Vivariums. See Terrariums

The **Vixen and her cub**
In Ginsburg, M. comp. One trick too many p39 **398.2**

The **Vizir who was punished**
In Lang, A. ed. Arabian nights p32-42 **398.2**

Vocabulary
Rand, A. Sparkle and spin **E**

Vocal music. See Carols; Folk songs; Hymns; Opera; Singing; Songs

Vocational and technical education—multimedia, Index to. See Index to vocational and technical education—multimedia

Vocational guidance. See Blind—Education; Occupations; also names of occupations, e.g. Nurses and nursing; and such headings as Law as a profession

Vocations. See Occupations

Vo-Dinh
The toad is the Emperor's uncle (4-6) **398.2**
Contents: The toad is the Emperor's uncle; Father Catfish; The snake and its benefactor; The ravens build a bridge; The clever earthworm; The eel and the porgy; The carp that became a dragon; The hare and the tiger; The tiger's stripes; That fourth leg of the dog; The little lizard's sorrow; The sand-carrier crab; The fly; The horse and the eighteen bandits; The crow's pearl; A cat is a cat is a cat; The golden buffalo; Dragons?
(illus.) Cassedy, S. comp. Birds, frogs, and moonlight **895.6**
(illus.) Coutant, H. First snow **Fic**
(illus.) Kirkup, J. The magic drum **398.2**

Voice
Kettelkamp, L. Song, speech, and ventriloquism (5-7) **808.5**
See also Speech

Voice in the jug. Credle, E.
In Credle, E. Tall tales from the high hills, and other stories p122-32 **398.2**

The **Voice of death**
In Lang, A. ed. The red fairy book p182-85 **398.2**

The **voice of liberty. Fisher, A.**
In Fisher, A. Holiday programs for boys and girls p77-88 **812**

The **voice of the children. Jordan, J. comp.** **810.8**

Voices from America's past. Morris, R. B. ed. **973**

Voight, Virginia Frances
Brave little hummingbird (2-4) **598.2**
Sacajawea (2-4) **92**

Volavková, Hana
(ed.) I never saw another butterfly. See I never saw another butterfly **741.9**

Volcanoes
Marcus, R. B. The first book of volcanoes & earthquakes (5-7) **551.2**
Matthews, W. H. The story of volcanoes and earthquakes (4-6) **551.2**

See also pages in the following books:

Branley, F. M. Shakes, quakes, and shifts: earth tectonics p24-28 (5-7) **551.4**
Lauber, P. This restless earth p45-67 (5-7) **551**
Matthews, W. H. The earth's crust p37-46 (5-7) **551**
Matthews, W. H. The story of the earth p49-62 (5-7) **551**
Perry, R. The Galápagos Islands p9-20 (5-7) **500.9**

See also names of volcanoes, e.g. Paricutin (Volcano)

The **Volga. Hall, E.** **947**

Volga River
Hall, E. The Volga (5-7) **947**

See also pages in the following books:

Nazaroff, A. The land and people of Russia p20-25 (5-7) **914.7**

Volkh's journey to the East. Almedingen, E. M.
In Colwell, E. ed. A second storyteller's choice p46-56 **372.6**

Volleyball

See pages in the following book:

Keith, H. Sports and games p373-86 (5-7) **796**

Volsunga saga

See pages in the following books:

Colum, P. The children of Odin p199-271 (5-7) **293**
The Story of Sigurd
In Lang, A. ed. The red fairy book p357-67 **398.2**
White, A. T. The Golden Treasury of myths and legends p134-63 (5-7) **292**

Von Frisch, Karl. See Frisch, Karl von

Von Frisch, Otto. See Frisch, Otto von

Von Grofé, Ferdinand Rudolph. See Grofé, Ferde

Von Linné, Carl. See Linné, Carl von

Von Richthofen, Manfred Albrecht, Freiherr. See Richthofen, Manfred Albrecht, Freiherr von

Von Schmidt, Erich
(illus.) Anderson, J. The haunting of America **398.2**
(illus.) Fleischman, S. By the Great Horn Spoon! **Fic**
(illus.) Fleischman, S. Chancy and the grand rascal **Fic**
(illus.) Fleischman, S. The ghost on Saturday night **Fic**
(illus.) Fleischman, S. Jingo Django **Fic**
(illus.) Fleischman, S. Mr Mysterious & Company **Fic**
(illus.) O'Connor, R. Sitting Bull: war chief of the Sioux **92**

Von Steuben, Friedrich Wilhelm Ludolf Gerhard Augustin, Baron. See Steuben, Friedrich Wilhelm Ludolf Gerhard Augustin, Baron von

Von Wartburg, Ursula. See Wartburg, Ursula von

Von Zitzewitz, Hoot. See Zitzewitz, Hoot von

Voorhies, Stephen J.
 (illus.) Kjelgaard, J. Explorations of Père Marquette **92**

Vorderwinkler, William
 (jt. auth.) Axelrod, H. R. Tropical fish in your home **639**

Vorse, Albert White
 On a glacier in Greenland
  In A St Nicholas anthology p258-63 **810.8**

Vosburgh, Leonard
 (illus.) Hine, A. ed. This land is mine **811.08**

Voting. See Elections; Suffrage

Voute, Kathleen
 (illus.) Mason, M. E. Caroline and her kettle named Maud **Fic**
 (illus.) Steele, W. O. Westward adventure **920**

The **voyage** below the water. Courlander, H.
 In Courlander, H. The piece of fire, and other Haitian tales p71-75 **398.2**

The **voyage** of Cud. Curtin, J.
 In Brown, M. ed. A cavalcade of sea legends p198-217 **808.8**

The **Voyage** of Maelduin
 In Garner, A. ed. A cavalcade of goblins p13-34 **398.2**

The **voyage** of the Dawn Treader. Lewis, C. S.
 See note under Lewis, C. S. The lion, the witch and the wardrobe **Fic**

The **voyage** of the Northern Light. Trowbridge, J. T.
 In A St Nicholas anthology p130-36 **810.8**

The **voyage** of the wee red cap. Sawyer, R.
 In Association for Childhood Education International. Told under the Christmas tree p163-71 **808.8**
 In Ward, W. ed. Stories to dramatize p219-24 **372.6**

A **voyage** to Brobdingnag. Swift, J.
 In Mayne, W. ed. William Mayne's Book of giants p177-94 **398.2**

A **voyage** to Lilliput; condensation. Swift, J.
 In Lang, A. ed. The blue fairy book p313-32 **398.2**

The **Voyage** to New Zealand
 In Brown, M. ed. A cavalcade of sea legends p194-97 **808.8**

Voyagers. See Explorers

Voyages and travels
 Buehr, W. The world of Marco Polo (4-6) **92**
 Marco Polo's adventures in China (5-7) **92**
 Murphy, B. B. Thor Heyerdahl and the reed boat Ra (4-7) **910.4**
 Villiers, A. Men, ships, and the sea (6-7) **910.4**
 See also pages in the following book:
 Johnson, E. ed. Anthology of children's literature p1101-36 **808.8**
  See also Adventure and adventurers;

Aeronautics—Flights; Discoveries (in geography); Explorers; Overland journeys to the Pacific; Scientific expeditions; Seamen; Voyages around the world; Whaling; also names of countries with the subdivision Description and travel, e.g. United States—Description and travel; also names of regions, e.g. Antarctic regions; and names of ships, e.g. Fox (Steam yacht)

Voyages around the world
 Graham, R. L. The boy who sailed around the world alone (5-7) **910.4**
 Israel, C. E. Five ships west; the story of Magellan (4-6) **92**
 Syme, R. Magellan, first around the world (4-6) **92**

The **voyages** of Christopher Columbus. Sperry, A. **92**

The **voyages** of Doctor Dolittle; excerpts. Lofting, H.
 In Lofting, H. Doctor Dolittle p77-80 **Fic**

Voyages to Mars. See Space flight to Mars

Voyages to the moon. See Space flight to the moon

Voyageurs National Park
 See pages in the following book:
 Melbo, I. R. Our country's national parks v 1 p319-34 (5-7) **917.3**

Vroman, Tom
 (illus.) Asbjörnsen, P. C. East of the sun and west of the moon, and other tales **398.2**

Vukub-Cakix
 In Garner, A. ed. A cavalcade of goblins p4-10 **398.2**
 See also Hero twins

Vultures
 Turner, A. W. Vultures (5-7) **598.2**
 See also pages in the following books:
 Earle, O. L. Scavengers p37-44 (3-5) **591.5**
 Hopf, A. L. Misunderstood animals p47-52 (4-7) **591.5**

W

WAGGS. See World Association of Girl Guides and Girl Scouts

WHO. See World Health Organization

Wabash and Erie Canal
 See pages in the following book:
 Franchere, R. Westward by canal p129-31 (5-7) **386**

Waber, Bernard
 An anteater named Arthur **E**
 A firefly named Torchy **E**
 The house on East 88th Street **E**
 Ira sleeps over **E**
 Lyle finds his mother **E**
 Lyle, Lyle, crocodile **E**
 You look ridiculous, said the rhinoceros to the hippopotamus **E**

Waciuma, Charity
 See pages in the following book:
 Ojigbo, A. O. comp. Young and Black in Africa p63-70 (6-7) **920**

Wee bannock—*Continued*
Wee bannock
In Jacobs, J. ed. More English folk and fairy tales p73-77 **398.2**
See also Bun; Gingerbread boy; Johnny-cake; Pancake

Wee Gillis. Leaf, M. **E**

Wee little woman
In The Tall book of nursery tales p49-50 **398.2**

Wee Meg Barnileg and the fairies. Sawyer, R.
In Sawyer, R. The way of the storyteller p205-16 **372.6**

The **Wee Red Man. MacManus, S.**
In MacManus, S. Hibernian nights p85-98 **398.2**

Wee Robin's Christmas Day
In Association for Childhood Education International. Told under the green umbrella p162-64 **398.2**

Wee, wee Mannie
In Jacobs, J. ed. More English folk and fairy tales p192-94 **398.2**
In Williams-Ellis, A. Fairy tales from the British Isles p20-23 **398.2**

Wee, wee woman
Wee little woman
In The Tall book of nursery tales p49-50 **398.2**

A **weed is a flower: the life of George Washington Carver. Aliki** **92**

Weeds
Dowden, A. O. Wild green things in the city (4-7) **582**
Hogner, D. C. Weeds (3-6) **632**
Podendorf, I. The true book of weeds and wild flowers (1-3) **582**
Wright, R. H. What good is a weed? (4-6) **581.5**
See also names of weeds, e.g. Dandelions

A **week of Sundays. Baker, M.**
In Gruenberg, S. M. ed. Favorite stories old and new p359-63 **808.8**

Weekly Record **015**

Weems, Mason Locke
See pages in the following book:
Haviland, V. ed. Yankee Doodle's literary sampler of prose, poetry, & pictures p40-44 **028.5**

The **weeping lass at the dancing place. Nic Leodhas, S.**
In Nic Leodhas, S. Twelve great black cats, and other eerie Scottish tales p41-49 **398.2**

Wegner, Fritz
(illus.) Jacobs, J. Jack the Giant-Killer **398.2**
Weighing & balancing. Srivastava, J. J. **389**
Weight and weightlessness. Branley, F. M. 531

Weight control

Fiction
Marshall, J. Yummers! **E**
Solot, M. L. 100 hamburgers **E**

Weightlessness
Branley, F. M. Weight and weightlessness (1-3) **531**

Weights and measures
Schlein, M. Heavy is a hippopotamus **E**
Srivastava, J. J. Weighing & balancing (1-3) **389**
See also Mensuration; Metric system

Weihs, Jean Riddle
Nonbook materials **025.3**

Weik, Mary Hays
The Jazz Man (3-5) **Fic**

Weil, Lisl
(illus.) Association for Childhood Education International. Told under the city umbrella **S C**
(illus.) Fisher, A. Human Rights Day **394.2**
(illus.) LeShan, E. What makes me feel this way? **152.4**
(illus.) Stevens, C. Your first pet **636.08**

Weilerstein, Sadie Rose
K'tonton arrives
In Association for Childhood Education International. Told under the Christmas tree p255-58 **808.8**
K'tonton takes a ride on a runaway trendel
In Association for Childhood Education International. Told under the Christmas tree p259-63 **808.8**

Weiner, Sandra
Small hands, big hands (4-7) **331.5**

Weingarten, Violet
The Ganges (4-6) **915.4**

Weir, Ruth Cromer
Sailing west to find the east
In Cavanah, F. ed. Holiday roundup p240-44 **394.2**

Weisberger, Bernard A.
Captains of industry. See Captains of industry **920**

Weisgard, Leonard
The beginnings of cities (6-7) **913.35**
Caldecott Medal acceptance paper
In Miller, B. M. ed. Caldecott Medal books: 1938-1957 p151-56 **028.5**
The Plymouth Thanksgiving (3-5) **974.4**
Treasures to see (1-4) **708**
(illus.) Brown, M. W. Country noisy book **E**
(illus.) Brown, M. W. Indoor noisy book **E**
(illus.) Brown, M. W. Nibble nibble **811**
(illus.) Bulla, C. R. The valentine cat **E**
(illus.) Bulla, C. R. White Bird **Fic**
(illus.) Campbell, E. Nails to nickels **737.4**
(illus.) Dalgliesh, A. The courage of Sarah Noble **Fic**
(illus.) Ferris, H. ed. Favorite poems, old and new **808.81**
(illus.) Fitch, F. M. A book about God **231**
(illus.) Franchere, R. Willa **Fic**
(illus.) Garelick, M. Look at the moon **811**
(illus.) Garelick, M. Where does the butterfly go when it rains **E**
(illus.) Haviland, V. Favorite fairy tales told in Norway **398.2**
(illus.) Hays, W. P. Pilgrim Thanksgiving **Fic**
(illus.) Joslin, S. Baby Elephant and the secret wishes **E**
(illus.) Joslin, S. Brave Baby Elephant **E**
(illus.) Kipling, R. How the leopard got his spots **Fic**
(illus.) Kipling, R. How the rhinoceros got his skin **Fic**

Wildsmith, Brian—*Continued*
The North Wind and the Sun (k-3)   398.2
The owl and the woodpecker   E
The rich man and the shoe-maker (k-2)   398.2
Squirrels (k-2)   599
(illus.) Blishen, E. comp. Oxford Book of poetry for children   821.08
(illus.) Brian Wildsmith's The twelve days of Christmas. See Brian Wildsmith's The twelve days of Christmas   E
(illus.) Mother Goose. Brian Wildsmith's Mother Goose   398.8
(illus.) Stevenson, R. L. A child's garden of verses (Watts, F.)   821
(illus.) Turner, P. Brian Wildsmith's Illustrated Bible stories   220.9

About
See pages in the following book:
Hoffman, M. ed. Authors and illustrators of children's books p412-16   028.5

Wilkins, Mary Eleanor
Pumpkin giant
In Davis, M. G. ed. A baker's dozen p81-100   372.6
In Ross, E. S. ed. The lost half-hour p35-44   372.6
The silver hen
In Ross, E. S. ed. The lost half-hour p158-71   372.6
For another title by this author see entry under Freeman, Mary Eleanor

Will
Finders keepers   E
Will I have a friend? Cohen, M.   E
"The will-o'-the-wisps are in town," said the bog witch. Andersen, H. C.
In Andersen, H. C. The complete fairy tales and stories p799-811   S C
The will of the Wise Man. MacManus, S.
In MacManus, S. Hibernian nights p160-73   398.2
Will you be my friend. Iwasaki, C.   E
Willa. Franchere, R.   Fic

Willard, Barbara
The Richleighs of Tantamount (4-7)   Fic

Willem, I, Prince of Orange. See William I, Prince of Orange

Willen, Patt
(illus.) Bley, E. S. The best singing games for all children of all ages   796.1
The willful child. Grimm, J.
In Grimm, J. The complete Grimm's Fairy tales p534-35   398.2

William and his kitten. Flack, M.
In Gruenberg, S. M. comp. Let's hear a story p150-60   808.8

William and Jane. Aldis, D.
In Association for Childhood Education International. Told under the blue umbrella p125-33   S C
In Gruenberg, S. M. ed. Favorite stories old and new p23-28   808.8

William Bradford of Plymouth Colony. Jacobs, W. J.   92

William I, the Conqueror, King of England
Hodges, C. W. The Norman Conquest (4-7)   942.02

William III, King of Great Britain
See pages in the following book:
Barnouw, A. J. The land and people of Holland p83-86 (5-7)   914.92

William of Malmesbury
The witch of Berkeley
In Hope-Simpson, J. ed. A cavalcade of witches p128-32   808.8

William of Orange. See William III, King of Great Britain

William I, Prince of Orange
See pages in the following book:
Barnouw, A. J. The land and people of Holland p58-62 (5-7)   914.92

William Tell and his son. Hürlimann, B.   398.2

William the Silent. See William I, Prince of Orange

Williams, Adrian
(illus.) Nayman, J. Atlas of wildlife   591.9

Williams, Albert
(illus.) Jordan, J. Fannie Lou Hamer   92

Williams, Barbara
Albert's toothache   E

Williams, Berkeley
(illus.) Chase, R. ed. Grandfather tales   398.2
(illus.) Chase, R. ed. The Jack tales   398.2

Williams, Bert
See pages in the following books:
Hughes, L. Famous Negro music makers p35-43 (5-7)   920
Rollins, C. Famous Negro entertainers of stage, screen, and TV p105-07 (5-7)   920
Rollins, C. H. They showed the way p146-49 (5-7)   920

Williams, Daniel Hale
See pages in the following books:
Hayden, R. C. Seven Black American scientists p26-43 (6-7)   920
Hughes, L. Famous American Negroes p57-60 (5-7)   920
Rollins, C. H. They showed the way p150-52 (5-7)   920

Williams, Francis A.
(illus.) Fowler, H. W. Kites   796.1

Williams, Garth
The chicken book   E
(illus.) Brown, M. W. Wait till the moon is full   E
(illus.) Carlson, N. S. The happy orpheline   Fic
(illus.) Garson, E. ed. The Laura Ingalls Wilder songbook   784
(illus.) Hoban, R. Bedtime for Frances   E
(illus.) Lindquist, J. D. The golden name day   Fic
(illus.) Schweitzer, B. B. Amigo   E
(illus.) Selden, G. The cricket in Times Square   Fic
(illus.) Selden, G. Harry Cat's pet puppy   Fic
(illus.) Selden, G. Tucker's countryside   Fic
(illus.) Sharp, M. Miss Bianca   Fic
(illus.) Sharp, M. The rescuers   Fic
(illus.) Stolz, M. Emmett's pig   E
(illus.) White, E. B. Charlotte's web   Fic
(illus.) White, E. B. Stuart Little   Fic
(illus.) Wilder, L. I. Little house in the big woods   Fic

Williams, Garth—*Continued*
(illus.) Zolotow, C. Do you know what I'll do? **E**

Williams, Gweneira M.
A kettle of brains
  In Burack, A. S. ed. One hundred plays for children p790-95 **808.82**
Timid Timothy: the kitten who learned to be brave
  In Gruenberg, S. M. comp. Let's hear a story p102-07 **808.8**

Williams, Harcourt
The Snooks family
  In Colwell, E. ed. A second storyteller's choice p104-06 **372.6**

Williams, Jay
Danny Dunn and the homework machine (3-6) **Fic**
The horn of Roland (4-6) **398.2**
Petronella (2-4) **Fic**
The practical princess (2-4) **Fic**
Raoul the owl
  In Untermeyer, B. ed. The Golden Treasury of children's literature p286-97 **808.8**

Williams, Jerome
Oceanography (5-7) **551.4**

Williams, Lee Ann
Shuttlesworth, D. E. Disappearing energy **333.7**

Williams, Margery
The velveteen rabbit (2-4) **Fic**
The velveteen rabbit; excerpt
  In Johnson, E. ed. Anthology of children's literature p613-15 **808.8**

Williams, Paul
(illus.) Place, M. T. Mountain man; the life of Jim Beckwourth **92**

Williams, Roger
  See pages in the following book:
Daugherty, S. Ten brave men p20-36 (5-7) **920**

Williams, Ted. See Williams, Theodore Samuel

Williams, Theodore Samuel
  See pages in the following book:
Libby, B. Baseball's greatest sluggers p64-89 (5-7) **920**

William's doll. Zolotow, C. **E**

Williams-Ellis, Amabel
Clever Oonagh
  In Greene, E. comp. Clever cooks p41-54 **398.2**
  In Mayne, W. ed. William Mayne's Book of giants p148-60 **398.2**
Fairy tales from the British Isles (5-7) **398.2**
Contents: Fifty red night-caps; Tom Tit Tot; The wee, wee mannie; The King, the Saint and the goose; Teeny-tiny; Happy Boz'll; Johnny-cake; The three little pigs; The changeling; Kate Crackernuts; Clever Oonagh; The Well of the World's End; The good old man; The hairy boggart; The false knight; The Black Bull of Norroway; Mr and Mrs Vinegar; The baker's daughter; The King of the Cats; The Cauld Lad of Hilton; A spadeful of earth; Cap o' Rushes; Hardy Hardback; The field of Boliauns; The fairy child; Mr Miacca; The secret room; White-faced Simminy; Jack and the beanstalk; The bear in the coach; Pengersec and the Witch of Fraddom; Mrs Mag and her nest; The magician and his pupil; The head of brass; Childe Rowland; Sir Gammer Vans; Old Bluebeard; The giants of Towednack;

Three sillies; The Lake Lady; Tamlane; Finlay the hunter; 'Water's locked'; The Devil and the tailor; The Red Ettin; The midnight hunt; The Laidly Worm of Spindlestone Heugh; A mouse from the Mabinogian
The giants of Towednack
  In Mayne, W. ed. William Mayne's Book of giants p138-47 **398.2**
The story of St George and the Dragon
  In Hoke, H. comp. Dragons, dragons, dragons p57-62 **398.2**

Williamsburg, Va.
  See pages in the following book:
Taylor, T. Rebellion town, Williamsburg, 1776 p29-37 (5-7) **973.3**

Willie Winkie. Leach, M.
  In Leach, M. Whistle in the graveyard p89-90 **398.2**

Willie's bad night. Lawson, R.
  In Arbuthnot, M. H. comp. The Arbuthnot Anthology of children's literature p481-83 **808.8**

Willis. Marshall, J. **E**

Willow
  In Garner, A. ed. A cavalcade of goblins p36-39 **398.2**

Willow plate, The legend of the. Tresselt, A. **398.2**

The willow-wren. Grimm, J.
  In Grimm, J. The complete Grimm's Fairy tales p705-08 **398.2**

The willow-wren and the bear. Grimm, J.
  In Grimm, J. The complete Grimm's Fairy tales p472-74 **398.2**
  See also Wren and the bear

Willy Winky. Andersen, H.
  In Andersen, H. Hans Andersen's Fairy tales p144-57 **S C**

Wilson, Barbara Ker
The faery flag of Dunvegan
  In Johnson, E. ed. Anthology of children's literature p229-33 **808.8**

Wilson, Charles Morrow
Geronimo (5-7) **92**

Wilson, Dagmar
(illus.) Gruenberg, S. M. comp. Let's hear a story **808.8**

Wilson, Erica
Fun with crewel embroidery (3-7) **746.4**

Wilson, Gilbert L.
Why the baby says "goo"
  In Gruenberg, S. M. ed. Favorite stories old and new p333-35 **808.8**

Wilson, Gilbert W.
Little Scar Face
  In Association for Childhood Education International. Told under the green umbrella p156-61 **398.2**

Wilson, Hazel
Last queen of Hawaii: Liliuokalani (4-6) **92**

Wilson, John
(illus.) Adoff, A. Malcolm X **92**
(illus.) Lexau, J. M. Striped ice cream **Fic**

Wilson, John MacKay
The doom of Soulis; adaptation. See Mayne, W. The doom of Soulis

Witch girl. Coatsworth, E.
  In Hoke, H. ed. Spooks, spooks, spooks
    p206-13   **S C**
Witch hare
  In De La Mare, W. ed. Animal stories p75-
    76   **398.2**
The witch in the pond. Harter, W.
  In Harter, W. Osceola's head, and other
    American ghost stories p57-61   **S C**
The Witch in the stone boat
  In Hardendorff, J. B. Witches, wit, and a
    werewolf p22-30   **S C**
  In Hoke, H. ed. Witches, witches, witches
    p197-204   **808.8**
  In Lang, A. ed. The yellow fairy book
    p274-78   **398.2**
The witch of Berkeley. William of Malmesbury
  In Hope-Simpson, J. ed. A cavalcade of
    witches p128-32   **808.8**
"The Witch of Endor"
  In Hope-Simpson, J. ed. A cavalcade of
    witches p168-71   **808.8**
The witch of Fourth Street. Levoy, M.
  In Levoy, M. The witch of Fourth Street,
    and other stories p 1-13   **S C**
The witch of Fourth Street, and other stories.
  Levoy, M.   **S C**
The witch of Lok Island. Masson, E.
  In Harper, W. comp. Ghosts and goblins
    p176-91   **394.2**
  In Hoke, H. ed. Witches, witches, witches
    p206-18   **808.8**
  See also Groac'h of the Isle of Loc
Witch of the Cumberlands. Stephens, M. J. **Fic**
Witch Wood. Bennett, A. E.
  In Hoke, H. ed. Spooks, spooks, spooks
    p13-20   **S C**
Witchcraft
  Kohn, B. Out of the cauldron (5-7)   **133.4**
  See also pages in the following book:
  Aymar, B. Laws and trials that created his-
    tory p54-64 (6-7)   **345.7**
    See also Demonology; Occult sciences;
    Witches

Fiction

Bellairs, J. The house with a clock in its walls
  (5-7)   **Fic**
Bennett, A. E. Little witch (3-5)   **Fic**
Fisher, L. E. The warlock of Westfall (5-7)
       Fic
Singer, I. B. The fearsome inn (4-6)   **Fic**
Snyder, Z. K. The witches of Worm (4-7) **Fic**

Witches
  Hoke, H. ed. Witches, witches, witches (5-7)
         808.8
  Hope-Simpson, J. ed. A cavalcade of witches
    (4-7)   **808.8**

  See also pages in the following book:
  McHargue, G. The impossible people p96-
    104 (5-7)   **398**

Fiction

Adams, A. A woggle of witches   **E**
Balian, L. Humbug witch   **E**
Coombs, P. Dorrie and the amazing magic
  elixir   **E**
Coombs, P. Dorrie and the birthday eggs   **E**

Coombs, P. Dorrie and the Blue Witch   **E**
Coombs, P. Dorrie and the goblin   **E**
Embry, M. The blue-nosed witch (1-4)   **Fic**
Estes, E. The witch family (1-4)   **Fic**
Manning-Sanders, R. A book of witches (3-6)
       398.2
Massey, J. The littlest witch   **E**
Peet, B. The whingdingdilly   **E**
Serraillier, I. Suppose you met a witch   **E**
Sleigh, B. Carbonel, the King of the Cats
  (4-6)   **Fic**
Stewart, M. The little broomstick (3-6) **Fic**
The witches of Worm. Snyder, Z. K.   **Fic**
Witches, pumpkins, and grinning ghosts.
  Barth, E.   **394.2**
The witches' ride. De Osma, L.
  In Arbuthnot, M. H. comp. The Arbuthnot
    Anthology of children's literature
    p407-08   **808.8**
  In Arbuthnot, M. H. comp. Time for old
    magic p273-74   **398.2**
  In Harper, W. comp. Ghosts and goblins
    p228-33   **394.2**
Witches, wit, and a werewolf. Hardendorff,
  J. B.   **S C**
Witches, witches, witches. Hoke, H. ed. **808.8**
The witch's brat. Sutcliff, R.   **Fic**
"The witch's curse." Alcott, L. M.
  In Hope-Simpson, J. ed. A cavalcade of
    witches p114-23   **808.8**
The witch's daughter. Bawden, N.   **Fic**
The witch's pumpkin. Cooper, E.
  In Burack, A. S. ed. One hundred plays
    for children p386-89   **808.82**
The witch's shoes. Olcott, F. J.
  In Harper, W. comp. Ghosts and goblins
    p192-94   **394.2**
  In Hoke, H. ed. Witches, witches, witches
    p219-20   **808.8**
The witch's skin. Alegría, R. E.
  In Alegría, R. E. The three wishes p86-89
         398.2
Witcracks. Schwartz, A. ed.   **398.6**
With a deep sea smile. Tashjian, V. A. ed. **372.6**
With a wig, with a wag. Cothran, J.
  In Tashjian, V. A. ed. With a deep sea
    smile p86-92   **372.6**
With all my heart; play
  In Smith, M. R. ed. 7 plays & how to pro-
    duce them p133-47   **792**
Withers, Carl
  (comp.) The American riddle book (5-7) **398.6**
  (ed.) I saw a rocket walk a mile (3-6) **398.2**
  (comp.) Riddles of many lands (5-7) **398.6**
  (comp.) A rocket in my pocket (3-6)   **398**
  A world of nonsense (4-7)   **398.2**
  Tales included are: The ship that sailed on water
  and on land; A trip to the sky; Old Wall Eyes;
  The mighty wrestlers; The clever boy; The remarkable
  ox, rooster, and dog; Big, big lies; The story without
  an end
Within the gates. Zei, A.
  In Arbuthnot, M. H. comp. The Arbuthnot
    Anthology of children's literature
    p772-75   **808.8**
Withrow, Dorothy E.
  Gateways to readable books   **028.52**

Wrightson, Patricia
Down to earth (5-7)   Fic
Down to earth; excerpt
  In Arbuthnot, M. H. comp. The Arbuth-
  not Anthology of children's literature
  p579-82   808.8
The powerful starer
  In Arbuthnot, M. H. comp. The Arbuth-
  not Anthology of children's literature
  p579-82   808.8
A racecourse for Andy (5-7)   Fic

About
See pages in the following book:
Townsend, J. R. A sense of story p204-11
                                                      028.5

Wrigley, Denis
(illus.) Northcott, C. Bible encyclopedia for
  children   220.3
(illus.) Northcott, C. People of the Bible
                                                      220.9

Wrigley, Elsie
(illus.) Cole, J. Fleas   595.7
(illus.) Rhine, R. Life in a bucket of soil 592
A wrinkle in time. L'Engle, M.   Fic
A wrinkle in time; excerpt. L'Engle, M.
  In Arbuthnot, M. H. comp. The Arbuthnot Anthology of children's literature
  p594-99   808.8
Writers. See Authors

Writing
  See also Alphabet; Ciphers; Cryptography; Cuneiform inscriptions; Hieroglyphics; Picture writing

History
Cahn, W. The story of writing (6-7)   411
Taylor, M. C. Wht's yr nm? (3-6)   411
  See also pages in the following book:
Neal, H. E. Communication p57-84 (5-7)
                                                      001.54

Written for children. Townsend, J. R.   028.5

Wuorio, Eva-Lis
Save Alice! (5-7)   Fic
To fight in silence (5-7)   Fic

Wurmfeld, Hope
(illus.) McGovern, A. Black is beautiful   811

Wyatt, Edgar
Cochise, Apache warrior and statesman (5-7)
                                                      92
Geronimo, the last Apache war chief (4-6) 92

Wycliffe, John
  See pages in the following book:
Hall, E. The land and people of Czechoslo-
  vakia p54-58 (5-7)   914.37

Wyeth, N. C.
(illus.) Johnson, E. ed. Anthology of children's literature   808.8

Wyler, Rose
The first book of science experiments (4-6)
                                                      507.2
Funny magic (1-3)   793.8
Magic secrets (1-3)   793.8
Prove it! (1-3)   507.2
Spooky tricks (1-3)   793.8
What happens if . . ? (2-4)   507.2
(jt. auth.) Ames, G. The earth's story   551

Wynar, Christine L.
Guide to reference books for school media
  centers   016

Wyndham, John
Chinese puzzle
  In Silverberg, B. ed. Phoenix feathers p56-
  80   S C

Wyndham, Lee
Mara, T. First steps in ballet   792.8

Wyndham, Robert
(ed.) Chinese Mother Goose rhymes (k-2)
                                                      398.8
Tales the people tell in China (3-6)   398.2
Contents: Discovery of salt; The wise man's pillow;
The marvelous pear seed; The young head of the
Cheng family; A gift of the unicorn; The man who
stole a rope; The borrowing of 100,000 arrows; The
man who sold a ghost; A warning from the gods;
Legend of how the ants came to earth; Stealing the
bell; The potter and the gate; Marking the boat
to locate the sword; The man who would know magic;
Ma Liang and his magic brush

Wyoming

Animals
  See Animals—Wyoming

Wyss, Johann David
Our first harvest
  ° *In* Martignoni, M. E. ed. The illustrated
  treasury of children's literature p446-
  49   808.8
The Swiss family Robinson (5-7)   Fic
The Swiss family Robinson; play. See
  Howard, V. The Swiss family Robinson—
  Rescued
The Wyvern. Henderson, B.
  In Hoke, H. comp. Dragons, dragons,
  dragons p199-210   398.2

X

The X cars. Lent, H. B.   629.22

X rays
  See pages in the following books:
Barr, G. Young scientist and the dentist p82-
  95 (5-7)   617.6
Berger, M. Animal hospital p73-78 (4-7)
                                                      636.089
Gallant, R. A. Explorers of the atom p29-37
  (6-7)   539.7

Xerxes, King of Persia
  See pages in the following book:
Collins, R. The Medes and Persians p138-48
  (6-7)   913.35

Xibalba. Roy, C.
  In Roy, C. The serpent and the sun p86-
  97   398.2

Y

Yallery Brown
  In Garner, A. ed. A cavalcade of goblins
  p42-51   398.2
  In Jacobs, J. ed. More English folk and
  fairy tales p28-36   398.2

DIRECTORY OF PUBLISHERS AND DISTRIBUTORS

A.L.A. American Library Association, 50 E Huron St, Chicago, Ill. 60611

APS Publications, Inc. APS Publications, Inc, 150 5th Av, New York, N.Y. 10011

Abelard-Schuman. See Crowell

Abingdon. Abingdon Press, 201 8th Av S, Nashville, Tenn. 37202

Addison-Wesley. Addison-Wesley Publishing Company, Inc, Reading, Mass. 01867

Am. Antiquarian Soc. American Antiquarian Society, 185 Salisbury St, Worcester, Mass. 01609

Am. Assn. for the Advancement of Science. American Association for the Advancement of Science, 1515 Massachusetts Av, N.W, Washington, D.C. 20005

Am. Council on Educ. American Council on Education, 1 Dupont Circle, N.W., Washington, D.C. 20036

Am. Forestry Assn. American Forestry Association, 1319 18th St, N.W, Washington, D.C. 20036

Am. Foundation for the Blind. American Foundation for the Blind, Inc, Publications Division, 15 W 16th St, New York, N.Y. 10011

Am. Heritage. American Heritage Publishing Company, Inc, 1221 Av of the Americas, New York, N.Y. 10020

Am. Heritage Press. See Am. Heritage

Anchorage Press. Anchorage Press, Inc, Cloverlot, Anchorage, Ky. 40223

Arco. Arco Publishing Company, Inc, 219 Park Av S, New York, N.Y. 10003

Ariel Bks. See Farrar, Straus

Aronson, J. Jason Aronson, Inc, 59 4th Av, New York, N.Y. 10003

Assn. for Childhood Educ. Association for Childhood Education International, 3615 Wisconsin Av, N.W, Washington, D.C. 20016

Assn. for Educational Communications and Technology. Association for Educational Communications and Technology, 1201 16th St, N.W, Room 227, Washington, D.C. 20036

Astor-Honor. Astor-Honor, Inc, 270 Madison Av, New York, N.Y. 10016

Atheneum Pubs. Atheneum Publishers, 122 E 42d St, New York, N.Y. 10017

Barnes, A.S. A. S. Barnes & Company, Inc, Forsgate Dr, Cranbury, N.J. 08512

Beginner Bks. Beginner Books, 201 E 50th St, New York, N.Y. 10022

Behrman. Behrman House, Inc, 1261 Broadway, New York, N.Y. 10001

Berkley Pub. Corp. Berkley Publishing Corporation, 200 Madison Av, New York, N.Y. 10016

Bobbs. Bobbs-Merrill Company, Inc, 4300 W 62d St, Indianapolis, Ind. 46206

Bowker. R. R. Bowker Company, 1180 Av of the Americas, New York, N.Y. 10036

Boy Scouts of Am. Boy Scouts of America, Supply Division, N Brunswick, N.J. 08902

Bradbury Press. Bradbury Press, Inc, 2 Overhill Rd, Scarsdale, N.Y. 10583

British Bk. Centre. British Book Centre, Inc, 153 E 78th St, New York, N.Y. 10021

Bro-Dart Foundation. Bro-Dart Foundation, P.O. Box 306, Montoursville, Pa. 17754

Cambridge. Cambridge University Press, 32 E 57th St, New York, N.Y. 10022

Camp Fire Girls, Inc. Camp Fire Girls, Inc, 1740 Broadway, New York, N.Y. 10019

Can. Lib. Assn. Canadian Library Association, 151 Sparks St, Ottawa, Ont. KIP 5E3, Canada

Caxton Ptrs. The Caxton Printers, Ltd, Caldwell, Idaho 83605

Chicorel Lib. Pub. Chicorel Library Publishing Corp, 275 Central Park W, New York, N.Y. 10024

Child Study Association of America/Wel-Met. See Child Study Press

Child Study Press. Child Study Association of America, 50 Madison Av, New York, N.Y. 10010

Children's Bk. Council. The Children's Book Council, Inc, 67 Irving Pl, New York, N.Y. 10003

Childrens Press. Childrens Press, 1224 W Van Buren St, Chicago, Ill. 60607

The Children's Science Book Review Committee. The Children's Science Book Review Committee, Longfellow Hall, Appian Way, Cambridge, Mass. 02138

The Children's Theatre Press. See Anchorage Press

Chilton Bk. Co. Chilton Book Company, Chilton Way, Radnor, Pa. 19089

Chilton Co. See Chilton Bk. Co.

Citation Press. Citation Press, 50 W 44th St, New York, N.Y. 10036

Collins. William Collins+World Publishing Company, Inc, 2080 W 117th St, Cleveland, Ohio 44111

Columbia Univ. Press. Columbia University Press, 562 W 113th St, New York, N.Y. 10025

Compton. F. E. Compton Company, 425 N Michigan Av, Chicago, Ill. 60611

Council on Interracial Books for Children. Council on Interracial Books for Children, 1841 Broadway, New York, N.Y. 10023

Coward-McCann. See Coward, McCann & Geoghegan

Coward, McCann & Geoghegan. Coward, McCann & Geoghegan, Inc, 200 Madison Av, New York, N.Y. 10016

Creative Educ. Soc. Creative Educational Society, Inc, 123 S Broad St, Mankato, Minn. 56001

Criterion Bks. Criterion Books, 666 5th Av, New York, N.Y. 10019

Crowell. Thomas Y. Crowell Company, Inc, 666 5th Av, New York, N.Y. 10019

Crowell-Collier Press. See Macmillan Pub. Co.

Crown. Crown Publishers, Inc, 1 Park Av, New York, N.Y. 10016

Day. The John Day Company, 666 5th Av, York, N.Y. 10019

Delacorte Press. Delacorte Press, 1 Dag Hammarskjold Plaza, New York, N.Y. 10017

Denison. T. S. Denison & Company, Inc, 5100 W 82d St, Minneapolis, Minn. 55437

Dial Press. The Dial Press, 1 Dag Hammarskjold Plaza, New York, N.Y. 10017

Dillon Press. Dillon Press, Inc, 510 S 3d St, Minneapolis, Minn. 55415

Dodd. Dodd, Mead & Company, 79 Madison Av, New York, N.Y. 10016

Doubleday. Doubleday & Company, Inc, 245 Park Av, New York, N.Y. 10017

Dover. Dover Publications, Inc, 180 Varick St, New York, N.Y. 10014

Dutton. E. P. Dutton & Company, Inc, 201 Park Av S, New York, N.Y. 10003

Educ. Film. Educational Film Library Association, 17 W 60th St, New York, N.Y. 10023

Education Today Co, Inc. Education Today Company, Inc, 530 University Av, Palo Alto, Calif. 94301

Educators Progress Service. Educators Progress Service, Inc, 214 Center St, Randolph, Wis. 53956

Elk Grove Press. See Children's Press

Encyclopaedia Britannica Educ. Corp. Encyclopaedia Britannica Educational Corporation, 425 N Michigan Av, Chicago, Ill. 60611

Enoch Pratt. Enoch Pratt Free Library, Publications, 400 Cathedral St, Baltimore, Md. 21201

Evans, M.&Co. See Lippincott

Farrar, Straus. Farrar, Straus & Giroux, Inc, 19 Union Sq W, New York, N.Y. 10003

Faxon. F. W. Faxon Company, Inc, 15 Southwest Park, Westwood, Mass. 02090

Fell. Frederick Fell Publishers, Inc, 386 Park Av S, New York, N.Y. 10016

Field Enterprises. Field Enterprises Educational Corporation, 510 Merchandise Mart Pl, Chicago, Ill. 60654

Five Owls Press. Five Owls Press, 67 High Rd, Wormley, Boxbourne, Herts, EN 10 6JJ, England

Fleet Press. Fleet Press Corporation, 160 5th Av, New York, N.Y. 10010

Follett. Follett Publishing Company, 1010 W Washington Blvd, Chicago, Ill. 60607

Forest Press. Forest Press, Inc, 85 Watervliet Av, Albany, N.Y. 12206

Four Winds. The Four Winds Press, 50 W 44th St, New York, N.Y. 10036

Friendship Press. Friendship Press, 475 Riverside Dr, New York, N.Y. 10027

Frontier Press. The Frontier Press Company, 250 E Town St, Columbus, Ohio 43215

Funk. Funk & Wagnalls Publishing Company, Inc, 666 5th Av, New York, N.Y. 10019

Gale Res. Gale Research Company, Book Tower, Detroit, Mich. 48226

Garden City Bks. See Doubleday

Garrard. Garrard Publishing Company, 1607 N Market St, Champaign, Ill. 61820

Girl Scouts of the United States of America. Girl Scouts of the USA, National Equipment Service, 830 3d Av, New York, N.Y. 10022

Golden Gate. See Childrens Press

Goldn Gate Junior Bks. See Childrens Press

Golden Press. Golden Press Publications, 850 3d Av, New York, N.Y. 10022

Grolier. Grolier, Inc, 575 Lexington Av, New York, N.Y. 10022

Grosset. Grosset & Dunlap, Inc, 51 Madison Av, New York, N.Y. 10010

Hall, G.K.&Co. G. K. Hall & Company, 70 Lincoln St, Boston, Mass. 02111

Hammond. Hammond, Inc, 515 Valley St, Maplewood, N.J. 07040

Harcourt. Harcourt Brace Jovanovich, Inc, 757 3d Av, New York, N.Y. 10017

Harper. Harper & Row, Publishers, 10 E 53d St, New York, N.Y. 10022

Harvard College Lib. See Walker & Co.

Harvey House, Inc, Publishers, Irvington-on-Hudson, N.Y. 10533

Hastings House. Hastings House, Publishers, Inc, 10 E 40th St, New York, N.Y. 10016

Hawthorn Bks. Hawthorn Books, Inc, 260 Madison Av, New York, N.Y. 10016

Hill & Wang. Hill & Wang, 19 Union Sq W, New York, N.Y. 10003

Holiday House. Holiday House, Inc, 18 E 53d St, New York, N.Y. 10022

Holt. Holt, Rinehart and Winston, Inc, 383 Madison Av, New York, N.Y. 10017

Horn Bk. Horn Book, Inc, 585 Boylston St, Boston, Mass. 02116

Houghton. Houghton Mifflin Company, 1 Beacon St, Boston, Mass. 02107

Hubbard Press. Hubbard Press, 1920 Waukegan Rd, Glenview, Ill. 60025

Human Sciences Press. Human Sciences Press, 72 5th Av, New York, N.Y. 10011

Instructor Publications. The Instructor Publications, Inc, P.O. Box 6099, Duluth, Minn. 55806

Int. Reading Assn. International Reading Association, 800 Barksdale Rd, Newark, Del. 19711

Interbk Inc. Interbook, Inc, 545 8th Av, New York, N.Y. 10018

Jugend und Volk Verlagsges. Verlag fuer Jugend und Volk, Tiefer Graben 7-9, Vienna, Austria

Kirkus Service. Kirkus Service, 60 W 13th St, New York, N.Y. 10011

Knopf. Alfred A. Knopf, Inc, 201 E 50th St, New York, N.Y. 10022

Kraus Reprint Co. Kraus Reprint Company, Route 100, Millwood, N.Y. 10546

Ktav. Ktav Publishing House, Inc, 120 E Broadway, New York, N.Y. 10002

Landers Associates. Landers Associates, P.O. Box 69760, Los Angeles, Calif. 90069

Larousse. Larousse & Company, Inc, 572 5th Av, New York, N.Y. 10036

Lerner Publications. Lerner Publications Company, 241 1st Av N, Minneapolis, Minn. 55401

Libs. Unlimited. Libraries Unlimited, Inc. Box 263, Littleton, Colo. 80120

Lion. Lion Books, 111 E 39th St, New York, N.Y. 10016

Lippincott. J. B. Lippincott Company, E Washington Sq, Philadelphia, Pa. 19105

Little. Little, Brown and Company, 34 Beacon St, Boston, Mass. 02106

London House & Maxwell. See British Bk. Centre

Longmans. See McKay

Lothrop. Lothrop, Lee & Shepard Company, 105 Madison Av, New York, N.Y. 10016

Luce, R.B. Robert B. Luce, Inc, 2000 N St, N.W, Washington, D.C. 20036

McGraw. McGraw-Hill Book Company, 1221 Av of the Americas, New York, N.Y. 10020

McKay. David McKay Company, Inc, 750 3d Av, New York, N.Y. 10017

Macmillan (N Y) See Macmillan Pub. Co.

Macmillan Educ. Corp. Macmillan Educational Corporation, 866 3d Av, New York, N.Y. 10022

Macmillan Professional Magazines, Inc. Macmillan Professional Magazines, Inc, 262 Mason St, Greenwich, Conn. 06830

Macmillan Pub. Co. Macmillan Publishing Company, Inc, 866 3d Av, New York, N.Y. 10022

Macrae Smith Co. Macrae Smith Company, 222 S 15th St, Philadelphia, Pa. 19102

Mark Press. Mark Press, 16 Park Pl, Waltham, Mass. 02154

Marsh Hall. Marsh Hall, Thurstonland, Huddersfield, HD 4 6XB, Yorkshire, England

Meredith. See Meredith Corp.

Meredith Corp. Meredith Corporation, 1716 Locust St, Des Moines, Iowa 50336

Merriam. G. & C. Merriam Company, 47 Federal St, Springfield, Mass. 01101

Messner. Julian Messner, 1 W 39th St, New York, N.Y. 10018

Mich. Assn. of School Librarians. Michigan Association of School Librarians, 401 S 4th St, Ann Arbor, Mich. 48103

Modern Lib. See Random House

Morrow. William Morrow & Company, Inc, 105 Madison Av, New York, N.Y. 10016

N.Y. Graphic. New York Graphic Society Ltd, 11 Beacon St, Boston, Mass. 02108

N.Y. Library Assn. New York Library Association, 60 E 42d St, New York, N.Y. 10017

N.Y. Pub. Lib. New York Public Library, Public Relations Office, 5th Av & 42d St, New York, N.Y. 10018

N.Y. Times Co. New York Times Company, Book Division, 330 Madison Av, New York, N.Y. 10017

Natl. Assn. for the Educ. of Young Children. National Association for the Education of Young Children, 1834 Connecticut Av, N.W, Washington, D.C. 20009

Natl. Council of Teachers of English. National Council of Teachers of English, 1111 Kenyon Rd, Urbana, Ill. 61801

Natl. Geographic Soc. National Geographic Society, 17 & M Sts, N.W, Washington, D.C. 20036

Natl. Information Center for Educational Media. National Information Center for Educational Media, University of Southern California, University Park, Los Angeles, Calif. 90007

Natl. Science Teacher's Assn. National Science Teacher's Association, 1742 Connecticut Av, N.W, Washington, D.C. 20009

Natl. Wildlife Federation. National Wildlife Federation, 1412 16th St, N.W, Washington, D.C. 20036

Natural Hist. Press. Natural History Press, 501 Franklin Av, Garden City, N.Y. 11530

Nelson. Thomas Nelson, Inc, 407 7th Av S, Nashville, Tenn. 37203

North American Pub. Co. North American Publishing Company, 134 N 13th St, Philadelphia, Pa. 19107

Norton. W. W. Norton & Company, Inc, 500 5th Av, New York, N.Y. 10036

Obolensky. See Astor-Honor

Oceana. Oceana Publications, Inc, Dobbs Ferry, N.Y. 10522

Ore. Educ. & Public Broadcasting Ser. Oregon Educational & Public Broadcasting Service, Div. of Oregon State System of Higher Education, Box 1097, Portland, Ore. 92707

Oxford. Oxford University Press, Inc, 200 Madison Av, New York, N.Y. 10016

Palo Verde Pub. Co. Palo Verde Publishing Company, 609 N 4th Av, Tucson, Ariz. 85705

Pantheon Bks. Pantheon Books, Inc, 201 E 50th St, New York, N.Y. 10022

Parents Mag. Press. Parents' Magazine Press, 52 Vanderbilt Av, New York, N.Y. 10017

Parnassus Press. Parnassus Press, 4080 Halleck St, Emeryville, Calif. 94608

Peabody College. George Peabody College for Teachers, Nashville, Tenn. 37203

Phaedrus, Inc. Phaedrus, Inc, 14 Beacon St, Boston, Mass. 02108

Phillips. S. G. Phillips, Inc, 305 W 86th St, New York, N.Y. 10024

Platt. Platt & Munk, 1055 Bronx River Av, Bronx, N.Y. 10472

Plays, Inc. Plays, Inc, 8 Arlington St, Boston, Mass. 02116

Potter, C.N. Clarkson N. Potter, Inc, 419 Park Av S, New York, N.Y. 10016

Prentice-Hall. Prentice-Hall, Inc, Route 9W, Englewood Cliffs, N.J. 07632

Press of Case Western Reserve Univ. The Press of Case Western Reserve University, Ltd, Frank Adgate Quail Bldg, Cleveland, Ohio 44106

Provincial Library Service. Provincial Library Service, 14th Floor, Mowat Block, Queen's Park, Toronto 182, Ont. Canada

Public Library of Cincinnati and Hamilton County. Exceptional Children's Division. Public Library of Cincinnati and Hamilton County, Exceptional Children's Division, 800 Vine St, Cincinnati, Ohio 45202

Putnam. G. P. Putnam's Sons, 200 Madison Av, New York, N.Y. 10016

Quadrangle Bks. See Quadrangle/The N.Y. Times Bk. Co.

Quadrangle/The N.Y. Times Bk. Co. Quadrangle/The New York Times Book Company, 10 E 53d St, New York, N.Y. 10022

Rand McNally. Rand McNally & Company, 8255 Central Park Av, Skokie, Ill. 60076

Random House. Random House, Inc, 201 E 50th St, New York, N.Y. 10022

Regnery. Henry Regnery Company, 180 N Michigan Av, Chicago, Ill. 60601

Reilly & Lee. See Regnery

Reinhold. See Van Nostrand-Reinhold

Rinehart. See Holt

Ronald. The Ronald Press Company, 79 Madison Av, New York, N.Y. 10016

Scarecrow. Scarecrow Press, Inc, 52 Liberty St, Metuchen, N.J. 08840

Schocken. Schocken Books, Inc, 200 Madison Av, New York, N.Y. 10016

School Library Assn. School Library Association, 150 Southampton Row, London WC 1, England

Scott. Scott, Foresman and Company, 1900 E Lake Av, Glenview, Ill. 60025

Scott, W.R. William R. Scott, Inc, 333 Av. of the Americas, New York, N.Y. 10014

Scribner. Charles Scribner's Sons, 597 5th Av, New York, N.Y. 10017

Scroll Press. Scroll Press, Inc, 129 E 94th St, New York, N.Y. 10028

Seabury. The Seabury Press, Inc, 815 2d Av, New York, N.Y. 10017

Simon & Schuster. Simon & Schuster, Inc, 630 5th Av, New York, N.Y. 10020

Singing Tree. Singing Tree Press, Book Tower, Detroit, Mich. 48226

Smith, P. Peter Smith, 6 Lexington Av, Gloucester, Mass. 01930

St Martins. St Martin's Press, Inc, 175 5th Av, New York, N.Y. 10010

Stackpole Bks. Stackpole Books, Cameron & Kelker Sts, Box 1831, Harrisburg, Pa. 17105

Steck-Vaughn. Steck-Vaughn Company, Box 2028, Austin, Tex. 78767

Sterling. Sterling Publishing Company, 419 Park Av S, New York, N.Y. 10016

Supt. of Docs. Superintendent of Documents, Government Printing Office, Washington, D.C. 20402

Taplinger. Taplinger Publishing Company, Inc, 200 Park Av S, New York, N.Y. 10003

Teachers College. Teachers College Press, Teachers College, Columbia University, 1234 Amsterdam Av, New York, N.Y. 10027

Temple Univ. Press. Temple University Press, Philadelphia, Pa. 19122

Thimble Press. The Thimble Press, Lockwood, Station Road, South Woodchester, Glos, GL5 5EQ, United Kingdom

Time-Life Bks. Time-Life Books, Time & Life Bldg, Rockefeller Center, New York, N.Y. 10020

Tuttle. Charles E. Tuttle Company, Inc, 28 S Main St, Rutland, Vt. 05701

U.S. Com. for UNICEF. Information Center on Children's Cultures. United States Committee for UNICEF, Information Center on Children's Cultures, 331 E 38th St, New York, N.Y. 10016

U.S. Govt. Ptg. Off. See Supt. of Docs.

Underhill, C.S. C. S. Underhill, P.O. Box 127, E Aurora, N.Y. 14052

Univ. of Calif. Press. University of California Press, 2223 Fulton St, Berkeley, Calif. 94720

Univ. of Chicago Press. University of Chicago Press, 5801 Ellis Av, Chicago, Ill. 60637

Univ. of Pittsburg Press. University of Pittsburgh Press, 127 N Bellefield Av, Pittsburgh, Pa. 15260

Vanguard. Vanguard Press, Inc, 424 Madison Av, New York, N.Y. 10017

Van Nostrand. See Van Nostrand-Reinhold

Van Nostrand-Reinhold. Van Nostrand Reinhold Company, 450 W 33d St, New York, N.Y. 10001

Viking. The Viking Press, Inc, 625 Madison Av, New York, N.Y. 10022

Walck, H.Z. Henry Z. Walck, Inc, 750 3d Av, New York, N.Y. 10017

Walker & Co. Walker & Company, 720 5th Av, New York, N.Y. 10019

Ward Ritchie Press. Ward Ritchie Press, 474 S Arroyo Pkwy, Pasadena, Calif. 91105

Warne. Frederick Warne & Company, Inc, 101 5th Av, New York, N.Y. 10003

Washburn. Ives Washburn, Inc, 750 3d Av, New York, N.Y. 10017

Watts, F. Franklin Watts, Inc, 730 5th Av, New York, N.Y. 10019

Westminster Press. The Westminster Press, Witherspoon Bldg, Philadelphia, Pa. 19107

Whitman, A. Albert Whitman & Company, 560 W Lake St, Chicago, Ill. 60606

Wilson, H.W. The H. W. Wilson Company, 950 University Av, Bronx, N.Y. 10452

Windmill Bks. Windmill Books, Inc, 201 Park Av S, New York, N.Y. 10010

Winston. See Holt

World Pub. See Collins

Young Scott Bks. See Addison-Wesley